The New York Times

guide to the best 1,000 movies ever made

UPDATED AND REVISED

The New York Times

THE FILM CRITICS OF THE NEW YORK TIMES

EDITED BY PETER M. NICHOLS

INTRODUCTION BY A. O. SCOTT

guide to the best 1,000 movies ever made

UPDATED AND REVISED

———— 🦅 ————

ST. MARTIN'S GRIFFIN 〽 NEW YORK

THE NEW YORK TIMES GUIDE TO THE BEST 1,000 MOVIES EVER MADE, UPDATED AND REVISED. Copyright © 2004 by The New York Times Company. All rights reserved. Printed in the United States of America. For information, address St. Martin's Press, 175 Fifth Avenue, New York, N.Y. 10010.

www.stmartins.com

The reviews that appear in this work were originally published in *The New York Times*.

Design by Nick Wunder

ISBN 0-312-32611-4

First published in the United States by Times Books in 1999

10   9

contents

preface

BY PETER M. NICHOLS

It was the evening of April 12, 1932, and *Grand Hotel* was about to open with Greta Garbo and John Barrymore. "Worshipers of the stars of the Hollywood firmament choked the sidewalk outside the Astor and also the theater lobby, while policemen afoot and on horse urged the throng to keep moving," Mordaunt Hall wrote in *The New York Times.* Chief critic of the paper, Hall was occasionally a reporter, too, and here he conveyed the electricity of a remarkable movie moment.

One advantage of a collection of film reviews spanning seven decades is that it reflects changing times as tellingly as it explores movies. In this book are one thousand complete film reviews from *The New York Times,* beginning in 1927 with *The Jazz Singer*, generally considered the first talkie, and running to the end of 2002. Along with each review is a cast box listing the leading players, production staff, and distribution companies. Almost every cast box has been expanded to include more information than appeared with the review when it originally ran. And over the years terminology changed, as cinematographers became directors of photography, and art designers turned into production designers. In some films, especially documentaries, some names and job slots are missing because there were no such positions or because the filmmakers simply did not fill in all the blanks.

The idea behind this book, of course, is to provide the film buff or anyone renting a video with as full an account of a movie as possible. But unedited reviews also leave no way to wriggle out of judgments made on deadline years ago. Are these really the one thousand best films? An impossible question, of course, but from the accumulated evidence, it's apparent that *Times* critics knew a great movie when they saw one. Their initials appear at the end of each review, along with the date the review appeared in *The Times.* A list of the critics' names and initials appears on page 2, following the list of all the movies in this guide.

The majority of movies in this book are among the "10 Best Films" chosen by critics at the end of each year. The lists appear in Appendix I. Not every film has a review in the book, however, since many films judged among the best in any one year have slipped off the pedestal. Taking their place among the one thousand are scores of films that have risen in common estimation to the point where they are generally considered among the best ever, though they weren't recognized as such by *Times* critics when they were released. For example, *Grand Illusion* (1937), *The Third Man* (1949), *The African Queen* (1951), *East of Eden* (1955), *Bonnie and Clyde* (1967), and *Chinatown* (1974) didn't make their respective "10 Best" lists but are included in the book. If that leaves a Times critic out on a limb at one time or another, so be it. Choosing "the best" of anything leaves room for endless argument, and readers undoubtedly will have their own additions and deletions.

For easy reference, Appendix II consists of the one thousand titles divided into ten categories, with each film listed chronologically within the category according to the year it was released. For foreign-language films, always a significant aspect of *Times* coverage, particularly since the mid-1960's, the country of origin is also given. (In Appendix III, foreign-language titles are listed according to country.) The body of the book consists of a straight alphabetical listing of the one thousand "best" films.

Finally, it should be noted that *The Times* frequently

reviewed many foreign films at least a year or two after their official release abroad. Often the film took a while getting to these shores. The most extreme case is Jean Renoir's *La Chienne* (The Bitch), which is dated 1931. The film "apparently has never been released here in an English-subtitled version," Vincent Canby wrote in his review in 1975. Well, better late than never.

Since this book was published in 1999, DVD has become far and away the best way to watch these films at home. Most are on disc and extra features—behind-the-scenes documentaries, commentaries by directors, additional scenes and the like—often add to the enjoyment. Titles that can't be found in video stores are usually available via mail order and on the Internet.

For this updated and revised edition, two new Times critics, A.O. Scott (see the Introduction, page xxiii) and Elvis Mitchell add their choices and reviews from 2000 through 2002. Once again, we thank Suzanne O'Connor of the *Times*'s culture department, who exercised prodigious patience and attention to detail in assembling the cast-and-credit boxes. (*The Times* changed the content and manner of presentation several times over the past five decades.) And thanks once more to Mitchel Levitas, the former director of book development of the *Times,* who organized this complex effort and kept it on track despite sudden threats of derailment from time to time.

list of movies

The year following the title of the movie is the year of its review unless otherwise indicated.

C

D

M

S

Y

Z

Introduction

BY A.O. SCOTT

The book you hold in your hands is often inconsistent, frequently self-subverting and, from time to time, utterly and stupefyingly wrong-headed. If it were not, I hasten to add, it would be pretty much useless, and not nearly as interesting as it is. Just as no director sets out to make a bad movie, so no critic sets out to render a faulty judgment, and most of us have sufficient pride to stand by our verdicts even as the taste of the majority and the opinion of history itself conspire to render them absurd. But however out-of-touch we may end up looking—or, for that matter, however prophetic—we know, as we type, dictate or email our copy for the morning paper, that the last word will not be ours. And so this volume is a collection of first words, some prescient, some premature, and worth a good deal less than the thousand pictures they describe. Though its title may invoke the authority of *The New York Times*, this collection is more likely to start arguments than to settle them, argument being one of the solemn duties of criticism and, more importantly, one of the great pleasures of movie-going.

As you browse through these thousand reviews, then, all of them originally published in *The Times* in the years since the start of the sound era, you may discern two related themes: the fallibility of even the most perspicacious critics (and *The Times*, it goes without saying, has never hired any other kind) and the durability of what appeared at the time of their release to be some of the cheapest, the silliest, the out-and-out strangest movies. For an example of the convergence of these these you need go no further than the letter B, where you will find the four paragraphs Frank S. Nugent devoted to *Bringing Up Baby* in the newspaper of March 4, 1938. Nugent was an engagingly honest about his own expectations and responses: writing about the hotly anticipated *Gone With the Wind* he confessed "we cannot get over the shock of not being disappointed; we had almost been looking forward to that." He could be an effortlessly funny writer, but *Baby*, Howard Hawks's definitively hilarious screwball comedy, left him in a rather ill humor. "After the first five minutes," he wrote, "we were content to play the game called 'the cliché expert goes to the movies' and we are not at all proud to report that we scored 100 percent." Nugent was willing to entertain the notion that some of his readers were less expert than he, but only facetiously: "Of course, if you've never been to the movies, *Bringing Up Baby* will be all new to you— a zany-ridden product of the goofy farce school. But who hasn't been to the movies?"

Who indeed? At the time, the art form had existed for a little more than a generation; movie reviews had been appearing in *The Times* for a scant quarter century, and talkies had been around for about a decade. But already, it seems, certain things had been done to death, to be resuscitated only on presumption of the audience's perpetual credulity. That much, of course, has not changed; there is surely no critic working today who has not emerged from the screening of a flaccidly naughty comedy or a sanctimoniously uplifting melodrama feeling something akin to Nugent's impatience. As often as not, now as then, the audience shrugs off the reviewer's vitriol and, at least for the few weeks of the picture's theatrical run, tolerates the stale, the familiar and the warmed over. And sometimes the passage of time, which turns novelty to cliché, can also turn cliché back into novelty. If you've never seen *Bringing Up Baby*, in other words (but who hasn't seen

Bringing Up Baby?), you may find yourself amazed at its freshness, its vigor, and its brilliance—qualities undiminished after 65 years and likely to withstand repeated viewings.

There are scores of movies that have outlived the opprobrium of critics and the indifference of audience to become classics, just as there are others that inspired critical rapture and lavish box office at first, only to fade from popular memory as time went by. Both kinds are represented here, as are films whose hold on the collective imagination has never faltered and films that have flickered in the perpetual half-light of cultish adoration. Movies have their fates, and the forces that determine those fates are as mysterious as they are complex, and as various as the movies themselves. Why are some pictures born as trash, only to reveal themselves, years later, to have been works of art all along? Why, on the other hand, do some arrive bedecked in the trappings of art only to end up in the cultural equivalent of flea market bins and curio shelves? Why do some flourish in the eternal sunshine of public adoration, thriving in the endless repetition of television and home-video, while others seem never to find the wide acceptance they deserve?

These are questions for philosophers. And while you will find many varieties of intelligence in these pages— the buoyant smarts of Frank Nugent, the judiciousness of Mordaunt Hall, the easy erudition of Bosely Crowther, the genial wisdom of Vincent Canby, the fierce skepticism of Renata Adler, the sober thoughtfulness of Roger Greenspun, the spirited brightness of Janet Maslin—you will not find much in the way of philosophical rumination. There simply has never been time. For many years, the paper's film critics followed the example of its theater reviewers, rushing back to the newsroom on opening night to compose their thoughts for the next morning's paper. Nowadays the deadlines are a little more forgiving, and reviewers may have as much as a week of reflection between the press screening and the day of release. (The reviews also tend to be longer.) But within that week there will be more movies to see, and the temptation to think deep thoughts or take a long view must be subordinated to the basic tasks of telling readers what the movie is about, and whether they should spend their time and money going to see it.

The performance of these task can sometimes feel like a chore. More often, as will be evident even in a causal perusal of these pages, it is a privilege and a joy. Who doesn't like going to the movies? A little more than a century after they were invented, movies remain the most protean and surprising of the arts. They come to us in every conceivable language, answering, sharpening, and sometimes frustrating our inexhaustible craving for narrative. The camera's eye can capture the grimmest realities and also conjure up the most lavish and extravagant fantasies; it can bring us closer to the world and provide a welcome escape from its rigors. Above all, cinema is a means of communication, a medium through which the range of human experience—the difficult emotions, the piquant absurdities, the heroic possibilities—is shared and expanded.

Favorite movies can be watched again and again, but there is nothing to match the thrill and surprise of seeing them for the first time, and it is this thrill—and, at times, the disappointed anticipation of it—that is captured here, a thousand times over. This list, revised for the new edition to make room for new movies, new critics, and the ongoing evolution of taste, presents the best movies of all time as they were seen for the first time, and thus offers fascinating glimpses of history. What was it like to see *Casablanca* in the first year of World War II, or *The Best Years of Our Lives* the year after the war had ended? How did it feel to be standing on the beach as the successive new waves of the 1960's and 70's—French, British, German, American—crashed ashore? While the *Times* critics only occasionally refer to events taking place offscreen or in other sections of the paper, you can frequently make out the shadowy newsreel images of the 20th century flickering between their lines.

And occasionally, lost in a thousand moments of reverie, we cast our eyes toward the horizon, and wonder how the pictures we are watching will look to future movie-goers. Musing on the decadent, marvelous spectacle of *Fellini Satyricon* and puzzling over its possible meanings, Vincent Canby concluded that "it is a surreal epic that, I confidently believe, will outlive all its interpretations." As will its 999 companions in this book, the moral of which, finally, is that while film critics are only human, the movies are divine.

key to critics

Renata Adler	R.A.
Eugene Archer	E.A.
D. J. R. Bruckner	D.J.R.B.
Tom Buckley	T.B.
Vincent Canby	V.C.
B. R. Crisler	B.R.C.
Bosley Crowther	B.C.
Richard Eder	R.E.
Walter Goodman	W.G.
Roger Greenspun	R.G.
Mordaunt Hall	M.H.
Donal J. Henahan	D.J.H.
Stephen Holden	S.H.
Caryn James	C.J.
Stanley Kauffman	S.K.
Hilton Kramer	H.K.
John T. McManus	J.T.M.
Janet Maslin	J.M.
Elvis Mitchell	E.M.
Frank S. Nugent	F.S.N.
Thomas M. Pryor	T.M.P.
Nora Sayre	N.S.
Harold C. Schonberg	H.C.S.
A. O. Scott	A.O.S.
Andre Sennwald	A.S.
Michael Stern	M.S.
Theodore Strauss	T.S.
Howard Thompson	H.T.
A. H. Weiler	A.W.

À NOUS, LA LIBERTÉ

Written (in French, with English subtitles) and directed by René Clair; cinematographer, Georges Périnal; edited by Mr. Clair and Rene Le Henaff; music by Georges Auric; art designer, Lazare Meerson; produced by Frank Clifford; released by SDFS Films. Black and white. Running time: 104 minutes.

With: Henri Marchand (Emile), Raymond Cordy (Louis), Rolla France (Jeanne), Paul Olivier (The Uncle), Jacques Shelly (Paul), Andre Micaud (The Foreman) and Germaine Aussey (Maud).

It is not astonishing that René Clair's picture, À Nous, la Liberté, which came to the Europa yesterday, mystified its first-night audience in Paris, for one might hazard that this French-language combination of fantasy and realism is like snapshots of a weird dream. The tale itself, M. Clair's own account of two prison pals, first inside and then away from jail, is sufficiently lucid, but the manipulation of the incidents is quite another matter. There is little real dialogue, music being often relied upon to do the "talking." The characters frequently give vent to their thoughts in song, whether they are behind the bars, in a factory, or in a banquet hall. And unlike M. Clair's previous hilarious contribution, *Le Million,* the humor in this new venture, despite its farcical nature, is provocative of thought rather than laughter.

À Nous, la Liberté is assuredly different from any other screen feature. It bristles with strange originality. It almost descends to slapstick in one sequence, but even that is set forth imaginatively. In contradistinction to the skittish happenings, there are the cleverly designed settings for the scenes in both the prison and the factory. This angle of the production is extraordinarily thorough, every detail having received most careful attention.

There have been unique introductory glimpses in many pictures, but M. Clair goes all one better by showing prisoners at work making toy horses, some of the inmates sticking legs into the wooden bodies, others doing the painting, and so forth. Emile and Louis, the principals in this fable, are among those at the long table with a moving section in the center. Following this the convicts are beheld at their evening meal, with the running centerboard on which are the salt, pepper, sugar, and bowls of food from which the prisoners help themselves.

It is really quite a dramatic sequence where Emile and Louis, armed with a grappling iron on the end of a rope, are ready to make their escape from their cell. The window bars have been neatly filed and the two men crawl out of their cell, ready to risk their necks by scaling a high wall. Louis, with the aid of his friend, succeeds in getting away, but before the unfortunate Emile can climb the wall he is caught by the keepers.

M. Clair arranges a neat way for Louis to avoid detection. The convict, once in the street, bowls over a speeding cyclist. While the dazed man is on the ground, Louis, who has disrobed down to his underwear, rides away on the bicycle. And then comes one of the few bits at which the spectators laughed. It is where Louis is greeted by a throng as the winner of the cycling race.

Putting to practice some of the ideas of prison,

Louis, in course of time, becomes a wonderfully wealthy phonograph manufacturer. His appearance is greatly changed by his prosperity. Eventually Emile is freed from prison, and without knowing that his former cellmate is managing director of the factory he succeeds in getting employment in the works. One day Emile is told that he must appear before the managing director, and to his astonishment he sees Louis, who is at first reluctant to admit his identity.

These ex-convicts have a high old time in the factory. In one episode a painting of Louis is used for fractious doings. The prison pals look at the painting and then they throw cakes from a buffet table at it, and they roar with laughter when Louis hurls a stone gin bottle through the center of the canvas.

Louis's labor-saving devices in the factory are beheld in many of the scenes, and in one of the latter interludes he caps all his other ideas by an invention whereby the phonograph parts are assembled automatically after going through a little tunnel.

As for the romantic side of the story, Emile, a dreamy sort of fellow most of the time, falls in love with a girl worker named Jeanne, but she is not interested in him. When Louis hears about this he insists on the match between the two, giving Jeanne's old uncle a check for her dowry. But nothing comes of this forced alliance.

The police ultimately learn that Louis is an escaped convict and he decides to flee with his pal. Louis stocks a bag with banknotes; but during a high wind the bag is blown off a table and opens, and soon the air is filled with 1,000-franc notes and also with the top hats of factory officials who are holding an open-air meeting.

In the final fade-out Louis and Emile have discovered liberty away from prison and work—they are happy tramps, glad to get a few sous with which to buy bread.

Henri Marchand gives a commendable performance as Emile, and Raymond Cordy is capital as the more vigorous Louis. Rolla France is pleasing as Jeanne, and Paul Olivier is excellent as the girl's uncle.
—*M.H., May 18, 1932*

ABOUT SCHMIDT

Directed by Alexander Payne: written by Mr. Payne and Jim Taylor: based on the novel by Louis Begley: director of photography. James Glennon: edited by Kevin Tent: music by Rolfe Kent: production designer. Jane Ann Stewart: produced by Harry Gittes and Michael Besman: released by New Line Cinema. Running time: 125 minutes.

With: Jack Nicholson (Warren Schmidt). Kathy Bates (Roberta Hertzel). Hope Davis (Jeannie). Dermot Mulroney (Randall Hertzel). Howard Hesseman (Larry). Len Cariou (Ray) and June Squibb (Helen Schmidt).

Of all the dramatic transformations Jack Nicholson has undergone in his 44-year screen career, none is more astonishing than his embodiment of a retired, widowed insurance executive from Omaha in Alexander Payne's film *About Schmidt.* Plodding in a weary, stiff-legged shuffle, his shoulders bowed, his features half-frozen into the guarded, sunken expression of someone who has devoted decades of thought to actuarial calculation, his character, Warren Schmidt, is a staid Middle American everyman who finds himself adrift at the precarious age of 66.

Warren may be the least colorful character Mr. Nicholson has ever played on the screen, and the role inspires this great actor's least flamboyant performance. The Mephistophelean eyebrows remain at half-staff, and the ferocious bad-boy grin that has illuminated many of his most famous roles with jagged lightning is stifled.

Instead of flash, what Mr. Nicholson brings to his role is a sorrowful awareness of human complexity whose emotional depth matches anything he has done in the movies before.

About Schmidt, which opens the 40th annual New York Film Festival tonight at Lincoln Center (it is to be released nationally in December), is much more than a character study of a man some might dismiss as bland. The third movie directed by Mr. Payne, who was born in Omaha and set his last film, *Election,* in the same territory, *About Schmidt* lays out an expansive, impressively even-handed vision of life in contemporary Middle America.

Like *Election,* in which a high school political contest became a microcosm of America's hyper-competitive political climate, this film (based on a novel by Louis Begley) reverberates outward in its social implications. The Warren Schmidts of this world and their friends and families, it suggests, constitute a quietly humming, stabilizing collective engine in American society. An out-of-date term that might still be applied to these decent middle-class folk who work hard, respect their neighbors, attend church and obey the law is the Silent Majority.

In *About Schmidt,* as in *Election* and *Citizen Ruth* (the first film this director created with his screenwriting partner, Jim Taylor), the team brilliantly reconciles a double vision of American life. While one eye gazes satirically at the rigid institutions and shopworn rituals that sustain a sense of order and tradition in the heartland, the other views those same institutions with a respectful understanding of their value.

This delicate balancing act echoes those sections of Jonathan Franzen's novel *The Corrections* that are set in a fictionalized St. Louis. The inhabitants of this comfortable, slightly shabby world may have their demons like everybody else, but they tend to keep their disappointment and self-pity inside.

Gregarious and trusting of their neighbors, they don't expect too much out of life and remember to count their blessings at the end of the day. The screenplay has a pitch-perfect ear for the kind of Middle American vernacular typified by one character's fervently emphatic observation about another who died: "She was a fine, fine woman."

Where *Election* was a comedy—along with *Best in Show* probably the finest American screen comedy of the last decade—*About Schmidt,* though often funny (a scene in which Warren tries to cope with a waterbed verges on slapstick), leans in a more bittersweet direction.

Peering into the future, Warren, who has spent his whole adult life calculating the life spans of others, contemplates his remaining years with a mixture of resignation, disappointment and impatience. Alone, with more time on his hands than he ever expected to have, he realizes with a mounting desperation that before he dies, he wants to feel he has made more of a difference in the world than he has so far.

What plunges Warren into this existential crisis is the sudden death of his wife, Helen (June Squibb), whom he discovers lying face down on the carpet she was vacuuming, felled by a cerebral hemorrhage. Earlier in the movie Warren has confessed in a voice over to harboring a growing, secret loathing of this stout, gray-haired woman he has been living with for 42

years. But with Helen gone, he finds himself helpless, unable to cook a meal or keep house. After flailing around for several weeks, he impulsively flees Omaha in the 35-foot Winnebago motor home he and his wife had planned to travel in once he retired.

As Warren barrels along the highway on a circuitous journey that eventually takes him to Denver to attend the wedding of his daughter, Jeannie (Hope Davis), it is impossible not to compare this excursion to the cross-country jaunt Mr. Nicholson made in *Easy Rider* 33 years ago. Where the earlier trip carried the actor into the sunrise of a drug-enlightened future, *About Schmidt* is a psychic journey into the twilight and the past.

True, the contemporary world the movie shows includes designer drugs, hot tubs and sexually emancipated older women. But it is still more like revisiting the 1950's than squinting into the new millennium.

In countless small ways the movie illustrates how Middle American culture absorbs innovation while remaining essentially unchanged in its solid (and some might say smug) sense of its own identity. Take the wedding, in which Jeannie, to her father's stifled fury, seals her vows with Randall Hertzel (Dermot Mulroney), an air-headed waterbed salesman with a penchant for losing his and other investors' shirts in get-rich-quick schemes.

Randall wears his hair in a mullet. His biggest fan is his garrulous twice-divorced mother, Roberta (Kathy Bates), who loudly informs Warren that the bond sealing the newlyweds' happiness is their "white hot" sex life. Her son, she boasts, inherited his healthy sex drive from her. And in one of the movie's funniest scenes, she terrifies Warren by plopping down next to him in a hot tub and waiting for the sparks to fly.

But despite such freewheeling flourishes, the wedding turns out be a conventional affair. As thin, wobbly voices serenade the bride and groom with Dan Fogelberg's "Longer" and Paul Stookey's "Wedding Song (There Is Love)," modern ballads that are every bit as kitschy as the vintage nuptial warhorses "I Love You Truly" and "Oh, Promise Me," the movie shows how the more things change, the more they stay the same.

Once Warren leaves Omaha, *About Schmidt* becomes a robust anecdotal road movie interspersed with voice-overs in which Warren composes letters to Ndugu, a 6-year-old Tanzanian boy he is sponsoring (to the tune of $22 a month) in response to a television pitch by an overseas charity. As Warren writes to the boy, he muses out loud, venting bottled-up frustrations no 6-year-old on any continent could begin to fathom.

If Warren is a decent, well-meaning individual, he is no paragon of psychological health. As a sympathetic woman he meets on the road observes, he is a "sad, sad man." His daughter, to whom he never paid much attention, resents him for his emotional absence over the years, and when he belatedly tries to mend the breach, he is coldly rebuffed. His urge to make a difference crystallizes in a fruitless, self-destructive effort to talk Jeannie out of marrying Randall, who he senses is not good enough for her.

What makes this exquisitely observed slice of American screen realism transcend itself is finally its moral sensibility. The movie's quest to discover how one ordinary person can make more of a difference turns out to be as serious as its title character's. The commonsense answer it comes up with, in a final scene so unassuming that it's almost a throwaway moment, is as simple and modest as it is profoundly moving.

—S.H., September 27, 2002

ABSENCE OF MALICE

Produced and directed by Sydney Pollack; written by Kurt Luedtke; cinematographer, Owen Roizman; edited by Sheldon Kahn; music by Dave Grusin; production designer, Terence Marsh; released by Columbia Pictures. Running time: 116 minutes.

With: Paul Newman (Gallagher), Sally Field (Megan), Bob Balaban (Rosen), Melinda Dillon (Teresa), Luther Adler (Malderone), Barry Primus (Wadell) and Josef Sommer (McAdam).

Sydney Pollack's recent movies have had a lot in common. In *The Way We Were,* in *Three Days of the Condor,* in *The Electric Horseman,* and now in *Absence of Malice,* Mr. Pollack has presented his own contemplative brand of lonely love story. These films may look like romances, but they're about people who never quite fall in love. The characters invariably come from two different worlds. As they meet and make their earnest but futile efforts to reach one another, the action remains cautious, thoughtful, and slow.

What Mr. Pollack's movies lack in momentum, they make up for in quiet gravity. Whether they work well (*The Way We Were*) or fail miserably (*Bobby Deerfield*), these films are soulful and serious, qualities that seem all too rare just now. There's some monotony to Mr. Pollack's approach, and an essential indecisiveness—each of these stories ends on a rueful note rather than a sharply dramatic one. Yet the intelligence of his work is unusual and rewarding, even when that work goes slightly awry.

Absence of Malice, which opens today at Loew's Tower East, would seem to have a tough, controversial subject, because it concerns itself with journalistic impropriety and a gangland killing. But this is a Sydney Pollack film before it's anything else, and it has the pensiveness to prove it. If other recent films have glorified the role of the investigative reporter, this is one that attempts to look closely and rather pessimistically at the profession.

Its heroine, Megan Carter, violates so many basic rules of journalism—from neglecting to check her story to sleeping with the man it is about—that it becomes impossible to view her behavior as representative. And yet, through Megan, the movie is able to raise a number of questions about reportorial tactics and the difference between what is accurate and what is true.

Megan (Sally Field) erroneously reports that Michael Gallagher (Paul Newman), a Florida liquor wholesaler whose father was a gangster, is implicated in the disappearance of a local labor leader. She has been tricked into doing this by a too-eager Government investigator (Bob Balaban) who knows that Gallagher is innocent but would like to pressure him into naming names. As the story grows more and more convoluted, Meg becomes what she describes as "involved" with Gallagher, and meanwhile does inestimable damage to a timid, devout Catholic woman (Melinda Dillon) who is not Gallagher's lover but his close friend.

Mr. Pollack's movies are often field days for the actors involved, and that is particularly true of *Absence of Malice.* Every performance from the large supporting cast—Mr. Balaban, Miss Dillon, Barry Primus, Josef Sommer, Don Hood, Luther Adler, and the scene-stealing Wilford Brimley, who is even more satisfyingly righteous at the end of this film than he was in the last moments of *The China Syndrome*—is extremely good. They're able to be because the scenes, as written by an ex-journalist, Kurt Luedtke, concentrate less heavily on moving the plot along than they do on giving everyone enough to do.

Even when the action seems wrongheaded—and it frequently does—the movie is richly textured and well played. Miss Field's big scene with Miss Dillon, for instance, shows the reporter behaving abominably from both a professional standpoint and a personal one, yet the sequence is a strong one anyhow. "I'm used to dealing with girlfriends," Miss Field says patronizingly, and proceeds to extract a painfully intimate confession from the other woman. She then threatens to print it, and has no patience for Miss Dillon's plea that this story will ruin her. "It's 1981. People will understand," Miss Field says carelessly. Nobody understands less than she.

Miss Field is in the unenviable position of having to play a hardboiled, unsympathetic woman whose behavior is sufficiently reckless to raise questions about whether she ought to be employed anywhere, let alone in a big-city newsroom. Even the scenes designed to make Megan more likable—as when Gallagher comes to visit her in the emptily modern apartment where she lives alone—don't soften the character, nor does the occasional misplaced kittenishness that Miss Field brings to the role. It doesn't help that the film's attitude about Megan's actions is understandably, but damagingly, indefinite. In another movie, someone like Megan might well be presented as a villain. In this one, a scene in which Gallagher wants to do her physical harm is tempered before it can get out of hand, even though his desire for a violent reprisal has become very understandable.

As for Gallagher, he is one of Mr. Newman's better characters in years, played so close to the vest that he never offers an extra syllable and eventually outsmarts everyone else in the story. Thanks to the plot's complexity and the painstaking fashion in which it is detailed for the audience, that seems quite an accomplishment. Even the foolish or misguided figures in the story are too thoughtful to be easily outsmarted.

—*J.M., November 19, 1981*

ADAM'S RIB

Directed by George Cukor: written by Ruth Gordon and Garson Kanin: cinematographer, George Folsey: edited by George Boemler: music by Miklos Rozsa: art designers, Cedric Gibbons and William Ferrari: produced by Lawrence Weingarten: released by Metro-Goldwyn-Mayer: Black and white. Running time: 101 minutes.

With: Spencer Tracy (Adam Bonner), Katharine Hepburn (Amanda Bonner), Judy Holliday (Doris Attinger), Tom Ewell (Warren Attinger), David Wayne (Kip Lurie), Jean Hagen (Beryl Caighn) and Hope Emerson (Olympia La Pere).

It has been seven years since Spencer Tracy and Katharine Hepburn played *Woman of the Year*, in which they got great good fun and wisdom out of a husband-wife rivalry. People still think of it fondly—including their studio, M-G-M, which obviously thought of it so fondly that it decided to try again. And that it has done, with equal humor and what should surely be comparable success, in *Adam's Rib*, a bang-up frolic, which came to the Capitol yesterday.

But don't let the basic resemblance lead you to suppose that you're going to see the same picture. And see it you certainly should. For not only have Ruth Gordon and Garson Kanin prepared a novel script for this new husband-wife fandango, but Metro has lined up a cast of brand-new supporting players which deserves a private triumph of its own. Headed by Judy Holliday, the girl who arrived sensationally as a Broadway stage performer in the Kanin farce *Born Yesterday*, and ably abetted by Tom Ewell, also from Broadway, this cast deserves as much credit as the wonderful Tracy-Hepburn team. With George Cukor deftly directing, one couldn't ask for more.

However, our first thanks this morning should go to the authors of the script, for they are the chief ones responsible for the pleasures of *Adam's Rib*. It is their delightful improvising on a nimble and fragile little tale of a violent courtroom rivalry between a lawyer-husband and his lawyer-wife that makes this current picture bounce and spin with thorough glee.

Taking a happy couple who are well settled in their careers and presumably wholly acquainted with each other's eccentricities, Miss Gordon and Mr. Kanin, who also are husband and wife, mix up their charming people by a far-fetched but clever device. They make the husband the prosecutor of a woman who has shot her spouse and they make the wife defense counsel for this miserably unhappy dame. And then they introduce a question of female equality between the two and let them fight it out roundly in the courtroom and in their home.

To be sure, the plot is a frail one and the argument is not profound. As a matter of fact, it gets quite fuzzy and vagrant as the picture goes along. And that is the one plain weakness of the whole thing: it is but a spoof, and the authors are forced to wild devices and shallow nonsense to wind it up. But en route they contrive some grand theatrics, which are all in the motion picture's range, to make for lively entertainment and passing comment on the home's felicities.

As we say, Mr. Tracy and Miss Hepburn are the stellar performers in this show and their perfect compatibility in comic capers is delightful to see. A line thrown away, a lifted eyebrow, a smile, or a sharp, resounding slap on a tender part of the anatomy is as natural as breathing to them. Plainly, they took great pleasure in playing this rambunctious spoof.

And Miss Holliday as the woman who slightly punctures her spouse for a bit of deliberate "cheating" and thus has to stand court trial is a simply hilarious representation of a dumb but stubborn dame. Her perfect New Yorkisms, her blank looks, her pitiful woes are as killingly funny—and as touching—as anything we've had in farce this year. Mr. Ewell as her husband is likewise deliciously droll, making of this loutish fellow a full-bodied character. David Wayne as a neighborly lounge-lizard is a glib but slightly too pat type, and Clarence Kolb makes some wonderful faces as a bewildered and unhappy judge.

Of *Adam's Rib* we might say, in short, that it isn't solid food but it certainly is meaty and juicy and comically nourishing.

—*B.C., December 26, 1949*

ADAPTATION

Directed by Spike Jonze: written by Charlie Kaufman and Donald Kaufman, based on the book *The Orchid Thief* by Susan Orlean: director of photog-raphy. Lance Acord: edited by Eric Zumbrunnen: music by Carter Burwell: production designer. KK Barrett: produced by Edward Saxon. Vincent Landay and Jonathan Demme: released by Columbia Pictures. Running time: 112 minutes.

With: Nicholas Cage (Charlie Kaufman/Donald Kaufman). Meryl Streep (Susan Orlean). Chris Cooper (John Laroche). Tilda Swinton (Valerie). Cara Seymour (Amelia). Brian Cox (Robert McKee). Judy Greer (Alice the Waitress). Maggie Gyllenhaal (Caroline). Ron Livingston (Marty) and Jay Tavare (Matthew Osceola).

More than once in the week after I saw *Adaptation,* I found myself suddenly awake in the middle of the night, pulse racing, fretting over the movie's intricate, fascinating themes. Since quite a few of the films I see have a decidedly soporific effect, those bouts of insomnia might in themselves be sufficient grounds for recommending this one. But my sleeplessness was edged with panic; it seemed to mirror the frantic anxiety that the hero of *Adaptation,* a screenwriter named Charlie Kaufman, suffers as he struggles to complete a script based on *The Orchid Thief* by Susan Orlean, a writer for *The New Yorker.*

At the paranoid hour of 3 in the morning, I wondered if Kaufman's towering writer's block might be contagious. As the deadline for this review approached, I pictured myself in his agitated state, pacing the floor in a sweat, muttering nonsense into a handheld tape recorder and then desperately stalling my impatient editors: "It's coming along. Really. You'll have something soon. No problem."

I realize that the fear of contracting writer's block from a fictional character is crazy, but in the brilliantly scrambled, self-consuming world of *Adaptation,* which opens today nationwide, it has a certain plausibility. After all, one of the movie's reigning conceits is that the boundary between reality and representations of it—between life and art, if you want—is highly porous, maybe even altogether imaginary. Another is that obsessive manias—for instance, the passion for certain forms of plant life that afflicts some of the characters—reproduce themselves like madly pollinating wildflowers.

According to the credits, someone named Charlie Kaufman did indeed write—or at least helped to write—the screenplay for *Adaptation,* which indeed is billed as based on "The Orchid Thief," the true story of a renegade horticulturalist, John Laroche. The encounters between Mr. Laroche and Ms. Orlean frame the book's excursions into Darwinian theory, Florida ecology and the history of orchid collecting. Many of these elements, by the way, are faithfully reconstructed in the movie. Mr. Kaufman's flailing attempts to honor the nuances and implications of Ms. Orlean's dense, elusive, intellectual mystery story are interwoven with a retelling of that story, until finally the two plots collide, overlap and blow each other to smithereens (along with the viewer's mind).

But all of this is much too straightforward. Yes *Adaptation* is, most obviously, a movie about itself, as gleefully self-referential an exercise in auto-deconstruction as you could wish. But it is also, more deeply, a movie about its own nonexistence—a narrative that confronts both the impossibility and the desperate necessity of storytelling, and that short circuits our expectations of coherence, plausibility and fidelity to lived reality even as it satisfies them. Common sense suggests that there could never be such a movie, but if there could, it would have to be one of the slipperiest, most fascinating and, by any sane reckoning, best movies of the year.

In their first collaboration, *Being John Malkovich,* Mr. Kaufman and Spike Jonze, the director of *Adaptation,* concocted a deft and dizzy trompe l'oeil brain teaser that, for all its kinetic inventiveness, had a surprising sweetness and intensity of feeling. Like *Adaptation,* it was a movie about creative insecurity, misbegotten love and the traps of identity. Its characters were drawn together by an itchy desire to shed their own skins, a longing made hilariously literal by their discovery of a secret passageway into Mr. Malkovich's brain.

Adaptation, picks up, literally, where *Malkovich* left off: on the set of the earlier picture, where Charlie Kaufman skulks around in a neurotic funk. But while Mr. Malkovich, in a cameo, reappears playing himself (a role for which he won the best supporting actor award from the New York Film Critics Circle), Mr. Kaufman is played here by Nicolas Cage. And so is the second credited screenwriter of *Adaptation,* Charlie Kaufman's twin brother, Donald.

Mr. Cage and Mr. Jonze share a casual, daredevil sensibility, and the two of them—or should I say the three of them?—pull off one of the most amazing technical stunts in recent film history. It's not just that Mr. Cage plays two fractious, unsettled characters, who each become more complicated as the picture vaults and scrambles toward its conclusion, or that Mr. Jonze manages to place them seamlessly together in the frame. It's more that these acts of bravura seem to be no big deal. For much of the movie, you are watching a single actor portray a prickly, tender sibling dynamic with himself, and yet after a while this astonishing feat seems as matter of fact as color film or synchronized sound (which were once, of course, astonishments in their own right).

Whether or not Donald Kaufman really exists (and there is not much evidence, other than this movie, that he does), he and his brother embody the antithetical impulses that haunt any writer. Charlie, nearly paralyzed by his dread of cliché and convention, sees his profession as an exacting, exalted search for truth. He wears his terrible awkwardness—with his would-be girlfriend (Cara Seymour), with a willowy producer (Tilda Swinton), with himself—like a badge of authenticity. The hapless Donald, who is freeloading at his twin's house, appears happily shallow and serenely untroubled by such concerns.

Although Charlie ridicules Donald's use of movie industry jargon ("Don't say industry," he snaps), Donald decides to try his hand at screenwriting. While his brother tears out his hair over *The Orchid Thief,* Donald churns out a serial-killer script so utterly derivative as to be a surefire six-figure sale (and sparks a happy, bawdy romance with a makeup technician played by Maggie Gyllenhaal).

He also attends seminars conducted by the screenwriting guru Robert McKee, whose rigorously structural approach to storytelling Charlie disdains. Later, in desperation, Charlie will turn to McKee, ripely impersonated by Brian Cox, for salvation, and will get an earful of self-help exhortation. "For God's sake, don't use a deus ex machina!," McKee thunders, perhaps fully aware that he is one.

Meanwhile, Susan Orlean (played with impish composure by Meryl Streep) falls in with Laroche (Chris Cooper), a haunted, antic autodidact who has been arrested for poaching rare orchids from a Florida swamp. The contrast of their backgrounds and temperaments, hinted at in Ms. Orlean's book, is wittily realized by Ms. Streep and Mr. Cooper, whose lank-haired, toothless charisma also resonates with Mr. Cage's improbable magnetism.

As the stories unfold in counterpoint, seesawing back and forth in time, ideas pop up like flowers blossoming crazily in timelapse photographs. It would be futile to try to account for all of them, but the effect is both exhilarating and a little stressful, like a graduate seminar in philosophy conducted by a slightly mad professor, and then edited down into an extralong episode of MTV's "Real World."

After it's over, you will want to keep arguing about it, if only in the relative safety of your own brain. The last part—what McKee's acolytes might call the "third act"—stages a formal death match between Donald's approach to storytelling and Charlie's, and sends Orlean and Laroche on to adventures undreamed of in the pages of *The New Yorker* (though they are, by Hollywood standards, perfectly predictable).

Some may find the ending rushed, inconclusive or cynical. I thought its lack of easy resolution was proof of the film's haphazard, devil-may-care integrity, and its bow to conventional sentiment a mark of sincerity.

At one point in *The Orchid Thief,* Ms. Orlean asks a park ranger named Tony why he thinks people find orchids so seductive. His answer matches both the nonchalance and the insight of this remarkable, impossible film: "Oh, mystery, beauty, unknowability, I suppose. Besides, I think the real reason is that life has no meaning. I mean, no obvious meaning. You wake up, you go to work, you do stuff. I think everybody's always looking for something a little unusual that can preoccupy them and help pass the time."

Charlie Kaufman could hardly have said it better, though perhaps his brother Donald might have.

—*A.O.S., December 6, 2002*

THE ADJUSTER

Written and directed by Atom Egoyan; director of photography, Paul Sarossy; edited by Susan Shipton; music by Mychael Danna; production designers, Linda Del Rosario and Richard Harris; produced by Camelia Frieberg; released by Orion Classics. Running time: 102 minutes.

With: Elias Koteas (Noah), Arsinée Khanjian (Hera), Maury Chaykin (Bubba), Gabrielle Rose (Mimi), Jennifer Dale (Arianne), David Hemblen (Bert), Rose Sarkisyan (Seta) and Armen Kokorian (Simon).

Atom Egoyan, the director of *The Adjuster,* takes quiet glee in laying out the individual elements of his film as if they were clues in a detective story or pieces of a puzzle. Mr. Egoyan, whose earlier *Speaking Parts and Family Viewing* employed a similar method, finds even greater satisfaction in the off-balance, mischievously witty way in which those pieces finally fit together.

With an approach like this, it isn't likely—or even necessary—that the final effect will be as fascinating as the deadpan, perfectly controlled manner in which the filmmaker permits information to be released. What matters is that Mr. Egoyan directs with utter confidence in a style that grows more polished and accessible with each new effort, and is unmistakably his own.

A fire scene. A screening room. A motel. A subway car, on which a rich woman makes herself available to a sobbing and thankful derelict. A brand-new house in the absolute middle of nowhere. These are some of the ingredients with which Mr. Egoyan, in typically solemn and elliptical fashion, allows *The Adjuster* to begin. Only gradually does the connective tissue begin to appear. The screening room is where Hera (the beautiful Arsinée Khanjian, who is this director's frequent leading lady and also his wife) works as a censor. The fire scene is where her husband, Noah (Elias Koteas), the insurance adjuster of the title, comforts a new client in a manner that is not entirely reassuring. As Noah is fond of saying, "You may not feel it, but you're in a state of shock."

Mr. Egoyan, who wrote the screenplay, has as much fun with his dialogue as he does in naming his characters. Noah is, he says, "just sorting things out, deciding what has value and what doesn't." Hera replies: "I know what you mean. It's the same thing I do."

The process of classification, as conducted by Hera and her intensely businesslike associates, is carried to bizarre extremes. (In long shot, in a library-like setting, Hera's colleagues are seen sifting gravely through enormous bins of porn.) Meanwhile, Noah goes to his own extremes in serving as a savior to those who have been figuratively cast adrift by disaster. A motel is populated solely by Noah's appreciative clients, some of whom go to extraordinary lengths to express their gratitude.

Noah makes house calls here not only for sexual purposes (at one point he discusses itemization and deductions while in the heat of passion) but also to study photographic evidence by which he reconstructs the value of his clients' past lives. "Was this a pure-bred?" he somberly asks two gay men who have lost their dog. "This is your bedroom?" he inquires studiously, when one of these men provocatively hands over a set of sexually explicit photographs. "These don't show too much of the background."

Also in the film and (it is eventually revealed) on a collision course with Noah and Hera are Bubba (Maury Chaykin) and Mimi (Gabrielle Rose), the wealthy couple who posed as derelict and dilettante on the subway and who go through numerous other dress-up games before the film is over. Bubba eventually becomes obsessed with the isolated house, as beached as the Ark, in which Noah and Hera live. "They have everything they want, or they have the means to have everything they want, but they don't know what they need," it is explained about Bubba and Mimi. "So they try different things, and this house is one of them." Having Mimi dress up as a cheerleader before a squad of utterly impassive, bored-looking football players turns out to be another.

The mournful music and the autumnal tone of *The Adjuster* allow Mr. Egoyan, a Cairo-born filmmaker of Armenian descent who now works in Canada, to incorporate all manner of mythological references, strange parallels, and even terrible puns into the film's seemingly serious mood. "I've had people with warts covering their entire soles," says a doctor who removes one from Hera's foot. The film also pays fairly serious attention to the question of why people sing in the shower.

That substance remains secondary to intriguing style here is borne out by the film's seemingly humorous listing of alphabetical categories of censorship from A through H. In fact, these guidelines, from the Ontario Board of Classification, are real. But in the blithely skewed context of Mr. Egoyan's film, they are made to seem otherwise.

The Adjuster will be shown tonight and tomorrow as part of the New York Film Festival.

—J.M., September 26, 1991

THE ADVENTURES OF ROBIN HOOD

Directed by Michael Curtiz and William Keighley; written by Norman Reilly Raine and Seton I. Miller, based on the novel *Ivanhoe* by Sir Walter Scott and the opera Robin Hood by De Koven-Smith; cinematographers, Sol Polito and Tony Gaudio; edited by Ralph Dawson; music by Erich Wolfgang Korngold; art designer, Carl Jules Weyl; produced by Hal B. Wallis; released by Warner Brothers. Running time: 102 minutes.

With: Errol Flynn (Robin Hood), Olivia de Havilland (Maid Marian), Basil Rathbone (Sir Guy of Gisbourne), Claude Rains (Prince John), Ian Hunter (Richard the Lion-Hearted), Eugene Pallette (Friar Tuck), Alan Hale (Little John), Melville Cooper (High Sheriff of Nottingham), Patric Knowles (Will Scarlett), Herbert Mundin (Much, the Miller's Son), Una O'Connor (Bess), Montagu Love (Bishop of Black Canon) and Robert Noble (Sir Ralf).

Life and the movies have their compensations and such a film as *The Adventures of Robin Hood*, which the Warners brought into the Music Hall yesterday, is payment in full for many dull hours of picture going. A richly produced, bravely bedecked, romantic and colorful show, it leaps boldly to the forefront of this year's best and can be calculated to rejoice the eights, rejuvenate the eighties, and delight those in between.

Few storybooks have been more brilliantly brought to life, page for page, chapter for chapter, derring-do for derring-do than this full-colored recounting of the fabulous deeds of legend's arch-archer, Sir Robin of Locksley. In Errol Flynn, Sir Robin of Sherwood Forest has found his man, a swashbuckler from peaked cap to pointed toe, defiant of his enemies and England's, graciously impudent with his lady love, quick for a fight or a frolic. Mr. Flynn is not the acrobatic Robin Douglas Fairbanks was some years ago. He doesn't slide down tapestries or vault his balustrades with the Fairbanks pere's abandon. But he moves swiftly when there's need and Guy of Gisbourne rues it.

Ay, and so do the Sheriff of Nottingham, that caitiff rogue, and Prince John whose Norman dogs are growling over Saxon bones while Lion-Hearted

Richard is captive of Leopold of Austria. Fortunate for England it was that Sir Robin became Robin Hood, the outlaw, and banded his merry men in Sherwood and robbed the rich to give to the poor. And fortunate for the Maid Marian was it to find such a wooer to free her from black-browed Sir Guy. And still more fortunate it was that Richard came home again, as John was seizing the throne, to acknowledge the men in Lincoln green, drive out the traitors, and celebrate the triumph of the gray goose shaft.

For here, romantics, is a tale of high adventure, wherein blood is spilled and arrows fly, villains scowl and heroes smile, swords are flashed and traitors die— a tale of action, pageantry, brave words, and comic byplay. Norman Reilly Raine and Seton I. Miller have studied their legend well and written of it knowingly. Michael Curtiz and William Keighley have kept that flavor in their direction, giving the action its head, turning their eye-pleasing Technicolor cameras upon the brightest episodes in Robin's bold career.

Nor can we find a fault with the cast. Friar Tuck, that gallant trencherman, has Eugene Pallette's gusty presence. Little John, who thwacked Robin's pate with the quarter-staff, is Alan Hale, and happily. Maid Marian has the grace to suit Olivia de Havilland. Much-the-Miller's Son has fallen to Herbert Mundin. And, on the side of villainy, we have such foilsports as Basil Rathbone as Guy of Gisbourne, Claude Rains as the treacherous Prince John, Melville Cooper as the blustering High Sheriff, Montagu Love as the evil Bishop of Black Canon. Deep-dyed they are, and how the children's matinees will hiss them! We couldn't. We enjoyed them all too much.

—*F.S.N., May 13, 1938*

AFFLICTION

Directed by Paul Schrader; written by Mr. Schrader, based on the novel by Russell Banks; director of photography, Paul Sarossy; edited by Jay Rabinowitz; music by Michael Brook; production designer, Anne Pritchard; produced by Linda Reisman; released by Lions Gate Films. Running time: 114 minutes.

With: Nick Nolte (Wade Whitehouse), Sissy Spacek (Margie Fogg), James Coburn (Glen Whitehouse), Willem Dafoe (Rolfe Whitehouse), Mary Beth Hurt (Lillian), Jim True (Jack Hewitt), Brigid Tierney (Jill) and Marian Seldes (Alma Pittman).

The powder keg in the small New Hampshire town has a name: Wade Whitehouse, keeper of the peace. As played with fierce, anguished intensity by Nick Nolte, who gives the performance of his career in Paul Schrader's quietly stunning new film, Wade works part time as Lawford's policeman and knows that his hardest job is policing himself. But during the devastating course of *Affliction,* Wade begins losing a lifelong struggle with his army of demons, and his carapace starts to crack. With gut-wrenching pity, the film watches pressures mount until Wade explodes.

Affliction is adapted, as "The Sweet Hereafter" was, from a penetratingly astute, grief-tinged novel by Russell Banks, whose stirring voice is much in evidence here. But its story is also well suited to Mr. Schrader, who finds in Wade's suffering a workaday *Taxi Driver* in the snow. Mr. Schrader coaxes forth the oppressive forces around Wade until they achieve microcosmic fullness, ranging from childhood beatings by his father to the covert economic rape of a working-class town. Though ponderous literary voice-overs (from Willem Dafoe as Wade's brother) provide armchair psychology, the film is about much subtler signposts on the road to destruction.

Forgoing any fanfare beyond the mournful strains of Michael Brook's score, Mr. Schrader has made a film that needs to be watched carefully. He gives it the deliberate plainness that makes every small exchange matter. It begins, for instance, with Wade trying to entertain his doleful little daughter Jill (Brigid Tierney) on Halloween. As they drive through Lawford, the girl (who is comfortable with neither the town nor her father) asks Wade if he ever engaged in Halloween vandalism and says she thinks that he used to be bad. Forcing the smile that will soon desert him, Wade tries to give a kindly, fatherly answer, but he can't. The voice of Wade's own raging father is still too loud.

In a shockingly savage performance, James Coburn rampages through the film as alcoholic Glen Whitehouse, the man who first cowed Wade into submission. Jumpy black-and-white flashbacks depict Glen's viciousness as this family's most fundamental fact of life and capture the terror of being a small boy at Glen's mercy. These glimpses of the past are juxtaposed with Wade's habit of not making waves, either on the job or with the few people who care about him, unless something pushes him off balance. The first such shove here: betrayal by Jill, who has her angry mother (Mary Beth Hurt) come rescue her from Wade's Halloween. "She never talks about you," Jill says with a shrug to Wade about his ex-wife.

Frozen into a posture of crucifixion as he plays crossing guard next morning, watching over every child except his own, Wade is further humiliated by a speeding hotshot in an expensive car. New money hovers around bleak little Lawford, as personified by this driver and his father-in-law. The older man, a powerful union official from Massachusetts, comes to Lawford just for the hunting, and on that very day is being guided through the woods by Jack Hewitt (Jim True), a smooth young man whose complacency rankles Wade. Alone with Jack, the union man is mysteriously killed, and suddenly Wade is one more inch off balance as he tries to investigate the shooting.

The most dangerous threat to Wade comes when, after trying to rekindle his relationship with a sweet, patient waitress named Margie (Sissy Spacek, luminous as ever), he takes her to his parents' home and stumbles into an unimaginable nightmare. Glen, now old and infirm but no less monstrous, is too chronically drunk to acknowledge the death of his wife upstairs, whom he always ignored anyway. Though Wade tries, with Margie's help, to deal sanely with Glen even when it comes to this catastrophe, it's too late. The son has been drawn within range of his father's blistering contempt, and finally made to face his longhidden fury. This time there will be no getting away.

Mr. Schrader guides *Affliction* through these momentous events in a spare, sorrowful spirit that exposes their universality. Like *The Sweet Hereafter,* a more meditative and elegant but less immediate, volcanic film, *Affliction* finds the deeper meaning in an all too believable tragedy. In Wade's story, of the strong trampling the weak and of a man suppressing every need and impulse until he collapses beneath his burden, *Affliction* succeeds in finding something larger than one man's misery. Like, *Hilary and Jackie, A Simple Plan, The General,* and *A Civil Action,* it turns dark truthfulness into the cinematic sentiment most worth celebrating this season.

—*J.M., December 30, 1998*

THE AFRICAN QUEEN

Directed by John Huston: written by James Agee and Mr. Huston, based on the novel by C. S. Forester: cinematographer, Jack Cardiff: edited by Ralph Kemplen: music by Allan Gray: produced by Sam Spiegel: released by United Artists. Running time: 105 minutes.

With: Humphrey Bogart (Charlie Allnut), Katharine Hepburn (Rose Sayer), Robert Morley (Reverend Samuel Sayer), Peter Bull (Captain of the Louisa), Theodore Bikel (First Officer of the Louisa) and Peter Swanick (German Army Officer).

Whether C.S. Forester had his salty British tongue in his cheek when he wrote his extravagant story of romance and adventure, *The African Queen,* we wouldn't be able to tell you. But it is obvious—to us, at least—that director John Huston was larking when he turned the novel into a film.

His lively screen version of it, which came to the Capitol yesterday with Katharine Hepburn and Humphrey Bogart in its two predominant roles, is a slick job of movie hoodwinking with a thoroughly implausible romance, set in a frame of wild adventure that is as whopping as its tale of offbeat love. And the main tone and character of it are in the area of the well-disguised spoof.

This is not noted with disfavor. Considering the nature of the yarn, it is hard to conceive its presentation in any other way—that is, in the realistic channels of the motion picture screen. For Mr. Forester's fable of love suddenly taking bloom in the hearts of a lady missionary and a Cockney rumpot while they're trying to escape down a German East African river in a wheezy steam-launch during World War I is so personally preposterous and socially bizarre that it would take a lot of doing to be made convincing in the cold, clear light of day. In the brilliance of Technicolor and with adventure intruding at every turn, any attempt at serious portrayal would be not only incongruous but absurd.

And so Mr. Huston merits credit for putting this fantastic tale on a level of sly, polite kidding and generally keeping it there, while going about the happy business of engineering excitement and visual thrills. His lady, played by Miss Hepburn with her crisp flair for comedy, is a caricature of a prissy female in her high choke collar, linen duster, and limp cloth hat. And his man, played by Mr. Bogart, is a virtual burlesque of the tropical tramp, just one cut—and that a very thin one—above the ripe meatiness of the clown. Not since Elsa Lanchester and Charles Laughton appeared in a very similar picture, *The Beachcomber,* several years ago, have the incongruities of social station and manners been so pointedly and humorously portrayed.

"Mr. Allnut—dear—what's your first name?" the lady politely inquires of her companion the morning after she has apparently submitted to him, in what is perhaps the screen's least lustful and least likely seduction scene. "Charlie," he beams, with melting coyness. It is that anomalous and droll.

Not all of it, however. Mr. Huston and his writer, James Agee, who assisted him in the preparation of the deliberately wordy script, have let the yarn slide onto the mud flats of heavy drama that Mr. Forester laid down, and while it is in that situation, they have let it become soggy in plot and mood. After running impossible rapids, eluding a German fort, and keeping the romance skipping nimbly on the sur face of sly absurdity, they have grounded their picture on a barrier of sudden solemnity and sanded it in with emotions that are neither buoyant nor credible. No wonder the fantastic climax that is abruptly and sentimentally contrived appears the most fulsome melodrama, unworthy of Mr. Huston and this film.

However, while it is skipping—and that is most of the time—there is rollicking fun and gentle humor in this outlandish *African Queen.* There's nothing subtle or moralistic, mind you, outside of the jesting display that nature's most formidable creature is a serene and self-righteous dame.

Without two accomplished players, Mr. Huston could never have achieved his highly audacious purpose of a virtually two-character film, but Miss Hepburn and Mr. Bogart are entirely up to their jobs, outside of their lack of resemblance to the nationals they're said to be. Robert Morley is briefly effective as the lady's missionary brother who conveniently dies, and Peter Bull struts and puffs for one sequence as the captain of a German gunboat on an African lake.

For the rest, there is beauty and excitement in the lush and colorful scenes of a broad and forbidding African river, its foaming white rapids and falls, and the various birds and animals that live on the banks and in the stream. Mr. Huston went right to Africa for this genuine atmosphere. While the hardships were said to be oppressive, he and his producer, S. P. Eagle [Sam Spiegel], have been repaid. Their picture is doubly provided with the insurance of popularity.

—B.C., February 21, 1952

L'AGE D'OR

Directed and edited by Luis Buñuel; written (in French, with English subtitles) by Mr. Buñuel and Salvador Dalí; cinematographer, Albert Dubergen; music by Richard Wagner, Felix Mendelssohn, Ludwig van Beethoven and Claude Debussy; produced by Le Vicomte de Noailles; released by Corinth Films. Black and white. Running time: 60 minutes.

With: Lya Lys (The Woman), Gaston Modot (The Man), Max Ernst (The Bandit Chief) and Pierre Prévert (Bandit).

DIARY OF A CHAMBERMAID

Directed by Luis Buñuel; written (in French, with English subtitles) by Mr. Buñuel, Jean-Claude Carrière and Octave Mirbeau, based on the novel by Mr. Mirbeau; cinematographer, Roger Follous; edited by Louisette Hautecoeur; production designer, Georges Wakhévitch; produced by Michel Safra and Serge Silberman; released by Ciné-Alliance. Running time: 101 minutes.

With: Jeanne Moreau (Celestine), Georges Géret (Joseph), Daniel Ivernel (Captain Mauger), Françoise Lugagne (Madame Monteil), Muni (Marianne), Jean Ozenne (Monsieur Rabour) and Michel Piccoli (Monsieur Monteil).

The New York Film Festival, persisting in its search for a sensation, dug into the vaults last night for *L'Age d'Or,* a much-censored thirty-four-year-old classic by Luis Buñuel.

It was an all-Buñuel evening at Philharmonic Hall,

with the outrageous old surrealistic comedy followed by his brand-new French version of *Diary of a Chambermaid.* This double dose of old-guard moviemaking drew a sellout crowd to both shows at the 2,500-seat auditorium, but disappointment was in the air.

Perhaps too much was expected from the celebrated Spanish director of *Viridiana* and *The Young and the Damned.* Teaming him with France's finest actress, Jeanne Moreau, sounded like a good idea, since her erotic gifts would seem an ideal complement to Mr. Buñuel's well-known penchant for perverse themes. No one was quite prepared for the tepid result.

As for L'Age d'Or, this widely discussed scandal film had been preceded by such a formidable critical reputation that it could scarcely have lived up to expectations.

This 1930 attack on the conventions of society, with particular emphasis on organized religion, was banned in most parts of the world. Its previous screenings abroad were mostly limited to private showings at film clubs and museums, but many critical histories accord it a high place.

The film is still an eye-opener. Its intentions are entirely clear from an early scene. A ceremony commemorating the founding of the Eternal City of Rome is interrupted by a pair of uninhibited lovers writhing in the mud. When the scandalized spectators pull them apart, the frustrated male gives a watching dog a well-aimed kick.

Mr. Buñuel and his coscenarist, none other than Salvador Dalí, have packed just about every surrealist symbol they could think of into this rebellious epic. Their lovers are prevented by society from satisfying their natural instincts.

Finally the hero, called to the telephone from a garden rendezvous, strides furiously to an upstairs window and throws out a donkey, a plow, a feather pillow, and an archbishop. A knowledge of Freud is not necessary to get the point.

Since the filmmakers are catholic in their protest, indiscriminately opposing all forms of social conventions rather than specific establishments, it is difficult to take offense. At this late date, the film's outstanding quality is not its defiance of traditional mores but its wit, which is savage, scabrous, and frequently hilarious. It is no more shocking than Dada.

If *L'Age d'Or* proved less than a sensation at Lincoln Center, it was in part because of its method of presentation. A French-language print was shown without subtitles, and a translator's voice barraged the auditorium over a loudspeaker, drowning the original soundtrack. It was not the happiest solution to the dubbing problem.

Sadly, the intervening decades seem to have weakened Mr. Buñuel's powers. His new adaptation of Octave Mirbeau's *Diary of a Chambermaid* suffers in comparison with the strange but memorable version Jean Renoir did with Paulette Goddard in 1946.

He has used the story of a worldly-wise domestic in a weird country household as a background for his comment on the changing French social structure before World War I. The provincial château is rife with old-fashioned quirks and perversions—a shoe fetishist, a servant-chasing master, a reluctant wife, a sinister overseer who rapes and murders a little girl.

A subdued Miss Moreau gives an able performance as the maid with idiosyncrasies of her own, but she is not aided by unsympathetic direction. Mr. Buñuel has photographed her harshly and scorned any background music that might accentuate her dramatic effects. It seems an ungrateful way to treat a brilliant star whose subtly modulated acting gives meaning to an unresolved and ambiguous script.

— *E.A., September 22, 1964*

AGUIRRE, THE WRATH OF GOD

Produced, written (in German, with English subtitles) and directed by Werner Herzog; director of photography, Thomas Mauch; edited by Beate Mainka-Jellinghaus; music by Popol Vuh; released by New Yorker Films. Running time: 90 minutes.

With: Klaus Kinski (Don Lope de Aguirre), Ruy Guerra (Don Pedro de Ursua), Del Negro (Brother Gaspar de Carvajal), Helena Rojo (Inez) and Cecilia Rivera (Flores).

In 1560, not quite twenty years after the death of Francisco Pizarro, who had conquered Peru for Spain, an elaborately provisioned party of conquistadores set out from Quito to find the land of El Dorado. It was a fearful journey first to cross the Andes but even worse on the other side. Those who didn't starve, drown, or die of fever in the Amazon jungles were in constant danger of being killed by Indians.

When it became apparent the entire expedition could not go on, a small task force was commissioned to continue down the Amazon for a week. In command were Pedro de Ursua and his aide, Lope de Aguirre, sometimes referred to in history books as Aguirre the Madman or Aguirre the Traitor. They never returned.

Exactly what happened afterward is unclear but it seems that Aguirre murdered Ursua, declared the little band's independence from Spain, and crowned a man named Fernando de Guzman, the ranking nobleman among them, "Emperor of El Dorado." He eventually murdered Guzman and was himself murdered by his own men when they at last reached South America's northeast coast.

This story, one of the more bizarre and bloody footnotes to the history of the Spanish conquests, is the basis for Werner Herzog's absolutely stunning 1972 German film, *Aguirre, the Wrath of God,* which opened yesterday at the D. W. Griffith Theater. The movie was shot by Mr. Herzog (*The Mystery of Kaspar Hauser, The Great Ecstasy of the Sculptor Steiner, Even Dwarfs Started Small*) on locations of breathtaking beauty (and, I must assume, of horrendous difficulty) in South America, but it's no ordinary, run-of-the-rapids adventure.

Aguirre, the Wrath of God is simultaneously a historical film (to the extent that it follows events as they are known) and a meditation upon history. Aguirre is truly mad, but as played by Klaus Kinski, whose crooked walk and undiluted evil recall Laurence Olivier's Richard III, he is the essential civilized man, a fellow who, in Mr. Herzog's vision of things, must be lunatic.

There's an eerie moment in the middle of the film when the Emperor, sitting in rags under an improvised shade on the makeshift raft that is carrying the party down the Amazon, picks at his fish dinner (the other men are starving) and thinks with satisfaction that his "empire" is now six times as large as Spain's. No matter that he too may never eat again, nor that his empire is jungle swamp, the sense of power is so intoxicating that it overwhelms all other considerations.

It's as if Mr. Herzog were saying that civilization—our assumption that we have conquered nature or even

come to some accommodation with it—is as ridiculous as the Emperor's pleasure.

From the film's opening sequence, when we see the conquistadores, their women (including Ursua's wife being carried in an elegant litter), and their Indian porters making their way down an Andean slope, looking like the inhabitants of an ant palace, to the concluding shots of Aguirre on his raft in the company of hundreds of tiny marmosets, Mr. Herzog views all the proceedings with fixed detachment. He remains cool. He takes no sides. He may even be slightly amused. Mainly he is a poet who constantly surprises us with unexpected juxtapositions.

The film is incredibly rich and lush looking. It is tactile. One can feel the colors of the jungle and see the heat. The conquistadores endure terrible trials—whirlpools, Indian attacks, rebellion within their own ranks—yet the mood of the film is almost languid. Ursua's faithful, loving wife, played by a classic beauty named Helene Rojo, throws no tantrums when her husband is executed. She watches and waits, and when the opportunity arises, she walks off to her own death in the jungle as if going to a tea.

Contrasting with this peculiar languor is the radiant madness of Aguirre, who hypnotizes his soldiers into following his wildest instructions, who sneers at men who seek riches when power and fame are all that matter, who aspires to be nothing less than the wrath of God, and who, at the end, is planning to create a new dynasty by marrying his dead daughter. He's mad but he's a survivor.

This is a splendid and haunting work.

—V.C., April 4, 1977

A.I.

Written and directed by Steven Spielberg: based on the screen story by Ian Watson and the short story "Super-Toys Last All Summer Long" by Brian Aldiss: director of photography, Janusz Kaminski: edited by Michael Kahn: music by John Williams: production designer, Rick Carter: costumes by Bob Ringwood: make up effects by Stan Winston: visual effects by Dennis Muren and Scott Farrar: practical effects by Michael Lantieri: conceptual art by Christopher Baker: produced by Kathleen Kennedy, Mr. Spielberg and Bonnie Curtis: executive producers, Jan Harlan and Walter F. Parkes; released by Warner Brothers Pictures. Running time: 140 minutes.

With: Haley Joel Osment (David), Jude Law (Gigolo Joe), Frances O'Connor (Monica Swinton), Sam Robards (Henry Swinton), Jake Thomas (Martin Swinton), Brendan Gleeson (Lord Johnson-Johnson), William Hurt (Professor Hobby), Jack Angel (Voice of Teddy), Robin Williams (Voice of Dr. Know) and Ben Kingsley (Narrator).

Steven Spielberg's career as a director has been one of almost profligate variety: from mechanical sharks to the Normandy invasion, from Indiana Jones to the Krakow ghetto, not to mention the slave ships, the angry dinosaurs and the second worst Pearl Harbor movie ever made. But every so often he comes back to the figure of a lonely boy facing the incomprehension and cruelty of the adult world, and when he does—most notably in *E.T.* and *Empire of the Sun*—it is with a feeling of coming home to emotions that lie beyond the reach of the ruthless sentimentality that has been his greatest weakness.

The vulnerability of children is of course a subject that invites maudlin excess. But Mr. Spielberg's needy lost boys dwell in a psychological limbo that elicits not only pity and protectiveness but also recognition. There is something irreducibly real about the sensitivity and curiosity of Eliot in *E.T.* and young Jim in *Empire*, and also about the primal resentment that troubles their smooth, eager faces. A central and nearly universal experience of childhood is to feel abandoned and betrayed by one's parents. The need to compensate for this loss is what forces us to grow up and what sends our fairy-tale alter egos off on their adventures.

A.I. is the best fairy tale—the most disturbing, complex and intellectually challenging boy's adventure story—Mr. Spielberg has made. Once again he asks us to identify with a young boy, exiled from the only home he knows and forced to find his way in a strange and unsympathetic world. Our bond with David (Haley Joel Osment) is complicated, however: he is not real at all but a sentient robot designed by a company called Cybertronics for the comfort and convenience of childless adults.

At the beginning, as an image of the ocean (a symbol of maternity) fills the screen, the soothing voice of

Ben Kingsley explains that an ecological catastrophe has left many of the earth's great cities underwater and that in the midst of widespread famine some places (like New Jersey, where the movie takes place) have sustained material prosperity by placing heavy restrictions on childbearing. David is the brainchild of a scientist named Allen Hobby (William Hurt), who theorizes that robots, once programmed with the capacity to love, will begin to develop an "inner life of metaphor and dreams" that will represent a qualitative advance beyond the outwardly lifelike robots called mechas that circulate among their human counterparts performing various services.

The wider dimensions of this future world become clear only later. The first third of *A.I.*, once some necessary exposition has been taken care of, introduces David into the home of Henry and Monica Swinton (Sam Robards and Frances O'Connor), whose only son, Martin (Jake Thomas), lies frozen and comatose in a hospital ward decorated with scenes from classic children's stories. At first Monica is repelled by David. Mr. Osment uses his wide blue eyes and ingratiating smile to suggest the uncanny creepiness of a living doll, and the film plays cleverly with the monstrous implications of its conceit. The fantasy that humans' replicas of themselves will come to life is more often than not—in the medieval legend of the golem, in Mary Shelley's *Frankenstein* and in countless horror films—a source of terror and anxiety. Fear is the underside of enchantment, and the spell of wonder *A.I.* casts is tinged with dread.

The mood of disquiet only deepens when Monica activates David's imprinting function, in effect flipping the one way switch that will make him love her unconditionally and eternally. His absolute and unwavering adoration—the way Mr. Osment utters the word mommy is both heart-rending and chilling—demands reciprocation.

Real children, it turns out, are more difficult to love. Martin, when he returns home, is sneaky and disobedient, sarcastic and manipulative. He urges Monica to read "Pinocchio" aloud at bedtime. "David will love it," he says with a knowing smirk. That Carlo Collodi story of a wooden puppet who turns into a real boy becomes a kind of scripture for David, and a rich source of images and allusions for *A.I.* (The version of the story most familiar to movie audiences, the Disney animated feature, seems not to have survived the great flood. This dream of the future has been brought to you, after all, by Warner Brothers and Dream Works, whose crescent-moon logo appears to decorate the bed where David and Martin sleep.)

Our startled discovery that we may prefer David to his quasibrother—he's perfect, after all—is an indication of how tangled and ambiguous the movie's themes are. If we all fall for David, and if, later, we side with his mechanical brethren against their human oppressors, are we affirming our humanity or have we been irrevocably alienated from it?

Tangled and ambiguous are not words one normally associates with Mr. Spielberg, who often pleases audiences by inviting them to be pleased with themselves. He tells you how to feel, and while you are usually powerless to resist his manipulations, you can always object to his moral bossiness.

But the experience of *A.I.* is different. The project was originally conceived by Stanley Kubrick, to whom the film is dedicated. Moments of homage are scattered through the movie: sly references to *A Clockwork Orange, The Shining,* and predominantly *2001: A Space Odyssey.* But on a deeper level Mr. Spielberg seems to be attempting the improbable feat of melding Kubrick's chilly, analytical style with his own warmer, needier sensibility. He tells the story slowly and films it with lucid, mesmerizing objectivity, creating a mood as layered, dissonant and strange as John Williams's unusually restrained, modernist score.

The mood shifts abruptly—and the picture becomes dreamier, funnier and intellectually riskier—when David is abandoned, along with his cybernetic teddy bear (with the voice of Jack Angel), in a dark forest. With exemplary childlike reasoning that bears out his creator's hunches, David conflates his own story with Pinocchio's and sets out to find the blue fairy who will transform him into a real boy. Joining him on his quest is a sex-slave mecha called Gigolo Joe, played with saucy, oily charm by Jude Law.

Once expelled from the cocoon of Henry and Monica's house—a scrupulously imagined retro-futuristic suburban palace, as if the Jetsons had shopped at Restoration Hardware—David plunges into the dystopian underside of this disconcertingly familiar future. He and Joe are captured by bounty hunters and herded into cages at a Flesh Fair, a combination revival meeting and monster-truck rally at which people express their hatred of mechas by blowing them up and dousing them with acid.

Presiding over the fair is Lord Johnson-Johnson (Brendan Gleeson), who styles his carnival a "celebration of life" devoted to "demolishing artificiality" and the securing of "a truly human future." "Originality without purpose is a white elephant," he rants.

The Flesh Fair sequence is a lacerating tug of war between thought and feeling, in which we are pulled to the side of Johnson-Johnson's victims even as we are forced to contemplate the truth of his statements. At this moment *A.I.* becomes not only an earnest meditation on the nature of humanity—and a more profound inquiry into the moral scandal of dehumanization than either *Schindler's List* or *Amistad*—but also a reflection on the paradoxical nature of cinematic illusion.

Movies are not real, and few moviemakers have been as adept at finding original ways to counterfeit human emotion as Mr. Spielberg. (The Flesh Fair might be a Dogma 95 pep rally, or a meeting of dyspeptic film critics protesting the movie's lavish and startling special effects, including the computer-enhanced broken-down robots doomed to destruction.) But here Mr. Spielberg confronts a crucial and difficult question: Do the virtual selves we project into the world, on screen and elsewhere, bring us closer to knowing who we are, or do they distract us from our search for that knowledge? "I am, I was," Joe says to David as they part company, asserting as a flat fact what the movie takes as unanswerable questions: What are we? What will we become?

"Stories are real," David insists to Monica before she leaves him to his fate. They aren't, of course. But stories that touch on the essential and unsolvable mysteries of who we are can nonetheless be true, and they are truest when they illuminate those mysteries while leaving them intact.

After the Flesh Fair and a tour of the artificial fleshpots of Rouge City (which looks like a fusion of the old Times Square and the new), David and Joe, with the help of Robin Williams's voice and William Butler Yeats's poetry come to the end of the earth, the half-submerged island of Manhattan. *A.I.* goes even further: on at least two occasions, it seems to be ending, only, like *2001,* to push into ever stranger territory, ultimately leaving the human world altogether.

The final scenes are likely to provoke argument, confusion and a good deal of resistance. For the second time the movie swerves away from where it seemed to be going, and Mr. Spielberg, with breathtaking poise and heroic conviction, risks absurdity in the pursuit of sublimity.

The very end somehow fuses the cathartic comfort of infantile wish fulfillment—the dream that the first perfect love whose loss we experience as the fall from Eden might be restored—with a feeling almost too terrible to acknowledge or to name. Refusing to cuddle us or lull us into easy sleep, Mr. Spielberg locates the unspoken moral of all our fairy tales. To be real is to be mortal; to be human is to love, to dream and to perish.

—*A.O.S., June 29, 2001*

AIRPLANE!

Written and directed by Jim Abrahams, David Zucker and Jerry Zucker; director of photography, Joseph Biroc; edited by Patrick Kennedy; music by Elmer Bernstein; produced by Jon Davison; released by Paramount Pictures. Running time: 88 minutes.

With: Kareem Abdul-Jabbar (Murdock), Lloyd Bridges (McCroskey), Peter Graves (Captain Oveur), Julie Hagerty (Elaine), Robert Hays (Ted Striker), Leslie Nielsen (Dr. Rumack), Lorna Patterson (Randy), Robert Stack (Kramer), Stephen Stucker (Johnny) and Barbara Billingsley (Jive Lady).

At a time when throwaway gags seem like a luxury in any film, *Airplane!* has jokes—hilarious jokes—to spare. It's also clever and confident and furiously energetic, and it has the two most sadly neglected selling points any movie could want right now: it's brief (only eighty-eight minutes), and it looks inexpensive (it cost about three million dollars) without looking cheap. *Airplane!* is more than a pleasant surprise, in the midst of this dim movie season. As a remedy for the bloated self-importance of too many other current efforts, it's just what the doctor ordered.

Like *Love at First Bite* or *Animal House, Airplane!*
has a cheerfully slapdash feeling. It also has a steadier comic attitude than either of these more chaotic movies, because it's set up primarily as a satirical disaster film. Shamelessly lifting the plot of *Zero Hour,* it tells what happens when the passengers on a flight to Chicago are poisoned by their fish dinners and the plane must be landed by shell-shocked veteran Ted Striker (Robert Hays), who has collected his battle scars in places called Drambuie and Daiquiri. Since then, Ted has developed what he calls "my drinking problem." Whenever he lifts a glass, he splashes its contents into his left eye.

Also on board the plane are the usual Noah's Ark disaster movie crew, with a difference. There is a stewardess (Lorna Patterson) who cries, at the height of the panic, "I've never been so scared—and besides, I'm twenty-six and I'm not married." There is a housewife who confides, seconds later, "I've never been so scared either—but at least I have a husband." There is a he-man Captain (Peter Graves) who heartily asks a little boy, "Joey, do you like movies about gladiators?" And there is the obligatory child en route to the Mayo Clinic for a transplant. A doctor at the Mayo Clinic is seen briefly at the beginning of the story. Behind his desk, the bookshelves are lined with jars of mayonnaise.

Airplane!, which opens today at the Baronet and other theaters, pokes fun at much more than disaster movies alone. Ted Striker tells, in flashback, of his days in the roughest, toughest bar in the Far East, where some of the world's meanest customers are seen lounging until "Stayin' Alive" comes on the jukebox; at that, everybody leaps into a *Saturday Night Fever* parody. There is also a *From Here to Eternity* takeoff, as Ted and his beloved Elaine (Julie Hagerty) lie in the surf, covered with seaweed and flanked by small animals. When an old-fashioned pair of lovers say farewell as the plane leaves, the departure scene suddenly seems set in a train station, with a kindly conductor counseling, "Better get on board, son." And when the plane is in danger, its every move is chronicled by newspaper headlines that appear much too speedily for the elapsed time. "Chicago Prepares for Crash Landing!" cries one. Says another, "Passengers Certain to Die!"

The authority figures of *Airplane!,* apparently cast for their thatchy hair and late-fifties television stardom, include Mr. Graves, Leslie Nielsen, Robert Stack, and Lloyd Bridges, all of them radiating a rib-tickling incompetence. Mr. Nielsen, who does a delightful job as the doctor on board, tells Striker, "Good luck, we're all counting on you," so many times that he's still saying it after the plane is down. Mr. Stack, as a hard-hearted fellow down at traffic control, replies angrily to a suggestion that the landing-field lights be turned on. "That's just what they're expecting us to do," he snarls.

No one in the large and talented cast of *Airplane!* does *anything* he or she might be expected to do, however. And that attitude extends to all aspects of the film, which has the happy, cluttered air of an old *Mad* magazine movie parody. The baggage-claim arrangement at the airport features passengers sitting wearily on a conveyor belt, looking in vain for their bags. The closing titles for the film list a credit for Charles Dickens as "Author of 'A Tale of Two Cities.'" When a passenger is offered a choice between "Smoking" and "No Smoking" and chooses "Smoking," he gets a ticket that appears to be on fire. Nothing is as it should be in *Airplane!* and thank goodness for that. Incidentally, watch for Ethel Merman in the Lieutenant Hurwitz role.

Airplane! is the work of the three-man team also responsible for *The Kentucky Fried Movie.* Jim Abrahams, David Zucker, and Jerry Zucker are credited as the film's cowriters and codirectors. And the Zuckers evidently make cameo appearances as a ground crew that guides a plane through the glass wall of a passenger lounge, in a bit that's all the funnier for lasting only a few seconds. The three of them have put together a much smoother movie than many solo directors have lately managed.

—*J.M., July 2, 1980*

ALADDIN

Directed by John Musker and Ron Clements; written by Mr. Clements, Mr. Musker, Ted Elliott and Terry Rossio; edited by H. Lee Peterson; music by Alan Menken, with lyrics by Howard Ashman and Tim Rice; production designer, R.S. Vander Wende; produced by Mr. Musker, Mr. Clements, Donald W. Ernst and Amy Pell; released by Walt Disney Pictures. Running time: 90 minutes.

With the voices of: Scott Weinger and Brad Kane (Aladdin), Robin Williams (Genie), Linda Larkin and Lea Salonga (Jasmine), Jonathan Freeman (Jafar), Frank Welker (Abu), Gilbert Gottfried (Iago) and Douglas Seale (Sultan).

Master, I hear and obey," said the Genie in the storybook version of *Aladdin,* and his comments seldom went further than that. For an exercise in contrast, consider the dizzying, elastic miracle wrought by Robin Williams, Walt Disney Pictures' bravura animators, and the Oscar-winning songwriting team of Alan Menken and Howard Ashman in *Aladdin,* the studio's latest effort to send the standards for animated children's films into the stratosphere.

It may be nothing new to find Mr. Williams, who provides the voice of a big blue Genie with a manic streak, working in a wildly changeable vein. But here are animators who can actually keep up with him. Thanks to them, the Genie is given a visual correlative to the rapid-fire Williams wit, so that kaleidoscopic visions of Groucho Marx, Arnold Schwarzenegger, William F. Buckley Jr., Travis Bickle, and dozens of other characters flash frantically across the screen to accompany the star's speedy delivery. Much of this occurs to the tune of "Friend Like Me," a cakewalking, showstopping musical number with the mischievous wit that has been a hallmark of Disney's animated triumphs.

If the makers of *Aladdin* had their own magic lamp, it's easy to guess what they might wish for: another classic that crosses generational lines as successfully as *Beauty and the Beast* did, and moves as seamlessly from start to finish. *Aladdin* is not quite that, but it comes as close as may have been possible without a genie's help. The fundamentals here go beyond first-rate: animation both gorgeous and thoughtful, several wonderful songs and a wealth of funny minor figures on the sidelines, practicing foolproof Disney tricks. (Even a flying Oriental rug is able to frolic, sulk, and move its thumb, which has evolved out of a tassel.) Only when it comes to the basics of the story line does *Aladdin* encounter any difficulties.

It may date back to the early eighteenth century, but the "Aladdin" story has a 1980's ring. Here is the ultimate get-rich-quick tale of an idle boy (a cute, raffish thief in Disney's modified version) who has the good luck to be designated the only person able to retrieve a magic, Genie-filled lamp from a subterranean cave. Once in possession of the lamp, the original Aladdin goes to work improving his fortunes. He acquires slaves, loot, and an extravagant dowry so as to win the hand of a princess, eventually ordering the Genie to build them a palatial home. Even in the movie version, this hero, who has been made more boyish and remains unmarried, dreamily tells his pet monkey: "Someday, Abu, things are going to change. We'll be rich, live in a palace, and never have any troubles at all."

Compared with the sounder underpinnings of *The Little Mermaid* and especially of *Beauty and the Beast*, this has an unfortunately shallow ring, as do the two teenage types on whom the story is centered. The blandly intrepid Aladdin (with the speaking voice of Scott Weinger) and the sloe-eyed Princess Jasmine (Linda Larkin), a nymph in harem pants, use words like "fabulous" and "amazing" to express unremarkable thoughts. (Jasmine's main concern is deciding whom she will marry.) Luckily, they are surrounded by an overpowering array of secondary characters who make the film's sidelines much more interesting than its supposed center. The scene-stealing monkey Abu (with noises supplied by Frank Welker) is a particular treat, as when he jealously mimics the Princess or otherwise comments on Aladdin's adventures.

As directed by John Musker and Ron Clements (the *Little Mermaid* team), *Aladdin* is a shade less smoothly paced than its recent predecessors. An opening number, "Arabian Nights," gets the film off to a grand start but ends sooner than viewers will wish. A sample lyric by the irreplaceable Mr. Ashman, who died of AIDS before completing this film's score:

> Oh I come from a land,
> From a faraway place,
> Where the caravan camels roam.
> Where they cut off your ear
> If they don't like your face.
> It's barbaric, but hey, it's home.

A lot of early exposition time is also used to explain the chicanery of Jafar (voice by Jonathan Freeman), the Sultan's evil vizier, whose chilling, bony features suggest a composite of Nancy Reagan (the animators have mentioned this as a deliberate reference, along with a more pointed one to Conrad Veidt in *The Thief*

of *Bagdad*) and Captain Hook. It's a long time before Mr. Williams's Genie makes his arrival, and some of the film's early moments—notably Aladdin's descent into a daunting, computer-animated cave—are on the scary side. But this *Aladdin* has so much in its favor that these drawbacks are truly minor. When it comes to Disney animators and children's films, this remains certain: nobody does it better.

What will children make of a film whose main attraction—the Genie himself—has such obvious parent appeal? They needn't know precisely what Mr. Williams is evoking to understand how funny he is. And the crazily antic pacing of the Genie's outbursts will be utterly familiar to small viewers, even if they can't identify a lightning-fast evocation of *The Ed Sullivan Show*. What will come through clearly to audiences of any age is the breathless euphoria of Mr. Williams's free associations, in which no subject is off-limits, not even Disney itself.

When Aladdin promises the Genie his freedom, the Genie mutters "Yeah, right" and turns into a nose-growing Pinocchio. Late in the story, the Genie cries out: "Aladdin! You've just won the heart of the Princess! What're you going to do next?" And the Genie even alludes to the centerpiece numbers of Disney's last two animated films by flashing an "Applause" sign after he sings "Friend Like Me," an heir apparent to the applause-getting "Under the Sea" (from *The Little Mermaid*) and "Be Our Guest" (from *Beauty and the Beast*). *Aladdin* actually has two of these sensationally playful songs, the other being "Prince Ali," in which Abu the monkey becomes Abu the elephant, and Aladdin struts his stuff on a grand scale.

Half the film's lyrics are by Tim Rice (*Evita* and *Jesus Christ Superstar*), whose style is so much more conventional than Mr. Ashman's that the difference is instantly apparent. But the collaboration between Mr. Rice and Mr. Menken has produced a lilting ballad, "A Whole New World," that provides the film with a pretty interlude. The soaring voice of Jasmine in this duet is provided by Lea Salonga, who sings with Brad Kane (as Aladdin) and offers more evidence of just how shrewdly this film has been put together.

Of special note are the warm, dark tones of the film's color palette and its playful allusions to Al Hirschfeld's drawings (in the many curving, seamless shapes of the Genie) and to Erté's designs (in the angular chic of Jafar). Among the many animators who made stellar contributions here, particular mention must be made of Randy Cartwright, who has nothing more to work with than a flying carpet, and turns it into a charming new fixture in Disney's Anthropomorphic Hall of Fame.

—*J.M., November 11, 1992*

ALEXANDER NEVSKY

Directed by Sergei Eisenstein and D. I. Vassillev: written (in Russian, with English subtitles) by Mr. Eisenstein and Pyotr Pavlenko: cinematographer. Edouard Tissé: music by Sergei Prokofiev: produced by Mosfilm: released by Artkino Films. Black and white. Running time: 107 minutes.

With: Nikolai Cherkassov (Prince Alexander Yaroslavich Nevsky). Nikolai Okhlopkov (Vassily Buslai). A. L. Abrikossov (Gavrilo Olexich) and D. N. Orlov (Ignat. Master Armorer).

After more than six years of unproductivity, not all of it voluntary, Sergei Eisenstein, the D. W. Griffith of the Russian screen, has returned to party favor and to public honors with *Alexander Nevsky,* a rough-hewn monument to national heroism which had its New World unveiling at the Cameo last night. This is the picture which saved Eisenstein's face, and possibly his hide, after his *Bezhun Lug* was halted after two years' shooting because of its allegedly unsympathetic treatment of the Communist revolution. It is the picture which prompted Josef Stalin to slap its maker on the back and exclaim, "Sergei, you are a true Bolshevik." And it is a picture, moreover, which sets up this morning an unusual problem in reviewing.

For Eisenstein's work can no more withstand the ordinary critical scrutiny, a judgment based on the refinement and subtlety of its execution than, say, the hydraulic sculpture and rock-blasting that Gutzon Borglum is dashing off on Mount Rushmore. Eisenstein is sublimely indifferent to detail, whether narrative or pictorial. His minor characters are as outrageously unidimensional as those Griffith created for *Intolerance* and *Birth of a Nation.* He is patently unconcerned about a change from night to day to night again during the space of a two-minute sequence, and if it

pleases him to bring on torchbearers at midday, simply because the smoke smudge is photographically interesting, he is not deterred by any thoughts of their illogic.

His concern, obvious from the start, is only with the broad outline of his film, its most general narrative and scenic contours, and with a dramatic conflict arising, not out of the clash of ideas or ideologies (although these have been unsubtly appended), but from the impact of great bodies of men and horse. His picture, whatever its modern political connotation, is primarily a picture of a battle and it must stand, or fall, solely upon Eisenstein's generalship in marshaling his martial array. And of his magnificent pictorial strategy there does not appear to be any question: it is a stunning battle, this reenactment of his of the beautiful butchery that occurred one winter's day in 1242, when the invading Teutonic knights and the serfs, mujhiks, and warriors of Novgorod met on the ice of Lake Peipus and fought it out with mace and axe, with pike and spear and broadsword.

The Russians won by might and strategy and the collapse of the ice under the weight of German armor, and Prince Alexander rings out the defiant charge, "Go home and tell all in foreign lands that Russia lives. Let them come to us as guests and they will be welcome. But if anyone comes to us with the sword he shall perish by the sword. On this the Russian land stands and will stand." So has Eisenstein discharged his party duty; and so the comrades at the Cameo cheered last night and out-thrust their chins at Hitler. Which is all right, too, since it pleases them.

But no propagandistic drum-beating is more than a muffled thump against the surge of Eisenstein's battle. Nor are his people much more than specks upon the bloody ice. Nikolai Cherkassov's Alexander is an exception, since both the role and its player are cast in the heroic mold. But the others, simply through their creator's indifference to their needs, are caricatures (like the Teuton priests), or gargoyles (like the traitors, spies, and enemy knights), or simpering nothings (like the little heroine), or mere focal points for watching the display of medieval arms (like the rival Russian soldiers). It is impossible not to admire Eisenstein's colossal unconcern with these refinements of filmmaking, not to marvel at his stylistic insistence that all people walk along a skyline, and not to wish, in the same breath, that more directors had his talent for doing great things so well and little things so badly.

—F.S.N., March 23, 1939

ALICE DOESN'T LIVE HERE ANYMORE

Directed by Martin Scorsese; written by Robert Getchell; director of photography, Kent L. Wakeford; edited by Marcia Lucas; music by Richard La Salle; production designer, Toby Rafelson; produced by David Susskind and Audrey Maas; released by Warner Brothers. Running time: 113 minutes.

With: Ellen Burstyn (Alice Hyatt), Kris Kristofferson (David), Alfred Lutter (Tommy), Harvey Keitel (Ben), Diane Ladd (Flo), Lelia Goldoni (Bea), Jodie Foster (Audrey), Valerie Curtin (Vera), Billy Green Bush (Donald), Lane Bradbury (Rita) and Vic Tayback (Mel).

Alice Hyatt (Ellen Burstyn) would seem to be up a creek. She lives in semi-urban New Mexico, married to a human slug who drives a soft-drink truck and who is so alienated from their twelve-year-old son, Tommy (Alfred Lutter), that when we first see the family together it seems as if the father is no more than a particularly unpleasant, demanding boarder. Suddenly and fortuitously everything changes. Donald, Alice's husband, is killed in a highway accident and Alice must take charge of her own life, which, until this time, she has always left in the care of others.

Martin Scorsese's *Alice Doesn't Live Here Anymore,* which opened yesterday at the Sutton Theater, is the fine, moving, frequently hilarious tale of Alice's first lurching steps toward some kind of self-awareness and self-sufficiency.

The story moves across the American Southwest as Alice and Tommy, their belongings stuffed into their station wagon, set off on the journey back to Alice's hometown of Monterey, California. The geography is familiar and mostly flat, strewn with motels, drive-in restaurants, taverns, service stations and diners—the bright, shiny artifacts of America's mobile optimism.

The interior landscape of the film is something else again. It's a Krazy Kat world where it's difficult to tell the difference between night and day, between robust laughter and hysterical tears, where the brick that hits you in the head may cause a slight concussion but may also knock some sense into you. The experience is scary but if you keep your wits about you, as Alice ultimately does, the chances are that things will work out. You'll get a slight purchase on survival, on life.

Alice Doesn't Live Here Anymore seems especially remarkable because it was directed by the man who first smashed into our consciousness with an entirely different kind of movie, *Mean Streets,* a male-dominated melodrama about life in New York's Little Italy.

Alice Doesn't Live Here Anymore is an American comedy of the sort of vitality that dazzles European film critics and we take for granted. It's full of attachments and associations to very particular times and places, even in the various regional accents of its characters. It's beautifully written (by Robert Getchell) and acted, but it's not especially neatly tailored.

It begins rather badly, with an unnecessary sequence showing Alice as a little girl, and then jumps forward to Alice's home life with her slob husband, played at such a high pitch you're not sure that Mr. Scorsese and the actors will be able to sustain whatever it is they are about. You don't know at first. It's a comedy that creeps up on you, somewhere near the Arizona state line, as Tommy begins to get on Alice's nerves by threatening to be carsick.

At the center of the movie and giving it a visible sensibility is Miss Burstyn, one of the few actresses at work today (another is Glenda Jackson) who is able to seem appealing, tough, intelligent, funny, and bereft, all at approximately the same moment.

It's Miss Burstyn's movie and part of the enjoyment of the film is in the director's apparent awareness of this fact, as in a sequence in which Alice is making a little extra money by singing and playing ersatz cocktail-piano in a roadside tavern. Alice is never going to bring show business to its knees, but the beer drinkers love her and Mr. Scorsese circles his camera around her as lyrically as if she were Ida Lupino knocking the customers dead in *Road House.*

Of equal but less spectacular importance are the supporting players, including the men. Although this is a movie that takes women seriously, and although it is essentially the chronicle of Alice's liberation, Mr. Scorsese has not shortchanged the actors, especially

Harvey Keitel, as a small-town sadist who traps Alice for a while; Kris Kristofferson, as the comparatively gentle rancher who wins her; and Alfred Lutter, as her son who, when the chips are down, is not at all bad.

Two other performances must be noted, those of Diane Ladd and Valerie Curtin as waitresses in a diner where Alice works. Their marvelous contributions in small roles are a measure of the film's quality and of Mr. Scorsese's fully realized talents as one of the best of the new American film-makers.

—V.C., January 30, 1975

ALICE'S RESTAURANT

Directed by Arthur Penn: written by Venable Herndon and Mr. Penn. based on the song "The Alice's Restaurant Massacree" by Arlo Guthrie: cinematographer. Michael Nebbia: edited by Dede Allen: music by Mr. Guthrie: produced by Hillard Elkins and Joe Manduke: released by United Artists. Running time: 111 minutes.

With: Arlo Guthrie (Arlo). Pat Quinn (Alice). James Broderick (Ray). Michael McClanathan (Shelly). Geoff Outlaw (Roger). Tina Chen (Mari-chan). Kathleen Dabney (Karin). William Obanhein (Officer Obie). Pete Seeger (Himself) and Shelley Plimpton (Reenie).

One of the definitions of grace is "the power or disposition to endure with patience the trials of the earthly state." Such grace is the leitmotiv of Arlo Guthrie's best-selling recording "The Alice's Restaurant Massacree," the long, cheerful, "talking blues" number in which Woody Guthrie's folk-singing son recounts in a wry, surreal monologue his actual confrontations with the law of Stockbridge, Massachusetts, and the draft board of New York City.

Grace is also manifest throughout the movie called *Alice's Restaurant,* which Arthur Penn, the director of *The Miracle Worker* and *Bonnie and Clyde,* has made with Arlo Guthrie starring as Arlo Guthrie and with the ballad as a frame. It's hardly an accident that the old evangelical hymn "Amazing Grace" ("How sweet the sound/That saved a wretch like me") keeps cropping up in this film—at a tent meeting, during church services, or in a line of dialogue. The film itself is a

hymn to the amazing grace of some of the most beautiful, funny, and affectionate wretches you're ever likely to meet in a movie.

Alice's Restaurant, which opened yesterday at the Festival and the Murray Hill Theaters, seems—on its surface—to be about Arlo's growing up, his short, disastrous college career, his relationships with his parents, and his friendships, particularly with Alice and Ray Brock, a young couple who live in a deconsecrated Stockbridge church, run a restaurant, and act as surrogate parents to a colony of hippies.

On a more profound level, it's about the America of the 1960's, which is like a dog being wagged by a tail pronounced "VEETnam," about the continuity between generations (as well as the gap), about the mindlessness of authoritarian systems, which it treats with gentle satire, about the responsibilities of love, which can be terribly painful, about the ceremonies of death—about almost everything, in fact, except Alice's restaurant.

Penn, who collaborated on the screenplay with Venable Herndon, has made a sort of folk movie—wise, fantastic, technically superb (especially the color photography by Michael Nebbia), sometimes wildly funny, sometimes touching in ways that are most agreeable because they are completely unforeseen. He mixes up real people who play themselves (Arlo, Stockbridge Police Chief William Obanhein, Pete Seeger), real people played by actors, including Pat Quinn and James Broderick, who play the Brocks, and composites of real-life characters played by both actors and real-life people.

They all are marvelous, including Chief Obanhein, who plays himself with such pleased and puzzled sincerity that he may be the most appealing villain since Captain Hook. Arlo, with his long, nappy hair and pale oval face, looks rather like a Dürer self-portrait. He is not an actor but he has a nice, dry wit and, like a good performer, he is always felt as a theatrical presence.

If the film has a flaw, it's that toward the middle the focus shifts from Arlo and his problems to the Brocks and theirs. As played by Miss Quinn, a lovely, dark-haired girl, and Broderick, who has the exuberance of a turned-on Y.M.C.A. instructor, the Brocks are very honest, generous people, so confident in the grace of their own love (they often ring the church bell to announce a successful mating) they feel they can spread their love among others, literally. Love, however, isn't infinitely regenerative. It can run out, like patience.

In an effort to renew their love (the real Brocks have since been divorced), Alice and Ray are remarried in a giant flower ceremony in their church. This final sequence of the film is tumultuously staged by Penn as if it were the climax of the Children's Crusade. It is full of color and music and bizarre costumes, and yet it is underscored by a sweet melancholy. One by one, their "children," including Arlo and his girl (Tina Chen), leave. It's the end of Alice and Ray's Stockbridge experiment.

In *Alice's Restaurant,* Penn has made a very loving movie, but the loving is not verbalized; it is sung and seen, in sequence after sequence. It is there when Arlo visits Woody, the old "citizen of the open road," now mute and dying in a hospital bed while Pete Seeger stands in the corner and plunks out the elder Guthrie's "The Pastures of Plenty." It is there in Arlo's funny encounter with a sniffly teenybopper (Shelley Plimpton) who wants to make it with Arlo because she's sure he'll be on an album some day, "like the Raspberry Wristwatch."

There is an extraordinarily cinematic funeral during a quiet New England snowfall, while Joni Mitchell sings "Songs to Aging Children." It may be self-conscious but it's also very beautiful. Not unexpectedly, the movie's flashiest and funniest sequence is Penn's visualization of "The Alice's Restaurant Massacree," Arlo's arrest and imprisonment for "litterin'," followed by his Army physical exam, which becomes a hilarious nightmare of things like spilled urine specimens and the filling out of incomprehensible forms.

Through it all, Arlo maintains amazing grace, which provides both the theme and the continuity for a very original movie whose structural weaknesses couldn't bother me less. With a film as interesting and fine as *Alice's Restaurant,* structural weaknesses, seen in proper perspective, simply become cinematic complexities to be cherished.

—*V.C., August 25, 1969*

ALIENS

Written and directed by James Cameron: based on a story by Mr. Cameron, David Giler and Walter Hill and on characters created by Dan O'Bannon and Ronald Shusett: director of photography, Adrian Biddle: edited by Ray Lovejoy: music by James Horner: production designer, Peter Lamont: produced by Gale Anne Hurd: released by Twentieth Century Fox. Running time: 137 minutes.

With: Sigourney Weaver (Ripley), Carrie Henn (Newt), Michael Biehn (Corporal Hicks), Paul Reiser (Burke), Lance Henriksen (Bishop), Bill Paxton (Private Hudson), William Hope (Lieutenant Gorman), Jenette Goldstein (Private Vasquez) and Al Matthews (Sergeant Apone).

The special-effects specialists are featured prominently in the credits that precede *Aliens,* and so they should be. Under the direction of James (*The Terminator*) Cameron, they have put together a flaming, flashing, crashing, crackling blow-'em-up show that keeps you popping from your seat despite your better instincts and the basically conventional scare tactics.

The sequel to the 1979 sci-fi shocker *Alien* opens today at the Warner Twin and other theaters. It's a touch less innovative than its predecessor, which introduced slimy "hostile organisms" that use humans as incubators and burst from people's stomachs at inopportune times, but it makes up in technique what it lacks in novelty. The effects, perils in outer space and in shadowy corners, quite overwhelm the skimpy script, which is loaded with gibberish uttered with authority: "Stand by to initiate release sequencer." When somebody says something sensible like "we're all in strung out shape," it sounds like a gag.

The plot, to use the word casually, starts with the rescue of Sigourney Weaver, who, you may recall, lost the rest of the crew of her spaceship to murderous monsters in *Alien.* She has spent the ensuing fifty-seven years loitering unconsciously in space, and no sooner does she get back to civilization, as it were, than off she goes again with a band of rough-looking, rough-talking, cannon-toting marines, of both sexes, to try to discover what happened to a colony of humans out there somewhere. Anybody who saw *Alien* can guess what has happened. The question is whether it will happen to Miss Weaver, the marines, and a little girl, the colony's sole survivor, who looks and acts like a Hollywood child actress. If that doesn't matter to you, forget the whole thing.

Miss Weaver's name in both movies is Ripley, and believe it or not, this smart good looker is a one-woman army. There is something inherently parodic about Warrant Officer Ripley, in a T-shirt, blasting away with a flame-spouting, grenade-launching weapon capable of wiping out a small zoo; it's a Rambo joke. But Miss Weaver does the job without cracking a smile.

Adrian Biddle's camera goes for the closest close-ups you've ever seen. They don't do much for anybody's complexion, but you can tell the pores from the beads of sweat on each marine's neck. When it comes to those aliens, however, the camera, understandably, doesn't get too close. It veers about, often at high speed to the quickened beat of the music, and what with all the movement and murky lighting, you can't get a sharp look at the creatures put together by Stan Winston, supervisor of "creature effects."

Although the aliens still have that nasty way of bursting through people's skin, mostly we meet them full-grown, with scales and coils and, my, what big teeth. Now they look like dragons, now like sea monsters or pterodactyls or a combination plate of lizard, bat, eel, and spider. The young aliens resemble agitated lobsters. I thought I saw an elephant trunk on the Big Mamma alien, who is too big to be blown away even by Miss Weaver's big gun, but it could have been something else. Anyhow, it wasn't anything you'd want clutching at your foot while you were trying to hang on to your spaceship and not be gulped into the void.

No monster movie with pretensions can do without a scene that stirs a twinge of compassion for the monsters. It might be just my wishful imagination, but I thought I detected an expression of anguish on Big Mamma, a prodigious breeder, as dozens of her extra-large eggs were getting badly cracked. But she could merely have been opening her glacierlike jaws to devour that little girl.

—*W.G., July 18, 1986*

ALL ABOUT EVE

Directed by Joseph L. Mankiewicz; written by Mr. Mankiewicz, based on the story "The Wisdom of Eve" by Mary Orr; cinematographer, Milton Krasner; edited by Barbara McLean; music by Alfred Newman; art designer, Lyle Wheeler and George W. Davis; produced by Darryl F. Zanuck; released by Twentieth Century Fox. Black and white. Running time: 138 minutes.

With: Bette Davis (Margo), Anne Baxter (Eve), George Sanders (Addison De Witt), Celeste Holm (Karen), Gary Merrill (Bill Simpson), Hugh Marlowe (Lloyd Richards), Thelma Ritter (Birdie) and Marilyn Monroe (Miss Casswell).

The good old legitimate theater, the temple of Thespis and Art, which has dished out a lot of high derision of Hollywood in its time, had better be able to take it as well as dish it out, because the worm has finally turned with a venom and Hollywood is dishing it back. In *All About Eve,* a withering satire—witty, mature, and worldly-wise—which Twentieth Century Fox and Joseph Mankiewicz delivered to the Roxy yesterday, the movies are letting Broadway have it with claws out and no holds barred. If Thespis doesn't want to take a beating, he'd better yell for George Kaufman and Moss Hart.

As a matter of fact, Mr. Kaufman and Mr. Hart might even find themselves outclassed by the dazzling and devastating mockery that is brilliantly packed into this film. For obviously Mr. Mankiewicz, who wrote and directed it, had been sharpening his wits and his talents a long, long time for just this go. Obviously, he had been observing the theater and its charming folks for years with something less than an idolator's rosy illusions and zeal. And now, with the excellent assistance of Bette Davis and a truly sterling cast, he is wading into the theater's middle with all claws slashing and settling a lot of scores.

If anything, Mr. Mankiewicz has been even too full of fight—too full of cutlass-edged derision of Broadway's theatrical tribe. Apparently his dormant dander and his creative zest were so aroused that he let himself go on this picture and didn't know when to stop. For two hours and eighteen minutes have been taken by him to achieve the ripping apart of an illusion which might have been comfortably done in an hour and a half.

It is not that his characters aren't full blown, that his incidents aren't brilliantly conceived, and that his dialogue, pithy and pungent, is not as clever as any you will hear. In picturing the inside story of an ambitious actress's rise from glamour-struck girl in a theater alley to flinty-eyed winner of the Siddons Prize, Mr. Mankiewicz has gathered up a saga of theatrical ambition and conceit, pride and deception and hypocrisy, that just about drains the subject dry.

Indeed, he has put so many characters—so many vivid Broadway types—through the flattening and decimating wringer of his unmerciful wit that the punishment which he gives them becomes painful when so lengthily drawn. And that's the one trouble with this picture. It beats the horse after it is dead.

But that said, the rest is boundless tribute to Mr. Mankiewicz and his cast for ranging a gallery of people that dazzle, horrify, and fascinate. Although the title character—the self-seeking, ruthless Eve, who would make a black widow spider look like a ladybug—is the motivating figure in the story and is played by Anne Baxter with icy calm, the focal figure and most intriguing character is the actress whom Bette Davis plays. This lady, an aging, acid creature with a cankerous ego and a stinging tongue, is the end-all of Broadway disenchantment, and Miss Davis plays her to a fare-thee-well. Indeed, the superb illumination of the spirit and pathos of this dame which this brilliant screen actress gives her merits an Academy Award.

Of the men, George Sanders is walking wormwood, neatly wrapped in a mahogany veneer, as a vicious and powerful drama critic who has a licentious list toward pretty girls; Gary Merrill is warm and reassuring as a director with good sense and a heart, and Hugh Marlowe is brittle and boyish as a playwright with more glibness than brains. Celeste Holm is appealingly normal and naive as the latter's wife and Thelma Ritter is screamingly funny as a wised-up maid until she is summarily lopped off.

A fine Darryl Zanuck production, excellent music, and an air of ultra-class complete this superior satire. The legitimate theater had better look to its laurels.

—*B.C., October 14, 1950*

ALL ABOUT MY MOTHER

Written (in Spanish, with English subtitles) and directed by Pedro Almodovar; director of photography, Alfonso Beato; edited by Jose Salcedo; music by Alberto Iglesias; production director, Esther Garcia; executive producer, Agustin Almodovar; released by Sony Pictures Classics. Running time: 100 minutes.

With: Penelope Cruz (Sister Rosa), Marisa Paredes (Huma Rojo), Candela Pena (Nina), Cecilia Roth (Manuela), Eloy Azarin (Esteban) and Antonia San Juan (Agrado).

When Pedro Almodovar gleefully established himself as "Spain's most reputable disreputable young filmmaker" (in Vincent Canby's words), it was the dizzy hilarity of *Women on the Verge of a Nervous Breakdown* that marked him as an avatar of outrageous, sexy humor. Eleven years later he is back at the New York Film Festival in a ravishingly different mode. The antic fizz and bold, theatrical exaggeration of his earlier work have blossomed (as was clear in the haunting 1997 *Live Flesh*) into a newly sophisticated style that is far more passionate, wise and deeply felt.

This year's New York Film Festival opens tonight with the marvelous *All About My Mother*, a whole new order of Almodovar extravaganza. It depends, as so many things do, upon the kindness of strangers. Starting at that place in Mr. Almodovar's great big heart where womanhood, artifice, Tennessee Williams, Truman Capote, and *All About Eve* collide, it weaves life and art into a rich tapestry of love, loss and compassion. This film's assorted females—real, theatrical or would-be—move past the nervous breakdown stage and on to something much more forgiving.

A Streetcar Named Desire plays a crucial role in the life of the film's heroine, a nurse named Manuela (Cecilia Roth). It is central to the film, too. Stellas and Stanleys abound throughout the story, beginning on the evening when Manuela celebrates the 17th birthday of her son, Esteban (Eloy Azarin), by accompanying him to a performance of the play in Madrid.

Esteban is so captivated by the evening's Blanche Dubois, the diva Huma Rojo (Marisa Paredes), that he waits for her in the street in hopes of an autograph. In a devastating sequence, filmed by Mr. Almodovar with the sweeping visual assurance that binds this film together so firmly, Manuela's beloved son is mowed down in the street. The camera stays wrenchingly with an Esteban's-eye view of the scene until Esteban is gone.

Because *All About My Mother* is about splendidly resilient women rather than wounded ones, it has already begun to entwine Manuela's shocking experience with a sense of drama. Manuela oversees donor organ transplants, and before the accident she has played the role of a widow in a hospital simulation. Now the moment is real, and the same two doctors who staged it with Manuela are really helping her to decide the fate of her son's heart. On the stage Blanche Dubois searches pitifully for her red heart-shaped jewelry box; in life Manuela leaves Esteban's heart beating in another man's body and goes on to fulfill her son's last wishes. And Mr. Almodovar, being to the weepie born, presents this womanly melodrama with an empathy to recall George Cukor's and an eye-dampening intensity to out-Sirk Douglas Sirk.

But when Manuela travels to Barcelona for her son's sake, the film enters a buoyant and generous new world. It was here, 20 years ago, that she and a senior Esteban first met, when they starred in *Streetcar*. And even though her husband has since become a larcenous femme fatale named Lola, Manuela wants to find him and tell him of her son's life and death.

She goes looking in a nefarious outdoor hangout called the Field, where prostitutes and their clients move in circles as if this were a merry-go-round, or a Fellini vision. What passes for vice in other contexts remains a source of wit and sweetness in Mr. Almodovar's work.

Charging into the story at this point, and bursting into the film like a drag supernova, is the irrepressible Agrado, played by a Spanish nightclub performer named Antonia San Juan. Algrado and Manuela turn out to be old friends from the days before Algrado had breasts, and soon she has taken Manuela under her wing. One by one, the women adrift through this story begin to help and restore one another, as when Agrado (in a pink Chanel suit) brings Manuela to the prostitutes' shelter where beautiful Sister Rosa (Penelope Cruz) ministers to the needy. The nun looks meek and devout, but it turns out that she knows Lola, too.

Working in a style he has called "screwball drama," Mr. Almodovar also brings in the two *Streetcar* actresses (who are stormy lovers) and lets the group of women gain sustenance as it grows. This film is lovingly dedicated to actresses who have played actresses (Gena Rowlands, Bette Davis, Romy Schneider), and

it celebrates the self-preservative instincts that can make an actress of anyone.

Huma and Nina (Candela Pena) have such a Kowalski-like battling relationship that Manuela is even called upon to play Stella onstage one night, which is something she can do by heart. There's a stroke of *All About Eve* here, but it comes without malice. Mr. Almodovar would rather show the power of artifice and impersonation to transcend ordinary truth.

Although Ms. San Juan's Agrado supplies a large share of comic relief, her most important moment in the film comes after a *Streetcar* performance is abruptly canceled. Agrado takes the stage and offers to tell the story of her life, which nearly clears the room. Then, in a funny yet prideful monologue, she recites chapter and verse on all the costly surgery and silicone that made her what she now appears to be. "It cost me a lot to be authentic," she says. And: "A woman is more authentic the more she looks like what she has dreamed for herself."

In *All About My Mother* the world of acting becomes a source of inspiration to women as they improvise their way through their own lives, with the kind of strength, passion and humor this filmmaker has always celebrated. Mr. Almodovar has expressed the idea of life as a divine form of acting before, but never with the kind of clarity and beauty that glitter here.

All About My Mother, his best film by far, is all about how tragedies of the flesh can yield renewal and hope despite the pain they leave behind, which is as clear an understanding of what makes movies tick as Mr. Almodovar will ever need. It's the crossover moment in the career of a born four-hankie storyteller of ever-increasing stature. Look out, Hollywood, here he comes.

—J.M., September 24, 1999

ALL QUIET ON THE WESTERN FRONT

Directed by Lewis Milestone; written by Del Andrews, Maxwell Anderson and George Abbott, based on the novel by Erich Maria Remarque; cinematographers, Karl Freund and Arthur Edeson; edited by Edgar Adams and Milton Carruth; music by David Broekman; art designers, Charles D. Hall and William R. Schmidt: produced by Carl Laemmle Jr.: released by Universal Pictures. Black and white. Running time: 140 minutes.

With: Lewis Ayres (Paul). George Summerville (Tjaden) and Beryl Mercer (Paul's Mother).

From the pages of Erich Maria Remarque's widely read book of young Germany in the World War, *All Quiet on the Western Front,* Carl Laemmle's Universal Pictures Corporation has produced a trenchant and imaginative audible picture, in which the producers adhere with remarkable fidelity to the spirit and events of the original stirring novel. It was presented last night at the Central Theatre before an audience that most of the time was held to silence by its realistic scenes. It is a notable achievement, sincere and earnest, with glimpses that are vivid and graphic. Like the original, it does not mince matters concerning the horrors of battle. It is a vocalized screen offering that is pulsating and harrowing, one in which the fighting flashes are photographed in an amazingly effective fashion.

Lewis Milestone, who has several good films to his credit, was entrusted with the direction of this production. And Mr. Laemmle had the foresight to employ those well-known playwrights, George Abbott and Maxwell Anderson, to make the adaptation and write the dialogue. Some of the scenes are not a little too long, and one might also say that a few members of the cast are not Teutonic in appearance; but this means but little when one considers the picture as a whole, for wherever possible, Mr. Milestone has used his fecund imagination, still clinging loyally to the incidents of the book. In fact, one is just as gripped by witnessing the picture as one was by reading the printed pages, and in most instances it seems as though the very impressions written in ink by Herr Remarque had become animated on the screen.

In nearly all the sequences, fulsomeness is avoided. Truth comes to the fore, when the young soldiers are elated at the idea of joining up, when they are disillusioned, when they are hungry, when they are killing rats in a dugout, when they are shaken with fear, and when they, or one of them, becomes fed up with the conception of war held by the elderly man back home.

Often the scenes are of such excellence that if they were not audible one might believe that they were actual motion pictures of activities behind the lines, in the trenches, and in No Man's Land. It is an expansive production with views that never appear to be cramped. In looking at a dugout one readily imagines a long line of such earthy abodes. When shells demolish these underground quarters, the shrieks of fear, coupled with the rat-tat-tat of machine guns, the bang-ziz of the trench mortars, and the whining of shells, it tells the story of the terrors of fighting better than anything so far has done in animated photography coupled with the microphone.

There are heartrending glimpses in a hospital, where one youngster has had his leg amputated and still believes that he has a pain in his toes. Just as he complains of this, he remembers another soldier who had complained of the same pain in the identical words. He then realizes what has happened to him, and he shrieks and cries out that he does not want to go through life a cripple. There is the death room from which nobody is said to come out, and Paul, admirably acted by Lewis Ayres, is taken to this chamber shouting, as he is wheeled away, that he will come back. And he does. The agony in this hospital reflects that of the details given by Herr Remarque.

In an early sequence there is the introduction of the tyrant corporal, Himmelstoss, who has no end of ideas to keep young soldiers on the alert, sometimes amusing himself by making them crawl under tables and then, during the day, ordering them to fall on their faces in the mud. Just as by reading the book, one learns, while looking at this animated work, to hate Himmelstoss. And one occasion when the audience broke their rapt stillness last night was with an outburst of laughter. This happened when Paul and his comrades lay in wait for the detested noncommissioned officer, and, after thrashing him, left him in a stagnant pool with a sack tied over his head.

Soldiers are perceived being taken like cattle to the firing line and then having to wait for food. There is the cook, who finds that he has enough rations for twice the number of the men left in the company, and when he hears that many have been killed and others wounded he still insists that these soldiers will only receive their ordinary rations. Here that amiable war veteran, Katczinsky, splendidly acted by Louis Wolheim, grabs the culinary expert by the throat and finally a sergeant intervenes and instructs the cook to give the company the full rations intended for the survivors and those who have either died or been wounded.

Now and again songs are heard, genuine melody that comes from the soldiers, and as time goes on Paul and his comrades begin to look upon the warfare with the same philosophic demeanor that Katczinsky reveals. But when the big guns begin to boom there are further terrors for the soldiers and in one of these Paul has his encounter with a Frenchman in a shell hole. Paul stabs the Frenchman to death and as he observes life ebbing from the man with whom he had struggled, he fetches water from the bottom of the shell hole and moistens the Frenchman's lips. It is to Paul a frightening and nerve-racking experience, especially when he eventually pulls from a pocket a photograph of the wife and child of the man he had slain.

Raymond Griffith, the erstwhile comedian who, years before acting in film comedies, lost his voice through shrieking in a stage melodrama, gives a marvelous performance as the dying Frenchman. It may be a little too long for one's peace of mind, but this does not detract from Mr. Griffith's sterling portrayal.

Another comedian, none other than George (Slim) Summerville, also distinguishes himself in a light but very telling role, that of Tjaden. It is he who talks about the Kaiser and himself both having no reason to go to war—the only difference, according to the soldier in the trenches, being that the Kaiser is at home. It is Tjaden who is left behind when the youngsters swim over to the farmhouse and visit the French girls.

Much has been made of the pair of boots and the soldier who wanted them and declared, when he got them from the man who passed on, that they would make fighting almost agreeable for anybody. Mr. Milestone has done wonders with this passage, showing the boots on the man and soon depicting that while they may have been comfortable and watertight, boots don't matter much when a shell with a man's name written on it comes his way.

The episodes are unfolded with excellent continuity and one of the outstanding ones is where Paul goes home and finds everything changed, including himself. He is asked by the same professor who had taught him, to talk to the new batch of pupils about the war. He remembers his enthusiasm for it when he enlisted in 1914 and he now knows how different are his impressions since he has been stringing barbed wire

under the dangerous glare of Very lights in No Man's Land. He knows what a uniform means, and believes that there is no glory at the front; all he has to say to the boys is hard and terse. He tires of the gray heads who think that they know something about war and prefers to cut his leave short and go back to the fighting area rather than listen to the arguments of those who have not been disillusioned by shells, mud, rats, and vermin.

During the intermission a curtain is lowered with "poppies, row on row," a glimpse of Flanders field. After that comes more grim battle episodes and more suffering of the men in the gray-green tunics.

All the players do capital work, but Beryl Mercer does not seem to be a good choice for the role of Paul's mother. This may be due, however, to having seen her relatively recently in the picturization of Sir James M. Barrie's playlet, *The Old Lady Shows Her Medals.*

Messrs. Milestone, Abbott, and Anderson in this film have contributed a memorable piece of work to the screen.

—M.H., April 30, 1930

ALL THAT HEAVEN ALLOWS

Directed by Douglas Sirk: written by Peg Fenwick. based on a story by Edna L. and Harry Lee: director of photography. Russell Metty: edited by Frank Gross: art director. Alexander Golitzen: music by Frank Skinner: produced by Ross Hunter: released by Universal-International. Running time: 89 minutes.

With: Jane Wyman (Cary Scott). Rock Hudson (Ron Kirby). Agnes Moorehead (Sara Warren). Conrad Nagel (Harvey). Virginia Grey (Alida Anderson). Gloria Talbott (Kay Scott). Hayden Rorke (Dr. Hennessy). Jacqueline deWit (Mona Plash). Leigh Snowden (Jo-Ann). Donald Curtis (Howard Hoffer). Alex Gerry (George Warren). Nestor Paiva (Manuel) and Forrest Lewis (Mr. Weeks).

One of those doleful situations so dear to the radio daytime serials is tackled in Universal's *All That Heaven Allows.* It is that or a well-to-do widow who falls in love with a noble nurseryman and then has to face the snide resentment of her collegiate children and her country-club friends.

Such a desperate domestic dilemma might conceivably be resolved by the lady's simply telling her offspring and her friends to go climb a tree—preferably a silver-tipped spruce, which is the sort her lover specializes in. But that would be too expeditious, too simple and logical. It would also be a violation of the professional heart-renders' rules.

And so, in this frankly feminine fiction, which came to the Mayfair yesterday all glittering in Technicolor and with Jane Wyman and Rock Hudson in the leading roles, Miss Wyman must reject Mr. Hudson with the wistful word that she can never be his, that she has an obligation greater than the tender call of love—which is the obligation of being a proper mother to her insufferable kids.

Whereupon the children have to show her that they only care about themselves, anyhow, and Mr. Hudson has to fall off a mountain and get a concussion of the brain before Miss Wyman sizes up the situation and does the inevitable thing.

Don't hold the actress responsible. The script was obviously written to bring her and Mr. Hudson, who made a popular twosome in the *Magnificent Obsession*, together again. Solid and sensible drama plainly had to give way to outright emotional bulldozing and a paving of easy clichés. What could a conscientious actress do when Director Douglas Sirk bathed her in lush autumnal colors and pulled all stops on the piano and violins?

Miss Wyman does her darndest. She smiles bravely, while her eyes show the hurt that only a woman who has loved (as they say) can understand. And when she surrenders to Mr. Hudson (as she does, we're bound to tell you, before the end), she does so with lady-like decorum and elegant restraint.

He, too, performs with perfect manners, barely speaking above a whisper most of the time and giving a sterling imitation of a rustic stalwart who is passionate for trees. It is true that he bears a slight resemblance to Li'l Abner of comic-strip fame, in his lumber-jackets and his pompadour hair-do, but that isn't inappropriate to this film.

In supporting roles, William Reynolds and Gloria Talbott are priggish as the kids, Agnes Moorhead is noisy as an old friend and Conrad Nagel is coy as an aging beau. Several others seem slightly uncomfortable in studiously country clothes and roles. A good bit of overdressing is evident throughout the show.

—B.C., February 29, 1956

ALL THE KING'S MEN

Produced and directed by Robert Rossen; written by Mr. Rossen, based on the novel by Robert Penn Warren; cinematographer, Burnett Guffey; edited by Al Clark; music by Louis Gruenberg; released by Columbia Pictures. Black and white. Running time: 109 minutes.

With: Broderick Crawford (Willie Stark), Joanne Dru (Anne Stanton), John Ireland (Jack Burden), John Derek (Tom Stark), Mercedes McCambridge (Sadie Burke), Shepperd Strudwick (Adam Stanton), Ralph Dumke (Tiny Duffy) and Anne Seymour (Lucy Stark).

Out of Robert Penn Warren's prize novel, *All the King's Men*, which was obviously based on the familiar rise and fall of the late Huey Long, Robert Rossen has written and directed, as well as personally produced, a rip-roaring film of the same title. It opened at the Victoria yesterday.

We have carefully used that descriptive as the tag for this new Columbia film because a quality of turbulence and vitality is the one that it most fully demonstrates. In telling a complicated story of a self-made and self-styled "red-necked hick" who batters his way to political kingdom in an unspecified southern state, the picture bounces from raw-boned melodrama into dark psychological depths and thrashes around in those regions until it claws back to violences again. Consistency of dramatic structure—or of character revelation—is not in it. But it has a superb pictorialism which perpetually crackles and explodes.

And because of this rich pictorialism, which embraces a wide and fluid scene, it gathers a frightening comprehension of the potential of demagoguery in this land. From ugly illustrations of back-room spittoon politics to wild illuminations of howling political mobs, it catches the dim but dreadful aspect of ignorance and greed when played upon by theatrics, eloquence, and bluff. It visions the vulgar spellbinders and political hypocrites for what they are and it looks on extreme provincialism with a candid and pessimistic eye.

In short, Mr. Rossen has assembled in this starkly unprettified film a piece of pictorial journalism that is remarkable for its brilliant parts. It clearly observes the beginnings of a Huey Long type of demagogue in an humble and honest lawyer fighting the "bosses" in a sleepy dirt-road town. It follows this disillusioned fellow as he gets the hang of politics and discovers the strange intoxication of his own unprincipled charm. And it wallows with him in egoism, corruption, and dictatorial power until he is finally shot down by an assassin when his triumphs appear uncontrolled.

All of these things, Mr. Rossen, as director, has pictured stunningly. His final episode of personal violence and mob hysteria is superb for savagery. But in his parallel endeavors to transfer from Mr. Warren's book some real understanding of the character, he has met with much less success. In fact, the whole middle section of the film, which is deeply concerned with the brutal impact of the fellow upon his wife, son, mistress, and friends, is a heavy confusion of dense dramatics that is saved from being downright dull only by the variety and vigor of pictorial detail.

And you may count as pictorial detail the performance which Broderick Crawford gives as the big, brawling, boisterous "hick" lawyer who makes himself a momentary "king." Mr. Crawford concentrates tremendous energy into every delineation he plays, whether it is the enthusiasm of a callow bumpkin or the virulence of a drunken demagogue. Although it is hard to know precisely why he gravitates and acts the way he does, he draws a compelling portrait, in two dimensions, of an egomaniac.

Less can be said for the other principal performers in the film—not because of their own shortcomings but because of the unresolved roles they play. Joanne Dru is a pretty, well-dressed cipher as the meaningless mistress of the man, and John Ireland is a loose-limbed, dead-panned puppet as a newspaper reporter who follows him around. Shepperd Strudwick fumbles vaguely with the passions of the doctor who assassinates the brute, and Mercedes McCambridge is picturesque but vagrant as a hard-boiled henchman in skirts. However, the various people who play cheap politicos, especially Will Wright and Ralph Dumke, are as genuine as pot-bellied stoves. As satellites to Mr. Crawford, in the raw, racy portions of the film, they help to bring color and excitement to this ironic *All the King's Men.*

—B.C., *November 9, 1949*

ALL THE PRESIDENT'S MEN

Directed by Alan J. Pakula; written by William Goldman, based on the book by Carl Bernstein and Bob Woodward; cinematographer, Gordon Willis; edited by Robert Wolfe; music by David Shire; production designer, George Jenkins; produced by Walter Coblenz; released by Warner Brothers. Running time: 138 minutes.

With: Dustin Hoffman (Carl Bernstein), Robert Redford (Bob Woodward), Jack Warden (Harry Rosenfeld), Martin Balsam (Howard Simons), Hal Holbrook (Deep Throat), Jason Robards (Ben Bradlee), Jane Alexander (Bookkeeper), Meredith Baxter (Debbie Sloan), Ned Beatty (Dardis), Stephen Collins (Hugh Sloan Jr.), Penny Fuller (Sally Aiken), John McMartin (Foreign Editor) and Robert Walden (Donald Segretti).

Newspapers and newspapermen have long been favorite subjects for moviemakers—a surprising number of whom are former newspapermen, yet not until *All the President's Men,* the riveting screen adaptation of the Watergate book by Carl Bernstein and Bob Woodward, has any film come remotely close to being an accurate picture of American journalism at its best.

All the President's Men, directed by Alan J. Pakula, written by William Goldman, and largely pushed into being by the continuing interest of one of its stars, Robert Redford, is a lot of things all at once: a spellbinding detective story about the work of the two *Washington Post* reporters who helped break the Watergate scandal, a breathless adventure that recalls the triumphs of Frank and Joe Hardy in that long-ago series of boys' books, and a vivid footnote to some contemporary American history that still boggles the mind.

The film, which opened yesterday at Loews Astor Plaza and Tower East Theaters, is an unequivocal smash-hit—the thinking man's *Jaws.*

Much of the effectiveness of the movie, which could easily have become a mishmash of names, dates, and events, is in its point of view, which remains that of its two, as yet unknown reporters—Carl Bernstein (Dustin Hoffman), highly competitive and a little more experienced than his partner, and Bob Woodward (Robert Redford), very ambitious and a dog for details.

It's through their eyes—skeptical, hungry, insatiably curious—that *All the President's Men* unfolds. It begins logically on the night of June 17, 1972, when five men were arrested in an apparent break-in at the headquarters of the Democratic National Committee in the Watergate complex in Washington, and continues through the spectacular series of revelations, accusations, and admissions of guilt that eventually brought the Nixon Presidency to its conclusion.

Like Bernstein and Woodward in the course of their investigation, the film maintains bifocal vision, becoming thoroughly absorbed in the seemingly unimportant minutiae out of which major conspiracies can sometimes be reconstructed, yet never for long losing sight of the overall relevance of what's going on. Although *All the President's Men* is first and foremost a fascinating newspaper film, the dimensions and implications of the Watergate story obviously give it an emotional punch that might be lacking if, say, Bernstein and Woodward had been exposing corruption in the Junior League.

Thus the necessity of the director's use of newsreel footage from time to time—the shots of President Nixon's helicopter making a night landing at the White House, which open the film; the television images of the President entering the House of Representatives, and of other familiar folk including former Attorney General John N. Mitchell, former Vice President Agnew, and, especially, Representative Gerald R. Ford in the course of his nomination of President Nixon at the 1972 Republican National Convention.

Though the film will undoubtedly have some political impact, its strength is the virtually day-by-day record of the way Bernstein and Woodward conducted their investigations, always under the supervision of a kindly avuncular Ben Bradlee (Jason Robards), the *Post*'s managing editor who (in this film) gives out advice, caution, and, occasionally, a "well-done," acting as Dr. Gillespie to their Dr. Kildares.

Mr. Redford and Mr. Hoffman play their roles with the low-keyed, understated efficiency required since they are, in effect, the straight men to the people

and the events they are pursuing. The film stays out of their private lives but is full of unexpected, brief, moving glimpses into the private lives of their subjects, including a frightened bookkeeper (Jane Alexander) for the Committee to Re-elect the President, Donald Segretti (Robert Walden), the "dirty tricks" man, and Hugh Sloan, Jr. (Stephen Collins), the committee treasurer, and his wife (Meredith Baxter).

The manners and methods of big-city newspapering, beautifully detailed, contribute as much to the momentum of the film as the mystery that's being uncovered. Maybe even more, since the real excitement of *All the President's Men* is in watching two comparatively inexperienced reporters stumble onto the story of their lives and develop it triumphantly, against all odds.

—V.C., April 8, 1976

AMADEUS

Directed by Milos Forman: written by Peter Shaffer. based on his play: cinematographer. Miroslav Ondricek: edited by Nena Danevic and Michael Chandler: music by Wolfgang Amadeus Mozart. Antonio Salieri and Giovanni Battista Pergolesi. conducted by Neville Marriner: choreography and opera staging by Twyla Tharp: art designers. Karl Cerny and Francesco Chianese: production designer. Patrizia Van Brandenstein: produced by Saul Zaentz: released by Orion Pictures. Running time: 158 minutes.

With: F. Murray Abraham (Antonio Salieri). Tom Hulce (Wolfgang Amadeus Mozart). Elizabeth Berridge (Constanze Mozart). Simon Callow (Emanuel Schikaneder). Roy Dotrice (Leopold Mozart). Christine Ebersole (Katerina Cavalieri). Jeffrey Jones (Emperor Joseph II). Charles Kay (Count Orsini-Rosenberg) and Kenny Baker (Parody Commendatore).

From the initial production of Peter Shaffer's *Amadeus* at the National Theater in London in 1979, through all of the refinements that preceded the play's New York premiere in 1980, and now, in the even more extensive rewriting and adjustments made by Mr. Shaffer for Milos Forman's handsome, music-filled screen version, one thing has remained constant and exhilarating.

That is Mr. Shaffer's ability to celebrate genius—in this case, that of Wolfgang Amadeus Mozart—in a fashion that is simultaneously illuminating, moving, and just. It's a major achievement, especially in films where genius is usually represented and dramatized as some kind of ill-humored, social eccentricity.

On film, the core of this extraordinary drama continues to be the paradox represented by Antonio Salieri who, as court composer to Joseph II, the Holy Roman Emperor, was Mozart's most ferocious adversary as well as the only person in Vienna to comprehend the magnificence of Mozart's gifts.

Very early in the film there's a marvelous moment when Salieri, played with immense, tragic humor and passion by F. Murray Abraham, hears for the first time the music of the young prodigy who has become the talk at the Hapsburg court in Vienna. In words that could only have been written by a playwright with a rare understanding of music, Salieri describes how the notes interact, one hanging over another, intersected by others, to bring out feelings of sweetness and pain that send Salieri rushing from the room in delirious panic.

"This was music I'd never heard before," says Salieri, whose face melts into ashen jelly. "It seemed to me the voice of God."

In *Amadeus,* which opens today at the Paramount and Tower East Theaters, we hear, almost as if for the first time, which is the way with great music, long, glorious passages from the operas, concertos, sonatas, and masses, and, through the obsession of Salieri, we come to understand something of their particular divinity. "If He did not want me to praise Him with music," the mad old Salieri says to an uncomprehending priest, "why did He give me the desire?"

As in the play, the frame of the film is Salieri's "confession," thirty-two years after the death of Mozart in 1791 at the age of thirty-five, about the events that led up to his—Salieri's—"murder" of the "obscene child" whom God had chosen to be his magic flute on earth. It is through Mozart, Salieri says in his rage, that God had poured music that, as Mr. Shaffer believes, is testimony that a divine spark can exist in mankind.

As directed for the stage by Peter Hall, *Amadeus* was a "black opera," a highly stylized phantasmagoria

that moved between past and present in a spectacular unit set, one that even comprehended the states of mind of old Salieri, the self-described patron saint of mediocrities, as he lay in the siege of memories of real events and those he has imagined.

Mr. Forman and Mr. Shaffer, acknowledging the differing demands of stage and screen, have opened up the play. They are able to include excerpts from the operas, which couldn't be shown on the stage, but they've also made a far more literal work.

Having been shot entirely in and around Prague—which stands in for Emperor Joseph II's Vienna—the movie looks wonderfully authentic. A centerpiece of the musical sequence is Prague's jewel-like Tyl Theater, where Mozart actually conducted the first performance of *Don Giovanni*. Never for a minute does this *Amadeus* seem like a filmed play.

Yet, for all of the right decisions, and in spite of the abundance of music, conducted by Neville Marriner, something also has been lost. Mr. Shaffer is a playwright of grand theatricality, and even when translated to film with intelligence and love, his work misses the particular rigors imposed by the limitations of the stage. This *Amadeus* is fascinating and it may be even more humane than the play, and though the impact is not necessarily less, it is decidedly different.

Mr. Abraham, whose first starring film role this is, is very fine as Salieri, initially secure—"Everybody liked me," he remembers, "and I liked myself"—and then increasingly lunatic as he plots Mozart's downfall.

A major but very effective switch in the film is the climactic sequence in which Salieri schemes to snatch "a bit of divinity" from the dying Mozart. As Mozart lies exhausted in bed, dictating the score of the Requiem Mass, the desperate Salieri takes down the notes in his own hand, in this fashion to pass off the work as his own. It may not be history, but it's the high point of this drama.

As Mozart, Tom Hulce, though extremely American in looks and voice, gets better and better as the drama progresses. He has the absolutely implacable self-assurance, the scatological humor, and the manic manner of the Mozart revealed in his letters, a fellow who can scribble some of the greatest music the world has ever heard amid rude jokes, with no self-consciousness about either.

Mozart's is not as interesting a role as that of Salieri. Mozart is never in doubt about his talents. The music is safely in his head—all he has to do is write it down. When, at last, he is sick and dying, though still not depleted, the defeat is only physical.

Most of the other performances are good, especially those of Jeffrey Jones, as the Emperor, and Roy Dotrice, as Mozart's exacting father, the "Commendatore" to his profligate son. Not so great is Elizabeth Berridge as Mozart's beloved Constanze—a large casting mistake. Miss Berridge is pretty and suitably silly, but it's probably not her fault that she suggests her native Westchester far more often than eighteenth-century Vienna.

The glimpses of the operas are so good that one wants to see more. They include *The Marriage of Figaro,* about which the Emperor complains that "there are too many notes," *The Abduction from the Seraglio* and *The Magic Flute,* and, in one of the film's most imaginative, most hallucinatory sequences, a parody version of *Don Giovanni,* whose obscenities, of course, delight the now ailing Mozart.

Mr. Forman, who created a highly original film out of the virtually formless stage production of Hair, has preserved the fascinating heart of Mr. Shaffer's play, and made it available to millions who might never enter a legitimate theater. Well done.

—*V.C., September 19, 1984*

AMARCORD

Directed by Federico Fellini; written (in Italian, with English subtitles) by Mr. Fellini and Tonino Guerra; director of photography, Giuseppe Rotunno; edited by Ruggero Mastroianni; music by Nino Rota; produced by Franco Cristaldi; released by Roger Corman/New World Pictures. Running time: 127 minutes.

With: Magali Noel (Gradisca), Bruno Zanin (Titta), Pupella Maggio (Titta's Mother), Armando Brancia (Father) and Giuseppe Lanigro (Grandfather), Luigi Rossi (The Lawyer).

Amarcord, which opened yesterday at the Plaza Theater, may possibly be Federico Fellini's most marvelous film. It's an extravagantly funny, sometimes dreamlike evocation of a year in the life of a small Italian coastal town in the 1930's, not as it literally was, perhaps, but as it is recalled by a director with a superstar's access to the resources of the Italian film industry and a piper's command over our imaginations.

When Mr. Fellini is working in peak condition, as he is in *Amarcord* (the vernacular for "I remember" in Romagna), he somehow brings out the best in us. We become more humane, less stuffy, more appreciative of the profound importance of attitudes that in other circumstances would seem merely eccentric if not lunatic.

Amarcord has close associations to Mr. Fellini's last two films, *The Clowns* and *Roma,* both memoirs of a sort, but the likeness turns out to be superficial on closer inspection. This new production combines the free form and make-believe splendor of those two films with the comic, bittersweet feeling for character and narrative we remember from some of his best films of the 1950's—*Variety Lights, The White Sheik, I Vitelloni,* and *Nights of Cabiria.*

Amarcord has a sort of narrator-host-master-of-ceremonies who watches over everything. He's called The Lawyer (Luigi Rossi) and is a scholarly, pedantic fellow with a fondness for historical dates that establish links between the present and a past that can be traced with some certainty to 268 b.c. From time to time The Lawyer turns up to talk to us directly, occasionally being pelted with vegetables or tin cans by the town loafers who find all his talk a bore.

The town in the film is not unlike the Adriatic resort inhabited by the young men in *I Vitelloni,* based on Rimini, where Mr. Fellini grew up. Yet there is now something magical, larger-than-life about the town, its citizens, and many of the things that happen to them.

There is no single central character, but an uproariously unruly procession of them. There are Titta (Bruno Zanin), a boy in his teens who could be the young Fellini; Titta's father (Armando Brancia), a terrible-tempered construction foreman who insists on wearing his Socialist tie every time the Fascists hold a local rally; Gradisca (Magali Noel), the town hairdresser, a silly, pretty, immaculately groomed (she even wears her saucy red beret to bed) femme fatale who dreams of Gary Cooper but settles down with a stodgy policeman.

There are also Titta's grandfather (Giuseppe Lanigro), a cheerful, foul-mouthed old man who remembers the joys of intercourse the way someone else might remember football scores, and Titta's crazy uncle (Ciccio Ingrassia), who, while on a picnic away from the asylum, climbs to the top of a tree and calls out his need for a woman. He is finally retrieved by one—a midget nun.

The movie is awash in the kind of poetic artifice that Mr. Fellini loves and that has become increasingly rare these days when most directors insist on working in actual locations.

Mr. Fellini is fascinated by movie studios, by makeup, by sets, by the work of the special-effects men, all of which are the materials of his kind of moviemaking. One of the most marvelous moments in *Amarcord* is also one of its most frankly fake, a scene in which the townspeople keep watch at night in rowboats and small cruisers, in what looks to be a cellophane sea, to herald the maiden voyage of the old Rex, which, when it appears, looms like some magnificent stage prop. We see what everyone else has been imagining.

This style has the effect of softening the edges of history, which is one of the things that memory also does. The arrogance and cruelty of the town's Fascists are certainly not diminished, but they are set at a distance, as if to be contemplated. A death is not made less poignant but it becomes a heartbreaking fact that has already been accepted.

Amarcord is as full of tales as Scheherazade, some romantic, some slapstick, some elegiacal, some bawdy, some as mysterious as the unexpected sight of a peacock flying through a light snowfall. It's a film of exhilarating beauty.

—*V.C., September 20, 1974*

AMÉLIE

Directed by Jean-Pierre Jeunet; written (in French, with English subtitles) by Guillaume Laurant and Mr. Jeunet; director of photography, Bruno Delbonnel; edited by Hervé Schneid; music by Yann Tiersen; produced by Claudie Ossard; released by Miramax Films. Running time: 120 minutes.

With: Audrey Tautou (Amélie), Mathieu Kassovitz (Nino Quicampoix), Rufus (Raphael Poulain),

Yolande Moreau (Madeleine Wallace), Arthus de Penguern (Hipolito), Urbain Cancellier (Collignon), Dominique Pinon (Joseph), Serge Merlin (Dufayel) and Flora Guiet (young Amélie).

Jean-Pierre Jeunet's *Amélie,* a sugar-rush of a movie, has what could be called meticulous clutter, a placement of imagery that covers every square centimeter of the screen. Mr. Jeunet's sense of humor gives the movie heart; his real affection for the medium can be seen in all the funny little curlicues and jottings around the action.

Amélie offers Mr. Jeunet a chance to show some flair without the brittle chill of his previous films like *Delicatessen* and *The City of Lost Children,* in which his imagination and heartlessness combined for the film version of felonious assault.

Amélie has a hypnotic sense of romance; it's a fable filled with longing, with a heroine who constantly flirts with failure. Just because the movie has the reflexes of a predatory animal doesn't mean it lacks a heart. (Or an audience. The picture is one of the biggest hits ever in France and will probably do well in the United States before its probable Oscar nomination—that is, if its American distributor, Miramax, has anything to say about it.)

Mr. Jeunet has made his own Paris through sets and computer-generated art for *Amélie.* He and Guillaume Laurant, with whom he wrote the script, tell the story of Amélie (Audrey Tautou) from her conception through her adult life, which is filled with the kind of offhand cruelty normally found in the novels of John Irving and Kurt Vonnegut. Her parents are described as "a neurotic and an iceberg," and part of Amélie's charm is that she is preternaturally levelheaded and survives her youth with her dark, glowing eyes wide open.

She has the innocent vitality of a silent-film star; with her helmet of gorgeous brunet hair, she is posed to suggest Louise Brooks from some angles. Mr. Jeunet directs his protagonist so that even when she is a child (played by Flora Guiet), each thought and impulse shines though her skin. (Ms. Tautou addresses the camera as if she were looking each viewer right in the eye; she has the crosshairs focus of a movie star.)

As a grown-up, Amélie, who works as a waitress,

tinkers in the lives of her friends. She scampers around like a woodland sprite, laying out elaborate stunts and practical jokes as payback for those who get on the wrong side of her buddies. When she falls in love with Nino (Mathieu Kassovitz), she can't be direct and let him know how she feels. Instead, she pulls him into an elaborate courtship dance that turns life in Paris into a game of Twister with a treasure hunt added to the mix. Nino, mouth agape, trails after Amélie, still the mystery woman to him, as she leaves clues about herself everywhere.

Mr. Jeunet soaks each frame with sepia and greens. The sepia indicates that *Amélie* takes place in a dreamscape Paris, and the wide-open streets come out of the French films of the 1930's, which already idealized France. The green gives the picture a trippy atmosphere, as if it had been dunked in absinthe. As a conception, the movie feels so scrubbed that it is on the sterile side.

And Mr. Kassovitz's presence underscores a pivotal deficit in *Amélie*. There are no people of color in this snow-globe version of Paris, and since Mr. Kassovitz is one of the few French directors to deal with racial tensions in his own work (the social drama *Hate*), the lack becomes impossible to ignore. Given that Mr. Jeunet used a black hero in *Alien: Resurrection*, he can't be blind to race. (Michael Haneke's *Code Inconnu*, due this month, is a hard-edged examination of racism in France, and a must.)

In *Amélie*, the fastidious complex of flesh and fantasy is a dazzling achievement. It has the impact of Wired magazine in its earliest days, when every single page looked like a ransom note put together by a kidnapper who had just downed a six-pack of Mountain Dew.

Mr. Jeunet is not the first French director to deal in pop-abstract terms; Louis Malle's *Zazie Dans le Métro* (1959) was the first influential example of eye-catching zest and was the story of a strong-willed princess-type, a plot point *Amélie* shares. Jean-Jacques Beineix's "Diva" (1981) was also a stylized tour, a walk through a punk Paris that is now as quaint as Mr. Jeunet's only-in-the-movies France. He painstakingly creates his urban vision with the same meticulousness that Amélie's neighbor, the painter Dufayel (Serge Merlin), does stroke-for-stroke recreations of Renoir paintings. (Dominique Pinon, a Jeunet regular who plays the jealous-guy Joseph in *Amélie*, is the shaved-head punk on the *Diva* poster.)

Perhaps after living under a studio's demands for a fourth-in-the-series *Alien* sequel, Mr. Jeunet decided to build his own universe from the ground up. Maybe, too, after the violence—spiritual and physical—of his earlier films, he wanted his latest tale to glisten with optimism. This balletic mix of whimsy and fairy tale could potentially err on the side of self-infatuation, but Mr. Jeunet moves so fast that the movie never stops to ogle its beautiful reflection.

Mr. Jeunet loves video stimulation. In a single scene, a television shows a man doing back flips while a friendly doggy runs in place on his stomach, an image replaced by the gospel whirlwind Sister Rosetta Tharpe, twanging her way through "Up Above My Head."

The film's pacing is athletic, though the pulse of the narrative is gradually slowed. By the climax, the movie segues into a rumination on loss and the perils of being too playful. When Dufayel straightens Amélie out, we see it in a monologue on videotape. Here Mr. Jeunet uses video as a device to demonstrate how Amélie has kept the world at arm's length, but the scene evokes "Krapp's Last Tape"; in close-up, Dufayel resembles Samuel Beckett. By this point, the director brakes the action so that thought, and possibly regret, can filter through.

The film's original French title was *Le Fabuleux Destin d'Amélie Poulain*, and Mr. Jeunet deflates the self-mocking pomposity of the title by the last third of the movie. Yet there is no denying that *Amélie* is, to paraphrase its title, fabulous.

—*E.M., November 2, 2001*

AMERICA, AMERICA

Produced, written and directed by Elia Kazan; based on the book by Mr. Kazan; cinematographer, Haskell Wexler; edited by Dede Allen; music by Manos Hadjidakis; released by Warner Brothers. Black and white. Running time: 176 minutes.

With: Stathis Giallelis (Stavros Topouzoglou), Frank Wolff (Vartan Damadian), Harry Davis

(Isaac Topouzoglou). Elena Karam (Vasso Topouzoglou) and Estelle Hemsley (Grandmother Topouzoglou).

Elia Kazan's Greek uncle, who was the first of his family to emigrate to the United States, is paid a splendid tribute by his nephew in the new film, *America, America.*

It is a tribute, expressed entirely in vivid, vigorous motion-picture terms, to the courage, tenacity, and foresight that drove the young man to fight his way out of a land of bondage in Turkey at the turn of the century and on to this land of freedom where his strength and his spirit might have full play. And since the recipient of the tribute might be any young immigrant of that day, the film is, indeed, not only a tribute but also a ringing ode to the whole great surging, immigrant wave.

An ode—that is what it is, precisely, for the story conveyed in this film, which opened last night at the Paris, is a minor odyssey that has the major connotations of a rich lyric-epic poem. It is a story as ancient as Homer, as modern as the dossier on the kid who has tried three times to enter this country as a desperate but clumsy stowaway. And in it is packed by Mr. Kazan all the longing, frustration, and ultimate joy of the tireless wanderer who seeks and finally finds his spiritual home.

Furthermore, the narrative construction of this lengthy account of the trek of a youth from darkest Asia Minor to the melting pot of New York is achieved with images that have poetic flavor. They have strong black-and-white pungency, the excitement and tension of strident language, the power and shock of mighty words. Along with the truly epic strophes of Manos Hadjidakis's musical score, they develop an assault upon the senses that may leave one completely overwhelmed.

One may also find one's senses exhausted by the sheer length and bulk of the film, which is based upon his uncle's true-life experiences and a fictional account of them that Mr. Kazan wrote. For the writer-director has been no less economical with the footage devoted to separate sequences than he has been with the miscellanea packed into the individual scenes.

All goes well when he is vividly describing the Turkish terror in Anatolia, the rugged region where the hero lives with his family and from which he is determined to escape. Mr. Kazan presents, at the outset, the sight of an abortive massacre that leaves no doubt of why his uncle wanted to get out of there.

And his brilliantly visualized description of the youth's sad encounter with a Turk who shamelessly preys upon his innocence and robs him of the few possessions with which he starts out from his home is as crisp and engrossing a sequence as anyone could wish.

But the movement begins to wax sluggish when Constantinople is reached and the youth gets involved with his uncle, cutthroat longshoremen, and treacherous prostitutes. And it wearisomely meanders through a folksy but too-long episode in which the lad finds himself suffocated by the rich family of a young woman he almost weds.

Mr. Kazan likewise gives too much attention to the shipboard experiences of the young man when he finally embarks for America. The lad's service as a gigolo to the wife of an elderly rug merchant is neither amusing nor wholly believable. And too much is made of the personal sacrifice a friend makes so the hero can get into the United States. The fine statement made by the picture doesn't need so much lush embellishment.

But, for all that, the sentiment surges when Ellis Island is finally reached and Mr. Kazan catches the poetry of immigrants arriving in America. With some masterfully authentic staging and a fitly hard-focus camera, he gives us as fine an understanding of that drama as the screen has ever had.

We must also be thankful to him for selecting a splendid cast to perform his colorful characters and for directing all of them so well. A Greek lad, Stathis Giallelis (pronounced STAH-this-Ya-lah-LEASE), is incredibly good as the determined hero, putting fire and spirit into the role, as well as a poignant revelation of the naïveté and gentleness of the youth.

Harry Davis and Elena Karam as his parents, Lou Antonio as the treacherous Turk, Salem Ludwig as his Constantinople uncle, Linda Marsh as his briefly affianced, and Paul Mann as her bearded, boisterous father are standouts in a cast that offers gemlike performances in even the smallest roles.

If Mr. Kazan's pictures weren't so overwhelmingly long and, consequently, so often redundant, it would be—what? Even finer than it is.

—B.C., *December 16, 1963*

THE AMERICAN FRIEND

Written (in English, French and German with English subtitles), produced and directed by Wim Wenders, based on the novel *Ripley's Game* by Patricia Highsmith; director of photography, Robby Muller; edited by Peter Przygodda; art directors, Heidi Ludi and Toni Ludi; music by Jurgen Knieper; released by New Yorker Films. Running time: 127 minutes.

With: Dennis Hopper (Tom Ripley), Bruno Ganz (Jonathan Zimmermann), Lisa Kreuzer (Marianne Zimmermann), Grard Blain (Raoul Minot), Nicholas Ray (Derwatt), Samuel Fuller (The American Mobster), Peter Lilienthal (Marcangelo), Daniel Schmid (Ingraham), Rudolf Schndler (Gantner), Sandy Whitelaw (Doctor in Paris) and Lou Castel (Rodolphe).

It's one of the peculiarities of contemporary film making that three of the most interesting American underworld movies of recent years have been made in West Germany by young German directors—two by Rainer Werner Fassbinder (*Gods of the Plague* and *The American Soldier*) and now one by Wim Wenders, *The American Friend,* which will be shown at the 15th New York Film Festival at Lincoln Center tonight at 9 and tomorrow at 3 P.M. The film will begin its regular commercial engagement Monday at the Cinema Studio.

Strictly speaking, all three are more important as comments on the genre than as demonstrations of it, though the tone of tragic-cool, which is essentially comic in Mr. Fassbinder's brilliantly slapdash films, is made so profound and desolate in "The American Friends" that the film can stand by itself.

Mr. Wenders describes *The American Friend* as "an entertainment film," by which, I assume, he means that unlike, say, his fine, icy adaptation of Peter Handke's *The Goalie's Anxiety at the penalty Kick* it's for mass audiences who demand narratives with more or less conventional beginnings, middles and ends. This is not quite true.

The American Friend, adapted from Patricia Highsmith's novel *Ripley's Game,* has those basic ingredients, plus a good deal of suspense, but it's almost as shy of easy explanation as *The Goalie's Anxiety at the Penalty Kick.* Like that film, too, *The American Friend* is obsessed with the idea of personal identity, which was slowly slipping away from the goalie during that earlier film, but which is the revelation in the new work.

The American Friend is about a young Hamburg picture-framer named Jonathan Zimmermann (Bruno Ganz), who is happily married and has a young son and who is perfectly ordinary except that he is suffering from a rare blood disease. He knows the disease will eventually be fatal, though doctors can't tell him whether he will live two days, a month or five years. The uncertainty gives him a kind of peace, a saintly sanity. He would call himself a moral man.

This peace and sanity is upset when Jonathan is approached by an insistent Frenchman who, promising to pay him handsomely and to help him obtain special medical treatment, asks him to come to Paris to assassinate a Mafia figure. Jonathan needs the money but the idea of killing seems inconceivable to him. Watching these negotiations, and advising the Frenchman while also establishing a friendship with Jonathan, is a mysterious American, Tom Ripley (Dennis Hopper), a fellow who wears a cowboy hat, looks ravaged by time though he's certainly not old, and who appears to be part of some sort of art-forging ring.

Little by little Jonathan Zimmermann finds himself being caught up in a series of outrageous circumstances that apparently have no connection to his earlier life. It's as if the promise of a huge sum of money, which would relieve his widow of financial worries, as well as the specialized medical treatment, derail the personality he thought he had. He kills once without remorse, and then finds he must accept a second assignment.

These are the bare bones of the story, which has almost nothing to do with the why of things and very little to do with the how. Instead it consists entirely of behavior observed from a privileged position, as was *The Goalie's Anxiety at the Penalty Kick.* We see Jonathan not as he is transformed into someone other, but as he strips down to his essential being. At least, that's how I read it.

Though it's fun, it's not always simple. Mr. Wenders has so spaced out sequences—consciously eliminating explanations—that he's left it up to us to read the film as we will from causes and effects.

One of the effects that most interests him is the friendship that grows up between Jonathan and the peculiar Tom Ripley, who moves through the film as he does from one continent to another, with supernatural ease. Ripley, which is the first decent role that Mr. Hopper has had in years, is the devil who buys Jonathan's soul, only to find that, eventually, their roles are, if not reversed, then rearranged. For a brief moment in between they are friends.

The American Friend, much superior to both Mr. Wenders's *Alice in the Cities* and *Kings of the Road,* is enigmatic if one insists on simple logic, which is not something that is terribly rare in movies, even bad ones. It is fascinating if you take it on its own terms. It is an extremely beautiful film, sometimes intentionally extravagant in visual detail, and acted with effectively insidious self-assurance by Mr. Hopper and with an appropriate sort of square intensity by Mr. Ganz, who was so good earlier this year in the German film version of *The Wild Duck.*

One reservation: Mr. Wenders's decision to cast the veteran Hollywood directors Nicholas Ray and Sam Fuller as two of the villains of the piece simply disturbs the flow of the film, if you recognize them, as I do. However, since I didn't recognize either Jean Eustache or Gerard Blain, the French directors, who also appear in the film, I suppose this won't seem especially important to most moviegoers.

—*V.C., September 24, 1977*

AMERICAN GRAFFITI

Directed by George Lucas: written by Mr. Lucas. Glora Katz and Willard Huyck: cinematographers. Ron Eveslage and Jan D'Alquen: edited by Verna Fields and Marcia Lucas: music by Karin Green: art designer. Dennis Clark: produced by Francis Ford Coppola and Gary Kurtz: released by Universal Pictures. Running time: 110 minutes.

With: Richard Dreyfuss (Curt). Ronny Howard (Steve). Paul Le Mat (John). Charlie Martin Smith (Terry). Cindy Williams (Laurie). Candy Clark (Debbie). Mackenzie Phillips (Carol). Wolfman Jack (Disc Jockey) and Harrison Ford (Bob Falfa).

At dusk the cars begin to congregate. The drivers, kids in their teens, meet and greet and happily insult one another. A few couples, going steady, may pair off. There is a high school dance, but there is also the lure of the main street to cruise up and down, exchanging pleasantries, looking for dates, for excitement, an impromptu race, even a little danger. Every radio in town is tuned in to Wolfman Jack with his line of eerie patter and all the latest hits—"Sixteen Candles," "The Book of Love" . . . It is early in the fall of 1962, somewhere in northern California.

Two of the boys, Curt Henderson and Steve Bolander, headed East to college, are uneasy at the prospect. John Milner, champion drag racer, is twenty-two—old enough to know he's headed nowhere, except up to the neon-lighted circle of Mel's Drive-In and perhaps down to the stillness of the automobile graveyard at the edge of town. Those are roughly the perimeters of George Lucas's *American Graffiti,* which examines that much of America as it lives for about twelve hours, from an evening to the following morning.

A lot happens. Steve (Ronny Howard) breaks up and makes up with Curt's sister Laurie (Cindy Williams). A younger boy, Terry, (Charlie Martin Smith) borrows Steve's Chevy, picks up a dizzy blonde (Candy Clark) for a night of horrendous misadventures, all greatly to her pleasure.

John (Paul Le Mat) enters the climactic drag race of his career. Curt (Richard Dreyfuss), the local intellectual, is almost inducted into the Pharaohs, the town gang. But Curt is following a vision, an elusive girl in a white Thunderbird who may have whispered "I love you." He never finds her. But when, in the morning, he takes off (via Magic Carpet Airlines), a white T-bird heads East on the road below. It is the only car we ever see leaving town.

American Graffiti exists not so much in its individual stories as in its orchestration of many stories, its sense of time and place. Although it is full of the material of fashionable nostalgia, it never exploits nostalgia. In its feeling for movement and music and the vitality of the night—and even in its vision in white—it is oddly closer to some early Fellini than to the recent American past of, say, *The Last Picture Show* or *Summer of '42.*

It is a very good movie, funny, tough, unsentimental. It is full of marvelous performances from actors (especially Candy Clark, Richard Dreyfuss, and Cindy Williams) hardly known for previous screen credits. But for me its excitement comes at least partly from its indication of what may be a major new career.

George Lucas, twenty-eight years old, has made one previous feature. It is a good science fiction film, *THX 1138,* about a closed, tranquilized future society, controlled by mysterious broadcast voices, and from which there is almost no escape. For all its apparent differences, *American Graffiti* really presents the obverse of that world—now beneficent, familiar; but also closed, tuned in to mysterious voices, and offering almost no means of escape.

The ways in which they are like each other are fascinating, and very much in keeping with the kinds of continuity the best directors have sustained from film to film. And somehow the persistence of an idea, reshaped and re-examined, gives me even greater joy than the specific pleasures of *American Graffiti.*

American Graffiti opened yesterday at the Sutton Theater.

—*R.G., August 13, 1973*

AN AMERICAN IN PARIS

Directed by Vincente Minnelli; written by Alan Jay Lerner; cinematographers, Alfred Gilks and John Alton; edited by Adrienne Fazan; music by George and Ira Gershwin; musical directors: Johnny Green and Saul Chaplin; choreography by Gene Kelly; art designers, Cedric Gibbons and Preston Ames; produced by Arthur Freed; released by Metro-Goldwyn-Mayer. Running time: 113 minutes.

With: Gene Kelly (Jerry Mulligan), Leslie Caron (Lise Bourvier), Oscar Levant (Adam Cook), Georges Guetary (Henri Baurel), Nina Foch (Milo Roberts), Eugene Borden (Georges Mattieu), Martha Bamattre (Mathilde Mattieu) and Mary Young (Old Woman Dancer).

Count a bewitching French lassie by the name of Leslie Caron and a whoop-de-do ballet number, one of the finest ever put upon the screen, as the most commendable enchantments of the big, lavish musical film that Metro obligingly delivered to the Music Hall yesterday. *An American in Paris,* which is the title of the picture, likewise the ballet, is spangled with pleasant little patches of amusement and George Gershwin tunes. It also is blessed with Gene Kelly, dancing and singing his way through a minor romantic complication in the usual gaudy Hollywood gay Paree. But it is the wondrously youthful Miss Caron and that grandly pictorial ballet that place the marks of distinction upon this lush Technicolored escapade.

Alongside this crisp and elfin youngster who plays the Parisian girl with whom the ebullient American of Mr. Kelly falls in love, the other extravagant characters of the romance seem standard and stale, and even the story seems wrinkled in the light of her freshness and charm. Mr. Kelly may skip about gaily, casting the favor of his smiles and the boon of the author's witticisms upon the whole of the Paris populace. Nina Foch may cut a svelte figure as a lady who wants to buy his love by buying his straight art-student paintings. And Oscar Levant may mutter wryly as a pal. But the picture takes on its glow of magic when Miss Caron is on the screen. When she isn't, it bumps along slowly as a patched-up, conventional musical show.

Why this should be is fairly obvious. Miss Caron is not a beauteous thing, in the sense of classic features, but she has a sweet face and a most delightful smile. Furthermore, she has winsomeness, expression, and youthful dignity—and she can dance like a gossamer wood-sprite on the edge of a petal at dawn.

When she and Mr. Kelly first meet in a Paris café, the previous routine of "bonjours" and "voilàs" and "mais ouis" is forgotten. Candor and charm invade the picture under Vincente Minnelli's helpful wand. And when they dance on a quai along the river, in the hush of a Paris night, to "Our Love Is Here to Stay," the romance opens and unrepressed magic evolves. Then, in the final, bursting ballet, which is done to a brilliant score of Gershwin music orchestrated with his *American in Paris* suite, the little dancer and Mr. Kelly achieve a genuine emotional splurge. It is Mr. Kelly's ballet, but Miss Caron delivers the warmth and glow.

And a ballet it is, beyond question—a truly cinematic ballet—with dancers describing vivid patterns against changing colors, designs, costumes, and scenes. The whole story of a poignant romance within a fanciful panorama of Paree is conceived and performed with taste and talent. It is the uncontested high point of the film.

Beside it such musical conniptions as Mr. Kelly and Mr. Levant giving out with "Tra-La-La," or Mr. Kelly doing a dance to "I Got Rhythm" with a bunch of kids, or Mr. Levant performing all the key jobs in a large symphonic rendition of Concerto in F are purely coincidental. And Georges Guetary's careful oozing of Gallic charm in "I'll Build a Stairway to Paradise" and "'S Wonderful" could well be done without. As a matter of fact, some of these numbers leave the uncomfortable impression that they were contrived just to fill out empty spaces in Alan Jay Lerner's glib but very thin script.

However, all things are forgiven when Miss Caron is on the screen. When she is on with Mr. Kelly and they are dancing, it is superb.

—B.C., October 5, 1951

THE AMERICANIZATION OF EMILY

Directed by Arthur Hiller; written by Paddy Chayefsky, based on the novel by William Bradford Huie; cinematographer, Philip Lathrop; edited by Tom McAdoo; music by Johnny Mandel; art designers, George W. Davis and Hans Peters; produced by Martin Ranshoff; released by Metro-Goldwyn-Mayer. Black and white. Running time: 117 minutes.

With: James Garner (Lieutenant Charles E. Madison), Julie Andrews (Emily Barham), Melvyn Douglas (Admiral William Jessup), James Coburn (Lieutenant Commander "Bus" Cummings), Joyce Grenfell (Mrs. Barham), Edward Binns (Admiral Thomas Healey) and Liz Fraser (Sheila).

If you can stand watching Julie Andrews playing a role in which she doesn't sing, but in which she does make some beautiful music with a delightfully unheroic man, then nothing should deter you from going as swiftly as you can to see *The Americanization of Emily*, which opened last night at Loew's State. (It opens today at the Tower East for a simultaneous run.)

Here is a film that not only gives the charming Miss Andrews a chance to prove herself irresistible in a straight romantic comedy but also gets off some of the wildest, brashest, and funniest situations and cracks at the lunacy of warfare that have popped from the screen in quite some time.

Indeed, when you think about it, you recognize the amazing fact that the comedy is more fascinating than the complementary byplay of romance and that James Garner as the antihero is more the wheelhorse than is the graceful female star.

It is Mr. Garner as the expert "dog robber"—or surefire aide—of an American admiral dwelling in somewhat gaudy luxury in a London hotel in 1944 who moves at the head of a skillful and deadly satiric thrust at the whole myth of war being noble and that "to die a hero is a glorious thing." And it is his taut and stalwart perseverance in acting an unregenerate coward that keynotes the yarn that Paddy Chayefsky has brilliantly adapted from a novel by William Bradford Huie.

What Mr. Garner is expressing in this sharply outspoken film, which conceals the deadly point of its thesis within some mischievously nimble farce, is that the philosophy of pacifism is the highest morality and that wars will be abolished only when people stop thinking it is noble to fight. "So long as valor is a virtue, we will have soldiers," he says in a speech in a scene with Miss Andrews and Joyce Grenfell as her mother, which has respectably Shavian overtones. It is to discredit this virtue that his character takes the attitude that dead heroes are simply dead men, less fortunate or commendable than living cowards.

This is, of course, a philosophy that shocks and initially repels the charming young English widow, a motor-pool driver, with whom he has an affair. But it even more seriously startles his gung-ho superiors when they start to execute their admiral's orders, conceived to elevate the image of the Navy, that a sailor must be "the first dead man on Omaha Beach."

It is a tense and sensitive area into which the comedy finally gets as it wildly propels its cowardly hero toward a cross-Channel landing craft and a lonely spot on the Normandy beachhead with a movie camera in his hands. There may be those who will find it distasteful after all that has gone before—the kidding of the Navy "brass" in London and the bouncing about of chairborne sailors in hotel beds.

But this deadly touch does put a climax to the serious implications of the film and provides an opportunity for resolving the previously faltering romance.

In addition to the splendid performances that Mr. Garner and Miss Andrews give—his with an edge of crisp sarcasm, hers with a brush of sentiment—there are dandy jobs by James Coburn as a swiveling "Annapolis man," Melvyn Douglas as the eccentric admiral, and Edward Binns as a solid hunk of "brass."

Also deft in small roles are Miss Grenfell, Keenan Wynn as a terrified swab, and Liz Fraser as a motor-pool driver who gladly accepts the Americans' silk stockings and Hershey bars.

Under Arthur Hiller's brisk direction of Mr. Chayefsky's script, which includes some remarkably good writing with some slashing irreverence, The *Americanization of Emily* comes out a spinning comedy that says more for basic pacifism than a fistful of intellectual tracts. It also is highly entertaining, and it makes a good case for pure romance.

—B.C., October 28, 1964

AMERICAN MOVIE

Directed by Chris Smith; director of photography, Mr. Smith; edited by Barry Poltermann, Jun Diaz and Mr. Smith; music by Mike Schank; produced by Sarah Price; released by Sony Pictures Classics. Running time: 104 minutes.

With: Mark Borchardt, Mike Schank, Monica Borchardt, Cliff Borchardt, Chris Borchardt, Alex Borchardt, Bill Borchardt, Ken Keen and Joan Petrie.

Meet Mark Borchardt, the funny, garrulous subject of the not-to-be-missed documentary *American Movie*. He's someone you won't soon forget. He has dedicated himself to making a no-budget black-and-white horror film that features homemade scarecrows and primitive acting, one that's not about to rival *The Blair Witch Project* in anything but the expletive department. But that doesn't matter. The point is that Mr. Borchardt cobbles together this project as if his life depended on it, because it does. Insightfully and stirringly, not to mention hilariously, *American Movie* shows why.

"The American Dream stays with me each and every day," Mr. Borchardt says when he speaks of his motivation. And he likes to drive past big, sterile new houses to illustrate what that dream means. But as captured here so intimately by Chris Smith, Mr. Borchardt is already living through a much darker and more authentically American story. As hard as he works to attain what he wants, he's struggling even harder to escape what he has.

Because *American Movie* is the rare documentary that combines a wildly charismatic subject with an elegant structure, it begins very simply, with the lanky, long-haired Mr. Borchardt talking about his big ambitions. ("If he is able to do even 25 percent of what he says, that is more than most people accomplish," a girlfriend later says of him.) Then the film starts to open, like a slow iris shot, onto the larger landscape of his life. When it comes to obstacles, he has a brother who announces that Mr. Borchardt would have been best suited for a factory job. And that's just for starters.

Mr. Smith, who made the film working closely with Sarah Price, builds a surprising amount of suspense and even shock into this documentary's gradual revelations about its subject. By the time Mr. Borchardt is seen doing a dead-end job at a cemetery and describing the worst kind of work he's ever been faced with, the film has built up an enormous amount of empathy and hope for him.

But even those parts of *American Movie* that display the most *Crumb*-like poignancy have their share of affectionate humor. Take Uncle Bill Borchardt, the only family member who might conceivably lend Mark any money. Mark Borchardt woos his uncle into the movie business by flashing a picture of a pretty young actress and announcing, "She wants to be in your movie, Bill." Almost before Bill can exclaim, "Oh, my gosh," he has been enlisted as the producer of *Coven*, which his nephew likes to mispronounce as KO-ven because he doesn't want it to rhyme with oven. When he gets an idea, he tends to stick with it all the way.

"I see great cinema in this," he says at one point, causing the woozy, pitifully fragile Bill to ask, "Cinnamon?" Mr. Smith has a wonderful ear for moments like that and does an expert job of extracting them from the 70 hours of film he originally shot.

Because Mr. Borchardt had been recruiting friends and relatives for projects like *The Creeps, I Blow Up* and *The More the Scarier III* since he was 14, everyone here is very comfortable with a camera rolling, and very revealing. Mr. Borchardt's friend Mike Schank, who seems to have wandered in dazed from a Kevin Smith movie, tells about a near-death experience on drugs. Then he giggles nervously and offers to tell some more. While Mr. Borchardt struggles to overcome a history of alcoholism, Mr. Schank goes him one better. He has an Alcoholics Anonymous sponsor who also drives him to Gamblers Anonymous meetings.

American Movie begins with Mr. Borchardt's ambition to make an autobiographical film called *Northwestern,* which is meant to be an ambitious exploration of his upbringing in Milwaukee. Since this soon proves to be a non-starter, he vows to raise the money for it by completing *Coven* and selling 3,000 video copies. It is soon revealed that this won't be easy, as Mr. Borchardt lies in the snow filming friends in black hooded capes ("Now you guys gotta look menacing!" he directs), bungles a scene in which a cabinet door is supposed to break on a friend's head, and otherwise shows why the road to a finished *Coven* is full of potholes.

By the time *American Movie,* opening today at Film Forum, completes its own mission, it has blossomed wonderfully into much more than a portrait of one fiendishly determined filmmaker. For anyone wondering where the spirit of maverick independent filmmaking has its source, you need look no further.

—*J.M., November 5, 1999*

AMORES PERROS

Directed and produced by Alejandro Gonzalez Inarritu; written (in Spanish, with English subtitles) by Guillermo Arriaga; director of photography, Rodrigo Prieto; edited by Mr. Gonzalez Inarritu, Luis Carballar and Fernando Perez Unda; music by Gustavo Santaolalla; production designer, Brigitte Broch; released by Lions Gate Films. Running time: 153 minutes.

With: Vanessa Bauche (Susana), Gael Garcia Bernal (Octavio), Umberto Busto (Jorge), Emilio Echevarria (El Chivo), Alvaro Guerrero (Daniel), Rodrigo Murray (Gustavo), Marco Perez (Romero), Jorge Salinas (Luis Miranda Solares) and Goya Toledo (Valeria).

When a director shifts gears as often as does Alejandro Gonzalez Inarritu, the man behind the emotionally rich debut film *Amores Perros,* you may wonder if he knows what he wants. He does, and this film is satisfying in many ways.

He is unashamed to immerse this tough-minded, episodic film noir in freshets of melodrama. Significantly, he knows the minute difference between being unashamed and being shameless, and because he knows how to keep things hopping—working from an intricate script by Guillermo Arrianga that has a novelistic texture—we watch a man with immaculate control of the medium.

The picture begins with a car chase through the streets of a Mexican city; there's a bleeding dog in the back seat, which certainly sounds shameless. Like everything else in *Amores,* a film in which nothing is what it seems, this is the kind of genre touch that Mr. Gonzalez Inarritu expands into something far more haunting.

The velocity of this first scene—in which Octavio (Gael Garcia Bernal, an actor with a wonderfully expressive face) drives his wounded dog to a veterinarian while fleeing revenge-crazed gunmen—may seem like something out of a silent film. But it still has a literal and emotional impact that knocks the breath of you. This may be one of the first art films to come out of Mexico since Bunuel worked there, and *Amores* has traces of Bunuel's romantic absurdism.

The setup of the stories—and the fact that a car wreck is at the center of the picture, an accident that changes of the lives of all of the principal characters—will inspire comparisons to *Pulp Fiction.* While *Amores* is often playful, it is certainly not glib; it's full of the heartbreak found in corridas, featuring an almost mythological suffering that owes much to the traditions of Mexico, with characters trapped in the undertow of Fate.

Many of the narrative details feel like loving gestures from a storyteller proud of the weight of folklore and of his story. The violence is fast and shocking: a shooting in a restaurant ends with blood dribbling onto a hot griddle, an image that could be a metaphor for the overheated emotions of the film.

Each of the film's three stories catches its characters at different times in their lives: the beginning, the middle and the end. In the first "Octavio and Susana," Octavio is in love with his thug-of-a-brother's wife, Susana (Vanessa Bauche). We're introduced to Susana as she walks distractedly down the street wearing a backpack and a schoolgirl's uniform. She rushes into the house and picks up her crying infant son, complaining to her mother-in-law that she has a math final to study for. Octavio stares longingly at her, and he's right: she is too good for his brother. But they're all kids scrambling for each other's attention.

Amores Perros, though it has an earthier meaning, could be translated as "Love's a Dog," and dogs play a big part in the story. Octavio ends up putting his dog, Cofi, on the dogfighting circuit after Cofi is attacked by a fighter's pit bull and triumphs. The unremitting brutality of the dogfights, in which the animals slam into each other and the sickening thud of their bodies is amplified, is something that has to be noted.

The sight of the dogs' bodies after the fights, fur matted with blood, sprawled on the concrete, will send a chill through even the most distanced viewers. (The canine carcasses look astonishingly real, though a tag at the end assures us that no animals were harmed in the making of the picture.) Dog lovers may be put off entirely by the fights.

A dog is an important element of "Daniel and Valeria," the story of a new relationship that curdles as it plays out. The middleaged Daniel (Alvaro Guerrero) has left his wife and daughter and moved into a love nest with Valeria (Goya Toledo), who can best be described as a spokesmodel; a towering billboard shot of her perfume ad can seen across the street from their new place.

Like all the stories this one teases us with a trick opening, before moving into a vignette that almost feels like an urban legend. Valeria's Lhasa apso dives into a hole in the floor, and we can hear the trapped dog scurrying back and forth and imagine the vermin feasting on its body.

Valeria is in a wheelchair—her car was struck by Octavio's, leaving her with a horribly damaged leg—and her inability to move and her wounded vanity change her behavior.

Amores feels like the first classic of the new decade, with sequences that will probably make their way into history. The picture has the crowded humidity of a telenovela, but Mr. Gonzalez Inarritu doesn't linger over the soap-operaish aspects. They're part of the fabric, an emotional tug that sends the characters to places they don't belong, though they know better.

As the last section, "El Chivo and Maru," unfolds, a devoted revolutionary turned street rat and assassin (the incredible Emilio Echevarria), who lives with his pack of dogs, seems to learn a lesson about not submitting to one's impulses. An unforgettable mark-of-Cain subplot, in more ways than one, arrives out of nowhere to deepen the hurt.

It's rare that a director can enter films with this much verve and emotional understanding. Mr. Gonzalez Inarritu loves actors, and his cast brings so many different levels of feeling to the picture that the epic length goes by quickly. *Amores Perros* vaults onto the screen, intoxicated by the power of filmmaking—speeded-up movement and tricked-up cuts that convey a shallow mastery of craft—but evolving into a grown-up love of narrative. In his very first film Mr. Gonzalez Inarritu makes the kind of journey some directors don't, or can't, travel in an entire career.

—*E.M., October 5, 2000*

ANASTASIA

Directed by Anatole Litvak: written by Arthur Laurents. based on Guy Bolton's adaptation of the play by Marcelle Maurette: cinematographer. Jack Hildyard: edited by Bert Bates: music by Alfred Newman: art designers. Andre Andrejew and Bill Andrews: produced by Buddy Adler: released by Twentieth Century Fox. Running time: 105 minutes.

With: Ingrid Bergman (Anastasia). Yul Brynner (Bounine). Helen Hayes (Empress). Akim Tamiroff (Chernov). Martita Hunt (Baroness von Livenbaum). Felix Aylmer (Russian Chamberlain). Sacha Pitoeff (Petrovin) and Ivan Desny (Prince Paul).

It is a long way round that the story of *Anastasia* has come in the course of arriving last evening on the Roxy's screen. This hypothetical drama of an actual European mystery woman who was believed by many to have been the daughter and sole survivor of the last of the Russian Czars was first a French play by Marcelle Maurette. Then it was adapted by Guy Bolton for the Broadway stage. Now it is shaped by Arthur Laurents into a romantic exercise for the screen.

But it has lost nothing in passage. If anything, it has gained pictorial scope and emotional dimensions in reaching the cinematic form. For Mr. Laurents has wisely given it geographical range, added strong scenes that the play barely suggested, and expanded the conflicts within the heroine. Anatole Litvak has smartly staged it for a fine projection of its human ironies. And it is played with keen sensitivity by Ingrid Bergman, Yul Brynner, and Helen Hayes.

This is not surprising. All of them have appropriate skills. And Mr. Litvak, of course, is no stranger to the emotional torments of fading royalty. It was his memorable French film, *Mayerling,* the poignant drama of Marie Vetserra and her Habsburg prince, that set the mark for royal romance in the movies and brought Mr. Litvak to Hollywood.

Now, in this tense and tender story of a woman who is literally snatched from death to be presented as the miracle survivor of the slaughter of the family of the Czar, he is dealing again with a drama that has to do with these royal chips on the human tide and wells from the deep and silent pockets of their pathetic loneliness.

With shrewd perception, Mr. Laurents and Mr. Litvak have realized and exposed the three fascinating facets of the fictionalized episode. The first is sheer melodrama: a plot by Russian expatriates to present a woman as the lost Anastasia to claim a fabulous inheritance. The second is stimulating mystery: is the woman presented truly she, or is she an innocent imposter with supernatural memory? And the third is genuine human drama, touched with inevitable romance: it is the drama of intimate feelings, torn by vicissitudes.

Each has been brought by Mr. Litvak into clear and exciting view, and all have been blended together into a tautly cohesive whole. The picture proceeds as one strong complex of melodrama, mystery, and romance, with no one incident providing the dominant portion, as it did on the stage. While the climactic meeting of the heroine and the Dowager Empress, her supposed grandmother, is intense, it is preceded and followed by incidents of contributing excitement and strength.

If the ending is slightly ambiguous and touched with a gloss of sentiment, that may be generously forgiven in gratitude for what has gone before.

Miss Bergman's performance as the heroine is nothing short of superb as she traces the progress of a woman from the depths of derangement and despair through a struggle with doubt and delusion to the accomplishment of courage, pride, and love. It is a beautifully molded performance, worthy of an Academy Award and particularly gratifying in the light of Miss Bergman's long absence from commendable films.

Miss Hayes's Dowager Empress is a sturdy, intense little dame, stubbornly realistic, yet containing a depth of sentiment. Her scene with her dubious granddaughter, which caps a sequence of excellent intrigues, is a beautiful exercise in acting. We only wish she seemed less Victorian.

Mr. Brynner, as the chief of the conspirators, is best when he is browbeating the girl, displaying his Slavic perseverance, and least impressive when he is itching with love. He also appears oddly youthful for a former Russian general, some ten years out of circulation, but he sure has the vigor for the role.

Martita Hunt walks away with minor honors in the amusing supporting role of a light-headed lady-in-waiting who still acts as if she is scuttling up and down backstairs. And Akim Tamiroff as a shady Russian banker, Ivan Desny as a flabby exiled prince, and Sacha Pitoeff as an unctuous conspirator are in fascinating form.

The color production is splendid, and the musical score is very good. Put this one in a class with *Mayerling.* It is that kind of high romantic film.

—B.C., December 14, 1956

ANATOMY OF A MURDER

Produced and directed by Otto Preminger; written by Wendell Mayes, based on the novel by Robert Traver; cinematographer, Sam Leavitt; edited by Louis Loeffler; music by Duke Ellington; art designer, Howard Bristol; released by Columbia Pictures. Black and white. Running time: 160 minutes.

With: James Stewart (Paul Biegler), Lee Remick (Laura Manion), Ben Gazzara (Lieutenant Manion), Arthur O'Connell (Parnell McCarthy), Joseph N. Welch (Judge Weaver), Eve Arden (Maida), Kathryn Grant (Mary Pilant), George C. Scott (Claude Dancer) and Orson Bean (Dr. Smith).

After watching an endless succession of court room melodramas that have more or less transgressed the bounds of human reason and the rules of advocacy, it is cheering and fascinating to see one that hews magnificently to a line of dramatic but reasonable behavior and proper procedure in a court. Such a one is *Anatomy of a Murder,* which opened at the Criterion and the Plaza yesterday. It is the best courtroom melodrama this old judge has ever seen.

Perhaps "melodrama" is the wrong word. Perhaps it would be better to say this is really a potent character study of a group of people involved in a criminal trial. For Otto Preminger, who produced and directed it from a script adapted by Wendell Mayes from the highly successful novel of Robert Traver (Judge John D. Voelker), has got as much fine illumination of the major personalities in this case as he has got strong suspense and pounding drama in the unfolding details of the trial.

Following the line of "Mr. Traver," even to the point of shooting all his film in the actual up-country of Michigan where the fictional murder case is set, Mr. Preminger has fittingly developed the sharp illusion of a realistic look, uninhibited and uncensored, at everything a small-town lawyer does to prepare and make a courtroom presentation of the defense of an accused murderer.

Neatly and with much local color, he finds the known facts in the case—that a moody young Army lieutenant has shot and killed a man, a tavern owner, whom the wife of the lieutenant says has raped her outside a trailer camp. Frankly, he drops the suspicion that the wife may be a bit on the shady side, that she may have been lying to the lieutenant and that he may be a mean, unstable type. And then, with this tempting information, he takes the case into court and achieves the succeeding revelation of character and conduct in that stringent atmosphere.

Actually, the major conflict and dramatic fascination from this point on is the battle of legal wits and personalities that is waged between the defense attorney and those of the prosecution, under the watchful eye of a shrewd, sardonic old judge. It is a beautifully drawn and maneuvered battle, full of neat little triumphs on each side, leading to a most exciting climax and clear exposures of the principal characters.

Most brilliantly revealed is the character of the lawyer for the defense, a part that is played by James Stewart in one of the finest performances of his career. Slowly and subtly, he presents us a warm, clever, adroit, and complex man—and, most particularly, a portrait of a trial lawyer in action that will be difficult for anyone to surpass.

On the bench as the judge, Joseph N. Welch of Boston, the lawyer who distinguished himself in the Army-McCarthy hearings, does an unbelievably professional job. He is delightful and ever so convincing. Mr. Preminger scored a coup in getting him.

George C. Scott as a prosecuting attorney makes the courtroom battle a deadly duel by offering himself as a skillful and unrelenting antagonist, and Brooks West as his standard-brand associate adds to the personal variety. Lee Remick treads beautifully a fine line between never-resolved uncertainties as the wife of the lieutenant and Ben Gazzara makes the latter role one of the haughty and haunting mysteries and ironies of the film.

Arthur O'Connell as a sozzled attorney and friend of Mr. Stewart, Eve Arden as the latter's secretary, Murray Hamilton as a witness for the state, and Kathryn Grant as a friend of the slain man turn in excellent jobs.

Outside of the fact that this drama gets a little tiring in spots—in its two hours and forty minutes, most of which is spent in court—it is well nigh flawless as a picture of an American court at work, of small-town American characters, and of the average sordidness of crime.

—*B.C., July 3, 1959*

THE ANGRY SILENCE

Directed by Guy Green: written by Bryan Forbes. based on a story by Michael Craig and Richard Gregson: cinematographer. Arthur Ibbetson: edited by Anthony Harvey: music by Malcolm Arnold: produced by Richard Attenborough and Mr. Forbes: released by Lion International Films. Black and white. Running time: 95 minutes.

With: Richard Attenborough (Tom). Pier Angeli (Anna). Michael Craig (Joe). Bernard Lee (Connolly). Geoffrey Keen (Davis). Laurence Naismith (Martindale) and Russell Napier (Thompson).

A bold, modern-times demonstration of the cozy, old-fashioned saw that an Englishman's home is his castle is bluntly and forcefully conveyed in the new British film, *The Angry Silence,* which came to the Sutton yesterday. Loaded with implications that cut deep to the heart of English life, especially among the working classes, it packs a lesson to be felt and thought about.

Specifically, this pregnant picture, which its star, Richard Attenborough, has produced in an independent association with its scriptwriter, Bryan Forbes, tells a slashing and sometimes shocking story of the ugly things that happen to a young English factory worker when he asserts his independence over the organized workers in his shop. But more than this, by implication, it says that the English working classes today are dull-witted, vicious, and sheeplike. At least, they are in this film.

If this far from flattering estimation appears to run counter to the traditional spirit of independence that supposedly flames in "this happy breed," it betokens the nature of the conflict that Mr. Forbes has chosen to describe, perhaps a little more sharply than general conditions justify.

His gaggle of workers in this instance is a pretty abominable lot, enslaved to a senseless slogan of "union solidarity." They vote for a strike that their shop chairman has secretly aggravated and engineered in cahoots with a shady outsider who might well be a sabotaging "red." Then, when they've staged their walkout (without the approval of their national, by the way), they behave like a bunch of goons and hoodlums toward the handful of members who have opted to stay in.

On the other hand, the hero, played by Mr. Attenborough, is a sensible, sober, sturdy, family-loving man. He can see no reason for a walkout, stays in (despite the raucous charge of being a "scab"), and reluctantly submits to the will of the strikers when his little knot of resisters evaporates.

But what really gets up his dander and causes him to defy the organization openly is a personal warning from the shop chairman that he had better not step out of line again. When the chairman—a hulking, brutish fellow, played powerfully by Bernard Lee—comes to his home to deliver this warning, he blasts the intruder's ears and heroically sends him hopping. That's what does it for him.

With a style of realism that is convincing and emotionally disturbing, too, the picture now displays the kind of vengeance the other workers wreak—how they scorn and abuse the nonconformist, keep him "in Coventry," and finally do bodily harm to his little son and injure him seriously.

At the end, there's a bit of melodrama to give retribution a chance and to suggest the chagrin and sorrow of some of the workers, but it does not absolve them from shame. They still look insensitive and unstable, as, by the way, does the boss of the factory (Laurence Naismith).

So energetic and compelling is the staccato style of Mr. Forbes's screenplay and the taut direction of Guy Green that one inclines to accept the actuality of this episode. And so simple and honest is the acting of Mr. Attenborough, of Geoffrey Keen as a decent personnel director, and of Pier Angeli as the hero's spunky wife, that one is immensely attracted to them and prejudiced to their case.

Equally, the pusillanimity and sideburned shoddiness of Michael Craig as a treacherous friend of the hero and the rank viciousness of Brian Bedford and Brian Murray as a couple of union punks are so strong that the mind is shaken by the notion that these types are general in Britain today.

It is well for one to recognize and remember that a particular and arbitrary set of circumstances has been organized in this film, which is one of the best of the year from Britain, lest one find oneself distrusting the entire working class.

—B.C., December 13, 1960

ANNA AND THE KING OF SIAM

Directed by John Cromwell; written by Talbot Jennings and Sally Benson, based on the biography by Margaret Landon; cinematographer, Arthur Miller; music by Bernard Hermann; art designers, Lyle Wheeler and William Darling; produced by Louis D. Lighton; released by Twentieth Century Fox. Black and white. Running time: 128 minutes.

With: Irene Dunne (Anna), Rex Harrison (The King), Linda Darnell (Tuptim), Lee J. Cobb (Kralahome), Gale Sondergaard (Lady Thiang), Mikhail Rasumny (Alak), Dennis Hoey (Sir Edward) and Tito Renaldo (Prince).

The noble and triumphant female, an ever-popular figure on the screen and always a particular favorite with audiences at the Music Hall, is exalted in the usual plushy manner but under circumstances which make for much appeal in the new picture at the nation's showplace, *Anna and the King of Siam*.

Based on the popular biography which Margaret Landon wrote of a lady who served as governess at the Siamese court eighty years ago, this film should be vastly attractive to those who respectably delight in the idealized picture of a female whose splendid qualities accomplish worthy ends. For Irene Dunne plays the fabled governess briskly and winsomely, and the whole pattern of her characterization is designed to show her strength of mind and will.

As the gentle and proud English widow who is considerably shocked and outraged at the feudal customs of Siam when she arrives there in 1862 to tutor the king's tribe of children—all sixty-seven of them—who stubbornly refuses to grovel before the masterful king and who spends several years in rather charming and occasionally brutal tilting with him, Miss Dunne makes a regular bandbox heroine. She carries her bonneted head high, demonstrates wit with pretty modesty, and eventually drops a tender, touching tear. Her lady is on a level with some that Greer Garson has played.

But it is really in the performance of Rex Harrison as the king and in the cunning conception of his character that the charm of the picture lies. For this king is a most exceptional person, as was well indicated in the book; he is strangely desirous for enlightenment and for progress, while preserving feudal rules. And his quaintly eccentric nature, his difficult comprehensions of new thought, his pride and his poignant humility supply the humor and appeal in this film. The fact that Mr. Harrison is able to play the role with rare personality and authority while wearing some of the silliest costumes droopy bloomers, spiked headgears, and silken jerkins—manifests the exceptional talent that he has. Casting this excellent British actor for this highly demanding role was most wise of Producer Louis D. Lighton. A more familiar star might well have botched it—good.

The script by Talbot Jennings and Sally Benson does not follow the line of the book, and certainly the extravagant decorations are a bit beyond the span of that report. Thus a few of the characters, such as Linda Darnell's Tuptim, a short-term harem favorite, and Gale Sondergaard's Lady Thiang, mother of the youthful heir-apparent, are elaborate and conventional "Hollywood." So, too, is the saccharine cuteness of some of the palace tots and Richard Lyon's stiffly self-conscious performance of the governess's own son.

John Cromwell, who directed, is responsible for much of the overdoing here. But Lee J. Cobb is quietly commanding as his majesty's chief minister and Mikhail Rasumny is amusing and attractive as a much put-upon court scribe. They contribute—along with Mr. Harrison—to the qualities which make this film worthwhile.

—B.C., June 21, 1946

ANNA CHRISTIE

Directed by Clarence Brown: written by Frances Marion. based on the play by Eugene O'Neill: cinematographer. William Daniels: edited by Hugh Wynn: art designer. Cedric Gibbons: released by Metro-Goldwyn-Mayer. Black and white. Running time: 86 minutes.

With: Greta Garbo (Anna). Charles Bickford (Matt). George F. Marion (Chris) and Marie Dressler (Marthe).

In her first talking picture, an adaptation of Eugene O'Neill's *Anna Christie,* the immensely popular Greta Garbo is even more interesting through being heard than she was in her mute portrayals. She reveals no nervousness before the microphone and her careful interpretation of Anna can scarcely be disputed. She is of the same nationality as Anna is supposed to be and she brings Anna to life all the more impressively through her foreign accent being natural, because it is something for which she does not have to strive.

Miss Garbo's voice from the screen is deep toned, somewhat deeper than when one hears her in real life. The low enunciation of her initial lines, with a packed theater waiting expectantly to hear her first utterance, came somewhat as a surprise yesterday afternoon in the Capitol, for her delivery is almost masculine. And although the low-toned voice is not what is expected from the alluring actress, one becomes accustomed to it, for it is a voice undeniably suited to the unfortunate Anna.

Unlike most of the film actresses in their debuts in talking films, Miss Garbo suits her actions to the words. She thinks about what she is saying and accompanies the lines with suitable gestures and expressions. There is no hesitancy in her speech, for she evidently memorized her lines thoroughly before going before the camera, and not in a single instance does she seem to be thinking about what she must say next, which has been the case in the first audible efforts of many of the male and female performers.

In her opening scene she enters the "ladies' entrance" of a wharf saloon in New York. Marthe, her father's mistress, a drink-sodden creature well on in years, is seated at a table endeavoring to satisfy an almost unquenchable thirst with a large glass of ale and lager. Marthe quickly realizes that the girl, who orders whisky and lights a cigarette, is Chris's daughter, from whom he had just received a letter. Chris knows nothing of his daughter's crimson career, and at that moment he has gone to eat soup and drink coffee to sober up for the meeting with the girl, whom he has not seen since she was five years old.

"You're me, forty years from now," says Anna to Marthe. The older woman lets the girl know that Chris believes his Anna to be an example of purity. When Chris, played by George Marion, who figured in the same role on the stage and in the excellent silent pictorial version of several years ago, enters the bar section of the saloon, he is heard and Marthe decides to go and collect her belongings from Chris's barge and make herself scarce.

Marie Dressler, who plays Marthe, may overact occasionally, but most of her performance is exceptionally clever. She, with all Marthe's bibulous nature, elicits sympathy for the dissolute woman and often she relieves the sordid atmosphere with effective comedy. Miss Dressler has done good work in audible screen offerings, but her speech, expressions, and her general gesticulations make this far and away her outstanding film characterization.

The nervous Chris is told that the girl he was expecting is in the room set apart for women. He enters and gazes upon the daughter he has not seen for fifteen years. After the preliminary greeting and explanations, he says that he thinks that it is a suitable occasion to be celebrated with a glass of port. So the girl who had imbibed spirits sips the glass of wine and subsequently is seen living on her father's coal barge.

Clarence Brown, who has directed a number of Miss Garbo's silent films, is also responsible for this audible picture. He depicts with marked ability the girl and the father renewing relations, without the old man ever suspecting his daughter's wayward life in the

middle West. Then Matt, the stoker, is washed up with others on a stormy sea and Chris resents this man's attentions to his daughter. Matt, impersonated by Charles Bickford, is a powerful physical specimen of humanity, who scoffs at Chris's interference. He falls in love with Anna, and during one interlude they are seen at Coney Island, where Matt has an opportunity of demonstrating his strength and his prodigious lung-power.

The reproduction of the voices was often much too loud yesterday afternoon, but the scenes of the altercation between Chris and Matt and those wherein Anna confesses to her florid past are a compliment to the screen, for these players make the most of their respective opportunities, especially Miss Garbo. Anna's scorching tirade against her father and her revelations of her scarlet days are delivered in a highly dramatic fashion. Matt's disappointment, his eventual return, and his satisfaction in knowing that Anna had at least never loved any other man but himself are equally satisfying.

Mr. Bickford succeeds splendidly with his portrayal of Matt. Mr. Marion's familiarity with the role does not diminish the importance of his present interpretation of the man who shakes his fist at that "Ole Devil Sea."

—M.H., March 15, 1930

ANNIE HALL

Directed by Woody Allen; written by Mr. Allen and Marshall Brickman; cinematographer, Gordon Willis; edited by Ralph Rosenblum and Wendy Greene Bricmont; art designer, Mel Bourne; produced by Charles H. Joffe and Robert Greenhut; released by United Artists. Running time: 93 minutes.

With: Woody Allen (Alvy Singer), Diane Keaton (Annie Hall), Tony Roberts (Rob), Carol Kane (Allison), Paul Simon (Tony Lacey), Colleen Dewhurst (Mom Hall), Shelley Duvall (Pam), Janet Margolin (Robin), Christopher Walken (Duane Hall), Donald Syminton (Dad Hall) and Helen Ludlam (Grammy Hall).

Alvy Singer (Woody Allen) stands in front of an orangey sort of backdrop and tells us, the movie audience, the joke about two women at a Catskill resort. "The food," says the first woman, "is terrible." "Yes," the second woman agrees, "and the portions are so small."

This, says Alvy Singer, is just about the way he feels about life. It's not great—in fact, it's pretty evenly divided between the horrible and the miserable—but as long as it's there, he wants more.

In this fashion, Woody Allen introduces us to the particular concerns of his fine new film, *Annie Hall*, a comedy about urban love and incompatability that finally establishes Woody as one of our most audacious filmmakers, as well as the only American filmmaker who is able to work seriously in the comic mode without being the least bit ponderous.

Because Mr. Allen has his roots as a writer of one-liners and was bred in television and nightclubs, standing up, it's taken us quite a while to recognize just how prodigiously talented he is, and how different he has always been from those colleagues who also make their livings as he once did, racing from Las Vegas to the Coast to Tahoe to San Juan, then back to Las Vegas. Among other things, he's the first major American filmmaker ever to come out of a saloon.

For all of Mr. Allen's growth as a writer, director, and actor, *Annie Hall* is not terribly far removed from *Take the Money and Run,* his first work as a triple-threat man, which is not to put down the new movie but to upgrade the earlier one. *Take the Money and Run* was a visualized nightclub monologue, as freely associated as an analysand's introspections on the couch.

This also is more or less the form of *Annie Hall,* Alvy Singer's freewheeling, self-deprecating, funny, and sorrowful search for the truth about his on-again, off again affair with a beautiful young woman who is as emotionally bent as he is. The form of the two films is similar, but where the first was essentially a cartoon, *Annie Hall* has the humane sensibility of comedy.

It is, essentially, Woody's *Scenes from a Marriage,* though there is no marriage, only an intense affair to which Alvy Singer never commits himself enough to allow Annie Hall (Diane Keaton) to give up her apartment and move in with him. Just why, we aren't told, though we can make guesses on the basis of the information furnished.

Alvy, who grew up as a poor Jewish boy in Brooklyn in a house under a Coney Island roller coaster, is chronically suspicious and depressed. It may have started when he was nine and first read about the expanding universe. What kind of faith can you have if you know that in a couple of billion years everything's going to fly apart? With the firm conviction that the scheme is rotten, Alvy becomes a hugely successful television comedian somewhat on the scale of—you can guess Woody Allen.

Annie Hall is no less ambitious and mixed up, but for other reasons that, we must assume, have to do with the kind of WASPy, Middle Western household where Mom and Dad tend guilts as if they were prize delphiniums.

As Annie Hall, Miss Keaton emerges as Woody Allen's Liv Ullmann. His camera finds beauty and emotional resources that somehow escape the notice of other directors. Her Annie Hall is a marvelous nut, a talented singer (which Woody demonstrates in a nightclub sequence that has the effect of a love scene), generous, shy, insecure, and so uncertain about sex that she needs a stick of marijuana before going to bed.

Alvy, on the other hand, embraces sex as if it were something that wouldn't keep, even when it means going to bed with a dopey reporter from *Rolling Stone* (Shelley Duvall in a tiny role). The most Alvy can do to meet Annie's fears is to buy a red lightbulb for the bedroom lamp. He thinks it's sexy.

Annie Hall moves back and forth in time according to Alvy's recollections, from his meeting with Annie on a tennis court, to scenes of his childhood, to a disastrous visit with her family in Chippewa Falls, to trips to Hollywood and scenes of reconciliations and partings in New York. Throughout there are explosively comic set-pieces having to do with analysis, Hollywood, politics, you-name-it, but the mood, ultimately, is somber, thoughtful, reflective.

One of Mr. Allen's talents as a director is his casting, and *Annie Hall* contains more fine supporting performances than any other American film this year, with the possible exception of *The Late Show* and *Three Women.* Most prominent are Paul Simon as a recording industry promoter, Carol Kane as Alvy's politically committed first wife, Tony Roberts as Alvy's actor-friend, Colleen Dewhurst as Annie Hall's mother, and Christopher Walken as Annie's quietly suicidal brother. That's to name only a few.

There will be discussion about what points in the film coincide with the lives of its two stars, but this, I think, is to detract from and trivialize the achievement of the film, which, at last, puts Woody in the league with the best directors we have.

—V.C., April 21, 1977

THE APARTMENT

Produced and directed by Billy Wilder; written by Mr. Wilder and I. A. L. Diamond; cinematographer, Joseph LaShelle; edited by Daniel Mandell; music by Adolph Deutsch; art designer, Alexander Trauner; released by United Artists. Black and white. Running time: 125 minutes.

With: Jack Lemmon (C.C. Baxter), Shirley MacLaine (Fran Kubelik), Fred MacMurray (J. D. Sheldrake), Ray Walston (Mr. Dobisch), David Lewis (Mr. Kirkeby) and Jack Kruschen (Dr. Dreyfuss).

You might not think a movie about a fellow who lends his rooms to the married executives of his office as a place for their secret love affairs would make a particularly funny or morally presentable show, especially when the young fellow uses the means to get advanced in his job.

But under the clever supervision of Billy Wilder, who helped to write the script, then produced and directed The Apartment, which opened at the Astor and the Plaza yesterday, the idea is run into a gleeful, tender, and even sentimental film. And it is kept on the side of taste and humor by the grand performance of Jack Lemmon in the principal role.

This Mr. Lemmon, whose stock went zooming last year with *Some Like It Hot,* takes precedence as our top comedian by virtue of his work in this film. As the innocent and amiable young bachelor who methodically passes around the key of his modest brownstone's front apartment among the sultans of the place where he is employed, he beautifully maintains the appearance of a lamb among ravening wolves. He has the air of a good-natured hermit who calls Grand Central Station his home.

His character does not like what he's doing. He would much prefer to stay in his bed on a rainy night when a sozzled sales executive telephones and demands the key. But he turns out, in line of duty,

when the hint of a promotion is flung, and he continues to oblige, confidentially, until the inevitably romantic trouble brews.

You can probably guess the reason. It is one of the elevator girls, for whom our fellow has worked up quite a fancy but whom he discovers is using the apartment with the head of personnel. Then he goes through an ordeal of worrying, especially after the girl has the rashness to choose the apartment for a suicide attempt on Christmas Eve. That makes for a sticky situation and a sharply ironic point of view on the perfidiousness of men with families playing around with the office girls.

Even in this dismal incident, Mr. Wilder and his coauthor on the script, I. A. L. Diamond, have managed to keep the action and the dialogue tumbling with wit. In the midst of a grim operation to get a pill-poisoned girl to come awake, they relieve the graveyard tension with trenchant and credible gags. And they bring the sentiment to focus with a wistful remark from the girl. "When you're in love with a married man, you shouldn't wear mascara," she says.

Mr. Wilder has done more than write the film. His direction is ingenious and sure, sparkled by brilliant little touches and kept to a tight, sardonic line. In addition to Mr. Lemmon's, there's a splendid performance by Shirley MacLaine, as the daffy girl who gets into a lot of trouble, and a good one by Fred MacMurray, as the wicked boss. Jack Kruschen makes a funny doctor-neighbor who mistakes Mr. Lemmon for a ladies' man, and Ray Walston and David Lewis are amusing (and slightly sordid) wolves.

Adolph Deutsch has contributed a light, sentimental accompanying score, and Joseph LaShelle, the cinematographer, has made the whole thing look quite stylish and metropolitan on the black-and-white large screen.

—B.C., June 16, 1960

APOCALYPSE NOW

Produced and directed by Francis Ford Coppola; written by Michael Herr, John Milius and Mr. Coppola; cinematographer, Vittorio Storaro; edited by Richard Marks; music by Carmine Coppola; art designer, Angelo Graham; released by United Artists. Running time: 139 minutes.

With: Marlon Brando (Colonel Kurtz), Robert Duvall (Lieutenant Colonel Kilgore), Martin Sheen (Captain Willard), Frederic Forrest (Chef), Albert Hall (Chief), Sam Bottoms (Lance), Larry Fishburne (Clean), Dennis Hopper (Photo Journalist), G. D. Spradlin (General), Harrison Ford (Colonel) and Jerry Zeismer (Civilian).

Scene: Day. Jungle. A small United States Army patrol boat pushes its way up a river overhung with dense foliage. The members of the crew make no comment on the burnt-out ribs of an American helicopter that remain stuck in a tree like the struts of a child's forgotten kite.

Scene: Day. Jungle. The little patrol boat cuts through the water with uncharacteristic speed, drawing behind it an exultant crew member on water skis. The brown-skinned farmers on the riverbank watch impassively.

Scene: Day. Jungle. The patrol boat stops to search a Vietnamese dugout filled with people and produce. Are they friends, enemies, or, as is most likely, simply uncommitted? No way to know. No language to communicate in. A young Vietnamese woman makes a sudden move to protect a particular crate. An American, armed with a machine gun, begins to fire. In several seconds these boat people are dead. The one survivor is a puppy.

Scene: Night. Jungle. The patrol boat, now deep in hostile territory, rounds a bend in the river to come upon a brilliantly floodlit stadium preparing to receive a U.S.O. troupe of Playboy bunnies.

In dozens of such scenes Francis Coppola's *Apocalypse Now* lives up to its grand title, disclosing not only the various faces of war but also the contradictions between excitement and boredom, terror and pity, brutality and beauty. Its epiphanies would do credit to Federico Fellini, who is indirectly quoted at one point.

Apocalypse Now, which opens at long last today at the Ziegfeld Theater, is not about any war but about the disastrous United States involvement in Vietnam, which, probably because it was disastrous, seems now to have been different, but was it really? The technology was as up-to-date as the taxpayers' billions could buy, but everything else was essentially the same. At its confused heart: a fearful hunger to survive. No matter what.

When it is thus evoking the look and feelings of the Vietnam War, dealing in sense impressions for which

no explanations are adequate or necessary, *Apocalypse Now* is a stunning work. It's as technically complex and masterful as any war film I can remember, including David Lean's *The Bridge on the River Kwai,* which comes to mind, I suppose, because both productions were themselves military campaigns to subdue the hostile landscapes in which they were made. *Kwai* was shot in Ceylon; *Apocalypse Now* in the Philippines, which became, for Mr. Coppola, his Vietnam, swallowing men, money, and equipment as voraciously as any enemy.

Apocalypse Now, though, wants to be something more than a kind of cinematic tone poem. Mr. Coppola himself describes it as "operatic," but this, I suspect, is a word the director hit upon after the fact. Ultimately, *Apocalypse Now* is neither a tone poem nor an opera. It's an adventure yarn with delusions of grandeur, a movie that ends—in the all-too-familiar words of the poet Mr. Coppola drags in by the bootstraps—not with a bang, but a whimper.

I realize that a movie's ending should not deny all that has gone before, but almost from the beginning of *Apocalypse Now* there have been portents that the film means to deal not only with the looks and expressions of war but also with such heavy things as the human condition, good, evil, fate, and various other subjects whose weight, in an earlier century, demanded that they be capitalized.

Mr. Coppola and John Milius, with whom he wrote the screenplay, have taken as their source material *Heart of Darkness,* Joseph Conrad's classic story about a mad ivory hunter in nineteenth-century Africa. This shadowy man, named Kurtz, comes to represent to Conrad's narrator, Marlow, all the terrible possibilities of a soul returned to some precivilized state. Conrad is rather vague about the terrible things that Kurtz is up to. We know only that he rules his local tribes with a bloody hand and charms them with his sorcery. The point of the story is Marlow's realization that Kurtz is a heretofore unrecognized aspect of himself, which, being known, is safely manageable.

Mr. Coppola and Mr. Milius have attempted to update Conrad, who really doesn't need updating, by placing this story more or less on top of the Vietnam War. Kurtz (Marlon Brando), whom we meet in the film's concluding section, is a renegade Green Berets officer who has taken refuge in the Cambodian jungles, where, to the fury of his superiors, he wages his own wars—for and against whom is left blurry—at the head of a group of ferocious Montagnard tribesmen.

The Marlow character is now a battle-scarred Special Services officer named Captain Willard (Martin Sheen), who is assigned by the commanding general to go into Cambodia, find Kurtz, and to "terminate" him "with extreme prejudice." This plot, which seems to have been imposed on the film from above, keeps interrupting the natural flow of Mr. Coppola's perfectly sound, sometimes incredibly beautiful, meditation upon war.

The major part of the film is occupied with Willard's adventures as he travels upriver in the small patrol boat provided by the Army. These sequences are often spellbinding, none more so than one in which Willard and his companions are forced to observe an assault on a Vietcong village by American fighter planes and helicopters under the command of an exuberantly manic officer who's also a surfing nut. This fellow, played with breathtaking force and charm by Robert Duvall, exhibits most of the qualities we miss in the foolish pretensions of the movie's Kurtz, whose actions and words, when they finally come, have little to do with the rest of the movie.

From time to time in the course of his upriver odyssey, Captain Willard muses on the nature of the man he seeks—soundtrack narration that makes one's flesh wet with embarrassment. When we hear Willard say, "Everything I saw told me that Kurtz had gone insane," it not only fails to establish any bond between the two men, it's also an understatement to break a camel's back.

With the exception of Mr. Brando, who has no role to act, the actors are superlatively right, beginning with Mr. Duvall and Mr. Sheen, and including Frederic Forrest, Albert Hall, Larry Fishburne, and Sam Bottoms, who play the members of the patrol boat's crew. Dennis Hopper, looking as wild and disconnected as ever, turns up briefly at the end as a freelance photographer who has fallen under Kurtz's spell, apparently because Kurtz reads T. S. Eliot aloud (though none too well).

Vittorio Storaro, who photographed *Last Tango in Paris,* among other fine films, is responsible for the extraordinary camerawork that almost, but not quite, saves *Apocalypse Now* from its profoundly anticlimactic intellectual muddle.

—*V.C., August 15, 1979*

APOLLO 13

Directed by Ron Howard: written by William Broyles Jr. and Al Reinert. based on the book *Lost Moon*, by Jim Lovell and Jeffrey Kluger: director of photography. Dean Cundey: edited by Mike Hill and Dan Hanley: music by James Horner. with vocal performance by Annie Lennox: production designer. Michael Corenblith: costumes by Rita Ryack: produced by Brian Grazer: released by Universal Pictures. Running time: 135 minutes.

With: Tom Hanks (Jim Lovell). Kevin Bacon (Jack Swigert). Bill Paxton (Fred Haise). Gary Sinise (Ken Mattingly). Ed Harris (Gene Kranz). Kathleen Quinlan (Marilyn Lovell) and Jean Speegle Howard (Blanch Lovell).

The line of dialogue that will be best remembered from Ron Howard's absolutely thrilling new *Apollo 13* is a slight variation on the truth. "Houston, we have a problem," says one of this film's three endangered astronauts, although "Houston, we've had a problem" is what Jim Lovell actually said. It's a small but important change, one more way that *Apollo 13* unfolds with perfect immediacy, drawing viewers into the nail-biting suspense of a spellbinding true story. You can know every glitch that made this such a dangerous mission, and *Apollo 13* will still have you by the throat.

Better even than Mr. Howard's sure hand with this fascinating material is his film's unexpected restraint. *Apollo 13* understands the difference between movie bravado and real courage, and it celebrates the latter in inspiring ways that have almost gone out of style. With Tom Hanks, wonderful again, as the Everyman in the driver's seat, *Apollo 13* isn't afraid of the stone-cold fear at the heart of this tale or of the intricate group effort needed to see it through. This film and its brave, believable characters are uplifting in ways that have nothing to do with a voyage to outer space.

We take it for granted today that there have been a hundred manned American space flights, and that an astronaut can remain in orbit almost unnoticed for a three-month stretch. But the weeklong adventure of the Apollo 13 crew unfolded in a very different atmosphere. In April 1970, the space program still aroused strong emotions: attention had begun to wane after the previous year's moon walk, but the nation found itself desperately receptive to the astronauts' unforeseen display of heroism after their flight became so perilous. *Apollo 13* doesn't mention Vietnam, but it doesn't have to. The war-weary climate of that time enhances this film's wishful, stirring faith in American know-how.

Like *Quiz Show*, *Apollo 13* beautifully evokes recent history in ways that resonate strongly today. Cleverly nostalgic in its visual style (Rita Ryack's costumes are especially right), it harks back to moviemaking without phony heroics and to the strong spirit of community that enveloped the astronauts and their families. Amazingly, this film manages to seem refreshingly honest while still conforming to the three-act dramatic format of a standard Hollywood hit. It is far and away the best thing Mr. Howard has done (and *Far and Away* was one of the other kind). Equally sound was casting his own mother (Jean Speegle Howard) as Jim Lovell's mother, a real corker. "Are you boys in the space program, too?" she sweetly asks the film's Buzz Aldrin and Neil Armstrong.

Apollo 13 makes it unsurprising that Jim Lovell ("no stranger to emergencies he," a television commentator says) would come from sturdy stock. Mr. Lovell is presented as a quietly gung-ho commander, the kind of man who tells his wife (played brightly and affectingly by Kathleen Quinlan) that he's going to the moon as if that's great news. For Mr. Lovell, on whose memoir, *Lost Moon* (written with Jeffrey Kluger), the film is based, it actually was: he had come tantalizingly close to the moon on the Apollo 8 flight and enthusiastically looked forward to a lunar landing. Instead, on a mission whose original flight plan was abruptly aborted, he was lucky to come home alive.

The science behind *Apollo 13* is detailed and specific, and the film conveys it with superb simplicity. Easy as it would have been to sling showy high-tech jargon, the screenplay (credited to William Broyles Jr. and Al Reinert) is gratifyingly terse and clear. With a pitch-perfect ear for NASA syntax ("Come on, rookie, park that thing"), the film stays informative while dealing with arcane facts that became matters of life and death. You may see no more dazzling display of ingenuity all year than the authentic way the film's NASA technicians scramble with cardboard and duct tape to make a square peg fit a round hole.

In terms of realism, nothing else here comes close

to the staggering fact that some of the film's zero-gravity scenes were shot aboard a KC-135 NASA plane on a steep parabolic orbit that earned it the nickname "vomit comet." Some may feel that Mr. Hanks, Kevin Bacon, and Bill Paxton, who play the astronauts so expertly, deserve something better than the usual end-of-the-year recognition for having even *taken* these roles.

These three stars (and their terrific backup teammates on the ground, especially Gary Sinise as Ken Mattingly, an astronaut benched at the last minute because of a measles scare, and Ed Harris as the nail-spitting flight commander, Gene Kranz) capture an extraordinary verisimilitude. No film about space travel has done a more realistic job of conveying the strangeness and exhilaration of such exploits, not to mention the terror summed up by Mr. Bacon's Jack Swigert: "If this doesn't work, we're not going to have the power to get home."

Crippled by the explosion of one of its oxygen tanks as it neared the moon, the spaceship Odyssey experienced sudden electrical failures that forced the astronauts to shut it down. They took refuge in their lunar exploration module, the Aquarius, which was neither built nor programmed to bring three men back to earth. Computer readjustments, navigational problems, lack of heat in space, fear of incineration on reentry, condensation that made the flight "a little like trying to drive a toaster through a car wash": all these troubles are grippingly dealt with in cinematically unconventional ways. When the guys in this film frantically get out their slide rules, they're executing a gutsier rescue than the maneuvers of any cape-wearing cartoon super-hero.

Thanks largely to Mr. Hanks's four-square presence here, the empathy factor for *Apollo 13* is through the roof. This actor's way of amplifying the ordinary side of an extraordinary character remains supremely fine-tuned. Playing the tough, commanding Jim Lovell is a substantial stretch for Mr. Hanks, but as usual his seeming ingenuousness overshadows all else about the role. There's not a false move to anything he does on-screen. Once again, he gives a performance that looks utterly natural and is, in fact, subtly new.

The other principal performances are equally staunch, giving vivid, likable impressions of characters whose rough edges have been only slightly smoothed. (The fact that Gene Kranz liked to start his day listening to John Philip Sousa marches, as reported in Andrew Chaikin's lucid Apollo overview, *A Man on the Moon,* is the kind of thing not dealt with by Mr. Harris's tight, steely performance.)

Also notable about *Apollo 13:* James Horner's rousing music, convincing rocket scenes that don't come from NASA, and an authentic glimpse of the role of television reporting during the Apollo crisis. The news media can be faulted for some of the behavior seen here, but Mr. Howard doesn't waste time taking those potshots. Truly, *Apollo 13* has better things to do.

—*J.M., June 30, 1995*

THE APOSTLE

Written and directed by Robert Duvall: director of photography. Barry Markowitz: edited by Steve Mack: music by David Mansfield: production designer. Linda Burton: produced by Robert Carliner: released by October Films. Running time: 148 minutes.

With: Robert Duvall (the Apostle E. F.). Farrah Fawcett (Jessie Dewey). Miranda Richardson (Toosie). John Beasley (Brother Blackwell). June Carter Cash (Mrs. Dewey Sr.) and Billy Bob Thornton (Troublemaker).

Euliss (Sonny) Dewey, played with foxy charm and volcanic energy by Robert Duvall in his lovely, heartfelt film *The Apostle,* is a man of the cloth. But the cloth from which this Pentecostal preacher is cut may seem familiar at first, at least in movie terms. As a white preacher whose specialty is rousing black churchgoers to a holy fury, Sonny does look like something of a flimflam artist. And behind the kindly manner and beatific smile we know there is a man with serious marital troubles. Does the equally devout Jessie (Farrah Fawcett) want to leave Sonny because of his wicked ways? Is Sonny's overbearing godliness merely a cynical trick?

If this were *Elmer Gantry,* that might indeed be its message. But *The Apostle* is something unusual in cinematic terms. It's a film that can create a full, fiery, warts-and-all portrait of Sonny without reducing him to any kind of stereotype. The exhilarating, touching Sonny is very much his own man, and earnest about

his mission. Even when fate deals him a career-ending crisis, Sonny rebounds by inventing new ways to do what he does best.

Clearly a man of strong passions, Sonny is driven wild by Jessie's new boyfriend and her reluctance to let Sonny see his children as often as he'd like. Then Jessie (played convincingly by Ms. Fawcett) really hits him where he lives. She tries using church bylaws to separate him from the ministry, and he responds by hitting her lover with a baseball bat. "I think he might be on the road to glory this time," Sonny says of the comatose man, as he stays a step ahead of the law by skipping town.

The real test of Sonny's character comes as he leaves with nothing, travels humbly ("It's a mansion on a hill!" he exclaims over the pup tent a stranger lends him) and tries starting life anew in a tiny Louisiana town. There in Bayou Boutté, Sonny does a wonderful job of building himself a new world, baptizing himself the Apostle E. F. It's a world of hard work, helping neighbors, and joyful preaching, which Mr. Duvall delivers with fiery, galvanizing energy. Of God giving Moses the Ten Commandments, Sonny exhorts: "He didn't give him twelve or fourteen. He gave him ten! And the Eleventh Commandment, thou shalt not shout—that does not exist!" Not for Sonny, that's for sure.

Mr. Duvall's unobtrusive direction moves the film at a leisurely pace that lets many scenes build the gentle, pleasing rhythms of small-town Southern life. And the film's church sequences also call for slow, mounting excitement, especially during the remarkable scene where Sonny preaches his heart out, knowing this sermon is liable to be his last.

The well-known, well-cast supporting players include Miranda Richardson as the married woman on whom Sonny turns the full blast of his charm; Billy Bob Thornton as a racist who demonstrates that when Sonny opens his mouth, he can do anything, and June Carter Cash as Sonny's mother. (Yes, she gets the chance to sing a hymn. There are also the stirring sounds of gospel choirs throughout the soundtrack.)

John Beasley is especially good as the retired black preacher who is suspicious of Sonny at first. "I tell you what," he says, "I'm going to keep my eye on you. And the Lord keep his eye on both of us. And we all three keep an eye out for the Devil."

The actors are first rate, but much screen time in

The Apostle is given to nonactors who give the film a sweetly believable tone and fill its churchgoing scenes with blazing heart and soul. A rare display of spiritual light on-screen.

—J.M., October 9, 1997

L'ARGENT

Written (in French, with English subtitles) and directed by Robert Bresson: based on a short story by Leo Tolstoy: directors of photography, Pasqualino de Santis and Emmanuel Machuel: edited by Jean-François Naudon: released by Marlon's Films. Running time: 90 minutes.

With: Christian Patey (Yvon). Sylvie van den Elsen (The Little Old Lady). Michael Briguet (Father of the Little Old Lady). Caroline Lang (Elise). Jeanne Aptekman (Yvette). Vincent Risterucci (Lucien). Beatrice Tabourin (The Female Photographer) and Didier Baussy (The Male Photographer).

That Robert Bresson, the veteran French director, is still one of the most rigorous and talented filmmakers of the world is evident with the appearance of his beautiful, astringent new film, *L'Argent,* which will be shown at the New York Film Festival in Lincoln Center today and tomorrow. Mr. Bresson does not make films casually—*L'Argent* is only his thirteenth since his first feature, *Les Anges du Péché (Angels of the Streets)*, was released in 1943.

The man who made *Diary of a Country Priest, Pickpocket,* and *Lancelot du Lac* is at the top of his very idiosyncratic form with *L'Argent,* which has nothing to do with the Émile Zola novel or Marcel L'Herbier's film adaptation of that novel. The Bresson film is inspired by a Tolstoy short story, and though I've never read it, I would assume that Mr. Bresson has turned it to his own purposes.

Set in contemporary France in an unidentified city that sometimes seems to be Paris but probably isn't, *L'Argent (Money)* is a serenely composed film that tells a ruthless tale of greed, corruption, and murder without once raising its voice. It goes beyond the impartiality of journalism. It has the manner of an official report on the spiritual state of a civilization for which there is no hope.

The narrative is mainly concerned with Yvon, a young truck driver framed by some bourgeois shopkeepers who identify him as the source of counterfeit notes. Because he has no criminal record, Yvon is given a suspended sentence, but he loses his job anyway. Soon he agrees to participate in a bank holdup to obtain money to support his wife and child.

The holdup fails and Yvon is packed off to jail, where things go from very bad to far, far worse. He loses all sense of compassion and, when he is paroled, he is beyond any redemption except God's.

Like all Bresson films, *L'Argent* can't be interpreted exclusively in social, political, or psychological terms. Mr. Bresson's characters act out dramas that have been in motion since the birth of the planet. He's not a fatalist, but he insists on recognizing inevitable consequences, given a set of specific circumstances.

L'Argent would stand up to Marxist analysis, yet it's anything but Marxist in outlook. It's far too poetic—too interested in the mysteries of the spirit.

As usual, Mr. Bresson has cast the film largely with nonprofessionals, a practice that contributes importantly to the film's manner. Christian Patey, the young man who plays Yvon, possesses the dark, almost pretty good looks of something idealized, apotheosized. He is not only Yvon, but also the representation of all innocents who have been betrayed by a system that rewards corruption.

Mr. Patey's is what amounts to a carefully designed nonperformance. He doesn't act his lines. He recites them as simply as possible, as do all the performers. They give the impression of traveling through the events of the narrative without being affected by them, which reduces any chance that the film will prompt sentimental responses.

The look of *L'Argent* accentuates this chilliness. The images have the clean, uncharacterized look of illustrations in the annual report of a large corporation. They are perfectly composed and betray no emotions whatsoever. This distance between the appearance of something and what it means is one of the methods by which the power of any Bresson film is generated.

L'Argent is not an easy film. It's tough but it's also rewarding, and it's the kind of film that justifies film festivals.

—V.C., September 24, 1983

ASHES AND DIAMONDS

Directed by Andrzej Wajda: written (in Polish. with English subtitles) by Mr. Wajda and Jerzy Andrzejewski. based on the novel by Mr. Andrzejewski: cinematographer. Jerzy Wojcik: edited by Halina Nawrocka: music by Aroclaw Radio Quintet: art designer. Roman Mann: produced by Film Unit KADR: released by Janus Films. Black and white. Running time: 105 minutes.

With: Zbigniew Cybulski (Maciek). Ewa Krzyzewska (Christine). Adam Pawlikowski (Andrzej). Waclaw Zastrzezynski (Szczuka) and Bogumil Kobiela (Drewnowski).

Deterioration in Poland as a consequence of World War II is a subject from which Andrzej Wajda, one of that country's best young film directors, has evidently found it hard to get away.

In his first feature film, *A Generation,* not yet released in this country, he examined the dismal condition of juvenile gangs in Poland after the war. In his subsequent *Kanal,* now showing at the New Yorker Theatre on upper Broadway, he reflected upon the painful happenings in the disastrous Warsaw uprising of 1944. Now, in his *Ashes and Diamonds,* which opened at the Fifth Avenue Cinema yesterday, he is doing a melancholy recapitulation on the political and social chaos at the end of the war.

As in his previous pictures, Mr. Wajda is putting forth here something more than a trenchant observation of a highly dramatic episode. While his action is set within the area of a small Polish city in one full day—the day of Germany's surrender—and mainly revolves around the efforts of a young resistance fighter to spot and assassinate a new Polish Communist leader, his camera takes in a shattering sweep of the litter of a lost and ruined country at the symbolic dawn of a new day.

There are greedy politicians in his round-up, smug and sharp-eyed fellows who pretend that a hastily arranged victory banquet is a welcome to their new political chief but wind up in the gray light of the morning reeling drunkenly to the off-key Polonaise.

There is a tough and tense resistance leader who will never say surrender or die and who makes his getaway into the darkness when he thinks that he has his murder plot arranged. There is the mellow, serene, paternalistic incoming commissar who grieves when he learns that his own son is one of a band of captured and condemned resistance troops. And there is the young, idealistic assassin who hesitates at dealing out more death and spends the long night of the vulgar banquet paying court and making love to a clear-eyed girl.

With the literary help of Jerzy Andrzejewski, upon whose novel this drama is based, director Wajda has shaped the story in strong and striking visual images. His sharply etched black-and-white action has the pictorial snap and quality of some of the old Soviet pictures of Pudovkin and Eisenstein. Facial expressions are highlighted, bodily movements are swift and intense, and the light that comes in from the outside in the shaky morning is as dense as luminous smoke.

Likewise, Wajda has created some vivid ideas through imagery—ideas that carry cynicism, melancholia, wistfulness, and shock. There is a beautiful scene of the killers remembering dead comrades at a bar, marking each recollection with a glass of brandy set aflame. There is a scene of the lovers wandering restlessly among ruins, coming upon a large crucifix dislodged and swaying perilously head down. And there's the idea conveyed with the shot commissar dying in his assassin's arms, and finally that of the young hero twitching convulsively to his death on a rubbish heap.

The mood of despair in this picture is as heavy as that in *Kanal,* but the film itself is much more searching and infinitely better performed. Zbigniew Cybulski as the hero is sensitive, attractive and alert—a lad with humor and compassion. One is strongly drawn to him. Ewa Krzyzewska as the barmaid with whom he has one last lyrical love looks like Gina Lollobrigida and acts decently to boot. Others, whose names are equally difficult, make vigorous and valid characters. The musical score is excellent and the English subtitles will do.

—B.C., May 30, 1961

THE ASPHALT JUNGLE

Directed by John Huston: written by Ben Maddow and Mr. Huston. based on the novel by W. R. Burnett: cinematographer. Harold Rosson: edited by

George Boemler; music by Miklos Rozsa; art designers, Cedric Gibbons and Randall Duell; produced by Arthur Hornblow Jr.; released by Metro-Goldwyn-Mayer. Black and white. Running time: 112 minutes.

With: Sterling Hayden (Dix Handley), Louis Calhern (Alonzo D. Emmerich), Jean Hagen (Doll Conovan), James Whitmore (Gus Minissi), Sam Jaffe (Doc Erwin Riedenschneider) and John McIntire (Police Commissioner Hardy).

Ever since W. R. Burnett's *Little Caesar* muscled into films with a quality of arrogance and toughness such as the screen had not previously known, this writer and this type of story—about criminals in the higher realms of crime—have been popular and often imitated, but *Little Caesar* has yet to be surpassed. However, we've got to say one thing: a lot of pictures have come close—and one of them is *The Asphalt Jungle,* also from a novel by Mr. Burnett.

This film, derived by Ben Maddow and John Huston from Mr. Burnett's book and directed by Mr. Huston in brilliantly naturalistic style, gives such an electrifying picture of the whole vicious circle of a crime—such an absorbing illustration of the various characters involved, their loyalties and duplicities, and of the minutiae of crime techniques—that one finds it hard to tag the item of exhibition repulsive in itself. Yet that is our inevitable judgment of this film, now on the Capitol's screen.

For the plain truth is that this picture—sobering though it may be in its ultimate demonstration that a life of crime does not pay—enjoins the hypnotized audience to hobnob with a bunch of crooks, participate with them in their plunderings, and actually sympathize with their personal griefs. The vilest creature in the picture, indeed, is a double-crossing cop. And the rest of the police, while decent, are definitely antagonists.

Furthermore, unlike *Little Caesar,* this picture does not expose any particular canker of society that has not often been displayed upon the screen. Its characters are ordinary criminals—a mastermind for a big jewel robbery, a safecracker, a hoodlum, a crooked lawyer, and other types of the underworld—none of them novel or distinguished in the disturbance of society by crime. Mr. Burnett, Mr. Huston, and this picture are merely concerned with the excitement of one case.

But, in that meager interest, we've got to hand it to the boys, particularly to Mr. Huston: they've done a terrific job! From the very first shot, in which the camera picks up a prowling thug, sliding along between buildings to avoid a police car in the gray and liquid dawn, there is ruthless authority in this picture, the hardness and clarity of steel, and remarkably subtle suggestion that conveys a whole involvement of distorted personality and inveterate crime. Mr. Huston's *The Maltese Falcon,* which brought him to the fore as a sure and incisive director, had nothing in the way of toughness on this film.

Likewise, the story construction, both with pen and camera, is of a most intriguing nature. Slowly the elements merge—here a thwarted vagrant, there a conniving cop, here a greasy bookmaker, and there an ex-convict with a plan. Smoothly and swiftly they're assembled until a masterful jewel robbery is afoot—a complex job of safecracking that will make you scream in suspense. And then comes the big double-dealing by the lawyer brought in to back the stunt, fireworks, flight into hideouts, and the slow, inexorable hunt of the police. Mr. Huston has filmed a straight crime story about as cleverly and graphically as it could be filmed.

And that's the way his actors have played it. Louis Calhern as the big lawyer who tries to pull a double cross and muffs it is exceptionally fluid and adroit and Sterling Hayden is surefire as a brazen hoodlum who just wants to go back home. Likewise Sam Jaffe does wonders as a coolheaded mastermind, James Whitmore is taut as a small "fixer," and John McIntire is crisp as a chief of police. But, then, everyone in this picture—which was produced, incidentally, by M-G-M—gives an unimpeachable performance. If only it all weren't so corrupt!

—B.C., June 9, 1950

L'ATALANTE

Directed by Jean Vigo; written (in French, with English subtitles) by Mr. Vigo and Albert Riera, based on a story by R. de Guichen; cinematographers, Boris Kaufman and Louis Berger; edited by Louis Chavance; art designer, Francis Jourdain;

produced by Jacques-Louis Nounez: released by Cine Classics. Black and white. Running time: 89 minutes.

With: Dita Parlo (Juliette). Jean Dasté (Jean). Michel Simon (Father Jules). Lefèvre (The Boy) and Giles Margarites (Traveling Salesman).

ZERO FOR CONDUCT

Produced, edited and directed by Jean Vigo: written (in French, with English subtitles) by Mr. Vigo: cinematographer, Boris Kaufman: music by Maurice Jaubert: released by Cine Classics. Black and white. Running time: 44 minutes.

With: Jean Dasté (Superintendent Hugnet). Robert La Fion (Superintendant Pete-Sec). Du Veron (Superintendent Dec-de-Gez). Delphin (Principal). Madame Emile (Mother Haricot) and Larive (Professor).

What the late Jean Vigo was attempting to illustrate back in 1933–34 when he made *Zéro de Conduite* and *L'Atalante,* the pair of Gallic importations which came to the Fifth Avenue Playhouse on Saturday, is nebulous and difficult to perceive today. Except for occasional moments of comedy, satire, and tender romance, these intellectual exercises should prove of high interest only to avid students of the cinema.

The earlier of the two, *Zéro de Conduite* (*Zero for Conduct*), a study of life in a French boarding school for boys, is a series of vignettes lampooning the faculty climaxed by a weird, dreamlike rebellion of the entire student body. These amorphous scenes, strung together by a vague continuity, may be art but they are also pretty chaotic.

L'Atalante, Vigo's last film, hews closer to the standard concept of moviemaking. It is, in sum, the story of a pair of honeymooners aboard a barge slowly making its way on the Seine. Life aboard the barge, satirically named for the fleet goddess, is tedious and dull for the young girl, who wants excitement.

She finds it when she deserts the boat to flirt with a stranger, a traveling salesman, and the aged barge hand seeks her out, and affects a reconciliation between the errant lady and her jealous barge-master husband. Here too, the action is episodic and diffuse but Michel Simon, as the dour and cat-loving barge hand lends a bit of comic relief to the pallidly poetic proceedings.

Count *Zéro de Conduite* and *L'Atalante* as examples of avant-garde pictures which have now become passé.

—A.W., June 23, 1947

ATLANTIC CITY

Directed by Louis Malle: written by John Guare: cinematographer, Richard Ciupka: edited by Suzanne Baron: music by Michel Legrand: production designer, Anne Pritchard: produced by Denis Heroux: released by Paramount Pictures. Running time: 104 minutes.

With: Burt Lancaster (Lou). Susan Sarandon (Sally). Kate Reid (Grace). Michel Piccoli (Joseph). Hollis McLaren (Chrissie). Robert Joy (Dave). Al Waxman (Alfie) and Robert Goulet (Singer).

Atlantic City, Louis Malle's fine new movie, may be one of the most romantic and perverse ghost stories ever filmed, set not in a haunted castle but in a haunted city, the contemporary Atlantic City, a point of transit where the dead and the living meet briefly, sometimes even make love, and then continue on their individual ways.

This Atlantic City, caught in the first excitement of the legalized gambling boom, is in a state of almost hysterical flux. Elegant, old-fashioned, ocean-front hotels are demolished before our eyes—collapsing gracefully in subdued long-shots—while new, even bigger, probably flimsier hotels rise to take their places.

Though much of the movie, a Canadian-French co-production, was obviously photographed on location, the film's Atlantic City is the particular creation of Mr. Malle, the director (*Pretty Baby; Lacombe, Lucien*), of John Guare, the playwright (*House of Blue Leaves, Bosoms of Neglect*) who wrote the screenplay, and of Richard Ciupka, who photographed it. It's a place of myth, of legends and dreams, most of them pretty tacky. It's beautiful and squalid and, like the movie itself, sometimes rueful and sometimes funny.

It's principally about Lou (Burt Lancaster), who dresses neatly in frayed old clothes and fondly remembers the hustling Atlantic City of forty years ago, when gambling was exhilarating because it was illegal and Lou was the associate of top mob figures. Lou is now reduced to running numbers in the ghetto and living in a soon-to-be-torn-down apartment house just off the Boardwalk. He also acts as the companion to and occasional lover of Grace (Kate Reid), who came to Atlantic City during World War II to compete in a Betty Grable look-alike contest and is now a bedridden shrew.

Lou rather loftily passes himself off as a former mob hit man who has become—he acknowledges with dignity—a has-been, when in fact Lou is a never-was. At the height of his career he was a mob gofer, an errand boy. He is also one of Mr. Lancaster's most remarkable creations, a complex mixture of the mingy and magnificent even when we see the vigor of the youthful Burt Lancaster showing through the real age.

Playing more or less opposite Mr. Lancaster is Susan Sarandon, as Sally, a pretty, no-nonsense young woman who works by night shucking clams at a seafood bar and during the day studies to become a casino employee. Her goal: to become the first female croupier in Monte Carlo. Chief among the other characters is Chrissie (Hollis McLaren), Sally's out-of-date flower-child sister who, without warning, descends on Sally accompanied by Sally's husband Dave (Robert Joy), a small-town punk who earlier ran off with Chrissie and made her pregnant.

When Chrissie and Dave arrive in Atlantic City, riding in the back of an open truck and looking like turn-of-the-century immigrants, Dave is also carrying a large amount of cocaine, stolen from the Philadelphia mob, which he attempts to sell in the Atlantic City underworld, with disastrous results.

The urbane Michel Piccoli appears in a tiny role that he turns into a memorable cameo, that of a casino manager who, on the side, runs the croupier school and attempts to instruct the ambitious Sally in some of the finer things of life, including opera and the French language.

Atlantic City is full of odd, sometimes disturbing juxtapositions of image, mood, and event. The opening of the film establishes this essential unpredictability that gives *Atlantic City* so much of its energy. The sequence begins as a close-up of a young woman, who appears to be as exhausted as she is beautiful, seen through a tenement window in golden lamplight. Methodically she massages her hands, arms, shoulders, and breasts with lemon halves. As the camera pulls back, the audience becomes aware—as she most certainly is—that she is being peeped at by an old man from an equally shabby room across the air shaft.

Thus is set the relationship between Sally, who uses the lemon juice to rid herself of the smell of clams, and old Lou—though at this point in their lives they haven't yet met. Before the film is over, Sally and Lou will have a short and, for Lou, idyllic love affair and Lou will get a chance to prove himself to be the man he never was when young.

There are other unexpectedly moving relationships—between Lou and the usually angry Grace; between Lou and the young, dope-dealing Dave, who thinks he's using Lou for his own ends and inadvertently provides the means and motives for Lou's salvation; and between the mean-tempered Grace and the innocent Chrissie, who goes into Grace's room to massage Grace's aching feet and stays on to preach her own brand of mysticism.

One of the sweetest sequences in the film is a conversation in which Grace offers to give the pregnant Chrissie the money to fly home to Canada—"that's if," says Grace, "you can get a seat belt around you." Replies Chrissie earnestly, "I never use seat belts. I don't believe in gravity." Chrissie does, however, believe in reincarnation. As she says of Dave, "He's had some pretty hard lives. He's gone all the way back to ancient Egypt. I've hardly been reincarnated at all."

Though there are two villains in the film, they are anonymous—the Philadelphia hoods who track Dave to Atlantic City. Like all of Mr. Malle's earlier work, the film regards its principal characters with a kind of detached serenity that prevents sentimentality from creeping in. It takes note of occasional, remarkable twists of fortune, such as the events that allow Lou his brief fling with Sally, but it never suggests that the ultimate fates of Lou and Grace and the other ghosts of the old Atlantic City, or of Sally and Chrissie and Dave, are going to be anything other than what each has already been prepared for. When the audience last sees Sally she is in a car stolen from the mobsters, speeding off into the sunrise as if headed straight for Monaco. She is a toughly determined young woman, but it's apparent that she's not likely to get even as far as Trenton.

Though Mr. Malle is French, his visions of America (in *Pretty Baby* and now *Atlantic City*), are neither that of a tourist nor that of the alien who, like Roman Polanski (*Chinatown, Rosemary's Baby*), seems to have learned how to fit in. His visions are his own. As in *Pretty Baby,* he is not dealing in reportage or sociology but in fiction of a high order, which is why *Atlantic City* seems both strange (I hesitate to use the word foreign) and absolutely right. Mr. Guare, as the writer, seems to have provided the director with a screenplay that seamlessly continues the concerns and style of the earlier Malle films.

All of the performances are excellent, from Mr. Lancaster, Miss Reid, Miss Sarandon, Miss McLaren, and Mr. Joy, right on down to Sean Sullivan, who appears in two marvelous, very short scenes as an elderly attendant in a washroom, one of Lou's cronies from the good old days.

Atlantic City, which opens today at Loew's Tower East, is a rich, gaudy cinema trip.

—V.C., April 3, 1981

AU REVOIR LES ENFANTS

Produced, written (in French, with English subtitles) and directed by Louis Malle; cinematographer, Renato Berta; edited by Emmanuelle Castro; music by Franz Schubert and Camille Saint-Saëns; released by Orion Classics. Running time: 104 minutes.

With: Gaspard Manesse (Julien Quentin), Raphaël Fejtö (Jean Bonnet), Francine Racette (Madame Quentin), Stanislas Carré de Malberg (François Quentin), Philippe Morier-Genoud (Father Jean), François Négret (Joseph) and François Berleand (Father Michel).

Louis Malle's Au *Revoir les Enfants* (*Goodbye, Children*) is based on an event that took place during January 1944, when the French writer and director, then twelve years old, was attending a Jesuit boarding school near Fontainebleau. At the end of the Christmas holidays, in the middle of the scholastic year, there appeared at the school three new boys, one of whom became the young Malle's chief competitor for scholastic honors and then, briefly, his best friend.

Several weeks later, this boy, as well as the two other newcomers who were also Jewish, was arrested by the Germans and, with the school's headmaster, a priest, disappeared.

It has taken Mr. Malle more than forty years to make *Au Revoir les Enfants*. He grew up, attended the Sorbonne, became an assistant to Jacques Cousteau (*Le Monde du Silence*) and went on to make his own series of often exceptional fiction and documentary films (*The Lovers; Phantom India; Murmur of the Heart; Human, Much Too Human; Lacombe, Lucien;* and *Atlantic City;* among others).

Every film that Mr. Malle made in those intervening years has been preparation for *Au Revoir les Enfants*. Like The Dead, which it resembles in no other way, it's a work that has the kind of simplicity, ease, and density of detail that only a filmmaker in total command of his craft can bring off, and then only rarely.

Au Revoir les Enfants, which opens today at Cinema 1, is a fiction film created out of memory and made tough by a responsible journalist's conscience. It's about life during the German Occupation of France, about being a bright, curious, rather privileged child, about growing up and, perhaps most important, about the compulsive need to find meaning, if not order, through recollection.

At the beginning of the film, Julien Quentin (Gaspard Manesse) is on a Paris railroad platform saying good-bye to his pretty mother before returning to school. He clings to her and weeps like a six-year-old, and when she points out that this parting is not, exactly, forever, he doesn't hesitate to announce—haughtily—that he detests her.

Yet she encourages his childish behavior. "I'd like to dress up like a boy and join you," she says and hugs him. "Then we could be together and nobody would know." It's a splendidly ambiguous moment, the sort that films don't often contain. It may be the first time that Julien senses the end of childhood. The last thing that a twelve-year-old boy wants is a boyhood pal who's actually his mother in knee-pants.

Julien is truculent in his initial encounters with the mysterious "new boy," Jean Bonnet (Raphaël Fejtö), who's considerably taller than he is and completely self-reliant. The new boy is given the bed next to Julien's in the dormitory. He attempts to be friendly, but Julien is wary.

"I'm Julien Quentin. Don't mess with me," is all that Julien will say at first. In the classroom Julien is jealous of the ease with which Jean answers questions. He's also baffled by Jean's indifference to gross insults, threats, and practical jokes, which, according to the code of adolescents, are supposed to prompt outrage.

Little by little, Julien's curiosity gets the better of him. The two boys, who share a passion for books, become inarticulate friends, which still doesn't stop Julien from going through his friend's locker, where he discovers the secret of Jean's identity. His real name: Jean Kippelstein. A day or two later, Jean asks his older brother, "What's a 'Yid'?"

Mr. Malle never gets in the way of this story of friendship, betrayal, and guilt. It's as if it were telling itself, rather than being recalled and composed by someone outside. The film attends to the daily routine of school life much the way Julien does, without noticing the things that will seem important only later, including the presence of the much despised Joseph.

Joseph (François Négret) is the school's runty, lame young kitchen helper, who supplies the boys with cigarettes and other black market items in return for the food the boys receive from home. Though the relationship of the naive, impressionable Julien and the exotic, martyred Jean is the focus of the film, Joseph is the film's catalyst, as well as its conscience.

Mr. Malle treats his young actors without condescension and they, in turn, respond with performances of natural gravity and humor. Most directors seem to go wrong when they attempt to recapture the way children behave and talk with each other when adults aren't around. Children in movies tend to become far brighter and more precocious than any children ever are. They are children remembered as we wish we had been. Mr. Malle never indulges this longing.

Au Revoir les Enfants remains utterly specific, which is why it's so moving without ever being sentimental. Though the action of the film covers only a few weeks, it seems (as it might to a child) to cover a lifetime. Not until the closing credits does Mr. Malle allow himself to take the long view. Not until then does everything we've seen begin to make the sense that Mr. Malle is just now coming to terms with.

Mr. Manesse and Mr. Fejtö are fine, but Mr. Négret is especially memorable as Joseph, who is a small, rich variation on the doomed farm boy in *Lacombe, Lucien*. The excellent supporting cast includes Francine Racette, as Jean's bewitching mother; Stanislas Carré de Malberg as Julien's worldly older brother, and Philippe Morier-Genoud, as the headmaster who, in one of the film's funnier moments, lectures a church full of well-heeled parents on the difficulties that a camel faces in passing through the eye of a needle.

—*V.C., February 12, 1988*

L'AVVENTURA

Directed by Michelangelo Antonioni; written (in Italian, with English subtitles) by Mr. Antonioni, Elio Bartolini and Tonino Guerra, based on a story by Mr. Antonioni; cinematographer, Aldo Scavarda; edited by Eraldo Da Roma; music by Giovanni Fusco; art designer, Piero Poletto; produced by Cino Del Duca; released by Janus Films. Black and white. Running time: 145 minutes.

With: Monica Vitti (Claudia), Gabriele Ferzetti (Sandro), Lea Massari (Anna), Dominique Blanchar (Giulia), James Addams (Corrado), Renzo Ricci (Anna's Father), Esmerelda Ruspoli (Patrizia) and Lelio Luttazi (Raimondo).

Watching *L'Avventura* (*The Adventure*), which came to the Beekman yesterday, is like trying to follow a showing of a picture at which several reels have got lost.

Just when it seems to be beginning to make a dramatic point or to develop a line of continuity that will crystallize into some sense, it will jump into a random situation that appears as if it might be due perhaps three reels later and never explain what has been omitted.

At least, that's how it strikes us.

What Michelangelo Antonioni, who wrote and directed it, is trying to get across in this highly touted Italian mystery drama (which is what we take it to be) is a secret he seems to be determined to conceal from the audience. Indeed he stated frankly to a reporter from this paper last week that he expects the customers to search for their own meanings. "I want the audience to work," he said.

That would be all right, if the director would help us a bit along the way, if he would fill in a few of the big potholes in this two-hour-and-twenty-five-minute film. But he doesn't. Like a breathless storyteller who has a long and detailed story to tell and is so eager to get on to the big doings that he forgets to mention several important things, Signor Antonioni deals only with what seems to interest him. He omits such little details as whatever happens to some key characters and why others turn up in certain places and do what they do.

For instance, it might be helpful if he would have the kindness to explain what gives on a curious, barren island, where his drama presumably begins. To this lava rock off the coast of Sicily he brings a peculiarly viperous group of jaded and selfish worldings in a conspicuously crowded little yacht. While they are wandering across its waste space, he has one of the party disappear—a sad young woman who has been having a bit of a dido with one of the handsome bachelors in the group.

What has happened to this poor young woman? Has she committed suicide? Has her lover stuffed her in a cozy crevice? Signor Antonioni never explains. He just keeps us there on that ugly island for what seems an interminable length of time while the party and police hunt for the body. Then he suddenly jumps the scene to Sicily, where the lover and another young woman in the party somehow meet on strangely disagreeable terms.

Has that prelude on the island been symbolic? Are the two, now isolated, meant to be the forlorn and exhausted relics of a social catastrophe? Maybe so, maybe not, but in a short time they are on anything but disagreeable terms. They are suddenly enthusiastic lovers, embracing frequently.

However, their affair does not run smoothly. They have doubts, anxieties, violent spats. One time they drive together into an empty city and look at the cold austere facade of a concrete church. ("These buildings are madness," the girl says.) They are lonely amid gay people.

One night the man stays away with another girl. The woman finds them together the next morning. They have a dismal reunion in the cheerless dawn.

Perhaps Signor Antonioni is saying something valuable in this. We would very much hate to think he isn't, for he has put a lot of craft into his film. His photography is exquisite—sharp and immensely picturesque. Much of it is shot on location, in the cities and countryside of Sicily, and there is a great deal of beauty and excitement in the pure composition of movement against architectural forms.

Signor Antonioni also has great skill in conceiving and conveying provocative isolated images. A shot of the woman walking from her first assignation past a lineup of ogling, leering men, or one of her running distractedly down an endlessly long hall to seek aid, flash vivid concepts of feeling. And the actors are all provocative types and interesting performers of the odd things they have to do.

Gabriele Ferzetti as the lover has a taut, tireless energy, and Monica Vitti, as his second mistress, is weirdly coquettish and intense. Lea Massari, Dominique Blanchar, and James Addams make odd sybarites—until they are dropped like hot potatoes. Several others fit into that class.

A wry musical score and soundtrack and English subtitles that seem inadequate contribute to the mystification of this picture, which won prizes in Europe. 'Tis strange.

Or maybe Signor Antonioni isn't out to prove anything—just to give us a weird adventure. Well, it gives us that.

—B.C., April 15, 1961

THE AWFUL TRUTH

Produced and directed by Leo McCarey; written by Vina Delmar, based on the play by Arthur Richman; cinematographer, Joseph Walker; edited by Al Clark; music and lyrics by Ben Oakland and Milton Drake; art designers, Stephen Goosson and Lionel Banks; released by Columbia Pictures. Black and white. Running time: 90 minutes.

With: Irene Dunne (Lucy Warriner), Cary Grant (Jerry Warriner), Ralph Bellamy (Daniel Leeson), Alexander D'Arcy (Armand Duvalle), Cecil Cunningham (Aunt Patsy), Molly Lamont (Barbara Vance) and Esther Dale (Mrs. Leeson).

The art of being Gallic, or bedroomish, in a nice way, is demonstrated with Celtic ingenuity (the principals are just interlocutorily divorced, not actually unwedded) and a technique which seems original, possibly because no one has dared to use it since the talkie revolution, in Leo McCarey's Columbia production *The Awful Truth,* at the Music Hall. To be frank, *The Awful Truth* is awfully unimportant, but it is also one of the more laughable screen comedies of 1937, a fairly good vintage year. Its comedy is almost purely physical—like that of the old Avery Hopwood stage farces—with only here and there a lone gag to interrupt the pure poetry of motion, yet its unapologetic return to the fundamentals of comedy seems, we repeat, original and daring.

Its obvious success with a modern audience is also rather disquieting. Just when it began to appear that an excellent case had finally been made out for spoken wit and adultness of viewpoint on the screen, the mercurial Mr. McCarey, who only a few months ago saddened us to the point of tears with his *Make Way for Tomorrow,* shocks us with a comedy in which speech is subsidiary, and maturity exists only to be deflated into abject juvenility. Though the film has a certain structural unevenness—some of the scenes having a terrific comic impact, others being a shade self-conscious—the final result is a picture liberally strewn with authentic audience laughs which appear to be just as unashamedly abdominal as they were in the days of Fatty Arbuckle.

The story is one that simply disintegrates under analysis. Its funniest scene, that of the dog, "Mr. Smith" (Asta of *The Thin Man*) playing hide-and-seek, and repeatedly dragging out the incriminating derby hat from where Irene Dunne has hidden it, is based on the purely farcical premise that it would really have mattered to Cary Grant, her estranged husband, if he had found its harmless owner in the drawing room, when he arrived. If any jest in dramaturgy is more ancient than the piling up of rival males in a lady's boudoir, it must antedate the Greeks—a fact which doesn't keep it from being pretty funny in *The Awful Truth.*

Miss Dunne and Mr. Grant, as the couple who get undivorced, and Ralph Bellamy as the rich respectable suitor from Oklahoma have fun with their roles, and the pleasure seems to be shared, on the whole, by the Music Hall audience.

—*B.R.C., November 5, 1937*

b

BABETTE'S FEAST

Directed by Gabriel Axel: written (in Danish and French. with English subtitles) by Mr. Axel. based on the short story by Isak Dinesen: cinematographer. Henning Kristiansen: edited by Finn Henriksen: music by Per Norgard and Wolfgang Amadeus Mozart: produced by Just Betzer and Bo Christensen: released by Orion Classics. Running time: 102 minutes.

With: Stéphane Audran (Babette). Birgitte Federspiel (Older Martine). Bodil Kjer (Older Filippa). Vibeke Hastrup (Younger Martine). Hanne Stensgard (Younger Filippa) Jarl Kulle (Older Lorenz Lowenhielm). Gudmar Wivesson (Younger Lorenz Lowenhielm). Jean-Philippe Lafont (Achille Papin) and Bibi Andersson (Lady from the Court).

Taking a longish tale, *Babette's Feast,* from Isak Dinesen's last collection, *Anecdotes of Destiny* (1958), Gabriel Axel has made a very handsome, very literary movie that does justice to the precision of the Dinesen prose, to the particularity of her concerns and to the ironies that so amused her.

What with the English subtitles that translate the Danish dialogue and soundtrack narration, one spends almost as much time reading *Babette's Feast* as watching it. Subtitles, under most circumstances, are simply a necessary intrusion. In this case, however, they have the effect of subtly amplifying the distinctive voice of the storyteller, who can make great leaps forward and backward in time without destroying the commanding unity of the tale. Dinesen is just offscreen throughout.

Babette's Feast is set in the second half of the nineteenth century on Denmark's remote Jutland coast, in a small fishing village whose most notable inhabitants are a fervent Protestant pastor and his two beautiful, pious daughters. Martine and Filippa. Mindful of their responsibilities to their father and his reformist mission, each daughter turns down a beloved suitor. Martine's is a young officer, Filippa's a famous French opera star who has been vacationing on the Jutland coast.

After their father's death the two young women slip into unmarried middle age, carrying on the pastor's work with saintly dedication. One night in the middle of a terrible storm, Babette (Stéphane Audran) turns up at their door, battered by weather and circumstances, and carrying a letter of introduction from Filippa's opera singer, now old and retired. Having lost both her husband and son in the Paris Commune, Babette, he explains, needs political sanctuary. He begs the sisters to take her in. The sisters, who are nearly penniless, accept Babette's offer to act as their unpaid housekeeper.

In time, Babette becomes an indispensable though ever enigmatic member of the household. Her Roman Catholicism is politely ignored. She brings order and efficiency to the sisters' lives as defenders of their father's aging flock, which, over the years, has become split by old grievances and jealousies. Babette cooks, cleans, washes, and sews, always remaining aloof and proud, at a distance from her benefactors.

All of this is by way of being the prelude to the film's extended, funny, and moving final sequence, a spectacular feast, the preparation and execution of which reveal Babette's secret and the nature of her sustaining glory.

It's not telling too much to report that this glory is Art—in Babette's case, a very special God-given talent. *Babette's Feast* is an affirmation of Art as the force by which, in the words of the old pastor (who never quite realized what he was saying) "righteousness and bliss," otherwise known as the spirit and the flesh, shall be reconciled.

Mr. Axel, a filmmaker new to me who has worked as much in France as in Denmark, treats the Dinesen text with self-effacing but informed modesty. The understated courage of the characters, the barren beauty of the landscape and, finally, the unexpected appearance of salvation are all effortlessly defined in images and language that reflect the writer's style— swift, clean, witty, and elegant.

Miss Audran dominates the movie in the same way that Babette takes charge of the sisters' household and the village. The actress is still one of the great natural resources of European films.

The beautiful Birgitte Federspiel, remembered from Carl Dreyer's classic, *Ordet,* appears as the older Martine and Bodil Kjer as the older Filippa. Jean-Philippe Lafont plays the expansive opera singer and Bibi Andersson is seen in a cameo role as a patron of the arts. Every member of the cast is excellent.

A note of caution: do not see *Babette's Feast* on an empty stomach. Before the film ends, the feast itself, which includes, among other things, fresh terrapin soup, quail in vol-au-vents, blinis, caviar, and baba au rhum, may drive you out to the nearest three-star restaurant. It could be a dangerously expensive evening.

—*V.C., October 1, 1987*

BABY DOLL

Produced and directed by Elia Kazan: written by Tennessee Williams. based on his story and stage play: cinematographer. Boris Kaufman: edited by Gene Milford: music by Kenyon Hopkins: released by Warner Brothers. Black and white. Running time: 114 minutes.

With: Karl Malden (Archie). Carroll Baker (Baby Doll). Eli Wallach (Silva Vacarro). Mildred Dunnock (Aunt Rose Comfort). Lonny Chapman (Rock). Eades Hogue (Town Marshall) and Noah Williamson (Deputy).

It looks as though the ghost of Tennessee Williams's *Streetcar Named Desire* has got bogged down in the mud of Erskine Caldwell's famous *Tobacco Road* in the screenplay Mr. Williams has written for Elia Kazan's *Baby Doll.*

For there is in this last picture, which opened at the Victoria last night with an elaborate benefit showing for the Actors Studio, a lot of the sort of personal conflict that occurred in Mr. Williams's former play taking place among characters in an environment in which Jeeter Lester would feel quite at home.

Mr. Williams again is writing tartly about decadence in the South in this film, which has drawn the condemnation of the Roman Catholic Church. His theme is the degeneration and inadequacy of old Southern stock, as opposed to the vital aggressiveness of intruding "foreigners." But where he was dealing with a woman of a certain culture in *A Streetcar Named Desire,* he is down to the level of pure "white trash" in this sardonic *Baby Doll.*

This is the major shortcoming of Mr. Williams's and Mr. Kazan's film. Its people are virtually without character, content, or consequence. Three of its four main people are morons or close to being same, and its fourth is a scheming opportunist who takes advantage of the others' lack of brains.

There is Archie Lee Meighan, the oafish owner of a broken-down country cotton gin, and his girl-wife, Baby Doll, an unmistakable victim of arrested development. Then there is Aunt Rose Comfort, an aged, pathetic simpleton, and there is wily Silva Vacarro, the "foreigner" who runs a rival cotton gin.

And what is the pertinent business with which the film is concerned? It is the uncovering by Vacarro that Archie Lee has set fire to his cotton gin. And how does he do this? By dallying unrestrainedly with Baby Doll, who has never submitted to her husband and is fair prey for Vacarro's game.

These are the people and the story, and unless they were shaped with utmost skill they would be something less than trifling; they would be unendurable. But no one can say that Mr. Williams is not a clever man with his pen. He has written his trashy, vicious people so that they are clinically interesting. And Karl

Malden, Carroll Baker, Mildred Dunnock, and Eli Wallach have acted them, under Mr. Kazan's superb direction, so that they nigh corrode the screen.

Archie Lee, played by Mr. Malden, is a man of immense stupidity, rendered the more offensive by his treachery and bigotry; and Baby Doll, played by Miss Baker, is a piteously flimsy little twist of juvenile greed, inhibitions, physical yearnings, common crudities, and conceits. Vacarro, played by Mr. Wallach, is dynamic, arrogant, and droll, and Aunt Rose Comfort, played by Miss Dunnock, is a pitifully patient, frightened freak.

What is more, they are done with withering candor. No ugliness of their lives is spared. And Mr. Kazan has staged the afternoon dalliance of Baby Doll and Vacarro with startling suggestiveness. While he pointedly leaves it uncertain whether the girl is actually seduced, there is no question that she is courted and riotously pursued. Mr. Kazan keeps the courtship bouncing between the emotional and the ludicrous. The nonchalance of the pursuer is its most entertaining grace.

But Mr. Kazan's pictorial compositions, got in stark black-and-white and framed for the most part against the background of an old Mississippi mansion, are by far the most artful and respectable feature of *Baby Doll*.
—*B.C., December 19, 1956*

BACK TO THE FUTURE

Directed by Robert Zemeckis; written by Mr. Zemeckis and Bob Gale; cinematographer, Dean Cundey; edited by Arthur Schmidt and Harry Keramidas; music by Alan Silvestri; art designer, Todd Hollowell; produced by Mr. Gale and Neil Canton; released by Universal Pictures. Running time; 116 minutes.

With: Michael J. Fox (Marty McFly), Christopher Lloyd (Dr. Emmett Brown), Lea Thompson (Lorraine Baines), Crispin Glover (George McFly), Thomas F. Wilson (Biff Tannen), Claudia Wells (Jennifer Parker), Marc McClure (Dave McFly) and Wendie Jo Sperber (Linda McFly).

The people in Robert Zemeckis's films have the great fun of living out their craziest daydreams.

And the crazier the better: Mr. Zemeckis, together with his screenwriting partner Bob Gale, has progressed from teenage kamikazes willing to risk anything to meet the Beatles (*I Wanna Hold Your Hand*) to salesmen ready to peddle any form of figurative snake oil (*Used Cars*) to a timid pulp novelist who travels to the tropics (*Romancing the Stone,* with a screenplay by Diane Thomas) and becomes her own most adventuresome heroine.

Mr. Zemeckis has now gone himself one better with *Back to the Future,* about a boy who wonders what his parents were like in their salad days and is miraculously given the chance to find out. What child wouldn't love the chance to tell the two lovestruck teenagers who will someday become his mother and father: "Hey, if you guys ever have kids and one of them, when he's eight years old, accidentally sets fire to the living room rug—go easy on him, willya?"

Back to the Future, which opens today at Loew's State and other theaters, takes this sweet, ingenious premise and really runs with it. In less resourceful hands, the idea might quickly have worn thin; it might have taken an uncomfortable turn, since the story's young hero must face the transformation of his plump, stern, middle-aged mother into a flirtatious young beauty. But Mr. Zemeckis is able both to keep the story moving and to keep it from going too far. He handles *Back to the Future* with the kind of inventiveness that indicates he will be spinning funny, whimsical tall tales for a long time to come.

The hero of the film is named Marty McFly, though his mother insists, when he ventures back in time thirty years, on calling him Calvin Klein. The film's observation that, in those days, a name sewn onto the back of one's pants was probably one's own is only one of the shrewd, rueful contrasts it draws between 1955 and the present day. Once Marty (played winningly by Michael J. Fox) steps into the specially equipped DeLorean owned by a mad scientist friend of his and floors the accelerator, he finds himself in a much simpler world. The neighborhood where he will someday live hasn't even been built. The local soda jerk thinks anyone who orders a Pepsi Free ("If you want a Pepsi you gotta pay for it!") is being a wise guy. The town's movie theater is playing a Ronald Reagan film, and when Marty announces that Mr. Reagan will be President some day, he is met with a stare of disbelief and a sarcastic remark about Vice President Jerry Lewis.

While keeping the film well stocked with similar witticisms and giving the production the muted, well-groomed look of 1950's advertising and television, Mr. Zemeckis keeps the film firmly anchored in McFly family history. Dad (Crispin Glover) is a nerd, while Mother (Lea Thompson) is a demure beauty; it should be noted that Mr. Glover and Miss Thompson are funny and credible both as parents and as teenagers.

But there is a danger that they will never meet, particularly since Marty's arrival has permanently altered their history. This, and Marty's decade-hopping rapport with the mad scientist (Christopher Lloyd) whose DeLorean he borrowed, keeps *Back to the Future* very busy indeed. Even so, it still manages to end with a surprise.

One of the most appealing things about *Back to the Future* is its way of putting nostalgia gently in perspective. Like Marty, Mr. Zemeckis takes a bemused but unsentimental view of times gone by. And he seems no less fascinated by the future, which is understandable. His own looks very bright.

—*J.M., July 3, 1985*

THE BAD AND THE BEAUTIFUL

Directed by Vincente Minnelli; written by Charles Schnee, based on a story by George Bradshaw; cinematographer, Robert Surtees; edited by Conrad A. Nervig; music by David Raksin; art designers, Cedric Gibbons and Edward Carfagno; produced by John Houseman; released by Metro-Goldwyn-Mayer. Black and white. Running time: 116 minutes.

With: Lana Turner (Georgia), Kirk Douglas (Jonathan), Walter Pidgeon (Harry Pebbel), Dick Powell (James Lee), Barry Sullivan (Fred), Gloria Grahame (Rosemary), Gilbert Roland ("Gaucho"), Leo G. Carroll (Henry Whitfield) and Vanessa Brown (Kay).

The widely circulated notion that there are monsters in Hollywood, aside and apart entirely from the grim and ghoulish get of Frankenstein, is given unqualified endorsement, with no reservations and no holds barred, in Metro's *The Bad and the Beautiful,* which came to the Music Hall yesterday. For the hero of this relentless saga is a Hollywood producer who is a heel, a West Coast, Noël Cowardish scoundrel, a perfect Kirk Douglas—type bum. And the fine job of drawing him and quartering him that is done in the course of two hours by a top staff of Metro dissectors is enough to make the blood run sour and cold.

First, they slit him down the middle and show, in considerable detail, how he blandly double-crosses a director who has helped him through his early struggling years. Then they lop off another portion and show, in even greater detail, how he drags and romances a sad young actress to glittering triumph and then gives her the air. Finally, with what's left, they show us how he baits a young author to Hollywood, then throws the guy's wife to a wolfish actor just so he'll be free to work on a script.

Through all of this gory demonstration of the miserable innards of a man, the doctors are also displaying the innards of Hollywood. They move from producers' offices to studio sets and screening-rooms, from cheap boarding houses to Beverly Hills mansions, from well-laden bars to beds, pretty well indicating—or suggesting—what goes on therein. They talk about "shooting on location," "going over the budget," "sneak previews," and "audience response," and they make a few jabs at movie critics, European directors, Pulitzer Prizes and such—all of them incidental nettles that get under the average Hollywood person's skin.

But, somehow, for all this probing and all this intimate looking around amid the realistic paraphernalia and artificial clutter of Hollywood, there does not emerge a clear picture of exactly how movies are made. It is a crowded and colorful picture, but it is choppy, episodic, and vague. And what is much more annoying, for all the carving and digging that are done in the producer's insides, it is still not discovered what makes this vicious fellow run.

To be sure, Charles Schnee's script makes some effort to explain him as the cynical son of a pioneer movie producer who has died broke and hated in Hollywood. And Kirk Douglas plays the fellow with all that arrogance in the eyes and jaw that suggest a ruthless disposition covering up for a hurt and bitter soul. But this doesn't justify his meanness or his broad inconsistencies. The fellow is a picturesque composite of Hollywood rumor—a prototype of many legends. But that's all he is. He's a cliché.

The same might be said of Lana Turner as the incredible girl who is raised from a drunken extra to staggering stardom by the willpower of this man. Frankly, she is no more convincing as the drunken extra than she is as the star. She is an actress playing an actress, and neither one is real. A howling act in a wildly racing auto—pure bunk—is the top of her speed.

As a veteran producer, Walter Pidgeon does give some notion, withal, of the squirming and agonizing that goes on in Hollywood. Barry Sullivan as the gypped director, Dick Powell as the misused novelist, Gilbert Roland as a lame-brained Latin actor, and Paul Stewart as a loyal publicist also perform with proper motions under Vincente Minnelli's crafty hand, and Leo G. Carroll is delicious in a bit as a British director.

John Houseman's skill as a producer is also evident in the slickness of this film. But certainly he and all the others who worked on it know much more about the subject of Hollywood egos and championship chumps than is revealed.

—*B.C., January 16, 1953*

BAD DAY AT BLACK ROCK

Directed by John Sturges; written by Don McGuire and Millard Kaufman, based on a story by Howard Breslin; cinematographer, William Mellor; edited by Newell P. Kimlin; music by André Previn; art designers, Cedric Gibbons and Malcolm Brown; produced by Dore Schary; released by Metro-Goldwyn Mayer. Running time: 81 minutes.

With: Spencer Tracy (John J. Macreedy), Robert Ryan (Reno Smith), Anne Francis (Liz Wirth), Dean Jagger (Tim Horn), Walter Brennan (Doc Velie), John Ericson (Peter Wirth), Ernest Borgnine (Coley Trimble), Lee Marvin (Doctor David), Russell Collins (Mr. Hastings) and Walter Sande (Sam).

Much the same sort of situation that prevailed in the memorable *High Noon* is apparent in *Bad Day at Black Rock,* which came yesterday to the Rivoli. And a comparable regard for personal valor is involved in this Metro CinemaScope film.

A stranger drops off a streamliner at a California desert whistle-stop. The local characters view him with suspicion and treat him with cruel hostility. They're not accustomed to strangers in this lonely, flea-bitten town. The streamliner hasn't stopped in four years, and apparently few people ever pass through.

Especially are they wary of this stranger when they discover that he is interested in a certain Japanese farmer who they tell him left town a few years back. They wonder if he is a detective, seeing how he noses around. And he, in turn, wonders darkly why everyone is so hostile toward him.

Slowly, through a process of guarded discourse, which Director John Sturges has built up by patient, methodical pacing of his almost completely male cast, an eerie light begins to glimmer. The Japanese was actually slain, and most of the townsmen were in on it. That's why they're so wary and on edge. And the stranger, whose mission is simply to deliver a war medal of a hero son to the Japanese, comes to suspect that he is in the midst of a gang of arrogant murderers.

Why these small-time tyrants, dominated by a simpering Robert Ryan, should assume it necessary to murder the stranger, whom Spencer Tracy plays, is a point that the script of Millard Kaufman never makes reasonable. Thus a small doubt as to the logic of the drama is left in a close attendant's mind.

But the menace of these swaggering desert roughnecks is nonetheless creeping and cold. And the battle that Mr. Tracy puts up to save his hide is dramatically taut. When he comes out, it is obvious that not only valor but justice has prevailed.

Quite as interesting as the drama, which smacks of being contrived, are the types of masculine creatures paraded in this film. Mr. Tracy is sturdy and laconic as a war veteran with a lame arm (which does not hamper him, however, in fighting judo style). Mr. Ryan is angular and vicious as the uneasy kingpin of the town, and Walter Brennan is cryptic and caustic as the local mortician with a streak of spunk.

Ernest Borgnine as a potbellied bully (he was Fatso in *From Here to Eternity*), Dean Jagger as a rumguzzling sheriff, Lee Marvin as a dimwitted tough, John Ericson as a nervous hotel clerk, and Russell Collins as a stationmaster are all good, too. The only female in the film is Anne Francis.

She is more fetching than felicitous in this environment. Above all, the gritty, dry-hot feeling of a rough-plank desert town, lying bare beneath the sun and a mountain backdrop, is got in color on the CinemaScope screen. Dore Schary, who produced this film for Metro, strove for drama in the pictorial scene. And that, quite as much as the drama of personal conflict, is what *Bad Day at Black Rock* has.

—B.C., February 2, 1955

BADLANDS

Produced, written and directed by Terrence Malick; cinematographers, Brian Probyn, Tak Fujimoto and Stevan Larner; edited by Robert Estrin; music by George Tipton; art designer, Jack Fisk; released by Warner Brothers. Running time: 95 minutes.

With: Martin Sheen (Kit), Sissy Spacek (Holly), Warren Oates (Holly's Father), Ramon Bieri (Cato) and Alan Vint (Deputy).

The time is late summer at the end of the 1950's and the place a small, placid town in South Dakota. The streets are lined with oak and maple trees in full leaf. The lawns are so neat, so close-cropped, they look crew-cut. Kit Carruthers (Martin Sheen) is twenty-five, a garbage collector who fancies his cowboy boots and his faint resemblance to James Dean. Holly Sargis (Sissy Spacek) is fifteen. Until she meets Kit, she hasn't much interest in anything except her dog and her baton, which she practices twirling in her front yard.

In Terrence Malick's cool, sometimes brilliant, always ferociously American film, *Badlands,* which marks Malick's debut as a director, Kit and Holly take an all-American joyride across the upper Middle West, at the end of which more than half a dozen people have been shot to death by Kit, usually at point-blank range.

Badlands was presented twice at Alice Tully Hall Saturday night, the closing feature of the 11th New York Film Festival that began so auspiciously with François Truffaut's *Day for Night.* In between there were a lot of other films, good and bad, but none as provocative as this first feature by Malick, a twenty-nine-year-old former Rhodes Scholar and philosophy student whose only other film credit is as the author of

the screenplay for last year's nicely idiosyncratic *Pocket Money.*

Badlands was inspired by the short, bloody saga of Charles Starkweather who, at age nineteen, in January, 1958, with the apparent cooperation of his fourteen-year-old girlfriend, Caril Fugate, went off on a murder spree that resulted in ten victims. Starkweather was later executed in the electric chair and Miss Fugate given life imprisonment.

Badlands inevitably invites comparisons with three other important American films, Arthur Penn's *Bonnie and Clyde* and Fritz Lang's *Fury* and *You Only Live Once,* but it has a very different vision of violence and death. Malick spends no great amount of time invoking Freud to explain the behavior of Kit and Holly, nor is there any Depression to be held ultimately responsible. Society is, if anything, benign.

This is the haunting truth of *Badlands,* something that places it very much in the seventies in spite of its carefully re-created period detail. Kit and Holly are directionless creatures, technically literate but uneducated in any real sense, so desensitized that Kit (in Malick's words at a news conference) can regard the gun with which he shoots people as a kind of magic wand that eliminates small nuisances. Kit and Holly are members of the television generation run amok.

They are not ill-housed, ill-clothed, or ill-fed. If they are at all aware of their anger (and I'm not sure they are, since they see only boredom), it's because of the difference between the way life is and the way it is presented on the small screen, with commercial breaks instead of lasting consequences.

Badlands is narrated by Holly in the flat, nasal accents of the Middle West and in the syntax of a story in True Romances. "Little did I realize," she tells us at the beginning of the film, "that what began in the alleys and by-ways of this small town would end in the badlands of Montana." At the end, after half a dozen murders, she resolves never again to "tag around with the hell-bent type."

Kit and Holly share with Clyde and Bonnie a fascination with their own press coverage, with their overnight fame ("The whole world was looking for us," says Holly, "for who knew where Kit would strike next?"), but a lack of passion differentiates them from the gaudy desperados of the thirties. Toward the end of their joyride, the bored Holly tells us she passed the time, as she sat in the front seat beside Kit, spelling out complete sentences with her tongue on the roof of her mouth.

Malick tries not to romanticize his killers, and he is successful except for one sequence in which Kit and Holly hide out in a tree house as elaborate as anything the M-G-M art department ever designed for Tarzan and Jane. Sheen and Miss Spacek are splendid as the self-absorbed, cruel, possibly psychotic children of our time, as are the members of the supporting cast, including Warren Oates as Holly's father.

One may legitimately debate the validity of Malick's vision, but not, I think, his immense talent. *Badlands* is a most important and exciting film.

—*V.C., October 15, 1973*

THE BAKER'S WIFE

Directed by Marcel Pagnol; written (in French, with English subtitles) by Mr. Pagnol, based on the novel *Jean Le Bleu* by Jean Giono; cinematographers, Georges Benoit, R. Lendruz and N. Daries; edited by Suzanne de Troeye; music by Vincent Scotto; produced by Robert Hakim and Raymond Hakim. Black and white. Running time: 130 minutes.

With: Raimu (Aimable, the Baker), Ginette Leclerc (Aurelie, the Baker's Wife), Charles Moulin (Dominique, the Shepherd), Robert Vattier (The Priest), Robert Bassac (The Schoolteacher) and Fernand Charpin (The Marquis).

On top of *Harvest,* which reverently told how the seed was sowed and the grain reaped, the French now have added an impious chapter about the flour, its baking, and *The Baker's Wife.* A perfectly scandalous story it is, too; the kind of story Frenchmen were born to tell—the French being, as our old schoolbooks used to explain, "a gay people, fond of dancing and light wines." Certainly no other breed could have told it so cutely, with such disarming good humor, with such tolerance and wit. It opened at the World Theatre last night and we commend it to you for many reasons, not the least being its proof that the French have not lost the gift of laughter and the ability to communicate it to others.

It seems that the new baker had a wife who ran off with the marquis's shepherd on the marquis's best horse. Now this was a calamity. The marquis thought highly of his horse, the baker thought still more highly of his wife, the village thought still, still more highly of the baker's bread which he, poor man, had not the heart to bake, so grieved he was. He went to the church for consolation and the stern young priest was preaching a highly moralistic, but unsympathetic, sermon about every wife's need for a Good Shepherd. He went to the tavern and he grew gloriously drunk and he mourned man's inhumanity to man. "I invited this fellow into my house for a cookie," he says, "and he took all I had." With a mean side glance at the curate, he compliments the Pope for his diplomacy in speaking only Latin—"the Italians couldn't understand him." Well, finally, they bring his wife back, and the marquis gets his horse, and the baker bakes again, with five extra loaves for the poor. The wife? Oh, she's forgiven. We've said this is a French picture.

Marcel Pagnol, the director who filmed *Harvest,* has adapted, written, and directed this one too, and with much the same appreciation of his material. His village vignettes are superb and completely revelatory, telling us all we need know about the village and its life, telling it so deftly we scarcely are conscious of his having bothered to describe it. And that is important, for it is the human background, more than the architectural, that must highlight his comedy of the community problem created by the scandalous—and terribly inconvenient—defection of the baker's wife. After all, even a righteous curate must have bread, and even a profligate marquis and a heretical schoolteacher; in the face of a common emergency they must set aside their normal enmity and combine against the foe: pantheists for once.

But the bulwark of the comedy, of course, is the baker himself, the great god Pan who goes by the name of Raimu. An Olympian clown Raimu, with an equatorial waistline, a buttony mustache, a foolscap of knitted wool, and the true clown's genius for pathos. There is something Chaplinesque about his inability to recognize the harshness of the world. His deception is comic, but it is tragic too; just as there is tragedy in his refusal to resent the mocking villagers who drunkenly bring him antlers. He tries to commit suicide, but that act was not of their doing; it was a bewildered recognition of the bitterness in his own soul, a gesture of despair wrung from his heart rather than by their deeds. It is this undercurrent of tragedy, this steadfast air of dignity that is at once the secret of his funniest scenes, the quality that prevents his film from toppling into farce and makes *The Baker's Wife* a true comedy and a delightful one.

—*F.S.N., February 27, 1940*

BALL OF FIRE

Directed by Howard Hawks: written by Charles Brackett and Billy Wilder, based on the story "From A to Z" by Mr. Wilder and Thomas Monroe: cinematographer, Gregg Toland: edited by Daniel Mandell: music by Alfred Newman: art designer, Perry Ferguson: produced by Samuel Goldwyn: released by RKO Radio Pictures. Black and white. Running time: 111 minutes.

With: Gary Cooper (Professor Bertram Potts), Barbara Stanwyck (Sugarpuss O'Shea), Oscar Homolka (Professor Gurkakoff), Henry Travers (Professor Jerome), S. J. Sakall (Professor Magenbruch), Tully Marshall (Professor Robinson), Leonid Kinskey (Professor Quintana), Richard Haydn (Professor Oddly), Aubrey Mather (Professor Peagram), Dana Andrews (Joe Lilac), Dan Duryea (Duke Pastrami), Ralph Peters (Asthma Anderson), Kathleen Howard (Miss Brag) and Mary Field (Miss Totten).

According to legend, Samuel Goldwyn has made some beautiful lapsi linguae in his time and has done things with the King's English that stand as a monument to his name. Maybe. But still Mr. Goldwyn can't be too touchy on that score, for now he has produced a picture which deliberately kicks the language around in a manner so colorful and lively that you can almost sense his tongue stuck in his cheek. *Ball of Fire* is the title of this wholly ingratiating lark, and so pleasant is its spoofing of the professorial pose, so comprehensive is its handling of the modern vernacular, and so altogether winning are Gary Cooper and Barbara Stanwyck in it that it had the customers jumping with enjoyment at the Music Hall yesterday.

Empirical is the adjective for the method by which it was derived—or maybe, in jellybean parlance, you'd rather say it was "dug." For not only have Charles

Brackett and Billy Wilder, the authors of the script, fetched their most flavorsome dialogue from the lingo of the day but they have borrowed their plot and their characters rather freely from here and there. Thus Mr. Cooper in the role of a literal encyclopedist working upon an analysis of current American slang is really just Mr. Deeds with a lot of book-learning. And Miss Stanwyck as the flashy nightclub singer who becomes his most fruitful source is strictly the Lady Eve with the same old apples to sell. And the story, which lets Mr. Cooper and a septet of academic pals give shelter to the fugitive Miss Stanwyck in their old-fashioned ivory tower, is frankly just an up-to-date version of *Snow White and the Seven Dwarfs*.

But who wants to be a Crabapple Annie about a little larceny like that. So long as it fits together and sends you, it's in the groove. And *Ball of Fire,* we assure you, makes with the words and the fun. Mr. Cooper may be a little loose-tooth in spots, but he gives a homespun performance such as only he can give. Miss Stanwyck is plenty yum-yum (meaning scorchy) in her worldly temptress role. S. J. Sakall, Richard Haydn, and Henry Travers stand out most among the seven "squirrely cherubs" who abet Mr. Cooper in studious pursuits and encourage him along the road of love, and Dana Andrews, Dan Duryea, and Allen Jenkins do handsomely in minor tough-boy roles.

As usual in a Samuel Goldwyn picture, the production is excellent, and Howard Hawks has kept the whole thing moving at accelerated pace for nigh two hours. That is an awfully long time to drag out a single-note plot, but, oddly enough, it works. Mr. Goldwyn has turned out a very nice comedy, indeed, and old Geoffrey Chaucer must be gulping rather limply at the bottom of his well.

—*B.C., January 16, 1942*

THE BALLAD OF CABLE HOGUE

Produced and directed by Sam Peckinpah: written by John Crawford and Edward Penney: director of photography, Lucien Ballard: music by Jerry Goldsmith: released by Warner Brothers. Running time: 113 minutes.

With: Jason Robards (Cable Hogue), Stella Stevens (Hildy), David Warner (Joshua), Strother Martin

(Bowen). Slim Pickens (Ben). Max Evans (Webb). L. Q. Jones (Taggart). Peter Whitney (Cushing). R. G. Armstrong (Quitner) and Susan O'Connell (Claudia).

To the mysteries, the complexities, the cruelties of Sam Peckinpah's American West (*The Deadly Companions*, 1961; *Ride the High Country*, 1961; *Major Dundee*, 1964; *The Wild Bunch*, 1969) there can now be added an elegy for laissez-faire capitalism, *The Ballad of Cable Hogue*, Peckinpah's gentlest, boldest, and perhaps most likable film to date. It is also thematically his most ambitious. For the story of Cable Hogue, who, left to die in the desert, bargains with God and is reborn from the dust, saved by a whirlwind that leads him to water, is hedged round with myth, with shadowy presences and distant voices, and with images of man's history from creation until—typically for Peckinpah—the coming of the automobile.

Cable sets out to convert God's gift to cash, shoots the first man who refuses him a dime for his water, stakes a claim, floats a loan, opens a stage stop (between the towns of Gilla and Deaddog), and settles in with the local hooker (a businesswoman of course), a very conspicuous American flag, and Joshua, an improbable young preacher who feels called to comfort young women, but who functions as the Angel of Death. Before he dies, most cheerfully and affectingly, Cable has suffered and killed, loved and prospered, turned legend and fact to personal fiction, and basically recognized when his time has come.

This is *The Ballad of Cable Hogue*, repeatedly dropping into music (pleasant and skillful music, much of it in songs), and committed to a rambling inclusiveness and preposterous shapeliness that seems proper to folk tale. For all its lapses—fast motion movie camera gimmicks, occasional fine writing, and a frequent indifference to the more ordinary demands of the plot—it is a film of a kind so tolerant of excess and so open to good feeling and invention that the faults remain individual and the virtues make up the sense of the whole.

I am less impressed with the inclusiveness of Peckinpah's iconography (from the evolutionary lizard at the beginning to the revolutionary automobiles at the end) than with the completeness of his understanding of the dramatic moment and of how actors, who are the life of the moment, relate. There is nobody in the cast not to praise, and Jason Robards especially joins a list of mature leading actors (Randolph Scott, Joel McCrea, William Holden) who have grown in depth and discipline under Peckinpah's direction. But it is Stella Stevens, at last in a role good enough for her, who most wonderfully sustains and enlightens the action. What she brings to her scenes with Jason Robards, especially to one midnight encounter before a long farewell, will tell you much of what you need to know about the best that can happen between a man and a woman.

—*R.G., May 14, 1970*

BAMBI

Directed by David D. Hand: written by Larry Morey and Perce Pearce. based on the story by Felix Salten: music by Frank Churchill and Edward H. Plumb: art designer. Thomas H. Codrick: produced by Walt Disney: released by RKO Radio Pictures. Running time: 70 minutes.

With the voices of: Bobby Stewart (Bambi). Peter Behn (Thumper). Stan Alexander (Flower) and Cammie King (Phylline).

The children at the Music Hall yesterday were content again; from all over the darkened house childish laughter broke forth continuously and once or twice childish tears and boohoos. For *Bambi* has come to town and with it the Music Hall has again become a children's fairyland. And after five long years of labor, Walt Disney's wizards have caught much of the breathless and breathtaking fantasy of Felix Salten's tremulous story of the little fawn who grew up in the woodland with his assorted playmates and finally became a great forest prince like his father. Mr. Disney, of course, has made some additions of his own—Thumper, the jovial rabbit who keeps saying the wrong things; Flower, the skunk with the inferiority complex; Friend Owl, the misanthrope of the treetops; and a score of other woodland phantoms. No child could ask for better company.

In colors that would surprise even the spectrum itself, Disney's cartoon craftsmen have re-created a woodland that shimmers and glows and darkens altogether magically. The wind over a green field, the morning light on the meadow, the hushed naves of the forest inhabited by all sorts of hidden folk, the artists have made with a simple and loving touch. In this enchanted sanctuary they have assembled a cast that grows up, comically discovers love, tells jokes, and plays pranks as only Disney's animals can. In the cycle of growth of Bambi and his friends the film catches much of the surprise of those seeing the world for the first time—Bambi's discovery that his feet were not meant for gambols on the winter "stiff water," his first awkward attempt to jump over a log, or Thumper's intense dislike for the "green stuff" his mother makes him eat with the clover blossoms.

It would be churlish to rebuke an effort that has caught so much startling beauty or that so often touches the heart with a humor that is both inventive and wise. And yet, for all its frequent gossamer loveliness, *Bambi* left at least one grown-up more than a little disappointed. For in re-creating Salten's fable Mr. Disney has again revealed a discouraging tendency to trespass beyond the bounds of cartoon fantasy into the tight naturalism of magazine illustration. His painted forest is hardly to be distinguished from the real forest shown by the Technicolor camera in *Jungle Book*. His central characters of Bambi and his parents—all the deer, in fact—are as naturalistically drawn as possible; only the little "character" actors such as Thumper, Friend Owl, or the moles are the "humanized" creations of fantasy. The free and whimsical cartoon caricatures have made way for a closer resemblance to life, which the camera can show better. Mr. Disney seems intent on moving from art to artiness.

For in trying to achieve a real-life naturalism as the camera does, Mr. Disney is faced with the necessity of meeting those standards, and if he does, why have cartoons at all? One cannot combine naturalism with cartoon fantasy. Because Bambi and his mother are naturalistically conceived, the fact that they speak like people becomes widely incongruous; because the stags are similarly drawn their stiff leaps across the meadow merely throw into relief the failure of pen and brush to catch the fluent movement of real photography. A waterfall that does not ripple with complete realism tears apart the illusion of a naturalistically contrived forest.

No doubt these considerations will seem academic to the children at the Music Hall, for *Bambi* is their picture and childhood sometimes has a literal mind. They will remember most, perhaps, those touches of humor such as the field mouse scurrying from one toadstool marquee to another for shelter in the rain, or the baby duck poking a webbed toe into the water and whistling, or the two little moles who bump heads when their underground trails cross. No doubt they even will forgive Mr. Disney for putting false eyelashes on his enticing female bunnies. For *Bambi* has the Disney stamp upon it and it has many a moment that brings a thrill of visual delight. But insofar as it reaches out into the world of actual beings it gives away its make-believe. In his search for perfection Mr. Disney has come perilously close to tossing away his whole world of cartoon fantasy. Meanwhile, of course, *Bambi* is going to please a great many people, for all our churlish exceptions.

—*T.S., August 14, 1942*

THE BAND WAGON

Directed by Vincente Minnelli; written by Betty Comden and Adolph Green; cinematographer, Harry Jackson; edited by Albert Akst; music by Adolph Deutsch; choreography by Michael Kidd; produced by Arthur Freed; released by Metro-Goldwyn-Mayer. Running time: 111 minutes.

With: Fred Astaire (Tony Hunter), Cyd Charisse (Gaby), Oscar Levant (Lester Marton), Nanette Fabray (Lily Marton), Jack Buchanan (Jeffrey Cordova), James Mitchell (Paul Byrd) and Robert Gist (Hal Benton).

That wonderful talent for satire which Betty Comden and Adolph Green possess and which was gleefully turned upon the movies in their script for last year's *Singing in the Rain* is even more gleefully let loose upon the present-day musical stage in their book for Metro's *The Band Wagon,* which rolled into the Music Hall yesterday. Joined with the equally nimble talents of Fred Astaire, Jack Buchanan, and Cyd Charisse and some tunes from the sterling repertory of Arthur Schwartz and Howard Dietz, this literate and witty combination herein delivers a show that respectfully bids for recognition as one of the best musical films ever made.

Don't look for anything resembling the memorable musical revue of the same name in which Mr. Astaire did quite nicely with the help of the Messrs. Schwartz and Dietz. Outside of three classic song numbers picked up from that sparkling revue—"Dancing in the Dark," "I Love Louisa," and the spirited "New Sun in the Sky"—there is none of it in this picture, saving the name and Mr. Astaire. Oh, yes—and one very incidental orchestral playing of "High and Low."

But that is more to the credit of Miss Comden and Mr. Green and all of the other people who have contributed to this brilliant Technicolor film. For theirs is a wholly original and intrinsic musical show that cleverly takes advantage of the old—and two new—Schwartz-Dietz tunes.

What it is, in essence, is just a very sophisticated turn on the old and completely hackneyed story of people putting on a show. Mr. Astaire, as a washed-up movie idol, returns to Broadway and is snagged to appear in a musical written by two zanies, played by Oscar Levant and Nanette Fabray. Trouble comes when Jack Buchanan, as a flamboyant genius-type, decides to produce their carefree item as a modern-day version of *Faust* and Miss Charisse, as the prima dancer, decides that Mr. Astaire is too old. He likewise gets the notion that she is decidedly too tall. And out of this clutch of complications the magic of a movie is evolved.

Take it from us, it is a honey—a genial and comprehending snipe at the rampant egos of theater people, their reckless excursions and alarums, and all of the manifold headaches that accompany the production of a show. It is also, by chance, a very touching appreciation of the nature of Mr. Astaire. If there is anything wrong with it as entertainment, it is too subtle about the theater for all to get.

However, that shouldn't matter too much, for the whole thing is so adroitly played under Vincente Minnelli's direction, with Mr. Buchanan stealing the show as the demoniac director and the others playing straight to his conceits that the humors are steady and abundant, both the obvious ones and those concealed.

And certainly the musical numbers are shaped to the champagne tastes of all, especially the terminal ballet number, which is a take-off on the literary works of such hard-boiled detective-fiction writers as the popular Mickey Spillane. Called "Girl Hunt," it is dazzling satire, in semi-surrealistic style, full of gunmen and sleek seductive vampires. And it is danced beautifully by Mr. Astaire and Miss Charisse. Oliver Smith's fantastic settings are striking in this number, too.

But they're all, in their moods, just as fetching—the song and dance that Mr. Astaire does, with the help of an unnamed Nubian, to the jaunty "Shine on Your Shoes"; the singing of "That's Entertainment," a new number, by Mr. Astaire, Mr. Buchanan, and Miss Fabray; or the dancing of Mr. Astaire and Mr. Buchanan to "I Guess I'll Have to Change My Plans."

Everything in this bulging picture, which Arthur Freed has luxuriously produced, exemplifies its rousing theme song. That's entertainment, indeed!

—B.C., July 10, 1953

BANG THE DRUM SLOWLY

Directed by John Hancock; written by Mark Harris, based on his novel; cinematographer, Richard Shore; edited by Richard Marks; music by Stephen Lawrence; production designer, Robert Gundlach; produced by Maurice and Lois Rosenfield; released by Paramount Pictures. Running time: 96 minutes.

With: Michael Moriarty (Henry Wiggen), Robert De Niro (Bruce Pearson), Vincent Gardenia (Dutch Schnell), Phil Foster (Joe Jaros), Ann Wedgeworth (Katie), Patrick McVey (Mr. Pearson), Tom Ligon (Piney Woods) and Heather Macrae (Holly Wiggen).

Except for some updating, and minimal plot simplification, John Hancock's *Bang the Drum Slowly* is a remarkably faithful rendering of the well-known baseball novel that Mark Harris wrote in 1955. It is one of those rare instances in which close adaptation of a good book has resulted in possibly an even better movie.

The story is simple enough. Bruce Pearson, a kid from Georgia and a catcher of no great quality for the New York Mammoths, is dying of Hodgkin's disease, incurable but, in his case, not yet debilitating. Nobody knows except his roommate and one friend, Henry Wiggen, and it is Henry's job not to tell—especially the team manager, Dutch Schnell—so that Bruce can play baseball through the last season that is left him on earth.

Henry leads the league in pitching, and sells insurance and writes books on the side. Everybody admires Henry and calls him "Author," except Bruce, who calls him "Arthur"—because he's a little too dense to get the name straight.

The film is more Henry's than Bruce's—Henry's and Dutch Schnell's. Henry conceals; Dutch wants to reveal. A rough diamond with a heart of coal, Dutch is the game, and the team, and the World Series bid. Henry must learn—lots of things, like why he is devoting his life to easing the end of his dopey roommate. But Dutch, though he hires a private detective to answer the same particular question, already has a vast store of general knowledge to hand.

Some of the film's greatest moments consist of his imparted wisdom, in certain locker-room speeches, like the "When I die the newspaper will write in their headline 'The Son of a Bitches of the World Have Lost Their Leader' " speech, or the "Go ahead you old Baltimore fly" speech—consisting largely of buzzing fly noises, all simultaneously translated into Spanish for the benefit of the Mammoths' Cuban third baseman.

Vincent Gardenia, a wonderfully professional New York stage actor who has had a fairly minor career in film, plays Dutch with a belligerent comic diligence that should constitute any director's dream performance. In his way, Michael Moriarty as Henry—clever, cautious, skilled at keeping secrets from himself—is almost as good.

And all the rest of the cast, from Robert De Niro, as Bruce, down to the least consequential team members who only stand and get photographed, seem to have been assembled out of a love for placing the right kinds of people in dramatic situations—a love that proves all over again that it is just as possible to make a movie in front of the camera as in the lab or the editing room.

John Hancock's background is mainly in the theater (he has had one previous feature: an entertaining but very mixed-up horror film called *Let's Scare Jessica to Death*), and that background shows to stunning advantage. We are not so used to performance—as opposed, say, to "presence"—in movie acting. But if Hancock prospers, as he should, we may get used to it. This will be everyone's good luck.

Bang the Drum Slowly (the title comes from the cowboy song "The Streets of Laredo") is ultimately a lament for the dying. But since that includes all of us, it would be unseemly to shed too many tears. Henry Wiggen doesn't cry; he peddles life insurance. And once he forces the Mammoths to sign a contract tying himself to Bruce—a necessary gesture, in a sense, accepting death—then he is free for the play of wits and character, the comedy, that takes up most of the film.

It's a gentle comedy; not gutless, but kind. Even Dutch Schnell is allowed his moments of second-rate decency. And since the Mammoths win the pennant and the series that year, everybody ends up happy—except Bruce, who ends up dead. The juxtaposition is ironic, but not too ironic.

Henry resolves never again to be brutal to people; but that was not his problem in the first place. If you want a major statement on man's fate, you'd better try another movie. This one pretends to no more insight than it has honestly earned. Its chief quality is not its pathos, but its beautiful, perhaps heroic, tact.

Bang the Drum Slowly opened yesterday at Cinema I.

—R.G., August 27, 1973

THE BANK DICK

Directed by Edward F. Cline; written by W. C. Fields; director of photography, Milton R. Krasner; edited by Arthur Hilton; art directors, Jack Otterson and Richard H. Riedel; music by Charles Previn; produced by Jack J. Gross; released by Universal Pictures. Black and white. Running time: 74 minutes.

With: W. C. Fields (Egbert Sousé), Cora Witherspoon (Agatha Sousé), Una Merkel (Myrtle Sousé), Evelyn Del Rio (Elsie Mae Adele Brunch Sousé), Jessie Ralph (Mrs. Hermisillo Brunch), Franklin Pangborn (J. Pinkerton Snoopington), Shemp Howard (Joe Guelpe), Richard Purcell (Mackley Q. Greene), Grady Sutton (Og Oggilby), Russell Hicks (J. Frothingham Waterbury), Pierre Watkin (Mr. Skinner), Al Hill (Filthy McNasty), George Moran (Cozy Cochran), Bill Wolfe (Otis) and Jack Norton (A. Pismo Clam).

No reflection is intended upon the appearance of W. C. Fields when we say that the great man has mellowed considerably, and for the best, since he was last among us in *My Little Chickadea* and, before that, in *You Can't Cheat An Honest Man*. Then he gave signs of degenerating into a pesky, cantankerous old fluff with a disposition as vile as that of a wolverine. But now, in Universal's *The Bank Dick,* which is current at the Palace, we welcome our old friend Bill back, as magnificently expansive as ever.

True, he is herein supported (technically speaking, of course) by an excellent cast of comics, including Franklin Pangborn, Una Merkel, Cora Witherspoon, Grady Sutton, and Harlan Briggs. But the gratifying thing is that Bill is at last given his muffin head again and is not compelled to tag along with such excess baggage as Mae West or even Charlie McCarthy. The picture belongs to him, and his name—or nom de plume—is stamped all over it.

To be sure, the suggestion of a story which Mahatma Kane Jeeves (or you know who) has contrived for himself is thinner than a dime and certainly no heavier. It tells of an indigent gentleman in a town called Lompoc, who accidentally captures a hold-up man and gets a job as a bank guard in reward. Then his troubles and temptations begin, and it looks as though his goose is nearly cooked, but another bank robber conveniently comes along and he again gets a chance to pull a coup.

With such a part to play around with, old Bill has the time of his life—growling, feinting, being official and forever preserving his fly-blown dignity. No one who fancies madcap comedy can reasonably afford to miss the spectacle of Bill creeping up and pouncing upon a kid with a cap-pistol in the bank; or of Bill solicitously attending a bank examiner whom he has fed a "Michael Finn"; or of Bill at the wheel of the car in which a desperate bandit is attempting to escape. "The resale value of this car," says Bill from the corner of his mouth, "is going to be practically nil when we get through with this trip."

In fact, for anyone who simply likes to laugh at the reckless manities of an inspired buffoon, we recommend *The Bank Dick*. It's great fun.

—*B.C., December 13, 1940*

BARFLY

Directed by Barbet Schroeder: written by Charles Bukowski: cinematographer, Robby Muller: edited by Eva Gardos: production designer, Bob Ziembicki: produced by Mr. Schroeder, Fred Roos and Tom Luddy: released by the Cannon Group. Running time: 100 minutes.

With: Mickey Rourke (Henry), Faye Dunaway (Wanda Wilcox), Alice Krige (Tully), Jack Nance (Detective), J. C. Quinn (Jim), Frank Stallone (Eddie), Sandy Martin (Janice), Roberta Bassin (Lilly) and Gloria LeRoy (Grandma Moses).

Barbet Schroeder, the French producer best known for his association with Eric Rohmer, infrequently directs films, but when he does, they're worth the long intervals between. It could be that being a producer is Mr. Schroeder's protective cover.

Nobody expects him to direct a new movie every eighteen months. He's too busy producing the work of others. In the meantime he can take all the time he wants preparing his own films, including More (1969), a sunlit romance of doomed drug addicts, and *General Idi Amin Dada* (1976), his spellbinding documentary about the former dictator of Uganda, a man as madly obsessed as any of the creatures in the director's fiction films.

Mr. Schroeder's latest is *Barfly,* his first American film and another not easily categorized movie that may be, I think, some kind of small, classic, one-of-a-kind comedy. One thing is sure: *Barfly,* in spite of its occasionally stomach-turning details, is not a tragedy— and it will invite anyone who says so to step into the alley.

Though it's set within the world of the seriously down-and-out in Los Angeles and is about people who are at the end of their ropes, *Barfly* somehow manages to be gallant and even cheerful. It has an admirably lean, unsentimental screenplay by Charles Bukowski, the poet laureate of America's misbegotten, a big, broad, mesmerizing performance by Mickey Rourke, and one by Faye Dunaway that rediscovers the reserves of talent that, in recent years, have been hidden inside characters who wear designer wardrobes and sleep masks.

As Henry Chinaski, Mr. Rourke has a lot of the seedy, insinuating charm of Dustin Hoffman's Ratso Rizzo in *Midnight Cowboy*. Henry, the Bukowski surrogate figure, is a part-time writer and full-time drink-cadger who frequently gets beaten senseless in boozy brawls. Some area of his face seems always to be swollen. His knuckles remain perpetually skinned. The way he hustles down a street, Quasimodo-like (though he has perfectly normal legs), one can feel the pain in his ribs.

Henry is not a conventional movie's idea of a drunk. His alcoholism isn't *Lost Weekend* instructive. It's far more insidious. He has no remorse for a life left behind, and he doesn't fall down or suffer blackouts. Throughout the long days and nights at the Golden Horn, a neighborhood bar just this side of Skid Row, he drinks only enough to maintain his easily wounded dignity. He's like a frigate bird hanging in the wind over the same patch of earth.

Though *Barfly* makes some half-hearted passes at explaining alcoholism as a way of dealing with life's pervasive second-rateness, it remains, for the most part, serenely above such paperback psychiatry. Mr. Bukowski and Mr. Schroeder are content simply to observe the minute, grotesque, hilarious details of the behavior of Henry and the other patrons of the Golden Horn—with respectful interest and amusement that never slop over into condescending compassion.

Barfly has the form of a vividly remembered vignette about several tumultuous days that almost (but not quite) change Henry's life. First there is his encounter with Wanda Wilcox (Miss Dunaway) who, though rather classily pulled together, is no less of a barfly than Henry and who, like him, has no particular past. Henry can't quite believe his good fortune when Wanda responds to him, scabby knuckles, dirty fingernails, filthy T-shirt, and all.

Wanda tells him she likes the cockiness of his walk. He also talks in an unusual way, affecting a kind of W. C. Fields drawl to say things Wanda's never heard before. When she asks him solemnly if he doesn't hate people, he thinks before he answers, "No, but I feel better when they're not around." In the society Wanda keeps, this is rare wit.

In fact, Henry is light years ahead of Wanda in the brain department. Her recognition of this is to her credit, even as she admits that, if another man comes along with a fifth of whisky, she'll go off with him. Though the movie never makes a big deal of it, Wanda is far more lost than the resilient Henry will ever be.

Their new, very edgy relationship is complicated by the arrival of Tully (Alice Krige), a pretty, rich, upper-crust patron of arts who wants to publish one of Henry's short stories in her literary magazine.

This is pretty much the so-called plot of *Barfly*. The film deals not in event but in the continuing revelation of character in a succession of horrifying, buoyant, crazy confrontations of barflies, bartenders, police, and other representatives of the world of the sober. Mr. Bukowski's dialogue is not only richly funny but, when Henry quotes his own writings, it's also compelling. There's a kind of courtly nobility about Henry that Mr. Schroeder appreciates.

The story of Henry and Wanda doesn't come to a conclusion. The movie seems to withdraw from it. At the end of another raucous night at the Golden Horn, Robby Muller's discreet camera pulls back from the bar and out the front door without interrupting the lives that have been recorded.

Note also the performances of J. C. Quinn as Henry's bartender friend, Frank Stallone as the mean-tempered bartender who can never resist yet another fight with Henry in the alley and, as some of the Golden Horn regulars, Sandy Martin, Roberta Bassin, Gloria LeRoy, Joe Rice, and Julie (Sunny) Pearson. Each one is memorable.

—*V.C., September 30, 1987*

BARRY LYNDON

Produced and directed by Stanley Kubrick: written by Mr. Kubrick, based on the novel by William Makepeace Thackeray: cinematographer, John Alcott: edited by Tony Lawson: music by Leonard Rosenman: production designer: Ken Adam: released by Warner Brothers. Running time: 184 minutes.

With: Ryan O'Neal (Barry Lyndon), Marisa Berenson (Lady Lyndon), Patrick Magee (Chevalier), Hardy Kruger (Captain Potzdorf), Gay Hamilton (Nora), Marie Kean (Barry's Mother) and Diana Koerner (German Girl).

Barry Lyndon, Stanley Kubrick's handsome, assured screen adaptation of William Makepeace Thackeray's first novel, is so long and leisurely, so panoramic in its narrative scope, that it's as much an environment as it is a conventional film. Its austerity of purpose defines it as a costume movie unlike any other you've seen.

Yet in the brilliance of its images the film surrounds you—the way good nineteenth-century novels do—with characters, events, and little discourses on the curious ways of a world in which folly is recognized as a legitimate form of self-achievement.

Don't be misled into thinking that *Barry Lyndon* is going to be a *Tom Jones* romp. The two films share a century (the eighteenth), one country (England), and the picaresque mode, but their concerns and styles are entirely different.

Barry Lyndon, which opened yesterday at the Ziegfeld and Baronet Theaters, might be most easily described as an eighteenth-century comedy of manners, though that doesn't do justice to what Mr. Kubrick has attempted, which is coolly to examine a world as strange and distant in its way as were the future worlds of 2001 and *A Clockwork Orange*.

Some people may have difficulty with its length (over three hours, and every minute necessary) and its deliberate pacing (which I find luxurious, like sinking into a fine long book). They make the film a rigorous experience unless you give yourself up to the director's method. Mr. Kubrick takes his own sweet time as he looks, examines, comments, enchants the eye frequently, but always remains a little distant. In a Kubrick film even genuine sentiments are so suspect that a scene that in any other director's film would be sentimental becomes almost malicious.

Barry Lyndon is about foolish, gallant overreaching. It's the story of the rise and fall of a poor, good-natured Irish opportunist, born Redmond Barry and later to take the name of *Barry Lyndon*, after his successful courtship of one of England's richest aristocrats, the widowed Lady Lyndon, a beautiful vaporous woman whose high station gives her the right to be boring. The film has a great deal to say about the privileges of class.

When we first meet Barry (Ryan O'Neal) he is a naive, headstrong young man without a bean but with a terrific crush on a female cousin, whose English suitor he shoots in a duel. This sends Barry off to the Seven Years War in Germany, first in the English Army, then the Prussian.

As is the fashion in such literature, no situation remains permanent, and Barry in the course of what the narrator describes as "a wandering and disconnected life," becomes, successively, a Prussian spy, a Continental gambler, a ladies' man and, finally, a husband to Lady Lyndon (Marisa Berenson). This, in the not-so-mock piety of the film, is his undoing.

Mr. Kubrick has spent a fortune on the film, and it shows, not only in the care that's been taken in locations (England, Ireland, and Germany), in the grand houses, and in the battle scenes, but also in the photography of John Alcott.

One of Mr. Kubrick's boldest decisions was to make the film as beautiful as it is. Good movies should not be too beautiful. It's thought to be distracting, if not a substitute for content. Yet the Alcott camerawork, which transforms scene after scene into something that suggests a Gainsborough or a Watteau, has the function of setting us apart from Barry's adventures, rather than tricking us into involvement.

Mr. O'Neal, who's on the screen throughout, is, I think, fine, too self-assured for his own good, growing increasingly reckless as the film progresses and, at the end, a surprised wreck. Among the supporting players, Murray Melvin (as Lady Lyndon's resident priest), Marie Kean (as Barry's ambitious mother), and Diana Koerner (as a pretty German fortune of war) are superb. Marisa Berenson splendidly suits her costumes and wigs.

As in every Kubrick film, the musical score is special indeed, though no one element in this film can stand apart from the others. They all fit together. *Barry Lyndon* is another fascinating challenge from one of our most remarkable, independent-minded directors.

—*V.C., December 19, 1975*

BARTON FINK

Directed by Joel Coen; written by Ethan Coen and Joel Coen; cinematographer, Roger Deakins; edited by Roderick Jaynes; music by Carter Burwell; production designer, Dennis Gassner; produced by Ethan Coen; released by Twentieth Century Fox. Running time: 116 minutes.

With: John Turturro (Barton Fink), John Goodman (Charlie Meadows), Judy Davis (Audrey Taylor), Michael Lerner (Jack Lipnick), John Mahoney

(W. P. Mayhew), Tony Shalhoub (Ben Geisler), Jon Polito (Lou Breeze), Steve Buscemi (Chet) and David Warrilow (Garland Stanford).

Joel and Ethan Coen's *Barton Fink* looked very good at Cannes this year, where, in the first sweep ever at the film festival, it was awarded the prizes for best film, best direction, and best performance by an actor. The news this morning: *Barton Fink* looks even better on home territory.

Barton Fink opens today at the Coronet Theater.

After three movies in which they seemed to be finding their bearings (*Blood Simple, Raising Arizona,* and *Miller's Crossing*), the Coens have at last produced an unqualified winner. Here is a fine dark comedy of flamboyant style and immense though seemingly effortless technique.

Barton Fink might possibly be classified as a satire on the life of the mind. There is no doubt that it is about the perils of the mind for someone as impressionable as Barton Fink (John Turturro). Barton is a pious, prissy New York playwright of very funny, unredeemed humorlessness, someone who has dedicated himself to creating "a living theater of, about, and for the Common Man."

The time is the early 1940's, just before World War II, when Clifford Odets and a number of other American playwrights were still riding high on a wave of poetic proletarianism.

After having written one Broadway hit, Barton, who resembles the hero of David Lynch's *Eraserhead*, goes to Hollywood to earn some big money and maybe, as he says, "to make a difference."

Barton's responsibilities to the Common Man weigh heavily on his skinny frame. He stays not at one of Los Angeles's fancier hotels but at the Earle, a downtown establishment ("For a Day or a Lifetime") whose Art Deco lobby and corridors give no hint of the Skid Row seediness of the rooms.

The Earle has a dreamlike emptiness to it when Barton arrives. His state of mind (and the things to come) are hinted at when the bellboy emerges from a trapdoor in the floor behind the reservations desk to sign him in. Barton, who devotes himself to theater of noble purpose, has clearly landed in hell.

Barton's adventures in Hollywood are a series of grotesquely funny confrontations as his writer's block becomes manifest and his panic accumulates. His first

assignment for Capitol Pictures is a wrestling movie "for Wally Beery."

"It's not a B picture; Capitol Pictures does not make B pictures," says Jack Lipnick (Michael Lerner), Capitol's squat, barrel-chested president, who seems to be a cross between Harry Cohn of Columbia and Louis B. Mayer of M-G-M.

It is, of course, a B picture, and Barton hasn't a clue as to how to start. His desperation mounts.

He is befriended by another Capitol writer, W.P. Mayhew (John Mahoney). A drunken Southern novelist of Faulknerian dimensions, Mayhew calls Hollywood "the great salt lick," and is first seen from the thighs down, kneeling on a handkerchief inside a toilet stall. In as gentlemanly a way as possible, he is vomiting.

There is also Mayhew's beautiful, wise, and self-assured "assistant," Audrey Taylor (Judy Davis), who is more than just a secretary or even a mistress. Her dread fate, on the night she comes to the Earle to help Barton with the Wally Beery treatment, is the center of the film's sly and elusive narrative.

More important to Barton than anyone else is Charlie Meadows (John Goodman), his next-door neighbor at the Earle. He's a big, gregarious insurance man who tells Barton, man-to-man, "You might say that I sell peace of mind."

The shirtsleeved Charlie is actually too good to be true, but Barton doesn't notice. All he sees is the beer belly, the sweat, the suspenders, the desperation to please. He's someone in whom Barton can confide.

"I write about people like yourself, Charlie," Barton announces to his new friend. "The simple working stiff." "Well," says the pleased Charlie, "I could tell you some stories." Later, his writer's block paralyzing his work on the Wally Beery picture, Barton talks to Charlie about the terrors and mysteries of the territory called the mind: "There's no road map for it."

Among other things, *Barton Fink* demonstrates just how fraught with danger that territory can be. It is one of the filmmakers' more comic conceits that Barton's socially conscious mind should be the crucible for a succession of such lurid and extravagant events.

The Coen brothers share credit for their screenplays, which are then produced by Ethan and directed by Joel. They are quoted as saying that they turned to the writing of *Barton Fink* when they found themselves blocked while working on the screenplay for *Miller's Crossing.* This seems completely plausible.

Barton Fink has the manner of a work that was written in a high old halcyon rush, of a screenplay that announced itself and took form without a lot of nervous pushing and probing to give it existence. It is seamless, packed with the sort of pertinent and priceless detail that can't be worried out of the mind piecemeal.

The dialogue from Barton's hit play, heard at the movie's beginning, is both wicked parody and pertinent to Barton's own overheated reveries.

The finished film, so vivid and startling, has the same coherence. The performances are virtually indistinguishable from the characters as written. It's difficult to tell where the roles leave off and the actors begin.

Mr. Turturro, the Cannes winner, is superb, but so are Mr. Goodman, Mr. Mahoney, Mr. Lerner, and Ms. Davis, as well as Jon Polito, who plays Jack Lipnick's Job-like yes-man; Steve Buscemi, who plays the Earle's eerie bellboy; and David Warrilow, who turns up as Barton's New York agent. Everybody deserves mention.

Each aspect of the film hits, from the production design by Dennis Gassner to the remarkable cinematography by Roger Deakins. The Coens' screenplay is the kind that encourages and accommodates spectacular camera gestures. These include point-of-view and overhead shots and moments when the camera becomes a kind of evil companion to the disintegrating Barton.

The camera nudges Barton to expect the worst when someone knocks at the door. It points to the wall where, suddenly, for no apparent reason, the wallpaper starts curling back, exposing a lazy rivulet of viscous ooze too disgusting to identify.

After observing some furtive lovemaking, the camera sneaks away from the couple on the bed, possibly in shame, moves into the bathroom and (in effect) disappears down the drain of the basin, like a silverfish when the light goes on.

It was said by some at Cannes that *Barton Fink* is a movie for people who don't like the Coen brothers' films. Not quite true. It's a film for those who were not sure that the Coens knew what they wanted to do or had the authority to pull off a significant work.

Barton Fink eliminates those doubts. It's an exhilarating original.

—*V.C., August 21, 1991*

THE BATTLE OF ALGIERS

Directed by Gillo Pontecorvo; written (in Italian, with English subtitles) by Mr. Pontecorvo and Franco Solinas; cinematographer, Marcello Gatti; edited by Mario Serandrei; music by Mr. Pontecorvo and Ennio Morricone; produced by Antonio Musu and Yacef Saadi; released by Rizzoli Film Distributors. Black and White. Running time: 120 minutes.

With: Yacef Saadi (Kader), Jean Martin (Colonel Mathieu), Brahim Haggiag (Ali La Pointe), Tommaso Neri (Captain Dubois), Fawzia El Kader (Halima), Michele Kerbash (Fathia) and Mohamed Ben Kassen (Little Omar).

A most extraordinary picture for an opener at the New York Film Festival was placed before the first-night audience in Philharmonic Hall last night. It is Gillo Pontecorvo's ferocious *The Battle of Algiers,* a starkly realistic reenactment of events as they substantially occurred between 1954 and 1957 in the rebellion against the French in the capital of Algeria.

It is extraordinary, first, that such a picture—such a literal and traditional account of intra-urban guerrilla warfare in a wasteful conflict that occurred so long ago—should have been picked to open a festival that has been kicked off in the last four years by noticeably avant-gardish and thematically exploratory films.

The supposition is that this departure was made because *The Battle of Algiers* is an uncommonly dynamic picture that has proved its pulling power at festivals. It pulled down the grand prize at Venice and the top award at London last year, and took a blue at Acapulco last winter. On the strength of this, it was acquired for commercial distribution in this country, and was booked to open here at Cinema II tonight.

What could have been more appropriate, then, than to have this much talked-about film rack up two premieres with one show at the New York festival?

But more extraordinary and therefore more commanding of lasting interest and critical applause is the amazing photographic virtuosity and pictorial conviction of this film. So authentically and naturalistically were its historical reflections staged, with literally thousands of citizens participating, in the streets and buildings of Algiers, that it looks beyond any question

81

to be an original documentary film, put together from newsreel footage, complemented by staged dramatic scenes.

Startling long shots of people and police fighting in the sun-drenched, tree-lined streets, so familiar and recognizable from the photographs of the Algerian strife; shattering close-ups of thunderous explosions in native quarters and crowded French cafés have all the concrete and vibrant "actuality" of newsreels made during the war.

Yet Mr. Pontecorvo assures us there's not a scrap of newsreel footage in his film—that he and his crews shot the whole thing very much after the facts, with native amateurs and a few professional actors playing the key and leading roles.

This becomes apparent as one follows the narrative account of the violent upsurge of rebellion in Algiers in 1954 and the establishment of a rebel stronghold in the Casbah, from which hit-and-run forays of snipers and women bomb-planters into the French section of the city are made. And it is clear, to anyone who remembers, when the French paratroopers move in and begin the systematic clean-out of the Casbah under the command of a Colonel Mathieu.

This lean and relentless officer, played by Jean Martin, is obviously not the colorful and memorable General Jacques Massu, whose 10th Paratrooper Division wiped out the rebel opposition in Algiers in 1957. But his manner is so intense and forceful, and his fairness and even respect for the resistance leaders are so well drawn, that one feels as though one is truly watching the spectacular and compassionate Massu.

Likewise, the roles of rebel leaders, played by Brahim Haggiag and Yacef Saadi, are done with such ferocity and fervor that they certainly convince me.

In its melodramatic structure, as well as its staging techniques, this film does have antecedents. The excellent *Four Days of Naples,* done with such documentary stylization by Mr. Pontecorvo's fellow Italian, Nanni Loy, back in 1962, is its immediate model. And the prototype for both of them, of course, is Roberto Rossellini's *Open City,* a classic neo-realistic film.

Essentially, the theme is one of valor—the valor of people who fight for liberation from economic and political oppression. And this being so, one may sense a relation in what goes on in this picture to what has happened in the Negro ghettos of some of our American cities more recently. The fact that the climax of the drama is actually negative, with the rebellion wiped out and its leaders destroyed, has immediate pertinence, too. But eventual victory for the Algerians—and therefore symbolic hope for all who struggle for freedom—is acknowledged in a sketchy epilogue.

I must also mention the very interesting and effective musical score prepared by Mr. Pontecorvo and Ennio Morricone for this vivid dramatic reportage.
—B.C., September 21, 1967

LE BEAU MARIAGE

Written (in French, with English subtitles) and directed by Eric Rohmer; cinematographer, Bernard Lutic, Romain Winding and Nicolas Brunet; edited by Cecile Decugis and Lisa Heredia; music by Ronan Girre and Simon des Innocents; produced by Margaret Menegoz; released by United Artists Classics. Running time: 97 minutes.

With: Béatrice Romand (Sabine), André Dussollier (Edmond), Féodor Atkine (Simon), Huguette Faget (Antique Dealer), Arielle Dombasle (Clarisse), Thamila Mezbah (Mother) and Sophie Renoir (Lise).

Like the major characters in most of Eric Rohmer's comedies, Sabine (Béatrice Romand), the heroine of Mr. Rohmer's new *Le Beau Mariage,* seems almost ordinary at first. She is pretty in a fresh but unspectacular way, articulate, and seemingly well adjusted to a kind of enlightened middle-class existence.

Part of the week Sabine works in an antique shop in Le Mans, where she lives with her younger sister and widowed mother, and the rest of the week she is in Paris, where she is studying—half-heartedly—for a degree in art history and carrying on a casual affair with a married painter named Simon.

One night as she and Simon are making love in his apartment, the telephone rings. The call is from his children, who are reporting, probably at their mother's suggestion, on some recent accomplishment, which the father attends to with patient pleasure. Sabine gets out of bed, dresses quickly and, when she finally has Simon's attention, announces that she is leaving, not for the night but for good.

By way of explanation she tells him she is getting

married. To whom? Sabine says she doesn't know. She hasn't yet met the man, but she has no doubt that she soon will. Sabine is fed up with a life of freedom and understanding.

This is more or less the jumping-off place for *Le Beau Mariage* (translated into English as *The Well-Made Marriage*), one of Mr. Rohmer's most charming and, in some ways, most compact comedies. The film reduces the relations between the sexes in twentieth-century Western civilization to the dimensions of Sabine's single-minded pursuit of Mr. Right in Le Mans and Paris and back again. Sabine might at first appear to be ordinary, but it soon becomes apparent that her ordinariness disguises a woman of quite extraordinary emotional tenacity and moral conviction.

Sabine is alternately sweet and ferocious as she puts into effect her plan to convince Edmond (André Dussollier), a handsome, thirtyish Parisian lawyer, that the two of them are made for each other, or at least as made for each other as any two people ever are— Sabine is a pragmatist. Edmond is at first amused and then alarmed.

One of the consistent rewards of Mr. Rohmer's films (*My Night at Maud's, Claire's Knee, Perceval,* among others) is that his characters never behave in ways made predictable by the second-rate fiction of others. Under any other circumstances Sabine would probably be intolerable in the way she dogs the trail of poor Edmond and refuses to take his lack of telephone calls as a sign of indifference, which, of course, it is.

Sabine is neither stupid nor arrogant. She is, rather, totally convinced of the utter reasonableness of what she's about. It's this reason, sometimes misapplied, that forever separates her—and other Rohmer characters—from the people who turn up in far more conventional romantic comedies.

Mr. Rohmer is one of the few filmmakers who can create convincingly intelligent characters, people whose thought processes are in some fashion demonstrated and not solely defined by the music they listen to or the books they say they have read. Unlike *My Night at Maud's* and *Claire's Knee,* there is little such name-dropping going on here. Sabine is certainly not an intellectual, but she is a remarkably self-aware, engaging woman with a no-nonsense approach to her life.

There is a revealing, very funny sequence in which Sabine runs into Claude, the first man she ever loved,

a fellow who is now a teacher and happily married to another teacher, and goes back to his apartment with him. For a few moments it seems as if they might make love, for old times, but they immediately become embroiled in an argument about Sabine's militantly proclaimed desire to get married and become a housewife.

The news astonishes Claude. What about her career? Does she want to become a hearth slave, ever dependent on her husband? What will happen to her need for self-expression? Sabine has answers for each of his questions and, moreover, makes them sound convincing.

The scope of *Le Beau Mariage* is limited, but everything within it is well-defined and magically, unexpectedly, illuminating. One has the feeling—rare in commercial films—of having met romantic characters who in no way deny the social and political complexities of the real world that exists just outside the view of the camera.

Miss Romand, who made her screen debut as the precocious teenager in *Claire's Knee,* has grown into immensely appealing womanhood and is a comedienne of the first order. Prominent in the excellent supporting cast is Arielle Dombasle as Clarisse, Sabine's best friend, a wise beauty who watches Sabine with a mixture of concern and amusement; Mr. Dussollier as the besieged Edmond; and Thamila Mezbah as Sabine's mother, who is shocked when she hears her daughter talking about chastity in terms that she, the mother, considers a hundred years out of date.

Le Beau Mariage, which opens today at the Cinema 2, is a witty, halcyon entertainment, especially in a season that has otherwise been notable mostly for extravagant overstatement and special effects.

—V.C., August 27, 1982

BEAUTIFUL PEOPLE

Written and directed by Jasmin Dizdar: director of photography, Barry Ackroyd: edited by Justin Krish: music by Garry Bell: production designer, Jon Henson: produced by Ben Woolford: released by Trimark Pictures. Running time: 107 minutes.

With: Charlotte Coleman (Portia Thornton). Charles Kay (George Thornton). Rosalind Ayres

(Nora Thornton). Roger Sloman (Roger Midge). Heather Tobias (Felicity Midge). Danny Nussbaum (Griffin Midge). Siobhan Redmond (Kate Higgins). Gilbert Martin (Jerry Higgins). Steve Sweeney (Jim). Linda Bassett (Sister) and Nicholas Farrell (Dr. Mouldy).

Beautiful People ends in a flurry of rapid cuts, with a series of perfectly ordinary moments: a man reads a picture book to a child; a family sets out on vacation. There is a wedding party, a birthday party, and a raucous game of cards around a hospital bed. Jasmin Dizdar's camera hurtles through these scenes like a child in a toy store, grabbing at every detail as though it were a shiny, precious prize. The screen hums with the vital cacophony of daily life, and glows with the thick, bright colors of human emotion—unspeakable pain, inexplicable loss, and sheer irrational pleasure at being alive.

And then the whiplash motion abruptly stops, as though interrupted, and the last thing we see before the credits roll is a wedding band on the hand of one of the card players. The ring comes to us as a found image, but it is also a resonant symbol of one of the movie's main themes: the desire for connection.

The final sequence is so powerful because the movie, which follows a scattered agglomeration of characters through multicultural London, has been unsparing in its attention to the ways human connections can fail. The man with the wedding ring is the hospital because, in the movie's opening scene, he was involved in a fistfight on a London bus. All we ever learn about him is that he is a Croat, and his antagonist, whom Britain's mischievous National Health Service bureaucracy has assigned to a neighboring bed, is a Serb from the same Bosnian village—unless it's the other way around.

"So you're a Serb and he's a Croat?" their kindly, officious nurse inquires, trying to discover why one has repeatedly tried to disconnect the other's oxygen lines and intravenous hookups. "No, no, no," her patient protests.

"It's completely different. I am Croat and he is Serb." And then, like schoolboys, they fall to arguing over who started it all.

Beautiful People, which takes place in 1993, acknowledges both the fundamental ridiculousness of the Bosnian civil war and its unassimilable horror. In another part of the same hospital, a young refugee in the late stages of pregnancy begs her obstetrician to kill the baby she is carrying, one conceived when she was gang-raped by Serbian soldiers. When the baby is born, its mother and her husband will name her Chaos.

Later a BBC foreign correspondent, tormented by survivor's guilt after his return from Srebenica, storms into a hospital demanding that someone amputate his legs. "I hope your mother and father end up in a U.N. safe haven," he says bitterly to the policeman who sends him home.

The journalist is soon told he's suffering from a disorder called Bosnia syndrome, which is basically Stockholm syndrome in reverse: a tendency to identify, morbidly and irrationally, with the victims of catastrophe.

Not that London itself doesn't offer ample opportunities for heartbreak. The doctor who tries to help the rape victim and her husband is powerless to stop the collapse of his own marriage. The headmaster of the school that the doctor's children attend cannot fathom why his son has taken up heroin and hooliganism. And another doctor, in love with one of her patients—also a refugee from the Balkan slaughter—must confront the snobbery and prejudice of her stuffy conservative family.

Yet this movie, which arranges torn lives into a gaudy collage of misery, is anything but grim. Its title—at once sarcastic and entirely sincere—recalls *High Hopes* and *Life Is Sweet,* Mike Leigh's mordant anatomies of social and familial dysfunction in late-Thatcherite London. Like Mr. Leigh in those films, Mr. Dizdar cuts between disparate and complementary stories to get at the density and complexity of contemporary urban life.

But even in his first feature film Mr. Dizdar, a naturalized British citizen who grew up in Bosnia and studied filmmaking in Prague, directs with extraordinary exuberance and self-confidence, in a style that combines documentary realism with a playful, improvisatory sense of formal possibility.

Beautiful People is not perfect. Because it is so heavily populated, some of its characters are rather thinly drawn, and some of its stories forced to unlikely conclusions. Among the upper and lower extremes of the British class system, the toffs and the yobs, so to speak, Mr. Dizdar eye for the particularities of character weakness, and he falls back on stereotypes. But the actors—none of them beautiful in the usual movie star way, and few of them likely to be familiar to American audiences—manage to play even the sketchier parts of Mr. Dizdar's script with intelligence and grace.

A few false notes are to be expected in a composition of such expansiveness and ambition. For all the sorrow it confronts; *Beautiful People* is, in the end, a boisterous love song—a funny valentine to London, to chaos and to human decency.

—*A.O.S., February 18, 2000*

BEAUTY AND THE BEAST

Directed by Jean Cocteau; written (in French, with English subtitles) by Mr. Cocteau, based on the fairy tale by Madame LePrince de Beaumont; cinematographer, Henri Alekan; edited by Claude Ibéria; music by Georges Auric; art designer, Christian Bernard; produced by André Paulvé; released by Lopert Films. Black and white. Running time: 90 minutes.

With: Jean Marais (Avenant/The Beast/The Prince), Josette Day (Beauty), Marcel André (The Merchant), Mila Parély (Adelaide), Nane Germon (Felicie) and Michel Auclair (Ludovic).

The oft-tried but seldom-known accomplishment of telling a familiar fairy tale with pure imagery and enchantment through the sensuous devices of the screen has been almost perfectly realized by the French poet-playwright, Jean Cocteau, in his beautifully measured French production of the old fable, *Beauty and the Beast*. Except that it isn't in color, this film which came to the Bijou yesterday is an eminent model of cinema achievement in the realm of poetic fantasy.

This should be understood, however: the achievement is on a definitely adult plane and the beauties of Cocteau's conception will be most appreciated by sophisticated minds. It is not the sort of picture that will send the children into transports of delight, unless they are quite precocious youngsters of the new progressive school.

For Cocteau has taken the old story of the beautiful country girl who goes to live as a hostage for her impoverished father in the palace of a terrifying beast, there to be treated with such kindness that she falls in love with the unhappy brute, and has used it as a pattern for weaving a priceless fabric of subtle images. In the style of his *Blood of a Poet,* though less abstract and recondite, it is a fabric of gorgeous visual metaphors, of undulating movements and rhythmic pace, of hypnotic sounds and music, of casually congealing ideas.

Freudian or metaphysician, you can take from it what you will. The concepts are so ingenious that they're probably apt to any rationale. From the long corridor of candelabra, held out from the walls by living arms, through which the wondering visitor enters the palace of the Beast, to the glittering temple of Diana, wherein the mystery of the Beast is revealed, the visual progression of the fable into a dream-world casts its unpredictable spell.

The dialogue, in French, is spare and simple, with the story largely told in pantomime, and the music of Georges Auric accompanies the dreamy, fitful moods. The settings are likewise expressive, many of the exteriors having been filmed for rare architectural vignettes at Raray, one of the most beautiful palaces and parks in all France. And the costumes, too, by Christian Berard and Escoffier, are exquisite affairs, glittering and imaginative, lacking only the glow of color, as we say.

As the Beast (and also as the Young Prince and as the churlish suitor of the heroine), Jean Marais has the grace of a dancer, the voice of a muffled baritone. Although his grossly feline makeup is reminiscent of some of the monsters of Hollywood (and could drive the little kiddies to hysterics), he wears it exceedingly well. And as Beauty, Josette Day is truly lovely, youthful, and delicate, a convincingly innocent maiden and student to the mysteries of life. Mila Parély is despicably vain and greedy as one of Beauty's bad sisters and Marcel André is nicely theatrical as her doting, ineffectual papa.

Studied or not for philosophy, this is a sensuously fascinating film, a fanciful poem in movement given full articulation on the screen.

—*B.C., December 24, 1947*

BEAUTY AND THE BEAST

Directed by Gary Trousdale and Kirk Wise; written by Linda Woolverton; edited by John

Carnochan; music by Alan Menken with songs by Howard Ashman and Mr. Menken; art designer, Brian P. McEntee; produced by Don Hahn; released by Walt Disney Pictures. Running time: 84 minutes.

With the voices of: Paige O'Hara (Belle), Robby Benson (Beast), Richard White (Gaston), Jerry Orbach (Lumiere), David Ogden Stiers (Cogsworth), Angela Lansbury (Mrs. Potts) and Bradley Michael Pierce (Chip).

Two years ago Walt Disney Pictures reinvented the animated feature, not only with an eye toward pleasing children but also with an older, savvier audience in mind. Disney truly bridged a generation gap with *The Little Mermaid,* bringing the genre new sophistication without sacrificing any of the delight.

It's not surprising that an attempt has been made to replicate that success with *Beauty and the Beast,* a film that takes a similar view of its audience and transfers some of the earlier film's most inspired staging ideas from an underwater setting to eighteenth-century France. But it is a surprise, in a time of sequels and retreads, that the new film is so fresh and altogether triumphant in its own right. Lightning has definitely struck twice.

With *Beauty and the Beast,* a tender, seamless, and even more ambitious film than its predecessor, Disney has done something no one has done before: combine the latest computer animation techniques with the best of Broadway. Here, in the guise of furthering a children's fable, is the brand of witty, soaring musical score that is now virtually extinct on the stage. *The Little Mermaid* was similarly a showcase for the extraordinary songwriting talents of Alan Menken and Howard Ashman, but this time the music is even more central. Broadway is as vital to this film's staging and characterizations as it is to the songs themselves.

Since *Beauty and the Beast* is a work of Disney animation, it also has its own traditions and its own purview. No live-action musical could ever match the miracles of anthropomorphism that occur here, or the fantastically sweeping scale. Nor could a live-action work achieve this mixture of elaborate, painstaking technique and perfect simplicity. Beauty and the Beast is filled with affectionate homages to the live-action

sources that have inspired it, and indeed those influences are strong. But its overriding spirit is all its own.

If this *Beauty and the Beast* is a long way from Jean Cocteau's 1947 black-and-white version, it's also a long way from the original fairy tale, which has been largely jettisoned in favor of a more timely story. This film's Beauty, called Belle, is the smartest, best-read person in a small provincial French town. As such, she is hotly pursued by Gaston, the lantern-jawed he-man who is initially the butt of the film's jokes and later becomes its villain. "The most beautiful girl in town," Gaston decides about Belle, in his booming bass tones. "That makes her the best. And don't I deserve the best?" Thoughts like that make *Beauty and the Beast* an amusingly clear product of its time.

Wandering through her village while reading a book, Belle becomes the focus of a spectacular opening number that captures the essence of this film's appeal. Bit by bit, the population trickles out to greet Belle and gossip about her, while she herself bemoans the small-mindedness of the place. This rousing number reaches such a flurry of musical counterpoint that it recalls sources as unlikely as *West Side Story,* while the direction builds energetically from quiet beginnings to a formidable finale. The directors, Gary Trousdale and Kirk Wise, have been plucked out of relative obscurity (i.e., a short film shown at Epcot Center) in one of many remarkable casting coups here, and they acquit themselves beautifully.

So does Robby Benson, the actor chosen out of far left field to provide the voice of the Beast. Mr. Benson's usually soft timbre has been so altered and amplified (by the growls of real panthers and lions) that it is virtually unrecognizable, but a crucial hint of gentleness remains. And his vocal performance, as an initially surly and frightening Beast who must be tamed by his household bric-a-brac before he can win Belle's love, is so convincing that it eradicates all memory of his mild manner.

That bric-a-brac, enchantingly cast and conceived, includes Angela Lansbury as the voice of Mrs. Potts, a kindly teapot and the mother of a snub-nosed little cup named Chip (Bradley Michael Pierce); Jerry Orbach as the surprisingly Chevalier-like voice of Lumiere, a debonair candelabrum; David Ogden Stiers as Cogsworth, a proper English clock; and a footstool that wags its tassels and barks like a dog. All of these inventions, along with others like a dust mop with the cap and beauty mark of a French chambermaid, join forces to define the film's idea of magic, especially when at last the objects' true natures are revealed.

"Be Our Guest," the lavish production number that is a dry-land answer to "Under the Sea" from *The Little Mermaid,* may not have the identical calypso charm, but it has just about everything else, including Busby Berkeley—style choreography carried out by dancing silverware. The jaunty Lumiere sings:

> *Soup du jour, hot hors d'oeuvres*
> *Why, we only live to serve*
> *Try the gray stuff, it's delicious*
> *Don't believe me? Ask the dishes!*

This demonstrates Mr. Ashman's gifts as an outstandingly nimble lyricist. His death from AIDS in March at age forty cut short a brilliant career, but the jubilant energy of his work will long live on.

Because of its wider ambitions, *Beauty and the Beast* is less intent on sweetness than on making its story's central point (which is slightly undercut when the Beast is ultimately revealed to be a paragon of bland handsomeness beneath his glowering exterior). It is more darkly forbidding and at times more violent than the average animated children's fable. But it also has more to say. Belle's intelligence and bravery are as well conveyed as the fatuousness beneath Gaston's handsome exterior, all of which gives the story a modern flavor. Paige O'Hara and Richard White, supplying the voices, do wonders in bringing Belle and Gaston to life.

Gaston is the subject of another outstanding song, a musical lambasting to a tune vaguely reminiscent of "Captain Hook," from *Peter Pan.* Mr. Menken's melodics, always buoyant and captivating, are familiar only in a way that bespeaks good sense and great taste. By far the songwriters' biggest triumph is the title song, which becomes even more impressive in view of the not-very-promising assignment to create a *Beauty and the Beast* theme song.

But the result is a glorious ballad, one that is performed in two versions, as both a Top Forty—style duet heard over the closing credits and a sweet, lilting solo sung by Ms. Lansbury during the film's most melt-

ingly lovely scene. For the latter, which also shows off the film's dynamic use of computer-generated animation, the viewer would be well advised to bring a hanky. And Mr. Menken should make room on the shelf where he keeps his Oscars.

—*J.M., November 20, 1991*

BED AND BOARD

Produced and directed by François Truffaut: written (in French. with English subtitles) by Mr. Truffaut. Claude de Givray and Bernard Revon: cinematographer. Nestor Almendros: art designer. Jean Mandaroux: released by Columbia Pictures. Running time: 95 minutes.

With: Jean-Pierre Léaud (Antoine). Claude Jade (Christine). Hiroko Berghauer (Kyoko). Barbara Laage (Executive Secretary). Daniel Ceccaldi (Mr. Darbon). Claire Duhamel (Mrs. Darbon) and Pierre Fabre (The Sneerer).

The new year is scarcely three weeks old, but I can't help believing that François Truffaut's latest Antoine Doinel comedy, *Bed and Board,* which opened yesterday at the Fine Arts Theater, will turn out to be one of the loveliest, most intelligent movies we'll see in all of 1971.

I realize that such a statement implies at least a certain amount of biased expectation concerning the several hundred other movies that have yet to open this year but, like Antoine Doinel himself, I'm what might be called an optimist with revisionist tendencies: I constantly hope that all movies will be great, but I'm never much surprised when they aren't.

Bed and Board, whose original French title is *Domicile Conjugal,* is the fourth in the cycle of Antoine Doinel films that was begun in 1959 with *The 400 Blows,* was continued in 1962 with "Antoine and Colette" (an episode in the *Love at 20* feature), and in 1969 with Stolen Kisses.

Because Jean-Pierre Léaud has literally grown up on the screen playing Antoine, whose adventures closely parallel those of Truffaut (both in real and fantasy life), and because each of the later films contains references to the preceding films, it's quite easy to regard the films as a rather high-class serial. This, however, does a disservice to the individuality of the films and ignores their interest as an extraordinary record of the development of one man's filmmaking sensibility.

The 400 Blows is a tough little movie, but it is full of the resiliency (and some of the excesses) of youth. "Antoine and Colette" is a summery idyll, while *Stolen Kisses* is autumnal, nostalgic. However *Bed and Board*, which is the story of the marriage of Antoine and Christine (whom Antoine courted intermittently throughout *Stolen Kisses*), is positively wintery. I don't mean that it is cold; rather that it looks like a movie made by a mature director for whom style has become content and who no longer worries about playing it safe.

Bed and Board is an exuberant domestic comedy that has quite a lot of unhappiness just beneath the surface. Antoine is no longer the totally lovable schlemiel he was in *Stolen Kisses*. Much of the time, he is self-centered, with the attention span of a fly. When Christine is having their baby, he is the last member of the family to get to the hospital. When she finds out about his affair with a beautiful Japanese girl, he is somewhat impatient because she is jealous. Eventually, when he becomes bored by his exotic mistress, it's Christine to whom he complains.

Antoine comes very close to being an outright rat, but, happily, he fails at this as he does at just about everything else he undertakes with such intensity.

Quite early in the film, Antoine, momentarily employed as a florist's assistant, conceives a hare-brained plan for tinting white carnations "an absolute red." When he tries out his experiment, by pouring some sort of lethal fluid into the water in which the flowers are standing, the water sizzles, clouds of smoke envelop the courtyard, and the flowers emerge looking as if they had been electrocuted.

In the failure of Antoine-the-chemist, there is the triumph of Antoine-the-human-spirit: Antoine will continue pursuing the absolute, even though he is aware he must fail.

Bed and Board, however, is never solemn. It is full of affection for the idiosyncrasies of that kind of petite bourgeoisie that only an outsider could love. The quartier in which Antoine and Christine live is inhabited by picturesque characters observed as much in French movies of the 1930's as (I suspect) in life of the 1960's. Truffaut has great fun reworking movie clichés and, in one brief episode, calls attention to his admiration for the work of Jacques Tati by bringing on Mr. Hulot himself.

There are, within the film, enough references to other movies, and to Truffaut's own life, to keep scholars busy for years. Claude Jade bears an unsettling resemblance to Catherine Deneuve, who has, of course, played a very important role in Truffaut's recent career. She is beautiful and simple and enchanting, even when she is getting on Antoine's nerves. Léaud, on the other hand, is somewhat off-putting, but I'm not sure if this is because of Léaud himself, who has not grown up with particular physical grace, or because of the way the role is written. There are times when Truffaut seems to be confessing to more sins than are really necessary.

Toward the end of the film, Antoine announces he is writing a novel about his unhappy childhood. It is only partially a gag, because it returns our thoughts to the very different world of *The 400 Blows*. However, it doesn't matter that you can't believe that this Antoine could focus his thoughts long enough to write a page of prose, much less a novel. It matters that you believe Truffaut, which I do—for *Bed and Board* is a kind of diary of thoughts, jokes, perceptions, movie routines, guilts, and aspirations, composed by one of our most complex filmmakers, who explores films while exploring himself.

—*V.C., January 22, 1971*

BEETLEJUICE

Directed by Tim Burton; written by Michael McDowell and Warren Skaaren, based on a story by Mr. McDowell and Larry Wilson; director of photography, Thomas Ackerman; edited by Jane Kurson; music by Danny Elfman; production designer, Bo Welch; produced by Richard Hashimoto, Mr. Wilson and Michael Bender; released by Warner Brothers. Running time: 92 minutes.

With: Alec Baldwin (Adam), Geena Davis (Barbara), Michael Keaton (Betelgeuse), Jeffrey Jones (Charles), Winona Ryder (Lydia), Sylvia Sidney (Juno), Catherine O'Hara (Delia) and Glenn Shadix (Otho).

Anyone whose idea of high wit can be achieved with bizarre latex facial makeup and extra eyeballs in unexpected places will at least admire *Beetlejuice* for its ingenuity. Tim Burton, who also directed *Pee-Wee's Big Adventure,* shows a keen grasp of preadolescent tastes in special effects (the weirder the better), pacing (illogical but busy), and comic constructs (only something incongruous, like people breaking into the Banana Boat song—"Day-O"—for no reason, is funnier than something rude).

But for other audiences *Beetlejuice,* which opens today at the Criterion Center and other theaters, is about as funny as a shrunken head—and it happens to include a few. The big joke here is death, since the film's principals are a cute young couple named Adam (Alec Baldwin) and Barbara (Geena Davis) who are killed as the story begins. These two immediately return as ghosts, but *Topper* this isn't; sophisticated spirit-world humor is hardly the order of the day. So dim are Adam and Barbara that he has trouble reading properly and they both require about twenty minutes' worth of not finding their reflections in mirrors to realize they're not precisely in the pink.

Adam and Barbara are horrified to find their rustic house sold to a group of fey, obnoxious New Yorkers who are a great deal more ghoulish than the ghosts themselves, and so they do what they can to haunt the place and scare the new owners away. They try severing their heads and so forth, but when the new owners shriek, it's only over the lack of closet space. Into the midst of this standoff rides Michael Keaton as the title character, a "bio-exorcist" who emerges from the grave determined to appall everyone as much as he possibly can. He does this much too well.

Elaborate as this sounds, there really isn't much plot here, only a parade of arbitrary visual tricks to hold the film together. Mr. Keaton, for instance, appears in one scene with a tiny carousel atop his head, bat-wings coming out of his ears, and huge, inflatable arms that turn into mallets. At another point, when asked if he can be scary, he sprouts Medusa-like snakes atop his head. And when he spins his head in another scene, he complains, "Don't you hate it when that happens?"

Mr. Burton, who seems to take his inspiration from toy stores and rock videos in equal measure, tries anything and everything for effect, and only occasionally manages something marginally funny, like a bureaucratic waiting room for the dead packed with very peculiar casualties (that shrunken head is one of them). His actors, not surprisingly, are limited by the stupidity of their material. Winona Ryder makes a good impression as the new owners' daughter, a girl much creepier than the ghosts themselves, and Glenn Shadix does what he can as their very arch decorator but, as the owners, Catherine O'Hara and Jeffrey Jones are made to behave as dopily as Mr. Keaton himself. To affirm this couple's status as bores, Dick Cavett and Robert Goulet appear as their friends.

—J.M., March 30, 1988

BEFORE NIGHT FALLS

Directed by Julian Schnabel; written by Cunningham O'Keefe, Lazaro Gomez Carriles and Mr. Schnabel, based on the autobiography of Reinaldo Arenas; directors of photography, Xavier Perez Grobet and Guillermo Rosas; edited by Michael Berenbaum; music by Carter Burwell, with additional music by Lou Reed and Laurie Anderson; production designer, Salvador Parra; produced by Jon Kilik; released by Fine Line Features. Running time: 125 minutes.

With: Javier Bardem (Reinaldo), Johnny Depp (Bon Bon and Lieutenant Victor), Andrea Di Stefano (Pepe Malas), Olatz Lopez Garmendia (Reinaldo's Mother), Olivier Martinez (Lazaro), Sean Penn (Cuco Sanchez) and Michael Wincott (Heberto Zorilla Ochoa)

Julian Schnabel's film *Before Night Falls* belongs to what might be called the life-is-but-a-dream school of biographical cinema in the way it hovers ethereally over its subject and conjures up fragments of his consciousness in brilliant, disconnected flashes. Adapted from a memoir by the exiled Cuban poet and novelist Reinaldo Arenas, this haunting film portrays that homosexual dissident writer as a desperate unfulfilled searcher for a lost heaven on earth that he experiences only briefly as a very young man. No sooner has he tasted the ecstasies of this pagan paradise than it is snatched away by the punishing, gray-faced Communist revolution.

Relentlessly persecuted for being gay and for having

his manuscripts smuggled out of the country and published abroad, Arenas eventually migrated to the United States along with thousands of other Cubans during the 1980 Mariel boatlift. But if exile brought him freedom, it provided little satisfaction. After living unhappily in Miami for a time (the film omits this period) Arenas settled in New York, where he committed suicide in 1990. (He was suffering from AIDS.) In his suicide letter he bitterly blamed Fidel Castro for all his troubles, including his death.

For all the pain and disappointment it encapsulates, *Before Night Falls* is far from a glum film. Like a deathbed dream it leapfrogs through Arenas's life, reconstructing crucial moments as a succession of bright, feverish illuminations. The movie, which the New York Film Festival is showing this evening and on Sunday at Alice Tully Hall, makes little attempt to psychoanalyze Arenas or to explain him. Instead it dips into his imagination, plumbing the sources of his art in scenes that evoke his closeness with nature and his obsession with sex.

Javier Bardem, the gifted Spanish actor who portrays Arenas (and who bears a striking physical resemblance to him) narrates the film (whose screenplay incorporates swatches of Arenas's posthumously published 1993 memoir) in a thickly accented English that is occasionally difficult to follow. The portrait it paints is of a slightly mad romantic who never recovers from the dashing of his illusions.

Freedom for Arenas didn't simply mean freedom of political expression; it was synonymous with his being a wild boy who claimed to have had 5,000 sexual encounters by age 25. When the Communist revolution on which he had pinned his inchoate boyhood hopes clamped down on Cuba's free-for-all sexual climate and threw homosexuals in prison camps, Arenas began to throw a lifelong tantrum. Liberation wasn't supposed to bring repression.

The film's early scenes of Arenas's dirt-poor childhood in Oriente province, where he was brought up by a single mother and his grandparents, are dizzyingly gorgeous, surreal evocations of a sopping semi-jungle environment where he played in mud holes and carved his early poems into trees. Childhood memories of torrential floods rushing across the landscape have a kind of a voluptuous majesty, and as Arenas matures, the movie returns again and again to images of water.

His happiest moments are his days spent lolling on the beach in male company and having indiscriminate sex everywhere and with everyone. One of his first boyfriends, Pepe (Andrea Di Stefano), a handsome bisexual stud and heartbreaker (who later betrays him), is held up as Arenas's erotic ideal, a rampantly priapic force of nature.

In these scenes the film deliciously evokes pre-Castro Cuba as a sensual endless summer of hot pliable flesh and lapping turquoise waters. Later, when Arenas escapes from prison, he steals out of his cell, squeezes through a fence, and dives into the ocean. Later still, in an unsuccessful attempt to flee Cuba, he floats out to sea on an inner tube.

While still a boy, the film recalls, Arenas desperately wanted to join the Communist guerrillas, and it skillfully weaves period color film clips of the revolutionary celebration with similarly grainy original scenes. No wonder then that when the revolution, which he had naïvely equated with personal salvation, repressed homosexuals and artists, he became its bitter, unforgiving enemy.

Before Night Falls skips lightly over Arenas's persecution and imprisonment. Thrown into an overcrowded jail teeming with murderers and rapists, he earns respect (and cigarettes) by writing letters for his illiterate fellow prisoners. In the most nightmarish scene he is thrown into solitary confinement in a cell, lighted with a single hissing bulb, that is so cramped he is unable to stand up straight.

Johnny Depp has flashy dual cameo roles as a transvestite who smuggles Arenas's rolled-up manuscripts out of prison and as a prison guard who uses sexual manipulation to secure Arenas's signature on a statement declaring his own writing to be worthless.

Once the film moves to New York, its colors dim, as though all the light had gone out of Arenas's life. As he becomes ill, he is dutifully attended by his companion Lazaro Gomes Garriles (Olivier Martinez). Long before Arenas kills himself (with pills and a plastic bag), his will to live appears to be spent. One of the movie's final and most resonant scenes intercuts images of the slums of New York with the grand but now crumbling architecture of contemporary Havana.

Before Night Falls is a larger, more emotionally sweeping film than Mr. Schnabel's 1996 movie debut, *Basquiat*. But like its predecessor it is essentially a painter's movie. Despite its copious narration, it often feels as if the words of the screenplay were scrawled onto the canvas as an afterthought.

Like many of Mr. Schnabel's paintings, this cinematic canvas is consciously heroic in its scale. Yet *Before Night Falls* is mercifully neither hagiographic nor politically strident. And for all the brutality Arenas endured in his life, the movie is surprisingly gentle and free of jarring shocks. If *Before Night Falls* doesn't give us Arenas's life as he actually experienced it, it offers penetrating glimpses into his life as he may have dreamed it.

—S.H., October 6, 2000

BEFORE THE RAIN

Written (in Macedonian, Albanian and English, with English subtitles) and directed by Milcho Manchevski; director of photography, Manuel Teran; edited by Nicolas Gaster; music by Anastasia; production designers, Sharon Lamofsky and David Munns; produced by Judy Counihan, Cedomir Kolar, Sam Taylor and Cat Villiers; released by Gramercy Pictures. Running time: 116 minutes.

With: Katrin Cartlidge (Anne), Rade Serbedzija (Aleksandar), Gregoire Colin (Kiril) and Labina Mitevska (Zamira).

In a sedate London restaurant, two people meet to discuss their marital troubles. They agree that they need more time, not realizing that there is no time left. In the background, away from the main action, an unexplained argument has begun to brew, as a waiter is taunted by an increasingly wild-eyed stranger. "Sir, I didn't do anything," the waiter insists to his boss. He appears to be right. It doesn't matter.

We will never know what the stranger's grievance was, only that it proved the point of Milcho Manchevski's devastating *Before the Rain:* that violence escalates organically and mysteriously, in ways that mean there can be no innocent bystanders in an explosive, hair-trigger world. In a film that unfolds unpredictably, with a Mobius-strip structure oddly like that of *Pulp Fiction,* the one constant becomes an air of foreboding. The birth of a lamb, a pregnant woman in a cemetery, the sight of a small boy toying with a

machine gun: any of these things may signal sudden disaster.

"War torn" is the preferred cliché for events occurring near Mr. Manchevski's native Macedonia, but this film takes a more intuitive view of violence than that. "War is a virus," suggests a doctor in the film, providing a suitably unruly model for the uncontrollable peril Mr. Manchevski explores. The rain of the title is the hard rain Bob Dylan described. And the Macedonian hilltop setting where much of the film unfolds is divided by such stubborn bitterness that different parts of the landscape experience different weather.

It's a red-letter occasion when two first-time directors with films as hugely effective as *Before the Rain* and Lee Tamahori's *Once Were Warriors* make their New York debuts on the same day. Of the two, Mr. Tamahori has the brute force, while Mr. Manchevski has the poetry. Working in a sophisticated, elliptical style, he joins filmmakers as disparate as Krzystof Kieslowski (*Red*) and Atom Egoyan (*Exotica*) in finding his story's deepest meaning in hauntingly oblique connections. Ideas that defy reason, like the immutability of hatred and violence, may be best approached this way.

Before the Rain, opening today at Lincoln Plaza, begins with and returns to a remote Macedonian monastery, which might seem a safe haven from random bloodshed. It starts off peacefully, with the sight of Kiril (Gregoire Colin), a beatific-looking young priest, working in a vegetable garden. When he returns to his bedroom, he finds a surprise: Zamira (Labina Mitevska), an Albanian girl with oddly close-cropped hair, is hiding there. There would be a language barrier between these two anyway, and there is the added obstacle of Kiril's vow of silence.

As the monks meet for prayers, death makes its entrance: armed Macedonian villagers have arrived, demanding to search the monastery in their hunt for Zamira, who they say is a killer. So edgy that they wind up machine-gunning a cat, these intruders do not see in Kiril the purity that is apparent to the audience. They soon rob him of any refuge he may have known as a young monk, leaving him absolutely adrift when the episode is over. Mr. Manchevski needs no more terrible image of an uncertain, treacherous world than the sight of Kiril lost at the end of this episode.

This opening section of the film is called "Words."

The next story that is told, "Faces," is seemingly separate and may or may not occur next in time. Set in London, it features Katrin Cartlidge (who was so memorable in *Naked,* and is fine again here) as Anne, who works in a photo agency. When first seen, Anne is idly looking at two bare chests, one Madonna's, the other that of a hollow-eyed, starving man. *Before the Rain* uses such juxtapositions with chilling authority, to powerfully ironic effect.

Anne has been involved with Aleksandar (Rade Serbedzija), a rakish Pulitzer Prize-winning Macedonian photographer with a weary view of war. "Peace is an exception, not a rule," Alex maintains. Meanwhile, Anne's mother accuses her daughter, who is pregnant, of a different sort of nonchalance. "No problem is so formidable that you can't just walk away from it," her mother says icily. In fact, *Before the Rain* proves an overwhelming argument for the opposite point of view.

Breaking off with Anne during the London sequence, Alex returns to his family for an episode called "Pictures." (Mr. Serbedzija, a formidably magnetic presence, seems much more at ease during the film's non-English-speaking segments.) Not having visited the place in sixteen years, he finds his home half-destroyed and armed friends and relatives, who are Macedonian Christians, patrolling the tiny village. Nearby, at a neighboring settlement, Albanian Moslems are doing likewise.

Alex's former sweetheart, who could be Anne in a different life, lives in the Moslem village and barely dares speak to him. That is not Alex's only reason for sensing how absurd and dangerous these divisions have become. Casually, he takes a weapon away from a half-naked boy and finds that the child's uncle looks angry. It's not clear whether the uncle thinks the boy was endangered or is simply irritated to see him lose his gun.

Mr. Manchevski's taste for ambiguity sometimes leads *Before the Rain* into blatant paradoxes, so that it does not unravel with quite the satisfying completeness that *Pulp Fiction* did; after this film circles back to its denouement, a minor narrative thread involving photographs of Kiril and Zamira is left deliberately unexplained. Neither the presence of such loose ends nor the film's slight straining of its rain metaphor diminishes the final impact of an overwhelming vision.

Transfixed in horror, *Before the Rain* watches the promise of violence seep into every last aspect of its narrative. Mr. Manchevski tells his story elegantly and leaves his audience with a warning too strong to be ignored.

—*J.M., February 24, 1995*

BEING JOHN MALKOVICH

Directed by Spike Jonze; written by Charlie Kaufman; director of photography, Lance Acord; edited by Eric Zumbrunnen; music by Carter Burwell; production designer, K. K. Barrett; produced by Michael Stipe, Sandy Stern, Steven Golin and Vincent Landay; released by USA Films. Running time: 112 minutes.

With: John Cusack (Craig Schwartz), Cameron Diaz (Lotte), Catherine Keener (Maxine), John Malkovich (Himself), Orson Bean (Dr. Lester) and Mary Kay Place (Floris).

Among the hits to emerge from this year's New York Film Festival—like Pedro Almodovar's *All About My Mother,* Kimberley Peirce's *Boys Don't Cry,* Mike Leigh's *Topsy-Turvy* and Kevin Smith's *Dogma*—none is more endearingly nutty than *Being John Malkovich.* None is more intriguingly prophetic, either. In this irresistible first feature by the stellar video director Spike Jonze, the reigning fears and obsessions of a technology-crazed, voyeuristic culture are given an even wilder workout than they got in *The Truman Show.* And the bizarre, masklike facade of today's lonely Everyman is again in the spotlight, even before Milos Forman's film about Andy Kaufman comes to town.

Mr. Jonze's film, with a terrific original screenplay by Charlie Kaufman, is not the first to explore the prospect of being able to sneak into the mind of another person. But Mr. Jonze's version is definitely the most fun. The innovative writer and director have come up with a contemporary fun-house ride that turns identity inside out and makes puppetry an all-important survival skill, which becomes a great boon to Craig Schwartz (John Cusack), the story's unwitting hero.

Craig, a puppeteer, is a shaggy-haired, dejected-looking fellow whose skill at pulling strings turns out to be much more valuable than he ever imagined.

Craig feels outclassed by the competition. (One of the film's many hilarious asides shows a rival staging *The Belle of Amherst* with a 60-foot Emily Dickinson.) And as he explains, "Nobody's looking for a puppeteer in today's wintry economic climate." So he takes his skilled fingers out to apply for a filing job, and finds himself in a most peculiar place: on floor 7[h] of an office building, where both rents and ceilings are low. This is the headquarters for the Lester Corporation, where Craig makes two life-altering discoveries. One is an imperious beauty named Maxine (Catherine Keener), whose response to being told in a restaurant that Craig is a puppeteer is to ask immediately for the check. The other is a doorway that leads to a long tunnel, which ends somewhere in John Malkovich's brain. (Mr. Malkovich more or less plays himself, but the movie gives him Horatio as a middle name.)

Why Mr. Malkovich? Perhaps because he is an actor with an obvious gift for self-mockery, and because his ever-tricky presence fits perfectly into the film's string-pulling scheme. Just to begin with, it's funny to find Craig turning up inside the Malkovich mind to find the actor eating toast and reading *The Wall Street Journal* in his Park Avenue apartment. (The viewer need know nothing more about Mr. Malkovich's life except that this probably isn't it.) And Mr. Malkovich is well up to such tasks as playing a whole roomful of assorted Malkoviches and doing a *Face/Off*-style Cusack imitation once Craig gets serious about invading the actor's privacy.

It's at about this revealing stage in the plotting that many a science fiction premise starts to fall apart. Not this one, however. Mr. Jonze's and Mr. Kaufman's inspired craziness leads into far greater complications as the film's other characters get in on the Malkovich game. While Ms. Keener, an established indie queen whose funny, alluring work here will make her much more widely appreciated, turns conniving Maxine into the object of everyone's affections, Cameron Diaz does a hilarious turn as Craig's frumpy wife, Lotte. Previously most thrilled by taking care of her pet chimpanzee, Lotte goes bananas over the gender-bending experience of inhabiting Malkovich's mind as he is seduced by Maxine. Soon she is making plans to discuss sexual reassignment surgery with her allergist and warning Craig, "Don't stand in the way of my actualization as a man."

Without spoiling what follows, let's just say that *Being John Malkovich* features a fine cast of dryly comic actors who are very much in on the joke. That can even be said of Charlie Sheen, who turns up for some wicked self-parody in a film that also features cameo appearances by Sean Penn, Brad Pitt, and the New Jersey Turnpike.

Also right on target are Orson Bean as the irrepressible entrepreneur, Dr. Lester, and Mary Kay Place as a secretary who is always, figuratively speaking, out to lunch. Carter Burwell's music is perfect for the film's artfully understated, fablelike tone. And Mr. Cusack is first rate as the man who asks the salient question, "Do you know what a metaphysical can of worms this portal is?" Though the movie is nimble and very funny, its serious answer is yes.

—*J.M., October 1, 1999*

BEING THERE

Directed by Hal Ashby; written by Jerzy Kosinski, based on his novel; cinematographer, Caleb Deschanel; edited by Don Zimmerman; music by Johnny Mandel; art designer, James Schoppe; produced by Andrew Braunsberg; released by United Artists. Running time: 130 minutes.

With: Peter Sellers (Chance), Shirley MacLaine (Eve Rand), Melvyn Douglas (Benjamin Rand), Jack Warden (President Bobby), Richard Dysart (Dr. Robert Allenby), Richard Basehart (Vladimir Skrapinov), Ruth Attaway (Louise), Dave Clennon (Thomas Franklin), Fran Brill (Sally Hayes) and Denise DuBarry (Johanna Franklin).

Being There is a stately, beautifully acted satire with a premise that's funny but fragile. Chance, the hero of Jerzy Kosinski's novel and now his screenplay, is a slow-witted innocent who has spent all his adult life in seclusion, working as a gardener and watching television. These two pursuits, and only these two, have shaped his notion of the rest of the world. *Being There* explains, among other things, how illiteracy, ignorance, and a sweet attitude can lead to riches, fame, and a glamorous social career.

Chance, who is played with brilliant understatement by Peter Sellers, is immediately mistaken for

Chauncey Gardiner, an aristocratic businessman (because he wears his former benefactor's elegant hand-me-down suits) and witty raconteur (because he laughs at other people's jokes). He is admired for his fluent knowledge of Russian; this comes from nodding knowingly at a Soviet diplomat at a party. Chance also advises the President, and appears on something like *The Tonight Show.* He has been commenting on how the changing of the seasons means that all is well in the garden, and everyone mistakes this for a metaphor about economics.

Hal Ashby directs *Being There* at an unruffled, elegant pace, the better to let Mr. Sellers's double-edged mannerisms make their full impression upon the audience. Mr. Sellers never strikes a false note, as he exhibits the kind of naïveté that the film's other characters mistake for eccentricity. Not knowing polite conventions, he answers even perfunctory questions ("Will you be seated?") with hilariously excessive enthusiasm ("Yes, I will!"). Not knowing figures of speech, he begins standing like a stork when a doctor advises him to keep his weight off one foot. Not knowing the answers to certain questions, he simply doesn't answer them. This impresses his new friends as reticence of the cagiest kind.

The other fine actors in *Being There*—Melvyn Douglas as a poignantly ailing rich man, Shirley MacLaine as his sexy, sprightly wife, Jack Warden as a suspicious President, and Richard Dysart as the sick man's quietly watchful doctor—conspire to accept Chance as a plausible figure, and thereby keep the story in motion. There is superb ensemble playing in *Being There,* particularly in scenes that bring Mr. Sellers and Mr. Douglas together. The timing is often so perfect that the film, at its very wittiest, strips conversation down to its barest maneuvers and stratagems.

The idea of Chance's miraculous success in the world is a slender one, though, and *Being There* eventually takes it farther than it will go. Chance's adventures begin to have a similar ring; the story doesn't so much progress as repeat itself after a while. And Mr. Ashby, who ruptures the film's exaggeratedly upper-crust mood with an early sequence of Chance in the ghetto, and with frequent doses of television noise, stays close to reality when the story most needs its air of the fantastic. The references to television begin delightfully, as when Mr. Ashby cuts from a jubilant mattress commercial to a man on his deathbed. But since the point

of these snippets is made early on and then reiterated quite a lot, the film at times begins to drag.

There's also something precious about Mr. Ashby's elaborate, solemn, approach to even the most airy and delicate aspects of Chance's story. But for the most part, *Being There,* which opens today at the Coronet, moves handsomely, and ingeniously, to make a whimsical dream of a story come true.

—*J.M., December 20, 1979*

BELLE DE JOUR

Directed by Luis Buñuel; written (in French, with English subtitles) by Mr. Buñuel and Jean-Claude Carrière, based on the novel by Joseph Kessel; cinematographer, Sacha Vierney; edited by Walter Spohr; art designer, Robert Clavel; produced by Robert Hakim and Raymond Hakim; released by Allied Artists. Running time: 100 minutes.

With: Catherine Deneuve (Severine Serizy), Jean Sorel (Pierre Serizy), Genevieve Pase (Madame Anais), Michel Piccoli (Henri Husson), Macha Maril (Renee), Francisco Rabal (Hyppolite) and Pierre Clémenti (Marcel).

Luis Buñuel's particular combination of religion, decay, and morbid eroticism has never been my absolutely favorite kind of cinema—although *Viridiana* was great, and people who say they have an interest in the arts, "if only the subject matter were not so depressing," are of a particularly philistine order of square. But *Belle de Jour,* which opened yesterday at the Little Carnegie, is a really beautiful movie, and somehow, letting the color in—this is Buñuel's first color film—has changed the emotional quality of his obsessions in a completely unpredictable way. All these clean, lovely, well-dressed people preparing for their unspeakable practices are very attractive; and *Belle de Jour* is, among other things, Buñuel's first comedy.

The story is a kind of fantasy cryptogram, with countless clues—verbal puns about cats, nonsense syllables, bells, speech with motionless lips, time cues, and so on—as to when we are in a fantasy, and whose. Catherine Deneuve plays the young, beautiful, but unresponsive wife of a French medical student, Jean Sorel. From a middle-age libertine, Michel Piccoli, she learns the address of a little brothel in Paris, where she goes—or where she appears to go—secretly every afternoon until five, and where, in a series of afternoons, a young gangster, played by Pierre Clémenti, falls in love with her. (Miss Deneuve, Sorel, Piccoli, and Clémenti are all used by Mag Bodard in Benjamin, and all but Mr. Clémenti will appear later this week in *The Young Girls of Rochefort*. They are excellent and they seem to have become a kind of cinema repertory company.)

At the brothel—a wonderfully middle-class household, run by a very kind, sensitive madam, played to perfection by Genevieve Page—Miss Deneuve accommodates a series of gentlemen of eccentric tastes: a jolly, but obligingly sadistic spherical candy manufacturer, an amiable single-minded Japanese, who hopes to pay with his credit card. Just as one thinks the whole movie is about to become a dreary series of sex tableaus by Jean Genet, a customer—a gynecologist in bellboy uniform, with whip—whose tastes we think we already fully understand, demands an inkwell. The movie becomes comic again.

The young gangster himself is marvelous; a grotesque parody on every young hero, Jean-Paul Belmondo in *Breathless* included, out of the milieu. And since, in the cinema daydream convention, almost anything goes, Buñuel is able to put in any number of sequences—a thundering herd of bulls, one of which is named Expiation while all the rest are called Remorse, a child refusing the sacrament—that have less of the ring of false profundity to them, since they appear in the minds of his characters this time, and not necessarily in Buñuel's own. The movie ends with a dark ambiguity about how we are to regard what has gone before, but every detail has been so carefully thought out that seeing it again is like seeing it in another key.

—*R.A., April 11, 1968*

BEN-HUR

Directed by William Wyler; written by Karl Tunberg, based on the novel by Lew Wallace; cinematographer, Robert Surtees; edited by Ralph E. Winters and John Dunning; music by Miklos Rozsa; art designers, William A. Horning and Edward Carfagno; produced by Sam Zimbalist; released by Metro-Goldwyn-Mayer; Running time: 212 minutes.

With: Charlton Heston (Judah Ben-Hur), Jack Hawkins (Quintus Arrius), Stephen Boyd (Messala), Haya Harareet (Esther), Hugh Griffith (Sheik Iderim), Martha Scott (Miriam), Sam Jaffe (Simonides) and Cathy O'Donnell (Tirzah).

Within the expansive format of the so-called "blockbuster" spectacle film, which generally provokes a sublimation of sensibility to action and pageantry, Metro-Goldwyn-Mayer and William Wyler have managed to engineer a remarkably intelligent and engrossing human drama in their new production of *Ben-Hur*.

Without for one moment neglecting the tempting opportunities for thundering scenes of massive movement and mob excitement that are abundantly contained in the famous novel of General Lew Wallace, upon which this picture is based, Mr. Wyler and his money-free producers have smartly and effectively laid stress on the powerful and meaningful personal conflicts that are strong in this old heroic tale.

As a consequence, their mammoth color movie, which opened at Loew's State last night, is by far the most stirring and respectable of the Bible-fiction pictures ever made.

This is not too surprising, when one considers that the drama in *Ben-Hur* has a peculiar relationship and relevance to political and social trends in the modern day. Its story of a prince of Judea who sets himself and the interests of his people against the subjugation and tyranny of the Roman master race, with all sorts of terrible consequences to himself and his family, is a story that has been repeated in grim and shameful contexts in our age. And where the parallels might be vague in the novel, which was first published, after all, away back in 1880, they could be made clearer in the film.

Significantly, they have been, both in Karl Tunberg's excellent screenplay and in Mr. Wyler's largely personal and close-to direction design. For, without stint, the interest is now focused on the character of Judah, son of Hur, and his emotional and spiritual development under the heavy shadows of tyranny, injustice, and hate. And his final emergence from these oppressions imposed and aggravated by a slave state is achieved through his observation of the example and teachings of Jesus.

This pertinent theme of the story is appropriately and grippingly conveyed in some of the most forceful personal conflicts ever played in costume on the giant screen. Where the excitement of the picture may appear to be in the great scenes, such as those of the ancient sea battle in which Ben-Hur is involved as a galley slave or those of his final contention with Messala, the Roman tribune, in a mammoth chariot race, the area of fullest engrossment is the scenes of people meeting face to face—Ben-Hur verbally clashing with Messala, a Roman soldier suddenly looking upon Jesus.

Here is where the artistic quality and taste of Mr. Wyler have prevailed to make this a rich and glowing drama that far transcends the bounds of spectacle. His big scenes are brilliant and dramatic—that is unquestionable. There has seldom been anything in movies to compare with this picture's chariot race. It is a stunning complex of mighty setting, thrilling action by horses and men, panoramic observation, and overwhelming dramatic use of sound.

But the scenes that truly reach you and convey the profound ideas are those that establish the sincerity and credibility of characters. Ben-Hur's encounters with his mother and his sister, who later become lepers during the time of their oppression, or his passing meetings with Jesus (who is, tactfully, never viewed in full face) are dignified and true. Likewise, the enactment of the Crucifixion is impressively personal, strong, and real. It is not done in an aura of gauzy reverence but has the nature of a dark political deed.

For the performance of his characters, Mr. Wyler has a cast that impressively delivers the qualities essential to their roles. Charlton Heston is excellent as Ben-Hur—strong, aggressive, proud, and warm—and Stephen Boyd plays his nemesis, Messala, with those same qualities, inverted ideologically.

Jack Hawkins as the Roman admiral who fatefully makes Ben-Hur his foster son, Haya Harareet as the Jewish maiden who tenderly falls in love with him, Hugh Griffith as the sheik who puts him into the chariot race, and Sam Jaffe as his loyal agent—these also stand out in a very large cast.

Much more could be said in praise of the technical quality of this film, which vastly surpasses the silent version of the same story released back in 1926. Space does not permit it. Otherwise this review would run too long, which is the one thing this picture does distressingly. Three hours and thirty-two minutes of it, not counting intermission, is simply too much of a good thing. The stimulated soul may be willing but the tormented flesh is weak.

—B.C., November 19, 1959

BERLIN ALEXANDERPLATZ

Directed by Rainer Werner Fassbinder; written (in German, with English subtitles) by Mr. Fassbinder, based on the novel by Alfred Döblin; cinematographer, Xaver Schwarzenberger; edited by Juliane Lorenz; music by Peer Raben; produced by Peter Marthesheimer; released by Teleculture Films. Running time: 930 minutes (15 hours, 20 minutes).

With: Gunter Lamprecht (Franz Biberkopf), Hanna Schygulla (Eva), Barbara Sukowa (Mieze), Gottfried John (Reinhold), Elisabeth Trissenaar (Lina), Brigitte Mira (Frau Bast), Karin Baal (Minna), Barbara Valentin (Ida), Roger Fritz (Herbert Virchow) and Franz Buchreiser (Meck).

The New York theatrical premiere of Rainer Werner Fassbinder's *Berlin Alexanderplatz,* the late German director's masterly, fifteen-and-a-half-hour television adaptation of Alfred Döblin's epic 1929 novel of postwar Berlin, stands to become one of the year's most important cinema events. Its importance goes far beyond the Fassbinder career, though we must now reevaluate that career in light of *Berlin Alexanderplatz,* a 1980 work that has the effect of being the coda we did not see in Fassbinder's final film, the lamentable *Querelle.*

When it was shown in Germany, *Berlin Alexanderplatz* was in thirteen segments, totaling thirteen-and-a-half hours, plus a two-hour epilogue. At the Lincoln Plaza Cinema it will be more or less parceled out to the public in three-hour chunks over a five-week period.

Totally impractical—at least from any levelheaded business point of view—is the way in which I saw the film, that is, in two sections, one lasting seven and a half hours, the other eight, on successive days.

In *Berlin Alexanderplatz* Fassbinder has created a

huge, magnificent melodrama that has the effective shape of a film of conventional length. There's never before been anything quite like it, possibly because no filmmaker of comparable stature has ever tried to work on such a grand scale, with the exception of Erich von Stroheim when he attempted to realize his vision of *Greed.*

Throughout his short but spellbinding career—more than thirty features between 1969 and 1982—Fassbinder concentrated on films that reflected his own idiosyncratic visions, while occasionally putting his talent in the service of the works of others, most successfully in his adaptations of Theodor Fontane's *Effi Briest* and Vladimir Nabokov's *Despair,* based on an English-language screenplay by Tom Stoppard. It's in this small group of adaptations that *Berlin Alexanderplatz* belongs, towering above all of the others.

Berlin Alexanderplatz is a serio-comic, two-volume epic about the life, death, and salvation of one Franz Biberkopf, a former transport worker who, when first met, is leaving prison after a four-year term for having beaten to death his prostitute-mistress in a drunken fury. The time is 1927 and Franz, a hulking, self-confident fellow given to sudden rages and quick remorse, makes a vow to himself to remain "decent."

It's not easy. There are no jobs open to him. For a while, he sells tie-clips on the street, becomes a vendor of the National Socialist newspaper *The People's Observer* though he has no use for the Nazis, flirts with anarchism, and finally becomes involved with a mob of crooks—comic but deadly parodies of the crooks in early Fritz Lang movies.

Fassbinder adds at least one important character and changes the tone of several others but otherwise sticks closely to the Döblin novel, in which Franz, moving from one mistress to the next, getting into one scrape after another, blames fate for his troubles instead of recognizing the rottenness of the world and double-crossing friends for what they are.

In the film's apocalyptic finale, Franz, mad as a hatter, has a long dialogue with Death, comparable to a jazzy sort of Dostoyevsky vision, in which Death lectures Franz on the need to look with his eyes and see, to listen with his ears and hear. In attempting to be "strong" and "decent," says Death, Franz has remained naive without being innocent.

As Death talks to Franz in New Testament terms, the movie also makes associations between Franz and Jeremiah, Job, and Abraham. Then, like Christ, Franz dies and is resurrected in the person of someone who looks exactly like Franz Biberkopf and has his papers in his pocket.

At the center of the film is the remarkable performance of Gunter Lamprecht as Franz. He is a large, doughy-looking fellow with small eyes, a big stomach, and a certain sweetness that makes understandable the loyalty he inspires in the series of women who live with him. Mr. Lamprecht must rant, rave, laugh crazily, booze, brawl, and never—not for a minute—be ridiculous while behaving in ridiculous ways.

Almost as important to the film is Gottfried John, a tall, lanky man whose features look to have been carved out of wood, who plays Reinhold, a pathological killer and stuttering ladies' man whom Franz persists in considering his very best friend.

Fassbinder has surrounded Mr. Lamprecht and Mr. John with virtually all of the members of his great stock company, whose familiar faces on this screen give the film the manner of a grand finale. They include Brigitte Mira, Irm Hermann, Ivan Desny, Volker Spengler, Udo Kier, and, especially, three actresses who are identified with the director's greatest work.

Hanna Schygulla (*Maria Braun*) is radiant—again—as the high-class prostitute and former mistress of Franz who continues to watch over him; Elisabeth Trissenaar (*The Stationmaster's Wife, In a Year of 13 Moons*) is one of Franz's more pliant mistresses; and Barbara Sukowa (*Lola*) is nothing less than superb as Mieze, a streetwalker, years younger than Franz, whose love for him prompts him to commit what becomes a mortal sin and leads to her death. Miss Sukowa gives a performance worthy of the young Lillian Gish.

Berlin Alexanderplatz was made into a German film in 1931 by Piel Jutzi. Mordaunt Hall, in reviewing Jutzi's *Berlin Alexanderplatz* in the May 11, 1933, issue of *The New York Times,* noted that it was "an adaptation of Alfred Döblin's two-volume novel, which is said to have been among those tossed to the flames yesterday in Berlin." Yet it survives, triumphantly.

—*V.C., August 10, 1983*

THE BEST YEARS OF OUR LIVES

Directed by William Wyler; written by Robert E. Sherwood, based on the novella *Glory for Me* by

MacKinlay Kantor: cinematographer. Gregg Toland: edited by Daniel Mandell: music by Hugo Friedhofer: art designers. George Jenkins and Perry Ferguson: produced by Samuel Goldwyn: released by the Samuel Goldwyn Company. Black and white. Running time: 172 minutes.

With: Myrna Loy (Milly Stephenson). Fredric March (Al Stephenson). Dana Andrews (Fred Derry). Teresa Wright (Peggy Stephenson). Virginia Mayo (Maria Derry). Cathy O'Donnell (Wilma Cameron). Hoagy Carmichael (Butch Engle). Harold Russell (Homer Parrish). Gladys George (Hortense Derry) and Roman Bohnen (Pat Derry).

It is seldom that there comes a motion picture which can be wholly and enthusiastically endorsed not only as superlative entertainment but as food for quiet and humanizing thought. Yet such a one opened at the Astor last evening. It is *The Best Years of Our Lives.* Having to do with a subject of large moment—the veteran home from war—and cut, as it were, from the heartwood of contemporary American life, this film from the Samuel Goldwyn studio does a great deal more, even, than the above. It gives off a warm glow of affection for everyday, down-to-earth folks.

These are some fancy recommendations to be tossing boldly forth about a film which runs close to three hours and covers a lot of humanity in that time. Films of such bulky proportions usually turn out the other way. But this one is plainly a labor not only of understanding but of love from three men who put their hearts into it—and from several others who gave it their best work. William Wyler, who directed, was surely drawing upon the wells of his richest talent and experience with men of the Air Forces during the war. And Robert E. Sherwood, who wrote the screenplay from a story by MacKinlay Kantor, called *Glory for Me,* was certainly giving genuine reflection to his observations as a public pulse-feeler these past six years. Likewise, Mr. Goldwyn, who produced, must have seen this film to be the fulfillment of a high responsibility. All their efforts are rewarded eminently.

For *The Best Years of Our Lives* catches the drama of veterans returning home from war as no film—or play or novel that we've yet heard of—has managed to do. In telling the stories of three veterans who come back to the same hometown—one a middle-aged sergeant, one an air officer, and one a sailor who has lost both hands—it fully reflects the delicate tensions, the deep anxieties, and the gnawing despairs that surely have been experienced by most such fellows who have been through the same routine. It visions the overflowing humors and the curious pathos of such returns, and it honestly and sensitively images the terrible loneliness of the man who has been hurt—hurt not only physically but in the recesses of his self-esteem.

Not alone in such accurate little touches as the first words of the sergeant's joyful wife when he arrives home unexpectedly, "I look terrible!" or the uncontrollable sob of the sailor's mother when she first sees her son's mechanical "hands" is this picture irresistibly affecting and eloquent of truth. It is in its broader and deeper understanding of the mutual embarrassment between the veteran and his well-intentioned loved ones that the film throws its real dramatic power.

Especially in the readjustments of the sailor who uses prosthetic "hooks" and of the airman who faces deflation from bombardier to soda-jerker is the drama intense. The middle-aged sergeant finds adjustment fairly simple, with a wife, two grown-up kids, and a good job, but the younger and more disrupted fellows are the ones who really get it in the teeth. In working out their solutions Mr. Sherwood and Mr. Wyler have achieved some of the most beautiful and inspiring demonstrations of human fortitude that we have had in films.

And by demonstrating frankly and openly the psychological blocks and the physical realities that go with prosthetic devices they have done a noble public service of great need.

It is wholly impossible—and unnecessary—to single out any one of the performers for special mention. Fredric March is magnificent as the sergeant who breaks the ice with his family by taking his wife and daughter on a titanic binge. His humor is sweeping yet subtle, his irony is as keen as a knife, and he is altogether genuine. This is the best acting job he has ever done. Dana Andrews is likewise incisive as the Air Forces captain who goes through a grueling mill, and a newcomer, Harold Russell, is incredibly fine as the sailor who has lost his hands. Mr. Russell, who actually did lose his hands in the service and does use "hooks," has responded to the tactful and restrained direction of Mr. Wyler in a most sensitive style.

As the wife of the sergeant, Myrna Loy is charmingly reticent and Teresa Wright gives a lovely, quiet performance as their daughter who falls in love with the airman. Virginia Mayo is brassy and brutal as the latter's two-timing wife and Cathy O'Donnell, a new, young actress, plays the sailor's fiancée tenderly. Hoagy Carmichael, Roman Bohnen, and Ray Collins will have to do with a warm nod. For everyone gives a "best" performance in this best film this year from Hollywood.

—B.C., November 22, 1946

BEVERLY HILLS COP

Directed by Martin Brest; written by Daniel Petrie Jr., based on a story by Mr. Petrie and Danilo Bach; cinematographer, Bruce Surtees; edited by Billy Weber and Arthur Coburn; music by Harold Faltermeyer; production designer, Angelo Graham; produced by Don Simpson and Jerry Bruckheimer; released by Paramount Pictures. Running time: 105 minutes.

With: Eddie Murphy (Axel Foley), Judge Reinhold (Detective Billy Rosewood), John Ashton (Sergeant Taggart), Lisa Eilbacher (Jenny Summers), Ronny Cox (Lieutenant Bogomil), James Russo (Mikey Tandino), Jonathan Banks (Zack) and Stephen Elliott (Chief Hubbard).

Beverly Hills Cop finds Eddie Murphy doing what he does best: playing the shrewdest, hippest, fastest-talking underdog in a rich man's world. An opening montage establishes the ghetto origins of Axel Foley, the Detroit policeman whom Mr. Murphy plays. But Axel turns out to be much more at home in the posh California settings where most of the film takes place. Cruising the streets of Beverly Hills in his jalopy, or strolling into hotels and restaurants in a well-worn sweatshirt, Axel maintains every bit of his cool. Far from being daunted, he enjoys the challenge. Axel's confidence never wavers, nor does his natural authority—and for that, audiences will love him.

Beverly Hills Cop, which opens today at Loews State and other theaters, is an even better showcase for Mr. Murphy's talents than *Trading Places* was, although it gets off to a shaky start. A Detroit prologue, combining an over-scored car chase sequence with the murder of Axel's best friend, is somewhat bungled; Martin Brest, the director, establishes the friendship in such brief and sodden terms that it's a wonder Axel cares at all about finding his buddy's killers. But track them he does, and the trail leads him to a Beverly Hills art gallery filled with hilarious modern sculpture. Searching out the owner, Mr. Murphy's Axel is soon booted through a plate-glass window. At that point, two blond policemen arrest him for disturbing the peace.

However, he easily establishes the upper hand. He takes up residence in an elegant hotel that was not expecting him, after loudly intimating that the desk clerk may be practicing racial discrimination and also announcing that he's in town to interview Michael Jackson. He also makes some inroads with the local police force, who get to know him after arresting him and following him around town, and who cannot help but admire his technique. Notwithstanding the title, Axel never does join the Beverly Hills police himself. But he manages to teach them a thing or two about how to invent fish stories, how to bend the rules, and why it's imperative that no one ever put a banana in the tailpipe of a patrol car.

Although *Beverly Hills Cop* is less strictly a comedy than *Trading Places* was, it loses nothing by allowing Mr. Murphy a broader role; his brashness is as well suited to detective work as to sweet-talking his way out of trouble. He comes closer than ever to being able to carry a film single-handedly, although this one surrounds him with an excellent supporting cast. Mr. Brest displays a particular talent for positioning just the right actors in small roles and letting them make their marks succinctly. John Ashton and Judge Reinhold are well teamed as a stuffy police sergeant and his more laissez-faire young partner, and Ronny Cox is suitably dumbfounded as the superior who can't quite understand why this Mr. Murphy's newcomer has the regulars on the ropes. Steven Berkoff makes a chilling villain named Victor Maitland, and Lisa Eilbacher is appealing as an old friend of Axel's who happens to be in Maitland's employ. The brief scenes in Maitland's art gallery are greatly enlivened by Bronson Pinchot, whose accent should baffle linguists everywhere. Mr. Pinchot even steals these scenes from Mr. Murphy, which can't have been easy.

Beverly Hills Cop was written by Daniel Petrie Jr., who co-wrote the story with Danilo Bach. The material never makes an overt issue out of Axel's blackness (indeed, the role was once intended for Sylvester Stallone), except on several occasions when Mr. Murphy slyly uses it as one more weapon in his conversational arsenal. However, the mere juxtaposition of a shabbily dressed Mr. Murphy and the film's staid Beverly Hills locations has great comic potential, in view of the star's unfailing superiority. To the extent that Mr. Murphy has a true costar here it is the city itself, which throws up a long parade of obstacles to his mission, and which seems a constant reproach to his renegade ways. But Mr. Murphy knows exactly what he's doing, and he wins at every turn.

—J.M., December 5, 1984

THE BICYCLE THIEF

Produced and directed by Vittorio De Sica; written (in Italian, with English subtitles) by Cesare Zavattini, based on the novel by Luigi Bartolini; cinematographer, Carlo Montuori; edited by Eraldo Da Roma; music by Alessandro Cicognini; art designer, Antonio Traverso; released by Mayer, Burstyn. Black and white. Running time: 90 minutes.

With: Lamberto Maggiorani (Antonio), Lianella Carell (Maria), Enzo Staiola (Bruno), Elena Altieri (The Medium), Vittorio Antonucci (The Thief), Gino Saltamerenda (Baiocco) and Fausto Guerzoni (The Amateur Actor).

Again the Italians have sent us a brilliant and devastating film in Vittorio De Sica's rueful drama of modern city life, *The Bicycle Thief.* Widely and fervently heralded by those who had seen it abroad (where it already has won several prizes at various film festivals), this heart-tearing picture of frustration, which came to the World yesterday, bids fair to fulfill all the forecasts of its absolute triumph over here.

For once more the talented De Sica, who gave us the shattering *Shoeshine,* that desperately tragic demonstration of juvenile corruption in postwar Rome, has laid hold upon and sharply imaged in simple and realistic terms a major—indeed, a fundamental and universal—dramatic theme. It is the isolation and loneliness of the little man in this complex social world that is ironically blessed with institutions to comfort and protect mankind.

Although he has again set his drama in the streets of Rome and has populated it densely with significant contemporary types, De Sica is concerned here with something which is not confined to Rome nor solely originated by postwar disorder and distress. He is pondering the piteous paradoxes of poverty, no matter where, and the wretched compulsions of sheer self-interest in man's desperate struggle to survive. And while he has limited his vista to a vivid cross-section of Roman life, he actually is holding a mirror up to millions of civilized men.

His story is lean and literal, completely unburdened with "plot," and written by Cesare Zavattini with the camera exclusively in mind. Based on a novel by Luigi Bartolini, it is simply the story of a poor working man whose essential bicycle is stolen from him and who hunts feverishly to find it throughout one day. The man is a modest bill-poster; he must have a bicycle to hold his newly found job; he has a wife and small son dependent on him; the loss is an overwhelming blow. And so, for one long, dismal Sunday he and his youngster scour the teeming streets of Rome, seeking that vital bicycle which, we must tell you, they never find.

That is the picture's story—it is as stark and direct as that, and it comes to a close with a fade-out as inconclusive as a passing nod. But during the course of its telling in the brilliant director's trenchant style, it is as full and electric and compelling as any plot-laden drama you ever saw. Every incident, every detail of the frantic and futile hunt is a taut and exciting adventure, in which hope is balanced against despair. Every movement of every person in it, every expression on every face is a striking illumination of some implicit passion or mood.

Just to cite a few episodes and crises, there is the eloquent inrush of hope when the workman acquires his bicycle after his wife pawns the sheets from their beds; there is the horrible, sickening moment when he realizes that the bicycle is gone, seized and ridden away before his own eyes by a thief who escapes in the traffic's swirl; there is the vain and pathetic expedition to hunt the parts of the bicycle in a second-hand mart; and there is the bleak and ironic pursuit of a suspect into a church during a mass for the poor. There are also lighter touches, such as a flock of babbling German seminarians rudely crowding the father and boy out of a shelter into the rain and a dash after the thief into a bordello, with the little boy compelled to remain outside.

Indeed, the whole structure of this picture, with its conglomeration of experiences, all interlocked with personal anguish, follows a classic plan. It is a plan in which the comedy and tragedy of daily life are recognized. As a matter of fact, both the story and the structure of this film might have been used by Charlie Chaplin in the old days to make one of his great wistful films, for *The Bicycle Thief* is, in essence, a poignant and bitter irony—the irony of a little fellow buffeted by an indifferent world.

As directed by De Sica, however, the natural and the real are emphasized, with the film largely shot in actual settings and played by a nonprofessional cast. In the role of the anguished workman, Lamberto Maggiorani is superb, expressing the subtle mood transitions of the man with extraordinary power. And Enzo Staiola plays his small son with a firmness that fully reveals the rugged determination and yet the latent sensitivity of the lad. One of the most overpowering incidents in the film occurs when the father, in desperation, thoughtlessly slaps the anxious boy. Lianella Carell is also moving as the mother—a smaller role—and Vittorio Antonucci is hard and shabby as the thief. He is the only professional in the large cast.

One further word for the music which has been aptly written and used to raise the emotional potential—the plaintive theme that accompanies the father and son, the music of rolling bicycles, and the "morning music," full of freshness and bells. De Sica has artfully wrapped it into a film that will tear your heart, but which should fill you with warmth and compassion. People should see it—and they should care.

Excellent English subtitles translate the Italian dialogue.

—*B.C., December 3, 1949*

THE BIG CHILL

Directed by Lawrence Kasdan: written by Mr. Kasdan and Barbara Benedek: director of photography. John Bailey: edited by Carol Littleton: production designer. Ida Random: produced by Michael Shamberg: released by Columbia Pictures. Running time: 104 minutes.

With: Tom Berenger (Sam). Glenn Close (Sarah). Jeff Goldblum (Michael). William Hurt (Nick). Kevin Kline (Harold). Mary Kay Place (Meg). Meg Tilly (Chloe). JoBeth Williams (Karen). Don Galloway (Richard). James Gillis (Minister) and Ken Place (Peter the Cop).

In the opening sequence of *The Big Chill*, Lawrence Kasdan's sweet, sharp, melancholy new comedy, seven friends, who went through the University of Michigan together and are veterans of the activist 1960's, meet at the funeral of one of their comrades, who has inexplicably committed suicide. The setting is a small Baptist church somewhere in the South.

The first speaker, the church pastor, rather helplessly concedes that he didn't know the man he must bury. He attempts to be fair to a memory he does not share, but everything he says comes out slightly wrong, as when he talks of the deceased's "seemingly random series of occupations," without then going on to disprove the "seemingly."

The mourning friends are constantly teetering between laughter and tears, which is the mood of this very accomplished, serious comedy, which will be shown tonight at Lincoln Center to start the 21st New York Film Festival.

The Big Chill, which begins its regular commercial engagement at the Paramount and other theaters next Thursday, is an unusually good choice to open this year's festival in that it represents the best of mainstream American filmmaking. Among other things, it's a reminder that the same people who turn out our megabuck fantasies are often capable of working even more effectively on the small, intimate scale of *The Big Chill.*

It's a particular achievement for Mr. Kasdan, who made a stunning directorial debut with *Body Heat,* which he also wrote, after writing the screenplays for *Continental Divide* and, with George Lucas, for *Raiders of the Lost Ark* and *The Empire Strikes Back.* Barbara Benedek shares *The Big Chill* writing credit with him.

The Big Chill is a somewhat fancy variation on John Sayles's *Return of the Secaucus Seven,* in that these sixties survivors all seem to have climbed higher in the seventies, so that their sense of dreams lost and ideals betrayed is sharper and, possibly, more romantically dramatic.

Meg (Mary Kay Place), having once been a dedicated public defender, has abandoned her poor and—she ruefully concedes—often guilty clients to become a successful corporation lawyer. Sam (Tom Berenger), a very nice guy and probably a second-rate actor, is the star of a popular television series that embarrasses him. Recalling the earnest fellow he used to be, he says solemnly, "At least once each show I try to put in something of value." Michael (Jeff Goldblum) wanted to become a novelist and has settled for the jazzy career of a writer for *People* magazine.

Harold (Kevin Kline) and Sarah (Glenn Close), who have fared better than any of their friends, live an enlightened suburban existence. He is the owner of a successful shoe-retailing company, and she is a physician. Karen (JoBeth Williams) says she is happy but is really bored to tears by the devotion of her husband, Richard (Don Galloway), a stranger to this group, and by the housewife she has become.

The most complicated member of the group is Nick (William Hurt), a Vietnam veteran who once enjoyed some fame as a psychologist on a West Coast radio call-in show but who now lives an aimless, rootless life supported by drugs. Completing the group at this postfuneral weekend is Chloe (Meg Tilly), the pretty, much younger woman, who was living with Alex, the dead man, at the time of the suicide and who is completely unconcerned by the specter of time's passing that haunts the rest.

As much as any one character can be the focus in a film of this sort, the enchantingly funny and direct Chloe is the center of the narrative. While the others are being mopey as they drive from the church to the cemetery, Chloe expresses her disappointment at having to ride in an ordinary car and not in the limousine with Alex's mother. Everything is still new to Chloe, including, she concedes, limousines. Later, as if to root out the genteel self-consciousness that has overtaken the mourning friends, she announces: "Alex and I made love the night before he died. It was fantastic!"

In the course of their weekend together in an extremely photogenic antebellum mansion outside Beaufort, South Carolina, the friends move from depression to high spirits, to boozy, druggy confessions, accusations, and revelations of long-hidden disappointments. By the end, several members of the group have made important decisions, which may or may not change their lives, while the others resume the routines they left the preceding Friday.

Mr. Kasdan is one of the finest of Hollywood's new young writers but *The Big Chill*, like *Body Heat*, demonstrates that he is a writer who works as much through images as through words. *The Big Chill* is packed with frequently witty visual information that sometimes contradicts and sometimes supports what the characters say about themselves. There's a wonderfully funny montage early in the movie in which we see each character as defined in the contents of his or her overnight bag. The soundtrack is loaded with sixties music that recalls, without sentimentality, everything the friends have grown away from.

The performances represent ensemble playing of an order Hollywood films seldom have time for, with the screenplay providing each character with at least one big scene. If the actors were less consistent and the writing less fine the scheme would be tiresome. In *The Big Chill* it's part of the fun.

Two reservations should be noted. The character of the dead Alex never comes through as vividly as it should. What does come through—a portrait of an exceptionally gifted, charming, dedicated man, whose life effectively stopped with the excitement and promise of the sixties—blends so thoroughly with that of Mr. Hurt's Nick that one can't be sure if this is the point or if it's a weakness in the conception.

Further, there is the matter of what happened to Nick in Vietnam. We are told on several occasions that his sexual life is over, but why is left for us to speculate about. It's never clear whether he has been physically or emotionally impaired, or both.

This might well be a reference to poor old Jake Barnes of Hemingway's *The Sun Also Rises,* a book that college students have been poring over for fifty years now in their fruitless search for clues to the exact nature of Jake's problem. Considering the frankness with which the characters in *The Big Chill* discuss everything else, this discretion is ridiculous.

—*V.C., September 23, 1983*

THE BIG CLOCK

Directed by John Farrow; written by Jonathan Latimer, based on the novel by Kenneth Fearing;

director of photography. Daniel L. Fapp: edited by LeRoy Stone: music by Victor Young: art directors. Roland Anderson. Hans Dreier. Albert Nozaki: produced by John Farrow and Richard Maibaum: released by Paramount Pictures. Black and white. Running time: 95 minutes.

With: Ray Milland (George Stroud). Charles Laughton (Earl Janoth). Maureen O'Sullivan (Georgette Stroud). George Macready (Steve Hagen). Rita Johnson (Pauline York). Elsa Lanchester (Louise Patterson). Harold Vermilyea (Don Klausmeyer). Dan Tobin (Ray Cordette). Harry Morgan (Bill Womack). Richard Webb (Nat Sperling). Elaine Riley (Lily Gold). Luis Van Rooten (Edwin Orlin). Lloyd Corrigan (Mckinley). Frank Orth (Burt) and Margaret Field (Second Secretary).

When you hear the musical chime at the end of this ticking review of the Paramount's *The Big Clock,* which opened at that theatre yesterday, it will be exactly the time for all devotees of detective films to make a mental memorandum to see it without possible fail. Note well, we make the stipulation that you should be a devotee of detective films and that you should have in your mind the mechanisms of precision peculiar to the cult. For this is a dandy clue-chaser of the modern chromium-plated type, but it is also an entertainment which requires close attention from the start.

Actually, in the manner of the best detective fiction these days, it isn't a stiff and stark whodunnit activated around some stalking cop. Nary a wise guy policeman clutters up the death-room or the clues. As a matter of fact, the policemen are not called in until the end. And the fellow who does the murder is known by the audience all along.

He's a dynamic publishing magnate, ruler of a realm of magazines and a double-dyed rogue who runs his business on the split-tick of a huge electric clock. In a mad, jealous moment, he kills his sweetie, a not very temperate young thing, and then calls upon the cagey editor of his crime magazine to find the man. Two circumstances make this ticklish. The clues have been rigged to make it look as though the murderer were another fellow. And the other fellow is—the editor.

Out of this cozy situation of a guy trying to square himself, even though he is thoroughly innocent and knows perfectly who the murderer is, Scriptwriter Jonathan Latimer and Director John Farrow have fetched a film which is fast-moving, humorous, atmospheric and cumulative of suspense. No doubt there are holes in the fabric—even a rip or two, perhaps—and the really precision-minded are likely to spot them the first time around. But the plot moves so rapidly over them and provides such absorbing by-play that this not-too-gullible observer can't precisely put his finger upon one. (That's why we urge your close attention—just to se if there is anything to catch.)

As the self-protection clue-collector, Ray Milland does a beautiful job of being a well-tailored smoothie and a desperate hunted man at the same time. Charles Laughton is characteristically odious as the sadistic publisher and George Macready is sleek as his henchman, while Maureen O'Sullivan is sweet as Ray's nice wife. Exceptional, however, are several people who play small but electric character roles: Elsa Lanchester as a crack-pot painter and Douglas Spencer as a barman, best of all. Miss Lancaster is truly delicious with her mad pace and her wild, eccentric laugh. A leg on somebody's "Oscar" is won by her with this role.

Indeed, some minor pedestal might be provided, too, for *The Big Clock,* a seventeen-jewel entertainment guaranteed to give a good—if not perfect—time.

—B.C., April 22, 1948

THE BIG DEAL ON MADONNA STREET

Directed by Mario Monicelli: written (in Italian. with English subtitles) by Suso Cecchi d'Amico. Agenore Incrocci. Furio Scarpelli and Mr. Monicelli: produced by Franco Cristaldi: released by United Motion Picture Organization. Black and white. Running time: 91 minutes.

With: Vittorio Gassman (Peppe). Marcello Mastroianni (Tiberio). Toto (Dante). Renato Salvatori (Mario). Rossana Rory (Norma). Carla Gravina (Nicoletta). Claudia Cardinale (Carmelina). Carlo Pisacane (Capanelle) and Tiberio Murgia (Ferribotte).

A longtime popular subject for vaudeville and music-hall farce, the butter-fingered burglar who thoroughly goofs while trying to rob a safe, is given a full-scale treatment and knocked out by a top name cast in the new Italian comedy, *The Big Deal on Madonna Street*. Directed by Mario Monicelli, one of the bright new directors on the Italian scene, this eventually explosive kit of cutups opened at the Fine Arts yesterday.

Obviously the film was calculated as an out-and-out parody of the French melodrama *Rififi*, which was a hit in Italy. For the "big deal" referred to in that title (which was not the Italian title, by the way) is the contemplated burglary of a smalltime jeweler's safe, and the fellows who conspire to do it try to lay out their plans in the same "scientific" fashion as did the robbers in that serious French film.

But, of course, they are not successful. In the first place, they have a terrible time getting all of their elements together and headed the same way. There's that nice fellow (Marcello Mastroianni) who has a wife temporarily in jail and so has to mind the baby, which takes a lot of would-be burglar's time. Then there's the former prizefighter (Vittorio Gassman) who finds himself much more interested in the maid in the apartment through which the burglars will have to travel than he is in the burglary itself.

There's the youngster (Renato Salvatori) who falls hopelessly and helplessly in love with the guarded sister of another of the conspirators (Tiberio Murgia), a Sicilian of hot and vengeful moods. There's the little shrimp (Carlo Pisacane) who is forever concentrating on food. And finally there is the "expert," a role that the wonderful Toto plays.

This "expert" acknowledged as a genius in the business of blowing safes, knows all the techniques, all the laws, all the loopholes, and all the slang words for the chisels and drills. He gives an exquisite lecture (which nobody quite understands). But he gracefully takes a powder when it comes time to do the job.

And when that time comes, everybody—everybody who is left—becomes all thumbs. They sneeze, drop their tools with a horrible clatter, they drill holes into water pipes that jet cold streams, and they set up a monstrous apparatus with which they laboriously punch through a wall—into an easily accessible adjoining room. At that point, in the cold, gray morning, they all give up and go home.

It may be a spoof on *Rififi* but its comedy is based on something much more universal and elementary. That is the humor of sheer clumsiness. Try as they do, these fellows cannot begin to overcome their woeful lack of criminal coordination and their obvious decency. They are like our old vaudeville comic, Tom Howard, who used to go through the same routine with a large sign reading "Burglar" safely pinned to his hat.

There are several dull stretches in this picture, which in Italy was called *I Soliti Ignoti,* a newspaper phrase that means "the usual unknown person," used with reference to the commission of a crime. And we must say that the English subtitles no more duplicate the linguistic quality of the rich Italian babble than the English title duplicates that idiom.

But it's still an essentially funny picture, artfully and joyously played. It's just too bad those incongruous, flat subtitles have to get in the way.

—*B.C., November 23, 1960*

THE BIG HEAT

Directed by Fritz Lang; written by Sydney Boehm, based on the serial story by William P. McGivern in *The Saturday Evening Post*; cinematographer, Charles Lang; edited by Charles Nelson; music by Daniele Amfiftheatrof; art designer, Robert Peterson; produced by Robert Arthur; released by Columbia Pictures. Black and white. Running time: 89 minutes.

With: Glenn Ford (Dave Bannion), Gloria Grahame (Debby Marsh), Jocelyn Brando (Katie Bannion), Alexander Scourby (Mike Lagana), Lee Marvin (Vince Stone), Jeanette Nolan (Bertha Duncan), Peter Whitney (Tierney) and Willis Bouchey (Lieutenant Wilkes).

D ice, Vice, and Corruption"—those are the inducements advertised on the marquee of the Criterion Theatre, where *The Big Heat* opened yesterday, and dice, vice, and corruption—especially corruption—are what you get a full share of in this Columbia crime melodrama, which has Glenn Ford as its taut, relentless star.

Say this for Fritz Lang, who directed, and Sidney

Boehm, who wrote the script: they haven't insulted their players by putting them in a game of tiddly-winks. The business that occupies their hero in this tale of criminals and crooked politics is gambling, conspiracy, extortion, murder, and a few other things. The police commissioner is the hireling of a steel-springed rackets boss. There are strata and sub-strata of underworldlings. Even the widow of a policeman is a bum.

In fact, it is in an endeavor to fathom the suicide of a seemingly honest policeman that Mr. Ford, as a detective, runs afoul of one or two little irregularities that cause his suspicions to hum. And the first thing you know, his nice detective, his home-loving family man, is mixed up in the stickiest lot of knavery since the Kefauver committee was on the air. His sweet wife, played by Jocelyn Brando, gets blown up outside his own home. He himself gets the air as a detective for yelling "murder!" And, indeed, he is all but killed. However, he cracks the crime ring and exposes the crooks and the thieves.

No matter about the implications of shady cops and political goons. The script is so vague in this department that no specific allusions may be found. The only concern of the filmmakers is a tense and eventful crime show, and this they deliver in a fashion that keeps you tingling like a frequently struck gong. Thanks to Mr. Lang's vivid direction, you grunt when Mr. Ford throws a punch. You wince when a cretin-faced Lee Marvin flings scalding coffee into Gloria Grahame's eyes. It isn't a pretty picture. But for those who like violence, it's fun.

Mr. Ford is in fine style as the hero—as angry and icy as they come—and Miss Grahame is intriguingly casual as the renegade girlfriend of a crook. Mr. Marvin and Alexander Scourby represent the criminal elements graphically, Miss Brando makes a briefly cosy housewife, and Jeanette Nolan plays the widow viciously.

But, then, this should not be surprising. Mr. Lang can direct a film. He has put his mind to it, in this instance, and he has brought forth a hot one with a sting.

—*B.C., October 15, 1953*

BIG NIGHT

Directed by Campbell Scott and Stanley Tucci: written by Joseph Tropiano and Mr. Tucci: direc-tor of photography. Ken Kelsch: edited by Suzy Elmiger: music by Gary DeMichele: production designer. Andrew Jackness: produced by Jonathan Filley: released by MGM-UA. Running time: 107 minutes.

With: Tony Shalhoub (Primo). Stanley Tucci (Secondo). Minnie Driver (Phyllis). Isabella Rossellini (Gabriella). Ian Holm (Pascal) and Campbell Scott (Bob).

The calendar says March, but that's hard to believe. On the evidence of the amazing abundance of clever, adventurous American comedies that have arrived here during the last two weeks, it's looking like Christmas in July.

March may have brought more witty new films than Hollywood delivers all year. Foremost among them is the dizzying *Flirting with Disaster,* a complete original and a film so fabulously funny you may find yourself still laughing days after it's over. And *Fargo* shows off the best of the Coen brothers' mischievously deadpan style. Meanwhile, at the top of the charts, the entertaining if not exactly groundbreaking *Birdcage* is the mainstream hit of the moment. There's also Spike Lee's *Girl 6,* uneven but thoroughly good-humored, offering its own brand of raunchy good cheer.

And the New Directors/New Films series (with a number of American selections that were also seen at January's Sundance Film Festival) has been an outstanding showcase for bright new films that fit no Hollywood formulas. Among them: *Welcome to the Dollhouse,* a knowing, caustic look at the life of a misfit seventh grader; *Denise Calls Up,* an all-too-modern romantic comedy staged entirely via computers and call waiting; and *Walking and Talking,* about best friends and their tiny, amusing tribulations. Sweetest of all is Stanley Tucci and Campbell Scott's *Big Night.*

The time is the late 1950's, the place the Paradise, a failing Italian restaurant in New York run by two irresistible brothers. Both are fiercely proud, and their culinary relationship is so close that each has opinions about how the other minces garlic or wields a salt shaker. Secondo (Mr. Tucci) is the front man, debonair and impeccable, humoring the few boorish customers that the restaurant is able to lure. As his name suggests, Primo (Tony Shalhoub) is the artist, hiding himself in the kitchen and muttering about crimes like "the rape of cuisine."

The Paradise is in so much trouble that Secondo, adjusting the flower pots by the front door or picking a cigarette butt off the sidewalk, has begun showing his quiet desperation. If business stays this bad, the brothers' move from Italy to New York may not work out. But Secondo tries everything, from asking for a bank loan to romancing a woman who might help him get a good price on discount liquor. Throughout it all, it's clear that the Paradise and all it stands for are Secondo's real loves.

Big Night, which has the simple, graceful arc of a short story, is about the brothers' last chance to keep the place alive. Opportunity arrives by means of Pascal (Ian Holm), their neighbor and rival, whose own Italian restaurant features meatballs and flambé dishes and a lounge singer performing "O Sole Mio." "The man should be in prison for the food he serves," Primo complains. But Pascal's place is wildly popular, while the Paradise struggles to remain afloat.

From his wood-paneled office lined with celebrity photographs, Pascal offers some advice: get Louis Prima and his band to dine at the Paradise and the place will make its reputation. Pascal even offers to call Prima and invite him to drop by. And with that, *Big Night* is off and running with a lovely delirium of dinner preparation. Like *Babette's Feast* and *Eat Drink Man Woman,* this is a film in which food is half the fun.

There's much more to *Big Night* than culinary ecstasy, although the filmmakers surely deliver that. (By the end of Primo's incredible meal, all the diners look weak with happiness, except for the one woman who sobs, "My mother was such a terrible cook!") What's most affecting here, beyond the vast charm of the two main characters, is the film's absolute faith in artistry and independence in a world that may not necessarily respect either one. The beauty of *Big Night* is that it can express all this in a wordless, eloquent coda devoted to nothing more monumental than cooking and eating eggs.

Both on-screen and off, *Big Night* is clearly a labor of love. Written by Mr. Tucci with his cousin, Joseph Tropiano, as a family homage of sorts, and directed by two talented actors who are also old friends, the film is loaded with brotherly affection and with warm, funny, and poignant evocations of a gentler time. From the white-glove elegance of the friends who form the dinner party to the proud ceremoniousness of the brothers' manners, *Big Night* thrives on small but impeccable touches. "Come on," complains Primo, to the greengrocer trying to sell him wilted basil. "Looks dead, like a wig."

Mr. Tucci, whose comically reserved performance is a complete delight, goes a long way toward single-handedly establishing the film's beguiling sensibility. Whether cooking with his necktie neatly over his shoulder, serving risotto colored like the Italian flag, or eyeing the unattainable fins of a new Cadillac, he captures a well-drawn and hugely sympathetic character. The interplay between Mr. Tucci and the excellent Mr. Shalhoub is no less perfect, with both actors sharing the taste for understatement. Just the way that Primo reacts, when advised by Secondo to stop making his visionary but labor-intensive risotto, is typical of the film's sang-froid. Primo thinks it over and then coldly agrees. O.K., he has a better idea. How about making hot dogs instead?

Big Night, directed with serviceable skill but loads of heart, fills out its story with supporting performances from Isabella Rossellini (as Pascal's glamorous girlfriend, secretly close to Secondo) and Minnie Driver (as Secondo's more reputable love interest). Both are charming, but neither has much more reason to be here than Mr. Scott, who turns up briefly and amiably as a Cadillac salesman. ("I detect an accent," he tells Secondo.) None of the minor characters does anything more vital than hang around till dinnertime. Who can blame them?

Also in *Big Night:* a timpano, a rare and backbreaking Italian delicacy that is the pièce de résistance during the extended dinner party sequence. Primo and Secondo, enchantingly in character, are moved to kiss and touch this drum-shaped, many-layered marvel when it comes out of the oven.

Big Night will be shown tomorrow and Sunday as part of the New Directors/New Films series. Eat before you go.

—*J.M., March 29, 1996*

THE BIG RED ONE

Written and directed by Samuel Fuller; director of photography. Adam Greenberg; edited by Morton Tubor; music by Dana Kaproff; produced by Gene Corman; released by United Artists. Running time: 113 minutes.

With: Lee Marvin (Sergeant), Mark Hamill (Griff), Robert Carradine (Zab), Bobby DiCicco (Vinci), Kelly Ward (Johnson), Siegfried Rauch (Schroeder), Stéphane Audran (Walloon), Serge Marquand (Rensonnet) and Charles Macaulay (General-Captain).

Samuel Fuller, the director of such obsessively self-absorbed, often shocking, sometimes foolish low-budget American melodramas as *China Gate, Underworld, U.S.A.,* and *Shock Corridor,* has been a cult figure for years. It's ironic that just as he's being recognized as one of the great primitives of American movies, he should come out with *The Big Red One,* a handsome, technically first-rate, almost leisurely recollection of the World War II experiences of five American soldiers, from the landings in North Africa in 1942 until the collapse of Germany in 1945.

Mr. Fuller is a nervy, no-nonsense Hollywood original. People on the order of Jean-Luc Godard, who cast Mr. Fuller in a small role in *Pierrot Le Fou,* and Wim Wenders, who used him in *The American Friend,* have often given Mr. Fuller credit for shaping their own, far more sophisticated, far more complex cinema styles.

However, *The Big Red One,* which opens today at Loew's State One and other theaters, is not a typical Fuller work. I can't be sure whether this is because more than ten years elapsed between its production and the last Fuller film, and Mr. Fuller, now approaching seventy, has become more mellow, or because the film, originally shot and edited by Mr. Fuller, was later cut by others to its present running time (though with Mr. Fuller's consent).

For a war movie, and one that contains a lot of graphic battle footage, *The Big Red One* (a reference to the arm patch of the First Infantry Division) is surprisingly cheerful, which has as much to do with the comic-book level on which Mr. Fuller deals with his characters as with their remarkably good fortune in surviving three years in the most bitterly fought war in history.

To speak of comic books in reference to Mr. Fuller is not automatically to put him down, but to describe what his characters and his movies look like. They don't contain many shadows. They are straightforward, blunt, on occasion unashamedly sentimental, and punctuated here and there with ironies of a subtlety that a three-year-old couldn't miss.

For Mr. Fuller, *The Big Red One* was a labor of love, a film he's been wanting to make for decades. Based on his own World War II experiences, the film is an attempt to show us a kind of war not often seen on the screen, that is, a war reduced to what can be seen from the point of view of the foot soldier who has no connections to headquarters or to decision making. To the extent to which Mr. Fuller succeeds in eliminating grand melodrama from *The Big Red One,* it is a most un-Fuller-like film.

The movie is a succession of small, deadly problems. It's about getting safely through the surf to the invasion beach, about finding and knocking out a hidden enemy gun, about being pinned to the beach by horrendous enemy fire, about moments of respite, about being exhausted and then plowing on some more. It is epic and episodic, and the characters exist only in relation to the events they find themselves in.

In addition to the sergeant (Lee Marvin), the characters are Zab (Robert Carradine), based on Mr. Fuller himself, a cigar-chewing young writer who talks in the short, stabbing sentences you can imagine Mr. Fuller once wrote when he wanted to be a novelist; Griff (Mark Hamill), a fine young soldier who suffers terrible bouts of battle fright; Vinci (Bobby DiCicco), a wise-cracking Sicilian-American soldier, and Johnson (Kelly Ward), who's much like the others except that he suffers from hemorrhoids.

The movie's battle footage is mostly small-scale but terrifically effective, especially in a sequence devoted to the 1944 landings at Omaha Beach in Normandy, which is as good as anything in *The Longest Day.* Mr. Fuller's characters aren't very interesting but, in this case, banality has a point. These really are ordinary guys and not the wildly representative ones seen in most Hollywood war movies. More important, one is always aware of the soldiers' sense of isolation even in the midst of battle and of the endlessness of their task. If they survive one battle, their only reward is to be able to fight another.

For Fuller buffs, there are more than a few Fullerisms in *The Big Red One,* including the soundtrack narration, spoken by Zab, which often has a decidedly purple tint. There's also a comic childbirth sequence inside a tank, successive sequences in which an American noncommissioned officer and a German noncom each say exactly the same things in answering their men's objections to war ("We don't murder. We kill our enemies."), and a recurring image of a wooden figure of Christ hanging from a cross, gazing empty-eyed over the carnage of a battlefield.

The performances are perfectly in line with the material, which is to say they are competent without being idiosyncratic in the least. Mr. Marvin gives the film weight and substance by being the only character at all memorable, mostly because he's older than the others and is easily identifiable. Mr. Carradine and Mr. DiCicco look so much alike that you are not always sure which is which until you remember that the one with the cigar is Mr. Carradine.

—V.C., July 18, 1980

THE BIG SKY

Produced and directed by Howard Hawks: written by Dudley Nichols, based on the novel by A. B. Guthrie Jr.: cinematographer, Russell Harlan: edited by Christian Nyby: music by Dimitri Tiomkin: art designers, Albert S. D'Agostino and Perry Ferguson: released by RKO Radio Pictures. Black and white. Running time: 140 minutes.

With: Kirk Douglas (Jim Deakins), Dewey Martin (Boone Caudill), Elizabeth Threatt (Teal Eye), Arthur Hunnicutt (Zeb Callaway), Steven Geray (Jourdonnais), Hank Worden (Poor Devil), Buddy Baer (Romaine) and Jim Davis (Streak).

Howard Hawks, a producer-director who obviously is deeply in love with the storied, pioneer West, again is proving his unabashed sentiment for sturdy men and rugged places in *The Big Sky,* a saga as long as the day and as big as all outdoors, which is being spun now at the Criterion. Mr. Hawks's source material is the finest on the subject and if he simply captured the muscular, surface effects and some of the scenic glories of A. B. Guthrie's novel he has done a viewer a real service.

For, in exploring the route of the trailblazers who left Kentucky and Tennessee to open the sweeping vistas and riches of the Northwest to the white trader and settler, he has not added another Western to film annals. *The Big Sky* is a Western in locale but not entirely in content. The purists will argue against changes in plot, characters, and shifting of emphasis on the story line wrought by Mr. Hawks and Dudley Nichols, his scenarist. But they should not debate the fact that they are examining a facet of history rarely touched on by the moviemakers and a part of our past rich in courage and adventure.

Mr. Hawks is still the craftsman who, in *Red River,* made a full-bodied and memorable legend of cattlemen on the Chisholm Trail. He has reconstructed in *The Big Sky* the tale of the restless Kentuckians, Jim Deakins and Boone Caudill, who, in 1830, forsook their wooded hills for St. Louis and the faraway virgin Indian territories; of that sage and lovely trapper-scout, Zeb Callaway (who is a composite of the Dick Summers and Zeb Callaway of the book); of that voyageur, Jourdonnais, irascible, but intrepid keelboat "patron," and his varied French crew, who rowed, poled, and hauled their small craft some 2,000 miles up the wide Missouri, the Platte, and the Cheyenne to trade for beaver pelts with the feared Blackfoot Indians. And, he has not ignored that hostage, Blackfoot princess, Teal Eye—whose eyes were like those of a blue wing teal—and her strange, almost wordless romance with Caudill.

Mr. Hawks and company have chosen to concentrate on one phase of the panoramic and powerful book but, as has been noted, he has given that phase a connoisseur's consideration. His principals are a lusty troupe who are not averse to tilting a jug continuously, to tavern brawling, to tangling with marauding Crow Indians and renegade whites in the pay of the fur company supporting the forts along their river route. In so doing they have retained the salty dialogue, including French, of the traders and they have even injected humor into such a normally morbid sequence as an amputation. The Indian attacks, of course, are howling successes.

Arthur Hunnicutt is outstanding as the buckskin-clad Zeb. He most closely approximates the type of "mountain man" described by the author, that rare man who had to leave civilization to live in a "big and wide country." Kirk Douglas is competent as the fearless but fun-loving Jim Deakins, who yearns for Teal Eye but is silent because she has eyes only for his friend. As that friend, Dewey Martin, a newcomer, makes Boone Caudill a tough, laconic youngster who is ready to brave dangers and the savage apple of his eye. Elizabeth Threatt is tall, dark, and handsome as that prize, a princess who has only Indian lines to speak. And Steven Geray, as the keelboat owner, pitches in with a properly accented portrayal.

Since he is a stickler for authenticity, Mr. Hawks should be credited with having shot his story in truly natural surroundings. The majestic sweep of rivers, mountains, passes, and woods of Grand Teton National Park is a sight to behold and a tribute to photography. He obviously has been unable to re-create plains black with buffalo, nor has he achieved a full sense of the vastness of the singing silences of that unblemished area.

The two-hour-and-twenty-minute running time of *The Big Sky* is much too long. Also, Mr. Hawks has not delved too deeply into the psychological urges and the dreams which drive the pioneer northwest. But the fact that he has indicated the flavor of the period, the beauty of an unsullied countryside, and, above all, the nature of some of those daring few is enough.

—*A.W., August 20, 1952*

THE BIG SLEEP

Produced and directed by Howard Hawks; written by William Faulkner, Jules Furthman and Leigh Brackett, based on the novel by Raymond Chandler; cinematographer, Sid Hickox; edited by Christian Nyby; music by Max Steiner; art designer, Carl Jules Weyl; released by Warner Brothers. Black and white. Running time: 118 minutes.

With: Humphrey Bogart (Marlowe), Lauren Bacall (Vivian), Martha Vickers (Carmen), Charles Waldron (General Sternwood), John Ridgely (Eddie Mars), Charles D. Brown (Norris), Regis Toomey (Bernie Ohls), Louis Jean Heydt (Joe Brody) and Elisha Cook Jr. (Harry Jones).

If somebody had only told us—the scriptwriters, preferably—just what it is that happens in the Warners' and Howard Hawks's *The Big Sleep*, we might be able to give you a more explicit and favorable report on this overage melodrama which came yesterday to the Strand. But with only the foggiest notion of who does what to whom—and we watched it with closest attention—we must be frankly disappointing about it.

For *The Big Sleep* is one of those pictures in which so many cryptic things occur amid so much involved and devious plotting that the mind becomes utterly confused. And, to make it more aggravating, the brilliant detective in the case is continuously making shrewd deductions which he stubbornly keeps to himself. What with two interlocking mysteries and a great many characters involved, the complex of blackmail and murder soon becomes a web of utter bafflement. Unfortunately, the cunning scriptwriters have done little to clear it at the end.

This is a frequent failing in films made from Raymond Chandler's books, as this one is; and if you haven't read the original, as we haven't, you are stuck. It is something about a detective who undertakes a job of private and perilous sleuthing for a decadent millionaire, mainly to save the old man's daughters from some blackmailers and bums. And since quite obviously the daughters are bums, too, it has a not very lofty moral tone.

Much of the terseness and toughness of Mr. Chandler's style has been caught in the movement and dialogue of William Faulkner's and Leigh Brackett's script. And Mr. Hawks, who produced and directed, has kept the action racy and raw. Everyone in the story, except the old father, seem to carry guns, which they use at one time or another with a great deal of flourish and éclat. And fists are frequently unlimbered, just to vary the violence. Students of underworld minutiae will find plenty of it here.

Through it all, Humphrey Bogart stalks his cold and laconic way as the resolute private detective who has a mind—and a body—made of steel. And Lauren Bacall (Mrs. Bogart) plays the older of the daughters languidly. (Miss Bacall is a dangerous looking female, but she still hasn't learned to act.) A dozen or so other actors play various tramps and tough guys acidly, and the whole thing comes off as a poisonous picture lasting a few minutes shy of two hours.

But, for all that, it's likely to leave you confused and dissatisfied. And, by the way, would somebody also tell us the meaning of that title, *The Big Sleep*.

—*B.C., August 24, 1946*

BILLY LIAR

Directed by John Schlesinger; written by Willis Hall and Keith Waterouse, based on the novel and play by Mr. Waterhouse; director of photography, Denys N. Coop; edited by Roger Cherrill; music by Richard Rodney Bennett; produced by Joseph Janni; released by Walter Reade Sterling, Inc. Running time: 98 minutes.

With: Tom Courtenay (Billy Fisher), Wilfred Pickles (Geoffrey Fisher), Mona Washbourne (Alice Fisher), Ethel Griffies (Florence), Finlay Currie (Duxbury), Gwendolyn Watts (Rita), Helen Fraser (Barbara), Julie Christie (Liz), Leonard Rossiter (Shadrack), Rodney Bewes (Arthur Crabtree), George Innes (Stamp), Leslie Randall (Danny Boon), Patrick Barr (Inspector MacDonald), Ernest Clark (Prison Governor) and Godfrey Winn (Disc Jockey).

Of course you remember Walter Mitty, James Thurber's timid little man who escaped from his humdrum existence by imagining himself involved in glorious fantasies. Well, the hero of *Billy Liar,* which came to the Coronet yesterday, is his British cousin—a wee less timid, but the same breed of cat.

Like Walter, he is a big nobody and lives in a middle-class home in a dismal Midlands city. Unlike Walter, he was a minor clerical job in a dreary funeral parlor and he dates girls whose horizons are limited mainly to wedding rings and four-room flats.

The only thing that saves him from madness—and saves this picture from being just one more of those angry-young-man British dramas—is his fertile ability to dream, to weave fantasies of himself as various heroes accomplishing bold and glamorous deeds.

He even has the ability to turn on the make-believe in the face of his friends and pompous superiors and stagger them with his mimicry. He is a card. He is also a bit of a sham.

As much as John Schlesinger, the director, gives him all the best of it in this film, which is based on a play and a novel that were both big London hits, and as much as the young star, Tom Courtenay, plays him appealingly, he is hollow, not only as a hero but as a dramatic character.

So long as he is badgering his parents, playing impudent practical jokes on his stiff-backed and humorless superiors, bouncing frantically back and forth between two girls to whom he is trying to keep attached as his finacées with one cheap engagement ring, he's a gay and amusing fellow, and Mr. Schlesinger succeeds in giving the film a mood of spontaneity and madness that is quite agreeable.

But when the fable slips into an issue of some considerable seriousness—at least, so far as the future of the hero is concerned—and it is solved, or allowed to crumble, in a cheerless denouement, I find it a dramatic contrivance that is theatrical and false. I do not think Mr. Courtney's hero—at least, the funny fellow we have seen being so-brisk and enterprising in the better part of the film—would turn out to be such a chicken, such a dismal stereotype. It seems that the authors and Mr. Schlesinger want to make him more pathetic than he is.

However, he's fun through most of the picture, even when you can't understand what he says—and, believe me, there are lots of times in this picture when English subtitles would be a help. The Midlands accent is that muddy! Helen Fraser and Gwendoyln Watts are pert and harsh as the chippies he courts with breathless ardor, and an actor named Wilfred Pickies—no fooling!—is appropriately sour as his old man.

Billy Liar is least convincing and least appealing when it attempts to expose a poignant truth.

—B.C., December 17, 1963

BILOXI BLUES

Directed by Mike Nichols; written by Neil Simon, based on his play; director of photography, Bill Butler; edited by Sam O'Steen; music by Georges Delarue; production designer, Paul Sylbert; produced by Ray Stark; released by Universal Pictures. Running time: 104 minutes.

With: Matthew Broderick (Eugene), Christopher Walken (Sergeant Toomey), Matt Mulhern (Wykowski), Corey Parker (Epstein), Markus Flanagan (Selridge), Casey Siemaszko (Carney), Michael Dolan (Hennesey) and Penelope Ann Miller (Daisy).

When first seen in *Biloxi Blues,* the movie, Eugene Morris Jerome is not, technically speaking, actually seen. He's an indistinct figure in the window of a World War II troop train. With more purpose than hurry, the train chugs across a broad, verdant American landscape, shimmering in the golden light of memory, as well as in the kind of humid, midsummer heat in which even leaves sweat. On the soundtrack: "How High the Moon."

In one unbroken movement, the camera swoops down and across time and landscape into a close-up of the ever-observant Eugene. He's headed for Biloxi, Mississippi, and basic training in the company of other recruits who, to his Brighton Beach sensibility, seem to have been born and bred under rocks.

They are Wykowski, Selridge, Carney, and Epstein, the usual American cross-section. They're an exhausted but still tirelessly obscene crew given to communication by insults—rudely frank comments about each other's origins, intelligence, odors, and anatomies. Says the voice of Eugene (Matthew Broderick), who has a would-be writer's way of stepping outside events to consider his own reactions to them: "It was hard to believe these were guys with mothers and fathers who worried about them. It was my fourth day in the Army, and I hated everybody so far."

It now seems as if the entire Broadway run of Neil Simon's 1985–86 hit play was simply the out-of-town tryout for the movie, which opens today at the Baronet and other theaters. However it came to be, *Biloxi Blues,* carefully adapted and reshaped by Mr. Simon, is a very classy movie, directed and toned up by Mike Nichols so there's not an ounce of fat in it.

Here is one adaptation of a stage piece that has no identity crisis. *Biloxi Blues* is not a movie that can't quite cut itself loose from the past, and never for a minute does it aspire to be anything but a first-rate service comedy. With superb performances by Mr. Broderick, who created the role of Eugene on Broadway, and Christopher Walken, who plays Mr. Simon's nearly unhinged, very funny variation on the drill sergeant of movie myth, *Biloxi Blues* has a fully satisfying life of its own.

In one brief but key sequence, the camera watches Eugene and his buddies as they watch the Abbott and Costello classic *Buck Privates.* The beautifully timed, low-comedy scene that so delights them continues to be funny in itself. It also helps to place *Biloxi Blues* in a very different movie-reality, in an Army that's racially segregated and in which ignorance and bigotry are the order, though, in hindsight, World War II remains the last "good war."

Biloxi Blues is about the education of Eugene Morris Jerome, who has three goals in life: to become a writer, to lose his virginity, and to fall in love. Even if, through some warp in time, we'd never before heard of Neil Simon, the existence of this first-person memoir would reveal how Eugene succeeded in his chosen craft. *Biloxi Blues* recalls how he made out in the sex and romance departments while also growing up.

It makes no difference that there's never any doubt that he will make out. That's a given. The pleasure comes in witnessing Mr. Simon and Mr. Nichols as they discover surprises in situations that one might have thought beyond comic salvation.

Beginning with young Richard, the lovesick poet in Eugene O'Neill's *Ah, Wilderness!,* would-be writer characters in the American theater have been sneaking off to brothels virtually nonstop. However, not one of those earlier adventures equals the nuttiness of Eugene's with a Biloxi woman (Park Overall) who, on the side, deals in perfume, stockings, black lace panties, and other items hard to find in a wartime economy. Says Eugene, "Do you sell men's clothing?"

There is also an idealized funniness in Eugene's sweet, tentative romance with a pretty Catholic girl (Penelope Ann Miller), who sends his head (and the camera) spinning. When she tells him that her name is Daisy, the delighted Eugene says that Daisy is the name of his favorite female character in fiction. Responds this no-nonsense Daisy, "Which one, Daisy Buchanan or Daisy Miller?"

Even more important are Eugene's relations with the other recruits, including the slobbish but pragmatic Wykowski (Matt Mulhern) and Selridge (Markus Flanagan), and especially Epstein, played by Corey Parker with seriously funny arrogance. Epstein is a young, bookish fellow with a delicate stomach and utter disdain for what people think.

Epstein serves as Eugene's conscience, but Eugene still can't bring himself to stand up for a fellow Jew: "Epstein sort of sometimes asked for it, but since the guys didn't pick on me that much, I just figured I'd stay neutral, like Switzerland."

Eugene's coming of age is sharpened in the film by

having Eugene, rather than Epstein, become the key figure in the recruits' late-night showdown with the crazy Sergeant Toomey.

As Sergeant Toomey ("You're not fighting men yet, but I'd put any one of you up against a Nazi cocktail waitress"), Mr. Walken gets his best role in a very long time, possibly since *Pennies from Heaven*. Mr. Broderick is wonderfully devious as a young man who's so taken by life's spectacle that he sometimes forgets he's a part of it.

As if he believed that a wisecrack left unspoken were a treasure lost forever, Eugene won't keep quiet. This is an endearing characteristic in Eugene but a problem in some of Mr. Simon's other works. *Biloxi Blues* is different. Mr. Nichols keeps the comedy small, precise, and spare. Further, the humor is never flattened by the complex logistics of movie-making, nor inflated to justify them.

Biloxi Blues is the second play of Mr. Simon's "Eugene trilogy," which begins with *Brighton Beach Memoirs* and ends with *Broadway Bound*. It may not be as good a play as *Broadway Bound* but, with *The Heartbreak Kid*, adapted from a Bruce Jay Friedman story, and *The Sunshine Boys*, it stands as one of the three best films Mr. Simon has yet written.

—*V.C., March 25, 1988*

THE BIRDS

Produced and directed by Alfred Hitchcock; written by Evan Hunter, based on a story by Daphne du Maurier; cinematographer, Robert Burks; edited by George Tomasini; music by Bernard Herrmann; production designer, Norman Deming; released by Universal Pictures. Running time: 120 minutes.

With: Tippi Hedren (Melanie Daniels), Rod Taylor (Mitch Brenner), Jessica Tandy (Mrs. Brenner), Suzanne Pleshette (Annie Hayworth), Veronica Cartwright (Cathy Brenner), Ethel Griffies (Mrs. Bundy), Charles McGraw (Sebastian Sholes), Ruth McDevitt (Mrs. McGruder) and Joe Mantell (Salesman).

Take in the birdbath and feeder! Beware the first robin of spring! A threat of unspeakable horror is latent in our feathered friends! At least, that is what Alfred Hitchcock is implying in his new film, *The Birds*, which is whirring and screeching with deafening uproar at the Palace and Sutton Theaters.

Making a terrifying menace out of what is assumed to be one of nature's most innocent creatures and one of man's most melodious friends, Mr. Hitchcock and his associates have constructed a horror film that should raise the hackles on the most courageous and put goose pimples on the toughest hide.

Whether Mr. Hitchcock intended this picture of how a plague of birds almost ruins a peaceful community to be symbolic of how the world might be destroyed (or perilously menaced) by a sudden disorder of nature's machinery is not apparent in the picture. Nor is it made readily clear whether he meant the birds to represent the classical Furies that were supposed to pursue the wicked on this earth.

I prefer to suspect the latter, although it isn't in Mr. Hitchcock's style to inject allegorical meanings or social significance in his films. But the context of the birds concentrating their fury upon a house in which a possessive and jealous mother hovers anxiously over her son is so obvious and fascinating that I rather lean to it.

There is also this further indication: a young woman who is made out to be the vaguely resentful ex-sweetheart of the son is killed by the birds in one of their onsets before they zero in on the mother's house. Evidently this young woman has been ridden with jealousy, too.

But whether or not it is intended that you should find significance in this film, it is sufficiently equipped with other elements to make the senses reel. Mr. Hitchcock, as is his fashion, has constructed it beautifully, so that the emotions are carefully worked up to the point where they can be slugged.

He begins, innocently, with a haughty San Francisco girl having a testy encounter in a bird shop with a man on whom she plays a practical joke. Then, mischievously, he leads her to the fellow's family home in a fishing village north of San Francisco to deliver an impudent present of two lovebirds.

Notice how clear and naturalistic the narrative elements are: a plausible confrontation, beautiful scenery, a literal enactment of a playful intrigue—all very nicely arranged.

Then, sneakily, Mr. Hitchcock tweaks us with a

tentative touch of the bizarre. The plausible is interrupted by a peculiar avian caprice. A seagull attacks the young woman. Flocks of angry gulls whirl in the air. A swarm of sparrows swoops down a chimney and whirrs madly through a living room. And, then, before we know it, he is flying in shock waves of birds and the wild, mad, fantastic encounter with a phenomenon of nature is on.

There may be no explanation for it (except that symbolic one, perhaps), but the fierceness and frightfulness of it are sufficient to cause shock and chills. And that is, no doubt, what Mr. Hitchcock primarily intends.

The cast is appropriate and sufficient to this melodramatic intent. Tippi Hedren is pretty, bland, and wholesome as the disruptive girl. Rod Taylor is stolid and sturdy as the mother-smothered son. Jessica Tandy is querulous as the mother, and pretty Suzanne Pleshette is pleasant but vaguely sinister as the old girlfriend.

There are the usual Hitchcock "characters" spotted through the film. And those birds! Well, you've never seen such actors! They are amazingly malevolent feathered friends.

—*B.C., April 1, 1963*

BIRDY

Directed by Alan Parker; written by Sandy Kroopf and Jack Behr, based on the novel by William Wharton; cinematographer, Michael Seresin; edited by Gerry Hambling; music by Peter Gabriel; production designer, Geoffrey Kirkland; produced by Alan Marshall; released by Tri-Star Pictures. Running time: 120 minutes.

With: Matthew Modine (Birdy), Nicolas Cage (Al Columbato), John Harkins (Doctor Weiss), Sandy Baron (Mr. Columbato), Karen Young (Hannah Rourke), Bruno Kirby (Renaldi), Nancy Fish (Mrs. Prevost), George Buck (Birdy's Father), Dolores Sage (Birdy's Mother), Robert L. Ryan (Joe Sagessa) and James Santini (Mario Columbato).

The most unusual thing about *Birdy*, William Wharton's novel about a boy who develops an overwhelming erotic fascination with avian life, is its lack of allegorical implications. The story of Birdy, who actually reaches the point of imagining that he has fathered a family of canaries, can be taken at face value. So can the parallel tale of Al, the boyhood friend who years later, after suffering grave wartime injuries, returns to coax the adult Birdy out of his madness.

Like Mr. Wharton's novel, Alan Parker's film of *Birdy*, which opens today at the Beekman Theater, works best when it concentrates on the friendship, and on Birdy's amazing eccentricities. The material is so odd and so powerful that its particulars are of much greater interest than its larger implications. It is some measure of just how compellingly Mr. Parker has set forth this tale that when, barely twenty minutes into the movie, Birdy and Al don feathered pigeon suits for a nocturnal adventure, the episode seems neither silly nor incredible. Birdy's intensity is so captivating, and Al's discomfiture so believable and funny, that their story becomes irresistibly involving.

The film takes the form of a series of flashbacks. Its present-day sections are set in a military hospital, where Al (Nicolas Cage) tries desperately to elicit some human response from his friend. Birdy (Matthew Modine) has finally transformed himself into one of the creatures of his dreams. He stares at Al with one eye, birdlike, and perches naked and motionless on the railing of his hospital bed. These scenes are contrasted with glimpses of the younger, happy-go-lucky Al, whose interests are girls and weight lifting, and the delicate, grinning Birdy, whose obsession has not yet drawn him away from human contact. Mr. Modine's performance is exceptionally sweet and graceful; Mr. Cage very sympathetically captures Al's urgency and frustration. Together, these actors work miracles with what might have been unplayable.

Mr. Parker has for the most part directed the film deftly and unobtrusively. Every so often, though, he introduces the kind of overstatement *Birdy* didn't need, as in a shot of Birdy lying Christlike on the floor of his hospital room. The disco music accompanying Birdy's first dream of flight, the adolescent sex scenes played bluntly for laughs, and the combative ending seem similarly unnecessary, as does the updating of the story from the World War II of the novel to the Vietnam era. Fortunately, the heavy-handedness is in limited supply. Most of *Birdy* is enchanting.

The film contains many brief but memorable vignettes, particularly those involving the boys' families; Sandy Baron is especially good as Al's blowhard father, and George Buck has a touching scene as Birdy's father, who works as a janitor at a school and is there cleaning bathrooms on the night his son attends a prom. In addition to its human players, *Birdy* has a large animal contingent, with some remarkable footage of canaries being hatched. To the extent that any film could translate Birdy's obsession into visual terms, this one has. Mr. Parker, in filling the film with animals and studying their motion without giving any of the canaries speaking lines (the book's Birdy has a winged "wife" who eventually begins talking to him), has been wise to leave well enough alone.

—*J.M., December 21, 1984*

BLACK NARCISSUS

Written, produced and directed by Michael Powell and Emeric Pressberger; based on the novel by Rumer Godden; cinematographer, Jack Cardiff; edited by Reginald Mills; music by Brian Easdale; released by Universal-International Pictures. Running time: 100 minutes.

With: Deborah Kerr (Sister Clodagh), Flora Robson (Sister Philippa), Jenny Laird (Sister Honey), Judith Furse (Sister Briony), Kathleen Byron (Sister Ruth), Esmond Knight (The Old General), Sabu (The Young General), David Farrar (Mr. Dean), Jean Simmons (Kanchi), May Hallatt (Angu Ayah), Eddie Whaley, Jr. (Joseph Anthony), Shaun Noble (Con), Nancy Roberts (Mother Dorothea) and Ley On (Phuba).

A curiously fascinating psychological study of the physical and spiritual tribulations that overwhelm five Protestant missionary nuns in the remote fastness of the Himalayas is unfolded with considerable dramatic emphasis in *Black Narcissus*. This English-made picture, presented yesterday by J. Arthur Rank and Universal-International at the Fulton Theatre in West Forty-sixth Street, is a work of rare pictorial beauty.

The awesome grandeur of the setting, a fantastic old palace perched on a mountainside 8,000 feet above the floor of India but still dwarfed by the snow-capped peaks of Kanchenjunga, is stunningly reflected in Technicolor. Indeed, the whole chromatic scheme of the picture is marvelous to behold, and the russet hues of sunset streaking through the dilapidated Palace of Mopu, where once wine flowed and harem ladies cavorted, is a brilliant achievement in color composition.

Michael Powell and Emeric Pressburger have come so close to executing a perfect fusion of all the elements of cinematic art—story, direction, performances, and photography—that one wishes they had hit upon a theme at once less controversial and more appealing than that of *Black Narcissus*. Not being familiar with Rumer Godden's novel, we don't know how closely the film adheres to its source. But that is of small consequence after all. What matters is that which they have imaged on celluloid, and that is an engrossing, provocative contemplation of the age-old conflict between the soul and the flesh.

Black Narcissus is a coldly intellectual morality drama tinged with a cynicism which has the effect of casting, as it were, a gratuitous reflection upon those who, regardless of sect, have forsaken worldly pleasures out of sheer religious devotion. This is so because the two dominant characters are basically frustrated women who seek solace in religion after unhappy romances.

One eventually is overcome by her desire for an agnostic Englishman who spurns her after she resigns from the Order of the Servants of Mary, a voluntary community of the Anglican Church. The triumph of the Sister Superior, who is known as Sister Clodagh, over worldly temptation is mitigated to a large extent by the ignoble failure of the mission at Mopu and the almost complete spiritual debilitation of the nuns as they journey back to the mother house in Calcutta.

If, as it appears, the intention of *Black Narcissus* is to demonstrate that religious zeal is dependent on suitable climatic and social surroundings, then history has already provided the answer to this thesis. All of the uncertainties that beset the nuns, who were invited by a beneficent potentate to establish a convent-school and hospital for his primitive people, are attributed to the barbaric magnificence of the country which, coupled with the high altitude and the constant, unnerving singing of the wind, produces deleterious physical and mental effects.

Black Narcissus is so brilliantly performed and expertly executed in the telling, however, that it holds one completely in its spell. Deborah Kerr is excellent as the overconfident, young Sister Superior who is humbled by adversities and eventually learns to serve the Order with her heart as well as her head, and Kathleen Byron plays the unfortunate Sister Ruth with a careful shading of emotion that bespeaks a talented artist. Hers is truly a magnificent performance. As Mr. Dean, the cynical British agent of the potentate, David Farrar combines a natural aptitude for acting with sturdy masculine features and the kind of physique that no doubt will send Hollywood agents scurrying after him.

While Messrs. Powell and Pressburger may have a picture that will disturb and antagonize some, they also have in *Black Narcissus* an artistic accomplishment of no small proportions.

—*T.M.P., August 14, 1947*

BLACK ORPHEUS

Directed by Marcel Camus; written (in Portuguese. with English subtitles) by Jacques Viot. based on the play *Orfeu da Conceicao* by Vinicius de Moraes; cinematographer. Jean Bourgoin: edited by Andree Feix. music by Antonio Carlos Jobim and Luiz Bonfa; produced by Sacha Gordine; released by Lopert Films. Running time: 100 minutes.

With: Breno Mello (Orpheus). Marpessa Dawn (Eurydice). Lourdes de Oliveira (Mira). Lea Garcia (Sarafina). Ademar Da Silva (Death). Alexandro Constantino (Hermes). Waldetar De Souza (Chico). Jorge Dos Santos (Benedito) and Aurino Cassanio (Zeca).

All tangled up in the madness of a Rio de Janeiro carnival, full of intoxicating samba music, frenzied dancing, and violent costumes, the Frenchman Marcel Camus presents us a melancholy tale in his color film, *Black Orpheus* (*Orfeu Negro*), which came to the Plaza yesterday.

It is a tragic story of a Negro chap and a Negro girl who meet at the time of the annual blowout, fall suddenly and rapturously in love, whirl through the night in a furious revel and fall off a cliff in the dawn. At least, the fellow falls off the cliff, holding the dead body of the girl in his arms. She has been killed the previous evening while trying to escape a scoundrel in a skeleton costume.

According to word from Paris and a somewhat involved program note, this samba drama is supposed to be based on the classic legend of Orpheus and Eurydice. Some parallels may be detected, but to us this seems an innocent conceit, unless you want to claim all sad love stories come from the same original source.

The parallels here are that Orpheus plays a guitar instead of a lute, his Eurydice is killed in fleeing a suitor and Orpheus goes to the morgue (instead of Hades) in search of her. Otherwise it is an arbitrary fable of love foiled in the midst of gaiety, not very well played by its main performers and therefore lacking in real emotional punch.

Breno Mello makes a handsome, virile Orpheus who glistens when covered with sweat, but he performs the role more as a dancer than as an actor trying to show a man in love. No real conviction of passion comes out of his furious posturing. A suspicion of affectation inevitably intrudes.

Conversely, the girl who plays Eurydice is an American dancer, Marpessa Dawn, and she conveys more forthright emotion than does the non-terpsichorean man. A pretty, frank face and a gentle manner that suggest absolute innocence gather an aura of wistfulness about her that filters down into a melancholy mood. This, at least, is appropriate and helpful for the accidental tragedy that ensues.

But it really is not the two lovers that are the focus of interest in this film; it is the music, the movement, the storm of color that go into the two-day festival. M. Camus has done a superb job of getting the documented look not only of the overall fandango but also of the buildup of momentum the day before.

He has got much more of a sense of turmoil in his minor characters—in the people surrounding the lovers and the wild, abandoned mobs in the streets. Lea Garcia is especially provoking as the loose-limbed cousin of the soft Eurydice, and Lourdes de Oliveira is lissome and wanton as the cast-off fiancée of Orpheus. Swarms of sinuous girls and children shimmy and race to the samba beat, which is insistent through most of the footage. That's what makes the picture alive.

Whether it proves what is concluded—that the poor are doomed to tragedy—is a point we strongly question. But it certainly does fill the ears and eyes.

The language spoken, incidentally, is Brazilian Portuguese, which is translated in English subtitles that completely lack the samba beat. A cat with a cool vocabulary should have been turned loose on them.

—*B.C., December 22, 1959*

BLACK ROBE

Directed by Bruce Beresford; written by Brian Moore, based on his novel; cinematographer, Peter James; edited by Tim Wellburn; music by Georges Delarue; production designer, Herbert Pinter; produced by Robert Lantos, Stephane Reichel and Sue Milliken; released by the Samuel Goldwyn Company. Running time: 100 minutes.

With: Lothaire Bluteau (Father Laforgue), Aden Young (Daniel), Sandrine Holt (Annuka), August Schellenberg (Chomina), Tantoo Cardinal (Wife of Chomina) and Frank Wilson (Father Jerome).

Of all the tales that make up the saga of France's seventeenth-century exploration and settlement of what was to be called Canada, one of the most heroic, brutal, and finally disastrous, is the story of the Huron Mission.

Founded and maintained by Jesuit priests at great cost in physical suffering to themselves and to the Hurons, the mission endured for two decades before it was abandoned in the early 1650's. The Jesuit plan had been to convert the stationary Huron tribes, whose members would then become missionaries to their nomadic Indian brothers.

The Hurons occupied the territories west of Lake Huron. They tolerated the proselytizing Jesuits without embracing them. They accepted the Christian faith whenever it was convenient and would later revert to their old ways.

The Jesuits developed their own tricks. They were not above surreptitiously baptizing a Huron baby while pretending to give it sips of sugared water. Epidemics, famine, and wars with the Iroquois eventually brought about the end of the mission and the end of the Huron nation. Piety backfired.

This epic story provides the background for Bruce Beresford's *Black Robe,* which opens today at the Beekman Theater.

Black Robe is no over-decorated, pumped-up boy's adventure yarn like *Dances with Wolves.* It is an attempt to find the drama in the confrontation of one Jesuit priest, full of burning faith but hopelessly naive, with both the horrors and the crude, atavistic splendors of the wilderness.

Young and well-born, the saintly Father Laforgue (Lothaire Bluteau) has come to New France to save the heathen and, if necessary, to become a martyr on behalf of God. His assignment: to make his way 1,500 miles west from the frontier town of Quebec to work at the newly established Huron Mission.

Most of the film is devoted to this journey, which begins with such high hopes in early autumn and ends in frozen midwinter, at what remains of the desolate mission. The film's subject is a grand one, but Mr. Beresford and Brian Moore, who adapted his own novel for the screen, never find a way to make Father Laforgue's spiritual journey as dramatic or photogenic as the physical one.

The movie was filmed entirely on spectacular Canadian locations, under weather conditions nearly as harsh as those that faced the early Jesuit missionaries. *Black Robe* looks great. The unspoiled majestic reaches of the Saguenay River stand in beautifully for those of the St. Lawrence nearly 350 years ago.

At the start of the journey, Father Laforgue's Algonquin escorts find him a figure of ridicule. After a dwarf Indian shaman joins the party, they begin to suspect that the Jesuit is some kind of devil.

The priest's self-assurance is not helped when his young French interpreter, Daniel (Aden Young), begins an affair with the pretty daughter of an Algonquin chief, who is also in the party. Father Laforgue, it seems, is himself subject to the desires of the flesh, which the Indians around him indulge at will without embarrassment.

There are also a mutiny and later the party's capture and torture by a band of Iroquois. A lot happens in the course of this journey, yet none of it is especially surprising or urgent. *Black Robe* has something of the manner of a series of dioramas in a museum of natural history.

The characters, as written and performed, are perfunctory functions of the plot. Mr. Bluteau, who played the title role in *Jesus of Montreal,* looks right as Father Laforgue, but the priest goes through the film simply responding to the world around him. He's a passive and rather wimpish figure instead of a hero-ically troubled one.

Yet *Black Robe* has its peripheral pleasures, which, because they are so seldom seen in movies, should not be underrated. It is historically authentic not only in its locations but also in the picture it gives of the conditions in which these people lived. Unlike the scenery, these conditions are not pretty.

As in *Dances with Wolves,* the Indians speak their own languages, translated by English subtitles that often are better than the English dialogue spoken by the French characters. "We'll cross that bridge when we come to it," says a priest early on when discussing the journey through the virgin wilderness to the Huron Mission.

—*V.C., October 30, 1991*

BLAZING SADDLES

Directed by Mel Brooks; written by Mr. Brooks, Norman Steinberg, Andrew Bergman, Richard Pryor and Alan Uger, based on a story by Mr. Bergman; director of photography, Joseph Biroc; edited by John C. Howard and Danford Greene; music by John Morris; production designer, Peter Wooley; produced by Michael Hertzberg; released by Warner Brothers. Running time: 93 minutes.

With: Cleavon Little (Bart), Gene Wilder (Jim), Mel Brooks (Governor Lepetomane/Indian Chief), Harvey Korman (Hedley Lamarr), Madeline Kahn (Lili Von Shtupp), Slim Pickens (Taggart), Dom DeLuise (Buddy Bizarre) and Alex Karras (Mongo).

Some film comedies, like Jacques Tati's *Playtime* and Woody Allen's *Sleeper,* stay with you after you've seen them. The humor, firmly rooted in the wilder contradictions of life, flourishes in the memory. Other comedies, like Mel Brooks's *Blazing Saddles,* the best title of the year to date, are like Chinese food. A couple of hours later you wonder where it went. You wonder why you laughed as consistently as you did.

Blazing Saddles, which opened yesterday at the Sutton Theater, is every Western you've ever seen turned upside down and inside out, braced with a lot of low burlesque, which is fine. In retrospect, however, one remembers along with the good gags the film's desperate, bone-crushing efforts to be funny. One remembers exhaustion, perhaps because you kept wanting it to be funnier than it was. Much of the laughter Mr. Brooks inspires is hopeful, before-the-gag laughter, which can be terribly tiring.

In short takes Mr. Brooks's comedy has rewarding shock, especially when he's being insulting or rude or when he is going too far in areas usually thought to be in bad taste. Throughout the film, Madeline Kahn does a marvelously unkind take-off on Marlene Dietrich, playing a dance-hall star named Lili von Shtupp who has a slight speech defect. When someone gives Lili a flower, she responds: "Oh, a wed wose! How womantic!" She also sings a song, "I'm Tired" (lyrics by Mr. Brooks), which lays waste for all time "Falling in Love Again."

The trouble is that *Blazing Saddles* has no real center of gravity. It has a story, something about a black sheriff (Cleavon Little) and his white sidekick (Gene Wilder) who save the town of Rock Ridge from land speculators, but as charming and funny as Mr. Little and Mr. Wilder are, the film's focus is split among the comic set pieces and the various eccentric supporting characters.

Some of these are very amusing in themselves: a bigoted preacher (Liam Dunn) who decries the fate of his town ("... our people scattered, our cattle raped ..."); a lecherous, near-sighted governor (Mr. Brooks), and a huge, beagle-brained desperado (Alex Karras) who has a fist fight with a horse.

The result of the film's short attention span is to make the smaller roles more effective than the larger ones. Harvey Korman, a gifted comic actor who is so fine as Carol Burnett's television costar, tries very hard to be funny as a crooked businessman and sometimes succeeds. But it's apparent that he's hard put to keep up with the movie's restless shifting from satire to parody to farce to blackout sketch.

Throughout *Blazing Saddles* I kept being reminded of *Sleeper,* both films being the work of men who had their first real successes as gag writers. Both worked for Sid Caesar, and both still appreciate the need for getting a joke to the audience fast and then moving on. However, *Sleeper* builds momentum through the continuing character played by Mr. Allen himself, and gives the impression of having been pared down to comic essentials.

Blazing Saddles has no dominant personality, and it looks as if it includes every gag thought up in every story conference. Whether good, bad, or mild, nothing was thrown out.

Mr. Allen's comedy, though very much a product of our Age of Analysis, recalls the wonder and discipline of people like Keaton and Laurel and Hardy. Mr. Brooks's sights are lower. His brashness is rare, but his use of anachronism and anarchy recalls not the great film comedies of the past, but the middling ones like the Hope-Crosby "Road" pictures. With his talent he should do much better than that.

—*V.C., February 8, 1974*

BLOODY SUNDAY

Written and directed by Paul Greengrass; director of photography, Ivan Strasburg; edited by Clare Douglas; music by Dominic Muldoon; production designer, John Paul Kelly; produced by Mark Redhead; released by Paramount Classics. Running time: 110 minutes.

With: James Nesbitt (Ivan Cooper), Tim Pigott-Smith (Maj. Gen. Robert Ford), Nicholas Farrell (Brigadier MacLellan), Gerard McSorley (Chief Supt. Lagan), Kathy Kiera Clarke (Frances), Allan Gildea (Kevin McCorry), Gerard Crossan (Eamonn McCann), Mary Mouldes (Bernadette Devlin) and Declan Duddy (Gerry Donaghy).

In the writer-director Paul Greengrass's magnetic and impassioned melodrama *Bloody Sunday,* the recreation of the 1972 outbreak of violence during a pro-I.R.A. civil-rights march in Londonderry, Northern Ireland, two contrasting points of view are presented immediately.

"In view of the adverse security situation in the province, all parades, processions and marches will be banned until further notice," maintains Maj. Gen. Robert Ford (Tim Pigott-Smith) of the British Army.

And the director frames the remarks of Ivan Cooper (James Nesbitt), a Protestant member of Parliament representing an Irish-Catholic district in Londonderry, as a response, though he's simply addressing his followers. "The British government have promised us reform, and all we've had is excuses and curfews," he says. (Later he says, "If we don't march, civil rights is dead in this city.")

The director presents the attitudes and the events leading to the horrible clash with a tense, self-aware propulsion—it's like a Brechtian newsreel. The opening alone is akin to guns being loaded and cocked—machinery readied for battle. The picture is dense with emotional and political conflict.

The director makes things move even faster by assembling it as a series of blackouts, and all the cuts build a charged thoughtfulness reminiscent of Costa-Gavras's *Z.* The level of accomplishment in the filmmaking is overwhelming, because in addition to the flash-cut boldness, it's an earthy epic like Gillo Pontecorvo's *Battle of Algiers.* For all the characters on screen, we can glimpse their hearts in their eyes.

Though the picture makes attempts at balance, it would be a mistake to say it has the even-handedness of a down-the-middle docudrama, because *Sunday* is clearly on the side of the 15,000 Irish-Catholic demonstrators who turned out to make a nonviolent point about their grievances at what they saw as discrimination by the Protestant majority in the Ulster Government. The real-life tragedy is that this was an occasion fated to be taken over by violence given the historical circumstances.

Mr. Greengrass's instincts led him to stage *Sunday* as a polemical version of *Romeo and Juliet,* with the underlying politics occupying the foreground. Gerry Donaghy (Declan Duddy), a teenager who hangs with a tough crowd and has been arrested for rioting previously, is in a romance with a Protestant girl, underscoring his homage to Shakespeare.

It's never a good sign in the movies when a crowd breaks into "We Shall Overcome," and the harsh, angry rendition by Cooper's marchers on the eve of the demonstration seals our awareness of imminent pain. The dramatic scheme of *Sunday,* which will be shown today and tomorrow at the Lincoln Center Film Festival and opens in New York on Friday, is established with deft simplicity, but the movie doesn't oversimplify the conflicts.

The anxious, energetic Cooper is constantly detoxifying squabbles between citizens and the police. Playing him, Mr. Nesbitt doesn't overdo the warm empathetic demeanor, either; his gaunt, gray face makes him a man-of-the-soil peacemaker.

Mr. Greengrass has an instinctive filmmaker's temperament—he invites the audience into the action with rolling, vertiginous hand-held camera movements. We run along with the action, and the moments of stillness provide only an uneasy quiet. It's impossible to see *Bloody Sunday* and not be reminded of the American civil-rights struggle, if only because the picture has subtly infused Cooper's behavior with gestures and nuances from his chief influence, the Rev. Dr. Martin Luther King Jr.

The paratroopers assigned to the area were untrained for their policing duties and were already in the midst of a volatile situation. They are as determined as Cooper, though their compasses have another setting, calling the Irish hooligans with a sneering disdain. Their paternalism is a little coarse. Dialogue by their leaders like "Tell the lads we want plenty of arrests today" is a challenge begging to be answered with violence.

"You will reap a whirlwind," Cooper says after the shooting has subsided and the body count of victims climbs—13 unarmed civilian marchers were killed when the British opened fire. And by the end, the depth of Greengrass's artistry is plain: he's made a movie called *Bloody Sunday* and kept the color red muted because the film is also about the rush of blood in the head that leads to violence.

—*E.M., October 2, 2002*

BLOW-UP

Directed by Michelangelo Antonioni; written by Mr. Antonioni, Tonino Guerra and Edward Bond, based on a story by Julio Cortázar; cinematographer, Carlo Di Palma; edited by Frank Clarke; music by Herbie Hancock and The Yardbirds; produced by Pierre Rouve and Carlo Ponti; released by Premier Pictures. Running time: 110 minutes.

With: David Hemmings (Thomas), Vanessa Redgrave (Jane), Sarah Miles (Patricia) and Verushka, Jill Kennington, Peggy Moffit, Rosaleen Murray, Ann Norman and Melanie Hampshire (Models).

It will be a crying shame if the audience that will undoubtedly be attracted to Michelangelo Antonioni's *Blow-Up* because it has been denied a Production Code seal goes looking more for sensual titillation than for the good, solid substance it contains—and therefore will be distracted from recognizing the magnitude of its forest by paying attention to the comparatively few defoliated trees.

This is a fascinating picture, which has something real to say about the matter of personal involvement and emotional commitment in a jazzed-up, media-hooked-in world so cluttered with synthetic stimulations that natural feelings are overwhelmed. It is vintage Antonioni fortified with a Hitchcock twist, and it is beautifully photographed in color. It opened at the Coronet last night.

It marks a long step for Mr. Antonioni, the Italian director whose style of introspective visualization has featured in all his Italian-language films from *L'Avventura* through *Red Desert,* and in all of which Monica Vitti has played what has amounted to a homogeneous gallery of alienated female roles. It is his first film in eight years without Miss Vitti. It is his first major film about a man. And it is his first film made in England and in English (except for one vagrant episode in his three-part *I Vinti,* made in 1952).

The fellow whose restlessness and groping interests Mr. Antonioni in this new film is a dizzyingly swinging and stylish freelance magazine photographer, whose racing and tearing around London gives a terrifying hint of mania. He can spend a night dressed up like a hobo shooting a layout of stark photographs of derelicts in a flophouse, then jump into his Rolls-Royce open-top and race back to his studio to shoot a layout of fashion models in shiny mod costumes—and do it without changing expression or his filthy, tattered clothes.

He can break off from this preoccupation and go tearing across the city in his car to buy an antique airplane propeller in a junk shop, with virtually the same degree of casualness and whim as he shows when he breaks off from concentrating on a crucial job in his darkroom to have a brief, orgiastic romp with a couple of silly teenage girls.

Everything about this feral fellow is footloose, arrogant, fierce, signifying a tiger—or an incongruously baby-faced lone wolf—stalking his prey in a society for which he seems to have no more concern, no more feeling or understanding than he has for the equipment and props he impulsively breaks. His only identification is with the camera, that trenchant mechanism with which he makes images and graphic fabrications of—what? Truth or Fantasy?

This is what gets him into trouble. One day, while strolling in a park, he makes some candid snaps of a young woman romancing with a man. The young woman, startled, tries to get him to give the unexposed roll of film to her. So nervous and anxious is she that she follows him to his studio. There, because she is fascinated by him and also in order to get the film, she submits to his arrogant seduction and goes away with a roll of film.

But it is not the right roll. He has tricked her, out of idle curiosity, it appears, as to why the girl should be so anxious. How is she involved?

When he develops the right roll and is casually studying the contact prints, he suddenly notices something. (Here comes the Hitchcock twist!) What is that there in the bushes, a few feet away from where the embracing couple are? He starts making blowups of the pictures, switching them around, studying the blow-ups with a magnifying glass. Is it a hand pointing a gun?

There, that is all I'm going to tell you about this uncommon shot of plot into an Antonioni picture—this flash of melodramatic mystery that suddenly presents our fellow with an involvement that should tightly challenge him. I will only say that it allows Mr. Antonioni to find a proper, rueful climax for this theme.

One may have reservations toward this picture. It is redundant and long. There are the usual Antonioni passages of seemingly endless wanderings. The interest may be too much concentrated in the one character, and the symbolistic conclusions may be too romantic for the mood.

It is still a stunning picture—beautifully built up with glowing images and color compositions that get us into the feelings of our man and into the characteristics of the mod world in which he dwells. There is even exciting vitality in the routine business of his using photographs—prints and blow-ups and superimpositions—to bring a thought, a preconception, alive.

And the performing is excellent. David Hemmings as the chap is completely fascinating—languid, self-indulgent, cool, yet expressive of so much frustration. He looks remarkably like Terence Stamp. Vanessa Redgrave is pliant and elusive, seductive yet remote as the girl who has been snapped in the park and is willing to reveal so much—and yet so little—of herself.

And Sarah Miles is an interesting suggestion of an empty emotion in a small role.

How a picture as meaningful as this one could be blackballed is hard to understand. Perhaps it is because it is too candid, too uncomfortably disturbing, about the dehumanizing potential of photography.

—B.C., December 19, 1966

BLUE COLLAR

Directed by Paul Schrader; written by Paul Schrader and Leonard Schrader, based on material by Sydney A. Glass; director of photography, Bobby Byrne; edited by Tom Rolf; music by Jack Nitzche; produced by Ron Guest; released by Universal Pictures. Running time: 110 minutes.

With: Richard Pryor (Zeke), Harvey Keitel (Harry), Yaphet Kotto (Smokey), Ed Begley Jr. (Bobby Joe), Harry Bellaver (Eddie Johnson), George Memmoli (Jenkens) and Lucy Saroyan (Arlene Bartowski).

Blue Collar, directed by Paul Schrader and written by him and his brother Leonard, is a film about which you are likely to have very mixed feelings. It is a sort of poor man's *On the Waterfront,* a movie that simply—often primitively—describes corruption in a Detroit auto workers' local with-out ever making the corruption a matter of conscience. Corruption is there. It exists. It's part of the system.

This emphasis on inevitability, which is one step away from complete passivity, may be the essential difference between a certain kind of pop culture today and that of the mid-fifties when Elia Kazan made his furious, idealized film about crooked locals on New York piers. The Kazan film dramatized one man's fight against corruption and made a hero of a fellow brave enough to testify before a crime commission.

At the end of *Blue Collar* we see a man more or less cornered into turning state's evidence. His testimony probably won't do any good. The movie even implies that his decision to testify may make him an unwitting tool of the system. His fate isn't especially tragic. It's a pop tune with a big beat.

At least, this is the way I reacted to *Blue Collar,* which opens today at three theaters. *Blue Collar* is the first film to be directed by Mr. Schrader, who was one of Hollywood's hottest young writers even before the appearance of *The Yakuza,* his first screenplay to be filmed. Since then he has been represented by *Taxi Driver, Obsession,* and *Rolling Thunder,* all movies containing a lot of highly cinematic violence and a certain amount of intellectual confusion. Is *Blue Collar* an action film or a meditation upon the American Dream? I suspect it wants to be both though it's not very serious at being either.

The movie is at its best in describing the quality of the day-to-day life of its three leading characters— Zeke (Richard Pryor), Jerry (Harvey Keitel), and Smokey (Yaphet Kotto), friends who work together on the assembly line at the automobile plant. Zeke, who is married, is irrepressibly rude and in debt to the Internal Revenue Service for claiming six children instead of his actual three. Jerry, also married, also is in debt and works two jobs to make ends meet. Smokey is the sophisticated one. An ex-con and a bachelor, he throws parties that he imagines Playboy would admire. All three work nonstop to afford the material comforts they've been told they deserve. Each in his own way is a very angry man.

Where *Blue Collar* starts to go awry is in its melodramatic plotting that has the three friends attempting to rob their union headquarters. Instead of a large amount of cash, they find a ledger that records the details of the union's loan-sharking activities. When they attempt to use this information as blackmail, the results are predictably disastrous—for the friends and for the movie that otherwise shows us a kind of existence seldom accurately depicted on the screen.

Everything in the characters' private lives looks right, from the pictures on the walls (and stuck into the corners of mirrors), to their color television sets, plastic slipcovers, and bowling costumes. You suspect that each item was bought yesterday on time and will be worn out tomorrow before the payments are completed.

The performances are excellent. Mr. Keitel's Jerry is all itchy ignorance, baffled by the circumstances in which he finds himself wanting to do the right thing but having no idea of what that is. Mr. Kotto's Smokey appears to be as much a matter of his sheer presence as it is of his cool, self-assured performance.

The center of the film, however, is Mr. Pryor who,

in *Blue Collar,* has a role that for the first time makes use of the wit and fury that distinguish his straight comedy routines. It's a sneakily funny performance right up to the film's angry, freeze-frame ending, which by this time is a mannerism that almost any film could do without.

Mr. Schrader's decision to use that freeze-frame calls attention to the phoniness that haunts the film at other moments. The scene in which a fussy I.R.S. man calls on Mr. Pryor is funny, but do I.R.S. men often make house calls at night? If the television programs that Mr. Keitel's family watches are always black programs, how did something like *Rhoda* become so popular? I'd even question whether the Keitel character, given the probable prejudices of a man in his position, would have two blacks as his only friends.

The movie, which is so accurate in other ways, manipulates life to create the sort of idealized, color-balanced reality we are force-fed by television.

—V.C., February 10, 1978

BLUE VELVET

Written and directed by David Lynch; director of photography. Frederick Elmes; edited by Duwayne Dunham; music by Angelo Badalamenti; production designer. Patricia Norris; produced by Fred Caruso; released by De Laurentiis Entertainment Group. Black and white. Running time: 120 minutes

With: Kyle MacLachlan (Jeffrey Beaumont). Isabella Rossellini (Dorothy Vallens). Dennis Hopper (Frank Booth). Laura Dern (Sandy Williams). Hope Lange (Mrs. Williams). Dean Stockwell (Ben). George Dickerson (Detective Williams). Priscilla Pointer (Mrs. Beaumont). Frances Bay (Aunt Barbara) and Jack Harvey (Mr. Beaumont).

Other directors labor long and hard to achieve the fevered perversity that comes so naturally to David Lynch, whose *Blue Velvet* is an instant cult classic. With *Eraserhead, The Elephant Man,* and *Dune* to his credit, Mr. Lynch had already established his beachhead inside the realm of the bizarre, but this latest venture takes him a lot further. Kinkiness is its salient quality, but *Blue Velvet* has deadpan humor too, as well as a straight-arrow side that makes its eccentricity all the crazier. There's no mistaking the exhilarating fact that it's one of a kind.

Blue Velvet, which opens today at the Baronet and other theaters, has a brilliant introductory sequence that sets the tone for the best of what will follow, and goes a long way toward excusing the worst of it. The place is Anywhere, U.S.A., or actually a place called Lumberton, where the local radio station devotes a lot of energy to log-related humor. (It is, among other things, "the town that *knows* how much wood a woodchuck chucks," and a place where the sound of the falling timber tells you the time.)

With Bobby Vinton on the soundtrack, Mr. Lynch presents the blue skies, trim flowerbeds, and sweet little houses of a suburbia so perfect that it looks surreal. It is surreal, but its surface is hardly impermeable. Mr. Lynch makes that clear almost immediately, by letting the camera dip down through a neat, weedless lawn, past a homeowner who has just had an apparent seizure, to observe the teeming hordes of insects living in the dirt.

Figuratively speaking, the film means to remain at bug's-eye level for nearly two hours, until it is ready to return to the surface for an ironically sunny coda. And if the sheer creepiness of that first descent seems a hard act to follow, Mr. Lynch is more than up to the challenge. Once the film's hero, Jeffrey Beaumont (Kyle MacLachlan), discovers a severed ear lying in the tall grass and begins tracing its origin, *Blue Velvet* begins ricocheting from one weird episode to another, propelled by the logic of a bad dream. These forays seem to grow even longer and stranger as the film progresses. *Blue Velvet* is overloaded with the kinds of piquant little details that would stand up nicely to the repeat viewings it will undoubtedly receive. When it comes to the larger points that might give its plot some semblance of rationality, though, it is sorely—and maybe even deliberately—lacking.

The ear, in brief, leads to a detective (George Dickerson) and his pretty, inquisitive daughter, Sandy (Laura Dern, who's as demure as Nancy Drew), who tells Jeffrey she "hears things—bits and pieces" about the severed article. Together, Sandy and Jeffrey trace matters to a torchy singer named Dorothy Vallens (Isabella Rossellini) who becomes the sweet, blond Sandy's erotic opposite in Jeffrey's imagination. Following Dorothy home to the Deep River Apartments, Jeffrey is, in the film's most startling extended episode, drawn into voyeurism, sadomasochism, and the unexplored dark side of his own character. In this sequence, he watches Miss Rossellini's Dorothy be tormented by the inimitable Dennis Hopper, who plays the most abusive, frightening psycho of his screen career. And that's really saying something.

Mr. Hopper and Miss Rossellini are so far outside the bounds of ordinary acting here that their performances are best understood in terms of sheer lack of inhibition; both give themselves entirely over to the material, which seems to be exactly what's called for. Both Miss Dern and Mr. MacLachlan—the *Dune* star who is the straight man of the piece, and resembles a young Robert Vaughn—do a fine job in a more controlled, normal mode that in its own way seems equally demented. The cinematography, by Frederick Elmes, has a constant edge, in both its exaggeratedly sunny stages and its murky ones.

For those with the temerity to follow it anywhere, *Blue Velvet* is as fascinating as it is freakish. It confirms Mr. Lynch's stature as an innovator, a superb technician, and someone best not encountered in a dark alley.

—*J.M., September 19, 1986*

BOB & CAROL & TED & ALICE

Directed by Paul Mazursky; written by Mr. Mazursky and Larry Tucker; director of photography, Charles Lang; music by Quincy Jones; produced by Mr. Tucker; released by Columbia Pictures. Running time: 104 minutes.

With: Natalie Wood (Carol), Robert Culp (Bob), Elliott Gould (Ted), Dyan Cannon (Alice), Horst Ebersberg (Horst), Lee Bergere (Emilio) and Donald Muhich (Psychiatrist).

Bob & Carol & Ted & Alice, a conventional comedy about the new morality, told in terms of the old, manages to be offensive for the least stimulating of reasons. It's not the occasional nudity (the breasts of some female extras, Natalie Wood's back, so thin and vulnerable from neck to coccyx), not the scenes of enlightened adultery, which actually are quite funny.

Rather, the movie is unpleasant because it acts superior to the people in it, which is no great feat because Bob and Carol and Ted and Alice are conceived as cheerful but humorless boobs, no more equipped to deal with their sexual liberation than Lucy and Desi and Ozzie and Harriet.

The movie, which will have a regular theatrical engagement here starting October 8, was shown twice last night at Lincoln Center's new Alice Tully Hall to open the seventh New York Film Festival.

I can't possibly imagine why the festival saw fit to program a film that is already assured of wide commercial release and, I would predict, of certain popularity. I've always assumed that one of the festival's principal purposes is to call attention to the work—by either new or established directors—that for various reasons might otherwise be missed in the commercial market. The festival has also, quite honorably, given valuable time and space to important works of the past that cast light on the present.

If *Bob & Carol & Ted & Alice* has any purpose in the festival, it is to show contemporary Hollywood's debt to television—to TV's comedy formulas, to its money, which has helped the major film companies survive, and to television's way of reassuring a mythical American middle class that its manners and morals are not becoming as unstuck as they seem in movies like *Alice's Restaurant* and *Easy Rider*.

Bob & Carol & Ted & Alice is the first directorial effort of Paul Mazursky, who also wrote the screenplay with Larry Tucker. The Mazursky-Tucker team, which originated when both were members of the Second City improvisational troupe, graduated from the Danny Kaye TV show, which they wrote for four years, to feature films this year with the screenplay for *I Love You, Alice B. Toklas.*

What they do—that is, knocking down straw men that already lean at a fearful tilt—they do well. The new film, set in that now familiar drive-in paradise, southern California, concerns two couples. One couple, Bob and Carol (Robert Culp and Natalie Wood), is grotesquely hip as only a middle-aged couple that has found love in pot and instant therapy can be.

Their best friends, Ted and Alice (Elliott Gould and Dyan Cannon), are somewhat more square and are aghast when, one night, Carol confides ecstatically that Bob has had an affair in San Francisco and loves her, Carol, so much, that he could tell her about it.

Ted is appalled that Bob should have talked; Alice is numb at the mere thought of the infidelity.

It isn't long, however, before Ted and Alice are making their own experiments that, in turn, progress to formal wife swapping. If you know your TV situation comedies, you probably have a pretty good idea how it all cops out. Mazursky and Tucker have updated the sort of wife versus husband confrontation in which thirty years ago Irene Dunne, to make Cary Grant jealous, used to simulate an affair with Ralph Bellamy. The only difference is that there's no need for simulation now that movies are playing the rating game.

Considering the limited range of material that relies on gags more than wit, the movie is decently performed, especially by Gould and Miss Cannon. Gould, whom I did not see in *The Night They Raided Minsky's,* registers just the proper amount of intellectual density to be very funny as the sort of man who'd wear his stretch socks to a group assignation. Miss Cannon delivers one of the film's really genuine moments in a disastrous, slip-filled session with a psychiatrist who, for once, is not played as a fool, although he is supremely, and hilariously, unflappable.

Mazursky's direction is straight, routine Hollywood, not at all personal, with the usual, obligatory, self-conscious helicopter shots, one love scene in a bathroom photographed—for no particular reason—from the ceiling, as if the camera had the eye of a temporarily liberated canary, and some not very sensual slow motion footage.

If this festival were being held in an otherwise movieless limbo, such as Anguilla, *Bob & Carol & Ted & Alice* might conceivably demand our attention. In a city as thoroughly saturated with movies and television as is New York, its presence in a film festival is simply an indulgence. Meanwhile, on to Bresson, Bergman, and von Stroheim, and even an antifilm by Godard.

—*V.C., September 17, 1969*

BOB LE FLAMBEUR

Written (in French, with English subtitles), directed and produced by Jean-Pierre Melville; director of photography, Henri Decae; edited by Monique Bonnot; production design by Claude Bouxin; music by Eddie Barclay; released by Triumph Releasing. Running time: 98 minutes.

With: Isabelle Corey (Anne). Daniel Cauchy (Paolo). Roger Duchesne (Bob Montagn). Guy Decomble (Inspector Ledru). André Garret (Roger). Gérard Buhr (Marc). Claude Cerval (Jean). Colette Fleury (Jean's wife). Simone Paris (Yvonne) and Howard Vernon (McKimmie).

Because the films of the late Jean-Pierre Melville, the French director whose spare, ironic work was much admired by the members of the Nouvelle Vague, are largely unknown in this country, his *Bob le Flambeur* (Bob the Gambler) should turn out to be one of the more delightful surprises of the New York Film Festival. The 1956 film, a festival retrospective selection, will be shown today in Alice Tully Hall at 12:30 P.M.

I've seen only three other Melville films—his version of Jean Cocteau's *Les Enfants Terribles* (originally released here as *The Strange Ones* in 1952) and two "policiers," *L'Aine des Ferchaux,* shown at the first New York Film Festival in 1963 as *Magnet of Doom,* and *Le Samourai,* released here in 1972 as *The Godson.*

That's scarcely enough material on which to base any important assumptions, especially because *Les Enfants Terribles* owes as much to Cocteau as to Melville, who died in 1972.

Melville's affection for American gangster movies may have never been as engagingly and wittily demonstrated as in *Bob le Flambeur,* which was only the director's fourth film, made before he had access to the bigger budgets and the bigger stars (Jean-Paul Belmondo, Alain Delon) of his later pictures.

It's a seemingly deadpan narrative about an incredibly cool, no longer young Paris gambler Bob Montagne (Roger Duchesne), a reformed bank robber who slouches around Pigalle in a Jean Gabin wardrobe (trenchcoat, fedora) making and losing pots of money in backroom card games, being kind to hookers and unkind only to pimps. Bob has his code. He lends money to barmaids, acts as the kindly, wise, surrogate father to the son of one of his comrades killed in a failed bank job and is, usually, the prince of all he sees. He's even much admired by a police inspector whose life he saved during a holdup.

Though *Bob le Flambeur* looks sober enough at the start, what with the grainy black-and-white photography and the expressionless voice-over narration (by Melville) describing a typical Montmartre dawn, it soon becomes apparent that Melville is sending up the ordinary conventions of the hood-picture.

The pretty young thing from the country, a girl named Anne (Isabelle Corey), who offers herself to Bob but is protected by him instead, is only too eager to slip into a life of depravity. Bob is superstitious, like all gamblers, but his superstitions never work out the way they're supposed to in movies.

The major part of the film is about Bob's carefully detailed attempt to make one last grand heist, the robbery of the safe in the Deauville Casino, a job that requires major financial backing and a gang big enough to occupy all of Brittany. Because at least half of Paris, including the police, are aware of what Bob is up to, the heist doesn't come off exactly as planned, but the heist is not a total failure.

Bob le Flambeur is a very funny, jaunty movie, and one can understand why Jean-Luc Godard, who was to make *Breathless* just three years later, admired it so much. Its realism is not the reality of life, but of the kind of movies that give shape to the disordered lives of the people who watch movies. Miss Corey is charming and Mr. Duchesne is nearly perfect, moving through his underworld with the sort of tacky élan that defines his morality.

—*V.C., September 26, 1981*

BODY HEAT

Written and directed by Lawrence Kasdan: director of photography. Richard H. Kline: edited by Carol Littleton: music by John Barry: produced by Fred T. Gallo: released by Warner Brothers. Running time: 113 minutes.

With: William Hurt (Ned Racine). Kathleen Turner (Matty Walker). Richard Crenna (Edmund Walker). Ted Danson (Peter Lowenstein). J. A. Preston (Oscar Grace). Mickey Rourke (Teddy Lewis). Kim Zimmer (Mary Ann) and Jane Hallaren (Stella).

Everything's just a little askew. Pretty soon people start thinking the old rules are no longer in effect." A character says that in *Body Heat,* though in this movie the old rules are the only ones that matter. Those rules—which say the world is a sultry, shadowy place full of characters motivated solely by lust and greed—have little to do with anything lifelike, and everything to do with the 1940's film noir classics from which *Body Heat* is skillfully, though slavishly, derived.

They don't make movies like that anymore—but oh, how they try. *Body Heat,* which opens today at the Loews State and other theaters, can lay some claim to a textbook perfection. Lawrence Kasdan, who wrote and directed the film, has learned the lessons of *Double Indemnity* and *The Postman Always Rings Twice* very well. And he hasn't confined himself strictly to the conventions of his material. While *Body Heat* involves murder, fraud, a weak hero led astray, and a seductive, double-dealing broad, it also incorporates something new: a sexual explicitness that the old films could only hint at.

When Ned Racine (William Hurt), the libidinous, slightly down-at-the-heels lawyer, who is the movie's hero, meets Matty Walker, she drives him wild. Matty (Kathleen Turner) is a rich and unhappily married beauty in a clinging white dress, and she means to arouse in Ned a sexual longing so powerful it will make him absolutely ruthless. When characters in forties movies experienced such lust, their passions were revealed to the audience only in oblique ways. But these are modern times.

Ned and Matty embark upon a sexual tryst that might be powerfully erotic were Mr. Kasdan not so concerned with his characters' posing. Their postures suggest what Ned and Matty may have been up to, and their dialogue is full of bold (Matty's) and more sly (Ned's) sexual patter. But most of the lovemaking is a matter of either promises or memories. Ned is seen breaking down a door to get to Matty, but there's barely so much as a memorable kiss on camera.

If there were any other chemistry at work between Ned and Matty, perhaps that wouldn't matter so. But sex is all-important to *Body Heat,* as its title may indicate. And beyond that there isn't much to move the story along or to draw these characters together. A great deal of the distance between them can be attributed to the performance of Miss Turner, who looks like the quintessential forties siren, but sounds like the soap-opera actress she is. Miss Turner keeps her chin high in the air, speaks in a perfect monotone, and never seems to move from the position in which Mr. Kasdan has left her. Yet her allure is supposed to be the magnet that leads Ned away from the straight and narrow.

Because Mr. Kasdan relies as heavily upon old-movie motives as he does upon old-movie wooden blinds and headlights seen through fog, his story is quite implausible on its own terms. Matty's selfishness might have a certain wicked grandeur if it came from Barbara Stanwyck, but coming from Miss Turner it just seems silly. So does Ned's fatal weakness, although Mr. Hurt does a wonderful job of bringing Ned to life. Once again, Mr. Hurt establishes himself as an instantly affable screen star, an actor who combines some of Dustin Hoffman's best qualities with some of Jeff Bridges's. He seems thoughtful, wry, and funny, yet he has a comfortable physical presence, too, and a friendliness that's uncomplicatedly disarming. As played by Mr. Hurt, Ned may not be the good-hearted fall guy the screenplay is about, but he's a likable enough leading character to hold the film together.

Mr. Kasdan demonstrates enough talent and thoroughness to breathe life into sections of the movie, particularly those parts that don't involve Miss Turner, who can deliver a line like "I love you and I need you and I want you forever" with perhaps less conviction than it has ever been delivered before. Mr. Hurt's key scene with Richard Crenna, as Miss Turner's very unwanted husband, is staged with unexpected energy, as are Mr. Hurt's encounters with a young hood (Mickey Rourke) and two buddies (Ted Danson and J. A. Preston).

Mr. Danson, as a lawyer, does the same little soft-shoe dance on several different occasions, and he is also established, rather pointedly, as virtually the only character in the movie who doesn't smoke. Matty, on the other hand, has a body temperature several degrees higher than normal and likes to wear red. Ned, whose life may go up in smoke, is first seen watching a fire, and he has a predilection for women in uniform. These are the kinds of touches an audience either loves or hates. But no audience ever finds them as interesting as the director who's seen fit to include them.

—*J.M., August 28, 1981*

BONNIE AND CLYDE

Directed by Arthur Penn: written by David Newman and Robert Benton: director of photography.

Burnett Guffey; edited by Dede Allen; music by Charles Strouse; art designer, Dean Tavoularis; produced by Warren Beatty; released by Warner Brothers. Running time: 111 minutes.

With: Warren Beatty (Clyde Barrow), Faye Dunaway (Bonnie Parker), Michael J. Pollard (C.W. Moss), Gene Hackman (Buck Barrow), Estelle Parsons (Blanche), Denver Pyle (Frank Hamer), Dub Taylor (Ivan Moss), Evans Evans (Velma Davis) and Gene Wilder (Eugene Grizzard).

A raw and unmitigated campaign of sheer press-agentry has been trying to put across the notion that Warner Brothers' *Bonnie and Clyde* is a faithful representation of the desperado careers of Clyde Barrow and Bonnie Parker, a notorious team of bank robbers and killers who roamed Texas and Oklahoma in the post-Depression years.

It is nothing of the sort. It is a cheap piece of bald-faced slapstick comedy that treats the hideous depredations of that sleazy, moronic pair as though they were as full of fun and frolic as the jazz-age cutups in *Thoroughly Modern Millie*. And it puts forth Warren Beatty and Faye Dunaway in the leading roles, and Michael J. Pollard as their sidekick, a simpering, nose-picking rube, as though they were striving mightily to be the Beverly Hillbillies of next year.

It has Mr. Beatty clowning broadly as the killer who fondles various types of guns with as much nonchalance and dispassion as he airily twirls a big cigar, and it has Miss Dunaway squirming grossly as his thrill-seeking, sex-starved moll. It is loaded with farcical holdups, screaming chases in stolen getaway cars that have the antique appearance and speeded-up movement of the clumsy vehicles of the Keystone Kops, and indications of the impotence of Barrow, until Bonnie writes a poem about him to extol his prowess, that are as ludicrous as they are crude.

Such ridiculous, camp-tinctured travesties of the kind of people these desperados were and of the way people lived in the dusty Southwest back in those barren years might be passed off as candidly commercial movie comedy, nothing more, if the film weren't reddened with blotches of violence of the most grisly sort.

Arthur Penn, the aggressive director, has evidently gone out of his way to splash the comedy holdups with smears of vivid blood as astonished people are machine-gunned. And he has staged the terminal scene of the ambuscading and killing of Barrow and Bonnie by a posse of policemen with as much noise and gore as is in the climax of *The St. Valentine's Day Massacre*.

This blending of farce with brutal killings is as pointless as it is lacking in taste, since it makes no valid commentary upon the already travestied truth. And it leaves an astonished critic wondering just what purpose Mr. Penn and Mr. Beatty think they serve with this strangely antique, sentimental claptrap, which opened yesterday at the Forum and the Murray Hill.

This is the film that opened the Montreal International Festival!

—B.C., April 14, 1967

BOOGIE NIGHTS

Written and directed by Paul Thomas Anderson; director of photography, Robert Elswitt; edited by Dylan Tichenor; music by Michael Penn; production designer, Bob Ziembicki; produced by Lloyd Levin, John Lyons, Mr. Anderson and Joanne Sellar; released by New Line Cinema. Running time: 152 minutes.

With: Mark Wahlberg (Dirk Diggler), Julianne Moore (Amber Waves), Burt Reynolds (Jack Horner), Don Cheadle (Buck Swope), John C. Reilly (Reed Rothchild), William H. Macy (Little Bill), Robert Ridgely (The Colonel), Ricky Jay (Kurt Longjohn), Philip Seymour Hoffman (Scotty) and Alfred Molina (Rahad Jackson).

Everything about *Boogie Nights* is interestingly unexpected, even the few seconds of darkness before the film's neon title blasts onto the screen. The director, Paul Thomas Anderson, whose display of talent is as big and exuberant as skywriting, seems to mean this as a way of telling viewers to brace themselves. Good advice.

Some of the most distinctive American films of recent years—*Pulp Fiction, The People vs. Larry Flynt, L.A. Confidential,* and now this one—have invoked a sleaze-soaked Southern California as an evilly alluring nexus of decadence and pop culture. *Boogie Nights* further ratchets up the raunchiness by taking porn movies and drug problems entirely for granted, and by fondly embracing a collection of characters who do the same.

The film's unofficial family group is immersed in exploitation movies, which becomes the same collective eccentricity that country music was for *Nashville.* Mr. Anderson, who begins his film spectacularly with a version of the great Copacabana shot from *Goodfellas,* has no qualms about borrowing from the best.

As the camera roams with incredible agility through a disco in the San Fernando Valley (in a long, bravura shot that Mr. Anderson apparently rehearsed and filmed in a single night), the movie introduces all of its major characters with thrilling ease. The godfather of this motley group is Jack Horner, porn auteur. ("Before you turn around you've spent maybe 20, 25, 30 thousand dollars on a movie!") Burt Reynolds rises to this occasion by giving his best and most suavely funny performance in many years. Like Jerry Lewis in *The King of Comedy,* he gives the role an extra edge by playing a swaggering, self-important figure very close to the bone.

In the disco on that first night, Jack's eyes alight on a busboy named Eddie, whom he pronounces "a seventeen-year-old piece of gold." Eddie, who has already learned to peddle himself to $10 customers, will soon become Jack's new star, thanks to his exceptional anatomy, about which he says, "Everyone's blessed with one special thing."

The movie's special gift happens to be Mark Wahlberg, who gives a terrifically appealing performance in this tricky role. Mr. Wahlberg must do many things here: attract all the film's other characters, rise credibly from naive kid to arrogant cokehead, behave as if he thinks Dirk Diggler (Eddie's nom de porn) is a really grand name. He does all this with captivating ingenuousness and not a single false move.

Eddie's room in his parents' unhappy home is covered with posters: bathing beauties, sports cars, martial arts, all the elements of his particular American dream. The movie's first hour watches him attain all this during the course of a hot, meteoric rise. Mr. Anderson has great fun with the mundaneness of his porn filmmakers, who remain unflappable almost all of the time, except for when they first see Eddie take off his pants.

Boogie Nights doesn't depict much nudity or sex (except during a lengthy sequence showing Eddie's first movie scene), but does make its point with sly, expert reaction shots of crew members watching Eddie, um, act. Among his colleagues: Julianne Moore, wonderful as the vaguely lost soul whom Jack has transformed into a porn queen (her studiously bad acting in moviemaking scenes is perfect); Don Cheadle as the aspiring cowboy who is much too nice for porn stardom; William H. Macy, in a wig borrowed from the Partridge Family, as the crew member whose wife enjoys embarrassing him most unmistakably; Philip Seymour Hoffman as Eddie's most ardent admirer; Robert Ridgely as the shady financier who, like Jack Horner, is so discreetly excited by young talent; Ricky Jay as the unflappable cameraman; and John C. Reilly as Eddie's main sidekick in this wild new world.

Mr. Reilly had a major role in *Hard Eight,* the twenty-seven-year-old director's only previous feature, which was slow and stagy in ways that gave no inkling of this. The film, which begins in 1977 (just in time for a dancing *Saturday Night Fever* homage), casually incorporates such milestones as Dirk Diggler's virtual baptism in a hot tub and the New Year's Eve gunfire that ends the 1970's with a bang. Then it's downhill, as video changes the porn world, and drugs transform its stars.

On the night when Eddie literally runs out of gas, Alfred Molina embodies total drug insanity as a rich, out-of-control freebaser who is the target of a robbery attempt. His terrifying meltdown announces once and for all, in a movie full of showstopping party sequences, that the party's over.

Yet the film's many intimations of how badly this bubble will burst, in a story drawn loosely from the career of the porn star John Holmes, never really coalesce. And since Mr. Anderson shows no interest in passing judgment on his characters, the film's extravagant two-hour thirty-two-minute length amounts to a slight tactical mistake. *Boogie Nights* has no trouble holding interest; far from it. But the length promises larger ideas than the film finally delivers.

Unlike *Nashville,* this crowded, entertaining ensemble film doesn't aspire to any epiphany. Mr. Anderson just sees a lot of good stories in this particular naked city, and he wants to tell them, with enormous flair.

So *Boogie Nights* invests much attention in enjoyable surface details: a Greek chorus of a jukebox ("Oh what a lonely boy!" sings a pop song when the son of Ms. Moore's character can't reach his mother at a party), witty film parodies, perfect period ephemera, and flashy costumes that are an evil treat. Mr. Anderson also has a fine ear for dialogue, especially at such absurd moments as when Eddie compares himself to Napoleon "in the Roman Empire" or when two coked-up porn actresses madly extol the joys of taking a pottery class. Madness it was. And now it is madly well preserved, forever after.

Boogie Nights, this year's fireworks event at the New York Film Festival, will be shown there tonight and Friday night. Its commercial run begins on Sunday.

—*J.M., October 8, 1997*

BORN ON THE FOURTH OF JULY

Directed by Oliver Stone: written by Mr. Stone and Ron Kovic. based on the book by Mr. Kovic: director of photography. Robert Richardson: edited by David Brenner: music by John Williams: production designer. Bruno Rubeo: produced by A. Kitman Ho and Mr. Stone: released by Universal Pictures. Running time: 145 minutes.

With: Tom Cruise (Ron Kovic). Kyra Sedgwick (Donna). Raymond J. Barry (Mr. Kovic). Caroline Kava (Mrs. Kovic). Jerry Levine (Steve Boyer). Frank Whaley (Timmy). Willem Dafoe (Charlie). Josh Evans (Tommy Kovic) and Jamie Talisman (Jimmy Kovic).

As a teenager in Massapequa, Long Island, in the 1960's, Ron Kovic believed in all of the right things, including God, country, and the domino theory. He was Jack Armstrong, the all-American boy, good-looking, shy around girls, and a surreptitious reader of *Playboy.* He was the archetypal son in a large archetypal lower-middle-class Roman Catholic family.

When he competed as a member of the high school wrestling team, he wanted to win, and when he lost a match, he wept. Winning was the way he measured his belief in himself. He didn't question the values that shaped his optimism.

On graduating from high school, he enlisted in the Marine Corps to fight in Vietnam. "Communists are moving in everywhere," he told his somewhat more skeptical classmates. Home and hearth were endangered. Ron Kovic, who really was born on the Fourth of July, was ready when his country called.

In 1968, during his second tour of duty in Vietnam, a bullet tore through his spinal column. He returned home a paraplegic, paralyzed from the waist down, emotionally as well as physically shattered. That was the beginning of a long, painful spiritual rehabilitation that coincided with his political radicalization.

By the time the war ended, Ron Kovic had become one of the most restless and implacable spokesmen for Vietnam Veterans Against the War. Childhood was forever gone.

Taking *Born on the Fourth of July,* Mr. Kovic's fine spare memoir about this coming of age, published in 1976, Oliver Stone has made what is, in effect, a bitter, seething postscript to his Oscar-winning *Platoon.*

It is a film of enormous visceral power with, in the central role, a performance by Tom Cruise that defines everything that is best about the movie. He is both particular and emblematic. He is innocent and cleancut at the start; at the end, angry and exhausted, sporting a proud mustache and a headband around his forehead and hippie-length hair.

Though ideally handsome, Mr. Cruise looks absolutely right, which is not to underrate the performance itself. The two things cannot be easily separated. Watching the evolution of his Ron Kovic, as he comes to terms with a reality for which he was completely unprepared, is both harrowing and inspiring.

Written by Mr. Stone and Mr. Kovic, the screenplay is panoramic, sometimes too panoramic for its own good. It covers Ron's childhood, his teenage years, his enlistment, the tour of duty in Vietnam, and his long recuperation in a Bronx veterans' hospital, an institution that makes Bedlam look like summer camp.

No other Vietnam movie has so mercilessly evoked the casual, careless horrors of the paraplegic's therapy, or what it means to depend on catheters for urination, or the knowledge that sexual identity is henceforth virtually theoretical.

One of the film's problems is that it becomes increasingly generalized as it attempts to dramatize Mr. Kovic's transformation from a wide-eyed Yankee Doodle boy to an antiwar activist.

The film is stunning when it is most specific. There is the nighttime mission when Ron's outfit slaughters a group of Vietnamese peasants in the belief that a Vietcong patrol has been ambushed.

In the confusion of a firefight, Ron shoots one of his own corporals through the neck. When he tries to confess to murder, he is given absolution by an officer who tells him that he is probably mistaken and that, anyway, these things happen.

Equally agonizing are the posthospital sequences when Ron returns to his well-meaning but bewildered family in Massapequa, where he is presented as the grand marshal of the annual Fourth of July parade. People are always trying to help. "I'm O.K.," he says, or "I'm all right" or "O.K. O.K." But there is no understanding.

There is a fine old family row when Ron comes home one night from the local bar, drunk, as has become his habit. In a fury, he pulls out the catheter. His mother calls him a drunk. His father tries to get him into his room. Ron cries out about his inoperative penis. His mother screams, "I will not have you use the word penis in this house."

The film turns less persuasive as Ron acquires his new political consciousness, possibly because, given everything that has gone before, the transformation is so obligatory to the drama. Mr. Stone's penchant for busy, jittery camera movements and cutting also do not help. Though they reflect Ron's earlier state of mind, they start to obscure the character of the man they mean to reveal.

Every member of the large cast is exemplary. It includes Raymond J. Barry and Caroline Kava as Ron's parents; Kyra Sedgwick as his high school girlfriend; Frank Whaley, who is especially good as a fellow vet, one of the few people with whom Ron can communicate when he comes home; and Cordelia Gonzalez as the Mexican whore who tries to persuade Ron that he's still a man.

The two stars of *Platoon* appear in cameo roles: Tom Berenger, as the marine who recruits Ron with his rousing pep talk at Ron's high school, and Willem Dafoe, as a fellow paraplegic vet Ron meets during a brief interlude in Mexico. An aging Abbie Hoffman, an icon of the Vietnam years, makes a sad, curious appearance, more or less playing himself during an antiwar demonstration set in the 1960's. (Hoffman committed suicide in April at the age of fifty-two.)

Born on the Fourth of July is a far more complicated movie than *Platoon*. It's the most ambitious nondocu-mentary film yet made about the entire Vietnam experience. More effectively than Hal Ashby's *Coming Home* and even Michael Cimino's *Deer Hunter,* it connects the war of arms abroad with the war of conscience at home.

As much as anything else, Ron Kovic's story is about the vanishing of one man's American frontier.

—*V.C., December 20, 1989*

BORN YESTERDAY

Directed by George Cukor; written by Albert Mannheimer, based on the play by Garson Kanin; cinematographer, Joseph Walker; edited by Charles Nelson; music by Frederick Hollander; produced by S. Sylvan Simon; released by Columbia Pictures. Black and white. Running time: 103 minutes.

With: Judy Holliday (Billie Dawn), William Holden (Paul Verrall), Broderick Crawford (Harry Brock), Howard St. John (Jim Devery), Frank Otto (Eddie), Larry Oliver (Congressman Hedges), Barbara Brown (Mrs. Hedges), Grandon Rhodes (Sanborn) and Claire Carleton (Helen).

Just in time to make itself evident as one of the best pictures of this fading year is Columbia's trenchant screen version of the stage play, *Born Yesterday*. More firm in its social implications than ever it was on the stage and blessed with a priceless performance by rocketing Judy Holliday, this beautifully integrated compound of character study and farce made a resounding entry at the Victoria yesterday.

On the strength of this one appearance, there is no doubt that Miss Holliday will leap into popularity as a leading American movie star—a spot to which she was predestined by her previous minor triumph in *Adam's Rib* as the tender young lady from Brooklyn who shot her husband (and stole the show). For there isn't the slightest question that Miss Holliday brings to the screen a talent for characterization that is as sweetly refreshing as it is rare.

Playing the wondrous ignoramus that she created on the stage—the lady to whom her crude companion rather lightly refers as a "dumb broad"—this marvelously clever young actress so richly conveys the attitudes and the vocal intonations of a native of the sidewalks of New York that it is art. More than that, she illuminates so brightly the elemental wit and honesty of her blankly unlettered young lady that she puts pathos and respect into the role.

But it must be said in the next breath that Miss Holliday doesn't steal this show—at least, not without a major tussle—for there is a lot of show here to steal. Not only has the original stage play of Garson Kanin been preserved by screenwriter Albert Mannheimer in all of its flavorsome detail—and that, we might add, is a triumph of candor and real adapting skill—but George Cukor has directed with regard for both the humor and the moral. And Broderick Crawford has contributed a performance as the merchant of junk who would build himself up as a tycoon that fairly makes the hair stand on end.

Where this role was given some humor and even sympathy on the stage, in the memorable performance of Paul Douglas, Mr. Crawford endows it with such sting—such evident evil, corruption, cruelty, and arrogance—that there is nothing amusing or appealing about this willful, brutish man. He is, indeed, a formidable symbol of the menace of acquisitive power and greed against which democratic peoples must always be alert. And that's why his thorough comeuppance, contrived by his newly enlightened "broad" amid the monuments of serene and beautiful Washington, is so winning and wonderful. In short, a more serious connotation has been given the role on the screen and Mr. Crawford plays it in a brilliantly cold and forceful style.

As the Washington correspondent hired to cultivate the junkman's girl—an enterprise which leads directly to her enlightenment and revolt—William Holden is tuned to perfection. He has dignity, diligence, and reserve and gives a romantic demonstration of tolerance and amorous regard. It might be added in this connection that Miss Holliday, while frankly gotten up in the most absurdly tasteless outfits, is not a repulsive dish.

Howard St. John also gives a clean performance as the lawyer reduced to shady deals on the part of the horseback-riding braggart for fat and corrupting fees. Frank Otto is droll as a henchman and Larry Oliver injects a bit of gall into the somewhat reduced and denatured role of a congressman.

With more room to move around in—meaning the city of Washington—and doing that in vivid fashion, *Born Yesterday* is reborn on the screen as a larger, stronger, more articulate, and even more appealing prodigy.

—B.C., December 27, 1950

LE BOUCHER

Written (in French, with English subtitles) and directed by Claude Chabrol; director of photography, Jean Rabler; edited by Jacques Gaillard; music by Pierre Jansen; produced by André Génoves; released by Cinerama Releasing. Running time: 93 minutes.

With: Stéphane Audran (Mademoiselle Hélène), Jean Yanne (Popaul), Antonio Passalia (Angelo), Roger Rudel (Grumbach), Mario Beccaria (Leon Hamel) and William Guerault (Charles).

Claude Chabrol's *Le Boucher* is a love story about a gentle, self-possessed butcher, Popaul (Jean Yanne), who may or may not spend his off-hours carving up young women in the woods, and a lovely school mistress, Mlle. Hélène (Stéphane Audran). The setting is the tiny village of Tremolat, not far from the Lascaux caves, but Mlle. Hélène is no ordinary small-town schoolmistress. She is a woman who obviously buys her clothes in Paris, who can smoke in the street—a Gauloise hanging from her mouth apache-style—without ever losing her chic, and who responds with genuine pleasure when a student writes in a theme that "it was so hot the air hurt you . . ."

Popaul and Mlle. Hélène meet at one of those exuberant, traditional wedding feasts at which they are the apparent but not unhappy outsiders. He is just out of the regular Army (where, as he says, he did a lot of butchering in Algeria and Indochina), and she has been living in a very feminine kind of sexual isolation ever since a love affair ended disastrously ten years earlier.

They make an odd but immensely appealing pair as he courts her with specially cut legs of lamb and as she draws him into her life by having him join her on mushroom hunts and as a participant in a school fete, for which she teaches the butcher an eighteenth-century court dance (one of the movie's most touching moments). On one excursion to the country, he asks her how she can do without a lover. "There are other ways," she answers. "Disgusting," says the butcher, and she laughs. Later he wonders what she would do if he tried to kiss her. "Nothing," she answers, adding, in a way that is both vulnerable and absolutely chilling, "but I wish you wouldn't."

Like all of Chabrol's recent films, Le Boucher has to do with decisions made moments too late, of love just missed like a train. It is also second only to the practically perfect *La Femme Infidèle* as the most elegant, most sorrowful of Chabrol's recent films, better than both the very stylish but geometric *Les Biches* and *Que La Bête Meure* (which will be released here as *This Man Must Die*).

I'm not sure that *Le Boucher* works for me on the level of psychological realism. I find it impossible to accept the suggestion that Chabrol ultimately makes, that is, that Mlle. Hélène could have saved the psychotic killer from himself had she not been afraid to love, and that, by withholding her love, she is in some way as much of a beast as he is, fit to be condemned to eternal loneliness.

Ironically, however, it is completely credible as romantic realism of the kind that has its models in Hitchcock's *Spellbound* and Lang's *Scarlet Street*. Although Chabrol will probably never attain the seeming spontaneity of his masters (he is simply too intellectual a filmmaker), he can excel both when it comes to creating deeply felt characters and their relationships with each other as well as with their environment.

The tempo and the temper and even the weather of the little town of Tremolat are very much a part of *Le Boucher* and of the lives of Popaul and Mlle. Hélène, who emotionally, anyway, pass in the course of the storm from late summer into irrevocable autumn. This is not to say the movie is without some conscious Hitchcockian details. Chabrol builds his suspense obliquely and although he uses blood sparingly, it is done with a sense of spectacle.

There is one particularly outrageous moment when a little girl, who has been on a group outing to the caves, sits beneath a cliff and unwraps her sandwich, only to have a large dollop of red fall on the bread. It's the first indication that the killer's been at work again and that his victim, dead but still warm as pie, is hidden above.

Le Boucher, however, is not primarily interesting as conventional mystery, which the film makes little effort to maintain after a certain point. Rather it's as a moving love story that it makes sense, and this because Chabrol has respect and admiration for his stars as performers and as characters. Yanne's Popaul, for example, who does such terrible things offscreen, is never seen on-screen as anything but completely sympathetic.

It's no casual coincidence that each of Chabrol's best movies recently has starred Miss Audran, who, in private life, is Mrs. Chabrol and, in public, is the most beautiful and enigmatic screen personality to emerge in France since the early appearances of Jeanne Moreau in the 1950's. In *Le Boucher* there is something about Miss Audran's intelligence, her wit, her style, and her wardrobe that makes her seem a very unlikely provincial schoolmarm, but (as it used to be with actresses like Garbo and Dietrich) it's this very unlikelihood that makes the character of Mlle. Hélène appear to be unique, thus special and worth caring about.

Le Boucher, which was shown Saturday night at the New York Film Festival, has not yet been acquired for commercial release.

—V.C., September 14, 1970

BOUND FOR GLORY

Directed by Hal Ashby; written by Robert Getchell, based on the autobiography by Woody Guthrie; director of photography, Haskell Wexler; edited by Pembroke J. Herring and Robert C. Jones; production design by Michael D. Haller; music by Leonard Rosenman; produced by Robert Blumofe, Harold Leventhal and Jeffrey M. Sneller; released by United Artists. Running time: 147 minutes.

With: David Carradine (Woody Guthrie), Ronny Cox (Ozark Bule), Melinda Dillon (Mary/Memphis Sue), Gail Strickland (Pauline), John Lehne (Locke), Ji-Tu Cumbuka (Slim Snedeger), Randy Quaid (Luther Johnson), Elizabeth Macey (Liz Johnson), Susan Vaill (Gwen Guthrie), Sarah Vaill (Gwen Guthrie), Alexandra Mock (Sue Guthrie) and Kimberly Mock (Sue Guthrie).

Like the guests of honor who won't be allowed entrance until the proper moment, the presence of Woody Guthrie hovers for a long time—felt but unheard—outside *Bound for Glory,* the film biography that Hal Ashby has made of one of America's greatest folk singers and composers. Then, at the film's end, as the final credits are unreeling, the slightly raspy voice of the real Woody Guthrie is invited in via the soundtrack.

The movie, which until that moment has solemnly recorded selected events of Woody's life in Depression America, comes suddenly to life in a medley of Guthrie songs sung by him and others. The songs are buoyant, funny, mocking. They are full of feelings that somehow elude the rest of the film, even though *Bound for Glory* has apparently been made with love and care and is virtually stricken by its social conscience.

The film, which opened yesterday at the Coronet, has a number of very good things going for it, in particular David Carradine's dry, haunted performance as the young Woody Guthrie who passes through the film more or less as if he were a camera, storing away impressions and emotions that only occasionally are allowed to erupt with dramatic force. Mr. Carradine may be taller and huskier than the real Woody, but he has the right look and manner—the reserve, skeptical squint, the texture of the countryman's skin.

Mr. Ashby and Haskell Wexler, his cameraman, have also been immensely successful in recreating the look of place and period from the drought-ridden Texas Panhandle of the 1930's, when rural America appeared to be returning to dust even before it had actually died, to the California fruit ranches and the "Hoovervilles" where Woody sang and attempted to organize the migrant workers.

What the film doesn't have much of is a screenplay. At least, it doesn't have a screenplay that matches with dramatic conviction the intensity and drive of its largely mysterious central character.

Woody Guthrie was a very odd duck, and certainly not easy to live with. At the height of the Depression, he abandoned his wife and two small daughters in Texas and took to the road, heading for California on foot and freight car. When he began to receive a little recognition as a country singer on a California radio station, he retrieved his family but abandoned them again. His feelings for "the people" never quite extended far enough to include his wife and children.

Robert Getchell, who wrote the screenplay based on Woody's autobiography, doesn't permit the screen Woody to sound any more articulate than your average, tongue-tied man-in-the-street interviewee.

"Seems to me something ought to be done about this," says the film's Woody early on, commenting on the disastrous conditions in the Texas dust bowl. Later, to explain why he had run away from home again, he says, "I had to touch the people again . . . The worst that can happen to a guy is to cut himself off from the folks."

Had this sort of talk been combined with more of Woody's music as the film unfolds, the result might not have seemed as ultimately barren and trivial as it now does, but Mr. Ashby didn't want *Bound for Glory* to be a musical. That's understandable, though to separate Woody from his music, as the film does to a great extent, is to separate us from a major portion of his experience.

Woody's music is galvanizing, upbeat, convinced of the possibilities for a better society, committed to change. Like Woody's impatience with social and political injustice, the music is unequivocal, decisive. The movie isn't.

It ambles through conventionally pitiful scenes of dust-bowl poverty and union-busting, and shows us Woody refusing to compromise his ideals to get along in show business. On only two occasions, however, do we have some sense of what drove the man.

One is an old-fashioned hoedown with a group of fruit pickers and the other is a sequence in which Woody, attempting to organize workers in a canning plant, is beaten up by company thugs. Both sequences make their points as much through music as through anything that happens.

Though Mr. Carradine's performance is almost the entire film, he receives fine support from the other actors, including Melinda Dillon, who plays both his abandoned wife and a singing partner named Memphis Sue, and Ronny Cox, who plays a fictionalized version of one of Woody's real-life sidekicks and mentors.

—*V.C., December 6, 1976*

BOYS DON'T CRY

Directed by Kimberly Peirce. written by Ms. Peirce and Andy Bienen: director of photography.

Jim Denault: edited by Lee Percy and Tracy Granger: music by Nathan Larsen: production designer, Mike Shaw: produced by Jeffrey Sharp, John Hart and Eva Kolodner: Pamela Koffler and Christine Vachon, executive producers: released by Fox Searchlight Pictures. Running time: 114 minutes.

With: Alison Folland (Kate), Alicia Goranson (Candace), Matt McGrath (Lonny), Peter Sarsgaard (John), Chloe Sevigny (Lana), Brendan Sexton 3d (Tom) and Hilary Swank (Brandon Teena).

Kimberley Peirce's stunning debut feature, *Boys Don't Cry,* tells the strange and resonant story of Brandon Teena, who despite being born Teena Brandon, went on to create a charismatic identity as an attractive young man. When Brandon was found out, raped and murdered, this tabloid-ready tale attracted the kind of omnivorous media attention that distorts the truth beyond recognition and milks reality dry.

Nonetheless, Ms. Peirce has found a way to tell it brilliantly, with *Badlands, Bonnie and Clyde,* and *In Cold Blood* among her inspirations, and with Theodore Dreiser's idea of American tragedy hauntingly reawakened. Here is one more trapped, small-town character who yearned for the freedom of a new life, reached for it recklessly and wound up paying a terrible price for that dream. Here, too, is the astonishing acting to make Brandon's story understandable.

Boys Don't Cry, a film much tougher and more transfixing than its wan title, understand that this is more than just biography. It reaches out to reveal something about all the lives that Brandon changed forever. At first it would seem that this whole film hangs on the inspired performance of Hilary Swank, a beautiful, lanky actress with *Beverly Hills 90210* to her credit and no residual vanity to come between herself and Brandon. And Ms. Swank, who deserves to be remembered at the end of the year for a devastating portrayal, does account for much of the film's credibility.

But this is an ensemble effort, one that draws as much upon Ms. Peirce's insightful overview, Jim Denault's streamlined cinematography and the cast's raw emotion to make it work. On a par with Ms. Swank's work is Chloe Sevigny's as Lana Tisdel, the nubile, luminous girlfriend who fell in love with Bran-

don's masculinity, facts notwithstanding. It was in Lana's nature to make that leap of faith.

Without sensationalism *Boys Don't Cry* does a remarkably good job of explaining the specifics of Brandon's role playing. (While the film compresses some of the data in a previous documentary, *The Brandon Teena Story,* it is cast and written with consideration for real people and facts.) And it sustains a note of stirring optimism for a long while. The viewer is easily caught up in the exhilaration of the former Teena, who moves from Lincoln, Neb., to the small town of Falls City, so her new persona as Brandon can be given free reign. Brandon's secret joy in discovering that he can meet and flirt with women is indeed touching and not merely a matter of sexual orientation. The film understands the seductive lure of creating a brand new identity and making it stick.

In a story too strange to be fiction, Brandon falls into a complicated new family. At its heart is Lana (Ms. Sevigny), who lives with her dissolute mother and has a proprietary old boyfriend, John Lotter (Peter Sarsgaard), still lurking around the house. Having already taken up with Lana's friend Candace (Alicia Goranson), Brandon fits in reasonably well as part of this extended family. But to John and his equally macho friend Tom, who are part of the town's group of "wall people" (named for loitering against the wall of the local Quik Stop), Brandon is a threat.

"It's not just about two stupid thugs who killed somebody," the film's habitually daring executive producer, Christine Vachon (*Kids, Happiness, Velvet Goldmine*) has said. "It's about these guys whose world is so tenuous and so fragile that they can't stand to have any of their beliefs shattered."

And *Boys Don't Cry,* whose villains are as affecting as their victims, understands the bullies' side of the story. By the time Teena's identity is discovered and the men who have been fooled by her want vengeance, the film has unveiled all the anger and frustration that goads them, even when, as they tell Teena chillingly, "You know you brought this on yourself."

Boys Don't Cry is never preachy or complacent in its depiction of its trapped small-town characters. But it sees the difference between wallowing in nothingness, a favorite Falls City pastime, and rising magically out of oblivion, as Brandon and Lana do so tenderly when they fall in love. Moving inexorably, and with great innate suspense, toward disaster, it still savors the visions of transcendence and escape that Brandon offered. Unlike most films about mind-numbing tragedy, this one manages to be full of hope.

—*J.M., October 1, 1999*

BOYZ N THE HOOD

Written and directed by John Singleton; director of photography, Charles Mills; edited by Bruce Cannon; music by Stanley Clarke; art designer, Bruce Bellamy; produced by Steve Nicolaides; released by Columbia Pictures. Running time: 107 minutes.

With: Ice Cube (Doughboy), Cuba Gooding Jr. (Tre Styles), Morris Chestnut (Ricky Baker), Larry Fishburne (Furious Styles), Angela Bassett (Reva Styles), Nia Long (Brandi) and Tyra Ferrell (Mrs. Baker).

*B*oyz N the Hood, John Singleton's terrifically confident first feature, places Mr. Singleton on a footing with Spike Lee as a chronicler of the frustration faced by young black men growing up in urban settings. But Mr. Singleton, who wrote and directed this film set in south central Los Angeles, has a distinctly Californian point of view. Unlike Mr. Lee's New York stories, which give their neighborhoods the finiteness and theatricality of stage sets, Mr. Singleton examines a more sprawling form of claustrophobia and a more adolescent angst. If Mr. Lee felt inclined to remake George Lucas's *American Graffiti* with a more fatalistic outlook and a political agenda, the results might be very much like this.

Boyz N the Hood spans seven years in the life of Tre Styles (Cuba Gooding Jr.), who in the film's first episode is seen idly discussing street crimes, and in its last is caught up in one such crime himself. Beginning with some sobering statistics detailing the homicide rate among black men in America, the film builds toward a deadly climax even while depicting its characters' best efforts to keep violence at bay.

Mr. Singleton may not be saying anything new about the combined effects of poverty, drugs, and aimlessness on black teenagers. But he is saying something familiar with new dramatic force, and in ways that a wide and varied audience will understand. His film

proceeds almost casually until it reaches a gutwrenching finale, one that is all the more disturbing for the ease with which it envelops the film's principals.

In the end, *Boyz N the Hood* asks the all-important question of whether there is such a thing as changing one's fate. If there is—and Mr. Singleton holds out a powerful glimmer of hope in the story's closing moments—then for this film's young characters it hinges on the attitudes of their fathers. Tre is a child of divorce, but he has two parents who are devoted to him, and in particular a father who takes over his son's upbringing at a critical age. At the start of the story, when Tre is ten years old, Furious Styles (Larry Fishburne) assumes custody of his only son, announcing that it is his responsibility to teach Tre to be a man.

Tre's mother, Reva (Angela Bassett), apparently independent and relatively successful, agrees to the change, perhaps because of the unsatisfactory way in which Tre is being reared. In his elementary school, a condescending white teacher delivers an irrelevant lecture on Pilgrims and Indians—"excuse me, the Native Americans," she wearily corrects herself—to her bored and restless black students. On the streets, Tre has learned to walk past skirmishes without even noticing them. He and his friends talk idly about street shootings, and about how bloodstains turn plasma-colored on pavement over time.

But from Tre's first day on the cozy, communal block of small houses where Tre's father lives, Furious does what he can to keep his son in line. Tre is assigned a chore when he first sets foot on his father's front lawn: "You the prince, I'm the king," is his father's joking credo. And later, even in times of crisis, Furious does a lot to sustain order. One especially gripping sequence shows Furious foiling a prowler in the house, as the camera pulls back abruptly through bullet holes in the front door.

Much of the conversation in *Boyz N the Hood* has to do with sex, and a lot of that talk is fearful. Mr. Singleton makes the connection between sex and reproduction foremost on everyone's mind, and a major factor in the destruction of these young characters' independence. Anyone can have sex, Furious tells Tre during a lecture on the facts of life, "but only a real man can raise his children." By the time Tre and his friends are high school seniors, the football hero Ricky Baker (Morris Chestnut) is already a father, and can feel the walls closing in. Ricky's brother, Doughboy (the rapper Ice Cube), filled with scowling contempt for the neighborhood and its foibles, has opted not for early fatherhood but for a life of crime.

Boyz N the Hood—the title, about these young men and their neighborhood, comes from one of Ice Cube's records—watches Tre, Ricky, and Doughboy navigate these perilous waters to the accompaniment of violent background sound. Police helicopters are such a constant presence that Brandi (Nia Long), Tre's girlfriend, who hopes to go to college, can barely get her homework done. Drive-by shootings between gang members are also part of the landscape. "Can't we have one night where there ain't no fight and nobody gets shot?" somebody finally says in frustration.

In this setting, the actors could easily disappear into speeches or stereotypes, but they don't; the film's strength is that it sustains an intimate and realistic tone. Mr. Fishburne, who is called upon to deliver several lectures, manages to do so with enormous dignity and grace, and makes Furious a compelling role model, someone on whom the whole film easily pivots. Mr. Gooding gives Tre a gentle, impressionable quality that is most affecting. Ice Cube, who sometimes mutters too gruffly to be heard, nonetheless has a humorous delivery and a street swagger that effectively brings the neighborhood to life. The women in the film, particularly Tyra Ferrell as the exasperated mother of Doughboy and Ricky, are often feisty and vibrant but play only minor roles. As the title indicates, the climate of violence, raunch, raw nerves, and adolescent longing in which this story unfolds is very much a man's world.

—*J.M., July 12, 1991*

BRAZIL

Directed by Terry Gilliam; written by Mr. Gilliam, Tom Stoppard and Charles McKeown; director of photography, Roger Pratt; edited by Julian Doyle; produced by Arnon Michan; released by Universal Pictures. Running time: 131 minutes.

With: Jonathan Pryce (Sam Lowry), Robert De Niro (Harry Tuttle), Michael Palin (Jack Lint), Kim Greist (Jill Layton), Katherine Helmond (Ida Lowry), Ian Holm (Kurtzmann), Bob Hoskins (Spoor) and Ian Richardson (Warren).

Terry Gilliam's *Brazil*, a jaunty, wittily observed vision of an extremely bleak future, is a superb example of the power of comedy to underscore serious ideas, even solemn ones. Brazil, which was not scheduled for 1985 release until the Los Angeles Film Critics Association voted it best film of the year, was slated, as of yesterday, to open on December 25 for one week in order to qualify for Academy Awards consideration. However, the opening was suddenly advanced, and it began its weeklong engagement today at Loew's New York Twin. It is scheduled to reopen on February 14.

Brazil may not be the best film of the year, but it's a remarkable accomplishment for Mr. Gilliam, whose satirical and cautionary impulses work beautifully together. His film's ambitious visual style bears this out, combining grim, overpowering architecture with clever throwaway touches. The look of the film harkens back to the 1930's, as does the title; *Brazil* is named not for the country but for the 1930's popular song, which floats through the film as a tantalizing refrain. The gaiety of the music stands in ironic contrast to the oppressive, totalitarian society in which the story is set.

The plot itself, from a screenplay by Mr. Gilliam, Tom Stoppard, and Charles McKeown, is rather thin; it exists mainly as an excuse to lead the viewer into various corners of an unexpectedly humorous Orwellian world. Mr. Gilliam's answer to Mr. Orwell's Winston Smith is one Sam Lowry, a gray-suited bureaucrat who has a forbidden love, a lively fantasy life, and a socialite mother. Ida Lowry (played hilariously by Katherine Helmond), who is constantly in the company of her in-house plastic surgeon, spends most of her time lunching with lady-friends and a bit of it worrying about her son's limited career. So Ida—whose fashion sense dictates that she wears hats that look very much like upside-down shoes—arranges a promotion for Sam. He winds up in an office so small that he has only half a desk and half a poster, sharing both with the bureaucrat next door. This change somehow propels Sam into a romance with a woman who may be a terrorist and into a series of hellish nightmares.

Much of the cleverness of *Brazil* has to do with its tiny details, the sense of how things work in this new society. Signs glimpsed in the background say things like "Loose Talk Is Noose Talk" and "Suspicion Breeds

Confidence," while television advertisements are for things like fashionable heating ducts "in designer colors to suit your demanding taste" (the production design makes sure that heating ducts are everywhere). Politeness counts for everything, as in an early scene where one hapless Mr. Buttle is arrested in his own living room, stuffed into what looks like a large canvas bag, and led away, never to be seen again. At least Mrs. Buttle is given a written receipt for her confiscated husband.

Harry Tuttle, the man the police were actually after until a large bug dropped into a computer and caused a typographical error, is played by Robert De Niro as a combination repairman and commando. Mr. De Niro has only the briefest of roles here, but he makes it count for a lot, as does Bob Hoskins as a sinister fellow passing himself off as a rival repairman. The friends of Sam's mother are also nicely played, particularly Shirley (Kathryn Pogson), who tells Sam shyly that she doesn't like him at all. Michael Palin is both ominous and funny as Sam's friend Jack Lint, and Jonathan Pryce is especially good as Sam. Giving his regards to Jack's twins and learning that they are triplets, Sam responds by saying "Triplets! How time flies."

Also in *Brazil* is Kim Greist as the pretty young woman who fascinates Sam in reality and in his dreams; in the latter, she has angelic blond hair and he appears as a magnificent winged silver creature swooping through the skies. Earlier in his career, Mr. Gilliam might have staged such a scene more facetiously, but here it has a real poignance. For all its fancifulness, *Brazil* and its characters seem substantial and real.

—*J.M., December 18, 1985*

BREAD, LOVE AND DREAMS

Directed by Luigi Comencini: written (in Italian. with English subtitles) by Ettore Margadonna and Mr. Comencini. based on a story by Mr. Margadonna: cinematographer. Arturo Gállea: music by Alessandro Cicognini: produced by Marcello Girosi: released by IFE. Black and white. Running time: 90 minutes.

With: Vittorio De Sica (The Marshal). Gina Lollob-

rigida (The Girl). Marisa Merlini (The Midwife). Roberto Risso (The Carabiniere) and Virgilio Riento (The Village Priest).

Although three basic stuffs of human sustenance are mentioned in *Bread, Love and Dreams,* the Italian comedy-romance that came to the Paris yesterday, comparatively little attention is paid to bread and dreams. The main concern of this attraction is the eager pursuit of love. And with handsome Vittorio De Sica playing the principal role—that of a middle-aged bachelor in quest of a companionable female friend—and pert Gina Lollobrigida playing one whom he pursues, the attention given to the subject is both artful and full of mischievous charm.

Such is the substance in a nutshell. A new marshal of military police—the famous Carabinieri—arrives at a hilltop village to assume command of the modest six-man garrison. There is not much to do in the place. Indeed, the principal pastime of the residents seems to be tending to other people's affairs. And so there is general excitement when the marshal begins to pursue, in a not altogether honorable fashion, the village's most notorious and bumptious girl.

It is a pursuit that is fraught with subtle aspects, for the marshal is bound to preserve the traditional authority and dignity that goes with his elevated rank. He must maintain his poise and position. He must act as beseems his middle age. And, especially, he must manage to conquer the insolence and resistance of the girl, who just happens to have her cap set for a younger member of the police.

How deftly and drolly Signor De Sica plays this amusing masculine role—how properly he poses, yet how slyly and adroitly he unbends—makes for the principal amusement in this somewhat formless and offhand film, which is built much more upon performance and implication than it is upon plot. Signor De Sica is a master of suggestion—the raised eyebrow, the lightly stroked mustache. He assembles, under his own "supervision," a wry and wistful character.

And Signorina Lollobrigida, who is a bumptious young lady anyhow, does a grand job of playing the graceless gamine whom he manfully pursues. She shrills at him in derision, she mocks his graceful pleasantries, and she fends off his tender advances with the most provocative shifts of her shapely frame. And yet there is in her performance a suggestion of poignancy, too. She, like Signor De Sica, symbolizes a tenuous pursuit.

Theirs are not the only good performances. Virgilio Riento as the parish priest, the other symbol of authority and dignity in the village, is excellent in an arch and crafty role, and Marisa Merlini is fetching as the midwife for whom the marshal eventually settles. Roberto Risso as the youthful policeman is a fine-looking, bashful lad, and Vittoria Crispo makes a couple of howlers as the frantic mother of the girl.

Bread, Love and Dreams is not a mighty or particularly meaningful film, but it is full of good, earthy entertainment, of regard for human nature—and for girls.

—B.C., September 21, 1954

BREAKER MORANT

Directed by Bruce Beresford: written by Mr. Beresford, Jonathan Hardy and David Stevens, based on the play by Kenneth Ross: cinematographer, Don McAlpine: edited by William Anderson: music by Phil Cuneen: produced by Matt Carroll: released by South Australian Film Company. Running time: 107 minutes.

With: Edward Woodward (Lieutenant Harry Morant), Jack Thompson (Major J. F. Thomas), John Waters (Captain Alfred Taylor), Bryan Brown (Lieutenant Peter Handcock) and Lewis Fitz-Gerald (Lieutenant George Witten).

Scapegoats of the Empire is the title of a book by someone who survived the affair on which *Breaker Morant,* a new Australian movie with a dependably old-fashioned manner, is based. The drama takes place in 1901, in South Africa, at the end of the Boer War. The action is confined almost exclusively to a trial, the outcome of which is a fait accompli. The mood of it recalls military drama of the 1950's, like Terence Rattigan's *Ross.* In this case, the gears move almost automatically. There's nothing unexpected here, but neither are there omissions of anything an audience might anticipate. As based on Kenneth Ross's play, *Breaker Morant* is a shapely and orderly kind of drama. Its greatest strength is that it delivers what it promises.

Breaker Morant, which opens today at Cinema I, is the story of how three Australian soldiers become sacrificial lambs. It follows them to their fates with a mixture of high moral dudgeon and propriety. Lieutenant Harry Morant, who earned the nickname of the title by being the best horse-breaker in his native Australia, is the victim of a British military that hasn't prepared itself for the decline of strict discipline. The guerrilla fighting that characterized this conflict amounts to what one character labels "a new kind of war—new war for a new century."

As the film soon explains, the Boers' guerrilla tactics have left the British unable to finish a war they have effectively won. So when Morant, to avenge the murder of a comrade at the Boers' hands, allows his men to take reprisals, the British see an opportunity to make an example of Morant without truly losing one of their own. Australia won't help him, either; having just become a Commonwealth, Morant's homeland is eager to rid itself of a frontier atmosphere. Allowing Morant to be condemned for his allegedly roughneck morals becomes the new Australian government's way of taking on a civilized veneer.

Most of the Australian films that have been released in America take place at the turn of the century. *Breaker Morant,* like many of these, accounts for this turbulent period in Australia's history by exaggerating the gentility that the characters and their countrymen have tried to adopt, in reaction to British rule. In this case, the result is a touchingly stiff-upper-lip approach to the events that occur in the courtroom. The events are so unfortunate and unjust that the film's air of restraint gives it a genuinely tragic dimension.

The director, Bruce Beresford, relying heavily on flashbacks to reconstruct the action, guarantees that the audience's sympathies are never anywhere but with Morant and his men. But he also, until late in the story, maintains both a tension and a coldness by letting the defendants keep a tight rein on their fear. Lieutenant Peter Handcock is allowed the occasional courtroom outburst, shouting, "You couldn't lie straight in bed!" to one witness and, "Anytime, mate!" to another. But young Lieutenant George Wilton stays silently terrified throughout, and Morant vents his rage only through sarcasm.

The three actors who play these condemned men— Edward Woodward as Morant, Bryan Brown as Handcock, and Lewis Fitz-Gerald as Witten—are all so good they make the movie as much a character study as a courtmartial. The same is true of Jack Thompson, as the country lawyer who becomes unexpectedly resourceful as he rises to their defense. Mr. Beresford's direction is at first so crisp that *Breaker Morant* appears headed for a familiar dead end—the land of stiff salutes, twitching mustaches, barked commands, and other staples of movies about the military.

But by the time it plays out its hand, this film has become genuinely, surprisingly affecting. And unspeakably sad.

—*J.M., December 22, 1980*

THE BREAKFAST CLUB

Written and directed by John Hughes; director of photography, Thomas Del Ruth; edited by Dede Allen; music by Keith Forsey; produced by Ned Tanen, Mr. Hughes and Michelle Manning; released by Universal Pictures. Running time: 95 minutes.

With: Emilio Estevez (Andrew Clark), Paul Gleason (Richard Vernon), Anthony Michael Hall (Brian Johnson), John Kapelos (Carl), Judd Nelson (John Bender), Molly Ringwald (Claire Standish), Ally Sheedy (Allison Reynolds), Perry Crawford (Allison's Father), Mary Christian (Brian's Sister), Ron Dean (Andy's Father), Tim Gamble (Claire's Father), Fran Gargano (Allison's Mother) and Mercedes Hall (Brian's Mother).

Five kids spending Saturday doing detention time in the high school library: it's not such a spine-tingling situation. But in *The Breakfast Club,* which he wrote and directed, John Hughes lets the kids challenge, taunt, and confront each other as if this were *Twelve Angry Men.* Personalities are dissected; tears are shed. The kids, each representing a different teen stereotype, come to understand each other. They strike up friendships. They denounce their parents. They decide that "when you grow up, your heart dies."

The offhand, knowing humor of Mr. Hughes's *Sixteen Candles* is supplanted here by a deadly self-importance, occasionally leavened with a well-timed gag or a memorable bit of teenage slang ("Yo, Waste-oid! You're not gonna blaze up in here," says one char-

acter, meaning "Don't smoke."). Fortunately, Mr. Hughes retains some of his earlier playfulness, and all of his talent for casting. There are some good young actors in *The Breakfast Club,* though a couple of them have been given unplayable roles.

Ally Sheedy, for instance, must do what she can with the part of an uncommunicative psycho who reveals herself to be a compulsive liar, then changes radically by the time the story is over. None of this is credible, but Miss Sheedy still manages to be appealing. Judd Nelson is in a much worse spot as the hoodlum in the group, since Mr. Hughes's screenplay makes him the story's only aggressor. He can't help but get on the other characters' nerves, and on the audience's, too.

Molly Ringwald and Anthony Michael Hall, reunited after *Sixteen Candles,* are the movie's standout performers as an affluent prima donna and a boy who cares about physics to the exclusion of all else. As the athlete who rounds out this predictable lineup, Emilio Estevez has an edgy physical intensity very reminiscent of his father, Martin Sheen. The five young stars would have mixed well even without the fraudulent encounter-group candor toward which *The Breakfast Club* forces them. Mr. Hughes, having thought up the characters and simply flung them together, should have left well enough alone.

—*V.C., February 15, 1985*

BREAKING AWAY

Produced and directed by Peter Yates; written by Steve Tesich; cinematographer, Matthew F. Leonetti; edited by Cynthia Scheider; music by Patrick Williams; released by Twentieth Century Fox. Running time: 100 minutes.

With: Dennis Christopher (Dave), Dennis Quaid (Mike), Daniel Stern (Cyril), Jackie Earle Haley (Moocher), Barbara Barrie (Mom), Paul Dooley (Dad), Robyn Douglass (Katherine), Hart Bochner (Rod) and Amy Wright (Nancy).

Breaking Away was made in Bloomington, Indiana, which is perhaps the film world's equivalent of left field. For that and other reasons, it's a classic sleeper. The cast is unknown, the director has a spotty history, and the basic premise falls into this year's most hackneyed category (unknown boxer/bowler/jogger hopes to become sports hero). Even so, the finished product is wonderful. Here is a movie so fresh and funny it didn't even need a big budget or a pedigree.

Breaking Away, which opens today at the Coronet and other theaters, has a sense of place that goes hand in hand with its sense of humor. In Bloomington, on the outskirts of Indiana University, four boys endure the confusion of being nonstudents—and pariahs of a sort—in a college town. The college kids, who seem privileged and carefree, instill the Bloomington boys with both an uneasy class-consciousness and a feeling that life is passing them by. As Mike (Dennis Quaid), the angriest of the four, remarks bitterly, "These college kids out here, they're never gonna get old. There'll always be new ones coming along."

While his father (Paul Dooley, who gives a fabulous supporting performance) sells used cars with names like Magna Cum Laude and Varsity Squad, Dave (Dennis Christopher) indulges in a form of escapism that's both hilarious and touching. Dave is a first-rate bicycle racer, which makes him an outsider in another way: the really top-notch bicyclists, the royalty who occasionally deign to visit Bloomington, are Italians. Dave, who is nothing if not enterprising, sees no choice but to try to become Italian too.

So he sings operatic arias as he rides, and feeds his cat out of a Cinzano ashtray. He uses Neapolitan Sunset cologne. He drives his father wild by crying "Ciao," and by conspiring with his mother (Barbara Barrie) to insinuate foreign dishes—"all them '-ini' foods, zucchini, and linguini and fettucine," Mr. Dooley shrieks—into the family's french fry–based diet. Mr. Dooley is finally driven to take out his frustrations on the family cat, whom he warns "Your name is Jake, not Fellini!"

The proof of Dave's success in transforming himself comes when he starts serenading a pretty college girl named Katherine (Robyn Douglass), who falls for the act, perhaps because she loves being called Caterine. But, much to the movie's credit, it follows Dave beyond these endearingly transparent efforts. In fact, it even passes the point at which he realizes that escaping his status as a town kid—"cutters," they're called—will require something more strenuous than whimsy. Halfway through the movie, the cutters begin in earnest to carve out an identity they can be proud of.

They pit themselves against the college boys, who are snobs, not fighters, and want a sporting contest, not a dangerous one. The movie culminates in a bike race that left at least one screening-room audience cheering. Screening-room crowds don't ordinarily cheer.

The cutters, who make very convincing misfits, are played by a well-chosen ensemble including Mr. Christopher, Mr. Quaid (Randy Quaid's younger brother, though he bears more resemblance to Jan-Michael Vincent), Daniel Stern, and Jackie Earle Haley. Mr. Stern's scarecrow manner and offbeat comic timing work very nicely here, as does Mr. Haley's almost dwarfish physical presence. Mr. Haley, who played the little blond androgyne in *The Day of the Locust* and then the most unmistakable juvenile delinquent among the Bad News Bears, has grown into an odd actor and a gifted one too.

Peter Yates, the director, has been euphemistically remembered as the director of *Bullitt* while he turned out more questionable offerings, such as *For Pete's Sake* and *The Deep* and *Mother, Jugs* and *Speed.* This time, to anyone who said it couldn't be done, Mr. Yates can say "Hah!" and point to a subtle and imaginative success. Much of the credit undoubtedly also goes to the screenwriter, Steve Tesich, whose keen feeling for Americana belies his childhood overseas. But perhaps his background accounts for why Mr. Tesich, who spent his first thirteen years in Yugoslavia and is now thirty-five, can render both the Middle Western settings and the boys' feeling sense of themselves as outsiders so beautifully.

As enjoyable as those scenes centering on the young actors are, it's always a pleasure to get back to Mr. Dooley and Miss Barrie, who are at the comic heart of the story, reflecting those aspects of Indiana life that seem most incapable of changing—and yet, by the end of the story, do give way. Midway through the movie, they have a particularly memorable love scene, in which Miss Barrie attempts to seduce her husband with her own wiles plus the Italian music he professes to hate.

All of this, not to mention a good dinner, goes to Mr. Dooley's head. And he is charmed beyond all reason when Miss Barrie removes the flower she's put in her hair. In response, he tempestuously rips the plastic pencil case out of his breast pocket. He doesn't know it, but this is the first sign that he'll be eating pizza by the end of the story.

—*J.M., July 18, 1979*

BREAKING THE WAVES

Written and directed by Lars von Trier; director of photography, Robby Müller; edited by Anders Refn; music by Joachim Holbek; production designer, Karl Juliusson; produced by Vibeke Windelv and Peter Aalbaek Jensen; released by October Films. Running time: 158 minutes.

With: Emily Watson (Bess), Stellan Skarsgard (Jan), Adrian Rawlins (Doctor), Katrin Cartlidge (Dodo) and Udo Kier (Man on the Trawler).

Risky does not begin to describe *Breaking the Waves,* the raw, crazy tour de force that is the frenzied highlight of the New York Film Festival this year. Courting and sometimes winning ridicule, daring to fuse true love with lurid exploitation and pure religious faith, the Danish director Lars von Trier has created a fierce, wrenchingly passionate film about the struggles of a shy young woman who is goodness personified. Truly, bells ring in heaven for a heroine like this.

Yet Mr. von Trier, the famously eccentric Danish director of *Zentropa* and *The Kingdom* (one of his current projects is a thriller filmed in yearly three-minute segments, which he plans to finish in 2004), also has no qualms about dragging his film's gentle Bess through the mud. With a plot that owes as much to the Marquis de Sade as it does to higher-minded sources, Mr. von Trier begins his film as a powerfully carnal love story and eventually leaves it, by his own description, "treading on the verge of kitsch."

A narrative path leading from the sincere to the ludicrous, then culminating in a final image of flabbergasting transcendence, gives *Breaking the Waves* its surprising power. The film's visceral effectiveness is heightened further by the intimacy of Robby Müller's vigorous handheld cinematography and by Mr. von Trier's formula-free affectations, which sustain their peculiar discipline while also indulging the filmmaker's every whim. "For more intellectual audiences the style will excuse the tears," Mr. von Trier has said mischievously about these tactics. "The intellectuals will be able to permit themselves to cry because the story is so refined."

Indeed, audiences for *Breaking the Waves* can be expected to spend an unusually long time studying the closing credits, regaining their composure after having been put through Mr. von Trier's wringer. The film's final impact is stunning enough to justify a few yawns and snickers along the way.

Set in the early 1970's in a tiny coastal Scottish village, effectively severed from the rest of the world, *Breaking the Waves* begins with the rhapsodic transformation of Bess (Emily Watson, making an astonishing screen debut) from a sheltered innocent into a passionate wife. Early in the film, this fragile creature is married to a hulking, handsome oil rig worker named Jan (Stellan Skarsgard) and falls in love beyond her wildest dreams. The frank carnality of these early scenes sets a tone of muscular physicality that is one of the film's essential attributes. It conveys the full range of Bess's happiness and gives horrific impact to the tragedy that follows.

Desperately attached to her new husband, Bess wails in grief when he sails back out to sea. Though she is considered simple-minded by her neighbors in this harsh, forbidding Calvinist community, Bess often expresses her longings with that animal intensity; she also articulates her prayers as two-way talks with a reproachful God. Chiding herself as unworthy in that stern voice, Bess still dares to pray for Jan's return. She gets her wish with the malevolent fatefulness of a ghost story or a campfire tale.

The audience must watch in horror as Mr. von Trier emphasizes every threatening clank of the oil machinery, and every glimpse of heedless playfulness from Jan and his friends. Then the accident occurs. Jan returns home grievously injured, and now he is suddenly bitter toward his bride. Jan sees Bess's sexuality as a mocking reminder of his loss.

So far this is melodrama; then it goes mad. With a pornographer's ingenuity, Jan thinks of a way to rekindle his own sexual vitality while testing Bess's devotion. Without Bess's help in this, he says he will die. So the film follows wide-eyed Bess off the deep end, through an odyssey involving red vinyl hot pants, degrading sex, and a brief, leering appearance by Udo Kier. Adrian Rawlins, who plays Jan's doctor, prompts an inadvertent laugh in his first scene just by looking handsome enough to signal where this new side of the plot is headed.

And as *Breaking the Waves* requires Bess to make her leap of faith, it demands one from the audience, too. It's necessary to follow this quirky, single-minded film into parts unknown, trusting that the risk will be rewarded.

As Mr. von Trier fades his images into bleak natural tones, he creates a chilly and forbidding isolation for his characters. The church elders seen in *Breaking the Waves* espouse conventional thoughts of duty and punishment, displaying more faith in damnation than they do in divine mercy. Mr. von Trier counters that rigidity with near-lunatic flourishes that prove hugely effective, if only because they burst redemptively into the film with sudden flashes of pop vitality. The occasional rainbow, rock song, or computer-enhanced vista comes as an anachronistic jolt in a story that despite its offshore oil drilling and nominal time period could almost be taking place a century or two earlier. Mr. von Trier whimsically punctuates the film with chapter headings, too.

Nothing about *Breaking the Waves* is more fortuitous than the choice of Ms. Watson, the former Royal Shakespeare Company actress who so fervently and glowingly embodies Bess. The role calls for a trusting, absolutely unguarded performance, and the film would have been destroyed by anything less. Ms. Watson creates Bess with a devastating immediacy, and she deeply rewards the camera's penetrating gaze. Also very good are Mr. Skarsgard as the sturdy masculine presence so vital to the story, and the coolly forceful Katrin Cartlidge as Bess's straight-talking, sensible sister-in-law. She represents the rationality that *Breaking the Waves* eventually leaves far behind.

Breaking the Waves will be shown tonight and Sunday as part of the New York Film Festival. Brace yourself, and check your skepticism at the door.

—*J.M., October 4, 1996*

BREATHLESS

Directed by Jean-Luc Godard; written (in French, with English subtitles) by Mr. Godard, based on a story by François Truffaut; cinematographer, Raoul Coutard; edited by Cécile Decugis; music by Martial Solal; art designer, Claude Chabrol; produced by Georges de Beauregard; released by Films Around the World. Black and white. Running time: 89 minutes.

With: Jean Seberg (Patricia Franchini), Jean-Paul Belmondo (Michel Poiccard), Liliane David (Liliane), Daniel Boulanger (Inspector), Jean-Pierre Melville (Parvulesco) and Henri-Jacques Huet (Berrouti).

As sordid as is the French film, *Breathless* (*À Bout de Souffle*), which came to the Fine Arts yesterday—and sordid is really a mild word for its pile-up of gross indecencies—it is withal a fascinating communication of the savage ways and moods of some of the rootless young people of Europe (and America) today.

Made by Jean-Luc Godard, one of the newest and youngest of the "new wave" of experimental directors who seem to have taken over the cinema in France, it goes at its unattractive subject in an eccentric photographic style that sharply conveys the nervous tempo and the emotional erraticalness of the story it tells. And through the American actress, Jean Seberg, and a hypnotically ugly new young man by the name of Jean-Paul Belmondo, it projects two downright fearsome characters.

This should be enough, right now, to warn you that this is not a movie for the kids or for that easily shockable individual who used to be known as the old lady from Dubuque. It is emphatically, unrestrainedly vicious, completely devoid of moral tone, concerned mainly with eroticism and the restless drives of a cruel young punk to get along. Although it does not appear intended deliberately to shock, the very vigor of its reportorial candor compels that it must do so.

On the surface, it is a story of a couple of murky days in the lives of two erratic young lovers in Paris, their temporary home. He is a car thief and hoodlum, on the lam after having casually killed a policeman while trying to get away with a stolen car. She is an expatriate American newspaper street vendor and does occasional stories for an American newspaper man friend.

But in the frenetic fashion in which M. Godard pictures these few days—the nerve-tattering contacts of the lovers, their ragged relations with the rest of the world—there is subtly conveyed a vastly complex comprehension of an element of youth that is vagrant, disjointed, animalistic, and doesn't give a damn for anybody or anything, not even itself.

The key is in the character that M. Belmondo plays, an impudent, arrogant, sharp-witted, and alarmingly amoral hood. He thinks nothing more of killing a policeman or dismissing the pregnant condition of his girl than he does of pilfering the purse of an occasional sweetheart or rabbit-punching and robbing a guy in a gentlemen's room.

For a brief spell—or, rather a long spell, for the amount of time it takes up in the film—as he casually and coyly induces his pensive girlfriend to resume their love affair, it does look as if there may be a trace of poignant gentleness in him, some sincerity beneath the imitation of a swaggering American movie star. But there isn't. When his distracted girl finally turns him in and he is shot in the street, he can only muster a bit of bravado and label his girl with a filthy name.

The girl, too, is pretty much impervious to morality or sentiment, although she does indicate a sensitive nature that has been torn by disappointments and loneliness. As little Miss Seberg plays her, with her child's face and closely cropped hair, she is occasionally touching. But she is more often cold and shrewd, an efficiently self-defensive animal in a glittering, glib, irrational, heartless world.

All of this, and its sickening implications, M. Godard has got into this film, which progresses in a style of disconnected cutting that might be described as "pictorial cacophony." A musical score of erratic tonal qualities emphasizes the eccentric moods. And in M. Belmondo we see an actor who is the most effective cigarette-mouther and thumb-to-lip rubber since time began.

Say this, in sum, for *Breathless:* it is certainly no cliché, in any area or sense of the word. It is more a chunk of raw drama, graphically and artfully torn with appropriately ragged edges out of the tough underbelly of modern metropolitan life.

—B.C., February 8, 1961

THE BRIDE WORE BLACK

Directed by François Truffaut; written (in French, with English subtitles) by Mr. Truffaut and Jean-Louis Richard, based on the novel by Cornell Woolrich (as William Irish); cinematographer, Raoul Coutard; edited by Claudine Bouché; music by Bernard Herrmann; art designer, Pierre Guffroy; produced by Marcel Berbert; released by Lopert Pictures. Running time: 107 minutes.

With: Jeanne Moreau (Julie), Jean-Claude Brialy (Corey), Michel Bouquet (Coral), Charles Denner (Fergus), Claude Rich (Bliss), Daniel Boulanger (Holmes) and Michel Lonsdale (Morane).

Even working lightly, on a film not his best in a genre not his own, François Truffaut is such a rare talent that one knows instantly, as soon as the credits for *The Bride Wore Black* appear on screen, that this is what movies are about, this is how they can be done, this is why so few people do them beautifully. The movie is technically a suspense and horror film—a tribute to Alfred Hitchcock, with whom Truffaut did a fascinating book of interviews last year—in which Jeanne Moreau murders a number of gentlemen. But Truffaut is such a poetic filmmaker that the film turns around and becomes, not at all Hitchcockian, but a gentle comedy and one of the few plausible and strange love stories in a long time.

Miss Moreau murders five men in all—Claude Rich, Michel Bouquet, Michael Lonsdale, Daniel Boulanger, and Charles Denner—and every one of them is a gem of characterization, lines witty and right, acting subtle and thought out, the decor of their lives and even the manner of their deaths inventive and expressive of personality. Miss Moreau herself, who is always dressed in black or in white (this is a color film) has to maintain a kind of Mademoiselle and Kriemhild deadpan in an uncharacteristically young unsensual role and does it fine. Alexandra Stewart as a schoolteacher, Jean-Claude Brialy as a friend, even Frederique and Renaud Fontanarosa playing musicians (which they are), every member of the cast gives a performance that makes other people's movies seem keyed loose and out of tune.

There are all kinds of little things: the look of fear that crosses the expression of Claude Rich when he thinks he is going to be pushed off a balcony, then the look of embarrassment over this silly fear, then his look as he falls; Michel Lonsdale's minute, self-satisfied nod toward his Légion d'Honneur lapel; a small, perfectly timed clapping of the hands, in a game of hide-and-seek by Christophe Brunot, a little boy from whom Truffaut gets the best child performance since Alain Cohen's in *The Two of Us.* (Ever since Jean-Pierre Léaud's performance in Truffaut's first film, *The 400 Blows,* the director has had a special gift with children.) The boy knows an adult is being misled; his behavior toward adults, suspicious, canny, stubborn, terrified, amused, is one of the most remarkable evocations of certain moments in certain childhoods on screen.

The photography is by Raoul Coutard—who also did Truffaut's *400 Blows, Jules and Jim,* and *Shoot the Piano Player!*—and it, too, is beautifully and carefully worked out. A sign of the absolute confidence one has in every moment of the film is that, although one of the killings is done by high-powered rifle, from a window to the street, the movie recovers from real associations to that act almost at once. Everything is so clearly the result of thought and wit; this is, for a change, a film in which it is pure pleasure to be alert. One does not want to review the refinements of the plot away. It is not a great, great picture but it is touching and fun at a level so much higher than other films that it is just a great relief to have it to see. The film opened yesterday at the Festival Theater.

—*R.A., June 26, 1968*

THE BRIDGE ON THE RIVER KWAI

Directed by David Lean; written by Michael Wilson, Carl Foreman and Pierre Boulle, based on the novel by Mr. Boulle; cinematographer, Jack Hildyard; edited by Peter Taylor; music by Malcolm Arnold; produced by Sam Spiegel; released by Columbia Pictures. Running time: 161 minutes.

With: William Holden (Shears), Alec Guinness (Colonel Nicholson), Jack Hawkins (Major Warden), Sessue Hayakawa (Colonel Saito), James Donald (Major Clipton), Geoffrey Horne (Lieutenant Joyce), Andre Morell (Colonel Green), Peter Williams (Captain Reeves) and John Boxer (Major Hughes).

There are actually two motion picture dramas— two strong, suspenseful issues—embraced in Sam Spiegel's exceptional film production, *The Bridge on the River Kwai.*

The first is a powerful personal drama of a conflict of wills between two military men, one the Japanese commander of a prisoner-of-war camp in the Burmese jungle and the other a British colonel brought there with a handful of his men. The second drama is a tingling action thriller that follows smoothly upon the resolution of the first. The crux of it is a bold maneuver to blow up a jungle railway bridge.

This mounting of drama upon drama in Mr. Spiegel's magnificent color film, which opened last night at the Palace for an extended two-a-day run, makes it more than a towering entertainment of rich variety and revelation of the ways of men. It makes it one of the niftiest bargains to be had on the screen this holiday.

Since both of the issues in this picture—the conflict of wills between two men and the subsequent contest to accomplish the destruction of the prisoner-built bridge—are loaded with mortal tension that holds the viewer in sweating suspense, it seems a shame that we have to give an inkling of the outcome of either one. But so much of the theme of the whole picture is conveyed in the resolution of the first that we have to tip you off to that one; the British colonel wins.

That is to say, he outfaces and outwits the camp commandant in compelling the latter's surrender on a military technicality. He refuses to permit himself or his officers to do manual labor on the building of the strategic bridge, as is brutally and illegally demanded by the snarling commandant. And for the first hour or so of the picture, he undergoes torture of a terrible, withering sort, until he catches his adversary in an ironic weakness and compels him to respect the military code.

He wins, but he wins at the expense of a shocking, significant compromise. He agrees to apply himself and officers as supervising engineers. He accepts the narrow technical victory with satisfaction and even pride, without regard for—or even apparent awareness of—the aid he will thus give the enemy. The building of the bridge for the one-track railway becomes the sole aim of this man with the one-track mind.

Here is the heart of this fine picture, here is its stark and potent theme: discipline and conformity are the obsession of the professional militarist. And upon this rising realization hinges all the subsequent drama and suspense as a small commando team inches into the jungle to destroy the colonel's precious bridge. Does the colonel actually stop his own countrymen? This one we will not reveal!

Brilliant is the word, and no other, to describe the quality of skills that have gone into the making of this picture, from the writing of the script out of a novel by the Frenchman Pierre Boulle, to direction, performance, photographing, editing, and application of a musical score.

David Lean has directed it so smartly and so sensitively for image and effect that its two hours and forty-one minutes seem no more than a swift, absorbing hour. In addition to splendid performance, he has it brilliantly filled with atmosphere—the atmosphere of war's backwash and the jungle—touched startlingly with humor, heart, and shock.

In the line of performance, Alec Guinness does a memorable—indeed, a classic—job in making the ramrod British colonel a profoundly ambiguous type. With a rigid, serene disposition, he displays the courage and tenacity of a lion, as well as the denseness and pomposity of a dangerously stupid, inbred snob. He shows, beneath the surface of a hero, the aspects of an inhuman fool. He gives one of the most devastating portraits of a militarist that we have ever seen.

As his Japanese opposite number, old Sessue Hayakawa is superb—brutal, stubborn, sluggish, an equally grotesque fool. Jack Hawkins is droll and determined as the British major who leads the commando raid and William Holden is delightfully gallant as an American sailor mixed up in this strange affair. James Donald, Geoffrey Horne, and Peter Williams are splendid as British army chaps, and a bunch of little Oriental females add spice as native porters on the raid.

A real bridge and natural settings in Ceylon have been exquisitely photographed by Jack Hildyard's color cameras.

Here is a film we guarantee you'll not forget.

—*B.C., December 19, 1957*

BRIEF ENCOUNTER

Directed by David Lean; written by Mr. Lean, Anthony Havelock-Allan and Noël Coward, based on his play *Still Life*; cinematographer, Robert Krasker; edited by Jack Harris; music by Sergei Rachmaninoff; produced by Mr. Coward; released by Prestige Pictures. Black and white. Running time: 86 minutes.

With: Celia Johnson (Laura Jesson), Trevor Howard (Dr. Alec Harvey), Cyril Raymond (Fred Jesson), Joyce Carey (Barmaid), Stanley Holloway (Station Guard), Valentine Dyall (Stephan Lynn),

Everley Gregg (Dolly Messiter), Margaret Barton (Beryl) and Dennis Harkin (Stanley).

An uncommonly good little picture—and one which is frankly designed to appeal to that group of filmgoers who are provoked by the "usual movie tripe"—is the British-made *Brief Encounter*, which opened on Saturday at the Little Carnegie Theatre as the first of so-called Prestige imports.

Being no more than an expansion of one of Noël Coward's one-act plays—the conversational *Still Life*, from his *Tonight at 8:30* group—it is plainly an intimate drama, limited in every respect to the brief and extremely poignant romance of a married woman and a married man. And virtually all of the action takes place in a railway waiting-room and in the small English town adjacent thereto, where the couple make their fleeting rendezvous.

That's all there is to the story—a quite ordinary middle-class wife, contentedly married and the mother of two children, meets a similarly settled doctor one day while on a weekly shopping visit to a town near that in which she lives. The casual and innocent acquaintance, renewed on successive weeks, suddenly ripens into a deep affection by which both are shaken and shocked. For a brief spell they spin in the bewilderment of conventions and their own emotional ties. Then they part, the doctor to go away and the wife to return to her home.

There are obvious flaws in the story. The desperate affection of the two develops a great deal more rapidly than the circumstances would seem to justify. And the cheerful obtuseness of the lady's husband is more accommodating than one would expect. But the whole thing has been presented in such a delicate and affecting way—and with such complete naturalness in characterization and fidelity to middle-class detail—that those slight discrepancies in logic may be easily allowed.

Under David Lean's fluid direction, Celia Johnson, who was memorable as the commander's wife in Mr. Coward's fine *In Which We Serve*, gives a consuming performance as the emotionally shaken lady in the case. Unprettified by makeup and quite plainly and consistently dressed, she is naturally and honestly disturbing with her wistful voice and large, sad saucer-eyes. And Trevor Howard, who has none of the aspects of a cutout movie star, makes a thoroughly credible partner in this small and pathetic romance. Excellent, too, as characters in a flat, middle-class milieu are Joyce Carey, Cyril Raymond, Everley Gregg, and Stanley Holloway.

—B.C., August 26, 1946

A BRIEF HISTORY OF TIME

Directed by Errol Morris: based on the book by Stephen Hawking: directors of photography, John Bailey and Stefan Czapsky: edited by Brad Fuller: music by Philip Glass: production designer, Ted Bafaloukos: produced by David Hickman: released by Triton Pictures. Running time: 80 minutes.

Help is at hand for everyone who, like me, plunked down $18.95 to buy Stephen Hawking's *Brief History of Time* only to realize, upon reaching page 11, that not a word had sunk in after page 5. *A Brief History of Time* has been its own black hole. It not only swallowed up enough of the curious to keep it on the best-seller lists for 100 weeks. It also seems to have prevented any reader from emerging to sound the alarm: brief the volume is, but also dangerously dense.

Errol Morris, a director of documentaries (*The Thin Blue Line, Gates of Heaven*), has come to the rescue of everyone who feels somehow inadequate for failing to mush on to the last page. Inspired by the book and working with the English physicist's cooperation, Mr. Morris has now made a film with the same alluring title. It opens today at the Lincoln Plaza Cinemas.

This *Brief History of Time* has its impenetrable moments, but it is also something of a delight. It functions both as an introduction to the work by Mr. Hawking and his associates in their search for a unified theory of physics, and as a most engaging portrait of him, the members of his family, his friends, and colleagues. They are variously serious, funny, brilliant, caustic, and, from time to time, eccentric in a way that evokes memories of more than one novel about England's academe.

Mr. Hawking's own story would be enough for any single film. A bright but lazy student, he was diagnosed as having amyotrophic lateral sclerosis (known as Lou Gehrig's disease in the United States) shortly after he went to Cambridge in the mid-1960's to work on his Ph.D. in theoretical physics. The illness, which is progressive and incurable, has now left him almost completely paralyzed. After a bout of pneumonia and a tracheotomy, he talks through a computer whose commands activate a voice synthesizer.

The film integrates Mr. Hawking's personal story with the story of his work on the unified theory, including his increasing ability to focus his mental energies while losing so much of his physical freedom. His mother speaks of the effect of the illness on his work, and of luck, something her son might associate with the random behavior of particles. "Everybody has disasters," she says, "and yet some people disappear and are never seen again."

The film moves easily among its dozens of interviews. This is surprisingly lively stuff, whether his sister is recalling Mr. Hawking's passion for board games and his mother is saying that board games are just a substitute for life, or his colleagues are attempting to explain the value of Mr. Hawking's work, his breakthroughs and his mistakes. Little by little some inkling of what the book is all about comes through, though certain terms (event horizons, singularities, imaginary time) still are not easily grasped.

There are moments when Mr. Hawking and his colleagues sound a bit like characters in a revue sketch from *Beyond the Fringe*. "I was thinking about black holes as I got into bed one night in 1970, shortly after the birth of my daughter Lucy." This is Mr. Hawking's way of introducing an insight he had about the behavior of collapsing stars and what might happen should they collide.

Later he recalls having made a proposal to an associate that "time and space are finite in extent, but they don't have any boundary or edge." He likens it to the earth's surface, which is finite in area though without boundaries. He then adds something that sounds very much like a physicist's joke: "In all my travels I have not managed to fall off the edge of the world."

A number of the Hawking theories are illustrated by beautifully executed graphics. Yet ideas seem less important to the film than being in the presence of agile minds at work, talking, speculating, theorizing, searching, questioning. *A Brief History of Time* is a kind of adventure that seldom reaches the screen, and it's a tonic.

—V.C., August 21, 1992

BRINGING UP BABY

Produced and directed by Howard Hawks; written by Dudley Nichols and Hagar Wilde, based on a short story by Mr. Wilde; cinematographer, Russell Metty; edited by George Hively; music by Roy Webb; art designer, Van Nest Polglase; released by RKO Radio Pictures. Black and white. Running time: 102 minutes.

With: Katharine Hepburn (Susan Vance), Cary Grant (David Huxley), Charlie Ruggles (Major Applegate), Barry Fitzgerald (Gogarty), May Robson (Mrs. Random), Walter Catlett (Constable Slocum), Fritz Feld (Dr. Lehman), Leona Robers (Mrs. Gogarty) and George Irving (Lawyer Peabody).

To the Music Hall yesterday came a farce which you can barely hear above the precisely enunciated patter of Miss Katharine Hepburn and the ominous tread of deliberative gags. In *Bringing Up Baby* Miss Hepburn has a role which calls for her to be breathless, senseless, and terribly, terribly fatiguing. She succeeds, and we can be callous enough to hint it is not entirely a matter of performance.

And the gags! Have you heard the one about the trained leopard and the wild leopard who get loose at the same time? Or the one about the shallow brook with the deep hole? Or the one about the man wearing a woman's negligee? Or the one about the Irishman who drains his flask and sees a wild animal which really is a wild animal?

You have? Surprising, indeed. But perhaps you haven't heard the one about the annoying wire-haired terrier who makes off with a valuable object and buries it somewhere and has the whole cast on his heels. That one, too? Well, then, how about the one where the man slips and sits on his top hat? Or the one where the heroine is trying to arouse a sleeper by tossing pebbles at his window and, just as he pokes his head out, hits him neatly with a bit of cobblestone? Or, getting back to the leopard who is the "baby" of the title, would

you laugh madly if a Charles Ruggles did a leopard-cry imitation as an after-dinner stunt and commented two minutes later upon the unusual echo?

Well, neither did we. In fact, after the first five minutes of the Music Hall's new show—we needed those five to orient ourselves—we were content to play the game called "the cliché expert goes to the movies" and we are not at all proud to report that we scored 100 percent against Dudley Nichols, Hagar Wilde, and Howard Hawks, who wrote and produced the quiz. Of course, if you've never been to the movies, *Bringing Up Baby* will be all new to you—a zany-ridden product of the goofy farce school. But who hasn't been to the movies?

—F.S.N., March 4, 1938

BROADCAST NEWS

Written, produced and directed by James L. Brooks; director of photography, Michael Ballhaus; edited by Richard Marks; music by Bill Conti; production designer, Charles Rosen; released by Twentieth Century Fox. Running time: 133 minutes.

With: William Hurt (Tom Grunick), Albert Brooks (Aaron Altman), Holly Hunter (Jane Craig), Robert Prosky (Ernie Merriman), Lois Chiles (Jennifer Mack), Joan Cusack (Blair Litton), Peter Hackes (Paul Moore), Christian Clemenson (Bobby) and Robert Katims (Martin Klein).

There once was a time when big news events had the power to stun and, sometimes, to cause a certain amount of anxiety. Wars, earthquakes, airplane crashes, stock market busts, mass-murder sprees, kidnappings, duplicity in positions of public trust, political assassinations. These things could upset daily routine. They were reminders of the precariousness of the existence we tend to take for granted.

Today, having harnessed the atom, we're well on the way toward the taming of fate or, at least, our perception of random events as presented on the home television screen. Today, thanks to the warmth and sincerity of Dan and Peter and Jane and Connie, we might even accept—with little more than informed concern—the imminent end of the world: after the bang, we'll have these messages from the sponsors and then tomorrow's weather.

Television news-as-entertainment is the very funny, occasionally satiric subtext of *Broadcast News,* the bright new comedy written and directed by James L. Brooks, with three smashing star performances by William Hurt, Albert Brooks, and Holly Hunter. *Broadcast News* opens today at the Coronet.

In his first film since his Oscar-winning *Terms of Endearment,* Mr. Brooks goes inside the offices and studios of the Washington bureau of a national television network to show us how things work. As exposés go, *Broadcast News* is gentle. It's far more amused than angry. Its wit is decently humane. It also says something about the pervasive nature of television that, although the subject is parochial, *Broadcast News* is no more or less arcane than *Miami Vice.*

The movie is mainly concerned with the fortunes of three ambitious colleagues.

Tom Grunick (Mr. Hurt) is on his way up as an anchor. When he arrives at his new Washington berth, he is, by his own admission, "no good at what I'm being a success at." He can't write. He has no experience as a newsman. Yet he's making a fortune. What he does have, in addition to good looks, is a lot of savvy on how to use the camera.

Seen sitting at his anchor desk in a big fat close-up, Tom Grunick can take information being fed to him (via a hidden head-mike from the control room) and translate it into an expression of a singularly magnetic public personality. Cool, intelligent, caring. Off camera, Tom Grunick is earnest, well meaning, none too well informed. On camera he's the soul of Walter Cronkite inhabiting the physique of a matinee idol.

Aaron Altman (Albert Brooks) is an old-fashioned reporter. He's his own best legman. He's a quick study and possesses the kind of curiosity that equips him to cover just about any kind of story. He's a successful on-camera reporter, the sort who, without missing a beat, can switch from a story about equal opportunity employment to one about a war veteran.

More than anything else, Aaron Altman wants to be an anchor. However, when the lights are on him, behind that great, photogenic, immaculate desk in the news studio, Aaron Altman, Pulitzer Prize—winning reporter, goes to pieces. He sweats like a weight lifter and projects the charm of an unsuccessful salesman of used cars.

Jane Craig (Miss Hunter) is a pretty, brainy young woman who's obsessed with her work as a producer of television news spots. She's smart enough to know news from filler material and how best to present it. She's one of those women sometimes thought to be too smart for her own good, and sometimes she has to agree. When the head of the network news division says, with a good deal of sarcasm, "It must be nice to always think you're the smartest person in the room," she replies, "No, it's awful."

The private lives of Tom, Aaron, and Jane are scarcely more than slight interruptions in their careers. They exist entirely within their jobs. In the course of *Broadcast News,* as the network goes through various upheavals, the three become emotionally involved in ways that would seem heartbreaking to people less ambitious. Here it's the material of high comedy.

Mr. Brooks's screenplay overstates matters both at the beginning of the film and at the end, with a prologue that strains to be cute and an epilogue that is just unnecessary. In between, however, the movie is a sarcastic and carefully detailed picture of a world Mr. Brooks finds fascinating and also a little scary.

Mr. Hurt, a most complicated actor, is terrific as a comparatively simple man, someone who's perfectly aware of his intellectual limitations but who sees no reason for them to interfere with his climb to the top. Miss Hunter, whose performance as the wife in *Raising Arizona* was lost in that film's comic frenzy, is a delight as a woman who at heart is quite satisfied to be liberated. Miss Hunter is a bit reminiscent of Debra Winger (who seems to be this year's role model for actresses) but is idiosyncratic enough to lend her own substance to the film.

As the fast-talking Aaron, Albert Brooks comes very close to stealing *Broadcast News.* Mr. Brooks, who has directed and starred in three genially oddball comedies of his own (the most recent being *Lost in America*), is more or less the conscience of *Broadcast News.*

Yet James Brooks, as this film's writer-director, has so balanced the movie that no one performer can run off with it. This would include Jack Nicholson, who makes a fine unbilled appearance as the network's star anchor from New York.

Mr. Brooks gives his characters the benefit of the doubt. Unlike stock figures, they can send themselves up. Says one reporter to another, "Would you tell a source you loved them just to get information?" The immediate response, "Yes," is followed by laughter all around. In fact, the question remains unanswered.

—*V.C., December 16, 1987*

BROTHER'S KEEPER

Produced, directed and edited by Joe Berlinger and Bruce Sinofsky: director of photography, Douglas Cooper: music by Jay Ungar and Molly Mason: released by Creative Thinking International. Running time: 104 minutes.

With: The Ward brothers, Madison County residents and Attorney Ralph A. Cognetti.

On June 6, 1990, William Ward, sixty-four years old, was found dead in the bed he had shared for most of his life with his brother, Adelbert, fifty-nine, known as Delbert, in the unheated shack on the upstate New York dairy farm where they lived with their brothers Roscoe, seventy, and Lyman, sixty-two. Bill suffered from several ailments, and the death was originally thought to have been the result of natural causes. An autopsy then suggested that there had been foul play.

After his interrogation by the state police, Delbert signed a confession to the effect that he had smothered Bill in his sleep in a mercy killing that had been sanctioned by the three surviving brothers. Until then the semiliterate brothers, always called "the Ward boys" in spite of their ages, were regarded as harmless eccentrics. With their long beards, unkempt hair, and disregard for personal hygiene, the brothers didn't have many friends in nearby Munnsville (population 499). "The smell might get the best of you," one woman reports. The Ward boys kept to themselves.

Yet when Delbert was arrested, his cousins, neighbors and even those Madison County people who didn't personally know him rose up to unite in his defense. Within a few of hours of the announcement of his arrest, they had collected the $10,000 needed for his bail. Their common belief was that the Delbert they knew, if only from a distance, was incapable of murder. There also was the conviction that Delbert had no idea what he was signing when he put his name to the confession.

Further, there was something like territorial pride

at work: the Ward boys might be oddballs, but they were Munnsville oddballs. It was all right for people in Munnsville to make fun of them, but woe to the outsiders who assumed that intimacy. Early in the case, two New York filmmakers began to record the developments as they occurred. The result is *Brother's Keeper,* the superb documentary opening today at the Film Forum.

Produced, directed, and edited by Joe Berlinger and Bruce Sinofsky, *Brother's Keeper* is not only the story of Delbert's arrest, the long months leading up to his trial and the trial itself. It's also about his family and about the community that found its identity by supporting him. It's a rich slice of Americana that would seem to belong to an earlier, pretelevision era, except that television comes to play a large part in Delbert's story. It's also about an aspect of life in rural America that's seldom seen by people who drive through it, and seldom if ever glimpsed in movies.

Mr. Berlinger, Mr. Sinofsky, and Douglas Cooper, the cameraman, start at the story's center and work out from there. They begin with portraits of the brothers as they go about their chores on the farm, and as they sit around their filthy, cluttered two-room house, sometimes talking, often not saying much at all. The focus becomes wider as the filmmakers talk to cousins and neighbors, including the man who came over shortly after Bill was found dead, and who reports that at six a.m., the body "was kind of cool, not cold, and his arm sort of flipsy."

There are interviews with members of the state police, with the people responsible for the prosecution, and with Ralph A. Cognetti, the Syracuse lawyer hired to defend Delbert. The filmmakers attend a noisy, convivial community dinner and square dance organized by the Delbert Ward Defense Fund. The affair also attracts television reporters who are seen giving their on-camera reports even as Delbert, no longer the recluse he once was and now something of a local celebrity, is happily do-si-doing in the background.

The case turns into a media event. Connie Chung comes to Munnsville. Mr. Cognetti speaks to a large schoolroom full of Delbert's supporters, telling them that he worries that Delbert will lose his plausibility if he becomes too fond of the limelight. Delbert demonstrates for the camera how the state police demonstrated to him how he had smothered Bill. The prosecution suggests that Bill was murdered as a result of an incestuous relationship between the brothers.

Yet nothing fazes Delbert's supporters, a number of whom are as surprisingly articulate as they are staunch. The camera pulls further and further back until, by the end, *Brother's Keeper* is a remarkably rich portrait of a man in the context of his family, his community, the law, and even the seasons.

The film inevitably raises more questions than it answers. Are the individual Ward boys genuinely slow-witted or, until this event, have they been hampered by their isolation and lack of formal schooling? To what extent, if any, was the case against Delbert trumped up? And to what extent was his community's increasing support a result of the media attention?

Like fine fiction, *Brother's Keeper* does not supply easy answers. It haunts the mind in the speculation it prompts.

—*V.C., September 9, 1992*

THE BUDDY HOLLY STORY

Directed by Steve Rash; written by Robert Gittler, based on the book by John Coldrosen; director of photography, Stevan Larner; edited by David Ble-witt; music by Joe Renzetti; production designer, Joel Schiller; produced by Fred Bauer; released by Columbia Pictures. Running time: 113 minutes.

With: Gary Busey (Buddy Holly), Don Stroud (Jesse), Charles Martin Smith (Ray Bob), Bill Jordan (Riley Randolph), Maria Richwine (Maria Elena Holly), Conrad Janis (Ross Turner) and Albert Powell (Eddie Foster).

There are a lot of actors in *The Buddy Holly Story*—some of them very nice—but the movie is really a one-man show. It's Gary Busey's galvanizing solo performance that gives meaning to an otherwise shapeless and bland feature-length film about the American rock-and-roll star who was killed in a plane crash in 1959.

The film, which opens today at the Criterion and other theaters, was made with the cooperation of Holly's widow, Maria Elena Holly, and may be a demonstration of why keepers of the flame are not the best people to have around when you're making a movie.

The Buddy Holly Story has a story of sorts, but it's a B-picture plot with all of the crises and villains discreetly removed, about the virtually unimpeded rise to the top, within three years, of a nice, gawky kid from Lubbock, Texas, who could express himself only through his music.

Buddy Holly was not Wolfgang Amadeus Mozart. What he expresses are not the contradictory impulses of a society of rare sophistication, but the pounding lusts and comic heartbreaks of people who have trouble dealing with any gratification not instant.

It may be argued that the film, written by Robert Gittler and directed by Steve Rash, reflects the essential simplicity of Holly's music, but that, I think, is to confuse simplicity with lack of technique, which is the manner of the film. Holly's music—including the dozen songs ("That'll Be the Day," "Well Alright," "Every Day," among others) that are reprised in the movie—is not especially complex but it expresses a kind of youthful vitality that has nothing much to do with the conventions of dopey moviemaking.

Which brings us to Mr. Busey, who's already been seen in *The Last American Hero, Thunderbolt and Lightfoot,* and, most recently, in *Straight Time,* as Dustin Hoffman's junkie pal. Mr. Busey, tall and slightly awkward, a fellow whose teeth appear to have been grown and not styled, has the look of middle America all over him. He's also capable of making articulate a character who remains inarticulate except in his music. He's not only an actor who possesses a center of gravity—of intelligence—but he's also a pop musician (professional name: Teddy Jack Eddy) who understands the mysterious (to the rest of us) transformation that takes place during a performance.

Don Stroud and Charles Martin Smith (*American Graffiti*) are effective and functional as Buddy Holly's two hometown pals who accompany him to stardom. Maria Richwine plays the Puerto Rican girl he marries, Gloria Irricari is her skeptical, watchful aunt (who doesn't trust musicians), and Paul Mooney, Gilbert Melgar, and George Simonelli show up as some of the other rock stars (Sam Cooke, Richie Valens, and Dion) whose careers crossed that of Holly.

Although *The Buddy Holly Story* can't be classified as a musical, it's a movie that comes alive only during the musical sequences, and these sequences, featuring Mr. Busey's transformed country-boy, are so good, so full of energy, they turn the material that frames them into wood.

—V.C., July 21, 1978

BULL DURHAM

Written and directed by Ron Shelton; director of photography, Bobby Byrne; edited by Robert Leighton and Adam Weiss; music by Michael Convertino; production designer, Armin Ganz; produced by Thom Mount and Mark Burg; released by Orion Pictures. Running time: 115 minutes.

With: Kevin Costner (Crash Davis), Susan Sarandon (Annie Savoy), Tim Robbins (Ebby Calvin "Nuke" LaLoosh), Trey Wilson (Skip), Robert Wuhl (Larry), William O'Leary (Jimmy), David Neidorf (Bobby) and Danny Gans (Deke).

*B*ull Durham is a film with spring fever, a giddy, playful look at life in baseball's minor leagues. The team on which it concentrates is the Durham, North Carolina, Bulls, but the film involves no person, team, or chewing tobacco with the Bull Durham name, so the title is slightly puzzling. It would be unsporting to mention this if there weren't many other misfires of a similar nature: dialogue that strains to be colorful, indiscriminately piled-on pop songs, plot developments that aren't followed through on, and minor aspects of motivation that are never known.

It's a lucky thing that the film, like the players it celebrates, knows better than to stake too much on ability alone. Even luckier, it has more than enough spirit and sex appeal to get by. In fact, *Bull Durham* has a cast that's much too attractive to need the kind of overheated sexual grandstanding that the writer and director Ron Shelton (who previously wrote *Under Fire*) insists upon. Brash but a little unsteady in his directing debut feature, Mr. Shelton has a way of overstating some things about these characters and leaving others bafflingly unsaid.

Bull Durham, which opens today at the Criterion and other theaters, sets up a romantic triangle involving Annie Savoy (Susan Sarandon) with two baseball players, Crash Davis and (Nuke) Laloosh (played by Kevin Costner and Tim Robbins, both of whom might well have accepted these roles on the strength of the character names alone).

Annie, who narrates the film, is a baseball enthusiast with a difference: she keeps a shrine to the sport in her home, ponders odd facts linking baseball with religion (that there are 108 beads on a rosary, for instance, and also 108 stitches in a baseball), and each year chooses a player to become the beneficiary of her own highly unconventional brand of home instruction. It might be said that Annie is an aging groupie. But Mr. Shelton, who shows her lashing one new recruit to her bed and reading him Walt Whitman, presents her as a muse.

Miss Sarandon turns Annie into such a dish that the distinction hardly matters, sashaying through the film in off-the-shoulder outfits and delivering much more advice on the game of baseball than any of the Bulls ever dreamed he'd want to hear. Annie's protégé for this particular season is the talented, extremely dim (and extremely funny, thanks to Mr. Robbins) rookie she nicknames "Nuke," who is every tutor's dream.

Nuke follows Annie's every suggestion, right down to her idea of having him wear a black garter belt under his uniform while he pitches. That way, Nuke explains dutifully to a teammate, he can "keep one side of my brain occupied when I'm on the mound, thus keeping the other side slightly off-center, which is where it should be for artists and players." Good student that he is, Nuke has understandable nightmares about the pitfalls of following Annie's advice a little too far.

Crash Davis arrives on the scene as an older player assigned to keep Nuke from self-destructing, but he quickly emerges as the kid's antithesis in every way. Crash had the brains that might have made him great, but he didn't have the talent; he was good, but not good enough. And he can understand Annie a lot better than Nuke can, possibly better than she understands herself.

Mr. Shelton manages to make these qualities seem pat and hazy simultaneously, and there are too many times when it's difficult to be sure where Crash stands; when he picks a barroom fight with Nuke at the beginning of the film, for instance, the sequence is directed so slackly that it's momentarily hard to be sure whether the fight is a trick or the real thing. Kevin Costner, whose wary, elusive manner in other films has sometimes been mistaken for blankness, this time seems a good deal more definite than the material itself.

Mr. Costner, who is well on his way to becoming a full-fledged matinee idol, does a lot with this role all the same.

Mr. Costner gives Crash a shrewd, knowing manner so effortless that it's easily mistaken for nonchalance, and a flirty, confident style that Annie inevitably begins to appreciate. The attraction between them need not have led to the elaborate antics Mr. Shelton produces: Crash and Annie dancing around her apartment in kimonos (twice), or cavorting in the bathtub, or collaborating on an impromptu pedicure. Each of them, and particularly Mr. Costner, knows how to make a small amount of suggestiveness go a lot farther than this.

Another thing these actors do is to camouflage the material's seamier side. "I mean, it wasn't the first time I went to bed with a man and woke up with a note," says Annie at one point, but her past history is handled with kid gloves. And Crash's professional status remains somewhat indistinct, so that he's neither a misguided winner nor the kind of resigned has-been played by Paul Newman in *Slap Shot,* that classic comedy of second-rate sports. The best of *Bull Durham* has some of that film's loose-jointed, iconoclastic physical humor. It also has the charming if belabored notion that baseball, love, poetry, and religion do indeed share common ground.

—*J M., June 15, 1988*

fast, well acted, written the way people talk. The plot is dense with detail about the way things work: hospitals, police, young politicians with futures, gangsters, airports, love affairs, traffic, dingy hotels. There are a lot of Negroes cast, for a change, in plausible roles. The setting, in San Francisco, is solidly there, and the ending should satisfy fans from *Dragnet* to Camus.

There are excellent chases, one around and under jet aircraft taking off by night, the other, by car, over the San Francisco hills. The car chase in particular is comic and straight. (Nobody drives better than Steve McQueen.) McQueen, quietly stealing a newspaper because he hasn't got the dime or exchanging just the right look with a Negro surgeon who understands, or even delivering a line that consoles and sums up the situation with his girl (played by Jacqueline Bisset) embodies his special kind of aware, existential cool— less taut and hardshell than Bogart, less lost and adrift than Mastroianni, a little of both.

The movie, which is in color (rather dark and yellow), was directed by Peter Yates and also features Don Gordon, Robert Duvall, Simon Oakland, Robert Vaughan (from U.N.C.L.E.), and Norman Fell (of the 87th Precinct). They and the minor characters are all fine, dry, and natural, as this particular detective form requires. Television has almost stolen the genre, or made it unserious, but *Bullitt* tightens and reclaims it for the movies. McQueen simply gets better all the time.

—*R.A., October 18, 1968*

BULLITT

Directed by Peter Yates; written by Alan R. Trustman and Harry Kleiner; based on the novel *Mute Witness* by Robert L. Pike; cinematographer, William A. Fraker; edited by Frank P. Keller; music by Lalo Schifrin; art designer, Albert Brenner; produced by Philip D'Antoni; released by Warner Brothers. Running time: 114 minutes.

With: Steve McQueen (Bullitt), Robert Vaughn (Chalmers), Jacqueline Bisset (Cathy), Don Gordon (Delgetti), Robert Duvall (Weissberg), Simon Oakland (Captain Bennett) and Norman Fell (Baker).

*B*ullitt, which opened yesterday at the Music Hall, is a terrific movie, just right for Steve McQueen—

BUS STOP

Directed by Joshua Logan; written by George Axelrod, based on the play by William Inge; cinematographer, Milton Krasner; music by Alfred Newman; produced by Buddy Adler; released by Twentieth Century Fox. Running time: 94 minutes.

With: Marilyn Monroe (Cherie), Don Murray (Bo), Arthur O'Connell (Virgil), Betty Field (Grace), Eileen Heckart (Vera), Robert Bray (Carl), Hope Lange (Elma), Hans Conreid (*Life* Photographer), Casey Adams (*Life* Reporter) and Henry Slate (Manager of the Nightclub).

*H*old onto your chairs, everybody, and get set for a rattling surprise. Marilyn Monroe has finally proved herself an actress in *Bus Stop.* She and the picture are swell!

This piece of professional information may seem both implausible and absurd to those who have gauged the lady's talents by her performances in such films as *Niagara, Gentlemen Prefer Blondes,* and even *The Seven Year Itch,* wherein her magnetism was put forth by other qualities than her histrionic skill. And it may also cause some skepticism on the part of those who saw the play by William Inge, from which the film is lifted, and remember Kim Stanley in the role.

But all you have to do to test our comment is to hop around to the Roxy, where the film, produced by Twentieth Century Fox and directed by Joshua Logan, opened yesterday. If you don't find Miss M. a downright Duse, you'll find her a dilly, anyhow.

For the striking fact is that Mr. Logan has got her to do a great deal more than wiggle and pout and pop her big eyes and play the synthetic vamp in this film. He has got her to be the beat-up B-girl of Mr. Inge's play, even down to the Ozark accent and the look of pellagra about her skin.

He has got her to be the tinseled floozie, the semi-moronic doll who is found in a Phoenix clip joint by a cowboy of equally limited brains and is hotly pursued by this suitor to a snowbound bus stop in the Arizona wilds. And, what's most important, he has got her to light the small flame of dignity that sputters pathetically in this chippie and to make a rather moving sort of her.

This may not sound too stimulating to those who prefer their Miss Monroe looking healthy and without anything flaming inside her, except a mad desire. But don't think because the little lady creates a real character in this film she or it are lacking in vitality, humor, or attractiveness.

Without too much literal attachment to the play of Mr. Inge, Mr. Logan and George Axelrod, the screenplaywright, have started proceedings well in advance of the bus stop where the drama and its strange romance come to a satisfactory head. They have brought their wild cowboy and their floozie together in a two-bit cabaret crowded with rodeo busters and reeking of raw inanity, and they have kept things in that area and on that level for a good part of the film.

This build-up of modern Western background and rodeo atmosphere allows for some lusty observation and ribald humor that is richly realized. With a

wondrous new actor named Don Murray playing the stupid, stubborn poke and with the clutter of broncos, blondes, and busters beautifully tangled, Mr. Logan has a booming comedy going before he gets to the romance. The flow from the general to the particular of such human ferment is logical and smooth.

A great deal is owed to Mr. Murray. His tempestuous semi-idiocy exploding all around a juvenile softness sets up a mighty force to be curbed by Miss Monroe. And the fact that she fitfully but firmly summons the will and the strength to humble him—to make him say "please," which is the point of the whole thing—attests to her new acting skill.

There are other fine performances in this picture. Arthur O'Connell is delightful as the cowboy's pal who big-brothers him with loving patience. Eileen Heckart is droll as the chippie's friend. Betty Field is robust as the bus-stop owner and Robert Bray is firm as the driver of the bus.

Mr. Logan has ranged from panoramic long shots to smothering close-ups in color and CinemaScope. His imagery is vigorous and audacious, the same as all the rest of his film.

—B.C., September 1, 1956

BUTCH CASSIDY
AND THE SUNDANCE KID

Directed by George Roy Hill; written by William Goldman; cinematographer, Conrad Hall; edited by John C. Howard; music by Burt Bacharach; art designer, Jack Martin Smith; produced by Paul Monash and John Foreman; released by Twentieth Century Fox. Running time: 112 minutes.

With: Paul Newman (Butch Cassidy), Robert Redford (The Sundance Kid), Katharine Ross (Etta Place), Strother Martin (Percy Garris), Henry Jones (Bike Salesman), Jeff Corey (Sheriff Bledsoe), George Furth (Woodcock), Cloris Leachman (Agnes) and Ted Cassidy (Harvey Logan).

Butch Cassidy and the Sundance Kid were real-life, turn-of-the-century outlaws who, in 1905, packed up their saddlebags, along with Sundance's mistress (a schoolteacher named Etta Place), and left the shrinking American West to start a new life, robbing banks in Bolivia.

According to the movie which opened yesterday at the Penthouse and Sutton Theaters, their decline and fall was the sort of alternately absurd and dreamy saga that might have been fantasized by Truffaut's Jules and Jim and Catherine—before they grew up.

Butch (Paul Newman) is so amiable that it's not until he gets to Bolivia, and is more or less forced to go straight, that he ever brings himself to shoot a man. Sundance (Robert Redford) behaves like the perpetual younger brother. Although confident of his own abilities, he always defers to Butch, whose schemes end in disaster more often than success. Etta (Katharine Ross) is the kind of total woman who can cook, keep house of sorts, seldom grumbles, and, if necessary, will act as third gun.

This is an attractive conceit and much of *Butch Cassidy and the Sundance Kid* is very funny in a strictly contemporary way—the last exuberant word on movies about the men of the mythic American West who have outlived their day. Butch and Sundance have the physical graces of classic Western heros, but all four feet are made of silly putty.

When they try to rob a train and blow open its safe, the dynamite charge destroys not only the safe but also the entire baggage car. When they can escape from a posse only by jumping from a high cliff into a raging rapids below, Sundance must admit ruefully that he doesn't know how to swim.

Later, in Bolivia, their first attempt at bank robbery almost fails when they forget a list of Spanish phrases not included in the ordinary tourist's guidebook: "This is a robbery." "Stand against the wall." "Put up your hands." Butch and Sundance are the fall guys of their time and circumstances, and also of their movie.

George Roy Hill (*Thoroughly Modern Millie, Hawaii*) who directed, and William Goldman, the novelist (*Boys and Girls Together*) and occasional scenarist (*Harper*), who wrote the original screenplay, have consciously mixed their genres. Even though the result is not unpleasant, it is vaguely disturbing—you keep seeing signs of another, better film behind gags and effects that may remind you of everything from *Jules and Jim* to *Bonnie and Clyde* and *The Wild Bunch.*

In the center of the movie is a lovely, five-minute montage—done in sepia still photographs of the period—showing Butch, Sundance, and Etta having a brief fling in New York and making the steamer passage to South America. The stills tell you so much about the curious and sad relationship of the three people that it's with real reluctance that you allow yourself to be absorbed again into further slapstick adventures.

There is thus, at the heart of *Butch Cassidy,* a gnawing emptiness that can't be satisfied by an awareness that Hill and Goldman probably knew exactly what they were doing—making a very slick movie. They play tricks on the audience, by turning a bit of melodrama into a comic blackout, and by taking shortcuts to lyricism as when we get an extended sequence showing Butch clowning on a bicycle for the benefit of Etta backed by full orchestra playing Burt Bachrach's latest. I admire Bachrach but he simply is not Georges Delarue, as Hill is not Truffaut; nor, for that matter, is Goldman.

There are some bothersome technical things about the movie (the camera is all zoom, zoom, zoom) but the over-all production is very handsome, and the performances fine, especially Newman, Redford, and Miss Ross, who must be broadly funny and straight, almost simultaneously. They succeed even if the movie does not.

—*V.C., September 25, 1969*

THE BUTCHER BOY

Directed by Neil Jordan; written by Mr. Jordan and Patrick McCabe, based on the novel by Mr. McCabe; director of photography. Adrian Biddle; edited by Tony Lawson; music by Elliot Goldenthal; production designer, Anthony Pratt; produced by Redmond Morris and Stephen Woolley; released by Warner Brothers. Running time: 106 minutes.

With: Eamonn Owens (Francie Brady). Fiona Shaw (Mrs. Nugent). Aisling O'Sullivan (Ma Brady). Stephen Rea (Da Brady). Alan Boyle (Joe Purcell). Sinead O'Connor (Virgin Mary) and Milo O'Shea (Father Sullivan).

Set in a picturesque Irish town and featuring a freckle-faced young hero in knee pants, *The*

Butcher Boy may look familiar at first. But as the real, disturbing nature of Neil Jordan's audacious film emerges, this story moves far outside the realm of the ordinary. Mr. Jordan's films at their best (*Mona Lisa, The Crying Game, Interview with the Vampire,* and now this) are perversely comfortable on such difficult terrain, contemplating the hidden extremes of human nature. The film maker's gift for genuinely shocking his audience is, for him, an essential way of telling the truth.

So consider Francie Brady, the rambunctious hero of the novel by Patrick McCabe on which this strange, astonishing film is based. The book's cover art shows a running stick figure, a bomb with a lighted fuse where his head ought to be, and that describes Francie perfectly. Pugnacious and brazen, Francie moves from boyish pranks to more twisted behavior in a story that culminates in startling violence. Among its lingering echoes is a hint of the childish viciousness lately seen in Jonesboro, Arkansas, as it eerily captures the thinking of a reckless, disaffected small-town boy.

Remarkably, almost every scene in the film is carried by Eamonn Owens's performance as Francie, though the star is an Irish schoolboy whose only previous international exposure was marching with his youth band in New York's 1995 St. Patrick's Day Parade.

Francie's high spirits fly in the face of acute family problems. His father (Stephen Rea, Mr. Jordan's frequent star) is a musician and a drunk, while Francie's mother (Aisling O'Sullivan) is prone to frightening mood swings and bitter quarrels with her husband. There are days when a picture of his parents on their honeymoon is all Francie has to sustain him, but he is not a twelve-year-old to suffer in silence. Roaming the town with a pal named Joe, Francie tries his hand at hooliganism while watching his parents' lives fall apart.

The focus of his hatred becomes a woman named Mrs. Nugent (Fiona Shaw), who puts on English airs and has had the effrontery to call Francie's father names. Though she appears infrequently in the film (always unfriendly, costumed in the same odious green), she becomes a handy fixture in Francie's imagination. The film enters that imagination in uncanny ways, so that it sees Mrs. Nugent and everyone else in the story through the eyes of a cheeky, raging adolescent. For instance, Francie never forgives his nemesis for alienating Joe's affections by bribing him with a gift of goldfish.

The Butcher Boy so effectively juggles two viewpoints, Francie's and the rest of the world's, that Mrs. Nugent emerges as both witchy tormentor and worried matron. Mr. Jordan, working from a screenplay he wrote with Mr. McCabe and capturing the quicksilver tone of this fine, tricky novel, does a remarkable job of entering Francie's thoughts without leaving the rest of the village behind. Ordinarily that might limit it to a tortured, sensitive perspective, but *The Butcher Boy* is full of surprises and gallows humor. "Yes, I do believe I shall be off on my travels," Francie tells himself as he prepares to run away from home during one of his parents' boozy fights.

In finding a visual equivalent for the book's flights of fancy, Mr. Jordan creates a riveting mixture of daydream and reality, steeped in the nostalgia of an early 1960's time frame. In the wake of *Michael Collins,* one of his few relatively conventional films, he again mounts a lavish production but keeps it unpredictable and expressive. The small-town mores of the era are conjured just by Francie's mock-cheerful chats with the local housewives, who treat him as harmless even in the face of mounting evidence to the contrary. Francie works for a butcher at one point, but that's not the sole source of the title.

Anecdotal and increasingly chilling, *The Butcher Boy* moves from its early prankster spirit into parts unknown with the help of many pungent background touches. The threat of atomic warfare looms constantly at the time of the Cuban missile crisis, although for Francie, atomic weapons, Communists, and space aliens are all part of the same danger. (Mr. Jordan invokes the bomb most effectively to suit the oddly jokey tone of Francie's transgressions.) Sinead O'Connor plays the vixenish Virgin Mary of the boy's daydreams in a film that sees religion through the boy's especially distorted lens. When Milo O'Shea, as a priest, makes sexual advances to Francie, he puts the boy in a bonnet more fitting to a child's fantasy than a grown man's.

Francie's wily, headstrong voice through all his tumultuous experiences—including work in peat bogs and electroshock therapy—is the film's own evidence of a free spirit. Never compromised by false piety or adult morality, it remains defiantly honest, startlingly pure. Francie uses the word garage for mental hospital, for instance, because his mother's breakdown reminds him of a car's and because he can't bear describing the real thing. When he fakes being good, he congratulates himself with boyish gusto. ("And the Francie Brady Not a Bad Bastard Anymore Award goes to— Great God, I think it's Francie Brady.") And many sad years later, with Mr. Rea playing an adult version of Francie, he remains a lost version of the same boy. As he asks his same too-radiant vision of the Virgin Mary, "What're you doing, Missus, still talking to the likes of me?"

—J.M., April 3, 1998

BYE BYE BRASIL

Written (in Portuguese with English subtitles) and directed by Carlos Diegues: director of photography. Lauro Escorel Filho: edited by Mair Tavres: music by Chico Buarque. Roberto Menescal and Dominguinhos: produced by Luiz Czarlos Bareto: distributed by Unifilm. Running time: 110 minutes.

With: Jos Wilker (Lorde Cigano). Betty Faria (Salome). Fabio Jinior (Cico). Zaira Zambelli (Dasdo). Principe Nabor (Swallow). Jofre Soares (Ze da Luz). Marcus Vincius (Gent). Jos Mara Lima (assistant). Emmanuel Cavalcanti (Mayor). Jos Mrcio Passos (Mayor's Assistant). Rinaldo Gines (Indian Chief). Carlos Kroeber (Driver). Oscar Reis (Smuggler). Rodolfo Arena (Peasant) and Catalina Bonakie (Widow).

Carlos Diegues's *Bye Bye Brasil* is a psychological inventory of a country on the verge of extraordinary economic and industrial development, a travelogue through a nation that doesn't yet exist.

A tiny troupe of tacky performers, who call themselves the Caravana Rolidei, mush their way by ancient truck from the arid, poverty-stricken Brazilian northeast to the seacoast at Belem, across the jungles on the trans-Amazonian highway to Brasilia and points in between. They are a magician-mind reader, a sultry rhumba dancer who hustles on the side, a naïve young man who plays the accordion, his very pregnant wife, and a mute black man who drives the truck and picks up small change hand-wrestling in roadside cafes.

Bye Bye Brasil, which will be shown at the New York Film Festival at Alice Tully Hall today at 9 P.M. and tomorrow at 2 P.M., is a curious, quiet, introspective sort of film, which pays attention to the changing nature of the Brazil that is paying increasingly less attention to these nearly extinct players.

Mr. Diegues, whose *Summer Showers* was seen in New York earlier this year, refuses to be alarmed by the advent of civilization or, as it's often represented in his film, by television, which now occupies the public for whom the members of the Caravana Rolidei once performed. Mr. Diegues makes no judgments and means for us to keep our wits about us in the face of tumultuous changes.

This is the film's recurring theme as it observes the emotional attachments that spring up between the various members of the traveling band.

Ciço, the accordion player, falls desperately in love with Salomé, the rhumba dancer, who is the mistress of Lord Gypsy, the troupe's leader and star. Lord Gypsy accepts Salomé's easy ways and himself has an untroubled affair with Ciço's wife, Dasdô, after her baby is born. In the course of their tour, Salomé and Dasdô become friends with no sense of rivalry.

Mr. Diegues appears to believe that nothing is quite as foolish or dangerous as passions out of control, perhaps in politics as well as in personal relationships. This is an odd, unusually temperate notion to come from a film maker who is one of the fathers of Brazil's "Cinema Novo," that group of young film makers who turned away from conventional film forms in the 1960's to start a cinema more responsive to the country's political and social needs.

Bye Bye Brasil is a most reflective film, nicely acted by its small cast and beautifully though not artily photographed in some remarkable locations. It is civilized.

—V.C., September 27, 1980

C

CABARET

Directed and choreographed by Bob Fosse; written by Jay Presson Allen, based on the musical *Cabaret* by Joe Masteroff, the play *I Am A Camera* by John Van Druten and the writings *Berlin Stories* by Christopher Isherwood; cinematographer, Geoffrey Unsworth; edited by David Bretherton; music by John Kander with lyrics by Fred Ebb; art designers, Jurgen Kiebach and Rolf Zehetbauer; produced by Cy Feuer; released by Allied Artists. Running time: 124 minutes.

With: Liza Minnelli (Sally Bowles), Michael York (Brian Roberts), Helmut Griem (Maximilian von Heune), Joel Grey (Master of Ceremonies), Fritz Wepper (Fritz Wendel) and Elisabeth Neumann-Viertel (Fräulein Schneider).

I doubt whether too many young women have had a fuller life in art than Christopher Isherwood's divinely decadent and infinitely appealing English girl adrift in Berlin in the early 1930's, Sally Bowles. She has gone from fiction to theater (*I Am a Camera*) and thence to film, then back to theater, a Broadway musical, and now again to film.

And though I haven't seen everything that came between, I have seen enough and heard enough to guess that Sally has fared best at first, in Isherwood's lovely, minor *Berlin Stories,* and at last, in Bob Fosse's new movie version of the musical *Cabaret,* which opened yesterday at the Ziegfeld Theater.

A lot has happened to Sally and her friends in the process. She is now an American (Liza Minnelli), while her young man, Brian (Michael York), is now British. There is another girl, a Jewish Berlin department-store heiress (Marisa Berenson), and a man for her (Fritz Wepper). In the midst of everything there appears a handsome German baron (Helmut Griem), who seduces both Sally and Brian and then drops them. Brian's bisexuality now has as much as Sally's accidental pregnancy to do with moving the plot, and it connects as well with a general theme of sick sexual ambiguity that runs through the film as a kind of working motif.

The master of sexual ambiguity, and the master of motifs is again Joel Grey, master of ceremonies at the Kit Kat Klub, the cellar cabaret where Sally sings and dances, and where everything, even the rise of the Third Reich, is "beautiful."

Cabaret is not so much a movie musical as it is a movie with a lot of music in it. Several numbers from the Broadway show have been dropped, and some new, and better ones added—by John Kander and Fred Ebb, the original composer and lyricist—and all for Miss Minnelli. Most of the music is limited to performance at the Kit Kat Club, and Fosse's approach has been not to open up but rather to confine, on a small and well-defined stage, as much of *Cabaret* as means to be musical theater.

Thus the film has a musical part and a nonmusical part (except for Miss Minnelli, none of the major characters sings), and if you add this to the juxtaposition of private lives and public history inherent in the scheme of the *Berlin Stories,* you come up with a structure of extraordinary mechanical complexity. Since everything has to do with everything else and the Cabaret is always commenting on the life outside it, the film sometimes looks like an essay in significant crosscutting, or associative montage. Occasionally this fails; more often it works.

Fosse makes mistakes, partly because his camera is a more potent instrument than he realizes, but he also makes discoveries—and *Cabaret* is one of those immensely gratifying imperfect works in which from beginning to end you can literally feel a movie coming to life.

The film gains a good deal from its willingness to isolate its musical stage—even to observe it from behind the heads of a shadowy audience in the foreground—so that every time we return to the girls and their leering master (by now, a superbly refined caricature) we return, as it were, to a sense of theater. And when at certain moments that theater is occupied only by Liza Minnelli, working in a space defined only by her gestures and a few colored lights, it becomes by the simplest means an evocation of both the power and fragility of movie performance so beautiful that I can think of nothing to do but give thanks.

Everybody in *Cabaret* is very fine, and meticulously chosen for type, down to the last weary transvestite and to the least of the bland, blond open-faced Nazis in the background. As for Miss Minnelli, she is sometimes wrong in the details of her role, but so magnificently right for the film as a whole that I should prefer not to imagine it without her.

With her expressive face and her wonderful (and wonderfully costumed) body she moves and sings with a strength, warmth, intelligence, and sensitivity to nuance that virtually transfixes the screen.

—*R.G., February 14, 1972*

THE CAINE MUTINY

Directed by Edward Dmytryk; written by Stanley Roberts, based on the novel by Herman Wouk; cinematographer, Franz Planer; edited by William Lyon and Henry Batista; music by Max Steiner; production designer, Rudolph Sternad; produced by Stanley Kramer; released by Columbia Pictures. Running time: 123 minutes.

With: Humphrey Bogart (Captain Queeg), José Ferrer (Lieutenant Barney Greenwald), Van Johnson (Lieutenant Steve Maryk), Fred MacMurray (Lieutenant Tom Keefer), Robert Francis (Ensign Willie Keith), Tom Tully (Captain DeVriess), E. G. Marshall (Lieutenant Commander Challee), Arthur Franz (Lieutenant Paynter), Lee Marvin (Meatball), Warner Anderson (Captain Blakely), Claude Akins (Horrible), Katharine Warren (Mrs. Keith), May Wynn (May) and Jerry Paris (Ensign Harding).

The job of compacting and containing Herman Wouk's *The Caine Mutiny* into two hours of color motion picture, with all the character and drama preserved, was one that compared in major aspects with the similar job on *From Here to Eternity*. And we're glad to report that Columbia Pictures and Producer Stanley Kramer have achieved this extraordinarily difficult endeavor with clarity and vigor, on the whole.

This tale of the tensions and turmoils among the officers and crew of a Navy destroyer-minesweeper in the Pacific in World War II is a compound of several personal dramas and conflicts of male temperaments, all drawn to a fine, explosive crisis during a violent typhoon at sea. At the core of its swirling rotation are the bravery and cowardice of men. These are the elements that stand out sharply and gauntly in this film, which was greeted by swarming patrons at the Capitol yesterday.

Unfortunately, screenwriter Stanley Roberts, in preparing the complicated script, endeavored to cram into the picture more of the novel than was required. He gave a great deal of attention to the completely extraneous love affair between Keith, a secondary junior officer, and the nightclub singer, May Wynn. This was both useless and artless. Whenever the love affair obtrudes, the genuine drama is sidetracked and the crisscrossing tensions are snapped.

Also, the structure of the story presented in Mr. Wouk's book was not entirely felicitous for the playing of a drama on the screen. Yet Mr. Roberts has endeavored to follow it faithfully. As a consequence, the naval court-martial that follows the howling typhoon, wherein the executive officer relieves the incompetent captain of command, becomes an anticlimax as it covers essentially the same ground and repeats the collapse of the captain that are visibly shown in the storm.

On the stage, this Caine mutiny court-martial is brilliant because it unfolds in the calm atmosphere of a courtroom the events that have gone before—events that are graphically enacted prior to the trial on the screen. The sole achievement of the trial in the picture is that of demonstrating the perfidy of one man—Lieutenant Tom Keefer. The audience already knows the captain's guilt.

This is a weakness of the picture that takes a lot of time, since more than twenty minutes are virtually wasted in building up to the thin theatrics at the end.

However, the body of the picture—the good, solid, masculine core—that has to do with the chafing of naval officers under a neurotic captain's command is salty, exciting, and revealing. And it is smartly and stingingly played by a cast of able performers, with Edward Dmytryk calling the turns.

Van Johnson as the blunt executive officer who commits the so-called act of mutiny does an excellent job of revealing the distress and resolution of this man, and Fred MacMurray is likewise fascinating as the modern "sea lawyer" who eggs him on. Humphrey Bogart's twitchy performance of the "by-the-book" Captain Queeg is a bit in the usual Bogart manner but, by and large, it is sound. Robert Francis as the romancing ensign, Tom Tully as the sloppy captain who precedes Queeg, and José Ferrer as the lawyer for the defendant in the court-martial are good. As it happens, the role of the lawyer has little body in the film.

Thanks to the help of the Navy, the shipboard business is on the beam, the blue-water shots of maneuvers are spanking, and the atmosphere is keen.

The Caine Mutiny, though somewhat garbled, is a vibrant film.

—*B.C., June 25, 1954*

CALIFORNIA SUITE

Directed by Herbert Ross: written by Neil Simon, based on his play: cinematographer, David M. Walsh: edited by Michael A. Stevenson: music by Claude Bolling: produced by Ray Stark: released by Columbia Pictures. Running time: 103 minutes.

With: Alan Alda (Bill Warren), Michael Caine (Sidney Cochran), Bill Cosby (Dr. Willis Panama), Jane Fonda (Hannah Warren), Walter Matthau (Marvin Michaels), Elaine May (Millie Michaels), Richard Pryor (Dr. Chauncy Gump) and Maggie Smith (Diana Barrie).

Neil Simon deals in the kind of lethal wisecracks—put-downs with dum-dum bullets for centers—that often have a way of destroying the wrong people. In the mouths of unknowing characters they are dangerous weapons, instruments for the sort of accidental suicides that demolish everything in the neighborhood. His wisecracks define a world of mighty desperation in which every confrontation, be it with a lover, a child, a husband, a friend, or a taxi driver, becomes a last chance for survival.

When he writes a work in which this desperation is built into the situations Mr. Simon can be both immensely funny and surprisingly moving. Such were *The Heartbreak Kid* and *The Sunshine Boys* and such is his new *California Suite,* which opens today at the National and Loews Tower East and is the most agreeably realized Simon film in years.

The screenplay was adapted by Mr. Simon from his four short plays, all set in the Beverly Hills Hotel in Beverly Hills, which were done on Broadway under the collective title of *California Suite* with the same actors tripling in several roles. For the movie Mr. Simon has intercut the stories, now played by eight stars, so that the film simulates the drive and cohesion of a single, seamless comedy.

Despite its title, *California Suite* is anything but a California movie. It's about as far as you can get from the Pacific Ocean if your heart is in New York. Though the locale is California, the sensibility is of New York—rude, fast-paced, uproariously blunt, and so insistently contemporary it could have been written tomorrow and (who knows?) out of date the day after.

Here is Mr. Simon in top form, under the direction of Herbert Ross, one of the few directors (in addition to Elaine May) who can cope with the particular demands of material that simultaneously means to be touching and so nonstop clever one sometimes wants to gag him. It all works in *California Suite,* not only because the material is superior Simon, but also because the writer and the director have assembled a dream cast.

Chief among these are Maggie Smith, who has her best screen role since *The Prime of Miss Jean Brodie,* and Michael Caine, who is seldom acknowledged as the fine actor he is, playing a celebrated English actress and her antique-dealer husband who come to Hollywood for the Oscar ceremony. After having wrestled so long with movie material that offered no real contest, Miss Smith now has a part that makes use of her unique gift for comedy that has its origins in things far from pleasant.

In the film's early scenes she is pricelessly funny, getting ready for her big night in a magnificent display of hope, panic, and despair, knowing that she doesn't have a snowball's chance of winning the Oscar, but listening eagerly to even the dimmest person who thinks she has. When, without melodramatic effort, the tale becomes an examination of a marriage that has slipped into compromised intimacy, she and Mr. Caine create characters of unexpected depth and compassion.

Jane Fonda and Alan Alda must deliver quintessential Simon dialogue, the sort that can undercut a comic situation of less importance than the one Mr. Simon has provided here. They are a long-divorced couple—he a successful Hollywood writer, she a confirmed New York career woman—who meet in Beverly Hills to discuss the future of their daughter, who has run away from her mother. Miss Fonda is superlative as the glib, semi-intellectual New Yorker whose only way of dealing with desperation is through sarcasm. Mr. Alda, playing it more or less straight, nicely complements her as the sort of man who doesn't have to be told when he's making a fool of himself. With him, that has been a conscious decision.

Walter Matthau and Elaine May play the principals in Mr. Simon's boisterous West Coast version of bedroom farce. He is an aging middle-class businessman, very much the conservative husband, whose one night alone in Los Angeles almost destroys his marriage after his brother presents him with the present of a prepaid hooker. Watching Mr. Matthau, as his wife awaits on the other side of the door, trying to pull pantyhose onto the rubbery form of a very drunk hooker, is one of the more cheerful moments of the entire movie season.

Richard Pryor and Bill Cosby appear as a pair of Chicago doctors who, with their wives, are sharing a vacation of the sort Mr. Simon cherishes. Everything goes wrong, including friendships. This sequence is the film's most frantic and, perhaps because of that, it runs out of breath before the end, but then no comedy can be completely perfect.

—*V.C., December 22, 1978*

CALLE 54

Directed by Fernando Trueba: director of photography. Jose Luis Lopez-Linares: edited by Carmen Frias: produced by Cristina Huete and Fabienne Servan Schreiber: released by Miramax Films. Running time: 105 minutes.

With: Paquito D'Rivera. Eliane Elias. Chano Dominguez. Jerry Gonzalez and the Fort Apache Band. Michel Camilo. Gato Barbieri. Tito Puente. Hilton Ruiz. Bebo Valdes. Chucho Valdes. Dave Valentin and Chico O'Farrill.

Sometimes, a critic wonders if a movie seen at a festival, where audiences are so eager to be moved by anything, will maintain its magic outside such a forgiving setting. *Calle 54,* Fernando Trueba's wonderful documentary tribute to Latin jazz, is even better on a second viewing because the film is such a pure expression of the director's love for the music, a love so infectious it should leave you elated.

The picture, which opens today at Lincoln Plaza, is bound to draw comparisons to *The Buena Vista Social Club,* if only for the subject matter. But this film, set in a variety of locales from New York to Europe, is a completely different take, not the work of archivists falling in love with a crumbling city and musicians with the grace of natural stars waiting to be rediscovered. *Calle 54* is closer in spirit to *The Last Waltz* in that it mounts a respectful staging of the songs by its performers with an ease and classiness not lavished on jazz since the black-and-white jazz shorts of the 1930's and 40's. That was probably the last time jazz musicians have been treated as well by the medium.

From on-the-run black-and-white hand-held camera work during which each musician offers a little bit of his history, *Calle 54* goes to extravagant color stage sets in which each performer does a number. If you have any knowledge of jazz, you're likely to squeal with happiness as you recognize the sidemen, who include Hilton Ruiz and Dave Valentin, backing the leaders. (They're all identified over the end credits.) If not, then you may just be swept away by the powerful talents and the unity of spirit. The pianist and composer Michel Camilo is seen preparing charts for some of his warm, fluid orchestral compositions; then he and his combo race through a gorgeous tune that should leave you slack-jawed.

If the soundtrack is not on sale in the lobby of every theater showing the film, then someone is suffering from fatal shortsightedness. Mr. Camilo will probably see a run on his entire catalog.

"I wrote this piece to be like a movie," says the saxophonist Gato Barbieri before he begins to play. One of the best-known performers in the film and renowned in the United States for the weary machismo of his forlorn wails on the *Last Tango in Paris* soundtrack, he still wears his big-brimmed slouch hat and, wrapped in dramatic shawls, resembles a South American widow from an Isabel Allende novel.

Mr. Barbieri mentions the names of filmmakers with whom he felt a kinship—Jean-Luc Godard, Luchino Visconti and the director of *Last Tango,* Bernardo Bertolucci—men who represent wildly different styles but who embraced danger and passion, as Mr. Barbieri does. He talks about dropping out of recording for an extended period, alluding to his unhappiness with the albums he released on A&M in the late 1970's. But this grand old tiger can still blow a hole in the ozone layer. His magnificence remains unabated.

So does that of the pianist Bebo Valdes, who plays duets with his son, Chucho. (Bebo is tickled by his son's avoirdupois, and Chucho's large hands span the keyboard like those of another Atlas of the keyboards, the Canadian giant Oscar Peterson, although Chucho plays with a much livelier attack.) Father and son reach into themselves for a performance that's fiery and heart-rending.

Tito Puente, who died this year, plays against a white background, sadly apropos, as if he were in rehearsals to play one of the lounges in heaven.

Puente flashes a mouthful of teeth that are the same dazzling white as the set as he grins and pounds his congas. In a brief interview he pays tribute to his inspiration, Dizzy Gillespie, whose work probably influenced many of the musicians seen and heard in *Calle 54.* Among them is the New York trumpeter Jerry Gonzalez, seen in sunglasses and leaning in a 47-degree-angle posture that suggest Miles Davis in one of his coolest Young Man With a Horn poses. His Fort Apache band shakes the house.

The film also introduces Eliane Elias, whose sound is flavored by Antonio Carlos Jobim and Lalo Schifrin, as well as the masterly Paquito D'Rivera and Cachao. At the Toronto Film Festival, the roster of *Calle 54* brought the audience to its feet after each number. (The delicacy of the sound recording is a marvel.) No doubt it'll send shivers of joy through crowds here, too.
—E.M., October 20, 2000

CAMELOT

Directed by Joshua Logan; written by Alan Jay Lerner; based on the musical by Mr. Lerner and Frederick Loewe and the novel *The Once and Future King* by T. H. White; cinematographer, Richard H. Kline; edited by Folmar Blangsted; music by Mr. Loewe; art designer, Edward Carrere; produced by Jack L. Warner; released by Warner Brothers. Running time: 178 minutes.

With: Richard Harris (King Arthur), Vanessa Redgrave (Guenevere), Franco Nero (Lancelot du Lac), David Hemmings (Mordred), Lionel Jeffries (King Pellinore), Laurence Naismith (Merlin) and Estelle Winwood (Lady Clarinda).

If ever there was a Broadway musical that cried for simple clarification and opening up of its story and its visual apparatus in a transfer to the screen, it was Alan Jay Lerner's and Frederick Loewe's melodious but murky *Camelot.*

That elaborate theatrical whimsy about the troubles of King Arthur with his wife and court, based on a charmingly eccentric and mischievous novel by T. H. White, was generally regarded by its critics as being a little too heavy and obscure in its trifling with the Arthurian legends for the kind of fanciful business it was about. It needed considerable fluffing and irreverent performing by the king and queen, originally Richard Burton and Julie Andrews, who was no fair lady, but King Arthur's wife.

Indeed, what it basically needed in its transfer to the screen was a drenching in cinema magic to remove all the dull and pretentious patches of realism and romantic cliché that kept it from sparkling in the theater. And that's what we all hoped it would have.

Well, it hasn't, alas. In the production that Jack L. Warner has engineered and Joshua Logan has directed, with Richard Harris and Vanessa Redgrave as the king and queen, it is still the same sort of clutter of supernaturalism ornately displayed with conventional romantic realism, all set to music, as it was on the stage—only more so, because of the extravagance of Warner Brothers and the massiveness of the Panavision screen. The picture opened last night at the Warner Theater.

Its effort to make us see King Arthur as a hopeful, enlightened idealist, inspired by the mystical Merlin, but disillusioned by his queen, Guenevere, and her well-advertised and disruptive love affair with his best knight, Lancelot, wavers between pseudo-Shavian satire and standard sentimental romance, with the latter more dominant than the satire, and nothing like as engaging and sincere.

When it is showing us Arthur shyly jousting with his bride-to-be and lyrically trying to persuade her of the felicities of Camelot, it seems to be on the verge of that magical kind of make-believe that is essential for these never-never people in an obviously never-never land. Mr. Harris seems reasonably suited to the evident eccentricity of this king, and Miss Redgrave seems beautifully in tune with the apparent female perversities of Guenevere.

Likewise, when both of them are taking the measure of the new boy, Lancelot, upon his precipitate arrival, full of boastful and pious conceits, it appears to be headed in the direction of an urbane, satiric spoof, especially when they all engage quite nicely in the tra-la-laing of "The Lusty Month of May."

But the moment that Lancelot bends gravely over the knight he has speared in the lists and urges life back into his body, to the amazement of all, especially Guenevere, the direction and character of the picture take a perceptible turn. From here on it is rather heavy going around the course of triangular romance, with occasional side excursions to the forest of Merlin, which is a grossly whimsey-whamsey Disneyland and vexingly unproductive of explanations for the indecisiveness of the king.

This mystical aspect of Arthur, which is never satisfactorily clarified, and Guenevere's dual devotion to him and to the easily diverted Lancelot, constitute the most formidable barrier to audience empathy. It is hard to feel cozy with people you simply don't under-

stand. If we're supposed to regard theirs as a clandestine ménage-à-trois, which is likely to be suspected from the campy way Mr. Harris sometimes performs, it isn't developed sufficiently to make it daring or interesting. The principals are as opaque and elusive as they were on the stage.

Miss Redgrave is the shiniest of them. She is almost dazzling at times, and joins most charmingly in rendering at least the convincing lip movements of her songs. Mr. Harris is broad and uneven, sometimes winning, more often brusque and on the verge of being boorish. Franco Nero is good as Lancelot, handsome, ingenuous, and eager—but, again, a romantic cliché.

For the rest, Lionel Jeffries is labored as the comical King Pellinore and David Hemmings is noxious as Mordred, the bastard son of Arthur, as he should be.

The music is played and sung with great charm, but the settings are vastly overdone—much too massive and vulgar for the delicacy and grace that should prevail. Mr. Logan has run to heavy close-ups of his characters that uncomfortably crowd the screen. Somehow, there isn't much magic in the insides of people's mouths, which is what we are shown too often. Nor is there enough in the film.

—*B.C., October 26, 1967*

CAMILLE

Directed by George Cukor; written by Zoe Akins, Frances Marion and James Hilton, based on the novel and play *La Dame aux camélias* by Alexandre Dumas; cinematographer, William Daniels; edited by Margaret Booth; music by Herbert Stothart; produced by Bernard Hyman; released by Metro-Goldwyn-Mayer. Black and white. Running time: 108 minutes.

With: Greta Garbo (Marguerite), Robert Taylor (Armand), Lionel Barrymore (Monsieur Duval), Elizabeth Allan (Nichette), Jessie Ralph (Nanine), Henry Daniell (Baron de Varville), Lenore Ulric (Olympe) and Laura Hope Crews (Prudence).

Having passed its fiftieth anniversary, *Camille* is less a play than an institution. Just as *Hamlet* is the measure of the great actor, so has the Dumas fils' classic become the ultimate test of the dramatic actress. Greta Garbo's performance in the new Metro-Goldwyn-Mayer version at the Capitol is in the finest tradition: eloquent, tragic, yet restrained. She is as incomparable in the role as legend tells us that Bernhardt was. Through the perfect artistry of her portrayal, a hackneyed theme is made new again, poignantly sad, hauntingly lovely.

George Cukor, the classicist of the Metro studios, has retained the full flavor of the period—France in the middle of the last century—without drenching his film with the cloying scent of a hothouse. *Camille,* under his benign handling and the understanding adaptation by Zoe Akins, Frances Marion, and James Hilton, is not the reverentially treated museum piece we half expected to see. Its speech has been modernized, but not jarringly; its characters, beneath the frill and ruffles of the fifties, have the contemporary point of view; its tragedy is still compelling, for the Lady of the Camellias must eternally be a tragic figure.

Miss Garbo has interpreted Marguerite Gautier with the subtlety that has earned for her the title, "first lady of the screen." Even as the impish demi-mondaine of the early sequences, she has managed to convey the impression of maturity, of a certain etherialism and spiritual integrity which raise her above her surroundings and mark her as one apart. Her love for Armand, dictating her flight from Paris and the protection of the Baron de Varville, becomes, then, less a process of reformation and regeneration than it is the natural realization of her true character; less a variation of life than a discovery of life.

To appreciate her complete command of the role, one need only study her approach to the key scenes of the drama. Where the less sentient Camille bides her time until the moment comes for her to tear her passions and the scenery to tatters, Garbo waits and then understates. It is her dignity that gives strength to her scene with M. Duval when he asks her to give up his son. It is because her emotions do not slip their leash—when you feel that any second they might—that saves her parting scene with Armand from being a cliché of renunciation. And, above all, it is her performance in the death scene—so simply, delicately, and movingly played—which convinces me that Camille is Garbo's best performance.

Robert Taylor is surprisingly good as Armand, a bit on the juvenile side at times, perhaps, but certainly not guilty of the traditional sin of the many Armands of the past—callowness. As the Baron de Varville, Henry Daniell is suavely perfect. It is a matter for rejoicing that a character, so clearly stamped for villainy, should receive, belatedly, some of the sympathy he deserved: Camille did, you know, treat him shamefully. From Jessie Ralph as Nanine, Lionel Barrymore as M. Duval, Lenore Ulric as Olympe, Laura Hope Crews as Prudence, and Rex O'Malley as Gaston we have received what we had every right to expect—good, sound, supporting performances. That they should have been noted at all, in view of Miss Garbo's brilliant domination of the picture, is high praise indeed.

—*F.S.N., January 23, 1937*

CAPTAINS COURAGEOUS

Directed by Victor Fleming; written by John Lee Mahin, Marc Connelly and Dale Van Every, based on the novel by Rudyard Kipling; cinematographer, Harold Rosson; edited by Elmo Veron; music by Franz Waxman with lyrics by Gus Kahn; art designer, Cedric Gibbons; produced by Louis D. Lighton; released by Metro-Goldwyn-Mayer; Black and white. Running time: 115 minutes.

With: Freddie Bartholomew (Harvey Cheyne), Spencer Tracy (Manuel), Lionel Barrymore (Disko), Melvyn Douglas (Mr. Cheyne), Charley Grapewin (Uncle Salters), Mickey Rooney (Dan), John Carradine (Long Jack), Oscar O'Shea (Cushman) and Jack La Rue (Priest).

Metro's *Captains Courageous,* which had its premiere at the Astor last night and will be shown henceforth on a two-a-day basis, is another of those grand jobs of moviemaking we have come to expect of Hollywood's most prodigal studio. With its rich production, magnificent marine photography, admirable direction and performances, the film brings vividly to life every page of Kipling's novel and even adds an exciting chapter or two of its own.

In tailoring the narrative to the starring dimensions of Freddie Bartholomew, the trio of adapters (John Lee Mahin, Marc Connelly, and Dale Van Every) had to trim several years from the age of Harvey Cheyne, changing him from a spoiled nineteen-year-old to a spoiled twelve-year-old. Except for that and a few pardonable additions, they have steadfastly followed the Kipling tale of an imperious and detestable young scamp who toppled from a liner's rail off the Grand Banks, was picked up by a Portuguese doryman from the schooner *We're Here,* and became a regular fellow during an enforced three-months fishing cruise.

Interesting as the early sequences are, with their telling revelation of Harvey's character, the picture does not really come alive until the cameras turn upon the *We're Here.* Then, in its depiction of the men and methods of the old Gloucester fleet, it takes on almost the quality of a documentary film, enriched by poetic photography of schooners spanking along under full sail, of dories being lowered into a running sea, and shading in, quite deftly, the human portraits of the fishermen with their quiet heroism and resignation, their Down East humor, and their stern code of decency.

The picture's character gallery is happily served. Young Master Bartholomew, who, frankly, never has been one of this corner's favorites, plays Harvey faultlessly, presenting at first as reptilian a lad as a miniature Basil Rathbone might have managed and bringing him around eventually to the grieving, bewildered small boy who has lost the one person he loved and cannot readily admit his father into the desolate sanctuary of his heart.

Spencer Tracy, as Manuel, the boy's idol, seemed curiously unconvincing in the beginning probably because the accent does not become him—but made the part his in time. Then there is Lionel Barrymore, who is a flawless Captain Disko, and Melvyn Douglas giving an understanding interpretation of the elder Cheyne, and John Carradine as Long Jack, Mickey Rooney as Dan, Charles Grapewin as Uncle Salters, and others equally assured.

Victor Fleming's direction has kept the tale flowing, Hal Rosson's photography has given it beauty, and excellent characterization has lent to it poignance. Metro can take pride in its production.

—*F.S.N., May 12, 1937*

CARMEN JONES

Produced and directed by Otto Preminger; written by Harry Kleiner, based on the book by Oscar Hammerstein 2d; cinematographer, Sam Leavitt; edited by Louis Loeffler; music by Georges Bizet; released by Twentieth Century Fox. Running time: 105 minutes.

With: Dorothy Dandridge (Carmen), Harry Belafonte (Joe), Olga James (Cindy Lou), Pearl Bailey (Frankie), Diahann Carroll (Myrt), Roy Glenn (Rum), Nick Stewart (Dink) and Joe Adams (Husky).

Carmen Jones, the opera *Carmen* of Bizet in an American Negro translation, which made quite a hit when it was tumbled onto a Broadway stage in 1943, is again a big musical shenanigan and theatrical tour de force in the giant-sized motion picture version that Otto Preminger delivered last night to the Rivoli.

Crowded with more Negro talent than you could catch on a Saturday night at the Harlem Apollo, turned out in colors that nearly blind you, and splashed across the Cinema-Scope screen, this lot of bamboozling by way of Bizet and Oscar Hammerstein 2d is a sex melodrama with longhair music and a mad conglomeration of bizarre show.

Do not go to it expecting to hear a fully integrated opera sung or see a particularly sensitive or intelligent Negro drama performed. Mr. Hammerstein's job of transferring the Bizet music and the story of Prosper Mérimée into an American locale and idiom was a sheer stunt of carpentry, and the product betrays from every angle its jerry-built incongruities.

The tale of the cigarette-maker Carmen and the Spanish cavalry soldier Don José is now a modern-day story of a parachute factory worker in the South and a stalwart G.I.—named Joe, naturally—who is about to go to flying school. And the Spanish toreador, Escamillo, is now Husky Miller, a prize-ring champ, who captures the favor of the Southern Carmen after she has seduced Joe and caused him to go AWOL.

In essence, it is a poignant story. It was in the opera of Bizet, and it is in the rich nostalgic folklore of the American Negro in the South. But here it is not so much poignant as it is lurid and lightly farcical, with the Negro characters presented by Mr. Preminger as serio-comic devotees of sex.

Carmen, performed by Dorothy Dandridge, is the most notable devotee—a slinky, hip-swinging, main-drag beauty with a slangy, come-hither way with men.

And, far from the desperate, tragic hunger for possession that Bizet's *Carmen* has, this cool, calculating little siren seems interested mainly in a good time.

Likewise the Joe of Harry Belafonte is an oddly static symbol of masculine lust, lost in a vortex of confusion rather than a nightmare of shame. He is the hero, but he is oddly unheroic in this noisily ridiculed role. Olga James as his ever-loving sweetheart is a wistful little comic figure, too, and Joe Adams as the arrogant Husky Miller is virtually a caricature of a bully-boy. Pearl Bailey's performance as Frankie, a roadhouse gal, is unrestrainedly broad, and around the fringes there are numerous and assorted Amos 'n' Andy characters.

The incongruity is pointed when these people break into song to the wholly surprising and unnatural aria airs from Bizet's opera. The tempos are alien to their spirits, the melodies are foreign to their moods, but they have at these classical numbers as though they were cutting rugs. And whatever illusions and exaltations the musical eloquence might remotely inspire are doused by the realistic settings in which Mr. Preminger has played his film.

As it happens, the music is sung well by dubbed-in voices for the three principals—Marilyn Horne's for Miss Dandridge, Le Vern Hutcherson for Mr. Belafonte, and Marvin Hayes for Mr. Adams. And the choruses have the color and vibrance that are standard with good Negro choirs. There is nothing wrong with the music—except that it does not fit the people or the words.

But that did not seem to make much difference to Mr. Hammerstein or Mr. Preminger. They were carried away by their precocity. The present consequence is a crazy mixed-up film.

B.C., October 29, 1954

CARNAL KNOWLEDGE

Produced and directed by Mike Nichols: written by Jules Feiffer: director of photography. Giuseppe Rotunno: edited by Sam O'Steen: production designer. Richard Sylbert: released by Avco Embassy. Running time: 96 minutes.

With: Jack Nicholson (Jonathan). Candice Bergen (Susan). Arthur Garfunkel (Sandy). Ann-Margret (Bobbie). Rita Moreno (Louise). Cynthia O'Neal (Cindy) and Carol Kane (Jennifer).

The young man standing in front of me in the line yesterday morning outside the Cinema I, where *Carnal Knowledge* opened, was quite unremarkable except for the fact that he was carrying a full set of golf clubs.

I have no idea what he was up to. Was the bag his security blanket? Did the clubs have sentimental value? Was the young man en route to a match? To his analyst? Was he about to knock over a cigarette machine? I only mention it because it is one of those odd, seemingly irrelevant but perfectly commonplace gestures that define so much of the visual and verbal comedy sense shared by Mike Nichols, who directed *Carnal Knowledge,* and Jules Feiffer, who wrote the original screenplay. In addition to being the toughest comedy since *Little Murders,* and the most imaginative comedy since *Catch-22, Carnal Knowledge* represents a nearly ideal collaboration of directorial and writing talents.

Coming as it does after Nichols's *Who's Afraid of Virginia Woolf?, The Graduate,* and *Catch-22,* there is a danger, I'm afraid, that *Carnal Knowledge* will be found disappointing by those who feel that a man's movies must be increasingly elaborate and long-focused if it's to be said that his career is progressing. This is just a variation on the old Hollywood myth to the effect that unless each succeeding film of an individual director is more expensive, and a bigger box-office success than the one before, the director must be on his way to Skid Row, or even retirement in Santa Monica.

Carnal Knowledge is nothing if not short-focused. Indeed, it's virtually a two-character film that devotes itself—with an exclusivity that is rare outside stag films, television commercials, and Japanese haiku—to a single subject: the sexual disasters of Jonathan (Jack Nicholson) and Sandy (Art Garfunkel), initially met when they are Amherst undergraduates in the 1940's, and finally abandoned as they enter bleak middle-age in the 1970's.

Because the sexual fantasies shared by Jonathan, the Don Juan in the crew sweater, and Sandy, the saddle-shoed intellectual (he has plans to read *The Fountainhead* and *Jean Christophe*), have their origins in post–World War II middle-class America, their defeats and their confusions, and their very occasional adjustments, are also a reflection of forty years of social and political history. However, to worry about this too much while watching *Carnal Knowledge* is to freight an essentially unpretentious movie—about men vs. women vs. men—with the very pretenses it seeks to avoid.

Much more than his *Little Murders,* Feiffer's screenplay for *Carnal Knowledge,* and Nichols's direction of it, evoke the form of Feiffer's cartoons. It is, in effect, a series of slightly mad dialogues between two people— seen a lot of the time individually in close-ups from which all extraneous background detail has been eliminated—that almost always lead to new plateaus of psychic misunderstanding and emotional hurt.

Although *Carnal Knowledge* is often pricelessly funny and accurate, it is about as warm and lovable as a confession made on an analyst's couch. That is to say that warmth and lovability are beside the point of the film, which is merciless toward both its men and its women in order to reach some kind of understanding of them, of their capacities for self-delusion, and for the casual infliction of pain.

More than any other film Nichols has made, *Carnal Knowledge* reminds me of his stage work at its best, particularly of the highly stylized *Luv* in which low comedy techniques were employed to illuminate material that might otherwise seem too cruel, or too antiheroic for a dramatic medium.

His recollections of the various decades—through decor and music and costume and language—is lovely, even to the choice of the unseen film playing on the telly when Jack Nicholson and Ann-Margret are having an epic battle in bed (*20,000,000 Sweethearts* with Dick Powell singing "I'll String Along with You"). They're the sort of lovers who go to bed with Frank Sinatra singing "Dreams" and wake up to Bach, which, for some reason, I associate with the affectations of the 1960's.

The performances are almost spectacularly right— Nicholson and Garfunkel, of course, but also Candice Bergen, as the Smith girl in plaid skirt and loafers whom Garfunkel marries; Ann-Margret, as "the girl in the airline commercial," a performance that attains a perfect balance between the character's desperation, her aggressiveness, and her surprising simplicity; and Cynthia O'Neal, as a New York career woman who,

according to Sandy, gives instructions in bed as if she were a drill sergeant.

By limiting their vision to a single aspect of human experience (I suppose you could also call it human endeavor), Nichols and Feiffer have made a movie that is not only very funny, but in a casual way—in the way of something observed in a half-light—more profound than much more ambitious films.

—*V.C., July 1, 1971*

CASABLANCA

Directed by Michael Curtiz: written by Julius J. Epstein. Philip G. Epstein and Howard Koch. based on the play *Everybody Goes to Rick's* by Murray Burnett and Joan Alison: cinematographer. Arthur Edeson: edited by Owen Marks: music by Max Steiner: art designer. Carl Jules Weyl: produced by Hal B. Wallis: released by Warner Brothers. Black and white. Running time: 102 minutes.

With: Humphrey Bogart (Rick). Ingrid Bergman (Ilsa Lund). Paul Henreid (Victor Laszlo). Claude Rains (Captain Louis Renault). Conrad Veidt (Major Strasser). Sydney Greenstreet (Señor Ferrari). Peter Lorre (Ugarte) and Dooley Wilson (Sam).

Against the electric background of a sleek café in a North African port, through which swirls a backwash of connivers, crooks, and fleeing European refugees, the Warner Brothers are telling a rich, suave, exciting, and moving tale in their new film, *Casablanca,* which came to the Hollywood yesterday. They are telling it in the high tradition of their hard-boiled romantic-adventure style. And to make it all the more tempting they have given it a top-notch thriller cast of Humphrey Bogart, Sydney Greenstreet, Peter Lorre, Conrad Veidt, and even Claude Rains, and have capped it magnificently with Ingrid Bergman, Paul Henreid, and a Negro "find" named Dooley Wilson.

Yes, indeed, the Warners here have a picture which makes the spine tingle and the heart take a leap. For once more, as in recent Bogart pictures, they have turned the incisive trick of draping a tender love story within the folds of a tight topical theme. They have used Mr. Bogart's personality, so well established in other brilliant films, to inject a cold point of tough resistance to evil forces afoot in Europe today. And they have so combined sentiment, humor, and pathos with taut melodrama and bristling intrigue that the result is a highly entertaining and even inspiring film.

The story, as would be natural, has its devious convolutions of plot. But mainly it tells of a tough fellow named Rick who runs a Casablanca café and of what happens (or what happened last December) when there shows up in his joint one night a girl whom he had previously loved in Paris in company with a fugitive Czech patriot. The Nazis are tailing the young Czech; the Vichy officials offer only brief refuge—and Rick holds the only two sure passports which will guarantee his and the girl's escape. But Rick loves the girl very dearly, she is now married to this other man—and whenever his Negro pianist sits there in the dark and sings "As Time Goes By" that old, irresistible feeling consumes him in a choking, maddening wave.

Don't worry; we won't tell you how it all comes out. That would be rankest sabotage. But we will tell you that the urbane detail and the crackling dialogue which has been packed into this film by the scriptwriters, the Epstein brothers and Howard Koch, is of the best. We will tell you that Michael Curtiz has directed for slow suspense and that his camera is always conveying grim tension and uncertainty. Some of the significant incidents, too, are affecting—such as that in which the passionate Czech patriot rouses the customers in Rick's café to drown out a chorus of Nazis by singing the "Marseillaise," or any moment in which Dooley Wilson is remembering past popular songs in a hushed room.

We will tell you also that the performances of the actors are all of the first order, but especially those of Mr. Bogart and Miss Bergman in the leading roles. Mr. Bogart is, as usual, the cool, cynical, efficient, and superwise guy who operates his business strictly for profit but has a core of sentiment and idealism inside. Conflict becomes his inner character, and he handles it credibly. Miss Bergman is surpassingly lovely, crisp, and natural as the girl and lights the romantic passages with a warm and genuine glow.

Mr. Rains is properly slippery and crafty as a minion of Vichy perfidy, and Mr. Veidt plays again a Nazi officer with cold and implacable resolve. Very little is demanded of Mr. Greenstreet as a shrewd black-market trader, but that is good, and Mr. Henreid is forthright and simple as the imperiled Czech patriot. Mr. Wilson's performance as Rick's devoted friend, though rather brief, is filled with a sweetness and compassion which lend a helpful mood to the whole film, and other small roles are played ably by S. Z. Sakall, Joy Page, Leonid Kinskey, and Mr. Lorre.

In short, we will say that *Casablanca* is one of the year's most exciting and trenchant films. It certainly won't make Vichy happy—but that's just another point for it.

—*B.C., November 27, 1942*

CAT ON A HOT TIN ROOF

Directed by Richard Brooks; written by Mr. Brooks and James Poe, based on the play by Tennessee Williams; cinematographer, William Daniels; edited by Ferris Webster; art designers, William A. Horning and Urie McCleary; produced by Lawrence Weingarten; released by Metro-Goldwyn-Mayer. Running time: 106 minutes.

With: Elizabeth Taylor (Maggie), Paul Newman (Brick), Burl Ives (Big Daddy), Jack Carson (Gooper), Judith Anderson (Big Mama), Madeleine Sherwood (Mae), Larry Gates (Dr. Baugh) and Vaughn Taylor (Deacon Davis).

An all-fired lot of high-powered acting is done in *Cat on a Hot Tin Roof*, the film version of the Tennessee Williams stage play, which came to the Music Hall yesterday. Burl Ives, Paul Newman, Elizabeth Taylor, Judith Anderson, Jack Carson, and two or three more almost work and yell themselves to pieces making this drama of strife within a new-rich Southern family a ferocious and fascinating show.

And what a pack of trashy people these accomplished actors perform! Such a lot of gross and greedy characters haven't gone past since Lillian Hellman's *The Little Foxes* went that way. The whole time is spent by them in wrangling over a dying man's anticipated estate or telling one another quite frankly what sort of so-and-so's they think the others are.

As a straight exercise in spewing venom and flinging dirty linen on a line, this fine Metro-Goldwyn-

Mayer production in color would be hard to beat. It is done by superior talents, under the driving direction of Richard Brooks, making even the driest scenes drip poison with that strong, juicy Williams dialogue. And before the tubs full of pent-up fury, suspicion, and hatred are drained, every major performer in the company has had a chance to play at least one bang-up scene.

The fattest and juiciest opportunities go to Mr. Newman, Miss Taylor, and Mr. Ives as the son, his wife, and the former's father (the Big Daddy of the lot), respectively. In their frequent and assorted encounters, they have chances, together and in pairs, to discourse and lash each other's feelings over the several problems of the family.

First there is the private problem of why this son and his wife do not have any children—and, indeed, why the young man shuns his wife. Why does he spend his time boozing, hobbling around his bedroom on a crutch, and reviling his wife, who quite obviously has the proclivities of that cat on the roof?

And, secondly, why does this young fellow resent and resist his old man, who as obviously wants to be pals with him and leave him his estate if he will only have kids?

Let it be said, quite frankly, that the ways in which these problems are solved do not represent supreme achievements of ingenuity or logic in dramatic art. Mr. Williams's original stage play has been altered considerably, especially in offering explanation of why the son is as he is. Now, a complicated business of hero-worship has been put by Mr. Brooks and James Poe in place of a strong suggestion of homosexuality in the play.

No wonder the baffled father, in trying to find out what gives, roars with indignation: "Something's missing here!"

It is, indeed. And something is missing in the dramatists' glib account of how the son gets together with his father in one easy discourse on love. But what is lacking in logical conflict is made up in visual and verbal displays of vulgar and violent emotions by everybody concerned.

Mr. Newman is perhaps the most resourceful and dramatically restrained of the lot. He gives an ingratiating picture of a tortured and tested young man. Miss Taylor is next. She is terrific as a panting, impatient wife, wanting the love of her husband as sin-

cerely as she wants an inheritance. Mr. Ives snorts and roars with gusto, Miss Anderson claws the air as his wife, and Mr. Carson squirms and howls atrocious English as their greedy, deceitful older son.

Madeleine Sherwood does a fine job as the latter's cheap, child-heavy wife and a quartet of unidentified youngsters insult the human race as their brats.

Lawrence Weingarten's production is lush with extravagance, which is thoroughly appropriate to the nature of *Cat on a Hot Tin Roof*.

—B.C., *September 19, 1958*

CATCH-22

Directed by Mike Nichols; written by Buck Henry, based on the novel by Joseph Heller; cinematographer, David Watkins; edited by Sam O'Steen; music by Fritz Reiner; production designer, Richard Sylbert; produced by Martin Ransohoff and John Calley; released by Paramount Pictures. Running time: 121 minutes.

With: Alan Arkin (Captain Yossarian), Martin Balsam (Colonel Cathcart), Richard Benjamin (Major Danby), Art Garfunkel (Captain Nately), Jack Gilford (Dr. Daneeka), Anthony Perkins (Chaplain Tappman), Paula Prentiss (Nurse Duckett), Martin Sheen (Lieutenant Dobbs), Jon Voight (Milo Minderbinder), Orson Welles (General Dreedle), Robert Balaban (Captain Orr), Buck Henry (Lieutenant Colonel Korn), Bob Newhart (Major Major) and Austin Pendleton (Colonus Moodus).

Panic, like some higher forms of grief and joy, is such an exquisite emotion that nature denies its casual recollection to all except psychotics, a few artists, and an occasional, pre-existential hero like Yossarian, the mad bombardier of Joseph Heller's World War II novel, *Catch-22*.

Once experienced by the normal neurotic, panic is immediately and efficiently removed from reality, twice removed, in fact, transformed into a memory of a memory. But Yossarian is not your normal neurotic. At the United States Air Force base on the tiny Mediterranean island of Pianosa, which Heller describes as a defoliated, shrunken, surreal Corsica, Yossarian lives in a state of perpetual, epic panic. For

Yossarian, a willing convert to paranoia, panic is a kind of Nirvana.

He is convinced that everyone wants him dead—the Germans, his fellow officers, Nurse Duckett, bartenders, bricklayers, landlords, tenants, patriots, traitors, lynchers, and lackeys. If they don't get him, Yossarian is aware that there are lymph glands, kidneys, nerve sheaths, corpuscles, Ewing's tumors, and possibly Wisconsin shingles that will.

Because mankind is conspiring in his death, and he wants to survive, Yossarian knows that the whole world is crazy—and he's absolutely right, almost, you might say, dead-on-target.

It's the special achievement of Heller's novel, as well as of Mike Nichols's screen version, that Yossarian's panic emerges as something so important, so reasonable, so moving, and so funny. In the peculiar, perfectly ordered universe of Pianosa, where the system of rewards and punishments is perfectly disordered, panic is positive and fruitful, like love.

Catch-22, which opened yesterday at the new Paramount Theater on Columbus Circle and at the Sutton Theater, is, quite simply, the best American film I've seen this year. It looks and sounds like a big-budget, commercial service comedy, but it comes as close to being an epic human comedy as Hollywood has ever made by employing the comic conventions of exaggeration, fantasy, shock, and the sort of insult and reverse logic that the late Lulu McConnell elevated to a fine, low art form on radio's *It Pays to Be Ignorant.*

I do have some reservations about the film, the most prominent being that I'm not sure that anyone who has not read the novel will make complete sense out of the movie's narrative line that Nichols and his screenwriter, Buck Henry, have shaped in the form of flashbacks within an extended flashback. Missing, too, are some relevant characters (ex-Pfc. Wintergreen, the dispassionate, God-surrogate who actually rules Pianosa) and relevant sequences, as when Chaplain Tappman learns to lie and thus makes his accommodation with the system.

Great movies are complete in themselves. *Catch-22* isn't, but enough of the original remains so that the film becomes a series of brilliant mirror images of a Strobe-lit reality.

Nichols and Henry, whose senses of humor coincide with Heller's fondness for things like the manic repetition of words and phrases, have rearranged the novel without intruding on it. Most of the film is framed by Yossarian's delirium (after he has been stabbed by what appears to be a German P.O.W.) and is played in the form of funny and sad blackout sketches.

These involve, to name just a few, Colonel Cathcart (Martin Balsam), whose dearest desire is to be featured in *The Saturday Evening Post;* Captain Nately (Art Garfunkel), the rich Boston boy who is fated to love a mean Roman whore, Major Major (Bob Newhart), the timid squadron commander, General Dreedle (Orson Welles), who likes to say "Take him out and shoot him" when people behave stupidly, Captain Orr (Robert Balaban), who practices crashing in preparation for an escape to Sweden, Milo Minderbinder (Jon Voight), the squadron's mess officer, a sort of one-man, free-enterprise convulsion, and glum old Doc Daneeka (Jack Gilford).

Each one is marvelous, but it is Alan Arkin as Yossarian who provides the film with its continuity and dominant style. Arkin is not a comedian; he is a deadly serious actor, but because he projects intelligence with such monomaniacal intensity, he is both funny and heroic at the same time.

The film is Nichols's third (*Who's Afraid of Virginia Woolf?, The Graduate*), so it may be safe to say now that he's something more than lucky. *Catch-22* is a giant physical production, even by Hollywood's swollen standards, but the complexities of the physical production never neutralize the personal comedy, even when Nichols has a bomber crash in flames as the background to a bit of close-up dialogue.

There are some things in the film that I wish he had resisted, such as images out of Fellini and a reference to Kubrick's use of "Zarathustra," which is also being used currently in a Swanson's Frozen Foods television commercial.

Nichols's cinematic style now looks almost classic, in comparison with *The Graduate.* There is not as much cutting within sequences; he uses real tracking shots; zooms are held to a minimum, and he remains, as he was before, one of our finest directors of a certain kind of controlled comic performance. With the exception of Elizabeth Taylor, nobody in a Nichols film is ever allowed to overreach himself.

Catch-22 is so good that I hope it won't be confused with what is all too loosely referred to as black comedy, which usually means comedy bought cheaply at the expense of certain human values, so that, for example, murder is funny and assassination is hilarious. *Catch-22,* like Yossarian, is almost beside itself with panic because it grieves for the human condition.

—*V.C., June 25, 1970*

CAVALCADE

Directed by Frank Lloyd: written by Reginald Berkeley, based on the play by Noël Coward: cinematographer, Ernest Palmer: edited by Margaret Clancy: music by Louis Francesco: produced by Winfield Sheehan: released by Fox. Black and white. Running time: 110 minutes.

With: Diana Wynyard (Jane Marryot), Clive Brook (Robert Marryot), Ursula Jeans (Fanny Bridges), Herbert Mundin (Alfred Bridges), Una O'Connor (Ellen Bridges) and Merle Tottenham (Annie).

It is a most affecting and impressive picture that the Fox studios have produced from Noël Coward's stage panorama, *Cavalcade.* It reached the Gaiety last night and, without having seen the original, one senses the genuine quality of the film and also the advantages that have been taken of the camera's far-seeing eye. Never for an instant is the story, which takes one through three decades of life in England, lost sight of, notwithstanding the inclusion of remarkable scenes of throngs in war and peace, and it is a relief to observe that the obvious is left to the spectator's imagination.

One sees England, merry and sad, belligerent and peaceful, an England with the characters speaking their minds. The atmosphere of London and elsewhere has been reproduced in a masterful fashion, from the days of the Boer War to the present time. In the early episodes one hears occasionally the sound of horses' hoofs on the streets and now and again an old four-wheeler puts in an appearance. Then there are familiar sights, including the pillar boxes, the lamp posts, flashes of the East End and Mayfair, including a distant view of the Houses of Parliament with Big Ben booming the hour.

This production was directed by Frank Lloyd, under the experienced supervision of Winfield Sheehan, who knows his London. In all its scenes there is a meticulous attention to detail, not only in the settings, which include one of Trafalgar Square during the armistice celebrations, but also in the selection of players. The principals are English and Clive Brook, Diana Wynyard, and Frank Lawton give conspicuously fine performances. Then there are also highly pleasing portrayals in lighter roles by Herbart Mundin, Una O'Connor, Beryl Mercer, and others.

It is a tale of joy and woe, chiefly concerned with the experiences of Robert Marryot and his wife, Jane, and embracing what happens to their children and their servants. It is unfurled with such marked good taste and restraint that many an eye will be misty after witnessing this production.

It begins with New Year's Eve in 1899, with the Marryots drinking their customary toast. Robert is to leave the following day for South Africa as an officer in the City Imperial Volunteers. Their butler, Alfred Bridges, impersonated by Mr. Mundin, who has joined up as a private, is leaving on the same troop ship. Mafeking is being besieged and it is questionable whether it can hold out much longer. Jane Marryot's brother is one of the officers in Mafeking.

Jane hates war and she dislikes even to see her two little boys playing with toy cannon and soldiers. The music of martial bands, with the inevitable "Soldiers of the Queen," gets on Jane's nerves. Months afterward, however, she is jubilant when her husband returns. There is some excellent comedy at this time afforded by Bridges and his wife, Ellen. All are glad the war is over. The next stirring moment happens when the news comes that Queen Victoria is dying. Subsequently the film is concerned with the Queen's funeral, seen by the characters (but not by the spectators) from a window in their home. The funeral march is heard and Jane comments on five kings being in one group of the procession.

The years roll by and Bridges and his wife are running a "pub," which is none too successful, due to the landlord imbibing too freely himself and being too generous to his customers. It ends with Bridges being fatally injured by being run over by a horse-drawn vehicle. One also hears from Fanny Bridges, his daughter, who later distinguishes herself as a dancer and eventually takes up singing the "blues."

Edward Marryot, one of the Marryots' sons, and Edith Harris go on their honeymoon as passengers aboard the *Titanic* and just a glimpse of a life-belt tells of their untimely ends. Without ever a hasty word between them, the Marryots console themselves that they still have one son, Joe.

Then comes 1914, with the first shock of the World War, its Zeppelins dropping bombs and the wounded being brought in by ambulance trains. Joe goes forth to fight and he returns on leave, after being the only remaining officer of his original battalion. It is just after he returns to the front that he is killed, but Jane and Robert Marryot are beheld drinking to each other's health when 1930, or is it 1932, is welcomed by the usual throngs singing "Auld Lang Syne." With its discordant and peaceful notes life goes on.

Miss Wynyard is excellent as Jane Marryot. She portrays her role with such sympathy and feeling that one scarcely thinks of her as an actress. Mr. Brook is at his best as Robert Marryot. Mr. Lawton is capital as Joe Marryot. In fact all in the large cast give a good account of themselves.

—M.H., January 6, 1933

THE CELEBRATION

Directed by Thomas Vinterberg; written (in Danish, with English subtitles) by Mr. Vinterberg and Mogens Rukov, based on an idea by Mr. Vinterberg; director of photography, Anthony Dod Mantle; edited by Valdis Oskarsdottir; produced by Birgitte Hald; released by October Films. Shown with a 15-minute short, Thomas Bardinet's *Let's Be Friends*, today at 6 P.M. and tomorrow at 9 P.M. at Alice Tully Hall as part of the 36th New York Film Festival. Running time: 106 minutes.

With: Ulrich Thomsen (Christian), Henning Moritzen (Helge), Thomas Bo Larsen (Michael) and Paprika Steen (Helene).

Though it dedicates itself to avoiding directorial egotism, in accordance with strict rules of the Danish filmmakers' collective known as Dogma 95, Thomas Vinterberg's *Celebration* is still a virtuoso feat. Five years out of film school and colossally assured, Mr. Vinterberg strips away the conventions of ordinary filmmaking (as per the group's manifesto) and furiously devises new, unfettered ways of telling a story. If the style of this group, which also includes the formidable trendsetter Lars von Trier, should ever become widely imitated, it risks looking as fresh as the Macarena. But at a time when filmmaking so often falls back on the familiar, its effect indeed manages to be excitingly inventive and pure.

Dogma 95, in brief: Look, Ma, no genre stories or superficial action. No special lighting or extra sound. No tarting up the location with props; no optical tricks; no camera work that isn't handheld. No black-and-white or flashbacks. And for the director, goodbye to an actual credit and so-called personal imprint. "My supreme goal is to force the truth out of my characters and settings," say the group's Vows of Chasity. "I swear to do so by all the means available and at the cost of any good taste and any esthetic considerations."

If this sounds like a stunt, it surely doesn't look that way in *The Celebration*. Choosing as his setting a grand château that is a family-owned hotel, Mr. Vinterberg presents a birthday reunion that becomes a black-tie psyche-bashing blowout with latter-day Shakespearean overtones.

The king of this event is Helge (Henning Moritzen), a prosperous patriarch turning sixty and presiding over longtime friends and rebellious children. The event begins with an excess of gentility ("Thanks for a lovely funeral," "Thank YOU!") and whirls into battle royal once an army of skeletons comes out of this family's closet. While the strictures on the film's direction may sound like the visual equivalent of a brown rice diet, Mr. Vinterberg instead shows off thrilling vitality.

Taking full advantage of the lack of restrictions on film editing, he hurtles the film forward in a manner that feels seamless but calls for immense skill. With terrific agility, he keeps the camera work vigorously mobile (the film was shot with a small video camera, then transferred to Dogma-ordained 35-millimeter format) and jump cuts with nimble grace. And all the ostensible limitations of this approach are transformed into opportunities. Unusual vantage points, close scrutiny of faces, and savvy editing juxtapositions create the story's palpable momentum. The confused hush at dinner after one shocking pronouncement creates much sharper emphasis than any garden-variety music cue would.

"It is quite a job being toastmaster tonight," remarks one guest, illustrating the power of understatement as a tactic here, too. Helge's son Christian

(Ulrich Thomsen) arrives at the party with the self-appointed mission of making his father own up to past sins. As the full house of guests settle in—including Michael (Thomas Bo Larsen), Christian's black-sheep brother, and their loose-cannon sister, Helene (Paprika Steen)—Christian prepares to tap his knife against his glass and make a terrible pronouncement. He plans to tell the assembled revelers about having been incestuously abused by Helge and that the death of Christian's twin sister, Linda, is on Helge's hands. But like the audience, Christian is in for some surprises. This crowd looks civilized, but it proves amazingly shockproof, too.

The Celebration, which easily accommodates allusions to both Cries and Whispers and The Godfather, features a large, credible cast all over the hotel, from patrician guests to flirtatious waitresses to Helene's American boyfriend (a black man whose presence brings out the considerable worst in this family) to a kitchen staff bent on settling old scores. They and Mr. Vinterberg (who wrote the screenplay with Mogens Rukov) succeed dizzyingly well in making this a party to remember.

—J.M., October 7, 1998

LA CÉRÉMONIE

Directed by Claude Chabrol; written (in French, with English subtitles) by Mr. Chabrol and Caroline Eliacheff, based on the novel *A Judgment in Stone*, by Ruth Rendell; director of photography, Bernard Zitzermann; edited by Monique Fardoulis; music by Mathieu Chabrol; produced by Marin Karmitz; released by New Yorker Films. Running time: 111 minutes.

With: Isabelle Huppert (Jeanne), Sandrine Bonnaire (Sophie), Jacqueline Bisset (Catherine Lelièvre), Jean-Pierre Cassel (Georges Lelièvre), Virginie Ledoyen (Mélinda Lelièvre) and Valentin Merlet (Gilles Lelièvre).

In *La Cérémonie,* the instant suspense classic that is Claude Chabrol's best thriller in more than a decade, the action unfolds in an elegant, isolated château whose inhabitants rely unduly on the comforts of the television screen. Upstairs, the maid watches junk in her room; downstairs, the rich, complacent owners are capable of planning a black-tie evening around a broadcast of *Don Giovanni*. And in between, danger lies in the social and cultural tensions that have made natural enemies of these separate classes.

So when the television offers a quick, teasing glimpse of Mr. Chabrol's own *Wedding in Blood,* everyone here ought to be paying the very closest attention. *La Cérémonie* shows off this filmmaker's graceful way of building tension in slow, subversive increments until violence erupts as a natural outgrowth of his characters' secret lives.

La Cérémonie, which takes its title from the ritual that precedes execution by guillotine, begins on a businesslike note. A beautiful, chic matron named Catherine Lelièvre (Jacqueline Bisset) is seen hiring a servant. The maid is Sophie, who seems an exceptionally stern and secretive individual. The intrepid actress Sandrine Bonnaire, who plays Sophie with bloodcurdling composure, has said that Mr. Chabrol suggested she think of her character as a vegetable. She chose to imagine herself as a stiff and featureless leek.

Catherine is cordial but mildly impatient with her new employee. The Lelièvres have had servant trouble before. (Mr. Chabrol is particularly adept at letting little facts like this stay tantalizingly half explained.) The family includes Georges (Jean-Pierre Cassel), a worldly patriarch, and Mélinda (ravishing young Virginie Ledoyen), his nineteen-year-old daughter by a previous marriage. The Lelièvres also have an adolescent son named Gilles (Valentin Merlet).

When Sophie arrives by train to begin her new job, she turns up on the wrong side of the tracks. This film takes quiet, devilish pleasure in every such hint of something awry. For instance, there is the impassive way that Sophie behaves around the Lelièvres, and how it contrasts with her coarse, ravenous manner when she's eating alone. There is the odd secret that emerges when Sophie visits a bakery on her day off; she can't count money and she can't read.

Surrounded by the daunting opulence of the Lelièvre house, Sophie feels the need for an ally. She accidentally finds one in Jeanne (Isabelle Huppert), the local postmistress, who is insolent, reckless, and even slightly unhinged. Jeanne is irrepressibly nosy, and she's happy to voice any rude thought that comes to mind. She's not quite a liar, but she has a way of getting her facts wrong, as when she confuses *Long*

Day's Journey into Night with a book by Céline. And Jeanne happens to loathe Georges Lelièvre. He loathes her, too.

La Cérémonie is based on *A Judgment in Stone,* a book by the crime writer Ruth Rendell, whose view of human nature is every bit as bighearted as Alfred Hitchcock's, and almost as fascinatingly macabre. This story has a chilling, lethal inevitability from the very start. But the artistry of *La Cérémonie* is in Mr. Chabrol's precise control of his material and in the way an intricate, unnerving bond is seen growing between Sophie and Jeanne. Ms. Huppert, who has more often played reserved characters like Sophie, is simply astonishing as the loose cannon capable of blowing up the film's small, tidy world.

There's plenty of social criticism implicit in the way the film contrasts these resentful women with the oblivious bourgeoisie. But Mr. Chabrol is much too astute to draw easy conclusions.

Class tensions fuel the intrigue, but some of these characters are much too peculiar to speak for anything beyond themselves. There's an extraordinary scene, for instance, in which Sophie and Jeanne have an impromptu birthday party and trade secrets, exchanging information that would send a more conventional thriller into overdrive.

Instead, Mr. Chabrol notices how each woman's recognition of the other as a soul mate cancels out any pangs of conscience. Nothing could be more unsettling than their secret little smiles. And this friendship is made to seem all the spookier when the women, so intensely drawn together, embrace each other often but don't bother with sexual love.

Within the sedate realm of the Lelièvres, Ms. Bisset glides demurely through the film and still manages to suggest that the highly unflattering things Jeanne says about her might be true. She and Mr. Cassel have exactly the right regal assurance to make this story work. So does Ms. Ledoyen, the star of the recent *A Single Girl,* whose very poised, impervious appearance strikes Jeanne as an affront.

There's a little scene in which Jeanne's car has broken down, Mélinda stops to help her, and Mélinda finds herself holding the grime-stained cloth that she used on the car. How would such a privileged young woman casually dispose of such a thing? It's a small exchange, but precisely the sort of moment that Mr. Chabrol can turn quietly devastating. From many

such building blocks, *La Cérémonie* is beautifully and wickedly made.

—*J.M., December 20, 1996*

CHAN IS MISSING

Produced and directed by Wayne Wang; written by Mr. Wang, Isaac Cronin and Terrel Seltzer; cinematographer, Michael Chin; edited by Mr. Wang; music by Robert Kikuchi-Yngojo; released by New Yorker Films. Black and white. Running time: 80 minutes.

With: Wood Moy (Jo), Marc Hayashi (Steve), Lauren Chew (Amy), Judi Nihei (Lawyer), Peter Wang (Henry the Cook), Presco Tabios (Presco) and Ellen Yeung (Mrs. Chan).

It cost less than $20,000 to produce. It's photographed in grainy black-and-white, mostly in San Francisco's Chinatown, with a cast composed entirely of Asian-American actors. Its title is *Chan Is Missing,* and it's a matchless delight.

It is, however, so small and modest in appearance that when you suddenly find yourself laughing with it helplessly, your first suspicion is that someone near you made the joke, not Wayne Wang, the Hong Kong–born, San Francisco-bred, thirty-one-year-old filmmaker who produced, directed, and edited *Chan Is Missing,* and cowrote the screenplay with Isaac Cronin and Terrel Seltzer.

The film will be shown today at the Festival Theater and tomorrow in the New Directors/New Films series. When it eventually goes into commercial release, I hope it will be in a small, modest way that will allow it to find an audience at its own civilized speed. It's a film to be discovered without hard-sell.

Chan Is Missing is about Jo (Wood Moy), a middle-age taxi driver with the face of an Oriental Job, and Jo's nephew Steve (Marc Hayashi), a restless, gabby young man who talks like Charlie Chan's No. 2 son overdosed on Richard Pryor. Jo and Steve, in an effort to get their own taxi medallion, have entrusted their savings—$4,000—to a fellow named Chan Hung, a wheeler-dealer from Taiwan who has apparently absconded with the loot.

Jo and Steve's search for Chan is conducted with

the self-aware solemnity of an especially inscrutable Philip Marlowe case, but the Chinatown through which they move hasn't much to do with Marlowe's world of shadowy sleaze. It's resolutely ordinary—a place of neat middle-class apartments, well-lit inexpensive restaurants, busy kitchens, language schools, sunny sidewalks, and one center for the elderly.

The more that Jo and Steve find out about Chan, the less they know. Chan's estranged wife, a haughty, thoroughly Americanized lawyer, dismisses Chan as a hopeless case, that is, as "too Chinese." There are reports that Chan: 1) has returned to Taiwan to settle a large estate, and 2) has important ties to Communist China. The clues grow curiouser and curiouser.

Chan seems to have played some part in a scuffle between rival political factions during a New Year's parade, when marchers sympathetic to Taipei locked flags with marchers sympathetic to Peking. Jo studies a newspaper photograph of the incident, looking for *Blow-Up* clues, before deciding that the photograph is of another scuffle entirely.

There are suggestions that Chan, who was guilty of a minor traffic violation the day he disappeared, is connected with an argument between two elderly Chinese in which one fellow shot the other dead—in a fit of temper. A visit to a center for the elderly reveals that Chan liked to tango and was nicknamed Hi-Ho, after the cookies he so loved. Chan's world is one of tumultuous contradictions and even more tumultuous anticlimaxes.

The pursuit turns up the existence of the obligatory "other woman," prompts telephoned warnings ("Stop asking questions about Chan"), which may possibly be calls to a wrong number, and, at one point, leads to an interview with a hip Chinese cook who wears a *Saturday Night Fever* T-shirt and morosely amuses himself by singing "Fry me to the moon."

Chan Is Missing is a very funny movie, but it's not a spoof of its characters or even of its so-called "mystery," which, like everything else in the film, is used to illustrate the film's quite serious concerns. These are identity, assimilation, linguistics, and what one hilariously earnest young woman, describing Chan's argument with the traffic cop, defines as "cross-cultural misunderstandings."

Chan Is Missing is not only an appreciation of a way of life that few of us know anything about; it's a revelation of a marvelous, completely secure new talent.

Mr. Wang, who went to college in San Francisco and has worked on theatrical and television films in Hong Kong and San Francisco, obtains superlative performances from Mr. Moy, Mr. Hayashi, and the dozens of other actors who appear in supporting roles. He never wastes a minute of his footage, which has the beauty of something functional transformed by being perfectly realized.

I would especially recommend paying attention to the closing frames of the film, a series of shots of Chinatown facades, suddenly seen devoid of people. This is not architecture arbitrarily tacked onto the film. Nor is it a conventional leave-taking. Rather, it's a final reminder of what Jo and Steve have learned in their search for Chan—that what isn't seen and what can't be proved must remain as important as things seen and proved. Not since the final frames of Luis Buñuel's *Tristana* has there been an ending so dazzling in its utter simplicity.

—*V.C., April 24, 1982*

CHARIOTS OF FIRE

Directed by Hugh Hudson; written by Colin Welland; director of photography, David Watkin; edited by Terry Rawlings; music by Vangelis Papathanassiou; art designer, Roger Hall; produced by David Puttnam; released by Warner Brothers. Running time: 123 minutes.

With: Ben Cross (Harold Abrahams), Ian Charleson (Eric Liddell), Nigel Havers (Lord Andrew Lindsay), Nicholas Farrell (Aubrey Montague), Ian Holm (Sam Mussabini), Sir John Gielgud (Master of Trinity), Lindsay Anderson (Master of Caius), Nigel Davenport (Lord Birkenhead), Cheryl Campbell (Jennie Liddell) and Alice Krige (Sybil Gordon).

Losing a dearly fought athletic contest may very well build character. But winning the contest can build self-confidence as well as character—there's no need to settle for less. This is one of the points made in *Chariots of Fire,* the unashamedly rousing, invigorating, but very clear-eyed evocation of values of the old-fashioned sort that are today more easily satirized than celebrated.

This makes *Chariots of Fire* as festive a film as one

could imagine to open the 19th New York Film Festival tonight. It will begin its regular commercial run tomorrow at the Cinema I.

Chariots of Fire is a celebration of a number of things, not the least of which is a kind of highly committed, emotionally involving drama that knows the difference between sentiment and sentimentality. It also introduces more than a half-dozen talents, mostly English, and celebrates the British film industry, which, with *The French Lieutenant's Woman* and now *Chariots of Fire,* is quite evidently in top form once again.

Chariots of Fire was conceived by David Puttnam, its producer, who commissioned the excellent original screenplay by Colin Welland and then assigned a man new to feature films, Hugh Hudson, to direct it. The film, virtually a succession of smashing debuts, is the story of the 1924 Olympics, particularly of two British track stars who helped win glory for God, King, and country—one furiously competitive young English Jew, a Cambridge student named Harold Abrahams, and one dedicated young Church of Scotland preacher, Eric Liddell, who says at one point to explain why he runs, "God made me devout and—He made me fast."

In the way that Eric Liddell runs to honor God, Harold Abrahams, the son of a Lithuanian immigrant who made a fortune in England, runs to become visible in the Anglo-Saxon society that pretends not to notice his Jewishness. They are splendid roles, splendidly performed by, respectively, Ian Charleson and Ben Cross. These actors are so good that one wonders why it's taken even this long for them to receive the kind of attention that each will certainly enjoy from this film forward.

Mr. Cross, handsome in a Byronic way, is tough, abrasive, and completely believable as the low-born but richly bred Cambridge student who fights for his rights with a mixture of extroverted charm and naked ambition, which shocks the Caius College dons.

Mr. Charleson's Eric Liddell is a fair-haired knight of the cross, so devoted to his mission that at a crucial moment just before the Paris Olympics, he doesn't hesitate to turn down—firmly but not too rudely— what he thinks to be a frivolous request by the Prince of Wales, Lord Birkenhead, and the other members of the British Olympic Committee.

Mr. Cross and Mr. Charleson are not, however, the film's only discoveries. The others include Nigel Havers and Nicholas Farrell, as two other key members of the British track team; Cheryl Campbell as Eric Liddell's equally devout sister, who'd rather have him preaching in China than running in Paris; and Alice Krige, who has the look and manner of a young Grace Kelly, as the London actress who falls in love with Harold Abrahams.

Supporting these newcomers are Ian Holm, who runs off with one of the fattest roles in the film, as Sam Mussabini, the Italian-Turkish track coach privately hired by Abrahams, and Sir John Gielgud and Lindsay Anderson—usually a director, who makes a brief, richly funny appearance as an actor—as the disapproving Cambridge dons.

Two excellent American actors, Brad Davis, the star of *Midnight Express,* and Dennis Christopher, of *Breaking Away,* play important cameo roles as the American athletes who are the major competition faced by the British runners.

It's to the credit of both Mr. Hudson and Mr. Welland that *Chariots of Fire* is simultaneously romantic and commonsensical, lyrical and comic. David Watkin's photography is very fine, and the track sequences—even to someone who has no real interest in track—are charged with poetry.

Though *Chariots of Fire* is mostly about the very privileged, it is so carefully balanced that it doesn't deny the realities of lives less privileged. It's an exceptional film, about some exceptional people.

—V.C., September 25, 1981

CHARLEY VARRICK

Produced and directed by Don Siegel; written by Dean Riesner and Howard Rodman, based on the novel *The Looters* by John Reese; cinematographer, Michael Butler; edited by Frank Moriss; music by Lalo Schifrin; art designer, Fernando Carrere; released by Universal Pictures. Running time: 111 minutes.

With: Walter Matthau (Charles Varrick), Joe Don Baker (Molly), Felicia Farr (Sybil Fort), Norman Fell (Mr. Garfinkle), Sheree North (Jewell Everett) Andy Robinson (Harman Sullivan) and John Vernon (Maynard Boyle).

An intelligent action melodrama is probably one of the most difficult kinds of film to make. Intelligence in this case has nothing to do with being literate, poetic, or even reasonable. It has to do with movement, suspense, and sudden changes in fortune that are plausible enough to entertain without challenging you to question basic premises. If you start asking whether such-and-such could really have happened, or if so-and-so would have acted in a certain way, the action film falls apart.

It also falls apart when it has the distasteful philosophical underpinnings that Don Siegel last year gave his *Dirty Harry*. The vigilante justice favored by that film made the violence truly shocking. There are no such problems with Siegel's new movie, the entertaining robbers-and-robbers action melodrama called *Charley Varrick,* which opened yesterday at the Loews State 2 and the Orpheum.

Charley Varrick (Walter Matthau) is a former air-circus pilot, supposedly turned legitimate crop duster, who makes his living robbing small banks in the Southwest.

By some dreadful fluke, when he and his associates stick up the bank in Tres Cruces, New Mexico, they get away not with the modest $15,000 or $20,000 they expected, but with more than three-quarters of a million dollars. The neat, unassuming little bank turns out to be a way station employed by the Mafia when it sends Las Vegas gambling money out of the country to be laundered.

There is a lot of violence in *Charley Varrick*—so much that I'm staggered by its comparatively benign PG rating. Yet its violence is less a disturbing reflection of any recognizable world than an essential part of the choreography of action melodrama in a make-believe world.

The fun in *Charley Varrick* is not sadistic, though there are cruel moments in it, but in watching Charley attempt to outwit both the cops and the Mafia. The casting of Matthau in this key role helps tremendously. Though Charley is tough enough to walk away from his wife's death (after the initial holdup) without showing much emotion, the character is inhabited—maybe even transformed—by Matthau's wit and sensitivity as an actor. If the role were played by someone else, *Charley Varrick* would be something else entirely.

With the exception of Charley and a sheriff, played by Norman Fell, who is pretty much a straight man, everyone in the movie is to a greater or lesser extent rotten: Charley's greedy young assistant (Andy Robinson), the Mafia hit man (Joe Don Baker), the owner of the Tres Cruces bank (John Vernon) and a photographer, very nicely played by Sheree North, who specializes in making fake passports on short notice.

Siegel has decorated the movie with a lot of colorful bit characters including a chatty, sex-obsessed old woman, but the action sequences give the film its content as well as style. The duel between a high-powered automobile and an ancient biplane at the end of the movie is what it's all about.

—*V.C., October 20, 1973*

CHICAGO

Directed and choreographed by Rob Marshall; written by Bill Condon, based on the musical play (book by Bob Fosse and Fred Ebb) and the play by Maurine Dallas Watkins; director of photography, Dion Beebe; edited by Martin Walsh; music by John Kander, lyrics by Mr. Ebb, original score music by Danny Elfman; production designer, John Myhre; produced by Martin Richards; released by Miramax Films. Running time: 108 minutes.

With: Renée Zellweger (Roxie Hart), Catherine Zeta-Jones (Velma Kelley), Richard Gere (Billy Flynn), Queen Latifah (Matron Mama Morton), John C. Reilly (Amos Hart), Lucy Liu (Kitty Baxter), Taye Diggs (Bandleader), Colm Feore (Harrison), Christine Baranski (Mary Sunshine), Dominic West (Fred Casely) and Chita Rivera (Nickie).

It's rare to find a picture as exuberant, as shallow—and as exuberant about its shallowness—as the director Rob Marshall's film adaptation of the Broadway musical "Chicago." It's the raw expenditure of energy and the canniness of the staging that should pull audiences in and keep them rooted. The fabulous bones of this oft-told tale have been picked over so often that there's no flesh left on them. But Mr. Marshall and the screenwriter Bill Condon get a terrifically sweet concoction out of this fabled skeleton.

The movie, set in Prohibition-era Chicago, is tough, brittle fun—a mouthful. Mercilessly adapted by Mr. Condon, who won an Oscar for his *Gods and Monsters* script, this *Chicago* has a connoisseur's appreciation of camp, which it treats as a dish best served cold. This, of course, is undoubtedly the best way to present a movie take on Bob Fosse's digressive musical version of *Chicago,* itself a song-and-dance spin on the 1926 play by Maurine Dallas Watkins.

Her original *Chicago* had made it to the screen twice, most notably as 1942's *Roxie Hart,* one of the finest comedies of that era. (A bit of intriguing trivia: *Roxie Hart* starred Ginger Rogers, but it wasn't a musical.) This new picture maintains the relentless spirit of Fosse's blunt suavity and the breathless, black-silk enthusiasm of Kander and Ebb's songs.

In other words, *Chicago* is as tough as Roxie (Renée Zellweger) turns out to be. Her Roxie is on trial on a murder charge, accused of killing a man (Dominic West) who took advantage of her. Mr. Marshall's movie makes her more of a victim initially, tumbling from a happy romp into the lurid terror of violation. His adaptation plays on the audience's affection for Ms. Zellweger's scrappy Kewpie-doll-with-a-heart image before exposing the knowing smirk and steel-jacketed ambition looming beneath Roxie's dimples. The picture saves her chameleon aspect for later, turning her spunky, spiky näif on her head: instead of spreading good will, she pimps for it. As the press coverage of Roxie's trial grows, her own sense of self inflates, she gets hooked on cheap, easy fame.

The retread nature of the material, centering on America's thrill-hungry, low-attention-span press and public, is undeniable. This hoary attack on sensationalism has been covered in almost every newspaper picture of the 1930's, from *Five Star Final* (1931) to *Nothing Sacred* (1937). Fosse heated up the action by making *Chicago* about predatory sex and wild justice.

Turning the tawdriness of Roxie's murder trial into a brash campaign for fame and allure, Fosse's *Chicago*—which jumped from one roof-raising number to another—broadcast the crass, manipulative motives of everyone involved. The sinewy, exposed skin of the dancers provided a jaw-plummeting contrast to the cold callousness of the characters.

Mr. Marshall and Mr. Condon try something different. This movie, choreographed by Mr. Marshall, may be accused of being inspired by Baz Luhrmann's *Moulin Rouge.* It cranks up the temperature by flashing more thigh than Kentucky Fried Chicken, gener-

ating excitement with bullet-timed editing and brassy, hip-shaking musical numbers that openly comment on what has come before as well as advancing the story.

Dennis Potter's *Pennies From Heaven,* with its cold-hearted Brechtian observational style, is a big influence, too. The trial and everything leading up to it are treated in Mr. Marshall's picture like backstage preparation. It provides standard dialogue exchanges for the cast members so their beady-eyed grasping is obvious. For the eruption of the musical numbers, the movie pops inside Roxie's head—the id-free world of her unconscious, where the songs are sung out and the dances are flung out.

Back in the real world, the competition grows between Roxie and Velma (Catherine Zeta-Jones) for the public's attention and constantly diminishing concentration. Velma is a jazz baby stage performer who is also doing time and anxious about being upstaged—especially when both her life and her public profile may be at stake. Mr. Condon may have also gone back to the prefatory material that Watkins wrote for her *Chicago,* which details a chunk of the actual history of the crimes that inspired the show.

Chicago was a tough movie to make. Fosse, laboring to get it done since he brought it to the stage in 1975, finally gave up on it; instead he transplanted some of the plot machinations and several of the show's lines to the movie *All That Jazz* (1979). His Expressionists-link dance style has turned up everywhere but the Christian Broadcasting Network in the interim. But Fosse's death in 1987 wasn't enough to derail a filmed *Chicago.* And with the exception of Wilma Flintstone, almost every female star of the last 20 years who ever sang a note—or dreamed of it—was mentioned as a possible star.

On first sight of Ms. Zeta-Jones in *Chicago* in her Louise Brooks wig and ruthless smile, it's hard not to be reminded of the limping musical she was seen rehearsing in last year's comedy *America's Sweethearts* with the same vocal equipment. But not since she used that martial form of Pilates to slither through a series of electronic alarms in *Entrapment* (1999) has she shown the kind of physicality she displays here. She pumps her majestic, long legs like the cylinders of a Corvette about to redline, but always knowing exactly when to stop short of throwing a piston.

Chicago has become more of Roxie's story, but that

doesn't stop Mr. Marshall from supplying its cast with moments to, as Fosse used to say, razzle-dazzle 'em. As the big-ticket defense lawyer and jury barometer Billy Flynn, Richard Gere has never been better, turning spoiled princeling arrogance into a witty revel. He splashes his winner's juice sparingly, and the movie's shift from acid reality to bitter, high-flying musical serves him best.

Queen Latifah, as the prison matron, has a number dripping with the honey of the young Bessie Smith. She and Mr. Gere are used for their bigger-than-life personae, and sudden pressure drops in those presences signal their duplicity. John C. Reilly is the opposite—the movie's conscience—as Roxie's long-suffering husband, and his baggy-pants "Mr. Cellophane" number is rueful and angry.

Chicago, which opens nationally today, is also a Broadway baby's joy, with snappy cameos of theater performers, including the lovable Christine Baranski, who seems to bring a cheering section with her. To be sure, it's not the type of picture that lingers, and obviously some of the sting-like-a-bee editing is a mercy to Ms. Zellweger, whose float-like-a-butterfly voice doesn't triumph over her my-left-foot dance skills.

The big finale featuring her and Ms. Zeta-Jones almost does what a jury can't: stop them cold. Until that scene, Ms. Zellweger's performance is alternately subtle and reptile; she can still win the day. Who would have expected Ms. Zellweger—and Miramax—to come through in a musical? And it's one of the few Christmas entertainments to run under two hours. Who couldn't love that?

—*E.M., December 22, 2002*

CHICKEN RUN

Directed by Peter Lord and Nick Park: written by Karey Kirkpatrick. based on a story by Mr. Lord and Mr. Park: director of photography. Dave Alex Riddett: edited by Mark Solomon: music by John Powell and Harry Gregson-Williams: produced by Mr. Lord. David Sproxton and Mr. Park: released by Dream Works Pictures. Running time: 86 minutes.

With the voices of: Phil Daniels (Fetcher). Lynn Ferguson (Mac). Mel Gibson (Rocky). Tony Haygarth (Mr. Tweedy). Jane Horrocks (Babs). Miranda Richardson (Mrs. Tweedy). Julia Sawalha (Ginger). Timothy Spall (Nick). Imelda Staunton (Bunty) and Benjamin Whitrow (Folwer).

*C*hicken Run, the first full-length feature from Aardman Animation, makes brainy use of Mel Gibson. It parodies Mr. Gibson's inane heroics in giving him a loud loose-cannon entrance.

He's the voice of Rocky the Flying Rooster, and he comes soaring into Tweedy's farm, where a grim set of henhouses look just like barracks and the residents, led by the . . . well, plucky Ginger (Julia Sawalha), are constantly trying to escape. Ginger is, anyway, and she has just been released again from the Tweedy version of solitary confinement when Rocky, arms flailing and screaming in an unusually uncomfortable version of flight, hits the yard.

He promises Ginger and her friends that he'll teach them to fly and save them from a life of squeezing out eggs for the awful Mrs. Tweedy (Miranda Richardson).

Based on the sympathy that *Chicken Run* will engender for chickens, it's probably good that McDonald's doesn't have a promotional tie-in. The sight of youngsters sobbing over Chicken McNuggets in a Happy Meal while their parents try to explain the food chain wouldn't be good for anybody. *Chicken Run* is, though, because like other efforts from the directors Nick Park ("Wallace and Gromit" and *Creature Comforts,* the 1989 Academy Award–winning short) and Peter Lord, who also produced this film, it flies in the face of brightly colored, blandly energetic song-filled animated features.

There's one forgettable song sequence, but like the other Aardman pieces that Mr. Park has directed, *Chicken Run* has that yearning for home that's at the heart of all good fables. There's a wistful calm in the gray skies of England, where all of Mr. Park's work is set, and his characters just want a comfortable place to rest their heads. Ginger dreams of lounging on grass instead of digging in the dirt in the Tweedy yards. (In the Wallace and Gromit shorts, Gromit, the poor thinking man's pooch, is constantly in danger of being tossed out of his home.)

Visually as depressively earth-toned as *Stalag 17* (which is also parodied in the film), the world created by Mr. Park and Mr. Lord will hypnotize the young who may have had a full dose of antic full-length cartoons. (It assumes that children are up for animation a little darker in spirit than what they're usually fed.) The movie rewards them for their rapt, quiet attention, and its use of modeled latex figures instead of drawn animation makes *Chicken Run* more realistic and far more vigorously dramatic.

The film is packed with the kind of detail that adults will like, too, with visual and verbal jokes that make references ranging from *Modern Times* to *Star Trek*. When the hens, following Rocky's daft flight instructions, are launched into the air, Fetcher (Phil Daniels), one of the farm's hustler mice, moans, "It's raining hen."

There aren't many directors of animation who make such effective use of a Dickensian landscape and have Mr. Park's ability to wrest laughs from situations that lean toward the tragic. Mr. Park and Mr. Lord use several motifs of the Wallace and Gromit shorts, including some unwieldy, potentially deadly machinery: Mrs. Tweedy has installed a chicken pie machine because egg production isn't bringing in the kind of revenue stream she wants.

Those expecting a breakthrough in animation storytelling may be a little disappointed, though. The DreamWorks influence has made *Chicken Run* a little safe; the Wallace and Gromit pictures provided more of an emotional roller coaster. And the presence of Mr. Gibson, even though he lends himself to satirizing his persona, provides comfort.

If it's the more subversive Nick Park you want or are unfamiliar with, seek out the Wallace and Gromit films, all of which are available and should be seen. There are other notable Aardman projects as well, including the fabulous and rambunctious "Rex the Runt" shorts, which can be found on the Atomfilms.com Web site.

But *Chicken Run* is by no means a letdown. It's immensely satisfying, a divinely relaxed and confident film. Mr. Park and Mr. Lord brilliantly integrate everyday objects into the story.

And this briskly paced epic—not a minute is wasted—uses their satirical take on British modesty and balmy superiority, exemplified here in a cranky former R.A.F. rooster, Fowler (Benjamin Whitrow). The directors have transferred all the deftness and talent of their shorter films into an artful big screen realization.

Ginger is ingenious and ambitious, and for a change the movie gives children a quick-thinking heroine who eventually realizes that she's responsible for her future.

More important, *Chicken Run* doesn't try to cram messages of uplift down its audience's gullet. It's a great eggscape from banality.

—*E.M., June 21, 2000*

LA CHIENNE

Directed by Jean Renoir; written (in French, with English subtitles) by Mr. Renoir and Andre Girard, based on the novel by Georges de la Fouchardière; cinematographer, Theodor Sparkuhl; edited by Denise Batcheff-Tual, Marguerite Renoir and Jean Renoir; art designer, Gabriel Scognamillo; produced by Charles David; released by Ajay. Black and white. Running time: 100 minutes.

With: Michel Simon (Maurice Legrand), Janie Marèze (Lulu), Georges Flamant (Dede), Madeleine Berubet (Adele Legrand), Galliard (Alexis Godard) and Jean Gehret (Dagodet).

This is neither a comedy nor a tragedy. It proves no moral at all. It's simply another story about He and She and 'The Other Guy.'"

So says, in effect, the master of ceremonies, the hand puppet that introduces Jean Renoir's 1931 classic, *La Chienne* (*The Bitch*), whereupon the camera moves across the apron of the miniature stage, through a cloth backdrop, and into the world of real-life Paris.

Maybe it's not an absolutely real-life Paris. The city we see is familiar in all its physical characteristics, but it is lit by the unique combination of compassion, wit, amusement, and surprise that this greatest of all French directors has brought to virtually every film he's ever made.

La Chienne will be screened as a retrospective entry at the New York Film Festival at Alice Tully Hall this afternoon and once again next Saturday. Of the seven festival films I've seen at this writing, it's the only one that can be recommended without reservation. It's fresh, funny, rude and gentle about the appalling consequences one faces if one has the gift of staying alive.

179

La Chienne, which apparently has never been released here in an English-subtitled version, is Renoir's first full-length sound film. It's based on the novel by Georges de la Fouchardière that was also made into quite a different movie, *Scarlet Street,* by Fritz Lang in 1945. The basic story lines of both films are approximately the same, but where the Lang is dark, violent and obsessive, the tone of the Renoir is contemplative and ironic. In spite of what the master of ceremonies says, *La Chienne* is a comedy in the best sense.

It's the not-really-so sad story of Maurice (Michel Simon), a painter on Sundays and a quiet, self-contained, somewhat comic figure of a bookkeeper the other six days. One night, Maurice, who is married to a perpetually furious shrew, meets a vulgar prostitute named Lulu (Janie Marèze). In the way of such tales, he falls desperately in love with Lulu and sets her up in a flat that is occupied mostly by Lulu and her pimp.

La Chienne is the tale of Maurice's degradation, his victimization, and his ultimate liberation, first through love, followed by violence, then by that curious, benign second sight that Renoir bestows upon characters who have the courage to survive.

The late Mr. Simon is superb as the bookkeeper who doesn't fit into any stereotype of henpecked husband. His Maurice is a man of many parts, including the will to indulge his pleasures and a remarkable resolution, when necessary. All of the performances are close to flawless, but it's Renoir's unseen presence one remembers most vividly, the man we saw on-screen, and recognized immediately, when he introduced the vignettes of his last film, *The Little Theater of Jean Renoir.*

—*V.C., September 27, 1975*

CHINATOWN

Directed by Roman Polanski: written by Robert Towne: cinematographer. John A. Alonzo: edited by Sam O'Steen: music by Jerry Goldsmith: production designer. Richard Sylbert: produced by Robert Evans: released by Paramount Pictures. Running time: 131 minutes.

With: Jack Nicholson (J.J. Gittes). Faye Dunaway (Evelyn Mulwray). John Huston (Noah Cross). Perry Lopez (Escobar). John Hillerman (Yelburton). Darrell Zwerling (Hollis Mulwray). Diane Ladd (Ida Sessions). Ray Jenson (Mulvehill) and Roman Polanski (Man with Knife).

Pin-striped suits, men's hair parted slightly off-center like Richard Arlen's, four-door convertible touring cars (not yet declared unsafe), official portraits of Franklin D. Roosevelt in public buildings, women with marceled hair and elegant slouches.

These are just some of the 1930's artifacts that decorate Roman Polanski's *Chinatown,* a new private-eye melodrama that celebrates not only a time and a place (Los Angeles) but also a kind of criminality that to us jaded souls today appears to be nothing worse than an eccentric form of legitimate private enterprise.

There's nothing wanton, mindless or (with one exception) especially vicious about the murders and assaults that J.J. Gittes (Jack Nicholson), a private detective who has heretofore specialized in matrimonial disputes, sets out to solve in *Chinatown.* No senseless massacres, no rapes, no firebombings of innocents.

In that far-off time—midway between the repeal of Prohibition and the inauguration of lend-lease—murderers, swindlers and blackmailers acted according to carefully premeditated plans. These plans, in turn, were always there for the uncovering by a Sam Spade or a Philip Marlowe or, in this case, a J.J. Gittes, a man whose name is repeatedly mispronounced as Gibbs, which is one of the burdens he learns to live with, along with a vulnerable nose.

This fixed order of things, of a cause for every effect, explains the enduring appeal of fiction like *Chinatown,* but it also is something of a test for the writer who comes after Dashiell Hammett and Raymond Chandler and who doesn't hesitate to evoke their memories and thus to invite comparisons.

Robert Towne, who adapted *The Last Detail* and wrote the original screenplay for *Chinatown,* is good but I'm not sure he's good enough to compete with the big boys. When Robert Altman set out to make Chandler's *The Long Good-bye,* he had the good sense to turn it into a contemporary film that was as much a comment on the form as an evocation of it.

Mr. Polanski and Mr. Towne have attempted nothing so witty and entertaining, being content instead to make a competently stylish, more or less thirtiesish movie that continually made me wish I were back seeing *The Maltese Falcon* or *The Big Sleep*. Others may not be as finicky.

Among the good things in *Chinatown* are the performances by Mr. Nicholson, who wears an air of comic, lazy, very vulnerable sophistication that is this film's major contribution to the genre, Faye Dunaway, as the widow of the film's first murder victim, a woman too beautiful to be either good or true, and John Huston, who plays a wealthy old tycoon whose down-home, sod-kicking manner can't quite disguise the sort of fanaticism displayed by Sidney Greenstreet in Mr. Huston's *Maltese Falcon*.

The plot is a labyrinth of successive revelations having to do with Los Angeles water reserves, land rights, fraud and intrafamily hanky-panky, climaxing in Los Angeles's Chinatown on a street that seems no more mysterious than Flatbush Avenue.

Mr. Polanski himself turns up in the film's most vicious scene, playing the half-pint hood who neatly slices one of J. J. Gittes's nostrils, thus requiring the detective to go through the rest of the picture with stitches that look like blood-encrusted cat's whiskers sticking out of his nose.

—*V.C., June 21, 1974*

CHLOË IN THE AFTERNOON

Written (in French, with English subtitles) and directed by Eric Rohmer; director of photography, Nestor Almendros; edited by Cecile Decugis; music by Arié Dzierlatka; art designer, Nicole Rachline; produced by Pierre Cottrell; released by Columbia Pictures. Running time: 97 minutes.

With: Bernard Verley (Frédéric), Zouzou (Chloë), Françoise Verley (Hélène), Daniel Ceccaldi (Gerard), Malvina Penne (Fabienne) and Babette Ferrier (Martine).

Frédéric (Bernard Verley), the hero of *Chloë in the Afternoon*, the last in Eric Rohmer's marvelous cycle of comedies, which he calls his *Six Moral Tales*, is happily married, but he is stumped: he's no longer capable of flirting with other women.

That's what he says, but he is not always trustworthy when he talks about himself. Never before in his life has he been so conscious of desirable women—on the train as he commutes from Saint-Cloud, in his Paris office, in the cafés. When he crosses a street, he attends to the passing women like a naturalist studying life in a rain forest. For a minute or two, he even falls in love with an unspectacular young saleswoman, apparently because she is so seriously insistent that he buy a shirt he doesn't want.

"I feel marriage closes me in, cloisters me, and I want to escape," he tells us on the soundtrack. "The prospect of happiness opening indefinitely before me sobers me. I find myself missing that time, not too long ago, when I could experience the pangs of anticipation. I dream of a life made of first loves, lasting loves."

Like Adrien in *La Collectionneuse*, Jean-Louis in *My Night at Maud's*, and Jérome in *Claire's Knee*, Frédéric must choose between love and desire, which Mr. Rohmer sometimes calls love-in-idleness. In *Chloë in the Afternoon*, desire takes the fairly ample shape of Chloë (Zouzou), a none too stable, not immediately prepossessing young woman out of his past. Chloë, who was once a successful model and the mistress of an artist with whom she went to America, has returned to Paris with boredom in her heart and a man named Serge she doesn't love.

Because Frédéric feels so secure in his marriage, because Chloë's interest flatters him, and because he is so incapable of flirting, he begins to see Chloë in the afternoons, just to talk, sometimes to advise her on her muddled affairs. He tells himself that because they have no commitments to each other, he can feel a freedom and excitement with her that he can't allow in his marriage. Quite surprisingly (at least to Frédéric), he finds himself wanting to go to bed with her.

Chloë in the Afternoon, which opened the 10th New York Film Festival last night and begins its commercial engagement today at the 68th Street Playhouse, is the perfect coda to those three of the Six Moral Tales that have already been released here (*Collectionneuse*, *Maud's*, and *Claire*, whose heroines are recollected in a comic reverie in the new film).

In *Chloë* Mr. Rohmer examines monogamous marriage as if it were the sum total of contemporary civilization: the thought of destroying it is natural but also to be resisted for the time being, at least until something better, more practical, comes along. It's a comedy of very funny, complex contradictions, between action and word, between image and sound.

Unfortunately, because American audiences must spend a great deal of their time reading the English subtitles that translate the French dialogue, *Chloë*, like the earlier Rohmer films, will probably be too easily classified as literate.

Much of the wit is verbal, and Mr. Rohmer's screenplay contains absolutely lovely passages, such as the one in which Frédéric describes his love of Paris and its crowds as being like his love for the sea. He says he is not engulfed or lost in the city. Instead, he rides its crest like a solitary surfer following the rhythm of a wave.

These passages are impressive, but the reading of them tends to distract the eye from seeing what's really happening on-screen: including Mr. Rohmer's way with actors. He seldom photographs them in close-up so that we must make our own choices about what sort of people they are, about what they're thinking, and whether or not we can trust them.

Although Mr. Rohmer's heroes inevitably opt for the comparatively celibate choice, his films succeed in being immensely erotic. When Nestor Almendros, Mr. Rohmer's superb cameraman, shows us a few square inches of Chloë's flesh, it has the suddenly tactile effect of a real—not an imagined—embrace. Most important, just because Mr. Rohmer keeps his focus short, clear, and precise, one sees deeply into the lives of his characters without the sort of pretentious distortions of most movies that deal in metaphors. Because Chloë is about what it says it is, it works on more profound levels.

—*V.C., September 30, 1972*

CHOCOLAT

Directed by Claire Denis; written (in French, with English subtitles) by Ms. Denis and Jean-Pol Fargeau; director of photography, Robert Alazraki; edited by Claude Merlin; music by Abdullah Ibrahim; art designer, Thierry Flamand; released by TFI Films. Running time: 105 minutes.

With: Isaach de Bankolé (Protée), Giulia Boschi (Aimee Dalens), François Cluzet (Marc Dalens), Cécile Ducasse (Younger France Dalens), Jean-Claude Adelin (Luc Segalen), Kenneth Cranham (Jonathan Boothby), Mireille Perrier (Adult France Dalens) and Jacques Denis (Detpich, the Coffee Planter).

The new French film *Chocolat* is so fine that a lot of people may want—or assume—it to be about more things than it is.

Chocolat recalls the last years of French West African colonialism through the memory of a young white woman who, in the late 1950's, grew up as the daughter of a district officer in Cameroon. Its view of black Africa is limited, but the entire film is of such clarity and authenticity of feeling that it doesn't deny the existence of other truths.

I liked *Chocolat* very much when I first saw it at last year's Cannes Film Festival. Now I think it is some kind of miniature classic.

The film, opening today at the Cinema Studio 2, is the first to be directed by the forty-one-year-old Claire Denis, who wrote the screenplay (with Jean-Pol Fargeau) drawing on her own childhood in what was then a French colony.

Chocolat begins in the 1980's. A young woman named France (Mireille Perrier), traveling around Cameroon with all she owns in a backpack, is diffident to the point of rudeness. One afternoon, she reluctantly accepts a ride from an affable middle-class black man and his small son. Her answers to their questions are given with effort.

Through the windows of the car, France looks at a familiar landscape. The quality of light, the heat, the sights, and the sounds haven't changed, only her connection to them. *Chocolat* slips sideways into France's mind and the past.

The young France (Cécile Ducasse), an alert, inquisitive little girl, lives with her mother and father in a large plain bungalow in the parched bush country, surrounded by black servants who are faceless except for Protée (Isaach de Bankolé). Though he is the house "boy," Protée has the splendid physique and the manner of a prince, someone taken hostage in war, waiting to be ransomed.

Protée is scrupulous in carrying out his assigned duties. He waits on table, makes beds, cleans the house, sometimes helps out in the garden. As France's parents seem not to see him, he does not allow himself to see them. He remains impassive, a distant if obedient figure. Only with France does Protée express himself.

Because France has no friends, Protée becomes, by default, her closest companion and ally. Each is in some way excluded from the more important activities of the main house. Though France is an embarrassment to Protée when she bosses him around in the nearby village, their friendship at home seems secure. They exchange mysterious riddles. Often they don't talk at all. They just sit.

When he offers her an ant sandwich—large live black ants embedded between two slices of buttered bread—it's both a dare and a gift. Neither of them laughs as she solemnly eats it.

Chocolat, which is said to be a 1950's slang expression that means "to get caught" as well as dark-skinned, is about the inevitable end of that friendship. It's also about France's mother and father, their friends and the curious people who pass through their lives and become, because of the isolation, their intimates, at least for a little while.

Some of the events the audience sees are drawn from France's memory. Some are the imaginings of the grown woman looking back, trying to piece things together. When an airplane makes a forced landing nearby, France's parents have to put up a house full of edgy, quarrelsome strangers, including a crude white coffee planter, traveling with his black mistress whom he does not acknowledge.

On another occasion, friends come to visit, bringing with them a handsome young Frenchman, Luc, described as a former seminary student who is traveling across Africa on foot. The bored wives look with longing at Luc, an early hippie, part of whose charm is being rude to everybody. Luc insists on eating with the servants and using their shower. He sneers at Protée, "You're even worse than the priests who raised you."

The nature of the relationship between France's parents reveals itself slowly, in details that can never be fully explained. A key to the film is a sudden, forbidden gesture, which the young France could never have witnessed, and which could only have been guessed by the woman she grew into.

Miss Denis's mastery of filmmaking technology, which is something that can be learned, is equaled by her splendid control of narrative, a more elusive talent. She is astonishing. There are no dark corners in the story. Everything that happens is vivid and clear, though subject to the kind of speculation that tantalizes and rewards.

Beginning with young Miss Ducasse and Mr. de Bankolé, all of the performances are peerless. Most prominent are Giulia Boschi and François Cluzet as France's parents. Jean-Claude Adelin as the hippie and Jacques Denis as the coffee planter.

Chocolat is among the best.

—*V.C., March 10, 1989*

THE CIDER HOUSE RULES

Directed by Lasse Hallstrom; written by John Irving, based on his novel; director of photography, Oliver Stapleton; edited by Lisa Zeno Churgin; music by Rachel Portman; production designer, David Gropman; produced by Richard N. Gladstein; released by Miramax Films. Running time: 125 minutes.

With: Tobey Maguire (Homer Wells), Charlize Theron (Candy Kendall), Delroy Lindo (Mr. Rose), Paul Rudd (Wally Worthington), Michael Caine (Dr. Wilbur Larch), Jane Alexander (Nurse Edna), Kathy Baker (Nurse Angela), Kieran Culkin (Buster), Kate Nelligan (Olive Worthington), Erykah Badu (Rose Rose) and Heavy D (Peaches).

It doesn't take a cryptographer to decipher the meanings in John Irving's sprawling picaresque allegories. But a reader who wants to savor them must be willing to suspend a psychoanalytic view of human nature descended from Freud through Oprah and surrender to an imagination that is more Dickensian than Freudian. Once you give up those expectations, a visit to the world according to Irving is a little like touring a parallel universe where fate is determined not so much by abusive parents as by wondrous tragicomic events beyond the realm of psychology.

I can't think of a better filmmaker to guide us through that world than Lasse Hallstrom, the director of *My Life as a Dog* and *What's Eating Gilbert Grape?,* two grown-up movies that share Mr. Irving's adult-child sensibility. In Mr. Hallstrom's lovely adaptation (with a screenplay by the author) of Mr. Irving's sixth novel, *The Cider House Rules,* the author's fantastical world of wonders and the director's tender-hearted compassion mesh into what is easily the finest film realization of an Irving novel.

The movie is really only a fragment of that novel, scaled down to conventional movie length, with numerous characters discarded and the story's time frame compressed from decades into a couple of years. The novel's exhaustive examination of abortion (both its moral and medical aspects) has been greatly softened.

What's left is a gentle, beautifully acted fable about a young man's journey into the world, his loss of innocence and his acquiring of values that reflect the lessons learned on his journey. The movie is also a blatant homage to *David Copperfield,* brief passages of which are read aloud to the children in St. Cloud's orphanage, the Maine institution where much of the story takes place during the height of World War II.

Finally, it is a sustained meditation on the dream of home sweet home that gnaws at the heart of its orphaned main character Homer Wells (Tobey Maguire) as well as the hearts of the other children who grow up in St. Cloud's. Some of the movie's most touching moments find the camera lingering over the faces of children silently pleading with angelic smiles and saucer eyes to be selected for adoption by couples who visit the institution in search of the perfect child.

It is here that Homer grows up under the tutelage of the good-hearted, tight-lipped Wilbur Larch (Michael Caine), the orphanage's omnipotent doctor who delivers the babies of unwed mothers and who also performs abortions on request. Although Homer never attends medical school, by the time he leaves St. Cloud's he knows both how to deliver and how to abort babies. One Dickensian message the movie hammers home is that growing up means coming to the realization that in a cosmic sense we are all orphans.

Although Dr. Larch is portrayed as a benign figure, the movie wonders about the consequences of his life-and-death decisions and his readiness to play God, and asks how anyone could presume to be so omnipotent. By giving the doctor a tragic flaw in his addiction to ether, it suggests that his need to escape facing full responsibility for his hubris is what finally undoes him. But the film implies even more forcefully that in order for our lives to mean anything at all, we sometimes have to play God, take charge and do what we believe is right.

When Homer is barely out of his teens, he leaves St. Cloud's to explore the big, wide world in a red roadster driven by Wally Worthington (Paul Rudd), a cocky young Army flyer whose beautiful blond fiancee, Candy Kendall (Charlize Theron), has just had an abortion at St. Cloud's. While Wally is away at war, Homer works as an apple-picker on his father's farm, and he and Candy fall in love.

Homer also becomes involved in the lives of the migrant workers who share a dormitory where the inane rules of conduct (the cider house rules) are posted on the wall. And in the movie's dramatic climax, he finds himself intervening in the tormented incestuous relationship of a character simply named Mr. Rose (Delroy Lindo) and his daughter Rose (the pop singer Erykah Badu) and eventually having to play God. The consequences of this act of conscience, however, are tragically ambiguous.

The Cider House Rules is an unabashedly sentimental movie that wants to pluck our heart strings, and now and then its tone (and its quiet but incessant soundtrack by Rachel Portman) turns cloyingly sweet. But the performances have an understated gravity and the screenplay a thematic consistency that largely avoid tawdry manipulation.

Anchoring the movie is Mr. Maguire's sober, wide-eyed Homer, a wounded, moon-faced innocent who, in leaving the institution that nurtured him, blindly follows his heart and finds fulfillment working outdoors. Even in simple apple picking, Homer feels he is obeying Dr. Larch's dictum (a recurrent theme in the movie) to "be of use."

Mr. Caine's portrayal of a Maine doctor (he has a perfect American accent and clipped New England delivery) is a coup for an actor who had seemed too often trapped in the roles of snake-eyes British lotharios, con men and other sleazeballs. Mr. Lindo's apple-picker is a towering human storm about to collapse on itself, and Ms. Badu's desperately agitated Rose is one of the year's sharpest screen acting debuts.

Oliver Stapleton's cinematography drenches the movie in an oak-gold 40's New England ambiance that is so intense you can almost taste the sour-apple pungency of the orchard air. That ambiance, along with the idealized romance of the gung-ho daredevil flyer and his honey-blond sweetheart, gives the film a slightly mythical quality that harmonizes with Mr. Irving's subtly literary screenplay and the director's soft-hearted child's-eye vision.

The need to be of use, the discovery that the official rules and real-life rules of how to behave rarely coincide—these and other life lessons that our innocent hero learns may sound like the tritest of homilies. But *The Cider House Rules* gives them the depth and emotional weight of earned wisdom.

—*S.H., December 10, 1999*

THE CITADEL

Directed by King Vidor; written by Ian Dalrymple, Frank Wead and Elizabeth Hill, with additional dialogue by Emlyn Williams, based on the book by A. J. Cronin; cinematographer, Harry Stradling; edited by Charles Frend; music by Louis Levy; art designers, Lazare Meerson and Alfred Junge; produced by Victor Saville; released by Metro-Goldwyn-Mayer. Black and white. Running time: 110 minutes.

With: Robert Donat (Andrew Manson), Rosalind Russell (Christine Manson), Ralph Richardson (Denny), Rex Harrison (Dr. Lawford), Emlyn Williams (Owen) and Penelope Dudley Ward (Toppy Leroy).

A. J. Cronin's *The Citadel* has been converted by Metro's British unit into one of the most satisfying screen dramas of the year. Although the film, like the novel, may be criticized for offering little new to those who have read *Arrowsmith,* it has the cinema's advantage over the printed word in the living backgrounds it creates, the vivid characterizations it establishes, its shrewd utilization of only the telling scenes of the book. Dr. Cronin's work, in consequence, is always appearing at its best, a circumstance which should flatter its author, is bound to delight his readers, and cannot fail to stamp the film version now showing at the Capitol as one of the great events of the season.

Since this is one of those hands-across-the-seas productions, wherein the Muse is prodded into action by the British quota requirements, the film becomes a happy illustration of Anglo-American accord, in the arts division at least. Dr. Cronin's adapters include Frank Wead of Hollywood and Ian Dalrymple of London; it is King Vidor of Hollywood who was in charge of directing the production in King George's England; Rosalind Russell is America's representative

in a cast which otherwise is soundly British and thoroughly sound. All of them, working in seemingly complete harmony, have achieved a picture which has the pace of a Hollywood production, the honest characterization typical of England's best films, and the sincerity and depth which are proper to no country but are in the public domain of drama.

It is not too disrespectful of Dr. Cronin to say that the film has tightened and heightened his dramatic story of a young Scots doctor who changes objectives in midcareer and has to be jolted back into the line of humble medical service again. A fault with the novel was that its characters were all black or white; a virtue of the film is that it has added the necessary shadings and gradations. Andrew Manson, M.D., has become a very human entity whether he is driving energetically through his silicosis researches in a Welsh mining town or deftly thumping a dowager's chest in the West End. Dr. Manson ceases to be a paragon, but neither is he a reprehensible monster when he accepts the easily gained income of a fashionable specialist.

King Vidor and his writing crew have caught the essence of *The Citadel* and, with their cast's magnificent assistance, have redistilled it in a series of striking episodes. Best of them, perhaps, are those dealing with the young doctor's arrival at the Welsh town where he meets Denny and, with him, blows up the pestilential sewer; where he brings life into a stillborn child and murmurs, almost unbelievingly, "Thank God! I am a doctor!" and where he makes his most abject proposal to the pretty school teacher (a scene, parenthetically, which we consider the most delightful in current screen history).

It wouldn't do to enumerate all the others. There are too many and it would destroy the effect. Our difficulty is not in recalling the best sequences, but in determining their responsibility. How much credit belongs to Director Vidor, to the quartet of adapters, to Dr. Cronin, to Robert Donat as Andrew Manson, to Miss Russell as his wife, to Ralph Richardson as Denny, to Emlyn Williams as Owen, the committeeman? Quite frankly, we do not know. Only this much is clear: it is a splendid transcription of a dramatic story, with strong performances to match a sensitive director's design. The result is a passionate affirmation of faith in the good physician, a passionate denunciation of the hypocritical, an appeal for broader medical service, and a lesson in humility.

So much is *The Citadel* which Metro's British unit has presented to the Capitol. We pause to inquire: is that Leo, or is it the British lion, which is growling so triumphantly from the M-G-M trademark?

—*F.S.N., November 4, 1938*

CITIZEN KANE

Produced and directed by Orson Welles; written by Mr. Welles and Herman Mankiewicz; director of photography, Gregg Toland; edited by Robert Wise and Mark Robson; music by Bernard Herrmann; art designers, Van Nest Polglase and Perry Ferguson; released by RKO Radio Pictures. Black and white. Running time: 119 minutes.

With: Orson Welles (Charles Foster Kane), Joseph Cotten (Jedediah Leland), Dorothy Comingore (Susan Alexander), Everett Sloane (Mr. Bernstein), Ray Collins (James W. Gettys) and George Coulouris (Walter Parks Thatcher).

Within the withering spotlight as no other film has ever been before, Orson Welles's *Citizen Kane* had its world premiere at the Palace last evening. And now that the wraps are off, the mystery has been exposed, and Mr. Welles and the RKO directors have taken the much-debated leap, it can be safely stated that suppression of this film would have been a crime. For, in spite of some disconcerting lapses and strange ambiguities in the creation of the principal character, *Citizen Kane* is far and away the most surprising and cinematically exciting motion picture to be seen here in many a moon. As a matter of fact, it comes close to being the most sensational film ever made in Hollywood.

Count on Mr. Welles; he doesn't do things by halves. Being a mercurial fellow, with a frightening theatrical flair, he moved right into the movies, grabbed the medium by the ears, and began to toss it around with the dexterity of a seasoned veteran. Fact is, he handled it with more verve and inspired ingenuity than any of the elder craftsmen have exhibited in years. With the able assistance of Gregg Toland, whose services should not be overlooked, he found in the camera the perfect instrument to encompass his dramatic energies and absorb his prolific ideas. Upon

the screen he discovered an area large enough for his expansive whims to have free play. And the consequence is that he has made a picture of tremendous and overpowering scope, not in physical extent so much as in its rapid and graphic rotation of thoughts. Mr. Welles has put upon the screen a motion picture that really moves.

As for the story which he tells—and which has provoked such an uncommon fuss—this corner frankly holds considerable reservation. Naturally we wouldn't know how closely—if at all—it parallels the life of an eminent publisher, as has been somewhat cryptically alleged. But that is beside the point in a rigidly critical appraisal. The blamable circumstance is that it fails to provide a clear picture of the character and motives behind the man about whom the whole thing revolves.

As the picture opens, Charles Kane lies dying in the fabulous castle he has built—the castle called Xanadu, in which he has surrounded himself with vast treasures. And as death closes his eyes his heavy lips murmur one word, "Rosebud." Suddenly the death scene is broken; the screen becomes alive with a staccato *March-of-Time*-like news feature recounting the career of the dead man—how, as a poor boy, he came into great wealth, how he became a newspaper publisher as a young man, how he aspired to political office, was defeated because of a personal scandal, devoted himself to material acquisition and finally died.

But the editor of the news feature is not satisfied; he wants to know the secret of Kane's strange nature and especially what he meant by "Rosebud." So a reporter is dispatched to find out, and the remainder of the picture is devoted to an absorbing visualization of Kane's phenomenal career as told by his boyhood guardian, two of his closest newspaper associates, and his mistress. Each is agreed on one thing—that Kane was a titanic egomaniac. It is also clearly revealed that the man was in some way consumed by his own terrifying selfishness. But just exactly what it is that eats upon him, why it is there and, for that matter, whether Kane is really a villain, a social parasite, is never clearly revealed. And the final, poignant identification of "Rosebud" sheds little more than a vague, sentimental light upon his character. At the end Kubla Kane is still an enigma—a very confusing one.

But check that off to the absorption of Mr. Welles in more visible details. Like the novelist Thomas

Wolfe, his abundance of imagery is so great that it sometimes gets in the way of his logic. And the less critical will probably be content with an undefined Kane, anyhow. After all, nobody understood him. Why should Mr. Welles? Isn't it enough that he presents a theatrical character with consummate theatricality?

We would, indeed, like to say as many nice things as possible about everything else in this film—about the excellent direction of Mr. Welles, about the sure and penetrating performances of literally every member of the cast, and about the stunning manner in which the music of Bernard Herrmann has been used. Space, unfortunately, is short. All we can say, in conclusion, is that you shouldn't miss this film. It is cynical, ironic, sometimes oppressive, and as realistic as a slap. But it has more vitality than fifteen other films we could name. And, although it may not give a thoroughly clear answer, at least it brings to mind one deeply moral thought: for what shall it profit a man if he shall gain the whole world and lose his own soul? See *Citizen Kane* for further details.

—B.C., May 2, 1941

CLAIRE'S KNEE

Written (in French, with English subtitles) and directed by Eric Rohmer; cinematographer, Nestor Almendros; edited by Cécile Decugis; produced by Pierre Cottrell; released by Columbia Pictures. Running time: 103 minutes.

With: Jean-Claude Brialy (Jerome), Aurora Cornu (Aurora), Béatrice Romand (Laura), Laurence De Monaghan (Claire), Michèle Montel (Madame Walter), Gérard Falconetti (Gilles) and Fabrice Luchini (Vincent).

Eric Rohmer's *Claire's Knee,* which opened yesterday at the 68th Street Playhouse, comes very close to being a perfect movie of some kind, something on the order of an affectionate comedy of the intellect that has no easily identifiable cinema antecedents except in other films by Mr. Rohmer, most notably *My Night at Maud's.*

It is the product of a literary sensibility, and it grows out of a literary tradition, but it is, first and foremost, a superlative motion picture. Like *Intolerance, My Darling Clementine, Rear Window* and *Le Gai Savoir*—movies I mention only because it resembles them not in the least—*Claire's Knee* could exist in no other form.

The film is the fifth in Rohmer's projected cycle of *Six Moral Tales,* each of which is designed as a variation on the theme of the man who, in love with one woman, feels drawn to another, whom he finally rejects in order to pursue the first, whom he may or may not win. Carlos Clarens, writing in *Sight and Sound,* has called this official schema "a snare for professional film decoders," and I agree.

The joys in Rohmer's Moral Tales exist not so much in the variations he works in, nor in contrasting one film with another, but in responding to the various levels of experience contained within each film. Of the three Moral Tales I've now seen, including *Maud* (the third) and *La Collectionneuse* (the fourth), which has not yet been released here, *Claire's Knee* is by far the most fascinating. It is both more easily accessible than *Maud,* and more complex, less of a conventional narrative and more of an emotional experience.

The setting is near Annecy in western France, not far from the Swiss border, a lovely, slightly out-of-fashion summer community that faces the overwhelming Alps across the Lake of Annecy. The time of the film is most exact: it opens on Monday, the 29th of June, and closes on Wednesday, the 29th of July. Among other things, the movie is all about the disciplines by which civilized man maintains his sanity, including the concept of time.

Jerome (Jean-Claude Brialy), a diplomat in his thirties, engaged to Lucinda whom he will join in Stockholm shortly, has come to Annecy to sell the villa where he spent his vacations as a boy. There by chance he meets an old friend, Aurora (Aurora Cornu), a beautiful, wise, amused novelist, with whom he's always been somewhat in love, and the two teenage daughters, Laura (Béatrice Romand) and Claire (Laurence De Monaghan) of the family Aurora is staying with.

Both Aurora and Jerome are, as they say, "in transit"—their real lives are elsewhere. Out of curiosity, and to amuse Aurora, who says she needs inspiration for a story, Jerome allows himself to become drawn to sixteen-year-old Laura, who, according to Aurora, is in love with him. Suddenly, however, he finds himself full of desire for the somewhat older Claire, specifically for her right knee, that "magnet" of his desire that, in another woman, might be located in the nape of the neck, the waist, or the hands.

If *Claire's Knee* can be said to have a story, it would relate, I suppose, to how Jerome succeeds, for one brief moment, in possessing Claire's knee. Through plot permutations I need not go into, Jerome's gesture of desire is accepted as one of consolation.

Claire's Knee unfolds like an elegant fairy tale in a series of enchanted and enchanting encounters, on the lake, in gardens heavy with blossoms, in interiors that look like Vermeers. Everything in this world has sharply defined edges, like the lake, which is not bordered by beach but by a manmade quay.

Jerome, Aurora, and Laura live according to sharply defined rules of behavior. Although they may seem romantic in that their conversation is mostly of love and friendship, this is, of course, a human activity of the most refined sort. When they explore their own emotions, test their feelings, and exercise aspects of their will, it is a sport for esthetes. For them, in spite of all their talk about being bored with love and suffocated by beauty, each polite meeting becomes as fraught with suspense and danger as a confrontation of gladiators.

Beneath this surface level, *Claire's Knee* is also about self-deception, about cruelty, about a certain kind of arrogance that goes with wisdom, and very much about sex. It is no accident that the beautiful, lean, comparatively stupid Claire, for whom Jerome conceives his "pure desire," is the only person in the movie enjoying, at the moment, a completely satisfactory, uninhibited sex life.

The film is as physically lovely as any I've seen in years, and the performances are of such variety and wit that they should remove forever the notion that Rohmer, with his literary sensibility, is not essentially a filmmaker. Everyone is fine, but I have special feeling for Miss Romand, who grows up in such mysterious and wonderful ways in front of the camera, and for Miss Cornu, a novelist and poet in real life, who comes close to being a total woman.

Claire's Knee is a difficult film to do justice to without overselling it. It is so funny and so moving, so immaculately realized, that almost any ordinary attempt to describe it must, I think, in some way diminish it.

—V.C., February 22, 1971

CLAUDINE

Directed by John Berry; written by Lester Pine and Tina Pine; director of photography, Gayne Rescher; edited by Louis San Andres; music by Curtis Mayfield; produced by Hannah Weinstein; released by Third World Cinema. Running time: 94 minutes.

With: Diahann Carroll (Claudine), James Earl Jones (Roop), Lawrence Hilton-Jacobs (Charles), Tamu Blackwell (Charlene), David Kruger (Paul), Yvette Curtis (Patrice), Eric Jones (Francis), Socorro Stephens (Lurlene), Adam Wade (Owen), C. Harrison Avery (Minister), Mordecai Lawner (Process Server), Elisa Loti (Miss Kabak) and Roxie Roker (Mrs. Winston).

Claudine (Diahann Carroll) has a number of problems, including a small Harlem apartment and six children, who are all that remain of two marriages and what the Welfare Department describes as two "consensual unions." Although she is on welfare, Claudine works clandestinely as a maid in the Riverdale section of the Bronx to give her kids something more than the bare necessities.

When Claudine falls in love with an exuberant, twice-married garbageman named Roop (James Earl Jones), matters become more complicated. Roop sees welfare as the ultimate indignity. Nothing short of castration. If he moves in with her, she can remain on welfare, but she must deduct everything he gives her. However, if he loses his job, he too must go on welfare whether he wants to or not. To top everything off, Roop is sued for the nonsupport of his own children and his salary is garnisheed.

Claudine, the comedy that opened yesterday at the De Mille and Fine Arts Theaters, has its own problems, including a tendency toward cuteness and a form that recalls television's worst situation comedies. You know the ones—about resourceful moms, dumb dads and smart-talking kids who can burp on cue.

The good news this morning is that *Claudine* manages to be very funny, in a couple of instances, triumphantly so.

The screenplay was written by Tina and Lester Pine, who also wrote *Popi,* which was quite awful except for Alan Arkin and some isolated wisecracks. Unlike *Popi,* however, *Claudine* succeeds in being comic without denying the realities of ghetto life.

It softens them a bit, perhaps. Not through fraud, but through the presence of the two larger-than-life characters played marvelously by Miss Carroll and Mr. Jones. Claudine and Roop are comic romantics of the most honorable, appealing sort, people who have a firm grasp on everything but themselves.

Miss Carroll is an exceptionally beautiful woman, but the beauty of this performance is in the force of her toughness and wit. It's in the furies she directs at the idiocies of her children, at the 16-year-old daughter who becomes pregnant by Abdullah (né Timmy) and at the 18-year-old son who arranges his own vasectomy to make sure he won't pollute the country with babies.

Mr. Jones turns Roop into a gargantuan clown, which is not to be confused with buffoon. Roop thinks he means it when he explains his job on the garbage truck by saying that he has consciously avoided success because losers are more popular. He's a huge tangle of contradictions, wise, foolish, self-pitying, thoughtful. It's by far the best thing Mr. Jones has ever done in films.

Part of the reason for this success, I suspect, is the director, John Berry, who made films in Hollywood (*He Ran All the Way*) before going to France in the nineteen-fifties, in the dark days of the Hollywood red scare. More recently, he has been directing Off Broadway, including *Boesman and Lena* with Mr. Jones. Though I would never mistake *Claudine* as anything but a film, it displays an attention to dramatic rhythm and to dialogue that is essentially theatrical.

Even the children are exceptionally good, especially a new actress named Tamu, playing the daughter who goes out one evening to learn how to meet people and hold her liquor and winds up first sick and, eventually, pregnant. Tamu has the kind of intensity touched with humor that one associates with the late Diana Sands.

Claudine is more than the sum of its performances, however. Two sequences are standouts. One, set in a welfare office, is simultaneously satiric and moving, because it is the first time that Claudine and Roop see themselves aligned against a common enemy, sinking into a marsh of red tape. I won't describe the last sequence in the film beyond noting that it achieves—and holds for not one second longer than it can be sustained—the level of true farce.

There are times when *Claudine* threatens to go as soft as a *Doris Day Show* rerun, when you are aware that some of its middle-class sensibilities don't quite fit. They seem borrowed from the white media. Then it recoups with the sort of line or gesture that makes this one of the few recent black films to reach beyond the black audience without, as far as I can tell, insulting it.

A word about the production auspices: *Claudine* is the first film to be made by a company called Third World Cinema, designed by its founders—Miss Sands, Ossie Davis, Mr. Jones, Rita Moreno and Hannah Weinstein, the producer—to make films, that not only give blacks, Puerto Ricans and other minorities substantial film-making roles but also improve the quality of the films themselves. *Claudine* is a very happy debut performance.

—*V.C., April 23, 1974*

THE CLOCKMAKER

Directed by Bertrand Tavernier; written (in French, with English subtitles) by Jean Aurenche and Pierre Bost, based on the novel *The Clock-maker of Everton* by Georges Simenon; cinematographer, Pierre William Glenn; edited by Armand Psenny; music by Philippe Sarde; released by Lira Films. Running time: 105 minutes.

With: Philippe Noiret (Michel Descombes), Jean Rochefort (Commissioner Guiboud), Jacques Denis (Antoine), William Sabatier (Lawyer) and Andree Tainsy (Madeleine).

Michel Descombes (Philippe Noiret) is a Lyons clockmaker by trade and by nature an observer of the rules. He waits for the "walk" sign before crossing the street, even when there are no cars and no policemen in sight. When he is asked if he is a widower he considers the question with care. His wife, he says, left him many years earlier, but she is now dead. Yes, he supposes, he is a widower at least technically. Michel is not a fussy or fearful man, but to the extent that he ponders the inner workings of his life, he values order and accuracy.

The Clockmaker, which opened yesterday at the Embassy 72d Street and Quad 4 Theaters, is a fine, precise, very moving account of what happens to Michel in a situation where order and accuracy have no application.

He wakes up one morning to learn that the son he has raised as a companion has murdered a factory foreman, burned the man's car and run off with a young woman whose existence Michel had never been aware of. Michel cooperates in the police investigation, but it's as if they were searching for a stranger.

The film, an adaptation of the Georges Simenon novel *The Clockmaker of Everton,* is a rather startling combination of old and new talents. Maybe reconciliation is the better word. The screenplay is by Jean Aurenche and Pierre Bost—who wrote the adaptation of *Le Diable au Corps* and are closely identified with the French cinema establishment of the 1940's against which the New Wave was a reaction—but it is the first feature to be directed by Bertrand Tavernier, a young French critic and film scholar who belongs to the post-New-Wave generation.

The Clockmaker was produced in 1973 and Mr. Tavernier has since made two more films, but this initial effort is a work of assurance and ease. It is both complex and simple in the way of a film that knows exactly what it's about—which is fathers and sons and the respect that is possible between them under even the worst of circumstances.

When Michel's son (Sylvain Rougerie) and his girl (Christine Pascal) are finally arrested, the young man refuses to give any motive for the crime, refusing even to allow his lawyer to make a point of the murdered man's having been a management spy and responsible for the young woman's having been discharged. "He was a pig," the son says, though not using the word in any political connection, and, "I'm sick of the same ones always winning."

Mr. Tavernier sets the film in an environment that is intensely political though the characters profess not to be. Says a cheery, foolish voice on the radio: "Polls show that eighty-nine percent of all Frenchmen are happy. Are you?" "France is peculiar," Michel is told by the friendly police commissioner (Jean Rochefort) assigned to the case. "Fifty million inhabitants, twenty million informers." Michel's best friend, a Communist, fumes against the complacency of France. Yet the son is no political activist. He has asserted himself in a way that remains mysterious to his father, who nevertheless comes to recognize and respect the boy's identity.

If anything gives away the youth of the director it's his use of quotations—literary quotations (Claudel, Céline), visual quotations from other films, quotations from the news, even reminiscences that are one of the principal ways in which the characters communicate. Events thus recalled establish links to the present and make it if not comprehensible at least tolerable.

Mr. Noiret gives a performance of the high caliber that we now take for granted from him, and Mr. Rochefort and Mr. Rougerie are almost as good in much smaller roles. More important, *The Clockmaker* introduces us to a fine new director.

—V.C., June 29, 1976

A CLOCKWORK ORANGE

Produced, written and directed by Stanley Kubrick; based on the novel by Anthony Burgess; director of photography, John Alcott; edited by Gill Butler; music by Walter Carlos; production designer, John Barry; released by Warner Brothers. Running time: 137 minutes.

With: Malcolm McDowell (Alex), Patrick Magee (Mr. Alexander), Adrienne Corri (Mrs. Alexander), Aubrey Morris (Deltoid), James Marcus (Georgie), Warren Clarke (Dim), Michael Tarn (Pulp), Sheila Raynor (Mum), Philip Stone (Dad), Miriam Karlin (Cat Lady) and Godfrey Quigley (Chaplain).

On the soundtrack we hear Henry Purcell's almost comically elegant "Music Composed for Queen Mary's Funeral." On the screen we see a closeup portrait of Alex (Malcolm McDowell), who, for a moment, is uncharacteristically still. The face looks floodlit, as if caught by one of those automatic photo machines in a bus station.

However, the eyes, one of which is ringed by false lashes, reveal an intelligence that is no less alive for being occupied, momentarily, with the kind of drug fantasies that Alex and his droogs are able to buy at the Kerova Milkbar, before going out into the London night in search of the old ultraviolence. There's always the chance they'll find a dirty old man to beat up, or some frightened devotchka for a malenky bit of in-out, in-out.

Thus begins *A Clockwork Orange,* Stanley Kubrick's adaptation of Anthony Burgess's perversely moral, essentially Christian novel about the value of free will, even if the choice exercised is to tear through the night robbing, raping, and battering the citizens until they lie helpless, covered with what Alex describes happily as "the real red vino," or krovvy.

In both English and Nadsat, the combination of Anglicized Russian, Gypsy, rhyming slang and associative words spoken by Alex and his teenage friends in what seems to be 1983, *A Clockwork Orange* is a great deal more than merely horror show—that is, Nadsat for good. It is brilliant, a tour de force of extraordinary images, music, words and feelings, a much more original achievement for commercial films than the Burgess novel is for literature, for Burgess, after all, has some impossibly imposing literary antecedents, including the work of Joyce.

The film, which opened yesterday at the Cinema I, is cast in the form of futurist fiction, but it is no spin-off from Mr. Kubrick's *2001,* nor is it truly futurist, if that means it is one of those things-to-come fantasies. More correctly it contemplates the nightmares of today, often in terms that reflect the 1950's and 1960's, out of which the Burgess novel grew. It is also—at least it seems to me—an essentially British nightmare (while *2001* was essentially American) in its attentions to caste, manners, accents, and the state of mind created by a kind of weary socialism.

The movie shows a lot of aimless violence—the exercise of aimless choice—but it is as formally structured as the music of Alex's "lovely lovely Ludwig Van," which inspires in Alex sadomasochistic dreams of hangings, volcanic eruptions, and other disasters.

Alex is a terrifying character, but also an intelligent, funny and pathetic one, whose spiritual crucifixion comes when, having been jailed for murder, he is subjected to the Ludovico Treatment. Alex is one of the early guinea pigs in a rehabilitation program that involves the conditioning of his responses, via the nonstop viewing of sex, horror and atrocity movies. At the end of two weeks, he is left as dumb and defenseless as a defanged, declawed animal.

Impulses to hate, anger, lust make him physically ill. He has become a model of good, "as decent a lad as you would meet on a May morning," but, as his fundamentalist prison chaplain points out, he is without a soul.

Under these circumstances, Alex's eventual return to his original "free" state becomes an ironic redemption, yet not much attention is paid to the fact that Alex the hood is as much a product of conditioning as was the denatured Alex, the product of aversion therapy.

However, I won't quibble over the point. *A Clockwork Orange* is so beautiful to look at and to hear that it dazzles the senses and the mind, even as it turns the old real red vino to ice: Alex and his friends having a rumble with a rival gang to the tune of Rossini's "The Thieving Magpie," or preparing a gang rape in the home of a definitely upper-class writer as Alex does a lyric soft-shoe (into the stomach and face of the writer), singing "Singin' in the Rain." That's the sort of thing that makes Alex feel all nice and warm in his guttywuts.

McDowell is splendid as tomorrow's child, but it is always Mr. Kubrick's picture, which is even technically more interesting than *2001.* Among other devices, Mr. Kubrick constantly uses what I assume to be a wide-angle lens to distort space relationships within scenes, so that the disconnection between lives, and between people and environment, becomes an actual, literal fact.

At one point in his therapy, Alex says: "The colors of the real world only become real when you viddy them in a film." *A Clockwork Orange* makes real and important the kind of fears simply exploited by other, much lesser films.

—*V.C., December 20, 1971*

CLOSE ENCOUNTERS OF THE THIRD KIND

Written and directed by Steven Spielberg; director of photography, Vilmos Zsigmond; edited by Mike Kahn; music by John Williams; production designer, Joe Alves; produced by Julia Phillips and Michael Phillips; released by Columbia Pictures. Running time: 135 minutes.

With: Richard Dreyfuss (Roy Neary), François Truffaut (Claude Lacombe), Teri Garr (Ronnie Neary), Melinda Dillon (Jillian Guiler), Cary Guffey (Barry Guiler), Bob Balaban (David Laughlin) and Lance Henriksen (Robert).

In the 1950's, the decade in which we fought the Korean War, witnessed the rise and fall of Senator Joseph R. McCarthy and fretted (along with Mort Sahl) about the atomic bomb's falling into the hands of Princess Grace and Prince Rainier, science fiction films enjoyed a new, lively popularity largely by feeding on our wildest nightmares. We watched movies in which planets fought wars with each other, worlds threatened to collide and a huge malignant carrot, a vegetable with a higher form of intelligence, landed at the North Pole.

A favorite theme was the invasion of earth by alien creatures who, nine times out of ten, were up to no good. The unholy immigrants in *The Invasion of the Body Snatchers* attempted to usurp earth by catching the souls of the incumbents in giant peapods, receptacles that suggested the work of an early Jasper Johns.

Sometimes the visitors were motivated by a territorial imperative—they were running out of air back home or there were no more materials for beer cans. Often the creatures were simply making mischief, though occasionally they expressed benign intentions. From Krypton came Superman to play the role of a supercharged savior whose work would never be done.

Klaatu, the impeccably space-suited, English-accented visitor in *The Day the Earth Stood Still*, wanted earthlings to stop fooling around and live in peace. The implied threat of Klaatu's "Or else . . ." might have struck some of us as galactal neofascism, but that was to read the film deeper than it was meant to go.

Steven Spielberg's giant, spectacular *Close Encounters of the Third Kind*, which opened at the Ziegfeid Theater yesterday, is the best—the most elaborate—1950's science fiction movie ever made, a work that borrows its narrative shape and its concerns from those earlier films, but enhances them with what looks like the latest developments in movie and space technol-

ogy. If, indeed, we are not alone, it would be fun to believe that the creatures who may one day visit us are of the order that Mr. Spielberg has conceived—with, I should add, a certain amount of courage and an entirely straight face.

Mr. Spielberg's tongue is not in his cheek, as was George Lucas's when he made *Star Wars,* the funniest, farthest-out kid-trip of this decade to date. *Star Wars* is virtually an anthology of all sorts of children's literature. *Close Encounters* is science fiction that means us to say, "this is the way it could be," though we don't for a minute forget that we're watching a movie almost entirely related to other movies—the ones that Mr. Spielberg, who's just thirty years old, grew up with, rather than a movie with its own poetic vision, like Stanley Kubrick's *2001.*

As he has demonstrated in *The Sugarland Express* and especially in *Jaws,* Mr. Spielberg is at his best as a movie craftsman, someone who seems to know by instinct (and after millions of hours of movie-watching) how best to put together any two pieces of film for maximum effect. He's serious about this—sensation as an end in itself, an interest that defines better than anything else his generation as moviegoers, music lovers, and moviemakers.

Close Encounters is most stunning when it is dealing in visual and aural sensations that might be described as being in the seventies Disco Style. The unidentified flying objects that both terrorize and enchant the citizens of Muncie, Indiana, early in the film, when the night sky is suddenly filled with blinking lights and several brilliantly colored shapes, each of which looks like a Portuguese man-of-war, make up an extraordinary psychedelic light show.

The disco manner is further suggested in the movie's use of sound, an almost nonstop confusion of voices, languages, technical jargon, weather, vehicles and (I sometimes suspect) gibberish, often so noisy that you can't hear yourself think.

Though *Close Encounters* is strictly a product of the seventies in its dress and manners, its heart is in the fifties. This is apparent from the first scene, when a squadron of World War II fighter planes, missing on a training mission more than thirty years earlier, suddenly turn up intact, as good as new, in the Mexican desert. In classic sci-fi manner, Mr. Spielberg's screenplay then cuts from this general introduction to the "mystery" to encounters with the mystery by individual folks in Muncie, homespun types like you and me who draw us into the adventure.

Mr. Spielberg's homespun types are mostly serviceable characters like Roy Neary, a blue-collar worker whose life is changed the night he spots the U.F.O.'s over Muncie. As do many of the others who shared his experience, Roy is obsessed by the memory, though his wife and three children think he is nuts. Another person similarly obsessed is a young mother, played by Melinda Dillon, whose four-year-old son appears to be in some kind of psychic connection with the U.F.O.'s.

Following this initial, quite magnificent display of the movie technicians' special-effects wizardry, *Close Encounters* settles down to crosscutting between scenes of Roy's seemingly lunatic efforts to find the U.F.O.'s again, and the efforts being made by an international team of scientists who are preparing themselves for the second coming (of the U.F.O.'s).

The film's two most arresting personalities are the four-year-old Indiana boy (played with marvelous lack of self-consciousness by Cary Guffey), who gets to take a trip into space, and the French scientist who is the chief of the international U.F.O. team. As this fellow, François Truffaut, making his acting debut in an American film, gives *Close Encounters* a kind of prophetic center and dramatic weight it would otherwise lack.

Mr. Spielberg's usually uncanny cinematic instincts fail him from time to time in the extended central section of the film. He attempts to give *Close Encounters* a substructure of both scientific and theological importance. That might have been fascinating if I'd had a chance to understand it. Since I didn't, it came across as rather high-toned mad-doctor stuff.

There's also a sequence set on a hillside in India with the French scientist and his team of experts that seems to have been rather badly staged. It's a mess, perhaps in the confusion of an expensive movie location trip.

The final thirty to forty minutes of the film, however, are what it's all about—and they are breathtaking: the close encounter of the third kind in which the earthlings and the alien creatures come together on a secret landing field in Wyoming. This sequence, as beautiful as anything I've seen since *2001,* has been deliberately designed to suggest a religious experience of the first kind. Whether or not you believe it, this climax involves the imagination in surprising, moving ways. This is a day in which the earth might have stood still.

Mr. Spielberg tempts fate (and the value of Columbia Pictures' stock) by briefly introducing us to the alien creatures, and it's the measure of his success that no one giggles. Is *Close Encounters* better or worse than *Star Wars?*—that's the boring question this morning. It's neither one. It's different, an achievement on its own.

—V.C., November 17, 1977

CLOSE-UP

Written, edited and directed by Abbas Kiarostami; director of photography, Ali Reza Zarrin-Dast; produced by the Institute for the Intellectual Development of Children and Young Adults; released by Zeitgeist Films. In Farsi, with English subtitles. Running time: 90 minutes.

With: Hossain Sabzian, Mohsen Makhmalbaf and Abbas Kiarostami (Themselves), Abolfazl Ahankhah (Father), Mehrdad Ahankhah and Manoochehr Ahankhah (Sons), Mahrokh Ahankhah and Nayer Mohseni Zonoozi (Daughters), Ahmed Reza Moayed Mohseni (Friend) and Hossain Farazmand (Reporter).

In one film after another, the great Iranian director Abbas Kiarostami twists around the equation that the author Neal Gabler calls "Life: The Movie" to make films whose aesthetic might be described as "The Movie: Life." Mr. Kiarostami's films frequently feature nonactors playing themselves in unglamorized reconstructions of actual events. And in his brilliant, knotty 1990 film *Close-Up,* which has its New York theatrical premiere today at the Screening Room, those reconstructions are seamlessly embedded in a documentary about the trial of Hossein Sabzian, a young man arrested on charges of fraud.

Close-Up is directed in a radically drab cinema-verite style that helps blur any difference between what is real and what is reconstructed. The movie is not always easy to watch. In one scene, the camera follows the course of a kicked piece of trash for a few seconds that seem nearly endless.

But if, on the surface, the movie appears to epitomize crude, seat-of-your-pants filmmaking, the raw aesthetic of *Close-Up,* which is not rated, is really one of its strengths. For like other Kiarostami films, it goes to risky extremes to remind us that what we are seeing is a movie.

Toward the end of the film, as the director and his cinematographer and sound engineer follow Mr. Sabzian in a post-trial sequence, their audio equipment malfunctions, and as the sound comes in and out, half of what we see is silent. The director's insistence on making us aware of filmmaking technology is part of a broader strategy to force us to contemplate the basic experience of moviegoing.

The serious, far-reaching joke of *Close-Up* is that Mr. Sabzian's fraud was his impersonation of a successful filmmaker, Mohsen Makhmalbaf. By pretending to be a director interested in filming the Ahankhahs, a well-to-do-family, Mr. Sabzian was able to insinuate his way into their lives and feel like a Somebody.

It all began by chance, when he was reading Mr. Makhmalbaf's book *The Cyclist,* while sitting next to Mrs. Ahankhah on a bus. After they struck up a conversation, he impulsively said he was the author, and one thing led to another. His deceit in some ways parallels John Guare's *Six Degrees of Separation,* in which a young man of meager means and dazzling charm convinces a prosperous Manhattan couple that he is the prep school–educated son of the actor Sidney Poitier.

After they find him out, the Ahankhahs accuse Mr. Sabzian of fraud because he borrowed money from them. Since he has thoroughly inspected their home in preparation for a film he says he is preparing, in which they will appear, they assume he has been planning to rob them.

But at the trial, it becomes evident that Mr. Sabzian had no plans to steal from his new friends. A dreamer who worships art, he insists that he pretended to be Mr. Makhmalbaf because it gave him status and self-esteem. At first, Mehrdad, one of the Ahankhahs' sons, doesn't believe him and accuses him of playing another role. But as Mr. Sabzian abjectly pleads his innocence to the judge and apologizes to the Ahankhahs, he cuts a compelling waifish figure.

It is Mr. Sabzian's poignancy that makes *Close-Up* much more than a clever reflection on film-versus-life as an endless hall of mirrors. A transcendent humanist in the tradition of the Italian neorealists and the Indian director Satyajit Ray, Mr. Kiarostami has made a film that looks into the heart of a man accused of a crime and, instead of evil, discovers only sweetness, longing and a sad confusion.

—*S.H., December 31, 1999*

CLUELESS

Written and directed by Amy Heckerling; director of photography. Bill Pope; edited by Debra Chiate; music supervision by Karyn Rachtman with music score by David Kitay; production designer, Steven Jordan; costume designer, Mona May; produced by Scott Rudin and Robert Lawrence; released by Paramount Pictures. Running time: 113 minutes.

With: Alicia Silverstone (Cher). Stacey Dash (Dionne). Brittany Murphy (Tai). Paul Rudd (Josh). Dan Hedaya (Mel). Donald Faison (Murray) and Elisa Donovan (Amber).

Alicia Silverstone makes a delectable teen queen in *Clueless,* a candy-colored, brightly satirical showcase for her decidedly visual talents. Thus far famous mostly for being famous (mostly in Aerosmith videos), Ms. Silverstone finally gives a film performance that clicks. As a pampered Beverly Hills clotheshorse, she's mostly a one-joke princess, but the joke happens to work. Even if *Clueless* runs out of gas before it's over, most of it is as eye-catching and cheery as its star.

The director, Amy Heckerling, also finds herself on friendly territory with the worst Californian academic talent this side of Ridgemont High. Surfer burnouts held center stage in that earlier comedy of Ms. Heckerling's, but this time she has gone hilariously upscale. Ms. Silverstone's Cher, a heroine who along with her friend Dionne (Stacey Dash) is "named after great singers of the past who now do infomercials," uses a computer to tell her when her clothes match and doesn't even let it go at that. "I don't rely on mirrors, so I always take Polaroids," Cher confides.

The setting is Bronson Alcott High School, which is not this film's only nod to the classics. Some of *Clueless* is actually lifted from Jane Austen's *Emma,* with Cher a mind-bendingly up-to-date version of the novel's matchmaking minx. Ms. Heckerling (who also wrote the film) deserves extra credit for doing that homework, but some of the modified Austen situations become a little improbable here. That's to be expected when characters who once paid endless polite visits to one another's country houses are now conducting business at the dinner table with their cellular phones.

Clueless is best enjoyed as an extended fashion show (kudos to the costume designer, Mona May) peppered with amusing one-liners, most of which Ms. Silverstone gets to deliver. On television violence: "There's no point in taking it out of shows that need it for entertainment value!" On Billie Holiday: "I *love* him!" On why she's a virgin: "You see how picky I am about my shoes, and they only go on my feet!"

Despite its literary quasi-pedigree, *Clueless* doesn't have much more than these scattered gags to keep it going. Recognizable characters like Cher's serious, disapproving stepbrother (Paul Rudd) or her seemingly hapless protégée (Brittany Murphy) are trotted out dutifully without being given much to do. But it's true that the tirelessly helpful instincts of Austen's Emma have been nicely translated into a contemporary idiom. "God, this woman is screaming for a makeover!" Cher decides about a dowdy teacher. "I'm her only hope."

While Miss Silverstone guides Cher through the witty costume changes that serve as character development, she's backed up by a solid supporting cast. Ms. Dash is especially appealing as Dionne, Cher's true soul mate, who upon finding someone else's hair extension in her boyfriend's car is most offended because the hair is polyester and looks cheap. Dan Hedaya is enjoyably gruff as the father whose litigation practice subsidizes Cher's expensive habit, and who has even bought her a car that she hasn't learned to park. "What's the point?" she reasons, "Everywhere you go, you've got valet."

—*J.M., July 19, 1995*

COAL MINER'S DAUGHTER

Directed by Michael Apted; written by Thomas Rickman, based on an autobiography by Loretta Lynn with George Vecsey; director of photography, Ralf D. Bode; edited by Arthur Schmidt; songs by various composers; released by Universal Pictures. Running time: 125 minutes.

With: Sissy Spacek (Loretta Webb/Lynn), Tommy Lee Jones (Doolittle "Mooney" Lynn), Levon Helm (Ted Webb), Phyllis Boyens (Clara "Clary" Webb), Bill Anderson Jr. (Webb Child), Foister Dickerson (Webb Child), Malla McCown (Webb Child), Pamela McCown (Webb Child), Kevin Salvilla (Webb Child), William Sanderson (Lee Dollarhide) and Beverly D'Angelo (Patsy Cline).

The obligatory scene in which the musician first performs in front of an audience: That's one of the many things that *Coal Miner's Daughter*, which opens today at the Rivoli, handles beautifully. Loretta Lynn, played with captivating daintiness by Sissy Spacek, climbs onto the stage at a Grange hall, at the urging of her husband. Her singing is wispy at first, but it grows clear and confident as she takes command of the stage. By the end of the number, she has found her footing and launched her career.

The audience is enthusiastic, but not so rapt as to make the scene unbelievable: there's a little less rustling in the crowd than there has been, and a few people begin gazing at the singer. That's all—that's enough. The point has been made, with the gentle touch that gives this movie its distinctive sweetness. *Coal Miner's Daughter* risks understating its story to make Loretta Lynn's biography part of a larger fabric and the gamble pays off.

Most of the film, the best part of it, depicts the world Miss Lynn grew up in, the world she both immortalized and lost when she became famous as a country music star. She grew up in Butcher Holler, Kentucky, a tiny place that has been faithfully reconstructed for the film, since Miss Lynn's fans have changed the real Butcher Holler from an unspoiled spot into a tourist attraction. She married at 13, and by 20 had four children. Neither her father nor her husband had much money, but poverty doesn't seem to have put her at any disadvantage. Her autobiography, upon which the movie is based, describes these early years as peaceful and uncomplicated, far more so than the times that followed.

This part of Miss Lynn's life has been preserved in the emphatic, folksy lyrics of her songs, and some of the movie's dialogue has that same home-spun sound. "You're my pride, girl—my shining pride," says Loretta's father, and, amazingly, the line isn't forced. "You'll just have to make up your mind, darlin', whether you're his daughter or my wife," says her husband, voicing another sentiment straight out of a song. Perhaps because Loretta doesn't answer these statements, or even ponder them unduly, the first part of the film takes place in the realm of clear choices and simple delights. The director, Michael Apted, has this tone so effortlessly that it's hardly noticeable—until, in the second half of the movie, it disappears.

Eventually, Miss Lynn's story moves her out of this fairy-tale world and into show business. And once she becomes a success, the old values suddenly aren't much help to her any more. This is a transition that the movie can't manage. Perhaps it should have ended at the Grand Ole Opry, where Loretta's dream is realized and her fate is sealed.

Instead, the film skims over her more recent history with a protective air, never making the big star as vivid as the little girl has been. The problem isn't simply one of candor (although Miss Lynn's book is considerably franker than the movie about what a strain her success has been). It's a matter of context. Loretta starts out as a tiny figure in the Kentucky landscape, one of many different elements in this story. The film wrenches her away and carries her off to a new setting that is far less complete, and less compelling.

Throughout the film, she searches for a home. Though the point is never stated, her elaborate Tennessee mansion looks like a strangely insubstantial version of the Kentucky cabin. At her father's grave—which her husband drives up to, appropriately, in a bulldozer—Loretta cries "I ain't gonna have no home now." "You got our home," the husband says, meaning to be soothing, but Loretta just weeps all the more. Mr. Apted presents some particularly delicate images to capture Loretta's uprootedness, as in a tableau of the singer, her husband and their four small children. The pose recalls Loretta and her siblings in Appalachia—but this time, the family is reflected in the glass window of a recording studio.

Coal Miner's Daughter features four extraordinary performances, each of them somewhat unexpected. Miss Spacek is luminous and lovely, easily outshining her previous work, as good as it has been. Even in the latter parts of *Coal Miner's Daughter,* in scenes that

may strike some viewers as a pale reminder of *Nashville* she holds her own. Tommy Lee Jones, as her husband, Doolittle, has a strength and humor that bring the film's love story to life, and he, too, quite outdoes his past performances. Beverly D'Angelo, who as Patsy Cline does her own singing (Miss Spacek sings too, very nicely), makes a brief but astonishingly sharp impression. And Levon Helm, playing Loretta's father, embodies all the quiet decency that gives this film its foothold. Mr. Helm was formerly a member of the Band, and he's at least as good an actor as he was a singer and drummer, which is saying quite a lot.

Like *Agatha* and the rock drama *Stardust,* other movies of Mr. Apted's, *Coal Miner's Daughter* does a better job of setting its scenes than of telling a story. Its characterizations and its atmosphere work better than the action, which becomes shapeless and, in the manner of biographies of living subjects, slightly cramped by good intentions.

—*J.M., March 7, 1980*

THE COLOR OF MONEY

Directed by Martin Scorsese: written by Richard Price, based on the novel by Walter Tevis: director of photography, Michael Ballhaus: edited by Thelma Schoonmaker: music by Robbie Robertson: production designer, Boris Leven: produced by Irving Axelrod and Barbara De Fina: released by Touchstone Pictures. Running time: 117 minutes.

With: Paul Newman (Eddie), Tom Cruise (Vincent), Mary Elizabeth Mastrantonio (Carmen), Helen Shaver (Janelle), John Turturro (Julian) and Bill Cobbs (Orvis).

Martin Scorsese's *Color of Money* picks up the character of Fast Eddie Felson twenty-five years after he walked out of Chalkie's pool hall into the exhausted dawn at the end of Robert Rossen's fine 1961 melodrama, *The Hustler.* In the person of Paul Newman, who received an Oscar nomination for his performance in the Rossen film, the former pool-hall hustler has aged with remarkable grace, his physical vitality intact and his view of the world less cynical than barroom-pragmatic.

Today Fast Eddie is a genial, silver-haired liquor

salesman, immaculately dressed in the leisure wear that spells "class" to his customers. He's a fund of the kind of stories that sound best when told late in the afternoon, over a shot glass of Wild Turkey with beer as a chaser, to whatever bartender is the last of his calls for the day.

Fast Eddie travels light in a big white Cadillac. In fact, he's a modern-day Flying Dutchman, a myth in polyester, doomed to move forever from one barroom to the next, never stopping very long in any one place for fear that his curse will catch up with him.

In *The Color of Money*, Mr. Newman and Mr. Scorsese dare to do something that few serious filmmakers ever attempt—that is, to give us an update on a character who was complete in his own time, place, and work.

The news this morning is that, against all odds, they've succeeded in creating a most entertaining, original film with its own, vivid, very contemporary identity and reason for being. Sharing honors with Mr. Newman, who appears certain to receive another Oscar nomination for his performance as this Fast Eddie, are Tom Cruise and Mary Elizabeth Mastrantonio, both of whom do their best work in films to date.

The *Color of Money*, which opens today at the Coronet and other theaters, is not a sequel to *The Hustler*. Mr. Scorsese's work is as different from the Rossen film as Michael Ballhaus's brilliant color photography is different from Eugene Shuftan's equally brilliant black-and-white work for Mr. Rossen.

The Hustler has a classic structure. It's about moral choices that are defined in black and white. As do the people in an Odets drama of the 1930's, Mr. Rossen's characters mean exactly what they say in well-shaped, passionately spoken speeches.

The *Color of Money* is not so clear-cut. It's set in another world, one full of deceptively bright neon colors but where motives are ambiguous. Its characters communicate in wisecracks that pass for wisdom. Their mostly inarticulated feelings are expressed in close-ups of such intensity they seem to rediscover the reason close-ups were invented.

In Richard Price's screenplay, which keeps only the title of Walter Tevis's second Eddie Felson novel, Fast Eddie has been away from pool for twenty-five years, ever since the climactic game in *The Hustler*. That was when Fast Eddie finally defeated the legendary Minnesota Fats (Jackie Gleason) and, in so doing, found himself blackballed from the game for life. In *The Color of Money*, Fast Eddie is lured back as the manager-mentor of Vincent Lauria (Tom Cruise), a gifted but naïve pool hustler well on his way to becoming the loser that the young Fast Eddie was a quarter-century ago.

Mr. Price's screenplay doesn't have the single-minded drive and satisfying shapeliness of the original film. It also doesn't have any draggy "Seventh Heaven" sentimentality in the form of Fast Eddie's very unlikely affair with the doomed, lame (emotionally and physically) Sarah (Piper Laurie).

Instead, *The Color of Money* is a comedy of character about Fast Eddie's relations with the ambitious young Vincent and Vincent's far brighter, tougher girlfriend, Carmen (Miss Mastrantonio). The film follows Fast Eddie, who has assumed a lot of the attributes of the gambler played by George C. Scott in *The Hustler*, as he attempts to prepare the younger man for the now-respectable, annual pool competition in Atlantic City.

Fast Eddie has words of advice for every occasion. Early on, he tells the swaggering Vincent, "You know when to say 'Yes,' when to say 'No,' and everybody goes home in a limousine." When Vincent doesn't seize the occasion to make a quick buck, Fast Eddie says simply: "That's the problem with mercy, kid. It just ain't professional."

What *The Color of Money* lacks in narrative shapeliness, it makes up for in the spectacle of three fully realized, if narrowly focused, characters as they play cat-and-mouse with one another. Mr. Price and Mr. Scorsese don't adequately prepare for the twist that ends the film, which is more emotionally soothing than believable. However, the journey to that conclusion—through a succession of pool halls, diners and motels between Chicago and Atlantic City—is most satisfying.

Mr. Newman appears to be having a ball as the aging but ever-resilient Fast Eddie. It's a wonderfully funny, canny performance, set off by the actor's intelligence that shines through the character without upstaging it. Mr. Cruise works successfully against his pretty-boy looks to find the comic, shortsighted nastiness that's at the center of the younger man.

The film's revelation is Miss Mastrantonio, whose performance as Al Pacino's sister in Scarface was hardly preparation for what she does here. Her Carmen is a neighborhood beauty on her way to the big-time, with or without the Cruise character. One of the better, funnier inventions of Mr. Price's screenplay is her recollection of the circumstances in which she met Mr. Cruise at a police station.

Among the supporting players, the standouts are Helen Shaver, who appears as the barmaid Fast Eddie seems permanently stuck on (for the moment) and John Turturro, as a pool hustler Mr. Cruise passes on his way to the top.

The Color of Money isn't *Mean Streets* or *Raging Bull*. It is, however, a stunning vehicle—a white Cadillac among the other mainstream American movies of the season.

—*V.C., October 17, 1986*

COME BACK, LITTLE SHEBA

Directed by Daniel Mann; written by Ketti Frings, based on the play by William Inge; cinematographer, James Wong Howe; edited by Warren Low; music by Franz Waxman; produced by Hal B. Wallis; released by Paramount Pictures. Black and white. Running time: 95 minutes.

With: Burt Lancaster (Doc Delaney), Shirley Booth (Lola Delaney), Terry Moore (Marie Buckholder), Richard Jaeckel (Turk Fisher), Philip Ober (Ed Anderson), Liza Golm (Mrs. Goffman) and Walter Kelley (Bruce).

Thanks to producer Hal Wallis and director Daniel Mann, who had the good sense not to tamper too much with the original play of William Inge, the screen version of *Come Back, Little Sheba*, which opened at the Victoria last night, makes as poignant and haunting a drama as was brought forth upon the stage. For this we may also be grateful to Burt Lancaster and Shirley Booth, who contribute two sterling performances in the picture's leading roles.

Kept pretty much within the four walls of the commonplace, middle-class home of the middle-aged, childless couple of whose wistful lives the drama treats, the film nonetheless succeeds in seeming to move a great deal and say a lot about the small and pathetic human frailty with which it is concerned.

Actually, the crux of the drama is nothing more than a crisis that occurs in the drab and monotonous relations of this uninspired husband and wife. Stirred into passion and rebellion by the proximity of amorous youth, represented by a young lady boarder and her callow, college-boy beau, the husband kicks over the traces of rigid temperance he has patiently held, abuses his wife for being a slattern, and takes a knife to her. Then, after this violent outburst, he docilely returns to his home, and the wife, badly shaken by the call-down, appears to make an effort to improve.

That is the substance of the drama, but around it there graphically turns a vastly suggestive panorama of two pathetically cramped and wasted lives. There is the wife, a dull and bulky shadow of a nineteen-twenties vamp, and the husband, a washed-out relic of a hopeful medical student gone to pot. And it is in the subdued illumination of these two characters through the amiable progress of the picture that its theatrical validity lies.

Enough cannot be said for the excellence of the performance Miss Booth gives in this, her first screen appearance—which, in itself, is something of a surprise. Her skillful and knowing creation of a depressingly common type—the immature, mawkish, lazy housewife—is visualization at its best. And the excellence of Mr. Lancaster as the frustrated, inarticulate spouse, weak-willed and sweetly passive, should not be overlooked. As on the stage, it is the tandem of these two performances that makes the show.

As the pretty and hot-blooded boarder, Terry Moore strikes precisely the right note of timeless and endless animalism and Richard Jaeckel is good as the boy who carnally pursues her. Philip Ober also does a first-rate job as a pillar of Alcoholics Anonymous who is the steady and reliable friend in need. One of the few excursions of the camera away from the home to look in on an A.A. meeting is one of the nicer bits of Americana in the film.

Come Back, Little Sheba may not go down in the books as a great American movie, but it is one of which all may be proud.

—*B.C., December 24, 1952*

COMING HOME

Directed by Hal Ashby; written by Waldo Salt and Robert C. Jones, based on a story by Nancy Dowd;

director of photography, Haskell Wexler; edited by Don Zimmerman; production designer, Michael Haller; produced by Jerome Hellman; released by United Artists. Running time: 127 minutes.

With: Jane Fonda (Sally Hyde), Jon Voight (Luke Martin), Bruce Dern (Captain Bob Hyde), Robert Ginty (Sergeant Dink Mobley), Penelope Milford (Viola Munson), Robert Carradine (Bill Munson), Willie Tyler (Virgil Hunt) and Ron Amador (Beany).

A group of young men in various stages of casual dress is playing pool. The single overhead light leaves deep shadows on the perimeter of the game to create a feeling of isolation and conspiracy. A man moves to the table, makes his shot, pulls back. As they play, the men argue about Vietnam. Someone says that if he had it all to do over again, he would. He believes in defending his country, he says. The others hoot with laughter. A second man sneers at the first fellow, though he understands the desperate need to justify what happened.

The men, each of whom is in a wheelchair or on a cot, are paraplegics, the visible detritus of the invisible war. Now isolated in the ward of a California veterans hospital, they conspire to come to terms with numbed bodies and memories composed of non sequiturs.

Thus begins Hal Ashby's *Coming Home,* Hollywood's most solemn and serious attempt yet to deal with the Vietnam experience in a commercial fiction film, which may well be an impossibility, at least the way Mr. Ashby and his associates have gone at the job.

Coming Home, which opened yesterday at the Cinema One, starts beautifully. As long as it observes the behavior of its troubled veterans, including the manic fury of one young man who finds himself falling in love with a hospital volunteer, the film has a kind of terse, tough documentary truth. But *Coming Home* is not really about paraplegia or the emotional chaos left behind by the Vietnam War. At first, it touches on these things and uses them (sometimes very movingly), and then slowly, disastrously, it reveals its true identity as a three-sided love story about two Vietnam veterans and the one woman who loves them both.

It's a fiction problem of the sort that prompts the dopiest of romantic resolutions, which also has the effect of transforming *Coming Home* into what used to be called a "woman's picture." Consider, dear reader, what poor Jane should do. Should she stay with the man to whom she's legally bound, but who's clearly a neurotic mess since he came home, even though he wasn't much better before he left? Or should she follow her heart with the other vet who, though paralyzed from the waist down, has taught her the joy of orgasms and who shares her newly raised political consciousness?

Jane is Jane Fonda, who plays the pivotal role of Sally Hyde and who, we are told, was the principal mover behind this film's production. The other major roles are played by Bruce Dern, as Sally's husband, a Marine captain who goes to Vietnam as a gung-ho type and returns a mentally shattered man, and by Jon Voight, as the paraplegic vet, the best role Mr. Voight has had in years, even when the movie more or less washes away from under him.

The trouble seems to be that *Coming Home* wants to be all things to as wide an audience as possible. It wants to condemn war. It wants to be a love story. It wants to record the kind of polarization that Vietnam prompted in people like Sally, who otherwise would never have come to any political commitment whatsoever. It looks like a house whose plans were drawn up to incorporate the favorite idea of each member of the family. Too many things have been tacked onto the main structure.

Though the screenplay is credited to Waldo Salt and Robert C. Jones, based on a story by Nancy Dowd (who wrote the quite remarkable screenplay for *Slap Shot*), other people reportedly made a lot of suggestions that went into the final work. This results in moments of arbitrary, patently phony plot twists and in subsidiary characters who inhabit the film as if they were decor, like the suicidal veteran (Robert Carradine) who hangs out in the paraplegic ward though his problems are obviously mental.

Mr. Dern's role is a sort of modified version of the nut he played in *Black Sunday,* though Miss Fonda and Mr. Voight are immensely appealing in the film's opening sequences, before they are required to do and say things that are gross and heavy-minded.

What's worse, though, is the general tone of Mr. Ashby's direction, which puts great store by period (1968) detail that is intrusive even when it's accurate. The soundtrack is a nonstop collection of yesterday's song hits (Beatles, Rolling Stones and so on), not one of which is allowed to pass without making some drearily obvious or ironic comment on the action on the screen. Mr. Ashby has poured music over the movie like a child with a fondness for maple syrup on his pancakes.

Coming Home is soggy with sound, just as, eventually, it becomes soggy with good if unrealized intentions.

—*V.C., February 16, 1978*

THE CONFORMIST

Directed by Bernardo Bertolucci; written (in Italian, with English subtitles) by Mr. Bertolucci, based on the novel by Alberto Moravia; director of photography, Vittorio Storaro; edited by Franco Arcalli; music by Georges Delarue; production designer, Ferdinando Scarfiotti; produced by Maurizio Lodi-Fe, released by Paramount Pictures. Running time: 110 minutes.

With: Jean-Louis Trintignant (Marcello), Stefania Sandrelli (Giulia), Dominique Sanda (Anna Quadri), Pierre Clementi (Lino Seminara), Gastone Moschin (Manganiello) and Enzo Tarascio (Professor Quadri).

Bernardo Bertolucci, who is associated with Italy's avant-garde because of such films as *Before the Revolution, Partner* and *The Spider's Stratagem,* (which was shown at the New York Film Festival Thursday night), has at last made a very middle-class, almost conventional (in the context of his other work) movie that turns out to be one of the elegant surprises of the current New York Film Festival.

The Conformist, an adaptation of the novel by Alberto Moravia and which was shown last night at Philharmonic Hall, is a superior chronicle film that equates the rise and fall of Italian Fascism, from the early 1920's until 1943, with the short, dreadful, very romantic life of Marcello (Jean-Louis Trintignant), a young man for whom conformity becomes a kind of obsession after a traumatic homosexual encounter in his youth.

That Bertolucci is aware of the fact that the equation of politics with sex is extremely complex is apparent in his having changed the Moravia ending in such a way that the entire film is ultimately modified by ambiguity. It is also apparent in Bertolucci's cinematic style, which is so rich, poetic and baroque that it is simply incapable of meaning only what it says—and which is, I think, a decided improvement over Moravia's sometimes tiresomely lean prose.

The movie, based on the first screenplay that Bertolucci has written without collaborators since *Before the Revolution,* is a series of nonsequential memories that are evoked in Marcello's mind as he and another Italian Fascist, a trigger man, drive through snowy French landscapes to attend the assassination of an exiled anti-Fascist who was once Marcello's philosophy professor. The time is 1936, and not the least of the film's extraordinary beauties is the way it recalls an era, from the looks of the clothes and the automobiles and the awful modern architecture and decor, to the sounds of its music and radio programs.

Marcello, pursued by the guilt of the attempted homosexual seduction when he was twelve (and which was climaxed by his shooting the man), has in turn pursued the illusion of adequacy. He has loved, courted and married a girl (Stefania Sandrelli) so commonplace as to be unique and he has given the Fascists such dedication that he doesn't hesitate to combine his honeymoon to Paris with an assignment to murder his former professor.

The movie is full of such curious coexistences, some of which align good alongside evil and others that reinforce or echo major themes. At one point, Marcello's blind friend, another staunch Fascist, points out (none too subtly, perhaps) that they are alike, that kind gravitates toward kind. This later gives a most peculiar perspective to Marcello's sudden infatuation with the professor's young wife, Anna, played by Dominique Sanda (*La Femme Douce*). Although Anna responds to him, it is almost immediately revealed that she is head over heels in love with Marcello's absurd wife.

Bertolucci will be faulted, I expect, for his rather loving depiction of all of the very photogenic details of upper middle-class decadence. It does get to be a bit much when Marcello goes to call on his mother and finds her in bed, asleep, at noon, wearing a feathered bedjacket, a mask over her eyes and waiting for a morphine fix to be administered by her Japanese chauffeur. (At the news conference following the showing of the film Thursday, Bertolucci said that the difference between his film and Visconti's *The Damned* is that *The Damned* is operatic, while his film is operettic, which is, in a way, quite right.)

There are excesses in the film, but they are balanced by scenes of such unusual beauty and vitality that I couldn't care less. I think particularly of a scene in which Marcello and his mother visit his father in the courtyard of a mental hospital that looks very much like a surreal Greek marketplace. It could be Oedipus and Jocasta come to call on a crazy Laius. There is another, absolutely marvelous sequence in a Parisian dance hall in which Anna and Marcello's wife dance a funny, more or less sapphic, tango.

The movie is perfectly cast, from Trintignant and on down, including Pierre Clementi, who appears briefly as the wicked young man who makes a play for the young Marcello. *The Conformist* is flawed, perhaps, but those very flaws may make it Bertolucci's first commercially popular film, at least in Europe where there always seems to be a market for intelligent, upper middle-class decadence.

—*V.C., September 19, 1970*

THE CONQUEST OF EVEREST

Directed by George Lowe; produced by Leon Clore, John Taylor and Grahame Tharp; released by United Artists. Running time: 90 minutes.

With: Alpine climbers.

The triumph of the motion picture camera as an instrument for capturing for all time the look, the "feel" and the excitement of the bold and brave adventures of man has seldom been more fitly demonstrated than it is in the British documentary film, *The Conquest of Everest,* which opened at the Fine Arts yesterday.

No need to give an explanation of what this nerve-tingling picture is about. It is the official film record of the ascent of Mount Everest last spring, accomplished by a group of British climbers with Nepalese porters and guides. But more than a slapdash compilation of incidentally taken photographs, picked up by the climbers at odd moments—as such records often are—this is a skillful visualization of drama of the most tremendous sort, filmed in magnificent color and edited, scored, and presented in brilliant style.

From the initial phases, in which are vividly described the painstaking preparations and testing of equipment for the trip—the eleventh assault on the world's highest mountain in a span of thirty years—to the climactic footage in which the conquest of the peak is explained, the viewer is engrossingly transported on an adventure of indescribable awe and thrill. The sense of a campaign by an army upon a citadel is conveyed, and the magnitude of the achievement is fully and stirringly revealed.

This reviewer must make the frank admission that he had never quite understood the attraction of mountain-climbing, an exercise of vast discomfort and mortal peril, nor the logic in the classic explanation of the late George Leigh-Mallory for attempting Everest: "Because it is there!" The doubtful and chilly satisfaction of planting a flag on a far-off, wind-whipped peak scarcely seemed worth the danger and the agonizing toil. But this picture gives some comprehension. It makes sharply and tangibly plain the bond of the robust group effort and the profound spiritual test involved.

We cannot attempt to tell in detail the countless stunning incidents contained—incidents that make up the fabric of a vastly absorbing enterprise. Such things as the grand planning of the project under the leadership of Sir John Hunt, the selection of the climbers, the arrival in Nepal, the rendezvous with the Sherpas, those indomitable little mountain men without whom a Himalayan expedition could not even take to the hills—these are important stages in the project that are expertly shown.

But it is when the sturdy band of climbers push up into the ice and snow, higher and higher and higher, to the face of the great Everest massif, where the wind howls with banshee terror and the soul of man is naked and alone—here is where this picture record takes on a rare magnificence. And the last grinding, staggering pictorialization of the final assault against the top of the world by a handful of heroes in the rarefied vastness is a photographic triumph beyond compare.

Actually, the terminal push by Sir Edmund Hillary and Tenzing, the Sherpa, to Everest's peak was not filmed, and this climactic leg of the assault is vocally described while the "goddess mother" is viewed in all her majesty and remoteness from a plane. But the lack of this critical footage, while disappointing, is not deplorable. The final triumph was that of the whole outfit, and that is what is manifest in this film. The tension and anxiety of the others all the way down the mountainside bespeaks the determination and courage that went into the peak climb.

The greeting for Sir Edmund and Tenzing as they return to the advance base on the grim South Col is one of the grandest, most throat-choking moments this reviewer has ever witnessed on a screen.

Beyond the extraordinary footage brought back by Thomas Stobart and George W. Lowe, credit must be extended for the editing and musical scoring of this film; for the commentary, written by Louis Macneice, which Meredith Edwards and members of the expedition speak, and for the tasteful restraint with which affection and pride are expressed throughout the film. Thanks to brave men and fine technicians, the experience of climbing Everest may be had for the price of a theater ticket. This is certainly the bargain of the year!

—*B.C., December 10, 1953*

CONTEMPT

Directed by Jean-Luc Godard: written (in French. with English subtitles) by Mr. Godard. based on the novel *A Ghost at Noon* by Alberto Moravia: cinematographer. Raoul Coutard: edited by Agnes Guillemot and Lila Lakshmanan: music by Georges Delarue: produced by Georges de Beauregard. Carlo Ponti and Joseph E. Levine: released by Embassy Pictures. Running time: 100 minutes.

With: Brigitte Bardot (Camille Javal). Jack Palance (Jeremy Prokosch). Michel Piccoli (Paul Javal). Giorgia Moll (Francesca Vanini) and Fritz Lang (Himself).

For a director who manipulates cinema as adroitly as does Jean-Luc Godard, and has as much feeling for the image and as much sense of pictorial style as he has, it would seem he could put his talents to more intelligent and illuminating use than he has been doing in his recent pictures—especially *Contempt*, which opened yesterday at the Lincoln Arts.

In this luxuriant color picture, which boasts Brigitte Bardot displaying her famous figure in the nude in a number of scenes, it appears he is aiming to tell us why a young French woman grows to hate her loving husband who is making a lot of money as a movie scriptwriter in Italy.

At least, that's the purport of the novel of Alberto Moravia on which the film is based—the novel known in Italy as *Il Disprezzo* and published in this country as *A Ghost at Noon*. And that's the direction in which the drama seems to tend about halfway through, when a burst of bitter bickering between the couple gives a hint of an ominous rift in their marital lute.

Up to this point, it is evident that the wife is confused and put out by her husband's unseemly condescension to an American producer for whom he's about to write a film. The husband has let this uncouth fellow make obvious passes at her. He has even pointedly left them alone together. The wife would like to know why.

It is also evident that she is disconcerted by her husband's flirtations with the girl who is the secretary of the producer. She is curious as to what is cooking here. And she is a little baffled about the project on which he is planning to embark.

It is a film to be titled *Odysseus,* directed by Fritz Lang—yes, the famous German-American director, who actually plays himself here. Obviously he and the producer have different ideas about how it should be done. The wife seems to be a bit puzzled as to which side her husband is on.

All of these things have been established when the couple start throwing verbal knives in their new, not yet furnished apartment in a stylish building in Rome. And the first thing you know they are arguing about whether they are still in love and whether the husband should go on with the project. This runs for a half hour or so, while they take baths, change clothes and so forth. The husband never takes off his hat.

The arguments continue when they go on location to Capri, only now they are further complicated by discussions over the interpretation of the film. What is to be the explanation of the relations of Odysseus and his wife, Penelope? The husband, Mr. Lang, and the producer can't resolve this point.

And neither can Mr. Godard make us understand why the wife in his drama suddenly tells her husband she has contempt for him and decides to leave. Has she lost faith in him? Is she bored? Or is she just fed up with watching him wearing his hat all the time?

Evidently, Mr. Godard has attempted to make this film communicate a sense of the alienation of individuals in this complex modern world. And he has clearly directed to get a tempo that suggests irritation and ennui.

His characters are specific. Miss Bardot as the wife is restless and erratic. She moves about nervously, wears wigs, takes baths and has a penchant for sunning herself or going swimming in the nude. The husband, played by Michel Piccoli, is conspicuously gross and crude, insensitive and intellectually uncertain. He is provoking and rude. Jack Palance makes the producer a horribly crass and brutal type. Mr. Lang plays himself with a nice tone of serenity, cultivation, and good sense.

The imagery, too, is specific. Mr. Godard sets interesting scenes, with provocative color combinations and a suggestive pictorial flow. But out of it all comes nothing—or very little that tells you why this wife is so contemptuous of her husband. Maybe he should be contemptuous of her!

The dialogue is spoken in English, French and Italian, jumbled up amusingly. Where they are necessary, English subtitles are used.

—B.C., December 19, 1964

THE CONVERSATION

Written and directed by Francis Ford Coppola; director of photography, Bill Butler; edited by Walter Murch and Richard Chew; music by David Shire; production designer, Dean Tavoularis; produced by Fred Roos; released by Paramount Pictures. Running time: 113 minutes.

With: Gene Hackman (Harry Caul), John Cazale (Stan), Allen Garfield (Bernie Moran), Frederic Forrest (Mark) and Cindy Williams (Ann).

Early last summer, it was comforting when one authority on wiretapping referred to the equipment used to eavesdrop on the Democratic National Committee's headquarters as "sloppy" and "amateurish." And Dick Gregory's reflection on the White House tapes is worth preserving: "Imagine feelin' so lonely and insignificant that you'd bug your own phone!" But yuks about bugging recede swiftly while you watch Francis Ford Coppola's *The Conversation,* which opened yesterday at the Coronet.

This extremely grim movie explores the character of a middle-aged surveillance wizard: a dedicated professional who prefers to "know nothing about human nature," or even about the people he's paid to spy on. Wedded to secrecy as a moral principle, he's the kind of man who lies down to neck with his shoes on—an acutely repressed solitary who repeats that he's not responsible for the outcome of his work.

He feels totally disconnected from the three murders that resulted from one of his assignments: "I just turned in the tapes." But he loathes even mild profanity, and when he confesses his sins to a priest, he includes failing to pay for some newspapers. It's an impressive portrayal by Gene Hackman: the inhibited laugh, the bland, bleak face with lips pressed flat together and chin drawn in, convey the ruthless stranger who knows our most intimate moments but won't react to them.

However, in the course of a routine job, he detects that a new murder's in the making. Against all resolve, he becomes involved—and desperately determined to forestall a possible killing. (His suspicions spring from what he's collected on tape—a powerful reminder of the photographer in Antonioni's *Blow-Up.*) The movie's plot is twisted by a cleverly deceptive use of sentimentality; people who sound soupy later turn out to have sinister intentions.

Suddenly, those whose guilt he has spotted turn his own technology against him: he himself is bugged and spied on. So he becomes the hunter at bay—frantic because he knows that some equipment is unbeatable. In a futile effort to protect his privacy, he finally trashes his own apartment—even smashing a statuette of the Virgin Mary (and finding nothing)—and winds up a victim of his craft.

It's a brilliant idea for a movie, and much of it works. But some of the action drags—perhaps because the style is so muted, so deliberately dry and cool, that suspense is partially muffled. The scenes where two different women fawn on Mr. Hackman are unconvincing, since they have to behave as though this grubby, uptight man were irresistible. And I'm mildly mystified by the casting of Cindy Williams as an executive's roving wife, since she appears far too prim and conventional to stray over any kind of boundary. But Alan Garfield is splendid as a boastful wiretapper, and there's a fine, nervy performance by John Cazale.

Mr. Coppola has certainly succeeded in making surveillance repulsive. While that's hardly a new notion, we can thank him for withering the last tendrils of romance: The dagger and the cloak have lost all dash—they're equally dangerous and dirty.

—*N.S., April 8, 1974*

COOL HAND LUKE

Directed by Stuart Rosenberg; written by Donn Pearce and Frank R. Pierson, based on the novel by Mr. Pearce; cinematographer, Conrad Hall; edited by Sam O'Steen; music by Lalo Schifrin; art designer, Cary Odell; produced by Gordon Carroll; released by Warner Brothers. Running time: 126 minutes.

With: Paul Newman (Luke), George Kennedy (Dragline), J. D. Cannon (Society Red), Lou Antonio (Koko), Robert Drivas (Loudmouth Steve), Strother Martin (Captain), Jo Van Fleet (Arletta), Clifton James (Carr), Morgan Woodward (Boss Godfrey) and Luke Askew (Boss Paul).

That traditional object of sorrow and compassion in American folk song and lore, the chain-gang prisoner, is given as strong a presentation as ever he has had on the screen in *Cool Hand Luke*, which opened at Loew's State last night. It will continue there and at Cinema I today.

Indeed, in my recollection, he has never been as forcefully revealed as a victim not only of the brutality and sadistic discipline of his captors, but also—and this is most important—of the indirect cruelty that comes from idolization in the eyes of his fellow prisoners and, finally, of himself.

This reticent young fellow who is picked up by the police at the beginning of this film and sent off to a correctional workcamp in what is evidently some Southern state for the minor offense of vandalizing parking meters is more than a conventional misused convict, more than a human being who is unjustly abused. He is a psychologically disturbed and complicated victim of his own self-ostracism and pride.

He is a curiously calculating loner, a terse and sarcastic misanthrope who treats his jailors with taciturn defiance and his fellow prisoners with cool contempt—at the start. He takes with bland endurance the kicks and proddings and verbal insults the skulking guards rain on him, and he smiles when his fellows ridicule him and haze him unmercifully.

But he has pride and the dignity of detachment grown out of some boyhood hurt, perhaps. He isn't a coward or weakling. So when things finally come to the point that he must fight the top-dog prisoner to a showdown, he does so gamely, ferociously, and defiantly until he drops.

That is the turning point for him, because from there on the top dog takes him in tow, makes him his boasted companion and, recognizing his superior skill and wit, backs him in poker games and, most impressively, in a refreshingly funny wager that he can eat fifty hard-boiled eggs.

This elevation does it. Now he is Cool Hand Luke, the idol of the sychophantic prisoners and the growing concern of the guards. He assumes bravura postures to demonstrate his contempt. And because it is expected of him, when he receives word that his mother has died he makes a break for freedom. He almost gets away, but is caught and returned.

The inevitable commitment to this pattern—other breaks, other returns, other and crueler beatings and tortures until his pride and will are destroyed—leads to the sad and grisly finish for this congenital fugitive—a fugitive not only from the chain gang, but also from society and, indeed, from life.

What elevates this brutal picture above the ruck of prison films and into the range of intelligent contemplation of the ironies of life is a sharp script by Donn Pearce and Frank R. Pierson, ruthlessly realistic and plausible staging and directing by a new man, Stuart Rosenberg, and splendid acting by Paul Newman and a totally unfaultable cast.

Mr. Newman is excellent, at the top of his sometime erratic form, in the role of this warped and alienated loner whose destiny it is to lose. George Kennedy is powerfully obsessive as the top dog who handles things his way as effectively and finally as destructively as does the warden or the guards. Strother Martin, Luke Eskew, Morgan Woodward and several others are blood-chilling as these red-necked brutes, and any number of others are fine as prisoners.

A special word of commendation must be said for Jo Van Fleet as Mr. Newman's mother, who, in one scene, in which she comes to visit him propped up in the back of a truck, does as much to make us comprehend the background and the emotional hang-up of the loner as might have been done in the entire length of a good film.

Mr. Rosenberg's skill with the camera, his sense of graphic imagery and cinema pace, and Conrad Hall's superb color photography merit conversation and awards.

—B.C., November 2, 1967

THE COUNT OF MONTE CRISTO

Directed by Rowland V. Lee; written by Philip Dunne, Dan Totheroh and Mr. Lee, based on the novel by Alexandre Dumas; cinematographer, Peverell Marley; edited by Grant Whytock; music by Alfred Newman; produced by Edward Small; released by United Artists. Black and white. Running time: 113 minutes.

With: Robert Donat (Edmond Dantes), Elissa Landi (Mercedes), Louis Calhern (De Villefort Jr.), Sidney Blackmer (Mondego), Raymond Walburn (Danglars), O. P. Heggie (Abbé Faria), William Farnum (Captain Leclere) and Georgia Caine (Mme. De Rosas).

In its third cinema reincarnation, *The Count of Monte Cristo,* which began an engagement at the Rivoli yesterday, is still as passionate and grand as the waves that crash against the grim battlements of the Château d'If. For almost two hours, a small eternity when the eyes are glued to a flashing screen, it unfolds the classic story of the revenge of Edmond Dantes. Building steadily and powerfully to its feverish climax, the new film is constantly refreshing the spectator with the variety and shouting impact of its episodes. What a scenario writer this man Dumas would have been! In dramatic invention and the cumulative architecture of its plot, *Monte Cristo* is made in heaven for the manufacturers of the costume film drama. Rowland V. Lee and his assistants have mounted it excellently, and Robert Donat, who was imported from England for the Edmond Dantes role, adds a welcome modern touch to the great chronicle with the cool and even-tempered brilliance of his performance.

This is none of your trivial stream of consciousness works. This is a walloping melodrama of revenge, conceived on the grand scale. Edmond Dantes is the superman who dedicates his life to the fulfillment of the biblical moral, "Vengeance is mine." To modern eyes the elaborate mystery of the count's movements has something of the aroma of what Mr. Shaw called Sardoodledum. Yet there is certainly vast fascination in watching the count as he spins his intricate web about his unsuspecting victims, driving the evil Mondego to suicide, whipping the treacherous Danglars into gibbering idiocy and having his final revenge on the crafty De Villefort in the climactic court scene. And so terrible are the years of this man's imprisonment in the dank fortress (you can even see the lime dripping from the ceiling of his cell) that the audience is with him to the hilt when he comes forth to avenge himself on the three who condemned him to a life in death.

France in the years of Napoleon's abortive coup d'état and the monarchy of the eighteenth Louis provides a picturesque background of costume and setting for the drama. Its progress on the screen is with the slow, bitter, and remorseless tread of Edmond Dantes himself. Especially admirable are the scenes in the Château d'If, the patient, year-by-year construction of the passage through the impregnable walls, the death of the old Abbé when the two prisoners are close enough to freedom to hear the sea outside and Edmond's miraculous escape. There is the stuff of superb detective romance in the Count's relentless investigations into the remote corners of the lives of his three enemies. The suspense of the audience, when finally the Count has arranged his marvelously ingenious traps, becomes one long ache.

This Robert Donat makes a splendid impression in his first American film appearance. His performance is lean, intelligent and quietly overwhelming, and it is unmarked by hysteria or the grand ham manner that the part invites. As the three rogues, Louis Calhern, Sidney Blackmer and Raymond Walburn are the devil's own brethren. The heroine in *Monte Cristo* is pretty small fry, but Elissa Landi gives her a handsome and gallant look. Although the cast is long, it would be ungrateful not to single out the work of Clarence Muse and Luis Alberni as the Count's faithful lieutenants and of O. P. Heggie as the old Friar Faria.

It is the private opinion of this department that pictures like *The Count of Monte Cristo* do not advance the art of the cinema. The modern world cries in a thousand voices for expression on the screen. But this is a whispered postscript to a report of genuine admiration. The new film is a first-class movie version of a classic novel.

—A.S., September 27, 1934

THE COUNTRY GIRL

Directed by George Seaton; written by Mr. Seaton, based on the play by Clifford Odets; cinematographer, John F. Warren; edited by Ellsworth Hoaglan; music by Victor Young; art designers, Hal Pereira and Roland Anderson; produced by William Perlberg; released by Paramount Pictures. Black and white. Running time: 104 minutes.

With: Bing Crosby (Frank Elgin), Grace Kelly (Georgie Elgin), William Holden (Bernie Dodd), Anthony Ross (Phil Cook) and Gene Reynolds (Larry).

Clifford Odets's poignant drama of a broken-down actor, his loyal wife and a misunderstanding stage director that he told in *The Country Girl,* has been put on the screen with solid impact—and with Bing Crosby in the actor role. This latter piece of offbeat casting is the most striking thing about the film, which Paramount delivered last evening to the Criterion.

For, with all the uncompromising candor of George Seaton's adaptation of the play and with all the intense, perceptive acting of Grace Kelly and William Holden in the other roles, it is truly Mr. Crosby's appearance and performance as the has-been thespian who fights and is helped back to stardom that hits the audience right between the eyes.

Mr. Odets's drama is a searching and pitiless thing. It cuts to the hearts of three people without mercy or concern for their deep shame. It eviscerates a middle-aged actor who has taken to self-pity and drink because of some canker in his confidence, which is, indeed, an occupational disease. And it lays bare the proud and bleak devotion of his sadly humiliated wife and the arrogance of the stage director who fails to grasp the shabby lie the actor lives.

Although the heroic character is inevitably the wife, who fights for her weak and sodden husband with the last store of energy in her weary frame, it is he—the degraded husband—who is the focus of attention here. And the force and credibility of the drama depends upon how he is played. That is why it is Mr. Crosby who merits particular praise, for he not only has essayed the character but also performs it with unsuspected power.

It is notable that his shabby actor is not so testy nor prone to smear his wife as was the cunning and cantankerous fellow Paul Kelly created on the Broadway stage. Mr. Crosby's fidgety defeatist is more the apologetic sort whose manner appeals for forgiveness and who only rarely explodes in rage. But he is nonetheless basically brutal as he torments his loyal "country girl" with his agonizing self-pity and his shamefully losing battles with his nerves.

Mr. Seaton, who wrote the screenplay and directed with a hand as firm as iron, has allowed him one dispensation to yank on the strings of the heart. He has made him a musical comedy actor, which is logical with Mr. Crosby in the role, and has given him several numbers by Harold Arlen and Ira Gershwin to sing.

One is an item called "The Pitchman," which is supposed to be from one of the actor's old shows and which he sings when he does an audition, through the good offices of the stage director, early in the film. But the more sentimental obtrusion is a ballad, "The Search Is Through," which is wrapped up with misty recollections of happier days and a little son who was killed. Naturally, Mr. Crosby tugs when the strings are in his hands.

But, for the most part, he plays the broken actor frankly and honestly, goes down to the depths of degradation without a bat of his bleary eyes and then brings the poor guy back to triumph in a chest-thumping musical show with a maximum of painful resolution and sheer credibility. There is no doubt that Mr. Crosby deserves all the kudos he will get.

So does the lovely Miss Kelly, who likewise will get her share of praise for the quality of strain and desperation she puts into the battered, patient wife. And Mr. Holden, too, merits approval for the stinging yet oddly tender way he plays the stage director—the man who gives the actor his break. Anthony Ross as a heartless producer and Gene Reynolds as a backstage myrmidon add the flavor of hard-grained reality to this trenchant, intense, and moving film.

The *Country Girl* comes along fitly as one of the fine and forceful pictures of the year.

—B.C., December 16, 1954

THE COUSINS

Produced, written (in French, with English subtitles) and directed by Claude Chabrol; cinematographer, Henri Decaë; music by Paul Misraki; released by Films-Around-The-World. Black and white. Running time: 112 minutes.

With: Gérard Blain (Charles), Jean-Claude Brialy (Paul), Juliette Mayniel (Florence), Claude Cerval (Clovis), Genevieve Cluny (Genevieve), Michelle Meritz (Yvonne), Corrado Guarducci (Italian Count) and Guy Decomble (Librarian).

Another morbid picture of the younger generation in France—this time the men and women students who attend college in Paris by day and carouse by night—is offered in the new French film, *The Cousins*, which opened at the Beekman yesterday.

It was written, produced, and directed by twenty-seven-year-old Claude Chabrol, whose recent picture, *Le Beau Serge*, contemplated the decadence and apathy of younger Frenchmen in the provinces.

To judge by both these pictures, which are in the stream of the "new wave" of French motion picture creation that recently brought us the brilliant *The 400 Blows*, M. Chabrol is the gloomiest and most despairing of the new creative men. His attitude is ridden with a sense of defeat and ruin. And if his cinema reporting is as reliable as it is clear-eyed, candid, and cruel, then others, as well as he, have good reason to be concerned about the youth of France.

For his evident conviction, as reflected most forcefully in *The Cousins*, is that a foul contamination has infected the nation's intellectual youth. It is more than a restlessness and frenzy; it is a deep cynicism that is expressed in absolute hedonism and a maudlin wish for death.

This is indicated with shocking candor in the most powerful part of this film, which represents a veritable orgy in the swanky apartment of a student of law. This fellow has given a room to his country cousin who is an innocent and optimistic youth, still tied to the apron-strings of his mother and extremely naive about girls.

Whether to educate this bumpkin, or simply because it is their customary behavior, the older cousin and one of his decadent playmates throw this Saturday night brawl, which for drinking and general carousing puts most Greenwich Village blowouts in the shade. And at the height of the orgiastic doings, the host puts a Wagner record on the hi-fi, turns out the lights, and appears among his guests carrying a candelabra, wearing a Nazi officer's cap and reciting a German poem.

Done as it is in a vivid fashion, this scene and the idea hit hard. The concept of the youth of the nation corrupted by the Nazi image is profound. And the progress of the film, from this point on, while not so forceful, conveys the hopeless thought that this cousin, who is obviously a leader among the students, is an inevitable influence for ruin. For he befouls a likely romance for his young cousin by himself taking over the girl, and he succeeds in destroying the morale of the youngster by cynically bluffing his way through his law exams.

M. Chabrol has more skill with the camera than he has with the pen, and his picture is more credible to the eye than it is to the skeptical mind. But it is not the less overwhelming, and it is beautifully played by much the same cast that performed for him in *Le Beau Serge*.

Jean-Claude Brialy is cold and brilliant, elegant and epicene, as the older cousin; Gérard Blain is soft and touching as the youth; and Juliette Mayniel is thoroughly provoking as the girl who is diverted from a pure romance. Claude Cerval as the decadent playmate and Corrado Guarducci as an Italian hedonist work to make the orgy something sinister and hard to forget.

—B.C., November 24, 1959

THE CRANES ARE FLYING

Produced and directed by Mikhail Kalatozov; written (in Russian, with English subtitles) by Victor Rozov, based on his play; cinematographer, Sergei Urusevsky; edited by M. Timofeyeva; music by Moisei Vaynberg; art designer, Y. Syidetelev; released by Warner Brothers. Black and white. Running time: 94 minutes.

With: Tatyana Samoilova (Veronica). Alexei Batalov (Boris). Vasily Merkuryev (Fyodor Ivanovich). Alexander Shvorin (Mark). Sonhola Kharitonova (Irina) and Konstantin Nikintin (Volodya).

Some things that many people may be surprised to find in a Soviet film are the warp and weft of *The Cranes Are Flying*, which came to the Fine Arts yesterday. These are a downright obsessive and overpowering revulsion to war and, in contrast, a beautifully tender, almost lyric, feeling for romantic love.

These two amazing expressions, so uncommon in Soviet films, which are more often given to extolling patriotic fervor and the lovable qualities of hydroelectric plants, are the particular thematic distinctions of this extraordinary prize-winning film, offered here under the cultural exchange agreement promoted by the Soviet Union and our Department of State.

Unusual, too, is the employment of a highly intimate, impressionistic style of cinematic narration to tell the story of a sensitive Moscow girl who weakens and is unfaithful to her sweetheart when he is at the front in World War II. Mikhail Kalatozov, the director, has harked back to a cinematic style that was popular in the days when Pudovkin and Dovzhenko were making heroic revolutionary films. It is a style used in silent pictures, full of angular shots and close-up views of running feet and anguished faces. But M. Kalatozov has brought it up to date to blend with sound and the overlapping idioms of modern screen reportage. It might be called neoromanticism, applied to a tragic tale.

The story is that of two lovers who are parted by the war—he a stalwart and patriotic fellow who willingly volunteers and marches off, while she, a wholesome maiden, remains behind and tends her hospital job. But under the strain of wartime torments, the loss of her family and her home in an air raid and the loneliness of waiting and not hearing from her beau, she submits to the latter's pianist cousin, who has got out of going to war. And, in the turmoil of the moment, she lovelessly marries him.

The illogic of this marriage is the most glaring fault of the plot, since it represents a conspicuous old-fashioned romantic cliché. But the twist does provide the solid basis for the heroine's subsequent despair and the high moral of the fable, which is that one should stay faithful to one's love.

Other familiar little details may be noted in the film, possibly signifying deliberate propaganda aims. For instance, an aged grandmother bestows upon the departing soldier the sign of the cross. The piano used by the musician is a Steinway. And family affections are strongly pronounced. But most genuine and touching is the emphasis on the steadfast love and devotion of the heroine for her sweetheart—and his for her, as caught in quick scenes at the front.

Thanks to Mr. Kalatozov's direction and the excellent performance Tatyana Samoilova gives as the girl, one absorbs a tremendous feeling of sympathy from this film—a feeling that has no awareness of geographical or political bounds. She is simply a fine, fecund-looking young woman torn from her lover by war. And he, played by Alexei Batalov, is a pleasant and credible young man moved by romantic impulses and shattered by fates outside himself.

Vasily Merkuryev as the soldier's father, Alexander Shvorin as the pianist and Alla Bogdanova as the grandmother make solid characters, too.

Strong music and good English subtitles to translate the Russian dialogue complete a moving drama that carries a message of love.

—*B.C., March 22, 1960*

CRIES AND WHISPERS

Produced, written (in Swedish, with English subtitles) and directed by Ingmar Bergman; director of photography, Sven Nykvist; edited by Siv Lundgren; music by Frederic Chopin and Johann Sebastian Bach; art designer, Marik Vos; released by New World Films. Running time: 95 minutes.

With: Harriet Andersson (Agnes). Ingrid Thulin (Karin). Liv Ullman (Maria/Her Mother). Kari Sylway (Anna). Erland Josephson (Doctor). George Arlin (Fredrik, Karin's Husband) and Henning Mortizen (Joakin, Maria's Husband).

Set in a tranquil autumn park is a handsome eighteenth-century Swedish manor house, every room of which is decorated in a shade of red. Walls, rugs, draperies, even the blankets in the bedrooms. Depending on the light, the red may look as dark as dried blood or as brilliantly scarlet as a new azalea.

The time is the turn of the century, at the end of a long night. Agnes (Harriet Andersson) awakens, moves her head fretfully from side to side on the pillow, then gets out of bed and goes to her desk. In her diary she writes: "It is early Monday morning and I am in pain."

Thus begins Ingmar Bergman's magnificent, moving and very mysterious new film, *Cries and Whispers,* with a focus so sharp that it seems to have the clarity of something seen through the medium of fever. Every sense has been heightened to a supernatural degree. Fears, wishes and suspicions never spoken occasionally rustle through the house like wind. We can even hear the newly dead talk, distantly and somewhat reproachfully, mindless of the rapidity with which physical decay sets in.

Agnes, in her late thirties, unmarried and with nothing much to show for her life except some rather ordinary watercolors of flowers, is dying of cancer, slowly and with great pain.

Attending her are her older sister, Karin (Ingrid Thulin), a drawn, angry woman who is married to a diplomat she loathes; her younger sister, Maria (Liv Ullmann), an extraordinary beauty, also married but not inhibited from extramarital affairs that help pass the time; and Anna (Kari Sylway), a peasant woman with a round, expressionless face, who is probably younger than Agnes but who acts like a mother to her.

When Agnes awakens in the night in pain, it is Anna who crawls into bed and holds her and fondles her until she drifts into sleep again.

Nothing that Bergman has done before is likely to prepare you for *Cries and Whispers* except in a comparatively superficial sense. Like all of his recent works, it's ever-aware of what I hesitate to call its filmicness. Sequences begin and end with close-up portraits of the character being considered. The color program of the film is designed to call attention to itself—the red interiors, a fondness for white costumes that is so insistent that the appearance of a gray dress seems to be a terrible omen, the periodic dissolves to the blank red screen.

All of these things are simply the methods by which Bergman dramatizes states of mind that have seldom been attempted, much less achieved, outside of written fiction. A lot, I'm afraid, will be made of the fact that *Cries and Whispers* moves, like *Persona,* in and out of reality and fantasy without easily defining either, though it must now be apparent that everything we see in Bergman is "real" to the extent that we see it and that it is meaningful to the characters and to us.

The movie is Bergman's *The Three Sisters,* not set in any recognizable provinces but in three overlapping wastelands of the soul. On the occasion of Agnes's dying, the three sisters come together again briefly, each life having already peaked. Each longs for the kind of communion they may or may not have had in childhood, though they remember having had it. Each realizes that it is now impossible.

Maria (Miss Ullmann, who here is one of the world's great beauties), more or less seduces the guilt-ridden Karin into believing that the two of them can recapture the intimacy of their youth; then the next day she forgets the promises made. After her death, Agnes implores Karin to help her until—I suppose you might say—she gets through to the other side. "I'm alive," screams Karin, "and I want nothing to do with your death!"

Because Bergman is a man who loves women without identifying with them, his film is full of the sort of wonder and speculation experienced by a tourist in a strange land that he knows well, but that will never be his own.

Only Bergman, I think, could get away with the scene in which Karin picks up the piece of a broken wine glass and slashes her genitals, in order to taunt her husband with her blood. And only Bergman could obtain the mixture of humor and sadness that floods the scene in which Maria's former lover, the local doctor now grown middle-aged, holds Maria in front of a mirror and charts for both their benefit the tiny lines that mark Maria's journey into laziness and indolence.

Cries and Whispers, which opened yesterday at the Cinema I, is not an easy film to describe or to endure. It stands alone and it reduces almost everything else you're likely to see this season to the size of a small cinder.

—V.C., December 22, 1972

CROSSFIRE

Directed by Edward Dmytryk; written by John Paxton, based on the novel *The Brick Foxhole* by Richard Brooks; cinematographer, J. Roy Hunt; edited by Harry Gerstad; music by Roy Webb; art

209

designers. Albert S. D'Agostino and Alfred Herman: produced by Adrian Scott: released by RKO Radio Pictures. Black and white. Running time: 86 minutes.

With: Robert Young (Finley). Robert Mitchum (Kelley). Robert Ryan (Montgomery). Gloria Grahame (Ginny). Paul Kelly (The Man). Sam Levene (Samuels). Jacqueline White (Mary Mitchell) and Steve Brodie (Floyd).

An unqualified A for effort in bringing to the screen a frank and immediate demonstration of the brutality of religious bigotry as it festers and fires ferocity in certain seemingly normal American minds is due to Producers Dore Schary, Adrian Scott and everyone else at RKO who had a hand in the making of *Crossfire*, which came to the Rivoli yesterday, For here, without hints or subterfuges, they have come right out and shown that such malice—in this case, anti-Jewish—is a dark and explosive sort of hate which, bred of ignorance and intolerance, can lead to extreme violence.

And an equally high mark for lacing this exceedingly thoughtful theme through a grimly absorbing melodrama is due the film's makers, too. For, again in a manner which advances the realistic techniques of the screen, they have blended both theme and storytelling in a cinematically stimulating way.

Slowly and apparently incidentally, the theme invades the plot, which seems, at its outset, to be more than a standard murder yarn. A man, suspected of a murder, refers to the victim as a "Jew boy"—that is all. A little later, this same man—an ex-soldier—lets slip some further anti-Jewish prejudice. And then the audience comes to realize, as does the district attorney probing the case, that here is the sole motive for the murder: a vicious and drunken hate.

But then, as this realization is shockingly brought to the fore, there emerges an equally strong resistance to the unmasking of the suspected man. That is the curious confusion which certain of his soldier pals created, out of sheer misguided loyalty, to prevent his unqualified arrest. And thus is evolved a drama in which intolerance, supported by loyalty, is pitted against social justice and the righteousness of humanity.

In developing this stinging drama, Director Edward Dmytryk has employed a slow, aggravatingly set tempo and a heavily shaded pictorial style. He has worked for moods of ominous peril to carry the hot ferocity suggested in the script which John Paxton has written from Richard Brooks's novel, *The Brick Foxhole*. Incidentally, the motive for murder which was brought out in the book has been changed for this present film version—and to remarkably advantageous effect.

Also, Mr. Dmytryk has handled most excellently a superlative cast which plays the drama. Robert Ryan is frighteningly real as the hard, sinewy, loud-mouthed, intolerant and vicious murderer, and Robert Mitchum, Steve Brodie and George Cooper are variously revealing as his pals. Robert Young gives a fine taut performance as the patiently questioning D.A. whose mind and sensibilities are revolted—and eloquently expressed—by what he finds. Sam Levene is affectingly gentle in his brief bit as the Jewish victim, and Gloria Grahame is believably brazen and pathetic as a girl of the streets.

Indeed, *Crossfire* would warrant an A for accomplishment all around if it weren't for an irritating confusion of detailed exposition at the start—a jumble of names and identities which oppress a watcher's mind—and for a few illogical police slips and occasional stretches of heavy talk. Some of the slow dramatic tension is lost through these unhappy faults. But they can be generally forgiven for a thematically articulate film.

—*B.C., July 23, 1947*

CRUMB

Directed by Terry Zwigoff: director of photography. Maryse Alberti: edited by Victor Livingston: music by David Boeddinghaus: produced by Lynn O'Donnell and Mr. Zwigoff. Running time: 119 minutes.

With: Robert Crumb. Beatrice Crumb. Charles Crumb. Max Crumb. Dana Morgan. Robert Hughes and Aline Kominsky.

When the cartoonist Robert Crumb was a little boy, he reveals in Terry Zwigoff's riveting documentary portrait, he was sexually attracted to Bugs Bunny, even carrying around a picture of this buck-toothed rabbit. Eventually it became crumpled and was all but destroyed after he had his mother iron it for him. At twelve, he developed a new fixation. He became erotically obsessed with the television character Sheena, Queen of the Jungle.

Although Mr. Crumb went on to create such famous modern cartoon characters as Fritz the Cat and Mr. Natural, and helped to found the underground-comic movement, Bugs Bunny and Sheena continued to reverberate through his art. Bugs Bunny's cheery irreverence was sharpened into a satirical sensibility that has been compared to Daumier and George Grosz. Sheena's descendants are the devouring Amazonian women portrayed in work that is often savagely misogynistic and pornographically explicit.

The cartoonist's memories of his childhood sexual fantasies are only the tip of the confessional iceberg in *Crumb,* which the New York Film Festival is showing this evening at Alice Tully Hall. Much more than a polite documentary profile of an artist's life and times, the film offers an astonishingly unguarded portrait of Mr. Crumb, who is fifty-one, and his seriously dysfunctional family. Just when you think the film couldn't probe any more intimately, it off-handedly reveals information about people's medications, bathroom habits and genitalia.

Long stretches of the film are devoted to the cartoonist's talented, mentally disturbed elder brother, Charles, who committed suicide recently. Calmed by medication, Charles, who never moved out of his mother's house, recalls the homicidal impulses he felt toward Robert when they were growing up. The film offers ample documentation to show that Charles was as talented an artist as Robert. But as his mental illness worsened, he gave up drawing.

A third brother, Max, is also interviewed. A self punishing ascetic and sometime artist who lives in San Francisco, he is shown preparing to meditate while lying bare-backed on a bed of nails. Neither of the artist's two sisters cooperated in the making of the film.

Mr. Crumb makes no bones about his anger at his late father and at American society in general. He readily admits that his urge to succeed was fueled by a desire for revenge. His father, a Marine Corps officer turned businessman, is remembered as a cold and tyrannical straight-arrow who remained aloof from his eccentric sons and stopped speaking to Robert after a colleague showed him some of his work. In high school, the cartoonist was a nerd who could not get a date. As his autobiographical drawings of his high school days illustrate, he was permanently wounded by his adolescent peers' rejection.

Although Mr. Crumb and his characters are widely identified with the hippie movement, and he concedes that many of his ideas grew out of experiments with LSD, he never lived the hippie lifestyle. He was far too much of a misanthropic loner.

The artist's grievances extend well beyond high-school pariahhood. Early in the film, he expresses enormous bitterness at the paltry sums he made for two of his most famous works: a poster bearing the slogan "Keep on Truckin'" and the cover art for Big Brother and the Holding Company and Janis Joplin's best-selling album *Cheap Thrills.* He is shown abruptly turning down an offer from Hollywood, which he resents for mutilating his character Fritz the Cat.

If *Crumb* were merely a behind-the-scenes portrait of the artist and his troubled family, it would exert a gothic sort of fascination. But the film does much more. It succeeds at showing how one man's psychic wounds contributed to an art that transmutes personal pain into garish visual satire. While the film's amazingly candid interviews with the artist, his friends, family members, and his current and former wives shed light on the sources of his work, the final leap from neurosis into artistic brilliance remains mysterious.

The art critic Robert Hughes calls Mr. Crumb "the Brueghel of the twentieth century." That may be overstating it. But the film's many examples of Mr. Crumb's work present a vision of American life as a phantasmagoric gallery of grotesques that is as gripping as it is harshly funny.

—S.H., September 27, 1994

CRY, THE BELOVED COUNTRY

Directed by Zoltan Korda: written by Alan Paton, based on his novel: cinematographer, Robert Krasker: edited by David Eady: music by R. Gallois-Montbrun: produced by Mr. Korda and Mr. Paton: released by Lopert Films. Black and white. Running time: 105 minutes.

With: Canada Lee (Stephen Kumalo), Charles Carson (James Jarvis), Sidney Poitier (Reverend Msimangu), Joyce Carey (Margaret Jarvis), Geoffrey Keen (Father Vincent), Michael Goodliffe (Martens), Edric Connor (John Kumalo) and Lionel Ngakane (Absalom).

Out of Alan Paton's beautiful and profound narrative, *Cry, the Beloved Country,* which is, of course, a classic tale of the crisscross of racial tensions in modern South Africa, producer-director Zoltan Korda, with Mr. Paton by his side, has made a motion picture of comparable beauty and power—a motion picture that exemplifies the novel and redounds to the credit of the screen. Filmed on the broad uplands of Natal, in the slums of Johannesburg, and in the London studios of Mr. Korda, and played by a wonderful cast, headed by Canada Lee and Charles Carson, this lovely and compassionate work had its American premiere at the Bijou Theatre last night.

Those who have read the novel or saw the musical play, *Lost in the Stars,* based upon it, done here in 1949, are aware that the essential characteristic of Mr. Paton's masterful approach to material of angry implications was one of patience and humility. Within the dramatic situation arbitrarily constructed by him—a situation emerging from the chaos of conflict between blacks and whites in the supercharged community of South Africa—there was latent dynamite, ready to burst into melodramatics at the touch of a wrathful pen. But Mr. Paton, through his years of experience with the tormenting problem of race, had proceeded from wrath and frustration to the wisdom that is evidenced in his work.

And it is this profundity of wisdom, this discipline of the mind and the easily excited emotions, that most distinctly and gratifyingly marks this pictorially eloquent and faithful rendering of the novel to the screen. Where Mr. Paton limned the aspects of racial segregation in temperate words and brought forth the tragedy of conflict in the spiritual suffering of two men, Mr. Korda has used his cameras to dwell but briefly upon the literal scene of squalor and corruption in South Africa and has caught his drama in personalities.

True, the perceptive director has not hesitated to show the miserable living conditions of the blacks in Johannesburg's slums or to indicate frankly the strict enforcement of the South African code of "Jim Crow." But he has made evident these aspects only to set his scene, to establish the oppressiveness of the climate, without having his cameras groan.

The particular interest of Mr. Korda, working trenchantly from a script prepared by Mr. Paton, is the dark and terrible passage of two men through the valley of grief and distraction into which they are plunged by a mutually calamitous act. One is a simple, God-fearing Negro Anglican priest who comes down from the sturdy hills of Natal to Johannesburg to seek his sister and his missing son, and who arrives too late to save the lost lad from murdering a respected white man. And the other is the father of the white man murdered by the old priest's son—a rigid and bigoted farmer from the same fertile hills of Natal.

Out of the shock and bewilderment, the passion and despair, of these two men; out of the purging of their resentments in the obliterating fires of their griefs, and out of the dismal demonstration of the ironies that touch human lives, Mr. Paton and Mr. Korda achieve the illumination of their theme—which is that society may emerge from the darkness of fear and hate when it, too, is shaken and purged by the counterpart of grief.

In this illumination, Mr. Korda depends upon the light that is generated in his characters, and no better assist can be imagined than that contributed by Mr. Lee and Mr. Carson. Mr. Lee, the American actor, does a profoundly moving job in capturing the dignity, the fervor, and the humility of the old Zulu priest, especially when he is shaken by disillusion and despair. He even conveys the impression of being indigenous to the environment in which he plays. And Mr. Carson is intensely compelling as the stubborn, inarticulate man who acquires understanding through his misery and through the discovered example of the dead son for whom he grieves.

In other roles, Joyce Carey is poignant as the farmer's gentle wife, Michael Goodliffe is intense as a reform school warden and Lionel Ngakane is meek as the old priest's son. Sidney Poitier makes evident deep conflicts in the role of a young Negro priest and Geoffrey Keen is quietly authoritative as the head of the mission with which he works. All of the people who play natives are uniformly excellent, conveying in poetic rhythms of voice and body the haunting rhythm of the book.

It is difficult to do proper justice to the fine qualities of this film or to the courage and skill of Mr. Korda in transmitting such a difficult and sobering theme.

—B.C., January 24, 1952

THE CRYING GAME

Written and directed by Neil Jordan: director of photography. Ian Wilson: edited by Kant Pan: music by Anne Dudley: production designer. Jim Clay: produced by Stephen Woolley: released by Miramax Films. Running time: 112 minutes.

With: Forest Whitaker (Jody). Miranda Richardson (Jude). Stephen Rea (Fergus). Adrian Dunbar (Maguire). Breffini McKenna (Tinker). Joe Savino (Eddie). Birdie Sweeney (Tommy). Jaye Davidson (Dil) Andre Bernard (Jane). Jim Broadbent (Col) and Ralph Brown (Dave).

Neil Jordan, the Irish writer and director of *The Company of Wolves* (1985), *Mona Lisa* (1986) and *The Miracle* (1991), is one of a kind. He makes melodramas that are often very funny, fantasies that are commonsensical, and moral fables that are perverse. At heart, he is a madly unreconstructed romantic. In his view, the power of love can work miracles of a kind that would send Freud back to his own couch.

All of these things are evident in Mr. Jordan's elegant new film, *The Crying Game*, which will be shown at the New York Film Festival tonight and tomorrow.

When the film's subplots, all of which are germane, are stripped away, *The Crying Game* becomes a tale of a love that couldn't be but proudly is, although even this love could be a substitute for another love that never quite was.

If I sound vague, it's partly because the film's producers have pleaded with reviewers not to reveal important plot twists, and partly because Mr. Jordan's screenplay reveals itself as if it were an onion being peeled. The nubbin of onion remaining at the end is important only as a memory of the initially unviolated bulb. More from me you will not get.

The love story that dominates the film is about Fergus (Stephen Rea), a sweet-tempered, naive Irish Republican Army terrorist, and Dil (Jaye Davidson), the snappy, almost beautiful London hairstylist who captures his heart. Fergus is living in England under an assumed name after a botched kidnapping in Northern Ireland. He's lonely and haunted by the events that forced him into exile.

Dil is like no one he's ever met before. Wearing a tight spangled dress and earrings that look like Christmas tree ornaments, she drinks margaritas and flirts with no thought of what her political responsibilities might be. When she gets up on the stage at her favorite pub, the Metro Bar, and sings the film's title song, Fergus is hooked. Dil is glamorous, witty, and capable of a depth of love that Fergus has never known before.

Their idyll is short-lived. His past and her present surface in a manner to tear them apart. Fergus's former comrades show up in London and, threatening harm to the unsuspecting Dil, force Fergus to participate in one last job, the assassination of an English judge.

The film's penultimate sequence is as bloody and brutal as the extended opening sequences set in Northern Ireland, as Fergus, assigned to guard an I.R.A. hostage, first begins to understand "the war" in human terms. Yet for all its sorrowful realism, *The Crying Game* believes in the kind of redemption not often seen in movies since the 1930's and 40's. At times the film comes close to trash, or at least camp, but it's saved by the rare sensibility of Mr. Jordan, who isn't frivolous.

The *Crying Game* is full of masks. Fergus and Dil wear them, as do the people who have shaped Fergus in Ireland, including his I.R.A. girlfriend, Jude (Miranda Richardson), and the English soldier (Forest Whitaker) he comes to know in Northern Ireland. The biggest mask is that worn by the film itself, which pretends to be about the love affair of Fergus and Dil, although it really has more esoteric matters on its mind, the strength of political commitment and the role-playing of life's fugitives.

The film is exceptionally well acted by Mr. Rea, in a big, very complex role, and by some of the subsidiary players, including Jim Broadbent, the writer and star of Mike Leigh's *Sense of History,* as the Metro bartender who functions as the matchmaker for Fergus and Dil. There are times when Mr. Whitaker's English accent sounds post-synchronized, but the performance is good.

Mr. Jordan's screenplay could have done without the cautionary tale about the frog that agreed to ferry the scorpion to the other side of the river, which is told twice, but is otherwise both efficient and ingenious. The physical production is as lush as the film's romantic longings.

—V.C., September 26, 1992

DAMN YANKEES

Produced and directed by George Abbott and Stanley Donen; written by Mr. Abbott, based on the play by Mr. Abbott and Douglas Wallop and the novel *The Year the Yankees Lost the Pennant* by Mr. Wallop; cinematographer. Harold Lipstein; edited by Frank Bracht; music by Jerry Ross and Richard Adler; choreography by Bob Fosse; production designers. William Eckart and Jean Eckart; released by Warner Brothers. Running time: 110 minutes.

With: Tab Hunter (Joe Hardy). Gwen Verdon (Lola). Ray Walston (Applegate). Shannon Bolin (Meg). Nathaniel Frey (Smokey). Jimmie Komack (Rocky). Rae Allen (Gloria). Robert Shafer (Joe Boyd). Jean Stapleton (Sister) and Albert Linville (Vernon).

Maybe you think that was a heat wave that hit town yesterday. We prefer to think it was Gwen Verdon making her debut hereabouts as a star in a film.

For her sizzling performance in *Damn Yankees*, the Technicolored screen version of the Broadway show that is serving to return the Roxy to a picture-and-stage-show policy, is one of the hottest and heartiest we've seen in a musical movie in years. And if that isn't what warmed the weather, it should certainly do a lot to warm you.

As the sultry handmaiden of the Devil who is given the critical job of vamping a Cinderella rookie on the Washington Senators into forgetting his old place by the home fire, Miss Verdon is wondrously repeating the role she played on the stage—and doing it in a fashion that is rare and refreshing on the screen.

While she isn't exactly constructed along the lines of a Brigitte Bardot or blessed with the sort of facial beauty that Elizabeth Taylor has, this long-legged, swivel-jointed siren manufactures her own strong brand of sex, even when she is gleefully lampooning all the basic techniques of the camp. Indeed, although brilliant as a dancer and at heating the atmosphere, her exceptional achievements in this picture are as a comedienne.

If you're one of those aging admirers of old Fanny Brice or Lucille Ball, you'll delight in discovering Miss Verdon is a little of both in this show in addition to being a dancer who is probably as deft as any now in films. When she sings "A Little Brains, a Little Talent," with appropriate dancing gestures to describe the assets that a lady should have to seduce a man, it is comedy of an order that is so many levels above the ordinary run of screen humor that it comes like a summer breeze. And when she travesties the techniques of seduction in "Whatever Lola Wants Lola Gets," she's as torrid as a West Indian wiggler and as funny as W. C. Fields.

Miss Verdon has the sort of fine, fresh talent that the screen badly needs these days.

But lest she seem to be the whole show, let us hasten to proclaim that there's a great deal more to *Damn Yankees* than this wonderful red-headed dame. Like the George Abbott stage show before it, it has class, imagination, verve, and a good many of the same performers who did so charmingly by it on Broadway.

Ray Walston is still the Devil, that sly, hissing little man who decides to fix it so the Senators can beat the

Yankees for the American League pennant and cause millions of people to go mad. Shannon Bolin is still the sweet and loving wife of the middle-aged Senators fan whom the Devil selects to change into a sensational "long-ball hitter" and plant on the Senators team. And Nathaniel Frey is still the genial, white-haired manager of the Senators.

Tab Hunter may not have the larynx that Stephen Douglass had as the original hero, but he has the clean, naive look of a lad breaking into the big leagues and into the magical company of a first-rate star. He is really appealing with Miss Verdon in the boogie-woogie ballet, "Two Lost Souls," which is done in a smoky, soft-lit setting and is the dandiest dance number in the film.

As for the obvious improvements over the show as it was done on the stage, there are genuine outdoor baseball sequences (including some sneak shots of the real Yankees at play) and an overall speed-up of movement and flexibility.

Mr. Abbott and Stanley Donen have codirected. While they have held to the format of the show on the stage they have given it cinematic treatment that is suitable in changes and pace. Most of the musical score is in the picture, well played and well sung. Mr. Abbott and Mr. Donen also were the producers. Warner Brothers is releasing the film.

If you can't get to see the World Series, get to see *Damn Yankees*. It's some show.

—*B.C., September 27, 1958*

THE DAMNED

Directed by Luchino Visconti: written (in Italian, with English subtitles) by Nicola Badalucco, Enrico Medioli and Mr. Visconti: directors of photography, Armando Nannuzzi and Pasquale De Santis: edited by Ruggero Mastroianni: music by Maurice Jarre: produced by Alfredo Levy and Ever Hagglag: released by Warner Brothers-Seven Arts. Running time: 155 minutes.

With: Dirk Bogarde (Friederich Bruckmann), Ingrid Thulin (Baroness Sophie von Essenbeck), Helmut Griem (Aschenbach), Helmut Berger (Martin von Essenbeck), Charlotte Rampling (Elisabeth Thall-man), Florinda Bolkan (Olga) and René Kolldehoff (Baron Konstantine von Essenbeck).

Luchino Visconti's *The Damned* may be the chef d'oeuvre of the great Italian director (*La Terra Trema, Rocco and His Brothers, Sandra*)—a spectacle of such greedy passion, such uncompromising sensation, and such obscene shock that it makes you realize how small and safe and ordinary most movies are. Experiencing it is like taking a whiff of ammonia—it's not conventionally pleasant, but it makes you see the outlines of everything around you with just a little more clarity.

The Damned, called *Götterdämmerung* in Europe, opens like *Buddenbrooks*—with so many characters introduced so quickly that one part of your mind will spend the rest of the movie just trying to sort them out, which is a rare treat since the decline of the novel-as-genealogy. It also draws on *Hamlet, Macbeth,* the legend of the Nibelungen, on recent history (as it might be fabricated in something like *True Detective*) and on Visconti's love for the grand cinematic gesture.

Its story is that of a Krupp-like German steel dynasty in the first two years (1933–1934) of Hitler's struggle to consolidate his power. It's not so much that the von Essenbecks symbolize Germany—they *are* Germany. The film does occasionally record events in real Germany—the burning of the books, assignations in squalid rooming houses and (for almost a quarter of an hour and with such loving detail that it almost wrecks the balance of the film) the "night of the long knives," when Ernst Röhm and most of his SA (Storm Troops) were assassinated by the SS (Elite Guard).

Most of *The Damned,* however, takes place within the huge, dark drawing rooms, the bedrooms, corridors, baths, and banquet halls of the Ruhr Valhalla where the von Essenbecks, surrounded by silent servants and as isolated as gods, struggle for control of "the factory," the power of the universe.

There's the old Baron, an aristocrat who has made no commitments to Hitler, but only because he regards Hitler with the distaste of a snob. There are also his son, Konstantin (René Kolldehoff), a follower of Röhm in matters sexual as well as political; a young cousin, Aschenbach (Helmut Griem), an SS man scheming to keep von Essenbeck arms from the SA; the Baroness Sophie (Ingrid Thulin), the widowed daughter-in-law who likes to see her son, Martin (Helmut Berger), the Baron's heir, dress up in extraordinarily convincing Marlene Dietrich drag; and Friedrich Bruckmann (Dirk Bogarde), a mortal who, with Sophie, plots to acquire the von Essenbeck fortune, power, and name.

If the film can be said to have a protagonist, I suppose it would be Bogarde who, after murdering the old Baron in his bed, finds himself finally destroyed in a bizarre reworking of classic consequences. Visconti, however, keeps the melodrama at such a distance and plays it at such a high pitch that there can't be much thought about protagonists and antagonists.

The Damned, while having validity as a political and social parable, is mind-blinding as a spectacle of fabulous corruption, detailed within the family organism that so fascinates Visconti. Like *La Terra Trema* and *Rocco and His Brothers,* Visconti's new film keeps the audience outside the spectacle, but the von Essenbecks, unlike the families in the earlier works, are not only a family—they create their own social milieu. Nothing that happens outside seems to matter much because despite our knowledge of history, we know that Germany's fate is the von Essenbecks'.

The film triumphs over a number of bothersome things, including too-quick transformations of characters, dialogue of epic flatness ("Complicity grows. I've accepted a ruthless logic and I shall never get away from it"), inconsistency of language (most of it is in English, but some is in German for no apparent reason), self-conscious references to great moments in history (the Reichstag fire), and scenes of melodrama that would strain even Wagner (as when Martin decides to "destroy" his mother by raping her).

All of the performances are excellent, but at least two are superb, that of Miss Thulin and Berger, a young Austrian actor who gives, I think, the performance of the year.

The Damned, however, is not a film that depends on dialogue or performance, but on Visconti's vision that capitalizes on what would be theatrical excesses in anyone else's work. He likes to begin scenes in close-up with one character talking to another, who may remain unseen, unknown, for minutes at a time. The entire film evokes a sense of makeup and masquerade, both physical and emotional. Color also is important. The first shot of the movie is a close-up of the orange flames of a blast furnace, after which the light seems to dim progressively to a twilight, set off by splotches of red, first a flower in a buttonhole, then Nazi armbands and flags and, finally, blood.

The Damned is a movie of great perversity—so intransigent that I think even von Stroheim would have liked it. It opened yesterday at the Festival Theater.

—V.C., December 19, 1969

DANCE WITH A STRANGER

Directed by Mike Newell; written by Shelagh Delaney; cinematographer, Peter Hannan; edited by Mick Audsley; music by Richard Hartley; production designer, Andrew Mollo; produced by Roger Randall-Cutler; released by Samuel Goldwyn Company. Running time: 102 minutes.

With: Miranda Richardson (Ruth Ellis), Rupert Everett (David Blakely), Ian Holm (Desmond Cussen), Matthew Carroll (Andy), Tom Chadbon (Anthony Findlater), Jane Bertish (Carole Findlater), David Troughton (Cliff Davis), Paul Mooney (Clive Gunnell) and Stratford Johns (Morrie Conley).

Like François Truffaut's *Peau Douce* (1964), the very good new English film titled *Dance with a Stranger* takes an utterly commonplace crime of passion and finds something very particular in it. Unlike Truffaut's hard-edged romantic drama, a fictional tale about the last, fatal liaison of a philandering literary celebrity, the new film, based on a true story, contains no characters who would have had any claim to fame except for the events that ended their story.

On July 13, 1955, Ruth Ellis, the former hostess of a rather sleazy late-night London establishment called the Little Club, and the mother of two young children, one of whom was born out of wedlock, was hanged for the murder of David Blakely, her young, somewhat better-born lover. Though Blakely had some notoriety as an automobile racer, it was still the kind of case, according to Shelagh Delaney, who wrote the screenplay, that newspapers headlined "Blonde Shoots Man in Hampstead." Ruth Ellis has gone into the archives not for what she did but for what the state did to her. She was the last woman in Britain to be sent to the gallows.

Dance with a Stranger, which opens today at the Paris Theater, is an unsentimental speculation on the events leading up to the murder, made fascinating by what seems—after the fact—to be their inevitability. Miss Delaney and Mike Newell, the director, are clearly appalled that Ruth should have been hanged, believing, I suspect, that it was less for her crime than for her way of life at a time when women were expected to remain squeaky clean. Ruth Ellis was the kind of woman who could be easily referred to as "that tart."

Dance with a Stranger is not a polemic. It's a beautifully acted cat-and-mouse story, in which Ruth Ellis, the otherwise tough-minded, pragmatic "good-time girl," loses her wits when she finds herself cornered by her love for a charming, totally unreliable man. When she finally strikes back, it has the effect of being not an aggressive act but the ultimate expression of her desperate masochism.

Giving the film its special edge is the striking performance of Miranda Richardson, a new English actress who makes her smashing film debut as Ruth Ellis. I've no idea what Miss Richardson looks like in real life, but in *Dance with a Stranger* she appears to be one of the more successful of the millions of young women who in the early 1950's modeled their hair color and their mannerisms on those of *Marilyn Monroe.*

Beneath the platinum rinse and the heavy makeup, Miss Richardson's Ruth Ellis is anything but innocent, though she isn't very bright when it comes to men. It's apparent to everyone, including Ruth's stolid, masochistic, would-be lover, Desmond Cussen (Ian Holm), that David Blakely (Rupert Everett) is bad news. He drinks too much, beats her up with regularity, and breaks dates without explanation. To Ruth, however, he remains an incredibly romantic figure, a representative of the aristocracy. In actuality, he's just another spoiled, middle-class young man who's indulged occasionally by a rich stepfather.

Almost as good as Miss Richardson are Mr. Everett (*Another Country*), who has the kind of dark, almost pretty good looks that turn women like Ruth into jelly, and Mr. Holm, who makes Desmond Cussen's obsession with Ruth as sadly comprehensible as Ruth's with David Blakely. Desmond is always around to pick up the pieces after Ruth's crises. He puts up the money to send Ruth's ten-year-old son, Andy (Matthew Carroll), to boarding school and, without knowing it, supplies the murder weapon.

Miss Delaney (*A Taste of Honey*) has written an effectively lean screenplay that has been directed with straightforward simplicity by Mr. Newell, best-known here for his direction of the television miniseries *Blood Feud.* The writer and the director have come up with some wonderfully vivid moments that define the central situation, including a scene in which a temporarily contrite David arrives unexpectedly at Ruth's flat and says that she has to marry him. "Why?" says Ruth. "Are you pregnant?"

In another scene, as the doggedly faithful Desmond watches her make up for the evening, she puts a pair of false eyelashes on him—an unspoken reference to David's handsomeness and his eyelashes that someone has earlier suggested are so long they must be fake. Watching impassively as things go increasingly wrong is young Andy who, looking forward to boarding school, is impressed most by the fact that all his clothes now have his name stitched in them.

The film is not always clear about David's exact station in life, nor about the influence his pre-Ruth friends have on him. In this way, he seems as shadowy to us as he is to Ruth. Nor does the film ever take the trouble to explain much about Desmond Cussen. We never learn how he makes the money he can spend on Ruth without expecting anything in return.

These, however, are not major criticisms. *Dance with a Stranger* is a startling and involving melodrama about the sort of banal crime that obsessed Truffaut, not only in *La Peau Douce* (*The Soft Skin*), but also in *The Woman Next Door* and, to a lesser extent, in *The Bride Wore Black.* I think he would have liked it.

—*V.C., August 9, 1985*

DANGEROUS LIAISONS

Directed by Stephen Frears; written by Christopher Hamilton, based on his play, adapted from the novel *Les Liaisons Dangereuses* by Choderlos de Laclos; director of photography, Philippe Rousselot; edited by Mick Audsley; music by George Fenton; production designer, Stuart Craig; produced by Norma Heyman and Hank Moonjean;

released by Warner Brothers. Running time: 118 minutes.

With: Glenn Close (Marquise de Merteuil), John Malkovich (Vicomte de Valmont), Michelle Pfeiffer (Madame de Tourvel), Swoosie Kurtz (Madame de Volanges), Keanu Reeves (Chevalier Danceny) and Mildred Natwick (Madame de Rosemonde).

Like the elaborate dresses into which she has been fitted with a good deal of help, the Marquise de Merteuil (Glenn Close) seems always about to burst, not because of any engineering failure but in anticipation of some delightful new viciousness, a plot of such subtlety that only she can appreciate it. She keeps control of herself and simply smiles.

In the fashion of the day, the Marquise's waist is cinched to the point where her generous bust has no place to go but up, and possibly out. It can't be comfortable but, among other things, the Marquise has learned that to be a successful woman in France in the 1780's, the last decade of the ancien regime, one has to put up with a certain amount of pain. The pleasure will follow.

Pleasure also follows a certain amount of time spent becoming accustomed to the stylized mannerisms of *Dangerous Liaisons,* Stephen Frears's handsome, intelligent adaptation of Christopher Hampton's London and Broadway play, *Les Liaisons Dangereuses.*

The source material is the classic 18th-century epistolary novel by Choderlos de Laclos, adapted and updated in 1959 by Roger Vadim as a vehicle for Gerard Philippe and Jeanne Moreau. (The Vadim film was not released here until 1961, after the censors demanded that the lighting in several scenes be dimmed to obscure the nudity.) Though I have fond, fuzzy memories of that film, I can't imagine that it could come anywhere near the Frears-Hampton version in terms of witty, entertaining, if occasionally overripe decadence.

Dangerous Liaisons, which opens today at the 68th Street Playhouse, is comparatively small in physical scope, having been filmed with a handful of actors, mostly indoors, though in some of France's most magnificent chateaus. Whenever it does go outside, it resolutely avoids looking at the conditions that, a few

years later, will result in the first great bloody revolution of the modern age.

Mr. Frears and Mr. Hampton resist the temptations of hindsight, as they also resist the unimaginative movie maker's desire to open up the play. Instead, *Dangerous Liaisons* unfolds as a kind of lethal drawing-room comedy with occasional more or less obligatory visits to various bedchambers. History's echoes are there, but they're heard mostly in the hollow sounds of footsteps on parquet floors.

At the center of the film are the Marquise de Merteuil and Vicomte de Valmont (John Malkovich), her rich aristocratic former lover, who now devote themselves to the pursuit of sexual liaisons, not necessarily for pleasure but for the power they confer on the one who is loved but does not love. Power is all. It's apparent in the film's opening sequence that, since Valmont still has a passion for the Marquise, she holds the advantage.

The Marquise has a plan: to even the score with a lover who has left her, she asks Valmont to seduce the man's virginal, convent-bred fiancee. Valmont has his own plan. He has set his sights on a faithful young wife whose husband is serving abroad. Valmont's idea of pleasure is to persuade the wife to surrender herself to him without, for a moment, abandoning her principles.

When seduction has become such a commonplace pastime, refinements in betrayal are immensely important.

The Marquise insists that Valmont undertake her mission and, to keep him interested, agrees to spend one night with him if he can prove that he has also been successful with the faithful wife. Valmont accepts, but he makes a fatal mistake. He falls in love along the way.

From time to time, Mr. Hampton's dialogue comes perilously close to camp, especially at the beginning. When the ear gets used to it and to actors for whom, like Mr. Malkovich, this sort of dialogue initially seems as foreign as Eskimo, the film takes off in the breathless pursuit of its scheming seducers.

Nothing Miss Close has done on the screen before approaches the richness and comic delicacy of her work as the Marquise. She was exceptionally good in *Fatal Attraction* but, compared with her elegant performance as the Marquise, her abandoned mistress in the earlier film is a dreadnought plowing across a sea no bigger than a bathtub.

The Marquise is a wonderfully written role of almost classical dimensions. When she spars with Valmont, finally admitting that her game is cruelty rather than betrayal, she assumes command of the movie, hanging onto it until the very last shot.

Valmont would not seem to be a role that Mr. Malkovich was born to play. He looks and sounds more like 20th-century Pittsburgh than 18th-century Paris. Yet once the shock of seeing him in powdered wigs recedes, he is unexpectedly fine. The intelligence and strength of the actor shape the audience's response to him. He's no mincing fop but a man caught in what is finally an unequal struggle.

Michelle Pfeiffer, whose brightly colored, contemporary beauty seems to have been muted by camera filters, is another happy surprise as the pure wife who is romantically swindled by Valmont. Equally good are Uma Thurman as the convent girl who takes to sin with enthusiasm, Swoosie Kurtz as her worried mother and the indefatigable Mildred Natwick as Valmont's old aunt.

The film looks great, in part, I assume, because of the contributions of Stuart Craig, the production designer, and Philippe Rousselot, the cameraman. *Dangerous Liaisons* seems to use a lot of two-shots, in which one character is seen instead of two, the rest of the image being filled with details of decor. For Mr. Frears (*My Beautiful Laundrette, Sammy and Rosie Get Laid*), environment doesn't have to be working-class to be important.

—V.C., December 21, 1988

DANIEL

Directed by Sidney Lumet: written by E.L. Doctorow. based on his novel *The Book of Daniel*: director of photography. Andrzej Bartkowiak: edited by Peter C. Frank: music by Bob James: production designer. Philip Rosenberg: produced by Burtt Harris: released by Paramount Pictures. Running time: 130 minutes.

With: Timothy Hutton (Daniel Isaacson). Edward Asner (Jacob Ascher). Mandy Patinkin (Paul Isaacson). Lindsay Crouse (Rochelle). Joseph Leon (Selig Mindish). Amanda Plummer (Susan Isaacson). Ellen Barkin (Phyllis Isaacson). Tovah Feldshuh (Linda Mindish). John Rubinstein (Robert Lewin). Maria Tucci (Lise Lewin) and Julie Bovasso (Frieda Stein).

As "the story of two generations of a family whose ruling passion is not success or money or love, but social justice," Sidney Lumet's film *Daniel*—thus described by Mr. Lumet and by E.L. Doctorow, whose screenplay is based upon his own novel—is a work of noble and unusual ambitions. That these ambitions become the film's most admirable element is a sign of just how difficult it must have been to bring this material to the screen, as well as an indication of problems that are more mundane.

As was the case with Mr. Doctorow's *Ragtime,* history and fiction are mingled here, in a manner that is innovative but that can also become confusing. Audiences not closely familiar with the case of Julius and Ethel Rosenberg may not be certain where they differ from Mr. Doctorow's Paul and Rochelle Isaacson, whose story is told here in highly compassionate terms (the film views their fate as abhorrent, though it does not speak explicitly to the question of their innocence or guilt). While it does not present a new argument about the Rosenbergs (as does the current book *The Rosenberg File: A Search for the Truth,* in which Ronald Radosh and Joyce Milton postulate the guilt of Julius Rosenberg and at least the complicity of his wife), its more bombastic passages amount to an indirect partisanship that will undoubtedly fuel the continuing controversy surrounding the case.

Daniel, which opens today at the Coronet Theater, incorporates its thinly fictionalized version of the Rosenberg story into a larger family drama: that of a son searching to determine the truth about his parents, and through this quest finally coming to terms with their values and their legacy. This material hardly lends itself to any standard movie treatment. Imagine a courtship scene between two young radicals, as the young man passionately lectures his future bride about the means of production, and you may have some idea of how idiosyncratic Daniel can be. With Paul Robeson singing on the soundtrack, and with its painstaking re-creations of rallies, Bronx neighborhood scenes, and college vignettes set in the late 1930's and early 40's, *Daniel* means to evoke a powerful sense of the radical left in that period. But its use of these memories, and of the passions they arouse, is less sure than its ability to conjure them up.

In Mr. Doctorow's novel *The Book of Daniel,* the title character is the grown son of the Isaacsons, who, like the Rosenbergs, have been convicted and executed for participating in a conspiracy to commit atomic espionage. The very narration of the novel, as Daniel tries to keep to the third person but frequently lapses into the first, is a measure of the intensity of his struggle. Daniel's bitterness throughout the book is a vital part of his efforts to come to terms with his parents' histories and with his own. The two generations are seen as closely intertwined, chiefly through anguish the son exhibits while he relives his parents' nightmare.

The film is less passionate and more ponderous, a work composed of much more disparate pieces. It begins with an extreme close-up of a scowling, furious Daniel (Timothy Hutton) as he recites a definition for electrocution, and this device is repeated periodically throughout the film (with Daniel explaining a different form of punishment in each instance). These scenes, which are all that remain of the narrator's tone, effectively capture Daniel's rage—but do not convey that his struggle is painful and continuing, and that he is in the process of change. As a result, much of the movie is angry and self-righteous, without sufficiently close links between Daniel's story and that of his parents, and without the sympathetic elements that make the novel a complex, human story, rather than a tract.

Mr. Doctorow's screenplay would seem to be a lot like his novel; indeed, many of the passages of dialogue are virtually the same. The trouble is that they have been transported whole, so that they now become overbearing speeches. Scene after scene in the film begins as a new supporting character—the cast, like the casts of most recent Lumet films, is enormous—launches into a windy and uninterrupted soliloquy. Mr. Lumet, far from keeping the histrionics in check, seems to have actively encouraged his actors to go for broke during each one's showstopping minute or two. The film's dramatic progress is repeatedly halted as actors in minor roles indulge themselves to the utmost, offering what are clearly meant to be bravura turns.

This isn't a film that can easily withstand so many interruptions, since its structure is already fragmented. In addition to intercutting Daniel's late-1960's story with that of his parents, Mr. Lumet also fractures time within the flashbacks; when the Isaacson family boards a bus to attend a Paul Robeson concert in Peekskill, New York (which would later develop into a riot), they aren't seen arriving until almost an hour later. Of course, this isn't forgetfulness on Mr. Lumet's part. It's consistent with a strategy of presenting all of the exposition early in the story and saving for last all the scenes that are unavoidably wrenching. The film ends with two lengthy, detailed electrocution sequences, followed by two funeral scenes, followed by a coda that cannot help being uplifting. This is moving, and then some—it's enough to make the audience feel clobbered.

Daniel has been directed in what is immediately recognizable as Mr. Lumet's recent style. There is somber, stylized lighting. There are plenty of long shots. And there is unusual casting, which is ordinarily one of the things this director does best. Here, though, there are too many moments in which the casting undercuts the film's plausibility. For instance, John Rubinstein does a good job as Daniel's stepfather, but he simply doesn't look much older than Mr. Hutton or than Amanda Plummer, who plays his sister. The members of the Isaacson family don't much resemble one another, either. And Lindsay Crouse, who as Rochelle has a Yiddish-speaking mother and a husband who in one scene dances around a room like Tevye, still has traces of the brogue she used as an Irish nurse in Mr. Lumet's *Verdict.*

Miss Crouse, along with Edward Asner as the Isaacsons' lawyer, gives the kind of heavy, sturdy performance that is the order of the day here. The few actors who attempt anything more offbeat—like Ellen Barkin, who has a scene-stealing presence in the tiny role of Daniel's wife—are left with little to do. Miss Plummer brings a frightening urgency to the role of Daniel's troubled sister, but she's almost too real and unpredictable for her surroundings here. Ilan M. Mitchell-Smith and Jena Greco do a good job playing childhood versions of Daniel and his sister. Mr. Hutton has some fine moments, particularly in the latter part of the movie. But his role, as written and edited, lacks context and continuity.

If the book succeeds in emerging finally as Daniel's story, the movie remains more focused on Paul and Rochelle. Miss Crouse and Mandy Patinkin—who has some very touching moments with Daniel as a boy, explaining the hidden radical messages in everything from a day at the beach to a Wheaties package—both work very hard at those key characterizations. And at the last minute the movie spoils it all.

When Rochelle says goodbye to her children, even the tiny daughter has been directed to walk across the room and pause dramatically while speaking. Their mother has hardly flown out the door when, seconds later, in rushes their father, behaving like a punch-drunk Jimmy Durante. These are the moments when the audience hardly needs to see showy acting, when instead it needs to believe it is seeing a family caught in an agony of unprecedented dimension.

—*J.M., August 26, 1983*

DANTON

Directed by Andrzej Wajda; written (in French, with English subtitles) by Jean-Claude Carrière, Mr. Wajda, Agnieszka Holland, Boleslaw Michalek and Jacek Gasiorowski, based on the play *The Danton Affair* by Stanislawa Przbyszewska; director of photography, Igor Luther; edited by Halina Prugar-Kelling; music by Jean Prodromides; art designers, Allan Starski and Gilles Vaster; produced by Margaret Menegoz; released by Triumph Releasing. Running time: 136 minutes.

With: Gérard Depardieu (Danton), Wojciech Pszoniak (Robespierre), Anne Alvaro (Eleanor Duplay), Roland Blanche (Lacroix), Patrice Chereau (Camille Desmoulins) and Emmanuelle Debever (Louison Danton).

Compared to the massive scale of the Russian Revolution, the French Revolution of 1789–95 seems almost to have been a chamber piece. Though armies supporting Louis XVI crossed France's border seeking to save the Bourbon monarchy, and though all of France eventually become involved in the bloodshed, the most decisive battles of the Revolution were fought in Paris, in the political clubs and on the streets.

In Paris, the Revolution's leaders, with the backing of the angry mobs, set policies that the rest of the country, left to their own devices, would probably have disowned, at least initially. The course of the Revolution was shaped by a small group of extraordinary men, all young, who started out as idealists, then became comrades and close friends, godfathers to one another's children. Within four years, they had split into factions as mortal enemies. Men did not hesitate to send to the guillotine former boon companions, now branded as traitors to the fatherland.

This peculiar, dreadful intimacy of a handful of remarkable personalities is vividly dramatized in *Danton*, Andrzej Wajda's fine, comparatively ascetic historical film that will be shown at the New York Film Festival at Lincoln Center today and tomorrow.

Chief among these personalities are Georges Danton and Maximilien Robespierre. Danton is the passionate, vulgar, not entirely honest man of the people, a hugely popular leader of the Revolutionary left who becomes increasingly moderate as the Revolution adopts policies of extermination. Robespierre, called "the incorruptible," is the small, fastidiously dressed, rigorously moral lawyer from Arras who, being convinced that Danton's moderation is a betrayal of the Revolution, engineers his trial and execution. "Robespierre, you will follow me within three months!" the furious Danton screams as he is hauled off to the guillotine and, as things turned out, he was absolutely right.

Danton, a Franco-Polish coproduction, was directed in France by Mr. Wajda from a screenplay by Jean-Claude Carrière, based on a stage play by Stanislawa Przybyszewska. Gérard Depardieu, who is, of course, a French actor, stars as the sympathetic Danton. Wojciech Pszoniak, a Polish actor, shares star billing as the thin-lipped voice of reason, Robespierre. That the Robespierrists, all of whom are seen as fanatics, some slightly less opportunistic than others, should be played by Polish actors, while the earthy, hearty, mostly honest Dantonists are played by French actors, is just one of the possible reasons why the Polish Government has not yet seen fit to release the film at home.

Without stretching things too much, I suppose, Mr. Wajda presents us with a Danton who is the articulate conscience of the Revolution, someone, perhaps, not entirely unlike Lech Walesa, the popular spokesman of Poland's Solidarity movement. On the other hand, Robespierre is seen as being completely removed from the practical needs and real feelings of the people, a stern father-figure of a dictator, a man who doesn't hesitate to approve the murder of thousands of people for the fatherland's ultimate good.

In an interview in *Le Monde*, Mr. Wajda denies all

associations between eighteenth-century France and twentieth-century Poland, though he does say that Danton represents the West and Robespierre the East.

Whether or not these associations hold true are beside the point of the film. *Danton* brilliantly illuminates one of the most fascinating periods of the French Revolution—those early months in 1794 when Danton, having been in self-imposed retirement in the country, returned to Paris to attempt to stop the Terror. Louis had been beheaded in January 1793. By October 1793, the Terror was picking up momentum, with the execution of Marie Antoinette, the liberal-thinking Duc D'Orleans, the chatty, letter-writing Madame Roland, and the leaders of the Girondists, the Revolution's moderates. In returning to Paris instead of fleeing the country, as his friends advised him to do, Danton knew he was leaving his head exposed to the guillotine.

In keeping with the chamber-piece nature of this Revolution, *Danton* is played out in a series of mostly small, intimate, beautifully defined confrontations between the robust, commonsensical Danton and the steely Robespierre. It's to Mr. Carrière's credit, as the screenwriter, that these scenes should be so truly dramatic and understandable, even, I suspect, to someone who has no special knowledge of or interest in the course of the Revolution.

It's to Mr. Wajda's credit that though his sympathies are clearly with Danton, played with all stops out by Mr. Depardieu, it is Robespierre, played with silky neuroticism by Mr. Pszoniak, who emerges as the film's most arresting, possibly tragic figure.

Not so effective are those scenes that attempt to place the personal-political drama in the context of a city and a nation in rebellion. There is something as perfunctory as there is obligatory about the crowd scenes. They remind me, in fact, of those Hollywood mobs, led by Blanche Yurka as Madame Defarge, that were out to get Charles Darnay in the 1935 *A Tale of Two Cities*. It also doesn't help that the French dialogue of the Polish actors, including Mr. Pszoniak, has not been especially well post-synchronized with the movements of the actors' lips.

Mr. Wajda and Mr. Carrière haven't exactly cleaned up Danton's reputation, but the bad things remain offscreen. There are references to the taking of bribes, to his love of women and property, and he himself asks forgiveness for having formed the notori-ous Committee of Public Safety, the body through which Robespierre came to control the country. Not emphasized at all is Danton's part in the September 1793 massacre in which mobs were encouraged to ransack Paris prisons and, without discrimination, murder everyone they could lay hands on as agents of the feared monarchist counterrevolution. Danton was not as clean as a hound's tooth.

What the film does most effectively is dramatize his later conviction that the Revolution's fury was itself a betrayal of the Revolution, as he says so eloquently in the trial that is the film's climax.

In addition to Mr. Depardieu and Mr. Pszoniak, the excellent cast includes Patrice Chereau as Danton's journalist-friend, Camille Desmoulins; Angela Winkler as Lucille Desmoulins, Camille's wife who followed him to the scaffold; Boguslaw Linda, as Saint Just; and Roger Planchon, who is particularly good as Fourquier Tinville, who prosecuted Danton and his associates in a rigged trial.

Danton is a major work from this major filmmaker.
—*V.C., September 28, 1983*

DARK EYES

Directed by Nikita Mikhalkov; written (in Italian, with English subtitles) by Alexander Adabachian, Mr. Mikhalkov and Suso Cecchi D'Amico, based on the stories "The Lady with the Dog," "The Name-Day Party," "Anna Around the Neck," and "My Wife" by Anton Chekhov; director of photography, Franco de Giacomo; edited by Enzo Meniconi; music by Francis Lai; art designers, Mario Garbuglia and Mr. Adabachian; produced by Silvia D'Amico Bendico and Carlo Cucchi; released by Island Pictures. Running time: 118 minutes.

With: Marcello Mastroianni (Romano), Silvana Mangano (Elisa), Marthe Keller (Tina), Elena Sofonova (Anna), Pina Cei (Elisa's Mother), Vsevolod Larienov (Pavel), Innokenti Smoktunovski (The Governor) and Roberto Herlitzka (The Lawyer).

Nikita Mikhalkov's *Dark Eyes,* tonight's convivial opening attraction of the 25th New York Film Festival at Lincoln Center, is both enchanting and enchanted, a triumph composed of seemingly irreconcilable contradictions.

Dark Eyes is—technically—a pastiche, but it has the manner of something freshly conceived. It's Russian to the core, yet much of it is set in Italy and its star is the matchless Marcello Mastroianni. It's a wise, ruefully funny Chekhovian comedy, though Chekhov did not write it. It takes one into a turn-of-the-century world that's as casually prescient as those of *The Three Sisters* and *Uncle Vanya,* without for a minute seeming to be.

Though it's about a man with the soul of an artist and the manner of a buffoon, about the man's abandoned aspirations and doomed love affairs, as well as about the heedless follies of the new European bourgeoisie, *Dark Eyes* is consistently exhilarating. In the steadfast resolve of a fellow who's an utter failure, it dramatizes a truly Chekhovian concept of comedy.

Like John Huston, Mr. Mikhalkov, best known here for *Slave of Love* and *Oblomov,* is an eclectic filmmaker who manages to honor his source material. In *Dark Eyes,* the Russian director borrows freely from four Chekhov stories, mostly from "The Lady with the Dog" and "The Name-Day Party," to create an original work that Chekhov would never have written.

The film begins and ends aboard a Mediterranean steamer en route to Italy from Greece. Romano (Mr. Mastroianni), a garrulous Italian fellow with frayed cuffs and the flush of an alcoholic, corners a Russian passenger, in the ship's saloon, and more or less pins down the stranger while he reminisces about the great, lost love of his life, a young Russian woman he met some years ago at an Italian spa.

In what is virtually a single, chronological flashback, Romano recalls his ironic downfall. It all began to go wrong, he remembers, at his wife's birthday party, at which point the film cuts to an earlier time and a huge estate in the Italian countryside.

The day is hot and still. People wander about the lawn. They play croquet. Elisa (Silvana Mangano), Romano's wife, attempts to attend to her duties as hostess while coping with the news that the family fortune may have been wiped out. Guests drink tea, eat strawberries, and gossip. Small boys in sailor suits run about making too much noise. Boredom is in the air. Worry is only partly disguised. During the afternoon's musicale, Elisa cannot sit without fidgeting.

Romano is no help to her. The once-promising student of architecture, who "had the luck to marry an heiress," has long since given up any idea of a career. Seduced by money, Romano has accepted his position as consort and court jester. In the course of this party, he makes a fool of himself to amuse the children, flirts half-heartedly with his bird-brained mistress (Marthe Keller) and sneaks off for a nap. At the end of the day, Romano is so exhausted he feels he must go away for a few weeks "to take the waters."

Dark Eyes is as much about the lost marriage of Romano and Elisa as it is about Romano's love for Anna (Elena Sofonova), the young Russian woman he meets at the spa and with whom, initially, he begins an affair just to pass the time. He doesn't find Anna especially interesting "physically," though he feels there is something "pure" about her. Back home, Romano can't get Anna out of his mind. Under the pretense of selling a newly patented process for the manufacture of unbreakable glass, Romano sets off for Russia to find Anna.

Mr. Mastroianni's remarkable performance, both heartbreaking and farcical, sets the tone for *Dark Eyes,* whose emotional landscape is as broad and rich as its physical terrain. The screenplay, by Alexander Adabachian and Mr. Mikhalkov "with the collaboration of Suso Cecchi D'Amico" makes astonishingly successful and intelligent use of the Chekhov material. Mr. Mikhalkov and his collaborators have folded key moments from "The Name-Day Party" into "The Lady with the Dog," borrowing from another tale, "Anna Around the Neck," for the substance of Anna's character, and taking inspiration from "My Wife" to arrive at their own conclusion.

The screenplay can be faulted only for being more shapely than Chekhovian, but then this is a movie, not a short story.

Though Mr. Mastroianni's performance is one of the highlights of his career, those by the other actors are almost in his league. Miss Sofonova, a beautiful, new young Russian actress, is both innocent and winning as the not completely naive Anna. Miss Mangano's Elisa is as complex as Mr. Mastroianni's Romano, while Miss Keller, trapped for too many years in sudsy romantic roles, is here revealed to be a comic actress of sweet, rare humor.

Occasionally (especially in the spa sequences) Mr. Mikhalkov's vision appears to have been unduly influenced by the style of Federico Fellini, possibly because the orchestrations make Francis Lai's soundtrack score sound uncomfortably like one by Nino Rota. There also are times when the lip-synching of the Italian dialogue is off. These are minor reservations. That the film is the work of a singular, very Russian artist, a man with a profound appreciation for his sources, is apparent throughout, from the indolent luxury of the great party scene until the final, elegant shot of the beloved Anna.

In one of the film's sharpest, funniest sequences, the dignitaries of a small provincial Russian city turn out to welcome Romano and his unbreakable-glass patent. The bewildered, love-sick Romano is celebrated as the town's first foreigner and the harbinger of the "new" Russia of "progress, prestige, and population increase." Possibly inspired by *Uncle Vanya* is the ridiculous madman who attacks Romano and begs him not to build the factory that must eventually spoil Russia's great rivers, forests, and streams.

In everything he wrote, Chekhov's sense of the future was as strong as his feeling for the past. The future existed in the commonplace world around him. Working today, Mr. Mikhalkov has access to hindsight, but he never allows himself to see more than the master felt instinctively, in his thoroughly Russian bones.

—*V.C., September 25, 1987*

DARK VICTORY

Directed by Edmund Goulding; written by Casey Robinson, based on the play by George Emerson Brewer Jr. and Bertram Bloch; cinematographer, Ernest Haller; edited by Williams Holmes; music by Max Steiner; art designer, Robert Haas; produced by David Lewis; released by Warner Brothers. Black and white. Running time: 105 minutes.

With: Bette Davis (Judith Traherne), George Brent (Dr. Frederick Steele), Humphrey Bogart (Michael O'Leary), Geraldine Fitzgerald (Ann King), Ronald Reagan (Alec) and Henry Travers (Dr. Parsons).

Bette Davis won an Academy Award last year for her performance in *Jezebel,* a spottily effective film. Now it is more than ever apparent that the award was premature. It should have been deferred until her

Dark Victory came along, as it did yesterday to the Music Hall. Miss Davis is superb. More than that, she is enchanted and enchanting. Admittedly it is a great role—rangy, full-bodied, designed for a virtuosa, almost sure to invite the faint damning of "tour de force." But that must not detract from the eloquence, the tenderness, the heartbreaking sincerity with which she has played it. We do not belittle an actress to remark upon her great opportunity; what matters is that she has made the utmost of it.

Dark Victory was not so well received when Tallulah Bankhead played it on Broadway four seasons ago. Those notoriously uncompromising gentlemen, the drama critics, found it and its star good in spots, like the vicar's egg. It ran six weeks and expired, presumably of nervous exhaustion. Simply on that evidence, the Warners must be complimented for making a better job of it. Casey Robinson's adaptation has distilled the drama of the play; Edmund Goulding's direction has fused it into a deeply moving unity; Miss Davis, Geraldine Fitzgerald and the rest of the players have made it one of the most sensitive and haunting pictures of the season.

It isn't, of course, entirely a happy theatrical occasion. The mascara was running freely at the Music Hall yesterday. For essentially the picture is simply a protracted death scene in which the heroine's doom is sealed almost in the first sequence. She is a gay, irresponsible member of the horsey Long Island set who has less than a year to live. She doesn't know it for a while, believing the operation on her brain has effected a permanent cure. But her surgeon knows the tumor will recur, cause blindness for a while, then death. And soon she discovers it, too—bitterly, just as she has discovered her love for the surgeon and his for her. It is a tragic romance: two gallant people bravely pretending that time is standing still and knowing deep down that they are lying.

A completely cynical appraisal would dismiss it all as emotional flimflam, a heartless play upon tender hearts by a playwright and company well versed in the dramatic uses of going blind and improvising on Camille. But it is impossible to be that cynical about it. The mood is too poignant, the performances too honest, the craftsmanship too expert. Miss Davis, naturally, has dominated—and quite properly—her film, but Miss Fitzgerald has added a sentient and touching portrayal of the friend, and George Brent, as the sur-

225

geon, is—dare we say?—surprisingly self-contained and mature. This once we must run the risk of being called a softy: we won't dismiss *Dark Victory* with a self-defensive sneer.

—*F.S.N., April 21, 1939*

DARLING

Directed by John Schlesinger; written by Frederic Raphael, based on a story by Mr. Raphael, Mr. Schlesinger and Joseph Janni; cinematographer, Ken Higgins; edited by James B. Clark; music by John Dankworth; art designer, Ray Simm; produced by Mr. Janni; released by Embassy Pictures. Black and white. Running time: 122 minutes.

With: Julie Christie (Dianna Scott), Dirk Bogarde (Robert Gold), Laurence Harvey (Miles Brand), Ronald Curram (Malcolm), Jose Luis de Villalonga (Prince Cesare) and Trevor Bowen (Tony Bridges).

Don't let the appellation *Darling,* which is the title of the sleek British film that had its world premiere yesterday at the Lincoln Arts and the Tower East, deceive you as to the true nature of its robust heroine. The word should be pronounced in this instance the way Tallulah Bankhead pronounces it when she is raking her vocal claws over someone she heartily detests.

The woman so nominated in this totally corrosive film, which director John Schlesinger has put together for distribution by Joseph E. Levine, is anything but a darling.

She is a selfish, ambitious, fickle wench whose tender and lovable qualities might be compared to those of a threshing machine. And the obvious purpose of the title is just to put an ironic tag on a film in which all the softer sentiments are blisteringly satirized.

Indeed one is finally brought to wonder whether love, which is often talked about in this tale of a London photographer's model who goes from bed to worse, is really understood and respected as anything but a four-letter word that is flung with the same frank abandon as several crude and insulting terms.

While *Darling* pretends to trace the story of this meagerly talented girl, who proceeds from an imma-

ture marriage into a series of shabby affairs—first with a television talker, then with a slick promotion man—and ultimately lands in a palazzo as the loveless wife of an Italian prince, it is really much more the destruction of a whole range of London social types than it is a sincere contemplation of a miserably misspent life.

And as such—as a slashing social satire and also a devastating spoof of the synthetic, stomach-turning output of the television-advertising age—it is loaded with startling expositions and lacerating wit. The screen never put forth types and dialogue more purple and frank than those here.

"What is wrong with England?" our television talker asks an assortment of picked-up people in a sidewalk interview, and their screamingly funny fumbles with elegant words and ideas are but a pleasant preface to the evidence that is displayed in the subsequent journeys and encounters of the gaudy heroine.

Aging and seedy title-bearers, vulgar and pushy new-rich, BBC intellectuals, the "dolce vita" set with its outspoken homosexuals and their grotesque confusions with sex, bumbling big-business nitwits, posey suburbanites—all are arrayed as examples of what is wrong with England today. It is a surface skim of an area, sarcastic without going deep—mischievous, devastating, sometimes disgusting and usually droll.

Actually, the screenplay, written by Frederic Raphael, no more reveals the several characters who move more or less to the fore than we assume will be revealed in the profile that is allegedly being assembled about the heroine for a slick magazine.

The heroine, as played by Julie Christie, is a vigorous, vivacious sort, full of feline impulses and occasional disarming charms, but uncommunicative of the urges that make her tick.

Why she tumbles so quickly for the television chap, whom Dirk Bogarde makes a curiously cryptic intellectual, is not explained. Is it love that passes between them? Is it status-seeking? Is it sex?

And why does she drift so casually to the high-living advertising man, played with élan by Laurence Harvey, after having an abortion and going home for a turn? We just have to put it down to *whimsy*—the same thing that takes her to Capri with a homosexual photographer or causes her to accept the Italian prince as a husband and inherit notoriety with him.

These are ambiguities of behavior that Mr. Schlesinger does not explore in his brilliantly graphic and fluid surface-skimming of the in-group social scenes and the multitude of characters in London, Paris, and Italy. His film is a documentation of implicit ironies rather than a discovery of why people act as they do. It is too long. It could be a half-hour shorter.

It has a dandy musical score by John Dankworth, and everyone in its large cast plays it splendidly. Mr. Schlesinger, best known as the director of *A Kind of Loving* and *Billy Liar,* has made a film that will set tongues to wagging and moralists to wringing their hands.

—*B.C., August 4, 1965*

DAVID COPPERFIELD

Directed by George Cukor; written by Howard Estabrook and Hugh Walpole, based on the novel by Charles Dickens; cinematographer, Oliver T. Marsh; edited by Robert J. Kern; music by Herbert Stothart; art designer, Cedric Gibbons; produced by David O. Selznick; released by Metro-Goldwyn-Mayer. Black and white. Running time: 133 minutes.

With: W. C. Fields (Micawber), Lionel Barrymore (Dan Peggotty), Maureen O'Sullivan (Dora), Madge Evans (Agnes), Edna May Oliver (Aunt Betsey), Roland Young (Uriah Heep), Lewis Stone (Mr. Wickfield), Frank Lawton (David, the Man) and Freddie Bartholomew (David, the Child).

I have in my heart of hearts," said Dickens, "a favorite child and his name is David Copperfield." The classic story of David's triumphs and sorrows, and of the amazing people who were his friends and enemies, has been made into a gorgeous photoplay which encompasses the rich and kindly humanity of the original so brilliantly that it becomes a screen masterpiece in its own right. The immortal people of *David Copperfield,* of whom G. K. Chesterton has said they are more actual than the man who made them, troop across the Capitol's screen like animated duplicates of the famous Phiz drawings, an irresistible and enormously heartwarming procession. It is my belief that this cinema edition of *David Copperfield* is the most profoundly satisfying screen manipulation of a great novel that the camera has ever given us.

Therein you will discover all the superb caricatures of blessed memory, led by a manly and heartbreaking David who is drawn to the life in the person of Master Freddie Bartholomew. Here are all the old scenes of David's adventures, Blunderstone and Yarmouth, Dover and Canterbury and London. Here are Peggotty, with no shape at all, and Aunt Betsey Trotwood, who expressed both her hatreds and her affections in the furioso manner, and poor Mr. Dick, who couldn't keep King Charles's head out of his writings, and bluff Dan Peggotty, who owned the heart of a child, and Barkis, who was willin', and Uriah Heep, who was 'umble, and dear Little Em'ly, and the terrible Mr. Murdstone and all the rest.

Lord bless us, and Micawber, the inconquerable Micawber, who inhabited a world of creditors and squashy souls, but sent his spirit soaring among the stars. Being himself pretty generally a spiritual descendant of Mr. Micawber, W. C. Fields manages with the greatest of ease to become one with his illustrious predecessor according to the directions laid down in the text of Dickens and the drawing of Phiz. The Fields Micawber is, as it ought to be, the one performance that is able to remain predominant among such splendors of character acting as Lennox Pawle's Mr. Dick, Edna May Oliver's Aunt Betsey, Roland Young's Uriah Heep, Lionel Barrymore's Dan Peggotty and both Master Bartholomew as David the boy and Frank Lawton as David the man. Being himself touched by madness and genius, Mr. Fields is similarly the only player in a notable cast who has the audacity to contribute anything of himself to these incredibly real people of Dickens. But when you have heard him in his lofty rhetorical flights, heard him in the speech that begins: "You perceive before you the shattered fragments of a temple that was once called man"; heard him say: "With renewed courage I again throw down the gauntlet to society," you will perhaps understand that Mr. Fields can do no wrong.

Naturally, it is the magnificent Micawber, the indigent aristocrat, the tool of circumstance, who dominates that most splendid scene in which the sniveling Uriah is brought to account for his treacherous conduct toward Mr. Wickfield. Striking his regal pose, with the verminous Uriah quaking before him, and the victims of Uriah's cupidity at his back, he declaims that memorable declaration of independence which begins: "In denouncing the most consummate villain that has ever existed, I ask no consideration for myself. I have been myself enmeshed in this villain's machinations. . . . I declare that Heep, and Heep only, of the firm of Wickfield & Heep, is the forger and the cheat!" Only a little below it in heroic stature place that other scene of liberation in which Aunt Betsey Trotwood tells the evil Murdstones exactly what she thinks of the way they behaved toward poor David.

Although it is a film of enormous length, according to screen standards—two hours and ten minutes—Hugh Walpole's screenplay has been arranged with such uncanny correctness, and each of the myriad episodes which go into the making of the varied canvas has been performed so perfectly, that the photoplay slips by in an unwearying cavalcade. It is astonishing to discover how very much of the novel has found its way to the screen. Some of it has been telescoped for brevity, some of it has been omitted out of sheer painful necessity, but the total impression is one of amazing completeness and accuracy. Pausing only once or twice for the briefest of subtitles, the work flows on its invincibly entertaining way from beginning to end.

Like Dickens himself, it is able to invest each character in this complex story with such a completeness of personality that none is too minor to take his place in the unforgettable gallery. Certainly it is in the great narrative tradition of the cinema. A new year that has already been enriched by several distinguished photoplays now adds a genuine masterpiece to its record with *David Copperfield.*

—*A.S., January 19, 1935*

DAVID HOLTZMAN'S DIARY

Produced, written and directed by Jimmy McBride; cinematographers, Michael Wadleigh, Paul Glickman and Paul Goldsmith; edited by Mr. McBride; released by New Yorker Films. Black and white. Running time: 74 minutes.

With: L. M. Kit Carson (David Holtzman), Eileen Dietz (Penny Wohl) and Lorenzo Mans (Pepe).

"Life as a work of art"—at least once a decade that ancient concept seduces some members of yet another generation, and inspires them to hash up their lives in the name of truth or beauty. Jim McBride's *David Holzman's Diary,* a totally delightful satire on "the blubber about cinéma vérité," mocks those ghastly reels from the 1960's, when various filmmakers immortalized themselves or their friends by trying and failing to be spontaneous. *Diary,* which derides directors who scorned imagination or invention while worshiping the camera, opened yesterday at the Whitney Museum of American Art.

Holzman, an earnest young Godard-hound, decides to film his life in order to understand it—and only succeeds in ruining it. As a voyeur, a gentle intruder into other people's lives, he can't understand that the filming makes his subjects feel self-conscious, or that "reality" is altered by the presence of his camera and his tape recorder and his lavalier mike, which he calls his "friends."

His girlfriend, who detests his moviemaking, finally leaves him because of it. He's already told us in a dry, flat voice that he really loves her, though he can't resist pointing out that she's "dirty, sloppy." Forlornly, he adds, "I don't quite get her sense of privacy." After she's gone, he argues that masturbation is an improvement on the real thing because "You can think of anything . . . *pigs.* Think of trains going in tunnels. Think of bagels. I mean, you're not limited to women."

However, his obsession with freezing everything on celluloid rarely allows him any other fantasies. He gives manic attention to every detail of his New York neighborhood, from derelict sofas on the street to the installation of matchstick bamboo blinds in a nearby apartment, and finally gets slugged by a cop for filming people through their windows.

Soon, we realize that the camera is his analyst. He tells it everything, and then grows furious because it doesn't answer him with "the right things," and also makes him "do things" that he wouldn't ordinarily do. Accusingly, he asks it, "What do you want?" Then he shouts at the lens that it hasn't helped him—just as a frustrated patient may denounce an all too silent psychiatrist.

Diary was made in 1967, and time has served it very well. We get a pungent flash on the past when a radio announces the numbers killed in the Newark riots, or refers to "the new Israel-Egyptian cease-fire," or quotes the Pentagon on the probable increase of American forces in Vietnam next year. But aside from politics, that period now seems a rather innocent one in retrospect, and the character of David Holzman (admirably played by L. M. Kit Carson) distills the eager naïveté that accompanied the zest for technology, deliberate inarticulation, and the mistrust of words, the vibes and the hoaxes and all the lighter put-ons of 1967.

At the end, Holzman is bitterly disappointed that his movie and his camera have taught him nothing—least of all how to control his life. The picture reminds me of the late A.J. Liebling's recollection of being twenty-three in Paris, when he felt that his life hinged on an impossible decision. Meanwhile, he was writing a novel about a twenty-three-year-old in Paris whose future hung upon an insoluble choice. When the character caught up with the day of his own life that he was describing, he couldn't finish the book. Jim McBride's movie evokes the spirit of Liebling's enormous laughter when he remarked that few diaries yield conclusions or solutions.

—*N.S., December 7, 1973*

DAWN OF THE DEAD

Written and directed by George A. Romero; director of photography. Michael Gornick; edited by Mr. Romero and Kenneth Davidow; music by the Goblins, with Dario Argento; produced by Richard P. Rubinstein; released by United Film Distribution Company. Running time: 125 minutes.

With: David Emge (Stephen). Ken Foree (Peter). Scott Reiniger (Roger) and Gaylen Ross (Francine).

Some people hate musicals, and some dislike westerns and I have a pet peeve about flesh-eating zombies who never stop snacking. Accordingly, I was able to sit through only the first fifteen minutes of *Dawn of the Dead,* George Romero's follow-up to *Night of the Living Dead,* which Mr. Romero directed in black and white in 1968. Since then, he has discovered color. Perhaps horror-movie buffs will consider this an improvement.

At the beginning of *Dawn of the Dead,* it was explained that the living dead were on the rampage, that there were a lot of them, and that they were hun-gry. It was also graphically demonstrated that the only way to kill one of these zombies permanently was to blow his or her head off, preferably in a nice, tight close-up. The few living souls who still remained were obviously fighting a losing battle, since their idea of a safe hiding place was a gas station outside of Harrisburg, Pennsylvania.

Mr. Romero is an acknowledged dean of this sort of thing, and he has been assisted this time by another red-meat magnate, Dario Argento. Mr. Argento, who most recently directed the less stomach-turning *Suspiria,* has provided a lot of thumpity-thump music for the soundtrack, along with his combo, the Goblins. On limited evidence, though, *Dawn of the Dead* didn't seem like anything that would send an audience home humming its theme song.

It was explained to me in the lobby, while a preview audience moaned and groaned, that this is the second installment in what Mr. Romero foresees as a trilogy, and that the bulk of *Dawn of the Dead* had been filmed in America's largest shopping mall and is full of satirical points about consuming. Whatever it may be full of, *Dawn of the Dead* opens today at the Gemini, the Rivoli, the U.A. 85th Street East, and other theaters.

—*J.M., April 20, 1979*

DAY FOR NIGHT

Directed by François Truffaut; written (in French with English subtitles) by Mr. Truffaut. Suzanne Schiffman and Jean-Louis Richard; cinematographer. Pierre-William Glenn; edited by Yann Dedet and Martine Barraque; music by Georges Delarue; art designer, Damien Lanfranchi; produced by Marcel Berbert; released by Warner Brothers. Running time: 120 minutes.

With: François Truffaut (Farrand). Jacqueline Bisset (Julie). Jean-Pierre Léaud (Alphonse). Valentina Cortese (Severine). Jean-Pierre Aumont (Alexandre). Dani (Liliana). Alexandra Stewart (Stacey) and Jean Champion (Bertrand).

Moviemaking is a strange business, says Severine (Valentina Cortese), an actress who steadies her nerves by sipping champagne on the set of *Meet*

Pamela, a rather tacky melodrama being made within François Truffaut's exhilarating new comedy about moviemaking, *Day for Night.*

"As soon as we grasp things," says Severine, "they're gone."

In one way and another, almost all of Truffaut's films have been aware of this impermanence, which, instead of making life and love seem cheap, renders them especially precious.

Worthy adventures are risky; they are headlong plunges into the unknown. Whether they end with a shotgun murder (*La Peau Douce*), middle-class boredom (*Bed and Board*), or total isolation (*Jules and Jim*) is not so important as the acceptance of the gamble itself. The quality of an experience cannot be measured by its duration or its end. Longevity is for redwood trees.

The original French title of *Day for Night* is *La Nuit Americaine,* which is what French moviemakers call the method by which a scene shot in daylight is made to look like night through the use of filters. *Day for Night* is a hilarious, wise and moving chronicle about the members of a crew who come together for seven weeks at the Victorine Studios in Nice to manufacture a movie, an illusion that is, for the period of its production, more important than life itself.

They include Ferrand (Truffaut), the director who observes at one point that making a movie is like a stagecoach trip through the old West ("At first you hope for a pleasant trip. Then you simply hope to reach your destination."); Julie (Jacqueline Bisset), the beautiful Hollywood star of the film within; Alphonse (Jean-Pierre Léaud), a nice, nut-brained young actor preoccupied by movies and women, in that order; Alexandre (Jean-Pierre Aumont), the aging male lead of the film within; and Severine (Miss Cortese), Alexandre's costar and former mistress, who is genuinely pleased for Alexandre when he reveals plans to settle down with his new young male lover.

Day for Night is Truffaut's fondest, most compassionate film, and although it is packed with references to films and film people (Welles, Vigo, Fellini, Buñuel, among others) and although it is dedicated to Lillian and Dorothy Gish, it's not a particularly inside movie. That is, it has great fun showing us how movies are made, how rain and snow are manufactured, how animals are directed (or not), how acts of God can affect a script, but its major concerns are people working at a profession they love, sometimes to the exclusion of everything else.

The movie people are different from you and me, Truffaut seems to say, but only in the intensity of their passions and in constantly having to differentiate between reality and its various reflections. Romantic alliances are always shifting. Infatuation is mistaken for love (and, for a moment, it may really be love). Severine becomes hysterical after fluffing half a dozen takes because the makeup girl is doubling as a maid in a brief scene. "In my day," she screams, "makeup was makeup, and an actress was an actress."

The performances are superb. Miss Cortese and Miss Bisset are not only both hugely funny but also hugely affecting, in moments that creep up on you without warning. It's no accident, I suspect, that the only characters who come close to being either evil (the jealous wife of the film's production manager) or uninteresting (Julie's doctor husband) are nonmovie people. In *Day for Night,* Truffaut is looking at the world from inside a glorious obsession: everyone outside looks a little gray and dim.

Day for Night, which begins its commercial engagement October 7 at the Festival Theater, was the opening attraction of the New York Film Festival last night at Lincoln Center. Never has the festival been so appropriately begun.

—V.C., September 29, 1973

THE DAY OF THE JACKAL

Directed by Fred Zinnemann: written by Kenneth Ross. based on the novel by Frederick Forsyth: director of photography. Jean Tournier: edited by Ralph Kemplen: music by Georges Delarue: art designers. Willy Holt and Ernest Archer: produced by John Woolf. David Deutsch and Julien Derode: released by Universal Pictures. Running time: 142 minutes.

With: Edward Fox (The Jackal). Michel Auclair (Colonel Rolland). Alan Badel (The Minister). Tony Britton (Inspector Thomas). Adrien Cayla-Legrand (The President). Cyril Cusack (The Gunsmith) and Derek Jacobi (Caron).

Except for its downbeat ending, Fred Zinnemann's thoroughly competent film version of *The Day of the Jackal* might lead one to believe that the life of a professional political assassin involves almost as much ground travel to and from airports as does an airline pilot's—but the assassin's work is much better paid.

The Jackal, the code name for the assassin played by Edward Fox, a man reported to have murdered both Trujillo and someone cryptically identified as "that fellow in the Congo," is hired by a group of former French Army officers, furious over the loss of Algeria, to assassinate President Charles de Gaulle. The fee: $250,000 down and another $250,000 on completion.

Frederick Forsyth's novel, which has been written for the screen by Kenneth Ross, belongs to a very special subcategory of fiction—one that leaves me cold but apparently fascinates two out of every three people in the Free World who can afford to buy adventure novels in hardback editions.

Because history has tipped us off that no one ever did assassinate De Gaulle, the suspense of the novel and the film must depend on our wondering just how the assassin is going to fail. This preordained failure also allows us to hope rather tentatively for his success. We can identify with him in a way that we certainly would not allow ourselves with an Oswald or a Ray.

The Day of the Jackal, which opened yesterday at the Loews State 2 and Orpheum Theaters, devotes itself entirely to this question of how—how the assassin operates and how he is ultimately caught.

It is virtually encyclopedic in describing the assassin's preparations, which involve a lot of flying back and forth between London, Paris, Vienna and Rome. We watch him doing research in libraries, ordering false identity papers, and buying specially made weapons as well as over-the-counter hair dyes. The details are minutely observed and, to me, just a bit boring. I keep thinking that although it could have happened, in this case it didn't.

Zinnemann's way with this material is cool, sober, and geographically stunning (the film was shot all over Europe at what looks to be a huge cost). Where Hitchcock would have made it funny, Zinnemann plays it straight (and perhaps dull), allowing himself only that margin of humor provided by the bureaucratic style of the good guys (cops and government functionaries), so that the funniest line of the film comes when

someone says of De Gaulle: "At ten he rekindles the eternal flame."

Edward Fox is a very natty-looking assassin, a role that requires a lot of walking around, getting in and out of cars, and puffing on cigarettes, but not much acting. In the supporting cast are some of the best actors in England and France, including Michel Lonsdale as a French supercop and Delphine Seyrig as a bossy baroness whom the assassin encounters en route to his date with destiny.

I've no doubt it will be a smash.

—V.C., May 17, 1973

THE DAY THE EARTH STOOD STILL

Directed by Robert Wise; written by Edmund H. North, based on a story by Harry Bates; cinematographer, Leo Tover; edited by William Reynolds; music by Bernard Herrmann; art designers, Lyle Wheeler and Addison Hehr; produced by Julian Blaustein; released by Twentieth Century Fox. Black and white. Running time: 92 minutes.

With: Michael Rennie (Klaatu), Patricia Neal (Helen Benson), Hugh Marlowe (Tom Stevens), Sam Jaffe (Dr. Barnhardt), Billy Gray (Bobby Benson) and Lock Martin (Gort).

Now, don't be alarmed, anybody, but one of those things is here again. We mean one of those awesome contraptions that comes whirring in from outer space, humming and glowing with energy like a gigantic neon sign, to settle to earth in fearful splendor and disembark creatures of such powers that they thoroughly belittle us mortals and put our worldly accomplishments to shame. The medium of its transmission is a film called *The Day the Earth Stood Still,* which Twentieth Century Fox delivered to the Mayfair yesterday.

Don't be alarmed, we confidently tell you, because, once this contraption is down and its pilots have emerged from its innards on the Ellipse in Washington, they turn out to be such decent fellows, so well-mannered and peacefully inclined, that you'd hardly expect them to split an infinitive, let alone an atom or a human head. Indeed, the more important of these creatures—the other is just a mere mechanical man—is in the nature of a superemissary, sent to earth from one of the planets to counsel peace. And so benign is his disposition, even when he arranges things so the flow of all the world's electricity is stopped for an awesome half-hour, that he inspires one more with admiration than with bewilderment or fear.

Such benignity in a creature from whom menace is expected, obviously, might sit rather well in a picture that is set in a fairly literal frame. But in a fable of such absurd assumptions as this one amusingly presents, cold chills might be more appropriate than lukewarm philosophy. One expects more—or less—than a preachment on political morality from a man from Mars.

Likewise, Michael Rennie, who plays this genteel soul, while charmingly suave and cosmopolitan, is likely to cause unguarded yawns. His manners are strangely punctilious for a fellow just off a space boat, and his command of an earthly language must have been acquired from listening entirely to the BBC. Nice chap, Mr. Rennie, but a bit on the soft side, don'tcha know.

His giant mechanical assistant, which someone named Lock Martin animates, is also oddly unmenacing, for all his grossness and his death-ray eye. We've seen better monsters in theater audiences on Forty-second Street. And the somewhat befuddled humans who react to these visitors perform with conspicuous coolness for persons so uniquely exposed. Sam Jaffe as an eminent scientist, Patricia Neal as a lady susceptible to love, and Billy Gray as a clean-cut American youngster are among those who can take it or leave it alone.

It is comforting, of course, to have it made plain that our planetary neighbors are much wiser and more peaceful than are we but this makes for a tepid entertainment in what is anomalously labeled the science-fiction field.

—*B.C., September 19, 1951*

DAYS OF HEAVEN

Written and directed by Terrence Malick; director of photography. Nester Almendros; edited by Billy Weber; music by Ennio Morricone; art designer. Jack Fisk; produced by Bert and Harold Brackman; released by Paramount Pictures. Running time: 92 minutes.

With: Richard Gere (Bill), Brooke Adams (Abby), Sam Shepard (The Farmer), Linda Manz (Linda), Robert Wilke (The Farm Foreman), Jackie Shultis (Linda's Friend), Stuart Margolin (Mill Foreman) and Tim Scott (Harvest Hand).

Some years ago Terrence Malick produced, wrote, and directed *Badlands,* a film that created a certain stir. Now comes *Days of Heaven,* which opened here. It stars Richard Gere, Brooke Adams, Sam Shepard and Linda Manz; it obviously has cost a lot of money; it is full of elegant and striking photography; and it is an intolerably artsy, artificial film.

At the beginning, it is as though this is going to be a film about European immigrants in the early days of President Wilson's presidency. Then it switches to the Texas Panhandle, where the buffalo roam and the deer and the antelope still play. Migrant workers, fleeing the big cities, help reap the wheat harvest of a young, wealthy farmer. There are all kinds of special effects, including a plague of locusts and a prairie fire. There is a romance, in which the girlfriend of a young worker, who poses as his sister, marries the farmer. What results is jealousy and murder.

But *Days of Heaven* never really makes up its mind what it wants to be. It ends up something between a Texas pastoral and *Cavalleria Rusticana.* Back of what basically is a conventional plot is all kinds of fancy, self-conscious cineaste techniques. The film proceeds in short takes: people seldom say more than two or three connected sentences. It might be described as the mosaic school of filmmaking as the camera and the action hop around, concentrating on a bit here, a bit there.

A young girl named Linda Manz—and a talented young lady she is—has a prominent part of the action. The voice-over that constantly runs through the film is hers; she comments on the action, something in the manner of a Greek chorus. The photography, beautiful as some of it is, is as self-conscious as the rest of the film. People are carefully arranged, frames are carefully composed; there are more silhouettes than in an old nickelodeon.

Anyway, the old cars and the biplane and triplane in an airplane sequence are fun.

A competent group of actors tries to deal with the farrago. Richard Gere, looking as though the genes of the young Gregory Peck and Montgomery Clift have gotten mixed up, gives a sturdy performance as Bill, even if he is too sophisticated to give the impression of a migrant worker.

Sam Shepard has the part of the farmer. He is the well-known playwright, the author of such interesting works as *Mad Dog Blues and Operation Sidewinder.* This appears to be his first acting assignment in a film. He has a tall, rangy figure, a broodingly intense quality, and his work comes as a welcome surprise.

Brooke Adams, as Abby, the hero's girlfriend, is not a conventionally pretty girl. She has something better: an elfin quality, a wonderfully expressive face, an ability to project. But the one who really steals the show is little Miss Manz, in her first film. She comes from New York, is seventeen, looks sixteen, acts in an unselfconscious manner, and nonchalantly takes in stride any crazy hop made by the football of life. She will have a big future. The minor roles in *Days of Heaven* are in good hands. But nobody can really overcome the nature of the material.

—*H.C.S., September 14, 1978*

DAYS OF WINE AND ROSES

Directed by Blake Edwards: written by J. P. Miller, based on his television play: cinematographer, Philip Lathrop: edited by Patrick McCormack: music by Henry Mancini: art designer, Joseph C. Wright: produced by Martin Manulis, released by Warner Brothers. Black and white. Running time: 117 minutes.

With: Jack Lemmon (Joe). Lee Remick (Kirsten). Charles Bickford (Arnesen). Jack Klugman (Jim Hungerford). Alan Hewitt (Leland). Tom Palmer (Ballefoy). Debbie Megowan (Debbie) and Maxine Stewart (Dottie).

Strong drink is a curse, screamed the zealot of the women's temperance unions years ago, as they sharply illustrated their warning with grim and gruesome displays of evil saloons, drunken fathers, sotted mothers and broken homes. And their messages were repeated in equally lurid temperance plays.

Today, the foes of strong waters are more subtle in how they attack this sometime accessory of social evil, and "alcoholic" is now the word that describes the problem drinker, rather than "drunkard," the term in other days. But there is still pretty much of the spirit of the old-time temperance plays in the dramas we've had upon this subject in recent years—such eloquent items as *The Lost Weekend* and *Come Back, Little Sheba,* to name two.

And the same goes for *Days of Wine and Roses,* which finally arrived yesterday to bring some postholiday sobriety to the Radio City Music Hall.

As much as this stark domestic drama, based on a television play by J. P. Miller, archly starts out to be a modern sophisticated romance in which hard-drinking boy meets soft-drinking girl, it doesn't stay long in that area—no longer than it takes its skillful stars, Jack Lemmon and Lee Remick, to set up two general characters.

Barely have they trod one measure of gaiety along the primrose path as a hard-pressed young advertising executive and his new, happy, sympathetic wife, than the husband is gravely overdrinking (to compensate for his insecurity) and the wife is beginning to drink with him so he won't feel resentful toward her. And before either we or they know it, they are both alcoholics—bums—fighting each other and the bottle and neglecting their lonely child.

From here on, the content is completely a grim, graphic, heart-rending account of the agony of these two people in the clutch of booze and the husband's painful struggle out of it with the help of Alcoholics Anonymous, while the wife is still battling at the end.

As a straight, ruthless visualization of an alcoholic's fate, with the bouts of delerium tremens and "dry-out" and all the rest, it is a commanding picture, and it is extremely well played by Mr. Lemmon and Miss Remick, who spare themselves none of the shameful, painful scenes. But for all their brilliant performing and the taut direction of Blake Edwards, they do not bring two pitiful characters to complete and overpowering life.

The couple in this picture, unlike the sot in *The Lost Weekend,* seemed to be horrible examples that we face objectively. We shudderingly watch them suffer, we do not really suffer with them. They are impressive performers in a temperance play, and in the background one senses the tinkle of "Father, Dear Father. Come Home to Me Now."

Charles Bickford is strong in a few scenes as the straight-laced father of the girl and Jack Klugman gives a good account of a compassionate member of A.A.

—*B.C., January 18, 1963*

THE DEAD

Directed by John Huston; written by Tony Huston, based on a short story in *The Dubliners* by James Joyce; director of photography, Fred Murphy; edited by Roberto Silvi; music by Alex North; production designer, Stephen Grimes; produced by Wieland Schulz-Keil and Chris Sievernich; released by Vestron Pictures. Running time: 83 minutes.

With: Anjelica Huston (Gretta), Donal McCann (Gabriel), Helena Carroll (Aunt Kate), Cathleen Delany (Aunt Julia), Dan O'Herlihy (Mr. Brown), Donal Donnelly (Freddy Malins) and Marie Kean (Mrs. Malins).

One by one we're all becoming shades," says Gabriel Conroy, looking out into Dublin's bleak winter dawn. Gretta, the wife he loves and suddenly realizes he has never known, lies asleep on the bed nearby. His own life now seems paltry: "Better pass boldly into that other world, in the full glory of some passion, than fade and wither dismally with age."

These words are spoken toward the end of *The Dead,* John Huston's magnificent adaptation of the James Joyce story that was to be the director's last film.

Some men pass boldly into that other world at seventeen. Huston was eighty-one when he died last August. He failed physically, but his talent was not only unimpaired, it was also richer, more secure and bolder than it had ever been. No other American filmmaker has ended a comparably long career on such a note of triumph.

The Dead and *Prizzi's Honor* (1985), Huston's altogether different, exuberantly melodramatic comedy, comprise a one-two punch quite unlike anything I can remember in movies. Who would have thought the old man had so much passion in him?

The Dead is so fine, in unexpected ways, that it almost demands a reevaluation of Huston's entire body of work. Like most American filmmakers of his generation, Huston depended largely on what Hollywood calls presold properties, on novels that had been published and plays that had been produced. Of his thirty-seven theatrical features, beginning with *The Maltese Falcon* in 1941, all but ten were adaptations.

The free-ranging restlessness of Huston's mind is seen in his choice of authors: B. Traven, Dashiell Hammett, Herman Melville, Richard Condon, Rudyard Kipling, Noel Behn, the fellows who wrote the Old Testament, W. R. Burnett, Flannery O'Connor, Malcolm Lowry and now (one might think the most difficult of all) James Joyce. It's not, however, just the variety of writers that's of interest but also the particular material.

The Dead, taken from *The Dubliners,* which was published in 1914, may be the finest story in the collection, but it has, it would seem, just two scenes, not much for a man who put such store by conventional narrative. The first scene, which lasts approximately an hour in the film, is the annual post–New Year's holiday party given by two elderly Dublin sisters, Kate and Julia Morkan, and their unmarried niece, Mary Jane.

Among the guests: the aunts' favorite nephew, Gabriel Conroy, and his wife, Gretta; a genial toper named Freddy Malins and his domineering, not completely disapproving mother; some single young ladies who are Mary Jane's music students; Mr. Brown (an aging, gently skeptical Protestant), a young man who is supposed to have the sweetest tenor in all Dublin; and Molly Ivors, a politically committed woman who twits the Irish-born-and-bred Gabriel about his fine English ways and affectations.

In the second scene, Gabriel and Gretta are in the hotel room they've taken for the night so they don't have to make the long drive to their home in the Dublin outskirts.

This is not exactly the material of which epics are made. However, Huston and his elder son, Tony, who did the immensely faithful adaptation, discover the rich narrative line that builds to the film's big, breathtaking coda. Like Joyce's story, the movie reveals itself with leisurely discretion in bits of observed behavior and overheard conversation, which initially seem as halt and illogical as Molly Ivors's criticism of Gabriel.

The Huston camera moves about the undistinguished, middle-class Morkan drawing room, where there's dancing before the banquet, as if it were a guest looking for a place to sit down. It seems to know everyone slightly but no one especially well. It attends to Aunt Kate, who worries about the condition in which Freddie Malins might turn up.

On the arrival of the Conroys, it pays more attention to Gabriel (Donal McCann), who frets about his after-dinner speech, than to Gretta (Anjelica Huston), who appears to be a serenely self-assured wife and mother. An amused Gretta tells the aunts about Gabriel's insistence that she wear galoshes. "Everyone on the Continent is wearing them," says Gabriel. The aunts are properly amazed, though they're not certain what galoshes are.

There are waltzes, with Mary Jane providing the music at the piano. Aunt Julia sings something by Bellini in an ancient, sweet-flat voice that reaches from a past no longer seen in her face. Freddy Malins is overcome with sentiment and goes on much too long telling her that she's never sounded better.

Mr. Grace recites a poem that everyone agrees is beautiful, even if the meaning of the words is not clear. At dinner there is small talk about the decline of opera in Dublin and about the generosity of monks who sleep in their coffins and pray for the salvation of all, even those not of the faith. "Like free insurance," says Mr. Brown.

At meal's end, in remarks preceding his toast to the three hostesses, Gabriel chooses literary quotations that aren't too highbrow. He speaks with some feeling of Irish hospitality, of traditions in danger of being lost, of the memories of other such parties. It's only later, when he and Gretta are alone in the chilly hotel room, that Gabriel understands exactly how inescapable and unrelenting the past continues to be.

Little by little, *The Dead* closes in on Gabriel and Gretta Conroy. The specific details accumulate, so that the movie's final sequence becomes a justification for everything that has gone before. Revealed with stunning forthrightness are the concerns that have earlier been obliquely touched on—the impermanence of all things, including love, the impossibility of escaping the past, particularly the dead who refuse to stay

buried in their country churchyards, and the relationship between the animate and inanimate in Nature, which is not to be understood, only accepted.

This remarkable sequence, in which the film's third-person narrative slips into the first person, has an emotional impact not easily described. It's not sentimental. In the way of any work of art, it's complete in itself.

That Huston should have dared search for the story's cinema life is astonishing. That he should have found it with such seeming ease is the mark of a master.

The production is close to faultless, from the camerawork of Fred Murphy, the production design of Stephen Grimes (in collaboration with Dennis Washington), and the costumes of Dorothy Jeakins, to the performances by the exceptional cast, which includes Helena Carroll and Cathleen Delany as the aunts, Donal Donnelly as the stewed Freddy Malins, Marie Kean as his mother, and Dan O'Herlihy as Mr. Brown. It's an ensemble performance, but Miss Huston and Mr. McCann must be the first among equals.

Mr. McCann, at the beginning as faceless as his character is indistinct, grows into a figure of besieged grace. The body sags but the spirit toughens. Miss Huston is splendid, a figure of such self-contained sorrow that it's difficult to believe she was ever Maerose Prizzi. Toward the end of the party sequence, there's a shot of her standing on the stairway in her aunts' house, her face partly hidden, listening to an unseen singer. Direction and performance are seamless in an image that exemplifies the achievement of this wonderful film.

The Dead opens today at the Cinema 1.
—V.C., *December 17, 1987*

DEAD CALM

Directed by Phillip Noyce; written by Terry Hayes, based on the novel by Charles Williams; director of photography, Dean Semler; edited by Richard Francis-Bruce; music by Graeme Revell; production designer, Grahan (Grace) Walker; produced by Mr. Hayes, Doug Mitchell and George Miller; released by Warner Brothers. Running time: 95 minutes.

With: Nicole Kidman (Rae Ingram). Sam Neill (John Ingram). Billy Zane (Hughie Warriner). Rod Mullinar (Russell Bellows). Joshua Tilden (Danny). George Shevtsov (Doctor) and Michael Long (Specialist Doctor).

Phillip Noyce's *Dead Calm* is an unsettling hybrid of escapist suspense and the kind of pure trash that depends on dead babies and murdered dogs for effect. In it, John and Rae Ingram (Sam Neill and Nicole Kidman) are a husband and wife alone on their yacht in still waters. They are joined by a classic intruder, the mysterious stranger, who in this case doesn't arrive nearly soon enough.

First, we hear about a car accident in which Rae was injured and their small son killed. This is the excuse Mr. Noyce needs to send his characters on their restful cruise, but he doesn't leave things there. He recreates one of Rae's nightmares, and we watch a beautiful little boy clutching a teddy bear smash through the windshield of the car. Dead Calm moves above this shoddy beginning and sinks back to its sleazy level a dizzying number of times.

Based on the Charles Williams novel, which did not have dead babies or dogs, the story has no surprises, but there are plenty of opportunities for psychological suspense. (In the late 1960's, Orson Welles shot an unfinished version, called *The Deep*.) When a lone man rows a dinghy from his stranded schooner to the Ingrams' yacht, John and the audience are instantly suspicious. All the signs of menace are there. The stranger is shot in a sinister manner from the back as he approaches. He turns slowly to reveal a handsome face whose expression seems to cry, "I am a sadistic murderer." He has the improbably innocent name of Hughie, and says that everyone else on his ship, the *Orpheus*, has been killed by botulism from a can of salmon.

John locks Hughie in a room and heads for the *Orpheus*. The villain breaks out, of course, knocks Rae unconscious and sends the yacht racing away. Meanwhile, back on the schooner, John bails water and discovers bodies for most of the film. This means that Mr. Neill, who was so strong as Meryl Streep's repressed husband in *A Cry in the Dark*, costars here with a drowning engine and a temperamental radio.

Mr. Noyce is an Australian director with a meandering career. His *Newsfront* appeared at the 1978

New York Film Festival, and his previous film, a supposedly steamy romance called *Echoes of Paradise*, opened in New York just a month ago and left in a mercifully short time.

Scene for scene, he is capable of creating terror. As Hughie, Billy Zane is every bit as repugnant as he is meant to be. But the film's pace is so flaccid that Hughie and Rae might be playing a sinister game of hide-and-seek. She locks him up; he breaks through another of the yacht's many cardboard-thin doors; she devises another shaky plan to shoot or stab or drug him. She is one tough but stupid heroine, who doesn't know enough to use the kitchen knife in her hand when Hughie's back is conveniently turned.

Her incompetence leaves time for Mr. Noyce to indulge in more tasteless excess. Rae seduces Hughie to save her life, her dog meets a peculiar and graphically violent end, and *Dead Calm,* which opens today at the Gemini Twin and other theaters, becomes disturbing for all the wrong reasons.

—*C.J., April 7, 1989*

DEAD END

Directed by William Wyler: written by Lillian Hellman, based on the Norman Bel Geddes production of the play by Sidney Kingsley: cinematographer, Gregg Toland: edited by Daniel Mandell: music by Alfred Newman: art designer, Richard Day: produced by Samuel Goldwyn: released by United Artists. Black and white. Running time: 93 minutes.

With: Sylvia Sidney (Drina). Joel McCrea (Dave). Humphrey Bogart ("Baby Face" Martin). Wendy Barrie (Kay). Claire Trevor (Francey). Allen Jenkins (Hunk) and Marjorie Main (Mrs. Martin).

Samuel Goldwyn's screen transcription of *Dead End,* as it came to the Rivoli Theatre last night, deserves a place among the important motion pictures of 1937 for its all-out and well-presented reiteration of the social protest that was the theme of the original Sidney Kingsley stage play.

As a picture of life in an East River dead-end street, where hopeless squalor rubs daily against Sutton Place elegance with no more salutary effect on either than mutual irritation, it is again an arresting, inductive consideration of the slum problem, a prima facie case for a revision of the social system. As a motion picture, however, it has technical faults, mainly its rigid adherence to the physical form of the play (seemingly a much too frugal use of so mobile an instrument as the camera), and its reshaping of the play's pivotal character to make him conform to the accepted cinema hero type.

But in spite of these relatively unimportant failings (both can be convincingly defended), the story of the frustrations and rebellions of the underprivileged people of *Dead End* has been brought smoothly and forcefully to the screen by an admirable cast.

Without ever moving off its one magnificent set, a disturbingly accurate conception of a typically contrasty block in the East Fifties, the camera seeks out Drina Gordon, her young orphan brother, Tommy, and his playmates: Dave Connell, sucked back into the environment after six valiant years of study to become an architect; Baby Face Martin, returning to visit the street after ten years as a marauding killer; Kay Burton, seeking retreat from unwholesome luxury in the fashionable apartment that towers above the tenements on the riverfront; and the other people of the teeming block.

The show undoubtedly belongs to the six incomparable urchins imported from the stage production whenever they are in view, but the camera occasionally leaves them to their swimming or to their boisterous horseplay to discover Drina, footsore after a day on the picket line, patching her worn shoe with paper; Dave and Kay, longing together for release from their respective imprisonments; Baby Face snarling at life after his mother's hateful denunciation and his disillusionment on finding that the girl, Francey, hadn't waited.

The character Dave, conceived in the original as an introspective cripple, is altered for Joel McCrea and simplified for the film audience in Lillian Hellman's adaptation. Here the conflict between the opposed products of the street, Dave and Baby Face, is physical and personal. There is an exchange of dissembled cunning for frank and righteous hatred, which is more suitable to McCrea's personality as the film audience knows him, and the film's climax is staged accordingly. Dave kills off the killer in a remorseless personal combat, instead of merely informing on him.

The salty street jargon of the noted youngsters, a feature that perhaps brought more people to the Belasco Theatre in the last two seasons than did the basic theme of the play, has necessarily been purged of its vulgarities, but it is still authentic New Yorkese and the highlight of the play.

Curtain calls are in order for all the principals, with as many as they'll answer to for the youngsters. Of the smaller parts, Claire Trevor's moment as Francey and Marjorie Main's flat-voiced hate as Martin's mother are memorable.

—*J.T.M., August 25, 1937*

DEAD MAN WALKING

Written and directed by Tim Robbins; based on the book by Sister Helen Prejean; director of photography, Roger A. Deakins; edited by Lisa Zeno Churgin; music by David Robbins; production designer, Richard Hoover; produced by Jon Kilik, Mr. Robbins and Rudd Simmons; released by Gramercy Pictures. Running time: 120 minutes.

With: Susan Sarandon (Sister Helen Prejean), Sean Penn (Matthew Poncelet), Robert Prosky (Hilton Barber), Raymond J. Barry (Earl Delacroix) and R. Lee Ermey (Clyde Percy).

The casting of Sean Penn as Matthew Poncelet, the convicted murderer on death row in Tim Robbins's quietly courageous drama about capital punishment, reveals a lot about this film's exceptional mettle. Mr. Penn isn't an actor who prompts automatic sympathy. He rarely invites any sympathy at all, and his unrepentant swagger says he wouldn't be caught dead trying. But his natural aloofness is what this role demands, since *Dead Man Walking* isn't about the effort to rescue a contrite convict from an unfair fate. It's a hard look at issues raised by the death penalty, and Mr. Penn's lean, mean performance makes those issues come furiously alive.

Based on an extraordinarily lucid and affecting memoir by Sister Helen Prejean, a nun from Louisiana, *Dead Man Walking* is an account of the author's eye-opening experiences on death row. It concentrates on her relationship with a man accused of taking part in the murders of two teenagers, who were abducted from a lovers' lane.

Mr. Penn's Matthew Poncelet (the characters have been renamed and slightly fictionalized from Sister Helen's version) admits he was present for the killings but says he didn't take part. That's still enough to make him a pariah and, to the parents of the murder victims, even worse. But as a matter of principle, Sister Helen risks opprobrium to become the spiritual adviser to this condemned man.

Already, the cards are stacked colossally high against Mr. Robbins's being able to make this material work. The crusading heroine who risks ostracism to do what's right is the stuff of self-righteous issue pictures, and so are some of the sentiments in the early sections of Mr. Robbins's screenplay. "When you were a child you were always bringing home strays," says Sister Helen's mother. "How can you sit there with that scum?" the father of one murder victim angrily inquires. And Sister Helen justifies her interest in Poncelet by stating a familiar credo: "Every person deserves respect."

But *Dead Man Walking* is so unmistakably principled that its truisms radiate the religious intensity they have for Sister Helen. As played by Susan Sarandon with an unforced decency to match the book's narrative voice, this is simply a woman who has the courage of her convictions. Sister Helen isn't looking for a crusade, but she finds one after someone asks her to become a pen pal to Poncelet, and after she makes a pilgrimage to Louisiana State Prison to meet him. This sullen, heavy-lidded convict is a hard man to ignore.

Affecting a thick Cajun accent and a carefully groomed look suggesting equal degrees of Elvis and Mephistopheles, Mr. Penn gives an astonishing performance and delivers exactly what *Dead Man Walking* needs. Nothing about him suggests an innocent victim, but his surliness is so magnetic and mercurial that it holds the viewer's interest. At the same time, Ms. Sarandon takes the kind of risk she took playing a stubbornly obsessed mother in *Lorenzo's Oil.* She's commandingly blunt, and she avoids cheapening her performance with the wrong kind of compassion. Her Sister Helen is repelled and alarmed by this man, but she's determined to help him anyway. That's what makes the film so unrelenting.

Dead Man Walking bears out its heroine's strongest statement of her ideals: "I'm just trying to follow the example of Jesus, who said every person is worth more than his worst act." It isn't strictly necessary to share either that belief or the film's fierce opposition to the death penalty to admire its impressive decency. Catapulting past this story's potential for sentimentality, the film explores the moral issues raised by the alliance between nun and convict. Where are the limits of her responsibilities as spiritual adviser? What does she owe to the families of the dead? Can there be reconciliation after such a terrible event? There's an echo of Mr. Penn's own conscience-stricken film *The Crossing Guard* in that last question.

Mr. Robbins's writing is at times too speechy in tackling these issues, but his direction is graceful and finally devastating. The film moves methodically toward the agonizing conclusion that is its raison d'être. And as it approaches that point, Mr. Penn's Poncelet undergoes some extraordinarily well-evoked changes, to the point at which the audience must ultimately adopt Sister Helen's view of him. The film's idea of Christian generosity is powerfully here in practice as well as in principle.

In addition to another of Mr. Penn's amazing self-transformations and Ms. Sarandon's terrific grit, *Dead Man Walking* is directed to overcome the film's obvious physical limitations. Though it isn't easy for Mr. Robbins to sustain visual interest in a nun and a convict who meet only for closely supervised visits, he finds unobtrusive ways of lending variety to their meetings.

Mr. Robbins also lets some sparks fly in scenes between Sister Helen and the victims' parents (R. Lee Ermey plays an outraged father, Raymond J. Barry a more complex one) and especially in Poncelet's stiff, excruciating visit with his mother and his brothers. "Some people are asking me about your funeral, and I get real angry and say 'He's not dead yet,'" the convict's mother awkwardly tells him. Poncelet is still a tough customer, but he's not tough enough to ignore that.

Mournful soundtrack music by Eddie Vedder, Bruce Springsteen, Patti Smith, Johnny Cash and others gives *Dead Man Walking* the somber grace notes it deserves.

—*J.M., December 29, 1995*

DEAD OF NIGHT

An anthology directed by Alfredo Cavalcanti, Charles Crichton, Basil Dearden and Robert Hamer; written by John Baines, Angus MacPhail and T. E. B. Clarke, based on stories by H. G. Wells, E. F. Benson, Mr. Baines and Mr. MacPhail; cinematographers, Jack Parker and Harold Julius; edited by Charles Hasse; music by George Auric; art designer, Michael Relph; produced by Michael Balcon; released by Ealing Studios and Universal Pictures. Black and white. Running time: 104 minutes.

With: Mervyn Johns (Walter Craig), Roland Culver (Eliot Foley), Frederick Valk (Dr. van Straaten), Anthony Baird (Hugh Grainger), Googie Withers (Joan Cortland), Hartley Power (Sylvester Kee) and Michael Redgrave (Maxwell Frere).

Such folks as like to drag their friends into the parlor, turn out the lights and swap tales of the weird and supernatural will certainly enjoy the new film at the Winter Garden, the British-made *Dead of Night.* For this is precisely a package of those curious and uncanny yarns designed to raise secret goose pimples and cause the mind to make a fast check on itself. And although the stories here related are probably familiar to all who are devotees of such mysticisms, they are tightly and graphically told.

The film begins with a fellow arriving at an English country house that he feels he has previously visited in a violent, repulsive dream. As a matter of fact, all of the people who are gathered there for the weekend were in his somnific experience and he is able to foretell what they will do. This sets him to worrying considerably, since his dream ended badly, he recalls, and he has a distinct premonition of dire and desperate events.

Whereupon other persons in the company are prompted to recollect such baffling psychic experiences as have happened in their lives. One chap recalls a fantastic presentiment that he once had—a vision of a hearse and unctuous driver—that saved him from a fatal accident. A girl recounts a fearful encounter with her fiancé which resulted from hallucinations inspired in him by an antique looking glass. And, finally, a practical psychologist tells the evening's most fascinating tale—his experience with a nutty ventriloquist who became jealous of his dummy and "murdered" the doll.

At the end of these cozy little memoirs, the dreamy fellow who started all the talk tries to murder the psychologist, slips into a mad, phantasmic whirl and suddenly awakes. He was dreaming. But the authors have managed a twist. To put it rather cutely, that's where you come in.

To make this weird anthology, producer Michael Balcon employed a quartet of able directors, two scriptwriters, and three original tales. He also gave employment to a large and capable cast that performs the elaborate episodes as though they might really have occurred. Michael Redgrave is most disturbing as the mad ventriloquist and Frederick Valk is invidiously eerie as the sober psychologist. Mervyn Johns, Hartley Powers, and Googie Withers are absorbing in other roles. *Dead of Night* is not a very solid picture, but it is good, heterodox "thriller" stuff.

—B.C., June 29, 1946

DEAD RINGERS

Directed by David Cronenberg; written by Mr. Cronenberg and Norman Snider, based on the book *Twins* by Bari Wood and Jack Geasland; director of photography, Peter Suschitzky; edited by Ronald Sanders; music by Howard Shore; production designer, Carol Spier; produced by Mr. Cronenberg and Marc Boyman; released by Twentieth Century Fox. Running time: 115 minutes.

With: Jeremy Irons (Beverly and Elliot Mantle), Geneviève Bujold (Claire Niveau), Heidi von Palleske (Cary), Barbara Gordon (Danuta), Shirley Douglas (Laura), Stephen Lack (Anders Wolleck), Nick Nicholas (Leo) and Lynne Cormack (Arlene).

The sleek, icy elegance of *Dead Ringers,* David Cronenberg's film about twin gynecologists teetering on the brink of madness, is unexpected. Both the director, whose past films include the much gorier *Scanners* and *Videodrome,* and the highly unusual subject suggest a more lurid approach. But Mr. Cronenberg, who has begun to emerge as a master of body-related horrific fantasy (his last film was *The Fly*) clearly understands that a small amount of medical mischief can be more unnerving than conventional grisliness. Even the film's opening credits, which present antiquated obstetrical drawings and strange medical instruments, are enough to make audiences queasy.

Who, then, will be drawn to this spectacle? Anyone with a taste for the macabre wit, the weird poignancy and the shifting notions of identity that lend *Dead Ringers* such fascination. And anyone who cares to see Jeremy Irons's seamless performance, a schizophrenic marvel, in the two title roles. Mr. Cronenberg has shaped a startling tale of physical and psychic disintegration, pivoting on the twins' hopeless interdependence and playing havoc with the viewer's grip on reality. It's a mesmerizing achievement, as well as a terrifically unnerving one.

Dead Ringers, which opens today at the National and other theaters, owes some of its inspiration to the case of the doctors Cyril and Stewart Marcus, who died in 1975; its nominal source is *Twins,* a 1977 novel by Bari Wood and Jack Geasland. Adapting the novel with Norman Snider, Mr. Cronenberg has preserved only a trace of the real Marcus story, preferring to invent a pathology of his own. The twins of *Dead Ringers* descend, as the Marcuses did, into drug addiction, physical squalor, and finally violence. But they do this with a cool, brittle detachment that makes their final decline so much more wrenching, and with a painful interweaving of identities that at times becomes as unsettling for the audience as it is for them.

The prologue to *Dead Ringers* shows the preadolescent Mantle brothers discussing sex wistfully, regretting the fact that it seems so, well, *personal.* Creatures that fertilize eggs underwater without physical contact have a much easier lot than humans, they agree. A neighborhood girl, who merely laughs at the brothers when they express sexual curiosity, sends them further along the path to a purely clinical approach, and the film's next scene finds them at medical school, where they invent an instrument that other doctors deem bizarre. Nonetheless, it helps to make their fortune, and the film's first 1988 scene finds the prosperous, urbane Mantles running a private clinic in Toronto. In one of the story's many ironies, these twins have chosen infertility as their specialty.

Though the twins are not often seen on the job, their contemptuous and sometimes nasty approach to their patients is made clear, as is their fondness for gamesmanship. The brothers enjoy changing places on occasion, especially when they embark upon an affair. Without his efforts, the dapper Elliot tells his more introverted brother Beverly, the latter would perhaps never have had any luck with women at all. But the twins' tricks prove to be no match for Claire Niveau (given real substance by Geneviève Bujold), a famous film star who arrives at the clinic as a patient, is promptly wooed by Elliot and is then passed on to Beverly. Claire becomes the means by which the twins' lifelong bond is destroyed.

One brother falls in love with her, and wants for the first time to keep something for his own. The other brother finds he cannot tolerate this betrayal. And Mr. Irons, who uses few conversational clues to establish which twin he is playing in any given shot, manages to make this conflict as dramatically sharp as it is psychologically riveting. It is always evident which personality Mr. Irons has adopted, a feat even more impressive than the formidable technical tricks that keep the viewer from detecting a split screen. What makes the performance(s) even better is that Mr. Irons invests these bizarre, potentially freakish characters with so much intelligence and so much real feeling.

The ghoulishness of *Dead Ringers* is kept very much in check, even as the story spirals downward. The film's cool, muted visual style helps see to that. There are very few departures from the expensive, high-tech look of the Mantles' clinic and their apartment. And the odd touches, when they do occur, are treated almost offhandedly. Nothing is said, for instance, about the fact that when the Mantles appear in the operating room, the doctors, nurses, orderlies, and patients are serenely draped in fabric that is blood red.

Among the film's more hauntingly strange developments are Beverly's invention of a new set of surgical devices, which frighten everyone who sees them, the brothers' growing identification with the Siamese twins Chang and Eng, and the drug addiction that finally leaves one brother utterly oblivious to his sibling's fate. The film's final image, like so many steps along the brothers' route to self-destruction, is not easily forgotten.

—*J.M., September 23, 1988*

DEATH IN VENICE

Produced and directed by Luchino Visconti: written (in Italian, with English subtitles) by Mr. Visconti and Nicola Badalucco, based on the novel by Thomas Mann: cinematographer, Pasquale De Santis: edited by Ruggero Mastroianni: music by Gustav Mahler, Ludwig von Beethoven and Modest Mussorgsky: art designer, Ferdinando Scarfiotti: released by Warner Brothers. Running time: 130 minutes.

With: Dirk Bogarde (Aschenbach), Bjorn Andresen (Tadzio), Silvana Mangano (The Mother), Luigi Battaglia (The Scapegrace), Romolo Valli (Hotel Manager), Mark Burns (Alfred, Aschenbach's Pupil), Nora Ricci (The Governess) and Marisa Berenson (Mrs. Aschenbach).

The first few minutes of *Death in Venice*, Luchino Visconti's heavily ornamented film adaptation of the Thomas Mann short story, are an almost perfect evocation of the scene Mann sets as the prelude to Gustav Aschenbach's marvelous doom.

On the soundtrack we hear what seem, at first, to be the echoes of one of Mahler's most lonely melodies—the adagietto of the Fifth Symphony, which is a kind of requiem for the living. A small, fat steamer moves across a windless sea, trailing coal smoke that hangs in the air like a long, thin shred of dirty cotton. The time could be either dawn or dusk. The light is bluish pink and very dim, and there is no clearly defined horizon.

In a chair on the deck of the steamer, Gustav Aschenbach, fastidiously bundled up in an overcoat and a muffler, tries to read but he cannot concentrate. He puts the book aside, and there is even something fastidious in this gesture of impatience, which is neat and prim and controlled.

There are several such sequences in the film, when Visconti, the most operatic of film directors, and Mann, the least operatic of prose writers, more or less overlap. Not so surprisingly, they are the most consequential sequences of the film, and, comparatively speaking, anyway, the least consequential of the story.

What Visconti has done is to turn *Death in Venice*, which is about many things, including an artist's abject yet triumphant capitulation to his senses, into a scenically baroque tale of an inhibited immoralist, a fussy old man who develops a mad crush on a beautiful youth, and thus, unwisely, stays on too long in a city that is dying of a secret pestilence.

Death in Venice, which opened yesterday at the Little Carnegie Theater, is so full of high-class effects, and pretends to be of such serious purpose, that it must, I feel, convince skeptics that movies are a second-rate art. By failing to communicate the complexity and intelligence of the Mann work—and by failing with such seeming cinematic style, it says that this is all that movies can do. They can go no further, no deeper, than the specific images.

This, of course, is nonsense. Movies can go further and deeper, as Visconti himself has shown in things like *The Damned* and *Rocco* and *His Brothers,* movies that worked in spite of, rather than through, their flamboyant effects.

Everything that isn't of an especially first order of importance in Mann's *Death in Venice* is emphasized and enlarged in the film. It never finds a substructure, that is, equivalent to Aschenbach's interior monologues that give the story its meaning. Instead, there are some rather clumsy flashbacks that sound like afterthoughts, in which Aschenbach and a friend debate whether the creation of beauty is a spiritual act, or proceeds from an abandonment to the emotions.

The movie has not been written and directed as much as it has been decorated, by Visconti's assumption that Mann was writing about Gustav Mahler (the film's Aschenbach is a composer, rather than a writer), by the extensive use of Mahler's music on the soundtrack, by the magnificent care that has been taken to re-create the look of the 1911 period, in costumes, in the Venice locale, in the color and even in the sounds.

It is also decorated by Bjorn Andresen, as the beautiful Polish boy with the face of a Botticelli angel who, according to Visconti's version, begins luring Aschenbach to his fate, with all of the innocence of a street hustler, from virtually their first encounter. But then the camera adores the boy quite as much as Aschenbach, which gives the movie a homosexual feeling that limits Mann's intent.

The movie is most spectacularly decorated by Dirk Bogarde's performance as the once-disciplined German artist. It is a performance full of right gestures—the precise walk, the sudden awarenesses of hidden intention that are marked by hopeless shrugs, the sly smiles, the hands to the face in embarrassment, and finally, the frail, dandified strut that marks Aschenbach's submission to his passion.

Curiously, even though the gestures are right, they seem calculated and rather empty, as if each had been carried one step too far. But Visconti overdoes everything in the film from the intimations of death, and the grotesque makeup Aschenbach sports toward the end of the film, to the great blobs of black hair dye that run down poor Aschenbach's face at the moment of death.

The movie becomes, eventually, an elegant bore, full of rather lovely things on the periphery—such as the sight of Silvana Mangano, as the cool Polish aristocrat, moving like a mother duck through the hotel dining room, followed by her stiff little daughters, forever mysterious. *Death in Venice* often looks right, but it's a vacant look. Instead of bringing the story to life, Visconti has, I'm afraid, embalmed it.

—*V.C., June 18, 1971*

DEATH OF A SALESMAN

Directed by Laslo Benedek; written by Stanley Roberts, based on the play by Arthur Miller; cinematographer, Franz Planer; edited by William Lyon and Harry Gerstad; music by Alex North; production designer, Rudolph Sternad; produced by Stanley Kramer; released by Columbia Pictures. Black and white. Running time: 115 minutes.

With: Fredric March (Willy Loman), Mildred Dunnock (Linda Loman), Kevin McCarthy (Biff), Cameron Mitchell (Happy), Howard Smith (Charley), Royal Beal (Ben), Don Keefer (Bernard), Jesse White (Stanley) and Claire Carleton (Miss Francis).

Now that Arthur Miller's *Death of a Salesman* has been brought by Stanley Kramer to the screen and Fredric March has been given the opportunity to play its difficult leading role, a great many more million people, not only in this country but in the world, will have a chance to see this shattering drama at what is probably its artistic best. That chance was initiated at the Victoria Theatre yesterday.

For, in every respect, this transference to the motion picture form enhances the episodic structure and the time-ranging nature of the play—which, in short, tells a grim, reflective story of the terrible self-delusions of a man and the tragic upset that his faking works on his wife and sons. Where the earlier performance of the drama on the stage used the syntax of the screen, with time and location shifting often with the wandering of the man's mind, such movement and flow are thoroughly natural and consistent in the cinematic form. Past and present are run together with perfect smoothness and striking clarity in the film.

Furthermore, Mr. Kramer's production is so faithfully transcribed and well designed that it stands as a nigh exact translation of Mr. Miller's play, both in its psychological candor and its exhibit of a bleak bourgeois milieu. Except for a few small omissions of dialogue lines and words, the drama is offered in toto, right down to its torturing graveyard scene. And the whole atmosphere of middle-class drabness, which was visually strained on the stage, is here given full exhibition in skimpy bedrooms, kitchens and backyards.

Indeed, one perceptible advantage of this performance of the drama on the screen is the sense of a broader frame of reference for the "salesman's" failure that it conveys. The locale is nominally Brooklyn and points adjacent thereto, but could happen in any American city and to anyone who lived by false ideals.

Mr. March's performance does a lot to illuminate this broader implication of the drama, for it fills out considerably the lack of humanity in the main character that Mr. Miller somehow overlooked and thus makes the character more symbolic of the frustrated "little man." The weakness of Mr. Miller's "salesman," in this corner's opinion, is a petty and selfish disposition, unredeemed by any outgoing love. Mr. March, by his personable nature, gives occasional fleeting glints of tenderness. Otherwise, he is the shabby, cheap, dishonest, insufferable big-talker of the play.

As the long-suffering wife of this faker, Mildred Dunnock is simply superb, as she was on the stage. Her portrayal of a woman who bears the agony of seeing her sons and husband turn out failures supports the one pretension of this drama to genuine tragedy. Cameron Mitchell and Kevin McCarthy are disturbingly shifty as the sons, and Howard Smith and Don Keefer do finely by the roles of close relatives that they played on the stage. Laslo Benedek's direction is commendable all the way.

Death of a Salesman is dismally depressing, but it must be acclaimed a film that whips you about in a whirlpool somewhere close to the center of life.

—*B.C., December 21, 1951*

THE DECALOGUE

A series of 10 related films. directed by Krzysztof Kieslowski: written (in Polish. with English subtitles) by Mr. Kieslowski and Krzysztof Piesiewicz: inspired by the Ten Commandments: directors of photography. Wieslaw Zdort (1). Edward Klosinski (2). Piotr Sobocinski (3 and 9). Krzysztof Pakulski (4). Slawomir Idziak (5). Witold Adamek (6). Dariusz Kuc (7). Andrzej Jaroszewicz (8) and Jacek Blawut (10): edited by Ewa Smal: music by Zbigniew Preisner: art director. Halina Dobrowolska: produced by Ryszard Chutkowski: released by New Yorker Films. Each film's running time: roughly 55 minutes.

With: Maria Koscialkowska (Zofia). Teresa Marczewska (Elzbieta). Henryk Baranowski (Krzysztof). Wojciech Klata (Pawel). Aleksander Bardini (Consultant). Olgierd Lukaszewicz (Andrzej). Daniel Olbrychski (Janusz). Maria Pakulnis (Ewa). Miroslaw Baka (Jacek). Krzysztof Globisz (Piotr). Maja Barelkowska (Majka). Ewa Blaszczyk (Hanka). Piotr Machalica (Roman) and Artur Barcis (Young Man in each segment).

For Krzysztof Kieslowski, the great Polish filmmaker who died four years ago, the answers to our most troubling questions about the meaning of life and death and the existence of God can be intuited only from riddles, signs, portents, coincidences and sudden, odd strokes of fate. On entering Kieslowski's somber but far from depressing cinematic world, we find ourselves in a place where everything from household objects to chance encounters with strangers is charged with a mysterious gravity and enigmatic sense of connection. But as powerfully as his films portray human pain and longing, they also convey the preciousness of life with a conviction that few other filmmakers have succeeded in bringing to the screen.

Among Kieslowski's films, including his celebrated *Red, White,* and *Blue* trilogy, the work that towers over everything is *The Decalogue* his 10-part, nearly 10-hour made-for-television series of reflections on the Ten Commandments. Although *The Decalogue* has been shown in New York by the Film Society of Lincoln Center and is available on home video, it is only just now having its commercial release in the city, at the Lincoln Plaza.

If its 10 parts inevitably vary in quality, in its entirety, the cycle—which was first shown on Polish television in 1988–89—stands as a masterwork of modern cinema, essential viewing for anyone who cares about the movies as a serious art form.

The Lincoln Plaza will present *The Decalogue* chronologically in one-week programs, each consisting of two parts, for the next five weeks.

Far from illustrating Old Testament laws with a thunderous drum-beating moralism, these 10 films, set mostly in the vicinity of a large, rather bleak apartment complex in Warsaw, might be described as metaphysical speculations. Without sermonizing or even trying to prove the existence of a divine power operating in the universe, these oblique dramatic parables imagine lives influenced by unseen forces whose intentions can't be predicted or even begun to be grasped.

The profound pleasures they offer derive not only from their deft metaphysical playfulness but also from their storytelling genius. In portraying touching, often anguished human quandaries (including adultery, murder, kidnapping and the death of a child) *The Decalogue* gives each tale the structure of a mathematical equation that almost but doesn't quite balance.

The cycle doesn't have a beginning, a center or a conclusive ending. The closest it comes to expressing the director's personal beliefs is probably in its brilliant eighth part, loosely inspired by the command "Thou shalt not bear false witness against they neighbor."

The central character Zofia (Maria Koscialkowska) a wise, kindly professor of ethics at the University of Warsaw, is paid a surprise visit by Elzbieta (Teresa Marczewska), a much younger, Polish-born American scholar who after having translated several of Zofia's books is returning to Poland to do research on the fate of Jewish survivors of World War II. Invited to sit in on one of Zofia's classes, in which the students debate and try to untangle knotty ethical conundrums, Elzbieta volunteers the story of a six-year-old Jewish girl, hidden in Warsaw by resistance fighters in 1943, who was brought for safekeeping to the home of a Roman

Catholic couple working against the Nazis. Instead of offering her refuge, the couple suddenly changed their minds and without explanation turned her away.

As Zofia listens to the story, in which no names are mentioned, her face crumples into a stricken mask, for she realizes that Elzbieta's story is autobiographical and that Zofia and her husband (now long dead) were the couple who rejected the girl. Later, when Zofia explains to Elzbieta the reasons for that rejection (they had just heard a false rumor that the people bringing the child to them were actually secret agents of the Gestapo), the questions that have haunted both women for more than four decades seem to have been answered and Elzbieta's shaky faith in humanity restored.

But the story has no pat happy ending. Zofia continues to believe that she and her husband made a terrible mistake in being willing (even when their lives seemed in imminent danger) to sacrifice the little girl's life. "Nothing is as important as the life of a child," she declares.

The words that the screenplay by Kieslowski and his collaborator and scenarist Krzysztof Piesiewicz put into the mouth of this wonderful character, who radiates such profound humanity, come as close as any in *The Decalogue* to expressing Kieslowski's own philosophy. All humans, she surmises, are born with goodness and evil, qualities that are summoned by situations, and everyone grows up knowing the difference. As for the existence of God (a word she prefers not to use), he exists in all of us, although we can choose to leave God behind. Those who make that choice, however, are condemned to a state of loneliness.

Although each part of *The Decalogue* is self-contained and may be viewed separately, the 10 have enough thematic connection so that when seen consecutively they build into a much larger and richer whole. Leitmotifs run throughout. One is the recurrent appearance of a silent young man in several episodes who gazes momentarily at the camera, an enigmatic, possibly angelic witness to the events being portrayed. And as in *Red, White,* and *Blue,* the color scheme of *The Decalogue* is loaded with symbolism that enhances the movie's many subtle, surreal touches.

The eighth part, in addition to voicing Kieslowski's ethical philosophy, recapitulates, in a student discussion, the story of Episode 2 ("Thou shalt not take the name of the Lord thy God in vain"), one of the most gripping in the cycle. Here, a prickly, embittered doctor who years ago lost his family in a tragic explosion, is asked to predict the fate of a patient—who seems to be near death—by the patient's wife, a professional musician, who is carrying another man's child. If her husband's chances of surviving are good, she explains, she will have an abortion. If not, she will have the baby and probably go off with her lover.

In this part, which includes the disturbing close-up image of a bee struggling frantically to extricate itself from a container of rusty water collected from a leaky pipe, Kieslowski contrives a miracle. As grim as he could be at times, the supremely evenhanded director could also conjure up a state of grace.

Echoing Zofia's statement about the importance of children, several other episodes are also concerned with their fate at the hands of adults. In Part 1 ("Thou shalt have no other gods before me") a university professor who believes that everything in life can be measured, teaches his young son how to use a computer. When the little boy decides to go skating, he calculates that the ice on the lake should be thick enough to support him. The professor learns tragically that nature isn't as orderly or predictable as his equations suggest. This moving story, which pits the boy's rationalist father against his religiously devout aunt as spiritual influences, is a classic fable of hubris. In one of its surreal twists, it also includes what appears to be a self-starting computer.

A more brutal struggle for a child is waged in Episode 7 ("Thou shalt not steal") in which a little girl brought up believing her grandmother is really her mother and her biological mother her sister is kidnapped by the younger woman, who was 16 when she gave birth and is now of college age. The situation gives us one of Kieslowski's more fiendishly clever equations by wondering which is the real kidnapper: the embittered teenage mother running off with the child or the grandmother who for selfish reasons arranged to make it look as though the baby were hers?

The Decalogue varies enough in tone to include some comedy and suspense as well as high drama and tragedy. Part 6 ("Thou shalt not commit adultery"), which was released in an expanded form under the title *A Short Film About Love,* is the relatively droll tale of a meek, virginal 19-year-old postal clerk who is a Peeping Tom and the beautiful woman across the courtyard on whom he obsessively spies.

Surveillance and voyeurism also haunt Part 9 ("Thou shalt not covet thy neighbor's wife") about a doctor diagnosed as incurably impotent, who encourages his beautiful wife to take a lover. When she does, he becomes jealous and suicidally depressed. It is one of several tales in the cycle in which women emerge as the wiser, nobler sex.

The final episode ("Thou shalt not covet they neighbor's goods") suggests a Hitchcockian interpretation of a De Maupassant tale, in its story of two brothers (one of whom is lead singer for a rock band that performs blasphemous songs) who discover that their just-deceased father amassed a priceless stamp collection. Each becomes increasingly paranoid that the other intends to steal it. Kieslowski makes no bones about it: greed is bad.

The consistency of performances by a sprawling cast that includes both well-known and obscure Polish actors is remarkable. Directing the cast, Kieslowski avoids even a hint of melodrama, and most of the performances are restrained and internalized to the brink of introspection. What we remember most are faces with complicated histories in which hardship and suffering are taken for granted, inner conflicts are continually flickering and an awareness of death shadows even the happiest smile.

Superficially at least, this world feels so different from here and now. In the United States, especially in this time of abundance when the gospel of eternal youth proliferates, we lull ourselves into believing that somehow life can be solved. And more and more of us seek to conceal or even erase the histories Kieslowski's camera locates in his actors' faces. As long as we can erase them, presumably we can live forever.

But *The Decalogue* also conveys the feeling that many of these people have lived more and know more about life than we do. They understand that in the best of all possible worlds fleeting glimpses of salvation are the most any of us can expect.

—S. H., June 29, 2000

DEEP END

Directed by Jerzy Skolimowski; written by Mr. Skolimowski, Jerzy Gruza and Boleslaw Sulik; cinematographer, Charly Steinberger; edited by Barrie Vince; art designer, Max Ott Jr.; produced by Helmut Jedele; released by Paramount Pictures. Running time: 90 minutes.

With: Jane Asher (Susan), John Moulder-Brown (Mike), Diana Dors (Lady Client), Karl Michael Vogler (Swimming Instructor), Christopher Sandford (The Fiancé), Louise Martini (Prostitute) and Erica Beer (The Baths Cashier).

The Polish director Jerzy Skolimowski has been making movies since 1964. He has had showings, especially film festival showings, from the beginning, and he has received a good deal of serious critical attention. But he has not, at least in this country, enjoyed great popularity even with the minuscule movie audience that supports in spirit, if not with cash, whatever really matters in the new and newest cinema.

One reason is that a time lag generally attaches to East European cinema which, like Skolimowski's, follows Western modes, and automatically renders the latest thing just a little old hat. But there are other reasons in the personality of the filmmaker himself, a penchant for fashionable rhetorical postures, a tendency toward surface obscurity without much real complexity underneath, an addiction to more strained anguish than most audiences—or even Skolimowski's own point of view—could really handle.

But *Deep End*, which opened yesterday at the Paris Theater, is a somewhat different and an altogether happier matter. At once funnier and more tragic, more serious and more relaxed, it is recognizably the work of its director in every frame—and at the same time the work of a director who has come to feel at ease with his insights and his own ways of developing them.

I'm not sure that I know why. Perhaps it is the calm of old age (Skolimowski is now pushing thirty-three); perhaps it is color (all the previous Skolimowski films to have played here were in moody black and white); perhaps it is London, where the film takes place; certainly it is at least in part the wonderful presence of John Moulder-Brown and Jane Asher as his hero and heroine.

Moulder-Brown plays Mike, a fifteen-year-old who takes his first job out of school as an attendant at a drab public bath and swimming pool in a run-down part of London. Miss Asher plays Susan, in her early twenties, the female attendant at the bath, who teaches

Mike the ropes and with whom he immediately falls in love. Neither her fiancé (Christopher Sandford) nor her lover (Karl Michael Vogler) nor her own bitter heart and tongue deter Mike. He makes himself into an irresistible nuisance, and a very attractive one as well, and he pursues Susan through thick and thin, from public play to private pleasures, to a somewhat sensational crisis that involves most of the not inconsiderable resources of their bathhouse.

The bath in *Deep End* is not so much a place for getting clean as a place for indulging fantasies, generally sexual, and Skolimowski, who drops symbols the way detective writers drop clues, is not about to ignore any of its possibilities. All through the film, the peeling blues and greens on the walls are being painted over with hot colors, mostly red, to match the growth of passion and to set things up for the climax, in which the decor is at least as important as the action—and indeed is inseparable from it.

Susan functions as cynical realist pandering to other people's fantasies (customers, lover, fiancé), and Mike, as supreme fantasist, who will alter any reality to make his dreams actual. Mike's innocence, decency, and lively good humor hide the fact that his is the crueler role. And his general incompetence makes it easy to ignore that in this environment the odds are wholly in his favor.

Like Truffaut's Antoine Doinel, to whom he owes a good deal, he muddles through. But unlike Antoine, what he muddles through to has only a nightmare relation to the cultural mainstream and the affectionate light of common day.

Although it has a strong and good story, *Deep End* is put together out of individual, usually comic routines. Many of these don't work, but many more work very well. A curious man in a kayak, Mike's adventure with a soccer-loving lady (Diana Dors), and a wonderful sequence in which Susan's fiancé takes her to a pornographic movie while Mike sits behind them molesting Susan—are among the best in a level that is very high indeed.

But for John Moulder-Brown and Jane Asher, I am lost in admiration. It is not so much that they give the performances of their careers—which are just beginning—as that they give the performances of Skolimowski's career. They take a vision that had been sober, fateful and heavily ironic and they help render it alert, subtle, graceful and sensitive to some of the loveliest gestures in recent films.

—R.G., August 11, 1971

THE DEER HUNTER

Directed by Michael Cimino; written by Deric Washburn, based on a story by Mr. Cimino, Mr. Washburn, Louis Garfinkle and Quinn K. Redeker; director of photography, Vilmos Zsigmond; edited by Peter Zinner; music by Stanley Myers; produced by Barry Spikings, Michael Deeley, Mr. Cimino and John Peverall; released by Universal Pictures. Running time: 183 minutes.

With: Robert De Niro (Michael), John Cazale (Stan), John Savage (Steven), Christopher Walken (Nick), Meryl Streep (Linda), George Dzundza (John) and Chuck Aspegren (Axel).

Michael Cimino's *The Deer Hunter* is a big, awkward, crazily ambitious, sometimes breathtaking motion picture that comes as close to being a popular epic as any movie about this country since *The Godfather*. Though he has written a number of screenplays, Mr. Cimino has only directed one other movie (the 1974 box-office hit, *Thunderbolt and Lightfoot*), which makes his present achievement even more impressive. Maybe he just didn't know enough to stop. Instead, he's tried to create a film that is nothing less than an appraisal of American life in the second half of the twentieth century.

I don't mean to make *The Deer Hunter* sound like *War and Peace* or even *Gone With the Wind*. Its view is limited and its narrative at times sketchy. It's about three young men who have been raised together in a Pennsylvania steel town, work together in its mill, drink, bowl and raise hell together, and then, for no better reason than that the war is there, they go off to fight in Vietnam.

The Deer Hunter, which opens today at the Coronet, is an update on the national dream, long after World War II, when America's self-confidence peaked, after the Marshall Plan, after Korea, dealing with people who've grown up in the television age and matured in the decade of assassinations and disbelief.

The three friends, all of Russian extraction, are Mike (Robert De Niro), Nick (Christopher Walken), and Steve (John Savage). Mike is the one who calls the tune for his friends. To the extent that any one of them has an interior life, it is Mike, a man who makes a big thing about hunting, about bringing down a deer with one shot. More than one shot apparently isn't fair. As codes go this one is not great, but it is his own.

Nick goes along with Mike, sometimes suspecting that Mike is eccentric, but respecting his eccentricities. Steve is the conventional one, whose marriage (a Russian Orthodox ceremony, followed by a huge, hysterical reception) occupies most of the film's first hour and sets out in rich detail what I take to be one of the movie's principal concerns—what happens to Americans when their rituals have become only quaint reminders of the past rather than life-ordering rules of the present.

Mr. Cimino has described his treatment of the three friends' war experiences as surreal, which is another way of saying that a lot of recent history is elipsized or shaped to fit the needs of the film. What is not surreal is the brutality of the war and its brutalizing effects, scenes that haunt *The Deer Hunter* and give point to the film even as it slips into the wildest sort of melodrama, which Mr. Cimino plays out against the background of the collapse of Saigon and the American withdrawal from Southeast Asia. It's Armageddon with helicopters.

Most particular and most savage is the film's use of Russian roulette as a metaphor for war's waste. It's introduced when the three friends, prisoners of war of the North Vietnamese, are forced by their captors to play Russian roulette with one another. The game crops up again in Saigon where, according to this film, it was played in back-street arenas rather like cock-fighting pits, for high-dollar stakes. These sequences are as explicitly bloody as anything you're likely to see in a commercial film. They are so rough, in fact, that they raise the question of whether such vivid portrayals don't become dehumanizing themselves.

More terrifying than the violence—certainly more provocative and moving—is the way each of the soldiers reacts to his war experiences. Not once does anyone question the war or his participation in it. This passivity may be the real horror at the center of American life, and more significant than any number of

hope-filled tales about raised political consciousnesses. What are these veterans left with? Feelings of contained befuddlement, a desire to make do and, perhaps, a more profound appreciation for love, friendship and community. The big answers elude them, as do the big questions.

Deric Washburn's screenplay, which takes its time in the way of a big novel, provides fine roles for Mr. De Niro, Mr. Walken and Mr. Savage, each of whom does some of his best work to date. Meryl Streep, who has long been recognized for her fine performances on the New York stage, gives a smashing film performance as the young woman, who, by tacit agreement among the friends, becomes Nick's girl but who stays around long enough to assert herself. In the splendid supporting cast are George Dzundza, Chuck Aspegren, Shirley Stoler and Rutanya Alda. The late John Cazale makes his last film appearance a memorable one as the kind of barroom neurotic who might at any moment go seriously off his rocker.

The film has been stunningly photographed by Vilmos Zsigmond, who provides visually a continuity that is sometimes lacking in the rest of the movie. *The Deer Hunter* is both deeply troubling and troublesome (for the manner in which Mr. Cimino manipulates the narrative), but its feelings for time, place and blue-collar people are genuine, and its vision is that of an original, major new filmmaker.

—V.C., December 15, 1978

THE DEFIANT ONES

Produced and directed by Stanley Kramer; written by Nathan E. Douglas and Harold Jacob Smith; cinematographer, Sam Leavitt; edited by Frederic Knudtson; music by Ernest Gold; production designer, Rudolph Sternad; released by United Artists. Black and white. Running time: 97 minutes.

With: Tony Curtis (John "Joker" Jackson), Sidney Poitier (Noah Cullen), Theodore Bikel (Sheriff Max Muller), Charles McGraw (Captain Frank Gibbons), Lon Chaney (Big Sam), King Donovan (Solly), Claude Akins (Mac) and Lawrence Dobkin (Editor).

A remarkably apt and dramatic visualization of a social idea—the idea of men of different races brought together to face misfortune in a bond of brotherhood—is achieved by producer Stanley Kramer in his new film, *The Defiant Ones*. Tony Curtis and Sidney Poitier are its title players. It opened at the Victoria yesterday.

Reminiscent of Mr. Kramer's early picture *Home of the Brave* in its candid presentment of racial conflict and resentment between Negroes and whites, it rips right into the subject with clawing ferocity and flails it about with merciless fury until all the viciousness in conflict is spent.

The story line is simple. Two convicts, a Negro and a white, escape into open country from an overturned prison van. They put a good deal of ground between them and the wreck before the bloodhound chase begins. The fateful hitch is that they hate each other and they are shackled together at the wrists by a heavy chain.

Thus, in a concrete situation that is sharpened and simplified by the contours of genuine outdoor settings and hard black-and-white camera work, Mr. Kramer has a strong, stark symbolization of an abstract truism. These two men, who think they are so profoundly different, are in basic respects the same. Each is the victim of cruel oppressions, each has his hopes and dreams and each, as a consequence of frustrations, has committed crime.

And this is the thought that Mr. Kramer, as director, tirelessly pounds throughout the film, with the help of a keen, sardonic screenplay by Nathan E. Douglas and Harold Jacob Smith. As his fugitives pause for brief recovery after perilous fording of streams, racing across open country, or hairbreadth escape from a mob, he has them slash at each other with bitter accusations that reveal with startling illumination their complete commonality. In the end, it is clear that they are brothers, stripped of all vulgar bigotry.

While he is clawing out this message, Mr. Kramer is also giving us a fast and exciting melodrama, with a manhunt and chase at its core. By a pattern of crisp, direct cutting and jumping back and forth from the fugitives to their pursuers, among whom there is also a little strife, he keeps the action moving.

It is nervous and suspenseful from the start. And a couple of major incidents, such as their capture and near-lynching by a mob and a cruelly ironic encounter with a young widow and her little boy, bring an accumulation of drama and diversion along the way.

Between the two principal performers there isn't much room for a choice. Mr. Poitier stands out as the Negro convict and Mr. Curtis is surprisingly good. Both men are intensely dynamic. Mr. Poitier shows a deep and powerful strain of underlying compassion. Mr. Curtis is the unregenerate "tough." His one weakness is a "Southern accent," which fluctuates comically.

In the ranks of the pursuers, Theodore Bikel is most impressive as a sheriff with a streak of mercy and justice, which he has to fight to maintain against a brutish state policeman, played by Charles McGraw. Lon Chaney gives a strong performance as an upright and fearless man who firmly deflates a lynch mob and Cara Williams is pathetic as the pretty and pliant young widow who almost snags a man.

With this forceful social drama, we are glad to see Mr. Kramer return to the kind of "idea" picturemaking he did when he was breaking his own trail.

—*B.C., September 25, 1958*

DELIVERANCE

Produced and directed by John Boorman; written by James Dickey, based on his novel; director of photography, Vilmos Zsigmond; edited by Tom Priestley; released by Warner Brothers. Running time: 109 minutes.

With: Jon Voight (Ed), Burt Reynolds (Lewis), Ned Beatty (Bobby), Ronny Cox (Drew), Billy McKinney (Mountain Man), Herbert Coward (Toothless Man), James Dickey (Sheriff Bullard), Ed Ramey (Old Man) and Billy Redden (Lonny).

James Dickey, who won the 1965 National Book Award for poetry and published his first novel, *Deliverance,* in 1970, has been described as a poet "concerned primarily with the direct impact of experience."

In *Deliverance,* he attempts to describe the direct impact of the experience of four Atlanta suburbanites—three of whom are less fit for hiking across a steep cornfield than for watching televised football—when they go on a weekend canoe trip that turns into a nightmare of the machismo mind.

Survival, says one of the characters helpfully (at least helpfully for those of us who suffer genetic deficiencies), is the name of the game. Together the members of the party shoot the white water and, individually, are assaulted by a couple of sodomy-inclined hillbillies, scale sheer cliffs using nothing more than what seem to be prehensile fingernails and fight death duels armed with bow-and-arrow before eventually finding their—well—deliverance.

The problem with the novel is that the perfectly legitimate excitement of the tall story is neutralized by a kind of prose that only Irving Wallace might envy (i.e., "She had great hands; they knew me"). Ordinarily, a film is much better suited than a novel for communicating the direct impact of experience, if only because the experience is immediate and unintellectualized, and you don't have to climb over picturesque semicolons to get from one statement of fact to another.

However, so many of Dickey's lumpy narrative ideas remain in his screenplay that John Boorman's screen version becomes a lot less interesting than it has any right to be. *Deliverance,* which opened yesterday at Loew's Tower East, is an action melodrama that doesn't trust its action to speak louder than words on the order of: "Sometimes you gotta lose yourself to find something." If anybody said that to me—seriously—in the course of a canoe trip I think I'd get out and wade.

This is a disappointment because the film contains some good things, including the look of the production, which was photographed by Vilmos Zsigmond, who did *McCabe and Mrs. Miller,* entirely on locations in rural Georgia in a kind of bleached color that denies any thoughts of romantic sentimentality. The white water sequences are smashingly vivid and untricky, as is Boorman's treatment of his characters who, much of the time, are kept in a middle distance—one that precludes a phony intimacy with them—until crucial moments when close-ups are necessary.

Best of all are the performances—by Jon Voight, as the thoughtful, self-satisfied businessman who rather surprisingly meets the challenge of the wilderness; Burt Reynolds, as the Hemingway hero who fails, through no real fault of his own, and Ned Beatty and Ronny Cox, as their two city friends whose total unsuitability for such a weekend venture is just one of

a number of unbelievable and unexplained points in the Dickey screenplay. I wouldn't get into a Central Park rowboat with either one, but then Dickey's story is schematic, and to make his points about the nature of man he had to deny the very realism that the film pretends to deal in.

—*V.C., July 31, 1972*

DESPERATELY SEEKING SUSAN

Directed by Susan Seidelman; written by Leora Barish; director of photography, Edward Lachman; edited by Andrew Mondshein; music by Thomas Newman; production designer, Santo Loquasto; produced by Sara Pillsbury and Midge Sanford; released by Orion Pictures. Running time: 104 minutes.

With: Rosanna Arquette (Roberta), Madonna (Susan), Aidan Quinn (Dez), Mark Blum (Gary), Robert Joy (Jim), Laurie Metcalf (Leslie), Anna Levine (Crystal) and Will Patton (Nolan).

Susan Seidelman, you should remember, is the young director who first came to attention three years ago with *Smithereens,* a wonderfully funny, independently financed, $80,000 first-feature about a pushy, punkish young woman named Wren and her adventures in the Day-Glo lower-depths of the East Village and blocks west. It's now apparent that *Smithereens* was not a fluke.

With *Desperately Seeking Susan,* her second feature, which opens today at Loew's Paramount and other theaters, Miss Seidelman successfully takes the long, potentially dangerous leap from the ranks of the promising independents to mainstream American moviemaking, her integrity, her talent, and her comic idiosyncrasies intact.

Desperately Seeking Susan, based on a good screenplay by a new writer named Leora Barish, is a terrifically genial New York City farce in which the lives of two very different young women become tangled in an Orlon web of lies, half-truths, and cross-purposes.

It's a fable that involves, among other unlikely things and people, a pair of stolen earrings that once belonged to Nefertiti; a gangster slain in Atlantic City; an earnest, uptight businessman who sells Jacuzzis and hot tubs and who stars in his own cheery television commercials; a professional hit man; amnesia and mistaken identity; a soberly commonplace magician; and a handsome young fellow who makes his living as the projectionist at a theater specializing in the B pictures of yesteryear.

The film's two charming, very funny stars are Rosanna Arquette, the blond chameleon most recently seen in John Sayles's *Baby, It's You* and in the television adaptation of Norman Mailer's *The Executioner's Song,* and Madonna, one of the hottest personalities in music videos, who here has her first major role in a theatrical film and carries it off with nervy ease, as if to echo the Jerry Leiber-Mike Stoller lament, "Is That All There Is?"

Miss Arquette's Roberta is a pampered, Fort Lee, New Jersey, princess, married to Gary, the Jacuzzi salesman and TV "star." Like Ibsen's Nora, magically transported to a condo-with-pool on the far side of the George Washington Bridge, Roberta gets fed up and leaves home, though, unlike Nora, she really doesn't mean to bang the door behind her.

What lures the romantically inclined Roberta away from her probably fake fireplace is a series of personal ads she has been following for some months, each headed "Desperately Seeking Susan," followed by a message from "Jim," who sets up the time and place for their next rendezvous. On impulse one afternoon, Roberta decides to spy on one such rendezvous in Battery Park, where, after a series of unfortunate misunderstandings and a bop on the head, she finds herself with no memory of who she is, though everybody seems to think she's Susan.

Madonna plays the real Susan, a slightly more focused variation on the eccentric, free-living heroine of Miss Seidelman's *Smithereens,* which is not to say that Susan is more conventional, only that the film surrounding her is. Susan is one of society's most winning bandits, but her crimes are essentially victimless. She has no pad of her own and sleeps around for convenience as much as for pleasure. Dressed in her miniskirts, rhinestone boots, and enough New Wave junk jewelry to start her own thrift shop, Susan looks like a piece of performance art on the hoof.

Through a succession of perfectly implausible coincidences—this is, after all, a farce—Roberta, the protected princess from Fort Lee, starts living a reasonable facsimile of Susan's wayward life. She is housed, against his better judgment, by Dez (Aidan Quinn), the projectionist, who is the best friend of Susan's main man Jim (Robert Joy), and works as the onstage assistant to the world's most optimistic, second-rate magician (Peter Maloney) in a Village club that would attract only the seediest of conventioneers.

Susan, aware that the mob might be after her for reasons she never worries about, eventually connects with Roberta's husband, Gary (Mark Blum), and Gary's sister, Leslie (Laurie Metcalf), who, her imagination expanded by exposé magazines, suspects that Roberta may be either a housewife-prostitute or a housewife-lesbian, and maybe both. Gary, dazzled by Susan's manners and glittery raiment, takes her back to Fort Lee, which seems as exotic to her as the Village is to Roberta.

It's no easy thing to keep this kind of farce spinning with seeming effortlessness and, toward the end, *Desperately Seeking Susan* becomes a little desperate itself. Miss Seidelman and Miss Barish never find that single, explosively funny, climactic confrontation scene in which all of the characters would converge for sudden recognition. The movie ends sweetly, but sort of piecemeal.

Miss Seidelman's principal talent is for bringing cockeyed characters to life with great good humor and no condescension, and she's as wicked about life in the new bohemia as in the new suburbia. *Desperately Seeking Susan* is full of funny, sharply observed details, reflected in Santo Loquasto's witty production design as well as in all of the dozens of individual performances. The cast is virtually a Players Guide to the variety of performing talent available in New York.

Miss Arquette and Madonna are delights, as is each member of the huge supporting cast, from Mr. Quinn, Mr. Blum, Mr. Joy, and Miss Metcalf, through Mr. Maloney, and down to those people who appear in split-second cameos, including Anne Carlisle, from *Liquid Sky,* and John Lurie, the star of *Stranger Than Paradise,* who is seen here as the silhouette of a musician behind a window shade.

Desperately Seeking Susan is not, however, an inside joke. It's a New York movie that, like Times Square at four A.M. or Central Park at high noon, is available to everyone.

—V.C., March 29, 1985

DESTRY RIDES AGAIN

Directed by George Marshall: written by Felix Jackson. Gertrude Purcell and Henry Myers. based on the novel by Max Brand: cinematographer Hal Mohr: edited by Milton Carruth: music by Frank Skinner: art designer Jack Otterson: produced by Joe Pasternak: released by Universal Pictures. Black and white. Running time: 94 minutes.

With: Marlene Dietrich (Frenchy). James Stewart (Thomas J. Destry Jr.). Charles Winninger (Wash Dimsdale). Mischa Auer (Boris Callahan). Brian Donlevy (Kent). Irene Hervey (Janice Tyndall). Una Merkel (Lily Belle Callahan) and Allen Jenkins (Gyp Watkins).

Typecasting, the bane of the film industry, has rarely been more successfully plied than by producer Joe Pasternak in his *Destry Rides Again* at the Rivoli. With a sweep of his Hungarian fist he has taken Marlene Dietrich off her high horse and placed her in a horse opera and has converted James Stewart, last seen as Washington's timid Mr. Smith, into the hard-hitting son of an old sagebrush sheriff. Such epics as Max Brand's tale of the coming of law and order to the frontier town of Bottleneck have been told often enough before. What sets this one off from its fellows, converts it into a jaunty and amusing chronicle, is the novelty of finding a Dietrich and a Stewart in it and playing it as wisely as though their names were Mr. and Mrs. Hoot Gibson.

It's difficult to reconcile Miss Dietrich's Frenchy, the cabaret girl of the Bloody Gulch Saloon, with the posed and posturing Dietrich we last saw in Mr. Lubitsch's *Angel*. Her *Blue Angel* comes closer to it. Once again she's hard and tough and painted to the margins of the pallette. She delivers such ballads as "Little Joe the Wrangler" and "The Boys in the Back Room" with quite the proper whiskey contralto effect. She cold-decks a poker sucker with complete nonchalance, tucks her earnings down her dress front and doesn't bat an eye when a cowhand murmurs "Thar's gold in them hills." (And where the Hays office was when that line sneaked through we'll never know, not that we mind it.)

The scene that really counts, though, is the catfight between Miss Dietrich's Frenchy and Una Merkel's outraged Mrs. Callahan. We thought the battle between Paulette Goddard and Rosalind Russell in *The Women* was an eye-opener; now we realize it was just shadow-clawing. For the real thing, with no holds barred and full access to chairs, tables, glasses, bottles, waterbuckets and as much hair as may be conveniently snatched from the opponent's scalp, we give you not *The Women,* but the two women who fight it out in the Bloody Gulch over a pair of Mischa Auer's pants.

Mr. Stewart is all right, too. He usually is. Here he's Destry, son of a fighting father, who comes to Bottleneck as Charles Winninger's deputy and almost breaks that old fire-eater's heart by professing a dislike for firearms. That, naturally, sets him down as a softy, in the opinion of Brian Donlevy and the rest of the thick-necked gentry of Bottleneck. It shouldn't fool you, though; with a name like Destry and a girl like Frenchy to lend him her rabbit's foot, Mr. Stewart couldn't very well help emerging as the hero of a rather heroic occasion. And he couldn't help being Mr. Stewart, turning in an easy, likable, pleasantly humored performance.

So there it is, a bit of the old West with a good bit of the old Dietrich in it; a tightly written, capitally directed show, with perfectly grand supporting performances by Samuel S. Hinds as Bottleneck's mayor, Mr. Donlevy as the chief villain, Mr. Winninger as the shirt-tucking sheriff, and Mischa Auer as a Russian cowboy. Good fun every minute of it, and another trophy for Mr. Pasternak.

—*F.S.N., November 30, 1939*

DIABOLIQUE

Produced and directed by Henri-Georges Clouzot: written (in French, with English subtitles) by Mr. Clouzot. Jerome Geronimi. Frederic Grendel and René Masson. based on the novel *Celle Qui N'etait Pas* by Pierre Boileau and Thomas Narcejac: cinematographer. Armand Thirard: edited by Madeleine Gug: music by Georges Van Parys: art designer: Leon Barsacq: released by Vera Films and United Motion Pictures. Black and white. Running time: 107 minutes.

With: Simone Signoret (Nicole Horner). Vera Clouzot (Christina Delasalle). Paul Meurisse (Michel

Delasalle). Charles Vanel (Inspector Fichet). Noel Roquevert (M. Herboux) and Thérèse Dorny (Mme. Herboux).

It is easy to see why the distributors of H.-G. Clouzot's French film, *Diabolique,* which opened last night at the Fine Arts with a benefit premiere for the Herald Tribune Fresh Air Fund, are earnestly asking audiences not to reveal how it ends. For this is one of the dandiest mystery dramas that has shown here in goodness knows when. To tell anybody the surprises that explode like shotgun blasts in the last reel is a crime that should be punishable by consigning of the culprit to an endless diet of grade-B films.

And it isn't only in the last reel that the surprises and the excitement are in evidence. The morbid fascination starts building before the picture is ten minutes gone. By the time it is rolling toward a climax it is spreading the most delicious chills. It is a pip of a murder thriller, ghost story and character play rolled into one.

True, at the start, it has the appearance of a typical French account of abnormality and sadism in a badly run boys' private school. The headmaster is a tyrant who bullies the students, his sickly wife and even his recognized mistress, who is one of the stoical teachers in the school. Everything seems to be set up for one of those ghastly little psychological tales of genteel mismating and frustration, when—bing!—the mischief begins.

First off, the wife and the mistress conspire to dispose of their mutual male, on the thoroughly acceptable conclusion that he is fit for nothing else but to be killed. And, in the coziest, clammiest fashion, they go about this interesting job, first drugging the old boy with tampered whiskey, then soaking him overnight, headdown, in a bathtub and later dumping his soggy body in the school swimming pool. Anyone at all familiar with the grisly, morbid style of M. Clouzot, whose *Wages of Fear* was a recent manifestation, may have some notion of how enjoyably this is done. The wife's qualms and the mistress's tenacity add to the sport and the suspense.

But this is only the beginning—the setting of the stage, as it were. M. Clouzot is himself unrelenting where a murder and a conscience are concerned. When the wife's sense of guilt and anxiety become so taut at the end of a few days that she demands that the pool be drained so the body may be discovered, he rigs it so the body isn't there! It is gone, disappeared, evaporated! But how—and by whose hand? And what ghostly presence arranges that the suit the husband was wearing is delivered, neatly pressed, the next day?

From here on the writer-director plunges us into a pool of blood-chilling mystifications and suffocating dreads. Who is the strange, unshaven fellow the wife encounters at the morgue when she goes to look at a body that has been fished out of the Seine? Why does one of the younger students insist that he has seen "the Head"? Whose shadowy face is that at a window in a recent school photograph?

Don't expect us to tell the secrets of this diabolical film. We wouldn't think of marring your pleasure of the series of neat surprises at the end. Let us merely assure you that the writing and the visual construction are superb and the performance by top-notch French actors on the highest level of sureness and finesse.

Vera Clouzot, the wife of the director, is a bundle of quivering nerves as the wife in the tale, and Simone Signoret is swift and icy as the mistress who plans everything. Paul Meurisse as the husband, Charles Vanel as the man at the morgue and Pierre Larquey as a foolish old schoolteacher are tops among the males. The settings are sharply realistic. This could be a journalistic account of a particularly gruesome murder mystery.

English subtitles translate the French.

—*B.C., November 22, 1955*

DIAL M FOR MURDER

Produced and directed by Alfred Hitchcock: written by Frederick Knott. based on his play: cinematographer. Robert Burks: edited by Rudi Fehr: music by Dimitri Tiomkin: art designers. Edward Carrere and George James Hopkins: released by Warner Brothers. Running time: 105 minutes.

With: Ray Milland (Tony). Grace Kelly (Margot). Robert Cummings (Mark). John Williams (Inspector Hubbard). Anthony Dawson (Captain Legate). Leo Britt (The Storyteller) and Patrick Allen (Pearson).

The elegant coils of murder drama that Frederick Knott contrived in his play, *Dial M for Murder,* a recent favorite on the Broadway stage, are given a proper twisting in the transmission of that play onto film. In the pliant hands of Alfred Hitchcock, past master at the job of squeezing thrills, the coils twine with sleek and silken evil on the Paramount's screen.

Let's understand at the outset that Mr. Knott's one-set play is a difficult chunk of melodrama for an hour-and-three-quarters-long cinema. All of its critical action logically takes place in one room, and its considerable plot development must necessarily evolve from lots of talk.

The dark machinations of a London husband to get his wife bumped off and then, failing that, to twist the evidence so that it looks as though she willfully murdered the man who tried to murder her are matters of wicked rationalization rather than physical activity. The thrills come in following a succession of dawnings in people's minds.

But Mr. Hitchcock has presented this mental material on the screen with remarkable visual definition of developing intrigue and mood. His actors unfold the drama in their very appearances and, as the chic and malevolent plot thickens, so do their various attitudes.

This is a technical triumph that Mr. Hitchcock has achieved—the tensing of interest and excitement with just a handful of people in a room. It is one for which he needed good actors. He has them—and the best of the lot is John Williams, late of the stage play, who is the detective who solves the sinister ruse.

Mr. Williams, a virtual stranger to movies, tosses knockouts with a flick of his mustache, a lifting of an eyebrow, or a mild exclamation of "oh!" Wisely, of course, Mr. Hitchcock has worked him in close camera range. It is as thrilling as watching Native Dancer just to see Mr. Williams perform. Ray Milland as the machinating husband is excitingly effectual in using expression, too, and Grace Kelly does a nice job of acting the wife's bewilderment, terror and grief. Anthony Dawson, also from the stage play, has the manners and appearance of a snake as the hired murderer. Robert Cummings is negative as a fiction-writing friend.

Excellent color and color combinations add to the flow and variety of the drama's moods. Shot for 3-D but offered here in "standard," the film is vividly pictorial right straight through.

—*B.C., May 29, 1954*

DIARY OF A COUNTRY PRIEST

Directed by Robert Bresson; written (in French, with English subtitles) by Mr. Bresson, based on the novel *Journal d'un Curé de Campagne* by Georges Bernanos; cinematographer, L. H. Burel; edited by Paulette Robert; music by Jean-Jacques Grunenwald; art designer, Pierre Charbonnier; produced by Léon Carré; released by Brandon Films. Black and white. Running time: 120 minutes.

With: Claude Laydu (The Priest of Ambricourt), Nicole Maurey (Louise), André Culbert (The Priest of Torcy), Jean Riveyre (The Count), Madame Arkell (The Countess) and Nicole Ladmiral (Chantal).

Sometimes it helps a little to be able to understand the motivations and maneuverings of the characters in a film. A few simple clues to their behavior do aid one to grasp what's going on. But these rather modest assistances are not provided—to this reviewer, at least—by the contents of Robert Bresson's *Diary of a Country Priest,* the French film that opened yesterday at the refurbished Fifth Avenue Cinema, formerly the Fifth Avenue Playhouse, down near Washington Square.

Despite the extraordinary closeness one has to the hero of this film—and Mr. Bresson gets his camera so close that you can study every bump on the young priest's sad face, every quiver and droop of his sick body, every gesture of his expressive hands, as he fumblingly tries to be a pastor to the people of a village parish in France—the scope of the personal relations and inner conflicts that agonize this man and hasten his death (of cancer) remains elusive and obscure.

What is the deep and dark misgiving that seems to be eating on him as he takes up his clerical duties in a curiously churlish little town? Why do the children torment him—especially one little girl, whose peculiarly sadistic taunting is never made reasonably clear? And what is this complicated business of a slyly adulterous count, his neurotic wife and their strange daughter, who seems to have some complex toward the priest?

Don't ask us. We followed the picture as closely as we could, ears open and eyes darting diligently over the English subtitles for the dialogue. And still we could not catch the pattern of the poor young priest's misery nor penetrate the veil of mysticism that strangely enshrouds the whole film.

This may not be blamed on M. Bresson. The late George Bernanos, who wrote the original story, which is the basis for the film, was one of those French Catholic authors whose concern was the abstract regions of the soul. And it is into these difficult regions that M. Bresson obviously has attempted to have his camera delve.

His cinema technique is brilliant. Reflective of the work of Carl Dreyer, the old Danish master of the close-up and the hard, analytical camera style, it is a compound of searching realism and a tempo of movement that approaches poetry. Thanks to fine photography and authentic backgrounds, this is a pictorially beautiful film.

And the performances are gauntly impressive. Claude Laydu as the tortured young priest gives such a sense of general suffering that he is literally painful to watch. Madame Arkell as the embittered countess is a credible sufferer, too. One long scene between these two characters, in which they talk out the tangles in their souls, is so mentally and physically agonizing that one feels exhausted when it's done. You may not know what has been accomplished, but you know you have been through an ordeal.

Others who play their parts fitly are André Guibert as an old priest, Jean Riveyre as the count, Nicole Maurey as his paramour and Nicole Ladmiral as the daughter of the count.

Perhaps those more closely familiar with the states of grace discussed in this film will be more alert to its meanings. This reviewer was completely confused.

—*B.C., April 6, 1954*

DIE HARD

Directed by John McTiernan; written by Jeb Stuart and Steven E. de Souza, based on the novel by Roderick Thorp; director of photography, Jan De Bont; edited by Frank J. Urioste and John F. Link; music by Michael Kamen; production designer, Jackson DeGovia; produced by Lawrence Gordon and Joel Silver; released by Twentieth Century Fox. Running time: 127 minutes.

With: Bruce Willis (John McClane), Bonnie Bedelia (Holly Gennaro McClane), Reginald Veljohnson (Sergeant Al Powell), Alan Rickman (Hans Gruber), Alexander Godunov (Karl), Paul Gleason (Dwayne T. Robinson), De'Voreaux White (Argyle) and William Atherton (Thornburg).

Die Hard, the movie that gambles a $5 million salary on Bruce Willis, has to be the most excessive film around. It piles every known element of the action genre onto the flimsy story of a New York cop who rescues hostages from a Los Angeles office tower on Christmas Eve. Partly an interracial buddy movie, partly the sentimental tale of a ruptured marriage, the film is largely a special-effects carnival full of machine-gun fire, roaring helicopters and an exploding tank. It also has a villain fresh from the Royal Shakespeare Company, a thug from the Bolshoi Ballet and a hero who carries with him the smirks and wisecracks that helped make *Moonlighting* a television hit. The strange thing is, it works: *Die Hard* is exceedingly stupid, but escapist fun.

The film's producers and director were also responsible for the Arnold Schwarzenegger hit *Predator*. Here they graft the Schwarzenegger-style comic hero onto Mr. Willis's boyish, mischievous *Moonlighting* persona and send this new creature sauntering into *The Towering Inferno*.

There is a slow half-hour at the start, when John McClane (Mr. Willis) lands in Los Angeles to visit his estranged wife (Bonnie Bedelia) and goes to her office Christmas party. Minutes later, a group of terrorists shows up, planning to steal six million dollars in bonds. The terrorists have to crack a difficult computer code before getting into the vault, so there is plenty of time for McClane to play hero.

Mr. Willis's true expertise is in banter, so the director, John McTiernan, shrewdly blends bursts of action with comic dialogue. McClane races up and down elevator shafts. He kills one terrorist, taking his machine gun and citizens' band radio. Now he can have a running conversation with Al, the sympathetic black cop who arrives first at the scene. Al (played by Reginald Veljohnson) becomes part of the only buddy film where the friends don't meet until the story is over.

Meanwhile, back in the executive suite, there is Hans, the ruthless terrorist leader in a very well-tailored suit. He is the film's best surprise, played by Alan Rickman, who was recently the seductive, manipulative Valmont in the Royal Shakespeare Company's stage production of *Les Liaisons Dangereuses.* Here, he makes Hans a perfect snake. "Who are you?" he superciliously asks McClane via radio. "Are you just another American who saw too many movies as a child?"

Well, yes, he did. McClane is a movie maverick, who asks to be called Roy, because he always liked Roy Rogers's fancy shirts. Here, he walks around in a sleeveless undershirt, a tattoo on his left bicep, getting sweatier and dirtier and bloodier by the minute. A great part of the film's appeal is in watching the down-and-dirty cop match wits with the aloof master criminal. The filmmakers even have the wit to play the "Ode to Joy" when Hans finally walks into the opened vault.

Die Hard, which opens today at the Baronet and Criterion Center, has more than its share of bloody moments and blasted bodies, and it has some abysmal scenes as well. The former ballet star Alexander Godunov is a conspicuous terrorist, jumping around the set in a basic black costume and flowing blond hair. As the brother of McClane's first victim, he gets to say things like "I want blood!" And when McClane realizes he has been too hard on his wife, he radios an unintentionally funny message to Al: "Tell her that she is the best thing that ever happened to a bum like me."

The final action sequence is not surprising, as F.B.I. helicopters buzz the rooftop and McClane swings down the side of the high-rise and crashes through a window. But the scenes move with such relentless energy and smashing special-effects extravagance that *Die Hard* turns out to be everything action-genre fans, and Bruce Willis's relieved investors, might have hoped for.

—*C.J., July 15, 1988*

DINER

Written and directed by Barry Levinson; director of photography, Peter Sova; edited by Stu Linder; music by Bruce Brody; art designer, Leon Harris; produced by Jerry Weintraub; released by Metro-Goldwyn-Mayer/United Artists. Running time: 110 minutes.

With: Steve Guttenberg (Eddie), Daniel Stern (Shrevie), Mickey Rourke (Boogie), Kevin Bacon (Fenwick), Timothy Daly (Billy), Ellen Barkin (Beth), Paul Reiser (Modell), Kathryn Dowling (Barbara) and Michael Tucker (Bagel).

Movies like *Diner*—fresh, well-acted and energetic American movies by new directors with the courage of their convictions—are an endangered species. They deserve to be protected, not to mention appreciated and enjoyed. *Diner* isn't lavish or long, but it's the sort of small, honest, entertaining movie that should never go out of style, even in an age of sequels and extravaganzas. It isn't perfect, mind you, but its very unevenness is part of its appeal. There's an excitement in watching a talented fledgling filmmaker take chances.

Diner, which opens today at the Festival, will sound at first like a genre movie in the still-fashionable *American Graffiti* mold. Like *American Graffiti*—or like *Porky's,* for that matter—it's set twenty-odd years ago, returns habitually to some hangout or restaurant and features male adolescents approaching adulthood while talking constantly about sex, to the tune of an incessant parade of hit records.

The resemblance ends there, however; *Diner* is much less carefree than any of its counterparts. The mood is echoed by the color scheme, which is almost entirely discouraging and drab. Only in one key scene do two of the characters find themselves outside of Baltimore's dingy confines, and in the middle of a sunny, bright, wide-open landscape in a wealthy suburb. Riding past them, on a horse, is a privileged, pretty girl. "You ever get the feeling that there's something going on that we don't know about?" one principal asks the other, and then they speed right back to the movie's dark everyday locales.

Barry Levinson, the film's writer and director, goes out on a limb with such touches, and there are scenes as bold as this one that backfire. But Mr. Levinson's feeling and enthusiasm for his youthful characters are unmistakable. And his excesses, like theirs, are easily forgiven.

Diner is about a group of high school buddies who, in 1959, are a year or two out of high school and just beginning to find their ways. Shrevie (Daniel Stern) has already fallen into an early marriage with a woman with whom, he confides to his pals, he cannot have a five-minute conversation. Sex is no longer a mystery to him, but he's already wistful for the time when it was.

His wife, Beth (Ellen Barkin), understands him so little that she cannot even figure out something as basic and important as how he keeps his records filed. At the end of a long domestic quarrel in which he has harangued Beth about the records, Shrevie, meaning to demonstrate his memory for trivia, shouts at Beth that he first met her in 1955—"and 'Ain't That a Shame' was playing when I walked in the door."

Another of the boys, Eddie (Steve Guttenberg), is about to marry a girl named Elyse, whom we hear about constantly but never see. Eddie is such a Baltimore Colts fan that he is insisting that their colors be the colors for his wedding. He's such a nervous bridegroom that he's demanding Elyse score higher than sixty-five on a sports quiz of Eddie's own making. If Elyse flunks, he says, he won't marry her. He isn't kidding. What will he do when she scores sixty-three?

The other principals are a rich, dissolute, loutish bad boy, Fenwick (Kevin Bacon) who, in one surprising private moment gets all the answers right while watching *College Bowl;* a smooth-talking Romeo (Mickey Rourke), who makes bets about everything, including his sex life, and who works as a beautician but who does better with girls if he tells them he's going to law school; and a nice, straight-arrow college boy (Timothy Daly), who can't persuade his pregnant girlfriend to get married to him. These characters are individually well drawn, and they're played beautifully. Mr. Levinson has found a first-rate cast, most of them unknown but few to be unknown for long.

Mr. Guttenberg and Mr. Stern have had previous film experience, but neither has had as good a role before. Mr. Bacon, who's worked on soap operas and Off Broadway, makes Fenwick a memorable mixture of rakishness and desperation. Mr. Rourke, who was outstanding as the jailbird demolition expert in *Body Heat,* has a much bigger role here and plays it superbly. Soft-spoken and sly, his ne'er-do-well hairdresser also turns out to be the sweetest character in the movie, and Mr. Rourke makes his kindness seem inviting and real.

Mr. Levinson varies the movie's mood greatly from scene to scene. Some sequences—like one at a strip club, where two of the boys get the band to play some jazz and everyone starts dancing—are pure fantasy, and don't look like anything else. Others—as when the group sits arguing heatedly over whether Frank Sinatra is better than Johnny Mathis—have a charmingly silly mundanity. So does a scene in which Shrevie, who works in a television store, tries to persuade one customer to buy a color set, even though the man says he once saw *Bonanza* in color and "the Ponderosa looked faked." Mr. Levinson isn't above sending his characters to see Troy Donahue and Sandra Dee at a local movie house, either. The nostalgic side of his material is played to the hilt.

But *Diner* has much more to it than that, and it doesn't seem to strive for the studied authenticity that other, similarly structured movies are after. When Mr. Levinson stages a school dance, it doesn't look quite like a real dance of 1959 vintage. The clothes are too dark, the steps aren't right, and the characters are faintly out of place. Mr. Levinson isn't just a man with a fond or encyclopedic memory for his own early years. He's someone trying to make sense of that time, not simply to remember it. In *Diner,* he makes a great deal of sense indeed.

—J.M., April 2, 1982

DINNER AT EIGHT

Directed by George Cukor; written by Edna Ferber, George S. Kaufman, Herman J. Mankiewicz, Frances Marion and Donald Ogden Stewart, based on the play by Ms. Ferber and Mr. Kaufman; cinematographer, William H. Daniels; edited by Ben Lewis; music by William Axt; art designers, Hobe Erwin and Fredric Hope; produced by David O. Selznick; released by Metro-Goldwyn-Mayer. Black and white. Running time: 113 minutes.

With: Marie Dressler (Carlotta Vance), John Barrymore (Larry Renault), Wallace Beery (Dan Packard), Jean Harlow (Kitty Packard), Lionel Barrymore (Oliver Jordan), Lee Tracy (Max Kane), Edmund Lowe (Dr. Wayne Talbot) and Billie Burke (Mrs. Oliver Jordan).

With its remarkable array of histrionic talent and with George Cukor at the helm, the film adaption of the play, *Dinner at Eight,* which was offered last night by Metro-Goldwyn-Mayer at the Astor, could scarcely help being successful. And it lives up to every expectation, even though a few of the unforgettable lines penned by George S. Kaufman and Edna Ferber have been lost in the general shuffle. The picture clings as closely as possible to the original, and the many opportunities along cinematic lines have been fully appreciated by Mr. Cukor and others responsible for the offering.

This *Dinner at Eight* has a cast of twenty-five, and among the players are most of the stellar lights of the Metro-Goldwyn-Mayer studios, besides a few borrowed from other companies. It is one of those rare pictures that keeps you in your seat until the final fade-out, for nobody wants to miss one of the scintillating lines.

It is a fast-moving narrative with its humor and tragedy, one that offers a greater variety of characterizations than have been witnessed in any other picture. Some are polished and others decidedly rough and ready. They range from Mrs. Oliver Jordan, the snobbish hostess, who is wrapped up in the dinner she is giving for Lord and Lady Ferncliffe, to the scheming Dan Packard and his wife, Kitty, who in the play was said to talk "pure spearmint." But there is a reason in all cases for inviting the guests.

A strong line of drama courses through the story notwithstanding the flip dialogue. The picture runs along with a steady flow of unusually well knit incidents, which are woven together most expertly toward the end. This is owing to the fine writing of Mr. Kaufman and Miss Ferber, and it might easily be said that the wonder would be that anybody could go askew in turning such a play into pictorial form.

Veteran players of the stage, who have since been won over to talking pictures, are the principal assets in this film. It is a great pleasure to behold Marie Dressler away from her usual roles, dressed in the height of fashion and given lines that aroused gales of mirth from the first-night audience.

Miss Dressler acts Carlotta Vance, the stage beauty of the mauve decade. Carlotta is a woman of much common sense who has a retort for every quip made to her. When one woman, obviously well on in years, hints that she was a child when she first saw Carlotta, the former actress ends the conversation by suggesting that they talk about the Civil War. Carlotta has her

Pekingese dogs, one of which boasts of the name of Tarzan.

Another stage favorite of old is Billie Burke, who appears as the handsome Mrs. Oliver Jordan. A week before the dinner in honor of the Ferncliffes, she is worrying about the affair, making sure that there will not be the slightest hitch. An orchestra is ordered, extra servants hired and, when the morning of the dinner comes around, an aspic in the form of a lion is made. Little does Mrs. Jordan think that her dinner is going to be a memorable fiasco.

Lionel Barrymore fills the part of Mr. Jordan, whose mind is more concerned about money matters and his steamship line than his wife's dinner. His brother John is cast as Larry Renault, the motion picture actor who brags of having earned $8,000 a week at one time, while he has only seven cents to his name.

The scenes depicting Dan Packard, played by Wallace Beery, and Kitty, his ash-blonde wife, acted by Jean Harlow, are filled with gruff fun. There is hardly a moment while they are at home when the air is not filled with acrimonious accusations and retorts. Kitty rather likes the idea of blossoming out in society, while Dan's heart is set on being a big gun in politics. Edmund Lowe impersonates Dr. Wayne Talbot, who is infatuated with Kitty, one of his patients.

Mrs. Jordan's state of mind can well be imagined when she hears over the telephone that the Ferncliffes are unable to attend the dinner as they are on their way to Florida. Added to this are other troubles, including the tragic end of Larry Renault, who, unknown to Mrs. Jordan, had had an affair with her daughter, Paula.

Miss Dressler is splendid as the wise Carlotta. Miss Burke's contribution to the story is all one could wish. She is the personification of an anxious hostess at one moment and subsequently a deeply disappointed woman. John Barrymore tackles his role with his usual artistry. His acting during Larry's last moments is most effective. Mr. Beery fits into the role of Dan Packard as though it were written especially for him and Miss Harlow makes the most of the part of Kitty. Lionel Barrymore is suave and sympathetic. Edmund Lowe does quite well as Dr. Talbot.

It was a grand evening, an entertainment that caused one to forget about the deluge outside.

—*M.H., August 24, 1933*

THE DIRTY DOZEN

Directed by Robert Aldrich: written by Lukas Heller and Nunnally Johnson. based on the novel by E. M. Nathanson: cinematographer. Ted Scaife: edited by Michael Luciano: music by Frank De Vol: art designer. William Hutchinson: produced by Raymond Anzarut: released by Metro-Goldwyn-Mayer. Running time: 149 minutes.

With: Lee Marvin (Major Reisman). Ernest Borgnine (General Worden). Charles Bronson (Joseph Wladislaw). Jim Brown (Robert Jefferson). John Cassavetes (Victor Franko). Richard Jaeckel (Sergeant Bowren). George Kennedy (Major Max Armbruster). Trini Lopez (Pedro Jiminez). Ralph Meeker (Captain Stuart Kinder). Robert Ryan (Colonel Everett Dasher-Breed). Telly Savalas (Archer Maggott). Donald Sutherland (Vernon Pinkley) and Clint Walker (Samson Posey).

A raw and preposterous glorification of a group of criminal soldiers who are trained to kill and who then go about this brutal business with hot, sadistic zeal is advanced in *The Dirty Dozen,* an astonishingly wanton war film, which opened last night at the Capitol and begins a dual engagement at the 34th Street East today.

It is not simply that this violent picture of an American military venture is based on a fictional supposition that is silly and irresponsible. Its thesis that a dozen military prisoners, condemned to death or long prison terms for murder, rape and other crimes, would be hauled out of prison and secretly trained for a critical commando raid behind the German lines prior to D-Day might be acceptable as a frankly romantic supposition, if other factors were fairly plausible.

But to have this bunch of felons a totally incorrigible lot, some of them psychopathic, and to try to make us believe that they would be committed by any American general to carry out an exceedingly important raid that a regular commando group could do with equal efficiency—and certainly with greater dependability—is downright preposterous.

And then to bathe these rascals in a specious heroic light—to make their hoodlum bravado and defiance of discipline, and their nasty kind of gutter solidarity, seem exhilarating and admirable—is encouraging a spirit of hooliganism that is brazenly antisocial, to say the least.

Finally, to put them to blasting and butchering a château filled with Nazi staff officers and their women, upon whom they parachute a few nights before D-Day, shooting and stabbing and setting fire to a lot of them locked in an air-raid shelter, and then carrying it on to interminable length, is a studied indulgence of sadism that is morbid and disgusting beyond words.

To be sure, Nunnally Johnson and Lukas Heller, who wrote the turgid script from a novel by E. M. Nathanson, have tried to justify certain absurdities along the way. They have dropped a hint that the American general who orders this grotesque adventure and a couple of his subordinate officers are a wee bit mad or depraved. And, from the way Ernest Borgnine plays the general and Robert Ryan and Robert Webber play the officers, one might truly get the idea that they are crazy or grossly incompetent or out to get Lee Marvin, who plays the major assigned to train the "Dirty Dozen."

Mr. Johnson and Mr. Heller have also built up a sprawling episode of a preinvasion war game in which the fellows prove themselves by capturing Mr. Ryan's headquarters as a way of justifying their competence. Actually, this whole maneuver is directed by Robert Aldrich in a vulgarly raucous, comic vein, and is so loaded in favor of the felons and their deceitful tactics that it proves nothing but the meretriciousness of the film.

And in that final raid on the Normandy château, an attempt to make it seem realistic and suspenseful by a careful preliminary verbal plotting of it in the script is blown to bits by the wildly abandoned and explosive style of Mr. Aldrich's staging.

There are some bizarre and bold performances, if one cares for that sort of thing. Mr. Marvin's taut, pugnacious playing of the major who whips the group into a fairly efficient team of killers is tough and terrifying. John Cassavetes is wormy and noxious as a psychopath condemned to death, and Telly Savalas is swinish and maniacal as a religious fanatic and sex degenerate. Charles Bronson as an alienated murderer, Richard Jaeckel as a hard-boiled military policeman and Jim Brown as a white-hating Negro stand out in the animalistic group.

The only women who appear, incidentally, are the German concubines at the château and a group of seven sleazy prostitutes with which the major generously rewards his raunchy mob of commandos after their exhausting training course. This little touch of "realism" is but another manifestation of the deliberate endeavor to make this a sadistic film.

One might wonder, at times, whether Mr. Johnson and Mr. Heller were not attempting a subtle exposition of the hideousness and morbidity of war—that is, until Mr. Aldrich sets the hoodlums to roaring and shooting guns. Then it is clear that the intent of this loud picture is just to delight and stimulate the easily moved.

—B.C., June 16, 1967

DIRTY HARRY

Produced and directed by Don Siegel; written by Harry Julian Fink, Rita M. Fink and Dean Riesner, based on a story by Ms. Fink and Mr. Fink; director of photography, Bruce Surtees; edited by Carl Pingitore; music by Lalo Schifrin; art designer, Dale Hennesy; released by Warner Brothers. Running time: 102 minutes.

With: Clint Eastwood (Harry), Harry Guardino (Bressler), Reni Santoni (Chico), Andy Robinson (Killer), John Larch (Chief), John Mitchum (DeGeorgio) and John Vernon (The Mayor).

The honorable and slightly anachronistic enterprise of the Don Siegel cops-and-crooks action movies over the last few years (*Madigan, Coogan's Bluff*) takes a sad and perhaps inevitable step downward in *Dirty Harry*, which opened yesterday at the Loew's State 2 and Loew's Orpheum theaters. There are moments in *Dirty Harry* that I would place above anything in the earlier films, but as a whole it makes less sense—or less interesting sense—than they do. And the grim devotion to duty that has always been the badge of Siegel's constabulary is here in Clint Eastwood's tough San Francisco plainclothesman, pushed beyond professionalism into a kind of iron-jawed self-parody.

"Dirty" is Harry's given epithet, and he carries it proudly enough. But he is really a knight in shining armor whose dirtiness is mostly rubbed on from the scummy world he keeps trying to wipe clean. From beginning to end he has an antagonist (Andy Robinson), a skillful sniper and a maniacal murderer of innocent young girls, cops, kids and Negroes, who means to hold the city to ransom for the lives of its inhabitants. However, he faces other problems. A full-scale bank robbery (lovely sequence) and high-jumping suicide attempt he foils, as it were, during coffee breaks. But against civil rights and civic administration he has few resources. In the long run it is the Mayor's office, Miranda and Escobedo, and the first ten amendments to the Constitution that deal him out and—professionally—do him in.

Of course he gets his man—more than once. But despite four known murders the man keeps walking away (limping a bit from Harry's strong right arm and rough right foot) because he has been searched without a warrant and apprehended with a little too much zeal. It is not the hard-hat sentiment that I find disturbing in all this so much as the dull-eyed insensitivity.

Dirty Harry fails in simple credibility so often and on so many levels that it cannot even succeed (as I think it wants to succeed) as a study in perversely complimentary psychoses.

What does succeed, and what makes *Dirty Harry* worth watching no matter how dumb the story, is Siegel's superb sense of the city, not as a place of moods but as a theater for action. There is a certain difficult integrity to his San Francisco, which is not so beautiful to look at, but is fantastically intricate and intriguing—a challenging menace of towers and battlements and improbable walls.

It is from the properties of such a theater that *Dirty Harry* creates its own feelings and makes its only real meaning, and occasionally even generates a curious misty atmosphere that owes nothing to vague imaginings and everything to a desperate awareness that for this world the only end of movement is in pain.

—R.G., December 23, 1971

DIRTY ROTTEN SCOUNDRELS

Directed by Frank Oz; written by Dale Launer, Stanley Shapiro and Paul Henning; director of photography, Michael Ballhaus; edited by Stephen A. Rotter and William Scharf; music by Miles Goodman; production designer, Roy

Walker: produced by Bernard Williams: released by Orion Pictures. Running time: 110 minutes.

With: Steve Martin (Freddy Benson). Michael Caine (Lawrence Jamieson). Glenne Headly (Janet Colgate). Anton Rodgers (Inspector Andre). Barbara Harris (Fanny Eubanks). Ian McDiarmid (Arthur) and Dana Ivey (Mrs. Reed).

Lawrence Jamieson (Michael Caine) is a haberdasher's dream, the sort of man who could make Oleg Cassini look like a panhandler. Lawrence wears clothes well, has a gourmet's palate, impeccable manners, and lives in splendor on the French Riviera in a magnificent villa overlooking the sea.

He's also a superior con artist. Most of the time he passes himself off as a prince in mufti, a deposed royal in need of money to liberate his homeland from the yoke of Communism. Rich women of a certain age find Lawrence irresistible.

Freddy Benson (Steve Martin) wears baggy gray trousers, a green T-shirt, and a Panama hat. He's a self-satisfied klutz who aspires to be a con artist. His ploy is to tell rich women that his grandmother needs an operation. Sometimes Freddy receives a "loan." More often it's the price of a meal, which, on the French Riviera, isn't necessarily modest. Compared with Lawrence, Freddy is small change.

At the beginning of *Dirty Rotten Scoundrels,* one of the season's most cheerful, most satisfying new comedies, Freddy is on a train en route to the South of France, trying to psych himself up to the task at hand. He asks himself why he shouldn't prey on women. Men, he reasons, suffer "more heart attacks than women, more strokes, and more prostate problems." Men are entitled to whatever they can get.

That thought prompts Freddy to grin with eager anticipation and utterly unwarranted confidence in his own malevolent schemes.

Freddy's mistake is to settle in the fictitious Riviera town of Beaumont-sur-Mur, which is Lawrence's exclusive turf. After some initial sparring, Freddy blackmails the elegant Lawrence into teaching him the tricks of the trade. They make a bet: the first man to swindle a woman out of $50,000 can keep the money and the territory.

All of this may sound familiar. *Dirty Rotten Scoundrels* is a remake of the 1964 comedy *Bedtime Story,* which was written by Stanley Shapiro and Paul Henning and which starred David Niven and Marlon Brando in the roles now being played by Mr. Caine and Mr. Martin.

Except for its title, the earlier film has receded from memory, but I can't imagine that it could have been anywhere near as entertaining as this blithe, seemingly all-new, laugh-out-loud escapade opening today at the Embassy 4 and other theaters.

Their comic methods are different, but from their first unequal encounter until the very last in a series of twist endings, Mr. Caine and Mr. Martin work together with an exuberant ease that's a joy to watch.

Don't mistake what Mr. Caine does with the work of a straight man like Jack Benny, whom he otherwise resembles not at all. Mr. Caine is a sneaky master of the pregnant reaction shot. This is a superb comic performance, seeming laid-back but larcenous in effect. Looking exceptionally fit, well-fed, and intimidatingly grand, Mr. Caine nearly walks off with the movie, mostly by appearing to be politely appalled by the gauche Freddy Benson.

Playing to (and for) his costar, Mr. Martin gives a performance of inspired goofiness. As an American innocent who sets out to bag big game with a BB gun, he is the last hilariously enfeebled embodiment of nineteenth-century frontier optimism. No matter how often his Freddy Benson fails, he's ever ready to get up, brush himself off and start all over again.

Lawrence announces loftily that he never takes advantage of the poor or the virtuous. Freddy likes nothing better than a sitting target. His career depends on it.

Dirty Rotten Scoundrels was directed by Frank Oz, one of the Muppet wizards who went on to make the film adaptation of *The Little Shop of Horrors,* and written by Dale Launer (*Ruthless People*), with equal credit going to Mr. Shapiro and Mr. Henning. Line by line, the dialogue isn't all that quotable, but there is consistently funny life on the screen. The film's comic timing is nearly flawless.

The object of the $50,000 bet between the two men is the pretty, gullible young Janet Colgate (charmingly played by Glenne Headly), known as "the American soap queen," a sitting target if there ever was one. Freddy attempts to play on her sympathies by passing himself off as a paralyzed naval officer on six weeks of "medical trauma leave."

He has been unable to walk, he explains, ever since his fiancée ran off with the television host of *Dance, U.S.A.*

The more urbane Lawrence, not to be outdone, identifies himself to the heiress as a famous Viennese psychiatrist, the only man in the world who is known to be able to cure such psychosomatic illnesses.

Among the other women who come into the lives of the desperate competitors are a romantic, husky-voiced Nebraska widow (Barbara Harris) and an Oklahoma millionairess (Meagen Fay). When the latter falls for Lawrence, she makes firm plans to have "the biggest royal wedding Tulsa has ever seen."

Each and every one of them is a delight. In this season of lazy, fat, mistimed, and misdirected comedies, exemplified by *Scrooged* and *Twins, Dirty Rotten Scoundrels* is an enchanted featherweight folly.

—*V.C., December 14, 1988*

THE DISCREET CHARM OF THE BOURGEOISIE

Directed by Luis Buñuel; written (in French, with English subtitles) by Mr. Buñuel and Jean-Claude Carrière; director of photography, Edmond Richard; edited by Helen Plemiannikov; music by Galaxie Musique; art designer, Pierre Guffroy; produced by Serge Silberman; released by Twentieth Century Fox. Running time: 100 minutes.

With: Fernando Rey (The Ambassador), Jean-Pierre Cassel (M. Sénéchal), Delphine Seyrig (Madame Thevenot), Stéphane Audran (Madame Sénéchal), Bulle Ogier (Florence), Paul Frankeur (M. Thevenot), Julian Bertheau (Bishop), Michel Piccoli (Home Secretary) and Muni (Peasant Girl).

As in a dream things go fearfully wrong for the characters in Luis Buñuel's brilliant (and brilliantly titled) new comedy, *The Discreet Charm of the Bourgeoisie,* but the Ambassador of Miranda and his Parisian friends, the Sénéchals and the Thevenots, and Mrs. Thevenot's sister, Florence, always manage to cope gracefully. On second thought, Florence is not quite as consistent as the others.

One martini and Florence is inclined to throw up—looking beautiful one minute and like a dead goose the next, her head dangling out the Ambassador's Cadillac window.

For the most part, however, the Ambassador, the Sénéchals, the Thevenots and Florence survive a series of magnificently bewildering circumstances, employing the kind of elegance, self-interest, delicacy, intelligence, rudeness and short attention spans that Buñuel apparently finds to be the power, the curse and the appeal of the European upper-middle class.

The world of *The Discreet Charm of the Bourgeoisie* is one of absolutely everything interrupted.

For some peculiar reason, every time the friends sit down to dine, odd things happen. An Army arrives or, just as the food is being served, a curtain goes up and the friends find themselves on a stage playing to an audience. "I don't know my lines," M. Sénéchal (Jean-Pierre Cassel) says with wild-eyed, middle-of-the-night fright.

When Mme. Thevenot (Delphine Seyrig) is at the flat of the Ambassador (Fernando Rey) for an afternoon tryst, her husband (Paul Frankeur) stops by—and you haven't seen such a flurry of garter belts and little white gloves in forty years of moviegoing. Things get so bad that fate even conspires to interrupt (though not permanently) the very profitable heroin smuggling operation that the Ambassador conducts with the help of M. Sénéchal and M. Thevenot.

One must, I suppose, talk about *The Discreet Charm of the Bourgeoisie* rather gravely. It is, after all, Buñuel's twenty-eighth feature since *L'Age D'Or* in 1929 but, except for *The Exterminating Angel* and *Belle de Jour,* he has never since employed the special freedom of Surrealism for such astonishing and lucid results.

Several years ago, Buñuel said of *The Exterminating Angel* that "its images, like the images in a dream, do not reflect reality, but create it." A lot of *The Discreet Charm of the Bourgeoisie* is made up of dreams—at times, of dreams within dreams, at other times, dreams that one person has dreamed that another dreamed. Sometimes they are just the dreams of a passerby. You've never seen so many wish fulfillments. However, much of it is not a dream, and all of it is real—the unique creation of a director who, at seventy-two, has never been more fully in control of his talents, as a filmmaker, a moralist, social critic and humorist.

One must talk about these things; yet they tend to

flatten the special exhilaration that *The Discreet Charm of the Bourgeoisie* inspires when you see it. That exhilaration has to do with the awareness that you're watching a genius at work through any number of indications, some almost minuscule.

Take, for example, the sort of small to-do that ensues when Mme. Sénéchal (Stéphane Audran) and Mme. Thevenot, with Florence (Bulle Ogier), go for afternoon tea at a fancy Paris hotel. Florence asks to change her seat. She can't stand looking at the cellist. "I hate cellos," she pouts. "Most orchestras have dropped them." Like others in her class, Florence is a woman in the thrall of cockeyed fashion.

Or take the character of the clergyman (Julien Bertheau). "You've heard of the worker priests?" he asks the astonished Mme. Sénéchal as he applies for the job of gardener. "Well, I'm a worker bishop."

In addition to being extraordinarily funny and perfectly acted, *The Discreet Charm* moves with the breathtaking speed and self-assurance that only a man of Buñuel's experience can achieve without resorting to awkward ellipsis. It was shown last night at the New York Film Festival and opens Sunday, October 22 at the Little Carnegie. As I have not said in several years: Don't miss it.

—V.C., October 14, 1972

DISRAELI

Directed by Alfred E. Green; written by Julien Josephson, based on the play by Louis Napoleon Parker; cinematographer, Lee Garmes; edited by Owen Marks; music by Louis Silvers; released by Warner Brothers. Black and white. Running time: 90 minutes.

With: George Arliss (Disraeli), Joan Bennett (Lady Clarissa Pevensey), Florence Arliss (Lady Beaconsfield), Anthony Bushell (Lord Deeford) and Ivan Simpson (Hugh Myers).

It would have done old Louis Parker's heart good last night to hear and see George Arliss in the Vitaphone version of his play, *Disraeli,* which was offered to an appreciative audience at Warner's Theater. For Mr. Arliss is on his mettle and he lends to the romantic conception of the great Jew an artistry and vigor that is a joy to behold.

Mr. Arliss is thoroughly familiar with this part, having played it many a time on the stage and then also in a silent picture. Here, in his first talking film, he realizes, evidently, that it is but one performance and it must be his best work. The picture was directed by Alfred Green, but Mr. Arliss cannot be denied the little touches he has insisted upon in this audible production.

Mr. Arliss's diction is smooth and he achieves the climaxes with a characteristic savoir faire. He becomes, through his experience with this play, a Disraeli that one does not question. It may seem strange that spies are ubiquitous in the prime minister's home, but that's what makes the story, and each time the farsighted statesman calls on his wit to cover an awkward situation, it is something one desires to acclaim.

In the picture with Mr. Arliss is that clever actor, Ivan Simpson, the valet of *The Green Goddess,* who in this current feature impersonates Hugh Myers, the sympathetic banker.

The tirade that Disraeli lets loose at the bumptious governor of the Bank of England is portrayed with a vehemence that calls for attention from every eye and ear in the theater. And when Disraeli virtually forces this Lord Probert to sign the document financing the Suez Canal venture, the governor of the Bank of England tosses aside the pen and declares that it is not right that any man should have such power.

A little while later Lady Beaconsfield comments on the power of the prime minister and Disraeli with a crafty smile says:

"But I haven't, you know."

There is the code Disraeli is presumed to have invented on the spur of the moment. It was sent in a message by the none-too-bright Lord Deeford from Egypt after the Myers check had been accepted, and it read:

"The celery is ready to cut."

Which being interpreted means that the huge deal had been consummated.

Disraeli takes a liking to Deeford in spite of the latter's youthful Oxonian political ideas. Mrs. Travers and her colleague in crime are desirous of ascertaining whether the prime minister has any intention of sending a representative to Egypt, and they ask Deeford, who refuses to say a word. When told of this, Disraeli tells Deeford that he might just as well have talked to Mrs. Travers for an hour, as his "silence was most eloquent."

The idea of this narrative is to show how Disraeli outwitted the Russians in the Suez Canal purchase and made Victoria an Empress. An early incident depicts a debate in the House of Commons, the interior of which, incidentally, is marvelously well reproduced. There is Gladstone attacking Disraeli and that prime minister is on his bench with his gray top hat tilted over his eyes. Disraeli lazily arises and punctures the oratory of the rival statesman.

The romantic side of this story is supplied by Joan Bennett as Lady Clarissa Pevensey and Anthony Bushell, who fills the role of Lord Deeford. Miss Bennett contributes a charming personality to her part. But it is Disraeli, who is never averse to being interrupted, who really brings about the match. He elects to send Deeford to Egypt because it is a mission, he explains, that requires either a brilliant man or one who is so honest that he is suspected of guile in his intentions.

Florence Arliss, Mr. Arliss's wife, plays Lady Beaconsfield, who is always thoughtful of her husband and his career. The story is told that one day she caught her finger in the carriage door, but covered the pain for fear that it might distress her husband in the House that night. Mrs. Arliss is sympathetic and human in this part.

There are glimpses of the prime minister's love of gardening and his peacocks are perceived decorating the lawn and the steps of his home. Mr. Green uses his camera also in other interludes to good advantage.

Disraeli's gentle epigrams lighten this pleasing picture. At the outset, when interrupted, Disraeli says that the less work a prime minister does, the fewer mistakes he makes.

The tonal quality of the voices is capital and Mr. Arliss betrays not the slightest anxiety concerning the propinquity of that frequently treacherous device, the microphone.

—M.H., October 3, 1929

DISTANT THUNDER

Directed by Satyajit Ray; written (in Bengali, with English subtitles) by Mr. Ray, based on the novel by Bibhuti Bhusan Bannerji; director of photography, Soumendu Roy; editor, Dulal Dutta; music by Mr. Ray; executive producer, Mrs. Sarbani Bhattacharya. Running time: 100 minutes.

With: Soumitra Chatterji (Gangacharan), Babita (Ananga), Sandhya Roy (Chhutki), Gobinda Chakravarty (Dinabandhu) and Romesh Mukerji (Biswas).

The Bengali countryside is almost heavy with color, with golds, yellows, umbers and especially with the greens of the rice fields. The village is tranquil. Caste is observed. It is part of the order of things. Occasionally groups of airplanes are heard overhead, but they are as remote as the war that, according to a village elder, "the king is fighting with the Germans and the Japanese." One villager reports the Germans have captured Singapore, but he is corrected. It's the Japanese who have captured Singapore, the man is told.

Aside from a shortage of kerosene, the war, at first doesn't seem to have much effect on the villagers in Satyajit Ray's fine, elegiac new film, *Distant Thunder* (*Ashani Sanket*). The movie, which has the impact of an epic without seeming to mean to, was shown last night at the New York Film Festival at Lincoln Center. It will be presented there again tonight.

Distant Thunder has all sorts of connections with Ray's great Apu Trilogy—its village setting, its leading actor, Soumitra Chatterji, who played the title role in *The World of Apu,* and its source material. The new film, like the Apu Trilogy, is based on a novel by Bibhuti Bhusan Bannerji. It is, however, very different from those early films.

It is the work of a director who has learned the value of narrative economy to such an extent that *Distant Thunder,* which is set against the backdrop of the "manmade" famine that wiped out five million people in 1943, has the simplicity of a fable.

Though its field of vision is narrow, more or less confined to the social awakening of a young village Brahmin and his pretty, naive wife, the sweep of the film is so vast that, at the end, you feel as if you'd witnessed the events from a satellite. You've somehow been able to see simultaneously the curvature of the earth and the insects on the blades of field grass.

Distant Thunder is about Gangacharan (Mr. Chatterji), the only Brahmin in his village, a solemn and rather pompous young man who accepts the responsibilities as well as the privileges of caste. As teacher, physician and priest he looks forward to the material rewards due him. When Ananga, his wife, asks him if he really can ward off cholera through spells, for which neighboring villagers will pay him handsomely, he replies that, in addition to the spells, he will pass on to the villagers the practical information from his hygiene encyclopedia.

As the war-induced rice shortage becomes increasingly acute, the tranquillity of the village is destroyed. Lifelong trusts are betrayed. Civil order falls apart. At the same time, the famine prompts some remarkable instances of love and compassion. The self-assured Gangacharan, who wears black-rim spectacles and carries a black umbrella, is at first angry when his wife proposes that she go to work to earn rice for them. Then he says quietly: "If we have to humble ourselves, it's best we do it together."

As the scramble to survive humiliates some of Ray's characters, it ennobles others, including Gangacharan who, toward the end, has begun to question the social system that he has always accepted as given and right. In the context of the film, this is a revolutionary conversion, and a most moving one.

Ray has chosen to photograph the film in rich, warm colors, the effect of which is not to soften the focus of the film but to sharpen it. The course of terrible events seems that much more vivid in landscapes of relentless beauty.

—*V.C., October 12, 1973*

DIVA

Directed by Jean-Jacques Beineix: written (in French. with English subtitles) by Mr. Beineix and Jean Van Hamme. based on the novel by Delacorta: director of photography. Philippe Rousselot: edited by Marie-Josephe Yoyotte and Monique Prim: music by Vladimir Cosma: art designer. Hilton McConnico: produced by Irene Silberman: released by United Artists Classics. Running time: 123 minutes.

With: Wilhelminia Wiggins Fernandez (Cynthia). Frederic Andrei (Jules). Richard Bohringer (Gorodish). Thuy An Luu (Alba). Jacques Fabbri (Saporta). Chantal Deruaz (Nadia) and Anny Romand (Paula).

*D*iva is an empty though frightfully chic-looking film from France. Though it means to be a romantic suspense-thriller, it has the self-consciously enigmatic manner of a high-fashion photograph, the kind that's irresistible to amateur artists who draw mustaches on the perfectly symmetrical faces of pencil-thin models in sables.

The movie, which has been very well received in Paris and elsewhere, is the first feature to be directed by Jean-Jacques Beineix who, possibly, has a rare sense of humor. At least, I can't believe that a film that contains the blazing newspaper headline "Who Stole Diva's Gown?" doesn't mean to be funny. However, the jokes are self-congratulatory in the manner of puns. They are less funny than interruptive.

It's difficult to say what *Diva* is about, though it has a lot of plot. First, there is a young messenger, Jules (Frederic Andrei), a sensitive-featured, obsessed fellow in his late teens who whizzes around Paris on his moped, delivering things and dreaming of Cynthia Hawkins (Wilhelminia Wiggins Fernandez), an American concert singer who is the toast of the town.

Cynthia, a slim, high-cheekboned woman who would look truly stunning in sables, has one idiosyncrasy—she will not make recordings. She believes that her art is that profound relationship between her and her audience during those fleeting moments when she is performing. To record her voice, she says, would be to recognize only half of the creative process.

The infatuated Jules goes to her concert one night and surreptitiously records Cynthia on a tape machine hidden on his person. Later, he adds insult to that injury, which is equated with rape, when he goes backstage to meet his idol and steals the white satin gown she had been wearing during the performance.

A secondary plot, which eventually engulfs the first one, is about the efforts of the police to crack a drug-and-prostitution ring headed by a Mr. Big. Mr. Big's girlfriend, just before she is murdered by the mob, makes a tape full of incriminating evidence, the cassette of which accidentally falls into Jules's possession. Thus, Jules suddenly finds himself pursued by a couple of the mob's nastier hit men, as well as by two ruthless agents of a Taiwan recording company, who threaten to market the pirated tape unless Cynthia agrees to sign a recording contract.

Mr. Beineix, I think, would like us to consider the differences between these two tapes and make something of it. I can't. It just seems to be more symmetry for its own sake.

There is more to the story, but none of it is as important to Mr. Beineix as style, and style as content has its limits when it's so pretty and mechanical. Nothing in the film is photographed straight-on. *Diva* is an anthology of affectations. The camera waltzes around as we sit pinned to our chairs. Everything is seen through glass, in mirrors, or as reflected from the surfaces of mud puddles. If a scene isn't shot from a low angle, it's shot from a chandelier. When all else fails, the lights are lowered to create a mood.

The best thing in the film is a wild though improbable chase through Paris—its streets, sidewalks and metros, with Jules on his cycle being pursued by a mob man on foot.

Style is the only consistent thing in *Diva*. Jules, who starts out as something of a psychopath, is an unwitting hero. His two eccentric friends, Gorodish (Richard Bohringer), who spends his time meditating in his lovely loft apartment, and Alba (Thuy An Luu), the pretty shoplifter who roller-skates around Gorodish's pad and lives with him, become the unlikely instruments of his salvation. And the celebrated Cynthia, against all common sense, sees the beauty within Jules's soul, perhaps because they both share an unbounded admiration for her talent.

The second best thing in *Diva* is Miss Fernandez, the Philadelphia-born soprano who is no actress yet, though she has great film presence. The other performers, especially young Mr. Andrei, Miss Luu and Mr. Bohringer, are as acceptable as they can be under these fancified circumstances.

Diva opens today at the Plaza.

—V.C., April 16, 1982

DIVORCE—ITALIAN STYLE

Directed by Pietro Germi: written (in Italian, with English subtitles) by Ennio De Concini, Alfredo Giannetti and Mr. Germi: cinematographer, Leonida Barboni: edited by Roberto Cinquini: music by Carlo Rustichelli: produced by Franco Cristaldi: released by Embassy Pictures. Black and white. Running time: 108 minutes.

With: Marcello Mastroianni (Ferdinando), Daniela Rocca (Rosalia), Stefania Sandrelli (Angela), Leopoldo Trieste (Carmelo Patane), Odoardo Spadaro (Don Gaetano) and Angela Cardile (Agnese).

Marcello Mastroianni, the Italian actor who had the leading role in *La Dolce Vita* and what seems like at least half the important Italian films of recent years, surpasses himself as a comedian in *Divorce— Italian Style,* a dandy satiric farce that opened at the Paris yesterday. And Pietro Germi, who directed and helped write the script, announces himself with this achievement as a master of farce in any style.

For here, in this nifty frolic about a bored Sicilian baron who plots to force his wife to compromise herself with another man so he can honorably shoot her and then marry a sixteen-year-old girl, the director and star have accomplished that very difficult and delicate thing of making murder seem an admirable ambition and the would-be murderer seem a sympathetic gent, all without violating reason or causing really serious moral offense.

To be sure, the assumption is outrageous—at least, to a non-Latin it is—that the "code of honor" might be craftily manipulated in order to "divorce" one's spouse. And the fact that the total population of a Sicilian city might be cunningly engineered into demanding and compelling the act of honor might seem beautifully and blissfully naive.

But Mr. Germi has managed to establish his thesis so well, with a wonderfully droll illumination of the slippery characters of the community, and he has worked out his plot so deftly, with his tongue obviously in his cheek, that the whole arrangement seems not only respectable but also devilishly ingenious.

Indeed, ingenuity is the striking directorial quality one notes in the charmingly smooth, efficient and flexible flow of the film. Mr. Germi is a genius with the sly twist. With the deft fluidity of the dissolves, he wittily mingles the images of his hero's murderous fantasies with the humdrum actuality of his torpid and henpecked home.

And he gets out of Mr. Mastroianni a performance

that hangs in one's mind as one of the most ingenious and distinctive comic characterizations that has lately been.

Not since Charlie Chaplin's beguiling Verdoux have we seen a deliberate wife-killer so elegant and suave, so condescending in his boredom, so thoroughly and pathetically enmeshed in the suffocating toils of a woman as Mr. Mastroianni is here. His eyelids droop with a haughtiness and ennui that are only dispelled when he looks with a gaze of lecherous longing at his teenage cousin, whom Stefania Sandrelli plays.

With his wife, played by Daniela Rocca, he is weary, disgusted and sad—until he is hit by the inspiration to arrange an Italian "divorce."

Then his crafty maneuverings to discover and place the right man in what might be accepted as a shameful situation with his wife, his tricky arrangements of tape recorders and his lining up the proper lawyer in advance—these all are deliciously ingenious and grandly diabolic and droll.

Even to begin to hint at what happens and how nicely and ironically it ends would be to endanger your enjoyment, but be sure the humor holds to the end.

Mr. Mastroianni's performance is thoroughly complemented by the humorous uxorial enthusiasm that Miss Rocca provides. Miss Sandrelli is fetching as the girl who captivates and Leopoldo Trieste is uproarious as the diffident and respectful "other man." Colorful and funny characterizations of Sicilian locals are turned in by Odoardo Spadaro, as the hero's father; Pietro Tordi, the silver-tongued lawyer; Bianca Castagnetta, the hero's mother; and several more.

The background music, very Sicilian and romantic, is wittily and wistfully used, and the English subtitles of Rick Carrier catch the humor of the lively dialogue.

This is one of the funniest pictures the Italians have sent along.

—B.C., September 18, 1962

DO THE RIGHT THING

Produced, written and directed by Spike Lee; director of photography, Ernest Dickerson; edited by Barry Alexander; music by Bill Lee, production designer, Wynn Thomas, released by Universal Pictures. Running time: 120 minutes.

With: Danny Aiello (Sal), Ossie Davis (Da Mayor), Ruby Dee (Mother Sister), Richard Edson (Vito), Giancarlo Esposito (Buggin Out), Spike Lee (Mookie), Bill Nunn (Radio Raheem), John Turturro (Pino), Paul Benjamin (M. L.), Frankie Faison (Coconut Sid), Robin Harris (Sweet Dick Willie), Sam Jackson (Mister Señor Love Daddy), Rosie Perez (Tina) and Roger Guenveur Smith (Smiley).

In all of the earnest, solemn, humorless discussions about the social and political implications of Spike Lee's *Do the Right Thing,* an essential fact tends to be overlooked: it is one terrific movie.

From the sinuous and joshing solo dance sequence, which begins the fable on the dawn of the hottest day of the summer in Brooklyn's Bedford-Stuyvesant section, until the mournful fadeout twenty-four hours later, *Do the Right Thing* is living, breathing, riveting proof of the arrival of an abundantly gifted new talent.

Mr. Lee has been edging up on us. First there was the slyly subversive comedy *She's Gotta Have It,* about a young woman who can be satisfied only by three men. Then there was *School Daze,* which examines intraracial prejudice in the terms of the old-fashioned college movie-musical, which, until Mr. Lee came along, had always been Wonder Bread–white and utterly brainless. Each film was by way of preparation.

With *Do the Right Thing,* which he wrote, produced, directed and stars in, Mr. Lee emerges as the most distinctive American multithreat man since Woody Allen.

The film, which opens today at the National Twin and other theaters, is the chronicle of a bitter racial confrontation that leaves one man dead and a neighborhood destroyed. The ending is shattering and maybe too ambiguous for its own good. Yet the telling of all this is so buoyant, so fresh, so exact and so moving that one comes out of the theater elated by the display of sheer cinematic wizardry.

Do the Right Thing is a big movie. Though the action is limited to one more-or-less idealized block in Bed-Stuy, the scope is panoramic. It's a contemporary *Street Scene.* It has the heightened reality of theater, not only in its look but also in the way the lyrics of the songs on the soundtrack become natural extensions of the furiously demotic, often hugely funny dialogue.

The film begins with disarming ease, introducing its dozen or so characters while Mister Señor Love

Daddy (Sam Jackson), the local disk jockey, wakens the citizenry from the storefront studio of Station W(e)L(ove)R(adio). The sun is scarcely up, but it is already steamy. "The color of the day is black," says Mister Señor Love Daddy, "to absorb some of those *rays!*"

The rummy old "Mayor" (Ossie Davis) arises to search for a can of Miller High Life. The unexcitable, skeptical Mookie (Mr. Lee), who works as a delivery man for Sal's Famous Pizzeria, sits on the side of his bed, counting his cash. Radio Raheem (Bill Nunn) is walking the street with his giant boom box blasting into consciousness everyone who has managed to sleep through Mister Señor Love Daddy.

In the Cadillac that eases to a stop in front of the pizzeria are Sal (Danny Aiello) and his sons, Pino (John Turturro) and Vito (Richard Edson). They haven't yet started work but the brothers are arguing about who must do what. Sal, who wants nothing but peace, threatens to kill someone before the day is over.

Other characters are introduced: Mother Sister (Ruby Dee), whose eye on the world is the window from which she monitors the street; Buggin Out (Giancarlo Esposito), a young man whose anger has no target as yet; Smiley (Roger Guenveur Smith), a retarded man with a bad stutter who hawks copies of what is apparently the only photograph ever taken of the Rev. Dr. Martin Luther King Jr. and Malcolm X together; and Tina (Rosie Perez), Mookie's pretty Puerto Rican girlfriend and the mother of his son, Hector.

Tina, who seldom stops talking, is impatient and loving at the same time. The only way she gets to see Mookie is by ordering pizzas.

There is also the three-man chorus M.L. (Paul Benjamin), Coconut Sid (Frankie Faison), and Sweet Dick Willie (Robin Harris). Protected by a small umbrella, they sit on the corner, backed by a brick wall of brilliant vermilion. When they aren't commenting on each other, they are commenting on the people around them, including the Korean operators of the fruit-and-vegetable shop across the street.

As the heat intensifies, so do the tempers. For a while potential fights are defused by good humor, but then the kidding starts to turn mean. Buggin Out asks Sal why the pizzeria is hung with photographs of Frank Sinatra, Sophia Loren and John Travolta, but no blacks. Says Buggin Out, "Rarely do I see any Italian-Americans eating here." He decides to organize a boycott of Sal's.

Mr. Lee's particular achievement is in building the tensions so gradually and so persuasively that the explosion, when it finally comes, seems inevitable. He doesn't deal in generalities. The movie is packed with idiosyncratic detail of character and event, sometimes very funny and sometimes breathtakingly crude.

Every now and then Mr. Lee pulls back from the narrative to present montages that characterize time, place and urban condition. Heat and noise are palpable in the juxtaposition of images scored by the Steel Pulse number "Can't Stand It." At another point, blacks, whites, Puerto Ricans and Koreans come forward in turn to recite a litany of bigoted epithets. At times, characters speak directly to the camera, as if in desperation to vent their rage.

None of this would have the impact it does if the film didn't also possess a solidly dramatic center in the well-meaning but fallible Sal. As written by Mr. Lee and played by Mr. Aiello, he is the film's richest, most complex character, his downfall as harrowing as the events that bring it about.

Mr. Lee is almost as good as a fellow who has been biding his time, good-naturedly slouching through life until the events of this day change him forever. Especially funny and affecting are Mookie's relationship with Tina and a love scene that is a temporary reprieve from all that is going on outside.

Tina, silent for the moment, lies on the bed in her darkened room. "Thank God for lips," says Mookie as he rubs an ice cube over her mouth. "Thank God for necks, thank God for kneecaps, for elbows, for thighs."

All of the other actors are fine, but some demand to be singled out: Mr. Edson, Mr. Turturro, Miss Perez, Mr. Esposito, Mr. Nunn, and—performing dual functions—Miss Dee and Mr. Davis. Miss Dee and Mr. Davis are not only figures within the film but, as themselves, they also seem to preside over it, as if ushering in a new era of black filmmaking.

Note should also be made of the camerawork of Ernest Dickerson, Wynn Thomas's production design and the original score by Bill Lee (the director's father), which makes a lot of witty comments on its own as it backs the narrative and provides the bridges between the musical recordings.

Do the Right Thing is a remarkable piece of work.
—*V.C., June 30, 1989*

DR. JEKYLL AND MR. HYDE

Produced and directed by Rouben Mamoulian; written by Samuel Hoffenstein and Percy Heath, based on the novel *The Strange Case of Dr. Jekyll and Mr. Hyde* by Robert Louis Stevenson; cinematographer, Karl Struss; edited by William Shea; art designer, Hans Dreier; released by Paramount Pictures. Black and white. Running time: 90 minutes.

With: Fredric March (Dr. Henry Jekyll/Mr. Hyde), Miriam Hopkins (Ivy Parsons), Rose Hobart (Muriel Carew), Holmes Herbert (Dr. Lanyan), Halliwell Hobbes (Brigadier General Carew), Edgar Norton (Poole), Arnold Lucy (Utterson), Colonel MacDonnell (Hobson) and Tempe Pigott (Mrs. Hawkins).

What with the audibility of the screen and the masterful photography, the new pictorial transcription of Stevenson's spine-chilling work, *Dr. Jekyll and Mr. Hyde,* emerges as a far more tense and shuddering affair than it was as John Barrymore's silent picture. True, the producers are not a little too zealous in their desire to spread terror among audiences, but while there are pardonable roamings from the original, there is in most instances a good excuse for making the scenes as they are in this current study.

Fredric March is the stellar performer in this bloodcurdling shadow venture. His makeup as Hyde is not done by halves, for virtually every imaginable possibility is taken advantage of to make this creature "reflecting the lower elements of Dr. Jekyll's soul" thoroughly hideous. Instead of being undersized or smaller than Dr. Jekyll, as in the Stevenson description, this repellent thing here is broader and taller. In physiognomy this Hyde has the aspects of an ape, with protruding teeth, long eyeteeth, unkempt thick hair leaving but a scant forehead, a broad nose with large nostrils, eyes with the lower part of the sockets pulled down, thick eyebrows and hairy arms and hands—a creature that would make the hairy ape of O'Neill's play a welcome sight.

Rouben Mamoulian, the director of this film, has gone about his task with considerable enthusiasm, and the way in which Jekyll changes into Hyde is pictured with an expert cunning, for it is a series of gradual exposures during which the changing face does not leave the screen. The first time the transition takes place it is effective, but it is still more so in subsequent sequences, for Hyde, who cannot return to his other self without the necessary prescription, in one episode is forced virtually to accomplish the transformation from the apish thing to his ordinary form at the point of a pistol before his friend Dr. Lanyan. It is about this time that Jekyll realizes that he assumed the frightening shape suddenly without swallowing his preparation, which in the first case brought about the change.

Mr. March's portrayal is something to arouse admiration, even taking into consideration the camera wizardry. As Dr. Jekyll he is a charming man, and as the fiend he is alert and sensual.

The producers have seen fit to include both a romantic theme and a sex influence in the course of the narrative, and toward the end one is apt to think that this story is to be given a happy ending. But this does not happen, for after having committed several murders, including the slaying of Ivy Parsons, a singer in a cabaret, Hyde runs amuck, wielding a heavy stick, leaping up on desks and shelves, and hurling vases at his pursuers until a Scotland Yard sleuth sounds his death knell with a bullet.

One of the many highly dramatic episodes is where Jekyll calls on his fiancée, Muriel Carew. After leaving her, one of the periodical transformations takes place and he reenters the Carew home and takes Muriel in his arms. Once she looks upon Hyde's awful physiognomy, she screams and faints. This results in the chase that leads to the death of the man. When breathing his last, the fearsome creature gradually changes from Hyde to Jekyll.

Miriam Hopkins does splendidly as the unfortunate Ivy. Rose Hobart is clever as the sympathetic Muriel. Holmes Herbert delivers a pleasingly restrained performance as Dr. Lanyan, and Halliwell Hobbes's portrayal of Muriel's father, General Carew, is another asset to this fine film. Edgar Norton, who plays Poole, Dr. Jekyll's faithful servant, is very much at home in the part, inasmuch as he acted it with Richard Mansfield.

The atmosphere, that of London in Stevenson's day, is quite pleasing. There are the gas lamps, old-fashioned feminine costumes and other details. Likewise the settings enhance the scenes, particularly those of the interesting twisted little byways.

—*M.H., January 2, 1932*

DR. STRANGELOVE OR:
HOW I LEARNED TO STOP
WORRYING AND LOVE THE BOMB

Produced and directed by Stanley Kubrick: written by Mr. Kubrick. Terry Southern and Peter George. based on the novel by Mr. George: cinematographer. Gilbert Taylor: edited by Anthony Harvey: music by Laurie Johnson: production designer. Ken Adam: released by Columbia Pictures. Black and white. Running time: 102 minutes.

With: Peter Sellers (Group Captain Lionel Mandrake/President Merkin Muffley/Dr. Strangelove). George C. Scott (General Buck Turgidson). Sterling Hayden (General Jack D. Ripper). Keenan Wynn (Colonel "Bat" Guano). Slim Pickens (Major T. J. "King" Kong). Peter Bull (Ambassador de Sadesky). Tracy Reed (Miss Scott) and James Earl Jones (Lieutenant Lothar Zogg).

Stanley Kubrick's new film, called *Dr. Strangelove or: How I Learned to Stop Worrying and Love the Bomb,* is beyond any question the most shattering sick joke I've ever come across. And I say that with full recollection of some of the grim ones I've heard from Mort Sahl, some of the cartoons I've seen by Charles Addams, and some of the stuff I've read in *Mad* magazine.

For this brazenly jesting speculation of what might happen within the Pentagon and within the most responsible council of the President of the United States if some maniac Air Force general should suddenly order a nuclear attack on the Soviet Union is at the same time one of the cleverest and most incisive satiric thrusts at the awkwardness and folly of the military that has ever been on the screen. It opened yesterday at the Victoria and the Baronet.

My reaction to it is quite divided, because there is so much about it that is grand, so much that is brilliant and amusing, and much that is grave and dangerous.

On the one hand, it cuts right to the soft pulp of the kind of military mind that is lost from all sense of reality in a maze of technical talk, and it shows up this type of mentality for the foolish and frightening thing it is.

In a top-level Air Force general, played by George C. Scott with a snarling and rasping volubility that makes your blood run cold, Mr. Kubrick presents us with a joker whose thinking is so involved with programs and cautions and suspicions that he is practically tied in knots.

It is he who is most completely baffled, bewildered and paralyzed when word comes through to Washington that a general in the Strategic Air Command has sent a wing of bombers off to drop bombs and that the planes cannot be recalled. It is he who has to answer to the President for this awesome "accident" when the President gathers his council in the War Room at the Pentagon. And it is he who looks the most unstable and dubious in the cause of peace when it begins to appear that the Russians have a retaliatory "doomsday device."

Some of the conversations in that War Room are hilarious, shooting bright shafts of satire through mounds of ineptitude. There is, best of all, a conversation between the President and an unseen Soviet Premier at the other end of a telephone line that is a titanic garble of nuttiness and platitudes.

Funny, too, in a mad way, is the behavior of the crew in one of the planes of the airborne alert force ordered to drop the bomb. The commander is a Texan who puts on a cowboy hat when he knows the mission is committed. Slim Pickens plays this role. He and Keenan Wynn as a foggy colonel are the funniest individuals in the film.

As I say, there are parts of this satire that are almost beyond compare.

On the other hand, I am troubled by the feeling, which runs all through the film, of discredit and even contempt for our whole defense establishment, up to and even including the hypothetical Commander in Chief.

It is all right to show the general who starts this wild foray as a Communist-hating madman, convinced that a "Red conspiracy" is fluoridating our water in order to pollute our precious body fluids. That is pointed satire, and Sterling Hayden plays the role with just a right blend of wackiness and meanness to give the character significance.

But when virtually everybody turns up stupid or insane—or, what is worse, psychopathic—I want to know what this picture proves. The President, played by Peter Sellers with a shiny bald head, is a dolt, whining and unavailing with the nation in a life-or-death spot. But worse yet, his technical expert, Dr.

Strangelove, whom Mr. Sellers also plays, is a devious and noxious ex-German whose mechanical arm insists on making the Nazi salute.

And, oddly enough, the only character who seems to have much common sense is a British flying officer, whom Mr. Sellers—yes, he again—plays.

The ultimate touch of ghoulish humor is when we see the bomb actually going off, dropped on some point in Russia, and a jazzy sound track comes in with a cheerful melodic rendition of "We'll Meet Again Some Sunny Day." Somehow, to me, it isn't funny. It is malefic and sick.

—*B.C., January 31, 1964*

DOCTOR ZHIVAGO

Directed by David Lean; written by Robert Bolt, based on the novel by Boris Pasternak; cinematographer, Freddie Young; edited by Norman Savage; music by Maurice Jarre; production designer, John Box; produced by Carlo Ponti; released by Metro-Goldwyn-Mayer. Running time: 197 minutes.

With: Omar Sharif (Yuri Zhivago), Julie Christie (Lara), Tom Courtenay (Pasha Antipov), Rod Steiger (Komarovsky), Geraldine Chaplin (Tonya Gromeko), Alec Guinness (Yevgrat Zhivago), Siobhan McKenna (Anna Gromeko), Ralph Richardson (Alexander Gromeko), Rita Tushingham (The Girl) and Adrienne Corri (Lara's Mother).

In the three hours and seventeen minutes (not counting intermission time) it takes to move Robert Bolt's dramatization of Boris Pasternak's *Doctor Zhivago* across the screen, a few rather major things happen. The First World War for one and the Russian Revolution for another. A whole social system is torn down and another of a harsh, dynamic nature is constructed to take its place.

Yet these things are only indicated in a few fine and fiercely acted scenes that are thrust suddenly through a fabric of personal drama and then are as quickly withdrawn. Such scenes as a devastating slaughter of socialist demonstrators in the streets of Moscow around 1910 or a clash of Czarist troops and Communist deserters on a frozen road toward the end of the war or a longer, more agonizing sequence of exiles being transported in a train to the distant regions of the Urals do suggest the boiling surge of violent change. And they are sharply illustrated on the large screen under the skillful direction of David Lean.

But the much greater part of this picture, which had its world premiere last night at the Capitol, is given to sentimental contemplation of the emotional involvement and private sufferings of a small group of bourgeois who are brutally unsettled and disrupted by the surrounding circumstances of change. And particularly is it given to the description of a passionate love affair between the gentle, courtly Dr. Zhivago and Lara, the lost, estranged wife of a Communist.

This sad love affair of two people who have come to their grim Gethsemane in a dismal town in the Urals after going through various personal trials in Moscow and elsewhere is the matter upon which Mr. Bolt has chosen to settle all the tensions of spiritual conflict and personal tragedy that are packed in the Pasternak novel. And this is the weakness of the film. Mr. Bolt has reduced the vast upheaval of the Russian Revolution to the banalities of a doomed romance.

No matter how heartbreaking he has made the backgrounds of the couple appear—with the doctor torn from a promising practice and from a lovely, loving wife by the brutal demands of the revolution and with Lara left on her own after a girlhood affair with an older lover and a marriage with a revolutionist. No matter how richly graphic these affairs have been made by Mr. Lean—and, believe me, he has made them richly graphic; the decor and color photography are as brilliant, tasteful, and exquisite as any ever put on the screen.

No matter how sweet and loving, idealistic and pitiable the handsome Dr. Zhivago is invariably made to seem by dark-eyed, intense Omar Sharif, and no matter how sad and brave the remarkable young Julie Christie makes the bold but confused Lara be, the long-drawn sadness of these two lovers is not enough for the crux of this film.

Furthermore, the necessities of drama—of action and suspense—are not served by the fact that these two people and some others are possessed by a strange passivity. As much as Dr. Zhivago obviously dreads and distrusts the onslaught of the vulgar revolution, he does not get his back up to it. He takes all its cruel oppressions with a solemn, uncomplaining wistfulness. Lara, too, is submissive to the irony of fate. This may be proper to their natures and faithful to Pasternak, but it makes for painfully slow going and inevitable tedium in a film.

Missing, too, in the doctor is that aura of genius that Pasternak evolved as the spiritual setting of the man and his poetry. Mr. Sharif's Zhivago is just an ordinary gent who seems to have no more poetry in him than an occasional jingle for a holiday. Thus it is startling and disturbing to see him sit down in the middle of the night toward the end of the film in that ice-box villa on the edge of the wintry and wolf-infested steppe and start writing poems to Lara that we are led to assume are great. I have a feeling it is fortunate they don't let us hear the poetry.

But his being a poet is the basis for the framing device in which Mr. Bolt has set his drama. The picture is begun and the story told with the half-brother of the doctor—a Soviet engineer, austerely played by Alec Guinness—trying to discover whether a Russian working girl (Rita Tushingham) is the lost daughter of Lara and Zhivago, now long dead. Neither the inquiry nor the device can be reckoned a success.

Successful, however, beyond question is the physical production of this film—the brilliant visual realization. As in *Lawrence of Arabia,* Mr. Lean has joined with Fred A. Young, his photographer, to create a superlative mise-en-scène. His pictorial stuff is tremendous, whether it be a snow-filled Moscow street or a burnished room full of Christmas celebrators or a great expanse of windy steppe or a train in the snow or a country cottage frosted with shimmering ice.

And he has got very good performances from Rod Steiger and Tom Courtenay—the former as the bourgeois opportunist who first seduces and later plagues Lara, and the latter as the thin-lipped revolutionary who is strangely and briefly loved by her. Geraldine Chaplin is shiny but vapid as Dr. Zhivago's band-box wife and Ralph Richardson is pompous and pathetic as his bumbling, bewildered father-in-law.

But all these people and others are but characters in a sad romance that seems almost as far away from Russia as the surging revolution seems from them. They are as fustian and sentimental as the music of Maurice Jarre that has a nostalgic balalaika tinkle. They are closer to Hollywood than to the steppes.

—*B.C., December 23, 1965*

DODSWORTH

Directed by William Wyler: written by Sidney Howard. based on his play adapted from the novel by Sinclair Lewis: cinematographer. Rudolph Maté: edited by Daniel Mandell: music by Alfred Newman: art designer. Richard Day: produced by Samuel Goldwyn: released by United Artists. Black and white. Running time: 90 minutes.

With: Walter Huston (Sam Dodsworth). Ruth Chatterton (Fran Dodsworth). Paul Lukas (Arnold Iselin). Mary Astor (Edith Cortright). David Niven (Lockert) and Gregory Gaye (Kurt von Obersdorf).

Brooks Atkinson, in his review of the play *Dodsworth,* on the morning of February 26, 1934, wrote: "Among the virtues of *Dodsworth,* place Walter Huston foremost." This morning, with Samuel Goldwyn's admirable film transcription of the drama on view at the Rivoli, we can but repeat Mr. Atkinson's summary. Mr. Huston still is foremost, lending a driving energy and a splendid virility to the character so clearly drawn in Sinclair Lewis's novel, and so brilliantly highlighted in Sidney Howard's dramatization of the book.

Mr. Howard, who must be considered Mr. Lewis's personal dramatic translator, has adapted his play to the screen with the seriousness of an author who has studied his work long and has weighed each comma before fitting it into his literary mosaic. He was not, then, in converting his play into a pattern for a motion picture, lightly to be turned from his conception of its dramatic sequence, its characterization or its speech. Mr. Goldwyn has had the wisdom to accept his judgment; William Wyler, the director, has had the skill to execute it in cinematic terms; and a gifted cast has been able to bring the whole alive to our complete satisfaction.

Dodsworth remains, through the years, a man we can understand and believe and respect. Mr. Huston deserves most of the credit for that by treating the character as it deserves: with sympathy, humor, delicacy, irony and crudity, all in their turn. It must be a studied characterization, but we never are permitted to feel that, for Mr. Huston so snugly fits the part we cannot tell where the garment ends and he begins.

We cannot feel the same about Fran Dodsworth—either as she is in the novel or as played by Fay Bainter on the stage or Ruth Chatterton in the current screen edition. There is a basic impossibility in Mr. Lewis's premise that she and Dodsworth could have been married for twenty years before his retirement and their tragic grand tour abroad which revealed her to him for what she was—a silly, shallow, age-fearing woman of ingrained selfishness and vulgarity. Fran, for all the skill of the Lewis-Howard writing and the deftness of Miss Chatterton's portrayal (one of her best, by the way), is just convincing fiction against Sam Dodsworth's unquestionable fact.

This is a minor note, an aside in a sense, which is offered less as a criticism than as a contrapuntal comment on a work which already has attained something of the stature of an American classic. The film version has done more than justice to Mr. Howard's play, converting a necessarily episodic tale, interrupted by fourteen curtains, into a smooth-flowing narrative of sustained interest, well-defined performance, and good talk.

If we had more words to use we should employ them to compliment Mary Astor for her alert and intelligent playing of the Edith Cortright role, and to acknowledge the excellence of Spring Byington and Harlan Briggs as the Pearsons, Paul Lukas as Arnold Iselin, Maria Ouspenskaya in the Baroness von Obersdorf role she had in the play, John Payne as Dodsworth's son-in-law, David Niven as Major Lockert and Gregory Gaye as Kurt.

—*F.S.N., September 24, 1936*

LA DOLCE VITA

Directed by Federico Fellini; written (in Italian, with English subtitles) by Mr. Fellini, Ennio Flaiano, Tullio Pinelli and Brunello Rondi, based on a story by Mr. Fellini, Mr. Flaiano and Mr. Pinelli; cinematographer, Otello Martelli; edited by Leo Catozzo; music by Nino Rota; art designer, Piero Gherardi; produced by Giuseppe Amato; released by Astor Films. Black and white. Running time: 180 minutes.

With: Marcello Mastroianni (Marcello Rubino), Walter Santesso (Photographer), Anouk Aimée (Maddalena), Adriana Moneta (The Prostitute), Yvonne Furneaux (Marcello's Mistress), Anita Ekberg (A Hollywood Star), Carlo Di Maggio (The Producer), Lex Barker (Robert), Alan Dijon (Frankie Stout) and Alain Cuny (Steiner).

Federico Fellini's *La Dolce Vita* (*The Sweet Life*), which has been a tremendous hit abroad since its initial presentation in Rome early last year, finally got to its American premiere at Henry Miller's Theater last night and proved to deserve all the hurrahs and the impressive honors it has received.

For this sensational representation of certain aspects of life in contemporary Rome, as revealed in the clamorous experience of a free-wheeling newspaper man, is a brilliantly graphic estimation of a whole swath of society in sad decay and, eventually, a withering commentary upon the tragedy of the overcivilized.

The critic is faced with a dilemma in attempting to assess and convey all the weird observations and intimations that abound in this titanic film. For Signor Fellini is nothing if not fertile, fierce and urbane in calculating the social scene around him and packing it onto the screen.

He has an uncanny eye for finding the offbeat and grotesque incident, the gross and bizarre occurrence that exposes a glaring irony. He has, too, a splendid sense of balance and a deliciously sardonic wit that not only guided his cameras but also affected the writing of his script. As a consequence there are scores of piercing ideas that pop out in the picture's nigh three hours and leave one shocked, amused, revolted, and possibly stunned and bewildered at the end.

Perhaps the best way to give the reader a hint as to the flavor of this work is to describe its amazing beginning. A helicopter is seen flying toward Rome with an uncertain object dangling beneath it by a rope. As the machine comes closer, we see the object is a statue of Jesus, arms outstretched as if in blessing, a sweet, sad expression on its face.

Casually, the whirring "chopper" flies past an ancient aqueduct, the modern machine and its strange burden looking incongruous against the ruin. On it goes past piles of buildings, the ugly postwar apartment houses on the fringe of Rome, and over the heads of a bevy of voluptuous females sunbathing in bikinis on a penthouse roof. Then alongside it comes a second helicopter bearing our young newspaper man and his persistent photographer recording the bizarre scene.

Here is the flavor of the picture and, in a fast glimpse, its theme. Dignity is transmuted into the sensational. Old values, old disciplines are discarded for the modern, the synthetic, the quick by a society that is past sophistication and is sated with pleasure and itself. All of its straining for sensations is exploited for the picture magazines and the scandal sheets that merchandise excitement and vicarious thrills for the mob.

This is Signor Fellini's comment, not put into words, of course, but fully illuminated in his accumulation of startling episodes. It is clear in the crazy experience of his questing newspaper man (played brilliantly by Marcello Mastroianni) with a visiting Hollywood movie star (enacted by Anita Ekberg with surprising personality and punch).

It comes through with devastating impact in an episode wherein two frightened kids are used to whip up a religious rally for the benefit of television. It is implicit in the contact of the hero with a strange and motley mob of jaded aristocrats and worldlings at an all-night party in a palace outside Rome.

It finally comes home to the hero (at least we think it does) when he sees his own pack of voracious photographers trying to make a sensation of the suicide of his most respected friend (Alain Cuny) for whom the "sweet life" becomes too grim. And it is evident in unmistakable symbols at a mammoth orgy the hero attends with a gang of depraved sensation seekers who face their loneliness and emptiness in the dawn.

Possibly Signor Fellini has rambled a bit in his film. Possibly he has strained logic and exaggerated somewhat here and there. (He has a character say "The public demands exaggeration," which does support the theme.)

In sum, it is an awesome picture, licentious in content but moral and vastly sophisticated in its attitude and what it says. An excellent cast performs it. In addition to those named above, Yvonne Furneaux as the hero's mistress, Anouk Aimée as a nymphomaniac, Annibale Ninchi as the hero's father, and Magali Noel as a nightclub chorus girl make most vivid impressions in a stupendous cast.

An all-purpose musical melody, as persistent and haunting as the memorable *Third Man* theme, is aptly played in the right places. The use of multilingual dialogue (the French and Italian translated with English subtitles) makes the yakkity-yak really sound like Rome. If the subtitles are insufficient, the picture itself speaks louder than any words.

—*B.C., April 20, 1961*

DONNIE BRASCO

Directed by Mike Newell; written by Paul Attanasio, based on the book by Joseph D. Pistone with Richard Woodley; director of photogrpahy, Peter Sova; edited by Jon Gregory; music by Patrick Doyle; production designer; Donald Graham Burt; produced by Mark Johnson, Barry Levinson, Louis DiGiaimo and Gail Mutrux; released by Tri-Star. Running time: 121 minutes.

With: Al Pacino (Lefty), Johnny Depp (Donnie), Michael Madsen (Sonny), Bruno Kirby (Nicky), James Russo (Paulie) and Anne Heche (Maggie).

There's a great little moment in the gangster film *Donnie Brasco* that shows Al Pacino preparing to meet the Godfather. Fine, we've seen that before. But this Mr. Pacino is different: aging, weary, drab, down on his luck though desperately eager to please. Trying to put his best foot forward, he stands dutifully amid a crowd of low-level Mafiosi. The boss walks by without giving him a look.

It's a sharp, clever encounter, overturning all manner of genre clichés and viewer expectations. And the crackling good *Donnie Brasco,* the best crime movie in a long while, is full of similar surprises as it leads Mr. Pacino and Johnny Depp through a fine-tuned tale of deception. Surprise No. 1: Mr. Depp's tremendous talent is no longer surprising. With this film his career reaches critical mass, turning an assortment of varied, offbeat roles into the trajectory of a major star.

Mr. Depp is not alone in being in the right place at the right time with *Donnie Brasco*. It's also an affirmation that the director, Mike Newell, has a gift for talkative, intelligent films that make his actors shine. Whether in sunny Italy (*Enchanted April*), mystical Ireland (*Into the West*), nuptial-mad England (*Four Weddings and a Funeral*), or now in the tacky realm of the American gangster, Mr. Newell can make the most out of tartly fine acting and good conversation. (His last film, *An Awfully Big Adventure,* failed miserably because its backstage theatrical milieu, arch tone and English accents traveled badly. It's worth a second look.)

Donnie Brasco is also a boon to Mr. Pacino, who brings such color and pathos to a story that automatically invokes the breadth of his own career. Whether in the mob (you know where) or undercover (*Serpico*), he has been here before as the brash young man, and now he graduates to the kind of senior status that is a character actor's field day. A whole world of second thoughts about the gangster's game can be found in the small strokes of his performance here. And Mr. Pacino's reward for passing a generational torch to Mr. Depp is the chance to team up with a young actor on the same wavelength. These two stars have such good, macho chemistry that their scenes together really shoot off sparks.

As Donnie Brasco, a man who doesn't exist, Mr. Depp turns tough so easily and charismatically that it's easy to forget he was ever Gilbert Grape or Edward Scissorhands. Donnie is actually Joe Pistone, the undercover F.B.I. agent who infiltrated the Bonnano family in the late 1970's and upon whose memoir Paul Attanasio's screenplay is based. (Mr. Attanasio, who wrote *Quiz Show,* is also in fine form.) Donnie's initial mission is to befriend Lefty Ruggiero, the over-the-hill hit man played by Mr. Pacino with a mixture of regret and indignation over his career progress. "Twenty-six guys I clipped," Lefty complains. "Do I get upped? No, they pass me by!"

The first meeting between Donnie and Lefty sets the tone for the long, artful two-man exchanges that separate this mob movie from the many others it resembles. In a bar, Donnie pretends to be a jewel expert and convinces Lefty that the new diamond Lefty just bought is fake. Without further ado Lefty scoops up Donnie, takes him to a different joint and confronts the seller, whom Donnie roughs up as a matter of mob etiquette. Before leaving with the seller's car in tow, Donnie stuffs some money in the man's mouth to pay a bar bill.

"Why'd you pay for that drink, Don?" Lefty asks paternally. "Wise guys *never* pay for a drink."

"You know something?" Donnie soon boasts, when he meets F.B.I. agents in a place the mob would never look (a kosher restaurant). "I got him. I got my hooks in the guy." But it's the other way around. Lefty begins fouling up the plan by welcoming and instructing

Donnie as his surrogate son, since Lefty's real son is no good. And Donnie grows increasingly fond of the irresistible Lefty. But the undercover man also knows, throughout *Donnie Brasco,* that Lefty will be the one to pay the price for Donnie's treachery when the F.B.I. scam is eventually exposed.

That prospect gives the film dramatic tension, as does the threat that Donnie's new mobster friends will catch him in a lie. There are well-timed bubbles of suspicion that deliberately stop the story, which otherwise has all the rowdy wise-guy color that its genre requires. Michael Madsen (just right as an imposing new boss), Bruno Kirby, and James Russo are the other gang members closest to Lefty and Donnie, and they share the small-time ethos that gives the film its distinctive flavor.

Even when—especially when—these guys strike it big and go from Brooklyn to Florida, they have no class. In one funny throwaway, they show up looking sporty in favorite loud polyesters and wind up in a melee on the tennis court, Mr. Newell may not have been at home in Brooklyn, but he is certainly enough of a humorist and anthropologist for this.

Mr. Depp moves through the film with a brand-new hardboiled grace to give it heat, and a more familiar conscience-stricken sensitivity to keep it interesting. Anne Heche does well with what could have been the thankless role of Joe Pistone's wife, who is left to mind three children and shovel snow for months at a time while Joe is busy being Donnie Brasco. One quick, impassioned visit is all this character-driven film needs to show why these two are still married. But as an added bonus, they are seen visiting a counselor together. Donnie is not exactly inclined to let a jargon-spouting therapist tell him what to do.

Like all gangster films, *Donnie Brasco* finally runs into unwelcome reality, turning cruel and bloody in ways that leave audience sympathy in the lurch. In the end it's a sordid and deadly story. But along the way, it's full of life.

—*J.M., February 28, 1997*

DON'T LOOK BACK

Directed by D.A. Pennebaker; production designer, James D. Bissell; released by Leacock-

Pennebaker. Black and white. Running time: 96 minutes.

With: Joan Baez, Donovan, Bob Dylan, Marianne Faithfull and Allen Ginsberg (Themselves).

It will be a good joke on us all if, in fifty years or so, Dylan is regarded as a significant figure in English poetry. Not Mr. Thomas, the late Welsh bard, but Bob, the guitar-picking American balladeer. One step toward the latter's canonization has been taken, in fact, in a full-length documentary, *Don't Look Back,* now at the 34th Street East Theater.

It is an absorbing film. Whether one is a member of the under-thirty set that regards Mr. Dylan as a spokesman, or one of the vanishing Americans over that age, this look into the life of a folk hero is likely to be both entertaining and occasionally disturbing.

Those who know the songs will hear them here ("The Times They Are A-Changing," "The Gates of Eden," and so on) both in formal concerts and in hotel-room improvisation sessions. It is in the ad hoc gatherings that one glimpses something of what gives Mr. Dylan his extraordinary appeal for young people.

We see him, this prickly, wary artist, almost dropping his guard as he jokes with the inner circle of his friends: Joan Baez; the English folk singer Donovan; Mr. Dylan's manager, Albert Grossman; and a few, a precious few, other intimates. The sequences that focus on Miss Baez provide the film some of its loveliest moments, letting one see her sad, somewhat weary but still Madonna-like beauty in flashes of repose and repartee. (One boy kids her affectionately: "She's got on one of those see-through blouses that you don't even wanna.")

But it is Bob Dylan that we came to see, and it is ultimately frustrating to discern so little of the man beneath the bushy hair, the dark glasses and the leather jacket. Even in what appear to be candid shots, the performer's public face is turned to the camera. Mr. Dylan parries and thrusts with interviewers (some of them impossibly square, of course, and therefore perfect targets for the put-on); he doggedly and sullenly resists attempts to probe his psyche. If he has ideas, he hides them. He and his pals can have fun but it is a special, hip fun that always threatens to turn to anger.

Technically the film, which was produced and directed by D.A. Pennebaker, uses the devices popularized by Richard Lester's Beatle movies. Handheld cameras zoom and stagger about. Fast cuts and purposely crude editing keep the pace lively. The happy frenzy of the Beatle films is never suggested, perhaps because Bob Dylan is anything but a blithe subject. There are a few obtrusively arty shots, but in the main the story is allowed to tell itself in fairly direct ways. In fact, despite its up-to-date camera techniques, *Don't Look Back* is in the tradition of the chronological, sequential documentary familiar to several generations of moviegoers.

Many scenes stick in one's mind, but it is often the people around the star who prove most fascinating. Mr. Grossman, the Buddha-like manager, helped to produce the film, and he moves through it like a hippier Hitchcock, impassively dickering with impresarios, oddly in tune with the Dylan ménage although he looks more like Andrés Segovia than a pop tycoon.

Much of the film affects an air of being unplanned, and one has the sensation at times of being allowed to peep on the private lives of public idols. This is probably only a directorial trick, but it is a realistic one. There are drinking bouts, brawls and near-brawls, confrontations with hotel managers trying to enforce the nocturnal peace and loud internecine rumbles over exactly who threw that water glass out the window. There is lots of uninhibited hard talk.

And one does go away with a few solid hints as to what Mr. Dylan is up to, desperately though he resists anything like a friendly embrace. At the end, after a wildly successful concert at London's Royal Albert Hall, we see the poet-balladeer and friends chuckling over the "anarchist" tag hung on him by British newspapers. Mr. Dylan seems delighted to have put on the meretricious press, and fades out, happily sad in the eternal youth's realization that nobody understands him.

—*D.J.H., September 7, 1967*

DOUBLE INDEMNITY

Directed by Billy Wilder; written by Mr. Wilder and Raymond Chandler, based on the novel by James M. Cain; cinematographer, John Seitz, edited by Doane Harrison; music by Miklos Rozsa and Cesar Franck; art designers, Hans Dreier and Hal Pereira; produced by Joseph Sistrom; released by Paramount Pictures. Black and white. Running time: 106 minutes.

With: Fred MacMurray (Walter Neff), Barbara Stanwyck (Phyllis Dietrichson), Edward G. Robinson (Barton Keyes), Porter Hall (Mr. Jackson), Jean Heather (Lola Dietrichson), Tom Powers (Mr. Dietrichson), Byron Barr (Nino Zachette), Richard Gaines (Mr. Norton) and Fortunio Bonanova (Sam Gorlopis).

The cooling system in the Paramount Theatre was supplemented yesterday by a screen attraction designed plainly to freeze the marrow in an audience's bones. *Double Indemnity* is its title, and the extent of its refrigerating effect depends upon one's personal repercussion to a long dose of calculated suspense. For the sole question in this picture is whether Barbara Stanwyck and Fred MacMurray can kill a man with such cool and artistic deception that no one will place the blame on them and then maintain their composure under Edward G. Robinson's studiously searching eye.

Such folks as delight in murder stories for their academic elegance alone should find this one steadily diverting, despite its monotonous pace and length. Indeed, the fans of James M. Cain's tough fiction might gloat over it with gleaming joy. For Billy Wilder has filmed the Cain story of the brassy couple who attempt a "perfect crime," in order to collect some insurance, with a realism reminiscent of the bite of past French films. He has detailed the stalking of their victim with the frigid thoroughness of a coroner's report, and he has pictured their psychological crackup as a sadist would pluck out a spider's legs. No objection to the temper of this picture; it is as hard and inflexible as steel.

But the very toughness of the picture is also the weakness of its core, and the academic nature of its plotting limits its general appeal. The principal characters—an insurance salesman and a wicked woman, which Mr. MacMurray and Miss Stanwyck play—lack the attractiveness to render their fate of emotional consequences. And the fact that the story is told in flashback disposes its uncertainty. Miss Stanwyck gives a good surface performance of a destructively lurid female, but Mr. MacMurray is a bit too ingenuous as

the gent who falls precipitately under her spell. And the ease of his fall is also questionable. One look at the lady's ankles and he's cooked.

The performance of Mr. Robinson, however, as a smart adjuster of insurance claims, is a fine bit of characterization within its allotment of space. With a bitter brand of humor and irritability, he creates a formidable guy. As a matter of fact, Mr. Robinson is the only one you care two hoots for in the film. The rest are just neatly carved pieces in a variably intriguing crime game.

—*B.C. September 7, 1944*

DOWN BY LAW

Written and directed by Jim Jarmusch; director of photography, Robby Müller; edited by Melody London; music by John Lurie and Tom Waits; produced by Alan Kleinberg; released by Island Pictures. Black and white. Running time: 107 minutes.

With: Tom Waits (Zadk), John Lurie (Jack), Roberto Benigni (Roberto), Nicoletta Braschi (Nicoletta), Ellen Barkin (Laurette), Billie Neal (Bobbie), Rockets Redglare (Gig), Vernel Bagneris (Preston), Timothea (Julie), L. C. Drane (L. C.) and Joy Houck Jr. (Detective Mandino).

Jim Jarmusch is an American original. He's as singular as "Bob" Frost, Sam Shepard and Nicholas Ray, each of whom is evoked—in one way and another—by Mr. Jarmusch's darkly comic, lighter-than-air *Down by Law,* which provides the 24th New York Film Festival with a truly festive opening tonight at Lincoln Center.

Like *Stranger Than Paradise,* which introduced Mr. Jarmusch to the American public in 1984, *Down by Law* wears a furrowed brow on its long face, which doesn't initially identify it as a comedy. However, Mr. Jarmusch's comedies, which might be described as existential shaggy-dog stories, look and sound like those of nobody else making movies in America today.

The act of watching one may even be therapeutic: it cleans the mind of all the detritus acquired while responding in the preconditioned ways demanded by most other films. *Down by Law* is an upper, though you probably won't realize this at first.

It's been photographed by Robby Müller in the rich, almost liquid, black-and-white tones that recall films like *The Big Heat* and *The Asphalt Jungle*. It's about three seemingly expendable misfits—a small-time pimp, an out-of-work disk jockey, and an indomitably cheerful Italian tourist, who seems to have disembarked in the wrong country without knowing it.

The setting is contemporary New Orleans, though the city looks as if it had recently been ransacked by Union armies, and the Louisiana bayou country, where chance encounters are as life-enhancing as they are life-threatening in the city.

When first met, in separate sequences, both the pimp, Jack (John Lurie), and the disk jockey, Zack (Tom Waits), are on their way to the slammer, though neither has any reason to know this yet.

Late at night, lying in bed in a sleazy room in the French Quarter, Jack listens without interest as his companion (Billie Neal) quotes her mother's analysis of America. "She used to say it's a big melting pot, because when you bring it to a boil, all the scum rises to the top."

More than a little bored, Jack is fair game when a man, whom he has no right to trust, arrives and offers to introduce him to a teen-age "Cajun goddess" who'd like to join his stable. The not-so-streetwise Jack trots off to the rendezvous, which turns out to have been set up by the vice squad.

In another bed, in another part of this same forest, the bewildered, out-of-work Zack is being harangued by his girlfriend (Ellen Barkin), at the end of which he says, tentatively, "I guess it's all over between us, Laurette?" Out in the street, retrieving his shoes from the gutter (where Laurette has tossed them), Zack is offered an easy $1,000. All he has to do is drive a Mercedes from one side of New Orleans to the other. The hitch is that the car, which turns out to be stolen, also contains a dead man in the trunk.

Jack and Zack are turning into sullen near-vegetables in the cell they share at the Orleans Parish prison when Roberto (Roberto Benigni) joins them. Unlike Jack and Zack, who proclaim their innocence, Roberto freely admits that he did kill the man he's accused of murdering, though it was in self-defense during a card game.

To Jack and Zack, Roberto is not only from another country, but another planet. His English is, at best, random. He's read all of the great American writers ("in Italian translation, of course"), including "Bob" Frost. He regards his murder charge only as something of a temporary delay, like bad weather at the airport.

Roberto is part clown, part genius. There's something of Papageno about him, especially as played by the irrepressible Mr. Benigni. He's simultaneously pragmatic and sophisticated. It's Roberto who plans the odd trio's successful escape from prison.

No more about the story should be revealed or, for that matter, can be revealed. There's even less "story" to *Down by Law* than to *Stranger Than Paradise*.

Down by Law is a fable of poetic density. It's so much of a piece that it's not easy to separate and identify the components that make the movie what it is. The performances by Mr. Lurie, Mr. Waits, and Mr. Benigni are extraordinary. However, they wouldn't exist had they not been photographed by Mr. Jarmusch and Mr. Müller in the kind of deep focus that permits the three to be on the screen at the same time, in the same frame. In this way they are able to act and react to one another—in a way that just isn't possible when the camera keeps intercutting between the actors.

Early on, Mr. Jarmusch's characters, and the world they inhabit, remind one of the plays of Sam Shepard, but the similarity is superficial. Unlike Mr. Shepard's characters, who have their roots in the theater of Ibsen, Mr. Jarmusch's travel light. They carry very little in the way of historical baggage. Their pasts are unimportant. They take their shapes from their present circumstances, and from the way they are seen by the camera in their environment—mostly at a comparatively cool distance.

Mr. Shepard's Americans have cut themselves loose from the safety of middle-class life, and must come to terms with their sense of dislocation. In *Down by Law*, Jack, Zack and Roberto seem to have been classless forever, floating always (as they are seen in the film) off the shore of a foreign land they've never known or understood, where a logical system of rewards and punishments still exists. They give us not the actuality of life but a dream impression.

The excitement of *Down by Law* comes not from what it's "about." Reduced to its plot, it is very slight. But the plot isn't the point. The excitement comes from the realization that we are seeing a true filmmaker at work, using film to create a narrative that couldn't exist on the stage or the printed page of a novel.

Down by Law works on the mind and senses in a completely different fashion. It's an unqualified delight, from its elegiacal opening shots to its unexpected last scene, which is funny in itself as well as a wicked pun on "Bob" Frost's now somewhat tired "Road Not Taken."

—*V.C., September 19, 1986*

DRACULA

Directed by Tod Browning: written by Garrett Fort. based on the play by Hamilton Deane and John Balderston and the novel by Bram Stoker: cinematographer. Kark Freund: edited by Milton Carruth and Maurice Pivar: music by Peter Ilich Tchaikovsky and Richard Wagner: art designer. Charles D. Hall: produced by Carl Laemmle Jr.: released by Universal Pictures. Black and white. Running time: 84 minutes.

With: Bela Lugosi (Count Dracula). Helen Chandler (Mina Seward). David Manners (John Harker). Dwight Frye (Renfield). Edward Van Sloan (Dr. Van Helsing). Herbert Bunston (Dr. Seward) and Frances Dade (Lucy Weston).

Count Dracula, Bram Stoker's human vampire, who has chilled the spines of book readers and playgoers, is now to be seen at the Roxy in a talking film directed by Tod Browning, who delights in such bloodcurdling stories. It is a production that evidently had the desired effect upon many in the audience yesterday afternoon, for there was a general outburst of applause when Dr. Van Helsing produced a little cross that caused the dreaded Dracula to fling his cloak over his head and make himself scarce.

But Dracula's evil work is not ended until Dr. Van Helsing hammers a stake through the Count's heart as he lies in his native earth in a box.

Mr. Browning is fortunate in having in the leading role in this eerie work, Bela Lugosi, who played the same part on the stage when it was presented here in October 1927. What with Mr. Browning's imaginative direction and Mr. Lugosi's makeup and weird ges-

tures, this picture succeeds to some extent in its Grand Guignol intentions.

As the scenes flash by there are all sorts of queer noises, such as the cries of wolves and the hooting of owls, not to say anything of the screams of Dracula's feminine victims, who are found with twin red marks on their white throats.

The Count is able to change himself into a vampire that flies in through the window and in this guise he is supposed to be able to talk to his victims, who are either driven insane or are so thoroughly terrified that they would sooner do his bidding than pay heed to those who have their welfare at heart. Martin, the keeper in the sanitarium in which an unfortunate individual named Renfield is under supervision, fires at the big bat with a shotgun, but, of course, misses.

To enhance the supernatural effect of this film there is a fog in many of the scenes. The first glimpses are of ordinary humans, but so soon as Renfield goes to the Transylvania castle of the Count, who lives on for centuries by his vampirish actions, there are bony hands protruding from boxes, rats and other animals fleeing, and corridors that are thick with cobwebs and here and there a hungry spider.

Most of the excitement takes place in Carfax Abbey and other places in England, the Count having traveled there to accomplish his bloodthirsty intentions. To start the grim work he causes all the ship's crew to go insane and commit suicide, but his subsequent activities are not as fruitful as he anticipates.

Helen Chandler gives an excellent performance as one of the girls who is attacked by the "undead" Count. David Manners contributes good work. Dwight Frye does fairly well as Renfield. Herbert Bunston is a most convincing personality. Charles Gerrard affords a few laughs as Martin.

This picture can at least boast of being the best of the many mystery films.

—*M.H., February 13, 1931*

THE DREAMLIFE OF ANGELS

Directed by Erick Zonca: written (in French. with English subtitles) by Mr. Zonca and Roger Bohbot. with the collaboration of Virginie Wagon: director of photography. Agnes Godard: edited by Yannick Kergoat: art director. Jimmy Vansteenkiste:

produced by Francois Marquis: released by Sony Pictures Classics. Running time: 113 minutes.

With: Elodie Bouchez (Isa). Natacha Regnier (Marie). Gregoire Colin (Chriss). Jo Prestia (Fredo) and Patrick Mercado (Charly).

This year's New York Film Festival concludes on a note of uncommon grace. *The Dreamlife of Angels,* to be shown on Sunday night at 8:30, begins simply and becomes a glimpse into an unexpected world. Though its two main characters, young Frenchwomen adrift and living hand to mouth, are rough-edged and scrappy, they wind up forming a bond of enormous delicacy. As that bond frays, this impassioned first feature by Erick Zonca reveals a soulful, moving vision of our shared responsibility for one another's lives.

In a film whose two stars jointly won best actress honors at Cannes this year, the most immediately unforgettable figure is Elodie Bouchez's Isa (short for Isabelle). At 21, she's a scruffy opportunist toting her backpack through Lille, raising pocket money by hustling religious pictures to passers-by. She takes a factory job as a seamstress, failing dismally but winding up with a fellow worker, Marie (Natacha Regnier) as her new best friend.

Marie couldn't care less about being a seamstress either. In a film that easily incorporates class struggle into its story and cares more about working-class experience than many a more openly political drama, she too lives strictly in the moment. Both women are at an adventurous age, looking for opportunity wherever they find it and working only because they must. Then, with the lovelorn blindness of a Dreiser heroine, Marie hitches her hopes to a wealthy man.

Mr. Zonca, who cares more about emotional fire than social realism, depicts Marie's love affair with furious intimacy. It begins in a most unexpected way. Isa and Marie have been happily taunting bouncers at a club, mostly just for sport; Marie even has an affair with one of them (a hefty biker, played with incongruous tenderness by Patrick Mercado). The women have also harassed smug-looking Chriss (Gregoire Colin), without realizing that he is the club's owner. One day Chriss spots slim, pretty Marie while she is shoplifting a jacket and saves her from arrest. Rebellious but also secretly impressed, Marie lets Chriss buy the jacket and buy her, too.

With her big, toothy grin and rough features, Ms. Bouchez's Isa looks like the plainer of the two women at first. But as she rises to the occasion of befriending the badly confused Marie, she takes on an astonishing radiance, a glow of stirring compassion. "She gave out an impression of serenity, grace and absolute confidence in life," Mr. Zonca has said of the young woman who inspired this story, and the luminous Ms. Bouchez (whose credits include Andre Techine's *Wild Reeds*) summons that same spirit magnificently here. In the subplot from which the title comes, Isa learns of a comatose young girl (whose apartment she and Marie happen to be sharing) and avidly makes herself the girl's guardian, sharing in her fate.

The Dreamlife of Angels escalates with frightening urgency as Marie loses her bearings. Wise in the ways of stubbornly wrongheaded love affairs, Mr. Zonca shows how sexually responsive she is to Chriss's cruelty, and how easily sexual desperation drives a wedge between the friends when Isa counsels caution. In scenes of tumultuous intimacy, he watches the two feisty heroines fight out their differences. The two actresses perform with overwhelming naturalness, as if utterly locked into this conflict. Mr. Zonca had them live together while making the film, and it shows.

In the end, this beautifully acted drama, as raw and immediate as it is heartfelt, describes much more than the fallout from friendship or a headstrong love affair. It leaves behind what Isa has discovered: the profound ties among the lives that are seen here, and the way those ties make sense of our world.

—J.M., October 9, 1998

DRESSED TO KILL

Written and directed by Brian De Palma: director of photography. Ralf D. Bode: edited by Jerry Greenberg: music by Pino Donaggio: production designer. Natalie Massara: produced by George Litto: released by Filmways. Running time: 105 minutes.

With: Michael Caine (Dr. Robert Elliott). Angie Dickinson (Kate Miller). Nancy Allen (Liz Blake). Keith Gordon (Peter Miller). Dennis Franz (Detective Marino). David Margulies (Dr. Levy) and Kenny Baker (Warren Lockman).

Inside his one body there have always been two Brian De Palmas. The personality hasn't been exactly split, since aspects of one side have always been evident in the other; yet until now the two Brian De Palmas seem to have functioned side-by-side only in uneasy peace.

There's the Brian De Palma who makes *Hi, Mom, Greeting* and *Home Movies,* exuberantly anarchic, essentially formless comedies full of low jokes and sometimes inspired satire. There's also the Brian De Palma who directed *Obsession, Carrie* and *The Fury,* psychological thrillers and horror films executed mainly in the manner of Alfred Hitchcock. The films of this Brian De Palma, who is what the French would call a cinéaste, a scholarly filmmaker of decisive style (though it's not necessarily all his own), are more fun for lively, isolated sequences than for any sustained effect.

Now with *Dressed to Kill,* it's apparent that the two Brian De Palmas can settle down to work together with most entertaining results. The film, which opens today at the Beekman and other theaters, is a witty, romantic, psychological horror film and it's almost as rewarding as a successful analysis.

Dressed to Kill is, appropriately, about a split personality, a furious transvestite who goes clomping around Manhattan in large high heels, a blond wig, dark glasses and a black raincoat, carrying a straight razor ready to slash any woman who arouses the man in him.

Among the people whose lives he touches in one way and another are Dr. Robert Elliott (Michael Caine), a psychiatrist with a fancy East Side office and the patients to go with it; Kate Miller (Angie Dickinson), a suburban matron whose sex life at home leaves her too much time for erotic fantasies; Peter Miller (Keith Gordon), her teenage son, who's also a science genius; Liz Blake (Nancy Allen), a sweet-looking Park Avenue hooker, who turns tricks to play the stock market; Detective Marino (Dennis Franz), who must track down the slasher; and Dr. Levy (David Margulies), another psychiatrist, more avuncular than and nowhere near as posh as Dr. Elliott, who has been treating a possibly homicidal transvestite.

Not too much stress should be placed on the logic within Mr. De Palma's screenplay, though it's adequate to the kind of entertainment *Dressed to Kill* is. Unlike *The Fury,* which was a collection of big, splashy, loosely strung-together set pieces, *Dressed to Kill* is one succeeding spectacular effect after another. The fun is not in logic but watching how Mr. De Palma successfully tops himself as he goes along, and the fun lasts from the sexy, comic opening sequence right through to the film's several endings.

Dressed to Kill is difficult to describe without giving away unmentionable things. However, I have a particular fondness for an extended, simultaneously funny and scary sequence, virtually without dialogue, in which Miss Dickinson's sexually deprived suburban matron goes to the Metropolitan Museum of Art and picks up a man who may or may not be a killer.

The movie owes a great deal to Hitchcock, perhaps too much for one to be able to judge it entirely on its own merits. It's possible that if one is a Hitchcock student, with a special knowledge of *Psycho* and *Vertigo,* one will resent all of the so-called quotes and references that Mr. De Palma includes in *Dressed to Kill.* But that, I think, is to underrate what the writer-director has pulled off in this case, which is not an imitation but a film made by someone who has studied the master and learned, in addition to style, something far more important, that is, a consistent point of view. Among other things, the De Palma camera appears to have an intelligence of its own.

Equally important, at least to those of us who have always favored the comic De Palma, *Dressed to Kill* is very funny, which helps to defuse the effect of the graphically photographed violence. In addition, the film is, in its own inside-out way, peculiarly moral. There's no other way to respond to the particular manner in which he resolves a sequence of highly satisfactory, illicit, afternoon lovemaking.

Dressed to Kill has weak points. Mr. De Palma sometimes tells us too much about what's going on in a character's mind, which is a stylistic affectation I'm sure he's perfectly well aware of. Also not satisfactory are some of the explanations about why someone won't or can't do the obvious thing, such as go to the police.

The movie, though, never forgets that it's meant to be fiction, even in the way it's photographed in the rich, vivid colors of Hollywood movies of the fifties. The result is a Manhattan (including its subways) that could have been constructed on some fantastic backlot.

The performers are excellent, especially Miss Dickinson, whose drawn, taut beauty says as much about her character as anything she actually does. Mr. Caine, after the disaster *The Island,* is in top form, and Miss Allen and Mr. Gordon are most appealing as strictly 1980's versions of what used to be called the ingénue and the juvenile.

Even the title is good.

—V.C., July 25, 1980

THE DRESSER

Produced and directed by Peter Yates: written by Ronald Harwood, based on his play: director of photography. Kelvin Pike: edited by Ray Lovejoy: music by James Horner: production designer. Stephen Grimes: released by Columbia Pictures. Running time: 118 minutes.

With: Albert Finney (Sir). Tom Courtenay (Norman). Edward Fox (Oxenby). Zena Walker (Her Ladyship). Eileen Atkins (Madge). Michael Gough (Frank Carrington). Cathryn Harrison (Irene) and Betty Marsden (Violet Manning).

The time is 1940, some months after Dunkirk but still more than a year before the United States's entry into World War II. The German Luftwaffe is reducing Britain's cities to rubble and Winston Churchill is rallying the citizens to meet their finest hour. Among those responding are the members of one of the seediest repertory companies ever assembled to carry the Bard to what Margot Metroland would call the lower orders, mostly in the provinces.

"I've been reduced to old men, cripples, and nancy boys," bellows Sir (Albert Finney), the troupe's increasingly confused old star, referring to his supporting players. Not only are all of the good actors in uniform but the theaters that Sir is accustomed to playing are being bombed out from under him. His world is vanishing but the ghosts that haunt Sir in these last days are not out of life but the memories of great roles.

"What is tomorrow night's play?" Sir, exhausted after a performance of *Othello,* asks Norman (Tom Courtenay), his faithful dresser, nanny and confidant.

"Lear," says Norman.

"How does it start?" says Sir.

The film that contains Sir and Norman is *The Dresser,* Ronald Harwood's screen adaptation of his 1981 Broadway play, which has been directed with immense affection for actors and acting by Peter Yates.

The Dresser is a very curious work. The movie itself isn't satisfying in a conventional way, but it is great fun if you are moved by actors and acting even when the mechanics of the playwrighting do not quite match the mechanics of the playing. This is not to underrate Mr. Harwood's work. These two roles didn't write themselves. Yet the characters thus created by Mr. Harwood and the two splendid actors have a rather limited emotional payoff within the eventually melodramatic circumstances of the film.

When *The Dresser* opened on Broadway with Mr. Courtenay as Norman and Paul Rogers as Sir, Mr. Courtenay received the greater part of the attention focused on the two star performances. It is one of the measures of the particular success of Mr. Yates's film version that Mr. Finney's Sir is every bit as riveting as Mr. Courtenay's Norman, and that the two actors, even if for a very brief time, give you a very flashy run for your money.

Though most of the film takes place inside the theater where an exhausted, emotionally ravaged Sir is preparing to play Lear for the 427th time, the film moves outside for a couple of quite marvelous scenes that open up the play without letting the life out of it.

There is one sequence in which the fussy, brandy-swigging Norman attempts to herd his raggle-taggle troupe from one train to another in a steam-filled station crowded with service people and other wartime travelers. His actors simply can't walk as fast as Norman. "Please," says the desperate Norman to the train's engineer, "Wait just a minute. They're old actors." The engineer refuses and the train starts up when from the far end of the platform comes the commanding voice of Sir. "Stop the train!" The train stops and Sir, his somewhat younger wife and the others are able to board.

In another, far more harrowing scene, a temporarily deranged Sir lurches through the streets of a provincial city, discarding his clothes, ranting against fate, vowing to give it all up and acknowledging his defeat, to the embarrassment and curiosity of the onlookers. All the time Norman is pursuing him, trying to protect the old man and to bring him back to some sort of sanity.

This is the film's recurring image— that of the mad

Lear crashing ever closer to the edge of the known world while the sorrowing Fool attempts to prevent inevitable disaster.

This works at first, but then the analogy between Lear and Fool and Sir and Norman gives out. Mr. Finney's Sir is a vain, irascible, funny, fascinating, actory turn, but he is not an especially tragic figure, and Mr. Courtenay's Norman is a sharp-tongued, loyal, heartbreakingly limited, backstage queen, a middle-aged man who moves from deceptively unthreatening camp mannerisms to serious ferocity within a single speech.

After a while one wonders why the other characters in their lives, including Sir's wife, known as Her Ladyship (Zena Walker), and Madge (Eileen Atkins), the manager of the troupe who has loved Sir for twenty years, really play such small roles in the disaster we witness. It's just possible that the relationship between Norman and Sir doesn't appear big and encompassing enough to exclude the others to the extent we see.

I am also somewhat perplexed about how we are supposed to feel about Sir as an actor. Early in his career, Mr. Harwood actually worked as a dresser for the late Donald Wolfit and wrote a popular biography of Wolfit, who, like Sir, spent many years playing the provinces. In 1947, in a London revue called—I think—"Sweetest and Lowest," Hermione Gingold got one of her biggest laughs by asking another cast member if he knew the difference between Laurence Olivier and Donald Wolfit. The answer, which brought down the house both times I saw the show: "Laurence Olivier is a tour de force. Donald Wolfit is forced to tour."

Not long after that, Wolfit won the London acclaim he had so long sought, playing *King Lear,* and went on to receive the knighthood denied to Sir. Yet though the other actors and the audiences within *The Dresser* sometimes talk about how great Sir has just been on stage, what the film audience sees are bits and pieces of performances that remind me, at least, of all of the jokes once told about Wolfit.

This is not important to one's enjoyment of *The Dresser.* It's only something to think about as you watch two terrifically gifted performers have an actor's field day with, of course, the aid and affection of the writer and the director.

—*V.C., December 6, 1983*

DRIVING MISS DAISY

Directed by Bruce Beresford; written by Alfred Uhry, based on his play; director of photography, Peter James; edited by Mark Warner; music by Hans Zimmer; production designer, Bruno Rubeo; produced by Richard D. Zanuck and Lili Fini Zanuck; released by Warner Brothers. Running time: 99 minutes.

With: Morgan Freeman (Hoke Colburn), Jessica Tandy (Daisy Werthan), Dan Aykroyd (Boolie Werthan), Patti LuPone (Florine Werthan), Esther Rolle (Idella), Joann Havrilla (Miss McClatchey) and William Hall Jr. (Oscar).

That car," says Miss Daisy, "misbehaved."

"Cars don't misbehave, Mama," says Boolie Werthan. "They have to be caused to misbehave."

That morning Miss Daisy (played by Jessica Tandy) had been inching out of her Atlanta driveway when the car suddenly zoomed back across the flower beds, up and over a small retaining wall, so as to teeter, with its rear end exposed, over her neighbor's yard.

Miss Daisy had put her foot on the gas instead of the brake, though Boolie (Dan Aykroyd) has the good sense not to accuse his mother of the obvious. She's not around the bend yet. Miss Daisy is in her seventies and has all her faculties. She has, however, reached a point where cars tend to misbehave when she is behind the wheel.

Against his mother's furious objections, Boolie decides it is time she had a man to drive for her. It is his great good fortune to find Hoke Colburn (Morgan Freeman), a black man in his sixties, a widower who is patient and has infinite tact and vast reserves of subversive wit.

Thus begins Bruce Beresford's gently opened-up screen version of *Driving Miss Daisy,* Alfred Uhry's fine Pulitzer Prize—winning play, which is still running Off Broadway at the John Houseman Theater.

Plays, especially small ones, do not always open up with ease on the big movie screen, but *Driving Miss Daisy* carries most of its cinematic options with great style. It is the most successful stage-to-screen translation since Stephen Frears turned Christopher Hampton's *Liaisons Dangereuses* into *Dangerous Liaisons.*

Mr. Uhry, who wrote the screenplay, has supplemented the play's three characters with people who are only talked about on the stage. They are introduced with care and so discreetly characterized that they do not impinge upon the central relationships that give the play its strength.

Mr. Uhry's job was easier than the task most playwrights face when doing stage-to-screen adaptations. His play is comparatively free of form to start with. It uses a minimum of props within a single all-purpose set that comes to represent Miss Daisy's house as well as locations all over Atlanta and its environs. To a certain extent, his play was already opened up.

Even so, there is an exhilarating, singularly theatrical lightness of touch that is often lost when these settings are made manifest in a movie. Mr. Beresford and Mr. Uhry, working in concert, see to it that the essential spirit of *Driving Miss Daisy* shines through the sometimes deadening effects of literalism.

This *Driving Miss Daisy* is small and pure and healthily skeptical as it chronicles, from a privileged position, the social changes taking place in the South between 1948 and 1973, and the remarkable twenty-five-year friendship that embraces those changes.

On one side is Miss Daisy, the rich Jewish widow who hates being called rich and loathes the whole idea of servants. "I don't have any privacy," she complains to Boolie. "It's like having children in the house."

On the other side is Hoke, who knows far more of the real world than Miss Daisy and remains steadfastly unsurprised by it.

To Hoke's amusement, Miss Daisy clings with tenacity to the memories of her humble beginnings on the wrong side of the tracks, and to her years as a schoolteacher. Among other things, she teaches him how to read. He teaches her about the world he inhabits, which, when the privileges are removed, is not so different from hers.

She is almost impossible to deal with in the early years, but Hoke plays her as if he were a benign angler. She finds fault everywhere. Hoke agrees with her and then goes on, in his resolute way, to show her up with such maddening delicacy that she cannot find fault.

Because she is Jewish and he is black, both are outsiders. Mr. Uhry does not press down too hard on this, though it is a fact of life that, at a key moment, provides an unexpected point of alliance. Miss Daisy and Hoke are as much outsiders for their age and sensibility as for anything else. Theirs is the friendship of equals.

So is the casting of the two central roles.

In her long career in films, Miss Tandy, always celebrated on the stage, has never had a role of a richness and humor to match Miss Daisy, and she brings to it her mastery of what might be called selective understatement. She is a spectacular accumulation of tiny obsessions and misconceptions. Miss Tandy creates a most particular woman, who is sometimes hilariously wrongheaded but almost always self-aware.

Her Miss Daisy possesses the kind of stubbornness that one hesitates to crack, since, underneath, there is something extremely fragile. Yet there is also a fierce intelligence that comes through, no more movingly than in the film's final sequence.

Mr. Freeman, who originated the role on the stage, eases through the movie with the sort of humor that has been earned after a lot of hard knocks. Though the character never appears to be tough, it's a tough performance. It is laid-back and graceful, the work of an actor who has gone through all of the possibilities, stripped away all of the extraneous details and arrived at an essence.

The two actors manage to be highly theatrical without breaking out of the realistic frame of the film.

Mr. Aykroyd gives a notably self-effacing performance as Boolie, a role that is in large measure a dramatic device, but also a lot more fully drawn than most dramatic devices in such plays. He is funny, loving and amazingly nonjudgmental, especially when it comes to his wife.

She is the fearfully nouveau riche Florine, played by Patti LuPone with just the right amount of heedless determination. (According to Miss Daisy, Florine's idea of heaven is socializing with Episcopalians.) Esther Rolle is also good in the brief role of Miss Daisy's cook and housekeeper.

Some of the ways in which the film has been opened up inevitably coarsen a very delicate work. It is difficult to believe that even Florine, who is, after all, the wife of Atlanta's businessman of the year, would cover her house with the kind of garish Christmas decorations that would look overwrought at Disney World. It's a cheap laugh.

Also a bit heavy-handed is a scene in which Miss

Daisy and Hoke, en route to Mobile, are stopped and questioned by a couple of redneck state troopers. Says one trooper to the other as Miss Daisy and Hoke go on their way. "An old Jew woman and an old nigger, taking off down the road together. What a sorry sight."

It is unnecessary. The movie is too good for that sort of reverse editorial comment.

—V.C., December 13, 1989

DROWNING BY NUMBERS

Written and directed by Peter Greenaway: director of photography. Sacha Vierny: edited by John Wilson: music by Michael Nyman: produced by Kees Kasander and Denis Wigman: released by Prestige Miramax Films. Running time: 114 minutes.

With: Joan Plowright (Cissie Colpitts 1). Juliet Stevenson (Cissie Colpitts 2). Joely Richardson (Cissie Colpitts 3). Bernard Hill (Madgett) and Jason Edwards (Smut).

The mind that embraces pure gamesmanship is rarely as fanciful as that of Peter Greenaway, who obviously plays by his own rules. Mr. Greenaway's love of puzzles, riddles, obscure references and obsessive schematization is truly astounding, but it is rarely matched by an equivalent interest in whatever has set these maneuvers in motion. He would be perfectly capable, it often seems, of staging an elaborate whodunit without bothering to determine whether anyone was ultimately to blame.

The visual appeal of Mr. Greenaway's work is unmistakable, as is the impression that something of great moment is under way. So his card castles become that much more remarkable when it becomes apparent that they are built on such thin air. This filmmaker's audacity, which is indeed formidable, has much more to do with testing the limits of his audience's patience, curiosity and tolerance for outrage than it does with intellectual challenge.

In Mr. Greenaway's *Drowning by Numbers,* which was made in 1988 and serves as a kind of dress rehearsal for his subsequent *The Cook, the Thief, His Wife and Her Lover*, there are three principal women, all of whom have the same name. Cissie Colpitts (who figured in Mr. Greenaway's 1980 film *The Falls*) now spans three generations, and in each incarnation she drowns her husband, after which she mourns him briefly before going on contentedly with her life. Meanwhile, each of the numbers from 1 to 100 is seen somewhere during the course of the film, whether on a laundry mark (3) or a herring (92, 93, 94) or a dead cow (78 and 79). The names of a hundred stars are also worked into the film. So are the last words of Gainsborough, Charles II, William Pitt and Lord Nelson.

It would be unsporting and also futile to ask why, since Mr. Greenaway's intentions never reveal themselves in full. Production notes for this film include the director's eight-page, single-spaced synopsis of what transpires, yet little of this is clearer on paper than it is on screen. "Smut is perturbed by the Skipping Girl's remarks about circumcision and asks Madgett questions prompted by a painting he's found of Samson and Delilah," goes a sample development. It's not difficult to absorb such an event, and the countless others like it, without developing any larger notion of what is under way.

If Mr. Greenaway operated strictly on the level of narrative, he would have little claim to an audience's attention, but his narratives are secondary anyhow. His films are indeed visually fascinating (since the 1985 *A Zed and Two Noughts,* they have been beautifully photographed by Sacha Vierny, who did so much fine work for Alain Resnais). And this one has a particularly seductive look, with a setting on the English coast and an inviting mixture of seashore and greenery. Mr. Greenaway's compositions are also hauntingly lovely even when marginally sickening, like the array of apples at the first murder scene, where insects and snails perch mysteriously amid the ripe fruit. Film-minded entomologists will note that the death's-head moth of *The Silence of the Lambs* can also be seen here, although Mr. Greenaway's film has the upper hand when it comes to bugs.

Working up to the mettle-testing extremes of *The Cook, the Thief, His Wife and Her Lover,* Mr. Greenaway this time includes Smut (Jason Edwards), the small boy who counts and celebrates road kills, collects insects and becomes obsessed with the dream of circumcising himself, which indeed comes true. There are also traces of the physical disgust—the revulsion for food and flesh—and the free-spirited nudity that help to foster the impression of a larger honesty, though none is particularly forthcoming.

Despite that, and despite its pervasive morbidity, *Drowning by Numbers* is a much more lighthearted work than its successor. It's also a film that affords its actors better and more wry roles than Mr. Greenaway usually provides. Joan Plowright, as the senior Cissie and the one who first kills her husband, presides over the film as a droll, knowing figure and provides a deadpan delivery well suited to the film's cryptic wit. She and Juliet Stevenson, a particularly poised and acerbic Cissie 2, indeed seem cut from the same cloth.

Joely Richardson, as the youngest Cissie, is more the innocent, even though her role is largely that of a homicidal nymph. The women in the film are treated far better than the men, who include Bernard Hill as the central male figure, a coroner named Madgett whose desire for all three Cissies is only heightened by their lethal proclivities. Mr. Greenaway's brand of feminism, one of the film's few discernible constructs, brings death or bodily harm to most of his male characters.

Drowning by Numbers is best watched as a fable made in the manner of a latter-day and even more debauched Lewis Carroll, replete with oddly staged contests like the cricket match involving dozens of players, odd rules and abundant masks. It is also filled with gaming equipment, compulsive collections, painterly references and a degree of intensive detail that holds the interest even when nothing else does. The film's tendency to be obscure is not helped by its soundtrack, which is occasionally muffled. But the music, composed by Michael Nyman around several bars of *Mozart's Sinfonia Concertante for violin, viola and orchestra,* is on a par with the glowing cinematography.

—*J.M., April 26, 1991*

DRUGSTORE COWBOY

Directed by Gus Van Sant Jr.; written by Mr. Van Sant and Daniel Yost, based on the novel by James Fogle; director of photography, Robert Yeoman; edited by Curtiss Clayton; music by Elliott Goldenthal; production designer, David Brisbin; produced by Nick Weschler and Karen Murphy; released by Avenue Pictures. Running time: 100 minutes.

With: Matt Dillon (Bob), Kelly Lynch (Dianne), James Le Gros (Rick), Heather Graham (Nadine), Beah Richards (Drug Counselor), Grace Zabriskie (Bob's Mother), Max Perlich (David) and William S. Burroughs (Tom the Priest).

Drugstore Cowboy, Gus Van Sant Jr.'s glum, absorbing film about a clan of heroin addicts who travel around the Pacific Northwest looting pharmacies of their supplies the way Bonnie and Clyde cleaned out banks, gives Matt Dillon the role of his career.

The young actor's mannerisms—his self-consciously surly machismo and outlawish posturing, which in other films can seem annoying—perfectly serve the role of Bob Hughes, the little band's superstitious leader. Bob's extended family of junkies includes his haughty wife, Dianne (Kelly Lynch), his dumb sidekick Rick (James Le Gros) and Nadine (Heather Graham), Rick's teenage girlfriend whose death from an overdose convinces Bob that he should kick heroin and leave his life of crime.

The film, which opens today at the Carnegie Hall Cinema, is based on an unpublished novel by James Fogle, who has served time for similar crimes. Set in 1971 in Portland, Oregon, it offers a cool-eyed vision of young addicts adrift during the twilight of the counterculture. Both in its delineation of character and in its evocation of an era when drug taking still carried an aura of hipness, the film rings deeply true. Its downbeat mood, underscored by Abbey Lincoln's haunting recording of "For All We Know," partakes of the same mood as such other relatively recent movies as *Round Midnight, Sid and Nancy* and *Patty Hearst.*

The way of life portrayed in the film is jarring in its abrupt changes of rhythms, as the somnolent lulls of consumption are broken by ferocious spasms of violence and paranoia. The film takes us so deeply into this shabby, transient world that we feel its texture—both its scary thrills and its bleak, fatalistic uncertainty. There are graphic scenes of the characters shooting up drugs and being rocked by waves of euphoria.

Drugstore Cowboy is the first major feature by Mr. Van Sant, a thirty-six-year-old director who lives in Portland. It fulfills the promise suggested by his grainy low-budget 1987 film, *Mala Noche,* which was also set in Portland and which dispassionately observed a skid-row liquor clerk's romantic fixation on a young Mexican migrant worker. As in *Mala Noche,* Mr. Van Sant, who collaborated on the screenplay for *Drugstore Cowboy* with Daniel Yost, neither glamorizes nor sharply censures his characters.

Mr. Dillon's Bob is alternately appealing and appalling. Even though he devotes all his energies to crime and addiction, he brings a certain swaggering savvy to his tasks. And when he successfully carries off a vicious practical joke on the police, one feels a reluctant twinge of approval. Dianne, whom Miss Lynch portrays with a steely authority, inspires the same ambivalent response. Except for her drug addiction, Dianne is a profoundly ordinary young woman. And the movie suggests that aside from its chemical highs, one appeal of the wayward life to Dianne is that it makes her feel special.

Because the characters are so self-absorbed and their lives so totally unproductive, there is an element of comic absurdity in their continual desperation. After Nadine dies, their motel happens to become the site of a convention of state policemen. With the place aswarm with overweight law officers in uniform, the urgent problem of removing the body is treated as deadpan black comedy.

Among the performances, the only false note is struck by the writer William S. Burroughs, who makes a cameo appearance near the end as a defrocked junkie priest who lives in the same hotel as Bob. Reflecting on the pull of heroin to Bob, who has taken a steady job and left his old life behind, the cadaverous Mr. Burroughs gives one of his standard performances, raving in a feverish monotone. His appearance slightly throws off the mood of a film that is otherwise a very impressive look into a dark subject.

—S.H., October 6, 1989

DUCK SOUP

Directed by Leo McCarey; written by Bert Kalmar, Harry Ruby, Arthur Sheekman and Nat Perrin; cinematographer, Henry Sharp; edited by LeRoy Stone; art designer, Hans Dreier and Wiard Ihnen; produced by Herman Mankiewicz; released by Paramount Pictures. Black and white. Running time: 70 minutes.

With: Groucho Marx (Rufus T. Firefly), Chico Marx (Chicolini), Harpo Marx (Brownie), Zeppo Marx (Bob Rolland), Racquel Torres (Vera Marcal), Louis Calhern (Ambassador Trentino) and Margaret Dumont (Mrs. Teasdale).

Those mad clowns, the Marx brothers, are now holding forth on the Rivoli screen in their latest concoction, *Duck Soup,* a production in which the bludgeon is employed more often than the gimlet. The result is that this production is, for the most part, extremely noisy without being nearly as mirthful as their other films. There are, however, one or two ideas in this sea of puns that are welcome, and Groucho, Chico, Harpo and Zeppo reveal their customary zeal in striving to get as much as possible out of these incidents.

Groucho is the latest of the performers to indulge in a mythical kingdom story, for he, as the more or less illustrious Rufus T. Firefly, after being referred to as possessing the statesmanship of Gladstone, the humility of Lincoln and the wisdom of Pericles, is made the dictator of Freedonia. Slapping the face of Ambassador Trentino, Sylvania's representative, means little to Firefly, even though it may result in war. As one might imagine, there is not only friction between Freedonia and Sylvania during most of this story, but also among other persons in the country ruled over by Groucho, or Mr. Firefly. Mrs. Teasdale, whose husband was a serious thinker who once held Firefly's job, is keen to see that Firefly gets full support from other worthies.

During one important juncture for Freedonia, one discovers that two of the brothers Marx—Chico and Harpo—have decorated their faces with black mustaches and spectacles, so that they look like doubles of Groucho. This gives the performers a chance for many stunts, including the idea that one of them is the reflection of the other in a mirror. The insanity persists until a third, or the real Groucho, appears on the scene, which yesterday aroused a torrent of laughter.

Another equally hilarious morsel is where the dumb Harpo does a Paul Revere ride for Freedonia's sake. It happens, however, that Harpo, unlike the original, has an eye for a pretty face, and therefore when he perceives a girl in the window the ride comes to an abrupt end. Wild activities ensue, however, for the husband of the young blonde turns up and Revere's imitator has to hide under the water in a bathtub. Subsequently, when the frightened husband has made himself scarce, Harpo thinks that it would be a good idea to bring his horse into the house.

In another episode Groucho works himself up into a state of frenzy over a supposed insult, and when Ambassador Trentino appears with a hope of avoiding war, Groucho again slaps Sylvania's envoy. A certain amount of fun is furnished by Harpo's being constantly busy with a pair of scissors. He cuts the tails off Trentino's well-tailored coat and also uses his shears to cut a panama hat in half and to despoil other articles of clothing.

Now and again the governmental activities in Freedonia are interrupted with music and song. Besides the characteristic work of the Marx brothers, Louis Calhern gives an adequate interpretation as Trentino. Margaret Dumont is satisfactory as the eminent Mrs. Teasdale and Edwin Maxwell officiates as secretary of war.

—M.H., November 23, 1933

THE DUELLISTS

Directed by Ridley Scott: written by Gerald Vaughan-Hughes, based on the story "The Duel" by Joseph Conrad: director of photography, Frank Tidy: edited by Pamela Powers: music by Howard Blake: art designer, Bryan Graves: produced by David Puttnam: released by Paramount Pictures. Running time: 101 minutes.

With: Keith Carradine (D'Hubert), Harvey Keitel (Feraud), Albert Finney (Fouche), Edward Fox (Colonel Reynard), Cristina Raines (Adele), Robert Stephens (General Treillard) and Tom Conti (Jacquin).

The Duellists, the first major film to open here this year, may well remain one of the most dazzling visual experiences throughout all of 1978. The movie, set during the Napoleonic Wars, uses its beauty much in the way that other movies use soundtrack music, to set mood, to complement scenes and even to contradict them. Sometimes it's almost too much, yet the camerawork, which is by Frank Tidy, provides the Baroque style by which the movie operates on our senses, making the eccentric drama at first compelling and ultimately breathtaking.

The Duellists, which opened yesterday at the Fine Arts Theater, is an adaptation of a Joseph Conrad story, "The Duel," which I haven't read. It's the first feature film by Ridley Scott, a young English director whose previous experience appears to have been entirely in the making of television commercials (though this doesn't show) and it was written by Gerald Vaughan-Hughes, whose work is also unfamiliar to me. However they collaborated, the result is a film that satisfies not because it sweeps us off our feet, knocks us into the aisles, provides us with visions of infinity or definitions of God, but because it is precise, intelligent, civilized and because it never for a moment mistakes its narrative purpose.

This is to recount the bizarre story of how the life of a young French officer named Armand D'Hubert (Keith Carradine) comes to be dominated by the obsession of a fellow officer, Gabriel Feraud (Harvey Keitel), who believes that D'Hubert has somehow impugned his honor. It begins in Strasbourg in 1801, the year Napolcon comes to power, and continues for the next fifteen years, throughout the Emperor's rise, fall and brief comeback as the two men accidentally meet in the course of various campaigns, each meeting culminating in a duel that D'Hubert cannot gracefully deny.

Though Feraud is clearly mad, there is no way that D'Hubert can avoid the challenges within the code of honor that defines the professional life of each. At Strasbourg, they fight with sabers, at Augsburg with what looks almost like broadswords. Once they meet on horseback. Another time pistols are the weapons. Every time they meet, each pares a little more off the other. It's as if they were whittling each other down to the bone, though the ending, which is a perfect short-story ending, makes it apparent that Feraud's obsession has had the effect of tempering the spiritual strength of the other man.

I assume that it's to the credit of Mr. Scott, the director, that after we once get over the shock of seeing Mr. Keitel and Mr. Carradine in the uniforms of

Napoleonic Hussars, we never again see anything anachronistic about these two most contemporary of American actors in such strange surroundings. They are splendid and are never once upstaged by such high-powered English acting talent as Albert Finney, Alan Webb, Robert Stephens, John McEnery, Meg Wynn Owen, Edward Fox and Jenny Runacre, who appear in supporting roles. Cristina Raines, a young American actress (*The Sentinel*), is charming in the small but important part of Mr. Carradine's young wife.

What one carries away from the film, though, is a memory of almost indescribable beauty, of landscapes at dawn, of overcrowded, murky interiors, of underlit hallways and brilliantly sunlit gardens. It's not a frivolous prettiness, but an evocation of time and place through images that are virtually tactile, and which give real urgency to this curious tale. It's marvelous.

—*V.C., January 14, 1978*

DUMBO

Directed by Ben Sharpsteen; written by Joe Grant and Dick Huemer, based on the story by Helen Aberson and Harold Pearl; music by Oliver Wallace and Frank Churchill, with lyrics by Ned Washington; art designers, Herb Ryman, Kendall O'Connor, Terrell Stapp, Donald Da Gradi, Al Zinnen, Ernest Nordli, Dick Kelsey and Charles Payzant; produced by Walt Disney; released by RKO Radio Pictures. Running time: 64 minutes.

With the voices of: Edward Brophy (Timothy Mouse), Herman Bing (Ringmaster), Verna Felton (Elephant), Sterling Holloway (Stork) and Cliff Edwards (Jim Crow).

Ladeez and gentlemen, step right this way—to the Broadway Theatre, that is—and see the most genial, the most endearing, the most completely precious cartoon feature film ever to emerge from the magical brushes of Walt Disney's wonder-working artists! See the remarkable baby elephant that flies with the greatest of ease. See the marvelous trick-performing animals in the biggest little show on earth. See the wonderland you first saw within the pages of story books. Ladeez and gentlemen, see *Dumbo,* a film you will never forget.

Maybe you think we are barking a little bit louder than we should. But this is a sober opinion, believe us, which takes into account the pristine freshness of *Snow White,* the sparkling beauty of *Pinocchio* and the rich, enchanting variety of the more recent *Fantasia.* For this time Mr. Disney and his genii have kept themselves within comfortable, familiar bounds. This time they have let their kindlier natures have more commanding play. This time they have made a picture that touches the very heart of sentiment. It may not be the most impressive feature that Mr. Disney has turned out, but it certainly is the most winsome, and the one that leaves you with the warmest glow.

Never did we expect to fall in love with an elephant. But after meeting up with Dumbo at the Broadway Theatre last night we have thoroughly transferred our affections to this package of pachyderm. Of course he isn't just a usual elephant. That wouldn't be Disney's style. Dumbo is a cunning little fellow—more lovable than Dopey, and likewise as dumb—with tiny, moleskin trunk, soft and trusting blue eyes, pin-cushiony contours and ears the size of flapping sails.

And with this funny object as their hero, Mr. Disney and his boys have told a tale of how he is born to Mrs. Jumbo, one of the circus "girls," and how he is cruelly ridiculed by all the gossipy old female elephants because of his oversized ears. So frigid, in fact, is their contempt that little Dumbo gets a positive complex. But along comes Timothy Mouse, who encourages the woebegone mite; together chance leads them to imbibe a tub of diluted champagne, and out of this fortunate accident Dumbo discovers that he can fly. Thus he becomes the flying elephant, the precocious pachyderm, and finally ascends to triumph over all the other elephants.

That gives but a meager impression of the charms you will find in *Dumbo.* For Mr. Disney has crammed it with countless of his fanciful delights. There is a truly brilliant sequence—one of the finest things that Disney has yet done—in which a phantasmagoria of pink elephants glide and mold through grotesque patterns and shapes after Dumbo has sipped the champagne. There is also that hilarious business in which the elephants build themselves into a pyramid, groaning and wobbling atop one another in ponderous and perilous suspense. There are Jim Crow, the loud and fancy sport who cackles, "Well, hush mah beak!" and his raffish crew of dusky satellites, the Messenger Stork who sings a jingle when he delivers *Dumbo* to Mrs. J. and Casey Jones Jr., the circus engine, which squeals and jumps forward whenever the rattling cars bump into him.

Very wisely, Mr. Disney has held the picture to an hour of running time, which is an excellent concession to young children, and he has not let any horror stuff slip in. That will be good news to many. But one problem is definitely posed. In the opening sequence of the picture, an army of storks are delivering babies to the circus animals. Modern parents are going to find that a tough phenomenon to explain.

Need we further mention that the color is excellent, that the musical score is good, that the story is neatly constructed and that the animation is perfect. Or shall we just say go see *Dumbo,* and guarantee you will agree with Jim Crow that you "been done seen about everything when you see an elephant fly."

—*B.C., October 24, 1941*

e

THE EARRINGS OF MADAME DE . . .

Directed by Max Ophüls; written (in French, with English subtitles) by Marcel Achard, Annette Wademant and Mr. Ophüls, based on the novel by Louise de Vilmorin; cinematographer, Christian Matras; edited by Borys Lewin; music by Oscar Straus and Georges Van Parys; produced by H. Baum and Ralph Baum; released by Arlan Pictures. Black and white. Running time: 105 minutes.

With: Charles Boyer (Monsieur De, the General), Danielle Darrieux (Madame De) and Vittorio De Sica (Baron Donati).

The French, who rarely are casual about l'amour, are being serious, tender and slightly ineffectual about a romantic triangle in *The Earrings of Madame De . . .*, a bittersweet confection that came from France to the Little Carnegie yesterday.

Like its turn-of-the-century decor and costuming, it is elegant and filled with decorative but basically unnecessary little items, which give it gentility and a nostalgic mood, but nothing much more substantial. The principals of the Parisian haut monde involved in this affair of the heart—a lady, her general-husband and her lover, naturally—are well behaved, but unfortunately their problem seems more important to the producers than to a viewer.

Although the romantic trials in which the trio becomes enmeshed are fundamentally simple, the earrings on which this yarn hangs lead an uncommonly complex existence. First, the lady of the title sells them back to the jeweler from whom her husband bought them as a wedding present. She then tells her spouse a white lie about losing them. The jeweler, fearful of a scandal, reports the truth to the confused husband, who retrieves the trinkets and, in turn, gives them to his mistress. That luckless dame gambles them away and a noble Italian diplomat snags them and, as may be guessed, turns up in Paris, is smitten by our heroine and donates the baubles to the lady as a token of his undying affection.

From here on in our Madame De and her paramour, whose love is real but unrequited, spend considerable time together and apart but always pining desperately. When, by either a quirk of passion or devotion to her husband, the lady decides to wear the gems again, her mate, a strangely observant gent, learns of the deception and there is the inevitable duel. Madame De, a frail sort at best, succumbs to a heart attack on the field of honor.

Three fine performers such as Charles Boyer, Danielle Darrieux and Vittorio De Sica contribute polished characterizations in the principal roles, but fail to give insouciance and bite to this standard, gossamer romance. Mlle. Darrieux, who is fetching in the many pretty, furbelowed costumes she wears, is a beautiful but ill-defined creature given to fits of vague illnesses. As her military husband, Charles Boyer is a handsome figure of a general who does, occasionally, inject Gallic nuance into gestures and speech. Sadly enough, Vittorio De Sica, as the lover who decides to step out of the picture, is afforded little opportunity to do more than be gallant. Although its charm is evident, the passion in this period piece is relegated, more often than not, to its French dialogue and English subtitles.

—*A.W., July 20, 1954*

EAST OF EDEN

Produced and directed by Elia Kazan: written by Paul Osborn. based on the novel by John Steinbeck: cinematographer. Ted McCord: edited by Owen Marks: music by Leonard Rosenman: art designers. James Basevi and Malcolm Bert: released by Warner Brothers. Running time: 115 minutes.

With: Julie Harris (Abra). James Dean (Cal Trask). Raymond Massey (Adam Trask). Burl Ives (Sam). Richard Davalos (Aron Trask). Jo Van Fleet (Kate). Albert Dekker (Will) and Lois Smith (Ann).

Only a small part of John Steinbeck's *East of Eden* has been used in the motion picture version of it that Elia Kazan has done, and it is questionable whether that part contains the best of the book.

It is the part that has to do with the conflict between the farmer, Adam Trask, and Cal, his son—the one who is obsessed with a sense of "badness" and jealousy toward his brother, whom his father loves. It also contains the later details of the career of the monstrous mother of the boys and the story of the sweetheart of brother Aron who forsakes him for the more exciting Cal.

Compressed in a script by Paul Osborn, which reduces the mother to little more than a black shrouded figure of a madam of a sporting house in a California town, this quarter-part of the novel is boiled down to a mere review of the coincidental way in which the conflict between the father and son is resolved.

Yet Mr. Kazan has at it in this picture that runs for two hours—and which opened last night at the Astor in a benefit performance for the Actors Studio—with such elaborate pictorial buildup and such virtuosity on his actors' parts that he gets across the illusion of a drama more pregnant than it is.

In one respect, it is brilliant. The use that Mr. Kazan has made of CinemaScope and color in capturing expanse and mood in his California settings is almost beyond compare. His views of verdant farmlands in the famous Salinas "salad bowl," sharply focused to the horizon in the sunshine, are fairly fragrant with atmosphere. The strain of troubled people against such backgrounds has a clear and enhanced irony.

Some of Mr. Kazan's interiors—especially his final scene in the bedroom of the father, where the old man is dying of a stroke—have a moodiness, too, that moves the viewer with their strongly emotional overtones. The director gets more into this picture with the scenery than with the characters.

For the stubborn fact is that the people who move about in this film are not sufficiently well established to give point to the anguish through which they go, and the demonstrations of their torment are perceptibly stylized and grotesque. Especially is this true of James Dean in the role of the confused and cranky Cal. This young actor, who is here doing his first big screen stint, is a mass of histrionic gingerbread.

He scuffs his feet, he whirls, he pouts, he sputters, he leans against walls, he rolls his eyes, he swallows his words, he ambles slack-kneed—all like Marlon Brando used to do. Never have we seen a performer so clearly follow another's style. Mr. Kazan should be spanked for permitting him to do such a sophomoric thing. Whatever there might be of reasonable torment in this youngster is buried beneath the clumsy display.

To a lesser degree, Julie Harris exaggerates the role of the country coquette who becomes serious and devotes herself to saving the anguished boy. Fortunately, she giggles herself out early, and then she settles down to acting like a young lady concerned for the fellow she loves.

Raymond Massey as the father, Adam, would be all right if one could understand his monumental severity and his persistent rejection of his son. His fanatical devotion to the Bible has been thoroughly watered down, and his peculiar sense of justice is more talked about than explained. Therefore his terrible obtuseness is mostly a lot of vexing show.

Richard Davalos as the sibling rival, Aron; Albert Dekker as a citizen of the town; Burl Ives as a philosophical sheriff; and Jo Van Fleet as the mother of the boys do what they have to do intensely, which goes for all the people in other roles.

In short, there is energy and intensity but little clarity and emotion in this film. It is like a great, green iceberg: mammoth and imposing but very cold.

—B.C., March 10, 1955

EASY LIVING

Directed by Mitchell Leisen; written by Preston
Sturges, based on a story by Vera Caspary; cinematography by Ted Tetzlaff; edited by Doane
Harrison; art directors, Hans Dreier and Ernst
Fegté; produced by Arthur Hornblow Jr.; released
by Paramount Pictures. Black and white. Running
time: 88 minutes.

With: Jean Arthur (Mary Smith), Edward Arnold
(J. B. Ball), Ray Milland (John Ball Jr.), Luis Alberni
(Mr. Louis Louis), Mary Nash (Jenny Ball), Franklin
Pangborn (Van Buren), Barlowe Borland (Mr. Gur-
ney), William Demarest (Wallace Whistling),
Andrew Tombes (Elwyn Hulgar), Esther Dale (Lil-
lian), Harlan Briggs (Mr. Higginbottom), William B.
Davidson (Mr. Hyde), Nora Cecil (Miss Swerf) and
Robert Greig (Butler).

That wasn't a WPA demonstration in West Forty-
third Street yesterday. It was Martha Raye's public storming the Paramount for a glimpse of the lady
"in person"—with an incidental eye for the new farce,
Easy Living, in which Preston (*Strictly Dishonorable*)
Sturges throws a Kolinsky coat around Cinderella and
lets slapstick take its course. It's a fairly exhausting
course, too, with more involvements than we care to
mention, with its cast frequently overwhelmed by the
Sennett touches (a Sennett touch usually produces a
"Whiff! Bang! Ouch!") and yet with enough sound
comedy to guide it into the charitable channels of
midsummer entertainment.

Certainly it is an unseasonable show; the very
thought of a Kolinsky, even of a sable, in this weather
is enough to counteract the indubitable charms of an
air-conditioning system. But otherwise the film is fabricated for summer when critical standards are presumed to be lower and when audiences are so bored
with people asking, "Is it hot enough for you?!" that
anything—even so absurd a farce as this—is likely to
come under the head of relief. And, in all fairness, the
film has its merits, notably Jean Arthur and Edward
Arnold, who have the gift of understating farce—if
that be possible.

Here, at any rate, we have Miss Arthur as a stenographer riding to work on a bus-top one morning when
tycoon Mr. Arnold flings his wife's newly purchased
coat out the window. Upon Miss Arthur's head it falls
and with it, in one of those farce-illogical chains of
circumstance, comes the reputation of being the
tycoon's mistress, her lodgment in the imperial suite
of the Hotel Louis (Luis Alberni, manager) and her
unbeknownst encounter with the tycoon's son, Ray
Milland, who has been earning a busboy's living in the
automat. Among the subsequent events are a bear raid
on steel, a riot in the automat and the acquisition of a
couple of friendly sheep dogs.

It doesn't, as any one can see, make much sense,
and a good bit of it is incredibly reminiscent of those
old custard pie and Keystone chase days. But yesterday
was warm, and Miss Arthur, Mr. Arnold and Mr. Milland tried hard and who are we to accuse them of
carrying comedy too far? The sensible thing would be
to take a cold shower and concede the Paramount a
wild, foolish and fairly amusing little number. Besides,
there is Miss Raye—in person.

—*F.S.N., July 8, 1937*

EAT DRINK MAN WOMAN

Directed by Ang Lee; written (in Chinese, with
English subtitles) by Mr. Lee, Hui-Ling Wang and
James Schamus; director of photography, Jong
Lin; edited by Tim Squyres; music by Mader; pro-
duced by Li-Kong Hsu; released by the Samuel
Goldwyn Company. Running time: 123 minutes.

With: Sylvia Chang (Jin-Rong), Winston Chao (Li
Kai), Chao-Jung Chen (Guo-Lun), Ah Leh Gua
(Mrs. Liang), Chin-Cheng Lu (Ming-Dao), Sihung
Lung (Mr. Chu), Yu-Wen Wang (Jia-Ning), Yu-
Chien Tang (Shan-Shan), Chien-Lien Wu (Jia-
Chien) and Kuei-Mei-Yang (Jia-Jen).

Eat Drink Man Woman, the delectable new film
from Ang Lee, the director of *The Wedding Banquet,* is about a father who has lost his joie de vivre. No
happier than Mr. Chu (Sihung Lung) are the three
beautiful daughters whose romantic lives are star-
crossed and who can't seem to escape their father's
spell. Mr. Chu, a widower, is considered a great man
in some circles, but at home it's another matter. Sun-

day dinner for father and daughters is a terrible ordeal. Family tensions run so high the participants can barely even eat.

It's possible that Mr. Lee, a warmly engaging storyteller under any circumstances, could have made the father a celebrated singer or dog trainer with equal ease. As it happens, he presents Mr. Chu as the greatest chef in Taipei, which not only makes the Sunday dinner sequence a spectacular affair but also turns *Eat Drink Man Woman* into an almost edible treat.

Wonderfully seductive, and nicely knowing about all of its characters' appetites, *Eat Drink Man Woman* makes for an uncomplicatedly pleasant experience. Its thoughts about its characters don't go much deeper than the bottom of a soup bowl, but those thoughts are still expressed with affection, wit, and an abundance of fascinating cooking tips. As in the comparably crowd-pleasing *Like Water for Chocolate,* this film's use of food is both voluptuous and serious, amplifying the story even as it offers an irresistible diversion. The film succeeds in presenting Mr. Chu's intricate cooking (rendered for the camera by three amazingly artful chefs) as an expression of larger traditionalism and as an endangered art.

Less audacious in subject matter than *The Wedding Banquet* (in which a gay man marries a woman to deceive his parents), *Eat Drink Man Woman* is more ambitious in other ways. It unfolds on a broader canvas, with each character's separate story given room to play out, and each used somehow to illustrate the film's title. "Food and sex," one character says succinctly, amplifying that four-ideogram phrase. "Basic human desires. Can't avoid them."

But each of this film's main characters is trying to avoid them, somehow. Mr. Chu, widowed sixteen years earlier, spends much of his time as a lonely homebody, cooking obsessively and even doing his daughters' laundry while they're at work. Finally finding someone on whom he can dote, Mr. Chu begins supplying exquisite multicourse lunches to little Shan-Shan (Yu-Chien Tang), a schoolgirl whose mother is a family friend. Her classmates are dazzled, all the more so because they are too young to realize that Mr. Chu's cooking is often flawed. Symbolically enough, he has lost the use of his taste buds, which seems all too fitting to the daughters, who view him as joyless and remote.

Equally joyless, in her own way, is Jia-Chien (Chien-Lien Wu), the most beautiful and successful of the young women. With a prominent job as an airline executive, an ex-lover she has sex with as a convenience and intentions to move into a new high-rise apartment building called Little Paris in the East, the gorgeous Jia-Chien radiates a brittle professionalism. Even less satisfied with her life is the eldest daughter, Jia-Jen (Kuei-Mei-Yang), a prim schoolteacher who has never recovered from an unhappy love affair. The youngest daughter, Jia-Ning (Yu-Wen Wang), delivers the most obvious reproach to her father and all he stands for. She is a counter clerk at a Wendy's.

Mr. Lee introduces a couple of other characters sure to shake up this family. Li Kai (Winston Chao), the handsome new executive at Jia-Chien's office, is certain to be trouble; Mrs. Liang (Ah-Leh Gua), a harpy newly returned to the neighborhood, has set her sights on Mr. Chu. And her best friend's boyfriend begins courting Jia-Ning with the kind of wry comic style that marks this film at its best. "I want to end this addiction to love," says this young man, who reads Dostoyevsky and rides a motorcycle, "but I'm too weak."

Many of these actors also appeared in *The Wedding Banquet* (and in Mr. Lee's first film, *Pushing Hands*). Well used as they all are (particularly Mr. Lung, whose performance has a true poignancy), they are understandably upstaged by such artifacts as a watermelon carved to resemble a decorative Chinese vase and a cooked green dragon-shaped delicacy draped across a dinner plate. At its best, though, the film warmly integrates food and humor, as in a lovely sequence that finds Mr. Chu summoned on an emergency basis by a crowd of frowning, toque-wearing chefs. The occasion is an important banquet, and the shark fin soup is simply shot. "The guy who bought the fins didn't know anything," someone explains. Mr. Chu solemnly studies this situation, then he saves the day.

Intermingling a sexual episode with a glimpse of Mr. Chu blowing air into a duck, Mr. Lee often makes his characters seem oblivious in certain basic ways. By the end of the film—a slightly false but happy ending, as in *The Wedding Banquet*—he has delivered enough last-minute surprises to belie that impression.

—*J.M., August 3, 1994*

EFFI BRIEST

Produced and directed by Rainer Werner Fassbinder: written (in German, with English subtitles) by Mr. Fassbinder, based on the novel by Theodor Fontane: cinematographer, Jürgen Jürges: edited by Thea Eymes: music by Camille Saint-Saëns: art designer, Kurt Raab: released by New Yorker Films. Black and white. Running time: 140 minutes.

With: Hanna Schygulla (Effi Briest), Wolfgang Schenk (Baron von Instetten), Ulli Lommel (Major Crampas), Lila Pempelt (Frau Briest) and Herbert Steinmetz (Herr Briest).

The setting is a handsome old country house outside Berlin in the 1890's, the home of a well-to-do upper-middle-class businessman, his wife and their seventeen-year-old daughter, Effi Briest. Effi, as played by the enchanting Hanna Schygulla, is all sunlit curls and radiant beauty, a combination of naïveté, native intelligence, forthrightness and willful self-interest.

When the somewhat older Baron von Instetten (Wolfgang Schenk), whom Effi doesn't know, asks for her hand, Effi is as happy as her ambitious mother. Several days before the wedding, though, she is apprehensive. She and her mother are taking the air, walking across a field of untended grass, when Effi stops short. "The baron," she says, "is a man of firm principles." Her mother agrees, pleased that a seventeen-year-old might grasp such a point. Effi, desolate for the briefest of moments, adds, "I have none at all."

Rainer Werner Fassbinder appends to *Effi Briest,* his film adaptation of Theodor Fontane's 1894 German novel, the subtitle: "Or many who have an idea of their possibilities and need nevertheless accept the prevailing order in the way they act, and thereby strengthen and confirm it absolutely." Mr. Fassbinder is being both funny and severe in the manner of the Fontane novel, which describes the decline and fall of Effi Briest after she has flouted convention not out of passion but boredom and whim.

Nothing seen earlier in the New Yorker Theater's current Fassbinder festival, where *Effi Briest* opened yesterday, quite prepares one for the special pleasures of this beautiful, ironic, intentionally literary-sounding film. It's an achievement of several kinds. In the way it uses language (narration as well as dialogue) it reminds me of both Robert Bresson's *Diary of a Country Priest* and François Truffaut's *The Wild Child.* It's visually beguiling—its cameramen having found shades of gray between black and white I'm not sure I've seen before—and it is performed by the Fassbinder stock company with the precision and style one seldom finds outside the legitimate theater.

Mr. Fassbinder made *Effi Briest* three years ago, and though I've no way of knowing for sure, I suspect one of the reasons he wanted to do it would be to show his critics that he was quite capable of putting his formidable talent to the service of someone else's work. His success is such that I think *Effi Briest* might well have pleased André Bazin, the late French critic who dared suggest that, in a film adaptation of a literary work, one picture was not necessarily worth one thousand words.

Mr. Fassbinder has certainly not been stingy with Fontane's words. They are spoken as dialogue, as the texts of letters, as chapter headings and as narration, which are the words of the author who, though all-seeing, is not as much a moralist as an observer. Fontane's attitude toward the events observed matches the cool—the dispassion—that has been method of such dissimilar Fassbinder films as *Katzelmacher, Mother Kusters Goes to Heaven, Chinese Roulette* and *The Bitter Tears of Petra Von Kant.*

Unlike Anna Karenina's and Emma Bovary's, Effi's problem is not that she loved—which she didn't—but that she carried on a harmless flirtation that, eventually, made her feel as guilty as her husband suspected her of being. The society of *Effi Briest* is as closed and airless as ancient Egypt's. In the tiny bourgeois community where she settles with the baron, the virtually uneducated Effi is regarded as (1) an atheist, (2) a deist, or (3) "a superficial Berliner."

In loneliness she responds to the courtship of a handsome young officer, Major Crampas (Uli Lommel), who is a bit of a rake, unhappily married, and fully aware of the baron's various ways of intimidating Effi into fidelity. The major also writes Effi letters that the foolish Effi preserves. Some years after the baron and Effi have moved to Berlin, the baron finds the letters and, to uphold his "duty to the community," challenges the major to a duel. The end is tragic, not because people die but because Effi ultimately believes guilt to be her duty.

The film is composed of short scenes, some almost subliminal, often separated by fades to a white that suggest the empty space on a page at the end of a chapter. Each member of the cast is superb, though Miss Schygulla is stunning in a role that bears little resemblance to her work in *Katzelmacher* and *Petra Von Kant*.

As the film understates its ideas, though at some length, the characters overstate their feelings in such a way that seems to prevent them from seeing the truth. It's in keeping that Effi, at wit's end toward the conclusion of the film, should say tearfully, "Too much is too much." She means "enough is enough," but she can't recognize the fact, thus to do something about it. It's the peculiar fate of the naïve Effi, in the words of the film's subtitle, to "strengthen and confirm the ruling order absolutely."

—*J.C., June 17, 1977*

8½

Directed by Federico Fellini: written (in Italian, with English subtitles) by Mr. Fellini, Tullio Pinelli, Ennio Flaiano and Brunello Rondi, based on a story by Mr. Fellini and Mr. Flaiano: cinematographer, Gianni Di Venanzo: edited by Leo Catozzo: music by Nino Rota: art designer, Piero Gherardi: produced by Angelo Rizzoli: released by Embassy Pictures. Black and white. Running time: 140 minutes.

With: Marcello Mastroianni (Guido Anselmi), Claudia Cardinale (Claudia/The Dream Girl), Anouk Aimée (Luisa Anselmi), Sandra Milo (Carla), Rosella Falk (Gloria Morin), Guido Alberti (The Producer), Barbara Steele (An Actress) and Jean Rougeul (The Writer).

If you thought Federico Fellini's *La Dolce Vita* was a hard-to-fathom film, random and inconclusive, wait until you see *8½*, his latest.

It opened yesterday at the handsome new Festival Theater, on 57th Street West of Fifth Avenue, and at the Embassy on Seventh Avenue and 46th Street.

Here is a piece of entertainment that will really make you sit up straight and think, a movie endowed with the challenge of a fascinating intellectual game. It has no more plot than a horse race, no more order than a pinball machine and it bounces around on several levels of consciousness, dreams and memories as it details a man's rather casual psychoanalysis of himself. But it sets up a labyrinthine ego for the daring and thoughtful to explore, and it harbors some elegant treasures of wit and satire along the way.

Cannily, Mr. Fellini has chosen a character he knows as the subject of his introspection. He has chosen a director of films. A person familiar with his nature might even suspect it is Mr. Fellini himself. And he has planted this character in a milieu of luxury and toil he knows so well that you sense that every detail of the canvas must be wrenched from his own experience.

The picture begins with this fellow sitting trapped in his car in a traffic jam, immobilized among a crowd of zombies that might be dead souls crossing the River Styx. Suddenly suffocating, he struggles wildly to be released. And the next thing—he's floating upward, out of the traffic jam and above a beach, where he is magically hauled back earthward by a kite-string tied to his leg.

Thus does Mr. Fellini notify us right away that he has embarked on a fanciful excursion with a man who has barely escaped death. By the obvious implications of his pictorial imagery this would be the only release from the stagnation and deadness he feels himself to be in.

Now the fellow comes to in bed in a luxurious health-resort hotel, attended by truculent physicians, needled by a nurse (who asks if she may borrow his typewriter), and watched by a hawklike little man who turns out to be a scriptwriter waiting to go to work with him. Reality is reestablished. We are among the living now.

But not for long. And, indeed, there is some question as to whether Mr. Fellini sees the old and antiquated people he parades at this health resort as actually living creatures. May not they, too, be dead and decayed, the relics and shells of a society that is struggling feebly and ironically to regain its health?

Anyhow, it is in this environment that the fellow, who is now identified as a famous movie director, tries to apply himself to preparing a new movie, while his mistress comes to stay nearby and swarms of idlers and job-hunters persistently keep after him.

But, alas, he cannot get going. He is full of anxieties, doubts, and disbelief in the value of movies. And, in this uncertain state, his mind takes to wandering off in memories and building fantasies.

He sees himself in his childhood. He visions painful experiences with priests. He goes from actual encounters with his mistress to recollections of his education in sex. The present, the past, and wishful thinking are wryly and poignantly blurred. (Last year we were at Marienbad, remember? Well, we're at Montecatini or some such place this year!)

However, Mr. Fellini does give us sufficient clues to the nature and problems of his fellow to lead us to understand—that is, if we have the patience and the prescience. And what we discover (at least, I do) is an outrageous egotist, a man of supreme romantic notions with a charmingly casual conceit who has been attended and spoiled by women ever since he was a tot.

One of the most delightful fabrications is a wild and robust fantasy in which the director sees himself as the master of a harem of all the women he has known (or desired) ordering them to do his bidding, slapping them with a whip, receiving their utter adulation in a state of complete harmony. And this is an adult variation of one of his cozy childhood memories.

Mr. Fellini has managed to compress so much drollery and wit, so much satire on social aberrations, so much sardonic comment on sex, and, indeed, when you come right down to it, even a bit of a travesty of Freud, that it pains me to note that he hasn't thought his film through to a valid end.

He has his erratic hero, whom Marcello Mastroianni plays in a beautifully bored and baffled fashion, suddenly become aware that the trouble with him is that he has always taken but never given love. And when he grasps this, he is able to get all the people he knows to join hands and get ready to make a fine movie on the set of a rocket launching pad.

This is a romantic sidestep—as romantic as the whole film, the title of which, incidentally, means simply Mr. Fellini's Opus 8½. (This is his seventh full-length film; he has also made three shorts.) And it leaves an uncomfortable feeling of letdown at the end.

But this is, in large part, compensated by much that is wonderful—by Mr. Fellini's tremendous pictorial poetry, his intimations of pathos and longing, his skill with the silly and grotesque; by some splendid and

charming performing—Sandra Milo as the mistress (she's a doll!), Guido Alberti as a producer, Anouk Aimée as the director's jealous wife, Claudia Cardinale as a "dream girl," and many, many more. There is also another delicious Nino Rota musical score.

So if Mr. Fellini has not produced another masterpiece—another all-powerful exposure of Italy's ironic sweet life—he has made a stimulating contemplation of what might be called, with equal irony, a sweet guy.

The English subtitles are good ones, but they miss the total substance of the Italian dialogue.

—B.C., June 26, 1963

EIGHT MEN OUT

Directed by John Sayles: written by Mr. Sayles, based on the book by Eliot Asinof: director of photography. Robert Richardson: edited by John Tintori: music by Mason Daring: production designer: Nora Chavooshian: produced by Sarah Pillsbury and Midge Sanford: released by Orion Pictures. Running time: 120 minutes.

With: John Cusack (Buck Weaver). Clifton James (Charles Comiskey). Michael Lerner (Arnold Rothstein). Christopher Lloyd (Bill Burns). John Mahoney (Kid Gleason). Charlie Sheen (Hap Felsch). David Strathairn (Eddie Cicotte). D. B. Sweeney (Shoeless Joe Jackson). Gordon Clapp (Ray Schalk). Richard Edson (Billy Maharg). Michael Mantell (Abe Attell). Kevin Tighe (Sport Sullivan). John Sayles (Ring Lardner) and Studs Terkel (Hugh Fullerton).

Of course John Sayles begins *Eight Men Out* with a little boy, with the kid who is the purest and most hopeful of baseball fans, the one whose subsequent plea, "Say it ain't so, Joe!" went down in history. *Eight Men Out* is the story of the 1919 World Series–fixing scheme that shattered the faith of this boy and so many others. As such, it's much more than a film about baseball. It's an amazingly full and heartbreaking vision of the dreams, aspirations and disillusionments of a nation, as filtered through its national pastime.

Eight Men Out, which opens today at Loews Tower East and other theaters, establishes its scope in a wonderfully edited (by John Tintori) opening ballpark scene that shows how many disparate elements Mr. Sayles will bring into play. There are the Chicago White Sox themselves, just on the verge of winning the pennant and in their full bloom of talent and optimism. There are the White Sox wives and children, bursting with pride, and the fans, whose excitement fills the air. There is also the team's owner, Charles Comiskey (Clifton James), whose stinginess is so extraordinary that he rewards his players for winning the pennant with bottles of flat champagne.

Also poised in the stadium, ready to bring about the White Sox's downfall, are the various speculators who know how many bets will be riding on this popular team. Realizing that the players' economic dissatisfaction contains the seeds of a big gambling win, these operators lay their plans to subvert the ballplayers one at a time. Ready to record and lament this sad story are the sportswriters, led by Hugh Fullerton (Studs Terkel) and Ring Lardner (played by Mr. Sayles), who wander through the film as a tiny Greek chorus. "Gamblers 8, baseball 0," they say in disgust at this scandal's sorry outcome.

In addition to viewing the events of the Black Sox debacle (as it became known) from so many different angles, Mr. Sayles also sees it with great generosity. The jaunty, deceptively upbeat *Eight Men Out* (with credits in which the camera rises blissfully heavenward, then falls again) resembles the filmmaker's earlier and more mournfully beautiful *Matewan,* not only in using many of the same actors but also in bringing such far-reaching sympathy to its story. *Eight Men Out* doesn't condemn the White Sox, and would be a far less interesting film if it did. Instead, it regards the players as unwitting losers caught by forces far more powerful than their own winning spirit. Some of the team members are depicted as more eager to take a tumble than others, but all are seen by Mr. Sayles as pawns in a losing game.

The actors have clearly been chosen very carefully, so that their faces alone speak eloquently of America's post–World War I self-image. The ballplayers, even those who prove quickest to betray their game, have strong, clear faces that radiate vitality and dedication, while the gamblers' various looks suggest the network of power, money and opportunism of which they are a part. The players' fine young faces grow ever cloudier and more downcast as the story proceeds.

One of Mr. Sayles's many talents is for drawing striking performances from actors who have never been nearly this memorable in other roles. *Eight Men Out* contains many such small marvels, particularly from John Cusack and David Strathairn as the film's closest approximation of tragic heroes. Mr. Cusack, as Buck Weaver, the team member who most strenuously resisted the fix scheme, conveys an idealism and disappointment that struggle within him visibly as the team's fortunes pivot back and forth. Mr. Strathairn, as the once-honest pitcher Eddie Cicotte, who suffers the story's most painful crisis of conscience, captures the full helplessness and misery of a man who sees no choice but to do what he knows is wrong.

There is in this material (with Mr. Sayles's screenplay based on Eliot Asinof's 1963 book) great potential for pious oversimplification, for viewing the White Sox as cardboard victims. Happily, Mr. Sayles avoids this easily, and breathes enormous humanity and variety into this story. The film's snappy manner, aside from capturing the spirit of postwar buoyancy and soon-to-be-lost innocence, also holds the attention handily, and Robert Richardson's cinematography creates a handsome and evocative look, making meticulous use of light and shadow. Chief among the director's other accomplishments are insuring that the World Series games are genuinely exciting, despite what the audience knows about their ultimate outcome, and making an extremely complicated plot full of bribes, counterbribes and double-crosses seem crystal clear.

Notable in the large and excellent cast of *Eight Men Out* are D. B. Sweeney, who gives Shoeless Joe Jackson the slow, voluptuous Southern naïveté of the young Elvis; Michael Lerner, who plays the formidable gangster Arnold Rothstein with the quietest aplomb; Gordon Clapp as the team's firecracker of a catcher; John Mahoney as the worried manager who senses much more about his players' plans than he would like to; and Michael Rooker as the quintessential bad apple. Charlie Sheen is also good as the team's most suggestible player, the good-natured fellow who isn't sure whether it's worse to be corrupt or be a fool. The story's delightfully colorful villains are played by Christopher Lloyd and Richard Edson (as the halfway-comic duo who make the first assault on the players), Michael Mantell as the chief gangster's extremely undependable right-hand man and Kevin

Tighe as the Bostonian smoothie who coolly declares: "You know what you feed a dray horse in the morning if you want a day's work out of him? Just enough so he knows he's hungry."

For Mr. Sayles, whose idealism has never been more affecting or apparent than it is in this story of boyish enthusiasm gone bad in an all too grown-up world, *Eight Men Out* represents a home run.

—*J.M. September 2, 1988*

THE ELEPHANT MAN

Directed by David Lynch; written by Christopher DeVore, Eric Bergren and Mr. Lynch, based on *The Elephant Man and Other Reminiscences* by Sir Frederick Treves and in part on *The Elephant Man: A Study in Human Dignity* by Ashley Montagu; director of photography, Freddie Francis; edited by Ann V. Coates; music by John Morris and Samuel Barber; production designer, Stuart Craig; produced by Jonathan Sanger; released by Paramount Pictures. Black and white. Running time: 125 minutes.

With: Anthony Hopkins (Frederick Treves), John Hurt (John Merrick), Anne Bancroft (Mrs. Kendal), John Gielgud (Carr Gomm), Wendy Hiller (Mothershead), Michael Elphick (Night Porter) and Hannah Gordon (Mrs. Treves).

The time is the late 1880's and the place is London, where the beau monde, the rich and fashionable as well as the mannered and the educated who aspire to higher things, live in a refinement that's all the more precarious for the assaults of the Industrial Revolution, which is wrecking the social order. Just beyond the elegant parks, malls and town houses is the real London of crowded, narrow streets, slums, factories and sweatshops, and the ever-present smoke, grime, noise and degradation.

In such a setting it's no surprise that a kind of sad, desperate genteelness was once equated with human dignity. To be kind and polite, in such a landscape, under such circumstances, when the masses were living in such squalor, were reassuring signs of orthodoxy to a threatened London Establishment.

This is one of the vividly unexpected impressions one carries away from *The Elephant Man,* David Lynch's haunting new film that's not to be confused with the current Broadway play of the same title, though both are based on the life of the same unfortunate John Merrick, the so-called Elephant Man, and both, I assume, make use of some of the same source materials. These include Sir Frederick Treves's *The Elephant Man and Other Reminiscences,* and *The Elephant Man: A Study in Dignity* by Ashley Montagu.

When he died in London in 1900, John Merrick was twenty-seven years old. Having been grotesquely deformed at birth from a disease called neurofibromatosis, with a head twice normal size, a twisted spine and a useless right arm, John Merrick made his living exhibiting himself in a freak show until he was saved by Frederick Treves, a London surgeon. The doctor provided a tranquil home for Merrick in the London Hospital, introduced him to society and later wrote his famous book.

The Elephant Man, which opens today at the Coronet, is the first major commercial film to be directed by Mr. Lynch, whose only previous feature is *Eraserhead,* a cult movie I've not seen but which, apparently, is also about an outsider. The new film was written by Christopher DeVore and Eric Bergren, with the later participation of Mr. Lynch. It's a handsome, eerie, disturbing movie.

The Elephant Man uses some of the devices of the horror film, including ominous music, sudden cuts that shock and hints of dark things to come, but it's a very benign horror film, one in which "the creature" is the pursued instead of the pursuer.

Unlike the play, in which the actor playing John Merrick wears no makeup, his unadorned face representing the beauty of the interior man, the audience thus being forced to imagine his hideous appearance, the movie works the other way around. John Hurt, as John Merrick, is a monster with a bulbous forehead, a Quasimodo-like mouth, one almost-obscured eye, a useless arm and crooked torso. It's to the credit of Christopher Tucker's makeup, and to Mr. Hurt's extraordinary performance deep inside it, that John Merrick doesn't look absurd, like something out of a low-budget science-fiction film.

But what we eventually see underneath this shell is not "the study in dignity" that Ashley Montagu wrote about, but something far more poignant, a study in genteelness that somehow suppressed all rage.

That is the quality that illuminates this film and makes it far more fascinating than it would be were it merely a portrait of a dignified freak. Throughout the film one longs for an explosion. That it never comes is more terrifying, I think, than John Merrick's acceptance of the values of others is inspiring.

The key sequence in the movie is when Dr. Treves, played with humane, quirky compassion by Anthony Hopkins, brings Merrick home to tea with Mrs. Treves in a perfectly ordered Victorian drawing room.

Merrick, looking like the fastidiously dressed Walrus in the Tenniel illustrations for "The Walrus and the Carpenter," is a most dainty guest. He speaks in the acquired accents of an English upper-class gentleman's gentleman, and has the same sort of manners. "They have such noble faces," he says of the Treves family photographs on the mantelpiece, and then shows his hosts a picture of his mother, a very pretty woman. "Yes," he acknowledges, "she had the face of an angel," adding so delicately that one can only suspect what depths of feeling are being ignored, "I must have been a great disappointment to her. I tried so hard to be good."

Mr. Hurt is truly remarkable. It can't be easy to act under such a heavy mask.

The movie covers Merrick's life from the time Dr. Treves finds him on exhibition, through a briefly peaceful time in Dr. Treves's care, interrupted when his former promoter kidnaps him and takes him off to France, and concludes after his return to Treves, when he becomes the pet of London's high society. The chief of his admirers is the actress, Mrs. Kendal, played in her best grand-lady style by Anne Bancroft, in scenes that are surprisingly affecting.

The physical production is beautiful, especially Freddie Francis's black-and-white photography. In addition to Mr. Hurt, Mr. Hopkins and Miss Bancroft, the classy supporting cast includes Dame Wendy Hiller, as the London Hospital's chief nurse, Sir John Gielgud, as the hospital's chief, and Freddie Jones as Bytes, the old rummy who exhibited John Merrick in freak shows.

—V.C., October 3, 1980

ELMER GANTRY

Directed by Richard Brooks; written by Mr. Brooks, based on the novel by Sinclair Lewis; cin-ematographer, John Alton; edited by Marjorie Fowler; music by André Previn; produced by Bernard Smith; released by United Artists. Black and white. Running time: 146 minutes.

With: Burt Lancaster (Elmer Gantry), Jean Simmons (Sister Sharon Falconer), Dean Jagger (William L. Morgan), Arthur Kennedy (Jim Lefferts), Shirley Jones (Lulu Bains), Patti Page (Sister Pachel), Edward Andrews (George Babbitt) and John McIntire (Reverend Pengilly).

Sinclair Lewis's *Elmer Gantry,* which shocked, amused, confounded but rarely bored readers back in 1927, has been lifted from the pages of the justifiably controversial novel and impressively transformed into an exciting film. The briskly paced drama of a religious opportunist, his colleagues and his times utilizes the tools of the motion picture in expert fashion.

The result, as exposed in color and old-fashioned, small screen at the Capitol Theatre yesterday, is a tribute to the artistry of Richard Brooks, the scenarist-director, and a fine cast. They make this story of the devil-may-care revivalist a living, action-packed, provoking screen study, largely devoid of the novel's polemics, that captures both the eye and mind.

Perhaps devoted readers blanch at the metamorphosis wrought here. The book, it may be recalled, followed Elmer Gantry all over the country for a long period of time. It did not hesitate in its condemnation of his charlatanry, his lusts, his adultery and, of course, his blatant opportunism both in sex and religion. And Mr. Lewis digressed often into pamphleteering that obscured his principal characters in a welter of bias and tub-thumping discussion. The book also paid copious attention to the many often colorful and often pitiful people affected by Gantry during his undulant career.

Mr. Brooks, an obviously dedicated artisan who has owned the property for some five years and shaped the script over the past two years, has made astounding but effective changes in the original. Many of the characters are gone, some have been changed completely, scenes have been shifted and emphasis on other principals has been raised or lowered. But Gantry and his company emerge, in essence, in bold, rough, sacrilegious but nearly always human, believable terms.

The Gantry we see now is not ordained, Baptist, Methodist or any other sect, but an expert spieler and a lusty, ribald drummer who sees a good thing in Sister Sharon Falconer's evangelical troupe and cons his way into her tent-tabernacle, her graces and her heart. And, in focusing only on this period in Gantry's peripatetic career, Mr. Brooks has given point and action to the sprawling, contentious work that was the novel.

This is not to say that it has been transformed into a simple adventure. It is a complex story running nearly two and a half hours, but its length is hardly noticeable since its many vignettes, each sharply presented, are joined into a theme that somewhat changes Gantry, Sister Falconer et al., from Lewis's conception but has them shape up as forceful, and often memorable, individuals. Perhaps the sleaziness of some forms of evangelism is not too pressing an issue these days but in *Elmer Gantry* it is made authentic and engrossing.

As Gantry, Burt Lancaster has one of his fattest roles and one to which he gives outstanding service. As has been noted, he is not quite Lewis's boy, but he is still the smirking, leering lecher who tells his fellow salesmen an off-color yarn with the same case that he thumps the Good Book and shouts the name of Jesus with amazing frequency. If he is not completely redeemed at the film's end, he indicates that his love for the ill-fated Sharon Falconer is real and not mere lust.

The character of Sister Falconer, as played by Jean Simmons, also has been subjected to change by Mr. Brooks. And for the better, too. In Miss Simmons's finely etched portrayal of the evangelist, the erstwhile Katy Jones of Shantytown, is a truly devout preacher of the Gospel. Her love of Gantry and death in the climactic conflagration that destroys the Waters of the Jordan tabernacle is a pointed and poignant lesson. Completely altered, too, is the character of Jim Lefferts, no longer a seminary classmate of Gantry but now a cynical reporter who, as played in serious but restrained style by Arthur Kennedy, evolves as a three-dimensional realist and not a type.

Shirley Jones certainly is different from the sweet heroine of *Oklahoma!* as the blonde, brash prostitute first violated by Gantry. And, the success-conscious George Babbitt, as neatly played by Edward Andrews; Dean Jagger's worried but purposeful manager of Sister Falconer; and Patti Page, as the tabernacle's choral soloist, add professional support to the principals.

Scenes in a brothel and a speakeasy and the salvation-hungry faces of the tabernacle crowds strikingly illuminate the excitement, the follies, the tawdriness and the tragedy of the era. Now, the mustiness of the printed page of 1927 is gone. This *Elmer Gantry* makes the age and the people vividly come alive.

—*A.W., July 8, 1960*

EMPIRE OF THE SUN

Directed by Steven Spielberg; written by Tom Stoppard, based on the novel by J.G. Ballard; director of photography, Allen Daviau; edited by Michael Kahn; music by John Williams; production designer, Norman Reynolds; produced by Mr. Spielberg, Kathleen Kennedy and Frank Marshall; released by Warner Brothers. Running time: 152 minutes.

With: Christian Bale (Jim), John Malkovich (Basie), Miranda Richardson (Mrs. Victor), Joe Pantoliano (Frank), Rupert Frazer (Jim's Father), Emily Richard (Jim's Mother) and Leslie Phillips (Mr. Maxton).

God playing tennis: that's what Jim Graham (Christian Bale), a privileged British schoolboy living in high colonial style in the pre-Pearl Harbor Shanghai of 1941, sees in one of his dreams. God taking a photograph: Jim thinks he sees that four years and seemingly several lifetimes later, as a starving, exhausted prisoner witnessing the brilliant light of the atomic bomb.

What transpires in between, the sweeping story of Jim's wartime exploits after he is separated from his family, is set forth so spectacularly in Steven Spielberg's *Empire of the Sun* that the film seems to speak a language all its own. In fact it does, for it's clear Mr. Spielberg works in a purely cinematic idiom that is quite singular. Art and artifice play equal parts in the telling of this tale. And the latter, even though intrusive at times, is part and parcel of the film's overriding style.

Yes, when Jim crawls through swampy waters he emerges covered with movie mud, the makeup man's kind; when he hits his head, he bleeds movie blood.

It's hard not to be distracted by such things. But it's also hard to be deterred by them, since that same movie-conscious spirit in Mr. Spielberg gives *Empire of the Sun* a visual splendor, a heroic adventurousness and an immense scope that make it unforgettable.

There are sections of *Empire of the Sun* that are so visually expressive they barely require dialogue (although Tom Stoppard's screenplay, which streamlines J. G. Ballard's autobiographical novel, is often crisp and clever). Its first half hour, for example, could exist as a silent film—an extraordinarily sharp evocation of Shanghai's last prewar days, richly detailed and colored by an exquisite foreboding. Jim is first seen singing in a church choir (the Welsh hymn "Suo Gan" will echo again hauntingly later in the story), then gliding through crowded streets in his family's chauffeur-driven Packard. At home, he asks his parents off-handed questions about the coming war. When the three of them, elaborately costumed, heedlessly leave home for a party on the other side of the city, it's clear that their days there are numbered just from the way the Chinese servants wave goodbye.

That first glimpse of the choirboys will prompt audiences to wonder which of these well-groomed, proper little singers is to be the film's leading man. Mr. Bale, who emerges from the choir by singing a solo, at first seems just a handsome and malleable young performer, another charming child star. But the epic street scene that details the Japanese invasion of the city and separates Jim from his parents reveals this boy to be something more. As Mr. Bale, standing atop a car amid thousands of extras and clasping his hands to his head, registers the fact that Jim is suddenly alone, he conveys the schoolboy's real terror and takes the film to a different dramatic plane. This fine young actor, who appears in virtually every frame of the film and ages convincingly from about nine to thirteen during the course of the story, is eminently able to handle an ambitious and demanding role.

Once *Empire of the Sun,* which opens today at the National and other theaters, follows Jim to the prison camp where he spends the duration of the war, it becomes slightly less focused. The pattern of events that occur within the camp is at times difficult to follow, in part because the emphasis is divided equally among so many different characters and episodes. When Mr. Spielberg—again, working almost without dialogue—outlines Jim's growing friendship with a Japanese boy from the airfield that adjoins the prison camp, or demonstrates Jim's profound respect for the Japanese pilots he sees there, the film takes on the larger-than-life emotional immediacy it seems designed for. But other episodes are less sharply defined. When Jim, who has proudly won his right to live in the American barracks, returns to the British camp in which he formerly lived, it takes a moment to remember why he's back—not because the motive is unclear, but because his departure from the one place and return to the other are separated by intervening scenes.

Still, there are many glorious moments here, among them Jim's near-religious experiences with the fighter planes he sees as halfway divine (in one nighttime scene, the sparks literally fly). And there is a full panoply of supporting characters, including Miranda Richardson, who grows more beautiful as her spirits fade, in the role of a married English woman who both mothers Jim and arouses his early amorous stirrings. It is the mothering that seems to matter most, for Jim's small satchel of memorabilia includes a magazine photograph of a happy family, a picture he takes with him everywhere. For a surrogate father, he finds the trickier figure of Basie (John Malkovich), a Yank wheeler-dealer with a sly Dickensian wit. Basie, who by turns befriends Jim and disappoints him, remains an elusive character, but Mr. Malkovich brings a lot of fire to the role. "American, are you?" one of his British fellow prisoners asks this consummate operator. "Definitely," Mr. Malkovich says.

Gone With the Wind is playing at the biggest movie theater in Shanghai when the Japanese are seen invading that city, and *Gone With the Wind* is a useful thing to remember. The makers of that film didn't really burn Atlanta; that wasn't their style. They, too, as Mr. Spielberg does, let the score sometimes trumpet the characters' emotions unnecessarily, and they might well have staged something as crazy as the *Empire of the Sun* scene in which the prisoners find an outdoor stadium filled with confiscated art and antiques and automobiles, loot that's apparently been outdoors for a while but doesn't look weatherbeaten in the slightest. Does it matter? Not in the face of this film's grand ambitions and its moments of overwhelming power. Not in the light of its soaring spirits, its larger authenticity and the great and small triumphs that it steadily delivers.

—*J.M., December 9, 1987*

ENEMIES, A LOVE STORY

Produced and directed by Paul Mazursky; written by Roger L. Simon and Mr. Mazursky, based on the novel by Isaac Bashevis Singer; director of photography, Fred Murphy; edited by Stuart Pappe; music by Maurice Jarre; production designer, Pato Guzman; released by Twentieth Century Fox. Running time: 119 minutes.

With: Ron Silver (Herman), Anjelica Huston (Tamara), Lena Olin (Masha), Margaret Sophie Stein (Yadwiga), Alan King (Rabbi Lembeck), Judith Malina (Masha's Mother), Rita Karin (Mrs. Schreier), Phil Leeds (Pesheles) and Elya Baskin (Yasha Kotik).

From a window in one of his apartments, the one in Coney Island, Herman Broder (Ron Silver) has an unobstructed view of the Wonder Wheel. It's a sight to which the camera often returns in *Enemies, a Love Story,* Paul Mazursky's deeply felt, fiercely evocative adaptation of Isaac Bashevis Singer's brilliantly enigmatic novel. Mr. Mazursky doesn't belabor the image, and he doesn't have to. The story itself has a sense of life's cyclical possibilities, of a bustling new world rising from the ashes, of hope and fatalism inseparably intermingled. Somehow, the giddy spectacle of this neon-lined amusement park artifact captures those paradoxes perfectly.

The year is 1949, the place New York and the characters, at least by some lights, very lucky. They have managed to survive the Holocaust, Herman himself by hiding for three years in a Polish hayloft with the help of a family servant named Yadwiga (Margaret Sophie Stein), whom he has since married out of gratitude.

To those who know Herman well, particularly Masha (Lena Olin), the shrewd, mercurial mistress with whom he shares a second residence in the Bronx, the fact that he escaped in this manner is very apt. "The truth is you're still hiding in the hayloft," Masha says, since Herman's double life does indeed call for furtiveness on a grand scale. As Mr. Singer puts it: "In Herman there resided a sorrow that could not be assuaged. He was not a victim of Hitler. He had been a victim long before Hitler's day."

Masha, whom Mr. Singer calls "the best argument Herman knew for Schopenhauer's argument that intelligence is nothing more than a servant of blind will," has survived internment in a concentration camp. As it turns out early in the story, so has Tamara (Anjelica Huston), an earlier wife with whom Herman had such a vexing marriage that the hayloft years almost came as a relief. When Tamara turns up in New York and traces Herman through a personal ad in a Yiddish newspaper, she proves to be as mocking as ever. "How do you manage it?" she asks of Herman's arrangement with the two other women. "Do you rush from one to the other?"

"I do my best," says Herman, with a self-effacing shrug. "It's not so easy."

Enemies, a Love Story, which opens today at the Gotham, handles this romantic triangle—and the quadrilateral it turns into once Tamara arrives on the scene—in an unexpected and not easily categorizable way. Like the best of Mr. Mazursky's work, it presents a very full spectrum of complicated and sometimes darkly funny emotions. Although the shadow of the Holocaust extends to cover everyone in the story, none of the characters are in any way typical; each has a psychic makeup that is idiosyncratic and distinct. In a story with so much potential for sentimentality and broad bedroom farce, it is surprising that there is none of either.

For Herman, these three romances are a source of as much anxiety as satisfaction. And Herman, uncommonly rakish for a character with a thick Yiddish accent, never attempts to be cavalier. Masha, for her part, begins the film as a sullenly voluptuous figure and grows to seem more and more haunted as the story goes on. Yadwiga, who dotes on Herman and treats him like the child he will not allow her to have, gradually emerges from her slavishness as the dimensions of Herman's secret life become known; when her former employer, Tamara, appears on her doorstep and dramatically proclaims herself to be dead, Yadwiga shrieks as if seeing a ghost. Tamara, as played by Ms. Huston, is a sweeping, embittered figure who turns out to know Herman a lot better than he knows himself.

The New York street and subway scenes in *Enemies, a Love Story,* in places like the Bronx, Brooklyn and the Lower East Side, have been given a vibrant glow by Fred Murphy's cinematography, but their vitality runs much deeper than that. The thriving Jewish culture that is seen in the background, along busy streets and even in dim, cramped apartment houses, becomes a sign of affirmation in contrast to the characters' terrible memories. As such, it's much more than scenery, and Mr. Mazursky clearly invests a lot of energy in staging these scenes well. Even in the hubbub of Coney Island, the film glimpses a New York filled with enough promise to do battle against the characters' pain.

The film missteps when it tries to get any closer to the characters' European memories. The few occasions when Herman imagines he sees Nazis in New York rupture what is otherwise a remarkably understated mood. Thoughts of the past are much better expressed by Masha when Herman takes her on an outing to a hotel in the Catskills, a setting to which Mr. Mazursky brings a particular dry touch. "Where are the Nazis? What kind of world is this without Nazis?" Masha marvels, looking at a sylvan lake.

Mr. Silver does a fine job conveying the guarded, desperate nature of a man about whom very little is finally known. Ms. Olin makes Lena a steamy and dangerous siren, as well as a tragic one. Ms. Huston, commanding as ever, gives the film its most drolly articulate voice, and Ms. Stein makes Yadwiga as touching in her dutifulness as she is sympathetically furious later on. The film's small performances are also quite good, with the casting of minor roles sometimes uncannily right. Alan King is perfect as the prosperous, highly assimilated rabbi who employs Herman as a ghostwriter ("this town is lousy with bookworms—everyone wants to be a ghostwriter," he declares).

Judith Malina, as a mother-in-law of Herman's, and Phil Leeds, as the wealthy philanthropist who finally blows the whistle on Herman's trigamy, manage to be both unpleasant and sweet in equal measure. Best of all is the director himself, briefly appearing as Masha's estranged husband, sipping tea from a glass in a cafeteria on the boardwalk. Mr. Mazursky makes himself the clearest embodiment of the turbulent, transitional world his film means to capture.

—*J.M., December 13, 1989*

LES ENFANTS DU PARADIS (CHILDREN OF PARADISE)

Directed by Marcel Carné: written (in French, with English subtitles) by Jacques Prévert: cine-matographers. Roger Hubert and Marc Fossard: edited by Henri Rust: music by Maurice Thiriet, Joseph Kosma and Georges Mouqué: art designers. Léon Barsacq. R. Cabutti and Alexander Trauner: produced by Fred Orain: released by Pathé Studios and Tricolore Films. Black and white. Running time: 194 minutes.

With: Jean-Louis Barrault (Baptiste Deburau), Arletty (Garance). Marcel Herrand (Lazenaire). Pierre Renoir (Jericho). Fabien Loris (Avril) and Etienne Decroux (Anselme Deburau).

The strong philosophical disposition of the French film director, Marcel Carné, to scan through the medium of cinema the irony and pathos of life—a disposition most memorably demonstrated in his great prewar film, *Quai des Brumes*—has apparently not been altered by the tragic experience of the last few years, as witness his most ambitious picture, *Les Enfants du Paradis*. For, in this long and fervid French picture, which was more or less clandestinely made during the Nazi occupation under circumstances of the most exacting sort—and which had its American premiere at the Ambassador Theatre yesterday—M. Carné is platonically observing the melancholy masquerade of life, the riddle of truth and illusion, the chimeras of la comédie humaine.

And if that sounds like a mouthful, you may rest emphatically assured that M. Carné has bitten off a portion no less difficult to chew. For his story concerns the crisscrossed passions of a group of Parisian theater folks—clowns, charlatans and tragedians—in the mid-nineteenth century. It is a story of the fatal attraction of four different men to one girl, a creature of profound and rank impulses, in the glittering milieu of the demimonde. And to render it even more platonic, he has framed this human drama within the gilded proscenium of the theater, as though it were but a pageant on the stage—a pageant to hypnotize and tickle the shrilling galleries, the "children of 'the Gods'."

Obviously such an Olympian—or classical—structure for a film presumes a proportionate disposition to philosophize from the audience. And it assumes a responsibility of dramatic clarity. Unfortunately, the pattern of the action does not support the demand. There is a great deal of vague and turgid wandering in

Les Enfants du Paradis, and its network of love and hate and jealousy is exceptionally tough to cut through. Its concepts are elegant and subtle, its connections are generally remote and its sad, fatalistic conclusion is a capstone of futility.

It is said that the film was considerably cut down into its present two-hour and twenty-four-minute length, which may account for the lesions in the pattern and for the disjunction of the colorful musical score. That would not account, however, for the long-windedness of Jacques Prévert's script, sketchily transcribed in English titles, and for the generally archaic treatment of Passion and Destiny.

Withal, M. Carné has created a frequently captivating film which has moments of great beauty in it and some performances of exquisite note. Jean-Louis Barrault's impersonation of the famous French mime, Baptiste Deburau, is magically moody and expressive, especially in his scenes of pantomime, although it is hard to perceive the fascination which he is alleged to have for the lady in the case. And as the latter, the beauteous Arletty intriguingly suggests deep mysteries in the nature of a richly feminine creature—but it is difficult to gather what they are. Pierre Brasseur is delightfully extravagant as a selfish, conceited "ham," Marcel Herrand is trenchant as a cutthroat and Louis Salou is brittle as a swell.

On the basis alone of performance and of its bold, picturesque mise-en-scène, *Les Enfants du Paradis* is worth your custom. What you get otherwise is to boot.
—*B.C., February 20, 1947*

THE ENGLISH PATIENT

Directed by Anthony Minghella; written by Mr. Minghella, based on the novel by Michael Ondaatje; director of photography, John Seale; edited by Walter Murch; music by Gabriel Yared; production designer, Stuart Craig; produced by Saul Zaentz; released by Miramax Films. Running time: 160 minutes.

With: Ralph Fiennes (Almasy), Juliette Binoche (Hana), Willem Dafoe (Caravaggio), Kristin Scott Thomas (Katharine Clifton), Naveen Andrews (Kip), Colin Firth (Geoffrey Clifton) and Julian Wadham (Madox).

Christmas in Cairo, 1938: an exquisite sequence in *The English Patient,* one of so many in this fiercely romantic, mesmerizing tour de force. In the courtyard of the British Embassy, soldiers sit at tables baking in the sun while a bagpipe plays "Silent Night." The heat is overwhelming. And the effect is one of dizzying incongruity, as if all the conventions of ordinary life had been suspended. The world has palpably been turned upside down.

Even more torrid than the weather is the erotic pull that draws Katharine Clifton, an elegant Englishwoman who is helping to preside over this party, to the ornate window behind which her handsome, obsessed lover hides. He longs to lure her away for one of the trysts that fill this haunting film with its intricate array of memories. "Swoon," he whispers ardently. "I'll catch you." She does swoon. No wonder.

The English Patient, a stunning feat of literary adaptation as well as a purely cinematic triumph, begins long after this love affair has come to a terrible end. The man of the title, who once pursued Katharine with such intensity, has been literally consumed by fire. Scarred beyond recognition, he lies in a bombed-out Tuscan monastery in the waning days of World War II and is tended by Hana, a luminous nurse. Hana performs near-miracles. So does Anthony Minghella's film as it weaves extravagant beauty around a central character whose condition is so grotesque.

The same was true for Michael Ondaatje's poetic and oblique 1992 novel, a winner of the Booker Prize. From the standpoint of film adaptation the book is hugely daunting, and not merely because its hero is disfigured and confined to his bed. "There are stories the man recites quietly into the room which slip from level to level like a hawk," Mr. Ondaatje wrote of the injured man sifting through his memories. This dreamlike, nonlinear tale moves in much the same way, swooping gracefully from past to present, from one set of lovers to another, from the contours of the body to the topography of the desert sands.

In love with the mystery of far-flung places, the book invokes geography, wartime espionage and consuming physical passion as it evocatively spans the globe. Mr. Minghella (whose *Truly, Madly, Deeply* and *Mr. Wonderful* are no preparation for this) manages to be astonishingly faithful to the spirit of this exotic material while giving it more shape and explicitness, virtually reinventing it from the ground up. He has described what he aspires to here as "epic cinema of a personal nature." With its immense seductiveness, heady romance and glorious desert vistas at the *Lawrence of Arabia* level, *The English Patient* imaginatively lives up to that description.

Like T. E. Lawrence, the English patient—actually the Hungarian Count Laszlo Almasy—comes to the desert as a cartographer and stays to find himself caught up in war. And Ralph Fiennes, as Almasy, makes himself the most dashing British actor to brood in such settings since the young Peter O'Toole. Though Mr. Fiennes plays the film's Tuscan scenes from beneath pale, bristly stubble and a mask of web-like scars (courtesy of Jim Henson's Creature Shop), he is often seen as a dazzling, elusive figure working with the Royal Geographical Society in remote corners of North Africa. The film's debonair side is so highly developed that the actors playing these adventurers wear dinner clothes from a tailor who dressed the Duke of Windsor.

As the burn victim confides in Hana (played with radiant simplicity by Juliette Binoche, as a woman recovering her own equilibrium), the details of this earlier life unfold. And the film, like Almasy himself, is most alive in the tempestuous past. *The English Patient* sets off sparks with the grand entrance of Katharine, played by Kristin Scott Thomas in a great career-altering change of pace. Ms. Scott Thomas's more restrained roles anticipate nothing of her sensual allure and glittering sophistication here.

Katharine descends grandly from the skies with an airplane and a husband (Colin Firth) at her disposal. "She was always crying on my shoulder for somebody," Geoffrey Clifton confides, without realizing that his wife and Almasy have become feverishly involved. "Finally persuaded her to settle for my shoulder. Stroke of genius." Meanwhile, Almasy's obsession does not escape the notice of Madox (Julian Wadham), his worldly friend and colleague. "Madox knows, I think," he tells Katharine. "He keeps talking about Anna Karenina. It's his idea of a man-to-man chat."

There is no time, while being swept away by the sheer magnetism of *The English Patient,* to complain that this kind of treachery is not earthshaking or new. The film has so many facets, and combines them in such fascinating and fluid style (with great polish from John Seale's cinematography, Stuart Craig's production design, Gabriel Yared's insinuating score and Walter Murch's adroit editing), that its cumulative effect is much stronger than the sum of its parts.

So in exchange for a sharp central story—or even one that is easily described—the film offers such indelible images as cave paintings of swimmers in the desert, a sandstorm of mysterious (and prophetic) fury as Almasy and Katharine are thrown together, and the English patient's great treasure, a well-worn, memento-filled volume of Herodotus. Even without that book, the film's reverence for history and literature would be very clear.

The film's parallels and layers also incorporate Caravaggio (Willem Dafoe), a wily Canadian thief whose fate is linked to Almasy's and whose name, like every other detail here, has been chosen with intriguing care. A more captivating character who receives shorter shrift is Kip (Naveen Andrews), the voluptuously handsome Sikh who defuses land mines and becomes gently involved with Hana. The spareness with which Mr. Ondaatje describes this liaison has a piercing loveliness that Mr. Minghella's film mirrors:

"She walks towards his night tent without a false step or any hesitation. The trees make a sieve of moonlight, as if she is caught within the light of a dance hall's globe. She enters his tent and puts an ear to his sleeping chest and listens to his beating heart, the way he will listen to a clock on a mine. Two A.M. Everyone is asleep but her."

The English Patient sees the eloquent delicacy in that passage and brings it to every frame.

—J.M., November 15, 1996

THE ENTERTAINER

Directed by Tony Richardson; written by John Osborne and Nigel Kneale, based on the play by Mr. Osborne; cinematographer, Oswald Morris; edited by Alan Osbiston; music by John Addison; art designers, Ralph Brinton and Ted Marshall; produced by Harry Saltzman; released by Continental Distributing. Black and white. Running time: 97 minutes.

With: Laurence Olivier (Archie Rice), Brenda de Banzie (Phoebe Rice), Joan Plowright (Jean),

Roger Livesey (Billy), Alan Bates (Frank), Daniel Massey (Graham), Albert Finney (Mick Rice), Shirley Ann Field (Tina) and Thora Hird (Mrs. Lapford).

As an antidote to all the bromides about show people being lovely folk, amusing, courageous, softhearted and dedicated to spreading sunshine in the world, we suggest that you see *The Entertainer,* Laurence Olivier's new film, based on the play by John Osborne, which opened at the Sutton yesterday. It pretty well shatters forever—or for the moment, at least—a fond belief.

Acting a tinhorn song-and-dance man in secondrate English music halls—a type for which lots of sweet nostalgia has been nicely concocted in recent years—Mr. Olivier, who might be regarded as the first gentleman of the British stage, brings forth a brilliant exposure of a cheap, sentimental theatrical fraud. And what he doesn't uncover about the people of the profession who live in "digs" and slosh through life in a sodden, aimless fashion, Brenda de Banzie and Roger Livesey do.

Possibly Mr. Osborne had something deep and wise in mind when he wrote *The Entertainer,* done here two years ago on the stage. Possibly he intended its ruthless and dismal exposé of a fading figure in a fast-declining pastime to be reflective of the position of Britain today, and its trailing of the tattered glories of vaudeville to suggest a greater passing of prestige.

There are certain intimations to support this. One son of its tarnished, middle-aged hoofer is a British soldier en route to the Suez to represent Queen and country when the drama begins. He is captured and his fate hangs in the balance all the while his old man is trying to save himself from ruin. Nothing comes of efforts to save him. Both are finished at the end.

Also there's a cogent bit of business in which the hoofer's wife and mundane relatives try to get him to forsake his bleak profession and move to Canada. He resists this practical suggestion. Why? Because "Bass's draught ale is not obtainable in the former Dominion." It's a bit of implication, if you please.

But for all that—or, rather, for whatever of that you are able to perceive—*The Entertainer* is a devastating picture of a hollow, hypocritical heel and of the pitiful people around him who are drowned in his grubby vanity. There is not a great deal of body to it.

The fellow himself is too shallow and cheap to be worth very much consideration or extensive sympathy. And the members of his family—with one exception—are generally stupid, unstable and dull.

Yet it works out to a fascinating picture, for one reason because of its superior illustrative performance and, for another, because of its striking mise-en-scène. Mr. Olivier is nothing short of brilliant as he runs the monotonous scale of turns and tricks of his shoddy entertainer, singing banal songs, pumping out endless off-stage wheezes and oozing absurd synthetic charm.

It is only in the moments of his triumph over a pathetically silly stagestruck girl, appropriately and even compassionately performed by Shirley Ann Field, or of sudden self-torturing confidence with his daughter, whom Joan Plowright plays, that our man affectingly exposes the emptiness of his soul. Mr. Olivier is terrific in what is not one of his more terrific roles.

Miss de Banzie is also excellent as his poor, confused, ineffectual wife, struggling to hang onto nothing and kid herself with an illusion of hope. Mr. Livesey does a fine job, mingling pathos with some pomposity, as a retired vaudevillian who succumbs to a fatal chance to return. Alan Bates is significantly flighty as a backstage son and Thora Hird gives a sharp impersonation of the vulgar mother of an ambitious girl.

Director Tony Richardson has imaged the cheapness of a seaside music hall, of grubby digs, and the midway surroundings in such a way as to have them all but smell. *The Entertainer* may not be an earthshaking or even an important film. But it is entertaining. It reeks of show business. At least, it is always "on."

—B.C., October 4, 1960

ENTRE NOUS

Directed by Diane Kurys; written (in French, with English subtitles) by Ms. Kurys and Alain Henry, based on the book by Ms. Kurys and Olivier Cohen; director of photography, Bernard Lutic; edited by Joele Van Effenterre; music by Luis Bacalov; production designer, Jacques Bufnoir; produced by Ariel Zeitoun; released by United Artists Classics. Running time: 110 minutes.

With: Miou-Miou (Madeleine), Isabelle Huppert (Lena), Guy Marchand (Michel), Jean-Pierre Bacri

(Costa). Robin Repucci (Raymond) and Patrick Bauchau (Carlier).

Neither of Diane Kurys's two previous films, *Peppermint Soda* (1977) and *Cocktail Molotov* (1980), gives any hint of the wonderfully sustained artistry that she demonstrates in *Entre Nous,* her very personal, moving new film that, all of a sudden, places her among those in the forefront of the commercial French cinema.

Entre Nous, which is titled *Coup de Foudre* in France, is something like Lawrence Kasdan's *Big Chill* in that it has the looks and manner of a conventional film but, in addition, has the sort of intelligence that seldom survives the smog of compromises in conventional filmmaking. *Entre Nous* will be shown at the New York Film Festival at Lincoln Center today and tomorrow.

Because *Entre Nous* is mainly about the friendship of two quite different women, each of whom eventually takes charge of her own life, the film may be in danger of being labeled feminist, which, I suppose, it is, at least in part. However, because the term is usually applied to consciousness-raising literature as glumly represented by films like Agnes Varda's *One Sings, the Other Doesn't,* the term doesn't do justice to the specific idiosyncrasies of Miss Kurys's work.

Entre Nous is not the sort of film that soothes by supplying upbeat answers. It doesn't have answers of any kind. Like all serious works of narrative fiction, it examines people in particular situations and makes some speculations about what it finds. After that, it's for each of us to interpret according to his own circumstances.

The time is 1942. Lena (Isabelle Huppert), a young Belgian Jew, is interned in southern France awaiting deportation to Germany. Unknown to her, she has caught the eye of a camp worker, Michel (Guy Marchand), a French Legionnaire, also Jewish, who is soon due for discharge. In a note slipped to her one day inside a piece of bread, Michel proposes to Lena. If she marries him, he writes, she'll be allowed to leave the camp. It's not especially romantic, but Michel is young and presentable and Lena is practical. She accepts.

Intercut with these early, tragislapstick adventures of Lena are scenes of the courtship and marriage of the bourgeois Madeleine (Miou-Miou), an art student whose young husband is killed in a partisan raid just a few months after their marriage.

The film then cuts forward to 1952 in Lyons, where Lena now lives with her two small daughters and the attentive, hardworking Michel, who has become the prosperous owner of a garage. One afternoon at a grade-school pageant, Lena meets Madeleine, now a mother with a small son and married to a good-looking rather feckless fellow named Costa (Jean-Pierre Bacri), a would-be actor.

Entre Nous is the minutely detailed story of the rare friendship that develops between the two women over the next few years as each faces a succession of crises that, at last, alter their lives. Lena, the more conventional of the two, slowly grows from a prematurely dowdy duckling into a sleek, smart, self-assured woman. She has never been in love with Michel, but they seem to have an exceptionally good marriage. They amuse each other and both are genuinely delighted in their children.

Madeleine's life with Costa is a good deal more bleak. He gets into one financial scrape after another, and the childish ways that once amused her are no longer funny. She's bored with Costa, sorry for—and a little bored by—her shy son, and wants desperately to start life over, preferably in Paris.

Entre Nous is not a movie-as-short story. It's a novel-sized film, the kind that is so perfectly realized in vivid incidents that, not until the end does one realize how big it is and how effortlessly it has covered so much social and psychological territory.

Like Mr. Kasdan, Miss Kurys is a first-rate writer with a director's vision and command of technique. The first quarter of the film—before Lena and Madeleine meet in Lyons—is virtually all exposition, but it is not only packed with detail, it is almost breathlessly suspenseful.

As admirable as the film's clear, unsentimental, long view of things are the beauty and the humor of many of its seemingly throwaway moments. It's marvelous about both the boredom and the joys of family life, about minor crises (when a child locks himself in a bathroom), and major ones, when, at last, a marriage is finally, irrevocably over. Late in the film there is a short but momentous scene aboard a night train to Paris that is stunning in its economy.

Miou-Miou, whom I don't think I've seen since she played the dyed blonde supermarket cashier in Alain

Tanner's *Jonah Who Will Be 25 in the Year 2000,* is an entirely new screen personality as the gravely pretty, dark-haired Madeleine. As written, this role leaves much for the audience to fill in or to speculate on, which is what Miss Kurys is doing in the film.

In the central role of Lena, which Miss Kurys says is based on her own mother, Miss Huppert is superb, better than she has been in years—strong, funny, self-assured. Audiences who only know her as a professional waif in things like *The Trout, Loulou, and Coup de Torchon,* won't recognize the authority in this fresh, unhackneyed performance.

Also extremely fine is Mr. Marchand as Michel, one of the most appealing boors ever to be found in a conventional movie. Mr. Bacri is also good as Madeleine's bewildered husband. Special mention must also be made of the excellent work Miss Kurys has obtained from Patricia Champane and Saga Blanchard as Lena's small daughters, and Guillaume de Guellec, who plays Madeleine's little boy.

Entre Nous is one of this festival's few unqualified hits.

—*V.C., October 8, 1983*

E.T. THE EXTRA-TERRESTRIAL

Directed by Steven Spielberg; written by Melissa Mathison; director of photography, Allen Daviau; edited by Carol Littleton; music by John Williams; production designer, James D. Bissell; produced by Mr. Spielberg and Kathleen Kennedy; released by Universal Pictures. Running time: 120 minutes.

With: Dee Wallace (Mary), Henry Thomas (Elliott), Peter Coyote (Keys), Robert Macnaughton (Michael), Drew Barrymore (Gertie), K. C. Martel (Greg), Sean Frye (Steve) and Tom Howell (Tyler).

The camera pans across a starry sky so clear that it has the effect of putting you in touch with the galaxies. When you lie on your back and stare into such a night sky, you feel as if you were tumbling upward through space. The camera slowly descends to earth to come to rest on a spaceship, its lights ablaze, comfortably settled in a clearing in a California forest. Small, Munchkin-sized creatures, whose abdomens glow on and off like those of fireflies,

attend to their tasks of gathering specimens of earth rocks and plant life.

Suddenly the visitors sense that they are about to be discovered. The alarm sounds. It's everyone back on board for an emergency takeoff that, unfortunately, leaves one crew member behind, marooned on a strange planet, without a friend to his generic name.

This is the eerie prefatory sequence to Steven Spielberg's *E.T. the Extra-Terrestrial,* an enchanted fantasy about the relationship of E.T. and the practical, staunch ten-year-old boy, Elliott (Henry Thomas), who discovers the frightened alien in the toolshed, befriends him and hides him in his bedroom.

With the best of intentions and the collaboration of his older brother, Michael (Robert Macnaughton), and his younger sister, Gertie (Drew Barrymore), Elliott attempts to aid and to domesticate E.T., who, though he's only a little taller than a coffee table, is both civilized and learned. More than anything else, the patient, gentle-natured E.T. wants to go home.

E.T. the Extra-Terrestrial, which opens today at Loews Manhattan Twin Cinema and other theaters, may become a children's classic of the space age. The film, directed by Mr. Spielberg and written by Melissa Mathison from an idea of Mr. Spielberg, freely recycles elements from all sorts of earlier children's works, including *Peter Pan* and *The Wizard of Oz. E.T.* is as contemporary as laser-beam technology, but it's full of the timeless longings expressed in children's literature of all eras.

Mr. Spielberg and Miss Mathison have taken the tale of Dorothy and her frantic search for the unreliable Wizard of Oz and turned it around, to tell it from the point of view of the Scarecrow, the Cowardly Lion and the Tin Woodman. Dorothy has become E.T., Kansas is outer space and Oz is a modern, middle-class real-estate development in California.

E.T. is not to be compared with Mr. Spielberg's *Poltergeist,* which is a child's ferocious nightmare re-created as a film. E.T. is a slick, spirited comedy about children's coping in a world where adults have grown up and away from innocence. Elliott, Michael, Gertie and their friends must protect E.T. from their elders, who are trying to catch E.T. to study him, to subject him to all sorts of unspeakable tests and, possibly, to dissect him like a frog.

It isn't difficult to fool Elliott's mother, Mary (Dee Wallace). She is a loving parent but so preoccupied by her recent separation from the children's father that when E.T. totters across the kitchen, she doesn't see him. It's more difficult outwitting the government security people, who have somehow gotten wind of E.T.'s presence. Then, too, there's E.T.'s terrible homesickness, which has all of the symptoms of a terminal disease.

Mr. Spielberg may not have photographed E.T. entirely at a child's eye-level, but the film gives that impression. It's a wise film without being smart-alecky, even if the children, when alone, talk a lot more vulgarly than many parents would be happy to hear.

The problems faced by Elliott, E.T. and the others are mostly comic ones. How to get E.T. out of the house, unseen, so that he can build a radar with which to communicate with his associates? The children wait till Halloween, throw a sheet over his head and lead him boldly through the front door. Once outside, E.T. finds the neighborhood alive with other creatures, some more familiar—children in costumes inspired by characters from *The Empire Strikes Back*—than others, children disguised as terrorists.

The most difficult problem is saving E.T.'s life, once the earth's polluted atmosphere has caught up with him, and just how this is accomplished, I'm not completely certain. There are some subtleties in the narrative toward the end that, I suspect, only a child will fully grasp.

The special effects, including flights through the air on ordinary bicycles, are beautifully realized. The best one of all is the E.T. itself, created by Carlo Rambaldi. E.T., who looks a lot like the creatures seen at the end of Mr. Spielberg's *Close Encounters of the Third Kind*, walks, talks, plays jokes, does tricks, gets tipsy and, at a crucial moment, even seems on the point of weeping a large, probably salt-free, tear.

Mr. Thomas, Mr. Macnaughton and Miss Barrymore give most appealing, modest performances of the sort we now associate with children in Spielberg films, especially with Cary Guffey in *Close Encounters of the Third Kind*.

A couple of minor reservations: John Williams's soundtrack music is beginning to sound just a tiny bit familiar, not all that different from the scores he has done for *Star Wars, Close Encounters* and *Raiders of the Lost Ark,* among others. Also, at the end of the film,

there is an all-out assault on the emotions that depends, it seems, more on the rising volume of this music than on the events portrayed. *E.T.* is good enough not to have to resort to such tricks.

—*V.C., June 11, 1982*

EUROPA, EUROPA

Directed by Agnieszka Holland: written (in German and Russian. with English subtitles) by Ms. Holland. based on the autobiography *Memoires* by Solomon Perel: director of photography. Jacek Petrycki: edited by Ewa Smal and Isabelle Lorente: music by Zbigniew Preisner: production designer. Allan Starski: produced by Margaret Mengoz and Artur Brauner: released by Orion Classics. Running time: 110 minutes.

With: Marco Hofschneider (Solomon Perel). Rene Hofschneider (Isaak). Piotr Kozlowski (David). Klaus Abramowsky (Solomon's Father). Michele Gleizer (Solomon's Mother) and Julie Delpy (Leni).

Running on tracks that predate Hitler's rise to power, the trolley car still passes through the Loaz ghetto, so its windows have been whitewashed to shield the eyes of Aryan riders from unwelcome sights. But a member of Hitler Youth surreptitiously creates a peephole, and through it he glimpses a terrible vision: the abject, suffering figure of his own mother. The woman he sees—he thinks she is his mother, though he cannot be positive—moves slowly through a landscape of utter misery. Her son, a Jew who has managed to pass himself off as a Nazi hero, can do nothing to alter her fate.

At moments like this, Agnieszka Holland's *Europa, Europa,* which opens today at the Lincoln Plaza Cinema, accomplishes what every film about the Holocaust seeks to achieve: it brings new immediacy to the outrage by locating specific, wrenching details that transcend cliché. Based on the memoirs of Solomon Perel, who survived the war through a variety of unusual subterfuges and is briefly seen offering a song of thanksgiving at the story's end, this film includes several remarkable episodes illustrating the strange events that shaped Mr. Perel's destiny and the full force of his terror and sorrow.

But much of the time, the truth here has a way of seeming stranger than fiction, largely because of Miss Holland's determinedly blithe directorial style. *Europa, Europa* has the pretty, sensitive look of a pastoral French romance even as it presents the most harrowing aspects of Mr. Perel's early years. Miss Holland's smooth direction is appealing and never fundamentally negates the essence of Mr. Perel's situation, but the result is a less ironic or complex film than must have been intended. The ingenuousness of the young hero, who was only a teenager at the time he found himself in the midst of a grave moral quandary, often feels bizarre in light of the events at hand.

Solly (Marco Hofschneider) comes from a close-knit family that is torn apart very early in the film, leaving him to fend for himself in an increasingly dangerous world. In 1938, on the eve of Solly's bar mitzvah, his home in a German city is disrupted by a pogrom that kills his sister, an event Miss Holland presents with wrenching simplicity and tact. Soon afterward, the Perels move to Lodz, Poland. But when war breaks out, the parents order their two younger sons to flee, and during the journey Solly is separated from his older brother. *Europa, Europa* is set forth as a linear, episodic story, punctuated by this and many other sad partings.

Solly makes his way east and winds up in a Soviet orphanage, where his identity as a Jew is still reasonably secure. Eminently adaptable, he learns to denounce religion as the opiate of the masses and to coexist with Christian classmates, despite the obvious tensions in the air.

But when the orphanage is bombed—marking another sad separation, since Solly has developed ties to the beautiful Stalinist who is his teacher—Solly is again adrift, and this time he lands in the hands of Nazi soldiers. They treat him royally, partly because of his usefulness as a Russian translator and partly because of his rosy, wide-eyed good looks. Typically, when the film presents a man claiming to be Stalin's son as a Soviet prisoner whom Solly interrogates, the incident has an indefinite, fairy tale quality, although it happens to be a slightly modified version of a real event.

The fact that Solly has been circumcised, in the Jewish ceremony that is seen at the film's outset, becomes critical to his survival, since this physical evidence is the only link to his Jewish heritage. The film pays considerable attention to his efforts to avoid being caught in showers, in bathrooms, and even in a sexual situation with a fresh faced young German girl (Julie Delpy) who admires him as a German hero. "If I ever catch a Jew, I'll cut his throat," she eventually tells him, in a manner that is offhanded but nonetheless certain to wreck their budding romance.

Presented with his personal copy of *Mein Kampf*, learning to swim in a swastika-decorated pool while wearing his army helmet and carrying his rifle, Solly eventually becomes a respected member of Hitler Youth; as such, he sits quietly through classroom lectures on how to identify Jews on sight and why "the Nordic man is the gem of this earth." The pressure of this new life eventually becomes unbearable, but Miss Holland does better at depicting the impossible aspects of Solly's outer circumstances than at probing his inner confusion.

The film's dream sequences, which involve Hitler and Stalin, are less affecting than the blunt outburst of emotion that Solly feels in the presence of his Aryan girlfriend's mother, at a moment when he simply can't stand the pressure of lying any longer. Mr. Hofschneider, whose performance is direct and impassioned as far as it goes, conveys Solly's raw panic and confusion much more effectively than the crisis of conscience that inevitably goes with them.

—*J.M., June 28, 1991*

EVERY MAN FOR HIMSELF

Directed by Jean-Luc Godard; written (in French, with English subtitles) by Jean-Claude Carrière and Anne-Marie Miéville; cinematographers, William Lubtchansky and Renato Berta; edited by Ms. Miéville and Mr. Godard; music by Gabriel Yared; art designer, Romain Goupil; produced by Alain Sarde and Mr. Godard; released by New Yorker Films. Running time: 87 minutes.

With: Isabelle Huppert (Isabelle Riviere), Jacques Dutronc (Paul Godard), Nathalie Baye (Denise Rimbaud) and Roland Amshutz (Second Customer).

It would be misleading to say that Jean-Luc Godard's brilliant new comedy, *Every Man for Himself*, the

French title of which is *Sauve Qui Peut/La Vie,* is the story of Paul, Denise and Isabelle. Though it's primarily about Paul, Denise and Isabelle, as well as about amorous bellboys, patient pimps, lecherous businessmen, opera singers who won't shut up, modern milkmaids and total strangers, it's not a story in any familiar way. Rather it's about this particular time and place in history as reflected in a series of cockeyed epiphanies and paradoxes.

Paul (Jacques Dutronc), a shrewd, good-looking young man with a strong sense of style and his own importance, which is paramount, works in a Swiss television station. He is separated from his wife and skeptical, twelve-year-old daughter, though they are on speaking terms. Denise (Nathalie Baye), who works with Paul and has been having an intense, quite unsatisfactory affair with him, is thinking about changing her life by a move to the country. The glamour has gone out of television for Denise. There must be more to life than trying to get hold of Marguerite Duras or, as she puts it tersely, "I want to do things, not just name them."

Isabelle (Isabelle Huppert), a country girl with a ravishingly pretty, poker face and the practicality of a peasant, has come to the city to make her living as a prostitute. This is not a fate worse than death for Isabelle, nor is she degraded by her work. She remains removed from it. In the way of a registered nurse, she's efficient and cool in every emergency.

Though Paul has his job as an anchor, he is without essential aims. He's drifting. Denise is restless, but has no clear notion how to improve things except to get up and move. Isabelle saves her money and, you suspect, she'll one day open a beauty parlor or a boutique. In the meantime, she hasn't the leisure to be happy or unhappy.

In the course of *Every Man for Himself,* whose English title was *Slow Motion* when it was shown at Cannes this year, Paul, Denise and Isabelle meet and, in various combinations, talk, argue, observe and make love, then separate. There are no thunderous emotional confrontations, but, by the end of the film, one's perceptions have been so enriched, so sharpened, that one comes out of it invigorated. *Every Man for Himself* leaves you with a renewed awareness of how a fine movie can clear away the detritus that collects in a mind subjected to endless invasions by clichés and platitudes and movies that fearlessly champion the safe or obvious position. It's a tonic.

Every Man for Himself will be shown at the New York Film Festival in Alice Tully Hall tonight and on Saturday. It will open its regular commercial engagement at the Cinema Studio 2 on Sunday.

At one point in the movie, the introspective Denise writes in her journal, "Something in the body arches its back against boredom and aimlessness," which is what Mr. Godard seems to do instinctively when he starts to make a movie. No matter how outrageous some of his public statements about filmmaking and filmmakers, he swoops and soars above and around his subjects with a grace that defies analysis. It's simply what he does, and does better than anyone else of his generation.

Every Man for Himself, his first theatrical film since *Tout Va Bien* in 1971, recalls the greatest of his "pre-revolutionary" films of the 60's—*Pierrot Le Fou, Vivre Sa Vie* and *Weekend,* and, being so completely controlled and disciplined, it may even be more effectively revolutionary than his Maoist movies. Dialectics on the soundtrack can be tuned out. When they are in the images, they pass directly into one's memory bank.

There's not a banal shot or a predictable moment in the film, which has an effect similar to that of poetry or good prose. It invites one to respond to familiar sights and sounds as if coming upon them for the first time. Watching the film is a process of discovery, sometimes funny, sometimes scary.

Though the three principals are given more or less equal time, Isabelle is clearly the film's focal point, whether she is participating in an elaborately choreographed foursome that suggests a Rube Goldberg contraption designed to make sex simple, or being kidnapped by her pimp, who must teach her a lesson. Isabelle has been holding out on him. The pimp is not cruel, but he is firm. As he spanks her in the back seat of his limousine he makes her repeat after him, "Nobody is independent, not whores, not typists, not duchesses, not servants, not champion tennis players."

Later, when Isabelle's young sister decides to turn tricks, Isabelle gives her pointers in return for 50 percent of the take.

Individual images as well as entire sequences are dense with detail. A bit of random violence seen in the background while Denise waits in a train station puts her restlessness into perspective. Without seemingly being aware of it, the movie conveys a terrific feeling of loss, of something gone forever, in Paul's relationship with his daughter. The film is not "about" fathers and daughters, but what it says, in passing, is more disturbing than some entire novels.

The film is unusually beautiful without being pretty; its style detached, except for those moments when the director calls attention to a look or a gesture through the use of stop-motion. Even then, it's not as if Mr. Godard were telling us what to think, but, rather, suggesting that we consider the possibilities. In this fashion each embrace of Paul and Denise—slowed down as a rapid succession of still photographs—becomes a possibly fatal collision. It's no wonder they're breaking up.

The actors are so much a part of the texture of the film that they can't be easily separated as performers' performances. *Every Man for Himself* is a single seamless endeavor, a stunning, original work about which there is still a lot to say, but there's time. I trust it will outlive us all.

—V.C., October 8, 1980

THE EXORCIST

Directed by William Friedkin; written by William Peter Blatty; directors of photography, Owen Roizman and Billy Williams; edited by Norman Gay, Jordan Leondopoulos, Evan Lottman and Bud Smith; music by Jack Nitzsche; production designer, Bill Malley; produced by Mr. Blatty; released by Warner Brothers. Running time: 121 minutes.

With: Ellen Burstyn (Mrs. MacNeil), Linda Blair (Regan), Max von Sydow (Father Merrin), Jason Miller (Father Karras), Lee J. Cobb (Lieutenant Kinderman), Jack MacGowran (Burke) and Mercedes McCambridge (Voice of the Demon).

The Georgetown dinner party being given by Chris MacNeil (Ellen Burstyn), a Hollywood movie actress making a film in Washington, is going beautifully, with diplomats, astronauts, senators and show people carrying on in high style. A movie director gets drunk and tries to beat up the butler while a swinging Jesuit priest plays the piano for a sing-along.

Everything is as it should be until Regan (Linda Blair), Chris's twelve-year-old daughter, appears in the middle of the drawing room in her nightdress. As Chris watches appalled, Regan fixes her eyes on the astronaut, urinates on the floor, and says:

"You're going to die up there."

That's more or less the first big scene in William Friedkin's film version of *The Exorcist*, a chunk of elegant occultist claptrap that opened yesterday at the Cinema I. However, lots of other peculiar things have gone on before. A statue in the Catholic church down the street has been desecrated. Little Regan's bed has been bouncing around so antically she's been unable to sleep at night, and there have been unexplained noises in the attic of Chris's Georgetown mansion.

The devil, it seems, for all his supposed powers, can't break and enter without sounding like Laurel and Hardy trying to move a piano.

The Exorcist, the story of the attempts to save the life of the demonically possessed Regan, is a practically impossible film to sit through, but not necessarily because it treats diabolism with the kind of dumb piety moviemakers once lavished on the stories of saints.

It establishes a new low for grotesque special effects, all of which, I assume, have some sort of religious approval since two Jesuit priests, who are listed as among the film's technical advisers, also appear in the film as actors.

Among the sights to which the audience is treated are Regan, her face contorted and parched by the devil inside, vomiting what looks to be condensed split-pea soup onto an exorcising priest, and her paroxysms of fury as she jabs a crucifix into herself and shoves her mother's head down under her bloodied nightgown. In the context of this kind of spectacular nonsense, a carefully detailed sequence showing the child undergoing an encephalogram is almost therapeutic.

William Peter Blatty, who produced the film and adapted his best-selling novel for the screen, has succeeded in leaving out very few of the kind of ridiculous details that, I suspect, would have earned a less expensive, more skeptical film an X rating instead of the R rating that mysteriously has been achieved.

The Exorcist is not an unintelligently put-together film, which makes one all the more impatient with it.

The producer and the director have gone whole hog on (and over) their budget, which included the financing of a location trip to Iraq to shoot a lovely, eerie prefatory sequence at an archeological dig that is, as far as I can see, not especially essential to the business that comes after.

The cast is made up of some excellent actors: Ellen Burstyn (who is becoming America's answer to Glenda Jackson), Max von Sydow as the old Catholic priest who also functions as chief exorcist, the late Jack Mac-Gowran as the director of the film within, Jason Miller as the priest who attains success through imitation of Jesus and Lee J. Cobb as a kindly Jewish detective.

The care that Mr. Friedkin and Mr. Blatty have taken with the physical production, and with the rhythm of the narrative, which achieves a certain momentum through a lot of fancy, splintery crosscutting, is obviously intended to persuade us to suspend belief. But to what end? To marvel at the extent to which audiences will go to escape boredom by shock and insult.

According to trade reports, *The Exorcist* cost about ten million dollars. The money could have been better spent subsidizing a couple of beds at the Paine-Whitney Clinic.

—*V.C., December 27, 1973*

THE EXTERMINATING ANGEL

Directed by Luis Buñuel; written (in Spanish, with English subtitles) by Mr. Buñuel and Luis Alcoriza, based on the play *Los Naufragos de la Calle de la Providencia* by José Bergamín; cinematographer, Gabriel Figueroa; edited by Carlos Savage; music by Alessandro Scarlatti and Pietro Dominico Paradisi; art designer, Jesus Bracho; produced by Gustavo Alatriste; released by Altura Films International. Black and white. Running time: 91 minutes.

With: Silvia Pinal (The Walkyrie), Jacqueline Andere (Señora Roc), Jose Baviera (Leandro), Augusto Benedico (Doctor), Luis Beristain (Cristián) and Antonio Bravo (Russell).

Did you ever have guests come to dinner and then, neglecting to go home, just hang around your apartment or house for days on end? If you haven't had the experience, you can imagine how awkward it would be—how taxing to the fragile bonds of friendship and to the facilities of your kitchen and home.

This is the situation that old social needler, Luis Buñuel, has imposed upon a wealthy host and hostess in their elegant Mexico City home in his film, *The Exterminating Angel,* which was presented at the Carnegie Hall Cinema yesterday. Only he has piled Pelion on Ossa in showing the consequences that might come from having a lot of pompous worldlings and social parasites pent up in one place.

He has smoothly brought together a chattering party of resplendent guests in a marble town house after the opera. He has fed them luxuriously, and then he has sat them down to listen to one of the ladies play the piano a bit.

When it comes time to leave, however, he won't let them out of the place. For some mysterious reason, no one can quite up and go. On one pretext or another, they dally and hesitate. Then, slowly and to their amazement, they find it impossible to leave. What's more, they now discover that all the servants save the butler have cleared out, and they are imprisoned and isolated in this magnificent, cheerless house.

In this situation, Mr. Buñuel manipulates the guests onto various successive levels of boredom, annoyance and hostility. They try to be genteel at the outset, but as the hours and then the days drag on, they start breaking up, pairing off, quarreling and finally acting like vicious animals.

One of the crabbier gentlemen has a heart attack and dies. His body is hustled into a closet and discreetly got out of the way. A couple—each engaged to be married to someone not there—try to sneak a little lovemaking. They become frustrated and commit suicide. An incestuous brother and sister fight with the host for a hidden box of morphine. And all the while, physical conditions are going from bad to worse.

Meanwhile, no one on the outside can get into this strangely shut-off house. The phenomenon of isolation is a seeming insoluble mystery.

But knowing Mr. Buñuel and his penchant for scourging society with allegorical whips, it is obvious that what he is showing us is a symbolical state of affairs. He is showing us the played-out privileged classes in all their stubborn sterility. He is letting us in on the secret of their shocking and shabby rotting away.

At the end he takes another of his characteristic swipes at the church. With his people finally released from their confinement, they go to a cathedral to give thanks. When the solemn service is over, they find—guess what!—they can't leave.

In his customary fashion, Mr. Buñuel stages this play with cumulating nervousness and occasional explosive ferocities. He whips up individual turmoils with the apt intensities of a uniformly able cast; and he throws in frequent surrealistic touches, such as a disembodied hand coasting across the floor, or a bear and a flock of sheep coming up from the kitchen, to give the viewer little hints of mental incongruities.

But my feeling is that his canvas is too narrow and his social comment too plain to keep our interest fixed upon his people and their barren stewing for an hour and a half. This is a case in which the ennui and frustration, so purposely conveyed, creep into the patience of the audience as fast as they suffuse the characters.

I suspect this realization is one reason why this film is only now being released commercially, after its initial showing as the first presentation of the New York Film Festival on its inauguration in 1963.

The dialogue is in Spanish with English subtitles.
—*B.C., August 22, 1967*

A FACE IN THE CROWD

Produced and directed by Elia Kazan; written by Budd Schulberg, based on his short story "The Arkansas Traveler"; cinematographers, Harry Stradling and Gayne Rescher; music by Tom Glazer; released by Warner Brothers. Black and white. Running time: 125 minutes.

With: Andy Griffith (Lonesome Rhodes), Patricia Neal (Marcia Jeffries), Anthony Franciosa (Joey Kiely), Walter Matthau (Mel Miller), Lee Remick (Betty Lou Fleckum), Percy Waram (Colonel Hollister) and Rod Brasfield (Beanie).

Budd Schulberg and Elia Kazan, the writer-director team whose *On the Waterfront* manifested the rare congeniality of their skills, are doing a brisk encore in tracing the phenomenal rise (and fall) of a top television "personality" in their new film, *A Face in the Crowd*. This sizzling and cynical exposure, which came to the Globe last night, also presents Andy Griffith as the key figure in his first screen role.

Like other debunking films before it that have gleefully discovered feet of clay on seemingly solid public idols, this one is more concerned with the nature and flamboyance of the idol than with the milieu and machine by which he is made. Lonesome Rhodes, the two-faced hero, is pretty much the whole show, and what he symbolizes in society is barely hinted—or discreetly overlooked.

From the outset, when he is picked up as a drunken guitar-playing tramp by a female television reporter in an Arkansas town, he progressively dominates the TV audience to which he is expandingly exposed, the advertising agency representatives and the big industrialist by whom he is employed. He even is coming close to dominating a political faction and a Presidential aspirant when the rug is suddenly pulled out from under him by his girlfriend, who throws a studio switch.

Meanwhile, he is demonstrating his eccentric personality—his gusto, his candor, his shrewdness, his moral laxity and his treachery. And, from the way his eyes narrow and his lips tighten, we gather he is demonstrating a thirst for power, when his loving and loyal discoverer decides that we've all had enough.

In a way, it is not surprising that this flamboyant Lonesome Rhodes dominates the other characters in the story and consequently the show. For Mr. Schulberg has penned a powerful person of the raw, vulgar, roughneck, cornball breed, and Mr. Griffith plays him with thunderous vigor, under the guidance of Mr. Kazan.

You know you are in the vicinity of someone who has white-lightning for blood when Mr. Griffith first hits old "Mama Git-tar" and howls his "Free Man in the Morning" song. And you know you are up against a trickster when he starts spouting amiable lies. Mr. Schulberg and Mr. Kazan spawn a monster not unlike the one of Dr. Frankenstein.

But so hypnotized are they by his presence that he runs away not only with the show but with intellectual reason and with the potentiality of their theme. Lonesome Rhodes builds up so swiftly that it is never made properly clear that he is a creature of the television mechanism and the public's own gullibility. He swings in an ever-widening orbit, as it were by his own energy and not by the recognized attraction and governance of a new magnetic field.

Everyone condescends to him—in the script of Mr. Schulberg, that is—instead of taking positive positions that would better represent reality. Patricia Neal as his doting discoverer, Paul McGrath as an advertising man, Percy Waram as a big manufacturer, Marshall Neilan as a scheming senator and Anthony Franciosa as a wise guy—all play their roles capably, but they're forced to behave as awed observers, not as flexible factors in the scheme of things.

As a consequence, the dominance of the hero and his monstrous momentum, driven home by a vast accumulation of TV detail and Mr. Kazan's staccato style, eventually become a bit monotonous when they are not truly opposed. Reality is proved by inadvertence. We finally get bored with Lonesome Rhodes. Thus the dubious device of having his girlfriend switch him on the air when he thinks he is finished with his program (and is scorning his public) is inane. This type would either have become a harmless habit or the public would have been finished with him!

Withal, he is highly entertaining and well worth pondering when he is on the rise.

—B.C., May 29, 1957

FACE TO FACE

Produced, written (in Swedish, with English Subtitles) and directed by Ingmar Bergman: cinematographer, Sven Nykvist: edited by Siv Lundgren: music by Wolfgang Amadeus Mozart: production designer, Anne Hagegörd: released by Paramount Pictures. Running time: 136 minutes.

With: Liv Ullman (Dr. Jenny Isaksson), Erland Josephson (Dr. Thomas Jacobi), Gunnar Björnstrand (Grandpa), Aino Taube-Henrikson (Grandma), Kari Sylwan (Maria), Sif Ruud (Elizabeth Wankel) and Sven Lindberg (Dr. Erik Isaksson).

In the first scene of *Face to Face*, Ingmar Bergman's beautiful, agonizing new film, Dr. Jenny Isaksson (Liv Ullmann), a psychiatrist with a firm grip on what she takes to be the real world, walks through the newly empty rooms of a house she is moving out of. As she looks about, we share her particular sense of unexpected space. The texture of the wooden floors is seen as if for the first time. The white walls are bright but neutral—simply impersonal backdrops after all. In the void there are echoes of Jenny's footsteps.

Lives—even the most carefully managed—are voids filled with echoes. The echoes accumulate. Sometimes when one least expects it the mind's tuning device, a kind of psychic censor, breaks down and the echoes cannot be sanely controlled. Forgotten moments from the past push into the present. Signals cross, messages overlap. The garble in the void is insupportable. There may be nothing else to do but to turn off.

Face to Face, which opened last night at the Beekman Theater, traces Jenny's sudden, breathtaking descent into despair, her unsuccessful suicide attempt and her apparent recovery. That is the shape of the film anyway. *Face to Face,* like all Bergman films, reaches out to contemplate all sorts of other things, from the more or less fixed, contemporary reality of Jenny's career, her marriage, family and friends, to the emotional anxieties, represented by the echoes from her past, that come out of the dark to overwhelm her.

As Jenny sits on her bed in a room filled with sunlight, and sets about the task of swallowing handfuls of sleeping pills, she tells us she feels neither fear nor sadness. She is instead cheerful, excited as if going on her first train trip.

Why does Jenny do it?

The only reservation I have about *Face to Face* is that Mr. Bergman, perhaps for the first time, is uncharacteristically explicit when it comes to laying out the reasons for Jenny's breakdown. In a series of dreams and waking hallucinations that form important sections of the film he takes us on a guided tour of a house of Jenny's subconscious, a journey through a house of horrors as immaculately tended as a Disneyland funhouse, and carefully laid out to save the biggest surprises for the last few minutes of the ride.

This Freudian literalness is surprising in that Mr. Bergman seems clearly to believe that psychiatry is, at best, a passing fad, something of a shell game, though his feelings are ambivalent. There are times when one suspects that his vision of the decline and fall of Jenny the Psychiatrist, with whom Ingmar Bergman the artist intensely identifies, is really the analysand's ultimate revenge on the analyst. Two things are going on at the same time. The patient is saying, "He's crazier than I," but "I am him."

In his preface to the published screenplay (somewhat expanded from what we see on the screen), Mr. Bergman admits that he's always been "extremely suspicious of dreams, apparitions, and visions, both in literature and in films and plays. Perhaps it's because mental excesses of this sort smack too much of being 'arranged.'"

He goes on to say that he thinks of the dreams in this film as being "extensions of reality," and thus, I suppose, not to be taken literally as dreams (if that's not too much of a confusion).

Whatever they are, when fitted together they give us a detailed psychiatric profile of Jenny's childhood when, orphaned as a result of an automobile accident, she was raised by her maternal grandparents, who were loving, strict and, on occasion, stupendously unfeeling.

The power of *Face to Face* is not in its case history. It's in the brilliant drama of an intelligent woman attempting to come to terms with all sorts of disappointments, which will never be made right, and contradictions that have to be reconciled. These are most movingly demonstrated in Jenny's relationship with her grandparents, especially her grandmother, who was an ogre in Jenny's childhood but whom we see, in old age, as a woman of profound gentleness and wisdom, being infinitely kind and patient to a husband who is fighting an angry losing battle with senility.

Almost ignored by the film is Jenny's husband, who is in America during most of the film and who, when we do see him, seems too priggish and dull ever to have interested a woman of Jenny's capabilities—though this may be because we are seeing him through the eyes of the woman who no longer loves him.

Face to Face is another tour de force for Miss Ullmann, who is nothing short of immense. I know of no other actress today who has at hand the reserves that enable her to move so effortlessly through such multiple levels of mood and feeling. But then nobody today except Mr. Bergman writes such roles for actresses. Erland Josephson, Miss Ullmann's costar in *Scenes from a Marriage,* is also fine in the much smaller but very affecting role of a man who might have loved Jenny but for one small impediment—his homosexuality.

With *Cries and Whispers* and *Scenes from a Marriage,* Mr. Bergman's newest film forms a trilogy quite distinct from his earlier though equally fascinating films. In these last three works, Mr. Bergman is more mysterious, more haunting, more contradictory than ever, though the style of the film has never been more precise, clear, levelheaded.

—V.C., April 6, 1976

FACES

Written and directed by John Cassavetes: cinematographer. Al Ruban: edited by Maurice McEndree and Mr. Ruban: music by Jack Ackerman: art designer. Phedon Papamichael: produced by Mr. McEndree: released by Continental Distributing. Black and white. Running time: 130 minutes.

With: John Marley (Richard Forst). Gena Rowlands (Jeannie Rapp). Lynn Carlin (Maria Forst). Fred Draper (Freddie). Seymour Cassel (Chet). Val Avery (McCarthy) and Dorothy Gulliver (Florence).

Faces, which was shown yesterday at the New York Film Festival, is incomparably better than John Cassavetes's first film, *Shadows,* and a really important movie about the American class, generation and marriage abyss. The film, which is in black and white, is part fine script, part inspired improvisation, about a middle-aged suburban couple (John Marley and Lynn Carlin) who separate for a night and sleep with a young prostitute (Gena Rowlands) and an oldish hippie (Fred Draper). The acting and characterization, down to the smallest role, are so strong and the scenes so original and sharp that the movie can be wildly funny without seeming at all satirical.

The young characters are trying to make contact, and the older people imagine that they are, but everything is lost in jokes, and formulas and self-annihilating routines. The camerawork is crude and highly imaginative. The movie is very blunt and relentless, sometimes redundant, at moments nearly unintelligible, but the entire effect is as of a high-strung, very bright documentary about the way things are.

—R.A., September 23, 1968

THE FAMILY GAME

Directed by Yoshimitsu Morita; written (in Japanese, with English subtitles) by Mr. Morita, based on the novel by Yohei Honma; cinematographer, Yonezo Maeda; edited by Akimasa Kawashima; art designer, Katsumi Nakazawa; produced by Shiro Sasaki and Yu Okada; released by The Film Society of Lincoln Center and The Film Department of the Museum of Modern Art. Running time: 107 minutes.

With: Yusaku Matsuda (Yoshimoto), Juzo Itami (Mumata), Saori Yuki (The Mother), Junichi Tsujita (Older Brother) and Ichirota Miyagawa (Shigeyuki).

"Everybody in my family is too much," says a voice on the soundtrack as, during the opening credits, we see the members of that family lined up, side by side, at the narrow, possibly imported Scandinavian dining table, noisily slurping their food and sticking elbows and arms into each other's faces. They are only four—father, mother, older brother and the hero-narrator, Shigeyuki, a misunderstood teenager—but they look like the figures in some dreadful, bourgeois parody of The Last Supper.

With these arresting images, Yoshimitsu Morita, a new young Japanese director, opens his wickedly funny The Family Game, a stylish, deadpan comedy about Japan's comparatively affluent, utterly direction-less, new middle class.

The Family Game is not always easy to follow, but it's almost always funny and, from the opening shots until the last, it's a visual adventure. The succession of brilliantly colored, often geometric compositions satirize the worst aspects of what might be called Japan's economic modernism. Mr. Morita, thirty-four years old, is clearly someone to watch.

It's fitting that The Family Game should be one of the opening attractions of this year's New Directors/New Films Festival sponsored by the Film Society of Lincoln Center and the Museum of Modern Art's Department of Film.

The family—it has no last name—lives in a high-rise apartment building in a flat that is spick-and-span and modern. On the walls there are one not-super Utrillo print and something that looks like a tacky souvenir bought in Cairo. Unfortunately the flat also is so tiny that no one has any privacy.

Shigeyuki's older brother has to walk through Shegeyuki's bedroom to get to his own. When mother and father want to have a private talk, they go downstairs and sit in their Toyota.

We never are told what father does for a living, but he makes enough money so that mother doesn't have to work—she amuses herself with leather crafts—and the sons can go to the good schools. Older brother does well at his studies but Shigeyuki is a disappointment. As the film opens, father and mother have just hired another in what has apparently been a long line of tutors for him.

The Family Game is mostly concerned with the confrontations between Shigeyuki and this new fellow, Yoshimoto, a good-looking, blandly arrogant, completely inscrutable university student who, having been promised a bonus if the boy's grades improve, is not about to fail at the job. At their first session Yoshimoto asks the boy to read something aloud, which the boy does with no interest whatsoever.

"You're cute," says the tutor, betraying no sarcasm. "All those pimples—the symbol of youth." He leans over and kisses the boy's pimply cheek.

Thus begins Shigeyuki's unsentimental education, which the tutor carries out largely by keeping the boy off balance. He sometimes encourages him with words but as often as not he ridicules him and slaps him around. Once, when Shigeyuki concedes that he is afraid of a fellow student, the tutor teaches the boy some karate basics.

Shigeyuki's grades do improve, but The Family Game isn't about Shigeyuki's immediate problems. It's about the futility of education unrelated to wisdom, about appliances that save time in which to do nothing, about urban landscapes from which all references to nature have been removed.

The film's next to last scene—a dinner to celebrate Shigeyuki's scholastic triumph—turns into a grotesquely funny shambles as the tutor, acting as sort of avenging angel, shows the family members exactly what he thinks of them. This one-man riot is the humanist's only response to the genteel inhumanism we've been witnessing throughout the film.

All of the performances are good but Ichirota Miyagawa is very good as the young Shigeyuki, and Yusaku Matsuda is wonderfully comic as the tutor.

In addition to directing, Mr. Morita adapted the screenplay from a novel by Yohei Honma. I assume he is also responsible for the extraordinary visual design, though Yonezo Maeda was the cameraman and Katsumi Nakazawa the art director. It's risky to make predictions on the basis of just one film, but *The Family Game* is so rich that Mr. Morita would seem to be one the most talented and original of Japan's new generation of filmmakers.

—*V.C., April 1, 1984*

FANNY AND ALEXANDER

Written (in Swedish, with English subtitles) and directed by Ingmar Bergman: cinematographer, Sven Nykvist: edited by Sylvia Ingemarsson: music by Daniel Bell, Benjamin Britten, Frans Heimerson, Robert Schumann and Marianne Jacobs: art designers, Anna Asp and Susanne Lingheim: produced by Jorn Donner: released by Embassy Pictures. Running time: 188 minutes.

With: Pernilla Allwin (Fanny Ekdahl), Bertil Guve (Alexander Ekdahl), Börje Ahlstedt (Carl Ekdahl), Harriet Andersson (Justina), Mats Bergman (Aron), Gunnar Björnstrand (Filip Landahl), Allan Edwall (Oscar Ekdahl), Ewa Fröling (Emilie), Bertil Guve (Alexander), Erland Josephson (Isak) and Jan Malmsjö (The Bishop).

Even as you watch Ingmar Bergman's new film, *Fanny and Alexander,* it has that quality of enchantment that usually attaches only to the best movies in retrospect, long after you've seen them, when they've been absorbed into the memory to seem sweeter, wiser, more magical than anything ever does in its own time. This immediate resonance is the distinguishing feature of this superb film, which is both quintessential Bergman and unlike anything else he has ever done before.

Fanny and Alexander is a big, dark, beautiful, generous family chronicle, which touches on many of the themes from earlier films while introducing something that, in Bergman, might pass for serenity. It moves between the worlds of reality and imagination with the effortlessness characteristic of great fiction as it tells the story of the quite marvelous Ekdahl family.

The time is 1907, and the setting is the provincial city of Uppsala. The Ekdahls represent all that is most civilized about the upper middle classes. The source of their money is commerce, but art is the center of their lives. Long before the start of the film, Oscar Ekdahl, a wealthy businessman, fell in love with and married Helena Mandelbaum, a beautiful stage actress, and built a theater for her in Uppsala.

When the film opens on Christmas Eve, the Ekdahl family is gathering for its annual holiday rituals. Helena, now old but still beautiful and a woman of great style, faces the festivities with less joy than usual. She's beginning to feel her age, and various members of the family worry her. Her eldest son, Oscar, who now manages the theater and whose wife, Emilie, is its star, is not looking well. Even though he's not a good actor, she notes dryly, he is insisting on playing the ghost in their new prouction of *Hamlet*.

Her second son, Carl, is a self-pitying failure, a professor who hates his career and loathes his servile, German-born wife. The youngest son, Gustav Adolf, is a bon vivant, a successful restaurateur with a pretty wife, who loves him dearly and finds his alliances with chambermaids only natural, in view of his inexhaustible sexual appetites.

Among the grandchildren, Helena's favorites are Alexander, who is a very solemn, sage ten, and Fanny, several years Alexander's junior, who are the children of Oscar and Emilie. Also virtually a member of the household is Isak Jacobi, a well-to-do antiques dealer and money lender who, years ago, was Helena's lover and, later, her husband's best friend. Time, in this film, is as soothing as it is relentless.

Fanny and Alexander follows the fortunes of the Ekdahl family for a little more than one tumultuous year, during which the ailing Oscar dies of a stroke and the newly widowed Emilie marries the local bishop, a stern, handsome prelate of the sort who preaches "love of truth" and whose severity his women parishioners find immensely erotic.

Though most of the film is seen through the eyes of Alexander, all of *Fanny and Alexander* has the quality of something recalled from a distance—events remembered either as they were experienced or as they are imagined to have happened. In this fashion Mr. Bergman succeeds in blending fact and fantasy in ways that never deny what we in the audience take to be truth.

Fanny and Alexander has the manner of a long, richly detailed tale being related by someone who acknowledges all of the terrors of life without finding in those terrors reason enough to deny life's pleasures.

"It is necessary and not in the least bit shameful," a slightly drunk Gustav Adolf says in the film's final, joyous sequence, "to take pleasure in the little world— good food, gentle smiles, fruit trees in bloom, waltzes." This happy occasion is the banquet celebrating the joint christening of his illegitimate daughter by the pretty chambermaid named Maj and Emilie's new daughter by the bishop. Says Gustav Adolf: "Let us be happy while we are happy. Let us be kind and generous and affectionate and good."

There are repeated references in *Fanny and Alexander* to this "little world," which in the film refers to the Ekdahls' theater, a place of melodrama, comedy, dreams, magic and moral order, in contrast to the increasing chaos of life outside.

The world of *Fanny and Alexander* also has its share of melodrama and comedy and magic and, finally, of moral order as it might be perceived by a teller of fairy tales.

The film's most riveting sequences are those that recount the unhappy adventures of Emilie, when at the request of her new husband, she takes Fanny and Alexander to live in the bishop's palace, carrying with them no possessions except the clothes they wear on their backs. The bishop's palace is a great, terrifying prison, a bleak mausoleum dominated by the scolding presences of the bishop's mother and unmarried sister and haunted by the ghosts of the bishop's dead wife and two dead daughters. How Fanny and Alexander are eventually rescued, and how the bishop meets his comeuppance, are among the most wondrous scenes Mr. Bergman has ever realized.

There's also an extraordinary sequence set in Isak's cluttered antiques shop where Fanny and Alexander are hidden after their rescue, especially a scene, set in the middle of the night, in which Alexander is convinced he's having a philosophical discourse with God.

In contrast are the exuberant Ekdahl family get-togethers, the love scenes, the moments of intimacy between Helena and old Isak. The ghost of the dead Oscar turns up frequently, sometimes just looking tired, sometimes worried about the way things are going. In one beautiful moment, Helena, alone in her summer house in the country, looks up to see Oscar watching her. Holding his hand in hers, she says with

infinite, sweet sadness: "I remember your hand as a boy. It was small and firm and dry."

The members of the huge cast are uniformly excellent, most particularly Gunn Walgren, as Helena; Ewa Fröling, who looks a lot like a young Liv Ullmann, as Emilie; Jan Malmsjö, as the tyrannical bishop, the character that, Mr. Bergman says, he most identifies with; Jarl Kulle, as the life-loving Gustav Adolf; Allan Edwall, as Oscar, both living and dead; Börje Ahlstedt, as Carl; Erland Josephson, as Isak; Harriet Andersson, as a ferocious maid who tends the children at the bishop's palace; Pernilla Wallgren, as Gustav Adolf's saucy mistress, and, of course, Bertil Guve, the remarkable young boy who plays Alexander, and Pernilla Allwin, who plays Fanny.

Fanny and Alexander, which opens today at the Cinema I and Cinema 3, is still another triumph in the career of one of our greatest living filmmakers.

—*V.C., June 17, 1983*

FANTASIA

Directed by Samuel Armstrong, James Algar, Bill Roberts, Paul Satterfield, Hamilton Luske, Jim Handley, Ford Beebe, Walt Disney, Norman Ferguson and Wilfred Jackson; written by Lee Blair, Elmer Plummer, Phil Dike, Sylvia Moberly-Holland, Norman Wright, Albert Heath, Bianca Majolie, Graham Keid, Paul Pearse, Carl Fallberg, Leo Thiele, Robert Sterner, John Fraser McLeish, Otto Englander, Webb Smith, Erdman Penner, Joseph Sabo, Bill Peet and George Stallings; music by Bach, Tchaikovsky, Dukas, Stravinsky, Beethoven, Ponchielli, Mussorgsky and Schubert, conducted by Leopold Stokowski; produced by Mr. Disney; released by RKO Radio Pictures. Running time: 120 minutes.

With: Deems Taylor (Narrator), Leopold Stokowski (Himself) and the Philadelphia Symphony Orchestra.

At the risk of being utterly obvious and just a bit stodgy, perhaps, let us begin by noting that motion picture history was made at the Broadway Theatre last night with the spectacular world premiere of Walt Disney's long-awaited *Fantasia*. Let us agree, as did almost everyone present on the occasion, that the sly and whimsical papa of Mickey Mouse, Snow White, Pinocchio and a host of other cartoon darlings has this time come forth with something that really dumps conventional formulas overboard and boldly reveals the scope of films for imaginative excursion. Let us temperately admit that *Fantasia* is simply terrific—as terrific as anything that has ever happened on a screen. And then let's get on from there.

For the vital report this morning is that Mr. Disney and his troop of little men, together with Leopold Stokowski and the Philadelphia Orchestra and a corps of sound engineers, have fashioned with music and colors and animated figures on a screen a creation so thoroughly delightful and exciting in its novelty that one's senses are captivated by it, one's imagination is deliciously inspired. In the same fresh, lighthearted spirit which has marked all their previous cartoons, Mr. Disney and the boys have gone aromping in somewhat more esoteric fields; they have taken eight symphonic numbers which are generally reserved for the concert halls, let Mr. Stokowski's band record them on multiple soundtracks and have then given them visual accompaniments of vast and spellbinding range. In brief, they have merged high-toned music with Disney's fantastic imagery.

What the music experts and the art critics will think of it we don't know. Probably there will be much controversy, and maybe some long hair will be pulled. Artistic innovations never breed content. But for this corner's money—and, we reckon, for the money of anyone who takes it in the blithe and wondrous spirit in which it is offered—*Fantasia* is enchanting entertainment. This is one time, we warrant, you won't want to listen to music with your eyes shut.

For, as mentioned, you need not expect the customary collaboration of film and music. From the beginning—from before the beginning, in fact, when vague shadows of musicians appear on the screen, when the sound of instruments being tuned is heard and when finally the theater lights go down and Deems Taylor steps up on the orchestra platform to introduce the show—it is obvious that this is a visual concert, with Mr. Taylor participating as commentator. It is, he explains, a representation of "designs and pictures and stories" that the selected music has inspired in the minds of a group of artists. Then Mr. Stokowski—or rather his shadow—dramatically ascends the podium, and the concert begins.

The first number is Bach's "Toccata and Fugue," illustrated abstractly on the screen with brilliant colors flowing and merging, lacy figures cometing through space, a skywriting cipher tracing patterns and sprays of falling stars. It is intended, obviously, to create the necessary mood of reverie, of immaterial detachment necessary to the complete comprehension and enjoyment of the entire program. At its conclusion, Mr. Taylor returns to explain the second selection—Tchaikovsky's "Nutcracker Suite"—and so the picture goes.

Space limitations prevent a detailed consideration of each number. But the high points cannot be overlooked. There is, for instance, the fragile and shimmering beauty of tiny fairies placing dewdrops on cobwebs in the first passage of the "Nutcracker Suite" and the lovable humors of the Chinese mushrooms dancing in the same selection; there is the familiar hectic comedy of Mickey Mouse in Dukas's "The Sorcerer's Apprentice," the titanic upheavals of the earth and the roaring battles of prehistoric animals in Stravinsky's "Rite of Spring," the winsome charm of baby fauns and sleek little centaurettes gamboling on pink fields of asphodel in Beethoven's "Pastoral Symphony," and the superb satire on ballet, with ostrich, hippopotamus and elephant performers, in Ponchielli's "Dance of the Hours." The final selections are Mussorgsky's "Night on Bald Mountain," visualized with a weird and terrifying assortment of skeletons, ghouls and imps swirling around the monstrous devil of the mountain, and then a solemn, liturgical illustration of Schubert's "Ave Maria."

Naturally, there are things about this film which one might readily criticize. The elaborate sound-projection system, of which there has been much talk, seems to possess many remarkable advantages, not least of which is its ability to "place" sounds. But it also amplifies them too much in certain passages—and that is hard on the ears. Also the length of the picture—more than two hours—tends to weary the senses, to dull one's receptiveness. Sometimes the color is too "pretty," especially in the "Pastoral," and frequently the dramatic action on the screen becomes so absorbing that the music, the primary music, takes an incidental place.

Both those are esthetic details that the majority will casually ignore. Mr. Disney said himself the other night that there are many problems he has yet to lick, that *Fantasia* is a frank experiment. Perhaps so, but it is also the most original and provocative film in some time. If you don't mind having your imagination stimulated by the stuff of Mr. Disney's fanciful dreams, go to see it. It's a transcendent blessing these days.

—*B.C., November 14, 1940*

FAREWELL MY CONCUBINE

Directed by Chen Kaige: written (in Mandarin, with English subtitles) by Lilian Lee and Lu Wei, based on the novel by Miss Lee: director of photography, Gu Changwei: edited by Pei Xiaonan: music by Zhao Jiping: production designer, Chen Huaikai: produced by Hsu Feng: released by Miramax Films. Running time 154 minutes.

With: Leslie Cheung (Dieyi), Zhang Fengyi (Xiaolou) and Gong Li (Juxian).

Chen Kaige's *Farewell My Concubine,* the Chinese epic that has proved so troublesome to the Communist authorities at home, is one of those very rare film spectacles that deliver just about everything the ads are likely to promise: action, history, exotic color, multitudes in confrontation, broad overviews of social and political landscapes, all intimately rooted in a love story of vicious intensity, the kind that plays best when it goes badly, which is most of the time.

Farewell My Concubine, which shared the top prize at this year's Cannes International Film Festival with *The Piano,* by Jane Campion, is a vastly entertaining movie. It's also one of such recognizably serious concerns that you can sink into it with pleasure and count it a cultural achievement.

The film will be shown at the New York Film Festival today and tomorrow. It will open commercially next Friday.

The time covered is 1925 through 1977. The setting is Beijing, earlier called Peking and, when not the national capital, Peiping. The film's title is taken from a favorite work in Chinese opera repertory, a tragic tale out of an ancient past that has become myth. It's about a concubine who's so loyal and true that rather than abandon her king as he faces military defeat, she chooses to dance for him one last time and then to cut her throat with his sword.

The opera is important to the film for several reasons. It is the work that makes stars of the two actors who are its principal characters, Dieyi and Xiaolou. It comes to dominate the professional lives of both men, and even to shape the emotional and sexual development of Dieyi, who is loved by the public for the women's roles he plays in the all-male opera company. The opera is also a reminder that in life, as in the story of the concubine and the king, each of us must take responsibility for his own fate.

Dieyi and Xiaolou meet as boys when both are apprenticed to an opera school. It is the mid-1920's, near the end of the period when warlords were the effective rulers of China. Dieyi, a pretty, gentle boy, is the son of a prostitute who dumps him at the school to get him out of the brothel. When the school's master initially refuses to accept Dieyi because he has six fingers on one hand, his mother takes an ax and chops off the extra digit.

During those first days at the school, which makes a Dickensian orphanage look like Disney World, the robust Xiaolou befriends Dieyi, initiating a relationship that becomes the obsessive center of Dieyi's life. As often happens in such fiction, crucial events in the friends' lives coincide with great public events that, in turn, shape their destinies.

In this way *Farewell My Concubine* interweaves the story of Dieyi and Xiaolou with the Japanese invasion of China in the 1930's, the surrender of the Japanese at the end of World War II, the rule of the Nationalist Government, the Chinese civil war, the victory of the *Communists* in 1949 and, finally, the Cultural Revolution (1966–1976) and its exhausted aftermath.

That's a lot of ground for any film to cover, but Mr. Chen and his screenwriters (Lilian Lee and Lu Wei) succeed with astonishing intelligence and clarity. For all of the complexities of its leading characters, *Farewell My Concubine* is not a subtle film. It's a long declarative statement, reporting complexities without in any way reflecting them, which ultimately distinguishes a film as thoroughly accomplished as this from a truly great one.

Instead of subtleties, *Farewell My Concubine* offers a physical production of grand scale and sometimes ravishing good looks, though those looks overwork the director's fondness for shooting through filtered lenses, glass, smoke, mist, gauze, fish tanks and flames. All of the sequences relating to Chinese opera are riveting, from the brutal discipline and training of the boys to their exquisite performances on the stage when they have grown up. Mr. Chen is a director who has as much command of the intimate moments as of the big scenes of crowds, chaos and confusion.

The film's central love story is actually a triangle: Dieyi, Xiaolou and Juxian, the beautiful, strong-minded prostitute whom Xiaolou, an aggressive heterosexual as an adult, marries to the furious resentment of his costar and boyhood friend. Dieyi drifts into a liaison with a rich, older opera patron. The costars break up their act on the night the Japanese enter Peiping. Yet when Xiaolou is arrested by the Japanese, it is Dieyi who sings a command performance for the occupation officers to win Xiaolou's release.

The movie is full of memorable scenes, including Xiaolou's courtship of Juxian while she's still working at the notorious House of Blossoms, and a harrowing sequence toward the end when the Red Guards successfully reduce their initially decent victims to desperate, panicked wrecks, each furiously denouncing old friends and lovers as counterrevolutionaries. It's a narrative of suicides, miscarriages, betrayals, drug addiction and sorrowful paradoxes: good intentions inevitably go wrong, which could be an observation about the Communist Revolution.

Leslie Cheung is exceptionally good as the adult Dieyi, a waif transformed into a glamorous star, a boy trained from adolescence to think of himself as a woman, and then scorned when he succeeds. He's bitchy, forever vulnerable, vain, and, in his own way, loyal to the end to his first and only love.

Zhang Fengyi's Xiaolou is equally effective, a man full of bravado but one whose sense of honor is seriously flawed. The film's most luminous presence is Gong Li (the gorgeous actress in *Raise the Red Lanterns),* who is splendid as Juxian. Hers is the movie's most sophisticated performance.

You don't have to be a China hand to understand why *Farewell My Concubine* has had the Beijing authorities climbing the walls. Though the evils it describes would not be denied by the present Communist regime, the film doesn't preach truisms. It celebrates the rights of the individual and the importance

of idiosyncrasy. Its treatment of the homosexual Dieyi is sympathetic to the point of being deeply romantic. *Farewell My Concubine* examines the activities of the Red Guards with such implacable fury that the criticism extends to the entire system itself, before and after the Cultural Revolution.

Probably the film's most maddening fault in the eyes of official Beijing, where no news is good news: It will bewitch audiences everywhere, people who have never before spent two consecutive moments thinking about the nature of the world's least-known major power.

—*V.C., October 8, 1993*

FAR FROM HEAVEN

Written and directed by Todd Haynes; director of photography, Edward Lachman; edited by James Lyons; music by Elmer Bernstein; production designer, Mark Friedberg; costumes by Sandy Powell; produced by Christine Vachon and Jody Patton; released by Focus Features. Running time: 107 minutes.

With: Julianne Moore (Cathy Whitaker), Dennis Quaid (Frank Whitaker), Dennis Haysbert (Raymond Deagan), Patricia Clarkson (Eleanor Fine), Viola Davis (Sybil) and James Rebhorn (Dr. Bowman).

At the beginning of *Far From Heaven,* the camera drifts downward toward the tidy streets of Hartford, through a screen of blood-red maple leaves. It is autumn 1957, and like the New England foliage, the people of Hartford are chilled into vivid, lurid color by the frost of middle-class, midcentury propriety. The bright clothes they wear, the baroque interiors of their houses, the jarring pastel tones of their enormous cars all stand in contrast to the constriction of their emotional lives and the narrow range of expression their bizarre, disconcertingly familiar world allows.

The visual and aural texture of Todd Haynes's ardent and intelligent new film provides a kind of subliminal commentary on its story of thwarted desire and soul-killing pretense. All of the wild, unruly feeling that the characters must repress pops to life around them, in every detail of Mark Friedberg's production design, Edward Lachman's painterly cinematography, Sandy Powell's delectable costumes and, above all, the great Elmer Bernstein's sobbing, swooping score.

Mr. Bernstein's music, which plays beneath nearly every scene, puts the melody in this melodrama, and Mr. Haynes, fading breathlessly from one scene to the next, reaches moments of operatic intensity that seem disproportionate to his tale of genteel bigotry and marital dysfunction. But that's the point of the movie, and the source of its troubling beauty. It suggests that the 50's facade of normalcy—represented by the routinized, orderly lives of Frank and Cathy Whitaker (Dennis Quaid and Julianne Moore)—concealed both incendiary passions and a ruthless social machinery devoted to their suppression.

Of course, this is hardly a new idea; it was, indeed, part of the era's understanding of itself. *Far From Heaven,* which opens today in New York and Los Angeles, is both a movie about the 50's and a tribute to some of the great movies of the 50's, in particular the Technicolor melodramas that Douglas Sirk made in collaboration with the producer Ross Hunter for Universal Pictures. (It happens that Focus Features, the distributor of Mr. Haynes's movie, is Universal's newly reorganized art-film subsidiary.)

Those pictures—including *Magnificent Obsession, Written on the Wind, Imitation of Life* and *All That Heaven Allows*—were popular with audiences in their day, but they were regarded with condescension by critics and other sophisticates suspicious of their soapy, maudlin extravagance. As was the case with so much postwar American popular culture, the subtlety and complexity of Sirk's art—in particular his subversive knack for tucking social criticism and psychological insight into stories governed by the constraints of the Production Code and the conventions of the tear-jerker—were appreciated only in retrospect, in part through Sirk's influence on later filmmakers, notably Ranier Werner Fassbinder.

Like Fassbinder, Mr. Haynes, whose previous features are *Poison, Safe* and *The Velvet Goldmine,* is interested both in updating Sirk and in reproducing his fluid, incandescent style. He wants, in effect, to appeal to that part of the audience that is flattered by knowing, analytical entertainments and, at the same time, to seduce us out of our intellectual cocoon into a state of pure, unbridled feeling—to bridge the gap between the Eisenhower-era housewives who were Sirk's original audience and the aesthetes who secured his belated entry into the auteurist pantheon.

This is a remarkable ambition, but also an eminently sensible one: the union of art and sensation, intellect and feeling, mass appeal and aesthetic refinement is something the movies are uniquely able to promise, and occasionally, when a filmmaker possesses the right mixture of calculation and compassion, able to deliver.

For a director who got his start working with Barbie dolls (in *Superstar,* his harrowing short film about the life of Karen Carpenter), Mr. Haynes is fiercely devoted to his actors. Ms. Moore, who played the unhappy suburban housewife in *Safe,* here plays a heartbreaking variation on the theme. At first, Cathy is almost a caricature of domestic fulfillment, driving her daughter home from ballet class in a sky-blue station wagon, planning her annual cocktail party with her best friend, Eleanor (the splendidly wicked Patricia Clarkson) and welcoming a reporter and a photographer from the local society pages into her meticulously decorated home.

But Mr. Haynes never mocks Cathy's happiness, even as he chronicles its unraveling. Though her face is framed by stiff curls and masked with rouge and lipstick, Ms. Moore (who was pregnant during the filming) glows with warmth, curiosity and goodness—the very qualities, Mr. Haynes suggest, that cause Cathy so much trouble.

Her life is complicated by the discovery of her husband's homosexuality and then (perhaps consequently) by her friendship with Raymond Deagan (Dennis Haysbert), a black gardener. Their relationship—chaste, but charged with mutual longing—and Frank's sexuality are, of course, matters that Sirk could have addressed only obliquely. But though he is more candid than he could have been in the 50's, Mr. Haynes refrains from tearing aside the veil of euphemism and hypocrisy that shrouds his characters' lives. For one thing, he is as fond of the language of the period as he is of its interior decoration; the dialogue he has written is highly stylized, at times almost to the point of Coen brothers campiness. Cathy scolds her son when he says things like "shucks" and "jeez," and Eleanor reels off a litany of insinuating synonyms for homosexual (the funniest of which turns out to be "wickedly successful Gotham art dealer").

But by observing—and even, to some extent, exaggerating—the decorum of the era, Mr. Haynes gives *Far From Heaven* an emotional impact that could not have been achieved by conventionally realistic means. The most casual moments are suffused with a feeling of emotional extremity; the air is as charged and threatening as it might be in a horror film. Everyone in this world seems terribly alone—Cathy increasingly so—and at the same time under constant surveillance, spied upon and gossiped about, an instant away from betrayal or ostracism.

The film's rawer moments—when Frank explodes into obscenity, when Cathy catches him kissing a man, when Raymond's young daughter is attacked by a group of white schoolboys—feel almost unbearably brutal. And the actors invest their smallest gestures with the weight of inexpressible feeling.

Mr. Quaid's handsome face is twisted with suffering and self-loathing, and his performance is all the more shattering because he thwarts our compassion. Frank's misery transmutes, all too easily, into cruelty directed at his wife. Mr. Haysbert is equally powerful in a performance that goes in the opposite direction. On the surface, Raymond is all reticence, decency and good manners—liberal Hollywood's dream of the noble, upwardly mobile Negro. But Mr. Haysbert and Mr. Haynes conspire to subvert this stereotype, too. Along with Viola Davis, who plays Cathy's housekeeper, they pay homage to Sirk's grandest, most radical picture, *Imitation of Life,* in which Juanita Moore took the cinema archetype of the selfless black servant and turned her into a human being.

And this, in effect, is what *Far From Heaven* accomplishes for all of its characters. It rediscovers the aching, desiring humanity in a genre—and a period—too often subjected to easy parody or ironic appropriation. In a word, it's divine.

—*A.O.S., November 8, 2002*

FARGO

Directed by Joel Coen; written by Joel Coen and Ethan Coen; director of photography, Roger Deakins; edited by Roderick Jaynes; music by Carter Burwell; production designer, Rick Heinrichs; produced by Eric Fellner, Tim Bevan, Ethan Coen and John Cameron; released by Gramercy Pictures. Running time: 95 minutes.

With: Frances McDormand (Marge Gunderson), Steve Buscemi (Carl Showalter), Peter Stormare (Gaear Grimsrud), William H. Macy (Jerry Lundegaard), Harve Presnell (Wade Gustafson), Kristen Rudrüd (Jean Lundegaard), John Carroll Lynch (Norm Gunderson) and Steve Park (Mike Yanagita).

Joel and Ethan Coen's new film is called *Fargo* even though most of it is set in Minnesota. Apparently the title is about something beyond geography. Testing limits, breaking boundaries, going too far: the Coen brothers' eclectic films, ranging from the great (*Barton Fink*) to the inscrutable (*The Hudsucker Proxy*), always manage to make that their guiding principle and secret weapon. They're road movies headed for the tricky unknown, and *Fargo* finds the Coens roaming exuberantly across their favorite terrain.

The Coens are at their clever best with this snowbound film noir, a crazily mundane crime story set in their native Midwest. Purportedly based on real events, it brings them as close as they may ever come—not very—to everyday life and ordinary people. Perversely, the frozen north even brings out some uncharacteristic warmth in these coolly cerebral filmmakers, although anyone seeking the milk of human kindness would be well advised to look elsewhere. The Coens' outlook remains as jaundiced as it was in *Blood Simple,* the razor-sharp 1984 debut feature that the much more stylish and entertaining *Fargo* brings to mind.

Fargo starts small and almost innocently—by the Coens' standards, anyhow. Only an opening title stating that this story has been told factually "out of respect for the dead" hints at the escalating mayhem that lies ahead. All we see at first is a beleaguered car salesman named Jerry Lundegaard (William H. Macy) hiring two hoods (Steve Buscemi and Peter Stormare) to kidnap his wife. He's in debt and needs ransom money from his father-in-law (Harve Presnell), who otherwise wouldn't give him the time of day.

These details are almost secondary to the film's more general interests: merrily evoking the singsong drabness of Midwestern life, and suggesting that this year's dominant film motif could well be Revenge of the Nerds. (*The Young Poisoner's Handbook* and the imminent *Welcome to the Dollhouse* and *I Shot Andy Warhol* all make fine, mordant use of a nerd's-eye point of view.) Certainly Jerry makes a milquetoast of a villain, what with the golf toys and matching pencils adorning his office or the galoshes and grocery bags that accompany him to a crime scene. Wide-eyed and mousy, played by Mr. Macy with fine panic-stricken timidity, he is left to handle the wild consequences of the kidnapping plot when it spins out of control.

The Coens (Joel directs; Ethan produces; both wrote this screenplay) fill *Fargo* with close encounters between the nerdy and the macabre. For instance, Jerry's wife (Kristin Rudrüd) is knitting in pink pajamas and watching perky morning television when her black-hooded kidnappers appear at the door. (She tries to fight them off by hurling a pastel-colored Princess phone.)

Even when events turn deadly, the Coens keep their emphasis on piquant weirdo details and let their mood remain impossibly light. *Fargo* is a crime tale in which somebody's foot is seen sticking out of a wood chipper. And the Coens can present that image so that its salient feature is the victim's white sock.

Fargo has as its centerpiece the gloriously unhip Marge Gunderson (Frances McDormand), exactly the rural chief of police whom Jerry Lundegaard deserves. Sometimes the camera gazes balefully at a huge statue of Paul Bunyan, but it's Marge who is this film's idea of a folk hero. Seriously pregnant, wearing a ruffled blouse or a hat with ear flaps, toddling intrepidly through the snow to investigate grisly crime scenes, Marge is this film's ace detective as well as its closest thing to a moral center. The film adores her, but it also has great fun with her lingo ("Oh, ya betcha, yah!") and with her ability to eat a hearty meal while in the presence of live bait.

Marge keeps up her domestic bliss with Norm "Son-of-a-Gunderson" (John Carroll Lynch), who paints ducks that he hopes are destined for stamps, while she also patiently pursues Jerry. And *Fargo* watches in morbid fascination as the net tightens around the film's foremost sap. Meanwhile, Mr. Buscemi's character becomes increasingly fed up with his fellow kidnapper, a stony blond who is a man of few words. (Consistent with the oddball tone, one of those words is "unguent.") When witnesses begin telling Marge about "a little guy, kind of funny look-

ing?" the net tightens around Mr. Buscemi's character, too.

As *Fargo* plays out the kidnapping and its aftermath, it sometimes turns grisly with the sharp ferocity that is another staple of the Coens' noir style. The violence is so quick it appears cartoonish, but there's no mistaking the fact that this tale is fundamentally grim. Yet the filmmakers' absurdist humor and beautifully honed storytelling give it a winning acerbity, a quirky appreciation of the sheer futility captured on screen. "There's more to life than a little money, you know," Marge tells a malefactor. "Don't you *know* that?" The characters in *Fargo* mostly wouldn't have a clue about what Marge means.

Even for filmmakers this idiosyncratic, the casting of *Fargo* is offbeat. But it works in creating a humorously drab universe where the minor characters contentedly do things like sweep slush or admire the local Radisson. Beyond Mr. Macy and Ms. McDormand, who are perfectly matched (their battles of wits are among the film's best scenes), *Fargo* makes good use of Mr. Buscemi in his cork-blowing mode, the physically daunting Mr. Stormare (from *Fanny and Alexander*), Steve Park as a very strange old friend of Marge's, and Mr. Presnell. Best known for *Paint Your Wagon* and absent from the screen for twenty-five years, Mr. Presnell has just the gruff, booming manner to explain why Mr. Macy, as his son-in-law, looks scared to death.

Fargo has been hauntingly photographed by Roger Deakins with great, expressive use of white-outs that sometimes make the characters appear to be moving through a dream. Roads disappear, swallowed up in a snowy void, making *Fargo* look eerily remote. As the title suggests, there is a steady sense of distance and uncharted territory. For all its exaggerated ordinariness, this film seems to start out where others leave off.

—*J.M., March 8, 1996*

FAST, CHEAP AND OUT OF CONTROL

Directed by Errol Morris: director of photography. Robert Richardson: edited by Shondra Merrill and Karen Schmeer: music by Caleb Simpson: production designer: Ted Bafaloukos: produced by Mr. Morris. Julia Sheehan. Mark Lipson and Kathy

Trustman; released by Sony Pictures Classics. Running time: 82 minutes.

With: Dave Hoover, George Mendoca, Ray Mendez and Rodney Brooks.

Errol Morris's delightfully exotic documentary *Fast, Cheap and Out of Control* explores the curious thoughts of four visionaries: a topiary gardener, a lion tamer, a robot scientist and an expert in the social behavior of naked mole rats. All are interesting, but certainly the most fascinating figure here is the man behind the camera. The director of *The Thin Blue Line* and *A Brief History of Time* remains a one-of-a-kind filmmaker capable of melding science, philosophy, poetry and sheer whimsy into an elaborate meditation on mankind's mysteries. He's as good a teacher as he is a filmmaker, which is saying a lot.

In *Fast, Cheap and Out of Control*, which takes its title from a hypothesis about sending robots out to explore the universe, Mr. Morris roams from garden to circus to laboratory in search of models for human behavior. He gracefully integrates conversations with four experts who, on first impression, would seem to have nothing in common. There is George Mendoca, who has spent his lifetime envisioning and pruning topiary animal shapes and who has learned to adapt his thinking to nature's patterns in the process. "This is all from memory," he explains overmodestly. "If you know what an animal looks like, you just start making the animal."

On the other end of the spectrum from natural to mechanical is Rodney Brooks, the M.I.T. robot scientist who smiles with a wild gleam in his eye when describing, say, how watching a group of ants haul a piece of breakfast cereal inspired one of his grander experiments. This display prompted him to consider the ants' collective pattern and whether such collaborative effort had a place in the robot world. Contraptions with bread-related names (Bran, Wonder, English Muffin) are seen skittering around his laboratory, giving life to this abstract theory.

Also here, and most entertaining about his research, is Ray Mendez, who wears a butterfly-patterned bow tie as he gleefully explains the ramifications of his mole rat studies. "This has got nothing to do with science," he says about his research into the creatures'

social patterns. "I look at it strictly from the point of view of self-knowledge."

Dave Hoover, a lion tamer, brings no less wisdom to bear upon the more practical problem of how to understand what a lion is thinking and how to avoid being eaten while inside a cage. A trio of lions with singed fur, having been coaxed by Mr. Hoover to leap through rings of fire at a circus, attest to the efficacy of his thinking.

Now anyone could find four offbeat experts and edit their observations into some kind of coherent whole. But Mr. Morris, in a film elegantly photographed by Robert Richardson (who has shot almost all of Oliver Stone's films) and scored with enchantingly weird music by Caleb Sampson, aspires to much more. Mr. Morris imaginatively weaves together his speakers' ideas to achieve a much larger overview than any of them achieves individually, and to make haunting connections among man, beast and machine. He starts simply and builds to unexpected metaphysical heights, expressed by images as simple, powerful and mysterious as circus elephants defying their elephant nature to walk upright in a line.

Fast, Cheap and Out of Control intersperses such eerily poetic images with flashes of the humor and even absurdity that come with life in an offbeat profession. ("They can nail you before you say oops," says Mr. Hoover about life with lions.) The film also relies on slow motion, odd angles and the special exaggeration of circus tricks to heighten its inquisitive spirit. The ultimate effect, not one often achieved on screen these days, is to illuminate and invigorate the viewer with a sense of mysterious possibility. "Does a bird fly better than a 747?" Mr. Brooks asks rhetorically. "Well, it depends on what you're trying to do."

Mr. Morris's latest intellectual adventure can be seen tonight at the New York Film Festival. (It opens commercially at the Film Forum on Friday.)

—J.M., September 30, 1997

THE FAST RUNNER (ATANARJUAT)

Directed by Zacharias Kunuk; written (in Inuktitut, with English subtitles) by Paul Apak Angilirq; director of photography, Norman Cohn; edited by Mr. Kunuk, Mr. Cohn and Marie-Christine Sarda; music by Chris Crilly; art director, James Ungalaaq;

produced by Mr. Angilirq. Mr. Cohn and Mr. Kunuk. released by Lot 47 Films. Running time: 172 minutes.

With: Natar Ungalaaq (Atanarjuat). Sylvia Ivalu (Atuat). Peter Henry Arnatsiaq (Oki). Lucy Tulu-garjuk (Puja). Madeline Ivalu (Panikpak). Pauloosie Qulitalik (Qulitalik). Eugene Ipkarnak (Sauri) and Pakkak Innukshuk (Amaqjuaq).

In standard histories of world cinema, the Inuit people of northern Canada figure mostly in connection with Robert J. Flaherty's *Nanook of the North,* an epochal silent documentary made in 1922. Eighty years later, the voices of the Inuit can at last be heard on screen. *The Fast Runner (Atanarjuat)* directed by Zacharias Kunuk and based on an ancient folk epic, is the first feature film made in the Inuktitut language by an almost entirely Inuit cast and crew. It was made, with financial assistance from the National Film Board of Canada, by Igloolik Isuma Productions. Mr. Kunuk founded this company in 1990 with Norman Cohn, the film's director of photography; Paul Apak Angilirq, who wrote the screenplay; and Pauloosie Qulitalik, a cast member, with the intention of expanding film and video productions in the aboriginal areas that now form the Canadian province of Nunavut.

All of this would be enough to make *The Fast Runner,* which will be shown tonight and tomorrow in the New Directors/New Films series at the Museum of Modern Art, a noteworthy film. It's always interesting when a hitherto unrepresented corner of the world shows up on the screen. Part of the wonder of the movies, even at this late date in their history, lies in their ability to acquaint us with cultures and places far removed from what we already know. The arrival of a movie that expands the scope of our experience, that immerses us in a radically different point of view, is always a welcome event, and such a movie does not necessarily have to be great to be interesting.

The Fast Runner, however, is not merely an interesting document from a far-off place; it is a masterpiece. Mr. Kunuk's film, which won the Caméra d'Or for best first feature at last year's Cannes International Film Festival, is much more than an ethnographic curiosity. It is, by any standard, an extraordinary film, a work of narrative sweep and visual beauty that hon-

ors the history of the art form even as it extends its perspective.

The myth that Eskimos have dozens of words for snow may have been discredited by linguists, but Mr. Cohn, using a widescreen digital video camera, has discovered at least a dozen distinct shades of white, from the bluish glow of the winter ice to the warm creaminess of coats made of polar bear fur. Shot over six months and taking place across a span of many years, *The Fast Runner* captures the movement of the seasons above the Arctic Circle and the ways climate and the migratory patterns of animals influenced the traditional Inuit way of life.

Although it has the close, intimate feel of the present tense—an effect partly of the hand-held video camera and the unaffected emotions of the actors— the film reconstructs those traditions rather than documenting them. You are so completely caught up in the codes and rituals of a nomadic, tribal society governed by complex ideas of honor and loyalty that it is easy to overlook the artistry that has put them before you. During the end credits, as if to remind the audience that this is not a documentary, the cast and crew are glimpsed in leather jackets and sunglasses, pushing sled-mounted cameras across the snow.

Though the story takes a while to establish itself, it has the clarity and power common to epics from the sagas of ancient Scandinavia to the westerns of the old Hollywood. The first half-hour, which turns out to be a prologue to the main narrative, is a little confusing, in part because it immediately plunges into arcane Inuit lore. "I can only say this story to someone who understands it," a voiceover says at the beginning, and what follows slowly creates the conditions for that understanding.

The people of Igloolik suffer under a shamanic curse that causes bad luck and dissension in their midst. Atanarjuat (Natar Ungalaaq), a child at the start of the movie, comes into a legacy of ill will when he falls in love with Atuat (Sylvia Ivalu), who has been promised to the chief's son, an arrogant hothead named Oki (Peter Henry Arnatsiaq). The rivalry between them is as violent and stirring as anything in Victor Hugo, and it fills the screen with a kind of outsize life-or-death passion that is all too rare in movies these days.

Because different camps and clans in the tribe depend on one another for survival, Atanarjuat and

Oki are continually butting heads—or, as in a ritual contest to decide who will marry Atuat, punching each other in the head. The tragic cycle of vengeance and cruelty consumes them for years, but *The Fast Runner* also abounds with humor and sensuality.

Mr. Kunuk has accomplished the remarkable feat of endowing characters from an old folk tale with complicated psychological motives and responses. The combination of dramatic realism and archaic grandeur is irresistibly powerful.

So is Mr. Zunuk's visual command. *The Fast Runner* includes some unforgettable sequences, shot in the smoky interiors of igloos, out on the ice and in fields of yellow grass and purple clover during the brief spring thaw. The most astonishing scene—during which Oki and his minions, after a brutal assault on their enemy's tent, pursue the naked, barefoot Atanarjuat across a vast expanse of ice—has already become something of a classic, a word that will quickly be bestowed on the film as a whole.

—A.O.S., March 30, 2002

FAT CITY

Directed by John Huston; written by Leonard Gardner, based on his novel; cinematographer: Conrad Hall; edited by Margaret Booth; music by Marvin Hamlisch; production designer, Richard Sylbert; produced by Ray Stark; released by Columbia Pictures. Running time: 100 minutes.

With: Stacy Keach (Tully), Jeff Bridges (Ernie), Susan Tyrrell (Oma), Candy Clark (Faye), Nicholas Colasanto (Ruben), Art Aragon (Babe), Curtis Cokes (Earl) and Sixto Rodriguez (Lucero).

In *Fat City*, John Huston's fine film version of Leonard Gardner's novel, life is having a cigarette and no match—then finding a match and getting slightly ill on the first puff.

Nothing quite works out the way it's supposed to. Before his first professional bout, eighteen-year-old Ernie Munger (Jeff Bridges) buys a sporty white dressing gown with a gold lamé collar and is knocked out after thirty-three seconds in the first round.

Tully (Stacy Keach), who could be Ernie twelve years later, by superhuman effort pulls himself up and out of Skid Row to return to the ring. He wins his comeback bout ("the most colorful fighter in northern California," his manager calls him a bit lamely), but he hasn't the endurance to follow through. He goes back to picking onions by day, spending his evenings in Skid Row bars and sleeping in flophouses.

This is grim material but *Fat City* is too full of life to be as truly dire as it sounds. Ernie and Tully, along with Oma (Susan Tyrrell), the sherry-drinking barfly Tully shacks up with for a while, the small-time fight managers, the other boxers and assorted countermen, upholsterers and lettuce pickers whom the film encounters en route, are presented with such stunning and sometimes comic accuracy that *Fat City* transcends its own apparent gloom.

It reminds me of the impatience I used to experience when it was the fashion (more than it is now) to categorize playwrights and novelists as either pessimistic or optimistic. Pessimism and optimism are beside the point of the compassion expressed in Mr. Gardner's screenplay without melodrama and without the kind of phony philosophizing that once framed the agitprop plays of Clifford Odets and others.

The film's vision is purposely limited. For at least some of its 113,000 residents, Stockton, California, where *Fat City* is set, probably is a place where things can work out. Situated in the rich San Joaquin Valley, where lettuce, onions, tomatoes and walnuts grow when most other parts of the country are under ice, Stockton is a thriving, go-getting modern American community.

Tully and Ernie and Oma, however, live on its dark side, which Huston shows us without ever indulging them or us, or for that matter, himself. Huston's affection for life's eccentrics, as well as its rejects and misfits, is legendary—so much so that it has sometimes seemed as if he had cast his films as if running a mission.

In *Fat City* he has kept himself under control. The result is one of the three or four most beautifully acted films seen so far this year. Keach and Bridges, who are comparatively known quantities, are splendid, but so are some faces that are new to me, including Nicholas Colasanto, Art Aragon, Curtis Cokes and especially Miss Tyrrell, who plays one of the first believable drunks I've ever seen on screen.

Mr. Gardner's screenplay, of course, is something quite special, full of the kind of dialogue that movies usually can't afford, that defines time, place, mood and character while seemingly going nowhere. Nobody ever manages to say exactly what's on his mind or, if he does, to admit it. "Is it my fault that you can't fit in?" screams Oma at her black lover in between her protestations of love for him in a crowded bar. At other times, the characters trade clichés as solemnly as marriage vows. "You're not fulfilled," Ernie says sadly to the girl he has just deflowered. "I *am* fulfilled," she answers without enthusiasm, working him carefully toward a proposal by making him feel a thorough cad.

For years, Huston has been fooling around with movies as if he weren't interested. *Fat City,* which opened yesterday at the Columbia II, shows us the director of *The Treasure of the Sierra Madre* and *The Asphalt Jungle* working with his old meticulousness but without recourse to either the comic or melodramatic crutches that have, in recent years, seemed to set the director apart from his films, as if to hide any real feelings.

—V.C., July 27, 1972

FATAL ATTRACTION

Directed by Adrian Lyne; written by James Dearden; director of photography, Howard Atherton; edited by Michael Kahn and Peter E. Berger; music by Maurice Jarre; production designer, Mel Bourne; produced by Stanley R. Jaffe and Sherry Lansing; released by Paramount Pictures. Running time: 121 minutes.

With: Michael Douglas (Dan Gallagher), Glenn Close (Alex Forrest), Anne Archer (Beth Gallagher), Ellen Hamilton Latzen (Ellen Gallagher), Stuart Pankin (Jimmy), Ellen Foley (Hildy) and Fred Gwynne (Arthur).

Years hence, it will be possible to pinpoint the exact moment that produced *Fatal Attraction,* Adrian Lyne's new romantic thriller, and the precise circumstances that made it a hit. It arrived at the tail end of the having-it-all age, just before the impact of AIDS on movie morality was really felt. At the same time, it was a powerful cautionary tale. And it played skillfully upon a growing societal emphasis on marriage and

family, shrewdly offering something for everyone: the desperation of an unmarried career woman, the recklessness of a supposedly satisfied husband, the worries of a betrayed wife. What's more, it was made with the slick, seductive professionalism that was a hallmark of the day.

Fatal Attraction, which opens today at the Paramount and other theaters, is a thoroughly conventional thriller at heart, but its heart is not what will attract notice. As directed by Mr. Lyne, who also made *9½ Weeks* and *Flashdance,* it has an ingeniously teasing style that overrules substance at every turn. Mr. Lyne, who displays a lot more range this time, takes a brilliantly manipulative approach to what might have been a humdrum subject and shapes a soap opera of exceptional power. Most of that power comes directly from visual imagery, for Mr. Lyne is well versed in making anything—a person, a room, a pile of dishes in a kitchen sink—seem tactile, rich and sexy.

That kitchen sink is quite literally thrown into the torrid romance of Dan Gallagher and Alex Forrest, played by Michael Douglas and Glenn Close, neither of whom has previously given off much heat in other roles. However, Mr. Lyne's handiwork transforms them into a convincingly passionate pair. The change in Miss Close is especially startling, with the witchy blond tendrils and hard, steady gaze that make her character so seductive and finally so frightening. She first meets Dan at a party, then at a weekend business meeting and after that Mr. Lyne toys luxuriantly with the viewer's expectations. In a film of his, even Miss Close's signaling Mr. Douglas to wipe some cream cheese off his nose during the meeting can have a remarkable charge.

It's raining after the meeting. Her umbrella works, his doesn't. He suggests they have a drink somewhere, and they do, and what happens after that is no surprise, nor is it made out to be any of Dan Gallagher's doing. His wife, who happens to be gorgeous and perfect (as played by Anne Archer, whose glamorous presence does a lot to make the extramarital affair seem unlikely), happens to be away for the weekend. So what does he do? He doesn't bother to resist, that's all. Audiences who saw the seduction coming will also see its by-product, a streak of persistence and vindictiveness from the woman who considers herself wronged. As in *Play Misty for Me,* still a classic of this genre, this spurned lover's pique becomes ever more terrifying as the film progresses. Most of her tricks are unsurprising, but they are unnerving anyway, so effectively does Mr. Lyne create the happy Gallagher family that Alex means to destroy. The film becomes more predictable and violent as it goes along, but at least one of her methods, having to do with the Gallaghers' search for a storybook house in the suburbs, is indeed ingenious.

Fatal Attraction provides some textbook examples of how to scare an audience even when the audience knows what's coming (though there's one final touch that's inexcusable). It also offers a well-detailed, credibly drawn romantic triangle that's sure to spark a lot of cocktail-party chatter. The fact that Dan Gallagher's home life seems so happy only makes matters more interesting, as does the film's refusal to explain him. It's even difficult to tell anything about this man's inner life from Mr. Douglas's performance, and that may be the point. He doesn't understand it either.

Contributing greatly to the film's success are a nicely direct screenplay by James Dearden, warmly handsome photography by Howard Atherton, a thoroughly credible production design by Mel Bourne and a wonderful and unaffected performance by Ellen Hamilton Latzen, who plays the Gallaghers' daughter.

—J.M., September 18, 1987

FATER OF THE BRIDE

Directed by Vincente Minnelli; written by Frances Goodrich and Albert Hackett, based on the novel by Edward Streeter; cinematographer, John Alton; edited by Ferris Webster; music by Adolph Deutsch; art designers, Cedric Gibbons and Leonid Vasian; produced by Pandro S. Berman; released by Metro-Goldwyn-Mayer. Black and white. Running time: 92 minutes.

With: Spencer Tracy (Stanley T. Banks), Joan Bennett (Ellie Banks), Elizabeth Taylor (Kay Banks), Don Taylor (Buckley Dunstan), Billie Burke (Doris Dunstan), Leo G. Carroll (Mr. Massoula), Moroni Olsen (Herbert Dunstan) and Melville Cooper (Mr. Tringle).

To the best of our knowledge, nobody has yet set out to compile a dependable set of statistics that would show whether marriages in this land have been to any extent discouraged by Edward Streeter's *Father of the Bride*. That is a job of social research which has apparently been overlooked by the scholarship-granting foundations—and it's probably just as well. For the likelihood is that such statistics would only prove that this wonderful book has merely terrified a few vulnerable parents and caused five million other folks to split their sides.

Such, we feel sure, will be the consequence—and the only consequence—of the equally wonderful film which M-G-M has now fashioned from Mr. Streeter's delightful book. For the film, while it packs all the satire of our modern tribal matrimonial rite that was richly contained in the original, also possesses all the warmth and poignancy and understanding that makes the Streeter treatise much beloved. Those who would check this estimation may do so at the Music Hall.

Frankly, this corner had anxieties as to how any studio would contrive to get the essential authenticity of *Father of the Bride* onto film. So many previous pretensions at mirroring our middle-class life have gone up in synthetic blazes that we definitely feared the worst. But obviously we reckoned on something less than a finely blended script from Frances Goodrich and Albert Hackett, on something cruder than the deft directorial hand of Vincente Minnelli and on someone less magnificent than Spencer Tracy in the title role. We might also add that we reckoned on something less than the excellent cast that supports Mr. Tracy in the effort and on a production nowhere near so exact.

From the moment the picture opens, with Mr. Tracy slumped wearily in a chair amid all the litter and leavings of a played out wedding feast, one can sense that the M-G-M craftsmen have got it off on the right foot, and from the moment he starts his peroration, you know he's the man for the job. There is recognizable back-break in that litter and there's a true edge to Mr. Tracy's voice. Here is the veritable image of the thoroughly squeezed father of the bride.

And all that succeeds as retrospection upon the events leading up to this collapse is utterly apt and consistent with the verities of normal family life. There's the staggeringly casual announcement by the daughter to her parents one night that she and a certain Buckley, an indistinguishable suitor, plan to wed. There's the midnight resentment of papa in his nice suburban home, the utter contentment of mama—

and then the sudden reversal of moods. There's the "fatherly talk" with Buckley to find out how he is fixed, and there's the nervous visit of the parents with the equally nervous father and mother of the intended groom. Indeed, there is in this picture every episode of any consequence in the book, all constructed to illustrate completely the vast hilarity of preparing a girl to wed. And all of them add up to something that is grandly funny, sharp and just a bit sad.

Throughout these demonstrations, Mr. Tracy conducts himself with precisely the air of self-importance that a bride's father likes to think he has, coupled with the mingled indignation and frustration that he is sure to acquire. Further, he has a capacity to show that warmth and tenderness toward his own that flavors with universal poignance the irony of the joke on him. As a father, torn by jealousy, devotion, pride and righteous wrath, Mr. Tracy is tops.

And right beside him are Joan Bennett as the typical mother of the bride, Elizabeth Taylor as the happy little lady and Don Taylor as the overshadowed groom. Nor far behind them are Moroni Olsen, Billie Burke, Leo G. Carroll, Melville Cooper and Rusty Tamblyn in other highly recognizable roles.

Yes, *Father of the Bride* is a honey of a picture of American family life. It shouldn't discourage matrimony but—well, this reviewer is certainly happy to have all sons.

—*B.C., May 19, 1950*

FELLINI SATYRICON

Directed by Federico Fellini: written (in Italian. with English subtitles) by Mr. Fellini. Bernardino Zapponi and Brunello Fellini. based on the fragment *Satyricon* by Gaius Petronius: cinematographer. Giuseppe Rotunno: edited by Ruggero Mastroianni: music by Nino Rota: art designer. Luigi Scaccianoce: produced by Alberto Grimaldi: released by United Artists. Running time: 120 minutes.

With: Martin Potter (Encolpius). Hiram Keller (Ascyltus). Max Born (Giton). Capucine (Tryphaena). Salvo Randone (Eumolpus). Magali Noel (Fortunata). Alain Cuny (Lichas). Lucis Bose (Suicide Wife). Tanya Lopert (Caesar). Gordon Mitchell (Robber) and Fanfulla (Vernacchio).

In almost every film Federico Fellini has ever made, the sea has occupied a very special place, sometimes as the ultimate barrier between confusion and understanding, sometimes as a kind of vast, implacable presence that dimly recalls protozoan origins. *La Strada, La Dolce Vita* and his newest, most tumultuous movie, *Fellini Satyricon,* all end by the edge of the sea.

Watching *Fellini Satyricon,* which opened yesterday at the Little Carnegie Theater, you suddenly realize that Fellini, unlike the creatures of his extraordinary imagination, has refused to be stopped by the sea. He has pushed on, and there are moments when he seems to have fallen over the edge into the cinema of the ridiculous. You ask yourself: Is this dwarf, or this albino hermaphrodite, or is this latest amputation, really necessary? However, he finally arrives, if not at understanding, then at a magnificently realized movie of his own—and our—wildest dreams.

There have already been lots of pious alarms sounded over the excesses of it all, statements to the effect that it is fascinating to look at, but . . . and debates about its profundity—all of which strike me as about as relevant as finding oneself on Venus and complaining that one's Boy Scout pocket compass doesn't work. Even though I feel the film does have meanings, including dozens Fellini himself may be unaware of, *Fellini Satyricon* is essentially its own justification, as is any work of art.

The film, which uses the director's name in the title to differentiate it from another Italian film based on the same source, is Fellini's adaptation of the satiric novel by Petronius Arbiter, written in the first century A.D. *Satyricon* has survived in such fragmentary form that all scholars do not necessarily agree whether it is a moral essay or simply a catalogue of the sexual achievements, most of them perverse, of its student-hero, Encolpius, his boy-lover, Giton, who has the constancy of a cloud, and his best friend.

Sometimes together, sometimes separately, Encolpius, Giton, and Ascyltus wander across the face of the Roman Empire, either participating in (often as victims) or just observing orgies, feasts, festivals, murders, abductions, you-name-it.

This is the first time that Fellini has based a feature

film on a borrowed source, which may be the reason why the movie, although as fragmented in continuity as the literary work, achieves a classic dimension that is new for Fellini. Paradoxically, it is also his most original film. Fellini has done nothing less than create a new world, a kind of subterranean Oz, a world of magic and superstition, without values, without government, without faith and almost totally without conscience. It has the quality of a drug-induced hallucination, being without past or future, existing only in a present that, at best, can be survived.

Fellini Satyricon also has the form of theater, of ritual, to such a degree that there is no difference between the reality of the film and the reality of a play-within-the-film or of the dryly comic legend of the Widow of Ephesus, which is pictured as it is being told by a storyteller at a sulphurous banquet.

This is made apparent from the very first frame, when Encolpius is discovered, back to camera, standing off to one side before a wall that is blank except for some odd graffiti. After a minute or two of rapid-fire, theatrically declaimed exposition, Encolpius turns to face the camera. From that moment on, Fellini fills in the blank wall. Quite literally, he turns his characters into art. The tale never ends. The film simply stops, in mid-sentence, as Encolpius, Giton, Ascyltus and all of the other Fellini phantoms take their places in the fragments of a lovely wall painting that overlooks a serene sea.

The most spectacular aspect of the film, which is essentially descriptive rather than narrative, is the decor, the color, for everything has been manufactured by Fellini. Like El Greco, Fellini scorns natural sunlight. Even exterior landscapes have been photographed in such a way as to suggest the exotic fraud of the steamy, hermetic interiors. When Encolpius goes to retrieve his beloved Giton, who has been purchased by an actor, you aren't sure for a moment whether he has wandered into life, or into a play, although everyone seems to be speaking Latin and not Italian.

Even Fellini's casual way of synchronizing dialogue with lip movements works here. Dialogue comes to sound like incantation, instead of information. The individual elements of the film are realized with such conscious style that all of the nonacting, as well as the scenes of violence, or of copulations performed by

persons fully clothed, have the effect of ritual, rather than the reality of some gaudy Italian spear-and-sandal epic, to which *Fellini Satyricon* is actually related, as all movies are related, though distantly.

The cast is a typical, multinational, Fellini mélange of amateurs and professionals, each one of whom exists principally as a face or just as a physical presence rather than as a performer. Most prominent are Martin Potter, an Englishman, and Hiram Keller, an American, who play Encolpius and Ascyltus and who might pass as a couple of Andy Warhol's tough-soft leading men. Max Born, a young Englishman who resembles Joan Collins in drag, is Giton, an existentical cupid as might be imagined by Genet.

Although all of the women in the film, with the exception of a patrician's wife (played by Lucia Bose), are harpies of terrifying scale, I don't think Fellini is pushing homosexuality, which he depicts with such noneroticism that the movie looks almost chaste.

Fellini Satyricon is no more about homosexuality, than it is about ancient Rome. It is a surreal epic that, I confidently believe, will outlive all its interpretations.

—V.C., March 12, 1970

LA FEMME INFIDÈLE

Directed and written (in French, with English subtitles) by Claude Chabrol: cinematographer, Jean Rabier: edited by Jacques Gaillard: music by Pierre Jansen: art designer, Guy Littaye: produced by Andre Genoves: released by Allied Artists. Running time: 98 minutes.

With: Stéphane Audran (Helene Desvallées). Michel Bouquet (Charles Desvallées). Maurice Ronet (Victor Pegala). Serge Bento (Bignon). Michel Duchaussoy (Police Officer Duval) and Guy Marly (Police Officer Gobet).

*L*a Femme Infidèle, which opened yesterday at the Little Carnegie, tells the story of a happy family that is somewhat upset when the husband murders his wife's lover but ultimately finds a yet richer harmony in the wife's new respect for her husband's initiative and prowess. In concept and execution, it is a film so calmly and thoughtfully perverse that it can have been born only in the unique cinematic imagination of Claude Chabrol.

Claude Chabrol (*The Cousins, Leda, Les Bonnes*) is a highly intelligent French New Wave director who, because he works in conventional forms (most of his movies are murder stories) has never excited the dedicated following that has maintained interest in his colleagues Godard and Truffaut. When he needed to, he made spy thrillers for money—and his commercial films look almost as personal as his art films. With *Les Biches* (1967), his reputation took a swing upward, at least in America, and *La Femme Infidèle* should establish him with audiences who may at last be open to what makes his vision strange and wonderful.

Chabrol once filmed a modern version of the Hamlet story in which Claudius was innocent and the only person left both alive and sane at the end was Ophelia. He doesn't see things the way most people do. He sees the same things, and he often sees them better (the handsome suburban house and the Paris apartment in *La Femme Infidèle* offer fine lessons in traditional interior decorating—with deep browns and blues and muted yellow greens), but he sees them as odd.

In the film, just before Charles (Michel Bouquet) bops Victor (Maurice Ronet), his wife's lover, over the head with a weighty little portrait bust, he discovers a keepsake on Victor's night table. It is a giant Zippo pocket lighter that he had given his wife on a wedding anniversary (although he is the one who smokes—to incredible excess), and the sight of this huge grotesquerie actually brings tears to his eyes and impels him to fight for his marriage by eliminating Victor.

For the most part, the world of *La Femme Infidèle* is resolutely good-looking. Chabrol fills his rooms with fresh flowers and with a sense of orderly livability. But the most subtle dislocations catch you up. The camera tracks with lyrical gravity—but with a little too much lyrical gravity, like a gesture so little in excess of the occasion that it would seem nearly perfect if you hadn't sensed that it was also slightly mad. Michel Bouquet for example, plays Charles with great suavity and grace—except that he stares intently, and I do believe he is a trifle cross-eyed. And though he is the image of a man born to be cuckolded (like a French Herbert Marshall), he happens to have a pretty good time with his wife.

So the plot of *La Femme Infidèle* makes even less sense than many Chabrol plots—which doesn't matter, because the meaning has less to do with sense than with sensibility. However, even in this context Charles's adventures in disposing of Victor's body (a long, entertaining sequence—and a tribute to Hitchcock's *Psycho*) have so little to do with the case as to mislead the moviegoer temporarily as to the kind of film he is watching.

But the moviegoer will be reassured when he returns his attention to the unfaithful wife herself. The actress is Stéphane Audran, Chabrol's own wife, and she is beautiful, though a little ironic. She controls a sense of social parody so sustained that her simple "Bonjour" becomes a major critique of French language and civilization.

Near the very end of the film, when she accidentally discovers that her husband has killed her lover, she destroys the evidence (no use; the police will come for him shortly) and then walks out to where he is working in his garden. As the camera travels with her, it watches in medium close-up while she composes the beginnings of a smile.

The making of that smile, enigmatic and discreet, must count as one of the finest small passages in the history of cinema—and in the lovely, disquieting art of Claude Chabrol.

—*R.G., November 10, 1969*

LA FEMME NIKITA

Written (in French, with English subtitles) and directed by Luc Besson; director of photography, Thierry Arbogast; edited by Olivier Mauffory; music by Eric Serra; production designer, Dan Weil; released by the Samuel Goldwyn Company. Running time: 117 minutes.

With: Anne Parillaud (Nikita), Jean-Hugues Anglade (Marco), Tcheky Karyo (Bob), Jeanne Moreau (Amande), Jean Reno (Nikita's Friend) and Jean Bouise (Chief of Intelligence).

The most popular film in France during the last twelve months has been *La Femme Nikita*, a slick, calculating mixture of French contemplativeness and American flying glass. Directed by Luc Besson, whose dazzling early ingenuity (in his austere science-fiction film *Le Dernier Combat*) subsequently gave way to high style and hot air (in *Subway* and *The Big Blue*), *La Femme Nikita* combines hip violence, punk anomie, lavish settings and an old-fashioned paean to the power of love.

These unlikely ingredients are held together by Mr. Besson's frankly commercial but agile direction, and by the strange and vicious Nikita (as played by the striking Anne Parillaud). Wearing chopped-off hair and a dazed expression, Nikita is first seen taking part in a drugstore robbery; more accurately, she is being dragged along for the ride. Yet for all her apparent blankness, Nikita is tough. In the aftermath of a lurid shoot-out, she emerges as the only member of her gang to have survived. And she manages to attack and kill several policemen before the incident is over.

Nikita (named for an Elton John song) is sentenced to a prison term, and then behaves so badly that she is administered what seems to be a lethal injection. But she wakes up anyway, asking angrily whether she has arrived in heaven. Not really, but she has stumbled onto something almost as promising: a second chance. Nikita is told she must learn to "read, walk, talk, smile and even fight" for the sake of her country.

Thus begins the glamorous part of *La Femme Nikita*, in which this previously unmanageable street punk is transformed into a chic, ladylike assassin. Nikita is equipped with makeup, high heels, a little black dress and pearls and sent to work her wiles in various high-risk situations. She is given tactical advice by Jeanne Moreau, who appears briefly as a beauty consultant and tells her of "two things that have no limit: femininity and the means of taking advantage of it." Nikita is also told to "smile when you don't know something: you won't be any smarter, but it's nice for the others."

The film, like Nikita herself, becomes more conventionally sleek and less interestingly bizarre as it moves along. The latter part of the story alternates between intrigue episodes (in one, Nikita dresses up as a hotel maid to deliver a poisoned room-service meal) and scenes that reveal Nikita's softer side. It turns out, not very surprisingly, that Nikita is susceptible to love. The film supplies both Bob (Tcheky Karyo), the government interrogator who becomes her Pygmalion, and Marco (Jean-Hugues Anglade), the charming supermarket checkout clerk who wins Nikita over while ringing up her ravioli.

Mr. Besson brings on Marco with typically broad flair. First he shows the coltish Nikita scrambling to figure out what to buy in a supermarket as she studies the other shoppers; then he makes a pleasant joke of Marco's incompetence when they meet. The ravioli dinner these two subsequently share in Nikita's unfinished apartment gracefully fades into a scene set six months later, when the place is furnished and the couple have set up housekeeping together. The smoothness with which these transitions are executed goes a long way toward making *La Femme Nikita* attractive.

Yet the film eventually loses sight of its heroine, and bogs down in fatuous speculation about her moral standing. She has, after all, committed various murders during the course of the story. But both Bob and Marco are willing to attach more weight to the way Nikita looks in an evening dress than to her lethal track record. Mr. Besson also betrays his initial conception of Nikita as brutal and remorseless by letting her melt into an ordinary figure, even a mundane one.

La Femme Nikita is best taken lightly and appreciated for the high-gloss effectiveness of Mr. Besson's methods. Among the film's most striking ingredients are the pumped-up violence of its shoot-out scenes, the sumptuous settings of a long Venetian sequence during which Nikita carries out a foreign assignment and Miss Parillaud herself, a nimble and dangerous-looking actress with a fashion model's leggy cachet. This actress makes Nikita a femme fatale in every way.

— *J.M., March 8, 1991*

THE FISHER KING

Directed by Terry Gilliam; written by Richard LaGravenese; director of photography, Roger Pratt; edited by Lesley Walker; music by George Fenton; production designer, Mel Bourne; produced by Debra Hill and Lynda Obst; released by Tri-Star Pictures. Running time: 135 minutes.

With: Jeff Bridges (Jack), Robin Williams (Parry), Mercedes Ruehl (Anne), Amanda Plummer (Lydia) and Michael Jeter (Homeless Singer).

The cry of contrition that is sounded in *The Fisher King* can be heard long after the film is over. In bringing a jaded late-1980's celebrity to the brink of destruction and then allowing him to do penance for his cynicism, this film strikes at the heart of something disturbingly real. That, apparently, was not enough for the filmmakers, who have feverishly piled on elements of whimsy, mythology and romance to what was never a simple concept in the first place. The likelihood of creating an unholy mess is further heightened by the throwing in of the Holy Grail.

Yet *The Fisher King,* directed by the ever-fanciful Terry Gilliam from an ingenious if loose-knit screenplay by Richard LaGravenese, is capable of great charm whenever its taste for chaos is kept in check. For every wild ride through Manhattan by an imaginary Red Knight trailing billows of flame, there is a small, comic encounter in a more down-to-earth mode.

The source of much of this appeal is obvious: the film's stars, particularly Jeff Bridges as a fallen radio star and Mercedes Ruehl as the sweetly flamboyant video-store owner who loves him, bring an emotional authenticity to material that could easily have had none. Only Robin Williams, as a gentle soul who has been left homeless and driven half-mad by grief, is allowed to chatter aimlessly, cavort naked in Central Park and generally go overboard.

The Fisher King begins stunningly well with a few glimpses of Jack Lucas (Mr. Bridges), a sleek, mean-spirited radio bully who is quite literally on top of the world. Seen in his fashionably dehumanized high-rise apartment, or in his limousine, sneering at a panhandler from behind dark glasses, Jack is instantly emblematic of the coldhearted excesses of his time. As the deejay sits in his bathtub, Mr. Gilliam, working with rare restraint, and Mr. Bridges, abandoning all traces of his usually ingratiating manner, create a chillingly indelible image of Jack's spiritual emptiness. His face caked eerily with a rejuvenating cosmetic mask, Jack tries repeatedly to master the line "Hey, forgive me!" for a possible role in a television show.

Moments later, Jack's career has ended and his quest for real forgiveness has begun. A deranged caller on Jack's radio show, taking his cue from the host's insults, has committed mass murder in a yuppie bar. When Jack is next seen, three years later, he is as demoralized and barren as the mythical figure for whom the film is named. He now looks disheveled and lives listlessly with Anne Napolitano (Ms. Ruehl), who has clearly not been successful in rekindling his spirits. The only things that attract Jack's notice are unfortunate ones, like the fact that the television series that

treated "Hey, forgive me!" as a comic punch line has gone on to become a hit without him.

Jack is at the end of his rope, almost literally, when he meets Parry (Mr. Williams), the colorful derelict who takes many of his cues from visions of "hundreds of the cutest little fat people floating right in front of me." Parry, who lives in a drab, industrial boiler-room setting that recalls the look of Mr. Gilliam's earlier Brazil, turns out to be a casualty of the yuppie-bar tragedy, and as such he holds forth the possibility of Jack's redemption.

So Jack begins devoting himself to rehabilitating Parry, which will turn out to be a two-pronged mission. He must help Parry win the woman he loves, a shy eccentric (Amanda Plummer) who is adorable to Parry even when she accidentally drops dumplings onto her lap. And he must reclaim the Holy Grail from the place where Parry is sure, in today's world, that it must reside: a billionaire's apartment on Fifth Avenue. "Who'd think you could find anything divine on the Upper East Side?" Parry wisecracks in typically facile style.

The screenplay's enthusiasm for the mythological aspects of the story is clearly genuine, and the central myth indeed seems apt in a modern setting. But *The Fisher King* still strains to accommodate it, perhaps because so much other antic activity is allowed to swirl around on the sidelines. Even though Mel Bourne's production design fuses the modern and the medieval in fascinating ways, the narrative itself often seems confused and cluttered.

The film's flights of fancy begin to derail its story line very soon after Jack's fall from grace, and by the tale's strange and equivocal last episodes this shapelessness has become exhausting. Mr. Gilliam, though working in a much more controlled style than usual, nonetheless often chooses to sustain a funhouse atmosphere at the expense of dramatic development. What emerges, in the end, are a clever premise that has been allowed to go awry and several performances that are lively and unpredictable enough to transcend the confusion. Mr. Bridges, always a fine intuitive actor, has never displayed a greater range.

Mr. Williams, when not off on any of his various tangents, brings a disarming warmth and gentleness to the fiendishly comic Parry. Ms. Ruehl again proves herself to be a fiery comedian graced with superb timing. Ms. Plummer gives the film's most restrained performance, which will provide some idea of the others.

And Michael Jeter is heartbreakingly funny in a brief turn as a frenetic gay singer who does a mean Ethel Merman impression and also momentarily works the thought of AIDS into the film's overripe atmosphere. The best parts of *The Fisher King* and its mad, whirling vision of modern life are those that see grief lurking just beneath the surface.

—*J.M., September 20, 1991*

FIST IN HIS POCKET

Written (in Italian, with English subtitles) and directed by Marco Bellocchio: cinematographer, Alberto Marrama: edited by Aurelio Mangiarotti: music by Ennio Morricone: art designer, Gisella Longo: produced by Ezio Passadore: released by Peppercorn-Wormser. Black and white. Running time: 105 minutes.

With: Lou Castel (Alessandro). Paola Pitagora (Giulia). Marino Mase (Augusto). Liliana Gerace (Mother). Pier Luigi Troglio (Leone) and Jennie MacNeil (Girlfriend).

*F*ist in His Pocket (for some reason someone has amputated a fist and a pocket from any likely translation of *I Pugni In Tasca*) is the first and strongest movie by the Italian director Marco Bellocchio (whose *China Is Near* was released earlier this year). It is sealed and stifling, gray and extremely powerful—about as attractive as somebody coughing wretchedly beside you on a subway. And as insistent. It is not for seeing on a day when you are celebrating something. On the other hand, on a day when you can face it, it is very much worth seeing.

The movie is about four people in an Italian provincial family, whose very existence drain the possibility for the happiness of a fifth, the oldest son. The mother of the family is a blind and whimpering widow, who collects dusty closets full of *Pro Familia* (a magazine she requires her sons to read to her) and who sits passively as the cat licks the food from her plate. Her youngest son is demented and misshapen, with an insectoid thorax and a moronic laugh; he steals spoonfuls of sugar from the sugar bowl.

Her middle son is only an epileptic, and her daughter—but for her isolation in the oppressive villa in which they live—is almost normal. But the quality of their lives is illustrated by what the oldest, healthiest son does for entertainment: he shoots rats at night on the town garbage dump. This son wants to get married; with his familial responsibilities, he does not have the freedom or the money to.

The middle son, as an act of intelligence and courage, decides to do himself and all the defective others in, so that his healthy brother can be free. He fails when he tries it in one fell swoop, but he does better when he works by degrees. He pushes his mother off a cliff. He drowns his younger brother in the bath. There are shots of wakes and the depressing snows of Northern Italy. It is morbid, and convincing and written exactly right, yet everyone who has ever thought for an instant that his only hope lay in doing somebody in can't help indulging in a small, dark Rickety, Tickety Tin.

The movie is absolutely true to the writhing, sordid and incestuous predicament of the family and yet it leaves each person touching, and even reasonable. The acting, on the part of Lou Castel, Paola Pitagora, Marino Mase, Liliana Gerace, Pier Luigi Troglio, and Jennie MacNeil is so convincing, as a unit, that it seems the family has been lifted from life, in a jar, intact. Miss Pitagora is particularly fine as the sister—horrified, guilty and yet aroused and released by what her brother has done. And Mr. Castel, as the brother Alessandro, epileptic and also choking on his desire to live, is remarkable—through a daring final scene in which he is required to have a terminal epileptic fit in time with the "Sempre Libera" aria from *La Traviata*.

What is strong and original in the picture is that it shows people just poor enough and just handicapped enough to be unfit to join the community of people for whom happiness is at all possible. One sees such people everywhere, in the cities and in the towns; everyone occasionally teeters far enough out of life to be among them. And yet they are very seldom effectively portrayed on film. In this line Bellocchio's talent is altogether new and powerful.

—*R.A., May 28, 1968*

FITZCARRALDO

Written (in German, with English subtitles) and directed by Werner Herzog: cinematographer:

Thomas Mauch: edited by Beate Mainka-Jellinghaus: music by Popol Vuh, Giuseppe Verdi, Vincenzo Bellini and Richard Strauss: art designer: Henning von Gierke: produced by Mr. Herzog and Lucki Stipetic: released by New World Pictures. Running time: 157 minutes.

With: Klaus Kinski (Brian Sweeney Fitzgerald-Fitzcarraldo), Claudia Cardinale (Molly), José Lewgoy (Don Aquilino), Miguel Angel Fuentes (Cholo), Paul Hittscher (Captain) and Huerequeque Enrique Bohorquez (Huerequeque).

Forget everything you've heard so far about Werner Herzog's *Fitzcarraldo,* which brings the 20th New York Film Festival to a metaphysically rowdy, upbeat end tonight at Lincoln Center. The film will be shown in Avery Fisher Hall and will open its regular commercial engagement tomorrow at the Paris Theater.

Fitzcarraldo may well be a madman's dream, but it's also a fine, quirky, fascinating movie. It's a stunning spectacle, an adventure-comedy not quite like any other, and the most benign movie ever made about nineteenth-century capitalism running amok.

There is a danger that one's perception of what is actually on the screen might be clouded by all of the publicity surrounding the film's lengthy production in the Peruvian Amazon basin, when Jason Robards had to leave because of illness, Mick Jagger because of other commitments and everyone had to put up with physical hardships that no film is worth.

Mr. Herzog, starting over from scratch with Klaus Kinski in the title role, finally completed the film so successfully that it is difficult to imagine what it might have been otherwise.

Don't be put off by the fact that Mr. Kinski, the most idiosyncratic of German actors, plays an Irishman, one Brian Sweeney Fitzgerald, known as Fitzcarraldo among the Spanish-speaking rubber barons whose company he keeps in turn-of-the-century Iquitos, Peru. Mr. Kinski is as Irish as sauerbraten, but then the rubber barons and other residents of Iquitos and the upper reaches of the Amazon also didn't speak German, as they do in *Fitzcarraldo. Fitzcarraldo* has its own reality.

This Fitzcarraldo is something of a nut and a laughing stock among the other Europeans who have swarmed into the Amazon to make their fortunes in the rubber boom. Wearing a soiled white planter's suit and his hair always standing on end, even after it has been brushed, Fitzcarraldo is an affront to civilized eyes and a jester to the Indians.

His attempt to build a trans-Andean railroad has collapsed after the laying of a few yards of tracks and the importing of a single locomotive to sit on them. When the film opens, he is busy losing whatever shirts he has left in the ice-making business in Iquitos. Financial failure of such consistency, at such a time, isn't easy. It must be pursued with dedication.

Fitzcarraldo's flaw—which is not exactly tragic—is that he has no interest in money for its own sake. He doesn't long for the luxuries of Manaus, the rubber capital of Brazil, whose newly rich burghers send their laundry to Portugal. Fitzcarraldo finds it difficult to pay attention to the petty details of business because he is interested only in what he will do with his profits, which, of course, never materialize.

Fitzcarraldo's goal is to make enough money to build an opera house in Iquitos, more rococo than the one in Manaus, and to import a company of singers headed by Enrico Caruso, whose records he plays on what looks to be RCA's first Victrola. In this wild endeavor he has the patient, loving support of Molly (Claudia Cardinale), the madam of the most popular brothel in Iquitos, who, in her own way, is touched by the madness that inspires Fitzcarraldo.

Though she appears only at the beginning and the end of the film, Molly sets the comic tone of the film that, incorrectly, is likely to be compared to Mr. Herzog's *Aguirre, the Wrath of God.* Although both films are set in the same part of the world, and both are scenically splendid and star Mr. Kinski, they are completely different works. The story of Fitzcarraldo and Molly is more reminiscent of *The African Queen,* but this analogy shouldn't be pursued. Where *The African Queen* is sweet, *Fitzcarraldo* is likely to be abrasive. It's not slick.

Supported by Molly's belief in him and by her bank account, Fitzcarraldo sets out to make a fortune by opening up a tract of rubber trees on a spread roughly the size of Belgium. The reason the land comes so cheap is that it is inaccessible, an inconvenience that Fitzcarraldo plans to eliminate by taking a large steamer up one jungle river, hauling it in one piece over a mountain and relaunching it in the river on the other side, which has access to his lands.

This is the film's magnificent centerpiece, in which Fitzcarraldo is joined by his ship's nearly blind European captain (Paul Hittscher), a giant Indian mechanic (Miguel Angel Fuentes), a drunken cook (Huerequeque Enrique Bohorquez), and hundreds of Indians who have their own inscrutable reasons for supporting the project.

These scenes are as extraordinary as Mr. Herzog intended them to be, but the movie contains more. There is the film's introductory sequence, in which Fitzcarraldo and Molly travel in a small open motorboat 1,200 miles down the Amazon from Iquitos to Manaus to hear Caruso—paddling the last mile or so with a single oar. For a few moments, we see the great Caruso (Costante Moret) on the Manaus stage in Verdi's *Ernani*, costarring with a masculine-looking Sarah Bernhardt (Jean-Claude Dreyfuss), who lipsyncs the lyrics being sung by a woman who is very visible in the orchestra pit.

I've no idea whether or not this is based on historical fact but, if not, it's a glorious invention. It's also far more satisfying than the movie's climactic sequence, which, probably because of production problems, appears to be composed of two sets of footage shot some months apart.

Miss Cardinale is not on-screen as long as one might wish, but she not only lights up her role, she also lights up Mr. Kinski. Molly's belief in Fitzcarraldo helps to transform Mr. Kinski into a genuinely charming screen presence. This adds a whole new dimension to an actor known primarily for playing megalomaniacal tycoons, international crooks and vampires. He is very fine. So, too, are the supporting actors, including José Lewgoy, a Brazilian actor who plays a genially sadistic Iquitos millionaire who supports Fitzcarraldo in order to witness some gaudy new failure.

Mr. Herzog did not set out to make what he calls "an ethnic film," and *Fitzcarraldo* is certainly no such thing. Yet the film, beautifully photographed by Thomas Mauch, is an exotic, visual treat. The Indians are a handsome people who remain remote and unexploited, though one of their beliefs—or, at least, a belief attributed to them—is appropriated by Mr. Herzog to make one of those points that, under the circumstances, might well have gone without saying. That is that "life is the illusion behind which lies the reality of dreams."

A small reservation to a big film.

—*V.C., October 10, 1982*

FIVE EASY PIECES

Directed by Bob Rafelson: written by Adrien Joyce, based on a story by Mr. Rafelson and Ms. Joyce: director of photography. László Kovacs: edited by Gerald Shepard and Christopher Holmes: music by Johann Sebastian Bach. Wolfgang Amadeus Mozart and Frédéric Chopin: produced by Mr. Rafelson and Richard Wechsler: released by Columbia Pictures. Running time: 96 minutes.

With: Jack Nicholson (Robert Eroica Dupea). Karen Black (Rayette Dipesto). Billy Green Bush (Elton). Fannie Flagg (Stoney). Sally Ann Struthers (Betty). Marlena MacGuire (Twinky). Lois Smith (Partita Dupea) and Helena Kallianiotes (Palm Apodaca).

*F*ive *Easy Pieces,* which played last night at Philharmonic Hall (the one American fiction movie in the regular events of this year's Film Festival) and opens today at the Coronet Theater, is the second feature of Bob Rafelson, a young director whose name will probably not be remembered in connection with his first film, *Head.*

Head suffered from its cast, the Monkees, and from an ad campaign that perhaps did more for the publicist than for the client (you may recall a month when New York was inundated with mysterious posterphotographs of John Brockman's head), but it was a better movie than most critics allowed—largely because it had at least as many ideas as it had technical resources and because it kept turning its excesses into playful but responsible style. *Head* was a movie that had nowhere to go except down, but in retrospect, doesn't seem all that bad.

I'm not sure how *Five Easy Pieces* will seem in retrospect—perhaps not all that good. It has its own redherring equivalent to John Brockman's head—in the folly of a title that everybody seems to find terribly provocative but that refers more logically to piano pieces for the beginner. And it has a trip—north to Alaska—which is part of a fairly elaborate central metaphor. And it is full of ideas, and a style—in this case, a rigorously deliberate and plain style—that is not less insistent than the canny exuberance of *Head.*

Five Easy Pieces is an open-ended story, like much recent American fiction, satiric in thrust (notice the names in the cast of characters) and elegiac in mood, about a young California oil worker (Jack Nicholson) who travels up to his family's island home on Puget Sound where he sees his dying father, makes a sexual conquest and visits his past—before heading further north.

By inclination the young man is very rootless-contemporary-American, with a country-and-western–loving mistress (Karen Black), beer in the refrigerator, and nights out at the bowling alley. But his family is well-off, musical, and eccentric; his brother and sister (Ralph Waite and Lois Smith) concertize; and he himself has given up a career—more or less in the name of aimless integrity. Before he seduces his brother's fiancée (Susan Anspach), he plays for her—an easy piece—but scorns her reaction: "I faked a little Chopin. You faked a little response."

Something of this exchange carries into my feeling about *Five Easy Pieces,* which at first appears to be rich with a quantity of felt life, but on reflection seems both more carefully studied and more coldly casual than profoundly understood. In all nonessentials it is moviemaking of a very high order. But scene by scene I find myself moving from sympathy, to admiration, to respect—for a performance, for László Kovac's evocative photography, or merely for the superior quality of the color film used in capturing the soft, wet, lovely ambience of the Pacific Northwest.

The acting is generally good, but except for Karen Black's pathetically appealing vulgarian, it lives in bits and pieces, rather than in a quality of sustained characterization. Almost everybody in *Five Easy Pieces* is a caricature but plays for all-round sentiment, and in context the one pointedly funny single-dimension role (Helena Kallianiotes as a tough lesbian hitchhiker on her way to Alaska to escape America's accumulated filth) looks like a tour de force.

Five Easy Pieces is built around a series of good-byes. As the central character divests himself of responsibilities, of people and possessions, finally of the coat off his back (rather too pointedly—just before hitching his own symbolic ride North) the film grows heavy with a kind of poignancy that for all its understatement leans heavily on a stock of quite unearned response.

Rafelson is expert at supporting this movement, and the film proceeds from scene to scene with a quiet competent modernism that bespeaks quality, but that more often begs than provides expression. Greater things seem always to be in the offing. But I think they are an illusion. *Five Easy Pieces* is a film that takes small risks and provides small rewards.

—*R.G., September 12, 1970*

THE FLAMINGO KID

Directed by Garry Marshall: written by Mr. Marshall and Neal Marshall, based on a story by Neal Marshall: director of photography, James A. Contner: edited by Priscilla Nedd: production designer, Lawrence Miller: produced by Michael Phillips: released by Twentieth Century Fox. Running time: 100 minutes.

With: Matt Dillon (Jeffrey Willis), Hector Elizondo (Arthur Willis), Molly McCarthy (Ruth Willis), Martha Gehman (Nikki Willis), Richard Crenna (Phil Brody), Jessica Walter (Phyllis Brody), Carole R. Davis (Joyce Brody), Janet Jones (Carla Samson), Brian McNamara (Steve Dawkins) and Fisher Stevens (Hawk Ganz).

Garry Marshall's *Flamingo Kid* is an ebullient, unsentimental *Summer of '42*, updated to the summer of 1963, about Jeffrey Willis (Matt Dillon), an upwardly mobile Brooklyn teenager whose father is a plumber and proud of it.

The film, which opens today at the Warner Twin and other theaters, is by far the best—and funniest—work yet done by Mr. Dillon, for whom Jeffrey Willis is a welcome change of character from the moody, brooding young men he's played in the past. With his flat-top crew cut, his utterly open though not unknowing expression—and wearing his somewhat square sports shirts, plus his ever-present pork-pie hat—Mr. Dillon creates a memorably comic hero. His Jeffrey Willis is not exactly Tom Jones, but even if *The Flamingo Kid* comes out of sitcom country, the character and the performance effortlessly rise above their origins.

The Flamingo Kid is also the best work yet done in theatrical films by Mr. Marshall, the television whiz who created, among other hit series, *Happy Days, Laverne and Shirley* and *Mork and Mindy.* The film has the kind of slickness one expects of the most popular television fare, but it also has a bit of the satirical edge of a film like Elaine May's *Heartbreak Kid.*

The screenplay, by Mr. Marshall and Neal Marshall, who is no relation, is set mostly in and around a busy, superbly garish Long Island cabana club, always referred to as "the El Flamingo." This is an overcrowded, sweaty playground for Long Island's nouveau riche, mostly nouveaux arrivals from Brooklyn, who spend their days getting dangerously tan, taking rumba lessons and playing nonstop games of gin rummy for huge stakes.

In the course of this one, minutely momentous summer, Jeffrey learns all about high life on that part of the south shore of Long Island that's just a Ping-Pong ball's toss from the Rockaways. Much to the fury of his practical, no-nonsense father, Arthur (Hector Elizondo), Jeffrey has turned down a summer job as a messenger for an engineering firm to become a parking lot attendant at the El Flamingo.

Under the benign guidance of the club's gin rummy champion, Phil Brody (Richard Crenna), who's made his money as a sports car dealer, Jeffrey advances from parking lot attendant to cabana boy and finds himself being groomed by Phil for a career "in sales," which would mean bypassing college. Jeffrey's blue-collar father is furious. On the other hand, Phil blithely points out that he himself didn't need a college education to reach the heights. Says Phil, as he takes Jeffrey for a spin in every young guy's dream of a red Ferrari: "Socrates rode around on a donkey."

Jeffrey's summer, which also includes a fairly chaste but tantalizing affair with a blond beauty (Janet Jones) from California, runs a conventional but unexpectedly witty course. The film is very good about Jeffrey's prickly relations with his family, particularly with his father, and about his education by the rich.

There's a very funny dinner at the Brodys' somewhat palatial Long Island residence where Jeffrey learns about tomato aspic, which he doesn't like. Neither does Phil, who yells across the table to his wife (Jessica Walter), "Phyllis, I don't want anything on my plate that moves!" Jeffrey also astonishes the Brody family by his unconscious habit of humming while he eats—he's the Glenn Gould of Brooklyn gourmets.

Beginning with Mr. Dillon's, there's not a bad or even middling performance in the film. Mr. Crenna and Miss Walter are extremely funny as the nouveau riche couple and Mr. Elizondo is excellent as Jeffrey's father, a role written and played with such understanding that the conventions never slip into clichés.

Garry Marshall, who has written and produced several theatrical films, and who made his debut as a director with *Young Doctors in Love,* here shows complete control of his material. Unlike something on the order of *The Cotton Club, The Flamingo Kid* never wanders around looking for itself. Every scene, every cut, every shift in mood demonstrates its efficiency.

—V.C., December 21, 1984

THE FLY

Produced and directed by Kurt Neumann; written by James Clavell, based on a story by George Langelaan; cinematographer, Karl Struss; edited by Merrill White; music by Paul Sawtell; art designers, Lyle Wheeler and Theobold Holsopple; released by Twentieth Century Fox. Running time: 94 minutes.

With: Al Hedison (Andre), Patricia Owens (Helene), Vincent Price (Francois), Herbert Marshall (Inspector Charas), Kathleen Freeman (Emma) and Charles Herbert (Philippe).

It flew in yesterday, *The Fly* did—and folks, hang on to your hair. This Twentieth Century Fox fantasy-thriller, which the company is advertising as the absolute end in horror, alighted at more than one hundred neighborhood theaters.

It does indeed contain, briefly, two of the most sickening sights one casual swatter-wielder ever beheld on the screen. At one point, the hooded hero discloses his head as that of a giant-size fly. And the climax, when this balcony-sitter nearly shot through the roof, is a fat close-up of a fly, with a tiny, screaming human's head, trapped by a spider on its web. To any random customer expecting a pleasant doze, watch out! Short as these two scenes are, there's no escaping them.

Otherwise, believe it or not, *The Fly* happens to be one of the better, more restrained entries of the "shock" school. As produced and directed by the late Kurt Neumann, with an earnest little cast headed by Al Hedison, Patricia Owens, and Vincent Price, this is a quiet, uncluttered, and even unpretentious picture, building up almost unbearable tension by simple suggestion.

Most of it takes place in and around the sunniest of homes, that of a highly likable young Montreal scientist, Mr. Hedison, his wife, Miss Owens and their youngster, Charles Herbert. One of the most appealing things about the picture is the pretty pleasantry and chilling contrast of the everyday setting, nicely framed in color and CinemaScope. Most appealing of all, however, is the compassion blended in with the suspense when something terrible happens in Mr. Hedison's basement laboratory.

This altruistic chap somehow has evolved a method of electronically disintegrating objects, then materializing them at a distance. Foolishly, he experiments with himself, a housefly intrudes, and—flash!—the man and the tiny creature have proportionately exchanged heads.

We learn this slowly, bit by bit, in the hysterically scribbled messages he feeds his terrified wife. The idea is to find the fly, still flitting about the premises, put the two of them back together in the original enclosure and turn on the juice again.

If this story, adapted by James Clavell from an original by George Langelaan, sounds like a sidesplitting howl, it doesn't play that way. Not with the shaking, hooded figure lunging at a blackboard for "Plees help—find fly—LOVE YOU."

The sight of Miss Owens, Master Herbert and Kathleen Freeman, the cook, stalking the little critters upstairs is enough to freeze anyone's blood. And even the "murder" flashback that spans the entire film finally clicks into place logically as a mercy killing.

This is quite a little picture. Even with the laboratory absurdities, it holds an interesting philosophy about man's tampering with the unknown. Mr. Marshall, as a police inspector, mumbles like a fly's drone. All the others, including Mr. Price as a family friend, are fine.

By deftly easing some nice people in and out of a situation as pathetic as it is horrible, Mr. Neumann has wrought the most originally suggestive hair-raiser since *The Thing.*

—*H.T., August 30, 1958*

FORCE OF EVIL

Directed by Abraham Polonsky: written by Mr. Polonsky and Ira Wolfert. based on Mr. Wolfert's novel *Tucker's People*: director of photography. George Barnes. edited by Art Seid and Walter Thompson: produced by Bob Roberts: released by Metro-Goldwyn-Mayer. Black and white. Running time: 78 minutes.

With: John Garfield (Joe Morse). Thomas Gomez (Leo Morse). Marie Windsor (Edna Tucker). Howland Chamberlain (Freddie Bauer). Roy Roberts (Ben Tucker). Paul Fix (Bill Ficco). Stanley Prager (Wally). Barry Kelley (Detective Egan). Paul McVey (Hobe Wheelock) and Beatrice Pearson (Doris Lowry).

It may be that *Force of Evil,* which opened at Loews State on Christmas Day, is not the sort of picture that one would choose for Yuletide cheer. It's a cold, hard, relentless dissection of a bitter, aggressive young man who lets himself get in too deep as the lawyer for a "policy racket" gang. And as such it is full of vicious people with whom the principal boy associates, it reeks of greed and corruption and it ends in death and despair.

But for all its unpleasant nature, it must be said that this film is a dynamic crime-and-punishment drama, brilliantly and broadly realized. Out of material and ideas that have been worked over time after time, so that they've long since become stale and hackneyed, it gathers suspense and dread, a genuine feeling of the bleakness of crime and a terrible sense of doom. And it catches in eloquent tatters of on-the-wing dialogue moving intimations of the pathos of hopeful lives gone wrong.

Written by Abraham Polonsky and Ira Wolfert from the latter's acid book, *Tucker's People,* about the numbers racket, and directed by Mr. Polonsky, it gets right at the matter or petty gambling from the bottom to the top. It gives a fair understanding of the vast and monstrous scale on which the numbers business is established. And it hints obliquely at political hook-ins.

But this isn't the main thing about it. Racketeers are still racketeers and the operation of numbers is special but not unique. The main thing about this picture is that it shows, in plausible terms, the disintegration of a character under the too-heavy pressure of his sense of wrong.

In their up-from-nothing lawyer who gets himself

in too deep on the moral excuse that he is doing it for his brother, a middle-aged man, Mr. Polonsky and Mr. Wolfert have some real things to show about the practical operation of the psychology of crime. And in the frenzied romance of this tough lawyer with a decent but daring little girl, they say something rather disturbing about lust for the dangerous and unknown.

They do it in startling situations and in graphic dialogue, in shattering cinematic glimpses and in great, dramatic sweeps of New York background. New to the business of directing, Mr. Polonsky here establishes himself as a man of imagination and unquestioned craftsmanship.

True, he was very fortunate in having John Garfield play the young lawyer in the story, for Mr. Garfield is his tough guy to the life. Sentient underneath a steel shell, taut, articulate—he is all good men gone wrong. And a new little actress named Beatrice Pearson is something of a lucky feature, too. With her innocent, worldly demeanor, her shyness yet forwardness, too, and a voice that would melt a pawnbroker, she points up the pathos in the tale.

But Mr. Polonsky's direction of Thomas Gomez, who does a fine, tense job as the small-time brother of the tough guy; of Roy Roberts, who plays Tucker, the big boss, and of half a dozen others shows that he has the stuff. In this particular picture, produced by Bob Roberts for Enterprise, we have a real new talent in the medium, as well as a sizzling piece of work.

—B.C., December 27, 1948

FOR WHOM THE BELL TOLLS

Produced and directed by Sam Wood; written by Dudley Nichols, based on the novel by Ernest Hemingway; cinematographer, Ray Rennahan; edited by Sherman Todd and John F. Link; music by Victor Young; production designer, William Cameron Menzies; released by Paramount Pictures. Running time: 170 minutes.

With: Gary Cooper (Robert Jordan), Ingrid Bergman (Maria), Akim Tamiroff (Pablo), Katina Paxinou (Pilar), Vladimir Sokoloff (Anselmo), Arturo de Córdova (Augustin), Mikhail Rasumny (Rafael) and Fortunio Bonanova (Fernando).

With such fidelity to the original that practically nothing was left out except all of the unmentionable language and the more intimate romantic scenes, Ernest Hemingway's wonderful novel of the Spanish civil war, *For Whom the Bell Tolls,* has been brought to the screen in all its richness of color and character. By and large, it is the best film that has come along this year, and its opening last night at the Rivoli was a truly deserving "event." For, in spite of its almost interminable and physically exhausting length—it takes two hours and fifty minutes to cover less than four days in a group of people's lives—and in spite of some basic detruncations of the novel's two leading characters, it vibrates throughout with vitality and is topped off with a climax that's a whiz.

As often is the case with pictures that are based upon popular works, a thorough comprehension of this one may depend on whether one has read the book. For the fundamental emphasis of the novel upon the rapturous and tragic love of Robert Jordan, the American dynamiter, and Maria, the orphaned Spanish girl, has been vitiated in large measure by the obvious blanks compelled by the Hays code. And as a consequence, the cosmic symbolism of their regenerative love, set against a background of violence and the impending prospect of death, will barely be comprehensible only to those who have read the book. To others the love of Robert and Maria will be little more than good boy-meets-girl.

But so much that was fine in the novel and so much that was humanly true have been faithfully reproduced in the picture that the other is not too greatly missed. Now the emphasis is primarily upon the conflict within the band of Loyalist Spanish guerrillas to whom Robert Jordan goes for aid in his perilous mission to blow up an enemy bridge. And the study of character among those Spaniards, the definition of the braves and the cowards, is the matter of absorbing interest for at least two-thirds of the film.

The rest is the tingling action-business of the calculated blowing of the bridge, which is as tense and vivid melodrama as anyone could normally stand. And this is preceded by a thrilling representation of the fight of El Sordo's little band against the troop of Nationalist cavalry which comes into the mountains to ferret them out.

Incidentally, the political sympathies of the characters are perfectly clear. The protagonists are plainly

345

antifascists, and this fact is, at one point, well expressed. However, the political confusion and ramifications of the civil war are as vague and strangely amorphous as they were in Mr. Hemingway's book.

In their fidelity to the novel, Dudley Nichols, who wrote the screenplay, and Sam Wood, who directed for Paramount, were overzealous, if anything, and lingered too long over matters which might have been profitably compressed. Mr. Nichols, in his script, caught the flavor and the spirit of the novel handsomely, and Mr. Wood gained an intimacy with the characters through constant close-ups which is well-nigh unique. The quality of their work is flawless. There is only too much of it.

However, the superb characterizations are the outstanding merit of the film. Gary Cooper as Robert Jordan and Ingrid Bergman as Maria are fine, though limited in their opportunities. Miss Bergman is perhaps a shade too gay. But Katina Paxinou as Pilar, the rugged Spanish woman who is the tower of strength, is a marvel of tenderness and violence, the Spanish peasant character in fluid mass. And Akim Tamiroff as Pablo is a masterpiece of dark and devious moods, as fine an expression of animal treachery and human pride as has ever been put on the screen.

Likewise, Vladimir Sokoloff as Anselmo, the aged man of iron; Joseph Calleia as El Sordo, the invincible; Mikhail Rasumny as Rafael, the gypsy clown; Fortunio Bonanova as Fernando, the realist; and many more perform excellently. The film is well worth seeing for its assorted characters alone.

And also it is produced as magnificently as any film has ever been. Photographed very largely in the High Sierras in Technicolor that is breathtakingly fine, it has the hard texture of granite, the rough and vivid colors of all outdoors. And some of the close shots of the characters have the brilliance of Goya paintings. By and large, it is a picture that offers many rewards. It's a shame, to put it bluntly, that in it art is so long and life so short.

—*B.C., July 15, 1943*

FORBIDDEN GAMES

Directed by René Clément; written (in French, with English subtitles) by Mr. Clément, Jean Aurenche and Pierre Bost, based on the novel *Les*

Jeux Inconnus by François Boyer; cinematographer, Robert Julliard; edited by Roger Dwyre; music by Narciso Yepes; art designer, Paul Bertrand; produced by Robert Dorfman; released by Times Film Corporation. Black and white. Running time: 102 minutes.

With: Brigitte Fossey (Paulette), Georges Poujouly (Michel), Lucien Hubert (Father Dolle), Suzanne Courtal (Mother Dolle), Jacques Marin (Georges Dolle), Laurence Badie (Berthe Dolle), Andre Wasley (Father Gouard), Amédée (Francie Goulard) and Louis Saintève (The Priest).

It had been the vague hope of many that the French would eventually come through with a film that would boom such shattering comment upon the tragedy and irony of World War II as their memorable *Grand Illusion* did for World War I. That hope at last has been realized. Such a film came along yesterday to the Little Carnegie. It is René Clément's *Forbidden Games* (*Jeux Interdits*).

A great deal of professional excitement was aroused in Europe by this film, and some of that bubbling excitement had been transmitted over here. For one thing, the film stirred howling protests last spring from visiting critics after a special screening at the Cannes Film Festival because it had not been selected as an official entry of France. For another, it almost got a fast brush at the subsequent Venice Festival, on the grounds that it wasn't eligible because it already had been shown at Cannes—and then, when it was accepted, it won the Venice Grand Prize. And, finally, it has been lambasted (as was inevitable) by certain elements abroad as a vicious and unfair picture of the peasantry of France.

All of this rambling excitement may have sounded excessive over here, especially in the light of some confusions at previous European festivals. But now that the film has been exhibited and its qualities revealed on this side, it may be reported confidently that the excitement is not only understandable but entirely justified. For *Forbidden Games* is a brilliant and devastating drama of the tragic frailties of men, clear and uncorrupted by sentimentality or dogmatism in its candid view of life.

As *Grand Illusion* found its area for comment upon the irony of war outside the actual range of warfare—

it was about war prisoners, you may recall—this film finds its area for comment upon the damage that has been done to humankind in the seemingly innocent realm of farmers and children in the undisturbed countryside. The towering symbol of the war's vast devastation is one little five-year-old girl. And her immediate world, as we see it, is mostly that of a French peasant's farm.

But out of these plain and modest elements, M. Clément, who directed and helped to write the script with Jean Aurenche and Pierre Bost from an original screen story by François Boyer, has fused a powerful drama that cuts a wide swath through the fields of man's ripe hopes and symbolizes the frustration that many Europeans must feel about war.

For the little girl of this story is a pitiful orphan of the war—a child who has seen her two parents and her little dog killed on the road while they were fleeing from the oncoming Germans and has found sanctuary in a peasant home and in the wonderfully sympathetic companionship of a slightly older peasant boy. The only thing is that this youngster has a fondness for the symbols of death—a fondness in which her new companion encourages and comforts her by killing other animals and burying them, with ceremonials, beside the grave of her dog. And the irony is that the peasants have no way to help with this strange attitude because, as is demonstrated, they are burdened and confused by their own pitiably ignorant, hypocritical and inhuman fixed ideas about death.

We will not attempt a recital of the shattering details of this haunting film—of the swiftness of its dramatic passage from the most tender and heart-tearing scenes of attachment between the naïve children to scenes of earthy and ghoulish comedy in which the remarkably credible peasants demonstrate their pathetic crudity. Nor can we express sufficient admiration for the brilliant acting of it—for the five-year-old girl, Brigitte Fossey, from whom M. Clément has got a performance that rips the heart out with its simplicity and sincerity; for a youngster named Georges Poujouly, who makes of the little boy not a creature of juvenile mischief but of spiritual magnificence; for Lucien Hubert, as the boy's peasant father; Suzanne Courtal, as the latter's wife, and for all the remaining actors in this extraordinary film.

All to be said at the moment is that M. Clément has brought forth a film that has the irony of a *Grand Illu-sion*, the authenticity of a *Harvest*, and the fineness of French films at their best.

—B.C., December 9, 1952

A FOREIGN AFFAIR

Directed by Billy Wilder: written by Charles Brackett. Mr. Wilder. Richard Breen and Robert Harari. based on a story by David Shaw: cinematographer. Charles Lang: edited by Doane Harrison: music by Frederick Hollander: art designers. Hans Dreier and Walter Tyler: produced by Mr. Brackett: released by Paramount Pictures. Black and white. Running time: 116 minutes.

With: Jean Arthur (Congresswoman Phoebe Frost). Marlene Dietrich (Erika Von Schluetow). John Lund (Captain John Pringle). Millard Mitchell (Colonel Rufus J. Plummer). Peter von Zerneck (Hans Otto Birgel) and Stanley Prager (Mike).

Maybe you think there's nothing funny about the current situation of American troops in the ticklish area of Berlin. And it's serious enough, heaven knows, what with the Russians pushing and shoving and the natives putting on their own type squeeze. But, at least, Charles Brackett and Billy Wilder have been happily disinclined to wax morose about the problems presented by occupation—and by "fraternization," specifically. Rather these two bright filmmakers have been wryly disposed to smile upon the conflicts in self and national interests that proximities inevitably provoke. And in their most recent picture, a comedy romance, called *A Foreign Affair,* they have turned out a dandy entertainment that has some shrewd and realistic things to say.

Congress may not like this picture, which came to the Paramount yesterday. And even the Department of the Army may find it a shade embarrassing. For the Messrs. Brackett and Wilder, who are not the sort to call a spade a trowel, as was eminently proved by their honest and hard-hitting film *The Lost Weekend,* are here making light of regulations and the gravity of officialdom in a smoothly sophisticated and slyly sardonic way.

Particularly, their interest is in how human beings behave when confronted by other human beings—

347

especially those of the opposite sex. And their logical conclusion is that, granted attractions back and forth, most people—despite regulations and even differences in language and politics—are likely to do toward one another that which comes naturally.

Taking as their point of observation an American Congresswoman in Berlin, accompanying a Congressional committee sent to investigate the morale of American troops, the Messrs. Brackett and Wilder have looked realistically upon the obvious temptations and reactions of healthy soldiers far from home. They have wisely observed that black markets are not repugnant to boys with stuff to trade and that frauleins are simply bobby-soxers with a weakness for candy bars. They have slyly remarked that Russian soldiers love to sing gymnastic songs and that Americans are nothing loath to join them of a quiet night in a smoky café. And especially have they noted that an American captain may actually fall in love with a svelte German nightclub singer and take her beneath his protective custody, even though she may have been the mistress of a former Nazi trump.

Of course, they have made these observations in a spirit of fun and romance. And the shame of the captain's indiscretion is honorably whitewashed in the end. But there is bite, nonetheless, in the comment which the whole picture has to make upon the irony of big state restrictions on the level of individual give-and-take.

Under less clever presentation this sort of traffic with big stuff in the current events department might be offensive to reason and taste. But as handled by the Messrs. Brackett and Wilder as producer and director of this film—and also as its principal writers—it has wit, worldliness and charm. It also has serious implications, via some actual scenes in bombed Berlin, of the wretched and terrifying problem of repairing the ravages of war. Indeed, there are moments when the picture becomes downright cynical in tone, but it is always artfully salvaged by a hasty nip-up of the yarn.

Much credit is due the performers. Jean Arthur is beautifully droll as the prim and punctilious Congresswoman who has her eyes popped open to the power of love. And John Lund is disarmingly shameless as the brash American captain. Millard Mitchell gives a trenchant imitation of a wise and sharp-eyed colonel in Berlin and three or four other fellows are richly amusing as just plain Joes.

But it is really Marlene Dietrich who does the most fascinating job as the German nightclub singer and the charmer par excellence. For in Miss Dietrich's restless femininity, in her subtle suggestions of mocking scorn, and in her daringly forward singing of "Illusions" and "Black Market," two stinging songs, are centered not only the essence of the picture's romantic allure, but also its vagrant cynicism and its unmistakable point.

—B.C., July 1, 1948

THE FORTUNE COOKIE

Produced and directed by Billy Wilder; written by Mr. Wilder and I. A. L. Diamond; cinematographer, Joseph LaShelle; edited by Daniel Mandell; music by André Previn; art designer, Robert Luthardt; released by United Artists. Black and white. Running time: 125 minutes.

With: Jack Lemmon (Harry Hinkle), Walter Matthau (Willie Gingrich), Ron Rich (Luther "Boom Boom" Jackson), Cliff Osmond (Mr. Purkey), Lurene Tuttle (Mother Hinkle), Judi West (Sandy) and Harry Holcombe (O'Brien).

Billy Wilder is a cranky, perhaps even dangerous, man. That is, he is an unregenerate moralist whose latest vision of the American Dream, titled *The Fortune Cookie,* is a fine, dark, gag-filled hallucination, peopled by dropouts from the Great Society. It arrived here yesterday at the Astor, Trans-Lux East and Murray Hill Theaters.

The Fortune Cookie is no more sunny—and, if possible, even less romantic—than *Kiss Me, Stupid,* Mr. Wilder's last film and a comedy of unrelieved vulgarity, but it has style and taste. It is also an explosively funny live-action cartoon about petty chiselers who regard the economic system as a giant pinball machine, ready to pay off to anyone who tilts it properly.

The chief chiselers are Walter Matthau, an ambulance-chasing legal eagle, and Jack Lemmon, his schnook brother-in-law, a television cameraman whom Matthau entices into an elaborate, one-million-dollar insurance swindle after Lemmon is slightly roughed up while covering a Cleveland Browns football game.

Hovering around them, like molting vultures, are Judi West, Lemmon's ex-wife who returns to the hearth following the scent of money; Lurene Tuttle, his termagant mother; and a grotesque assortment of nieces and nephews, doctors, nurses and private eyes.

What makes them funny is that they see themselves at the center of a constantly expanding universe that, Mr. Wilder seems to say, is roughly the size of Cleveland and made of dreams of Thunderbirds, fur jackets, two-week trips to Florida, even a wife—or, just about anything that money can buy.

Mr. Matthau, with eyes that are in a perpetual squint of calculation, makes a fine figure of a comic villain—bushy-browed, chop-licking, impudently optimistic even in the face of disaster. He looks, in fact, like the cat in the Tom & Jerry cartoons as he persuades Mouse Lemmon to go along with the caper: "What's wrong?" he snarls. "Insurance companies have so much money—they have to microfilm it!"

Mr. Lemmon, in turn, is the perfect knucklehead, a guy with a wet noodle for a spine, who can't help being sentimental about a girl even while she's picking his pockets. As this broad, and that's just what she is, Miss West is almost perfect, a dyed blonde, totally devoid of warmth and humor. The only approximation of decency in the film is Ron Rich, the Negro ballplayer, who considers himself responsible for Mr. Lemmon's bogus injuries. But even he is flawed—his very decency makes him a noble simpleton.

Mr. Wilder, having set his story in a black-and-white world of sleazy apartments and cluttered offices, then tells it in terms of gags, both verbal and visual, that come at us as if from a machine gun. As Mr. Matthau closes his rolltop desk, the top keeps rolling right onto the floor. He threatens to sue United Fruit for not labeling every banana skin as possibly harmful to the health.

The film has also been beautifully cast with the kind of immediately identifiable characters we used to know and love in the old two-reelers. There are, for example, the smug gumshoe, played by Cliff Osmond; the fishy-eyed Viennese specialist, played by Sig Ruman; and the battle-axe nurse, without whom no hospital would be complete, played by Maryesther Denver.

While the superb performance of Mr. Matthau dominates the film, there is always behind him the specter of Mr. Wilder, coolly upbraiding us for our foibles. There may also be a final irony in the ending, brought about when Mr. Lemmon simply refuses to carry on with the fraud any longer. It isn't so much that virtue triumphs—just that the chiselers—and perhaps also Mr. Wilder and I. A. L. Diamond, his co-writer—ran out of tricks.

—V.C., October 20, 1966

THE 400 BLOWS

Produced and directed by François Truffaut; written (in French, with English subtitles) by Mr. Truffaut and Marcel Moussy, based on a story by Mr. Truffaut; cinematographer, Henri Decae; edited by Marie-Joseph Yoyotte; music by Jean Constantin; art designer, Bernard Evein; released by Janus Films. Black and white. Running time: 93 minutes.

With: Jean-Pierre Léaud (Antoine Doinel), Patrick Auffey (Rena), Claire Maurier (Madame Doinel), Albert Rémy (Mr. Doiel) and Guy Decomble (The Teacher).

Let it be noted without contention that the crest of the flow of recent films from the "new wave" of young French directors hit these shores yesterday with the arrival at the Fine Arts Theatre of *The 400 Blows* (*Les Quatre Cents Coups*) of François Truffaut.

Not since the 1952 arrival of René Clément's *Forbidden Games*, with which this extraordinary little picture of M. Truffaut's most interestingly compares, have we had from France a cinema that so brilliantly and strikingly reveals the explosion of a fresh creative talent in the directorial field.

Amazingly, this vigorous effort is the first feature film of M. Truffaut, who had previously been (of all things!) the movie critic for a French magazine. (A short film of his, *The Mischief Makers,* was shown here at the Little Carnegie some months back.) But, for all his professional inexperience and his youthfulness (twenty-seven years), M. Truffaut has here turned out a picture that might be termed a small masterpiece.

The striking distinctions of it are the clarity and honesty with which it presents a moving story of the troubles of a twelve-year-old boy. Where previous films on similar subjects have been fatted and fictionalized with all sorts of adult misconceptions and senti-mentalities, this is a smashingly convincing demonstration on the level of the boy—cool, firm and realistic, without a false note or a trace of goo.

And yet, in its frank examination of the life of this tough Parisian kid as he moves through the lonely stages of disintegration at home and at school, it offers an overwhelming insight into the emotional confusion of the lad and a truly heartbreaking awareness of his unspoken agonies.

It is said that this film, which M. Truffaut has written, directed and produced, is autobiographical. That may well explain the feeling of intimate occurrence that is packed into all its candid scenes. From the introductory sequence, which takes the viewer in an automobile through middle-class quarters of Paris in the shadow of the Eiffel Tower, while a curiously rollicking yet plaintive musical score is played, one gets a profound impression of being personally involved—a hard-by observer, if not participant, in the small joys and sorrows of the boy.

Because of the stunningly literal and factual camera style of M. Truffaut, as well as his clear and sympathetic understanding of the matter he explores, one feels close enough to the parents to cry out to them their cruel mistakes or to shake an obtuse and dull schoolteacher into an awareness of the wrong he does bright boys.

Eagerness makes us want to tell you of countless charming things in this film, little bits of unpushed communication that spin a fine web of sympathy—little things that tell you volumes about the tough, courageous nature of the boy, his rugged, sometimes ruthless, self-possession, and his poignant naïveté. They are subtle, often droll. Also we would like to note a lot about the pathos of the parents and the social incompetence of the kind of school that is here represented and is obviously hated and condemned by M. Truffaut.

But space prohibits expansion, other than to say that the compound is not only moving but also tremendously meaningful. When the lad finally says of his parents, "They didn't always tell the truth," there is spoken the most profound summation of the problem of the wayward child today.

Words cannot state simply how fine is Jean-Pierre Léaud in the role of the boy—how implacably dead-panned yet expressive, how apparently relaxed yet tense, how beautifully positive in his movement, like a pint-sized Jean Gabin. Out of this brand-new youngster, M. Truffaut has elicited a performance that will live as a delightful, provoking and heartbreaking monument to a boy.

Playing beside him, Patrick Auffay is equally solid as a pal, companion in juvenile deceptions and truant escapades.

Not to be sneezed at, either, is the excellent performance that Claire Maurier gives as the shallow, deceitful mother, or the fine acting of Albert Rémy, as the soft, confused and futile father, or the performance of Guy Decomble, as a stupid and uninspired schoolteacher.

The musical score of Jean Constantin is superb, and very good English subtitles translate the tough French dialogue.

Here is a picture that encourages an exciting refreshment of faith in films.

—B.C., November 17, 1959

FRANKENSTEIN

Directed by James Whale: written by Garett Fort. Francis Edwards Faragoh. John L. Balderston and Robert Florey. based on the novel by Mary Wollstonecraft Shelley and the play by Peggy Webling: cinematographer. Arthur Edeson: edited by Maurice Pivar and Clarence Kolster: music by David Broekman: art designer. Charles D. Hall: produced by Carl Laemmle Jr.: released by Universal Pictures. Black and white. Running time: 71 minutes.

With: Colin Clive (Frankenstein). Mae Clarke (Elizabeth). John Boles (Victor). Boris Karloff (The Monster). Edward Van Sloan (Dr. Waldman). Dwight Frye (The Dwarf). Frederick Kerr (The Baron). Lionel Belmore (The Burgomaster). Michael Mark (Peasant Father) and Marilyn Harris (Maria the Child).

Out of John L. Balderston's stage conception of the Mary Shelley classic, *Frankenstein,* James Whale, producer of *Journey's End* as a play and as a film, has wrought a stirring Grand Guignol type of picture, one that aroused so much excitement at the

Mayfair yesterday that many in the audience laughed to cover their true feelings.

It is an artistically conceived work in which Colin Clive, the Captain Stanhope of the London stage production of the R. C. Sherriff play, was brought from England to act the role of Frankenstein, the man who fashions a monster that walks and thinks. It is naturally a morbid, gruesome affair, but it is something to keep the spectator awake, for during its most spine-chilling periods it exacts attention. It was Carl Laemmle, head of Universal, the firm responsible for this current picture, who presented Lon Chaney in *The Hunchback of Notre Dame,* and while, as everybody knows, Quasimodo was a repellent sight, he was a creature for sympathy compared to the hideous monster in this *Frankenstein.* Boris Karloff undertakes the Frankenstein creature and his makeup can be said to suit anybody's demands. He does not portray a robot but a monster made out of human bodies, and the reason given here for his murderous onslaughts is that Frankenstein's Man Friday stole an abnormal brain after he had broken the glass bowl containing the normal one. This Frankenstein does not know.

No matter what one may say about the melodramatic ideas here, there is no denying that it is far and away the most effective thing of its kind. Beside it *Dracula* is tame and, incidentally, *Dracula* was produced by the same firm, which is also to issue in film form Poe's *Murders in the Rue Morgue.*

There are scenes in Frankenstein's laboratory in an old windmill, somewhere in Germany, where, during a severe electric storm, the young scientist finally perceives life showing in the object on an operating table. It is not long after that the monster walks, uttering a sound like the mooing of a cow. And then ensues the idea that while Frankenstein is proud of the creature he has made and boasts loudly about his achievement, he soon has reason to fear the brute, and in course of time it attacks Frankenstein's faithful servant, a bowed and bent little man, and kills him.

The scenes swing here and there to the Baron, Frankenstein's father, efficiently acted by Frederick Kerr, to those of a friend named Victor, played by John Boles, and to Elizabeth, Frankenstein's fiancée, portrayed by Mae Clarke. This is a relief, but they are all anxious about what Frankenstein is doing. They learn at the psychological moment, and have then still greater anxiety for Frankenstein.

Imagine the monster, with black eyes, heavy eyelids, a square head, huge feet that are covered with matting, long arms protruding from the sleeves of a coat, walking like an automaton, and then think of the fear in a village, and especially of the scientist, when it is learned that the monster has escaped from the windmill. It is beheld parading through the woods, sitting down playing with a little girl, and finally being pursued by a mob with flaming torches, for apparently fire is the only thing that causes the monster to hesitate.

The sounds of the cries of the pursuers and the strange noises made by the monster add to the disturbing nature of the scenes, and in a penultimate episode there is the struggle between the monster and Frankenstein. As a concession to the motion picture audience, Frankenstein is not killed, but he is badly injured. Two endings were made for this production, and at the eleventh hour it was decided to put in the one in which Frankenstein lives, because it was explained that sympathy is elicited for the young scientist and that the spectators would leave disappointed if the author's last chapter was adhered to.

As for the monster, he is burned when the villagers set fire to the windmill. From the screen comes the sound of the crackling of the blazing woodwork, the hue and cry of the frightened populace, and the queer sounds of the dying monster.

Mr. Clive adds another fine performance to his list. He succeeds in impressing upon one the earnestness and also the sanity of the scientist, in spite of Frankenstein's gruesome exploits. Lionel Belmore gives an easy performance as the town burgomaster. Miss Clarke, Edward Van Sloan and Dwight Frye also serve well.

—M.H., December 4, 1931

THE FRENCH CONNECTION

Directed by William Friedkin: written by Ernest Tidyman, based on the book by Robin Moore: director of photography, Owen Roizman: edited by Jerry Greenberg: music by Don Ellis: art designer, Ben Kazaskow: produced by Philip D'Antoni: released by Twentieth Century Fox. Running time: 104 minutes.

With: Gene Hackman (Jimmy "Popeye" Doyle), Fernando Rey (Alain Charnier), Roy Scheider (Buddy Russo), Tony Lo Bianco (Sal Boca), Marcel Bozzufi (Pierre Nicoli), Frédéric de Pasquale (Devereaux) and Bill Hickman (Mulder).

The ads say that the time is just right for an out-and-out thriller like this, and I guess that you are supposed to think that a good old kind of movie has none too soon come around again. But *The French Connection,* which opened yesterday at Loew's State 2 and Loew's Orpheum, is in fact a very good new kind of movie, and that in spite of its being composed of such ancient material as cops and crooks, with thrills and chases, and lots of shoot-'em-up.

It concerns a very large shipment of unusually pure heroin that has been hidden somewhere in a late-model Lincoln Continental for transport from Marseilles to New York City. Once in New York, it must, of course, be sold. And the point of sale becomes the point of ultimate encounter between the shipment's proprietor, a suave, civilized, elusive Frenchman (Fernando Rey), and a narcotics squad detective (Gene Hackman) who knows that a big deal is in the works and means to make a kill.

The Hackman characterization, one of the most successful in his career, and the only one that is allowed to emerge in much detail, virtually defines the attitude of *The French Connection.* Hard-nosed, pork-pie-hatted, vulgar, a tough cop in the latest measure of a fine tradition, he exists neither to rise nor to fall, to excite neither pity nor terror—but to function. To function in New York City is its own heroism, and the film recognizes that, but it is not the heroism of conventional gesture, and so even the most conventional excitements of *The French Connection* carry with them a built-in air of fatigue.

I don't mean that they are not exciting. *The French Connection* is a film of almost incredible suspense, and it includes, among a great many chilling delights, the most brilliantly executed chase sequence I have ever seen. But the conditions for the suspense (indeed, the conditions of the chase—to intercept a hijacked elevated train) carry with them the potential for failure not of this particular action, but of all action in the great doomed city that is the film's real subject. From the moment, very early on, when Hackman first pistol-whips a black pusher, you know that the world

is cursed and that everybody playing out his allotted role is cursed along with it.

In a more pretentious and less perceptive film, destinies might have turned tragic. In *The French Connection* they become all but invisible. The whole movie has slightly the look of being background material, or maybe excellent precredit material, for another movie. It moves at magnificent speed, and exhausts itself in movement. The central characters repeatedly appear as if out of the city's mass and then disappear into it again—a superb conception for an action of difficult pursuit, but one that never allows the luxury of personal identification.

That is why only Gene Hackman surfaces as a character, although there are the fragments of many good performances—seen as if across the street, outside the window, or at the other end of the subway platform. There are also faults: a murder too many, some shaky motivation among the bad guys, a degree of coldness that perhaps even exceeds the requirements of the cold intelligence that controls the film.

But *The French Connection* is mostly a credit to everyone who helped shape it. This would include Ernest Tidyman, who wrote the screenplay and who also wrote *Shaft;* Owen Roizman, the cinematographer; and William Friedkin, a director whose previous work (*The Birthday Party, The Night They Raided Minsky's,* etc.) may not have prepared anyone for the excellence of this.

—R.G., October 8, 1971

FRENZY

Produced and directed by Alfred Hitchcock; written by Anthony Shaffer, based on the novel *Goodbye Piccadilly, Farewell Leicester Square* by Arthur La Bern; director of photography, Gil Taylor; edited by John Jympson; released by Universal Pictures. Running time: 116 minutes.

With: Jon Finch (Richard Blaney), Barry Foster (Robert Rusk), Barbara Leigh-Hunt (Brenda Blaney), Anna Massey (Babs Milligan), Alec McCowen (Chief Inspector Oxford), Vivien Merchant (Mrs. Oxford), Billie Whitelaw (Hetty Porter) and Clive Swift (Johnny Porter).

Alfred Hitchcock will be seventy-three on August 13, but like Luis Buñuel, whom he otherwise resembles but slightly, his talent is only enriched by the advancing years that make most directors fearful and insecure. In the last twelve years he has given us, among other things, *The Birds, Topaz* (really a one-film anthology of Hitchcock work), and now *Frenzy,* which is his fifty-fifth film as a director since 1922.

Frenzy is Hitchcock in the dazzling, lucid form that is as much the meaning as the method of his films. For Hitchcock the mastery of style and the perfection of technique are the expressions of a passion that might prompt other men to seek cancer cures, or to construct completely nonutilitarian towers out of pieces of broken glass and bottle tops.

Frenzy, which opened yesterday at the Palace, Murray Hill and other theaters, is a passionately entertaining film set in a London that, except for the color photography, seems not too different from the setting of his earliest pictures, including *The Lodger.*

Like that 1926 film about a Jack the Ripper, *Frenzy* has to do with a sex-crazed, homicidal maniac who, in this case, does away with his victims (all women) with a necktie around the throat. As the newspaper headlines scream about The Necktie Killer, bodies turn up everywhere—in the Thames, in the backs of potato trucks, even sitting at their office desks, understandably somewhat disheveled.

The mystery of *Frenzy,* however, is not who the killer is (which is revealed quite early on) but how Hitchcock is going to maintain our interest in what is essentially a trite situation: the problem of the decent enough fellow, Richard Blaney (Jon Finch), a former R.A.F. ace whom bad luck has reduced to bartending, who becomes the chief suspect when his ex-wife is murdered.

Hitchcock does it with a marvelously funny script by Anthony Shaffer, with a superb English cast that is largely unknown here, and with his gift for implicating the audience in the most outrageous acts, which, as often as not, have us identifying with the killer. In one agonizing sequence, we are put into the position of cheering on (well, almost) the maniac, who has only a few minutes in which to retrieve an identifiable tiepin from the clenched fingers of his most recent victim.

Were Hitchcock less evident throughout the film, *Frenzy* would be as unbearable as it probably sounds when I report that the killer has to break the fingers of the corpse. Yet it is something more than just bearable because never for a minute does one feel the absence of the storyteller, raising his eyebrows in mock woe. That pressure is apparent in a spectacular, seemingly unbroken camera movement that takes us, with the camera, down the stairs of the killer's apartment, out the front door, to a position across the street.

It is apparent in the way Hitchcock plays fast but not necessarily loose with film time, that is, in the way he indulges himself in exploring the details of a single murder, yet manages to cover the hero's long court trial in approximately ninety seconds.

It is also there in the exposition delivered in counterpoint to a hilariously inedible, gourmet dinner, served up to the chief inspector (Alec McCowen) by his prescient wife (Vivien Merchant). She disputes the facts he has had to feed us, while cheerily feeding him pig's feet he can't eat. "Women's intuition," she says cheerfully, "is worth more than laboratories. I don't know why you don't teach it in police colleges."

For *Frenzy,* Hitchcock has assembled one of his best casts, including Finch, Barry Foster, Miss Merchant, McCowen, and particularly, Anna Massey (Raymond Massey's daughter), who plays a remarkably sexy London barmaid without being especially beautiful.

"We haven't had a good sex murderer since Christie," says someone in the film of the necktie killer, and *Frenzy* is the first good movie about a sex murderer since *Psycho.*

—V.C., June 22, 1972

FRIENDLY PERSUASION

Produced and directed by William Wyler; written by Michael Wilson, based on the novel by Jessamyn West; cinematographer. Ellsworth Fredericks; edited by Robert Swink. Edward A. Biery and Robert Belcher; music by Dimitri Tiomkin; art designer; Ted Haworthy; released by Allied Artists. Running time: 137 minutes.

With: Gary Cooper (Jess Birdwell). Dorothy McGuire (Eliza Birdwell). Marjorie Main (Widow Hudspeth). Anthony Perkins (Josh Birdwell).

Richard Eyer (Little Jess), Robert Middleton (Sam Jordan) and Phyllis Love (Mattie Birdwell).

Who would have thought the story of a Quaker family living on a farm in southern Indiana at the time of the Civil War would make for a winning motion picture in which a spurt of stirring drama and suspense would top comedy, quaintness and charm? The likelihood of such a setup was frankly hard to foresee.

Yet producer-director William Wyler has come up with just this surprise in his colorful *Friendly Persuasion,* which opened at the Music Hall yesterday. And what is more, he has got into this treatise on the old-time manners and basic beliefs of the Society of Friends a lot of homely precept and a touching display of the nobility of man.

Inspired by a lovely group of stories by Jessamyn West and spurred by the sympathetic talents of Gary Cooper and Dorothy McGuire, Mr. Wyler has brought forth a picture that is loaded with sweetness and warmth and as much cracker-barrel Americana as has been spread on the screen in some time.

For the most part, his *Friendly Persuasion* is nothing more than a loosely woven account of the amiable rural adventures of the Birdwell family, a quaint clutch of Indiana Quakers, and their robust neighbors and friends. There are five Birdwells—Papa and Mama, whom Mr. Cooper and Miss McGuire play; one daughter, Mattie; and two sons, Josh and Little Jess. There is also a pet goose, Samantha; a horse out in the barn (she is traded for a somewhat faster stepper during the course of proceedings); and various cows.

In the way of neighbors, there are Sam Jordan, whom Robert Middleton plays; his son Gard, who is a suitor for Mattie; and an assortment of stiff-backed friends. And, of course, there are all those people at Meeting and at the country fair, not to mention the riotous Widow Hudspeth, who is played by Marjorie Main.

With this assortment of people, Mr. Wyler (still inspired by Miss West) has a grand time showing how lively spirit bubbles out of Quaker austerity. Mama is a gentle Quaker preacher, so she formally disapproves of Papa racing his mare against Sam Jordan's, but she secretly enjoys the pell-mell buggy rides. And when Papa brings home a wheezy organ that he has recklessly bought at the fair, she finally succumbs to persuasion and allows him to keep it upstairs.

So it goes with the well-adjusted family, little bickers and reserved displays of love, until Morgan's Raiders appear on the horizon and son Josh wants to shoulder a gun. Then Mama abhors the bent toward violence and Papa delves deeply in his soul to find justification for the breaking of faith by his son. Mr. Wyler, in a tautly staged sequence that matches *The Red Badge of Courage* for shock and gore, resolves the zeal of the young warrior. And all is happy at the end.

What he achieves in this picture is acquaintance with solid characters whose lives are happily ordered by a simple morality and genuine love. In their very naïveté and simplicity there is a soothing serenity. And in all their surroundings, Mr. Wyler has got so much warm rusticity, which is richly enhanced by color, that it makes you feel mellow and good. Except for a modern theme song that is sung as an introduction by Pat Boone and sneaks in on various occasions, you wouldn't think you were within years of video.

While top honors go to the performances of Mr. Cooper and Miss McGuire, who are wonderfully spirited and compassionate in their finely complementary roles, a great deal of admiration must go to Anthony Perkins as Josh. He makes the older son of the Birdwells a handsome, intense and chivalrous lad. Richard Eyer is delightful and natural as the rambunctious Little Jess, while Phyllis Love is electrical as Mattie and Mark Richman is nice as her suitor, Gard. Walter Catlett, Russell Simpson and Joel Fluellen are good in lesser character roles.

As they put it in *Friendly Persuasion,* thee should be pleasured by this film.

—*B.C., November 2, 1956*

FROM HERE TO ETERNITY

Directed by Fred Zinnemann; written by Daniel Taradash, based on the novel by James Jones; cinematographer, Burnett Guffey; edited by William A. Lyon; music by George Duning; art designer, Cary Odell; produced by Buddy Adler; released by Columbia Pictures. Black and white. Running time: 118 minutes.

With: Burt Lancaster (Sergeant Milton Warden), Montgomery Clift (Robert E. Lee Prewitt), Deborah Kerr (Karen Holmes), Frank Sinatra (Angelo Maggio), Donna Reed (Alma Lorene), Philip Ober (Captain Dana Holmes) and Mickey Shaughnessy (Leva).

Out of *From Here to Eternity,* a novel whose anger and compassion stirred a postwar reading public as few such works have, Columbia and a company of sensitive hands have forged a film almost as towering and persuasive as its source. Although it naturally lacks the depth and fullness of the 430,000 words and 850 pages of the book, this dramatization of phases of the military life in a peacetime army, which was unveiled at the Capitol yesterday, captures the essential spirit of the James Jones study. And as a job of editing, emending, rearranging and purifying a volume bristling with brutality and obscenities, *From Here to Eternity* stands as a shining example of truly professional moviemaking.

As may be surmised, credit for this metamorphosis cannot be localized. The team of scenarist, director, producer and cast has managed to transfer convincingly the muscularity of the basically male society with which the book dealt; the poignance and futility of the love lives of the professional soldiers involved, as well as the indictment of commanding officers whose selfishness can break men devoted to soldiering. They are trapped in a world they made and one that defeats them. Above all, it is a portrait etched in truth and without the stigma of calculated viciousness.

Although the incisive script fashioned by Daniel Taradash sidesteps such matters as the shocking "Stockade" chapters of the book, it fundamentally cleaves to the author's thesis. Set in Schofield Barracks in Oahu, Hawaii, in the months preceding the attack on Pearl Harbor, it is the tragic story of the youthful Private Robert E. Lee Prewitt, hardheaded Kentuckian whose convictions are strong enough to force him to forgo his passionate devotion to both the bugle and prizefighting despite the knowledge that his superior officer, Captain Dana Holmes, and his crew of athletes will give him "The Treatment."

It is the story, also, of First Sergeant Milton Warden, top kick of the company, a rough-hewn pillar of strength whose know-how guides and supports the pompous and philandering captain and the admiring contingent of G.I.'s in his command. It is the tale of sinewy Angelo Maggio, enlisted man from the sidewalks of New York, whose brave revolt against the confinements of the Army system ends in tragedy. And it is the account of the ill-fated affair between Karen Holmes, the captain's wife, and Sergeant Warden, as well as the romance of Private Prewitt and Lorene, whose charms were purveyed in Mrs. Kipfer's New Congress Club.

Credit Fred Zinnemann with an expert directorial achievement in maintaining these various involvements on equal and lucid levels. While each yarn is pertinent and commands attention, the conflicts of its principals are fayed neatly into a compact whole. And the climactic strafing of Schofield Barracks is a fittingly explosive finish to the two hours of uncluttered drama culled from an immense and sometimes sprawling work of fiction.

Fortunately the cast members measure up to their assignments. In Burt Lancaster, the producer has got a top kick to the manner born, a man whose capabilities are obvious and whose code is hard and strange but never questionable. He is a "thirty-year man" respected by his superiors and the G.I.'s with whom he fights and plays. His view of officers leaves him only with hatred of the caste although he could easily achieve rank, which would solve his romantic problem. But he is honest enough to eschew it and lose the only love he has known.

Montgomery Clift adds another sensitive portrait to an already imposing gallery with his portrayal of Prewitt. Since he has blinded a man in the ring, no carefully planned scheme of harassment will get him in again. And, since he considers it a slight when he has been passed over as a bugler who once played taps at Arlington National Cemetery, he deems it his right to be "busted" from corporal to conform to his credo that "if a man don't go his own way, he's nothin'."

Although it is a deviation from the norm, Frank Sinatra is excellent in the nonsinging role of Angelo Maggio, a characterization rich in comic vitality and genuine pathos. Deborah Kerr, heretofore the genteel lady in films, contributes a completely tender stint as the passionate Karen Holmes, defeated by a callous mate and a fruitless marriage, who clings to a doomed love.

355

While Donna Reed is not precisely the picture of a lady of the evening, her delineation of Lorene, wracked between a desire to be "proper" and her anomalous affair with Prewitt, is polished and professional. Although Philip Ober's weak captain is a comparatively slight and shallow role, the company of G.I.'s and the Schofield Barracks, where some of the film was shot, gave the drama and the authenticity required.

From Here to Eternity is being shown on a wide screen and with Stereophonic sound. It does not need these enhancements. It has scope, power and impact without them.

—*A.W., August 6, 1953*

THE FUGITIVE

Directed by John Ford; written by Dudley Nichols, based on the novel *The Power and the Glory* by Graham Greene; cinematographer, Gabriel Figueroa; edited by Jack Murray; music by Richard Hageman; art designer, Alfred Ybarra; produced by Mr. Ford and Merian C. Cooper; released by RKO Radio Pictures. Black and white. Running time: 104 minutes.

With: Henry Fonda (A Fugitive), Dolores Del Río (An Indian Woman), Pedro Armendáriz (Lieutenant of Police), J. Carrol Naish (Police Informer), Leo Carrillo (Chief of Police), Ward Bond (El Gringo) and Robert Armstrong (Sergeant of Police).

Out of the flood of pictures which opened on Broadway yesterday emerges in monolithic beauty John Ford's *The Fugitive*. For here, in this strange and haunting picture, now showing on the Victoria's screen, is imaged a terrifying struggle between strength and weakness in a man's soul, a thundering modern parable on the indestructibility of faith, a tense and significant conflict between freedom and brute authority.

It is difficult to fashion in a few lines an indication of the nature of this film because of its violent eccentricities and its crashing overtones. But it is enough to say, at the moment, that Mr. Ford has accomplished in it a true companion piece to *The Informer,* which he directed some years back.

In fact, there are strong resemblances between the two finely imaged films, since *The Fugitive* is also a picture about a frenzied spiritual flight. It is, in brief, the story of a young priest's bewildered attempts to carry on his humble ministrations in a land where the church has been banned and still avoid apprehension by the brutal totalitarian police.

Like *The Informer,* however, it is much more than a melodramatic "chase," although the vigorous accumulation of terror of a physical hue and cry has not been missed. Taking place, supposedly, in a fictitious Latin American land, which has been appropriately pictured by filming in Mexico, Mr. Ford has made *The Fugitive* a symphony of light and shade, of deafening din and silence, of sweeping movement and repose. And by this magnificent ordering of a strange, dizzying atmosphere, he has brewed a storm of implications of man's perils and fears in a world gone mad.

The script, prepared by Dudley Nichols from a novel by Graham Greene, is a workmanlike blueprint for action, failing only to define the deeper indecision of the hero as it was apparently conceived by Mr. Greene. And the performances are all of them excellent, from the anguished straining of Henry Fonda as the priest to Ward Bond's stony arrogances as an American gangster "on the lam." Dolores Del Rio is a warm glow of devotion as an Indian Magdalene and Pedro Armendáriz burns with scorching passion as a chief of military police. The musical score by Richard Hageman is a tintinnabulation of eloquent sounds.

Let us thank Mr. Ford for giving us, at this late date, one of the best films of the year.

—*B.C., December 26, 1947*

FULL METAL JACKET

Produced and directed by Stanley Kubrick; written by Mr. Kubrick, Michael Herr and Gustav Hasford, based on the novel *The Short Timers* by Mr. Hasford; director of photography, Douglas Milsome; edited by Martin Hunter; music by Abigail Mead; production designer, Anton Furst; released by Warner Brothers. Running time: 118 minutes.

With: Matthew Modine (Private Joker). Adam Baldwin (Animal Mother). Vincent D'Onofrio (Private Pyle). Lee Ermey (Gunnery Sergeant Hartman). Dorian Harewood (Eightball). Arliss Howard (Cowboy). Kevyn Major Howard (Rafterman) and Ed O'Ross (Lieutenant Touchdown).

More than any other major American filmmaker, Stanley Kubrick keeps to his own ways, paying little attention to the fashions of the moment, creating fantastic visions that, in one way and another, are dislocated extensions of the world we know but would prefer not to recognize.

The best Kubrick films—*Lolita, Dr. Strangelove, 2001, A Clockwork Orange* and *Barry Lyndon*—are always somewhat off-putting when first seen. They're never what one has expected. No Kubrick film ever immediately evokes the one that preceded it. Yet it's so distinctive that it can't be confused with the work of any other director.

Though the general public couldn't care less, this can be infuriating to anyone who wants to be able to read a filmaker's accumulated body of work as if it were a road map leading to some predetermined destination. As movie follows movie, the Kubrick terrain never becomes familiar. You drive at your own risk, confident only that the director has been there before you.

Full Metal Jacket, Mr. Kubrick's harrowing, beautiful and characteristically eccentric new film about Vietnam, is going to puzzle, anger and (I hope) fascinate audiences as much as any film he has made to date. The movie, opening today at the National and other theaters, will inevitably be compared with Oliver Stone's *Platoon,* but its narrative is far less neat and cohesive—and far more antagonistic—than Mr. Stone's film.

Like *The Short Timers,* Gustav Hasford's spare, manic novel on which it is based, the Kubrick film seems so utterly reasonable that one doesn't initially recognize the lunacies recorded so matter-of-factly. The film is a series of exploding boomerangs. Just when you think you can relax in safety, some crazed image or line or event will swing around to lodge in the brain and scramble the emotions.

Full Metal Jacket is closer in spirit to Francis Coppola's *Apocalypse Now,* even if it has none of the mystical romanticism of the Coppola film in either its text or physical production. However, lurking just off-screen, there's always the presence of Mr. Kubrick, a benign, ever mysterious Kurtz, who has come to know that the only thing worse than disorder in the universe is not to recognize it—which is, after all, the first step toward understanding and, possibly, accommodation.

Disorder is virtually the order of *Full Metal Jacket,* whose pivotal character, Private Joker (Matthew Modine), the narrator of the novel, wears a peace symbol on his battle fatigues and, on his helmet, the slogan "Born to Kill." Disorder is also there in the structure of the film itself.

Full Metal Jacket is divided into two parts, which at first seem so different in tone, look and method that they could have been made by two different directors working with two different cameramen from two different screenplays. Only the actors are the same. Part of the way in which the movie works, and involves the audience, is in its demand that the audience make the sudden leap to the seemingly (but far from) conventional battle scenes in Vietnam, which conclude the film, from its flashily brilliant first half, set in the Marine Corps boot camp at Parris Island, South Carolina.

Though Mr. Modine's Private Joker, a humanist in the process of being permanently bent by the war, provides the film with its center, the poetically foul-mouthed Gunnery Sergeant Hartman (Lee Ermey) is the film's effective heart, giving terrifying life to *Full Metal Jacket* long after he has left the scene and the film has moved on to Vietnam.

Sergeant Hartman is a Marine "lifer," a machine whose only purpose is to turn the soft, half-formed young men who arrive at Parris Island into killers without conscience. There's no nonsense that he's doing it for the men's own good. Everything is made subordinate to "the corps," to which end the recruits are humiliated, beaten, exhausted, tricked, lied to, subjected to racial slurs and drilled, constantly drilled, physically and psychologically.

They recite by rote creeds, prayers and obscene couplets intended to detach them from all values from the past. On Christmas they sing "Happy birthday, dear Jesus," and laugh at their own impertinence. They sleep with their rifles, to which they've been ordered to give girls' names. The training is a kind of ecstatic, longed-for washing of brain and body, defined by Mr. Kubrick in a succession of vignettes so vulgar and so outrageous that one watches in hilarity that, boomerang-like, suddenly returns as shock and sorrow.

The effect of this part of the film, photographed and played with an unnatural cleanliness that reflects the nature of the training itself, is so devastating that one tends to resist the abrupt cut to Vietnam, where order is disorder and truth is simply a matter of language. At one point Private Joker, who has become a Marine combat correspondent, respectfully notes that henceforth "search and destroy" missions are to be described as "sweep and clear." The landscape is lunar. Even the sky is a different color.

Though the first half seems complete in itself, the point of *Full Metal Jacket* is made only through the combat mission that ends the film in the ruins of the city of Hue, which, as seen by Mr. Kubrick, is both a specific place and the seat of judgment for all that's gone before. Sergeant Hartman's ghost looks on.

The performances are splendid. Mr. Modine (*Birdy, Mrs. Soffel, Streamers*) must now be one of the best, most adaptable young film actors of his generation. The film's stunning surprise is Mr. Ermey, a leathery, ageless, former Marine sergeant in real life. He's so good—so obsessed—that you might think he wrote his own lines, except that much of his dialogue comes directly from Mr. Hasford's book, adapted by the novelist with Mr. Kubrick and Michael Herr (*Dispatches*). Note with admiration Vincent D'Onofrio, who plays a hopelessly overweight Parris Island recruit who turns himself into Sergeant Hartman's most dedicated student.

Full Metal Jacket is not without its failed inspirations. A series of television "interviews" with battle-worn marines suggests a different, simpler, more obvious kind of movie. Some jokes intended to appall are just jokes: "How do you manage to shoot women and children?" "Easy. You don't lead them so far." It sounds as if it's been said many times before, but that could also be the point.

Not for Mr. Kubrick is location shooting in the Philippines or Thailand. Since the early 1960's, he has lived and worked in England, where he created his own, very particular Vietnam locations for *Full Metal Jacket.* They're otherworldly. They don't match expectations, any more than the narrative does. They are,

however, utterly true to a film of immense and very rare imagination.

—V.C., June 26, 1987

THE FULL MONTY

Directed by Peter Cattaneo: written by Simon Beaufoy: director of photography, John de Borman: edited by Nick Moore and Dave Freeman: music by Anne Dudley: production designer, Max Gottlieb: produced by Uberto Pasolini: released by Fox Searchlight Pictures. Running time: 90 minutes.

With: Robert Carlyle (Gaz), Tom Wilkinson (Gerald), Mark Addy (Dave), Steve Huison (Lomper), Paul Barber (Horse), Hugo Speer (Guy), Lesley Sharp (Jean), Emily Woof (Mandy) and William Snape (Nathan).

Improbable smiles dot the ads for noncomedies from *Mrs. Brown* to *In the Company of Men,* but in fact this summer at the movies has been no laughing matter. Not until *The Full Monty,* the irresistible tale of unemployed steelworkers in Sheffield, England, who contrive a bold moneymaking scheme. Shy, gruff or paunchy as they are, these middle-aged men are persuaded to try stripping to raise funds and bolster damaged self-esteem. Brightly acted and casually hilarious, *The Full Monty* exploits this gimmick in witty, trenchant ways that are always generous, never cruel.

Put women in this situation and it turns sour instantly. But the hunk-free cast of *The Full Monty* gives it loads of nonchalant humor, serious social underpinnings and a wonderfully incongruous edge. As played by Robert Carlyle, the scrappy little actor who nearly stole *Trainspotting* as Begbie, the ringleader, named Gaz, hatches a crazy plot while remaining a pragmatist. He has a child to support, no job, a limited range of skills and a willingness to learn new tricks. Like putting down his lighted cigarette before trying to wiggle out of his shirt.

One clever touch in *The Full Monty,* a splendid feature debut for both its director (Peter Cattaneo) and writer (Simon Beaufoy), is the stabilizing presence of Gaz's young son. If a boy of about ten is privy to his father's striptease scheme, how bad can it be? Awful:

the boy watches in deadpan disbelief as his father and a few friends prepare (sidesplittingly) to risk embarrassment on every level. "Give us a chance!" one of them protests. "I'll bet even Madonna has difficulty getting her shoes and socks off!"

Gaz hatches the get-solvent-quick scheme after sneaking into a club and watching women go wild over male dancers. The women behave with such masculine aggressiveness that it's enough to make an unemployed steelworker feel "extincto," as Gaz puts it. So he and Dave (Mark Addy), a bashful but cooperative friend, begin recruiting unlikely talent. In the obligatory bad audition sequence, which turns devilishly funny here, one man prepares to imitate Donald O'Connor dancing up a wall. (The camera looks elsewhere while the audience hears a well-timed thud.) Another man, upon undressing, is greeted by Gaz and company with the exclamation, "Gentlemen, the lunchbox has landed."

Dave, who is so hapless that he sets off a store's security alarm by pocketing a single piece of candy, is sent to procure research materials. He comes back with a videotape of *Flashdance,* which the men watch studiously. "She's nifty on her pins," one of them says about Jennifer Beals's dancing steelworker. Still, he can't get past the fact that Flashy (as he calls her) looks like a lousy welder.

As *The Full Monty,* which takes its title from a slang phrase for total nudity, guides these men toward their own form of flashdancing, it displays tenderness and respect on a par with its great good humor. The film understands that joblessness is a humiliation well beyond nakedness, but it also revels in the sight of downtrodden ex-workers learning to enjoy their new freedom.

Beyond Gaz, played with stellar presence and acerbic charm by Mr. Carlyle, the film's most winning character is Gerald (Tom Wilkinson), an aging ex-foreman with a distinguished look. Partly to escape his wife's ornamental lawn gnomes, Gerald winds up in a show of solidarity with the men he once supervised. To his own surprise, he becomes as dedicated as the others to the new art of (in the words of one) "jiggin' about in the buff."

With foolproof appreciation for the absurdity of this situation, Mr. Cattaneo uses Gerald's pink, flowery-wallpapered living room for a mock-momentous scene in which the men peel down to their underwear for the first time. "Well, no looking," Dave warns. "And no laughing, ya bastards."

No laughing at *The Full Monty?* Sorry. Not a chance.

—*J.M., August 13, 1997*

FUNNY FACE

Directed by Stanley Donen; written by Leonard Gershe, based on his musical *Wedding Day*; cinematographer, Ray June; edited by Frank Bracht; music by George Gershwin, Ira Gershwin, Roger Edens and Mr. Gershe; choreography by Fred Astaire and Eugene Loring; art designers, George W. Davis and Hal Pereira; produced by Mr. Edens; released by Paramount Pictures. Running time: 103 minutes.

With: Audrey Hepburn (Jo), Fred Astaire (Dick Avery), Kay Thompson (Maggie Prescott), Michel Auclair (Professor Emile Flostre), Robert Flemyng (Paul Duval) and Dovima (Babs).

Spring flounced her skirts and breezed blithely into the Music Hall yesterday with as truly appropriate a seasonal program as has been there in many a year. Along with the annual Easter pageant and other cheery entertainment on the stage, there is Paramount's conspicuously vernal musical picture, *Funny Face,* which teams Fred Astaire and Audrey Hepburn in a delightfully balmy romance. Nothing so colorful and glittering is likely until the bunny lays its eggs.

Indeed, it is reasonable to reckon that you won't see a prettier musical film—or one more extraordinarily stylish—during the balance of this year. If you do you may count yourself fortunate, for this is a picture with class in every considerable department on which this sort of picture depends.

Let's begin with the songs of George and Ira Gershwin, which are from their musical comedy of the same title, produced thirty years ago. That's the oldest thing in the picture, barring Mr. Astaire and perhaps the simple Cinderella story, which is basically as old as the hills. Yet they have more lilt and frolic in them than if they had been written last year. And even the Cinderella story has its contemporary charm.

It is (this comes after the music) a purely coincidental tale of a drab little Greenwich Village salesgirl who is grabbed by a pertinacious troupe of style-magazine super-worldlings, whisked off to Paris and turned into a dazzling super-dress model, with whom the blasé photographer falls in love. But she can't stay out of those smoky cellars where the long-haired intellectuals hive—not until one bearded cultist shows he's interested in more than her mind.

For all the simplicity of that fable, Leonard Gershe, who prepared the script, has made it spin by being lightly satiric of all the la-de-da of the dress trade, while taking a few good-natured tumbles out of the breast-beating Existentialists. And Roger Edens, the talented producer, and Stanley Donen, the director, have turned the whole thing into a lovely phantasm made up of romance, tourism and chic.

This is its major magnificence—appropriate decor and visual style that lend to the Cinderella story a modern-Cinderella atmosphere. The gentlemen have figured, probably rightly, that there is nothing more illusory in our times than the costly adornment of females. And from that they have taken their cue.

The eye is intoxicated with exquisite color designs and graphic production numbers that are rich in sensory thrills. There's one done by the principals in a darkroom, with the faint cherry-red glow of a ruby light keying the shadowy movement that goes with the singing of the title song. (The final shot is a dazzling close-up of Miss Hepburn's face against the dead-white negative frame.) And there's another tenebrous number done in a Paris dive, with red and green lights blotching the darkness, that has a terrific mood.

Finally we come to the acting (and singing and dancing), which are elegant, too, but not quite as elegant as the rest of it, due partly to a certain gentleman's age. Miss Hepburn has the meek charm of a wallflower turned into a rueful butterfly, and Mr. Astaire plays her lens-hound suitor softly, as if afraid to turn on too much steam. Even so they make very nice music with such graceful Gershwin numbers as "He Loves and She Loves," "'S Wonderful" and the title song.

Kay Thompson, the brittle café singer, is fantastic and fun as a style-magazine director, and Robert Flemyng and Michel Auclair are good as a couple of Paris characters in the only other roles that amount to anything.

A lot of fine outdoor shots were made in Paris—in the springtime and in the rain. If you try hard, you can smell horse-chestnut blossoms. That is the sort of film this is.

—B.C., March 29, 1957

FUNNY GIRL

Directed by William Wyler; written by Isobel Lennart, based on the play and book by Ms. Lennart; director of photography. Harry Stradling; music by Jule Styne; edited by William Sands and Maury Winetrobe; production design by Gene Callahan; produced by Ray Stark; released by Columbia Pictures and Rastar Productions. Running time: 151 minutes.

With: Barbra Streisand (Fanny Brice). Omar Sharif (Nick Arnstein). Kay Medford (Rose Brice). Anne Francis (Georgia James). Walter Pidgeon (Florenz Ziegfeld). Lee Allen (Eddie Ryan). Mae Questel (Mrs. Strakosh). Gerald Mohr (Branca). Frank Faylen (Keeney). Mittie Lawrence (Emma). Gertrude Flynn (Mrs. O'Malley) and Penny Santon (Mrs. Meeker).

It is a great credit to the talent of Barbra Streisand that one keeps hoping, for three long solid hours with intermission, that *Funny Girl* will turn out to be something—an old-fashioned musical, a new-fashioned musical, a successful adaptation of the Broadway show, anything with just that breath of the genuine that makes you have a good time, or want to cry at moments, or respond as one does to musicals with excellent scores and great entertainers in them. Instead, the movie is an elaborate, painstaking launching pad, with important talents of Hollywood, from the director, William Wyler, on down, treating Barbra rather fondly, improbably and even patronizingly, as though they were firing off a gilded broccoli. Miss Streisand's talent is very poignant and strong, but the movie almost does her in.

Almost every shot is held too long, every pointless scene is interminable, sometimes shots are held just to let you know the scene has come to an end. Fanny Brice isn't there, Nicky Arnstein isn't there, the live garish period of the Ziegfeld Follies isn't there. Arnstein, in particular, instead of being the special, small-time gangster that the story requires, has been cast—presumably for an audience in a small-town typing pool—as an exotic seducer (Omar Sharif). Everyone around Miss Streisand, in fact, has been cast in stereotype, so that one's attention is continuously drawn to a subdrama, whether Miss Streisand is making good, whether she is going to be a movie star in the great old tradition of stars. This kind of scrutiny puts the audience in a calculating frame of mind, and even Miss Streisand turns off at moments and becomes mannered or absent-minded.

The film has something a little condescending about it—as though there were some special virtue in making a movie star out of someone who is not likely to be whistled at on Main Street or featured in cold-cream commercials. I thought if one more joke or whimsical, self-deprecating reference was made to Miss Streisand's looks—and for most of the movie she looks great—some European filmmaker, accustomed to people with faces, moods and expressions of their own, ought to liberate the Criterion, where *Funny Girl* opened yesterday, from these apologetic, brouhaha incarnations of *I Can Get It for You Wholesale*'s Miss Marmelstein.

Miss Streisand doesn't need any of this. When she is singing—in a marvelous scene on roller skates—when she throws a line away, or shrugs, or looks funny or sad, she has a power, gentleness and intensity that rather knocks all the props and sets and camera angles on their ear. There is something, too, about the poignance of a particular kind of ambition that is dated and almost nostalgic now

—R.A., *September 20, 1968*

FURY

Directed by Fritz Lang; written by Bartlett Cormack and Mr. Lang, based on the story "Mob Rule" by Norman Krasna; cinematographer, Joseph Ruttenberg; edited by Frank Sullivan; music by Franz Waxman; art designers, Cedric Gibbons, William A. Horning and Edwin B. Willis; produced by Joseph L. Mankiewicz; released by Metro-Goldwyn-Mayer. Black and white. Running time: 90 minutes.

With: Sylvia Sidney (Katherine Grant), Spencer Tracy (Joe Wilson), Walter Abel (District Attorney), Bruce Cabot (Kirby Dawson), Edward Ellis (Sheriff) and Walter Brennan ("Bugs" Meyers).

Let it be said at once: *Fury,* which came to the Capitol yesterday, is the finest original drama the screen has provided this year. Its theme is mob violence, its approach is coldly judicial, its treatment as relentless and unsparing as the lynching it portrays. A mature, sober and penetrating investigation of a national blight, it has been brilliantly directed by the Viennese Fritz Lang, bitingly written by Norman Krasna and Bartlett Cormack and splendidly performed by Spencer Tracy, Sylvia Sidney, Walter Abel, Edward Ellis and many others. It should appeal mightily to those of you who look to Hollywood—forlornly most of the time—for something better than superficial, dream-world romance.

Mr. Krasna's story, elemental in its simplicity, is yet an encyclopedia of lynch law. It permits us to study this great American institution from every angle and from points of vantage provided by Mr. Lang's unquestionable camera genius. We see it as the victim sees it, as the mob sees it, as the community sees it, as the law sees it, as the public sees it. We see a lynching, its prelude and its aftermath, in all its cold horror, its hypocrisy and its cruel stupidity; and it disgusts us and fills us with shame for what has been done, and is being done, in our constitutional republic.

The case of Joe Wilson is fictitious and it is laid in a nonexistent midwestern city; yet the case of Joe Wilson is typical of all lynch outrages, wherever committed. The Joe Wilson of *Fury* is a gasoline station owner, driving happily down a byroad to meet the girl he plans to marry. It is a day they have awaited for years. The world is bright, men are good, justice prevails. Then a deputy sheriff, with leveled shotgun, stops the car. "Weren't letting grass grow under yer tires, were ye? Illinois license plates, too!" The tragedy has begun.

There had been a kidnapping. A few shreds of evidence are enough to lodge Wilson in the county jail at Strand, held for further investigation. Rumors spread through the town. The knaves and the righteous, the loafers and the business men, convert Wilson from suspect to swaggering criminal. The mob storms the jail, beats down the sheriff and his deputies and, unable to reach the prisoner, sets the building afire.

Wilson's sweetheart arrives in time to see him being burned alive as men gape, as a woman holds her child aloft to get a better view, as an ogling youth pauses between bites of a frankfurter and roll. Call this the prelude.

Fury has been objective so far; now it goes beneath the surface of the news reports and considers a lynching in terms of community reaction and the law. Strand returns to righteousness. The responsible business men agree that it was a "Community, not an Individual thing"; they pledge themselves to cover up. The women quote the minister: "Some things are better forgiven and forgotten." But the law, handicapped by hypocrisy and perjury, moves to punish the mob leaders; twenty-two citizens of Strand go on trial for their lives; and Joe Wilson, who had miraculously escaped, sits by his radio and hears them perjure themselves. His enjoyment is keen and his course of action clear to him: he is legally dead, legally murdered; he will let his legal killers stand a legal trial, get a legal sentence and a legal death.

The trial proceeds and its outcome will not be divulged here; but you will see in it a reenactment of hundreds of lynch trials that have been held, of thousands that might have been held to determine the guilt of the men and women responsible for the six thousand-odd lynchings in this country during the last forty-nine years. And it is a trial scene written in acid, a searing commentary upon a national disregard for the due processes of law and order that finds flower in such organizations as Detroit's Black Legion and kindred "100 percent American" societies.

This has been a completely enthusiastic report, and such was our intention. Hollywood rarely bothers with themes bearing any relation to significant aspects of contemporary life. When it does, in most cases, its approach is timid, uncertain or misdirected. *Fury* is direct, forthright and vehement. That it is brilliantly executed as well makes it all the more notable.

Cinematically it is almost flawless. Mr. Lang, director of *Metropolis* and *M,* had been in Hollywood almost two years before Metro-Goldwyn-Mayer permitted him to make this picture. It was worth waiting for. Nor can we fail to salute its cast for their sincere and utterly convincing performances. Mr. Tracy's bitter portrait of Joe Wilson, Miss Sidney's moving portrayal of the sweetheart, Walter Abel's District Attorney, Edward Ellis as the Sheriff, Bruce Cabot as the town bully, Frank Albertson and George Walcott as Wilson's brothers, Walter Brennan's loose-mouthed rustic deputy—all of these, and others, have a share in the glory of *Fury*.

—F.S.N., June 6, 1936

g

GALLIPOLI

Directed by Peter Weir: written by David
Williamson, based on a story by Mr. Weir: director
of photography, Russell Boyd: edited by William
Anderson: music by Brian May: production
designer, Wendy Weir: produced by Robert Stigwood and Patricia Lovell: released by Paramount
Pictures. Running time: 110 minutes.

With: Mark Lee (Archy), Bill Kerr (Jack), Ron Gra-
ham (Wallace Hamilton), Harold Hopkins (Les
McCann), Charles Yunupingu (Zac), Heath Harris
(Stockman), Gerda Nicolson (Rose Hamilton),
Brian Anderson (Angus) and Mel Gibson (Frank
Dunne).

A young athlete takes a dare. A handsome runner
in the first bloom of youth, he agrees to race
barefoot against a bully on horseback, even though the
odds are stacked hopelessly against him—and even
though an important contest he has been training for
is only days away. He cuts his feet badly while outrun-
ning the horse, but not even the bruises can lessen his
bravado. So when the day of the major race arrives, he
runs triumphantly. And when he decides, on this same
day, to enlist in the army, he does so with the same
reckless, buoyant self-confidence that induced him to
compete with the horse and to court disaster.

Peter Weir's *Gallipoli,* which opens today at the
Baronet, follows this young Australian and others like
him to the fateful World War I battle of the title.
Beginning with the footrace, and ending with the
amphibious military maneuver that proved so catastrophic for the British and Australian forces, the film
approaches the subject of war so obliquely that it can't
properly be termed a war movie. Besides, it is prettier
than any war film has ever been, which makes its emotional power something of a surprise. Mr. Weir's work
has a delicacy, gentleness, even wispiness that would
seem not well suited to the subject. And yet his film
has an uncommon beauty, warmth, and immediacy
and a touch of the mysterious, too.

Touches of the mysterious are certainly Mr. Weir's
stock in trade; in *The Last Wave* and *Picnic at Hanging
Rock,* the bewildering, magical elements outweigh all
else. In the more sweeping *Gallipoli,* he relies successfully on a greater naturalism, so that the story of his
young soldiers has the easy, uncomplicated momentum of a tale of action.

Yet the more elusive images, though infrequent, are
those for which the film is best remembered. The soldiers are first fired upon while they are bathing, and
Mr. Weir's underwater shot of these surprised, naked
young swimmers in reddening water is one of his
loveliest and his most disturbing. So is the image of
the night landing at Gallipoli, with boats full of soldiers waiting quietly, utterly in limbo, enveloped in a
blue mist.

Much of *Gallipoli* has the ring of a chronicle of
boyish exploits, albeit an unusually good-looking and
sweet one. Archy (Mark Lee), the handsome blond
runner of the opening scene, becomes fast friends
with Frank (Mel Gibson), a more ironic, less golden-
limbed fellow, who happens also to be a track star.
Together, they journey from rural Australia to Perth,
traveling across blindingly white desert (another of
Mr. Weir's striking images) to reach the post where

they plan to enlist. Their path also leads to Cairo, where Mr. Weir stages a long sequence of soldiers' experiencing their last carefree moments at the bazaar, a sequence at once comic and touching. Mr. Weir, whose other films have had their share of mumbo-jumbo, shows himself here to be well able to work in a forthright and engaging manner.

He is also very successful with his actors. Mr. Lee, with no previous film experience and sunny good looks, makes a very serviceable Archy, and Mr. Gibson shows wit, ingenuity and range as Frank. A number of small roles are well handled, even those that suffer from the sentimentality Mr. Weir imposes on some portions of the story. Bill Hunter, as a major who brings a bottle of champagne off to war (a gift from his wife, for him to drink on their anniversary), is most effective despite the maudlin side to his role. So are David Argue, Robert Grubb and Tim McKenzie, the various young players whose primary job here is to await a terrible end.

Much of *Gallipoli* has a full-blown, almost romantic style more akin to that of *My Brilliant Career* than to *Breaker Morant,* another Australian film dealing with that country's military history. There's nothing pointed in Mr. Weir's decorous approach, even when the material would seem to call for toughness. But if the lush mood makes *Gallipoli* a less weighty war film than it might be, it also makes it a more airborne adventure.

—J.M., August 28, 1981

GANDHI

Produced and directed by Richard Attenborough; written by John Briley; directors of photography, Billy Williams and Ronnie Taylor; edited by John Bloom; music by Ravi Shankar; art designers, Robert Laing, Ram Yedekar and Norman Dorme; released by Columbia Pictures. Running time: 188 minutes.

With: Ben Kingsley (Mahatma Gandhi), Candice Bergen (Margaret Bourke-White), Edward Fox (General Dyer), John Gielgud (Lord Irwin), Trevor Howard (Judge Broomfield), John Mills (The Viceroy), Martin Sheen (Walker) and Rohini Hattangady (Kasturba Gandhi).

True greatness cannot be hidden behind mere ordinariness. Some subjects are so pervasively great that no film, given a certain level of intelligence on the part of the people who make it, can fail to catch something of the essence.

Such a subject is Mohandas K. Gandhi (1869–1948), the great Indian political leader who used nonviolent resistance to win the Indian subcontinent's freedom from the British Empire, and who lived to see that dream split in the partition of India and Pakistan.

On independence day in August 1947, when someone used the word "congratulations," Gandhi is reported to have said that condolences would be more in order. Six months later, Gandhi, who was born a Hindu but who preached the brotherhood of men under one God, was assassinated in Delhi by a Hindu fanatic. His is one of the great stories of modern times.

Gandhi, produced and directed by Richard Attenborough (*Oh! What a Lovely War, Young Winston*), is a big, amazingly authentic-looking movie, very sincere and aware of its responsibilities in the panoramic manner of a giant post office mural. It has huge, rather emotionless scenes of spectacle that are the background for more or less obligatory historical confrontations in governors' palaces and, best of all, for intimate, small-scale vignettes from Gandhi's life. The film follows him from his days as a young lawyer in South Africa, through the evolution of his political activism and asceticism, until his death at the age of seventy-nine.

Gandhi, which opens today at the Ziegfeld Theater, is most effective when it is being most plain and direct, like Gandhi himself. In Ben Kingsley, the young Anglo-Indian actor who plays the title role, the film also has a splendid performer who discovers the humor, the frankness, the quickness of mind that make the film far more moving than you might think possible.

Mr. Kingsley, a member of London's Royal Shakespeare Company, looks startlingly like Gandhi. But this is no waxworks impersonation. It's a lively, searching performance that holds the film together as it attempts to cover nearly half a century of private and public turmoil.

Neither Mr. Attenborough nor John Briley, who wrote the screenplay, are particularly adventurous filmmakers. Yet in some ways their almost obsessively middle-brow approach—their fondness for the gestures of conventional biographical cinema—seems self-effacing in a fashion suitable to the subject. Since Roberto Rossellini is not around to examine Gandhi in a film that would itself reflect the rigorous self-denial of the man, this very ordinary style is probably best.

Gandhi is least effective when it is dealing with historical events and personages, especially British personages, who are portrayed by such as John Gielgud, Edward Fox, John Mills, Trevor Howard and Michael Hordern. Some of them come very close to being cartoons, the sort of Englishmen who are always identified by having either a teacup or a whiskey glass in hand. The people who play Lord Mountbatten, India's last viceroy, and Lady Mountbatten look remarkably lifelike but sort of stuffed.

Somewhat better are the Indian actors who play Pandit Nehru (Roshan Seth), Mohammed Ali Jinnah (Alyque Padamsee), and Gandhi's wife, Kasturba (Rohini Hattangady). Athol Fugard, the South African playwright, has one brief, effective scene as General Smuts. Ian Charleson of *Chariots of Fire* has a small part as one of Gandhi's early English supporters, and Martin Sheen turns up from time to time as an American newspaper reporter. Candice Bergen is on hand at the end as Margaret Bourke-White, the *Life* magazine photographer.

Though *Gandhi* is long—more than three hours—it is full of scenes that catch the emotions by surprise. Among them are the funny, bitter sequence in which Gandhi is booted out of his first-class railroad seat in South Africa, a suddenly angry encounter with his wife when she haughtily refuses to clean the latrines at an ashram, and a scene in which Gandhi basks in the adoration of Margaret Bourke-White and threatens to teach her how to spin.

Also moving is an early scene in South Africa when Gandhi, long before he adopted the loincloth as his only dress, beams proudly at his small, immaculately tailored sons. "I'm so proud of them," he says. "Perfect little English gentlemen!"

The film portrays the political events from 1915 until independence in broad, "You Are There" style, sometimes with real dramatic impact, as in the protests over the government's salt monopoly, but sometimes perfunctorily, considering the awful nature of the events. This is particularly true of the film's handling of the Amritsar massacre of 1919 when British troops were ordered to fire on hundreds of unarmed Indians.

Considering its length, *Gandhi* should probably be allowed its small share of silly lines. Gandhi: "Who's that fellow?" Friend: "Young Nehru. He may amount to something someday." These are small lapses but they shouldn't happen in a film project that was undertaken—as this one was by Mr. Attenborough—as a special mission.

Of more overall importance is the possibility that the film will bring Gandhi to the attention of a lot of people around the world for the first time, not as a saint but as a self-searching, sometimes fallible human being with a sense of humor as well as of history. "I have friends," he says to Margaret Bourke-White at one point, "who are always telling me how much it costs to keep me in poverty."

—*V.C., December 8, 1982*

GANGS OF NEW YORK

Directed by Martin Scorsese; written by Jay Cocks, Steven Zaillian and Kenneth Lonergan, based on a story by Mr. Cocks; director of photography, Michael Ballhaus; edited by Thelma Schoonmaker; music by Howard Shore; production designer, Dante Ferretti; produced by Alberto Grimaldi and Harvey Weinstein; released by Miramax Films. Running time: 165 minutes.

With: Leonardo DiCaprio (Amsterdam Vallon), Daniel Day-Lewis (Bill the Butcher), Cameron Diaz (Jenny Everdeane), Liam Neeson (Priest Vallon), Jim Broadbent (Boss Tweed), John C. Reilly (Happy Jack), Henry Thomas (Johnny) and Brendan Gleeson (Monk McGinn).

Gangs of New York, Martin Scorsese's brutal, flawed and indelible epic of 19th-century urban criminality, begins in a mudwalled, torchlighted cavern, where a group of warriors prepare for battle, arming themselves with clubs and blades and armoring themselves in motley leather and cloth. Though this is Lower Manhattan in 1846, it might as well be the Middle Ages or the time of Gilgamesh: these warlike rituals have an archaic, archetypal feeling.

And the participants are aware of this. As the members of various colorfully named Irish gangs emerge into the winter daylight of Paradise Square (a place long since given over to high-rises and resurrected here on the grounds of the vast Cinecitta studio complex in Rome), their native-born Protestant enemies greet them with an invocation of "the ancient laws of combat." The ensuing melee turns the new-fallen snow pink with blood and claims the life of Priest Vallon (Liam Neeson), an Irish gang chieftain whose young son witnesses the carnage.

Sixteen years later, the boy, whose name is Amsterdam, has grown into Leonardo DiCaprio, his wide, implacable face framed by lank hair and a wispy Van Dyke. He returns from a long stint in the Hell Gate Reformatory to his old neighborhood, the Five Points, and finds it ruled by his father's killer, Bill Cutting (Daniel Day-Lewis), known as the Butcher, a swaggering monster who has turned the anniversary of Priest's death into a local holiday.

Like a figure out of Jacobean theater or a Dumas novel, Amsterdam is consumed by the need for revenge. With the help of a boyhood friend (Henry Thomas), he infiltrates the Butcher's inner circle, becoming a surrogate son to the man who assassinated his father and who now, in accordance with those ancient laws, venerates Priest's memory.

The New York evoked in Amsterdam's voice-over is "a city full of tribes and war chiefs," whose streets are far meaner than any Mr. Scorsese has contemplated before. The Butcher has formed an alliance of convenience with Boss Tweed (Jim Broadbent), the kingpin of Tammany Hall, and together they administer an empire of graft, extortion and larceny that would put any 20th-century movie gangster or political boss to shame. Rival fire companies turn burning buildings into sites of rioting and plunder; crowds gather to witness hangings, bare-knuckled boxing contests and displays of knife throwing.

As new immigrants, from Ireland and elsewhere, pour off the ships in New York harbor, they are mustered into Tweed's Democratic Party and then, since they lack the $300 necessary to buy their way out, into the Union Army. Occasionally a detachment of reform-minded swells will tour the Points, availing themselves of the perennial privileges of squeamish titillation and easy moral superiority. This anarchic inferno is, in Amsterdam's words, not so much a city as "a cauldron in which a great city might be forged."

And in recreating it, Mr. Scorsese has made a near-great movie. His interest in violence, both random and organized, is matched by his love of street-level spectacle. His Old New York is a gaudy multiethnic carnival of misrule, music and impromptu theater, a Brueghel painting come to life. Though the details of this lawless, teeming, vibrant milieu may be unfamiliar, we nonetheless instinctively recognize it, from the 19th-century novels of Dickens and Zola, from samurai movies and American westerns and from some of this director's previous films.

Most notably in *Mean Streets, Goodfellas, The Age of Innocence* and *Casino,* Mr. Scorsese has functioned as a kind of romantic visual anthropologist, fascinated by tribal lore and language, by half acknowledged codes of honor and retribution and by the boundaries between loyalty and vengeance, between courtesy and violence, that underlie a given social order.

As in *Casino* and *The Age of Innocence,* the setting of *Gangs* is sometimes more interesting than the story. At 2 hours 45 minutes, the film, deftly edited by Mr. Scorsese's frequent collaborator Thelma Schoonmaker, moves swiftly and elegantly. It is never dull, but I must confess that I wish it were longer, so that the lives of the protagonists, rather than standing out in relief against a historical background, were more fully embedded within it. The quasi-Oedipal struggle between Amsterdam and Bill is meant to have a mythic resonance, but that makes it the most conventional element in the picture.

The relationship between the two men is triangulated by Jenny Everdeane (Cameron Diaz), a flame-haired thief (and a protégée of Bill's) who catches Amsterdam's eye and steals his lucky religious medallion. But like Sharon Stone in *Casino,* Ms. Diaz ends up with no outlet for her spitfire energies, since her character is more a structural necessity—the linchpin of male jealousy—than a fully imagined person. The limitations of her role point to a more serious lapse, which is the movie's lack of curiosity about what women's lives might have been like in Old New York.

Like Tony Soprano's crew in the V.I.P. room at the Bada Bing, Bill and his minions spend a lot of time cavorting with half-naked prostitutes, which is fair (and for all I know accurate) enough. But all the glum evocation of lost fathers makes you wonder if any of these guys had mothers, and you wonder what a typical household in the Five Points might have looked like. (Though I, like just about everyone else had been waiting impatiently for *Gangs* I almost wish Mr. Scorsese and his screenwriters had been delayed long enough to take account of *Paradise Alley*, Kevin Baker's new novel about the draft riots of 1863, in which some of the events touched on in this movie are perceived through women's eyes.)

These objections should not detract from an appreciation of what Mr. Scorsese and his cast have done. Mr. DiCaprio and Ms. Diaz may be too pretty for the neighborhood, but one should hardly hold their being movie stars against them; they are smart, eager and intrepid actors as well. For his part Mr. Day-Lewis positively luxuriates in his character's villainy and turns Bill's flavorsome dialogue into vernacular poetry.

He understands the Shakespearean dimensions of the character and has enough art to fill them out. Surrounded by Irish brogues and deracinated British accents, Mr. Day-Lewis has the wit to speak an early version of Noo Yawkese, making the Butcher the butt of a marvelous historical joke: this bigoted, all-but-forgotten nativist, it turns out, bequeathed his speech patterns to the children of the immigrants he despised.

Gangs of New York is an important film as well as an entertaining one. With this project, Mr. Scorsese has made his passionate ethnographic sensibility the vehicle of an especially grand ambition. He wants not only to reconstruct the details of life in a distant era but to construct, from the ground up, a narrative of historical change, to explain how we—New Yorkers, Americans, modern folk who disdain hand-to-hand bloodletting and overt displays of corruption—got from there to here, how the ancient laws gave way to modern ones.

Such an ambition is rare in American movies, and rarer still is the sense of tragedy and contradiction that Mr. Scorsese brings to his saga. There is very little in the history of American cinema to prepare us for the version of American history Mr. Scorsese presents here. It is not the usual triumphalist story of moral progress and enlightenment, but rather a blood-soaked revenger's tale, in which the modern world arrives in the form of a line of soldiers firing into a crowd.

The director's great accomplishment, the result of three decades of mulling and research inspired by Herbert Asbury's *Gangs of New York*—a 1928 book nearly as legendary as the world it illuminates—has been to bring to life not only the texture of the past but its force and velocity as well. For all its meticulously imagined costumes and sets (for which the pro-

duction designer, Dante Ferretti, surely deserves an Oscar), this is no costume drama.

It is informed not by the polite antiquarianism of Merchant and Ivory but by the political ardor of someone like Luchino Visconti, one of Mr. Scorsese's heroes. *Senso,* Visconti's lavish 1953 melodrama set during the Italian Risorgimento (and his first color film), is one of the touchstones of *My Voyage to Italy,* Mr. Scorsese's fascinating, quasi-autobiographical documentary on postwar Italian cinema.

Though *Gangs of New York* throws in its lot with the rabble rather than the aristocracy, it shares with *Senso* (and also with *The Leopard,* Visconti's 1963 masterpiece) a feeling that the past, so full of ambiguity and complexity, of barbarism and nobility, continues to send its aftershocks into the present. It shows us a world on the brink of vanishing and manages to mourn that world without doubting the inevitability or the justice of its fate.

"America was born in the streets," the posters for *Gangs* proclaim. Later, Amsterdam Vallon, in the aftermath of the draft riots, muses that "our great city was born in blood and tribulation." Nobody as steeped in film history as Mr. Scorsese could offer such a metaphor without conjuring the memory of D. W. Griffith's *Birth of a Nation,* and Griffith, along with John Ford and others, is one of the targets of Mr. Scorsese's revisionism.

In Griffith's film, adapted from *The Clansman,* a bestselling novel by Thomas Dixon, the American republic was reborn after Reconstruction, when the native-born whites of the North and South overcame their sectional differences in the name of racial supremacy. Ford's myth of American origins—which involved the subjugation of the frontier and the equivocal replacement of antique honor by modern justice—also typically took place after the Civil War.

In *Gangs,* which opens nationwide today, the pivotal event in our history is the riot that convulsed New York in July of 1863. While this emphasis places the immigrant urban working class at the center of the American story—a fairly radical notion in itself—the film hardly sentimentalizes the insurrection, which was both a revolt against local and federal authority and a vicious massacre of the black citizens of New York.

The rioters are seen as exploited, oppressed and destined to be cannon fodder in a war they barely understand, but they are far from heroic, and the vio-

367

lence of the riots makes the film's opening gang battle seem quaint and decorous. What we are witnessing is the eclipse of warlordism and the catastrophic birth of a modern society. Like the old order, the new one is riven by class resentment, racism and political hypocrisy, attributes that change their form at every stage of history but that seem to be as embedded in human nature as the capacity for decency, solidarity and courage.

This is historical filmmaking without the balm of right-thinking ideology, either liberal or conservative. Mr. Scorsese's bravery and integrity in advancing this vision can hardly be underestimated.

This movie was a long time in the making, but its life has barely begun. Now that the industry gossip about it has subsided, let us hope that a more substantial discussion can start. People who care about American history, professionally and otherwise, will no doubt weigh in on the accuracy of its particulars and the validity of its interpretation; they will also, I hope, revisit some of their own suppositions in light of its unsparing and uncompromised imagining of the past. I said earlier that *Gangs of New York* is nearly a great movie. I suspect that, over time, it will make up the distance.

—*A.O.S., December 20, 2002*

THE GARDEN OF THE FINZI-CONTINIS

Directed by Vittorio De Sica; written (in Italian, with English subtitles) by Cesare Zavattini, Vittorio Bonicelli and Ugo Pirro, based on the novel by Giorgio Bassani; cinematographer, Ennio Guarnieri; edited by Adriana Novelli; music by Manuel De Sica; art designer, Giancarlo Bartolini; produced by Gianni Hecht Lucari and Arthur Cohn; released by Cinema V. Black and white. Running time: 95 minutes.

With: Dominique Sanda (Micol), Lino Capolicchio (Giorgio), Helmut Berger (Alberto), Fabio Testi (Malnate) and Romolo Valli (Giorgio's Father).

The garden of the Finzi-Continis, owned by a rich, intellectual Jewish-Italian family, is a sylvan sanctuary in the ducal town of Ferrara in 1938. Outside its walls, the good gentile citizens of Ferrara parade Fascist banners and slogans and prepare for war, but these things are barely acknowledged by the Finzi-Continis, who have their gardens and woods, a huge main house, a smaller but still imposing summer lodge and a private tennis court.

When the tennis club, observing Mussolini's new anti-Semitic laws, drops the Finzi-Continis from its rolls, Micol Finzi-Contini (Dominique Sanda) and her brother, Alberto (Helmut Berger), make a tentative gesture toward ending their aristocratic isolation. They invite friends—gentiles as well as Jewish—into their sanctuary to play tennis on long, lovely, hot summer afternoons. Micol is paid romantic court by Giorgio (Lino Capolicchio), the narrator of the film, a nice young Jewish boy, but she has midnight assignations with Malnate, a gentile whom she can never marry.

There are no commitments in such liaisons, and although Micol and Alberto are fond of their friends, they are different from them, even from their Jewish friends. They are aware of something that is apparent to no one else. They are dying but will do nothing about it.

The Garden of the Finzi-Continis, adapted from Giorgio Bassani's highly regarded novel (which I have not read), is certainly the best film that Vittorio De Sica has made in years, but the shabby habits he acquired when directing such things as *Sunflower* and *A Place for Lovers* keep intruding upon this new, much more ambitious work to render it less affecting than it has every right to be.

Mr. De Sica's way with end-of-an-era romance is to shoot almost everything in soft focus, as if he didn't trust the validity of the emotions in what seems to be a perfectly decent screenplay. The film's mood of impending doom is not discovered by the viewer, but imposed on him, by a syrupy musical score and by a camera that keeps panning to and from the sky, and shots of the sun, seen through the same sort of treetops that hover over the actors in the world of Newport cigarettes.

This is particularly frustrating because it has the effect of constantly reducing and denying the complexities of the characters and the performances. One suspects that Miss Sanda's Micol is a very special person—wise, sensuous and possessed with some kind of awful foresight—yet, in the context of popular movie fiction, she seems simply willful and cruel. When the movie means to hint, as it does that Micol and Alberto are something more than just fond siblings, it does so with such bluntness that any ambiguity seems merely arbitrary storytelling.

All of the other major performances are similarly reduced in dimension—Helmut Berger's tubercular Alberto, who is literally dying; Fabio Testi's Malnate, a gentile as doomed as the Finzi-Continis; and Lino Capolicchio's Giorgio, through whose eyes we watch the downfall of the Finzi-Continis, aristocrats fatally anesthetized against the realities of the world around them.

The Garden of the Finzi-Continis, which opened yesterday at the Plaza Theater, is a very melancholy movie, but its sentiments are essentially those contained on Micol's 78 r.p.m. recording of Tommy Dorsey's "Getting Sentimental Over You." They are prettily expressed but not profoundly moving.

—*V.C., December 17, 1971*

GAS FOOD LODGING

Written and directed by Allison Anders; based on the novel *Don't Look and It Won't Hurt* by Richard Peck; director of photography, Dean Lent; edited by Tracy S. Granger; music by J Mascis; production designer, Jane Ann Stewart; produced by Daniel Hassid, Seth M. Willenson and William Ewart; released by IRS Releasing. Running time: 100 minutes.

With: Brooke Adams (Nora), Ione Skye (Trudi), Fairuza Balk (Shade), James Brolin (John Evans), Robert Knepper (Dank), David Lansbury (Hamlet), Donovan Leitch (Darius) and Jacob Vargas (Javier).

The Film Forum has brought more excitement to moviegoing in the past two weeks than Hollywood has delivered all summer. The theater's second fine sleeper in a row, after Carl Franklin's *One False Move,* is Allison Anders's debut feature *Gas Food Lodging,* a look at three vibrant, restless women in a dusty Western town.

Imagine *The Last Picture Show* shot in color and shaped by a rueful feminine perspective, in a place where women are hopelessly anchored while the men drift through like tumbleweed. The becalmed town of Laramie, New Mexico, is the setting in which Nora (Brooke Adams), a hardworking waitress with a knowing, generous grin, has tried to bring up her two unruly daughters.

The older one, Trudi (Ione Skye), has turned defiantly trampy by the time the film begins, trying hard to hurt her mother while inflicting even greater pain upon herself. The younger and more hopeful girl, Shade (Fairuza Balk), loses herself in campy Mexican movie romances that tell her something about noble, long-suffering women in a cruel world.

The father in this family is long gone, and the mother and daughters spend too much time in indirect efforts to replace him. Trudi, an angry bombshell played with enormous delicacy and openness by Ms. Skye, fails miserably at drowning her sorrows with the town's loutish teenage boys. Nora has had her own share of dead-end encounters, enough to prompt one of her daughters to shout, "I think you just hate men," though that is clearly not the whole story.

Shade, thinking that finding a mate for her mother may offer some sort of family panacea, actually arranges a blind date (in an extremely funny dinner scene staged in the family's cramped mobile home) between Nora and a man with whom she has already had a long, deflating affair. Each of the three principals has learned the hard way that Laramie is a small town. Although the self-sufficiency of its heroines is always apparent, *Gas Food Lodging* pivots upon the arrival of various male strangers on this desolate scene. Although Ms. Anders (whose screenplay is based on a novel by Richard Peck) has to rely twice on introducing characters when one finds another crying, the meetings are felicitous and the tears very easy to understand. But *Gas Food Lodging* takes a wry, upbeat view of its principals, despite the enormous obstacles that face them and despite the absurdity of their plight. The fact that Shade is sweet on a boy who wishes she were more like Olivia Newton-John, or that Nora can stagger out of her trailer at dawn and bump into a possible Mr. Right, only heightens these women's justly whimsical view of the world.

Ms. Anders keeps her film expertly balanced between quiet despair and a sense of the miraculous, as manifested by the big, open skies and glorious sunrises and sunsets (with cinematography by Dean Lent) that punctuate the story.

When Trudi experiences a transforming romance with a sincere English geologist (Robert Knepper) who is passing through town, the consummation of the affair is staged unforgettably in a cave shimmering with eerie blue light.

Shade's burgeoning friendship with a shy Mexican boy (Jacob Vargas) takes an unexpected turn when his mother, who is deaf, motions for the couple to join her in an impromptu modern dance. At that particular moment the film overworks its sense of wonder, but most of the time Ms. Anders's instincts are uncannily right. *Gas Food Lodging* is a big film in a small setting, a keenly observed character study of women who don't know their own strength. The film shows how they find that strength and heal old wounds, discovering great reserves of grace and hope in the process.

There is nothing traditionally uplifting here, nor any cause for getting out one's handkerchief (at least until the story's closing moments); Ms. Anders directs in a spare, laconic style that keeps the material from degenerating into soap opera. But there are subtly etched characters, effortlessly fine performances and a moving story that is not easily forgotten.

Also in *Gas Food Lodging,* playing a small but crucial role, is James Brolin, who perfectly embodies the kinds of hopes and disappointments this story is all about.

Donovan Leitch, Ms. Skye's brother, appears as one of the landmarks in Shade's life, a window dresser with a taste for peculiar pop artifacts. A pair of psychedelic platform shoes that turn up prominently in a couple of scenes could easily have belonged to Mr. Leitch's namesake and father.

—*J.M., July 31, 1992*

GASLIGHT

Directed by George Cukor; written by John Van Druten, Walter Reisch and John L. Balderston, based on the play *Angel Street* by Patrick Hamilton; director of photography, Joseph Ruttenberg; edited by Ralph E. Winters; art director, Cedric Gibbons; music by Bronislau Kaper; produced by Arthur Hornblow Jr.; released by Metro-Goldwyn-Mayer. Black and white. Running time: 114 minutes.

With: Charles Boyer (Gregory Anton), Ingrid Bergman (Paula Alquist), Joseph Cotten (Brian Cameron), Dame May Whitty (Miss Thwaites), Angela Lansbury (Nancy Oliver), Barbara Everest (Elizabeth Tompkins), Emil Rameau (Maestro Mario Guardi), Edmund Breon (General Huddleston), Halliwell Hobbes (Mr. Muffin), Tom Stevenson (Williams), Heather Thatcher (Lady Dalroy), Lawrence Grossmith (Lord Dalroy) and Jakob Gimpel (Pianist).

That dark and shivering study of Victorian villainy which has been shaking the boards of Broadway for more than two years under the title of *Angel Street* is now doing similar violence to the Capitol Theater's screen, where it arrived yesterday under the no more illuminating title of *Gaslight*. But don't let that mellow come-on fool you, all ye who enter here. Prepare yourselves rather for a lengthy and restless stretch on tenterhooks. For Metro has given a pungent production to the Patrick Hamilton play. It has used Ingrid Bergman and Charles Boyer in the dominant roles of the distraught wife and her wicked spouse. And it has pulled such a ticklish assortment of melodramatic camera tricks that the audience was giggling with anxiety at a performance yesterday.

Maybe we shouldn't tell you what it is all about, even though that knowledge is rather general with theatergoers by now. But we can, at least, slip the information that the study is wholly concerned with the obvious endeavors of a husband to drive his wife slowly mad. And with Mr. Boyer doing the driving in his best dead-pan hypnotic style, while the flames flicker strangely in the gas jets and the mood music bongs with heavy threats, it is no wonder that Miss Bergman goes to pieces in a most distressing way. Both of these popular performers play their roles right to the hilt.

Nice little personality vignettes are interestingly contributed, too, by Joseph Cotten as a stubborn detective, Dame May Whitty and Angela Lansbury as a maid. But it must be stated frankly that the film doesn't match the play, mainly because of circumstances of an ambiguous physical sort. The play, by its rigid confinement within the limitations of one room, prevades the spectator with the horror and frustration of a claustrophobic mood. One is dragged imperceptibly right up there into that room and made to experience the same emotions as the bewildered and fear-driven wife. But the very flexibility of the camera, the constant cutting away from that one scene, induces the audience to take a comfortably objective point of view. Much of the fearful immediacy of the play is sadly lost in the film.

—B.C., May 5, 1944

GATE OF HELL

Directed by Teinosuke Kinugasa; written (in Japanese, with English subtitles) by Mr. Kinugasa, based on a play by Kan Kikuchi; cinematographer, Kôhei Sugiyama; music by Yasushi Akutagawa; produced by Masaichi Nagata; released by Daiei Films. Running time: 89 minutes.

With: Machiko Kyô (Lady Kesa), Kazuo Hasegawa (Moritoh), Isao Yamagata (Wataru), Koreya Senda (Kiyomori) and Yataro Kurokawa (Shigemori).

Out of Japan has come another weird and exquisite film—this one in color of a richness and harmony that matches that of any film we've ever seen. It is a somber and beautiful presentation of a thirteenth-century legendary tale, smoothly and awesomely unfolding behind the volcanic title, *Gate of Hell.* Under the sponsorship of the Japan Society, it opened last night at the Guild.

It is hard to convey in simple language the moving qualities of this lovely film, which, among other things, was the winner of the grand prize at the Cannes film festival last spring. The secret, perhaps, of its rare excitement is the subtlety with which it blends a subterranean flood of hot emotions with the most magnificent flow of surface serenity. The tensions and agonies of violent passions are made to seethe behind a splendid silken screen of stern formality, dignity, self-discipline and sublime esthetic harmonies. The very essence of ancient Japanese culture is rendered a tangible stimulant in this film.

The story itself is quite simple—neither so complex nor abstruse as the stories of Rashomon and Ugetsu, recent imports from postwar Japan. It is the story of a thirteenth-century warrior—a handsome and proud

samurai—who falls in love with a dainty Japanese lady whom he aids and saves during a palace revolt and later requests in marriage, only to learn that she already is wed. Burning with a mad desire for her, he besieges her in her happy married state and causes her such shame and sorrow that she commits suicide.

It is simple, and yet the strain and anguish that develop as the story moves on—out of the violence and turbulence of the initial insurrection into a consideration of the turbulence that occurs amid seemingly peaceful surroundings in a man's and a woman's hearts—are as gripping and full of silent terror as they might be in a more elaborate plot. The individual frustration that a social form imposes is the gist of its timeless tragedy.

How Teinosuke Kinugasa, who wrote the screenplay and directed this film, has achieved such extraordinary emotional impact is a matter of true wizardry. His use of color (Eastman) as applied to the Japanese scene, with such economy in his composition and such texture and color subtleties in his materials, is on a level that renders it comparable to the best in Japanese art. And his use of music and physical movements has a weird eloquence and grace that are profound.

One could rhapsodize for a whole column on the beauty and excitement of individual scenes—a shot of a coral-colored temple ranked with white-kimonoed priests by a blue sea; a sequence reenacting a horse race, full of feudal pomp and panoply; a truly bewitching vision of a pale lady in a blossom-pink robe twanging the strings of a strange musical instrument in a quiet Japanese home.

And one could write reams of lush enthusiasm for the porcelain beauty and electrifying grace of Machiko Kyô, the lady of *Rashomon and Ugetsu,* who is the heroine here. For it is she, with her great power of suggestion with a minimum of gesture and a maximum use of the tiny mouth and eyes, who conveys the sense of sadness and despair that suffuses this film.

Kazuo Hasegawa as the proud and insistent samurai is powerful, too, in his vigorous, vain formality and Isao Yamagata is quietly compelling as the dignified husband of the harassed heroine.

There is much to be got from this picture—much to savor and deeply enjoy. English subtitles, which oddly glisten, carry the sense of the dialogue.

—B.C., December 11, 1954

A GEISHA

Directed by Kenji Mizoguchi: written (in Japanese, with English subtitles) by Yoshikata Yoda, based on a story by Mr. Matsutaro Kawaguchi: cinematographer. Kazuo Miyagawa: edited by Mitsuji Miyata: music by Ichiro Saito: art designer. Kazumi Koike: distributed by New Yorker Films. Black and white. Running time: 87 minutes.

With: Michiyo Korgure (Miyoharu). Ayako Wakao (Eiko). Seizaburô Kawazu (Kusuda). Chieko Naniwa (Chimi) and Eitarô Shindô (Sawamoto).

To the extent that any Japanese film directors can be well known in this country, Akira Kurosawa and Yasujiro Ozu have made it. Yet Kenji Mizoguchi, who died in 1958 and who may well be one of the greatest filmmakers of all time, remains relatively obscure, even to those audiences for whom such obscurity is usually a certification of honor.

Kurosawa had the luck to make a couple of films that found comparatively large American audiences (*Rashomon, Seven Samurai*) while Ozu, though not as well known as Kurosawa, became something of a small fashion early in the decade with the release of many of his later films.

To date, fewer than ten Mizoguchi works have received commercial engagements in New York, and though each has been critically acclaimed, especially *Ugetsu, Sansho the Bailiff* and *Utamaro and His Five Women,* there's never been a continuing Mizoguchi audience. Every time we receive a new-old Mizoguchi, he must be rediscovered.

Mizoguchi's *A Geisha,* which is having its New York theatrical premiere today at the Film Forum, was made in 1953. Unlike most of the other Mizoguchis we've seen here, it is set in its own time, 1953, in Kyoto, though it shares with the director's period films the quality of being incredibly beautiful without being particularly, foolishly pretty.

The story is about the friendship of two women, Miyoharu (Michiyo Korgure), an older geisha bound by a tradition that no longer holds, and Eiko (Ayako Wakao), a sixteen-year-old girl whom Miyoharu agrees to sponsor and train as a geisha after the death of Eiko's mother, a former geisha who'd been Miyoharu's friend. Though Mizoguchi's film makes only two quick trips outside Kyoto's teahouses and geisha houses, the film is as much about the social revolution taking place in 1953 occupied Japan as it is about the emotional relationship between the two women.

From the beginning, it's apparent that the young Eiko is not going to be a conventional, subservient geisha. After a class in which the teacher has told her pupils that the geisha is a work of art, like Noh drama and the tea ceremony, Eiko wonders whether the new Japanese constitution doesn't guarantee a geisha the right to say no to a patron. The other young women giggle, but Eiko is serious.

It's evidence of the system of balances that always operate in a Mizoguchi film that as Eiko is wondering about the geisha's constitutional rights, the geisha's role is being corrupted. In postwar Japan, the geisha, who had once been a highly skilled entertainer, was being called upon with increasing frequency to perform the duties of the not necessarily skilled prostitute.

It's a trend that the older Miyoharu resists, more or less passively, while Eiko does battle. When her would-be patron takes the two women on a trip to Tokyo, Eiko refuses to perform the duties she does in the teahouse. "I serve at parties," she says, "I'm a lady."

This doesn't put off the man. He makes a lunge at her, wrestles her to the floor, plants a big kiss on her mouth, to which Eiko responds by biting his lip so badly the fellow has to be hospitalized. Because of the scandal, the two women are blackballed by all of Kyoto's teahouses. Miyoharu is confused, worried, though she doesn't blame the younger woman. Says Eiko, in effect, "If that's what being a geisha means, then I don't want it."

The charm of *A Geisha* is the compassionate but completely unsentimental way it regards the two women's friendship, as well as the manner in which this friendship changes and deepens as their responsibilities, each to the other, are acknowledged. Miyoharu is much the more interesting of the two, but it is the younger Eiko who is more often right.

Though the landscape of the film is restricted to a small, rather exotic quarter in Kyoto, *A Geisha* is far from esoteric. The scope is narrow and the focus is deep.

The two actresses who dominate the film are splendid, as are several other performers, especially Chieko Naniwa, who plays the not unkind but money-minded doyenne of Kyoto's geishas, and Eitarô Shindô, who plays Eiko's father.

A Geisha is actually a remake, being based on a film Mr. Mizoguchi made in 1936 that, to my knowledge, has never been released here, yet the 1953 version is far from being dated. One can say that the best, most intelligent film about women to be seen here in the last twelve months was a film made twenty-five years ago.

—V.C., June 1, 1978

THE GENERAL

Written, directed and produced by John Boorman: director of photography. Seamus Deasy: edited by Ron Davis: music by Richie Buckley: production designer. Derek Wallace: released by Sony Pictures Classics.

With: Brendan Gleeson (Martin Cahill). Maria Doyle Kennedy (Frances). Angeline Ball (Tina). Eamon Owens (Young Cahill) and Jon Voight (Inspector Ned Kenny).

No doubt John Boorman's canny, elegant new film, *The General*, about the notorious Irish thief Martin Cahill, hits unusually close to home for the filmmaker. The real Mr. Cahill actually did hit Mr. Boorman's home some years ago, and he stole the gold record that had been awarded the director for "Dueling Banjos," from *Deliverance*. Now Mr. Boorman has his chance to return the favor, and what a chance it is. He tells this tale of an Irish underworld original with an unerring instinct for the captivating detail. And he presents this film (photographed by Seamus Deasy) in such seductively beautiful black and white that it has the visual precision of a photo essay. The black-and-white tones (shot on color stock) are so rich that the ski masks of burglars wind up looking like velvet.

Mr. Boorman begins this story, a much more familiar one in Ireland than it is here, with the brutal end of Cahill's career. (He died in 1994, caught not by the police who had dogged him for years but by the Provisional I.R.A.) He then deftly traces the basis for Cahill's formidable reputation. Nicknamed after General Douglas MacArthur, he showed a taste for larceny at an early age (and is played as a boy fleetingly by Eamon Owens, fiery young star of *The Butcher Boy*). Mr. Cahill's biographer, Paul Williams, maintains that when Cahill tried to enlist in the Navy at fifteen,

in 1964, and filled out an application, "Martin chose the position of bugler. Unfortunately, due to his difficulties in school, he misread the word as 'burglar.'" Somehow a star criminal was born.

Always fascinated and sometimes aghast, *The General* watches Martin develop his trademark style. As played magnificently by Brendan Gleeson, who bears an amazing resemblance to the real Cahill, he had a modus operandi often bordering on pure mischief. Cahill went to such great lengths to hide his face from public view that he is most often seen in photographs hiding inside the hood of a ski parka. He presided over an unusual two-house domestic arrangement that involved both his wife (Maria Doyle Kennedy) and her sister, Tina (Angeline Ball), presented here as understanding and even understandable. Unlike most films based on true stories whose real participants are alive, well and legally represented, *The General* doesn't seem to pull its punches about its surviving characters. Mr. Boorman, working in top form with a keenly acerbic overview, has written the film so sharply that the facts speak well for themselves.

With his police nemesis, Inspector Ned Kenny, beautifully embodied by Jon Voight as a staunch, weary Javert who knows all Cahill's tricks, Cahill becomes for Mr. Boorman a figure of compelling controversy as well as a source of great crime tales. So the beauty of a jewel heist, which is presented here in all its crafty planning, is carefully placed in the shadow of its larger implications. As Kenny tells Cahill, he may be a smart thief but he has put 100 employees at the jewelry company out of work. In one of the film's most startling juxtapositions, Cahill punishes one of his own men so savagely that the act becomes part of his legend. Then he takes this same man to a hospital, having decided that the punishment was unwarranted. Mr. Boorman's great skill in unifying *The General* lies in creating a big, blustery, most unlikely hero whose nature so easily embraces both these extremes.

Tricky crime sequences here are especially well staged, and make fine use of Cahill's rampant contradictions. The most brazen (and famous) of these found Cahill playing the art lover, and with his band of henchmen spiriting off a cache of treasures, including a Vermeer, offering their own priceless opinions about the artwork, and carefully leaving the "Please Do Not Touch" sign undisturbed.

—J.M., October 2, 1998

GENERAL DELLA ROVERE

Directed by Roberto Rossellini; written (in Italian, with English subtitles) by Mr. Rossellini, Sergio Amidei, Diego Fabbri and Indro Montanelli, based on a story by Mr. Montanelli; cinematographer, Carlo Carlini; edited by Anna Maria Montanari and Cesare Cavagna; music by Renzo Rossellini; art designer, Piero Zuffi; produced by Moris Rossellini; released by Continental Distributing. Black and white. Running time: 130 minutes.

With: Vittorio De Sica (Bardone/Grimaldi), Hannes Messemer (Colonel Mueller), Vittorio Caprioli (Banchelli), Giuseppe Rossetti (Fabrizio), Sandra Milo (Olga), Anne Vernon (Valeria) and Baronessa Barzani (Contessa della Rovere).

Roberto Rossellini is back on the high dramatic plane of his historic *Open City* and similarly powerful *Paisan* with his new film, *General della Rovere,* which opened at the Paris yesterday. What is more, he has Vittorio De Sica to lend his skill to the principal role. The consequence is a communication to rank with the best of Italian films.

As he was in those two great postwar pictures, Signor Rossellini is again in the torn and terrible environment of his country toward the end of World War II. He has turned back the clock to those dark days when his country, experiencing defeat, was still occupied by the hated Nazis, who were stubbornly continuing the war. He has once more recalled the haunting anguish of his people's frustration and shame, their shattering demoralization and physical misery.

But he has also done the same thing he did in *Open City* and *Paisan.* He has turned the spotlight of his brilliant talent upon the isolated and unsung heroes of those times. He has caught in the clear eye of his camera the dauntless and gritty qualities of those impassioned resistance fighters who would not yield, even in prison and faced with death. He has shown, in the experience of one man, how the example of these heroes in defeat could inspire an ultimate emulation and a sense of moral victory.

His principal character is a gambler, a shifty and shameless gent who finds himself in dire circumstances in Genoa. The debts of his degenerate way of living have compelled him to scratch for funds in every dishonest and ignoble way conceivable. He preys upon the credulity and sentiment of prostitutes, and he takes money from frantic people for pretending to try to get their loved ones out of Nazi jails.

His most brazen and cowardly surrender of his integrity, however, comes when he agrees, for a promised reward and sanctuary in Switzerland, to participate in a dirty Nazi plot. He lets himself be put in a political prison impersonating a certain General della Rovere, a prize resistance leader only a few Nazis know has been secretly killed. By this treacherous deception, he is supposed to find out all he can about the identity and importance of other prisoners and serve in time as a valuable hostage.

But during his stay in prison several things occur to unsettle his greed and cynicism. He sees how other prisoners behave—little men with no claim to importance save their hatred of the Nazis and their devotion to Italy. He discovers the satisfaction of being respected and admired. And he receives a loving, loyal letter from the unknowing widow of the man he is supposed to be.

What this does to his spirit and how he faces up to the inevitable test of his self-respect and courage are the dramatic resolutions of this fine film.

It would be easy to say that the story is melodramatic, at least in part (as was *Open City*), and that some details are implausible. (It is rather surprising that no one spots the bogus general as a fraud.) It also would be forgivable to notice that Signor De Sica inclines to clown a bit in some of the involvements when humor is not the mood.

But on the whole the drama is terrific, accumulating and deepening as it goes along, until the final scene in the prison has a heartrending, nerve-twisting power, and Signor De Sica's performance, ranging from shifty and glib to dignified and laconic, is a beautiful thing.

But Signor Rossellini, working from a fine script by Sergio Amidei, Diego Fabbri and Indro Montanelli, elicits beautiful performances from everyone. As the Nazi colonel who devises and enforces the plot, Hannes Messemer is a picture of potent but reluctant efficiency. Vittorio Caprioli is fine as the most heroic prisoner and Baronessa Barzani is excellent in one scene as the general's wife. Giovanna Ralli and Sandra Milo are vivid as prostitutes.

The English subtitles do justice to the Italian dialogue, but that's about all.

—*B.C., November 22, 1960*

GENEVIEVE

Produced and directed by Henry Cornelius: written by William Rose: cinematographer. Christopher Challis: edited by Clive Donner: music by Larry Adler: choreography by Eric Rogers: released by Universal International Pictures. Running time: 86 minutes.

With: John Gregson (Alan). Dinah Sheridan (Wendy). Kenneth More (Ambrose Claverhouse). Kay Kendall (Rosalind Peters). Geoffrey Keen (First Speed Cop). Harold Siddons (Second Speed Cop). Joyce Grenfell (Hotel Proprietress) and Arthur Wonter (Elderly Gentleman).

On the strength of the current mania that some restless people have for automobiles of ancient vintage—what are fondly called "veteran cars"—a British producer-director, Henry Cornelius, has made a film that may cautiously be recommended as one of the funniest farce comedies in years. It is a thoroughly delirious little scramble that goes by the name of *Genevieve,* and anyone who doesn't get around to see it is going to miss a delightful movie ride.

Genevieve, we might add, is the term of affection by which the picture's heroine is known—said heroine being a Darracq roadster, vintage of 1904. But it covers much more than the stout body of an aged automobile. It covers a package of nimble mischief on the Sutton Theatre's screen.

What happens in *Genevieve* is simple: A nice young fellow who owns this antique car enters it, as has been his custom, for the annual London-to-Brighton Commemoration run. Along with half a hundred other veteran car maniacs in England, he anticipates the festive outing with bounding enthusiasm and joy. So does his pal—a jovial peacock—who owns a Spyker of the same year. But the wife and the lady friend of these fellows—well, they have a different point of view!

These poor females, dragged along by their menfolk as ballasting passengers, see the whole thing as juvenile madness on the part of overgrown kids. Bump and bounce through the peaceful English country in a couple of wheezy motorcars? Sheer idiocy and physical torture, to their way of thinking! But they go.

And so, on the run down to Brighton and then, on the breathless chase home, when the two pals, vexed

at each other, race for a bet of £100, the dear ladies alternately cheer and heckle, badger and spur their crazy men, complicating with emotional explosives the howlingest lot of popping and banking you've ever seen.

If that sounds suspiciously Keystonic, in the old Mack Sennett vein, rest assured that something more has been added by Mr. Cornelius and scriptwriter William Rose. For these gentlemen, whose humor is as impish as that of any of the postwar British jackanapes, are here interested in something a bit more basic than an ancient motorcar race. They are interested in the running of the sexes, the clatter and bang of jealousies, the hissing of tempermental punctures, the road-testing of true love.

Being extremely urbane fellows, as well as gentlemen of wit, they have gone about stating their interest with absolute impiousness and skill. They have no shame in proclaiming that an exhilarated husband and wife may be at one another's throats one minute and at one another's lips the next. A delicious sense of the erratic runs all through the film.

And the wit is not wasted on dullards, for the cast that Mr. Cornelius has to play this gay exposé of exuberance is blessed with awareness and charm. John Gregson is the dedicated owner of the mellow and sedate Genevieve. He also is the husband of a spirited helpmate, whom lovely Dinah Sheridan plays. Kenneth More is the blithe and cocky owner of the Spyker 1904, and Kay Kendall is the trim and stylish model whom he takes along for the weekend run. The four of them give as delightful a performance of romance and farce, cleverly intermingled, as anyone could wish.

Add to this a most merry and witty harmonica accompaniment, which Larry Adler composed and plays, and a fine Technicolor production, with the London-to-Brighton countryside as the scene, and you have the complete accomplishment of a ding-dong entertainment film.

—B.C., February 16, 1954

GENTLEMEN PREFER BLONDES

Directed by Howard Hawks: written by Charles Lederer. based on the play by Anita Loos and Joseph Fields: cinematographer. Harry Wild: edited by Hugh S. Fowler: music by Lionel Newman: art designers. Lyle Wheeler and Joseph C. Wright: produced by Sol C. Siegel: released by Twentieth Century Fox. Running time: 91 minutes.

With: Jane Russell (Dorothy). Marilyn Monroe (Lorelei). Charles Coburn (Sir Francis Beekman). Elliott Reid (Malone). Tommy Noonan (Gus Esmond). George Winslow (Henry Spofford 3d). Marcel Dalio (Magistrate). Taylor Holmes (Gus Esmond Sr.) and Norma Varden (Lady Beekman).

A sideline exchange of conversation, tossed off early in *Gentlemen Prefer Blondes,* the new Twentieth Century Fox musical with Jane Russell and Marilyn Monroe as its stars, gives a pretty fair indication of the fundamental aspects of this film, which bumped and gyrated broadly into the Roxy yesterday.

Says one bug-eyed fellow to another as the Misses Russell and Monroe do a languid parade up the gangplank of the Le Havre–bound *Ile de France:* "If this ship hit an iceberg and sank, which one would you save?" To which his admiring companion gurgles: "Those girls couldn't drown."

That subtle backlash of burlesque banter not only tags the brand of wit that flows with old-fashioned charm through the picture, but pointedly explains the buoyancy and survival of the young ladies in this bumptious film. For the simple fact is that the conveyance in which they are bravely embarked takes water almost from the beginning and sinks lower and lower as it goes. Along toward the end, it wholly flounders and sinks dismally into those depths reserved for the wreckage of screenplays that haven't the structure or the steam. But the Misses Monroe and Russell, with their famous charms and airy graces, keep bobbing like chips on a wave.

Credit their happy survival not so much to the inventions in the script, which was casually scribbled by Charles Lederer from the musical comedy by Joseph Fields and Anita Loos, or to the rambling and random direction of the oddly assigned Howard Hawks. Credit it simply to the well-defined construction and the outgoing natures of the girls, to one or two rampant song numbers, and the Technicolor flash of the ladies' clothes.

For the screenplay contrived by Mr. Lederer is less the classic saga of two smart dames, which was originally played beneath this title, than it is a silly tale of two dumb dolls. And Mr. Hawks's direction is uncomfortably cloddish and slow. Whatever there was of Miss Loos's memorable Lorelei Lee, the blonde whose hobby was money back in the easy-salad days, is lost, strayed, or possibly stolen in the foolish stunts set for Miss Monroe. And the gags pulled out for Miss Russell are devoid of character or charm.

Except for one plush production number, in which Miss Monroe sings that candid refrain, the theme song of the gold diggers, "Diamonds Are a Girl's Best Friend," there is not much class in this picture. The humor is mainly in such things as Miss Monroe's finding it difficult, for anatomical reasons, to squeeze her way through a porthole, or she and Miss Russell, conspiring to pull the pants off a gentleman friend. And the music is figured in such numbers as Miss Russell's violent chant to he-man love, sung for a bunch of squirming athletes, or in her rendering of a torrid shimmy in a French court.

Neither do the gentlemen in this dido—Charles Coburn, as a babbling diamond king, Tommy Noonan, as a dunce with lots of money and Elliott Reid, as the one who loses his pants—come up with anything other than usual helpings of slightly stewed corn.

And yet, there is that about Miss Russell and also about Miss Monroe that keeps you looking at them even when they have little or nothing to do. Call it inherent magnetism. Call it luxurious coquetry. Call it whatever you fancy. It's what makes this a—well, a buoyant show.

—B.C., July 16, 1953

GEORGY GIRL

Directed by Silvio Narizzano: written by Margaret Forster and Peter Nichols. based on the novel by Miss Forster: cinematographer. Ken Higgins: edited by John Bloom: music by Alexander Faris: art designer. Tony Woollard: produced by Otto Plaschkes and Robert A. Goldston: released by Columbia Pictures. Black and white. Running time: 100 minutes.

With: James Mason (James). Alan Bates (Joe). Lynn Redgrave (Georgy). Charlotte Rampling (Meredith). Bill Owen (Ted). Clare Kelly (Doris). Rachel Kempson (Ellen) and Denise Coffey (Peg).

There is a moment a little more than halfway through *Georgy Girl* when Lynn Redgrave, the improbably fey heroine, complains that "God always has another custard pie up his sleeve."

The pity of it is that the same cannot be said of the director, Silvio Narizzano. His solution when the going gets gummy, which it does more than occasionally in this perverse fairy tale, is to have Alan Bates strip down to his Jockey shorts or beyond (three times) or make a flying leap into a lustful embrace (I lost count), neither of which is quite as funny as a pie in the face.

There are genuinely comic moments in this film, which opened yesterday at the Fine Arts—Miss Redgrave reaching deep into her leather pouch of a handbag to bring forth a tiny shower of confetti for her just-married friends; James Mason trying to hide his joy as he marches, in time to a military dirge, to view the mortal remains of his unloved wife; Mr. Bates stiffening his lip and downing his doubts before hurling himself across a London street to keep a Registry Office appointment that will make an honest woman of Charlotte Rampling.

But to say that these moments are too few is not really the point. They just do not seem to belong in the same film with the sometimes tragic, sometimes bathetic, and oftentimes sordid scenes they relieve—like the one in which Miss Rampling raises a voice, not at all enfeebled by a difficult confinement, to tell her friend, her husband and the whole cockeyed world that she doesn't want the baby.

The trouble with *Georgy Girl* is that it is an unsuccessful translation of the Cinderella fantasy—by way of an intervening novel—into the angry-young-man idiom of twentieth-century London. It is perverse because the heroine runs from the arms of her Carnaby Street prince into a marriage with her fairy godfather, a switch that might have both enchanted and succeeded if Mr. Narizzano had decided—once and for all—whether he wanted to be Walt Disney or Tony Richardson.

What does enchant is the cast: Miss Rampling, who even in her most sulky moments is lovely to look at; Mr. Mason, who pauses, as he always has, for a deep breath before every speech but is most engaging as a new kind of Humbert Humbert; Mr. Bates, who almost always convinces that his highjinks and high spirits are genuine; and Miss Redgrave, an ugly duck-

ling of a girl who never gets even close to becoming a swan, but who has a heart-winning attractiveness her mugging cannot quite conceal.

Miss Redgrave—daughter of Sir Michael Redgrave and Rachel Kempson (who has a minor role in *Georgy Girl*) and younger sister of the Vanessa you met in *Morgan!*—cannot be quite as homely as she makes herself in this film. Slimmed down, cosseted in a couture salon, and given more of the brittle, sophisticated lines she tosses off with such abandon here, she could become a comedienne every bit as good as the late Kay Kendall.

—*M.S., October 18, 1966*

GET CARTER

Directed by Mike Hodges; written by Mr. Hodges, based on the novel *Jack's Return Home* by Ted Lewis; director of photography, Wolfgang Suschitzky; edited by John Trumper; music by Roy Bud; production designer, Ashton Gordon; produced by Michael Klinger; released by Metro-Goldwyn-Mayer. Running time: 112 minutes.

With: Michael Caine (Jack Carter), Ian Hendry (Eric Paice), Britt Ekland (Anna), John Osborne (Cyril Kinnear), Tony Beckley (Peter), George Sewell (Con McCarty), Geraldine Moffat (Glenda), Dorothy White (Margaret), Rosemarie Dunham (Edna), Alun Armstrong (Keith), Bryan Mosley (Cliff Brumby), Glynn Edwards (Albert Swift), Bernard Hepton (Thorpe) and Terence Rigby (Gerald Fletcher).

Jack Carter (Michael Caine) is a fastidious, small-time London hood, a natty dresser who reinforces himself with vitamin pills and wipes his silverware before eating. When he takes the train to Newcastle to investigate his brother's mysterious death, he passes the trip reading Raymond Chandler's *Farewell, My Lovely*, published here in 1940.

A little later, as Carter swigs a scotch in a mob-owned Newcastle pub, a lady, who probably wishes she looked like the young Lauren Bacall (but is disqualified by both pounds and pores), belts out the great, old (1941) Ralph Freed-Burton Lane number, "How About You?" Among other unlikely things, she likes New York in June—and Franklin Roosevelt's looks give her a thrill.

Within the next 48 hours, Carter goes to bed with a lonely landlady, past her prime, and the beautiful, neurotic mistress of a mob chief; he uncovers a racket in stag films, one of which stars his niece; he gets fingered and shot at, discovers a brutal murder and finally himself commits a couple that are in the style of ritual executions.

All of this may sound crushingly familiar, but I hope you'll read on, for the thing that makes *Get Carter* persistently and consistently interesting, even when it's not especially artful, is that it does a good deal more than simply recall the fiction, and the fictional attitudes, of an earlier era.

By contrasting the Chandler mythography with the facts of the dismal life of its protagonist, *Get Carter* manages to evoke a sense of irony that is both entertaining and complex, when the plot itself is simply breathless and confused. These successes, I assume, are the work of Mike Hodges, a 38-year-old British television director, who directed and wrote the movie (an adaptation of Ted Lewis's novel, *Jack's Return Home* as his first theatrical effort.

Chandler used to bristle when critics categorized his novels as murder mysteries, arguing that although some of his characters did commit murders, there was no mystery involved. Instead, he said, they murdered for sex or money, and, of course, they were brought to heel by that most durable of underpaid private eyes, Philip Marlowe.

The lovely irony of this movie is that although Jack Carter sees himself as a sort of latter-day Marlowe, he more closely resembles one of Chandler's minor characters, a petty crook with delusions of grandeur.

Marlowe's impulses were first fired by a fat fee, plus expenses, while Carter operates in the completely romantic fashion of someone for whom fiction has provided standards that have no relation to life. Although we are told that his brother loathed him, and that Carter is probably the real father of his "niece," Carter's private crime spree loftily is motivated by revenge of an order that would—I think—be incomprehensible to the realistic Marlowe.

Caine, Hodges, and the large cast obviously have had a great deal of fun reworking the stylized conventions of an ancient genre—the car chases, the mysterious appearances of various Mr. Bigs, violence

suddenly punctuated by moments of absurd sentiment, the contemporary variations on the wise-guy dialogue of 30 years ago. I should admit that I had trouble differentiating between the several villains and never did understand the resolution, which is, I suspect, a lot less interesting than that of *The Big Sleep,* but I just don't know.

The film opened yesterday at the Victoria, the 86th Street East and other theaters around town. It's definitely worth the time of the sentimentalists.

—V.C., March 4, 1971

GET OUT YOUR HANDKERCHIEFS

Written (in French, with English subtitles) and directed by Bertrand Blier; director of photography, Jean Penzer; edited by Claudine Merlin; music by Georges Delarue, Wolfgang Amadeus Mozart and Franz Schubert; art designer, Eric Moulard; produced by Paul Claudon; released by New Line Cinema. Running time: 108 minutes.

With: Gérard Depardieu (Raoul), Patrick Dewaere (Stephane), Carole Laure (Solange), Riton (Christian Beloeil) and Michel Serrault (Neighbor).

I have trouble looking at the light side of Bertrand Blier's *Get Out Your Handkerchiefs,* a comedy with a heroine who isn't altogether funny. Here is a woman who barely speaks, never thinks, spends most of her time scrubbing and knitting, is completely available (and indifferent) to any man who wants her, and will be happy only when she is at last made pregnant. She has so little will of her own that a thirteen-year-old boy can persuade her to have sex with him by pointing out that he'll "have to wait five, six years for another chance like this." Arguably, she is an object of mystery. But by the same argument, so is a seashell or a goldfish or an ashtray.

Here, as with his earlier *Going Places,* Mr. Blier stops me dead. I never had a clear or reasonable response to that film; I tuned out during a sequence in which two young men petulantly shot a female hairdresser with whom they were both involved, wounding her in the leg, and the woman was such a compliant dimwit that she didn't mind. Compared to that, the scene that showed Jeanne Moreau committing suicide by shooting herself in the genitals was a positive picnic.

Mr. Blier's penchant for depicting behavior like this is certainly daring, but whether it amounts to anything truly provocative is another matter. Genuinely challenging an audience is one thing, and simply upsetting it is something else. At least in my case, Mr. Blier at his most outrageous doesn't elicit much more than fleeting, if heartfelt, indignation.

In fairness, in *Get Out Your Handkerchiefs* he also elicits a great many laughs, and that's certainly more than could be said for *Going Places.* This time, the same two actors (Gérard Depardieu and Patrick Dewaere) play the same kind of oversized, irrepressible children, floundering around a woman whose true nature eludes them. She (Carole Laure) is the wife of one of them (Mr. Depardieu), but she's been depressed and uncommunicative for a while. Marriage being whatever it is today, her husband decides she needs another man to cheer her up, and recruits Mr. Dewaere in a restaurant.

Their ostensible pursuit of the wife's happiness launches the two men on a series of adventures that makes them seem ever more boyish, until they encounter an adolescent (Riton) who is infinitely wiser and manlier than they. Ever more overshadowed by him, they find their high spirits and their connection with the wife both waning.

Until it takes this fairly solemn turn, the film is an exuberant and highly inventive comedy, filled with the very funny quirks of these characters' lives. The Dewaere character has a collection of every Pocket Book ever printed, and can recite any title if he's given the serial number. The wife quietly knits matching sweaters for half the men in the movie. When Mr. Depardieu first strikes a bargain with Mr. Dewaere, he promises that if Mr. Dewaere accepts the wife as a gift he will become Mr. Depardieu's pal, "and when a man is my pal he can ask for anything." Without the wife, though, "there wouldn't be much to ask me for."

Both of these actors are at once knowing and funny, and their camaraderie can be wonderful to watch; Mr. Depardieu in particular projects an innocence so strenuous it takes on a demonic edge. Miss Laure does an amusing-enough deadpan, but she's so opaque her charm eventually wears thin.

Riton, the child actor, does a fine job, but there's something disconcerting about his prematurely mournful expression. Mr. Blier's device of setting his boyish adults in opposition to an adult boy has a certain cleverness. But his casting such a dolorous child merely calls too much attention to the patness of this part of the scenario, and to its pretension.

Similarly, a late-night dormitory scene involving a number of small boys is shot with such overweening poignancy that it's out of sync with most of the film's airier mood. Mr. Blier has a habit of strong-arming his audience in one scene, and letting his characters drift amiably in the next. That halting quality was effective enough in *Going Places,* but *Get Out Your Handkerchiefs* is a much more substantial and sophisticated effort, in which even the slightest technical clumsiness is notably out of place.

—*J.M., December 18, 1978*

GHOST WORLD

Directed by Terry Zwigoff; written by Mr. Zwigoff and Daniel Clowes, based on Mr. Clowes's comic book series; director of photography, Affonso Beato; edited by Carole Kravetz; music by David Kitay; production designer, Edward T. McAvoy; produced by Lianne Halfon, John Malkovich and Russell Smith; released by United Artists. Running time: 111 minutes.

With: Thora Birch (Enid), Scarlett Johansson (Rebecca), Steve Buscemi (Seymour), Brad Renfro (Josh), Bob Balaban (Enid's Father), Illeana Douglas (Roberta) and Teri Garr (Maxine).

I have often complained, aloud and in print, about the sorry state of America's youth, at least as they are depicted in movies. A year ago, I wrote an article bewailing the decline of two genres dear to my reluctantly adult heart: the high school or college campus romantic comedy and the coming-of-age melodrama. My despair, happily, was premature. This year has brought, along with a flood of worse-than-average blockbusters, some better-than-average growing-up movies (including *Save the Last Dance* and *Crazy/Beautiful*) as well as two—Jim McKay's *Our Song* and John Singleton's *Baby Boy*—that miraculously transcend the conventions of the subject matter while avoiding cheap laughs and exploitative moralizing.

Terry Zwigoff's *Ghost World,* loosely adapted from a novel-length comic book by Daniel Clowes, continues this hopeful trend. It's surely the best depiction of teenage eccentricity since *Rushmore,* and its incisive satire of the boredom and conformity that rule our thrillseeking, individualistic land, and also its question mark ending, reminded me of *The Graduate.* With all due respect to Mike Nichols, Simon and Garfunkel, and Mrs. Robinson, I like *Ghost World* better.

Over the past 15 or 20 years, comic book artists and writers like Mr. Clowes, Harvey Pekar, the Hernandez brothers and R. Crumb (the subject of Mr. Zwigoff's wonderful 1995 documentary) have explored the tedium and mystery of contemporary American life with more wit and insight than most novelists or filmmakers.

The original *Ghost World* captures the slack rhythms and tiny surprises of daily experience with a precision that would seem hard to replicate on screen. But instead of following the book frame by frame, Mr. Zwigoff and Mr. Clowes (who collaborated on the screenplay) have added new, sharper story lines and fashioned a tighter narrative framework. Mr. Zwigoff's unhurried editing and his subtle sense of composition approximates Mr. Clowes's clean, quiet, black-and-white drawings without seeming arch or arty.

The cast, faced with the challenge of making those drawings breathe and move, brings Mr. Clowes's sad world of loneliness and disaffection to vivid comic life. Thora Birch, whose performance as Lester Burnham's alienated daughter was the best thing about *American Beauty,* plays a similar character here, with even more intelligence and restraint.

Enid is a recent high school graduate who lives with her father (Bob Balaban) in a small apartment in Los Angeles and spends her days with her best friend, Rebecca (Scarlett Johansson), hanging out in coffee shops and record stores. Their main activity, though, is mocking—with a callow conviction worthy of Holden Caulfield—the phoniness and hypocrisy that surrounds them. Enid's capacity for scorn is unlimited: her plucked eyebrows might illustrate a dictionary entry for "supercilious," and her quiet voice shoots darts of sarcasm in every direction.

Nor does she lack targets in a landscape of retro-50's diners, pretentious latte mills, a remedial high school art class (taught by Illeana Douglas with dead-on manic gooeyness) and an endless stream of obnoxious pseudo-bohemian losers. When boys gravitate to the less rigorously misanthropic (and conventionally prettier) Rebecca, Enid scares them away with her glowering superiority. One of the film's narrative threads charts the growing distance between the two friends, as Rebecca gravitates toward a maturity that Enid regards as a fatal compromise.

In her dogged search for authenticity amid the fakery that surrounds her, Enid befriends a middle-aged record collector named Seymour (Steve Buscemi). His obsession with obscure popular culture and his grumpy disconnection from just about everything else ("I can't relate to 99 percent of humanity") fascinate her; he seems like a kindred spirit, the grown-up version of herself.

But Seymour's own view of himself is colored by a sense of self-loathing and failure. While Enid's estrangement from everything and everyone is in part a youthful pose, his is rooted in the pain and frustration of unfulfilled adulthood.

Their relationship is the key to the movie's sensibility. Mr. Zwigoff and Mr. Clowes never waver in their sympathy for Enid and often share in her withering contempt for the world around her. The movie makes fun of ignorant video store clerks and highbrow cineastes, educators and parents, the politically correct and the politically incorrect.

But the filmmakers, despite their solidarity with Enid, also allow us to see the limitations and the dangers of her attitude, which is ultimately self-protective, cruel and a little cowardly. As the movie gathers momentum, we see that Enid faces a delicate predicament, a crisis much more real and familiar than the usual senior-prom agonies. Can she hold on to her critical intelligence and her skepticism without succumbing to bitterness? Can she find her way in the world without being swallowed up in it?

By the end of *Ghost World,* we have some reason for hope. The movie's last third gracefully gathers the off-hand observations and shaggy-dog episodes that have accumulated along the way into a skein of comic misunderstanding. But even as the story seems to satisfy the generic requirements of comedy—disasters are narrowly averted, misunderstandings explained away—the filmmakers never cheat us with false promises of everlasting happiness, a prospect that Enid would surely find appalling even if she had any reason to believe in it.

We're not sure, as we say our fond good-bye, what will become of her—and how could we be? She's 17, with—to revert to guidance counselor jargon—her whole life ahead of her. We do know she has a knack for drawing and a collector's eye for the precious odds and ends, human and material, that our culture is quick to cast aside as junk. So maybe she'll grow up to be a highbrow comic book artist like her creator. That would be fine, but I'd encourage her (still in guidance counselor mode) to consider a different direction. With her impossibly high standards, her cranky disposition, and her unshakable (and quite justified) belief in the superiority of her judgments, she'd make a great film critic.

—*A.O.S., July 20, 2001*

GIANT

Directed by George Stevens; written by Fred Guiol and Ivan Moffat, based on the novel by Edna Ferber; cinematographer, William Mellor; edited by William Hornbeck, Fred Bohanan and Philip W. Anderson; music by Dimitri Tiomkin; production designer, Boris Leven; produced by Mr. Stevens and Henry Ginsberg; released by Warner Brothers. Running time: 201 minutes.

With: Elizabeth Taylor (Leslie Benedict), Rock Hudson (Bick Benedict), James Dean (Jett Rink), Carroll Baker (Luz Benedict 2d), Jane Withers (Vashti Smythe), Chill Wills (Uncle Bawley), Mercedes McCambridge (Luz Benedict), Sal Mineo (Angel Obregon 3d), Dennis Hopper (Jordan Benedict 3d) and Paul Fix (Dr. Horace Lynnton).

Apparently the subject of Texas is so large and provocative that no one can get going on it without taking a large amount of time. Producer-director George Stevens demonstrates the point. In his much-touted color film version of Edna Ferber's big Texas novel, *Giant,* which opened last night at the Roxy with a benefit showing for the Muscular Dystrophy Associations, Inc., he takes three hours and seventeen minutes to put his story across. That's a heap of time to go on about Texas, but Mr. Stevens has made a heap of film.

Hewing pretty closely to the content of Miss Fer-

ber's agitating tale of contemporary Texas cattle barons and nouveau riche oil tycoons, Mr. Stevens and his able screenplay writers, Fred Guiol and Ivan Moffat, have contrived a tremendously vivid picture-drama that gushes a tawdry tragedy. And Mr. Stevens has made it visual in staggering scenes of the great Texas plains and of passion-charged human relations that hold the hardness of the land and atmosphere.

In strong swipes of outdoor realism and audaciously close-to interplay of invariably violent emotions among its lively characters, *Giant* gives an almost documentary picture of how oil exaggerated and confused the virtually feudalistic ways of living of the old Texas landowners and cattlemen. It visions the change of social standards from rugged individuality to the massive and vulgar acceptance of running in plutocratic herds. It does not wax moralistic. It simply presents what has occurred—or what Miss Ferber and Mr. Stevens tell us is the reason that Texas is as it is today.

Perhaps because Mr. Stevens has attempted to include in his film the full content of Miss Ferber's story and then a good bit more, it does have a way of becoming a trifle rambling and overwrought at times. Dramatic emphasis changes from one to another theme.

At the start, we have the story of the sudden and incongruous love of a well-bred Virginia beauty and the raw-boned Texan who owns the great Reata ranch. Then we have a conflict between the beauty and the razor-backed sister of her spouse when she weds him and moves to Texas and to a gaunt Victorian house on the empty range.

In order, there follow a passionate rivalry between the owner of Reata and a surly hand who later becomes the most vulgar of the new crop of oil millionaires; an interlocking contemplation of Jim Crow treatment of local Mexicans; and finally a set of climaxes in which each theme is more or less resolved.

But despite the confusion of issues, the whole picture flows rapidly and is a series of fascinating episodes that illuminates its complexities. Thanks to Mr. Stevens's brilliant structure and handling of images, every scene and every moment is a pleasure. He makes "picture" the essence of his film.

Such things as the great ranch house standing in the midst of an empty plain, or the death of a booted Texas woman on a big horsehair sofa in a hollow room, or the coming in of an oil gusher or the funeral of a Mexican boy killed in the war are visioned by Mr. Stevens with superlative artistry. And his final show of the oil baron raving drunkenly in an empty banquet hall is an eloquent presentation of the irony and idiocy of it all.

Under Mr. Stevens's direction, an exceptionally well-chosen cast does some exciting performing. Elizabeth Taylor as the ranchman's lovely wife, from whose point of observation we actually view what goes on, makes a woman of spirit and sensitivity who acquires tolerance and grows old gracefully. And Rock Hudson is handsome, stubborn and perverse but oddly humble as her spouse.

However, it is the late James Dean who makes the malignant role of the surly ranch hand who becomes an oil baron the most tangy and corrosive in the film. Mr. Dean plays this curious villain with a stylized spookiness—a sly sort of offbeat languor and slur of language—that concentrates spite. This is a haunting capstone to the brief career of Mr. Dean.

Others, too, are excellent—Chill Wills as an old Texas type, Jane Withers as a plump and uncouth heiress, Mercedes McCambridge as a bitter, cold old maid, Charles Watts as a hypocritical windbag and Carroll Baker as a spirited Texas deb.

Dimitri Tiomkin's music lends a thumping accompaniment.

Giant, for all its complexity, is a strong contender for the year's top-film award.

—*B.C., October 11, 1956*

GIGI

Directed by Vincente Minnelli; written by Alan Jay Lerner; based on the play by Anita Loos and the novel by Colette; cinematographer, Joseph Ruttenberg; edited by Adrienne Fazan; music by Frederick Loewe, with lyrics by Mr. Lerner; production designer, Cecil Beaton; produced by Arthur Freed; released by Metro-Goldwyn-Mayer. Running time: 116 minutes.

With: Leslie Caron (Gigi), Maurice Chevalier (Honoré Lachaille), Louis Jourdan (Gaston Lachaille), Hermione Gingold (Madame Alvarez), Eva Gabor (Liane D'Exelmans), Jacques Bergerac (Sandomir), Isabel Jeans (Aunt Alicia) and John Abbott (Manuel).

There won't be much point in anybody trying to produce a film of *My Fair Lady* for awhile, because Arthur Freed has virtually done it with *Gigi,* which had a grand premiere at the Royale last night.

On an obviously blank-check commission from Metro-Goldwyn-Mayer, which has long had the notion that money is just something you spend on musical films, he has taken a popular Colette novel, already done as a French movie and a Broadway play, and placed it coyly in the hands of two wizards, Alan Jay Lerner and Frederick Loewe. Maybe Mr. Freed didn't realize it, but they just happen to be the gentlemen who wrote the book, lyrics, and music for *My Fair Lady,* now in its third year on Broadway.

Also, by possible coincidence, he had Cecil Beaton do the production design, costumes, and scenery, for presentation in color and CinemaScope. Mr. Beaton just happens to be the gentleman who designed the *My Fair Lady* costumes.

And what do you think they've come up with? Well, you will probably be amazed—as we're sure Mr. Freed was—to discover they've come up with a musical film that bears such a basic resemblance to *My Fair Lady* that the authors may want to sue themselves.

We began to perceive it faintly almost at the start with the colorful introduction of the lively heroine. She's a bright little teenage tomboy living in Paris at the century's turn and highly resistant to the notion, insisted upon by her grandmother and great-aunt, that she should grow up.

Particularly is she resistant to their intention that she should learn all the graces and qualities of a lady so that she may become an accomplished courtesan. The idea of love repels her. She even sings a little song indicating her disgust with Parisians.

Does this remind you of anyone?

Then, as the picture continues and the hero is clearly built up as an elegant, blasé young bachelor with an amiable indifference toward the child, it is plain that he's being set for dazzling when the butterfly bursts from the cocoon. It does and he is—all in the spirit of good, racy, romantic fun. And to clinch it, he sings a song called "Gigi," which lets it be generally known that he's grown accustomed to her face and other allurements. It is a strikingly reminiscent tune.

But don't think this point of resemblance is made in criticism of the film, for *Gigi* is a charming entertainment that can stand on its own two legs. It is not only a charming comprehension of the spicy confection of Colette, but it is also a lovely and lyrical enlargement upon that story's flavored mood and atmosphere.

Mr. Beaton's designs are terrific—a splurge of elegance and whim, offering fin de siècle Paris in an endless parade of plushy places and costumes. And within this fine frame of swanky settings, Vincente Minnelli has marshaled a cast to give a set of performances that, for quality and harmony, are superb.

Leslie Caron, the little lady who helped to make *Lili* a memorable film, gets something of the same sort of magic of youthful rapture as the heroine in this. Louis Jourdan is suave as the hero who holds out against her blossoming charms, and Maurice Chevalier is wonderfully easy as a mellowing boulevardier.

As the grandmother and great-aunt, Hermione Gingold and Isabel Jeans give elaborately humorous exhibitions of the airs and attitudes of ancient dames; Eva Gabor is posh as a passing mistress, and John Abbott is droll as a valet.

Of Mr. Loewe's musical numbers, "Gigi" is probably the best, though M. Chevalier makes something quite beguiling of "Thank Heaven for Little Girls." He also imbues with cheerful poignance "I'm Glad I'm Not Young Anymore," and he and Miss Gingold sing a duet of wit and wisdom to "I Remember It Well." You will also find reminiscent the vastly colorful "Waltz at Maxim's."

Perhaps Messrs. Lerner, Loewe and Beaton have stolen *Gigi* from themselves, but they have no reason to regret or disguise it. They've left their *Lady* fingerprints for all to see.

—*B.C., May 16, 1958*

GIMME SHELTER

Directed by David Maysles, Albert Maysles and Charlotte Zwerin; edited by Ellen Gifford, Robert Farren, Joanne Burke and Kent McKinney; music by the Rolling Stones; released by Cinema V. Black and white. Running time: 90 minutes.

With: The Rolling Stones (Mick Jagger, Charlie Watts, Keith Richards, Mick Taylor, Bill Wyman), Melvin Belli and others.

Let it bleed, let it bleed, in sound and image, and in the hyped syntax of rock criticism.

The Rolling Stones are here, pursuing their grail, live on film, dead on film, drenched in the boreal red (read "rage") of a portable spotlight. (A gelatin mask over the face of fact.) They are phantoms that, in great, pointillist close-ups, when you squint your eyes, become the conceptualizations of yesterday's Pop mystery, which is, in reality—there is reality at the end of every trip—a memory collage of newspaper headlines, of rumored truths, of the titles of best-selling albums. Drug raps. Death embraced in a swimming pool. Sympathy for the devil. Also love. Love.

"Gonna get us a little satisfaction," sings Mick Jagger and generations scream their ecstasy. In this masochistic subculture, a threat is a promise. The lithe, graceful, tubular physique, wearing a mad Uncle Sam hat of red, silver, and blue stripes and stars (forever, for us) moves in and out of the focus of the camera, which cannot make up its mind whether it adores Mick Jagger or loathes him, whether it is an instrument of exploitation or a victim of it.

This is more or less the beginning of *Gimme Shelter,* the filmed record of the last leg of the Rolling Stones' 1969 American tour, a movie that can only be described adequately in the kind of awful Pop prose that stitches together instant contradictions. "An ugly, beautiful mass" is the way one man described the audience at an early Stones concert in the East, and this pretty much holds true for the film, which opened yesterday at the Plaza Theater. It's true, that is, if you can regard it simply as a neutral record of fact. I'm afraid I can't.

Although *Gimme Shelter* is photographed and edited with all the skill that I've admired in earlier "direct cinema" films by David and Albert Maysles and Charlotte Zwerin, particularly *Salesman,* it is touched by the epic opportunism and insensitivity with which so much of the rock phenomenon has been promoted, and written about, and with which, I suspect, the climactic concert at Altamont was conceived.

If you remember, the Stones ended their tour,

just one year ago, at the Altamont Speedway in Alameda County, California, with a "free" concert that was publicized as a way of their saying thank you, America. It was a mess in every respect. Two locations declined the honor before the speedway was found. Approximately 300,000 people showed up, but the only security arrangements were those made with the Hell's Angels, who agreed to keep order for $500 worth of free beer. No less than four persons were killed, including one gun-carrying young man who was stabbed to death by an Angel on camera.

As was the movie about the Woodstock festival, *Gimme Shelter* was a part of the event it recorded, being, in fact, a commissioned movie, the proceeds from which are to help the Stones pay the costs of the free concert (although they grossed a reported $1.5 million from the other, nonfree concerts on their tour). Thus, the movie that examines the Stones, and the Altamont manifestation, with such a cold eye, seems somehow to be examining itself.

The Maysles and Miss Zwerin have used the murder of Meredith Hunter to give shape to their film, which cuts back and forth between the chaotic preparations for Altamont and a couple of concerts that preceded it. There are flash-forwards showing the Stones watching a monitor of the Altamont events, after they happened. There also are flashbacks showing Melvin Belli, the San Francisco lawyer, who looks like Jim Backus on an ego trip and who shuns publicity wherever he can find it, negotiating for the use of Altamont while surrounded by reporters, who act as if they were covering the Paris talks.

There are occasional, not terribly revealing sequences showing the Stones at their leisure, punctuated by shots that zoom in on bizarre details, such as one Stone's snakeskin boot and another's cougar-tooth earring. When the Maysles finally get us to Altamont, they don't disappoint us. We see the Angels beating people with lead-tipped pool cues and then, finally, the murder, which is shown twice (once in slow motion).

There is quite a lot of music and performing in *Gimme Shelter,* some of it beautifully recorded, but it is not a concert film, like Woodstock. It is more like an end-of-the-world film, and I found it very depressing.
—*V.C., December 7, 1970*

THE GIRL CAN'T HELP IT

Directed by Frank Tashlin: written by Mr. Tashlin and Herbert Baker: director of photography, Leon Shamroy: edited by James B. Clark: art director, Leland Fuller and Lyle R. Wheeler: music by Bobby Troup: produced by Mr. Tashlin: released by 20th Century Fox. Running time: 99 minutes.

With: Tom Ewell (Tom Miller), Jayne Mansfield (Jerri Jordan), Edmond O'Brien (Marty Murdock), Henry Jones (Mousie), John Emery (Wheeler), Juanita Moore (Maid) and, as themselves, Julie London, Fats Domino, the Platters, Abbey Lincoln, Little Richard and his Band, Eddie Fontaine.

The recognized fact that women are shaped somewhat differently from men is the only apparent justification for Jayne Mansfield's being in Twentieth Century-Fox *The Girl Can't Help It,* which came to the Roxy yesterday. Miss Mansfield has a figure that is so different it's hard to believe, but what she can do in the way of acting, beyond wiggle and squirm, remains to be seen.

True, her failure to give a demonstration in this her first film starring role, arrived at from "bit" parts in movies via a freakish foray on the Broadway stage, may not be her fault entirely. (Let's give her the benefit of several doubts.) It may be the fault of Frank Tashlin, who produced, directed and helped to write this film.

Apparently, Mr. Tashlin was so staggered by Miss Mansfield's shape that he couldn't get his mind off the subject—nor the camera, nor even the picture's plot. His script is concerned entirely with the theatrical advancement of a dame whose figure is so phenomenal that it yanks people's eyes right out of their heads. And his penchant for placing the camera and Miss Mansfield (whenever she's on the screen) in such a relation as to pinpoint the phenomenon approaches the grotesque.

Even so, and for all the other obstacles, such as Tom Ewell and Edmond O'Brien, that are put in the way of the blonde actress' demonstrating her histrionic skill, it definitely looks as though the lady has a long way to go to be a Duse. Her range, at this stage, appears restricted to a weak imitation of Marilyn

Monroe. And the fact that it is imitation, rather than trenchant parody, is revealed by Miss Mansfield's gaucheness with such broad things as powder-room jokes. She stumbles all over several that Mr. Tashlin has coyly scattered through the film.

A hint of her limitation is given in something other than the plot, which comes to the hopeless conclusion that she can do nothing more than make weird sounds. It is tipped by the fact that the picture is heavily padded with singers and rock 'n' roll bands, which swiftly take over at frequent intervals when the principals appear at their wits' ends.

Among these makers of music are The Treniers, Little Richard and his Band, The Chuckles, Gene Vincent and His Blue Caps, Johnny Olenn and Fats Domino. The vigor with which they grab the spotlight and beat out their agonized tunes reminds one of the way alert bullfighters rush into the ring when a companion is being gored.

Julie London is also shoved on briskly to act a mawkish charade as Mr. Ewell's unforgettable sweetheart, while singing "Cry Me a River," a tear-drenched song.

As for the masculine performing of Mr. Ewell and Mr. O'Brien, who play the press agent of Miss Mansfield and her ex-gangster sponsor, respectively, it is bleary-eyed, broad and boisterous. They are just what you'd expect mere men to be when placed at the hopeless disadvantage that Mr. Tashlin has concocted for them here.

Sure, the scenery is splashy and sporty in color and CinemaScope. But the show is as meager and witless as a cheap pinup magazine joke.

— *B.C., February 9, 1957*

GIRL WITH A SUITCASE

Directed by Valerio Zurlini: written (in Italian, with English subtitles) by Leo Benvenuti, Piero De Bernardi, Enrico Medioli, Giuseppe Patroni-Griffi, Giuseppe Bennati and Mr. Zurlini based on a story by Mr. Zurlini; cinematographer, Tino Santoni; edited by Mario Serandrei; music by Mario Nascimbene; art designer, Flavio Mogherini; produced by Maurizio Lodi-Fe; released by Ellis Film Company. Black and white. Running time: 111 minutes.

With: Claudia Cardinale (Aida), Jacques Perrin (Lorenzo), Corrado Pani (Marcello) and Luciana Angelico (Aunt Martha).

A very sensitive and shaky area between purity and vice, between the innocence of childhood and the guilt and shame of the abandoned and corrupt, is explored with exceptional intelligence and great emotional sympathy in the Italian film, *Girl with a Suitcase (La Ragazza con la Valigia)*, which opened at the Pix and the Trans-Lux Normandie yesterday. And a new girl, Claudia Cardinale, who appears briefly as the young wife in the currently showing *Rocco and His Brothers,* leaps to well-deserved prominence in it.

The social and emotional complication that provides the dramatic terrain for this absorbing and moving exploration is one that has been pursued in any number of previous pictures, from Europe and Hollywood. Joan Crawford used to be discovered in it, over and over again.

It is that of a girl of poor background, no talent or assets save good looks and the kind of conspicuous femininity that inevitably attracts predaceous men, honestly and stubbornly trying to preserve her self-respect, to keep herself fairly decent and avoid sliding into straight commercial vice. It is a social and emotional complication that invites the cliché twist and happy end.

But in this finely disciplined instance, the temptation has been shunned, the pattern of the obvious has been avoided and reality has been confronted. Valerio Zurlini, the director, who also helped write the script, has faced up to the cruel, sad fact that heaven does not always protect the working girl.

In shaping his story, however, he has chosen a beautiful way for discovering the irony and poignance in the plight of his vulnerable girl. He has brought her in contact with a youngster, the teenage brother of a rich and selfish lout who has brutally deceived her, and shaped a brief and charming idyll with this boy—an idyl of tenderness and torment that has to end in violence and shame.

The course of this oddly mismatched romance, this innocent attraction between a girl of tawdry background and experience and a well-bred, virginal, lonely boy, is the heart-throbbing body of the drama and the delicate area in which Signor Zurlini accomplishes the most perceptive and brilliant realizations of his theme.

In the diffident meeting of the youngsters (for the girl is little more than a child who has been through a lot of ugly ordeals), in the charmingly secret ways they expand their innocent acquaintance as the boy makes the proud and gallant move of ensconcing the girl in a hotel where she can have her first taste of luxury—with these tender details the director is beautifully sensitive and sure.

And in his first stunning notification to the boy that there is pain in this game—a haunting scene in which the youngster tensely sits by and watches the girl dance with wolves at the hotel—he reaches the most penetrating and electrifying moment in the film.

It is in these areas, too, that Signorina Cardinale and Jacques Perrin, who plays the boy, display the most fragile, subtle facets of their characters (and of themselves). Signorina Cardinale has the body and the movements of a standard sex symbol, but she has a flexibility of mood and expression that give her a wide and provocative emotional range. Her girl has a common exterior but an uncommon, human inwardness.

M. Perrin, boyish and pliant, with deep, expressive eyes and an ability to make his face speak volumes of age-old feeling when it is firm and motionless, brings across a heartbreaking knowledge of the hard road to manhood for a boy. He reminds one most nostalgically of the young, fine Gérard Philipe.

In the latter part of the picture, the melodramatics explode and a vicious and not-too-lucid climax for the hopeless dilemma is achieved. In this area, the elements are more obvious and the secondary characters more patly played by Carlo Hinterman as a jealous bandleader and Riccardo Garrone as a male on the prowl.

But even here the grasp is solid and the theme is implicitly resolved. Signor Zurlini has turned out a picture that should be received as well as his star.

A fine musical score by Mario Nascimbene, which employs the harpsichord in the tender and idealistic moments, as against jazz explosions in harsh moods, enhances the feeling of the drama. The English subtitles do their job.

—*B.C., September 12, 1961*

THE GLEANERS AND I

Directed by Agnes Varda. commentary (in French with English subtitles) by Ms. Varda. directors of photography. Stephane Krausz. Didier Rouget. Didier Doussin, Pascal Sautelet and Ms. Varda. edited by Ms. Varda and Laurent Pineau: music by Joanna Bruzdowicz: produced by Cine Tamaris: released by Zeitgeist Films. Running time: 82 minutes.

The Gleaners and I takes its title, and some of its inspiration, from an 1867 painting by Jean-Francois Millet that shows three women in a wheat field, stooping to pick up sheaves and kernels left behind after the harvest. The image is well known; it appears in the *Larousse Dictionary of the French Language* alongside the definition of the verb "glaner" (to glean). The painting itself, which hangs in the Musee d'Orsay in Paris, shows up early in Agnes Varda's wonderful new documentary, thronged by camera-wielding tourists.

The painting—or, more accurately, the activity it depicts—sent Ms. Varda, a warm, intrepid woman in her early 70's and one of the bravest, most idiosyncratic of French filmmakers, on a tour of her own. From September 1999 until May of this year, she crisscrossed the French countryside with a handheld digital video camera and a small production crew, in search of people who scavenge in potato fields, apple orchards and vineyards, as well as in urban markets and curbside trash depositories. Some are motivated by desperate need, others by disgust at the wastefulness all around them and others by an almost mystical desire to make works of art out of things—castoff dolls, old refrigerators, windshield wipers—that have been thrown away without a second thought.

Ms. Varda, their patient interlocutor, also sees herself as a gleaner in her own right. (The film's French title, *Les Glaneurs et la Glaneuse,* makes this plain.) She plucks images and stories from the world around her, finding beauty and nourishment in lives and activities the world prefers to ignore. She is a constant, funny presence in the film, providing piquant voice-over narration and allowing herself visual and verbal digressions on the state of her aging hands, the water damage on her ceiling and her portable camera's dancing lens cap.

She is also an indefatigably curious, skeptical and sympathetic observer. *The Gleaners and I* is both a diary and a kind of extended essay on poverty, thrift and the curious place of scavenging in French history and culture. The patrons of a provincial bar explain the difference between gleaning and picking; a magistrate in black robes stands in a cabbage field and cites the section of the French penal code (Article R-26.10) and the royal edict of Nov. 2, 1554, that establish the right to glean. This bureaucratic side of the national temperament is also embodied by an apple farmer who explains the system he has developed for registering and licensing those who wish to gather his unharvested fruit.

For all its gentle humor—there is a hilarious dispute about just how many oysters one is allowed to gather after a storm—Ms. Varda's film uncovers a subterranean world of poverty and loneliness in the midst of plenty. An elderly peasant woman recalls the old days, when, as in Millet's painting, gleaning was a communal activity, festive and sociable even as it was backbreaking. Now, Mr. Varda notes, people scavenge alone, and they gather not only agricultural surplus but supermarket trash as well.

And yet *The Gleaners and I* is never depressing. Even at their most desperate—a former truck driver, fired for drinking on the job, who lives in a shabby trailer; a group of disaffected young people who vandalize hulking trash bins—Ms. Varda's gleaners retain a resilient, generous humanity that is clearly brought to the surface by her own tough, open spirit.

The film is studded with found metaphors and serendipitous insights, like the collection of heart-shaped potatoes Ms. Varda brings home from her travels. They're coarse, homely objects, misshapen and flecked with dirt, unmarketable in the view of the potato growers. But their poetic value is self-evident. "I'm something of a leftover myself," Ms. Varda remarked to journalists covering the New York Film Festival, where *The Gleaners and I* will be shown tomorrow night. This was a charming bit of modesty. She's a treasure.

—A.O.S., September 30, 2001

THE GOALIE'S ANXIETY AT THE PENALTY KICK

Directed by Wim Wenders; written (in German, with English subtitles) by Mr. Wenders and Peter Handke, based on the novel by Mr. Handke; cinematographer, Robby Müller; edited by Peter Przygodda; music by Jurgen Knieper; produced by Peter Genee; released by Bauer International. Running time: 101 minutes.

With: Arthur Brauss (Josef Bloch), Kai Fischer (Hertha Gabler), Erika Pluhar (Gloria T.), Libgart Schwartz (Anna), Marie Bardischewski (Maria) and Michael Toost (Salesman).

When we first see Josef Bloch (Arthur Brauss), the goalie, he is isolated in a long shot at the far end of the soccer field. The frantic activity of the game at the other end of the field has no apparent relation to him. He walks around impatiently. He wipes his hands. He is a lean man, all tendons that have been tense so long that even the most ordinary gesture seems to be a kind of tic.

Suddenly the game closes in on him and Josef Bloch, who has been waiting for this moment, fails to prevent the score. He displays no impatience with himself, no bitterness, no visible emotion whatsoever. For, as we learn in Wim Wenders's superlative screen version of Peter Handke's novel *The Goalie's Anxiety at the Penalty Kick*, Josef Block has been disconnected.

This precise and beautiful German film, directed by Mr. Wenders and written by him and Mr. Handke, was originally shown in New York at the Museum of Modern Art's 1972 New Directors/New Films series, but it is only now having its commercial premiere at the Film Forum, where it opened yesterday.

Like the Handke novel, the film will be described—incorrectly, I think—as dispassionate, which is not to see the film, or the book, for its style, which is about as self-effacing as a style can be without disappearing entirely. However, *The Goalie's Anxiety at the Penalty Kick* is seething with feelings that are so ambiguous, so terrifying, that like Josef Bloch, the film can recognize them only obliquely as if trying to put a good face on things by refusing to make a fuss.

The Goalie's Anxiety at the Penalty Kick is a carefully composed, unhysterical record of one man's coming apart. At the end of his last game, Josef Bloch wanders aimlessly around a Vienna that is both familiar to him and as strange as the inside of a beehive. He drinks. He plays the jukebox. He sleeps. He gets mugged. He picks up a girl and goes to her apartment at the edge of an airfield. They make love. The next morning they have breakfast. He thinks he sees ants in the teapot. He strangles her. He leaves. He buys a newspaper and gets on a bus. . . .

Those sentences suggest the tempo of the film, but not its impact on the viewer who, by being required to fill in explanations the filmmakers resolutely refuse to give, becomes drawn into Josef Bloch's madness in a way that leaves one breathless and high. It's as exciting as any conventionally successful and high-suspense film.

Mr. Handke's novels—he is perhaps better known here as a playwright—have been associated with France's nouveau roman and the work of Alain Robbe-Grillet. The methods are similar, but there is a major, crucial difference. Mr. Robbe-Grillet's novels and films seem bent on demonstrating the boredom of alienated man by turning their backs on the reader and boring him into a stupor. *The Goalie's Anxiety* is also about disconnection, but the novelist's impulse is furious, rather than bored. His work has the vigor of a revolutionist.

Since *The Goalie's Anxiety* was first shown in New York, Mr. Wenders has been represented by two later films seen at the New York Film Festival, *Alice in the Cities* and *Kings of the Road,* but because neither has had the force and cool beauty of this film, I would assume he needs a collaborator of Mr. Handke's discipline and intellectual enthusiasm.

The Goalie's Anxiety doesn't contain one redundant shot or unnecessary camera movement. For the most part, the camera seldom moves. It is content to record the actors walking into and out of a frame, more or less in the passive manner of Josef Bloch as he regards the odd behavior of himself and of the strangers in the world around him.

This simplicity, as opposed to the fancy photography and the modish fragmentation of time and image favored by Mr. Robbe-Grillet (*L'Immortelle, The Man Who Lies*), has the effect of making us see people, objects, and bits of action with a clarity so stunning that they come to have for us as much menace and mystery as they have for the mad Josef Bloch.

The Goalie's Anxiety at the Penalty Kick is a remarkable, fascinating film, one that suggests, among many other things, that the nouveau film, if indeed there is

to be such a thing, will be plain, unadorned, direct, not an accumulation of fashionable mannerisms.

—V.C., January 14,1977

THE GO-BETWEEN

Directed by Joseph Losey; written by Harold Pinter, based on the novel by L. P. Hartley; cinematographer, Gerry Fisher; edited by Reginald Beck; music by Michel Legrand; art designer, Carmen Dillon; produced by John Heyman and Norman Priggen; released by Columbia Pictures. Running time: 118 minutes.

With: Julie Christie (Marian), Alan Bates (Ted Burgess), Dominic Guard (Leo Colston as a Boy), Margaret Leighton (Mrs. Maudsley), Michael Redgrave (Leo Colston as a Man), Michael Gough (Mr. Maudsley), Edward Fox (Hugh Trimingham), Richard Gibson (Marcus) and Simon Hume-Kendall (Denys).

When Leo Colston, who will be thirteen on the 27th, goes to visit his classmate at Brandon Hall in July of 1900, the elegant Maudsley family receives him with that special graciousness reserved for poor but well-bred boys, the sort who live with widowed mothers in small, neat cottages, far enough away so as not to be social embarrassments.

The first evening Mrs. Maudsley asks Leo to escort her into the great dining room. "And so," she says, looking vague but kind, "you are a magician." "Not really," Leo tells her modestly, "only at school." However, Marcus Maudsley has already told admiring stories about how Leo can effect spells, and once so cursed two bullying older boys that they fell off a roof with near-fatal results.

Marian Maudsley, who is about to become engaged to a viscount, teases Leo and, when she is particularly bored, she flirts with him. Then, when it's apparent that Leo is about to expire in the heat of his only suit, a heavy winter thing, she takes him into town and buys him an entire new outfit, of superb Lincoln green.

Leo falls hopelessly in love with Marian and, without quite knowing what he is doing, he becomes the secret letter carrier for Marian and Ted Burgess, the tenant farmer with whom she is conducting business that Leo doesn't really want to think about.

While I have some reservations about *The Go-Between,* directed by Joseph Losey and adapted by Harold Pinter from L. P. Hartley's novel, I think it's quite safe to say that it's one of the loveliest, and one of the most perfectly formed, set and acted films we're likely to see this year.

The Go-Between is the third collaboration of Losey and Pinter and, like both *The Servant* and *Accident,* it is a kind of horror story, this time located in a world in which caste and manners have yet to be seriously questioned. There is something immensely appealing about this world—of great estates, of tea parties, of novels read aloud on the lawn, of a dog named Dry Toast, of croquet and faceless servants and cricket matches—and it serves to enrich a drama that is, on close inspection, somewhat less complex and more simplistic than the production that's been given it.

The film begins as a nostalgic reminiscence ("The past is a foreign country—they do things differently there") and slowly evolves, through flashes forward to an approximate present, into a classic Freudian case history about the traumatized adolescent, and about the sterile adult he becomes.

The story is seen entirely through the eyes of Leo, played with lovely comic candor by Dominic Guard as the boy, and by Michael Redgrave, looking as plump and healthy, and as impotent, as some kind of religious celibate, as the old man. It is not, however, Leo's trauma that commands attention, but the picture of the golden society through which the boy moves, and the beautifully defined ambiguity of the relationships of the adults that tower above him.

The cast is splendid and I'm afraid that any listing I may give will sound like a sort of half-baked inventory of superlatives. To cite just a few: Julie Christie, cool and passionate and cruel and sweet, as the heiress who is the principal instrument of Leo's destruction; Alan Bates, as the tenant farmer she loves and whom she meets in the hayloft at teatime; Margaret Leighton, as the mother who is not without feeling, but puts manners first; and Edward Fox, as the viscount who apparently accepts the scandal since, after all, "nothing is ever a lady's fault."

The production that Losey has designed for Pinter's screenplay is close to perfect, with never a shot, a camera angle, nor a cut from one scene to another that is not synchronized to the structure of the whole. Long views of meadows and skies are not simply scenic constables, but memories of events seen fifty years later. When the camera moves in for a close-up—I remember especially vividly one of Miss Leighton on the verge of hysteria—the effect is of the kind of complex, contradictory kind of revelation that only a movie camera can capture.

The Go-Between, which won the Grand Prize at this year's Cannes Festival and opened yesterday at the 68th Street Playhouse, is full of those contradictions that make both life and movies interesting. It's an idyll about murder, a charming tale of casual cruelty, and a terrifying picture of an innocent love. It's one of the few new movies, in fact, that I can recommend without any real qualifications.

—*V.C., July 30, 1971*

THE GODFATHER

Directed by Francis Ford Coppola: written by Mario Puzo and Mr. Coppola. based on the novel by Mr. Puzo: director of photography. Gordon Willis: edited by William Reynolds. Peter Zinner. Marc Laub and Murray Solomon: music by Nino Rota: production designer. Dean Tavoularis: produced by Albert S. Ruddy: released by Paramount Pictures. Running time: 175 minutes.

With: Marlon Brando (Don Vito Corleone). Al Pacino (Michael Corleone). James Caan (Sonny Corleone). Richard Castellano (Clemenza). Robert Duvall (Tom Hagen). Sterling Hayden (McCloskey). Diane Keaton (Kay Adams) and Talia Shire (Connie Corleone Rizzi).

Taking a best-selling novel of more drive than genius (Mario Puzo's *The Godfather*), about a subject of something less than common experience (the Mafia), involving an isolated portion of one very particular ethnic group (first-generation and second-generation Italian-Americans), Francis Ford Coppola has made one of the most brutal and moving chronicles of American life ever designed within the limits of popular entertainment.

The Godfather, which opened at five theaters here yesterday, is a superb Hollywood movie that was photographed mostly in New York (with locations in Las Vegas, Sicily, and Hollywood). It's the gangster melodrama come of age, truly sorrowful and truly exciting, without the false piety of the films that flourished forty years ago, scaring the delighted hell out of us while cautioning that crime doesn't (or, at least, shouldn't) pay.

It still doesn't, but the punishments suffered by the members of the Corleone Family aren't limited to sudden ambushes on street corners or to the more elaborately choreographed assassinations on thruways. They also include lifelong sentences of ostracism in terrible, bourgeois confinement, of money and power, but of not much more glory than can be obtained by the ability to purchase expensive bedroom suites, the kind that include everything from the rug on the floor to the pictures on the wall with, perhaps, a horrible satin bedspread thrown in.

Yet *The Godfather* is not quite that simple. It was Mr. Puzo's point, which has been made somehow more ambiguous and more interesting in the film, that the experience of the Corleone Family, as particular as it is, may be the mid-twentieth-century equivalent of the oil and lumber and railroad barons of nineteenth-century America. In the course of the ten years of intra-Mafia gang wars (1945–1955) dramatized by the film, the Corleones are, in fact, inching toward social and financial respectability.

For the Corleones, the land of opportunity is America the Ugly, in which almost everyone who is not Sicilian or, more narrowly, not a Corleone, is a potential enemy. Mr. Coppola captures this feeling of remoteness through the physical look of place and period, and through the narrative's point of view. *The Godfather* seems to take place entirely inside a huge, smoky, plastic dome, through which the Corleones see our real world only dimly.

Thus, at the crucial meeting of Mafia families, when the decision is made to take over the hard drug market, one old don argues in favor, saying he would keep the trade confined to blacks—"they are animals anyway."

This is all the more terrifying because, within their isolation, there is such a sense of love and honor, no matter how bizarre.

The film is affecting for many reasons, including the return of Marlon Brando, who has been away only in spirit, as Don Vito Corleone, the magnificent, shrewd old Corleone patriarch. It's not a large role, but he is the key to the film, and to the contributions of all of the other performers, so many actors that it is impossible to give everyone his due.

Some, however, must be cited, especially Al Pacino, as the college-educated son who takes over the family business and becomes, in the process, an actor worthy to have Brando as his father; as well as James Caan, Richard Castellano, Robert Duvall, Al Lettieri, Abe Vigoda, Gianni Russo, Al Martino and Morgana King. Mr. Coppola has not denied the characters' Italian heritage (as can be gathered by a quick reading of the cast), and by emphasizing it, he has made a movie that transcends its immediate milieu and genre.

The Godfather plays havoc with the emotions as the sweet things of life—marriages, baptisms, family feasts—become an inextricable part of the background for explicitly depicted murders by shotgun, garrote, machine gun, and booby-trapped automobile. The film is about an empire run from a dark, suburban Tudor palace where people, in siege, eat out of cardboard containers while babies cry and get underfoot. It is also more than a little disturbing to realize that characters, who are so moving one minute, are likely, in the next scene, to be blowing out the brains of a competitor over a white tablecloth. It's nothing personal, just their way of doing business as usual.

—*V.C., March 16, 1972*

THE GODFATHER, PART II

Produced and directed by Francis Ford Coppola: written by Mr. Coppola and Mario Puzo, based on the novel by Mr. Puzo: directed of photography. Gordon Willis: edited by Peter Zinner: Barry Malkin and Richard Marks: music by Nino Rota: production designer, Dean Tavoularis: released by Paramount Pictures. Running time: 200 minutes.

With: Al Pacino (Michael Corleone), Robert Duvall (Tom Hagen), Diane Keaton (Kay Corleone),

Robert De Niro (Vito Corleone). John Cazale (Fredo Corleone). Talia Shire (Connie Corleone Rizzi). Lee Strasberg (Hyman Roth) and Michael V. Gazzo (Frankie Pentagelli).

The only remarkable thing about Francis Ford Coppola's *The Godfather, Part II* is the insistent manner in which it recalls how much better his original film was. Among other things, one remembers *The Godfather*'s tremendous narrative drive and the dominating presence of Marlon Brando in the title role, which, though not large, unified the film and transformed a super-gangster movie into a unique family chronicle.

Part II, also written by Mr. Coppola and Mario Puzo, is not a sequel in any engaging way. It's not really much of anything that can be easily defined.

It's a second movie made largely out of the bits and pieces of Mr. Puzo's novel that didn't fit into the first. It's a Frankenstein's monster stitched together from leftover parts. It talks. It moves in fits and starts but it has no mind of its own. Occasionally it repeats a point made in *The Godfather* (organized crime is just another kind of American business, say) but its insights are fairly lame at this point.

The Godfather, Part II, which opened yesterday at five theaters, is not very far along before one realizes that it hasn't anything more to say. Everything of any interest was thoroughly covered in the original film, but like many people who have nothing to say, *Part II* won't shut up.

Not the least of its problems is its fractured form. *Part II* moves continually back and forth in time between two distinct narratives. It's the story of the young Vito Corleone (who grew up to be played by Marlon Brando in the first movie) seen first around the turn of the century in Sicily and then in 1917 in New York, where he's played by Robert De Niro, and it's the story of Vito's son, Michael, played again by Al Pacino, the new Mafia don who sets out to control Las Vegas in the late 1950's.

One story doesn't necessarily illuminate the other. It's just additional data, like footnotes. I can't readily imagine what Mr. Coppola and Mr. Puzo were trying to do, except to turn their first film into a long parenthesis that would fit between the halves of the new movie.

Even if *Part II* were a lot more cohesive, revealing, and exciting than it is, it probably would have run the risk of appearing to be the self-parody it now seems.

Looking very expensive but spiritually desperate, *Part II* has the air of a very long, very elaborate revue sketch. Nothing is sacred. The photography by Gordon Willis, so effective originally, is now comically fancy—the exteriors are too bright and glowy while the interiors are so dark you wonder if these Mafia chiefs can't afford to buy bigger light bulbs.

Nino Rota's old score keeps thumping away like a heavenly jukebox. The performers, especially those repeating their original roles, seem locked into waxily rigid attitudes. Mr. Pacino, so fine the first time out, goes through the film looking glum, sighing wearily as he orders the execution of an old associate or a brother, winding up very lonely and powerful, which is just about the way he wound up before. Mr. De Niro, one of our best young actors, is interesting as the young Vito until, toward the end of his section of the film, he starts giving a nightclub imitation of Mr. Brando's elderly Vito.

There are a couple of notable exceptions. Lee Strasberg, the head of the Actors Studio, makes an extraordinarily effective screen debut as Hyman Roth, the powerful Jewish mobster (reportedly modeled on Meyer Lansky) with whom Michael attempts to take over the Havana rackets under the Battista regime. Mr. Strasberg's Roth is a fascinating mixture of lust, ruthlessness, and chicken soup. Michael V. Gazzo, the playwright (*A Hatful of Rain*), is also superb as a Corleone captain who crosses the Family. Another more or less nonpro, G. D. Spradlin (a former politician, according to publicity sources) is absolutely right as a crooked, very WASPish United States Senator from Nevada.

The plot defies any rational synopsis, but it allows Mr. Coppola, in his role as director, to rework lots of scenes that were done far better the first time: family reunions, shoot-outs, ambushes and occasional dumb exchanges between Don Michael Corleone and his square, long-suffering wife, Kay (Diane Keaton). "Oh, Michael," says the slow-to-take-offense Kay when Michael is about to sew up the Vegas rackets, "seven years ago you told me you'd be legitimate in five years."

Part II's dialogue often sounds like cartoon captions.

—V.C., December 13, 1974

GOING MY WAY

Produced and directed by Leo McCarey; written by Frank Butler and Frank Cavett, based on a story by Mr. McCarey; cinematographer, Lionel Lindon; edited by Leroy Stone; music by Robert Emmett Dolan, with songs by Johnny Burke and James Van Heusen; art designers, Hans Dreier and William Flannery; released by Paramount Pictures. Black and white. Running Time: 130 minutes.

With: Bing Crosby (Father Chuck O'Malley), Risë Stevens (Jenny Linden), Barry Fitzgerald (Father Fitzgibbon), James Brown (Ted Haines Jr.), Jean Heather (Carol James), Elly Malyon (Mrs. Carmody), Frank McHugh (Father O'Dowd), Stanley Clements (Tony Scaponi), Gene Lockhart (Haines Sr.), Porter Hall (Mr. Belknap) and Fortunio Bonanova (Tomaso Bozanni).

Having hit about as high in his profession as any average man would hope to hit—and that is to say the top notes in the musical comedy league—Bing Crosby has switched his batting techniques (or had it switched for him) in his latest film, *Going My Way*. And—would you believe it?—old Bing is giving the best show of his career. That's saying a lot for a performer who has been one of the steadiest joys of the screen. But, in this Leo McCarey film, now at the Paramount, he has definitely found his sturdiest role to date.

For in this, Mr. Crosby's first picture with a comparatively serious dramatic theme—and also the first in which his singing is not heavily depended upon—he has been beautifully presented by Mr. McCarey, who produced and directed the film. And he has been stunningly supported by Barry Fitzgerald, who plays one of the warmest characters the screen has ever known. As a matter of fact, it is a cruel slight to suggest that this is Mr. Crosby's show. It is his and Mr. Fitzgerald's together. And they make it one of the rare delights of the year.

For *Going My Way* is the story—rich, warm, and human to the core—of a progressive young Catholic priest who matches his wits and his ideas with those of the elderly pastor of a poor parish—a parish that the young priest is tacitly sent to conduct. It is the story of new versus old customs, of traditional age versus youth. And it is a story of human relations in a simple, sentimental, honest vein.

But it is far from a serious story—in the telling, anyhow. It is as humored and full of modern crackle as a Bing Crosby film has got to be. From the moment that Mr. Crosby shows up at St. Dominic's Church in a faded athletic costume to face the breathless skepticism of Mr. Fitzgerald until the final (and somewhat obvious) fadeout, when Mr. Crosby goes away in the night—the parish's treasury replenished and Mr. Fitzgerald comfortably wrapped in his old mother's arms—it is a delightful and witty case of sparring, with perfect dignity, between the two men.

There is the beautiful moment when Mr. Fitzgerald, while displaying his parish garden to the young priest, exclaims that it is a wonderful place to meditate and then adds, slyly, "You do—meditate?" There is the charming scene in which Mr. Crosby escorts the weary old gentleman to his bed, and then is surprised to discover that the reverent ancient likes "a drop of the craiture" now and then. And there is that simply exquisite sequence in which Mr. Fitzgerald goes off in a huff because Mr. Crosby is testing the neighborhood roughnecks in a vocal rendering of "Three Blind Mice."

Yes, there are musical passages in the picture. They come when Mr. Crosby occasionally sings a modern song bearing the title of the picture, another new air, and a couple of old timers. They also come—and more magnificently—when Risë Stevens, who is trickily worked in, sings an aria from *Carmen*, "Ave Maria," and the title song, too. And Mr. Crosby and the Robert Mitchell Boy Choir (dressed up like neighborhood kids) do very amusingly by a number called "Swinging on a Star."

The only criticism of the production—and of the excellent script that Frank Butler and Frank Cavett wrote—is that it runs to an excess. It is more than two hours long. And in that time there are certain stretches when the momentum somewhat lags. But otherwise no exceptions are taken. In addition to Mr. Crosby and Mr. Fitzgerald, Frank McHugh, Miss Stevens, Jean Heather and Stanley Clements—especially the latter as a genial tough—give thoroughly good performances. They enrich this already top-notch film with a vigorous glow of good spirit. *Going My Way* is a tonic delight.

—B.C., May 3, 1944

GOLDFINGER

Directed by Guy Hamilton; written by Richard Maibaum and Paul Dehn, based on the novel by Ian Fleming; cinematographer, Ted Moore; edited by Peter Hunt; music by John Barry; production designer, Ken Adam; produced by Harry Saltzman and Albert R. Broccoli; released by United Artists. Running time: 112 minutes.

With: Sean Connery (James Bond), Gert Fröbe (Goldfinger), Honor Blackman (Pussy Galore), Shirley Eaton (Jill Masterson), Tania Mallett (Tilly Masterson), Harold Sakata (Oddjob), Bernard Lee (M), Martin Benson (Solo), Cec Linder (Felix Leiter) and Lois Maxwell (Miss Moneypenny).

Old Double-Oh Seven is slipping—or, rather, his scriptwriters are. They are involving him more and more with gadgets and less and less with girls. This is tediously apparent in *Goldfinger*, the latest movie adventure of James Bond, the dauntless sleuth of Ian Fleming's detective fiction, whom Sean Connery so handsomely portrays.

In this third of the Bond screen adventures, which opened last night at the DeMille and goes continuous today at that theater and the Coronet, Agent 007 of the British Secret Service virtually spurns the lush temptations of voluptuous females in favor of high-powered cars and tricky machines.

That is to say, he virtually spurns them in comparison to the way he went for them in his previous cinematic conniptions, *Dr. No* and *From Russia with Love*. In those fantastic fabrications, you may remember, he was constantly assailed by an unending flow of luxurious, exotic, and insatiable girls. And, being the sort of omnipotent and adaptable fellow he is, he did what he could to oblige them in the course of pursuing his sleuthing chores.

But in this most gaudy of his outings—the most elaborate and fantastic to date—he manages to bestow his male attentions on only a couple of passing supplicants. One is a pliant little number who expires early, sealed in a skin of gold paint, and the other is a brawny pilot who remarkably resembles Gorgeous George. Neither is up to the standard of femininity usually maintained for Mr. Bond.

Why this neglect of his love life is difficult to imagine—except that Mr. Bond's off-handed conquests were always open to a certain amount of doubt, a certain amount of skepticism as to how much of a Lothario he actually is. Indeed, they have often intimated a bland contempt for, or, at least, a slippery spoof of the whole notion of masculine prowess. One might question whether Bond really likes girls.

So maybe his careful scriptwriters have played down that overly amorous side, delicately displacing dolls with automation and beautiful bodies with electronic brains. Anyhow, what they give us in *Goldfinger* is an excess of science-fiction fun, a mess of mechanical melodrama, and a minimum of bedroom farce.

It is good fun, all right, fast and furious, racing hither and yon about the world as Double-Oh Seven pursues the intrigues of a mysterious financier named Goldfinger, who is criminally tampering with the gold reserves of Britain and the United States.

Meeting his quarry in a crooked card game on the terrace of a hotel in Miami Beach, he follows him to a golf club outside London, trails him to a gold refinery in the Swiss Alps, and then is captured by him and flown to America to be an inside observer of a fantastic raid on Fort Knox. En route, the fellow has some lively set-tos, exercises smashing ingenuity and meets that Amazonian pilot, whom he conquers after a deadly judo match.

As usual, Mr. Connery plays the hero with an insultingly cool, commanding air, providing a great vicarious image for all the panting Walter Mittys in the world. Gert Fröbe is aptly fat and feral as the villainous financier, and Honor Blackman is forbiddingly frigid and flashy as the latter's aeronautical accomplice.

In lesser roles, Shirley Eaton is delectable as the girl who is quickly painted out, and Harold Sakata is traditionally sinister as a mute Oriental who is adept at throwing a razor-brimmed hat.

Of course, the high point of the picture is the climactic raid on Fort Knox with the intent of blowing it up and contaminating its hoard of gold with a nuclear bomb. It is spinningly staged and enacted, drenched in cliff-hanging suspense. But somehow, by the time it gets to this point—well, we've had Mr. Bond.

—B.C., December 22, 1964

GONE WITH THE WIND

Directed by Victor Fleming. George Cukor and Sam Wood; written by Sidney Howard. Jo Swerling. Charles MacArthur. Ben Hecht. John Lee Mahin. John Van Druten. Oliver H. P. Gerrett. Winston Miller. John Balderston. Michael Foster. Edwin Justus Mayer. F. Scott Fitzgerald and David O. Selznick. based on the novel by Margaret Mitchell; cinematographers. Ernest Haller. Ray Rennahan and Lee Garmes; edited by Hal C. Kern and James E. Newcom; music by Max Steiner; choreography by Frank Floyd and Eddie Prinz; art designers. Lyle Wheeler and Hobe Erwin; produced by Mr. Selznick; released by Metro-Goldwyn-Mayer. Running time: 220 minutes.

With: Vivien Leigh (Scarlett O'Hara). Clark Gable (Rhett Butler). Leslie Howard (Ashley Wilkes). Olivia de Havilland (Melanie Hamilton). Hattie McDaniel (Mammy). Thomas Mitchell (Gerald O'Hara). Barbara O'Neil (Ellen O'Hara). Butterfly McQueen (Prissy). Ona Munson (Belle Watling). Alicia Rhett (India Wilkes). Rand Brooks (Charles Hamilton). Harry Davenport (Doctor Meade). Carroll Nye (Frank Kennedy). Laura Hope Crews (Aunt Pittypat). Oscar Polk (Pork) and Eddie Anderson (Uncle Peter).

Understatement has its uses too, so this morning's report on the event of last night will begin with the casual notation that it was a great show. It ran, and will continue to run, for about three hours and forty-five minutes, which still is a few days and hours less than its reading time and is a period the spine may protest sooner than the eye or ear. It is pure narrative, as the novel was, rather than great drama, as the novel was not. By that we would imply you will leave it, not with the feeling you have undergone a profound emotional experience, but with the warm and grateful remembrance of an interesting story beautifully told. Is it the greatest motion picture ever made? Probably not, although it is the greatest motion mural we have seen and the most ambitious filmmaking venture in Hollywood's spectacular history.

It—as you must be aware—is *Gone With the Wind*, the gargantuan Selznick edition of the Margaret Mitchell novel which swept the country like Charlie McCarthy, the "Music Goes 'Round," and similar inexplicable phenomena; which created the national emergency over the selection of a Scarlett O'Hara and which, ultimately, led to the $4,000,000 production that faced the New York public on two Times Square fronts last night, the Astor and the Capitol. It is the picture for which Mr. Gallup's American Institute of Public Opinion has reported a palpitantly waiting audience of 56,500,000 persons, a few of whom may find encouragement in our opinion that they won't be disappointed in Vivien Leigh's Scarlett, Clark Gable's Rhett Butler or, for that matter, in Mr. Selznick's Miss Mitchell.

For, by any and all standards, Mr. Selznick's film is a handsome, scrupulous, and unstinting version of the 1,037-page novel, matching it almost scene for scene with a literalness that not even Shakespeare or Dickens were accorded in Hollywood, casting it so brilliantly one would have to know the history of the production not to suspect that Miss Mitchell had written her story just to provide a vehicle for the stars already assembled under Mr. Selznick's hospitable roof. To have treated so long a book with such astonishing fidelity required courage—the courage of a producer's convictions and of his pocketbook, and yet, so great a hold has Miss Mitchell on her public, it might have taken more courage still to have changed a line or scene of it.

But if Selznick has made a virtue of necessity, it does not follow, of necessity, that his transcription be expertly made as well. And yet, on the whole, it has been. Through stunning design, costume and peopling, his film has skillfully and absorbingly recreated Miss Mitchell's mural of the South in that bitter decade when secession, civil war and reconstruction ripped wide the graceful fabric of the plantation age and confronted the men and women who had adorned it with the stern alternative of meeting the new era or dying with the old. It was a large panel she painted, with sections devoted to plantation life, to the siege and the burning of Atlanta, to carpetbaggers and the Ku Klux Klan, and, of course, to the Scarlett O'Hara about whom all this changing world was spinning and to whom nothing was important except as it affected her.

Some parts of this extended account have suffered a little in their screen telling, just as others have profited by it. Mr. Selznick's picture-postcard Tara and Twelve Oaks, with a few-score actors posturing on the premises, is scarcely our notion of doing complete justice to an age that had "a glamour to it, a perfection, a symmetry like Grecian art." The siege of Atlanta was splendid and the fire that followed magnificently pyrotechnic, but we do not endorse the superimposed melodramatics of the crates of explosives scorching in the fugitives' path; and we felt cheated, so ungrateful are we, when the battles outside Atlanta were dismissed in a subtitle and Sherman's march to the sea was summed up in a montage shot. We grin understandingly over Mr. Selznick's romantic omission of Scarlett's first two "birthings," and we regret more comic capital was not made of Rhett's scampish trick on the Old Guard of Atlanta when the army men were rounding up the Klansmen.

But if there are faults, they do not extend to the cast. Miss Leigh's Scarlett has vindicated the absurd talent quest that indirectly turned her up. She is so perfectly designed for the part by art and nature that any other actress in the role would be inconceivable. Technicolor finds her beautiful, but Sidney Howard, who wrote the script, and Victor Fleming, who directed it, have found in her something more: the very embodiment of the selfish, hoydenish, slant-eyed miss who tackled life with both claws and a creamy complexion, asked no odds of anyone or anything—least of all her conscience—and faced at last a defeat which, by her very unconquerability, neither she nor we can recognize as final.

Miss Leigh's Scarlett is the pivot of the picture, as she was of the novel, and it is a column of strength in a film that is part history, part spectacle, and all biography. Yet there are performances around her fully as valid, for all their lesser prominence. Olivia de Havilland's Melanie is a gracious, dignified, tender gem of characterization. Mr. Gable's Rhett Butler (although there is the fine flavor of the smokehouse in a scene or two) is almost as perfect as the grandstand quarterbacks thought he would be. Leslie Howard's Ashley Wilkes is anything but a pallid characterization of a pallid character. Best of all, perhaps, next to Miss Leigh, is Hattie McDaniel's Mammy, who must be

personally absolved of responsibility for that most "unfittin'" scene in which she scolds Scarlett from an upstairs window. She played even that one right, however wrong it was.

We haven't time or space for the others, beyond to wave an approving hand at Butterfly McQueen as Prissy, Thomas Mitchell as Gerald, Ona Munson as Belle Watling, Alicia Rhett as India Wilkes, Rand Brooks as Charles Hamilton, Harry Davenport as Doctor Meade, Carroll Nye as Frank Kennedy. And not so approvingly at Laura Hope Crews's Aunt Pitty, Oscar Polk's Pork (bad casting), and Eddie Anderson's Uncle Peter (oversight). Had we space we'd talk about the tragic scene at the Atlanta terminal, where the wounded are lying, about the dramatic use to which Mr. Fleming has placed his Technicolor—although we still feel that color is hard on the eyes for so long a picture—and about pictures of this length in general. Anyway, "it" has arrived at last, and we cannot get over the shock of not being disappointed; we had almost been looking forward to that.

—*F.S.N., December 20, 1939*

THE GOOD, THE BAD AND THE UGLY

Directed by Sergio Leone: written (in Italian. with English subtitles) by Mr. Leone and Luciano Vincenzoni: director of photography. Tonino Delli Colli: edited by Eugenio Alabiso and Nino Baragli: production design by Carlo Simi: music by Ennio Morricone: produced by Alberto Grimaldi: released by United Artists. Running time. 161 minutes.

With: Clint Eastwood (Blondie. The Man With No Name). Lee Van Cleef (Sentenza). Eli Wallach (Tuco). Aldo Giuffré (Union Captain). Luigi Pistilli (Father Pablo Ramirez). Rada Rassimov (Maria). Enzo Petito (Storekeeper) and John Bartha (Sheriff).

"The burn, the gouge, and the mangle" (its screen name is simply inappropriate) must be the most expensive, pious and repellent movie in the history of its peculiar genre. If 42d Street is lined with little pushcarts of sadism, this film, which opened yesterday at the Trans-Lux 85th Street and the DeMille, is an entire supermarket.

The plot—and in their eagerness to mutilate someone, the writers continually lose track of it—seems to run as follows:

A man whose pseudonym is Bill Carson, and who owns a clam-shaped snuffbox, knows the whereabouts of $200,000. Three characters, Burn (Clint Eastwood), Gouge (Lee Van Cleef) and the Mexican, Mangle (Eli Wallach)—whose names in the film are Joe, Sentenza, and Tuco, respectively—are anxious to get hold of it. Ultimately, Clint Eastwood gets it. The action takes place in the West during the Civil War. That is all. It lasts two and a half slow hours.

The movie entitled *The Good, the Bad and the Ugly* forgets all about Bill Carson for an hour. Then, he makes a brief appearance, rolling his one eye (any number of characters in the movie have lost an eye, or an arm, or a leg or two legs), and dies, covered with blood and flies and making rasping noises, in incredible agony. Before expiring, he divulges the location of the cemetery in which the money is buried to Mangle, and the gravesite to Burn.

The sole purpose of the snuffbox is to enable Gouge to jam Mangle's fingers quite painfully in it. Gouge himself is missing a joint of a finger on his gun hand. The camera dwells on this detail lovingly.

Eli Wallach, as the Mexican, has a wound over his left eye, which heals and reopens throughout the film for no apparent reason. He is throttled three times, sun-scorched, and once so severely beaten by Van Cleef that anyone who would voluntarily remain in the theater beyond this scene (while he might be a mild, sweet person in his private life) is not someone I should care to meet, in any capacity, ever.

Wallach rolls his eyes, makes hideous gastrointestinal noises to convey shades of emotion, and laughs incessantly. Among his feldspar teeth, there is one capped with what looks like a molten paper clip. He also forgets, from time to time, what sort of ethnic part he is playing; and particularly when he is called upon to shout, his Mexican is laced with Riverdale.

Van Cleef's acting consists of displaying a stubble of beard and narrowing his eyes. Aside from various other shootings and beatings he administers, he shoots one man through a salad bowl (although most of the movie takes place in arid country, there are an awful lot of salads and vegetables) and another through a pillow. In the end, he is shot.

There is scarcely a moment's respite from the pain. Most of the scars and wounds are administered about the face, and even Eastwood, as the hero, spends a good part of the movie with his face blistered. His face and voice are expressionless throughout.

Several of the actors are Italian, and their voices are dubbed. There are some irrelevant battle scenes, as though, near the end of the movie, the writers and the director, Sergio Leone, hoped that it might pass for antiwar. "Never so many men who were wasted so badly," Eastwood says. And there is a completely meaningless sequence with a bridge—as though it might pass for "San Luis Rey" or "Kwai." Sometimes, it all tries to pass for funny.

The film is the third of a trilogy, (*A Fistful of Dollars* and *A Few Dollars More* preceded it.) There are immortal lines in the special context. One, just when it appears there is going to be a nonviolent moment in the film, from an officer who is preaching against brutality: "Sergeant," he begins, "gangrene is eating my leg away. Also my eye." Another, when Eastwood surprises Wallach in the bathtub: "Put your drawers on and take your gun off," he says.

—*R.A., January 25, 1968*

THE GOOD EARTH

Directed by Sidney Franklin: written by Talbot Jennings. Tess Slesinger and Claudine West. based on the novel by Pearl S. Buck and the stage adaptation by Owen Davis and Donald Davis: cinematographer. Karl Freund: edited by Basil Wrangell: music by Herbert Stothart: art designers. Cedric Gibbons. Harry Oliver and Arnold Gillespie: produced by Albert Lewin and Irving Thalberg: released by Metro-Goldwyn-Mayer. Black and white. Running time: 138 minutes.

With: Paul Muni (Wang). Luise Rainer (O-Lan). Walter Connelly (Uncle). Tilly Losch (Lotus). Charley Grapewin (Old Father) and Jessie Ralph (Cuckoo).

Once again Metro-Goldwyn-Mayer has enriched the screen with a superb translation of a literary classic. Its film of Pearl Buck's *The Good Earth,* which had its premiere at the Astor Theatre last night, is one of the finest things Hollywood has done this season or any other. While it has taken some liberties with the novel's text, it has taken none with its quality or spirit. The performances, direction and photography are of uniform excellence, and have been fused perfectly into a dignified, beautiful, and soberly dramatic production.

The making of *The Good Earth*, according to our Hollywood historians, was one of the most chaotic ventures in the annals of an industry in which chaos is the normal state of affairs. The picture was four years in preparation and production. It was begun by one director, George Hill, and completed by another, Sidney Franklin. Its early sequences were supervised by Irving Thalberg, and upon his death the production was entrusted to his associate, Albert Lewin.

The cast and script were forever being revised. The picture was edited and reedited. Some 2,000,000 feet of film were exposed in China, to be used in process shots and for atmosphere; another 700,000 or 800,000 feet were taken in Hollywood. Out of it all emerged a picture 12,450 feet long, running two and a half hours, costing (it is whispered respectfully) $3,000,000.

These things are mentioned less in ridicule than in awe, for there is no hint of behind-the-scenes chaos or conflict in the orderly and serenely smooth narrative film that was presented at the Astor last night. The picture has an easy rhythm, graciously suited to Miss Buck's chronicle of the founding of the House of Wang Lung. If its pace is leisurely, it has the valid excuse of dealing with a quiet theme. If it lingers upon details, it is because they richly deserve attention. It is the commonplaces in the life of Wang Lung and O-Lan, his wife, rather than the high points, that fascinate us.

Metro's script, written by Talbot Jennings, Tess Slesinger and Claudine West, parallels the action of the book in so many respects that a synopsis of the story, at this late date, is likely to be repetitious. Miss Buck's theme, of course, was the peasant's love for the land. It was that simple, unquestioning earthworship that was the talisman of Wang the farmer. Away from his land, he was as other men; on it, he was strong and upright and dignified. *The Good Earth* is the story of Wang's devotion to the land and the tragedy that threatened to overwhelm him when he neglected it.

The picture has chosen the best of Miss Buck's sequences. Wang's touchingly comic appearance at the Great House to claim his slave girl bride, O-Lan; their working of his farm; the famine that drove them south; the looting of the manor which permitted them to return to their farm; Wang's prosperity and his taking of a young second wife; his neglect of O-Lan; the discovery of the illicit romance between his younger son and the second wife—these are plucked straight from the novel.

The picture invents a new climax, a terrifying locust plague that threatens to destroy his crops and makes Wang realize that the land and O-Lan means more to him than being the lord of the Great House. It may be a theatrical conclusion, but it has been brilliantly photographed and provides a dramatic finale to a dramatic film.

The performances, which probably should have been mentioned before, are collectively splendid. Luise Rainer is tragically real as O-Lan, bringing to life the pathetic slave girl who was so modest yet so indomitable, so generous and selfless and loyal. Paul Muni, flawless in the early sequences, seemed to me to step out of his Chinese character in the post-famine episodes, talking, walking, reacting more as Muni than as Wang Lung. Walter Connolly makes the gambling uncle an ingratiating old rascal. Tilly Losch is graceful and dainty as the second wife, Lotus. Wang's sons are soundly portrayed by Roland Lui and Keye Luke. The others—Charles Grapewin as the senile grandfather, William Law as the gateman, Jessie Ralph, Olaf Hytten, and Suzanna Kim—are worthy of the company.

Metro was a long while getting around to it, but in *The Good Earth* it has something to show for its time and money—and for ours. The picture does full justice to the novel, and that is the highest praise one can give it.

—*F.S.N., February 3, 1937*

GOODBYE, MR. CHIPS

Directed by Sam Wood; written by R. C. Sherriff, Claudine West, Eric Maschwitz and Sidney

Franklin, based on the novel by James Hilton; director of photography, Freddie Young; edited by Charles Frend; music by Richard Addinsell; art designer, Alfred Junge; produced by Victor Saville; released by Metro-Goldwyn-Mayer; Black and white. Running time: 114 minutes.

With: Robert Donat (Charles Chipping), Greer Garson (Katherine Ellis), Terry Kilburn (John/Peter Colley), John Mills (Peter Colley as a young man), Paul Henried (Max Staefel), Judith Furse, (Flora) and Lyn Harding (Dr. Wetherby).

Metro's Leo and the British lion still are on the very best of terms, a fact most pleasantly demonstrated last night when M-G-M's London-made version of *Goodbye, Mr. Chips* had its premiere at the Astor. James Hilton's sentimental tribute to the English public school system and to its institutional Mr. Chipping of Brookfield has been rather tenderly done. Alexander Woollcott and the other authorities who have been quoted in the ads may be guilty of whooping up its merits overmuch, but basically they are right: It is a serene, heartwarming and generally satisfactory film edition of an edifyingly sentimental novelette. Like the story, the film is nostalgic: if we never knew a Mr. Chips, we should have known him. He belongs to every young man's past.

The Mr. Chips of the Hilton biography was the somewhat dull young pedant who came to Brookfield's ivy-grown walls in his twenties, took quiet root there, languished miserably for a decade or two and then, under the tender cultivation of a woman's hand, became such a human, quizzical and understanding person that all Brookfield eventually began to regard him as an institution. He cracked academic jokes, reminded undergraduates at his teas that he had caned their grandfathers, took a philosophic view of wars and small boys' appetites for walnut cakes, was a bit of bore and a bit of an idol. That was Mr. Chips.

Metro and its British aides have dealt with the chronicle affectionately, almost as though the centuried tradition and ingrained snobbery of the English public school system were our own. They have given the picture its properly leisurely pace, have adapted the novel carefully so as not to rend the gossamer fabric of its idealization, have valiantly—and, on the whole, successfully—kept its sentimentality within bounds. The book one muses over respectfully in the quiet of a study is apt to be coarsened, cheapened in its mutation to the imagery of the screen. The film of *Goodbye, Mr. Chips* is not entirely an exception. Some parts of it are brought home with eye-blackening vigor. But on the whole it is admirable and right and comes honestly by its emotionalism.

Credit for that must be divided. Mr. Hilton's adapters obviously have stenciled each page of their script with a "handle with care" and there is evidence that director Sam Wood, Robert Donat, Greer Garson, and the rest heeded their injunction. They have played out the drama at their own leisurely pace, which was the appropriate tempo. They have taken no unforgiveable liberties with the story, none at all with characterization, none with setting or atmosphere. Mr. Hilton, after all, had merely sketched in his drama, notched the highlights of its action, summarized the dialogue. The picture has no difficulty in using two hours to retell a story that was scarcely above short-story length. Mr. Chips is worth its time.

Particularly is he worth it with Mr. Donat's portrait of him. It is an incredibly fine characterization, not merely for its ability to make its convincing transition from young schoolmaster to octogenarian institution, but for its subtle underlining—if underlining can be subtle—of the dramatic moments in an essentially undramatic life. Chips was a reticent person. Like an iceberg, two-thirds of him always was subsurface. Mr. Donat has wisely understated him, played him softly, doubled his poignance. It is only in his crochety years, when he is scampering across the campus in his tattered robe, that Chips seems a trifle overdrawn, a fraction on the cute and overacted side. But that is just an impression and not deep enough to discredit an otherwise flawless performance.

Miss Garson's Katherine—the assertive young woman who changed the dour Mr. Chipping into the lovable Mr. Chips—is altogether believable and quite entrancing. Mr. Hilton deserves no credit for her at all. He simply said that she was captivating and lively, that she soon had Chips, the boys, and the masters worshiping at her feet. Authors have a habit of inventing people like that, merely saying they are so and so, and not bothering to prove it. But Miss Garson manages to fit the bill; more, to make it seem to do her an injustice. Her Katherine is one of the nicest people we would hope to meet anywhere. When she dies, we hate to have the picture continue without her.

The others are as good, in their way, as the script lets them be, or as Mr. Hilton might have wished. Terry Kilburn appears as the fresh-faced Peter Colleys—first, second, and third; Paul Henried is splendid as the German instructor; there are shrewd supporting bits by Louise Hampton as Mrs. Wickett, Milton Rosmer as Chatteris, Lyn Harding as Wetherby. As Katherine remarks to Chips, "What a nice lot they are!" And somehow that suits the picture. What a nice one it is!

—F.S.N., May 16, 1939

GOODFELLAS

Directed by Martin Scorsese; written by Nicholas Pileggi and Mr. Scorsese; based on the book *Wiseguy* by Mr. Pileggi; director of photography, Michael Ballhaus; edited by Thelma Schoonmaker; production designer, Kristi Zea; produced by Irwin Winkler; released by Warner Brothers. Running time: 146 minutes.

With: Robert De Niro (James Conway), Ray Liotta (Henry Hill), Joe Pesci (Tommy DeVito), Lorraine Bracco (Karen Hill), Paul Sorvino (Paul Cicero), Frank Sivero (Frankie Carbone), Tony Darrow (Sonny Bunz) and Mike Starr (Frenchy).

Some guys grow up wanting to design computer games, fly space missions, or play for the New York Knicks. Henry Hill always wanted to be a gangster. Like Martin Scorsese, who, from any early age, wanted to make movies, Henry Hill realized his grand ambition.

The two dreams come together with exuberant results in *Goodfellas*, Mr. Scorsese's breathless and brilliant new film, adapted by him and Nicholas Pileggi from Mr. Pileggi's best-selling book, *Wiseguy*.

As *Wiseguy* is possibly the best, least romanticized, and chilliest book in any library devoted to real-life Mafia manners, *Goodfellas* is both the most politically serious and most evilly entertaining movie yet made about organized crime. As cinema, it ranks alongside Mr. Scorsese's classics, *Taxi Driver* and *Raging Bull*.

Henry Hill, raised in the Brownsville-East New York section of Brooklyn, began his career early. In 1955, when he was eleven, Hill was running errands for the Euclid Avenue Taxicab and Limousine Service, which was something more than just a cab stand. It was the unofficial clubhouse for members of the local underworld and their hangers-on: bookmakers, politicians, off-duty cops, policy runners, union officers and aging hit men, among others.

It was also one of the many business fronts of Paul Vario, a mobster on the rise within the Luchese crime family. Vario took a liking to young Hill. Unlike Vario's own sons, Hill was an eager and efficient gofer. If he was sent out for coffee, he brought it back hot.

When Hill's school notified his parents that their boy was not attending classes, Vario's associates roughed up the postman. There were no longer any letters from the school arriving at the Hill house. The trouble was that there was no mail at all, which prompted Hill's mother to complain to the Post Office.

Over the next twenty years, Vario treated Hill like a son. The young man became one of Vario's most trusted "mechanics." He was a driver, companion, messenger, confidant, strong-arm man, student of rackets and natural-born wheeler-dealer. He had just one flaw.

Though his mother was Sicilian, his father was Irish. Hill could never be a "made man" within the Sicilian organization. He was privy to just about every one of the mob's scams, thefts and assassinations, but he was forever denied the status that pure blood would have allowed him.

This was Hill's seriocomic-tragic flaw and, later, his value to the Federal Bureau of Investigation. People who look with longing through a window see more than those who are inside.

Mr. Pileggi says it was Hill's point of view that interested him when, in 1981, he was approached by Hill's lawyers to write the story of the gangster, who had entered the F.B.I.'s witness-protection program. Hill was then about to testify against everyone in his adult life who had been nearest and dearest to him.

Hill "knew a great deal about the world in which he had been raised," Mr. Pileggi writes, "but he spoke about it with an odd detachment, and he had an outsider's eye for detail."

It is this detachment and these details, seemingly so commonplace as they are recalled by the film's Henry

Hill (Ray Liotta) and his wife, Karen (Lorraine Bracco), that help to make *Goodfellas* such a singular and, in an upside-down way, such a riotous movie.

Francis Coppola's two *Godfather* movies are full of noble despair and sentiment. This, they say, is the American Dream gone onto rocks the size of Gibraltar. The emotions are operatic. Jonathan Demme's *Married to the Mob* turns Mafiosos into characters out of a Preston Sturges comedy.

Both director's visions are legitimate. Mr. Scorsese's is something else.

Goodfellas looks at the mob without making any apparent comment of its own. As it adopts the flat tone of Henry, its principal narrator, it also reflects Henry's jittery and driven concerns. It moves from sequence to sequence with slightly crazed speed, as if anticipating one of the cocaine highs that, finally, were to be Henry's undoing.

Mr. Scorsese and Mr. Pileggi can't quite get the entire book onto the screen, but they succeed in preserving a remarkable number of the details.

There are young Henry's initial encounters at the cab stand with Vario, called Paulie (Paul Sorvino), his later hectic courtship of Karen, a nice Jewish girl who admits to being turned on by Henry's guns (and who is, toward the end, turned on by his cocaine), and, most important, his friendships with his mob partners, Jimmy Conroy (Robert De Niro) and Tommy DeVito (Joe Pesci).

The jealous Karen is always furious about Henry's girlfriends. "Friday night at the Copa was for the girlfriends," Henry says on the soundtrack at one point. "Saturday night was for the wives." Yet girlfriends are not Karen's competition. She is, instead, up against Henry's addiction to the excitement, power and perks of his job and his life, in which his associates come first.

Paulie functions as his true father. Jimmy and Tommy are his true brothers.

Some brothers.

Tommy is clearly psychotic. For laughs he shoots a barroom gofer in the foot and, later, when the gofer talks back, he shoots him through the heart. Jimmy seems steadier. At sixteen, he was a hit man for Paulie but, as Henry recalls later, "What Jimmy really loved to do was steal."

Jimmy's truck hijackings are just rehearsals for what would become the mob's greatest heist, the Lufthansa robbery at Kennedy Airport in 1978. The size of the Lufthansa haul turned everyone a bit giddy, leading to a series of murders that eventually doomed them all. Greed eats away at lifelong friendships. The only thing that survives is the instinct for self-preservation.

Goodfellas looks and sounds as if it must be absolutely authentic. It's not just the New York settings in which the film was photographed, or the barrooms and diners and nightclubs in which the guys hang out. It isn't even the throwaway bits of sociology the audience hears. Recalling her introduction into mob society, Karen says, "Almost all the sons were named Peter or Paul and all the wives named Marie."

The authenticity exists in the unimaginative ordinariness of the violent lives it depicts. These guys "wack" an associate with ease and then stop by Tommy's mother's house to pick up a shovel. The old lady insists on feeding them.

She scolds Tommy for not finding a nice girl. Tommy says, "I find a nice girl every night." Laughter. Boys will be boys.

It's not all fun. One night they have to drive upstate to dig up a body they thought was safely disposed of. It seems that the burial ground has been sold for condominiums. The body, only partially decomposed, smells worse than they could have imagined. Details. Details.

Paulie and his pals buy a Queens restaurant, steal it blind, and burn it down to collect the insurance.

It is the mobsters' ferocious pettiness and the smallness of their aspirations that are so terrifying in *Goodfellas*. This may be the most cautionary aspect of the film. After all, America made them.

More than any earlier Scorsese film, *Goodfellas* is memorable for the ensemble nature of the performances. Mr. De Niro, Mr. Liotta, Mr. Pesci, and Mr. Sorvino shine together, though Mr. Pesci's material is the flashiest. Miss Bracco is equally good, but so is the role. The movie has been beautifully cast from the leading roles to the bits.

There is flash also in some of Mr. Scorsese's directorial choices, including freeze-frames, fast cutting, and the occasional long tracking shot. None of it is superfluous. The film's rhythms are built into the shape of the narrative, whose penultimate sequence is a Keystone Kops comedy for adults.

Goodfellas doesn't end. It crashes, with Henry, into

the sobriety of the straight world. It disturbs, and even makes one think.

—*V.C., September 19, 1990*

GOSFORD PARK

Directed by Robert Altman; written by Julian Fellowes, based on an idea by Mr. Altman and Bob Balaban; director of photography, Andrew Dunn; edited by Tim Squyres; music by Patrick Doyle; production designer, Stephen Altman; produced by Mr. Altman, Mr. Balaban and David Levy; released by USA Films. Running time: 137 minutes.

With: Eileen Atkins (Mrs. Croft), Bob Balaban (Morris Weissman), Alan Bates (Jennings), Charles Dance (Raymond, Lord Stockbridge), Stephen Fry (Inspector Thompson), Michael Gambon (Sir William McCordle), Richard E. Grant (George), Tom Hollander (Lt. Cmdr. Anthony Meredith), Derek Jacobi (Probert), Kelly Macdonald (Mary Maceachran), Helen Mirren (Mrs. Wilson), Jeremy Northam (Ivor Novello), Clive Owen (Robert Parks), Ryan Phillippe (Henry Denton), Camilla Rutherford (Isobel McCordle), Maggie Smith (Constance, Countess of Trentham), Geraldine Somerville (Louisa, Lady Stockbridge), Kristin Scott Thomas (Lady Sylvia McCordle), Sophie Thompson (Dorothy), Emily Watson (Elsie) and James Wilby (The Hon. Freddie Nesbitt).

Robert Altman's film *Gosford Park* is a melt-in-your-mouth hunk of 12-layer English spice cake that will appeal to anyone who feels a nostalgic pang for the long-running British television series *Upstairs, Downstairs,* or for the cozy whodunits of Agatha Christie. Made with an all-star, mostly British cast, it is a virtuoso ensemble piece to rival the director's *Nashville* and *Short Cuts* in its masterly interweaving of multiple characters and subplots.

The film, set in November 1932, takes place on a grand country estate where well over a dozen aristocrats and their servants gather for a weekend shooting party during which their host, Sir William McCordle (Michael Gambon), is murdered. The mystery genre lends *Gosford Park* a tidy symmetry lacking in earlier Altman epics, but it also forces the movie to fall into a formula.

Anglophiles will gleefully wallow in the baronial splendor of the setting and in the movie's canny eye for period detail, including everything from dinner place settings to vintage cars to the rituals of the shoot. The performances, for the most part, are so pitch-perfect that you needn't pay close attention to the film's complicated plot to have fun. English snobbery and class envy have always provided vicarious enjoyment when ogled from a safe distance. The vision of Maggie Smith as Constance, the Countess of Trentham, peering down her nose while dispensing barbed little pearls of imperious condescension and cruelty to one and all is almost sinfully delicious.

So is the sight of Kristin Scott Thomas as Sir William's icy wife, Lady Sylvia. Early in the movie we learn that she and her younger sister, Louisa (Geraldine Somerville), cut cards to determine which of the two, who come from an impoverished but titled family, would snag Sir William, a self-made millionaire described by one character as "a hardhearted randy old sod."

If Sir William thinks nothing of pawing at every young woman who catches his fancy, Lady Sylvia, who disdainfully mocks her husband for being interested only in money and fiddling with his guns, has a more discreetly roving eye. Setting her sights on a handsome young valet (Ryan Phillippe), she zeroes in with the predatory sangfroid of the truly entitled. When she requests delivery of a glass of warm milk at 1 A.M., at which time she promises to be "wide awake," there is no mistaking what she wants.

On the surface *Gosford Park* may appear to be little more than an elaborate, star-studded PBS-ready mystery yarn. But under its opulent surface it is programmatically subversive of the very thing it pretends to be. *Upstairs, Downstairs,* you may recall, was a reassuring Edwardian soap opera in which the beneficent ruling class dispensed noblesse oblige to the true-blue servants, and everybody was reasonably settled and happy.

Gosford Park, which was written by Julian Fellowes from a concept by Mr. Altman and the actor Bob Balaban, portrays a similar milieu as a Darwinian shark tank of money grubbing, social climbing and scurrilous gossip in which upstairs and downstairs are treacherously intertwined.

Those with titles might be described as the idle (and embittered) not-so-rich. One aristocrat who has married money, has already squandered his wife's inheritance and having no use for her any longer, now despises her. Another, who faces financial ruin, desperately pleads with Sir William to invest in his ridiculous scheme to sell boots to the Sudanese.

For all her grand airs, the Countess of Trentham (who is Lady Sylvia's aunt) is dependent for her livelihood on an allowance from Sir William, which he threatens to take away. Sir William's fortune didn't come from banking but from factories that are described as sweatshops, in which he relentlessly preyed on his young female workers.

The pains of World War I, which ended fourteen years earlier, still throb. Those who fought that war wear a halo of valor, while a secret shame accrues to those who did not.

Hatreds and rivalries abound both upstairs and below, and sexual shenaningans cross class boundaries. They are pretty much taken for granted as long as discretion is maintained. The movie's truth teller and most likable character, Elsie (Emily Watson), is the head housemaid whose affair with Sir William is common knowledge, although it is never spoken of.

The movie throws in a hall-of-mirrors wrinkle in its choice of three of the guests: a discreetly gay American movie producer, Morris Weissman (Mr. Balaban), researching his newest movie, *Charlie Chan in London;* his ambitious, bisexual boyfriend, Henry Denton (Mr. Phillippe), an actor posing as a Scottish valet; and the English matinee idol Ivor Novello (Jeremy Northam). Novello was a real life movie star who also composed numerous English hit songs in a Noel Coward style. A running subtext of the film is the collision and mutual exploitation of two far-flung fantasy worlds: aristocratic England and Hollywood.

As much as the presence of a movie star and a Hollywood producer titillates some of the aristocrats, they also envy and look down on their American guests, wearing their snobbery as armor. Mr. Balaban's producer has some of the screenplay's most telling lines about the relationship between these two worlds.

"How do you put up with these people?" Weissman asks Novello, who replies with a smile, "You forget I earn my living by impersonating them." When Novello sits at the piano and sings his songs evoking the upper-class milieu as a charmed never-never land of romance and wit, the servants practically swoon, while the aristocrats affect utter disinterest. When Weissman is discussing casting on the telephone to Hollywood, the name Claudette Colbert is dropped, and he asks, "Is she affected or is she British?"

When it comes to portraying the upper class, *Gosford Park* succeeds in having its cake and eating it too. While demolishing the *Upstairs, Downstairs* myth of kindness toward those of lower station, it allows these jaded, chilly malcontents to retain a patina of supercilious glamour.

In the spirit of democracy, the movie is as attentive to its downstairs characters as to those upstairs. Helen Mirren is especially fine s the head housekeeper, Mrs. Wilson, a woman so resigned to her lot in life that she is able to say proudly and with only a trace of bitterness: "I'm the perfect servant. I have no life." As Mrs. Croft, who runs the kitchen and carries on a bitter rivalry with Mrs. Wilson, Eileen Atkins is equally incisive.

Gosford Park is far more satisfying as social satire than as a mystery.

To foreshadow a crime, the camera lingers portentously on bottles labeled "poison." And when murder is committed, the movie resorts to the cliché of photographing a suspect from the knees down. The criminal investigation is perfunctory, and the police inspector (Stephen Fry) the movie's least compelling character. The final revelations, when they pour out, feel like the hoary contrivances of a 19th-century melodrama.

But when *Gosford Park* is not adhering to a formula, which is most of the time, it is at the top its game. The screenplay is so amazingly concise that if you watch the film more than once (which I would advise), you'll find barely a word has been wasted. Almost every sentence conveys crucial information, but in a deceptively offhand style that's so light it feels like casual banter. And the director's trademark style of overlapping dialogue that is never "speechy" in a theatrical sense adds to the overall sense of naturalness.

What makes the achievement of *Gosford Park* all the more remarkable is that Mr. Altman is 76. If the movie's cool assessment of the human condition implies the dispassionate overview of a man who has seen it all, the energy that crackles from the screen suggests the clear-sighted joie de vivre of an artist still deeply engaged in the world.

—*S.H., December 26, 2000*

THE GRADUATE

Directed by Mike Nichols: written by Calder Willingham and Buck Henry. based on the novel by Charles Webb: cinematographer. Robert Surtees: edited by Sam O'Steen: music by Dave Grusin: production designer. Richard Sylbert: produced by Lawrence Turman: released by Embassy Pictures. Running time: 105 minutes.

With: Anne Bancroft (Mrs. Robinson). Dustin Hoffman (Ben Braddock). Katharine Ross (Elaine Robinson). William Daniels (Mr. Braddock). Murray Hamilton (Mr. Robinson). Elizabeth Wilson (Mrs. Braddock). Brian Avery (Carl Smith) and Walter Brooke (Mr. Maguire).

Suddenly, here toward the year's end, when the new films are plunging toward the wire and the prospects of an Oscar-worthy long shot coming through get progressively more dim, there sweeps ahead a film that is not only one of the best of the year, but also one of the best seriocomic social satires we've had from Hollywood since Preston Sturges was making them.

It is Mike Nichols's and Lawrence Turman's devastating and uproarious *The Graduate,* which came yesterday to the Lincoln Art and the Coronet.

Mark it right down in your datebook as a picture you'll have to see—and maybe see twice to savor all its sharp satiric wit and cinematic treats. For in telling a pungent story of the sudden confusions and dismays of a bland young man fresh out of college who is plunged headlong into the intellectual vacuum of his affluent parents' circle of friends, it fashions a scarifying picture of the raw vulgarity of the swimming-pool rich, and it does so with a lively and exciting expressiveness through vivid cinema.

Further, it offers an image of silver-spooned, bewildered youth, standing expectantly out with misgiving where the brook and the swimming-pool meet, that is developed so wistfully and winningly by Dustin Hoffman, an amazing new young star, that it makes you feel a little tearful and choked up while it is making you laugh yourself raw.

In outline, it may sound skimpy and perhaps a little crude—possibly even salacious in a manner now common in films. For all it is, in essence, is the story of this bright but reticent young man who returns from an Eastern college to his parent's swanky home in Beverly Hills, gets seduced rather quickly by the restless wife of his father's law partner, then falls in love with the lady's daughter and finds himself helplessly trapped in a rather sticky dilemma until he is able to dislodge himself through a familiar romantic ploy.

That's all. And yet in pursuing this simple story line, which has been adorned with delicious incidents and crackling dialogue in the screenplay by Calder Willingham and Buck Henry, based on a novel by Charles Webb, the still exploring Mr. Nichols has done such sly and surprising things with his actors and with his camera—or, rather, Robert Surtees's camera—that the overall picture has the quality of a very extensive and revealing social scan.

With Mr. Hoffman's stolid, deadpanned performance, he gets a wonderfully compassionate sense of the ironic and pathetic immaturity of a mere baccalaureate scholar turned loose in an immature society. He is a character very much reminiscent of Holden Caulfield in J. D. Salinger's *Catcher in the Rye.*

And with Anne Bancroft's sullenly contemptuous and voracious performance as the older woman who yearns for youth, Mr. Nichols has twined in the netting the casual crudeness and yet the pathos of this type.

Katharine Ross, another comparative newcomer, is beautifully fluid and true as the typical college senior daughter whose sensitivities are helplessly exposed for brutal abrasion by her parents and by the permissive society in which she lives. Murray Hamilton is piercing as her father—a seemingly self-indulgent type who is sharply revealed as bewildered and wounded in one fine, funny scene. And William Daniels and Elizabeth Wilson fairly set your teeth on edge as the hotcha, insensitive parents of the lonely young man.

Enhancing the veracity of the picture is first-rate staging in true locations and on well-dressed sets, all looking right in excellent color. And a rich, poignant musical score that features dandy modern folk music, sung (offscreen, of course) by the team of Simon and Garfunkel, has the sound of today's moody youngsters—"The Sound of Silence," as one lyric says.

Funny, outrageous, and touching, *The Graduate* is a sophisticated film that puts Mr. Nichols and his associates on a level with any of the best satirists working abroad today.

—*B.C., December 22, 1967*

GRAND HOTEL

Directed by Edmund Goulding; written by William A. Drake, based on his play and the novel *Menschen im Hotel* by Vicki Baum; cinematographer, William Daniels; edited by Blanche Sewell; art designer, Cedric Gibbons; released by Metro-Goldwyn-Mayer. Black and white. Running time: 115 minutes.

With: Greta Garbo (Grusinskaya), John Barrymore (The Baron), Joan Crawford (Flaemmchen), Wallace Beery (Preysing), Lionel Barrymore (Otto Kringelein), Jean Hersholt (Senf), Robert McWade (Meierheim), Purnell B. Pratt (Zinnowitz), Ferdinand Gottschalk (Pimenov), Rafaela Ottiano (Suzette), Morgan Wallace (Chauffeur), Tully Marshall (Gerstenkorn) and Edwin Maxwell (Dr. Waltz).

For the first showing last night of the film of Vicki Baum's stage work, *Grand Hotel,* those worshipers of the stars of the Hollywood firmament choked the sidewalk outside the Astor and also the theater lobby while policemen afoot and on horse urged the throng to keep moving. And from across Broadway blinding beams of light added to the general excitement.

Inside the theater it was for a time difficult to move but very slowly, for many of those who had tickets pressed into the aisles and behind the orchestra seats with the evident hope of catching a glimpse of one or another cinema celebrity. But once microphone music came from the stage the spectators hastened to their places and soon the introductory scene of the much talked-of motion picture was emblazoned on the screen. It was that of the telephone operators in the Grand Hotel and the pushing and shouting was a thing of the past.

It is a production thoroughly worthy of all the talk it has created and the several motion picture luminaries deserve to feel very proud of their performances, particularly Greta Garbo and Lionel Barrymore. So far as the direction is concerned, Edmund Goulding has done an excellent piece of work, but occasionally it seems as though he relies too much on close-ups. Nevertheless he has sustained a steady momentum in darting here and there in the busy hostelry and working up to an effective dramatic pitch at the psychological moment. In all, the picture adheres faithfully to the original and while it undoubtedly lacks the life and depth and color of the play, by means of excellent characterizations it keeps the audience on the qui vive.

It is indubitably a capital subject to bring to the screen, for it benefits by the sweeping scope of the camera and in swaying from room to room and from the lobby to the telephone switchboard, Mr. Goulding gives some markedly fine photographic effects. But it should be stated that in one scene he permits an extremely gruesome idea to creep in. This will probably be eliminated at some of the future exhibitions.

Miss Garbo, of course, impersonates the dancer, Grusinskaya, played on the stage by Eugénie Leontovich. Miss Garbo, possibly appreciating that she was supported by a galaxy of efficient performers, decided that she would do her utmost to make her role shine. And she succeeds admirably. She is stunning in her early scenes and charming in the love scene with Baron Geigern, portrayed by John Barrymore with his usual savoir faire. And later, wearing a chinchilla coat, she is gay and lighthearted, for love has beckoned to the temperamental dancer. Grusinskaya leaves the screen hopeful of meeting the Baron at the railroad station, but the audience knows that the good-natured and sympathetic thief has met his doom at the hands of the ignoble Preysing, a part acted by Wallace Beery.

It fell to Lionel Barrymore's lot to play Otto Kringelein, the humble bookkeeper who decides in an introductory scene that, as he has not long to live, he will go out of this world in a blaze of glory. Mr. Barrymore brings out every possible note of this sensitive person, who talks with bated breath to the Baron, entertains with champagne and caviar, loathes his employer, the hard-fisted, sensual Preysing, for whom he has worked for a pittance. He is going to die and therefore what cares he if Preysing discharges him? But, instead of passing away, he entrains for Paris with the attractive stenographer, Flaemmchen, who is seen in the person of Joan Crawford. Through Mr. Barrymore's skillful interpretation one gleans the satisfaction this obsequious human adding machine has in hobnobbing with people of the world and in living in the corner suite of the Grand Hotel. Mr. Barrymore is superb when he, as Kringelein, finds himself tipsy, tipsy but elated. If ever an actor got under the skin of a character, Mr. Barrymore does here.

And, although Miss Garbo and Lionel Barrymore deliver talented portrayals, it does not mean that any aspersion is to be cast at the work of others in the cast. Miss Crawford, for instance, is splendid as Flaemmchen. She, too, does all that is possible to vie with the others in the cast. Then there is John Barrymore as the Baron. Nobody could hope to see such a type better acted. This Baron is handsome, a little sly, eager for money, but always thoughtful and friendly when it comes to his association with Kringelein. He steals Kringelein's wallet, but, when he hears Kringelein bewailing his loss, he "finds" the wallet, and how glad is Kringelein!

As for Mr. Beery, it may seem that while his performance does not quite compare with that of Siegfried Rumann, the stage Preysing, it is nevertheless a very worthy characterization. Mr. Beery is sufficiently ponderous and forbidding as Preysing, but in having to assume a German accent he is not quite in his element. But those who did not see Mr. Rumann will undoubtedly decide that Mr. Beery's performance is good enough.

No review of this picture would be complete without a mention of the genuinely pleasing work of Ferdinand Gottschalk, who acts the loyal underling of Pimenov. Lewis Stone also does well as Dr. Otternschlag and Jean Hersholt is up to his usual high standard as the porter, Senf, whose chief interest during the running of the story is the condition of his wife, who finally gives birth to a child as the story comes to a close. And it is Dr. Otternschlag who is given to saying that "people come and people go, and nothing ever happens in the Grand Hotel."

And the audience has seen manslaughter, gambling, a baron bent on stealing pearls, love affairs, a business deal, and various other doings. And "nothing ever happens"!

—M.H., April 13, 1932

GRAND ILLUSION

Directed by Jean Renoir; written by Mr. Renoir and Charles Spaak, based on a story by Mr. Renoir; cinematographer, Christian Matras; edited by Marguerite Renoir; music by Jerome and Joseph Kosma; art designer, Eugène Lourie; produced by Raymond Blondy; released by World Pictures Corporation. Black and White. Running time: 95 minutes.

With: Jean Gabin (Marechal), Pierre Fresnay (de Boeldieu), Erich von Stroheim (Von Rauffenstein), Dalio (Rosenthal) and Dita Parlo (Peasant Woman).

Surprisingly enough, in these combustible times, the French have produced a war film under the title *Grand Illusion.* It served to reopen the Filmarte last night and it serves to warn the British that they no longer have a monopoly upon that valuable dramatic device known as understatement. Jean Renoir, the film's author and director, has chosen consistently to underplay his hand. Time after time he permits his drama to inch up to the brink of melodrama: one waits for the explosion and the tumult. Time after time he resists the temptation and lets the picture go its calmer course.

For a war film it is astonishingly lacking in hullabaloo. There may have been four shots fired, but there are no screaming shells, no brave speeches, no gallant toasts to the fallen. War is the grand illusion and Renoir proceeds with his disillusioning task by studying it, not in the front line, but in the prison camps, where captors and captives alike are condemned to the dry rot of inaction. War is not reality; prison camp is. Only the real may survive it.

Renoir cynically places a decadent aristocrat, a German career officer, in command of the camp; he places his French counterpart among the prisoners. Theirs is an affinity bred of mutual self-contempt, of the realization of being part of an outgrown era. The other prisoners are less heroic, but more human. They are officers, of course, but officers of a republic, not an aristocracy. One is Marechal, ex-machinist; another is Rosenthal, a wealthy Jew. Von Rauffenstein, the German commandant, held them both in contempt. The elegant Captain de Boeldieu respected them as soldiers, admired them as men, faintly regretted he could not endure them as fellow beings.

So it becomes a story of escape, a metaphysical escape on de Boeldieu's part, a tremendously exciting flesh-and-bone escape on the part of Marechal and Rosenthal. Renoir's narrative links the two adventures for a while, but ultimately resolves itself into a saga of flight. As an afterthought, but a brilliantly executed one, he adds a romance as one of his French fugitives finds shelter in the home of a young German widow. The story ends sharply, with no attempt to weave its threads together. It is probably the way such a story would have ended in life.

Renoir has created a strange and interesting film, but he owes much to his cast. Erich von Stroheim's appearance as von Rauffenstein reminds us again of Hollywood's folly in permitting so fine an actor to remain idle and unwanted. Pierre Fresnay's de Boeldieu is a model of gentlemanly decadence. Jean Gabin and Dalio as the fugitives, Dita Parlo as the German girl, and all the others are thoroughly right. The Filmarte is off to a good beginning.

—*F.S.N., September 13, 1938*

THE GRAPES OF WRATH

Directed by John Ford: written by Nunnally Johnson. based on the novel by John Steinbeck: cinematographer. Gregg Toland: edited by Robert Simpson: music by Alfred Newman: art designers. Richard Day and Mark Lee Kirk: produced by Darryl F. Zanuck: released by Twentieth Century Fox. Black and white. Running time: 129 minutes.

With: Henry Fonda (Tom Joad). Jane Darwell (Ma Joad). John Carradine (Casey). Charley Grapewin (Grampa). Dorris Bowdon (Rose of Sharon). Russell Simpson (Pa Joad). O. Z. Whitehead (Al). John Qualen (Muley). Eddie Quillan (Connie) and Zeffie Tilbury (Granma).

In the vast library where the celluloid literature of the screen is stored there is one small, uncrowded shelf devoted to the cinema's masterworks, to those films which by dignity of theme and excellence of treatment seem to be of enduring artistry, seem destined to be recalled not merely at the end of their particular year but whenever great motion pictures are mentioned. To that shelf of screen classics Twentieth Century Fox yesterday added its version of John Steinbeck's *The Grapes of Wrath*, adapted by Nunnally Johnson, directed by John Ford, and performed at the Rivoli by a cast of such uniform excellence and suitability that we should be doing its other members an

injustice by saying it was "headed" by Henry Fonda, Jane Darwell, John Carradine, and Russell Simpson.

We know the question you are asking, have been asking since the book was acquired for filming: Does the picture follow the novel, how closely, and how well? The answer is that it has followed the book; has followed it closely, but not with blind, undiscriminating literalness; has followed it so well that no one who has read and admired it should complain of the manner of its screen telling. Steinbeck's language, which some found too shocking for tender eyes, has been cleaned up, but has not been toned so high as to make its people sound other than as they are. Some phases of his saga have been skimped and some omitted; the book's ending has been dropped; the sequence of events and of speeches has been subtly altered.

The changes sound more serious than they are, seem more radical than they are. For none of them has blurred the clarity of Steinbeck's word-picture of the people of the Dust Bowl. None of them has rephrased, in softer terms, his matchless description of the Joad family's trek from Oklahoma to California to find the promised land where work was plenty, wages were high and folk could live in little white houses beside an orange grove. None of them has blunted the fine indignation or diluted the bitterness of his indictment of the cruel deception by which an empty stewpot was substituted for the pot of gold at the rainbow's end. And none of them has—as most of us feared it might—sent the film off on a witch-hunt, let it pretend there had just been a misunderstanding, made it end on the sunrise of a new and brighter day.

Steinbeck's story might have been exaggeration; at least some will take comfort in thinking so. But if only half of it were true, that half still should constitute a tragedy of modern America, a bitter chapter of national history that has not yet been closed, that has, as yet, no happy ending, that has thus far produced but two good things: a great American novel (if it is truly a novel) and a great American motion picture.

Its greatness as a picture lies in many things, not all of them readily reducible to words. It is difficult, for example, to discuss John Ford's direction, except in pictorial terms. His employment of camera is reportage and editorial and dramatization by turns or all in one. Steinbeck described the Dust Bowl and its farmers, used page on page to do it. Ford's cameras turn off a white-striped highway, follow Tom Joad scuffling through the dust to the empty farmhouse, see through Muley's eyes the pain of surrendering the land and the hopelessness of trying to resist the tractors. A swift sequence or two, and all that Steinbeck said has been said and burned indelibly into memory by a director, a camera, and a cast.

Or follow the Joads in their piled-up, rattling, wheezing truck along Highway 66, and let the Russian realists match if they can that Ford shot through the windshield, with three tired faces reflected in it and the desert through it. Or the covered wagon's arrival at the first of a series of Hoovervilles, with a litter of humans and dogs and crates in its path, and the eloquence of their mute testimony to poverty and disillusion and the degradation of the human spirit. We could mention a score of others, but they would mean no more unless you, too, had seen the picture. Direction, when it is as brilliant as Mr. Ford's has been, is easy to recognize, but impossible to describe.

It's simpler to talk about the players and the Nunnally Johnson script. There may be a few words of dialogue that Steinbeck has not written, but Mr. Johnson almost invariably has complimented him by going to the book for his lines. A sentence from one chapter is made to serve a later sequence; sometimes Ma Joad is saying things the preacher originally said; sometimes Tom is borrowing Ma's lines. But they fit and they ring true, and that applies, as well, to Mr. Johnson's reshuffling of the Steinbeck sequences, his coming to the end of the saga before Steinbeck was willing to punch out the final period.

And if all this seems strange for Hollywood—all this fidelity to a book's spirit, this resoluteness of approach to a dangerous (and, in California, an especially dangerous) topic—still stranger has been the almost incredible rightness of the film's casting, the utter believability of some of Hollywood's most typical people in untypical roles. Henry Fonda's Tom Joad is precisely the hot-tempered, resolute, saturnine chap Mr. Steinbeck had in mind. Jane Darwell's Ma is exactly the family head we pictured as we read the book. Charles Grapewin's Grampa cannot be quite the "heller" we met in the novel: the antiprofanity dictums bothered him more than the rest of them, but Mr. Grapewin's Gramp is still quite an old boy.

We could go on with this talk of the players, but it would become repetitious, for there are too many of them, and too many are perfect in their parts. What we've been trying to say is that *The Grapes of Wrath* is just about as good as any picture has a right to be; if it were any better, we just wouldn't believe our eyes.

—F.S.N., *January 25, 1940*

THE GREAT DICTATOR

Written, directed and produced by Charles Chaplin; cinematographers, Roland Totheroh and Karl Struss; edited by Willard Nico; music by Meredith Willson; art designer, J. Russell Spencer; released by United Artists. Black and white. Running time: 127 minutes.

With: Charles Chaplin (Adenoid Hynkel, Dictator of Tomania/A Jewish Barber), Jack Oakie (Benzini Napaloni, Dictator of Bacteria), Reginald Gardiner (Schultz), Henry Daniell (Garbitsch), Billy Gilbert (Herring), Grace Hayle (Mme. Napaloni), Carter de Haven (Bacterian Ambassador), Paulette Goddard (Hannah), Maurice Moscovich (Mr. Jaeckel), Emma Dunn (Mrs. Jaeckel), Bernard Gorcey (Mr. Mann) and Paul Weigel (Mr. Agar).

Now that the waiting is over and the shivers of suspense at an end, let the trumpets be sounded and the banners flung against the sky. For the little tramp, Charlie Chaplin, finally emerged last night from behind the close-guarded curtains which have concealed his activities these past two years and presented himself in triumphal splendor as *The Great Dictator*—or you know who.

No event in the history of the screen has ever been anticipated with more hopeful excitement than the premiere of this film, which occurred simultaneously at the Astor and Capitol Theatres; no picture ever made has promised more momentous consequences. The prospect of little "Charlot," the most universally loved character in all the world, directing his superlative talent for ridicule against the most dangerously evil man alive has loomed as a titanic jest, a transcendent paradox. And the happy report this morning is that it comes off magnificently. *The Great Dictator* may not be the finest picture ever made—in fact, it possesses several disappointing shortcomings. But, despite them, it turns out to be a truly superb accomplishment by a truly great artist—and, from one point of view, perhaps the most significant film ever produced.

Let this be understood, however: it is no catchpenny buffoonery, no droll and gentle-humored social satire in the manner of Chaplin's earlier films. *The Great Dictator* is essentially a tragic picture—or tragicomic in the classic sense—and it has strongly bitter overtones. For it is a lacerating fable of the unhappy lot of decent folk in a totalitarian land, of all the hateful oppression that has crushed the humanity out of men's souls. And, especially, it is a withering revelation, through genuinely inspired mimicry, of the tragic weaknesses, the overblown conceit, and even the blank insanity of a dictator. Hitler, of course.

The main story line is quite simple, though knotted with many complications. A little Jewish barber returns to his shop in the ghetto of an imaginary city (obviously Berlin) after a prolonged lapse of perception due to an injury in the World War. He does not know that the state is now under the sign of the double cross, that storm troopers patrol the streets, that Jews are cruelly persecuted and that the all-powerful ruler of the land is one Hynkel, a megalomaniac, to whom he bears—as a foreword states—a "coincidental resemblance." Thus, the little barber suffers a bitter disillusionment when he naively attempts to resist; he is beaten and eventually forced to flee to a neighboring country. But there he is mistaken for Hynkel, who has simultaneously annexed this neighboring land. And pushed upon a platform to make a conqueror's speech, he delivers instead a passionate appeal for human kindness and reason and brotherly love.

Thus the story throws in pointed contrast the good man against the evil one—the genial, self-effacing, but courageous little man of the street against the cold, pretentious tyrant. Both are played by Chaplin, of course, in a highly comic vein, beneath which runs a note of eternal sadness. The little barber is our beloved Charlie of old—the fellow with the splay feet, baggy pants, trick mustache and battered bowler. And, as always, he is the pathetic butt of heartless circumstances, beaten, driven but ever-prepared to bounce back. In this role Chaplin performs two of the most superb bits of pantomime he has ever done—one during a sequence in which he and four other characters eat puddings containing coins to determine which shall sacrifice his life to kill the dictator, and the other a bit in which he shaves a man to the rhythm of Brahms's Hungarian Rhapsody.

But it is as the dictator that Chaplin displays his true genius. Whatever fate it was that decreed Adolf Hitler should look like Charlie must have ordained this opportunity, for the caricature of the former is devastating. The feeble, affected hand salute, the inclination for striking ludicrous attitudes, the fabulous fits of rage and violent facial contortions—all the vulnerable spots of Hitler's exterior are pierced by Chaplin's pantomimic shafts. He is at his best in a wild, senseless burst of guttural oratory—a compound of German, Yiddish, and Katzenjammer double-talk; and he reaches positively exalted heights in a plaintive dance that he does with a large balloon representing the globe, bouncing it into the air, pirouetting beneath it—and then bursting into tears when the balloon finally pops.

Another splendid sequence is that in which Hynkel and Napaloni, a neighboring dictator, meet and bargain. Napaloni, played by Jack Oakie, is a bluff, expansive creature—the anthesis of neurotic Hynkel—and the two actors contrive in this part of the film one of the most hilarious lampoons ever performed on the screen. Others in the cast are excellent—Paulette Goddard as a little laundry girl, Henry Daniell as a Minister of Propaganda, Billy Gilbert as a Minister of War—but Oakie ranges right alongside Chaplin. And that is tops.

On the debit side, the picture is overlong, it is inclined to be repetitious, and the speech with which it ended—the appeal for reason and kindness—is completely out of joint with that which has gone before. In it Chaplin steps out of character and addresses his heart to the audience. The effect is bewildering, and what should be the climax becomes flat and seemingly maudlin. But the sincerity with which Chaplin voices his appeal and the expression of tragedy which is clear in his face are strangely overpowering. Suddenly one perceives in bald relief the things that make *The Great Dictator* great—the courage and faith and surpassing love for mankind which are in the heart of Charlie Chaplin.

—B.C., October 16, 1940

GREAT EXPECTATIONS

Directed by David Lean; written by Mr. Lean, Anthony Havelock-Allan, Cecil McGivern, Kay Walsh and Ronald Neame, based on the novel by Charles Dickens; cinematographer, Guy Green; edited by Jack Harris; music by Walter Goehr; production designer, John Bryan; produced by Mr. Neame; released by Universal International Pictures. Black and white. Running time: 118 minutes.

With: John Mills (Mr. Pip), Anthony Wager (Young Pip), Valerie Hobson (Estella), Jean Simmons (Young Estella), Bernard Miles (Joe Gargery), Francis L. Sullivan (Jaggers), Finlay Currie (Magwitch), Alec Guinness (Herbert Pocket), John Forrest (Young Herbert) and Martita Hunt (Miss Havisham).

If there is any lingering necessity of inspiring more Charles Dickens fans—not to mention more fans for British movies—the thing that should certainly do the job is the film made from *Great Expectations*, which came to the Music Hall yesterday. For here, in a perfect motion picture, made in England (where it should have been made), the British have done for Dickens what they did for Shakespeare with *Henry V*; they have proved that his works have more life in them than almost anything now written for the screen.

Not that there haven't been previous delightful and inspiring Dickens films. *David Copperfield* was a winner a dozen years ago. And, from away back in antiquity we recall a memorable, silent *Oliver Twist*, while, more recently than either, came a sugar-cured *Christmas Carol*. But, somehow, the fullness of Dickens, of his stories and characters—his humor and pathos and vitality and all his brilliant command of atmosphere—has never been so illustrated as it is in this wonderful film, which can safely be recommended as screen storytelling at its best.

That may sound slightly excessive to the fireplace-and-slippers Dickens fans, who seldom propose *Great Expectations* as one of the novelist's most distinguished works. They might have asked for something stronger in the way of a narrative. But the everyday moviegoer—and even the casual reader of Dickens's books—will not recognize any weakness in either the structure or the characters of this film. For, despite necessary elisions and compressions of favorite scenes, the picture is so truly Dickens—so truly human and noble in its scope—that the quality of the author is revealed in every shot, in every line. Mid-nineteenth-century England—and a thrilling story—are crowded on the screen.

Are you familiar with this story—the story of little Pip, the poor orphan boy who is accosted on the lone and shiverin' marshes one fateful night by Magwitch, the granite-faced convict, escaped from the nearby hulks, whom Pip, in fear and compassion, befriends before the felon is caught and returned? Do you remember the contrivance by which Pip is later sent to "play" in the great, musty house of mad Miss Havisham; how he meets his love, Estella, there and is thus inspired with the ambition of becoming "a gentleman"? And do you recall how, years later, Pip is actually endowed with handsome means by a mysterious benefactor, how he goes to London and becomes a fancy blade and then suddenly runs into such adventures as only the nimble mind of Dickens could contrive?

Even if you do remember, it shouldn't lessen your enjoyment in the least from this glowing illumination of the warm and deliciously surprising tale. For the smooth team of Anthony Havelock-Allan, David Lean, and Ronald Neame have caught it right down to the last shiver of a frightened youngster or the haughty flash in Estella's eye. A script that is swift and sure in movement, aromatic English settings and costumes, and superlatively sensitive direction and acting are conjoined to make a rich and charming job. And a musical score of exceptional taste and understanding contributes too.

In the large cast of unsurpassed performers, John Mills, of course, stands out, since his is the paramount opportunity to play the grown-up Pip. He makes of this first-personal character such a full-bodied, gracious young man that Pip actually has more stature here than he has in the book. And little Anthony Wager, as the boy Pip, is so beautifully quiet and restrained, yet so subtly revealing of spirit, that he is certain to win every heart. Neither space nor words are sufficient to praise adequately the rest—the thundering Francis L. Sullivan as Jaggers, the shrewd solicitor; the sparrow-like Ivor Bernard as Wemmick, his Old

Bailey clerk; the beautiful Valerie Hobson as the perverse Estella grown up and the arrogant little Jean Simmons as this mettlesome creature as a girl; the tremendously comic Alec Guinness as Herbert Pocket, Pip's mad-hatter friend; or Finlay Currie as the beetling old Magwitch; or Martita Hunt as mad Miss Havisham. Nor have we space or words to give more than a deeply grateful salute to Bernard Miles for making of Joe Gargery, the blacksmith, a vivid memory, nor to mention a half-dozen others who are magically Dickensian in bits.

But we must say that all of them have managed to frame a Dickens portrait gallery to the life and to make real a tale of humble virtue elevated above snobbery and hate. It is such a tale as is enriching, for both young and old, in this day, and we offer as unforgettable some of its richest scenes. Like memorable moments from the novel, we will long cherish in our mind Pip's comical fight with the "pale young gentleman" that day at Miss Havisham's, or the desperate race to board the packet on the lower reaches of the Thames, with only the splash of water and the cry of gulls to break the tension of the scene. And always will we remember the sweetness in Joe's loving voice as he pours out his heart to his idol, "Dear old Pip, old chap!"

—B.C., May 23, 1947

THE GREAT MCGINTY

Written and directed by Preston Sturges; cinematographer, William Mellor; edited by Hugh Bennett; music by Frederick Hollander; art designers, Hans Dreier and Earl Hedrick; produced by Paul Jones; released by Paramount Pictures. Black and white. Running time: 81 minutes.

With: Brian Donlevy (Dan McGinty), Muriel Angelus (Catherine McGinty), Akim Tamiroff (The Boss), William Demarest (The Politician), Allyn Joslyn (George) and Thurston Hall (Maxwell).

In the trade they call them "sleepers"—these pictures that come drifting in without benefit of much advance publicity and that turn out delightful surprises. And if ever one came along to jolt the snoozers right out of their seats it is *The Great McGinty,* which

blew into the Paramount yesterday with all the spontaneous combustion and pyrotechnic display of an old-time Tammany parade through the streets of the lower East Side. Ladies and gentlemen and registered voters of this fair metropolis, here is a picture that really captures the rowdy spirit of corrupt politics, that makes titanic sport of the brazen peculations of grafting opportunists, and that reflects by innuendo the indifference of the American "sucker" during that pre-Depression period which one smart writer has called the "era of wonderful nonsense."

There was a time—and that not so long ago—when such good-natured elbow-rubbing, even upon the screen, with crooked political bosses, ward heelers, and profligate officios might not have been so amusing for the local constituents. But now, with graver matters to concern us and with a more comfortable sense of civic security, it is sublimely easy to laugh at the shameless tricks and vulgarities of out-and-out political buccaneers. It is good satiric fun to hear a grafter piously explain that "you've got to pay somebody to protect you from human greed." And it is highly amusing farce to see a tough and enterprising bum rise from a bread line of weeping Willies to become a mayor and briefly, a state governor by virtue of magnificent crookedness.

At least, it is in *The Great McGinty,* which Preston Sturges has written and directed for Paramount with a coarse and racy wit, a superior acceleration of action, and a flavor as pungent and infectious as the fumes of a red-fire torch. The story is simple, in the main. A bartender in a "banana port" dive tells it by way of flashback to a suicide-inclined customer—the story of how he rose from the bread line to the job of "collector" for a political boss because he "repeated" at the polls and was handy with his mitts; how he became an alderman and later a "reform" mayor; how he married his secretary just for appearances and because, as the boss put it, "marriage is the most beautiful setup amid the sexes"; how he fell in love with his wife, went on to the governorship, crossed the boys by threatening to go straight, and took a terrific fall. When he finishes the story, one of his listeners calls him a bald-faced liar. And he doesn't deny it. But he has saved a man from suicide—and Mr. Sturges has had a lot of fun.

Much praise must be bestowed on Brian Donlevy for his masterful comprehension of McGinty, who starts out as a plain dumb palooka and grows into a thoughtful man. Akim Tamiroff, too, as the boss gives a surprisingly restrained and incisive portrayal. Both catch the satiric points in their roles with consistent brilliance. Muriel Angelus is a beautiful contrast as the refined and level-headed wife, William Demarest makes a gem of a brassy ward heeler, and a whole troupe of shrewdly chosen "bit" players give authentic life and gusto to this ribald account of mudlarking. You won't make a mistake, believe us, if you stuff the ballot box for *The Great McGinty*.

—B.C., August 15, 1940

THE GREATEST SHOW ON EARTH

Produced and directed by Cecil B. DeMille; written by Fredic M. Frank, Barre Lyndon and Theodore St. John, based on a story by Mr. Frank, Mr. St. John and Frank Cavett; cinematographers, George Barnes, Peverell Marley and W. Wallace Kelley; edited by Anne Bauchens; music by Victor Young; art designers, Hal Pereira and Walter Tyler; released by Paramount Pictures. Running time: 153 minutes

With: Betty Hutton (Holly), Cornel Wilde (Sebastian), Charlton Heston (Brad), Dorothy Lamour (Phyllis), Gloria Grahame (Angel), James Stewart ("Buttons," a Clown), Henry Wilcoxon (Detective), Lyle Bettger (Klaus), Lawrence Tierney (Henderson) and Emmet Kelly, Cucciola, Antoinette Concello and John Ringling North (as Themselves).

It is difficult to be certain, in the case of *The Greatest Show on Earth,* whether Mohammed has gone to the mountain or the other way around. That is to say, there is some question whether Cecil B. DeMille or the Ringling Brothers and Barnum & Bailey Circus deserves the major credit for this film. Everything in this lusty triumph of circus showmanship and movie skill betokens the way with the spectacular of the veteran Mr. DeMille. And yet the bright magic that is in it flows from the circus as it was photographed for real. One of them must have done the honors. We honestly can't tell you which.

But this we can tell you for certain: Two American institutions have combined to put out a piece of entertainment that will delight movie audiences for years. Sprawling across a mammoth canvas, crammed with the real-life acts and thrills, as well as the vast backstage minutiae that make the circus the glamorous thing it is, and glittering in marvelous Technicolor—truly marvelous color, we repeat—this huge motion picture of the big top is the dandiest ever put upon the screen. There may be some valid hesitation to tag it the greatest show on earth. But what is currently showing at the Music Hall is great.

Of course, as we say, it is circus—it is glamour and sentiment, romance and razzle-dazzle, excitement and daredeviltry. And the story that is told in its passage is shaped to these elements, having been written on order for the smart showman, Mr. DeMille. It isn't penetrating. It certainly is not profound. It is simply a romance of the circus, which makes no dramatic claims.

Briefly, it is the story of the circus's "big boss," who has sawdust for blood and puts the circus and its welfare above all else; his girlfriend, a glamorous "flyer"; a handsome, daredevil aerialist; a clown who is wanted for murder; an elephant trainer; his heartless girl; and several more. And in the unraveling of it, the handsome aerialist takes a terrible fall, the girl spurns her jealous mahout and the circus train is wrecked. In the familiar tradition, however, the show must go on. And out of some real DeMillian wreckage, it rises to play the next day.

But it isn't so much the story that carries the thing along—though don't let us give the impression that we underestimate its place. And don't let us lead you to imagine that it is poorly or thoughtlessly played. Believe us, it takes real smart playing and direction to put such stuff across. And that is what all the actors give it—Charlton Heston as the "big boss," Betty Hutton as the "flyer," Cornel Wilde as the handsome aerialist, James Stewart as the clown, Lyle Bettger as the elephant trainer and Gloria Grahame as his girl, not to mention many others who eagerly get in their oars.

The captivation of this picture is in the brilliance with which it portrays the circus and all its movement, not as a mere performing thing but, as Mr. DeMille says in the narration, as a restless and mobile giant. All of the wonderful excitement of this mammoth caravan pulling out of winter quarters in Florida, with the animals and wagons loaded on the trains, the bells clanging, the people rushing, and that old Coast Line engine whistling "all aboard" has been captured in fine pictorial crispness. And then the imagery of arriving in a town, rolling to the lot, spreading the canvas, raising the tents, and getting ready for the show have the authority and the impact of a top documentary film. Even the intercut glimpses of the circus in performance have power, though many will find them familiar and—like the circus itself—too long.

However, to Mr. DeMille's credit—and to the credit of his cutter, be it said—the montage effects in this picture are dynamically superb. The old master, who has previously fashioned his pictures in realms of make-believe, has here invaded an appropriate reality and has done himself and it proud.

Indeed, on the strength of this picture, we suspect they will henceforth have to refer to the circus as that of Ringling Brothers and Barnum & Bailey–Cecil B. DeMille. They all of them worked together. "Get with it," as the hands say!

—*B.C., January 11, 1952*

GREEN FOR DANGER

Produced and directed by Frank Launder and Sidney Gilliat: written by Mr. Gilliat and Claude Guerney. based on the novel by Christianna Brand: cinematographer. Wilkie Cooper: edited by Thelma Myers: music by William Alwyn: production designer. Peter Proud: released by Eagle-Lion Films. Black and white. Running time: 91 minutes.

With: Sally Gray (Nurse Freddi Linley). Trevor Howard (Dr. Barnes). Rosamund John (Nurse Sanson). Alastair Sim (Inspector Cockrill). Leo Genn (Mr. Eden). Megs Jenkins (Nurse Woods). Judy Campbell (Sister Bates) and Moore Marriott (Postman Higgins).

The British have sent over another humdinger of a baffler in *Green for Danger,* which settled down yesterday at the Winter Garden for what should turn out to be a comfortable stay. Once again the director-producer combination of Sidney Gilliat and Frank Launder have laid deftly humorous hands on the subject of murder. And, while they manage to keep the

spectator chuckling most of the time, they never for a moment lose sight of a mystery film's prime purpose—that is, to intrigue and startle the onlooker.

What more could one ask? In the case of *Green for Danger* one could reasonably request just a bit more justification for the solution, which, truth to tell, is bewildering. The story unfolds in the form of a report by a Scotland Yard inspector to his superior anent a series of murders that happened in the hospital at Heron's Park between buzz bomb attacks.

This Inspector Cockrill is the most engaging detective the screen has had since Nick Charles was young. He's a bumptious creature all right, but not overbearing, for the angular Alastair Sim plays him with just the right touch of sardonic wit and an air of casual authority that is altogether captivating.

The interrogation of an operating room staff by Cockrill after the mysterious death of a patient while being anaesthetized and the subsequent murder in the operating room of the head nurse after she claims to know the patient did not die accidentally is a delightfully gruesome bit of business. Cockrill's bland accusations set the five witnesses to suspecting each other, with consequences that are best left unmentioned here.

Through the tangled skein of the mystery runs a three-cornered romance of better than average interest involving two of the doctors and a pretty nurse. These roles are well performed by Trevor Howard, Leo Genn, and Sally Gray, and Rosamund John brings conviction to the part of a nurse whose nerves are at the breaking point.

Green for Danger will give the aisleside sleuths a better workout than they have had for months and it also will rest easily with those who are content just to sit back and let the story resolve itself, for the melodrama is nicely spiced with dry humor.

—*T.M.P., August 8, 1947*

GREGORY'S GIRL

Written and directed by Bill Forsyth: cinematographer. Michael Coulter: edited by John Gow: music by Colin Tully: art designer. Adrienne Atkinson: produced by Clive Parsons and Davina Belling: released by Samuel Goldwyn Company. Running time: 91 minutes.

With: Gordon John Sinclair (Gregory). Dee Hepburn (Dorothy). Chic Murray (Headmaster). Jake D'Arcy (Phil). Alex Norton (Alec). John Bett (Alistair). Robert Buchanan (Andy) and William Greenlees (Steve).

A lot of movies are easy to resist, including those in which a major character is dying of cancer, two or more characters are beheaded on screen, or when the entire plot depends on someone's not going to the police in the second scene. Extremely rare is the movie that is irresistible. Offhand, I can think of only two kinds, one being any Billy Wilder film costarring Jack Lemmon and Walter Matthau.

The other is any movie containing a small boy who has been warned that he is going to run out of perversions before he is twelve years old, a lost penguin, a football player who makes a winning goal and is hugged and kissed not only by teammates but also by members of the opposing team, plus the following bit of wisdom: "Foreplay is great as long as you know it's leading up to something. Otherwise, it's just fooling around."

Bill Forsyth's *Gregory's Girl*, which opens today at the Lincoln Plaza Theater, contains all these things and more. It is, by definition, irresistible.

This enchanting comedy, made in Scotland and only the second feature to be written and directed by Mr. Forsyth, who is thirty-three years old, is one of the cheeriest unsentimental reports on the human condition since François Truffaut's *Small Change,* which it recalls because it, too, is almost entirely concerned with teenagers and their juniors.

Further, like Mr. Truffaut, Mr. Forsyth accepts nothing at face value. No character, emotion, gesture, or response is too commonplace not to be reexamined and, in the process, miraculously seen anew. In this fashion, what might have been an ordinary comedy about the perils and pressures of growing up is transformed into something as exotic as a visit to another planet, a place that looks and sounds familiar but whose gravitational pull is about one-tenth of Earth's.

Gregory's Girl is set outside Glasgow in the carefully tended but not antiseptic "new town" of Cumbernauld. Gregory (Gordon John Sinclair) is, by American standards, a bit square for a fellow of sixteen, but that's understandable. Cumbernauld is not exactly a place where teens swing.

As the film begins, Gregory is facing a midteen crisis. He is growing very tall very quickly and he finds it difficult to concentrate on, among other things, his position on the football team. It comes as no great surprise to him when a pretty, athletic girl named Dorothy (Dee Hepburn) tries out for the team and takes his spot, so that Gregory is demoted to goalie. Gregory couldn't care less. He has never been much committed to football and, for the first time in his life, he has fallen in love. With Dorothy. Her triumphs on the field balance his dismal failures. That's the sort of fellow Gregory is.

To find out whether Dorothy ever becomes Gregory's girl, you will have to see the film, and when you do you will also meet some of the most eccentric and engaging characters to inhabit any movie in a long time.

Among these is Gregory's ten-year-old sister Madeline (Allison Forster), Gregory's Rock of Gibraltar, a fount of common sense, still more interested in food than boys but beloved by one contemporary and admired from afar by a somewhat more mature boy who exclaims, "Ten years old . . . with the body of a woman of thirteen!"

There are also Gregory's best friend, Steve (William Greenlees), a student who bakes pastries for the school with the passion that Dorothy devotes to football; Andy (Robert Buchanan), Gregory's second-best friend, a fellow who is so hopeless with girls that he attempts to pick them up by asking, "Did you know that when you sneeze, it comes out your nose 180 miles an hour?"; and the school's headmaster (Chic Murray), an odd sort of pedagogue who appreciates the airiness of good pie crust and likes to play the harmonium.

In addition there are Phil Menzies (Jake D'Arcy), the harried football coach who learns to adjust to Dorothy's extremely physical presence; Susan (Clare Grogan), a pretty girl who begins as a runner-up in the Gregory Sweepstakes; Gregory's dad (David Anderson), a driving instructor whom we see only once, when one of his pupils almost runs over Gregory; and the aforementioned person in the penguin suit who, throughout the film, wanders the school's hallways forever in search of something unstated.

Though Mr. Forsyth's dialogue frequently echoes the kind of mad reasonableness we associate with Jules Feiffer, and though Gregory and his sister, Madeline, are distant kin to Holden and Phoebe

Caulfield, *Gregory's Girl* is a movie with an original, distinct personality. It floats effortlessly over its landscape, seeing all from a marvelously cockeyed perspective all its own.

—*V.C., May 26, 1982*

THE GRIFTERS

Directed by Stephen Frears: written by Donald Westlake: director of photography. Oliver Stapleton: edited by Mike Audsley: music by Elmer Bernstein: production designer. Dennis Casner: produced by Martin Scorsese. Robert Harris and James Painten: released by Miramax Films. Running time: 119 minutes.

With: Anjelica Huston (Lily Dillon), John Cusack (Roy Dillon), Annette Bening (Myra Langtry), Pat Hingle (Bobo Justus), Henry Jones (Simms), Michael Laskin (Irv), Eddie Jones (Mints), J. T. Walsh (Cole) and Charles Napier (Hebbing).

Lily, Roy and Myra.

Operating alone, each is a comparatively harmless swindler. When they are put together in Stephen Frears's new film titled *The Grifters*, they become a viciously entertaining parody of a trinity: mother, son, and unrepentant Mary Magdalene. The ghosts that hover over them are unholy jokesters.

Lily Dillon (Anjelica Huston) gives the impression of being as hard as nails. It's the platinum blond hair, which doesn't match the rest of her. The platinum hair is a disguise that has become permanent.

In fact, Lily's features are as finely drawn as those of a Modigliani model, and as impassive.

Lily works hard for a big-time bookie. It's not the sort of job that provides health-care benefits, but the money is serious and it's always in cash.

Lily lives the life of a loner, driving around the country in a brown-and-gold Cadillac. She goes from racetrack to racetrack, putting down large bets at the last minute to change the odds to favor her employer.

Roy Dillon (John Cusack) is a small-time con artist who, with his oval baby face and squinty eyes, looks like a variation on the same Modigliani model that suggested Lily. He should. He is Lily's son, born when she was fourteen years old and passed off as her brother as he was growing up.

Roy sticks to Los Angeles, where he spends his days scamming a few bucks here and there as the mood hits him. His favorite con is to trick bartenders into giving him change for a twenty-dollar bill when he hands them a ten.

Roy's manner is smooth and self-assured. The desk clerk at his residential hotel says of him fondly, "He could be a congressman." Yet there is something bent about Roy. His ambitions are small.

Myra (Annette Bening) is another sort entirely. She has been in the big time and wants to work her way back. She is an all-American beauty with the kind of radiant smile that, placed on billboards, convinces the consuming public that the pause that refreshes will not also rot the teeth.

Myra looks like an angel, and uses her body as if it were a Visa card: to pay the rent, to obtain credit from a jeweler, and even with Roy, whom she sleeps with to convince him that they could be a winning team.

In his American film debut, Mr. Frears, the English director (*My Beautiful Laundrette* and *Dangerous Liaisons,* among others), has made a smashing variation on the sort of movie that people mean when they ask why Hollywood doesn't make movies the way they used to.

The Grifters, adapted and effortlessly updated by Donald Westlake from Jim Thompson's 1963 novel, is taut, tough, and funny, and, at the end, sorrowful to a degree that takes the breath away.

Lily and Roy haven't seen each other in eight years when Lily arrives in Los Angeles to carry out a series of business commissions. More or less for the sake of old times, almost as if they had once been a team, Lily looks up Roy to see how the world is treating him. She arrives none too soon.

Having been badly punched by a bartender the day before, Roy is in terrible shape. He is doubled over, bleeding internally. Lily gets him to the hospital where the doctors manage to straighten things out, just in time, and where Lily meets Myra. Lily doesn't like Myra on sight. It takes Myra a little longer to size up Lily.

Lily hangs around the hospital during Roy's convalescence. Having given him life twice, as she puts it, she doesn't want him throwing himself away on a cheap piece of merchandise like Myra. She also recognizes that a timid grifter, which Roy is, is a failed grifter.

In her uncharacteristic anxiety about Roy, Lily messes up a big racetrack score, which suggests to her boss, Bobo (Pat Hingle), that she may be stealing from him.

Lily, who is so officious and commanding with Roy, becomes another person with Bobo. She doesn't talk back. She agrees with everything Bobo says to the point of seeming abject. Bobo kids her along. Is she skimming money off the top? She shrugs girlishly. "Maybe" she says, "a little."

But, says Bobo in effect, that is a sort of safety valve, isn't it? She agrees shyly. Bobo asks why. Says Lily, as if being coached by her first-grade teacher, "If he ain't stealing a little, he's stealing a lot."

Bobo seems pleased by Lily's performance, and then humiliates her in a way that will leave a large, very evident scar for the rest of her life. Lily doesn't even complain about that. In the trunk of her car she has a secret compartment full of reasons not to.

Among other things, the movie gives new currency to the expressive, redolently seedy word "grifter," which is apparently an amalgam of "graft" and "drift." According to some etymologists, the word was coined to describe two-bit swindlers and gamblers who once followed carnivals and circuses through the American heartland.

Lily, Roy, and Myra are new-day grifters but, like their prototypes, they are nearsighted. All of their plans are short-term. There is never any thought of consequences. In the case of this trio, the consequences are fatal.

Working from Mr. Westlake's first-rate screenplay, Mr. Frears has made a gritty, hard-boiled melodrama that is also an examination of the genre. It's as much about the muddled private lives of these grifters as it is about their professional expertise.

Though Lily, Roy, and Myra function on the fringes of society, their methods and ambitions are really not so different from those of the straight world. Each is tireless in the pursuit of ease.

Myra is also too crafty for her own good.

Miss Bening, who was miscast as the scheming Madame de Merteuil in Milos Forman's *Valmont,* is absolutely right as a bright-eyed, giggly, amoral young woman who has possibly never had a generous or spontaneous thought in her life.

Miss Bening has something of the angelic looks of Michele Pfeiffer and the comic style and low-down sexiness of Kathleen Turner. It is a terrific combination.

One of the film's highlights is a hilarious flashback in which Myra recalls her success as one half of a team that conned greedy, oil-rich Texans out of small fortunes.

Mr. Cusack is equally good as the reserved, deeply troubled Ron, a fellow who knows his limitations and is prepared to stick by them until he is compromised by both Myra and Lily. It's not an easy role, but Mr. Cusack gives it both strength and, more difficult in the circumstances, pathos.

Miss Huston is again spectacular. Not since *The Dead* has she had a role of such eerie complexity, nor given a performance that was so haunting. Though Lily is a sly, unpleasant woman, out always for the main chance, Miss Huston discovers the sadness within that comes close to true tragedy.

In addition to Mr. Hingle, the super supporting cast includes J. T. Walsh as Myra's partner in her Texas days; Henry Jones as the folksy desk clerk at Roy's hotel; Eddie Jones as Roy's grifting mentor; and Charles Napier as a swindled Texas millionaire.

There are a couple of points in the film at which plausibility is stretched, but forget them. They do no damage.

From the opening sequences, which establish Lily, Roy, and Myra, sometimes in a screen split three ways, *The Grifters* moves with swift unsentimental resolve toward a last act as bleak as any in recent American screen literature.

In a less skillful work, it would be a downer. *The Grifters* is so good that one leaves the theater on a spellbound high.

—*V.C., December 5, 1990*

GROUNDHOG DAY

Directed by Harold Ramis: written by Danny Rubin and Mr. Ramis. based on a story by Mr. Rubin: director of photography. John Bailey: edited by Pembroke J. Herring: music by George Fenton: production designer. David Nichols: produced by

Trevor Albert and Mr. Ramis: released by Columbia Pictures. Running time: 103 minutes.

With: Bill Murray (Phil), Andie MacDowell (Rita), Chris Elliott (Larry), Stephen Tobolowsky (Ned), Brian Doyle (Buster), Marita Geraghty (Nancy) and Angela Paton (Mr. Lancaster).

In *Groundhog Day,* playing a formerly smug weatherman who finds himself condemned to relive one Feb. 2 over and over again in Punxsutawney, Pa., Bill Murray explains his feelings to two bleary-eyed, beer-drinking locals. "What would you do if you were stuck in one place and everything was exactly the same and nothing that you did mattered?" he asks despairingly. The two strangers listen very sympathetically. They didn't have to be trapped by a magic spell to know what he means.

That glimmer of recognition is what makes *Groundhog Day* a particularly witty and resonant comedy, even when its jokes are more apt to prompt gentle giggles than rolling in the aisles. The story's premise, conceived as a sitcom-style visit to the Twilight Zone, starts out lightweight but becomes strangely affecting. Phil Connors, Mr. Murray's amusingly rude Pittsburgh television personality, surely deserves to be punished for his arrogance. But who in the audience hasn't ever wished time would stand still and offer a second, third, or even a 20th chance?

The jaded Phil, a perfect character for Mr. Murray, begins the story sounding terminally smooth. He refers to himself as "talent," and addresses a fellow newscaster as "Hairdo." He sneers at Punxsutawney and is contemptuous of his own charming producer (Andie MacDowell) and darkly funny cameraman (Chris Elliott). He even delivers pleasant-sounding insults to the proprietors of the bed-and-breakfast where he is staying, not realizing he may be staying there forever.

As directed breezily by Harold Ramis (who wrote the screenplay with Danny Rubin), *Groundhog Day* employs the sort of time-bending trickery that worked so well for *Back to the Future.* Thus, Phil finds himself revisiting the recent past and coming face to face with people not fully aware of his special powers. On the first Feb. 2, he is cheerfully odious to everyone he meets, including an insurance salesman named Ned (Stephen Tobolowsky, hilarious as the quintessential pest). But as time goes by—or doesn't—Phil begins to try out different gambits, testing the limits of his plight. He learns that he can do nothing bad enough to keep himself from waking up under the same flowered quilt, listening to Sonny and Cher sing "I Got You, Babe" on the clock radio at 6 A.M. Not even smashing the radio to bits will make them shut up.

Wildly frustrated at first, Phil gradually begins to treat his plight as a learning experience. He can, for instance, take enough piano lessons to impress Ms. MacDowell's enchanting Rita, once he realizes how wrong he was to treat her badly. One of the film's many repetitive sequences shows Phil on a date with Rita, learning so much about her that he can begin sounding like a mind reader and passing himself off as the perfect mate. "You couldn't *plan* a day like this!" Rita finally sighs happily. "Well, you can," says Phil. "It just takes an awful lot of work."

The film makes the most of the sentimental possibilities in Phil's rehabilitation. (Viewers who notice Phil ignoring a panhandler on his first Groundhog Day will surely know where that setup is headed.) But it also has fun with the nihilism. Phil eagerly explores every self-destructive possibility now open to him, from jumping off buildings to smoking cigarettes to overeating and refusing to floss; at one point he even casually robs an armored truck, just to see if he can. "Well, what if there *is* no tomorrow?" he anxiously asks someone. "There wasn't one today!"

Mr. Murray is back in top form with a clever, varied role that draws upon the full range of his talents. As in *Scrooged,* he makes a transition from supreme cynic to nice guy, and this time he does so with particularly good grace. Half Capra and half Kafka, the story of *Groundhog Day* presents golden opportunities, particularly in the gently romantic scenes with Ms. MacDowell. Mr. Murray is as believable and appealing at these moments as he is flinging insults. Ms. MacDowell, a warm comic presence and a thorough delight, plays a modern working woman while also reminding viewers that this is at heart a fairy tale. As Phil tries one desperate tactic after another, fairy tale fans will be way ahead of him, knowing what it takes to break a spell.

—*J.M., February 12, 1993*

THE GUNFIGHTER

Directed by Henry King: written by William Bowers. William Sellers. Nunnally Johnson (uncredited) and André De Toth (uncredited). based on a story by Mr. Bowers: cinematographer. Arthur Miller. edited by Barbara McLean: music by Alfred Newman: art designers. Lyle Wheeler and Richard Irvine: produced by Mr. Johnson: released by Twentieth Century Fox. Black and white. Running time: 84 minutes.

With: Gregory Peck (Jimmy Ringo). Helen Westcott (Peggy Walsh). Millard Mitchell (Sheriff Mark Strett). Jean Parker (Molly). Karl Malden (Mac). Skip Homeier (Hunt Bromley). Anthony Ross (Charley) and Verna Felton (Mrs. Pennyfeather).

The addicts of Western fiction may find themselves rubbing their eyes and sitting up fast to take notice before five minutes have gone by in Twentieth Century Fox's *The Gunfighter,* which came to the Roxy yesterday. For suddenly they will discover that they are not keeping company with the usual sort of hero of the commonplace Western at all. Suddenly, indeed, they will discover that they are in the exciting presence of one of the most fascinating Western heroes as ever looked down a six-shooter's barrel.

Sure, the dark, dusty horseman of this fiction, played shrewdly by Gregory Peck, is personally remote and laconic, just as most Western buckos are, and he's a dangerous man with a pistol—the acknowledged "top gun of the West." Furthermore, he has no hesitation to put a lead slug through the heart of a reckless upstart who tries to jump him in the very first scene of the film. But the uncommon thing about him is that he hates to shoot. He is trying, in fact, to shun trouble in the most determined way. Only, the young, foolish "squirts" in every barroom won't let him pursue his peaceful way. They want to outdraw the famous "bad man." That's the gamut he has to run.

And it is along this line of presentation that Nunnally Johnson has contrived, as a consequence, one of the tautest and most stimulating Westerns of the year. For a fine script by William Bowers and William Sellers brings this gent to a rare rendezvous with destiny in a Western frontier town, with vengeful pursuers behind him and a faint, hopeful future before. And good writing, good direction and good acting in this chronological span of a couple of hours provides some of the slickest, sharpest drama that you will get in this type of film.

We're not going to tell you what happens, but we will say that in this town is the wife of the noted gunfighter whom he hasn't seen for years—and who now isn't sure she wants to see him, on account of their unsuspecting son. There is also a firm-handed sheriff who used to ride with the gunfighter in the old days but who won't let this sentimental friendship obstruct him in upholding peace. There is a gun-happy youngster here also; a man with a fanatical passion for revenge; a little boy—and those three angry brothers of the kid shot back there in that saloon.

Shuffling these people together, along with a lot of incidents of humorous, dramatic, sentimental and even poignant quality, director Henry King and Mr. Johnson have fetched an intriguing film that actually says a little something about the strangeness of the vainglory of man. And through Mr. Peck's fine performance, a fair comprehension is conveyed of the loneliness and the isolation of a man with a lurid name.

Contributing to the distinction and high entertainment of this film are Millard Mitchell as the sheriff—a wonderfully crisp and tangy role; Skip Homeier as the youngster in quest of the gunfighter's scalp; Karl Malden as a bartender; and at least a half-dozen more. To name them, indeed, would be to run down the length of a very large cast.

To be sure, one might offer the opinion, in a solemn analysis of the full credibility of this picture, that the gunfighter might have stayed clear of trouble and consequent danger if he had merely kept out of bars. But that is a sober assumption, if it's true what they say of the frontier. And, besides, such restraint would have denied us an arresting and quite exciting film.

—B.C., June 24, 1950

GUNGA DIN

Produced and directed by George Stevens: written by Joel Sayre and Fred Guiol. based on a story by Ben Hecht and Charles MacArthur. inspired by the poem by Rudyard Kipling: cinematographer.

Joseph August: edited by Henry Berman and John Lockert: music by Alfred Newman: art designers. Van Nest Polglase and Perry Ferguson: released by RKO Radio Productions. Black and white. Running time: 117 minutes.

With: Cary Grant (Cutter). Victor McLaglen (MacChesney). Douglas Fairbanks Jr. (Ballantine). Sam Jaffe (Gunga Din). Eduardo Ciannelli (Sufi Khan). Joan Fontaine (Emmy). Montagu Love (Colonel Weeks). Robert Coote (Higginbotham). Abner Biberman (Cheta) and Lumsden Hare (Major Mitchell).

With a poet in the credit lines, it is hardly surprising that *Gunga Din* (at the Music Hall) should turn about to be as jaunty as a Barrack Room Ballad, as splendid as a Durbar, as exciting and at times as preposterous as a Pearl White serial. Thanks to the collaboration of the late Mr. Kipling, who wrote for the cinema without knowing it, it moves with all the discipline, dash, and color of a vanished time, when Mr. Disraeli was Prime Minister and the empire had a good conscience. Although its mid portions tend to sag a bit under the weight of Victorian destiny, it blossoms at both ends into sequences of magnificently explosive action.

All movies, as a matter of fact, should be like the first twenty-five and the last thirty minutes of *Gunga Din,* which are the sheer poetry of cinematic motion. Not that the production as a whole leaves anything to be desired in lavishness and panoramic sweep. The charge of the Sepoy Lancers, for example, in the concluding battle sequence, is the most spectacular bit of cinema since the Warner Brothers and Tennyson stormed the heights of Balaklava. In fact the movies at their best really appear to have more in common with the poets than with plain, straightforward, rationally documented prose.

Though the picture draws heavily on the Ballads for atmosphere and inspiration, and doesn't scruple to use Kipling himself, the brilliantly talented young war correspondent, as a minor character (it seems he dashed off the famous poem in time for the commandant to read it over the water carrier's grave), the only historical or literary authority for it seems to have been an original story by Ben Hecht and Charles MacArthur. In this case, "original" may be

taken to signify that the story is quite unlike other predecessors in the same genre, except possibly *The Lives of a Bengal Lancer, Beau Geste, The Lost Patrol,* and *Charge of the Light Brigade.* The parallels—some of them doubtless unavoidable—may be charitably excused on the ground that two memories are better than one.

As for Gunga Din himself, it seems rather a pity that he should receive fourth billing in his own picture. Yet for all the dash cut by the three stars, Cary Grant, Victor McLaglen and Douglas Fairbanks Jr., it is the humble, ascetic, stooped, yet somehow sublime, figure of Sam Jaffe that one remembers. "An' for all 'is dirty 'ide, 'e was white, clear white, inside, when 'e went to tend the wounded under fire," said the poet, and the sentiment, Victorian and patronizing as it may be, echoes in the heart. There is infinite humility, age-old patience, and pity, in the way old Din kneels to offer water to the living and the dying. And, though bent under the weight of his perspiring water-skin, his agility in dodging bullets is marvelous to behold. As Sam Jaffe plays him, Gunga Din is not only a better man than any in the cast; he should be a serious contender for the best performance of the year.

Even at those points where the script seems to lose its sense of direction, George Stevens always admirably retains his own. At its best, it is an orchestration, taut with suspense and enriched in the fighting scenes with beautifully timed, almost epigrammatic bits of "business" and a swinging gusto that makes of every roundhouse blow a thing of beauty. Mr. Fairbanks leaps from roof to roof like his esteemed sire; Mr. McLaglen in his uniform struts intemperately; Cary Grant clowns even beneath the lash of the cult of Thugs, even with a bayonet wound in his vitals. As Guru, high priest of the killer cult, whose attempted ambush of the British troops is foiled by the heroic and suicidal bugling of good old Din, Eduardo Ciannelli has stepped straight from an old-fashioned serial.

And the hills, meanwhile, swarm with costume extras, resound with the boom of obsolete artillery, dance together in a rich confusion of tartans, turbans and the monotonous, martial tunes of the bagpipes. Victoria Imperatrix! Involuntarily, we feel the tears start.

Although *Gunga Din* is not an adult picture, when it gets going you might as well try to question the ideology of a parade of Seaforth Highlanders. Our own impulse was to run along happily beside it, dodging between the solemn grown-up legs that line the way, occasionally skipping rope. Another thing we like about it is the way it shoves romance (Joan Fontaine) resolutely aside when the bugles blow and the stallions begin to whinny. Who cares about all the mush stuff when there's a good battle in prospect somewhere over beyond Cuckoo Cloudland in the Kyber Pass?

—*B.R.C., January 27, 1939*

HAIL THE CONQUERING HERO

Produced, written and directed by Preston Sturges; cinematographer, John Seitz; edited by Stuart Gilmore; music by Werner R. Heymann; art designer, Hans Dreier; released by Paramount Pictures. Black and white. Running time: 101 minutes.

With: Eddie Bracken (Woodrow Truesmith), Ella Raines (Libby), Bill Edwards (Forrest Noble), Raymond Walburn (Mayor Noble), William Demarest (Sergeant), Jimmy Dundee (Corporal), Georgia Caine (Mrs Truesmith) and Franklin Pangborn (Chairman of Committee).

Don't ever let anyone tell you that Preston Sturges is just a maker of madcap films, of gloriously impudent satires that are basically frivolous withal. Mr. Sturges is just about the sharpest and most rational Hollywood Magus on the job—a fellow with a searching way of looking at the follies of us rather silly folks. And now that his *Hail the Conquering Hero* has come to the Paramount, you can see this beyond any question that might persist from his former excellent films. For this riotously funny motion picture, this superlative small-town comedy, is also one of the wisest ever to burst from a big-time studio.

Where Mr. Sturges was spoofing the sacred realm of maternity in his recent comic broadside, *The Miracle of Morgan's Creek,* and where he has cracked at other idols in his previous antic films, he is mauling the fetish of the Hero in his latest screen masterpiece. He is kidding the old American penchant for reverencing martial renown, and he is showing the ironic danger of snatching at demagogues. On the side, he is laughing his head off at what someone has called our "cult of Mom" and is making some rather saucy sport with the good old "Mother" refrain.

But in a nice way! No ponderous sermonizing is reckoned in Mr. Sturges's style. When he slashes at human foibles, he does so with benevolence in his heart. And when he is most keenly cutting the mush from our fondest shibboleths, he spirals his blade with a flourish that is equally designed to get a laugh.

There is nothing mean or deceitful about the hero in this present gay satire. He is just a small-town youngster with a loving regard for his mom and respect for the memory of his father who died a brave marine in the last war. And so it is readily forgivable that he should write to the folks back home that he fought with the marines in the Solomons, although he was really discharged from the corps for hay fever. It is only when a sextet of actual heroes from Guadalcanal hear his appealing story in a San Francisco bar that they decide, in a soapy wave of sentiment, to return him as a conqueror to his mom.

And thus it is that Woodrow—Woodrow Lafayette Pershing Truesmith, that's his name—alights from the train in his hometown with medals and ribbons all over his uniformed chest and with his six insistent sponsors shoving him on as an honor guard. Only Woodrow, and even less his sponsors, are not prepared for the welcome he receives—and certainly not for the dilemma that is riotously precipitated thereby. For not only do the home folk welcome Woodrow in a hero-worshiping mob but they pay off the mortgage on his mom's house and want to make him the reform mayor

of the town. The manner in which the frantic youngster gets out of this dish of dangerous soup, squares
himself with his girl and proves his honesty is the
charming and trenchant traffic of the film.

It is vain to attempt an indication of the sharpness
of verbal wit and the vigor of visual expression that
Mr. Sturges, as writer and director, has produced. The
picturesque bedlam of images with which he conveys a
welcoming crowd cannot be put down in words, for
instance, nor can his sardonic slant on a political mob.
And the electric flow of his dialogue has to be heard to
be enjoyed. Suffice it to say that his method is motion-
picture making in the truest sense.

As the trumped-up young hero, Eddie Bracken,
remembered from *The Miracle of Morgan's Creek,* gives
a squarely hilarious imitation of a thunderstruck
human football, and his more solemn shows of sincerity are affecting to a tearful degree. William Demarest,
who is Mr. Sturges's image, makes a grandly cynical
sergeant of marines, and Jimmy Dundee is incomparably amusing as a tough corporal with a hallowed awe
for moms. Raymond Walburn makes a devastating figure of a fatuous political windbag, and Franklin Pangborn gives a classic representation of a harassed master
of ceremonies. Ella Raines, Arthur Hoyt and many
others are perfect in a finely ordered cast.

A good many motion pictures have had bold and
penetrating things to say. But Mr. Sturges smiles—
nay, laughs—when he says his. Hail the conquering
hero, indeed!

—*B.C., August 10, 1944*

HAIR

Directed by Milos Forman; written by Michael
Weller, based on the musical play by Gerome
Ragni, James Rado and Galt McDermot; director of
photography, Miroslav Ondricek; edited by Alan
Hein, Lynzee Klingman and Stanley Warnow;
music by Mr. McDermot with lyrics by Mr. Ragni
and Mr. Rado; choreography by Twyla Tharp; pro-
duction designer, Stuart Wurtzel; produced by
Lester Persky and Michael Butler; released by
United Artists. Running time: 118 minutes.

With: John Savage (Claude), Treat Williams
(Berger), Beverly D'Angelo (Sheila), Annie Golden
(Jeannie), Dorsey Wright (Hud), Don Dacus
(Woof), Cheryl Barnes (Hud's Fiancée), Richard
Bright (Fenton), Nicholas Ray (General), Charlotte
Rae (Party Guest) and Miles Chapin (Steve).

One might think that because *Hair* was so much
the contemporary artifact when it opened on
Broadway ten years ago, its time as a movie would
have come and gone. Lifetimes of lifestyles have been
junked in the interim. We all know people who for
years wore their hair in the modified Medusa-bob of
Gerome Ragni but who now look as neat as Otto Preminger, or who experimented with grass and then quietly returned to the known pleasures of booze, or who
once marched on the Pentagon with the enthusiasm
they now display in Central Park, jogging around the
Reservoir. *Hair* should be old hat, but the good news
this morning is that it's not.

Milos Forman's screen version, which opens today
at the Ziegfeld Theater, is a rollicking musical memoir, as much a recollection of the show as of the
period, a film that has the charm of a fable and the
slickness of Broadway show biz at its breathless best.

This *Hair* is not to us what the original Joseph Papp
and the Broadway productions were to their audiences. There's no pretense that it has anything to do
with today except to antecede it. It no longer feels the
need to shock us with the once highly publicized curtain scene in which the cast stripped down to the buff
to confront the audience in lights so dim we could
have been watching Julia Child on a bum picture tube.

The Galt McDermot score, with lyrics by Mr.
Ragni and James Rado (who wrote the book for the
stage show and starred in it), is as sweet as an album of
golden oldies but far livelier and wittier than most.
You may think you can't listen to "Aquarius" even
once more without doing yourself damage, but give it
a chance. It frames the film with good feelings that
include a dozen other numbers that still have the
power to surprise and amuse us.

Most important, Mr. Forman and Michael Weller,
who wrote the script, have found an easy, loose, very
winning screen equivalent to the show's illusive narrative about a naif named Claude who, en route to Vietnam, shares a few halcyon days with a group of
hippies in Central Park. Mr. Weller's inventions make
this *Hair* seem much funnier than I remember the
show's having been. They also provide time and space

for the development of characters who, on the stage, had to express themselves almost entirely in song.

The film moves in and out of its principal Central Park location—to Wall Street (for Claude's induction in the Army), to the suburbs (for a classic low-comedy confrontation between the hippies and society's stuffed shirts), and to an Army base in Nevada (where the hippies follow Claude to say good-bye but, instead, effect an unwitting change in the plans of the United States Government).

Mr. Forman, who won an Oscar for his direction of *One Flew Over the Cuckoo's Nest,* has long had an affection for the American counterculture of the sixties. In *Hair* he has been able to express it with an exuberance that was never completely convincing in *Taking Off.* He also manages to keep the fantasy aloft so that we accept the music and the dancing (choreography by Twyla Tharp) without worrying about the realism that so often keeps film musicals earthbound.

The contributions of Miroslav Ondricek, a fellow Czechoslovak who was Mr. Forman's cameraman here, and of the members of the cast are of immense value. John Savage, so good in *The Deer Hunter,* is very funny as the naive Claude, but then the entire cast is superb, especially Treat Williams as Berger, the hippie leader, and Beverly D'Angelo as Sheila, the society girl who joins the tribe.

The film has several things that are not super. The big production number based on the title song—staged in a jail—is total confusion, and there are times when the itchy fingers of the editor prevent us from getting the full effect of what the dancers are doing. Mostly, though, the film is a delight.

—*V.C., March 14, 1979*

HAMLET

Produced and directed by Laurence Olivier; written by Alan Dent, based on the play by William Shakespeare; cinematographer, Desmond Dickinson; edited by Helga Cranston; music by William Walton; production designer, Roger Furse; released by Two Cities Films. Black and white. Running time: 155 minutes.

With: Laurence Olivier (Hamlet), Eileen Herlie (The Queen), Basil Sydney (The King), Jean Simmons (Ophelia), Felix Aylmer (Polonius), Norman Wooland (Horatio) and Terence Morgan (Laertes).

It may come as something of a rude shock to the theater's traditionalists to discover that the tragedies of Shakespeare can be eloquently presented on the screen. So bound have these poetic dramas long been to the culture of our stage that the very thought of their transference may have staggered a few profound diehards. But now the matter is settled; the filmed *Hamlet* of Laurence Olivier gives absolute proof that these classics are magnificently suited to the screen.

Indeed, this fine British-made picture, which opened at the Park Avenue last night under the Theatre Guild's elegant aegis, is probably as vivid and as clear an exposition of the doleful Dane's dilemma as modern-day playgoers have seen. And just as Olivier's ingenious and spectacular *Henry V* set out new visual limits for Shakespeare's historical plays, his *Hamlet* envisions new vistas in the great tragedies of the Bard.

It is not too brash or insensitive to say that these eloquent plays, in their uncounted stage presentations, have been more often heard than seen. The physical nature of the theater, from the time of the Globe until now, has compelled that the audiences of Shakespeare listen more closely than they look. And, indeed, the physical distance of the audience from the stage has denied it the privilege of partaking in some of the most intimate moments of the plays.

But just as Olivier's great *Henry* took the play further away by taking it out into the open—and thereby revealed it visually—his *Hamlet* makes the play more evident by bringing it closer to you. The subtle reactions of the characters, the movements of their faces and forms, which can be so dramatically expressive and which are more or less remote on the stage, are here made emotionally incisive by their normal proximity. Coupled with beautiful acting and inspired interpretations all the way, this visual closeness to the drama offers insights that are brilliant and rare.

Further, a quietly moving camera that wanders intently around the vast and gloomy palace of Elsinore, now on the misty battlements, now in the great council chamber, now in the bedroom of the Queen, always looking and listening, from this and from that vantage point, gives the exciting impression of a silent observer of great events, aware that big things are impending and anxious not to miss any of them.

Actually, a lot of material that is in the conventional *Hamlet* text is missing from the picture—a lot of lines and some minor characters, notably those two fickle windbags, Rosencrantz and Guildenstern. And it is natural that some fond Shakespearians are going to be distressed at the suddenly discovered omission of this or that memorable speech. But some highly judicious editing has not done damage to the fullness of the drama nor to any of its most familiar scenes. In fact, it has greatly speeded the unfolding of the plot and has given much greater clarity to its noted complexities.

Hamlet is nobody's glass-man, and the dark and troubled workings of his mind are difficult, even for Freudians. But the openness with which he is played by Mr. Olivier in this picture makes him reasonably comprehensible. His is no cold and sexless Hamlet. He is a solid and virile young man, plainly tormented by the anguish and the horror of a double shock. However, in this elucidation, it is more his wretched dismay at the treachery of his mother than at the death of his father that sparks his woe. And it is this disillusion in women that shapes his uncertain attitude toward the young and misguided Ophelia, a victim herself of a parent's deceit.

In the vibrant performance of Eileen Herlie as the Queen is this concept evidenced, too, for plainly she shows the strain and heartache of a ruptured attachment to her son. So genuine is her disturbance that the uncommon evidence she gives that she knows the final cup is poisoned before she drinks it makes for heightened poignancy. And the luminous performance of Jean Simmons as the truly fair Ophelia brings honest tears for a shattered romance that is usually a so-what affair.

No more than passing mention can be made at this point of the fine work done by Norman Wooland as Horatio and by Basil Sydney as the King, by Felix Aylmer as Polonius, Terence Morgan as Laertes and all the rest. Perfect articulation is only one thing for which they can be blessed. A word, too, of commendation for the intriguing musical score of William Walton and for the rich designing of Roger Furse must suffice. In the straight black-and-white photography which Mr. Olivier has wisely used—wisely, we say, because the study is largely in somber mood—the palace conceived for this *Hamlet* is a dark and haunted palace. It is the grim and majestic setting for an uncommonly galvanic film.

—B.C., September 30, 1948

HAMLET

Directed by Michael Almereyda: screen adaptation by Mr. Almereyda, based on the Shakespeare play: director of photography, John de Borman: edited by Kristina Boden: music by Carter Burwell: production designer, Gideon Ponte: produced by Andrew Fierberg and Amy Hobby: released by Miramax Films. Running time: 112 minutes.

With: Ethan Hawke (Hamlet), Kyle MacLachlan (Claudius), Diane Venora (Gertrude), Liev Schreiber (Laertes), Julia Stiles (Ophelia), Bill Murray (Polonius), Karl Geary (Horatio), Steve Zahn (Rosencrantz), Dechen Thurman (Guildenstern), Sam Shepard (Ghost), Jeffrey Wright (Gravedigger) and Robin MacNeil (Player King).

It is curious; one never thinks of attaching *Hamlet* to any special locale," the critic Kenneth Tynan once wrote of Shakespeare's tragedy, and the director Michael Almereyda has brilliantly seized upon that by rooting his voluptuous and rewarding new adaptation of the play in today's Manhattan. The city's contradictions of beauty and squalor give the movie a sense of place—it makes the best use of the Guggenheim Museum you'll ever see in a film—and New York becomes a complex character in this vital and sharply intelligent film.

Mr. Almereyda contours the material to his own needs, even though he was inspired by the 1987 *Hamlet Goes Business,* a deadpan update by the renegade Finnish director Aki Kaurismaki. This *Hamlet* is also set in the corporate world, where Claudius (Kyle MacLachlan) has risen to the top of the Denmark Corporation.

But where Mr. Kaurismaki presented his take as a slapstick tragedy that bordered on sadism, Mr. Almereyda layers his cool-to-the-touch version with a luxuriant paranoia compounded by the constant deployment of video cameras and listening devices.

Often shaded in lush, soothing hues of blue, *Ham-*

let exudes an intoxicating masochism in which half the cast is battling despondency and the other half has the glint of imminent insanity. As insightfully played by Diane Venora, Hamlet's mother, Gertrude, is in danger of breaking down into a fine, distraught powder from the outset. In this version, the melancholy of Hamlet (Ethan Hawke) over the death of his father is almost a state of grace; it gives him a sense of purpose that the other characters lack.

Mr. Almereyda has created a new standard for adaptations of Shakespeare, starting with an understanding of the emotional pull of the material that corresponds with its new period and setting. Hamlet's soliloquies are now interior monologues except for the "To be or not to be" speech, which he delivers in a Blockbuster video store, using the blue in the company logo and the word "Action" emblazoned on the shelves to fit in with the mood and color of the rest of the picture.

The director's rigorous trimming has a boldness and vivacity that makes this version exhilarating while leaving Shakespeare's language and intent intact. The use of colors—its palette is red, green and the aforementioned blue—is a visual manifestation of the streamlining. This movie will send shivers of happiness through audiences because it's one of the few American productions of *Hamlet* constructed around the rhythms of the actors, giving each scene a different pulse.

Mr. Almereyda plays to his performers' strengths, and it's awe inspiring. The truly revelatory performance comes from the ravaged dignity that Bill Murray lends Polonius, a weary, middle aged man whose every utterance sounds like a homily he should believe in and perhaps did many years ago. Mr. Murray takes the bemused hollowness he first discovered in sketch comedy and gives it a worn, saddened undercurrent; it's what those bullying cynics he plays in comedies would be like in real life after about 20 years. The speech Polonius gives to his son, Laertes (Liev Schreiber), has a truth that "Death of a Salesman" can only aspire to and certifies Mr. Murray—who's been giving fully shaped performances in bad or little-seen movies for years—as one of the finest actors currently working. "Madam, I use no art at all," he says at one point, and it's true; he uses apparent artlessness to achieve art.

It's not just Mr. Murray and Ms. Venora who are worth watching. Mr. MacLachlan's Claudius has a hail-fellow-well-met shallowness, a blandness tinged with creeping ambition. Mr. Schreiber is all lovely Old World elegance; he uses his resonant, trained voice to find the injured quality of lines like "You wound me, sir," and offers a classical turn in the midst of the modernity. Steve Zahn plays Rosencrantz as slacker-weasel with a blurry twang that is just what's called for here. And Karl Geary is a steadfast, affecting Horatio.

Conceptually, *Hamlet* has all the goods and then some. Oddly enough, the title character is a little lacking in complication. Mr. Hawke's laudable commitment to the project was obviously responsible for getting it made, and his feline transparency would appear to be right for a Hamlet wrestling with the urge to kill Claudius and avenge his father's death.

But this Hamlet, wearing knit caps that make him look like a lost member of the Spin Doctors, is mired in an arrested adolescence that infantilizes him. For this conception to be fully realized, Hamlet's interior monologues shouldn't so fully mirror what's going on with him outwardly; a contrast would have provided some tension. Mr. Hawke's moping slows things down too much, and a clip from a James Dean movie playing behind him emphasizes the self-pitying aspect.

Julia Stiles plays Ophelia, and this may be the first time in her brief film career that this wildly talented young actress has seemed immature. *Hamlet* exploits her youth effectively: Polonius laces up her sneakers as he addresses her. But Ms. Stiles seems too much a child and often can't get her footing as the production sprints past her. Her natural on-screen empathy does allow for several moments that get under the skin: Ophelia plunges into an azure pool, imagining her death; she's often photographed at some of the most beautiful fountains and water spouts in New York. And when distraught, she dissolves into sobs, flinging Polaroids as if they were flower petals; it's heart-rending. The scenes she has with Mr. Hawke with a conventional and definable give-and-take also serve her well.

Little of Mr. Almereyda's previous films (*Another Girl, Another Planet, Nadja*), which are often dizzy with promise, suggested that he had the technique and imagination he brings to bear here. It's incredibly satisfying to see a director grow in the ways that he has. The *Romeo and Juliet* director Baz Luhrmann fired his camera out of the barrel of a gun, and the overdirected velocity was a moviemaker's equivalent of a collection of nervous tics; Mr. Almereyda's audacity comes in problem solving, one of the true functions of a director.

Whereas Mr. Luhrmann's dazzle is all from the outside, Mr. Almereyda goes to the heart of things and has given Shakespeare a distinctively American perspective. *Hamlet* is a movie about urban isolation and the damage it causes, using corrupted wealth as a surrogate for stained royalty.

To develop the distrust and miscommunication—a contemporary spin on the Shakespearean theme of people being out of touch with their natural environments—bits of dialogue are filtered through other sources, like overheard phone conversations. Mr. Almereyda's use of technology is fascinating and well thought out; Hamlet's dead father (Sam Shepard), for example, is first glimpsed on video screens. Hamlet's "get thee to a nunnery" speech to Ophelia becomes an unrelenting tantrum; it follows her home and continues to attack her when she turns on her answering machine.

You'll also catch snatches of material out of the corner of your eye, like Jeffrey Wright's cameo as the Gravedigger singing "All Along the Watchtower," a piece of pop music that was made for Shakespeare: "There must be some kind of way out of here, said the Joker to the Thief."

So much of the play is pleasurably recast—like a snapshot of Fortinbras on a television screen as the Player King, now a news anchor, wraps things up—that Mr. Almereyda has created a hunger for more. In so many ways, *Hamlet* is a palpable hit, or it should be.

—E.M., May 12, 2000

HANDLE WITH CARE

Directed by Jonathan Demme; written by Paul Brickman; director of photography, Jordan Cronenweth; edited by John F. Link 2d; music by Bill Conti; produced by Shep Fields, Frederick Field and Mr. Brickman; released by Paramount Pictures. Running time: 96 minutes.

With: Paul Le Mat (Solder), Candy Clark (Pam), Bruce M. Gill (Dean), Hobert S. Blossom (Papa Thermodyne), Charles Napier (Chrome Angel) and Ann Wedgeworth (Dallas Angel).

Most of the principals in Jonathan Demme's *Handle with Care* have citizens' band radios, and these people careen into one another's lives just as easily as they interrupt one another's broadcasts. The visual editing of the film is very much like its sound editing, so scenes become short and fragmented, like loosely overheard snatches of conversation. The radio conceit also provides the film with a unifying notion, because each character has a real name and a C.B. "handle," with separate identities for each. One of the characters even spells this out, though the point is hard to miss: "Everybody in this town is somebody they're not supposed to be."

Handle with Care, which was originally released in other cities under the title *Citizen's Band,* is so clever that its seams show. Mr. Demme's tidiest parallels and most purposeful compositions are such attention-getters that the film has a hard time turning serious for its finale, in which characters who couldn't communicate directly come to understand one another at long last.

The film will be shown tonight in Alice Tully Hall at Lincoln Center as part of the New York Film Festival and again tomorrow.

Even though the film's energy and its intelligence are at war with each other all the way through, their incompatibility is eminently engrossing. The structure is thoughtful, and some of the imagery is so calculated it seems chilly; on the other hand, the film's surface is flippant and funny, full of talented performers in whimsical, open-ended roles. It's easy to see why *Handle with Care* was too scrambled to succeed during its first go-round. It's even easier to see that the film deserves a second chance.

The characters include a bigamous trucker (Charles Napier) and his two wives (Marcia Rodd and Ann Wedgworth), who first meet on a bus in one of the funniest sequences here; after comparing family photos and then weeping their eyes out, the wives begin to wonder if they aren't related. Another triangle includes two competitive brothers (Paul Le Mat and Bruce McGill) and their mutual sweetheart (Candy Clark), who is forced, by an otherwise-graceful screenplay, to tell one of them "I'm a woman, not a trophy."

There is also a squealy, roly-poly hooker who operates out of a mobile home, and who laments, "Now with that gol-darned fifty-five-mile limit, nobody's got time for nothin'." There is the brothers' drunken old dad, who is forever threatening to eat the family dog. And there are a wide variety of crackpots on the airwaves, who become Mr. Le Mat's prey after he decides to do his civic duty by eliminating all improperly used C.B.'s with a baseball bat.

The plot may operate on the premise that wackiness is its own reward, but Mr. Demme's direction is decidedly, almost jarringly, on the serious side. When Mr. Le Mat and Miss Clark, whose affair has been on and off the rocks, finally get back together, Mr. Demme manages to make a high school setting look like a chapel, shooting up at the couple and letting a light bulb shower them with beatific rays. The composition has a life of its own, almost more life than it needs, and it has very little bearing on the characters as we've come to know them. But it's a stunning composition just the same.

—*J.M., September 30, 1977*

HANNAH AND HER SISTERS

Written and directed by Woody Allen: director of photography. Carlo Di Palma: edited by Susan E. Morse: production designer. Stuart Wurtzel: produced by Robert Greenhut: released by Orion Pictures. Running time: 106 minutes.

With: Woody Allen (Mickey). Michael Caine (Elliot). Mia Farrow (Hannah). Carrie Fisher (April). Barbara Hershey (Lee). Lloyd Nolan (Hannah's Father). Maureen O'Sullivan (Hannah's Mother). Daniel Stern (Dusty). Max von Sydow (Frederick) and Dianne Wiest (Holly).

From the first soaring notes of Harry James's trumpet playing "You Made Me Love You," which is heard behind the opening credits, until the series of reconciliation scenes that bring the film to a close, Woody Allen's *Hannah and Her Sisters* is virtually non-stop exhilaration—a dramatic comedy not quite like any other, and one that sets new standards for Mr. Allen as well as for all American moviemakers.

It isn't meant to demean Mr. Allen's earlier films, or to imply that he has here reached some sort of end,

to say that *Hannah and Her Sisters* is the movie he's been working toward ever since *Annie Hall, Interiors,* and *Manhattan.* It's both a summation of a career to date, as well as a window on a career to come. It's warmhearted, wise, and fiercely funny, demonstrating a rigorous command of a talent that, in the manner of Jack's prodigious beanstalk, won't stop growing. The film opens today at the Beekman and other theaters.

Like *Interiors, Hannah and Her Sisters* is an intensely felt family drama about three very different but emotionally dependent sisters, as well as about their parents, husbands, lovers, and friends. Like *Annie Hall* and *Manhattan,* it's also an utterly contemporary romantic comedy of almost classic shapeliness. Its Forest of Arden is the island of Manhattan, and, though no one wears an actual disguise, it's full of desperate dissembling, not all of it innocent.

Hannah (Mia Farrow) is the eldest sister and, possibly because of her age, the strongest. She's a successful actress who's given up her career to become a fulltime, Central Park West earth mother—as wife to Elliot and mother to their children and to her twins from her first marriage.

Holly (Dianne Wiest), the brightest, is the troubled, aimless middle sister, a would-be actress, a would-be caterer and a would-be writer. The youngest is Lee (Barbara Hershey), a perennial student who frequently falls in love with her teachers. Lee is so radiantly pretty and seemingly so in command of herself that one learns with shock she's a recovered alcoholic, though, after the fact, this seems to be perfectly credible.

In addition to Elliot (Michael Caine), a financial adviser to rock musicians, the men in their lives include Frederick (Max von Sydow), the much older painter with whom Lee lives (and for whom she is a rebellious Galatea), and Mickey Sachs (Mr. Allen), a successful, hypochondriacal television producer, formerly married to Hannah and sometime suitor of Holly.

Remaining very much a part of the sisters' lives, for better and worse, are their parents (Lloyd Nolan and Maureen O'Sullivan), who somehow never realized their initial promise as an acting couple and who today live in precarious peace with each other and their failed hopes, doing the odd show in Rochester and the occasional television commercial. "They liked the idea of having children," says Lee at one point, "but they were never very interested in raising them."

Hannah and Her Sisters has the narrative scope of a novel. Beginning with a big, festive family celebration—a Thanksgiving dinner at which Elliot finds himself falling in love with the not-unwilling Lee—the film covers several years in the lives of its six principal characters, moving effortlessly from the mind of one into another. Mr. Allen's most surprising achievement is the manner by which he has refracted his own, very pronounced screen personality into the colors of so many fully realized characters that stand at such a far remove from the filmmaker.

His cast serves him well. Miss Farrow's wise, self-assured Hannah is as radical a departure from the waif of *The Purple Rose of Cairo* as that waif is from the brassy doll of *Broadway Danny Rose*. Miss Wiest and Miss Hershey are no less splendid. A key scene, in which the camera circles the three sisters sitting at a table in a French restaurant for lunch, is emotionally packed (within the film) as well as a celebration of the actresses themselves.

It's a measure of the way the film works that Mr. Caine has never before been so seriously comic, nor Mr. Allen so comically serious. We've seen the grandly neurotic, possibly suicidal side of Mr. Allen's Mickey Sachs in other films, but never the genuinely (if still comically) compassionate lover he also becomes here. One of the great scenes in all of the Allen oeuvre must be the one in *Hannah* in which—in a single, unbroken take—Mickey Sachs, against his better judgment, finds himself courting the emotionally unreliable Holly in a Tower Records shop.

Mr. von Sydow's role is comparatively brief but brilliantly done. Frederick is a dour, legitimately witty man. In a marvelous class by themselves are the still beautiful Miss O'Sullivan and the late Mr. Nolan, particularly in a sequence in which the audience—and their characters—get a glimpse at the deeply troubled truth of their marriage. Giving big performances in small, vividly written roles are Sam Waterston, Daniel Stern, Carrie Fisher, Tony Roberts and Joanna Gleason.

As photographed by Carlo Di Palma, *Hannah and Her Sisters* is as stunning to look at as is *Interiors*, though the content is far livelier and far less self-conscious.

With this film, it's apparent that Mr. Allen has become the urban poet of our anxious age—skeptical, guiltily bourgeois, longing for answers to impossible questions, but not yet willing to chuck a universe that can produce the Marx Brothers.

—*V.C., February 7, 1986*

HAPPINESS

Written and directed by Todd Solondz; director of photography, Maryse Alberti; edited by Alan Oxman; music by Robbie Kondor; production designer, Therese Deprez; produced by Ted Hope and Christine Vachon; released by Good Machine. Running time: 135 minutes.

With: Jane Adams (Joy Jordan), Elizabeth Ashley (Diane Freed), Dylan Baker (Bill Maplewood), Lara Flynn Boyle (Helen Jordan), Ben Gazzara (Lenny Jordan), Jared Harris (Vlad), Philip Seymour Hoffman (Allen), Louise Lasser (Mona Jordan), Jon Lovitz (Andy Kornbluth), Camryn Manheim (Kristina), Marla Maples (Ann Chambeau), Rufus Read (Billy Maplewood) and Cynthia Stevenson (Trish Maplewood).

"Don't worry," coos the famous, successful, beautiful sister. "I'm not laughing at you, I'm laughing with you."

A look of dismay. "But I'm not laughing," the other sister replies.

It has taken only two films, *Welcome to the Dollhouse* and now *Happiness,* for Todd Solondz to establish his as one of the most lacerating, funny and distinctive voices in American film. In his hands, passive aggression is a deadly weapon, right there in the arsenal alongside perky suburban decor and easy-listening songs. (*Happiness* deploys both "You Light Up My Life" and "Mandy.") Yet kitschy Americana does not apparently interest him as a target for sardonic potshots. It interests him as a matter of proportion. There are people out there who are more bothered when a child's Tamagotchi dies than when a clean-cut relative turns out to be a serial pederast. Mr. Solondz wants to know how they tick.

In *Happiness,* a much bigger film than his first and another murderous comedy of manners, Mr. Solondz gets even closer to the bone. His natural tendency to make audiences squirm leads him into material that wouldn't be mentioned in many other films; here, it's linked to the eating of ice cream sundaes. But Mr. Solondz doesn't seem to be straining for shock value when he turns the man in the sunny family portrait on the wall into the man who drugs his family's dessert. (His purpose: an assault on the son's young friend.) He fills *Happiness* with enough misery to make its most outrageous joke its title—and with enough true, unexpected tenderness to warrant this view of the world.

Happiness revolves around the lives of three sisters and observes their romantic lives with enough acid precision to make it a *Bob and Carol and Ted and Alice* for totally dysfunctional times. Helen (Lara Flynn Boyle) is the glamour girl, the celebrity writer who complains: "I hate Saturday nights. Everybody wants me. You have no idea." One look at her and you're meant to hate her along with Allen (Philip Seymour Hoffman), her timid neighbor. Allen makes obscene phone calls so furtively that one of the funniest things in the film is watching him try to switch gears and behave normally ("Seen the playoffs last night?") with the guys at the office.

Helen's sister Joy, played with hilarious tremulousness by Jane Adams, is the dartboard in a family that also includes chirpy Trish (Cynthia Stevenson). Trish looks as pert as her name suggests and has a wonderful time pitying Joy's single status. ("Just because you've hit thirty doesn't mean you can't be fresh anymore!") But the film, which also features Louise Lasser and Ben Gazzara as the suitably unhappy parents of this brood and Jon Lovitz and Jared Harris as the funniest of Joy's Mr. Wrongs, veers right out of situation comedy and into what was once the unspeakable when it gets to Trish's husband. He (Dylan Baker, in a brave and chilling performance) is known as Dr. Maplewood by the little boys who look up to him.

In depicting this doctor, who lives a secret life of shame and prurience, and talks so matter-of-factly about male sexuality with his son (Rufus Read) that *Happiness* was dropped by its original distributor (October Films, owned by Universal), Mr. Solondz lives up to his growing reputation for shock value. There can be no more shocking view of the doctor than an understanding one. And in the same way he made viewers share the junior high school humiliations of *Welcome to the Dollhouse*, Mr. Solondz calmly draws his audience into sharing the doctor's ordeal.

Not without humor, of course. When Dr. Maplewood tells his therapist that his latest dream of shooting up a public park ends without suicide, the therapist remarks, "You see this as something positive?" This sequence is shot with an imaginative crane maneuver by Maryse Alberti, who also gives such visual flair to Todd Haynes's *Velvet Goldmine.* It's a shot that pulls away from the doctor's bland exterior until it reaches parts unknown. This funny yet frightening film works the same way.

—*J.M., October 9, 1998*

A HARD DAY'S NIGHT

Directed by Richard Lester; written by Alun Owen; cinematographer, Gilbert Taylor; edited by John Jympson; music by John Lennon and Paul McCartney; art designer, Ray Simm; produced by Walter Shenson; released by United Artists. Black and white. Running time: 83 minutes.

With: John Lennon (John), Paul McCartney (Paul), George Harrison (George), Ringo Starr (Ringo), Wilfrid Brambell (Grandfather) and Norman Rossington (Norm).

This is going to surprise you—it may knock you right out of your chair—but the new film with those incredible chaps, the Beatles, is a whale of a comedy.

I wouldn't believe it either, if I hadn't seen it with my own astonished eyes, which have long since become accustomed to seeing disasters happen when newly fledged pop-singing sensations are hastily rushed to the screen. But this first fiction film of the Beatles, entitled *A Hard Day's Night,* which exploded last night at the Astor, the Trans-Lux East, and other theaters hereabouts, has so much good humor going for it that it is awfully hard to resist.

In the first place, it's a wonderfully lively and altogether good-natured spoof of the juvenile madness called "Beatlemania," the current spreading craze of otherwise healthy young people for the four British lads with the shaggy hair.

The opening shots, behind the credits, are of three of the fellows running ahead of a mob of howling admirers chasing after them as they break away from a theater where they have played a singing engagement

429

and race for a waiting train. And all the way through the picture, there are frenzied episodes of the Beatles' encounters with squealing fans and with reporters who ask silly questions, all in a facile, witty vein.

But more than this, it's a fine conglomeration of madcap clowning in the old Marx Brothers' style, and it is done with such a dazzling use of camera that it tickles the intellect and electrifies the nerves.

This is the major distinction of this commercially surefire film: It is much more sophisticated in theme and technique than its seemingly frivolous matter promises. With practically nothing substantial in the way of a story to tell—nothing more than a loosely strung fable of how the boys take under their wings the wacky old grandfather of one of them while preparing for a London television show—it discovers a nifty little satire in the paradox of the old man being more of a problem, more of "a troublemaker and a mixer," than the boys.

"'e's a nice old man isn't 'e?" notes one of the fellows when they first meet Granddad on a train. And another replies, with courteous unction, which parodies the standard comment about the Beatles themselves, "'e's very clean."

This line, which runs through the picture, may be too subtle for the happily squealing kids who will no doubt be its major audience, but the oldsters may profitably dig. And, of course, everybody will be able to enjoy the rollicking, madcap fun.

There's no use in trying to chart it. It comes in fast-flowing spurts of sight gags and throwaway dialogue that is flipped about recklessly. Alun Owen, who wrote the screenplay, may have dug it all out of his brain, but Richard Lester has directed at such a brisk clip that it seems to come spontaneously.

And just one musical sequence, for instance, when the boys tumble wildly out of doors and race eccentrically about a patterned playground to the tune of their song "Can't Buy Me Love," hits a surrealistic tempo that approaches audio-visual poetry.

Sure, the frequent and brazen "yah-yah-yahing" of the fellows when they break into song may be grating. To ears not tuned to it, it has moronic monotony. But it is always relieved by pictorial compositions that suggest travesties—or, at least, intelligent awareness of the absurdity of the Beatle craze.

Unless you know the fellows, it is hard to identify them, except for Ringo Starr, the big-nosed one, who does a saucy comic sequence on his own. But they're all good—surprisingly natural in the cinema-reality style that Mr. Lester expertly maintains. And Wilfrid Brambell as the old man is dandy, a delightfully comic Irishman. Many others are also funny.

It is good to know there are people in this world, up to and including the major parties, who don't take the Beatles seriously.

—*B.C., August 12, 1964*

HARLAN COUNTY, U.S.A.

Directed by Barbara Kopple; cinematography by Tom Horwitz, Kevin Keating, Flip McCarthy, Phil Parmet, Hart Perry; editing by Nancy Baker, Mirra Bank, Lora Hays, Mary Lampson; music by Hazel Dickens, Merle Travis; produced by Barbara Kopple; released by Cinema 5. Running time: 103 minutes.

Coal miners are a permanent underground in more than the literal sense. They trouble any society they support: Like feet, the more they are weighed down by their owners the more pain they give.

In East Germany and Poland the authorities treat them with a special deference. Even in its harsher times the Franco regime was never able to stop them from striking. Laws against assembly were useless. A hammer would stop a mile below ground; the man in the next chamber would go to see what the matter was; the silence would spread and a line of stubborn, blackened men came to the surface and stayed until the government could figure out some way of getting them back down.

Miners' strength, their assertiveness and solidarity are based largely on their economic power; and where coal-mining becomes marginal to the economy of a region, they lose much of their ability to fight. There is another factor, though. Miners in their tunnels, vulnerable to explosions, cave-ins and destroyed lungs, weigh on a society's conscience as well as its economy. Their grievances command an instinctive respect.

One of the reasons for the defeat of Prime Minister Edward Heath in Britain two years ago was a widespread feeling that in choosing the miners as the target for his austerity fight he had picked just the wrong target.

Harlan County, U.S.A., to be shown tonight and tomorrow at the New York Film Festival in Alice Tully Hall, is a full-length documentary of the year-long strike carried on by the miners at the Brookside works in eastern Kentucky. It has flaws, some of them considerable, but it is a fascinating and moving work. Its strength lies chiefly in its ability to illuminate the peculiar frightfulness and valor of coal-mining, and made it clear just why coal miners can never be rightly treated as a less than a very special case.

Barbara Kopple and her photographers have got right inside the life of the miners and their families in their long struggle against the operators of the Brookside mine and its parent company, the Duke Power Company. It is a brilliantly detailed report from one side of a battle that caused one death, several shootings and a flood of violent bitterness; and that brought back to Harlan County memories of the much-bloodier coal strikes of the early 1930's.

The strike began after the miners voted to join the United Mine Workers of America—which had lost its hold in eastern Kentucky—and the owners refused to sign a standard UMW contract. It was not until more than a year later—after the violence had claimed the life of one striker—that Duke Power, under strong pressure from federal mediators, agreed to sign.

The film shows the picketing, the use of state troopers to keep the road open for nonstrikers, the confrontations, a shooting, the efforts of the strikers and their families to remain organized and united through the long year. It intercuts old footage from the 1931 strike, where five miners were killed. It also details the successful battle of reformers to oust the old national leadership of the UMW; and the support given to the Harlen County strike by the new leadership under Arnold R. Miller.

Some of the thematic interweaving is awkward, but this is more than made up for by the extraordinary intimacy Miss Kopple has achieved with the strikers and with the bitter life of the strike. There is an old miner, lungs torn by coal dust, who makes our chests hurt as he talks. There are frightening scenes of tight-lipped strikebreakers, guns openly displayed rushing through the pickets. There is a terrifying night scene where shots are fired and we see the leader of the strike-breakers brandishing a pistol in the cab of his pickup truck. There is a heartbreaking scene where the mother of the slain miner collapses at his wake. There is much more, equally good.

The film is entirely partisan. Considering that the company's refusal to sign a contract was condemned by the National Labor Relations Board as a pretext not to recognize the union and considering that the film itself is forthrightly an effort to see the struggle through the miners' own eyes, this is no real drawback. Perhaps there is some skimping: it is something of a cinematic trick to film the president of Duke Power in such tight close-up that his face completely fills the screen.

More serious are the sometimes questionable ways in which the film advances its message: that the Harlan strike is only part of a struggle, and that the miners must go on struggling and striking. The instance I am thinking of comes in its suggestion that the reformist leadership of the UMW may have sold out in 1974—after the Harlan County strike was over—by recommending acceptance of a national mine contract that curtails local strikes.

The film does not call this a sellout—it uses no narration at all and conveys its message by its editing—but all reactions of individual miners that it shows before the vote are negative. Yet the membership ratified the contract by 44,000 to 34,000. The film states this, to be sure; yet somehow all the faces we have learned to admire during the long Harlan County struggle seem to push us to feel toward Mr. Miller the same way we felt toward the recalcitrant mine owners.

—*R.E., October 15, 1976*

HARRY AND TONTO

Produced and directed by Paul Mazursky; written by Mr. Mazursky and Josh Greenfeld; cinematographer, Michael Butler; edited by Richard Halsey; music by Bill Conti; production designer, Ted Haworth; released by Twentieth Century Fox. Running time: 115 minutes.

With: Art Carney (Harry), Ellen Burstyn (Shirley), Chief Dan George (Old Indian), Geraldine Fitzgerald (Jessie). Larry Hagman (Eddie) and Arthur Hunnicutt (Wade).

At the Wedding of the Generations in 1972—when Allen Ginsberg and others decided that it was time to end "youth chauvinism" and performed a symbolic marriage between all the young and all the old in Miami Beach—it was pleasing to hear the poet chanting "the generation war is at an end" while people of all ages danced and sang around his stepladder by the sea. There were quite a few conversations that focused on what the old and the very young have in common—in a society that deeply distrusts both.

Some of the same spirit pervades *Harry and Tonto,* which opened yesterday at the Plaza Theater. Harry (Art Carney) is an independent seventy-two-year-old who demands freedom and privacy and welcomes almost any chance to expand his experiences. Evicted from his building on the Upper West Side, he feels a kinship with King Lear: "He gave up his real estate, too." The police finally have to carry him out in a chair. Then, this devout New Yorker recoils from a dreary suburban existence with his son's family, and strikes out on a voyage across the country.

Paul Mazursky, director and coauthor of *Bob & Carol & Ted & Alice,* and author and director of *Blume in Love,* directed *Harry* from the novel he wrote with Josh Greenfeld. The result is an anecdotal chronicle of Harry's encounters with various individuals, including his now semisenile first love—played with batty precision by Geraldine Fitzgerald—and an Indian chief whom he meets in jail. Mr. Carney maintains a gentle dignity and resilience throughout, though he has to address too many of his lines to a cat named Tonto. His scenes with two benign young performers (Melanie Mayron and Joshua Mostel) nicely emphasize his agelessness.

The narrative of this sympathetic movie wobbles on the edge of sentimentality, though there are only a few sticky moments. But—unlike the novel, which moved swiftly—it has been directed at far too slow a pace, which means that the comic possibilities and the social comment have been diminished. The muted style robs the picture of the liberating point it's meant to make: that imaginative energy transcends the generations.

—N.S., August 13, 1974

A HATFUL OF RAIN

Directed by Fred Zinnemann: written by Michael V. Gazzo and Alfred Hayes. based on the play by Mr. Gazzo: cinematographer. Joseph MacDonald: edited by Dorothy Spencer: music by Bernard Hermann: art designers. Lyle Wheeler and Leland Fuller: produced by Buddy Adler: released by Twentieth Century Fox. Black and white. Running time: 109 minutes.

With: Eva Marie Saint (Celia Pope). Don Murray (Johnny Pope). Anthony Franciosa (Polo). Lloyd Nolan (John Pope Sr.). Henry Silva (Mother). Gerald O'Laughlin (Church) and William Hickey (Apples).

The gruesome—indeed, repulsive—subject of narcotics addiction, long taboo in motion pictures until recent revisions were made in the screen's production code, is opened for an honest exploration in Twentieth Century Fox's *A Hatful of Rain,* made from the stage play of Michael Vincente Gazzo. It came to the Victoria yesterday.

The sum of it is a harrowing picture of what it means for a man to be a slave of the dope habit—what it costs in money, in anguish and in hurt to those he loves.

Most effective of its achievements is the emotional intensity it builds up, as it closely and candidly traces the behavior of a young married man, caught in the trap of addiction since he was hospitalized after fighting in Korea. This is developed through full exposure of his shattering contacts with the "pushers" from whom he gets narcotics; his loving brother, who knows of his plight and secretly but vainly tries to help him; his doting father, who doesn't know or understand; and his pregnant wife, who is also ignorant of his addiction and bewildered by his eccentricities.

Significantly, Mr. Gazzo and Alfred Hayes, who helped him write the picture's script, under the supervision of producer Buddy Adler and director Fred Zinnemann, have played down the more spectacular aspects of personal enslavement to narcotics—the fearful spasms that come with the hunger and especially the way the stuff is got into the blood. Obviously, they and Mr. Zinnemann have calculated that these are the things of which sensational melodramas, not straight and thoughtful tragedies, are made.

Also, the writers have avoided exploring the narcotics traffic beyond the level of the shrewd and heartless "pushers" who sell the "fixes" to the helpless addicts for crushing sums.

Less wisely, they have neglected to make it entirely clear how their hero, a sympathetic figure, came to be addicted to dope; what goes with him, his father and his brother; and why it is that his loyal wife has never dreamed that something more than "another woman" was the cause of his eccentricity. A clarification of these matters would give the drama more firm authority.

But certainly, within the framework of the simplified plot, they have contrived a tremendously taut and true description of human agony and shame, of solicitude and frustration and the piteousness of tangled love. And it is so directed by Mr. Zinnemann and acted by an excellent cast that every concept and nuance of the story is revealed.

In the hard black-and-white pictorial pattern that Mr. Zinnemann has employed, the characters stand out genuinely, in a state of emotional nakedness. They loom honestly against a background of a low-cost housing project in New York and swirl in the cold, impersonal eddies of the windy streets of the East Side. Except that Mr. Zinnemann had some trouble matching shots of snow-draped streets with others bereft of snow, he has got the character of the city unalteringly.

Though Don Murray as the addict is most impressive in the versatility with which he rings a "junkie's" baffling changes, the surest acting is done by Eva Marie Saint. Her portrait of the pregnant wife is tender, poignant, brave, and haunting beyond words. As the brother, Anthony Franciosa is a bit on the artificial side, but Lloyd Nolan is appropriately heavy and intellectually slow as the "old man." Henry Silva, Gerald O'Loughlin and William Hickey are variously sinister as the "pushers" who harass and brutalize the victim.

Make no mistake: this is a striking, sobering film.

—B.C., July 18, 1957

THE HEARTBREAK KID

Directed by Elaine May; written by Neil Simon, based on a story by Bruce Jay Friedman; director of photography, Owen Roizman; edited by John Carter; music by Garry Sherman; art designer, Richard Sylbert; produced by Edgar J. Scherick; released by Twentieth Century Fox. Running time: 104 minutes.

With: Charles Grodin (Lenny), Cybill Shepherd (Kelly), Jeannie Berlin (Lila), Eddie Albert (Mr. Corcoran), Audra Lindley (Mrs. Corcoran), William Prince (Colorado Man), Augusta Dabney (Colorado Woman) and Mitchel Jason (Cousin Ralph).

Elaine May's *A New Leaf,* her first film as a director, was a charming, slightly nutty film with some awkward moments in it. *The Heartbreak Kid,* her second, is a first-class American comedy, as startling in its way as was *The Graduate*. It's a movie that manages the marvelous and very peculiar trick of blending the mechanisms and the cruelties of Neil Simon's comedy with the sense and sensibility of F. Scott Fitzgerald.

It begins as a rather familiar New York Jewish comedy about the marriage of Lenny (Charles Grodin), a wide-eyed, completely self-absorbed young man who sells sporting goods, and Lila (Jeannie Berlin), who makes the (it turns out to be) terrible mistake of saving herself for Lenny until their wedding night. "Was it as good as you'd thought?" Lila asks in the dark of their Virginia motel room. "Exactly," says Lenny. "Exactly or better?" Lila insists. "Better!" he cries in desperation.

As Lenny recalls their wedding trip later: "I had my doubts in Virginia. . . . I was pretty sure in Georgia."

Most of their honeymoon takes place in Miami Beach, where Lenny, wearing his matching swimming trunks and beach shirt, meets and falls wildly in love with a beautiful blond WASP from Minnesota named Kelly (Cybill Shepherd). Lila, who has gotten fearfully sunburned their first day, stays in their hotel room—a loud, reproachful voice inside a mound of Solarcaine.

The Heartbreak Kid, which opened yesterday at the Sutton, is the story of Lenny's efforts to unload Lila and to pursue Kelly to Minnesota. It suggests Fitzgerald's *Winter Dreams* updated to 1972, but now the poor boy from the wrong side of the tracks is a New York Jew, and the unattainable Judy Jones is, ironically and perhaps tragically, all too attainable.

The film succeeds in being equally merciless to the

unfortunate Lila, who eats Milky Ways in her wedding bed and dribbles egg salad down her chin at breakfast, and to the magnificent-looking Kelly, whose idea of wit is the snarling retort: "How do you expect me to think when I'm listening?" Not even Fitzgerald, I think, would have had the chutzpah to have his Judy Jones say to a man who'd just divorced his wife for her: "Gee! I'm really flattered!"

The film, adapted by Neil Simon from a story by Bruce Jay Friedman, is full of more recent echoes, especially in the performance of Jeannie Berlin, Miss May's daughter, who looks, sounds, and acts exactly as her mother did as recently as yesterday. It recalls the great performing years of Nichols and May, as does so much of the dialogue, especially when Lenny, dining with Kelly's parents in their huge, clapboard ice palace in Minnesota, tries to say nice things about the "plain" food. Food in New York, he expains, "is exotic but not honest. There's nothing *dishonest* about these potatoes. There's no *deceit* in that cauliflower . . ."

Charles Grodin inevitably recalls Dustin Hoffman in *The Graduate,* but I hope he won't be faulted for it. It's a perfomance of completely controlled enthusiasms and puzzlements. As the object of his unreasonable passion, Miss Shepherd succeeds in the fairly unusual feat of being lovely, bitchy and funny, all more or less simultaneously, and Eddie Albert, in the comparatively small role of her father, is a model of superbly comic, quite understandable outrage.

The Heartbreak Kid occasionally goes for laughs without shame (which is what has always bothered me about Simon's brand of New York comedy), but behind the laughs there is, for a change, a real understanding of character—which is something that, I suspect, can be attributed to Miss May. The film is an unequivocal hit.

—V.C., December 18, 1972

HEARTLAND

Directed by Richard Pearce; written by Beth Ferris, based on the books and papers of Elinore Randall Stewart; director of photography, Fred Murphy; edited by Bill Yahraus; music by Charles Gross; art designer, Carl Copeland; produced by Beth Ferris and Michael Hausman; released by Filmhaus Production. Running time: 96 minutes.

With: Rip Torn (Clyde Stewart), Conchata Ferrell (Elinore Randall Stewart), Barry Primus (Jack), Lilia Skala (Grandma Landauer), Megan Folsom (Jerrine) and Jane Amy Wright (Clara).

There are two very different ways of recalling the lives of the pioneers who settled America's frontiers and carried civilization westward. One way is to remember the terrible physical hardships that had their equivalents in the settlers' psychological dislocations and disorders. By far the more popular method is to recall the pluck and perseverance that overcame all obstacles and made America great. There's nothing wrong with this method, though it does tend to be sentimental, prompting us to grieve for an innocence that probably never was.

The nicest thing about *Heartland,* a new low-budget, uncommonly beautiful film written by Beth Ferris and directed by Richard Pearce, is that even though it celebrates the people of the American frontier, with emphasis on the women, it largely avoids sentimentality. The screenplay, based on the real-life story of Elinore Randall Stewart, is about an impoverished Denver widow who, in 1910, moves from the comparative ease of the city to the wilds of Burntfork, Wyoming, to become the housekeeper for a taciturn Scottish rancher named Stewart. With her small daughter from her first marriage, and with Stewart, whom she eventually married, Mrs. Stewart survived just about everything the frontier could throw at her.

Though Mr. Pearce has made documentaries and features for television and was the cameraman for Peter Davis's Oscar-winning *Hearts and Minds,* this is his first theatrical feature as a director. It is also Miss Ferris's first theatrical screen credit as a writer. Together they have made an unusually accomplished work.

Heartland, which was shot entirely in Montana under what must have been difficult circumstances, has the benefit of three remarkable performances—by Rip Torn, as the dour rancher, a man whose humor, though buried, is as real as his courage, by Conchata Ferrell, as the no-nonsense housekeeper, a big, hearty woman who is strong without being tough and by young Megan Folsom, as her small daughter, who looks a bit the way Peggy Ann Garner did in *A Tree Grows in Brooklyn.*

Because the seasons are as important as anything that happens in them, the photography by Fred Murphy is much a part of the film's success. Mr. Murphy seems to have achieved his effects with high color contrasts that are never too bright and that have the texture of early black-and-white photography.

Heartland doesn't entirely avoid the clichés of the genre. It may be time to declare a moratorium on the slaughter of pigs on camera to indicate the fundamental laws that rule the farm. Also, there must be ways to celebrate the so-called miracle of life without forcing us to endure both human and animal births.

Most of the time, though, *Heartland* is firm and realistic in its appreciation of its people and the quality of their lives.

—V.C., August 23, 1981

HEARTS OF DARKNESS: A FILMMAKER'S APOCALYPSE

Written and directed by Fax Bahr and George Hickenlooper: director of photography, Vittorio Storaro: edited by Michael Greer and Jay Miracle: music by Todd Boekelheide: production designer, Dean Tavoularis: produced by George Zaloom and Les Mayfield: released by Triton Pictures. Running time: 96 minutes.

With: Francis Ford Coppola, Robert Duvall, Dennis Hopper, Frederic Forrest, John Milius, Martin Sheen and others.

There have been few sharper portraits of the filmmaker as alchemist than *Hearts of Darkness: A Filmmaker's Apocalypse,* in which Francis Ford Coppola is seen struggling with hellish logistical problems, wild-card actors, freak accidents and other unseen demons, then ultimately pulling a miracle out of his hat. Previously seen on Showtime, *Hearts of Darkness* opens today at the Film Forum. It's well worth close scrutiny on a large screen.

The filming of Mr. Coppola's *Apocalypse Now* in the Philippines, mostly in 1977 and '78, presented rare opportunities for a journalistic fly on the wall, opportunities rendered that much more interesting when the fly turned out to be Eleanor Coppola, the director's wife. Mrs. Coppola, who earlier wrote about her experiences in an account called *Notes,* shot some documentary material while the film crew was on location, and had close access to the events that tormented her husband. She was also well acquainted with the particular brand of high-strung creative ferment that is Mr. Coppola's stock in trade, and that in the case of *Apocalypse Now* tested the limits of his capacity for courting disaster.

"We were in the jungle, there were too many of us, we had access to too much money, too much equipment—and little by little we went insane," Mr. Coppola is heard saying, at one of the many times either he or his wife equates the filmmaker's experience with the journey into spiritual torment described in Joseph Conrad's "Heart of Darkness," upon which *Apocalypse Now* was loosely based. Grandiose as that parallel may sound, this documentary by Fax Bahr and George Hickenlooper lends it credence. The cast and crew of *Apocalypse Now* clearly came apart at the seams during the 238 days of principal photography, as a result of strain, isolation, considerable drug use and, of course, the weight of Mr. Coppola's ambitions. "My greatest fear is to make a really pompous film on an important subject, and I am making it," he is overheard saying on his wife's tape recording of one of his phone calls.

Interviewed recently, Mrs. Coppola observed that the making of *Apocalypse Now* became for her husband "a metaphor for a journey into self: he has made that journey and is still making it." Fortunately, this documentary is usually a lot more specific as to just what journey the director was on, and what obstacles he faced.

Assuming control of a long-deferred project, one that had once been planned by Orson Welles (before *Citizen Kane*) and that Mr. Coppola himself expected to make before *The Godfather,* he declared plans for a relatively modest $13 million undertaking. Among the things that destroyed any hope of such simplicity or economy were a major monsoon, civil unrest in the Philippines, the firing of one leading man (Harvey Keitel) and the serious heart attack suffered by his replacement (Martin Sheen), and the eleventh-hour arrival of a colossally unhelpful Marlon Brando, whose haunting appearance in the finished film is revealed here as a major triumph of mind over matter.

Sitting bare-chested in the jungle, talking a mile a minute about his grand plans, Mr. Coppola was clearly as much affected by chemical influences and creative pressures as anyone in his cast or crew. A directorial command like "Everyone land in the rice paddies and we'll have a meeting," as the Wagnerian helicopter assault on a Vietnamese village was being filmed, helps to convey the sheer unreality of the situation. So do genial claims by the screenwriter, John Milius, that the film was meant to resemble *The Odyssey,* with its Playboy bunnies substituting for sirens (Mr. Coppola at times preferred to call it "The Idiodyssey"). Never being exactly sure what he was after, Mr. Coppola planned to "take John's screenplay and kind of mate it with whatever happened in the jungle."

What happened was that the actors got high and improvised endlessly. Mr. Sheen, who says he seldom touched alcohol, appeared drunk and naked in a wrenchingly painful Saigon hotel room scene he barely remembered shooting; the actors' call sheets, according to Frederick Forrest, often summoned the performers for nothing more precise than "scenes unknown." Dennis Hopper, arriving to play a photojournalist late in the film, appeared so cheerfully incoherent that the director could tease him about forgetting his lines: "It's not fair to forget 'em if you never knew 'em!"

Interspersing present-day interviews with the principals with Mrs. Coppola's on-location scenes, this film saves for last the director's most staggering challenge: figuring out what to do when Marlon Brando arrived grossly overweight (to play a version of Conrad's skeletal Kurtz), unfamiliar with "Heart of Darkness" and determined to hold up production with days' worth of discussion about his character. In desperation, Mr. Coppola is heard weighing his alternatives and finally deciding it's best simply to let Mr. Brando improvise and hope something usable will emerge.

"See, I not only have to come up with a scene, but it has to be the right shape to fit into the jigsaw puzzle," Mr. Coppola is heard saying. And astonishingly, Mr. Brando's scenes delivered exactly what the film needed, in a remarkable display of an actor's ability to achieve magical effects in purely intuitive ways.

Even allowing for the aggrandizing nature of a film largely shot by his wife, Mr. Coppola emerges from this portrait in legitimately heroic terms. He may have brought on much of the trouble and confusion, and he may not always have reacted to crises in the nicest ways ("If Marty *dies* I want to hear everything is OK until I say Marty is dead!" he exclaims, when threat-

ened with a shutdown after Mr. Sheen's heart attack.) But he also provided the inspiration and the vision to cut through utter chaos and create perhaps a better film than the one he originally imagined. *Hearts of Darkness* shows how it was done.

—*J.M., November 27, 1991*

HEAT AND DUST

Directed by James Ivory; written by Ruth Prawer Jhabvala, based on her novel; director of photography, Walter Lassally; edited by Humphrey Dixon; music by Richard Robbins; production designer, Wilfred Shingleton; produced by Ismail Merchant; released by Universal Pictures. Running time: 130 minutes.

With: Christopher Cazenove (Douglas Rivers), Greta Scacchi (Olivia), Julian Glover (Mr. Crawford), Susan Fleetwood (Mrs. Crawford), Patrick Godfrey (Dr. Saunders), Jennifer Kendal (Mrs. Saunders) and Shashi Kapoor (The Nawab).

India changes a person," someone says in *Heat and Dust,* just as other travelers from the West have been saying in fiction about India for the last one hundred or so years. What makes the old line so poignant in this fine new film is the understanding that the changes wrought by India aren't necessarily accidental, involuntary, or even very mysterious. Instead, they've been sought out by generations of tourists, some less heedless than others, who, as often as not, are infatuated by an idea of India long before they set foot on the subcontinent.

Heat and Dust, which opens today at the Paris Theater, is Ruth Prawer Jhabvala's wise, multilayered, essentially comic adaptation of her own novel for her longtime screen collaborators, James Ivory, the director, and Ismail Merchant, the producer. *Heat and Dust* may be their most thoroughly satisfying collaboration since their first film, *The Householder* (1963), and their second, *Shakespeare Wallah* (1965).

The new movie, demonstrating a sort of literary complexity that seldom works well on the screen, cuts back and forth between two parallel stories separated by nearly sixty years. At the heart of the first, set in the mid-1920's, is Olivia (Greta Scacchi), a pretty, well-born young Englishwoman, the wife of a very proper British civil servant, who falls into a disastrous affair with the local reigning prince (Shashi Kapoor), a charming, apparently completely corrupt nawab.

Framing the story of Olivia is that of Anne (Julie Christie), the granddaughter of Olivia's sister. Anne not only represents today's liberation movement, she might also be one of its victims in ways she doesn't acknowledge. After an unhappy affair at home, Anne comes to India to research the story of her long-dead great-aunt Olivia. With her files of old letters and a tape recorder for interviews, Anne settles down in Satipur with a middle-class Indian family that, by chance, lives in the house where Olivia and Douglas (Christopher Cazenove), her husband, acted out their unhappy tale.

Heat and Dust derives its comic power from the differences between Olivia and Anne, and the similarities that Anne, who is also a romantic, more or less forces into being. In the way that it is played, Anne's affair with her young Indian landlord (Zakir Hussain) is cheerful and none too serious. It's just that the landlord is at hand when she needs someone.

Miss Christie, who makes too few movies, is lovely and commonsensical as Anne. Her intelligence perfectly reflects that of the film itself. As the lost Olivia, Miss Scacchi, an Italian-born, English-bred actress new to films, dominates *Heat and Dust*. She looks a little like Susan Sarandon but has her own kind of not completely suppressed fire. It's a good role, exceptionally well played. Mr. Kapoor, who has made a number of Merchant-Ivory productions, is both funny and mysterious as the nawab, whose perfect manners may be the mask of either a fool or a villain.

Mrs. Jhabvala's screenplay is full of rich characters. There is Harry (Nickolas Grace), a blythe young Englishman who appears to be a permanent guest at the palace of the nawab, for whom he is an intimate companion and court jester. Harry is the sort of man who says of the riots that swept Satipur in the 1920's, "When all these things began to happen, I just ran away to Olivia's and asked her to play some Schumann."

There are also a stern English doctor (Patrick Godfrey) who abhors Olivia's behavior and condemns her publicly; the doctor's weepy wife, very nicely played by Jennifer Kendal, who was so good in the Merchant-Ivory-Jhabvala *Bombay Talkie*; and the imperious

begum, the nawab's chain-smoking mother, played by the beautiful Madhur Jaffrey, first seen in *Shakespeare Wallah*.

If the contemporary story is not as involving as that of Olivia and the nawab, it's partly because the contemporary problems are far more prosaic. It's as if the passage of time that witnessed the independence of India and its partition, as well the introduction of jet travel for the budget-minded, had neutralized all possibility of heroic romance. When Olivia runs away from her adoring English husband, who is, after all, a decent fellow, the act is political as well as personal. When Anne invites her landlord into her bed, it's simply convenient.

Next to Anne, the most appealing character in the contemporary story is Chid (Charles McCaughan), a breezy American hippie who has come to India to find truth nearly twenty years after such quests were fashionable. Instead of finding truth, Chid ruins his liver. Walter Lassally, who has photographed most of the recent Merchant-Ivory films, does an exceptionally handsome job on this one.

Mr. Ivory and Mrs. Jhabvala have been working together so long that it's difficult for an outsider to know exactly who contributed what to any of their collaborations. Together, over the years, they have evolved a kind of ironic, civilized cinema that doesn't quite correspond to anyone else's. Of all their collaborations, none has been more graceful, funny, literate or entertaining than *Heat and Dust*.

—V.C., September 15, 1983

HEATHERS

Directed by Michael Lehmann; written by Daniel Waters; director of photography, Francis Kenney; edited by Norman Hollyn; music by David Newman; production designer, Jon Hutman; produced by Denise Di Novi; released by New World Pictures. Running time: 102 minutes.

With: Winona Ryder (Veronica), Christian Slater (J. D.), Shannen Doherty (Heather Duke), Lisanne Falk (Heather McNamara), Kim Walker (Heather Chandler), Penelope Milford (Pauline Fleming), Glenn Shadix (Father Ripper), Lance Fenton (Kurt Kelly), Patrick Labyorteaux (Ram), Jeremy Applegate (Peter Dawson) and Jon Matthews (Rodney).

Heather is the name of choice at Westerburg High School, the name that signifies power, popularity, and unlimited license to make mischief. The rules of the game are established in an early scene in *Heathers,* in which a trio of girls named Heather cruise the school cafeteria with a reluctant handmaiden named Veronica (Winona Ryder) in tow. They taunt some classmates, flirt with others, compliment others on their clothes. This sequence has a bright look, a buoyant style, and an utterly vicious spirit, giving *Heathers* the air of a demonic sitcom.

Heathers, a first feature directed by Michael Lehmann, is as snappy and assured as it is mean-spirited. Its originality extends well beyond the limits of ordinary high school histrionics and into the realm of the genuinely perverse. And for as long as Mr. Lehmann and the screenwriter, Daniel Waters, have the temerity to sustain the film's bracingly nasty tone, *Heathers* is legitimately startling. As one of the film's characters puts it, "The extreme always seems to make an impression."

Heathers, which opens today at Loews New York Twin and other theaters, shares Veronica's misgivings about the three beautiful, bitchy Heathers (Shannen Doherty, Kim Walker, and Lisanne Falk) and their collective modus operandi. Veronica, who wears a monocle as she scribbles furious little diary entries about the Heathers' exploits, doesn't much like her friends' predilection for dirty tricks, but she goes along with them out of a sense of obligation. It takes a mysterious gun-toting newcomer named J. D. (Christian Slater) to nudge Veronica into a different set of activities altogether.

The diabolical J. D., played by Mr. Slater as an exact teenage replica of Jack Nicholson, goads Veronica into playing out her little resentments against the other girls. When the wickedest of the Heathers, Heather Chandler (Miss Walker), pushes Veronica too far, J. D. helps her get even. He suggests slipping Heather a drink laced with kitchen cleaner, and he draws upon Veronica's proven talents as a forger to craft the appropriate suicide message. "People think just because you're beautiful and popular, life is easy and fun," Heather/Veronica writes. "No one understood that I had feelings too." Because this note makes use of the word "myriad," the teachers at Westerburg are very much impressed.

Exhilarated by this murderous prank, J. D. and Veronica raise the ante. So Westerburg's next two teenage "suicides" are a pair of lame-brained football heroes against whom Veronica has a valid grudge. J. D., who likes planting appropriate props at the scenes of these crimes, leaves a bottle of mineral water this time, maintaining that in Ohio this constitutes strong evidence that the two football players were in love. It is at about this point that the gorgeous, petulant Veronica begins to wonder just what is going on.

And it's at about this point that the film loses its nerve, demanding that Veronica wake up to the awfulness of what J. D. has done. Since he has largely acted on her half-conscious wishes, this turnabout isn't entirely convincing, and it undermines the film's earlier relentlessness. *Heathers* finally reestablishes Veronica as a nice normal girl, but it does this at the expense of its earlier toughness. In any case, the film's hard-edged satire lasts a long while before it finally winds down.

Mr. Lehmann's spiky sensibility is evident in the film's jauntily sardonic style and in its cast of clever and attractive young actors. Miss Ryder, in particular, manages to be both stunning and sympathetic as the watchful Veronica, and she has the glamorous presence of a promising new star. Miss Walker makes the meanest Heather suitably monstrous, and Mr. Slater is effectively insinuating in a role that needn't have been so narrow. Too often, J. D.'s function is only to smirk at Veronica and egg her on.

Mr. Waters's screenplay has a devilish ear for the clichés of teenage conversation. "Great pâté, but I have to motor if I want to be ready for that funeral," says Veronica to her unlistening, happily oblivious parents.

—*J.M., March 31, 1989*

HEAVY TRAFFIC

Written and directed by Ralph Bakshi; cinematography. Ted C. Bemiller and Gregg Heschong; edited by Donald W. Ernst; music by Ray Shanklin and Ed Bogan; characters created by Mr. Bakshi; produced by Steve Krantz; released by American International Pictures. Running time: 76 minutes.

With: Joseph Kaujman (Michael), Beverly Hope Atkinson (Carole), Frank De Kova (Angie), Terri

Haven (Ida), Mary Dean Lauria (Molly), Jacqueline Mills (Rosalyn) and Lillian Adams (Rosa).

In the glass top of a pinball machine the figures start to materialize, like emanations from the mind of a player obsessed with a game that can only end in "TILT." They strut, creep, hobble out into the squalid streets—these characters whose passing miseries become the substance of *Heavy Traffic*, Ralph Bakshi's animated movie, a cruel, funny, heartbreaking love note to a city kept alive by its freaks, and always, always dying.

There is Michael, the shy young cartoonist, fed by his Jewish mother, prodded by his Italian father, whose chief ambition is to make it big with his bosses in the Mafia. There is Shorty, the legless bar bouncer, hopelessly in love with the gorgeous black barmaid, Carole, whom Michael also loves and courts with gift cartoon strips from afar. The drag queen Snowflake looks for true affection, but chases brutal boyfriends, who always find him out. Everyone tends toward tragedy, with gobs of tears, and sometimes buckets of blood—like the stoical godfather whose head is riddled with bullets, and *still* he finishes his plateful of spaghetti.

Not everyone's ending is so conclusive. For example, when Rosalyn Schecter, the freckle-faced neighborhood seductress, falls off a tenement rooftop (victim of a small miscalculation in Michael's fumbling attempt to lose his virginity), she never hits the ground. She is saved halfway down by a clothesline, where throughout the picture she remains, totally naked, somewhat embarrassed and upside down, hanging by a big toe.

Bakshi's subject is really the city, New York City, the sum of his many characters' lives, and yet desolate, depopulated. Generally it looks as if news of some impending disaster had reached everybody in time to leave New York deserted—except for the creatures in the movie, who live together in the shadow of a doom they don't understand but somehow express. At one point Michael goes to the movies, and he sits utterly alone in a cavernous Broadway theater while on the screen, in actual film clips, Harlow stars with Gable in *Red Dust*. It's like always being haunted by the ghost of yourself, a familiar, unshakable terror.

Bakshi's sources range from Alfred Hitchcock to Edward Hopper (both very openly quoted) and his

resources seem almost limitless. Often he places his cartoon characters over photographed back-projection footage of the city at night—some of it very old, like a seamy memory of the 1950's. The characters themselves, the drawings, are rich, vigorous, full of comic-book vitality and exaggeration. People who felt that his earlier feature, *Fritz the Cat*, merely debased a cherished original, can now judge Bakshi's development of his own material. I think that development is as brilliant as anything in recent movies—as brilliant and, in its own improbable way, as lovely and as sad.

Heavy Traffic opened yesterday at the Penthouse and the 86th Street and 59th Street Twin 1 theaters.

—R.G., August 9, 1973

HEIMAT

Directed by Edgar Reitz; written (in German, with English subtitles) by Mr. Reitz and Peter Steinbach; cinematographer, Gernot Roll; edited by Heidi Handorf; music by Nikos Mamangakis; art designer, Franz Bauer; produced by Mr. Reitz, Joachim von Mengershausen and Hans Kwiet; released by Artificial Eye. Black and white. Running time: 924 minutes (16 hours).

With: Marita Brever, Michael Lesch, Dieter Schaad, Karin Kienzler, Eva Maria Bayerswaltes, Rüdiger Weigang and Karin Rasenach.

Last weekend and this, New York audiences have been lining up at the Museum of Modern Art to see Edgar Reitz's massive, beautifully realized new German film, *Heimat*, which, in a running time of almost sixteen hours, chronicles in minute detail the life and times of one small Rhineland village from 1919 to 1982. The film, financed mostly by television interests, has been shown both on television and in theaters in Germany. It's virtually certain to receive some sort of theatrical release in this country before going to television, thus following the pattern set by the 1983 American release of Rainer Werner Fassbinder's masterly, fifteen-and-one-half-hour adaptation of Alfred Doblin's *Berlin Alexanderplatz*.

Ten days ago, a lot of television viewers sat through *A.D.*, the sometimes riotously solemn, five-part, ten-hour, post-Crucifixion biblical epic, conceived and written by Vincenzo Labella and Anthony Burgess as a sequel to their 1977 collaboration, *Jesus of Nazareth,* directed by Franco Zeffirelli.

These productions follow the huge critical and popular success of *The Jewel in the Crown,* the fifteen-hour English miniseries, adapted from Paul Scott's *Raj Quartet,* presented on public television by *Masterpiece Theater.* Though the best of these marathon movies (*Brideshead Revisited; I, Claudius; The Barchester Chronicles*) have been coming from abroad, American entrepreneurs have not been snoozing on the sands of Malibu. They've been getting into the act with *The Winds of War* (seven segments, eighteen hours), *Roots* (eight segments, twelve hours), *Roots—The Second Generation* (seven segments, fourteen hours), and *Shōgun* (five segments, twelve hours).

So far, the only film director of a stature comparable to Fassbinder to attempt one of these maxi-movies is Ingmar Bergman, who originally made *Scenes from a Marriage* to be shown on Swedish television in six episodes of fifty minutes each. I missed the original but, having seen his theatrical version, which he edited down to a superlatively condensed, three-hour length, I can only suspect that the miniseries might have been a bit overwrought.

Something revolutionary is taking place in the narrative cinema. That "something" is possibly comparable to the development of the modern novel by Defoe, Richardson, and Fielding in the early eighteenth century, when refinements in printing techniques made books available to the general public. Until then, books were out of economic reach for most people, not, as any author knows, because the writers were greedy and were being overpaid, but because the physical production of books was such a slow, tedious, and expensive process. Suddenly, with a public ready to read and able to buy, a new kind of popular literature evolved.

Now the Television Age is making possible a new kind of film—the maxi-movie—one that, for both better and worse, is bound to effect changes both in cinema esthetics and in our expectation of movies. The still-unknown factor in this revolution is the effect of the increasingly ubiquitous home video cassette player, which allows the public to rent films as easily as books, and for far less money than three or four people would pay to see a movie in a theater.

A spot-check of several Manhattan video stores reveals that although a number of these maxi-movies, or miniseries (including both *Berlin Alexanderplatz* and *I, Claudius*) are available on cassettes, the demand for them is not overwhelming. The same people who will decline dinner party invitations to stay home to watch the latest installment of *The Jewel in the Crown* are not, apparently, rushing out to pick up cassettes of those miniseries they missed when originally telecast. However, even if these maxi-movies still have to prove themselves at the video store, their popularity on television has been so established that, in time, they must affect the narrative cinema as we have come to know it.

The length of theatrical feature films was never fixed by God, but the length we've come to accept has unmistakably determined how theatrical films operate on our senses. The limitations imposed on filmmakers by that length have also prompted them to develop a kind of narrative shorthand that is a part of the cinema art. It is more than a little ironic that television, whose information-packed commercials demonstrated that audiences will accept all sorts of ellipses, is now demonstrating that they will also accept maxi-movies like *The Jewel in the Crown* and *Brideshead.* Running times are relative. Any audience's powers of concentration are flexible.

When Edwin S. Porter's *Great Train Robbery* was being prepared for release in 1903, there was some fear that nickelodeon audiences simply would not have the interest or physical stamina to sit still for one "feature" of this unusual length—eleven minutes.

The Great Train Robbery became a smash, a true movie milestone. Its audiences not only sat still, enchanted by the suspense of this made-in-New Jersey "Western," but they couldn't wait for more, which they soon got. When D. W. Griffith's *Birth of a Nation* had its premiere at the *Liberty Theater* here on March 3, 1915, a *New York Times* reporter, with some awe, wrote the next day that it "takes a full evening for its unfolding and marks the advent of the two-dollar movie." *The Birth of a Nation* actually only takes a little over two and one-half hours to unfold, but for the next sixty-five years, the movies that dared exceed that length were the exceptions, and the vast majority were much, much shorter.

Erich von Stroheim composed *Greed* to have a running time of something like nine hours but, when it opened in New York in 1924, the studio moguls, using hacksaws, had pared it down to something less than three hours.

In Paris in 1927, Abel Gance tried to get away with a nearly five-hour *Napoleon,* but he, too, was overwhelmed by his producers, who cut it to shreds. It wasn't until 1981 that New Yorkers had the opportunity of seeing the Gance masterpiece in something approximating its original form, a 240-minute version reconstructed by Kevin Brownlow. David O. Selznick was going against all custom in 1939 when he made *Gone With the Wind* with a running time of three hours and forty-two minutes, plus intermission.

It wasn't whim that dictated movie running times of anywhere from sixty-two minutes to, rarely, nearly two hours during the 1930's, 40's, and into the 50's. It was business. In those decades, the double feature program was the standard mode of presenting films, and if those programs ran more than three hours, it cut down on the turnover.

Moviemakers didn't necessarily suffer. The exhilaration we experience while watching the classics of those years is at least partially the result of their remarkable, strictly enforced, narrative economy. Preston Sturges's greatest films never run much more than an hour and a half—*The Lady Eve* ninety-seven minutes, *Sullivan's Travels* ninety-one minutes, and *The Palm Beach Story* ninety minutes. In 1946 David Lean squeezed most of *Great Expectations*—a candidate for a miniseries or a maxi-movie if there ever was one—into a most satisfactory 118 minutes.

In the 1960's, movie producers, faced with competition from television and the collapse of the double-feature system, allowed movies to get longer and longer to give the public its money's worth. Most directors and writers didn't know what to do with this freedom, though Mr. Lean's *Lawrence of Arabia,* released in 1962, still seemed comparatively short with a running time of 222 minutes.

Just how flabby most films—especially comedies—could get, when their directors were left to follow their own courses, was all-too-well demonstrated that same year with Stanley Kramer's 154-minute *It's a Mad, Mad, Mad, Mad World.* This is a staggering example of inflation when one considers that Buster Keaton's *General* (1927), one of the two or three greatest film comedies of all time, runs just seventy-four minutes.

The limitations imposed on filmmakers in those long-gone decades played a major part in how the best directors developed their individual styles. To make the kinds of movies he wanted, Alfred Hitchcock had to pack every frame of film with information that a later director, with more time at his disposal, might spread over a series of separate sequences. A very particular kind of film language was found.

However, brevity in itself means nothing. Artists throughout the ages have allowed themselves to use whatever amount of time they wanted. Wagner's *Ring* cycle could not be coherently reduced, nor could Eugene O'Neill's *The Iceman Cometh.* Proust's *Remembrance of Things Past* is not a series of novels. It's a life's work, a complete world created from memory and imagination. It succeeds through the painstaking accumulation of details that cannot be abbreviated.

In recent years, avant-garde artists in the theater and films have frequently used time as a weapon in their assault on established bourgeois esthetics—and it's an intimidating weapon if not always a successful one. Most relentless have been Robert Wilson in his theater pieces (*The Life and Times of Joseph Stalin*) and Hans-Jurgen Syberberg, whose seven-and-a-half-hour *Our Hitler* (1980) left me euphoric. However, I'm not sure whether this was because of the images I'd witnessed on the screen, and the emotions they evoked, or because of the hypnotic state they'd left me in, after sitting all that time in one spot, watching a minimal spectacle.

The new maxi-movies/miniseries are not, by the stretch of anybody's imagination, avant-garde. Their roots are in radio soap operas and the television soaps that followed, their chief appeal being that they are unending. These soap operas, and their slightly more sophisticated, prime-time, once-a-week, television spinoffs (*Dallas, Dynasty,* and *Falcon Crest*) are necessarily shapeless. It doesn't make any difference at what point one comes in on their stories or leaves them—they flow on forever, stopping not when some particular dramatic point has been reached but only when the ratings drop off.

The best of the maxi-movies/miniseries are something else entirely. They do have shape, and they have the luxury in which to explore and develop a sense of time, place, character, and narrative in a manner that has not before been available in the theater or films. Their manner is not only literary but literary in a leisurely, nineteenth-century manner. This is what's "new" about them, and potentially most exciting. It's no accident that the most successful of these series have been based on novels that, if not always of the highest literary quality, were immensely popular with the public.

It's no accident, too, that hardly anybody remembers the names of the people who have written and directed these presentations. This is possibly because, as in the case of *Brideshead, I, Claudius* and *The Barchester Chronicles,* it seems as if the films' auteurs were the actual authors, which is a kind of compliment to the filmmakers, though not a very flattering one.

It's also because, with the exception of *Berlin Alexanderplatz* and *Scenes from a Marriage,* the films have not been made with an easily recognizable style.

What makes the new, nearly sixteen-hour *Heimat* so invigorating, even when one has seen it, as I did, in two nearly equal, mammoth chunks on two successive days, is that here is a gigantic film with a life of its own. *Heimat* is an original. It doesn't depend on literary credentials earned earlier. Mr. Reitz, whose other films I don't know, is not a director of the striking idiosyncrasies of a Fassbinder or a Bergman, but he has succeeded in making an epic film from his own passion and imagination. It's also a film that could not possibly fit into a more conventional three- or even four-hour format.

There are times when *Heimat* does dawdle, especially at the beginning. However, by the time one reaches the second half of the film, one is suddenly aware that the early, rather plodding lack of cinema sophistication is, in fact, a reflection of the saga itself, which becomes increasingly sophisticated as it goes along. Mr. Reitz's screenplay, written with Peter Steinbach, follows the fortunes of the members of one peasant-farmer family from the end of World War I, through the days of the Weimar Republic, the rise of Hitler, World War II, the collapse of the Third Reich, up to and through the postwar economic miracle.

It's not a masterpiece, but it's a monumental achievement in the narrative form of the popular cinema, and it immediately identifies Mr. Reitz as a formidable, new (to us) director. Like a soap opera, *Heimat,* which is translated as "homeland," has its fair share of sudden deaths, automobile accidents, mysterious disappearances, unrequited loves, abortions, reconciliations, and illegitimate births. It also has behind it a true artist's personal vision, which is realized in dozens of memorable performances and scenes that separate art from soap opera. By the time it ends, its shape is apparent and its effect is invigorating.

The problem: What is the best way to see it? Few people have the time or the interest to devote two days of their life to one film. Somewhat more feasible is watching it in four four-hour chapters, one a week for four weeks, in the manner in which *Berlin Alexanderplatz* was shown here theatrically. The easiest way is to watch it is in the now-accepted miniseries format on television, even though one won't be able to appreciate fully the film's technical beauty, especially the photography by Gernot Roll.

By far the most convenient way, of course, is to watch it at home, on your own video cassette recorder, going through it at your own speed as you would any very long novel.

However you do it, you won't be disappointed. Among other things, *Heimat* could be one of the seminal works in a new cinema form that is not better than the conventional forms we're used to, just different. Because the cinema hasn't really changed that much in the last fifty years, that's news.

—V.C., April 14, 1985

THE HEIRESS

Produced and directed by William Wyler; written by Ruth and Augustus Goetz, based on their play and the novel *Washington Square* by Henry James; cinematographer, Leo Tover; edited by William Hombeck; music by Aaron Copland; art designers, John Meehan and Harry Horner; released by Paramount Pictures. Black and white. Running time: 115 minutes.

With: Olivia de Havilland (Catherine Sloper), Montgomery Clift (Morris Townsend), Ralph Richardson (Dr. Austin Sloper), Miriam Hopkins (Lavinia Penniman), Vanessa Brown (Maria), Mona Freeman (Miriam Almond), Ray Collins (Jefferson Almond), Betty Linley (Mrs. Montgomery) and Selena Royle (Elizabeth Almond).

Not many film producers are able to do the sort of thing that William Wyler has done with *The Heiress,* the mordant stage play of two seasons back.

For Mr. Wyler has taken this drama, which is essentially of the drawing room and particularly of an era of stilted manners and rigid attitudes, and has made it into a motion picture that crackles with allusive life and fire in its tender and agonized telling of an extraordinarily characterful tale. This film, with Olivia de Havilland playing the title role, was delivered by Mr. Wyler (and Paramount Pictures) to the Music Hall yesterday.

Moving about, in the first place, in a fine house in Washington Square, which was tacitly represented on the stage by one elegant set, and then going out from that center to other places for colorful scenes, Mr. Wyler has got for the drama plenty of space in which to move around. More than that, with the help of his writers, Ruth and Augustus Goetz, who adapted the play originally from a novel by Henry James, he has chopped up the play's continuity into a fluid succession of scenes that have the advantage of contrasts in movement and physical mood.

But most particularly, Mr. Wyler, who also directed the film, has given this somewhat austere drama an absorbing intimacy and a warming illusion of nearness that it did not have on the stage. He has brought the full-bodied people very closely and vividly to view, while maintaining the clarity and sharpness of their personalities, their emotions, and their styles.

As a consequence, the conflict that this story is basically built upon—the struggle between a timid daughter and her willful father over the suitor of the girl—becomes an impassioned and arresting clash of immediate minds and a locking of adult emotions that we can expressly comprehend. And the burning and then the bitter experience of the girl with the deceitful man is filled with pervasive nuances that it could not reveal at long range.

For some reason, Mr. Wyler and his writers have softened the shock of the most explosive moments in this tale of a hundred years ago. The father, a suave and clever person is not quite the sadist that he was—nor as nebulously psychopathic as he appeared—on the stage. Here, in the rich and sleek performance that Sir Ralph Richardson gives, he is a socially disciplined parent calculating the protection of his child—a cautious and masterful person whom you cannot help but admire. As a consequence, his critical resistance to his daughter's precarious romance is not as precisely diabolic as it might profitably be.

Likewise, the soft and pliant nature that Miss de Havilland gives to the shy and colorless daughter is much less shatterable by shock, and her ecstasies and her frustrations are much more open than they appeared on the stage, where Wendy Hiller performed her with significant restraint. Thus her emotional reactions are more fluent and evident, which has forced Mr. Wyler to abandon her poignant breakdown at the shock of being deceived. On the whole, however, her portrayal of the poor girl has dignity and strength.

As the mercenary suitor, Montgomery Clift seems a little young and a wee bit too glibly modern in his verbal inflections and attitudes. But he brings a vast deal of vitality and romantic charm to the role. Likewise, Miriam Hopkins is delightful as the girl's impulsive aunt and Betty Linley is exquisitely touching in one scene as the sister of the man. John Meehan's expensive settings have exceptional refinement and taste. *The Heiress* is one of the handsome, intense, and adult dramas of the year.

—B.C., October 7, 1949

HENRY V

Directed by Laurence Olivier and Reginald Beck; written by Alan Dent and Mr. Olivier, based on the play by William Shakespeare; cinematographer, Robert Krasker; edited by Mr. Olivier and Mr. Beck; music by William Walton; art designer, Paul Sheriff; produced by Mr. Olivier and Filippo Del Giudice; released by United Artists. Running time: 127 minutes.

With: Laurence Olivier (King Henry V), Robert Newton (Ancient Pistol), Renee Asherson (Princess Katharine), Esmond Knight (Fluellen), Leo Genn (The Constable of France) and Felix Aylmer (Archbishop of Canterbury).

Out of Will Shakespeare's rather turgid *Chronicle Historie of King Henry the Fifth*—more concisely and conveniently titled for this occasion simply *Henry V*—a fine group of British film craftsmen and actors, headed by Laurence Olivier, have concocted a stunningly brilliant and intriguing screen spectacle, rich in theatrical invention, in heroic imagery, and also gracefully regardful of the conventions of the Elizabethan

443

stage. They have further achieved the full eloquence of Shakespeare's tribute to a conquering English king in this Theatre Guild–sponsored motion picture, which opened at the City Center last night.

The reason for choosing this chronicle out of all the bard's better-known plays for production in Britain during wartime has not been mentioned by Mr. Olivier. But the enticement is fairly apparent: there was provided in *Henry V* a most tempting and timely opportunity for expansive cinematic display. The mounting and execution of the battle of Agincourt, which is the play's and the film's central drama, offered a spectacle too gorgeous to resist. And the theme of traditional English triumph on the Continent was appropriate to the day.

Certainly the story in this chronicle could not have lured Mr. Olivier too much, nor could the chance to explore a complex character have been the bait to draw him on. For the reasons for Henry's expedition against France, as laid down in the play, are neither flattering to him nor to his churchly counselors. The bishops conspire to urge Henry to carry his claims against France in order to distract the Commons from confiscating their lands; and Henry apparently falls for it, out of sheer royal vanity and greed. His invasion of France is quite clearly a war of aggrandizement, and his nature appears slightly naive when he argues the justice of his cause.

But that, of course, is Shakespeare; and Mr. Olivier and his editor, Reginald Beck, have not attempted to change it. They have simply cut large chunks out of the play, especially the plot of the traitors, to get at the action and the meat. Thus reduced of excessive conversations (though it might have been trimmed even more), they have mounted the play with faithful service to the spirit and the word. That service is as truly magnificent as any ever given to a Shakespearean script, both in visual conception and in the acting of an excellent cast.

The film begins as a picturization of a performance at the Globe Theatre, with the arrival of the Elizabethan audience and preparation backstage. For students of Shakespearean stagecraft, this introduction is fascinating. And the early scenes are played within the confines and on the stages of the picturesque "wooden O." Then, as the Chorus advises to "eke out our performance with your mind," the character of the visualization lapses into naturalistic style, but with the

scenes still played in the foreground against painted backdrops, as though seen through an invisible proscenium arch. This technique permits the embroidery of the motion-picture screen with images that have the texture of rich and silken animated tapestries.

It is only when the action develops to the night before Agincourt, in the quiet and vigilant camp of the English, that a realistic style is employed, and here Mr. Olivier has directed for action on a broad, spectacular scale. The night scenes in the camp are tense and thoughtful, as Henry, incognito, moves about, musing on war with his nervous soldiers. And then the violence explodes as the ringing, racing battle of Agincourt is fought in all its medieval pomp. The tumult of the armorers' preparations, the stretch of bowmen, and the clash of steel-casqued knights is vividly recreated. Not since *The Birth of a Nation* do we recall a more thrilling and eerie charge of horsemen than the charge of the knights in *Henry V*.

This emphasis upon the spectacular has not absorbed Mr. Olivier to the point of neglecting the subtleties and eloquence of Shakespeare's verse and prose. And Mr. Olivier's own performance of Henry sets a standard for excellence. His majestic and heroic bearing, his full and vibrant use of his voice, create a kingly figure around which the other characters rightly spin. And Leslie Banks, in the role of the Chorus, is his match in eloquence. Due and sufficient credit cannot be given the entire excellent cast, but mention must be made of Harcourt Williams's splendid portrait of the senile King of France, Max Adrian's pompous mincing as the Dauphin, and Robert Newton's posturing as the clown Pistol. Renee Asherson is also very lovely and gracefully piquant in two scenes as the Princess Katharine, whose conversations are almost wholly in French.

Mr. Olivier has leaned perhaps too heavily toward the comic characters in the play—at least, for American audiences, which will find the dialects a little hard to get. The scenes with the Welsh and Irish captains are too parochial for our taste. And certainly the writing-in completely of the Falstaff deathbed scene, with the echoing voice of Harry carrying over from *Henry IV, Part Two,* is obviously nonessential and just a bit grotesque.

However, in all other matters—in the use of music, in the brilliance of costumes (which appear most remarkably exciting in the Technicolor employed), in toning the whole film to the senses—Mr. Olivier has done a tasteful job. Thanks to him and to all those who helped him, we have a glowing "touch of Harry in the night."

—B.C., June 18, 1946

HENRY V

Directed by Kenneth Branagh; adapted by Mr. Branagh, based on the play by William Shakespeare; director of photography, Kenneth MacMillan; edited by Mike Bradsell; music by Pat Doyle; production designer, Tim Harvey; produced by Bruce Sharman; released by the Samuel Goldwyn Company. Running time: 135 minutes.

With: Kenneth Branagh (Henry V), Derek Jacobi (Chorus), Ian Holm (Fluellen), Christian Bale (Boy), Judi Dench (Mistress Quickly), Paul Scofield (French King), Emma Thompson (Katherine), Geraldine McEwan (Alice) and Michael Williams (Williams).

Kenneth Branagh has done it.
Who is Kenneth Branagh?

He's the young Belfast-born actor and director, best known here for his recent appearance in the ghastly *Fortunes of War* miniseries on television, who has transformed what initially seemed to be a lunatic dare into a genuine triumph. Mr. Branagh has made a fine, rousing new English film adaptation of Shakespeare's *Henry V*, a movie that need not apologize to Laurence Olivier's 1944 classic.

The Branagh version, opening today at the Paris Theater, is comparatively small. It's almost pocket-size, but it is big enough to encompass the emotional impact of the extraordinary text as acted by the mostly superlative actors.

In addition to Mr. Branagh, who plays the title role under his own direction, the cast includes Ian Holm as Fluellen, Brian Blessed as Exeter, Paul Scofield as the King of France, Judi Dench as Mistress Quickly, Derek Jacobi as the Chorus, Emma Thompson as Princess Katherine, and Geraldine McEwan as her companion.

Some comparisons between old and new cannot be avoided.

The Olivier film, produced at the height of World War II, when the British withdrawal from Dunkirk was still a bleeding wound, is a heroic spectacle, a celebration of monarchy as well as a reminder of Britain's place on the European Continent.

There was contemporary political point to its pageantry and pomp, to its magnificent battle scenes, and to its depiction of Henry's French enemies as representative of an effete society, no match for the staunch islanders who journeyed to France only to do their duty for king and country.

Olivier's *Henry V* is a splendid film that is also splendid propaganda.

The Branagh *Henry* is something quite other. There is little pageantry and less pomp. No fancy sets. The lighting is kept dim in the interiors and when the film moves outside, the skies are gray and air has the chill and damp of late fall, after the sun has lost its warmth.

The spectacle is nil. The battlefields are muddy and so messy that it's impossible to be quite sure which are the English and which are the French, though the carnage is explicit. The French are no more effete than the English.

This may or may not be historically accurate, but it does rob the Branagh film of an explanation for the remarkable English victory at Agincourt, in which the tiny English expeditionary force defeated a French army ten times its size. It seems that God really was on the side of the English.

Mr. Branagh keeps the focus short. Most of the film appears to have been photographed in medium shots or close-ups. As a result, the emphasis of this *Henry* is less on politics and statecraft than on the complex nature of the ambitious young Henry and how he wrestles with the demands of kingship.

This is where Mr. Branagh's film is most affecting. His Henry is tight-lipped and steely but also immensely intelligent. One correctly senses that when he was the carousing Prince Hal, bosom friend to Falstaff, the role was never more than the consciously adopted disguise for the king who was to be.

That his former drinking companions never understood this is less a reflection on the king than an indication of their own wishful naïveté.

Mr. Branagh's Henry has psychological heft and intellectual weight. He is not a nice man, but great kings are not required to be nice. Henry's awareness of all of these things is what makes him the fascinating character he is.

Though Mr. Branagh has severely pruned the text, nothing vital appears lost. It's a tougher text than Olivier's. Henry's vivid threats before Harfleur, when he threatens that the English will leave every woman raped and every babe dead, is not the sort of thing that the Olivier version wanted to emphasize.

Some of Mr. Branagh's interpolations are not great. Falstaff, played by Robbie Coltrane, appears in a couple of flashbacks, material purloined from *Henry IV.* The point of the flashbacks is to recall Henry's former loyalties. They are a mistake. Mr. Coltrane is not on the screen long enough to create any true idea of Falstaff's magnificence. Instead, he simply looks like a woozy Santa Claus.

The play's two greatest sequences remain great in the modest manner in which Mr. Branagh presents them, that is, the scene in which Henry prowls about the English camp during the long night before Agincourt, and then his rousing St. Crispin's Day speech the next morning.

The battle scenes, seen in a succession of close-ups, are chaotic and so exhausting that as the film slips into slow motion it seems to be sympathetic fatigue. One does not have to be an Anglophile to be moved by Mr. Branagh's Henry when in the late afternoon after Agincourt he turns bewildered to the French herald and asks which side has carried the day.

In addition to Mr. Branagh's excellent, not especially lyric performance, those that stand out include Mr. Holm's Fluellen, Mr. Blessed's Exeter, and Miss Dench's Mistress Quickly. The tavern scenes are otherwise pretty awful, but when Mistress Quickly describes Falstaff's death, the movie recoups.

Note also the quietly sturdy performance of Christian Bale, the young man who played the lead in *Empire of the Sun,* as Falstaff's Boy, a tiny but important role.

—*V.C., November 8, 1989*

HENRY FOOL

Written, directed and produced by Hal Hartley; director of photography, Michael Spiller; edited by Steve Hamilton; music by Mr. Hartley; production designer, Steve Rosenzweig; released by Sony Pictures Classics. Running time: 138 minutes.

With: Thomas Jay Ryan (Henry Fool), James Urbaniak (Simon Grim), Parker Posey (Fay), Maria Porter (Mary), James Saito (Mr. Deng) and Kevin Corrigan (Warren).

The affectless precision of Hal Hartley's previous work is absolutely no preparation for the brilliance and deep resonance of his *Henry Fool.* Here is a great American film that's no more likely than *Nashville* to turn up on the American Film Institute's Top 100 hit parade (where *Rocky* outranks *The Searchers*) but will linger where it matters: in the hearts and minds of viewers receptive to its epic vision.

Without forsaking the clean, spare look and hyperrealistic clarity that are so much his own, Mr. Hartley moves into a much larger realm than those of his earlier works. This film aspires to be a meditation on (among other things) art, trust, loyalty, politics, and popular culture. With utter simplicity, and with unexpectedly intense storytelling, it achieves all that and more.

Shot so beautifully by Michael Spiller that its squalid Queens settings assume an instant mythic quality, *Henry Fool* is a perfect modern parable. It begins with the utter degradation of Simon Grim (James Urbaniak) and the mysterious appearance of a stranger who may be his salvation. "Get up off your knees!" orders *Henry Fool* (Thomas Jay Ryan, a stage actor making a swaggeringly good screen debut) barging into the basement apartment in Simon's house and instantly taking up residence. Henry's arrival would be Faustian even if it were not, thanks to the basement hearth, greeted by a fiery glow.

The scarecrow-thin, owlish Simon (the haunting Mr. Urbaniak bears a deliberate resemblance here to young Samuel Beckett) works as a garbageman and takes heaps of abuse from much of the neighborhood. That includes his heavily medicated mother (Maria Porter) and his slatternly sister Fay (played with deadpan, nonchalant wit by Parker Posey in one of her best roles). Simon is so silent that his response to this literally and figuratively Grim existence is a mystery until Henry urges him to write down his thoughts.

Henry describes his own huge, unpublished work,

known variously as "my opus" or "my confession," with supreme grandiosity. "It's a philosophy," he tells Simon. "A poetics. A politics, if you will. A literature of protest. A novel of ideas. A pornographic magazine of truly comic-book proportions." The work's mystique comes from Henry's cagey unwillingness to let anyone see it.

Simon's writing also remains hidden at first (and always wisely hidden from the audience). But as it starts to emerge, its effects are astonishing. The mute girl at the local World of Donuts, this story's cultural and culinary mecca, reads a few words, and she suddenly sings. A girl who once bullied him becomes a literary groupie in a beret. A waitress with conservative political leanings is offended. "You brought on my period a week and a half early, so just shut up!" complains Fay, after typing Simon's manuscript.

When the Board of Education denounces Simon's poem as scatological (in a film that insists on a few wild gross-outs of its own), Simon and Henry share a proud handshake. "An honest man is always in trouble," Henry has announced early in the story, and an honest artist is, too.

Genius and celebrity eventually shift the story's balance in wry ways. There's an especially droll sequence devoted to the world of publishing, where slick young executives insist on thinking way beyond mere books. The effect of a right-wing political candidate on the neighborhood's sleaziest character (Kevin Corrigan) points to another wave of the future. But the tension between Simon's utter seriousness and Henry's big dreams always remains the story's central concern, especially after Simon learns more about Henry's past. "To be honest, my ideas, my writing, they've not always been received well—or even calmly," Henry eventually confesses.

Henry Fool is its own testament to the power of words, even as it merges the fortunes of its characters in a wonderfully ambiguous final gesture. Mr. Hartley's splendidly articulate screenplay (which won a prize at Cannes this year) is as exacting as his visual style. Even more than its story of private genius and public opinion, the dialogue itself offers proof that every word matters. All the film's characters speak with utter honesty about matters both large and small, and sometimes make a major virtue of understatement. As in: "Look, Simon, I made love to your mother about half an hour ago, and I'm beginning to think it wasn't such a good idea."

Visually, *Henry Fool* shows off such fine compositional sense that there's not a paint streak on a wall that doesn't tie in with some other part of the frame. There are no casual details and absolutely no clutter. Props are where Mr. Hartley finds them, to the point where a stack of huge tires, a gumball machine, or a garden hose can be as arresting as another film's elaborate set. Everything the camera sees is present for a reason.

—*J.M., June 19, 1998*

HERE COMES MR. JORDAN

Directed by Alexander Hall; written by Sidney Buchman and Seton I. Miller, based on the play *Heaven Can Wait* by Harry Segall; cinematographer, Joseph Walker; edited by Viola Lawrence; music by Frederick Hollander; art designer, Lionel Banks; produced by Everett Riskin; released by Columbia Pictures. Black and white. Running time: 93 minutes.

With: Robert Montgomery (Joe Pendleton), Evelyn Keyes (Bette Logan), Claude Rains (Mr. Jordan), Rita Johnson (Julia Farnsworth), Edward Everett Horton (Messenger 7013) and James Gleason (Max Corkle).

There is going to be heaven to pay when the folk around St. Peter's gate see *Here Comes Mr. Jordan*, but who cares? For in the new film at the Music Hall Columbia has assembled its brightest people for a delightful and totally disarming joke at heaven's expense. Even the celestial guardians, it seems, can make an occasional mistake. And just because Messenger 7013 was overanxious to make a good impression on the boss, Joe Pendleton had to win the world's boxing championship in another man's body. A fantastic story? Well, we got it from Max Corkle, Joe's manager, who was there at the time. And if you don't believe us, just go to the Music Hall and see for yourself. Because *Here Comes Mr. Jordan* is gay, witty, tender and not a little wise. It is also one of the choicest comic fantasies of the year.

Joe was plenty sore about the whole thing, and who could blame him? Here he was, "in the pink of condition," as he kept telling Mr. Jordan afterward, and all set to take the championship, until Messenger 7013, who collected souls from a "place called New Jersey," gave him his ticket to heaven fifty years before his time. The fact that Joe's earthly remains were taken from the crashed plane and cremated made it difficult for Mr. Jordan to make amends. It didn't make things easier that when they looked over some of the bodies to be "shortly available" Joe was disgruntled and choosy. When a man's soul is intent on the world's championship he has to have a body that's in the pink.

Well, after a few tries, Joe did get his body, the championship, and even a tidy little blonde that he'd met a couple of transmigrations back. Heaven, and especially Messenger 7013, breathed easier. But don't ask us to explain everything that happened. Even Corkle, we're afraid, never got things straight. It was pathetic when for the first time in his life he thought heaven was handing him a sure thing in a fighter and he was anxiously discussing his forty percent with a man who wasn't there. Pathetic and hilariously funny.

However you look at it, *Here Comes Mr. Jordan* is rollicking entertainment. Sidney Buchman and Seton Miller, who wrote the script, and Alexander Hall, who directed it, have had the rare sense to keep the comedy where it belongs—in the characters and situations rather than in a series of double exposures and process shots of ectoplasmic spooks. The performances, with the exception of the distaff side, are tops. Robert Montgomery's dazed prizefighter keeps his place secure as one of the screen's deftest comedians. Jimmy Gleason again steals the film's most comic scene as the manager with cosmic premonitions. Claude Rains, as Mr. Jordan, has all the kindly authority of an archangel. And save a line for Edward Everett Horton, the peripatetic Messenger 7013, who started it all.

Meanwhile, if all the heavenly guardians are as obliging and convivial as those in *Here Comes Mr. Jordan,* we know why Little Eva couldn't wait.

—*T.S., August 8, 1941*

HIGH AND LOW

Directed by Akira Kurosawa: written by Eijir Hisaita, based on the novel *King's Ransom* by Ed McBain: cinematography by Choichi Nakai and Takao Sato: music by Masaru Sato: produced by Ryuzo Kikushima and Tomoyuki Tanaka: released by Toho Company. Running time: 143 minutes.

With: Toshiro Mifune (Kingo Gondo). Tatsuya Nakadai (Chief Detective Tokura). Kyoko Kagawa (Reiko Gondo). Tatsuya Mihashi (Kawanishi. Gondo's secretary). Isao Kimura (Detective Arai). Kenjiro Ishiyama (Chief Detective Taguchi). Takeshi Kato (Detective Nakao). Takashi Shimura (Chief of Investigation Section). Jun Tazaki (Kamiya). Nobuo Nakamura (Ishimaru). Ynosuke It (Baba). Tsutomu Yamazaki (Ginjir Takeuchi). Minoru Chiaki (first reporter). Hiroshi Unayama (Detective Shimada) and Eijir Tono (factory worker).

Let's give fervent thanks for *High and Low,* one of the best detective thrillers ever filmed, arriving yesterday at the Toho Cinema. Where from? Japan, of all places, and from the devastating hand of that great director, Akira Kurosawa. Here is one import—for suspense fans and students of moviecraft—that simply must be seen.

Using, of all things, Ed McBain's strictly American novel, *King's Ransom,* as a source, Mr. Kurosawa and two co-scenarists have transferred the kidnaping yarn from Manhattan to Yokohama, using a fine cast headed by the famous Toshiro Mifune.

The result is a sizzling, artistic crackerjack and a model of its genre, pegged on a harassed man's moral decision, laced with firm characterizations and tingling detail and finally attaining an incredibly colorful crescendo of microscopic police sleuthing. Crime, believe us, doesn't pay in Yokohama—not in the end.

From the very fade-in, when Mr. Mifune, as a prosperous business executive, tangles with his stockholders in his suburban home, the quiet wizardry of the director is apparent in the chessboard groupings framed by the superb photography of Choichi Nakai and Takao Saito.

The stage is set here, literally and leisurely, for a menacing telephone call and a crucial decision. Shall the bristly, self-made hero use his fortune to subjugate his hostile partners or to ransom his chauffeur's son, mistakenly kidnaped for his own?

Mr. Kurosawa takes his time in these opening scenes, in the precise confinement of a two-room setting, with Mr. Mifune attended by his anxious wife, Kyoko Kagawa, the groveling chauffeur, Yutaka Sada, and two extremely alert detectives, Tatsuya Nakadai and Kenjiro Ishiyama.

About here, some viewers may wonder if the gifted director has blandly glued the whole film indoors. Not on your life.

The action with the two detectives suddenly fans out across the bustling metropolis. The chase is on and the dazzling scenes that follow, with the entire police force scientifically sifting skimpy evidence, make masterful use of pure movie technique.

Mr. Kurosawa's galvanic use of a train for the ransom-tossing, for instance, makes the one in *The Lady Vanishes* seem like the Toonerville Trolley. Bit by bit, in such things as a crackling newspaper, the stillness of a coastal villa, a small boy's drawing and a brilliantly spangled kaleidoscope of Yokohama's lower depths, Mr. Kurosawa has composed a remarkable movie mosaic, both spine-tingling and compassionate.

As the suave chief inspector, Mr. Nakadai almost steals the show. Almost. It belongs, of course, to the man who made it. Anyway—since we can't say it in Japanese—bravo!

—H.T., *November 27, 1963*

THE HIGH AND THE MIGHTY

Directed by William A. Wellman; written by Ernest K. Gann, based on his novel; cinematographers, Archie Stout and William Clothier; edited by Ralph Dawson; music by Dimitri Tiomkin; art designer, Alfred Ybarra; produced by Robert Fellows and John Wayne; released by Warner Brothers. Running time: 147 minutes.

With: John Wayne (Dan Roman), Claire Trevor (May Holst), Laraine Day (Lydia Rice), Robert Stack (Sullivan) and Jan Sterling (Sally McKee).

The nervous strains and terrors among the passengers and crew of an airliner that loses an engine while flying between Honolulu and San Francisco are what you get in hot abundance in the new Wayne-Fellows film, *The High and the Mighty,* that arrived yesterday in color and CinemaScope at the Paramount. Loaded with touches of lumpy humor and assorted heavy sentiments, it rocks and buffets and bounces across the wide screen for more than two hours, spitting fire, tossing propellers and strewing emotional wreckage all over the place.

To say that the drama concocted by Ernest K. Gann from his own popular novel of the same name is a bit on the synthetic side, is to offer an observation that is wholly superfluous. Synthesis is the essence of this sort of melodramatic yarn, which visions the reactions of many characters in the face of impending catastrophe. The question is, how authentic and legitimate does it appear. The answer is that most of it seems entirely artificial and contrived.

This is not to say it lacks excitement. Mr. Gann writes an incident-crowded yarn and William A. Wellman directs it with the vigor and snap he's always shown. The business of airplanes departing, of motors catching fire in the air, of passengers getting excited, and of pilots desperately battling their controls is stuff with which Mr. Wellman is thoroughly and capably at home. And he makes all such business in this picture have a direct effect on the nerves.

But the characters and their personal dramas—well, they're the sort that hang on strings in the prop room of any studio and are animated in conformance with a code. There's the brittle dame and her husband, played by Laraine Day and John Howard, returning home with the intention of getting a divorce. There's the blowhard theatrical producer, Robert Newton; the chicken-livered playboy, David Brian; the demoralized atomic scientist, Paul Kelly; the gallant lady of much circulation, Claire Trevor. Close to a dozen others make up the passenger list. All are fabricated characters—and that is the way they are played. The hot crucible of their experience firms their moral fibers, of course.

Of the four crewmen, John Wayne makes the best show as a veteran pilot, second in command, who has the coolness and courage to knock some clear sense into the muddled head of the captain, Robert Stack. Mr. Stack is a dreary sort of psychopath to be commanding a trans-Pacific plane, and Wally Brown makes the navigator an utter incompetent. William Campbell as the fourth in the "office" is just another flyboy, that's all.

Despite several terrible technical bobbles, such as the opening outward of a passenger door while the plane is in flight, Mr. Wellman has made his airports and instrument panels look businesslike. But the picture does not conduce to flying. It shows what every jittery novice dreams and dreads.

—B.C., July 1, 1954

HIGH ART

Written and directed by Lisa Cholodenko; director of photography, Tami Reiker; edited by Amy E. Duddleston; music by Shudder to Think; production designer, Bernhard Blythe; produced by Dolly Hall, Jeff Levy-Hinte and Susan A. Stover; released by October Films. Running time: 96 minutes.

With: Ally Sheedy (Lucy Berliner), Radha Mitchell (Syd), Patricia Clarkson (Greta), Gabriel Mann (James) and Anh Duong (Dominique).

High Art is an attention-getting debut feature by Lisa Cholodenko, the rare filmmaker to acknowledge Calvin Klein ads as part of her creative inspiration. She mentions the ads for their subtext rather than their style. Interested in the collision between naturalistic, highly personal photography and cool commerce, she makes her film's main character a once-celebrated photographer named Lucy Berliner, who is played by Ally Sheedy in a fierce, tricky performance that is the film's strongest element. Spooked by fame, Lucy long ago retreated from the art world to live a reclusive, druggy life in an apartment that has become a louche mecca for her lesbian friends.

The uninspired plot device of a plumbing emergency brings baby-faced Syd (Radha Mitchell) into Lucy's spider web. It happens that Lucy lives directly upstairs from Syd and her boyfriend, and that Lucy has a leaky tub. It also happens that Syd is bored with the boyfriend and that she works as a new recruit at *Frame,* a desperately chic photography magazine. Wowed by Lucy's hidden world and fascinated by her images, Syd fastens on the idea of drawing Lucy out of seclusion and putting her in touch with *Frame's* editors (among them David Thornton). It is coyly mentioned in passing that the magazine's queen bee (Anh Duong, a painter and ex-model) used to be a receptionist at *Interview.*

Syd's professional seduction of Lucy is complicated by Lucy's sexual gamesmanship with Syd. Ms. Sheedy's haunting, wily character is visibly at war with herself even as she flirts with Ms. Mitchell's pretty young thing. Guarded, bony, startlingly intense, Lucy finds herself intrigued by Syd and the opportunity she offers: to shake off the heroin haze and dare to start life anew. Complicating Lucy's interest in Syd is her longtime relationship with Greta (Patricia Clarkson), the washed-up German actress who drips world-weary glamour and drops Fassbinder's name as often as she can.

Thus Ms. Cholodenko fills her story with novel ingredients and offbeat possibilities, held together by the magnetic pull of Lucy's life. The question of what a professional comeback might do to her is enough to give *High Art* some drama, and so is the delicate balance of power between a jaded artist and a bright-eyed ingenue. But the film sacrifices any hope of raw edges and real emotion to its own chic sensibility, which is so studiously alluring that it overwhelms the story. In its own fashionably nonchalant way, *High Art* proves every bit as sleek as *Frame,* the film's emblem of poisonous commerce corrupting creative purity.

By the time it reaches an ending of contrived inevitability, *High Art* has felt the burden of its own pretensions. Lucy's noble superiority to the world of slick images is undercut by the unrelenting attractiveness of the film's visual style. *High Art* affects a spare naturalism that looks worlds away from anything authentic, with an emphasis on studied simplicity and flattering light. Though some of the characters are so lost in drugs that even their sexual experiences remain incomplete, the film depicts them with incongruous (rather than revealing) clarity. A voyeuristic charge accompanies these scenes of stylish abandon.

To their credit, the actors immerse themselves deeply in the film's self-conscious aura. Ms. Sheedy reinvents herself as a tough, fascinating presence, while Ms. Mitchell's earnest bewilderment also serves the story well. Ms. Clarkson, in a devilish turn, is all the comic relief this film needs as a walking (or keeling over) reminder of the Fassbinder demimonde. Her Greta is all that's needed to show how these women got lost in a world that time passed by.

—J.M., June 12, 1998

HIGH HOPES

Written and directed by Mike Leigh: director of photography. Roger Pratt: edited by John Gregory: music by Andrew Dixon: production designer. Diana Charnley: produced by Simon Channing-Williams and Victor Glynn: released by Skouras Films. Running time: 110 minutes.

With: Philip Davis (Cyril). Ruth Sheen (Shirley). Edna Dore (Mrs. Bender). Philip Jackson (Martin). Heather Tobias (Valerie). Lesley Manville (Laetitia) and David Bamber (Rupert).

A traveler from the country who is lost in London wanders into the flat shared by Cyril (Philip Davis) and Shirley (Ruth Sheen), and he has such a hard time going home that they wind up nicknaming him "E.T." It's easy to see why the stranger, only a minor character drifting through Mike Leigh's *High Hopes,* is so drawn to these two. Cyril and Shirley, who travel about in matching motorcycle leathers, are an utterly spontaneous and unpretentious duo, which sets them in marked contrast to everyone else in Mr. Leigh's astute socioeconomic satire.

The title seemingly refers to Cyril and Shirley's optimism, a sentiment that often seems badly misplaced in view of Mr. Leigh's larger portrait of the England of Margaret Thatcher, for whom Shirley has named her prickliest cactus. The spirit of self-interest can be found everywhere in the film, even in the principals' figurative backyard.

High Hopes revolves loosely around the various members of Cyril's family, who represent a wide range of economic conditions. Cyril himself is defiantly impecunious, working as a messenger and refusing Shirley's persistent pleas that they have a child. On the other hand, Cyril's sister, Valerie (Heather Tobias), is loudly and aggressively nouveau riche, with a red sports car and an Afghan hound that wears a sweater. A less self-conscious form of poverty than Cyril's is represented by his mother (Edna Dore), a quietly dejected woman now on the eve of her seventieth birthday. The run-down row house where she lives is in a neighborhood where gentrification has begun, and the yuppies next door do not take kindly to such a shabby old lady.

Although *High Hopes* is mostly a gentle, reflective, and personable comedy of manners, it turns sharply funny at the sight of these new neighbors. "I thank God every day I've been blessed with such beautiful skin," says the wife, Laetitia (Lesley Manville); for his part, her husband, Rupert (David Bamber), declares, "What made this country great is a place for everyone, and everyone in his place."

On one unfortunate occasion, when the ever-more-forgetful old woman loses her money and keys, the neighbors are thrown together with hilarious results. Laetitia, visibly annoyed when the old lady asks to use her bathroom, soon warms to this conversational opportunity. She suggests that Cyril's mother has no business occupying such a large house, and asks her, "Do you have all your original features?" By this she means fireplaces and such, but Cyril's mother is understandably confused.

It seems only fitting that a film containing Rupert and Laetitia should also include a visit to the grave of Karl Marx, where Cyril and Shirley wonder what exactly has gone wrong in their society until a group of Asian tourists interrupts their reverie. The later part of the film, which takes an abruptly more serious tone than its opening, is a serious contemplation of Cyril and Shirley's frustration. There is no better setting for this than the house of Cyril's shrieking sister, the indescribably vulgar setting for the old woman's wretched seventieth birthday party. Cyril winds up stealing an imitation-gold banana as a kind of trophy.

High Hopes manages to be enjoyably whimsical without ever losing its cutting edge. Mr. Leigh, who works with his actors in a quasi-improvisatory way, succeeds especially well in creating the impression that rarely, if ever, does anyone in the film understand anyone else's point of view. The exceptions to this rule are Cyril and Shirley, who understand each other perfectly but in matters regarding their future can seldom agree. Though the actors are all good, Miss Sheen, a wonderfully empathetic actress with a flair for comic understatement, is outstanding.

High Hopes will be shown tonight and tomorrow as part of the New York Film Festival.

—*J.M., September 24, 1988*

HIGH NOON

Directed by Fred Zinnemann: written by Carl Foreman. based on the story "The Tin Star" by

John W. Cunningham: cinematographer. Floyd Crosby: edited by Elmo Williams and Harry Gerstad: music by Dimitri Tiomkin: production designer. Rudolph Sternad: produced by Stanley Kramer: released by United Artists. Black and white. Running time: 85 minutes.

With: Gary Cooper (Will Kane). Thomas Mitchell (Jonas Henderson). Lloyd Bridges (Harvey Pell). Katy Jurado (Helen Ramirez). Grace Kelly (Amy Kane). Otto Kruger (Percy Mettrick). Lon Chaney (Martin Howe) and Henry Morgan (William Fuller).

Every five years or so, somebody—somebody of talent and taste, with a full appreciation of legend and a strong trace of poetry in their soul—scoops up a handful of clichés from the vast lore of Western films and turns them into a thrilling and inspiring work of art in this genre. Such a rare and exciting achievement is Stanley Kramer's production, *High Noon,* which was placed on exhibition at the Mayfair yesterday.

Which one of several individuals is most fully responsible for this job is a difficult matter to determine and nothing about which to quarrel. It could be Mr. Kramer, who got the picture made, and it could be scriptwriter Carl Foreman, who prepared the story for the screen. Certainly director Fred Zinnemann had a great deal to do with it and possibly Gary Cooper, as the star, had a hand in the job. An accurate apportionment of credits is not a matter of critical concern.

What is important is that someone—or all of them together, we would say—has turned out a Western drama that is the best of its kind in several years. Familiar but far from conventional in the fabric of story and theme and marked by a sure illumination of human character, this tale of a brave and stubborn sheriff in a town full of do-nothings and cowards has the rhythm and roll of a ballad spun in pictorial terms. And, over all, it has a stunning comprehension of that thing we call courage in a man and the thorniness of being courageous in a world of bullies and poltroons.

Like most works of art, it is simple—simple in the structure of its plot and comparatively simple in the layout of its fundamental issues and morals. Plotwise, it is the story of a sheriff in a small Western town, on the day of his scheduled retirement, faced with a terrible ordeal. At ten thirty in the morning, just a few minutes after he has been wed, he learns that a dreaded desperado is arriving in town on the noon train. The bad man has got a pardon from a rap on which the sheriff sent him up, and the sheriff knows that the killer is coming back to town to get him.

Here is the first important question: Shall the sheriff slip away, as his new wife and several decent citizens reasonably urge him to do, or shall he face, here and now, the crisis that he knows he can never escape? And once he has answered this question, the second and greater problem is the maintenance of his resolution as noon approaches and he finds himself alone—one man, without a single sidekick, against a killer and three attendant thugs; one man who has the courage to take on a perilous, righteous job.

How Mr. Foreman has surrounded this simple and forceful tale with tremendous dramatic implications is a thing we can't glibly state in words. It is a matter of skill in movie writing; but, more than that, it is the putting down, in terms of visually simplified images, a pattern of poetic ideas. And how Mr. Zinnemann has transmitted this pattern in pictorial terms is something that we can only urge you to go yourself to see.

One sample worth framing, however, is the brilliant assembly of shots that holds the tale in taut suspension just before the fatal hour of noon. The issues have been established, the townsfolk have fallen away, and the sheriff, alone with his destiny, has sat down at his desk to wait. Over his shoulder, Mr. Zinnemann shows us a white sheet of paper on which is scrawled "last will and testament" by a slowly moving pen. Then he gives us a shot (oft repeated) of the pendulum of the clock, and then a shot looking off into the distance of the prairie down the empty railroad tracks. In quick succession, then he shows us the tense faces of men waiting in the church and in the local saloon, the still streets outside, the three thugs waiting at the station, the tracks again, the wife of the sheriff waiting and the face of the sheriff himself. Then, suddenly, away in the distance, there is the whistle of the train and, looking down the tracks again, he shows us a whisp of smoke from the approaching train. In a style of consummate realism, Mr. Zinnemann has done a splendid job.

And so has the cast, under his direction. Mr. Cooper is at the top of his form in a type of role that has trickled like water off his back for years. And Lloyd Bridges as a vengeful young deputy, Katy

Jurado as a Mexican adventuress, Thomas Mitchell as a prudent townsman, Otto Kruger as a craven judge, and Grace Kelly as the new wife of the sheriff are the best of many in key roles.

Meaningful in its implications, as well as loaded with interest and suspense, *High Noon* is a Western to challenge *Stagecoach* for the all-time championship.
—*B.C., July 25, 1952*

HIGH SIERRA

Directed by Raoul Walsh: written by John Huston and W. R. Burnett. based on the novel by Mr. Burnett: cinematographer. Tony Gaudio: edited by Jack Killifer: music by Adolph Deutsch: art designer. Ted Smith: produced by Mark Hellinger: released by Warner Brothers. Black and white. Running time: 100 minutes.

With: Ida Lupino (Marie). Humphrey Bogart (Roy Earle). Alan Curtis ("Babe"). Arthur Kennedy (Red). Joan Leslie (Velma). Henry Hull ("Doc" Banton) and Henry Travers (Pa).

We wouldn't know for certain whether the twilight of the American gangster is here. But the Warner Brothers, who should know if anybody does, have apparently taken it for granted and, in a solemn Wagnerian mood, are giving that titanic figure a send-off befitting a first-string god in the film called *High Sierra,* which arrived yesterday at the Strand. Yessir, Siegfried himself never rose to more heroic heights than does Mr. Humphrey Bogart, the last of the great gunmen, when, lodged on a high mountain crag with an army of coppers below, he shouts defiance at his tormentors ere his noble soul take flight. It's truly magnificent, that's all.

As a matter of fact—and aside from the virtues of the film itself—it is rather touching to behold the Warners pay such a glowing tribute, for no one has made a better thing out of the legendary gangster than they have. No one has greater reason to grow nostalgic about the bad boys of yesterday who, as one of the characters in *High Sierra* reverently remarks, are "all either dead or doing time now in Alcatraz." So, indeed, we are deeply moved by this honest payment of respects to an aging and graying veteran of the

1930's banditti who makes his last stand his best. Somehow, it seems quite fitting.

Of course, that is exactly the way the Warners and everyone concerned intended it should seem. For the story that is told is that of a notorious holdup man who is sprung out of an Illinois prison by an old gangland pal who wants him in California for a big job. But the gunman has got some ideas about freedom and the joy of living. He wants to marry a simple little girl he meets on the road heading West; he wants to do good things because, you see, he really has a good heart.

Well, you know what that means. It's just as old "Doc" Banton tells him ("Doc" being the quack who tends "Big Mac"). He says, "Remember what Johnny Dillinger said about guys like you and him; he said you're just rushing toward death—that's it, you're rushing toward death." And that's the truth. For the big holdup job gets messed up by a couple of "jitterbugs" who are assisting on it, the girl turns out a great disappointment, the gunman is rendered a fugitive with a moll and a dog who love him, and finally he is brought to bay on that peak in the High Sierras. And there he dies gallantly. It's a wonder the American flag wasn't wrapped about his broken corpse.

As gangster pictures go, this one has everything—speed, excitement, suspense, and that ennobling suggestion of futility that makes for irony and pity. Mr. Bogart plays the leading role with a perfection of hard-boiled vitality, and Ida Lupino, Arthur Kennedy, Alan Curtis, and a newcomer named Joan Leslie handle lesser roles effectively. Especially is Miss Lupino impressive as the adoring moll. As gangster pictures go—if they do—it's a perfect epilogue. Count on the old guard and Warners: they die but never surrender.
—*B.C., January 25, 1941*

THE HILL

Directed by Sidney Lumet: written by Ray Rigby and R. S. Allen. based on their play: cinematographer. Oswald Morris: edited by Thelma Connell: music by Art Noel and Don Pelosi: art designer. Herbert Smith: produced by Kenneth Hyman: released by Metro-Goldwyn-Mayer: Black and white. Running time: 122 minutes.

With: Sean Connery (Joe Roberts). Harry Andrews (Sergeant Major Wilson). Ian Hendry (Sergeant Williams). Ian Bannen (Sergeant Harris). Alfred Lynch (George Stevens) and Ossie Davis (Jacko King).

An aspect of military activity that is usually bypassed on the screen, except in such infrequent items as the little independent film, *The Brig,* is exposed in intensely graphic detail in Sidney Lumet's *The Hill,* a different kind of war film that came to the Sutton yesterday. That is the way men are treated in a military stockade—not one for prisoners of war but one for soldiers who have been condemned to punishment by their own officers.

In this long and unrelenting documentation of the kind of brutal, sadistic discipline meted out by the staff of a British military prison in North Africa during World War II, Mr. Lumet and a cast that must surely have suffered torment simply making this film have come up with a sobering revelation that inhumanity is not unique with the enemy.

By following the dismal fortunes of five soldiers brought to this stockade—men of varying types and courage—and noting especially the way these men behave when they are confronted with the camp's special torture, a great pile of sand and rock they are made to climb and descend in the withering desert heat, the director truly makes the viewer suffer almost as much as do the men. It is almost as much a test of the audience as it is of the prisoners.

After an hour or so of showing torture, the fire point of the drama is reached with death from exhaustion and nervous breakdown of one of the five men. Then the strongest of the lot—a hard-mouthed tankman, played by Sean Connery—determines to lodge a charge of murder against the most brutal of the staff, and this is the instigation that thrusts the drama to its bruising, ironic end.

Actually, the structure of the drama is no different from that of numerous prison films. The distinction is in the revelation of usually heroic characters being thus abused and in the smashing realism of Mr. Lumet's fierce imagery.

Harry Andrews is devastating as the sergeant major who runs the stockade—a stiff, controlled, tough administrator who is a real professional military

man—and Ian Hendry is brilliantly sinister as the evil sergeant who precipitates the crisis.

Mr. Connery is stark and sturdy as the usual underdog hero—quite a departure from the flashiness of his characterization of James Bond. Ossie Davis as a West Indian Negro who finally rebels, tears off his clothes, resigns from the army, struts out in his skivvies, and defies the staff, has the best scene and plays it superbly. It is a flamboyant gesture that draws a great audience response, but it is actually more theatrical than it is plausible.

Other men are excellent—Jack Weston, Roy Kinnear, and Alfred Lynch as the remaining members of the quintet and Ian Bannen and Michael Redgrave as staff more kindly disposed toward the prisoners. But unfortunately Mr. Lumet has engineered so much noise, shouting, screaming and babbling of myriad British accents through the film, that it is difficult to hear what anyone is saying.

However, it isn't what you hear but what you see that hurts.

—B.C., October 4, 1965

HIROSHIMA, MON AMOUR

Directed by Alain Resnais: written (in French. with English subtitles) by Marguerite Duras: cinematographers. Sacha Vierny and Michio Takahashi: edited by Henri Colpi. Anne Sarraute and Jasmine Chasny: music by Georges Delarue: production designer. Esaka Mayo: produced by Samy Halfon: released by Zenith International. Black and white. Running time: 88 minutes.

With: Emmanuelle Riva (She). Eiji Okada (He). Stella Dassas (Mother). Pierre Barbaud (Father) and Bernard Fresson (German Lover).

If Alain Resnais, producer-director of *Hiroshima, Mon Amour,* may be classified a member of the French "new wave," then he also must be listed as riding its crest. For his delicately wrought drama, which had its local premiere at the Fine Arts Theatre yesterday, is a complex yet compelling tour de force—as a patent plea for peace and the abolition of atomic warfare, as a poetic evocation of love lost and momentarily found, and as a curiously intricate but intriguing montage of thinking on several planes in Proustian style.

Although it presents, on occasion, a baffling repetition of words and ideas, much like vaguely recurring dreams, it, nevertheless, leaves the impression of a careful coalescence of art and craftsmanship.

With the assistance of Marguerite Duras, one of France's leading symbolic novelists (*The Sea Wall, Moderato Cantabile*), as well as the Nipponese technicians involved in this Franco-Japanese coproduction, M. Resnais is not merely concerned with the physical aspects of a short (two-day) affair between a Gallic actress, in Hiroshima to make a film, and a Japanese architect. He also explores the meanings of war, the woman's first love, and the interchange of thoughts as they emerge during the brief but supercharged romantic interlude.

A viewer, it must be stated at the outset, needs patience in order to appreciate the slow but calculated evolvement of the various levels of the film's drama, despite its fine, literal English subtitles. Neither M. Resnais nor Mlle. Duras are direct in their approach.

For the first fifteen minutes, our lovers, in intimate embrace, seemingly are savoring the ecstacies of their moment. Simultaneously, however, they are discussing Hiroshima, the 200,000 dead, the remembrance (shown in harrowingly stark newsreel and documentary footage of that monumental holocaust) of that frightful period in history. It is, in striking effect, an oblique but vivid reminder of the absolutes of love and death.

As his parable progresses, however, M. Resnais reveals through his principals, both of whom indicate that they are happily married, that our love-wracked heroine has been through a similar situation before. This elegiac affair is the sudden outgrowth of her previous liaison during World War II in her native Nevers, with a young German soldier, an act for which she was ostracized both by Nevers's citizens and her parents. Now, fourteen years later, she divulges in tortured snatches of remembrance that she is again suddenly, experiencing that initial, exquisite happiness.

It is here, when the pain of memory forces the actress to refer to her Japanese vis-à-vis as if he were the German of her "amour impossible," that Mlle. Duras's script becomes slightly bewildering. Also in the final quarter of the film, when the distracted lovers merely state and restate their devotion and indecision, the drama drops into unnecessary romantic vagueness and repetition.

Mlle. Duras's screenplay is, of course, largely a woman's point of view, one in which the nuances of love, physical and ephemeral, are dissected to a faré-thee-well. Despite this overemphasis, Emmanuelle Riva, a French actress who is making her screen debut in *Hiroshima, Mon Amour,* gives each word and phrase meaning and tenderness.

Since she and her partner are, in effect, the only two important players in the picture, it is notable that Mlle. Riva, a pale, blonde, wan type whose large eyes mirror beautifully the variations in her emotions, gives her heavy assignment professional polish and expression. Eiji Okada, as her confused lover, is obviously cast in a less weighty role, but the dark-haired, intense Mr. Okada, speaking French in strange, Oriental accents, nevertheless lends dignity and understanding to the characterization.

There is no doubt now that M. Resnais has chosen his proper metier. As a director who set himself an extremely difficult task, he expertly sustains the fragile moods of his theme most of the way. He also illustrates a rare expertise in his ability to show flashbacks, to intercut scenes of France and Hiroshima (where the picture was filmed) of today and yesterday and to draw the most from his principals and the factual footage he uses.

This offering represents the first feature film M. Resnais has done, although he has won a niche for himself with such documentaries as the Picasso *Guernica,* and others, not yet shown here publicly, like *Nuit et Brouillard* (*Night and Fog*), which deals with concentration camps. If *Hiroshima, Mon Amour* is any yardstick, M. Resnais seems to have assured himself a niche in the feature film field, too.

—A.W., May 17, 1960

HIS GIRL FRIDAY

Produced and directed by Howard Hawks; written by Charles Lederer, based on the play *The Front Page* by Ben Hecht and Charles MacArthur; cinematographer, Joseph Walker; edited by Gene Havlick; music by M.W. Stoloff; art designer Lionel Banks; released by Columbia Pictures. Black and white. Running time: 92 minutes.

With: Cary Grant (Walter Burns), Rosalind Russell (Hildy Johnson), Ralph Bellamy (Bruce Baldwin), Gene Lockhart (Sheriff Hartwell), Helen Mack (Mollie Malloy), Ernest Truex (Bensinger) and Porter Hall (Murphy).

They've replated *The Front Page* again, have slapped *His Girl Friday* on the masthead and are running it off at the Music Hall as a special woman's edition of the frenzied newspaper comedy Hecht and MacArthur first published back in 1931. Hildy Johnson is a girl reporter. She has just been divorced from managing editor Walter Burns and is threatening to take the night train to Albany, to matrimony, and to Bellamy (Ralph). The celebrated curtain line about the so-and-so's stealing the watch has gone by the board—the State Censor Board—but they have another just as cute if you can hear it.

That goes for most of the picture: the lines are all cute if you can hear them, but you can't hear many because everyone is making too much noise—the audience or the players themselves. Hysteria is one of the communicable diseases and *His Girl Friday* is a more pernicious carrier than Typhoid Mary. It takes you by the scruff of the neck in the first reel and it shakes you madly, bellowing hoarsely the while, for the remaining six or seven. Before it's over you don't know whether you have been laughing or having your ears boxed. The veriest bit on the strenuous side, if you follow us.

Charles Lederer, who wrote the adaptation, has transposed it so brilliantly it is hard to believe that Hecht and MacArthur were not thinking of Rosalind Russell, or someone equally high-heeled, when they wrote about the Hildy Johnson who once had a printer's ink transfusion from a Machiavellian managing editor and never again could qualify as a normal human being. It was a wild caricature, of course, and, if there ever were newspaper people like that, they went into limbo when Hecht and MacArthur, Gene Fowler, Joel Sayre and Nunnally Johnson died (journalistically) and went to Hollywood. Still, caricatures are fun if you don't have to put up with them too long and if they don't insist on being taken too seriously.

Under Howard Hawks's direction, the cast has acknowledged the clamoring script with performances that are hard, brittle, and strained to the breaking point, if not somewhat beyond, as though they were waiting for the camera to look the other way so they

could collapse with honor. Cary Grant's Walter Burns is splendid, except when he is being consciously cute. Mr. Bellamy's woebegone insurance man, Gene Lockhart's Sheriff Hartwell, Ernest Truex's sob-brother, Helen Mack's Mollie Malloy, John Qualen's Earl Williams, and—most especially—Billy Gilbert's governor's messenger, Joe Pettibone, are faces that stand out in the swirling hubbub.

Except to add that we've seen *The Front Page* under its own name and others so often before we've grown a little tired of it, we don't mind conceding *His Girl Friday* is a bold-faced reprint of what was once—and still remains—the maddest newspaper comedy of our times.

—*F.S.N., January 12, 1940*

THE HOMECOMING

Directed by Peter Hall; written by Harold Pinter, based on his play; cinematographer, David Watkin; edited by Rex Pike; production designer, John Bury; produced by Ely A. Landau; released by American Film Theater. Running time: 111 minutes.

With: Cyril Cusack (Sam), Ian Holm (Lenny), Michael Jayston (Teddy), Vivien Merchant (Ruth), Terence Rigby (Joey) and Paul Rogers (Max).

Harold Pinter's rabid comedy *The Homecoming* has been turned into a movie of astonishing dynamism by Peter Hall, who also directed the original London and Broadway productions, with six extraordinary English actors who, with one exception, appeared in the play on the stage. The film, the second offering in the American Film Theater series, opened yesterday at selected theaters.

The Homecoming is Pinter's most tumultuous full-length play, as menacing as *The Birthday Party,* as mysterious as *Old Times,* but so full of wild, essential life that questions about its meaning seem secondary if not superfluous.

One need not define life when one can point to it, which is what Pinter is doing in *The Homecoming,* with marvelous control of exaggerated language and gesture that have the effect of a fluoroscope. Pinter keeps giving us glimpses of interior furies that most of us prefer not to acknowledge in the daytime.

For some peculiar reason, these glimpses are often hilariously funny. It may be that we laugh at the outrageous behavior of the members of the Cockney family in *The Homecoming* for the same reason that we laugh at the terrible things that happen to characters in slapstick comedy, because it's happening to them and not to us.

The film, as far as I can tell from a reading of the stage text, is a practically untouched adaptation of the play, though Hall's camera never seems to intrude on the life of the play. It never embarrasses the actors by exposing them to be what they are. Most of the action continues to take place in the barren parlor of the North London house ruled by foul-mouthed old Max (Paul Rogers), the patriarch of a clan now reduced to three: his sons, Lenny (Ian Holm) and Joey (Terence Rigby), and his younger brother, Sam (Cyril Cusack), a chauffeur for a private firm.

Max is losing his grip. He roams the house as purposely as a convict trying to hide the aimlessness of his confinement. Lenny, a small-time pimp and a dandy, ridicules him and calls him an old prat. Joey, somewhat simpleminded, doesn't understand him and thinks mostly of going to the top as a boxer, just as soon as he masters the arts of defense and attack.

The fastidious Sam, when he isn't busy washing dishes, which greatly irritates Max, suggests that he might once have had an affair with Max's late wife, Jesse. Max's moods wander, like a mind, often in midspeech. He remembers Jesse fondly and then says: "She wasn't such a bad woman. Even though it made me sick just to look at her rotten stinking face, she wasn't a bad bitch."

Into this totally male pride come Max's eldest son, Teddy (Michael Jayston), a professor of philosophy at an American university, and his wife Ruth (Vivien Merchant). While Teddy watches with apparent complacency, the members of his family transform Ruth into a whore, a role with which she is not entirely unfamiliar and that she is willing to accept, as long as she is given a written contract.

The film is so much of an entity, so beautifully integrated, that its spell is never broken, not even with one intermission. The mood begins with the bigger-than-life noises we hear behind the opening credits—someone rummaging through a drawer that seems to contain everything from silverware and carpenter's tools to salvaged paperclips that no one will ever use—and does not let up until a final tableau that is both theatrical and cinematic.

Hall goes outside the house just once, when Ruth takes a late-night walk, but even the street we see her walk down is as sealed off from humanity as the interior of the house. It's not that we sense that other lives are not being lived elsewhere in Pinter's world, but rather that those lives are simply reflections and extentions of those Pinter has chosen to show us.

—V.C., November 13, 1973

HOOP DREAMS

Directed by Steve James: director of photography, Peter Gilbert: edited by Frederick Marx, Mr. James and Bill Haugse: music by Ben Sidran: produced by Mr. Marx, Mr. James and Mr. Gilbert: released by Fine Line Features. Running time: 171 minutes.

With: Steve James, William Gates, Arthur Agee, Emma Gates, Sheila Agee and Gene Pingatore.

At a high point in his young career, Arthur Agee, a fourteen-year-old basketball player at St. Joseph High School in Chicago, stands on the court with his idol, Isaiah Thomas. The NBA star is visiting his old school, and as Arthur goes one-on-one with his hero, the boy flashes a smile as big and joyous as any you've ever seen.

Four years later, Arthur's classmate William Gates, who also dreams obsessively about playing in the National Basketball Association, has progressed to the Nike All-America basketball camp, where college coaches look over high school players. Spike Lee visits and tells the students a cold-blooded truth: They are being used and the one way to protect themselves is to know it. "The only reason you are here is because you can make their schools win and they can make a lot of money," Mr. Lee says of the coaches. "This whole thing is about money." It is the kind of valuable advice boys like Arthur and William, from poor black neighborhoods, hear all too rarely.

Hoop Dreams is a brilliantly revealing documentary that follows Arthur and William through high school to their first year of college. Along the way it raises many potent questions, none more difficult than this: How can you encourage the kinds of dreams that transform Arthur's face while keeping harsh reality in sight?

The filmmakers, Steve James Frederick Marx and Peter Gilbert, spent four and a half years with the boys and their families, acquiring 250 hours of film. Their fascinating, suspenseful film turns the endless revision of the American dream into high drama. The story begins when Arthur and William are actively recruited by St. Joseph, a mainly white Roman Catholic school with a major basketball program. Just as the boys' paths seem settled—William is heading for a dazzling college career and pro prospects, while Arthur is spiraling downward—they face abrupt changes. *Hoop Dreams* is the profound social tale of these two emblematic boys, who are sucked into a system ready to toss them aside, disillusioned and uneducated, the minute they stumble on the basketball court.

Hoop Dreams will close the New York Film Festival on Sunday night, the first documentary ever to do so. (It will open in New York next Friday and around the country on October 21.) It is a daring choice for the prestigious closing-night slot because the movie, though finely made, is not about bravura filmmaking. Instead, *Hoop Dreams* affirms the role of film as a medium for exploring social issues. And like any important documentary, this one raises crucial questions beyond what is on-screen. How does the camera change the subjects' behavior? How well can the filmmakers, who are white, see beyond the stereotypes of poor black kids and their broken families?

Though it tries, *Hoop Dreams* doesn't find the complex people behind the stereotypes often enough; as viewers, we remain sympathetic voyeurs rather than intimates. The film's great achievement is to reveal the relentless way in which coaches and recruiters refuse to see Arthur and William as anything other than social clichés.

Arthur lives in the Cabrini-Green housing project with his parents and siblings. In the course of the film, Arthur's parents break up and get together again, and his father overcomes a crack addiction after serving time in prison. William lives with his single mother and older brother in a slightly better neighborhood. Both families are too dream-besotted themselves to offer good advice.

William's older brother, Curtis, failed in his own college basketball career and has invested his dreams in his brother. Arthur's father also missed out on a college career, and says of his son with a confidence that is eerily shortsighted, "I don't even think about him not making it."

St. Joseph seems the way to a pro career. Both boys are given partial scholarships, though they read at a fourth-grade level. Gene Pingatore, the head coach, who never lets the boys forget that he launched Isaiah Thomas, is the distillation of all the white coaches and recruiters in the film. He talks a good game about caring for the boys' future, but over and over the film captures his hideously callous behavior. The strongest proof is what happens to Arthur.

Arthur doesn't shine in sports or academics. "I've just never been around a lot of white people, but I can adjust," he says. When he starts behaving badly in class, Coach Pingatore tells the camera Arthur is reverting to the influence of "his environment." Arthur is tossed out of St. Joseph in the middle of his sophomore year because his family owes $1,500 in back tuition.

Two years later, when Arthur needs his freshman transcript to graduate from the local public school, St. Joseph's holds the records hostage until the Agees arrange to make monthly payments on the back tuition. In a brutal documentary moment, St. Joseph's finance director condescends to Mr. and Mrs. Agee, who act amazingly grateful for the chance to pay the old debt. The subjects could not have guessed what a painful impression they would all make.

William has financial problems, too. But he has raised his reading level and done well on the varsity team. St. Joseph's finds a private sponsor to take care of his share of the tuition.

Primed for success, William becomes the more articulate and vibrant of the two, with Arthur seeming guarded and shy. Then William injures his knee, and the camera closes in on his impassive face as the doctor says he might have to sit out a year. It's hard to guess how much of his stoicism is an act for the audience.

Arthur's mother becomes the warmest and fullest character, because she is the only one we see looking past the camera and talking to the person behind it. After celebrating Arthur's eighteenth birthday, she learns he has been cut off welfare, even though he is still a full-time student. "Do you all wonder sometime how am I living?" she asks, clearly talking to a person and not posterity. In all those hours of film, there were certainly other, unused moments when the barrier of the camera was broken down, but Sheila Agee must have done that a lot. She encourages her son, wears a Detroit Pistons sweatshirt and triumphantly passes a course to become a nurse's assistant. Yet she is plainly furious at St. Joseph's for what she considers the broken promises that let her son down and temporarily shattered his self-confidence.

In shaping *Hoop Dreams* into a dramatic two-hour-and-fifty-one-minute narrative, the filmmakers do an expert job of demonstrating the pressures and excitement surrounding the boys. Both have crowds cheering as they take last-minute shots in do-or-die games that might lead to the state championship.

By his junior year, William is getting dozens of letters from big-time basketball schools like Georgetown. One letter offers the lure, "We play on national television." Yet his grades have fallen so much he might be ineligible to play in college; he has fathered a child. He later recalls that when he went to Coach Pingatore for help dealing with his family, he was told, "Write them off."

Arthur, who has grown taller and wears a stylish fade haircut, has regained some confidence. But he has had a few weak seasons and hears from places like Mineral Area Junior College in Missouri. When he visits there, he finds they have no dorms. They do have an isolated house for the basketball team; six of the school's seven black students live there.

What is most disturbing about *Hoop Dreams* is that no one seems willing or equipped to help William and Arthur navigate between their dreams and reality. When William says wearily toward the end of the film, "Basketball is my ticket out of the ghetto," it sounds as if he is parroting a phrase that has been drilled into him, as if an alien has taken over his mind.

The story behind *Hoop Dreams* is not over, either. The TNT cable channel is planning to remake the story as a fictional movie for television. A book based on transcripts from the interviews will be released in the spring. Meanwhile, William and Arthur are now college seniors, William at Marquette University and Arthur at Arkansas State.

The National Collegiate Athletic Association has ruled, despite the filmmakers' appeals, that neither the boys nor their families may receive any money from the sale of the film because they would lose their amateur status and their scholarships. And just last week,

St. Joseph High School filed a civil suit for defamation against the filmmakers and the distributor, Fine Line Features.

Despite all the drama on- and offscreen, a particularly quiet moment best captures the life lesson of *Hoop Dreams* and is the scene most likely to have audiences cheering. William, about to graduate from St. Joseph's, tells Coach Pingatore of his college plans. "I'm going into communications," he says, "so when you come asking for donations, I'll know the right way to turn you down."

—*C.J., October 7, 1994*

HOPE AND GLORY

Written, produced and directed by John Boorman; director of photography, Philippe Rousselot; edited by Ian Crafford; music by Peter Martin; production designer, Anthony Pratt; released by Columbia Pictures. Running time: 112 minutes.

With: Sebastian Rice Edwards (Bill), Geraldine Muir (Sue), Sarah Miles (Grace), David Hayman (Clive), Sammi Davis (Dawn), Derrick O'Connor (Mac), Susan Woolridge (Molly), Jean-Marc Barr (Bruce) and Ian Bannen (Grandfather).

It's difficult to imagine anyone's remembrance of World War II as idyllic, but it's not impossible. In John Boorman's radiant *Hope and Glory*, the autobiographical hero is a young boy of just the right age, humor, and sensitivity to savor the adventure of which he finds himself a part.

The horror of war intrudes only intermittently into the London suburb where Bill (Sebastian Rice Edwards) and his family live. And when war does make its presence felt, it's often in unexpected ways: not just the burning houses and the scattered shrapnel, but also the German flier who parachutes into this street of identical row houses, surveys the crowd of neighbors, and calmly lights a cigarette before being led off, by a local constable, through someone's vegetable garden. It takes a young boy to marvel at the strangeness of all this, and a skilled filmmaker to recall it so clearly and so sweetly.

Mr. Boorman, the director of films including *Point*

Blank, *Deliverance,* and *The Emerald Forest,* has never shown anything like this temperament before. But *Hope and Glory* has an invitingly nostalgic spirit and a fine eye for the magical details that a little boy might notice. There is the incident involving fish, for example, after Bill's mother, Grace, has moved the family to a house on the Thames owned by her parents, who named their other daughters Faith, Hope and Charity. On one oddly peaceful day in this lovely setting, Bill and his little sister are sent by their wildly eccentric grandfather to catch fish, and warned not to come home empty-handed. The children have tried and failed, and are ready to despair, when a bomb blast kills every fish in the vicinity, thus providing an odd form of salvation.

Hope and Glory manages to be warmly personal without being private in the least. The details that are mystifying, like the fact that a sign in front of Bill's house names the place "Bhim-tam," are no less baffling to young Bill than they might be to a viewer (Mr. Boorman explains, in an autobiographical note introducing the film's published screenplay, that he himself never knew what this sign at his parents' house meant, either). Neither the local atmosphere nor the family history seems at all remote, and Mr. Boorman makes the film seem open and involving at every turn. Right from the scene establishing young Bill's first awareness of war—which comes in the form of sudden quiet when every lawnmower stops working on a Sunday afternoon, as the radio announcement is made—the film maintains an eccentric, childlike viewpoint that holds its audience's attention.

The key figures in Bill's life are almost all women, which is another of the film's peculiarities. Chief among them are his sturdily courageous mother (played by Sarah Miles, who's a good deal less excitable here than she is in other roles) and the rebellious teenage sister (Sammi Davis, who's especially fine) who creates a new crisis every day. From the film's rosy vantage point, the war is seen as having frightened and inconvenienced these relatives without much altering the essential pettiness of their daily lives, and from this the film derives a lot of its humor. There is bleakness, perhaps, in the carefully constructed view of Bill's mother and an old flame sharing a picnic on a beach, right next to the line of barbed wire, there to fend off enemy frogmen. But there's also

a comic aspect, and Mr. Boorman has managed to capture both without diminishing either.

Hope and Glory has a luminous look and a period feeling that's both unusual and convincing, to which Shirley Russell's costumes are a particularly key contribution. The ensemble acting is uniformly entertaining (Ian Bannen, as Bill's foxy Grandpa, is especially so), and the pacing almost dreamlike, as befits a reverie. The film's ending is especially sweet, affirming the boyish sense of wonder and bemusement that informs it all.

Hope and Glory will be shown tonight and Sunday as part of the New York Film Festival. It opens at the Baronet next Friday.

—*J.M., October 9, 1987*

HOTEL TERMINUS: THE LIFE AND TIMES OF KLAUS BARBIE

Produced and directed by Marcel Ophuls: directors of photography. Michael Davis. Pierre Boffety. Reuben Aaronson. Wilhelm Rosing. Lionel LeGros. Daniel Chabert and Paul Gonon: edited by Albert Jurgenson and Catherine Zins: released by Samuel Goldwyn Company. Running time: 267 minutes.

With: Klaus Barbie and various associates and friends.

Marcel Ophuls's *Hotel Terminus: The Life and Times of Klaus Barbie* begins with a deceptive sense of restraint and calm. In the opening sequence, a friend of Mr. Barbie's recalls a New Year's Eve party at which the former Gestapo officer took offense at some disrespectful remarks made about Hitler. The friend was amused that Mr. Barbie still might find some subjects not funny.

Cut to Lyons, where three former members of the French Resistance are playing pool and talking about Mr. Barbie's forthcoming trial for crimes against humanity, committed in and around Lyons in 1944 and 1945.

The aging Frenchmen now seem philosophical. Terrible things were done, that's true, but it was all such a long time ago. One fellow recalls that he was a fifteen-year-old bellboy at the Hotel Terminus when it was the Gestapo headquarters in Lyons. Were the Germans good tippers? They were, he says with a smile, "but we also cheated them a bit."

Sitting in front of a Christmas tree, a former American intelligence agent does his best to appear at ease and cooperative. He talks to Mr. Ophuls in a friendly, now-that-you-mention-it manner.

Oh, yes, he says, he certainly did use Mr. Barbie, no doubt about that. He worked with him closely, in fact, but he never had the feeling that Mr. Barbie was the sort of man who might be guilty of atrocities. Mr. Barbie was such a devilishly clever fellow that he wouldn't have to lower himself. A very old German farmer remembers Klaus as a boy he called "Sonny."

This early testimony is almost genial.

Yet *Hotel Terminus: The Life and Times of Klaus Barbie* quickly gathers the force and the momentum of a freight train that will not be stopped or sidetracked. It is inexorable in its pursuit of truth, not just about Barbie the "butcher of Lyons," but about the moral climate of his world and of ours today.

This spellbinding, four-and-a-half-hour film will be shown at the New York Film Festival today and on Saturday. It starts a commercial engagement Sunday at the Cinema Studio.

In form, *Hotel Terminus* is much like Mr. Ophuls's classic *Sorrow and the Pity* (1970), a vivid, harrowing, minutely detailed recollection of France under the German occupation as it was experienced in and around the town of Clermont-Ferrand. Like *The Sorrow and the Pity*, the new film is composed of dozens and dozens of interviews, each of which evokes another narrative within the principal narrative.

These accumulate, finally, to create a vast historical panorama far beyond the scope of conventional movie fiction. At the center there is the unprepossessing figure of Mr. Barbie himself, self-described as "privileged to act as a small but active member of the Führer's following."

A boyhood friend recalls Mr. Barbie as a good pal. In addition, he is, variously, "a Nazi idealist"; a man who would fondle a cat one minute and beat up a young girl the next; and a Nazi survivor who, in the immediate postwar years, was employed by American intelligence, both for his own talents and those of his informants, a network, one man says, stretching "from Portugal to Moscow." Mr. Barbie was a con artist who sold snake oil to his American benefactors.

At the end of his career, in South America before his extradition to Europe in 1983, he was a tireless hustler and deadly crackpot, wheeling and dealing in Bolivia and Peru where he was an active member of the German business communities, hobnobbing with politicians, arms dealers, and drug traffickers.

The witnesses to Mr. Barbie's life and times include his victims, his colleagues in the Gestapo (who are less defensive than his colleagues in American intelligence), veterans of the French Resistance, collaborators, historians, janitors, businessmen, leftists, rightists, neighbors, journalists and the film's most enigmatic character, Jacques Vergès, the man who defended Mr. Barbie at his trial last year.

The method is the same that Mr. Ophuls used in *The Sorrow and the Pity,* but *Hotel Terminus* is very different from that film and from Claude Lanzmann's *Shoah. The Sorrow and the Pity* is meditative, a sad but even-tempered film that can find pathos in the desperately frightened face of a woman, a collaborator, having her head shaved in front of an angry mob.

Shoah is almost unbearably mournful, not only because of the graphic testimony recalled so matter-of-factly by Mr. Lanzmann's witnesses, but also because there's scarcely a frame of film that doesn't suggest the manner by which time softens the past. *Shoah* says that some things must not be forgotten, but distance blurs the image and, no matter how we try to remember it, pain recedes. The images of a concentration camp as it looks today—a peaceful, ghostly, park-like setting with well-tended grass—are metaphors for the impermanence of all things, including memory.

In *Hotel Terminus* Mr. Ophuls is anything but meditative. He's angry and sarcastic and, as the film goes on, he becomes increasingly impatient. He argues with reluctant witnesses. He pushes his camera into a stranger's face and laughs when the stranger refuses to cooperate. (One such stranger is an ex-president of Bolivia, caught as he's putting out his garbage.)

The tempo of the crosscutting between witnesses speeds up, on occasion so maddeningly that one forgets the identity of the speaker. At times, it seems as if the director were telling some self-serving interviewee to stop all this nonsense and come clean. At other times, he appears to fear that he simply won't be able

461

to get everything in. The more he digs, the more he finds.

Mr. Ophuls is not dealing with some vague, comfortingly abstract concept of guilt, but with provable guilt, which includes guilt by association, by stupidity, by naïveté, and, most of all, by deed.

The film is rich with the details of how people look, sound, and behave, and with the details of middle-class decor, from the rugs on the floor to the pictures on the walls. There are plenty of things a film cannot do, but no novelist could possibly set a scene with the inventorying eye of the Ophuls camera.

Hotel Terminus leaves certain questions unanswered, but that's all right too. One longs to learn more about the rabidly anticommunist René Hardy, twice acquitted of charges that he betrayed his Resistance comrades, and about Mr. Vergès, who attempted to defend Mr. Barbie by equating Nazi atrocities with France's colonial policies. In any case, the questions are raised.

The Barbie trial is something of an anticlimax in the film, as it was in fact when Mr. Barbie refused to take the stand. Yet *Hotel Terminus* proceeds to its conclusion with the breathtaking relentlessness of superior fiction. It's a fine, serious work by a filmmaker unlike any other. Great.

—*V.C., October 6, 1988*

THE HOURS

Directed by Stephen Daldry: written by David Hare. based on the novel by Michael Cunningham: director of photography. Seamus McGarvey: edited by Peter Boyle: music by Philip Glass: production designer. Maria Djurkovic: produced by Scott Rudin and Robert Fox: released by Paramount Pictures. Running time: 110 minutes.

With: Nicole Kidman (Virginia Woolf). Julianne Moore (Laura Brown). Meryl Streep (Clarissa Vaughan). Stephen Dillane (Leonard Woolf). Miranda Richardson (Vanessa Bell). John C. Reilly (Dan Brown). Jack Rovello (Richie). Toni Collette. (Kitty). Ed Harris (Richard Brown). Allison Janney (Sally Lester). Claire Danes (Julia Vaughan) and Jeff Daniels (Louis Waters).

In *The Hours* Nicole Kidman tunnels like a ferret into the soul of a woman besieged by excruciating bouts of mental illness. As you watch her wrestle with the demon of depression, it is as if its torment has never been shown on the screen before. Directing her desperate, furious stare into the void, her eyes not really focusing, Ms. Kidman, in a performance of astounding bravery, evokes the savage inner war waged by a brilliant mind against a system of faulty wiring that transmits a searing, crazy static into her brain.

But since that woman is the English writer Virginia Woolf (a prosthetic nose helps Ms. Kidman achieve an uncanny physical resemblance), her struggle is a losing battle. On March 28, 1941, Woolf, hounded by inner voices while in the throes of her fourth breakdown, put a stone in her pocket and drowned herself in the Ouse River near the English country house she shared with her husband, Leonard. And in the opening scene of *The Hours,* the eloquent, somber screen adaptation of Michael Cunningham's meditation on that suicide (it won the 1998 Pulitzer Prize for fiction), Woolf scrawls an anguished farewell letter to her husband, then hurries into the muddy water like Joan of Arc embracing the fire, accompanied by the churning, ethereal strains of Philip Glass's score.

The deeply moving film, directed by Stephen Daldry (*Billy Elliot*) from a screenplay by David Hare that cuts to the bone, is an amazingly faithful screen adaptation of a novel that would seem an unlikely candidate for a movie. A delicate, layered reflection that skips around through time, *The Hours,* which opens today in New York, is Mr. Cunningham's homage to Woolf's first great novel, *Mrs. Dalloway,* published in 1925.

Woolf's novel details a day in the life of Clarissa Dalloway, a conventional upper-class Englishwoman giving a party, who experiences nagging intimations of the more adventurous life she might have led. On the same day, Septimus Warren Smith, a character in the novel whom she never meets but with whom she shares some of the same observations, commits suicide. Five years ago *Mrs. Dalloway* was adapted into a shallow, unsatisfying film starring Vanessa Redgrave. In accomplishing the virtually impossible feat of bringing to the screen that novel's introspective essence, the director and the screenwriter of *The Hours*

462

have righted a wrong, albeit by proxy, through Mr. Cunningham's intuitive channeling.

A central idea animating *Mrs. Dalloway* and embodied in its stream-of-consciousness language is that people who never meet, like Clarissa Dalloway and Septimus Warren Smith, are connected by experiencing the same external events. *The Hours* extends that idea through the decades to celebrate the timelessness of great literature by placing the author, her fictional alter ego and two of her latter-day readers in the same sphere of consciousness.

Interweaving flashbacks from Woolf's life as she was writing *Mrs. Dalloway* with scenes from the lives of Laura Brown (Julianne Moore), a Southern California housewife and mother in 1951, and Clarissa Vaughan (Meryl Streep), a New York book editor living in contemporary Greenwich Village, their stories blend into a lofty, mystical theme and variations on Woolf's novel.

Laura, who is depressed and agitated, is reading *Mrs. Dalloway* on the same day she is baking a birthday cake for her husband, Dan (John C. Reilly), a blunt, hale World War II veteran who dotes on her and barely notices her anguish. Observing and absorbing Laura's distress is her timid, fiercely clinging young son, Richie (Jack Rovello). While baking the cake, Laura receives a surprise visit from a brightly perky neighbor, Kitty (Toni Collette), who is about to go into the hospital to be tested for cancer and admits she's frightened.

Meanwhile, in New York, Clarissa Vaughan (named after Woolf's character) is planning a celebration for her closest friend, Richard Brown (Ed Harris), a poet in the advanced stages of AIDS who has just won a prestigious award. As the movie folds these stories together, it emerges that Richard is Laura's grown-up son. And in a huge risk that pays off, the movie gives the dying poet a sudden flashback to the scared little boy he was (and fundamentally still is). Another bold surreal touch imagines Laura lying on a bed that's suddenly engulfed by the river that took Woolf.

Clarissa and Richard were lovers when they were younger, but both eventually chose partners of the same sex. Richard had a long affair with Louis Waters (Jeff Daniels), now a college professor in San Francisco, who shows up for the celebration of the award. Clarissa has lived for years with a woman, Sally Lester (Allison Janney), and has a college-age daughter, Julia (Claire Danes), from an unknown sperm donor.

Woolf herself was attracted to both men and women, and although her literary alter ego, Mrs. Dalloway, is married to a member of Parliament, on the day of the party her mind darts back to a kiss exchanged with another woman years earlier. In the movie, Woolf's sister Vanessa Bell (Miranda Richardson) visits from London with her family. And Woolf, in a moment of panic, plants a desperate, passionate kiss on Vanessa's mouth. In California, Laura Brown spontaneously reaches out to Kitty with a lingering kiss that is more than polite.

Some of the movie's most wrenching moments show Leonard Woolf (Stephen Dillane) frantically reaching out to his troubled wife and being rebuffed. It's not that the Woolfs don't love each other, but the agony Virginia is enduring can't be touched by love or reason. These moments bring home the film's deepest and most intimidating insight about the essential aloneness of the individual and its feminist corollary: that appearances to the contrary, women in their deepest selves do not and should not define themselves in terms of men.

Clarissa is the most grounded character, probably because she has been the truest to her instincts and has the most love to give back. When Richard, whose good days have dwindled to none, accuses Clarissa (whom he calls Mrs. Dalloway) of forcing him to stay alive, it's obviously true. Mr. Harris, more than matching his tumultuous performance in *Pollock,* creates a wrenching, incendiary portrait of a man ravaged with illness, who thrashes with rage and bitterness, his emotions burning out of control like a torched oil slick on a contaminated lake.

Ms. Streep's frayed, moody Clarissa is no hovering, haloed angel of mercy but an intensely self-aware, vulnerable urbanite worn down by her efforts to do the right thing. Through Ms. Streep's performance, the movie captures, like no film I can remember, the immediate, continuing interaction of experience and memory in the instinctive human drive to infuse the moment with meaning and value.

Ms. Moore's Laura, although a reader, lacks Clarissa's or Richard's literary armament and is the more vulnerable for it. A wistful, frightened creature embarrassed by her own china-doll fragility, she longs to escape a life that feels all wrong but has little notion of where to go or what to do. Ms. Moore brings to the role the same luminous demureness that colors her portrayal of an innocent, well-meaning Connecticut housewife whose world shatters in *Far From Heaven*.

All these brooding, complicated people are prototypical Woolfian figures blessed and afflicted with the same feverish imaginations, perplexing ambiguities and brightly etched memories of their younger, more hopeful selves. Yet for all its sexual complexity, *The Hours* is not really about sex. The film, like the novel, is a sustained meditation on connection, human possibility, the elusive dream of happiness and the sometimes seductive call of death.

Although suicide eventually tempts three of the film's characters, *The Hours* is not an unduly morbid film. Clear eyed and austerely balanced would be a more accurate description, along with magnificently written and acted. Mr. Glass's surging minimalist score, with its air of cosmic abstraction, serves as ideal connective tissue for a film that breaks down temporal barriers.

Appropriately it is Woolf who has the definitive final word on the questions lurking in the backs of the minds of the film's characters with their flickering life forces.

Leonard Woolf, querying his wife about her decision to kill off a character in *Mrs. Dalloway*, asks her why.

She answers carefully, "Someone has to die that the rest of us should value life more."

—S.H., December 27, 2002

HOUSEHOLD SAINTS

Directed by Nancy Savoca; screenplay by Ms. Savoca and Richard Guay, based on the novel by Francine Prose; director of photography, Bobby Bukowski; edited by Beth Kling; production designer, Kalina Ivanov; produced by Mr. Guay and Peter Newman; released by Fine Line Features. Running time: 124 minutes.

With: Tracey Ullman (Catherine Falconetti), Vincent D'Onofrio (Joseph Santangelo), Judith Malina (Carmela Santangelo), Michael Rispoli (Nicky Falconetti), Victor Argo (Lino Falconetti) and Michael Imperioli (Leonard Villanova).

After Nancy Savoca made *True Love*, her wonderfully funny and candid-looking film about a Bronx wedding, she surely could have taken the traditional route to Hollywood. *True Love* was so promising that it could have allowed Ms. Savoca to make films much bigger and blander, but instead she has retained her idiosyncratic tastes. Her third film, after the 1990 *Dogfight*, is *Household Saints*, a warm, rueful, thoroughly peculiar tale set in Little Italy. The story is filled with strange, homespun miracles, and this single-minded little film could be counted as one of them.

Adapted with exceptional skill from the novel by Francine Prose (Ms. Savoca wrote the screenplay with her husband, Richard Guay), *Household Saints* spans three generations in two small Italian families. Those families are brought together with the help of a card game and a butcher shop. "Man deals, and God stacks the deck," says one character, who happens to be a ghost. He aptly describes the film's view of spiritual matters.

Ms. Savoca, who has a way of magnifying small, unglamorous events until they become unaccountably magical, sees a supreme inevitability in the occurrence that begins this story. It is a hot summer night, and Joseph Santangelo (Vincent D'Onofrio), a sly young butcher, wins Catherine Falconetti (Tracey Ullman) in a pinochle game. He bets her father a blast of cold air from the Santangelo meat locker, and in the process he casts a kind of spell. The film actually suggests that everything about this couple's destiny, and the odd life of their fiercely devout daughter, Teresa (Lili Taylor), was determined the moment Joseph opened that freezer.

Ms. Prose's novel makes a clear connection between the Falconetti family, renowned for its bad luck, and Maria Falconetti, the haunting star of Carl Dreyer's 1928 film *The Passion of Joan of Arc*. (Catherine, an avid reader of Silver Screen magazine as the story begins in the late 1940's, recalls vaguely that one of her relatives was once an actress.) Since Teresa will later strive for sainthood in her own way, the link is interesting and inexplicable, as are many of the film's background motifs. Ms. Savoca underscores certain quirky details—the sudden resuscitation of house plants, the amazing importance of sausage in the lives of the Santangelos—without overexplaining them. The film, like its fundamental subject, works in mysterious ways.

The fourth major figure in *Household Saints,* a film whose minor roles are also very well cast, is Carmela, Joseph's witch of a mother. Played with gleeful nastiness by Judith Malina, she uses the full force of her many superstitions to make Catherine miserable, once she realizes that her son is hell-bent on having this lank-haired, sullen girl. Joseph has suddenly become determined to marry Catherine, not only because he has won her but also because her virginity and drabness intrigue him somehow.

The film includes a long, entertainingly wretched dinner sequence during which the two families meet and Carmela offers some unmistakably hostile opinions about Catherine's cooking. The old woman also boasts of having been so poor she "picked shells out of the garbage at Umberto's Clam House—and believe me, I made a delicious soup!" "When?" her son wants to know.

An unexpectedly tender wedding night scene between Joseph and his sulky bride gives *Household Saints* one of its occasional opportunities to burst into pure fantasy. Others come from *Madama Butterfly,* which is an intense preoccupation for Catherine's half-crazy brother (Michael Rispoli). Carmela has her own fanciful side, conversing with her dead husband and becoming certain that Catherine, once she becomes pregnant, will give birth to a chicken. Carmela forces Catherine to pray that this will not happen. Somehow the old woman's religious devotion becomes a curse in its own right. After Carmela dies, an event quickly followed by the first flourishes of color in the dim apartment she has shared with the newlyweds, her spirit somehow reasserts itself through their baby, Teresa.

Ms. Taylor gives an eerie, radiant performance as the teenage Teresa, who yearns to join a convent and is thwarted by her parents. Although Ms. Taylor doesn't appear until an hour and a quarter into the film, she dominates it the rest of the way. And by the time Teresa experiences a miraculous vision of Jesus as she obsessively irons her boyfriend's shirt, it's clear that *Household Saints* is too single-minded to concern itself with credibility in the usual sense. The director is able both to handle the fancifulness of her material and to evoke the pop-cultural background of the early 1970's with a few well-chosen strokes. The latter touches underscore Teresa's utter isolation from the ordinary world.

Household Saints, an offbeat, involving story told with perfect confidence, is credibly acted despite the difficulty of its central roles. Ms. Ullman, who remains deliberately subdued, and especially Mr. D'Onofrio, who makes a warm and subtle butcher, manage to evolve convincingly over time. Ms. Malina turns her character's meanness into a comic virtue. Ms. Taylor strikes a note of fascinating ambiguity, which is just what the film requires. Equally effective in a smaller role is Michael Imperioli as the young man who cares for Teresa but is dumbfounded when he sees beyond her beatific smile.

—J.M., September 15, 1993

HOUSE OF GAMES

Directed by David Mamet; written by Mr. Mamet, based on a story cowritten with Jonathan Katz; director of photography, Juan Ruiz Anchia; edited by Trudy Ship; music by Alaric Jans; production designer, Michael Merritt; produced by Michael Hausman; released by Orion Pictures. Running time: 102 minutes.

With: Lindsay Crouse (Margaret Ford), Joe Mantegna (Mike), Mike Nussbaum (Joey), Lilia Skala (Dr. Littauer), J. T. Walsh (Businessman), Willo Hausman (Girl with Book) and Karen Kohlhaas (Prison Ward Patient).

Quite early in *House of Games,* David Mamet's entertaining, deadpan, seriocomic melodrama about con artists, there's a backroom poker game that sets the tone for everything that comes after.

Though the players could withdraw at any point, they don't, this being a serious game. Raises are seen, and raised again. The pot accumulates. "Everybody stays. Everybody pays," says the dealer. Tensions mount and tempers shorten like fuses burning in slow motion. Somebody must be bluffing, and somebody must lose, though there's nothing in the book that says the bluffer must lose or that the best hand wins.

That's the fascination of this insidiously addictive game in which the loser, if he plays his cards right, takes all. It's also the fun of the film with which Mr. Mamet, poker player and Pulitzer Prize–winning playwright, makes a fine, completely self-assured debut directing his original screenplay. Sometimes he's bluffing outrageously, but that's all right too.

In movies, as in poker, it's not always what you do but the way you do it. Or, as they say around the poker table, "A man with style is a man who can smile."

In *House of Games* a lot of other things are said, some of them unintentional howlers. "You need joy!" says a psychoanalyst to a woman in need, as if prescribing a detergent. But there's also the scam expert who reasons: "We all gotta live in an imperfect world. I acted atrociously, but I do that for a living." The movie never goes so far wrong that it can't retrieve its illusions.

House of Games will be shown tonight at Avery Fisher Hall, closing the 25th New York Film Festival with a presentation in which expectations are fulfilled. The film begins its regular commercial engagement here Wednesday at the D. W. Griffith Theater.

With *House of Games* it's clear that Mr. Mamet not only knows exactly how he wants his work to sound, but also how it should look. Though photographed on location in Seattle, *House of Games* contains no easily identifiable landmarks, no tourist attractions.

The movie remains ambiguously, mysteriously dislocated, not to give the impression that the setting is Anycity, U.S.A., but to emphasize the banality of place to its particular characters. For the sorts of things that occupy them, one city is as good as another. They're not the sort of people who look at scenery. They're floaters.

New to this world is Margaret Ford (Lindsay Crouse), a successful, severely stylish psychoanalyst, author of the new best-seller, *Driven,* a series of studies of obsessive behavior. Through one of her patients, a compulsive gambler who's alternately suicidal and abusive ("You do nothing. This whole thing is a con game"), Margaret decides to investigate the world of crooked gamblers, swindlers and confidence men, possibly for a new book.

Her initially reluctant docent is Mike (Joe Mantegna), a smooth-talking fellow of indeterminate age who appears to have learned how to be sincere by practicing in front of a mirror. Except for his gift of gab, everything about Mike is slightly bogus, his anger as well as his cool. His facial expressions never quite match what he says but, for Margaret, this is his charm as well as his value. He's also a fund of arcane information and, as a reader of character, as good as any analyst.

Not much more can be reported without revealing the twists, turns, and reversals by which *House of Games* proceeds. Mr. Mamet's screenplay builds much like a whopping-good poker game in which the stakes become so high that the players, having invested so much, can't afford to pull out. One may have reservations about the film's ending, but the ending, I suspect, was the point toward which the writer was aiming before he put one word to paper.

There'll be further reservations about the film's style, which has something of Mike's sincerity about it. It's deliberately artificial, which is both comic and scary. The sometimes very funny, bizarre Mamet dialogue is spoken in intense monotones, a manner designed to call attention to itself.

Yet one hears the words as if they were italicized. Mostly this works extraordinarily well, though there are times, especially when the camera comes in for a tight close-up on the speaker, when the artifice wears thin. One sees the actor within the character who is speaking the lines, as well as the man, just offscreen, who wrote the screenplay and is monitoring everything the actor does.

Though *House of Games* is not of the dramatic heft of the playwright's *American Buffalo* and *Glengarry Glen Ross,* the screenplay is the first true Mamet work to reach the screen, and the direction illuminates it at every turn. Both Miss Crouse and Mr. Mantegna and the supporting actors, including Mike Nussbaum, J. T. Walsh and Steve Goldstein, are splendidly in touch, not only with character but also with the sense of the film.

Early in *House of Games,* guns are produced, in effect, onstage. According to the rules of theater, guns, once produced, must be used. Though Mr. Mamet abides by the rules, don't be put off by that. *House of Games,* the vision of a secure moviemaker, is a wonderfully devious comedy.

—*V.C., October 11, 1987*

HOW GREEN WAS MY VALLEY

Directed by John Ford; written by Philip Dunne, based on the novel by Richard Llewellyn; cinematographer, Arthur Miller; edited by James B.

Clark: music by Alfred Newman: art designer. Richard Day: produced by Darryl F. Zanuck: released by Twentieth Century Fox. Black and white. Running time: 118 minutes.

With Walter Pidgeon (Mr. Gruffydd). Maureen O'Hara (Angharad). Donald Crisp (Gwilym Morgan). Anna Lee (Bronwen). Roddy McDowall (Huw). John Loder (Ianto). Sara Allgood (Mrs. Morgan). Barry Fitzgerald (Cyfartha) and Patric Knowles (Ivor).

The majesty of plain people and the beauty that shines in the souls of simple, honest folk are seldom made the topics of extensive discourse upon the screen. Human character in its purer, humbler aspects is not generally considered enough. Yet out of the homely virtues of a group of Welsh mining folk—and out of the modest lives of a few sturdy leaders in their midst—Darryl Zanuck, John Ford and their associates at Twentieth Century Fox have fashioned a motion picture of great poetic charm and dignity, a picture rich in visual fabrication and in the vigor of its imagery, and one which may truly be regarded as an outstanding film of the year. *How Green Was My Valley* is its title, and it opened last night at the Rivoli.

Persons who have read the haunting novel by Richard Llewellyn from which the story is derived will comprehend at its mention the deeply affecting quality of this film. For Mr. Ford has endeavored with eminent success to give graphic substance to the gentle humor and melancholy pathos, the loveliness and aching sentiment, of the original. And Mr. Zanuck has liberally provided with the funds of his studio a production that magnificently reproduces the sharp contrasts of natural beauties and the harsh realities of a Welsh mining town. In purely pictorial terms, *How Green Was My Valley* is a stunning masterpiece.

If, then, it fails to achieve a clear dramatic definition and never quite comes across with forceful, compelling impact this must be charged to the fact that the spirit of the original is too faithfully preserved. Mr. Llewellyn was recounting the sessions of sweet, silent thought wherein an old man was summoning the remembrance of happy things past—the fond recollections of his youth and his cheerful home on a Welsh hillside, his father and mother and brothers, and the joys and griefs of those who lived by the pit. His was a story told in reverie, episodically, running through a period of years.

And that is the form of the screenplay that Phillip Dunne has prepared. With several alterations but no major changes in the tale, this is the story of the Morgans, a Celtic mining clan, as seen through the eyes of Huw, the youngest of the brood. It is the story of Huw's "dada," a strong but gentle man; his mother, a sweet and tireless woman who loved her large family with all her heart; his hot-tempered, fearless brothers and his beautiful sister who married not wisely but well; of the pastor, Mr. Gruffydd, who inspired Huw with spiritual zeal and a thirst for knowledge, but never gained his own desire. And it is, by implication, the story of a good people's doom, the story of how the black coal wrung so perilously from the fair earth darkens the lives of those who dig it and befouls the verdant valley in which they live.

And that is the weakness of this picture. For in spite of its brilliant detail and its exquisite feeling for plain, affectionate people, it never forms a concrete pattern of their lives. Opportunities for dramatic intensity, such as that in which Huw saves his mother's life, are deliberately thrown away. And the obvious climactic episode, in which Huw's father is killed in the mine, is nothing more than a tragic incident that brings the story to a close. Apparently the intention was to have the film follow the formless flow of life. But an audience finds it hard to keep attentive to jerky episodes for the space of two hours.

However, you can never expect to see a film more handsomely played. Little Roddy McDowall, who has had only one previous small role in Hollywood, is superb as the boy Huw, with his deeply sensitive face and shy but stalwart manner. No one that we can think of could bring more strength and character to the difficult role of Gwilym Morgan than Donald Crisp, and Walter Pidgeon plays Mr. Gruffydd as a true, simple, forthright man of God. Excellent, too, are Sara Allgood as the mother, Maureen O'Hara as the beautiful Angharad, who marries the wrong man, Anna Lee as loyal Bronwen, and a cast too numerous to mention. Only Morton Lowry as Mr. Jonas, the teacher, and Marten Lamont as the husband of Angharad are permitted to overplay.

More than a word should be said for the perfect reproduction of a stone colliery, stone houses and chapel built in the Ventura hills of California especially for this film. And more than a mere nod accorded to the beautiful Welsh choral singing so generously spaced through it. If only the structure of the story were as sound as everything else, there is great (as the Welsh idiom has it) that this picture would be. As a matter of fact, there is fine that this picture is, anyhow.

—B.C., October 29, 1941

HOW TO MARRY A MILLIONAIRE

Directed by Jean Negulesco: written by Nunnally Johnson, based on the play *The Greeks Had a Word for It* by Zoë Akins and the play *Loco* by Dale Eunson and Katherine Albert: cinematographer, Joseph MacDonald: edited by Louis Loeffler: music by Alfred Newman and Cyril J. Mockridge: art designers, Lyle Wheeler and Leland Fuller: produced by Mr. Johnson: released by Twentieth Century Fox. Running time: 95 minutes.

With: Marilyn Monroe (Pola), Betty Grable (Loco), Lauren Bacall (Schatz Page), David Wayne (Freddie Denmark), Rory Calhoun (Eben) and Cameron Mitchell (Tom Brookman).

In the lingo of merchandising there is a neat word— "packaging"—for the business of putting up a product in a container of deceptive size and show. And that, in a manner of speaking, is the word for what Twentieth Century Fox has done in fetching an average portion of very light comedy in its *How to Marry a Millionaire*.

Around a frivolous story of the maneuvering of three dumb blondes to hook themselves wealthy husbands, regardless of the usual ardent urge, the Fox boys have tossed the imposing wrapper of their new wide-screen CinemaScope and put the whole thing forth as an opportunity in entertainment that you can't afford to miss. Within the mammoth dimensions of their giant-economy-size screen, they have dribbled a moderate measure of conventional, wisecracking fun. As premiums, to take up the air space, they have put Betty Grable, Marilyn Monroe and Lauren Bacall. And that constitutes the bargain package. It is obtainable at Loew's State and the Globe.

Why beat around the bush about it? This chuckle-some account of how three girls—all of them beautiful New York models—go gunning for rich old bucks looks even more skimpy and trivial on the big panel screen than it is. Plucked from a play by Zoë Akins, *The Greeks Had a Word for It*—which was done as a film with Madge Evans, Ina Claire and Joan Blondell long years ago—it does find some nimble, obvious humor in the hardworking efforts of the dames and in the wriggling evasions of their nominated prey.

Miss Grable, as a breezy huntress who cuts out a skittish gent, Fred Clark, and shamelessly pursues him right up to his snowbound lodge in Maine, is the funniest of the ladies. And she does work the simple running gag of thinking she is going to an Elks convention for as much meager jest as it contains. Her offscreen capitulation to a forest ranger, Rory Calhoun, is by far the most sensible and painless bit of feminine behavior in the film.

As the hardheaded "brain" of the trio, Miss Bacall has a cold and waspish way of regimenting her playmates or plunging for the heart of William Powell, and her last-minute switch to Cameron Mitchell is a grudging and cheerless giving-in.

However, the baby-faced mugging of the famously shaped Miss Monroe does compensate in some measure for the truculence of Miss Bacall. Her natural reluctance to wear eyeglasses when she is spreading the glamour accounts for some funny farce business of missing signals and walking into walls. As the gentlemen of her favor, Alex D'Arcy and David Wayne throw a slight bit of comical flavor into the thinness of the film.

But the substance is still insufficient for the vast spread of screen that CinemaScope throws across the front of the theater, and the impression it leaves is that of nonsense from a few people in a great big hall.

It is true that producer Nunnally Johnson, who also wrote the script, and Jean Negulesco, who directed, have attempted to fill the mammoth screen with extravagant scenic adornments and some fine panoramic displays. Some shots of the New York skyline as seen from the Upper Bay, of La Guardia and Kansas City airports, and of snow-covered timberland (in Maine) are visually exciting. The color, when firm, is very good. But the total effect of these glimpses is one of proud but nonessential showing off.

As a matter of fact, these cut-in pictures seem almost as unmatched and remote as some excellent footage, included on the program, showing a bit of Britain's Coronation parade. The straight panoramic picturization of masses of marching troops in the drizzle of a famous day in London is more stirring than the feature film.

Likewise, a Disney cartoon item, titled *Toot, Whistle, Plunk and Boom,* manifests more fulfillment of the wide screen than does *How to Marry a Millionaire.* A stretch of playing by the Fox symphonic orchestra is static, pretentious and dull.

One thing more: it is painfully evident that some of the technical "bugs" of CinemaScope, such as the tendency to jump out of focus and the "washing" of color at the end of shots, are still doing mischief in the system. Until these are cleared, at least, it is difficult to pass judgment on the comfort and harmony of the device.

—*B.C., November 11, 1953*

HOWARDS END

Directed by James Ivory; written by Ruth Prawer Jhabvala, based on the novel by E.M. Forster; director of photography, Tony Pierce-Roberts; edited by Andrew Marcus; music by Richard Robbins; production designer, Luciana Arrighi; produced by Ismail Merchant; released by Sony Pictures Classics. Running time: 145 minutes.

With: Vanessa Redgrave (Ruth Wilcox), Helena Bonham Carter (Helen Schlegel), Emma Thompson (Margaret Schlegel), Prunella Scales (Aunt Juley), Sam West (Leonard Bast), Anthony Hopkins (Henry Wilcox), James Wilby (Charles Wilcox), Jemma Redgrave (Evie Wilcox), Nicola Duffett (Jacky Bast) and Barbara Hicks (Miss Avery).

It's time for legislation decreeing that no one be allowed to make a screen adaptation of a novel of any quality whatsoever if Ismail Merchant, James Ivory and Ruth Prawer Jhabvala are available, and if they elect to do the job. Trespassers should be prosecuted, possibly condemned, sentenced to watch *Adam Bede* on *Masterpiece Theater* for five to seven years.

In case you've been living inside a pinball machine for the last several decades, Mr. Merchant, the pro-

ducer; Mr. Ivory, the director and Mrs. Jhabvala, the writer, are the team responsible for, among other films, the screen adaptations of Henry James's *Bostonians,* E. M. Forster's *Room with a View,* and Evan S. Connell's *Mr. and Mrs. Bridge.*

They triumph again with their entertaining, richly textured film translation of Forster's fourth novel, *Howards End,* opening today at the Fine Arts.

Like the novel, which was published in 1910, the film is elegant, funny and romantic. Though intensely serious in its concerns, it is as escapist as a month in an English countryside so idyllic that it probably doesn't exist.

Forster is not passé, but time has played tricks on his work. The shapeliness of his prose and his plotting still satisfies. The wit remains piercing and seemingly painless. "All men are equal," he writes in *Howards End,* "all men, that is to say, who possess umbrellas."

Yet our world is now so different from Forster's that we follow the drawing-room war in *Howards End,* seen in the confrontation of the two high-minded Schlegel sisters with the members of the rich, acquisitive Wilcox family, as if it were a fantastic spectacle, a time out of time.

Howards End, set at the end of the Edwardian era, doesn't even dimly perceive World War I, to say nothing of World War II, the Holocaust, the Bomb, and the possibility of the planet's extinction. The stakes being fought over in this film are high, but no one is killed, with the exception of poor Leonard Bast, and he scarcely counts (this is a Forster irony), since he is of the lower orders.

It's easy for us to shake our heads with Forster over the inequities built into England's class system, although that same system provides the stability of the structure in which such drawing room wars can be fought. Forster was a social critic capable of savagery, but for today's film audiences, *Howards End* is so much fun that it becomes a guilty pleasure. Thank heaven for inequities.

Although Leonard Bast (Sam West), a rather dull bank clerk who aspires to culture, is the unwitting instrument for the story's optimistic resolution, he is at the center of the film only when he is invited to call by the brainy Margaret Schlegel (Emma Thompson) and her younger, prettier, more headstrong sister, Helen (Helena Bonham Carter).

The Schlegel sisters are well-bred, well-read, music-loving people for whom the life of the mind is as natural as fine food and drink. Their serene London existence is forever destroyed by the richer, cruder, altogether (it seems at first) more dynamic Wilcoxes, whom they have met (before the film starts) while on a holiday abroad.

Sticking to the novel with unhurried fidelity, Mrs. Jhabvala's screenplay traces Helen's brief, doomed infatuation with the younger Wilcox son, Paul (Joseph Bennett). There follows the friendship of Margaret with the otherworldly Ruth Wilcox (Vanessa Redgrave), mother of Paul and two other children and wife to Henry (Anthony Hopkins). After Ruth's death, Margaret marries Henry, whom Helen sees to be a barbarian, if a very rich one.

The war that ensues has as its main issue Henry Wilcox's high-handed treatment of the dopey Leonard Bast and Leonard's good-natured, tarty wife, Jacky (Nicola Duffett), who, it turns out, had once been Henry's mistress.

Standing first as decor, then as a concept, is Howards End, the Wilcox family's comfortable old country house, which Forster saw as a symbol of England. It is Forster's conceit that the house must fall if the Schlegels, the Wilcoxes and the Basts cannot somehow be reconciled within Howards End. The grace with which this is accomplished is just one of the delights of this film, which is nothing if not symmetrical.

Though full of plot, Howards End is a comedy of character, expertly realized in performances that match any on the screen now or in the recent past.

Ms. Thompson, who was a charming asset to Henry V and Dead Again, both directed by her husband, Kenneth Branagh, comes into her own as the wise, patient Margaret Schlegel. Hers is the film's guiding performance. Ms. Thompson even manages to be beautiful while convincingly acting the role of a woman who is not supposed to be beautiful, being all teeth and solemn expressions.

The film is also a breakthrough for Ms. Bonham Carter. No more the pouty ingénue, she here gives a full-length portrait of a pretty young woman who, disappointed by life, gathers a sort of mad force as she ages and proudly assumes the role of one of society's outcasts.

Mr. Hopkins is splendid and easy as the Edwardian era's equivalent to a corporate raider, outwardly tough and willful but, at heart, almost fatally fragile. Miss Redgrave is not on the screen long, but hers is also a strong performance as a woman not quite in touch with the quotidian world. She looks grandly haggard, as she is supposed to, while her niece, Jemma Redgrave (daughter of Corin Redgrave), is very comic as her spoiled Wilcox daughter. Prunella Scales bustles through the movie as the Schlegel sisters' managerial aunt.

That Mr. Ivory and Mrs. Jhabvala work well together is not exactly news. What continues to astonish is Mrs. Jhabvala's magical way of putting herself in the service of another writer's work, preserving as she distills. The film unfolds chronologically. No narrator is used. Yet the Forster voice is heard in virtually every scene, chatting, being discreetly sarcastic, sometimes sounding worried and, at other times, laughing with pleasure.

Like all Merchant-Ivory productions, Howards End looks terrific, the colors mostly muted, the light dim. Occasionally the physical opulence does become excessive, as with the wisteria, which may be all nature's doing. Yet there is so much wisteria clinging to the roof and walls of Howards End that the place would seem in danger of collapse, no matter how the characters pair off to save England.

That's an extremely minor reservation. Howards End need apologize only for its bracing high spirits and the consistency of its intelligence. A great pleasure.

—V.C., March 13, 1992

HUD

Directed by Martin Ritt; written by Irving Ravetch and Harriet Frank Jr., based on the novel Horseman, Pass By by Larry McMurtry; cinematographer, James Wong Howe; edited by Frank Bracht; music by Elmer Bernstein; art designers, Hal Pereira and Tambi Larsen; produced by Mr. Ritt and Mr. Ravetch; released by Paramount Pictures. Black and white. Running time: 112 minutes.

With: Paul Newman (Hud Bannon), Melvyn Douglas (Homer Bannon), Patricia Neal (Alma), Brandon de Wilde (Lon Bannon), John Ashley (Hermy) and Whit Bissell (Burris).

Any film with a title as cryptic and ugly-sounding as *Hud* better have more to recommend it than its name. So, take it from me, *Hud,* which came to the Paramount and the Coronet yesterday, does have more—so much more, in every aspect—that it shapes up now as this year's most powerful film.

This is a daring endorsement for a picture in which the principal character is a heel and the setting is the Texas cow country that we've seen a thousand times (or more) in films. But the heel in this instance is different. He's more than a stock Western brute, banging the bar for red-eye and sneaking out to steal cattle in the dark.

This heel, named Hud, is a rancher who is fully and foully diseased with all the germs of materialism that are infecting and sickening modern man. He is a nineteen-sixties specimen of the I'm-gonna-get-mine breed—the selfish, snarling smoothie who doesn't give a hoot for anyone else.

And the place where he lives is not just Texas. It is the whole of our country today. It is the soil in which grows a gimcrack culture that nurtures indulgence and greed.

Here is the essence of this picture that Martin Ritt and Irving Ravetch have produced and Mr. Ritt has directed in a powerfully realistic style. While it looks like a modern Western, and is an outdoor drama, indeed, *Hud* is as wide and profound a contemplation of the human condition as one of the New England plays of Eugene O'Neill.

As a matter of fact, the structure of it is close to the spare and simple lines of one of those great O'Neill dramas—say, *Desire Under the Elms.* For the human elements are simply Hud, the focal character, with his aging father, a firm and high-principled cattleman, on one hand, and Hud's seventeen-year-old nephew, a still-growing and impressionable boy, on the other. The conflict is simply a matter of determining which older man will inspire the boy. Will it be the grandfather with his fine traditions or the uncle with his crudities and greed?

It would not be proper to tell which influence prevails. Nor is that answer essential to the clarification of this film. The striking, important thing about it is the clarity with which it unreels. The sureness and integrity of it are as crystal-clear as the plot is spare.

Mr. Ritt, working from an excellent screenplay that Mr. Ravetch and Harriet Frank Jr. wrote from a novel by Larry McMurtry, has caught the whole raw-boned atmosphere of a land and environment lying between nature and cheap urbanity, between the vastness of yesterday's open country and the closeness of the claptrap of tomorrow. And with a fine cast of performers, he has people who behave and talk so truly that it is hard to shake them out of your mind.

Paul Newman as Hud is tremendous—a potent, voracious man, restless with all his crude ambitions, arrogant with his contempt, and churned up inside with all the meanness and misgivings of himself.

And Melvyn Douglas is magnificent as the aging cattleman who finds his own son an abomination and disgrace to his country and home. It is Mr. Douglas's performance in the great key scene of the film, a scene in which his entire herd of cattle is deliberately and dutifully destroyed at the order of government agents because it is infected with foot-and-mouth disease, that helps fill the screen with an emotion that I've seldom felt from any film. It brings the theme of infection and destruction into focus with dazzling clarity.

As the young fellow, Brandon de Wilde is eloquent of clean, modern youth—naïve, sensitive, stalwart, wanting so much to be grown up. And Patricia Neal is brilliant as the lonely housekeeper for these men. She is a rangy, hard-bitten slattern with a heart and a dignity of her own.

There is also much else that is excellent: the camerawork of James Wong Howe, the poignant musical score of Elmer Bernstein, the insinuating use of natural sounds. They merge in an achievement that should be honored as a whole.

In spite of the title, *Hud* has it. That's all you have to know.

—*B.C., May 29, 1963*

HUEY LONG

Directed by Ken Burns: written by Geoffrey C. Ward: directors of photography. Mr. Burns and Buddy Squires: edited by Amy Stechler Burns: music by John Colby and Randy Newman: produced by Mr. Burns and Richard Kilberg: released by Florentine Films. Running time: 88 minutes.

With: David McCullough (Narrator).

The depressed late 1920's and early 1930's produced some remarkable American characters, including the Reverend Charles E. Coughlin, the radio priest from Detroit whose sermons were less religious than political, and Dr. Francis E. Townsend, the elderly Long Beach, California, physician whose "Townsend Plan" was a kind of crackpot preview of what eventually came into being as Social Security. The times were tough then and a desperate citizenry was ready to listen to almost anybody with a plan—or even a promise.

The most extraordinary—and successful—of these angry, ambitious populists was Huey Long (1893–1935), who came out of a small parish in Louisiana, first to become governor and then United States senator. By his carefully affected, often crude, country manners, by his wit and by his real brilliance, Mr. Long captured the loyalty and the votes of the poor and the disenfranchised of Louisiana, putting together a political machine that might well have won him a chance to run for the White House had he not been assassinated in September 1935.

Ken Burns's fine, feature-length documentary, *Huey Long,* beautifully evokes not only "the Kingfish," as Mr. Long styled himself after the character on the *Amos 'n' Andy* radio show, but also the social and economic conditions that produced the man, described by Franklin D. Roosevelt, when he was the Democratic Party's nominee for president, as "one of the two most dangerous men in the country"—the other being Douglas MacArthur.

Huey Long will be shown at the New York Film Festival today and tomorrow.

Mr. Burns has created a remarkably comprehensive portrait of a man, a time, and a place by using old newsreel footage, a series of especially revealing, contemporary interviews with people on the order of Arthur M. Schlesinger Jr., the historian, the journalists I. F. Stone and Mrs. Hodding Carter, and the novelist Robert Penn Warren, whose novel *All the King's Men* was inspired by the rise and fall of Huey Long. Supplementing this material are other interviews with Louisianians who still remember Huey Long with affection and respect.

When Mr. Long became governor, Louisiana was about as backward as any state in the union, with a high illiteracy rate, fewer than 300 miles of paved roads, and no bridges across the Mississippi River. No one could deny that Mr. Long did, in fact, bring Louisiana into the twentieth century, but at a cost that few people, except Mr. Long and his supporters, could defend.

Mr. Long did build bridges and highways, and he did provide free textbooks to the public schools, but in the process graft and corruption became a way of life in Louisiana. Civil liberties were all but suspended, especially for Mr. Long's opponents. It's estimated that every $100 million worth of highways cost the taxpayers $150 million.

Mr. Schlesinger comments, "His methods outweighed the good he did." And someone else says of Mr. Long just after he won his election to the state capitol, "The governor-elect is so agreeable that when a leaf blew onto his desk one morning, he signed it."

Despite Mr. Long's down-home fascism, his demagogy, his endorsement of corruption and his vanity, the man, as seen from this vantage point, remains amazingly vital and appealing. This may be the most important lesson to be learned from Mr. Burns's meticulously researched, graceful, funny and disturbing film.

—*V.C., September 28, 1985*

HUSBANDS AND WIVES

Written and directed by Woody Allen; director of photography, Carlo Di Palma; edited by Susan E. Morse; production designer, Santo Loquasto; produced by Jack Rollins and Charles H. Joffe; released by Tri-Star Pictures. Running time: 107 minutes.

With: Woody Allen (Gabe Roth), Mia Farrow (Judy Roth), Judy Davis (Sally), Sydney Pollack (Jack), Juliette Lewis (Rain), Liam Neeson (Michael), Lysette Anthony (Sam), Benno C. Schmidt Jr. (Judy's Ex-husband), Christi Conaway (Shawn Grainger), Timothy Jerome (Paul), Ron Rifkin (Rain's Analyst), Blythe Danner (Rain's Mother) and Brian McConnachie (Rain's Father).

Well, then, what about the movie?

Woody Allen's *Husbands and Wives* is a very fine, sometimes brutal comedy about a small group of contemporary New Yorkers, each an edgy, self-analyzing achiever who goes through life without much joy, but who finds a certain number of cracked satisfactions along the way.

The film is Mr. Allen's uproarious answer to Ingmar Bergman's far more solemn but no less bleak *Scenes from a Marriage.* It's also an ensemble piece acted to loopy perfection by a remarkable cast headed by Judy Davis, Sydney Pollack, Mia Farrow, Juliette Lewis, Liam Neeson and Mr. Allen, who's also the writer, director and ringmaster, as well as his own best friend.

In a crunch, Mr. Allen comes through for himself.

With *Husbands and Wives* he has made a movie that's so strong, wise and exhilarating that it should be able to weather the chaos of accusations, gossip, public statements and dirty jokes attending its release. Whether this was the right time to open *Husbands and Wives* nobody yet knows, although the kind of attention being given to the very noisy split of Mr. Allen and Ms. Farrow has never sold tickets in the past.

People with insatiable appetites for the lubricious details of scandal are not the most loyal moviegoers. The sort of information they want is supplied by newspapers, magazines and television. They demand facts, or their loose facsimiles. A movie, after all, is fiction, and with fiction you can never be sure what really happened. Or, as a bright student of creative writing says in *Husbands and Wives,* writing (meaning fiction) "is just a trick."

Or is it? That's the question that haunts this new movie and sometimes clouds the screen. If *Husbands and Wives* were less of an achievement, it might be impossible to watch. It's sorrowful enough without real life butting in.

Husbands and Wives is actually scenes from two marriages, one on the rocks as the film begins, the other in a kind of stasis, set in a uniformly upscale Manhattan where the apartments are big, book-lined and comfortable, the corporate suites ultramodern, the halls of academe ivied and the restaurants quiet enough to permit sustained conversation. The characters all work at endeavors that are immensely profitable, prestigious or celebrated (as with fame).

Gabe Roth (Mr. Allen) is a novelist and short-story writer who teaches at Columbia. He and Judy (Mia Farrow), an editor at an art magazine, have been married for ten years. Their best friends are Jack (Mr. Pollack), a successful businessman who is an epically

clumsy, impotent philanderer, and Sally (Ms. Davis), whose work for the Landmarks Preservation Commission does not fill the void left by her bored husband.

In the film's stunning opening sequence Jack and Sally arrive at the Roths' apartment on their way out to dinner. In the course of a single extended take, which has the appearance of something shot by the handheld camera of a documentary filmmaker, Jack and Sally cheerfully announce that they are separating, and then stand by as the camera tries to keep up with the donnybrook that follows.

Gabe and Judy are shocked. Judy goes from shock to fury. She's ready to throw something. Gabe tells her mildly that it isn't their business. "Of course it's our business!" Judy yells. She works herself into a first-rate tantrum and disappears into the bedroom. "Please don't not support us," Sally says. Jack looks embarrassed for his friends.

Husbands and Wives follows the moral muddles and emotional crises of Jack, Sally, Judy and Gabe over the next year and a half as the friends fight, schmooze, separate, take lovers and, in a way, reconcile. The film's form is freer than anything Mr. Allen has attempted in the past, although it's more successful for what it achieves than for its consistency.

At the beginning, *Husbands and Wives* appears to be some kind of simulated cinema verité. All of the characters, usually alone but sometimes in couples, take time out to be interviewed by the offscreen director of what one assumes to be the film-within. The testimony, as heartbreaking as it is hilarious, is interrupted by jump cuts within close-ups, as if the editor were eliminating the repetitions and nonessential information.

Yet there are other times when the audience is clearly watching things that no filmmaker would be allowed to photograph. The movie becomes a narrative presented by an omniscient observer. This form (could it be Mr. Allen in a postmodern mode?) disturbs, but it works for sometimes devastating results. Carlo Di Palma is the brilliant cinematographer. *Husbands and Wives* goes beneath the surface of things in a way few movies ever do. The story spins dizzily on.

Mr. Pollack's human, klutzy Jack realizes his dream: he moves in with his much younger aerobics instructor, Sam (Lysette Anthony), whom Gabe labels a cocktail waitress. Jack admits that she's not Simone de Beauvoir. She's a vibrant young beauty who is into health and astrology, and who talks too much at parties with his older friends. Sometimes Jack loses a serious temper.

Judy introduces Sally to Michael (Mr. Neeson), a young, good-looking, intensely sincere editor who wants very much to be married. Judy, who fancies Michael herself, is not pleased that Michael falls for Sally, while Sally makes him miserable.

Sally must be one of the most endearingly impossible characters Mr. Allen has ever written, and Ms. Davis nearly purloins the film. If Michael asks Sally how she liked their dinner, she says that she loved it, that it was superb, but that she'd like to teach the chef how to make a proper Alfredo sauce. She tells him the Mahler symphony was divine, but the second movement too slow. Michael kisses her. Sally responds, then breaks away. "Metabolically," she says, "it's not my rhythm."

Ms. Farrow's Judy is also a rich and contradictory character. Her former husband, one of the film-within's peripheral witnesses (played by the former president of Yale University, Benno C. Schmidt Jr.), describes her with lethal accuracy as "passive-aggressive." She's someone with a will of steel who pretends to be helpless. Yet she is also the one character in the film who seems to have her eyes open, if sometimes with a vengeance.

In the early scenes, she whines to Gabe about wanting a child. He points out that she already has a daughter from her first marriage. Aren't she and he enough as they are? She says no. He accuses her of the worst kind of deceit, of telling him that she's using a diaphragm when she isn't. Later, when he says that he's changed his mind about a baby, she refuses. "This is crazy," Gabe says. "I'm urging you to have a baby I don't even want!" Judy leaps at him in rage. Her point has been made.

In the meantime, Gabe has been seeing one of his students, Rain (Juliette Lewis), a pretty, uncommonly self-possessed would-be writer, named by her mother for Rainer Maria Rilke. Rain sets about to seduce Gabe, who has always been drawn to what he describes as "kamikaze women"—that is, women who "crash into you," possibly to take you down in flames with them.

Rain's twenty-first-birthday party at her family's penthouse becomes a major romantic moment for Gabe. There's a grandly operatic thunderstorm. The lights go out. Candles are lighted. The wine is vintage stuff. Gabe and Rain are alone. She asks him to kiss her on the mouth. "Why is it," he says, "that I'm hearing $50,000 worth of psychotherapy dialing 911?"

Fact? Fiction? Fantasy? Who cares? This sort of material is better analyzed by the critical biographer than by either the gossip columnist or the film critic. What is far more disturbing (because of current events) is the role Mr. Allen has given Ms. Farrow, that of a woman who is both tenacious and unforgiving. Judy gets what she wants. Ms. Farrow is funny and more than a little frightening. The performance is superb. Yet the role now seems mean-spirited. This Judy is a waif with claws. A year ago, no one would have seen anything except the fiction. Today, that's not possible.

Husbands and Wives—the entire Allen canon, for that matter—represents a kind of personal cinema for which there is no precedent in modern American movies. Even our best directors are herd animals. Mr. Allen is a rogue: he travels alone. This species is not unknown in Europe. Consider Federico Fellini and *8½* and *City of Women.* Or François Truffaut and the devastating *La Peau Douce,* made at a time when his own marriage was in difficulty. *La Peau Douce* is about a husband whose jealous wife calmly blows his head off with a shotgun. The man had been unfaithful but, the film seems to ask, does infidelity really deserve this? Truffaut photographed much of that film in his own apartment.

Husbands and Wives is the thirteenth collaboration of Mr. Allen and Ms. Farrow and, it must be assumed, the last. Too bad, we say, but, as Ms. Farrow's Judy tells Gabe in the film, life is change. Like life, all relationships have their beginnings, middles and ends. Not to recognize that natural law is to attempt to stop the planets.

As it plays today, *Husbands and Wives* may appear self-serving. Mr. Allen's Gabe is the one who suffers most. In the film's poignant last scene, played to the film-within's interviewer, Gabe says, "I blew it," then, at the very end: "Can I go? Is this over?"

—*V.C., September 18, 1992*

THE HUSTLER

Produced and directed by Robert Rossen; written by Sidney Carroll and Mr. Rossen, based on the novel by Walter Tevis; cinematographer, Eugene Schufftan; edited by Dede Allen; music by Kenyon Hopkins; production designer, Harry Horner; released by Twentieth Century Fox. Running time: 134 minutes.

With: Paul Newman (Eddie Felson), Jackie Gleason (Minnesota Fats), Piper Laurie (Sarah Packard), George C. Scott (Bert Gordon), Myron McCormick (Charlie Burns) and Michael Constantine (Findlay).

Dad always said stay out of poolrooms, and obviously he was right, to judge by what one sees in *The Hustler,* which came to the Paramount and the Seventy-second Street Playhouse yesterday. For the characters one meets in the succession of sunless and smoky billiard halls (to use a more genteel term for them) that are tenanted in the course of this tough film are the sort to make your flesh creep and whatever blood you may have run cold.

Indeed, one character says in the beginning that a poolroom looks like a morgue and "those tables are the slabs they lay the stiffs on."

We're glad we took the good advice of Dad.

But this doesn't say the weird assembly of pool players, gamblers, hangers-on, and hustlers—especially the hustlers—that they used to call "pool sharks" in our youth, are not fascinating and exciting to watch at a safe distance from the screen. They're high-strung, voracious and evil. They talk dirty, smoke, guzzle booze and befoul the dignity of human beings. At least, the hustlers' wicked betting managers do. They have a consuming greed for money that cancels out charity and love. They're full of energy and action.

That's the virtuous quality of this film.

Under Robert Rossen's strong direction, its ruthless and odorous account of one young hustler's eventual emancipation is positive and alive. It crackles with credible passions. It comes briskly and brusquely to sharp points. It doesn't dawdle with romantic nonsense, except in one brief unfortunate stretch.

Along about midway, after its hero has been washed out in a herculean game and has sneaked away into a cheap New York apartment with a fortuitously picked-up girl, it does mush about a bit with chitchat anent the deep yearnings of the heart and the needful direction a man takes to get onto solid ground.

But even in this mushy area, Mr. Rossen and Sidney Carroll have provided their characters with dialogue that keeps them buoyant and alive. And soon they are potently projected into the world of the realists again—into a brutally cynical connivance and a gorge-raising sweep to an ironic end.

There may not be much depth to the hero, whom Paul Newman violently plays with a master's control of tart expressions and bitterly passionate attitudes. Nor may there be quite enough clarity in the complicated nature of the girl, whom Piper Laurie wrings into a pathetic and eventually exhausted little rag. But they're both appealing people, he in a truculent, helpless way and she in the manner of a courageous, confused and uncompromising child.

The real power is packed into the character of an evil gambler, whom George C. Scott plays as though the devil himself had donned dark glasses and taken up residence in a rancid billiard hall. Mr. Scott is magnificently malefic. When he lifts those glasses and squints, it is as though somebody had suddenly put a knife between your ribs.

Jackie Gleason is also excellent—more so than you first realize—as a cool, self-collected pool expert who has gone into bondage to the gambling man. His deceptively casual behavior in that titanic initial game conceals a pathetic robot that you only later perceive.

Myron McCormick is touchingly futile as a tinhorn manager and Murray Hamilton, too, is effective in the brief role of a wealthy billiards buff. Michael Constantine, Carl York, and Jake LaMotta are colorful as poolroom types.

The Hustler is not a picture to take the children to see, but it is one a father might wisely recommend to a restless teenage son.

An appropriately nervous jazz score keeps the eardrums sharp.

—*B.C., September 27, 1961*

I KNOW WHERE I'M GOING

Written, produced and directed by Michael Powell and Emeric Pressburger; cinematographer, Erwin Hillier; edited by John Seabourne; music by Allan Gray; art designer, Alfred Junge; released by Universal International Pictures. Black and white. Running time: 91 minutes.

With: Wendy Hiller (Joan Webster), Roger Livesey (Torquil MacNeil), Finlay Currie (Ruairidh Mor), Pamela Brown (Catriona), Valentine Dyall (Mr. Robinson), Petula Clark (Cheril), Walter Hudd (Hunter), George Carney (Mr. Webster) and Duncan Mackechnie (Captain Lochinvar).

The Archers, which is a corporate way of saying Michael Powell and Emeric Pressburger, have scored another bullseye. Last week this English writing-directing team gave us the artistically exciting *Black Narcissus*. Yesterday they sent to the Sutton Cinema, on East Fifty seventh Street, one of the most satisfying screen romances of many a season. *I Know Where I'm Going* is boy-meets-girl, but developed in an adult, literate style—a sort of romantic suspense drama that is as beautifully performed as it is beautifully written and directed.

Wendy Hiller, back on the screen for the first time since *Major Barbara* (1941), is giving a facile, captivating portrayal of a materialistic young woman who believes that money is the springboard to all earthly happiness. She is expertly assisted by Roger Livesey as a British naval officer who would convince her otherwise and a host of lesser-known players, each of whom

appears to have been chosen for his or her particular role with meticulous care. These minor characters are fully rounded personalities, and what they have to say and do exerts considerable influence upon the destiny of the principals. In other words, *I Know Where I'm Going* is a striking example of the ensemble precept of moviemaking.

At twenty-six, Joan Webster is represented as a girl who had always known where she was going in life. And, as the story gets under way, she is going from London to the Island of Kiloran, in the Hebrides, to marry an elderly and wealthy industrialist. A storm maroons her for eight days on the Isle of Mull in the company of the personable naval officer and other Highland folk, and for the first time in her life Miss Webster begins to live with her heart as well as her head. This simple story line is developed with considerable imagination, wit and emotional insight into a thoroughly enjoyable and exhilarating romantic experience.

Practically all of *I Know Where I'm Going* unfolds on the rugged, picturesque Isle of Mull, and the Scottish inhabitants and their customs are exquisitely depicted. The whole atmosphere of the film is alive with the sound of whining wind and the crashing of angry waves on the rocky coast, the ghosts of ancient, kilted clansmen standing silent watch over abandoned castles and the skirling of bagpipes.

One of the most fascinating sequences of the picture is the Ceilidh ("Kayley"), an ancient Highland song and dance ritual, held in honor of a couple celebrating their sixtieth wedding anniversary. Much of the song and conversation is carried on in Gaelic at the Ceilidh, and though unintelligible to most American moviegoers, one would not want it otherwise, for therein lies the true flavor of the people.

I Know Where I'm Going will be a treat for discriminating moviegoers, but it will not hold much appeal for those who may expect any violent emotional display. For the characters in this picture are solid, normal and mature human beings and their experiences are far from spectacular. But they are intensely interesting people in their own quiet way.

—*T.M.P., August 20, 1947*

I REMEMBER MAMA

Produced and directed by George Stevens: written by DeWitt Bodeen, based on the play by John Van Druten and the novel *Mama's Bank Account* by Kathryn Forbes: cinematographer, Nicholas Musuraca: edited by Robert Swink and Tholen Gladden: music by Roy Webb: art designers, Albert S. D'Agostino and Carroll Clark: released by RKO Radio Pictures. Black and white. Running time: 134 minutes.

With: Irene Dunne (Mama), Barbara Bel Geddes (Katrin), Oscar Homolka (Uncle Chris), Philip Dorn (Papa), Cedric Hardwicke (Mr. Hyde), Edgar Bergen (Mr. Thorkelson), Rudy Vallee (Dr. Johnson), Barbara O'Neill (Jessie Brown), Florence Bates (Florence Dana Moorhead), Peggy McIntyre (Christine), June Hedin (Dagmar), Steve Brown (Nels) and Ellen Corby (Aunt Trina).

Kathryn Forbes's tender memories of a childhood in San Francisco and of her wonderful ex-Norwegian grandma, projected through *Mama's Bank Account* into the stage success *I Remember Mama,* are now to be had upon the screen, stretched out to full visual proportions and performed by an excellent cast. Like the book and the play before it, the film, at the Music Hall—also called *I Remember Mama*—should prove irresistible.

For producer-director George Stevens has transferred the John Van Druten play, via a freewheeling script by DeWitt Bodeen, in all its genial personality to the screen. Within the same architectural framework that was effectively used for the play—that is, a series of reflections (or flashbacks) of a youthful

author's thoughts—he has woven a pictorial fabric of humorous and poignant episodes in the lives of a remarkably good-natured family of Norwegian-Americans. And with a cast of Hollywood performers, all of them new to the roles (with the single exception of Oscar Homolka), he has caught the pristine glow of character.

Since there is nothing essential in the picture of later invention than the contents of the play, it would take a heretical reviewer to criticize its substance and scheme. Here is the same Hanson family—Mama, Papa and the kids—in their Larkin Street house in San Francisco, still struggling cheerfully to make ends meet. Here is immaculate Katrin, Mama's mainstay and her Boswell-to-be, watching the flow of family happenings while diffidently taking part in them. Here is little sister Christine with her impishness and her pets and her case of mastoiditis, which gives Mama her most potent chance to "mom."

Here, too, are Brother Nels and Papa and Sister Dagmar, the last impeccable, and the three aunts and Mr. Torkelson "from der funeral parlor" and, definitely, Uncle Chris. Here is Mr. Hyde, the English boarder who reads to the family at night. And above all, here is Mama, superb and infallible, mothering her brood with infinite kindness, understanding and intensity.

Already proved substantial show-stuff beyond the shadow of an ultraskeptic's doubts, this material wants only tactful handling to achieve its deserved success. And Mr. Stevens has assured this with unfaltering control of the directorial reins. His soft scenes are never too sloppy—not even the death of Uncle Chris (with its nod to matrimony and morality) or the scene where Mama sings her lullaby. And the humor is kept in an area of reasonable levity, without any obvious endeavors to force or "milk" the laughs.

Furthermore, in the frequent brief excursions of the family outside their home—and particularly in the frantic glimpses of their breathless pumping up (and down) Larkin Street hill—Mr. Stevens has added such touches as relate these people to an outside world that by the nature of the story is only vaguely acknowledged to exist.

As Mama, the wheelhorse of the family, Irene Dunne does a beautiful job, in a blonde, braided wig and in dresses that actually appear to be worn. Handling with equal facility an accent and a troubled look,

Miss Dunne has the strength and vitality, yet the softness, that the role requires. As Katrin, the oldest daughter, Barbara Bel Geddes plays most often as in a trance, hypnotized by Mama and sheer Beauty, but that fits with the general atmosphere. Likewise, Philip Dorn as Papa and Peggy McIntyre and June Hedin as the girls have the air of angels, for all their charming attitudes.

However, Mr. Homolka, who plays the bombastic Uncle Chris, gives to it all the bluff and blunder that was in this decidedly "hammy" gent. And Ellen Corby's twittering as the simpleton Aunt Trina brings the humor within regions where it can be readily understood. Edgar Bergen's Mr. Thorkelson is also a comic delight and Sir Cedric Hardwicke makes a small thing but a good one out of Mr. Hyde.

If one were to venture a comment in a critical vein on this film, it might be that the pace is too leisurely, in spots, and the story too long. But those are common objections to personal reminiscences. In the darkness of a theater it is not impolite to doze.

—B.C., March 12, 1948

I WANT TO LIVE!

Directed by Robert Wise; written by Nelson Gidding and Don Mankiewicz, based on the letters of Barbara Graham; cinematographer, Lionel Lindon; edited by William Hornbeck; music by Johnny Mandel; art designer, Ted Haworth; produced by Walter Wanger; released by United Artists. Black and white. Running time: 120 minutes.

With: Susan Hayward (Barbara Graham), Simon Oakland (Ed Montgomery), Virginia Vincent (Peg), Theodore Bikel (Carl Palmberg), Wesley Lau (Henry Graham), Philip Coolidge (Emmett Perkins), Lou Krugman (Jack Santo), Joe De Santis (Al Matthews), Raymond Bailey (Warden) and James Philbrook (Bruce King).

Susan Hayward has done some vivid acting in a number of sordid roles that have called for professional simulation of personal ordeals of the most upsetting sort. But she's never done anything so vivid or so shattering to an audience's nerves as she does in Walter Wanger's sensational new drama, *I Want to Live!*

In this arresting prison picture, which came to the Victoria yesterday, and which is based on the actual experience of a West Coast woman named Barbara Graham, Miss Hayward plays a candid B-girl who gets hooked on a murder rap, is railroaded to a conviction and condemned to die in the gas chamber. While waiting for execution, she is compelled to endure a grim succession of legal maneuverings that put the Chinese water torture to shame.

Finally, when all the petitions and appeals that might save her have failed, she is marched into the gas chamber and—we might as well tell you—put to death.

It's a miserable set of circumstances that Nelson Gidding and Don Mankiewicz have arranged to show the ultimate dilemma into which impeccable persons can be plunged when legal trickery and newspaper pressure are thrown against them in this jazzed-up age. And it's a brutal and gruesome ordeal they have concocted for Miss Hayward to perform as the heroine waits in prison for the possible reprieve that never comes.

This latter ordeal, which is extended through the entire second half of this two-hour film, is by far the most harsh and devastating—and, indeed, most original—phase of it. And that is easily understandable, for it is realism of a sort seldom shown.

The pace is swift through the first half, as the picture beats out in fast-cut style and to interrupted jazz rhythms the story of how the heroine is caught with a pair of suspected murderers and condemned on rigged evidence. But it slows to a solemn, deadly tempo as she languishes anxiously in a cell, awaiting a correction of injustice, and then is ominously removed to the death house at San Quentin where she plays out her ghastly last ordeal.

And ghastly is what you have to call it, for the death-house phase of this film is a harrowing synthesis of drama and cold documentary detail. As the minutes tick off and the tension of last-gasp appeals is sustained through the pacing of death-house formalities against the image of the nearby telephone, attendants go through the grisly business of preparing the gas chamber for its lethal role. Anyone who can sit through this ordeal without shivering and shuddering is made of stone.

And Miss Hayward plays it superbly, under the consistently sharp direction of Robert Wise, who has shown here a stunning mastery of the staccato realistic style. From a loose and wisecracking B-girl she moves onto levels of cold disdain and then plunges down to depths of terror and bleak surrender as she reaches the end. Except that the role does not present us a precisely pretty character, its performance merits for Miss Hayward the most respectful applause.

Others are excellent in small roles—Lou Krugman and Philip Coolidge as crooks, Joe De Santis as the heroine's last attorney, Simon Oakland as a newspaper man, Raymond Bailey as the San Quentin warden, Theodore Bikel as a psychiatrist, and several more. John Mandel has provided a slangy and insinuating jazz score that is played by the Gerry Mulligan combo. That, too, is deeply in the groove.

I Want to Live! is a picture to shake you—and give you pause.

—*B.C., November 19, 1958*

IF . . .

Directed by Lindsay Anderson: written by David Sherwin. based on a story *The Crusaders* by Mr. Sherwin and John Howlett: cinematographer. Miroslav Ondricek: edited by David Gladwell: music by Marc Wilkinson: production designer. Jocelyn Herbert: produced by Michael Medwin and Mr. Anderson: released by Paramount Pictures. Running time: 111 minutes.

With: Malcolm McDowell (Mick). David Wood (Johnny). Richard Warwick (Wallace). Christine Noonan (The Girl). Robert Swan (Rowntree). Hugh Thomas (Denson). Guy Ross (Stephans) and Peter Jeffrey (Headmaster).

If . . . is so good and strong that even those things in the movie that strike me as being first-class mistakes are of more interest than entire movies made by smoothly consistent, lesser directors. Lindsay Anderson's second feature (his first, *This Sporting Life,* was released here in 1963) is a very human, very British social comedy that aspires to the cool, anarchic grandeur of Godard movies like *Band of Outsiders* and *La Chinoise.*

As an artist, however, Anderson, unlike Godard, is more ageless than young. He was born in 1923. His movie about a revolution within a British public school is clear-eyed reality pushed to its outer reaches. The movie's compassion for the individual in the structured society is classic, post-World War II liberal, yet *If . . .* is also oddly nostalgic, as if it missed all that sadism and masochism that turned boys into adolescents for life.

Mick and his two roommates, Johnny and Wallace, are nonconforming seniors at College House, a part of a posh boarding school that is collapsing under the weight of its 1,000-year history.

"Cheering at college matches has deteriorated completely," warns the student head of College House.

"Education in Britain," says the complacent headmaster a little later, "is a nubile Cinderella, sparsely clad and often interfered with."

As the winter term progresses through rituals that haven't varied since the Armada, Mick, Johnny and Wallace move mindlessly toward armed rebellion. On Speech Day, armed with bazookas and rifles, they take to the roofs and stage a reception for teachers, students and parents—and at least one Royal Highness—comparable to that given by Mohammed Ali to end the control of the Mamelukes.

I can't quarrel with the aim of Anderson and David Sherwin, who wrote the screenplay, to turn the public school into the private metaphor, only with the apparent attempt to equate this sort of lethal protest with what's been happening on real-life campuses around the world. Revolution as a lifestyle, as an end in itself, is the fundamental form of *La Chinoise,* but it's confusing and too grotesque to have real meaning attached to what is otherwise a beautifully and solidly constructed satire. In such a conventional context, the revolutionary act becomes one of paranoia.

Anderson, a fine documentary moviemaker, develops his fiction movie with all the care of someone recording the amazing habits of a newly discovered tribe of aborigines. The movie is a chronicle of bizarre details—Mick's first appearance wearing a black slouch hat, his face hidden behind a black scarf, looking like a teenage Mack the Knife; the hazing of a boy by hanging him upside down over (and partially in) a toilet bowl; and a moment of first love, written on the face of a lower form student as he watches an older boy whose exercises on the crossbar become a sort of mating dance.

As a former movie critic, Anderson quite consciously reflects his feelings about the movies of others in his own film. *If . . .* , an ironic reference to Kipling's formula for manhood, uses a lot of terms most recently associated with Godard. There are title cards between sequences ("Ritual and Rebellion," "Discipline," etc.), and he arbitrarily switches from full color to monochromatic footage, as if to remind us that, after all, we are watching a movie. There is also an enigmatic girl (Christine Noonan), a waitress picked up at the Packhorse Café, who joins the revolt. Miss Noonan suggests a plump, English, mutton-chop version of Anna Karina, even without looking much like Miss Karina.

Less successful are visualized, split-second fantasies—or what I take to be fantasies. When the three boys are told to apologize to the chaplain for having attacked him during a cadet field corps exercise, the headmaster withdraws the chaplain's body from a morgue-like drawer. The fantasies just aren't very different from a crazy, believable reality in which a master's inhibited wife wanders nude through a deserted dormitory, lightly caressing objects that belong to the boys.

The movie is well acted by a cast that is completely new to me. Especially good are Malcolm McDowell (Mick), who looks like a cross between Steve McQueen and Michael J. Pollard, Richard Warwick (Wallace), Peter Jeffrey (the headmaster), Robert Swan (the student leader) and Mary McLeod (the lady who likes to walk unclothed)

If . . . , which opened yesterday at the Plaza Theater, is such an interesting movie (and one that I suspect will be very popular) that the chances are there will not be another six-year gap between Anderson features. After making *This Sporting Life*, Anderson worked in the British theater and turned out two shorts, *The White Bus* and *The Singing Lesson,* which will be shown here at the Museum of Modern Art April 30.

—*V.C., March 10, 1969*

IKIRU

Directed by Akira Kurosawa; written (in Japanese, with English subtitles) by Mr. Kurosawa, Hideo Oguni and Shinobu Hashimoto; cinematographer, Asakazu Nakai; music by Fumio Hayasaka; art designer, So Matsuyama; produced by the Toho Company; released by Brandon Films. Black and white. Running time: 140 minutes.

With: Takashi Shimura (Kanji Watanabe), Miki Odagiri (Toyo), Nobuo Kaneko (Mitsuo), Kyoko Seki (Kazue), Kamatari Fujiwara (Ohno), Minosuke Yamada (Saito) and Makoto Kobori (Kiichie Watanabe).

For a varied and detailed illustration of middle-class life in contemporary Japan, with a good deal of caustic social comment and extra thick sentiment thrown in, Akira Kurosawa's *Ikiru* (*To Live*), that opened at the Little Carnegie yesterday, is the best of the series of Japanese films that Thomas J. Brandon has shown at that theater in the last several weeks. It is also the most expressive in its cinematic style, and if it weren't so confused in its storytelling, it would be one of the major postwar films from Japan.

As it stands, it is a strangely fascinating and affecting film, up to a point—that being the point where it consigns its aged hero to the great beyond. Then the last third (or forty-five minutes) of it is an odd sort of jumbled epilogue in which the last charitable act of the deceased man is crudely reconstructed in a series of flashbacks that are intercut with the static action of a tedious funeral.

The essential drama of the picture is that of an aging widower, a petty government official who has done nothing but shuffle papers and pass the buck for thirty years. Then, on the shattering discovery that he has cancer and has only a few months to live, he fearfully and frantically endeavors to make up for all the life and gratification he has lost.

In company with a disenchanted novelist, he tours the fleshpots of Tokyo, seeking joy in girls and liquor. That doesn't do any good. Then he tries to arrange for a calm retirement with his much adored son and daughter-in-law. They misunderstand his dilemma and rebuff him, which breaks his heart. A poignant attempt to have a friendship with a cheerful young woman does not succeed. Finally, he turns to a project of civic improvement that has been held up by government red tape for years, and it is upon this that he is working when he dies.

If the drama were clearly completed in continuity, it would be a proper progression to a climax with char-

481

acter and force. For the pathos of loneliness and searching in a friendless and meretricious world is brought out with vivid illustration in the first two-thirds of this film. And the idea of misunderstanding and callous disregard for other men that is the charge brought against the government officials could be continued to a straight ironic end.

It's that long-drawn, funereal maundering by the dead man's family and dull associates, all of them drinking and talking and showing their pettiness, that is the anticlimactic death of the film.

Even so, in this flat phase, Kurosawa often flashes that cinematic style of sharp reportage and introspection of his characters that distinguishes his films. He patiently studies his people, gives them plenty of time to move and surrounds them with rich and meaningful details in composing the comment of a scene. As a consequence, you see more human nature and more Japanese customs in this film—more emotion, personality and ways of living—than in most of the others that have gone before.

Particularly does Takashi Shimura give a deep and exhaustive notion of a man tormented by frustration and the dread of approaching death. Unquestionably, Shimura, who was the woodcutter in *Rashomon,* measures up through his performance in this picture with the top film actors anywhere. Miki Odagiri as the girl he seeks as a companion, Nobuo Kaneko as his unfeeling son, and Yunosuke Ito as the novelist are also remarkably good.

Although the English subtitles are somewhat pallid against the bottom margins of this black-and-white film, they are generally decipherable and sufficient to convey the thought of the Japanese dialogue.

—*B.C., January 30, 1960*

I'M ALL RIGHT, JACK

Directed by John Boulting; written by Frank Harvey. Alan Hackney and Mr. Boulting, based on the novel *Private Life* by Mr. Hackney; cinematographer, Mutz Greenbaum; edited by Anthony Harvey; music by Ken Hare and Ron Goodwin; produced by Roy Boulting; released by Lion International Films. Black and white. Running time: 105 minutes.

With: Peter Sellers (Fred Kite). Ian Carmichael (Stanley Windrush). Terry-Thomas (Major Hitchcock). Richard Attenborough (Sidney De Vere Cox). Dennis Price (Bertram Tracepurcel). Margaret Rutherford (Aunt Dolly) and Irene Handl (Mrs. Kite).

Of all the unlikely subjects for successful satirizing on the screen—organized labor and management in modern industry—the British Boulting brothers, John and Roy, have picked it for their film *I'm All Right, Jack.* And what do you know!—they have run it into the brightest, liveliest comedy seen this year.

Much like their *Private's Progress,* which took a decidedly scandalous view of life in the British Army during World War II, this new satire at the Guild Theatre plays absolutely devastating hob with the obstructive tactics of trade unions—and with the intrigues of management, too.

As a matter of fact, most of the characters in this delightfully sharp and rowdy farce are the same as were in *Private's Progress,* only grown a little longer in the tooth. There's Ian Carmichael, the private, still a naive and dizzy gentleman, seeking a place to dispose his peacetime talents and finding it as a laborer in a missile-making plant.

There's Richard Attenborough, the Cockney schemer, now become a dapper man of affairs, and Dennis Price, the art-purloining major, now the head of the arms factory. These two arch and practiced connivers are joined in a clearly crooked plot, with Marne Maitland as a shifty-eyed Mohammedan, to mulct an unnamed Arab country on a big arms deal.

And whom do you think these fine industrialists have as the labor-relations manager in their plant? None other than bucktoothed Terry-Thomas, the snarling major in that other film. He's the frenzied but foxy fellow who is now stuck with the patience-fraying job of dealing with the bland, lint-picking workers and spying on their time-wasting toils.

However, someone new has been added—an outsider to complicate the lives of these memorable and mischievous war buddies and make their best-laid schemes gang agley. He is a stalwart and solemn-faced shop steward, a provokingly pompous, priggish type. And he is played so sensationally by Peter Sellers that the whole film is made to jump and throb.

Truly, it's hard to tell you what it is that Mr. Sellers does to make this figure of a union fanatic devastatingly significant and droll. Up to the point of his entrance, the comedy runs along in an innocent, charming fashion, poking fun at the British upper class and making a mockery of modern manufacturing and merchandising, somewhat in the manner of Charlie Chaplin's *Modern Times*.

But when Mr. Sellers strides into the picture at the head of a shop committee, breathing fire and rattling off union specifications in an educated Cockney tone of voice, it is as if Mr. Chaplin's Great Dictator has come upon the scene. He is all efficiency, righteous indignation, monstrous arrogance and blank ineptitude. He is the most scathing thing that union labor has ever had represent it on the screen. He is also side-splittingly funny, as funny as a true stuffed shirt can be.

We're not going to try to tell you how it all comes out; how Mr. Carmichael, with the best intentions, upsets the labor apple cart and precipitates a strike that puts a spoke in the conniving management's scheme and how this arouses the nation and compels a television panel show, in which the honest Mr. Carmichael exposes labor and management alike.

All we'll say further is that John Boulting, Frank Harvey and Alan Hackney have written a script that is one of the liveliest in a long time, although loaded with cryptic British slang; that Mr. Boulting has directed it briskly; that Margaret Rutherford, Irene Handl, Liz Fraser, and Victor Maddern play it finely, along with all those mentioned above—and that this is a picture that only members of the National Association of Manufacturers, the unions, and a few million other Americans should be sure to see.

—*B.C., April 26, 1960*

IMITATION OF LIFE

Directed by Douglas Sirk; written by Eleanore Griffin and Allan Scott, based on the novel by Fannie Hurst; director of photography, Russell Metty; edited by Milton Carruth; art directors, Alexander and Richard H. Riedel; music by Frank Skinner; produced by Ross Hunter; released by Universal-International. Running time: 125 minutes.

With: Lana Turner (Lora Meredith), John Gavin (Steve Archer), Sandra Dee (Susie, age 16), Robert Alda (Allen Loomis), Susan Kohner (Sarah Jane, age 18), Dan O'Herlihy (David Edwards), Juanita Moore (Annie Johnson), Karin Dicker (Sarah Jane, age 8), Terry Burnham (Susie, age 6), John Vivyan (young man), Lee Goodman (photographer), Ann Robinson (Showgirl), Troy Donahue (Frankie), Sandra Gould (Annette) and David Tomack (Mr. McKenney).

For positive verification of the old French saying, "The more things change, the more they are the same," consider the new film at the Roxy. It is Universal's *Imitation of Life*.

Twenty-five years ago, a picture of the same title, based upon the then popular Fannie Hurst novel, opened at the same theatre. Its star was Claudette Colbert. It was in black-and-white. And the reviewer for this paper tagged it "the most shameless tearjerker of the fall."

Yesterday's arrival at the Roxy has Lana Turner as its star. It happens to be in vivid color, and a few details in the story have been changed. But otherwise this modernized remake of Miss Hurst's frankly lachrymose tale is much the same as its soggy predecessor. It is the most shameless tearjerker in a couple of years.

Once more, it circulates a story of the hazards of motherhood at the stage when one's children—in this case daughters—are growing up and preparing to enter the world.

There are two mothers in the situation—and no fathers, by the way; no parents of masculine gender to confuse the rich flow of mother love. One is a lovely young widow who aspires to a theatrical career and somewhat neglects her growing daughter in gaining great success in that field. (In the former film and in the novel, she was a tycoon in pancake flour, but the point was the same: she concentrated on a self-aggrandizing career.)

The other mother is a Negro and is the first mother's loyal maid. She doesn't neglect her daughter, but she has a serious problem on her hands. Her daughter is markedly light-skinned and, as she grows up, she wants to pass for white—so much so that she repudiates her mother and eventually runs away. Thus the poor woman's heart is broken, in the midst of her employer's lush success. The contrast of the mother's compensations from their differing daughters is the story's irony,

As you may sense from this outline, the emotional potentialities are strong, and no reluctance, restraint or artful prudence has been exercised in banging them across. The screenplay by Eleanore Griffin and Allan Scott puts the issue positively, and, to make sure there's no vagueness in the dialogue, it is written in basic clichés.

"Tell her I know I was selfish—and if I loved her too much, I'm sorry—but I didn't mean to cause her any trouble. She was all I had." Thus speaks the mother on her deathbed about the daughter who ran away. That is the tenor of the writing—and the simplified feeling—in this film.

As for the Negro mother's funeral, which is the climactic episode, it is a splurge of garish ostentation and sentimentality. Mahalia Jackson is recruited to do a full-voiced wail of "Trouble of the World," while a church is packed with principals and extras who sob noisily and dab at their eyes. And, of course, the wayward daughter who wants to be white shows up at the end and throws herself on the coffin, crying for mama piteously.

Under Douglas Sirk's direction, which is manifested by that episode, Miss Turner and all the others act unreally and elaborately. Miss Turner as the actress, Sandra Dee as her daughter (at 16), Juanita Moore as the Negro mother, Susan Kohner as her daughter (at 18), John Gavin as a suitor of Miss Turner, Robert Alda as her agent in the theatre and Dan O'Herlihy as a doting playwright do not give an imitation of life. They give an imitation of movie acting at its less graceful level twenty-five years ago.

—B.C., April 18, 1959

IN COLD BLOOD

Produced and directed by Richard Brooks; written by Mr. Brooks, based on the book by Truman Capote; director of photography. Conrad Hall; edited by Peter Zinner; music by Quincy Jones; art designer. Robert Boyle; released by Columbia Pictures. Black and white. Running time: 134 minutes.

With: Robert Blake (Perry Smith). Scott Wilson (Dick Hickock). John Forsythe (Alvin Dewey). Paul Stewart (Reporter). Gerald S. O'Loughlin (Harold Nye). Jeff Corey (Hickock's Father) and John Gallaudet (Roy Church).

The public hazard in the kind of random violence that is occurring in our communities these days as part of the alarming upsurge of wild, neurotic crime is envisioned in terrifying images in the film Richard Brooks has made from Truman Capote's celebrated reporting of a Kansas murder case, *In Cold Blood*. This excellent quasidocumentary, which sends shivers down the spine while moving the viewer to ponder, opened at Cinema I yesterday.

Substantially, the film is a reenactment in electrifying cinematic terms of the essential events in the case record of that gruesome and mystifying crime in which four members of the modest Clutter family were slaughtered in their home near Holcomb, Kansas, by two ex-convicts, Richard Hickock and Perry Smith, one night in 1959.

It is a faithful and absorbing demonstration of how the police, with very few clues and no initial inkling of a motive, patiently investigated the crime while the killers were boldly making an escape into Mexico; how the case was eventually broken, the killers fortuitously caught, then tried, convicted and executed in a Kansas prison in 1965.

Since most of this is now common knowledge, thanks to the circulation of Mr. Capote's book, and since the culpability of the murderers is specified early in the film, the excitement generated in the viewer is not over who committed the murders, but why. Why did two who had originally intended robbery, and who had not committed murder before, suddenly come to the point of slaughtering four innocent persons in cold blood? And what does this single explosion of violence indicate as to society's pitiable vulnerability to the kooks that are loose in the land?

This pervasive concern with the natures and the backgrounds of the two young men who commit the murders and are therefore the symbols of the forces of evil in this dramatic scan accounts for the considerable alteration that Mr. Brooks has made in the substance and structure of Mr. Capote's book.

With a proper disregard for the extraneous, he has dropped out much of the detail of life in the community of Holcomb that Mr. Capote so patiently inscribed, and he has swiftly introduced his two marauders and brought them to the driveway of the Clutter home on that fateful night.

Then, with a rip in the sequence that is characteristic of the nervous style of the film—it is done with frequent flashbacks and fragmentations of continuity—he cuts to the interior of the Clutter home on the morning after the crime and the discovery of the bodies by the housemaid (but unseen by the camera), to her shrieking horror.

Thus the evident hideousness and mystery of what occurred is craftily withheld until the flow of the film has encompassed the investigations by the police, the getaway of the fugitives and their visit to Mexico (during all of which we are treated to grim reflections of their blighted early years), and their capture in Las Vegas, by an extraordinary fluke.

Not until they're brought back to Holcomb do we get in a confession by Smith, a graphic reconstruction of what happened in the house that awful night, and here Mr. Brooks exercises his most admirable skill and good taste. For without once actually showing the raw performance and effects of violence, the shooting and the knifing, he builds up a horrifying sense of the slow terror and maniacal momentum of that murderous escapade.

He makes us see the arrogance of the marauders, the astonishment and disbelief of the awakened Clutters, the fury of the robbers when they find there is no expected hoard of money and the piteous terror of the victims when they know their lives are to be taken. But, best of all, he makes us understand, on the basis of what he has shown us about these hoodlums earlier in the film, why their wild, smashing outburst of vengeance is inevitable.

From here on, the course of the picture—the barely sketched-in trial, the languishing of the men in prison while their case goes through endless appeals, and finally their execution—is but the ironic playing out of society's ritualistic compensation for damage already done. The final scene of the hanging, which is realistically done, is like some medieval rite of retribution. It leaves one helplessly, hopelessly chilled.

I have not emphasized the vivid realism and literal quality of this film, that are the product of Mr. Brooks's sharp direction and the black-and-white photography of Conrad Hall; nor have I nailed down the subtle revelations and variations in the performances of Robert Blake and Scott Wilson in the principal roles. Their abilities to demonstrate the tensions, the torments and shabby conceits of the miserable criminals, give disturbing dimension to their roles.

As dogged investigators, John Forsythe, John Gallaudet, Jim Lantz and others manifest the terminal functioning of the law; Paul Stewart is dry as a reporter and John McLiam plays Mr. Clutter pitiably.

There is sure to be comparison of this picture with the controversial *Bonnie and Clyde,* which is also about two killers who are brought to their doom. That one, subjective and romantic, does not hold a candle, I feel, as a social illumination, to this one, which is objective and real.

—*B.C., December 15, 1967*

IN THE BEDROOM

Directed by Todd Field. written by Mr. Field and Robert Festinger. based on the short story "Killings" by Andre Dubus: director of photography. Antonio Calvache: edited by Frank Reynolds: music by Thomas Newman: produced by Mr. Field. Ross Katz and Graham Leader: released by Miramax Pictures. Running time: 130 minutes.

With: Sissy Spacek (Ruth Fowler). Tom Wilkinson (Matt Fowler). Nick Stahl (Frank Fowler). Marisa Tomei (Natalie Strout). William Mapother (Richard Strout). William Wise (Willis Grinnel). Celia Weston (Katie Grinnel). Karen Allen (Marla Keyes). Frank T. Wells (Henry). W. Clapham Murray (Carl). Justin Ashforth (Tim). Terry A. Burgess (District Attorney). Jonathan Walsh (Father McCasslin). Diane E. Hamlin (Davis's Assistant) and Camden Munson (Jason Strout).

The typical American movie is so committed to noisy spectacle and shameless emotional button-pushing that when a film as profoundly quiet as *In the Bedroom* comes along, it feels almost miraculous, as if a shimmering piece of art had slipped below the radar and through the minefield of commerce.

This perfectly observed, wrenchingly acted drama about a middle-class New England couple coping with the murder of their 21-year-old son cuts to the quick.

Its portrait of grief, rage, jealousy, flawed justice and revenge in a Maine lobstering town zeroes in on its characters' tragic flaws, yet refuses to condemn them. It reminds us that, like it or not, the capacity to commit a crime of passion is part of being human.

As the movie follows Matt and Ruth Fowler (Tom Wilkinson and Sissy Spacek) dragging themselves through the crushingly empty weeks after their son's murder, it finds in the hovering silences between words a depth of sorrow and stifled fury that few films have ever conveyed. The director Todd Field, who adapted the film from a story by Andre Dubus, understands that the essence of violence has little to do with Hollywood fireballs and the splatter of exploding bodies. It can accumulate over time and can be discerned in people's clenched, drawn faces and choked-back words.

Neither the killing itself nor the domestic disturbances that lead up to it are shown in the film, yet it sustains an awful sense of foreboding and dread of the inevitable. Its final disquieting message suggests that middle-class gentility is only a shallow veneer that circumstances can strip away; that the most perfect revenge can be far from sweet; that our darkest passions after discharging themselves may still never fully subside.

It is a message that seems especially pertinent since the events of Sept. 11. The terrorist attacks on the World Trade Center and the Pentagon left many Americans who had previously considered themselves gentle, nonviolent sorts unapologetically thirsting for eye-for-an-eye retaliation.

In the Bedroom begins with a romantic idyll in which the Fowlers' golden son, Frank (Nick Stahl), runs through a field with his slightly older girlfriend, Natalie Strout (Marisa Tomei), and they tumble blissfully into the grass. Frank—a handsome, careless architecture student, home for the summer—is considering postponing his fast-track career plans to go into the lobster business, in which he has a temporary job that he loves. Natalie is a working-class woman with two young children who is separated but still not divorced from her abusive husband, Richard (William Mapother), a former high school athlete who can't seem to get his life together.

Matt and Ruth are at odds over their son's relationship. While Matt, a prosperous local doctor, takes a vicarious enjoyment in the affair, Ruth sees Natalie as a threat to her son's future and makes no bones about

her disapproval. A proud, refined woman, highly competent but slightly cold, she teaches Eastern European folk songs to a high school chorus.

All these tensions tug at one another beneath the placid surface of a family picnic—the film's brilliant set piece—in which the dominant atmosphere is one of collective well-being. It is only when Richard makes an unexpected appearance that the tensions surface and warning signs flash. Although Richard wants desperately to reunite with Natalie, she has no interest in a reconciliation. But Richard can't leave her alone. And after several skirmishes, he sneaks into a back door of the house where she is staying with her children and Frank, and shoots him to death in the kitchen.

At first, the killing seems to be an open-and-shut case for which Richard stands to serve life imprisonment. But at the hearing, when Natalie truthfully testifies that she didn't actually see the shooting, an indictment for manslaughter appears likely, with Richard having to serve only a few years' time.

The Fowlers are outraged. And the anguished heart of the film explores their growing anger and frustration at what seems to be an imminent miscarriage of justice. Ruth, rigid and defiant, is the more furious of the two. The Fowlers browbeat the district attorney, and turn to their best friends, the Grinnels (William Wise and Celia Weston) as emotional allies.

As the Fowlers go about their daily business in Camden, their small town, their anger is continually pricked by glimpses of the killer, who has been released on bail.

When they can no longer bury their feelings, Matt and Ruth turn on each other, each blaming the other for Frank's death. The mutual bitterness they dredge up in one of the most emotionally brutal scenes of domestic strife ever filmed, is really the accumulated muck of any long-term relationship, When they've exhausted themselves, they can at least cling to each other in a way they hadn't before.

At this point the story makes a huge and dangerous leap. Late one night, as Richard is leaving his job in a bar on the outskirts of town, Matt appears and forces him into a car at gunpoint. It is the first step in an ingenious plan for revenge that involves kidnapping Richard and transporting him to a remote cabin in the Maine woods.

While an ordinary movie might have hardened its heart and milked the rest of the story for easy suspense and a cheap emotional payoff, *In the Bedroom* remains true to its commitment to explore every nuance of its characters' emotional lives by turning the tables. It finds Matt's mission every bit as ominous as Richard's crime. The outcome leaves a deeply bitter taste.

In the Bedroom is the directorial debut of Mr. Field, who wrote the screenplay with Rob Festinger. Phrase by phrase, image by image, it is an astonishingly rich, detailed and grimly moving piece of work. Ms. Spacek's performance is as devastating as it is unflashy. With the slight tightening of her neck muscles and a downward twitch of her mouth, she conveys her character's relentlessness, then balances it with enough sweetness to make Ruth seem entirely human. It is one of Ms. Spacek's greatest performances.

Mr. Wilkinson's shambling New England doctor is so quintessentially American in look and manner that you'd never guess he was a British Shakespearean actor. Ms. Tomei's ruined, sorrowful Natalie is easily her finest screen role.

The picturesque windburned town is as much a character as any individual, and the movie—which takes us aboard a lobster boat, visits the local cannery and stops in at stores and restaurants—almost makes us feel part of the community. It also reveals its pronounced class divisions.

In the Bedroom belongs to a handful of small, hardy North American films, among them *The Sweet Hereafter, Affliction,* and *You Can Count on Me,* whose flinty-eyed realism cuts against prevailing Hollywood froth. As small as their audiences may be, these are the films that stand the best chance of one day being regarded as classics. *In the Bedroom* is as good as any of them.

—S.H., November 23, 2001

IN THE HEAT OF THE NIGHT

Directed by Norman Jewison; written by Stirling Silliphant, based on the novel by John Ball; cinematographer, Haskell Wexler; edited by Hal Ashby; music by Quincy Jones; art designer, Paul Groesse; produced by Walter Mirisch; released by United Artists. Running time: 109 minutes.

With: Sidney Poitier (Virgil Tibbs), Rod Steiger (Bill Gillespie), Warren Oates (Sam Wood), Lee Grant (Mrs. Leslie Colbert), James Patterson (Purdy), Quentin Dean (Delores Purdy) and Larry Gates (Eric Endicott).

The hot surge of racial hate and prejudice that is so evident and critical now in so many places in this country, not alone in the traditional area of the Deep South, is fictionally isolated in an ugly little Mississippi town in the new film, *In the Heat of the Night,* which opened at the Capitol and the 86th Street East yesterday.

Here the corrosiveness of prejudice is manifested by a clutch of town police and a few weaseling nabobs and rednecks toward a Negro detective from the North who happens to be picked up as a suspect in a white man's murder while he is passing through town. But the surge of this evil feeling is also manifested by the Negro himself after he has been cleared of suspicion and ruefully recruited to help solve the crime. And in this juxtaposition of resentments between whites and blacks is vividly and forcefully illustrated one of the awful dilemmas of our times.

But here Norman Jewison has taken a hard, outspoken script, prepared by Stirling Silliphant from an undistinguished novel by John Ball, and, with stinging performances contributed by Rod Steiger as the chief of police and Sidney Poitier as the detective, he has turned it into a film that has the look and sound of actuality and the pounding pulse of truth.

The line of its fascination is not so much its melodramatic plot. It is not in the touch-and-go discovery by the detective of who it was who bumped off that prominent northern industrialist in town to start an integrated mill, or in the gantlet of perils of bodily injury from snarling rednecks that Mr. Poitier constantly runs. Actually, the mystery story is a rather routine and arbitrary one and it is brought to a hasty conclusion in a flurry of coincidences and explanations that leave one confused and unconvinced.

The fascination of it is in the crackling confrontations between the arrogant small town white policeman, with all his layers of ignorance and prejudice, and the sophisticated Negro detective with his steely armor of contempt and mistrust.

It is in the alert and cryptic caution with which these two professional cops face off, the white man arrogant and rueful but respectful of the black man's evident skill and the latter enraged and disgusted by the other's insulting attitudes.

And it is in the magnificent manner in which Mr. Steiger and Mr. Poitier act their roles, each giving physical authority and personal depth to the fallible human beings they are.

Fascinating, too, are the natures and details of other characters who swarm and sweat through a crisis in a believable Mississippi town—Warren Oates and Peter Whitney as raw cops, William Schallert and Larry Gates as powerful whites, Scott Wilson as a renegade redneck and Quentin Dean as a slippery little slut.

The end of it all is not conclusive. It does not imply that the state of prejudice and antagonism in the community is any different from what it was at the start. But it does suggest that a rapport between two totally antagonistic men may be reached in a state of interdependence. And that's something to be showing so forcefully on the screen.

—B.C., August 3, 1967

THE INFORMER

Directed by John Ford: written by Dudley Nichols. based on the novel by Liam O'Flaherty: cinematographer. Joseph August: edited by George Hively: music by Max Steiner: art designers. Van Nest Polglase and Charles Kirk: produced by Cliff Reid: released by RKO Production Company. Black and white. Running time: 91 minutes.

With: Victor McLaglen (Gypo Nolan). Heather Angel (Mary McPhillip). Preston Foster (Dan Gallagher). Margot Grahame (Katie Madden). Wallace Ford (Frankie McPhillip) and Una O'Connor (Mrs. McPhillip).

John Ford, who earned our gratitude last season with *The Lost Patrol,* has made an astonishing screen drama out of Liam O'Flaherty's novel *The Informer.* Having no patience with the childlike rigmarole of routine film manufacture, he recites Mr. O'Flaherty's realistic drama of the Dublin slums with bold and smashing skill. In his hands *The Informer* becomes at the same time a striking psychological study of a gutter Judas and a rawly impressive picture of the Dublin

underworld during the Black and Tan terror. It would not be strictly accurate to say that the photoplay unlooses the O'Flaherty work on the Music Hall's screen without compromise. But within his obvious limitations, Mr. Ford has achieved one of the finest dramas of the year.

There is something just a bit sinister about the way Victor McLaglen becomes brilliant under Mr. Ford's guidance. If you remember Mr. McLaglen in *The Lost Patrol,* you may not be surprised to learn that he makes something stark and memorable out of the stupid giant in *The Informer* who betrays his best friend to the Black and Tans for £20. The animal cunning of the man, his transparent deceits and his naive belief in his powers of deception are woven into the fabric of a character that is worthy of the pen of a Dostoyevsky. Amid the murk and drizzly mists in which the drama is played out, he becomes some dreadful and pathetic creature of darkness. Although the photoplay makes you understand why *informer* is the ugliest word in an Irishman's vocabulary, there is a tragic quality in this man's bewildered terror.

The cycle of Gypo Nolan's torment, from his betrayal, through his frantic spree with the blood money, to his death under the revolutionary guns, is enclosed within the twelve hours of a rainy night. When Frankie McPhillip comes down from the hills to visit his mother, it is partly hunger and partly a vague notion to flee with his sweetheart to America that makes Gypo walk into Black and Tan headquarters and claim the price that is on his friend's head. From that time until his death he is scourged by conscience and fear. He goes to the McPhillip home intending to divert suspicion from himself by attending the wake, and there he begins the strange behavior which finally betrays him to the organization. He numbs his tortured nerves with liquor and surrounds himself with underworld sycophants. He cannot drink too much or spend his money too quickly. At the court of inquiry he bears false witness against an innocent man, not knowing that he himself is on trial for his life. He dies at last, an abject coward, after he has been routed from his sweetheart's house.

It is one of the minor faults of *The Informer* that Katie, Gypo's companion, has been made into a conventional motion picture sweetie who pleads for his life as he lies hidden in her room. That is dramatically false, since Mr. O'Flaherty emphasizes the utter loneliness of an Irishman who has betrayed the cause, the traitor whom nobody will shield. It also struck this column that some judicious slicing in the middle section of the film would improve its tempo.

Under Mr. Ford's shrewd and sensitive direction there are excellent performances by Wallace Ford as the hunted Frankie McPhillip, by Una O'Connor as his sorrowing mother, by Donald Meek as the man whom Gypo accuses and by May Boley as the Madame Betty of the establishment where Gypo carouses. J. M. Kerrigan is amusing as a crafty tout, and Preston Foster, as the revolutionary commandant, does what he can with a role that was richer in the novel than it is on the screen.

—A.S., May 10, 1935

INHERIT THE WIND

Produced and directed by Stanley Kramer: written by Nathan E. Douglas and Harold Jacob Smith, based on the play by Jerome Lawrence and Robert E. Lee: cinematographer, Ernest Laszlo: edited by Frederic Knudston: music by Ernest Gold: production designer, Rudolph Sternad: released by United Artists. Black and white. Running time: 127 minutes.

With: Spencer Tracy (Henry Drummond), Fredric March (Matthew Harrison Brady), Gene Kelly (E. K. Hornbeck), Florence Eldridge (Mrs. Brady), Dick York (Bertram T. Cates), Donna Anderson (Rachel Brown), Harry Morgan (Judge), Elliott Reid (Davenport), Philip Coolidge (Mayor) and Claude Akins (Reverend Brown).

While the basic conflict is intellectual in the new film, *Inherit the Wind*—freedom of inquiry clashes with the slavery of dogmatic thought—it is one that can be made dramatic in a straight confrontation of two men, one a tough, agile advocate of freedom and the other a staunch, shrewd supporter of the mental block. This is the triumph of the picture that Stanley Kramer has made and that opened yesterday at the Astor and the redecorated Trans-Lux Eighty-fifth Street.

For with a dramatic face-off between Spencer Tracy and Fredric March, the two unsurpassable

actors persuaded to play the roles, Mr. Kramer has wonderfully accomplished not only a graphic fleshing of his theme but he also has got one of the most brilliant and engrossing displays of acting ever witnessed on the screen.

It is not an unmentionable secret that the stage play, *Inherit the Wind,* of Jerome Lawrence and Robert E. Lee, upon which this picture is based, was a thinly disguised reenactment of the famous trial of John T. Scopes—called the "monkey trial" by some newspapers—that took place in Dayton, Tennessee, in 1925. Nor is it a point to be avoided that its principal courtroom antagonists were supposed to be Clarence Darrow, the defense attorney, and William Jennings Bryan.

The latter is made more apparent, if not more explicit, in the film by Mr. March's extraordinary makeup and assumption of the mannerisms of Bryan. His fine simulation of a bald dome, a fringe of flowing hair, and a way of tightening his lips and making gestures and nervous flutters with a palm-leaf fan are vividly recollective of the "silver-tongued orator" who made the air ring with his phrases in support of the fundamentalist interpretation of the Bible at the Dayton trial.

But the accuracy of the resemblance is mainly a dividend for those who remember what Bryan looked like. The artistic virtue of it is that it gives a stunning comprehension of a proud, pompous, demagogic man, full of dogmatic assertion and theatrical flourishes who stands serenely encircled by ignorance until the locks of his own mind are forced.

As the man who accomplishes this forcing, by dint of his intelligence, tenacity, patience, inspiration and adroitness at verbal argument, Mr. Tracy does not endeavor to do a resemblance to Darrow, but he gives a fine, forceful simulation of a strong, homespun advocate of good sense. He is, of course, the lawyer who defends the young schoolteacher charged with violating the state law forbidding the teaching of Darwin's theory of evolution.

As courtroom antagonists, Mr. Tracy and Mr. March strike continuous sparks that fall into the highly volatile tinder of surroundings that richly represent a community of generally ignorant, bigoted people supercharged with emotion over the trial. All of this, too, is recreated by Mr. Kramer with colorfulness and clarity, so that humor as well as grassroots toughness is piled with insensitivity.

Conspicuous in the surroundings are assorted small-town types and several characters closely related to the principals. There is the young man on trial, a hayseed hero, played stalwartly by Dick York, a fire-snorting fundamentalist minister, performed robustly by Claude Akins, and the latter's tormented daughter, played tautly by Donna Anderson. There's the wife of the fundamentalist lawyer, whom Florence Eldridge quietly makes a beautifully ladylike dispenser of compassion and loyalty, and there's a nimble newspaper reporter, played briskly and glibly by Gene Kelly.

Some changes have been made by Nathan E. Douglas and Harold Jacob Smith in writing the play into a script. Some academic and theological points have been blunted, the carnival atmosphere of the trial pointed up. But the essential conflict of the principals is precisely what it was, and it grows in tempestuousness and tension until it is the big dramatic thing.

When the two men come to their final showdown and the barrier of dogma is breached, it is a triumphant moment for human dignity—and for Mr. Tracy and Mr. March.

—B.C., October 13, 1960

THE INSIDER

Directed by Michael Mann; written by Eric Roth and Mr. Mann, based on the article "The Man Who Knew Too Much" by Marie Brenner; director of photography, Dante Spinotti; edited by William Goldenberg, Paul Rubell and David Rosenbloom; music by Lisa Gerrard and Pieter Bourke; production designer, Brian Morris; produced by Mr. Mann and Pieter Jan Brugge; released by Touchtone Pictures. Running time: 155 minutes.

With: Al Pacino (Lowell Bergman), Russell Crowe (Jeffrey Wigand), Christopher Plummer (Mike Wallace), Michael Gambon (Thomas Sandefur), Diane Venora (Liane Wigand), Bruce McGill (Ron Motley), Philip Baker Hall (Don Hewitt), Lindsay Crouse (Sharon Tiller) and Gina Gershon (Helen Caperelli).

Late in *The Insider* the tobacco industry whistle-blower Jeffrey Wigand sits despondently in a hotel room and contemplates the steep price of what he has done. The setting is somber except for the bright pastoral mural on the wall behind him, looking like a window onto an unsullied, unattainable world. Then the image begins to roil and morph, and it turns into a vision of the home and family that Mr. Wigand has lost. This is a flashy visual effect, but it's also one that piercingly captures the man's state of mind. And although Michael Mann is a filmmaker whose stylistic brio has a way of overpowering his subject matter, this time he strikes a balance, and he gets it right.

Mr. Mann has directed *The Insider* with a pulse-quickening panache that heightens the tensions within its story. In describing Mr. Wigand's progress from a staid corporate existence into a risky and unpredictable one, the film entails both visual and moral vertigo. Once Hollywood had a favorite folk tale: that the lone truth teller battling political or corporate evil would triumph, however bitterly, when the facts became known. But in the chillingly contemporary world of *The Insider* it's not that simple. Almost every character in the story is compromised by business considerations. And in the film's vision of television news reporting, moral relativism is a big part of playing the game.

The film centers on CBS's *60 Minutes* and does the kind of muckraking that would ordinarily be that program's own province. The connection between CBS and Mr. Wigand's revelations—that the Brown & Williamson Tobacco Company knew that cigarette smoking was addictive even as it sought new ways to make nicotine deliver more of a kick—is a producer named Lowell Bergman.

In the film Mr. Bergman keeps a portrait of Cesar Chavez on display, mentions that Herbert Marcuse was his mentor ("major influence on the New Left in the 1960's") and otherwise calls attention to his political credentials. "How did a radical journalist from *Ramparts* magazine wind up at CBS?" he is asked. He replies modestly: "I still do the tough stories. *60 Minutes* reaches a lot of people."

The film's casting stacks the deck to lionize Mr. Bergman, even while that casting also makes for dramatic fireworks. Christopher Plummer does an acute Mike Wallace impersonation, summoning all the mannerisms familiar to television audiences, including Mr. Wallace's canny way of listening. And Russell Crowe, a subtle powerhouse in his wrenching evocation of Mr. Wigand, takes on the thick, stolid look of the man he portrays.

On the other hand, Mr. Bergman is glamorized into a crusading Al Pacino and becomes the only beacon of rectitude to be found here. But *The Insider* is a movie about shadows, not absolutes. And it would have reached deeper if its Mr. Bergman weren't so self-righteous a hero.

The Insider, as written by Eric Roth (*Forrest Gump*) and Mr. Mann, suspensefully lays out the facts of its story. It begins as Mr. Wigand surreptitiously reveals what he has learned as a chemist for Brown & Williamson: Its cigarettes are designed to deliver an extra-quick fix of nicotine despite obvious health risks. Sensing that Mr. Wigand may be a loose cannon, the company's chief executive (played commandingly by Michael Gambon) binds Mr. Wigand to a strict confidentiality agreement.

But as the pressure on him begins to mount, Mr. Wigand finds his situation becoming intolerable. "Can you imagine," he asks Diane Venora, as the wife who will soon be walking out on him, "me coming home from some job and feeling good at the end of the day?"

Along comes *60 Minutes,* with promises to give Mr. Wigand's charges a public airing, but with too much corporate baggage to let that happen. *The Insider* offers an account of how the program wound up sidestepping the confidentiality agreement to interview Mr. Wigand and exposing him to threats of retaliation, only to bail out on running the interview when it ran afoul of CBS's larger interests. What emerge as controversial here are not the facts themselves but the ways in which *The Insider* uses docudrama ethics to draw its close-up views of CBS's inner workings.

The movie is about telling the truth, and yet at times it seems manipulative itself, as when it presents Mr. Wallace confessing his innermost thoughts about his career and reputation.

This venerable television star could have been captured just as fully in the scene that finds him venting outrage at Gina Gershon's smooth corporate lawyer. "Mike?" he thunders when she addresses him. "Mike? Try Mr. Wallace."

The Insider is still sleek, gripping entertainment with a raw-nerved, changeable camera style that helps to amplify its meaning. So what if, when Mr. Bergman finds himself feeling betrayed and alone, he happens to be standing in the turquoise waters of some tropical hideaway? And so what if when the Wigand story pushes him to the edge, the film visualizes this picturesquely as the Gulf Coast of Mississippi?

There are stunningly evocative images here, like perilous nighttime scenes at a golf driving range and in the Wigand backyard, with dramatic meaning only heightened by their obvious beauty. This is the kind of movie in which Mr. Bergman can make a phone call and reach somebody who happens to be in the cockpit of a Lear jet. Thanks to the dazzling cinematography of Dante Spinotti (whose other Mann films include *Heat* and *The Last of the Mohicans*) visual interest is not a problem.

The Insider, by far Mr. Mann's most fully realized and enthralling work, features brief, sharply etched performances from Bruce McGill as a Mississippi prosecutor raging in a courtroom, Lindsay Crouse as Mr. Bergman's wife and Philip Baker Hall as the *60 Minutes* executive who labels Mr. Bergman an anarchist and a fanatic. Each of these characters contributes memorably to the film's troubling resolution and to Mr. Bergman's verdict on the emblematic crisis within *the Insider.* As he puts it regretfully, "What got broken here doesn't go back together again."

—J.M., November 5, 1999

INTERNAL AFFAIRS

Directed by Mike Figgis; written by Henry Bean; director of photography, John A. Alonzo; edited by Robert Estrin; music by Mr. Figgis, Anthony Marinelli and Brian Banks; production designer, Waldemar Kalinowski; produced by Frank Mancuso, Jr.; released by Paramount Pictures. Running time: 115 minutes.

With: Richard Gere (Dennis Peck), Andy Garcia (Sergeant Raymond Avila), Nancy Travis (Kathleen Avila), Laurie Metcalf (Sergeant Amy Wallace), Annabella Sciorra (Heather), Richard Bradford (Grieb), William Baldwin (Van Stretch) and Michael Beach (Dorian).

Mike Figgis's films could be watched at any hour, but they're really best suited to the middle of the night. With only two theatrical features to his credit, the terrific 1988 sleeper *Stormy Monday* and now *Internal Affairs,* a dizzying police thriller, Mr.

Figgis has established himself as a master of steamy sex appeal and brooding, nocturnal murk.

Logic and character development take a distinct back seat, in Mr. Figgis's scheme of things, to sheer overheated atmosphere. No one in either of these films seems ever to blink. Every relationship has some physical component, whether it's the charged camaraderie between a male police detective and his female partner or the grasping and slapping that heighten an exchange between two male friends. Dresses are short, tempers even more so. And every man on the force in *Internal Affairs* seems to have a beautiful, restless, tousle-haired wife.

Richard Gere at first seems an odd choice for the role of Dennis Peck, a stalwart officer of the Los Angeles Police Department. But it soon becomes clear that part of what Peck does is pay attention to all those tousle-haired women. *Internal Affairs* gradually reveals that Peck is a great deal more diabolical than he initially appears, and that he may, in fact, be one of the rottenest movie cops in memory. That he is also supposed to be the serene father of eight children (with a ninth on the way), a man who has been married either three or four times (the number seems to vary from scene to scene), is just one indication of the film's cheery disregard of credibility.

Andy Garcia, with a police department brush cut to match Mr. Gere's, appears as Peck's nemesis, a detective newly assigned to the department's internal affairs division in charge of investigating in-house indiscretions. As Raymond Avila, Mr. Garcia teams up with a somberly magnetic new partner named Amy Wallace (Laurie Metcalf) and immediately begins to notice some peculiarities about Dennis Peck's private life. It develops that Peck is able to support all of his various families in relatively high style, and that Peck's close friends on the force also live well beyond their official means.

The ensuing investigation gravitates further and further away from the facts of the case, until it begins to seem as if no one on the LAPD does a lick of work, that sexual taunting is what makes the world go round and that every seemingly happy marriage is an accident waiting to happen. Raymond Avila at one point finds his own wife, Kathleen (Nancy Travis), lunching secretly with Dennis Peck. At another point, he turns up at the museum where she stages exhibitions of risqué video art, and finds her talking about Luis Buñuel's *Belle du Jour*.

Simply by virtue of its being a police thriller, *Internal Affairs* is less original than *Stormy Monday,* which had an unusual mix of characters and a novel setting in the waterfront music clubs of Newcastle, England. Mr. Figgis, a sometime musician who once again contributes part of his film's score, has attempted something more conventional this time, but he still invests it with purring, libidinous energy and a lot of heat.

The last part of the story, turning gory and feverish, winds up going way overboard. Even then, the film's energy level remains enjoyably high. The cast is well chosen and attractive, with Ms. Metcalf particularly good in her supporting role; also good is Annabella Sciorra, the star of *True Love,* who plays the small and mostly thankless role of Dennis Peck's latest wife. The very appealing Mr. Garcia has an intense, studied cool that is nicely offset by bilingual outbursts. And Mr. Gere makes the most of Peck's smiling villainy, giving him a powerful physical presence and a dangerous, unpredictable edge.

Henry Bean's screenplay has no fear of the farfetched, along with a tendency toward excessive jive. But it does mark the first time one screen character has screamed "You selfish yuppie!" at another. The screenplay also raises countless unanswered questions, one of which has to do with how one character happens to wind up with another character's underwear. Surely the film's biggest mystery is how Dennis Peck, with so many children, still manages in one scene to have a long, uninterrupted and carefree conversation with his wife while she is in the bathtub.

Internal Affairs is, for the dim movie season that is traditionally January, an unusually bright light.

—*J.M., January 12, 1990*

THE IPCRESS FILE

Directed by Sidney J. Furie; written by Bill Canaway and James Doran, based on the novel by Len Deighton; cinematographer, Otto Heller; edited by Peter Hunt; music by John Barry; production designer, Ken Adam; produced by Harry Saltzman; released by Universal Pictures. Running time: 108 minutes.

With: Michael Caine (Harry Palmer), Nigel Green (Dalby), Guy Doleman (Major Ross), Sue Lloyd

(Jean), Gordon Jackson (Jock Carswell) and Aubrey Richards (Radcliffe).

It doesn't take a detective to figure out Harry Saltzman's game and to calculate what's brewing in his British spy film, *The Ipcress File*.

Having picked up a tidy packet as coproducer of the James Bond films and having found what appears to be a booming market for pictures about daredevil sleuths (vide Jean-Paul Belmondo's as well as Sean Connery's), he is obviously trying to start another with a good-looking chap named Michael Caine in this double-o-sevenish picture, which came to the Coronet yesterday.

And in one respect he has succeeded. He has built up the proper atmosphere in which a daredevil-challenging mystery might conceivably occur and a dauntless and daring detective might acceptably take wing.

His Techniscope setting of London, in which this espionage thriller takes place, is full of rich and mellow colors and highly official goings-on behind dark-paneled doors in old, gray buildings and in cozy bachelor digs and gentlemen's clubs.

An air of mystery and menace to the very balance of scientific power seems to surround the pressing problem Civil Intelligence has to solve regarding the curious kidnapping and brainwashing—or braindraining, as they call it—of a slew of distinguished scientists. And the chaps who have to solve it seem eminently qualified.

There's Dalby, chief of Civil Intelligence, a bristly-mustached, guardsman type, quivering with efficiency and sarcasm as played by Nigel Green. There's Ross, chief of Military Intelligence, who has curiously passed the buck, and, in Guy Doleman's slippery portrayal, seems not quite worthy of trust.

There's Carswell, the canny Scot analyst who assembles the Ipcress file and is strangely bumped off shortly after. Gordon Jackson performs well in the role.

And, finally, there's Harry Palmer, the key sleuth, played by Mr. Caine, not to mention several lesser secret agents, including one strange, incongruous girl.

Yes, there's everything here to charge the large screen with the toniest spy-film atmosphere, and the director, Sidney J. Furie, has added to it with his flashy camera style.

Fast, fluid, candid shooting; startling close-ups of telephones, traffic lights, train wheels; eyes and faces seen through slits in doors make for sheer physical excitement and a feeling of things happening. *The Ipcress File* is as classy a spy film as you could ask to see.

But somehow Len Deighton's story of this running down of a gang of scientist body snatchers gets confusingly out of hand as it tumbles and swirls in the direction of a gadgeted sweatbox in which the hero's mental reflexes are relentlessly conditioned under stress.

Suspense and even attention are allowed to lag by the script that Bill Canaway and James Doran have written. There are too many yawning holes in it.

And for all Mr. Caine's casual manner—for all his scholarly and amiable air—he just doesn't ooze the magnetism that would make him an irresistible sleuth. He is simply too much of an esthete. He loves Mozart, cooking and books as much as he loves—well, temptation of the sort introduced by Sue Lloyd.

There may be a place in the affections of some filmgoers for a genteel cop—for one who can cook up a stew as well as a turmoil. But this one will never take the place of Bond.

—*B.C., August 3, 1965*

IT HAPPENED ONE NIGHT

Directed by Frank Capra; written by Robert Riskin, based on the story "Night Bus" by Samuel Hopkins Adams; cinematographer, Joseph Walker; edited by Gene Havlick; music by Louis Silvers; art designer, Stephen Goosson; produced by Harry Cohn; released by Columbia Pictures. Black and white. Running time: 105 minutes.

With: Clark Gable (Peter Warne), Claudette Colbert (Ellie Andrews), Walter Connolly (Alexander Andrews), Roscoe Karns (Mr. Shapeley) and Jameson Thomas (King Westley).

There are few serious moments in *It Happened One Night*, a screen feast which awaits visitors to the Radio City, and if there is a welter of improbable incidents these hectic doings serve to generate plenty of laughter. The pseudosuspense is kept on the wing until a few seconds before the picture ends, but it is a foregone conclusion that the producers would never dare to have the characters acted by Clark Gable and Claudette Colbert separated when the curtain falls.

In this merry romance, which is an adaptation of a magazine story by Samuel Hopkins Adams, Peter Warne (Mr. Gable) and Ellie Andrews (Miss Colbert) enjoy the discomforts of a long-distance bus ride; they also experience the pain of hitchhiking and the joys of tourist camps. Besides these glimpses, one beholds Alexander Andrews searching for his daughter in an airplane, expostulating with secretaries and sleuths because he is unable to find the missing girl, incidentally an heiress.

Warne is one of those crack newspaper men frequently discovered in Hollywood's spacious studios. He does not hesitate to tell his superiors in outbursts of slang precisely what he thinks of them, even though his finances at the time are at a low ebb. Ellie is an obstinate young person, who to spite her father has become the wife (in name only) of a dashing young man named King Westley. She finds herself virtually a prisoner on her father's yacht and, in the introductory scenes, she is on a hunger strike. Soon afterward she darts from her cabin to the deck, leaps overboard and swims for Florida and freedom.

It is while she is on her way from Miami to New York that she encounters Warne, an audacious person. To make matters more interesting, the producers or the author decide that the fiery Ellie must have her suitcase stolen. As days go by, Warne and Ellie experience the pangs of hunger and, at one period, they have to content themselves with a meal of raw carrots.

It Happened One Night is a good piece of fiction, which, with all its feverish stunts, is blessed with bright dialogue and a good quota of relatively restrained scenes. Although there are such flighty notions as that of having Ellie running away from a marriage ceremony when the guests—and particularly King Westley—had expected to hear her say "I will"; or those depicting Warne volleying vituperation over the telephone at his city editor; there are also more sober sequences wherein Warne and Ellie spread cheer to the audience, notwithstanding their sorry adventures with little or no money.

Miss Colbert gives an engaging and lively performance. Mr. Gable is excellent in his role. Roscoe Karns affords no little fun by his flirtatious conduct on board a bus. Walter Connolly is in his element as Ellie's father and Alan Hale gives a robust portrayal of an artful owner of a flivver.

—M.H., February 23, 1934

IT'S A GIFT

Directed by Norman Z. McLeod; written by Jack Cunningham and W. C. Fields, based on the play *The Comic Supplement* by J. P. McEvoy and a story by Charles Bogle (W. C. Fields); cinematographer, Henry Sharp; art designer, Hans Dreier; produced by William LeBaron; released by Paramount Pictures. Black and white. Running time: 73 minutes.

With: W. C. Fields (Harold Bissonette), Baby LeRoy (Baby Dunk), Kathleen Howard (Amelia Bissonette), Jean Rouverol (Mildred Bissonette), T. Roy Barnes (Insurance Salesman) and Julian Madison (John Durston).

Perhaps if the W. C. Fields idolators continue their campaign on his behalf over a sufficient period of years his employers may finally invest him with a production befitting his dignity as a great artist. In the meantime such comparatively journeyman pieces as *It's a Gift* will serve very adequately to keep his public satisfied. Although the Roxy's new Fields picture is seldom equal in comic invention to the master's possibilities, it does keep him on the screen almost continuously, and it permits him to illuminate the third-rate vaudeville katzenjammer of the work with his own quite irresistible style of humor. To the student of comedy who is able to tell a great funnyman from a merely good one, that is a way of saying that *It's a Gift* is the first "must" assignment to the new year.

You ought to be informed that the slightly phony name of Charles Bogle, which appears among the credits as the author of the story, is really Mr. Fields himself, lurking modestly in the corridors of Paramount's Writer's Row. This time he is the vague and fumbling Mr. Bissonette, who is the proprietor of a small-town general store as well as the helpless victim of a shrewish wife. *It's a Gift* tells how Mr. Bissonette, after being badgered and hounded beyond his generous powers of endurance, finally boards a rattletrap flivver with his family and sets off across the country to a California orange plantation that he has purchased with the proceeds of his late uncle's will.

That is approximately a skeleton of the narrative and as usual it is singularly useless as a guide to Mr. Fields's behavior. *It's a Gift* immerses the veery, adenoidal, and bulbous-nosed star in a variety of situations that he promptly embroiders into priceless and classic comic episodes. You find him torturing the laws of logic and gravitation in his efforts to shave himself while being annoyed by his young daughter. There is the extended account of his futile struggles to catch some sleep on the porch after he has been driven from his bedroom by Mrs. Bissonette's constant nagging. With the one exception of Charlie Chaplin, there is nobody but Mr. Fields who could manage the episode with the blind and deaf man in the store so as to make it seem genuinely and inescapably funny instead of just a trifle revolting. Then, with Baby LeRoy for his straight man, he goes quite mad during the infant's extensive operations in the store, finally closing up shop in despair and leaving behind him a sign explaining that the store is closed on account of molasses.

The great man's assistants in the new comedy provide him with excellent foils. As the nagging wife Kathleen Howard is so authentic as to make Mr. Fields's sufferings seem cosmic and a little sad despite their basic humor. As the thick witted grocery clerk, Tammany Young is an effective lunkhead, and Charles Sellon, as the blind man, is quite as irresistible as he was last month as the wheelchair invalid in *Bright Eyes*. The fact is that Mr. Fields has come back to us again and *It's a Gift* automatically becomes the best screen comedy on Broadway.

—*A.S., January 5, 1935*

IT'S A WONDERFUL LIFE

Produced and directed by Frank Capra: written by Frances Goodrich, Albert Hackett, Mr. Capra and Jo Swerling, based on the story "The Greatest Gift" by Philip Van Doren Stern; cinematographers, Joseph Walker and Joseph Biroc; edited by William Hornbeck; music by Dimitri Tiomkin; art designer, Jack Okey; released by RKO Radio Pictures. Black and white. Running time: 129 minutes.

With: James Stewart (George Bailey), Donna Reed (Mary Hatch), Lionel Barrymore (Mr. Potter), Thomas Mitchell (Uncle Billy), Beulah Bondi (Mrs. Bailey), Frank Faylen (Ernie), Ward Bond (Bert), Harry Travers (Clarence), H. B. Warner (Mr. Gower) and Gloria Grahame (Violet).

The late and beloved Dexter Fellows, who was a circus press agent for many years, had an interesting theory on the theater that suited his stimulating trade. He held that the final curtain of every drama, no matter what, should benignly fall upon the whole cast sitting down to a turkey dinner and feeling fine. Mr. Fellows should be among us to see Frank Capra's *It's a Wonderful Life,* which opened on Saturday at the Globe Theatre. He would find it very much to his taste.

For a turkey dinner, with Christmas trimmings, is precisely what's cooking at the end of this quaint and engaging modern parable on virtue being its own reward. And a whole slew of cozy small-town characters who have gone through a lot in the past two hours are waiting around to eat it—or, at least, to watch James Stewart gobble it up. For it is really Mr. Stewart who does most of the heavy suffering in this film, and it is he who, in the end, is most deserving of the white meat and the stuffing.

That is because Mr. Capra, back from the war, has resumed with a will his previously manifest penchant for portraying folks of simple, homely worth. And in this picture about a young fellow who wants to break away from his small-town life and responsibilities but is never able to do so because slowly they close in upon him, Mr. Capra has gone all out to show that it is really a family, friends and honest toil that make the "wonderful life."

His hero is a personable fellow who wants to travel and do big things but ultimately finds himself running a building-and-loan association in a one-horse town, married and locked in constant struggle with the greedy old banker of the town. And when it finally looks as though the banker is about to drive him to ruin, he makes what appears a brash endeavor to take his own baffled life. Whereupon a heavenly messenger providentially intercedes and shows him, in fanciful fashion, what the town would have been like without him. The vision is so distressing that he returns to his lot with boundless joy—and is saved, also providentially, by the financial assistance of his friends.

In composing this moralistic fable, Mr. Capra and his writers have tossed in a great abundance of colloquial incidents and emotional tangles of a mistful, humorous sort. The boyhood of his hero, the frolic at a high school dance, the clumsy pursuit of a courtship—all are shown in an entertaining way, despite the too frequent inclinations of everyone to act juvenile and coy. And the heavier sections of the drama are managed in a tense, precipitate style.

As the hero, Mr. Stewart does a warmly appealing job, indicating that he has grown in spiritual stature as well as in talent during the years he was in the war. And Donna Reed is remarkably poised and gracious as his adoring sweetheart and wife. Thomas Mitchell, Beulah Bondi, H. B. Warner, and Samuel S. Hinds stand out among the group of assorted small-town characters who give the picture variety and verve. But Lionel Barrymore's banker is almost a caricature of Scrooge, and Henry Travers's "heavenly messenger" is a little too sticky for our taste.

Indeed, the weakness of this picture, from this reviewer's point of view, is the sentimentality of it—its illusory concept of life. Mr. Capra's nice people are charming, his small town is a quite beguiling place and his pattern for solving problems is most optimistic and facile. But somehow they all resemble theatrical attitudes rather than average realities. And Mr. Capra's "turkey dinners" philosophy, while emotionally gratifying, doesn't fill the hungry paunch.

—*B.C., December 23, 1946*

JAILHOUSE ROCK

Directed by Richard Thorpe: written by Nedrick Young and Guy Trosper: director of photography. Robert J. Bronner: edited by Ralph E. Winters: art directors. Randall Duell and William A. Horning: music by Roy C. Bennett. Jerry Leiber. Aaron Schroder. Abner Silver. Mike Stoller. Sid Tepper. Ben Weisman: produced by Pandro S. Berman: released by Metro-Goldwyn-Mayer. Running time: 96 minutes.

With: Elvis Presley (Vince Everett). Judy Tyler (Peggy Van Alden). Mickey Shaughnessy (Hunk Houghton). Vaughn Taylor (Mr. Shores. narrator). Jennifer Holden (Sherry Wilson). Dean Jones (Teddy Talbot) and Anne Neyland (Laury Jackson).

Jailhouse Rock a Metro-Goldwyn-Mayer showcase for Elvis Presley, opening yesterday on the Loew's neighborhood circuit, carries ol' El all the way from the hoosegow to Hollywood, where our boy turns into a sour, spoiled (millionaire) apple. A pal beats some sense back into him though.

This, the third Presley picture, reverentially produced by Pandro S. Berman and directed by Richard Thorpe, also features two talented performers, Mickey Shaughnessy and Judy Tyler. The former plays a kind of Luther Billis of a state pen, who should be forgiven for developing his young cellmate's talent. Although she isn't allotted one single note here. Miss Tyler is the lovely little brunette from Broadway's *Pipe Dream*, tragically killed after making her film debut.

For reasons best known to Guy Trosper, who wrote the script, these two delightfully capable people are forced to hang onto the hero's flying mane and ego for the entire picture.

Here's what happens. Defending a frail lady barfly, Elvis conks a bully and draws a brief sentence for manslaughter. Toughened considerably, he later forms a record company with Miss Tyler, as the money and fame roll in. "Uh got wars [wires] 'n' letters from all over the wurl'," he gloats at one point. Presley fans may not like the idea of his being a churlish, egotistical wonder boy of television and the screen for a good half of the picture.

Elvis stays front and center, of course, muttering his lines sheepishly, and wooing Miss Tyler by collapsing like a rag doll and hooking a chin on her shoulder.

The sound technicians must have closed in, for this time most of his singing can actually be understood. And in two numbers, "Treat Me Nice" and the title song, done as a convict jamboree, Elvis breaks loose with his St. Vitus specialty. Ten to one, next time he'll make it—finally getting those kneecaps turned inside out and cracking them together like coconuts. Never say die, El.

—*H.H.T., November 14, 1957*

JAWS

Directed by Steven Spielberg: written by Peter Benchley and Carl Gottlieb. based on the novel by Mr. Benchley: director of photography. Bill Butler: edited by Verna Fields: production design by Joe Alves: music by John Williams: produced by David

Brown and Richard D. Zanuck: released by Universal Pictures. Running time: 124 minutes.

With: Roy Scheider (Police Chief Martin Brody). Robert Shaw (Quint). Richard Dreyfuss (Matt Hooper). Lorraine Gary (Ellen Brody). Murray Hamilton (Mayor Larry Vaughn). Carl Gottlieb (Ben Meadows) and Jeffrey Kramer (Deputy Leonard Hendricks).

If you are what you eat, then one of the sharks in *Jaws* is a beer can, half a mackerel and a Louisiana license plate. Another is a pretty young woman, a cylinder of oxygen, a small boy, a scout master and still more. The other characters in the film are nowhere nearly so fully packed.

Jaws, which opened yesterday at three theaters, is the film version of Peter Benchley's best-selling novel about a man-eating great white shark that terrorizes an East Coast resort community, which now looks very much like Martha's Vineyard, where the film was shot.

It's a noisy, busy movie that has less on its mind than any child on a beach might have. It has been cleverly directed by Steven Spielberg (*Sugarland Express*) for maximum shock impact and short-term suspense, and the special effects are so good that even the mechanical sharks are as convincing as the people.

Jaws is, at heart, the old standby, a science-fiction film. It opens according to time-honored tradition with a happy-go-lucky innocent being suddenly ravaged by the mad monster, which, in *Jaws* comes from the depths of inner space—the sea as well as man's nightmares. Thereafter *Jaws* follows the formula with fidelity.

Only one person in the community (the chief of police) realizes the true horror of what has happened, while the philistines (the mayor, the merchants and the tourism people) pooh-pooh his warnings. The monster strikes again. An expert (an oceanographer) is brought in who confirms everyone's wildest fears, at which point the community bands together to hire an eccentric specialist (a shark fisherman) to secure their salvation.

If you think about *Jaws* for more than 45 seconds you will recognize it as nonsense, but it's the sort of nonsense that can be a good deal of fun if you like to have the wits scared out of you at irregular intervals.

It's a measure of how the film operates that not once do we feel particular sympathy for any of the shark's victims, or even the mother of one, a woman who has an embarrassingly tearful scene that at one point threatens to bring the film to a halt. This kind of fiction doesn't inspire humane responses. Just the opposite. We sigh with relief after each attack, smug in our awareness that it happened to them, not us.

In the best films characters are revealed in terms of the action. In movies like *Jaws,* characters are simply functions of the action. They're at its service. Characters are like stage hands who move props around and deliver information when it's necessary, which is pretty much what Roy Scheider (the police chief), Robert Shaw (the shark fisherman) and Richard Dreyfuss (the oceanographer) do.

It may not look like much but it puts good actors to the test. They have to work very hard just to appear alive, and Mr. Scheider, Mr. Shaw and Mr. Dreyfuss come across with wit and easy self-assurance.

It's not their fault if they are upstaged by the mechanics of the fiction. That, too, is the way *Jaws* was meant to be. Mr. Spielberg has so effectively spaced out the shocks that by the time we reach the spectacular final confrontation between the three men and the great white shark, we totally accept the make-believe on its own foolishly entertaining terms.

—*U.C., June 21, 1975*

THE JAZZ SINGER

Directed by Alan Crosland: written by Alfred A. Cohn and Jack Jarmuth. based on the play *Day of Atonement* by Samson Raphaelson: cinematographer. Hal Mohr: edited by Harold McCord: music by Louis Silvers: released by Warner Brothers. Black and white. Running time: 88 minutes.

With: Al Jolson (Jakie Rabinowitz/Jack Robin). May McAvoy (Mary Dale). Warner Oland (Cantor Rabinowitz). Eugenie Besserer (Sara Rabinowitz). Bobby Gordon (Jakie at 13) and Otto Lederer (Moishe Yudelson).

In a story that is very much like that of his own life, Al Jolson at Warners' Theatre last night made his screen debut in the picturization of Samson Raphaelson's play *The Jazz Singer,* and through the interpolation of the Vitaphone the audience had the rare opportunity of hearing Mr. Jolson sing several of his own songs and also render most effectively the Jewish hymn "Kol Nidre."

Mr. Jolson's persuasive vocal efforts were received with rousing applause. In fact, not since the first presentation of Vitaphone features, more than a year ago at the same playhouse, has anything like the ovation been heard in a motion picture theater. And when the film came to an end Mr. Jolson himself expressed his sincere appreciation of the Vitaphoned film, declaring that he was so happy that he could not stop the tears.

The Vitaphoned songs and some dialogue have been introduced most adroitly. This in itself is an ambitious move, for in the expression of song the Vitaphone vitalizes the production enormously. The dialogue is not so effective, for it does not always catch the nuances of speech or inflections of the voice so that one is not aware of the mechanical features.

The Warner Brothers astutely realized that a film conception of *The Jazz Singer* was one of the few subjects that would lend itself to the use of the Vitaphone. It was also a happy idea to persuade Mr. Jolson to play the leading role, for few men could have approached the task of singing and acting so well as he does in this photoplay. His "voice with a tear" compelled silence, and possibly all that disappointed the people in the packed theater was the fact that they could not call upon him or his image at least for an encore. They had to content themselves with clapping and whistling after Mr. Jolson's shadow finished a realistic song. It was also the voice of Jolson, with its dramatic sweep, its pathos and soft slurring tones.

One of the most interesting sequences of the picture itself is where Mr. Jolson as Jack Robin (formerly Jakie Rabinowitz) is perceived talking to Mary Dale (May McAvoy) as he smears his face with black. It is done gradually, and yet the dexterity with which Mr. Jolson outlines his mouth is readily appreciated. You see Jack Robin, the young man who at last has his big opportunity, with a couple of smudges of black on his features, and then his cheeks, his nose, his forehead and the back of his neck are blackened. It is also an engaging scene where Jack's mother comes to the Winter Garden and sees him for the first time as a blackface entertainer.

There is naturally a good deal of sentiment attached to the narrative, which is one wherein Cantor Rabinowitz is eager that his son Jakie shall become a cantor to keep up the traditions of the family. The old man's anger is aroused when one night he hears that Jakie has been singing jazz songs in a saloon. The boy's heart and soul are with the modern music. He runs away from home and tours the country until through a friend he is engaged by a New York producer to sing in the Winter Garden. His debut is to be made on the Day of Atonement, and, incidentally, when his father is dying. Toward the end, however, the old cantor on his deathbed hears his son chanting the "Kol Nidre."

Some time afterward Jack Robin is perceived and heard singing "Mammy," while his old mother occupies a seat in the front row. Here Mr. Jolson puts all the force of his personality into the song as he walks out beyond the footlights and, sometimes with clasped hands, he sings as if to his own mother.

The success of this production is due to a large degree to Mr. Jolson's Vitaphoned renditions. There are quite a few moments when the picture drags, because Alan Crosland, the director, has given too much footage to discussion and to the attempts of the theatrical manager (in character) to prevail upon Jack Robin not to permit sentiment to sway him (Jack) when his great opportunity is at hand. There are also times when one would expect the Vitaphoned portions to be either more subdued or stopped as the camera swings to other scenes. The voice is usually just the same whether the image of the singer is close to the camera or quite far away.

Warner Oland does capable work as Cantor Rabinowitz. May McAvoy is attractive, but has little to do as Mary Dale. In most of her scenes Eugenie Besserer acts with sympathetic restraint.

Cantor Josef Rosenblatt contributes an excellent Vitaphoned concert number in the course of the narrative.

—*M.H., October 7, 1927*

JEAN DE FLORETTE

Directed by Claude Berri; written (in French, with English subtitles) by Mr. Berri and Gérard Brach, based on the novel by Marcel Pagnol; director of photography, Bruno Nuytten; edited by Arlette Langmann, Hervé de Luze and Noëlle Boisson;

music by Jean-Claude Petit; production designer, Bernard Vezat; produced by Pierre Grunstein; released by Orion Classics. Running time: 122 minutes.

With: Yves Montand (César Soubeyran), Gérard Depardieu (Jean de Florette), Daniel Auteuil (Ugolin), Elisabeth Depardieu (Aimée), Ernestine Mazurowna (Manon) and Marcel Champel (Pique-Rouffigue).

Get ready to binge.

Claude Berri's four-hour, two-part screen adaptation of Marcel Pagnol's epic, two-part Provençal novel, published under the collective title of *L'Eau des Collines* (*Water of the Hills*), is going to be irresistible.

That's if *Jean de Florette,* the first of the two films, is any indication—and there's no reason to suppose that it isn't. Here's the kind of exuberant, French Midi, melodramatic comedy that no one has successfully brought off since Pagnol himself made *César* (1936), which, with *Marius* and *Fanny,* constitutes the Pagnol *Marseilles Trilogy.* (I exclude Jean Renoir's Midi films. They remain incomparable.)

Jean de Florette stars Gérard Depardieu, a fine new actor named Daniel Auteuil and Yves Montand (in the role of his career) in a peasant tale of money, property, duplicity and greed, which is nothing if not colorful while miraculously avoiding the merely picturesque. It's also the most enjoyable, most canny feature-length "preface" in the history of the cinema.

It may be that television's miniseries are making us more polite and docile these days. I can't recall ever having walked out of a movie theater with the same mixture of satisfaction and anticipation as I did when I left the screening of *Jean de Florette,* which, even if ripe with narrative, doesn't quite stand on its own.

Though the films were made at the same time on a marathon, nine-month shooting schedule in the South of France, they are being released here separately, as they were in France. *Jean de Florette,* opening today at the Paris, will be followed later this year by *Manon des Sources* (*Manon of the Springs*), which is not a true sequel but, in fact, the rest of the story.

Jean de Florette is set in the 1920's, in the beautiful, forbiddingly arid hills thirty or so miles north of Marseilles but light-years away in terms of manners and habits. With *Manon of the Springs,* it's a tale of Dickensian shapeliness about a rich, proud farmer, César Soubeyran (Mr. Montand), who, unmarried and childless, schemes with Ugolin (Mr. Auteuil), his nephew and heir, to acquire the only property in the district to possess a functioning spring.

When he dies, César wants to leave behind an orchard "that's like a cathedral," but there can be no orchard, or no flower farm (Ugolin's plan), without the spring.

The scheme begins with the inadvertent murder of the coveted property's irascible old owner and proceeds to the carefully planned deception of the foolish, earnest young man who inherits the farm and who, instead of selling it, decides to settle down there. Unknown to the heir, Jean de Florette, his acquisitive neighbors have stopped up the spring.

Jean, a postal clerk from the city, is played by Mr. Depardieu with a humpback and a sweet, alert, nineteenth-century faith in progress through knowledge. He arrives to take up residence with his young wife, Aimée (Elisabeth Depardieu), who's a former opera singer, their small daughter, Manon (Ernestine Mazurowna), and a library of self-help books on agriculture.

Jean is a terrifically winning character, romantic and hardworking. He also drinks too much and is fatally self-confident. He's no match for the wily César and the younger Ugolin, who, if left to his own devices, would probably have been won over by Jean's innocence and helped him.

Mr. Montand's César, who's said to dominate *Manon of the Springs,* remains on the edges of *Jean de Florette* as, with a clear conscience, he enthusiastically stage-manages what turn into terrible events. The physically formidable Mr. Depardieu successfully disappears inside the naïve, ambitious former postal clerk, and Mr. Auteuil's Ugolin, who seems to be almost retarded at first, emerges as a man of essential decency that fails.

All of the performances, like the characters, are rich without being quaint. The Midi landscapes are magnificent through the seasons. Mr. Berri tempts fate by borrowing the film's musical theme from Verdi (*La Forza del Destino*), which puts a great load onto the tangled narrative and, from time to time, almost flattens it.

Yet Mr. Berri's control remains sure and firm. Jean

de Florette has the delicacy of something freshly observed. It's so good that one needn't be ashamed of escaping into its idealized if harsh and rocky world.

—*V.C., June 26, 1987*

JERRY MAGUIRE

Written and directed by Cameron Crowe; director of photography, Janusz Kaminski; edited by Joe Hutshing; music by Danny Bramson; production designer, Stephen Lineweaver; produced by James L. Brooks, Laurence Mark, Richard Sakai and Mr. Crowe; released by Tri-Star Pictures. Running time: 135 minutes.

With: Tom Cruise (Jerry Maguire), Cuba Gooding Jr. (Rod Tidwell), Renee Zellweger (Dorothy Boyd), Kelly Preston (Avery Bishop), Jonathan Lipnicki (Ray Boyd), Jerry O'Connell (Frank Cushman), Jay Mohr (Bob Sugar), Todd Louiso (Chad the Nanny), Regina King (Marcee Tidwell), Bonnie Hunt (Laurel Boyd) and Beau Bridges (Star Athlete's Father).

When Jerry Maguire, looking like Tom Cruise at his considerable best, shows up unexpectedly at the house of his admiring young business assistant, he mentions that he has suddenly split up with his fiancée. Jerry turns his back to Dorothy (Renee Zellweger) as he says this, just long enough for her jaw to drop.

It's a lovely little moment, and *Jerry Maguire* is loaded with them: bright, funny, tender encounters between characters who seem so winningly warm and real. As such, it recalls not only the two other sweetly appealing films written and directed by Cameron Crowe (*Say Anything* and *Singles*), but also the great shaggy-dog storytelling style of James L. Brooks (*Broadcast News*), one of its producers. So *Jerry Maguire* moves unpredictably through its tale of comeuppance and redemption, but it never loses its bearings. Disarming acting, colorful writing and true generosity of spirit keep it right on track.

Mr. Cruise could have been too big a star for this becomingly modest movie, but Mr. Crowe makes clever use of his leading man's golden-boy aspect. Jerry Maguire, when first we meet him, is all about appearances anyhow. He looks great, talks fast and cares not one whit about the sports stars he represents as a high-powered agent. "Listen, there's no proof of anything except this guy is a sensational athlete," Jerry tells the police on behalf of one client. Jerry also tries sweet-talking the son of a football player when the boy pleads: "Mr. Maguire, this is his fourth concussion. Shouldn't *somebody* get him to stop?"

Unfortunately for Jerry, he is not quite cad enough for this line of work. One night he writes a ringing declaration of principle that wins him the applause of his colleagues; it also soon brings him the chance to be fired in a crowded restaurant by his former protégé. The film finds some humor in the speed-dialing war between Jerry and his rival (Jay Mohr) to hang on to clients, but its real strength is not in satirizing the corporate realm. Mr. Crowe's great talent is for creating a glow of intimacy around tentative young characters as they find themselves falling in love.

When Dorothy is seen on an airplane, eavesdropping avidly as Jerry tells a boastful story, she seems resigned to living in another universe from men like this. (The flight attendant emphasizes that point by closing the curtain between Dorothy's rear cabin and Jerry's seat up front.) Besides, Dorothy has a cute little son (Jonathan Lipnicki) and later explains that she's trying to raise a man, not find one. Yet Ms. Zellweger's open, eager, unconventionally pretty face suggests that miracles are in the offing.

This refreshing actress (who has had small film roles before but now arrives in a big way with *Jerry Maguire* and *The Whole Wide World*, opening just after Christmas) is an inspired choice to play opposite a dreamboat of Mr. Cruise's stature. Her fetching ordinariness, which happens to be quite extraordinary, brings him down to earth in ways no movie queen could manage. And it affirms the film's sense of freedom. The basic appeal of *Jerry Maguire,* pure midlife crisis played with a younger cast, is in watching Jerry become liberated from the rat race and discover a richer new life in the real world.

Since *Jerry Maguire* is a romantic comedy, it handles this transition with exuberant humor. There's an uproariously funny performance from Cuba Gooding Jr. as the one client Jerry is able to hang on to, a loudmouthed showoff who demands big money and refuses the offer of a towel in the locker room. ("No, I air-dry.") Nothing about Mr. Gooding's earnest roles before (in films including *Boyz N the Hood*) is preparation for the hilarity he generates here.

Also scene-stealingly good is Bonnie Hunt, who plays Dorothy's wisecracking sister and is wary when she hears about Jerry. "O.K., but he better not be good-looking," she warns, just before Mr. Cruise appears.

In addition, this film's strong cast includes Regina King as the football player's hard-boiled wife. ("Why don't you be the first man in your family not to use that word, and then we'll let you live," she warns her son.) Kelly Preston makes a brief but memorable appearance as Jerry's shark of a fiancée from his big-shot days. Jerry O'Connell and Beau Bridges (in an unbilled appearance) play a star athlete and his father who sit in a room full of brand-new sneaker boxes trying to decide the young man's big-ticket future.

Todd Louiso has some funny moments as the cranky male nanny to Mr. Lipnicki, whose little lisp and precocious manner have made him perfect for television commercials. He's also dependably adorable here, though the film relies too readily on his antics sometimes. This six-year-old does show a remarkable rapport with the film's two leads, and he has some fine scenes with Mr. Cruise once Jerry tries to start a new career with Dorothy by his side.

Then, when work begins to mix with romance, Jerry expresses some uneasiness and even mentions sexual harassment and Clarence Thomas. "I may not sue," Dorothy says sweetly.

Having just walked through *Mission: Impossible* in colorlessly heroic mode, Mr. Cruise does some of his best real acting here. It's a complicated role, one that requires him to master the manner of a blowhard (he often points with both index fingers) while suggesting the better, hidden side of Jerry that is ready to be coaxed out. And to the film's credit, Jerry's evolution isn't that simple. He didn't entirely hate being a high roller, and he doesn't always see his comedown as spiritual progress.

Still, his kinder side always shows through. There's a nice little moment when Jerry tries to sing along with his car radio but keeps finding the wrong songs. The Rolling Stones's "Bitch" just isn't Jerry Maguire.

Mr. Crowe, who started out as a teenage journalist writing about rock music, has arrived as a screenwriter and director with a distinctively touching, quirky style. And he still has his mojo working: *Jerry Maguire* shares

with his earlier films the benefits of an exceptionally well-used, tuneful pop score.

—J.M., *December 13, 1996*

JOHNNY GUITAR

Directed by Nicholas Ray; written by Philip Yordan, based on the novel by Roy Chanslor; director of photography, Harry Stradling; edited by Richard L. Van Enger; art director, James W. Sullivan; music by Victor Young; produced by Herbert J. Yates; released by Republic Pictures. Running time: 110 minutes.

With: Joan Crawford (Vienna), Sterling Hayden (Johnny "Guitar" Logan), Mercedes McCambridge (Emma Small), Scott Brady (Dancin' Kid), Ward Bond (John McIvers), Ben Cooper (Turkey Ralston), Ernest Borgnine (Bart Lonergan), John Carradine (Old Tom), Royal Dano (Corey), Frank Ferguson (Marshal Williams), Paul Fix (Eddie), Rhys Williams (Mr. Andrews) and Ian MacDonald (Pete).

In *Johnny Guitar,* a Republic Western, which came to the Mayfair yesterday, Joan Crawford plays essentially the role that Van Heflin played in *Shane.* She is the law-abiding squatter who stakes a claim and builds a simon-pure saloon on land that greedy Mercedes McCambridge says should be kept open for cattle range. The only big difference in the character, as plainly rewritten for her, is that now it falls in love with the ex-gunfighter, whom Sterling Hayden here plays.

But this condescension to Miss Crawford and her technically recognized sex does nothing more for the picture than give it some academic aspects of romance. No more femininity comes from her than from the rugged Mr. Heflin in *Shane.* For the lady, as usual, is as sexless as the lions on the public library steps and as sharp and romantically forbidding as a package of unwrapped razor blades.

Too bad, because there were possibilities in this stenciled but workable plot and in the lush accumulation of performers that Republic put into the film. However, neither Miss Crawford nor director

502

Nicholas Ray has made it any more than a flat walk-through—or occasional ride-through—of western clichés.

There's the rivalry between Miss Crawford's and Miss McCambridge's gangs and then there's a sub-rivalry between Mr. Hayden and Scott Brady, Miss Crawford's bad-boy friend. There's a great deal of talk and a little shooting, and at one point Miss Crawford is almost lynched—looking in this situation like a figure in a waxworks of famous crimes.

That's about all there is to it. Miss McCambridge screeches nastily and Mr. Hayden gallumps about morosely as though he'd rather play the guitar. The color is slightly awful and the Arizona scenery is only fair.

Let's put it down as a fiasco. Miss Crawford went thataway.

—B.C., May 28, 1954

THE JUDGE AND THE ASSASSIN

Directed by Bertrand Tavernier; written (in French, with English subtitles) by Mr. Tavernier, Jean Aurenche and Pierre Bost; cinematographer, Pierre-William Glenn; edited by Armand Psenny; music by Philippe Sarde; art designer, Antoine Roman; produced by Raymond Danon; released by Libra Films. Running time: 130 minutes.

With: Philippe Noiret (Judge Rousseau), Michel Galabru (Sergeant Joseph Bouvier), Isabelle Huppert (Rose), Jean-Claude Brialy (Attorney Villedieu), Renée Faure (Madame Rousseau) and Cecile Vassort (Louise Lesueur).

In the early sections of Bertrand Tavernier's *The Judge and the Assassin*, the killer of the title is most frequently seen in pastoral settings, often atop mountain peaks, where he babbles to himself or shouts rapturously to the heavens. The judge, on the other hand, is distinctly an indoor creature. A denizen of drawing rooms, an orderly bourgeois who lives with his mother, the judge is neither prepared nor equipped to understand a roaming, vicious murderer who preys on teenage shepherdesses.

Mr. Tavernier's reflective, exquisitely detailed film, which opens today at the Film Forum, is partly an examination of the extended encounter between these two men, which is set in Lourdes in 1893. More essentially, it is a portrait of a particular era in French history. In the same climate of intolerance in which the Dreyfus case has been tried, in which Zola's name is mentioned scornfully and often, Judge Rousseau (Philippe Noiret) takes on the task of deciding whether the murderer, Sergeant Joseph Bouvier (Michel Galabru), is a madman or a fraud.

It is not Mr. Tavernier's aim to make this suspenseful or titillating; the murders occur off-camera, and the question of Bouvier's guilt is so easily answered that it needn't be raised. Instead, Mr. Tavernier concentrates on setting forth the history of the case, and on pondering its ramifications. He accomplishes this so richly and so cleverly that the murder story itself becomes quite secondary.

As the movie begins, Bouvier shoots both himself and Louise, a woman who won't marry him (and whose sixteen-year-old sister won't marry him, either). Neither is mortally wounded, and Bouvier is sent to an asylum for a very brief stay. When the doctors are ready to release him, he protests that it may be too soon, but they don't care to listen. "If we can't cure a simple mental disease in three months," they say, "there's no hope for modern medicine."

So Bouvier goes on his way, savagely killing shepherds and shepherdesses all across France. Judge Rousseau makes his first appearance in the film reviewing the grisly case history with his mother, who sits placidly through accounts of one grotesque mutilation after another. The report of one young woman disemboweled with a scythe, for instance, does nothing to dismay Rousseau's mother—but she is dismayed at the last crime on the list. Not because it's exceptionally vicious, but because it took place near Lourdes.

In Lourdes, after Bouvier is apprehended, the judge examines him over and over, trying to determine whether the man's claims of insanity are to be believed. When Bouvier insists on having his photograph in the newspaper, the judge takes this as a sign that the man isn't mad. On the other hand, Bouvier shows little sympathy for his victims. "But you made your victims suffer horribly," the judge maintains. That is nothing, says Bouvier, compared to the way he himself has suffered, wandering under the hot sun with two bullets still not removed from his head. By this time, Bouvier has also begun equating himself with Christ and with Joan of Arc.

Mr. Tavernier's *The Clockmaker* and his *Let Joy Reign Supreme* belong to the same period as this 1975 film, which ranks with either of those and stands far above the more recent *A Week's Vacation* or *Spoiled Children*.

Even the best of Mr. Tavernier's work exists at a slight but definite emotional distance from the viewer. *The Judge and the Assassin* is a film more apt to be admired or reflected upon than to provoke any more urgent response. But a good deal of admiration is in order.

Mr. Noiret is expert as ever, but the real surprise here is Mr. Galabru. His Bouvier is a vibrant, humorous figure and also one whose agony seems terribly real. Mr. Galabru remains unexpectedly moving in the role even as Bouvier's story becomes more and more of an abstraction, his destiny more and more of a fait accompli. Even in his ravings, he manages to maintain an odd dignity.

Also in the film is Isabelle Huppert, as the judge's working-class mistress and a woman who becomes the brunt of much of his frustration about the case. As passive as she is beautiful, Miss Huppert is sometimes seen in abrupt close-ups, as if to create the impression that her responses are more emphatic and less impenetrable than they might otherwise appear.

—J.M., August 25, 1982

JUDGMENT AT NUREMBERG

Produced and directed by Stanley Kramer: written by Abby Mann: cinematographer. Ernest Laszlo: edited by Frederic Knudtson: music by Ernest Gold: production designer. Rudolph Sternad: released by United Artists. Black and white. Running time: 189 minutes.

With: Spencer Tracy (Judge Dan Haywood). Burt Lancaster (Ernst Janning). Richard Widmark (Colonel Tad Lawson). Marlene Dietrich (Madame Bertholt). Maximilian Schell (Hans Rolfe). Judy Garland (Irene Hoffman). Montgomery Clift (Rudolf Petersen). Ray Teal (Judge Curtiss Ives). Alan Baxter (General Merrin). William Shatner (Captain Byers) and Ed Binns (Senator Burkett).

On the point of the fundamental issue in the Nazi war guilt trials that were held in Nuremberg, Germany, after World War II, Stanley Kramer, the producer-director, has pinned a powerful, persuasive film. It is *Judgment at Nuremberg* and it opened at the Palace last night.

This issue, deceptively simple in basic moral terms but highly involved and perplexing when set against hard realities, is the question of how much responsibility and guilt the individual must bear for crimes committed or condoned by him on the order and in the interest of the state.

Viewed, as it is in this picture, with potent reasoning and sympathy being thrown on the side of the Germans who claimed innocence of the Nazi crimes out of ignorance and national expediency, it emerges as a double-edged issue when the interest of those who seek justice is raised, they are urged to compromise their own moral principles and shirk responsibility.

But, with the logic and fervor of advocates for humanity—and with the clarity and firmness of the judges who sat in the Nuremberg trials—Mr. Kramer and his incisive scriptwriter, Abby Mann, have kept the issue exalted. They have cut through the specious arguments, the sentiments for mercy and the reasonings for compromise, and have accomplished a fine dramatic statement of moral probity. They have used the motion picture to clarify and communicate a stirring, sobering message to the world.

Appropriately, Mr. Kramer has centered the bulk of the action in this film at the focal point of the philosophical conflict, the courtroom at Nuremberg. And he and Mr. Mann have whacked the drama out of a familiar, fundamental clash—that of a hammering prosecutor and an obdurate lawyer for the defense. Over all, and as the catalyst of the issue, they have an American judge, the symbol of legalistic fair play and the arbiter of the rights of man.

With a sharp sense of inherent drama, they have made the defendants in their case (which is not, be it said, a documentation of any one of the Nuremberg trials, but a composite of several that most nearly resembles the so-called "justice" or "Alstoetter" case) a quartet of former German judges, all of them supposedly sworn to uphold the ideals of justice. Thus judge is being judged in this trial.

As the case progresses, Mr. Kramer and Mr. Mann

rely less on evidence than argument to ignite the explosive ideas. They have one poignant German witness, played touchingly by Montgomery Clift, testify to his sterilization on the order of one of the judges on trial. They have another—a fat young hausfrau whom Judy Garland makes amazingly real—tell a horrifying tale of trumped-up charges of "racial contamination" against an elderly Jew.

But the sparks really fly when Richard Widmark as the American colonel prosecuting the case strikes boldly and with flashing indignation at the character of the men on trial and their defense is flung back with flinty firmness by their counsel, performed masterfully by Maximilian Schell. It is in these fiery exchanges that the drama comes alive and the judge, played superbly by Spencer Tracy, is challenged most tryingly.

Meanwhile, cut in with the court action, are interesting interludes describing the American judge's endeavors to understand the German people. Through the widow of a German general, whom Marlene Dietrich makes most sensitive and sad, he gets the aloof, aristocratic anti-Nazi point of view. From concert, café, and beerhall visits, he (and the audience) get the effect of the old-time, untroubled German culture and deceptive sentiment.

In the end, the accumulating drama collides with the issue head-on when the principal defendant, played weakly by Burt Lancaster, acknowledges his guilt. Then the tension is drawn to resolution in a question of compromise for the sake of not offending the German people, needed in the "Cold War." And the judges make their ruling honestly.

Within the scope and depth of this picture, which runs for something more than three hours, there are many disturbing intimations and revealing performances. There are questions of the moral responsibility of political and religious powers, thoughts on the weaknesses of people and some shocking looks at concentration camp films. Ray Teal gives a dandy performance as a highly conservative judge; Alan Baxter is sharp as an American general who urges clemency.

The major weakness, perhaps, of the whole thing is that it is inevitably compressive and sometimes glib. The strength and wonder of it is that it manages to say so much that still needs to be said.

—*B.C., December 20, 1961*

JU DOU

Directed by Zhang Yimou, in collaboration with Yang Fengliang; written (in Mandarin, with English subtitles) by Lui Heng; edited by Du Yuan; music by Zhao Jipin; produced by Zhang Wenze, Yasuyoshi Tokuma and Hu Jian; released by Miramax Films. Running time: 94 minutes.

With: Gong Li (Ju Dou), Li Baotian (Tian Qing), Li Wei (Jinshan), Zhang Yi (Tinabi as Child) and Jian Zhen (Tiabi as Boy).

The most dazzling element in *Ju Dou* is the everyday work of its characters. In a Chinese village in 1920, a beautiful young woman named Ju Dou is married off to a belligerent older man who owns a factory where fabric is dyed. Though this weighty film is about the sins of the fathers, the oppression of women and passion challenging tradition, cheerful-looking banners of ruby, sapphire and topaz-colored cloth are hung to dry in the open air. They fly in the background as perpetual suggestions of the beauty that exists here only in stolen, illicit moments.

This visually stunning backdrop is one of the saving features of *Ju Dou,* which will be shown at the New York Film Festival tonight at 7:15 and tomorrow at 9:45. For though the story is filled with drama including Ju Dou's adulterous liaison with her husband's middle-aged adopted son, the illegitimate birth of their own child, a self-induced abortion, several murder attempts and two vengeful acts of arson—the film is curiously calm, slow and dispassionate.

Much of that effect is due to the circumspect, ritualistic traditions of Chinese art. Much is due to the emotionally flat approach of Zhang Yimou, who directed this film as well as *Red Sorghum,* which closed the 1988 festival. As he was in *Red Sorghum,* an imagistically flashy but much more didactic work about a young widow (Gong Li, who also plays Ju Dou) and the workers in her wine factory, here Mr. Zhang is a social critic who choreographs actions and images at the expense of emotions. Individual scenes jump out in brilliantly conceived moments. Beaten by her impotent husband because she has not borne a son, Ju Dou appeals to the lonely Tian Qing. When she discovers a peephole through which he watches her bathe, she is at first appalled. Later, she uses his voyeurism as a way to

505

display the bruises that cover her body. By Western standards, it is a scene of extraordinary discretion and a mere shade of titillation. But by Chinese standards, both the character and the film are startlingly bold.

It is characteristic of Mr. Zhang's metaphorical approach that when Ju Dou and Tian Qing make love, the director cuts away to show a bolt of blood-red cloth unraveling in a vat of dye, establishing a major, recurring image. The old husband, eventually paralyzed from the waist down and reduced to crawling on the ground and propelling himself around in a bucket on wheels, will try to push Ju Dou's child into a vat. And years later the child himself, an adolescent disgusted with gossip about his mother's adultery and enraged at Tian Qing, will take his own violent revenge in a scene that involves the same vat of red dye associated with his conception.

All these neat images, all this obvious Oedipal wrangling, result in a film more intriguing to think and talk about than to watch. *Ju Dou* is one of the first major films to be made in the repressive, post-Tiananmen Square period by the daring group of Chinese film makers known as the Fifth Generation. Beginning his story in the 1920's and ending it in the 1930's, Mr. Zhang situates it safely in the pre-Communist period; yet his criticism of the ancient traditions that force Ju Dou to despair clearly reverberates through much of 20th-century Chinese history. *Ju Dou* is an intellectually and artistically brave film. Asking for dramatic power and psychological depth as well may be expecting too much.

—C.J., September 22, 1990

JULES AND JIM

Directed by François Truffaut; written (in French, with English subtitles) by Mr. Truffaut and Jean Gruault, based on the novel by Henri-Pierre Roché; cinematographer, Raoul Coutard; edited by Claudine Bouche; music by Georges Delarue; produced by Marcel Berbert; released by Janus Films. Running time: 115 minutes.

With: Jeanne Moreau (Catherine), Oskar Werner (Jules), Henri Serre (Jim), Marie Dubois (Thérèse), Vanna Urbino (Gilberte), Sabine Haudepin (Sabine), Boris Bassiak (Albert), Kate Noelle (Birgitte), Anny Nelsen (Lucie) and Christiane Wagner (Helga).

François Truffaut, the French director whose first film, *The 400 Blows,* was a strong, sensitive study of a boy's rebellion (and a first powerful thrust of the French "new wave"), has come up with something quite different in his third film (his second to be shown here). He has come up with an arch and arty study of the perversities of woman and the patience of man in this *Jules and Jim,* which opened at the Guild yesterday.

At least, that is putting it as clearly as one can in a few well-chosen words—and almost as clearly as he does in a continual, complex, babbling flow of same. For not only is woman evasive and enigmatic in this film, M. Truffaut himself is quite as shifty and puzzling as its agile cinematist.

Taking his cue from a novel by Henri-Pierre Roché, who was in his seventies when he wrote it and therefore should have known whereof he wrote, Truffaut is endeavoring to express (and presumably let us know) what it's like when two happy fellows fall in love with one whimsical girl. To put it quickly and crisply, it is charming, exciting and sad.

He begins with a lively, spicy look-in on Paris around 1912 and upon the bachelor escapades of his two heroes, two young bohemians, Jules and Jim. They are cheerful, inseparable companions. Jules is German, Jim is French. They even find enjoyment in their casual exchanges of girls.

Then they meet a young woman who becomes more than a passing pal of theirs. She becomes, after certain gay frivolities, the focal point in their lives. And from here on, the text of the drama, as well as its character and tone, becomes reflective, philosophic, strangely resigned and sad.

For with the young woman's capricious marriage to Jules, there begins a long series of sexual and emotional adjustments among them that extend over a period of years. And it ends in a tragic occurrence and a wistful resignation to life.

The fascination in M. Truffaut's telling of this curious relationship is not so much in the personal conflicts. They are deviously intellectualized—talked and talked over so deeply that they become academic and strangely sterile. It is in the involved and artful structure of the scenic elements and in the demonstrations of personalities.

Jeanne Moreau is as variable as a prism that gives off lights and glints as she puts into the role of the woman a bewitching evanescent quality. Oskar Werner gives a haunting presentation of the cerebral nature of Jules, and Henri Serre makes a vivid, melancholy, and finally tragic figure of Jim. Little Sabine Haudepin is winning as the daughter of Jules, and Boris Bassiak is rather funny as a marginal lover.

Actually, the emotional content is largely carried in the musical score, which Georges Delarue has constructed as a dominant element in the film. It and the lengthy conversations and intrusions of a commentator's voice, which are translated in English subtitles that are tedious to read, impart to the film a perceptible aural character that is odd for a film of an artist as "cinematic" as M. Truffaut.

—B.C., April 24, 1962

JULIET OF THE SPIRITS

Directed by Federico Fellini; written (in Italian, with English subtitles) by Mr. Fellini, Tullio Pinelli, Ennio Flaiano and Brunello Rondi, based on a story by Mr. Fellini and Mr. Pinelli; cinematographer, Gianni De Venanzo; edited by Ruggero Mastroianni; music by Nino Rota; art designer, Piero Gherardi; produced by Angelo Rizzoli; released by Rizzoli Film Distributors. Running time: 148 minutes.

With: Giulietta Masina (Giulietta), Mario Pisu (Husband), Sandra Milo (Susy), Caterina Boratto (Mother), Luisa Della Noce (Addie), Sylva Koscina (Sylva) and Lou Gilbert (Grandfather).

Are your eyes in good condition, able to encompass and abide some of the liveliest, most rococo resplendence ever fashioned in a fairyland on film? And are your wits so instructed and sharpened that you can sit for more than two hours and enjoy a game of armchair psychoanalyzing in a spirit of good, bawdy fun?

If they are, then you are ripe for the experience— and an Experience is exactly what it is—of seeing Federico Fellini's and Giulietta Masina's new film, *Juliet of the Spirits,* which opened at the RKO 58th Street last night. (It continues there and will also be at the RKO 23d Street and the New Embassy, beginning today.)

Never before—or maybe not since Moss Hart's *Lady in the Dark,* which was made into a dazzling motion picture with Ginger Rogers in 1944—has the matter of a woman's psychic nature been so generously examined and explained or so sumptuously illustrated in rich, symbolistic Freudian terms.

Mr. Fellini has reared back and truly passed a cinematographic miracle in this gaudy, surrealistic rendering of the fantasies of a wealthy bourgeois wife when her mind is aroused by the suspicion that her husband is cheating on her.

Vividly outsized observations of normal happenings in her everyday life, such as a visit from her mother and two sisters, are followed by nightmares, and these are followed by reverie recollections of painful childhood experiences, until the days and nights of the troubled woman are haunted by the spirits she has loosed.

Soon she is seeing herself going to the office of a private eye (who bears a surprising resemblance to a curious character that comes from the sea in one of her dreams) to arrange for some spying on her husband. And then she is ascending into a tree, to elude a couple of young fellows, with the fancy courtesan who lives next door. Eventually she turns up at an orgy arranged by this neighborly type, and finally she is— but why tell what happens and spoil Mr. Fellini's gaudy game?

Maybe you'll be able to find a pattern in the jumble of dreams and fantasies that the whimsical Miss Masina sees through her various kinds of eyes. Actually her psychological problem is not too elusive or complex. She is inhibited and repressed by an assortment of rather clearly defined experiences.

Her mother (Caterina Boratto) is an elegant, domineering type—at least, as her daughter sees her; her sisters (Sylva Koscina and Luisa Della Noce) are saucy, superior sibling rivals; her husband (Mario Pisu) is a man of splendid appearance and manners and highly provoking disregard.

Did that childhood experience, when old grandpa (Lou Gilbert) leaped up on the stage and interrupted a school play to prevent her from being elevated as a martyred saint, leave a lasting scar on her psyche? Naturally it did. And how come the gaudy next-door neighbor (Sandra Milo) looks so much like the bareback rider in the circus with whom Grandpa was presumably having an affair? (At least, as Giulietta sees it, they flew pretty wide and free.)

It isn't necessary that you fit the pieces too snugly to enjoy the film. Mr. Fellini is not trying to resolve a mystery. He is trying primarily to give you an exciting experience on the screen, generated by a bold conglomeration of visual and aural stimuli. And that he does, with becoming accretions of humor and poignancy.

Miss Masina may not be as winning and heartbreaking as she was in *Nights of Cabiria* and *La Strada,* which Mr. Fellini, her husband, also did. Nor may this film have the sweep and significance of Mr. Fellini's *La Dolce Vita* or *8½.* The actress is still appealing, in her innocent, Harry Langdon way, and something quite human and tender is said about loneliness in the film.

The whole cast performs delightfully, and it includes, in addition to those named, Valentina Cortese as a fey friend, José de Villalonga as a romantic Spanish type, Waleska Gert as a frenzied medium and a couple of dozen more.

This being Mr. Fellini's first feature-length color film, it should be said that he uses the palette most astonishingly. And, finally, the whole thing is accompanied by a brilliant Nino Rota score, which blends the spirit of the circus and sadness with electronic style and taste.

—B.C., November 4, 1965

JUNIOR BONNER

Directed by Sam Peckinpah; written by Jeb Rosebrook; cinematographer. Lucien Ballard; edited by Robert Wolf; music by Jerry Fielding; art designer. Ted Haworth; produced by Joe Wizan; released by Cinerama. Running time: 100 minutes.

With: Steve McQueen (Junior Bonner). Robert Preston (Ace Bonner). Ida Lupino (Elvira Bonner). Ben Johnson (Buck Roan). Joe Don Baker (Curly Bonner). Barbara Leigh (Charmagne). Mary Murphy (Ruth Bonner) and Bill McKinney (Red Terwiliger).

The old West, whose passing was so beautifully recalled by Sam Peckinpah in *The Wild Bunch* and *The Ballad of Cable Hogue,* never really died. It lives on—at least on weekends and holidays—as a particularly robust kind of regional show business, the circuit rodeo, whose actors travel in beat-up Chrysler convertibles, their horses transported in trailers attached to rear bumpers.

"Motel cowboys" is the way someone describes them in Peckinpah's funny and elegiac new film, *Junior Bonner,* which continues Peckinpah's preoccupation with what might be called reluctant past-primeness, that quality of being about to find oneself over-the-hill (and not liking it a bit).

Junior Bonner (Steve McQueen), pushing forty and no longer an especially successful circuit contestant, returns to his hometown of Prescott, Arizona, to compete in the annual rodeo. It's no accident that he's still called Junior. As his personality gives a definition to the name, the name, in the way that names do, has shaped his life.

His father, Ace (Robert Preston), a former rodeo star, hasn't settled down in Prescott as much as he's allowed himself to be hemmed in by it. Ace seldom calls on Junior's mother (Ida Lupino) and instead of working, he boozes it up, rides occasionally and dreams of emigrating to Australia to prospect for gold.

Supporting the family is another son, Curly Bonner (Joe Don Baker), a high-pressure developer of real estate, the sort of businessman who does his own folksy television commercials and, in the course of the two days covered by the film, tries to talk Junior into becoming a salesman for Reato Rancheros ("home on the range retirement").

"You're as genuine as a sunrise," says Curly, and Junior belts him through their mother's living room window.

Junior Bonner, based on an excellent original screenplay by Jeb Rosebrook, is Peckinpah in the benignly comic mood that, I suspect, is much more the natural fashion of this fine director than is the gross, intellectualized mayhem of his recent *Straw Dogs. Junior Bonner* is about a man at a critical point in his life—will Junior be able successfully to ride a mean old black bull named Sunshine? Yet there is something as essentially comic as serious about the nature of the challenges Junior faces, including one, early in the film, in which he is more or less faced down by a man driving a huge scoopshovel. For just a fraction of a second you are aware that Junior is considering a gesture of sentimental lunacy—he wants to ram it with his car.

The thing that distinguishes *Junior Bonner,* however, is not necessarily its broad streak of romanticism, but its affection for all of the Bonners, including the cheerfully venal Curly and his pretty wife (Mary Murphy), who spends most of her time putting other people down. At a family dinner the night before the rodeo, she turns on Junior and snaps: "There never was a horse that couldn't be rode and there never was a cowboy that couldn't be throwed."

The movie seems to amble through its narrative with no great purpose until a moment, toward the end, when all of the Bonners—father, mother, sons, daughter-in-law and grandchildren—find themselves holding an odd reunion in an extremely crowded barroom. Like a lot of families, the Bonners love one another and find it completely impossible to live together. The scene's climax: an uproarious barroom brawl in which absolutely no one is hurt.

The movie is made to order for both McQueen and Preston, but the loveliest performance is that of Miss Lupino, whose first screen appearance this is in something like seventeen years. *Junior Bonner,* which looks like a rodeo film and sounds like a rodeo film, is a superior family comedy in disguise.

It opened yesterday at the Penthouse, the 59th Street Twin No. 1, and the RKO 86th Street Twin No. 1 Theaters.

—V.C., August 3, 1972

KAGEMUSHA

Produced and directed by Akira Kurosawa: written (in Japanese, with English subtitles) by Mr.
Kurosawa and Masato Ide: directors of photography, Kazuo Miyagawa, Takao Saitô, Asakazu Nakai
and Masaharu Ueda: music by Shinichiro Ikebe: art
designer, Yoshiro Muraki: released by Twentieth
Century Fox. Running time: 160 minutes.

With: Tatsuya Nakadai (Shingen Takeda/Kage-
musha) Tsutomu Yamazaki (Nobukado Takeda),
Kinichi Hagiwara (Katsuyori), Jinoachi Nezu
(Sohachiro Tsuchiya) and Shuji Otaki (Masakage
Yamageta).

With *Kagemusha,* his twenty-seventh feature,
Akira Kurosawa, the great Japanese director,
returns to the samurai form that originally brought
him international popularity to match the acclaim he
received from critics around the world. Yet *Kagemusha*
is a far, far different kind of film from *Seven Samurai,
Yojimbo,* and *The Throne of Blood,* Mr. Kurosawa's
Japanese interpretation of *Macbeth.*

Kagemusha is probably the director's most physically elaborate, most awesome film, full of magnificent
views of lines of mounted soldiers slowly crossing
grand landscapes or galloping along seashores, against
sunsets of a magnificence that seems to foreshadow
the end of the world. *Kagemusha* is majestic, stately,
cool and, in many of its details, almost abstract. It
appears very much to be the work of a director who,
now seventy years old, is no longer concerned with the
obligations of conventional drama or even with moral

questions. He is, instead, contemplating history, not as
something to be judged but, rather, acknowledged
and, possibly, understood.

The time is the mid-sixteenth century when three
warlords are competing for the domination of Japan
and, in turn, laying much of the country to waste.
Kagemusha, which translates as "the shadow of the
warrior," refers to a petty thief (Tatsuya Nakadai) who
is saved from crucifixion because of his resemblance to
Shingen Takeda, also played by Mr. Nakadai, the
strongest of the three warlords. When Shingen
Takeda succumbs to a sniper's bullets, his followers
hush up his death and put Kagemusha on the warlord's throne, hoping his presence will forestall attacks
by their enemies.

Kagemusha is partly the story of the thief who
slowly acquires the grandeur and vision of the man he
is impersonating, partly the story of Shingen's ambitious son, whose claims to leadership had been ignored
by his father and partly the story of the evolution of
modern Japan. However, Mr. Kurosawa allows no one
of these stories to dominate. *Kagemusha,* though so
elegantly directed that even perfunctory shots (say, the
arrival of a messenger) seem integral to the film's ritual, has no more narrative drive than an entry in an
encyclopedia.

Indeed, the first fifteen minutes of the film contain
so much exposition about who is doing what to whom
that the average moviegoer may well despair. And
because the dying Shingen has a younger brother who
has also impersonated him, a good hour may pass
before one is absolutely certain which of the three
lookalikes is on the screen. The movie frequently cuts
away to scenes in the enemy camps, but if you're fol-

lowing the subtitles, you may not always know where you are.

About halfway through *Kagemusha* it becomes apparent that the specific details are less important than the overall panorama, the accumulation of scenes of court politics, of Kagemusha growing into his role and of furious, life-and-death battles, all of which are observed as if from another planet.

The great battle that concludes the film is one of the strangest I've ever seen on the screen, if only because none of the major characters is more than an observer to the battle that will determine his fate. Kagemusha, once again an outcast, dressed in rags, watches the battle from the station of someone not allowed into the club. Even Shingen's son, now in command, observes the carnage from a safe distance, according to custom, sitting on a camp chair. What we see is not a battle that holds us in suspense, but the progress of something over which we have no control, like someone else's revolution.

In *Kagemusha* Mr. Kurosawa contemplates tumult in brilliant individual images of battle, of bodies falling, of great bands of nameless men advancing to their deaths. When, at the end, the camera pans across the quiet battlefield, we see the occasional figure of a dying soldier or a horse attempting to stand, only to fall back, collapsed, finished and forgotten. What one carries away from this film is not any pret-tified idea of the dignity of man but of man in impotent relation to historical forces over which he has little if any control.

There is beauty in *Kagemusha* but it is impersonal, distant and ghostly. The old master has never been more rigorous.

—V.C., October 6, 1980

THE KILLERS

Directed by Robert Siodmak: written by Anthony Veiller and John Huston, based on a story by Ernest Hemingway: cinematographer, Elwood Bredell: edited by Arthur Hilton: music by Miklos Rozsa: art designers, Jack Otterson and Martin Obzina: produced by Mark Hellinger: released by Universal Pictures. Black and white. Running time: 102 minutes.

With: Burt Lancaster (Swede), Ava Gardner (Kitty Collins), Edmond O'Brien (Riordan), Albert Dekker (Colfax), Sam Levene (Lieutenant Lubinsky) and Jack Lambert (Dum Dum).

Back in the gangster-glutted twenties, Ernest Hemingway wrote a morbid tale about two gunmen waiting in a lunchroom for a man they were hired to kill. And while they relentlessly waited, the victim lay sweating in his room, knowing the gunmen were after him but too weary and resigned to move. That's all the story told you—that a man was going to be killed. What for was deliberately unstated. Quite a fearful and fatalistic tale.

Now, in a film called *The Killers,* which was the title of the Hemingway piece, Mark Hellinger and Anthony Veiller are filling out the plot. That is, they are cleverly explaining, through a flashback reconstruction of the life of that man who lay sweating in his bedroom, why the gunmen were after him. And although it may not be precisely what Hemingway had in mind, it makes a taut and absorbing explanation as unreeled on the Winter Garden's screen.

For the producer and writer have concocted a pretty cruel and complicated plot in which a youthful but a broken-down prizefighter treads a perilous path to ruin. Mobsters and big-time stickup workers get a hold on him, and a siren of no mean proportions completely befouls his career. In the end, we perceive that the poor fellow—who is bumped off in the first reel, by the way—was the victim of love misdirected and a beautiful double cross.

This doesn't prove very much, obviously, and it certainly does not enhance the literary distinction of Hemingway's classic a bit. But, as mere movie melodrama, pieced out as a mystery that is patiently unfolded by a sleuthing insurance man, it makes a diverting picture—diverting, that is, if you enjoy the unraveling of crime enigmas involving pernicious folks.

With Robert Siodmak's restrained direction, a new actor, Burt Lancaster, gives a lanky and wistful imitation of a nice guy who's wooed to his ruin. And Ava Gardner is sultry and sardonic as the lady who crosses him up. Edmond O'Brien plays the shrewd investigator in the usual cool and clipped detective style, Sam Levene is very good as a policeman and Albert Dekker makes a thoroughly nasty thug. Several other characters are sharply and colorfully played. The tempo is slow and metronomic, which makes for less excitement than suspense.

—B.C., August 29, 1946

THE KILLING FIELDS

Directed by Roland Joffe; written by Bruce Robinson, based on the magazine article "The Death and Life of Dith Pran" by Sydney Schanberg; director of photography, Chris Menges; edited by Jim Clark; music by Mike Oldfield; production designer, Roy Walker; produced by David Puttnam; released by Warner Brothers. Running time: 139 minutes.

With: Sam Waterston (Sydney Schanberg), Dr. Haing S. Ngor (Dith Pran), John Malkovich (Al Rockoff), Julian Sands (Jon Swain), Craig T. Nelson (Military Attaché), Spalding Gray (United States Consul), Bill Paterson (Dr. Macentire) and Athol Fugard (Dr. Sundesval).

On January 20, 1980, *The New York Times Magazine* published a remarkable memoir, "The Death and Life of Dith Pran," by Sydney Schanberg, then *The Times*'s metropolitan editor and today a *Times* columnist but who, from 1972 until 1975, was *The Times*'s correspondent in Cambodia, covering the decline and fall of the United States-backed Lon Nol regime in its civil war with the Communist Khmer Rouge forces.

Mr. Schanberg received the 1976 Pulitzer Prize and a number of other awards for his pieces filed from Phnom Penh, but not until "The Death and Life of Dith Pran" was he able, at last, to come to terms with the experience he had lived through and that, subsequently, haunted him.

Not for nothing does the magazine piece carry the subhead, "A Story of Cambodia."

"The Death and Life of Dith Pran" is, in Mr. Schanberg's words, about Cambodia "as a nation pushed into the war by other powers, not in control of its destiny, being used callously as battle fodder, its agonies largely ignored as the world focused its attention on neighboring Vietnam."

That's a large subject but Mr. Schanberg was finally able to comprehend it—and to allow us to share that comprehension—in his moving, precisely detailed recollection of a single friendship. The friend was Dith Pran, his Cambodian assistant for three years, the man who saved his life and those of several other correspondents when the victorious Khmer Rouge occupied Phnom Penh. Mr. Schanberg's agony was that he was not able to protect Mr. Dith when the Khmer Rouge began their systematic purge of all educated Cambodians and especially those who had worked with the Americans during the previous regime.

While Mr. Schanberg and other Western correspondents were still in sanctuary in the French Embassy in Phnom Penh in 1975, Dith Pran slipped out of the compound and disappeared. In the years that followed, almost everybody except Mr. Schanberg, who returned to New York, eventually assumed Dith Pran to be dead, one of the estimated three million out of seven million Cambodians who were either massacred by the Khmer Rouge or died of starvation or disease.

That Dith Pran did survive provided the shape and the heart of the Schanberg memoir.

All this needs saying by way of introduction to *The Killing Fields,* the ambitious, serious new film that, with great care and respect, has been based on "The Death and Life of Dith Pran."

In most of its surface details, *The Killing Fields* is a faithful adaptation, acted with self-effacing honesty by Sam Waterston as Mr. Schanberg, Dr. Haing S. Ngor—himself a Cambodian refugee—as Mr. Dith, and by the members of the large, meticulously chosen cast. Photographed mainly on location in Thailand in jungles, paddy fields and cities made to appear ravaged, the movie looks amazingly authentic. There's not a cheap shot in the entire film.

Yet something vital is missing, and that's the emotional intensity of Mr. Schanberg's first-person prose. The movie is diffuse and wandering. It's someone telling a long, interesting story who can't get to the point.

The Killing Fields, which opens today at the Cinema 1, is less a cinematic equivalent to the original than a movie about those experiences. It's a story told in the third person that attempts to make conventional, dramatic order out of the highly dramatic, harrowing, emotional disorder of the memoir. Bruce Robinson's screenplay makes clumsily explicit those subtly implicit feelings of doubt and guilt by which Mr. Schanberg's recollections of Dith Pran become, in fact, "a story of Cambodia."

Mr. Robinson and Roland Joffe, the director, never successfully dramatize the particularity of the events that, over an extended period of time, describe the rare nature of that friendship. It takes such a long, godlike view of things that often we're never sure what or whom the movie is about. Mr. Waterston's Schanberg is on screen most of the time but the camera, instead of convincing us that it's seeing events through his eyes, keeps looking over him to the wartime panorama beyond. The story is there but not the personal impact.

The film begins in 1973 and, with a lot of technical virtuosity, creates a vivid picture of the last, desperate months of the Lon Nol Government. There are Mr. Schanberg's discoveries of the terrible "miscalculations" by which innocent Cambodians are bombed to oblivion by United States planes, the increasing panic and high-handedness of American representatives in Phnom Penh and, finally, the abandonment of Phnom Penh.

Mr. Schanberg makes arrangements for the safe evacuation of Mr. Dith's wife and children, and when he, with a handful of other correspondents, elects to remain in the capital, Mr. Dith stays, too.

This decision, which puts Mr. Dith's life on the line, comes to haunt Mr. Schanberg. It also becomes so curiously overstated by the film that it seems that the meaning of the friendship, for dramatic expediency, has been vastly oversimplified and thus, in a way, underrated.

The film is most effective when it takes leave of Mr. Schanberg and follows Mr. Dith's dogged attempts to stay alive after he leaves Phnom Penh. At one point he is put into a forced labor camp where he survives on lizards and scorpions and by sucking the blood from living water buffaloes. Though tortured, he refuses to die. There's a good but never fully developed sequence in which he's befriended by a provincial Khmer Rouge official who trusts Mr. Dith to get his small son to the safety of Thailand.

The movie is not easy to watch. The massacres by which the Khmer Rouge attempt to reduce the population to manageable size—and to change the character of the country—are graphically depicted. Prisoners, individually and in odd lots, are shot casu-

ally. Sometimes they're simply beaten to death—it saves bullets. In a nightmare scene near the end, the exhausted Mr. Dith finds himself stumbling through a paddy field whose dikes are composed of human bones.

The performances are uniformly fine. Mr. Waterston possesses the strength, humor and compassion of the increasingly obsessed Mr. Schanberg, and Dr. Ngor, who's never acted before, reveals an extraordinary screen presence as the resilient Mr. Dith. Prominent in the supporting cast are Julian Sands, Craig T. Nelson, Spalding Gray, Bill Paterson, Athol Fugard and John Malkovich, though, with the exception of Mr. Malkovich, who plays a prickly sort of news cameraman, the roles are mostly functions of the plot.

Unfortunately, the most moving aspect of *The Killing Fields* is not the friendship, which should be the film's core, but the fact that the friendship never becomes as inspiriting as the one Mr. Schanberg recalled in his own searching, unhackneyed prose.

—*V.C., November 2, 1984*

KIND HEARTS AND CORONETS

Directed by Robert Hamer; written by Mr. Hamer and John Dighton, based on the novel by Roy Horniman; cinematographer, Douglas Slocombe; edited by Peter Tanner; music by Wolfgang Amadeus Mozart; art designer, William Kellner; produced by Michael Balcon; released by Eagle Lion Films. Black and white. Running time: 105 minutes.

With: Dennis Price (Louis), Valerie Hobson (Edith), Joan Greenwood (Sibella) and Alec Guinness (The Duke/The Banker/The Parson/The General/The Admiral/Young Ascoyne/Young Henry/Lady Agatha).

An abundance of Alec Guinness, the delightfully clever young man who racked up a personal triumph in *The Cocktail Party* this past season on Broadway, is probably the first inducement to which the local community will respond in the cunning new British picture, *Kind Hearts and Coronets*. For in this delicious little satire on Edwardian manners and morals, which had its American premiere at the Trans-

Lux Sixtieth Street yesterday, the sly and adroit Mr. Guinness plays eight Edwardian fuddy-duds with such devastating wit and variety that he naturally dominates the film.

And why not? The protean Mr. Guinness as eight members of a ducal clan that must be got around by a young kinsman bent upon becoming the duke is so deft in his brief impersonations, so sharp and trenchant in his economical thrusts, that with this one film he should garner three or four awards for fine support.

But don't let this obvious admiration for Mr. Guinness obscure the fact that the picture itself is a sparkling and sometimes devilishly cutting jest or that the other performers in it are of excellent quality, too. Indeed, Dennis Price as the young man who coolly undertakes a monstrous scheme of killing off all his kinfolk in order to succeed to the family coronet is as able as Mr. Guinness in his single but most demanding role, and Joan Greenwood and Valerie Hobson are provocative as women in his life.

Credit must also be given to Robert Hamer and John Dighton, who wrote the script, to Mr. Hamer, who capably directed and to Michael Balcon, who produced. And, since we are flinging bouquets, we might as well toss one, wistfully, to our old friend, Sacha Guitry, whose prewar films are much resembled by this work.

As a matter of fact, there is so much about *Kind Hearts and Coronets*—so much in subject and in spirit—that is reminiscent of Guitry's *The Story of a Cheat* that a person of suspicious nature might suspect that it had been thereby inspired. In the first place, the narrative pattern is the same as that of the memorable French film, the story being told—and narrated—as the recollections of a candid scoundrel. And, in the second place, the whole development of the scoundrel's calculated career—in this case, of civilized murder—is described in the finest spirit of Gallic wit.

You see, it is all so refined and proper. The instincts and conduct of the young man who aspires to the eminence of a dukedom, from which he seems hopefully removed by the precedence of several relatives and an indiscreet marriage that his mother made, are elegant and impeccable. He does everything in the most considerate way—even to polishing off one of his kinsmen, a windy general, by putting dynamite in his caviar. And his deference to the etiquette of concourse with the ladies is past compare.

Most scathing, however, of the incidents (to put it mildly) that this gentleman completes is that of the dignified poisoning of an aged vicar, member of the ducal clan. And it is in this sardonic depiction that Mr. Price and Mr. Guinness achieve the supremacy of their satire. Mr. Price, for this episode disguised as a touring bishop, and Mr. Guinness as a shriveled clergyman pull off as withering a comment on English stuffiness as one will ever see. Furthermore, it is in absolute good humor, which is the saving grace of the whole film.

For the fact is that such a story of unmitigated contempt for the fundamental laws of society could only be tolerable when played as a spoof—a spoof on the highest level of cultivated humor and device. And that, thanks to all who made this picture—and to Mr. Guinness's incredible skill at vivid impersonation—is what this picture is.

—*B.C., June 15, 1950*

THE KING AND I

Directed by Walter Lang; written by Ernest Lehman, based on the musical by Oscar Hammerstein 2d and Richard Rodgers, from the book *Anna and the King of Siam* by Margaret Landon; cinematographer, Leon Shamroy; edited by Robert Simpson; music by Mr. Rodgers, with lyrics by Mr. Hammerstein; choreography by Jerome Robbins; art designers, Lyle Wheeler and John DeCuir; produced by Charles Brackett; released by Twentieth Century Fox. Running time: 133 minutes.

With: Deborah Kerr (Anna), Yul Brynner (The King), Rita Moreno (Tuptim), Martin Benson (Kralahome), Terry Saunders (Lady Thiang), Rex Thompson (Louis Leonowens), Carlos Rivas (Lun Tha), Patrick Adiarte (Prince Chulalongkorn), Alan Mowbray (British Ambassador) and Geoffrey Toone (Ramsay).

Whatever pictorial magnificence *The King and I* may have had upon the stage—and, goodness knows, it had plenty, in addition to other things—it has twice as much in the film version that Twentieth Century Fox delivered last night to the Roxy. It also has other things.

515

It has, first of all, the full content of that charmingly droll and poignant "book" that Mr. Hammerstein crystallized so smartly from Margaret Landon's *Anna and the King of Siam*. Every bit of the humor and vibrant humanity that flowed through the tender story of the English schoolteacher and the quizzical king is richly preserved in the screenplay that Ernest Lehman has prepared. And it is got onto the screen with snap and vigor under the direction of Walter Lang.

It has, too, the ardor and abundance of Mr. Rodgers's magnificent musical score that rings out as lyrically and clearly as those clusters of Siamese bells. Most of the memorable numbers are here and are beautifully done, from "I Whistle a Happy Tune" to the zealous and rollicking "Shall We Dance?" And the few that have been omitted—the slave girl Tuptim's "My Lord and Master" is one, and another is Anna's acrimonious "Shall I Tell You What I Think of You?"—are not missed in the general extravagance of melody and decor.

Also, it has the great advantage of a handsome and talented cast, headed by the unsurpassed Yul Brynner and lovely Deborah Kerr. Mr. Brynner, whose original performance of the volatile King of Siam was so utterly virile and commanding that he took possession of the role, repeats it here in a manner that the close-in camera finds fresh with pride and power. Mr. Brynner has a handsomeness of features and a subtlety of expression that were not so evident on the stage.

His comprehension of the tyrant whose passionate avidity for "scientific" knowledge and enlightenment often clashes with his traditional arrogance and will is such that there come from his performance all sorts of dazzling little glints of a complex personality battling bravely and mightily for air. The king is the heart of this story, and Mr. Brynner makes him vigorous and big.

But Miss Kerr matches him boldly. Her beauty, her spirit and her English style come as close to approximating those of the late Gertrude Lawrence as could be, and the voice of Marni Nixon adds a thrilling lyricism to her songs. The point of the story, as all know, is that you should never underestimate a woman's power. Miss Kerr makes it trenchant and enjoyable. She and Mr. Brynner are a team.

Rita Moreno as the lovelorn Tuptim and Carlos Rivas as her Burmese beau are relegated to small roles, but they handle them gracefully and manage to put a

haunting poignance into "We Kiss in a Shadow," the lovers' song. Terry Saunders is attractive as the "first wife," Patrick Adiarte is trim as the young prince and Martin Benson does very nicely with the abbreviated role of the prime minister.

However, as we said in the beginning, it is the pictorial magnificence of the appropriately regal production that especially distinguishes this film. Done with a taste in decoration and costuming that is forceful and rare, the whole thing has a harmony of the visuals that is splendid in excellent color and CinemaScope. The imagery is beautifully climaxed in the "Little Hut of Uncle Thomas" ballet, which sort of wraps up the quaintness, the humor and the exquisite delicacy of the issues in this fine film.

If you don't go to see it, believe us, you'll be missing a grand and moving thing.

—B.C., June 29, 1956

KING KONG

Directed by Merian C. Cooper; written by James Ashmore Creelman and Ruth Rose, based on a story by Mr. Cooper and Edgar Wallace; cinematographers, Eddie Linden, Vernon Walker and J. O. Taylor; edited by Ted Cheesman; music by Max Steiner; art designers, Carroll Clark, Al Herman and Van Nest Polglase; special effects by Willis O'Brien, E. B. Gibson, Marcel Delgado, Fred Reese, Orville Goldner, Carroll L. Shepphird, Mario Larrinaga and Byron L. Crabbe; produced by Mr. Cooper and Ernest B. Schoedsack; released by RKO Pictures. Black and white. Running time: 100 minutes.

With: Fay Wray (Ann Redman), Robert Armstrong (Denham), Bruce Cabot (Driscoll), Frank Reicher (Englehorn), Sam Hardy (Weston), Noble Johnson (Native Chief), James Flavin (Second Mate), Steve Clemento (Witch King) and Victor Long (Lumpy).

At both the Radio City Music Hall and the RKO Roxy, which have a combined seating capacity of 10,000, the main attraction now is a fantastic film known as *King Kong*. The story of this feature was begun by the late Edgar Wallace and finished by Merian C. Cooper, who with his old associate, Ernest B.

Schoedsack, is responsible for the production. It essays to give the spectator a vivid conception of the terrifying experiences of a producer of jungle pictures and his colleagues, who capture a gigantic ape, something like fifty feet tall, and bring it to New York. The narrative is worked out in a decidedly compelling fashion, which is mindful of what was done in the old silent film *The Lost World*.

Through multiple exposures, processed "shots" and a variety of angles of camera wizardry, the producers set forth an adequate story and furnish enough thrills for any devotee of such tales.

Although there are vivid battles between prehistoric monsters on the island that Denham, the picture-maker, insists on visiting, it is when the enormous ape, called Kong, is brought to this city that the excitement reaches its highest pitch. Imagine a fifty-foot beast with a girl in one paw climbing up the outside of the Empire State Building, and after putting the girl on a ledge, clutching at airplanes, the pilots of which are pouring bullets from machine guns into the monster's body.

It often seems as though Ann Redman, who goes through more terror than any of the other characters in the film, would faint, but she always appears to be able to scream. Her body is like a doll in the claw of the gigantic beast, who in the course of his wanderings through Manhattan tears down a section of the elevated railroad and tosses a car filled with passengers to the street. Automobiles are mere missiles for this Kong, who occasionally reveals that he relishes his invincibility by patting his chest.

Denham is an intrepid person, but it is presumed that when the ape is killed he has had quite enough of searching for places with strange monsters. In the opening episode he is about to leave on the freighter for the island supposed to have been discovered by some sailor, when he goes ashore to find a girl whom he wants to act in his picture. In course of time he espies Ann, played by the attractive Fay Wray, and there ensues a happy voyage. Finally, through the fog, the island is sighted and Denham, the ship's officers and sailors, all armed, go ashore. It soon develops that the savages, who offer up sacrifices in the form of human beings to Kong, their super-king, keep him in an area surrounded by a great wall. Kong has miles in which to roam and fight with brontosauri and dinosaurs and other huge creatures.

There is a door to the wall. After Denham and the others from the ship have had quite enough of the island, Kong succeeds in bursting open the door, but he is captured through gas bombs hurled at him by the white men. How they ever get him on the vessel is not explained, for the next thing you know is that Kong is on exhibition in Gotham, presumably in Madison Square Garden.

During certain episodes in this film Kong, with Ann in his paw, goes about his battles, sometimes putting her on a fifty-foot high tree branch while he polishes off an adversary. When he is perceived on exhibition in New York he is a frightening spectacle, but Denham thinks that he has the beast safely shackled. The newspaper photographers irritate even him with their flashlights, and after several efforts he breaks the steel bands and eventually gets away. He looks for Ann on the highways and byways of New York. He climbs up hotel façades and his head fills a whole window, his white teeth and red mouth adding to the terror of the spectacle.

Everywhere he moves he crushes out lives. He finally discovers Ann, and being a perspicacious ape, he decides that the safest place for himself and Ann is the tower of the Empire State structure.

Needless to say that this picture was received by many a giggle to cover up fright. Constant exclamations issued from the Radio City Music Hall yesterday. "What a man!" observed one youth when the ape forced down the great oaken door on the island. Human beings seem so small that one is reminded of Defoe's *Gulliver's Travels*. One step and this beast traverses half a block. If buildings hinder his progress, he pushes them down, and below him the people look like Lilliputians.

Miss Wray goes through her ordeal with great courage. Robert Armstrong gives a vigorous and compelling impersonation of Denham. Bruce Cabot, Frank Reicher, Sam Hardy, Noble Johnson and James Flavin add to the interest of this weird tale.

—M.H., March 3, 1933

KING LEAR

Directed by Peter Brook: written by Mr. Brook. based on the play by William Shakespeare: director of photography. Henning Kristiansen: edited by Kasper Schyberg; production designer, George Wakhevitch; produced by Michael Birkett; released by Altura Films International. Black and white. Running time: 137 minutes.

With: Paul Scofield (King Lear), Irene Worth (Goneril), Jack MacGowran (Fool), Alan Webb (Duke of Gloucester), Cyril Cusack (Duke of Albany), Patrick Magee (Duke of Cornwall), Robert Lloyd (Edgar), Tom Fleming (Earl of Kent), Susan Engel (Regan), Annelise Gabold (Cordelia), Ian Hogg (Edmund), Barry Stanton (Oswald) and Soren Eluns Jensen (Duke of Burgundy).

Having missed the *King Lear* that was staged here seven years ago by Peter Brook with the Royal Shakespeare Company, I'm unable to compare it with Mr. Brook's film version, which also stars Paul Scofield and Irene Worth and opened yesterday at the Paris Theater.

Thus happily unburdened of the need to make comparisons, I can simply state that this is a *King Lear* of splendor and shock. Mr. Brook's screen adaptation, filmed in a kind of primeval black-and-white, mostly in the wintery dune country of Denmark's Jutland Peninsula, is set in a time and place where the sun seems to be receding not because of any seasonal course but because the entire universe is moving toward an exhausted end.

Mr. Brook's film career has been wildly variable, including the fine, witty screen adaptation of his own production of *Marat/Sade,* as well as the really dreadful Vietnam improvisation called *Tell Me Lies. King Lear* is, I think, Brook at his manic best. It triumphantly ignores both romantic and naturalistic traditions to achieve something akin to the so-called new theater in film terms.

It is not an easy film to watch. It has the relentless single-minded purpose of a prophet of doom. It also, from time to time, goes quite mad itself with cinematic effects, but it is so magnificently acted and so bravely conceived that I, for one, am willing to forgive these trespasses.

Mr. Brook's production is, I'm told, largely prompted by an essay, "King Lear or Endgame" by the Polish critic Jan Kott, who sees Lear as a Shakespearean tragedy of the grotesque, "an ironic, clownish morality play" that "makes a mockery of all eschatolo-

gies: of the heaven promised on earth, and the heaven promised after death."

In this conception, there is no need to worry about psychological truths. It doesn't concern itself with why a king, even one approaching senility, would arbitrarily carve up his kingdom and parcel it out among his three daughters on the basis of their love for him, nor why he could so arbitrarily disinherit the one daughter who loves him best for speaking sanely. These are simply the fateful mechanics by which Lear is set free in a universe that is quite as cold and terrifying as that in which Beckett's characters find themselves trapped in ash cans.

The people in Brook's *Lear* inhabit a kind of visual wasteland and live in places that look like frontier forts, and, except for the opening sequences, they have no subjects, only attending soldiers and servants. There is no music in this land, only crude sound effects, like those of the wheels of the rough wooden carts that serve as royal carriages.

What is most remarkable to me is that the director has been able to get so much of the beautiful text on the screen, so purely, through techniques that usually either overwhelm the language or make it preposterously theatrical. He uses lots of giant close-ups, individual zoom shots that separate the lines of a soliloquy and even a handheld camera that at times can barely keep up with the tumultuous action. With the exception of the tempest scenes, which seem to have been shot through a pot of Vaseline and lit with H-bomb flashes, everything works to enhance the meaning of the play.

Of course, Brook has an extraordinary cast. This is no all-star assembly but an ensemble. No one, perhaps, but Scofield could withstand the camera's close scrutiny so effectively. His Lear, who looks like a Michelangelo God somehow fallen to earth, is a life force at the end of his rope. Most importantly, he speaks the lines as if they'd just been created—with intelligence and surprise.

Everyone is equally fine, but special mention must be made of Irene Worth (Goneril), Jack MacGowran (the Fool), Alan Webb (the Duke of Gloucester), Susan Engel (Regan) and Tom Fleming (the Earl of Kent). I question some small bits of business (does Goneril really manage to kill herself by banging her head against a rock?) but not the overall effect.

Toward the close of the film, as Lear's world collapses into piles of corpses (Cordelia, the Fool, Goneril, Regan, Gloucester, almost everyone), the images become more and more pale, until, as Lear himself sinks slowly into death, the screen goes completely white. It is truly an end. Lear dies grotesquely, but unhumiliated, which, according to Brook, is as much of a victory as can ever be achieved by a magnificent clown.

—*V.C., November 23, 1971*

THE KING OF COMEDY

Directed by Martin Scorsese; written by Paul D. Zimmerman; director of photography, Fred Schuler; edited by Thelma Schoonmaker; music by Robbie Robertson; production designer, Boris Leven; produced by Robert Greenhut; released by Twentieth Century Fox. Running time: 108 minutes.

With: Robert De Niro (Rupert Pupkin), Jerry Lewis (Jerry Langford), Diahnne Abbott (Rita), Sandra Bernhard (Masha), Ed Herlihy (Himself), Lou Brown (Bandleader) and Liza Minnelli (Herself)

It would be difficult to describe Martin Scorsese's fine new film, *The King of Comedy,* as an absolute joy. It's very funny, and it ends on a high note that was, for me, both a total surprise and completely satisfying. Yet it's also bristly, sometimes manic to the edge of lunacy and, along the way, terrifying. It's not an absolute joy by a long shot but, in the way of a film that uses all of its talents to their fullest, it's exhilarating.

The King of Comedy, which opens today at the Coronet, is most easily categorized as satire. Though television and instant celebrity are two of its principal targets, it has less in common with something like Paddy Chayefsky's *Network* than with Susan Seidelman's *Smithereens.*

Like Wren, the aggressive groupie in *Smithereens,* Rupert Pupkin, the hero of *The King of Comedy,* wants to be celebrated and famous. However, unlike Wren, who has no talent for anything and knows it, Rupert is convinced that he is a great comedian, nothing less than "the king of comedy," which is what he calls himself.

As played by Robert De Niro, in one of the best,

most complex and most flamboyant performances of his career, Rupert Pupkin represents the apotheosis of all that is most commonplace in America's increasingly homogenized society. For Rupert, immortality is a series of boffo one-liners.

Though there is a little bit of almost every film Mr. Scorsese has ever made in *The King of Comedy,* including even *Taxi Driver* and *Raging Bull,* this new work is an original. Its excellent screenplay, written by Paul D. Zimmerman, a former film critic for *Newsweek,* is witty and, even in Rupert's hilarious fantasy sequences, tough. Like all good movies, the film has the measure of the times that produced it.

When we first meet Rupert Pupkin, there is little to distinguish him from all of the other pushy, half-crazed, lovesick fans who wait for their idols outside stage doors, furiously demanding autographs and as likely to turn vicious as they are to swoon with ecstasy at the merest brush with celebrity. Rupert's idol is Jerry Langford, a late-night television talk show host played—with brilliant solemnity—by Jerry Lewis. *The Jerry Langford Show* is obviously modeled on Johnny Carson's, but the Langford character and well-corseted figure suggest the offstage Bob Hope.

Rupert pursues the defenseless Jerry Langford with the single-minded intensity of the true psychotic. When all other avenues to the achievement of his goal—a ten-minute guest spot on *The Jerry Langford Show*—fail, Rupert and his equally obsessed sidekick, Masha (Sandra Bernhard), a rich groupie with an East Side mansion, decide to kidnap Jerry and to hold him for one of the weirdest ransoms in the history of narrative films.

More of the story you need not know.

One of the ways in which *The King of Comedy* works so effectively is in the viewer's uncertainty whether it's going to wind up as terrifyingly as is always possible. It's full of laughs, but under all of the comic situations is the awful suspicion that our laughter is going to be turned against us, like a gun.

Mr. Zimmerman's screenplay is ungraciously hilarious when it focuses its attention on pure showbiz, as when, in one of Rupert's fantasies, he attempts, with the gravity of a Barbara Walters, to explain the sources of his comic routines. I also cherish its throwaway lines: Rupert, lying in wait for Jerry Langford in a fancy network waiting room, keeps staring at the ceiling. "Is it cork?" he asks, being suave. Says the bored receptionist: "I don't know. Is it dripping on you?"

519

Though the film is Mr. De Niro's from start to finish, all of the members of the cast are impeccable, including Mr. Lewis; Miss Bernhard, who is new to films and may be one of the decade's comic finds; Diahnne Abbott, as Rupert's skeptical, sometime girlfriend; Catherine Scorsese (the director's mother), as Rupert's mother, who remains a quarrelsome, off-screen voice throughout; Shelley Hack, as the sort of beautiful, cool network secretary who could give lessons in the art of the elegant put-down. Among the real-life personalities who turn up as themselves are Tony Randall, Victor Borge and Dr. Joyce Brothers, who doesn't seem to have any idea that, under these circumstances, she's a not-very-kind joke.

With *The King of Comedy,* Mr. Scorsese again confirms his reputation as one of the most authentic, most original voices of his film generation.

—*V.C., February 18, 1983*

THE KING OF MARVIN GARDENS

Produced and directed by Bob Rafelson: written by Jacob Brackman, based on a story by Mr. Brackman and Mr. Rafelson: director of photography, Laszlo Kovacs: edited by John F. Link: art designer, Toby Rafelson: released by Columbia Pictures. Running time: 103 minutes.

With: Jack Nicholson (David Staebler), Bruce Dern (Jason Staebler), Ellen Burstyn (Sally), Julia Anne Robinson (Jessica) and Benjamin "Scatman" Crothers (Lewis).

Picture Atlantic City in winter. The leaden sky, the sea, the deserted boardwalk, the Convention Hall, a few old souls shuffling through the shabby decay of the grand hotels—picture these easy images of indefinable sadness, and you almost won't need a movie. You certainly won't need a movie like *The King of Marvin Gardens,* which played last night in the New York Film Festival and opens tomorrow at the Columbia I theater.

You will not find Marvin Gardens on a map. You will find it on a Monopoly board—between Water Works and Go to Jail—and its king, Jason Staebler, you will find in some country of the mind known best to desperate scenarists. Jason (Bruce Dern), an artist, a

visionary, dreams of buying an island ("Off the coast of Hawaii") but actually fronts for a mob in Atlantic City, where he occupies some hotel rooms with his girl, Sally (Ellen Burstyn), and his other girl, Sally's stepdaughter, Jessica (Julia Anne Robinson).

To Jason comes David (Jack Nicholson), also an artist, his kid brother. David is supposed to help finalize the Pacific island plans, but actually he oversees the insubstantial kingdom of Jason until its tragic, but less than inevitable, end.

David is a late-night FM radio personality, a philosopher, a novelist manqué, who speaks his fables into a tape recorder for future broadcast. "Nobody reads anymore . . . Good-bye, written word! . . . And I crave an audience . . . So I have chosen this form . . ." Sometimes "this form" finds David without anything to say, and the tape recorder sits there as reproachfully as any typewriter with a blank sheet of paper. *The King of Marvin Gardens* is thus the first movie to deal sincerely with a new artistic malady: tape-recordist's block.

There are no dialogue blocks, however, and the film simply swarms with meaningful phrases, like: "That's what I mean by being committed to somebody."

"You mean, sleepwalking along on somebody's else's life!"

I'm afraid I have made it seem that *The King of Marvin Gardens* is mostly the fault of its screenplay—by Jacob Brackman—whereas it is really just as much the fault of its direction—by Bob Rafelson. Rafelson's kind of poetic realism, an accuracy in the treatment of unexpected settings, looked like quality to some in *Five Easy Pieces* two years back. Now it looks like the most pretentious of tired clichés, a low-keyed but very empty bombast exploiting rather than exploring its themes of failed dreams and tawdry realities.

—*R.G., October 13, 1972*

KISS OF THE SPIDER WOMAN

Directed by Hector Babenco: written by Leonard Schrader, based on the novel by Manuel Puig: director of photography, Rodolfo Sanchez: edited by Mauro Alice: music by John Neschling and Wally Badarou: art designer, Clovis Bueno: produced by David Weisman: released by Island Alive. Running time: 119 minutes.

With: William Hurt (Luis Molina). Raul Julia (Valentin Arregui). Sonia Braga (Leni Lamaison/Marta/Spider Woman). José Lewgoy (Warden). Milton Goncalves (Pedro) and Miriam Pires (Mother).

Kiss of the Spider Woman begins with a theatrical-sounding homosexual describing the plot of an old movie ("her petite ankle slips into the perfumed water") for the benefit of his prison cellmate, a political radical. There is nothing in this seemingly frivolous, beautifully staged opening to betray the film's tremendous reserves of seriousness and passion. Nor are there sufficient clues in the previous film careers of the director, Hector Babenco (the highly praised *Pixote*), or the two stars, William Hurt and Raul Julia, to anticipate the stature of the work they do here. *Kiss of the Spider Woman* is a brilliant achievement for all of them, staged with the perfect control and fierce originality that make it one of the best films in a long while.

Mr. Hurt won a well-deserved best actor award at the Cannes Film Festival for a performance that is crafty at first, carefully nurtured and finally stirring in profound, unanticipated ways. What starts out as a campy, facetious catalogue of Hollywood trivia becomes an extraordinarily moving film about manhood, heroism and love. As Luis Molina, the storyteller who keeps his cellmate Valentin Arregui entertained with pulp movie fiction, Mr. Hurt is first seen wrapping a red towel around his head as a turban, the better to impersonate the female star of the film he is describing. The red scarf he ties around his neck in the climactic sequence is both a reminder of his earlier character and a sign of the completeness of his transformation.

Kiss of the Spider Woman, which opens today at Cinema I, has been adapted by Leonard Schrader from Manuel Puig's unusually structured novel with an imaginativeness that amounts to absolute fidelity. The book, which contains no physical description whatsoever and establishes its characters entirely through what they think and say, intermingles dialogue between the cellmates, footnotes referring obliquely to their psychological makeup and the lengthy recapitulations of movie plots that punctuate their conversation. All of these things manage somehow to form a seamless narrative, one that has been made even more so on the screen.

The initial disparity between Valentin and Molina (as they address one another) becomes a dichotomy between superficiality and seriousness. Molina is quite literally a window dresser who has been jailed for molesting minors, whereas Valentin is a political prisoner. Valentin tells Molina, "Your life is as trivial as your movies"; Molina replies, "Unless you have the keys to that door, I will escape in my own way, thank you." Mr. Puig typically couches the debate between them in mundane, even homey terms. When Molina offers his cellmate some extra food, Valentin snaps, "I can't afford to get spoiled." Molina argues that one must take what life offers. Valentin replies self-righteously that what life offers him is his cause, and that its nobility makes everything secondary. "What kind of a cause is that," asks the sly Molina, "a cause that won't let you eat an avocado?"

The grace with which the film establishes the growing affection between these two, a fondness that tempers their ideological dispute to the point at which they understand one another completely, is given an element of suspense by the possibility of Molina's treachery. It is this that makes Mr. Hurt's performance so exquisitely poised. When his face sags, sick with fear, during a telephone conversation late in the story, the extent of his earlier artifice becomes visibly apparent. Before that, his Molina is by turns coy, flirty, confessional and entertaining, offering only the tiniest indications of where his true loyalties may lie. His face, for all its quicksilver changes of expression, remains essentially opaque. Only gradually do his actions—this is a film that manages to derive a scene of astonishing tenderness from one character's violent indigestion—begin to override his histrionics. Mr. Hurt also succeeds in making the campy, flamboyant aspects of Molina's homosexuality seem credible and metaphorical in equal measure.

If Mr. Hurt has never been so daringly extroverted on the screen before, Mr. Julia has never been so restrained. And they meet halfway in a manner that is electrifying. Their teamwork, choreographed with a relentless, escalating rhythm by Mr. Babenco, never falters, which is made all the more remarkable by the fact that it is frequently interrupted. Several films-within-the-film, illustrating Molina's movie descriptions and starring the Brazilian actress Sonia Braga as a satirically elegant grande dame, serve as refracted images of the main action, couching the larger film's concerns with love and honor in witty, deliberately clichéd terms. Mr. Babenco, whose tough, unsparing *Pixote* was so impressive, weaves all these elements together in ways that reveal whole new reserves of precision, sophistication and even humor.

Kiss of the Spider Woman unfolds slowly at first, building gradually and carefully until its momentum becomes urgent and palpable. From its droll, playful opening to its transcendent coda, it has the mark of greatness from beginning to end.

—*J.M., July 26, 1985*

KLUTE

Directed by Alan J. Pakula: written by Andy Lewis and Dave Lewis: cinematographer. Gordon Willis: edited by Carl Lerner: music by Michael Small: art designer. George Jenkins: produced by Mr. Pakula. C. Kenneth Deland and David Lange: released by Warner Brothers. Running time: 114 minutes.

With: Jane Fonda (Bree Daniel). Donald Sutherland (John Klute). Charles Cioffi (Cable). Roy Scheider (Frank Ligourin) and Dorothy Tristan (Arlyn Page).

Six months after his best friend has unaccountably disappeared and nobody official has been able to find him, John Klute, a small-town cop, sets out for New York City to question Bree Daniel, a call girl to whom the missing man has allegedly written obscene letters and who is the only possible clue to his disappearance.

This is the initial proposition to Alan Pakula's *Klute,* which opened yesterday at the Cinerama Theater, and which ought to be called "Bree" (or maybe "Miss Daniel") because it is really about her and her problems—one of which happens to be a psychopathic killer.

Bree Daniel (Jane Fonda) likes her job, and she's good at it, but she's trying, without luck, to act on the stage. "Why do I still want to trick?" she asks her analyst. Her analyst, a most helpful woman, replies, "What is the difference? You're *successful* as a call girl; you're not successful as an actress. . . ." Which is not strictly true, for Bree, who is a kind of Method call girl, really does act when she tricks, and never more ambitiously than for a favorite customer, a seventy-year-old garment cutter ("I'm all he's got") to whom she recalls the old-world glamour he has never known:

"Cannes was rather amusing. . . . We played baccarat and chemin de fer. . . ." There was an intriguing older man. "Nobody could tell me whether he was an exiled prince—or a mercenary. . . ." And so on (all the while delicately stripping) in a manner better realized by Genet in *The Balcony,* a work of somewhat different intentions.

The actual intentions of *Klute* are not all that easy to spot, though I think they have more to do with its intellectual aspirations than with its thriller plot. For this is a thriller in which even the climactic terror (as contrived a terror as any I've seen) seems more like interpersonal relations than climactic terror, and the psychopathic killer, hooked on self-analysis, keeps a wire recording of his latest murder, as if to carry his guilt around in his pocket.

At one point in her way through the nightmare of her life Bree takes drugs. Klute (Donald Sutherland), who by this time has grown pretty attached to his only clue, patiently sees her through her withdrawal until she is cured—and then suddenly her apartment, which had been a mess until then, appears all waxed floors and newly discovered fireplace, in a good-taste tenement restoration semitraditional that may be a key to the soul of *Klute.*

Pakula, when he is not indulging in subjective camera, strives to give his film the look of structural geometry, but despite the sharp edges and dramatic spaces and cinema presence out of *Citizen Kane,* it all suggests a tepid, rather tasteless mush.

The acting in *Klute* seems semi-improvisitory, and in this Jane Fonda, who is good at confessing, is generally successful. Everybody else merely talks a lot, except for Sutherland, who scarcely talks at all. A normally inventive actor, he is here given precisely the latitude to evoke a romantic figure with all the mysterious intensity of a youthful Calvin Coolidge.

—*R.G., June 24, 1971*

KNIFE IN THE WATER

Directed by Roman Polanski: written (in Polish. with English subtitles) by Mr. Polanski. Jerzy Skolimowski and Jakub Goldberg: cinematographer. Jerzy Lipman: music by Krzysztof Komeda:

produced by Stanislaw Zylewicz; released by Kanawha Films. Black and white. Running time: 94 minutes.

With: Leon Niemczyk (Andrzej), Jolanta Umecka (Christine) and Zygmunt Malanowicz (The Young Man).

The odd sort of personal hostility that smolders in many men who have trouble asserting their egos in this complex modern world is casually, cryptically and even comically dissected by the probing camera of Roman Polanski in his *Knife in the Water,* which opened at the Beekman yesterday.

This strange little film from Poland, which was one of the more popular among the twenty-one multinational features shown at the First New York Film Festival last month, is the first of that lot of offbeat pictures to be presented commercially here. And it eminently justifies the interest in its acid contents and in the techniques of its young director that it stirred.

Using his naturalistic camera as though it were an outsized microscope set up to observe the odd behavior of three people completely isolated for twenty-four hours aboard a weekend pleasure boat, Mr. Polanski evolves a cryptic drama that has wry humor, a thread of suspense, a dash of ugly and coruscating evil—and also a measure of tedium because of the purposeful monotony of its pace.

What he has done, as coauthor as well as director, is merely place these people—an edgy, snarling husband, his cool and calmly critical wife and a surly and sassy young hitchhiker whom they have picked up en route to their boat—within the controlled confinement of a trim little sailing sloop and there has them work out their aggressions and their sly sexual rivalries.

From their first harsh exchange of hostilities as they almost collide on the road, the husband and his virtually shanghaied passenger casually taunt each other and contend to show their superior skills and prowess, while the smirking wife silently observes. The husband vaunts himself as a sailor and mocks the clumsiness of the youth; the latter shows off his agility with a murderous switchblade knife.

Comical and trifling at the outset, these rivalries between the two men appear to be no more consequential than the jostling of two hostile kids, daring one another to step over a line. And the casual goings and comings of the pretty young wife about the boat, innocently but very seductively patched in a two-piece bathing suit, appear no more pertinent to the wrangling than the picnic lunch she serves.

But Mr. Polanski is sneaky. In carefully guarded ways, he has the competition become more vicious, the distraction of the woman more intense, until suddenly he has a situation where hostilities flare into hate and the two men vie with each other in a series of water shenanigans that thinly veil their lethal inclinations and the hideous possibilities of death.

In this situation, he flashes the chemistry of sex—the natural bestowal by the woman of her token of sympathy upon the more pathetic of these rivals and then her ultimate display of contempt for both immature male creatures. It makes for a neat ironic twist.

As I say, the style is so casual and random at the start that the clambering of only three people about a sailboat tends to become monotonous. And unless one is quickly perceptive of the subtle drama Mr. Polanski is about, the use of attending their behavior may be disastrously missed.

But the performances are engaging. Leon Niemczyk is mephitic and intense as the nasty husband, Zygmunt Malanowicz is dry and droll as the young man, and Jolanta Umecka is obligingly attractive and provokingly scornful as the wife. The decor is entertaining, if you can overlook the facts that the sailing is laughably sloppy and that there are no other boats on the lake.

Once you realize that this is a devilish dissection of man in one of his more childish and ridiculous aspects, you should get some laughs and tingles out of it.

It is too bad about that Polish dialogue. The English subtitles are good.

—*B.C., October 29, 1963*

KRAMER VS. KRAMER

Directed by Robert Benton; written by Mr. Benton, based on the novel by Avery Corman; director of photography, Nestor Almendros; edited by Jerry Greenberg; music by Henry Purcell and Antonio Vivaldi; production designer, Paul Sylbert; produced by Stanley R. Jaffe; released by Columbia Pictures. Running time: 105 minutes.

With: Dustin Hoffman (Ted Kramer). Meryl Streep (Joanna Kramer). Jane Alexander (Margaret Phelps). Justin Henry (Billy Kramer). Howard Duff (John Shaunessy). George Coe (Jim O'Connor). JoBeth Williams (Phyllis Bernard) and Bill Moor (Gressen).

There may be no place in the world that seems quite as civilized and reassuring as Manhattan's East Side—when you're feeling good and have money in your pocket. It's expensive but value is given. It's a privilege simply to look into the windows of Madison Avenue boutiques that keep their doors bolted against customers who don't measure up. The sidewalk musicians on Fifth Avenue play Purcell and Vivaldi and one never has to travel very far to find a restaurant where the food is worth the king's ransom it costs. Unlike those on the West Side, most of the apartment building doormen on the East Side wear uniforms that differentiate them from the muggers. Everything seems forever.

When things are going wrong, though, Manhattan's East Side immediately reflects the unhappiness of an upwardly mobile people who have no idea where they're going or why. Everything is ridiculously expensive. Walls are thin and ceilings low. Cabdrivers are rude. Husbands are self-centered and unreliable and wives, who have been urged to realize themselves, start by seeing an analyst. As rats command the sewers, vaguely understood fears run amok through the corridors of the fancy new high-rises above.

This is the hermetic world of Robert Benton's fine, witty, moving, most intelligent adaptation of Avery Corman's best-selling novel, *Kramer vs. Kramer,* which opens today at Loews Tower East and other theaters.

Kramer vs. Kramer is a Manhattan movie, yet it seems to speak for an entire generation of middle-class Americans who came to maturity in the late 60's and early 70's, sophisticated in superficial ways but still expecting the fulfillment of promises made in the more pious Eisenhower era.

Ted Kramer (Dustin Hoffman) is a self-described take-over guy who left Brooklyn for Manhattan's East Side and is speeding to the top at his advertising agency. Everything in his life is working out as planned. When *Kramer vs. Kramer* opens, the elated Ted has just been handed his agency's most valued new account. As he says a few minutes later, this has been one of the five best days of his life.

It is with some surprise, then, that he returns home to find his wife, Joanna (Meryl Streep), jaw-set and teary-eyed, determined to depart forever, leaving Ted not only with an entire ad presentation to prepare for the next day but also with their six-year-old son, Billy (Justin Henry), to take care of. Ted is not someone who always gets his priorities straight.

Kramer vs. Kramer is one of those rare American movies that never has to talk importantly and self-consciously to let you know that it has to do with many more things than are explicitly stated. It's about fathers and sons, husbands and wives, and most particularly, perhaps, about the failed expectations of a certain breed of woman in this day and age.

Though much of *Kramer vs. Kramer* is occupied with the growing relationship between the abandoned father and son, through tantrums and reconciliations and playground accidents, the central figure is that of the movingly, almost dangerously muddled mother, played by Miss Streep in what is one of the major performances of the year. Joanna is not an easily appealing character, especially when she returns after eighteen months of therapy in California and seeks legal custody of the child she walked out on.

Though beautiful, intelligent, well-educated and no more than casually self-assertive at the start, she grows into one of those fiercely determined people who talks about "finding" herself even as we—and she—suspect there may be nothing to find except another series of compromises. She seems to be a woman in transit to disappointment. Maybe not. She's not a character who can be conveniently categorized, and she is fascinating.

Mr. Hoffman is splendid in one of the two or three best roles of his career. It's a delicately witty performance, funny and full of feeling that never slops over into the banal, which is the greatest danger faced by an actor who must play most of his scenes with a small boy who is as down-to-earth and pragmatic as Justin Henry. There is no way that Mr. Hoffman can avoid being upstaged when Billy, watching his father make a mess of French toast, says carefully, "I don't like it folded."

Kramer vs. Kramer is densely packed with such beautifully observed detail. It is also superbly acted by its supporting cast, including Jane Alexander, Howard Duff and George Coe.

The man responsible for the photography is the gifted Nestor Almendros, whose earlier credits include Terrence Malick's *Days of Heaven,* François Truffaut's *The Story of Adele H.,* and Eric Rohmer's *Clair's Knee,* among other things. The Manhattan he shows us is familiar enough but we see a lot more than a series of pretty surfaces.

—*V.C., December 19, 1979*

L.A. CONFIDENTIAL

Directed by Curtis Hanson; written by Brian Helgeland and Mr. Hanson, based on the novel by James Ellroy; director of photography, Dante Spinotti; edited by Peter Honess; music by Jerry Goldsmith; produced by Arnon Milchan, Mr. Hanson and Michael Nathanson; released by Warner Brothers. Running time: 136 minutes.

With: Kevin Spacey (Jack Vincennes), Russell Crowe (Bud White), Guy Pearce (Ed Exley), James Cromwell (Dudley Smith) and Kim Basinger (Lynn Bracken).

Curtis Hanson's resplendently wicked *L.A. Confidential* is a tough, gorgeous, vastly entertaining throwback to the Hollywood that did things right. As such, it enthusiastically breaks most rules of studio filmmaking today. Brilliantly adapted from James Ellroy's near-unfilmable cult novel, it casts anything-but-A-list stars (yet) in a story with three leading men, no two of whom can be construed as buddies. It embroils them in a cliché-free, vigorously surprising tale that qualifies as true mystery rather than arbitrary thriller and that revels in its endless complications. Take a popcorn break and you'll be sorry.

L.A. Confidential roams the full expanse of Mr. Ellroy's 1950's Los Angeles, a film noir paradise of smoldering evil and knee-weakening glamour with a dirty little secret behind every palm tree. As conjured first by the author and then by a film uncannily faithful to his prose style (though it deftly shrinks the convoluted plot), this is a place best symbolized by its favorite forms of corruption. Mobsters, drugs, brutally racist cops and wish-fulfilling whores made to resemble movie stars all conspire to drag the film through the gutter while, in terms of achievement, it reaches for the stars.

With perfect timing, *L.A. Confidential* also contemplates what it calls "sinnuendo," the leering tabloid mentality that speaks to this story's secret dreams. Danny DeVito embodies this as a gleeful Sid Hudgens (a character whom Mr. Hanson has called "the Thomas Edison of tabloid journalism"), who is the unscrupulous editor of a publication called *Hush-Hush* and winds up linked to many of the other characters' nastiest transgressions. Sid's flawless cynicism sets the tone not only for the film's ersatz movie-star elegance but also for its police, who often share his ethical constructs. "Don't start trying to do the right thing, boy-o," a police official tells one of his men, in the razor-sharp language of Mr. Ellroy's sinewy characters. "You haven't had the practice."

The essential questions throughout this captivating film are whether and how anyone will rise above its quagmire. Since the answer must be yes (some genre rules are inviolable), *L.A. Confidential* leavens its vice with affecting tenderness. Bud White (Russell Crowe) may be a thug and bruiser, but he melts at the white satin vision of Lynn Bracken (Kim Basinger), a call girl whose face, hair, costumes and bungalow are meant to conjure thoughts of Veronica Lake. The film's valid idea of good old-fashioned steam heat is to have Lynn lead Bud into her real bedroom—the one filled with mementoes of her native Arizona—at dawn.

Late in *L.A. Confidential,* in a scene for which viewers will be endlessly grateful, a character being interrogated finally gives a brief synopsis of the plot. That's no easy matter. But among its main points are that Bud, like Mr. Ellroy (as described in his fine, wrenching memoir, *My Dark Places*), is fiercely bothered by acts of violence against women. Ed Exley (Guy Pearce), his priggish colleague on the police force, will do anything for his own advancement. And Jack Vincennes (Kevin Spacey), who dines out on being the police adviser to a television show like *Dragnet,* often finds himself right up Sid Hudgens's alley. When they conspire to set up movie stars on vice charges, Sid gets the story. Jack gets to preen while making the arrest.

The crime that envelops all these characters is a mysterious massacre at a coffee shop called the Nite Owl. The investigation, which makes a hero of Exley, leads to three black men. Having sanctioned the Christmastime beating of Mexican prisoners at police headquarters, the Los Angeles Police Department cannot be accused of undue racial sensitivity, and indeed there is more to the Nite Owl matter than anyone first imagines. Since *L.A. Confidential* is not a story to waste time on innocent victims, the search for the three black men yields a separate, heinous crime of its own.

Without strain or affection, *L.A. Confidential* recalls *Chinatown* in drawing an entire socioeconomic cross-section and elaborate web of corruption out of an investigation that starts small. This time, high up on the food chain resides Pierce Patchett (David Strathairn), who finances his taste for modern architecture with a business interest in the oldest profession. Among the film's other privileged characters are a district attorney (Ron Rifkin) who is a tabloid headline waiting to happen, and a ruefully knowing police captain, James Cromwell, a long way from *Babe,* is mordantly good in the latter role.

Mr. Hanson, who is himself a long way from *The Hand That Rocks the Cradle, Bad Influence,* and *The River Wild,* and who now brings the dark side of his earlier work to dazzling fruition, achieves casting coups both large and small. Mr. Spacey is at his insinuating best, languid and debonair, in a much more offbeat performance than this film could have drawn from a more conventional star. And the two Australian actors, tightly wound Mr. Pearce and fiery, brawny Mr. Crowe, qualify as revelations. Both performances should send viewers off to the video store, with Mr. Crowe's past credits including *Romper Stomper, Virtuosity,* and *The Quick and the Dead.* The bigger surprise

is Mr. Pearce, who was better known for his Abba jokes as Felicia in *The Adventures of Priscilla, Queen of the Desert.*

Much of the strength of *L.A. Confidential* (which also makes the most of Ms. Basinger in her worldly calendar-girl role) comes from tiny roles, of which there are many. Mr. Hanson relies on strong, unfamiliar faces—a strange bereaved mother, a cynical coroner—to etch the film's story points and underscore its fundamental power to surprise. Though film noir revivals are often wearily derivative, this one casts a long shadow of its own.

Mr. Ellroy, as adapted by Mr. Hanson and Brian Helgeland, makes his long-overdue burst into movies as an indelibly smart, acerbic voice. The dialogue throughout the film is rewardingly concise and dark. "Looks like his bodyguard had a conflict of interest," somebody says of a corpse. Or: "You have any proof?" "The proof got his throat slit." Or (on the verge of the film's climactic shoot-out, furious even by Hong Kong standards): "All I ever wanted was to measure up to my father." "Here's your chance."

Or: "You're like Santa Claus with a list, Bud. Except everyone on it's been naughty."

—*J.M., April 19, 1997*

LACOMBE, LUCIEN

Produced and directed by Louis Malle; written (in French, with English subtitles) by Mr. Malle and Patrick Modiano; director of photography, Tonino Delli Colli; edited by Suzanne Baron; music by Django Reinhardt, Andre Claveau and Irene de Trebert; art designer, Ghislain Uhry; released by Twentieth Century Fox. Running time: 141 minutes.

With: Pierre Blaise (Lucien), Aurore Clément (France), Holger Lowenadler (Albert Horn), Thérèse Gieshe (Bella Horn), Stéphane Bouy (Jean-Bernard de Boisin) and Loumi Iacobesco (Betty Beaulieu).

*L*acombe, Lucien, the title of Louis Malle's fine, uncompromising new film, is a statistic, a name on a list, someone unknown, without identity. Which is pretty much the way Lucien Lacombe, age seventeen, sees himself in June 1944.

Lucien (Pierre Blaise) is a strong, square-jawed, none-too-bright country boy living in southwest France during the Nazi occupation. He scrubs floors in the hospital of a small provincial city and makes occasional visits to his home, a farm now run by the landlord who has become his mother's lover while his father is a prisoner of war.

Lucien is a hunter, usually by necessity and now and then for sport. He shoots rabbits and wrings the necks of chickens, which are food for the dinner table, but sometimes he can't resist going after a yellow warbler with his slingshot. The bird means nothing to him. Proving the excellence of his aim does.

In *Lacombe, Lucien,* Mr. Malle asks us to contemplate Lucien as he chooses, it seems accidentally, his course toward destruction. After being turned down for membership in the Underground in his native village because he's too young, Lucien more or less slips into total collaboration with the French arm of the German police, the only club that will accept him, at just that point in history when it's apparent to even the densest minds that the Germans are beaten.

The film, which was shown at Alice Tully Hall on Saturday and Sunday evenings, will open in a theater here in mid-October.

Lacombe, Lucien is Mr. Malle's toughest, most rueful, least sentimental film. Like the extraordinary Marcel Ophuls documentary, *The Sorrow and the Pity,* the film refuses to identify heroes and villains with certainty. That, Mr. Malle seems to say, is to oversimplify issues and to underrate the complexity of the human experience.

Mr. Malle is adamant on these points. It's very difficult for anyone of my (World War II) generation to understand a collaborationist, which the director-writer underscores by allowing Lucien scarcely any saving graces. When hunting rabbits, he has the impassive face of a killer. Once taken into the police force, he becomes as impossibly arrogant as only the ignorant can be. He coolly witnesses torture procedures as if the system had nothing to do with him.

Instinctively, however, he finds himself attracted to the household of a once-famous, rich Paris tailor, an aristocratic Jew named Albert Horn (Holger Lowenadler), who is in hiding with his ancient mother and pretty daughter, France (Aurore Clément), in Lucien's town.

Armed with a machine gun, his official police

passes and gifts such as confiscated champagne, as well as with a monumental insensitivity, Lucien invites himself into the lives of these refugees. Lucien bullies them, makes a fool of himself and suddenly falls in love with France.

The difficulty of the task that Mr. Malle has set for himself by focusing on Lucien is manifest in two magnificent scenes that are the highlights of the film. In one, Mr. Horn turns his elegant, exhausted eyes on Lucien and warns that he doesn't need Lucien to make him appreciate his daughter. "We're both fragile," he says. In the other scene, France clings to Lucien, who doesn't come up to her instep in any way, and damns the fact of being a Jew. Her degradation is complete.

A more sentimental director would, I'm sure, have made this film the story of the Horns. They are marvelous, gallant creatures, and both Mr. Lowenadler and Miss Clément are superb.

By fixing the sights of the film on Lucien, Mr. Malle and Patrick Modiano, who worked with him on the screenplay, force us to considerations of more agonizing import. We never know how Lucien got that way, only that the times made possible his short, disastrous season in the sun. With the liberation, Lucien once again becomes a statistic.

Lacombe, Lucien is easily Mr. Malle's most ambitious, most provocative film, and if it is not as immediately affecting as *The Fire Within* or even the comic *Murmur of the Heart,* it's because—to make his point—he has centered it on a character who must remain forever mysterious, forever beyond our sympathy.

—V.C., *September 30, 1974*

THE LADY EVE

Written and directed by Preston Sturges, based on the story "The Faithful Heart" by Monckton Hoffe: cinematographer. Victor Milner: edited by Stuart Gilmore: music by Sigmund Krumgold: art designers. Hans Dreier and Ernst Fegté: produced by Paul Jones: released by Paramount Pictures. Black and white. Running time: 97 minutes.

With: Barbara Stanwyck (Jean/The Lady Eve). Henry Fonda (Charles Pike). Charles Coburn ("Colonel" Harrington). Eugene Pallette (Mr. Pike).

William Demarest (Ambrose "Muggsy" Murgatroyd), Eric Blore (Sir Alfred McGlennan Keith), Melville Cooper (Gerald) and Martha O'Driscoll (Martha).

Now there's no question about it: Preston Sturges is definitely and distinctly the most refreshing new force to hit the American motion pictures in the past five years. The fact was thoroughly apparent—but almost too good to believe—when his rowdy comedy, *The Great McGinty,* came along last summer. Further corroboration was given it by his *Christmas in July.* And now, with *The Lady Eve,* which arrived yesterday at the Paramount, Mr. Sturges is indisputably established as one of the top one or two writers and directors of comedy working in Hollywood today. A more charming or distinguished gem of nonsense has not occurred since *It Happened One Night.*

Superlatives like that are dangerous, but superlatives like *The Lady Eve* are much too rare for the careful weighing of words. And much too precious a boon in these grim and mirthless times. For this bubbling and frothy comedy-romance, which Mr. Sturges has whipped up for Paramount, possesses all the pristine bounce and humor, all the freshness and ingenuity, that seem to have been lacking from movies since away back—we don't know when. Suddenly the art of comedy-making is rediscovered in the most matter-of-fact place.

For actually Mr. Sturges has taken one of the stock stories off the movies' middle shelf—the old one about the man who falls in love with a lady of unsuspected sin—and has given it such humorous connotation and such a variety of comic invention that it sparkles and cracks like a pretty right out of a brand-new box. The lady, to be sure, is not a sinner with a great big capital S; she is just a delightful cardsharp who happens to be working the boat that picks up a wealthy young scientist fresh out of the Amazon jungle. And the way he falls for her—and eventually she for him—is a matter of magnificent consequence with Mr. Sturges directing it.

Of course, there is the inevitable unmasking, the forlorn and vindictive farewell; but the lady has her day—and recompense for her broken heart—when she returns to delude the young man as an English noble miss. *The Lady Eve,* in other words. And the screaming honeymoon sequence that Mr. Sturges has devised for the two in a flower-decked Pullman compartment is one of the most deliciously funny scenes ever put into a motion picture. Now you guess how it ends.

The secret of Mr. Sturges's distinctive style is yet to be analyzed, but mainly it is composed of exceedingly well turned dialogue, a perfect sense for the ridiculous in the most mundane and simple encounters and generous but always precise touches of downright slapstick. No less than six flat falls are taken by the hero in this piece. And the manner in which action is telescoped and commented upon by fast and hilarious glimpses is cinema at its very best. You'll not see anything better than the suggestion of a whirlwind courtship that wins the Lady Eve.

Likewise, Mr. Sturges has a genius for picking his casts. No one could possibly have suspected the dry and somewhat ponderous comic talent that is exhibited by Henry Fonda as the rich young man. And Barbara Stanwyck as the lady in the case is a composite of beauty, grace, romantic charm and a thoroughly feminine touch of viciousness. Other beautiful performances are contributed by Charles Coburn as a wry and lovable cardsharper, William Demarest as hard-boiled bodyguard and gentleman's man, Eugene Pallette as a much-abused tycoon and Eric Blore as a confidence worker.

But the picture is mainly Mr. Sturges's, and to him the chief credit is due. Perhaps it is somewhat academic to hail him as the American René Clair, but there is a delightfully reminiscent suggestion of that gentleman's early verve in his work. Mr. Sturges writes with a skimming but penetrating touch. He may have sacrificed a rib to the cause, but he has done the old Adam proud in his creation of *The Lady Eve.*

—B.C., February 26, 1941

THE LADY VANISHES

Directed by Alfred Hitchcock; written by Alma Reville, Sidney Gilliat and Frank Launder, based on the novel *The Wheel Spins* by Ethel Lina White; cinematographer, Jack Cox; edited by Alfred Roome and R.E. Dearing, music by Louis Levy; produced by Edward Black; released by Metro-Goldwyn-Mayer. Black and white. Running time: 97 minutes.

With: Margaret Lockwood (Iris Henderson). Michael Redgrave (Gilbert). Paul Lukas (Dr. Hara). Dame May Whitty (Miss Froy). Cecil Parker (Mr. Todhunter). Linden Travers (Mrs. Todhunter) and Naughton Wayne (Caldicott).

Just in under the wire to challenge for a place on the year's best ten is *The Lady Vanishes* (at the Globe), latest of the melodramatic classics made by England's greatest director, Alfred Hitchcock. If it were not so brilliant a melodrama, we should class it as a brilliant comedy. Seeing it imposes a double, a blessedly double, strain: When your sides are not aching from laughter your brain is throbbing in its attempts to outguess the director. Hitch occasionally relents with his rib-tickling, but his professional honor would not brook your catching up with his plot.

A lady vanishes on a train. One moment she was sitting there, plump, matronly, reading a needlework magazine, answering to the name and description of Miss Froy, governess, London-bound from the Tyrol. The next, she was gone. And the young woman in the compartment, awakening from her doze, was solemnly assured by her neighbors that they had seen no Miss Froy. A brain specialist aboard suggests that Miss Froy was a hallucination induced by the blow she had received when a flower box fell on her head at the station.

The young man who had been one of the avalanche-bound guests at the inn was skeptical, too, but offered to help. The two Englishmen aboard didn't want to be involved; they were eager to reach England in time for the cricket finals. The pacifist was afraid his reputation might suffer; he obviously was traveling with a woman not his wife.

Still, there was something about Miss Froy. When we first saw her she was being serenaded (odd for a woman her age) by an elderly porter in the Tyrolean inn. And then, although she didn't know it, a pair of shadowy hands knotted about the porter's neck and he died. Besides, she was standing beside the young woman at the station when someone pushed the flower pot off the roof. Could that have been meant for Miss Froy? Yet it doesn't seem quite credible for everyone in the train to enter a conspiracy about her—conductors, dining room stewards, a countess, a noted surgeon, a music hall performer, a nun, two cricket-mad Englishmen, a woman in tweeds. (Mr.

Hitchcock, a very old Nick of a St. Nich, is laughing fit to kill.)

Well, there's the puzzle, and we cannot conceal our admiration over the manner in which Mr. Hitchcock and his staff have pieced it together. There isn't an incident, be it as trivial as an old woman's chatter about her favorite brand of tea, that hasn't a pertinent bearing on the plot. Everything that happens is a clue. And, having given you fair warning, we still defy you to outguess that rotund spider, Hitch. The man is diabolical; his film is devilishly clever.

His casts are always neglected by reviewers, which isn't fair, especially since he has so perfect a one here. Honors belong, of course, to his priceless cricketers, Caldicott and Charters—or Naughton Wayne and Basil Radford—whose running temperature about "how England is doing" makes the most hilarious running gag of the year. Margaret Lockwood and Michael Redgrave as the puzzled young woman and her ally are just the sort of pleasant, intelligent young people we should expect to find going through a casual Hitchcock gesture to boy-meets-girl.

The others are equally right—Dame May Whitty as the surprising Miss Froy, Paul Lukas as the specialist, Cecil Parker, Linden Travers—in fact, all the others. Did we say *The Lady Vanishes* was challenging the best ten? Let's amend it: the bid has been accepted.

—*F.S.N., December 26, 1938*

LADYBIRD, LADYBIRD

Directed by Ken Loach; written by Rona Munro; director of photography, Barry Ackroyd; edited by Jonathan Morris; music by George Fenton; production designer, Martin Johnson; produced by Sally Hibbin; released by Samuel Goldwyn Productions. Running time: 102 minutes.

With: Crissy Rock (Maggie). Vladimir Vega (Jorge). Sandie Lavelle (Mairead). Mauricio Venegas (Adrian) and Ray Winstone (Simon).

Ken Loach's *Ladybird, Ladybird* asks viewers to imagine what it is like for Maggie (Crissy Rock) to open a newspaper one day and see a photograph of a boy in need of adoptive parents. "I've never had much love," says the caption. "Can you give me some now?" The photograph is of Maggie's own son.

Maggie, the central figure in this raw, wrenching film based on a true story, is first seen as a mother of four who has no children. English social service agencies have seen fit to take all of them away. And those agencies are not presented as simply villainous. Maggie's history is troubling enough to yield different opinions on whether she is a fit parent for her children.

Mr. Loach knows better than to present Maggie's story as a mere case of bureaucratic injustice, even though it escalates into exactly that before it is over. His interest goes beyond the black-and-white outline of such a horrific situation, and into the harrowing gray reality. *Ladybird, Ladybird* is a tough, utterly absorbing film even at moments when it seems to skirt some of the fine points of Maggie's difficulties. It's not necessary to see her as a pure victim to appreciate the hellishness of her ordeal.

The film begins as Maggie, who looks like a heavier, blowsier Susannah York, meets Jorge (Vladimir Vega), a gentle Paraguayan immigrant. After he approaches her in a karaoke bar, she tells him about her past. Raised by an abusive father, she had four children by four different men, at least one of whom also had a violent temper; he is seen savagely beating Maggie with a beer can during one of the film's flashbacks. The four children are a racially mixed group. Racial prejudice can be seen as contributing to Maggie's uneasy relations with various social workers, most of whom are white.

But Maggie's biggest problem with these authorities is Maggie herself. One night she makes an inexcusable mistake, leaving her children home alone while she goes out on a singing engagement. She locks them in the apartment, supposedly for their own protection. A fire breaks out. One boy is badly burned, and the whole group is summarily removed from Maggie's care and classified "At Risk" by government agencies.

Maggie's subsequent behavior makes matters worse. One night, she shows up late to visit the burned boy in his foster home, expressing surprise that he is already in bed at eight thirty. Volatile and quarrelsome, she instantly picks a fight with the foster mother, and then barges in to visit her son. Insisting on changing his bandage, she is so clumsy that she hurts him. Whatever has made Maggie this distraught, the fact is

that she has become her own worst enemy. She screams at any authority figure who comes to visit her, badly compounding the communications failure on all sides.

Ladybird, Ladybird watches Maggie fall into a love affair with the patient, generous Jorge, who does his best to get her back on her feet. It then watches, first with hope and then with horror, as Maggie and Jorge prepare for a new start with a child of their own. The social service workers who once expressed concern over whether Maggie was "coping" (a favorite word here) have lost patience, and they become more invasive. And Maggie goes to war with an increasingly brutal bureaucracy, in a series of struggles that take some unimaginably ghastly turns.

One of these events takes place in a hospital room and is so wrenching that it makes a nurse cry. *Ladybird, Ladybird* is extremely upsetting at such moments, fully sharing Maggie's hopelessness and grief. Although a closing title says Maggie's life took a positive turn after the events seen here, the film does little to give credence to that possibility. By the end of the story, her fate has come to seem irremediably bleak, and Mr. Loach has stirred a fierce sense of outrage. The facts presented here are devastatingly cruel. The final impression is that somehow it needn't have been so.

Does it matter that Mr. Loach has altered the names and characteristics of his film's two principals? Or that a "based on a true story" credit makes it possible to eliminate unpleasant facts? No: even if Jorge tends toward saintliness and the question of Maggie's real competence as a mother remains unexamined, the film has honesty and immediacy on its own dramatic terms. Mr. Loach incorporates enough ambiguity to keep his story painfully lifelike, and he finds scorching social realism beyond the bare facts of this tale.

Ladybird, Ladybird, which takes its title from the nursery rhyme about children in peril, is acted with passionate intensity by Ms. Rock. She rails terrifyingly at those around her in some of the film's most disturbing scenes. An imposing actress of mercurial range, she also displays a warm intimacy in scenes with Mr. Vega, whose sympathetic presence softens Jorge's Prince Charming role.

Ladybird, Ladybird will be shown tonight and tomorrow as part of the New York Film Festival.

—*J.M., October 7, 1994*

LAMERICA

Directed by Gianni Amelio; written (in Italian, with English subtitles) by Mr. Amelio, Andrea Porporati and Alessandro Sermoneta; director of photography, Luca Bigazzi; edited by Simona Paggi; music by Franco Piersanti; produced by Mario and Vittorio Cecchi Gori; released by New Yorker Films. Running time: 120 minutes.

With: Enrico Lo Verso (Gino), Michele Placido (Fiore), Carmelo Di Mazzarelli (Spiro) and Piro Milkani (Selimi).

Gianni Amelio's magnificently humane *Lamerica* takes place in 1991 in an Albania visibly coming apart at the seams. After nearly fifty years in isolation under the Communist dictatorship headed by Enver Hoxha and his successor, Ramiz Alia, Europe's poorest country is in turmoil, led by a socialist government that will hold power for only one year. Meanwhile, the streets are strewn with rubble and the populace is volatile and anarchic. It is either a scene of devastation or a land of opportunity, depending on one's point of view.

Lamerica begins with two Italian entrepreneurs who hope to turn Albania's misery into a private windfall. The prosperous Fiore (Michele Placido) and his slick assistant, Gino (Enrico Lo Verso), expect to start a dummy corporation, open a bogus shoe factory and exploit the economic possibilities. This scheme follows a familial pattern of sorts, since twenty years earlier Gino's father and Fiore tried a similar scam with electronics in Nigeria. Fiore's outlook has become no less patronizing since then. "The Albanians are like children," he says. "If an Italian said 'The sea is made of wine,' they'd drink it."

Fiore and Gino's idea requires the use of an Albanian figurehead for their company. And it is here that the fiscal plans start collapsing, and this spare, supremely eloquent film takes flight. From a labor camp that once housed political prisoners, they commandeer the most helpless-looking wretch they can find, a man so withdrawn and confused that they can even park him in an orphanage for safekeeping. This old man (Carmelo Di Mazzarelli) is named Spiro and is lost in the past. When asked his age, in one of the film's most profoundly startling moments, he signals with his hands that he is twenty. Fifty years in prison have slipped his mind.

What happens next becomes a potent reminder of Mr. Amelio's equally astonishing *Stolen Children*, in which Mr. Lo Verso played a carabiniere reluctantly forced to escort two children on a journey across Italy. Directed in the same lucid, simple, beautifully refurbished neorealist style, *Lamerica* sends Mr. Lo Verso on another spiritual journey. Surprising as it is to see this actor's open, guileless features obscured by yuppie accouterments, the film has something else in mind for him. Separated from Fiore and sent off to watch Spiro, he is gradually stripped of everything that identifies him as a wealthy Italian carpetbagger. Instead, Gino is forced to become part of Albania's upheaval and to discover the world anew.

Albania is an inspired setting for *Lamerica,* a film that proceeds matter-of-factly until it escalates to capture a far-reaching poetic vision of immigrant experience. (The title is meant to be an illiterate Italian immigrant's spelling of America, to which Mr. Amelio's grandfather immigrated from Italy after World War II.) The film makes a clear connection between Albania in the 1990's and postwar Italy: both nations were economically devastated and reeling from the effects of dictatorship. One out of eight Albanians emigrated during the period the film describes, just as many Italians left Italy along with Mr. Amelio's grandfather.

These were the postwar conditions from which Italian neorealism emerged, exposing the personal hardships wrought by political strife and finding hope and bravery in the daily struggles waged by ordinary people. So this time Mr. Amelio reinvents neorealism with an especially acute sense of history. A young Italian like Gino, interested only in newfound prosperity and oblivious to the lessons of the past, has a lot to learn from Albania's troubles.

Lamerica describes Gino's journey through this landscape with documentary precision. Nonprofessional actors play most roles, and real events that the filmmaker observed in Albania—like the sight of a hip-hopping Albanian waif, energized by the sudden onslaught of pop culture via previously unavailable Italian television—have been incorporated into the film.

The film's synthesis of fact and fiction is gracefully achieved, as in placing Gino on a jam-packed truck transporting would-be immigrants to an Albanian port city. The scene is galvanized by the sad, dramatized fate that befalls one passenger, but its conversation and impossible crowding seem real.

Mr. Lo Verso once again shows himself to be a touchingly naive everyman, a mournfully handsome actor whose face seems effortlessly revealing. His carefully shaded performance melds the arrogance of new prosperity with the broadening, unwanted emergence of a wider worldview. Without a false note anywhere, he also establishes the right prickly intimacy with Mr. Mazzarelli, an eighty-year-old retired Sicilian fisherman with no acting experience. The ease with which Mr. Amelio creates an impromptu father-son bond between these two is a sign of this filmmaker's bracingly unsentimental compassion.

Mr. Amelio, whose earlier films (including the more arid 1990 *Open Doors*) have been well received without reaching a large audience, deserves to emerge from this year's New York Film Festival much more widely known.

—*J.M., October 4, 1995*

THE LAST AMERICAN HERO

Directed by Lamont Johnson: written by William Roberts, based on articles by Tom Wolfe: director of photography, George Silano: edited by Tom Rolf and Robbe Roberts: music by Charles Fox: art designer, Lawrence G. Paull: produced by Mr. Roberts and John Cutts: released by Twentieth Century Fox. Running time: 100 minutes.

With: Jeff Bridges (Elroy Jackson Jr.), Valerie Perrine (Marge), Geraldine Fitzgerald (Mrs. Jackson), Ned Beatty (Hackel), Gary Busey (Wayne Jackson), Art Lund (Elroy Jackson Sr.) and Ed Lauter (Burton Colt).

Lamont Johnson's *The Last American Hero* has a source in an *Esquire* article Tom Wolfe wrote several years ago about a stock-car racer and automobile customizer named Junior Johnson. The source isn't very close, however, and the film, with its hero, Junior Jackson (Jeff Bridges), hasn't too much to do with the subject of Wolfe's famous article. It hasn't too much to do with the mystique of automobile racing either—though it is full of automobiles and races. It does have to do with human relations, with the choice between a private and a public life, with the meaning of imprisonment, with the ways in which a souped-up hot rod is like a Carolina moonshiner's still.

Junior's dad (Art Lund) makes the moonshine. Really committed to his trade, by now almost friends with the revenue agent who keeps tossing him in jail, he is a man of great character and gentle sadness whose way of life is pushing him into an extreme of privacy literally hidden down inside his native earth. Junior's spirit of independence, equally fierce, has no such luck. In a sense he must rise, taking nothing with him—not his friends, not even his own car—as success encloses him in its own forms of isolation.

The outline of this progress is conventional. But the terms developed for it in *The Last American Hero* are serious and rich and sometimes very beautiful.

Strictly for its car racing, the film isn't so exciting. But you might say the same for Howard Hawks's stock-car movie, *Red Line 7000* (1965), which from this distance begins to look like one of the important films of the last decade. But Hawks did care about the world of the drivers and their women, and he used car racing to express the stoical pessimism typical of his later work. Johnson withdraws from all that, to concentrate on individual solutions and moments of personal exploration. In this he is aided by stunning performances from Bridges, from Lund, from Geraldine Fitzgerald as Junior's mother, from Ed Lauter as the factory-team manager to whom Junior must finally sell himself, from Valerie Perrine as the girl for Junior—and for any other driver in the circuit.

Miss Perrine—known only, and rather spectacularly, for her performance in *Slaughterhouse Five*—has an interesting role. Quite obviously cast as the fickle prize of fame, she becomes humanly more appealing as she is revealed to be more tawdry, more helplessly disloyal—to just about everybody, even herself. *The Last American Hero* is a film of many regrets but no great bitterness. And its freedom from easy ironies and from any kind of condescension is one clue to its value.

The movies of Lamont Johnson (*The McKenzie Break, The Groundstar Conspiracy,* etc.) continue to impress me for their intelligence, their good B-movie toughness, their care and grace in performance. *The Last American Hero* opened yesterday at neighborhood

theaters. That means that it may not be around long—
and it is worth seeing.

—*R.G., July 28, 1973*

THE LAST EMPEROR

Directed by Bernardo Bertolucci; written by Mark
Peploe, Mr. Bertolucci and Enzo Ungari, based on
*From Emperor to Citizen, the Autobiography of
Pu Yi;* director of photography, Vittorio Storaro;
edited by Gabriella Cristiani; music by Ryuichi
Sakamoto, David Byrne and Cong Su; art design-
ers, Gianni Giovagnoni, Gianni Silvestri and Maria
Teresa Barbasso; produced by Jeremy Thomas;
released by Columbia Pictures. Running time: 160
minutes.

With: John Lone (Pu Yi), Joan Chen (Wan Jung),
Peter O'Toole (Reginald Johnston), Yin Ruocheng
(The Governor), Victor Wong (Chen Pao Shen),
Dennis Dun (Big Li), Ryuichi Sakamoto (Amakasu),
Maggie Han (Eastern Jewel), Lisa Lu (Tzu Hsui)
and Richard Vuu (Pu Yi, age 3).

Pu Yi (1906–1967), the last Manchu emperor of
China, came to the Dragon Throne at the age of
two and some months. Four years later, the prince
regent, Pu Yi's father, was forced to abdicate all imperial authority to republican forces. The boy-emperor
continued to stay on in lonely, unreal splendor in Beijing's Forbidden City for another decade or so. He was
attended by 1,500 eunuchs, the various members of
his extended household, their hangers on, and, toward
the end, by Reginald Johnston, his faithful and sometimes acerbic British tutor, a Scot with a deep admiration for Chinese civilization and nothing but ridicule
for salvation-mongering Christian missionaries.

In the 1920's, supported by his huge private fortune, Pu Yi and his beautiful empress, nicknamed
Elizabeth, accompanied by his secondary wife, were
kicked out of the palace and moved to the port city of
Tianjin. For a few years they carried on in what was
seen as heedless, high-style decadence in the foreign
enclave.

In the 1930's, the Japanese, who sought to legit-
imize their hold on Manchuria, returned Pu Yi and his
family to their Manchu homeland where, until the end
of World War II, he reigned as the Japanese puppet-
emperor of the new state of Manchuko. After the war,
he spent five years in a Russian prison, testified against
his former Japanese allies in the Tokyo war crimes trials, was repatriated to China and, after ten years of
reeducation, was paroled as *Mr.* Pu Yi. At the time of
his death he was a park attendant in Beijing.

These are the bare facts of a quite extraordinary life
lived by someone who seems to have been a most commonplace person. Pu Yi was an accident of meteorol-
ogy, the calm, rather empty center of the political
hurricane that was blowing around him and that
defined his place in history. Pu Yi was a cipher compared to the remarkable characters who, in one way or
another, shaped his life and modern China—Tzu
Hsui, the old, ferocious Empress Dowager, who
brought the boy to the throne and promptly died, and
the mutually warring revolutionaries, Sun Yat-sen,
Chiang Kai-shek and Mao Zedong.

With the exception of the Empress Dowager, who
makes one brief but riveting appearance, none of the
major figures in this immense drama appear in
Bernardo Bertolucci's arthritic, occasionally spectacular new film, *The Last Emperor.* If it were a more poetically conceived movie, one might respond to
everything of consequence that is not on the screen.
That's not easy when most of what we do see and hear
is of such ordinariness. The movie would appear to
share Pu Yi's severely limited experience of—and
curiosity about—the world.

The Last Emperor, written by Mark Peploe "with"
(as the credits say) Mr. Bertolucci, may have been
inhibited by the enormousness of its subject, and even
by the apparently enthusiastic support of China, which
acted as host to Mr. Bertolucci, his cast and production crew. This isn't a movie that could offend any political biases, except maybe those of Chiang Kai-shek.

The director was given access to some magnificent
locations within the Forbidden City as well as elsewhere in China and Manchuria. When the screenplay
calls for thousands of extras, there are thousands of
extras on the screen. One assumes that all of the costumes, props and random historical references are
authentic. The eye is frequently entertained, while the
center of the screen remains dead.

The Last Emperor is like an elegant travel brochure.
It piques the curiosity. One wants to go. Ultimately
it's a letdown.

The film opens in 1950, with the return to China of Pu Yi (John Lone) as a war criminal. Thereafter the movie jumps awkwardly forward and back in its attempt to account for more than fifty years of the emperor's utterly passive life. Big scenes recall the boy's first (and last) encounter with the Empress Dowager (Lisa Lu), his acclamation as emperor and something of his pampered, artificial childhood.

The movie picks up momentum with the arrival in 1919 of his tutor, Reginald Johnston (Peter O'Toole). Though Johnston seems to have been a most interesting fellow in real life, both incurably romantic and fastidiously British, Mr. Peploe's screenplay freights him with a lot of factual information to speak as dialogue, but nothing much in the way of character.

The curious (to Westerners) mating customs of Chinese monarchs are reported with care. Wan Jung (Joan Chen), Pu Yi's bride, is seen as a woman of some spirit who quickly adopts an opium habit to the disgust of her husband. When the movie attempts to characterize the bored lives of Pu Yi and Wan Jung in Tianjin, *The Last Emperor* looks briefly very much like *The Conformist*.

Lots of cocktails are drunk. In the middle of the afternoon, Pu Yi leans against the piano in a hotel dining room and croons "Am I Blue," while Wan Jung trades sapphic sallies with Eastern Jewel (Maggie Han), a young woman dressed in a leather flying suit.

"I'm a Japanese spy and I don't care who knows it," announces the decadent Eastern Jewel. The fact that Eastern Jewel was a real character, a Manchu princess executed after the war as a traitor, doesn't inspire the director to make her seem to be anything more than an outtake from an earlier Bertolucci film.

Mr. O'Toole rattles off his lines with speed and what often seems to be a comic disregard for what they mean. From time to time, when he must register a certain ineffable sadness, he enunciates each word as if it were a pearl, which it isn't. This is not a great performance. Somewhat better are Mr. Lone, Miss Chen, Miss Lu and Richard Vuu, who plays Pu Yi as a three-year-old and looks angelic.

The Last Emperor, which opens today at Cinema 1, works most effectively as an illustrated introduction to modern Chinese history. It contains just enough information to send one looking for *From Emperor to Citizen,* Pu Yi's autobiography, which is the basis of the film. Other helpful books include Henry McAleavy's

Dream of Tartary, also a life of Pu Yi, and Reginald Johnston's own account of his years in China, *Twilight in the Forbidden City.*

—*V.C., November 20, 1987*

THE LAST METRO

Directed by François Truffaut: written (in French. with English subtitles) by Mr. Truffaut. Jean-Claude Grumberg and Suzanne Schiffman: director of photography. Nestor Almendros: edited by Martine Barraqué-Curie: music by Georges Delarue: produced by Jean-José Richer: released by United Artists. Running time: 133 minutes.

With: Catherine Deneuve (Marion Steiner). Gérard Depardieu (Bernard Granger). Heinz Bennent (Lucas Steiner). Jean Poiret (Jean-Loup Cottins). Andréa Ferréol (Arlette Guillaume). Sabine Haudepin (Nadine Marsac) and Maurice Risch (Raymond Boursier).

François Truffaut's *The Last Metro* is a dazzlingly subversive work. The film has the form of a more or less conventional melodrama, about a small Parisian theater company during the 1942–44 Nazi occupation, though the film's methods are so systematically unconventional that it becomes a gently comic, romantic meditation on love, loyalty, heroism and history. Not since Lubitsch's *To Be or Not to Be* has there been such a triumphantly unorthodox use of grim material that usually prompts movies of pious, prefabricated responses.

The film will be shown at Avery Fisher Hall tonight to conclude the 18th New York Film Festival, and will go into commercial release here later this year.

The Last Metro is a melodrama that discreetly refuses to exercise its melodramatic options. It's also a love story that scarcely recognizes its lovers. Though the setting is a legitimate theater, the Theatre Montmartre, it's not an "inside theater" movie. Contrary to what the program for the New York festival says, *The Last Metro* does not do for the theater what *Day for Night* did for the cinema.

Day for Night is a lyrical human comedy that finds an almost perfect metaphor for life in the shooting of the film-within-the-film, that is, if life could be speeded up to run at the rate that film runs through a movie camera.

The Last Metro is about a particular time in history. Its Theatre Montmartre is a refuge—actual in the case of one character, and psychological for the others. The theater provides them survival.

Chief among the characters are Marion Steiner (Catherine Deneuve), the Theatre Montmartre's beautiful, levelheaded star and manager; her husband Lucas Steiner (Heinz Bennent), formerly the manager and director of the theater, who has gone underground to escape deportation; Bernard Granger (Gérard Depardieu), Marion's new leading man, a former Grand Guignol actor who is getting his first major break at the Montmartre; Jean-Loup, the theater's stage director, a gallant, unflamboyant homosexual; Arlette (Andréa Ferréol), the costume designer, and Nadine Marsac, the Theatre Montmartre's ambitious, gutsy ingenue, played by Sabine Haudepin who, seventeen years ago, played the small daughter of Catherine and Jules in *Jules and Jim*.

The Last Metro may be unique among Mr. Truffaut's films in that it contains a villain, a character beyond any redeeming except, possibly, by God. He is Daxiat, based on the real-life, Nazi-sympathizing, Jew-baiting Paris drama critic who, during the occupation, exercised such power that he was, at one point, on the verge of taking control of the Comédie Française.

As played by Jean-Pierre Richard, he recalls some of the great World War II villains played by the young Walter Slezack. Says Marion Steiner of one of Daxiat's reviews, "He signed it but it reads like an anonymous letter."

The focal point of the film is the Theatre Montmartre's production of the French translation of a Norwegian play, *La Disparue* (*The Woman Who Disappeared*). From what we see of it, *La Disparue* appears to be one of those star vehicles, so popular in the 20's, 30's and 40's, in which leading ladies suffered anguish, including amnesia, talked at great length about love (which they felt they had to deny themselves) and often swooned.

The content of *La Disparue*, however, is of no more moment than that of *Meet Pamela*, the rather awful-sounding film that was being produced in the course of *Day for Night*. *The Last Metro* is about the manner in which the Theatre Montmartre actors approach their work, their shifting relations with each other and the way in which each responds to the condition of being "occupied."

The Last Metro doesn't dwell on the horrors of Nazi-encouraged French anti-Semitism, which flourished during the occupation, but it is haunted by those horrors. They are there in the sorrowful love scenes of Marion and Lucas Steiner, which are among the loveliest moments in all of Mr. Truffaut's works, and in what seem to be throwaway scenes, as in a chance encounter Marion has at Gestapo headquarters with a young French woman who has been playing both sides to go on living.

The movie, which was photographed by Nestor Almendros, even looks haunted and a bit hungry. The colors are mostly muted. The streets of Paris have the cramped look of streets shot in a studio, which recalls the look of films of forty years ago and reflects the feeling of restriction of life in an occupied zone.

Without going into specific details, I'd also like to commend the shape of the film, which effectively covers the two years of the occupation and leads to a conclusion that, for sheer, bold theatricality, may remind you of the end of Luis Buñuel's *Tristana*.

Tristana doesn't pop into the mind by chance. It's not since *Tristana* that Miss Deneuve has had a role to match that of Marion Steiner, a woman of intelligence, backbone and the kind of beauty that, you believe, would have made her a star of the Paris stage. With her hair done up in a style I associate with Danielle Darrieux, Miss Deneuve is elegant without being frosty, grand without being great lady-ish. It's a star performance of a star role.

The entire cast is splendid, including Mr. Depardieu, as much for the control he exercises throughout most of the film as for the strength he displays in the film's big scene. Heinz Bennent, the father of *The Tin Drum's* David Bennent, is also noteworthy in the role that Paul Henreid might have played forty years ago, but without Mr. Bennent's humor.

It takes a little while to catch the tempo of the film, but pay attention. *The Last Metro* is about lives surrounded by melodrama, being lived with as little outward fuss as possible. The courage goes without saying, or is acknowledged only obliquely. When the Theatre Montmartre's cheerfully rotund stage manager says in sudden fury, "I'm not a nice fat man!" the anger expressed is on the other side of a heroic front.

—*V.C., October 12, 1980*

537

THE LAST PICTURE SHOW

Directed by Peter Bogdanovich; written by Mr. Bogdanovich and Larry McMurtry, based on the novel by Mr. McMurtry; director of photography, Robert Surtees; edited by Donn Cambern; production designer, Polly Platt; produced by Stephen J. Friedman; released by Columbia Pictures. Black and white. Running time: 118 minutes.

With: Timothy Bottoms (Sonny Crawford), Jeff Bridges (Duane Jackson), Cybill Shepherd (Jacy Farrow), Ben Johnson (Sam the Lion), Cloris Leachman (Ruth Popper), Ellen Burstyn (Lois Farrow), Eileen Brennan (Genevieve), Clu Gulager (Abilene), Sam Bottoms (Billy), Sharon Taggart (Charlene Duggs), Randy Quaid (Lester Marlow) and Bill Thurman (Coach Popper).

Peter Bogdanovich's fine second film, *The Last Picture Show,* adapted from Larry McMurtry's novel by McMurtry and Bogdanovich, has the effect of a lovely, leisurely, horizontal pan shot across the life of Anarene, Texas, a small, shabby town on a plain so flat that to raise the eye even ten degrees would be to see only an endless sky.

In an unbroken arc of narrative, beautifully photographed (by Robert Surtees) in the blunt, black-and-white tones I associate with pictures in a high school yearbook, the film tells a series of interlocking stories of love and loss that are on the sentimental edge of *Winesburg, Ohio,* but that illuminate a good deal more of one segment of the American experience than any other American film in recent memory.

It is 1951, the time of Truman, of Korea, of Jo Stafford, of *I, the Jury* as a best-selling paperback, when tank-town movie houses like the Royal Theater had to close because the citizens of Anarene, like most other Americans, were discovering, in television, a more convenient dream machine that brought with it further isolation from community—a phenomenon analyzed by Philip Slater, the sociologist, as America's pursuit of loneliness.

The Last Picture Show is not sociology, even though it is sociologically true, nor is it another exercise in romantic nostalgia on the order of Robert Mulligan's *Summer of '42.* It is filled with carefully researched details of time and place, but although these details are the essential decor of the film, they are not the essence. It is a movie that doesn't look back; rather, it starts off and ends in its own time, as much as does such a completely dissimilar, contemporary story as that of *Sunday, Bloody Sunday.*

The Last Picture Show is about both Anarene and Sonny Crawford, the high school senior and football cocaptain (with his best friend, Duane Jackson, of the always-defeated Anarene team), through whose sensibilities the film is felt. As Bogdanovich seldom takes his story very far from Anarene, he sees *The Last Picture Show* entirely in terms of the maturation of Sonny, in the course of the emotional crises and confrontations that have become the staples of all sorts of American coming-of-age literature, from *Penrod* to *Peyton Place* and *Portnoy's Complaint.*

They are familiar staples, but they are treated with such humor, such sympathy and, with the exception of a few overwrought scenes, reticence that *The Last Picture Show* becomes an adventure in rediscovery—of a very decent, straightforward kind of movie, as well as of—and I rather hesitate to use such a square phrase—human values.

Timothy Bottoms, who gave most of his performance in *Johnny Got His Gun* as a voice on the soundtrack for the mummy-wrapped, quadruple-amputee hero, is fine as Sonny Crawford, but then I liked just about everyone in the huge cast.

This includes Jeff Bridges (son to Lloyd, younger brother to Beau), as Duane; Cybill Shepherd, as the prettiest, richest girl in town, who is almost too bad to be true; Cloris Leachman, as the coach's wife, who gives Sonny some idea of what love might be; Ellen Burstyn (who was so good in *Alex in Wonderland*), as a tough, Dorothy Malone type of middle-aged beauty (middle-aged? she's all of forty!) who is one of the few people in Anarene to have recognized what life is and come to terms with it; and Ben Johnson, as the old man who most influences Sonny's life.

I do have some small quibbles about the film. Bogdanovich and McMurtry have done everything possible to get the entire novel on screen, yet they have mysteriously omitted certain elements, such as Sonny's family life—if any—and the reasons why the coach's wife is such a pushover for a teenage lover. The movie is, perhaps, too horizontal, too objective.

I didn't see Bogdanovich's first film, *Targets,* but *The Last Picture Show* indicates that Bogdanovich, the movie critic, had already taken Jack Valenti's advice when, last winter, the film industry spokesman described critics as physicians who should heal themselves—by making movies—if they wanted to be taken seriously as critics. Bogdanovich has.

The Last Picture Show was screened at the New York Film Festival Saturday and opened yesterday at the new Columbia I Theater. My only fear is that some unfortunates are going to confuse it with Dennis Hopper's *The Last Movie,* to which *The Last Picture Show* is kin only by title.

—V.C., October 4, 1971

THE LAST SEDUCTION

Directed by John Dahl; written by Steve Barancik; director of photography. Jeffrey Jur; edited by Eric L. Beason; music by Joseph Vitarelli; production designer. Linda Pearl; produced by Jonathan Shestack; released by October Films. Running time: 110 minutes.

With: Linda Fiorentino (Bridget Gregory). Peter Berg (Mike Swale). J. T. Walsh (Frank Griffith). Bill Nunn (Harlan) and Bill Pullman (Clay Gregory).

A hired assassin, an innocent fall guy, and a husband and wife intent on killing each other made a sterling film noir spectacle out of *Red Rock West,* John Dahl's recently released sleeper. Now Mr. Dahl, whose work will never again fall into the sleeper category, is back with *The Last Seduction,* which makes his earlier miscreants look like a collection of cream puffs. *Red Rock West* was memorably smart and steely. But it's a walk in the park picking buttercups compared with this.

Nothing else about *The Last Seduction* is as polite or colorless as its title. Certainly not Bridget Gregory (Linda Fiorentino), the hot, slinky monster who is this film's central character. There were 1940's noir heroines with Bridget's brand of undiluted self-interest, but she also throws in a few tricks from the *Basic Instinct* school of interpersonal relations. Only in the insect or animal worlds are there comparable models for feminine behavior. And the female praying mantis is nicer to her mates than Bridget is to the men in this movie.

It takes about five minutes for Mr. Dahl to establish Bridget's breathtaking ruthlessness, as she robs her husband Clay (Bill Pullman) of the proceeds from a drug deal. Maybe she does this because Clay treated her a little badly, and maybe she's just ready for new scenery. Anyway, Bridget takes the money and leaves New York City, winding up in Beston, a friendly little town near Buffalo. No one in Beston has ever seen anything like Bridget, and neither have you.

Both Mr. Dahl, who directs this film with stunning economy, and Ms. Fiorentino, whose performance is flawlessly hard-boiled, exult in the sheer wickedness of Bridget's character. What makes this easy to do are Bridget's stony seductiveness and her spellbinding talent for getting exactly what she wants. For instance, she soon appropriates Mike Swale (Peter Berg), a naive Beston resident who's wowed by Bridget's drop-dead sophistication. Their meeting alone, with Bridget unceremoniously unzipping Mike's pants in a crowded barroom, is guaranteed to make every man in the audience squirm. And wonder what's next.

Bridget, now using the name Wendy, lures Mike into one half of an intense affair. (She herself remains maddeningly aloof.) Meanwhile, she puts down a few tentative roots in Beston, despite the fact that the neighbors' neighborliness is enough to make her cringe. She rents a house in suburbia (Mr. Dahl has great fun with that little contrast) and finds a job at the insurance company where Mike works. But she wants to keep their relationship a secret, so she slaps Mike when he tries talking to her at the office. "A woman loses fifty percent of her authority when people find out who she's sleeping with," Bridget declares.

Bridget will not be mistaken for a crusading feminist. Her outlook is much too selfishly pathological to have a political edge, and her glamour is too scarily seductive. Besides, Bridget is a more darkly fascinating anomaly, with old-style killer instincts along with a liberated aggressiveness that suits the present day. The audience can only sit back and watch in astonishment as Bridget embroils Mike in an intricate, deadly scheme that harks back to James M. Cain, while also doing her best to keep Clay off her trail.

Red Rock West had a mostly nocturnal look and eventually bogged down under the weight of its genre affectations. *The Last Seduction,* which opens today at Sony Village Theater VII, looks sunnier and sounds less derivative. That's because its malice is so nonchalant and springs from the depths of Bridget's character, not from the machinations of an overloaded plot. Steve Barancik's clever screenplay builds up carefully and delivers a perfect payoff, one that suits the story while also acknowledging Bridget's very special toughness.

"Why do I have to turn off the lights?" Mike asks, when Bridget tries to give him orders about how to commit a murder. But of course that's the heart of any noir-based love story.

"Pop psychology," she answers. "Let yourself know you've finished an unpleasant chore."

The Last Seduction, a devilishly entertaining crime story with a heroine who must be seen to be believed, is as satisfying an ensemble piece as *Red Rock West.* J. T. Walsh, who was also in *Red Rock,* shows up as Bridget's lawyer and asks her the question on every mind: "Anyone check you for a heartbeat lately?" Mr. Pullman is especially good as a man who really did deserve to be married to Bridget, and clearly gave as good as he got while the union lasted, with all the dark humor that job demanded.

Mr. Berg is gently appealing and makes the perfect chump, which is no small compliment in such a story. And Bill Nunn has some fine scenes as the private investigator who thinks he can get the best of Bridget. Maybe male praying mantises feel that way, too.

Mr. Dahl's early admirers will find the promise of *Red Rock West* (and one other film, *Kill Me Again*) furthered by a gripping story and a tight, suspenseful directorial style, not to mention a heroine who's literally to die for. Mr. Dahl was good to begin with, and now he's badder and better.

—*J.M., October 26, 1994*

LAST TANGO IN PARIS

Directed by Bernardo Bertolucci; written (in French, with English subtitles) by Mr. Bertolucci and Franco Arcalli, based on a story by Mr. Bertolucci; director of photography, Vittorio Storaro; edited by Mr. Arcalli; music by Gato Barbieri; produced by Alberto Grimaldi; released by United Artists. Running time: 125 minutes.

With: Marlon Brando (Paul), Maria Schneider (Jeanne), Jean-Pierre Léaud (Tom), Giovanna Galetti (Prostitute) and Maria Michi (Rose's Mother).

The feelings of love, anguish and despair that erupt all over the place in Bernardo Bertolucci's new film, *Last Tango in Paris,* are so intense, so consuming, that watching the film at times comes close to being an embarrassment.

Last Tango in Paris is all about romantic love, but its expressions are the sometimes brave, sometimes wildly foolish-looking Lawrentian gestures of an intense sexual passion that goes as far as it can and then collapses, in physical and emotional exhaustion. The movie is sad, but it's also hugely funny, occasionally when it doesn't mean to be.

The film is about Paul (Marlon Brando), a middle-aged American of obscure antecedents who has been living in Paris for seven years with his wife, the beautiful patronne of a second-rate hotel. When the film opens, the wife has just committed suicide and Paul is coolly setting up an apartment with a girl whose name he does not want to know, whose feelings he does not want to hear, for afternoons of pure, absolutely free sexual encounters.

A most willing partner (and victim) is Jeanne (Maria Schneider), a pretty, comically independent girl who, on her hours off, returns to her mother, the widow of an army colonel, and to her fiancé (Jean-Pierre Léaud). The latter is a movie nut in the process of starring Jeanne in a cinema verité film.

The center of the film is composed of the extraordinary Paul-Jeanne encounter sessions, during which she, first, demands to know more about him, after which the tables slowly turn. Little by little Paul reveals himself as the widower of a woman he loved in spite of her other lovers, freely admitted and even discussed.

Last Tango in Paris is most affecting when it's most ambiguous, cross-breeding tragic melodrama with elegant satire. When, eventually, Paul tries to explain himself, and the despair that drove him into the affair with the girl, the movie goes so surprisingly banal that not even Bertolucci's magnificently rich physical production, or Brando's courageous performance, can make it seem as important as we want it to be.

I use the word *courageous* carefully. For Brando, like Bertolucci, has pulled out all the stops without fear of looking absurd, as when, toward the end, he runs drunkenly through a proper Paris dance hall pursuing the frightened girl, whom he has admitted to himself he now loves.

Bertolucci's courage is expressed in his undertaking a film of such poetic ambitions and being as successful as he has been. After the success of the comparatively conventional *The Conformist,* he might easily have preferred to play it safe. He hasn't. He has made a film that, on one viewing, leaves me somewhat cool—and determined to see it again.

Bernardo Bertolucci's *Last Tango in Paris* is a beautiful, courageous, foolish, romantic and reckless film and Bertolucci is like a diving champion, drunk on enthusiasm, who dares dive from the high board knowing well that the pool is half empty. The stunt comes off, but the dive is less grand than we might expect from what we've heard and read, and especially from what we know of Bertolucci. I mention this at the outset because the film is being so overpraised (and overpriced) that many disappointed people may be reluctant to indulge its failures, thus to miss its achievements, which are considerable.

Last Tango in Paris is the movie romance of the 1970's, at least of that portion of the 1970's we have seen so far. It carries its ideas of love and sexuality not to the limits of conceivable time, but to the limits of last year—the era of Norman Mailer, Germaine Greer, "J," airplane goggles, porno films and revolutionary semantics. It's not the film's boldness that shocks, amuses and fascinates us, but its topicality.

It's what in the 1960's (a decade not great for jargon) would have been called, lamely, a Now film. It's so Now, in fact, that you better see it quickly. I suspect that its ideas, as well as its ability to shock or, apparently, to arouse, will age quickly. This is not true, I think, of the superlative production by Bertolucci, nor of the extraordinary performance by Marlon Brando who plays a role that does not simply identify him with his own time, as did his roles in *A Streetcar Named Desire* in the 1940's and *On the Waterfront* in the 1950's. It also makes him a Pop spokesman, tough, irreverent, mocking, as well as an incurable sentimentalist.

The finest things about *Last Tango in Paris* are the set scenes, riotous, furious, frenzied celebrations of the differences between men and women. Oddly enough, I found them more funny, occasionally more embarrassing, even more philosophical, than

erotic. The intensity of Brando's anger and humor, and the desperation with which he sets out to insulate himself from the world through this affair, are very special to behold. His language—crude, witty, magnificently vulgar—and the stories that tumble out in the form of random monologues are unlike anything we've ever heard on the screen before. It sounds tough as hell, which explains, I think, why the film's full-blown, almost old-fashioned romanticism goes unnoticed. In spite of all the simulated sex, everything in the film is touched by exotic fancy.

The look of the film, too, is pure romance—lots of dusky, autumnal golds and blue-grays, long, graceful camera movements, scenes shot through frosted glass or against fractured mirrors and a soundtrack that carries music on the order of a high-class, though not classical, Muzak. When Bertolucci scores one of Paul and Jeanne's encounters with what sounds like a Hawaiian love song, you know he must be kidding. Or is he? I don't think he is.

The film's revealed mysteries let us down. They aren't grand enough for violence and humiliation and the intimacies we've been asked to share until then. Behind the raised consciousness of *Last Tango in Paris* there's a little bit of the simplistic foolishness of *Love Story,* which people thought was old-fashioned but was topical enough to make a zillion dollars. *Last Tango,* touted as something completely new, will, I predict, make a zillion dollars for the very same reason.
—V.C., February 2, 1973

THE LAST TEMPTATION OF CHRIST

Directed by Martin Scorsese; written by Paul Schrader, based on the novel by Nikos Kazantzakis; director of photography, Michael Ballhaus; edited by Thelma Schoonmaker; music by Peter Gabriel; production designer, John Beard; produced by Barbara De Fina; released by Universal Pictures. Running time: 164 minutes.

With: Willem Dafoe (Jesus), Harvey Keitel (Judas), Barbara Hershey (Mary Magdalene), Harry Dean Stanton (Saul/Paul), David Bowie (Pontius Pilate), Andre Gregory (John the Baptist) and Tomas Arana (Lazarus).

Nikos Kazantzakis's radical, revisionist novel *The Last Temptation of Christ* redefines divinity through choice. It suggests that if Jesus accepted his destiny triumphantly, in full awareness of another alternative, his spiritual example was thus greatly enhanced by a human dimension. "That part of Christ's nature which was profoundly human," Mr. Kazantzakis wrote in his introduction to this startling volume, "helps us to understand him and love him and to pursue his Passion as though it were our own."

Martin Scorsese's film adaptation of this 1951 novel, which opens today at the Ziegfeld, is also informed by a concept of choice, and the choices the filmmaker has made cover a wide spectrum. He has elected to shun the conventions of biblical cinema, underscore the contemporary implications of Mr. Kazantzakis's story, create a heightened historical context for Jesus' teachings and emphasize the visceral aspects of his experience as well. Though the choices that shape this exceptionally ambitious, deeply troubling and, at infrequent moments, genuinely transcendent film are often contradictory, they create an extra dimension. Mr. Scorsese's evident struggle with this material becomes as palpable as the story depicted on the screen.

Faith and sacrifice, guilt and redemption, sin and atonement—these are forceful elements in many of Mr. Scorsese's earlier films, from *Mean Streets* (1973) to *Taxi Driver* (1976) to *Raging Bull* (1980). And these works have established their director as perhaps the most innately religious of major American filmmakers, certainly one of the best. But paradoxically, the film that finds Mr. Scorsese in such close proximity to the heart of his earlier concerns is often strikingly less spiritual than its secular equivalents. It seems possible, indeed understandable, that for him this monumental subject has had a daunting effect.

The director does not seem constrained by the episodes setting forth Mr. Kazantzakis's most daring constructs; if anything, it is these seemingly irreverent and sometimes very bloody sequences that generate the film's most spontaneous and powerful scenes. *The Last Temptation of Christ* begins with a voice-over (its tone reminiscent of Harvey Keitel's opening inner monologue in *Mean Streets*) that presents Jesus as a tormented, worried individual. Soon afterward, he is seen assisting in the crucifixion of a fellow Jew, an act that makes him the object of universal scorn. He is

doing this, he then explains, in a passage that typifies the film's unconventional tactics, because he fears and dreads his messianic destiny. Perhaps he would rather invoke God's wrath than His love.

Soon afterward, he appears transfixed by guilt, sorrow and even longing in the presence of Mary Magdalene (played in fiery style by a tattoo-wearing Barbara Hershey) as he watches her engage in prostitution with an international array of clients. Pained, awkward and self-analytical in these early moments ("What if I say the wrong thing? What if I say the right thing?"), the film's Jesus changes markedly as the story progresses. He is seen addressing and conquering his doubts until he at last attains a joyful acceptance of his role.

The promise held forth by the film's beginning, a promise to use drastic and unexpected ideas as a means of understanding Jesus' inner life, gradually gives way to something less focused. Though this handsome film was made on a small budget and a streamlined scale, it's big enough to wander from the central thread of its story. The opening sequences, which are abruptly strung together, are closely connected with Jesus' internal struggle, but they give way to a less emotionally compelling central section in which miracle after miracle is reenacted. This part of the film, working as a kind of greatest hits sequence in which Jesus heals the sick, turns water to wine and raises a handsome young Lazarus from the grave, functions as pageantry without much passion.

A lot of the film has this stilted, showy quality, since it's often more apt to announce its ideas than to illustrate them. In contrast with the real spiritual torment conveyed by many of Mr. Scorsese's other characters, his version of Jesus is a controlled, slightly remote figure, despite the screenplay's many allusions to his pain. Fortunately, Willem Dafoe has such a gleaming intensity in this role, so much quiet authority, that the film's images of Jesus are overwhelming even when the thoughts attributed to him are not. As photographed by Michael Ballhaus and staged by Mr. Scorsese, with many aspects of religious painting in mind, some of the film works better on a visual level than a verbal one. Many of the tableaux that come to life here, like the elaborate Palm Sunday scene, are altogether breathtaking.

The dialogue that accompanies these moments amounts to one of the film's great incongruities, since the language (in a screenplay by Paul Schrader) is often as intentionally flat as the imagery is starkly glorious. Peering out through various odd-looking beards and wigs are actors so identifiable and eccentric that they often upstage the material: Though David Bowie makes a strikingly urbane Pontius Pilate, Andre Gregory as a chattering John the Baptist and Harry Dean Stanton as a fast-talking Saul (who becomes Paul) have a more distracting effect. So does Harvey Keitel, with red hair and an enlarged nose to play an eminently down-to-earth Judas, whose betrayal of Jesus is one of the many events that this film reenvisions. When a lion appears to Jesus in the desert and asks, in the voice of Mr. Keitel, "Don't you rekonnize me?" the film is in danger of becoming silly.

And yet, despite such maladroit moments, *The Last Temptation of Christ* finally exerts enormous power. What emerges most memorably is its sense of absolute conviction, never more palpable than in the final fantasy sequence that removes Jesus from the cross and creates for him the life of an ordinary man. Though this episode lasts longer than it should and is allowed to wander far afield, it finally has the mightily affirmative, truly visceral impact for which the whole film clearly strives. Anyone who questions the sincerity or seriousness of what Mr. Scorsese has attempted need only see the film to lay those doubts to rest.

—J.M., August 12, 1988

THE LAST WALTZ

Directed by Martin Scorsese; directors of photography, Michael Chapman, Laszlo Kovacs, Vilmos Zsigmund, David Myers, Bobby Byrne, Michael Watkins and Hiro Narita; edited by Yeu-Bun Yee and Jan Roblee; music by The Band and others; produced by Robbie Robertson; released by United Artists. Running time: 120 minutes.

With: Bob Dylan, Joni Mitchell, Neil Diamond, Emmylou Harris, Neil Young, Van Morrison, Ron Wood, Muddy Waters, Eric Clapton, The Staples, Ringo Starr, Dr. John and The Band.

Martin Scorsese had the makings of a better-than-average concert movie at his disposal when he made *The Last Waltz*, but the film is full of evidence that Mr. Scorsese had something more ambitious in mind. One exquisitely edited sequence of the Band performing "The Weight," filmed on a soundstage by cameras that sway and rotate with the music, infuses the interaction of a rock band with more joy and lyricism than any other rock film has ever approached. A guest appearance at the concert by the singer Van Morrison, now paunchy and balding but triumphantly galvanizing just the same, makes for a moment rich with both euphoria and regret.

Mr. Scorsese's decision to train his cameras more closely on the musicians' faces than on their instruments leads to an unexpected examination of the physical and emotional costliness of their craft, and of the element of acting that's an integral part of any kind of live performance. Indeed, Mr. Scorsese manages to turn Rick Danko, the Band's bassist, into a veritable double for one of the director's favorite actors, Robert De Niro.

The Last Waltz, which opens today at the Ziegfeld Theater, is Mr. Scorsese's record of a 1976 Thanksgiving concert given by the Band—and several of their most famous friends, like Joni Mitchell, Neil Young, Muddy Waters, Eric Clapton and Bob Dylan—to mark the group's farewell to live performing.

However definite the show's raison d'être may have been, though, its spirit remains strangely ambiguous. Members of the Band, interviewed by Mr. Scorsese afterward in footage that is interspersed among the songs, speak about the performance almost noncommittally, and their offhandedness is contagious.

If this wasn't a particularly sad or celebratory occasion for them, it can't mean much to the viewer either, unless one approaches the film with a full set of memories of the principals in better days. A peculiarly myopic view of the aging process is also required, if one is to find *The Last Waltz* unusually stirring. The life of a rock star may be more draining than the life of a Maytag repairman, but when the film tries to milk too much from every last sign of wear and tear, it comes dangerously close to self-importance and self-pity.

One of the Band's most fascinating idiosyncrasies has always been its combination of a strong group identity with the virtual anonymity of individual members. The group identity has also been powerfully visual, reinforced by album cover photographs that make the musicians out to be woodsy and austere, so deliberately antiquated looking that they summon up an impression of simpler times.

The Last Waltz takes pains to introduce them as individuals, in interviews that are slack at times but occasionally very winning. Other group members explain, for instance, that in their early days the bashful organist Garth Hudson demanded $10 a week from each of them, ostensibly for music lessons. Only later, they realized that the classically trained Mr. Hudson was too embarrassed to tell his family he was working as a rock-and-roller, and was instead claiming to have found a few teaching jobs.

The interviews are uneven, but their function is to amplify. On the other hand, the setting for the concert—an elegant stage backed by drapes and candelabra—is mightily incongruous with the Band's group identity, and the mismatch is more disruptive than illuminating. A guest appearance by the very Las Vegasy Neil Diamond, one of whose albums was recently produced by the Band's leader, Robbie Robertson, is so jarring and unwelcome that the movie takes minutes to recover. And Mr. Scorsese's efforts to stir up a distinct visual style for the film, a style that might somehow have compensated for the curious lack of sentiment that marks all but the film's final half-hour, are so half-hearted and sporadic they become almost maddening.

Just think of the rich visual eloquence with which Mr. Scorsese was able to invest a simple Checker cab in *Taxi Driver,* and just notice that all he supplies here are a waltzing couple behind the credits and some smoke clouds. Given that, you can't help realizing that for all its impressive musical accomplishments, *The Last Waltz* is a great lost opportunity. There is a dazzling array of talent on display here, and the film surely has its memorable moments. But it articulates so little of the end-of-an-era feeling it hints at—and some of Mr. Scorsese's accomplishments have been so stunning—that it's impossible to view *The Last Waltz* as anything but an also-ran.

—*J.M., April 26, 1978*

LAURA

Produced and directed by Otto Preminger; written by Jay Dratler. Samuel Hoffenstein. Elizabeth Reinhardt. Ring Lardner Jr. and Jerry Cady. based on the novel by Vera Caspary: cinematographer. Joseph La Shelle: edited by Louis Loeffler: music by David Raksin: production designer. Thomas Little: released by Twentieth Century Fox. Black and white. Running time: 88 minutes.

With: Gene Tierney (Laura Hunt). Dana Andrews (Mark McPherson). Clifton Webb (Waldo Lydecker). Vincent Price (Shelby Carpenter). Judith Anderson (Ann Treadwell). Dorothy Adams (Bessie Clary) and James Flavin (McAvity).

When a murder mystery possessing as much sustained suspense, good acting and caustically brittle dialogue as *Laura,* which opened yesterday at the Roxy, comes along it might seem a little like carping to suggest that it could have been even better. As the story of a strangely fascinating female who insinuates herself into the lives of three very worldly gents, much depends, of course, upon the lady herself. This is made quite evident in the beginning of the story when considerable interest and curiosity is generated over the murder of Laura Hunt, and the two rivals for her affections make quite a to-do about her intriguing attributes to an inquiring detective.

Yes, you get the idea that this Laura must have been something truly wonderful. Now, at the risk of being unchivalrous, we venture to say that when the lady herself appears upon the scene via a flashback of events leading up to the tragedy, she is a disappointment. For Gene Tierney simply doesn't measure up to the word portrait of her character. Pretty, indeed, but hardly the type of girl we had expected to meet. For Miss Tierney plays at being a brilliant and sophisticated advertising executive with the wild-eyed innocence of a college junior.

Aside from that principal reservation, however, *Laura* is an intriguing melodrama. Suspects are plentiful enough, if not too pointed, and Vera Caspary gives the whole riddle an added measure of complexity by having the supposed corpse turn up very much alive at about the halfway mark. Her reappearance was quite timely, too, for it was becoming obvious that even the detective was coming under Laura's spell—a situation which doesn't present itself every day in crime novels, much less on the screen.

Clifton Webb, making his film debut in *Laura* as the acid-tongued columnist, Waldo Lydecker, is sophistry personified. His incisive performance is, however, closely matched by that of Dana Andrews as the detective. Mr. Andrews is fast proving himself to be a solidly persuasive performer, a sort of younger-edition Spencer Tracy. Other performances are contributed by Vincent Price, Judith Anderson and Dorothy Adams. Only Miss Tierney seems out of key. Perhaps if Laura Hunt had not had such a buildup, it would have been different. Anyway, the picture on the whole is close to being a top-drawer mystery.

—T.M.P., October 12, 1944

THE LAVENDER HILL MOB

Directed by Charles Crichton: written by T. E. B. Clarke: cinematographer. Douglas Slocombe: edited by Seth Holt: music by Georges Auric: art designer. William Kellner: produced by Michael Balcon: released by Universal International Pictures. Black and white. Running time: 82 minutes.

With: Alec Guinness (Holland). Stanley Holloway (Pendlebury). Sidney James (Lackery). Alfie Bass (Shorty). Marjorie Fielding (Mrs. Chalk) and Edie Martin (Miss Evesham).

That genius for civilized humor possessed by Britain's Ealing Studios, where they have tossed off such dexterous rib-ticklers as *Passport to Pimlico* and *Kind Hearts and Coronets,* has been wound up again and set humming in a jolly trifle called *The Lavender Hill Mob,* which served last night to open the new Fine Arts Theatre on Fifty-eighth Street, between Park and Lexington Avenues.

Jot it down as a picture that you will find it best to see at a moment when your mood is mellow and your sense of righteousness is slightly askew. For here again is a frolic that, like *Kind Hearts and Coronets,* indulges a serene and casual tolerance for undisguised lawlessness in man. And once again Alec Guinness, who played eight roles in *K. H. and C.,* delivers himself of one character that is as wickedly droll as Halloween.

In this disdain of pious precept, which was written by T. E. B. Clarke, the scandalously nimble-witted humorist who has been responsible for several of Ealing's recent gems, Mr. Guinness plays a mousy bank clerk who conceives and engineers a mammoth plot to steal and smuggle a hoard of gold bullion out of England to France. But no varlet, he—not by a long shot! Though his bank clerk may look a timid sort, peering out from behind his steel-rimmed glasses and from beneath his conventional bowler hat, he burns with a bold and gleeful fever to satisfy his fiendish greed. And though he trembles and gulps in the doing of desperate deeds, he is undismayed.

Indeed, he is much more aggressive than his fortuitous partners in crime who have an uncomfortable disposition to fold up when the going is rough. At least, this is true of his initial and most congenial associate, a genteel but windy high-binder, whom Stanley Holloway riotously plays. It is he who goes off in all directions when the two smugglers get to France and discover that their gold, cast in the image of little Eiffel Towers, is being sought by English schoolgirls as souvenirs. And it is he whom Mr. Guinness has to rally to a desperate pursuit that takes them back across the Channel to England and to the dire threat of Scotland Yard.

We cannot describe in too great detail the adventures that Mr. Clarke has contrived to make both amusement and excitement out of the whackiest crime story of the year. Neither can we suggest too broadly the impious fun that is poked at the practical ways of policemen, because the fun itself is far from broad. And certainly we aren't going to tell you how the whole jolly business shakes out in a wild auto chase through London that stirs the shades of the Keystone Kops.

Suffice it to say that Charles Crichton has directed the whole thing with a touch of polite and gentle mockery applied to wholehearted farce; that Mr. Guinness and Mr. Holloway are deliciously adroit in their roles; and that Sidney James and Alfie Bass support them with comparable slyness as a pair of henpecked crooks. Except for a couple of places, there is no hilarity in *The Lavender Hill Mob.* But its humors are so ingenious and persistent that it is one big chuckle from beginning to end.

—B.C., October 16, 1951

LAWRENCE OF ARABIA

Directed by David Lean: written by Robert Bolt. based on *The Seven Pillars of Wisdom* by T.E.

Lawrence: cinematographer, Freddie Young: edited by Anne V. Coates: music by Maurice Jarre: art designer, John Stoll: produced by Sam Spiegel: released by Columbia Pictures. Running time: 220 minutes.

With: Peter O'Toole (Lawrence), Alec Guinness (Prince Feisal), Anthony Quinn (Auda Abu Tayi), Jack Hawkins (General Allenby), Jose Ferrer (Turkish Bey), Anthony Quayle (Colonel Brighton), Claude Rains (Mr. Dryden), Arthur Kennedy (Jackson Bentley), Donald Wolfit (General Murray), Omar Sharif (Sherif Ali) and I. S. Johar (Gasim).

Like the desert itself, in which most of the action in *Lawrence of Arabia* takes place, this much-heralded film about the famous British soldier-adventurer, which opened last night at the Criterion, is vast, awe-inspiring, beautiful with ever-changing hues, exhausting and barren of humanity.

It is such a laboriously large conveyance of eye-filling outdoor spectacle—such as brilliant display of endless desert and camels and Arabs and sheiks and skirmishes with Turks and explosions and arguments with British military men—that the possibly human, moving T. E. Lawrence is lost in it. We know little more about this strange man when it is over than we did when it begins.

Sure, a lean, eager, diffident sort of fellow, played by blue-eyed Peter O'Toole, a handsome new British actor, goes methodically over the ground of Lawrence's major exploits as a guerrilla leader of Arab tribesmen during World War I. He earnestly enters the desert, organizes the tribes as a force against the Turks for the British, envisions Arab unity and then becomes oddly disillusioned as the politicians move in.

Why Lawrence had a disposition to join the Arab tribes, and what caused his streak of sadism, is barely hinted in the film. The inner mystery of the man remains lodged behind the splendid burnoosed figure and the wistful blue eyes of Mr. O'Toole.

The fault seems to lie first in the concept of telling the story of this self-tortured man against a background of action that has the characteristic of a mammoth Western film. The nature of Lawrence cannot be captured in grand Super-Panavision shots of sunrise on the desert or in scenes of him arguing with a shrewd old British general in a massive Moorish hall.

The fault is also in the lengthy but surprisingly lusterless dialogue of Robert Bolt's overwritten screenplay. Seldom has so little been said in so many words.

There are some great things in the picture—which runs, incidentally, for three hours and forty minutes, not counting intermission. There is some magnificent scenery, barbaric fights, a mirage in the desert that is superb (the one episode in the picture that conveys a sense of mystery). And there are some impressive presentations of historic characters.

Alex Guinness as the cagey Prince Feisal, Anthony Quinn as a fierce chief, Omar Sharif as a handsome Arab fighter, and Jack Hawkins as General Allenby stand out in a large cast that is ordered into sturdy masculine ranks by David Lean.

But, sadly, this bold Sam Spiegel picture lacks the personal magnetism, the haunting strain of mysticism and poetry that we've been thinking all these years would be dominant when a film about Lawrence the mystic and the poet was made. It reduces a legendary figure to conventional movie-hero size amidst magnificent and exotic scenery but a conventional lot of action film clichés.

It is, in the last analysis, just a huge, thundering camel opera that tends to run down rather badly as it rolls on into its third hour and gets involved with sullen disillusion and political deceit.

—*B.C., December 17, 1962*

A LEAGUE OF THEIR OWN

Directed by Penny Marshall: written by Lowell Ganz and Babaloo Mandel, based on a story by Kim Wilson and Kelly Candaele: director of photography, Miroslav Ondricek: edited by George Bowers: music by Hans Zimmer: production designer, Bill Groom: produced by Robert Greenhut and Elliot Abbot: released by Columbia Pictures. Running time: 124 minutes.

With: Tom Hanks (Jimmy Dugan), Geena Davis (Dottie Hinson), Lori Petty (Kit Keller), Madonna (Mae Mordabito), Rosie O'Donnell (Doris Murphy), Megan Cavanagh (Marla Hooch), Tracy Reiner (Betty Horn), Bitty Schram (Evelyn Gardner), Ann Cusack (Shirley Baker), Jon Lovitz (Ernie Capadino) and Bill Pullman (Bob Hinson).

In 1943 at the height of World War II, when women well over voting age could still be called girls, Philip K. Wrigley, of the Chicago Cubs, and other prominent baseball figures got together to form the non-profit All-American Girls Professional Baseball League. It was a stopgap idea. Its aim: to fill the vacuum if, as seemed possible, the major league clubs lost too many of their players to the armed services.

As things turned out, the major leagues never had to shut down, but the women's league survived until 1954.

Taking this footnote to baseball history, the director, Penny Marshall, and the screenwriters, Lowell Ganz and Babaloo Mandel, have made *A League of Their Own,* which must be as rare as a day in August when the sky is clear, the humidity low, and the temperature hovers in the mid-70's.

Though big of budget, *A League of Their Own* is one of the year's most cheerful, most relaxed, most easily enjoyable comedies. It's a serious film that's lighter than air, a very funny movie that manages to score a few points for feminism in passing.

The film's focus is the Rockford (Illinois) Peaches, one of the four clubs that made up the league in its problematical first season. As imagined by Ms. Marshall and her associates, the Peaches are a gallant and somewhat rum crew.

Their star: Dottie Hinson (Geena Davis), a cracker-jack catcher and a dependable hitter who is so beautiful that she winds up on the cover of *Life* magazine. On the mound is Dottie's younger sister Kit (Lori Petty). She has a terrific arm but tends to go to pieces when at bat. It's a sibling thing—she gets rattled by Dottie's advice and can't resist swinging at the high ones. Keeping things lively in center field is pint-size Mae Mordabito (Madonna), informally known as All the Way Mae, who finds pro baseball preferable to taxi dancing.

Coaching the Peaches, at first with great reluctance, is Jimmy Dugan (Tom Hanks), a former major league hero disabled by booze and unreliable knees. Jimmy is a tobacco-chewing slob with his own manner of expressing himself. He's a guy who doesn't hesitate to urinate in front of his players in their locker room. During their disastrous first game, he lounges in the dugout, snoozing in rye-induced oblivion.

Though *A League of Their Own* is an ensemble piece, meaning that each performer relates to and enriches the others, Mr. Hanks is first among the equals. His Jimmy

Dugan is a priceless, very graceful eccentric. With his work here, there can be no doubt that Mr. Hanks is now one of Hollywood's most accomplished and self-assured actors. Having put on weight for the role, he even looks jowly and over-the-hill.

While the women on the field are knocking themselves out to achieve fame and glory in a league that embraces just three Midwestern states, the film never strains to get a laugh or make a point. It adopts a summer pace as it follows Dottie, Kit, Mae and their teammates from what is, in effect, boot camp to the league's first world series, in which the Peaches face the Racine (Wisconsin) Belles.

The players' training includes not only practice on the field, but also intense sessions at a charm school where they are drilled in table manners, dress, makeup, posture and general deportment. In addition to public apathy, the league's backers have to overcome furious editorials warning against the threatened "masculinization" of the players.

Mr. Ganz and Mr. Mandel, whose earlier collaborations include the screenplays for *City Slickers* and *Splash,* have written a dozen rich roles, which Ms. Marshall has filled with a dream cast. Ms. Davis, who reportedly arrived on the set well after her colleagues had been practicing, comes across as a no-nonsense ball player, which reflects Dottie's no-nonsense approach to her career in the women's league. Dottie hasn't any intention of staying with the game when her husband returns from overseas.

She's a Peach with attitude. When a teenage boy comes on to her ("What say we get in the back of the car and you make a man of me?"), her reply is, "What say I smack you around?" She doesn't have the last word, though. His wistful answer: "Can't we do both?"

Not since *Desperately Seeking Susan* has Madonna had a role that fits her public personality as well as Mae, an opinionated, operational fighter who's not about to pay too much attention to training rules when it comes to men. It's not a big role, but it is choice.

The film's most unexpected performance is that of Ms. Petty. She has true comic radiance as an awestruck, loving younger sister who would often like to murder the paragon to whom she's so closely related. It's a performance that could shape her career.

Among the excellent supporting players are Rosie

O'Donnell, as Madonna's sidekick and a former dance hall bouncer; Megan Cavanagh, a heavy heavy-hitter from rural Colorado who's too shy even to smile so that anyone will notice; Garry Marshall (the director's brother and a director in his own right), who plays the fictional equivalent to Philip K. Wrigley (the character manufactures candy bars, not gum); and Bill Pullman, as Dottie's soldier-husband.

On-screen too short a time is Jon Lovitz, formerly of *Saturday Night Live,* who plays Ernie Capadino, the weary talent scout for the new league. As he delivers his finds to their training center, Ernie says: "Hey, cowgirls, see the grass? Don't eat it."

A League of Their Own has its share of obligatory lines. At a sentimental moment, Jimmy Dugan must say, "There's no crying in baseball." He must also define the game for the women: "Baseball is what gets inside you. It's what lights you up."

A League of Their Own is so good that it can accommodate such stuff and still leave one admiring its skill, humor, and all-American enthusiasm.

—V.C., July 1, 1992

LEAVING LAS VEGAS

Directed by Mike Figgis: written by Mr. Figgis. based on the novel by John O'Brien: director of photography. Declan Quinn: edited by John Smith: music by Mr. Figgis: production designer. Waldemar Kalinowski: produced produced by Lila Cazès and Anne Stewart: released by United Artists. Running time: 112 minutes.

With: Nicolas Cage (Ben). Elisabeth Shue (Sera). Julian Sands (Yuri) and Valeria Golino (Terri).

Ben Sanderson, played devastatingly by Nicolas Cage in *Leaving Las Vegas,* is something other than the usual movie drunk. Nothing about him offers golden opportunities to the Good Samaritan. Already in the terminal stages of alcoholism as the film begins, Ben seems to sense his fate and want to face it in his own way, with crazy bravado and a whiff of desperate romance. This small, searing film watches transfixingly as Ben plays out his final hand.

As directed by Mike Figgis, who makes a long overdue return to the sultry intensity of his *Internal Affairs*

and *Stormy Monday,* Leaving Las Vegas has the daring to suspend judgment about Ben's downward spiral. This film simply works as a character study, pitilessly well observed and intimately familiar with its terrain. Mr. Figgis based his screenplay on a novel by John O'Brien, who committed suicide two weeks after learning that his book would be made into a movie. Mr. O'Brien's father describes the novel as his son's suicide note, which does not seem a farfetched claim.

But *Leaving Las Vegas* is far less dolorous than might be expected. Passionate and furiously alive, it is brightened by the same unlikely bonhomie that has long kept Ben afloat. First seen gaily loading up a shopping cart at the liquor store, Ben has a courtly charm that is as beguiling as it is erratic. He can move from high spirits to furniture-smashing rage in a matter of seconds, but he never has trouble getting attention.

The film begins with an exceptional bender, following Ben through the last gasps of his career in Los Angeles. He turns obnoxious in a restaurant, name-dropping about Dickie Gere and annoying the movie executives he meets. He tries to pick up a woman in a bar. ("You've been drinking all day," remarks the woman, played by Valeria Golino. "But of course!" Ben replies.) He goes to a strip club, gets so drunk he can barely see the dancers, and takes home a prostitute who steals his wedding ring. He wakes up on his kitchen floor, having passed out in front of an open refrigerator.

For Ben, this appears to have been an ordinary day.

Leaving Los Angeles after being fired from his job, Ben moves on to the city of the title, a very different place from the coarse, brassy setting for *Showgirls.* This Las Vegas is a neon apparition, beautifully evoked by otherworldly contrasts and lurid nocturnal light. (The cinematography is by Declan Quinn, whose work is as subtly distinctive as it was in *Vanya on 42d Street.*) And here he meets Sera, whose very name (as in "que será") suggests some kind of cosmic shrug. Sera (Elisabeth Shue), a Las Vegas prostitute, has somehow been waiting her whole life for a man like this.

As he did in his fine, fluid earlier films (before being sidetracked by the unaccountably listless *Mr. Jones* and *The Browning Version*), Mr. Figgis gives his narrative a musical dimension. A sometime musician who composed this film's jazzy score, Mr. Figgis uses a haunting soundtrack (with several vocal numbers performed by Sting) to turn this into a sustained, moody reverie. Indeed, the film's musical effectiveness minimizes some of its dramatic contrivance, especially where Sera is concerned. Ms. Shue gives a daring and affecting performance, but she's essentially playing one more whore with a heart of gold.

The awkward device of letting Sera talk about herself on a therapist's couch doesn't give her much added depth, though her troubles with a sleazy Latvian pimp (Julian Sands, with a flamboyant accent) add some color. And the screenplay's attempt to create an eleventh-hour crisis for Sera seems false, too. For all Ms. Shue's warmth, in the kind of gutsy, unflinching role that often goes to Jennifer Jason Leigh, *Leaving Las Vegas* never rings entirely true as a bleak love story. Ben clings to Sera as a last straw, but he's still a man alone.

Mr. Cage digs deep to find his character's inner demons while also capturing the riotous energy of his outward charm. The film would seem vastly more sordid without his irrepressible good humor.

At the same time, without overworking the pathos of Ben's situation, *Leaving Las Vegas* fully conveys the health risks of gulping vodka in the shower, crashing onto a glass coffee table or otherwise lurching through life with Ben's particular abandon. A man who spends $500 for a prostitute's hour-long visit to his $29 hotel room (with "complimentary bar of soap" and lucky aces over the headboard) is a man beyond caring about the future.

—J.M., October 27, 1995

THE LEOPARD

Directed by Luchino Visconti; written (in Italian, with English subtitles) by Mr. Visconti, Suso Cecchi D'Amico, Pasquale Festa Campanile, Enrico Medioli and Massimo Franciosa, based on the novel *Il Gattopardo* by Giuseppe Tomasi di Lampedusa; cinematographer, Giuseppe Rotunno; edited by Mario Serandrei; music by Nino Rota; art designer, Mario Garbuglia; produced by Goffredo Lombardo; released by Twentieth Century Fox. Running time: 165 minutes.

With: Burt Lancaster (Prince Don Fabrizio Salina, The Leopard), Alain Delon (Tancredi), Claudia Cardinale (Angelica Sedara), Rina Morelli (Princess Maria Stella), Paolo Stoppa (Don Calogero Sedara) and Lucilla Morlacchi (Concetta).

The film that Luchino Visconti and his star, Burt Lancaster, have made from Giuseppe di Lampedusa's fine novel *The Leopard* is a stunning visualization of a mood of melancholy and nostalgia at the passing of an age.

Sentiment and sadness whisper through it like the soft Mediterranean breeze that flutters the curtains in the windows of the palace in the stark Sicilian hills, on the outskirts of Palermo, as the unhurried story begins. They waft through the slow and stately tableaux of incidents in the stilted, baroque life of a noble Sicilian family in the mid-nineteenth century.

They even rustle in the laughter of young people who are the inheritors of the change that the Risorgimento of Garibaldi is allegedly bringing to the land. And they hang like a softly soaking vapor over the great, gaudy end-of-an-era ball that takes up the last forty minutes of this two-hour-and-forty-minute film.

For the one thing that Mr. Visconti has been able to do magnificently—and it's the only thing I imagine he figured he could possibly do with the shimmering, atmospheric material of Mr. di Lampedusa's book—is translate in terms of brilliant pictures, almost like paintings, the autumnal mood of change and decay that the onrush of social revolution brought to one family and to the spirits of one strong man.

Faithful to the contours of the novel, he hasn't attempted to intrude into this handsome color picture, which opened at the Plaza last night, any more sense of the melodrama of Garibaldi's conquest of Sicily than a few lurid shots of fiery Redshirts fighting Bourbons in the narrow Palermo streets. Neither have he and his scenarists told us any more about the nature of the Risorgimento than simply that it freed and elevated a middle class.

All that he gives us in this picture in the way of plot and dramatic clash are loose suggestions of the personal accommodations to the pressures of the revolution that the prince and his family have in mild confrontations of the prince with members of the middle class. And since the supreme accommodation is to accept the marriage of a nephew with a girl of the bourgeoisie who is both beautiful and wealthy, the hardship does not appear great.

But the quality of the presentation is not in a running display of plotted, emotional crises. It is in a slow, rhythmic, tempered account of the yielding of the prince to changes that he realizes are inevitable, but perhaps not as gracious as he would have them, and that is why he is sad.

It is in the superb illustration of a special way of life, elaborate and luxurious, but confined by rigid restraints, surrounded by lush decoration but internally cramped and dour. And it is in the interesting suggestions of the nature of the prince, the soi-disant Leopard of the title, played by Mr. Lancaster.

Got up in sideburns and tailcoats, plug hats and canes, the American star gives a physically forceful presentation of the massive, imperious man on whom the mood of melancholy descends most heavily at the ball. He is mighty in moments of anger, harsh in his sarcastic bursts, and amazingly soft and sympathetic when the call is for tenderness.

But unfortunately Mr. Lancaster does have that blunt American voice that lacks the least suggestion of being Sicilian in the English-dialogue version shown here. And either the role lacks the humor—the gentle irony—of di Lampedusa's prince or Mr. Lancaster does not get it, which is a most regrettable miss.

Alain Delon is also handsome and physically correct as the prince's high-spirited nephew, but there isn't enough body in the role, not enough self-assertion to make it truly meaningful. And the American voice that speaks for him is not appropriate.

As for Claudia Cardinale in the role of the bourgeoise girl this young man chooses to marry, she is strangely, almost grotesquely made up to look and act like a gypsy in the earlier scenes, and in the later she is rendered so stylish and compelled to act so subdued that a curiously uneven character and social significance come from her.

Paolo Stoppa as her father, the crude, pushy mayor of a Sicilian town, is unmistakably vulgar, however, and Romolo Valli as the prince's personal priest and Serge Reggianni as a small-town traditionalist have the proper air of minor snobs. Lucilla Morlacchi as the prince's daughter, Rina Morelli as his wife, and Mario Girotti as an aristocratic suitor blend perfectly with the atmosphere.

For the most part, Nino Rota's music provides a rich melodic surrounding for the pictorial magnificence, and a heretofore unknown Verdi waltz that is played at the ball at the finish appropriately supplements this remarkably vivid, panoramic and eventually morbid show.

I just wonder how much Americans will know or care about what's going on, how much we will yield to a nostalgia very similar to that in *Gone With the Wind*.
—B.C., August 13, 1963

THE LETTER

Directed by William Wyler; written by Howard Koch, based on the play by W. Somerset Maugham; cinematography by Tony Gaudio; edited by George Amy and Warren Low; art director, Carl Jules Weyl; music by Max Steiner; released by Warner Brothers. Black and white. Running time: 95 minutes.

With: Bette Davis (Leslie Crosbie), Herbert Marshall (Robert Crosbie), James Stephenson (Howard Joyce), Frieda Inescort (Dorothy Joyce), Gale Sondergaard (Mrs. Hammond), Bruce Lester (John Withers), Elizabeth Inglis (Adele Ainsworth), Cecil Kellaway (Prescott), Doris Lloyd (Mrs. Cooper), Willie Fung (Chung Hi) and Tetsu Komai (Head Boy).

Director William Wyler was remarking recently that the final responsibility for a picture's quality rests solely and completely upon the shoulders of the man who directs it. His, said he, is the liability if an actor's performance is at fault; he is the one to censure—or to thank—for the finished effect, since it is the director, after all, who makes the picture and okays it.

Mr. Wyler spoke at a most propitious moment. For seldom has this theory been more clearly and more flatteringly supported than it is by his own screen version of Somerset Maugham's play, *The Letter,* which was delivered yesterday at the Strand. Indubitably Mr. Wyler must be grateful to Bette Davis, James Stephenson, Herbert Marshall and an excellent cast for doing as he told them; obviously Mr. Maugham supplied him with a potent play, out of which Howard Koch fashioned a compact script. But the ultimate credit for as taut and insinuating a melodrama as has come along this year—a film which extenuates tension like a grim inquisitor's rack—must be given to Mr. Wyler. His hand is patent throughout.

For the story told in *The Letter* is not an especially bold or novel one. Theatregoers who saw Katharine Cornell perform it a dozen years ago on the stage or Jeanne Eagels play it in 1929 on the screen will agree. It is the morbid tale of the wife of an English rubber planter in the Malay States who kills a man, presumably in defense of what is known as her honor. As the tedious inquest proceeds, however, it becomes known to her lawyer that a letter is in existence—a letter written by the woman to the dead man on the day of the deed—which fatally incriminates her. And thus the desperate and degrading task of the woman and her lawyer is to get this letter away from the native girl who owns it, the widow of the murdered man, and thereby to prevent complications. The manner in which this is done and what happens after fill out the substance of the story.

It is an evil tale, plotted with an eye to its torturing effects. And Mr. Wyler has directed the film along those lines. With infinite care, he has created the dark, humid atmosphere of the rubber country. At a slow, inexorable pace, he has accumulated the details. His camera generally speaks more eloquently than anyone in the picture—when, for instance, it finds a dead body lying in a rubber-curing shed or picks up the lacquered face of the native woman or focuses significantly upon the tinkling decorations in a Chinese room. The tensile strength of Mr. Wyler's suspense is incredible.

And his actors, too, have been directed for the distillation of somber moods. Miss Davis is a strangely cool and calculating killer who conducts herself with reserve and yet implies a deep confusion of emotions. James Stephenson is superb as the honest lawyer who jeopardizes his reputation to save a friend—a shrewd, dignified, reflective citizen who assumes a sordid business with distaste. He is the strongest character in the film, the one person who really matters. And Sen Yung plays a smart Oriental clerk with illuminating candor, Herbert Marshall is properly negative as the unsuspecting husband and Gale Sondergaard cryptically conveys through appearance and attitudes only the enigmatic menace of the native woman.

Only the end of *The Letter* is weak—and that is because of the postscript which the Hays office has compelled. The play ended with the freed wife return-ing to her poor husband, who knows that she doesn't love him, that she has killed the man she loves. But they must go on living together. That was the trenchant irony of the whole story, the sardonic victory of the Orient over the Occident. The Hays office demand for "compensating moral values" makes Miss Davis pay for her criminal deed with her own violent death. It is a feeble conclusion.

But, never mind—the picture as a whole is insured against that that. It is fine melodrama, in short. Postman Wyler has rung the bell—several times.

—B.C., November 23, 1940

A LETTER TO THREE WIVES

Directed by Joseph L. Mankiewicz; written by Mr. Mankiewicz and Vera Caspary, based on the novel by John Klempner; cinematographer, Arthur Miller; edited by J. Watson Webb Jr.; music by Alfred Newman; art designers, Lyle Wheeler and J. Russell Spencer; produced by Sol C. Siegel; released by Twentieth Century Fox. Black and white. Running time: 103 minutes.

With: Jeanne Crain (Deborah Bishop), Linda Darnell (Lora May Hollingsway), Ann Sothern (Rita Phipps), Kirk Douglas (George Phipps), Paul Douglas (Porter Hollingsway), Barbara Lawrence (Babe), Jeffrey Lynn (Brad Bishop), Connie Gilchrist (Mrs. Finney) and Thelma Ritter (Sadie).

Within the absorbing contents of *A Letter to Three Wives*, Joseph L. Mankiewicz is peddling some pretty good wisdom and advice. The wisdom, tucked off in corners of this tripaneled comedy-romance, is that love is a volatile something that can quickly evaporate unless it is constantly guarded with understanding and care. And the advice, angled mainly to the ladies, is never to speak harsh words (or such) to their true-loving husbands who may leave them and never return.

Indeed, it is just such a prospect—the prospect of hubby taking off—that suddenly confronts the three mesdames of the title in the Music Hall's new film. Just as they're starting out one morning to take some kids on a riverboat picnic, these three country-club wives in a small town get a letter from a local friend.

The friend very graciously informs them that she is eloping with the husband of one. Provokingly, however, she fails to tell them the husband of which.

And so, while these three anxious ladies are shanghaied all day with the kids, they have plenty of time to wonder—and reflect on their married lives. The one who snagged her helpmate while he was a sailor and she a Wave has little more to disturb her than the thought that she lacks sufficient "class." But the one who is a radio writer and has been letting her mind get rather blunt has the disquieting realization that she has fallen a bit beneath her spouse. And the third one—the hard-boiled gold digger who deliberately roped her hard-boiled man—has the frightening knowledge that, while she loves him, they have each let the other down.

Thus, in the reflections of these ladies, Mr. Mankiewicz cleverly evolves an interesting cross-sectioned picture of the small-town younger married set. And as writer as well as director, he has capably brought forth a film that has humor, skepticism, satire and gratifying romance.

The fact that so many paces are put on display in this film forewarns that a certain unevenness is likely to occur. And it must be admitted frankly that the whole thing is not in perfect time. The earlier phases are draggy and just a bit obvious. And because this is so, the episodes involving Jeanne Crain as the ex-Wave and Ann Sothern as the radio writer do less to enhance those stars.

But the final romantic remembrance—that of the hard-boiled wife—is a taut and explosive piece of satire, as funny and as poignant as it is shrewd. And it is played with coruscating vigor by Linda Darnell in the gold digger role and by Paul Douglas as the rough-cut big shot whom she tangles with using frank and ancient wiles. Indeed, this one rough-and-tumble between Mr. Douglas and Miss Darnell is deliciously rugged entertainment, the real salvation of the film.

For in it are also included Connie Gilchrist as Miss Darnell's old ma and Thelma Ritter as a beer-guzzling neighbor with remarkable and funny things to say. And the blatherskite performances of these two, punctuated with rowdy backhand swipes, give a wonderful shanty-town setting to a vulgar yet pathetic romance.

It wouldn't be fair to tell you whose husband it is that runs away. But the outcome is thoroughly satisfactory—and so is the film—by us.

—*B.C., January 21, 1949*

LES LIAISONS DANGEREUSES

Directed by Roger Vadim; written (in French, with English subtitles) by Mr. Vadim, Roger Vailland and Claude Brulé, based on the novel by Choderlos de Laclos; director of photography, Marcel Grignon; edited by Victoria Mercanton; music by Theolonious Monk and Jack Murray; released by Astor Pictures. Black and white. Running time: 106 minutes.

With: Gérard Philipe (Valmont), Jeanne Moreau (Juliette), Jeanne Valérie (Cecile), Annette Vadim (Marianne), Simone Renant (Volange) and Jean-Louis Trintignant (Danceny).

Note that the title and credits at the beginning of *Les Liaisons Dangereuses* are superimposed upon a chessboard on which the chessmen are obviously in play. Here is the tip-off to the nature of this supposedly naughty French film that followed hot on the heels of *La Dolce Vita* into Henry Miller's Theatre last night.

As much as the international chitchat about this updated eighteenth-century tale of bedroom shenanigans among the haute monde had led us to be prepared for something racy and appropriately informal in the line of Gallic amour, it turns out to be a rather solemn, ritualistic and dispassionate display of strictly tactical maneuvers in a bored game of musical beds.

Nor does the deceptive darkening of the prints in a couple of shots of notably underdressed young women account for the flatness of the film. We saw it first with these shots lighted and can assure you their candor added naught. A couple of store-window dummies without drapery might get the same effect.

For the dreary fact is that Roger Vadim, who directed and helped to write the script, has presented a volatile subject with a tired and aimless attitude. Where the novel of Choderlos de Laclos, upon which the script is based, offers a startling insight into the manners of a social stratum in a stilted age, this film offers no more than a wan look at a jaded married couple playing games in a modern void.

The premise is that this couple, figures in the diplomatic world, have a casual domestic arrangement. Each may have as many love affairs as he or she wishes (or can handle), so long as neither falls in love. This has led them to a series of adventures with various lovers and mistresses that is made about as graphic and absorbing at the outset as the conventional swapping of pieces at the beginning of a game of chess.

Then, in the middle section, the husband is captivated by a virtuous young married woman who will not bend to his bland seductive moves. He pursues her amid the gay surroundings of a sparkling Swiss ski resort, while deftly seducing another youngster as a roundabout favor to his wife (it seems that this youngster has snagged for marriage the wife's latest gentleman friend). Meanwhile, the wife is seducing this youngster's secret loverboy.

Sounds fast, you may think—maybe frisky, in the manner of the memorable *La Ronde,* which also happened to feature the talents of the late Gérard Philipe. But it isn't. Except in a few places where M. Vadim lets M. Philipe make his amorous maneuvers with a slight trace of elegant poker-faced farce, the going is slow and somber, serious and stark, as though lovemaking under these conditions were entirely academic and dull.

The mood is also burdened by the heaviness of the wife, who is made a quite nasty, noxious creature by bulgy-eyed Jeanne Moreau. Together, these two performers, acting with an air of decadence, seem at times to be a couple of odd psychotics, betraying further an aimless attitude. And the morbid mood is completed when the husband does fall in love with the virtuous young woman, finally wins her, and brings on a melodramatic doom.

The mood is neither brightened nor bettered by Annette Vadim in the role of the virtuous young woman. She's a sad one, without beauty, chic or charm—just another little heavy-lipped French girl with a mop of messy hair. And Jeanne Valérie as the youngster who lets herself be seduced with a minimum of resistance or resentment has the quality of a naughty, silly child.

The English subtitles lack distinction, as does the French dialogue.

M. Vadim brings off a stalemate in this dull exhibition of boudoir chess.

—*B.C., December 19, 1961*

THE LIFE AND DEATH OF COLONEL BLIMP

Produced, written and directed by Michael Powell and Emeric Pressburger; cinematographers, Jack Cardiff and Georges Périnal; edited by John Seabourne; music by Allan Gray; released by Archers Productions. Running time: 163 minutes.

With: Roger Livesey (Clive Candy), Deborah Kerr (Edith Hunter/Barbara Wynne/Johnny Cannon), Anton Walbrook (Theo Kretschmar-Schuldorff), Jan van Loewen (Indignant Citizen), David Hutcheson (Hoppy), Valentine Dyall (Von Schonborn) and Carl Jaffe (Von Reumann).

Colonel Blimp, that grandiose representative of pomposity and mental stagnation so eloquently characterized in David Low's drawings, has been interred with loving care and a touch of delightful impudence in the British Technicolor picture, *The Life and Death of Colonel Blimp,* which opened last night at the Gotham. Michael Powell and Emeric Pressburger, the authors, directors and producers, have fashioned an impressive, if not always consistent, entertainment in depicting the development of a typical Blimp-type British officer from his shining hour as a Boer War hero, complete with Victoria Cross, to his utter bewilderment by modern military methods.

Roger Livesey was an ideal choice for the leading role, Clive Candy. His transformation from a spirited young officer to a bluff "damn it all man" type of lovable old warhorse is a gem of florid makeup and characterization. It may be that Mr. Livesey's uncompromising British inflection will prove baffling, perhaps even annoying, in the film's early stages, but it grows upon one and becomes just right as Clive Candy progresses in years, girth and befuddlement.

The brash young man, who fought a duel with a Prussian officer in 1902, became friends with his opponent, and sportingly let him walk off with a beautiful English governess in Berlin, was growing old in the ways of the world even in the warfare of 1914–18. But it is not until 1939 rolls around that General Candy has unknowingly become a mental ancient. Even in retirement as head of the home guard he is out of step, a well-intentioned blunderer whose ultimate embarrassment comes when he is unceremoniously captured in a Turkish bath with his staff during practice maneuvers. "But war doesn't start till midnight," he thunders in pathetic confusion at his blitz-wizened captors.

Covering a span of more than two-score years is a

mighty undertaking, even in a picture that runs two and a half hours, and it is not surprising that *Colonel Blimp* bogs down for considerable stretches. But by scrupulous attention to detail the Messrs. Powell and Pressburger have achieved several distinguished individual scenes that will long remain in fond memory. One in particular is the dueling sequence, which is done with elaborate protocol and ceremony. Yet even this delightful episode could have used some careful pruning.

Anton Walbrook gives a completely winning performance as the Prussian officer. And while he finally emerges as a disciple of the "good German," the authors are careful to point out that his reformation comes only after he has been thoroughly trampled upon by his own country and children. Through the picture Deborah Kerr, a lovely and talented actress, plays three different ladies in the general's life with remarkable dexterity. Several worthy performances are contributed by A. E. Matthews, James McKechnie and John Laurie among others. *Colonel Blimp* is as unmistakably a British product as Yorkshire pudding and, like the latter, it has a delectable savor all its own.

—*T.M.P., March 30, 1945*

LIFE IS SWEET

Written and directed by Mike Leigh; director of photography, Dick Pope; edited by Jon Gregory; music by Rachel Portman; production designer, Alison Chitty; produced by Simon Channing-Williams; released by October Films. Running time: 102 minutes.

With: Alison Steadman (Wendy), Jim Broadbent (Andy), Claire Skinner (Natalie), Jane Horrocks (Nicola), Stephen Rea (Patsy), Timothy Spall (Aubrey) and David Thewlis (Nicola's Lover).

*L*ife *Is Sweet,* opening today at the Angelika Film Center, is a very special new English comedy by Mike Leigh, the English director whose *High Hopes,* one of the hits of the 1988 New York Film Festival, revealed him to be a filmmaker not quite like any other.

Among other things, Mr. Leigh makes movies in which the actors participate in the creative process,

discovering and refining their characters in the course of long rehearsal periods. Such collaboration would have sent Hitchcock into permanent retirement.

It obviously works for Mr. Leigh, whose gently cockeyed movies are so rich with character that they seem beyond ordinary invention. His films prompt the kind of excitement that comes only when experiencing something new or, at least, something new in the context of other movies.

Like *High Hopes,* an overtly political film about life in Britain under the Thatcher government, *Life Is Sweet* is as much about a particular time and place as it is about the characters. Though virtually nothing is said about politics, *Life Is Sweet,* whether consciously or not, evokes the end of the Thatcher era, before a new era has been defined, when times are neither good nor bad and life is shaped by routine.

Filmed entirely in the North London suburb of Enfield, *Life Is Sweet* is a contemplative comedy about people who aren't. Chiefly it's about the members of one lower-middle-class family: Wendy (Alison Steadman), a pretty woman of early middle age who laughs too much; her husband, Andy (Jim Broadbent), a good-natured fellow and professional cook; and their redheaded twin daughters, Natalie (Claire Skinner), who has found her calling as a plumber, and Nicola (Jane Horrocks), who says she wants to "write" (but doesn't) and stays home all day.

The family lives in comparative peace in a row house that Andy has never finished off properly. The front stoop still lacks the trellis he promised to build. Yet for al fresco dining, the backyard is furnished with an umbrella table and the sort of molded plastic chairs that can be stacked easily.

Wendy is determinedly cheerful as she goes about her various self-assigned tasks. She works in a shop that sells children's clothes (many of them pretty ghastly) and is an enthusiastic aerobics instructor to a class of tubby little girls. She is a good wife and mother, but also an edgy one.

Money, though not a pressing problem, is ever a concern. There is also the difficulty with Nicola, who lives in a perpetual grouch. When Wendy suggests that she ought to eat something since it's lunchtime, Nicola's response is a lofty "What's lunchtime? A convention."

In the course of the several days of *Life Is Sweet,* the sharp-tongued Nicola is revealed to be a secret bulimic. Her passion for chocolate also plays a part in her love life, though her boyfriend (David Thewlis) would prefer to have sex in a more conventional way.

Andy, who wants to be his own boss, takes the family savings and buys a used snack trailer. He plans to become one of those fellows who go from neighborhood to neighborhood, ringing a bell and selling hot coffee and sandwiches. "Gilt-edged," says the man who sells the trailer. "You can't go wrong." The family members are appalled.

Nothing much goes right for the family, though nothing goes terribly wrong, except for their friend Aubrey (Timothy Spall). He is a cook who opens his own French restaurant, the Regret Rien. Its decor features a stuffed cat's head on the wall, a birdcage hanging from the ceiling to recall the spirit of Edith Piaf (nicknamed "the sparrow"), and candles stuck into empty wine bottles "for that bistro effect."

Several choice items on Aubrey's menu: prune quiche, boiled bacon consommé and tongue in a rhubarb hollandaise sauce.

Life Is Sweet, a title that should not be taken as irony, demands that the audience accept its meandering manner without expectations of the big dramatic event or the boffo laugh. It is very funny, but without splitting the sides.

The film moves easily from the broad jokes about Aubrey's restaurant to Nicola's scenes of very real desperation. At the center of it all is the substantial but not simply characterized relationship between Wendy and Andy. The movie regards them fairly, at their own level, without trying to be nice to them.

Life Is Sweet is also an actor's field day. Miss Steadman, Mr. Broadbent, Miss Horrocks, Mr. Thewlis and the others are a joy to watch, both for the vigor of their performances and for the immense satisfaction they seem to have had in getting those characters together. *Life Is Sweet* is a movie that breathes.

—V.C., October 25, 1991

THE LIFE OF EMILE ZOLA

Directed by William Dieterle; written by Norman Reilly Raine, Heinz Herald and Geza Herczeg, based on the story by Mr. Herald and Mr. Herczeg; cinematographer, Tony Gaudio; edited by Warren Low; music by Max Steiner; art designer, Anton Grot; produced by Henry Blanke; released by Warner Brothers. Black and white. Running time: 123 minutes.

With: Paul Muni (Emile Zola), Gale Sondergaard (Lucie Dreyfus), Joseph Schildkraut (Captain Alfred Dreyfus), Gloria Holden (Alexandrine Zola), Donald Crisp (Maitre Labori), Erin O'Brien-Moore (Nana) and John Litel (Charpentier).

The Warners, who have achieved the reputation of being Hollywood's foremost triflers with history, paid their debt to truth last night with the presentation of *The Life of Emile Zola* at the Hollywood Theatre. Rich, dignified, honest and strong, it is at once the finest historical film ever made and the greatest screen biography, greater even than *The Story of Louis Pasteur* with which the Warners squared their conscience last year.

Like *Pasteur,* the picture has captured the spirit of a man and his times; unlike *Pasteur*—and this is the factor that gives it preeminence—it has followed not merely the spirit but, to a rare degree, the very letter of his life and of the historically significant lives about him. And, still more miraculously, it has achieved this brilliant end without self-consciousness, without strutting glorification, without throwing history out of focus to build up the importance of its central figure.

Literature knows Zola as the author of *Nana* and a score of other novels that crusaded, during a sociologically dark age in France, in behalf of the oppressed and the unenlightened. History knows him more dramatically as the man who cried out, so all the world could hear, against the famous perversion of justice that was the Dreyfus case. *The Life of Emile Zola*, is the story of both those men—the crusading novelist, the Dreyfus defender—and it is a story told with dramatic strength, with brilliant language and with superb performances.

Paul Muni's portrayal of Zola is, without doubt, the best thing he has done. Fiery, bitter, compassionate as the young novelist; settled, complacent, content to rest from the wars in his later years; then forced into the struggle again, although he resisted it, when the Dreyfus cause whispered to his conscience—Mr. Muni has given us a human and well-rounded portrait. It would have been simple to have stuffed the character with glory, to have presented Zola as charging happily into a battle in which he had everything to lose and nothing, personally, to gain. The true story was the more dramatic one and the Warners—by which I mean their writers—had the wisdom to follow it. Zola, when he thundered the "I Accuse" message that eventually exposed the army conspiracy against Dreyfus, was no longer an individual; he truly had become, as Anatole France later said of him, "a moment of the conscience of Man."

That was the essence of Zola—that he was not a man, but an instrument of freedom, truth and social justice. There is something infinitely touching in the contrast of the physical Zola and the spiritual Zola. One a human, frail, pathetic, at times a quaint figure; but behind him always, in his writings and utterances, the steadfast tread of truth on the march and our grateful knowledge, with him, that "nothing will stop her." And that has been written into the film, just as it has been written into history, and when a picture has that spiritual surge it has realized the best the cinema can accomplish.

Against the impressive bulk of its virtues, the few defects are negligible. True, the film could have been trimmed. True, the Mme. Dreyfus role, played by Gale Sondergaard, is an illustration of a part built up from nothing and even then scarcely able to get off the ground. True, there are sequences—like the Anatole France speech at Zola's bier and Zola's reading of his "I Accuse" editorial—which are pictorially static and offer nothing (although I think it is a great deal) but poetic language beautifully read. True, the picture skirts the real issues behind the Dreyfus case (the word "Jew" is never uttered) and skips recklessly over the political, racial background of the plot.

But these are little against a great and valuable and stirring film document. There is not space here for a full inventory of its assets, but mention must be made of the eloquent script turned out by Norman Reilly Raine, Heinz Herald and Geza Herczeg; of William Dieterle's majestic direction; and of such principal members of the cast as Mr. Muni, Joseph Schildkraut as Dreyfus, Donald Crisp as Maitre Labori, Vladimir Sokoloff as Cezanne, Erin O'Brien-Moore as Nana, Henry O'Neill as Colonel Picquart and Louis Calhern as Major Dort. The others are scarcely less worthy and another of 1937's "best ten" has arrived.

—*F.S.N., August 12, 1937*

LIFE WITH FATHER

Directed by Michael Curtiz: written by Donald Ogden Stewart. based on the play by Howard Lindsay and Russel Crouse and the book by Clarence Day Jr.: cinematographers. J. Peverell Marley and William V. Skall: edited by George Amy: music by Max Steiner: art designer. Robert Haas: produced by Robert Buckner: released by Warner Brothers. Running time: 118 minutes.

With: William Powell (Father). Irene Dunne (Vinnie). Elizabeth Taylor (Mary). Edmund Gwenn (Reverend Dr. Lloyd). ZaSu Pitts (Cora). Jimmy Lydon (Clarence). Emma Dunn (Margaret). Martin Milner (John). Johnny Calkins (Whitney). Derek Scott (Harlan) and Moroni Olsen (Dr. Humphries).

A round-robin of praise is immediately in order for all those, and they were many indeed, who assisted in filming *Life with Father*. All that the fabulous play had to offer in the way of charm, comedy, humor and gentle pathos is beautifully realized in the handsomely Technicolored picture, which opened yesterday at the Warner (formerly the Hollywood) Theatre. William Powell is every inch Father, from his carrot-patch dome to the tip of his button-up shoes. Even his voice, always so distinctive, has taken on a new quality, so completely has Mr. Powell managed to submerge his own personality. His Father is not merely a performance; it is character delineation of a high order and he so utterly dominates the picture that even when he is not on hand his presence is still felt.

The Warner Brothers have kept faith with both the letter and the spirit of the play fashioned by Howard Lindsay and Russel Crouse from the late Clarence Day's memoirs of his father. Most of the action still takes place in the living room of the Day residence, 420 Madison Avenue. The atmosphere of the period, 1883, is recaptured with all the rich flavor of a Currier & Ives print, even though Father's "damns" have been excised. But his thunderous "oh, gads!" and explosive "what in tarnations" are carefully preserved in the screenplay written by Donald Ogden Stewart. However, while the camera provides a scope and fluidity of action that necessarily was missing on the stage, the benefits thus derived are more of a pictorial than a dramatic nature, for the pace of the story always accelerates when the camera is simply reproducing scenes as done on the stage.

It sounds a bit absurd to be saying after all these years—eight to be exact—that *Life with Father* is the perfect family entertainment and that in it most everyone will notice a resemblance to something in his own family life. But that's the way it is, and perhaps there are some latecomers who would like to know just a little about this domestic classic. Actually, *Life with Father* is not so much a story as it is a reflection of little incidents that agitate a short-tempered, despotic parent. They are the kind of crises peculiar to family life, where a prudent husband and father of four sons attempts to run his home on a businesslike basis. While Father goes into a towering rage at the slightest provocation, stamping his feet at the breakfast table when the coffee isn't right, he is at heart a very kind, tolerant and sympathetic old man (and we use that term most affectionately).

For all his bluff and independence, Father would be lost without his patient, understanding wife, and one feels genuinely sorry for him in his hour of anxiety when mother lies ill upstairs and the doctors give him small comfort. It is almost unpardonable not to have mentioned Irene Dunne before this because she interprets Vinnie Day with charm, wit, and an exactness that perfectly complement Mr. Powell's Father. The way she finally cajoles her rebellious husband into making the journey up to Audubon Park to submit to the baptismal rites that his parents had somehow overlooked is handled by Miss Dunne with great charm and feminine wile.

The four Day boys—all redheads, naturally—are pleasingly played by Jimmy Lydon, the eldest, who has a crush on the visiting Mary Skinner; Martin Milner as John, the inventor; Johnny Calkins as Whitney, who would rather play baseball than study his catechism; and Derek Scott as little Harlan, who worries about meeting his unbaptized father in heaven. Elizabeth Taylor is very appealing as Mary Skinner, and other fine performances are contributed by Edmund Gwenn as the Reverend Dr. Lloyd, ZaSu Pitts as Cousin Cora and a string of maids too numerous to mention here.

Life with Father has been expertly staged by the resourceful Michael Curtiz, who has made certain that none of the essential comedy is overdrawn. The Warner Brothers can be proud of a job well done and the rest of us thankful that a classical slice of Americana has been preserved intact.

—*T.M.P., August 16, 1947*

LIKE WATER FOR CHOCOLATE

Produced and directed by Alfonso Arau; written (in Spanish, with English subtitles) by Laura Esquivel, based on her novel; cinematographers, Emmanuel Lubezki and Steven Bernstein; edited by Carlos Bolado and Francisco Chiu; music by Leo Brower; art designers, Marco Antonio Arteaga, Mauricio DeAguinaco and Denise Pizzini; released by Miramax Films. Running time: 113 minutes.

With: Lumi Cavazos (Tita), Marco Leonardi (Pedro), Regina Torné (Mama Elena), Mario Iván Martínez (John Brown), Ada Carrasco (Nacha), Yareli Arizmendi (Rosaura), Claudette Maillé (Gertrudis) and Pilar Aranda (Chencha).

Food and passion create a sublime alchemy in *Like Water for Chocolate,* a Mexican film whose characters experience life so intensely that they sometimes literally smolder. The kitchen becomes a source of such witchcraft that a fervently prepared meal can fill diners with lust or grief or nausea, depending upon the cook's prevailing mood.

This film, a lively family saga that is centered on forbidden love and spans several generations, relies so enchantingly upon fate, magic and a taste for the supernatural that it suggests Gabriel García Márquez in a cookbook-writing mode. (The best-selling Mexican novel by Laura Esquivel, who also wrote the screenplay, interweaves the fanciful story of *Like Water for Chocolate* with actual recipes.) Whether you approach this swift, eventful tale on the culinary or the cinematic level, prepare for a treat.

Like Water for Chocolate, which opens today, is the story of Tita (Lumi Cavazos), whose way of connecting cuisine with strong emotion truly begins at birth. Tita is born on a kitchen table to a mother who weeps so profusely, a narrator maintains, that the residue of

557

her tears yields an enormous bag of salt. This formidable mother, known as Mama Elena (Regina Torné), has endured her share of hardships and is determined to make her youngest child do the same. She decrees that Tita, the last of three daughters, must always serve her and therefore can never marry.

Years later, as a shy and watchful young woman, Tita attracts the attention of Pedro (Marco Leonardi). This is one of many romantic events that the film casts in amusingly food-related terms, as the narrator explains that when Tita felt Pedro's gaze on her shoulders, "she understood exactly how raw dough must feel when it comes into contact with boiling oil."

Pedro asks for Tita's hand in marriage, but his request is denied by Mama Elena. But she persuades him to marry Rosaura (Yareli Arizmendi), one of Tita's older sisters, instead. Pedro agrees to this empty marriage as a means of staying close to his beloved. But the idea of his marrying Rosaura is roundly criticized, once again by means of a culinary metaphor. "You can't just exchange tacos for enchiladas!" a household servant declares with indignation. Of course, she turns out to be right.

Tita herself is typically acquiescent, resigned to her role as a dutiful spinster. But then, with the help of Nacha (Ada Carrasco), the elderly cook who presides over the story before and after her death as spiritual adviser, Tita works on a wedding meal. Somehow, when saturated with Tita's tears, the food becomes so infused with her longing and frustration that the wedding guests are overcome. All are simultaneously taken sick, mourning for their own lost loves.

Like Water for Chocolate takes its title from a Mexican method of making hot chocolate by boiling and reboiling water with cocoa, until this substance becomes sweetly overagitated, much as Tita herself feels in the presence of her new brother-in-law. In one of the film's most wildly imaginative episodes, Tita pricks her fingers on thorns and thus turns a meal of quails cooked in rose-petal sauce into the pure physical embodiment of her desire for Pedro. At this point in the story, food is described as "voluptuously, ardently fragrant and utterly sensual," and ordinary nourishment is truly beside the point.

The effects of this dish are so potent that Gertrudis (Claudette Maillé), Tita's other sister, feels her temperature rise and rushes to an outdoor shower to cool off. The dinner has so overheated Gertrudis that her body actually gives off smoke. Then the boards surrounding the shower catch fire and Gertrudis is carried off naked by one of Pancho Villa's soldiers, who has also fallen under the quail-and-rose-petal spell. Incidentally, Gertrudis's eventual fate establishes the story's faith in feminine power as a force that extends well beyond the kitchen.

Miracles like that of the quail and roses are presented almost matter-of-factly by the film's producer and director, Alfonso Arau, who acted in *El Topo* and *The Wild Bunch.* (Mr. Arau is also the husband of Ms. Esquivel.) His direction can be seen as refreshingly plain, especially in light of the curious events the film often depicts, events that work best without stylistic flourishes. Strong passions produce sparks and lightning; a colossal knitted bedspread that expresses Tita's misery takes on epic proportions; one party scene somehow carries the celebrants twenty years forward in time. All of this is presented with the simplicity of a folktale, with exaggerated events blending effortlessly into those that seem real.

Miss Cavazos's performance as Tita is reticent and sly, perfectly in keeping with the film's muted manner. Tita never overreacts, preferring to bide her time and marvel silently at outward events that confirm her intuition. Mr. Leonardi, as the person who shares many of Tita's thoughts, enhances the film's romantic mood while also evolving from object of desire to petulant brother-in-law. Miss Torné carries Mama Elena's sternness to a suitably fierce extreme.

Also appearing in the story, eventually to bedevil Mr. Leonardi's Pedro, is John Brown (Mario Iván Martínez), the doctor whose American Indian heritage has made him privy to a whole different strain of folklore. It is he who compares the human spirit to a box of matches, suggesting how sad life can be if those matches are allowed to grow soggy. The film itself eagerly embraces the opposite notion, presenting a torrid, slow-burning love affair and never losing its own bright, original flame.

—*J.M., February 17, 1993*

LILI

Directed by Charles Walters; written by Helen Deutsch, based on the story by Paul Gallico; cinematographer. Robert Planck; edited by Ferris

Webster; music by Bronislau Kaper; art designers, Cedric Gibbons and Paul Groesse; produced by Edwin H. Knopf; released by Metro-Goldwyn-Mayer. Black and white. Running time: 81 minutes.

With: Leslie Caron (Lili Dautier), Mel Ferrer (Paul Berthalet), Jean-Pierre Aumont (Marc), Zsa Zsa Gabor (Rosalie), Kurt Kasznar (Jacquot), Amanda Blake (Peach Lips), Alex Gerry (Proprietor), Ralph Dumke (Mr. Corvier), Wilton Graff (Mr. Tonit) and George Baxter (Mr. Erique).

At last, the simplicity and freshness that the little French actress, Leslie Caron, showed in her screen debut in *An American in Paris* has been captured again in a film. This time it is in Metro's *Lili* that the elfin and winsome dancing star with the odd little face and the mobile figure once more demonstrates her youthful charm. And the consequence is that she helps *Lili* to be a lovely and beguiling little film, touched with the magic of romance and the shimmer of masquerade.

To be sure, it is not she entirely who deserves admiration and praise for the sweetness of this little picture, now at the TransLux Fifty-second Street. Helen Deutsch, who composed its fairy fable from a story by Paul Gallico about an orphan girl and a puppeteer in a French carnival deserves her portion of the praise, for she has put together a frankly fanciful romance with clarity, humor and lack of guile. Charles Walters, who prepared the simple dances and directed, deserves his portion, too, and Edwin H. Knopf, who produced for Metro, should likewise take a bow. He has maintained a touch of quiet authority and a unity of design in the whole thing.

Certainly the various craftsmen who designed the carnival sets, as spangled and gay in Technicolor as such things invariably are, the fellows who did the tinkling music and the others who moved the puppets and such, as well as those who handled the filter lenses on the color cameras, should get a nod. It is in the pictorial mountebankery and the waltzing music of the accordions, written by Bronislau Kaper, that a good bit of charm resides.

And, of course, we are not overlooking the attractiveness of Jean-Pierre Aumont as the amiable carnival magician with whom the little orphan first falls in love; nor the razzle and dazzle of Zsa Zsa Gabor as this

gentleman's assistant and secret wife, nor the poignant austerity and confusion of Mel Ferrer as the crippled puppeteer. They all contribute personal tone and color, as do Kurt Kasznar as a loyal friend to the pitiful puppetmaster and others in lesser roles.

But we still must return to Miss Caron as the focus of warmth and appeal in this delicate entertainment that relies very largely on her charm. For it is her patent air of naive credence, her bright smiles and the softness of her voice that win full belief and affection for her lonely orphan girl. It is her childish manner with the puppets that seals the fragile bond of wistful communication that forms the critical hinge of the plot. And it is her grace and beauty in the ballets and her initial singing of the song, "Hi-Lili, Hi-Lo," that give vitality to these otherwise banal little things.

Thank goodness, it's not necessary to wonder what *Lili* would be without Miss Caron. She's in it and it's a lovely little picture. Let's hope she may have many more.

—B.C., March 11, 1953

LITTLE BIG MAN

Directed by Arthur Penn; written by Calder Willingham, based on the novel by Thomas Berger; cinematographer, Harry Stradling, Jr.; edited by Dede Allen; music by John Hammond; production designer, Dean Tavoularis; produced by Stuart Millar; released by National General Pictures. Running time: 147 minutes.

With: Dustin Hoffman (Jack Crabb), Faye Dunaway (Mrs. Pendrake), Martin Balsam (Allardyce T. Merriweather), Richard Mulligan (General George A. Custer), Chief Dan George (Old Lodge Skins), Jeff Corey (Wild Bill Hickok), Aimee Ecclés (Sunshine), Kelly Jean Peters (Olga), Carole Androsky (Caroline) and Robert Little Star (Little Horse).

Little Big Man, the film adaptation of Thomas Berger's epic comic novel, is Arthur Penn's most extravagant and ambitious movie, an attempt to capture the essence of the American heritage in the funny, bitter, uproarious adventures of Jack Crabb, an irritable, 120-odd-year-old gentleman who may or may not have been the sole survivor of Custer's Last Stand.

The film, which opened yesterday at the Paramount and Sutton Theaters, tries to cover too much ground, even though Calder Willingham's script eliminates or telescopes events and characters from the Berger novel. Often it is not terribly funny, at just those moments when it tries the hardest, and it sometimes wears its social concerns so blatantly that they look like war paint.

There is little lyricism in it of the kind that bewildered criticism of *Bonnie and Clyde* and that blurred the bleak edges of *Alice's Restaurant*.

All of these things are true, and yet *Little Big Man*—both in spite of and because of these failings—is an important movie by one of our most interesting directors. It is also one of the maybe half-dozen American movies of this year that won't make you ponder the possibility of a subsidy plan to pay filmmakers not to work.

Little Big Man is Mr. Penn's tough testament to the contrariness of the American experience as witnessed by the durable Mr. Crabb, played mostly by Dustin Hoffman in various amounts of makeup, and by two younger actors who impersonate Crabb while growing up.

It was Crabb's quite extraordinary fate to be captured by the Cheyennes at the age of ten, raised by them as a brave, rescued by the whites at the age of fifteen and then to spend the next twenty years surviving two marriages, bankruptcy, sometime careers as an Indian scout and con artist, alcoholism, a brief period as a suicidal hermit and, finally, General Custer's ill-timed decision to push on into the territory of the Little Big Horn.

The film has the circular form of encounters with friends or relatives that Jack has somehow lost earlier along the way. Thus his huge, gritty sister Caroline, who had abandoned him in the Cheyenne camp years before when she learned (to her disappointment) that she wasn't going to be raped, later turns up to teach him to be the fastest gun in the West. Mrs. Pendrake (Faye Dunaway), the not-so-respectable wife of a preacher, is met again in a Black Hills bordello, where she philosophizes about her work: "This life is not only sinful, it's not much fun."

Met again too are his first wife, a quiet Swedish girl who reappears as an Indian's noisy squaw, and Allardyce T. Merriweather (Martin Balsam), a patent medicine salesman who loses parts of his body (an ear,

a hand, a leg) the way other people lose small change. Most important, however, are the reencounters with his Cheyenne family, presided over by the ancient chief, Old Lodge Skins (Chief Dan George), through whose eyes Jack Crabb watches the virtual extinction of "human beings," which is what the Cheyennes call themselves.

These sequences, beautifully photographed (for a change, in the American West and not Spain), are both the most significant and, at times, the least successful. Mr. Willingham never quite gets the hang of how Indians should talk in English meant to represent Cheyenne. "My son," says Old Lodge Skins to a recently returned Jack, "to see you again makes my heart soar like a hawk," and the movie, which has been putting down a romantic view of history, seems to be putting down itself, and all movies in which Indians talk movie English.

Mr. Penn obviously takes seriously the vanishing of the race that managed to give Jack "a vision of a moral order in the universe," but he is more likely to end a scene with a pratfall than a prayer, often going even further than Mr. Berger did to secure laughs, which are not always there. It is apparently Mr. Penn's aim to be more outrageously comic than the novel in order to be as essentially serious.

When the mixture of violence and something akin to slapstick does work, as it does in the climactic battle at the Little Big Horn (with Custer, amid the bodies, ranting on about General Grant's drinking habits), it is lovely and sad and profoundly crazy. When Old Lodge Skins can't quite succeed in willing his own death ("Sometimes the magic works, sometimes it doesn't"), the effect, like the inflection in which the speech is read, is that of borrowed Yiddish humor.

Mr. Hoffman is one of our two best young character actors (the other is Jon Voight) and although there are peculiar traces of both Ben Braddock and Ratso Rizzo in his Jack Crabb, he is fine, as is just about everybody in the huge cast, including the Indians, some of whom are real and some of whom are aspiring members of the Screen Actors Guild.

Little Big Man is a movie composed of such contradictions, about epic contradictions, as at some middle period of life, when Jack finds himself being attacked by his Cheyenne family. An American soldier shoots Jack's attacker and, on the soundtrack, the ancient Crabb says simply, "An enemy had saved my life by shooting my best friend." The old man and the movie then move on to other things.

—*V.C., December 15, 1970*

LITTLE CAESAR

Directed by Mervyn LeRoy; written by Robert N. Lee, Darryl F. Zanuck, Francis Edward Faragoh and Robert Lord, based on the novel by W. R. Burnett; cinematographer, Tony Gaudio; edited by Ray Curtiss; music by Erno Rapee and Leo F. Forbstein; art designer, Anton Grot; produced by Hal B. Wallis; released by Warner Brothers. Black and white. Running time: 80 minutes.

With: Edward G. Robinson (Cesare Enrico Bandello, "Little Caesar"), Douglas Fairbanks Jr. (Joe Massara), Glenda Farrell (Olga Strassoff), William Collier Jr. (Tony Passa), Ralph Ince (Diamond Pete Montana), George E. Stone (Otero) and Thomas Jackson (Lieutenant Tom Flaherty).

Little Caesar, based on W. R. Burnett's novel of Chicago gangdom, was welcomed to the Strand yesterday by unusual crowds. The story deals with the career of Cesare Bandello, alias Rico, alias Little Caesar, a disagreeable lad who started by robbing gasoline stations and soared to startling heights in his "profession" by reason of his belief in his high destiny.

The production is ordinary and would rank as just one more gangster film but for two things. One is the excellence of Mr. Burnett's credible and compact story. The other is Edward G. Robinson's wonderfully effective performance. Little Caesar becomes at Mr. Robinson's hands a figure out of Greek epic tragedy, a cold, ignorant, merciless killer, driven on and on by an insatiable lust for power, the plaything of a force that is greater than himself.

Douglas Fairbanks Jr., as Rico's pal, who brings about his friend's downfall by trying to live a decent life away from his old haunts, is miscast, and in addition suffers by comparison with the reality of Mr. Robinson's portrayal. At times Mr. Fairbanks talks and acts like the cheap Italian thug he is supposed to represent, but more often he is the pleasant, sincere youth who has been seen to so much better advantage elsewhere.

Little Caesar comes to the big town and joins Sam Vettori's gang, one of the two principal "mobs" in that city. Both gangs are under the supervision of Pete Montana, who in turn owes his allegiance to a mysterious "Big Boy," the king of the underworld. Early in his career Little Caesar plans and executes a raid on a cabaret protected by the rival gang, and in so doing kills a crime commissioner. Thereafter, step by step, he ousts Vettori, Pete Montana and the rival gang leader, and soon only "Big Boy" bars his way to complete mastery of the city's underworld.

His pal, Joe Massara, is threatened with the fatal "spot" because he knows too much, and that young man's sweetheart turns state's evidence. The "mob" is broken and scattered, and Little Caesar is cornered and killed by a crafty detective's appeal to the gangster's vanity.

Glenda Farrell is excellently authentic as Massara's "moll," and William Collier Jr. contributes a moving performance in a minor role. Thomas Jackson as the detective is also noteworthy.

—*M.H., January 10, 1931*

THE LITTLE FOXES

Directed by William Wyler; written by Lillian Hellman, based on her play; additional dialogue by Arthur Kober, Dorothy Parker and Alan Campbell; cinematographer, Gregg Toland; edited by Daniel Mandell; music by Meredith Willson; art designer Stephen Goosson; produced by Samuel Goldwyn; released by RKO Radio Pictures. Black and white. Running time: 115 minutes.

With: Bette Davis (Regina Giddens), Herbert Marshall (Horace Giddens), Teresa Wright (Alexandra Giddens), Richard Carlson (David Hewitt), Patricia Collinge (Birdie Hubbard), Dan Duryea (Leo Hubbard) and Charles Dingle (Ben Hubbard).

Lillian Hellman's grim and malignant melodrama, The Little Foxes, which had the National Theatre's stage running knee-deep in gall and wormwood the season before last, has now been translated to the screen with all its original viciousness intact and with such extra-added virulence as the relentless camera of director William Wyler and the tensile acting of Bette

Davis could impart. As presented at the Music Hall yesterday, under the trademark of Samuel Goldwyn, *The Little Foxes* leaps to the front as the most bitingly sinister picture of the year and as one of the most cruelly realistic character studies yet shown on the screen.

No one who saw the play need be reminded that Miss Hellman was dipping acid straight when she penned this fearful fable of second-generation carpetbaggers in a small Southern town around 1900. Henrik Ibsen and William Faulkner could not together have designed a more morbid account of interfamily treachery and revoltingly ugly greed than was contained in Miss Hellman's purple drama of deadly intrigue in the Hubbard clan. And with a perfect knowledge of the camera's flexibility, the author and Mr. Wyler have derived out of the play a taut and cumulative screen story which exhales the creepy odor of decay and freezes charitable blood with the deliberation of a Frigidaire.

Frankly, there is nothing pretty nor inspiring about this almost-fustian tale of Regina Giddens's foxiness in planting figurative knives in her own deceitful brothers' backs, of her callous neglect of her good husband when he is dying of a heart attack, all because she wants to grab the bulk of the family's rising fortune for herself. The whole suspense of the picture lies in the question of who's going to sink the last knife. Even the final elopement of Regina's appalled daughter, for whom the film conveniently provides a nice romance, adds little more than a touch of leavening irony. Regina is too hard a woman to mourn much for anything.

Thus the test of the picture is the effectiveness with which it exposes a family of evil people poisoning everything they touch. And this it does spectacularly. Mr. Wyler, with the aid of Gregg Toland, has used the camera to sweep in the myriad small details of a mauve decadent household and the more indicative facets of the many characters. The focus is sharp, the texture of the images hard and realistic. Individual scenes are extraordinarily vivid and compelling, such as that in which the Hubbard brothers plot a way to outdo their sister, or the almost unbearable scene in which Regina permits her husband to struggle unassisted with death. Only when Mr. Wyler plays obvious tricks with mirrors does a bit of pretension creep in.

And Miss Davis's performance in the role which Tallulah Bankhead played so brassily on the stage is abundant with color and mood. True, she does occasionally drop an unmistakable imitation of her predecessor, she performs queer contortions with her arms like a nautch-dancer in a Hindu temple, and generally she comports herself as though she were balancing an Academy "Oscar" on her high-coiffed head. But the role calls for heavy theatrics; it is just a cut above ten-twent'-thirt'. Miss Davis is all right.

Better than that, however, are the other members of the cast. Charles Dingle as brother Ben Hubbard, the oldest and sharpest of the rattlesnake clan, is the perfect villain in respectable garb. Carl Benton Reid as brother Oscar is magnificently dark, sullen and undependable. Patricia Collinge repeats her excellent stage performance as the faded flower of the Old South who tips the jug. Teresa Wright is fragile and pathetic as the harassed daughter of Regina. Dan Duryea is a shade too ungainly as Oscar's chicken-livered son, and Herbert Marshall is surprisingly British for a Southerner born and bred, but both fill difficult roles well.

The Little Foxes will not increase your admiration for mankind. It is cold and cynical. But it is a very exciting picture to watch in a comfortably objective way, especially if you enjoy expert stabbing-in-the-back.

—*B.C., August 22, 1941*

LITTLE FUGITIVE

Written and directed by Ray Ashley, Morris Engel and Ruth Orkin: cinematographer, Mr. Engel: edited by Ms. Orkin and Lester Troeb: music by Eddy Manson: produced by Mr. Engel and Mr. Ashley: released by Joseph Burstyn Inc. Black and white. Running time: 75 minutes.

With: Richie Andrusco (Joey), Rickie Brewster (Lennie), Winnifred Cushing (The Mother), Jay Williams (Pony Ride Man), Will Lee (Photographer), Charlie Moss (Harry) and Tommy De Canio (Charlie).

Little Fugitive, a shoestring film production, which opened at the Normandie yesterday under the auspices of Joseph Burstyn, dealer in cinema gems, might best be described as a candid study of a seven-year-old Brooklyn kid, done with a motion picture camera in Coney Island and points adjacent thereto. As such, it gives a wondrous illustration of the eccentricities of a small boy, adrift on his own resources in a tinny and tawdry mob playground. And its subject—a tad named Richie Andrusco—is so abounding in little-boy charm that his random adventures in the picture suggest more substance than is actually there.

For the simple fact is that this small item, which was put together by a group of young folks whose previous experience had been as still photographers and freelance journalists, is essentially a documentation of juvenile fancy and caprice, hung upon a mere situation, with slight dramatic conflict and form. And what there is of the latter is so unskillfully performed that it does not bear criticism as a finished professional job.

The heart and the body of the picture are the views of this little boy as he rambles around Coney Island, cut loose from his family and quite alone. His older brother and the latter's playmates have pulled a mean trick on him: they have made him think he has murdered his brother, and in terror he has fled.

But his terror is not long-lasting. Once at large on "the island's" teeming range, he abandons himself to the luxury of indulging his boyish whims. He stuffs himself with hot dogs, rides on the merry-go-round (because of his passion for cowboys) and tries various throwing and batting games. Then he discovers the big thrill—the two-for-a-quarter pony ride. Only now he has run out of money and has to collect pop bottle "empties" to pay his way.

All of this is observed in charming detail through the clever and watchful cameras of Morris Engel, Ray Ashley and Ruth Orkin, who wrote, produced, directed and sold the thing. The alertness and style of their photography are clearly reflective of the demands of the picture-magazine layout. And that is what they've mobilized in this film.

We are not criticizing that, mind you. A day at Coney Island with a small boy, torn between curiosity and survival, can be—and is—a lot of fun. And the small boy in this instance is so expressive and unconcerned, thanks to the obvious toil of his photographers, that it is a treat to be with him. Thanks, also, to a musical soundtrack, which Lester Troeb has conceived and supervised with a harmonica as the sole instrument, the frolic has a light, informal mood.

But the limits must be perceived and mentioned—there is little conception of drama in this trick, and the mere repetition of adventures tends eventually to grow

dull. The little boy, while natural and instinctive, portrays no problem of youth. If anything, he is a blissfully commonplace little animal. And his brother, played by Rickie Brewster, is an equally commonplace kid. The issue is purely fortuitous. Their anxieties are as mild as the summer rain, which pelts the beach and the boardwalk for a climactic moment in the film.

All hail to *Little Fugitive* and to those who made it. But count it a photographer's triumph with a limited theme.

—B.C., October 7, 1953

THE LITTLE KIDNAPPERS

Directed by Philip Leacock; written by Neil Paterson; cinematographer, Eric Cross; edited by John Trumper; music by Bruce Montgomery; produced by Sergei Nolbandov and Leslie Parkyn; released by United Artists. Black and white. Running time: 93 minutes.

With: Duncan Macrae (Grandaddy), Jean Anderson (Grandma), Adrienne Corri (Kirsty), Theodore Bikel (Willem Bloem), Jon Whiteley (Harry), Vincent Winter (Davy), Francis De Wolfe (Jan Hooft, Sr.), James Sutherland (Arron McNab) and John Rae (Andrew McCleod).

The clear and candid natures of children, so seldom captured fairly on the screen—mainly because adult film people tend to artificialize the little dears—usually make for charming entertainment when they are set down honestly and simply in a valid tale. And that they are in *The Little Kidnappers*, which opened yesterday at the Trans-Lux Sixtieth Street.

If this report seems to wax ecstatic about this thoroughly unpretentious British film, which was photographed in Scotland but has Nova Scotia as its fictional locale, it is because it gives off such a genuine and gratifying picture of kids in a story that measures so truly their natural instincts against grown-up attitudes.

The people who made this little treasure obviously were disinclined to be romantic about children—or, indeed, about the human race. Their singular aim was to reckon the possible blunders that may occur when anyone is driven by a deep fixation—particularly when a child is driven by the urge to love.

And so their simple story of the hurrah that happens when two orphan lads, living with their stern grandparents, innocently "kidnap" a baby because they have been forbidden to have a dog as an object for their affections is just a straight, humorous, poignant account of true but misguided devotions, on the part of the old folks as well as the boys.

A lot of the charm is in the telling. Neil Paterson, who wrote the script, and Philip Leacock, who directed, went back fifty years into a locale and era of austere living for a distinctively flavored atmosphere. Their stern Nova Scotian farmers are Scottish by descent, with manners and morals as rigid as their strangely chiseled speech. The grandfather is a Spartan elder, as zealous as the old abolitionist, John Brown, whom he strongly resembles with his long beard. He is rigorously played by Duncan Macrae. And the grandmother, played by Jean Anderson, is a quiet, long-suffering soul, dutiful to her husband. She is the feeble link with the boys.

Against these gritty characters, the warmth and freshness of the lads comes forth with an overpowering radiance. Jon Whiteley as the older of the two is a fragile but firm-minded youngster, and Vincent Winter as the five-year-old is a natural, beguiling little fellow with a Scottish accent that gives music to his words. The concept of these little boys as examples to older folks of the purity of affection is put forth firmly, without mawkishness or gush.

Adrienne Corri and Theodore Bikel play a lean and anguished romance touchingly. They and others help make *The Little Kidnappers* an extraordinarily true and winning film.

—B.C., September 2, 1954

LITTLE VERA

Directed by Vasily Pichul; written (in Russian, with English subtitles) by Mariya Khmelik; director of photography. Yefim Reznikov; edited by Yelena Zabolotskaya; music by Vladimir Matetsky; produced by Gorky Film Studios; released by International Film Exchange. Running time: 110 minutes.

With: Natalya Negoda (Vera) andrei Sokolov (Sergei). Yuri Nazarov (The Father). Lyudmila Zaitseva (The Mother) andrei Fomin (Andrei). Aleksandr Alekseyev-Negreba (Viktor). Aleksandra Tabakova (Chistiakova) and Aleksandra Linkov (Mikhail Petrovich).

The camera pans across a bleak industrial landscape of factories, smokestacks, warehouses, rows of identical apartment blocks. On the soundtrack can be heard the occasional call of a dove mixed with the noises of urban intercourse. There is a sense of activity, purpose and routine, of the heavy momentum that carries a great modern society from one day to the next, possibly forever.

Cut to a small, exceptionally pretty young woman as she stands on the tiny balcony of one of those apartment blocks, leaning on the rail in cheeky boredom. She is Vera and she is definitely not forever. With the exception of her surprising spirit, everything about her will soon wear out or be cheerfully forgotten, including her dark glasses, the gum she is chewing and the loud rock music she's listening to.

Because Vasily Pichul's *Little Vera* is a Russian film, I suppose that Vera must be analyzed as a political statement, a startling indication of just how open Mikhail S. Gorbachev's new Russian society actually is.

But *Little Vera* is so funny, so abrasive and so true that it transcends newsworthiness. It stands on its own. It also suggests that in Mr. Pichul, its twenty-eight-year-old director, and in Mariya Khmelik, who wrote the screenplay, the Russians have a pair of first-rate new filmmakers who will soon be internationally known.

Little Vera will be shown tonight and tomorrow at the Museum of Modern Art in the New Directors/New Films series.

Vera, played with remarkable comic authority by Natalya Negoda, is not doomy enough to be classified as seriously alienated. Underneath the punk hairstyle that her parents have learned not to criticize, she's bright, quick, and commonsensical, adrift in a world where everyone else appears to be traveling a set course. Vera is just out of school and about to take a job with the telephone company.

In the meantime, she waits around. When she can, she hangs out with her girlfriends, picking up boys. She shares a cramped, working-class apartment with her father, who is a decent sort until he drinks (when he turns into a slob), and her mother, a once pretty woman who works too hard at her job and spends her exhausted off hours fretting. The arbiter of family disputes is Vera's older brother, Viktor, a doctor who lives in Moscow and who is telephoned every time Vera does something wrong, which is constantly.

Her mother and father panic when Vera acknowledges she's having an affair with a good-looking young student named Sergei, whom she met one night after a public dance that turned into a rock riot.

Sergei represents sophistication to Vera. He is laid-back, cool, completely sure of himself. At his initial meeting with Vera's parents, a formal Sunday dinner, he turns up wearing Bermuda shorts. During the meal, bored by the conversation, he grabs Vera's hand and walks out.

When Sergei very casually suggests that maybe he and Vera should marry, her parents immediately insist that he move in with them, which is when the trouble really starts.

Little Vera is a far cry from *Moscow Does Not Believe in Tears*, the schmaltzy Russian romantic comedy that won the foreign language Oscar some years ago, though not because of its partial nudity and its awareness that people sometimes enjoy sex out of wedlock.

Little Vera is less critical and daring than honest and frank. More important, it doesn't simplify or attempt to explain the contradictory natures of the characters. They're not exactly Chekhovian, but they are complex, sometimes self-deluding and almost always, at some point, most engagingly comic.

Miss Negoda's Vera is an enchanting creature. She's willful, sweet, a little silly and essentially honest. She has a laugh that is a fishwife's cackle, which, like Elizabeth Taylor's, is all the more infectious for having no apparent relation to the beauty from which it issues. Miss Negoda could be the discovery of the year.

She receives excellent support from the other cast members, especially Andrei Sokolov as the debonair Sergei, and Yuri Nazarov and Lyudmila Zaitseva as her parents.

Little Vera will be opening a regular commercial run at the Lincoln Plaza on April 14. Go.

—*V.C., March 31, 1989*

LITTLE WOMEN

Directed by George Cukor; written by Sarah Y. Mason and Victor Heerman, based on the novel by Louisa May Alcott; cinematographer, Henry Gerrard; edited by Jack Kitchin; music by Max Steiner; art designer, Van Nest Polglase; produced by Kenneth MacGowan; released by RKO Radio Productions. Black and white. Running time: 117 minutes.

With: Katharine Hepburn (Jo), Joan Bennett (Amy), Paul Lukas (Fritz Bhaer), Frances Dee (Meg), Jean Parker (Beth), Edna May Oliver (Aunt March), Douglas Montgomery (Laurie), Henry Stephenson (Mr. Laurence), Spring Byington (Marmee), Samuel Hinds (Mr. March), Mabel Colcord (Hannah), John Davis Lodge (Brooke) and Nydia Westman (Mamie).

As vital, sympathetic and full of the joie de vivre as one could hope for, Jo, the Jo of *Little Women*, is to be seen in the person of Katharine Hepburn in the cinematic translation of Louisa May Alcott's immensely popular novel of the March family. Amy, Beth, Meg and other characters step from the book to the screen and retell this story of the sixties. They may be but mere shadow images with voices, but they are a lovable group, and the picture gains much by the hoop skirts and other fashions of those days of yesteryear.

The easygoing fashion in which George Cukor, the director, has set forth the beguiling incidents in pictorial form is so welcome after the stereotyped tales with stuffed shirts. It matters not that this chronicle is without a hero, or even a villain, for the absence of such worthies, usually extravagantly drawn, causes one to be quite contented to dwell for the moment with human hearts of the old-fashioned days. The film begins in a gentle fashion and slips away smoothly without any forced attempt to help the finish to linger in the minds of the audience.

Little Women is just as honest in its story as Jo's nature. It is stimulating to hear Jo sing out: "Look at me, World, I'm Jo March, and I'm so happy." She is the personification of sincerity, a thorough human being. Vice is unknown to her, or to the story for that matter. Imagine a picture concerned merely with the doings of a healthy-minded family! Miss Hepburn steps up the ladder, if anything, by her interpretation of Jo. She talks rather fast at times, but one feels that Jo did, and after all one does not wish to listen to dialogue in which every word is weighed when the part is acted by a Katharine Hepburn.

A delightful moment or so here is when Miss Hepburn acts two roles in the March family amateur theatricals. She is first the mustachioed villain, and right afterward, sans mustache and with a blonde wig, she is the spirit of chivalry, the handsome hero. Also during rehearsals there is the enjoyable bit where Jo tries so hard to teach Amy how to faint, but Amy prefers to save herself from bruises from many falls rather than perform realistically. Miss Hepburn goes darting through this picture without giving one a moment to think of her as other than Jo.

Joan Bennett as Amy first appears standing on a bench, in the schoolroom, with a sign around her neck reading: "I am ashamed of myself." She is very pretty, this Amy, and she often amuses the audience and irritates Jo with her catch-as-catch-can wrestling with words of three syllables. "Fastidious" is a favorite word with her, but she employs it instead of "fascinating." There are many other slips of the tongue that Amy inflicts on her Marmee and her sisters. Miss Bennett's interpretation is one of her very best.

How disappointing it is to Jo and how glad Amy is to go abroad with old Aunt March! This crabbed old lady is cleverly acted by Edna May Oliver. Jo, however, is philosophical and later she is thankful that she is with Beth when the latter is very ill. Aunt March is an ogre who has a good-natured side. And speaking of Aunt March reminds one of Mr. Laurence, the man who lives in marble halls and is played so excellently by Henry Stephenson.

Paul Lukas adds to the charm of the picture by his performance of Fritz Bhaer, the ingratiating Teuton who revels in music and takes Jo to the opera when she is in New York. Frances Dee plays Meg, who is more prosaic than Jo. Miss Dee does very well by the role. But, it is not necessary to tally all the players, for from Miss Hepburn's talented character study to the least important role, all the members of the cast make the most of their opportunities.

—*M.H., November 17, 1933*

LITTLE WOMEN

Directed by Gillian Armstrong: written by Robin Swicord, based on the novel by Louisa May Alcott: director of photography, Geoffrey Simpson: edited by Nicholas Beauman: music by Thomas Newman: production designer, Jan Roelfs: produced by Denise Di Novi: released by Columbia Pictures. Running time: 115 minutes.

With: Winona Ryder (Jo March), Gabriel Byrne (Friedrich Bhaer), Trini Alvarado (Meg March), Samantha Mathis (Older Amy March), Kirsten Dunst (Younger Amy March), Claire Danes (Beth March), Christian Bale (Laurie), Eric Stoltz (John Brooke), John Neville (Mr. Laurence), Mary Wickes (Aunt March) and Susan Sarandon (Mrs. March).

S ome books are so familiar reading them is like being home again," Jo March observes in the new film version of Louisa May Alcott's classic novel. She's talking about Shakespeare, but we all know *Little Women* is a book like that, one of the most seductively nostalgic novels any child ever discovers. As the gold standard for American girlhood, it lingers in our collective consciousness as a wistful, inspiring memory. Ladies, get out your hand-hemmed handkerchiefs for the loveliest *Little Women* ever on screen.

Gillian Armstrong's enchantingly pretty film is so potent that it prompts a rush of recognition from the opening frame. There in Concord, Mass., are the March girls and their noble Marmee, gathered around the hearth for a heart-rendingly quaint Christmas Eve. Stirring up a flurry of familial warmth, Ms. Armstrong instantly demonstrates that she has caught the essence of this book's sweetness and cast her film uncannily well, finding sparkling young actresses who are exactly right for their famous roles. The effect is magical. And for all its unimaginable innocence, the story has a touching naturalness this time.

Remember that these are fresh-faced teenagers who wassail and embroider. They put on little plays for at-home entertainment; they live out the pieties of "Pilgrim's Progress"; they talk passionately about music and literature. ("Your spelling's atrocious," Jo snaps at Amy, her princessy younger sister. "Your Latin's absurd.") The Marches' rare neighborliness and generosity are enough to heartstrings by summoning a world more benign than our own. Even when this film becomes family viewing on home video, watched with a passivity so different from the no-tech, active atmosphere of the March household, its idealism will come through.

The direction by Ms. Armstrong, who long ago summoned memories of *Little Women* with *My Brilliant Career* (1978), is sentimental without being saccharine. And the filmmaker is too savvy to tell this story in a cultural and historical vacuum. So this *Little Women* has ways of winking at its audience, most notably when the tomboyish, intellectually ambitious Jo March reveals that she has cut off and sold her mane of hair. "Jo, how could you?" wails Amy. "Your one beauty!" Well, this Jo is Winona Ryder and the joke is that she has beauty to spare, along with enough vigor to dim memories of Katharine Hepburn in the now badly dated 1933 George Cukor version. Ms. Armstrong reinvents *Little Women* for present-day audiences without ever forgetting it's a story with a past.

Once the March sisters have made their introductory embraces—and these are girls who embrace, never just hug—the four familiar personalities emerge. Ms. Ryder, whose banner year also includes a fine comic performance in *Reality Bites,* plays Jo with spark and confidence. Her spirited presence gives the film an appealing linchpin, and she plays the self-proclaimed "man of the family" with just the right staunchness.

The perfect contrast to take-charge Jo comes from Kirsten Dunst's scene-stealing Amy, whose vanity and twinkling mischief make so much more sense coming from an 11-year-old vixen than they did from grown-up Joan Bennett in 1933. Ms. Dunst, also scarily effective as the baby bloodsucker of *Interview With the Vampire,* is a little vamp with a big future.

Amy undergoes a jarring personality change when, after a four-year forward leap in the story, she grows up into the more ladylike Samantha Mathis. Meanwhile, Trini Alvarado captures the ladylike composure of Meg, the oldest and most marriageable of the sisters. Miss Alcott joked that the second half of her book ought to be called "Wedding Marches" for its way of realizing these young women's ambitions with a quick succession of nuptials and babies.

As written by Robin Swicord, this *Little Women* works overtime to balance such recidivist plotting with the occasional feminist mouthful, mostly spoken by Susan Sarandon's exceedingly prim mother figure. This version emphasizes the "marm" in "Marmee" with an excess of instructional dialogue that echoes the thinking of Alcott's progressive Concord parents. So the film makes reference to transcendentalism and raises Marmee's political consciousness a few notches.

("I so wish I could give my girls a just world. I know you'll make it a better place.") While the sentiments are admirable, the stridency can be irritating, especially since the film's moral tenor is never far from its surface.

There are also men in *Little Women*. As they were on the page, they're a bit secondary. Ms. Armstrong deals with that difficulty by casting attractive actors to breathe life into shapeless roles. So the handsome Christian Bale makes a dreamboat out of Laurie, the boy next door to the March family. (If viewers have trouble understanding why Jo wouldn't marry him, Miss Alcott's readers had the same problem.) Gabriel Byrne does his best with the thankless, tedious part of Professor Bhaer, the shy older man who courts Jo and is one of the book's nonautobiographical figures.

Eric Stoltz makes a puckish John Brooke, Laurie's tutor, even if he's the one actor here who seems to have wandered in from a later century. The March girls also have a father, but he is away as a Civil War chaplain when the story begins. Not even the joyful tears that mark his return make it credible that there really is an important man around this house.

Speaking of tears, Claire Danes is given the job of coaxing forth great torrents in the role of Beth, the doomed angel of the March family. While no reader of Miss Alcott's ever saw Beth through the valley of the shadow of death dry eyed, the film's Beth is its one relatively ineffectual character. Ms. Danes, the disarming star of television's *My So-Called Life,* does a fine job. But Beth is a quiet character, and the film has become too diffuse by the time it bids her farewell. Once the sisters leave home and hearth, Ms. Armstrong has more trouble keeping the story's strands together than she did when the girls were part of a single pretty picture.

Little Women also has a larger visual attractiveness, with picturesque views of Orchard House (the real Alcott home) and pristine, snowy Canadian scenery to suggest the rest of Concord. Indoor scenes have the warm glow of candlelight, and the production design is appealing without excess, in keeping with the Marches' limited means. The film's buoyant good looks stop just this side of trouble. One more violet painted on a teacup would have been too much.

—*J.M., December 21, 1994*

THE LIVES OF A BENGAL LANCER

Directed by Henry Hathaway; written by Waldemar Young, John L. Balderston, Achmed Abdullah, Grover Jones and William Slavens McNutt, based on the novel by Major Francis Yeats-Brown; cinematographer, Charles Lang; edited by Ellsworth Hoagland; music by Milan Roder; art designer, Hans Dreier; produced by Louis D. Lighton; released by Paramount Pictures. Running time: 109 minutes.

With: Gary Cooper (Captain McGregor), Franchot Tone (Lieutenant Forsythe), Richard Cromwell (Lieutenant Stone), Sir Guy Standing (Colonel Stone), C. Aubrey Smith (Major Hamilton), Monte Blue (Hamzulia Khan), Kathleen Burke (Tania Volkanskaya), Colin Tapley (Lieutenant Barrett), Douglas Dumbrille (Mohammed Khan), Akim Tamiroff (Emir) and Jameson Thomas (Hendrickson).

Borrowing the title of Mr. Yeats-Brown's Indian odyssey of four or five years ago, the filmmakers have invented a heroic narrative of Kiplingesque adventure around Khyber Pass, which began an engagement yesterday at the Paramount. The cinema *Lives of a Bengal Lancer* is as joyous in its gunplay as it is splendid and picturesque in its manufacture, and it proves to be consistently lively despite its great length. Anticipating the kind of upper-crust sneers that a free screen adaptation of a literary work is sure to suffer, its makers are careful and even eager to clarify their intentions, although they slightly diminish the effect of their apologies by referring to the book as a novel.

In its exciting and somewhat blood-chilling account of the gallant band of fighting men who guard the northern frontier of England's empire in India, the work is in the vigorously romantic tradition of Kipling and Talbot Mundy. While it usually manages to avoid Kipling's fatally objectionable preoccupation with the white man's burden, it is so sympathetic in its discussion of England's colonial management that it ought to prove a great blessing to Downing Street. Mr. Yeats-Brown himself may be a trifle astonished to discover that a ravishing Russian spy has found her way into the story. Happily, though, the photoplay ignores her most of the time. With an adventurous delight that is tempered by a grim respect for the fighting qualities of the Afridi, it plunges into the dashing stuff of border patrols, guerrilla warfare, Afghan torture methods and the honor of the regiment. Henry Hathaway, the director, executes a skillful and convincing blend of the studio scenes and the authentic atmospheric films made in India several years ago by a Paramount expedition headed by Ernest Schoedsack.

Not with the Kipling roughneck does *The Lives of a Bengal Lancer* deal, but with the well-bred Englishmen who are gentlemen as well as officers of the king. Thus you find Sir Guy Standing being superbly cold as the colonel who preserves his detachment toward the ordinary human emotions even when his son is in hourly danger of having his eyes put out by the ingenious Afghans who have captured him. In the same spirit Gary Cooper and Franchot Tone, rather than betray the route of the ammunition train to their captors, submit with cool nonchalance to the curious Afghan custom of shoving lighted slivers under the fingernails of tightlipped captives. The tale tells of Lieutenant Stone (Richard Cromwell), the unseasoned son of the commander of the Bengal Lancers, who is so angered by his father's cool passion for discipline that when he is captured by the Afghans he decides to give away military secrets rather than uphold the honors of the corps in the torture chamber. In the great battle in the fortress, though, he acquits himself heroically.

Since all this may give you the impression that the film is overly insistent upon the military phases of life among the lancers, you ought to be informed that it is equally successful in its humor. There are first-rate performances by Sir Guy Standing as the stern disciplinarian, by Gary Cooper as the dour and surly Scotsman, by Franchot Tone as his flippant comrade and by young Mr. Cromwell as the weakling of the outfit. A number of skillful actors lurk behind turbans and Afghan beards. *Lives of a Bengal Lancer* is a superb adventure story and easily the liveliest film in town.

—*A.S., January 12, 1935*

LIVING IN OBLIVION

Written and directed by Tom DiCillo; director of photography, Frank Prinzi; edited by Camilla

Toniolo; music by Jim Farmer; production designer, Therese Deprez; produced by Michael Griffiths and Marcus Viscidi; released by Sony Pictures Classics. Running time: 91 minutes.

With: Steve Buscemi (Nick Reve), James Le Gros (Chad Palomino), Catherine Keener (Nicole), Dermot Mulroney (Wolf), Danielle von Zernick (Wanda), Peter Dinklage (Tito), Rica Martens (Cora) and Tom Jarmusch (Driver).

An inspired choice opens this year's New Directors/ New Films series tonight: *Living in Oblivion*, Tom DiCillo's wonderfully funny behind-the-scenes look at the perils of filmmaking, no-budget style. While he nominally presents the directing process as a series of hellish travails, Mr. DiCillo captures such delicious mischief that his indictment becomes a valentine.

Smart, raffish and wickedly playful, *Living in Oblivion* sets the perfect tone for this annual series, which is presented jointly by the Film Society of Lincoln Center and the Museum of Modern Art at the museum. Mr. DiCillo winds up celebrating filmmaking so wittily that he's sure to encourage other, newer directors to follow suit.

He himself isn't so new. A former actor and cinematographer (he shot Jim Jarmusch's *Stranger Than Paradise*), Mr. DiCillo directed one previous feature, the quirkily deadpan *Johnny Suede*. That film starred Brad Pitt, who will be on more than a few minds as *Living in Oblivion* unfolds. This comedy's pièce de résistance is the behavior of Chad Palomino (James Le Gros), the hot young heartthrob who has deigned to appear in a modest film by Nick Reve (Steve Buscemi).

"I'm watchin' you, buddy, like a hawk!" the hipper-than-thou Chad declares on his arrival. "I wanna *learn* from you!" (Officially, Mr. DiCillo has denied that this character's diffident dude-hood has anything to do with that of his previous leading man. This may be the moment to mention that when a reporter asked Mr. Pitt, who was charming in *Johnny Suede*, what sort of character he played in that film, he reportedly said: "He's just an idiot trying to figure out how he can sit comfortably in a chair.")

Anyway, Chad's more typical roles are "a rapist that Michelle Pfeiffer falls in love with" and "a sexy serial killer that shacks up with Winona Ryder." So why is he wreaking havoc on Nick's little set? Let's just say that Mr. DiCillo is current enough to make sure the answer involves Quentin Tarantino.

Chad's antics are only part of the trouble that plagues Nick, whose black-and-white nightmare gives *Living in Oblivion* its opening salvo. In a half-hour sequence that Mr. DiCillo first intended as a self-contained short, an actress named Nicole (Catherine Keener, another *Johnny Suede* star) is forced to repeat the same scene with her "mother" over and over again, while mishaps ruin every take. There's nothing new about seeing a shot go fuzzy or a sound boom lurch comically into a close-up, but Mr. DiCillo turns the sheer accumulation of such screwups into something maddeningly funny.

He's helped enormously by Mr. Buscemi, an actor who ordinarily plays wide-eyed lunatics and whose edginess proves just right for this situation. Displaying endless patience and a touching, possibly misplaced optimism about his own artistry, Mr. Buscemi's Nick plays peacemaker despite all the internecine strains that plague his crew. It's achievement enough that Nick can handle Wolf (Dermot Mulroney), a sight-gag of a cameraman who wears beret, armband, black leather vest and a truckload of fake bravado. "I love the shot; hell, I *designed* it," he says of one scene.

Eminently reasonable as he verges on panic, Nick must also contend with Wanda (Danielle von Zernick), a cutthroat assistant director who sweetens noticeably when Chad appears; Cora (Rica Martens), an actress who's rather a mystery guest; a driver (Tom Jarmusch) loaded with free advice; and various crew members with plans to make their own films, perhaps with roles for either Nicole or Chad. As for those two, they become just well enough acquainted to turn their on-camera romance into a catastrophe. Among the many authentic lessons about filmmaking Mr. DiCillo has learned is that real-life love scenes have a way of turning troublesome on screen.

The film divides itself into three segments, the best of which is the central episode featuring Chad. For all his casual glad-handing ("LLLLobo!" he calls Wolf), Chad turns out to be a ruthless scene-stealer, sneakily outmaneuvering his director, cameraman and costar until he's forced to make the ultimate power play ("I'll pay for it myself!"). Mr. Le Gros is such an utter treat that when he makes his departure, the film never recovers from that loss.

The last third raises serious doubts about Nick's artistry as he stages a dream sequence involving Tito (Peter Dinklage), a dwarf in powder-blue formal dress. Tito can't get his scene right, perhaps because he resents being stereotyped. "Have you ever had a dream with a dwarf in it?" he asks Nick irritably. If Nick had a good answer for that, he might be making something better than *Living in Oblivion,* the hopeless film-within-a-film we see here.

As for Mr. DiCillo's own *Living in Oblivion,* it has the freshness and spontaneity that signal a labor of love. The subject matter may be narrow and in-jokey, but the finished film is broadened by infectious good humor, not to mention delightful ensemble acting that keeps its energy high. Inhabiting a tiny world that becomes seductively real, the performers display a shared sense of purpose as they convey the hair-raising perils of creative endeavor.

In a perfect coda, Mr. DiCillo shows just which longings each of his characters entertain. Whether they crave love, glory (an award "for the best film ever made by a human being"), or just lunch, all of them have somehow put their faith in filmmaking. And filmmaking this liberating may just answer their prayers.

—J.M., March 17, 1995

LOCAL HERO

Written and directed by Bill Forsyth: cinematographer. Chris Menges: edited by Micheal Bradsell: music by Mark Knopfler: production designer. Roger Murray-Leach: produced by David Puttnam: released by Warner Brothers. Running time: 111 minutes.

With: Burt Lancaster (Happer). Peter Riegert (Mac). Fulton Mackay (Ben). Denis Lawson (Urquhart). Norman Chancer (Moritz). Peter Capaldi (Oldsen). Rikki Fulton (Geddes) and Alex Norton (Watt).

Genuine fairy tales are rare; so is filmmaking that is thoroughly original in an unobtrusive way. Bill Forsyth's quirky, disarming *Local Hero* is both, and it's also proof that Mr. Forsyth's other feature film released here, *Gregory's Girl,* was more than a happy accident. The Glasgow-born Mr. Forsyth has put Scottish comedy on the map, for whatever that's worth. He has also developed a dryly whimsical style, very close to a deadpan at times, that allows the strangest events or personages to glide by almost unnoticed. *Local Hero* contains a mermaid, an enchanted village and a possibly magical rabbit. No undue fuss is made about any one of them.

Local Hero, which opens today at Cinema 1, doesn't begin on a very promising note. It starts in Houston, a place toward which Mr. Forsyth, who wrote and directed the film, has no outstandingly fresh attitude. The tale begins at the headquarters of gigantic Knox Oil, where it is learned—at a meeting in which everyone present has to whisper, because Felix Happer (Burt Lancaster), the board chairman, is snoozing—that the company plans to replace a charming little Scottish fishing village, called Ferness, with an oil refinery.

A Knox employee called Mac MacIntyre (Peter Riegert) is delegated to fly to Ferness to buy the place, and he is chosen because his name makes it sound as if he's well suited to the chore. MacIntyre isn't a Scot; he's the son of Hungarian immigrants who thought MacIntyre was an American name. That makes about as much sense as anything else that goes on here.

Once MacIntyre arrives in Scotland, odd things start to happen—nothing dramatic, nothing you can put your finger on, but undeniably strange. He and a traveling companion, a young Scottish employee of Knox named Danny Oldsen (Peter Capaldi), are en route to Ferness when their car hits a rabbit in a heavy fog. They stop the car in the middle of the road and sleep inside. The next morning, the fog is gone, the rabbit is sitting in the backseat, and the travelers are ready to proceed. But something indefinable has changed. It's as though they have entered into a dream.

Certainly the postcard-perfect town of Ferness has its delightfully dreamlike qualities. Every time Mac and Danny venture out of their inn, the same motorcyclist barrels by and nearly runs them down. The inn itself is managed by Gordon Urquhart (Denis Lawson), who also functions as the accountant next door, and who has a different personality to suit each job. (The accountant is unctuous, the innkeeper vaguely rude.) There is an omnipresent baby whose parents are never identified; a black African minister named Macpherson with an all-white congregation; a lone punk-rock groupie with a red-blue-and-green teased hairdo; and two beautiful women who probably function as muses, named Stella and Marina (Jennifer Black and Jenny Seagrove). Marina swims with exceptional grace. She has, as Danny notices but doesn't mention when he kisses her knee one afternoon, webbed feet.

Ferness casts its spell over Mac, who arrives there jealously guarding his battery-powered briefcase, and eventually becomes one of the place's more relaxed denizens. It ought to have a similar effect on the audience, and seduce the viewer just as gradually. The charm and humor of *Local Hero* are so very understated that they may seem elusive at first, but they are undeniably powerful.

The less Mr. Forsyth explains, the more appealingly odd the movie seems, and it manages to be open-ended but not annoyingly cryptic. Besides, even the occasional bits of information about the townspeople aren't very helpful. The more you find out about Ferness—why, say, the entire population of the village is seen sneaking out of the church as MacIntyre, who has come to buy the church, momentarily turns his back—the less you know.

The best thing that Mr. Forsyth does with actors is to induce them to behave as though nothing would surprise them. Everyone here has that air, particularly Mr. Riegert. His performance, which begins as a sendup of young corporate hotshots' demeanor, winds up as that of the movie's straightest straight man, the one who'll barely blink when someone else squirts lemon in his eye. Mr. Lancaster is less steadily present, appearing mostly at the film's beginning and at its end, but he brings with him sufficient authority when, say, he descends on Ferness out of the skies (via helicopter) and immediately begins ordering everyone around. Of course, Ferness isn't the sort of place where anyone takes orders terribly seriously.

Local Hero is a funny movie, but it's more apt to induce chuckles than knee-slapping. Like *Gregory's Girl,* it demonstrates Mr. Forsyth's uncanny ability for making an audience sense that something magical is going on, even if that something isn't easily explained.

—*J.M., February 17, 1983*

LOLA

Directed by Rainer Werner Fassbinder; written (in German, with English subtitles) by Peter Märthesheimer, Pea Fröhlich and Mr. Fassbinder; cinematographer, Xaver Schwarzenberger; edited by Juliane Lorenz; music by Peer Raben; art designer, Rolf Zehetbauer; produced by Horst Wendlandt; released by United Artists. Running time: 113 minutes.

With: Barbara Sukowa (Lola), Armin Mueller-Stahl (Von Bohm), Mario Adorf (Schuckert), Matthias Fuchs (Esslin), Helga Feddersen (Hettich), Karin Baal (Lola's Mother) and Ivan Desny (Wittich).

On the screen, before the opening credits of Rainer Werner Fassbinder's *Lola,* we see a black-and-white still photograph of Konrad Adenauer, Chancellor of West Germany from 1949 until 1963. He is caught in a position of awkward repose on a couch, half-sitting, half-lying, his head resting against his right hand as he strains to hear a reel-to-reel tape machine at his side.

The chancellor could be listening to Bach or Mozart, to some official transcriptions of one sort or another, or even to the contemporary music that we hear on the soundtrack. One thing is certain; he is not hearing the truth of what is going on in West Germany where, as Lola understands it, the free-enterprise system is running amok. The fat little bourgeois foxes are spoiling the vines in the fields, the buildings in the cities and everything else they can acquire through kickbacks, payoffs, fraud and, possibly, murder.

With this bold, swift, black-and-white image, which becomes partly obscured by the film's jazzy credits printed in lavender, cerise and yellow, does the still-astonishing Fassbinder begin *Lola,* one of the last films completed before his death in June at the age of thirty-six. Like *The Marriage of Maria Braun,* and almost the equal of that great film, *Lola* is a bitter, brisk, sometimes abruptly moving satire about the West German economic "miracle" of the fifties.

Lola, which opens today at the Lincoln Plaza Cinema 1, is also, after the fact, infinitely more sad than I would have thought possible. Here is the work not of someone who was on the point of burning himself out, as many of us interpreted his untimely death, but

571

of a major filmmaker in midcareer, at the peak of his form, refining his methods and chancing new ones in the ebullient manner of someone who has decades of work ahead of him.

The inspiration for the Fassbinder screenplay, written in collaboration with Peter Märthesheimer and Pea Fröhlich, is Josef von Sternberg's 1930 classic, *The Blue Angel,* in which Emil Jannings's inhibited old schoolteacher is lured to rack, ruin and madness by the siren-charms of Marlene Dietrich's sleazy cabaret singer. However, the similarities between the two films are nothing if not superficial.

The time of *Lola* is 1955, and the setting is a small German city where the politicians and businessmen, especially the city's leading building contractor, are busily and profitably "developing" all possible resources. Into their midst comes von Bohm (Armin Mueller-Stahl), the newly appointed building commissioner. The middle-aged von Bohm, well-born and handsome, stumps the crooked gang down at city hall as much by his elegant manners as by his cool, detached idealism.

At the city's most splendid cabaret-whorehouse, where the city fathers hang out after hours, Schuckert (Mario Adorf), the hustling building contractor, complains about the situation—with a good deal of awe—to Lola (Barbara Sukowa), the star performer at the cabaret, on stage and upstairs.

Lola, a yellow-haired beauty with the manner of a Marilyn Monroe without hangups, is Schuckert's mistress and mother of his illegitimate child. She is as ambitious as everyone else in town and is amused that Schuckert, whom she calls a pig and frequently means it, should be intimidated by von Bohm. She is also miffed that Schuckert should think that just because she is a whore she couldn't attract the interest of an aristocrat like von Bohm. She bets Schuckert some champagne that she can get von Bohm to kiss her hand in public.

Shortly after that, as von Bohm is participating in a local ceremony honoring the German Army, Lola drives up to the scene in a bright red roadster, gets out and, looking like a million American dollars in her couture clothes, extends a dainty, white-gloved hand to von Bohm, who kisses it.

One thing leads to another. Their courtship begins and is continued in out-of-the-way spots, Lola, of course, never revealing her profession or that her staunchly genteel mother is von Bohm's housekeeper.

Though *Lola* is told in the lean style of a political caricaturist—of someone more interested in exposing the rottenness of a system than in exploring the psychological complexities of character—the film is unexpectedly rich in the emotional details of the lives of von Bohm and especially Lola. She is genuinely attracted to von Bohm but never loses sight of her goal, which is to become one of "them," a member of the haute bourgeoisie. How she achieves this, and the effect it has on the sensitive but not silly von Bohm, are the film's major surprises.

Miss Sukowa, who can also be seen in Margarethe von Trotta's *Marianne and Julianne,* is a smashing new German actress, one who can be as funny and sweet and sexily abandoned as she is beautiful.

In the film's big "recognition" scene, when von Bohm comes into the cabaret to discover her real identity, Miss Sukowa's Lola does a riotous song-and-dance number that appears to be straight out of *Gilda.* Yet, minutes (in screen time) before, in an otherwise empty country chapel, she and von Bohm have sung a canon together in a scene of legitimate if mixed-up pathos.

Mr. Mueller-Stahl, Mr. Adorf and everyone else in the large cast, many of whom are new to Fassbinder films, are excellent. The film, though, remains the unmistakable work of its director.

One of the more striking aspects of *Lola* is Fassbinder's extraordinary use of color. Scenes are sometimes shot in the subtle ways of chiaroscuro and sometimes with the blatancy of a piece of Pop art, as when, near the end, von Bohm is always seen in an electric-blue light and Lola is drenched in pinky-lavender, even when they share the same film frame. I don't think this should be overanalyzed but, like Lola itself, enjoyed for the sheer, joyous effrontery of it.

—*V.C., August 4, 1982*

LOLA MONTES

Directed by Max Ophüls: written (in French, with English subtitles) by Mr. Ophüls, Jacques Natanson, Franz Geiger and Annette Wademant, based on the novel *La Vie Extraordinaire de Lola Montes* by Cecil Saint-Laurent; cinematographer, Christian Matras; edited by Madeleine Gug; music by Georges Auric; art designers, Jean d'Eaubonne and Willy Schatz; produced by Albert Caraco; released by Brandon Films. Running time: 110 minutes.

With: Martine Carol (Lola Montes), Peter Ustinov (Circus Master), Anton Walbrook (King of Bavaria), Ivan Desny (James), Will Quadflieg (Liszt) and Oskar Werner (Student).

This is the second time that the program director has selected Max Ophüls's last film, *Lola Montes*, for showing at the New York Film Festival. At the first festival in 1963, while the main event was being held at Philharmonic Hall, the 1955 movie was screened at the Museum of Modern Art as part of a series devoted to films that had been overlooked in American commercial release.

Last night *Lola Montes* finally made it to Philharmonic Hall. It is such an extraordinary movie, a movie-movie, in effect, that its repeat showing is worth the risks involved in the rather dubious precedent set. It is not only Ophüls's last film (he died in 1957), but it is also an eye-expanding summation of the lush, romantic style.

Ophüls makes the story of Lola Montes (Martine Carol), the successful nineteenth century courtesan (if only so-so Spanish fandango dancer), into a visually dazzling, ironic commentary on celebrity. It is set in the frame of a gaudy American circus where Lola is not the sideshow, but the main event, a sort of big time Evelyn Nesbitt who, in a series of opulent *tableaux vivants*, reenacts the high points of her life (principally, her love affairs) while she remembers the actual events. Thus, curiously, the carnival is real; the actual events are fantasy.

The late Miss Carol, with her hair dyed jet black, is a cold, stony-faced sphinx throughout, but I'm not sure this really detracts from the movie, which is really a tableau in itself. Ophüls did such flamboyant things with his CinemaScope color camera that the ripely romantic spell might have been broken by a more human presence.

A very young Peter Ustinov is fine as the ever-so-lightly malignant circus master and a very young

Oskar Werner is good as one of Lola's lovers, a student who spirits her out of Bavaria, which is in a state of revolution largely of her causing.

—*V.C., September 23, 1968*

LOLA

Directed by Stanley Kubrick; written by Vladimir Nabokov, based on his novel; cinematographer, Oswald Morris; edited by Anthony Harvey; music by Nelson Riddle; art designer, Bill Andrews; produced by James B. Harris; released by Metro-Goldwyn-Mayer. Black and white. Running time: 152 minutes.

With: James Mason (Humbert Humbert), Shelley Winters (Charlotte Haze), Peter Sellers (Clare Quilty), Sue Lyon (Lolita Haze), Marianne Stone (Vivian Darkbloom) and Diana Decker (Jean Farlow).

How did they ever make a movie of *Lolita?* The answer to that question, posed in the advertisements of the picture, which arrived at the Loew's State and the Murray Hill last night, is as simple as this. They didn't.

They made a movie from a script in which the characters have the same names as the characters in the book, the plot bears a resemblance to the original and some of the incidents are vaguely similar. But the *Lolita* that Vladimir Nabokov wrote as a novel and the *Lolita* he wrote to be a film, directed by Stanley Kubrick, are two conspicuously different things.

In the first place, the character of Lolita, the perversely precocious child who had such effect on the libido of the middle-aged hero in the book, is not a child in the movie. She looks to be a good seventeen years old, possessed of a striking figure and a devilishly haughty teenage air. The distinction is fine, we will grant you, but she is definitely not a "nymphet." As played by Sue Lyon, a newcomer, she reminds one of Carroll Baker's *Baby Doll*.

Right away, this removes the factor of perverted desire that is in the book and renders the passion of the hero more normal and understandable. It also renders the drama more in line with others we have seen.

Older men have often pined for younger females. This is nothing new on the screen.

Further, the structure and the climate of the movie are not the same as those of the book. The movie starts with the melodramatic incident that brings the novel to a close, then flashes back to the beginning and tells its story in a decreasingly humorous vein. Thus the viewer is warned by this weird preface that the ending is going to be grim. The device tends to shade the early satire and pulls the punch from Mr. Nabokov's curious tale.

But once this is said about the movie—and once the reader has been advised not to expect the distractingly sultry climate and sardonic mischievousness of the book—it must be said that Mr. Kubrick has got a lot of fun and frolic in his film. He has also got a bit of pathos and irony toward the end. Unfortunately, there are some strange confusions of style and mood as it moves along.

The best part comes early in the picture when Mr. Nabokov and Mr. Kubrick are making sport of their hero's bug-eyed infatuation with Lolita and his artful circumvention of her mother. Here the satire is somewhat gross but booming, assisted greatly by a wonderfully deft job of comical fumbling by Shelley Winters, who makes the mother a sublimely silly sort. James Mason as the gulping, amorous hero and Peter Sellers as a sly, predacious cad floating around the edges are at their best in this part of the film.

The switch to a more provocative passage or phase is introduced by a sharp paradoxical juxtaposition of humorous and ghoulish images (to which Mr. Kubrick appears partial), which starts the odd romance of man and girl. And from this, again, we are taken through a hauntingly poignant hospital scene, played brilliantly by Mr. Mason, into the solemn, tedious finish of the tale.

The changes are disconcerting, and Mr. Kubrick inclines to dwell too long over scenes that have slight purpose, such as scenes in which Mr. Sellers does various comical impersonations as the sneaky villain who dogs Mr. Mason's trail. But, for all that, the picture has a rare power, a garbled but often moving push toward an offbeat communication. And Miss Lyon makes a shallow, heartless girl. This is not the novel *Lolita,* but it is a provocative sort of film.

—B.C., June 14, 1962

LONE STAR

Written, directed and edited by John Sayles; director of photography, Stuart Dryburgh; music by Mason Daring; production designer, Dan Bishop; produced by R. Paul Miller and Maggie Renzi; released by Castle Rock Entertainment. Running time: 138 minutes.

With: Chris Cooper (Sam Deeds), Elizabeth Peña (Pilar), Miriam Colon (Mercedes Cruz), Matthew McConaughey (Buddy Deeds), Kris Kristofferson (Charley Wade), Clifton James (Mayor Hollis Pogue), Frances McDormand (Bunny), Ron Canada (Otis Payne), Joe Morton (Delmore Payne), Eddie Robinson (Chet Payne), Gabriel Casseus (Young Otis) and Beatrice Winde (Minnie Bledsoe).

The great, stirring epic *Lone Star* stands as a peak in the career of John Sayles, who already has such admirably serious films to his credit. Long admired for the independence and quiet intelligence of his work, Mr. Sayles this time delivers a vibrant history lesson about a Texas border town.

Gratifyingly complex and beautifully told, this tale explores a huge array of cultural, racial, economic and familial tensions. In the process, it also sustains strong characters, deep emotions and clear dramatic force. Plain and forthright as it looks, *Lone Star* winds up with a scope and overview rarely attempted in American films today, which makes its success that much more exemplary. Every moment of the film, from the quiet foreshadowing of its first scene to a magnificently apt ending, is utterly right.

Sometimes decent but didactic in his earlier work (including *Matewan, Eight Men Out, Passion Fish,* and *The Secret of Roan Inish*), Mr. Sayles this time displays nothing but soft-spoken grace. And he handles this film's dozens of significant characters and the many interwoven strands of its story line with ease. As writer, director and editor of *Lone Star* (the fluid editing is a particular asset, letting the story glide seamlessly between past and present), he assures the viewer that this film's many elements will converge in ways that are meaningful and moving. Indeed, *Lone Star* exists so far outside the province of slam-bang summer movies that it seems part of a different medium and a different world.

The place is Frontera, Texas, a sleepy little town on the Rio Grande. And the film's first sight is that of two army officers cataloguing fauna in the nearby desert. ("You live in a place, you should know something about it," one of them says.) In the process, they unearth what are probably the remains of Charley Wade (Kris Kristofferson), who in 1957 was the town's bullying sheriff. In the present day, the crime will be investigated by Sheriff Sam Deeds (Chris Cooper), whose father, Buddy (Matthew McConaughey), was Charley Wade's deputy and is now the prime suspect in Charley's murder.

This crime story, while well told, serves *Lone Star* more as pretext than plot. Sending Sam Deeds off to explore the past, the film also examines Sam's troubled memories of life in his father's shadow and looks at the Frontera where Buddy once wielded great power, especially over its black and Hispanic citizens. Drawn into this exploration are whole families of other characters, and their pasts are tied to Buddy Deeds in ways that are made clear by the film's stunning denouement. In each of these stories, parents and children display stubborn, warring ways of looking at the past.

So Delmore (Joe Morton), the rigid black colonel newly put in charge of the local army base, is estranged from Otis (Ron Canada), who runs the only local bar where black soldiers feel welcome. Del's attitude is not softened by the fact that Otis happens to be his father, nor is he able to behave less rigidly with Chet (Eddie Robinson), his own son.

As the film moves smoothly among dozens of characters, in a style Mr. Sayles also used somewhat more stiffly in *City of Hope,* the viewer also meets Pilar (Elizabeth Peña), Chet's history teacher.

"What are we seeing here, Chet?" she asks sternly, finding her student more interested in drawing cartoons than in studying Texas's violent past. "Uh, everybody's killing everybody else," Chet answers hastily. Pilar can hardly accuse him of missing the point.

It happens that Pilar, as Mr. Sayles gradually lets the audience know, is Sam Deeds's first love, and that as teenagers they were kept apart by both Buddy Deeds and Mercedes Cruz (Miriam Colon), Pilar's stern, prosperous mother. Shades of the past color the

film's portrait of Mercedes as well as its long view of Sam and Pilar, who are able to rekindle their romance with surprising passion. It's worth mentioning that Mr. Sayles films a startlingly tender bedroom scene between these two without nudity or graphic sex and without failing to communicate that they are deeply in love.

In Sam and Pilar, *Lone Star* finds not only a romance, but also an embodiment for its central ideas: about crossing borders, challenging the past, escaping the burden of history. These themes echo everywhere in a film that eloquently weaves together the multifaceted life of Frontera and grasps the importance of race or privilege or politics in every transaction.

From a parents' meeting at school to negotiations over the town's new jail to Charley Wade's ruthless bullying of local minorities, the film effortlessly incorporates a broad political awareness into its drama. One of its most subtly spellbinding scenes finds Del interrogating a young black private over her drug use, and finding his own view of the army changed by a single conversation.

This long, spare, contemplatively paced film, scored with a wide range of musical styles and given a sunbaked clarity by Stuart Dryburgh's cinematography, is loaded with brief, meaningful encounters like that one. And it features a great deal of fine, thoughtful acting, which can always be counted on in a film by Mr. Sayles. Though none of the actors are given much screen time, a remarkable number of them create fully formed characters in only a few scenes.

Mr. Kristofferson does a superb, unflinching job as the film's personification of racist evil; Mr. Canada and Clifton James (as the mayor) capture the tensions between Frontera's black and white characters as well as a certain brotherhood under the skin. Mr. Morton and Ms. Colon both illustrate the high price of repressing one's true nature, though nobody here has the two-dimensional nature of a symbolic figure. All the film's characters are flesh and blood.

Mr. Cooper brings grit and dignity to the film's pivotal role, perfectly in keeping with the film's tacit style. The sultry Ms. Peña gives an especially vivid performance as the character who is most unsettled by shadows of the past. The film is greatly helped by the fact that neither of these two looks or acts like a movie star and that they blend effortlessly into the texture of small-town life. *Lone Star* does glimpse flashes of Hollywood magnetism in Mr. McConaughey, who makes a riveting impression even though he appears only briefly. Buddy Deeds is meant to be feared and imagined more than he is seen.

Also outstanding are Gabriel Casseus playing Otis as a proud young black man in 1957, when it was clearly dangerous to behave that way, and Frances McDormand as Sam's jumpy, overmedicated ex-wife. Tiny roles are also memorably etched, as in the brief appearance by Beatrice Winde as the widow of a principal in a murder case, an old lady busily playing a Game Boy. Sam introduces himself politely, but she remembers Buddy too well to resist a wisecrack: "Sheriff Deeds is dead, honey. You just Sheriff Junior."

Lone Star is about watching a whole town, and perhaps a whole society, emerging from such long shadows.
—*J.M., June 21, 1996*

THE LONELINESS OF THE LONG DISTANCE RUNNER

Produced and directed by Tony Richardson: written by Alan Sillitoe, based on his story: cinematographer. Walter Lassally: edited by Anthony Gibbs: music by John Addison: art designer. Ted Marshall: released by Continental Distributing. Black and white. Running time: 104 minutes.

With: Michael Redgrave (Governor Warden). Tom Courtenay (Colin Smith). Avis Bunnage (Mrs. Smith). Peter Madden (Mr. Smith). James Bolam (Mike). Julia Foster (Gladys). Topsy Jane (Audrey) and Dervis Ward (Detective).

With a title as odd and bewitching as that of the new British film *The Loneliness of the Long Distance Runner,* which opened last night at the Baronet Theater, it is a bit of a letdown to find another go-round with an angry young man.

But he's an angry young man with a difference, this surly, skinny lad, whom we first meet as he is being trucked off to a Borstal reform school out of a tawdry Nottingham home. He is strangely without resolution, ambition or even hope. He is simply a heedless social rebel. And he is as much so at the end of the picture as he is when it begins.

Indeed, if anything, he is more so—more stoked up with anger and defiance at the reasonable efforts of the reformers to get him to be good and conform. The governor of the school has urged him to develop himself in the cross-country run so he can represent the institution in an unprecedented track meet with a swanky school. Indeed, the governor has suggested that if he works hard and trains himself well, he may some day represent England in the Olympic Games.

But what does this truculent youngster do when the race is run—the race for which he has so sternly, stoically and solitarily trained? He stops a hundred yards from the finish, when he is comfortably ahead, and lets all the other runners beat him.

That's how defiant he is.

Precisely what is proved by this conclusion that Alan Sillitoe has given to the film (and originally gave to his short story, on which his script is based) is left to the startled viewer to analyze. But Mr. Sillitoe and the director, Tony Richardson, have thrown out a few general clues.

They have gone into clear and vivid details about the depressing life of their boy, and they have laced these into the sequence of the drama in a most artful way as his free-flowing recollections while he is out on lonely morning training runs.

They have showed his disgust with his mother after his working-class father died and she squandered the bit of insurance a crass employer paid. They have showed his pitiful endeavors to find some happiness with a chum and a couple of girls, and then described his spontaneous impulse to rob a bakery.

In all these strongly pictured details, sympathy is directed to the boy, who is played with extraordinary sharpness and nervous energy by Tom Courtenay.

On the other hand, they have managed in a very creditable but clearly angled way to expose the masters of the reform school as sadists, incompetents, or snobs. The governor, played by Michael Redgrave, is a tweedy traditionalist impressed by the opportunity to play games with a starchier class. The school psychiatrist (Alex McGowan) is a fumbling zealot for the psychological test and the "phys ed" instructor (Joe Robinson) is a bullnecked brute. Other men at the penal institution are realistically tough.

So if one assumes from this picture that its curious conclusion proves the hero is grandly independent in his contempt for society, one may be close to the thesis of Mr. Sillitoe. His heart—or the heart of the picture—does warm most fondly to the boy.

While this show of compassion may not sit comfortably with those who distrust social agitation and too easy sympathy, it must be said that a splendid presentation is made by Mr. Richardson. His film has a vivid, compelling air of reality, an attractive compression of details, and an exciting cinematic flow. He has the all-seeing camera instinct of the new British "documentary" school, which overlays ugliness of background with foreground beauty of character and poetry.

Avis Bunnage is excellent as the mother—hard and cold yet pathetic and sad—and many others convey convincing slum types in this angry, disquieting film. Unfortunately, the crude midland accents are hard to understand. The antagonism toward British institutions appears extended even to the British tongue.

—B.C., October 9, 1962

LONG DAY'S JOURNEY INTO NIGHT

Directed by Sidney Lumet: written by Mr. Lumet, based on the play by Eugene O'Neill: cinematographer, Boris Kaufman: edited by Ralph Rosenblum: music by André Previn: production designer, Richard Sylbert: produced by Ely Landau and Jack J. Dreyfus Jr., released by Embassy Films. Black and white. Running time: 174 minutes.

With: Katharine Hepburn (Mary Tyrone), Ralph Richardson (James Tyrone Sr.), Jason Robards, Jr. (James Tyrone Jr.), Dean Stockwell (Edmund Tyrone) and Jeanne Barr (Cathleen).

Regardless how much torment of troubled souls is potentially packed into the dense and combustible words of Eugene O'Neill's *Long Day's Journey Into Night,* the final test of this great drama is in how it is presented and played. The actors and, behind them, the director, are the fallible factors.

Scarcely could this be demonstrated more impressively than it is in the generally stunning motion picture rendering of it that was given its world premiere last night in the new Loew's Tower East at Third Avenue and 72d Street.

More than the pouring forth of language is an essential here, more than the sharply apt projection of expressions and attitudes. These are standard requirements of a proper performance on the stage.

But now comes the added requirement of fitting the play to the screen, confining its almost-three-hour action in the physical bounds of one set, obtaining cinematic momentum with nothing more than the clash of characters. For the producers of the film have firmly held to the letter and limits of the play.

Except that the taut and testy Tyrones—father, mother, and two adult sons—are initially introduced in a family wrangle on the lawn of their Connecticut summer home, the entire evolution of this small wrangle—which develops into an exposé and a shattering clash of all the skeletons in their closets and continues on into the depths of night—is played in the stuffy confines of the first floor of the house.

Yet, cloistered in these confines and bound to every long scene in the script (some scenes, if you'll pardon the mention, are overlong on the stage), the actors expound vast ire and anguish in dizzying bursts of voice and mood. Under the direction of Sidney Lumet, they charge the place with electricity.

That is, on the whole they do so. They develop an overall sense of deep disquiet within the passionate individuals and an acrid air of smoldering savagery. But just as the O'Neill script is marked by sharp rises and falls of the spirits and moods of his volatile people, close reflections of his own family, the performances of the actors are marked by unevenness.

Most controlled and magnificent is Ralph Richardson in the devastating role of the aging father and matinee idol. His explicit awareness and command of the fatal ambivalence of this old rascal, his voluminous, flowing sentiment, and his terrible, corroding canker of pride and insecurity are brilliantly drawn. The performance reaches an absolute peak in the long scene in which he tells his younger son of the glories and satisfactions of his youth.

Mr. Richardson makes, beyond question, the most tragic figure on the screen.

Katharine Hepburn is tricky and uneven in the difficult role of the wife and mother in this divided family—probably because she has too much to do. In the moments of deepest anguish, she is vibrant with hot and tragic truth, an eloquent representation of a lovely woman brought to feeble, helpless ruin. But she is put to so much repetition in the first hour or so of the film, in hinting at the ultimate revelation that narcotics have her hooked, that she strains her own gifts of airy acting and the patience of workaday folks.

A little less of Miss Hepburn would help the film.

On the other hand, Jason Robards Jr. could give it a little more—at the start, anyhow. His performance and his character do not take form until the thundering scene with his brother, when he drunkenly rips the kid apart. Then he suddenly bursts like a volcano with the hot lava in the character.

Dean Stockwell, as the kid brother, is, alas, a minus quantity—a feeble representation of a restless, consumptive youth. He is out of his class with the others. What a shame that he has to come on and try to express his poetic nature right after Mr. Richardson has played his biggest scene!

Jeanne Barr counterpoints Miss Hepburn's maundering rather nicely in one scene as a maid.

One might wish that the action were more mobile, that Mr. Lumet had been able to use his camera to a lot more purpose, such as he does in one deeply touching shot where he follows the aging Tyrone down a long hall and comes upon him alone in the dining room. One might wish, too, that the bits of mood music that are heard from time to time did not startle one with the impression that they were coming from someone playing a piano in another room.

But these are marginal observations. For what they have set out to do, Mr. Lumet and the producer, Ely Landau, have given us a fine, fair picture of a tough and maybe tedious O'Neill play.

—B.C., October 10, 1962

THE LONG GOODBYE

Directed by Robert Altman: written by Leigh Brackett. based on the novel by Raymond Chandler: director of photography. Vilmos Zsigmond: edited by Lou Lombardo: music by John Williams: produced by Jerry Bick: released by United Artists. Running time: 112 minutes.

With: Elliott Gould (Philip Marlowe). Nina van Pallandt (Eileen Wade). Sterling Hayden (Roger Wade). Mark Rydell (Marty Augustine) and Henry Gibson (Dr. Verringer).

In *The Long Goodbye,* Robert Altman, a brilliant director whose films sometimes seem like death wishes (*Brewster McCloud*), attempts the impossible and pulls it off.

Using a screenplay by Leigh Brackett, freely adapted from Raymond Chandler's 1953 novel, he has successfully transported Philip Marlowe, Chandler's private eye whose roots are in the depressed, black-and-white 1930's, to the overprivileged, full-color seventies in the person of Elliott Gould, who is nothing if not a child of our time.

The film, which opened yesterday at the Trans-Lux East, is Altman's most entertaining, most richly complex film since *M*A*S*H* and *McCabe* and *Mrs. Miller.* It's so good that I don't know where to begin describing it. Perhaps at the beginning:

The nighttime view from a hillside high above Los Angeles is great, but inside the apartment you feel as if you're at the bottom of a well. It looks as if it had been furnished by San Quentin. There are smudges on the wall next to the bed where Philip Marlowe sleeps fully clothed and in desperate need of a shave.

A large, pushy yellow cat meows for something to eat, awakening Marlowe, who displays a cranky sort of affection for an animal that doesn't deserve it. When Marlowe tries to interest the cat in a plate of old cottage cheese, unconvincingly updated with a raw egg, the cat gives him a look that ought to have stuck at least four inches out of his back.

There is nothing for Marlowe to do but go to the supermarket to buy some canned cat food, even though it's three A.M. by the clock and in his soul.

It's the beginning of a crucial time for this particular Philip Marlowe, who, in spite of a lot of evidence to the contrary, persists in believing that not all relationships need be opportunistic or squalid.

When Marlowe returns from the supermarket, he meticulously pastes the label from a can of the cat's favorite brand over a substitute, but the cat is not fooled. It walks off, furious. A minute later Terry Lennox (Jim Bouton), an old friend of Marlowe's, shows up and asks Marlowe to drive him to the Mexican border. Terry, a part-time hood and full-time pretty boy, explains that someone has murdered his wife and the cops certainly won't accept his innocence. Marlowe does.

Almost immediately Marlowe is arrested by the police as an accessory to murder, roughed up by the associates of the syndicate boss (Mark Rydell), who suspects Marlowe of stealing $350,000, and invited to find the drunken novelist-husband (Sterling Hayden) of a tall, beautiful self-assured blonde (Nina van Pallandt), who looks like the promises made in a Coppertone ad.

Curiously enough, Gould's Marlowe, lonely, usually shabby, with a wit that is less often turned outward than inward onto himself, does not seem an anachronism in the world of contemporary freaks. That was the gnawing problem with Paul Newman, superman tough in the screen adaptation of Ross MacDonald's *Harper,* and the fatal flaw in *Marlowe,* Paul Bogart's adaptation of Chandler's *The Little Sister,* in which James Garner played it for laughs.

Gould's Marlowe is entirely different from Humphrey Bogart's (*The Big Sleep*) and Dick Powell's (*Farewell, My Lovely* and the 1954 TV adaptation of *The Long Goodbye*). Gould's Marlowe is not especially tough. He's a bright, conscientious but rather solemn nut, a guy who hopes for the best but expects the worst, having experienced the social upheavals, the assassinations, and the undeclared war of the sixties.

Altman, Miss Brackett (who collaborated with William Faulkner on the script for *The Big Sleep*), and Gould have had the courage to create an original character and almost an original story that, by being original, does more to honor Chandler's skills than would any attempt to make a forties movie today.

There are lots of eloquent references to Chandler in Altman's method, which is to pack the screen with more bizarre visual and aural detail than can be easily taken in at one sitting. There are also references in the appreciation of California decor, luxurious as well as tacky, and in the throwaway lines and uniformly excellent characterizations, including two by actors who will surprise you, Nina van Pallandt and Jim Bouton.

Don't be misled by the ads, *The Long Goodbye* is not a put-on. It's great fun and it's funny, but it's a serious, unique work.

—*V.C., October 29, 1973*

THE LONG GOOD FRIDAY

Directed by John Mackenzie; written by Barrie Keeffe; director of photography. Phil Meheux; edited by Mike Taylor; produced by Barry Hanson; released by Embassy Pictures. Running time: 114 minutes.

With: Bob Hoskins (Harold). Helen Mirren (Victoria). Dave King (Parky). Bryan Marshall (Harris). Derek Thompson (Jeff). Eddie Constantine (Charlie). Paul Freeman (Colin). Leo Dolan (Phil). Kevin McNally (Irish Youth). Patti Love (Carol). P. H. Moriarty (Razors). Ruby Head (Harold's Mother). Charles Cork (Eric). Olivier Pierre (Chef). Pierce Brosnan (First Irishman). Daragh O'Malley (2nd Irishman). Karl Howman (David Brian Hall (Alan). Alan Ford (Jack). Dave Ould (Don). Paul Kember (Ginger). Bill Moody (Boston) and Alan Devlin (Priest).

Don't be flustered by the beginning of *The Long Good Friday,* the rough-edged British gangster film that opens today at the Baronet. If you can't make sense of the first scenes, you won't be alone. John Mackenzie, the film's director, has plenty of flair for etching disturbing portraits of rich, modern-day London hoodlums operating in a 30's Chicago style. When one character in the film invokes the St. Valentine's Day Massacre, the reference is a very fitting one. Though its plot contains much that's new, *The Long Good Friday* is a swift, sharp-edged gangster story in a classic mold.

For all his skill with action and atmosphere, Mr. Mackenzie isn't nearly as good at holding the plot together, or even at keeping the audience abreast of what's going on. Even after its intrigue has been explained, the movie has no shortage of loose ends. But that isn't the major drawback it sounds like. *The Long Good Friday* has a lot to recommend it, chiefly in the fine performances of Bob Hoskins, as an underworld kingpin, and Helen Mirren as his very shrewd, curiously admirable partner in crime.

Though the film starts by introducing 15 characters in as many minutes, it soon becomes centered on Harold Shand, a blunt, squarely built mobster with a haircut suggesting Caesar's. He spends much of his time, rather incongruously, on a yacht in the Thames. Harold has a big real-estate deal brewing with an American Mafia counterpart (Eddie Constantine), but he's also got trouble. On the Friday of the title, somebody tries to bomb a couple of his clubs and successfully murders two of his men. The film sketches an intimate, memorable portrait of Harold as it follows his search to find out who his enemy may be.

Harold emerges as an unexpectedly captivating man, even in a movie that concentrates on his savagery. In a scene that shows him rounding up all possible suspects and hanging them, upside-down from meat hooks to interrogate them, Harold still maintains his aplomb. Mr. Hoskins makes him as clever and understandable as he is abhorrent. Not even a scene in which Harold suddenly attacks one of his underlings with a bottle costs him the audience's sympathy. The outburst is vicious and frightening, but it's as much of a shock to Harold as it is to the viewer.

Mr. Mackenzie has directed for television, and there are traces of that in his technique. The film is paced methodically, with its action in intervals, as much to prod the audience's attention as to advance the story. He also seems to indulge in a fair amount of obfuscation for obfuscation's sake; there are plenty of plot points that could have been better handled straightforwardly than they have been in Mr. Mackenzie's jumbled, stylized manner.

But he is very clearly a director of energy and originality, and he makes this a surprising, suspenseful drama. *The Long Good Friday* charts a perilous course through a world of powerful people, ghastly acts of vengeance and ominously shifting fortunes.

—J.M., April 2, 1982

THE LONG VOYAGE HOME

Directed by John Ford; written by Dudley Nichols, based on the plays *The Moon of the Caribbees, In the Zone, Bound East for Cardiff* and *The Long Voyage Home* by Eugene O'Neill; cinematographer, Gregg Toland; edited by Sherman Todd; music by Richard Hageman; art designer, James Basevi; produced by Walter Wanger; released by United Artists. Black and white. Running time: 105 minutes.

With: John Wayne (Ole Olsen), Thomas Mitchell (Aloysius Driscoll), Ian Hunter (Smitty), Barry Fitzgerald (Cocky), Wilfrid Lawson (Captain), Mildred Natwick (Freda), John Qualen (Axel Swanson) and Ward Bond (Yank Joe Sawyer).

Out of Eugene O'Neill's four short plays of the sea, and under the haunting title of one, *The Long Voyage Home,* John Ford has truly fashioned a modern Odyssey—a stark and tough-fibered motion picture which tells with lean economy the never-ending story of man's wanderings over the waters of the world in search of peace for his soul. It is not a tranquilizing film, this one which Walter Wanger presented at the Rivoli Theatre last night; it is harsh and relentless and only briefly compassionate in its revelation of man's pathetic shortcomings. But it is one of the most honest pictures ever placed upon the screen; it gives a penetrating glimpse into the hearts of little men and, because it shows that out of human weakness there proceeds some nobility, it is far more gratifying than the fanciest hero-worshiping fare.

Mr. Ford has ever been noted for his muscular realism on the screen, for the rich and authentic flavor with which he imbues his films. And in *The Long Voyage Home* he has had an exceptional opportunity to exercise not only his talents but also his avowed affections. For the story is that of the tough crew of the British tramp freighter *Glencairn* on a present-day voyage from the West Indies, via an American port, to London in a rusty old tub loaded deep with highly explosive ammunition. And the loose and unresolved plot concerns the characters and reactions of the men in the face of lurking danger and their various bewildered impulses. Given a theme of this sort, Mr. Ford is a man inspired.

Although the O'Neill plays were written separately and with only the same characters and locale to give them unity, Mr. Ford and his scenarist, Dudley Nichols, have pulled them together handsomely. From *The Moon of the Caribbees* they have taken their departure—the departure of the S.S. *Glencairn* and its lusty, rum-soaking crew—and proceeded on through the dramatic incidents contained in *Bound East for Cardiff, In the Zone,* and, eventually, the poignant episode of frustration presented in *The Long Voyage Home.* If the film does lack a conventional dramatic pattern, it is mainly because of this episodic construction. And this lack may be disturbing to some.

But the very essence of the theme lies exactly in its inconclusiveness, in deliberate fumbling onward toward a goal which is never reached, toward a peace which is never attained. Yank, the iron-muscled pal of the Irishman, Driscoll, dies at sea, but even in death he dreams of the land. Smitty, the outcast aristocrat, goes to his doom with a defiant gesture at the world which has overpowered him. Driscoll is lost to another ship, and the remaining members of the *Glencairn*'s crew—with the exception of Olson, who does go home—creep back to sea after a spree in London. In the end, they are Mother Carey's chickens, and the only home they can ever know is the restless deep.

And this is the endless story which Mr. Ford has told with magnificent sharpness. His ship is really made of iron and his actors are really tough. Thomas Mitchell as the roaring, truculent Driscoll; Barry Fitzgerald as the viperish steward, Cocky; John Wayne as the gentle, powerful Olson; Ian Hunter as Smitty, the heartsick; and Wilfred Lawson, Ward Bond, and all the rest are truly excellent. Suffice it to say that women only appear briefly in this odyssey, and then exclusively as agents of evil. For *The Long Voyage Home* is a story of men, of eternal suffering in a perilous trade, of life and tragic death in the dirty, heroic little cargo boats that sail the wet seas 'round.

— B.C., October 9, 1940

THE LONGEST DAY

Directed by Ken Annakin, Andrew Marton and Bernhard Wicki; written (in English and German, with English subtitles) by Cornelius Ryan, based on his book, with additional episodes by Romain Gary, James Jones, David Pursall and Jack Seddon; cinematographers, Jean Bourgoin, Henri Persin, Walter Wottitz and Guy Tabary; edited by Samuel E. Beetley; music by Maurice Jarre; art designers, Ted Haworth, Leon Barsacq and Vincent Korda; produced by Darryl F. Zanuck; released by Twentieth Century Fox. Black and white. Running time: 180 minutes.

With: John Wayne (Lieutenant Colonel Benjamin Vandervoort), Robert Mitchum (Brigadier General Norman Cota), Richard Todd (Major John Howard), Red Buttons (Private John Steele), Richard Beymer (Private Dutch Schultz), Robert Ryan (Brigadier General James M. Gavin), Mel Ferrer (Major General Robert Haines), Henry Fonda (Brigadier General Theodore Roosevelt), Paul Anka, Fabian, Tommy Sands, Robert Wagner (American Rangers), Eddie Albert (Colonel Tom Newton), Sean Connery (Private Flanagan), Ray Danton (Captain Frank), Steve Forrest (Captain Harding), Gerd Froebe (Sergeant Kaffeklatsch), Leo Genn (Brigadier General Parker), Henry Grace (General Dwight D. Eisenhower), Jeffrey Hunter (Sergeant Fuller), Alexander Knox (Major General Walter Bedell Smith), Roddy McDowall (Private Morris), Sal Mineo (Private Martini), Edmond O'Brien (General Raymond O. Barton), Ron Randell (Joe Williams), Rod Steiger (Destroyer Commander), Tom Tryon (Lieutenant Wilson), Stuart Whitman (Lieutenant Sheen), Richard Burton (Royal Air Force Pilot), John Gregson (British Padre), Peter Lawford (Lord Lovat), Kenneth More (Captain Colin Maud), Christian Marquand (Commander Philippe Kieffer), Hans Christian Blech (Major Werner Pluskat), Curt Jurgens (Major General Gunther Blumentritt), Paul Hartmann (Field Marshal Gerd von Rundstedt) and Werner Hinz (Field Marshal Erwin Rommel).

Just as Cornelius Ryan put into vivid words the sweeping drama of the Normandy invasion in his book, *The Longest Day*, Darryl F. Zanuck and a large team of associates have made that drama surge again upon the screen in a three-hour film, replete with "name" performers, which opened at the Warner Theater last night.

All of the massive organization of that most salient invasion of World War II, all the hardship and bloodiness of it, all the courage and sacrifice involved, are strongly and stalwartly suggested in the mighty mosaic of episodes and battle-action details that are packed into this film.

From the climactic concentration of Allied forces along the English coast, ready to launch the invasion in early June, 1944, to a few sample incidents at nightfall on D-Day, June 6, the immensity and sweep of the great battle to crack the Nazis' hold on France are portrayed.

There's the highly suspenseful moment when General Eisenhower has to make the fateful decision as to whether the invasion will go or have to be postponed. There's the nervousness and impatience of officers waiting the word, the restlessness and time-killing pastimes of soldiers poised to go.

And then there's the breathless excitement of the

Pathfinders being sent by air to parachute into Normandy at midnight to light the way for the following paratroops; the tension and terror of the airborne strike of Canadians to secure the critical Orne River bridge; the violence and confusion of the experiences of elements of the American 82d and 101st Airborne Division before dawn around Ste.-Mère-Église.

As daylight comes, there is the thunder of the first landing craft piling in on the fortress-fringed Normandy beaches, the bloody battles along the fire-raked strands of the Utah and Omaha sectors, fought by the Americans, and the assaults upon Sword, June, and Gold by the British and Canadians. There's the smashing fight of French commandos to capture the seaside town of Ouistreham and the terrible climb by American Rangers up the sheer cliffs of Point-du-Hoc. And there's a lot about French Resistance people fighting behind the main assaults.

Nor are the Germans neglected. Indeed, the picture begins with the cameras glimpsing their activities and anxieties behind the Atlantic Wall. Field Marshal Rommel is here to state the tension of German uncertainty and to cue in the picture's main title with his famous prediction as to "the longest day." And then, all the way through, the bickerings and bunglings of the German generals, from von Rundstedt down, are interlarded, historically and dramatically.

With Spartan restraint, Mr. Zanuck and the several people who worked on the script (including Mr. Ryan) and the fellows who helped direct resisted the possible temptation to put more into this film than a sweeping cross section of the battle—or battles—to land in Normandy. They avoided any inclination to go behind the scenes, to indulge in incidental flashbacks, or establish characters. Thus all that one sees in the three hours are the fighting men (and a few women) and the things they do in the course of one deadly, terrifying, and most momentous day.

No character stands out particularly as more significant or heroic than anyone else. John Wayne is notably rugged as Colonel Vandervoort, the dogged officer of the 82d who hobbled through D-Day on a broken ankle, using a rifle as a crutch. Robert Mitchum is tough as General Cota, who led his men of the 29th Division onto Omaha Beach and then off it after a day of deadly pounding by forcing a breach of the Vierville roadblock.

Red Buttons is very effective as paratrooper John Steele, who watched the pitiful slaughter of many of his buddies in the town square of Ste.-Mère-Église while hanging from the church steeple in the harness of his parachute. Richard Beymer does well as a young soldier who wanders dazedly through the whole thing, never connecting with his outfit and never firing a shot. And dozens of other actors are convincing (and identifiable) in roles that call for infrequent appearances (or only single shots) in the film.

Intelligently, the picture has been photographed in black-and-white to give a virtual newsreel authenticity to the vivid, realistic battle scenes. And the illusory aspect of reality has been achieved in other respects, notably in the use of their own languages by the Germans and the French, with English subtitles appended to translate what they say.

The total effect of the picture is that of a huge documentary report, adorned and colored by personal details that are thrilling, amusing, ironic, sad. It makes no conclusive observation, other than the obvious one that war is hell and that D-Day was a gallant, costly triumph for the Allied forces, not for any one man.

It is hard to think of a picture, aimed and constructed as this one was, doing any more or any better or leaving one feeling any more exposed to the horror of war than this one does.

—B.C., October 5, 1962

LOOK BACK IN ANGER

Directed by Tony Richardson; written by Nigel Kneale, based on the play by John Osborne; cinematographer, Oswald Morris; edited by Richard Best; music by Chris Barber; art designer, Peter Glazier; produced by Harry Saltzman; released by Warner Brothers. Black and white. Running time: 115 minutes.

With: Richard Burton (Jimmy Porter), Claire Bloom (Helena Charles), Mary Ure (Alison Porter), Edith Evans (Mrs. Tanner), Gary Raymond (Cliff Lewis), Glen Byam Shaw (Colonel Redfern), Phyllis Neilson-Terry (Mrs. Redfern) and Donald Pleasence (Hurst).

The fury and hate that John Osborne was able to pack into a flow of violent words in his stage play, *Look Back in Anger,* are not only matched but also documented in the film that the original stage director, Tony Richardson, has made from that vicious play.

In a rush of pictorial reinforcement that leads one to suspect Mr. Richardson was just itching for the cinema medium to fill the background and heighten the fever of the play, the passion of the characters now comes at you through the drab and depressing milieu of a genuine British Midlands city and the sweatiness of an ugly slum.

The film, produced in England by Harry Saltzman, opened here last night at the Forum and Baronet Theatres with benefit showings for the March of Dimes.

In our eyes, the principal character in this ferocious account of the emotional vandalism committed by what is popularly known as an "angry young man" is still a conventional weakling, a routine crybaby who cannot quite cope with the problems of a tough environment and, so, vents his spleen in nasty words. And the two women who let him run over them, his wife and his mistress, still seem to us to be strangely gullible creatures, a little self-piteous themselves.

But, at least, in this cacaphonic picture, which has a sort of metallic clatter and bang and a throbbing, eccentric jazz tempo that is picked up from time to time on the soundtrack, Mr. Richardson does provide us with a sense of the dismal atmosphere, the prevalence of social stagnation, that helps to frustrate our young man.

The long accumulation of middle-class smugness against which he fitfully rebels by blowing a jazz trumpet at a Saturday-night hot spot and blasting the Sabbath dawn is brilliantly illustrated by shots of people going to church in the rain and by glimpses of rows of ugly houses and streets in which grimy youngsters play. And the piteousness of his occupation as the keeper of a candy stall is conveyed in a stinging little drama of discord with the market superintendent.

Mr. Richardson uses his camera in a hard, crisp documentary style that recalls the way Carol Reed used one in his memorable *The Stars Look Down.*

In getting performances from his actors, Mr. Richardson repeats the quality of the play. Richard Burton is frenzied to the point of mania as the husband who hates the agony of life. His tirades are eloquent but tiring, his breast beatings are dramatic but dull, and his occasional lapses into sadness are pathetic but endurable.

Mary Ure makes a touching slavey as his nerve-jangled, fear-cluttered wife, representing the female frustration that can come in a tortured atmosphere. And Claire Bloom is delightful, sharp and catty as the neighboring friend who won't take the blowhard's guff—until, by a curious reversal, she succumbs to his pathos and falls in love with him.

Gary Raymond, as a genial, weakling Welsh friend, is the most agreeable actor in the film, and Edith Evans is amusing but mystifying as an ancient huckster's wife.

The jazz score provided by Chris Barber and his band and the trumpet playing Pat Halcox does on behalf of Mr. Burton are exciting and helpful to the whole.

—B.C., September 16, 1959

LOST HORIZON

Produced and directed by Frank Capra: written by Robert Riskin. based on the novel by James Hilton: cinematographers. Joseph Walker and Elmer Dyer: edited by Gene Havlick and Gene Milford: music by Dmitri Tiomkin: art designer. Stephen Goosson: released by Columbia Pictures. Black and white. Running time: 138 minutes.

With: Ronald Colman (Robert Conway). Jane Wyatt (Sondra). Edward Everett Horton (Lovett). John Howard (George Conway). Thomas Mitchell (Barnard) and Margo (Maria).

Metro-Goldwyn-Mayer has no corner on the large-scale production market as Columbia Pictures proved last night when it presented its film of James Hilton's *Lost Horizon* at the Globe. There, and for the balance of its two-a-day run, is a grand adventure film, magnificently staged, beautifully photographed, and capitally played. It is the second outstanding picture of the season—the first, of course, being *The Good Earth*—and, unless the Ides of March are particularly portentous this year, it need have no fear of being omitted from the golden brackets of anyone's "best ten" list.

Columbia is supposed to have spent $2,000,000 on the picture. That may or may not be true, $2,000,000 being a round and round-eyed sum even in Hollywood. But there is no denying the opulence of the production, the impressiveness of the sets, the richness of the costuming, the satisfying attention to large and small detail which makes Hollywood at its best such a generous entertainer. We can deride the screen in its lesser moods, but when the West Coast impresarios decide to shoot the works the resulting pyrotechnics bathe us in a warm and cheerful glow.

Robert Riskin, who wrote the adaptation, has not deviated markedly from Mr. Hilton's novel. Miss Brinklow, the missionary, has been metamorphosed into Gloria (Isabel Jewell), a tubercular of frankly dubious respectability. Mallinson, the nonconformist, has become Robert Conway's younger brother, still unadaptable to the serene climate of Shangri-La. Edward Everett Horton has found his way into the story as a prissy paleontologist (and comic relief). Mr. Hilton's Manchu princess—the young woman who really was seventy years old—has been hyphenated, splitting into Margo, who loves young Conway, and Jane Wyatt, authentically youthful, who has a romance with the elder brother (Ronald Colman).

But those are minor changes and, all things considered, for the better. The rest of the story Mr. Riskin has yielded intact to Frank Capra, the director; to Joseph Walker and Elmer Dyer, his cameramen; to Stephen Goosson, the art director; and to Dmitri Tiomkin, who wrote the score. It has been a perfect offscreen collaboration which, with the cast's aid, has transcribed in vividly cinematic terms Mr. Hilton's romantic tale of a hidden paradise in Tibet.

The picture opens with a rush on that wild scene of revolution in Baskul when Conway—England's potential Foreign Secretary—shepherds the last of the beleaguered whites into a roomy transport plane and gives his pilot the "go-ahead" for Shanghai. But shanghaied, not Shanghai, is the word, for their pilot has been killed and a grim Mongolian has them in charge, flying them high over the unknown mountains of Tibet to the hill-locked lamasery of Shangri-La, where disease is unknown, people live for centuries, and where the High Lama is building a storehouse of civilization against that time when man, in his brutality and greed, has destroyed all civilized things.

The plane trip, its crash, the shuddering climb along the narrow ledge leading to the hidden valley, their meeting with the genial Chang are dramatic events, piled one atop the other so swiftly that we found ourselves wondering how long we—and Mr. Capra—could stand the pace. Fortunately there is a respite after Conway has his first encounter with the High Lama. The tempo is quieter then, gently tracing the effect of Shangri-La upon the world-weary Englishman, upon the fugitive American investment banker, upon the diseased and disillusioned Gloria, upon the timorous fossil expert (who had been a bit of a fossil himself).

Young Conway alone is unchanged, impatient to be back to the civilization outside, dramatically convincing his brother that Shangri-La is mad. The penultimate scenes are as vivid, swift, and brilliantly achieved as the first. Only the conclusion itself is somehow disappointing. But perhaps that is inescapable, for there can be no truly satisfying end to any fantasy.

Speaking belatedly of the cast, there is nothing but unqualified endorsement here of Mr. Colman's Conway, of Mr. Horton's Lovett, of Thomas Mitchell's grand performance as the fugitive from the police, of Isabel Jewell's Gloria, H. B. Warner's moderately philosophic Chang, Jane Wyatt's attractive Sondra, and Margo's Maria. That leaves Sam Jaffe's portrayal of the High Lama, and that leaves me of a mixed opinion. Mr. Jaffe's makeup is grotesque and horrible and solid; the High Lama of Mr. Hilton's novel was mystic, ethereal, almost Christlike. Yet the High Lama must be weird to make credible Conway's suspicion that he might be mad. Mr. Jaffe certainly is weird enough. I really don't know. Maybe he should have used less makeup.

Mr. Capra was guilty of a few directorial clichés, but otherwise it was a perfect job. Unquestionably the picture has the best photography and sets of the year. By all means it is worth seeing.

—F.S.N., March 4, 1937

LOST IN AMERICA

Directed by Albert Brooks; written by Mr. Brooks and Monica Johnson; director of photography. Eric Saarinen; edited by David Finfer; music by Arthur B. Rubinstein; production designer. Richard

Sawyer: produced by Marty Katz: released by Warner Brothers. Running time: 91 minutes.

With: Albert Brooks (David Howard), Julie Hagerty (Linda Howard), Maggie Roswell (Patty), Michael Greene (Paul Dunn), Tom Tarpey (Brad Tooley) and Garry K. Marshall (Casino Manager).

David Howard is all ready for his promotion. He's bought a new house. He's discussed upholstery with the Mercedes-Benz salesman. He's even asked all his friends whether they think he deserves to be a senior vice president; they do. So all that remains is the formal meeting with his boss. When it doesn't come off exactly as planned, David finds himself screaming, "Now let's bring in Allen Funt and end this thing!"

But the boss isn't kidding. He's given the job to another man. David tries his best to look on the bright side in explaining this to his wife, Linda. "He'll buy that boat I had to look at in that stupid catalogue for three years," David says. "And it'll crash in Catalina and seals will eat him."

But after the initial shock, David has an inspiration. They'll sell the house! They'll sell the cars! They'll buy a mobile home and wander wherever the impulse takes them. "Linda, this is just like *Easy Rider,* only now its *our* turn," David says. And off they go in their brand-new Winnebago, leaving Los Angeles to the tune of "Born to Be Wild."

A yuppie mid-life crisis is in the offing, and Mr. Brooks has made it the basis for *Lost in America,* an inspired comedy in his own drily distinctive style. If Mr. Brooks isn't often laugh-out-loud funny, that's largely because so much of what he has to say is true. *Lost in America* follows the Howards, played by Mr. Brooks and Julie Hagerty, from a quiet dissatisfaction with their upwardly mobile lives ("Nothing's changing anymore . . . we've just stopped," Linda says) to an even bleaker realization of what their options may be. That it manages to find so much humor in so dismal a progression is amazing indeed.

The doggedness of Mr. Brooks's screen persona is his foremost survival skill, and as such it's part of his appeal. Applying his executive training, he finds himself eager to argue with anyone in his new capacity as a self-proclaimed social dropout. When Linda has too big a night in Las Vegas, for instance, David makes a stab at persuading the casino owner (Garry K. Marshall) that a

show of generosity would be good for the place's image. This doesn't work. Neither do any of the other conversational gambits that have left David unqualified for anything but his previous job in advertising and his subsequent one as a grade-school crossing guard.

Mr. Brooks and Monica Johnson have written *Lost in America* as a one-man show that both embraces and lacerates the character Mr. Brooks plays. That attitude is more realistic than self-contradictory, given their droll, uncompromising vision of David's life and its limitations.

—*J.M., February 15, 1985*

THE LOST WEEKEND

Directed by Billy Wilder: written by Charles Brackett and Mr. Wilder, based on the novel by Charles R. Jackson: cinematographer, John Seitz: edited by Doane Harrison: music by Miklos Rozsa and Giuseppe Verdi: art designers, Hans Dreier and Earl Hedrick: produced by Mr. Brackett: released by Paramount Pictures. Black and white. Running time: 101 minutes.

With: Ray Milland (Don Birnam), Jane Wyman (Helen St. James), Philip Terry (Wick Birnam) and Doris Dowling (Gloria).

The stark and terrifying study of a dipsomaniac which Charles R. Jackson wrote so vividly and truly in his novel, *The Lost Weekend,* has been brought to the screen with great fidelity in every respect but one: the reason for the "dipso's" gnawing mania is not fully and convincingly explained. In the novel, the basic frustration which drove the pitiable "hero" to drink was an unconscious indecision in his own masculine libido. In the film, which bears the same title and which came to the Rivoli on Saturday, the only cause given for his "illness" is the fact that he has writer's cramp. That is, he can't make himself accomplish a burning ambition to write.

However, this single shortcoming is a minor detraction, at worst, from a shatteringly realistic and morbidly fascinating film. For Paramount's ace brace of craftsmen, Billy Wilder and Charles Brackett, have done such a job with their pens and their cameras as puts all recent "horror" films to shame. They have also achieved in the process an illustration of a drunkard's misery that ranks with the best and most disturbing character studies ever put on the screen. *The Lost Weekend* is truly a chef d'oeuvre of motion-picture art.

In imaging the gruesome details of five days in the life of a chronic "lush"—five days during which this poor unfortunate is on one of his periodic "bats"—the Messrs. Brackett and Wilder have been as graphic and candid in their report as was Mr. Jackson in his novel—and that was almost too candid to bear. They have picked up their man at that moment when he is thirsting desperately for another go at his bottle, have indexed the dogged stratagems by which he evades his watchful brother and his sweetheart in getting at some booze, and then they have followed his debauch through a series of episodes which scarcely have a parallel as reflections of mortifying shame. These include his unblushing importunities of a bartender, begging for drinks; a horribly humiliating encounter when he is caught stealing money from a woman's purse; a racking walk along New York's Third Avenue, trying to pawn a typewriter for some cash; and a staggeringly ugly experience in the Bellevue alcoholic ward. A bout of delirium tremens is also made blood-chillingly real—in a sharp, photographic comprehension, not with the usual phantasmagoric tricks.

Most impressive throughout the picture is the honesty with which it has been made. It seems a case history documentation in its narrative and photographic styles. Mr. Wilder, who helped write and directed it, brought his camera and leading player to New York for those scenes which convey the grim relation of the individual to the vast, unknowing mass. And he kept a sharp tone of actuality in all of his studio work. The film's most commendable distinction is that it is a straight, objective report, unvarnished with editorial comment or temperance morality.

And yet the ill of alcoholism and the pathos of its sufferers are most forcefully exposed and deeply pitied, thanks also to the playing of Ray Milland. Mr. Milland, in a splendid performance, catches all the ugly nature of a "drunk," yet reveals the inner torment and degradation of a respectable man who knows his weakness and his shame. Jane Wyman assumes with quiet authority the difficult role of the loyal girl who loves and assists the central character—and finally helps regenerate him. (This climactic touch is some-

what off key—like the "cute" way in which the two meet—but it has the advantage of relieving an intolerable emotional strain.) Howard da Silva is tough and ironic as a disapproving bartender, Frank Faylen is glib as a sadistic male nurse, and Philip Terry plays the brother meekly and well.

We would not recommend this picture for a gay evening on the town. But it is certainly an overwhelming drama which every adult moviegoer should see.

—B.C., December 3, 1945

LOVE

Directed by Karoly Makk; written (in Hungarian, with English subtitles) by Tibor Dery, based on two of his novels; cinematographer, Janos Toth; edited by Gyorgy Sivo; music by Andras Mihaly; art designer, Jozsef Romvari; produced by Mafilm; released by Ajay. Running time: 92 minutes.

With: Lili Darvas (Old Lady), Mari Torocsik (Luca) and Ivan Darvas (Janos).

*L*ove tells the story of a young Hungarian woman whose husband has been arrested by the secret police and who eases the last months of his ancient bedridden mother with the fantastic tale that her son is in America seeing to the completion and premiere of his own motion picture.

In her youth, the old woman was used to some wealth and frivolous luxury, and to maintain the appearance of wealth and luxury, the daughter-in-law gives up her time, her energy, and most of her material possessions. Love thus deals not only with several kinds of love, but also with a history of heroic, exceptionally skillful devotion.

Sustaining the illusions of middle- and upper-class old folk has been the concern of many Eastern European movies over the years. But I find *Love* unique, not because it breaks new ground, but because it has such superb appreciation of emotions and responses already understood.

Subtle, rich, reserved, even elegant, it is a beautiful movie. Although never sentimental, it is about sentiment and also about a code of values. Surrounded by her books and mementos, propped and somewhat pampered on her bed, the old woman all but dreams her life away. A great and intelligent beauty in her youth (and, as played by Lili Darvas, a greatly refined beauty in old age), she relives her past and imagines the present as if it were the past; she asks after her doctor—so she may discuss Goethe with him in German.

Meanwhile, her son, serving ten years for his politics, sits in prison. And his wife scrimps and patches, humors the old woman, and puts the best face possible on the seeping ruin of her own life. An actress named Mari Torocsik plays the wife, a marvelously controlled and complete characterization, with an open-eyed and by no means uncomplaining gallantry.

Ultimately the wife and the mother-in-law have everything in common—even to jealousy in their love for the same man—but they share nothing so much as a standard of conduct and of feeling that I should want to call aristocratic, and that is one of the loveliest manifestations of romantic imagination I have seen on the screen.

Hungarian movies sometimes look like a demonstration of everything you could possibly learn in film school. Karoly Makk's direction of *Love* is also full of technical resourcefulness, but a resourcefulness fully in the service of the drama, and therefore not assertive of its own virtuosity. It is a deeply proportionate film, and it earns its insights, its feelings, and, finally, its happiness.

R.G., March 23, 1973

LOVE AFFAIR

Produced and directed by Leo McCarey; written by Delmer Daves and Donald Ogden Stewart, based on a story by Mildred Cram and Leo McCarey; cinematographer, Rudolph Maté; edited by Edward Dmytryk and George Hively; music and lyrics by B. G. DeSylva, Harold Arlen and Ted Koehler; art designer, Van Nest Polglase; released by RKO Production Company. Black and white. Running time: 87 minutes.

With: Irene Dunne (Terry Mackay), Charles Boyer (Michel Marnay), Maria Ouspenskaya (Mme. Marnay), Lee Bowman (Kenneth), Astrid Allwyn (Lois) and Maurice Moscovich (Cobert).

Leo McCarey, who directs so well it is almost anti-social of him not to direct more often, has created another extraordinarily fine film in *Love Affair,* which the Music Hall brought in yesterday. Like other McCarey pictures, this one has the surface appearance of a comedy and the inner strength and poignance of a hauntingly sorrowful romance. It is a technique or a mood creation developed, we suspect, out of Mr. McCarey's past experiments, ranging from *Ruggles of Red Gap* through *Make Way for Tomorrow* to *The Awful Truth.* The formula would be comedy plus sentiment plus X (which is Mr. McCarey himself) equal such things as *Love Affair.*

As coauthor, director, and producer, he must be credited primarily for the film's success, but almost as large a measure of acknowledgment belongs to Irene Dunne and Charles Boyer for the facility with which they have matched the changes of their script—playing it lightly now, soberly next, but always credibly, always in character, always with a superb utilization of the material at hand. Scarcely less effective has been the contribution of the small supporting cast: Maria Ouspenskaya, Lee Bowman, Astrid Allwyn, Maurice Moscovich, and the few bit players who have added their priceless touches of humor and pathos.

The love affair Mr. McCarey and his company are considering is the unexpectedly idyllic romance between the jaded man of the world, Michel Marnay, and the younger, but almost equally skeptical, Terry Mackay. Both of them were affianced elsewhere, not exactly for money (although that was part of the picture), but because they reasoned they might as well marry money if they had to marry at all. Then, suddenly, they met on shipboard, flirted since it amused them, parted unheroically when it occurred to them that news of an indiscretion might reach the ears of their respective future mates, and discovered, almost as surprisingly, that they were in love.

It is a discovery apt to alter the behavior of a couple of people who had been playing with life. Subtly, Mr. McCarey alters his style to meet the emergency. He finds it amusing that Michel should become a sign painter, Terry a nightclub singer as they put themselves on probation for six months to determine whether they are worthy of marriage. But he finds it touching, too. And, although he keeps reminding himself (and his audience) that life is a comedy, he finds tragedy in the accident that overtakes Terry on her way to the marriage rendezvous and pity in the misunderstanding that keeps his lovers apart so long.

In a sense, his film is a triumph of indirection, for it does one thing while seeming to do another. Its immediate effect is comedy; its afterglow is that of a bittersweet romance. A less capable director, with a less competent cast, must have erred one way or the other—either on the side of treacle or on that of whimsy. Mr. McCarey has balanced his ingredients skillfully and has merged them, as is clear in retrospect, into a glowing and memorable picture.

—*F.S.N., March 17, 1939*

LOVE AND DEATH

Written and directed by Woody Allen; director of photography. Ghislaine Clouquet; edited by Ralph Rosenblum; music by Sergei Prokofiev; art designer. Willy Holt; produced by Jack Rollins and Charles H. Joffe; released by United Artists. Running time: 85 minutes.

With: Woody Allen (Boris). Diane Keaton (Sonja). Feodor Atkins (Mikhail). Yves Barsace (Rimsky). Lloyd Battista (Don Francisco). Brian Coburn (Dimitri). Henry Czarniak (Ivan) and Despo Diamantidou (Mother).

Boris Grushenko (Woody Allen), the most reluctant Russian patriot ever to take up an arm against Napoleon, sits in his prison cell awaiting execution. At the instigation of his wife, Sonja (Diane Keaton), the sort of young woman who likes to debate moral imperatives, Boris had plotted the assassination of the French general and gotten caught.

Boris, like Sonja, is of philosophical bent. As death approaches, as it has been doing throughout his life, Boris muses:"Every man has to go sometime . . . but I'm different. I have to go at six A.M. It was five A.M., but I have a good lawyer."

Love and Death, which opened yesterday at the Sutton and Paramount Theaters, is Woody Allen's grandest work. It's the film (as he said somewhere) that God tried to stop, a sweeping, side-splitting spectacle of Europe at war, of clashing armies, and of Boris's puny

attempts to remain neutral, if not to evade the draft. At the height of one battle, Boris hid in the muzzle of a cannon.

Love and Death is Woody's *War and Peace,* written in English by Woody Allen, which may or may not be a nom de plume for the late Constance Garnett, and filmed on locations where it all did not happen, in Hungary and France. It's Woody's homage to Tolstoy, Kierkegaard, Eisenstein, Groucho Marx, Bob Hope, and maybe even Robert Z. Leonard. It looks terrific. You might say that it looks like a million, except that is probably a million or so less than it cost.

Besides being one of Woody's most consistently witty films, *Love and Death* marks a couple of other advances for Mr. Allen as a filmmaker and for Miss Keaton as a wickedly funny comedienne. Miss Keaton here plays a warped kind of Natasha. At first she is married to a rich, elderly, odoriferous herring merchant while happily carrying on with most of St. Petersburg's available males, and then, after a brief widowhood, she becomes Boris's wife, who loves him as if he were a brother.

"Sex without love is an empty experience," she solemnly tells Boris when he first makes advances. Boris ponders that a moment and suggests, "But as empty experiences go, it's one of the best."

The professional Woody Allen character, compounded of equal parts of optimism and pessimism, leavened by cowardice and a ready access to fractured philosophical jargon and literary allusions, has never before been as completely utilized as he is in *Love and Death.* If Woody's early films had the flavor of his nightclub monologues, this new one suggests the parodies he writes for *The New Yorker* magazine, fully expanded to film form and annotated with movie references.

Love and Death evokes not only *War and Peace* but also *The Brothers Karamazov,* especially in the mystical experiences that Boris has been prone to all his life. The first time was when he was a boy of twelve (played by Alfred Lutter 3d of *Alice Doesn't Live Here Anymore*) and met Death, whom he prodded to answer one key question: Are there any girls? Woody's vision of the Grand Inquisitor is a guy who wears a white sheet and goes about the daily routine in a methodical, conscientious way, sort of like mankind's gardener.

Most prominent in the large supporting cast are Olga Georges-Picot, as a sultry countess who, briefly, falls head over heels in love with Boris; James Tolkan, who plays Napoleon as if Napoleon were Roman Polanski; and Jessica Harper, as a mopy society girl who doesn't want to get married, just divorced.

—*V.C., June 11, 1975*

A LOVE IN GERMANY

Directed by Andrzej Wajda; written (in German, with English subtitles) by Mr. Wajda, Boleslaw Michalek and Agnieszka Holland, based on the book by Rolf Hochhuth; cinematographer, Igor Luther; edited by Halina Prugar-Ketling; music by Michel Legrand; art designers, Allan Starski, Gotz Heymann and Jurgen Henze; produced by Arthur Brauner; released by Triumph Releasing. Running time: 107 minutes.

With: Hanna Schygulla (Paulina Kropp), Marie-Christine Barrault (Maria Wyler), Armin Mueller-Stahl (Mayer), Elisbeth Trissenaar (Elsbeth Schnittgens), Daniel Olbrychski (Wiktorczyk) and Piotr Lysak (Stanislaw Zasada).

As she demonstrated in Ettore Scola's witty mediation on the French Revolution, *La Nuit de Varennes,* Hanna Schygulla will survive the death of Rainer Werner Fassbinder. It was Fassbinder who originally discovered her and for whom she made a whole series of extraordinary films, from the early *Katzelmacher* through *Effi Briest* and, perhaps the best of them all, *The Marriage of Maria Braun.*

Now, in Andrzej Wajda's *Love in Germany,* she gives what must be called a triumphant performance, one that ranks with the best of her work with Fassbinder, in a film that must be the most romantic ever made by Mr. Wajda, the great Polish director whose best films, from *Ashes and Diamonds* through *Man of Marble* and the recent *Danton,* have always been shaped by his political conscience.

A Love in Germany, which will be shown at the New York Film Festival at Alice Tully Hall tonight and tomorrow, is certainly full of political concerns, but it's also a story about a love so all-consuming that

its consequences seem less tragic than liberating, politically as well as emotionally. Though it's nowhere near as sexually explicit and violent as Nagisa Oshima's *In the Realm of the Senses, A Love in Germany* recalls the monomaniacal, self-obsessed passions of the Japanese film.

The screenplay, written by Mr. Wajda with Boleslaw Michalek and Agnieszka Holland, is based on a novel I haven't read by Rolf Hochhuth, best known here as the German playwright who, in the 1960's, offended just about everybody at least part of the time with his unflattering portraits of Pope Pius XII in *The Deputy* and Winston Churchill in *Soldiers.*

A Love in Germany is set during World War II in the small German town of Brombach, sometime before the eventual collapse of the Third Reich was even suspected by most citizens. The children of Brombach happily suck on lollipops decorated with sugar swastikas. The news from the fronts isn't yet so hopeless that the deaths in battle of husbands and fathers can't be accepted as noble sacrifices in the cause of the fatherland.

In Brombach, everybody knows everybody else's business, and as long as certain activities—those that don't actually threaten the tiny community—aren't flaunted, most people look the other way. Thus almost everyone, from her neighbors to the mayor, are aware that Paulina Kropp (Miss Schygulla), the mother of a small son and whose husband is away in the army, has something more than a passing interest in Stanislaw (Piotr Lysak), the handsome, much younger Polish prisoner of war who has been billeted in Brombach as a kind of boy-of-all-work.

Paulina runs a small, well-stocked grocery store, where she is assisted in the heavy work from time to time by Stanislaw, who lives across the street with an elderly couple. There is every indication that Paulina loves her absent husband, but the affair with Stani, as she calls him, is something quite other, a passionate sexual liaison that comes to dominate every aspect of her life.

Both Paulina and Stani are aware that sexual relations between German nationals and P.O.W.'s are forbidden by a law, which decrees the death penalty for the foreigner and imprisonment for the German. Yet Paulina and Stani become increasingly careless about hiding their relationship. Paulina, especially, seems to exult in it. Her happiness makes her euphoric.

Before a rendezvous with Stani in the woods on the outskirts of Brombach, she drops by the local pharmacy and, after making a few innocuous purchases in front of her friends, boldly asks the pharmacist for a condom. As the affair progresses to the consternation of her closest friends, her fever makes her ever less cautious. When Stani comes by in the middle of the day, she virtually tears his clothes off in the front window of the ever-unlocked shop. It isn't long before the lovers are informed upon by a neighbor who covets Paulina's very profitable little business.

Nobody, especially the army officer in charge of the prosecution, wants to see the case through to its inevitable end. Stani's death sentence can be avoided if it can be proved—or certified—that he is actually German. But Stani refuses to be thus "Germanized" in a bogus physical exam. If Paulina will testify that she was raped, she also might avoid the consequences. The manner in which each lover embraces fate is both exhilarating and terrible. Love so self-destructive is so rare that it appears ludicrous to everyone not a party to it.

This is the secret of the film, and one that perhaps no actress except Miss Schygulla could make so sexually vivid and even so politically important. Miss Schygulla's Paulina is a grandly heedless character, and though Stani, nicely played by Mr. Lysak, seems at first to be something of a victim of her passion, he too achieves a kind of heroic stature as the film moves to its foregone conclusion.

Mr. Wajda has cast the film impeccably. The supporting players include such stars as Marie-Christine Barrault, as the neighbor who wants Paulina's shop; Elisabeth Trissenaar, as Paulina's best friend who finally refuses to condone the affair; Armin Mueller-Stahl, as the officer who desperately tries to save the lovers; Daniel Olbrychski, as one of Stani's fellow P.O.W.'s; and Bernhard Wicki, as Brombach's civilian doctor who craftily avoids being a participant in the prosecution.

A Love in Germany initially appears to be an uncharacteristic Wajda work. Love of this kind has seldom if ever interested him in the past. Yet *A Love in Germany* may be one of his most effective films, evoking, effortlessly, large, haunting associations from a small set of extremely specific circumstances.

—*V.C., October 2, 1984*

LOVE IN THE AFTERNOON

Produced and directed by Billy Wilder; written by Mr. Wilder and I. A. L. Diamond, based on the novel *Ariane* by Claude Anet; cinematographer, William Mellor; edited by Leonide Azar; music by Franz Waxman; art designer, Alexander Trauner; released by Allied Artists. Black and white. Running time: 130 minutes.

With: Gary Cooper (Frank Flannagan), Audrey Hepburn (Ariane Chavasse), Maurice Chevalier (Claude Chavasse), John McGiver (Mr. X), Van Doude (Michel) and Lise Bourdin (Madame X).

The pedestal on which the reputation of Ernst Lubitsch has been sitting all these years will have to be relocated slightly to make room for another one. On this one we'll set Billy Wilder. Reason: *Love in the Afternoon*.

Not that our friend Mr. Wilder hasn't already manifested himself a likely successor to Lubitsch as a creator of gay comedy. Nine years ago he filed his motion with his writing and direction of *The Emperor Waltz*. And, most recently, with Sabrina, he mounted the Lubitsch pedestal. But now, with his latest romance, which came to the Paramount and the Plaza yesterday, he needs share his old pal's perch no longer. He's got a pedestal of his own!

For this grandly sophisticated romance, which Mr. Wilder and I. A. L. Diamond have penned, with a courteous nod to a novel by a Frenchman named Claude Anet, is in the great Lubitsch tradition, right down to the froth on the champagne, with a couple of fine additional "touches" that Mr. Wilder may wholly claim.

Like most of Lubitsch's chefs-d'oeuvre, it is a gossamer sort of thing, so far as a literary story and a substantial moral are concerned. A little French girl—a cello player and daughter of a private eye—matches wits with a formidable American roué in his suite in the Paris Ritz Hotel. That is to say, she matches techniques in the art of tangling someone in love. There is little more to the story. And, come to think of it, there is not a shred of moral.

But, boy, what a charming lot of detail Mr. Wilder and Mr. Diamond have contrived to keep their unmoral story going for a couple of minutes over two hours! And what delightful performances Audrey Hepburn and Gary Cooper give as the cleverly calculating couple who spar through the amorous afternoons!

In the manner of Lubitsch, Mr. Wilder employs a distinctive style of subtle sophisticated slapstick to give the fizz to his brand of champagne. His settings are elegant and solid—strictly Place Vendome. Indeed, the whole film was made in Paris, where *je ne sais quoi* is in the air. His people appear fairly likely—Miss Hepburn most certainly so and Mr. Cooper a reasonable facsimile of a composite playboy millionaire.

But, slowly, easy flirtation flows into ever so gentle farce. Waiters scramble about with pails of champagne and gypsy musicians play the "Fascination Waltz." Mood-drenched, seductive lovemaking becomes a wickedly funny routine. And, the first thing you know, the old seducer winds up with the gypsy musicians in a Turkish bath!

That's all we'll tell you about it. No use even trying to explain. This is tongue-in-cheek Mr. Wilder offering Cinderella to a deft Don Juan, she coming from music school in ermine and he padding about without his shoes. Both the performers are up to it—archly, cryptically, beautifully. They are even up to a sentimental ending that is full of the mellowness of afternoon.

Maurice Chevalier as the gumshoe father—the private eye from whose abundant files the little lady gets so much instruction in the lore of sophisticated love—also gives a warm, adroit performance. And John McGiver is a charming surprise as a clumsy, pistol-packing husband who goes gunning for the seducer of his wife.

Let's say a word, too, for the gypsies—those poker-faced gentlemen who saw their violins and play a dumb Greek chorus to one of the funniest seductions in years.

This film was produced by Mr. Wilder for Allied Artists—in black-and-white. It is a hit.

—*B.C., August 24, 1957*

LOVELY AND AMAZING

Written and directed by Nicole Holofcener; produced by Anthony Bregman. Eric d'Arbeloff and Ted Hope: director of photography. Harlan Bosmajian; edited by Rob Frazen; music by Craig Richey: production designer. Devorah Herbert: released by Lions Gate Films. Running time: 91 minutes.

With: Catherine Keener (Michelle Marks). Brenda Blethyn (Jane Marks). Emily Mortimer (Elizabeth Marks). Dermot Mulroney (Kevin McCabe). Jake Gyllenhaal (Jordan). Raven Goodwin (Annie). Clark Gregg (Bill) and James Le Gros (Paul).

Nicole Holofcener's smart, acidic comedy *Lovely and Amazing* zeroes in on contemporary narcissism and its fallout with a relentless, needling accuracy that illustrates exactly the way some people allow their personal insecurities and tics to poison their intimate relationships. Almost to a person, the film's mostly female characters are afflicted by our society's obsession with looks, to the degree that they never stop finding fault with themselves in the mirrors of their infinitely self-critical minds.

Take Elizabeth Marks (Emily Mortimer), a slender, attractive actress who is the younger of two sisters, both in their 30's. After being rejected for a role in a soap opera for not being sexy enough, Elizabeth sleeps with Kevin McCabe (Dermot Mulroney), the vain, handsome actor who would have played her lover on the series. Afterward, Elizabeth, who is fixated on the loose flesh on her upper arms, insists on posing nude for Kevin so he can deliver a point-by-point critique of her physical flaws.

After much coaxing, he obliges with a careful, detached analysis that doesn't mention those offending arms until Elizabeth calls his attention to them. Yes, he agrees, much to her perverse satisfaction; they're a little flabby. Kevin, for his part, worries out loud about the condition of his abdominals and frets that his personal trainer helped him to accumulate bulk instead of the leanness he desired.

One way of looking at this movie by the creator of the much admired 1996 comedy *Walking and Talking* is to see it as a West Coast answer to *Sex and the City*. The difference between that popular HBO series, several episodes of which Ms. Holofcener has directed, and the film is that the movie methodically strips away the high-gloss glamour and erotic joie de vivre. There is no Mr. Big to get excited about. The men in *Lovely and Amazing* are too self-absorbed and worn down by petty domestic squabbling to indulge in the sort of giddy screwball sparring that lends the sexual combat in *Sex and the City* a spicy romantic zest.

The particular psychic malaise examined by the movie seems to be an ingrained family trait of the Markses, a West Coast clan of high-strung women led by Jane (Brenda Blethyn), a divorced matriarch who is something of a diva. Rounding out the clan are her two grown daughters, Michelle (Catherine Keener) and Elizabeth, and Jane's recently acquired black eight-year-old adopted daughter, Annie (Raven Goodwin), whose biological mother was a crack addict.

In the first scenes of the movie, which opens today in New York and Los Angeles, Jane is preparing for liposuction (uninsured, at a cost of $10,000) to remove ten pounds of fat from her waist. Most of the drama takes place after the operation, when Jane develops complications and has to remain in the clinic, relying on her reluctant grown-up daughters to fill in as surrogate mothers for Annie.

Michelle is an artist who designs cute little nothings like spindly miniature chairs for sale in gift shops. When a potential vendor turns her down, Michelle, who admits she has a problem with anger, storms out of the store in a fury. And as her career languishes, her husband, Bill (Clark Gregg), who installs personal sound systems for rich people, is increasingly annoyed by her refusal to contribute to their family income.

The couple has a young daughter whose delivery by natural childbirth Michelle has turned into a self-aggrandizing shtick almost as abrasive as her blunt complaints about Bill's lack of interest in sex. When she finally agrees to take a job at a one-hour photo shop, she does so in a begrudging way that can only stir up more mutual resentment. Complicating matters is the avid sexual interest Michelle's gawky seventeen-year-old boss, Jordan (Jake Gyllenhaal), takes in her. She is flattered and angry enough at her husband to make the foolish mistake of responding.

Elizabeth's relationship with her steady boyfriend, Paul (James Le Gros), a nature writer, isn't any happier. She continually snipes at him for his indifference to her career anxieties, most of which revolve around her looks and sex appeal. Instead of lavishing affection on Paul, she diverts it into caring for stray dogs. Of the three daughters,

Annie seems the most grounded, although she's overweight. As the movie goes along, the little girl absorbs her adoptive family's neuroses and begins acting strangely.

Michelle, the film's most fully realized and compelling character, is the kind of role Ms. Keener has played before (most notably in *Your Friends and Neighbors* and *Being John Malkovich*), to the point that she has begun to represent a contemporary type. Headstrong, brutally candid, radiating a free-floating hostility that seems to stem from some deep, gnawing disappointment (especially in men), she is the embodiment of what might be called a postfeminist malcontent.

As smart and observant as it is, *Lovely and Amazing* doesn't really go anywhere. Ms. Holofcener's sharp, witty dialogue shows an ear acutely tuned to the edgy, competitive nuances of contemporary banter, and the movie expertly evokes the rivalry percolating just below the surface of the Markses' relationships. But once family members have weathered their personal crises, little seems to have changed.

The movie's title is ironic. When Jane tells Elizabeth she's lovely and amazing, her daughter doesn't believe it, even though it's obviously true.

—S.H., June 28, 2002

LOVE ON THE RUN

Directed by François Truffaut: written (in French, with English subtitles) by Mr. Truffaut. Marie-France Pisier, Jean Aurel and Suzanne Schiffman: director of photography, Nestor Almendros: edited by Martine Barraque-Curie: music by Georges Delarue: art designer, Jean-Pierre Kohut-Svelko: produced by Les Films du Carrosse: released by New World Pictures. Running time: 94 minutes.

With: Jean-Pierre Léaud (Antoine Doinel), Marie-France Pisier (Colette), Claude Jade (Christine), Dani (Liliane), Dorothée (Sabine), Rosy Varte (Colette's Mother), Julien Bertheau (Monsieur Lucien) and Daniel Mesguich (The Librarian).

François Truffaut's *Love on the Run*, which opens today at the Coronet, is the fifth film and, Mr.

Truffaut says, the last in his extraordinary Antoine Doinel series that began twenty years ago with *The 400 Blows.* Mr. Truffaut said the same thing in 1971 when *Bed and Board,* the fourth Doinel film, was released, but this time there's good reason to believe him. There's no place left to go for either Antoine, still played by Jean-Pierre Léaud, or for Mr. Truffaut, who has here made a movie that spells a more absolute end than death for a favorite character. The film is also an examination of principles—a unique essay on the methods and purposes of romantic comedy.

We've all seen actors over the years deal with age on the screen, some, with the aid of surgery, becoming miraculously more youthful looking while all around them disintegrated. Yet never before have we had the same director, the same actor, and the same character evolve, more or less naturally, over such an extended period of time.

After *The 400 Blows,* which introduced Antoine as the thirteen-year-old juvenile delinquent, there were the "Colette" sequence from *Love at Twenty* (1963), in which Antoine courted the spirited Marie-France Pisier but won only the affection of her parents; *Stolen Kisses* (1969), in which Antoine, discharged without honor from the army, pursued the music student, Christine (Claude Jade); and *Bed and Board* (1971), in which the marriage of Antoine and Christine fell apart as the self-interested Antoine sought a literary career and extra-marital affairs.

Love on the Run picks up Antoine and Christine on the morning that their no-contest divorce becomes final. Neither Antoine nor Christine is especially upset by this development. Christine has learned to live without Antoine and Antoine is busily involved in a new affair with Sabine, a pretty, bright young woman played by Dorothée, a new actress who looks a lot like the younger Claude Jade and like Catherine Deneuve, who has also figured in Mr. Truffaut's career.

That same evening Antoine runs into Colette, again played by Marie-France Pisier, who is now a lawyer and still a woman with a mind of her own, which is to say that she has Antoine's number. By one of those coincidences that tie such comedies together, Colette's lover, a librarian, turns out to be the brother of Antoine's Sabine, which leads to a certain amount of misunderstanding of no real importance.

You should be told here, however, that there's very little in the way of conventional story to *Love on the Run,* whose screenplay is jointly credited to Mr. Truffaut, Miss Pisier, Jean Aurel, and Suzanne Schiffman.

It is, instead, a series of sequences in which everyone takes stock—the now serenely self-aware Christine, the beautiful, sensitive, funny Colette, as well as the perplexed Antoine. They take stock in great swatches of flashbacks lifted from *The 400 Blows* (black-and-white), "Colette," (sepia), and *Stolen Kisses* and *Bed and Board* (both in color).

This method is initially disturbing. If you know the films well—as I do—it seems that Mr. Truffaut has ransacked his own archives in the manner of the television vultures who put together omnibus features with titles such as *The Hollywood Sirens* or *The Silver Age of the Golden Screen.* The bits and pieces—like Antoine's interview with the psychiatrist from *The 400 Blows*—are too good to be used in this fashion. The new context doesn't do them justice. It also appears to be lazy moviemaking.

Then, too, I wonder if people who do not know the earlier films will make any sense at all of *Love on the Run.* It's rather like opening a new book and skipping immediately to the epilogue.

But if you admire Mr. Truffaut, I urge you to stay with *Love on the Run,* which is this brilliantly, comically authoritative French director's analysis of his own work. I don't think any other filmmaker of his stature has ever attempted such a thing, certainly not in public with a feature film.

While Antoine, Christine, and Colette relive their earlier entanglements, Mr. Truffaut makes it clear that his identification with Antoine/Léaud has grown from one based on concern, fondness, and superficial likenesses to one having to do with a philosophy of life and art. Antoine's stories—the ones he acts out in these films as well as the ones he wants to write as a novelist—are so totally concerned with the processes and emotions of falling in love that he's continually surprised when the affairs are suddenly over.

Whether by design or accident, the Antoine films have always taken a dim view of those romantic comedies that insist that the stereotypical boy and girl, having met, lost each other, and met again, will live happily ever after. In the past Mr. Truffaut has shied away from such unequivocal cheeriness.

In *Love on the Run* he is expressing doubts. At one point the pragmatic Sabine says to Antoine with a good deal of patience, "Why impose despair on everyone else while you go around enjoying life?"

Mr. Truffaut ends *Love on the Run* in the only optimistic way he will permit himself. When Sabine and Antoine decide to stay together, they acknowledge that the decision may be a mistake and that it may end badly, but they agree to pretend that it's forever. For Mr. Truffaut to pretend is a major commitment.

I hope this analysis doesn't make *Love on the Run* seem tediously schematic. Once you get its rhythm it is great fun—full of the wit, the humanity, and the kind of mysterious references that separate Truffaut comedies from those of all other directors. It also offers a ravishing performance by Marie-France Pisier and very charming ones by Claude Jade and Dorothée.

Mr. Léaud is something else. He's exactly right but it's impossible now to identify the actor apart from the role. Seeing him as an obsessively selfish, unfeeling adult is a disappointment. He isn't as interesting or appealing as he used to be. As do some childhood friends, Antoine Doinel has grown away from us.

—V.C., April 6, 1979

LOVER COME BACK

Directed by Delbert Mann; written by Stanley Shapiro and Paul Henning; cinematography by Arthur E. Arling; edited by Maerjorie Fowler; art directors, Robert Clatworthy and Alexander Golitzen; music by Frank De Vol; produced by Martin Melcher and Stanley Shapiro; released by Universal-International. Running time: 107 minutes.

With: Rock Hudson (Jerry Webster), Doris Day (Carol Templeton), Tony Randall (Peter Ramsey), Edie Adams (Rebel Davis), Jack Oakie (J. Paxton Miller), Jack Kruschen (Doctor Linus Tyler), Ann B. Davis (Millie), Joe Flynn (Hadley), Howard St. John (John Brackett), Karen Norris (Kelly), Jack Albertson (Fred), Charles Watts (Charlie), Donna Douglas (Deborah) and Ward Ramsey (Hodges).

If you thought *Pillow Talk* was a "sleeper" when it popped up in 1959 as a comedy hit uniting Rock Hudson and Doris Day, wait till you see their latest, *Lover Come Back,* which came like a freshet of fluent fun and fancy into the Music Hall yesterday. *Pillow Talk* was but a warm-up for this springy and spirited surprise, which is one of the brightest, most delightful satiric comedies since *It Happened One Night.*

That may sound like a pretty tall order for a picture that candidly contains other echoes from that previous picture, not just Mr. Hudson and Miss Day. One of these is Stanley Shapiro, who helped to write *Pillow Talk.* He also helped to write this one (and, furthermore, co-produced). The fact that he is repeating as script writer for the same stars is no cause for sneers or suspicions. Mr. S. is a wizard with words.

Neither is there reason for skepticism or anguish in the fact that he is here following a somewhat similar storyline. That is to say, Mr. Hudson is again made out to be a wicked rake who deliberately disguises his identity in order to trick Miss Day, and she, poor dear, is once more made out to be a little gull who innocently falls for his deception, until—well, that's the point, friends! Until—!

Furthermore, Tony Randall, who was a big asset in that previous film, is an even bigger one—indeed, a character of major comic consequence—in this.

But don't let the seeming appearance of a hackneyed attempt at a repeat cause you to give it the go-by, for Mr. Shapiro and Paul Henning have contrived a script that has some of the sharpest and funniest situations you could wish and some of the fastest, wittiest dialogue that has spewed out of a comedy ears. And Delbert Mann has directed with such energy and at such a pace that *Lover Come Back* is the shortest hour-and-three-quarter film we've ever seen.

As *Pillow Talk* made Texas the butt of its faint satiric thrust, *Lover Come Back* fires its satire at a larger target—Madison Avenue. And it fires it with such precision and relentless velocity that it is questionable whether another pasting of advertising will ever be made again.

There is no use in trying to tell you of its comical ins and outs, its beautifully plotted situations, its deftly planted sight gags and its stimulating employment of that old-fashioned thing, cinema. Be it enough to tell you that Mr. Hudson and Miss Day are cast as account executives of rival advertising agencies in New York and are thrown into mortal competition for a critical account.

It happens that the account is a completely nonexistent one. It is for a product called VIP, which Mr. Hudson has dreamed up but which has not materialized and Mr. Randall, the bumbling head of his agency, has unwittingly put on the air.

But that is a part of the story we haven't got time to describe. Suffice it again to say that it is tremendously droll.

Anyhow, the point is that Mr. Hudson, whom Miss Day has never seen, must keep her away from the inventor, whom he has got to invent something to fit the name, until it is invented—that is, to keep her from getting the VIP account. And to do this he archly poses as the inventor himself—as shy, noble Dr. Linus Tyler, who has never, alas, been kissed.

Well, that's the main situation—Miss Day goes in hot pursuit of the slyly deceptive Mr. Hudson, and you can imagine whither that leads. That's right, it leads almost directly to the area of pillow talk. And what happens when it gets there remains for you to see. It's enough to make a fellow never want to believe another ad.

Mr. Hudson and Miss Day are delicious, he in his big, sprawling way and she in her wide-eyed, pert, pugnacious and eventually melting vein. Mr. Randall makes a wonderful nitwit who is drenched in psychiatry, and Jack Kruschen is richly comic as the smoke-pot who finally invents VIP. Edie Adams as a nightclub cutie and Jack Oakie as a manufacturer she helps to woo for Mr. Hudson's benefit are hilarious in their bits.

Altogether, this picture, in bright color, is one you had better not miss, unless you want to be that party-misfit who hasn't seen the funniest picture of the year.

The stage show includes the Corps de Ballet; Gil Dova, a juggling comedian; the Melodaires, a singing group; a piano sextette and the Rockettes.

—B. C., February 9, 1962

THE LOVERS

Written (in French, with English subtitles) and directed by Louis Malle: based on the novel *Point de Landemain* by Dominique Vivant: cinematographer. Henri Decaë: edited by Léonide Azar: music by Johannes Brahms and Alain Derosnay: production designers. Bernard Evein and Jacques Saulnier: produced by Nouvelles Editions des Films: released by Zenith International Film Corporation. Running time: 90 minutes.

With: Jeanne Moreau (Jeanne Tournier). Alain Cuny (Henri Tournier). José-Luis de Villalonga (Raoul Torres). Jean-Marc Bory (Bernard Langlois). Judith Magre (Maggie) and Gaston Modot (The Servant).

Having been preceded by both the fanfare of honors and the stigma of censorship, *The Lovers,* which came to the Paris Theatre from France yesterday, is less a bombshell than a letdown.

For the import, a prize-winner at the Venice Film Festival, which also reportedly was struck down by bans in several other European areas, evolves only as a truly tender and compassionate examination of a sudden torrid love affair. Unfortunately, it is weighted down by an abundance of saccharine and obvious preliminaries so dear to the hearts of the confessional magazine readers.

But Louis Malle, the twenty-eight-year-old writer-director, a prime exponent of the so-called "new wave" of young French film artists now enjoying popularity, certainly has been explicit and incisive in his handling of the film's major sequences. His principals—Jeanne Moreau, portraying a bored young matron who is suddenly and explosively catapulted into the grandest of passions by an equally youthful archaeologist, played by Jean-Marc Bory—appear to be as close to authentic amour as is possible on screen.

Spokesmen for the film's distributors admit that the film has been cut here and there so that the local version and the feature currently engrossing Parisians may not be exactly alike. This, it would appear, is of small moment. M. Malle, who served as a cameraman on the noted documentary *The Silent World,* proves again that he is no stranger to film techniques.

With the aid of simple but pointed dialogue, his shots of the lovers meeting by chance in a moonlit garden, walking hand in hand through fields and forest, by a millwheel to the sounds of a gurgling stream, and making love in a drifting boat and in the quiet of a manor house are strangely beautiful evocations of love.

However, a viewer is forced through a succession of introductory, uninspired, familiar scenes to establish the film's central action. Our heroine, it appears, is drawn to Paris from her country manse in Dijon because her husband, a sullen and introspective newspaper publisher, is closer to his business than the business of romance. The light of her life in the City of Light is a well-bred, rich polo player and she is almost ready to heed his flowery blandishments when she conveniently meets our hero en route home to a party. And, an observer is forced to wonder, despite the poetic, off-screen narration, is love at first sight ever as precipitous as presented here.

In Mlle. Moreau, however, M. Malle has the services of one of France's top-flight performers to judge by her contribution to *The Lovers*. The actress, to put it into a nutshell, is superb. As a woman torn by conventions, a need for love, a knowledge of the superficialities of the Parisian haute monde, and her ecstatic discovery of romantic fulfillment for which she sacrifices home, husband, and child, Mlle. Moreau seems to be living, rather than playing, a role.

M. Bory is handsome and, on occasion, an understanding mate for her. Alain Cluny is properly dour and suspicious as the husband, and José-Luis de Villa-longa, as the polo enthusiast, and Judith Magre, as Mlle. Moreau's pleasure-loving Parisian friend, are simply glib and attractive.

In short, M. Malle should be eternally grateful to both Mlle. Moreau and the film's evocative and torrid emotional sequences. Without them, *The Lovers* is a tedious and tepid affair.

—*A.W., October 27, 1959*

LOVES OF A BLONDE

Directed by Milos Forman: written (in Czech. with English subtitles) by Jaroslav Papousek. Ivan Passer. Mr. Forman and Vaclev Sasek: cinematographer. Miroslav Ondricek: edited by Miroslav Hajek: music by Evzen Illin: art designer. Karel Cernyapousek: produced by Barrandov. Ceskoslovensky: released by Prominent Films. Black and white. Running time: 88 minutes.

With: Hana Brejchova (Andula). Vladimir Pucholt (Milda). Antonin Blazejovsky (Tonda). Josef Sebanek (Boy's Father) and Milada Jezkova (Boy's Mother).

Now that Milos Forman's Czechoslovak film, *Loves of a Blonde,* has attained a lively reputation and a considerable audience want-to-see by virtue of its

explosive premiere showing at the recent New York Film Festival, the beginning of its regular engagement at the Sutton yesterday is almost an anticlimax in the trajectory of its interesting career.

Everybody seems to know about it from the generally fine and full reviews it received after its festival showing. Mr. Forman has had his day in the sun of the admiring gaze of interviewers and movie buffs hereabouts. And the rising stock of Czechoslovak pictures has taken another jump because of it.

There's not much more for me to say about it in the way of critical report than I said here on September 13. It is a delightfully simple and sure account of the way in which a romance-starved young woman warily surrenders herself to a visiting piano player on the night of a factory-town dance and then, acting on his casual invitation, follows him to his home in Prague.

What she finds there—two nervous parents, scolding and clucking over their son and treating his romantic peccadilloes as though they were the naughty acts of a little boy—provides the surprising material for a beautifully droll denouement that is laced with tender traces of youthful poignancy.

The notable thing about it is its frank inconclusiveness—its clear incidental indications that romance is perpetually pursued by young people seeking that something that can never be found totally. It is hopeful—but realistic. And full of delicious characters.

Most winning, of course, are the two young people, played with natural ingenuousness by Hana Brejchova and Vladimir Pucholt, but humorous and touching, too, are Milada Jezkova and Josef Sebanek, as the parents of the boy, and three fellows (not listed in the credits) who are army reservists at the dance. The maneuvers of these three citizen-soldiers attempting to pick up three factory girls, including the blonde of the title, are comedy of the grandest sort. Human comedy, I think they call it. Such is *Loves of a Blonde.*

—*B.C., October 27, 1966*

LOVING

Directed by Irvin Kershner: written by Don Devlin. based on the novel by J. M. Ryan: director of photography. Gordon Willis: edited by Robert Lawrence: music by Bernardo Segall: production designer. Walter Scott Herndon: produced by Mr.

Devlin: released by Columbia Pictures. Running time: 89 minutes.

With: George Segal (Brooks), Eva Marie Saint (Selma), Janis Young (Grace), Nancie Phillips (Nelly), Sterling Hayden (Lepridon), Keenan Wynn (Edward), David Doyle (Will), Paul Sparer (Marve), Andrew Duncan (Willy) and Sherry Lansing (Susan).

Irvin Kershner (*A Fine Madness, The Luck of Ginger Coffey*) seems to specialize in directing movies about men who have to rush to keep up with themselves. In his best film so far, *Loving*, which opened yesterday at the Cinema Rendezvous and Loew's New Ciné, he has not only a hero in a hurry, but also an actor who while he runs can react with precision, depth, and endless good sense.

Loving isn't only George Segal's movie. There is nobody in the very large supporting cast I should want to fault. But its world is so greatly an extension of the character Segal creates that I cannot happily imagine the film without him.

Segal plays a commercial artist with wife (wonderful Eva Marie Saint) and kids in Westport, and mistress and contacts in New York. He is in the midst of losing his mistress, winning a major account, acquiring a new house, keeping up appearances, satisfying his desires, pleasing clients, asserting his independence—and somehow keeping at bay the success that seems in danger of settling the precarious imbalance of his life.

It is a comic situation, being, like most comedy, a few footnotes to the course of human misery. Segal's particular brand of despair; his completeness, rather than brilliance, as an actor (he occasionally throws away good lines, but he always redeems the bad ones); his body's energy and his face's mobility; his ability not simply to move but to inhabit the space in which he moves—constitute a superior method of interpreting the ordinary world.

In a sense, the very banality of the film's anecdote allows George Segal the fullest scope for his intelligence—just as it forces Irvin Kershner's attention for once to upper middle-class normality, with greatly satisfying results.

Loving is wholly a New York (or, more accurately, greater metropolitan area) movie. Like the best New York movies, it is strong on reality—not local color, but localized attitudes and occupations. To his everlasting glory, Kershner never condescends toward the profession of commercial art, but, instead, understands it as effort, anxiety, and independence—as the essence of self-employment and not as personal sellout. The film ultimately reveals less about suburban morals, its advertised subject, than about the morality of making do, its real subject. It succeeds beautifully with the details of how we live, and fails only in the forced mechanics of its major scenes.

The giant Fairfield County cocktail party that climaxes *Loving*, and in which the all-seeing eye of closed-circuit television exposes Segal in a multiple sexual betrayal more comic than cataclysmic, is neither as funny nor as painful as it should be.

The fault lies partly with the hero, whose life is supposed to fall in shambles, but who, like other Irvin Kershner failures, is essentially a success. But it lies also with the construction of the sequence—too obvious, too repetitious, even too sloppy to convey the sense of inexorable coincidence that is the soul of this kind of fiction.

I suspect insensitive, or merely expeditious editing, which in many places subverts the film's graceful advances and lovely dislocations of mood. For in the direction of actors, judgment about scenes, and everything that happens in the camera, *Loving* is a fine and gratifying film.

—R.G., March 5, 1970

LUST FOR LIFE

Directed by Vincente Minnelli; written by Norman Corwin, based on the novel by Irving Stone; cinematographers, Freddie Young and Russell Harlan; edited by Adrienne Fazan; music by Miklos Rozsa; art designers, Cedric Gibbons, Hans Peters and Preston Ames; produced by John Houseman; released by Metro-Goldwyn-Mayer. Running time: 122 minutes.

With: Kirk Douglas (Vincent van Gogh), Anthony Quinn (Paul Gauguin), James Donald (Theo van Gogh), Pamela Brown (Christine), Everett Sloane (Dr. Gachet) and Niall MacGinnis (Roulin).

Clearly, the most dramatic feature of the life of Vincent van Gogh was the difference between his painting, which was forceful and sunny and warm, and the character of his disposition, which was clouded by dark and maddening moods. This contrast of coloration in the product and person of the man is more vivid and tantalizing than anything that happened in his career, including the celebrated episode of his slicing off his own ear.

Thus, it is gratifying to see that Metro-Goldwyn-Mayer, in the persons of producer John Houseman and a crew of superb technicians, has consciously made the flow of color and the interplay of compositions and hues the most forceful devices for conveying a motion picture comprehension of van Gogh.

In *Lust for Life,* the film biography which had its world premiere last night at the Plaza Theatre in a benefit for the Metropolitan Museum of Art's Student Fellowship fund, color dominates the dramatization—the color of indoor sets and outdoor scenes, the color of beautifully reproduced van Gogh paintings, even the colors of a man's tempestuous moods. These pictorial color continuities, planned like a musical score, have more effect upon the senses than the playing of Kirk Douglas in the leading role.

That does not discredit the acting of Mr. Douglas or the quality of the script prepared by Norman Corwin from a novel by Irving Stone. Both the script and the performance of this picture have a striking integrity in putting forth the salient details and the surface aspects of the life of van Gogh.

The tortuous career of the artist is recounted faithfully, from his experiences as an evangelist in a Belgian mining district to his ultimate suicide. The brutal rebuff of his love is in it, the turmoil of his affair with a prostitute, the uncertainty of his life in Paris, and the explosiveness of his residence in Arles with Gauguin. The incidents of the painter's manifestations of insecurity and emotional torment are well arranged, and Mr. Douglas performs them with superior intensity, variety, and yet restraint.

What is more, and especially fascinating, is the remarkable resemblance he bears to the famous self-portraits of the artist which are discreetly but prominently displayed.

As Gauguin, the friend but ultimate irritant to van Gogh, Anthony Quinn also gives a splendid concept of a disordered creative man, and James Donald is quiet and affecting as the sympathetic brother of van Gogh. A score or more other actors and actresses offer, in brief supporting roles, some notion of the many people that touched the life of the lonely man.

But the quality of the spiritual suffering of the sick and self-doubting van Gogh is difficult to bring to full expression in conventional histrionics or words—of which, incidentally, there are many, perhaps too many, in this film. And so Mr. Houseman and Vincente Minnelli, the director, have wisely relied upon color and the richness and character it gives to images to carry their tortured theme. The cold grayness of a mining district, the reds of a Paris café, the greens of a Provençal village, or the golden yellows of a field of ripening grain—these are the stimuli that give us a sensory knowledge of the surroundings that weigh upon van Gogh and reflect the contrasting umbers and purples of the sad and fated man.

—B.C., September 18, 1956

598

M

Directed by Fritz Lang; written (in German, with English subtitles) by Mr. Lang, Thea von Harbou, Paul Falkenberg, Adolf Jansen and Karl Vash, based on an article by Egon Jacobson; cinematographers, Fritz Arno Wagner and Gustav Rathje; edited by Mr. Falkenberg; music by Edvard Grieg; produced by Seymour Nebenzal; released by Foremco Pictures Corporation. Black and white. Running time: 117 minutes.

With: Peter Lorre (The Murderer), Ellen Widmann (The Mother), Inge Landgut (The Child), Gustav Gründgens (The Safebreaker), Fritz Gnass (The Burglar) and Fritz Odemal (The Card Sharper).

Based on the fiendish killings which spread terror among the inhabitants of Düsseldorf in 1929, there is at the Mayfair a German-language pictorial drama with captions in English bearing the succinct title *M,* which, of course, stands for murder. It was produced in 1931 by Fritz Lang and, as a strong cinematic work with remarkably fine acting, it is extraordinarily effective, but its narrative, which is concerned with a vague conception of the activities of a demented slayer and his final capture, is shocking and morbid. Yet Mr. Lang has left to the spectator's imagination the actual commission of the crimes.

Peter Lorre portrays the Murderer in a most convincing manner. The Murderer is a repellent spectacle, a pudgy-faced, pop-eyed individual who slouches along the pavements and has a Jekyll-and-Hyde nature. Little girls are his victims. The instant he lays eyes on a child homeward bound from school, he tempts her by buying her a toy balloon or a ball. This thought is quite sufficient to make even the clever direction and performances in the film more horrible than anything else that has so far come to the screen. Why so much fervor and intelligent work was concentrated on such a revolting idea is surprising.

It is unfurled in a way that reveals Mr. Lang and Thea von Harbou, his wife, evidently studied what happened in Düsseldorf during the score of atrocious murders, which incidentally caused young women to go about armed with pepper in case they were picked out by the slayer as possible victims. In the film the Commissioner of Police is given instructions to track the murderer down. He goes about his work in a systematic fashion, but when another crime is perpetrated he is talked to heatedly over the telephone by his superior.

So far as the film spectator is concerned, there is no mystery concerning the criminal. He is perceived looking into a mirror, making grimaces at himself, and later dawdling along the street, looking into shop windows. He has a habit of whistling a few bars of a tune, and apparently it is something he has little control over, for this whistling is actually responsible for his capture.

Mr. Lang has the adroit idea of having thugs, pickpockets, burglars, and highwaymen eventually setting about to apprehend the Murderer. His crimes are making things too hot for them and, bad as they are, they are depicted as being almost sympathetic characters compared to the Murderer. Every criminal in the town is told by the chief crook to be on the lookout for anybody who looks suspicious. Beggars and peddlers, as well as the thieves and swindlers, are all eager to catch the Murderer.

It is not astonishing that anybody doing a kindly turn for a child is suspected of being the criminal. A harmless individual is almost mobbed by hysterical women and enraged men. Meanwhile the Murderer is at large and has boastfully written of his last crime to the newspapers. The letter is analyzed. It was written evidently on a rough wooden table, and the sleuths draw circles about the map of the town as they widen their search.

But his capture does not come about through the minions of the law. It is a blind man, a peddler of toy balloons, who gives the alarm. He had sold a balloon a few days before to the man who had whistled the notes of an operatic tune. Suddenly the blind man several days later hears the melody whistled again, and it dawns upon him in a few seconds that the Murderer is passing. He gives the alarm, and in the course of the chase a youth, who had marked in chalk the letter "M" on his hand, slaps the suspect on the back.

There is a wild chase, the crooks being eager to get their man. They are willing to risk being held for crimes, and when the Police Commissioner understands from a prisoner that he and others were following the Murderer, the official is so stunned that he lets the cigar he is smoking drop from his mouth. One perceives the panting Murderer trying to get the lock off a door, his eyes wilder than ever, and perspiration dripping from his forehead. But the frantic, shrieking man is finally captured by the thieves, and a most interesting series of scenes is devoted to his trial. He bleats that he is a murderer against his will, whereas those before him commit crime because they want to. A thief presides at the trial. The Murderer has counsel, who says that the Murderer needs a doctor more than punishment. Then the Murderer is handed over to the police and the mother of one of the fiend's little victims declares that the death of the man will not give her back her child.

It is regrettable that such a wealth of talent and imaginative direction was not put into some other story, for the actions of this Murderer, even though they are left to the imagination, are too hideous to contemplate.

—*M.H., April 3, 1933*

MAD MAX

Directed by George Miller: written by Mr. Miller and James McCausland, based on a story by Mr.

Miller and Byron Kennedy: director of photography, David Eggby: edited by Tony Paterson and Clifford Hayes: music by Brian May: art designer, Jon Dowding: produced by Mr. Kennedy: released by American International, a Filmways Company. Running time: 90 minutes.

With: Mel Gibson (Max Rockatansky), Joanne Samuel (Jessie), Hugh Keays-Byrne (Toecutter), Steve Bisley (Jim Goose), Tim Burns (Johnny the Boy) and Roger Ward (Fifi Macaffee).

Along with such pests as jackrabbits and kangaroos, Australia "a few years from now" is being afflicted by predatory motorcycle gangs. An elite leather-clad highway police force has been established to oppose them.

This is the flimsy plot line of *Mad Max,* which opens today at the Embassy 5, but it provides an adequate framework for some vivid chase-and-crash sequences across the unpopulated outback and a heavy dose of sadism with obvious homosexual overtones.

The title figure is a relatively normal member of the police force, played by Mel Gibson, who decides to take the law, such as it is, into his own hands after his wife, played by Joanne Samuel, is dreadfully injured and their young son is murdered by the bikers.

He sets his jaw like Clint Eastwood in *Dirty Harry,* gets a supercharged black speedster out of the police garage, and with a sawed-off shotgun in his holster wreaks a terrible vengeance. In the final sequence, for example, he gives the last survivor of the motorcycle gang his choice of sawing his own leg off or being burned to death.

Mad Max is ugly and incoherent, and aimed, probably accurately, at the most uncritical of moviegoers. It's worth noting that much of the rudimentary dialogue in this Australian film has been dubbed from "strine," the thick dialect of the subcontinent, into country-and-western English. You can tell because the lip movement and sound are often slightly out of synchronization.

—*T.B., June 14, 1980*

THE MADNESS OF KING GEORGE

Directed by Nicholas Hytner: written by Alan Bennett, based on his play *The Madness of*

George III: director of photography. Andrew Dunn: edited by Tariq Anwar: music adapted from George Friederich Handel by George Fenton: production designer. Ken Adam: produced by Stephen Evans and David Parfitt: released by the Samuel Goldwyn Company. Running time: 105 minutes.

With: Nigel Hawthorne (George III). Helen Mirren (Queen Charlotte). Ian Holm (Willis). Amanda Donohoe (Lady Pembroke). Rupert Graves (Greville). Julian Wadham (Pitt) and Rupert Everett (Prince of Wales).

All the world's a stage for King George III, the royally irrepressible ruler who holds sway throughout *The Madness of King George*. While there's much to admire in Nicholas Hytner's splendid screen adaptation of Alan Bennett's neo-Shakespearean play (*The Madness of George III*), this exuberant tragicomedy is first and foremost a superb showcase. The monarch is a corker, and he commands almost all the attention.

Grandly played by Nigel Hawthorne, who repeats his stage role with a stunningly mercurial display of wit, pathos, and fiery emotion, this wily King is a figure to be reckoned with even when his powers decline. It was under the stormy reign of George III (1760–1810) that England's monarchy lost a substantial degree of its authority to Parliament, while England itself lost the United States (or "the place we mustn't mention," as it's called in the film). As for George himself, he began losing his reason periodically in 1788, when the film takes place, and was deemed quite mad during the last ten years of his monarchy.

Mr. Bennett's drama finds him at a critical juncture, still in control but well aware of the "catalogue of regal nonconformities" he presents to courtiers and loved ones. For all his comic fireworks, Mr. Hawthorne poignantly captures the King's understanding that his power may be slipping, that he may not be able to halt that process, and that a long list of adversaries eagerly awaits his decline.

The star, the filmmaker, and the playwright find something universal in the ways this embattled man fends off the inevitable, using every behavioral weapon in his arsenal to keep his enemies at bay. In the process, they also enjoy the essential hollowness of

keeping up appearances in royal fashion. "Smile at the people," King George exhorts his family, with a puckishness that certainly resonates today. "Wave to them. Let them see that we're happy. That's why we're here."

The early part of the film offers broadly entertaining displays of how this cagey, mocking King uses royal prerogatives to frazzle those around him. There is the music recital he attends, sweeping in to hear "Greensleeves" played on bells and then declaring: "Fascinating stuff, what-what? Let's have it again!" There is the fact that he refuses to let pregnant women be seated during this cultural ordeal, announcing: "If everybody who's having a baby wants to sit down, next thing it'll be everybody with gout."

There are his ways of addressing the Queen sweetly as "Mrs. King," though he is also capable of accusing her of sleeping with their son. There is his sudden decision to rouse his servants for a run at sunrise, announcing: "Six hours' sleep is enough for a man, seven for a woman, and eight for a fool!" There is the visit to a barnyard where the King, who regards himself as a farmer, has a nice, companionable chat with a tiny pig.

Events like these convince those closest to King George that it may be time to question his authority. And Mr. Hytner, the prodigiously talented stage director (of *Carousel* and *Miss Saigon*) who directed *King George* for London's Royal National Theater and now makes a vigorous film debut, has no trouble explicating this chicanery in colorful, entertaining fashion. *The Madness of King George* mixes the ebullience of *Tom Jones* with a pop-theatrical royal back-stabbing that is reminiscent of films like *The Lion in Winter*. That makes it a deft, mischievous, beautifully acted historical drama with exceptionally broad appeal.

Mr. Bennett explicates a convoluted governmental crisis in ways that are both lucid and sly. Challenged on all sides by Prime Minister William Pitt (Julian Wadham); a Member of Parliament, Charles James Fox (Jim Carter); and his own son, the scheming Prince of Wales (a flamboyantly memorable Rupert Everett), this King even winds up reading Shakespeare aloud with his Lord Chancellor one day. "*King Lear*—is that wise?" asks the Lord Chancellor, who has been enlisted to play Cordelia. "I had no idea what it was about, sir," the King's physician replies.

Mr. Bennett certainly knows what *King Lear* is about, but he is content with only an echo or two; for all its intimations of loss, *The Madness of King George* is largely lighthearted. Much of this film devotes itself to subsidiary matters like the abysmal medical practices to which the King is subjected once his condition becomes cause for concern. Typical of the film's contemporary asides is the declaration by one of the King's aides, a man named Fortnum, that he's tired of bedpan duty and thinks going off to Piccadilly to start a provision company might be a good career move. This film loves making hay out of hindsight.

The Madness of King George begins blithely and takes on substance as the King appreciates his own frailty, especially after he is forced to become a patient of Dr. Willis (Ian Holm). This doctor effectively scares the King back to his senses, understanding the problem at a time when ordinary doctors regarded even a physical examination as an impertinence. (The King's malady was eventually thought to be porphyria, a metabolic imbalance whose symptoms include mental disturbance.) Dr. Willis remarks that there are unhinged individuals who imagine themselves to be king. "He *is* the King," he says of his royal patient. "Where shall his fancy take refuge?"

As Mr. Hytner and Mr. Bennett follow that fancy so engagingly, *The Madness of King George* also thrives on the talents of a fine supporting cast. Helen Mirren makes a patient and formidable Queen, tolerating even the King's overt lunges at Lady Pembroke (Amanda Donohoe), her lady-in-waiting. "Did we ever forget ourselves?" King George asks Lady Pembroke, during a spell when the madness has subsided and he can assess his life with uncharacteristic calm. "Because if we did, I should like to remember."

As that suggests, this film eventually sounds grace notes that signal acceptance and understanding, even of facts that were heretofore unbearable. "We must get used to it," King George eventually sighs about the nation formed from his American colonies. "I have known stranger things. I once saw a sheep with five legs."

—*J.M., December 28, 1994*

THE MAGIC FLUTE

Directed by Ingmar Bergman; written (in Swedish, with English subtitles) by Mr. Bergman, based on the opera *Die Zauberflöte* by Wolfgang Amadeus Mozart and Emanuel Schikaneder; cinematographer, Sven Nykvist; edited by Siv Lundgren; music by Mozart; production designer, Henny Noremark; produced by Mans Reutersward; released by Svergies Radio/TV2. Running time: 135 minutes.

With: Ulrik Gold (Sarastro), Josef Köstlinger (Tamino), Erik Saedén (Speaker), Birgit Nordin (Queen of the Night), Irma Urrila (Pamina), Håkan Hagegård (Papageno) and Elisabeth Erikson (Papagena).

It's grand opera. It's a Freemasonry fable. It was made for Swedish television and reportedly cost about $650,000, which would barely cover the expenses of a Hollywood motorcycle movie. It's based on a work with a magnificent score but with a libretto whose second act seems to have forgotten how the first act started.

Yet Ingmar Bergman's screen version of Mozart's *The Magic Flute,* which opened at the Coronet yesterday, is an absolutely dazzling film entertainment, so full of beauty, intelligence, wit, and fun that it becomes a testimonial not only to man's possibilities but also to his high spirits.

All of the best Bergman films have been about some aspect of love (often its absence), but *The Magic Flute* is virtually an act of it.

It is, first and foremost, Mr. Bergman's exuberant tribute to Mozart's genius, with full, amused recognition of the inconsistencies in the Schikaneder libretto. Mr. Bergman hasn't set out to interpret *The Magic Flute* but rather to present it as it originally was, bursting with the life of an exquisite stage production as it would look within the physical limitations of an eighteenth-century court theater.

This approach recalls the Laurence Olivier production of *Henry V,* though there are marked differences. The Bergman *Flute* begins as if it were simply the record of a single performance of the opera on a golden summer evening in a theater set in a royal park. During the overture the camera scans the faces in the contemporary audience, all of whose members, with several obvious exceptions, look exceptionally, particularly Swedish. The recurring expression of the film itself is that of an enraptured little girl (said to be the director's daughter) as she watches the opera unfold.

As the overture ends and the curtain goes up, the camera slides over the footlights into a magical world of painted backdrops and other eighteenth-century stage conventions. Unlike the Olivier *Henry V*, the Bergman *Flute* never moves through the painted backdrops into a realistic world beyond. Though the film, after having established its stage conventions, enlarges upon them and, once or twice, abandons them when it suits the director's purpose, the Bergman production is virtually a hymn in praise of theatricality and the efficacy of art.

At the opera's intermission, the camera catches Tamino and Pamina, the opera's two young lovers, playing chess in a dressing room, while the evil Queen of the Night smokes languidly under a backstage "no smoking" sign. Mr. Bergman, who loves Mozart and the theater, has special fondness for the performers who work so hard for our joy.

The Magic Flute was first performed in a theater near Vienna on September 30, 1791, just a few weeks before Mozart died. Though *Don Giovanni* is the grandest of Mozart's operas, *The Magic Flute* is the more ideally romantic, the work of a man who, while dying, was able to compose the kind of profoundly lyrical and witty music that almost convinces a lot of people—including me—that opera should begin and end with Mozart.

Mr. Bergman treats the odd Schikaneder libretto fairly straight, neither apologizing for it nor patronizing it. Tamino, the young prince who, in the first scene, is charged by the Queen of the Night with the rescue of her daughter from the wicked sorcerer, Sarastro, winds up by becoming a member of Sarastro's mystical priesthood, the members of which are the protectors of truth, beauty, and wisdom. Somewhere near the end of the first act, the Queen of the Night has become the villainess of the piece, and *The Magic Flute* has turned into what was, in its day, quite bold propaganda for Freemasonry.

I hesitate to say even this much about the story of *The Magic Flute* since it gives no indication of the opera's phenomenal beauty and good humor. Reduced to its showbiz essentials, it's about the triumph of the perfect love of Tamino and Pamina, the daughter of the vengeful Queen of the Night, with the help of a little magic and a lot of steadfastness of purpose.

The aural quality of the production is superb. Mr. Bergman recorded the music before he began shooting the film, thus allowing the actors to lip-synch the lyrics (which are in Swedish, not German) instead of belting them out on-camera. The system works beautifully because of technological magic I don't understand and because the actors are lip-synching their own voices.

He has also found singers who both look and sound right, including his Tamino (Josef Köstlinger), who resembles a prince in a Maxfield Parrish mural, and a beautiful Pamina (Irma Urrila), who looks like a young Liv Ullman. He is especially fortunate, too, in his choice of a Papageno (Håkan Hagegård) who manages to be simultaneously robust and comic without ever being opera-silly.

The film is full of memorable moments, some moving, as in the first-act Pamina-Papageno duet, and some gravely funny, as when three little boys in a festively decorated eighteenth-century balloon caution Tamino to be steadfast, silent, and wise, which are probably the three things that any three little boys you or I know would find most difficult to do. The camera, in close-up, never misses a gesture.

Make no mistake: This *Magic Flute* is no uneasy cross-breed of art forms. It's a triumphant film in its own right.

—*V.C., November 12, 1975*

THE MAJOR AND THE MINOR

Directed by Billy Wilder; written by Charles Brackett and Mr. Wilder, based on the play *Connie Goes Home* by Edward Childs Carpenter and the story "Sunny Goes Home" by Fannie Kilbourne; cinematographer, Leo Tover; edited by Doane Harrison; music by Robert Emmett Dolan; art designers, Hans Dreier and Roland Anderson; produced by Arthur Hornblow Jr.; released by Paramount Pictures. Black and white. Running time: 100 minutes.

With: Ginger Rogers (Miss Applegate), Ray Milland (Major Kirby), Rita Johnson (Pamela), Robert Benchley (Mr. Osborne), Diana Lynn (Lucy Hill), Edward Fielding (Colonel Hill) and Lela Rogers (Mrs. Applegate).

Nobody thinks much of it when little girls use mama's clothes to play dress-up. But when a full-grown young lady dons a kid's clothes to play a little girl, it makes a delightful idea for a very cunning film. At least, it has in the case of Paramount's *The Major and the Minor,* which came to the Paramount Theatre yesterday—mainly because Ginger Rogers is the lady who dons the clothes, and also because Billy Wilder and Charles Brackett are two fast boys with a script.

Sly boys they are, too. You'd never dream the Hays office would permit a scene of rather intimate proximity between Miss Rogers and Ray Milland in a Pullman car. Yet youth is the age of innocence, as the Messrs. Wilder and Brackett know. And so they have managed to put by a deliciously risqué contretemps—and a continuously teasing complication—by simply passing the lady off as a little girl. "Don't worry," says Mr. Milland, "it's just like traveling with your grandfather or uncle." But it isn't—not by a long shot. And that is the devilish charm of this film.

For *The Major and the Minor* is really just a cute twist on the mistaken-identity gag, which starts with a homesick young lady, short of the necessary cash, trying to ride half-fare back to Iowa by dressing herself to look like a kid. En route she falls in with a major who teaches at a boys' military school—the major in whose Pullman compartment she breathlessly seeks refuge—and the remaining ambiguous involvements, both on train and at the school, turn on the natural assumption that she is a little girl.

But it takes more than a twist to make a picture, and that's where the Messrs. Wilder and Brackett have come in—by writing a script which effervesces with neat situations and bright lines. For instance, little girls have "button trouble"; the authors have not forgotten that. And little girls who are really grown-up ladies are likely to be uncommonly "filled out." Miss Rogers's reply to this objection is, "Ma says we have some sort of gland trouble." Also there comes a time when certain facts must be imparted to young girls. The opportunity the authors have provided Mr. Milland to convey this knowledge, via moths, is one of the priceless moments in the film. The gentlemen have written—and Mr. Wilder has directed—a bountiful comedy-romance.

And Miss Rogers and Mr. Milland have played it with spirit and taste. Never once does either permit the suggestion of a leer to creep in. Dogged out in pigtails and hair-ribbons, with her face shiny and her legs crossing swords, Miss Rogers gives a beautiful imita-

tion of a Quiz Kid imitating Baby Snooks. And in those moments when romance brightly kindles, she is a soft and altogether winning miss. Put this down as one of the best characterizations of her career.

Credit Mr. Milland, too, with making a warm and nimble fellow of the major, and all the rest of the cast for doing very well with lively roles. Robert Benchley is another genial numbskull, Rita Johnson is something of a cat, Diana Lynn is a frightening younger maiden, and a host of lads are very amusing school cadets.

But it's the minor, after all, that matters, and she is completely tops. "You know, Susu," says Mr. Milland, "you're a very precocious child." Miss Rogers has the right rejoinder. "You bet I am!" You bet she is.

—*B.C., September 17, 1942*

MAJOR BARBARA

Directed by Gabriel Pascal. Harold French and David Lean; written by Anatole de Grunwald and George Bernard Shaw, based on the play by Mr. Shaw; cinematographer, Ronald Neame; edited by Charles Frend; music by William Walton; production designer, Vincent Korda; produced by Mr. Pascal; released by United Artists. Black and white. Running time: 121 minutes.

With: Wendy Hiller (Major Barbara Undershaft), Rex Harrison (Adolphus Cusins), Robert Morley (Andrew Undershaft), Robert Newton (Bill Walker), Emlyn Williams (Snobby Price), Sybil Thorndike (Mrs. Baines), Deborah Kerr (Jenny Hill) and David Tree (Lomax).

Produced in a war-wracked England against odds which only the stiffest courage could lick, Gabriel Pascal's delightful picture version of Bernard Shaw's *Major Barbara* has finally arrived in this country, and opened yesterday at the Astor Theatre. To call it a manifest triumph would be arrant stinginess with words. For this is something more than just a brilliant and adult translation of a stimulating play, something more than a captivating compound of ironic humor and pity. This is a lasting memorial to the devotion of artists working under fire, a permanent proof for posterity that it takes more than bombs to squelch the English wit. It is as wry and impudent a satire of conventional morals and social creeds as though it had been made in a time of easy and carefree peace. It is, in short, a more triumphant picture than any the British have yet sent across.

To be sure, the major part of *Major Barbara* is more than thirty-five years old—that is, the play which Mr. Shaw presented to the London stage in 1905. Long ago it was acted on Broadway—in 1915 and again in 1928. And the still abundant Shavian idolaters know it like the backs of their hands. Yet for all its comparative antiquity, for all our long acquaintance with its theme, it still has the cogent vitality of an essay struck off only yesterday. It comes to grips with a problem—the problem of the human soul versus poverty—which is quite as perplexing today as it was back in 1905. And it is this major part of *Major Barbara* which Mr. Pascal has fully and faithfully brought to the screen.

As a matter of fact, this screen version probably does better by the play than was ever done by it on the stage, even with Mr. Shaw cracking the whip. For, according to most of the recorders, it was static and wordy on the stage, inclining to sag in those stretches where the author shook most weight out of his pen. By some careful and thoroughly respectful editing, by moving his cameras artfully about and by badgering Mr. Shaw into writing two or three new connecting sequences, Mr. Pascal has given the film that terseness and illusion of motion which films must have. In the process he has pointed the wit which crackles in Mr. Shaw's lines and has made more apparent the conflict which is joined rather loosely in the play.

If, by a possible chance, it should not prove too popular all around, the reason will probably be that Mr. Shaw's wit is still too nimble and his reasoning too bold and abstruse. It takes a powerful lot of listening to follow his logistic line, and the intellect is addressed much more vigorously than are the romantic sentiments. In the previous Shaw film, *Pygmalion,* which Mr. Pascal also produced, an essentially personal complication was impishly satirized. In this one the issue is much broader and cuts across more vital social lines.

Major Barbara, the earnest young daughter of the cannon-maker, Andrew Undershaft, is a morally righteous creature who is zealous about saving souls, and through her work in the Salvation Army she feels her efforts properly spent. And the drama—or what there is of it—in the picture is obliquely derived through Barbara's disillusion with the Army when she finds it will take money from her dad; and then from her final persuasion that poverty is the greatest crime of all, that money properly administered is essential to the softening of the soul.

It is in this exquisite social paradox that Mr. Shaw's agile wit finds much fun, and also a share of poignant feeling for the idealistic girl who must be shown. He is, of course, at his best when putting words into the mouth of Undershaft, the sardonic philosopher, or poking around among the riff-raff of a London East End shelter. It is definitely Mr. Shaw's film.

But Mr. Pascal, who has directed, and his completely superlative cast have brought it to vibrant life. Wendy Hiller plays Major Barbara with all the starry-eyed exaltation, all the heartbreak and eventual relief of a girl who endures a real soul-shattering trial. Robert Morley is deliciously satanic, profoundly suave, and tender, too, as the devil's disciple, Undershaft. Rex Harrison plays Adolphus Cusins, Barbara's professorial fiancé, with buoyant good humor, and Robert Newton pretty near wins the acting prize with his trenchant performance of Bill Walker, an East End bully whose soul is too tough for salvation. Other fine performances are given by Donald Calthrop as a wretched down-and-outer, Emlyn Williams as an unctuous deadbeat, Marie Ault as a shrill and wrinkled tosspot, and Torin Thatcher as a fighting soul saver.

And, likewise, a word must be spoken for the acting of Mr. Shaw himself. In a highly amusing and deeply affecting introduction which the bearded author speaks for his film, he irrevocably presents himself as a warm, genial, altogether winning exponent of the human race. Perhaps the old fellow has a temper; perhaps he is as cantankerous as he used to try to be. But thanks to this little preface—and to the greater joy we have found in his works—G.B.S. can rest assured that his triumph is complete.

—*B.C., May 15, 1941*

MAKE WAY FOR TOMORROW

Produced and directed by Leo McCarey: written by Vina Delmar. based on the novel *The Years Are So Long* by Josephine Lawrence and the play by Helen and Nolan Leary: cinematographer. William Mellor: edited by LeRoy Stone: music by Victor

Young and George Antheil; art designers, Hans Dreier and Bernard Herzbrun; released by Paramount Pictures. Black and white. Running time: 91 minutes.

With: Victor Moore (Barkley Cooper), Beulah Bondi (Lucy Cooper), Fay Bainter (Anita Cooper), Thomas Mitchell (George Cooper), Ray Mayer (Robert Cooper) and Barbara Read (Rhoda Cooper).

Leo McCarey's *Make Way for Tomorrow,* which sardonically delayed its Criterion premiere until the eve of Mother's Day, has three qualities rarely encountered in the cinema: humanity, honesty, and warmth. These precious attributes, nurtured and developed by the best script Vina Delmar has written, by Mr. McCarey's brilliant direction, and by the superb performances of Victor Moore, Beulah Bondi, and the rest, have produced an extraordinarily fine motion picture, one that may be counted upon to bid for a place among the "ten best" of 1937.

Based upon Josephine Lawrence's novel *The Years Are So Long* and the dramatization by Helen and Nolan Leary, the film considers, and courageously does not attempt to solve, the familiar but never commonplace problem of an old couple who, unable longer to support themselves, must depend upon the bounty of their children.

Here it is Bark and Lucy Cooper, whose home has been foreclosed and whose savings have been exhausted by four years of an unemployment which obviously is to be permanent, who are compelled to call upon their five sons and daughters for aid. They had hoped to be kept together, preferably in a place of their own. But George and his wife have a daughter to put through college; Nellie's husband couldn't see that he ever had contracted to support his in-laws; Robert did not amount to much; Cora's husband barely provided for his own brood; Addie was out in California.

So Bark and Lucy had to be separated for the first time in fifty years. She comes to New York to live with George and Anita, sharing their daughter's bedroom; Bark goes to Cora, 300 miles away. "Don't you worry; everything will work out all right," the children said. "Well, it never has," Bark replied. And, of course, it never does. The children are not intentionally cruel, nor are the old folk deliberately being nuisances. It is

just that each stands in the other's way and there's nothing they can do about it.

Although the conclusion is tragic and the burden of its story is somber, the film is by no means an unrelieved exercise in melancholy. Mr. McCarey is too much a comedy director for that and Victor Moore too great a comedian to be overwhelmed by his first "serious" role in years. There is a deal of laughter in the trivia of Bark's and Lucy's lives with their children; a deal of gaiety and warming fun in their second honeymoon before it ends in a heartbreak.

If one must mention Lucy's pathetic phone call from Bark, one must also refer to her comic disruption of Anita's bridge class. If you gulp a bit when Bark and his crony, the storekeeper, read Lucy's letter from New York, you also will chuckle delightedly when the cantankerous old boy growls insults at the young doctor they have called in for him. And, by the time the film has run its course, you will have come to know its characters well and grown to love a few of them. Mr. Moore's Bark and Miss Bondi's Lucy and Maurice Moscovitch's Mr. Rubens are in that group. But you must respect, too, the children's point of view, so perfectly expressed by Fay Bainter as Anita, Thomas Mitchell as George, Elisabeth Risdon as the sharp Cora, Barbara Read as the rebellious granddaughter and—well, call it a grand cast.

—*F.S.N., May 10, 1937*

MALCOLM X

Directed by Spike Lee; written by Arnold Perl and Mr. Lee. based on the book *The Autobiography of Malcolm X* as told to Alex Haley; director of photography, Ernest Dickerson; edited by Barry Alexander Brown; music by Terence Blanchard; production designer, Wynn Thomas; produced by Marvin Worth, Mr. Lee, Monty Ross, Jon Kilik and Preston Holmes; released by Warner Brothers. Running time: 199 minutes.

With: Denzel Washington (Malcolm X), Angela Bassett (Betty Shabazz), Al Freeman Jr. (Elijah Muhammad), Delroy Lindo (West Indian Archie), Albert Hall (Baines), Spike Lee (Shorty), Theresa Randle (Laura), Kate Vernon (Sophia), Lonette McKee (Louise Little), Tommy Hollis (Earl Little),

James McDaniel (Brother Earl), Ernest Thompson (Sidney), Jean LaMarre (Benjamin 2X), Bobby Seale (Speaker Number One), Al Sharpton (Speaker Number Two), Christopher Plummer (Chaplain Gill), Karen Allen (Miss Dunne), Peter Boyle (Captain Green) and William Kunstler (Judge).

Malcolm X lived a dozen different lives, each in its way a defining aspect of the black American experience from nightmare to dream. There was never any in-between for the man who was initially called Malcolm Little, the son of a Nebraska preacher, and who, when he died, was known by his Muslim name, El-Hajj Malik El-Shabazz. Malcolm traveled far, through many incarnations, to become as much admired as he was feared as the black liberation movement's most militant spokesman and unrelenting conscience.

Malcolm was already something of a myth when he was assassinated at the Audubon Ballroom in New York on February 21, 1965, just three months short of his fortieth birthday. The publication later that year of *The Autobiography of Malcolm X,* his remarkably vivid testament written with Alex Haley, eventually consolidated his position as a great American folk hero, someone whose life speaks with uncanny pertinence to succeeding generations, white as well as black.

Taking the autobiography and a screenplay by Arnold Perl that was begun more than twenty years ago (Perl died in 1971), Spike Lee has attempted the impossible and almost brought it off. His new *Malcolm X* is not exactly the equal, or even the equivalent, of the book, but it's an ambitious, tough, seriously considered biographical film that, with honor, eludes easy characterization.

Malcolm X will offend many people for all the wrong reasons. It is neither so inflammatory as Mr. Lee's statements about it would have you believe nor so comforting as might be wished by those who would call a halt to speculation concerning Malcolm's murder. It is full of color and exuberance as it tells of life on the streets in Boston and New York, but it grows increasingly austere when Malcolm is arrested for theft and sent to prison, where he finds his life's mission. The movie becomes proper, well mannered, and somber, like Malcolm's dark suits and narrow ties, as it dramatizes his rise in the Nation of Islam, founded by Elijah Muhammad.

Mr. Lee treats the Nation of Islam and its black separatist teachings seriously, and, just as seriously, Malcolm's disillusionment when Elijah Muhammad's fondness for pretty young secretaries is revealed. When, after his split from the Nation of Islam, Malcolm goes on his pilgrimmage to Mecca, the film celebrates his new insight into racial brotherhood, which makes his assassination all the more sorrowful.

In the film's view, a god has been recognized, then lost.

Mr. Lee means for *Malcolm X* to be an epic, and it is in its concerns and its physical scope. In Denzel Washington it also has a fine actor who does for *Malcolm X* what Ben Kingsley did for *Gandhi.* Mr. Washington not only looks the part, but he also has the psychological heft, the intelligence, and the reserve to give the film the dramatic excitement that isn't always apparent in the screenplay.

This isn't a grave fault, nor is it singular. Biographical films, except those about romantic figures long since dead like *Lawrence of Arabia,* carry with them responsibilities that tend to inhibit. Mr. Lee has not been inhibited so much as simultaneously awestruck and hard pressed.

Malcolm X is frank about what it sees as the murder conspiracy, which involves a combination of people representing the Nation of Islam and the Federal Bureau of Investigation. Yet in trying to cover Malcolm's life from his boyhood to his death, it sometimes seems more breathlessly desperate than cogently revealing.

The movie picks up Malcolm's story in the 1940's on his arrival in wartime Boston as a bright but square teenager from rural Michigan. Malcolm eagerly falls in with the wrong crowd, initially represented by Shorty (Mr. Lee), a street hustler who shows him how to dress (a pearl gray zoot suit) and introduces him to the fast set at the Roseland Ballroom. Malcolm learns how to lindy and how to wheel and deal. He discovers women and drugs. In addition to his attachment to Laura (Theresa Randle), a sweet young black woman, he develops a far steamier liaison with a thrill-seeking young white woman, Sophia, played by Kate Vernon, who looks a lot like Carroll Baker in her *Baby Doll* days.

As the film moves forward from the forties, it suffers spasms of flashbacks to Malcolm's childhood in Nebraska and Michigan. These are so fragmented that they may mean nothing to anyone who hasn't read the autobiography. They also don't do justice to the early experiences themselves, especially to Malcolm's time in a white foster home where he excelled in school and was encouraged by well-meaning adults who did not hesitate to refer to him as a "nigger."

Mr. Lee is very good in his handling of individual sequences, but until very near the end, *Malcolm X* fails to acquire the momentum that makes everything that happens seem inevitable. The film goes on and on in a kind of reverential narrative monotone.

The story of Malcolm X is fraught with pitfalls for any moviemaker. Mr. Lee is creating a film about a man he admires for an audience that includes those who have a direct interest in the story, those who may not have an interest but know the details intimately, and those who know nothing or only parts of the story. It's a tricky situation for anyone committed to both art and historical truth.

Mr. Lee's method is almost self-effacing. He never appears to stand between the material and the audience. He himself does not preach. There are no carefully inserted speeches designed to tell the audience what it should think. He lets Malcolm speak and act for himself. The moments of confrontational melodrama, something for which Mr. Lee has a particular gift, are quite consciously underplayed.

In this era of aggressive anti-intellectualism, the film's most controversial subtext might not even be recognized: Malcolm's increasing awareness of the importance of language in his struggle to raise black consciousness. Vaguely articulated feelings aren't enough. Ideas can be expressed only through a command of words.

Before Mr. Lee came to the *Malcolm X* project, other people had worked on it. In addition to Perl's screenplay, there were adaptations by James Baldwin, David Mamet, Calder Willingham, David Bradley, and Charles Fuller. In retrospect, it's easy to see what their difficulties might have been.

Though the autobiography is full of characters and incidents, they are only peripheral to the larger story of Malcolm's awkward journey toward intellectual and spiritual enlightenment. Then, too, Malcolm's life ended before the journey could be said to have been completed. This is not the sort of thing movies accommodate with ease.

Malcolm X never bursts with the free-flowing energy of the director's own fiction, but that's a reflection of the genre, the subject, and Mr. Lee's sense of mission. Though the film is being promoted with all sorts of merchandise on the order of T-shirts and baseball caps, the one item that promotes it best is the new book *By Any Means Necessary: The Trials and Tribulations of the Making of Malcolm X,* by Mr. Lee with Ralph Wiley, published by Hyperion.

In addition to the screenplay, the book has an extensive report on the research Mr. Lee did before starting the production. Among the people he interviewed was the Reverend Louis Farrakhan, who succeeded Elijah Muhammad as the head of the Nation of Islam. It was apparently a polite encounter, but Mr. Lee remains sharp, skeptical, and uninhibited. He's not a reporter to let anyone else have the last word. It's this sort of liveliness that is most missed in the film.

The real triumph of *Malcolm X* is that Mr. Lee was able to make it at all. As photographed by Ernest Dickerson and designed by Wynn Thomas, the movie looks as authentic as any David Lean epic. The large cast of featured players, including Al Freeman Jr., who plays Elijah Muhammad, and Angela Bassett, who plays Malcolm's wife, Betty Shabazz, is supplemented by, among others, Al Sharpton, Christopher Plummer, Bobby Seale, William Kunstler, and Peter Boyle in cameo roles.

Nelson Mandela, photographed in Soweto, appears at the end to speak a kind of benediction.

—*V.C., November 18, 1992*

THE MALTESE FALCON

Directed by John Huston; written by Mr. Huston, based on the novel by Dashiell Hammett; cinematographer, Arthur Edeson; edited by Thomas Richards; music by Adolph Deutsch; art designer, Robert Haas; produced by Henry Blanke; released by Warner Brothers. Black and white. Running time: 100 minutes.

With: Humphrey Bogart (Samuel Spade), Mary Astor (Brigid O'Shaughnessy), Gladys George (Iva Archer), Peter Lorre (Joel Cairo), Barton MacLane (Detective Lieutenant), Lee Patrick (Effie Perine), Sidney Greenstreet (Kasper Gutman), Ward Bond (Detective Polhaus), Jerome Cowan (Miles Archer) and Elisha Cook Jr. (Wilmer Cook).

The Warners have been strangely bashful about their new mystery film, *The Maltese Falcon,* and about the young man, John Huston, whose first directorial job it is. Maybe they thought it best to bring both along under wraps, seeing as how the picture is a remake of an old Dashiell Hammett yarn done ten years ago, and Mr. Huston is a fledgling whose previous efforts have been devoted to writing scripts. And maybe—which is somehow more likely—they wanted to give everyone a nice surprise. For *The Maltese Falcon,* which swooped down onto the screen of the Strand yesterday, only turns out to be the best mystery thriller of the year, and young Mr. Huston gives promise of becoming one of the smartest directors in the field.

For some reason, Hollywood has neglected the sophisticated crime film of late, and England, for reasons which are obvious, hasn't been sending her quota in recent months. In fact, we had almost forgotten how devilishly delightful such films can be when done with taste and understanding and a feeling for the fine line of suspense. But now, with *The Maltese Falcon,* the Warners and Mr. Huston give us again something of the old thrill we got from Alfred Hitchcock's brilliant melodramas or from *The Thin Man* before he died of hunger.

This is not to imply, however, that Mr. Huston has imitated anyone. He has worked out his own style, which is brisk and supremely hardboiled. We didn't see the first *Falcon,* which had Ricardo Cortez and Bebe Daniels in its cast. But we'll wager it wasn't half as tough nor half as flavored with idioms as is this present version, in which Humphrey Bogart hits his peak. For the trick which Mr. Huston has pulled is a combination of American ruggedness with the suavity of the English crime school—a blend of mind and muscle—plus a slight touch of pathos.

Perhaps you know the story (it was one of Mr. Hammett's best) of a private detective in San Francisco who becomes involved through a beautiful but evasive dame in a complicated plot to gain possession of a fabulous jeweled statuette. As Mr. Huston has adapted it, the mystery is as thick as a wall and the facts are completely obscure as the picture gets under way. But slowly the bits fall together, the complications draw out, and a monstrous but logical intrigue of international proportions is revealed.

Much of the quality of the picture lies in its excellent revelation of character. Mr. Bogart is a shrewd, tough detective with a mind that cuts like a blade, a temperament that sometimes betrays him, and a code of morals which is coolly cynical. Mary Astor is well-nigh perfect as the beautiful woman whose cupidity is forever to be suspect. Sidney Greenstreet, from the Theatre Guild's roster, is magnificent as a cultivated English crook, and Peter Lorre, Elisha Cook Jr., Lee Patrick, and Barton MacLane all contribute stunning characters. (Also, if you look closely, you'll see Walter Huston, John's father, in a bit part.)

Don't miss *The Maltese Falcon* if your taste is for mystery fare. It's the slickest exercise in cerebration that has hit the screen in many months, and it is also one of the most compelling nervous-laughter provokers yet.

—*B.C., October 4, 1941*

A MAN FOR ALL SEASONS

Produced and directed by Fred Zinnemann: written by Robert Bolt and Constance Willis. based on the play by Mr. Bolt: cinematographer. Ted Moore: edited by Ralph Kemplen: music by Georges Delarue: production designer. John Box: released by Columbia Pictures. Running time: 120 minutes.

With: Paul Scofield (Sir Thomas More). Wendy Hiller (Alice More). Leo McKern (Thomas Cromwell). Robert Shaw (King Henry VIII). Orson Welles (Cardinal Wolsey). Susannah York (Margaret More). Nigel Davenport (Duke of Norfolk). John Hurt (Richard Rich). Corin Redgrave (William Roper). Vanessa Redgrave (Anne Boleyn). Colin Blakely (Matthew) and Yootha Joyce (Averil Machin).

Fred Zinnemann has done a fine job of putting upon the screen the solid substance of *A Man for All Seasons,* Robert Bolt's play about Sir Thomas More, and in doing so he presents us with an awesome view of a sturdy conscience and a steadfast heart.

Within such magnificent settings as only England itself could provide to convey the resplendence and color of the play's sixteenth-century mise-en-scène, and with Paul Scofield playing Sir Thomas as he did so superbly on the stage, Mr. Zinnemann has crystallized the essence of this drama in such pictorial terms as to render even its abstractions vibrant. The film opened at the Fine Arts last night.

I lay stress upon the screen, because the play is essentially a showing of just one prolonged conflict of wills, one extended exposition of a man's refusal to swerve from his spiritual and intellectual convictions at the insistence of his King. And such ideological disagreements are difficult to state in visual terms, no matter how pyrotechnic the proponents and opponents may be.

It is to Mr. Zinnemann's credit that he has not allowed his excellent cast to resort to pyrotechnics, except in the singular case of Robert Shaw's tempestuous performance of the unbalanced Henry VIII. Mr. Shaw is permittedly eccentric, like the sweep of a hurricane—now roaring with seeming refreshment, now ominously calm, now wild with wrath—as he shapes a frightening portrait of the headstrong, heretical King who demands that More give acquiescence to his marriage with Anne Boleyn.

But Mr. Scofield is brilliant in his exercise of temperance and restraint, of disciplined wisdom and humor, as he variously confronts his restless King or Cardinal Wolsey, who is played by Orson Welles with subtle, startling glints of poisonous evil that, in this day, are extraordinary for him. Mr. Scofield is equally disciplined and forceful in his several dialectical duels with the King's advocate, Thomas Cromwell, who is played by Leo McKern with truly diabolical malevolence, or in his playful discourses with his son-in-law, William Roper, whom Corin Redgrave makes a bit of a fop.

In fact, it is this delineation of More's sterling strength and character, his intellectual vigor and remarkable emotional control, that endow this film with dynamism in even its most talky scenes. And, heaven knows, it is talky—full of long theological discourses and political implications that you must know your history to understand.

Likewise, it is repetitive in tracing the painful course of More to his final showdown before a rigged high court, where he is betrayed by a young Judas, and thence to the merciful block. And along this route, some of his sessions, especially with Master Rich, the sycophant of John Hurt, who betrays him, are much too involved and difficult.

But throughout, Mr. Scofield manages to use the glowing words of Mr. Bolt and his own histrionic magnificence to give a luminescence and power, integrity and honor, to this man who will not "yes" his King. And he also gets some deep emotion in his ultimate farewell scene with his stalwart wife, played by Wendy Hiller, and his daughter, played (too softly) by Susannah York.

It is notable that Mr. Bolt, in writing his own screenplay, has dropped the Common Man, who was a glib and ubiquitous character of vulgar wit and cynicism on the stage. By this stroke, he has eliminated the built-in point of view of the commonality to these grand monarchial intrigues that was helpful to a balance of the whole.

Moreover, the staging of the drama on the screen in a naturalistic style, with authentic medieval locations and sharply detailed sets designed by John Box, removes it from the ambience of philosophical reflection achieved in the abstract set of the stage production and puts it in the aspect of historical literalness. Both of these significant changes put a burden of stark illusion on the film.

I would say that the film misses the humor and pragmatism of the Common Man, and it sacrifices some scope of vision with the loss of the abstract set. But it gains great pictorial conviction with the naturalistic style and the beautiful color photography of Ted Moore.

A Man for All Seasons is a picture that inspires admiration, courage, and thought.

—B.C., December 13, 1966

MAN HUNT

Directed by Fritz Lang; written by Dudley Nichols, based on the novel *Rogue Male* by Geoffrey Household; cinematographer, Arthur Miller; edited by Allen McNeil; music by Alfred Newman; art designers, Richard Day and Wiard Ihnen; produced by Kenneth McGowan; released by Twentieth Century Fox. Black and white. Running time: 105 minutes.

With: Walter Pidgeon (Captain Alan Thorndike), Joan Bennett (Jerry), George Sanders (Major Quive-Smith), John Carradine (Mr. Jones), Roddy

McDowall (Vaner), Ludwig Stossel (Doctor), Frederic Worlock (Lord Risborough) and Heather Thatcher (Lady Risborough).

A great many folks in the world have toyed fondly with the dream of taking a potshot at Hitler from some convenient blind. It is a beguiling chimera in which one's helpless vehemence may find release—a chimera which is easily embellished with all sorts of lurid prospects. So, inevitably, it has been adopted as the point of departure for a grim, suspenseful film turned out by Twentieth Century Fox under the compelling title of *Man Hunt* and released at the Roxy yesterday.

If you are one of the people who have entertained that desperate thought, you shouldn't miss this film. For it tells of an English big-game hunter who, shortly before the outbreak of the present war, conceives the fantastic notion of simply stalking Hitler for sport. When he has his gun trained on the quarry, however, and is debating with himself whether to shoot, he is apprehended by guards and hauled before the Gestapo. The remainder of the picture tells with stark and terrifying ruthlessness how an attempt is made by the Nazis to use him as an international scapegoat, how he miraculously escapes and makes his way back to England, and how he is hounded even there by his cold and merciless pursuers. It is a sinister tale, with a surprising ending which fairness compels us to conceal.

For its keen and vivid contrast of British and Nazi temperaments—its interesting analysis of the so-called sportsman's code—*Man Hunt* rates somewhat above the run of ordinary "chase" films. In that respect, it projects certain subtle psychological overtones. But basically, of course, it is a straight melodrama composed of one long "chase"—a modern adaptation of the ancient "law of flight." And, as such, we feel that it doesn't fulfill its possibilities completely.

It is a film which is handsomely made and directed by Fritz Lang with unremitting intensity. Mr. Lang has also achieved the difficult task in such films of creating an illusion of actuality. Walter Pidgeon plays the leading role of the English huntsman—or rather the hunted—with superior sinew and integrity; George Sanders makes a hard and treacherous Nazi agent; even Joan Bennett handles the role of a Cockney streetwalker with delicacy, and the remainder of the cast is up to scratch.

But the script which Dudley Nichols prepared from a novel by Geoffrey Household—the popular novel *Rogue Male*—has holes in it. For one, the Nazi Gestapo has been endowed with incredible ubiquity. Sly agents are all over the place, and always taking the right turn. For another, the design of the Nazis upon the hunted man after he has escaped is never made properly clear. If it is merely that they want him to sign a paper, why couldn't his signature be forged? And finally, why should he worry after he arrives safely in England? It is preposterous to think he'd be sent back to Germany for trial.

To be sure, Mr. Nichols has attempted to plug up these holes with reasons, but every one of them leaks. And, as a consequence, you constantly feel that the "chase" is entirely contrived. Exciting? Yes, it is. But convincing? No. Somehow you just keep on asking, "For goodness sake, what makes Captain Thorndike run?"

—*B.C., June 14, 1941*

THE MAN WHO CAME TO DINNER

Directed by William Keighley; written by Julius J. Epstein and Philip G. Epstein, based on the play by George S. Kaufman and Moss Hart; cinematographer, Tony Gaudio; edited by Jack Killifer; music by Frederick Hollander; art designer, Robert Haas; produced by Jerry Wald and Jack Saper; released by Warner Brothers. Black and white. Running time: 112 minutes.

With: Bette Davis (Maggie Cutler), Ann Sheridan (Lorraine Sheldon), Monty Woolley (Sheridan Whiteside), Richard Travis (Bert Jefferson), Jimmy Durante (Banjo), Reginald Gardiner (Beverly Carlton), Billie Burke (Mrs. Stanley) and Elisabeth Fraser (June Stanley).

Just in time to slip under the wire as the niftiest comedy of 1942 (to date), the Warners' meticulous screen version of the George S. Kaufman—Moss Hart play, *The Man Who Came to Dinner*, kept an appointment at the Strand yesterday and pealed off more concentrated merriment than did the New Year's bells. Anyone who happened to miss the original acid-throwing antic on the stage—and anyone, for that matter, who happened not to have missed it—should pop around, by all means, and catch the cinematic reprise. For here, in the space of something like an hour and fifty-two minutes, is compacted what is unquestionably the most vicious but hilarious cat-clawing exhibition ever put on the screen, a deliciously wicked character portrait and a helter-skelter satire, withal.

Perhaps motion-picture audiences, in their oft-alleged innocence, will fail to perceive the mimicry supposedly implied in this film—the fact that the leading character, according to the Broadway Nestors, is but a thinly veiled impersonation of a writer and critic of portly frame who lectures for fabulous tributes and is called the Towncrier on the air. Maybe they won't even get it. But, if they don't, it makes no nevermind, for the probing is so incisive that a lot of ladies might be shocked otherwise. And, anyhow, it is a character which capably stands on its own feet.

Or should we say a character which sits on its own laurels? For the story, as everyone remembers, is that of a famous gadabout who takes an injurious tumble on the steps of a Medalia, Ohio, home and then spends three hectic weeks as a wheelchair tyrant within that house, bulldozing the permanent residents, flooding the living room with claptrap worldliness, and meddling with particular chicanery in the romance between his secretary and a local journalist. On this latter intrigue, you remember, hangs the wildly complicated plot.

The Messrs. Kaufman and Hart wrote the play very much in the image of a river of incidents and wisecracks plunging over a precipice. And the Warners have smartly filmed it at the same fluid, headlong tempo, keeping virtually all of the action flexing within the four walls of one room and making only such slight alterations as decent modesty compelled.

Also, the Warners were most wise when they finally decided to cast Monty Woolley in the title role which he so handsomely played on the stage. For Mr. Woolley makes *The Man Who Came to Dinner* a rare old goat. His zest for rascality is delightful, he spouts alliterations as though he were spitting out orange seeds, and his dynamic dudgeons in a wheelchair are even mightier than those of Lionel Barrymore. A more entertaining buttinsky could hardly be conceived, and a less entertaining one would be murdered on the spot.

One palm should be handed Bette Davis for accepting the secondary role of the secretary, and another palm should be handed her for playing it so moderately and well. Ann Sheridan, too, as an actress of definitely feline breed, gives a tartly mannered performance, and Jimmy Durante plays Jimmy Durante with so much gusto that it is just as well for our diaphragms that his part is comparatively brief. He's a killer while in there, though. And Reginald Gardiner, Billy Burke, Grant Mitchell, Mary Wickes, a new young actor named Richard Travis, and a cast which is perfect to a man assist most competently.

The picture as a whole is a bit too long and internally complex for 100 percent comprehension, considering the speed at which it clips. But even if you don't catch all of it, you're sure to get your money's worth. It makes laughing at famous people a most satisfying delight.

—*B.C., January 2, 1942*

THE MAN WHO LOVED WOMEN

Directed by François Truffaut; written (in French, with English subtitles) by Mr. Truffaut, Michel Fermaud and Suzanne Schiffman; cinematographer, Néstor Almendros; edited by Martine Barraqué-Curie; music by Maurice Jaubert; released by Cinema V. Running time: 119 minutes.

With: Charles Denner (Bertrand Morane), Brigitte Fossey (Geneviève Bigey), Nelly Borgeaud (Delphine Grezel), Leslie Caron (Vera) and Geneviève Fontanel (Hélène).

Bertrand Morane (Charles Denner) is a bachelor in his early forties. He lives in Montpellier in southern France, where he makes a decent if not great living in a testing laboratory. Bertrand is polite, intelligent, and sensitive, but mostly he is obsessed by women. Pretty ones, beautiful ones, plain ones, old ones, young ones. There are also one he never sees (the voice of the telephone operator who awakens him in the morning) and one he hasn't seen for many years—his mother.

When Bertrand dies, which is the way François Truffaut begins his lighthearted, wise new comedy, *The Man Who Loved Women*, the mourners who push through the winter chill to the cemetery are, without exception, women. Though Bertrand was obsessed by women and though he might have felt guilty about using them at times, it is not an untypical Truffaut reversal that Bertrand was as much used by them, not meanly but, after all, a man who loves women with such persistence (which is not to be confused with fidelity) is rare these days, worthy of having attention paid.

In this new film, Mr. Truffaut's sixteenth feature since *The 400 Blows* in 1959, the director is working in a vein usually thought to be frivolous to examine the serious, primary game that men and women play, an ancient pastime whose rules are changing, as one of his characters notes. I suppose there's always been a little of the late Ernst Lubitsch in all Truffaut comedies, though I wouldn't want to have to prove it, but there is more than I've ever seen before in *The Man Who Loved Women.*

It's full of the double-edged wit of the self-aware. Although it's a comedy about the sexes, it's less sexist, essentially, than Agnes Varda's liberation ode, *One Sings, the Other Doesn't.* I don't mean to impose a heavier burden on *The Man Who Loved Women* than it can carry, but the Truffaut comedy, in the way it appreciates women in their infinite variety and understands what they're up against, is infinitely more liberated than most liberated films, which reduce women to abstract concepts.

Enough of that sort of talk, though.

The movie is a supremely humane, sophisticated comedy that is as much fun to watch for the variations Mr. Truffaut works on classic man-woman routines as for the routines themselves. The narrative line is so gossamer-thin it barely sustains the sentence that describes it: Bertrand, in his memoirs, completed shortly before he's killed in an accident, remembers all the women he's loved, and a number he hasn't, trying in this fashion to understand why he has never been able to settle down.

There are, among others, Nicole, the theater usher who first caught his attention by the seductive noise of one silk-stockinged leg crossing the other; Hélène, a woman of his age who turns him down because she's attracted only to young men; Liliane, the headstrong waitress with whom he never slept and who, he says, is his "evidence that a man and a woman can be just friends."

Most hilariously there is Delphine (Nelly Borgeaud), a married woman whose deepest passions are unlocked by the unsuspecting Bertrand and who has a way of maneuvering him into situations in which they are threatened with public exposure. "Oh," says the overheated Delphine, tearing off her clothes in the car, "the things you make me do!"

There is also—in the film's most marvelous, most surprising sequence—an encounter with Vera, beautifully played by Leslie Caron, a woman with whom he had an extended affair some years before. It's a scene that lasts no more than four or five minutes, but it's so remarkably well played and written that an entire love affair, from the beginning to the middle and the end, is movingly evoked through what is really just exposition.

The film's style is so economical it seems almost terse. The flashback to Bertrand's childhood, in which the boy was made the go-between for his mother in her affairs, suggests the young Antoine of *The 400 Blows,* while Bertrand's funny, sweet encounter with a little girl he finds crying on a stairway recalls the Antoine of *Love at Twenty.* Bertrand asks the little girl why she's crying and finally gets her to concede that there is a certain amount of pleasure in being so unhappy, which makes her brighten immediately.

Brigitte Fossey plays Bertrand's literary editor, the one person, you feel, who might have straightened him out if she had taken him as seriously as he had begun to take her. Perhaps not. The film is open-ended on this.

Charles Denner is very, very funny as Bertrand, a fellow who has the same single-minded purpose as the rat exterminator he played in *Such a Gorgeous Kid Like Me,* as well as the delicacy of touch of Antoine Doinel on his best behavior.

It's not the Truffaut way to make movies that contain flat statements. Like almost every film he's ever done, *The Man Who Loved Women* considers some of the aspects and manifestations of love and then shakes its head—in a mixture of wonder, delight, and sadness.

—*V.C., October 1, 1977*

THE MAN WHO WASN'T THERE

Directed by Joel Coen; written by Joel Coen and Ethan Coen; director of photography. Roger

Deakins: edited by Roderick Jaynes and Tricia Cooke: music by Carter Burwell: production designer. Dennis Gassner: produced by Ethan Coen: released by USA Films. Running time: 112 minutes.

With: Billy Bob Thornton (Ed). Frances McDormand (Doris). Michael Badalucco (Frank). James Gandolfini (Big Dave). Katherine Borowitz (Ann Nirdlinger). Jon Polito (Creighton Tolliver). Scarlett Johansson (Birdy Abundas). Richard Jenkins (Walter Abundas) and Tony Shalhoub (Freddy Riedenschneider).

In *The Man Who Wasn't There* Billy Bob Thornton plays Ed Crane, a barber plying his trade in Santa Rosa, Calif., in 1949. The title is only slightly overstated. In this silver-gray film noir world, Ed at first seems as substantial as a shadow or the smoke from his unfiltered cigarettes. (He smokes so many of them that the movie deserves a surgeon general's warning to go with its M.P.A.A. rating.) He is content to work the second chair in his brother-in-law's barber shop and to go home to a bungalow on a shady street, where he lives in passionless matrimony with Doris (Frances McDormand), who keeps the books at a local department store.

On second thought, "content" is a bit of a stretch. Ed's dominant emotional state is a kind of baffled depression. Mr. Thornton's downturned mouth and deeply creased brow make Ed a spectator of his own uneventful life. Fallen arches kept him out of service in the war, and it seems unlikely he will see any kind of action on the home front. But then, in a small, ineffectual attempt to overcome his own passivity, Ed allows himself to be suckered by a garrulous traveling salesman (Jon Polito), who is looking for investors in a dry-cleaning venture.

To raise the capital, the barber decides to blackmail Doris's boss (James Gandolfini), with whom she is having an affair. Ed's small, sad act of protest against the meaninglessness of his own existence sets in motion a series of large and small disasters that have a curiously paradoxical effect. The closer Ed comes to utter ruin, the more alive he seems, and his downcast, expressionless countenance begins to glow with something like beatitude.

Also paradoxically, Mr. Thornton endows this shadow-man with extraordinary presence. Ed has very little to say to the big talkers who surround him, and Mr. Thornton's voice-over narration, playing over shots of his motionless face, emphasizes the character's essential alienation. The intense stillness of that face becomes the film's center of gravity, just as the increasingly animated voice becomes its propulsive force. Ed's blankness, which only Doris really appreciates, makes him easy to misread. "He is modern man," proclaims a slick Sacramento lawyer (Tony Shalhoub), who uses the Heisenberg uncertainty principle as a courtroom tactic. ("They got this guy over in Germany. Franz something. Or maybe it's Werner.")

"Do you know what you are, Mr. Crane," asks Birdy Abundas (Scarlett Johansson), a high school student whose piano playing becomes a source of solace for Ed in his times of trouble. "You're an enthusiast." This judgment is nearly as misguided as the sexual overture that follows, but it surely applies to Joel and Ethan Coen, who have followed the tall-tale Depression-era silliness of *O Brother, Where Art Thou* with this somber, comical visit to the paranoid universe of late-40's noir.

It's probable that most filmmakers love making movies, but few of them express this love with such voracious, crazy ardor. The brothers are a pair of brilliant oxymorons: shaggy-dog formalists, at once obsessed with every detail and apt to let their stories run wild. *The Man Who Wasn't There* moves with the stately grace of the Beethoven that decorates the soundtrack, but it is also a hectic grab bag of cold war Americana: flying saucers, pulp magazines, rayon shirts and porcelain coffee cups.

Last May the movie shared the director's prize at Cannes with David Lynch's *Mulholland Drive*. Like Mr. Lynch, the Coens have used the noir idiom to fashion a haunting, beautifully made movie that refers to nothing outside itself and that disperses like a vapor as soon as it's over. The critique of this kind of filmmaking is obvious enough: not only is there more to life than movies, there's more to movies than making reference to other movies. But in the case of *The Man Who Wasn't There,* it is possible to put such objections aside and luxuriate in the intelligent movie-ness of the experience.

The Coens are routinely praised, sometimes backhandedly, for their smarts, but they don't get enough credit for their generosity. *The Man Who Wasn't There* is full of delightful idiosyncrasies and surprising bits of acting. The Coen regulars—Mr. Polito, Ms. McDormand and Michael Badalucco, who plays Ed's gabby brother-in-law—all do terrific work twisting period types into odd new shapes, and Ms. Johansson, Mr. Gandolfini and Richard Jenkins (as Birdy's grieving, drunken father) are all terrific.

But Mr. Thornton is the Pole Star—or perhaps the black hole—around which everything else turns. At times the movie seems like a collaboration between the actor and Roger Deakins, the cinematographer who has shot the last five Coen brothers movies. Mr. Deakins's mastery of the focal and textural possibilities of black-and-white recalls old Hollywood masters like the prolific James Wong Howe and like Gregg Toland, who shot *Citizen Kane* and *The Best Years of Our Lives*. He is as eclectic as the Coens themselves. In one breathtaking sequence a family reunion in the Northern California countryside transports us from the gloom of film noir into the bleached sunshine of Italian neo-realism. But his camera work is especially tailored to the lines of Mr. Thornton's face and the comb tracks in his silvery hair. The rest of the movie, with its corkscrew plot and whiplash reversals, may fade quickly and pleasantly from memory, but that face remains emphatically there.

—A.O.S., October 31, 2001

THE MAN WITH THE GOLDEN ARM

Produced and directed by Otto Preminger; written by Walter Newman and Lewis Meltzer; based on the novel by Nelson Algren; cinematographer, Sam Leavitt; edited by Louis Loeffler; music by Elmer Bernstein; production designer, Joseph Wright; released by United Artists. Black and white. Running time: 119 minutes.

With: Frank Sinatra (Frankie), Eleanor Parker (Zosh), Kim Novak (Melly), Arnold Stang (Sparrow), Darren McGavin (Louie), Robert Strauss (Schwiefka) and John Conte (Drunky).

Why there should be any question about showing *The Man with the Golden Arm*, the new film about drug addiction that has been denied a screen Production Code seal, is—as the King of Siam said—a puzzlement. (It opened at the Victoria last night, despite that parochial disapproval, since it has been passed by the New York censor board.)

To the eyes of this watchful reviewer, this cleaned-up version of the Nelson Algren tale, which Otto Preminger has produced and directed and which has Frank Sinatra as its star, is nothing more than a long, torturous picture of one man's battle to beat a craving for dope. And there is nothing more bold or shocking in it than a few shots of this guy writhing on the floor.

To be sure, there is one pregnant sequence in which the character, tormented to the point where he can no longer fight off his craving (from which he had thought himself "cured"), pops around to the place of a "pusher" and pops down five dollars for a "fix." (A "fix" in the lingo of the "junkies"—or addicts—is a shot of dope.) The "pusher" gets out a pinch of powder, a hypodermic needle, a spoon, and some other uncertain paraphernalia, preparatory to administering the drug. The next thing you see is him arranging to punch the needle in the character's arm. Then you see just the eyes of Mr. Sinatra as the drug presumably enters him.

We understand some footage that was in this sequence has been cut—footage that showed the mixing of the powder in water and the heating of it in the spoon. This was cut, we understand, to avoid trouble over instructing in the methods of taking dope. But either way, what you see or what you don't see is not likely to create anything—outside of the hardened addicts—but a revulsion toward the habit of drugs.

In short, for all the delicacy of the subject and for all the pathological shivers in a couple of scenes, there is nothing very surprising or exciting about *The Man with the Golden Arm*. It is a pretty plain and unimaginative look-see at a lower-depths character with a perilous weakness for narcotics that he miraculously overcomes in the end. *The Lost Weekend* was much more arresting and shocking in its study of a drunkard.

Mr. Sinatra gives a plausible performance as the "junkie" who drifts back to the stuff when the pressures get too heavy for him after his return to his old haunts from taking "the cure." His old haunts consist of the cheap spots in a big town—Chicago, perhaps—where he is a professional dealer for a floating poker game. One smoky session in a backroom with the card sharps is more exciting than all the stuff about dope.

But the others in the cast are less effective. Eleanor

Parker as an uncertain dame who manages to hang on to the hero by feigning a crippling illness is the least. She looks and talks like a well-bred, well-kept lady—living in a slum. Mr. Preminger weakened his film immensely by not having her a realistic drab.

Kim Novak makes a strangely pallid figure as the nightclub girl who finally helps the hero toss "the monkey off his back" merely by locking him in her room for a couple of days, and Darren McGavin is a stock oily villain as the peddler of the dope. Arnold Stang as a feeble-minded lackey, Robert Strauss as a cheap gambling tout, and John Conte as a suitor to Miss Novak are standard types from gangster films.

—B.C., December 16, 1955

THE MANCHURIAN CANDIDATE

Directed by John Frankenheimer; written by George Axelrod, based on the novel by Richard Condon; cinematographer, Lionel Lindon; edited by Ferris Webster; music by David Amram; art designers, Richard Sylbert and Philip Jefferies; produced by Howard W. Koch; released by United Artists. Black and white. Running time: 126 minutes.

With: Frank Sinatra (Bennett Marco), Laurence Harvey (Raymond Shaw), Janet Leigh (Rosie), Angela Lansbury (Raymond's Mother), James Gregory (Senator Iselin) and John McGiver (Senator Jordan).

With the air full of international tension, the film *The Manchurian Candidate* pops up with a rash supposition that could serve to scare some viewers half to death—that is, if they should be dupes enough to believe it, which we solemnly trust they won't.

Its story of a moody young fellow who was captured by the Communists during the Korean campaign and brainwashed by them to do their bidding as a high-level assassin when he gets home to America is as wild a piece of fiction as anything Alfred Hitchcock might present, but it could agitate some grave imaginings in anxious minds these days, especially since it is directed and acted in a taut and vivid way.

Presumably it was intended as a thriller with over-tones of social and political satire—a deliberate double-barreled shot at the vicious practice of brainwashing, whether done by foreign militarists or by fanatical politicians working on the public here at home. That was the evident purpose of the novel by Richard Condon, on which it is based.

But somewhere along in the turning of the novel into the film that opened yesterday at the Astor, at the Trans-Lux 85th, and at some thirteen other theaters in the metropolitan area, the figure of the Communist-triggered killer loomed out of all proportion to the ridiculous United States senator who is set up as his thematic counterpart.

The menace of this fellow, the hypnotized hero with a gun waiting to do the bidding of the Moscow Frankensteins, becomes so ominous and pervasive that the rabid red-baiting senator—his stepfather, managed by his mother—becomes no more than a dunce, a joke. Whatever chance of balanced satire and ironic point there might have been in the subtle equating of these two firebrands is lost in the script of George Axelrod.

Also the basic suppositions, which might be more tolerable in a clearly satiric context, are extremely hard to take as here put forth. We are asked to believe that, in three days, a fellow could be brainwashed to the point that two years later, he would still be dutifully submissive to his brainwashers' spell. And the nature of the plot and its key figure here in this country, when finally revealed, are so fantastic that one is suspicious of the author's sincerity.

With that said, however, it must be added that the film is so artfully contrived, the plot so interestingly started, the dialogue so racy and sharp, and John Frankenheimer's direction so exciting in the style of Orson Welles when he was making *Citizen Kane* and other pictures that the fascination of it is strong. So many fine cinematic touches and action details pop up that one keeps wishing the subject would develop into something more than it does.

Laurence Harvey is impressive as the killer—a darkly moving evil force—until he has to perform the nonsense that is worked out for him at the end. Frank Sinatra is slightly overzealous and too conspicuous with nervous tics to carry complete conviction as the army major (also a brainwash victim) who breaks the case. But Angela Lansbury is intense as the killer's mother, James Gregory is vulgar and droll as the senator (modeled after Joseph R. McCarthy), and Khigh Dhiegh plays a villain handsomely.

With so much in it that examples a dynamic use of the screen, it is too bad that *The Manchurian Candidate* has so little to put across.

—*B.C., October 25, 1962*

MANHATTAN

Directed by Woody Allen; written by Mr. Allen and Marshall Brickman; director of photography, Gordon Willis; edited by Susan E. Morse; music by George Gershwin; production designer, Mel Bourne; produced by Charles H. Joffe; released by United Artists. Black and white. Running time: 96 minutes.

With: Woody Allen (Isaac Davis), Diane Keaton (Mary Wilke), Michael Murphy (Yale), Mariel Hemingway (Tracy), Meryl Streep (Jill), Ann Byrne (Emily), Karen Ludwig (Connie), Wallace Shawn (Jeremiah), Bella Abzug (Guest of Honor), Frances Conroy (Shakespearean Actress) and Mark Linn-Baker (Shakespearean Actor).

As California is our idealized future, a place where there is no downtown because the suburbs have moved in instead of out, hip Manhattan represents our idealized present. Existence in Manhattan is so fleeting that one sometimes wishes one could predate oneself, as do the weekly magazines, in this way to avoid life's litter basket, for a few days, anyway.

Manhattan, Woody Allen's extraordinarily fine and funny new film, is about many things, including a time and place where fashion probably blights more lives, more quickly, than any amounts of booze, drugs, radioactive fallout, and saturated animal fats. In this Manhattan, it's no longer a question of keeping up, but of staying ahead. The person on this week's cover is a leading candidate for next year's feature story that asks, "Whatever happened to . . . ?"

To survive in alien landscapes, animals develop bizarre defense mechanisms, often at a certain cost. Ostriches can run fast, but they are unable to fly. Sharks have teeth like the slicing blade in a Cuisinart, yet if they take a stationary snooze, their lungs fill with water and they drown. They must always keep moving.

This is pretty much the fate of a number of people who move through and around the Manhattan of Isaac Davis (Mr. Allen), a successful comedy writer who quits his television job to write a novel. As Isaac Davis is Mr. Allen's most fully realized, most achingly besieged male character, so is *Manhattan* his most moving and expansive work to date. It's as serious as *Interiors*—if one must use that often foolish word— but far less constricted and self-conscious. In *Manhattan,* Mr. Allen is working in a milieu he knows well and with characters he understands and appreciates, especially when they are drowning.

In addition to being the director and coauthor— with Marshall Brickman—of the film, Mr. Allen is its most important presence. He gives *Manhattan* a point of reference just as he did ten years ago when the character he played was named Virgil Starkwell in *Take the Money and Run.* How Virgil and Woody have grown!

Manhattan moves on from both *Interiors* and *Annie Hall,* being more effectively critical and more compassionate than the first and more witty and clear-eyed than the second. There is a sense of applied romance here, especially in the soundtrack use of some of the lushest melodies ever written by George Gershwin, as well as in Mr. Allen's decision to have Gordon Willis photograph *Manhattan* in the kind of velvety black-and-white I associate with old M-G-M films like *East Side, West Side* and *The Bad and the Beautiful.* The movie looks so good that it looks unreal, which, in this day and age of film and fashion, is to go so far out that you're back in.

Manhattan is, of course, about love, or, more accurately, about relationships. Among those who are attempting to relate to Isaac Davis are Mary Wilke (Diane Keaton), a journalist who carries on like an Annie Hall who has been analyzed out of her shyness into the shape of an aggressively neurotic woman doomed to make a mess of things, and Tracy (Mariel Hemingway), a beautiful, seventeen-year-old nymphet with a turned-down mouth and a trust in her forty-two-year-old lover, Isaac, that is also doomed. In addition, there is Yale (Michael Murphy), Isaac's best friend, who hands Mary over to Isaac for as long as it suits his (Yale's) purposes.

On the fringe of the film, observing the events with the grim determination of someone who has made a decision that must be stuck by, is Isaac's former wife, Jill (Meryl Streep), who left Isaac and, with their small son, moved in with her female lover, in such circumstances to write a best-selling book about her life titled *Marriage, Divorce and Selfhood.*

Manhattan, which opens today at the Baronet and other theaters, is mostly about Isaac's efforts to get some purchase on his life after he initiates a breakup with his illegal, teenage mistress—a marvelous scene set at a soda fountain, with Tracy slurping down a large malted while her life goes smash—and his attempt to forge a relationship with the deeply troubled Mary Wilke. Unlike all of his friends except the still-learning Tracy, Isaac believes in monogamy. "I think people should mate for life," he says, "like pigeons and Catholics."

What happens is not the substance of *Manhattan* as much as how it happens. The movie is full of moments that are uproariously funny and others that are sometimes shattering for the degree in which they evoke civilized desolation.

The screenplay is so vivid you may feel as if you've met characters who are only references in the dialogue. One of these is Mary Wilke's psychiatrist, Donny, who calls her up at three A.M. and weeps. The on-screen characters are beautifully played by, among others, Mr. Murphy and Miss Streep. Miss Keaton and Miss Hemingway are superb—the effect of Miss Hemingway's performance being directly responsible for the unexpected impact of Mr. Allen's penultimate moment in the film, which should not be described here.

I suspect there will be much more to say about *Manhattan* in the future. Mr. Allen's progress as one of our major filmmakers is proceeding so rapidly that we who watch him have to pause occasionally to catch our breath.

—*V.C., April 25, 1979*

MANON OF THE SPRING

Directed by Claude Berri; written (in French, with English subtitles) by Mr. Berri and Gérard Brach, based on the novel *L'Eau des Collines* by Marcel Pagnol; director of photography, Bruno Nuytten; edited by Geneviève Louveau and Hervé de Luze; music by Jean-Claude Petit; production designer, Bernard Vézat; produced by Pierre Grunstein; released by Orion Classics. Running time: 113 minutes.

With: Yves Montand (César Soubeyran), Daniel Auteuil (Ugolin), Emmanuelle Béart (Manon), Hippolyte Girardot (Bernard Oliver), Elisabeth Depardieu (Aimée) and Gabriel Bacquier (Victor).

Seeing *Manon of the Spring* four months after having been thoroughly enchanted by *Jean de Florette* is like going back to bed in an attempt to continue an interrupted dream. Sleep may come, but the dream is gone.

Manon of the Spring, which opens today at the Plaza, is the conclusion of Claude Berri's two-part adaptation of Marcel Pagnol's epic novel of Provence, *L'Eau des Collines* (*Water of the Hills*), shot as one film but, because of the nearly four-hour running time, released as two. Now, after the fact, I can say with hindsight's irritating authority that *Jean* and *Manon* only work when seen in immediate succession, in their proper chronological sequence.

Because *Jean de Florette* is still playing at the Lincoln Plaza 3, this can be done with the aid of jogging shoes—the Plaza, on East 58th Street, being a decent intermission's trot from the Lincoln Plaza, on Broadway at 63d Street.

That *Manon of the Spring* makes little narrative sense on its own isn't surprising. The two films are, in fact, a single story of duplicity, greed, and fatally crossed purposes, spanning a decade. What is unexpected is how much *Manon* depends on the manner, style, and pacing so carefully established by Mr. Berri in *Jean de Florette.*

Even when you know the story thus far, you may suffer the bends when you suddenly drop into *Manon of the Spring* after having been away from the rarefied, peasant atmosphere of *Jean de Florette* for even a couple of weeks. Without the overture and what, in effect, are the work's first three acts, which were provided by *Jean, Manon* plays the way an opera libretto reads in a dim, close-to-the-floor, aisle light.

Ten years later, Manon, now grown into untamed womanhood, lives in the grotto with Baptistine, the well-keeper, and tends her goats. One day Ugolin, who, with his wealthy uncle, César, had earlier connived to ensure Manon's late father's failure as a farmer, chances upon the nubile Manon as she bathes in a mountain pool.

Ugolin falls hopelessly in love with the maiden as, peering over a rock, he watches her dance uninhibitedly about the pool, accompanying herself on a harmonica. Unknown to him, Manon has given her heart to Bernard, the handsome young schoolteacher, whose knife she found on a hillside. Meanwhile, the childless César urges Ugolin to marry and have children, unaware (along with everyone else in the movie) that Manon is Ugolin's first cousin once removed.

There's more—much, much more—to this particular libretto, which also involves conversations overheard on barren hillsides (which seem as congested as Times Square), people hiding behind bushes unseen by people who stare straight at them, and letters sent but never received (the old blame-the-postman plot ploy). When Manon loses her hair ribbon in the vast acreage where her goats roam, it's immediately found by Ugolin, who sews it to the nipple of his left breast.

The events in *Manon of the Spring* are no more wildly melodramatic than those in *Jean de Florette* but, without the indoctrination provided by *Jean*, the second film functions as a mean-spirited review of the first. Helping to prompt this reaction is Mr. Berri's frequent use, on the soundtrack, of a soaring theme borrowed from Verdi's *Forza del Destino*. The movie is stuffed with cues for arias that are never heard.

The first film succeeds because it works slowly. With the deliberation of a nineteenth-century novel, *Jean de Florette* establishes its time and place (the mid-1920's in the hills above Marseilles), its peasant characters, their particular sense of community, their codes of honor, the arid feeling of the terrain, and even a sense of the weather, often equated with fate.

Jean de Florette has its own rhythm, which is beautifully reflected in the performances of Yves Montand as the wily old César, Daniel Auteuil as the simple-minded Ugolin, and, in particular, Gérard Depardieu, as the humpbacked Jean de Florette, who disappears from the narrative at the end of the first film.

Manon picks up the story in midstream. Seen by itself, it has no rhythm. It's a last act, which, without the buildup, is more hysterical than one can easily take. It's too busy dealing with events to have time for character. The performances of Mr. Montand and Mr. Auteuil remain splendid but unsupported. A cal-culated picturesqueness also shows through, especially in the casting of Emmanuelle Béart as Manon. Miss Béart is an elegant beauty who looks about as much like a goatherd as Catherine Deneuve in a promo for Chanel perfumes.

See *Manon* if you must find out what happens next—as I did. But you will certainly enjoy it more if you take the time to enter its world gradually, by seeing *Jean de Florette* just before. Otherwise, it's a huge anticlimax.

—*V.C., November 6, 1987*

MARRIAGE—ITALIAN STYLE

Directed by Vittorio De Sica; written (in Italian, with English subtitles) by Eduardo De Filippo, Renato Castellani, Antonio Guerra, Leo Benvenuti and Piero De Bernardi, based on the play *Filumena Marturano* by Mr. De Filippo; cinematographer, Roberto Gerardi; edited by Adriana Novelli; music by Armando Trovajoli; art designer, Carlo Egidi; produced by Carlo Ponti; released by Embassy Films. Running time: 102 minutes.

With: Sophia Loren (Filomena Marturano), Marcello Mastroianni (Domenico Soriano), Aldo Puglisi (Alfredo), Tecla Scarano (Rosalie), Marilu Tolo (Diane) and Pia Lindstrom (Cashier).

Whenever Vittorio De Sica gets together with Sophia Loren to make a motion picture, something wonderful happens. It did when he directed her in *Gold of Naples, Two Women, Yesterday, Today and Tomorrow,* and now it's happened again, in *Marriage—Italian Style.*

The something wonderful that's happened is the conception and projection of a film so frank and free and understanding of a certain kind of vital woman—and man, too—that it sends you forth from the theater feeling you've known her—and him—all your life.

Significantly, the actor they have to play the man is Marcello Mastroianni, who warmed up with them for this film in that memorably heat-producing comedy *Yesterday, Today and Tomorrow.* And the total combination is so congenial to the material at hand that it adds up to the achievement of one of the dandiest films of the year.

It opened last night at the Festival Theater with a gala benefit premiere, and it starts regular performances today at that theater and the Tower East.

Let's have clear, first, that the title, *Marriage—Italian Style,* doesn't give a precise comprehension of the dramatic situation in this film. It isn't exactly a marriage that is placed under candid scrutiny. It is more in the nature of what you might call a domestic relationship. And it isn't the sort that can loosely be labeled Italian-style. It specifically happens in Naples, which is known to be a quite unusual place, where the people are highly individual and may have bizarre relationships.

This one is in that category. It is a tacitly respected one between a prosperous middle-class merchant and a woman who was a prostitute. That is the subtle difficulty. She is eminently marriageable, and the merchant has generously allowed her to assume the functions and prerogatives of a wife—which is to say, he has promoted her from the bordello to an apartment of her own and then to the respectable environment of his tyrannical mother's home.

He has let her keep house for his mother. He has let her help run his shop. And he has obviously given her the comfort of his companionship. But, because of her slightly indelicate background, he has never made her his legal wife, nor has he let her inhabit his bedroom. He has kept her in a maid's room down the hall.

All things considered, the merchant is entirely satisfied. He has a comfortable domestic setup and can roam around as he will. But not so Filomena, the mistress and ex-prostitute. As the years go on, she hankers for respectability. And especially she wants to give her three sons, whom she has supported and raised secretly—three sons by assorted fathers—the advantage of a name.

This is the seriocomic issue in this wonderfully flamboyant film—how can Filomena force the merchant to marry her? How can she make the big transition from wife in practice to wife in name? How can she bridge the formidable chasm of social propriety?

I shan't go into details—how she first tricks her man into marrying her on the pretense of being at death's door and then, when he charges her with fraud and gets the marriage annulled on those grounds, informs him that one of her sons is his, thus piquing his egotism. But she won't tell him which son it is.

What Mr. De Sica has constructed, with the help of a small army of scriptwriters, including Eduardo De Filippo, who wrote the original play, is a rich and delicious confrontation of two ebullient and vivid characters, each exhibiting a whole range of qualities and foibles of his or her sex.

Miss Loren is delightfully eccentric, flashy, and formidable, yet stiff in her middle-class rigidity and often poignant in her real anxieties. And Mr. Mastroianni is marvelous as the elegant, egotistical male, wanting to eat his cake and have it, which, of course, is impossible.

They are brilliantly supported. Aldo Puglisi is vastly comical as a valet and domestic factotum whose associations with the mistress are never made quite clear. Tecla Scarano does a fine job as an efficient, hand-clasping maid, and Giovanni Ridolfi, Vito Moriconi, and Generoso Cortini are excellent as the sons. Note, too, that Pia Lindstrom plays a nubile and delectable shop girl—one of the merchant's passing fancies. You must know who Pia is.

Here again is another of those colorful reflections of Italian life, with lively music and good English subtitles to translate the flood of Italian dialogue.

—*B.C., December 21, 1964*

THE MARRIAGE OF MARIA BRAUN

Directed by Rainer Werner Fassbinder; written (in German, with English subtitles) by Peter Märthesheimer, Pea Fröhlich and Mr. Fassbinder; based on an idea by Mr. Fassbinder; cinematographer, Michael Ballhaus; edited by Juliane Lorenz and Franz Walsch; music by Peer Raben; art designers, Norbert Scherer, Helga Ballhaus, Claude Kottmann and George Borgel; produced by Michael Fengler; released by New Yorker Films. Running time: 120 minutes.

With: Hanna Schygulla (Maria Braun), Klaus Löwitsch (Hermann Braun), Ivan Desny (Willi), Gisela Uhlen (Mother), Günter Lamprecht (Hans) and Hark Bohm (Senkenberg).

Hitler's Germany is not just collapsing; it's being pulverized from above, though life goes on. Hermann Braun (Klaus Lowitsch), a private in the German Army, and his pretty young fiancée, Maria

(Hanna Schygulla), are exchanging their vows in a registrar's office when the air raid becomes increasingly fierce. The small room shudders and shakes, but the ceremony continues. There is an especially loud boom and, when a window shatters, the witnesses bolt for the door, followed by the registrar.

The furious Hermann, followed by Maria, runs after the registrar, and together they tackle him. Lying flat on the pavement, the terrified registrar between them, bricks and mortar falling all around them, Hermann and Maria are at last made man and wife.

It's a monstrously funny scene—Armageddon as screwball comedy. Only Rainer Werner Fassbinder, the prodigiously talented young West German director (*In a Year of 13 Moons, Effi Briest,* and so on) would dare begin a movie about total dissolution with a sequence dramatizing the end of the known world. Where can one go from there?

Mr. Fassbinder's *The Marriage of Maria Braun* goes on in epic—and epically funny—fashion to trace the rise of postwar Germany in the story of the single-mindedly faithful Maria Braun who becomes, in the words of one of her friends, "the Mata Hari of the economic miracle." Never underestimate the power of a woman who loves her husband.

After their marriage, Hermann returns to the Russian front where he is reported missing in action. Maria, at first, refuses to believe it. She gets a job in a bar catering to American G.I.'s, but stays true to Hermann until her brother-in-law returns from a prisoner-of-war camp to testify that Hermann is, indeed, dead.

Maria drifts into an affair with a black American soldier named Bill, a generous, cheerful, pudgy fellow by whom she becomes pregnant. But wait—Hermann is not dead!

As such things tend to go in the realm of farce, Hermann returns one evening just as Maria and Bill are preparing to make love. Maria, with the logic she uses in all crises, explains that although she likes Bill, she loves Hermann. There is a scuffle. Maria hits Bill over the head with a bottle, and in less time than it takes to write these words, Hermann has been packed off to prison and Maria has set off to make a fortune, which the two of them will share when he is released.

Watching *The Marriage of Maria Braun,* you come to realize that the economic miracle couldn't have happened without either United States aid or Maria Braun. Her steadfast loyalty, her determination, and her total disregard of consequences can move mountains of economic and emotional debris.

The Marriage of Maria Braun may be Mr. Fassbinder's most perfectly realized comedy to date, though the movie's last three minutes remain, for me, utter confusion. Everything I have to say about the movie excludes those final moments, about which I will say nothing out of respect for (and fear of) those letter writers who don't go to see Hamlet because they know how it all turns out.

The Marriage of Maria Braun is both an epic comedy and a romantic ballad, two not especially friendly forms that become seamlessly one in the sweet, tough, brilliantly complex performance of Hanna Schygulla, who is becoming for Mr. Fassbinder what Stéphane Audran once was for Claude Chabrol and Anna Karina was for Jean-Luc Godard.

Miss Schygulla, the bored, gum-chewing amateur tart of *Katzelmacher* and the elegantly doomed heroine of *Effi Briest,* is the kind of enchanted actress who, at any one moment in a Fassbinder movie, is the sum of all its parts, plus a little more. Though she always remains inside the film (she's not a bravura sort), she effectively represents everything it's about. This, I suppose, has as much to do with her looks and gestures as it does with the mechanics of a particular performance. Whatever it is, it's splendid and mysterious.

Something of the same can be said for the film, which, though it often proceeds as if it were a slapstick comedy, is frequently touching in a way that isn't a Fassbinder characteristic. One reason, I suspect, is that there isn't a single, easily defined villain in the entire film. Maria, Hermann, and Oswald (Ivan Desny), the rich textile manufacturer who becomes Maria's lover and her introduction to the world of Big Business, are, each one, coping as well as they can with absolutely terrible fates. It's not as if they were sentimental optimists. They are, instead, rather like children who are determined to believe in Santa Claus long after they know better.

The German-language screenplay, written by Peter Märthesheimer and Pea Fröhlich, with additional dialogue by the director, is the most accomplished of any Fassbinder film I've yet seen, with the exception of Tom Stoppard's for Despair. It's of that incredible sharpness that cuts through to the bone without giving immediately apparent pain. Very scary though funny.

The Marriage of Maria Braun will be shown at the

New York Film Festival in Avery Fisher Hall tonight, thus ending this year's festival in the most appropriate way—by reminding us of the still immense possibilities of movies made by masters.

—V.C., October 14, 1979

MARRIED TO THE MOB

Directed by Jonathan Demme; written by Barry Strugatz and Mark R. Burns; director of photography, Tak Fujimoto; edited by Craig McKay; music by David Byrne; production designer, Kristi Zea; produced by Kenneth Utt and Edward Saxon; released by Orion Pictures. Running time: 103 minutes.

With: Michelle Pfeiffer (Angela De Marco), Matthew Modine (Mike Downey), Dean Stockwell (Tony "the Tiger" Russo), Mercedes Ruehl (Connie Russo), Alec Baldwin (Frank "Cucumber" De Marco), Joan Cusack (Rose), Ellen Foley (Theresa), O-Lan Jones (Phyllis), Anthony J. Nici (Joey De Marco), Sister Carol East (Rita "Hello Gorgeous" Harcourt) and David Johansen (The Priest).

Jonathan Demme is the American cinema's king of amusing artifacts: blinding bric-a-brac, the junkiest of jewelry, costumes so frightening they take your breath away. Mr. Demme may joke, but he's also capable of suggesting that the very fabric of American life may be woven of such things, and that it takes a merry and adventurous spirit to make the most of them. In addition, Mr. Demme has an unusually fine ear for musical novelty, and the sounds that waft through his films heighten the visual impression of pure, freewheeling vitality. If making these films is half as much fun as watching them, Mr. Demme must be a happy man.

Married to the Mob, which opens today at Loews New York Twin and other theaters, is much more lightweight than Mr. Demme's wonderful *Something Wild,* but it's in the same exuberant vein. As usual, the director has found himself the perfect theme song, which in this case is "Mambo Italiano," sung by Rosemary Clooney. Close your eyes while this plays during the opening credits and you may well visualize the entire film ahead of time, from its quiet opening in a chandelier-filled corner of Long Island to the climactic sequence set in the Honeymoon Suite of the Eden Roc Hotel in Miami Beach.

In telling a story that hinges on stereotypical Italian gangsters, Mr. Demme conjures up a comic garishness that is really something special. He makes this even funnier by underscoring the aspects of mob-related home life that are, by these standards, utterly mundane. As the wife of "Cucumber" Frank De Marco (Alec Baldwin), the film's heroine Angela (Michelle Pfeiffer) has a home life fraught with problems, not the least of which is wondering how her philandering husband got his nickname. For instance, there's a revolver in the kitchen drawer, in easy reach of the couple's young son (Anthony J. Nici), who's in any case too busy running a three-card monte game in the backyard to notice.

There are other mob wives (Joan Cusack, O-Lan Jones, Ellen Foley, and Mercedes Ruehl) who pronounce themselves Angela's friends "whether you like it or not." And there's the fact that, as Angela puts it to Frank, "Everything we wear, eat, or own fell off a truck." No wonder Angela looks pink-eyed and weepy most of the time.

Frank and an associate are first seen in business suits, waiting for a commuter train as if this were second nature to them. They are there to assassinate another mobster, who is also dressed as if headed for an office job. That same evening, after having neatly knocked off their target, the two hit men meet with the rest of their mob family and are congratulated on "a beautiful ride." The setting for this is a place called the King's Roost, where each arriving mobster gives a pat on the cheek—a hard pat on the cheek—to a doorman who wears a full suit of armor. Mr. Demme has a great eye for this sort of detail.

The head of the family is Tony the Tiger (Dean Stockwell), who enters the place grandly bestowing big tips and pieces of his wardrobe—a silk scarf here, a vicuña coat there—on everyone in sight. Later in the evening, when Frank makes the mistake of fooling around with the waitress whom Tony has given a diamond necklace, Tony calmly makes Angela a widow.

This becomes the film's excuse for saying goodbye to mob life (after a funeral presided over by the singer David Johansen as a solemn priest) and embarking on a journey of discovery. It follows Angela as she moves to the Lower East Side, searches tremulously for a job, and winds up putting her beautician's skills to use at a place called Hello Gorgeous (run by Sister Carol East, the reggae singer who gave *Something Wild* such a terrific send-off). Unbeknownst to Angela, she does all this under the surveillance of a zany F.B.I. man (Matthew Modine) whose real target is Tony the Tiger. Just because Tony was seen kissing Angela at her husband's funeral, and later gave her various gifts covered in gilt wrap, red hearts, and white lovebirds, the F.B.I. thinks Angela may help the agents nail their man.

With a screenplay by Barry Strugatz and Mark R. Burns, *Married to the Mob* works best as a wildly overdecorated screwball farce, given an extra spin by the subplot that sends Connie, Tony's wife (Miss Ruehl), into the most hilarious of jealous rages. It also plays as a gentle romance, and as the story of a woman trying to reinvent her life. Unlike *Something Wild,* which sent its two chief characters on a true voyage into the unknown and turned each of them inside out before it was over, *Married to the Mob* has no real breakout quality. A closing montage, composed of glimpses of scenes that have evidently since been cut, suggests there may at some point have been more to it, but the finished film remains amiably thin.

Though Mr. Demme's *Something Wild* stars, Jeff Daniels and Melanie Griffith, set off palpable fireworks once the film threw them together, Miss Pfeiffer and Mr. Modine don't connect in the same way. Mr. Modine, a very likable actor, brings a nicely bemused quality to his role, but he doesn't have the game, nutty side suggested by the screenplay. Miss Pfeiffer, who looks utterly ravishing in outfits that set the teeth on edge, turns Angela's plight into something funny, but she seems eminently sane even when the movie does not. Appealing as they are, the two leads are readily upstaged by Miss Ruehl and, especially, by Mr. Stockwell. His shoulder-rolling caricature of this suave, foppish, and thoroughly henpecked kingpin is the film's biggest treat.

Married to the Mob also draws upon the talents of David Byrne, whose score drifts mischievously through the film, and Tak Fujimoto, Mr. Demme's longtime cameraman, who can imbue the ghastliest settings with full-bodied, jubilant good looks. The Eden Roc's Honeymoon Suite, which, if the film can be believed, has golden dolphins on the walls and tufts

of turquoise fluff on the bedspread, is a challenge even for him.

—*J.M., August 19, 1988*

THE MARRYING KIND

Directed by George Cukor; written by Ruth Gordon and Garson Kanin; cinematographer, Joseph Walker; edited by Charles Nelson; music by Hugo Friedhofer; art designer, John Meehan; produced by Bert Granet; released by Columbia Pictures. Black and white. Running time: 92 minutes.

With: Judy Holliday (Florence Keefer), Aldo Ray (Chet Keefer), Madge Kennedy (Judge Carroll), Sheila Bond (Joan Shipley), John Alexander (Howard Shipley), Rex Williams (George Bastian), Phyllis Povah (Mrs. Derringer) and Peggy Cass (Emily Bundy).

The simple domestic problems of a young married couple in New York—he a post office worker and she an ex-secretary—have been treated with cheerfulness and wisdom in the clever and facile script Ruth Gordon and Garson Kanin have written for Columbia's *The Marrying Kind.* And the wonderfully fluent talents of that grand actress, Judy Holliday, and an equally potent new actor by the name of Aldo Ray have been put by director George Cukor to the incarnation of this script into what will undoubtedly stand up as one of the happiest entertainments of the year. It had its opening performance at the Victoria yesterday.

Think it not curious if we don't seem to be as sidesplittingly impressed with the hilarities in this picture as its promotion might lead you to expect. Hilarity is in it—hilarity of the best—as would be almost mandatory in any picture with Miss Holliday. But the charming and lastingly affecting thing about *The Marrying Kind* is its bittersweet comprehension of the thorniness of the way that stretches out for two young people after they have taken the marriage vows.

Thorniness isn't apparent at the start, we'll concede—and that's a cut not alone to the pattern of this picture but to the realism of its view. The present is full of sunshine as our two young people meet in Central Park and, before they know it—he, at least—are saying, "I do." It is also loaded with laughter when they light up their first private home—an apartment in Peter Cooper Village—and start being man and wife.

There is even hilarity in their squabbling over such a ridiculous thing as his getting tight at a party and paying too much attention to a blonde. And humor, less strident but tender, is in their confusion and dismay when a radio jackpot-show calls them and dangles that bright, elusive prize.

But *The Marrying Kind* is not so funny when tragedy strikes the little home and a good bit of mutual understanding and sacrifice are required. And it is in this phase of the story that Miss Gordon and Mr. Kanin have conveyed the poignancy of frustrations that make marriage so challenging. It is here that they prove their moral—that the natural and ever-hopeful chase after glittering, material ambitions is a wistful and endless dream.

Although the form of the picture is a good bit on the obvious side, with the two frustrated spouses telling their story to a judge, Miss Gordon and Mr. Kanin have made it most palatable by wittily having the narrator tell a different story from that which is played on the screen. Thus when the husband tells his story of how he met his future wife, the facts as he narrates them are not entirely in accord with what is shown. "It so happens I remember it different," Miss Holliday primly says.

Also the rather sharp transition from the hilarity of gentle farce to the tension of sober drama may be a bit abrupt for easy assimilation, but the development is sound and the contrast in mood and comprehension elevates the significance of the film.

Naturally, everybody is eagerly anxious to know how well Miss Holliday's performance stands up with her one in *Born Yesterday*. Have no dread on that score. Her portrayal of an average New York girl—a girl who makes her marriage resolution, "I'm gonna think a half hour every day," to the utter bewilderment of her mother, who wants to know what she's going to think about—is beautifully textured and colored with expressions, modulations of voice, and a good bit more outgive of emotion than was evident in her other role.

But the big surprise of this picture is the talent of Mr. Ray in presenting a richly appealing and naturally complicated young man. Not handsome but sturdy in appearance, and possessed of a melting, husky voice, he has a gift for flowing humor and straight-faced

pathos that is almost beyond belief. His winning performance of the husband is a great factor in this film.

Under Mr. Cukor's fine direction, others turn in superb performances, too—Madge Kennedy as the judge, John Alexander as a wealthy brother-in-law, Mickey Shaughnessy as another in-law, Rex Williams as a friend, and many more. The colorful performance of much of the exterior work in New York enhances the happy illusion of actuality.

This reviewer has fond recollections of King Vidor's old film *The Crowd,* which was also about the frustrations of a young married couple in New York. *The Marrying Kind* compares to it and that's the nicest compliment we can pay.

—*B.C., March 14, 1952*

MARTY

Directed by Delbert Mann; written by Paddy Chayefsky, based on his television play; cinematographer, Joseph La Shelle; edited by Alan Crosland Jr.; music by Roy Webb; art designers, Ted Haworth and Walter M. Simonds; produced by Harold Hecht; released by United Artists. Black and white. Running time: 91 minutes.

With: Ernest Borgnine (Marty), Betsy Blair (Clara), Esther Minciotti (Mrs. Pilletti), Augusta Ciolli (Catherine), Joe Mantell (Angie), Karen Steele (Virginia), Jerry Paris (Thomas), Frank Sutton (Ralph), Walter Kelley (The Kid) and Robin Morse (Joe).

No matter what the movie people may say or think about television, they have it to thank for *Marty,* which came to the Sutton yesterday.

This neat little character study of a lonely fellow and a lonely girl who find each other in the prowling mob at a Bronx dance hall and get together despite their families and their friends was originally done as a TV drama, and its present transposition to the screen has been accomplished by its TV director, Delbert Mann, as his first film achievement.

The transfer is well worth a tribute, for *Marty* makes a warm and winning film, full of the sort of candid comment on plain, drab people that seldom reaches the screen. And Ernest Borgnine as the fellow and Betsy Blair as the girl—not to mention three or four others—give performances that burn into the mind. Except for a rather sudden ending that leaves a couple of threads untied and the emotional climax not quite played out, it is a trim and rewarding show.

In essence, this ninety-minute playlet, which Paddy Chayefsky has prepared from his own TV original, is just a good-natured, wistful kicking around of some of the socially awkward folkways of the great urban middle class. The hero, a stocky, moon-faced butcher, is thirty-four years old—unmarried, uninspired, unimaginative, and lost in boredom and loneliness. He lives with his quaint Italian mother and he spends dull time with his equally helpless friends whose ideal of femininity is a busty pickup, whose intellectual level is Mickey Spillane.

Into the life of this fellow—at the Stardust Dance Hall on a Saturday night—comes a not young, not glamorous schoolteacher who is as bleakly bored and lonely as he. She, too, has known the ignominy and the anguish of being shunned. She, too, has just about exhausted any hope of getting a mate. And even though our hero gallantly assures her "You're not really as much of a dog as you think you are," she needs much more than assurance. By the standards of the Bronx set, she's a dog.

There is the simple situation. Lonely boy meets lonely girl. Lonely boy takes lonely girl to meet his mama and then he takes her home. All the next day, he bears the criticism of his suddenly jealous mother and his friends. Then he conquers his torpor and telephones her. That is the end of the film.

But within the dramatic time-lapse of a little more than twenty-four hours, our hero breaks through the inhibitions of his fearful and inferior attitudes. He poignantly recognizes someone just as lost and desperate as he. And he amusingly and bravely grabs for her over the pitiful scoffing of his friends.

Mr. Chayefsky's script is loaded with accurate and vivid dialogue, so blunt and insensitive in places that it makes the listener's heart bleed while striking a chord of humor with its candor and colorfulness. And Mr. Mann's excellent staging has got the feel and the flavor of the Bronx, where all of the picture's exteriors and many of its interiors were filmed.

As for Mr. Borgnine's performance, it is a beautiful blend of the crude and the strangely gentle and sensitive in a monosyllabic man. It is amazing to see such a performance from the actor who played the Stockade sadist in *From Here to Eternity*. And Miss Blair is wonderfully revealing of the unspoken nervousness and hope in the girl who will settle for sincerity. The two make an excellent team.

As the disquieted mother of the hero, Esther Minciotti is superb, and Augusta Ciolli is devastating as a grimly dependent aunt. Jerry Paris is briefly amusing as the aunt's conscience-smitten son, and Joe Mantell is funny and incisive as the hero's pal. With all the others they present a dandy study in this Harold Hecht—Burt Lancaster film.

—B.C., April 12, 1955

MARY POPPINS

Directed by Robert Stevenson; written by Bill Walsh and Don DaGradi, based on the "Mary Poppins" books by P. L. Travers; cinematographer, Edward Colman; edited by Cotton Warburton; music by Richard M. Sherman and Robert B. Sherman; art designers, Carroll Clark and William H. Tuntke; produced by Walt Disney and Mr. Walsh; released by Buena Vista Pictures. Running time: 140 minutes.

With: Julie Andrews (Mary Poppins), Dick Van Dyke (Bert), David Tomlinson (Mr. Banks), Glynis Johns (Mrs. Banks), Ed Wynn (Uncle Albert), Reginald Owen (Admiral Boom), Hermione Baddeley (Ellen), Elsa Lanchester (Katie Nana), Arthur Treacher (Constable Jones), Karen Dotrice (Jane Banks) and Matthew Garber (Michael Banks).

That wonderful English nursemaid, Mary Poppins, who has charmed millions of children (and grown-ups) throughout the world since she first entered literary service under the encouragement of Miss P.L. Travers in 1934, has finally been embodied in a movie. And a most wonderful, cheering movie it is, with Julie Andrews, the original Eliza of *My Fair Lady,* playing the title role and with its splices and seams fairly splitting with Poppins marvels turned out by the Walt Disney studio.

In case you are a Mary Poppins zealot who dotes on her just as she is, don't let the intrusion of Mr. Disney and his myrmidons worry you one bit. Be thankful for it and praise heaven there are such as they still making films. For the visual and aural felicities they have added to this sparkling color film—the enchantments of a beautiful production, some deliciously animated sequences, some exciting and nimble dancing, and a spinning musical score—make it the nicest entertainment that has opened at the Music Hall this year.

And, of course, if you know Mary Poppins, you know that no one would dare to try to fool around with her appearance and her staunch individuality. Even the great Mr. Disney would find himself being subdued by a prim nanny flying through his window and warning crisply, "That will be quite enough of that."

This is the genuine Mary Poppins that comes sailing in on an east wind, her open umbrella canted over on the starboard tack, to take on the care of the Banks children, Jane and Michael, in their parents' London home, and vastly uplift the spirits of that father-dominated family.

It is she, played superbly by Miss Andrews, with her button-shoed feet splayed out to give her an unshakable footing and a look of complete authority, who calmly proceeds to show her charges that wonders will never cease and that there's nothing like a spoonful of sugar to sweeten the nastiest medicine. And it is she, with her unrelenting discipline and her disarmingly angelic face, who fills this film with a sense of wholesome substance and the serenity of self-confidence.

But don't think that Mary Poppins is simply a nursery martinet. She is a wonderfully agile spirit with a gift for expansion and fun. To her, it is not the least amazing that she can fly with an umbrella, slide upstairs on banisters on which ordinary people slide down, walk through chalk drawings on the pavement into glittering magical worlds, and take her young charges along with her, to their surprise and delight.

And it is in the performances of these wonders that Mr. Disney and his people assist in their most felicitous fashion. Flying characters are easy for them. There's nothing at all unusual about sliding a nanny upstairs. And when it comes to surrounding live persons with adorable animated cartoons, they are, of course, the past masters. They are close to their best in this film.

By far the most fanciful passage is a winning one in which Mary Poppins, her two young people, and Bert, the sidewalk artist and match-seller, pass into a cartoon wonderland where barnyard animals frolic. And there's a tinkling carousel, on the horses of which the four voyagers go bouncing off on adventuresome jaunts.

To a thoroughly rollicking musical number, "Jolly Holiday," they get mixed up in a cartoon fox-hunt, with a darling Irish fox, and ride on into the Derby horse race, which, needless to say, Mary Poppins wins.

Maybe it's our imagination, but there's something about the tunes that Richard M. and Robert B. Sherman have written for this film that reminds us of the tunes in *My Fair Lady*. And also the Edwardian costumes and the mellow London settings recollect that hit. A brilliant ballet in which Miss Andrews and Dick Van Dyke as Bert scatter and leap with a gang of sooty chimney-sweeps on the London rooftops is reminiscent, too. The comparison is not unflattering to either. *Mary Poppins* is a fair-lady film.

Bouquets don't go only to Miss Andrews. Mr. Van Dyke is joyous as Bert, the gay and irrepressible street merchant who is the companion of Mary Poppins and the kids. The latter, performed by Karen Dotrice and Matthew Garber, are just as they should be, and their parents—appropriately eccentric—are done beautifully by David Tomlinson and Glynis Johns.

Ed Wynn is grand as Uncle Albert, who soars up to the ceiling when he laughs, and Reginald Owen makes of Admiral Boom, the nautical neighbor, a natural caricature. Hermione Baddeley, Elsa Lanchester, and Arthur Treacher are droll in smaller roles. Robert Stevenson has directed with inventiveness and a true Mary Poppins flair.

Of course, it is sentimental. And, as Mary Poppins says, "Practically perfect people never permit sentiment to muddle their feelings." But being not practically perfect, I find it irresistible. Plenty of other adults will feel the same way. And, needless to say, so will the kids.

—B.C., September 25, 1964

M*A*S*H

Directed by Robert Altman; written by Ring Lardner Jr., based on the novel by Richard Hooker; cinematographer, Harold Stine; edited by Danford B. Greene; music by Johnny Mandel; art designers.

Jack Martin Smith and Arthur Lonergan; produced by Ingo Preminger; released by Twentieth Century Fox. Running time: 116 minutes.

With: Donald Sutherland (Hawkeye). Elliott Gould (Trapper John). Tom Skerritt (Duke). Sally Kellerman (Major Hot Lips). Robert Duvall (Major Frank Burns). Jo Ann Pflug (Lieutenant Dish). René Auberjonois (Dago Red). Roger Bowen (Colonel Henry Blake). Gary Burghoff (Radar O'Reilly). David Arkin (Sergeant Major Vollmer). Michael Murphy (Me Lay). Fred Williamson (Spearchucker). Kim Atwood (Ho Jon). John Shuck (Painless Pole) and G. Wood (General Hammond).

To my knowledge Robert Altman's *M*A*S*H* is the first major American movie openly to ridicule belief in God—not phony belief; real belief. It is also one of the few (though by no means the first) American screen comedies openly to admit the cruelty of its humor. And it is at pains to blend that humor with more operating room gore than I have ever seen in any movie from any place.

All of which may promote a certain air of good feeling in the audience, an attitude of self-congratulation that they have the guts to take the gore, the inhumanity to appreciate the humor, and the sanity to admire the impiety—directed against a major who prays for himself, his Army buddies, and even "our Commander in Chief."

Actually *M*A*S*H*, which opened yesterday at the Baronet, accepts without question several current pieties (for example, concern for a child's life, but not a grown man's soul), but its general bent is toward emotional freedom, cool wit, and shocking good sense.

Based upon a barely passable novel of the same name (the title stands for Mobile Army Surgical Hospital, but "MASH," of course, stands for a few other things as well). *M*A*S*H* takes place mostly in Korea during the war. However, aside from the steady processing of bloody meat through the operating room, the film is not so much concerned with the war as with life inside the Army hospital unit and especially with the quality of life created by the three hot-shot young surgeons (Donald Sutherland, Elliott Gould, and Tom Skerritt) who make most things happen.

But, unlike *Catch-22*, with which it has already been incorrectly compared (I mean the novel, not the legendary unfinished movie), *M*A*S*H* makes no profoundly radical criticism either of war or of the Army. Although it is impudent, bold, and often very funny, it lacks the sense of order (even in the midst of disorder) that seems the special province of successful comedy. I think that *M*A*S*H*, for all its local virtues, is not successful. Its humor comes mostly in bits and pieces, and even in its climax, an utterly unsporting football game between the MASH unit and an evacuation hospital, it fails to build toward either significant confrontation or recognition. At the end, the film simply runs out of steam, says good-bye to its major characters, and calls final attention to itself as a movie—surely the saddest and most overworked of cop-out devices in the comic film repertory.

Robert Altman's method has been to fill the frame to a great depth with overlapping bits of action and strands of dialogue. The tracking camera serves as an agent of discovery. To a very great degree, *M*A*S*H* substitutes field of view for point of view, and although I think this substitution has a lot to do with the movie's ultimate weakness, the choice is not without its intelligent rewards.

Insane announcements over the hospital's intercom system, Japanese-accented popular American songs from Armed Forces Radio in Tokyo, bungling corpsmen, drivers, nurses—and again and again the brilliantly understood procedures of the operating room—come together to define the spirit of the film.

In one brief night scene, some MASH-men and the chief nurse meet to divide the winnings of the football game. In the distance, a jeep drives by, carrying a white-shrouded corpse. The nurse glances at it for a second, and then turns back to her happy friends—and we have a momentary view of the ironic complexities of life that *M*A*S*H* means to contain.

The entire cast seems superb, partly, I think, because Altman (whose previous work, largely on television, I do not know) knows exactly where to cut away.

Among the leads, Elliott Gould suggests the right degree of coolly belligerent self-containment, but Donald Sutherland (in a very elaborate performance) supports his kind of detachment with vocal mannerisms that occasionally become annoying. Sally Kellerman plays the chief nurse, Major Hot Lips Houlihan—and how she earns her name is the funniest and nastiest sequence of the film. Her character changes—from comic heavy to something like romantic lead—but *M*A*S*H* really has no way of handling character change, so she mostly fades into the background.

Early in the film she is the butt of some dreadfully humiliating gags, and with her expressive, vulnerable face, she is disturbing to laugh at. It is as if she had returned from some noble-nonsense war movie of the 1940's to suggest an area of human response that the masterly sophistications of *M*A*S*H* are unaware of.

—*R.G., January 26, 1970*

THE MATCH FACTORY GIRL

Produced, directed, written (in Finnish, with English subtitles) and edited by Aki Kaurismaki; director of photography, Timo Salminen; released by Kino International. Running time: 70 minutes.

With: Kati Outinen (Iris), Elina Salo (Mother), Esko Nikkari (Stepfather), Vesa Vierikko (Man), Reijo Taipale (Singer) and Silu Seppälä (Brother).

For Aki Kaurismaki, the writer and director who has two films in the New York Film Festival, being laconical and deadpan is high art. Is his native Finland as dreary as it seems in his movies, he was asked at a press conference? Smoking a cigarette and drinking a bottle of beer, the director answered in a monotone, "It's a wonderland." He is obviously the prototypical Kaurismaki character: a droll personality stingy with words yet offering vast irony through his impassive presence.

The characters in his latest films start out being more morose than their creator, but they get over it. In one, the downtrodden heroine of *The Match Factory Girl* spends most of the film looking pathetic and sad, with excellent cause. But a glimmer of a smile crosses her face when she dilutes rat poison in water, for reasons the audience will soon discover. The film is a magnificent conclusion to a trilogy about Finnish working-class heroes that includes *Shadows in Paradise* and *Ariel*. This virtuosic work is heartbreaking until it turns outrageously funny.

The director's style is ruthlessly pared down, every scene edited to its core, every detail perfected, every lingering shot of an empty room used to good effect. Yet Mr. Kaurismaki's buoyant energy fends off any hint of a mannered or minimalist approach, and he keeps viewers trailing after him by unsettling every expectation. Having made eight smashingly original films in seven years, Mr. Kaurismaki's range and depth seem to be growing all the time.

The Match Factory Girl begins with a log in a factory and follows the stages by which wood emerges as a box of matches. At the end of this long mechanical chain is a pair of hands hovering over a conveyor belt, making certain the mailing labels are stuck securely on the boxes. The hands belong to Iris, a wan blonde with circles under her eyes whose life threatens to remain as mundane and sterile as her job.

She pays rent to sleep on the couch in the apartment of her mother and stepfather, who do little more than eat and smoke. She puts on blue eyeshadow, goes to a dance, and at the end of the evening is the only woman left sitting against the wall. And in a small act of heroism, she defies her parents and takes part of her paycheck to buy a cheap-looking red-flowered dress in which she is finally asked to dance.

As Iris, Kati Outinen has a slight, angelic smile as she rests her head on this strange man's shoulder. Her beautiful, unsentimental performance is all the more remarkable because so far Iris has not said a word on camera. No one, in fact, says very much in this film. Music and noise are everywhere, but dialogue is a luxury in Mr. Kaurismaki's spare esthetic.

Iris is no saint; she sleeps with the stranger that night and later finds herself in the kind of mess that makes her want to poison ratty humans. And the more rebellious she becomes, the more Mr. Kaurismaki provokes viewers to cheer her anti-social behavior. Iris is the most deeply realized and affecting character in the Finnish trilogy.

—*C.J., October 3, 1990*

MAYERLING

Directed by Anatole Litvak; written (in French, with English subtitles) by Joseph Kessel and Irma Von Cube, based on the novel *Idyl's End* by Claude Anet; cinematographer, Armand Thirard; edited by Henri Rust; music by Arthur Honegger; released by Pax Film. Black and white. Running time: 96 minutes.

With: Charles Boyer (Archduke Rudolph of Austria). Danielle Darrieux (Baroness Marie Vetsera). Suzy Prim (Countess Larisch). Jean Dax (Emperor Franz Joseph). Gabrielle Dorziat (Empress Elizabeth) and Debucourt (Count Taafe).

So much depends on the viewpoint. When Maxwell Anderson contemplated the Mayerling tragedy in *The Masque of Kings* last season he gave scarcely more than superficial consideration to the romance between the Crown Prince Rudolph and the Baroness Marie Vetsera. What interested him more and motivated his drama was the political struggle, the clash between an impetuous liberal and an unyielding symbol of the old order. When Rudolph ultimately committed suicide over the body of his beloved Marie in the hunting lodge at Mayerling we could not feel it was all for love. There had been too many other conflicts, too many other defeats. The Vetsera affair was merely the capstone.

Mayerling, the French film version of the same puzzling affair, which moved into the reopened Filmarte Theatre last night, simplifies the tragedy by stating it in purely romantic terms. There is a suggestion of intrigue, of political maneuvering, of Rudolph's restless ambition to be something more than a court wastrel. But from the moment he meets the lovely Vetsera until that when he stands, a grief-bowed Romeo, before the still form of his Viennese Juliet, it is a love story—completely and beautifully a love story. They are the only people in their world; the rest are shadows; and when the shadows grow too black, they leave it.

It is, in my opinion, the proper approach to the almost legendary tragedy. By contrast, Mr. Anderson's play was cluttered up with fiction and brave, theatrical speeches and hollow emotions. Here, through Anatol Litvak's superb assembling of scenes and through the matchless performances of Charles Boyer as Rudolph and the unbelievably lovely Danielle Darrieux as Vetsera, we are carried breathlessly along an emotional millrace, exalted and made abject as the dramatist directed. It is impossible to remain aloof, to regard the romance dispassionately. There is no resisting the fire that players, writer, and director have struck from the screen.

An admissable objection is that the early scenes, while making a great show of illustrating the political cross-currents in the court of Franz Joseph, actually tell us nothing about the Crown Prince's interests or purposes; and, having served that doubtful end, are forgotten completely when the young Baroness Vetsera appears. They serve only to introduce Rudolph as a man consumed by stifled ambitions, distrustful, reckless, weary, and debauched. Knowing him so well, we know, too, that Vetsera, whom he meets incognito and who innocently loves him for his stricken self, is his only salvation from madness.

Claude Anet, who wrote the novel from which the film is derived, has not seen fit to complicate their romance—as Anderson did—by suggesting that Vetsera actually was hired by the Emperor to spy upon his son. There were obstacles enough in the path: the Archduchess Stephanie, whom Rudolph had married by his father's command; his inability to obtain a divorce; the objections of Franz Joseph to the continuation of their affair; the fears of Vetsera's mother and brother. *Mayerling*'s solution to the riddle of the hunting lodge is that it was murder and suicide, by agreement. History inclines as much to that theory as to any other.

And so from France has come another great photoplay, superbly produced, poetically written—the cadence of the French is beautiful even though one does not understand it—and faultlessly played. Miss Darrieux, since lured by Universal to Hollywood, has a cameo-like perfection of feature and a limpid serenity of manner which make her portrayal of the tragic young Baroness one of the hauntingly charming performances of the year. Mr. Boyer has never been better and there are others—Suzy Prim as the Countess Larisch, Jean Dax as the Emperor, in fact all the others—who have contributed to the creation of an irresistible love story.

—*F.S.N., September 14, 1937*

McCABE AND MRS. MILLER

Directed by Robert Altman; written by Mr. Altman and Brian McKay, based on the novel *McCabe* by Edmund Naughton; cinematographer, Vilmos Zsigmond; edited by Lou Lombardo; music by Leonard Cohen; production designer, Leon Ericksen; produced by David Foster and Mitchell Brower; released by Warner Brothers. Running time: 120 minutes.

With: Warren Beatty (John Q. McCabe), René Auberjonois (Sheehan), John Schuck (Smalley), Bert Remsen (Bart Coyl), Keith Carradine (Cowboy), Julie Christie (Constance Miller), William Devane (The Lawyer), Corey Fischer (Mr. Elliott) and Shelley Duvall (Ida Coyl).

In the course of Robert Altman's new film, *McCabe and Mrs. Miller*, there is a shot of Warren Beatty steaming off a drunk in an old-fashioned wooden bathtub, his arms draped along the sides, his eyes closed, and his bearded face hanging limply forward. When such a shot prompts the woman behind you to hiss—with the excitement of someone who has spotted Rod McKuen at the Russian Tea Room—"He looks just like Jesus!" you may be sure you're in the presence of a movie of serious intentions. Shots that make the characters look just like Jesus don't happen by accident.

The intentions of *McCabe and Mrs. Miller* are not only serious, they are also meddlesomely imposed on the film by tired symbolism, by a folk-song commentary on the soundtrack that recalls not the old Pacific Northwest but San Francisco's hungry i, and by the sort of metaphysically purposeful photography that, in a tight close-up, attempts to discover the soul's secrets in the iris of an eye and finds, instead, only a very large iris.

Such intentions keep spoiling the fun of what might have been an uproarious frontier fable about a small-time gambler named McCabe (Beatty), a frizzy-haired whore named Mrs. Miller (Julie Christie), and the systematic destruction of their small, free American enterprise by Big Business, with the not so innocent cooperation of organized religion.

When McCabe first comes to the bleak little mining town of Presbyterian Church, it doesn't seem as God-forsaken as not yet discovered by God, for whom a church is under construction. It's a scenic mess of squalid shacks, bordered by an even more squalid ghetto for Chinese laborers.

McCabe, a man of common sense but very little arithmetic, sets out to bring civilization to Presbyterian Church in the form of a casino and a three-bed bordello. He doesn't do very well, however, until he is joined by Mrs. Miller, who has the heart of a bookkeeper, the aspirations of a madam, and connections with a house in Seattle. They make a marvelous, prac-

tical team, and are immensely successful until The Company moves to take over their businesses, via assassination when it becomes apparent McCabe won't sell.

There is one moment in the film that achieves, I think, just the right balance between comedy and satire that Altman seeks, unsuccessfully, for the entire film. McCabe, who is not exactly keen on being murdered, asks the help of a lawyer who lectures him on the American way and cheerfully concludes: "If men stop dying for freedom, freedom itself will be dead!" When poor McCabe gets hoodwinked into believing he's protecting free enterprise by accepting a show-down with the hired killers, the contemporary allusions become rather thick.

I don't automatically object to contemporary allusions, but I prefer to find them myself, and *McCabe and Mrs. Miller* is so busy pointing them out to us that the effect is to undercut its narrative drive and the dignity of its fiction. Dignity may sound like a curious word to use in this case, but the characters of *McCabe and Mrs. Miller*, as written and as played, do have an essential dignity that is very real and honest. Beatty's gambler-turned-businessman is a truly comic, clay-footed entrepreneur, and Miss Christie's tough-talking whore is about as appealing as that sentimental character can be until she's required to drift off into opium oblivion, a woman-turned-into-society's-victim.

As in *M*A*S*H* and *Brewster McCloud,* Altman fills his screen with sometimes exceptionally vivid detail, such as the casually viewed fight between a knife-wielding prostitute and her customer, the over-heard small talk between miners standing at the bar, and the physical growth of the Presbyterian Church in the course of the film.

As *McCabe and Mrs. Miller* progresses, however, there is also an increasing suspicion that these details are loaded with ulterior motives, which have not as much to do with the time and place of the film as with its pretensions. One thing the movie does have in beautiful and extraordinary abundance is weather—rain, snow, sleet, wind (it was photographed on location in Canada), which is most attractive, especially to someone who spends most of his life looking at the world through windows sealed for air-conditioning.

—V.C., June 25, 1971

MEAN STREETS

Directed by Martin Scorsese: written by Mr. Scorsese and Mardik Martin: cinematographer. Kent Wakeford: edited by Sidney Levin: produced by Jonathan T. Taplin: released by Warner Brothers. Running time: 110 minutes.

With: Robert De Niro (Johnny Boy). Harvey Keitel (Charlie). David Proval (Tony). Amy Robinson (Teresa). Richard Romanus (Michael). Cesare Danova (Giovanni). Victor Argo (Mario) and George Mammoli (Joey).

No matter how bleak the milieu, no matter how heartbreaking the narrative, some films are so thoroughly, beautifully realized they have a kind of tonic effect that has no relation to the subject matter. Such a film is *Mean Streets,* the third feature film by Martin Scorsese, the once-promising young director (*Who's That Knocking at My Door?* and *Boxcar Bertha*) who has now made an unequivocally first-class film.

Mean Streets, which was shown last night at the New York Film Festival in Alice Tully Hall, has a lot in common with *Who's That Knocking at My Door?*, Scorsese's first feature released here four years ago. It is set almost entirely in New York's Little Italy, where Scorsese grew up. Its hero is a second-generation Italian-American, a young man whose nature is a warring mixture of religious guilt, ambition, family loyalty, and fatalism.

Charlie (Harvey Keitel) is a nice, clean-cut petty hood, a sort of trainee-executive in the syndicate controlled by his Uncle Giovanni (Cesare Danova), an Old World gangster full of cold resolve and ponderous advice ("Honorable men go with honorable men"). Charlie makes collections for his uncle and aspires to take over a restaurant whose owner is deeply in debt to Giovanni.

Early on, however, it's apparent that Charlie is not quite ruthless enough to succeed in the Lower East Side territory that defines his world. He has made the mistake of falling in love with Teresa (Amy Robinson), an Italian-American girl who has epilepsy and is therefore out of bounds. He also feels almost maniacally responsible for Johnny Boy (Robert De Niro), Teresa's simpleminded brother who traffics with loan sharks, suicidally.

When Charlie tries to flee the territory, with Teresa and Johnny Boy, crossing over the bridge to Brooklyn in a borrowed car, the results are predictable. It's as if an astronaut had decided to take a space walk in a gray flannel suit.

Mean Streets, which has a screenplay by Mr. Scorsese and Mardik Martin, faces its characters and their world head-on. It never looks over their shoulders or takes a position above their heads in order to impose a self-conscious relevance on them. There is no need to. It is Scorsese's talent, reflected in his performers, to be able to suggest the mystery of people and place solely in terms of the action of the film.

This may seem simple but it's one of the fundamentals of filmmaking that many directors never grasp. Bad films need mouthpieces to tell us what's going on.

Mean Streets, which was shot entirely on its New York locations, unfolds as a series of seemingly casual incidents—barroom encounters, pickups, fights, lovers' quarrels, and small moments of introspection—that only at the end are seen to have been a narrative of furious drive.

De Niro (*Bang the Drum Slowly*) has an exceedingly flashy role and makes the most of it, but Keitel, modest, honorable, and doomed, is equally effective as the hood who goes right, and hates himself for his failure.

Mean Streets will be screened at Alice Tully Hall again this evening. It opens its commercial engagement at the Cinema One Theater on October 14, and deserves attention as one of the finer American films of the season.

—*V.C., October 3, 1973*

MEET ME IN ST. LOUIS

Directed by Vincente Minnelli: written by Irving Brecher and Fred Finklehoffe. based on the stories by Sally Benson: cinematographer. George Folsey: edited by Albert Akst: music by George Stoll: choreography by Charles Walters: art designers. Cedric Gibbons and Lemuel Ayers: produced by Arthur Freed: released by Metro-Goldwyn-Mayer. Running time: 113 minutes.

With: Judy Garland (Esther Smith). Margaret O'Brien (Tootie Smith). Mary Astor (Mrs. Smith).

Lucille Bremer (Rose). Marjorie Main (Katie). Harry Davenport (Grandpa) and Tom Drake (John Truett).

Now that the style for family albums in the theater has been charmingly set by Broadway's perennial *Life With Father,* Metro has taken the cue and has turned out a comparably charming movie in virtually the same period style. It is a warm and beguiling picturization based on Sally Benson's memoirs of her folks, *Meet Me in St. Louis,* and it came to the Astor yesterday. Let those who would savor their enjoyment of innocent family merriment with the fragrance of dried-rose petals and who would revel in girlish rhapsodies make a beeline right down to the Astor. For there's honey to be had inside.

And it isn't just the clang-clang-clanging of "The Trolley Song" that will ring in your energized ears, despite the rather frightening impression you may have got from the radio. Nor is it, indeed, the musical phases of the film that are most likely to allure. Except for maybe half a dozen numbers which Judy Garland melodically sings—and which have been planted like favors in a bride's cake—this is mostly a straight family lark, covering a year of rare activity in a house heavily peopled with girls. And, as such, it is fraught with such dilemmas as are peculiar to that fair, bewildering tribe.

For this is a free and genial recount of events in the home of the Smiths, who are staunchly devoted to St. Louis, during the year 1903–1904. There are long-suffering papa and mama, four daughters, a saucy elder son, grandpa (who is something of a crackpot), and a tautly tyrannical maid. And the tempests which occur in this large hen-roost derive from such grand necessities as meeting the right boy at the right time and not moving to New York.

There is the charming and homely incident when elder sister Rose anticipates a proposal of marriage from her hopefully "intended" in New York and has to take the call amidst the whole brood over the goose-necked telephone.

There is the equally terrifying episode when sister Esther biffs the boy next door because she thought he had walloped little Tootie, who was skylarking all the time. And, for the younger fry, there is the thoroughly bewitching and fay experience of this same little fanciful Tootie on a windy Halloween.

All of these bits of family humor—and several more in the same vein—are done in a manner calculated to warm and enthuse the heart. The Smiths and their home, in Technicolor, are eyefuls of scenic delight, and the bursting vitality of their living inspires you like vitamin A. Miss Garland is full of gay exuberance as the second sister of the lot and sings, as we said, with a rich voice that grows riper and more expressive in each new film. Her chortling of "The Trolley Song" puts fresh zip into that inescapable tune, and her romantic singing of a sweet one, "The Boy Next Door," is good for mooning folks.

Little Margaret O'Brien makes a wholly delightful imp of Satan as Tootie, and Lucille Bremer is lovely and old-fashioned as Rose, the nubile sis. Marjorie Main as Katie, the maid, Harry Davenport as Grandpa, and Tom Drake as the boy next door are only three of the several excellent members of the cast.

Vincente Minnelli, in his direction, has got all the period charm out of ladies dressed in flowing creations, gentlemen in straw "boaters" and ice-cream pants, rooms lush with golden-oak wainscoting, ormolu decorations, and red-plush chairs. As a comparable screen companion to *Life With Father,* we would confidently predict that *Meet Me in St. Louis* has a future that is equally bright. In the words of one of the gentlemen, it is a ginger-peachy show.

—*B.C., November 29, 1944*

MELVIN AND HOWARD

Directed by Jonathan Demme: written by Bo Goldman: director of photography. Tak Fujimoto: edited by Craig McKay: music by Bruce Langhorne: production designer. Toby Rafelson: produced by Art Linson and Don Phillips: released by Universal Pictures. Running time: 95 minutes.

With: Jason Robards (Howard Hughes). Paul Le Mat (Melvin Dummar). Mary Steenburgen (Lynda Dummar). Michael J. Pollard (Little Red). Pamela Reed (Bonnie Dummar) and Gloria Grahame (Mrs. Sisk).

It would be difficult to a imagine a better way to begin the 18th New York Film Festival than with the showing tonight of Jonathan Demme's sharp, engaging, very funny, anxious comedy, *Melvin and Howard,* a satiric expression of the American Dream in the closing years of the twentieth century, as old debts are being called in and life has become a series of repossessions.

Mr. Demme has now made five films, but on the basis of just two of them, *Handle with Care* (sometimes called *Citizen's Band*) and *Melvin and Howard,* he is clearly a social satirist in the tradition of Preston Sturges. He's a filmmaker with a fondness for the absurdities of our existence and for people who have no idea that they're "little" or teetering on the edge of disaster. Or, as Melvin Dummar says with impatience when his wife points out they are poor, "We're not poor! Broke, maybe, but not poor!"

Melvin and Howard is the story of Melvin Dummar, the filling station attendant who surfaced not long after the death of Howard Hughes as one of the principal beneficiaries of Hughes's fortune in what became known as "the Mormon will." Mr. Dummar's story was that one night, some years earlier, he had picked up a filthy old vagrant in the desert, driven him to Las Vegas, and paid no attention to the geezer's claims that he was Howard Hughes. This was the ingenuous way Melvin explained why the famous eccentric had reached out from the grave to shower him with riches.

Though the courts never admitted the Mormon will for probate, Mr. Demme and Bo Goldman, his screenwriter, take Melvin's tale at face value and present the movie as Melvin's wildest dream. The comic catch is that this wild dream is essentially so prosaic. It's also touched with pathos since Melvin—in spite of himself—knows that it will never be realized. This is the story of his life.

The film opens with the midnight encounter of Melvin (Paul Le Mat) and Howard (Jason Robards) in the desert. En route to Las Vegas, Melvin almost drives Howard out of his mind by singing a song of his own composition, "Santa's Souped-Up Sleigh," which has lyrics as well as what Melvin calls "dramatic narration." Howard is not an eccentric for nothing. He is eventually charmed by the young man.

The desert encounter is the preface for the film itself, which is concerned with Melvin's hilariously crisis-ridden life, with his two marriages to and two divorces from the pretty, sweetly nutty Lynda (Mary Steenburgen), his marriage to the slightly more practical Bonnie (Pamela Reed), his uncertain rise as a milkman, his dreams of becoming a yachtsman, and his career as the operator of a debt-ridden service station in Willard, Utah, where he's living with Bonnie when word of the Mormon will reaches him.

Melvin's dream may be prosaic but Mr. Demme's film is not. It's dense with sometimes priceless detail, including a wedding in a Reno "wedding chapel" to the tune of "The Hawaiian War Chant" and a sequence set in a Reno bar where one of the topless go-go dancers bumps and grinds conscientiously with one arm in a plaster cast.

When Lynda wins $10,000 on a television game show called *Easy Street* the couple immediately purchases a $45,000 house, which, all too soon, is repossessed along with a fancy automobile and a thirty-five-foot cabin cruiser Melvin has also bought "as an investment." One of the nicer moments in the movie is a shot of the wayward Melvin, sitting in his cabin cruiser, which is sitting on a trailer, attached to his car, in his backyard, as he radios the Coast Guard to obtain the latest marine weather forecast.

Though the movie is consistently, comically skeptical, it's never cruel. When Lynda, grinning in the lunatic manner she knows television expects, does a lead-footed tap dance on *Easy Street,* we don't laugh at her but with her and her great good fortune to have gotten on the show in the first place. One of Melvin and Lynda's reconciliations, via telephone, is effected when she tells him she's been reading a book, *The Magic of Believing,* which is helping her find herself. She admits, though, it's difficult to practice its principles. "Don't worry," says Melvin. "They didn't burn down Rome in a day."

As he did for *Handle with Care,* Mr. Demme has assembled a cast of first-rate character actors. Mr. Le Mat plays Melvin with the gentle but optimistic expectancy of someone playing a slot machine. Miss Steenburgen is enchanting as Lynda, as is Pamela Reed as the somewhat more patient Bonnie. Michael J. Pollard and Gloria Grahame are not used to the best of their abilities, but their presences add comic tone to the picture. Even the children are good, especially Elizabeth Cheshire as Melvin and Lynda's daughter Darcy, who recalls the Peggy Ann Garner of *A Tree Grows in Brooklyn.*

Mr. Robards is not on the screen very long but, looking like something out of a benign nightmare, he is the mythical figure that gives point to the entire fantasy.

Mr. Demme is a lyrical filmmaker for whom there is purpose in style. When, early in the film, the camera appears to loosen its moorings to float upward to give a broad view of Melvin's camper set in the middle of a junkyard, within a desolate desert landscape, the film is considering the nature of the fantasy even as it is relating it.

There is a problem in that *Melvin and Howard* has no real resolution. In Preston Sturges's films it was quite possible for the boob to triumph. History—real life—interferes with Melvin's dream, but this also reflects the difference between the optimism of American movies forty years ago and the tempered pessimism of today's.

Melvin and Howard is commercial American moviemaking of a most expansive, entertaining kind.
—V.C., September 26, 1980

MEMORIES OF UNDERDEVELOPMENT

Written (in Spanish, with English subtitles) and directed by Tomás Gutierrez Alea; based on the novel *Memorias del Subdesarrollo* by Edmundo Desnoes; director of photography, Ramón Suarez; edited by Nelson Rodriquez; music by Leo Brower; produced by the Instituto Cubano del Arte e Industria Cinematograficos; released by Transcontinental Films. Running time: 104 minutes.

With: Sergio Corrieri (Sergio), Daisy Granados (Elena), Eslinda Nuñez (Noemi) and Beatriz Ponchara (Laura).

The time is 1961, not long after the Bay of Pigs, and Sergio (Sergio Corrieri), the hero of Tomás Gutierrez Alea's superb Cuban film, *Memories of Underdevelopment,* moves through Havana as if he were a scuba diver exploring the ruins of a civilization he abhors but cannot bear to leave. The world he sees is startlingly clear. It is also remote. The sounds he hears are his own thoughts.

"Everything happens to me too early or too late," says Sergio, an intellectual in his late thirties whose

critical faculties have effectively rendered him incapable of any action whatsoever. After his estranged wife and his mother and father have fled to Miami, with the other bourgeoisie, he thinks he will write the novel he has always thought about, but then Sergio's standards are too high to allow him to add to the sum total of civilization's second-rateness. He finds himself blocked.

Perhaps if the revolution had happened earlier, he tells himself, he might have understood.

Sergio makes half-hearted little efforts to maintain his old ways. He picks up Elena (Daisy Granados), a pretty, bird-brained girl who wants to be an actress, and he tries to educate (he says "Europeanize") her. He takes her to art galleries and buys her books but her brain remains unreconstructed and birdlike. "She doesn't relate to things," he tells himself. "It's one of the signs of underdevelopment."

He takes Elena on a sightseeing tour of Hemingway's house. "He said he killed so as not to kill himself," Sergio remembers, looking at some mounted antlers. "In the end he could not resist the temptation."

Even suicide is beyond Sergio. All he can do is observe, much of the time through the telescope on the terrace of a penthouse apartment he must give up, sooner or later.

Memories of Underdevelopment is a fascinating achievement. Here is a film about alienation that is wise, sad, and often funny, and that never slips into the bored and boring attitudes that wreck Antonioni's later films. Sergio is detached and wary, but around him is a hurricane of life.

Gutierrez Alea was forty when he made *Memories* (in 1968), and he is clearly a man, like Sergio, whose sensibilities are European. Yet unlike Sergio, and unlike the director of *Eclipse* and *Red Desert,* he is so full of passion and political commitment that he has even been able to make an essentially pro-revolutionary film in which Castro's revolution is observed through eyes dim with bafflement.

The result is hugely effective and moving, and it is complete in the way that very few movies ever are. I haven't read Edmundo Desnoes's original novel (published here in 1967 as *Inconsolable Memories*), but I like the fact that Desnoes apparently likes the film that, in his words, had to be "a betrayal" of the book to be a good film. Gutierrez Alea, says the author, in the film's program notes, "objectivized a world that was shapeless in my mind and still abstract in the book. He added social density. . . ."

Memories of Underdevelopment was one of the films scheduled to be shown here last year at the aborted Cuban Film Festival. It finally opened yesterday at the First Avenue Screening Room where it will play one week and then, I hope, it will move to another theater for the long run it deserves.

—*V.C., May 18, 1973*

THE MEMORY OF JUSTICE

Directed and produced by Marcel Ophuls: chief editor, Inge Behrens: director of photography, Mike Davis: sound recording, Anthony Jackson: executive producers, Max Palevsky and Hamilton Fish 3rd, in coproduction with Polytel International: released by Paramount Pictures. Running time: 278 minutes.

With: Yehudi Menuhin, Telford Taylor, Karl Donitz, Albert Speer, Daniel L. Ellsberg, Barbara Keating, Mr. and Mrs. Robert Ransom and Mr. Ophuls.

Like his earlier *The Sorrow and the Pity,* which examined the behavior of the French during the Nazi occupation, Marcel Ophuls's *The Memory of Justice* expands the possibilities of the documentary motion picture in such a way that all future films of this sort will be compared to it. *The Sorrow and the Pity* and *The Memory of Justice* have set standards and created expectations that even Mr. Ophuls himself may not always meet, as in *A Sense of Loss,* his film about Northern Ireland, that was just as elusive as its subject. Mr. Ophuls doesn't deal in paltry material.

The Memory of Justice is monumental, though not only because it goes on for a demanding four hours and thirty-eight minutes, plus an intermission. It also marks off, explores, calls attention to, and considers, tranquilly, without making easy judgments, one of the central issues of our time: collective versus individual responsibility.

The starting point is an evocation of the 1946–47 Nuremberg war crimes trials, through newsreels and interviews with surviving defendants, prosecutors,

defending attorneys, and witnesses, that leads to a consideration of French tactics in the fight to keep Algeria and America in action in Vietnam.

"I go on the assumption," says Yehudi Menuhin early in the film, "that everyone is guilty." But that sort of readiness to accept responsibility, simply by being a member of mankind, evades the truth that Mr. Ophuls seeks here.

The ethical questions are timeless but the subject is particular, and it's through the accumulation of particularities that *The Memory of Justice* makes its impact. More than forty persons are interviewed by Mr. Ophuls, and a dozen more key figures are seen speaking for themselves in old newsreel footage.

Hermann Göring and Rudolf Hess whisper on the prisoners' bench in the Nuremberg courtroom. A United States Army psychiatrist recalls that their small talk in court could, indeed, be small, such as comparing the marks they'd received on their Army I.Q. tests.

An old farmer in Schleswig-Holstein remembers the Nazi era fondly. It was a time of law and order in the land. When reminded of the concentration camps and the mass murder of the Jews, he pauses, says: "Oh, that was not right. That was something else." General Telford Taylor discusses his role in preparing the Allied case at Nuremberg, setting precedents he still believes in, then talks about Vietnam and "the degeneration of standards under the pressure of war."

Admiral Karl Dönitz, to whom Hitler bequeathed the Third Reich in its death throes, today denies any knowledge of anything "dark" about Hitler, and describes as "politics" a speech in which he parroted the official anti-Semitic line.

Albert Speer, urbane, still handsome, has survived to become a kind of professional guilt assumer. He confesses easily in best-selling books and to movie cameras, but is the confession any less genuine for sounding slick? I'm not sure. When he says, "Long before the Jews were killed, it was all expressed in my buildings," *The Memory of Justice* becomes the memory of guilt. That he's so glib need not lessen the sincerity. After all, we can remember feeling pain but we don't again experience it as we remember. Perhaps some such protective device is at work in Speer.

Some people accept responsibility. They embrace it, like Mr. Speer. Others refuse to acknowledge anything but ignorance. Of the average German, one young German woman says of her parents' generation, "They deliberately didn't try to find out what was going on." Daniel L. Ellsberg, talking about "American war criminals" of Vietnam, sounds almost as glib as Mr. Speer.

Others are accidental victims. An aging German actress recalls life as a Nazi exile in Hollywood. The widow of a German general tells how her husband committed suicide rather than sign the death sentence of a group of Catholic priests. Barbara Keating talks proudly, with great feeling, of her husband, who was killed in Vietnam, and Mr. and Mrs. Robert Ransom, with the same feeling, regret that they hadn't urged their son, who was also killed there, to refuse to serve.

There is absolutely no way to condense this material. Its effect is cumulative. People who are equally sincere totally disagree. Discussions of moral positions suddenly turn into narratives-within-narratives of the most personal sort, as when someone like Colonel Anthony Herbert, now retired, recalls how he finally refused to be a part of a war he considered immoral. Individual responsibility still exists. It still counts.

Mr. Ophuls is very much a presence in *The Memory of Justice,* sometimes on the screen as the interviewer, shaping the film by his commitment to search through the past to discover the present. Perhaps because he himself was an exile from Nazi Germany, the son of an exile (Max Ophüls), and is married to a German woman who (in the course of this film) recalls her membership in the Hitler Youth, *The Memory of Justice* seems an especially personal, urgent work.

The Memory of Justice is long but it rivets the mind and the emotions so consistently that I can think of a dozen ninety-minute movies far more difficult to endure. It will be shown at the New York Film Festival at Alice Tully Hall today and again Saturday. It opens its commercial engagement at the Beekman Theater on Sunday.

—V.C., October 5, 1976

THE MEN

Directed by Fred Zinnemann; written by Carl Foreman; cinematographer, Robert de Grasse; edited by Harry Gerstad; music by Dimitri Tiomkin; produced by Stanley Kramer; released by United Artists. Black and white. Running time: 85 minutes.

With: Marlon Brando (Ken), Teresa Wright (Ellen), Everett Sloane (Dr. Brock), Jack Webb (Norm), Richard Erdman (Leo), Arthur Jurado (Angel), Virginia Farmer (Nurse Robbins), Dorothy Tree (Ellen's Mother) and Howard St. John (Ellen's Father).

A fine and arresting film drama about paraplegic veterans of the war—about men whose battle injuries have left them paralyzed below the waist—has been brought to the screen by Stanley Kramer in his independent production *The Men,* which was fittingly presented at the Music Hall yesterday. And a trenchant and stinging performance as one of these disabled men who struggles against his bleak frustrations toward a calm readjustment to life is given in it by Marlon Brando, making his screen debut after his notable Broadway triumph in *A Streetcar Named Desire.*

Much has been lucidly written about the paraplegic vets, numbering some 2,500, who are residuals of the war. And much has been done to place them normally in the public's inquisitive eye. Sports events in which paraplegics in their wheelchairs have played normal teams have been held to accustom the public to the capacities of these "immobilized" men, and in many other ways their abilities as participants in society have been revealed. But nothing yet demonstrated has so fully realized and portrayed—at least, to the public's comprehension—the inner torments, the despairs, the loneliness, and the possible triumphs of a paraplegic as this picture does.

In a firm, forthright, realistic study of a group of paralyzed men, and especially of one young fellow who seems more stubborn and frustrated than the rest, Mr. Kramer and his associates have tactfully but frankly exposed the bitter and ironic aspects of being paralyzed below the waist. They have caught the raw human anguish of bedridden and wheelchair-saddled men, the tensions and friendships and grim humors of a paraplegic hospital ward. And in tracing the course of a stark romance between their hero and a loyal, noble girl they have got a moving comprehension of the confused feelings of a paraplegic's wife.

Much of this picture was photographed and practically all of it was derived at the Birmingham Veterans Hospital near Los Angeles. Here producer Kramer and scriptwriter Carl Foreman lived for several weeks, and here director Fred Zinneman recruited some of the minor players in his cast. So there is no wonder that a striking and authentic documentary quality has been imparted to the whole film in every detail, attitude, and word.

But the major accomplishment of these artists is the simplicity and eloquence with which they have shown the fundamental conflicts in a paraplegic's readjustment to life—the terrible, pathetic reluctance to give up hoping for a "return" and the forcing of the head to take over the life of the dead, immobile legs. And in these demonstrations they have coincidently achieved an understanding of doctors, nurses, parents, sweethearts, and wives.

Mr. Brando, as the veteran who endures the most difficult time, is so vividly real, dynamic, and sensitive that his illusion is complete. His face, the whole rhythm of his body, and especially the strange timbre of his voice, often broken and plaintive and boyish, are articulate in every way. Out of stiff and frozen silences he can lash into a passionate rage with the fearful and flailing frenzy of a taut cable suddenly cut. Or he can show the poignant tenderness of a doctor with a child.

Excellent, too, are Richard Erdman, Arthur Jurado, and Jack Webb as three varied paraplegics, each a full, rich character in himself, and especially Everett Sloane as the doctor who understands, cajoles, badgers, and leads the men. And Teresa Wright, while a mite too wistful and wispy as the girl in the case, conveys the essential compassion and solidity that is necessary to the role.

Stern in its intimations of the terrible consequences of war, this film is a haunting and affecting, as well as a rewarding, drama to have at this time.

—B.C., July 21, 1950

MÉNAGE

Written (in French, with English subtitles) and directed by Bertrand Blier; director of photography, Jean Penzer; edited by Claudine Merlin; music by Serge Gainsbourg; produced by René Cleitman; released by Cinecom Pictures. Running time: 84 minutes.

With: Gérard Depardieu (Bob), Michel Blanc (Antoine), Miou-Miou (Monique), Bruno Cremer (Art Collector), Jean-Pierre Marielle (Depressed Man), Michel Creton (Pedro) and Caroline Sihol (Depressed Woman).

Bertrand Blier never seemed much of a fabulist in the past, but his *Ménage* puts its characters through the kinds of buoyantly kaleidoscopic changes one might associate with a fairy tale. It's an extraordinarily spry and witty film from a director who, on the evidence of *Going Places* and *Get Out Your Handkerchiefs*, has never regarded charming his audiences as much of a priority. Indeed, Mr. Blier has said in interviews that it disappoints him when his films fail to provoke indignation. So in terms of sheer shock value, *Ménage* may seem some slight comedown (though this director, whose great love of sexually explicit dialogue has not left him, will never be accused of gentility). In all other respects, it is Mr. Blier's most satisfying work.

One of the best things about *Ménage* is its elusiveness, a quality that might have served this director well in the days when his unbridled misogyny was being given free reign (*Going Places* now seems, if anything, even more mean-spirited than it did in 1973). Indeed, the new film sustains its brilliantly elliptical tone from beginning to end.

To the extent that it's about anything, it's about relationships between men and women and, more particularly, between men and men. But what matters most here is the incessant change. Mr. Blier creates three characters, all sexual stereotypes, and flings them vigorously into a series of comic variations that become wilder and wilder as *Ménage* progresses. These shifts are relatively subtle at first, but Mr. Blier, who wrote and directed the film, manages continually—and hilariously—to keep on raising the ante.

When we first meet them, the three principals are a miserable married couple and a flamboyant thief. The small, bald, pasty-looking Antoine (Michel Blanc) and his dejected wife, Monique (Miou-Miou), are broke, and they appear thoroughly fed up with each other when big, raffish Bob (Gérard Depardieu) storms his way into their lives. He meets them in a cafeteria and begins, quite literally, to shower them with money. He tells them, none too facetiously, that he himself enjoys a state of grace.

He works every one of his seductive wiles on the couple, teaching them to break into houses as festively as he does; instead of ransacking homes, the three raid closets and refrigerators and wine cellars, turning their adventures into a long, if somewhat morose, party. Bob teaches his new friends the ropes in his own idiosyncratic way, telling them, for instance, that it's best to go barefoot on marble floors and wear shoes on carpet. "It's a matter of harmony," Bob explains.

Bob's purpose in all this becomes gradually apparent: it's Antoine that he's after. He woos this tiny, mousy fellow tirelessly, as Antoine goes from outright disapproval ("Isn't this guy kinda strange?"), to apprehensiveness over Bob's persistence, to real annoyance once Bob starts pursuing Monique as well. Furious, Antoine winds up telling the delighted Bob that he's just going to have to choose.

The quick, uproarious process by which Bob breaks down Antoine's resistance would be enough for most films, but for this one it's only the beginning. Bob and Antoine become the unlikeliest of lovers, serenaded at one point by gypsy violins. Monique, played by Miou-Miou as the most comically disgruntled of Mr. Blier's feminine doormats, grows unhappy with sleeping at the foot of Bob and Antoine's bed. She longs for a real home, she says, and presto! the threesome is in a little hilltop fortress of an apartment, setting up housekeeping. There, Bob berates Monique about her deficiencies in dusting and works even harder to get Antoine just where he wants him. There are several more sudden, unexpected turns of events before the film reaches an ending that must be seen to be believed.

Mr. Blier's pacing is so light and swift that *Ménage* escalates too speedily for the audience to stop and think, which may be just as well; the director's sheer playfulness is the film's greatest asset, and it's not the sort of thing that calls for close analysis. *Ménage* is best enjoyed for the bold, cartoonish craziness with which Mr. Blier leaps from point A to point Z, and for the absolute rightness of the three leading performances.

Mr. Depardieu, at his beefiest here and looking more comically brutish than ever, is himself the film's single funniest image, as he parades about in tiger-striped briefs with a very large galleon tattooed over his breast. When he coos to the wary Antoine that "I've waited, quivering . . ." or declares, "I'll make you a princess," he does it with a perfect earnestness that is all the more outrageous. Mr. Blanc is the ideal foil, and the actor on whose credibility the entire film pivots; he manages to be entirely convincing throughout the many and varied paces through which Mr. Blier puts him. And Miou-Miou, though as blank as she was in *Going Places* or as Carol Laure was in *Get Out Your Handkerchiefs*, manages to bring an ironic dimension to the woman's role here. In a film of Mr. Blier's, that's a triumph.

—J.M., October 1, 1986

METROPOLITAN

Written and directed by Whit Stillman; director of photography, John Thomas; edited by Christopher Tellefsen; music by Tom Judson; produced by Mr. Stillman, Brian Greenbaum and Peter Wentworth; released by New Line Films. Running time: 98 minutes.

With: Carolyn Farina (Audrey Rouget), Edward Clements (Tom Townsend), Christopher Eigeman (Nick Smith), Taylor Nichols (Charlie Black), Allison Rutledge-Parisi (Jane Clarke), Dylan Hundley (Sally Fowler), Isabel Gillies (Cynthia McLean), Bryan Leder (Fred Neff), Will Kempe (Rick Von Sloneker), Elizabeth Thompson (Serena Slocum) and Stephen Uys (Victor Lemley).

I think we're all in a sense doomed," says Charlie Black, who takes the long view.

The time is three a.m. The members of the self-styled Sally Fowler Rat Pack ("the S.F.R.P.," for short) are sitting around the living room of Sally's parents' Park Avenue apartment. It's the kind of apartment where, because there's only one to a floor, the elevator opens directly into the marble-floored foyer.

On this night, Charlie, the philosopher, coins the acronym "UHB" (Upper Haute Bourgeoisie) to describe their class. "It's ridiculous to refer to someone like Averell Harriman as a yuppie."

One night is just like every other during the Manhattan debutante season, which is supposed to be fun, but sometimes isn't. The will to have fun runs out in the wee small hours, when the evening's dance is over but it's still too early to go home.

Fred Neff, drunk again, snoozes in a chair. Cynthia McLean is both haughty and bored when someone states flatly that there is no God. "I know no such thing," says Cynthia. She probably hasn't thought about it a lot but, otherwise, why would there be a St. Thomas's Episcopal Church?

Because there is an acute shortage of escorts, Tom Townsend, who is red-haired and as tightly buttoned up as his dress shirt, is invited into the group. Tom tries to mask his diffidence by saying that he doesn't believe in debutante balls. "I got an invitation and had nothing better to do, so I came." "That's true of most of us," says Sally, though it's not true at all.

The four debutantes and their escorts, who are the principal characters in Whit Stillman's fine new social comedy, *Metropolitan,* would rather die than miss one of the dances in the packed Christmas season set, according to a screen card, "not so long ago."

Nick Smith, the group's social commentator, says that it's untenable to say that one doesn't believe in debutante balls, and then go to them. Tom describes himself as a follower of Fourier (Charles, that is, the early nineteenth-century social reformer). "You're a Marxist?" "No," says Tom, "a socialist."

As the party splits up in the chill Manhattan dawn, Audrey Rouget, the most introspective member of the pack, calls out to Tom through the cab window, "Good luck with your Fourierisme." A very tentative, very rocky romance begins.

Taking a small, extremely privileged group of young people, Mr. Stillman has written and directed a comedy that has a most unparochial wit and sense of fun. *Metropolitan* is a comedy of manners of a very high order.

Audrey (Carolyn Farina), Tom (Edward Clements), Cynthia (Isabel Gillies), Charlie (Taylor Nichols), Nick (Christopher Eigeman), and the others often see no further than the next night's invitation. Yet the movie places them in context with such alertness and intelligence that there's no mistaking the author's vision. He neither sentimentalizes their confusions nor sends them up. He sees this special Manhattan world through the good satirist's bifocal lenses.

The film will be shown at the Museum of Modern Art today and tomorrow as part of the New Directors/New Films series. It will, I'm sure, be going into commercial release in the not too distant future.

Of the principal characters, Tom is the most lost and most earnestly self-deceiving. He goes to a proper prep school, but is something of an alien. He lives not on the East Side but on the Upper West Side (with his divorced mother) and describes his relationship with his father as being especially good. "We always have lunch when I'm in town."

Yet when he drops by his father's East Side apartment during this vacation, his father and stepmother have fled to Santa Fe, New Mexico, without leaving a forwarding.

Which may explain Tom's positive opinions on virtually everything, including Jane Austen. Audrey loves *Mansfield Park.* Tom thinks it's rot. When it turns out that he has only read Lionel Trilling on *Mansfield Park,* he explains that he much prefers good literary criticism to novels. That way, he says, you get both the novel and what to think about it.

Like Jane Austen, Mr. Stillman severely restricts his characters' field of action, which is sometimes combat. They define themselves in large part by what they say and do after the ball, usually in Sally Fowler's parents' living room. Audrey sets her hopes on Tom, but Tom still hasn't recovered from his "affair" with the mostly offscreen Serena Slocum (Elizabeth Thompson).

Serena is a femme fatale who is also, as is said more than once, "basically a nice person." Serena is currently involved with Rick Von Sloneker, who is slightly older than the others and is the bête noir of the male members of the S.F.R.P.

Nick, especially, loathes Rick and concocts the story of how Rick ruined a young woman named Polly Perkins. Polly met him at a bad time, he says. "During the summer, she started feeling depressed. It was partly getting over her thing about horses." Cynthia, cheerfully styled "a slut" by her peers, defends Rick in a way that makes it clear she wants him for herself.

It is one of Mr. Stillman's many accomplishments that when Rick (Will Kempe) shows up, he is everything that is expected and arrogantly more.

Some of the young actors seem awkward at first. Whether they actually improve during the film, or whether the self-consciousness is integral to the method of the ensemble performance, it's difficult to tell. However it happens, the actors are a uniformly engaging lot.

Particularly funny are Mr. Nichols, as the pessimistic Charlie, who talks of doom and downward mobility, and Mr. Eigeman's Nick, who has a snap judgment for every occasion. "The Surrealists were just a bunch of social climbers," he announces at one point and, at another, "Easthampton seagulls are morons."

Mr. Stillman's screenplay never directly acknowledges its pathos. The Old Manners still count. He is discreet. There's a wonderfully forlorn sequence near the end when Tom and Charlie try to rent a car to drive to Easthampton to save the honor of the young woman they both love. Neither, however, has a driver's license. That is one of the penalties for being brought up in Manhattan.

They do the only thing they can: they take a cab.

Almost as important and funny as Mr. Stillman's dialogue is the so-called society music on the soundtrack. It's composed largely of breathless cha-cha-chas and hard-edged versions of standard fox trots.

It seems tradition that everything is played at the same tempo, always a little too fast, as if to keep the young men from getting any sneaky ideas, and the debutantes all aglow around the neck and forehead, even in the palms of their hands.

—V.C., March 23, 1990

MIDNIGHT

Directed by Mitchell Leisen: written by Charles Brackett and Billy Wilder. based on a story by Edwin Justus Mayer and Franz Schulz: director of photography. Charles Lang: edited by Doane Harrison: art directors. Hans Dreier and Robert Usher: music by Frederick Hollander: produced by Arthur Honblow Jr.: released by Paramount Pictures. Black and white. Running time: 94 minutes.

With: Claudette Colbert (Eve Peabody). Don Ameche (Tibor Czerny). John Barrymore (Georges Flammarion). Francis Lederer (Jacques Picot). Mary Astor (Helene Flammarion). Elaine Barrie (Simone). Hedda Hopper (Stephanie). Rex O'Malley (Marcel Renaud). Monty Woolley (Judge) and Armand Kaliz (Lebon).

The ice went out of the river at the Paramount yesterday, and Spring came laughing in with *Midnight,* one of the liveliest, gayest, wittiest, and naughtiest comedies of a long hard season. Its direc-

tion, by Mitchell Leisen, is strikingly reminiscent of that of the old Lubitsch. Its cast, led by Claudette Colbert, Don Ameche, John Barrymore, and Francis Lederer, is in the best of spirits. Its script, by too many authors to mention, is a model of deft phrasing and glib narrative joinery; and its production, while handsome, never has been permitted to bulk larger than its players. The call is for three cheers and a tiger: the Paramount is back on Broadway again.

The *Midnight* of the title is the fatal hour that strikes for every Cinderella, the moment when the coach will change back into a pumpkin, the ballroom dress will fall into rags and the prince charming discover the smudge of soot, or fried egg, on the changeling's cheek. But the clock doesn't strike when the film's midnight comes; out, instead, pops a cuckoo with a clarion call to humor. Things go hilariously to smash, but not Cinderella. Even the fairy godmother—in this case, John Barrymore—blinks amazedly at his protégé's carryings-on. When Miss Colbert plays Cinderella she doesn't depend on a magic wand; a slapstick and a bludgeon are handier, and funnier.

It begins with the arrival in Paris on a rainy night of a young woman with one evening gown to her back, and not too much of it to it. In a matter of moments she has met a cab-driver named Czerny, crashed a society musicale and has been "set up"—to use the Park Avenue phrase—in the Ritz by a prankish, yet practical, millionaire with instructions to break up, by intervention, the affair between his wife and an irrepressibly romantic man about town. Miss Colbert's "Baroness Czerny"—a title by courtesy of the cabby—is beautiful bait, and everything goes smoothly until midnight and even more smoothly, in a comic sense, thereafter.

Usually these things fall apart of their own complications; this one has the marvelous air of being bolstered by them. There is the business of the cab-drivers' posse; there is the business of Cinderella being baffled by the godmother's magic wand; there is the business of Cabby Czerny's heroic attempts to expose the fraud and being considered a lunatic; there is the bit in which Mr. Barrymore impersonates a three-year-old; there is the complication attending the discovery that the non-wed Czernys will have to be divorced.

We could mention other zany bits, but it wouldn't

help. It is really too daffy to be synopsized. You'll have to take our word for it that it's fun. Most of the credit, of course, belongs to Miss Colbert. She has superb command of the comic style, can turn a line or toss a vase with equal precision. Mr. Barrymore, the Gehrig of eye-brow batting, rolls his phrases with his usual richly humorous effect, and Mr. Ameche and Mr. Lederer were quite as helpful. All of them have made it a happy occasion. Pictures like *Midnight* should strike more often.

—*F.S., April 6, 1939*

MIDNIGHT COWBOY

Directed by John Schlesinger; written by Waldo Salt, based on the novel by James Leo Herlihy; cinematographer, Adam Holender; edited by Hugh A. Robertson; music by John Barry; production designer, John Robert Lloyd; produced by Jerome Hellman; released by United Artists. Running time: 119 minutes.

With: Dustin Hoffman (Ratso), Jon Voight (Joe Buck), Sylvia Miles (Cass), John McGiver (Mr. O'Daniel), Brenda Vaccaro (Shirley), Barnard Hughes (Towny), Ruth White (Sally Buck) and Viva (Gretel McAlbertson).

Joe Buck is six feet tall and has the kind of innocence that preserves dumb good looks. Joe Buck fancies himself a cowboy, but his spurs were earned while riding a gas range in a Houston hamburger joint. Ratso Rizzo, his buddy and part-time pimp from the Bronx, is short, gimpy, and verminous. Although they are a comparatively bizarre couple, they go unnoticed when they arrive at one of those hallucinogenic "Village" parties where the only thing straight is the booze that no one drinks. Everybody is too busy smoking pot, popping pills, and being chic. Joe Buck, ever-hopeful stud, drawls: "I think we better find someone an' tell 'em that we're here."

Trying to tell someone that he's there is the story of Joe Buck's life—twenty-eight years of anxiety and dispossession fenced off by Priapian conquests that always, somehow, leave him a little lonelier than he was before. Joe is a funny, dim-witted variation on the lonely, homosexual dream-hero who used to wander

disguised through so much drama and literature associated with the 1950's.

Midnight Cowboy, which opened yesterday at the Coronet Theater, is a slick, brutal (but not brutalizing) movie version of James Leo Herlihy's 1965 novel. It is tough and good in important ways, although its style is oddly romantic and at variance with the laconic material. It may be that movies of this sort (like most war movies) automatically celebrate everything they touch. We know they are movies—isolated, simplified reflections of life—and thus we can enjoy the spectacle of degradation and loss while feeling superior to it and safe.

I had something of this same feeling about *Darling,* which was directed by John Schlesinger and in which Julie Christie suffered, more or less upwardly, on her way to fame and fortune in a movie as glossy as the life it satirized. There is nothing obviously glossy in *Midnight Cowboy,* but it contains a lot of superior laughter that has the same softening effect.

Schlesinger is most successful in his use of actors. Dustin Hoffman, as Ratso (his first movie performance since *The Graduate*), is something found under an old door in a vacant lot. With his hair matted back, his ears sticking out, and his runty walk, Hoffman looks like a sly, defeated rat and talks with a voice that might have been created by Mel Blanc for a despondent Bugs Bunny. Jon Voight is equally fine as Joe Buck, a tall, handsome young man whose open face somehow manages to register the fuzziest of conflicting emotions within a very dim mind.

Waldo Frank's screenplay follows the Herlihy novel in most of the surface events. Joe Buck, a Texas dishwasher without friend or family, comes to New York to make his fortune as a stud to all the rich ladies who have been deprived of their rights by faggot eastern gentlemen. Instead, he winds up a half-hearted 42d Street hustler whose first and only friend is a lame, largely ineffectual con artist.

As long as the focus is on this world of cafeterias and abandoned tenements, of desperate conjunctions in movie balconies and doorways, of catchup and beans and canned heat, *Midnight Cowboy* is so rough and vivid that it's almost unbearable. Less effective are abbreviated, almost subliminal fantasies and flashbacks. Most of these are designed to fill in the story of the young Joe Buck, a little boy whose knowledge of life was learned in front of a TV set while his grandmother, good-time Sally Buck, ran a Texas beauty parlor and lived with a series of cowboy-father images for Joe.

Schlesinger has given his leads superb support with character actors like Ruth White (Sally Buck), John McGiver, Brenda Vaccaro, Barnard Hughes, and Sylvia Miles. Miss Miles is especially good as the aging hooker Joe picks up under the mistaken impression she is a society lady. The one rather wooden performance, oddly, is that of superstar Viva, who plays a "Village" zombie with none of the flair she exhibits in Andy Warhol's improvisations.

Midnight Cowboy often seems to be exploiting its material for sensational or comic effect, but it is ultimately a moving experience that captures the quality of a time and a place. It's not a movie for the ages, but, having seen it, you won't ever again feel detached as you walk down West 42d Street, avoiding the eyes of the drifters, stepping around the little islands of hustlers, and closing your nostrils to the smell of rancid griddles.

—*V.C., May 26, 1969*

MINNIE AND MOSKOWITZ

Written and directed by John Cassavetes; directors of photography. Alric Edebns. Michael D. Margulies and Arthur J. Ornitz; edited by Frederic Knudtson; produced by Al Ruban; released by Universal. Running time: 114 minutes.

With: Gena Rowlands (Minnie Moore). Seymour Cassel (Seymour Moskowitz). Val Avery (Zelmo Swift). Timothy Carey (Morgan Morgan). Katherine Cassavetes (Sheba Moskowitz). Elizabeth Deering (Girl). Elsie Ames (Florence). Lady Rowlands (Georgia Moore). Holly Near (Irish). Judith Roberts (Wife). Jack Danskin (Dick Henderson) and Eleanor Zee (Mrs. Grass).

*M*innie *and Moskowitz,* John Cassavetes's sixth and, in many ways, most ambitious film, is also his friendliest, in the dish-throwing, door-pounding, exclamation-pointed manner of a comic strip. Every frame depicts a bodily assault or an exchange of angry words, representing love.

Because it means to be so friendly, and because

Mr. Cassavetes has exercised imagination and discipline that lift the film out of the neo-realist rut of *Husbands* and *Faces,* I wish I liked *Minnie and Moskowitz* more than I do. It's as open and vulnerable as someone who tells an elaborate ethnic joke, in an accent that isn't very authentic, with a point that isn't very funny.

The fact is that although I admired specific things about the film, I never laughed very much and only felt slight, distant tremors of the joy that, I assume, rocked everyone connected with the movie during its production.

Minnie and Moskowitz is a contemporary fairy tale about a youngish, eccentric, parking lot attendant (Seymour Cassel), who is essentially a middle-class Jewish prince in hippie disguise, and the very beautiful, mixed-up, middle-class gentile princess (Gena Rowlands), whose hand he wins in what is certain to be an idyllic, Maggie-and-Jiggs sort of marriage.

They meet in a parking lot when Moskowitz steps in (and is immediately flattened) as he attempts to stop Minnie's blind date from beating her up. Thereafter, Mr. Moskowitz, when he isn't pushing Minnie around to prove how much he loves her, gets pushed around by people trying to protect Minnie. They scream at each other, share sudden moments of tenderness, and spend what seems to be an extraordinary amount of time ordering and eating in roadside lunch stands.

Mr. Cassavetes's use of exaggerated slapstick gestures to underscore the loneliness and fears of his characters is more interesting in theory than funny or moving in actual fact. This may well have to do with the heavy literalness with which the supposedly comic brawls rephotographed (people do get hurt that way), and with the apparent disparity between the characters and their environments.

Minnie, for just one example, works at the Los Angeles County Museum and lives in a posh, book-lined duplex, yet she seems to have the mental equipment of Edgar Kennedy's bird-brained wife in those old two-reelers. It doesn't quite fit.

To the extent that the material allows them to be, Mr. Cassel and Miss Rowlands are most appealing. However, all of the performances are quite special and this, I think, is Mr. Cassavetes's strongest point.

As an actor, he appreciates actors and their mysterious art, as well as their awful dependency on the work of others. This explains why he casts his films so abundantly, using very fine actors in what are practically throw-away roles, or would be throwaway roles in the film of a less fond director.

Minnie and Moskowitz is loaded with small, sometimes lovely, sometimes oddball bits, by people like Tim Carey (as a nut in an all-night restaurant), Val Avery (as Minnie's aggressive blind-date), and even by members of the Cassavetes-Rowlands families. Two of the best performances of the film are given by the director's mother, Katherine Cassavetes, as Moskowitz's indulgent Jewish mum, and Mrs. Cassavetes's mother, Lady Rowlands, as Minnie's very starchy, WASPy parent.

Minnie and Moskowitz, which opened yesterday at the Cinema II, does reverse one usual movie procedure in that it improves as it goes along, instead of falling apart. Like Minnie and Moskowitz themselves, the movie attempts to fight its way out of the lower depths, but it's not as lucky as its prince and princess.
—*V.C., December 23, 1971*

THE MIRACLE OF MORGAN'S CREEK

Produced, written and directed by Preston Sturges: cinematographer, John Seitz: edited by Stuart Gilmore: music by Leo Shuken: art designers, Hans Dreier and Ernst Fegte: released by Paramount Pictures. Black and white. Running time: 99 minutes.

With: Eddie Bracken (Norval Jones), Betty Hutton (Trudy Kockenlocker), Diana Lynn (Emmy Kockenlocker), William Demarest (Officer Kockenlocker), Porter Hall (Justice of the Peace) and Emory Parnell (Mr. Tuerck).

The watchmen for the usually prim Hays office certainly permitted themselves a Jovian nod when confronted with the irrepressible impudence of Preston Sturges' *The Miracle of Morgan's Creek.* For a more audacious picture—a more delightfully irreverent one—than this new lot of nonsense at the Paramount has never come slithering madly down the path. Mr. Sturges, who is noted for his railleries of the sentimental, the pompous, and the smug in his clas-

sics, *The Great McGinty, Sullivan's Travels,* and *The Lady Eve,* has hauled off this time and tossed a satire which is more cheeky than all the rest. He has spoofed that most sacred institution, that most unapproachable mystery—motherhood.

Truly! It's hard to imagine how he ever got away with such a thing, how he ever persuaded the Hays boys that he wasn't trying to undermine all morals. Not only does he boldly make mad Christmas over a fact of approaching maternity but he frankly satirizes the sort of marriage that is significantly featured by a shotgun. No coying around with tiny garments in this one, no awaiting the event with bated breath. Mr. Sturges takes the euphemism "trouble" in its literal definition—but yes! Our only explanation of how he did it is a simple, disarming one: he made the film so innocently amusing, so full of candor, that no one could take offense.

Obviously Trudy Kockenlocker was inspired by generous motives beyond reproach when she got her 4-F idolater, Norval Jones, to drop her off at the servicemen's dance that fateful night. Obviously Trudy had no idea that the lemonade was spiked and that the big, noisy Private Ratziwatzi wasn't there to play post office. Obviously poor little Trudy was as much shocked as anyone would be when she discovered her unfortunate condition after that hazy night. And obviously Norval, though anguished at the thought of her heedless mistake, found the occasion propitious to offer himself as the father of her child-to-be.

That would seem a logical solution. But Mr. Sturges, being the satirist that he is, could not have anything as easy, as obvious, and as unfunny as that. And so the particular problem in *The Miracle of Morgan's Creek* is not how to find a willing husband but how to get hitched to him. Herein arise the complications and a delightful switch on the shot-gun wedding gag. Herein occurs the dilemma which runs contrary to logical rule. Fortunately, Mr. Sturges has a solution. The "miracle" which sets all things right is a beautiful touch of extravagance that is the liveliest spoof of all.

Mr. Sturges as author and director is thoroughly up to his stinging style in this film. Situations spark, dialogue crackles, and his camera works like a playful Peeping Tom. And from all of the actors he gets performances that make them look like inspired comedians. Betty Hutton is bird-brained as Trudy, Eddie Bracken is frantic as Norval, and William Demarest is

a tower of indignations as confused Mr. Kockenlocker. Diana Lynn, as a fourteen-year-old sister, is
full of wise, superior advice, and a large cast of ever-
ready actors do a lot of funny things outlandishly.

Maybe the humor is forced a little, and it may be
slightly difficult at times to understand precisely what
in heck is going on. But that doesn't make any difference. At those times, you can catch your breath.

—B.C., January 20, 1944

MIRACLE ON 34TH STREET

Directed by George Seaton: written by Mr.
Seaton. based on a story by Valentine Davies: cinematographers. Charles Clarke and Lloyd Ahern:
edited by Robert Simpson: music by Cyril J. Mockridge: art designers. Richard Day and Richard
Irvine: produced by William Perlberg: released by
Twentieth Century Fox. Black and white. Running time: 96 minutes.

With: Edmund Gwenn (Kris Kringle). Maureen
O'Hara (Doris Walker). John Payne (Fred Gailey).
Gene Lockhart (Judge Henry X. Harper). Natalie
Wood (Susan). Porter Hall (Mr. Sawyer). William
Frawley (Politician). Jerome Cowan (District Attor-
ney Mars) and Philip Tonge (Mr. Shellhammer).

For all those blasé skeptics who do not believe in
Santa Claus—and likewise for all those natives
who have grown cynical about New York—but most
especially for all those patrons who have grown weary
of the monotonies of the screen, let us heartily recommend the Roxy's new picture, *Miracle on 34th Street*.
As a matter of fact, let's go further: let's catch its spirit
and heartily proclaim that it is the freshest little picture in a long time, and maybe even the best comedy
of this year.

If that sounds like wild enthusiasm for a picture
devoid of mighty stars and presented without the
usual red-velvet-carpet ballyhoo, let us happily note
that it is largely because this job isn't loaded to the
hubs with all the commercial gimmicks that it is such
a delightful surprise. Indeed, it is in its open kidding
of "commercialism" and money-grubbing plugs that
lies its originality and its particularly winning charm.

What would you think, to put it plainly, if you ran

across an old man who not only looked like Kris
Kringle but confidently claimed that he was? And
what would you think, more specifically, if you were
an executive of Macy's store, employing the old man
to lure the kiddies before Christmas, and caught him
sending customers to Gimbel's, down the street?
Would you see in this merchandising technique a
"friendly policy," as Mr. Macy does, or would you figure the old fellow crazy and a menace, as does a sour
psychiatrist?

Well, if you were Valentine Davies and George
Seaton, who wrote the story and script of *Miracle on
34th Street* for Twentieth Century Fox, you would
give free rein to the latter point of view and you would
get the old man before the Supreme Court on a question of his sanity. You would, for the sake of the story
and an uncommonly fascinating jest, call for a formal
court decision as to whether there is actually a Santa
Claus. And, furthermore, you would demand substan-
tiation that this old fellow is the true Santa himself—
and you would then go ahead and prove it by the
highest authority in the land. By doing so, you would
not only gladden the hearts of all New York but you
would bring a young couple to matrimony and you
would lift a little girl's doubts.

At least, that is what Mr. Davies and Mr. Seaton
have done in their bright yarn. And, appropriately, in
this buoyant spirit, Mr. Seaton has directed it. He has
got Edmund Gwenn to play Kris Kringle with such
natural and warm benevolence that, if ever the real
Santa wants to step down, Mr. Gwenn is the man for
the job. His candor with Mr. Macy, an awesome
tycoon, his charm with little Sue, and his genuine attitude of generosity toward everybody are cherishable in
this dark day.

Good, too, are Maureen O'Hara and John Payne,
as the lady and gent who help Mr. Kringle spread sunshine. And most amusing are little Natalie Wood as
the child who has been trained to sniff at Santa and
Gene Lockhart as the much embarrassed judge. Porter
Hall is a tangle of malice as the big-business psychiatrist and at least a dozen others are delightful in small
roles or bits. Scenes shot in actual New York settings
add credibility to the film.

As a lesson in merchandising not only store products but good-will, this *Miracle on 34th Street* is a
dandy. Does Macy's tell Gimbel's? It should!

—B.C., June 5, 1947

THE MIRACLE WORKER

Directed by Arthur Penn; written by William Gibson, based on his play and the book *The Story of My Life* by Helen Keller; cinematographer, Ernest Caparros; edited by Aram Avakian; music by Laurence Rosenthal; art designers, George Jenkins and Mel Bourne; produced by Fred Coe; released by United Artists. Black and white. Running time: 106 minutes.

With: Anne Bancroft (Annie Sullivan), Patty Duke (Helen Keller), Victor Jory (Captain Keller), Inga Swenson (Kate Keller), Andrew Prine (James Keller) and Kathleen Comegys (Aunt Ev).

The absolutely tremendous and unforgettable display of physically powerful acting that Anne Bancroft and Patty Duke put on in William Gibson's stage play *The Miracle Worker* is repeated by them in the film made from it by the same producer, Fred Coe, and the same director, Arthur Penn. The picture opened at the Astor and the Trans-Lux Fifty-second Street yesterday.

But because the physical encounters between the two in their strongly graphic roles of trained nurse and deaf-and-blind pupil seem to be more frequent and prolonged than they were in the play and are shown in close-ups, which dump the passion and violence right into your lap, the sheer rough-and-tumble of the drama becomes more dominant than it was on the stage.

Indeed, one may well leave this picture with the feeling that the triumph achieved by Annie Sullivan with the child Helen Keller (which are the roles the two actresses play) was more a matter of muscle over sinew than of a strong mind over a raw, young, uncurbed will. One may well feel that Annie has just been winner in three falls out of five.

This has advantages and disadvantages in working toward the aim of a powerful emotional experience, which is the obvious object of the film. It is clear that the bold decision the stalwart young Annie makes when she arrives at the Southern home of the Kellers to try to train their desperately afflicted child is that she must go about it with the brute force one would apply to the breaking of a head-strong colt.

To "disinter the soul" of the youngster from the depths of the little animal that darkness and silence since infancy have cruelly made of her, the nurse sees it will take more than patience. It will take miraculous skill and energy. That's what she gives to the project. Thus the bruising encounters between the two, even from their first meeting—the knock-down-and-drag-out fights in which the child wildly bucks against the efforts of the nurse to reach her mind with crude hand signs—are intensely significant of the drama and do excite strong emotional response.

But the very intensity of them and the fact that it is hard to see the difference between the violent struggle to force the child to obey (which is the nurse's first big achievement) and the violent struggle to make her comprehend words makes for sameness in these encounters and eventually an exhausting monotony. This is the disadvantage of so much energy.

However, Miss Bancroft's performance does bring to life and reveal a wondrous woman with great humor and compassion as well as athletic skill. And little Miss Duke, in those moments when she frantically pantomimes her bewilderment and desperate groping, is both gruesome and pitiable. Inevitably, the young actress has grown since she did the play and she now is a shade too uncomfortably formidable as an adversary for the nurse.

Mr. Penn, who directed with great vigor, has also let Victor Jory play the father of the child a bit too harshly and loudly for the already loud tone of the whole, and Inga Swenson performs the mother a bit too softly and winsomely, in turn. Andrew Prine is impressively malicious and caustic as a grown-up half brother.

On one point, we file a strong objection. That is the flummery at the end that has the barely communicative youngster signaling a handy "I love you" to the nurse. This seems a trick by Mr. Gibson to work a hackneyed heart tug into the film, which by this time has either got you with its concept of humane conquest or it hasn't got you at all. Pathos is superfluous at this point, and such sophistication is unthinkable.

—*B.C., May 24, 1962*

LES MISÉRABLES

Directed by Richard Boleslawski; written by W. P. Lipscomb, based on the novel by Victor Hugo;

cinematographer. Gregg Toland; edited by Barbara McLean; music by Alfred Newman; produced by Darryl F. Zanuck; released by Twentieth Century Pictures and United Artists. Black and white. Running time: 108 minutes.

With: Fredric March (Jean Valjean), Charles Laughton (Javert), Cedric Hardwicke (Bishop Bienvenu), Rochelle Hudson (Big Cosette), Marilynne Knowlden (Little Cosette), Frances Drake (Eponine) and John Beal (Marius).

It is an affirmation of the timeless quality of *Les Misérables* that the magnificent film edition of Victor Hugo's nineteenth-century classic bears the hallmark of Twentieth Century Pictures. Despite its costumed surfaces, this odyssey of the greatest manhunt in literature possesses a topical significance in 1935 as real and moving as it did in 1862, and it is as undated as man's inhumanity to man. The underground reports from Hollywood are often capricious, but they have not deceived us this time. The photoplay at the Rivoli Theatre is unbelievably thrilling in all the departments of its manufacture, and it makes for a memorable experience in the cinema. You will surely be hearing about it for a long time.

In a work which represents the perfect collaboration of many talents, it is difficult to award the laurel adequately. But we can come pretty close by applauding Richard Boleslawski for his direction, Gregg Toland for his remarkable photography, W. P. Lipscomb for a screenplay which is a model of telescopic rewriting, and the distinguished performances of Fredric March and Charles Laughton.

Despite the rich kaleidoscopic variety of the drama, it is always at bottom the story of the hunted and the hunter—of Valjean, the tragic and eternally defeated man, and Javert, the eternal policeman, who had to pursue his quarry down the nights and down the days, and even down the labyrinthine ways of his own mind, because the law was his religion, his blood, and his life. It is one of the great merits of Mr. Lipscomb's screenplay that it brings Valjean and Javert down to the end of the story together, eliminating the anticlimax of Valjean's death. Thus the drama fades out powerfully with Valjean free at last, and Javert a suicide in the nearby Seine for the sin of mercy, for which he could atone only by forfeiting his own life.

If your memory is as bad as mine, you will not resent being reminded that the lifetime purgatory of Jean Valjean began when he stole a loaf of bread to feed his sister's starving family. For that breach of the law in the France of 1800 he was condemned to the galleys for ten years (it was five in the book). His penalty was increased because of his rebellious conduct, and when he was turned loose, theoretically a free man, he found his independence a cruel mockery because everyone's hand was turned against him. The Bishop Bienvenu alone sheltered him. When Valjean made off with the good man's silverware and was dragged back by the police the bishop saved the wretched Valjean from another spell in the galleys by pretending that the theft actually was a gift. Valjean never forgot the bishop's kindness. In the years that followed, although he became a sainted man out of his sufferings, the implacable Javert tracked him down, uprooted him, sent him fleeing. Even when Valjean spared his enemy's life on the barricades, Javert pursued him, because the pursuit was a disease in him which only death could conquer.

Charles Laughton is an actor of such brilliant range that it is foolhardy to estimate any single performance of his in relation to the ones which have gone before. But his Javert, the cropped head, the hideous trembling of the lips, the relentless monotone of his behavior, is one of the great screen portraits. After *Les Misérables* has been nationally circulated, the chances are that Mr. Laughton will not be safe on the streets. Mr. March's Valjean is a flawless thing, strong and heartbreaking. It reveals Mr. March as a screen player of enormous resource when, as on this occasion, he is properly cast. There are numerous minor performances of note, chief among them being Sir Cedric Hardwicke's as the Bishop Bienvenu, Florence Eldridge's as the tragic Fantine, and little Marilynne Knowlden's as Fantine's child. *Les Misérables* bulks impressively among the most notable contributions to the talking screen and it is sure to be remembered when the time comes to appraise the 1935 cinema. It deserves to run for months at the Rivoli.

—A.S., April 22, 1935

THE MISFITS

Directed by John Huston; written by Arthur Miller; cinematographer, Russell Metty; edited by

George Tomasini: music by Alex North: art designers. Stephen Grimes and William Newberry: produced by Frank E. Taylor: released by United Artists. Black and white. Running time: 124 minutes.

With: Clark Gable (Gay Langland). Marilyn Monroe (Roslyn Taber). Montgomery Clift (Perce Howland). Thelma Ritter (Isabelle Steers). Eli Wallach (Guido). James Barton (Old Man). Estelle Winwood (Church Lady). Kevin McCarthy (Raymond Taber) and Dennis Shaw (Young Boy).

There is this to be said for the people that Clark Gable, Marilyn Monroe, et al., play in John Huston's new film, *The Misfits,* which came to the Capitol yesterday: they are not what you might call status seekers or organization men. They are simply lowdown variations of the old-fashioned genus tramp.

They are nice tramps, it's true—chummy fellows and equally chummy girls, cowboys, garage mechanics, and assorted divorcées, who happen to gravitate together in Reno, Nevada, that toddling town, and soak up a little whiskey before taking off to catch some mustangs in the hills. They are scatterbrained, whimsical, lonely, and, in the case of the character of Miss Monroe, inclined to adore all living creatures and have a quivering revulsion to pain.

They are amusing people to be with, for a little while, anyhow. But they are shallow and inconsequential, and that is the dang-busted trouble with this film.

Right at the start, Arthur Miller, who wrote the original script, drops a hint of what is coming and the line that the film is going to take. "Cowboys," he has a jolly woman, played by Thelma Ritter, say, "are the last real men in the world, but they're as reliable as jackrabbits." And that's it.

Everyone in this film is unreliable, wild, slightly kookie. As William Saroyan once put it, "There's no foundation all the way down the line."

Mr. Gable is a leathery old cowboy with a realistic slant on most plain things, but even he has to go a little nutty and sentimental at the end. Eli Wallach as a rolling-stone mechanic is a bundle of impulses and appetites, sometimes very funny, sometimes repulsive and sad. Montgomery Clift as a vagrant rodeo rider is as slug-nutty as they come, equally cavalier toward injuries and toward his gnawing loneliness for his mom. And Miss Monroe—well, she is completely blank and unfathomable as a new divorcée who shed her husband because "you could touch him but he wasn't there."

Unfortunately for the film's structure, everything turns upon her—the congregation of the fellows, like a pack of dogs, the buildup of cross-purposed courtships, and the sentimental backflip at the end. But there is really not much about her that is very exciting or interesting. Mr. Miller makes a pass at explanation. He has someone tell her: "When you smile, it's like the sun coming up."

Toward the end, something happens. The three fellows go into the hills to catch wild horses to sell for dog meat, and the divorcée goes along. The wrangling is vivid and thrilling and everyone is having a good time, until the woman discovers what the horses are being captured for. Then she kicks up such a ruckus—and Mr. Huston lets his cameras show so much of the pitiful plight of the creatures—that the screen is full of shock and the audience is left in breathless horror until she persuades Mr. Gable to let the horses go.

It has something to do with her sense of freedom. What, we wouldn't know.

So that's what's wrong with this picture. Characters and theme do not congeal. There is a lot of absorbing detail in it, but it doesn't add up to a point. Mr. Huston's direction is dynamic, inventive, and colorful. Mr. Gable is ironically vital. (He died a few weeks after shooting was done.) Miss Ritter, James Barton, and Estelle Winwood are amusing in very minor roles, and Alex North has provided some good theme music.

But the picture just doesn't come off.

—B.C., February 2, 1961

MISSING

Directed by Constantin Costa-Gavras: written by Donald Stewart and Mr. Costa-Gavras, based on the book *The Execution of Charles Horman* by Thomas Hauser: director of photography. Ricardo Aronovich: edited by Françoise Bonnot: music by Vangelis: production designer. Peter Jamison: produced by Edward Lewis and Mildred Lewis: released by Universal Pictures. Running time: 122 minutes.

With: Jack Lemmon (Ed Horman), Sissy Spacek (Beth Horman), Melanie Mayron (Terry Simon), John Shea (Charles Horman), Charles Cioffi (Captain Ray Tower), David Clennon (Consul Phil Putnam), Richard Venture (United States Ambassador) and Jerry Hardin (Colonel Sean Patrick).

In addition to making movies that galvanize the emotions in ways that can be simultaneously fascinating and infuriating, Costa-Gavras, the Greek-born, French filmmaker (*Z, The Confession*), also has a knack for stirring up publicity from the most unlikely sources.

In 1973 his *State of Siege,* which accused an official of the United States Agency for International Development of teaching torture methods to repressive right-wing regimes in Latin America, was booked into the Kennedy Center for the Performing Arts in Washington, for a gala showing by the American Film Institute. At the last minute the showing was canceled when someone decided that it might not be an especially appropriate film for presentation under such auspices.

Now *Missing,* Mr. Costa-Gavras's latest film, which is about the 1973 kidnap and murder in Chile of Charles Horman, a young, Harvard-educated, counterculture journalist, is opening today at the Beekman Theater, two days after the release of a most unusual statement by the State Department. The department takes issue with a number of facts in the film and just about all of its conclusions.

It is the belief of Mr. Costa-Gavras, as well as of Thomas Hauser, the lawyer who wrote the book on which the film is based, that young Mr. Horman was executed by Chilean authorities, probably with the tacit approval of some United States representatives on the scene, because he had knowledge of United States involvement in the military coup that had overthrown the Marxist government of Dr. Salvador Allende Gossens, the Chilean President.

About the only fact not in dispute is that Mr. Horman, immediately after the coup, somehow became one of the victims of the roundup and execution of hundreds of Chilean left-wing activists and sympathizers.

Mr. Costa-Gavras seems to ask for such controversy. The film opens with a statement to the effect that *Missing* is "a true story" and that all of "the incidents and facts are documented." If all of the incidents and facts are really documented, then it should follow that the conclusions drawn cannot be open to too much question. This is something that I think even Mr. Costa-Gavras would not say, though by the end of the film, there is certainly no doubt about what he thinks.

Further complicating these questions is that *Missing* is Mr. Costa-Gavras's most beautifully achieved political melodrama to date, a suspense-thriller of real cinematic style, acted with immense authority by Jack Lemmon, as Charles Horman's father, Ed Horman, and Sissy Spacek as Charles's wife, Beth. The screenplay, by Mr. Costa-Gavras and Donald Stewart, is a model of its kind, in which Ed and Beth's search for Charles is developed in a series of scenes that seamlessly join past and present actions into a nonstop, forward-moving narrative.

The center of the film is the political awakening of Ed Horman, who comes to Chile to help Beth, though he suspects that Charles has gone under cover for some reason that is beyond his comprehension. "If he had stayed home," says Ed, who is well-to-do and politically conservative, as well as a practicing Christian Scientist, "this wouldn't have happened."

Ed calls Charles "almost deliberately naive" for his identification with underdogs. Says the beleagured Beth, "We're just two normal, slightly confused people trying to connect with the entire enchilada."

Charles, played with modest simplicity by John Shea, comes to life in the flashbacks. He's a dedicated, somewhat guilt-ridden heir to a privileged America, a young man who reads *The Little Prince* for literary inspiration and whose optimism is unshakable. If not deliberately naive, he's the kind of unsophisticated saint one always wants to believe in.

Ed and Beth's search for Charles involves a succession of chilling encounters with politely patronizing United States embassy and consular officials, as well as with members of the Chilean Government. The major villains are vaguely identified United States military people, especially a Captain Ray Tower (Charles Cioffi), who befriends Charles, and a young American woman named Terry Simon (Melanie Mayron), whom Charles meets when the two are marooned in the resort town of Viña del Mar during the coup, unable to return to Santiago.

If *Missing* were only an inventory of the details of

Charles's life and disappearance, it wouldn't have the terrific emotional impact that it has. Mr. Lemmon and Miss Spacek are superb, however, and their increasing respect and fondness for each other as the story unfolds gives *Missing* an agonizing reality.

Mr. Costa-Gavras also knows Chile, where he filmed State of Siege during the Allende regime— *Missing* was shot in Mexico—and he is particularly successful in evoking the looks, sounds, and feelings of a society in upheaval.

There's a stunning sequence in Santiago when Beth, unable to get home before curfew, spends an endless night hiding in an alley, hearing in the distance gunfire and other sounds not easily identified. At one point a terrified white horse goes galloping down an otherwise deserted street, pursued by soldiers firing random shots from a speeding jeep. In this sequence as elsewhere, the camera work by Ricardo Aronovich is very fine indeed.

Whether or not its facts are verifiable, *Missing* documents, in a most moving way, the raising of the political consciousness of Ed Horman, who has, until this devastating experience, always believed in the sanctity of his government and accepted its actions and policies without question.

In view of the film's opening contention of being a true story, the care that Mr. Costa-Gavras takes not ever to identify Chile by name is a bit disingenuous. The cities are clearly named and identified. Also a bit disingenuous is the way the film never bothers to give a good answer to the question of why the Chilean— and possibly the American—authorities found it necessary to liquidate Charles Horman while allowing the safe departure from Chile of Terry Simon. Terry, after all, is privy to all the supposedly damaging information Charles gathered in Viña del Mar.

These are valid questions to raise about a film that is so fine that one wants it to be above reproach.

—V.C., February 12, 1982

MR. AND MRS. BRIDGE

Directed by James Ivory; written by Ruth Prawer Jhabvala, based on the novels *Mr. Bridge* and *Mrs. Bridge* by Evan S. Connell; director of photography, Tony Pierce-Roberts; edited by Humphry Dixon; music by Richard Robbins; production designer, David Gropman; produced by Ismail Merchant; released by Miramax Films. Running time: 127 minutes.

With: Paul Newman (Walter Bridge), Joanne Woodward (India Bridge), Saundra McClain (Harriet), Margaret Welsh (Carolyn Bridge), Kyra Sedgwick (Ruth Bridge), Blythe Danner (Grace Barron), Austin Pendleton (Mr. Gadbury) and Robert Sean Leonard (Douglas Bridge).

Realistic is an accurate though hardly adequate way of describing Evan S. Connell's two exceptionally fine novels about the same upper-middle-class American marriage, *Mrs. Bridge* (1959) and *Mr. Bridge* (1969), which have now been turned into a singularly bold, weird, and offbeat movie titled *Mr. and Mrs. Bridge*. It opens today at the Cinema I in Manhattan.

The film's gallant perpetrators are the same team that found the cinematic centers of Henry James's Bostonians and E. M. Forster's *Room with a View*: Ismail Merchant, the producer; James Ivory, the director; and Ruth Prawer Jhabvala, the writer.

The chances are that Mr. Merchant, Mr. Ivory, and Mrs. Jhabvala will again be accused of rampant Masterpiece Theaterism, but never will that charge have been more loosely and wrongheadedly entered.

Mr. and Mrs. Bridge, in which Paul Newman and Joanne Woodward give the most adventurous, most stringent performances of their careers, is many odd things, but it certainly isn't safe or soothing or culturally self-congratulatory in the manner that Masterpiece Theaterism seems to imply.

Mr. and Mrs. Bridge is so deceptively clean and sunny, so anticlimactic from beginning to end, so subliminally subversive that it will probably send a lot of people out of the theater in a fury expressed by yawns.

Bear with it, though. The film is a vigorous, witty, satiric attempt to give dramatic shape to two aggressively anti-dramatic prose works. The "Bridge" novels take American realism to its outer limits. They exist just this side of the border where real life becomes surreal. In the borrowed idiom of our day, they might be called nouveau.

Mrs. Bridge and *Mr. Bridge* read almost as if they were inventories. Characters, behavior, and events, even inner thoughts, are presented in a series of laconic scenes with an uninflected clarity that has the effect of making the familiar look suddenly exotic, sometimes dangerous.

The reader must find his own bearings, as if lost at midnight in a landscape that is only occasionally illuminated by a bolt of lightning. Mr. Connell's realism is disorienting, something quite different from the orderly narratives of William Dean Howells, Booth Tarkington, and Sinclair Lewis.

The most serious charge that can be brought against Mr. Ivory and Mrs. Jhabvala is that they delight in and respect the original works too much. *Mr. and Mrs. Bridge* insists on being faithful in the terms of a medium where fidelity doesn't count.

The novels are set in Kansas City in those years between World Wars I and II when the great heartland of America was still serenely white, Protestant, and God-fearing (at least publicly), and when even people who had nothing were still obedient to the money and manners of others. The lives of Walter and India Bridge are placid. Fortune has been good to them. As far as they know, they love each other.

He is a successful lawyer who, by working six and sometimes seven days a week, has been able to provide handsomely for India and their three children. He is a conservative, bigoted son of the nineteenth century, a man with an opinion about everything.

She is reluctant to express an opinion about anything. For much of their marriage, India has accepted Walter's authority in all matters. She is only vaguely aware that something may be missing.

At one sorrowful moment in the novel *Mr. Bridge*, Walter realizes that he has never experienced joy. He has been joyful. He has been pleased, also sexually satisfied, but joy is something alien to him.

When such hints of desolation arise, Walter goes to his safe-deposit box and feels the texture of the stocks and securities that will protect India and the children after he is gone.

Mrs. Bridge and *Mr. Bridge* are obsessed with the observable facts of mundane existence. Melodrama is usually avoided but, when it does appear, it is seen at a remove. A suicide or a murder is reported as something that has happened elsewhere.

The surface of the novels thus remains apparently pacific. Life appears to go on, unchanged, though there is always the eerie, barely audible whisper, "Or does it?"

The remarkable thing about *Mr. and Mrs. Bridge* is

that the filmmakers have been able to preserve Mr. Connell's sense of exactitude in a medium composed of images that are always particular anyway. It's not the look of things that counts here, but the curious, often unexplained emphasis on the commonplace, which suggests the mystery within the familiar.

It takes a while to get the rhythm of the film, which, like the novels, is composed of short, sometimes abrupt vignettes that are never explained or generalized.

If, as in the novels, the vignettes were titled, they might include "On Becoming an Eagle Scout," "Caught in the Grip of the Garage Doors," "Harriet and Her Felon," "Ruth Takes a Sun Bath," "The Mirrors in European Hotels," "Leda and the Reluctant Swan," and "The Tornado at the Country Club."

On the night of their anniversary, Walter takes India to dinner at the country club. A tornado alert becomes a take-cover command. The other diners flee to the basement. Walter refuses to abandon his food. The sky darkens. The wind roars. India is paralyzed with fear but Walter continues to butter his biscuits.

Later he says, "For twenty years I've been telling you when something will or will not happen."

Walter's ideas are fixed. When their younger daughter, Carolyn (Margaret Welsh), a student at the University of Kansas, announces that she wants to marry a fellow student, Walter is appalled. "State universities," he says, "are jampacked with opportunists."

India is no great mind and knows it. She wants to improve herself.

She takes art lessons from a tentative little man (Austin Pendleton) who, years later, turns up at her back door selling Doberman, the magazine. She reads *The Theory of the Leisure Class*. When they go to Europe on a Grand Tour, she experiences an unanalyzable epiphany when she comes upon the "Winged Victory of Samothrace" in the Louvre.

India is bewildered but not exactly unhappy. Her teenage son, Douglas (Robert Sean Leonard), treats her as if she were an idiot. She is baffled by her elder daughter, Ruth (Kyra Sedgwick), who goes off to New York to become an actress.

One of her two best friends is Mabel Ong (Gale Garnett), who attends the weekly bridge luncheons in mannish suits and ties and talks about culture. The other is the profoundly unhappy Grace Barron (Blythe Danner), who drinks too much and one night, during a cocktail party, accidentally sets fire to a friend's Cadillac.

Mr. Newman and Miss Woodward are splendid. There is a reserve, humor, and desperation in their characterizations that enrich the very self-conscious flatness of the narrative terrain around them. For that matter, all of the performances are exceptionally good, and if Miss Danner and Mr. Pendleton stand out, it's because their roles are especially memorable.

Like life, the movie proceeds as if there will be no end. Yet everything that happens is full of omens of disaster. "Love, respect, human decency—some things never change," Walter tells Ruth, at just that point in American history when everything has begun to change irrevocably.

Mr. and Mrs. Bridge is wise and funny and just a little bit scary. Though it's an adaptation, it has the manner of a true original.

—V.C., November 23, 1990

MR. DEEDS GOES TO TOWN

Produced and directed by Frank Capra; written by Robert Riskin, based on the story "Opera Hat" by Clarence Budington Kelland; cinematographer, Joseph Walker; edited by Gene Havlick; music by Howard Jackson; art designer, Stephen Goosson; released by Columbia Pictures. Black and white. Running time: 115 minutes.

With: Gary Cooper (Longfellow Deeds), Jean Arthur (Babe Bennett), George Bancroft (MacWade), Lionel Stander (Cornelius Cobb), Douglass Dumbrille (John Cedar) and Raymond Walburn (Walter).

Frank Capra and Robert Riskin, who are a complete production staff in themselves, have turned out another shrewd and lively comedy for Columbia Pictures in *Mr. Deeds Goes to Town*, which opened yesterday at the Radio City Music Hall. The directing-writing combination which functioned so successfully in *It Happened One Night* and *Broadway Bill* has spiced Clarence Budington Kelland's story with wit, novelty, and ingenuity. And, spurred along by the capital performances of Gary Cooper, Jean Arthur, Lionel Stander, Douglass Dumbrille, and the

rest, the picture moves easily into the pleasant realm reserved for the season's most entertaining films.

Longfellow Deeds is the hero of the occasion and Longfellow Deeds becomes one of our favorite characters under the attentive handling of Mr. Cooper, who is proving himself one of the best light comedians in Hollywood. Mr. Deeds is the poet laureate of Mandrake Falls, Vermont. He writes greeting-day verses, limericks, and Edgar Guestian jingles with equal facility, and he plays the tuba in the town band. Then an uncle dies, leaving his $20,000,000 estate to the Vermont innocent, and Mr. Deeds, slightly dazed but unimpressed by his sudden riches, is tossed willy-nilly and tuba into scheming New York.

Crooked lawyers beset him, the board of the opera elects him chairman, a girl reporter gains his confidence and then headlines him as the "Cinderella Man." Crushed, derided, deceived, and disillusioned, the lean Longfellow prepares to share the wealth by establishing a collective farm colony and then, cruelest jest of all, he is hauled before a lunacy commission and only by the narrowest of margins and the love of Miss Arthur, the repentant sob sister, escapes being adjudged a manic depressive.

If this is the story in outline, it does not attempt to capture the gay, harebrained, but entirely ingratiating quality of the picture. To appreciate that, you will have to watch Mr. Cooper struggling with the tuba, Mr. Stander fighting off apoplexy, Raymond Walburn (that most perfect gentleman's gentleman) raising his voice against an echo, and, ultimately, the scene of the lunacy commission's hearing which is as perfect a spoof of alienists and expert testimony as the screen has presented. It is on this rousingly comic note that the picture ends, and the memory of it should be enough to erase the vague impression we got that the film had bogged down for a time in mid-career.

—F.S.N., April 17, 1936

MR. HULOT'S HOLIDAY

Directed by Jacques Tati; written (in French and English, with English subtitles) by Mr. Tati, Pierre Aubert, Jacques Lagrange and Henri Marquet; cinematographers, Jacques Mercanton and Jean Mousselle; edited by Suzanne Baron, Charles Bretoneiche and Jacques Grassi; music by Alain

Romans: production designer. Henri Schmitt: produced by Fred Orain and Mr. Tati: released by G.B.D. International Films. Black and white. Running time: 85 minutes.

With: Jacques Tati (Mr. Hulot). Nathalie Pascaud (Martine). Michèle Rolla (The Aunt). Valentine Camax (The Old Maid). Louis Perrault (The Boatman). André Dubois (The Colonel). Lucien Fregis (The Hotel Proprietor) and Raymond Carl (The Waiter).

Much the same sort of visual satire that we used to get in the "silent" days from the pictures of Charlie Chaplin, Buster Keaton, and such as those is supplied by the Frenchman Jacques Tati in his gay *Mr. Hulot's Holiday,* which exploded with merriment last evening at the Fine Arts Theatre. Being about the vacation of a clumsy fellow at a French seaside resort, it is thoroughly appropriate to the season and should be with us well into the fall.

M. Tati, a music-hall comedian, is not entirely unknown in these parts, having put in one charming appearance a few years back in a little film called *Jour de Fête.* But the modest distribution of that picture was nothing to what it deserved, so it still remains for many moviegoers to make the acquaintance of M. Tati through his new film.

What they will find in this comedian is a long-legged, slightly pop-eyed gent whose talent for caricaturing the manners of human beings is robust and intense. In *Jour de Fête,* he grandly kidded the notion of crisp efficiency inspired in a French village postman by an American documentary film. In this one, he kids the behavior of people at a summer hotel, particularly a brisk and gauche young bachelor, which he himself agilely plays.

There is really no story to the picture. That is usual with M. Tati's films. The whole thing is simply a series of comic mix-ups and casual caricatures, revealing how solemnly and strenuously people go about the job of enjoying themselves.

The dialogue, in French and English, is at a minimum, and it is used just to satirize the silly and pointless things that summer people say. Sounds of all sorts become firecrackers, tossed in for comical point. Music is used for commentary. The gags are played mainly to the eye.

As the picture's author and director, as well as its energetic star, M. Tati goes in for wild invention and occasional piracy. His running gag of an elderly couple who stroll through the picture aimlessly and are always first at the table is mischievously inspired. His climactic misadventure, wherein he, as a near-sighted dope, accidentally sets off all the fireworks, is as old as the Keystone Kops.

So is his disastrous struggle with a collapsible boat, or his being catapulted into the water by a tow-rope when it is snapped taut. But they are none the less funny confusions, as is a burlesque tennis game or a bit of crazy racing after a runaway car.

From M. Tati's arch performance there emerges a comic character—the amiable butterfingered nitwit bouncing around a summer hotel. And from several of the other performers—notably Nathalie Pascaud as a blonde, André Dubois as a retired Army person, and Lucien Fregis as the hotel manager—there come glints of human nature that are humorous and memorable.

Perhaps *Mr. Hulot's Holiday* extends a bit longer than it should. As such things do, it inclines to repetition. But most of it is good, fast, wholesome fun.

—B.C., June 17, 1954

MISTER ROBERTS

Directed by John Ford and Mervyn LeRoy: written by Frank S. Nugent and Joshua Logan. based on the play by Thomas Heggen and Mr. Logan and the novel by Mr. Heggen: cinematographer. Winton C. Hoch: edited by Jack Murray: music by Franz Waxman: art designer. Art Loel: produced by Leland Hayward: released by Warner Brothers. Running time: 123 minutes.

With: Henry Fonda (Lieutenant Roberts). James Cagney (The Captain). William Powell (Doc). Jack Lemmon (Ensign Pulver). Betsy Palmer (Lieutenant Ann Girard). Ward Bond (CPO Dowdy). Phil Carey (Mannion). Ken Curtis (Dolan). Nick Adams (Reber) and Harry Carey. Jr. (Stefanowski).

Now hear this! Another twenty-one-gun salute is hereby accorded *Mister Roberts* and the raffish, rough, and lovable World War II gobs who landed at the Music Hall yesterday. The motley complement of that ungainly Navy cargo "bucket," the *Reluctant,* who first sailed the Pacific in the novel by the late Thomas Heggen and then were transferred to the Broadway stage for a justifiably long cruise, now have emerged triumphantly in the complimentary full dress of CinemaScope and color. It was a trip worth making. Like its predecessors, this version of *Mister Roberts* is a strikingly superior entertainment.

Although it is obliquely ribald now, it is still hilarious. Again, it is wonderfully sentimental and touchingly perceptive about its civilian seamen caught in the backwash of a war they neither saw nor fully comprehended. And, while this long voyage now gives them room to roam, the script by Frank Nugent and Joshua Logan has not deviated from the dramatization to any great extent.

Mister Roberts once again pictures life aboard a "bucket" that tiresomely traffics between the islands of Tedium and Apathy with side trips to Monotony. The story revolves, as it always did, around the quietly towering figure of this supply vessel's cargo officer—Lieutenant Roberts, whose liaison with the crew is the essence of understanding.

Although he desperately longs for a berth on a fighting ship, he remains their strong bulwark against the stupidity and tyrannies of the captain, who sees in Roberts's know-how the means to a promotion. And it is also concerned with Roberts's unselfish sacrifice for his men and the final, tragic achievement of his goal.

But director John Ford (forced to quit by illness) and Mervyn LeRoy, who took up the directorial reins, as well as the scenarists and producer Leland Hayward, are not purveying static drama. The hatreds, dissensions, boredom, and the captain's fanaticism are not the bucket's sole cargo. It is loaded to the gunwales with screamingly funny scenes which, in several instances, are visual improvements on the play.

Count among these the crew's riotous return from its first liberty ashore in months; the mad general quarters alarm sounded by the frantic captain when his treasured palm tree is tossed overboard by Mr. Roberts; the sailors' long-distance discovery, via binoculars, of the charms of nurses; and the inventive Ensign Pulver's happy destruction of the ship's laundry with a home-made, giant firecracker.

Since Henry Fonda already has earned his stripes as Mr. Roberts on stage, it should be noted that he does not simply give the role a professional reading. It now appears as though he *is* Mr. Roberts. It evolves as a beautifully lean and sensitive characterization, full of dignity and power.

Although James Cagney's portrait of the captain has little shading, he still comes across as a petty, ludicrous, but viciously dictatorial figure. Jack Lemmon's Ensign Pulver is a broad delineation of the amorous misfit anxious to please his idol Roberts. He exhibits the explosive ebullience of a kid with a live frog in his britches. And William Powell's ship's doctor also is a bit of fortunate casting. His polished portrayal of the middle-aged, ennui-filled medico is subdued and effective.

The *Reluctant*'s large crew, including such salty stalwarts as Ward Bond, Phil Carey, and Ken Curtis, rates good conduct medals for comparatively small but muscular stints. And the bevy of nurses, led by Betsy Palmer, are decorative in brief appearances.

To *Mister Roberts* and all hands involved in one of the season's greatest pleasures: "Well done!
—A.W., July 15, 1955

MR. SMITH GOES TO WASHINGTON

Produced and directed by Frank Capra; written by Sidney Buchman, based on the novel *The Gentleman from Montana* by Lewis R. Foster; cinematographer, Joseph Walker; edited by Gene Havlick and Al Clark; music by Dimitri Tiomkin; art designer, Lionel Banks; released by Columbia Pictures. Black and white. Running time: 125 minutes.

With: Jean Arthur (Saunders), James Stewart (Jefferson Smith), Claude Rains (Senator Joseph Paine), Edward Arnold (Jim Taylor), Guy Kibbee (Governor Hopper), Thomas Mitchell (Diz Moore) and Eugene Pallette (Chick McGann).

Scorning such cinemacerated branches of the government as the FBI, the Army, Coast Guard, and Department of State which, by usage, have become Warner exclusives anyway, Columbia's Frank Capra has gone after the greatest game of all, the Senate, in *Mr. Smith Goes to Washington,* his new comedy at the Music Hall. In doing so, he is operating, of course, under the protection of that unwritten clause in the

Bill of Rights entitling every voting citizen to at least one free swing at the Senate. Mr. Capra's swing is from the floor and in the best of humor; if it fails to rock that august body to its heels—from laughter as much as injured dignity—it won't be his fault but the Senate's and we should really begin to worry about the upper house.

For Mr. Capra is a believer in democracy as well as a stouthearted humorist. Although he is subjecting the Capitol's bill-collectors to a deal of quizzing and to a scrutiny which is not always tender, he still regards them with affection and hope as the implements, however imperfect they may be, of our kind of government. Most directors would not have attempted to express that faith otherwise than in terms of drama or melodrama. Capra, like the juggler who performed at the Virgin's shrine, has had to employ the only medium he knows. And his comedy has become, in consequence, not merely a brilliant jest, but a stirring and even inspiring testament to liberty and freedom, to simplicity and honesty, and to the innate dignity of just the average man.

That may seem altogether too profound a way of looking at Mr. Capra's Mr. Smith, who is blood brother of our old friend, Mr. Deeds. Jefferson Smith came to Washington as a short-term senator. He came with his eyes and mouth open, with the blessing of the Boy Rangers and a party boss's prayer that he won't tumble to the graft clause in the bill the senior senator was sneaking into law. But Senator Smith tumbled; dazedly, because he couldn't quite believe the senior senator was less than godlike; helplessly, because the aroused political machine framed him four ways from Sunday and had him up for expulsion before he could say Jack Garner. But the right somehow triumphs, especially when there's a canny young secretary on Senator Smith's side to instruct him in the ungentle art of the filibuster and preserve his faith, and ours, in democracy.

If that synopsis is balder than the Capitol's dome, it is because there is not space here for all the story detail, the character touches, the lightning flashes of humor and poignance that have gone into Mr. Capra's two-hour show. He has paced it beautifully and held it in perfect balance, weaving his romance lightly through the political phases of his comedy, flicking a sardonic eye over the Washington scene, racing out to the hinterland to watch public opinion being made

and returning miraculously in time to tie all the story threads together into a serious and meaningful dramatic pattern. Sidney Buchman, who wrote the script, has his claim on this credit, too, for his is a cogent and workmanlike script, with lines worthy of its cast.

And there, finally, Mr. Capra has been really fortunate. As Jefferson Smith, James Stewart is a joy for this season, if not forever. He has too many good scenes, but we like to remember the way his voice cracked when he got up to read his bill, and the way he dropped his hat when he met the senior senator's daughter, and the way he whistled at the senators when they turned their backs on him in the filibuster. (He just wanted them to turn around so he could be sure they still had faces.) Jean Arthur, as the secretary—lucky girl being secretary to both Deeds and Smith—tosses a line and bats an eye with delightful drollery. Claude Rains, as the senior senator, Edward Arnold, as the party steamroller, and Thomas Mitchell, as a roguish correspondent, are splendid all.

Have we forgotten to mention it? *Mr. Smith* is one of the best shows of the year. More fun, even, than the Senate itself.

—*F.S.N., October 20, 1939*

MRS. MINIVER

Directed by William Wyler; written by Arthur Wimperis, George Froeschel, James Hilton and Claudine West, based on the book by Jan Struther; cinematographer, Joseph Ruttenberg; edited by Harold F. Kress; music by Herbert Stothart, with song "Midsummer's Day" by Gene Lockhart; art designers, Cedric Gibbons and Urie McCleary; produced by Sidney Franklin; released by Metro-Goldwyn-Mayer. Black and white. Running time: 134 minutes.

With: Greer Garson (Mrs. Miniver), Walter Pidgeon (Clem Miniver), Teresa Wright (Carol Beldon), Dame May Whitty (Lady Beldon), Reginald Owen (Foley), Henry Travers (Mr. Ballard) and Richard Ney (Vin Miniver).

It is hard to believe that a picture could be made within the heat of present strife which would clearly, but without a cry for vengeance, crystallize the cruel effect of total war upon a civilized people. Yet that is what has been magnificently done in Metro's *Mrs. Miniver,* which came to the Music Hall yesterday. Perhaps it is too soon to call this one of the greatest motion pictures ever made; perhaps its tremendous impact is too largely conditioned by one's own immediate association of one's torn heart with the people so heroically involved. But certainly it is the finest film yet made about the present war, and a most exalting tribute to the British, who have taken it gallantly.

For this is not a war film about soldiers in uniform. There are no bloody land battles in it; no armies clash by night, except for the unseen armadas which drone in the moonlit sky. This is a film about the people in a small, unpretentious English town on whom the war creeps up slowly, disturbing their tranquil ways of life, then suddenly bursts in devastating fury as the bombs rain down and the Battle of Britain is on. This is a film of modern warfare in which civilians become the front-line fighters and the ingrained courage of the people becomes the nation's most vital strength. This is a film in which a flower show is as pregnant of national spirit as Dunkerque.

Only the title and leading characters—and some of the rural charm, it is true—have been taken from Jan Struther's sketches of prewar English life. For the story itself tells entirely of the Miniver family after the war begins—of the lovely and gentle Mrs. Miniver, of her tall and whimsical husband, Clem, of the three charming Miniver children—Vin, the Oxford student, and Judy and Toby, the tots. And it tells of proud old Lady Beldon and her gracious granddaughter, Carol, who falls in love with Vin very naturally, and of Mr. Ballard, the stationmaster who grows the rose which he names for Mrs. Miniver, and of Foley, the air raid warden and greengrocer.

It tells of all these good people and many more in the town of Belham. It tells about Vin joining the air force and later marrying Carol; about Clem being wakened in the night to take his motor launch down the Thames and then on across to Dunkerque to help save the British Army. It tells how Mrs. Miniver catches a German flier who has been brought down and how she reads Toby to sleep with *Alice in Wonderland* in an Anderson shelter on a bomb-filled night, "remembering her own child life and the happy summer days." It tells of the Beldon flower show and of how Mr. Ballard wins the prize. But, above all, it tells

most eloquently of the humor and courage of these people under fire. And the climax is a shattering revelation that it is they, as well as the soldiers, who fight this war.

One cannot speak too highly of the superb understatement and restraint exercised throughout this picture. The four writers who prepared the script have given it a natural, literate quality which matches the very best work in their craft and have admirably blended light and humor with pathos and tragedy. And William Wyler has directed with a sensitivity that rarely shows in films. Every episode is made a full experience, with rich and vibrant overtones. The pulse of real humanity beats strong throughout the film.

Greer Garson's performance as Mrs. Miniver glows with compassion and womanly strength. Her encounter with the German flier conveys as fine an emotional conflict as you'll ever see—on the screen, anyhow. Walter Pidgeon is a real inspiration to masculine stamina and resource as Clem. And Dame May Whitty, Teresa Wright, Henry Travers, Richard Ney, and everyone in the cast—not forgetting the youngsters, Christopher Severn and Clare Sandars—are excellent.

Two years ago yesterday Winston Churchill gave his memorable address: "We shall go on to the end. . . . We shall never surrender." It was most propitious that *Mrs. Miniver* should open on that anniversary. One seeing it can understand why there was no doubt in Mr. Churchill's mind.

—*B.C., June 5, 1942*

MON ONCLE D'AMÉRIQUE

Directed by Alain Resnais; written (in French, with English subtitles) by Jean Gruault, based on the works of Henri Laborit; director of photography, Sacha Vierny; edited by Albert Jurgenson; music by Arié Dzierlatka; art designer, Jacques Saulnier; produced by Philippe Dussart; released by New World Pictures. Running time: 123 minutes.

With: Gérard Depardieu (Rene Ragueneau), Nicole Garcia (Janine Garnier), Marie Dubois (Thérèse Ragueneau), Nelly Borgeaud (Arlette Le Gall), Pierre Arditi (Zambeaux) and Philippe Laudenbach (Michel Aubert).

To a greater or lesser extent, all fiction is a study of human behavior. What distinguishes *Mon Oncle d'Amérique,* Alain Resnais's fine, funny new French comedy, is the film's mock-grave suggestion that human behavior isn't quite as mysterious as we like to pretend it is and that, indeed, most of the terrible things that happen to us need not be inevitable.

It's the proposition of Mr. Resnais and his collaborator, Dr. Henri Laborit, the French medical doctor and behavioral scientist, that our lives won't change until we understand the brain itself, something that Dr. Laborit has been studying for several decades.

Mon Oncle d'Amérique, which opens today at the Paris Theater, is an exhilarating fiction that takes the form of a series of dramatic essays about three highly motivated, extremely mixed-up persons. They are René Ragueneau (Gérard Depardieu), a successful textile company executive who is suddenly faced with the loss of his career; Jean Le Gall (Roger Pierre), an ambitious politician with a desire for total power, both private and public; and Janine Garnier (Nicole Garcia), Jean's mistress and a would-be actress who makes a noble sacrifice only to find that, like most noble sacrifices, it's a self-defeating gesture.

Mon Oncle d'Amérique is a chatty movie, rather like the kind of nineteenth-century novel in which the author is always chiming in to comment on what's happening and to make observations that instruct and amuse. In this case, the author is Dr. Laborit, whom we see being interviewed in his laboratory by Mr. Resnais. The doctor, one of the people responsible for the development of drugs to control the emotions, is the wise, literate, unflappable host, a sort of Gallic Alistair Cooke, and *Mon Oncle d'Amérique* is the show.

Of major concern to Dr. Laborit is the manner in which people inhibit their primal urges to dominate their landscapes and everyone around them. Mr. Depardieu, in one of his best performances to date, is especially comic and appealing as René, a good, practicing Catholic, a stalwart fellow who has left the family farm to make a career in industry, who has a decent wife and family and an unquestioned faith in the future, a fellow who is, in short, totally unprepared for the stresses and strains when they come. Being a civilized man, René doesn't fight back. He develops ulcers, a perfect disability for a man whose hobby is haute cuisine.

Jean, the politician, doesn't hesitate to leave his wife and children when he falls in love with Janine, but all the time he's living with Janine he is plagued by kidney stones. When Jean's wife comes to Janine and says she's dying of cancer, Janine sends Jean back to his wife, only to learn later that she's been tricked. Emotional blackmail is the common currency of their lives.

Almost any description of *Mon Oncle d'Amérique* tends to make it sound solemn though, in fact, it's immensely good-humored and witty. Mr. Resnais and Jean Gruault, the screenwriter (whose credits include *Jules and Jim, The Wild Child,* and *Les Carabiniers,* among others), neither patronize their characters nor make fun of them. They appreciate them and sympathize with their tangled lives even as we see René, Jean, and Janine behaving with the predictability of laboratory mice.

Miss Garcia is charming as the spunky, seemingly independent Janine, whose finally acknowledged fury with her lover brings the movie to a liberating conclusion. Even Roger Pierre's Jean, the only character in the film who is essentially nasty, is comic in the righteous way he attempts to justify self-absorption.

Mon Oncle d'Amérique is Mr. Resnais's most successful film in years, his best since *La Guerre est Finie* in 1966. It brightens a truly dreary season.

—V.C., December 17, 1980

MONA LISA

Directed by Neil Jordan; written by Mr. Jordan and David Leland; director of photography, Roger Pratt; edited by Lesley Walker; music by Michael Kamen; production designer, Jamie Leonard; produced by Stephen Woolley and Patrick Cassavetti; released by Island Pictures. Running time: 104 minutes.

With: Bob Hoskins (George), Cathy Tyson (Simone), Michael Caine (Mortwell), Clarke Peters (Anderson), Kate Hardie (Cathy), Robbie Coltrane (Thomas), Zoe Nathenson (Jeannie) and Sammi Davies (May).

Neil Jordan's *Mona Lisa* is classy kitsch. It's as smooth and distinctive (and, ultimately, as insubstantial) as the old Nat (King) Cole recording of the song, which gives the film its title and a lot of its mood. It's also got high style, so you needn't hate yourself for liking it.

Though *Mona Lisa* opens today at the Cinema 1, it's the sort of movie that might be best watched at three A.M., on a small screen, while sitting alone in an anonymous bar, nursing a warm glass of beer, feeling sorry for the world and even sorrier for yourself. When you think about it afterward, it's utterly preposterous.

The setting is London. George (Bob Hoskins) is a short, bullet-shaped, petty hood with a nasty temper. He talks tough and knows how to handle himself in the sleazy, violent world he inhabits. His masculinity is a serious business as well as his protection.

Underneath all, however, George is almost fatally sentimental. He's also as genteel as the lace doily that, in a working-class house, protects the back of the easy chair from the grease Dad puts on his hair.

George has been around—at the start of *Mona Lisa* he's just finished serving a seven-year prison term—but there are some things he simply cannot tolerate. It's what George can't tolerate that provides the film with its ending (and its letdown).

Mona Lisa is a romantic kind of shaggy-dog fable about the unlikely relationship that grows up between George and Simone (Cathy Tyson), the tall, beautiful, reed-thin black hooker to whom he's assigned as a chauffeur by his mob boss. At first George is cool to Simone, whom he dismisses as just another "black tart."

As George drives Simone from one high-paying assignment to the next, he's alternately haughty and sarcastic, but there's no slur that Simone hasn't heard before, said more effectively, by someone else. She's always in control of herself. George is humiliated when she criticizes his flashy taste in clothes, but he also admires her combination of utter streetwise frankness and elegant manners. Before long, he's in love with her.

As if to certify his feelings for Simone, he tells his pal Thomas that Simone is a lady. "I thought you said she was a tart," says the always logical Thomas. "She is," says George, "but she's also a lady."

When Simone asks George to find a fifteen-year-old prostitute named Cathy, who'd been Simone's only friend when she was still walking the streets, George risks life and limb in a hunt through London's underworld that becomes, in his eyes, a quest for the Holy Grail.

Like *The Company of Wolves,* Mr. Jordan's series of spectacularly ornamented variations on the story of Little Red Riding Hood, *Mona Lisa* is as much about the telling of tales as about the tales being told. George and his friend Thomas, who deals in bizarre stolen goods (including plastic Jesus figures that can be lighted within), pass the time making up mystery stories for each other. Each insists on logic in the other's tales, as well as on endings that tie up all loose threads.

Mona Lisa itself becomes George's story, lived by him to be judged eventually by Thomas. This is more interesting as an idea for a movie than it is to watch as a movie, possibly because it has the effect of denying the immediate emotional importance of just about everything that happens within the film.

Mona Lisa is less a true film noir than a comment on one. It's as bloodless as an abstract theory. However, though *Mona Lisa* is hardly ever involving, it is fun to watch, mostly for its performances.

As good as Mr. Hoskins is, and he is splendid (he shared the best-actor award at this year's Cannes Film Festival for his work in this film), he doesn't carry *Mona Lisa* alone. Miss Tyson (the English-born niece of Cicely Tyson) has a magical film personality, which, here, is beautiful, intelligent, and hard as nails. In their scenes together, Mr. Hoskins and Miss Tyson come very close to making the preposterous appear to be both significant and moving.

In a comparatively small role, that of Mortwell, the coolly vicious chief of a gang of London pimps and blackmailers, Michael Caine adds his own class to the melodrama. Behaving (initially) as if he were removed from the events we are seeing, Mr. Caine seems to be visiting the film with as much reluctance as Mortwell deals with the troubles caused him by George and Simone. The actor's presence shapes the film as much as anything he's required to say or do.

Also very good are Kate Hardie, as a teenage hooker-junkie at the end of her rope; Clarke Peters, as a black pimp; and Robbie Coltrane, as George's eccentric, fable-spinning friend.

Mona Lisa looks terrific. It has Nat (King) Cole on the soundtrack. It has vividly realized characters behaving in unexpected ways. Yet the excitement doesn't build—it runs down. It's like watching the departure of an ocean liner. After all of the initial excitement, you're left on the dock, alone, wondering what all the fuss was about.

—V.C., June 13, 1986

MONSIEUR VERDOUX

Produced and directed by Charles Chaplin: written by Mr. Chaplin, based on an idea by Orson Welles: cinematographers, Roland Totheroh and Curt Courant: edited by Willard Nico: music by Mr. Chaplin: art designer, John Beckman: released by United Artists. Black and white. Running time: 125 minutes.

With: Charles Chaplin (Henri Verdoux/Varney/ Bonheur/Floray/Narrator), Mady Correll (Mona Verdoux), Allison Roddan (Peter Verdoux), Robert Lewis (Maurice Bottell), Audrey Betz (Martha Bottell) and Martha Raye (Annabella Bonheur).

It has been seventeen years since Charles Chaplin's controversial film *Monsieur Verdoux* was released to what was perhaps the most antagonistic critical and public reception ever accorded a Chaplin film.

Mr. Chaplin had recently been through the unpleasant and unsympathetic experience of being sued by Joan Barry as the father of her child. Although the suit was decided in Mr. Chaplin's favor, it had brought him disagreeable notoriety. He was also under fire from patriotic organizations that attacked him for what they charged were his left-wing political sympathies.

Under these circumstances, it was not surprising that the film, which has to do with a comical fellow who marries women and then murders them for their insurance, should have been coolly and suspiciously regarded. People picketed the few theaters around the country in which it was shown. In many places, the bookings were canceled. It was banned in Memphis.

After a succession of difficult experiences, it was withdrawn from release in this country and it had not been shown in a single revival—until its arrival yesterday in the series of Chaplin films at the Plaza Theater.

The engagement now permits all those people who did not get to see it seventeen years ago and all those who have been hearing about it as one of the great Chaplin films through all these years to see for themselves what a superior sardonic comedy it is—and also to estimate how unjust was the bitter discrimination against it.

For *Monsieur Verdoux* is an engrossingly wry and paradoxical film, screamingly funny in places, sentimental in others, sometimes slow and devoted to an unusually serious and sobering argument. This is that the individual murderer—"the small businessman in murder," as the protagonist says—is regarded as a criminal, but the big businessman, the munitions manufacturer, and the professional soldiers who contribute to murder on a mass scale are given great honors and monetary rewards.

This theme is carried out by Mr. Chaplin in the role of Monsieur Verdoux, an ex–bank clerk in France who becomes a Bluebeard, a bigamist who murders his multiple wives in order to get the money to support his crippled wife and his little boy.

It is a classic performance by Mr. Chaplin, dapper and silver-haired, and he is fitly supported by a good cast, headed by Martha Raye. Miss Raye, as the most obnoxious and indestructible of the wives, is howlingly funny.

You shouldn't miss *Monsieur Verdoux.*

—B.C., July 4, 1964

MONSTERS, INC.

Directed by Pete Docter, with Lee Unkrich and David Silverman: written by Andrew Stanton and Daniel Gerson, based on a story by Mr. Docter, Jill Culton, Jeff Pidgeon and Ralph Eggleston: supervising technical director, Thomas Porter: edited by Jim Stewart: music by Randy Newman: production designers, Harley Jessup and Bob Pauley: produced by Darla K. Anderson: released by Walt Disney Pictures and Pixar Animation Studios. Running time: 88 minutes.

With the voices of: John Goodman (James P. Sullivan), Billy Crystal (Mike Wazowski), Mary Gibbs (Boo), Steve Buscemi (Randall Boggs), James Coburn (Henry J. Waternoose), Jennifer Tilly (Celia), Bob Peterson (Roz), John Ratzenberger (Yeti) and Frank Oz (Fungus).

Freaks, mutants and misshapen creatures shambling off to work—no, it's not a documentary about rush hour on the New York subway system. This is the premise of Pixar's newest brightly colored, computer animated feature, *Monsters, Inc.*

Pixar Animation Studios has now so streamlined the process that you may find yourself eagerly awaiting the release of *Monsters* on video so you can take in all the myriad visual jokes planted all over the frame, a form of visual invention that adds an extra tickle to the picture. Not that *Monsters* needs it; in a final reversal of events, Pixar has given Disney, which financed the film, the last leg up by stealing the style and speed of Warner Brothers cartoons, which used to ridicule Disney's do-gooder ethos.

The breakneck wit of *Monsters, Inc.* covers a lot of ground and makes fun of everything from the paranoid thrillers of the 1970's (this could be *The Parallax View* for kids) to the self-mythologizing needs of the mass media as well as the cartoon form. The opening credits evoke the clean lines and bop dizziness of UPA, the studio responsible for *Gerald McBoing-Boing* in the 1950's. No big deal is made of this, though; the joke is dropped and *Monsters* streaks along.

Monsters, Inc. is a company that sends kids screaming into their parents' bedrooms; it employs the creatures that ominously lurk inside closets and give children the frights. Closets are the entry into the regular world from the creatures' own home universe. The impetus to create fear comes out of self-interest; in Monstropolis, the freakazoid parallel dimension in which the monsters live, children's screams are used as a power source. But that power is drying up because kids don't scare so easily anymore.

One Monsters, Inc. employee still exceeds his mandated scare quota: Sullivan (the voice of John Goodman), a furry blue-and-purple giant whose design specs may have come from a 70's dorm room. His best pal is his one-man crew, Mike (Billy Crystal), a bouncy, bile-green little guy who would have a chip on his shoulder if he had shoulders; the ovoid Mike is one big eye with a really big mouth, arms and legs. (You'll choke on laughter as he tries to slip in his single, hubcapsize contact lens.)

Sullivan is the champ, and his boss and mentor, Mr. Waternoose (James Coburn), sums up Sully's technique for a group of auditioning monsters. "It's all about presence, about how you enter the room," Waternoose pontificates, and this authoritative twaddle spoofs the kind of thing heard on "Inside the Actors Studio."

Like any classic cartoon character, Mike is a textbook case of manic depression. He zooms from high to lows to tantrums faster than any three-year-old, even Boo (Mary Gibbs), the three-year-old human who puts all of Monstropolis, and specifically Sully and Mike, in danger.

Any artifact from the human world is a contaminant; when one hapless monster returns from a scare jaunt with an innocent-looking sock caught on his fur, he's attacked by a decontamination team, a group that subjects him to a special group of terrors to keep Monstropolis sterile. (This may be an unfortunate time to joke about a threat of contamination, but the rubber-suited mop-up squad—latex tight over their odd shapes—is a great sight gag.) When Boo enters Monstropolis, panic erupts and it's up to Sully and Mike to return her without being blamed for the mishap.

"Loch Ness, Big Foot, they all have one thing in common—banishment," Mike sputters, mentioning the ultimate punishment. And they have to stay out of the way of their vile competitor, Randall (Steve Buscemi), who lives to overtake Sully's fabulous stats.

This all leads to a chase that features slamming closet doors leading to many locations; maybe it's why Boo's decalspattered door looks like a portal from *Laugh-In*, because the doors all lead to other jokes. And the alternative-energy conclusion itself could make another movie. For a movie about an energy crisis, there hasn't been a film in years to use creative energy as efficiently as *Monsters, Inc.*; this is one clean-burning engine that doesn't waste a joke or a thought. The hot hues of the picture's color scheme are thought through; the shininess makes the film look as if it's set in an overly bright factory.

Portions of the movie bring to mind the 1989 film *Little Monsters,* in which a little boy found a netherworld of creatures under his bed, though here (as in some parts of *Little Monsters*), many of the inhabitants may have been inspired by the bug-eyed doodles of Ed (Big Daddy) Roth, whose *CARtoons* magazine regulars could all be like Mike. (Otherworldly denizens piling into bedrooms through a closet are a salute to Terry

Gilliam's *Time Bandits*; all the worlds constructed by Pixar are a perpetual tribute to Mr. Gilliam's gleeful eye-candy assaults.)

Monsters gets a little sticky in the end, which is apparently axiomatic, since feature-length cartoons are required to celebrate childhood in a rather square way. *Monsters* takes some mild shots at the jaded little members of its target audience, but it doesn't really want to upset them or their parents.

Pixar has created a genre that others merely imitate, and while they may do a creditable job—*Shrek* from Dream Works, for example—they don't get all the small touches right, like the thunderous and jazzy score of *Monsters*. The composer Randy Newman shows touches of Carl Stalling, whose brass construction kept Bugs Bunny and his clique moving.

Monsters may also be compared a little unfavorably with the director John Lasseter's Pixar work, including the *Toy Story* movies and *A Bug's Life*. It took Mr. Lasseter a while to achieve something like the ending of *Toy Story 2,* when Buzz the astronaut and Woody the cowboy talk like a couple of heroes from a John Ford western closing out a film; there was a surprising iconic majesty, with earned emotional attachment because of what they endured.

The *Monsters, Inc.* director, Peter Docter, makes his own inroads. He knows how funny it is to get the matching basso rumbles from Mr. Goodman and Mr. Coburn as a de facto father-and-son pair. He knows that older viewers—and *Monsters, Inc.* will have more than its share—will enjoy Mr. Crystal's recycling of the put-upon Jersey screech of one of his old *Saturday Night Live* characters, the sour-faced masochist Willie, who talked about how much he hated getting a potato peeler stuck up his nose.

Mr. Docter; his story co-creators, Jill Cultan, Jeff Pidgeon, and Ralph Eggleston; and the screenplay writers, Andrew Stanton and Daniel Gerson, get in a few digs at *Toy Story* and turn the fake-looking humans of computer animation into a canny joke early on. And they must be amused about persuading Disney to finance a comedy that is, finally, about anticorporate behavior. (A good inside bit: for years Mr. Buscemi has joked that he's never made a movie he could see with his family.)

What makes *Monsters, Inc.* so wonderful is that it's about scream deficit, yet all great cartoons are powered by screams. It's a tribute to noise, so how can you not fall in love with it?

—E.M., November 2, 2001

MOONLIGHTING

Written and directed by Jerzy Skolimowski; director of photography. Tony Pierce-Roberts; edited by Barrie Vince; music by Stanley Myers and Hans Zimmer; production designer. Tony Woollard; produced by Mark Shivas and Mr. Skolimowski; released by Universal Pictures. Running time: 97 minutes.

With: Jeremy Irons (Nowak). Eugene Lipinski (Banaszak). Jiri Stanislaw (Wolski) and Eugeniusz Haczkiewicz (Kudal).

Working in a style that appears to have little connection with any of his earlier films, including the French-language Le Départ and the English-language *The Shout,* Jerzy Skolimowski, the Polish filmmaker who has been living in England for years, has made a new film of the sort of introspective intensity seldom achieved on the screen. Movies journey into men's minds at some peril.

Moonlighting, which will be shown at the New York Film Festival today and tomorrow, possesses such clarity of vision and simplicity that it seems to have been made in one uninterrupted burst of creative energy. It's a small, nearly perfect work of its kind.

Moonlighting is about exile, not in the abstract but in the particular situation of a young Pole named Nowak (Jeremy Irons), who has gone to London from Warsaw with four colleagues to remodel a mews house for a wealthy Polish businessman, a commuter between Warsaw and London. The time is early December 1981. Being younger and apparently better educated than the others, as well as the only man in the group who speaks English, Nowak is the foreman. He is the man responsible, the decision maker, the keeper of discipline, the one with the money.

Nowak is apolitical. He is a pragmatist who deals with particular problems as they arise. And because he is the only one who speaks English, he is the only one of the group we get to know. The others keep to themselves, and though they are cheerful enough, they are not especially friendly.

The crew has four weeks in which to do the job, which begins as an exotic lark in a foreign land. A first visit to a London supermarket is better than a trip to Disneyland. The men, who have been given £20 as their recreation budget for the four weeks, blow it all, plus another £20, on the purchase of a second-hand color television set. Almost immediately the set breaks down.

Several days later, Nowak learns of the military upheaval in Warsaw, the declaration of martial law, and the confrontation between the Government and Solidarity. Nowak's concerns are not necessarily for Solidarity—he is not a member—but for his wife and family.

He doesn't tell his crew what has happened. They cannot get back to Warsaw anyway. Because the men cannot read the newspapers and have no access to television, Nowak takes it upon himself to keep them in the dark. It's not difficult. They have no money and no way of making contact with the neighbors.

As the days go on, Nowak finds himself increasingly isolated from his comrades as well as from the shopkeepers and building suppliers with whom he deals. His few random attempts to connect with the English are unsuccessful. The money begins to run out. When Nowak's bicycle is stolen, he steals someone else's. To keep up their food supply, he becomes expert at shoplifting at the supermarket.

Nowak presses the men to work harder and harder. When it seems that the job won't be completed in time, he sets his watch—the only one in the house—forward a couple of hours every night. The men arise at three a.m. thinking it is five a.m. The apolitical Nowak has slipped into the role of party chairman, decreeing what the men shall know and what shall be withheld from them, all for their own good.

The film doesn't utter a single pious or even impious thought about politics from beginning to end. Yet it is far more political than documentaries about identifiably political subjects. The movie works entirely through Nowak's day-to-day existence, through his own emotional panic and through the practical ways that he attempts to deal with his isolation.

Moonlighting is virtually a one-character film, and Mr. Irons, so fine in *The French Lieutenant's Woman*,

is remarkably effective as Nowak. Occasionally, he speaks his thoughts on the soundtrack, but far more often Mr. Skolimowski's camera successfully expresses what Nowak is thinking and feeling. It's a rigorous experience, relieved only occasionally by irony. The movie makes one work, but it's a rare kind of work and immensely rewarding.

Moonlighting is far above anything Mr. Skolimowski has ever done before. It may be a coincidence—maybe not—that two of the best films ever made about exile have been made by Polish directors, this film and Roman Polanski's mysteriously underrated *The Tenant*. It's a sorrowful subject.

—*V.C., September 26, 1982*

MOONSTRUCK

Directed by Norman Jewison: written by John Patrick Shanley: director of photography. David Watkin: edited by Lou Lombardo: music by Dick Hyman: production designer. Philip Rosenberg: produced by Patrick Palmer and Mr. Jewison: released by Metro Goldwyn-Mayer. Running time: 102 minutes.

With: Cher (Loretta Castorini). Nicolas Cage (Ronny Cammareri). Vincent Gardenia (Cosmo Castorini). Olympia Dukakis (Rose Castorini). Danny Aiello (Johnny Cammareri). Julie Bovasso (Rita Cappomaggi). John Mahoney (Perry). Louis Guss (Raymond Cappomaggi) and Feodor Chaliapin Jr. (Loretta's Grandfather).

The moon hits your eye like a big pizza pie in *Moonstruck,* and a lot of other things do too. *Moonstruck* is so heavily ethnic that it begins with Dean Martin's rendition of "That's Amore," and there's plenty more where that came from. With its accordion music, its bits of dialect, and its love of opera (a key segment of the story unfolds at a Metropolitan Opera performance of *La Bohème*), *Moonstruck* clearly means to celebrate all things Italian. However, it creates the false but persistent impression that most of the people who made it have never been closer to Italy than, perhaps, Iowa.

Moonstruck, which opens today at the Sutton and

other theaters, was directed by Norman Jewison, who may just be the Sir Richard Attenborough of light comedy. However, it offers further proof that Cher has evolved into the kind of larger-than-life movie star who's worth watching whatever she does. This time, she plays frumpy, which for Cher just means longer hems and a little gray in her hair. Those who wait for a Cinderella-like transformation will not be disappointed.

Cher also has what's supposed to be a comically heavy Brooklyn accent for her role as Loretta Castorini, who has a large, old-fashioned family and a job in a funeral parlor. As the film begins, Loretta becomes engaged to Johnny Cammareri, a doltish nice-guy type played by Danny Aiello (in addition to Castorinis and Cammareris, there are also several Cappomaggis in the screenplay by John Patrick Shanley). Loretta is a widow, it develops. She's also the kind of woman who can explain that her first husband was run over by a bus in an utterly uninterested tone of voice.

Right after the marriage proposal—delivered in a crowded Italian restaurant with a lot of fuss about whether Johnny will kneel in his good suit—Johnny goes to Italy to see his dying mother and instructs Loretta to find his brother Ronny. This turns out to be Nicolas Cage, who has a role so awful that it's hard to know whom to blame. Ronny is a slob. He works stoking the oven in a bakery (as he describes the job, it's "sweat and sweat and sweat, and shove this stinkin' dough in and out of this hot hole in the wall!"). Ronny is also missing a hand, which he lost when Johnny came to see him years earlier and Ronny, lost in conversation, forgot to keep an eye on the bread slicer. It's impossible to tell whether this is supposed to be funny, but the film does carry a "Mr. Cage's Hand Design" credit for Eion Sprott.

The process whereby Loretta and Ronny fall in love is a lot less appealing than the large-family drama unfolding around the Castorinis' kitchen table (over which there is an extremely harsh, glaring light). Among the actors playing Loretta's older relatives are Julie Bovasso, Feodor Chaliapin, Jr., Vincent Gardenia (as the father who spends much of the time listening to Vikki Carr sing "It Must Be Him"), and Olympia Dukakis, who has a comic sourness to match Cher's and manages to have some good moments.

The title refers to one relative's theory that the full moon can make people wildly romantic, make them behave in wonderful, unpredictable, crazy ways. Not crazy enough.

—J.M., December 16, 1987

THE MORE THE MERRIER

Produced and directed by George Stevens; written by Robert Russell, Frank Ross, Richard Flournoy and Lewis R. Foster, based on a story by Mr. Russell, Mr. Ross and Garson Kanin; cinematographer, Ted Tetzlaff; edited by Otto Meyer; music by Leigh Harline; art designers, Lionel Banks and Rudolph Sternad; released by Columbia Pictures. Black and white. Running time: 104 minutes.

With: Jean Arthur (Connie Milligan), Joel McCrea (Joe Carter), Charles Coburn (Benjamin Dingle), Richard Gaines (Charles J. Pendergast), Bruce Bennett (Evans), Frank Sully (Pike) and Clyde Fillmore (Senator Noonan).

Columbia hit a gem of a notion when it got the bright idea of having George Stevens make a comedy based on wartime housing conditions in Washington. For *The More the Merrier,* which is the consequence—and which skipped into the Music Hall yesterday—is as warm and refreshing a ray of sunshine as we've had in a very late spring. Maybe the trials of living in the nation's capital are not as humorous as seen herein. To judge by reports from present inmates, they're not having anything like the fun or the encounters with gay adventure as are enjoyed by Jean Arthur and Joel McCrea. But, no matter how tough conditions, they are cozy, as Charles Coburn says. Washington makes some curious bedfellows. And so does *The More the Merrier.*

For this is a harum-scarum fable about a Washington "government girl" who rents half of her four-room apartment to a daffy old gentleman, who in turn rents half of his half to a winning and eligible young man. (How the young lady got the apartment in the first place is never explained.) And thereupon starts a succession of mad and confusing incidents. The young lady is a stickler for system. She is also half-heartedly engaged to the assistant regional coordinator of something known as the OPL. But after a week of living in a four-room apartment with two strange males, she is neither—but she is something much better. We leave you to guess what that is.

Four writers—one of whom was Frank Ross, the husband of Miss Arthur—prepared the script, and theirs (to judge by the product) was a genuine labor of love. Their situations are not especially novel but the approach is joyous and their dialogue has the zip and spontaneity of impromptu and unrehearsed wit. And Mr. Stevens has brilliantly directed in the same offhand, impulsive style. He has one early sequence in this picture which matches that kitchen scene in *Woman of the Year*.

As the sorely put-upon little lady, Miss Arthur plays with spirit and with charm. Her indignations have the quality of those of a bantam hen and her nervous submission to the advances of Mr. McCrea are a tickling delight. He, in turn, plays the young man with amusing bumptiousness. But it is Mr. Coburn who really is the comical crux of the film and he handles the job in fine fettle. As a "well-to-do, retired millionaire," he follows the dictum of Admiral Farragut and barges blithely into jams "full steam ahead." You'll love Mr. Coburn's Benjamin Dingle if you have a heart in your breast.

And you'll love *The More the Merrier* if you have a taste for fun. It even makes Washington look attractive—and that is beyond belief.

—B.C., May 14, 1943

MORGAN!

Directed by Karel Reisz: written by David Mercer, based on the television play *A Suitable Case for Treatment* by Mr. Mercer: cinematographers, Larry Pizer and Gerry Turpin: edited by Victor Proctor and Tom Priestley: music by John Dankworth: art designer, Philip Harrison: produced by Leon Clore: released by Cinema V. Black and white. Running time: 97 minutes.

With: Vanessa Redgrave (Leonie), David Warner (Morgan Delt), Robert Stephens (Charles Napier), Irene Handl (Mrs. Delt), Newton Block (Mr. Henderson) and Nan Munro (Mrs. Henderson).

Not since Alec Guinness played Gulley Jimson in *The Horse's Mouth* and vitalized that sly bohemian scapegrace with charm and poignancy have we seen an artistic nonconformist as wild as David Warner's Morgan Delt, the infernal hero of *Morgan!* which came to the Sutton yesterday. Neither have we seen one as appealing and pathetic, in his brash, obnoxious way, as the fellow Karel Reisz flings at us in this howlingly funny British film.

But be on your guard against him and don't let him lead you astray into the realms of sublime escapist fancies he creates for himself. For the fact of the matter is that Morgan is some kind of a maladjusted nut, and too close an identification with him might leave you feeling inclined toward idiocy.

Morgan has a thing for gorillas. He dotes upon them. He collects all sorts of simian paraphernalia, and evidently he paints pictures with simian motifs that are popular with the London art set. So strong, indeed, is his involvement that he even looks a little bit like an ape, with his prognathous jaw, his shaggy hairdo, and his Irish sweater that hangs to his knees.

Most significant is the fact that Morgan has dreams and fantasies. He visions himself as a gorilla swinging freely and happily in the trees. He even mixes his passion for gorillas with an enthusiasm for Marxist politics. Once, while visiting the grave of Karl Marx with his Cockney mum, he sees the bust of Marx turn into the head of an ape.

Slowly, admiringly, reverently, he begins to thump his chest, which draws a shocked rebuke from his old lady. "Morgan, that's disrespectful," she says.

Thus you can understand why Morgan, with this sense of primitive power, is sadly put down when his young wife, rich and saucy, gets a divorce from him. You can perceive why he bridles at the cruel thought of her taking another mate—especially since this mate is his art dealer and presumably his good friend. And you can appreciate, when you discover the coziness of this ex-wife, why it is that Morgan fights so fiercely and unconventionally to keep from losing her.

It is a thoroughly funny movie that the heretofore serious Mr. Reisz, who directed *Saturday Night and Sunday Morning*, has made from a sparkling screenplay by David Mercer, which he in turn adapted from his own television play. But it is really much more than funny, much more than a swiftly moving farce. Within its absurdities is satire on some of the sad immaturities of our day.

Morgan, in dark glasses and a Dutch cap, vaulting

the high wall of his locked home and startling his ex-mate in the garden with an innocent and cheery "I'm back!" is a figure of fearful implications. He is a terse, precocious child ("a gifted idiot," as somebody puts it), with the body and the sex drives of a man. He will stop at nothing in his fiendish invention of games—games to foil his rivals and to escape the stuffy adult world—to get what he wants, in essence, or to heck with everything.

Blithely he sets a detonator under his ex-wife's bed in the gleeful expectation that it will cause an explosion when she and her lover lie down. Casually, he and a wrestler (Wally the Gorilla) kidnap her and take her to a Welsh lake where he visions their relation as that of Tarzan and his mate. And, finally, he drops in on her wedding to the other man wearing a suit and carrying an image in his rolled mind of the thundering King Kong.

Morgan is eerily symbolic of arrested development—in intellect and emotions, everything but sex. And Mr. Warner plays him so that he is terrifying and droll, crafty and pathetic. He is a beatnik with a broken heart.

Others are equally engaging and symbolic in their minor ways. Miss Redgrave is positively smashing as the flighty young wife who gets away—beautiful, pliant, voracious, childlike, immature, and yet alert to the necessity of breaking the Morgan mold. Robert Stephens is coy and killing as the irritated lover who pouts to the persistent ex-husband: "She's had enough of you; it's my turn now." And Irene Handl is a darling as the Cockney mum. Arthur Mullard as Wally the Gorilla and several others are gorgeous, too.

The only perilous thing about *Morgan!* is that it may cause us all to have a bit too much sympathy for beatniks and their childishness in a vicious world.

—*B.C., April 5, 1966*

THE MORTAL STORM

Directed by Frank Borzage: written by Claudine West Andersen Ellis and George Froeschel. based on the novel by Phyllis Bottome: cinematographer. William Daniels: edited by Elmo Veron: music by Edward Kane: art designers. Cedric Gibbons and Wade B. Rubottom: produced by Sidney Franlin: released by Metro-Goldwyn-Mayer. Black and white. Running time: 100 minutes.

With: Margaret Sullavan (Freya Roth). James Stewart (Martin Breitner). Robert Young (Fritz Marberg). Frank Morgan (Professor Roth). Robert Stack (Otto Von Rohn). Bonita Granville (Elsa) and Irene Rich (Mrs. Roth).

At last and at a time when the world is more gravely aware than ever of the relentless mass brutality embodied in the Nazi system, Hollywood has turned its camera eye upon the most tragic human drama of our age. In Metro's *The Mortal Storm,* which opened yesterday at the Capitol, a grim and agonizing look is finally taken into Nazi Germany—into the new Nazi Germany of 1933, when Hitler took over the reins and a terrible wave of suppression and persecution followed. And, on the basis of recorded facts and the knowledge that its drama is authentic, this picture turns out to be one of the most harrowing and inflammatory fictions ever placed upon the screen.

There is no use mincing words about it: *The Mortal Storm* falls definitely into the category of blistering anti-Nazi propaganda. It strikes out powerfully with both fists at the unmitigated brutality of a system which could turn a small and gemütlich university community into a hotbed of hatred and mortal vengeance, which could separate the loving members of a family and hound two free-thinking young people into flight from their homeland and to death. It gives no quarter to the antagonists; from clear-eyed and apparently upright young men, they suddenly become heartless sadists at nothing more than the call of their leader's name, the infectious chant of a song. There is no question of why they become such. The fact that they are is assumed as a premise.

But so violent is the oppression meted out by the Nazis and so bitter and hopeless is the fate of those against whom it is aimed that even the spiritual satisfaction which might be derived from a story of heroic suffering is seriously impaired, especially in the light of current headlines. As propaganda, *The Mortal Storm* is a trumpet call to resistance, but as theatrical entertainment it is grim and depressing today.

The story, as indicated, is a familiar and personal one. An eminent "non-Aryan" professor in a German university—presumably Munich—lives in comfort and honor amid his family and students until Hitler comes to power. Then, because he refuses to deny a scientific fact about human blood, he is sent to a concentration camp. His two stepsons become Nazis, his home is broken up. But his daughter and a former young man of the locality hold out against the rising tide. They are finally driven to flight, and, the house which was once filled with love and "gracious living" is left empty and desolate.

Although this tragic account has been pieced together out of a seven-year-old record of human suffering, the excellence of the production which Metro has given it—and the inherent forcefulness of a visual presentation—imbue *The Mortal Storm* with a sharp and seemingly contemporary reality. It is magnificently directed and acted. James Stewart and Margaret Sullavan bring to vibrant and anguished life the two young people who resist the sweeping system. Frank Morgan as the professor is superior as a gentle but resolute humanist. Robert Young plays the unsympathetic role of a Nazi zealot with convincing ostentation but limited penetration of the character. And fine performances also are given by Maria Ouspenskaya, Irene Rich, Bonita Granville, and many others.

The Mortal Storm is a passionate drama, struck out of the deepest tragedy, which is comforting at this time only in its exposition of heroic stoicism. As the oppressed professor says, "I've never prized safety, either for myself or my children. I've prized courage."

—B.C., June 21, 1940

MOTHER

Directed by Albert Brooks; written by Mr. Brooks and Monica Johnson; director of photography. Lajos Koltai; edited by Harvey Rosenstock; music by Marc Shaiman; production designer. Charles Rosen; produced by Scott Rudin and Herb Nanas; released by Paramount Pictures. Running time: 104 minutes.

With: Albert Brooks (John Henderson). Debbie Reynolds (Beatrice Henderson). Lisa Kudrow (Linda) and Rob Morrow (Jeff Henderson).

Out comes the lava lamp. Up go the Jimi Hendrix and *Barbarella* posters. And suddenly the twice-divorced, forty-ish John Henderson (Albert Brooks), who has insisted on moving into the house of his none-too-welcoming mother (Debbie Reynolds), is right back where he belongs. The same can happily be said for Mr. Brooks, whose humor thrives delightfully in this hothouse of Freudian confusion. He brings vast reserves of quarrelsome, hairsplitting hilarity to the story of a man going mano à mano with his sweet little mom.

Mom looks darling, but she sure fights dirty. She's played divinely by Ms. Reynolds, who shows off both acting expertise and apparent training at the International Mothers' School for Passive-Aggressive Bedevilment of Children.

"There are two kinds of mothers on the planet," Mr. Brooks has said about this scarily insightful comedy. "The first kind thinks that every single thing their children do is perfect and their children are God's gift to the world. And then there's the other kind. This is about the other kind."

So Beatrice Henderson is the type to affect a sunnily imperturbable attitude when John, a writer of science-fiction books with names like *The Day There Was No Earth,* seeks her support. "How's the book?" she asks one day, talking on a speaker phone, which, as she likes to mention, has been given to her by John's more successful brother. "A lot of people think I should write a sequel," John says. "To what?" Beatrice asks pleasantly.

Wary as he should be of moving back onto this battlefield, John is still excited about his little experiment. So he drives home gaily from southern California to Sausalito, accompanied by a special new version of "Mrs. Robinson" that describes the Henderson family. (I'd quote the lyrics, but they're too good to spoil. They were written by Mr. Brooks and Monica Johnson, longtime collaborators who also wrote the drily hilarious screenplay.)

When he arrives, he gets a greeting that signals what is to come. "You know I'm happy to see you," insists Beatrice. "Now why didn't you want to stay in a hotel?"

Mr. Brooks, whose films are too few and far between, lost some of his comic focus in the elaborate contrivances of his 1992 *Defending Your Life.* But this time he's working under optimum conditions in a spare, essentially two-character story with a new neurosis lurking behind every corner. *Mother,* which opens on Christmas Day and was produced by Scott Rudin and Herb Nanas, has the high gloss of Mr. Rudin's productions, but it's a lot nuttier than it looks.

Even in Beatrice's refrigerator Mr. Brooks finds endless inspiration; fighting about food has clearly been a favorite activity in this household. This film's two most priceless scenes involve an exploration of the super-thrifty Beatrice's frozen salad, snowy sherbet, etc., and a mother-son trip to the grocery store. There, Beatrice introduces John to the neighbors by saying: "Oh, this is my son. The other one."

The beauty of *Mother* is that while they stroll the aisles with a shopping cart, John and Beatrice work out the very essence of their lifelong struggle, even if they appear to be arguing only about the price of peanut butter. (There would be no *Seinfeld* strain of humor on television without Mr. Brooks's pioneering approach to yuppie psycho-trivia.) There's a full history of the Henderson family in the way Beatrice skimps and her son likes to splurge. "Because that's what I want to do," John insists over one purchase. "I want an experience where we throw away ninety-one cents together."

Faced with this assault on her solitude, Beatrice retreats into such rigidity that she makes John keep his groceries on his own side of the refrigerator. ("It's like *It Happened One Night* for food," he says.) And John does his best to rattle her by, for instance, trying to buy her something at Victoria's Secret and taking her to the zoo. Mom is at her most candid when John sees the same elephant he used to visit in his boyhood and this beast, famed for its memory, doesn't seem to remember him. "He might remember you," Beatrice points out. "He might not like you."

Working out a regression so complete that John even has a fight with his brother in John's boyhood bedroom, *Mother* winds up showing a surprising degree of insight without compromising its deft, badgering comic tone. Beatrice starts the film as a quintessentially deflating parent seen strictly through her son's eyes, but she's a fully formed character by the time *Mother* is over.

Mr. Brooks's reluctant admiration for this character comes through in his fine, prickly performance as clearly as it does on the page. He's often content to stand by gallantly and let Ms. Reynolds work her scene-stealing wiles.

Also perfectly in tune with Mr. Brooks's deadpan style are Rob Morrow, slyly good as the facile younger brother who bought his mother's favor with speaker phones until John decided to make a pest of himself. Mr. Morrow, most amusingly, is seen going to pieces in the face of this provocation. And Lisa Kudrow makes a brief, cheery appearance in her *Friends* dumb-bunny mode as the kind of woman whom John is afraid he'll have to date if he's single. She's definitely enough to send a middle-aged baby back home.

—*J.M, December 24, 1996*

MOULIN ROUGE

Produced and directed by John Huston; written by Anthony Veiller and Mr. Huston, based on the novel by Pierre LaMure; cinematographer, Oswald Morris; edited by Ralph Kemplen; music by Georges Auric; art designer, Paul Sheriff; released by United Artists. Running time: 123 minutes.

With: José Ferrer (Toulouse-Lautrec/The Count de Toulouse-Lautrec), Colette Marchand (Marie Charlet), Zsa Zsa Gabor (Jane Avril), Suzanne Flon (Myriamme), Katherine Kath (La Goulue), Muriel Smith (Aicha), Harold Gasket (Zidler) and Claude Nollier (Countess de Toulouse-Lautrec).

If the measure of the quality of a motion picture merely boils down to how much the screen is crowded with stunning illustration, then John Huston's *Moulin Rouge* well qualifies for consideration as one of the most felicitous movies ever made. For this fictionalized dramatization of the checkered life of Toulouse-Lautrec, the fin-de-siècle French painter whom José Ferrer primly portrays, is a bounty of gorgeous color pictures of the Parisian café world at the century's turn and of beautifully patterned compositions conveying sentiments, moods, and atmosphere.

With the help of an army of artists, which included Ossie Morris, his cameraman; his art director, costume designer, and a "special color consultant," Eliot Elisofon, Mr. Huston has brilliantly accomplished what emerges unquestionably to be the most vivacious and exciting illustration of bohemian Paris ever splashed upon the screen. From the fairly intoxicating opening, with dancers swirling in the smoky haze and the overcrowded climate of the wine-colored Moulin Rouge, to the last poignant sequence wherein Lautrec sees these same dancers ghosting through the rooms of his family's château near Albi as he lies on his painful deathbed, the exquisiteness of the illustration is superlative and complete.

A color-dazed mind fairly totters with the riot of images that remain, floating and whirling through the memory, after an initial viewing of this film. They emerge with distinct definition—the can-can dancers in a foam of pantaloons, black-stockinged legs pointing skyward, and skirts in pastel shades; a street of the Latin Quarter at night with the golden round of a gaslight faintly dusting Lautrec's dark and cruelly dwarfed form; a flower vendor's cart on a Paris morning; acrobats under the dome of the circus roof; foxhunters riding across French meadows; dawn on a bridge over the Seine.

Mr. Huston has got a motion picture in which the eyes are played upon with colors and forms and compositions in a pattern as calculated as a musical score. And the sheer stimulation is not only charming but it develops a flow of emotional response within the bewitched beholder that is keyed, indeed, to the plot. For instance, the color transition from rich and ruddy tones and from vivid and sparkling details in the scenes in the Moulin Rouge to the soft and subdued lights and shadows of Lautrec's studio is more evocative of feeling than the acting that is done. And the demoniac suggestion in the green tone that hovers around a scene in which Lautrec prepares to commit suicide is more depressing than is Mr. Ferrer.

As a matter of fact, the performance which this talented actor gives in a story that is highly sentimental is pretty much the creation of a mere facade. His Lautrec is a gross and grotesque figure, with his black beard, his priggish pince-nez, his thick lips, his burly body, and his pitifully truncated legs. (Mr. Ferrer has used an ingenious harness to simulate the painter's deformity.) And his acting, which is done very largely with his bodily poses and his eyes, does little more, in their limited employment, than ditto the absurdity and pathos of this facade.

The fault is not his entirely. Mr. Huston and Anthony Veiller's script is a not very fluent or plausible rework of the old *Of Human Bondage* theme. The self-depreciating artist falls in love with a gutter girl whose harsh but inevitable treatment of him makes it impossible for him to accept unselfish love. The lushly romantic fabrication is not only a simplification of the facts of Lautrec's life but it is in the realm of personal torment that is all too familiar on the screen.

However, it must be said that Colette Marchand does a quick but excruciating job of revealing the sharp, metallic spirit and the helpless weaknesses of the gutter girl. Less can be said for the handsome but surface performance of Suzanne Flon as the elegant, idealized woman who respectfully loves the little man. Katherine Kath and Muriel Smith as café dancers, Harold Gasket as the proprietor of the Moulin Rouge, and Zsa Zsa Gabor as the famous chanteuse, Avril, are vastly colorful, however, in their roles.

And color, of course, is the big thing in this film on the Capitol's screen—color that flows in a creation that quite o'ershadows the famous painter's poster art.
—B.C., *February 11, 1953*

THE MOUTHPIECE

Directed by James Flood and Elliott Nugent; written by Earl Baldwin and Joseph Jackson, based on the play by Frank J. Collins; cinematographer, Barney McGill; edited by George Amy; released by Warner Brothers. Black and white. Running time: 90 minutes.

With: Warren William (Vincent Day), Sidney Fox (Celia), Aline MacMahon (Miss Hickey), William Janney (John) and John Wray (Barton).

As a crafty and imaginative lawyer whose clients are crooks, Warren William gives a fine and forceful portrayal in *The Mouthpiece*, a picture which reached the Winter Garden last night. This film, the story of which is based on a play by Frank J. Collins, sweeps along swiftly from a tragic beginning to a highly dramatic climax, and most of the time Mr. William is on the screen. The character he plays, according to the author, was inspired by incidents in the life of a notorious New York lawyer.

Mr. William is master of his role throughout all his scenes. Whether he as Vincent Day is drunk or sober, flirting with women, arguing with crooks and gunmen, or indulging in theatrical tricks before a jury, he is ever the character. He as Day begets sympathy by his good looks, his facility in speech, his courage, and his knowledge of human nature. It is really one of the outstanding interpretations that has been contributed to the screen. Mr. William is ably supported by Miss Sidney Fox, Aline MacMahon, Ralph Ince, and others.

First there is a sequence wherein a man is about to be electrocuted. As an assistant district attorney, Day is responsible for the man's conviction. The real murderer finally confesses to the crime, but efforts to stop the execution of the innocent man fail. This brings about Day's resignation and he goes from bad to worse as a drunkard, until one day he listens to the advice of a bartender and soon becomes a prosperous lawyer for men of the underworld.

One episode in a courtroom reveals Day questioning a witness, an ex-pugilist with a faulty memory, who boasts that nobody like the lawyer could ever take him unawares and knock him out. The witness leaves the stand and a second later Day sends a blow to his chin that knocks him unconscious. The jury then brings in a verdict favoring Day's client.

On another occasion, Day, wishing to prove that a so-called poison is harmless, drinks a vial of the concoction before the jury, having been informed that it takes three-quarters of an hour to have effect. Again he wins an acquittal for his man, but immediately afterward he hurries to a physician.

A quaking embezzler enters the spacious offices occupied by Day and confesses that he has stolen some $90,000 from his employer for whom he worked as cashier. Day asks how much he has left and is told that there is $40,000 in a briefcase. The lawyer is soon on the wire talking to the thief's employer, who has heard of him as a blackleg lawyer. Soon this individual comes to Day's office and is told about his cashier's peculation and Day argues the employer into signing an agreement not to prosecute the thief. Day returns to the employer $30,000 and keeps the remaining $10,000 as his fee.

This employer goes to the district attorney to ask for Day's arrest, but he is warned that he has compounded a felony in signing the agreement. And Day sticks to the $10,000.

Miss Fox impersonates a naive little typist named Celia, who attracts Day's attention. In vain he endeavors to make her his mistress, and she scorns him and his money. But later it is for this girl that Day meets his end by bullets from a gangster's machine gun

because he was instrumental in sending one of their number to prison.

Miss MacMahon plays Miss Hickey, Day's knowledgeable secretary, who knows the strength and weakness of her employer. Miss MacMahon gives a strikingly good interpretation of her part. Miss Fox is excellent as the winsome girl who is so trustful and honorable. Ralph Ince is capital as J. B., the crook's agent, and Guy Kibbee is up to his usual high standard as a bartender.

—M.H., April 21, 1932

MUCH ADO ABOUT NOTHING

Directed by Kenneth Branagh; adapted by Mr. Branagh, based on the play by William Shakespeare; director of photography, Roger Lanser; edited by Andrew Marcus; music by Patrick Doyle; production designer, Tim Harvey; produced by Mr. Branagh, David Parfitt and Stephen Evans; released by Samuel Goldwyn Company. Running time: 111 minutes.

With: Denzel Washington (Don Pedro), Kenneth Branagh (Benedick), Emma Thompson (Beatrice), Michael Keaton (Dogberry), Robert Sean Leonard (Claudio), Keanu Reeves (Don John), Richard Briers (Leonato), Brian Blessed (Antonio), Kate Beckinsale (Hero), Imelda Staunton (Margaret) and Phyllida Law (Ursula).

Kenneth Branagh, the nervy young Belfast-born actor and director, has done it again. In 1989 he challenged Laurence Olivier's lordly reputation by making his own very fine, dark, and dour pocket-sized *Henry V* to stand alongside the classic Olivier film. Now he has accomplished something equally difficult. He has taken a Shakespearean romantic comedy, the sort of thing that usually turns to mush on the screen, and made a movie that is triumphantly romantic, comic, and, most surprising of all, emotionally alive.

The Branagh *Much Ado About Nothing* is a dreamlike house party set in and around a magnificent Tuscan villa in the erotic heat of an Italian summer. The period is not specified, although it seems to be a distant, vaguely Renaissance past. As can happen during a month of well-fed indolence in the country, connections to the outside world are forgotten. Time stops. Life becomes a pursuit of pleasure: eating, drinking, dancing, making love.

Mr. Branagh, Emma Thompson, Denzel Washington, Keanu Reeves, and Michael Keaton head the strong British-American cast. In most instances, the actors find just the right manner in which to play out a comedy of passionate love affairs, misunderstandings, renunciations, and reconciliations. Mr. Branagh has cut and rearranged the text. Yet the omissions will not be evident to anyone whose only earlier contact with the play in performance was a second-rate theatrical performance to snooze through. The film uncovers a radiant heart.

The movie celebrates the artifice of the play and finds the humanity within it, which is not easy to do in these days of meta-realism. It's not by chance that there have been far fewer attempts to film Shakespeare's comedies than his tragedies and histories. The camera is merciless to such conventions of Elizabethan comedy as disguises, gender reversals, garrulous country bumpkins, and the notion that someone is not hiding in the hedge where his feet are clearly visible.

By shifting the locale of *Much Ado* from Messina to a sunlit country estate, which is as removed from the ordinary world in spirit as it is in place, Mr. Branagh sidesteps the whole notion of reality. The reality of the film is its language, its characters, and its characters' perceptions. Disbelief melts with the pre-credit sequence.

The voice of Beatrice (Ms. Thompson) is heard against a black screen as she reads the mocking words; "Sigh no more, ladies, sigh no more/Men were deceivers ever/One foot in sea and one on shore/To one thing constant never." The lights come up on a picnic. Beatrice and her friends are thus passing a lazy afternoon when news comes of the imminent arrival of the victorious Don Pedro, Prince of Aragon (Denzel Washington), and his men on their way home from the wars. The prince has asked to spend some time at the villa of her uncle, Leonato (Richard Briers), the governor of Messina.

Everything that happens later is promised in the sequence that follows. Behind the credits, through what appears to be a zoom lens, Don Pedro and his soldiers are seen as they approach on horseback, jouncing rhythmically up and down in their saddles in slow motion, as if anticipating sexual unions still to be negotiated. It's a wonderfully funny poetic conceit, setting the tone for the film and everything it's about. It also alerts the ear to a text far more sensual than movie audiences are accustomed to hearing when paying their high-culture dues to Shakespeare.

Much Ado About Nothing casts the battle of the sexes in the form of an elegant dance, but it's a dance that goes uproariously to pieces after the proper introductory measures. At the center are Beatrice, an acid-tongued beauty and skeptic, and Benedick (Mr. Branagh), a young lord whose self-esteem denies the possibility of his ever finding a woman worthy of him. When the story begins, the mutually antagonistic, perfectly matched Beatrice and Benedick have already battled to a stalemate that only a rude trick by their friends can end.

Hero (Kate Beckinsale) and Claudio (Robert Sean Leonard) are more conventional lovers. She is Leonato's virginal, dutiful daughter who, in the manner of midsummer masques like *Much Ado,* falls in love with Claudio as immediately and completely as he with her. Love at first sight, though, is full of dangers. The stalwart Claudio is brave on the battlefield, but he so loses his reason in love that he can be easily gulled into believing that Hero is a strumpet. As quickly as he falls in love, his love seems to turn to loathing, but he waits until the wedding ceremony to denounce her.

More or less presiding over these perilous revels is Don Pedro, who, in the majestic presence of Mr. Washington, is a benign, wise, but lonely prince. Don Pedro is much taken with Beatrice, but though tempted to become a participant in the dance, he remains aloof. Benedick is his friend, and his subjects come first. Mr. Washington is amazingly good as an idealized Shakespearean monarch, the sort of character that sleeps on a page but comes to life when played by a charismatic actor.

In a review of a London production of *Much Ado* just ninety-five years ago, George Bernard Shaw took exception to what he described as Beatrice's "conscientious gambolling," which he found exhausting. The same sort of objection might be made to the pumped-up pacing of Mr. Branagh's production. There are times when one longs for him to pull back the camera, not only from the alternating close-ups that turn some of the Beatrice-and-Benedick exchanges into tennis matches, but also from the generalized dither of the big scenes.

Everyone seems to smile too much and to laugh too quickly. Yet I also suspect that if it weren't for this helium-high manner, Mr. Branagh would not be able to discover the moments of pathos that, by contrast, unexpectedly illuminate the comedy and give it value. Benedick's suddenly abject, intensely felt admission of his love for Beatrice, in a chapel during one of their otherwise barbed arguments, takes the breath away. Because it is such a surprise amid the tumult, it has an emotional impact I've never before experienced in Shakespeare, on stage or screen.

Ms. Thompson is enchanting. Looking gloriously tanned and windblown, wearing the kinds of gauzy slip-ons that today would be for après-swim in Majorca, she moves through the film like an especially desirable, unstoppable life force. Her submission to Benedick is as moving as his submission to her. Mr. Branagh is not your average Benedick. He's no supercilious aristocrat. For all of his intellectual affectations, he has his feet planted on earth.

Ms. Thompson and Mr. Branagh are such a terrifically engaging couple that even the differences in their accents work. Hers is traditional English upper-class; his is more contemporary, representative of a newly classless, English-hip generation. It would seem to indicate that this Beatrice and Benedick still have things to learn from each other.

One of Mr. Branagh's boldest maneuvers was to save Mr. Keaton from the limbo of Batman and to cast him as Dogberry, the bumbling constable who discovers the plot to slander Hero. Mr. Keaton's scenes aren't really funny, but they fascinate. Dogberry's malapropisms ("Comparisons are odorous") are like jokes in grand opera: tedious. As Mr. Keaton plays him, he is a fat, slobbish, menacing oaf. When he enters and exits, he mimes the galloping of a child who rides a broomstick pretending to be riding a horse.

It's as if Mr. Branagh, knowing that conventional low-comedy routines would not prompt anything but empty laughter, had opted to create a kind of surreal diversion.

Black-bearded, heavy-lidded, Keanu Reeves is elegantly handsome and speaks his lines with authority as Don John, Don Pedro's evil half-brother. As Hero and Claudio, Ms. Beckinsale and Mr. Leonard look right and behave with a certain naive sincerity, although they often seem numb with surprise at hearing the complex locutions they speak. Giving excellent performances in supporting roles are Brian Blessed and Phyllida Law, who, offscreen, is the mother of Ms. Thompson and the mother-in-law of the director.

Mr. Branagh has done well by everyone, particularly Shakespeare. This *Much Ado About Nothing* is a ravishing entertainment.

—V.C., May 7, 1993

MULHOLLAND DRIVE

Written and directed by David Lynch; director of photography, Peter Deming; edited by Mary Sweeney; music by Angelo Badalamenti; production designer, Jack Fisk; produced by Ms. Sweeney, Alain Sarde, Neal Edelstein, Michael Polaire and Tony Krantz; released by Universal Focus. Running time: 146 minutes.

With: Justin Theroux (Adam), Naomi Watts (Betty and Diane), Laura Harring (Rita and Camilla), Ann Miller (Coco), Robert Forster (Detective McKnight) and Dan Hedaya (Vincenzo).

While watching *Mulholland Drive*, you might well wonder if any film maker has taken the cliché of Hollywood as "the dream factory" more profoundly to heart than David Lynch. The newest film from the creator of *Blue Velvet* and *Twin Peaks* is a nervy full-scale nightmare of Tinseltown that seizes that concept by the throat and hurls it through the looking glass.

By surrendering any semblance of rationality to create a post-Freudian, pulp-fiction fever dream of a movie, Mr. Lynch ends up shooting the moon with *Mulholland Drive*. Its frenzied final forty-five minutes, in which the story circles back on itself in a succession of kaleidoscopic Chinese boxes, conveys the maniacal thrill of an imagistic brainstorm.

The notion of Hollywood as the world capital of corrupt, twisted fantasy is hardly new, thanks to Nathanael West, Raymond Chandler, Roman Polanski and countless others. But in wrestling with that notion, Mr. Lynch makes an extraordinary leap to embrace the irrational. Its sheer audacity and the size of its target make the director's earlier eviscerations of idyllic American oases and the rot beneath them seem comparatively petty. In taking on Hollywood, of course, Mr. Lynch is biting a hand that has fed him off and on, even though the Hollywood depicted by the film is a dream world that bears only a passing resemblance to the everyday film business of corporate yuppie sharpshooters.

Mr. Lynch's distillation of Hollywood vibrates weirdly between the present and the pop cultural climate of forty years ago. It is a place where a ludicrous monster in a bear costume hides behind a graffiti-spattered Denny's-like restaurant. In Mr. Lynch's Hollywood, authoritarian moguls of the Otto Preminger type still assert an imperial will in offices that feel like giant mausoleums.

Mr. Lynch's women also hark back to the perfectly coiffed blond heroines of Alfred Hitchcock's *Vertigo* and *Marnie,* while the music of Angelo Badalamenti, his favorite composer, is a Mannerist echo of Hitchcock's musical main man, Bernard Herrmann. The shiny pink songs that jingle through *Mulholland Drive* are the glittery baubles of forty years ago sung by Connie Stevens and Linda Scott. As in *Blue Velvet,* a Roy Orbison ballad (*Crying,* sung stunningly a cappella and in Spanish by Rebekah Del Rio) supplies an expressionistic flourish.

Mulholland Drive, which the New York Film Festival is showing tonight and tomorrow afternoon at Alice Tully Hall (it opens commercially on Monday), is a fascinating example of how a great film can evolve out of adversity. Begun as a pilot for an open-ended series much like *Twin Peaks,* it was reconfigured into a feature film after being rejected for television. That history is embodied in the structure of the movie, which begins as a leisurely contemporary film noir with surreal touches, then suddenly changes its form and blasts off toward outer (or is it inner?) space.

During its first one hundred minutes, *Mulholland Drive* lays out a network of interwoven plots revolving around a car crash, several murders, and the problems besetting a young hotshot director. The opening scene finds a slinky brunette (Laura Harring) dressed up for a party in the backseat of a car that pulls to a stop on Mulholland Drive overlooking Los Angeles's glittering lights. As the sinister driver and his pal turn and instruct

the woman to step out of the vehicle, it is slammed from behind by a car packed with drunken revelers and bursts into flame. Emerging from the wreckage before the police arrive, the backseat passenger walks away, the sole survivor. Except for a case of amnesia, she appears miraculously unscathed. Descending into the city, she takes refuge in a plush empty apartment.

Hours later, Betty (Naomi Watts), a blond ingénue, who has just arrived in Los Angeles, appears and finds the amnesiac survivor taking a shower. The apartment belongs to Betty's aunt, who works in the film business and has lent it to her niece while she's away on location. Betty, who traveled from Deep River, Ontario, is a likably gushy caricature of a naïve Hollywood hopeful and, as it turns out, a fine actress.

The strange woman, who brought a bag stuffed with money and a strange blue key with her from the car, doesn't know who she is and takes the name Rita (from Rita Hayworth) off a poster in the apartment advertising *Gilda.* Betty befriends Rita, and they spend half the film acting like Nancy Drew trying to figure out Rita's true identity. When they share a bed, their friendship flares into passion. Their tender love scenes lend the film a tint of lush romanticism.

Another strand of the plot involves Adam (Justin Theroux), a young director whose newest project is mysteriously taken over by the studio, which insists he hire an unknown named Camilla Rhodes for the coveted female lead. Adam receives more instructions from a waxen human relic dressed in western gear known only as the Cowboy.

Just when *Mulholland Drive* has acquired so many layers that its pieces seem impossible to reconcile, it leaves its complicated past behind and plunges into an alternate reality. A corpse that Betty and Rita discovered while sleuthing is magically resurrected by the Cowboy as the elusive Diane Selwyn, whom they were seeking for information.

Betty now all but disappears from the movie, and Ms. Watts portrays Diane, a hardened, strung-out vixen who suggests what Betty might become after living in Hollywood too long. Or might Diane be real and Betty be a fantasy projection of what she might have been? When Ms. Harring appears at the door of Diane's ratty bungalow, she is now Camilla Rhodes, the indifferent temptress with whom Diane is desperately and miserably in love.

From here on, watching *Mulholland Drive* is a little

like peering into the semidarkness from the front car of a runaway subway train tunneling furiously into the earth as if sucked toward some unknowable hell. Much of the foregoing is recycled in feverish, fleeting images that are often disconnected, and those that aren't disjointed have a nightmarish relationship. There is the suggestion that all the turmoil stems from one ruthless actress's murderous obsession to land the lead female role in Adam's movie, but that's only hinted at.

For *Mulholland Drive* finally has little to do with any single character's love life or professional ambition. The movie is an ever-deepening reflection on the allure of Hollywood and on the multiple role-playing and self-invention that the movie-going experience promises. That same promise of identity loss extends to the star-making process, in which the star can disappear into other lives and become other people's fantasies. What greater power is there than the power to enter and to program the dream life of the culture. Who needs continuity if you can disappear into a dream?

Since these questions are being pondered by a master surrealist reexamining his own obsessions and personal iconography, *Mulholland Drive* ranks alongside Fellini's 8½ and other auteurist fantasias as a monumental self-reflection.

Looked at lightly, it is the grandest and silliest cinematic carnival to come along in quite some time: a lurching journey through one filmmaker's personal fun house. On a more serious level, its investigation into the power of movies pierces a void from which you can hear the screams of a ravenous demon whose appetites can never be slaked.

—*S.H., October 6, 2001*

MURMUR OF THE HEART

Written (in French, with English subtitles) and directed by Louis Malle; cinematographer, Ricardo Aronovich; edited by Suzanne Baron; music by Charlie Parker, Sidney Bechet, Gaston Frèche and Henri Renaud; art designers, Jean-Jacques Caziot and Philippe Turlure; produced by Vincent Malle and Claude Nedjar; released by Nouvelle Editions. Running time: 118 minutes.

With: Léa Massari (Clara Chevalier), Benoit Ferreux (Laurent Chevalier), Daniel Gelin (The Father), Marc Winocourt (Marc), Fabien Ferreux (Thomas) and Michel Lonsdale (Father Henri).

The directorial career of Louis Malle has followed a general though by no means spectacular decline from the time ten years ago, when he was widely regarded as a major hope of the French New Wave, to the present, when he is scarcely regarded at all. After an initial outburst of such highly individual and charmingly perverse conceits as *The Lovers* (1958) and *Zazie dans le Métro* (1960), he has descended, through bouts of quality and commerce, to his latest film, *Le Souffle au Coeur,* in which the major purpose of perversity is to charm.

The point is not that *Le Souffle au Coeur* is a terrible movie—though it isn't very good—but that it could probably have been made with as much distinction by any of those directors, all equally anonymous, who specialize in urban romantic comedy (or tragedy) of a sophistication that is supposed to be peculiarly French. *Le Souffle au Coeur* is comedy, and I guess its sophistication is a bit peculiar.

Its hero is the fifteen-year-old son (Benoit Ferreux) of upper-middle-class parents, who is passing into maturity and who discovers that for sexual initiation as for everything else, a mother is a boy's best friend. It is, I should say, a happy incest movie, with the addition of a somewhat nervous morality requiring a) that the boy no sooner have his mother than he must rush out to take the nearest unrelated teenage girl, thereby proving his normality, and b) that his mother's joyful experience cancel out a previous extramarital affair, so that she returns to hearth and home. A family that plays together stays together.

Léa Massari is the mother, and it is important that she is beautiful, vivacious, generally affectionate, fantastically youthful—and not French. Indeed, so much is made of her warm Italian temperament that I suspect the working of a kind of national-character protectionism. Although Benoit Ferreux receives from Malle's camera the greater glamour treatment (he has sensitive good looks, but seems reserved to the point of placidity), Miss Massari is more properly the film's star. In a different kind of movie out of a different tradition I think she might have managed the major performance that ever since I first saw her (as the lost girl in *L'Avventura*) she seems to have promised.

Nothing in *Le Souffle au Coeur* seems very necessary but perhaps the most pleasantly gratuitous element is the time, the early 1950's. Except for references to Indochina, styles of dress, and styles of jazz, Malle has kept period authenticity to a gratifying minimum. But he has indulged himself in two minor characters, the boy's older brothers (Marc Winocourt and Fabien Ferreux). Lying, cheating, stealing, drinking, wenching, and insulting their elders, they are the very incarnation of 1950's juvenile delinquency. Of course they seem terribly classic and lovable. But in their genuinely outrageous vitality they are also the best reminder of the imaginative world Louis Malle used to inhabit—and can still, when the inspiration strikes.

Le Souffle au Coeur played Saturday night at the Vivian Beaumont Theater, the last selection in the New York Film Festival. Under the title *Murmur of the Heart,* it opened yesterday at the Little Carnegie.

—*R.G., October 18, 1971*

MUTINY ON THE BOUNTY

Directed by Frank Lloyd, written by Talbot Jennings, Jules Furthman and Carey Wilson, based on the novels *Mutiny on the Bounty* and *Men Against the Sea* by Charles Nordhoff and James Norman Hall; cinematographer, Arthur Edeson; edited by Margaret Booth; music by Herbert Stothart; art designers, Cedric Gibbons and Arnold Gillespie; produced by Irving Thalberg; released by Metro-Goldwyn-Mayer. Black and white. Running time: 132 minutes.

With: Charles Laughton (Bligh), Clark Gable (Christian), Franchot Tone (Byam), Herbert Mundin (Smith), Eddie Quillan (Ellison), Dudley Digges (Bacchus), Donald Crisp (Burkitt) and Henry Stephenson (Sir Joseph Banks).

The weird and wonderful history of H.M.S. *Bounty* is magnificently transferred to the screen in *Mutiny on the Bounty,* which opened at the Capitol Theatre yesterday. Grim, brutal, sturdily romantic,

made out of horror and desperate courage, it is as savagely exciting and rousingly dramatic a photoplay as has come out of Hollywood in recent years. The Nordhoff-Hall trilogy was, of course, born to be filmed, and Metro-Goldwyn-Mayer has given it the kind of production a great story deserves. As the sadistic master of the *Bounty,* the barbarous madman who was half god and half devil, Charles Laughton has the perfect role, and he plays it perfectly. Frank Lloyd, well remembered for *The Sea Hawk* and *Cavalcado,* has performed a distinguished job of direction. For all its great length, this is just about the perfect adventure picture.

The film concentrates on the first two volumes of the trilogy, *Mutiny on the Bounty* and *Men Against the Sea,* and touches only slightly on the fate of the mutineers as they prepare to face permanent exile with their Tahitian women on the uncharted Pitcairn Island. If the work has a flaw, it stems from Metro's characteristic prodigality. This is a crowded and fascinating canvas, but the film tends to become slack and dissipate some of its terrifying power because of the sheer burden it imposes on the spectator of watching the screen for more than two hours.

The history of the celebrated naval case will not suffer if I summarize it briefly. In 1787 H.M.S. *Bounty,* commanded by the able but intolerably savage Lieutenant Bligh, left England bound for Tahiti. The spirit of revolt grew among both officers and men during the voyage as Bligh's mania for discipline increased in fury. Discharging her cargo at Tahiti, the *Bounty* was sailing for home when Christian, the second-in-command, led the mutinous sailors and seized the ship. Bligh and eighteen loyal men were set adrift with the ship's launch in mid-Pacific, while the triumphant mutineers put back to Tahiti.

Miraculously Bligh took his open boat 3,600 miles across the ocean to the Dutch East Indies, a feat that is almost unparalleled for skill and courage in nautical annals. In the photoplay, though not in fact, Bligh commands the second British ship which pursues the mutineers and is wrecked in the futile search. Midshipman Byam and several other loyal seamen who were forced to accompany the rebels were returned to England for trial. Condemned with the rest, Byam, in the film, is pardoned after an eloquent speech in which he informs the court-martial of the conditions which drove Christian and the crew to mutiny.

Mr. Laughton's performance as the incredible Bligh is a fascinating and almost unbearable portrait of a sadist who took rapturous delight in watching men in pain. We get the full horror of his personality early in the film when a seaman, convicted of striking an officer, is ordered to be lashed on every vessel in the fleet. Brought to the *Bounty,* he is discovered to be already dead from his previous floggings, but Bligh, observing the cold letter of the regulations, insists that the corpse receive the appointed forty lashes in full view of his officers and men. His penalties for minor offenses are the judgments of a maniac. From the swish of the lash he derives a lewd joy.

Bligh's reign of terror on the *Bounty* is described with such relish that in time you discover yourself wincing under the lash and biting your mouth to keep from crying out. Yet, on the astounding odyssey in the small boat, Bligh becomes a man of heroic stature, fiercely guiding the rudder through the ocean wastes while his men lose their senses from thirst and hunger. I could have wished that these superb sequences telling of Bligh's indomitable will to live and find vengeance had been extended at the expense of the romantic business on Tahiti. At the court-martial the film punishes Bligh by submitting him to the contempt of his fellow officers. History, kinder to this amazing man, discloses that he rose to be an admiral in the King's navy.

There are numerous performances of excellence under the relentless eye of Mr. Laughton, notably Clark Gable as the rebellious second-in-command, Franchot Tone as the humane midshipman Byam, Dudley Digges as the magnificently drunk ship's doctor, Herbert Mundin as a timorous mess boy, Eddie Quillan as a victim of the press gang, and a dozen others. *Mutiny on the Bounty* contains the stuff of half a dozen adventure pictures. It is superlatively thrilling.

—A.S., November 9, 1935

MY BEAUTIFUL LAUNDRETTE

Directed by Stephen Frears: written by Hanif Kureishi: cinematographer. Oliver Stapleton: edited by Mick Audsley: music by Ludus Tonalis: production designer. Hugo Luczyc-Whyhowski: produced by Sarah Radclyffe and Tim Bevan: released by Orion Classics. Running time: 93 minutes.

With: Daniel Day-Lewis (Johnny). Saeed Jaffrey (Nasser). Roshan Seth (Papa). Gordon Warnecke (Omar). Shirley Anne Field (Rachel). Rita Wolf (Tania). Richard Graham (Genghis). Winston Graham (Jamaican One) and Dudley Thomas (Jamaican Two).

Don't be put off by the title, which makes it sound like a failed French farce. *My Beautiful Laundrette,* written by Hanif Kureishi and directed by Stephen Frears, is the first real sleeper of the year.

The film, which opens today at the Embassy 72nd Street Theater, is a rude, wise, vivid social comedy about Pakistani immigrants in London, particularly about the initially naive, university-age Omar (Gordon Warnecke) and Omar's extended family of wheeler-dealers and unassimilated layabouts.

"Take my advice," says Omar's Uncle Nasser (Saeed Jaffrey) early in the film, "there's money in muck." Omar heeds his uncle and enlists the aid of Johnny (Daniel Day-Lewis), a Cockney mate from his school days. Together, Omar and Johnny set out to revitalize "Churchill's," a failing laundromat, owned by Nasser, in a seedy section of London where enthusiastic, hustling immigrants are at odds with alienated, disenfranchised natives.

Like the film itself, the relationship between Omar and Johnny is not quite as simple as it initially seems. Both men are outsiders. In the years since he and Omar were first friends, Johnny has drifted from one jobless limbo to the next. When Omar meets him again, Johnny is affecting a punk haircut and, with his pals, bashing Pakistanis, mostly because there's nothing better to do.

It gradually becomes clear why Johnny has agreed to give up his street life to join Omar, who, being a Pakistani, isn't easily explained to his Cockney pals. Johnny is bored with his own aimlessness. He never quite admits it, but he'd like to get ahead in the world. Further, and most important, he's in love with Omar, something that Omar responds to and, like the hustler he's becoming, uses to his own advantage.

My Beautiful Laundrette, however, is much more than a comedy about a couple of male lovers who go into the laundromat business. It's about Omar's father (Roshan Seth), a successful journalist in Pakistan but who in England, where he has raised his son, spends all day in bed drinking vodka and railing against the system. "Oh, dear," he might say in his fastidious, upper-class accent, "the working class is a great disappointment to me."

It's also about Uncle Nasser's most proud possession—his English mistress, Rachel (Shirley Anne Field), a tarty, good-hearted woman who genuinely loves Nasser; Nasser's furiously jealous Pakistani wife (Charu Bala Choksi), who finally resorts to witchcraft (which works); and Tania (Rita Wolf), Nasser's pretty daughter, who feels neither Pakistani nor English.

Had *My Beautiful Laundrette* been written by anybody but the London-born Mr. Kureishi, whose father was Pakistani and mother was English, the film would possibly seem racist. He's merciless to his Pakistani characters, especially to Omar. However, he's merciless in the way of someone who creates characters so complex they can't be easily categorized as good or bad.

The film's most sympathetic as well as most stubbornly faithful characters are English. Johnny is a man of almost unbelievable patience and reserves of decency—qualities that Mr. Day-Lewis realizes in a performance that has both extraordinary technical flash and emotional substance. It's Mr. Kureishi's comic paradox that his upper-class Pakistani immigrants have become the exploiters in a land that once exploited them.

Mr. Warnecke, whose first film role this is, is wonderfully insidious as Omar. Also fine are Mr. Jaffrey, recently seen in both *Gandhi* and *A Passage to India*, and Mr. Seth, who played Nehru in *Gandhi*.

Mr. Frears made his theatrical film debut as a director fifteen years ago with Albert Finney's *Gumshoe*, a cheerful sendup of private-eye movies. Since then he has made only *The Hit*, which was not a hit, apparently preferring to work in television, for which *My Beautiful Laundrette* was originally intended. That *My Beautiful Laundrette* could have been conceived as a film for the small screen describes—better than anything else I can think of—the vast difference between American and English television.

My Beautiful Laundrette has the broad scope and the easy pace that one associates with our best theatrical films. It puts its own truth above the fear of possibly offending someone. Without showing off, it has courage as well as artistry. There are moments when key narrative points are obscure, and when characters behave in a way that has been dictated not by plausibility but the effect it will create. Toward the end, it threatens to fly apart.

It doesn't. *My Beautiful Laundrette* is a fascinating, eccentric, very personal movie.

—*V.C., March 7, 1986*

MY DARLING CLEMENTINE

Directed by John Ford; written by Samuel G. Engel and Winston Miller, based on a story by Sam Hellman from the novel *Wyatt Earp, Frontier Marshall* by Stuart N. Lake; cinematographer, Joseph MacDonald; edited by Dorothy Spencer; music by Cyril J. Mockridge and David Buttolph; art designers, James Basevi and Lyle Wheeler; produced by Mr. Engel; released by Twentieth Century Fox. Black and white. Running time: 97 minutes.

With: Henry Fonda (Wyatt Earp), Linda Darnell (Chihuahua), Victor Mature (Doc Holliday), Walter Brennan (Old Man Clanton), Tim Holt (Virgil Earp), Cathy Downs (Clementine), Ward Bond (Morgan Earp) and Alan Mowbray (Granville Thorndike).

Let's be specific about this: The eminent director John Ford is a man who has a way with a Western like nobody in the picture trade. Seven years ago his classic *Stagecoach* snuggled very close to fine art in this genre. And now, by George, he's almost matched it with *My Darling Clementine*.

Not quite, it is true—for this picture, which came to the Rivoli yesterday, is a little too burdened with conventions of Western fiction to place it on a par. Too obvious a definition of heroes and villains is observed, and the standardized aspect of romance is too neatly and respectably entwined. But a dynamic composition of Western legend and scenery is still achieved. And the rich flavor of frontiering wafts in overpowering redolence from the screen.

In this particular instance, Mr. Ford and Twentieth Century Fox are telling an oft-repeated story from the treasury of Western lore. It's the story of that famous frontier marshal who "cleaned up" Tombstone, Arizona—Wyatt Earp. And if that doesn't place him precisely in the history catalogue, rest assured that he's been a model for film heroes ever since the days of William S. Hart. And since legend is being respected, as well as the conventions of the screen, it is the story of Wyatt's dauntless conquest of a gang of rustlers and a maiden's heart.

But even with standard Western fiction—and that's what the script has enjoined—Mr. Ford can evoke fine sensations and curiously captivating moods. From the moment that Wyatt and his brothers are discovered on the wide and dusty range, trailing a herd of cattle to a far-off promised land, a tone of pictorial authority is struck—and it is held. Every scene, every shot is the product of a keen and sensitive eye—an eye which has deep comprehension of the beauty of rugged people and a rugged world.

As the set for this film, a fine facsimile of frontier Tombstone was patiently built in the desert of Monument Valley, and it was there that Mr. Ford shot most of the picture. And he is a man who knows that Westerns belong, in the main, out of doors. When he catches a horseman or a stagecoach thumping across the scrubby wastes, the magnificences of nature—the sky and desert—dwarf the energies of man. Yet his scenes of intensity and violence are played very much to the fore, with the rawness and meanness of the frontier to set his vital human beings in relief.

And the humans whom Mr. Ford imagines are not the ordinary stereotypes of films, no matter how hackneyed and conventional the things they are supposed to do. Henry Fonda, for instance, plays a Wyatt Earp such as we've never seen before—a leathery, laconic young cowpoke who truly suggests a moral aim. Through his quiet yet persuasive self-confidence—his delicious intonation of short words—he shows us an elemental character who is as real as the dirt on which he walks.

And Walter Brennan is completely characteristic as the scabby old desert rattlesnake whose villainous murder of Wyatt's brother sets off the dramatic fireworks. Even the mawkish fabrication of a young doctor gone to seed and turned bad man (who later turns a good man) is soundly played by Victor Mature—not to mention the several rawhide buckos who twirl guns and hide behind beards, who are played by such competent actors as Tim Holt, Don Garner and Ward Bond. Mr. Ford is less knowing with the females.

Linda Darnell makes a pinup of a trull, and Cathy Downs is simply ornamental as a good little girl from back East.

However, the gentlemen are perfect. Their humors are earthy. Their activities are taut. The mortality rate is simply terrific. And the picture goes off with several bangs.

—B.C., December 4, 1946

MY DINNER WITH ANDRÉ

Directed by Louis Malle: written by Wallace Shawn and André Gregory: director of photography. Jeri Sopanen: edited by Suzanne Baron: music by Allen Shawn: production designer, David Mitchell: produced by George W. George and Beverly Karp: released by New Yorker Films. Running time: 110 minutes.

With: Wallace Shawn (Wally). André Gregory (André). Jean Lenauer (Waiter) and Roy Butler (Bartender).

Wally (Wallace Shawn), wearing an oversize raincoat, mushes morosely along a street in SoHo in a chilly evening light. Wally, a playwright who takes acting jobs when he can get them to make ends meet, is on his way to a posh restaurant to have dinner with André (André Gregory), the innovative theater director (Off Off Broadway's *Alice in Wonderland* at his Manhattan Theater Project) who was Wally's first mentor.

Wally, as he tells us on the soundtrack, is not really looking forward to the evening. He and André haven't seen each other in some years and Wally is not sure what he's going to find.

He's heard stories about André's dropping out, periodically leaving a beloved wife and children to go off to Tibet and such places to talk to trees. He's agreed to dine with André only at the urging of a mutual friend who had recently come upon André "in some odd corner of town," sobbing uncontrollably, apparently because he had been so moved by the line in Ingmar Bergman's *Autumn Sonata* in which a character says, "I could always live in my art, but never in my life."

Thus begins Louis Malle's very funny, extremely

special new film, *My Dinner with André,* which will be shown at Alice Tully Hall at the New York Film Festival today and on Saturday. It will open its regular commercial engagement at the Baronet Theater on Sunday.

My Dinner with André is just that, nearly two hours of talk about theater, art, life, electric blankets, and Western Civilization, over dinner, during which André rattles on at enthusiastic length about his search for himself in the forests of Poland, the dunes of the Sahara, the heaths of Scotland, the mountains of India, and on the estate of Richard Avedon on Long Island. Wally asks questions and registers his amazement with "wows" and "goshes" and "Gods."

André is morose as he explains why he temporarily gave up the theater. His theatrical experiments were either self-defeating or impossible, as when he once suggested that the actress playing Agawe in his production of *The Bacchae* at Yale carry around a real severed head secured from the New Haven morgue. The actress flatly refused.

The talk is not exactly Shavian but it's sometimes so provocative or nutty or freewheeling that one would like to butt in. André has been obsessed with getting in touch with original feelings. People are robots, he's convinced, reacting in expected ways to expected situations. Everyone is on automatic pilot. Everybody responds only to what he wants. The forest, except in Jerzy Grotowski's Poland, is not to be seen for the trees.

André at first seems to be an impossibly self-centered kook. He speaks in the latest jargon and for all the pain he talks about feeling, he's dressed in the most fashionably casual way. Money clearly is no problem.

As the dinner progresses, though, he becomes a most winning character, and I use the word character advisedly. For although André Gregory is playing André Gregory and Wallace Shawn is playing Wally Shawn, *My Dinner with André,* put together from hundreds of hours of tapes of conversations between Mr. Shawn and Mr. Gregory, is fiction and the characters, modeled on their real selves, are fictitious characters.

It's the achievement of Mr. Malle, the director of *Atlantic City, Pretty Baby,* and a lot of other very fine, conventional movies, that he has successfully turned his two real-life personalities into actors capable of representing themselves. That's not easy. It must be added, however, that not all of the talk is so fascinating that one's interest doesn't flag. It might be better if it were a conversation heard at the next table, one on which one could tune in and out at will.

At times *My Dinner with André* suggests a reunion of Christopher Robin (Mr. Gregory) and Winnie-the-Pooh (Mr. Shawn) thirty years after each has left the nursery to pursue separate careers in the theater. Mr. Gregory, older, originally more practical, has sought truth in ways that must strike a lot of us, including Mr. Shawn, as crazily if wonderfully self-indulgent.

Mr. Shawn's Pooh, however, is just what you might think Pooh would grow up to be—still filled with wonder and curiosity about mundane things, capable of finding joy in daily tasks of utmost banality, thinking that a trip to the top of Everest to find oneself is somewhat expensive when he, Pooh, is convinced he might find himself quite as easily in the cigar store next door. Wally, like Pooh, is also candid enough to say at one point, with polite exasperation, "I really don't know what you're talking about."

And that, possibly, is the reason that this film is often so invigorating, and why these two men respond to each other so well. Wally's practical ordinariness as a man, the mild-mannered fellow who lies within the "raging beast" he seems to be as a playwright, is a perfect sounding board for the restless André. As André sees himself more clearly through Wally's self-awareness, Wally must examine his own delight in, say, a home-cooked meal with his friend Debby (on one of the nights when Debby isn't working as a waitress to support the two of them), through André's sometimes hilarious adventures in self-expression, here and abroad.

My Dinner with André is not a conventional movie, but it is a movie. However, I wouldn't advise anyone to see it after a satisfyingly big dinner. It's easier to watch other people eat, and to listen to other people talk, when one is hungry.

—V.C., October 8, 1981

MY FAIR LADY

Directed by George Cukor; written by Alan Jay Lerner, based on the musical by Mr. Lerner and Frederick Loewe and the play *Pygmalion* by

George Bernard Shaw: cinematographer. Harry Stradling: edited by William Ziegler: music by Mr. Loewe: production designers. Gene Allen and Cecil Beaton: produced by Jack L. Warner: released by Warner Brothers. Running time: 170 minutes.

With: Audrey Hepburn (Eliza). Rex Harrison (Henry Higgins). Stanley Holloway (Alfred Doolittle). Wilfrid Hyde-White (Colonel Pickering). Gladys Cooper (Mrs. Higgins). Jeremy Brett (Freddie). Theodore Bikel (Zoltan Karpathy). Mona Washbourne (Mrs. Pearce). Isobel Elsom (Mrs. Eynsford-Hill) and John Holland (Butler).

As Henry Higgins might have whooped, "By George, they've got it!" They've made a superlative film from the musical stage show *My Fair Lady*—a film that enchantingly conveys the rich endowments of the famous stage production in a fresh and flowing cinematic form. The happiest single thing about it is that Audrey Hepburn superbly justifies the decision of the producer, Jack L. Warner, to get her to play the title role that Julie Andrews so charmingly and popularly originated on the stage.

All things considered, it is the brilliance of Miss Hepburn as the Cockney waif who is transformed by Professor Henry Higgins into an elegant female facade that gives an extra touch of subtle magic and individuality to the film, which had a bejeweled and bangled premiere at the Criterion last night.

Other elements and values that are captured so exquisitely in this film are but artful elaborations and intensifications of the stage material as achieved by the special virtuosities and unique flexibilities of the screen.

There are the basic libretto and music of Alan Jay Lerner and Frederick Loewe, which were inspired by the wit and wisdom in the dramatic comedy *Pygmalion* of George Bernard Shaw. With Mr. Lerner serving as the screen playwright, the structure and, indeed, the very words of the musical play as it was performed on Broadway for six and a half years are preserved. And every piece of music of the original score is used.

There is punctilious duplication of the motifs and patterns of the decor and the Edwardian costumes and scenery, which Cecil Beaton designed for the stage. The only difference is that they're expanded. For instance, the Covent Garden set becomes a stunningly populated market, full of characters and movement in the film; and the embassy ball, to which the heroine is transported Cinderellalike, becomes a dazzling array of regal splendor, as far as the eye can reach, when laid out for ritualistic emphasis on the Super-Panavision color screen. Since Mr. Beaton's decor was fresh and flawless, it is super-fresh and flawless in the film.

In the role of Professor Higgins, Rex Harrison still displays the egregious egotism and ferocity that he so vividly displayed on the stage, and Stanley Holloway still comes through like thunder as Eliza's antisocial dustman dad.

Yes, it's all here, the essence of the stage show—the pungent humor and satiric wit of the conception of a linguistic expert making a lady of a guttersnipe by teaching her manners and how to speak, the pomp and mellow grace of a romantic and gone-forever age, the delightful intoxication of music that sings in one's ears.

The added something is what Miss Hepburn brings—and what George Cukor as the director has been able to distill from the script.

For want of the scales of a jeweler, let's just say that what Miss Hepburn brings is a fine sensitivity of feeling and a phenomenal histrionic skill. Her Covent Garden flower girl is not just a doxy of the streets. She's a terrifying example of the elemental self-assertion of the female sex. When they try to plunge her into a bathtub, as they do in an added scene, which is a wonderfully comical creation of montage and pantomime, she fights with the fury of a tigress. She is not one to submit to the still obscure customs and refinements of a society that is alien to her.

But when she reaches the point where she can parrot the correct words to describe the rain in Spain, she acknowledges the thrill of achieving this bleak refinement with an electrical gleam in her eyes. And when she celebrates the male approval she receives for accomplishing this goal, she gives a delightful demonstration of ecstasy and energy by racing about the Higgins mansion to the music of "I Could Have Danced All Night."

It is true that Marni Nixon provides the lyric voice that seems to emerge from Miss Hepburn, but it is an excellent voice, expertly synchronized. And everything Miss Hepburn mimes to it is in sensitive tune with the melodies and words.

Miss Hepburn is most expressive in the beautiful scenes where she achieves the manners and speech of a lady, yet fails to achieve that one thing she needs for a sense of belonging—that is, the recognition of the man she loves.

She is dazzlingly beautiful and comic in the crisply satiric Ascot scene played almost precisely as it was on the stage. She is stiffly serene and distant at the embassy ball and almost unbearably poignant in the later scenes when she hungers for love. Mr. Cukor has maneuvered Miss Hepburn and Mr. Harrison so deftly in these scenes that she has one perpetually alternating between chuckling laughter and dabbing the moisture from one's eyes.

This is his singular triumph. He has packed such emotion into this film—such an essence of feeling and compassion for a girl in an all too-human bind—that he has made this rendition of *My Fair Lady* the most eloquent and moving that has yet been done.

There are other delightful triumphs in it. Mr. Harrison's Higgins is great—much sharper, more spirited, and eventually more winning than I recall it on the stage. Mr. Holloway's dustman is titanic, and when he roars through his sardonic paean to middle-class morality in "Get Me to the Church on Time," he and his bevy of boozers reach a high point of the film.

Wilfrid Hyde-White as Colonel Pickering, who is Higgins's urbane associate, Mona Washburn as the Higgins housekeeper, Gladys Cooper as Higgins's svelte mama, and, indeed, everyone in the large cast is in true and impeccable form.

Though it runs for three hours—or close to it—this *My Fair Lady* seems to fly past like a breeze. Like Eliza's disposition to dancing, it could go on, for all I'd care, all night.

—B.C., October 22, 1964

MY LEFT FOOT

Directed by Jim Sheridan; written by Mr. Sheridan and Shane Connaughton, based on the book by Christy Brown; director of photography, Jack Conroy; edited by J. Patrick Duffner; music by Elmer Bernstein; art designer, Austen Spriggs; produced by Noel Pearson; released by Miramax Films. Running time: 103 minutes.

With: Daniel Day-Lewis (Christy Brown), Ray McAnally (Mr. Brown), Brenda Fricker (Mrs. Brown), Hugh O'Conor (Young Christy Brown), Fiona Shaw (Dr. Eileen Cole), Ruth McCabe (Mary), Adrian Dunbar (Peter), Eanna MacLiam (Benny) and Cyril Cusack (Lord Castlewelland).

Born in 1932 with cerebral palsy, the ninth of the twenty-two children his parents would eventually have (thirteen survived), Christy Brown grew up as an archetypal member of Dublin's working class—painfully poor, often deprived of essentials, yet also miraculously resilient.

Christy's body was both twisted and paralyzed. He was unable to communicate through recognizable speech. With his lips pulled over to one side, his eyes wobbling upward in their sockets, he spoke in a series of guttural syllables that would be translated by his mother.

Because he had the use of only his left foot, he was able to get around with difficulty, sometimes in a home-made wooden pramlike vehicle, pulled by his pals, and later in a wheelchair. People who had no idea they were being cruel referred to him within his hearing as an "idiot" and a "half-wit."

Through the uninhibited, unselfconscious love of his family, and the patience of his doctors, Christy learned how to be understood when he talked and to express himself first as a painter and then as a writer. His mind was fertile, restless, questing, and, it seems, surprisingly romantic.

With the more than ordinarily prehensile toes of his left foot, he could hold a paint brush, turn door knobs, type stories, play records, do almost everything, in fact, except cut his throat with a straight razor (tried once in a low moment).

My Left Foot is an intelligent, beautifully acted adaptation of Christy Brown's first book, published in 1955, the initial chapter in a series of semi-autobiographical works in which he recalled his own most particular coming of age. The film will be shown at the New York Film Festival today and tomorrow.

My Left Foot is a very successful example of the sort of triumph-over-adversity screen literature that Americans have tended to sentimentalize and prettify in such movies as *The Other Side of the Mountain* and *Mask. My Left Foot,* shot in Ireland with Irish and English talent, may not be entirely unsentimental, but its emotions are expressed within a social context that gives them a tough texture.

My Left Foot might have been even better if it had been even more caustic. That, however, would have been a different movie from the one that Jim Sheridan has directed from a screenplay written by him and Shane Connaughton, with the exemplary Daniel Day-Lewis playing the adult Christy Brown and Hugh O'Conor playing Christy as a boy.

It's never easy judging the work of actors in such singular and grotesque circumstances. Technical facility can go a long way toward the creation of what appears to be a performance. Thus it takes a while for the full measure of Mr. Day-Lewis's work in *My Left Foot* to be appreciated.

At first he is so explicitly deformed that it seems rude to stare at him, which might be just the sort of reaction that Christy would use to gain an advantage over a stranger. He is an exceptionally complicated man. He has long since moved beyond the longings, expressed by the protagonists in *Mask* and *The Elephant Man,* to be like other people.

Christy knows that he will always be different, but that doesn't prevent him from attempting to realize himself as completely as other men. How he does this, and at what cost, provides *My Left Foot* with its narrative shape. The film is a series of flashbacks from a gala benefit at which Christy is being honored and where he meets the young woman he will eventually marry.

Though he is not on screen as long as Mr. Day-Lewis, Mr. Conor is equally good as the young Christy, a furious intelligence lurking inside a body that is all twitches and spasms, whose muscles are clenched as tightly as his emotions.

The fine supporting cast is headed by Brenda Fricker and Ray McAnally as Christy's parents, Ruth McCabe as the young woman Christy falls in love with, and Fiona Shaw as the doctor who is largely responsible for the education of the older Christy.

Though *My Left Foot* is blunt and tough in its presentation of Christy's handicaps, it avoids any direct criticism of the handicapped world into which he is born, one in which his mother spends most of her time being pregnant, in which poverty is as likely to make the spirit ugly as beautiful, and in which the church always has the last word.

There is one funny-terrible scene in which a priest lectures the young, almost completely immobilized Christy on the evils of the flesh and the possibility of eternal damnation after the boy has been found with a dirty magazine.

Most of the time, though, *My Left Foot* is polite, nonjudgmental. The film ends with Christy's marriage in 1972. It does not mention that he choked to death while having dinner in 1981. He was forty-nine years old.

—*V.C., September 23, 1989*

MY LIFE AS A DOG

Directed by Lasse Hallström: written (in Swedish, with English subtitles) by Mr. Hallström, Reidar Jonsson, Brasse Brännström and Per Berglund, based on the novel by Mr. Jonsson: cinematographers, Jörgen Persson and Rolf Lindström: edited by Christer Furubrand and Susanne Linnman: music by Björn Isfält: art designer, Lasse Westfelt: produced by Waldemar Bergendahl: released by Svensk Filmindustrie. Running time: 101 minutes.

With: Anton Glanzelius (Ingemar), Tomas von Bromssen (Uncle Gunnar), Anki Lidén (Mother) and Melinda Kinnaman (Saga).

When left to his own devices, Ingemar Johansson is a most winning adolescent—skeptical, introspective, curious, trying earnestly to bring order out of nature's chaos. As played by eleven-year-old Anton Glanzelius in Lasse Hallström's 1985 Swedish film *My Life as a Dog,* Ingemar even looks unfinished. His forehead's too high for the rest of his face, and his eyes too small. Physically as well as emotionally, he's still in transit.

The trouble with *My Life as a Dog* is that too often it imposes an alien sensibility upon the boy, requiring that he behave in a way that adults can too easily identify as charming. *My Life as a Dog* is a movie with a split point of view.

Sometimes (especially in its funnier moments) it recalls the gravity with which François Truffaut remembered childhood. At other times, however, it suggests a 1980's variation on the prettified, idealized, sentimental view of kids favored by the Hollywood producers who made fortunes with Jackie Coogan,

Jackie Cooper, Shirley Temple, Margaret O'Brien and their lesser spinoffs.

My Life as a Dog will be shown in the New Directors/ New Films series at the Museum of Modern Art today and tomorrow. It will begin a regular commercial engagement here in May.

As adapted by Mr. Hallström, Reidar Jonsson, and two other collaborators from a novel by Mr. Jonsson, the film covers a crucial year in Ingemar's life, when, in addition to the storms of puberty, he must face the fact that his mother is dying of tuberculosis.

As much as he loves his mother (and his daydreams are full of poetic visions of her, accompanied by the sound of her uninhibited laughter), he seems always to be failing her. Ingemar and his older brother both mean well, but ordinary horseplay inevitably turns noisy and nasty when she's trying to sleep. When Ingemar is taken to the hospital to see her for what may be the last time, all he can say is that he's planning to buy her a toaster for Christmas.

In these moments, *My Life as a Dog* is funny and true and moving, as it also is when, on the soundtrack, he confides something of his philosophy for surviving from one day to the next: "You have to compare all the time—to get a distance on things." What's the good of being the first dog in space, he asks, if, like Russia's Laika, you wind up starving to death? How can a liver transplant be described as "successful" if the patient doesn't pull through? He ponders the meaning of a bus-train accident that leaves six people killed and fourteen injured. He's fascinated by statistics.

The character possesses an honesty and rigor that the rest of the film would seem to deny. Too many of the things that happen to Ingemar are intended to be "cute." Inevitably, these sequences are seen not through the boy's eyes but through those of the filmmakers, including one sequence in which Ingemar is humiliated for his participation in a sex-education "lecture" given by an older friend in a woodshed.

Mr. Glanzelius gives a firm and wise performance as the determined, mostly unsmiling Ingemar, whose namesake's unexpected 1959 heavyweight championship victory over Floyd Patterson brings the film to its conclusion. There also are good contributions by Anki Lidén as Ingemar's mother, Tomas von Bromssen as Ingemar's uncle (whose favorite song is the Swedish version of "Oh What a Lovely Bunch of Coconuts"), and Didrik Gustavsson, as a bedridden old man who likes to listen to Ingemar read the copy in the corset ads in a mail-order catalog.

My Life as a Dog looks as pretty as a picture, which, in this case, is too pretty for its own good.

—V.C., March 24, 1987

MY MAN GODFREY

Produced and directed by Gregory La Cava: written by Morrie Ryskind. Eric Hatch and Mr. La Cava. based on the novel *1101 Park Avenue* by Mr. Hatch: cinematographer. Ted Tetzlaff: edited by Ted J. Kent: music by Charles Previn: art designer. Charles D. Hall: released by Universal Pictures. Black and white. 1936. Running time: 94 minutes.

With: William Powell (Godfrey Park). Carole Lombard (Irene Bullock). Alice Brady (Angelica Bullock). Gail Patrick (Cornelia Bullock). Jean Dixon (Molly). Eugene Pallette (Alexander Bullock). Alan Mowbray (Tommy Gray). Mischa Auer (Carlo). Robert Light (Faithful George) and Pat Flaherty (Mike).

Rushing the calendar, the Radio City Music Hall has decided to have its April Fool's Day in September. With Universal's compliments, it presented yesterday the daffiest comedy of the year. *My Man Godfrey,* from the novel by Eric Hatch, is on the order of the *Three-Cornered Moon* of a few seasons ago—except that it is slightly more insane. There may be a sober moment or two in the picture; there may be a few lines of the script that do not pack a laugh. Somehow we cannot remember them. It's nonsense, of course, but it's something to relish on a damp September morn.

Perhaps you have not read the Hatch novel. Then you are not acquainted with the Bullocks. There is Mrs. Bullock (Alice Brady does her magnificently) who speaks in a stream of exclamation points and has a sad-eyed and voracious protégé, Carlo. There is Cornelia (Gail Patrick will serve), with a vicious temper and an ingrained snobbery. There is Irene, the cow-eyed, who has a one-track mind with grass growing over its rails. It is not a fair portrait of Carole Lombard, but she rises beautifully to the role. There is Mr. Bullock (Eugene Pallette), who glares at his Fifth

Avenue ménage and wonders whether he is going crazy or the people around him are.

And, naturally, there is Godfrey. We thought of calling him William Powell, but this isn't Mr. Powell, it's Godfrey. He was the forgotten man that the skirted Bullocks set out to find during a scavenger hunt. They already had goats, Japanese goldfish, corsets, tennis racquets, and a monkey. Cornelia found Godfrey first. He was living in a shack colony of the unemployed on the city dumps near the East River. Godfrey pushed Cornelia into an ash pile. But Irene won him over, captured the loving cup in the scavenger hunt, and rewarded Godfrey with a job. "Do you know how to buttle?" she asked, and Godfrey became a butler for the Bullocks.

That is the way it begins. Godfrey, we learn later, is a Harvard man, momentarily gone to seed, but like most Harvard men he is a thoroughly irresistible chap, equally capable of dealing with Mrs. Bullock's pixies (she sees them on morning-afters), with Cornelia's attempt to plant a pearl necklace on him, with Mr. Bullock's financial difficulties, or the plight of his former co-squatters in the waterfront jungle. But not, we hastily add, with the forthright emotional processes of that bovine divinity (or vice versa), Irene, who is somewhat surer than death or taxes. Godfrey, when we leave him, is being led to the slaughter and it's enough to bring tears to the eyes of an Eli.

Mr. Hatch has assisted in the writing of the screen version of his novel and he has preserved admirably the feather-brained quality of his book. Gregory La Cava has directed the piece with his customary feeling for comedy and, to the work of the players previously mentioned, has been added a cheerful contribution by such reliable clowns as Alan Mowbray, Mischa Auer, Jean Dixon, Franklin Pangborn, and Ed Gargan. The sum of it is that *My Man Godfrey* is an exuberantly funny picture.

—F.S.N., September 19, 1936

MY NIGHT AT MAUD'S

Written (in French, with English subtitles) and directed by Eric Rohmer: cinematographer. Nestor Almendros: edited by Cécile Ducugis: art designer. Nicole Rachline: produced by Pierre Cottrell: released by Pathé Pictures. Black and white. Running time: 105 minutes.

With: Jean-Louis Trintignant (Jean-Louis). Françoise Fabian (Maud). Marie-Christine Barrault (Françoise). Antoine Vitez (Vidal) and Leonide Kogan (Concert Violinist).

Eric Rohmer's *Ma Nuit Chez Maud* (literally, *My Night at Maud's*) is so French and so Catholic—as well as so fine—that it should prove irresistible to certain Americans, especially to those of us who, having been raised in a puritan tradition, have always been a little in awe of the Roman Church's intellectual catholicism. The French film was shown last night at Alice Tully Hall and will be repeated there tomorrow evening. To my way of thinking, it's the first new film to be seen at the current New York Film Festival that achieves with elegance and eloquence the goals it has set for itself.

Elegance and eloquence may seem like strange words to use about a film that was photographed entirely in black and white in a French provincial city in the dreariness of winter (mostly in ordinary interior settings) and that concerns four seemingly commonplace people, none of whom renounces a throne or even possesses an inflammatory political pamphlet.

I'd even go so far as to call *Ma Nuit Chez Maud* civilized, except for the fact that that adjective usually recalls some boring film adaptation of a Lillian Hellman play in which people talk canned wisdom as they move from fireplace to settee to French windows, all the while anticipating some melodramatic disaster.

Ma Nuit Chez Maud is the first Rohmer feature to be seen in this country. Rohmer, a forty-year-old *Cahiers du Cinéma* critic, directed one of the episodes in the omnibus feature *Six in Paris,* which was shown at the 1965 New York Film Festival (and which, frankly, I don't remember). This new film is described as the third feature in a projected cycle called *Six Moral Tales,* of which four have now been completed. Each is a variation on a single situation: a man who is in love with one woman meets and spends some time with another woman, whom he finds supremely attractive, but with whom he does not consummate the affair.

The hero of *Ma Nuit Chez Maud* is Jean-Louis (Jean-Louis Trintignant), an engineer in his early thirties, a solitary but not a lonely sort, a man who at first seems to be something of a prig. He isn't. He just values himself too much—in the best sense—to waste time on superficial sexual or social experiments. Within his abiding Roman Catholicism, he also believes he will ultimately meet and marry the right girl, who will not only be Catholic but also blond.

By chance one night, he runs into an old friend, a philosophy professor and Marxist atheist, who introduces him to Maud (Françoise Fabian), a divorcée and skeptic (this is the sort of movie in which people's philosophical attitudes are made as immediately apparent as are the birthrights in Shakespeare's histories). Maud, beautiful, wise, tells him about her marriage, her dead lover, her husband's mistress (a lovely young Catholic girl), and tries unsuccessfully to seduce him. The very next day, Jean-Louis meets the girl for whom he has been looking—which is not quite the end of a tale that is as ironic as it is moral.

Rohmer's achievement in *Ma Nuit Chez Maud* is that he has been able to make so much talk so unaffectedly cinematic. Although a quick dip into Pascal's *Pensées* would not hurt before seeing the film, there is so much wit-in-context that it is not absolutely necessary. Most refreshing is the sight and sound of four characters who are articulate, interested, informed, educated, amused, vulnerable, totally free of epigrams, and aware of their identities. Their only concern is the manner in which they will realize those identities, and whether it will be by choice, predestination, or simple luck.

The film is beautifully played, that is, as written, which is almost as if it were music. The camera literally and figuratively never looks down or up at the characters. It faces them straight on, the better to catch some completely unexpected moments of intimacy and humor.

Ma Nuit Chez Maud is set in Clermont, a town of something over 100,000 citizens, southwest of Paris, where Pascal was born in 1623. For more data, you'll have to search your own *Pensées*, and the film, both of which might be most agreeable.

—V.C., September 24, 1969

MY OWN PRIVATE IDAHO

Written and directed by Gus Van Sant Jr.; directors of photography, Eric Alan Edwards and John Campbell; edited by Curtiss Clayton; production designer, David Brisbin; produced by Laurie Parker; released by Fine Line Features. Running time: 105 minutes.

With: River Phoenix (Mike Waters), Keanu Reeves (Scott Favor), James Russo (Richard Waters), William Richert (Bob Pigeon), Rodney Harvey (Gary), Chiara Caselli (Carmella), Jessie Thomas (Denise), Mike Parker (Digger), Grace Zabriskie (Alena), Flea (Budd), Tom Troupe (Jack Favor) and Udo Kier (Hans).

With *My Own Private Idaho,* his third feature, Gus Van Sant Jr. makes a big bold leap to join Jim Jarmusch and the Coen brothers in the front ranks of America's most innovative independent filmmakers.

My Own Private Idaho is essentially a road movie that, in its subversive way, almost qualifies as a romantic comedy except that its characters are so forlorn. The film itself is invigorating—written, directed, and acted with enormous insight and comic élan.

It will be presented at the New York Film Festival today and tomorrow and is scheduled to open its regular commercial engagement on Sunday.

Like Sam Shepard's plays, *My Own Private Idaho* is set in a contemporary American West inhabited by people who have lost touch with a past perhaps best left unexplored. Their attempts to connect with the present are tentative, desperate, and usually doomed. For most, the cost of the connection is too high, being beyond their mental and emotional means.

My Own Private Idaho is about two very different male hustlers who cross paths on Portland, Oregon's, skid row, become close friends for a while, then separate.

Mike Waters (River Phoenix) is a good-looking, none-too-bright young fellow, the product of a dramatically dysfunctional family, whose career opportunities are affected by his narcolepsy. Mike has a terrible tendency to fall asleep, suddenly and deeply, when faced with a situation in which he can't cope.

A very different sort is Scott Favor (Keanu Reeves), who has the manners, self-assurance, and handsomeness associated with an idealized preppie. He is an untroubled bisexual who operates according to a carefully planned agenda. Scott comes from a rich family and stands to inherit a fortune. His father is the mayor of Portland.

He hustles not because he has to but to satisfy his ego, to infuriate his father, and to make his own apparent salvation, when he comes into his money, just that much more dramatic. Scott is rigorous and a bit spooky in his resolve. His aim: to become a pillar of the community and maybe, someday, even mayor.

This is the frame of the movie, which Mr. Van Sant wrote and directed and which operates according to an agenda as carefully structured as Scott's, though never as baldly stated.

The movie opens on a stretch of two-lane blacktop highway somewhere in the vast lonely landscape of Idaho. Wearing a wool stocking cap and a wool jacket and carrying a small duffle bag, Mike Waters stands at the side of the road, at loose ends. Which way to go? As often happens at such times, Mike is overwhelmed by sleep.

The movie more or less wakes up in Seattle, where Mike is pliantly responding to a male customer. He's still without direction. There's another customer who asks him to act out an elaborate domestic fantasy. Mike docilely complies.

Moving on to Portland, he is picked up by a woman who takes him back to an imposing mansion in the suburbs. Mike: "Do you live here?" The woman: "Yes." Mike: "I don't blame you." This, however, is a somewhat different kind of job. There are already two other hustlers there. Something about the looks of the woman prompts Mike to drop into a heavy snooze again.

Though Mike and Scott have seen each other around, this is how they become pals. Scott carries the sleeping Mike out of the house, covers him with his own dark blue blazer, and leaves him on the suburban lawn.

Back on skid row, they become something of a pair. Scott introduces Mike to an inner circle of skid row hustlers and their hangers-on. In particular, there is Bob Pigeon (William Richert), a big, fat, hard-drinking old drifter who has a fondness for young men but seldom the money to pay for them.

Bob talks grandly. Metaphors are his medium. Bob was once in love with Scott, and Scott used the older man as his teacher and protector in the demimonde. Mr. Van Sant is not subtle about it: Bob is Falstaff to Scott's Prince Hal. There is even an elaborate variation on Shakespeare's Gadshill caper, in which Falstaff becomes the butt of Hal's carefully orchestrated joke-robbery.

Mr. Van Sant's control is such that the movie accommodates the artifice of this allusion without embarrassment and, indeed, to its own profit. Of more immediate importance to the success of the film, though, is the odd relationship between Scott and the hapless Mike.

Scott, who has nothing better to do at the moment, agrees to help Mike search for his long-lost mother, last heard from somewhere in Idaho.

In the course of this journey, which begins on a stolen motorcycle and is the sad lost heart of the film, the two young men move from Portland to Idaho to Italy and back to Portland, though now going their separate ways.

Like the narcoleptic Mike, the movie initially seems to be without direction. It appears to drift from one casual encounter to the next, getting what it can from the passing connections, some of them very funny, others harrowing, until time runs out. When the film abruptly reaches its end, the conclusion is seen, in hindsight, to have been inevitable from the opening frame.

My Own Private Idaho is as blunt, uncompromising, and nonjudgmental as Mr. Van Sant's two earlier films, *Drugstore Cowboy* and *Mala Noche,* but the scope is now broader and the aspirations more daring.

Too much should not be made of the free use of Falstaff, Hal, and the two *Henry IV* plays. It's a nervy thing to do, and it works as far as it goes. Mr. Van Sant's evocation of the world in which Mike and Scott briefly connect is what *My Own Private Idaho* is all about.

The movie, photographed by Eric Alan Edwards and John Campbell, has a beautiful autumnal look and a way of seeming to take its time without actually wasting it.

The performances, especially by the two young stars, are as surprising as they are sure. Mr. Phoenix (*Dogfight*) and Mr. Reeves (of the two *Bill and Ted* comedies) are very fine in what may be the two best roles they'll find in years. Roles of this density, for young actors, do not come by that often.

Mr. Richert, best known as the director of the one-of-a-kind *Winter Kills* (1976), is not fat enough to be even a weight-conscious Falstaff, but he clearly enjoys acting.

At no point in the course of the film is mention made of AIDS. The omission is so marked that it must be deliberate. It's not enough to assume that all these guys practice safe-sex because Mike is once seen carrying a condom. It could be that Mr. Van Sant means the film to be a fable set in its own privileged time.

Whatever the explanation, AIDS simply does not exist in *My Own Private Idaho*.

—V.C., September 27, 1991

MY 20TH CENTURY

Written (in Hungarian, with English subtitles) and directed by Ildiko Enyedi; director of photography, Tibor Mathe, edited by Maria Rigo; music by Laszlo Vidovszky; production designer, Zoltan Labas; produced by Gabor Hanak and Norbert Friedlander; released by Aries Film Releasing. Black and white. Running time: 104 minutes.

With: Dorotha Segda (Dora/Lili/Their Mother), Oleg Jankowski (Z), Peter Andorai (Thomas Alva Edison) and Gabor Mate (X).

My 20th Century, a new Hungarian film written and directed by Ildiko Enyedi, is a number of wondrous things.

It's a bracing combination of wit, invention, common sense, and lunacy. It's a gravely comic meditation on civilization at the turn of this century. It's also about light and shadow and electricity, Thomas Alva Edison, movies, and what it's like to be Hungarian in a world where no one is quite sure where Hungary is.

More specifically, it is about the adventures of identical twin girls, Dora and Lili, born in 1880 in Budapest to the kind of chilly poverty in which D. W. Griffith might have placed Dorothy and Lillian Gish. One Christmas Eve, when the waifs are out on the snowy streets selling matches, each is snatched away by a different dirty old man.

When they are next seen (both played by a charm-ing actress named Dorotha Segda), it is New Year's Eve, 1899. Dora is a fashionably dressed con artist, sipping the champagne of a corrupt culture aboard the Orient Express. The somewhat more plain Lili is a dedicated anarchist, riding in third class with a cage of carrier pigeons concealed beneath her petticoats.

Each unaware of the other's existence, they go about their tasks. Dora seduces men, whether they are pompous aristocrats, handsome officers, or elevator boys, mostly out of boredom, sometimes for pleasure.

The innocent Lili reads books (*The Laws of Mutual Assistance in Nature*) and skips around Budapest, exchanging the password ("Rosewater"), passing inscrutable messages, and delivering bombs.

My 20th Century is surprising, but it is even more impressive when one realizes that it is the first feature by Miss Enyedi, who is thirty-five years old. For very good reason she was awarded the 1989 Cannes Festival's Caméra d'Or, given to the best debut film.

The comedy will be shown as part of the New Directors/New Films Series at the Museum of Modern Art today and tomorrow.

My 20th Century jumps from one setting to the next with the speed of an early silent film more concerned with visual effect than with tiresome logic. It moves from Menlo Park, New Jersey, to Budapest, from Paris to Hamburg, from the jungles of Burma back to Budapest. A handsome mystery man, who seems to be a professor of life, wanders in and out of the sisters' lives, unaware that there are two of them.

Along the way, Miss Enyedi takes time out to attend a hilariously misogynous lecture by a man who insists that he believes that women should have the vote. There is also a story about a jungle-born chimpanzee who recalls how his curiosity landed him in the zoo, and another about a dog who outwits the people studying him in a laboratory.

Dear old Edison, not entirely happy with what he has wrought, makes brief appearances throughout the film. At the beginning he attends a spectacular Menlo Park fair where the light bulb is celebrated. One woman, staring at the strange object, is warned, "Careful, the magnetism will pull out your hairpins." Incandescent light illuminates without providing answers.

The film looks terrific. *My 20th Century*, photographed by Tibor Mathe, must be one of the most handsome black-and-white films since Federico

Fellini's *8½.* It is also enormously good humored in its curiosity about virtually everything, including the way women dressed at the turn of the century. The performances are similarly invigorating.

Miss Segda has the shrewd, changeable screen personality of a young, very pretty Hanna Schygulla. Her politically committed Lili is especially appealing, and no more so than when she vows that "the mothers of the future will make dynamite instead of coffee." Lili is no more accurate in predicting the future than she is in tossing bombs.

—V.C., March 17, 1990

MY UNCLE

Produced and directed by Jacques Tati; written (in French, with English subtitles) by Mr. Tati, Jacques Legrange and Jean l'Hote; cinematographer, Jean Bourgoin; edited by Suzanne Baron; music by Franck Barcellini and Alain Romans; art designers, Henri Schmitt and Pierre Etaix; released by Continental Distributing. Running time: 110 minutes.

With: Jacques Tati (Mr. Hulot), Jean-Pierre Zola (Mr. Arpel), Adrienne Servantie (Mrs. Arpel), Alain Becourt (Gerard), Lucien Fregis (Mr. Pichard) and Betty Schneider (Betty).

France's incomparable Jacques Tati is having himself a barrel of fun making sport of mechanized living in his first new film since *Mr. Hulot's Holiday.* This one, entitled *My Uncle* (*Mon Oncle*), opened at the Baronet and guild yesterday, and it is so contrived by M. Tati that the audience can have a barrel of fun, too.

Casting himself as Mr. Hulot, the bouncy bachelor whose brainless joie de vivre entangled him in numerous mad adventures in his previous film, M. Tati is now loosing this blithe spirit in a modern mechanized home and in a mechanically antiseptic factory devoted to turning out plastic hose. Being of cheerful disposition and assuming his audience is, too, he finds nothing but pomposity and nonsense in these gadgeted and push-buttoned realms.

And of those there is a plenty to confront the serene vivacity of the breezy Mr. Hulot, sweeping about with his pipe as a cutwater and up on his loose-jointed toes. In the home, which belongs to his sister and his overweight brother-in-law, there are buttons that start fireless cookers, and electric eyes that open doors. There's a fish fountain in the modern garden that spouts a stream of water when guests arrive, and there are all sorts of sanitary features and inscrutable tables and chairs.

But, particularly, there are the adults, whose lives seem patterned to all this gadgetry, and there's a nephew, aged ten, whose tastes and interests are more attuned to Uncle Hulot's relaxed world.

In this latter environment, which is the ordinary one of cobbled streets and old buildings in a Paris suburb, M. Hulot is happily at home. And it is perfectly clear from the picture that M. Tati is more at home there, too. For the truth of it is that *My Uncle* is more natural and richly comical when it is bouncing around in the world of Hulot than it is in the mechanized realms.

For all M. Tati's slapstick thwacking at the ultra-modern boobs (and he winds up and lets go most stoutly when a garden-party gathering is exposed), he gets his most genuine humor out of the old house in which Hulot lives, out of his neighbors, the market-stall keepers, the expansive street sweeper, and the local dogs. It is in the company of these people, much like those with whom he spent his holiday, that Hulot exudes supreme good nature and not just bewilderment and alarm.

Obviously, Hulot's nephew, played by Alain Becourt, is most congenial with them, too.

Facing it squarely, *My Uncle* is perceptibly contrived when it lingers too long and gets too deeply into the dullness of things mechanical. After you've pushed one button and one modernistic face, you've pushed them all. Mr. Hulot is the focus of amusement, not electrical doors and machines that squeeze out plastic hose. Anyhow, this sort of kidding was done superbly more than twenty-five years ago by René Clair in *A Nous la Liberté* and afterward by Charlie Chaplin in *Modern Times.*

M. Tati, as his own producer, coauthor, and director, has arranged a handsome setting for his acting, and he has given himself a cast of colorful and adroit supporting players, all nonprofessionals. The film is in excellent color and it has a gay but somewhat monotonous musical score.

It is being shown at the Baronet with English subtitles and at the Guild with dubbed English dialogue. Fortunately, most of the humor is expressed in situations and pantomine.

—B.C., November 4, 1958

THE NAKED GUN: FROM THE FILES OF POLICE SQUAD!

Directed by David Zucker; written by Jerry Zucker, Jim Abrahams, David Zucker and Pat profit; director of photography, Robert Stevens; edited by Michael Jablow; music by Ira Newborn; production designer, John J. Lloyd; produced by Robert K. Weiss; released by Paramount Pictures. Running time: 89 minutes.

With: Leslie Nielsen (Lieutenant Frank Drebin), Priscilla Presley (Jane Spencer), Ricardo Montalban (Victor Ludwig), George Kennedy (Captain Ed Hocken), Nancy Marchand (Mayor of Los Angeles) and Charlotte Zucker (Ludwig's Secretary).

The proudly sophomoric comedy style of the Zucker-Abrahams-Zucker writing team, responsible for *Airplane!*, *Top Secret!*, and now (with Pat Proft) *The Naked Gun: From the Files of Police Squad!*, is funniest when it's hardest to second-guess. But this time, in a scattershot detective parody that's a spinoff of the team's television series, things are relatively sane.

It will help if, while watching *The Naked Gun* at Embassy 1 or other neighborhood theaters, viewers can assume a mental age of about fourteen. The jokes will seem fresher that way, and they will also, much to the writers' credit, seem screamingly funny at times. Bathroom jokes, giddy repetition, and calamitous pratfalls are the sine qua non of this kind of humor, but *The Naked Gun* gives such things an unexpected sophistication. Much of this can be attributed to the dapper presence of Leslie Nielsen who, as Lieutenant Frank Drebin, manages to bring something heroic to the role of a perfectly oblivious fall guy.

First seen at a meeting of hostile world leaders in Beirut, Lebanon ("And don't ever let me catch you guys in America!" he shouts to look-alikes representing Idi Amin, Yasir Arafat, Muammar el-Qaddafi, and others), Drebin returns to Los Angeles and finds himself on the hunt for a diabolical businessman named Victor Ludwig (Ricardo Montalban). Drebin, who is more or less outsmarted by Ludwig's tank of expensive fighting fish, isn't much of a match for the man himself.

Nor can he keep up with Drebin's beautiful assistant, Jane Spencer (Priscilla Presley), who has a gift for the double entendre and an unfortunate habit of walking into things. *The Naked Gun* is so good-natured that it brings out the funny side of performers who, like Miss Presley, have never seemed to have much sense of humor in the past. Also in the cast, and equally well used, are George Kennedy as Drebin's friend and superior, Nancy Marchand as the Mayor of Los Angeles, and Charlotte Zucker, who is David and Jerry Zucker's mother.

David Zucker, who directed *The Naked Gun*, has given it a cheerful, messy style that never quite matches the ebullience of the writing. But high spirits may be all that a film like this really needs.

One of the more inspired visual gags is the standard young-and-in-love montage that finds Mr. Nielsen and Miss Presley frolicking prettily together and experiencing quite a few physical mishaps themselves. This sequence ends with a small credit in its lower left-hand corner, making it suitable for use on MTV. Later on, once he and Miss Presley have begun their photogenic romance, she tells him, "I'm a very lucky woman." "So am I," Mr. Nielsen earnestly replies. It's impossible not to see that coming, but it's equally impossible not to laugh.

—*J.M., December 2, 1988*

NASHVILLE

Produced and directed by Robert Altman; written by Joan Tewksbury; cinematographer, Paul Lohmann; edited by Sidney Levin and Dennis M. Hill; music by Richard Baskin; released by Paramount Pictures. Running time: 159 minutes.

With: David Arkin (Norman), Barbara Baxley (Lady Pearl), Ned Beatty (Delbert Reese), Karen Black (Connie White), Ronee Blakley (Barbara Jean), Timothy Brown (Tommy Brown), Keith Carradine (Tom Frank), Geraldine Chaplin (Opal), Shelley Duvall (L.A. Joan), Henry Gibson (Haven Hamilton), Scott Glenn (Private Glenn Kelly), Jeff Goldblum (Tricycle Man), Barbara Harris (Albuquerque), Michael Murphy (John Triplette), Lily Tomlin (Linnea Reese), Keenan Wynn (Mr. Green) and James Dan Calvert (Jimmy Reese).

Robert Altman's *Nashville* is the movie sensation that all other American movies this year will be measured against. It's a film that a lot of other directors will wish they'd had the brilliance to make and that dozens of other performers will wish they'd had the great good fortune to be in.

It should salvage Mr. Altman's reputation in Hollywood as a director who makes movies only for the critics, and it could well be the high point in the careers of a number of its performers, who may never again be so ideally presented in roles that utilize their special gifts with such affection. What will Ronee Blakley or Henry Gibson or Lily Tomlin or Barbara Harris do for encores? It's a tough question but not an unhappy one.

Nashville, which opened yesterday at the Baronet and Cinema II Theaters, is a panoramic film with dozens of characters, set against the country-and-western music industry in Nashville. It's a satire, a comedy, a melodrama, a musical. Its music is terrifically important—funny, moving, and almost nonstop.

It's what a Tennessee granddaddy might call a real toe-tapper of a picture.

There are so many story lines in *Nashville* that one is more or less coerced into dealing in abstractions. *Nashville* is about the quality of a segment of Middle American life. It's about ambition, sentimentality, politics, emotional confusion, empty goals, and very big business in a society whose citizens are firmly convinced that the use of deodorants is next to godliness.

Nashville doesn't make easy fun of these people. It doesn't patronize them. Along with their foolishness, it sees their gallantry. At the beginning of the film when Henry Gibson as Haven Hamilton, Nashville's biggest male star, records "200 Years," a patriotic song in honor of the Bicentennial ("We must be doing something right/To last 200 years"), the movie is amused by the song's maudlin sentiments and rhyme schemes, and by Haven's recording-studio tantrums. But it also appreciates the song's stirring beat and the vast, earnest public for whom it will have meaning.

The film, which has an original screenplay by Joan Tewksbury, who collaborated with Mr. Altman in adapting *Thieves Like Us,* has a well-defined structure, while individual sequences often burst with the kind of life that seems impossible to plan, though that may be to underrate Miss Tewksbury's contributions and those of the extraordinary cast. I have no idea where the director and the writer leave off and the performers take over.

Whoever is responsible, *Nashville* comes across as a film of enormous feeling. It's compounded of moments that tingle the spine, as when Lily Tomlin, who makes a spectacular dramatic debut in the film as a gospel singer and the mother of two deaf children, patiently draws forth a story from her twelve-year-old son, in words and sign language, about a swimming test he's just passed.

At the end of the film Barbara Harris, as a perpetually disheveled, very unlikely aspirant to country-and-western stardom, almost tears the screen to bits with a gospel version of a song heard earlier ("It Don't Worry Me") that concludes the narrative in a manner that is almost magical.

Ronee Blakley, a composer-singer who came to Mr. Altman's attention when she attempted to interest him in some of her songs, dominates the film, as much as it can be dominated by any one performer, as Barbara

Jean, Nashville's beautiful, fragile, country-and-western princess—a rural girl who's hit it big and throughout the film sinks deeper and deeper into emotional panic.

The stunning effect of her performance has as much to do with Miss Blakley's talents as singer-composer-actress and her particular beauty as with Barbara Jean's role in the events the film records.

Nashville is an immense collaboration, a timely coming together of all sorts of resources, including those of twenty-five-year-old Richard Baskin, who arranged and supervised the music, much of it written by the people who perform it.

In addition to Miss Blakley and Mr. Gibson, this includes Karen Black, who wrote two songs and has a fine sequence as Nashville's No. 2 female star, and Keith Carradine, who plays a cad of a rock singer and who wrote two songs, "I'm Easy" and "It Don't Worry Me," which, with Miss Blakley's "My Idaho Home," are three of the film's best.

Nashville has some weak spots. Geraldine Chaplin turns up as a visiting British Broadcasting Corporation reporter of such gross idiocy she'd probably have trouble getting a job on a shopping guide. A couple of sequences in the middle of the movie just mark time, but usually everything works, to make *Nashville* the most original, provocative, high-spirited film Mr. Altman has yet given us.

—*V.C., June 12, 1975*

NATIONAL LAMPOON'S ANIMAL HOUSE

Directed by John Landis; written by Mr. Landis, Douglas Kenney and Chris Miller; director of photography, Charles Correll; edited by George Folsey Jr.; music by Elmer Bernstein; art director, John J. Lloyd; produced by Ivan Reitman and Matty Simmons; released by Universal Pictures. Running time: 109 minutes.

With: Tom Hulce (Larry Kroger), Stephen Furst (Kent "Flounder" Dorfman), Mark Metcalf (Doug Neidermeyer), Mary Louise Weller (Mandy Pepperidge), Martha Smith (Barbara Jansen), James Daughton (Greg Marmalard), Kevin Bacon (Chip Diller), John Belushi (John "Bluto" Blutarsky), Douglas Kenney (Stork), Chris Miller (Hardbar), Bruce Bonnheim (B. B.), Karen Allen (Katy), James Widdoes (Robert Hoover), Tim Matheson (Eric "Otter" Stratton) and Peter Riegert (Donald "Boon" Schoenstein).

It's Rush Week of 1962 at Faber College, where "Knowledge is Good" was the founder's most memorable witticism. The classiest fraternity on campus—the one to which the editor of the *Daily Bavarian* belongs—is wowing potential pledges with an elaborate show of gentility and a pianist who can play "Tammy." But right next door, at the eyesore that is the Delta House, something a little less civilized is going on.

The Deltas are the kind of guys who bash beer cans against their foreheads, wheel their dates home in shopping carts and think they know the words to "Louie, Louie," which they will sing in off-key unison at less than the slightest provocation. Needless to say, they will not be having a very good year. The brother who racks up a 1.2 grade point average will be the brightest of the bunch, and the house Romeo will be reduced to gearing his visits to a nearby girls' school to the obituary notices. Pretending to be the grieving fiancé of a dead coed is evidently a successful, if pitiable, gambit.

National Lampoon's Animal House is by no means one long howl, but it's often very funny, with gags that are effective in a dependable, all-purpose way. The movie works hard to supply something for the broadest possible audience, instead of aiming only at the viewer who'd like to watch John Belushi—as the Delta who knows the fewest words of more than one syllable—eating Jell-O with his fingers.

Animal House is too cheerfully sleazy to be termed tame, but the filmmakers have been smart enough to leaven each gross-out with an element of innocent fun. Even the action-packed finale amounts to nothing more dangerous than the spectacle of all heck breaking loose.

Except for Mr. Belushi, who mugs like crazy and spills a wide variety of substances all over himself, the actors tend to be as clean-cut and dopey as the movie's setting. Tim Matheson is a particularly self-congratulatory Joe College who whistles "Peter and the Wolf" as he loiters in a women's dorm; Stephen

Furst does some very successful scene-stealing as the house blimp.

And Thomas Hulce is appropriately dim playing the first guy in the frat to be offered a reefer, by the obligatory hyper-hip English professor (Donald Sutherland, in a throwaway role). "O.K., so that means our whole solar system could be one tiny atom in the fingernail of some other giant being," Mr. Hulce postulates, while under the influence. Then he breaks out in uncontrollable giggles.

At its best, in moments like this, the movie isn't strictly satirical, because it doesn't need to be. The film makers have simply supplied the appropriate panty-girdles, crew-neck sweaters, frat-house initiation rites and rituals of the toga party, and let all that idiocy speak—very eloquently, and with a lot of comic fervor—for itself.

—*J.M., July 28, 1978*

NATICNAL VELVET

Directed by Clarence Brown: written by Theodore Reeves and Helen Deutsch, based on the novel by Enid Bagnold: cinematographer. Leonard Smith: edited by Robert J. Kern: music by Herbert Stothart: art designers. Cedric Gibbons and Urie McCleary: produced by Pandro S. Berman: released by Metro-Goldwyn-Mayer. Running time: 125 minutes.

With: Mickey Rooney (Mr. Taylor). Donald Crisp (Mr. Brown). Elizabeth Taylor (Velvet Brown). Anne Revere (Mrs. Brown). Angela Lansbury (Edwina Brown). Jackie Jenkins (Donald Brown). Juanita Quigley (Marvolia Brown) and Arthur Treacher (Race Patron).

In the true spirit of Christmas, the Music Hall is showing rare good will not only toward human beings but toward animals in its current bill. For both the holiday stage show and the new picture, which opened there yesterday, are abundant in sympathy and benevolence toward creatures of two and four legs. The stage show offers jovial acquaintance with some entertainers in the latter class, and the new film, *National Velvet,* should be a joy to all right-minded folks. For this fresh and delightful Metro picture,

based on Enid Bagnold's novel of some years back, tells by far the most touching story of youngsters and of animals since Lassie was coming home.

Indeed, in its simple comprehension of the faith and affection of youth it is likely more tender and affecting than even the story of Lassie was. And it certainly is more exciting in its vivid, dramatic display. For this story of two English youngsters, the daughter of a butcher and a youthful vagabond, who train a magnificent sorrel gelding to run in the Grand National Steeplechase, is rich in the gentleness and confidence that only young people truly have. And it speaks, through the tenderness of children, of the more benevolent spirit that is in man.

All right, it is highly unlikely that two youngsters could do such a thing as acquire a headstrong hunter and turn him into a steeplechasing star by training him over the hills and fences of the rolling English Downs. It is far-fetched to say that these tyros could put their unknown jumper in the Grand National, and even more presumptive to imagine that the girl could ride him to win. But that doesn't mean that the fancy isn't pleasant to contemplate and that this contemplation of it isn't a wholly captivating one.

For Clarence Brown, directing the picture, has kept it out in the open as much as he could and has got an air of wind-swept freedom and candor all the way through. His scenes on the Downs, with the broad sea in the background, are lovely in the color that is used, and the section of the film showing the race course and the meet at Aintree are spectacular. As a matter of fact, a more exciting horse race than that shown in this film has never been represented on the screen, in our memory, anyhow. All the thrill and heart-stopping tension of watching the horses top jumps in soaring flights, go down in sickening shambles, or keep on pounding toward the next is captured here.

Mr. Brown has also drawn some excellent performances from his cast, especially from little Elizabeth Taylor, who plays the role of the horse-loving girl. Her face is alive with youthful spirit, her voice has the softness of sweet song, and her whole manner in this picture is one of refreshing grace. Mickey Rooney is also affecting, though somewhat less airily so, as the boy who helps her train her jumper and gains a new and happy outlook thereby. Anne Revere and Donald Crisp are splendid as the little girl's mother and dad, and a large cast of other performers creates a genial country air most winningly. (For folks who like juvenile cuteness there is little Jack Jenkins as the family tike.)

As the mother of Velvet puts it, "Everyone should have a chance at a breathtaking piece of folly at least once in his life." That chance is now open to anybody who has the price of admission to the Music Hall.

—*B.C., December 15, 1944*

NETWORK

Directed by Sidney Lumet; written by Paddy Chayefsky; cinematographer, Owen Roizman; edited by Alan Heim; music by Elliott Lawrence; production designer, Philip Rosenberg; produced by Howard Gottfried; released by United Artists. Running time: 120 minutes.

With: Faye Dunaway (Diane Christenson), William Holden (Max Schumacher), Peter Finch (Howard Beals), Robert Duvall (Frank Hackett), Wesley Addy (Nelson Chaney), Ned Beatty (Arthur Jenson), Darryl Hickman (Bill Herron), Beatrice Straight (Louise Schumacher) and Marlene Warfield (Laureen Hobbs).

After a long and rewarding career with the UBS Television network as one of America's most respected news commentators, Howard Beale (Peter Finch) is being given the sack. Because his ratings have begun to slip and his show's share of the national audience is nil, this heir to the ideals of Edward R. Murrow has been found wanting. He's obsolete. The night after receiving the bad news, Howard signs off the air by urging his viewers to tune in to his final show next week. He will, he says cheerily, commit suicide on camera.

The next night, against the better judgment of his employers, Howard is allowed to go back on the air to apologize. Instead, he launches into a tirade full of obscenities about the dreary quality of American life in general and corporate television's inhumanity in particular. More apoplexy in the UBS board room, but Howard Beale has just catapulted himself into a new career as television's biggest new star. He's also flipped, being certifiably insane.

Network, written by Paddy Chayefsky and directed by Sidney Lumet, is about the fall, rise, and fall of Howard Beale and about television's running horrendously and hilariously amok. It's about dangerous maneuvers in the executive suites and about old-fashioned newsmen like Max Schumacher (William Holden), who have scruples and are therefore impotent. It's also about Arab oil, conglomerates, and new-fashioned hucksters like Diana Christensen (Faye Dunaway), a television executive whose sensitive reading of the viewing audience ("the American people are turning sullen") prompts her to put a seeress on the eleven o'clock news (to predict what will happen tomorrow) and to promote the lunatic coming-apart of Howard Beale as America's most popular personality since Will Rogers.

Network, which opened yesterday at the Sutton Theater, is, as its ads proclaim, outrageous. It's also brilliantly, cruelly funny, a topical American comedy that confirms Paddy Chayefsky's position as a major new American satirist. Paddy Chayefsky? Major? New? A satirist? Exactly.

Mr. Chayefsky, who made his name initially as television's poet of the small and everyday, has evolved through work like *The Latent Heterosexual* and *The Hospital* into one of our very, very few card-carrying satirists with access to the mass market. His humor is not gentle or generous. It's about as stern and apocalyptic as it's possible to be without alienating the very audience for which it is intended.

Which leads me to wonder what it will mean when *Network* becomes—as I'm sure it will—a huge commercial hit with, one assumes, the same audiences whose tastes supposedly dictate the lunacies that Mr. Chayefsky describes in *Network.* Could it be that Mr. Chayefsky has not carried his outrage far enough or that American audiences are so jaded that they will try anything once, say, *Network* or Russian roulette? I'm not sure.

I expect that a lot of people will sniff at the film on the ground that a number of the absurdities Mr. Chayefsky and Mr. Lumet chronicle so carefully couldn't happen, which is to miss the point of what they're up to. These wickedly distorted views of the way television looks, sounds, and, indeed, is, are the satirist's cardiogram of the hidden heart, not just of television but also of the society that supports it and is, in turn, supported.

Network has soft moments. A scene in which the

aging, philandering Mr. Holden finally walks out on Miss Dunaway, predicting emotional disaster for such a heartless creature, is of a dopey sentimentality that belongs to another movie, even though both characters are completely credible. Miss Dunaway, in particular, is successful in making touching and funny a woman of psychopathic ambition and lack of feeling.

Robert Duvall, the superb Dr. Watson in *The Seven-Per-Cent Solution,* is fine as the network hatchet man, subservient only to the head of the conglomerate that owns the network. This fellow, a folksy messiah beautifully played by Ned Beatty, is the mouthpiece for some of Mr. Chayefsky's bluntest thoughts about the current state of the wealth of nations.

Network can be faulted both for going too far and not far enough, but it's also something that very few commercial films are these days. It's alive. This, I suspect, is the Lumet drive. It's also the wit of performers like Mr. Finch, Mr. Holden, and Miss Dunaway. As the crazy prophet within the film says of himself, *Network* is vivid and flashing. It's connected into life.

—V.C., November 15, 1976

NEVER ON SUNDAY

Written (in French, with English subtitles), produced and directed by Jules Dassin: cinematographer, Jacques Natteau: edited by Roger Dwyre: music by Manos Hadjidakis: released by United Artists. Black and white. Running time: 97 minutes.

With: Melina Mercouri (Ilya), Jules Dassin (Homer), Georges Foundas (Tonio), Titos Vandis (Jorgo), Mitsos Liguisos (The Captain), Despo Diamantidou (Despo) and Dimos Starrenios (Poubelle).

Perhaps the most amiable serpent ever to glide onto the screen and attempt to entice an innocent woman away from a life of heroic sin is presented to us by Jules Dassin, with himself in the serpent's role, in his new picture, *Never on Sunday,* which came to the Plaza yesterday.

From the moment he enters smiling into a Piraeus (Greece) café and proclaims to a mob of happy Greek boozers that he is an American tourist in search of the Truth, he makes a most genial companion. One

almost wishes, for his sake, that he could accomplish the purpose he embarks on, which is the moral reformation of a prostitute.

But if he accomplished his purpose, it would be a most disappointing ending for the mischievous paradox that Mr. Dassin so neatly and nimbly handles in this gay Greek-American comedy.

Dismiss from your mind the anxiety that he is trucking with licentiousness by seeming to bestow the laurel upon the oldest profession in the world or that he is belittling the virtues of purity and reasonableness by having them lose out in the end. One might succumb to that suspicion, if one took this picture seriously. But seriously is the last way you should take this droll and robust spoof.

When Mr. Dassin's tourist, who acknowledges himself to be a student of ancient Greek culture and a minor philosopher, tries to discover the secret of the departed glory of Greece in Melina Mercouri's carefree and big-hearted prostitute, he plunges headfirst into the whirling ambiguity of the modern Greeks.

His doxy, supposedly descended from the inventors of logic and harmony, is by far the most illogical, unharmonious individual he has ever run across. On weekdays she may be the bubbling sweetheart of all the sailors and shipyard workers in Piraeus, but on Sundays she's a true and virtuous patron of the ancient Greek tragedies.

However, her comprehension of these heady classics is not the same as that of her would-be instructor or of students throughout the centuries. She is quite convinced that Medea is a fine and noble woman, deceived by men, and that Oedipus Rex is a fellow who loves his mother very much. She won't believe Medea kills her children. After all, don't they come out on the stage for curtain calls? And she is quite convinced that everybody goes off to the seashore at the end of every play.

It is the bouncing and beaming expansiveness with which Miss Mercouri endows this woman and the patience with which Mr. Dassin tries to urge her to simmer down, to assume a little moral decorum, and abandon some of her nonintellectual and professional whims, that make for tremendous good humor in the often lusty episodes of this film. There are plenty of expansive Greek gentlemen to help make them droll and lusty, too.

In addition to Miss Mercouri and Mr. Dassin,

both of whom are superb—she in a flashy, forceful fashion and he in a Chaplinesque vein—there is Georges Foundas, who plays a cheerful, hot-blooded Italian-Grecian swain, and Titos Vandis, who is delightful as a dull-witted champion of the girl. Mitsos Liguisos is sly and mellow as a seaport amoralist, and Dimos Starrenios is blond and billowy as an antagonistic prostitute.

The music of Manos Hadjidakis is lively; Miss Mercouri sings one affecting song and suits the mood. While one might take some minor exception to the occasional illogic of the script, it's no use, since illogic is the human disposition most frankly acknowledged and happily applauded in this film.

—*B.C., October 19, 1960*

NIGHT MOVES

Directed by Arthur Penn; written by Alan Sharp; director of photography, Bruce Surtees; edited by Dede Allen; music by Michael Small; production designer, George Jenkins; produced by Robert M. Sherman; released by Warner Brothers. Running time: 100 minutes.

With: Gene Hackman (Harry Moseby), Susan Clark (Ellen), Jennifer Warren (Paula), Edward Binns (Ziegler), Harris Yulin (Marty Heller), Kenneth Mars (Nick), James Woods (Quentin) and Melanie Griffith (Dolly Grastner).

Arthur Penn's *Night Moves,* the director's first film since the epic *Little Big Man* five years ago, is an elegant conundrum, a private-eye film that has its full share of duplicity, violence, and bizarre revelation, but whose mind keeps straying from questions of pure narrative to those of the hero's psyche.

Over the years we have come to expect our private eyes to be somewhat seedy and second-rate, beer-drinking loners with their own secrets to hide. But that seediness, as well as the decency that lurked beneath, has always been in the service of the genres. One never worried about Philip Marlowe's mental health; one does about Harry Moseby's. In fact, Harry is much more interesting and truly complex than the mystery he sets out to solve.

This is the only way I can explain my mixed feelings about *Night Moves,* which opened yesterday at Loew's State 2, the Trans-Lux 85th Street, and other theaters. Harry Moseby (Gene Hackman), his wife Ellen (Susan Clark), and the assorted characters he encounters in the film seem to deserve better than the quality of the narrative given them.

I can't figure out whether the screenplay by Alan Sharp was worked on too much or not enough, or whether Mr. Penn and his actors accepted the screenplay with more respect than it deserves.

When we first meet Harry, he is taking on a classic missing-persons case. It's to find the nymphomaniac daughter of a once beautiful Hollywood actress. The daughter, who is only sixteen, has been competing with Mummy for boyfriends.

The girl also stands to inherit the trust fund from which Mummy now gets a sizable income. Why does Mummy seek the return of the child, whom she clearly detests?

The plot thickens, but in the wrong ways. Harry discovers his wife is having an affair, and we learn that Harry had a terrible childhood, that he has trouble facing things squarely (as a knight moves in chess?), and that for one reason or another, he wants to face things squarely in this particular case. It'll prove something, you see.

In addition to the performances of Mr. Hackman and Miss Clark, *Night Moves* features two others of note, by Jennifer Warren, as a beautiful, enigmatic drifter Harry meets in the Florida keys, and by Melanie Griffith, as the not-so-missing person. They all are more or less realistic, believable characters.

However, they are forced to behave and react in the completely unbelievable ways demanded of private-eye fiction, when people we know to be sensitive and caring can walk away from a new corpse as casually as if it were a minor social indiscretion. After a while it just seems absurd.

—*V.C., June 12, 1975*

THE NIGHT OF THE HUNTER

Directed by Charles Laughton; written by James Agee, based on the novel by Davis Grubb; director of photography Stanley Cortez; edited by Robert Golden; art director, Hilyard Brown; music by Walter Schumann; produced by Paul Gregory;

released by United Artists. Black and white. Running time: 93 minutes.

With: Robert Mitchum (Rev. Harry Powell). Shelley Winters (Willa Harper). Lillian Gish (Rachel Cooper). James Gleason (Birdie Steptoe). Evelyn Varden (Icey Spoon). Peter Graves (Ben Harper). Don Beddoe (Walt Spoon). Billy Chapin (John Harper). Sally Jane Bruce (Pearl Harper) and Gloria Castillo (Ruby).

A weird and intriguing endeavor to put across something more in the way of a horror story involving children than the mere menace of a bogeyman is made in *The Night of the Hunter*, a film based on the novel of Davis Grubb and directed by Actor Charles Laughton, which came to the Mayfair yesterday. Paul Gregory produced this audacious film.

The trenchant and troubling proposition they are obviously aiming to convey is that being a child in the midst of sordid adults is a terrible experience. Innocent, sweet and trusting youngsters are sorely torn in a world of greed and hate. Withal, the authors assure us, the strength of little children abides.

This is a difficult thesis to render both forceful and profound in an hour and a half of tangled traffic with both melodramatic and allegorical forms. And the fact that Mr. Laughton, undertaking his first film directorial job, has not brought forth a wholly shattering picture is easy to understand.

The story that Mr. Grubb provided is a dark and horrifying account of the torment a fake evangelist inflicts upon a couple of kids. In a frenzy to discover where a hanged bank robber has hidden $10,000 in stolen bills, this perambulating back-country preacher insinuates himself into the home of the robber's family, marries his moronic widow, murders her and then persecutes her kids (the only ones who know where the money is hidden) until he drives them forth into the world.

All this has been crisply compacted into clear screen drama by the late James Agee and it put forth under the direction of Mr. Laughton in stark, rigid visual terms. The locale is crushingly rural, the atmosphere of "the sticks" is intense, and Robert Mitchum plays the murderous minister with an icy unctuousness that gives you the chills. There is more than malevolence and menace in his character. There is a strong trace of Freudian aberration, fanaticism and iniquity.

Credit Mr. Laughton with a clever and exceptionally effective job of catching the ugliness and terror of certain ignorant, small-town types. He has got out of Shelley Winters a grueling performance as the vapid widow and wife. The scene of the wedding-night of Miss Winters and the preacher is one of the most devastating of its sort since Von Stroheim's *Greed*. And Evelyn Varden's and Don Beddoe's performances as village gossips and busy-bodies are edged with a sharp and treacherous cruelty that shows through the appearance of homely farce.

But unfortunately the story and the thesis presented by Mr. Grubb had to be carried through by Mr. Laughton to a finish—and it is here that he goes wrong. For the evolution of the melodrama after the threatened, frightened children flee home, angles off into that allegorical contrast of the forces of Evil and Good. Strange, misty scenes composed of shadows and unrealistic silhouettes suggest the transition to abstraction. When the children find sanctuary in the home of a little old lady who befriends orphans, the idea comes across. The preacher, pursuing, is the Devil; the little old lady is Goodness and Love.

All this is handled with obvious pretense. Lillian Gish is sweet but whispy in the role of the benefactress of orphans, and Billy Chapin and Sally Jane Bruce, who are fine as the youngsters through most of the picture, become posey and incredible in the later scenes. The toughness of the grain of the story goes soft and porous toward the end. The conclusion is an uncontestable statement that children, God bless them, will endure.

—B.C., September 30, 1955

NIGHT OF THE LIVING DEAD

Directed and edited by George Romero: written by John A. Russo. based on a story by Mr. Romero: cinematographer. Mr. Romero: production designer. Vincent Survinski: produced by Russell Streiner: released by Continental Films. Black and white. Running time: 90 minutes.

With: Judith O'Dea (Barbara). Russell Streiner

(Johnny), Duane Jones (Ben), Karl Hardman (Harry Cooper), Keith Wayne (Tom), Judith Ridley (Judy) and Marilyn Eastman (Helen Cooper).

Night of the Living Dead is a grainy little movie acted by what appear to be nonprofessional actors, who are besieged in a farmhouse by some other nonprofessional actors who stagger around, stiff-legged, pretending to be flesh-eating ghouls.

The dialogue and background music sound hollow, as if they had been recorded in an empty swimming pool, and the wobbly camera seems to have a fetishist's interest in hands, clutched, wrung, scratched, severed, and finally—in the ultimate assumption—eaten like pizza.

The movie, which was made by some people in Pittsburgh, opened yesterday at the New Amsterdam Theater on 42d Street and at other theaters around town.

—*V.C., December 5, 1968*

A NIGHT TO REMEMBER

Directed by Roy Ward Baker; written by Eric Ambler, based on the book by Walter Lord; cinematographer, Geoffrey Unsworth; edited by Sidney Hayers; music by William Alwyn; art designer, Alex Vetchinsky; produced by William MacQuitty; released by Rank Films. Black and white. Running time: 123 minutes.

With: Kenneth More (Herbert Lightoller), Anthony Bushell (Captain Rostron), Jane Downs (Mrs. Lightoller), James Dyrenforth (Colonel Gracie), Michael Goodliffe (Thomas Andrews), David McCallum (Bride), Kenneth Griffith (Phillips), Richard Leech (Murdoch), Alec McCowen (Cottan), Tucker McGuire (Mrs. Brown), Laurence Naismith (Captain Smith), Russell Napier (Captain Lord), Jack Watling (Boxhall), Harold Goldblatt (Guggenheim), Helen Misener (Mrs. Straus) and Meier Tzelniker (Mr. Straus).

*E*ven though the tragic story of the sinking of the *Titanic* is an old and oft-repeated one, it still makes for tense, exciting, and supremely awesome drama on the screen. In the British-made film, *A Night to Remember,* which opened at the Criterion last night, it is given as fine and convincing an enactment as anyone could wish—or expect.

Based on material assembled in a recent book of the same name by Walter Lord, with certain additions, subtractions, and reinforcements of some dramatic points, it puts the story of the great disaster in simple human terms and yet brings it all into a drama of monumental unity and scope.

Beginning with crisp descriptions of the launching of the great ship and of her festive departure from Southampton on her maiden voyage to America in April, 1912, the picture impressively introduces the predominant member of its cast—the magnificent and majestic vessel, which was considered unsinkable. And then it effectively pinpoints individuals among its passengers and crew who will be conspicuous and significant in the drama.

Before the great ship hits the iceberg that is to send it and the majority of the voyagers to their doom, the screen playwright, Eric Ambler, and the director, Roy Baker, introduce the most immediate and obvious villain in the drama. It is the ship *Californian* and her incredibly obtuse captain. This vessel, lying within sight of the *Titanic* when she hits and founders, is not taken to the stricken liner's aid. The grave stupidity of the *Californian's* captain is made to appear the most agonizing blunder in the whole résumé of mistakes, which has been portrayed in previous films and on television.

For the rest, this remarkable picture is a brilliant and moving account of the behavior of the people on the *Titanic* on that night that should never be forgotten. It is an account of the casualness and flippancy of most of the people right after the great ship has struck (even though an ominous cascade of water is pouring into her bowels); of the slow accumulation of panic that finally mounts to a human holocaust; of shockingly ugly bits of baseness, and of wonderfully brave and noble deeds.

The outstanding performer (only because he is given most to do) is Kenneth More, who plays Officer Lightoller with brisk assurance and stirring vitality. His evidences of competence, compassion, and unfailing bravery are in the best tradition of British seamanship.

Laurence Naismith as the *Titanic's* captain, Frank Lawton as the chairman of the White Star Line who shows the white feather in the crisis, John Merivale as a courageous young father who puts his wife and three small children into a boat, and any number of others make memorable persons in small roles. The natural suspense built into each one magnetizes them. They catch and hold your interest unremittingly.

A Night to Remember conveys this intensely and unforgettably.

—*B.C., December 17, 1958*

A NIGHTMARE ON ELM STREET

Written and directed by Wes Craven; director of photography, Jacques Haitkin; edited by Rick Shaine; music by Charles Bernstein; production designer, Gregg Fonseca; produced by Robert Shaye and Sara Risher; released by New Line Cinema. Running time: 91 minutes.

With: John Saxon (Lieutenant Thompson), Ronee Blakley (Marge Thompson), Heather Langenkamp (Nancy Thompson), Amanda Wyss (Tina Grey), Nick Corri (Rod Lane), Johnny Depp (Glen Lantz) and Robert Englund (Freddie Krueger).

In *A Nightmare on Elm Street,* several teenagers start sharing the same dream in which a long-dead child murderer attempts to carry on his mission from the far side of the grave. That he succeeds for a while should come as no surprise to anyone who keeps up with horror films, especially those in which the mortality rate among sexually active teenagers is always alarmingly high.

John Saxon and Ronee Blakley play—with suitable, furrow-browed seriousness—the parents of the young woman the monster would most love to kill. Her name is Nancy (Heather Langenkamp) and she's pretty and bouncy enough to be a terrific cheerleader. The monster is played by Robert Englund, but what he looks like is anybody's guess, since he wears a lot of masks that are about as scary as those worn by extremely small trick-or-treaters on Halloween.

The film was written and directed by Wes Craven, whose earlier films, *The Last House on the Left* and *The Hills Have Eyes,* specialized in graphically depicted mayhem and gore.

A Nightmare on Elm Street, which opens today at the National and other theaters, puts more emphasis on bizarre special effects, which aren't at all bad.

—*V.C., November 9, 1984*

Directed by Bernardo Bertolucci; written by Franco Arcalli, Bernardo Bertolucci and Giuseppe Bertolucci; director of photography, Vittorio Storaro; edited by Mr. Arcalli; music by Ennio Morricone; art designer, Ezio Frigerio; produced by Alberto Grimaldi; released by United Artists, Twentieth Century Fox and Paramount Pictures. Running time: 245 minutes.

With: Burt Lancaster (Alfredo Berlinghieri/Grandfather), Romolo Valli (Giovanni), Anna-Maria Gherardi (Eleonora), Laura Betti (Regina), Robert De Niro (Alfredo Berlinghieri/Grandson), Dominique Sanda (Ada) and Gérard Depardieu (Olmo Dalco).

Bernardo Bertolucci's *1900* is a four-hour, five-minute (plus intermission) movie that covers approximately seventy years of Italian social and political history, from 1901, the year Verdi died and peasants were still in bondage to the landowners, to the 1970's, when a capitalist movie producer would put up millions of dollars to make a film such as *1900,* which is essentially a Marxist romance. This is progress of a very particular sort.

The film begins beautifully, uproariously, as a realistic, three-generation, the-mansion-and-the-shanties family saga and then slowly congeals into the overblown attitudes of a political pageant, so positive and upbeat it's difficult to believe it comes from a land whose problems are a tiny bit more complex than those of Oz.

Before the family saga becomes a political statement, Mr. Bertolucci (*Last Tango in Paris, The Conformist, Before the Revolution*) presents us with a series of heavy-breathing and, I'm afraid, unintentionally comic sequences that more or less define current fashions of decadence as seen in movies made by European left-wing intellectuals.

Aristocrats, they tell us, are impotent. They loll around, lift fingers only when wrapped around champagne glasses, dance during the daytime, and, when being really wicked, sniff cocaine. The Italian Fascists (one could also read the German Nazis) have more strength, being bourgeois. They torture animals, sodomize little boys, exploit epileptic females, and murder children and widows.

Aristocrats and fascists can be nasty, all right, but the sad fact is that, though in movies like this they are no more believable than the politicized peasants, they are more cinematically decorative.

1900 will be shown twice today at Alice Tully Hall at Lincoln Center. It is scheduled for commercial release in this version (not always happily dubbed into English) later this month or next.

This 245-minute version of *1900* is not to be confused with the five-and-one-half-hour version that was shown at the 1976 Cannes festival, nor with the five-hour, ten-minute version that was later released in Europe, nor with the four-and-one-half-hour version that Mr. Bertolucci once said was as short as the film could possibly be, before giving his full approval to this even shorter version.

At one point or another, each of these versions has been approved by the young Italian director, who is not only talented and ambitious, but also flexible, so much so that when one looks at the film now one brings to it a certain amount of skepticism. How could a film that he once insisted on showing in its five-and-a-half-hour length be cut almost ninety minutes without losing entire sequences? A spokesman for the director insists, however, that nothing of importance has been eliminated.

If this is the case, and I've no reason to doubt the director's representative, it seems to reinforce one's suspicion that as grandly conceived as *1900* was, it has always lacked a guiding vision of real vitality and strength. It's a shapeless mass of film stock containing some brilliant moments and a lot more that are singularly uninspired.

Everything of real interest and epic sweep occurs in the film's first half, which introduces us to members of the land-owning Berlinghieri family, headed by the old patriarch Alfredo, robustly played by Burt Lancaster, and the Dalco family, who farm the Berlinghieri estate and whose patriarch is old Leo, played with a kind of severe passion by Sterling Hayden. The stage for the subsequent events is set when Alfredo and Leo each are presented with a grandson born on the same day, the one to grow up to be a dilletantish Robert De Niro and the other to be a passionate union organizer and Marxist, played by Gérard Depardieu.

The early lives of the two young men, their relationships to their families and to each other, are beautifully and movingly detailed, but as the years overtake them, so do Mr. Bertolucci's political purposes overtake the film.

Even in a film that runs more than four hours, Mr. Bertolucci still hasn't the time to give us more than posterlike sequences relating to the rise of unionism and Mussolini's Fascists. People that once were characters become points of view, a conscious decision on the part of the filmmaker who names his prototypical Fascist, the Berlinghieri estate's foreman, Attila, a role that Donald Sutherland plays in modified Casanova makeup and with such melodramatics he doesn't seem to have heard that Verdi really is dead.

Equally outrageous is Laura Betti as Mr. De Niro's aristocratic cousin who, disappointed in love, throws in her lot with Attila and his blackshirts. The other major role in the film is Dominique Sanda's as Mr. De Niro's highborn French wife, portrayed as an initially hedonistic type who wears clothes magnificently, especially evening dresses and various kinds of fur pieces, but who takes to drink when her husband won't come out firmly against the Fascists.

Mr. Lancaster has some fine moments early in the movie, including a tough, shocking, but eloquent scene in which the old man comes to realize that he can't have his way with a pretty little peasant girl who says to him matter-of-factly, "You can't milk a bull."

Even the boys who play Mr. De Niro and Mr. Depardieu as children are good. Once the film moves into the 1920's, only Mr. Depardieu's character maintains interest and identity. Mr. De Niro behaves as if he were making up his character as he went along, doing busy, Actors' Studiolike things that suggest he is sending up both the character and the film. It's his first bad performance.

The English dubbing doesn't relieve the feeling that the film has been patched together. Although all of the English-speaking actors have dubbed in their own lines, the dialogue often sounds as if it were an English translation of an Italian libretto. And the voices of the non-English actors are awful. Sometimes you suspect that only one man is playing all the peasants, each of whom sounds like a troll at the bottom of a well.

1900 is not an uninteresting failure, but being a failure, it looks arrogant. Mr. Bertolucci took risks as great with *Last Tango*. I realize that because he succeeded there, the quality that now looks like arrogance is basically not much different from the courage he displayed in the earlier film. That's what happens when you fail.

—*V.C., October 8, 1977*

NINOTCHKA

Produced and directed by Ernst Lubitsch: written by Charles Brackett. Billy Wilder and Walter Reisch. based on a story by Melchior Lengyel: cinematographer. William Daniels: edited by Gene Ruggiero: music by Werner R. Heymann: art designers. Cedric Gibbons and Randall Duell: released by Metro-Goldwyn-Mayer. Black and white. Running time: 110 minutes.

With: Greta Garbo (Ninotchka). Melvyn Douglas (Count Leon d'Algout). Ina Claire (Duchess Swana). Sig Rumann (Iranoff). Felix Bressart (Buljanoff). Alexander Granach (Kopalski). Bela Lugosi (Commissar Razinin). Gregory Gaye (Count Rakonin). Rolfe Sedan (Hotel Manager). Edwin Maxwell (Mercier) and Richard Carle (Gaston).

Stalin won't like it. Molotoff may even recall his envoy from Metro-Goldwyn-Mayer. We still will say Garbo's *Ninotchka* is one of the sprightliest comedies of the year, a gay and impertinent and malicious show which never pulls its punch lines (no matter how far below the belt they may land) and finds the screen's austere first lady of drama playing a dead-pan comedy role with the assurance of a Buster Keaton. Nothing quite so astonishing has come to the Music Hall since the Rockefellers landed on Fiftieth Street. And not even the Rockefellers could have imagined M-G-M getting a laugh out of Garbo at the U.S.S.R.'s expense.

Ernst Lubitsch, who directed it, finally has brought the screen around to a humorist's view of those sober-sided folk who have read Marx but never the funny page, who refuse to employ the word "love" to describe an elementary chemico-biological process, who reduce a spring morning to an item in a weather chart, and who never, never drink champagne without reminding its buyer that goat's milk is richer in vitamins. In poking a derisive finger into these sobersides, Mr. Lubitsch hasn't been entirely honest. But, then, what humorist is? He has created, instead, an amusing

panel of caricatures, has read them a jocular script, has expressed—through it all—the philosophy that people are much the same wherever you find them and decent enough at heart. What more could anyone ask?

Certainly we ask for little more, in the way of thoroughly entertaining screen fare, than the tale of his Ninotchka, the flat-heeled, Five-Year-Plannish, unromantically mannish comrade who was sent to Paris by her commissar to take over the duties of a comically floundering three-man mission entrusted with the sale of the former Duchess Swana's court jewels. Paris in the spring being what it is and Melvyn Douglas, as an insidious capitalistic meddler, being what he is, Comrade Ninotchka so far forgot Marx, in Mr. Lubitsch's fable, as to buy a completely frivolous hat, to fall in love, and, after her retreat to Moscow, to march in the May Day parade without caring much whether she was in step or not.

If that seems a dullish way of phrasing it, we can only take refuge in the adventitious Chinese argument that one picture is worth a million words. Mr. Lubitsch's picture is worth at least a few thousand more words than we have room for here. To do justice to it we should have to spend a few hundred describing the arrival of the Soviet delegation in Paris where they debate the merits of the Hotel Terminus (a shoddy place) and the Hotel Clarence where one need push a button once for hot water, twice for a waiter, thrice for a French maid. Would Lenin really have said, as Comrade Kopalski insisted, "Buljanoff, don't be a fool! Go in there and ring three times."

We should need a few hundred more to describe the Paris tour of Ninotchka, under Mr. Douglas's stunned capitalistic guidance; the typically Lubitsch treatment of a stag dinner party, with the camera focused on a door and only the microphone capable of distinguishing between the arrival of a cold meat platter and that of three cigarette girls on the hoof; the Moscow roommate's elaboration of the effect of a laundered Parisian chemise upon the becottoned feminine population of an entirely too-cooperative apartment house.

For these are matters so cinematic, so strictly limited to the screen, that newsprint cannot be expected to do justice to them, any more than it could do full justice to Miss Garbo's delightful debut as a comedienne. It must be monotonous, this superb rightness of Garbo's playing. We almost wish she would handle a scene badly once in a while just to provide us with an opportunity to show we are not a member of a fan club. But she remains infallible and Garbo, always exactly what the situation demands, always as fine as her script and director permit her to be. We did not like her "drunk" scene here, but, in disliking it, we knew it was the writer's fault and Mr. Lubitsch's. They made her carry it too far.

We objected, out of charity, to some of the lines in the script: to that when Ninotchka reports: "The last mass trials were a great success. There are going to be fewer but better Russians"; and to that when the passport official assures the worried traveler she need not fret about the towel situation in Moscow hotels because "we change the towel every week." But that is almost all. The comedy, through Mr. Douglas's debonair performance and those of Ina Claire as the duchess and Sig Rumann, Felix Bressart, and Alexander Granach as the unholy three emissaries; through Mr. Lubitsch's facile direction; and through the cleverly written script of Walter Reisch, Charles Brackett, and Billy Wilder, has come off brilliantly. Stalin, we repeat, won't like it; but, unless your tastes hew too closely to the party line, we think you will, immensely.
—F.S.N., *November 10, 1939*

NOBODY'S FOOL

Written and directed by Robert Benton; based on the novel by Richard Russo; director of photography, John Bailey; edited by John Bloom; music by Howard Shore; production designer, David Gropman; produced by Scott Rudin and Arlene Donovan; released by Paramount Pictures. Running time: 112 minutes.

With: Paul Newman (Sully), Jessica Tandy (Miss Beryl), Bruce Willis (Carl Roebuck), Melanie Griffith (Toby Roebuck), Dylan Walsh (Peter), Pruitt Taylor Vince (Rub Squeers), Gene Saks (Wirf), Josef Sommer (Clive Peoples Jr.), Catherine Dent (Charlotte), Alexander Goodwin (Will) and Elizabeth Wilson (Vera).

You hear Paul Newman before you see him in *Nobody's Fool*, yelling affectionately to Jessica Tandy as his landlady, Miss Beryl. With the raspiness his voice has taken on recently and the irreverence that has always been part of his charm, he shouts: "Still alive in there, old lady? Didn't die in your sleep, did you?" Then he sits in her living room chair to put on his work boots, which isn't easy. He has a bad knee that is getting worse and an occasional off-the-books job working construction for Carl Roebuck (Bruce Willis), who owes him money. He lives alone in the apartment above Miss Beryl's, and at sixty he is running out of time for his life to turn out all right. It says everything about Mr. Newman's performance, the single best of this year and among the finest he has ever given, that you never stop to wonder how a guy as good-looking as Paul Newman ended up this way.

As Donald Sullivan, called Sully by everyone except Miss Beryl, Mr. Newman does look good, even with a limp and muddy work clothes. But he plays Sully from the inside out. Though the character's humor carries traces of earlier Newman heroes, the effect is as natural as if Sully had watched *Butch Cassidy* or *Cool Hand Luke* and decided on a strategy: take life as it comes and face it down with a wisecrack.

Mr. Newman's approach—without cheap sentiment or self-pity—is matched by the film itself, exquisitely directed by Robert Benton and adapted by him from Richard Russo's novel. On screen as in the book, *Nobody's Fool* has the rich texture of a nineteenth-century novel, as if Thackeray's *Vanity Fair* were transported to the blue-collar town of North Bath in upstate New York.

Instead of glamour, Bath has the Iron Horse, the local bar where Sully and his perpetually losing lawyer (Gene Saks) bet on the outcome of *The People's Court* on television. There are tenement houses behind chain-link fences and a banner across Main Street that promotes the town as the future home of the Ultimate Escape Theme Park. Bath is the kind of place people usually try to escape, but *Nobody's Fool* is the nearly plotless story of those who stay. In a series of lifelike small encounters, some comic and some deeply emotional, Sully discovers how many people count on him.

They include his friend and coworker Rub Squeers (Pruitt Taylor Vince), who has far more loyalty than intelligence. There is Miss Beryl, who doesn't have much use for her son, Clive (Josef Sommer), the local banker. "He isn't my son; they switched bassinets at the hospital," she says tartly at Thanksgiving dinner with his business associates. In one of her last performances, Ms. Tandy is perfection, spry without being cute.

Sully flirts with Carl's wife, Toby (Melanie Griffith), who knows her husband is messing around with his secretary but can't seem to kick him out for good. She is a woman whose beauty is almost ready to fade, and her relationship with Sully has the ease and electricity of an attraction bound to go nowhere.

Throughout the film, Sully's past unfolds gracefully, as the pieces fall into his line of vision. An important part of the past literally drives into view while Sully is hitchhiking, and his son, Peter (Dylan Walsh), stops on the road. Peter has just been fired from his job as a college English teacher in West Virginia, and has driven with his wife and two small sons to spend Thanksgiving with Sully's ex-wife, the fastidious Vera (Elizabeth Wilson).

Peter is the one character let down by the screenplay. Every word he says seems to express anger at the way Sully abandoned the family when Peter was a baby. His dialogue goes beyond what an injured son might say, and lands in the area of clumsy exposition, even in a comic scene in which Peter helps his father knock out a Doberman and steal a snowblower.

The theme of redeeming yourself in someone's love works better and with greater subtlety in Sully's scenes with his grandson, Will (Alexander Goodwin). "Want to drive?" Sully asks the boy, putting him on his lap as they drive his old red pickup truck and revealing the easy charm that has made Sully a survivor.

A lesser problem is the feeling that something is slightly off in Sully's relationship with Toby. In fact, the film has cut out the character who balanced her in the novel, a married woman named Ruth with whom Sully has had a long on-and-off affair. Ruth's absence plagues the film like a phantom limb, making Sully more isolated; stranding him without a sex life and perhaps making him more acceptable to mainstream movie audiences.

But these are slight flaws in a film in which almost everything works. John Bailey photographs Bath with brisk, natural clarity. Mr. Willis uses smarminess to good effect, and Mr. Vince and Mr. Saks create two different but equally touching small-town failures.

Nobody's Fool opens on Christmas Day. In its elegiac final scene, Ms. Tandy walks toward her kitchen to make tea, still lively and clearheaded. Sully is asleep in her chair, physically back where he started but emotionally several leaps ahead. If *Nobody's Fool* is often heartbreaking in its sense of loss, it is also hopeful in the strength of its emotions and the sheer beauty of its performances.

—C.J., December 23, 1994

NORMA RAE

Directed by Martin Ritt; written by Irving Ravetch and Harriet Frank Jr.; director of photography, John A. Alonzo; edited by Sidney Levin; music by David Shire; produced by Tamara Assayev and Alex Rose; released by Twentieth Century Fox. Running time: 114 minutes.

With: Sally Field (Norma Rae), Beau Bridges (Sonny), Ron Leibman (Reuben), Pat Hingle (Vernon), Barbara Baxley (Leona), Gail Strickland (Bonnie Mae), Morgan Paull (Wayne Billings) and Robert Broyles (Sam Bolen).

Because so much of today's American labor movement seems to be too big and complicated to be easily understood, too rich to have time for the impoverished, and so powerful that its interests are as vested as those of any industry, stories about the early days of trade unionism have become expressions of a deep-seated, romantic longing. When the issues dividing labor and management can be clearly drawn, there is nothing quite as satisfying as collective effort to fight oppression. Workers are children of nature, born without sin. Bosses are devils. In such times faith can flourish. Salvation is not an abstract concept—it's a three-year contract.

These are sentiments that Martin Ritt, the director, and Irving Ravetch and Harriet Frank Jr. (Mrs. Ravetch), his screenwriters, understand and fervently evoke in their often stirring new film, *Norma Rae*. The movie, which opens today at Loews State 1 and other theaters, also provides Sally Field with the plum role of her career, an opportunity to demonstrate once and for all that she is an actress of dramatic intelligence and force, someone who no longer need be referred to in terms of her television credits.

As Norma Rae, a small-town Southern mill worker, a widow with one legitimate child and another born out of wedlock, a resilient young woman of no great education but a lot of common sense, Miss Field gives a performance that is as firm and funny as the set of her glass jaw—and just as full of risk. It's a role loaded with the kind of sentimental temptations that might sidetrack a lesser performer. Miss Field, though, has found its tough truth and stuck to it. The performance, which gives dimension to the film, may well be the one that those of other actresses are measured against this year.

Norma Rae does not take place in the dim dark past of trade unionism. It is set in today's rural South, where the idea of collective bargaining is considered roughly on a par with membership in a Communist cell. After all—though the movie doesn't stress this— the highly publicized industrial boom in the post-World War II South was largely the result of the cheaper (nonunion) wages that lured manufacturers away from the Northeast and mid-Atlantic states.

Norma Rae is about the efforts of one young New Yorker, a glib, fast-talking Jewish organizer named Reuben Marshasky (Ron Leibman) to bring justice to the tiny town where Norma Rae, her father (Pat Hingle), her mother (Barbara Baxley), her husband-to-be, Sonny (Beau Bridges), and virtually everyone else are dependent upon the cotton mill, the town's only industry.

The film's principal appeal, though, is not the manner in which this uphill struggle is fought and won, but in the way that Mr. Ritt, his writers, and his cast reveal the natural resources of the characters—their grit, their emotional reserves, and their complex feelings for one another. The politics of the film are worthy but they are never as surprising as the people, especially Norma Rae, whose personality is defined in her often comic, sometimes brutal, sometimes touching encounters with ex-husbands, lovers, children, parents, strangers.

The film, which was shot in Alabama, places its characters in a recognizable social context that neither parodies nor patronizes them. In short, swift, effective scenes *Norma Rae* dramatizes the limits imposed on imaginations by both poverty and tradition. Norma Rae's father is as wary of the union as any stockholder. Her mother, on the edge of deafness because of the noise in the weaving room where she works, is apathetic. At the first opportunity Sonny leaves the mill and takes a job in a service station. Without the efforts

of Reuben Marshasky and this one particular woman, life would have gone on as before.

Norma Rae is not without blemish. Mr. Ritt and the Ravetches, who've been collaborating on films since *Hud* and *The Long Hot Summer,* persist in equating the awakened social conscience with literature not always of the highest order. It's an endearing but dopey conceit that I associate first with the work of Clifford Odets. When Norma Rae is having her consciousness raised, it's signaled by the report that she's reading Dylan Thomas—offscreen. The platonic affair between Norma Rae and Reuben, played by Mr. Leibman in the television-breezy manner of his *Kaz* role, is given more time than her rocky, equally interesting relationship with her husband, a role that Mr. Bridges invests with more heft than seems to have been written into the script.

There's also an unintentionally hilarious scene in which we see some local codgers sitting around a general store whittling, but they whittle with a ferocity that seems less down-home than *Saturday Night Live.*

These are small objections. *Norma Rae* is a seriously concerned contemporary drama, illuminated by some very good performances and one, Miss Field's, that is spectacular.

—*V.C., March 2, 1979*

NORTH BY NORTHWEST

Produced and directed by Alfred Hitchcock: written by Ernest Lehman: cinematographer, Robert Burks: edited by George Tomasini: music by Bernard Herrmann: production designer, Robert Boyle: released by Metro-Goldwyn-Mayer. Running time: 136 minutes.

With: Cary Grant (Roger O. Thornhill), Eva Marie Saint (Eve Kendall), James Mason (Phillip Vandamm), Jessie Royce Landis (Clara Thornhill), Leo G. Carroll (Professor), Philip Ober (Lester Townsend) and Josephine Hutchinson (Handsome Woman).

Since he is a peripatetic operative who loves to beat about the bush while beating about the countryside, director Alfred Hitchcock and a covey of willing and able traveling companions have made *North by*

Northwest, which was unveiled at the Music Hall yesterday, a suspenseful and delightful Cook's Tour of some of the more photogenic spots in these United States.

Although they are involved in lightning-fast romance and some loose intrigue, it is all done in brisk, genuinely witty, and sophisticated style. With Mr. Hitchcock at the helm, moving *North by Northwest* is a colorful and exciting route for spies, counterspies, and lovers.

The director and Ernest Lehman, his scenarist, are not, to put a fine point on it, really serious about their mystery. With a tongue-in-cheek attitude and a breezy sense of humor, they are off in high gear right at the beginning as they spin the somewhat improbable yarn of a successful, handsome Madison Avenue executive, who is mistaken for a Federal intelligence man by foreign agents and forcibly pushed into a succession of macabre situations that shock, amaze, perplex, and anger our once-debonair hero.

Mr. Hitchcock, who, as has been noted, knows that travel is both fun and broadening, quickly shifts his cast from such locales as the Oak Room of the Plaza Hotel and the modernistic interiors of the United Nations Headquarters, to the fancy confines of the Twentieth Century Limited, to the posh Ambassador East Hotel in Chicago, to a vast, flat Midwest cornfield, and finally to the giant faces of the presidents sculptured on Mount Rushmore high above Rapid City, South Dakota.

The complications are introduced with about the same rapidity as the ever-changing scenery. Our beleaguered hero, it appears, is being harried by the villains who want to dispatch him because he seems to be on to their skulduggery. It is, of course, merely a case of mistaken identity, an illusion the Federal boys are desperate to maintain.

In any event, Mr. Hitchcock, et al., take time out now and again to stop strewing red herrings and inject a funny scene here and there, such as one involving our drunken hero in a local hoosegow, or to point up the quickly burgeoning romance between him and the blonde Mata Hari who apparently is aiding the dastards chasing him. Their interlude, to the sounds of slick, romantic dialogue, in a train drawing room, for example, is guaranteed to send viewers' temperatures soaring. The lines and the expert manipulation of the

principals are tributes to the outstanding talents of Messrs. Lehman and Hitchcock.

Cary Grant, a veteran member of the Hitchcock acting varsity, was never more at home than in this role of the advertising-man-on-the-lam. He handles the grimaces, the surprised look, the quick smile, the aforementioned spooning, and all the derring-do with professional aplomb and grace. In casting Eva Marie Saint as his romantic vis-à-vis, Mr. Hitchcock has plumbed some talents not shown by the actress heretofore. Although she is seemingly a hard, designing type, she also emerges both the sweet heroine and a glamorous charmer.

Jessie Royce Landis contributes a few genuinely humorous scenes as Mr. Grant's slightly addle-pated mother. James Mason is properly sinister as the leader of the spy ring, as are Martin Landau, Adam Williams, Robert Ellenstein, and Josephine Hutchinson, as members of his malevolent troupe. And Leo G. Carroll is satisfyingly bland and calm as the studious intelligence chief.

Perhaps they and Messrs. Hitchcock and Lehman are kidding, after all. Their climax is a bit overdrawn and there are a few vague spots along the way. But they do lead us on the year's most scenic, intriguing, and merriest chase.

—*A.W., August 7, 1959*

NOTHING BUT THE BEST

Directed by Clive Donner; written by Frederic Raphael, based on the short story "The Best of Everything" by Stanley Ellin; cinematographer, Nicolas Roeg; edited by Fergus McDonell; music by Ron Grainer; art designer, Reece Pemberton; produced by David Deutsch; released by Royal Films. Running time: 99 minutes.

With: Alan Bates (Jimmy Brewster), Denholm Elliott (Charlie Prince), Harry Andrews (Mr. Horton), Millicent Martin (Ann Horton), Pauline Delany (Mrs. March) and Godfrey Quigley (Coates).

The contents of *Nothing but the Best,* a barbed bundle from Britain that opened at Cinema I yesterday, may not be entirely new but they sparkle with gags, wit, and an educated, gratifying irreverence for status and sex.

The uninhibited troupe responsible for these terribly British gibes are fully aware of *Room at the Top* and the fact that they are not the first to kid the Establishment. Nevertheless, they have fashioned a carefree, cocky comedy blithely seasoned with murder that is both biting and debonair and, above all, entertaining.

Clive Donner, the director known here for his sensitive stint on *The Caretaker,* and a fine cast headed by Alan Bates, who was featured in *The Caretaker,* waste little time in exposing cracks in the caste system. As the color cameras focus on the fashionable London offices of Horton House, the hero, his eye cocked upward, is at the foot of the ladder in the real-estate business and society. "There's only room for one at the top," he cannily observes, and adds, this is "a filthy, stinking world but there are some smashing things in it."

Among the "smashing" stepping stones are the pert telephone lassie he can use on his way up or to the boudoir; his man-hungry landlady; his rough-and-ready or upper-crust clients; the boss's fathead of a would-be titled son-in-law; and, finally, the pretty daughter of the boss and a wise operator in her own posh field.

Since he is too shrewd to ignore the fact that his rough edges will not pass Mayfair's tests, he latches on—with the aid of the longest arm of coincidence you ever saw—to a playboy down on his luck, who proceeds to smooth those edges for a price. When that price becomes a mite too steep he blandly dispatches his mentor with the old school tie, no less, and then proceeds to marry the boss's daughter.

There are enough complications for several plots that are best left undivulged, but suffice it to say that the top of the ladder is always shaky and frightening. However, Mr. Donner and company, it might be noted, apparently never heard of the "crime must be punished" dictum so dear to our moviemakers. A viewer is left with a curiously titillating feeling that, for once, a charming conniver may get away with it.

As the conniver, Alan Bates is a delight. Benign, quizzical, restrained, and wryly humorous, he is hardly villainy incarnate. Instead, he projects a picture of winning boyish endeavor in a rough milieu that is captivating simply because the tongue in his cheek is so

obvious. Denholm Elliott, as the outcast who is his ill-fated mentor in the social graces, is haughtily impervious to his fall from grace and makes an equally charming scoundrel.

As the boss's daughter, Millicent Martin, who is comparatively new to American audiences (she is in the British *That Was the Week That Was* TV series) is auburn-haired, pretty, petite, and as designing as the climber she sets her cap for. Like the other principals, she is coolly proficient in delivering the clipped, arrogant, but funny dialogue of the upper classes with natural hauteur. Harry Andrews is properly bluff and patrician as her father, who heads Horton House. Pauline Delany adds a sharply etched portrait of the overly sexed landlady, and a variety of supporting players chip in with casual but polished bits that give color and giggles to the briskly-paced proceedings.

A word must be said for a hunt ball scene that is a sardonic illustration of the supercharged change in these once-stuffy affairs. This one is filled with twisting couples and wisps of unrelated conversation that are both effervescent and delightful. The same might be attributed to Ron Grainger's musical score, which is both tuneful and makes a droll commentary on the action.

Nothing but the Best may not be the best in its genre but it certainly proves that Britain's younger moviemakers can rib themselves and their times in extremely diverting style. They should have little trouble finding room at the top.

—*A.W., July 14, 1964*

NOTORIOUS

Produced and directed by Alfred Hitchcock; written by Ben Hecht; cinematographer, Ted Tetzlaff; edited by Theron Warth; music by Roy Webb; art designers, Albert S. D'Agostino and Carroll Clark; released by RKO Radio Pictures. Black and white. Running time: 101 minutes.

With: Cary Grant (Devlin), Ingrid Bergman (Alicia Huberman), Claude Rains (Alexander Sebastian), Louis Calhern (Paul Prescott), Madame Konstantin (Mrs. Sebastian), Reinhold Schünzel (Dr. Anderson), Moroni Olsen (Walter Beardsley), Ivan

Triesault (Eric Mathis), Alex Minotis (Joseph), Wally Brown (Mr. Hopkins) and Sir Charles Mendl (Commodore).

It is obvious that Alfred Hitchcock, Ben Hecht, and Ingrid Bergman form a team of motion-picture makers that should be publicly and heavily endowed. For they were the ones most responsible for *Spellbound,* as director, writer, and star, and now they have teamed together on another taut, superior film. It goes by the name of *Notorious* and it opened yesterday at the Music Hall. With Cary Grant as an additional asset, it is one of the most absorbing pictures of the year.

For Mr. Hecht has written and Mr. Hitchcock has directed in brilliant style a romantic melodrama which is just about as thrilling as they come—velvet smooth in dramatic action, sharp and sure in its characters, and heavily charged with the intensity of warm emotional appeal. As a matter of fact, the distinction of *Notorious* as a film is the remarkable blend of love story with expert "thriller" that it represents.

Actually, the "thriller" elements are familiar and commonplace, except in so far as Mr. Hitchcock has galvanized them into life. They comprise the routine ingredients of a South American Nazi-exile gang, an American girl set to spy upon it, and a behind-the-scenes American intelligence man. And the crux of the melodramatic action is the peril of the girl when the nature of her assignment is discovered by one of the Nazis whom she has wed.

But the rare quality of the picture is in the uncommon character of the girl and in the drama of her relations with the American intelligence man. For here Mr. Hecht and Mr. Hitchcock have done a forthright and daring thing: they have made the girl, played by Miss Bergman, a lady of notably loose morals. She is the logically cynical daughter of a convicted American traitor when she is pressed into this job of high-echelon spying by the confident espionage man. The complication is that she and the latter fall passionately and genuinely in love before the demands of her assignment upon her seductive charms are revealed. And thus the unpleasant suspicions and the lacerated feelings of the two as they deal with this dangerous major problem form the emotional drama of the film.

Obviously, that situation might seem slightly old-fashioned, too. But Mr. Hecht and Mr. Hitchcock have here treated it with sophistication and irony.

There is nothing unreal or puritanical in their exposure of a frank, grown-up amour. And Miss Bergman and Mr. Grant have played it with surprising and disturbing clarity. We do not recall a more conspicuous—yet emotionally delicate—love scene on the screen than one stretch of billing and cooing that the principals play in this film. Yet, withal, there is rich and real emotion expressed by Miss Bergman in her role, and the integrity of her nature as she portrays it is the prop that holds the show.

Mr. Grant, who is exceptionally solid, is matched for acting honors in the cast by Claude Rains as the Nazi big-wig to whom Miss Bergman becomes attached. Mr. Rains's shrewd and tense performance of this invidious character is responsible for much of the anguish that the situation creates. Reinhold Schünzel and Ivan Triesault are good, too, as Nazi worms, and a splendid touch of chilling arrogance as a German mother is added by Madame Konstantin. Louis Calhern and Moroni Olsen are fine in minor American roles.

Check up another smash hit for a fine and experienced team.

—B.C., August 16, 1946

NOW, VOYAGER

Directed by Irving Rapper; written by Casey Robinson, based on the novel by Olive Higgins Pouty; cinematography by Sol Polito; edited by Warren Low; art director, Robert M. Haas; music by Max Steiner; produced by Hal B. Wallis; released by Warner Brothers. Black and white. Running time: 117 minutes.

With: Bette Davis (Charlotte Vale), Paul Henreid (Jerry Durrance), Claude Rains (Dr. Jaquith), Gladys Cooper (Mrs. Henry Windle Vale), Bonita Granville (June Vale), John Loder (Elliot Livingston), Ilka Chase (Lisa Vale), Lee Patrick (Deb McIntyre), Franklin Pangborn (Mr. Thompson), Katharine Alexander (Miss Trask), James Rennie (Frank McIntyre) and Mary Wickes (Nurse Dora Pickford).

Although it carries a professional bedside manner, *Now, Voyager,* Bette Davis's latest tribulation at the Hollywood, contains not a little quackery. For two hours of heartache and repeated renunciation, Miss Davis lays bare the morbidities of a repressed ugly duckling who finally finds herself as a complete woman. From the original novel, Casey Robinson has created a deliberate and workmanlike script which more than once reaches into troubled emotions. Director Irving Rapper has screened it with frequent effectiveness. But *Now, Voyager,* either because of the Hays office or its own spurious logic, endlessly complicates an essentially simple theme. For all its emotional hair-splitting, it fails to resolve its problems as truthfully as it pretends. In fact, a little more truth would have made the film a good deal shorter.

In a personal study of the sort which Miss Davis has accepted as her forte, the film tells the story of an unattractive, hysterical girl enslaved by maternal tyranny and how through the ministrations of a psychiatrist, and even more through an abortive love affair on a southward cruise, she finally emerges from the dark chrysalis of her neurosis into the light of day. But the man whose love restores her is himself unhappily married to a woman he dares not hurt, and his own child has been victimized by the insecurity of an unsettled home. After several renunciations, Miss Davis and Paul Henried, as the married lover, form a curious partnership to aid the child. Violently in love with each other, they enter a platonic relationship in which Miss Davis keeps the child and Mr. Henried keeps his unwanted wife.

It is in these endless renunciations that the story moves from a direct and common-sense dramatic treatment into a prudish fantasy. Chained to a personal unhappiness, the lover's refusal to consummate his love for Miss Davis itself becomes a suspicious symptom. His nobility is phony—in his self-enforced martyrdom he is no less neurotic than the woman he has helped to bring to life. And certainly the final solution is more explosive than the original problem. Two people continually resisting their affection for one another while raising a child in partnership opens whole vistas of new neuroses.

Miss Davis plays the young woman, high-lighting her progress, to emotional maturity with the decision and accuracy of an assured actress. Claude Rains offers a polished and even-tempered performance as the psychiatrist. But Gladys Cooper's tyrannical downger is arbitrarily written and acted, and Paul

Henried never brings into focus the ambiguously conceived character of the lovelorn husband. Although *Now, Voyager* starts out bravely, it ends exactly where it started—and after two lachrymose hours.

—T.S., October 23, 1942

LA NUIT DE VARENNES

Directed by Ettore Scola: written (in French, with English subtitles) by Sergio Amidei and Mr. Scola: director of photography, Armando Nannuzzi: edited by Raimondo Crociani: music by Armando Trovajoli: produced by Renzo Rossellini: released by Triumph Films. Running time: 133 minutes.

With: Marcello Mastroianni (Casanova), Jean-Louis Barrault (Nicholas Edme Restif de la Bretonne), Hanna Schygulla (Countess Sophie de la Borde), Harvey Keitel (Thomas Paine), Jean-Claude Brialy (Monsieur Jacob), Daniel Gélin (De Wendel) and Andréa Ferréol (Madame Adelaide Gagnon).

The great historical pageant that is Ettore Scola's *La Nuit de Varennes* unfolds with supreme ease. It begins with a series of casual coincidences and weaves them brilliantly into a vision of one of the most important moments in French history, a vision not the least bit limited by the specifics of its place and time.

The time is the French Revolution, and the occasion is the flight of the royal family from Paris to the small town of Varennes, where they will be captured and sent back to their deaths. But the feeling is utterly modern, or perhaps it's timeless. The key issues of the film are the issues of any era. And the humor and generosity with which Mr. Scola presents them are correspondingly enduring.

La Nuit de Varennes, which opens today at the Lincoln Plaza 3, begins as an Italian theatrical troupe offers re-enactments of Revolutionary scenes to the people of Paris, two years after the fact. It quickly shifts, with a rhythm and reason that are all its own, to the night of the King's flight as it introduces Nicholas Edme Restif de la Bretonne (Jean-Louis Barrault), the writer who documented many of the events of the Revolution, and one of a number of historical personages who will follow in Louis XVI's wake.

During a scene in a bordello, sketched by Mr. Scola

with an earthy humor that figures throughout the film, Restif learns from a maid at the Royal Palace that the King may be attempting to escape from Paris. He follows along and soon becomes part of a group of travelers that includes one of the Queen's ladies-in-waiting (Hanna Schygulla), the wealthy industrialist De Wendel (*Daniel Gélin*), an Italian opera singer (Laura Betti), a wealthy widow (Andréa Ferréol), a prissy hairdresser (Jean-Claude Brialy), and others. Also eventually in the group, last but hardly least, are Casanova (Marcello Mastroianni) and Thomas Paine (Harvey Keitel).

All sides of the day's issues are represented within this entourage, with the foremost ideological rift between the progressive Restif and Casanova, now an elderly gentleman who declares: "I miss the sweeter times of yore, when all was harmony and light." However, *La Nuit de Varennes* is not a film about conflict, and it has no villains. It approaches the forces at work in the revolution evenhandedly—with compassion for the peasants whose uprising is about to begin, and also with regret about the violent change that is on its way. Mr. Scola sees change as something that is forever necessary and forever incomplete, which means that only one or two characters in the film regard the imminent revolution with any overriding idealism. Idealism in this film is very much a young man's attitude, and most of the characters are old enough to have a broader, more tolerant worldview.

The historical characters speak in the voices that might be expected of them (Casanova "On his throne or not, no king ever made me miss a meal"), but they're never in any danger of becoming puppets. The screenplay, by Mr. Scola and the late Sergio Amidei, never overstates the historical importance of any one event or individual. And so it accomplishes the small miracle of letting these figures exist, in equal measure, as characters within this story and as archetypes or legends. The small talk here is never small (the industrialist, telling a fellow voyager about the day he saw a worker fold his arms and refuse to do his job, calls this "the most terrifying sight I ever saw"). But it is wonderfully casual at some times, quietly resonant at others, and always exquisitely delivered. If *La Nuit de Varennes* offered nothing more than the ensemble acting on display, it would be major and memorable on that basis alone.

Of all the fine performances here, Mr. Mastroianni's is the most dazzling, because he plays the vainest of men without bringing any of his own vanity to the role. This Casanova is on his last legs, rueful about the ways in which his body now disappoints him and yet forever interrupting conversations to powder his nose. He's also a wonderfully gallant figure, and never one of whom the film makes fun; the friendship that develops between Casanova and Restif is one of the most moving things here. Miss Schygulla, whose lady-in-waiting is filled with serene faith in the crumbling order, brings an astonishing composure to her performance, and in her last scene Mr. Scola uses that quality stunningly. Mr. Keitel, Mr. Barrault, and the rest of a cast that also includes Jean-Louis Trintignant are superb too. Mr. Trintignant plays the timid deputy mayor of Varennes who keeps the royal family in his home, worrying about his hospitality even as he agrees to have them sent back to Paris.

Mr. Scola's direction of *La Nuit de Varennes* isn't overly elegant or schematic, and the film is all the fresher for that. His style is flexible without the slightest trace of gimmickry. When he sees the need for an odd lighting effect or a historical footnote, he simply tosses these things into a narrative that is otherwise simple, beautiful, and straightforward. So Casanova can interrupt the story to tell us, while wearing a wool bonnet and sipping soup or tea, why he wasn't very well known at the time the action takes place (his fame, he confides, came with the memoir "published after my death, which, as you all know, occurred in 1798"). And the key figure of Restif can, at the end of the film, stride out of the past and into the present—which, as a representative of a work that both encapsulates and transcends history, is most assuredly where he belongs.

—*J.M., February 16, 1983*

THE NUN'S STORY

Directed by Fred Zinnemann; written by Robert Anderson, based on a book by Kathryn C. Hulme; cinematographer, Franz Planer; edited by Walter Thomson; music by Franz Waxman; art designer, Alexander Trauner; produced by Henry Blanke; released by Warner Brothers. Running time: 149 minutes.

With: Audrey Hepburn (Sister Luke/Gabrielle Van Der Mal). Peter Finch (Dr. Fortunati). Edith Evans (Mother Emmanuel). Peggy Ashcroft (Mother Mathilde). Dean Jagger (Dr.Van Der Mal). Mildred Dunnock (Sister Margharita). Beatrice Straight (Mother Christophe) and Patricia Collinge (Sister William).

From Kathryn Hulme's novel *The Nun's Story,* which gives an amazing account of a young Belgian woman's experiences in becoming and being a nursing nun, screenwriter Robert Anderson and director Fred Zinnemann have derived an equally amazing motion picture of an extraordinary dedicated life. It, too, is called *The Nun's Story,* it has Audrey Hepburn in the leading role, it is in exquisite color, and it opened yesterday at the Music Hall.

To characterize this handsome picture as a conventional drama or romance or perhaps as an odd adventure story is a perilous thing to do, for it doesn't fit any category in an easy and obvious way. For at least the first hour of its more than two hours—two hours and twenty-nine minutes, to be exact—it is in the nature of a documentary picture of how a young woman becomes a nun.

Quietly, beautifully, and sensitively, it images and describes the entrance of the heroine into a nunnery and the stages by which she comes to her final vows. Through the mouth of a mother superior, whom Edith Evans powerfully plays, it articulates the philosophy and spiritual stress in the formation of a nun—the purposes of the rules of silence, obedience, poverty, and chastity, and the point of the most difficult surrender of liberty, memories, and will.

And then, through the radiant-eyed Miss Hepburn, it firmly details and reveals the effects of this rigorous education on one sensitive young body and soul. This account is substantial preparation for the drama of practical testing that ensues.

For the subsequent narrative of this picture, which literally and vividly conveys the young nun as a nurse to the Belgian Congo and puts her through harsh experiences there, expands into a scorching exposition of a deeply personal and private tug-of-war between a wish to respect the ingrained discipline and a spirit to rebel in the young nun.

The throb of fecund life in the Congo, the pressure of her daily routines, and constant incisive criticism of her religious practices from an attractive and agnostical medical man combine to disturb and upset her. A couple of violent incidents shock her mind. And a slight case of tuberculosis obviously strains her holy ties. When she is ultimately sent back to Belgium and is denied the right to avenge her slain father by serving as a nurse with the Belgian underground in World War II, she finds herself unable to endure the discipline of her order and is granted her wish to be released.

In a brilliant synthesis of idea and pictorial imagery, which includes stunning contrasts of color, the tempo of action, and moods, Mr. Zinnemann has made this offbeat drama describe a parabola of spiritual afflatus and deflation that ends in a strange sort of defeat. For the evident point of this experience is that a woman gains but also loses her soul, spends and exhausts her devotion to an ideal she finds she cannot hold.

In the role of the nun, Miss Hepburn is fluent and luminous. From her eyes and her eloquent expressions emerge a character that is warm and involved. Miss Evans, Patricia Collinge, Peggy Ashcroft, Mildred Dunnock, Beatrice Straight, and several more are variously fine as other sisters (or mothers superior), and Peter Finch gives a strong, taut performance as the tropical physician. Dean Jagger is tender and affecting as the father of the young nun.

A major musical score by Franz Waxman completes the artistry of this thoroughly tasteful film.

—B.C., June 19, 1959

ODD MAN OUT

Produced and directed by Carol Reed: written by F. L. Green and Robert C. Sherriff, based on the novel by Mr. Green: cinematographer, Robert Krasker: edited by Fergus McDonell: music by William Alwyn: production designer, Roger Furse: released by Universal International Pictures. Black and white. Running time: 116 minutes.

With: James Mason (Johnny O'Queen), Kathleen Ryan (Kathleen), Robert Newton (Lukey), Robert Beatty (Dennis), Cyril Cusack (Pat), Roy Irving (Murphy) and Dan O'Herlihy (Nolan).

The creative combination of James Mason, popular British star, and Carol Reed, the brilliant director of such films as *Night Train* and *The Stars Look Down,* is sure to attract wide attention to the new British picture, *Odd Man Out,* which had its American premiere at Loew's Criterion yesterday. And the further fact that it is fashioned from a novel by F. L. Green which is current catnip for thriller readers will not hurt the film's draw one bit—all of which is peculiarly propitious, for *Odd Man Out* is a picture to see, to absorb in the darkness of the theater and then go home and talk about.

Especially is it rewarding in its first two-thirds or so, when the galvanic talents of its director are most excitingly demonstrated on the screen. For in this part of the picture, the story and Mr. Reed are concerned almost exclusively with a matter that gives his camera its most auspicious range. This is the desperate endeavor of a wounded man to escape the police in the night-shrouded alleys of an Irish city after committing a murder for a political cause.

Being a graduate master of the cinematic "chase," Mr. Reed has constructed this grim coursing like nothing he has ever done before. From the moment he joins with his protagonist in the upstairs room of a Belfast slum, plotting a factory robbery in order to raise funds for a rebel "cause," he has colored and paced this terrible manhunt with the precision of a thundering symphony. The taut stickup of the bookkeepers, the uncalculated shooting of one, the critical wounding of the chieftain, his fall from the getaway car, and then his first panicky flight to cover in an air-raid shelter are swiftly and throat-catchingly achieved. Follows, then, the fugato passages as the partisans of the missing chief attempt to make perilous contact with him and he stumbles forth from his hiding place under cover of night.

All of this part of the picture—the horrible groping in the murk and the rain, the harrowing contacts with terrified people, the desperation of brushes with the police—is terrifically tense and dramatic on a purely visual-emotional plane, and Mr. Reed can be glowingly commended for his artistry in movement and mood. This part of his picture bears most favorable comparison with that classic film, *The Informer,* which John Ford directed several years ago.

But the latter phases of the picture, while peculiarly challenging to thought, lose the compactness and impetus of this prime and precise portion. For here the focus is expanded and the protagonist is shelved for long spells while the author and, perforce, the director go searching for a philosophy of life. In the backwaters of the city and in the ways of a span of characters, they seek for some vague illumination of the meanings of charity and faith. Through a priest, a mad portrait painter, a crafty derelict, and, especially, the girl who loves and believes in the murderer, they endeavor to throw some light. But Mr. Green and R. C. Sherriff have fumbled this portion of the script, and whatever it is they are proving—if anything—is anybody's guess.

Also, in switching attention from the manhunt to these cryptic characters, they have rudely relieved the protagonist of the illustrative role. As the fugitive, Mr. Mason gives a terrifying picture of a wounded man, disheveled, agonized, and nauseated, straining valiantly and blindly to escape. But the oblique dramatic construction, as the picture draws toward the end, neglects the responsibility of dramatizing the movements of his mind. Clarification of the moral— or the sympathy—is not achieved by him.

Nor is it achieved by the others, no matter how finely they represent peculiar and picturesque people. Kathleen Ryan is beautiful as the girl, cool, statuesque, and stoical, but it is difficult to fathom her thoughts. W. G. Fay, the great Abbey Theatre veteran, is deeply affecting as the priest and F. J. McCormick apes his famous "Joxer" Daly (of *Juno and the Paycock*) as the sniveling derelict. Allowance must be made for specious writing in the performance which Robert Newton gives as the wild-eyed and drunken painter. But Denis O'Dea is sobering as a constable and Robert Beatty, Kitty Kerwin, and many others are as richly and roundly Irish as Patty's pig.

Granting its terminal confusions, *Odd Man Out* is still a most intriguing film. And, even if you can't perceive its wherefores, you should find it a real experience.

—*B.C., April 24, 1947*

OF MICE AND MEN

Produced and directed by Lewis Milestone: written by Eugene Solow. based on the novel by John Steinbeck: cinematographer. Norbert Brodine: edited by Bert Jordan: music by Aaron Copland: art designer. Nicolai Remisoff: released by United Artists. Black and white. Running time: 107 minutes.

With: Burgess Meredith (George). Betty Field (Mae). Lon Chaney Jr. (Lennie). Charles Bickford (Slim). Roman Bohnen (Candy). Bob Steele (Curley). Noah Beery Jr. (Whit). Oscar O'Shea (Jackson). Granville Bates (Carlson) and Leigh Whipper (Crooks).

His biographers report that John Steinbeck's pet aversions are Hollywood and New York. Happily the feeling is not reciprocated. Hollywood, which brought his *Grapes of Wrath* so magnificently to the screen, has been no less reverent toward the strangely dramatic and compassionate tale that Steinbeck called *Of Mice and Men*. And New York, unless we have miscalculated again, will endorse its film version, at the Roxy, as heartily as it has endorsed the film of the Joads. The pictures have little in common as narrative, but they have much in common as art: the same deft handling of their material, the same understanding of people, the same ability to focus interest sharply and reward it with honest craftsmanship and skill.

Of Mice and Men is news no longer. It has the familiarity of a widely sold novelette, of a successful play that won the New York Drama Critics Circle award as the best American contribution to the 1937–38 season. It would be idle, we think, to say that it has found new meaning, new depth, new significance as a film. Nor should such added value be required. Lewis Milestone, who directed it; Eugene Solow, who adapted it; and Burgess Meredith, Lon Chaney Jr., Betty Field and the others who have performed it, have done more than well in simply realizing the drama's established values. *Of Mice and Men* need not have been better as a play than it was as a novelette; it need not be better as a picture, so long as it is just as good.

Book and play have been followed as literally as the screen demands and the Hays office permits. There is a short prologue; the camera enlarges the play's vista to include the fields where the barley-buckers worked, the messroom, the town café where the hands might spend their wages; but nothing has been added that does not belong, nothing has been removed that was important to the proper telling of the story. If we must be reduced to comparisons we should say the film has been better cast in almost every role: young Mr. Chaney does not quite erase the memory of Broderick Crawford's Lennie, but Mr. Meredith's George is an improvement on the flat, recitative interpretation by the play's Wallace Ford, and Miss Field is superb (an abused but useful word) as Mae.

Mr. Steinbeck wrote, as you probably are aware, the pathetic, fate-ridden drama of two bindle stiffs who dreamed, and kindled other men's dreams, of owning their own little ranch and living off "the fatta the lan'." George used to talk about it to Lennie, and Lennie, whose mind wasn't clear "on accounta he'd been kicked in the head by a horse," used to crow with delight at the notion of having to tend the rabbits and be permitted to stroke their soft fur. Lennie liked the feel of smooth things, but he was so strong his touch killed them—a bird, a mouse, a white-and-brown puppy, and finally Mae, the foreman's wife, who had silky hair. So the posse went out to hunt him down, and George knew he had to find Lennie first to tell him again about the time they'd have their own little place—and to hold a gun to the back of his happily nodding head.

In summary this has a cruel, bizarre, ridiculous sound. But it doesn't seem that way on the screen. Tragedy dignifies people, even such little people as Lennie, George, Candy, and Mae. Mr. Steinbeck and his adapters have seen the end all too clearly, the end of George's dream and Lennie's life. With sound dramatic instinct they have not sought to hasten the inevitable, or stave it off. Doom takes its course and bides its moment; there is hysteria in waiting for the crisis to come. And during the waiting there is the rewarding opportunity to meet some of Steinbeck's interesting people, to listen to them talk, to be amused or moved by the things they say and do. For here again, as in *Grapes of Wrath,* we have the feeling of seeing another third, or thirtieth, of the nation, not merely a troupe of play-actors living in a world of make-believe.

No small share of that credit belongs to the men and the one young woman Hal Roach has recruited for his production. Miss Field has added stature to the role of the foreman's wife by relieving her of the play's box-office-conscious order that she behave like a hoyden. Mae, in the film, is entitled to some respect—and never more so than in the splendid scene she has with Lennie when they share a cross-purposed soliloquy. Bob Steele's Curley, Leigh Whipper's Crooks (the only

carry-over from the play), Roman Bohnen's Candy, Charles Bickford's Slim, and the others have been scarcely less valuable in their several ways. We noted but one flaw in Mr. Milestone's direction: his refusal to hush the off-screen musicians when Candy's old dog was being taken outside to be shot. A metronome, anything, would have been better than modified "Hearts and Flowers." And that's the only fault we can find with Mr. Steinbeck's second Hollywood-to-New York contribution.

—*F.S.N., February 17, 1940*

OKLAHOMA!

Directed by Fred Zinnemann; written by Sonya Levien and William Ludwig, based on the musical by Richard Rodgers and Oscar Hammerstein 2d, from the play *Green Grow the Lilacs* by Lynn Riggs; cinematographer, Robert Surtees; edited by Gene Ruggiero; music by Mr. Rodgers; choreography by Agnes De Mille; production designer, Oliver Smith; produced by Arthur Hornblow Jr.; released by Magna Films. Running time, 145 minutes.

With: Gordon MacRae (Curly), Gloria Grahame (Ado Annie), Gene Nelson (Will Parker), Charlotte Greenwood (Aunt Eller), Shirley Jones (Laurey), Eddie Albert (Ali Hakim), James Whitmore (Carnes), Rod Steiger (Jud Fry) and Barbara Lawrence (Gertie).

At long last, *Oklahoma!,* the great Richard Rodgers-Oscar Hammerstein 2d musical show, which ran for more than five years on Broadway, has been brought to the motion picture screen in a production that magnifies and strengthens all the charm that it had upon the stage.

Photographed and projected in the new process known as Todd-AO, which reflects the images in color from a wide and deep Cinerama-like screen, the ever-popular operetta was presented before an invited audience at the Rivoli last night. It will be shown at two more invitation "premieres" tonight and tomorrow night. Then it begins its two-a-day public showings on Thursday at the Rivoli.

Inevitably, the question which leaps to every mind

is whether the essential magnificence and gusto of the original has been retained in the sometimes fatal operation of transfer to the screen. And then the question follows whether the mechanics of Todd-AO, which is being inaugurated with this picture, are appropriate to articulate this show.

To the first question, there is only one answer: under the direction of Fred Zinnemann—and, we might add, under the hawkeyed observation of Messrs. Rodgers and Hammerstein—a full-bodied *Oklahoma!* has been brought forth in this film to match in vitality, eloquence, and melody any musical this reviewer has ever seen.

With his wide-angle cameras catching backgrounds of gen-u-wine cornfields and open plains, red barns, yellow farmhouses, and the blue sky full of fleecy clouds, Mr. Zinnemann has brought into the foreground all the warm, lively characters that swarm through this tale of the Oklahoma Territory and sing and dance its songs. By virtue of the sweeping motion picture, he has obtained a fresh, open-air atmosphere to embrace the same rollicking romance that tumbled upon the stage. And because he had the fine assistance of choreographer Agnes De Mille, he has made the dances and ballet of the original into eloquent movements that flow beneath the sky.

In Gordon MacRae he has a Curly, the cowboy hero of the tale, who is wonderfully relaxed and unaffected (to this reviewer's delighted surprise). And in Shirley Jones, a strawberry-blonde newcomer, he has a Laurey, the girl Curly courts, so full of beauty, sweetness, and spirit that a better Laurey cannot be dreamed. Both have excellent voices for the grand and familiar Rodgers' tunes. They are best, as one might hope and reckon, in the lyrical "People Will Say We're in Love."

Charlotte Greenwood's rangy Aunt Eller is an unmitigated joy. She has added a rare quality of real compassion to the robust rusticity of the role. And Gene Nelson's lanky Will Parker is a deliciously light-footed, dim-witted beau to the squeaky and occasionally pretentious Ado Annie of Gloria Grahame.

Rod Steiger's Jud Fry is less degenerate and a little more human and pitiful than he is usually made, while Eddie Albert's Ali Hakim is the least impressive figure in the film. Both characters have been abbreviated, and a song of each has been dropped.

As for the "Out of My Dreams" ballet, with James Mitchell and Bambi Linn dancing the roles of Curly and Laurey, it is an exquisitely fluid and colorful thing, expansive and imagistic. The dancing boys and girls are as lithe as reeds. In colorful costumes and hairdos, they are pumpkin-seed-country come to town!

To the question of whether the dimensions and the mechanism of Todd-AO are appropriate to the material, one can only say that the generous expanse of screen is fetching, but the system has disconcerting flaws. The distortions of the images are striking when the picture is viewed from the seats on the sides of the Rivoli's orchestra or the sides and rear of its balcony. Even from central locations, the concave shape of the screen causes it to appear to be arched upward or downward, according to whether one views it from the orchestra or the balcony.

While a fine sense of depth is imparted with some of the outdoor scenes—notably one looking down the rows of a cornfield and in a thrilling sequence of a horse-and-wagon runaway—the third-dimensional effect is not insistent. The color in the present film is variable. Some highly annoying scratches are conspicuous in many otherwise absorbing scenes.

However, the flaws in mechanism do not begin to outweigh a superlative screen entertainment, which is endowed with excellent sound and runs for two hours and twenty-five minutes, with a ten-minute pause for air.

—B.C., October 11, 1955

OLIVER TWIST

Directed by David Lean; written by Mr. Lean and Stanley Haynes, based on the novel by Charles Dickens; cinematographer, Guy Green; edited by Jack Harris; music by Arnold Bax; produced by Ronald Neame; released by United Artists. Black and white. Running time: 105 minutes.

With: John Howard Davies (Oliver Twist), Robert Newton (Bill Sikes), Alec Guinness (Fagin), Kay Walsh (Nancy), Francis L. Sullivan (Mr. Bumble), Henry Stephenson (Mr. Brownlow), Ralph Truman (Monks) and Anthony Newley (The Artful Dodger).

At long last, the much controverted British film of *Oliver Twist* has got to the American public, past the protests of pressure groups and the prerequisites of the Production Code administrators, who compelled that some scenes showing Fagin be cut. And now that it is calmly and comfortably settled at the Park Avenue Theatre, where it opened yesterday, it is safe to proclaim that it is merely a superb piece of motion picture art and, beyond doubt, one of the finest screen translations of a literary classic ever made.

That is not put forth lightly nor without consideration of the fact that the original creation of the producers has been judiciously trimmed. To meet the objections of those critics who felt that Fagin was portrayed a bit too obviously for complacence along the pictorial lines of a notorious anti-Semitic stereotype, some considerable footage in which the character appeared in the original has been dropped and particularly a section demonstrating his instruction of young thieves has been telescoped.

But, as one who has seen the picture in both its original and its present lengths, this reviewer can confidently assure you that its quality has not been impaired—nor, indeed, has the character of Fagin been appreciably Bowdlerized. Except in so far as the appearance of Fagin in point of time has been reduced, his motivating influence and his impact upon the story has been preserved.

And that is both just to the purpose of the producers and considerate of those who might take reasonable exception to an excessive portrayal of a stereotyped Jew. For, of course, the character of Fagin and the fact that he is a Jew (though that is never mentioned in the picture) are mere part and parcel of the whole canvas of social injustice and degradation which is so brilliantly filled out in Charles Dickens's great work. And it is this extraordinary canvas, this vast picture of the poverty and greed which oppressed nineteenth-century England, that has been magnificently reproduced in this film.

Indeed, the simile of a canvas is an appropriate one to apply to this fine drama which David Lean has directed and Ronald Neame has produced. (They are the gentlemen, incidentally, who did Dickens's *Great Expectations* before this.) For the visual design of the picture and its striking photography have the rare characteristics of fine painting in their brilliant creation of mood. And within the narrow range of lights and shadows there have been captured an infinity of tones. Pictorial design and execution are as important as the characters here.

In the opening scene, for instance, against a montage of gathering storm clouds, bare branches, and rain-swept waters, Mr. Neame establishes the somber mood in which the poor boy who is later known as Oliver comes into the world. And in all of the subsequent episodes—in the dismal workhouse scenes, in the scenes of Oliver's apprenticeship to Sowerberry, the undertaker; in the scenes of London, to which the youngster flees; and in the whole visual elaboration of the underworld in which he is caught—there is an extraordinary richness of flavor, suggestion, and atmosphere.

Along with this graphic achievement, Mr. Neame and Mr. Lean have contrived to present the story and characters of Dickens with incredible fidelity. In a youngster named John Howard Davies, who has already been seen hereabouts in a film called *The Rocking Horse Winner* (which he made subsequent to this), they have a frail, sensitive, spirited little fellow who is Oliver Twist to a T. All of the poignancy, courage, and humor of the famous orphan are projected by him.

Robert Newton's Bill Sikes is a hoodlum of contemptible cunning and fear, Kay Walsh is pathetic as Nancy, and Ralph Truman makes a dark and vicious Monks. Francis L. Sullivan is tremendous as Mr. Bumble, the workhouse warden who is full of stupidity and greed, and Henry Stephenson is warm and gentle as Mr. Brownlow, the old gentleman who gives Oliver a happy home.

As for Alec Guinness's performance as Fagin, it is a vastly clever one—harsh, ugly, sly, and unwholesome, yet curiously appealing withal. In the strange sort of loyalty and kindness that are shown by the ghetto Jew toward the poor boys he obviously exploits, an affinity of social outcasts is implied. And when Fagin screams at the rabble which finally closes in on him, "What right have you to butcher me?", the moral of the story is expressed. It is society that is indicted as the real villain in *Oliver Twist*.

—B.C., *July 31, 1951*

LOS OLVIDADOS

Directed by Luis Buñuel: written (in Spanish, with English subtitles) by Mr. Buñuel and Luis Alcoriza: cinematographer. Gabriel Figueroa: edited by Carlos Savage: music by Gustavo Pittaluga: art designer, Edward Fitzgerald: produced by Oscar Dancigers: released by Meyer-Kingsley. Black and white. Running time: 88 minutes.

With: Estela Inda (The Mother), Alfonso Mejia (Pedro), Roberto Cobo (Jaibo), Jesus Navarro (The Lost Boy), Miguel Inclan (The Blind Man) and Alma Fuentes (The Young Girl).

A brutal and unrelenting picture of poverty and juvenile crime in the slums of Mexico City is presented in *The Young and the Damned,* a Mexican semi-documentary that was put on yesterday at the Trans-Lux Fifty-second Street. Although made with meticulous realism and unquestioned fidelity to facts, its qualifications as dramatic entertainment—or even social reportage—are dim.

For it is obvious that Luis Buñuel, who directed and helped write the script, had no focus or point of reference for the squalid, depressing tale he tells. He simply has assembled an assortment of poverty-stricken folk—paupers, delinquents, lost children, and parents of degraded morals—and has mixed them all together in a vicious and shocking mélange of violence, melodrama, coincidence, and irony.

To be sure, Mr. Buñuel does attract unstinted sympathy for a boy who appears the most pathetic victim of the state in which he lives. This lad is the son of a mother who has long since abandoned him, who resists his feeble bids for affection, and who gives herself to his partner in crime. Bullied and dominated by the latter, the boy is led into murder and other crimes and finally is murdered by his partner, who appears some sort of irredeemable psychopath.

Mr. Buñuel also assaults us with visual details of poverty and crime that will stagger the most case-hardened and make the timids' hair stand on end. The vicious badgering of a blind beggar and the ruthless beating of a cripple by a gang of boys are only minor indiscretions. The frenzied flaying to death of chickens is the cue for the beating to death of humans by the bully. The suggestion of madness is plain.

But why there should be this wild coincidence of evil and violence is not explained, nor is any social solution even hinted, much less clarified. A foreword merely states that the correction of this problem of poverty and delinquency is left to the "progressive forces" (whatever they are) of our times.

In the role of the bully, Roberto Cobo is a slashing creature of harsh depravities, while Alfonso Mejia is boyish and touching as the lad who is lonely and doomed. Estela Inda is metallic as the mother, Miguel Inclan is repulsive as the blind man, and a youngster named Alma Fuentes is appealing as a girl of the slums.

This picture, under its original title of *Los Olvidados,* previously was shown at the Cinema 48 without English subtitles. It is well provided with same in its present showing.

—*B.C., March 25, 1952*

ON THE BEACH

Produced and directed by Stanley Kramer: written by John Paxton and James Lee Barrett, based on the novel by Nevil Shute: cinematographers, Giuseppe Rotunno and Daniel Fapp: edited by Frederic Knudtson: music by Ernest Gold: production designer, Rudolph Sternad: released by United Artists. Black and white. Running time: 134 minutes.

With: Gregory Peck (Dwight Towers), Ava Gardner (Moira Davidson), Fred Astaire (Julian Osborn), Anthony Perkins (Peter Holmes), Donna Anderson (Mary Holmes), John Tate (Admiral Bridie) and Lola Brooks (Lieutenant Hosgood).

There is an initial impulse to say of Stanley Kramer's *On the Beach,* the new film that he and John Paxton have refined from the novel of Nevil Shute, that it is concerned with the imagined annihilation of all mankind on this earth, the slow poisoning of the last pocket of surviving humans by radioactive fallout from a nuclear war.

And that would be absolutely accurate, so far as the situation and plot are concerned. For the crisis in this deeply moving picture, which opened at the Astor last night—and in theaters in seventeen other places all around the world—is that which confronts a group of people in Australia in 1964 as they helplessly await the inexorable onset of a lethal cloud of atomic dust.

Death and complete annihilation of the human race are certainly the menaces that hang over all the characters in this film. They are specified at the beginning in the most candid and awesome terms.

A nuclear war someone started (it is never clarified who) has caused fallout that has completely decimated the entire northern hemisphere. Now the fallout is slowly drifting southward; the last people in Australia have five months to enjoy what is left of living and prepare themselves for the end.

So, as they grasp the situation, as an American submarine and its crew go north as far as Alaska in hopes of finding a clearing atmosphere, and as the final days come upon them (when they learn there is no hope), the ever-present realization of themselves—and the audience—is death.

Yet the basic theme of this drama and its major concern is life, the wondrous thing that man's own vast knowledge and ultimate folly seem about to destroy. And everything done by the characters, every thought they utter and move they make, indicates their fervor, tenacity, and courage in the face of doom.

The American submarine captain will not accept that his wife and children are dead, a young Australian naval lieutenant and his wife look forward to having a second child, a worldly and blasé woman who has wasted life tries to find true love, a seasoned and cynical atomic scientist tunes his cherished possession, a racing car.

In putting this fanciful but arresting story of Mr. Shute on the screen, Mr. Kramer and his assistants have most forcibly emphasized this point: life is a beautiful treasure and man should do all he can to save it from annihilation, while there is still time.

To this end, he has accomplished some vivid and trenchant images that subtly fill the mind of the viewer with a strong appreciation of his theme. The sequence in which the American submarine goes north to Point Barrow, then comes back by deadened San Francisco and puts a well-protected man ashore in empty San Diego to investigate a curious radio signal that comes from there, gives a tremendous comprehension of the waste of an unpeopled world. And scenes of life in Australia, which follow, point up the joy of carrying on. Even a nerve-tingling sequence representing a suicidal auto race impresses the viewer with the wisdom of man's being careful of his hide.

Mr. Kramer has brilliantly directed a strong and responsive cast, headed by Gregory Peck as the submarine commander and Ava Gardner as the worldly woman who craves his love. Miss Gardner is remarkably revealing of the pathos of a wasted life. Fred Astaire is also amazing as the cynical scientist, conveying in his self-effacing manner a piercing sense of the irony of his trade.

Anthony Perkins as the young lieutenant, Donna Anderson as his delicate wife, John Tate as an Australian admiral, and Lola Brooks as his loyal aide are among the many excellent listed and unlisted actors in the film.

A fine musical score, which leans heavily on the famous Australian tune, "Waltzing Matilda," has been contributed by Ernest Gold, and the fine black-and-white camera work of Giuseppe Rotunno merits a final word.

The great merit of this picture, aside from its entertaining qualities, is the fact that it carries a passionate conviction that man is worth saving, after all.

—*B.C., December 18, 1959*

ON THE TOWN

Directed by Gene Kelly and Stanley Donen; written by Adolph Green and Betty Comden, based on the musical play by Mr. Green, Ms. Comden and Leonard Bernstein, from the ballet *Fancy Free* by Jerome Robbins; cinematographer, Harold Rosson; edited by Ralph E. Winters; music by Leonard Bernstein, Robert Edens, Saul Chaplin and Conrad Salinger; choreography by Mr. Kelly and Mr. Donen; art designers, Cedric Gibbons and Jack Martin Smith; produced by Arthur Freed; released by Metro-Goldwyn-Mayer. Running time: 98 minutes.

With: Gene Kelly (Gabey), Frank Sinatra (Chip), Betty Garrett (Brunhilde Esterhazy), Ann Miller (Claire Huddesen), Jules Munshin (Ozzie), Vera-Ellen (Ivy Smith), Florence Bates (Madame Dilyovska), Alice Pearce (Lucy Shmeeler) and George Meader (Professor).

The Music Hall pulled the wrappings off its Christmas show yesterday and revealed a delightful entertainment for all ages, sexes, and seasonal moods. It is Metro's crackling screen version of the musical, *On the Town,* and a more appropriate all-purpose Yuletide picture would be hard to fashion or find. Gaiety, rhythm, humor, and a good, wholesome dash of light romance have been artfully blended together in this bright Technicolored comedy. The holidays should be nicer for having *On the Town* around.

Actually, some major changes have been made in the amiable show which caused such a buzz when it opened on Broadway five years ago. The story has not been altered; it is still the same fast and dizzy thing that Adolph Green and Betty Comden, the scriptwriters, originally wrote for the stage. That is to say, it is the story of three sailors who hit New York on a twenty-four-hour leave with two intentions: to see the sights and meet three girls. And it still satisfies these intentions with conspicuous success. No need to change that story. It is one which the screen understands.

But some of the original Broadway numbers have been dropped and some new ones have been put in, not without possible annoyance to some who liked the show the way it was. The beautiful "Lonely Town" number, sung by the hero, has gone by the board, and so has the fast and dazzling ballet, "Gabey in the Playground of the Rich." Two or three other songs and dances have likewise disappeared, to make way for substitutions. As good—or better? Maybe yes, maybe no.

However, the overall picture flits and frolics with the same carefree delight as did the popular original— and with equal originality, too. Gene Kelly and Stanley Donen, who directed under the eye of Arthur Freed, have actually found some fresh capers for screen musical comedy. They have cleverly liberated action in the manner of the musical stage and they have engineered sizzling momentum by the smart employment of cinema techniques.

From the moment the picture opens, in the actual Brooklyn Navy Yard, with the three sailors cutting off for New York, the whole thing precipitately moves, with song, dance, comedy, and romance ingeniously interwoven and performed. With Mr. Kelly playing the role of the principal tar, the excellence of the masculine dancing is immediately guaranteed. And with Vera-Ellen playing the little Manhattanite whom he meets—Miss Turnstile, the Subway Cinderella—his vis-à-vis is assured.

These two are deliciously coupled in the singing and dancing of "Main Street" and a new Leonard Bernstein ballet number, "A Day in New York." As another of the tars, Frank Sinatra finds his soulmate and comedy relief in Betty Garrett, who plays a taxi

driver with an obvious Sinatra yen. Together they comically warble the familiar "Come Up to My Place," "You're Awful" (a phrase of endearment!), and join jovially in "Prehistoric Man." This latter is a new item which has been neatly contrived for Ann Miller and giggly Jules Munshin, who comprise the third duo. Assisted further by Florence Bates and Alice Pearce in lesser roles, these six very spirited young people have great fun from *On the Town.* And so do we.

—B.C., December 9, 1949

ON THE WATERFRONT

Directed by Elia Kazan: written by Budd Schulberg, based on an original story by Mr. Schulberg and suggested by the series of Pulitzer Prizewinning articles by Malcolm Johnson: cinematographer. Boris Kaufman: edited by Gene Milford: music by Leonard Bernstein: art designer. Richard Day: produced by Sam Spiegel: released by Columbia Pictures. Black and white. Running time: 108 minutes.

With: Marlon Brando (Terry Malloy). Eva Marie Saint (Edie Doyle). Karl Malden (Father Barry). Lee J. Cobb (Johnny Friendly). Rod Steiger (Charley Malloy). John Hamilton ("Pop" Doyle). Pat Henning ("Kayo" Dugan). Leif Erickson (Glover) and James Westerfield (Big Mac).

A small but obviously dedicated group of realists has forged artistry, anger, and some horrible truths into *On the Waterfront,* as violent and indelible a film record of man's inhumanity to man as has come to light this year. And, while this explosive indictment of the vultures and the meek prey of the docksides, which was unveiled at the Astor yesterday, occasionally is only surface dramatization and an oversimplification of the personalities and evils of our waterfront, it is, nevertheless, an uncommonly powerful, exciting, and imaginative use of the screen by gifted professionals.

Although journalism and television already have made the brutal feudalism of the wharves a part of current history, *On the Waterfront* adds a graphic dimension to these sordid pages. Credit for this achievement cannot be relegated to a specific few. Scenarist Budd Schulberg, who, since 1949, has lived with the story stemming from Malcolm Johnson's crusading newspaper articles; director Elia Kazan; the principals headed by Marlon Brando; producer Sam Spiegel; Columbia, which is presenting this independently made production; Leonard Bernstein, who herein is making his debut as a movie composer; and Boris Kaufman, the cinematographer, convincingly have illustrated the murder and mayhem of the waterfront's sleazy jungles.

They also have limned a bestial and venal boss longshoreman; the "shape-up" by which only his obedient, mulct, vassals can earn a day's pay; the hard and strange code that demands that these sullen men die rather than talk about these injustices, and a crime commission that helps bring some light into their dark lives.

Perhaps these annals of crime are too labyrinthine to be fully and incisively captured by cameras. Suffice it to say, however, that while Mr. Kazan and Mr. Schulberg have not dug as deeply as they might, they have chosen a proper and highly effective cast and setting for their grim adventure. Moving cameras and crews to the crowded rookeries of Hoboken's quayside, where the film was shot in its entirety, they have told with amazing speed and force the story of Terry Malloy, ex-prizefighter and inarticulate tool of tough, ruthless, and crooked labor leader, Johnny Friendly. The labor leader is an absolute unregenerated monarch of the docks who will blithely shake down his own men as well as ship owners; he will take cuts of pay envelopes and lend his impecunious union members money at usurious rates and he will have his pistol-toting goons dispatch anyone foolish enough to squeal to the crime commission attempting to investigate these practices.

It is the story also of one of these courageous few about to "sing" to the commission—a luckless longshoreman unwittingly set up for the kill by Terry Malloy, who is in his soft spot only because his older brother is the boss's slick, right-hand man. It is the tale of Terry's meeting with the dead man's agonized sister and a fearless, neighborhood priest, who, by love and reason, bring the vicious picture into focus for him. And, it is the account of the murder of Terry's brother; the rampaging younger man's defiant testimony before the commission; and the climactic bloody battle that wrests the union from the boss's tenacious grasp.

Journalism may have made these ingredients familiar and certainly more inclusive and multidimensional, but Mr. Kazan's direction, his outstanding cast, and Mr. Schulberg's pithy and punchy dialogue give them distinction and terrific impact. Under the director's expert guidance, Marlon Brando's Terry Malloy is a shatteringly poignant portrait of an amoral, confused, illiterate citizen of the lower depths who is goaded into decency by love, hate, and murder. His groping for words, use of the vernacular, care of his beloved pigeons, pugilist's walk and gestures, and his discoveries of love and the immensity of the crimes surrounding him are highlights of a beautiful and moving portrayal.

In casting Eva Marie Saint—a newcomer to movies from TV and Broadway—Mr. Kazan has come up with a pretty and blond artisan who does not have to depend on these attributes. Her parochial school training is no bar to love with the proper stranger. Amid scenes of carnage, she gives tenderness and sensitivity to genuine romance. Karl Malden, whose importance in the scheme of this drama seems overemphasized, is, however, a tower of strength as the militant man of the cloth. Rod Steiger, another newcomer to films, is excellent as Brando's fearful brother. The pair have a final scene that is a harsh and touching revelation of their frailties.

Lee J. Cobb is muscularly effective as the labor boss; John Hamilton and Pat Henning are typical "longshoremen," gents who look at home in a hold; and Tony Galento, Tami Mauriello, and Abe Simon—erstwhile heavyweight boxing contenders, who portray Cobb's chief goons—are citizens no one would want to meet in a dark alley. Despite its happy ending, its preachments, and a somewhat slick approach to some of the facets of dockside strife and tribulations, *On the Waterfront* is moviemaking of a rare and high order.

—A.W., July 29, 1954

ONE FALSE MOVE

Directed by Carl Franklin; written by Billy Bob Thornton and Tom Epperson; director of photography, James L. Carter; edited by Carole Kravetz; music by Peter Haycock and Derek Holt; produced by Jesse Beaton and Ben Myron; released by IRS Releasing. Running time: 105 minutes.

With: Bill Paxton (Dale "Hurricane" Dixon). Cynda Williams (Fantasia "Lila"). Billy Bob Thornton (Ray Malcolm) and Michael Beach (Pluto).

Carl Franklin's first feature, *One False Move,* says as much about where Mr. Franklin is headed as about where he has been. Although he works within the idiom of a conventional crime story, telling of three violent drug dealers running from the law, Mr. Franklin delivers the kind of symmetry, surprise, and detail that easily transcend the limits of the genre. It's clear that this new filmmaker could work well with other types of material and on a much more ambitious plane. Thanks to the thoughtfulness and promise he displays this time, he undoubtedly will.

Too bad it would be unfair to describe the closing image of *One False Move,* since this film's resolution lifts it so far above ordinary film noir fatalism. Despair, terrible irony, and the sudden chance of redemption combine to end the story on a wrenching, altogether satisfying note.

This conclusion is light-years away from the ugly episode with which the film begins: three deceptively mild-mannered desperadoes terrorize people at a party, then butcher their victims. The viciousness of the attack and the banality of the motive—drugs and money—threaten to consign *One False Move* to the realm of mindless exploitation.

But something is different. The criminals are an unusual bunch. Fantasia (Cynda Williams), the soft-voiced beauty who served as a decoy, has a more complex conscience than might be expected. Pluto (Michael Beach), the stony mastermind of the operation, combines the look of a polite accountant with an incongruous taste for savagery. Ray (Billy Bob Thornton, who wrote the screenplay with Tom Epperson) is Fantasia's lover and a mouthpiece with a mad-dog temper, but his ability to intimidate the other two is not all it seems. The racial makeup of the group is equally unexpected: Pluto is black, Ray is white, Fantasia (who had a black mother and a white father) somewhere in between.

These three travel from Los Angeles back to Star City, Arkansas, where they plan to touch base with relatives. The film seems to expand along the way. Mr. Franklin, carefully balancing and manipulating his cast's racial makeup, sets up a parallel threesome in the form of a white Southern sheriff, Dale (Hurri-cane) Dixon (Bill Paxton), and a team of detectives from Los Angeles, one black, one white, who quietly ridicule Dale and his folksy ways. Dale does not need this extra pressure. He is already so tightly wound that he defiantly leaves a ten dollar bill at a coffee shop to pay a twelve dollar check. The film is about what happens when these opposing forces—Ray, Pluto, Dale, and the constantly surprising Fantasia, who was once a Star City small-town girl named Lila—finally collide.

Mr. Franklin's measured pacing and James L. Carter's meticulous cinematography give *One False Move* a clear, bold, angular look reminiscent of many other nouveau noir films, especially *Blood Simple,* the one that put the Coen brothers on the map. But the acting style here is warmer and less self-conscious than that implies. Ms. Williams carries a large part of the narrative burden and makes the gentle-sounding, deadly Lila a riveting modern counterpart to the familiar good-bad noir heroine. Mr. Paxton captures all Dale's regret about his past and uncertainty about his future. Both Mr. Beach and Mr. Thornton convey great menace with a minimum of effort.

Of particular note in *One False Move,* which opens today at the Film Forum, are a tense, well-staged encounter between the runaways and a highway patrolman in a convenience store, and the reunion of Lila and her brother in the perfect Hitchcockian setting, a crossroads beside an open field. That scene, like symmetries involving children in *One False Move* and even the conspicuous use of whippoorwill calls as harbingers, points to a director who knows the effects he wants and knows precisely how to achieve them.

—J.M., July 17, 1992

ONE FLEW OVER THE CUCKOO'S NEST

Directed by Milos Forman: written by Lawrence Hauben and Bo Goldman. based on the novel by Ken Kesey and the play by Dale Wasserman: cinematographer. Haskell Wexler. William A. Fraker and Bill Butler: edited by Richard Chew. Lynzee Klingman and Sheldon Kahn: music by Jack Nitzsche: production designer. Aggie Guerard Rodgers: produced by Saul Zaentz and Michael Douglas: released by United Artists. Running time: 129 minutes.

With: Jack Nicholson (R.P. McMurphy), Louise Fletcher (Nurse Ratched), William Redfield (Harding), Will Sampson (Chief Bromden), Brad Dourif (Billy Bibbit), Marya Small (Candy), Delos V. Smith Jr. (Scanlon), Mimi Sarkisian (Nurse Pilbow), Dean R. Brooks (Dr. Spivey), Scatman Crothers (Turkle), Danny DeVito (Martini), William Duell (Sefelt), Sydney Lassick (Cheswick), Christopher Lloyd (Taber) and Louise Moritz (Rose).

People like Randle Patrick McMurphy are foregone conclusions. You gather together at random any twelve men, and one of them will eventually surface as the group's Randle Patrick McMurphy, the organizer, the spokesman, the leading hell-raiser and free spirit, the man who accepts nothing at face value and who likes to shake up the system, sometimes just because it's there. The quality of Randle Patrick McMurphy depends entirely on the intensity of his opposition.

Before the start of *One Flew Over the Cuckoo's Nest,* Milos Forman's film version of Ken Kesey's 1962 novel, Randle Patrick McMurphy (Jack Nicholson) was strictly small potatoes, his life distinguished by nothing except carelessness.

One assumes him to have been a quick-witted, but none-too-bright fellow whose vanity, drinking, whoring, and short temper have earned him a minor police record consisting mostly of assault-and-battery complaints, concluding with a conviction for statutory rape. The girl, who said she was nineteen, was only fifteen.

When we first meet Randle, he has served two months of his six-month sentence and has managed to get himself transferred to the state mental hospital for psychiatric observation, figuring that life in the loony bin would be easier than on the prison farm. It's the beginning of the end for Randle, but the ferocity of the system imposes on him a kind of crazy grandeur.

One Flew Over the Cuckoo's Nest, which opened yesterday at the Sutton and Paramount Theaters, is a comedy that can't quite support its tragic conclusion, which is too schematic to be honestly moving, but it is acted with such a sense of life that one responds to its demonstration of humanity if not to its programmed metaphors.

Once in the bin, Randle becomes the self-proclaimed champion of the rights of the other ward patients, his adversary being Nurse Ratched, a severe, once-pretty woman of uncertain age who can be sympathetic and understanding only in ways that reinforce her authority. Nurse Ratched represents the System that all Randles must buck.

As played by Louise Fletcher and defined in the screenplay by Lawrence Hauben and Bo Goldman, the film's Nurse Ratched is a much more interesting, more ambiguous character than in Mr. Kesey's novel, though what we take to be her fleeting impulses of genuine concern only make the film's ending that much more unbelievable.

One Flew Over the Cuckoo's Nest is at its best when Mr. Forman is exercising his talents as a director of exuberant comedy that challenges preconceived notions of good taste. It's not too far from the mark to describe Randle as a sort of Mister Roberts who finds himself serving aboard the U.S.S. *Madhouse.* It's to Mr. Forman's credit that the other patients in the ward, though suffering from all sorts of psychoses, are never patronized as freaks but are immediately identifiable as variations on ourselves, should we ever go over the edge of what's called sanity.

Mr. Nicholson slips into the role of Randle with such easy grace that it's difficult to remember him in any other film. It's a flamboyant performance but not so overbearing that it obscures his fellow actors, all of whom are very good and a few of whom are close to brilliant, including William Redfield (as an egghead patient who talks grave nonsense), Will Sampson (as a deaf-mute Indian), and Brad Dourif (as a young man with a fatal mother complex).

There are some unsettling things about *One Flew Over the Cuckoo's Nest.* I suspect that we are meant to make connections between Randle's confrontation with the oppressive Nurse Ratched and the political turmoil in this country in the 1960's. The connection doesn't work. All it does is conveniently distract us from questioning the accuracy of the film's picture of life in a mental institution where shock treatments are dispensed like aspirins and lobotomies are prescribed as if the mind's frontal lobes were troublesome wisdom teeth.

Even granting the artist his license, America is much too big and various to be satisfactorily reduced to the dimensions of one mental ward in a movie like this.

—*V.C., November 20, 1975*

ONE FOOT IN HEAVEN

Directed by Irving Rapper; written by Casey Robinson, based on biography by Hartzell Spence; cinematographer, Charles Rosher; edited by Warren Low; music by Max Steiner; produced by Robert Lord; released by Warner Brothers. Black and white. Running time: 106 minutes.

With: Frederic March (William Spence), Martha Scott (Hope Morris Spence), Beulah Bondi (Mrs. Lydia Sandow), Gene Lockhart (Preston Thurston), Elisabeth Fraser (Eileen Spence at 18), Harry Davenport (Elias Samson), Laura Hope Crews (Mrs. Preston Thurston) and Grant Mitchell (Clayton Potter).

You might not think that the life of an insignificant preacher and the simple, homely problems he shoulders at the head of his family and flock could furnish sufficient material for one of the finest pictures of the year. But that only goes to show how limited our expectations have become. For out of Hartzell Spence's deeply affectionate biography of his ministerial father, William Spence, the Warners have derived a cheerful and warmly compassionate film, an excellent character study, and an adult entertainment on the screen. Imagine *Life with Father* in a parsonage, with the modifications that locale would compel, and you have a fair approximation of the better part of *One Foot in Heaven,* which opened at the Music Hall yesterday.

Naturally this amiable narrative of the Reverend Mr. Spence's service to the Lord is more devoutly motivated than was the late Clarence Day's memorial to his dad. The Reverend Mr. Spence was humble after all, and his spiritual duty came above all else. But in other essential respects he was very much akin to Papa Day—he was stubborn, he was honest, he was practical, and his sense of humor made his life a joy. And the story which Casey Robinson has prepared for the screen about him is surprisingly similar in structure to that which Crouse and Lindsay wrote for Mr. Day.

For One Foot in Heaven is simply a beautifully balanced account of the life of the Reverend Mr. Spence, beginning with his call to the Methodist ministry as a young man after he was about to embark on a medical career; his marriage to an understanding woman; their experiences in various parsonages; their humorous and touching difficulties in raising their children on virtually nothing a year, and finally climaxed by the good man's bitterest trial in attempting to build a new church for his flock.

That is the simple story. But it is studded with such eloquent detail—the trepidation and courage inspired by that first ministry; the reversion of the father from the Methodist discipline when he takes his son to see a Bill Hart movie, the anger and dismay aroused by a parsonage with a leaky roof—that it all adds up to a brilliant and revealing pattern of life.

And Frederic March and Martha Scott, under the superbly lucid and restrained direction of Irving Rapper, infuse with warm and sentient life the characters of William Spence and his wife. Mr. March is truly excellent as a man of stout conviction and resolute faith—a man who is not above a bit of honest chicane when it is a matter of coaxing a new Tree of Jesse window out of a parishioner or disposing of an unmelodious choir, but who is blessed with a deep humanity and walks in paths of righteousness all his life. Miss Scott abets him magnificently as his loyal and loving mate—a woman of fine sensibilities who endures the humiliations of a poor parson's wife and offers her comprehending self as the patient foil to his willful outbursts. Beulah Bondi, Gene Lockhart, Harry Davenport, and a cast too numerous to name all give impressive performances as characters met along the way.

A picture of this nature might all too easily drift off into maudlin sentiment, but Mr. Rapper has kept it well within the bounds of reality. Only the final sequence, in which Mr. March plays "The Church's One Foundation" on the new carillon and the citizens all look up with beaming faces, slips into mawkishness. But that may be excused. For a fine and brilliant picture precedes it. *One Foot in Heaven* is a rich experience.

—*B.C., November 14, 1941*

ONE HOUR WITH YOU

Directed by Ernst Lubitsch and George Cukor; written by Samson Raphaelson, based on the play *Only a Dream* by Lothar Schmidt; cinematographer, Victor Milner; edited by William Shea;

music by Oscar Straus and Richard Whiting; art designer. Hans Dreier; produced by Mr. Lubitsch; released by Paramount Pictures. Black and white. Running time: 80 minutes.

With: Maurice Chevalier (Dr. André Bertier). Jeanette MacDonald (Colette Bertier). Genevieve Tobin (Mitzi Olivier). Charles Ruggles (Adolph). Roland Young (Professor Olivier). George Barbier (Police Commissioner). Josephine Dunn (Mademoiselle Martel). Richard Carle (Detective). Charles Judels (Policeman) and Barbara Leonard (Mitzi's Maid).

Through the connivance of Adolphe Zukor and Ernst Lubitsch, Maurice Chevalier's prepossessing shadow was presented last night in a picture reveling in the title of *One Hour with You*, at both the Rivoli and the Rialto. If the gathering in the latter theater laughed as much as that in the former house, then it was a jolly hour or so in the two places.

This latest Lubitsch production, aided by M. Chevalier and his supporting cast, is filled with scintillating wit of the Parisian variety. The story is an adaptation of Lothar Schmidt's play, *Only a Dream,* which served Mr. Lubitsch years ago for his first American production, *The Marriage Circle.* But, with the French entertainer, and the fact that it is an audible production, it makes for a far better show than the old silent film. Mr. Lubitsch has played fast and loose with the story as it was in the old days, but the salient features remain virtually the same. There are moments when the audience giggled in expectation, and other incidents aroused hearty mirth. As it is now, *One Hour with You* is a kind of operetta, with some of the lines in rhyme and occasional outbursts of song. The fair and graceful Jeanette MacDonald is in her element in this offering and among others who give a good account of themselves are Genevieve Tobin, Charles Ruggles, and the ever amusing Roland Young.

It is quite obvious throughout this film that Mr. Lubitsch's nimble mind has been busy not only in the direction of the subject but also in the handling of the script. For instance, in the course of the proceedings, M. Chevalier as Dr. André Bertier finds himself tempted by Mitzi, the dainty wife of Professor Olivier, to go out on the balcony after dinner.

Mitzi frankly admires Bertier and she mischie-vously unties his white tie, which is extremely awkward for him as he cannot tie a bow. Then the wicked Mitzi prances out into the garden and Bertier plucks leaves off a plant to see whether he shall stay where he is or follow her. To follow her wins, so off he goes and soon one perceives that the bow has been tied, not around Bertier's neck, no never, but around Mitizi's ankle. Hence when Colette, Bertier's wife, very indignant and frightfully jealous, comes upon the scene the errant Bertier has no tie at all. But photography can accomplish wonders and soon he is quite presentable.

The trouble with Colette is that she never for an instant suspects Mitzi of flirting with her husband, for Mitzi is her best friend. Try to avoid Mitzi as much as he will, poor Bertier is constantly finding himself her rather unwilling victim. She thinks that she will be ill and calls up Dr. Bertier and Colette insists that her husband go and attend to Mitzi. And Bertier knows full well that all Mitzi desires is to flirt.

Professor Olivier (Roland Young) is not blind to his wife's flighty conduct. In fact, he has her trailed by a sleuth and in due time presents Bertier with a full report of what happened at certain periods of one evening. Hence Bertier thinks that he must tell all to Colette, who, be it known, never for a moment suspects him of being the guilty party in the mysterious affair Mitzi is supposed to be having. The shock to Colette is a rude one, but there happens to have been a near affair between herself and Adolph, played by Mr. Ruggles.

This production is magnificently mounted with amazing attention to every small detail. The changing of place cards at a dinner table is sufficient to arouse heaps of merriment, and likewise the chats Bertier has with the audience, whom he takes into his confidence, but decides for himself, believing that they would do just as he does.

Some of the music for this production was composed by Oscar Straus. Among the songs are "We Will Always Be Sweethearts," rendered by M. Chevalier and Miss MacDonald; "One Hour with You," "What Would Do?" and "What a Little Thing Like a Wedding Ring Can Do."

M. Chevalier is as enjoyable as ever. There is his smile and also his stare—a stare of discomfort when he is dumbfounded. But whether he is solemn or laughing, he is always engaging. Miss MacDonald is charming as Colette, and Genevieve Tobin gives a very pleasing performance as the flirt, Mitzi. Josephine Dunn does well as Mlle. Martel, and George Barbier appears as a commissaire de police. Richard Carle is entrusted with the role of a sleuth.

One Hour with You is an excellent production, with Lubitsch and Chevalier at the top of their form.

—*M.H., March 24, 1932*

ONE NIGHT OF LOVE

Directed by Victor Schertzinger: written by S. K. Lauren. James Gow and Edmund H. North. based on a story by Dorothy Speare and Charles Beahan: cinematographer. Joseph Walker: edited by Gene Milford: music by Louis Silvers. Mr. Schertzinger and Gus Kahn: art designer. Stephen Gossen: produced by Sara Risher: released by Columbia Pictures. Black and white. Running time: 84 minutes.

With: Grace Moore (Mary Barrett). Tullio Carminati (Guilio Monteverdi). Lyle Talbot (Bill Houston). Mona Barrie (Lally). Jessie Ralph (Angelina). Luis Alberni (Giovanni). Andres De Segurola (Galuppi) and Rosemary Glosz (Frappazini).

Besides shining as a successful prima donna in the rendition of several opera arias, Grace Moore, in her new picture, *One Night of Love,* also proves herself to be quite an expert comedienne. This film, which attracted unusual crowds to the Radio City Music Hall yesterday, is an enjoyable light diversion, one worthy of the charm and talent of its stellar performer.

Victor Schertzinger, the director, whose hobby is composing music, has handled this amiable narrative in a sympathetic and imaginative manner. And, although Miss Moore won high favor by her performances in her previous screen works, *A Lady's Morals* and *New Moon,* she shows greater confidence than ever in this current vehicle. She is decidedly fortunate in having Tullio Carminati play opposite her, for, as a celebrated Italian maestro, he senses precisely what is demanded of him.

After the reels and reels of torch singers and crooners, it is indeed a joyous relief to listen to the delightful melodies in this film. If the incidents are never really serious, they do often succeed in imparting some idea of the hard work involved in learning to sing and also in giving a conception of the possible trials an impresario may experience through the volatile temperament of his charge.

There are several very clever episodes, a noteworthy one coming in an early part of the film, soon after Mary Barrett (Miss Moore) has arrived in Italy. Mr. Schertzinger turns his camera on various windows at which one sees and hears the students contributing to a veritable bedlam of noise, either by singing or playing the piano, the violin, the cello and other instruments. Suddenly Mary appears at her balcony and lifts her voice in song, with the result that all the practicing ceases and the instruments are turned to accompanying her. Later Mary and her companions in poverty sing themselves out of paying the rent, for it happens that the landlady was once an aspiring singer. On this occasion they win her admiration and sympathy by rendering the sextet from *Lucia.*

Later, Mary is perceived in a cellar cabaret, to which the great impresario, Giulio Monteverdi, goes. He already has a handsome young woman as a student, but it chances that admiration, affection, or perhaps it is love, has interfered with their work. In fact, Monteverdi forgets about instruction when he gazes into the brunette's bright eyes. Here, however, in the unpretentious cabaret, is a girl with a voice which has, as one might surmise, wonderful possibilities.

Soon the brunette is thrown aside for Mary, who, notwithstanding certain surprises, eventually learns that Monteverdi's intentions are strictly honorable. There ensues a steady and severe course in operatic training and for months Mary is not given a chance to sing a note. She is told to exercise, sometimes at touching her toes without bending her knees. She has breathing exercises and diaphragm tests, all of which afford merriment to the audience.

The picture is photographed with considerable artistry. There are kaleidoscopic flashes which give a definite impression of both the passage of time and what is happening. There are also suggestions of work—singing in provincial theaters and traveling from place to place.

It is Monteverdi's intention never to let his charge smoke, drink, or even have much dinner. While he regales himself with tasty dishes, all poor Mary is permitted to order is Melba toast and spinach. Hence, it

722

is not surprising that she almost abandons her career when a wealthy young American appears on the horizon. Monteverdi wanted no affection between himself and his pupil, but it is obvious at one stage of the proceedings that Mary and Monteverdi will not be able to keep to the positions of instructor and student very much longer.

Miss Moore's singing is most pleasing. Among the arias she renders is one from *Carmen* and another from *Madame Butterfly*. Mona Barrie does well as Lally, the attractive brunette. Andres de Segurola performs well in a minor role, and so does the dependable Luis Alberni.

—M.H., *September 7, 1934*

ONE POTATO, TWO POTATO

Directed by Larry Peerce; written by Raphael Hayes and Orville H. Hampton, based on a story by Mr. Hampton; director of photography. Andrew Laszlo; edited by Robert Fritch; music by Gerald Fried; produced by Sam Weston; released by Cinema V. Black and white. Running time: 92 minutes.

With: Barbara Barrie (Julie Cullen Richards), Bernie Hamilton (Frank Richards), Richard Mulligan (Joe Cullen), Harry Bellaver (Judge Powell), Marti Mericka (Ellen Mary), Robert Earle Jones (William Richards), Vinette Carroll (Martha Richards) and Sam Weston (Johnny Hruska).

Modestly conceived and executed by a pair of movie tyros and cheered and honored at the recent Cannes Film Festival, *One Potato, Two Potato*, which arrived yesterday at the Murray Hill, Embassy, and other theaters, deserves its accolades and yet, like life itself, disturbingly shows its imperfections.

In simply mirroring cancerous injustices stemming from an interracial marriage, a terrible quandary is starkly, if patly, pictured. Gnawing doubts remain after the film's climactic decision is made, but this festering problem of our flawed society, which could have been depicted sordidly and sensationally, is, instead, often made moving in basically honest terms.

The newcomers involved—Larry Peerce, the director, and Sam Weston, the producer—have not achieved anything new cinematically nor have they presented the problem in exceptional dramatic fashion. Nevertheless, they engage a viewer by the restraint and decency of their approach. They have focused sharply on an as yet unrelieved bigotry that should gain sympathy from audiences willing to understand and appreciate these traumas.

Their drama is set against the court action for the custody of a girl, the daughter of a white woman who divorced her husband after he had left her, and who is now married to a Negro. The meeting of these two lonely coworkers in a local plant, their blossoming love, and their marriage is developed quietly and tenderly.

The story is realistically pointed in showing the initial resistance of the Negro's family to the marriage and their subsequent change of attitude. And, finally, it concentrates on the return of the errant first husband, his demand for custody, and the upstanding, harassed judge's decision to turn the child over to him.

It is here that *One Potato, Two Potato*—a title adopted from the juvenile jingle of choosing—becomes debatable, even impossible to accept. The first husband is portrayed as an unstable dreamer and wanderer who has never outgrown youthful irresponsibilities. The love and understanding of the well-bred Negro husband and his hard-working farmer parents toward their son's white wife and her child is made crystal-clear. The judge is presented as an extremely dedicated arbiter whose soul-searching and hesitancy to make a quick cold judgment are all too apparent. It seems unlikely that he would not have decided to keep a good home and family intact following his investigations under the circumstances portrayed.

A viewer is also left with doubts that the first husband would suddenly turn up after four years in South America to demand his daughter, as is flatly stated here. But in filming their sad tale in the small, well-kept confines of Painesville, Ohio, the producers have enhanced the documentary quality of their drama.

They have derived truly warm, evocative vignettes that are not only authentic but also touching. One vividly recalls the subdued playful courting in the town square that starts with a child's game and ends with a groping but love-filled embrace. The final scene of the parting of mother and daughter poignantly blends the youngster's fright and shock with a blind outburst of fury and tears that is neatly played against the mother's anguished helplessness.

As the mother, Barbara Barrie, who won an acting award at Cannes, justifies the prize with a portrayal that is perceptively naturalistic. She is timid, worried, and, finally, feminine in the extreme as a woman fighting against impossible odds in defense of her love and family.

As the Negro husband, Bernie Hamilton, in keeping with the documentary treatment of the theme, is properly subdued and dignified, except for a moment of uncontrolled anger.

Richard Mulligan, a tall, blond, handsome newcomer to films, is tense and sincere but unconvincing as the first husband. As the daughter fated by fate and the law, Marti Mericka is a realistically ordinary, nice child. And Robert Earle Jones and Vinette Carroll are proud but awkward as the Negro's parents.

One Potato, Two Potato is woefully loose in conviction and reasoning. It does not soar on wings of artistry in keeping with its strong subject. But it speaks out resolutely on a generally shunned social theme that is a credit to the courage of its producers and the team that made it.

—A.W., July 30, 1964

ONE, TWO, THREE

Produced and directed by Billy Wilder; written by Mr. Wilder and I. A. L. Diamond, based on the play *Egy. Ketto. Harom* by Ferenc Molnar; cinematographer. Daniel Fapp; edited by Daniel Mandell; music by André Previn; art designer. Alexander Trauner; released by United Artists. Black and white. Running time: 115 minutes.

With: James Cagney (C. R. McNamara), Horst Buchholz (Otto Ludwig Piffl), Pamela Tiffin (Scarlett Hazeltine), Arlene Francis (Phyllis McNamara), Lilo Pulver (Ingeborg), Howard St. John (Mr. Hazeltine), Hanns Lothar (Schlemmer) and Lois Bolton (Mrs. Hazeltine).

It is too bad the present Berlin crisis isn't so funny and harmless as the one Billy Wilder and I. A. L. Diamond have whipped up in their new movie, *One, Two, Three*. And it is too bad it can't be settled so briskly and pro-Americanly as James Cagney settles the one in this picture, which came to the Astor and the Fine Arts yesterday.

For the crisis is nothing more serious than the marriage of a rich American girl, daughter of a top man in Coca-Cola, to a communistic East Berlin boy. And the settlement of it by Mr. Cagney, who plays the Coca-Cola manager in West Berlin, is as easy, in a roundabout fashion, as threading the maze of a typical American farce.

Of course, there is more to the crisis than the mere marriage of a girl and boy. She happens to be a birdbrained tourist and the apple of her Georgian daddy's eye. When he finds out about the marriage, he is likely to burst several bottling-machines. And Mr. Cagney, who is supposed to be responsible for her in Berlin, is, meanwhile, bucking for a better job.

So, you see, what the crisis amounts to for Mr. Cagney is getting the marriage annulled, getting rid of the East Berlin hothead and getting Scarlett (that's her name) safely home. And then, when it's suddenly discovered that little Scarlett is blissfully with child, it's a matter of reclaiming Otto (that's the husband) out of the East Zone and making a presentable capitalist-type out of him.

In such a pregnant situation, one might naturally assume that Mr. Wilder and Mr. Diamond, distinguished humorists, would be making some sharp political jokes. They are. The very name of Coca-Cola in the context of American go-getting as represented by Mr. Cagney in this crisis is a mischievous joke in itself. Communist slipperiness and bombast are farcically portrayed, and German pigheadedness and heel-clicking are matters for running gags.

But the sharpness of wit and satire is less conspicuous than the magnitude and speed of the obvious jokes and comic action as they pour through the film like a cascade. There is nothing subtle about it, least of all about Mr. Cagney's role, which is that of the deus ex machina (or "mein fuehrer," as his wife refers to him). It is simply a matter of moving very fast and getting lots of things done, from sales pitching for Coca-Cola to an automobile chase through East Berlin.

With all due respect for all the others, all of whom are very good—Pamela Tiffin, a new young beauty, as Scarlett; Horst Buchholz as the East Berlin boy, Lilo Pulver as a German secretary, Leon Askin as a Communist stooge, and several more—the burden is carried by Mr. Cagney, who is a good 50 percent of the show. He has seldom worked so hard in any picture or had such a browbeating ball.

His fellow is a freewheeling rascal. His wife (Arlene Francis) hates his guts. He knows all the ways of beating the rackets and has no compunctions about their use. He is brutishly bold and brassy, wildly ingenious, and glib. Mr. Cagney makes you mistrust him—but he sure makes you laugh with him.

And that's about the nature of the picture. It is one with which you can laugh—with its own impudence toward foreign crises—while laughing at its rowdy spinning jokes.

—*B.C., December 22, 1961*

ONLY ANGELS HAVE WINGS

Produced and directed by Howard Hawks; written by William Rankin, Eleanore Griffin and Jules Furthman, based on a story by Mr. Hawks; cinematographers, Joseph Walker and Elmer Dyer; edited by Viola Lawrence; music by Dimitri Tiomkin; art designer, Lionel Banks; released by Columbia Pictures. Black and white. Running time: 121 minutes.

With: Cary Grant (Geoff Carter), Jean Arthur (Bonnie Lee), Richard Barthelmess (Bat MacPherson), Rita Hayworth (Judy), Thomas Mitchell (Kid Dabb), Allyn Joslyn (Les Peters), Sig Rumann (Dutchy) and Victor Kilian (Sparks).

Howard Hawks, whose aviation melodramas must, we suspect, drive airline stock down from two to three points per showing, has produced another fatality littered thriller in *Only Angels Have Wings* (even the title is ominous) which opened yesterday at the Music Hall. This once, however, Mr. Hawks has charitably transferred his operations base to Ecuador, presumably having exhausted his local sources, not to mention the patience of the commercial transport people.

In Ecuador, in the banana port of Barranca, he has indulged himself and the vicarious adventurers in the audience in a delightful series of crack-ups, close-shaves, and studiously dramatic speeches. It is all very exciting and juvenile.

Barranca, says Mr. Hawks, is a sultry little spot boasting a general store and bar, a swampy landing field, and Cary Grant as operations manager for a junky airline which must maintain a regular schedule for six months to obtain the mail subsidy. Flying conditions are rarely better than impossible. There are the Andes, there is a narrow pass with clawing crags, and a group of pilots who seem to be proud targets for all the slings and arrows of outrageous fortune, chiefly of feminine origin.

We particularly marveled at one sequence in which a flyer, grounded by failing eyesight, breaks another's arm in a fight and soon is helping probe a bullet from the commander's shoulder. That is known as piling it on.

Not content with this fell setup, Mr. Hawks, as author, has chosen to add a few dramatic and romantic complications. Miss Arthur enters the scene as a stranded showgirl, and a less convincing showgirl than Miss Arthur would be hard to find. Enter, too, Richard Barthelmess as a pilot with a black blot on his record and a wife who, by some strange coincidence, used to be Mr. Grant's fiancée.

The brew stirs slowly, as is the way with two-hour shows, tending toward silly romanticism in its dialogue, but moving splendidly whenever the plot's wheels leave the ground and take off over the Andes.

Few things, after all, are as exciting as a plane in flames, or the metallic voices of a pilot in a fog shrouded plane and the chap in the radio room, or a screaming power dive, or the wild downward swoop of a plane taking off from a canyon's rim.

Mr. Hawks has staged his flying sequences brilliantly. He has caught the drama in the meeting of a flier and the brother of the man he killed. He has made proper use of the amiable performing talents of Mr. Grant, Miss Arthur, Thomas Mitchell, Mr. Barthelmess, Sig Rumann, and the rest. But when you add it all up, *Only Angels Have Wings* comes to an overly familiar total. It's a fairly good melodrama, nothing more.

—*F.S.N., May 12, 1939*

OPEN CITY

Produced and directed by Roberto Rossellini; written (in Italian, with English subtitles) by Sergio Amidei. Federico Fellini and Mr. Rossellini. based on a story by Mr. Amidei and Alberto Consiglio: cinematographer. Ubaldo Arata: music by Renzo Rossellini: released by Mayer-Burstyn. Black and white. Running time: 105 minutes.

With: Marcello Pagliero (Manfredi). Aldo Fabrizi (Don Pietro). Anna Magnani (Pina). Vito Annicchiarico (Marcello). Maria Michi (Marina Mari) and Harry Feist (Captain Bergmann).

It may seem peculiarly ironic that the first film yet seen hereabouts to dramatize the nature and the spirit of underground resistance in German-held Europe in a superior way—with candid, overpowering realism and with a passionate sense of human fortitude—should be a film made in Italy. Yet such is the extraordinary case. *Open City* (*Citta Aperta*), which arrived at the World last night, is unquestionably one of the strongest dramatic films yet made about the recent war. And the fact that it was hurriedly put together by a group of artists soon after the liberation of Rome is significant of its fervor and doubtless integrity.

For such a picture as *Open City* would not likely be made under normal and established conditions. In the first place, it has the windblown look of a film shot from actualities, with the camera providentially on the scene. All of its exterior action is in the streets and open places of Rome; the interior scenes are played quite obviously in actual buildings or modest sets. The stringent necessity for economy compelled the producers to make a film that has all the appearance and flavor of a straight documentary.

And the feeling that pulses through it gives evidence that it was inspired by artists whose own emotions had been deeply and recently stirred. Anger, grim and determined, against the Germans and collaborationists throbs in every sequence and every shot in which the evil ones are shown. Yet the anger is not shrill or hysterical; it is the clarified anger of those who have known and dreaded the cruelty and depravity of men who are their foes. It is anger long since drained of astonishment or outrage.

More than anger, however, the feeling that flows most strongly through the film is one of supreme admiration for the people who fight for freedom's cause. It is a quiet exaltation, conveyed mainly through attitudes and simple words, illuminating the spirit of devotion and sacrifice. The heroes in *Open City* are not conscious of being such. Nor are the artists who conceived them. They are simple people doing what they think is right.

The story of the film is literal. It might have been taken from the notes of any true observer in occupied Europe—and, indeed, is said to have been based on actual facts. It is the story of an underground agent who is cornered by the Germans in a certain quarter of Rome and who barely escapes them until he is informed upon by his own girlfriend. In the course of his flight he necessarily involves his resistance friends: a printer of an underground newspaper, his wife-to-be and her small son, and a neighborhood priest who uses his religious office to aid freedom's cause. The woman is killed during a raid on an apartment, the captured resistance leader is tortured to death, and the priest is shot when he refuses to assist the Germans with any information.

All these details are presented in a most frank and uncompromising way which is likely to prove somewhat shocking to sheltered American audiences.

Yet the total effect of the picture is a sense of real experience, achieved as much by the performance as by the writing and direction. The outstanding performance is that of Aldo Fabrizi as the priest, who embraces with dignity and humanity a most demanding part.

Marcello Pagliero is excellent, too, as the resistance leader, and Anna Magnani brings humility and sincerity to the role of the woman who is killed. The remaining cast is unqualifiedly fine; with the exception of Harry Feist in the role of the German commander. His elegant arrogance is a bit too vicious—but that may be easily understood.

—*B.C., February 26, 1946*

OPERATION CROSSBOW

Directed by Michael Anderson: written by Ray Rigby. Derry Quinn and Emeric Pressburger: based on a story by Duilio Coletti and Vittoriano Petrilli: cinematographer. Erwin Hillier: edited by Ernest Walter: music by Ron Goodwin: art designer. Elliot Scott: produced by Carlo Ponti: released by Metro-Goldwyn-Mayer. Running time: 116 minutes.

With: Sophia Loren (Nora), George Peppard (John Curtis), Trevor Howard (Professor Lindemane), John Mills (Boyd), Richard Johnson (Duncan Sandys), Tom Courtenay (Robert Henshaw), Jeremy Kemp (Phil Bradley) and Anthony Quayle (Bamford).

Outside of the fact that it is an odd one to turn up as the "Easter film" at the Music Hall, *Operation Crossbow* is a beauty that no action-mystery-spy movie fan should miss. It is a grandly engrossing and exciting melodrama of wartime espionage, done with stunning documentary touches in a tight, tense, heroic story line. And even though its terminal pyrotechnics may seem a bit far from the mood of the "Glory of Easter" pageant and the vernal stage show that opened at the hall yesterday, it does end piously and quietly on a note of hope for the peaceful future of mankind.

It is, to put it quite simply—much more simply than the film itself is put—a story, part fact and part fiction, of how a complex British espionage team (which includes an inevitable American), acting under the secret direction of Duncan Sandys, discovers and scouts and finally blows up the deadly rocket bases in Nazi Germany and finally knocks out an underground factory from which a rocket to hit New York is about to be launched.

That is the substance of it, but that does not begin to tell the staggering complexity of its details and the swift precision with which they are interlocked. Richard Imrie, Derry Quinn, and Ray Rigby have put together a script that fairly bristles with assorted activities.

From the mellow cabinet room of the Prime Minister at 10 Downing Street, whence a grim, brooding Winston Churchill (Patrick Wymark) dispatches Duncan Sandys (Richard Johnson) to look into this business of secret weapons being constructed in Nazi Germany, *Operation Crossbow* skyrockets directly to the technical planning stage, to the business of preparation and training, and then, spang, into Germany!

It deftly counterpoints the tough recruitment of a team of Allied experts who will do the crucial spying and sabotaging behind the enemy lines against some brilliantly re-enacted drama of the Nazi efforts to launch their V-1 rockets, then their V-2's. It briskly builds up a realization of the urgency of the enterprise by pounding the eyes and ears of the audience with intercuts of the damage these missiles do. And then it completes the excitement with the tracing and the tying of the many strands of adventures and calamities of the fellows who drop into Germany.

There's the American, played by George Peppard, who has the most activity and suspense, including a touch-and-go brush with the widow of the German scientist whose identity he has assumed. The widow is played intensely by a black-wigged Sophia Loren. There's a Netherlander, played by Tom Courtenay, who is caught rather early along, and there's a wonderfully dry British agent who comes along later. He is played deliciously by Jeremy Kemp.

Behind these there's a slew of apt supporters—Lilli Palmer as a German innkeeper, John Mills as the chief of M.I. 6, Sylvia Syms as a photo interpreter, Maurice Denham as a Royal Air Force general, Richard Todd as a shrewd intelligence officer, Trevor Howard as an unregenerate skeptic, and many more.

The Nazis are played expertly by such old hands at this always juicy task as Paul Henreid, Helmut Dantine, Karl Stepanek, and Barbara Rueting, who is impressive as the test pilot of the V-1 flying bomb.

The whole thing is shot in excellent color, under the fine direction of Michael Anderson, who is best remembered for his direction of *Around the World in 80 Days*. And a strong illusion of actuality is got by having the Nazi characters speak German and using English subtitles to translate their dialogue.

Everything flows together swiftly in one fine, free, and finally fictional sweep, and the whole thing blows up much more brightly and credibly than did *The Guns of Navarone*.

—B.C., April 2, 1965

THE OPPOSITE OF SEX

Written and directed by Don Roos: director of photography. Hubert Taczanowski: edited by David Codron: music by Mason Daring: production designer. Michael Clausen: produced by David Kirkpatrick and Michael Besman: released by Sony Pictures Classics. Running time: 100 minutes.

With: Christina Ricci (Dedee Truitt), Martin Donovan (Bill Truitt), Lisa Kudrow (Lucia), Lyle Lovett

(Carl Tippett), Johnny Galecki (Jason), Ivan Sergei (Matt Mateo) and William Scott Lee (Randy).

Christina Ricci has morphed enchantingly from wicked little Wednesday of the *Addams Family* comedies into Lolita's evil twin. Voluptuous and scheming in Don Roos's gleefully acerbic comedy *The Opposite of Sex,* she plays the nasty little baggage named Dedee whose sexual chicanery and self-interest know no bounds. Neither does Mr. Roos's barbed humor as he mocks preconceptions about straight and gay lifestyles with total abandon, rude epithets and all. What redeem the film's surface bitterness are sharp observations, laceratingly funny dialogue, and something Dedee claims to find especially loathsome: a secret heart of gold.

Dedee narrates this busily plotted, nicely unpredictable sex comedy with a sarcastic edge. ("If you think I'm just plucky and scrappy and all I need is love, you're in over your head," she tells the audience right off the bat.) Trying out little tricks on her listeners whenever she feels like it, she explains how she left home in Louisiana to barge in on Bill (Martin Donovan), her levelheaded half brother. Bill is the kind of schoolteacher who, when finding rude graffiti about himself on a bathroom wall, corrects its faulty grammar. Bill is also gay, and his happy, stable relationship with Matt (Ivan Sergei) gives Dedee her first chance to pounce.

Stacked little Dedee doesn't so much seduce Matt as plop down in a bathing suit and bully him into giving heterosexuality a try. Soon she is pregnant and has run off with both Matt and a chunk of her half brother's savings, prompting an anti-Dedee backlash from the film's colorful array of supporting characters. Funniest and most touching of these is Lisa Kudrow's Lucia, the sister of Bill's previous lover, who died of AIDS. (Dedee insists on referring to him as "Tom the dead guy.") Ms. Kudrow sustains her expert *Friends* timing in a role that's a marked departure: a lonely, spinsterish schoolteacher who expresses her jealousy of others' happiness in especially funny ways.

"I never knew my father," Dedee tells her, by way of explaining the liaison with Matt. "And you really think this is a good way to make up for it?" Lucia inquires. To Matt's claims that he is now bisexual, Lucia snaps: "Please, I went to a bar mitzvah once. That doesn't make me Jewish."

Lucia and Bill, played with cool, quiet strength by Mr. Donovan, wind up joining forces in pursuit of Dedee, whom Lucia calls "the human tabloid." They track her to another city and spy on her with yet another lover. "That can't be good for the baby," muses Lucia, peering through a window. "Not only that, she's gonna smoke a cigarette after," adds Bill. And what about Matt, who by now is being cuckolded? ("He made his bed, he can lie in it." "If there's room.")

Well into this comedy of unspeakably bad manners (Dedee's, anyway), the wisecracks are outweighed by gratifyingly tenderhearted developments. Mr. Roos, making his directorial debut (after strong screenwriting credits including *Boys on the Side, Love Field,* and *Single White Female*), guides his lonely, smart-talking characters into relationships none ever thought possible.

This makes for a happy ending even if Dedee winds up throwing something at the camera. And the film's resolution gracefully repudiates all its poisonous talk, especially the stream of small-minded slurs about gay life that come from Dedee. Essentially generous, *The Opposite of Sex* winds up showing rotten little Dedee how little sense there is in stereotypes, and how varied and surprising love can be.

Also in *The Opposite of Sex* are Lyle Lovett as an accommodating policeman and Johnny Galecki as a gay student who tries to blackmail Bill after Matt vanishes. "For all I know, you killed him," the boy insists. "For all you know," Bill replies evenly, "I'm just getting started."

—*J.M., May 29, 1998*

ORDINARY PEOPLE

Directed by Robert Redford; written by Alvin Sargent, based on the novel by Judith Guest; director of photography, John Bailey; edited by Jeff Kanew; music adapted by Marvin Hamlisch; produced by Ronald L. Schwary; released by Paramount Pictures. Running time: 124 minutes.

With: Donald Sutherland (Calvin), Mary Tyler Moore (Beth), Judd Hirsch (Berger), Timothy Hutton (Conrad), M. Emmet Walsh (Swim Coach), Elizabeth McGovern (Jeannine) and Dinah Manoff (Karen).

The Jarretts are of the WASP family now common in most parts of the continental United States. They are Calvin Jarrett, a successful tax lawyer, Beth, his immaculately pretty wife, who runs the family as if life were something to be organized like a tennis tournament, and eighteen-year-old Conrad, their surviving son, fourteen months younger than Bucky Jarrett, who died a year and a half earlier.

The Jarretts are ordinary people, but they are extraordinarily privileged. They live in upper-middle-class splendor in Lake Forest, still Chicago's poshest suburb, and though the Jarretts don't live on a scale comparable to that of the "old" Lake Forest families, whose pre–World War I fortunes had their origins in meat packing, banking, railroading, and mail-order retailing, they inhabit a beautiful house that is much too big for them, have two cars, a country-club membership, and can afford vacations anywhere in the world whenever it suits them.

In her spare, efficient, best selling novel, Judith Guest, seemingly without trying, dissected the contemporary white Anglo-Saxon Protestant psyche when, by accident, such perfect order is destroyed. Recently achieved economic and social privilege is no defense against emotional chaos. Privilege is a plywood treehouse in a hurricane.

The very real achievement of Robert Redford, who makes his directorial debut with *Ordinary People,* and of Alvin Sargent, who meticulously adapted Miss Guest's novel for the screen, is that the Jarretts become important people without losing their ordinariness, without being patronized or satirized. *Ordinary People,* which opens today at the Loews Tower East, is a moving, intelligent, and funny film about disasters that are commonplace to everyone except the people who experience them. Not since Robert Benton's *Kramer vs. Kramer* has there been a movie that so effectively catches the look, sound, and temper of a particular kind of American existence.

The Jarretts are not only ordinary people, they are also "nice" people. They wear the right clothes, read the right books, eat the right things, and misbehave discreetly. They put great store in self-control, as much in the privacy of their own house as abroad in the company of friends or strangers. The problem is that such niceness and control cannot accommodate the fears, furies, and resentments occasioned when things go to pieces.

At the start of *Ordinary People,* young Conrad Jarrett (Timothy Hutton) has been home from the hospital for just a month and is trying very hard to resume life—school, the swimming team, the glee club—as if, five months earlier, he hadn't attempted suicide by slashing his wrists. Anyone looking at Conrad can tell that he is a wreck. He doesn't eat. He's nervous and he's too quick to say whatever he knows his mother and father want to hear.

Though Calvin (Donald Sutherland) worries about Conrad, he is unable to do much more than be enthusiastic in response to everything Conrad says. Beth (Mary Tyler Moore) resolutely pretends that there's nothing wrong with her son. She goes about her daily routine of golf, tennis, bridge, and committee meetings with the determination not of someone living the good life in suburbia, but of a woman climbing Everest. Her jaw is set. She doesn't look back or down.

She's quite right when she says at one point, "We'd have been all right if there hadn't been any mess."

The Jarretts' "mess" was the accidental drowning of Bucky Jarrett one summer afternoon when he and Conrad were sailing together on Lake Michigan. Bucky, the strong one, gave up and drifted away from the overturned boat. Conrad survived, in guilt and sorrow, but when he realized he couldn't be the son Bucky was, he chose suicide.

More than five months after the suicide attempt, Conrad is in even worse shape than before. His mother, he tells the psychiatrist, will never forgive him for, among other things, having ruined the bathroom rug when he cut his wrists. "She had to pitch it out," he says. "They even had to regrout the tile floor."

In several ways, Mr. Redford's film is far more effective than the novel. It's difficult to write about people who cannot talk to each other because writing is itself a kind of talking. Mr. Redford's film demonstrates this lack of communication, the inability to express affection, in scenes of sometimes overwhelming pathos—a Christmas Day gone all to hell for Conrad when his mother, as if in reflex, refuses to have her picture taken with her son.

Though *Ordinary People* focuses on the rehabilitation of Conrad, mostly through the efforts of a wise, understanding, quick-witted psychiatrist, played by Judd Hirsch, the film's most interesting character is Beth Jarrett, a Bonwit Teller lady hanging onto her sanity by fingertips made of steel.

Miss Moore is remarkably fine, simultaneously delicate and tough and desperate. The only reason she doesn't dominate the film is that all the other performances are equally good. Mr. Hutton is excellent in the difficult role of the deeply troubled boy, a nascent jock who, had there been no accident, might have gone through life always in second place and growing nothing much more than a slight paunch. Mr. Sutherland realizes his best film role in years, playing a fellow who, filled with love for both his wife and his son, is angrily accused by each of fence-sitting, of being weak and indecisive when he's really the only one in the family with some idea of what is wrong.

The supporting roles are splendidly handled by Mr. Hirsch, by a sweet newcomer named Elizabeth McGovern, as the girl who falls in love with Conrad despite Conrad's conviction that he is a no-good kid, and by Dinah Manoff, in the brief but splashy role of a young woman who shared Conrad's time in the psychiatric hospital.

Mr. Redford's appreciation for his actors is apparent, but it is also disciplined. *Ordinary People* doesn't look like any director's first movie. With the exception of fleeting flashbacks, which are necessary, I suppose, for exposition, the film's manner is cool, gentle, reserved. It never forces the emotions. It watches them erupt and allows us to make of them what we will, that is, until the last few minutes.

Though the film's ending approximates the novel's, it doesn't play very well on the screen. It's ordinary in the least interesting cinematic way. That, however, may be nit-picking. *Ordinary People* is otherwise so good—so full of rare feeling—that it would be presumptuous for a critic to attempt to re-edit it.

—*V.C., September 19, 1980*

OSSESSIONE

Directed by Luchino Visconti; written (in Italian, with English subtitles) by Mario Alicata, Antonio Pietrangeli, Gianni Puccini, Giuseppe De Santis and Mr. Visconti, based on the novel *The Postman Always Rings Twice* by James M. Cain; cinematographers, Aldo Tonti and Domenico Scala; edited by Mario Serandrei; music by Giuseppe Rosati; art designer, Gino Rosati; produced by Libero Solaroli; released by ICI Roma. Black and white. Running time: 112 minutes.

With: Clara Calamai (Giovanna), Massimo Girotti (Gino), Juan De Landa (The Husband), Elio Marcuzzo (Lo Spagnuolo) and Dhia Cristani (Anita).

Although there are almost as many definitions of Italian neorealism as there are Italian neorealist films, Luchino Visconti's first feature, *Ossessione,* made in 1942, is generally accepted as having launched the movement whose name was later applied to the work of Antonioni, Rossellini, De Sica, and others.

The film, which will be presented today at the New York Film Festival at Alice Tully Hall and again on Tuesday, is being shown here in a 35mm print for the first time. Earlier showings in the United States had been prohibited because Mr. Visconti had, without permission, helped himself to James M. Cain's novel, *The Postman Always Rings Twice,* the rights to which were owned by M-G-M, the studio that later filmed it in 1946 with John Garfield and Lana Turner under Tay Garnett's direction.

Comparing the Visconti *Ossessione* with the Garnett *Postman* is to stand a production of *Traviata* next to a McDonald's television commercial, which is not meant to underrate the American film that is as effectively steamy, tough, and terse as the Hollywood law allowed in those days.

Mr. Visconti follows with remarkable fidelity the Cain story about the handsome young drifter and the youngish wife who, driven by their sexual passion and greed, murder the woman's old husband to get his money and his business, a combination hamburger stand and filling station.

Ossessione today looks to be an extraordinarily majestic, elegant, and romantic movie to have started anything labeled neorealism. There is even something grand about the bleakness of the Italian landscapes, to say nothing of the mood. When the illicit lovers, Gino (Massimo Girotti) and Giovanna (Clara Calamai), are exchanging lustful glances at the dinner table, the soundtrack rumbles with the sounds of distant thunder and frantic cries of caged farm animals. Under these circumstances, one is disappointed that the characters don't sing.

Ossessione, which also launched the late Mr. Visconti's remarkable film career, may be slow-going to the uninitiated, but it's historical importance is not to be denied.

—V.C., October 2, 1976

OTHELLO

Produced and directed by Orson Welles; written by Mr. Welles, based on the play by William Shakespeare; cinematographers, Anchise Brizzi, G. R. Aldo, George Fanto, Oberdan Troiani and Alberto Fusi; edited by Jean Sacha, John Shepridge, Renzo Lucidi and William Morton; music by Angelo Francesco Lavagnino; art designer, Alexander Trauner; released by United Artists. Black and white. Running time: 90 minutes.

With: Orson Welles (Othello), Michael MacLiammoir (Iago), Suzanne Cloutier (Desdemona), Robert Coote (Roderigo), Hilton Edwards (Brabantio) and Michael Lawrence (Cassio).

How much of Shakespeare's *Othello* you are likely to be able to perceive in Orson Welles's motion picture version of it, which came to the Paris yesterday, is something this dazzled reviewer would not like to have to guarantee. Shakespeare himself, set down before it, might have a tough time recognizing his play.

For the great Mr. Welles apparently decided, when he set out to make and play this film in the authentic locale of Venice some six or eight years ago, that the text and even the plot of the original were incidental to the dark and delirious passions enclosed in its tormented theme. That theme is, of course, the tragic downfall of a man racked by jealousy, aroused by the treacherous rumor-mongering and conniving of an ungrateful friend.

What matters it that Othello bears a sense of social stigma in the play, based on the fact that he is an alien, a professional soldier, and, particularly, a dark-skinned Moor? What matters it that Iago, his villainous and deceitful "friend," hates him because he fancies Othello has captivated his wife? These are details and motivations that have been completely overlooked by Mr. Welles. All that he seems to find intriguing are the currents of hate and villainy.

And so this extraordinary picture, which took more than three years to make and equally as long—or longer—to re-dub and prepare for showing here, is strictly an un-literate, inarticulate, and hotly impressionistic film, full of pictorial pyrotechnics and sinister, shadowy moods.

Let's be completely forthright about the talent revealed by Mr. Welles. He has a wonderful skill at image-making but a blind spot where substance is concerned. For instance, he makes of the murder of Desdemona a chilling nightmarish display of stark faces, frenzied movements, architectural compositions, and shifting lights, cut into a montage with accompanying music and screams. But he backs up this hot, erratic action with little feeling for character or regard for the genuine human torment that is implied in this melodramatic display.

It would be hard to improve upon this rendering of *Othello* for sheer mise-en-scène. Mr. Welles has got Venice and Cyprus (or what passes for Cyprus) down to the ground. All the urbanity and stony beauty of the great Adriatic port and the island of Othello's triumph are made sharply visual in this film.

But, alas for the import of the drama! It is mainly spectacle—elaborate, expensive, complicated—with no continuity, meaning, or soul. Mr. Welles's own dusky Othello is a towering shadow of a man, monstrous in his pictorial movements but as hollow and heartless as a shell. And Michael MacLiammoir's Iago, which should be the sparkplug and fuse of the play, is not only vague in behavior but also almost impossible to understand. You can't expect much from an Iago when you can't hear the little that he says.

Suzanne Cloutier's Desdemona is a beautiful, frail, and gauzy girl who might be tremendously moving if you could sense her in relation to her man. But Mr. Welles has kept her an image of feminine anguish and nothing more. Her grief and the tragedy of her murder are purely theatrical displays. Robert Coote's Roderigo and the Cassio of Michael Lawrence are almost undistinguishable figures in a decidedly unclear plot.

There are flashes of brilliant suggestion in this tumbled, slurred, and helter-skelter film. But they add up to nothing substantial—just a little Shakespeare and a lot of Welles.

—B.C., September 13, 1955

OUR TOWN

Directed by Sam Wood; written by Thornton Wilder, Frank Craven and Harry Chandlee, based on the play by Mr. Wilder; cinematographer, Bert Glennon; edited by Sherman Todd; music by Aaron Copland; production designers, William Cameron Menzies and Harry Horner; produced by Sol Lesser; released by United Artists. Black and white. Running time: 90 minutes.

With: Frank Craven (Mr. Morgan, the Narrator), William Holden (George Gibbs), Martha Scott (Emily Webb), Fay Bainter (Mrs. Gibbs), Beulah Bondi (Mrs. Webb), Thomas Mitchell (Dr. Gibbs), Guy Kibbee (Editor Webb) and Stuart Erwin (Howie Newsome).

There is reason to take hope this morning, to find renewed faith and confidence in mankind—and, incidentally, in the artistry of the screen. For the film version of Thornton Wilder's prize-winning play, *Our Town,* opened yesterday at the Music Hall, and a more tonic and reassuring avowal of the nobility which resides in just plain folks—and the capacity for expression possessed by the screen—has not come this way in longer than we care to recall.

Mr. Wilder's play, which opened on Broadway in the winter of 1938, was a profoundly affecting drama, almost too sharply poignant in its exposure of human joy and grief for endurance. Gently but without stint, it lay bare the human heart and revealed the defenseless impulses of that member. As a play it was done without scenery, thus evoking the most fragile imagery; and, for this reason, it seemed almost too spiritual for transference to the screen. But now that producer Sol Lesser has had the insight to put it onto film—and to do so almost scene for scene and word for word—it is apparent that a finer original screenplay could scarcely have been written.

For this is not an ordinary picture, not a straight-away plotted-story film. This is a picture which utilizes the fullest prerogatives of the camera to participate as a recognized witness to a simple dramatic account of people's lives, not just to spy on someone's fictitious emotions. On the stage there was a character, known as the stage manager, who conducted the action of the play; on the screen, a small-town druggist acts as guide and narrator on a leisurely tour of a little New Hampshire town. He introduces characters who speak directly to the camera—or to the audience—and he takes time out to make incidental remarks himself. Once he places his hand before the lens to stop a sequence and introduce another. The camera thus becomes animate, not just a recording machine. It is an exciting technique, used occasionally before—by Sacha Guitry notably—and enhances the scope of the screen tremendously.

The story of *Our Town,* of course, is quite simple, but more powerful because of its simplicity. It is the story of several people living in Grovers Corner, New Hampshire, during the early years of this century. And chiefly it is the story of a boy and girl, children of neighboring parents, who fall in love, get married and have a child.

But because of the technique employed we are permitted to see these people in their entirety; we see them in their normal daily tasks, we hear the thoughts which run through their minds and, at the end, we behold the dream of death and survival of the soul which is dreamed by the girl who is soon to become a mother. It is, in short, a comprehensive penetration of the hearts of these good people, an external glance at the toils and humors of their humdrum lives and an internal revelation of their sorrows which brings, as Matthew Arnold said, "the eternal note of sadness in."

Not enough can be said for the courage of Mr. Lesser in producing a picture in this fashion, nor enough for the excellent contributions of everyone involved. Frank Craven as the druggist and narrator is the perfect New England Socrates—honest, sincere, and profound. Martha Scott, as the young girl, is lovely and vibrant with emotion, and William Holden plays the boy with a clean and refreshing youthfulness. Excellent projections of small-town characters are given by Beulah Bondi, Thomas Mitchell, Fay Bainter, Guy Kibbee, Stuart Erwin, and a host of other folks. And Sam Wood has caught in his direction all the flavor of small-town life, with exciting visual elaborations upon the theme. Likewise the score by Aaron Copland offers a subtle tonal response to the vagrant moods.

We hesitate to employ superlatives, but of *Our Town* the least we can say is that it captures on film the simple beauties and truths of humble folks as very few pictures ever do; it is rich and ennobling in its plain philosophy—and it gives one a passionate desire to enjoy the fullness of life even in these good old days of today.

—B.C., June 14, 1940

OUT OF THE PAST

Directed by Jacques Tourneur: written by Geoffrey Homes, Frank Fenton and James M. Cain, based on the novel *Build My Gallows High* by Mr. Homes: cinematographer, Nicholas Musuraca: edited by Samuel E. Beetley: music by Roy Webb: art designers, Albert S. D'Agostino and Jack Okey: produced by Warren Duff: released by RKO Radio Pictures. Black and white. Running time: 97 minutes.

With: Robert Mitchum (Jeff), Jane Greer (Kathie), Kirk Douglas (Whit), Rhonda Fleming (Meta Carson), Richard Webb (Jim), Steve Brodie (Fisher), Virginia Huston (Ann), Paul Valentine (Joe), Dickie Moore (The Kid) and Ken Niles (Eels).

There have been double- and triple-crosses in many of these tough detective films, and in one or two Humphrey Bogart specials they have run even higher than that. But the sum of deceitful complications that occur in *Out of the Past* must be reckoned by logarithmic tables, so numerous and involved do they become. The consequence is that the action of this new film, which came to the Palace yesterday, is likely to leave the napping or unmathematical customer far behind.

Frankly, that's where it left us. We were with it, up to a point, and enjoying the rough-stuff and the romance with considerable delight and concern. For this story of an ex-private detective who is shanghaied from a quiet, prosaic life to get involved with his old criminal associates is intensely fascinating for a time. And it is made even more galvanic by a smooth realistic style, by fast dialogue, and genuine settings in California and Mexican locales.

But after this private detective has reencountered an old girl friend (who originally double-crossed him after luring him to double-cross his boss, whom she had shot) and the two get elaborately criss-crossed in a plot to triple-cross our boy again, the involutions of the story become much too complex for us. The style is still sharp and realistic, the dialogue still crackles with verbal sparks, and the action is still crisp and muscular, not to mention slightly wanton in spots. But the pattern and purpose of it is beyond our pedestrian ken. People get killed, the tough guys browbeat, the hero hurries—but we can't tell you why.

However, as we say, it's very snappy and quite intriguingly played by a cast that has been well and smartly directed by Jacques Tourneur. Robert Mitchum is magnificently cheekly and self-assured as the tangled "private eye," consuming an astronomical number of cigarettes in displaying his nonchalance. And Jane Greer is very sleek as his Delilah, Kirk Douglas is crisp as a big crook, and Richard Webb, Virginia Huston, Rhonda Fleming, and Dickie Moore are picturesque in other roles. If only we had some way of knowing what's going on in the last half of this film, we might get more pleasure from it. As it is, the challenge is worth a try.

—B.C., November 26, 1947

THE OUTLAW JOSEY WALES

Directed by Clint Eastwood: written by Philip Kaufman and Sonia Chernus, based on the book *Gone to Texas* by Forrest Carter: director of photography, Bruce Surtees: edited by Ferris Webster, music by Jerry Fielding: production designer, Tambi Larsen: produced by Robert Daley: released by Warner Brothers. Running time: 137 minutes.

With: Clint Eastwood (Josey Wales), Chief Dan George (Lone Watie), Sondra Locke (Laura Lee), Bill McKinney (Terrill), John Vernon (Fletcher), Paula Trueman (Grandma Sarah) and Sam Bottoms (Jamie).

Each time Clint Eastwood, in *The Outlaw Josey Wales*, kills someone, or is about to kill someone, or is on the verge of some other major policy decision, he spits. This is to establish the character.

Mr. Eastwood has established several pints of character by the time he rides off into the sunset fully two hours and seventeen minutes after the movie begins. A number of other characters are established by devices every bit as worn and dribbly.

A hard-luck but winsome Indian girl repeatedly gets knocked off her feet or worse; a sneaky boatman cringes and leers; a spry old woman bustles about with a broom, shrills out hymns, and grabs a rifle to shoot marauders; a doe-eyed young woman opens her eyes reindeer-size to convey fear, passion, or bashfulness; a young follower of the outlaw manages three distinct and radiant deathbed scenes on one bullet hole.

The Outlaw Josey Wales, which opened yesterday at various local theaters, is a soggy attempt at a post–Civil War western epic. Josey Wales, a peaceable Missouri farmer, has his farm burned and his wife and child killed by Unionist freebooters. He joins a gang of Confederate marauders, goes through the war—conveyed briefly by a montage of war shots—mows down a platoon of Union soldiers, and flees to Texas with a price on his head and an array of vicious lawmen and bounty hunters after him.

It is a long exodus, in the course of which Wales kills a great many people and, despite his contention that he wants to travel alone, picks up a whole variegated convoy of stock characters.

They are tedious companions on such a long trip, especially because most of them—Paula Trueman as the old woman, Sondra Locke as the doe-eyed daughter, Sam Bottoms as Wales's dying follower—overact beyond belief. Their lines don't help them. "Clouds are the dreams floating across the sky of your mind," doe-eyes tells Wales.

Will Sampson, who played the Indian in *One Flew Over the Cuckoo's Nest,* and another Indian in *Buffalo Bill,* does a blue-painted Navajo chieftain and gets to say, among other things: "Your words of death carry iron." Mr. Sampson has specialized in displaced-Indian roles. As a real warrior Indian he seems embarrassed.

Playing a civilized Indian who attaches himself to Wales, Chief Dan George has moments of dry humor and whole stretches of damp whimsy. Mr. Eastwood, as indicated earlier, doesn't act; he spits. He is also the director.

The movie tends to muffle and sell short whatever points it may be trying to make. There seems to be a ghost of an attempt to assert the romantic individualism of the South against the cold expansionism of the North. Every Unionist is vicious and incompetent, whereas Wales, despite his spitting, is really a perfect gentleman.

There is something cynical about this primitive one-sidedness in what is not only a historical context, but happens also to be our own historical context. To the degree a movie asserts history, it should at least attempt to do it fairly.

—*R.E., August 5, 1976*

THE OVERLANDERS

Written and directed by Harry Watt; cinematographer, Osmond Borradaile; edited by Leslie Norman and Inman Hunter; music by John Ireland; produced by Michael Balcon and Ralph Smart; released by Ealing and Universal Pictures. Black and white. Running time: 91 minutes.

With: Chips Rafferty (Dan McAlpine), John Nugent Howard (Bill Parsons), Daphne Campbell (Mary Parsons), Jean Blue (Mrs. Parsons), Helen Grieve (Helen Parsons), John Fernside (Corky), Peter Pagan (Sinbad) and Frank Ransome (Charlie).

Vividly reminiscent of Merian C. Cooper's and Ernest Schoedsack's old film, *Grass,* which recounted with documentary brilliance the migrations of a Persian nomad tribe in search of pasture land for their cattle, is the British-Australian film entitled *The Overlanders,* which opened at the Rialto last night. And that is because this real-life drama, which was written and directed by Harry Watt, is not only based upon a similar subject but is in much the same cinematic style.

Based on the actual experience of northern Australian cattlemen who drove their herds across that continent in 1942 to keep them from the Japanese invaders, this epic picture reenacts the adventures of one hardy "plant" of drovers, represented as the first, on that stern and exceedingly perilous 1,600-mile trek. It follows the trials and sudden crises of this brave little nondescript band, headed by a rugged old-timer and including a mother and two young girls, as they trail their "mob" of clumsy cattle across the barren and dusty wastes, evading disasters by ingenuity and constantly worrying about water and forage for their beasts. And it concludes with the successful delivery of the cattle to the Queensland corrals, the pretty termination of a minor romance, and the northward departure of the drovers for another herd.

Although the story is fictional in structure, mounting through various episodes to a stirring climax in which the cattle are kept from stampeding by the drovers on foot, the film has been made in such a fashion within the actual Australian locales that it has all the visual authority of a photographic record of a literal trek. Mr. Watt, who is impressively remembered for his direction of such British war films as *London Can Take It* and *Target for Tonight,* has employed the "documentary method" for great pictorial and dramatic effect. And he has handled a group of native actors to point convincingly their personalities.

In the role of the rugged boss drover, Chips Rafferty, an experienced Australian star (he was seen in *10,000 Horsemen*), does a cool and masterful job. His face is lean, his voice is gravelly, he sits a horse with magnificent know-how, and he can crack a bull-whip at a herd of cattle with the lash of a palm tree in a gale. John Fernside and John Nugent Howard are also sturdy as drovers in the "plant," and Daphne Campbell, a former nursing orderly, looks and acts the real thing as a young cowgirl. Other pick-up actors are as right as the band's battered camp gear.

This film was made at the order of Michael Balcon, head of Ealing Studio in London, for the purpose of presenting a true picture of Australian life. It had the complete cooperation of the Commonwealth and state governments, and was filmed in remote localities where native beauty and character prevail. To the credit of all who worked on it, but especially of Mr. Watt, it is not only an impressive picture of Australia but it is an exciting and captivating entertainment as well.

—B.C., December 20, 1946

THE OX-BOW INCIDENT

Directed by William A. Wellman; written by Lamar Trotti, based on the novel by Walter Van Tilburg Clark; cinematographer, Arthur Miller; edited by Allen McNeil; music by Cyril J. Mockbridge; art designers, Richard Day and James Basevi; produced by Mr. Trotti; released by Twentieth Century Fox. Black and white. Running time: 75 minutes.

With: Henry Fonda (Gil Carter), Dana Andrews (Donald Martin), Mary Beth Hughes (Rose Mapen), Anthony Quinn (Juan Martines), William Eythe (Gerald Tetley), Harry Morgan (Art Croft) and Jane Darwell (Ma Grier).

An ugly study in mob violence, unrelieved by any human grace save the futile reproach of a minority and some mild post-lynching remorse, is contained in *The Ox-Bow Incident,* which was delivered to the Rivoli on Saturday by Twentieth Century Fox in as brazen a gesture as any studio has ever indulged. For it is hard to imagine a picture with less promise commercially. In a little over an hour, it exhibits most of the baser shortcomings of men—cruelty, blood-lust, ruffianism, pusillanimity, and sordid pride. It shows a tragic violation of justice with little backlash to sweeten the bitter draught. And it puts a popular actor, Henry Fonda, in a very dubious light. But it also points a moral, bluntly and unremittingly, to show the horror of mob rule. And it has the virtue of uncompromising truth.

The story is really no more than a single episode—an incident, as the title says—which is supposed to have occurred in Nevada back in 1885. But it might have happened any place, for that matter, and at almost any time. A rancher is reportedly killed by cattle-rustlers and a mob gathers to seek revenge. Rancor, lust, and curiosity fan a reckless fire. A deputy sheriff swears a posse; a demagogue takes command. And the self-assumed guardians of justice go tearing off into the hills to do their will. In the dark of night, they capture three men who are driving a herd. On the basis of circumstantial evidence, they assume these three are their prey. And, in a lather of hot brutality which takes no heed of the signs of innocence—nor of the valiant but do-nothing protests of a handful of clear-thinking men—the mob pulls a triplet lynching. When it is over, they learn that the "murdered" man still lives.

William Wellman has directed the picture with a realism that is as sharp and cold as a knife from a script by Lamar Trotti which is beautifully brief with situations and words. And an all-round excellent cast has played the film brilliantly. The manner in which Mr. Wellman has studied his characters is a lesson in close-up art. And the terror which he has packed into that night "trial," with the ruthless lynchers glowering around a mountain fire while the doomed men face their fate in pitiful misery, is drama at its cruel and cynical best.

A heart-wringing performance by Dana Andrews as the stunned and helpless leader of the doomed trio does much to make the picture a profoundly distressing tragedy, while Frank Conroy's performance of the demagogue (all rigged out in a Confederate officer's uniform) imparts to it a perceptive significance which is good to keep in mind. Mr. Fonda is cryptic and bitter as one of the stauncher holdouts for justice, while Harry Davenport and Leigh Whipper are more affecting emotionally as champions of the right. Mary Beth Hughes has been pulled in for one brief, ironic scene with Mr. Fonda which gives a justification for his mood. And the rest of the cast can take bows for small but impressive roles.

The Ox-Bow Incident is not a picture which will brighten or cheer your day. But it is one which, for sheer, stark drama, is currently hard to beat.

—*B.C., May 10, 1943*

PAINT YOUR WAGON

Directed by Joshua Logan: written by Alan Jay
Lerner and Paddy Chayefsky, based on the musi-
cal by Mr. Lerner and Frederick Loewe: cine-
matographer, William A. Fraker: edited by Robert
C. Jones: music by Mr. Loewe: choreography by
Jack Baker: production designer, John Truscott:
produced by Mr. Lerner: released by Paramount
Pictures. Running time: 166 minutes.

With: Lee Marvin (Ben Rumson). Clint Eastwood
(Pardner). Jean Seberg (Elizabeth). Harve Presnell
(Rotten Luck Willie). Ray Walston (Mad Jack Dun-
can). Tom Ligon (Horton Fenty). Alan Dexter (Par-
son). William O'Connell (Horace Tabor) and Ben
Baker (Haywood Holbrook).

Paint Your Wagon, which began its roadshow
engagement at Loew's State II last night, is an amiable, $20-million musical. That's a high price to pay
for something that is more an expression of good
intentions than evidence of sustained cinematic
accomplishment. However, because amiability is never
in overabundant supply, especially in Hollywood
super-productions, the movie can be enjoyed more
often than simply tolerated.

In some ways, in fact, the very weaknesses of *Paint
Your Wagon* are its virtues. There is something quite
cheerful about its book, which is so casual that it stops
being a story after intermission and becomes, instead,
a frame for some amusing, comedy "set pieces." Its
three stars—Lee Marvin, Clint Eastwood and Jean
Seberg—are not singers by the stretch of anybody's

imagination, but they are appealing performers and
they come on with such legitimate, graceful good
humor that they disarm the sort of criticism
demanded by more aggressive personalities.

Paint Your Wagon, which made its Broadway debut
in 1951, was never one of Lerner and Loewe's major
works. It falls behind *Brigadoon, Gigi*, and, of course,
My Fair Lady, but its score is miles ahead of those of
most of the other musicals of the 1950's, except those
by Cole Porter and by Rodgers and Hammerstein,
who somehow discovered the terrifying secret of
transforming sugar into gold.

Working from an adaptation by Paddy Chayefsky,
Alan Jay Lerner, the screenwriter, and Joshua Logan,
the director, have abandoned Lerner's original Broadway book while retaining the locale, a rustic mining
camp, fearfully short of females, during the height of
the California gold rush. What there is of a coherent
story concerns Ben Rumson (Marvin), a boozy old
prospector given to gargantuan fits of melancholy; his
best friend, Pardner (Eastwood), an equally tough but
younger, comparatively prim prospector; and Mrs.
Elizabeth Woodley (Miss Seberg), the No. 2 wife of a
passing Mormon whom Rumson buys for $800 and
marries in what is, in effect, a claim-staking ceremony.
"You are hereby granted exclusive title to Mrs. Elizabeth Woodley," says the "preacher," "and to all her
mineral resources."

When Rumson leaves town for several days on
community business (to kidnap a wagonload of what
are referred to, respectfully, as "French tarts"), Rumson's wife and his best friend fall in love. This crisis is
resolved by the older man taking the younger one into
the marriage partnership, which proves satisfactory to

all concerned—and works so pleasantly that it short-stops dark considerations of rather peculiar psychological implications. All of this takes place in the first half of the film and is just about the sum and substance of the so-called book.

The score, which is supplemented by a couple of new songs by André Previn, who comes close to capturing what seems like an antique style, is lovely in a high-class schmaltzy way. Marvin talks his numbers well, especially "Wand'run Star." Eastwood sort of croons his in an early Frankie Avalon mode ("I Still See Elisa," "I Talk to the Trees," and, the best of all, "Goldfever") and Miss Seberg rather decently lip-syncs someone else's voice ("A Million Miles Away Behind the Door").

The cast also includes a real singer, Harve Presnell (*The Unsinkable Molly Brown*), whose one great number, "They Call the Wind Maria," shows up the nonsingers for what they are. However, although they are nonsingers, they are real stars, which, I believe, is more important.

Structurally—and stylistically—the film looks like something Logan might be trying out in New Haven—twenty years ago. Although the movie was shot entirely on some spectacularly beautiful Oregon locations, the scenery never has much more effect than would theatrical backdrops. The musical numbers aren't particularly well integrated into the story. They more or less "happen." There is hardly anything that resembles choreography, but there are a lot of boisterous processions, town meetings, and such, all of which rock with the sort of rousing, somewhat artificially hearty masculinity that marked Logan's biggest stage hits, *South Pacific* and *Mister Roberts.*

Logan and Lerner aren't afraid to include the irrelevant as long as it is funny. The high point of the second half of the film is an extended sequence in which Marvin introduces an eager young man (Tom Ligon) of pious background to the joys of No Name City, the gold town that has turned into the Sodom of the Sierras. This sort of looseness eventually works against the film's carefully engineered climax, in which No Name City literally disappears into the earth of its own greed. The Sodom and Gomorrah parallels are neither profound nor funny. One is simply stunned by the obvious physical effort of the filming.

Most of the time, however, *Paint Your Wagon* is very easy to take, as amiable as Marvin, Eastwood, and

Miss Seberg, whose contemporary movie presences give an old property brand-new cool.

—V.C., October 16, 1969

PAISAN

Directed by Roberto Rossellini; written (in Italian, with English subtitles) by Sergio Amidei, Federico Fellini, Mr. Rossellini and Annalena Limentani, based on stories by Victor Haines, Marcello Pagliero, Mr. Amidei, Mr. Fellini, Mr. Rossellini, Klaus Mann and Vasco Pratolini; cinematographer, Otello Martelli; edited by Eraldo Da Roma; music by Renzo Rossellini; produced by Mr. Rossellini, Rod F. Geiger and Mario Conti; released by Mayer-Burstyn. Running time: 120 minutes.

With: Carmela Sazio (Carmela), Robert Von Loon (Joe from Jersey), Benjamin Emanuel, Raymond Campbell, Harold Wagner, Albert Hinze, Merlin Berth, Mats Carlson and Leonard Penish (American Soldiers), Dots M. Johnson (American M.P.), Alfonsino (A Boy in Naples), Maria Michi (Francesca) and Gar Moore (Fred).

Roberto Rossellini, the young Italian who first swam into our ken as the director of that fine Italian picture, *La Citta Aperta* (*Open City*), has now come forth with a film which, in many aspects, marks a milestone in the expressiveness of the screen. *Paisan* is the title and it opened at the World yesterday.

It is useless to attempt an explanation, in familiar and concrete terms, of its basic theme and nature, for it is not an ordinary film—neither in form nor dramatic construction nor in the things it has to say. In some ways, it is the antithesis of the classic "story film," and certainly it throws off glints of meaning which are strangely unfamiliar on the screen. Possibly for some persons who are accustomed to the routine sort of film, it will be completely bewildering and leave a sad sense of emptiness. But at least it cannot fail to rattle the windowpanes of your eyes. And for many it will crash into the consciousness and leave the emotions limp.

For, in a series of six dramatic incidents which supposedly occurred during the Allied war campaign in

Italy—random incidents, with no connection, except by war—Mr. Rossellini constructs a terrifying picture of the disillusion, the irony, the horribleness of strife. More than that, he bluntly shows the tragic chasms which open between good people under circumstances of war and, without saying so, he makes evident the gaunt, sad thing that life is in a world of hate and killing.

The first incident involves an American patrol in Sicily. One soldier is shot; an Italian girl is blamed and killed—yet, a few minutes before, she has been listening, sensing and sympathizing without comprehending, while the soldier talked to her of his family back home. That is all.

The second incident is equally cryptic. An American Negro M.P. in Naples gets drunk, sings his sadness to a little street urchin, has his shoes stolen by the boy and tries to get them back next day, only to discover the horrible squalor in which the little fellow lives.

And so on through the picture. There is an episode involving a Roman streetwalker and a heartsick "Joe"; one referring to the Partisans in Florence and an American nurse who hopes to meet an old lover there. Then there is a curious little incident in a Franciscan monastery in the Apennines and a final, cynical decimation of Italian partisans and American O.S.S. men in the marshy, bleak delta of the River Po.

As we say, there is no dramatic pattern in which all of these incidents are tied, yet the cumulative impact of them achieves an oddly disturbing effect. And the remarkable thing is that each incident is played for understatement straight through, with classic climaxes avoided and the anti-climax almost obviously applied. The consequence is a curious climate which accumulates as the film goes on—a climate such as that in the eye of a hurricane, windless and airless, in which all tragedy suddenly seems futile and flat. This is the ultimate expression which Mr. Rossellini has accomplished in his film.

The manner of its accomplishment is in his memorable "documentary" style, with this curious truncation of episodes. Through actuality photography, with an almost completely "pick-up" cast, including many Americans, he has developed a tremendous naturalness. And a musical theme of great pathos, running through the episodes, clinches the effect.

In Italian, "paisan" has the meaning of the common term "bud" in our tongue. Even the title is ironic. This is a film to be seen—and seen again.

—B.C., *March 30, 1948*

THE PALM BEACH STORY

Written and directed by Preston Sturges; cinematographer, Victor Milner; edited by Stuart Gilmore; music by Victor Young; art designers, Hans Dreier and Ernst Fegte; produced by Paul Jones; released by Paramount Pictures. Black and white. Running time: 90 minutes.

With: Claudette Colbert (Gerry Jeffers), Joel McCrea (Tom Jeffers), Mary Astor (Princess), Rudy Vallee (John D. Hackensacker 3d), William Demarest (First Member), Franklin Pangborn (Manager), Robert Dudley (Wienie King), Sig Arno (Toto) and Jack Norton (Second Member).

It's a shame that Preston Sturges the writer and Preston Sturges the director of loco films didn't get a little better acquainted before they—or, collectively, he—put the final and finishing touches on *The Palm Beach Story*, which came to the Rivoli last night. If so, we might now be exulting over another of those delicious comedies such as this ambidextrous young gentleman has been giving us for the last couple of years. But, as it is, Mr. Sturges's "write" hand has let his somewhat more deft one down; his fiction this time is much too barren of bright surprises for a bold directorial splurge. And, as a consequence, *The Palm Beach Story* never really becomes the romp it aims to be. Except for some helter-skelter moments, it is generally slow and garrulous.

Perhaps Mr. Sturges was trying to see how thin he could slice it and still get by. Perhaps he was making an experiment in conversational comedy. Anyhow, he is short on action and very long on trivial talk in this mildly satiric little fable about a young wife who leaves her baffled spouse because she has the odd notion that he can get along better without her, goes to Florida intending to divorce him, and there encounters a fabulously rich gent who finally plays Fairy Godfather in the conventional story-book way.

It is, in fact, so short on action that the one or two flashes of it herein stand out as gleaming oases amid

739

verbal aridity. By far the best part of the picture—in fact, the only part up to Sturges's style—is that wherein Claudette Colbert, playing the fanciful wife, beats a free ride toward Florida in a club car with the boys of the Ale and Quail outing society. Here, at least, Mr. Sturges has exercised his fine talent for revelry and has whipped up a beautiful confusion of shotguns blasting, bird dogs howling, and glass breaking.

But otherwise his paper-thin story is told pretty much in dialogue, which is neither remarkably witty nor very precise in its point. And the few promising complications which occasionally take form are permitted to fade without toppers. Mr. Sturges, it seems, just didn't try.

Miss Colbert makes a gallant effort to give an airy performance, mostly with words, and Joel McCrea appears blankly bewildered, which is quite understandable. Rudy Vallee is the picture's biggest surprise, in the role of a stuffy millionaire—John D. Hackensacker 3d—which he performs with amusing pomposity. Mary Astor shrills and waves her hands wildly as the millionaire's multi-married sister, and the usual mob of Sturges's favorite actors are in for supporting roles.

But they barely support *The Palm Beach Story*. It sags all around them and itself. It should have been a breathless comedy. But only the actors are breathless—and that from talking so much.

—B.C., December 11, 1942

THE PARALLAX VIEW

Produced and directed by Alan J. Pakula; written by David Giler and Lorenzo Semple Jr., based on the novel by Loren Singer; director of photography, Gordon Willis; edited by Jack Wheeler; music by Michael Small; production designer, George Jenkins; released by Paramount Pictures. Running time: 102 minutes.

With: Warren Beatty (Brady), Paula Prentiss (Lee Carter), William Daniels (Austin), Walter McGinn (Jack), Hume Cronyn (Rintels) and Kelly Thordsen (L. D.).

It's difficult not to feel a certain amount of suspense when you see a man standing below a huge hydro-electric dam, as blandly unaware of danger as a near-sighted pigeon walking across the Belt Parkway. The man doesn't know that at any minute several hundred thousand tons of water are going to come roaring out of the spillway, most likely onto his head.

Since the man is Warren Beatty, the star of *The Parallax View*, and since the film is more or less just beginning, you know he can't be fatally clobbered. The suspense comes from wondering how he's going to escape, as in old-time movie serials.

A little later Mr. Beatty, who plays a reporter investigating a political assassination conspiracy, is lured aboard a commercial airliner that is ostensibly headed for Denver, though we know that his appointment could be in Samarra: The villains have stashed a timebomb aboard the plane. Will he get back to earth safely? Check your watch.

The Parallax View, which opened yesterday at the Cinema 1, is the sort of suspense melodrama that travels a horizontal course from beginning to end. The thrills don't mount as the film goes on. They don't even accumulate. Once they are experienced, they dissolve so thoroughly that by the end you're likely to feel as cheated as I did.

The movie, which was directed by Alan J. Pakula, never rewards the attention we give it with anything more substantial than a few minor shocks.

Neither Mr. Pakula nor his screenwriters, David Giler and Lorenzo Semple Jr., display the wit that Alfred Hitchcock might have used to give the tale importance transcending immediate plausibility. The moviemakers have, instead, treated their central idea so soberly that they sabotage credulity.

Without giving away the plot, the idea, simply stated, is that there is somewhere in this country a giant corporation dedicated to training and putting out for hire misfits and malcontents who have been elevated to professional assassins.

According to this film, the Parallax Corporation has a recruiting program as thorough as that of General Motors, and much more paternal. Parallax seems to be vaguely right-wing, but the movie is fuzzy on this. It's also fuzzy on logistics. If, as is shown, Parallax insists on eliminating not only contracted targets but also all possible witnesses, as well as witnesses of witnesses, it would seem the population could, theoretically, be reduced by half in eighteen months.

This may be taking the movie more seriously than

is intended, but to treat a political assassination conspiracy merely as a subject for fun is frivolous.

In addition to Mr. Beatty, the cast includes Paula Prentiss as a TV news reporter, Hume Cronyn as a harassed city editor, and a number of other good actors. *The Parallax View* is not the kind of movie that depends on unusual performances, or even asks for them.

—*V.C., June 20, 1974*

A PASSAGE TO INDIA

Directed by David Lean; written by Mr. Lean, based on the play by Santha Rama Rau and the novel by E. M. Forster; cinematographer, Ernest Day; edited by Mr. Lean; music by Maurice Jarre; production designer, John Box; produced by John Brabourne and Richard Goodwin; released by Columbia Pictures. Running time: 163 minutes.

With: Judy Davis (Adela Quested), Victor Banerjee (Doctor Aziz), Peggy Ashcroft (Mrs. Moore), James Fox (Richard Fielding), Alec Guinness (Godbole) and Nigel Havers (Ronny Heaslop).

After watching the first public performance of Santha Rama Rau's dramatization of his *Passage to India* at Oxford in 1960, E. M. Forster, then eighty-one years old, walked onto the stage to express his pleasure with the performance.

"How good the actors were," said Forster. "And how pleased I am that there were so many of them. I am so used to seeing the sort of play which deals with one man and two women. They do not leave me with the feeling I have made a full theatrical meal . . . they do not give me the experience of the multiplicity of life."

Later, as P. N. Furbank reports in his fine biography, *E. M. Forster: A Life,* Forster called "absurd" the play's review in *The Times* of London that described it as being about "the incompatibility of East and West." According to Forster, he was really concerned with "the difficulty of living in the universe."

Forster, who died in 1970, might be equally pleased by most of David Lean's respectful, handsome new screen version, which cites as its sources the play as well as the novel. The film is very much "a full theatrical meal," and one that conveys a lot of "the multiplicity of life" one seldom sees on the screen these days.

Mr. Lean's *Passage to India,* which he wrote and directed, is by far his best work since *The Bridge on the River Kwai* and *Lawrence of Arabia* and perhaps his most humane and moving film since *Brief Encounter.* Though vast in physical scale and set against a tumultuous Indian background, it is also intimate, funny, and moving in the manner of a filmmaker completely in control of his material. Mr. Lean shares with Forster an appreciation for the difficulties involved in coping with the universe.

Because of the reputation the novel has acquired as a classic since its publication in 1924, one tends to forget what a smashingly good story it is—a grandly sorrowful muddle that becomes a mystery for the saddest, nastiest of reasons.

Set in the fictitious provincial city of Chandrapore in the 1920's, when the British raj was being threatened by the king-emperor's increasingly impatient Indian subjects, *A Passage to India* is essentially a story of what can happen as a result of a succession of wrongheaded decisions and dreadful misunderstandings, of trust either given too easily or withheld far too long.

Though the initial scenes are set in London, the film really begins with the arrival in Chandrapore of the uncommonly wise, kind, and sensitive Mrs. Moore (Peggy Ashcroft), who has come out from England to visit her son Ronny Heaslop (Nigel Havers), the British magistrate, and to chaperon Adela Quested (Judy Davis), the proper young Englishwoman to whom Ronny is unofficially engaged.

Almost immediately the liberal-minded Mrs. Moore and Adela are upset by the cloistered life of the small, hopelessly genteel British colony at Chandrapore. They are appalled by the attitudes of their compatriots toward the Indians and by the total lack of interest in what Mrs. Moore and Adela keep referring to as "the real India." They have scarcely settled in at Chandrapore before Adela is speaking about the possibility of "adventures," to which Mrs. Moore, similarly excited, adds that "adventures do occur, but not punctually."

They refuse to fall into the routine of cricket, polo, and afternoons at the club followed by the other members of this British station. With the help of the local school superintendent, Richard Fielding (James Fox),

Mrs. Moore and Adela attempt to break the invisible raj-barrier.

Through Fielding, they meet an eccentric old Brahmin scholar, Professor Godbole (Alec Guinness), whose words of wisdom, being inscrutable, they hang onto with delight, and an earnest, eager-to-please young Moslem medical doctor named Aziz (Victor Banerjee), a hard-working, financially impoverished widower who both admires and loathes the British in Chandrapore.

Aziz, who must be one of fiction's most appealing and brave comic heroes, gets carried away by the unexpected friendliness of Mrs. Moore and Adela at a small tea party. He invites them, along with Fielding and Professor Godbole, to go on an elaborate outing he cannot afford, a daylong picnic to the Marabar Caves, always called "extraordinary," though for reasons that no one can satisfactorily explain. The caves are not beautiful. They contain no sculpture or wall carvings and have absolutely no religious significance. Their importance seems to predate time.

The disastrous consequences of this outing, which occurs early in the film, set up everything that comes after, including an uproarious, agonizing courtroom melodrama during which Aziz is accused of the rape of the once dazzled, now nearly catatonic, Adela.

What happened in the Marabar Caves? That question pursued Forster throughout his life, and he always avoided answering.

In Mr. Lean's screenplay, which in most ways is remarkably faithful to the novel—it includes large swatches of very funny Forster dialogue—there is no longer much of a mystery. The audience knows, or at least thinks it knows, exactly what happened in the caves, which makes poor Aziz's trial even more outrageous than it is in the novel.

This conscious decision on Mr. Lean's part subtly distorts the original, but it also emphasizes some surprising revelations about Adela. Even more peculiar is Mr. Lean's decision to withhold from the audience a scene in the novel that explains Mrs. Moore's seemingly uncharacteristic actions preceding Aziz's trial. Though he has made A Passage to India both less mysterious and more cryptic than the book, the film remains a wonderfully provocative tale, full of vivid characters, all played to near perfection.

At the film's center is Mr. Banerjee's superb performance as Aziz, a mad mixture of foolishness, bravery,

honor, and anger. Miss Davis, the young Australian actress who first caught American attention in *My Brilliant Career,* is far prettier than Forster's Adela, but she has a particular presence—like that of a younger, less abrasive Glenda Jackson—that helps make the film work. The film's tone is set by the splendid Miss Ashcroft's Mrs. Moore, whose self-assurance slowly ebbs as events and life overwhelm her.

Mr. Guinness doesn't exactly underact. There are times when his performance comes perilously close to a Peter Sellers impersonation, but still he's invigorating company. Equally good in less flamboyant roles are Mr. Fox and Mr. Havers, and the members of the huge supporting cast.

The film contains a rather major flaw, one that keeps a very good film from being great. Though *A Passage to India,* which opens today at the Ziegfeld Theater, is essentially a dark comedy of manners, Mr. Lean sometimes appears to think of it as a romance. In this he's being as wrongheaded as the unfortunate Adela. This is the only explanation for the terrible Maurice Jarre score, which contradicts the images and sounds like a reworking of the music he wrote for Mr. Lean's unsuccessful *Ryan's Daughter.* This score has nothing to do with Forster, India, the time, or the story, but it has everything to do with moviemaking in the 1960s, when soundtrack music first became a major element in the merchandising of movies, including Mr. Lean's *Dr. Zhivago.*

—V.C., December 14, 1984

THE PASSION OF ANNA

Written (in Swedish, with English subtitles) and directed by Ingmar Bergman; cinematographer, Sven Nykvist; edited by Siv Kanalv; production designer, P. A. Lundgren; produced by Lars-Owe Carlberg; released by United Artists. Running time: 100 minutes.

With: Liv Ullmann (Anna Fromm), Bibi Andersson (Eva), Max von Sydow (Andreas Winkelman), Erland Josephson (Elis Vergerus), Erik Hall (Johan Andersson) and Sigge Furst (Verner).

Andreas Winkelman (Max von Sydow) is repairing the roof of the cottage in which he lives as a literate hermit. At one point, he stares off at the sun that hangs low and dim—with its edges made ragged by a telephoto lens—in the Scandinavian sky. Suddenly the sun disappears into the gray-blue haze, but it's as if Andreas had willed it invisible, much as he has tried to will himself invisible without taking the ultimate step.

With this lovely image, Ingmar Bergman begins *The Passion of Anna,* which opened yesterday at the Festival Theater and is the concluding film in the "island" trilogy that includes *Hour of the Wolf* and *Shame.* As in *Hour of the Wolf,* the von Sydow-Bergman character is again pursued by demons, but they are real this time—demons of pride, loneliness, and defeat. As in *Shame,* he is again framed against a world of war and violence, although the war is miniaturized and distanced (as a fleeting television image from Vietnam) and the violence is the work of a madman who roams the island ritualistically hanging a dog, cutting the throats of sheep, and setting horses on fire.

In *The Passion of Anna,* Andreas is as much victim as culprit. Living in solitude on the island, after having been abandoned at some earlier time by his wife, Andreas is drawn into a friendship with Elis (Erland Josephson), a successful architect; Eva (Bibi Andersson), his wife, and Anna (Liv Ullmann), their best friend, who is recovering from an automobile accident in which she, the driver, survived her husband and child.

Andreas first has an affair of convenience with Eva, a sad, pretty woman who loves her husband but feels unneeded by him. Later, he shares his cottage with Anna, a voluptuous woman who prattles on about the necessity of striving for spiritual perfection and about the "wholeness" of her lost marriage, although Andreas is perfectly aware of the fact that the marriage was a disaster, that her husband had tried, unsuccessfully, to leave her. Andreas has come upon a letter in Anna's purse in which her husband had warned that her unreasonable demands would lead first to "mental and psychical violence," and then to physical violence. The letter was signed "Andreas," which was also the name of Anna's husband.

Quite relentlessly, Anna's passion leads to the defeat of the second Andreas and, at the end, there is every indication that she will continue to go through life like some overzealous Christian missionary, preaching salvation and leaving behind her a trail of lies, compromises, confusion, and violence.

The Passion of Anna is one of Bergman's most beautiful films (it is his second in color), all tawny, wintry grays and browns, deep blacks, and dark greens, highlighted occasionally by splashes of red, sometimes blood. It is also, on the surface, one of his most lucid, if a film that tries to dramatize spiritual exhaustion can be ever said to be really lucid. However, like all of Bergman's recent films, it does seem designed more for the indefatigable Bergman cryptologists (of which I am not one) than for interested, but uncommitted filmgoers.

For example, I am curious about, but am unable to speculate on, the reasons Bergman persists in using the same names for his female characters who are not the same. The names of Eva and Anna turn up in *Shame* and *The Silence,* and the names of all his leading female characters in *The Silence, Persona, Hour of the Wolf, Shame,* and *The Passion* begin with an A or an E, which are the letters tagged on to the name of the von Sydow character in *The Passion.*

Does this mean something? I think not, but it is there. I also have the feeling that Bergman, who has a marvelous way of setting his scene and introducing his characters, especially the peripheral ones, becomes, in his role of film creator, rather like one of his own heroes. The director circles in closer and closer to the heart of the film, finally to find a void, or a secret so private that we can only guess its meaning.

Getting to the heart of it, however, can be stimulating, and involves its own kind of mounting suspense as one grasps at casual remarks for clues. Elis, the architect, is an amateur photographer, fascinated by faces. When he shows his work to Andreas, he says, with resignation: "I don't imagine that I reach into the soul with these photographs. [They can show] only an interplay of forces."

Of the four principal characters, Andreas is the one on screen the most, and the one least known. He has been in prison (for forgery, striking a policeman) and he has been married, but all we know of the marriage (via a flashback) is that his wife has accused him of having "cancer of the soul . . . you have tumors all over you." He does, however, talk at length about things like "the freedom to be humiliated."

It is somewhat ironic that Bergman, the great humanist, insists that his heroes suffer so profoundly from abstract malaises that they seem positively superhuman.

There is no confusion in *The Passion of Anna* between reality and fantasy—it is all fantasy. That, at least, is the effect of a device by which, at four points in the film, he steps back and asks each of his principal actors about his conception of the role he is playing. The result is not so much enlightenment as it is an expression of Bergman's appreciation to his stars, particularly von Sydow, Miss Ullmann, and Miss Andersson, who have contributed so much to so many of his films.

They are all superb here, and Bergman gives each of them extraordinary moments of cinematic truth, monologues of sustained richness and drama that are the hallmarks of Bergman's best work, when the camera, without moving, records the birth of a character largely through facial expression and dialogue.

I must admit that ever since *Persona* I've had trouble distinguishing between Miss Ullmann and Miss Andersson (at a certain point, all Bergman actresses look like Jessica Tandy). However, I shall always remember a scene in *The Passion* in which Miss Andersson, a little bit tight on wine, recalls her introduction to God, illustrated in one of her children's book as a handsome old man hovering just above the earth.

She is asked if she still believes in Him. She looks at her husband hesitantly and asks: "Do I?" As in all Bergman films, such moments cut through all the abstractions and make *The Passion of Anna* as vivid and moving as you demand that it be.

—*V.C., May 29, 1970*

PATHER PANCHALI

Produced and directed by Satyajit Ray: written (in Bengali, with English subtitles) by Mr. Ray, based on the novel by Bibhutibhushan Bandyopadhyaa: cinematographer, Subrata Mitra: edited by Dulal Dutta: music by Ravi Shankar: art designer, Banshi Chandra Gupta: released by Edward Harrison. Black and white. Running time: 112 minutes.

With: Kanu Banerji (The Father), Karuna Banerji (The Mother), Subir Banerji (Apu), Runki Banerji (Durga as a Child), Uma Das Gupta (Durga as a Young Girl) and Chunibala Devi (Old Aunt).

The Indian film, *Pather Panchali* (*Song of the Road*), which opened at the Fifth Avenue Cinema yesterday, is one of those rare exotic items, remote in idiom from the usual Hollywood film, that should offer some subtle compensations to anyone who has the patience to sit through its almost two hours.

Chief among the delicate revelations that emerge from its loosely formed account of the pathetic little joys and sorrows of a poor Indian family in Bengal is the touching indication that poverty does not always nullify love and that even the most afflicted people can find some modest pleasures in their worlds.

This theme, which is not as insistent or sentimental as it may sound, barely begins to be evident after the picture has run at least an hour. And, in that time, the most the camera shows us in a rambling and random tour of an Indian village is a baffling mosaic of candid and crude domestic scenes.

There are shots of a creaky old woman, a harassed mother, her lively little girl, and a cheerful husband and father who plainly cannot provide for his small brood. There are scenes, as familiar as next-door neighbors, of the mother trying to get the child to eat, washing clothes, quarreling with the husband, or pushing the child toward school.

Satyajit Ray, Indian artist, who wrote the screenplay and directed this film, provides ample indication that this is his first professional motion picture job. Any picture as loose in structure or as listless in tempo as this one is would barely pass as a "rough cut" with the editors in Hollywood.

But, oddly enough, as it continues—as the bits in the mosaic increase and a couple of basically human and dramatic incidents are dropped in, such as the pitiful death of the old woman and the sickness and death of the little girl—the poignant theme emerges and the whole thing takes a slim poetic form. By the time it comes to its sad end, it has the substance of a tender threnody.

Much of the effect is accomplished by some stunningly composed domestic scenes, well performed—or pictured—by an excellent Indian cast, and exquisitely photographed by Subrata Mitra in tastefully filtered blacks and whites. And a finely conceived and sympathetic original musical score, composed by Ravi Shankar, in which native instruments are employed, sets the whole sad story in the frame of a melancholy mood.

Karuna Banerji is touching as the mother who is most distressed by poverty and Uma Das Gupta is lovely and sensitive as the girl. Chunibala Devi is fantastically realistic and effective as the aging crone and Subir Banerji is wistful and beguiling as the small son of the family.

As we say, it is quite exotic. The dialogue often sounds like a Gramophone record going at high speed. English subtitles barely make some sense. But there are lovely little threads in the strange fabric. It's a film that takes patience to be enjoyed.

—B.C., September 23, 1958

PATHS OF GLORY

Directed by Stanley Kubrick; written by Mr. Kubrick, Calder Willingham and Jim Thompson, based on the novel by Humphrey Cobb; cinematographer, Georg Krause; edited by Eva Kroll; music by Gerald Fried; art designer, Ludwig Reiber; produced by James B. Harris; released by United Artists. Black and white. Running time: 86 minutes.

With: Kirk Douglas (Colonel Dax), Ralph Meeker (Corporal Paris), Adolphe Menjou (General Broulard), George Macready (General Mireau), Wayne Morris (Lieutenant Roget), Richard Anderson (Major Saint-Auban), Joseph Turkel (Private Arnaud), Timothy Carey (Private Ferol) and Peter Capell (Colonel Judge).

Credit Kirk Douglas with having the courage to produce and appear in the screen dramatization of a novel that has been a hot potato in Hollywood for twenty-two years. That is Humphrey Cobb's *Paths of Glory,* a shocking story of a shameful incident in World War I—the court-martial and execution of three innocent French soldiers on charges of cowardice, only to salve a general's vanity.

Obviously, this is a story—based on an actual occurrence, by the way—that reflects not alone on France's honor but also on the whole concept of military authority. Yet Mr. Douglas has made a movie of it—an unembroidered, documentary-like account—with himself playing the role of an outraged colonel who tries vainly to intercede. It opened at the Victoria yesterday.

To a certain extent, this forthright picture has the impact of hard reality, mainly because its frank avowal of agonizing, uncompensated injustice is pursued to the bitter, tragic end. The inevitability of a fatal foul-up is presented right at the start, when an ambitious general agrees to throw one of his regiments into an attack that he knows has little chance to succeed. And it looms with ever mounting horror as he orders an example to be made of three men picked at random from the thwarted attackers and dogs them unmercifully to their doom.

All this is shown with shattering candor in this film, which was shot in Germany and was directed by Stanley Kubrick, who also helped to write the screenplay with Jim Thompson and Calder Willingham. The close, hard eye of Mr. Kubrick's sullen camera bores directly into the minds of scheming men and into the hearts of patient, frightened soldiers who have to accept orders to die.

Mr. Kubrick has made it look terrific. The execution scene is one of the most craftily directed and emotionally lacerating that we have ever seen.

But there are two troubling flaws in this picture, one in the realm of technique and the other in the realm of significance, which determine its larger, lasting worth.

We feel that Mr. Kubrick—and Mr. Douglas—have made a damaging mistake in playing it in colloquial English, with American accents and attitudes, while studiously making it look as much as possible like a document of the French Army in World War I. The illusion of reality is blown completely whenever anybody talks.

Mr. Douglas exudes tremendous passion as the colonel who tries to stave off a sacrifice, but he speaks with the same kind of English that he used in *Gunfight at the O.K. Corral.* Adolphe Menjou is a bit more clipped and Gallic as a staff general who plays sly politics, but George Macready acts and speaks the vengeful general as if he were a slimy Harvard man. Ralph Meeker, Joseph Turkel, and Timothy Carey play the doomed poilus (remember that fine word?) with the swagger, slouches, and speech slurs of assorted G.I.'s in World War II. Emile Meyer is perhaps least effective (when he speaks) in the role of a French priest.

As for the picture's significance, it comes to an inconclusive point. Its demonstration of injustice is like an exhibit in a bottle in a medical museum. It is grotesque, appalling, nauseating—but so framed and

745

isolated that, when you come away, you are left with the feeling that you have been witness to nothing more than a horribly freakish incident.

Also, merely as a footnote—what a picture to open on Christmas Day!

—B.C., December 26, 1957

PATTON

Directed by Franklin J. Schaffner; written by Francis Ford Coppola and Edmund H. North, based on the books *Patton: Ordeal and Triumph* by Ladislas Farago and *A Soldier's Story* by General Omar N. Bradley; director of photography, Fred Koenekamp; edited by Hugh S. Fowler; music by Jerry Goldsmith; art designers, Urie McCleary and Gil Parrondo; produced by Frank McCarthy and Frank Caffey; released by Twentieth Century Fox. Running time: 170 minutes.

With: George C. Scott (General George S. Patton Jr.), Karl Malden (General Omar N. Bradley), Michael Bates (Field Marshal Sir Bernard Law Montgomery), Edward Binns (Major General Walter Bedell), Lawrence Dobkin (Colonel Gaston Bell), John Doucette (Major General Lucian K. Truscott), James Edwards (Sergeant William George Meeks) and Frank Latimore (Lieutenant Colonel Henry Davenport).

"My favorite general," Dwight Macdonald wrote during World War II, "is George S. Patton Jr. Some of our generals, like Stilwell, have developed a sly ability to simulate human beings. But Patton always behaves as a general should. . . . He wears special uniforms, which, like Goering, he designs himself and which are calculated, like the ox horns worn by ancient Gothic chieftains, to strike terror into the enemy (and into any rational person, for that matter)."

In much the same way, *Patton: A Salute to a Rebel* is likely to strike terror into any rational person who refuses—perhaps absurdly—to believe that war is man's most noble endeavor. The movie, which opened last night at the Criterion Theater, is a huge, initially ambivalent but finally adoring, Pop portrait of one of the most brilliant and outrageous American military figures of the last one hundred years.

It's both fascinating and appalling, the sort of extravagant, technically superior spectacle that only a big Hollywood movie company could afford to make, and the story of a man about whom only the Establishment could become genuinely sentimental.

Patton, the movie keeps telling us, is "a magnificent anachronism," "a sixteenth-century man lost in the twentieth century," a man who damn well loved war, was surprised and somewhat taken aback when men near to him were killed, who wrote poetry, quoted the Bible, had the political instincts of a California grape, and was, according to those who knew him best, basically decent.

Indeed, in this movie in which he is portrayed as a near-schizophrenic, he so touches General Omar Bradley (Karl Malden), that Bradley seems to have gone through World War II looking always as if he were about to weep over the sheer, lovable cussedness of the man.

The most refreshing thing about *Patton* is that here—I think for the first time—the subject matter and the style of the epic war movie are perfectly matched. War was, for Patton, his destiny and sometimes great fun. Thus the big, magnificently staged battle scenes (photographed in marvelous, clear, deep focus), are not giving the lie to a film that, like *The Longest Day,* would have us believe piously that war is hell.

Under Franklin J. Schaffner's superior direction (as well as under the supervision of what I assume to have been a number of assistant directors, second unit men, and technical advisers), the key incidents in Patton's campaigns from North Africa and Sicily to his extraordinary post D-Day dash across France are reproduced as giant, largely impersonal panoramas. The destruction of life is viewed from observation posts and mulled over later in bivouacs that, more often than not, are splendid, confiscated palaces.

For Patton, with his sense of déjà vu—his conviction that in earlier lives he had fought in ancient Greece, at Carthage, at Moscow—war was a kind of timeless abstraction, unconnected to specific causes and effects.

The movie takes much the same point of view of Patton, seeing him as a man of the ages whose genius as a tactician excused his vanities, his ignorances, and his seeming mental instability (as when, in Sicily, he began slapping shell-shocked soldiers for their cowardice).

Schaffner and his scriptwriters, Francis Ford Coppola and Edmund H. North, were obviously aware of the problems they faced in trying to transform Patton into a figure who would be as comprehensible today, if not quite as sympathetic, as Ringo Starr.

They open the film with a sort of overture that liberals can view as pure camp, and Patton fans will interpret as pure inspiration. Patton (George C. Scott) stands in the middle of a stage, dwarfed by a huge, almost Rauschenberg American flag, addressing us, the people in the movie audience who are his troops. "All Americans love the sting of battle," he says cheerfully. "That's why we've never lost a war. . . ."

Throughout the rest of the episodic film, there are other suggestions that Schaffner and company have quite mixed feelings about Patton, but they are ultimately denied by the epic (reverential) treatment.

There are also strong hints that the film shares Patton's distrust of the Russians (they are boors), the British (Montgomery is played as a smiling fool), and what might be his admiration for the Germans (General Jodl is the only person who believes that Eisenhower would not be stupid enough to sack a general as great as Patton just for slapping a soldier).

Although the cast is large, the only performance of note is that of Scott, who is continuously entertaining and, occasionally, very appealing. He dominates the film, even its ambiguities, although he never quite convinced me that Patton, by any stretch of the imagination, could be called a rebel against anything except the good, gray, dull forces of bleeding heart liberalism.

—V.C., February 5, 1970

THE PAWNBROKER

Directed by Sidney Lumet; written by David Friedkin and Morton Fine, based on the novel by Edward Lewis Wallant; cinematographer, Boris Kaufman; edited by Ralph Rosenblum; music by Quincy Jones; art designer, Richard Sylbert; produced by Roger Lewis and Philip Langner; released by Allied Artists. Black and white. Running time: 114 minutes.

With: Rod Steiger (Sol Nazerman), Geraldine Fitzgerald (Marilyn Birchfield), Brock Peters (Rodriguez), Jaime Sanchez (Jesus Ortiz), Thelma Oliver (Ortiz's Girl), Marketa Kimbrell (Tessie) and Baruch Lumet (Mendel).

Although the tragic character that Rod Steiger powerfully plays in the solemn new film, *The Pawnbroker,* is very much a person of today—a survivor of Nazi persecution who has become detached and remote in the modern world—he casts, as it were, the somber shadow of the legendary, ageless Wandering Jew. That is the mythical Judean who taunted Jesus on the way to Calvary and was condemned to roam the world a lonely outcast until Jesus should come again.

For this is a dark and haunting drama of a man who has reasonably eschewed a role of involvement and compassion in a brutal and bitter world and has found his life barren and rootless as a consequence. It is further a drama of discovery of the need of man to try to do something for his fellow human sufferers in the troubled world of today.

To view this remarkable picture, which opened yesterday at the Cinema Rendezvous, the Beekman, and the RKO 23d Street, as merely a mordant melodrama of a displaced European Jew who runs a pawnshop in New York's Harlem and is caught up in some evil doings there is to miss the profound dilemma and melancholy of its central character and the broader significance of his detachment and inability to adjust.

This man, played by Mr. Steiger with a mounting intensity that carries from a state of listless ennui to a point of passion where it seems he's bound to burst, has good enough reason for detachment. He has been through the horror of the concentration camps, has lost his immediate family, has seen his best friend tortured and killed. This terrible traumatic experience has left him intellectually drained and emotionally numb. He has a fitful affair with his friend's widow but looks on people as "rejects, scum."

A strange accumulation of events on an anniversary stirs him to painful recollections and causes old words to flash through his mind. An attempt by a woman welfare worker to strike up a friendship with him agitates his resentment with memories of a happier life. The wish of a Puerto Rican Negro assistant to get his help in learning the trade fires him to a violent outburst against the meaninglessness of everything—everything, that is, except money. And an effort by an anguished prostitute to offer her body to him causes him to recall the horrible experience of seeing his wife stripped and raped by prison guards.

It is a shattering excess of mental torment and deep self-pity this man must endure, and it shifts him to a level of awareness that lets him see his present life in previous terms. He sees the people on New York's crowded subways as lost souls headed for the concentration camps, the vicious gangsters who actually own his pawnshop as counterparts of Nazi racketeers.

But it is not until he sees his young assistant—Jesus Ortiz is significantly his name—shot dead by holdup hoodlums during a courageous attempt to protect him that he senses the shame of his detachment. Then he slams his hand down on a paper spike to inflict upon himself the stigmata and acknowledge his burden of grief and guilt.

It is not an ennobling picture that Roger H. Lewis and Philip Langner have produced and Sidney Lumet has directed. It is a picture of the shabbiness of man—of the misused, debilitated hero, as well as those among whom he lives. And the whole thing is staged and presented to convey and emphasize the meanness of those environments that would breed such shabbiness.

With the seasoned camera of Boris Kaufman, Mr. Lumet has ruthlessly searched some of the most hideous aspects of Harlem and middle-class life around New York. He has brilliantly intercut flashes of the horrors of the concentration camps with equally shocking visualizations of imprisonment in a free society. And he has clearly implied in terms of picture the irony of resemblances.

In certain respects, the suppurant screenplay of David Friedkin and Morton Fine departs from the feverish novel of the late Edward Lewis Wallant on which it is based. The detail of medical experiments upon the hero by the Nazis has been removed, thus freeing Mr. Steiger from the onus of playing the character as a sort of golem, as in the book. Now he can make the sad survivor a solid man in command of his own fate, driven with acerbity and cynicism but compelling an eventual sympathy.

Others of the cast are likewise striking—Geraldine Fitzgerald as the woman who tries in a wistful and clumsy fashion to draw the poor man from his obvious loneliness; Jaime Sanchez as the spry Negro assistant who teeters lightly on the fringes of crime; Thelma Oliver as the latter's loyal sweetheart who makes her

living as a tawny prostitute; Brock Peters as a brutal Harlem crime boss; and many more, including fine old Juano Hernandez in one of the several good small roles.

In his zeal to make sure the point is carried, Mr. Lumet lets his picture run too long. He might have cut out or held down some grim stretches that make for redundancy. But he and his sponsor, Ely Landau, are to be honored for even attempting this most uncommon film, which projects a disagreeable subject with power and cogency.

—B.C., April 21, 1965

PAYDAY

Directed by Daryl Duke; written by Don Carpenter; cinematographer, Richard C. Glouner; edited by Richard Halsey; music by Ed Bogas; produced by Martin Fink and Mr. Carpenter; released by Cinerama Releasing. Running time: 103 minutes.

With: Rip Torn (Maury Dann), Ahna Capri (Mayleen Travis), Elayne Heilveil (Rosamond McClintock), Michael C. Gwynne (Clarence McGinty) and Jeff Morris (Bob Tally).

The pursuit of that ultimate all-American pop-culture artifact, the road movie, continues. And it is not likely to be delayed for long by the emergence of *Payday*, an account of two nights and a day in the life of one Maury Dann, a country-and-Western singer journeying not too successfully up from Alabama to Nashville.

To appreciate the road movie, or the spirit of the road movie, you must refine your sensibilities—until you become a connoisseur of main streets, motel rooms, roadhouse parking lots, and of the dawn rising warmly over superhighways in the Southeast. To such taste *Payday* offers some nourishment—perhaps too much. In other respects it is very thin.

Indeed, a feeling very close to exhaustion, a kind of psychic emptiness, pervades the film. Maury Dann arranges play dates, bullies his entourage, hunts quail, visits his feeble pill-popping mom, picks up one girl and drops another, gets into real trouble with the cops, and drives off into the morning—on the lift from one dose of amphetamines too many. It should mean

748

something, or say something about a quality of life ("quality of life" is surely the film's subject); and yet it all seems unrealized, unrelated—like illustrative material for a movie not yet made.

To some extent this stems from a screenplay that seems curiously unattached to its material. But Daryl Duke's direction is a good deal less forceful than it needs to be, and though he clearly has some feeling for the atmosphere of the road, his approach to dramatic events ranges from hopeful uncertainty to downright miscalculation.

Rip Torn seals off the character of Maury Dann—a compound of meanness, gentleness, opportunism, enthusiasm, and desperation—as if covering an inner complexity that he never quite persuades us he possesses. The two girls, Ahna Capri and Elayne Heilveil, are pretty awful. This leaves the locations, all in Alabama, and very nice, and a collection of authentic-seeming minor players. It is probably a function of what's wrong with the movie that its happiest moments are provided by Michael C. Gwynne, who plays Maury Dann's business manager, and plays him for simple efficiency.

Payday opened yesterday at the Forum, the Juliet 2, and the Murray Hill theaters.

—*R.G., February 23, 1973*

PELLE THE CONQUEROR

Directed by Bille August; written (in Danish, with English subtitles) by Mr. August, based on the novel by Martin Andersen Nexö; director of photography, Jörgen Persson; edited by Janus Billeskov Jansen; music by Stefan Nilsson; art designer, Anna Asp; produced by Per Holst; released by Miramax Films. Running time: 160 minutes.

With: Max von Sydow (Lasse), Pelle Hvenegaard (Pelle), Erik Paaske (Manager), Kristina Tornqvist (Anna) and Morten Jørgensen (Trainee).

Bille August's *Pelle the Conqueror* is not for people who prefer to take showers. It's for the person who likes to get into a movie as if it were a long hot bath. To hurry it would be to miss its method and its point.

The Danish film, which won the Golden Palm, the top prize, at this year's Cannes Festival, is a vividly recreated, minutely detailed panorama of a particular time (the turn of the century), place (rural Denmark), and circumstance (life on a great farm) in the course of the four seasons. The observer is Pelle (Pelle Hvenegaard), a staunch, wide-eyed Swedish boy who has come to Denmark with his aging, destitute, and widowed father, Lasse (Max von Sydow).

Lasse has promised his son that Denmark will be a land of opportunity, a place of plentiful jobs, where pork is served on Sundays and butter is spread on bread. Instead Lasse and Pelle are lucky to be hired as little better than indentured servants, underpaid, underfed, and overworked.

For the illiterate Lasse, who drinks too much and has no spine to fight, the farm is the end of the line. For Pelle, it is his introduction to an adult world in which rewards and punishments are thoroughly scrambled and arbitrary power is exercised by the few. Mr. August's screenplay is adapted from the first part of Martin Andersen Nexö's Danish novel in which Pelle, when he grows up, goes on to become a union leader.

Pelle the Conqueror will be shown at the New York Film Festival tonight and tomorrow.

One of the scandals at the Cannes festival was that Mr. von Sydow did not win the best-actor award, which went to Forest Whitaker for his work in Clint Eastwood's *Bird*. The Whitaker performance is acceptable, possibly limited by its rather commonplace context. The von Sydow performance is in a category by itself. It is another highlight in an already extraordinary career, and quite unlike anything that American audiences have seen him do to date.

Lasse is a refinement of the sort of fraudulent, washed-up, but deep-down noble boxer that Wallace Beery exuberantly overacted in *The Champ,* a film that *Pelle* doesn't otherwise resemble, except in its close-up of the father-son relationship. Mr. von Sydow is something splendid to see as the boozy, weak-willed, loving Lasse. Though it is a rich performance, full of wit and humor, it is never broad or self-serving.

It is also the backbone of the movie, which sometimes looks too big in terms of landscapes, weather, and the crowds of people on screen to have come from the comparatively small though clearly vital Danish film industry. *Pelle* has a kind of Dickensian appreciation for narrative, being packed with subplots perceived in the melodramatic terms of an adolescent boy's imagination.

Among the many subsidiary characters, there are the parvenu landowner whose philandering has driven his wife to drink and, finally, to stronger measures of revenge; a malformed boy who is Pelle's age and who dreams of joining a circus as a freak; a kind, sex-starved widow who is partial to Lasse; and another woman, a boisterous farmhand who turns Lasse down as a suitor on the grounds that he's too old to be "dangerous."

Mr. August never indulges the pathos that is built into the story, which is to his credit as a disciplined filmmaker, though it also keeps the film at a slight remove from the audience. One is never unaware that this is a very long movie. Mr. August brings a cool twentieth-century sensibility to what is, at heart, a piece of passionate nineteenth-century fiction.

As played by Mr. Hvenegaard, who looks a bit like the young Dickie Moore in Hollywood's old *Oliver Twist*, Pelle is idealized without being softened. Mostly, he is a camera, receiving the images of a childhood that will eventually shape the course of his life.

The scale of the physical production is most impressive. Mr. August and Jörgen Persson, the cinematographer, avoid the picturesque, which is not to say that *Pelle* isn't a beautiful film. It's just that its looks are more than skin deep.

—V.C., September 30, 1988

THE PEOPLE VS. LARRY FLYNT

Directed by Milos Forman; written by Scott Alexander and Larry Karaszewski; director of photography, Philippe Rousselot; edited by Christopher Tellefsen; production designer, Patrizia von Brandenstein; produced by Oliver Stone, Janet Yang and Michael Hausman; released by Columbia Pictures. Running time: 129 minutes.

With: Woody Harrelson (Larry Flynt), Courtney Love (Althea Leasure Flynt), Edward Norton (Alan Isaacman), Donna Hanover (Ruth Carter Stapleton), Brett Harrelson (Jimmy Flynt), Richard Paul (The Rev. Jerry Falwell), Vincent Schiavelli

(Chester), Crispin Glover (Arlo), Miles Chapin (Milo), James Cromwell (Charles Keating) and James Carville (Simon Leis).

This year's New York Film Festival concludes with *The People vs. Larry Flynt,* a blazing, unlikely triumph about a man who is nobody's idea of a movie hero. Smart, funny, shamelessly entertaining, and perfectly serious too, Milos Forman's film describes the *Hustler* publisher and his many liberties, civil and otherwise. Above all, the film emerges as an object lesson in open-mindedness, winning a reluctant respect for its main character's right to crude self-expression just as Mr. Flynt has won his days in court.

"I would love to be remembered for something meaningful," opines the film's Larry Flynt, played with devilish charm by Woody Harrelson as a maverick vulgarian who embodies capitalism at its most unabashed, tapping into something shocking but real in the American spirit. Thanks to the acerbic wit and crusading intelligence of Mr. Forman's film, he actually will.

This film's savvy treatment of a potentially unpalatable character is on a par with that of *Ed Wood,* also written superbly by Scott Alexander and Larry Karaszewski. These writers make their mark so fast that the prologue to *The People vs. Larry Flynt* is enough to dispel doubt. In the backwoods of Kentucky in 1952, ambitious little Larry is seen peddling moonshine to a quivering old drunk, who hands the boy what looks like his last two dollars. Nobody forces him; he hands that money over willingly. It's free enterprise even if it isn't pretty.

Larry next throws a jug at his sleeping father, accusing him of drinking up the profits. He's no angel.

By the early 1970's, at the start of a career that this lean and eventful film turns into a flamboyant roller-coaster ride, Larry is running a dismal little strip club in Cincinnati. Here and throughout the film, Mr. Forman uses humor expertly to deflate sensationalism without avoiding the essence of Larry's big marketing idea. The film includes some nudity but handles it with what, under the circumstances, looks like remarkable discretion.

Hustler magazine is born soon after Larry meets Althea Leasure, the young bisexual stripper who joins Larry on the road to success. Courtney Love, who makes a smashing Althea, marches purposefully into the film and makes it clear that Mr. Harrelson's Larry has met his match. As eager and uninhibited as Larry is, Ms. Love's sultry, funny Althea is soon a loud voice among the seedy cronies who join in his new publishing venture. The film's scenes describing their creative efforts are as amusing as the moviemaking episodes in *Ed Wood.*

Althea, proposing a pornographic photo spread based on *The Wizard of Oz:* "And there's Toto maybe, even?"

One coworker: "Althea, I think maybe some things are sacred."

Larry: "Shut up! Althea, that is the best thing I ever heard!"

Once *The People vs. Larry Flynt* has had its mischievous fun describing the crassness behind *Hustler,* it takes on its real subject: the question of why a free society need tolerate provocations like this. Edward Norton, so good in *Primal Fear,* articulates the film's cogent if not really controversial First Amendment arguments as he plays a composite character, the long-suffering lawyer who defends Mr. Flynt on a wide range of charges.

"I'm your dream client!" Flynt insists, after the lawyer quits in protest over his obnoxious courtroom antics. "I'm the most fun, I'm rich, and I'm always in trouble."

The real Mr. Flynt plays a judge in one scene, sitting near Mr. Harrelson just long enough to remind the audience that a beaming, attractive Larry Flynt is very much a movie invention. But the film stops prettifying its main character as it depicts the shooting that left him paralyzed from the waist down, his subsequent drug addiction with Althea in Bel Air ("I ought to move to a place where perverts are welcome!" Larry decides, as the film cuts to the mountainside Hollywood sign) and his various run-ins with devout Christianity.

One of the odder tangents to this story is Mr. Flynt's encounter with Ruth Carter Stapleton, President Jimmy Carter's sister (played by Donna Hanover, Mayor Giuliani's wife). Larry is influenced by her just long enough to have an epiphany ("Where'd you learn that damn word?" Althea asks suspiciously) and devote *Hustler* disastrously to religious porn. (Sample idea: "Adam and Eve getting it on in the Garden of Eden.")

Later on, Larry's baiting of the Rev. Jerry Falwell (Richard Paul) creates the case that brings this film to its logical destination: the Supreme Court.

The People vs. Larry Flynt is a film that can comfortably accommodate both Justice Scalia's comments on satire and libel and the loony, trashy extravagance of the Flynts living high on the hog. Patrizia von Brandenstein's production design is a marvel of bad taste rendered beautifully, and the costumes by Theodore Pistek and Arianne Phillips are fittingly bold.

Mr. Flynt, after all, is a man who wore a star-spangled diaper for one court appearance. When Althea goes to seed, she begins looking more and more like Courtney Love, but Ms. Love's performance is far too good to confuse one well-tended image with the other.

Philippe Rousselot's expert cinematography gives this film's wide range of settings a glamorous consistency. Among the actors whose deadpan delivery keeps the film at a witty distance from its hero are Brett Harrelson, Vincent Schiavelli, Crispin Glover and Miles Chapin as Larry's dim, shock-proof employees. James Carville feigns indignation as a prosecutor horrified by *Hustler.* James Cromwell plays Charles Keating, who accuses Larry Flynt of "the destruction of the soul of our country" while himself playing an instrumental role in the savings and loan scandal.

The film knows which is worse.

—*J.M., October 12, 1996*

PERSONA

Produced, written (in Swedish, with English subtitles) and directed by Ingmar Bergman; cinematographer, Sven Nykvist; edited by Ulla Ryghe; music by Lars-Johan Werle; production designer, Bibi Lindström; released by Lopert Films. Black and white. Running time: 81 minutes.

With: Bibi Andersson (Nurse Alma), Liv Ullmann (Actress Elisabeth Vogler), Margaretha Krook (Woman Doctor), Gunnar Björnstrand (Mr. Vogler) and Jorgen Lindstrom (Boy).

Once again, Ingmar Bergman is bringing us into contact with two strangely troubled women and exploring the sensitive movements of their minds in his new Swedish film, *Persona,* which came to the Festival Theater yesterday. And once again he is inviting (or compelling) his public to engage in studious efforts at interpretation or simply outright involvement of themselves, empathically and esthetically, and let the egos and ids fall where they may.

The latter would seem the better purpose with which to approach this lovely, moody film which, for all its intense emotionalism, makes some tough intellectual demands. For its evident contemplation of a singular phenomenon of transfer of personality between an older mental patient and her pretty, lonely nurse is rich in poetic intimations of subconscious longings and despairs, and it is likely to move one more deeply as poetry than as thought.

Indeed, it appears from the way Mr. Bergman begins his film that he wants us to absorb it as experience conveyed through the mechanical techniques of this illusion-creating medium, rather than as transmitted reality. He wants us to understand clearly that we are looking at images that have their own personal connotations, according to the conditioning of the individual viewer.

He starts his picture literally inside a projection-machine—the arc-light hissing on, the film chattering with its intermittent movement through the gate, images flashing from the blank screen, conventional symbols or ideographs, such as a comic cartoon or a close-up of a hand being pierced by a spike, then shots of the faces of old people lying on slabs under sheets—all indications of the convictions compelled by mechanical images.

One small body lying inert under a seeming shroud, is finally summoned to movement by a persistently ringing telephone (this is an aural symbol), and rises to reveal itself as the boy from Mr. Bergman's *The Silence.* He scans a face that comes to form on an opaque screen, runs his hand over the image as though trying to understand it through the sense of touch. The effort is evidently unrewarding.

Thus the emotional experience is introduced.

It is that of a capable young trained nurse, who is given the delicate job of attending a famous actress. The latter has had a trauma of some sort, which has rendered her mute and caused her to withdraw from the world. The two go to spend the summer alone in a cottage by the sea. Here, by some curious osmosis of the actress's attitudes, the nurse takes on her personality and the actress takes on that of the nurse.

At least, I think that's the idea—though, as I say, interpretation is tough, and the impression one gets from the relations of these two images of troubled women may be different. The important thing is that Mr. Bergman has magnificently and sensitively composed a veritable poem of two feminine spirits exchanging their longings, repressions, and mental woes against a background of natural beauty and the atmosphere of the sea.

As Mr. Bergman himself has written, "Our work in films begins with the human face," and he has composed much of *Persona* with close-ups of the fascinating faces of Liv Ullmann and Bibi Andersson. Miss Ullmann is the silent patient, whose reactions are in moody pantomime, and Miss Andersson is the nurse, whose strange outpourings come in clouded expressions and many words. One slight drawback with this picture is that so much is said with words which, especially for us who have to read them in English subtitles, inject a lot of literary imagery. For instance, there is a lengthy monologue in which the nurse describes a bizarre sexual encounter she and another young woman had with two boys on a beach one summer, from which the nurse became pregnant. It is done with remarkable simplicity and dignity, but it is verbal stimulation, whether listened to or read.

Much finer, more vivid in the medium, is a visual enactment of a dream—or whatever, perhaps a sheer "experience"—in which the two women almost embrace.

That's it. Miss Ullmann and Miss Andersson just about carry the film—and exquisitely, too. The actress's husband is played in one brief scene by Gunnar Björnstrand, and Margaretha Krook is very minor as a psychiatrist.

At the end, which is inconclusive, the film goes back into the projection machine and we are left with the haunting wonder: Was this something that happened, or a dream?

—B.C., *March 7, 1967*

PERSUASION

Directed by Roger Michell: written by Nick Dear, based on the novel by Jane Austen: director of photography. John Daly: edited by Kate Evans: music by Jeremy Sams: production designers. William Dudley and Brian Sykes: produced by

Fiona Finlay: released by Sony Pictures Classics. Running time: 103 minutes.

With: Amanda Root (Anne Elliot), Ciaran Hinds (Captain Wentworth), Susan Fleetwood (Lady Russell), Corin Redgrave (Sir Walter Elliot), Phoebe Nicholls (Elizabeth Elliot), Fiona Shaw (Mrs. Croft), John Woodvine (Admiral Croft), Samuel West (Sir William Elliot), Sophie Thompson (Mary Musgrove), Emma Roberts (Louisa Musgrove) and Victoria Hamilton (Henrietta Musgrove).

Persuasion stands in Jane Austen's career as *The Winter's Tale* does in Shakespeare's: it is a lyrical, autumnal story of lost love, with the unexpected reward of a happy ending. The heroine of *Persuasion*, Anne Elliot, tossed away love at the age of nineteen, convinced by the sound maternal advice of her friend Lady Russell that a penniless naval officer was no match for the daughter of a baronet.

The story begins eight years later, when Anne is twenty-seven and therefore on the verge of nineteenth-century spinsterhood. Perfectly portrayed by Amanda Root in Roger Michell's lovely and subtle film, Anne is a plain, thin-lipped, intelligent woman who wears a perpetual look of worried resignation. The boundless possibilities she foresaw at nineteen seem to have vanished, though her love for Frederick Wentworth remains. When the newly rich Wentworth and her well-born cousin William reenter her small social circle, *Persuasion* throws Anne Elliot one, and maybe two, late chances at marriage.

Though *Persuasion* is not the most dramatic of Austen's novels, it may be the most deeply felt; written during her final illness, it was published in 1818, a year after her death. Similarly, the subdued Anne is not the most immediately endearing of her heroines, but she is the most mature and possibly the most poignant and autobiographical. Anne is the sane center around which Austen constructs the most bitter and redeeming of her social satires.

All this is brilliantly captured by Mr. Michell, with the screenwriter Nick Dear and a cast completely in sync with Austen's warm but piercing style. Their *Persuasion* is profoundly truthful in many ways: in its sense of emotional longing; in its natural, unglamorized visual beauty, ranging from drawing rooms to the sea; in its fidelity to the delicate tone of Austen's satire

and romance. Made for British television, *Persuasion* opens today at the Paris Theater.

The Elliot family includes Anne's vain father, Sir Walter (Corin Redgrave), and her self-important older sister, Elizabeth (Phoebe Nicholls). They have been living beyond their means at lavish Kellynch Hall. The film's pitch-perfect tone and impeccable casting become clear early on, when the Elliots learn they will have to live more modestly. Sir Walter and Elizabeth each say "Retrench?" with such contempt and precision that it seems the foulest word ever to be uttered in the King's English. Yet retrench they must, heading off to fashionable Bath while leasing Kellynch Hall to Admiral Croft and his wife, who happens to be Wentworth's sister.

Anne stays behind near Kellynch with her younger, married sister, Mary Musgrove, smartly played by Sophie Thompson as the comic embodiment of a good person who is also a silly little snob. Susan Fleetwood as the wrongheaded Lady Russell, and John Woodvine and Fiona Shaw as the amiable Crofts also turn functional types into credible individuals.

But Ms. Root and Ciaran Hinds as Wentworth form the powerful center of the film. Ms. Root makes Anne sad but never self-pitying or forlorn. The chatterbox Mary has repeated Wentworth's comment that he would never have recognized Anne, she is so changed. Anne tries hard to hide a love she believes can never now be returned. Her ability to signal unspoken emotions is matched by Mr. Hinds, whose sternly handsome face expresses the pain and distrust that linger after Anne's old rejection.

Mr. Michell is a theater director who also made the sharp BBC miniseries *The Buddha of Suburbia*. Mr. Dear has worked primarily in theater as well, so it is a wonderful surprise that they have made this highly literary novel so successfully cinematic. The camera becomes the visual equivalent of Austen's rich, commenting voice, and though it cannot be a complete replacement, it is a more than serviceable one. The camera slyly glances at Mary's sisters-in-law, the infatuated Louisa and Henrietta Musgrove, when the possibility of Frederick's marriage is discussed. And the film's visual design captures the world as Austen saw it. The women wear no makeup. The characters dine in darkness dramatically lighted by candles, or walk by the sea in translucent sunlight. On a walk in the woods, the serious Anne wears a deep green cloak while the frivolous Musgrove women all wear red. Only the pompous characters look artificial, notably the Elliots' garish rich relatives, the Dalrymples.

And when Anne joins her father and sister at Bath, Sir Walter notices that she looks better. She does appear softer, less pale and drawn. How much that has to do with the flattery of her inscrutable cousin William (Samuel West), and how much with Wentworth's proximity, creates the story's final suspense. Though the lack of Austen's voice means that Anne is defined by her broken heart for too long, by the end her strong voice and willful character emerge.

This is the first of the season's two major Austen adaptations, with Emma Thompson coming in *Sense and Sensibility* at Christmas. *Persuasion* is the more difficult to tackle, and this version is as successful as one of Austen's neatly contrived marriages. The film offers the same pleasures as an Austen novel, as the audience sinks into a comforting, orderly world where life-shattering disruptions are handled with elegant ease.

—*C.J., September 27, 1995*

LE PETIT THÉÂTRE DE JEAN RENOIR

Directed by Jean Renoir; written (in French, with English subtitles) by Mr. Renoir; cinematographer, Georges Leclerc; edited by Geneviève Winding; music by Joseph Kosma and Jean Wiener; production designer, Gilbert Margerie; produced by Pierre Long; released by Phoenix Films. Running time: 100 minutes.

With: Nino Fornicola (The Bum), Minny Monti (The Female Bum), Roger Trapp (Max Vialle), Marguerite Cassan (Emilie), Pierre Olaf (The Husband), Jacques Dynam (The Second Husband), Jeanne Moreau (The Singer), Françoise Arnoul (Isabelle), Fernand Sardou (Duvallier), Jean Carmet (Feraud) and Dominique Labourier (The Maid).

It has taken almost five years for Jean Renoir's marvelous *Le Petit Théâtre de Jean Renoir* (*The Little Theater of Jean Renoir*) to obtain a commercial release in New York, and now that it is here, I trust it will be around for a long, long time. It will be shown at the First Avenue Screening Room today and tomorrow and then open a regular engagement there next Thursday.

Le Petit Théâtre is as much a cause for celebration as an act of it, by one of the greatest of all film directors, who will mark his eightieth birthday this September. It is precise, witty, and luminous, and it stands just a little apart from time in the way of a work by an artist whose career spans the better part of a century.

Le Petit Théâtre was originally commissioned for French television. It is composed of three short comedies plus an outrageously funny, between-the-acts performance by Jeanne Moreau as a beautiful, deadpan, turn-of-the-century Parisian music-hall singer who, like Zola's Nana, takes her talent a lot more seriously than her audiences may be able to.

The director himself, the Octave in *Rules of the Game,* now older and in his own character as master of illusion, introduces the acts on screen, standing over one of those miniature theaters that any child would give up a month of Saturdays to own.

As Renoir gives credit to his "collaborator" on the first sketch (Hans Christian Andersen), the camera moves away from him over the tiny footlights into the "real" world of the theater. Back and forth we go until, at last, in the concluding sequence, the players, at a critical moment, release us from our commitments to them by turning toward the camera to bow from the apron of Jean Renoir's little theater.

The moment is both playful and exceptionally moving because, like so many other moments within the film, it recalls Renoir's blessed preoccupation with performance, with theater, as a means of getting a fix on life, if only for a little while.

The opening sequence, "The Last Christmas Dinner," is another adaptation—or variation really—of the Andersen story from which Renoir made *La Petite Marchande d'Allumettes* in 1928. It's about two ancient panhandlers, an old man and an old woman (in place of the match girl), and their last Christmas Eve on the bank of the Seine, being covered by snow that doesn't melt, warding off the cold that doesn't penetrate. Renoir deliberately exploits the artificiality of sets and circumstances to upstage any sentimentality that would interfere with true sentiment.

The second sequence is a comically mad opera, complete with singing choruses, arias, and sudden deaths, called "The Electric Waxer," about a woman fatally obsessed with the shine on her parquet floor. It is played with hilarious self-absorption by Marguerite Cassan, who has the superb nuttiness of the late Florence Lake, and by Pierre Olaf, as her unfortunate husband.

The last sequence, "Le Roi d'Yvetot," is set in the Midi of so many of Renoir's earlier films and concerns the "revolution" effected by an elderly landowner (Fernand Sardou), his pretty young wife (Françoise Arnoul), and her young lover (Jean Carmet) when they find themselves quite happy in spite of conventions.

This sequence in particular has the cheerful, sunny look that distracted a lot of critics in the 1930's from seeing the tougher side of Renoir's comedies. The compromises effected by his characters are amusing but there's always the realization that they've never been lightly made.

Something of this same awareness is apparent in many of the comedies of François Truffaut (who has described himself as one of Renoir's children), especially in *Stolen Kisses* and *Bed and Board,* films that, like a number of Renoir's, have on occasion been incorrectly labeled lightweight.

Le Petit Théâtre gives this mostly empty season a big boost. It looks like a work in miniature, but because the scale is perfect one never thinks about physical size. The movie is as big or small as our minds and emotions make it.

—*V.C., May 3, 1974*

PETULIA

Directed by Richard Lester; written by Larry Marcus and Barbara Turner, based on the novel *Me and the Arch Kook Petulia* by John Haase; cinematographer, Nicolas Roeg; edited by Anthony Gibbs; music by John Barry; production designer, Tony Walton; produced by Raymond Wagner; released by Warner Brothers. Running time: 105 minutes.

With: Julie Christie (Petulia), George C. Scott (Archie), Richard Chamberlain (David), Arthur Hill (Barney), Shirley Knight (Polo), Pippa Scott (May), Kathleen Widdoes (Wilma) and Joseph Cotten (Mr. Danner).

Petulia is a strange, lovely, nervous little film, very jaggedly cut (by Richard Lester, who also directed *Help!* and *How I Won the War*) so that the parts don't quite match and the plot is almost scattered through. It begins with a rich, married, kooky waif, played by Julie Christie, propositioning a tired divorced surgeon, played by George C. Scott, at a San Francisco charity ball. The waif kook at the top type is becoming a little worn, and Petulia isn't as inventive a character as Morgan or Holly Golightly—she only arrives with a tuba and bruises at Scott's apartment quite early one morning—and yet there is something awfully nice about this film.

For one thing, George C. Scott and Miss Christie are such human and inhabited actors. Early in the movie, when it seems the whole thing is going to expire in flat, heavy, whimsy, Petulia says to the surgeon, "I'm going to marry you, Archie." Very soon after that one begins to care about them, hopes they will marry, fights the story as, with its own peculiar pace, it keeps turning up odd little plot fragments. Archie's friends, Barney and Wilma (played by Arthur Hill and Kathleen Widdoes), understanding nothing, show him films of himself and his former wife, in hopes of a reconciliation. Then, in a single line it turns out their own marriage is a nightmare.

A few moments, and the whole life and atmosphere of a hospital are there intact; another fragment and one knows just what Archie's life was like with his wife Polo (Shirley Knight); what it is like with his mistress (Pippa Scott); a short scene on a boat and the quality of Petulia's marriage is clear (her husband, played by Richard Chamberlain, simply throws her an orange and once jumps a mile); her father-in-law (Joseph Cotten) visits her bedside and a whole kind of Californian, a surface-calm nightmare of the far right is on screen; Polo's relic of a new lover; Archie's relationship with his sons—everything is illuminated very fast, economically but separately, as though someone had deliberately shattered a perfectly formed and crafted film.

The story of Archie and Petulia is there, too, although the movie itself seems to forget it from time to time: whether a bored man will risk the relative order of his life for this violent and poetic idyll; whether she will take on the risks of the normal. Like that. Very odd. There is some very good music by The Grateful Dead, Big Brother and the Holding Company, and other groups. There is just too much talent in Lester's use of his own skittish comic techniques for serious purposes to miss. The movie opened yesterday at the Plaza Theater.

—R.A., June 11, 1968

THE PHILADELPHIA STORY

Directed by George Cukor; written by Donald Ogden Stewart and Waldo Salt, based on the play by Philip Barry; cinematographer, Joseph Ruttenberg; edited by Frank Sullivan; music by Franz Waxman; art designers, Cedric Gibbons and Wade B. Rutbottom; produced by Joseph L. Mankiewicz; released by Metro-Goldwyn-Mayer. Black and white. Running time: 112 minutes.

With: Cary Grant (C.K. Dexter Haven), Katharine Hepburn (Tracy Lord), James Stewart (Macaulay Connor), Ruth Hussey (Elizabeth Imbrie), John Howard (George Kittredge), Roland Young (Uncle Willie), John Halliday (Seth Lord), Mary Nash (Margaret Lord) and Virginia Weidler (Dinah Lord).

All those folks who wrote Santa Claus asking him to send them a sleek new custom-built comedy with fast lines and the very finest in Hollywood fittings got their wish just one day late with the opening of *The Philadelphia Story* yesterday at the Music Hall. For this present, which really comes via Metro-Goldwyn-Mayer, has just about everything that a blue-chip comedy should have—a witty, romantic script derived by Donald Ogden Stewart out of Philip Barry's successful play; the flavor of high-society elegance, in which the patrons invariably luxuriate; and a splendid cast of performers headed by Katharine Hepburn, James Stewart, and Cary Grant. If it doesn't play out this year and well along into next they should turn the Music Hall into a shooting gallery.

It has been a long time since Hollywood has spent itself so extravagantly, and to such entertaining effect, upon a straight upper-crust fable, an unblushing apologia for plutocracy. Money and talent are mostly going these days into elaborate outdoor epics and rugged individualist films. It is like old times to see one about the trials and tribulations of the rich, and to have Miss Hepburn back, after a two-year recess, as

another spoiled and willful daughter of America's unofficial peerage, comporting herself easily amid swimming pools, stables, and the usual appurtenances of a huge estate.

For that is what she is—and does—in the Messrs. Stewart's and Barry's pleasant dissertation upon a largely inconsequential subject, that subject being the redemption of a rather priggish and disagreeable miss. The writers have solemnly made her out as a frigid and demanding sort of person—one of "a special class of American females: the married maidens"—who has divorced her first husband and is preparing to take unto herself another simply because she doesn't understand her own psyche. But an amusing complication, whereby an ink-smeared journalist and a girl photographer turn up to "cover" her wedding for a "snoop" magazine, leads to a strange exposure of her basic hypocrisy, and she remarries the proper man to the proper effect.

Truthfully, the psychology of the story is as specious as a spiel, and, for all the talk about the little lady being "a sort of high priestess to a virgin goddess," etc., she is and remains at the end what most folks would call a plain snob. But the way Miss Hepburn plays her, with the wry things she is given to say, she is an altogether charming character to meet cinematically. Someone was rudely charging a few years ago that Miss Hepburn was "box-office poison." If she is, a lot of people don't read labels—including us.

But she isn't the only one who gives a brilliant performance in this film. James Stewart, as the acid word-slinger, matches her poke for gibe all the way and incidentally contributes one of the most cozy drunk scenes with Miss Hepburn we've ever seen. Cary Grant, too, is warmly congenial as the cast-off but undefeated mate, and Ruth Hussey, Virginia Weidler, Roland Young, and Mary Nash add much to the merriment.

Provided you have a little patience for the lavishly rich, which these folk are, you should have great fun at *The Philadelphia Story*. For Metro and director George Cukor have graciously made it apparent, in the words of a character, that one of "the prettiest sights in this pretty world is the privileged classes enjoying their privileges." And so, in this instance, will you, too.

—B.C., December 27, 1940

THE PIANIST

Directed by Roman Polanski: written by Ronald Harwood. based on the book by Wladyslaw Szpilman: director of photography. Pawel Edelman: edited by Hervé De Luze: music by Wojciech Kilar: production designer. Allan Starski: produced by Mr. Polanski. Robert Benmussa and Alain Sarde: released by Focus Features. Running time: 149 minutes.

With: Adrien Brody (Wladyslaw Szpilman). Emilia Fox (Dorota). Michael Zebrowksi (Jurek). Ed Stoppard (Henryk). Maureen Lipman (The Mother). Frank Finlay (The Father). Jessica Kate Meyer (Halina). Julia Rayner (Regina). Ruth Platt (Janina) and Thomas Kretschmann (Capt. Wilm Hosenfeld).

Roman Polanski's new movie, *The Pianist,* is based on the memoirs of Wladyslaw Szpilman, a star of Polish radio and cafe society in the 1930's and a member of Warsaw's assimilated Jewish middle class, who lived through the Nazi occupation and the Warsaw ghetto. Szpilman's recollections, published shortly after the war, offer, like other such books, a deeply paradoxical impression of the Holocaust. Accounts of survival, that is, are both representative and anomalous; they at once record this all but unimaginable historical catastrophe and, without intentional mendacity or inaccuracy, distort it.

The reason for this could not be simpler. Most of the intended victims of Nazi genocide did not survive; the typical Jewish experience in 1940's Europe was death. One of the main genres that allow later generations access to this time thus presents an inevitably unrepresentative picture of it.

We naturally identify with the protagonists of these books, and the characters based on them in movies and plays, and so imagine that we would have been among the lucky ones, even if the real odds suggest otherwise. (We also comfort ourselves in the vain belief that, had we been there, we would have bravely defied the Nazis, risking our own well-being to help their victims.) When it is not treated with the uneasy sentimentality reserved for miracles, survival—whether through dumb luck, resilience, the kindness of strangers or some combination of these—is often viewed with a deep and bitter sense of the absurd.

Mr. Polanski, who was a Jewish child in Krakow when the Germans arrived in September 1939, presents Szpilman's story with bleak, acid humor and with a ruthless objectivity that encompasses both cynicism and compassion. When death is at once so systematically and so capriciously dispensed, survival becomes a kind of joke. By the end of the film, Szpilman, brilliantly played by Adrien Brody, comes to resemble one of Samuel Beckett's gaunt existential clowns, shambling through a barren, bombed-out landscape clutching a jar of pickles. He is like the walking punchline to a cosmic jest of unfathomable cruelty.

Perhaps because of his own experiences, Mr. Polanski approaches this material with a calm, fierce authority. This is certainly the best work Mr. Polanski has done in many years (which, unfortunately, is not saying a lot), and it is also one of the very few nondocumentary movies about Jewish life and death under the Nazis that can be called definitive (which is saying a lot). And—again paradoxically—this is achieved by realizing the modest, deliberate intention to tell a single person's story, to recreate a specific and finite set of events. (Ronald Harwood's script does take some necessary liberties with Szpilman's account, but these seem justified by the demands of movie storytelling.)

The ambition to produce a comprehensive vision—a single spectacle adequate to the Holocaust—ultimately defeated Steven Spielberg's admirable and serious *Schindler's List.* Mr. Polanski, in staging a narrow, partial slice of history, has made a film that is both drier and more resonant than Mr. Spielberg's.

One of Mr. Polanski's trademarks is what might be called (to continue multiplying paradoxes) a humane sadism. He has always been fascinated by what happens to weak, ordinary people—Mia Farrow in *Rosemary's Baby,* for instance, or Jack Nicholson in *Chinatown*—when they are intruded upon by evil forces more powerful than they, and he punishes his actors, peeling back their vanity to make them show the face of humanity under duress.

One of Mr. Brody's most appealing features—from *King of the Hill* ten years ago through such varied and underseen pictures as *Restaurant, Summer of Sam,* and *Bread and Roses* more recently—is his quick-witted, almost smart-alecky cockiness. His Szpilman, in the first section of *The Pianist,* has the gait of a self-satisfied dandy and the smug smile of a man who takes charm and good fortune as his birthright. As he plays piano in a broadcast studio, an explosion rattles the building. He ducks, wipes some plaster off his sleeve, and keeps playing. Later Szpilman refuses to allow the widespread panic at the German invasion to interfere with more pressing matters, like the seduction of a star-struck young woman named Dorota (Emilia Fox).

History, the occupying Germans and Mr. Polanski then conspire to wipe the smirk off his face. The Nazi takeover is followed by a swift, brutal chronicle of violation and humiliation as the Szpilman family are stripped of their possessions, their dignity (the elderly father, played by Frank Finlay, is beaten by a German soldier for daring to use the sidewalk), and their home. With the other Jews of Warsaw, they are herded into the ghetto, a captive labor force subject to continual culling by disease, starvation, and the random violence of their tormentors.

Mr. Polanski, working in Poland for the first time in 40 years (and also in Prague), reconstructs the look and rhythm of life in the ghetto with care and sobriety. You feel the dread and confusion of the inhabitants, and you also observe their intuitive, futile attempts to master the situation—circulating underground newspapers, smuggling contraband through the walls, and quietly arming themselves for resistance.

The survival instinct is shown to exist in a weird, numb state that combines defiance and resignation. And Szpilman's evasion of death involves a curious combination of pluck, passivity, and arrogance. He is the only member of his family who avoids being shipped to the extermination camps, and he later manages to escape from the ghetto altogether. During the 1943 ghetto uprising, he is locked in a secure apartment in the gentile part of the city, and he watches helplessly from the window as the partisans begin their brave, doomed resistance to the German occupiers.

From this moment forward *The Pianist*—which opens today in New York and Los Angeles—becomes a tour de force of claustrophobia and surreal desperation, and Mr. Polanski ruthlessly strips his Szpilman down to the bare human minimum. He is neither an especially heroic nor an entirely sympathetic fellow, and by the end he has been reduced to a nearly animal condition—sick, haggard, and terrified. But then the film's climax offers the most dramatic paradox of all: a glimpse of how the impulses of civilization survive in the midst of unparalleled barbarism. When I first saw this film last spring in Cannes (where it won the Golden Palm), I thought Szpilman's encounter, in the war's last days, with a music-loving Nazi officer (Thomas Kretschmann) courted sentimentality by associating the love of art with moral decency, an equation the Nazis themselves, steeped in Beethoven and Wagner, definitively refuted. But on a second viewing, the scene, scored to the ravishing, sorrowful music of Chopin, was a painful and ridiculous testament to just how bizarre the European catastrophe of the last century was.

Szpilman may have been the butt of a monstrous joke, but the last laugh—appropriately deadpan—was his. "What will you do when this is over?" the officer asks. "I'll play piano on Polish radio," Szpilman replies. Which is exactly what he did until his death two years ago.

—A.O.S., December, 27, 2002

THE PIANO

Written and directed by Jane Campion: director of photography, Stuart Dryburgh: edited by Veronika Jenet: music by Michael Nyman: production designer, Andrew McAlpine: produced by Jan Chapman: released by Miramax Films. Running time: 120 minutes.

With: Holly Hunter (Ada). Harvey Keitel (Baines). Sam Neill (Stewart). Anna Paquin (Flora). Kerry Walker (Aunt Morag) and Genevieve Lemon (Nessie).

Don't let the mountains of superlatives that have already been heaped on *The Piano* put you off. Jane Campion's nineteenth-century love story lives up to its advance notices. Prepare for something very special.

The Piano is much like its remarkable heroine, Ada (Holly Hunter), a mute (but not deaf) young Scots widow who, with her nine-year-old daughter, travels to the New Zealand bush to marry a man she has never met. Ada's husband-to-be calls her "stunted." The film looks deceptively small, but in character it's big and strong and complex. Here's a severely beautiful, mysterious movie that, as if by magic, liberates the romantic imagination.

The Piano will be shown at Avery Fisher Hall tomorrow night, an especially celebratory choice to close this year's New York Film Festival, and will open its commercial run here on November 19. It could be the movie sensation of the year.

You know you're in uncharted cinema territory early on. Ada and Flora (Anna Paquin), her pretty but gnomelike child, are dumped onto a wild New Zealand beach and then abandoned by the ship that's brought them halfway around the world. With their crated belongings (including Ada's beloved piano) spread around them on the sand, the mother and daughter spend the night alone, huddled inside a sort of tent made out of one of Ada's hoop skirts.

This is how they're found the next morning by Stewart (Sam Neill), the well-meaning but dangerously unimaginative man who has ordered Ada by mail; Baines (Harvey Keitel), an illiterate settler with a nose tattooed Maori-style; and the Maori tribesmen hired as bearers.

The confusion of emotions of the moment is echoed in the confusion of languages being spoken: English, Maori (translated by English subtitles), and the sign language by which Ada instructs Flora what to say to the others. When Ada and Flora want privacy, they both sign, which is also translated by subtitles. *The Piano* is full of secrets.

When a pushy woman later pumps Flora for information about her mother's inability to speak, the girl spins a wondrous tale. Her parents, according to Flora, were German opera singers, renowned and celebrated. One day they were caught in a terrible storm in the forest. Suddenly a bolt of lightning struck her father, who went up in flames, a veritable torch. From that day to this, Flora concludes with gravity, her mother has never said a word.

In fact, it's as good an explanation as any for Ada's singular incapacity.

More important, *The Piano* is the story of the heedless and surprising sexual passion that eventually erupts to unite the grossly crude Baines and the seemingly remote and reserved Ada, whose marriage to Stewart hasn't been a happy one. Things had begun badly when Stewart refused to transport her piano inland to their house.

Sometime later, Baines acquires the piano (still sitting on the beach) from Stewart for eighty acres of land. Baines retrieves the piano, then offers to return it to Ada if she will teach him how to play. He asks for one lesson for each key. They haggle, finally agreeing on one lesson for each black key.

In this way begins one of the funniest, most strangely erotic love stories in the recent history of film. Ada seems not at all surprised when, at the beginning of the first lesson in Baines's shack, he admits that he really doesn't want to learn how to play. Rather, he says, "there are things I'd like to do while you play." It begins by his having her lift her skirts a few inches as she sits at the piano. He stretches out on the floor, looking up.

One lesson leads to another. Soon he's proposing that she lie with him on his bed, fully clothed, the act to be the equivalent of five keys, or five lessons. Ada says ten keys. Baines agrees. Meanwhile, Flora, who is told to stay outside during the lessons, becomes curious when the piano falls silent. She peeks, but holds her tongue for the time being.

There are things, though, that even this worldly child finds too much. One day when Stewart asks her where her mother has gone, Flora, with the wrath of an Old Testament prophet, shouts, "To hell!"

Like *Sweetie*, Ms. Campion's marvelous first feature, *The Piano* is never predictable, though it is seamless. It's the work of a major writer and director. The film has the enchanted manner of a fairy tale. Even the setting suggests a fairy tale: the New Zealand bush, with its lush and rain-soaked vegetation, is as strange as the forest in which Flora says her mother was struck dumb.

Trips through this primeval forest are full of peril. When Ada goes off to her first assignation with Baines, she appears to be as innocent as Red Riding Hood. Yet this Red Riding Hood falls head over heels in love with the wolf, who turns out to be not a sheep in wolf's clothing, but a recklessly romantic prince with dirty fingernails.

Not the least of Ms. Campion's achievements is her ability to communicate the heady importance of sexual and romantic feelings to both Ada and Baines. Their love is a simultaneous liberation. The director's style is spare. No swooping camera movements over naked, writhing bodies. The camera observes the lovers from a distance, from the points of view of the spying child and then of the spying, fascinated, and furious Stewart. It's as if the camera respected the lovers' privacy but felt compelled to show us what the others see.

Along with everything else, there is great wit in *The Piano*.

The film's effect is such that it's almost impossible to consider the contributors separately. The four principal performances are extraordinary: Ms. Hunter, with her plain, steely beauty and intelligence; Mr. Keitel, so robust and intense in what could be an Oscar performance; Mr. Neill, earnest and forever baffled; and the tiny Ms. Paquin, who is so sure of herself that she doesn't seem to be a child of this world.

The physical production, smashingly photographed by Stuart Dryburgh, is elegant without fanciness, which is the mark of Ms. Campion's work. She takes the breath away not by conventionally spectacular effects, but by the simple audacity of her choices about where to put the camera and what to show.

At one point we are staring at a vast, virgin beach, as it might have looked at the beginning of time. The next minute the camera is staring down into the contents of a teacup, seen in close-up. In such ways Ms. Campion somehow suggests states of mind you've never before recognized on the screen.

—*V.C., October 16, 1993*

PICKUP ON SOUTH STREET

Directed by Samuel Fuller; written by Mr. Fuller from a story by Dwight Taylor; cinematographer, Joseph MacDonald; edited by Nick DeMaggio; art directors, George Patrick and Lyle R. Wheeler; music by Leigh Harline; produced by Jules Schermer; released by Twentieth Century Fox. Black and white. Running time: 80 minutes.

With: Richard Widmark (Skip McCoy), Jean Peters (Candy), Thelma Ritter (Moe), Murvyn Vye (Capt. Dan Tiger), Richard Kiley (Joey), Willis Bouchey (Zara), Jerry O'Sullivan (Enyart) and Harry Carter (Dietrich).

It looks very much as though someone is trying toout-bulldoze Mickey Spillane in Twentieth Century Fox's *Pickup on South Street,* which came to the Roxy yesterday. For this highly embroidered presentation of a slice of life in the New York underworld not only returns Richard Widmark to a savage, arrogant role, but also uses Jean Peters blandly as an all-

comers' human punching-bag. Violence bursts in every sequence, and the conversation is slangy and corrupt. Even the genial Thelma Ritter plays a stool-pigeon who gets her head blown off.

Indeed, the climate is so brutish and the business so sadistic in this tale of pickpockets, demireps, informers, detectives and Communist spies that the whole thing becomes a trifle silly as it slashes and slambangs along, and the first thing you know its grave pretenses are standing there, artless and absurd. This exposure is further assisted by an exaggerated interplay with sex and some sequences in which the hard-boiled surface is riddled with pistol shots of farce.

At one moment, Mr. Widmark as a grifter who has "dipped" Miss Peters's purse and removed there from a strip of film containing priceless secrets, which she is delivering to Communist spies, is smothering the lady with hot kisses (this is a few minutes after she has discovered him in his lair). The next moment he is slapping her with her handbag and knuckle-dusting the side of her jaw. Oddly enough, this is treatment that Miss Peters seems to adore. She not only thrills to his caresses (of both sorts), but comes back for more.

And Mr. Widmark is not the only person who studiously beats her up. Her Communist playmate, Richard Kiley, knocks her around from time to time. Particularly does he abuse her along toward the end of the film, when he begins to suspect a slight betrayal.

Miss Peters is a sight with a black eye, not to mention assorted contusions here and there on her beautiful mug.

As for the amiable Miss Ritter, in view of her sweet congeniality as a practicing stool-pigeon, it is doubly distressing to see her quickly and savagely destroyed by a wicked young man with a gun. There is something about the destruction of Miss Ritter that punches a hole in the film.

But then, there are so many punctures in the fabric of this lurid, midnight tale that one further item of violence is no more than the nick of a pin. Sam Fuller, who wrote it and directed, appears to have been more concerned with hiring a barrage of sensations than with telling a story to be believed. Sensations he has in abundance and, in the delivery of them, Mr. Widmark, Miss Peters, Miss Ritter and all the others in the cast do very well. Murvyn Vye as a cynical detective is particularly caustic and good, and several other performers in lesser roles give the thing a certain tone.

The nonsense collapses, however, when the crooks are fired with patriotic zeal and scrub clean their dark police records by helping in the capture of the spies. This is a sweet exaggeration that might outrage even Mr. Spillane.

—*B.C., June 18, 1953*

THE PILLOW BOOK

Written and directed by Peter Greenaway: director of photography. Sacha Vierny: edited by Chris Wyatt and Mr. Greenaway: production designers. Wilbert van Dorp and Andrée Putman: produced by Kees Kasander: released by Cinepix Film Properties. Running time: 126 minutes.

With: Vivian Wu (Nagiko) and Ewan McGregor (Jerome).

Ritual, eroticism, poetry, and snobbery are the cornerstones of the tenth-century Japanese text that inspires Peter Greenaway's rapturously perverse new film. Since these are also essential aspects of Mr. Greenaway's own work, the match is phenomenally apt. *The Pillow Book* finds the filmmaker at his most atypically seductive, creating a spellbinding web of cruel elegance and intricate gamesmanship, exploring the exotic, haunting beauty of the bizarre.

This film's stylish surface makes it significantly more palatable than the other, chillier cinematic exercises (among them *Drowning By Numbers* and *The Cook, The Thief, His Wife and Her Lover*) for which Mr. Greenaway is known. Fetishism intact, he turns his sophisticated attention to what Sei Shonagon, the Heian courtesan whose haunting, eloquent journal entries form the thousand-year-old Japanese classic known as *The Pillow Book,* called "the delights of flesh and literature." As she put it, "I have had the good fortune to enjoy them both equally." The film, in its far kinkier fashion, means to do the same.

Mr. Greenaway's *Pillow Book* is no antique: set essentially in the present, it centers on a young woman (Vivian Wu) in the grip of a peculiar erotic obsession. Nagiko, the film's heroine (and the probable real name of Sei Shonagon), is the daughter of a calligrapher who lovingly painted words and characters on her skin during her childhood. And when she grows up to become a fashion model, she needs to recapture this experience. The film, which derives more sensuality from delicate brush strokes than many others find in conventional sex scenes, embroils Nagiko in a revenge scheme against an exploitative publisher while she tries to find a calligrapher-lover who can gratify her desires.

Naturally (and of course also unnaturally), Mr. Greenaway takes this conjunction of flesh and text to all possible extremes. The complex aural and visual style of *The Pillow Book* involves rectangular insets that flash back to Sei Shonagon (a kind of Windows 995) and illustrate the imperious little lists that made her sound like the Diana Vreeland of tenth-century tastes. ("Elegant things: A white coat worn over a violet waistcoat. Duck eggs . . . A rosary of rock crystal . . . a pretty child eating strawberries.")

Such inserts also capture simultaneous actions or visual commentary or different perspectives on the same experience, while the soundtrack ranges from an eerily repeated pop song to somber chants. Through this elaborate format, the filmmaker's preternatural fastidiousness easily exerts its fascination.

Mr. Greenaway's stylistic and cerebral interests are somewhat overshadowed by the film's preoccupation with bare bodies. After Nagiko has spent half the film inviting men to write on her, she is prompted to pick up her own brush and make a manuscript of Jerome, the first lover who truly captivates her. Jerome's affair with the publisher further inflames Nagiko and inspires her to create the monumental, subtly mischievous body-painting project that is the film's wicked pièce de résistance.

Jerome is played with charming insouciance by Ewan McGregor of *Trainspotting,* in what is sure to be seen as a classic before-I-was-famous turn. Entirely naked during much of this performance, and filmed with unswerving intensity, Mr. McGregor is elaborately painted and decorated before meeting the kind of physically ghastly, intellectually piquant fate that is a frequent Greenaway flourish. Magnetic as he is, Mr. McGregor gets fifth billing for what is actually the closest thing here to a male leading role.

As *The Pillow Book* carries its strange preoccupations to their fullest expression, it's clear at times that the emperor is as naked as the actors who bear Nagiko's writing. A core of surprising banality lies at the heart of this daughter's drive to reinvent and avenge her father, but then plot is never the essence of

Mr. Greenaway's work. The film is best watched as a richly sensual stylistic exercise filled with audaciously beautiful imagery, captivating symmetries, and brilliantly facile tricks. Traces of the filmmaker's supercilious misanthropy, as in his views of vulgar Americans and the Yiddish language, are also part of this mix.

The Pillow Book has been stunningly photographed by Sacha Vierny, renowned for his work with Mr. Greenaway and Alain Resnais, in a manner that emphasizes its wide spectrum of moods and extraordinary visual cachet. Elegantly minimal production design and an array of meticulously chosen objects and artifacts heighten the film's unflagging perfectionism and its truly rarefied allure.

—*J.M., June 6, 1997*

PILLOW TALK

Directed by Michael Gordon: written by Stanley Shapiro and Maurice Richlin, based on a story by Russell Rouse and Clarence Greene: cinematographer, Arthur E. Arling: edited by Milton Carruth: music by Frank De Vol: art designers, Alexander Golitzen and Richard Riedel: produced by Ross Hunter and Martin Melcher: released by Universal Pictures. Running time: 110 minutes.

With: Rock Hudson (Brad Allen), Doris Day (Jan Morrow), Tony Randall (Jonathan Forbes), Thelma Ritter (Alma), Nick Adams (Tony) and Julia Meade (Marie).

A nice, old-fashioned device of the theater, the telephone party line, serves as a quaint convenience to bring together Rock Hudson and Doris Day in what must be cheerfully acknowledged one of the most lively and up-to-date comedy-romances of the year. *Pillow Talk* is the item, and it was dually presented last night at the Palace and the new Murray Hill Theatre, 160 East Thirty-fourth Street.

"Bring together" may be slightly ambiguous and misleading to describe the precise liaison that the telephone accomplishes here, for the first result of the two principals' sharing the same line is a cool and remote antipathy. Miss Day as a fashionable interior decorator and Mr. Hudson as a successful songwriter in New York initially insult each other as unidentified voices at either end of their party line.

Particularly, Miss Day hates Mr. Hudson because every time she picks up her phone she hears him burbling the same corny love song to an amazing variety of cooing girls. And he hates her because her angry interruptions convey an image of an envious old maid.

But once the romantic songwriter gets a secret peek at Miss Day and realizes how wrong is his impression, the "bringing together" begins, and the telephone and Mr. Hudson's impersonation of an ardent Texan are combined to push the romance from there.

It is really the clever, witty screenplay that Stanley Shapiro and Maurice Richlin have prepared from a story by Russell Rouse and Clarence Greene that accounts for much of the sparkle in this film. Their devices are crisp, their dialogue funny, and their cinema mechanics are neat. Frequent clever use of a split screen make for fresh and appropriate drolleries. With a CinemaScope screen to play on, they and director Michael Gordon have much fun.

And this fun is transmitted to the audience in an easy and generous flow of ingeniously graphic situations and nimble repartee. The opportunity for the tricky songwriter to court the lady through a wicked pretense of being a high-minded Texan is in Mr. Hudson's groove, and he carries off the delicate deception with surprising dexterity.

"You give me a real warm feeling," he softly drawls to Miss Day, "like a potbellied stove on a frosty morning."

What girl could resist that line?

Well, certainly not the young lady played fiercely and smartly by Miss Day, who has a delightful way of taking the romantic offensive against a man. Her dudgeons are as chic and spectacular as her nifty Jean Louis clothes, and her fall for Mr. Hudson's deceptions is as graceful as a ski-run down a hill. Singing is kept to a minimum, but Miss Day does cut loose a couple of times, very pleasantly, as usual. Perry Blackwell also sings two bistro songs.

In support of Miss Day and Mr. Hudson are Thelma Ritter as an alcoholic maid and Tony Randall as a disappointed suitor, than whom no others could be more droll. Nick Adams as a wolfish Harvard senior almost steals one sequence from Miss Day, and Marcel Dallio, Allen Jenkins, and Lee Patrick are fun in a couple of scenes.

Color and some likeable music brighten this pretty film, which has a splendid montage of New York in it. Thank Universal for the boon.

—B.C., October 7, 1959

THE PINK PANTHER

Directed by Blake Edwards; written by Mr. Edwards and Maurice Richlin; cinematographer, Philip Lathrop; edited by Ralph E. Winters; music by Henry Mancini; art designer, Fernando Carrere; produced by Martin Jurow; released by United Artists. Running time: 113 minutes.

With: David Niven (Sir Charles), Peter Sellers (Inspector Jacques Clouseau), Capucine (Simone Clouseau), Claudia Cardinale (Princess Dale), Brenda de Banzie (Angela Dunning) and Fran Jeffries (Greek "Cousin").

Even if Peter Sellers weren't lying in a hospital bed recovering from a heart attack said to have been brought on by prolonged overwork, it would give us the willies to see the amount of labor he does in Blake Edwards's farce, *The Pink Panther*, which came to the Music Hall yesterday.

Seldom has any comedian seemed to work so persistently and hard at trying to be violently funny with weak material. Although Mr. Sellers plays but one role in this progressively more nonsensical film—that of a French detective on the trail of a phantom jewel thief, he goes at it with as much effort as he gave to *The Mouse That Roared* or, at least, to *The World of Henry Orient,* in which he just appeared at the hall.

He bumps into things. He stumbles blindly over doorsills and edges of rugs. He walks clumsily into his own bedroom without sensing what's under his own bed. (It happens to be David Niven as his wife's lover, who is nonchalantly lying there with a couple of champagne glasses, waiting casually for the coast to clear.)

This is the key to the character that Mr. Sellers plays—a detective who is so blind and stupid that he never dreams, let alone perceives, that his wife is carrying on with the very jewel thief he so archly and industriously seeks. And the measure of it as humor is the way Mr. Sellers has to work to make it frenetically funny, which indeed, it occasionally is.

But only occasionally. That's the trouble. It promises so much at the start, when we all go to Cortina d'Ampezzo, a winter resort in the Alps, where so many flashy people are gathered and the scenery and parties so plush that how can it help but be the next place for the phantom to strike.

Here, for a while, Mr. Sellers makes his stupid detective quite a joke, especially in one lengthy sequence in which he is preparing to retire with his wife. No one could be more solicitous and patient in humoring a woman's whims, even down to trying resignedly to play her to sleep with a violin. But the humor drains out of it quickly. By the time the shenanigans swing to a downright slapstick sequence of door-slamming and scuttling under the bed by two impudently interloping fellows in the detective's own bedroom, the fun has become too labored and Mr. Sellers too clearly has to force.

And that's what's wrong with the picture. Mr. Edwards's and Maurice Richlin's script is a basically unoriginal and largely witless piece of farce carpentry that has to be pushed and heaved at stoutly in order to keep on the move. Mr. Sellers does his part resolutely and so does Mr. Niven in the role of the charming, seductive phantom who is posing as a British peer.

But the women involved are too lazy—or perhaps Mr. Edwards has failed to give them any better direction than he has given them a script. Capucine, the tall and frosty clotheshorse, is utterly mirthless as the wife, and Claudia Cardinale is dour and sluggish as an Oriental princess who owns a priceless gem, which is known as the "Pink Panther," thus accounting for the tag. Their limpid and listless endeavors to fall in with the spirit of farce are almost painful and pathetic. They simply wear some handsome gowns of Yves St. Laurent.

As for Robert Wagner as a nephew of the phantom who pops in from Hollywood to offer a little boudoir competition, he is, well, let's just say superfluous.

But there is one thing about this picture that is clever and joyous, at least. That is a cartooned pink panther that runs through the main titles at the start making mischief with the lettering, insistently getting in the way. He is so blithe and bumptious, so sweet and entirely lovable, that he's awfully hard to follow. It's questionable whether the picture does.

—B.C., April 24, 1964

PINOCCHIO

Directed by Ben Sharpsteen and Hamilton Luske; written by Ted Sears, Webb Smith, Joseph Sabo, Otto Englander, William Cottrell, Erdman Penner and Aurelius Battaglia, based on the fairy tale by Carlo Collodi; music and lyrics by Leigh Harline, Ned Washington and Paul J. Smith; art designers, Charles Philippi, Hugh Hennesy, Dick Kelsey, Terrell Stepp, John Hubley, Ken Anderson, Kendall O'Connor, Thor Putnam, McLaren Stewart and Al Zinnen; produced by Walt Disney; released by RKO Radio Pictures. Running time: 88 minutes.

With the voices of: Dick Jones (Pinocchio), Christian Rub (Gepetto), Cliff Edwards (Jiminy Cricket), Evelyn Venable (The Blue Fairy), Walter Catlett (J. Worthington Foulfellow), Frankie Darro (Lampwick), Charles Judels (Stromboli the Puppetmaster) and Don Brodie (Barker).

If Westbrook Pegler could write (as he did write in January, 1938) that Walt Disney's *Snow White* was the happiest event since the armistice, we can report confidently this morning that Mr. Disney's *Pinocchio* is the happiest event since the war. His second feature-length cartoon, three years in the making and the occasion of the Center Theatre's return to the cinema's ranks, is a blithe, chucklesome, witty, fresh, and beautifully drawn fantasy which is superior to *Snow White* in every respect but one: its score. And, since its score is merry and pleasant, if not quite so contagiously tuneful as the chorals of the seven little men who really weren't there, we shall not have it stressed to *Pinocchio*'s disparagement. It still is the best thing Mr. Disney has done and therefore the best cartoon ever made.

Seeing a Disney work in action always is more fun than analyzing it, for charm is a quality even Barrie could not define and charm is the pulsating, radiant, winning something that shines through this latest Disney creation and makes it so captivating. It isn't at all self-conscious or calculating, like the charm of the matinee idol or honeyed radio voice; it seems almost too spontaneous for us to credit the fact that every bit of it was conceived, weighed, worked out during a three-year gestation period in a cartoon factory. At the risk of being, of all hateful words, sentimental, we would say *Pinocchio* is the work of men of goodwill and good fellowship. From Disney down to his least inker, animator, or air-brush wielder, we sense a guild of craftsmen smiling over their drawing boards and paintpots, delighted with the make-believe world they are creating.

The make-believe here, of course, is basically of Collodi's imagining. It was his notion, in a quaint and moral-pointing fairy tale, to tell of a long-nosed boy-like puppet, dubbed Pinocchio by Gepetto, the wood-carver, who was brought to life by the Blue Fairy but told he could not be a real little boy until he had acquired truth, courage, and unselfishness. To assist him in his quest, she provided him with a conscience in the form of a cricket—Jiminy Cricket to Mr. Disney's fantastic crew—and there were adventures with a cruel puppetmaster, encounters with a wicked Fox and a Cat, a bewitched sojourn on Pleasure Island, where wayward little boys turned into jackasses, and, finally, an exciting descent to the ocean's floor to rescue poor Gepetto from the belly of a whale. All grist, obviously, to the Disney mill.

And he has had an impish, a scampish, a quizzical and disarmingly whimsical time with it from the moment his Jiminy Cricket (who acts as a debonair tourist guide through this wonderland) opens the pages of his fantasy to that, at the very end, when Figaro, the kitten, jumps into the goldfish bowl to plant an ecstatic and suspiciously fishy kiss on the cupid's-bow lips of Cleo, the kittenish goldfish. For all these curious folk and all their curious adventures have been drawn with Mr. Disney's invariably quick eye to amusing characterization and humorous detail, with his usual relish for a sly little joke, with his habitual enjoyment of telling whoppers and making them seem just as natural as a cricket in spats.

His Jiminy Cricket, as you might have guessed, is the Dopey of *Pinocchio,* and for just the opposite reasons. He's smart as a cricket and twice as chirpy. It's something to hear him rap with his cane on the teeth of Monstro the Whale and demand admittance into the Blue Grottoed belly where Gepetto, perched on the rail of a swallowed derelict, is manfully fishing for tuna. It's something, too, to see the expression of annoyance drift across his face, glacier-like, when Gepetto's clocks begin to hammer out the seconds he meant to pass in sleep. "Quiet," he bellows, like an assistant director, and every pendulum freezes in mid-swing. No question about it, Jiminy Cricket has a commanding presence and the droll voice of Cliff Edwards, who can burlesque a tenor with the worst of them.

But it isn't easy to call Jiminy the only favorite. Pinocchio is a fresh little cuss, Cleo the Goldfish is a dream, and Figaro the kitten is the kind of kitten only Disney's men could draw, exact to the whistling purr, the wicked side-glance, the bewildered and hurt look when the hand that has been scratching its neck suddenly is withdrawn. You'll like Mr. Disney's cast, from cricket to Monstro, from kitten to Fox, from Gepetto to goldfish.

Technically, and we hate to be technical at a time like this, it answers every one of the objections raised when *Snow White* was shown. The drawing is finer, with none of the line-straying noticeable when Prince Charming and his Cinderella took the screen. The handling of shadows and highlights is surer, and the color—lovely as it was in Disney's first cartoon feature—is immeasurably lovelier here. We note, too, with vast admiration, evidences of true direction—freer use of camera in panning, zoom shot, and dollying, so that the vantage point is not fixed but travels to and from and with the subjects in its range. Some uses of it are cute, too—like the camera's hopping toward a scene when little Jiminy is telling us how he hopped over to take a look in Gepetto's window.

But that's enough about technique. Its refinement was inevitable, for Mr. Disney is a notorious perfectionist; we've no doubt he is dissatisfied still and will have even greater marvels for us in his *Fantasia,* the next of his promised features. What really matters, and all that matters, this morning is that *Pinocchio* is here at last, is every bit as fine as we had prayed it would be—if not finer—and that it is as gay and clever and delightful a fantasy as any well-behaved youngster or jaded oldster could hope to see.

—*F.S.N., February 8, 1940*

PIXOTE

Directed by Hector Babenco; written (in Portuguese, with English subtitles) by Mr. Babenco and Jorge Durán, based on the novel *Infancia Dos Martos* by José Louzeiro; cinematographer, Rodolfo Sánches; edited by Luiz Elias; music by John Neschling; art designer, Clovis Bueno; produced by Paulo Francini; released by Palace Films. Running time: 127 minutes.

With: Marília Pera (Sueli), Jardel Filho (Sapatos Brancos), Rubens de Falco (Juiz), Elke Maravilha (Debora) and Tony Tornado (Christal).

*P*ixote, the third feature film by the Argentine-born Brazilian director Hector Babenco, is a finely made, uncompromisingly grim movie about the street boys of São Paulo, in particular about Pixote—which, according to the program, translates roughly as "Peewee."

Pixote looks to be about sixty years old, though he's actually no more than ten or eleven. He may yet be growing, but one can't be sure. Clearly São Paulo's slums, backstreets, pinball parlors, whorehouses, and reform schools are not providing much nourishment. He is still learning how to snatch purses, roll drunks, deal in dope and murder, but the physical part of him seems permanently fixed in withered puberty.

How much of this is a performance and how much is the manner in which Mr. Babenco uses his actor, I've no idea. What is apparent from the beginning of *Pixote* to its pathetic end, though, is that Fernando Ramos Da Silva, who plays Pixote, has one of the most eloquent faces ever seen on the screen. It's not actually bruised, but it looks battered. The eyes don't match, as if one eye were attending to immediate events and the other were considering escape routes. It's a face full of life and expression and one that hardly ever smiles.

The film will be shown at the Museum of Modern Art today and tomorrow, concluding the annual New Directors/New Films series sponsored by the Film Society of Lincoln Center and the museum's department of film.

The movie that *Pixote* most quickly brings to mind is Luis Buñuel's classic *Los Olvidados,* though Mr.

Babenco doesn't possess the dark Buñuel humor nor does he attempt to imitate Mr. Buñuel's air of detachment, which has the effect of making credible horrors that are beyond the ken of most of us.

Mr. Babenco looks at his juvenile vagrants at eye level, in close-up, as if he were one of them, making no judgments on their behavior, seeing no further into the future than they do, accepting everything that occurs and always being slightly surprised that doomed schemes are doomed to fail.

This obviously is the manner of the film, not its substance, which is a mixture of outrage at social conditions and awe that within such lives traces of real humanity are still to be found.

Pixote has the conviction of a documentary, though Mr. Babenco adapted the screenplay from a novel by José Louzeiro. It records the unsentimental education of Pixote when, in one of the periodic police sweeps, he is packed off to a juvenile detention center where he witnesses rape, blackmail, and other forms of intimidation by the other kids, and arbitrary punishment, including murder, by the bored, underpaid, and sometimes sadistic attendants.

When he finally breaks out of the place, his associates are Lilica (Jorge Juliao), an effeminate boy who is always falling in love with Mr. Wrong; Dito (Gilberto Moura), a macho kid who throws Lilica over for a sick, aging São Paulo streetwalker; and Diego (José Nilson Dos Santos), who is closest in age and disposition to Pixote.

Among the characters they meet on the outside are Cristal, a drug-dealer with a fancy car and a fondness for young boys, who crazily commissions them to make a drug delivery in Rio de Janeiro, and Sueli (Marília Pera), the worn-out streetwalker for whom they procure and whose customers they occasionally rob. In one of the film's more lighthearted moments (comparatively speaking), the kids hold up one of Sueli's customers, force him into the trunk of his car, which they then drive off to a park where they celebrate by dancing, to music furnished by the car radio turned to top volume, and by becoming exceedingly drunk. No day ever has a tomorrow.

The performances are almost too good to be true, but Mr. Da Silva and Miss Pera are splendid. *Pixote* is not for the weak of stomach. A lot of the details are tough to take, but it is neither exploitative nor pretentious. Mr. Babenco shows us rock-bottom, and because he is an artist, he makes us believe it as well as all of the possibilities that have been lost.

—*V.C., May 5, 1981*

A PLACE IN THE SUN

Produced and directed by George Stevens; written by Michael Wilson and Harry Brown, based on the novel *An American Tragedy* by Theodore Dreiser and the play by Patrick Kearney; cinematographer, William Mellor; edited by William Hornbeck; music by Franz Waxman; art designers, Hans Dreier and Walter Tyler; released by Paramount Pictures. Black and white. Running time: 122 minutes.

With: Montgomery Clift (George Eastman), Elizabeth Taylor (Angela Vickers), Shelley Winters (Alice Tripp), Anne Revere (Hannah Eastman), Raymond Burr (Marlowe), Herbert Heyes (Charles Eastman) and Keefe Brasselle (Earl Eastman).

Although the term "remake" is, for some strange reason, shunned by the Coast's artisans as something vile, a stigma better left unheralded, Hollywood, Paramount, and George Stevens, producer-director, in particular, can point with pride to *A Place in the Sun*. For this second screen edition of Theodore Dreiser's monumental novel, *An American Tragedy*, which was unveiled at the Capitol last night, is a work of beauty, tenderness, power, and insight. And, though Mr. Stevens, his scenarists and cast have switched its time and setting to the present and avoided extreme concentration on the social crusading of the book, *A Place in the Sun* emerges as a credit to both the motion-picture craft and, we feel reasonably certain, the author's major intentions.

Out of Dreiser's often murky and turgid tale of the twenties, now the present—the stream of words in *An American Tragedy*, as has been noted many times previously, was not easy to navigate—scenarists Michael Wilson and Harry Brown have distilled the essence of tragedy and romance that is both moving and memorable. Retained, too, in this two-hour drama—representing the painstakingly edited end result of hundreds of thousands of feet of material shot—are characterizations which cleave to the Dreiser originals.

And it is a tribute to deft dramatization that the young principals are projected as fully as the maelstrom of life in which they are trapped and with which they are unable to cope.

One may argue that Mr. Stevens has given only surface treatment to the society which appears to propel George Eastman to his tragic end and accentuated his love affairs and groping for a higher rung in the social ladder. That, it becomes apparent, is basically captious. George Eastman is obviously an intelligent youth whose background has not equipped him for anything better than menial endeavor. So it is not surprising that he grasps at the opportunity to work in his rich uncle's factory. And it is not surprising that the lonely, brooding young man, ignored by his rich relatives, will find an answer to his crying need for companionship in his drab, unlettered, and equally lonely coworker, Alice Tripp.

The forces pushing young Eastman to the final, horrible retribution are obvious and a tribute to the naturalism of Dreiser as the youth is suddenly exposed to the overwhelming opulence of his family and Angela Vickers, to whose love and beauty he succumbs. Since his basic upbringing—a composite background of unbending Evangelism and slums from which he chose to escape—does not permit him to callously desert Alice—now frantic with the knowledge that she is bearing his child—he takes surreptitious steps to remedy his untenable position. This phase of his ordeal (and Alice's) is a wholly tasteful and compelling handling of a delicate situation. The questions of his morals and intrinsic cowardice here are placed squarely in the eyes of the viewer.

With similar integrity, the drama depicts Alice's drowning and the subsequent mounting terror and confusion of her lover, faced with the enormity of the tragedy and the reiteration of the insidious thought that while he did not commit murder he must have willed it. And George Eastman, grappling with a transgression he cannot fully comprehend, is a pitiful, yet strangely brave individual as he explains his act and convictions in court. Despite his weaknesses he is a strong figure who admits in his death cell that "I wanted to save her but I just couldn't." He takes on stature as does his love for Angela whom he tells: "I know something now I didn't know before. I'm guilty of a lot of things—of most of what they say I am."

There may be some belief that Montgomery Clift, as the tortured George Eastman, is not nearly the designing and grasping youth conceived by Dreiser. But his portrayal, often terse and hesitating, is full, rich, restrained, and, above all, generally credible and poignant. He is, in effect, a believable mama's boy gone wrong.

Equally poignant is Shelley Winters's characterization of the ill-fated Alice. Miss Winters, in our opinion, has never been seen to better advantage than as the colorless factory hand, beset by burgeoning anxieties but clinging to a love she hopes can be rekindled. Elizabeth Taylor's delineation of the rich and beauteous Angela also is the top effort of her career. It is a shaded, tender performance and one in which her passionate and genuine romance avoids the bathos common to young love as it sometimes comes to the screen.

And, under Mr. Stevens's expert direction, Raymond Burr, as the doggedly probing district attorney, and Anne Revere, as Clift's mother, a mission worker who feels that the blame for her son's crime is partly hers, as well as most of the supporting players, contribute fitting bits to an impressive mosaic. Despite the fact that this version of Dreiser's tragedy may be criticized—academically, we think—for its length or deviations from the author's pattern, *A Place in the Sun* is a distinguished work, a tribute, above all, to its producer-director and an effort now placed among the ranks of the finest films to have come from Hollywood in several years.

—A. W., August 29, 1951

PLACES IN THE HEART

Written and directed by Robert Benton: director of photography. Nestor Almendros: edited by Carol Littleton: music by John Kander and Howard Shore: production designer. Gene Callahan: produced by Arlene Donovan: released by Tri-Star Pictures. Running time: 110 minutes.

With: Sally Field (Edna Spaulding). Lindsay Crouse (Margaret Lomax). Ed Harris (Wayne Lomax). Amy Madigan (Viola Kelsey). John Malkovich (Mr. Will). Danny Glover (Moze). Yankton Hatten (Frank). Gennie James (Possum) and Lane Smith (Albert Denby).

Out of the memories of his boyhood in Waxahachie, Texas, during the Great Depression, and within the unlikely tradition of the old-fashioned "mortgage" melodrama, Robert Benton has made one of the best films in years about growing up American. Its title is *Places in the Heart,* which is misleading in its sentimentality, for the film itself, though full of sentiment, demonstrates in every other way the writer-director's built-in junk-detector.

Places in the Heart, which opens today at the Coronet Theater, is a movie about the process of remembrance, as well as about the events remembered. The terrible harshness of some of the events recalled has been softened by time, which also has invested those events with mythic importance. *Places in the Heart* is a family tale handed down from one generation to the next, full of wonder and longing and love.

The time is 1935, and the setting is the small town of Waxahachie and the gentle Texas countryside surrounding it. When her husband is killed in an accident, Edna Spaulding (Sally Field) finds herself, after fifteen years of marriage, with two small children to support, a farm on which the bank is about to foreclose, less than $200 in the bank, and no talent for anything except cooking and keeping house, which, for the self-employed, paid no more then than it does now.

Places in the Heart is the moving and often funny story of how Edna Spaulding, through hard work, grit, and a certain amount of luck, manages to see things through. Edna, as beautifully played by Miss Field, has a lot of the steadfastness that distinguished the actress's Oscar-winning performance in *Norma Rae.* However, Edna is also a much less sophisticated personality, whose growth, in the course of the film, reflects an almost nineteenth-century faith in the possibilities of the American system, not as the system was, but as one wanted to believe it to be.

As a title, *Places in the Heart* is also misleading in that it befogs the disciplined nature of the movie, which sees time and place with a critical eye and reserves its affection for the remarkable people who survived hardships that were at first beyond their imaginations. Like the best work of Jean Renoir and François Truffaut, *Places in the Heart* never denies the existence of the void that lies just beyond the film's horizon, and which infuses even the sunlit scenes with tension and foreboding.

In addition to Edna Spaulding, the principal characters include her sister Margaret (Lindsay Crouse), who supports herself, her smooth-talking, philandering husband, Wayne (Ed Harris), and their child by working as a beautician; Viola Kelsey (Amy Madigan), Margaret's best friend, who has slipped into an extramarital affair with Wayne; Mr. Will (John Malkovich), Edna's misanthropic, blind boarder; Edna's two small children (Yankton Hatten and Gennie James); and, probably most important, Moze (Danny Glover), a black hobo who stops by the farm one evening looking for work, steals the silver, and winds up teaching Edna how to plant and harvest cotton.

With the exception of one spectacular sequence in which a tornado tears through Waxahachie and another sequence involving the Ku Klux Klan, the film moves through a series of rather ordinary events, discovering in them not clichés but essential meanings. The strong, sweet emotions aroused by close relationships, among friends as well as among family members, are revealed with unaffected clarity and a sense of surprise. Considering the stinginess manifest in so many aspects of our lives, the existence of such decency is as unexpected as it is welcome.

Each member of the large cast is fine, but especially noteworthy are the performances of Miss Field, Miss Crouse, Mr. Malkovich, most recently seen on the New York stage in *Death of a Salesman* and *True West,* and Mr. Glover, who was so fine in the Broadway production of Athol Fugard's *Master Harold . . . and the Boys.*

The film was photographed entirely in and around Waxahachie by Nestor Almendros, Mr. Benton's gifted cameraman on *Kramer vs. Kramer* and *Still of the Night.* They have given the film the idealized look of the work by some of the better, now-anonymous painters who, supported by Federal subsidies during the Depression, traveled around the country covering the walls of public buildings, in small towns and large, with murals that weren't always flattering to the people who commissioned them.

Places in the Heart is a tonic, a revivifying experience right down to the final images, which, like those at the end of Luis Buñuel's *Tristana,* carry us back to the very beginning of the cycle of these particular lives.

—V.C., September 21, 1984

PLATOON

Written and directed by Oliver Stone: director of photography. Robert Richardson: edited by Claire Simpson: music by Georges Delarue: production designer. Bruno Rubeo: produced by Arnold Kopelson: released by Orion Pictures. Running time: 111 minutes.

With: Tom Berenger (Sergeant Barnes). Willem Dafoe (Sergeant Elias). Charlie Sheen (Chris). Forest Whitaker (Big Harold). Francesco Quinn (Rhah). John C. McGinley (Sergeant O'Neill). Richard Edson (Sal). Kevin Dillon (Bunny). Reggie Johnson (Junior) and Keith David (King).

Nothing that Oliver Stone has done before—including *Midnight Express,* for which he wrote the screenplay, and *Salvador,* which he wrote and directed—is preparation for the singular achievement of his latest film, *Platoon,* which is possibly the best work of any kind about the Vietnam War since Michael Herr's vigorous and hallucinatory book *Dispatches.*

For that matter, *Platoon,* opening today at Loews New York Twin and Astor Plaza, is not like any other Vietnam film that's yet been made—certainly not like those revisionist comic strips *Rambo* and *Missing in Action.* Nor does it have much in common with either Francis Coppola's epic *Apocalypse Now,* which ultimately turns into a romantic meditation on a mythical war, or Michael Cimino's *Deer Hunter,* which is more about the mind of the America that fought the war than the Vietnam War itself.

Much like Mr. Herr's *Dispatches,* this vivid, terse, exceptionally moving new film deals with the immediate experience of the fighting—that is, with the life of the infantryman, endured at ground level, in heat and muck, with fatigue and ants and with fear as a constant, even during the druggy hours back in the comparative safety of the base.

Life becomes very simple in such circumstances: "we" are "grunts" and "they" are "gooks." That's reason enough to kill or be killed. However, since the announced enemy remains invisible most of the time or, when visible, without particular character, an entire hierarchy of other, more comprehensible enemies

emerges from the ranks of one's comrades. Sanity is not a state of mind but a pair of dry socks. Objectives don't have names. They're numbered coordinates, drawn on a very small map from which the rest of the world has vanished.

Mr. Stone, himself a Vietnam vet, observes the war through the short focus of a single infantry platoon, fighting somewhere near the Cambodian border in 1967. It's meant as praise to say the film appears to express itself with the same sort of economy that used to be employed in old, studio-made action movies—B-pictures in which characters are largely defined through what they do rather than what they say.

That's only the impression, since the grunts in *Platoon* do talk quite a lot, though for the most part, they don't get too literary, nor do they explain too much. They are so exceedingly ordinary that they sometimes jump off the screen as if they were the originals for all the clichéd types that have accumulated in all earlier war movies.

There's the fellow who says with cheerful reason that, if you're going to get killed in Vietnam, it's better to get killed in the first couple of weeks. Otherwise, you just waste time worrying about it. There's also the young, out-of-his-depth officer who does the best he can to talk his men's language but, when he leaves their recreation hut, must say, as if exiting from the frat house, "I gotta run. I'll catch you guys later."

At the center of the film is Chris Taylor, a new arrival who dropped out of college to enlist, a fact that strikes the rest of the platoon as profoundly, comically irrational. Chris, beautifully played by Charlie Sheen, is about as close as *Platoon* ever gets to a literary mouthpiece—he writes letters home to his grandmother, which we hear on the soundtrack, and in which he always—politely—sends regards to his mother and father.

Chris is idealized but without sentimentality. Part of him remains unknown and private, at least until the final minutes of the film, when Mr. Stone unfortunately feels called upon to have Chris say what has been far more effectively left unsaid.

The platoon's most important figures are two NCO's, each an exhausted, self-aware veteran of earlier Vietnam tours: the facially scarred Sergeant Barnes (Tom Berenger), who has somehow become committed to the war, which is all he has left, and Sergeant Elias (Willem Dafoe), whom the war has made as eerily gentle as Barnes is brutal. The two men, long-time friends, loathe each other.

Throughout the action of the film, the sergeants are fighting their own war for the loyalty of the men. It's a measure of how well both roles are written and played that one comes to understand even the astonishing cruelty of Barnes and the almost saintly goodness of Elias. Each has gone over the edge.

Another measure of the film is the successful way Mr. Stone has managed to create narrative order in a film that, at heart, is a dramatization of mental, physical, and moral chaos. *Platoon* gives the impression at first of being only a little less aimless than the men, whose only interest is staying alive or, as Chris Taylor puts it, of remaining "anonymous," meaning safe.

Yet the tension builds and never lets up (until the anti-climactic final moments). Somewhere in the second half of the film, there's a sequence of astonishing, harrowing impact that sort of ambles into a contemplation of how a My Lai massacre could have happened. It's not easy to sit through, not only because it's grisly but also because, all things considered, it's so inevitable.

Mr. Stone's control over his own screenplay is such that *Platoon* seems to slide into and out of crucial scenes without ever losing its distant cool. He doesn't telegraph emotions, nor does he stomp on them. The movie is a succession of found moments. It's less like a work that's been written than one that has been discovered, though, as we all probably know, screenplays aren't delivered by storks. This one is a major piece of work, as full of passion as it is of redeeming, scary irony.

The members of the supporting cast are no less fine than the principal players, and no less effective, often, for being almost anonymous. Two particular standouts are Kevin Dillon, Matt's younger brother, who has the flashy role of a certifiable, homicidal maniac with a baby face, and Keith David, who plays Mr. Sheen's best friend, a black soldier who may be the only sane man in the platoon.

Platoon is a Vietnam film that honors its uneasy, complex, still haunted subject.

—*V.C., December 19, 1986*

PLAY MISTY FOR ME

Directed by Clint Eastwood; written by Jo Heims and Dean Riesner, based on a story by Mr. Heims; director of photography, Bruce Surtees; edited by Carl Pingitore; music by Dee Barton; art designer, Alexander Goljtzen; produced by Robert Daley; released by Universal Pictures. Running time: 102 minutes.

With: Clint Eastwood (Dave), Jessica Walter (Evelyn), Donna Mills (Tobie), John Larch (Sergeant McCallum), Irene Hervey (Madge) and James McEachin (Al Monte).

Director Clint Eastwood's first movie is the story of a California disk jockey (Eastwood) who one night meets Evelyn (Jessica Walter), a good-looking devoted listener who has always called to ask that he play Erroll Garner's "Misty" for her, and begins what is to be a short-term casual affair without complications.

But Evelyn has a personality quirk, a little violent streak that shows as obstinate possessiveness when she is happy and as homicidal mania when she is not. The disk jockey has a real girl (Donna Mills), and Evelyn's response to her is a one-woman reign of terror that threatens most of the circumstance and provides all the suspense of *Play Misty for Me,* which opened yesterday at neighborhood theaters.

Both the circumstance—the handsome bachelor, the minor glamour and attractive loneliness of the media people, the relaxed nights and entrancing days, the scenery and life style of the Monterey Peninsula—and the suspense recall other, better movies. And it is sad that this film, with its locale and some of its moods out of *Vertigo* and its central obsessional action almost an inversion of Preminger's wonderful *Laura* should echo so briefly in the imagination.

It is not simply that the movie fails to make sense. A lot of good movies are weak on sense—though they don't often require a leading man to be quite so dense for quite so long in interpreting the behavior of a psychotic leading woman. But they must not be weak in sensibility, in that logic of emotional response that is the real motive power of the atmospheric thriller.

Play Misty for Me begins to fail with its opening

title sequence, Eastwood's scenic drive from an isolated shore-side retreat to his radio station in Carmel—where each shot in the long, lyrical montage seems to count for less than the one that preceded it, until the car simply comes to a stop in a confusion of place and time that a broadcast voice on the soundtrack has to clear up.

The failure is never redeemed, and it extends even to the character of Evelyn, who begins as mystery and loses a bit with each appearance until she ends as mere knife-wielding mechanism for plot that happens to need a girlish monster.

The movie goes down with her, and I think the fault lies with Clint Eastwood the director, who has made too many easy decisions about events, about the management of atmosphere, about the treatment of performances—including the rather inexpressive one of Clint Eastwood the actor, who is asked to bear more witness to a quality of inwardness than his better directors have yet had the temerity to ask of him.

His best director, Don Siegel, makes his film acting debut here as a bartender named Murphy. Siegel is pretty good, but he's no Murphy. He looks decidedly Greek.

—R.G., November 4, 1971

THE PLAYER

Directed by Robert Altman; written by Michael Tolkin, based on his novel; director of photography, Jean Lepine; edited by Geraldine Peroni and Maysie Hoy; music by Thomas Newman; production designer, Stephen Altman; produced by David Brown, Nick Wechsler and Mr. Tolkin; released by Fine Line Features. Running time: 123 minutes.

With: Tim Robbins (Griffin Mill), Greta Scacchi (June Gudmundsdottir), Fred Ward (Walter Stuckel), Whoopi Goldberg (Detective Avery), Peter Gallagher (Larry Levy), Brion James (Joel Levison), Cynthia Stevenson (Bonnie Sherow), Vincent D'Onofrio (David Kahane), Dean Stockwell (Andy Civella), Richard E. Grant (Tom Oakley), Sydney Pollack (Dick Mellen), Lyle Lovett (Detective DeLongpre) and Dina Merrill (Celia);

with cameos by Buck Henry, Julia Roberts, Jack Lemmon, Marlee Matlin, Harry Belafonte, Anjelica Huston, Nick Nolte, Bruce Willis and others.

Robert Altman has not really been away. Yet his new Hollywood satire titled *The Player* is so entertaining, so flip, and so genially irreverent that it seems to announce the return of the great gregarious filmmaker whose *Nashville* remains one of the classics of the 1970's.

Taking Michael Tolkin's clever and knowing screenplay, which Mr. Tolkin adapted from his own novel, Mr. Altman has made the kind of "in" Hollywood film that will be comprehensible to just about anybody who goes to movies or who simply reads about them.

The Player is a Hollywood morality tale, appropriately skin-deep. It's no apocalyptic *Day of the Locust,* but a send-up of Hollywood spelled out in the broad terms that can be easily understood by the deal makers at the top, men and women who are so pressed for time that they prefer their stories synopsized, orally if possible.

It is also a tale of murder and mystery, though not a murder-mystery. There's no mystery about who commits the murder, only about the circumstances that make the crime inevitable. At the film's center is the head of production at a large studio, Griffin Mill (Tim Robbins), who is first met as he listens to a series of screenplay proposals that set the movie's tone.

Among them is Buck Henry's pitch for *The Graduate, Part 2,* which is the story of Ben Braddock and Elaine Robinson, who, twenty-five years after their elopement, are living with Mrs. Robinson. "I like it, I like it," says Griffin. Another fellow outlines a rather complicated story that Griffin tries to paraphrase: "Like *The Gods Must Be Crazy,* except that the Coke bottle is a television actress?"

Griffin's life is precarious. Production executives have notoriously short careers at any one company. There are rumors that a new young genius named Larry Levy (Peter Gallagher) is being hired with the obvious intent of replacing him. This aggravates another situation, which, at any other time, might not have come to obsess him the way it does now.

Griffin has picked up a poison-pen-pal. Every day or two he receives an anonymous card from someone whom he has apparently, in the jargon of American business, failed to get back to. The notes are cryptic, threatening his life. Apprehensive that he will become a laughingstock if he reports his fears, Griffin does a little detective work. He finally identifies the suspect as a screenwriter whom, indeed, he did fail to get back to.

When the writer turns up dead in an alley following a meeting with Griffin, the production chief becomes a suspect. What to do? Among other things, Griffin falls hopelessly in love with the writer's live-in lover. She is June Gudmundsdottir (Greta Scacchi), a painter from, she says, Iceland, which might explain her fondness for the color blue, though not for the isolated words that appear in her paintings.

"I like words and letters," she tells Griffin, "but I'm not crazy about complete sentences." It is also her opinion that her dead lover was "uniquely untalented."

In addition to its other identities, *The Player* is a love story, but one set in the very particular world of moviemaking, which is why Griffin is initially drawn to June as an outsider. Yet everyone seems to turn a little strange when brought into the Hollywood orbit. Among others there are the police who are investigating the writer's murder, including one cop who is a fan of *Freaks,* and Detective Avery (Whoopi Goldberg), who seems to find anything Griffin says ridiculously funny.

If *The Player* were more plot-oriented, Detective Avery might be described as playing Police Inspector Petrovich to Griffin's Raskolnikov, but the film has no intention of replaying *Crime and Punishment* on any level. To do so would be to crack the film's completely self-absorbed, comic facade.

Indeed, there is not really that much of a story to *The Player,* though it is breezy fun. The film is a grand Hollywood fresco that depicts the eccentric passion of Griffin Mill as he goes to his destiny, sometimes godlike and sometimes like a bewildered amoral pilgrim. Mr. Altman paints everything large, with lots of color and overlapping sound, whether the locale is a studio boardroom, a screening room, a cocktail party for the A list, or a dressed-to-the-nines Hollywood gala.

The members of the huge cast seem to be having a great night out on the town. They respond with enthusiasm to Mr. Altman's generosity, whether the roles are large or small, whether they play cameos or dress-extras. In addition to Ms. Goldberg and Mr. Gal-

lagher, the main featured actors are Fred Ward, Cynthia Stevenson, Vincent D'Onofrio, Sydney Pollack, Dean Stockwell, and Richard E. Grant. Mr. Robbins and Miss Scacchi are securely funny in the central roles, though attention is often drawn from them by the dozens of "names" who come and go around them.

A few of them: Julia Roberts, Jack Lemmon, Marlee Matlin, Harry Belafonte, Anjelica Huston, Nick Nolte, and Bruce Willis. Like a Renaissance master, Mr. Altman has a way of filling the frame of large crowd scenes with the faces of friends and associates who will be familiar to anyone who knows the neighborhood.

As a satire, *The Player* tickles. It doesn't draw blood. It says nothing about Hollywood that Hollywood insiders don't say with far more venom in their hearts. Mr. Altman's most subversive message here is not that it's possible to get away with murder in Hollywood, but that the most grievous sin, in Hollywood terms anyway, is to make a film that flops.

The Player looks to be a hit.

—*V.C., April 10, 1992*

PLAYTIME

Produced and directed by Jacques Tati: written (in English. French. German and Japanese. with English subtitles) by Mr. Tati and Jacques Legrange: directors of photography. Jean Badal and Andreas Winding: edited by Gerard Pollicand: music by Francis Lemarque and James Campbell: production designer. Eugène Roman: released by Continental Films. Running time: 108 minutes.

With: Jacques Tati (Mr. Hulot). Barbara Dennek (Young Stranger). Marc Monjou (The False Hulot) and George Faye (The Architect).

Playtime, which opened yesterday at the Festival Theater, is Jacques Tati's most brilliant film, a bracing reminder in this all-too-lazy era that films can occasionally achieve the status of art.

Playtime is a gloriously funny movie about a Paris so modern it does not yet exist, a Paris composed entirely of streets like our Avenue of the Americas, hemmed in by efficiently beautiful glass-and-steel tow-

772

ers in which, if we are quick about it, we may see momentary reflections of Sacre Coeur, the Arch of Triumph, or the Eiffel Tower.

It is a city inhabited almost entirely by tourists and their shepherd-guides who are spreading a terrible pox among the natives. It is not an immediately fatal disease but it makes everyone behave with the kind of frigid competence affected by airline stewardesses and reservation clerks.

Not even nuns are immune. Their heels click importantly as they glide across marbleized floors. A receptionist—a man so ancient that he could be a veteran of Verdun—operates a complex of computer buttons designed to announce a visitor's arrival in an office building. The old man does his best and the machine bleeps and gurgles successfully. It is the world of Kubrick's *2001* without the metaphysics and without Richard Strauss.

Playtime, which was made in 1967 and is only now being released in this country, is Tati's most free-form comedy to date, as well as his most disciplined, even more so than *Traffic,* which was made in 1971 but was seen here last winter.

It is virtually three major set pieces, or acts. The first act is set at Orly Airport, where we pick up some American tourists who arrive in a single, all-expenses-paid clump. The second is more or less devoted to a trade fair, where the tourists cross paths with Tati's Mr. Hulot.

The last act, a kind of neon-lit Gotterdammerung—is set in a posh nightclub whose opening night turns into the sort of chaos that civilizes. Everything goes wrong, including the air-conditioning, but in going wrong, life is somehow restored to the tourists as well as the natives.

You may well recognize the shape of the film, which is a variation on the favorite comedy theme about the family that inherits a lot of money, tries to put on fancy airs, loses its soul, and only finds itself again when the fortune is taken away.

However, it is not the shape of the film or its cheerful philosophy that are important. Rather it is the density of the wit. It is the gracefulness of the visual gags that flow one into another, nonstop, in a manner that only Tati now masters.

Mr. Hulot is still the nominal focal point of the comedy, particularly in the trade-fair sequence, but he is less in evidence in *Playtime* than in any other Hulot

feature. The film is even further removed from character than was *Traffic.* It observes not persons, but social clusters, in a manner that serves curiously to humanize group action and response instead of to dehumanize the individual.

However, don't waste time analyzing *Playtime* too much. It can easily withstand such critical assaults, but they serve to distract attention from the film's immense good humor, from, for example, the closing sequence that shows us a Parisian traffic circle that has been turned into a giant lazy Susan, serving, among other things, the sacred cause of inefficiency.

In addition to everything else, *Playtime* is a reckless act of faith—by Tati in himself. He photographed it in 70mm (though it is being shown here in 35mm), and he invested not only huge amounts of time in it, but also his own money. As anyone connected with films can tell you, this is certifiable madness.

The movie business is supposed to exist so that people other than its artists can lose their shirts in it, thereby to gain things that are called (by those who can use them) tax-loss carry-forwards. I hope *Playtime* will make Tati very rich so that at some future time he can use a tax-loss carry-forward.

—*V.C., June 28, 1973*

POINT BLANK

Directed by John Boorman: written by Alexander Jacobs, David Newhouse and Rafe Newhouse, based on the novel *The Hunter* by Richard Stark: cinematographer, Philip Lathrop: edited by Henry Berman: music by Johnny Mandel: art designers, George W. Davis and Albert Brenner: produced by Judd Bernard and Irwin Winkler: released by Metro-Goldwyn-Mayer. Running time: 92 minutes.

With: Lee Marvin (Walker), Angie Dickinson (Chris), Keenan Wynn (Yost), Carroll O'Connor (Brewster), Lloyd Bochner (Frederick Carter), Michael Strong (Stegman) and John Vernon (Mal Reese).

This much must be said for *Point Blank,* the crime melodrama that came in a blaze of gunfire and color into the DeMille and the Coronet yesterday: it is a spectacularly stylized and vividly photographed film that hints at some of the complex organization and hideous inhumanity of the modern-day underworld. It also has Lee Marvin performing a vengeful criminal out to get his cut of the swag from the connivers who have kept it from him in a viciously cold and stubborn mood.

John Boorman, a newcomer who directed this relentless, diabolic account of an escaped convict's hunting down and killing of the rascals who get in his way, has done an amazing job of getting the look and smell of Los Angeles into the texture of his picture and weaving it together in a tangled, cryptic way that is likely to engross the viewer without enlightening or edifying him.

He has also got some taut and tough performances from Carroll O'Connor, John Vernon, Keenan Wynn, and Michael Strong as assorted underworld characters and from Angie Dickinson as a moody mistress of thugs.

But, holy smokes, what a candid and calculatedly sadistic film it is! What a sheer exercise in creeping menace and crashing violence for their surface shock effects! It evolves on a shadowy social level and develops no considerate moral sense. Mr. Marvin is out to get his money by hitting, cutting with bottles, dumping men off roofs, and shooting them—and he does. He is a thorough antihero, a killer who must kill or be killed.

This is not a pretty picture for the youngsters—or, indeed, for anyone with delicate taste.

—B.C., September 19, 1967

POLTERGEIST

Directed by Tobe Hooper; written by Steven Spielberg, Michael Grais and Mark Victor, based on a story by Mr. Spielberg; director of photography, Matthew F. Leonetti; edited by Michael Kahn; music by Jerry Goldsmith; production designer, James H. Spencer; produced by Mr. Spielberg and Frank Marshall; released by Metro-Goldwyn-Mayer/United Artists. Running time: 115 minutes.

With: Craig T. Nelson (Steve Freeling), Jobeth Williams (Diane Freeling), Beatrice Straight (Dr. Lesh), Dominique Dunne (Dana Freeling), Oliver Robins (Robbie Freeling), Heather O'Rourke (Carol Anne Freeling), Michael McManus (Ben Tuthill) and Virginia Kaiser (Mrs. Tuthill).

More than any other Hollywood filmmaker of his generation, Steven Spielberg has preserved the wonderment of childhood while growing up to make the sort of movies he always loved as a child, but bigger and better and far more imaginative. He's a brilliant technician who still has doubts about the dark.

His *Close Encounters of the Third Kind* was the last, dazzling word on sci-fi fantasies, not about the end of the world but about the beginning of a benign new one. *Raiders of the Lost Ark* is every cliffhanging adventure film ever made, wrapped up into one hilarious odyssey, but with few of the anticlimaxes usual in such films.

Now, in *Poltergeist,* coproduced by Mr. Spielberg, directed by Tobe Hooper, and based on Mr. Spielberg's original story, he has come up with a marvelously spooky ghost story that may possibly scare the wits out of very small children and offend those parents who believe that kids should be protected from their own, sometimes savage imaginations.

I suspect, however, that there's a vast audience of teenagers and others who'll love this film. Indeed, *Poltergeist* often sounds as if it had been dictated by an exuberant twelve-year-old, someone who's sitting by a summer campfire and determined to spin a tale that will keep everyone else on the edges of their knapsacks far into the night.

Poltergeist, which opens today at the Cinerama and other theaters, is full of creepy, crawly, slimy things that jump out from the shadows. It contains playful ghosts and mean ones. It's a film in which childhood wishes and fears are made manifest, as in the image of a gnarled, long-dead tree, something to climb during the day and play in, but which, at night, casts scary shadows on a child's bedroom wall.

Poltergeist is like a thoroughly enjoyable nightmare, one that you know that you can always wake up from, and one in which, at the end, no one has permanently been damaged. It's also witty in a fashion that Alfred Hitchcock might have appreciated. Offhand, I can't think of many other directors who could raise goose bumps by playing "The Star-Spangled Banner" behind a film's opening credits.

The setting is an ordinary, quintessentially middle-class, new California subdivision called Cuesta Verde, where every house looks alike and comes equipped with the same vast assortment of appliances. Every family in Cuesta Verde is more or less on the same social, economic, and book-club level.

However, it's to the credit of Mr. Spielberg and Mr. Hooper, and to the screenplay by Mr. Spielberg, Michael Grais, and Mark Victor, that though the members of the Freeling family are typical, they aren't the nonentities one usually finds in such movies. This is as much a reflection of the manner of the movie as it is of the characters.

Steve and Diane Freeling (Craig T. Nelson and Jobeth Williams) are in their thirties, happily married, doing all right financially, and the parents of three children, a daughter in her mid-teens (Dominique Dunne), a son several years younger (Oliver Robins), and a ten-year-old daughter, Carol Anne (Heather O'Rourke). Carol Anne, a small, blond beauty, becomes the innocent hostage of the occult forces that, one night, come flying out of the untended television set.

It's one of the nicer variations on the film's ghost theme that the Freelings, though baffled by this visitation, are not initially panicked. Diane Freeling is enchanted when she finds that she can play games with the unseen creatures, rather as if they were to be treated as rare pets.

Suddenly, however, for reasons that are finally explained, they turn mean. All hell breaks loose, requiring the services first of an intelligent, somewhat embarrassed psychologist (Beatrice Straight), who moonlights as a parapsychologist, and eventually those of a most eccentric exorcist, a tiny woman played by Zelda Rubinstein, whose last film assignment was in *Under the Rainbow*.

Further details of the plot should not be revealed. More important are the film's extraordinary technical effects, by which we are made to see and experience the terrible assaults these angry spirits make on the Freelings, sometimes occupying their minds as well as their house. These effects are often eerie and beautiful but also occasionally vividly gruesome.

The structure of the film is not perfect. It seems to have two endings. This isn't because there are two, but because the film's exorcism rite is so spectacular that one really isn't prepared for still another confrontation, which doesn't quite measure up to the first one.

Miss Williams, still better known as a New York stage actress than as a film actress, is charming as the beleaguered Mom, a modern sort of woman who isn't above smoking a little marijuana after the kids are safely tucked into bed. Mr. Nelson is also good as the stalwart but not stolid father, and the children are excellent, especially Miss O'Rourke. The style of the film is probably best exemplified by the performances of Miss Straight and Miss Rubinstein, who play it absolutely without facetiousness, though with great good humor, and never look silly.

There's some controversy about the individual contributions to the film made by Mr. Spielberg and Mr. Hooper, best known as director of *The Texas Chainsaw Massacre*. I've no way of telling who did what, though *Poltergeist* seems much closer in spirit and sensibility to Mr. Spielberg's best films than to Mr. Hooper's.

—V.C., June 4, 1982

PONETTE

Written (in French, with English subtitles) and directed by Jacques Doillon; director of photography, Caroline Champetier; edited by Jacqueline Fano (Leconte); music by Philippe Sarde; production designer, Henri Berthon; produced by Alain Sarde; released by Arrow Releasing. Running time: 92 minutes.

With: Victoire Thivisol (Ponette), Xavier Beauvois (The Father), Claire Nebout (Aunt), Matiaz Bureau (Matthias), Delphine Schiltz (Delphine) and Marie Trintignant (The Mother).

One of the most irrevocable emotional blows that could befall a small child is the sudden death of a parent. The four-year-old title character of Jacques Doillon's heartbreaking film, *Ponette,* has survived a car crash that killed her mother and left the little girl with a broken arm. In the film's opening scene, her father (Xavier Beauvois) is taking Ponette (Victoire Thivisol) to live with an aunt (Claire Nebout), who has two children roughly Ponette's age. As the forlorn child with a cast on her arm clutches Yoyotte, her beloved doll, her father sternly explains to his tearful, disbelieving daughter that her mother is not coming back.

This poignant French film is so extraordinarily sensitive to the emotional landscape of childhood that only the hardhearted will not feel a vestigal tug of childish terror of parental loss and abandonment. But for all the sadness it bares, *Ponette* is far from a tear-drenched portrait of helpless suffering. If Ponette, thrown into a new environment, stubbornly clings to the notion that her mother might somehow return from the dead, she is also healing and growing up in spite of herself.

Ponette is acted with such a remarkable lack of self-consciousness by a cast made up largely of children that stretches of the fictional movie have the look and spontaneity of a documentary on children observed through one-way glass. Especially in scenes set in a nursery school that Ponette attends with her two young cousins, Matthias and Delphine, the movie captures a young child's indeterminate sense of time. Along with the fitful rhythms of children's outdoor play, it conveys the sense of almost every moment being one of discovery and every activity an initiation—so much so that you experience anew what it felt like to be four or five.

A scene in which three young children dare one another to take turns hiding alone inside a dumpster with the lid pulled down is an emotional roller coaster. One moment you want to cry out for the children to stop playing such a scary and potentially dangerous game. But when they sail through it a tiny bit more sure of themselves than before, you applaud this tiny step toward independence and the conquering of fear. In another scene, Ponette is cruelly taunted by a playmate who tells her it was her meanness that caused her mother's death. Although Ponette is reduced to tears, she fights back and stands up for herself.

The director also skillfully uses Ponette's anguished situation to pose unanswerable questions about God, Jesus, the afterlife, and the relation of religion to superstition. Having weighty theological issues filtered through the imagination of a bereaved child makes them seem fresh in a way that no adult debate ever could. As Ponette listens to the grown-ups' contradictory explanations of where her mother went, all translated in the careful protective language that adults adopt when talking to children, she absorbs them, then improvises her own religious rituals based on her emotional needs. These scenes are a humorous reminder of the susceptibility of children to religious indoctrination. As Ponette is fed the basics of Christianity, the question that perplexes her the most concerns the resurrection of Jesus. If Christ can come back from the grave, she asks, why can't her beloved mother?

Near the end of *Ponette,* the little girl visits her mother's grave and begins scratching in the ground to try to unearth her mother. At this point, the naturalistic movie makes a huge, unexpected leap into the mystical that could be taken as a hokily sentimental betrayal. However it's taken, it doesn't spoil the purity of what has come before.

—S.H., May 23, 1997

THE POSTMAN (IL POSTINO)

Directed by Michael Radford: written (in Italian, with English subtitles) by Anna Pavignano. Mr. Radford. Furio Scarpelli. Giacomo Scarpelli and Massimo Troisi. based on the novel *Burning Patience* by Antonio Skarmeta: director of photography. Franco Di Giacomo: edited by Roberto Perpignani: music by Luis Enrique Bacalov: production designer. Lorenzo Baraldi: produced by Mario and Vittorio Cecchi Gori and Gaetano Daniele: released by Miramax. Running time: 113 minutes.

With: Massimo Troisi (Mario). Philippe Noiret (Pablo Neruda). Maria Grazia Cucinotta (Beatrice). Linda Moretti (Rosa) and Renato Scarpa (Telegraph Operator).

Mario Ruoppolo (Massimo Troisi) is the gentlest of men, a lonely soul resigned to the monotony of life on a quiet Italian island. All that changes with the arrival of Pablo Neruda (Philippe Noiret), who suddenly becomes the island's resident celebrity. Exiled from his native Chile for political reasons, Neruda has a transforming effect on the ruggedly beautiful setting where *The Postman* (*Il Postino*) takes place. He becomes an unlikely friend to Mario, who blossoms so beautifully under Neruda's influence that he discovers the idea of poetry as if it were new.

As a rueful, warmly affecting film featuring a wonderful performance by Mr. Troisi, *The Postman* would be attention-getting even without the sadness that overshadows it. This Neapolitan actor, also a writer and director and much better known to Italian audiences than to viewers here, postponed a heart operation while he finished work on this pet project. He died (at the age of forty-one) the day after principal photography was completed.

Succinctly dedicated "To Our Friend Massimo," *The Postman,* which was directed by Michael Radford, is an eloquent but also wrenching tribute to Mr. Troisi's talents. The comic unease that he brought to this performance clearly has a component of real pain. But that hint of unease suits Mario's wide-eyed, wistful look and his slow, often dryly funny demeanor. When Mario is first hired to deliver Neruda's mail, he has so little else to do that he spends time breaking in his postman's hat so that it won't give him a headache.

"That's a little trick of ours," he says knowingly to his father, a fisherman, who is one of the main reasons there has not been much poetry in Mario's life. They live together in bleak, drafty quarters, where Mario probably dreams of better things while his father slurps soup out of the pot.

So the younger man is delighted to find a low-paying, not-too-promising job delivering mail to Neruda, who is the only local resident literate enough to be getting letters. Mario must bicycle to see Neruda at the remote hilltop outpost the writer shares with a woman, whom he treats grandly and addresses as "Amor."

"He's a poet," Mario confides to his sole post office colleague once he overhears that. "That's how you can tell."

At first, Mario's expeditions to see Neruda are cautious and polite, with Mr. Troisi engaged in amusing rehearsals for each brush with greatness. (Behind this handsome actor's hangdog expression and leisurely manner, there is slyly superb comic timing.) Then the postman begins to grow bold. He'd like a better autograph than the "Regards, Pablo Neruda" that his first request elicits. He'd like to know what makes Neruda tick. He might even like to be a poet himself.

Naturally, this story is too good to be true. *The Postman* is based on a novel, *Burning Patience,* by Antonio Skarmeta, in which the postman was a teenage boy. Anyway, the postman is a fiction, and Neruda's real home during the early 1950's (when the story takes place) was on Capri, a less undiscovered place than this film's delightfully sleepy setting. But what's most clearly a fiction here is the effect that Mario's lovely naïveté has on Neruda himself. Touched by the younger man's guilelessness, the writer is moved to show Mario that life on the island doesn't need the services of a visiting poet. It already has a poetry of its own.

The Postman would be awfully cloying if it hammered home that notion too insistently. In fact the thought is expressed with gentle grace, and it is tempered by other, wittier effects of Neruda's presence. There's a sweetly romantic subplot about Mario's insistence that poetry have some practical application. He wants it to win him the beautiful Beatrice (Maria Grazia Cucinotta), who's not much of a reader but likes being compared to a butterfly.

There's the hilarious way Beatrice's aunt is scandalized by such tactics, which she doesn't quite understand but does know are dangerous. And there's the sobering moment when Mario grasps what he must look like to a man of Neruda's celebrity. "I lived in complete solitude with the most simple people in the world," Neruda eventually tells a newspaper interviewer. Those simple people aren't entirely flattered by that description. Mario's reaction is more complicated, with a disillusionment that is also the measure of how profoundly Neruda has changed him.

Mr. Noiret, the superb French actor who is such a sturdy presence, has so much of the right lumbering gravity for Neruda that his performance is hardly hurt by being dubbed into Italian. He accomplishes the major feat of making Neruda's side of this tale plausible, and gives his love of poetry real immediacy on screen.

And Mr. Noiret is magnetic enough to account for the villagers' debate about the essence of Neruda's appeal. Mario and his postal superior spend a lot of time noticing how many female correspondents this outspoken Communist poet and politician seems to have. Mario thinks this must make Neruda "the poet loved by women," but his boss finds that embarrassing and staunchly corrects it. Neruda, he proclaims, is "the poet loved by the people."

Still, neither he nor Mario nor anything else about *The Postman* can resist the romance of Neruda. And those letters from the ladies just won't quit. The boss is finally forced to modify his position. "Even the women are interested in politics in Chile," he concedes.

—*J.M., June 14, 1995*

THE POSTMAN ALWAYS RINGS TWICE

Directed by Tay Garnett: written by Harry Ruskin and Niven Busch, based on the novel by James M. Cain: cinematographer, Sidney Wagner: edited by George White: music by George Bassman: art designers, Cedric Gibbons and Randall Duell: produced by Carey Wilson: released by Metro-Goldwyn-Mayer. Black and white. Running time: 113 minutes.

With: Lana Turner (Cora Smith), John Garfield (Frank Chambers), Cecil Kellaway (Nick Smith), Hume Cronyn (Arthur Keats), Leon Ames (Kyle Sackett), Audrey Totter (Madge Gorland), Alan Reed (Ezra Liam Kennedy) and Jeff York (Blair).

The long hesitation of the Hays office to permit a motion picture to be made from James M. Cain's plainspoken novel, *The Postman Always Rings Twice,* is proved an unnecessary caution by the film which came to the Capitol yesterday. For *The Postman,* as evidenced in this treatment, makes a sternly "moral" picture on the screen, without in the least evading the main line or the spirit of the book. It also comes off a tremendously tense and dramatic show, and it gives Lana Turner and John Garfield the best roles of their careers.

Actually, there is nothing so sensational about the story *The Postman* tells. It is strictly a crime-and-punishment saga, and it has been told on the screen before, notably in the film version of Mr. Cain's own *Double Indemnity.* But the picture achieves its distinction through the smart way in which it has been made and through the quality of its representation of two passion-torn characters.

Carey Wilson, who produced it for Metro, stuck close to the realistic style of the novel in picturing this story of a young bum and a temptatious blonde who kill the husband of the latter and then find you can't "monkey with murder" profitably. He and Tay Garnett, the director, shot much of the action out-of-doors—or, at least, around a solid reproduction of a California roadside lunchstand—in establishing the sordid liaison between the feverish hobo and the girl. And then, where the script called for action inside the lunch-stand, in court, and jail, they gave these scenes all the tough-grained texture of actuality.

Furthermore, Niven Busch and Harry Ruskin preserved in their well-constructed script the terseness and flavor of dialogue that was striking in Mr. Cain's book. The buildup of incident and character has the rhythm of a throttled-down machine, and the moments of cold, deliberate violence suddenly burst with accelerated force. Also, without illustrating any of the bluntly carnal scenes of the book, the authors, actors, and director have suggested sensual tensions thoroughly.

Too much cannot be said for the principals. Mr. Garfield reflects to the life the crude and confused young hobo who stumbles aimlessly into a fatal trap. And Miss Turner is remarkably effective as the cheap and uncertain blonde who has a pathetic ambition to "be somebody" and a pitiful notion that she can realize it through crime. Cecil Kellaway is just a bit too cozy and clean as Miss Turner's middle-aged spouse. He is the only one not a Cain character, and throws a few scenes a shade out of key. But Hume Cronyn is slyly sharp and sleazy as an unscrupulous criminal lawyer, Leon Ames is tough as a district attorney, and Alan Reed plays a gumshoe role well.

In its surface aspects, *The Postman* appears no more than a melodramatic tale, another involved demonstration (two hours in length) that crime does not pay. But the artistry of writers and actors have made it much more than that; it is, indeed, a sincere comprehension of an American tragedy. For the yearning of weak and clumsy people for something better than the stagnant lives they live is revealed as the core of the dilemma, and sin is shown to be no way to happiness.

—B.C., May 3, 1946

PRETTY BABY

Produced and directed by Louis Malle: written by Polly Platt. based on a story by Ms. Platt and Mr. Malle: director of photography, Sven Nykvist: edited by Suzanne Baron: music by Jerry Wexler: released by Paramount Pictures. Running time: 109 minutes.

With: Brooke Shields (Violet), Keith Carradine (Bellocq), Susan Sarandon (Hattie), Frances Faye (Nell), Antonio Fargas (Professor), Matthew Anton (Red Top) and Diana Scarwid (Frieda).

In a high panoramic shot we look over the roofs of a city at night. The opening title card tells us it's Storyville, New Orleans, 1917. From the far distance we hear a steamboat's whistle, followed by a few notes on a blues trumpet. The mood is of impending loss, of the kind of bone-deep loneliness that is particular to the middle of the night.

There's a sudden cut to the rapt face of a little girl. Just offscreen there are moans that could be either of pain or of ecstasy. Violet, the child, watches with both terror and excitement as her mother gives birth. The mother screams. The midwife gives reassuring instructions, and downstairs the nightly parties go on.

The setting is Nell's place, one of the fancier brothels in the New Orleans tenderloin, and the bed might be the same one where Violet herself was born twelve years before, the daughter of Hattie, one of Nell's best "girls," and of a father no longer known. Like her new half brother, Violet is what used to be called a "trick baby."

In this fashion Louis Malle takes us inside the hermetic world of *Pretty Baby,* an almost incredibly romantic, autumnally beautiful movie that looks at life in a Storyville whorehouse with the unsurprised curiosity and boredom of a child who's never known anything else. Mr. Malle, the French director (*The Lovers, Murmur of the Heart,* and *Lacombe, Lucien*), has made some controversial films in his time but none, I suspect, that is likely to upset convention quite as much as this one—and mostly for the wrong reasons.

Though the setting is a whorehouse, and the lens through which we see everything is Violet, who, in the course of the film, herself becomes one of Nell's chief attractions, *Pretty Baby* is neither about child prostitution nor is it pornographic.

The film, which opens today at the Coronet, is about the last days of Storyville, just before the New Orleans city fathers bowed to the reformers and closed down one of the most notorious redlight districts in the country. It is also a sad, essentially tender memoir about Violet's brief liaison and marriage with an obsessed photographer named Bellocq, a character based—but very loosely—on Ernest J. Bellocq, the physically misshapen, hydrocephalic photographer whose portraits of Storyville whores are now recognized as the work of a unique artist.

Mr. Malle and Polly Platt, with whom he collaborated on the screenplay, have largely avoided judgmental attitudes by looking out at the world through Violet's eyes. They've also softened the contours of what was probably very sordid history by making a film of dazzling physical beauty. Sven Nykvist's camera is as obsessed as Bellocq's with texture, light, shade, line, expression.

When one realizes that Keith Carradine's Bellocq is actually the center of the film, *Pretty Baby* becomes a parable about art and life, about the artist who makes the mistake of falling in love with his subject, a creature who is, in effect, his own creation. Mr. Carradine gives a haunting and haunted performance, as someone sentenced by his obsession always to be observer and interpreter, never a full participant.

I've no idea whether or not Brooke Shields, the breathtakingly beautiful twelve-year-old model who plays Violet, can act in any real sense, but Mr. Malle uses her brilliantly. As Gloria Swanson said of silent stars in *Sunset Boulevard,* "We had faces then," and Miss Shields has a face that here transcends the need to act.

She is, in quick succession, willful and funny, sly and stupid. At one minute she's a child with her first doll. Next she is grotesque in full makeup as she repeats by rote lines meant to excite a customer—"Why, I can feel the steam inside me, right through my dress"—or pathetic as she excitedly awaits the outcome of a whorehouse auction, the highest bidder to win her favors.

The consistent coolness of Mr. Malle's view prevents the movie from seeming to be exploitative. There is one key shot that, I think, defines this method, when, during the auction for Violet, the camera stays on the not quite impassive face of "the Professor" (Antonio Fargas), the black pianist who entertains Nell's drawing-room guests. As Mr. Fargas listens to the bids, we have, for just a fraction of a moment, a glimpse of what all this means in terms of life in the outside world, which is infinitely sad but far, far removed.

Both Mr. Fargas and Susan Sarandon, who plays Violet's mother, give fully realized performances but Frances Faye, who plays old Nell, the madam, is so bad that you can't believe it's not intentional. Has her dialogue been postsynchronized? It has that disconnected sound. Miss Faye seems properly tough, but it's a toughness of another era. Toward the end of the film, too, the narrative continuity seems to go astray. Have key scenes been cut to assure the film's rating?

These, though, are niggling questions to ask of something that is in every other way the most imaginative, most intelligent, and most original film of the year to date.

—*V.C., April 5, 1978*

PRIDE AND PREJUDICE

Directed by Robert Z. Leonard; written by Aldous Huxley and Jane Murfin, based on the play by Helen Jerome and the novel by Jane Austen; cinematographer, Karl Freund; edited by Robert J. Kern; music by Herbert Stothart; art designers, Cedric Gibbons and Paul Groesse; produced by Hunt Stromberg; released by Metro-Goldwyn-Mayer. Black and white. Running time: 117 minutes.

With: Greer Garson (Elizabeth Bennet), Laurence Olivier (Dr. Darcy), Mary Boland (Mrs. Bennet), Edna May Oliver (Lady Catherine de Bourgh), Maureen O'Sullivan (Jane Bennet), Ann Rutherford (Lydia Bennet), Frieda Inescort (Miss Bingley), Edmund Gwenn (Mr. Bennet) and Karen Morley (Charlotte Lucas).

If your fancy would be for a picture of a charming and mannered little English world which has long since been tucked away in ancient haircloth trunks—a quaint but lively world in which young ladies were mainly concerned with dances and ribboned bonnets and the light in a guardsman's eye, and matrons had the vapors and worried only about marrying off their eligible daughters—then the picture for you is *Pride and Prejudice,* which came yesterday to the Music Hall. For this, by your leave, we proclaim the most deliciously pert comedy of old manners, the most crisp and crackling satire in costume that we in this corner can remember ever having seen on the screen.

Jane Austen, who wrote the story way back at the turn of the nineteenth century, was an independent miss with a quick and affectionate eye for the nice little foibles of her frivolous age. Tolerantly, she comprehended the harmless absurdities of her middle-class provincial society, the trembling and dithering that went on in a household full of girls when a likely bachelor hove into the vicinity. And she had an incomparable wit, and a facility with the pen to put down all she saw and felt in one of the most delightful of English novels.

And with an instinct such as Hollywood can seldom boast, Hunt Stromberg and his associates have managed to turn out a film which catches the spirit and humor of Miss Austen's novel down to the last impudent flounce of a petticoat, the last contented sigh of a conquering coquette. With no more of a plot than Miss Austen herself provided, they have told the simple but continuously captivating story of the five Bennet sisters in quest of husbands, of their frankly scheming mother, their wisely unmeddlesome father, of Darcy and Bingley and the treacherous Wickham. The whole thing has been accomplished through a steady flow of superlative wit—most of it out of the novel and some of it supplied by Aldous Huxley and Jane Murfin—which puts a snapper on almost every scene; and also through a consistently artful inventiveness of detail and a keen appreciation of the subtleties of Miss Austen's characters.

It isn't often that a cast of such uniform perfection is assembled. Greer Garson is Elizabeth—"dear, beautiful Lizzie"—stepped right out of the book, or rather out of one's fondest imagination: poised, graceful, self-contained, witty, spasmodically stubborn, and as lovely as a woman can be. Laurence Oliver is Darcy, that's all there is to it—the arrogant, sardonic Darcy whose pride went before a most felicitous fall. Mary Boland is a completely overpowering Mrs. Bennet, a silly but determined mother hen to a brood of exquisitely fluffy chicks, which includes Maureen O'Sullivan, Ann Rutherford, and Heather Angel. And Edmund Gwenn, Edna May Oliver, Frieda Inescort, and Bruce Lester do handsomely in their respective roles. Only Melville Cooper as Mr. Collins and Marsha Hunt as Mary Bennet permit their characterizations to degenerate into burlesque. Robert Z. Leonard's direction is the touchstone.

Pictures played in costume often have an artificial air. But for pure charm and romantic diversion, for bubbling and wholesome life, we most heartily recommend this exquisite comedy about the elegant young gentleman who was proud and the beautiful young lady who was prejudiced. Both are as real as any two young people you know today.

—*B.C., August 9, 1940*

THE PRIDE OF THE YANKEES

Directed by Sam Wood; written by Jo Swerling and Herman Mankiewicz, based on a story by Paul Gallico; cinematographer, Rudolph Maté; edited by Daniel Mandell; music by Leigh Harline; production designer, William Cameron Menzies; produced by Samuel Goldwyn; released by RKO Radio Pictures. Black and white. Running time: 127 minutes.

With: Gary Cooper (Lou Gehrig), Teresa Wright (Eleanor Gehrig), Babe Ruth (Himself), Walter Brennan (Sam Blake), Dan Duryea (Hank Hannemann), Elsa Janssen (Mom Gehrig), Ludwig Stossel (Pop Gehrig), Virginia Gilmore (Myra), Bill Dickey (Himself), Ernie Adams (Miller Huggins) and Pierre Watkin (Mr. Twitchell).

So many hundreds of persons loved Lou Gehrig with a devotion that few men know and literally thousands of others held him in such true regard that the film biographers of the modest and valiant ball player assumed an obligation too ticklish for casual approach. But no one can say that Samuel Goldwyn has not been respectful of its due. In a simple, tender, meticulous, and explicitly narrative film, Mr. Goldwyn and his associates have told the story of Buster Lou with sincere and lingering affection, in face of which dramatic punch has been subdued. It is called *The Pride of the Yankees,* and it opened at the Astor last night—and also, for a single performance, in forty neighborhood theaters hereabout.

For months Mr. Goldwyn had seen to it that the word generally got around that this was not to be so much the story of Lou Gehrig, the great ball player, as of Lou Gehrig, a fine and humble man. That advice was absolutely on the level. For *The Pride of the Yankees* is primarily a review of the life of a shy and earnest young fellow who loved his mother, worked hard to get ahead, incidentally became a ball player for two reasons—because he loved the game and also needed the cash—enjoyed a clumsy romance which eventually enriched his life, and then, at the height of his glory, was touched by the finger of death.

It is, without being pretentious, a real saga of American life—homely, humorous, sentimental, and composed in patient detail. But, by the very nature of its subject, it lacks conflict till well on toward its end. And that is its principal weakness as a dramatic film. For the youth and early manhood of Lou Gehrig, according to this account, were picturesque without being too difficult, beset by shyness more than anything else. And the same was true of his ripe years and his romance—at least, in this film. It is not until illness leads the "Iron Man" into the valley of the shadow that this story of his life becomes dramatic. Illness and death are the only adversaries faced by Lou.

In view of the fact that a good three-quarters of this more than two-hour-long film is devoted to genial details, it inclines to monotony. This is further aggravated by the fact that the details are repetitious in themselves. Lou shows his mother that he loves her, not once but many times, and his coy and playful frisking with his wife becomes redundant after a while.

Furthermore, sports fans will protest, with reason on their side, that a picture about a baseball player should have a little more baseball in it. Quite true, this one has considerable footage showing stands and diamonds of the American League, with Lou at bat, running bases and playing the initial bag. What is shown is accurate. But it is only shown in glimpses or montage sequences, without catching much of the flavor or tingling excitement of a tight baseball game. Fans like to know what's the inning, how many are on, and how many out. At least, the score.

This underemphasis of Gehrig's profession is partially excused by the fact that Gary Cooper, who plays the great hero, doesn't look too good slamming or scooping 'em up. Mr. Cooper is perfectly able when it comes to playing the diffident, homespun man, and his performance in the touching final sequence—the presentation of the Gehrig tribute—is excellent. He even bears a slight resemblance to the "Iron Man," especially about the eyes. But when he's in there snagging the hot ones, he isn't likely to be mistaken for the real Lou.

The cast is superb, however, and does handsomely under Sam Wood's direction. Elsa Janssen and Ludwig Stossel are delightful humans as Ma and Pop Gehrig, and Teresa Wright has a lovely, gracious quality as Mrs. Lou. Walter Brennan, Dan Duryea, and Ernie Adams are a credit to Hollywood in lesser roles, and Babe Ruth—the real old Babe—roars and wrangles titanically in a couple of scenes playing himself. A few other old-time Yankees—Bill Dickey, Mark Koenig, and Bob Meusel—are in the background as local scenery, and Dickey gets a chance to slug a guy.

As a baseball picture—in which Veloz and Yolanda, for some reason, dance—*The Pride of the Yankees* is not anything to raise the blood-pressure. But as a simple, moving story with an ironic heart-tug at the end, it serves as a fitting memorial to the real Lou, who called himself the "luckiest man alive."

—*B.C., July 16, 1942*

PRINCE OF THE CITY

Directed by Sidney Lumet: written by Jay Presson Allen and Mr. Lumet. based on the book by Robert Daly: director of photography. Andrzej BartKowiak: edited by John J. Fitzstephens: music by Paul Chiahara: produced by Burtt Harris. released by Orion Pictures and Warner Brothers. Running time: 167 minutes.

With: Treat Williams (Ciello). Jerry Orbach (Gus Levy). Richard Foronjy (Joe Marinaro). Don Billett (Bill Mayo). Kenny Marino (Dom Bando). Carmine Caridi (Gino Mascone). Anthony Page (Raf Alvarez). Norman Parker (Rick Cappalino). Paul Roebling (Brooks Paige). Bob Balaban (Santi-massino). James Tolkan (District Attorney Polito). Steve Inwood (Mario Vincente). Lindsay Crouse (Carla Ciello). Matthew Laurance (Ronnie Ciello) and Tony Turco (Socks Ciello).

Although Sidney Lumet's *Prince of the City* has an atmosphere deeply redolent of crime and corruption, very few specific misdeeds are ever shown on the screen. They don't have to be. Mr. Lumet's film offers such a sharply detailed landscape, such a rich and crowded portrait, that his characters reveal themselves fully by the ways they move, eat, speak, listen, or lie.

The lying is terribly important, because so many different styles of dissembling are on display here, and because there is no one in the story who isn't forced into dishonesty sooner or later. Danny Ciello, the film's title character, is a man who sets out to tell the truth and winds up the very worst liar of all. Danny, a swaggering young police detective, doesn't see himself as a crusading hero when he decides to gather evidence of police corruption, early in the story. And he doesn't

see himself entirely as a villain when his revelations bring catastrophe to his friends. Danny appears to regard himself as someone who expected to undertake something simple, only to find the task so complicated that it might prove to be impossible. The progress of this energetic, hugely ambitious, and finally sprawling movie is very like Danny's own.

Prince of the City, which opens today at Cinemas 1, 2, and 3, begins as a crisp, thrilling adventure, as Danny embarks recklessly on his journey into unknown territory. The borders of his own world are delineated beautifully. In just a few short scenes—Mr. Lumet's economy in parts of this film is simply dazzling—we glimpse the cops who are Danny's devoted friends, the family that is overlooked for the sake of his career, the bullying, pugnacious manner in which he conducts himself and the dangerous intensity with which he embraces tragedy.

In a scene with two junkies, Danny finds himself both hating and relishing his power over these people, and perhaps secretly savoring his own invulnerability. This may be part of what leads him to work as an informer, and it may not. When Danny decides to begin taperecording his conversations with crooked cops and mobsters, he takes a step the film never fully accounts for—any more than Robert Daley's book could explain Robert Leuci, the ex-detective upon whose story the movie is based. But though Danny's presence is what binds the movie together, he doesn't dominate the action, and his motives aren't vitally important. The film concentrates much more compellingly on the human backdrop for Danny's action than it does on his inner workings.

Prince of the City has an enormous cast of incidental characters; no one, aside from Treat Williams as Danny, has a large role in a film this densely populated. And yet the brief characterizations are so keenly drawn that dozens of them stand out with the forcefulness of major performances. As Danny begins to drift away from the life he's familiar with, the landmarks of his voyage become a lawyer here, a mobster there, all of them instantly in focus thanks to carefully chosen sets, costumes and mannerisms, and thanks to casting that is superb. Though Mr. Lumet is clearly concerned with the moral ramifications of Danny's behavior, he establishes them better through the specifics of the actors' behavior than he does through more generalized debate.

The film is finally indecisive about the rectitude of Danny's actions, and it means to be. A key scene late in the book, with Mr. Leuci giving courtroom testimony against the cop to whom he was closest (called Gus Levy here, and played wonderfully by Jerry Ohrbach) would have made a heel out of Danny in the audience's eyes, and its omission is revealing. But Mr. Lumet's choice to suspend judgment, provocative at first, becomes troublesome—especially in the last of the film's nearly three hours, when his direction has wandered as far from its initial briskness as Danny has from his own safe berth. In avoiding the danger of jumping to a facile conclusion about Danny, Mr. Lumet heads off so far in the opposite direction that he ends the film on a disappointing, inconclusive note. So much evidence has been presented, so many lawyers have trooped across the screen, so much time has been devoted to the question of Danny's essential honesty that a verdict is in order—if not from a moral standpoint, then from a dramatic one.

Much of the burden of the movie's uncertainty falls upon Mr. Williams, whose performance must fill in those directorial omissions. Accordingly, he does his best work in the early part of the story, when his effort is most collaborative with Mr. Lumet and with the other actors. Mr. Williams, like the character he plays, is better off in company than he is alone; he brings a playful, arrogant, effectively brazen quality to Danny's maneuverings. And his rapport with the hoods in the story (Ron Karabatsos, Tony Munafo, and Ron Maccone are the most memorable of a very strong lineup) is so easy that it speaks volumes about his seedy side.

With the lawyers, especially with Norman Parker as the first to win his trust, Paul Roebling as a WASP who confounds him and Bob Balaban as a fussy, vindictive prosecutor, Danny is nervous in a way that's equally revealing. With his police friends (among them Mr. Ohrbach, Carmine Caridi, and Richard Foronjy) he shows the devotion of a lover, much more of it than he shows to his rock-solid wife (Lindsay Crouse). But as he wanders far from the people and places that have been familiar, Danny becomes less vivid. On unsteady ground (several scenes in which Danny loses his former allies are set aboard ferry boats), he registers a very touching fearfulness. But Mr. Williams, competent and plausible throughout the film and sometimes much better than that, never brings to Danny's lonely moments the

depth or importance that might make him more tragic than confused. And the last part of the film leaves him little to do except fall further and further into limbo.

Prince of the City begins with the strength and confidence of a great film, and ends merely as a good one. The achievement isn't what it first promises to be, but it's exciting and impressive all the same.

—J.M., August 19, 1981

THE PRISONER

Directed by Peter Glenville; written by Bridget Boland, based on her play; cinematographer, Reginald Wyer; edited by Frederick Wilson; music by Benjamin Frankel; art designer, John Hawkesworth; produced by Vivian A. Cox; released by Columbia Pictures. Black and white. Running time: 91 minutes.

With: Alec Guinness (The Prisoner), Jack Hawkins (The Interrogator), Raymond Huntley (The General), Jeanette Sterke (The Girl), Ronald Lewis (The Guard), Kenneth Griffith (The Secretary), Gerard Heinz (The Doctor), Mark Dignam (The Governor) and Wilfrid Lawson (The Jailor).

The great skill and charm of Alec Guinness in light and comical roles have obstructed somewhat the general knowledge that he is a dramatic actor of rare competence—a fact not too clearly demonstrated in his performance heretofore on the screen. But with the opening of his new film, *The Prisoner*, at the Plaza on Saturday, this range of Mr. Guinness's talent is brilliantly and movingly revealed.

For he plays, in this grim and gripping drama—which also happens to be an equally revealing motion picture, one of the best of the year—a role of tremendous emotional and intellectual complexity. And he does so with such clarity and feeling that it strikes the very marrow in your bones.

What he is playing precisely is a cardinal of the Roman Catholic Church who is arrested and charged with treason in one of the present European "police states," and then is put through such a psychological ordeal that he makes a full and degrading "confession" at a shamelessly staged public "trial." It is a role that demanded great courage, as well as comprehension and skill.

But before we appear to give all credit to Mr. Guinness, let us hastily say that the drama and its execution are beautifully done in every way. With a trenchant script by Bridget Boland (first done as a play on the London stage); strong direction by Peter Glenville, who is making his debut as a film director with this job; and fine performances by Jack Hawkins and Wilfrid Lawson, it is only fair that they should be directly mentioned.

In form, this is a psychological drama—a picture of the conflict of two minds, that of the cardinal and that of his interrogator, whom Mr. Hawkins plays. And it is in the marking of the slow deterioration of the cardinal's spirit and will under the relentless and calculated pressure of questions and physical distress that the cold, almost morbid fascination and tension of the drama reside.

But this is more than just an exercise of poking into the back corners of a man's mind, with all the ugly details of prison living, until the key to his fatal weakness is found. All of this is immensely absorbing. But this picture gets across a great deal more about the subtleties of human experience and behavior than is wrapped in a mere "third degree."

The weakness of the cardinal, when discovered, turns out to be his humility, not his pride, as is at first suspected by the interrogator. He lives—he has reached his clerical eminence—without fully understanding himself. And when the interrogator rips his secret from him, with the skill of a psychoanalyst, and uses it to force his "confession," much is hinted about mental and spiritual things.

Much is also said about the character and the dignity—or lack of dignity—of men who live under the rule of political tyrants, of the brutal techniques of the "police state." Mr. Hawkins reveals the terrible torment of a brilliant man whose skill is forced to corruptive use. Mr. Lawson as a jailer, Raymond Huntley as a general, and Gerard Heinz as a doctor are excellent, too. A subplot depicting the romance of a youthful jailer and a political fugitive's wife offers a further glint of terror and revulsion.

This is a film that will make you shiver—and think.

—B.C., December 12, 1955

THE PRIVATE LIFE OF HENRY VIII

Directed by Alexander Korda: written by Lajos Biro and Arthur Wimperis: cinematographer, Georges Périnal: edited by Harold Young and Stephen Harrison: music by Kurt Schroeder: art designer, Vincent Korda: produced by Mr. Korda and Ludovico Toeplitz: released by United Artists. Black and white. Running time: 97 minutes.

With: Charles Laughton (Henry VIII), Robert Donat (Thomas Culpeper), Lady Tree (Henry's Old Nurse), Binnie Barnes (Catherine Howard), Elsa Lanchester (Anne of Cleves), Merle Oberon (Anne Boleyn), Franklin Dyall (Thomas Cromwell), Miles Mander (Wriothesly) and Wendy Barrie (Jane Seymour).

Charles Laughton, whose shadow is scurrying around the country in several pictures, including *The Sign of the Cross,* in which he gave his clever conception of Nero, is at the top of his form in the title role of *The Private Life of Henry VIII,* which was directed in London by the Hungarian Alexander Korda. The current work, which is now at the Radio City Music Hall, was not always received with unstinted praise on the other side of the Atlantic, because, although it was admittedly a clever production, some of the critics resented the buffooning of the fiery and amorous monarch. But in this country it probably will be enjoyed heartily without any such reservations, for it is a really brilliant if suggestive comedy.

Mr. Laughton not only reveals his genius as an actor, but also shows himself to be a past master in the art of make-up. In this offering he sometimes looks as if he had stepped from the frame of Holbein's painting of Henry. He appears to have the massive shoulders and true bearded physiognomy of the marrying ruler. Mr. Laughton may be guilty of caricaturing the role, but occasionally truths shine in the midst of the hilarity. He gives an admirable idea of Henry's vanity and also of his impetuousness, his sense of humor, his courage, and fear. There is Laughton's amusing twist of his mouth and nose when he outwits, as Henry thinks, other persons in his entourage. This Henry is seldom able to conceal his actual thoughts. If he admires a woman, not only she knows, but everybody else. If he dislikes anything, as he does the appearance of Anne of Cleves, he almost groans.

He has a distinctive gait and glories in his strength. He also lays claim to being the best card player in England. When he laughs, the laughter of others is heard, gradually increasing in volume, until all subordinates are laughing with their respective superiors. The wives who lose their heads apparently cause him concern only until the execution is over.

Catherine Howard is the real beauty of his mates. She appears at a banquet and is about to sing, when Henry asks her if she knows "What Shall I Do For Love?"—one of his own compositions. Fortunately she is able to sing the ballad and it is quite evident that Henry has lost his heart. But it chances that the frightful Anne of Cleves is about to leave the Continent for England. Henry trusts that she will not risk the Channel crossing, but she turns up with her very plain maids-in-waiting. Her English is broken and her face scarcely prepossessing. But it is not her desire to please Henry. All she wants is not love, but money—two palaces and a generous income for life. She plays cards with Henry, and, boast as he may of his ability at the game, he loses. And the rapacious Anne refuses to trust him for a hand or two. He has to go forth and borrow crowns from his courtiers.

Before Anne reaches England, Henry thinks that he will visit the apartment of the dainty Catherine Howard. He walks stealthily along the corridors, but his silhouette is beheld and there roars forth the command "The King's Guard!" He takes another direction and again the order is heard. Just as a soldier is about to shout it a third time Henry puts his hand over the man's mouth and then succeeds in knocking on Catherine's door.

"Who's there?" asks Catherine.

"Henry," answers the man of many moods nervously.

"Henry who?" comes from the inside.

"The King," replies the visitor, meekly.

It is a great relief to Henry when Anne consents to a divorce and he is exuberant when he finds the way clear to make Catherine Howard his wife.

It is a remarkably well-produced film, both in the matter of direction and in the settings and selection of exterior scenes. There are several lovely glimpses of old structures, including the Tower of London. No knives and forks were used in that day and therefore the always scrupulously dressed monarch thinks nothing of devouring a chicken in his hands and tossing the bones to the floor.

The performances of the supporting players are uniformly good, especially the portrayal of Elsa Lanchester, who in private life is Mrs. Laughton. She is excellent as the fine little business woman, Anne of Cleves. Binnie Barnes is able and charming as Catherine Howard.

—M.H., October 13, 1933

PRIZZI'S HONOR

Directed by John Huston: written by Richard Condon and Janet Roach, based on the novel by Mr. Condon: director of photography, Andrzej Bartkowiak: edited by Rudi Fehr and Kaja Fehr: music by Alex North: production designer, J. Dennis Washington: produced by John Foreman: released by Twentieth Century Fox. Running time: 129 minutes.

With: Jack Nicholson (Charley Partanna), Kathleen Turner (Irene Walker), Robert Loggia (Eduardo Prizzi), John Randolph (Angelo "Pop" Partanna), William Hickey (Don Corrado Prizzi), Lee Richardson (Dominic Prizzi), Michael Lombard (Filargi "Finley") and Anjelica Huston (Maerose Prizzi).

Like Woody Allen's *Purple Rose of Cairo,* the only other great American movie of 1985, John Huston's *Prizzi's Honor* delivers a kind of high most commonly associated with controlled substances, or with works of art of liberating imagination.

From start to finish, this exhilarating adaptation of Richard Condon's phantasmagorical and witty novel—set inside the world of the Mafia—ascends, plunges, and races around hairpin curves, only to shoot up again and dive over another precipice. *Prizzi's Honor* does to *The Godfather* what Henry Fielding's *Joseph Andrews* did to Samuel Richardson's *Pamela.* It locates the deliriously comic center within all sentimentality. The melodrama is a breathless roller-coaster ride through a small part of the American Dream that has all the aspects of a funhouse, but it's a funhouse in which the skeletons that jump out at you are still quite fresh. The lye continues to drip from their extremities.

Charley Partanna (Jack Nicholson) is an earnest, efficient, unquestioning member of Brooklyn's powerful Prizzi family, a sub-boss and super hitman, as well as the particular favorite of old Don Corrado Prizzi (William Hickey). The Don held Charley in his arms at Charley's baptism. When Charley was a boy, the Don gave Charley his first pair of brass knuckles, and when it came time for Charley's initiation into the family, it was the Don who mixed his blood with that of the younger man.

Prizzi's Honor, which opens today at the Sutton and other theaters, is the story of how Charley Partanna, ever faithful as he moves into paunchy middle age and a man who doesn't aspire above his station, suddenly has greatness thrust upon him. The circumstances of Charley's unexpected elevation cannot possibly be synopsized here. They involve a series of explosively surprising double-, triple-, and quadruple-crosses that boggle the mind as they delight it, and which, I should add, all make sense when one unravels the movie from back to front.

Mr. Condon's paranoid epiphanies remain intact in the screenplay, written by him and Janet Roach, and directed by Mr. Huston with a humanely funny gusto that recalls two of his earlier classics, *The Man Who Would Be King* (1975) and *Beat the Devil* (1964). That *Prizzi's Honor* is in no other way similar to those two films simply demonstrates the extraordinary, continuing vitality of this amazing filmmaker, now seventy-eight and never better.

Two people in particular play key roles in the drama of Charley's journey to the top. Irene Walker (Kathleen Turner) is not only from the other side of the tracks but the other side of the continent. Los Angeles-bred and an expert in international finance, the stunningly beautiful Irene initially appears to have little in common with Charley.

She dresses with the ease and taste of old, respectable money. Charley catches a brief glimpse of her at the gaudy church wedding of the Don's granddaughter and is immediately, near-fatally hooked. Following a whirlwind, bicoastal courtship, plus a couple of jolting revelations about Irene's past, including the fact that she's really a simple little Polish girl who Americanized her name, Charley marries her and, with one thing and another, seems about to compromise the honor of the Prizzis.

The other woman—and what an Other Woman she is!—is Maerose Prizzi (Anjelica Huston), the Don's elder granddaughter, who disgraced the family and has been permanently exiled to Manhattan because, while engaged to Charley, she ran off to have a brief affair with another man.

Maerose makes her living in interior decoration, for which she has a philosophy: "Everyone sees shapes differently, but color is forever." She's tall, aristocratic looking, and always elegantly groomed. However, when she opens her mouth, the Brooklyn accent that comes out—like Charley's—sounds as if she'd never left Red Hook. It's wildly thick, but *Prizzi's Honor* is the sort of movie in which too much is good, and much too much even better.

Maerose is a wonderful character, far darker and more complex than is indicated by her self-deprecating wisecracks ("I'm a family scandal. I gotta reputation to keep up"). She's a riveting presence and if Miss Huston, the daughter of the director, doesn't get an Oscar nomination for this performance, I'll be very surprised.

Some of the other characters in Charley's life are his doting, benign father, Angelo Partanna, the Don's consigliere, a role played with laid-back style by John Randolph, and with an accent somewhat less pronounced than Mr. Nicholson's; Dominic Prizzi (Lee Richardson), the Don's elder son, who has a bad heart, a short temper, and takes care of the day-to-day business of the family; and Eduardo Prizzi (Robert Loggia), the Don's younger son and, being the most Americanized, the family front man and lawyer.

All of the performers are fine, but the four principals, including Miss Huston, are terrific. Mr. Nicholson's work is as good as anything he's ever done. His Charley grows dramatically within the film, as he evolves from being a strictly faithful "family" man into a leader who can think on his feet and make his own unorthodox business decisions. Miss Turner blends the steaminess of her performance in *Body Heat* with the comedy of *The Man with Two Brains* to create a kind of meta-enchantress Hollywood doesn't often produce anymore.

Controlling the destinies of all of them is the frail figure of Mr. Hickey's ferociously practical, wise, infinitely patient old Don, which is the role and the performance of Mr. Hickey's career to date. As one unforeseen lunatic event succeeds another, Mr. Hickey's dying Don, his intelligence unimpaired, seems actually to melt into his clothes, like the Wicked Witch at the end of *The Wizard of Oz.*

Also superior are the photography of Andrzej Bartkowiak, the production design by Dennis Washington, and the Alex North score, which makes liberal use of Puccini, though never to tease out a teardrop.

Admirers of Mr. Condon may be glad to know that great chunks of the original Condon dialogue are as alive on-screen as on the page. "Do I ice her? Do I marry her?" Charley asks at one point, wondering whether he can trust a woman he thinks he loves. Says Maerose, "Just because she's a thief and a hitter don't mean she ain't a good woman in all other departments."

I shall also cherish the film's last line, which deserves to be remembered around campfires, cocktail parties, or club meetings, wherever favorite lines of movie dialogue are recalled: "Holy cow, Charley, just tell me where you want to meet!"

—*V.C., June 14, 1985*

THE PRODUCERS

Written and directed by Mel Brooks; cinematographer, Joseph Coffey; edited by Ralph Rosenblum; music by John Morris; art designer, Charles Rosen; produced by Sidney Glazier; released by Embassy Pictures. Running time: 88 minutes.

With: Zero Mostel (Max Bialystock), Gene Wilder (Leo Bloom), Dick Shawn (LSD), Kenneth Mars (Franz Liebkind), Estelle Winwood ("Hold Me, Touch Me" Old Lady), Renee Taylor (Eva Braun), Christopher Hewett (Roger De Bris), Lee Meredith (Ulla) and Andreas Voutsinas (Carmen Giya).

The Producers, which opened yesterday at the Fine Arts Theater, is a violently mixed bag. Some of it is shoddy and gross and cruel; the rest is funny in an entirely unexpected way. It has the episodic, revue quality of so much contemporary comedy—not building laughter, but stringing it together skit after skit, some vile, some boffo. It is less delicate than Lenny

Bruce, less funny than *Doctor Strangelove,* but much funnier than *The Loved One* or *What's New, Pussycat?*

It begins with Zero Mostel, overacting grotesquely under the direction of Mel Brooks, the famous 2,000-Year-Old Man and writer-narrator of the Academy Award–winning cartoon *The Critic.* Mostel, as a producer who gets investors by giving old ladies "their last thrill on the way to the cemetery," is first shown in silhouette through the glass door to his office, as he nuzzles one of his elderly ladies. That is the last time. We next see him rolling about with them, being chased by them, making lewd conversation with them, and generally being as gross and unfunny as only an enormous comedian bearing down too hard on some frail, tasteless routines can be.

Gene Wilder, who plays the young bookkeeper who inspires Mostel to oversubscribe with backers a show that will close after a single night (leaving Mostel and Wilder with the amount that has been oversubscribed), is wonderful. Last seen as the young man who was stolen—along with his car and his fiancée—by Bonnie and Clyde, he plays his present part as though he were Dustin Hoffman being played by Danny Kaye. Going through long, infinitely variegated riffs and arpeggios of neuroticism, he blushes and gasps, "I'm hysterical," and grins shyly and fondles his security blanket. He is forced to be as loud and as fast as Mostel (and as the crude and incredibly amateurish cutting). But he's fine.

There is a great scene when the deal between them is consummated at night in front of Lincoln Center, and all the fountains soar at once. They decide to produce *Springtime for Hitler,* a play by a helmeted Nazi in Yorkville, a play true to "the Hitler you loved, the Hitler you knew, the Hitler with a song in his heart." They hire a transvestite director, whose plays have never lasted beyond the first rehearsal. There is a lovely conversation with the director's roommate, played by Andreas Voutsinas as a prancing young person in black slacks, black turtleneck, beads, and a beard curled up in front like the toe of a dancing slipper. As leading man, they hire a mind-blown hippie played by Dick Shawn. (At the audition for the part, he has sung a grand hippie song.) Mostel hires for himself a blond receptionist who does not speak English and who, when told to go to work, begins to dance frenetically.

Strangely enough, the first act of *Springtime for*

Hitler: A Gay Romp with Adolf and Eva in Berchtes-gaden is the funniest part of this fantastically uneven movie. The Gestapo chorines, the opening number, "Look Out, Here Comes the Master Race"—well, it loses absolutely everything in transcription. But there is just enough talent and energy to keep this blackest of collegiate humors comic. Barely.

Then, the movie makes a terrible and irreversible mistake. It allows the audience onscreen to find the play funny. This turned the real audience in the theater off as though a fuse had blown. Hardly anyone laughed again. Partly, it must be admitted, because *Springtime for Hitler* itself gets less funny at this point (even Shawn becomes quite weak). But mainly, because there is nothing like having your make-believe audience catch on to a joke—and a joke that absolutely capsizes the plans of your leading characters—to make your real audience really hostile to you.

The ending, when all the comic props are supposed to be in motion—Mostel conning, Wilder hysterical, German fanatic, girl dancing, etc.—goes better than one might think. On the whole, though, *The Producers,* leaves one alternately picking up one's coat to leave and sitting back to laugh.

—R.A., March 19, 1968

PSYCHO

Produced and directed by Alfred Hitchcock: written by Joseph Stefano. based on the novel by Robert Bloch: cinematographer. John L. Russell Jr.: edited by George Tomasini: music by Bernard Herrmann: production designers. Joseph Hurley and Robert Clatworthy: released by Paramount Pictures. Black and white. Running time: 109 minutes.

With: Anthony Perkins (Norman Bates). Janet Leigh (Marion Crane). Vera Miles (Lila Crane). John Gavin (Sam Loomis). Martin Balsam (Milton Arbogast). John McIntire (Sheriff Chambers) and Lurene Tuttle (Mrs. Chambers).

You had better have a pretty strong stomach and be prepared for a couple of grisly shocks when you go to see Alfred Hitchcock's *Psycho,* which a great many people are sure to do. For Mr. Hitchcock, an old

hand at frightening people, comes at you with a club in this frankly intended bloodcurdler, which opened at the DeMille and Baronet yesterday.

There is not an abundance of subtlety or the lately familiar Hitchcock bent toward significant and colorful scenery in this obviously low-budget job. With a minimum of complication, it gets off to a black-and-white start with the arrival of a fugitive girl with a stolen bankroll right at an eerie motel.

Well, perhaps it doesn't get her there too swiftly. That's another little thing about this film. It does seem slowly paced for Mr. Hitchcock and given over to a lot of small detail. But when it does get her to the motel and apparently settled for the night, it turns out this isolated haven is, indeed, a haunted house.

The young man who diffidently tends it—he is Anthony Perkins and the girl is Janet Leigh—is a queer duck, given to smirks and giggles and swift dashes up to a stark Victorian mansion on a hill. There, it appears, he has a mother—a cantakerous old woman—concealed. And that mother, as it soon develops, is deft at creeping up with a knife and sticking holes into people, drawing considerable blood.

That's the way it is with Mr. Hitchcock's picture—slow buildups to sudden shocks that are old-fashioned melodramatics, however effective and sure, until a couple of people have been gruesomely punctured and the mystery of the haunted house has been revealed. Then it may be a matter of question whether Mr. Hitchcock's points of psychology, the sort highly favored by Krafft-Ebing, are as reliable as his melodramatic stunts.

Frankly, we feel his explanations are a bit of leg-pulling by a man who has been known to resort to such tactics in his former films.

The consequence in his denouement falls quite flat for us. But the acting is fair. Mr. Perkins and Miss Leigh perform with verve, and Vera Miles, John Gavin, and Martin Balsam do well enough in other roles.

The one thing we would note with disappointment is that, among the stuffed birds that adorn the motel office of Mr. Perkins, there are no significant bats.

—B.C., June 17, 1960

THE PUBLIC ENEMY

Directed by William A. Wellman: written by Kubec Glasmon. John Bright and Harvey Thew.

based on the story "Beer and Blood" by Mr. Bright; cinematographer. Dev Jennings; edited by Ed McCormick; music by David Mendoza; art designer. Max Parker; produced by Darryl F. Zanuck; released by Warner Brothers. Black and white. Running time: 83 minutes.

With: James Cagney (Tom Powers). Jean Harlow (Gwen Allen). Edward Woods (Matt Doyle). Joan Blondell (Mamie). Beryl Mercer (Ma Powers). Donald Cook (Mike Powers) and Mae Clarke (Kitty).

It is just another gangster film at the Strand, weaker than most in its story, stronger than most in its acting, and, like most, maintaining a certain level of interest through the last burst of machine-gun fire. That was not the intention of the Warners, whose laudable motive it was to have *The Public Enemy* say the very last word on the subject of gang pictures. There is a prologue apprising the audience that the hoodlums and terrorists of the underworld must be exposed and the glamour ripped from them. There is an epilogue pointing the moral that civilization is on her knees and inquiring loudly as to what is to be done. And before the prologue there is a brief stage tableau, with sinuous green lighting, which shows a puppet gangster shooting another puppet gangster in the back.

The Public Enemy does not, as its title so eloquently suggests, present a picture of the war between the underworld and the upperworld. Instead the war is one of gangsters among themselves, of sensational and sometimes sensationally incoherent murders. The motivation is lost in the general slaughter at the end, when Matt and Tom, the hoodlums with whose career of outlawry the picture is concerned, die violently.

Edward Woods and James Cagney, as Matt and Tom respectively, give remarkably lifelike portraits of young hoodlums. The story follows their careers from boyhood, through the war period, and into the early days of prohibition, when the public thirst made their peculiar talents profitable. Slugging disloyal bartenders, shooting down rival beermen, slapping their women crudely across the face, strutting with a vast self-satisfaction through their little world, they contribute a hard and true picture of the unheroic gangster.

The audiences yesterday laughed frequently and with gusto as the swaggering Matt and Tom went through their paces, and this rather took the edge off the brutal picture the producers appeared to be trying to serve up. The laughter was loudest and most deserved when the two put a horse "on the spot," the reason being that the animal had had the temerity to throw Nails Nathan, the gang leader.

There is a reminder of newspaper headlines toward the close when Tom, lying wounded in a hospital, is kidnapped and murdered. The acting throughout is interesting, with the exception of Jean Harlow, who essays the role of a gangster's mistress. Beryl Mercer as Tom's mother, Robert Emmett O'Connor as a gang chief, and Donald Cook as Tom's brother, do splendidly.

—A.S., April 24, 1931

PULP FICTION

Written and directed by Quentin Tarantino; director of photography. Andrzej Sekula; edited by Sally Menke; music by Karyn Rachtman; production designer. David Wasco; produced by Lawrence Bender; released by Miramax Films. Running time: 149 minutes.

With: John Travolta (Vincent Vega). Bruce Willis (Butch). Samuel L. Jackson (Jules). Harvey Keitel (Wolf). Uma Thurman (Mia). Christopher Walken (Koons). Maria de Medeiros (Fabienne). Amanda Plummer (Honey Bunny). Rosanna Arquette (Jody). Ving Rhames (Marsellus Wallace). Tim Roth (Pumpkin). Eric Stoltz (Lance) and Quentin Tarantino (Jimmie).

Ever since Quentin Tarantino's *Pulp Fiction* created a sensation at this year's Cannes Film Festival, where it won top honors (the Palme d'Or), it has been swathed in the wildest hyperbole. In fact, it has sparked an excitement bound to look suspect from afar. It must be hard to believe that Mr. Tarantino, a mostly self-taught, mostly untested talent who spent his formative creative years working in a video store, has come up with a work of such depth, wit, and blazing originality that it places him in the front ranks of American filmmakers.

But tonight, as *Pulp Fiction* opens this year's New

York Film Festival at Lincoln Center, the proof is on the screen.

What proof it is: a triumphant, cleverly disorienting journey through a demimonde that springs entirely from Mr. Tarantino's ripe imagination, a landscape of danger, shock, hilarity, and vibrant local color. Nothing is predictable or familiar within this irresistibly bizarre world. You don't merely enter a theater to see *Pulp Fiction;* you go down a rabbit hole.

This journey, which progresses surprisingly through time as well as through Los Angeles and environs, happens to be tremendous fun. But it's ultimately much more than a joy ride. Coming full circle at the end of a tight, deliberate two and three-quarter hours, *Pulp Fiction* leaves its viewers with a stunning vision of destiny, choice, and spiritual possibility. The film needn't turn explicitly religious to reverberate when one character escapes death on a motorcycle labeled "Grace."

Remarkably, all this takes place in a milieu of obscenity-spouting, petty hoodlums, the small-timers and big babies Mr. Tarantino brings to life with such exhilarating gusto. *Reservoir Dogs,* the only other film he has written and directed (he also wrote *True Romance* and has a story credit on *Natural Born Killers*), offered only a glimmer of the high style with which he now conjures lowlifes. It also prefigures some of the chronology tricks that shape the much more ambitious *Pulp Fiction.*

Reservoir Dogs attained well-deserved notoriety for its violence, especially in an expert but excruciating sequence involving the playful torture of a policeman. In the less gory *Pulp Fiction,* where the disturbing scenes (from stories by the director and Roger Avary) are tempered by wild, impossible humor, it's especially clear that there is method to Mr. Tarantino's mad-dog moments. He uses extreme behavior to manipulate his audience in meaningful ways.

Surprisingly tender about characters who commit cold-blooded murder, *Pulp Fiction* uses the shock value of such contrasts to keep its audience constantly off-balance. Suspending his viewers' moral judgments makes it that much easier for Mr. Tarantino to sustain his film's startling tone. When he offsets violent events with unexpected laughter, the contrast of moods becomes liberating, calling attention to the real choices the characters make. Far from amoral or cavalier, these tactics force the viewer to abandon all preconceptions while under the film's spell.

Consider Christopher Walken's only scene in the film, in which he plays a military officer and delivers a lengthy monologue explaining how he happened to come by a gold watch, which he is now presenting to a little boy named Butch. The speech builds teasingly to an outrageous punch line, after which Mr. Tarantino knows just when to quit, moving on to the story of the adult Butch (Bruce Willis). Anyone surprised to be laughing at the gross-out gold-watch anecdote will be even more surprised to admire the noble side of the sadomasochistic episode in which Butch is soon embroiled.

Butch's story is the second of three vignettes presented here, though the order in which the tales are told on-screen proves not to be the order in which they actually occur. In addition, the film is framed by opening and closing coffee-shop scenes that turn out to dovetail. Far from confusing his audience, Mr. Tarantino eventually makes the film's time scheme crystal clear, linking episodes with dialogue that may sound casual but sticks indelibly in memory. When a man named Pumpkin (Tim Roth) offhandedly addresses a waitress as "Garçon!" it's not easily forgotten.

Trapped together in absurd predicaments, splitting conversational hairs about trivia that suddenly comes into sharp focus, Mr. Tarantino's characters speak a distinctive language. The bare bones of the stories may be intentionally ordinary, as the title indicates, but Godot is in the details. So the first episode, "Vincent Vega and Marsellus Wallace's Wife," finds Vincent (John Travolta) and his partner, Jules (Samuel L. Jackson), debating emptily and pricelessly while preparing to embark on a professional mission. Their profession is killing. Jules, easily the more thoughtful of the two (it's no contest), likes to recite Ezekiel's prophecy against the Philistines to scare those who are about to die.

Like all of Mr. Tarantino's characters, these two are more appealing than they have any right to be. They're all also worried, in Vincent's case with good reason. Vincent has been recruited to take out Mia Wallace (a spirited Uma Thurman) while her husband (Ving Rhames), the impassive kingpin he and Jules work for, is out of town. Marsellus is rumored to have had a man thrown out of a fourth-story window for massaging Mia's feet.

The date makes for a deliriously strange evening, featuring a drug-related mishap (involving a fine group of miscreants, among them Eric Stoltz and Rosanna Arquette) and a dance contest at a fantasy restaurant called Jack Rabbit Slim's. This set, spectacularly photographed by Andrzej Sekula with a 1950's motif dreamed up by Mr. Tarantino, is so showy and hallucinatory that it leaves poor Vincent in a daze. When he finally tells Mia what he has heard about that foot massage, Mr. Tarantino proves he can write clever, sardonic women on a par with his colorful men. "When you little scamps get together, you're worse than a sewing circle," says the mischievous, glittery-eyed Mia.

Mr. Travolta's pivotal role, which he acts (and even dances) with immense, long-overlooked charm, is one measure of why Mr. Tarantino's screenplays are an actor's dream. Mr. Travolta, Mr. Jackson and Mr. Willis may all sound like known quantities, but none of them have ever had quite the opportunities this material offers. Mr. Jackson, never better, shows off a vibrant intelligence and an avenging stare that bores holes through the screen. He also engages in terrific comic teamwork with Mr. Travolta. Mr. Willis, whose episode sags only slightly when it dwells on Fabienne (Maria de Madeiros), his baby-doll girlfriend, displays a tough, agile energy when placed in the most mind-boggling situation.

The third story, "The Bonnie Situation," finds Harvey Keitel playing a suave sanitation expert named Wolf, whose specialty is unwanted gore. "Now: you got a corpse in a car minus a head in a garage," Wolf says. "Take me to it." Lest this sound too hard-boiled, consider details, like the fact that Wolf is first glimpsed in black tie, at what looks like a polite party that happens to be under way at eight A.M. And that Mr. Tarantino turns up wearing a bathrobe and offering everyone coffee. Small pleasantries don't count for much here, but at least they're mentioned, as when Wolf brusquely gives Vincent orders about cleaning up after the corpse. "A please would be nice," Vincent complains.

Pulp Fiction is the work of a filmmaker whose avid embrace of pop culture manifests itself in fresh, amazing ways. From surf guitar music on the soundtrack to allusions to film noir, television, teenage B-movies, and Jean-Luc Godard (note Ms. Thurman's wig), *Pulp Fiction* smacks of the second-hand. Yet these references are exuberantly playful, never pretentious. Despite its fascination with the familiar, this film itself is absolutely new.

Mr. Tarantino's audacity also extends to profane street-smart conversation often peppered with racial epithets, slurs turned toothless by the fact that the film itself is so completely and amicably integrated. When it comes to language, *Pulp Fiction* uses strong words with utter confidence, to the point where nothing is said in a nondescript way. High praise, in this film's argot, has a way of sounding watered down if it's even printable. But "Bravo!" will have to do.

—*J.M., September 23, 1994*

THE PURPLE ROSE OF CAIRO

Written and directed by Woody Allen; director of photography, Gordon Willis; edited by Susan E. Morse; music by Dick Hyman; production designer, Stuart Wurtzel; produced by Robert Greenhut; released by Orion Pictures. Running time: 84 minutes.

With: Mia Farrow (Cecilia), Jeff Daniels (Tom Baxter/Gil Shepherd), Danny Aiello (Monk), Stephanie Farrow (Cecilia's Sister), Ed Herrmann (Henry), John Wood (Jason), Deborah Rush (Rita), Van Johnson (Larry), Zoe Caldwell (The Countess), Eugene Anthony (Arturo), Ebb Miller (Bandleader), Karen Akers (Kitty Haynes), Annie Joe Edwards (Delilah), Milo O'Shea (Father Donnelly) and Dianne Wiest (Emma).

Everything about Cecilia (Mia Farrow) is tinged with melancholy, including the time—the depressed 1930's—and the place, a drab little New Jersey town where even the sunlight looks gray. Her husband, Monk (Danny Aiello), a big, short-tempered lug, isn't a bad sort, really, and, like almost every other man in town, he's out of a job and not looking for work. However, when he's had a few beers, he's inclined to push her around a bit.

Cecilia presents her objections to Monk in the form of extremely tentative observations: "All you do is drink and play dice and I wind up getting smacked."

Replies Monk with reason: "I always warn you first." Cecilia is even a failure as a waitress in the town's single, very greasy spoon.

It's no wonder that Cecilia, like millions of other Americans of her time, finds life on the silver screen not only preferable to—but more real than—the world around her. One day, after going through a bad patch at the diner and with Monk, she is sitting in the Jewel Theater, watching something called *The Purple Rose of Cairo* for the umpteenth time, when the film's handsome, four-square juvenile, a pith-helmeted character named Tom Baxter (Jeff Daniels), steps down from the screen and into Cecilia's life. As Cecilia later confides to her sister, "I just met a wonderful man. He's fictional, but you can't have everything."

This is the real *Purple Rose of Cairo,* which is the title of Woody Allen's new comedy, as well as of the movie within it.

To be blunt about it, *The Purple Rose of Cairo* is pure enchantment. It's a sweet, lyrically funny, multilayered work that again demonstrates that Woody Allen is our premier filmmaker who, standing something over five feet tall in his sneakers, towers above all others.

The Purple Rose of Cairo, which opens today at the Beekman Theater, is as fine as anything he's ever done, from *Take the Money and Run, Annie Hall,* and *Manhattan,* through *Zelig* and *Broadway Danny Rose.* Quite possibly, it is his best. I'd even go so far as to rank it with two acknowledged classics, Luis Buñuel's *Discreet Charm of the Bourgeoisie* and Buster Keaton's *Sherlock Junior,* both of which it recalls though in no way imitates.

It also recalls Mr. Allen's own small classic of a story, "The Kugelmass Episode," about a professor of humanities who becomes so infatuated with Madame Bovary that he finds himself inside the Flaubert novel making mincemeat of the plot line.

Though Mr. Allen does not actually appear in *The Purple Rose of Cairo,* his work as the film's writer and director is so strong and sure that one is aware of his presence in every frame of film. It doesn't overwhelm the contributions of the others, but illuminates them, particularly the glowing, funny performance of Miss Farrow. It's as if this wonderful actress, in spite of her English stage credits and all of her earlier films, was finally awakened only when Mr. Allen cast her in *A Midsummer Night's Sex Comedy, Zelig,* and, most spectacularly, *Broadway Danny Rose.*

Her Cecilia, a waif of backbone and conviction, also possesses a liberating streak of recklessness. Another woman might have questioned her own sanity when discovering herself in the company of the dashing, fictional Tom Baxter, whose sunny disposition is only briefly troubled when he finds that a restaurant won't accept the stage money he has in his pocket. Cecilia questions nothing. As might a true Surrealist, she accepts the illogical as the natural order of things. So does the exuberant Tom, who exclaims after their first kiss, "How fascinating! You make love without fading away!"

Although this is, after all, a movie, the way of true love cannot run smoothly. For one thing, the other characters in the film-within-the-film, abandoned when Tom Baxter left the story, cannot proceed. The members of this cast of stranded actors, beautifully played by John Wood, Zoe Caldwell, Van Johnson, Milo O'Shea, and Ed Herrmann, among others, sit around on the screen in various stages of boredom and panic. The actor who plays the headwaiter within the movie welcomes the chance to step out of character and do a little tap dance.

Meanwhile, the film's producer (Alexander H. Cohen) and a small army of Hollywood executives swoop down on the small town. One man suggests that if Tom Baxter won't go back onto the screen, they should withdraw the film from release and take the loss. They then summon Gil Shepherd, the actor playing Tom Baxter, in an attempt to get him to persuade Cecilia to persuade Tom to return to the movie.

As the complications multiply and become increasingly Pirandellian, only Cecilia keeps her wits about her.

My admiration for Mr. Allen extends to everyone connected with *The Purple Rose of Cairo*—all of the actors, including Mr. Daniels, Mr. Aiello, Dianne Wiest, and the players within the film within; Stuart Wurtzel, the production designer, and particularly Gordon Willis, the director of photography, who has great fun imitating the look of the movie Cecilia falls in love with, as well as in creating a style fitting to the depressed times that frame the interior film.

I'll go out on a limb: I can't believe the year will bring forth anything to equal *The Purple Rose of Cairo.*

At eighty-four minutes, it's short, but nearly every one of those minutes is blissful.

—V.C., March 1, 1985

PYGMALION

Directed by Anthony Asquith and Leslie Howard; written by George Bernard Shaw, W. P. Lipscomb, Cecil Lewis, Ian Dalrymple and Mr. Asquith, based on the play by Mr. Shaw; cinematographer, Harry Stradling; edited by David Lean; music by Arthur Honegger; art designer, Laurence Irving; produced by Gabriel Pascal; released by Metro-Goldwyn-Mayer. Black and white. Running time: 96 minutes.

With: Leslie Howard (Henry Higgins), Wendy Hiller (Eliza Doolittle), Wilfrid Lawson (Alfred Doolittle), Marie Lohr (Mrs. Huggins), Scott Sunderland (Colonel Pickering) and David Tree (Freddy).

To put a completely straight face upon the matter, *Pygmalion,* which had its premiere at the Astor last night, marks the debut of a promising screenwriter, George Bernard Shaw. This Mr. Shaw, for many years identified with the legitimate theater, the rotogravure section, and the Letters-to-the-Editor columns, appears to have had little difficulty adapting himself to the strange new medium of the cinema. The difficulty, in fact, may be in the cinema's adapting itself to Mr. Shaw. His jocular boast, in the jocular preface to his picture, is that he intends to teach America what a "film should be like." But that sounds more revolutionary than it is; it is as optimistic as his wish that everyone see *Pygmalion* at least twenty times.

Mr. Shaw is not revolutionizing the cinema in *Pygmalion* any more than he revolutionized the theater when he first put his comedy on in London in 1914. It caused a "bloody" scandal then, but Mrs. Pat Campbell and Sir Herbert Beerbohm Tree were able to ride over it. The film version is no more startling, providing you keep a straight face upon the matter, for the camera is frequently flushing a covey of actors from a conversational thicket and Mr. Shaw sometimes is caught chuckling so hard behind his whiskers that it isn't quite clear what has been making him laugh. All this, of course, providing one keeps a straight face upon the matter.

But *Pygmalion* is not a comedy for straight faces, and anyone who puts one on at the Astor should have his theater-going credentials examined and his sense of humor sent off for repairs. In the Shaw repertory, it is not one of the major items, so need not be taken too seriously. Taken lightly, as befits it, the comedy trips light from the tongue of any troupe—stage or screen—which has the grace to memorize its lines, to say them well and with appropriate gesture, while a good director clears or clutters up his sets and adds the precious element of timing.

In each of these rather statistical particulars, Mr. Shaw's first film has been most happily served—although we reserve the right to enter a qualifier or two later. His story of a modern Pygmalion, a phonetics expert named Henry Higgins, who molds the common clay of Eliza Doolittle, cockney flower girl, into a personage fit to meet an Archduchess at an embassy ball, has been deftly, joyously told upon the screen. That instinct for comedy might have been expected of a Higgins by Leslie Howard, or a dustman by Wilfrid Lawson, or a Mrs. Higgins by Marie Lohr. It comes almost more satisfyingly, since unexpected, in the magnificent Eliza of Wendy Hiller.

Miss Hiller is a Discovery. (She deserves the capital.) We cannot believe that even Mr. Shaw could find a flaw in her performance of Pygmalion's guttersnipe Galatea. Eliza is the bedraggled cabbage leaf gruff Professor Higgins takes into his home, feeds, clothes, bathes (by proxy, of course), and teaches so that she can pass for a gentlewoman at the embassy ball and thereby win his wager. And as Eliza, who progresses from the "Garn, I'm a good girl, I am" days to those poignant ones when she is cat-clawing at her creator's eyes, Miss Hiller is so perfectly right that we wonder how either Mrs. Pat Campbell or Lynn Fontanne (of the Theatre Guild production) could have touched her.

The picture has rung a few changes on the play. The embassy ball is a new sequence, instead of an off-stage incident, and has been worked with suspense, comedy, and fresh dramatic interest. The Dustman is not entirely the towering comic figure he was. His plaintive speech about being the victim of middle-

793

class morality has been retained, naturally; but they lopped him off a trifle at the end. Professor Higgins's methods of phonetics instruction are added comic devices, and the scene at the Higgins tea party, when Eliza is getting a dress rehearsal for her social debut, has been enriched by some added Shavian dialogue.

"In Hampshire, Hereford, and Hartford, hurricanes rarely ever happen," says Eliza dutifully, hitting her "h's" carefully. That is just before she starts telling about her aunt who drank gin like mother's milk and was "done in" by the fond folks at 'ome.

Mr. Shaw truly has taught the American filmmakers something. He is showing them how valuable a writer can be, how unnecessary it is to drape romantic cupids over a theater's marquee, how wise it is to permit a leading man an occasional session of cruelly masculine ranting. But he must learn, too, not to let his cameras freeze too often upon a static scene. And he might have improved upon the film's conclusion—just as he might have bettered that of the play. But that's beside the point, which is that Pygmalion is good Shaw and a grand show.

—*F.S.N., December 8, 1938*

QUADROPHENIA

Directed by Franc Roddam; written by Dave Humphries, Martin Stellman, Mr. Roddam and Pete Townshend; director of photography, Brian Tufano; edited by Mike Taylor; music by the Who; production designer, Simon Holland; produced by Roy Baird and Bill Curbishley; released by World Northal. Running time: 120 minutes.

With: Phil Daniels (Jimmy), Mark Wingett (Dave), Philip Davis (Chalky), Leslie Ash (Steph), Garry Cooper (Pete), Toyah Wilcox (Monkey), Sting (Ace), Trevor Laird (Ferdy) and Gary Shall (Spider).

The results of my (highly) informal survey about *Quadrophenia* have been tabulated. They show that most moviegoers think this is either a concert film or a rock opera, or that the title refers to a quadrophonic soundtrack. Not true. This is a dramatic film, one that's gritty and ragged and sometimes quite beautiful. It happens to incorporate rock songs, and to be saddled with a silly title. Though it's by no means a movie for everyone, *Quadrophenia* is something very special. It demands—and deserves—some special allowances.

Quadrophenia, which opens today at the Paramount and other theaters, is set in England in 1964, and populated by Mods and Rockers, warring bands of teenagers who speak with such thick accents that American audiences may find their conversation indecipherable. For this and other reasons, the film—which is a hit in England—hasn't traveled well.

But its foreignness has perverse advantages, helping to recast situations that might seem commonplace in an American end-of-adolescence movie, and making them just remote enough to seem fresh. A gifted new director, Franc Roddam, lends the film a clarity of emotion that keeps it from becoming too confusing.

The story is derived very, very loosely from an album by the Who. This album was an ambitious undertaking: it described a teenage boy, Jimmy, who was so acutely sensitive to social pressures that he developed the four-way schizophrenia of the title. Jimmy's condition was illustrated, rather than described, by four separate melodies—one associated with each member of the Who that eventually merged into one transcendent theme. The specific ending of the album called for Jimmy to swim out to sea and scale an enormous rock. Unfortunately for the current film, which does some floundering at the finale, Ken Russell borrowed that scene for *Tommy* several years ago.

But *Quadrophenia,* as directed and cowritten by Mr. Roddam, is perhaps too raw to have culminated with pie-in-the-sky. Jimmy, played by a wonderfully avid-looking actor named Phil Daniels, is a cheerful, unexceptional fellow, by no means the Who's hypersensitive hero. He is seen squabbling with his parents, partying with his Mod friends, working at a mailroom job that's both dead-end and dull. These episodes, which are carried by the boisterous enthusiasm of an excellent cast, combine to form a slice-of-life movie that feels tremendously authentic in its sentiments as well as its details.

The Mods-and-Rockers aspect of the story might seem to date the material. But Mr. Roddam is as concerned with the general experience of adolescence as he is with these particular groups of people. And he is able, in re-creating the seaside riots between these rival gangs, to capture a fierce, dizzying excitement that epitomizes a kind of youthful extreme. Jimmy, who is so electrified by his new identity as a Mod that he makes a quick, thrilling sexual conquest while the fighting is going on, may never again feel so fully at the height of his powers. *Quadrophenia* fills the moment with equal elements of regret and celebration.

In a barely memorable shot at the beginning of the story, Jimmy is seen to be walking away from a cliff— a cliff from which, at the end of the movie, he appears to jump to his death. This disastrous attempt at a flashback damages the movie, which finally seems to be concerned with nothing more morbid than the end of this boy's flaming youth. The last minutes of the film are further weakened by some last-minute interjections of the Who's music, which has until now figured into the story more delicately.

Images of the group, up until this point, have been ghostly and ubiquitous. Their records play in party scenes; their posters and photographs decorate walls; Jimmy watches the band on television while his parents complain. Jimmy himself looks considerably like the Who's Pete Townshend, and he has the gawkiness that Mr. Townshend has made such memorable use of in the course of his career.

When Jimmy, in one of the film's most stunning set-pieces, dives into a crowd of dancers at a seaside resort, as much to vent his frustration as to attract attention, the spirit resembles that of an early Who concert—the kind that concluded with Mr. Townshend's furiously smashing his guitar.

Among the fine supporting performances in *Quadrophenia,* on a par with Mr. Daniels's superb Jimmy, is Raymond Winstone's Kevin, an old school friend Jimmy runs into in a public bath. When they put their clothes on, Jimmy realizes that his friend has become a Rocker; later, they share a conversation about how important it is to join the right group so you won't be like everybody else. Leslie Ash is suitably heartbreaking and heartless as the most popular of the female Mods, and the actors playing Jimmy's closest friends are affecting, too. The movie includes a hilarious turn by the Ace, the prettiest and surliest blond Mod, who turns out to be a bellhop on the side. The Ace is played by Sting, who is lead singer of a widely praised new band, the Police.

—*J.M., November 2, 1979*

THE QUIET MAN

Directed by John Ford: written by Frank S. Nugent and Richard Llewellyn. based on the story by Maurice Walsh: cinematographer. Winton C. Hoch: edited by Jack Murray: music by Victor Young: art designer. Frank Hotaling: produced by Merian C. Cooper: released by Republic Pictures. Running time: 129 minutes.

With: John Wayne (Sean Thornton). Maureen O'Hara (Mary Kate Danaher). Barry Fitzgerald (Michaleen Flynn). Ward Bond (Father Lonergan). Victor McLaglen ("Red" Will Danaher). Mildred Natwick (Mrs. Tillane) and Frances Ford (Tobin).

Before appraising *The Quiet Man,* which came to the Capitol yesterday, we ought to make one or two matters clear. John Ford, who directed it, was born in Maine but christened Sean Aloysius O'Feeney. Also he admits that he has assiduously studied the Irish for forty years, that he doesn't know a thing about them, and that he has "never met an Irishman" with whom he could agree. All of which apparently doesn't make a bit of sense at all. For it is obvious that in *The Quiet Man,* he actually went to the Emerald Isle with some of his veteran players, then enlisted some Abbey Theatre stalwarts before turning his Technicolor cameras on those fine bhoyos and colleens, a rollicking tale, and the green, dewy countryside to come up with as darlin' a picture as we've seen this year.

As we were saying, Mr. Ford, and Frank S. Nugent, his scenarist, who used Maurice Walsh's story to arrive at a dialogue that is as tuneful as a lark's song, have themselves a rollicking time. It is not an involved tale that is being told. It is merely the story of Sean Thornton, who was born in Inisfree, went to Pittsburgh, where he became a steel mill hand and a prizefighter and where he killed a man in the ring, a happenstance that drove him back to his birthplace seeking peace of mind and quiet.

So, it is on a "soft spring morning" that he turns

up—on the train that is always about two or three hours late—hoping to buy the cottage where he was born. At this point, he runs afoul of Will Danaher, a broth of a lad, a squire thwarted in his courtship of the rich Widow Tillane, and—the Saints preserve us!—the brother of Mary Kate, a red-haired spitfire and the prettiest colleen in the county. It is obvious, of course, that our hero will fall in love with Mary Kate and that her brother will stand in the way. But through the good offices of a wily marriage broker, the priest, the vicar, and the townspeople who have been itching to see Will take a fall, the "yank" takes his bride.

This, however, is not the point Mr. Ford and company are trying to make. This is no fine romance. Sean is unacquainted with Irish customs that call for a girl to come to a man with a dowry. And, obviously a man who won't fight for his wife's dowry is no man at all. And Mr. Ford's thoroughly comic and enjoyable accented use of those customs in his film is its substance.

The pair's courting, under the watchful eye of the matchmaker, is low but lovely comedy. The scene in which Mary Kate tries to pour her troubles into the ear of Father Lonergan, who has just hooked the salmon he's been trying to land for years, is explosively funny, and the climatic fight between Sean and his brawny brother-in-law is corny but as lengthy and thoroughly satisfactory as any donnybrook ever screened. The fact that the whole village is betting on the slugging match—with time out for a couple pints of porter for the principals at Pat Cohan's bar—gives it native charm, as does the family friendship that follows the battle.

Let it be said, too, that *The Quiet Man* is not entirely muscular. Mr. Ford has gotten superb visual effects from meadows, tilled fields, and streams of the village of Cong in County Mayo as well as other areas in Eire. And, since he is a sentimental man, he has adorned the scene and story with enough airs to make even a poteen-filled tenor reach for High C. "The Wild Colonial Boy" should make a man's eyes mist and "Galway Bay" and "The Young May Moon" should gladden the heart too.

Of course, Mr. Ford did not film *The Quiet Man* in Ireland in its entirety but his cast acts as though they had never been anywhere else. John Wayne is a quiet man who turns into a properly irate citizen dragging his wife over half the green countryside to prove his love. Maureen O'Hara is beautiful as his flame-haired love, who has a fiery temper to match her tresses. Barry Fitzgerald is superb as the matchmaking-bookmaker whose throat is always dry and whose quips are constant. Victor McLaglen is fine as the pig-headed, strong-boy brother, and Arthur Shields, as the vicar; Ward Bond, as Father Lonergan; Mildred Natwick, as the Widow Tillane; and the many Abbey players fit the story as neatly as a hand around a glass. Let's face it. Mr. Ford is in love with Ireland, as is his cast, and they give us a fine, gay time while they're about it.

—A.W., August 22, 1952

RAGING BULL

Directed by Martin Scorsese; written by Paul Schrader and Mardik Martin, based on the book by Jake La Motta with Joseph Carter and Peter Savage; director of photography, Michael Chapman; edited by Thelma Schoonmaker; production designer, Gene Rudolf; produced by Irwin Winkler and Robert Chartoff; released by United Artists. Running time: 129 minutes.

With: Robert De Niro (Jake La Motta), Cathy Moriarty (Vickie La Motta), Joe Pesci (Joey), Frank Vincent (Salvy), Nicholas Colasanto (Tommy Como), Theresa Saldana (Lenore), Frank Adonis (Patsy) and Mario Gallo (Mario).

Taking as his starting point the troubled life of Jake La Motta, the tough New York City kid who slugged his way to the world middleweight boxing championship in 1948 and then went on to lose almost everything, Martin Scorsese (*Mean Streets, Alice Doesn't Live Here Anymore, Taxi Driver*) has made his most ambitious film as well as his finest. Though *Raging Bull* has only three principal characters, it is a big film, its territory being the landscape of the soul.

The film, which opens today at the Sutton and Cinerama 1, is far too particular to be conveniently classified as either a fight movie or a film biography. Though it pays careful attention to the factual details of Mr. La Motta's career, it is a movie with a resonant life and style of its own.

It's exceedingly violent as well as poetic and, finally, humane in the way of unsentimental fiction that understands that a life—any life—can only be appreciated when the darkness that surrounds it is acknowledged. There's scarcely a minute in *Raging Bull* that isn't edged by intimations of mortality.

Jake La Motta, played by Robert De Niro in what may be the performance of his career, is a titanic character, a furious original, a mean, inarticulate, Bronx-bred fighter whom the movie refuses to explain away in either sociological or psychiatric terms, or even in terms of the Roman Catholicism of his Italian-American heritage. He is propelled not by his milieu, his unruly id, or by his guilts, but by something far more mysterious.

Just what that is, I'm not at all sure, nor is the movie, but *Raging Bull* comes close to some kind of truth when, toward the end, Jake, now over-the-hill, gone to flab and possibly deranged, is thrown into a Miami jail on a morals charge. Full of self-pity and unfocused rage, he beats his head against the wall of his cell. "Why, why, why?" he bellows, and then whimpers, "I'm not an animal." It's a risky moment that pays off. Though there's not one sequence in the film when he hasn't behaved like an animal, Jake, like all the rest of us, is the kind of animal who can ask a question.

Raging Bull, which has an unusually intelligent screenplay by Paul Schrader and Mardik Martin, covers Mr. La Motta's life from his earliest attempts to get a title fight in 1941, through the period when he was barred from the ring for throwing a fight on behalf of the mob, his winning of the crown, his final defeat by Sugar Ray Robinson, followed by his dwindling career as a nightclub personality. The story is told in flashbacks, framed by Jake's preparations for an appearance at the Barbizon Plaza Hotel Theater in 1964 in *An Evening with Jake La Motta,* with readings from Paddy Chayefsky, Budd Schulberg, and Shakespeare, among others. A peculiarly mid-century American purgatory.

Though it's a movie full of anger and nonstop physical violence, the effect of *Raging Bull* is lyrical. To witness Jake's fury is to swing through the upper atmosphere of the emotions. It's breathtaking and a little scary. This has to do both with Mr. De Niro's performance and with the film's literary and visual style.

Most of *Raging Bull* appears to have been shot (beautifully, by Michael Chapman) in black-and-white, with the exception of a splash of crimson in the title credits and several sequences of 8mm color home-movies that provide bridges within the narrative. The fight sequences are sometimes shown in gritty, realistic detail and sometimes in a series of stills. The world, when it is seen by Jake, is observed in slow motion—ghostly sequences that are in poignant contrast to the noisy chaos in which most of his life is lived. With an effortlessness that is as rewarding as it is rare in films. *Raging Bull* moves back and forth between the objective point of view and the subjective.

Too much will be made, probably, of Mr. De Niro's remarkable physical transformations for the role, by means of makeup as well as by putting on fifty pounds of weight for the latter part of the film. I've always been skeptical of this sort of thing—Shelley Winters has done it too often for too little effect. It's an integral part of this performance, however. In his decline, Jake La Motta seems to disappear into his flesh, as if seeking to scratch an interior itch that will be forever out of reach.

Giving him superb support are two new performers, Joe Pesci, who plays Jake's younger brother Joey, and Cathy Moriarty, a beautiful young blond woman who has never acted before. Miss Moriarty comes across with the assurance of an Actors Studio veteran as Jake's second wife, Vickie. Either she is one of the film finds of the decade or Mr. Scorsese is Svengali. Perhaps both.

There are lots of points on which one might quibble. Jake's rehabilitation after being barred from fighting is glossed over too quickly to make much realistic sense. The entire film is played at such high pitch it may well exhaust audiences that don't come prepared.

And, at the heart of the film, there is the mystery of Jake himself, but that is what separates *Raging Bull* from all other fight movies, in fact, from most movies about anything. *Raging Bull* is an achievement.

—*V.C., November 14, 1980*

RAIDERS OF THE LOST ARK

Directed by Steven Spielberg; written by Lawrence Kasdan, based on a story by George Lucas and Philip Kaufman; directors of photography, Douglas Slocombe and Paul Beeson; edited by Michael Kahn; music by John Williams; production designer, Norman Reynolds; produced by Frank Marshall; released by Paramount Pictures. Running time: 115 minutes.

With: Harrison Ford (Indiana Jones), Karen Allen (Marion), Wolf Kahler (Dietrich), Paul Freeman (Belloq), Ronald Lacey (Toht), John Rhys-Davies (Sallah), Denholm Elliott (Brady), Anthony Higgins (Gabler) and Alfred Molina (Satipo).

From the first moments, when the star-circled mountain in the Paramount Pictures logo fades into a similarly shaped, fog-shrouded Andean peak, where who knows what awful things are about to happen, *Raiders of the Lost Ark* is off and running at a breakneck pace that simply won't stop until the final shot, an ironic epilogue that recalls nothing less than *Citizen Kane.* That, however, is the only high-toned reference in a movie that otherwise devotes itself exclusively to the glorious days of the B-picture.

To get to the point immediately, *Raiders of the Lost Ark* is one of the most deliriously funny, ingenious, and stylish American adventure movies ever made. It is an homage to old-time movie serials and back-lot cheapies that transcends its inspirations to become, in effect, the movie we saw in our imaginations as we watched, say, Buster Crabbe in *Flash Gordon's Trip to Mars* or in Sam Katzman's *Jungle Jim* movies.

The film, which opens today at Loews Astor Plaza and other theaters, is the result of the particularly happy collaboration between Steven Spielberg, its director, and George Lucas, who is one of its executive producers and who, with Philip Kaufman, wrote the original story on which Lawrence Kasdan's screenplay is based.

As Mr. Lucas's *Star Wars* helped itself to all sorts of myths, folk tales, and characters from children's fiction and fused them into a work of high originality, and as Mr. Spielberg's *Close Encounters of the Third Kind* made sweetly benign a kind of science-fiction film that had turned paranoid, *Raiders of the Lost Ark* refines its tacky source materials into a movie that evokes memories of moviegoing of an earlier era but that possesses its own, far more rare sensibility.

The film, which is often pricelessly funny but never a sendup, is about Indiana Jones (Harrison Ford), a two-fisted professor of archeology with a knack for landing in tight situations in some of the earth's more exotic corners, and his sometimes girlfriend Marion Ravenwood (Karen Allen), the daughter of a world-famous archeologist who, when we first meet her, is running a lowdown bar in remotest Nepal. Just how Marion has come to be running a gin mill in Nepal is never explained, but *Raiders of the Lost Ark* is great fun as much for the things it explains as for the explanations it withholds.

The time is 1936, which not only attaches *Raiders of the Lost Ark* to the films it remembers but also makes possible its fondly lunatic plot, which is about the attempts of Indiana Jones and Marion, at the behest of the United States Government, to find the lost Ark of the Covenant before a team of Nazi archeologists can lay their hands on it.

Hitler, who is described as being obsessed with the occult, is hellbent on finding the Ark, which once contained the Ten Commandments as handed down to Moses on their originally inscribed tablets. The Ark is reported variously (1) to confer magical powers on the person who possesses it, (2) to be "something that man was not meant to disturb," being "not of this world" and, more picturesquely, (3) as "a radio for speaking to God." No wonder Indiana and Marion risk life and limb every ninety seconds to prevent the Ark from finding its way to Berlin!

After their initial reconciliation in Nepal, following Indiana's narrow escape from death in the Andes, Indiana and Marion fly on to Egypt where there is every reason to believe the Nazis are about to uncover the Ark in a long-buried temple called the Well of Souls. Even before they reach the actual dig, however, there are fearsome obstacles to be overcome in Cairo, including attempted assassinations, a successful kidnapping, and a fate worse than death for Marion at the hands of a renegade French archeologist named Belloq (Paul Freeman).

More of the plot you should not know, though it gives nothing away to reveal that Indiana and Marion, either singly or together, must face such tests of their endurance as confinement in an ancient tomb with thousands of asps and cobras, an attack by poisoned darts, a plate of poisoned dates, torture with a red-hot poker, being tied up in a vehicle that explodes before our very eyes, and a superchase in which Indiana, on horseback, attempts to catch a Nazi truck convoy carrying the newly found lost Ark to Cairo for transshipment to Berlin.

The film's climax, in which the powers of the Ark are demonstrated to one and all, is almost as dazzling a display as the one that brings *Close Encounters* to its climax.

Mr. Harrison and Miss Allen are an endearingly resilient, resourceful couple, he with his square jaw, his eyes that can apparently see out of the back of his head and his ever-present fedora, and she with her Brooke Adams-Margot Kidder beauty, her ability to out-drink, shot glass for shot glass, Nepal's toughest barflies, her ever-ready sarcasm, and her ability to screech without losing her poise.

Mr. Spielberg has also managed to make a movie that looks like a billion dollars (it was filmed in, among other places, Tunisia, France, England, and Hawaii) yet still suggests the sort of production short-cuts we associate with old B-movies. The Cairo we see on the screen is obviously a North African city but, also obviously, it's not Cairo. There's not a pyramid in sight. My one quibble with Mr. Spielberg is that he didn't insert a familiar, preferably unmatching stock shot of Cairo into the scene to make sure we got the point. Sam Katzman would have insisted on it but, I suppose, we can't have everything. Just almost everything.

—*V.C., June 12, 1981*

RAIN MAN

Directed by Barry Levinson; written by Ronald Bass and Barry Morrow; based on a story by Mr. Morrow; director of photography, John Seale; edited by Stu Linder; music by Hans Zimmer; production designer, Ida Random; produced by Mark

Johnson; released by Metro-Goldwyn-Mayer/ United Artists. Running time: 128 minutes.

With: Dustin Hoffman (Raymond Babbitt), Tom Cruise (Charlie Babbitt), Valeria Golino (Susanna), Jerry Molen (Dr. Bruner), Jack Murdock (John Mooney), Michael D. Roberts (Vern) and Ralph Seymour (Lenny).

When Charlie Babbitt (Tom Cruise), a fast-talking automobile salesman in Los Angeles, returns to Cincinnati for his father's funeral, he finds that he has inherited a pocket watch and a 1949 Buick Roadmaster convertible. The pocket watch and Roadmaster are in mint condition, and Charlie had been estranged from his father for years, but still he is disappointed.

The disappointment turns to fury when Charlie learns that his father's three-million-dollar fortune has been left to Raymond (Dustin Hoffman), Charlie's autistic older brother of whose existence he has been completely ignorant. To get his hands on the money, Charlie kidnaps the helpless Raymond, who has been confined to an institution, and sets off for Los Angeles, aiming to have himself declared Raymond's legal guardian.

Rain Man, directed by Barry Levinson from the screenplay by Ronald Bass and Barry Morrow, is both a road movie and the oddest of this year's brother-movies in which one brother, a sophisticated hustler, and the other, an innocent abroad, realize they are good for each other.

The difference, however, is that Mr. Hoffman's innocent exists in a neverending mental twilight, lit by occasional flashes of lightning. Raymond is not only autistic, which doctors say is the result of metabolic and neurological disorders, he is also an autistic savant.

Though he goes through life preoccupied by self, obsessed by routine, and hedged in by inexplicable anxieties, he is also capable of feats beyond the powers of genius. He can't make emotional contact with the people around him but, given a few hours, he memorizes the Cincinnati telephone book, "A" through "G." He glances at a pile of matches and correctly calculates their total number.

For Mr. Hoffman, *Rain Man* is a star's dream of a role.

From the moment Raymond comes onto the screen, a slight, small buttoned-up figure, avoiding eye contact, speaking in tight little sentences that match the steps he takes, Mr. Hoffman demands that attention be paid to his intelligence, invention, and research as an actor.

The performance is a display of sustained virtuosity but, like Raymond, it makes no lasting connections with the emotions. Its end effect depends largely on one's susceptibility to the sight of an actor acting non-stop and extremely well, but to no particularly urgent dramatic purpose.

The performance is so remarkable, in fact, that it overwhelms what is otherwise a becomingly modest, decently thought-out, sometimes funny film. For reasons I don't quite understand, the dead-seriousness of Mr. Hoffman's efforts don't add heft to *Rain Man.* In much the way that Raymond stays detached, the performance seems to exist outside the film but, instead of illuminating *Rain Man,* it upstages the work of everyone else involved.

This is partly because Raymond remains pretty much the same exotic creature from the beginning to the end. He can't change in any important measure. He can only reveal additional aspects of himself as the movie goes along.

The film's true central character, though he's not the center of attention, is the confused, economically and emotionally desperate Charlie, beautifully played by Mr. Cruise, even when he is put into the position of acting as straight-man to his costar. It may be no accident that Charlie (and Mr. Cruise) manage to survive *Rain Man* as well as they do. Charlie is a lot like the edgy, self-deluding heroes who have turned up in other Levinson films, most memorably as played by Richard Dreyfuss in *Tin Men.*

The brothers' "road" adventures begin with their first abortive attempt to leave Cincinnati. At the last minute, Raymond refuses to board the airplane on which they are booked, citing the airline's safety record. The only airline he'll consider is Australia's Qantas, which, of course, doesn't fly between Cincinnati and Los Angeles.

Charlie puts Raymond into the Roadmaster and they start to drive, but even driving has its problems. They spend several days in a Midwestern motel because Raymond won't go outside when it rains.

By the time they reach Las Vegas, Charlie has realized that Raymond has special mental skills. After instructing Raymond in the basics of blackjack, Charlie takes him into a casino for the sort of results any gambler would die for.

These scenes are funny, but the humor becomes uncomfortable when Charlie decides that Raymond should learn something about women. In a scene that duplicates the one played by Danny DeVito and Arnold Schwarzenegger in *Twins,* Charlie teaches Raymond how to dance. This appears to be stretching Raymond's potential for growth since, early on, the point has been made that he hates being touched.

The supporting cast is headed by Valeria Golino, the Italian actress who made her American film debut in *Big Top Pee-wee.* She's very good but the movie, a star vehicle, hasn't much time for her.

Rain Man opens today at the Paramount and other theaters.

—*V.C., December 16, 1988*

RAISE THE RED LANTERN

Directed by Zhang Yimou; written (in Mandarin, with English subtitles) by Ni Zhen, based on the novel *Wives and Concubines* by Su Tong; cinematographer, Zhao Fei; edited by Du Yuan; music by Zhao Jiping; art designer Cao Jiuping; produced by Chiu Fu-Sheng; released by Orion Classics. Running time: 125 minutes.

With: Gong Li (Songlian), Ma Jingwu (Chen Zuoqian), He Caifei (Meishan), Cao Cuifeng (Zhuoyun), Jin Shuyuan (Yuru), Kong Lin (Yan'er), Ding Weimin (Mother Song) and Cui Zhihgang (Dr. Gao).

Songlian (Gong Li), the college-educated beauty who arrives at a feudal manor house at the outset of Zhang Yimou's *Raise the Red Lantern,* insists on carrying her own suitcase, which is virtually the last act of independence she will be permitted during the course of the story. Forced by her stepmother into what is essentially the life of a concubine, Songlian has agreed to become the fourth wife of a feudal patriarch, a man so regal that each of his wives presides over her own separate home.

Mr. Zhang, while acknowledging this man's importance, deliberately ignores him. *Raise the Red Lantern,* a beautifully crafted and richly detailed feat of consciousness-raising and a serious drama with the verve of a good soap opera, is strictly about the women who manage to live under this arrangement. Ruled by elaborate rituals, the wives spend their days waiting to be chosen for the night by their mutual husband, whose ways of signaling his choice include assigning a special foot massage to the woman he likes best. "If you can manage to have a foot massage every day, you'll soon be running this household," wife No. 2 (Cao Cuifeng) tells the new arrival.

As in his earlier *Ju Dou* (which, like this film, was an Oscar nominee for best foreign film), Mr. Zhang works with an exquisite simplicity that broadens the universality of his work. Steeped as it is in the specifics of privileged life in 1920's China, *Raise the Red Lantern* is also filled with instantly familiar figures, from the gloriously malicious and spoiled wife No. 3 (He Caifei), a former opera singer who manages to play Camille whenever her husband visits his new bride, to the resentful maid (Kong Lin) who proves extremely treacherous to her new mistress.

The film, very knowing about its characters' particular personalities and the ways they intersect, even becomes quietly comic when Mr. Zhang stages dinner scenes among the four wives, each of whom has a maid standing in silent attendance. Progressively younger and more beautiful, the wives are united in quiet resentment of the man they call "the master." Yet the situation demands that each one try her best to win his approval. From the plain, motherly wife No. 1 to the trophy types who are the most recent additions, these women reveal a lot about the man who married them, while also providing a fairly hellish vision of life without the option of divorce. Songlian, who initially views the wives' intrigue with detachment, eventually learns to assess her rivals' abilities and fight fire with fire.

Directing in a quiet, observant style, Mr. Zhang begins the film—which opens today at the Lincoln Plaza Cinemas—by introducing Songlian to the household and its customs. The title ritual, like that of the foot massage, is meant to signal the husband's nightly sexual predilection, and is performed with elaborate fanfare. On the night she arrives, the passageway to Songlian's house is lined with red lanterns as her new husband tells her "I like it bright and formal." The next morning, Songlian gazes in the mirror with a look of pure disgust and shame.

Subtly exploring the politics of power and control, *Raise the Red Lantern* traces Songlian's growing canniness once she becomes accustomed to the strictures governing her new life. It eventually becomes a tale of treachery in some quarters and solidarity in others, with a narrative that yields several surprising shifts of character. Songlian learns, among other things, not to trust her first impressions, and not to lose track of who her real enemies are.

Gong Li, also the star of *Ju Dou* and Mr. Zhang's *Red Sorghum,* is a stunningly handsome actress of strong, stately bearing. In this role, she reveals unexpected sharpness as well as great depths of dignity and sorrow. Also fine are Ms. Cao as the wife eventually revealed to have "a Buddha's face and a scorpion's heart," and Ms. Kong as the disloyal maid whose lot is ultimately even more pitiable than her mistress's. Ms. He, as the opera singer who sets the film's tragic ending in motion, cogently demonstrates the film's attitudes about divisiveness, solidarity, and oppression.

Raise the Red Lantern, based on a novel called *Wives and Concubines* by Su Tong, is as visually striking as it is dramatically effective. Mr. Zhang makes evocative use of clear, simple colors, from the lanterns themselves to the blue of the house's rooftops at twilight. And he captures a detailed visual sense of the rituals governing Songlian's new life. (Ceremonial black lantern covers are employed when one of the wives commits a shameful transgression.) The house itself, hauntingly photographed, becomes a perfect visual metaphor for Songlian's plight. Vast, rambling, and strangely empty, it has developed the look of a prison by the film's closing moments.

—*J.M., March 20, 1992*

RAISING ARIZONA

Directed by Joel Coen: written by Ethan Coen and Joel Coen: director of photography. Barry Sonnenfeld: edited by Michael R. Miller: music by Carter Burwell: production designer. Jane Musky: produced by Ethan Coen: released by Twentieth Century Fox. Running time: 94 minutes.

With: Nicolas Cage (H. I.). Holly Hunter (Ed). Trey Wilson (Nathan Arizona Sr.). John Goodman (Gale). William Forsythe (Evelle). Sam McMurray (Glen). Frances McDormand (Dot). Randall "Tex" Cobb (Leonard Smalls). T. J. Kuhn (Nathan Jr.) and Lynn Dumin Kitei (Florence Arizona).

H. I. McDonough (Nicolas Cage), called "Hi," is a big, sincere oaf whose vocabulary is full of words and phrases he's picked up from reading magazines while serving time as a nonpaying guest of the state of Arizona. He's highly motivated, but in the wrong direction. When first seen in Joel and Ethan Coen's new comedy, *Raising Arizona,* he is one of the state's most faithful recidivists.

Hi's weakness is the all-American "convenience store" that, at any hour of day or night, can be held up for a six-pack of beer, a pair of pantyhose, a package of bubble gum, or cash. However, every time he pulls a job (with an unloaded gun), he's caught, tried and sentenced, serves a few months for what's called "rambunctious behavior," and is paroled, only to repeat the cycle.

Over the years of his recidivism, Hi develops an increasingly sentimental attachment for Edwina (Holly Hunter), called "Ed," the young police photographer in charge of mug shots at the pen. Ed is pretty in the flawed way of someone who always looks worried. If Hi's weakness is convenience stores, Ed's is unreliable men.

After being paroled for the third or fourth time, Hi proposes to Ed. They're married, settle down in a weedy trailer park and seem ecstatically happy, with Hi working in a sheet-metal plant and Ed pursuing her career in prison photography. Observes Hi on the soundtrack, "Ed rejoiced that my lawless days were over."

All of this is background information for the real business at hand in *Raising Arizona,* and is presented in a very extended (about ten minutes) pre-credit sequence. This promises a lot more than is ever delivered in the film, which opens today at the Beekman Theater.

Raising Arizona is the second feature by the Coen brothers, the filmmaking team whose flashy, neo-Hitchcockian *Blood Simple* caused a stir at the 1984 New York Film Festival. The Coens collaborate on their scripts, which are then directed by Joel and produced by Ethan. They're nothing if not knowledgable about films, as well as talented—up to a point.

At the long-delayed, actual beginning of *Raising*

Arizona, Hi and Ed are living in a marital bliss marred only by the news that they can't have a baby of their own. Because of Hi's prison record, they're also denied the right to adopt. With no other way out, they decide to help themselves to one of the quintuplets recently born to the wife of Nathan Arizona Sr., the king of a statewide empire of unpainted furniture and bathroom-fixture outlets.

They reason that, with five babies, the Arizonas wouldn't miss just one. Says Ed, her brow furrowed as usual, "They have more than they can handle, anyway."

Nathan Arizona is not unlike the hard-sell huckster played by Mr. Cage in *Peggy Sue Got Married*—a Crazy Eddie–type for whom pleasure is business. He has the Coens' best lines and, as played by Trey Wilson, exemplifies the implacable nuttiness that's missing in much of the rest of the film. Asked by a reporter if it's true that his son has been kidnapped by UFO's, Nathan, who sounds like the Great Gildersleeve, says sorrowfully, "Don't print that, son. If my wife reads that, she'll lose all hope."

Also very funny are Hi and Ed's best friends, Glen and Dot (Sam McMurray and Frances McDormand). Though they already have a batch of children of their own, they feel the need of a baby so strongly that they aren't above trying to blackmail Hi and Ed to acquire the purloined Nathan Arizona Jr.

The other subsidiary characters aren't nearly as much fun. They include a couple of escaped convict brothers, surnamed Snopes in a jokey reminder of Faulkner's Yoknapatawpha County, and a motorcycle-riding goon who shows up out of nowhere to help the Arizona family locate Junior. In addition to this utterly pointless reference to the *Road Warrior* films, *Raising Arizona* also "quotes" from *Carrie, Badlands,* and, I suspect, from other movies I didn't immediately recognize.

When Jean-Luc Godard and François Truffaut did this sort of thing twenty-five years ago, it served as an affirmation of their regard for works too long unrecognized. It announced pride in what then seemed to be an arcane heritage. Today it seems mostly a film-school affectation, which is a major problem with *Raising Arizona.* Like *Blood Simple,* it's full of technical expertise but has no life of its own.

The Coens' screenplay has a lot of funny, raffish ideas in it, and it has been well cast, even down to T. J. Kuhn, who appears as Nathan Arizona Jr., and to the other babies who play his siblings. However, the direction is without decisive style. *Raising Arizona* has the manner of a Jonathan Demme film— say *Handle with Care* or *Melvin and Howard*—directed by someone else. Its automobile chases are appropriately frantic, but they've been shot and edited with the kind of clumsiness that television producers try to cover up with laugh tracks.

Mr. Cage and Miss Hunter, who should carry the movie, go at their roles with a tenacity that the film itself never makes adequate use of. They less often prompt spontaneous pleasure than the recognition that they're supposed to be funnier and more endearing then they manage to be. *Raising Arizona* may well be a comedy that's more entertaining to read than to see.

—V.C., March 11, 1987

RAN

Directed by Akira Kurasawa: written (in Japanese, with English subtitles) by Mr. Kurasawa, Hideo Oguni and Masato Ide, based on the play *King Lear* by William Shakespeare: cinematographers, Takao Saito, Masaharu Ueda and Asakazu Nakai: edited by Mr. Kurosawa: music by Toru Takemitsu: production designers, Yoshiro Muraki and Shinobu Muraki: produced by Masato Hara and Serge Silberman: released by Orion Pictures. Running time: 160 minutes.

With: Tatsuya Nakadai (Hidetora Ichimonji), Akira Terao (Taro), Jinpachi Nezu (Jiro), Daisuke Ryu (Saburo), Mieko Harada (Lady Kaede), Yoshiko Miyazaki (Lady Sue) and Kazuo Kato (Ikoma).

It would be difficult to imagine a more appropriate way to open the 23d New York Film Festival than with the two showings, which are scheduled for tonight at Lincoln Center, of Akira Kurosawa's *Ran* (*Chaos*), a film of the sort of grandeur that brings to mind Griffith's *Birth of a Nation, Napoléon Vu par Abel Gance,* and Eisenstein's *Ivan the Terrible.*

Though big in physical scope and of a beauty that suggests a kind of drunken, barbaric lyricism, *Ran* has the terrible logic and clarity of a morality tale seen in tight close-up, of a myth that, while being utterly specific and particular in its time and place, remains ageless, infinitely adaptable.

Kurosawa resists the description of *Ran* as his "version" of *King Lear,* in the manner of his free, 1957 adaptation of *Macbeth,* titled *Throne of Blood.* However, he won't have an easy time disentangling his film from Shakespeare.

According to Kurosawa, *Ran* had its initial inspiration in the true story of a sixteenth-century Japanese warlord, which, as he worked on it, became increasingly associated in his imagination with the titanic fall of Shakespeare's Lear. There certainly are major differences between *Lear* and *Ran,* but there also are enough parallels to prompt comparisons, which may not always be illuminating. *Ran,* at least as read in the English subtitles that translate the Japanese dialogue, is not a piece of dramatic literature. It's a visual masterwork whose manners, which sometimes look old-fashioned, recall virtually the entire history of epic cinema.

Kurosawa's "Lear" is Hidetora, the head of the Ichimonji clan, a once-ruthless, now-exhausted warlord who has spent his entire life subjugating his rivals and consolidating a vast dominion that he now, at the age of seventy, wants to turn over to his three sons, on whose kindness he depends. Taro and Jiro, the two older sons, both ambitious, agree to their father's terms and swear loyalty to him and to each other. When Saburo, the youngest son, points out that by so dividing the lands, Hidetora is setting up conditions that will inevitably lead to disaster, the furious father sends Saburo into exile.

Unlike *Kagemusha,* Kurosawa's rather difficult-to-follow 1980 film, which the director has called a "dry run" for the more elaborate and expensive *Ran,* the politics and relationships in the new film are, though complex, always comprehensible. As in *King Lear,* what, under other, far more ordinary conditions, would simply be a family squabble becomes a meditation on the human condition.

By far the most interesting figure in this drama is not the foolish, pathetic old Hidetora, but his daughter-in-law Lady Kaede, the wife of his oldest son and principal heir, Taro. It's Kaede, the revenge-seeking daughter of one of the lords conquered by Hidetora, who urges her husband to humiliate his father, to disband his father's retinue, and to assume full control of the family in his own name.

Later, when Jiro, the second son, murders Taro, Kaede loses no time in staking her claims to Jiro, whom she seduces initially with her womanliness and then, when he shows signs of weakness, by holding a knife to his throat.

Kaede is as implacable as she is beautiful. In one of the film's more extraordinary scenes, she stands by while Jiro, at her insistence, gives orders to an aide to bring to them the head of Jiro's legal wife, "properly salted" so that it won't decompose during the long ride between castles. Kaede has no desire to be a concubine. She wants status as well as the power. She's a combination of Goneril, Regan, and Lady Macbeth, with a little bit of Barbara Stanwyck's Phyllis Dietrichson from *Double Indemnity.*

As played by Tatsuya Nakadai, Hidetora is not exactly a towering Lear, at least at the start. Mr. Nakadai seems initially too slight a man to have accomplished all the terrible deeds attributed to him. However, as the drama progresses, the actor seems to grow in stature, which has as much to do with what Mr. Nakadai does as with the increasingly phantasmagorical nature of the film itself.

Cast out by his faithless sons, wandering, quite mad, across a volcanic plain, accompanied by Kyoami, his androgynous "Fool," Mr. Nakadai's Hidetora becomes an awesome, wraithlike figure. There is no attempt to play on sentiment. Hidetora is an angry ghost of someone not yet dead, a being who has looked in at the window of death and had it slammed in his face.

When, toward the end, he cries out, "I have tales to tell, forgiveness to ask," everything we see—nature, landscapes, lighting, ominous cloud formations—conspires to allow the primal drama to leap over the inhibitions of the English subtitles to create a moment of remarkable cinema.

The most memorable of the supporting performances are those of Mieko Harada, as the gloriously vicious, single-minded Lady Kaede, and of Peter, the stage name of the young transvestite actor-singer who plays Hidetora's Fool, not as an especially loving companion but as someone as trapped by fate as his master.

The film's physical spectacle is astonishingly fine, the battle scenes so well integrated into the strong, inevitable story line that they never seem to become arbitrary set pieces—specialty numbers—the work of second-unit directors who know more about horses than actors. It's also meant as praise when I say that *Ran* is very much an old man's movie—Kurosawa is seventy-five years old. (Hideo Oguni and Masato Ide, who collaborated with Kurosawa on the screenplay are, respectively, eighty-one and sixty-five.) Here is a film by a man whose art now stands outside time and fashion.

Ran, which will open here commercially in December, is a film that couldn't possibly have been made at any earlier period in this great director's career.

—V.C., September 27, 1985

THE RAPTURE

Written and directed by Michael Tolkin; director of photography, Bojan Bazelli; edited by Suzanne Fenn; music by Thomas Newman; production designer, Robin Standefer; produced by Nick Wechsler, Nancy Tenenbaum and Karen Koch; released by Fine Line Features. Running time: 102 minutes.

With: Mimi Rogers (Sharon), David Duchovny (Randy), Patrick Bauchau (Vic), Kimberly Cullum (Mary), Will Patton (Sheriff Foster), Terri Hanauer (Paula), Dick Anthony Williams (Henry) and James Le Gros (Tommy).

By night Sharon (Mimi Rogers) leads a life of studied decadence, a response to the perfect emptiness of her days. When not tethered to her anonymous job as a telephone operator, she engages in mate-swapping sex with strangers, doing so in the impersonal confines of a friend's furniture store. "What if things go out of control?" asks a prospective partner at the start of one such event. "What's control got to do with it?" Sharon tauntingly replies.

"I think he wants to know if you have any limits," suggests Vic (Patrick Bauchau), the friend who joins Sharon for these sexual adventures and whose own motives have more to do with libido than self-loathing. "I haven't found them yet," Sharon says.

But in *The Rapture,* Michael Tolkin's fierce, frightening exploration of religious faith pushed to the breaking point, she finds those limits with the force of a revelation. Without warning, Sharon wakes up in the middle of the night in a frenzy of disgust. She orders a male acquaintance out of the bed she now says is unclean; she showers, flosses, changes the sheets, and declares herself reborn. "I need a new direction in my life," Sharon says. "There is a God. I know it."

The Player, Mr. Tolkin's scathing novel about a Hollywood executive who commits murder as a quasi-logical extension of his professional life, looks mild in comparison with what he has in mind this time. At first, that is belied by the eerily matter-of-fact manner in which he presents Sharon's conversion. Now she smiles more. She speaks of her new faith with serene self-assurance. She speaks of it so much that she begins to log seven-minute conversations with people calling her for directory assistance, which causes her supervisor to complain. "Henry, God made me an information operator for a reason," she tells him smoothly.

All of Sharon's friends marvel at this transformation, particularly Vic, who thinks at first that she must have found a new man. "Is he as bad a boy as I am?" Vic slyly inquires. "I think you should meet Him," Sharon replies. When her meaning begins to dawn on Vic, his leer evaporates and he tells Sharon to wake him when it's over.

But it doesn't end. Sharon, who always glimpsed what she thought were vague warning signs that the world was in peril, now becomes sure that Armageddon is near. And she aligns herself with a cult of like-minded individuals. All have had similar visions; all follow the teachings of a strange, oracular young boy, all wait with quiet certitude for what they know will come. In this, Mr. Tolkin is chillingly far away from the kind of movie theology that suggests the Apocalypse can be held at bay by a Terminator, that death is just a second chance, or that heaven is filled with thoughtful angels attending to the love lives of those on earth.

The very brazenness of his having made a main-stream film about religious faith is nothing beside the lengths to which Mr. Tolkin takes this story, once Sharon is forced to put her beliefs to what is truly the ultimate test. The last part of *The Rapture,* in which Sharon's new-found complacency is undone by matters of life and death, is, cinematically shocking in ways that, say, Freddy Krueger never dreamed of. Very likely many members of Mr. Tolkin's audience have not dreamed of them either.

The essence of this film's effectiveness lies there in

the fact that its deeply troubling ideas about theology are tailored to a contemporary audience, one that may be as impervious to the subject as Sharon is in the film's early scenes. "If everybody's getting this dream," she asks with representative modern cynicism, "how come it isn't on the news?"

Despite the seemingly unquestioning, even proselytizing tone of the scenes detailing Sharon's conversion, *The Rapture* succeeds in maintaining a subtle editorial distance from its subject. The immensity of that distance becomes devastatingly apparent in a tough, thoughtful ending that will not soon be forgotten.

All of *The Rapture* is, in its own way, as overweeningly ambitious as those visually demanding final episodes. And at times Mr. Tolkin lacks the wherewithal to realize his ideas as fully as he might have. Sharon herself, though played fervently by Ms. Rogers, is as much a theoretical construct as a flesh-and-blood individual, and her inner life in matters not linked to spirituality remains unexplored. The conspiratorial hints of a coming Apocalypse risk sounding silly when, say, whispered about during an office coffee break. The film's special effects budget does not begin to approach what would have been needed for a Hollywood-worthy climax. The flat, simple expository style is at times inadequate to the mysticism of the characters. None of this matters much in light of the fact that Mr. Tolkin has made a stark, daringly original film that viscerally demonstrates the courage of its convictions.

Also notable about *The Rapture* are David Duchovny as the slightly more dubious mate who joins Sharon in her quest for faith, Will Patton as the policeman who encounters her at a very late stage in her spiritual evolution, and Kimberly Cullum as the little daughter who becomes a sweetly terrifying reflection of her parents' unwavering thoughts. *The Rapture* will be shown tonight and tomorrow as part of the New York Film Festival.

—*J.M., September 30, 1991*

RASHOMON

Directed by Akira Kurosawa; written (in Japanese, with English subtitles) by Shinobu Hashimoto and Mr. Kurosawa, based on the short story "Yabu no Naka" and the novel *Rasho-Mon* by Ryunosuke Akutagawa; cinematographer, Kazuo Miyagawa; music by Fumio Hayasaka; art designer, So Matsuyama; produced by Jingo Minoura; released by RKO Radio Pictures. Black and white. Running time: 90 minutes.

With: Toshiro Mifune (The Bandit), Machiko Kyo (The Woman), Masayuki Mori (The Man), Takashi Shimura (The Firewood Dealer), Minoru Chiaki (The Priest), Kichijiro Ueda (The Commoner), Fumiko Homma (The Medium) and Daisuke Kato (The Police).

A doubly rewarding experience for those who seek out unusual films in attractive and comfortable surroundings was made available yesterday upon the reopening of the rebuilt Little Carnegie with the Japanese film, *Rasho-Mon*. For here the attraction and the theater are appropriately and interestingly matched in a striking association of cinematic and architectural artistry, stimulating to the intelligence and the taste of the patron in both realms.

Rasho-Mon, which created much excitement when it suddenly appeared upon the scene of the Venice Film Festival last autumn and carried off the grand prize, is, indeed, an artistic achievement of such distinct and exotic character that it is difficult to estimate it alongside conventional story films. On the surface, it isn't a picture of the sort that we're accustomed to at all, being simply a careful observation of a dramatic incident from four points of view, with an eye to discovering some meaning—some rationalization—in the seeming heartlessness of man.

At the start, three Japanese wanderers are sheltering themselves from the rain in the ruined gatehouse of a city. The time is many centuries ago. The country is desolate, the people disillusioned, and the three men are contemplating a brutal act that has occurred outside the city and is preying upon their minds.

It seems that a notorious bandit has waylaid a merchant and his wife. (The story is visualized in flashback, as later told by the bandit to a judge.) After tying up the merchant, the bandit rapes the wife and then—according to his story—kills the merchant in a fair duel with swords.

However, as the wife tells the story, she is so crushed by her husband's contempt after the shameful violence and after the bandit has fled that she begs her husband to kill her. When he refuses, she faints. Upon recovery, she discovers a dagger which she was holding in her hands is in his chest.

According to the dead husband's story, as told through a medium, his life is taken by his own hand when the bandit and his faithless wife flee. And, finally, a humble wood-gatherer—one of the three men reflecting on the crime—reports that he witnessed the murder and that the bandit killed the husband at the wife's behest.

At the end, the three men are no nearer an understanding than they are at the start, but some hope for man's soul is discovered in the willingness of the wood-gatherer to adopt a foundling child, despite some previous evidence that he acted selfishly in reporting the case.

As we say, the dramatic incident is singular, devoid of conventional plot, and the action may appear repetitious because of the concentration of the yarn. And yet there emerges from this picture—from this scrap of a fable from the past—a curiously agitating tension and a haunting sense of the wild impulses that move men.

Much of the power of the picture—and it unquestionably has hypnotic power—derives from the brilliance with which the camera of director Akira Kurosawa has been used. The photography is excellent and the flow of images is expressive beyond words. Likewise the use of music and of incidental sounds is superb, and the acting of all the performers is aptly provocative.

Machiko Kyo is lovely and vital as the questionable wife, conveying in her distractions a depth of mystery, and Toshiro Mifune plays the bandit with terrifying wildness and hot brutality. Masayuki Mori is icy as the husband and the remaining members of the cast handle their roles with the competence of people who know their jobs.

Whether this picture has pertinence to the present day—whether its dismal cynicism and its ultimate grasp at hope reflect a current disposition of people in Japan—is something we cannot tell you. But, without reservation, we can say that it is an artful and fascinating presentation of a slice of life on the screen. The Japanese dialogue is translated with English subtitles.

—*B.C., December 27, 1951*

RE-ANIMATOR

Directed by Stuart Gordon; written by Mr. Gordon, Dennis Paoli and William J. Norris; director of photography, Mac Ahlberg; edited by Lee Percy; art director, Robert A. Burns; music by Richard Band; produced by Brian Yuzna; released by Empire Pictures. Running time: 86 minutes.

With: Jeffrey Combs (Herbert West), Bruce Abbott (Dan Cain), Barbara Crampton (Megan Halsey), David Gale (Dr. Carl Hill), Robert Sampson (Dean Alan Halsey), Gerry Black (Mace), Carolyn Purdy-Gordon (Dr. Harrod), Peter Kent (Melvin the Re-Animated), Barbara Pieters (Nurse), Ian Patrick Williams (Swiss Professor), Bunny Summers (Swiss Doctor) and Al Berry (Dr. Gruber).

*R*e-Animator has as much originality as it has gore, and that's really saying something. Stay away if you haven't a special fondness for severed body parts, or an unflinching curiosity about autopsy scenes; this one takes place mostly at the morgue, and it doesn't leave a thing to the imagination. But as directed by Stuart Gordon, a television and stage director making his feature debut, *Re-Animator* has a fast pace and a good deal of grisly vitality. It even has a sense of humor, albeit one that would be lost on 99.9 percent of any ordinary moviegoing crowd.

Based on stories by H. P. Lovecraft, *Re-Animator*, which opens today at the U.A. Twin and other theaters, tells of Dr. Herbert West, a medical student whose pet project is resuscitating the dead. He accomplishes this by injecting them with a fluorescent chartreuse serum, which causes any corpse to spring to life in an outstandingly terrible temper. Dr. West, played with supreme priggishness and just the right scary countenance by Jeffrey Combs, is first seen attempting this in the swift prologue that ably introduces the movie; then, after a credit sequence propelled by a Bernard Herrmannesque score, he looks for new guinea pigs. The hapless Rufus, a cat belonging to Dr. Daniel Cain, has some very unpleasant things happen to him after Dr. West answers an advertisement and becomes Dr. Cain's new roommate.

Re-Animator isn't just another mad doctor movie; it soon moves on to the point where the serum has caused much more trouble than could have been anticipated, and Dr. West has progressed from the story's villain to one of its nicer, more level-headed characters. Unfortunately, he often has the bad judgment to inject his serum into bodies larger and stronger than his own, or even, on one occasion, into a body that happens to be in parts. This latter development leads to a sequence, which is nothing if not unusual, in which an evil doctor attempts to ravish Dr. Cain's cute young girlfriend (Barbara Crampton), even though he happens, quite literally, to have gone to pieces a few scenes before.

All of this, ingenious as it may be and much as it will redound to Mr. Gordon's credit in hard-core horror circles, is absolutely to be avoided by anyone not in the mood for a major bloodbath.

—J.M., October 18, 1985

REAR WINDOW

Produced and directed by Alfred Hitchcock; written by John Michael Hayes, based on the short story "It Had to Be Murder" by Cornell Woolrich; cinematographer, Robert Burks; edited by George Tomasini; music by Franz Waxman; art designers, Hal Pereira and Joseph MacMillan Johnson; released by Paramount Pictures. Running time: 112 minutes.

With: James Stewart (Jeff), Grace Kelly (Lisa Fremont), Wendell Corey (Thomas J. Doyle), Thelma Ritter (Stella) and Raymond Burr (Lars Thorwald).

The boorish but fascinating pastime of peeking into other people's homes—a thing that New York apartment dwellers have a slight disposition to do—is used by director Alfred Hitchcock to impel a tense and exciting exercise in his new melodrama, *Rear Window,* which opened last night at the Rivoli.

Setting his camera and James Stewart in an open casement that looks out upon the backyards and opposite buildings of a jumbled residential block off lower Fifth Avenue, the old thrill-billy has let the two discover a tingling lot about the neighbors' goings-on, including what appears to be a grisly murder by a sullen salesman across the way.

Mr. Hitchcock is nobody's greenhorn. When he takes on a stunt of this sort—and stunt it is, beyond

question, not dissimilar from his more restricted *Rope*—he may be counted on to pull it with a maximum of buildup to the punch, a maximum of carefully tricked deception and incidents to divert and amuse.

This time he does it with precision. He and the writer of his script, John Michael Hayes, have concocted what might aptly be described as a *Street Scene* of middle-class content, viewed from the back instead of the front. The major observer of his drama—the fellow whom Mr. Stewart plays—is a world-roving news photographer who is confined to a wheelchair for the moment by a broken leg. And his rear-window observations range from two sunbathing girls on a roof to the unseen but grimly indicated death of the salesman's wife.

The old master scans his action shrewdly. A glimpse of a ballet dancer here, stretching herself and spinning briskly around her apartment in scanty attire; a look there into the cluttered warren of a discouraged pianist, then, slyly, an inkling of the salesman's mysterious pursuit. Back in the apartment of the hero, he casually and cleverly suggests a bit of a personal involvement with a lovely, determined girl. And again, the glance of the camera ranges the rear-window view.

Mr. Hitchcock's film is not "significant." What it has to say about people and human nature is superficial and glib. But it does expose many facets of the loneliness of city life and it tacitly demonstrates the impulse of morbid curiosity. The purpose of it is sensation, and that it generally provides in the colorfulness of its detail and in the flood of menace toward the end.

The performances are in keeping. Mr. Stewart does a first-class job, playing the whole thing from a wheelchair and making points with his expressions and eyes. His handling of a lens-hound's paraphernalia in scanning the action across the way is very important to the color and fascination of the film.

Grace Kelly as the beautiful model who loves him and joins in the game of spying upon a likely killer is fascinating, too. Thelma Ritter as a nurse who drops in daily, Wendell Corey as a dull professional sleuth, and Raymond Burr as the unsuspecting salesman, who is spied upon, perform with simple skill.

As in *Dial M for Murder,* Mr. Hitchcock uses color dramatically. Without any gory demonstrations, he strongly suggests the stain of blood. In the polychromes seen from a rear window on steaming hot summer days and nights, and in the jangle and lilt of neighborhood music, he hints of passions, lust, tawdriness, and hope.

—B.C., August 5, 1954

REBECCA

Directed by Alfred Hitchcock: written by Robert E. Sherwood and Joan Harrison and adapted by Philip MacDonald and Michael Hogan. based on the novel by Daphne du Maurier: cinematographer, George Barnes: edited by James Newcom and Hal C. Kern: music by Franz Waxman: art designer, Lyle Wheeler: produced by David O. Selznick: released by United Artists. Black and white. Running time: 130 minutes.

With: Laurence Olivier (Maxim de Winter). Joan Fontaine (Mrs. de Winter). George Sanders (Jack Flavell). Judith Anderson (Mrs. Danvers). Nigel Bruce (Giles) and Reginald Denny (Frank Crawley).

Before getting into a review of *Rebecca,* we must say a word about the old empire spirit. Hitch has it— Alfred Hitchcock, that is, the English master of movie melodramas, rounder than John Bull, twice as fond of beef, just now (with *Rebecca*) accounting for his first six months on movie-colonial work in Hollywood. The question being batted around by the cineastes (hybrid for cinema-esthetes) was whether his peculiarly British, yet peculiarly personal, style could survive Hollywood, the David O. Selznick of *Gone With the Wind,* the tropic palms, the minimum requirements of the Screen Writers Guild, and the fact that a good steak is hard to come by in Hollywood.

But depend on the native Britisher's empire spirit, the policy of doing in Rome not what the Romans do, but what the Romans jolly well ought to be civilized into doing. Hitch in Hollywood, on the basis of the Selznick *Rebecca* at the Music Hall, is pretty much the Hitch of London's *Lady Vanishes* and *The Thirty-Nine Steps,* except that his famous and widely publicized "touch" seems to have developed into a firm, enveloping grasp of Daphne du Maurier's popular novel. His directorial style is less individualized, but it is as facile and penetrating as ever; he hews more to the original

story line than to the lines of a Hitch original; he is a bit more respectful of his cast, though not to the degree of close-up worship exacted by Charles Laughton in *Jamaica Inn.* What seems to have happened, in brief, is that Mr. Hitchcock, the famous soloist, suddenly has recognized that, in this engagement, he is working with an all-star troupe. He makes no concession to it and, fortunately, vice versa.

So *Rebecca*—to come to it finally—is an altogether brilliant film, haunting, suspenseful, handsome, and handsomely played. Miss du Maurier's tale of the second mistress of Manderley, a simple and modest and self-effacing girl who seemed to have no chance against everyone's—even her husband's—memories of the first, tragically deceased Mrs. de Winter, was one that demanded a film treatment evocative of a menacing mood, fraught with all manner of hidden meaning, gaited to the pace of an executioner approaching the fatal block. That, as you need not be told, is Hitchcock's meat and brandy. In *Rebecca* his cameras murmur "Beware!" when a black spaniel raises his head and lowers it between his paws again; a smashed China cupid takes on all the dark significance of a bloodstained dagger; a closed door taunts, mocks, and terrifies; a monogrammed address book becomes as accusative as a district attorney.

Miss du Maurier's novel was an "I" book, its story told by the second, hapless Mrs. de Winter. Through Mr. Hitchcock's method, the film is first-personal too, so that its frail young heroine's diffident blunders, her fears, her tears are silly only at first, and then are silly no longer, but torture us too. Rebecca's ghost and the bluebeard room in Manderley become very real horrors as Mr. Hitchcock and his players unfold their macabre tale, and the English countryside is demonridden for all the brightness of the sun through its trees and the Gothic serenity of its manor house.

But here we have been giving Mr. Hitchcock and Miss du Maurier all the credit when so much of it belongs to Robert Sherwood, Philip MacDonald, Michael Hogan, and Joan Harrison, who adapted the novel so skillfully, and to the players who have re-created it so beautifully. Laurence Olivier's brooding Max de Winter is a performance that almost needs not to be commented upon, for Mr. Olivier last year played Heathcliffe, who also was a study in dark melancholy, broken fitfully by gleams of sunny laughter. Maxim is the Heathcliffe kind of man and Mr.

Olivier seems that too. The real surprise, and the greatest delight of them all, is Joan Fontaine's second Mrs. de Winter, who deserves her own paragraph, so here it is.

Rebecca stands or falls on the ability of the book's "I" to escape caricature. She was humiliatingly, embarrassingly, mortifyingly shy, a bit on the dowdy side, socially unaccomplished, a little dull; sweet, of course, and very much in love with—and in awe of—the lord of the manor who took her for his second lady. Miss du Maurier never really convinced me anyone could behave quite as the second Mrs. de Winter behaved and still be sweet, modest, attractive, and alive. But Miss Fontaine does it—and does it not simply with her eyes, her mouth, her hands, and her words, but with her spine. Possibly it's unethical to criticize performance anatomically. Still we insist Miss Fontaine has the most expressive spine—and shoulders!—we've bothered to notice this season.

The others, without reference to their spines—except that of Judith Anderson's housekeeper, Mrs. Danvers, which is most menacingly rigid—are splendidly in character: George Sanders as the blackguard, Nigel Bruce and Gladys Cooper as the blunt relatives, Reginald Denny as the dutiful estate manager, Edward Fielding as the butler and—of course—Florence Bates as a magnificent specimen of the ill-bred, moneyed, resort-infesting, servant-abusing dowager. Hitch was fortunate to find himself in such good company but we feel they were doubly so in finding themselves in his.

—*F.S.N., March 29, 1940*

REBEL WITHOUT A CAUSE

Directed by Nicholas Ray; written by Stewart Stern, based on Irving Shulman's adaptation of the story "The Blind Run" by Dr. Robert M. Lindner; cinematographer, Ernest Haller; edited by William Ziegler; music by Leonard Rosenman; production designer, William Wallace; produced by David Weisbart; released by Warner Brothers. Black and white. Running time: 111 minutes.

With: James Dean (Jim), Natalie Wood (Judy), Jim Backus (Jim's Father), Ann Doran (Jim's Mother), Rochelle Hudson (Judy's Mother), William Hopper (Judy's Father), Sal Mineo (Plato), Corey Allen (Buzz), Dennis Hopper (Goon), Edward Platt (Ray) and Steffi Sidney (Mil).

It is a violent, brutal, and disturbing picture of modern teen-agers that Warner Brothers presents in its new melodrama at the Astor, *Rebel Without a Cause*. Young people neglected by their parents or given no understanding and moral support by fathers and mothers who are themselves unable to achieve balance and security in their homes are the bristling heroes and heroines of this excessively graphic exercise. Like *Blackboard Jungle* before it, it is a picture to make the hair stand on end.

The foremost of these youthful characters, played by the late James Dean, Natalie Wood and Sal Mineo, are several social cuts above the vocational high school hoodlums in that previous film. They are children of well-to-do parents, living in comfortable homes and attending a well-appointed high school in the vicinity of Los Angeles. But they are none the less mordant in their manners and handy with switch-blade knives. They are, in the final demonstration, lonely creatures in their own strange, cultist world.

Screenwriter Stewart Stern's proposal that these youngsters would be the way they are for the skimpy reasons he shows us may be a little hard to believe. Mr. Dean, he says, is a mixed-up rebel because his father lacks decisiveness and strength. "If he only had the guts to knock Mom cold once," Mr. Dean mumbles longingly. And Miss Wood is wild and sadistic, prone to run with surly juveniles because her worrisome father stopped kissing her when she was sixteen.

As for Mr. Mineo, he is a thoroughly lost and hero-searching lad because his parents have left him completely in the care of a maid.

But convincing or not in motivations, this tale of tempestuous kids and their weird ways of conducting their social relations is tense with explosive incidents. There is a horrifying duel with switchblade cutlery between the reluctant Mr. Dean and another lad (Corey Allen) on a terrace outside a planetarium, where the youngsters have just received a lecture on the tininess of man. There is a shocking presentation of a "chicky run" in stolen automobiles (the first boy to jump from two autos racing toward the brink of a cliff is a "chicken" or coward). And there's a brutal scene in which three hoodlums, villainous schoolboys in black-leather jackets and cowboy boots, beat up the terrified Mr. Mineo in an empty swimming pool.

Set against such hideous details is a wistful and truly poignant stretch wherein Mr. Dean and Miss Wood, as lonely exiles from their own homes, try to pretend they are happy grown-ups in an old mansion. There are some excruciating flashes of accuracy and truth in this film.

However, we do wish the young actors, including Mr. Dean, had not been so intent on imitating Marlon Brando in varying degrees. The tendency, possibly typical of the behavior of certain youths, may therefore be a subtle commentary but it grows monotonous. And we'd be more convinced by Jim Backus and Ann Doran as parents of Mr. Dean if they weren't so obviously silly and ineffectual in treating with the boy.

There is, too, a pictorial slickness about the whole thing in color and CinemaScope that battles at times with the realism in the direction of Nicholas Ray.

—B.C., October 27, 1955

RED

Directed by Krzysztof Kieslowski; written (in French, with English subtitles) by Krzysztof Piesiewicz and Mr. Kieslowski; director of photography, Piotr Sobocinski; edited by Jacques Witta; music by Zbigniew Preisner; production designer, Claude Lenoir; produced by Marin Karmitz. Running time: 95 minutes.

With: Irène Jacob (Valentine), Jean-Louis Trintignant (The Judge), Frédérique Feder (Karin) and Jean-Pierre Lorit (Auguste).

In the dense, archly mysterious films of Krzysztof Kieslowski, bold but ineffable patterns shape the characters' lives. Coincidences, missed opportunities, overbearing visual clues, and strange, haunting parallels: all of these contribute to a gradually emerging sense of destiny. Stories develop like photographs in a darkroom. They are sharply defined only in retrospect, when the process is complete.

So it is with *Three Colors,* the schematic, madly audacious trilogy that is Mr. Kieslowski's latest work, after *The Double Life of Véronique.* (Claiming to be through with filmmaking, the fifty-three-year-old Mr. Kieslowski also insists that it will be his last.)

The arrival of *Red,* this series' last installment, is an event in its own right. (It will be shown tonight and tomorrow as part of the New York Film Festival.) In fact, *Red* succeeds so stirringly that it also bestows some much-needed magic upon its predecessors, *Blue* and *White.* The first film's chic emptiness and the second's relative drabness are suddenly made much rosier by the seductive glow of *Red.*

Not for nothing is red the warmest of these three colors, which Mr. Kieslowski has taken from the French flag. Nor is it unhelpful that "Fraternité," the theme that follows "Liberté" and "Égalité" in his series, is potentially the most engaging of his subjects. *Red* gets an additional leg up from the presence of two exceptionally fine actors, Irène Jacob and Jean-Louis Trintignant, who are perfectly suited to playing polar opposites here. They act their roles in an intricate story of friendship and deliverance while also serving as tuning forks for the director's larger intuitions.

"I feel something important is happening around me," one of them says, describing the gripping, legitimately portentous mood Mr. Kieslowski captures best. As the earlier films (particularly *Blue*) made clear, such thoughts can have a hollow ring when not borne out by a larger meaning. The greatest virtue of Red is its profound sense of purpose. At last, making the whole trilogy transcend the sum of its parts, Mr. Kieslowski abandons the merely cryptic in favor of real consequence.

In addition to being the best-acted of these three films, *Red* is the one that weaves the most enveloping web. Working more assuredly and less arbitrarily than he did at the series' start, Mr. Kieslowski plays deftly with the crossed wires that either connect or separate his principals in mysterious ways.

Early in the film, a literal image of telephone cable is enough to question what it means for these characters to communicate. When Valentine (Ms. Jacob) makes a phone call to her lover, Michael, a phone is seen ringing in the apartment of Auguste (Jean-Pierre Lorit), who lives across the street from Valentine. Why? Valentine and Auguste do not precisely know each other. But maybe they do, or should, or will. Mr. Kieslowski is particularly expert this time in constructing puzzling, overlapping patterns that bind lonely people together. A higher order can be glimpsed, quite movingly, beyond such bonds.

Satisfying even on the level of gamesmanship, with the filmmaker reaching new heights of mischievous color-coding, *Red* is bolstered by a more deeply contemplative side. Valentine, the young model whose very name evokes the title color, accidentally makes contact with a bitter ex-judge (Mr. Trintignant), who lives in a Geneva suburb called Carouge. Many of the film's encounters are unwitting, with characters moving like ships passing in the night, but Valentine meets the judge through a direct collision.

After her car hits the judge's dog, she carries it to his house, finding herself face-to-face with a cruel recluse who rejects his own pet and spends time spying electronically on his neighbors. One of these is Karin, whose romance with Valentine's neighbor Auguste will turn out to be a strange echo of events in the judge's life. Karin has a telephone job dispensing "personal weather forecasts" for travelers, which is wittily appropriate. Even when their paths intersect, these characters remain separate enough to require their own individual weather.

The idea of fraternity emerges through Valentine's highly charged encounters with the judge. Though not a love story in any conventional sense, *Red* is very much about the redemptive power of love. Ms. Jacob, the enchanting star of *The Double Life of Véronique*, once again displays a lovely, eager naturalness that encompasses all the complexities of this director's work. Mr. Trintignant, moving from brusqueness to tenderness, transforms himself memorably, and in the process communicates real fraternity, an acceptance and generosity that go beyond the bounds of ordinary romance.

Red, which is itself filled with echoes and foreshadowing (greatly heightened by Zbigniew Preisner's insinuating music), culminates in a ferry crossing. As a red advertising billboard of Valentine becomes a prophecy, she is brought together with the principals from *Blue* and *White.* This juxtaposition of destinies, which is not made to tie up narrative loose ends, is satisfying without being pat. Speaking hauntingly of new beginnings, it raises the wish that Mr. Kieslowski, now working at the height of his enigmatic powers, would take his own advice.

—J.M., October 4, 1994

THE RED BADGE OF COURAGE

Directed by John Huston; written by Mr. Huston and Albert Band, based on the novel by Stephen Crane; cinematographer, Harold Rosson; edited by Ben Lewis; music by Bronislau Kaper; art designers, Cedric Gibbons and Hans Peters; produced by Gottfried Reinhardt; released by Metro-Goldwyn-Mayer. Black and white. Running time: 69 minutes.

With: Audie Murphy (The Youth), Bill Mauldin (The Loud Soldier), John Dierkes (The Tall Soldier), Royal Dano (The Tattered Man), Arthur Hunnicutt (Bill Porter), Tim Durant (The General), Douglas Dick (The Lieutenant) and Robert Easton Burke (Thompson).

There are few, if any, old men now living who know from experience the exact look and "feel" of a battle in the War Between the States. Such knowledge, so common to so many until a few years ago, must now be derived from descriptions that are vivid in so many texts; from old photographs of battles, such as those that Matthew Brady made; and from the wells of imagination that have been fed by countless legends and tales.

Certainly a classic description, not only of a battle in full blast but of the tormenting fears and emotions of an untried youth in the ranks, is Stephen Crane's *The Red Badge of Courage,* which says all that ever need be said about the terror of a man first entering battle, no matter which side he's on or in what war. Now, thanks to Metro and John Huston, *The Red Badge of Courage* has been transferred to the screen with almost literal fidelity. It opened here at the Trans-Lux Fifty-second Street yesterday.

Don't expect too much from it in the way of emotional punch—at least, not as much as is compacted in Mr. Crane's thin little book. For, of course, Mr. Crane was conveying the reactions of his hero to war in almost stream-of-consciousness descriptions, which is a technique that works best with words. When it is a matter of telling precisely how a young soldier feels at a time, for instance, when awaiting an enemy attack or when wandering behind the lines after lamming, it is easier to do so with words than with a camera going around with the soldier and frequently looking at his face.

This is a technical problem Mr. Huston has not been able to lick, even with his sensitive direction, in view of his sticking to the book. Audie Murphy, who plays the Young Soldier, does as well as anyone could expect as a virtual photographer's model upon whom the camera is mostly turned. And his stupefied facial expressions and erratic attitudes when grim experiences crowd upon him suggest what goes on in his mind. These, coupled with the visual evidence of all that surrounds him and all he sees, plus the help of an occasional narration that sketchily tells us what he feels, do all that can be expected to give us the inner sight of Mr. Crane's book.

But the major achievement of this picture is the whole scene it re-creates of a battlefield near the Rappahannock (Chancellorsville) from the soldier's point of view—the ragged and nondescript infantry, the marches, the battlelines, the din, the dust, the cavalry charges, the enemy surging out of the clouds of smoke, and the pitiful, wretched lines of the wounded reaching and stumbling toward the rear. Mr. Huston, who made *San Pietro*, one of the great documentaries of World War II, can conceive a Civil War battle, and he has done so magnificently in this film.

Furthermore, he has got the sense of soldiers in that long-ago day and war—their looks, their attitudes, their idioms—as suggested in the writings of the times. John Dierkes, as the Tall Soldier; Bill Mauldin as the loud, uneasy one; and Douglas Dick as the Lieutenant stand out in a small but excellent cast. All are the sort of soldiers that one's mind envisions on those battlefields.

Also, Mr. Huston has captured and etched vividly most of the major encounters of the hero that Mr. Crane described—the heartbreaking death of the Tall Soldier, the stunning blow on the head— all but the shocking discovery of the rotting corpse in the woods. This is out of the picture as it is being shown here, probably out of deference for the squeamish.

But, in most respects, Mr. Huston has put *The Red Badge of Courage* on the screen, and that means a major achievement that should command admiration for years and years.

—*B.C., October 19, 1951*

RED RIVER

Produced and directed by Howard Hawks; written by Borden Chase and Charles Schnee, based on the novel *The Chisholm Trail* by Mr. Chase; cinematographer, Russell Harlan; edited by Christian Nyby; music by Dimitri Tiomkin; art designer, John Datu Arensma; released by United Artists. Black and white. Running time: 125 minutes.

With: John Wayne (Thomas Dunson), Montgomery Clift (Matthew Garth), Joanne Dru (Tess Millay), Walter Brennan (Groot), Coleen Gray (Fen), John Ireland (Cherry), Noah Beery Jr. (Buster), Chief Yowlachie (Quo), Harry Carey Sr. (Melville) and Harry Carey Jr. (Dan Latimer).

Up to a point in *Red River*, which came to the Capitol yesterday, this opus is on the way toward being one of the best cowboy pictures ever made. And even despite a big letdown, which fortunately comes near the end, it stands sixteen hands above the level of routine horse opera these days. So strap on your trusty six-shooters and race to the windswept Capitol, you lovers of good old Western fiction. It's roundup and brandin' time!

From the moment this Howard Hawks super-special fades in on the open Western plains and picks up a wagon-train of settlers heading out toward the perilous frontier, it's plain that you're in for a picture with the genuine tang of the outdoors. For the beauty and scope of that first look is an unmistakable tip that Mr. Hawks has used real Western scenery for its most vivid and picturesque effects. And from the moment (right at the beginning) that John Wayne and Walter Brennan cut away from the train and strike off for their own realms, you know that you're riding with stout men.

That's the big thing about this picture: for at least two-thirds of the way, it's a down-to-earth story of cowpokes and the tough, dangerous lives they used to lead. It's the story of a great migration of a cattle herd, said to be the first, from the breeding grounds in Texas to Kansas, along the Chisholm Trail. And it's the story of a desperate contention between two strong-minded men, a hard-bitten veteran and a youngster—or Mr. Wayne and Montgomery Clift.

So long as it sticks to cow-herding and the gathering clash between these two—a clash brought on by disagreement as to whether they should try the untrod trail—it rings with the clang of honest metal and throbs with the pulse of real life. For Mr. Hawks has filled it with credible substance and detail, with action and understanding, humor and masculine ranginess. He has made it look raw and dusty, made it smell of beef and sweat—and he has got a stampede of cattle in it that makes you curl up with terror in your seat.

He has also got several fine performances out of a solidly masculine cast, topped off by a withering job of acting a boss-wrangler done by Mr. Wayne. This consistently able portrayer of two-fisted, two-gunned outdoor men surpasses himself in this picture. We wouldn't want to tangle with him. Mr. Clift has our admiration as the lean and leathery kid who does undertake that assignment, and he carries it off splendidly. As other rawhided cowhands, Mr. Brennan, John Ireland, and Paul Fix gabble and gripe and act like cowpokes in a thoroughly entertaining way.

They do, that is, up to the sad point when the cattlemen meet a wagon train which is being besieged by Indians and help beat the redskins off. Then the cowboys—and the picture—run smack into "Hollywood" in the form of a glamorized female, played by Joanne Dru. For she is the typical charmer, with a voice like Dorothy McGuire's, and the havoc she plays with the hero—and with the contents—is almost complete. The characters turn into actors and the story turns into old stuff. It ends with the two tenacious cowboys kissing and making up.

—B.C., October 1, 1948

THE RED SHOES

Produced and directed by Michael Powell and Emeric Pressburger; written by Mr. Powell, Mr. Pressburger and Keith Winter; cinematographer, Jack Cardiff; edited by Reginald Mills; music by Brian Easdale; choreography by Robert Helpmann; art designers, Hein Heckroth and Arthur Lawson; released by Eagle-Lion Films. Black and white. Running time: 133 minutes.

With: Anton Walbrook (Boris Lermontov), Marius Goring (Julian Craster), Moira Shearer (Victoria Page), Robert Helpmann (Ivan Boleslawsky), Leonide Massine (Ljubov), Ludmilla Tcherina (Boronskaja), Esmond Knight (Livy), Jean Short (Terry), Gordon Littman (Ike), Austin Trevor (Professor Palmer), Eric Berry (Dimitri) and Irene Browne (Lady Neston).

Over the years, there have been several movies in which attempts have been made to capture the spirit and the beauty, the romance and the enchantment of the ballet. And, inevitably, in these pictures, ballets have been performed, a few times with charm and sincerity but more often—and unfortunately—without. However, there has never been a picture in which the ballet and its special, magic world have been so beautifully and dreamily presented as the new British film, *The Red Shoes*.

Here, in this unrestricted romance, which opened at the Bijou yesterday, is a visual and emotional comprehension of all the grace and rhythm and power of the ballet. Here is the color and the excitement, the strange intoxication of the dancer's life. And here is the rapture and the heartbreak which only the passionate and the devoted can know.

In certain respects the whole picture which Michael Powell and Emeric Pressburger made seems to have the construction and the flow of a romantic dance. For not only is the story a frankly sentimental affair, true to the staunchest conventions of triumphal love and bitter tears, but it is played by a splendid cast of actors who have the grace and the pace of dancers themselves. Indeed, many of them are dancers, as is natural, and they frequently perform, so that the rhythm and movement of their dancing transmits easily into the dramatic scenes.

And, for that matter, the story—it being about an English girl who devotes herself to a famous ballet company, becomes its star, and then falls in love—is a symbolic realization of the theme of the principal ballet, which is based on Hans Christian Andersen's fable of the little girl who is bewitched by her red dancing shoes.

If there is one objection to the picture, it is that the story plays too long, with much involvement and redundance in a comparatively simple plot. There is no need to have the impresario, even though he is a charming martinet, reiterate with such monotony that dancing and love don't mix. And despite the beauties of the settings and the fascinations of the theater, it is wearying to see so much Monte Carlo and so much of the ebb-and-flow backstage.

However, the story is still beguiling, having been written with eloquence and taste, and the performance of Anton Walbrook as the impresario is winning, nonetheless. He gives such a wonderful picture of a forceful, inspired, creative man with a beautiful flair for the dramatic that his overfrequent presence can be borne.

And, at least, the length of the picture—a good bit over two hours, not counting an intermission—permits an abundance of dance, which is the particular glory and excitement in this film. Numerous bits and pieces of famous and popular ballets are handsomely and tactfully intruded. And the main ballet, "The Red Shoes," is given a full-length performance, playing for about twenty minutes on the screen.

The cinema staging of this ballet, conceived in cinematic terms, is a thrilling blend of movement, color, music, and imagery. For it quickly evolves from the confines of the limited settings of the stage into sudden and fanciful regions conceived in the dancer's mind. And here some spectacular decor and some fresh choreography, arranged by Robert Helpmann, spark impressions that are vivid and intense.

As the leading ballerina and the romantic heroine of the film, Moira Shearer is amazingly accomplished and full of a warm and radiant charm. Leonide Massine is wonderfully comic in a completely fantastic style as her dancing partner and ballet master, and his dancing (of his own creation) is superb. Mr. Helpmann and Ludmilla Tcherina dance and act remarkably well, too, and Esmond Knight, Albert Basserman, and Eric Berry are good in minor roles. Only Marius Goring, as the young composer who steals the heroine's heart, vaguely distressed this observer. Too flamboyant and insincere.

Much could be said of the whole decor, which is set off to brilliant effect by properly used Technicolor, and the music of the ballet. Much could be said of the direction of Mr. Powell and Mr. Pressburger. But right now we must be contented with repeating that *The Red Shoes* is one you must see.

—B.C., *October 23, 1948*

REDS

Produced and directed by Warren Beatty; written by Mr. Beatty and Trevor Griffiths; director of photography. Vittorio Storaro; edited by Dede Allen and Craig McKay; music by Stephen Sondheim and Dave Grusin; production designer. Richard Sylbert; released by Paramount Pictures. Running time: 200 minutes.

With: Warren Beatty (John Reed). Diane Keaton (Louise Bryant). Edward Herrmann (Max Eastman). Jerzy Kosinski (Grigory Zinoviev). Jack Nicholson (Eugene O'Neill). Paul Sorvino (Louis Fraina). Maureen Stapleton (Emma Goldman) and Nicholas Coster (Paul Trullinger).

The Scott Joplin ragtime tune behind the opening credits of Warren Beatty's *Reds* recalls the sounds of pre-World War I America as they were heard then, when Greenwich Village was still a new Bohemia, free love was a way of life for the adventurous, new ideas were shaping the arts, and radical politics were more a matter of theory than practice. As the ragtime music fades out, voices fade in, contemporary voices that form a bridge to the past. "Was that in 1917 or 1913?" asks one. "I'm beginning to forget." "You know," another voice acknowledges, "things go and come back." "Were they Socialists?"

One by one the faces that belong to these voices appear on the screen, seen in close-up against a luminously black void. Some are familiar—Rebecca West's, Henry Miller's, Adela Rogers St. Johns's—and all are very old (some have died since the interviews were filmed). Some are lined with the cobwebs of long life. Other faces, like Miller's, are as wrinkle-free as stretched parchment. Each in some way remembers that earlier time, if only, like George Jessel, who wears his U.S.O. uniform, to become confused. Jessel cannot remember whether the great anarchist and anti-World War I activist was named Emma Goldberg or Emma Goldman.

These are the Witnesses—there are more than two dozen of them—who make up a kind of Greek chorus, the members of which appear from time to time throughout *Reds* to set the film in historical perspective, as much by what they remember accurately as by their gossip and by what they no longer recall. It's an extraordinary device, but *Reds* is an extraordinary film, a big romantic adventure movie, the best since David Lean's *Lawrence of Arabia,* as well as a commercial movie with a rare sense of history.

The focal point of *Reds,* which Mr. Beatty produced, wrote (with Trevor Griffiths), directed, and acts in, is the love affair and marriage of John Reed, the flamboyant American journalist and radical sympathizer, and Louise Bryant, the Portland, Oregon, dentist's wife who, in 1915, fled from her husband and middle-class conventions to follow Reed to Greenwich Village and her own desperately longed-for emancipation.

The film, which begins with a montage of Reed's exploits while covering Pancho Villa in Mexico in 1913, moves from Portland to Greenwich Village; to Provincetown, Massachusetts, where Reed and Louise helped form the famous Provincetown Players with Eugene O'Neill and others; to France, before United States entry into the war; and finally to Russia, where Reed and Louise were covering the successful Bolshevik Revolution of 1917. Theirs is the kind of story that only a third-rate novelist would dare make up.

Though very long—more than three hours plus intermission—and broad in physical scale, *Reds* has at its center two remarkable characters—Reed, the perennial undergraduate who used wars and revolutions as his personal raw material, but whose commitment to social and political change led him to risk everything on behalf of the world Communist movement; and Louise Bryant, an incurable romantic who, in the course of her association with Reed, became her own tragic heroine.

Mr. Beatty is fine as Reed, full of youthful enthusiasm, arrogance, and the dedication of a convert, but Diane Keaton is nothing less than splendid as Louise Bryant—beautiful, selfish, funny, and driven. It's the best work she has done to date.

Most prominent in the supporting cast are Jack Nicholson as the young O'Neill, with whom Louise had an affair at the same time she was living with Reed; Maureen Stapleton, marvelous and earthy as Emma Goldman; Jerzy Kosinski, the novelist, who is very, very good as Grigory Zinoviev, the smarmy Bolshevik who may have helped push Reed to a disillusion with Communism never fully verified; and

Edward Herrmann, as Reed's friend and editor, Max Eastman.

Most astonishing is the way the movie, which abounds with Great Moments of History, including the Bolshevik takeover of the Winter Palace in Petrograd, avoids the patently absurd, even as Reed and Louise, drunk on the excitement of the successful revolution they've just witnessed, make love in a cold Petrograd flat to the strains of "The Internationale." The secret, I think, is that the film sees Reed and Louise as history's golden children, crass and self-obsessed but genuinely committed to causes they don't yet fully understand.

There are times when the movie falters—a reconciliation between Louise and Reed on a French battlefield, which never happened and seems drawn from an old Hollywood picture; a terrible decision by Mr. Beatty to cut to a close-up of a cute, sympathetic puppy when Reed is distraught and crying after one of Louise's periodic departures; and a long montage depicting the *Doctor Zhivago*–like hardships of Louise's second journey to Russia to join Reed in 1920, the year of his death.

These, however, are minor faults in a large, remarkably rich, romantic film that dramatizes—in a way that no other commercial movie in my memory has ever done—the excitement of being young, idealistic, and foolish in a time when everything still seemed possible.

The film's scenes of epic events (actually photographed in Finland and Spain) are stunning, but so are the more intimate moments, including a stuffy Portland dinner party where Reed and Louise are formally introduced; the Greenwich Village sequences in which Reed and Louise enjoy their newly found, mutual love; and a hilarious sequence in Provincetown in which Louise, not a born actress, plays the lead in the early O'Neill play called *Thirst.* Says O'Neill to Louise: "I wish you wouldn't smoke during rehearsals. You don't act as if you're looking for your soul but for an ashtray."

Students of history may argue over some of the film's ellipses, and film students may delight in pointing out cinema "quotes," shots that recall scenes from other movies, but they will be missing the point of a film of great emotional impact. The technical credits are superior, including Vittorio Storaro's photography and the mind-boggling editing job done by a crew headed by Dede Allen and Craig McKay.

Only the very narrow-minded will see the film as Communist propaganda. Though Reed remained at his death a card-carrying Communist and was buried in the Kremlin, the movie is essentially as ideological as the puppy that whimpers when Louise stalks out. *Reds* is not about Communism, but about a particular era, and a particularly moving kind of American optimism that had its roots in the nineteenth century.

The film, which opens today at the Astor Plaza and Coronet, sees this time as if through the wrong end of a telescope, the image being startlingly clear and distant and, finally, very sad. This mood is most effectively evoked in the testimony of the Witnesses, by one woman who recalls how Louise badgered her for a fur coat, by Rebecca West's talk of old lovers, by Henry Miller's suggestion that someone like Reed, who was so concerned with the world's problems, "either had no problems of his own or refused to recognize them."

Then there's the incredibly beautiful moment when the Witness Heaton Vorse, who looks as ancient as the sands of Cape Cod, jauntily sings the old song "I Don't Want to Play in Your Yard," to cue in a Provincetown revel in which the youthful, incredibly beautiful Louise, surrounded by friends and lovers, sings the same song, which suddenly becomes a lament.

Reds is an extremely fine film.

—*V.C., December 4, 1981*

THE REMAINS OF THE DAY

Directed by James Ivory: written by Ruth Prawer Jhabvala. based on the novel by Kazuo Ishiguro: director of photography. Tony Pierce-Roberts: edited by Andrew Marcus: music by Richard Robbins: production designer. Luciana Arrighi: produced by Mike Nichols. John Calley and Ismail Merchant: released by Columbia Pictures. Running time: 134 minutes.

With: Anthony Hopkins (Stevens). Emma Thompson (Miss Kenton). Christopher Reeve (Lewis). James Fox (Lord Darlington). Peter Vaughan (Father). Hugh Grant (Cardinal). Tim Pigott-Smith (Benn) and Patrick Godfrey (Spencer).

In the late 1930's, in a stately home of England called Darlington Hall, Stevens (Anthony Hopkins) is the butler. He's the supreme commander of a vast staff that includes the housekeeper, the underbutlers, the cooks, the maids, the footmen, the scullery helpers, even those people who work outside the great house. As the members of his staff are expected to serve him, so Stevens serves his master, Lord Darlington (James Fox). He serves without question. Or, as he says at one point, "It's not my place to have an opinion."

Stevens is not just any butler. Through a combination of hard work, long hours, denial of his own needs, and carefully blinkered intelligence, Stevens has become what his peers would acknowledge to be a great butler. In his world he's the equivalent to Lord Darlington, someone who, when the chips are down, is to be trusted. Stevens is a man of honor and dignity, which become for him, as for the intensely dim-witted Lord Darlington, fatal flaws.

Taking this rather arcane story, adapted from Kazuo Ishiguro's award-winning novel, Ismail Merchant, the producer; James Ivory, the director and Ruth Prawer Jhabvala, the writer, have made *The Remains of the Day* a spellbinding new tragicomedy of high and most entertaining order. Here is an exquisite work that could become a quite unlikely smash.

Nothing that Mr. Merchant, Mr. Ivory and Ms. Jhabvala have done before—not even *The Bostonians, A Room with a View,* or *Howards End*—has the psychological and political scope and the spare authority of this enchantingly realized film.

The Remains of the Day, like the novel, is nothing if not metaphoric. Stevens is the proudly subservient, pre–World War II English working class. Darlington Hall is England. Stevens's fierce determination to serve, and the satisfaction it gives him, are the last, worn-out gasps of a feudal system that was supposed to have vanished centuries before.

The film also has its roots in history. The people who gather around Lord Darlington recall the members of the so-called "Cliveden set." These were the high-minded, sometimes fascist-leaning, thoroughly wrongheaded English Tories who, in the years before Munich and the partition of Czechoslovakia in 1938, worked so hard to accommodate Hitler and to pre-serve England's rigid social hierarchies.

In one of the film's nastiest, most vicious scenes, Lord Darlington allows two of his guests to ask Stevens about his views on German war reparations and other international matters of the day. Says the mannerly Stevens in response to each question, "I'm sorry, sir, but I'm unable to be of assistance in this matter." Lord Darlington's friends have proved their point; universal suffrage is an appalling waste of time.

Yet history and metaphors never get in the way of the film's piercing social and psychological comedy. *The Remains of the Day* is so lucid and so minutely detailed that it has its own triumphant life, which is enriched by other associations without being depend-ent on them. Among other things, the film offers rivet-ing, almost documentarylike sequences showing how such great houses once functioned, how dozens of guests were accommodated, how elaborate meals were prepared, how the servants preserved order among themselves through their own hierarchies.

Stevens, as wondrously played by Mr. Hopkins, is a very strange romantic hero. He's fussy, uptight, humorless, and seemingly asexual. As improbable as it might seem, *The Remains of the Day* is a love story, possibly two love stories. It is most immediately about the edgy relationship of Stevens and Miss Kenton (Emma Thompson), the beautiful, lively, and very efficient housekeeper whom he hires after the previous housekeeper runs off with the underbutler.

In spite of her beauty, Miss Kenton wins the sober-sided Stevens's support. She's obviously motivated by a strong need for work and would appear to be com-monsensical. "I know from my own experience," she tells him early on, "how the staff is at sixes and sevens when they start marrying each other." In the months that follow, it's clear that Miss Kenton is drawn to the commanding, cool Stevens.

Yet Stevens allows nothing to come between him and his duties, which is just another way of saying between him and Lord Darlington. There isn't any-thing either overtly or covertly sexual about their rela-tionship. They are servant and master, but it's a relationship so satisfactory to both, each in a different way, that it subsumes the sexual and even the romantic.

Stevens worships Lord Darlington, a well-meaning twit of dangerously serious ambitions to serve England and save it from war as Hitler consolidates his hold on Germany. Darlington Hall becomes the center of all sorts of unofficial diplomatic conferences that, Stevens understands, will decide the fate of Europe. It is through Lord Darlington that Stevens, whether he's planning a banquet for forty or passing port in the library, sees himself as serving history. When his mas-ter is accused of being a Nazi sympathizer of possibly treasonous proportions, Stevens's world also collapses.

This is not giving away the plot. Lord Darlington's awesome naïveté is made known early in the film, which unfolds in a series of flashbacks from 1958, shortly after Lord Darlington's death and the sale of Darlington Hall. The hall's purchaser is Lewis (Christopher Reeve), a rich American who, as a United States Congressman, participated in one of Lord Darlington's peace-now conferences just before Munich.

The film begins when Stevens, having been given a week's holiday by Lewis, as well as the use of the old Daimler, sets off on a journey to the west of England. His goal: to see Miss Kenton, now Mrs. Benn, who he believes is ready to come back to Darlington Hall since the failure of her twenty-year marriage. As Stevens rolls majestically through the rolling countryside, his adventures prompt a shattering reevaluation of his life.

Harold Pinter wrote an earlier screen adaptation of the novel, but it's difficult to imagine how anyone could improve on Ms. Jhabvala's screenplay and Mr. Ivory's direction of it. Though the collaborators are sometimes less indirect than Mr. Ishiguro, the film retains the sense of the novel and is as rich in texture and incident.

In Ms. Thompson's performance, which suggests Miss Kenton's desperate, aching sexuality, the film makes coherent a passion not really believable in the novel. Ms. Thompson is splendid, even to the way Miss Kenton's carefully acquired upper-class accent, which she uses while in service at Darlington Hall, slips a few notches when she's met twenty years later.

Mr. Fox and Mr. Reeve head the fine supporting cast, which also includes notable work by Peter Vaughan, as Stevens's fearful old father; Hugh Grant as Lord Darlington's godson, an aristocrat who becomes a caustic critic of the politics of appeasement; and Tim Pigott-Smith, who plays Miss Kenton's hus-band, a very good role that isn't even in the book.

In the way that *The Remains of the Day* looks grand without being overdressed, it is full of feeling without being sentimental. Here's a film for adults. It's also about time to recognize that Mr. Ivory is one of our finest directors, something that critics tend to overlook because most of his films have been literary adaptations. It's the film, not the source material, that counts. *The Remains of the Day* has its own, securely original cinematic life.

—*V.C., November 5, 1993*

REPO MAN

Written and directed by Alex Cox: director of photography, Robby Müller: edited by Dennis Dolan: music by Tito Larriva and Steven Hufsteter: art designer, J. Rae Fox: produced by Jonathan Wacks and Peter McCarthy: released by Universal Pictures. Running time: 92 minutes.

With: Harry Dean Stanton (Bud), Emilio Estevez (Otto), Tracey Walter (Miller), Olivia Barash (Leila), Sy Richardson (Lite), Susan Barnes (Agent Rogersz), Fox Harris (J. Frank Parnell) and Tom Finnegan (Oly).

Repo Man, the first feature to be written and directed by a bright new filmmaker named Alex Cox, is a most engaging reprieve from Hollywood's general run of laid-back comedies of simulated nastiness and half-baked nonchalance.

Repo Man, which opens today at the Eighth Street Playhouse, is the real thing. It's a sneakily rude, truly zany farce that treats its lunatic characters with a solemnity that perfectly matches the way in which they see themselves. It's a neo-Surreal, southern California fable, set in a landscape inhabited by failed punk rockers, automobile-repossession men who behave as if they were the knights errant of capitalism, some creatures from outer space, as well as a television evangelist who preaches against "godless Communism abroad and liberal humanism at home." At its end, there's nothing less than an ascension to heaven in a 1964 Chevy Malibu.

The innocent Percival who wanders through this not entirely mythological world is Otto (Emilio Estevez), a self-described white suburban punk who, though he wears an earring and the prescribed haircut, can't make it with his disenchanted peers. He snarls a lot and attempts to look alienated, but he has a dreadful weakness. Otto keeps getting interested and not only interested but involved.

After one mishap and another, Otto winds up working as a "repo man" for the Helping Hands Acceptance Company, a seedy repossession outfit, whose star employee is a veteran named Bud (Harry Dean Stanton). Bud, who assumes responsibility for Otto's education, is a fast-talking, beat-up-looking guy with a worry line for every vehicle repossessed and a word of wisdom for every eventuality. "A repo man's life is always intense," he might say after a near-fatal accident on the highway, or, apropos of something else, "The more you drive, the less intelligent you get." That Bud is never entirely sober contributes to the general air of cheerful incoherence.

Exactly what happens in *Repo Man*—I suppose it should be called the narrative—can't be easily synopsized, which is one of the film's failings. However, most of what happens is very funny, including Alex's anything-but-sentimental affair with Leila (Olivia Barash), a pretty young woman, who for reasons never made clear is convinced that the aforesaid 1964 Chevy Malibu contains the bodies of four aliens in its trunk. "We must find it right away," she says with desperation, "or they could turn into moosh."

It's not easy reasoning with someone like Leila or, for that matter, with anything that happens in the film, which at times seems like a cross between *Close Encounters of the Third Kind* and *Used Cars.* What is clear, however, is that Mr. Cox, a young Englishman, who studied at the film school of the University of California at Los Angeles, is a movie-maker of wit and vision.

Repo Man is full of throwaway sight gags—odd bits of business seen at the corner of the film frame—and its soundtrack is sometimes as dense with bizarre non sequiturs as the soundtrack on a Robert Altman film. All of the performances are good, but those of Mr. Stanton and Mr. Estevez are excellent.

Repo Man frequently seems to be as zonked as Mr. Stanton's cocaine-sniffing Bud. It's not a big-budget *Ghostbusters* of a movie, but it's very entertaining, and though it's rude in an R-rated way, it has the good taste never to promise more than it can deliver.

—*V.C., July 6, 1984*

REPULSION

Directed by Roman Polanski; written by Mr. Polanski, Gerard Brach and David Stone; cinematographer, Gilbert Taylor; edited by Alastair McIntyre; music by Chico Hamilton; art designer, Seamus Flannery; produced by Gene Gutowski; released by Royal Films. Black and white. Running time: 104 minutes.

With: Catherine Deneuve (Carol Ledoux), Ian Hendry (Michael), John Fraser (Colin), Patrick Wymark (Landlord), Yvonne Furneaux (Helen Ledoux), Renee Houston (Miss Balch) and Helen Fraser (Bridget).

An absolute knockout of a movie in the psychological horror line has been accomplished by Roman Polanski in his first English-language film. It is the British-made, French-played *Repulsion* and it opened here Saturday.

Prepare yourself to be demolished when you go to see it—and go you must, because it's one of those films everybody will soon be buzzing about. It's the *David and Lisa*—only better—of this newspaper strike. To miss it would be worse than missing *Psycho*, if you've a taste for this sort of thing.

For it is more than just a tale of mounting horrors that moves its heroine—a beautiful, sex-repressed French girl living in London—from a state of mental woe into a stage of dithering madness and then to the dark extremity of murdering a brace of fellows who happen into the lonely apartment in which she is hidden.

It is also a haunting adumbration of a small but piercing human tragedy, and it is almost a perfect specimen of a very special cinema-sound technique.

Mr. Polanski, you'll remember, is the young director who made the Polish film *Knife in the Water*. In that one, he proved his ability to penetrate and expose the alien and angry impulses of the subconscious mind. Here he goes even further into the dank and murky chambers of the brain to discover the hideous demons that sometimes take possession there.

The brain of which the demons take possession in this progressively more horrendous film is that of a young manicurist, played by Catherine Deneuve, the slim girl whose radiant blond beauty is crucial, for the weird and agitating mystery here is why a girl of such fascinating beauty should be as hostile as she is toward men.

Creepingly, Mr. Polanski exposes this mystery by showing us first the tortured nature of his heroine—how she holds off an ardent young suitor, how she fiercely resents and hates the lustful lover of her older sister with whom she shares a London flat; and then he continues the exposure with a detailed and gruesome account of the crumbling of her mind while she is staying in the apartment alone and how she murders, first, her innocent suitor and then the lecherous landlord when they unwittingly invade the fetid place.

But the final, poignant revelation is in an old family photograph, which shows the two sisters when they were children, that is picked up by the camera at the end.

This subtlety is characteristic of the structure and realization throughout. Mr. Polanski builds a towering drama with a skillful mesh of incidental stimuli. The dressed carcass of a rabbit on a platter becomes a monstrous symbol as the picture goes along. Small cracks in the walls of the apartment flow into crunching indicators of the heroine's crumbling mind.

Distortions in the rooms of the apartment tacitly reveal her mental state. Phantom arms that punch through the walls and seize her visualize her nightmare insanity.

And with sound, too, Mr. Polanski weaves a fabric of tremendous effects.

Miss Deneuve is simply splendid in the central role—secretive in nursing her obsession, and starkly sad in her insanity. Yvonne Furneaux, who played the mistress of the hero in *La Dolce Vita,* also does a splendid job as the subtly contentious older sister, and Ian Hendry is properly crude as the latter's lover. Patrick Wymark plays the landlord vulgarly, and John Fraser is sugary as the suitor who is rewarded with a clout on the head.

Within the maelstrom of violence and horror in this film, Mr. Polanski has achieved a haunting concept of the pain and pathos of the mentally deranged. He has delivered undoubtedly one of the best films of the year.

—B.C., *October 4, 1965*

RESERVOIR DOGS

Written and directed by Quentin Tarantino: director of photography andrzej Sekula: edited by Sally Menke: music by Karyn Rachtman: production designer. David Wasco: produced by Lawrence Bender: released by Miramax Films. Running time: 99 minutes.

With: Harvey Keitel (Mr. White). Tim Roth (Mr. Orange). Michael Madsen (Mr. Blonde). Chris Penn (Nice Guy Eddie). Steve Buscemi (Mr. Pink). Lawrence Tierney (Joe Cabot). Randy Brooks (Holdaway). Kirk Baltz (Marvin Nash). Eddie Bunker (Mr. Blue) and Quentin Tarantino (Mr. Brown).

It's been an unusually good year for the discovery of first-rate new American film directors: Barry Primus (*Mistress*), Nick Gomez (*Laws of Gravity*), Allison Anders (*Gas Food Lodging*), and Carl Franklin (*One False Move*), among others. Now add to the list the name of Quentin Tarantino, the young writer and director of *Reservoir Dogs,* a small, modestly budgeted crime movie of sometimes dazzling cinematic pyrotechnics and over-the-top dramatic energy. It may also be one of the most aggressively brutal movies since Sam Peckinpah's *Straw Dogs.*

Reservoir Dogs is about a Los Angeles jewelry store robbery masterminded by a tough old mob figure named Joe Cabot (Lawrence Tierney). The principal characters are introduced in an extended precredit sequence in which the thieves are seen relaxing over lunch sometime before the job.

The camera looks on with the indifference of a waitress who expects no tip. One guy holds forth on the meaning of the lyrics of popular songs, with special emphasis on the oeuvre of Madonna. His discoveries are no more profound than those of academe, but his obscene jargon, which disgusts some of his colleagues, is refreshingly blunt and more comprehensible than any deconstructionist's. It's a brilliant scene-setter.

Cut to the initial postcredit sequence, just after the heist has been carried out and two of the hoods, played by Harvey Keitel and Tim Roth, are fleeing the scene. Mr. Keitel is at the wheel of the car while Mr. Roth lies across the back seat, bleeding badly and clutching his stomach as if to hold in the organs. Something obviously went wrong. One of the hoods became panicky during the holdup and began shooting. It's also apparent that the police had been tipped off. Mr. Roth begs to be taken to a hospital, or just dumped somewhere near a hospital, but Mr. Keitel refuses. They go on to the warehouse where the gang members were to meet according to the original plan.

Though all of the film's contemporary action takes place inside this warehouse, *Reservoir Dogs* cuts back and forth in time with neat efficiency to dramatize the origins of this soured caper. One of the elements of old Joe's plan was the anonymity of the men he hired for the job, to protect them from one another and from the police.

To this end he gave them noms de crime (Mr. White, Mr. Pink, Mr. Orange, and so on), which especially offends the man dubbed Mr. Pink, who thinks it makes him sound like a sissy. In the course of the film, some of the men do reveal their real names, which leads to a certain amount of confusion for the audience when the men are talking about characters who are offscreen.

Though small in physical scope, *Reservoir Dogs* is immensely complicated in its structure, which for the most part works with breathtaking effect Mr. Tarantino uses chapter headings ("Mr. Blonde," "Mr. Orange," etc.) to introduce the flashbacks, which burden the film with literary affectations it doesn't need. Yet the flashbacks themselves never have the effect of interrupting the flow of the action. Mr. Tarantino not only can write superb dialogue, but he also has a firm grasp of narrative construction. The audience learns the identity of the squealer about midway through, but the effect is to increase tension rather than diminish it.

Reservoir Dogs moves swiftly and with complete confidence toward a climax that matches *Hamlet*'s in terms of both the body count and the sudden, unexpected just deserts. It's a seriously wild ending, and though far from upbeat, it satisfies. Its dimensions are not exactly those of Greek tragedy. *Reservoir Dogs* is skeptically contemporary. Mr. Tarantino has a fervid imagination, but he also has the strength and talent to control it.

Like *Glengarry Glen Ross,* another virtually all-male

production, *Reservoir Dogs* features a cast of splendid actors, all of whom contribute equally to the final effect. Among the most prominent: Mr. Keitel, whose moral dilemma gives the film its ultimate meaning; Steve Buscemi, as the fellow who has thought long about the messages in Madonna's songs; Mr. Roth, the English actor who gives another amazing performance as a strictly American type; Chris Penn, as Mr. Tierney's son and heir; Michael Madsen, as a seemingly sane ex-con who isn't; and Mr. Tierney, who more or less presides over the movie.

The film also marks the American debut of Andrzej Sekula, the Polish-born director of photography. Mr. Sekula's work here is of an order to catapult him immediately into the front ranks. One of the principal reasons the film works so well is the sense of give-and-take that is possible only when two or more actors share the same image. Mr. Sekula and Mr. Tarantino have not been brainwashed by television movies. They don't depend on close-ups. Reservoir Dogs takes a longer view.

Pay heed: *Reservoir Dogs* is as violent as any movie you are likely to see this year, but though it's not always easy to watch, it has a point.

—*V.C., October 23, 1992*

THE RETURN OF MARTIN GUERRE

Produced and directed by Daniel Vigne: written (in French. with English subtitles) by Mr. Vigne and Jean-Claude Carrière: cinematographer. André Neau: edited by Denise de Casabianca: music by Michel Portal: art designer. Alain Negre: released by European International Distribution. Running time: 111 minutes.

With: Gérard Depardieu and Bernard Pierre Donnadieu (Martin Guerre). Nathalie Baye (Bertrande de Rols). Roger Planchon (Jean de Coras). Maurice Jacquemont (Judge Rieux) and Isabelle Sadoyan (Catherine Boere).

This is, as they say, a true story. In 1549 a young peasant named Martin Guerre disappeared from the small village of Artigat in the foothills of the Pyrenees in southwestern France. He left behind his wife of seven years, Bertrande de Rols; a young son; his parents; and other members of a large, comparatively prosperous family.

All had not been going well for Martin, who seems to have been something of a misfit and a joke. He was able to consummate his marriage only after the village priest had exorcised his "demons." The day before Martin vanished, his father had accused him of stealing and selling several sacks of family grain.

Eight years later, after his parents had died, Martin Guerre returned to Artigat to reclaim his wife and property. Bertrande greeted him warmly, and no one questioned his identity, though he had changed considerably for the better. The villagers delighted in his stories of army life and were dazzled by the fact that he had learned how to read and write. He fathered two more children, one of whom died, and worked his farm hard and profitably.

This new life was without incident until the appearance in Artigat of three vagabonds, who identified Martin as Arnaud du Thil, a young man who had soldiered with the real Martin, who, they said, was alive and living in Flanders. None of this would have caused a serious stir until the day that Martin asked his uncle to account for how he had handled his property while Martin was away. Shortly after, the uncle filed suit against Martin, charging him with being an imposter.

All of this is by way of being an introduction to *The Return of Martin Guerre,* a fine new French film that retells the tale that has already served as the basis for novels, plays, and operettas. Writers of history and fiction are forever indebted to one Jean de Coras, the Toulouse parliamentary counselor appointed to handle the case and who later wrote a detailed account of Martin Guerre's two trials, which are the center of the film.

The Return of Martin Guerre, which opens today at the 68th Street Playhouse, is social history of an unusually rich sort. It has a quality of immediacy to equal Le Roy Ladurie's extraordinary book *Montaillou,* in which Mr. Ladurie reconstructs the social life of a French village in the fourteenth century.

As directed by Daniel Vigne, a French filmmaker new to American audiences, and as written by him and Jean-Claude Carrière, *The Return of Martin Guerre* has the kind of shapeliness that one associates more often with fiction than fact. However, though it resolves the mystery of Martin Guerre, it also leaves room in which to speculate on the nature of life in sixteenth-century Artigat, on its institutions—especially the church—on family ties, on the sanctity of marriage, property, and money.

Gérard Depardieu, who has recently been in danger of becoming a parody of his own striking screen personality, is superb as the returned veteran. The hulking Depardieu looks the way a sixteenth-century peasant should look or, as Mr. Vigne has said in an interview, he's one of the few contemporary actors who wouldn't be a sight gag in the period costumes. His is a beautifully executed performance, its power always controlled and not, as sometimes happens with Mr. Depardieu, exercised for its own flamboyant sake.

Almost as good and, in her own way, almost as mysterious is Nathalie Baye as the wife, whose fidelity is rewarded when Martin returns as a far better husband than when he left. Chief among the excellent supporting actors are Roger Planchon, who plays Jean de Coras, the investigator who is too wise to be shocked by the trials' revelations, and Maurice Barrier, as the uncle who initiates the court actions against Martin.

Most of the film was photographed in southwestern France, not far from Artigat, which André Neau, the cameraman, has lighted to suggest the tones of amber, olive, and umber associated with Bruegel's paintings of sixteenth-century village life. Michel Portal's original score, like the performances and the dialogue, avoids sounding archaic, without being anachronistic.

Like *La Nuit de Varennes*, *The Return of Martin Guerre* is a period film that, without seeming effort, speaks to our moment.

—V.C., June 10, 1983

REUBEN, REUBEN

Directed by Robert Ellis Miller; written by Julius J. Epstein, based on the novel by Peter DeVries and the play *Spofford* by Herman Shumlin; director of photography, Peter Stein; edited by Skip Lusk; music by Billy Goldenberg; production designer, Peter Larkin; produced by Walter Shenson; released by Twentieth Century Fox. Running time: 101 minutes.

With: Tom Conti (Gowan McGland), Kelly McGillis (Geneva Spofford), Roberts Blossom (Frank Spofford), Cynthia Harris (Bobby Springer), E. Katherine Kerr (Lucille Haxby), Joel Fabiani (Dr. Haxby), Lois Smith (Mare Spofford), Rex Robbins (C. B. Springer) and Kara Wilson (Edith McGland).

The character of Gowan McGland is pure Peter DeVries, and *Reuben, Reuben*, adapted from the DeVries novel by Julius J. Epstein and directed by Robert Ellis Miller, is one of the most buoyantly satiric fables yet made from a DeVries work. It's a small, unpushy movie of rare wit.

Gowan McGland is an epic mess of underemployed talent. He's a nonwriting Scottish poet who has chosen to exile himself in the rich, fiercely quaint, exurban Connecticut community of Woodsmoke. Gowan gives an occasional lecture, drinks nonstop, and makes love to bored, middle-aged women who come to him in his shabby digs at the Dew Drop Inn. For pocket money he steals the tips left for waiters in the expensive restaurants his wealthy patrons take him to.

In his baggy brown tweed suit, the only one he owns, he looks like the human manifestation of a hangover. It would seem he bathes only on the equinoxes and only on those that fall on a Saturday. He suffers a terminal case of what he frankly calls laziness but which one of his more literary-minded mistresses calls sloth.

As played by Tom Conti, the English actor who was applauded for his performance in *Whose Life Is It Anyway?* on Broadway, Gowan is a wonderfully engaging character. Like Joyce Cary's Gulley Jimson, he's someone who's great fun to watch but who'd be impossible to share even a county with.

Reuben, Reuben, which is taken mostly from the central portion of the DeVries novel and from a stage adaptation written by Herman Shumlin, is about several months in the life of Gowan McGland, whose surname is no accident, during which his squalid existence is brightened by a tawny blonde named Geneva Spofford (Kelly McGillis). As Mr. DeVries knew, though the movie doesn't admit it, Geneva's extraordinary youth and beauty mask the soul of a shrew. That, however, is the story that follows Gowan's in the DeVries novel.

Gowan's other conquests include Bobby Springer (Cynthia Harris), the head of the local women's club, and Lucille Haxby (E. Katherine Kerr), the wife of a celebrated dentist. If the film has any clear-cut moral, it's that you shouldn't make love to the wife of a dentist, not if the dentist is jealous and not if you have a bad dental situation.

Teeth play a large part in poor Gowan's problems. His teeth are in terrible shape. When he's not in actual pain, he's worrying about losing the last upper tooth that can support a permanent bridge. Says Gowan at one point, "I've always seen myself as backing toward the grave, tooth by tooth, poem by poem." Since Gowan has virtually ceased to write, you might think that he thinks he'll live forever.

Mr. Epstein clearly has a fondness for Mr. DeVries's language. The *Reuben, Reuben* screenplay is full of—without being overstuffed with—good lines. It has the kind of appreciation for the oddness of words you seldom find in films.

Early in the movie there's a monologue by Frank Spofford (Roberts Blossom), Geneva's eccentric grandfather, who refuses to describe himself as "merely" a chicken farmer. "There's nothing 'mere' about chicken farming," he says, a line that more or less forces us to think about chicken farming, for a minute, anyway.

Reuben, Reuben, which opens today at the Sutton Theater, works very quietly, obliquely. It has the class of the veteran craftsmen who made it, including Mr. Miller, the director of *The Heart Is a Lonely Hunter,* and Mr. Epstein, whose credits reach back to 1935. Either alone or in collaboration, Mr. Epstein has written such films as *Four Daughters, Mr. Skeffington,* and *Casablanca,* which was done with his twin brother, Philip G. Epstein, and Howard Koch.

That the film suggests something of the quality of the sort of English films we used to see in the 1960's is also understandable. The producer is Walter Shenson, the American filmmaker who, during a long residence in England, produced such memorable films as *The Mouse That Roared, A Hard Day's Night,* and *Help.*

Mr. Conti is fine in a big, rich role, but the members of the large supporting cast are equally good in roles that are sometimes far too brief. The landscape is filled with some of New York's best performers, including Miss Kerr, Miss Harris, Mr. Blossom, Lois Smith, and Scott Coffey, among others. As the younger woman in Gowan's life, Miss McGillis, an actress new to films, looks to be a find.

Though *Reuben, Reuben* is thoroughly enjoyable, and as stylishly acted as any American film of the year, it does have a problem that, I suspect, is built-in. As we see it, the life of Gowan McGland is a little too sweetly funny to support the film's eventual shape. Had it been nastier and more cruel, we might feel that what happens is both inevitable and arbitrary, a contradiction embraced by great comedy. As it is, *Reuben, Reuben* turns out to be a joke, the kind that, like a pun, calls attention to itself and seems to be at the expense of the audience.

—*V.C., December 19, 1983*

REVERSAL OF FORTUNE

Directed by Barbet Schroeder; written by Nicholas Kazan, based on the book by Alan M. Dershowitz; director of photography, Luciano Tovoli; edited by Lee Percy; music by Mark Isham; production designer, Mel Bourne; produced by Edward R. Pressman and Oliver Stone; released by Warner Brothers. Running time: 110 minutes.

With: Glenn Close (Sunny von Bülow), Jeremy Irons (Claus von Bülow), Ron Silver (Alan M. Dershowitz), Annabella Sciorra (Carol), Uta Hagen (Maria), Fisher Stevens (David Marriott) and Christine Baranski (Andrea Reynolds).

That was my body," says the voice of the comatose Sunny von Bülow (Glenn Close) on the soundtrack at the beginning of Reversal of Fortune. Looking as still as death but serene and, somehow, very rich, she lies in bed in a hospital room, attached to machines that efficiently feed and cleanse her system.

"I never woke from this coma, and never will," she goes on. "I could remain this way for a very long time." There is just the slightest hint of a pause, and then the kicker: "Brain dead and body better than ever."

This figure of a woman who is alive but not living is the haunted central image of *Reversal of Fortune,* the lively, provocative, exquisitely acted screen adaptation of Alan M. Dershowitz's book about high society's real-life von Bülow case.

Mr. Dershowitz is the Harvard law professor and aggressive, outspoken lawyer who seems to specialize in unpopular causes. In 1982, after Claus von Bülow had been convicted on two counts of assault with intent to murder his wife, Martha, also called Sunny, Mr. von Bülow hired Mr. Dershowitz to prepare his appeal.

To those who followed the court case only in fits and starts, and even to those who followed it with the delighted fidelity of *Dallas* fans, there appeared to be no doubt about Mr. von Bülow's guilt. It was the kind of case to which one really didn't have to pay attention in order to have an informed opinion.

Mrs. von Bülow was immensely rich. Mr. von Bülow wasn't. She was the prototypical American heiress who, like a Henry James heroine, had gone to Europe to find an aristocratic husband.

The first was Prince Alfred von Auersperg, by whom she had two children, and the second was Mr. von Bülow, whose name originally was Claus Borberg but who later took his mother's maiden name. He seems to have adopted the "von" at the insistence of his bride when he married Martha Crawford von Auersperg. They had one child.

Mr. von Bülow, a wellborn Dane, had been brought up in England by his mother after the Germans occupied Denmark during World War II. He went to Cambridge, became an apprentice barrister, moved in society, and, at one point, was an aide to J. Paul Getty, the American billionaire.

During the period that ended when his wife went into her second mysterious coma, which turned out to be irreversible, Mr. and Mrs. von Bülow had been talking about divorce, and he was involved in an affair that she knew about. Mr. von Bülow was not famous for his discretion or his common touch. He was reported to be as arrogant and haughty as a middle-European nobleman in a grade-B movie.

Before the first trial in Newport, Rhode Island, the script of the case had been written, if not in a court, then in some of the most dearly held assumptions of American literature, from nineteenth-century novels to twentieth-century tabloid journalism and Hollywood movies.

As written by Nicholas Kazan and directed by Barbet Schroeder, the new film is, in the unusual breadth of its concerns, a serious, invigorating American comedy about class, money, greed, and, most important, the possibility of justice in the American criminal court system.

What makes it so instructively entertaining is the pivotal character of Claus von Bülow, played by Jeremy Irons within an inch of his professional life. It's a fine, devastating performance, affected, mannered, edgy, though seemingly ever in complete control. Mr. Irons comes very close to being too good to be true.

The accent is upper-class English, perhaps with a touch of Danish still buried within, overlaid with English twit. He seems someone very easy to dismiss, not easy to care about. He's a joke.

When Alan Dershowitz (Ron Silver) goes to meet Claus in his Park Avenue apartment, shortly after the first trial, Claus greets him in the manner of a constitutional monarch putting a new Minister of Fisheries at ease: "Professor Dershowitz, hello, hello, hello. How good of you to come."

The entire initial interview is a little unreal. Claus admits that the evidence produced at the trial was damning but, he charmingly reassures Alan: "I am innocent. You have my word as a gentleman." Among the things to which he does admit is that he has tremendous admiration for the Jewish people.

Gentlemen's words don't mean much in the world in which Alan practices. Nor, really, does guilt or innocence. Issues of law are the point. Alan isn't the sort of lawyer who becomes friendly with his clients. Nor is he often surprised by them, but it does happen.

Somewhat later Alan makes a perfunctory comment about the severity of Claus's thirty-year prison sentence. Claus replies with majesty, "For a man who twice tried to murder his wife, anything less would be monstrous."

That line and a number of others come directly from the Dershowitz book, which Mr. Kazan has turned into one of the most satisfying courtroom dramas in years. Forget the trumped-up superficial nonsense of *Presumed Innocent*. This "presumed guilty" tale is far more rewarding.

In fact, very little of *Reversal of Fortune* takes place in a courtroom, though it plays as if it were being put before a judge and jury. The movie, like the book, is the story of how Alan and a large team of assistants, including some of his law students, set about to appeal the first verdict and win a new trial for Claus.

It is fascinating stuff and all the more dramatic because of the ambiguous nature of the defendant. The film wouldn't have half the emotional and intellectual punch if the audience, going in, was already convinced that Claus was nothing more than an aging Peter Pan.

His innocence or guilt is, theoretically anyway, not the film's concern, though the audience probably will come to agree with the findings of his lawyers.

The drama of the film, as of Mr. Dershowitz's book, results from the investigation that reveals the essential sloppiness of so much of the circumstantial evidence that convicted Claus.

There is the crucial testimony (later found to be in error) of Sunny's dour, possessive German maid, Maria, played by the great Uta Hagen.

It is further found that evidence had been withheld at the first trial and some evidence tampered with, or "improved," by person or persons unknown. Most important are the findings relating to the needle with which Claus is accused of having injected Sunny with a near-lethal shot of insulin.

This is the "mystery" part of the film, and it is first-rate, but as Sunny remarks on the soundtrack, "It's easy to forget all this is about me."

That can happen in the course of a criminal trial. The victim is only one piece of evidence among many. It doesn't happen in the film. Though *Reversal of Fortune* is a courtroom drama, Mr. Schroeder and Mr. Kazan never forget the time and place that help to shape the events.

The movie can't possibly make use of all of the legal details that give heft to the book, but it presents a witty and vivid picture of the characters and their lives. Even the decision to have the forever-muted Sunny narrate her story works as literary license. It also enriches the portrait of the sad, bemused woman who says: "I liked to be in bed. I didn't much like anything else."

The private lives of Sunny and Claus, their children, and his lovers are presented with a great deal of care (various laws must be observed) but with a lot of insight. The way the very rich live seems always to be full of surprises, above and beyond those having to do with the consumption of alcohol and drugs.

In one of the flashbacks, the audience is treated to the picture of Claus preparing to get into bed with Sunny, who likes the room to be very cold. He wears a wool cap, a sweater, socks, and a scarf. At the dinner table Sunny wolfs down not oysters and champagne but an oversize ice cream sundae.

Beginning with Mr. Irons's, all of the principal performances are terrific, including those of Miss Close, who hovers over the film more often than she is in it, Miss Hagen, and Christine Baranski, who plays Claus's second mistress, Andrea Reynolds.

If Mr. Irons's Claus von Bülow gives the film its satiric tone, Mr. Silver's Alan Dershowitz gives it its energy and its singularly tough, unsentimental conscience.

It's easy to accept Mr. Silver as the man who, in his book, admits that access to a lot of money saved Mr. von Bülow. Mr. Dershowitz then adds, "Reform efforts should be directed not at reducing the justice available to the rich, but at raising the standard of justice for all."

There is a high degree of sometimes shocking intelligence running through *Reversal of Fortune*.

It's common to just about all of the films made by Mr. Schroeder, the gifted, not easily categorized French producer and director. Mr. Schroeder's last movie, *Barfly,* was set in Los Angeles, on the other side of the American continent, at the other end of the social scale, on Skid Row. *Reversal of Fortune* is a perfect American companion piece.

—V.C., October 17, 1990

RICHARD III

Produced and directed by Laurence Olivier; written by Mr. Olivier, Alan Dent, Colley Cibber and David Garrick, based on the play by William Shakespeare; cinematographer, Otto Heller; edited by Helga Cranston; music by William Walton; production designer, Roger Furse; released by London Films. Running time: 158 minutes.

With: Sir Laurence Olivier (Richard III), Sir Ralph Richardson (Buckingham), Sir John Gielgud (Clarence), Claire Bloom (Lady Anne), Sir Cedric Hardwicke (King Edward IV), Alec Clunes (Hastings), Pamela Brown (Jane Shore), Mary Kerridge (Queen Elizabeth), Norman Wooland (Catesby) and Helen Haye (Dutchess of York/Queen Mother).

The measure of Sir Laurence Olivier's genius for putting Shakespeare's plays on the screen is beautifully and brilliantly exhibited in his production and performance of *Richard III.*

This latest of Sir Laurence's films from Shakespeare, done in colors of which a Rembrandt might be proud and projected in the large-screen VistaVision that gives the pictures strong clarity and depth, opened last night at the Bijou with a benefit for the Actors Fund of America.

Richard III was shown on the National Broadcasting Company television network from 2:30 to 5:30 P.M. It marked the first time that a motion picture had its premiere on the two media on the same day. More important, however, was the fact that this was television's longest theatrical presentation on record, according to NBC spokesmen.

The three-hour entertainment, which surpassed such previous lengthy offerings as the two-hour *Peter Pan,* was televised over 146 stations in forty-five states. Although NBC officials could not estimate the number of viewers late last night, network representatives earlier in the week thought it possible that 25,000,000 persons would see the telecast.

Only a small fraction of these viewers saw the Technicolor *Richard III* in its various hues, since only about 25,000 color TV sets are in use throughout the country.

The millions of TV viewers saw a slightly abbreviated version of Shakespeare's classic than was offered at the Bijou. Some two or three minutes were cut from the film's original two-hour-and-forty-minute running time.

Video viewers were spared such scenes as the decapitation of Hastings, the murder by suffocation of the child princes in the Tower, and the climactic stabbing and death agonies of Richard III.

The first consideration in a production of *Richard III* is the quality of the portrayal of the title character. All other considerations—the substance and placing of the scenes, the staging, the lesser characterizations—are secondary to this.

For Richard, the dark, misshapen monster of the English House of York in those medieval years when it was waging the War of the Roses with the stubborn Lancasters, is the towering focal figure in this complex drama of plots and murders at court. And the way he is played makes all the difference in how the whole thing comes off.

Sir Laurence's Richard is tremendous—a weird, poisonous portrait of a super-rogue whose dark designs are candidly acknowledged with lick-lip relish and sardonic wit. Heavily made-up with one dead eyelid, a hatchet nose, a withered hand, a humped back, a drooping shoulder, and a twisted, limping leg, he is a freakish-looking figure that Sir Laurence so articulates that he has an electric vitality and a fascinatingly grotesque grace. A grating voice, too, is a feature of his physical oddity.

More important to the character, however, is the studiousness and subtlety with which Sir Laurence builds up tension within him as his mischiefs and crimes accumulate. From a glib and egotistical conniver at the outset of the play, when he confides his clever purpose to the audience and hypocritically woos Lady Anne, he becomes a cold and desperate tyrant after he has ordered Clarence and Hastings dispatched and faces up to the horror of slaying the little princes in the Tower.

And then, toward the end, when his conscience parades before his eyes the morbid ghosts of all his pitiful victims on the eve of the battle of Bosworth Field, he is lost of all feeling save terror and a horrible dread of his fate.

Sir Laurence, as director as well as actor, has clearly and artfully contrived to emphasize Richard's isolation and his almost pathetic loneliness. He sets him apart from the others, by cinematic design as well as by mood. Even when intimately plotting with Buckingham, his bland confederate, he seems alone. No wonder one feels some sorrow for him—for this dark gangster of another age—when he dies on the ground, thrashing in torment, with spears sticking in him like a pig.

Since he presents us a Richard who is vivid, exciting, and sound in his psychological complication (he's a man who makes his aggressions awfully clear!), Sir Laurence may be readily forgiven some slight liberties with Shakespeare's text. He opens the picture, for instance, with the coronation of Richard's brother, Edward IV, which is not in the play but which does help to set the regal scene and the dramatic plan. He has eliminated characters. He shows us Edward's mistress in the flesh (she is only mentioned by Shakespeare). And he has used some helpful lines that were added to the play by Colley Cibber, an eighteenth-century thespian.

Also, Sir Laurence has seen to it that none of the other characters has quite the air of importance—or vitality and definition—that Richard has.

Sir Ralph Richardson's Buckingham, for instance, seems quite mild and complacent for a man who would ally himself so cold-bloodedly with Richard's unconscionable schemes. Likewise, Sir John Gielgud's Clarence, Alec Clunes's Hastings, and Sir Cedric Hardwicke's Edward seem peculiarly shallow and ineffectual as experienced intriguers. Their performing and speaking are impeccable, like that of English gentlemen, but their stature is not impressive. They are shadowed by Richard's silhouette.

Most forceful of the ladies is Mary Kerridge as Edward's queen. She fully conveys a wife's anxiety and a mother's helpless grief. Claire Bloom as Lady Anne, the nubile widow who falls for Richard's sham romance, is lovely, but gives slight definition or plausibility to this skimpy role. Helen Haye as the aged queen mother quietly symbolizes despair, and Pamela Brown is impressively silent but suggestive as Edward's mistress, Jane Shore.

The staging in all respects is brilliant, the sets and costumes illustrate the violent age, and the musical score creates climates in the breathing of strings and lutes. Some interesting techniques of cinema have been used to get strong effects (as with close-ups and moving shadows) that could not be got on the stage.

The battle of Bosworth Field is modest, as such things go in films, but here again Sir Laurence has seen to it that Richard is not pictorially overwhelmed. Enough violence has already happened to sate the bloodthirsty, anyhow. It sets up just sufficient opposition to give climactic irony to the line (introduced by Cibber) that the doomed king wryly speaks as he goes forth to suffer his inevitable destruction:

"Conscience avaunt! Richard's himself again!"

Richard III represented perhaps the biggest financial gamble taken by NBC. Although the network paid $500,000 last June for the right to televise the drama, which is not a record price for a show, it had to wait six months before General Motors came forward to sponsor it.

General Motors reportedly paid $425,000 for the privilege. The full rate for air time was about $200,000, and the company is sharing the price paid by NBC for the film.

NBC also shares in the theater income of *Richard* in the United States. It will receive a maximum of $300,000 if the film reaches a gross of $350,000.

—*B.C., March 12, 1956*

RIDE THE HIGH COUNTRY

Directed by Sam Peckinpah; written by N. B. Stone Jr.; cinematographer, Lucien Ballard; edited by Frank Santillo; music by George Bassman; art designer, George W. Davis; produced by Richard E. Lyons; released by Metro-Goldwyn-Mayer. Running time: 94 minutes.

With: Joel McCrea (Steve Judd), Randolph Scott (Gil Westrum), Mariette Hartley (Elsa), Ronald Starr (Heck Longtree), R. G. Armstrong (Joshua Knudsen) and James Drury (Billy Hammond).

As for yesterday's new double bill in neighborhood theaters, *The Tartars* (Orson Welles and Victor Mature) is trash and *Ride the High Country* (Joel McCrea and Randolph Scott) is a perfectly dandy little Western.

Let's take care of history first, at least according to Metro-Goldwyn-Mayer, which sponsored the Italian-made color spectacle. Big it is—and loud—and gory, and the biggest thing in sight is Mr. Welles as an evil barbarian chief. At this point in his career he looks like a walking house.

At any rate, Mr. Welles and Mr. Mature, as a noble Viking landlubber, slug it out, as do their yowling armies, trailed by such people as Folco Lulli, Bella Cortez, Luciano Marin, and Arnaldo Foa. The last two are quite persuasive. As for the dubbed English, one variation has the "poor Slavs" called "slobs." At least that's what it sounds like in *The Tartars*.

In contrast, Metro's uncluttered Western supplement is a downright pleasure to watch. Take two corn-belt veterans like Mr. McCrea and Mr. Scott, give them a very tangy script (by N. B. Stone Jr.), a trim supporting cast, and a good director (Sam Peckinpah), and you have the most disarming little horse opera in months.

From the opening scene, when the two stars, as a couple of prairie old-timers, start reminiscing about wilder and woolier days, the picture projects a steady, natural blend of wisdom and humor. Excellently photographed in color against some lovely natural vistas, the picture finds the seasoned derelicts and their young partner, Ronald Starr, protecting a gold shipment (for a change) and salvaging an innocent girl, Mariette Hartley, from a lusty mining camp.

Symbols of a waning era who eventually clash over right and wrong, Messrs. McCrea and Scott mesh perfectly, with the latter getting the drollest lines—and there are plenty.

In the humor department, the entire film is spur-sharp, though the broad antics of the villains, a cutthroat quartet, could have been toned down somewhat. On the other hand, the salty grotesqueness of a saloon wedding (stunningly tinted) is pure gold. The final line caps the picture like a bottletop.

The two young people are quite good, especially Miss Hartley, a newcomer with real promise. R. M. Armstrong and Edgar Buchanan also contribute telling bits. We know little about the director and scenarist, but Mr. Peckinpah and Mr. Stone certainly have what it takes. And so, if anybody ever doubted it, do a couple of leathery, graying hombres named McCrea and Scott.

—*B.C., June 21, 1962*

RIFIFI

Directed by Jules Dassin; written (in French, with English subtitles) by Mr. Dassin, René Wheeler and Auguste Le Breton, based on the novel by Mr. Le Breton; cinematographer, Philippe Agostini; edited by Roger Dwyre; music by Georges Auric; art designer, Auguste Capelier; produced by René G. Vuattoux; released by United Motion Picture Organization. Black and white. Running time: 117 minutes.

With: Jean Servais (Tony Stephanois), Carl Mohner (Jo), Robert Manuel (Mario), Perlo Vita (Cesar), Marie Sabouret (Mado), Janine Darcey (Louise) and Claude Sylvain (Ida)

Do you want to see a tough gangster picture? Do you want to see a crime film that makes the characters of Mickey Spillane seem like sissies and, at the same time, gives you the thrill of being an inside participant in a terrific Parisian robbery? Then go to see *Rififi*, which opened at the Fine Arts last night. This is perhaps the keenest crime film that ever came from France, including *Pepe le Moko* and some of the best of Louis Jouvet and Jean Gabin.

Jules Dassin, former Hollywood director, adapted and directed this job about the planning and execution of the nighttime robbery of a swanky English jewelry shop in the Rue de Rivoli. Mr. Dassin, under the name of Perlo Vita, also plays one of the leading roles.

But there is more than just a rundown on a robbery in this beautifully fashioned black-and-white film. It has a flavor of crooks and kept women and Montmartre "boîtes" that you can just about smell. And after the robbery there follows a second crisis when another gang tries to get the swag by kidnapping the small son of one of the jewel thieves and holding him until the robbers kick in.

The robbery itself is terrific—a good solid half-hour in which the four thieves who have planned it with precision get into the apartment above the jewelry store and then, with the skill and calculation of expert engineers, cut their way down into the office and into the formidable safe.

Mr. Dassin has staged it like a ballet. Not a word is spoken by the thieves in that half-hour, which represents the better part of a night—from midnight until six A.M. in elapsed time. But he has paced it and checked it against a wristwatch until you in the audience almost scream when somebody accidentally touches a piano key or a little thing goes wrong.

What makes it particularly vital is that Mr. Dassin has already introduced his thieves in a way that puts you very much on their side. There is the brains of the gang, a tough "square-shooter," played tautly and grimly by Jean Servais. Then there is his younger disciple, a handsome and muscular family man and father of the boy later kidnapped. Carl Mohner plays him attractively. Next there is an amiable Italian who has a carefree, voluptuous doll. He is Robert Manuel. And, finally, there is the fellow who is the expert at cracking safes. He is a little rascal whose weakness is women. That is Mr. Dassin.

Once the robbery is completed, you are still frankly rooting for them—and that's what makes the intrusion of the rivals so outrageous and menacing. The terror is intensified by the climate of brutality that surrounds the leader of the rival gang, a nightclub owner, played by Marcel Lupovici, a cold, dark thug. Vice hangs like smoke in his clip joint. There is prostitution, dope. (Boy, what would they have done to this picture if it had been put up to Hollywood's Production Code!)

But there is also a poetry about it—and a poetic

justice, too. Mr. Dassin has got the tender beauty of Paris at dawn, when there is no one stirring but milkmen, street cleaners, gendarmes—and thieves. And he has ended his film with a feeling for the pathos of the comédie humaine that would do justice to a story with a more exalting theme.

Rififi compares more than favorably with the memorable Hollywood film *The Asphalt Jungle.* It has spawned a new genre of films in France. The dialogue is well translated in English subtitles which say everything but the dirty words.

—B.C., *June 6, 1956*

THE RIGHT STUFF

Directed by Philip Kaufman: written by Mr. Kaufman, based on the book by Tom Wolfe: director of photography. Caleb Deschanel: edited by Glenn Farr. Lisa Fruchtman. Stephen A. Rotter. Tom Rolf and Douglas Stewart: music by Bill Conti: production designer. Geoffrey Kirkland: produced by Irwin Winkler and Robert Chartoff: released by Warner Brothers. Running time: 192 minutes.

With: Sam Shepard (Chuck Yeager). Scott Glenn (Alan Shepard). Ed Harris (John Glenn). Dennis Quaid (Gordon Cooper). Fred Ward (Gus Grissom). Barbara Hershey (Glennis Yeager). Kim Stanley (Pancho Barnes). Veronica Cartwright (Betty Grissom). Pamela Reed (Trudy Cooper). Scott Paulin (Deke Slayton). Charles Frank (Scott Carpenter). Lance Henrikson (Wally Schirra) and Donald Moffat (Lyndon B. Johnson).

*T*he Right Stuff, Philip Kaufman's rousing, funny screen adaptation of Tom Wolfe's book about Project Mercury and America's first astronauts, is probably the brightest and the best rookie/cadet movie ever made, though the rookies and cadets are seasoned pilots and officers.

The film almost makes one glad to be alive in spite of famines, wars, and even the "greenhouse effect," which, if the Environmental Protection Agency is correct, means that the entire earth is inside its own space capsule that's rapidly overheating. *The Right Stuff* is full of short-term pleasures that yield to doubts only after the film is over.

Although the film, which opens today at the Beekman and other theaters, focuses mainly on the care, feeding, training, and exploitation of the astronauts, its most commanding figure is not an astronaut but a great test pilot, Chuck Yeager, who exemplifies everything represented by the title.

Mr. Yeager, who in 1947 became the first man in the world to break the sound barrier, was not a member of Project Mercury, but his story, in the film as in the book, more or less frames those of the astronauts. Systematically testing himself as well as his planes or, in the jargon of the space trade, "pushing the outside of the envelope," Mr. Yeager was the man against whom any pilot who thought he had the right stuff measured himself.

As played by Sam Shepard, the tall, lanky playwright-actor, the film's Chuck Yeager seems also to personify the reason and sanity that came close to being lost in the United States' hysterical drive first to catch up with the Soviet Union's space program and then to surpass it. Both as the character he plays and as an ironic screen presence, Mr. Shepard gives the film much well-needed heft. He is its center of gravity.

The three astronauts who come most vividly to life in the film are John Glenn (Ed Harris), the "clean Marine" who made this country's first successful orbital flight (and who today is the Democratic Senator from Ohio seeking his party's presidential nomination); Alan Shepard (Scott Glenn), the first American to ride a space capsule in suborbital flight; and Gordon Cooper (Dennis Quaid), the comically self-confident astronaut whose successful orbital flight brought Project Mercury to its conclusion.

Much was made of Mr. Wolfe's accomplishment in finding the astronauts' idiosyncrasies that give the lie to the handsome, cookie-cutter profiles that were promoted, especially in Life magazine, during the life of Project Mercury in the late 1950's and early 1960's. Like the book, the movie strips away the nonsense to find—underneath the nonsense—men who are not really much different from their official portraits.

It's true that not all of the other astronauts were taken by the pieties that flowed so effortlessly from John Glenn's lips during his public appearances publicizing Project Mercury. It's also true that we see Alan

Shepard violently objecting when Glenn attempts to scold the other astronauts for hell-raising and womanizing after hours. The astronauts use four-letter words and tell scatological jokes. We are even given indications that the marriage of Gordon and Trudy Cooper (Pamela Reed) is not as happy as it might be.

Yet these men remain virtually flawless heroes, almost too good, decent, and brave to be true, and it's a measure of how successful the movie is that one is inclined to believe it. The movie doesn't say it, but it's difficult to look at *The Right Stuff* without thinking that they represent the last gasp of nineteenth-century American WASPdom.

Because they are generally so perfect, the movie's most appealing astronaut is Gus Grissom (Fred Ward), who made Project Mercury's second suborbital flight, the one that ended in something of a mess when the capsule's hatch was prematurely blown and the capsule lost. Does or doesn't Gus Grissom have the right stuff? This impertinent question keeps the movie from becoming the unadulterated paean to American heroism and know-how it might otherwise have been.

The Right Stuff is very long—over three hours—but it has to be to cover the ground and space it must. Mr. Kaufman's screenplay is very efficient in the way it introduces so many characters and then crosscuts among them without confusion or repetition. The domestic lives of John Glenn, Gordon Cooper, and Gus Grissom are movingly detailed. Best of all, the flight footage is remarkably convincing, from Shepard's first suborbital flight, when a full bladder threatened the entire operation, through Glenn's three orbits of the earth, and his perilous descent, and, finally, Chuck Yeager's last flight, his near-fatal attempt to set a new speed record in the NF-104 airplane.

Some things are not so good. The early desert sequences at Muroc, now Edwards Air Force Base, are so poetically photographed one gets the impression that the sun seldom sets in this desert but hangs always at five P.M. There is a perfunctory, service-comedy jokiness about urine specimens and barium enemas during flight training. The movie sees all government officials as idiots, especially a couple of recruiters played by Jeff Goldblum and Harry Shearer. Though President Eisenhower is treated with a sort of dim respect, Lyndon B. Johnson, seen first as the Senate

majority leader and then as vice president, is made to look like a publicity-seeking buffoon. As played by Donald Moffat, who looks enough like the late politician to make a career impersonating him in revues, the movie's Lyndon Johnson is a character taken out of context.

More troublesome is the gingerly way the movie deals with the exploitation of the astronauts, particularly their deal with Time Inc. that gave *Life* magazine exclusive rights to their stories. Is one correct in assuming that the astronauts saw this as simply their due, their financial reward for celebrityhood, another glorious benefit provided by this land of opportunity? One can't be sure.

Very clear, however, is the meaning of the final sequence in which the film crosscuts between the heroic Chuck Yeager, testing his NF-104 over the California desert, and the astronauts in Texas, captured symbols of heroism, attending a gaudy, Lyndon Johnson-hosted barbecue that stars them alongside Sally Rand, the fan dancer.

There's not a weak performance in the entire film. In addition to those actors already mentioned, I'd like to cite Barbara Hershey, who plays Chuck Yeager's wife, Glennis; Mary Jo Deschanel, as Annie Glenn; Veronica Cartwright, as Betty Grissom, a wife who has very mixed feelings about the treatment of her husband; and Kim Stanley as Pancho Barnes, the tough-talking owner of the desert saloon that becomes a hangout for pilots at Edwards Air Force Base.

—*V.C., October 21, 1983*

RISKY BUSINESS

Written and directed by Paul Brickman; directors of photography, Reynaldo Villalobos and Bruce Surtees; edited by Richard Chew; music by Tangerine Dream; produced by Jon Avnet and Steve Tisch; released by Warner Brothers. Running time: 98 minutes.

With: Tom Cruise (Joel), Rebecca De Mornay (Lana), Curtis Armstrong (Miles), Bronson Pinchot (Barry), Raphael Sbarge (Glenn), Joe Pantoliano (Guido), Nicholas Pryor (Joel's Father), Janet Carroll (Joel's Mother), Shera Danese (Vicki) and Richard Masur (Rutherford).

Although Paul Brickman's *Risky Business* shows an abundance of style, you would be hard pressed to find a film whose hero's problems are of less concern to the world at large. Joel Goodsen (Tom Cruise) is an affluent suburban teenager, sex-starved yet smug, whose erotic daydreams begin to come true, once his parents go on vacation and leave him to hold the fort.

Joel's rebellion starts slowly, as he downs a glass of expensive Scotch with his TV dinner, but it escalates in a hurry. Eventually, he winds up operating an impromptu brothel, as well as driving his father's $40,000 car into the drink. Even feats like these manage to work to Joel's advantage.

As written and directed by Mr. Brickman, *Risky Business* is part satire, part would-be suburban poetry, and part shameless showing off. Mr. Brickman's talents are evident, but they're unevenly applied to this material; he's as capable of a slow, loving shot of a lawn being watered as of a witticism that's original and wry. The best things in *Risky Business,* opening today at the Sutton and other theaters, really are fresh, like Joel's fantasy of finding the house surrounded by the police as a man with a megaphone warns "Get off the baby-sitter!" On the other hand, there are too many moments when Mr. Brickman's pretensions fly out of control.

The casting is especially erratic. Joel's suburban parents, played by Nicholas Pryor and Janet Carroll, are crude caricatures. And a few of his friends are terrifically unappealing, speaking too slowly and savoring every nuance of some less than fascinating dialogue. On the other hand, Rebecca De Mornay is disarming as a call girl who looks more like a college girl, and who figures importantly in Joel's clean-cut daydreams. Mr. Cruise makes Joel's transformation from straight arrow to entrepreneur about as credible as it can be made.

Mr. Brickman, who favors a lot of portentous, panning camera motions, occasionally interjects something really unexpected, like the music that blares wildly when Joel starts his father's sports car, then stops abruptly as the car stalls. One funny moment, also tied to the music (the film has a highly effective rock score, with electronic incidental music by Tangerine Dream), has Joel bursting out of his dull workaday personality by suddenly grabbing a candlestick, then a fireplace poker, and pretending he's one very raunchy rock star.

Mr. Brickman, who wrote the screenplay for Jonathan Demme's *Handle with Care,* makes his directing debut here, and it's both promising and exasperating. Though his film can be all too knowing at times, it lacks much irony or distance where the real importance of either Joel or his situation is concerned.

However, *Risky Business* improves as it goes along—once it gets past, say, Joel's solemnly presented fantasy of a girl in a shower who asks him to wash her back, thus making him three hours late to take the college boards and ruining his future. This sequence begins the movie, and it seems to be rendered altogether seriously. Only toward the end—when Joel sinks the Porsche, or when his mother discovers that her beloved crystal egg has been cracked (Joel finds himself using it as a sort of football)—are these sorts of tragedies seen in any kind of perspective.

—*J.M., August 5, 1983*

RIVER'S EDGE

Directed by Tim Hunter; written by Neal Jimenez; director of photography, Frederick Elmes; edited by Howard Smith and Sonya Sones; music by Jurgen Knieper; production designer, John Muto; produced by Sarah Pillsbury, Midge Sanford and David Streit; released by Island Pictures. Running time: 99 minutes.

With: Crispin Glover (Layne), Keanu Reeves (Matt), Ione Skye Leitch (Clarissa), Daniel Roebuck (Samson), Dennis Hopper (Feck), Joshua Miller (Tim), Roxana Zal (Maggie), Josh Richman (Tony), Phil Brock (Mike) and Danyi Deats (Jamie).

The generation gap, as revealed in Tim Hunter's bitter and disturbing new film, *River's Edge,* is the thing that divides Samson (Daniel Roebuck) and Feck (Dennis Hopper). Long ago, Feck murdered his girlfriend—but he lived to regret it, and the killing has made him a crazy, desperate loner, a hermit who keeps an inflatable party doll as his only companion. Samson is younger, calmer, and very different. As the film begins, Samson has just strangled a young woman who said something unpleasant about his mother. He doesn't regret it; in fact, he doesn't feel a thing.

River's Edge, which opens today at the Baronet, is about the anomie of Samson and his friends in the face of this inexplicable violence. Their reaction is so casual that it comes as a shock. After an opening scene depicting a tough-looking boy named Tim throwing his sister's favorite doll into a river, and another in which Samson sits beside the body of a young woman named Jamie, it develops that twelve-year-old Tim (Joshua Miller) has seen Samson commit the crime. It also develops that for Tim, Samson's act isn't much different from his own. Tim accosts Samson, tells him what he knows, and then asks for some drugs. It's as simple as that.

Later on, when Samson (who is nicknamed John) tells his school friends what he's done, they are only slightly more concerned. They think he is joking. So he shows them Jamie's body, over which Mr. Hunter's camera lingers time and again during the film, as if to try to summon something from the audience that the characters themselves do not feel. The sight of the body, and the suggestion that their classmate Jamie has been raped as well as strangled, is only marginally more upsetting for Jamie's girlfriends than it is for the boys.

Though the girls are a little more worried about the etiquette of the situation—most specifically, about whether to tell the police—the whole group of Jamie and Samson's peers remains surprisingly calm. *River's Edge* is about their sincere, bewildered efforts to grasp the difference between killing a doll and killing a person, and about the audience's own efforts to understand how any amount of drug taking and parental indifference can induce this kind of stupor.

As he demonstrated in *Tex,* Mr. Hunter has an extraordinarily clear understanding of teenage characters, especially those who must find their own paths without much parental supervision. But the S. E. Hinton story for that film is a great deal more innocent than this one, and a lot more easily understood. While Mr. Hunter retains his ear for adolescent dialogue (the screenplay is by Neal Jimenez) and his eye for the aimless, restless behavior of these characters, neither he nor we can easily make the necessary leap to understand their casualness about Samson's crime. That Mr. Hunter is brave enough to avoid easy moralizing and easy explanations finally makes his film harder to fathom.

Much of *River's Edge*—which is based on several actual incidents, especially one in northern California—is acted with utter conviction by a fine and largely unknown young cast. But the uncertain conceptions of a few key characters are damaging, especially that of Layne, who in his confusion becomes Samson's accomplice. Layne thinks himself more daring than his classmates, and without question he is more stoned. That leads him to conclude that loyalty to Samson is the only practical option. Samson and Jamie were both friends, he reasons, but it is Samson who's still alive and needs support. This is the film's key moral position, but it is explicated cartoonishly by Crispin Glover, who makes Layne a larger-than-life caricature and creates a noisy, comic impersonation instead of a lifelike character. Nor does it help that one of the film's other moral polarities comes from a sixties-minded, hipper-than-thou schoolteacher who declares, "We took to the streets and made a difference!" To his bored, jaded eighties high-school students, this kind of self-righteousness makes no sense at all.

Most of the performances are as natural and credible as the ones in *Tex,* with Mr. Roebuck a sad and helpless figure as Samson, and Keanu Reeves affecting and sympathetic as Tim's older brother; a different kind of generation gap already exists between these two, and the threat of fratricide between them leads to the film's most frightening confrontation. The ravishing Ione Skye Leitch (daughter of the singer Donovan) seems convincingly troubled as the character who must wonder why she feels more watching television tragedies than she does about her dead friend. And Mr. Hopper, whose scenes with the party doll ought to be thoroughly ridiculous, once again makes himself a very powerful presence. For better or worse, Mr. Hopper is back with a vengeance.

Though its midwestern locale and lower socioeconomic stratum give it a different setting, *River's Edge* shares something with Bret Easton Ellis's *Less Than Zero,* a novel that is also full of directionless, drugtaking teenage characters who are without moral moorings and left entirely to their own devices. This is as chilling to witness as it is difficult to dramatize, if only because at their centers these lives are already so empty.

—*J.M., May 8, 1987*

THE ROAD WARRIOR

Directed by George Miller: written by Terry Hayes. Mr. Miller and Brian Hannant: director of photography. Dean Semler: edited by David Stiven. Tim Wellburn. Michael Balson and Michael Chirgwin: music by Brian May: art designer. Graham Walker: produced by Byron Kennedy: released by Warner Brothers. Running time: 94 minutes.

With: Mel Gibson (Max). Bruce Spence (Gyro Captain). Vernon Wells (Wez). Emil Minty (Feral Kid). Mike Preston (Pappagallo). Kjell Nilsson (Humungus). Virginia Hey (Warrior Woman) and Syd Heylen (Curmudgeon).

Never has a film's vision of the post-nuclear-holocaust world seemed quite as desolate and as brutal, or as action-packed and sometimes as funny, as in George Miller's apocalyptic *The Road Warrior,* an extravagant film fantasy that looks like a sado-masochistic comic book come to life.

The film stars Mel Gibson, the New York-born, Australian-bred actor (*Gallipoli, Tim*) who played the title role in Mr. Miller's *Mad Max,* to which, as I understand it, *The Road Warrior* is a sequel.

As *The Road Warrior* begins, World War III has just ended. Civilization has died. So have coherence and trust and hope. Max (Mr. Gibson) recalls the gritty, haunted quality of the young Steve McQueen. He's a sort of high-octane Lancelot who, accompanied by a loyal dog of extremely high I.Q., drives his old, perfectly preserved, souped-up hot-rod across the parched landscape of the Australian outback, not in search of the Holy Grail, but of gasoline. Gasoline allows Max to continue his furious, existential journey, which is virtually nonstop, from nowhere to nowhere. When the world has come to an end, there's no place else to go.

The Road Warrior, written by Terry Hayes and Mr. Miller with Brian Hannant, is not exactly fine art, but, in its stripped-down, cannily cinematic way, it's one of the most imaginative Australian films yet released in this country. It has no pretensions to do anything except entertain in the primitive, occasionally jolting fashion of the first nickelodeon movies, whose audiences flinched as streetcars lumbered silently toward the camera.

The film will be shown at the Festival Theater today in the New Directors/New Films series.

Existence in *The Road Warrior* is reduced to an unending, two-lane, blacktop highway that stretches from one horizon to the next, the landscape empty of houses or trees or any other sign of life except an occasional wrecked vehicle. While stopped to check out an abandoned tractor-trailer for gasoline, Max has his first encounter with some members of an especially vicious gang of post-holocaust, motorcycle-riding vandals.

These are the followers of the Humungus, a ferocious body-builder type who, like his associates, affects the sort of drag sold today in leather "specialty" shops—studded jacket, wristbands, posing strap, plus a leather mask. Like the film and almost everything in it, the Humungus and his friends represent the kind of cross-century cultural pollination favored in comic books.

They ride motorcycles but they fight with pikes, maces, and crossbows. The good guys in the film, a group of comparatively civilized types who run a small refinery in the middle of the wasteland, fight with boomerangs and flame throwers. The junk heap of this film contains the remains of more than one civilization.

Like Alan Ladd's Shane, Max, the loner, finds himself more or less coerced into helping the civilized oil refinery people. The Humungus and his friends have surrounded the refinery and threaten to level it and debauch everyone in it unless the gasoline is turned over to them. There are several bloody show-downs that finally lead up to a desperate break for freedom, in which the "good" pioneers are pursued down life's highway by the Humungus and his associates. This spectacular chase involves a trailer truck, a school bus, other vehicles of every sort, plus a home-made helicopter.

The Road Warrior doesn't have much time for women, who play decidedly inferior roles in this wilderness, especially in the camp of the vandals. The most evil of the Humungus's followers is another huge brute who rides around on his bike, snarling psychotically, with his pretty blond boyfriend hanging on to his waist. The women in the refinery compound fare somewhat better, but Max is apparently too busy remembering the unthinkable to have any time for romantic or even sexual thoughts.

Beside Max, the Humungus, whose face is never seen, and the Wild Angel and his mute boyfriend, the only other clearly identifiable characters in the film are the jaunty fellow (Bruce Spence) who pilots the small helicopter and comes to act as Max's faithful servant, and a small, scruffy little boy (Emil Minty) who plays Brandon de Wilde to Mr. Gibson's Alan Ladd.

The Road Warrior never means to be more than an adult-oriented kiddie fantasy, but it's an exceptionally witty exercise of that kind.

—*V.C., April 28, 1982*

ROBOCOP

Directed by Paul Verhoeven; written by Edward Neumeier and Michael Miner; director of photography, Jost Vacano; edited by Frank J. Urioste; production design by William Sandell; music by Basil Poledouris; produced by Arne Schmidt; released by Orion Pictures. Running time: 103 minutes.

With: Peter Weller (Officer Alex J. Murphy/Robo-Cop), Nancy Allen (Officer Anne Lewis), Dan O'Herlihy (The Old Man), Ronny Cox (Richard Jones), Kurtwood Smith (Clarence Boddicker), Miguel Ferrer (Robert Morton), Robert DoQui (Sergeant Warren Reed), Ray Wise (Leon Nash), Felton Perry (Johnson), Paul McCrane (Emil Antonowsky), Jesse D. Goins (Joe Cox), Del Zamora (Kaplan), Calvin Jung (Steve Minh), Rick Lieberman (Walker) and Lee de Broux (Sal).

If it's violence you're after, *RoboCop,* now showing at the National and other theaters, gives full value. In his first American movie, Paul Verhoeven, a Dutch director (*Soldier of Orange*), doesn't let the furiously futuristic plot get in the way of the flaming explosions, shattering glass and hurtling bodies.

Everything's constantly on the move in this movie full of camera tricks and computer tricks; if you glance away, chances are you'll miss somebody being blown away. Fortunately, the victims of the hand-held cannons that everybody shoots at everybody else take so long dying that you have plenty of time to enjoy their pain. When a baddie goes crashing into a toxic-waste tank, he not only staggers out looking hideous, but staggers on and on, getting hideouser and hideouser.

RoboCop (Peter Weller, well hidden) is an armored and computerized Galahad created by a sinister security company. He walks like Godzilla and shakes off shells like the tank the Army wishes it had. He was a good Detroit cop named Murphy before he was demolished by a gang of real bad guys led by a sadist (Kurtwood Smith). Only Murphy didn't quite die; there was a little piece of human memory inside the armor. So we have here a variation on the part-man-part-monster genre, except that this monster is programmed to enforce the law; he knows when and where a crime is being committed and can see through walls. The glitch is he's also been programmed not to go after the security company biggies.

Humor glimmers amid the mayhem. One of the many final shootouts is between RoboCop and ED 209 (ED stands for "enforcement droid"), a hulking klutz of a robot who can't do anything right. RoboCop's crime-busting techniques are funny if you don't mind how the criminal's body gets busted in the process. Jost Vacano's camera finds a particularly droll point of view in a men's room. And periodically, a happy pair of television anchorfolk pops up to deliver news of the latest disaster at such popular Detroit spots as the Lee Iacocca Elementary School. They break for a commercial for a product called Nukem, which comes with a warranty.

The plot, in case you need a respite, involves a corporate vice president (Ronny Cox) who is in cahoots with the bad guys, and another executive (Miguel Ferrer) who is in cocaine-sniffing decadent. Is that meant to be a comment on big business? Don't worry about it. Whatever may have been in the minds of the writers, Edward Neumeier and Michael Miner, has more trouble emerging from Mr. Verhoeven's sizzling battles than poor Murphy does from his robosuit.

—*W.G., July 17, 1987*

ROCCO AND HIS BROTHERS

Directed by Luchino Visconti; written (in Italian, with English subtitles) by Mr. Visconti, Suso

Cecchi D'Amico. Pasquale Festa Campanile. Massimo Franciosa. Enrico Medioli and Vasco Pratolini. based on the novel *The Bridge of Ghisolfa* by Giovanni Testori: cinematographer. Giuseppe Rotunno: edited by Mario Serandrei: music by Nino Rota: art designer. Mario Garbuglia: produced by Giuseppe Bordogni: released by Astor Pictures International. Black and white. Running time: 175 minutes.

With: Alain Delon (Rocco). Renato Salvatori (Simone). Annie Girardot (Nadia). Katina Paxinou (Rosaria). Roger Hanin (Morini). Paola Stoppa (Boxing Impresario). Duzy Delair (Luisa) and Claudia Cardinale (Ginetta).

A fine Italian film to stand alongside the American classic, *The Grapes of Wrath,* opened last night at the Beekman and the Pix on Forty-second Street. It is Luchino Visconti's *Rocco and His Brothers* (*Rocco e i suoi fratelli*), and it comes here garlanded with laurels that are quite as appropriate in this context as they are richly deserved.

For there is in this strong and surging drama of an Italian peasant family's shattering fate in the face of the brutalizing forces of unfamiliar modern city life a kind of emotional fullness and revelation that one finds in the great tragedies of the Greeks—a quality that was potent and conspicuous in the comparable *Grapes of Wrath.*

No minor or purely chance conditions affect and derange the simple lives of the Lucanian mother and her five sons who assemble in Milan at the beginning of the film. A destiny as sure and universal as the one that altered the life of Ruth, the displaced Moab maiden who stood in tears amidst the alien corn, or transformed the lives of the pioneers who pierced the American frontier, tangles and tears the living patterns of the people in this film and strains and distorts their gentle natures into forms that are pathetic and grotesque.

To be sure, the incidents that trigger the changes in the lives of these people who arrive in the big northern city with bags of oranges and thrill at their first glimpse of snow were arbitrary selections by the five men who wrote the script, but the point is that any alien incidents would eternally alter their lives. That is

the subterranean rumble that Signor Visconti makes one feel.

The fact that it is a little triumph for one of the brothers as a prizefighter with a sleazy stable that introduces the taint of callous commercialism and urban brutality into the bosom of the family is of incidental concern. This is but symptomatic of the inevitable condition of change. And events that snowball upon this triumph—the fighter's harboring of a prostitute, her switch to another brother (Rocco), the jealousy this foments, and the whole horrible rift in family feelings and loyalties it precipitates—are but the consequential workings of an ageless destiny.

At least, that is how Signor Visconti has clearly conceived his film and that is what his brilliant handling of events and characters makes one feel. There's a blending of strong emotionalism and realism to such an extent that the margins of each become fuzzy and indistinguishable.

In the strongest single sequence, for instance—the sequence in which the vicious brother rapes the reformed prostitute and budding sweetheart before the gentle Rocco's eyes and then slugs it out with the poor fellow all through the gaunt and ugly night—the reality of the defilement is so powerfully saturated with the emotional dam-burst of the brothers that the sequence is one raw experience, a vast tangle of cold fact and hot feeling, which is what all strong experience usually is.

And it is with this sensitive understanding that the whole film is played, in accord with the lush Italian nature and with the fullest emotional capacities of man. Alain Delon as the sweet and loyal Rocco, the brother who emerges from deep pain to shoulder the burden of his wayward brother and the family responsibilities, is touchingly pliant and expressive, but it is Renato Salvatori, as the bum, who fills the screen with the anguish of a tortured and stricken character. His raw and restless performance is overpowering and unforgettable.

The French actress Annie Girardot is likewise striking as the piteous prostitute, torn between a feral animalism and a longing for tender, honest love. She, too, is an interesting symbol of the brutalizing forces of urban life, and what happens to her at the finish is a meaningful irony.

As the warm, superstitious, helpless mother, Katina

Paxinou babbles and wails her love and anguish with great natural liberality, and Spiros Focas, Max Cartier, and Rocco Vidolazzi are rich and credible as other assorted sons. Claudia Cardinale, a new Italian starlet, is impressive as the oldest son's new wife, and Roger Hanin is appropriately unwholesome as a corrupt operator in the boxing world.

A haunting musical score by Nino Rota, top man in Italy in this field, puts a highly important aural background behind this three-hour-long, never-lagging film, which is being shown here with English subtitles, fairly good ones, for the Italian dialogue.

—*B.C., January 28, 1961*

ROGER AND ME

Written, produced and directed by Michael Moore; directors of photography, Christopher Beaver, John Prusak, Kevin Rafferty and Bruce Schermer; edited by Jennifer Beman and Wendy Stanzler; released by Miramax Films. Running time: 83 minutes.

With: Rhonda Britto (The Bunny Lady), Steve Wilson (The Tourism Chief), Michael Moore (Narrator) and Roger Smith, Ronald Reagan, Miss America, Pat Boone, Anita Bryant, the Reverend Robert Schuller, Bob Eubanks and Deputy Fred Ross (Themselves).

America has an irrepressible new humorist in the tradition of Mark Twain and Artemus Ward. He is Michael Moore, the writer, producer and director of the rude and rollicking new documentary feature *Roger and Me*. Much in the manner of those nineteenth-century forebears, Mr. Moore celebrates the oddities of the American frontier, once defined by the historian F. J. Turner as "the meeting place of savagery and civilization, where democracy is strengthened."

The American frontier of tall tales and garrulous fables has long since been developed into extinction. Mr. Moore's frontier is his hometown, Flint, Michigan, population 150,000, the birthplace of General Motors. As a result of the closing of various G.M. plants and the elimination of 40,000 jobs, Flint has become one of the more embarrassing eyesores in the landscape of what is supposed to be a booming American economy.

All sorts of attempts have been made to save Flint. "Just when things were beginning to look bleak," Mr. Moore recalls on the soundtrack, "Ronald Reagan arrived in Flint and took twelve workers out for a pizza." Somebody walked off with the pizzeria's cash register, though it's unclear whether the two events were connected.

When *Money* magazine named Flint "the worst place to live in America," ABC planned to devote an entire *Nightline* show to the subject. The program was canceled at the last minute. The television power truck had been stolen.

Depressing figures and nutty anecdotes bubble out of *Roger and Me* nonstop, leaving the frequently appalled audience roaring with laughter, the kind of response that Twain would cherish.

Roger and Me, which does not yet have a commercial distributor, will be shown at the New York Film Festival today and tomorrow.

The film takes its title from Mr. Moore's attempts to reach Roger Smith, the G.M. chairman. Mr. Moore's plan is to take Mr. Smith on a tour of Flint and to persuade him of G.M.'s responsibility in attending to the problems of the unemployed. A modest goal, it seems, though Mr. Moore knows as well as anybody that it's not a goal that stands any chance of being achieved. It is, however, a wonderful premise for an angry, biased, witty movie.

The portly, beady-eyed Mr. Moore, as sharp and sophisticated a documentary filmmaker as has come on the scene in years, manifests a down-home wonder at the world's idiocies. With a toothpick stuck in the corner of his mouth, wearing a down jacket, jeans, and the sort of cap that should have the name of a feedlot on it, he stalks the G.M. chairman in the assorted sanctuaries of the seriously rich and powerful.

He shows up at the G.M. offices in Detroit, where he has some hilarious, comparatively polite arguments with security guards and public relations people, who bite their lips as they try desperately to hang on to their well-paid cool.

He is hustled out of both the Grosse Point Yacht Club and the Detroit Athletic Club. He attends the annual G.M. stockholders' meeting and successfully gets the microphone, only to be cut off. On the dais, Mr. Smith brags to an associate about the fleetness with which he managed to avoid the embarrassment, not realizing that *his* microphone is still on.

Roger and Me is stuffed with such remarkable "found" moments, which are not really found at all. They may be unplanned, but only a filmmaker thoroughly at ease with his subject, and aware of various possibilities, is going to be in a position to find those moments.

They include Mr. Moore's not terribly warm encounter with Mr. Smith at a reception following the G.M. chairman's annual "Christmas message," a scene crosscut with the Christmas Eve eviction of an unemployed G.M. worker.

To save their city after the G.M. pullout, the Flint city fathers approve a series of schemes that sound as if they'd come out of the head of Evelyn Waugh, reborn as a Flint booster. They spend $13 million to build a Hyatt Regency Hotel and $100 million or so more for a theme park called AutoLand, both of which quickly go broke. They attempt to boost morale by bringing in Pat Boone and Anita Bryant to perform for the tired masses. The television evangelist the Reverend Robert Schuller is paid a reported $20,000 to tell his audience, "You can turn your hurt into a halo."

After photographing a radiant Miss Michigan in a Flint parade waving to crowds standing in front of closed stores, Mr. Moore tries to get her reaction to Flint's ever-present poverty. Her smile vanishes as she tries to show concern. Does she have any message for the people of Flint? The smile returns. "Just keep your fingers crossed for me as I go for the gold!" Miss Michigan did, indeed, become Miss America that year (1988).

Mr. Moore is clearly someone who believes that poverty and corporate neglect are sins, and he doesn't pull his punches. He doesn't appeal to easy sentiment. He demolishes the television personality Bob Eubanks, of *The Newlywed Game*, just by letting him talk on and on.

Mr. Moore makes no attempt to be fair. Playing fair is for college football. In social criticism, anything goes, as it goes triumphantly in *Roger and Me*.

—*V.C., September 27, 1989*

ROMAN HOLIDAY

Produced and directed by William Wyler; written by Dalton Trumbo, Ian McLellan Hunter and John Dighton, based on a story by Mr. Hunter; cinematographers, Franz Planer and Henri Alekan; edited by Robert Swink; music by Georges Auric; art designers, Hal Pereira and Walter Tyler; released by Paramount Pictures. Black and white. Running time: 119 minutes.

With: Gregory Peck (Joe Bradley), Audrey Hepburn (Princess Anne), Eddie Albert (Irving Radovich), Hartley Power (Mr. Hennessy), Harcourt Williams (Ambassador), Margaret Rawlings (Countess Vereberg), Tulio Carminati (General Provno) and Paolo Carlini (Mario Delani).

There has been a long hiatus between that day when history wore a rose, when princesses and knights-errant in mufti could get into a lovely scrape or two, and when the movies could do something about it. That day apparently has passed. For *Roman Holiday,* which arrived at the Music Hall yesterday, is a royal lark in the modern idiom about a regal but lonely young thing who has her moment of happiness with an adventurous newspaperman. It is a contrived fable but a bittersweet legend with laughs that leaves the spirits soaring.

Call *Roman Holiday* a credit to William Wyler's versatility. The producer-director, who has been expending his not inconsiderable talents on worthy but serious themes, is herein trying on the mantle of the late Ernst Lubitsch and making it fit fairly well. He certainly is dealing with the formal manners of ultra-high society and, if the unpolished common man is very much in evidence, too, it does not matter because his cast and the visually spectacular backgrounds of Rome, in which this romantic excursion was filmed, also are necessary attributes to this engaging story.

A viewer with a long memory might recall some plot similarities between *Roman Holiday* and *It Happened One Night.* This is not important. Mr. Wyler and his associates have fashioned a natural, tender, and amusing yarn about the heiress to the throne of a mythical kingdom who is sick unto death of an unending schedule of speeches, greetings, and interviews attendant on her goodwill tour and who suddenly decides to escape from these bonds of propriety. Her accidental meeting with Joe Bradley, the American journalist, and the night she spends in his apartment are cheerful, untarnished, and perfectly believable happenstances in which romance understandably begins to bloom.

The director and his scenarists, Ian McLellan Hunter and John Dighton, have sensibly used the sights and sounds of Rome to dovetail with the facts in their story. Since the newspaperman is anxious to get the exclusive rights to the princess's adventures in the Eternal City, and since he is also anxious to keep her in the dark as to his identity, a Cook's Tour of the Eternal City is both appropriate and visually edifying.

This is not a perfunctory trip. Mr. Wyler and his camera crew have distilled chuckles as well as a sightseeing junket in such stops as the princess getting a new coiffure; a perfectly wild motor-scooter ride through Roman streets, alleys, and marketplaces winding up with a session in a police station; and an uproarious dance on one of the barges on the Tiber that terminates with the princess and her swain battling and escaping from the sleuths sent to track her down. The cameras also have captured the raucous sounds and the varied sights of a bustling, workaday Rome; of sidewalk cafés, of the Pantheon, the Forum, and such various landmarks as the Castel Sant' Angelo and the rococo, mirrored grandeur of the Colonna, Brancaccio, and Barberini Palazzi.

Although she is not precisely a newcomer to films, Audrey Hepburn, the British actress who is being starred for the first time as Princess Anne, is a slender, elfin, and wistful beauty, alternately regal and childlike in her profound appreciation of newly-found, simple pleasures and love. Although she bravely smiles her acknowledgment of the end of that affair, she remains a pitifully lonely figure facing a stuffy future. Gregory Peck makes a stalwart and manly escort and lover, whose eyes belie his restrained exterior. And it is altogether fitting that he eschews the chance at that exclusive story, considering the circumstances.

Eddie Albert is excellent as the bewildered, bewhiskered, and breezy photographer who surreptitiously snaps the unwitting princess on her tour. Hartley Power, as the bureau chief of Mr. Peck's news agency; Paolo Carlini, as an amorous barber; Claudio

Ermelli, as a janitor; Alberto Rizzo, as a timorous cabbie; Harcourt Williams, Tullio Carminati, and Margaret Rawlings, as Miss Hepburn's official aides; and an echelon of actual Rome correspondents help give the proceedings authenticity and flavor. It is a short holiday in which they are involved but an entirely pleasureable one.

—A.W., August 28, 1953

ROMEO AND JULIET

Directed by George Cukor; written by Talbot Jennings, based on the play by William Shakespeare; cinematographer, William Daniels; edited by Margaret Booth; music by Herbert Stothart; art designer, Cedric Gibbons; choreographer, Agnes De Mille; produced by Irving Thalberg; released by Metro-Goldwyn-Mayer. Black and white. Running time: 127 minutes.

With: Norma Shearer (Juliet), Leslie Howard (Romeo), John Barrymore (Mercutio), Edna May Oliver (Nurse), Basil Rathbone (Tybalt), C. Aubrey Smith (Lord Capulet) and Andy Devine (Peter).

Metro the Magnificent has loosed its technical magic upon Will Shakespeare and has fashioned for his *Romeo and Juliet* a jeweled setting in which the deep beauty of his romance glows and sparkles and gleams with breathless radiance. Never before, in all its centuries, has the play received so handsome a production as that which was unveiled last night at the Astor Theatre. All that the camera's scope, superb photography, and opulent costuming could give it has been given to it here. Ornate but not garish, extravagant but in perfect taste, expansive but never overwhelming, the picture reflects great credit upon its producers and upon the screen as a whole. It is a dignified, sensitive, and entirely admirable Shakespearean—not Hollywoodean—production.

That distinction is important. Heretofore the screen has placed an evil brand upon the Shakespearean plays it attempted to produce. Its Shakespearean tradition has been uncertain and largely one of failure. Twenty years ago Theda Bara played in one version of *Romeo and Juliet;* Beverly Bayne and Francis

X. Bushman were the lovers in another. Ignoring these period pieces, relics of the early silent era, we come to the Pickford-Fairbanks *Taming of the Shrew* (with additional dialogue by Sam Taylor) and to the Warners' *A Midsummer Night's Dream,* which impressed me, at least, as a pretentious and overstuffed fantasy.

It is obviously impossible to discuss Metro's *Romeo* in terms of such predecessors. It would be equally unjust to treat it in the prescribed fashion of drama critics: virtually ignoring the production and estimating the play by the performances. Here the production is fully as important as the acting, and one's appraisal of the players must be an individual and personal opinion arrived at without application of the yardstick of stage tradition by which we measure our Romeos and Juliets. There is no precedent for this version, no stage or screen tradition to guide us in our consideration of the picture. Logically, if not chronologically, it is the first Shakespearean photoplay.

Hastening, then, into our report: Metro has translated the play into sheerly cinematic terms. It has omitted about a fourth of the verse—sometimes at the behest of the Hays office, which disapproves of Elizabethan English, more often because it was repetitious or in explanation of action which the stage cannot show, but which the screen can and does. The best-known passages, however, have been spared: the balcony scene has lost a line or two, but Mercutio's ode to Queen Mab is intact. The Nurse once again is called a bawd and speaks like a female Rabelais. No "additional dialogue" has been added. So much for the mechanics of the script.

In scene and motion, the screen has gloriously released the play from the limitations of the stage. The brawl in the Cathedral Square of Verona splashes over a few acres; the masque at the Capulets' home is brilliantly colorful; the balcony scene, no longer confined to a miniature window and painted garden, has a lush midnight beauty of physical things which merges graciously with the spoken rapture of the lovers' lines. Verona, in brief, and all the places within it have spread beyond painted canvas and stiffly standing props to come alive in their proper proportion, tone, and hue. In such matters the screen is beyond the reach of the boards and footlights. Shakespeare would have gloried in the medium.

But there is more to *Romeo* than mechanical perfection, and if we seem to have delayed unduly in reporting upon Leslie Howard's Romeo, Norma Shearer's Juliet, and the others, it is because the best news should be kept to the last. Considering the performances en masse, they are splendid. Here and there we can expect imperfections; Miss Shearer was not at her best in the balcony scene, Mr. Howard came a cropper in a few of his soliloquies—there must be some inherent antagonism between the screen and soliloquy—Conway Tearle was a bit on the declamatory side as the Prince of Verona.

Fortunately we need not value a performance as the proverb instructs us to judge a chain. With more pleasure, and with a sense that this memory will endure the longer, do we recall Miss Shearer's tender and womanly perverse Juliet during her farewell scene with Romeo before his flight to Mantua. Bright, too, is the recollection of her surrender to uncertainty, fear, and suspicion before swallowing the potion, and of that scene in which she finds her lover dead beside her in the tomb. Miss Shearer has played these, whatever her earlier mistakes, with sincerity and effect.

Mr. Howard is a pliant and graceful Romeo, overly weak perhaps in those moments when his hot blood should have boiled and he shared some of Mercutio's fiery spirit. But as a wooer and whisperer of Shakespeare's silver-sweet lines, he is as romantic as any lady on a balcony might desire.

And then, of course, there is John Barrymore, reveling—poseur that he is—in the role of flamboyant Mercutio and dying with dignity and a Shakespearean pun on his lips. And Basil Rathbone, a perfect devil of a Tybalt, fiery and quick to draw and an insolent flinger of challenges. No possible fault there. And Edna May Oliver, the very Nurse of the Bard's imagining; droll, wise, impish in her humor, and such a practical romanticist at that. She is grand. And Andy Devine as Peter—"I do bite my thumb, Sir!"—and spoken like a true Elizabethan clown with a frog's voice and canary's heart. For the rest a blanket salute: to C. Aubrey Smith for an admirable Capulet, to Reginald Denny for a carelessly proper Benvolio, to Ralph Forbes as a gallant and fond Paris, to Violet Kemble Cooper for a brisk and matronly Lady Capulet, to Henry Kolker for a troubled Friar Laurence.

Talbot Jennings has adapted the play wisely, and George Cukor has directed it as briskly as the quality of the tragedy permits and the pageantry of the picture will bear. We reach the end of the film with this realization: the screen is a perfect medium for Shakespeare; whether Shakespeare is the perfect scenarist for the screen remains uncertain. Metro's film of *Romeo and Juliet* is a lovely thing; if it should not be well received the fault will not be Hollywood's. It will mean only that Shakespeare has become a literary exercise or a matter for a drama cult's admiration. Somehow we cannot believe that.

—F.S.N., August 21, 1936

ROMEO AND JULIET

Directed by Franco Zeffirelli; written by Mr. Zeffirelli, Masolino D'Amico and Franco Brusati, based on the play by William Shakespeare; cinematographer, Pasqualino De Santis; edited by Reginald Mills; music by Nino Rota; production designer, Lorenzo Mongiardino; produced by Anthony Havelock-Allan and John Brabourne; released by Paramount Pictures. Running time: 138 minutes.

With: Olivia Hussey (Juliet), Leonard Whiting (Romeo), Milo O'Shea (Friar Laurence), Murray Head (The Chorus), Michael York (Tybalt), John McEnery (Mercutio), Pat Heywood (The Nurse), Natasha Parry (Lady Capulet), Robert Stephens (Prince of Verona) and Keith Skinner (Balthazar).

Franco Zeffirelli's *Romeo and Juliet* is a lovely, sensitive, friendly popularization of the play—the lovers, Leonard Whiting and Olivia Hussey, as young and full of life as they ought to be, Italy of its time there intact, a lot made of the relationship between Romeo and Mercutio, beautifully played by John McEnery. The prose suffers a bit, sounding more like *West Side Story* than perhaps it ought to. In the classic speeches, one begins to worry about diction and wish the modern would recede and let Shakespeare play through.

But the scenes, the ball, the duels, are so beautifully thought out and staged that things I had not noticed—the puppy play character of the duels at first—become extraordinary, temporally present, and remote. But for the poetry, and the fine archaic dignity of Romeo and Juliet, the story could be taking place

next door. It is the sweetest, the most contemporary romance on film this year.

There are fine, unanachronistic songs by Nino Rota and Eugene Walter, and scenes so human, social, and derived from Dutch and Italian painting schools that it is a joy to watch, if not quite to listen to.

Romeo and Juliet, when racked with sobs, go on too long, particularly since the crying does seem forced. Pat Heywood, as the nurse, seems too bawdy, cold, and almost terrifying—in the way that characters in Disney movies suddenly become uncanny, and haunt children's dreams. But these were clearly Zeffirelli's conscious choices and there is so much else that leads one to agree with what he does that he may be right in these uncomfortable choices, too.

There is a softly homosexual cast over the film—not just with Romeo and Mercutio, but with Juliet's bodice being much too tight, or a kind of Greek attention lavished on Romeo in the bedroom scene. And yet Romeo, his face not quite yet integrated, and Juliet, with a special lady quality of lust, work absolutely right—as do Natasha Parry, as the classic beauty, Lady Capulet, or Robert Stephens, as the wise, liberal Prince of Verona. Milo O'Shea plays Friar Laurence, rather as a modern, radical-understanding dean.

It wouldn't be surprising if this film, with all its youth-adult misses of contact, and its failure of the bureaucratic post, should become the thing for young people to see. The business of locating Shakespeare so firmly in a place, some scenes, and bodies, but not in language quite, is worrying. But the movie, which opened yesterday at the Paris Theater, is done with full awareness of the way it works, and it works touchingly.

—R.A., October 9, 1968

ROOM AT THE TOP

Directed by Jack Clayton; written by Neil Paterson, based on the novel by John Braine; cinematographer, Freddie Francis; edited by Ralph Kemplen; music by Mario Nascimbene; art designer, Ralph Brinton; produced by John Woolf and James Woolf; released by Romulus Films. Black and white. Running time: 115 minutes.

With: Laurence Harvey (Joe Lampton), Simone Signoret (Alice Aisgill), Heather Sears (Susan

Brown). Sir Donald Wolfit (Mr. Brown). Ambrosine Phillpotts (Mrs. Brown). Donald Houston (Charles Soames) and Raymond Huntley (Mr. Hoylake).

The cynical, disenchanted, and footloose postwar youths of England, who justifiably have been termed "angry," never have been put into sharper focus than in *Room at the Top*. The British-made import, which was unveiled at the Fine Arts Theatre yesterday, glaringly spotlights them in a disk of illumination that reveals genuine drama and passion, truth as well as corruption. Although it takes place 3,000 miles away, it is as close to home as a shattered dream, a broken love affair, or a man seeking to make life more rewarding in an uneasy world.

Unlike John Osborne, who, in *Look Back in Anger,* merely shouted the sensitive younger Britishers' fiery protests against class distinctions and other contemporary English inequities, John Braine, out of whose brilliant first novel this careful dissection was made, is more adult and scientifically observant about a grievous malaise. Mr. Braine, Neil Paterson, the scenarist, and Jack Clayton, who did a superb job in directing an excitingly effective cast, are angry, too. But they see the picture whole. They are basically moral people who know that, come what may, a price must be paid for revolt sometimes.

As has been noted, Mr. Braine is concerned with a type of schemer whose accent may be exotic but one who is becoming more and more symbolic of the restless young men of the world. In this case, he is Joe Lampton, born to poverty in a North Country manufacturing town but determined to catapult himself out of a world he never made or wanted. As a civil servant in another city, he meets the nubile and naive daughter of the richest tycoon, who represents the prize and escape he has been waiting for. But this is a consummation not easily achieved. And, when thrown into the orbit of a married woman, ill-used, worldly-wise, anxiously groping for real affection, it is fairly obvious that he will succumb first to lust and then to genuine love.

That this dual affair is doomed to tragedy is inevitable. But the artisans who fashioned this shaky triangle are neither crude nor insensitive. Joe is a calculating, shrewd, and realistic campaigner, yearning for wealth and the opportunity to rid himself of low-caste stigma through marriage with the heiress to a great fortune. He is, however, also pictured as a man

in whom all conscience has not been killed. He is a hero without medals and one mourning defeat when he should be enjoying victory.

The director and scenarist also have shown us a multidimensional figure in the married woman he is forced to reject, a deed that indelibly underlines the sadness, desperation, and tragedy that surrounds these truly ill-fated lovers. And they have done equally well by the rich, sheltered young girl he marries at long last, an untutored youngster wholly engulfed by the sweetness, wonder, and uneasiness of first love and sex.

A prudish observer perhaps might be shocked by some of the drama's explicit dialogue and situations, but these, too, are adult and in context. One also might be thrown by the thick, Yorkshire-like accents of the cast, which strike foreign and harsh on American ears. A viewer might take exception to the slowness of pace as this somber play is first exposed.

But these are minor faults that are heavily outweighed by the superb performances of Simone Signoret, as the married woman clutching at her last chance at happiness, and Laurence Harvey, the seemingly selfish schemer, who discovers that he cannot destroy all of his decency. Heather Sears is gentle, fresh, and properly naive as the heiress he is forced to marry; and Sir Donald Wolfit, as her outspoken, self-made millionaire father; Donald Houston, as Mr. Harvey's roommate and confidant; and Hermione Baddeley, as Miss Signoret's trusted friend, are among those supporting players who add distinctive bits to an engrossing picture.

Jack Clayton's vigorous and discerning direction has involved them in more than just a routine romantic drama. *Room at the Top* may be basically cheerless and somber, but it has a strikingly effective view.

—*A. W., March 31, 1959*

A ROOM WITH A VIEW

Directed by James Ivory: written by Ruth Prawer Jhabvala. based on the novel by E. M. Forster: director of photography. Tony Pierce-Roberts: edited by Humphrey Dixon: music by Richard Robbins: production designers. Gianni Quaranta and Brian Ackland-Snow: produced by Ismail Merchant: released by Cinecom International Films. Running time: 115 minutes.

With: Maggie Smith (Charlotte Bartlett), Helena Bonham Carter (Lucy Honeychurch), Denholm Elliott (Mr. Emerson), Julian Sands (George Emerson), Daniel Day-Lewis (Cecil Vyse), Simon Callow (Mr. Beebe), Judi Dench (Miss Lavish), Rosemary Leach (Mrs. Honeychurch), Rupert Graves (Freddy Honeychurch) and Patrick Godfrey (Mr. Eager).

Lucy Honeychurch would seem to be the quintessential well-brought-up young woman of Edwardian England. She's pretty, polite, and minds her elders, who believe in the efficacy of manners and the class system. In the genteel world in which Lucy has been raised, people are what they appear to be. Yet Lucy is seething with unrecognized passions. Says the startled clergyman, Mr. Beebe, when he hears Lucy playing Beethoven on the piano, "If she ever takes to living as she plays, it will be very exciting—both for us and for her."

For most of A Room with a View, E. M. Forster's third novel (1908), Lucy Honeychurch does her best not to live as she plays. While on a holiday in Florence, chaperoned by Charlotte Bartlett, her maiden cousin, Lucy has no idea that she's fallen in love with the socially unsuitable George Emerson. In the course of a picnic, the handsome, commonsensical young George, carried away by Lucy and the Tuscan scenery, has kissed her cheek—and turned Lucy's world onto its ear.

Lucy Honeychurch could be the giddy aunt to the hermetically sealed Adela Quested, who causes all the fuss in Forster's Passage to India (1924). Lucy is as self-deceiving as Adela and, with the highest of ladylike resolve, nearly ruins her own life as well as the lives of everyone around her. Yet she doesn't. Lucy isn't a tragic character.

Because common sense triumphs, A Room with a View is not only uncharacteristically benign for Forster, but also blithely, elegantly funny, which is a fit description of the first-rate film adaptation that opens today at the Paris.

As they've been doing now for over twenty years, Ruth Prawer Jhabvala, who wrote the screenplay for A Room with a View; James Ivory, who directed it; and Ismail Merchant, the producer, have created an exceptionally faithful, ebullient screen equivalent to a literary work that lesser talents would embalm.

The Merchant-Ivory-Jhabvala Room with a View is like a holiday out of time. It's a journey into another dimension as it travels from the dangerously seductive settings of Florence, with its foul smells and Renaissance glories, to the more serene landscapes of England, where undeclared wars are fought over teacups. Back home, Lucy compounds her "muddle" by becoming engaged to the supposedly suitable Cecil Vyse, who is far more in love with himself and his own responses to "Art" than he is with now increasingly restive Lucy.

A Room with a View is full of rich roles, splendidly acted by a cast made up of both newcomers and familiar performers like Maggie Smith and Denholm Elliott, who seem to keep getting better and better with time. Miss Smith plays Charlotte, Lucy's high-minded but meddlesome cousin, the sort of woman whose worst foible is gossip and not, as she claims, "the prompt settling of accounts." Very much her match is Mr. Elliott, who plays George Emerson's father, a retired socialist newspaperman and the only character in the film who is capable of expressing his feelings directly.

The real star of the film, though, is the very beautiful Helena Bonham Carter, seen here recently in the title role of Lady Jane. As Lucy Honeychurch, Miss Bonham Carter gives a remarkably complex performance of a young woman who is simultaneously reasonable and romantic, generous and selfish, and timid right up to the point where she takes a heedless plunge into the unknown.

Spectacular, too, is a new young actor named Daniel Day-Lewis, who plays the insufferable Cecil Vyse with a style and a wit that are all the more remarkable when compared to his very different characterization in My Beautiful Laundrette. Julian Sands, who played the English photographer in The Killing Fields, is equally good as the utterly straightforward George Emerson.

Among the noteworthy supporting performers are Judi Dench as Miss Lavish, the ubiquitous "female novelist" Lucy meets in Florence; Simon Callow as a clergyman, Mr. Beebe; and Rosemary Leach as Lucy's mother.

The film, photographed by Tony Pierce-Roberts, looks terrific, but maybe more important than anything else is the narrative tone. Mr. Ivory and Miss Jhabvala have somehow found a voice for the film not unlike that of Forster, who tells the story of *A Room with a View* with as much genuine concern as astonished amusement. That's quite an achievement.

—V.C., March 7, 1986

THE ROSE TATTOO

Directed by Daniel Mann; written by Tennesse Williams, based on his play and adapted by Hal Kanter; cinematographer, James Wong Howe; edited by Warren Low; music by Alex North; art designers, Hal Pereira and Tambi Larsen; produced by Hal B. Wallis; released by Paramount Pictures. Black and white. Running time: 117 minutes.

With: Anna Magnani (Serafina Delle Rose), Burt Lancaster (Alvaro Mangiacavallo), Marisa Pavan (Rosa Delle Rose), Ben Cooper (Jack Hunter), Virginia Grey (Estelle Hohengarten), Jo Van Fleet (Bessie) and Sandro Giglio (Father De Leo).

That fine Italian actress Anna Magnani, whom American audiences know best from such fine Italian films as *Open City* and *The Miracle,* has a triumphant field day in her first Hollywood and English-speaking film. It is *The Rose Tattoo,* from the play of Tennessee Williams. It opened at the Astor last night.

They say that Mr. Williams wrote the play with Miss Magnani in mind. Her performance would indicate it, for she fits the role—or it fits her—like skin. As the robust Italian-born widow of a truck driver in an American Gulf Coast town, where she baffles her friends with her endless mourning and her Spartan watchfulness over her teenage daughter, who is ripe for love, she splays on the screen a warm, full-bodied, tragic-comic character. And she is grandly assisted by Burt Lancaster in the second lead—and the second half—of the film.

Note well that Mr. Lancaster does not appear until the tale is nigh half told. This has particular significance in the pattern of the film. For the first half of it is a somber and sometimes even morbid account of a woman's idolization of a dead husband whom everyone but she seems to know was unfaithful to her. And because Miss Magnani is so ardent and intense in conveying the bleakness of this grief, this whole segment of the picture has a curious oppressiveness, which is barely lightened by the squalling and brawling that she either excites or engineers.

It is in the second half of the picture—when Mr. Lancaster appears as an ebulliently cheerful but stupid trucker who wants to assist the widow to a little fun—that the dismal atmosphere starts clearing and The Rose Tattoo bursts into flower. And it is in this second half that Miss Magnani displays her talents most winningly.

Let us be candid about it: there is a great deal more happening inside the widow's psychological frame than either she understands or Mr. Williams has bothered to analyze in the play or film. It is clear that she has a strong sex complex which stems from a lot of possible things, including her deep religious training. This is not discussed and barely hinted on the screen. Thus one must make one's own decision about the character's complete validity and the logic of her eventual conversion to a natural life and the acceptance of her daughter's love affair.

But, logical or not, Miss Magnani makes the change from dismal grief to booming joy such a spectrum of emotional alterations and personality eccentricities that—well, who cares! She overwhelms all objectivity with the rush of her subjective force. From the moment she and her new acquaintance get together for a good old-fashioned weep (for no particular reason except that they are both emotional), and then go on to obvious courting in a clumsy, explosive, guarded way, Miss Magnani sweeps most everything before her. And what she misses Mr. Lancaster picks up.

The exquisiteness of those two as sheer performers—just for instance, the authority with which she claps her hand to her ample bosom or he snags a runaway goat—would dominate the picture, if the rest of the cast were not so good, and Daniel Mann as the director did not hold them under tingling, taut control. Marisa Pavan as the sensitive, nubile daughter; Ben Cooper as the decent sailor whom she craves; Virginia Grey as a tawdry ex-mistress; and Sandro Giglio as a gentle priest head a group of supporting players that gives this picture—much of which was shot in Key West—a quality of utter authenticity. Producer Hal Wallis has afforded it the best.

We can add only that Miss Magnani speaks English—with an accent—charmingly. Her widow may be a slight enigma, but she—with her eyes and those hands to lend eloquence to her expression—is not hard to understand.

—B.C., December 13, 1955

ROSEMARY'S BABY

Directed by Roman Polanski; written by Mr. Polanski, based on the novel by Ira Levin; cinematographer, William A. Fraker; edited by Sam O'Steen and Bob Wyman; music by Krzysztof Komeda; production designer, Richard Sylbert; produced by William Castle; released by Paramount Pictures. Running time: 136 minutes.

With: Mia Farrow (Rosemary Woodhouse), John Cassavetes (Guy Woodhouse), Ruth Gordon (Minnie Castevet), Sidney Blackmer (Roman Castevet), Maurice Evans (Hutch), Ralph Bellamy (Dr. Sapirstein), Patsy Kelly (Laura-Louise), Elisha Cook, Jr. (Mr. Nicklas) and Charles Grodin (Dr. Hill).

If a person exhibits paranoid symptoms these days it would seem common decency not to report him, at least, to the persons he claims to be persecuted by, and when Mia Farrow tells what is, after all, a highly plausible story to her obstetrician in *Rosemary's Baby*, it seems wrong of him to deliver her straight to a coven of witches that has designs on her baby. Lord knows how many cases of extremely accurate reporting are cured each day by psychiatrists.

The story, based on a novel by Ira Levin, and written and directed by Roman Polanski (*Repulsion, Knife in the Water*), makes absolute sense in several ways. It is a horror film, not very scary. There are several false frights—a closet door opening ominously to reveal a vacuum cleaner, a letter in a dead woman's hand that reads "I can no longer associate myself," dropped objects in a dark cellar at the Dakota on West 72d Street. But the only really jumpy second occurs when Miss Farrow speaks suddenly and startles a reading witch.

It is a fantasy of the What could have happened to me while I was asleep sort, What did I do when I was drunk, How do I know I'm awake now, What if everyone is lying to me, What am I really pregnant with—not as effective as it might be, because it is a little hard to imagine more than two or three people conspiring in a single pregnancy. And it is a highly serious lapsed-Catholic fable, going on the assumption that God is dead to imagine a Nativity for the dark powers.

The story concerns a young couple, Miss Farrow and John Cassavetes, who move to the Dakota—as likely a place for horrors as any—where Miss Farrow ultimately has reason to believe that her husband, in return for success in his career as an actor, has arranged something with the people next door for her forthcoming child. Ruth Gordon overplays one rouged, elderly witch, with clear joy and overlapping, mutually interrupting sentences. Sidney Blackmer plays her smooth old husband. In the conception scene, there is a whole crew of aging, naked others. Maurice Evans has a small part as a friend, who tries to warn her and is put into a coma.

Miss Farrow is quite marvelous, pale, suffering, almost constantly on-screen in a difficult role that requires her to be learning for almost two hours what the audience has guessed from the start. One begins to think it is the kind of thing that might really have happened to her, that a rough beast did slouch toward West 72d Street to be born. Everyone else is fine, but the movie—although it is pleasant—doesn't quite work on any of its dark or powerful terms.

I think this is because it is almost too extremely plausible. The quality of the young people's lives seems the quality of lives that one knows, even to the point of finding old people next door to avoid and lean on. One gets very annoyed that they don't catch on sooner. One's friends would have understood the situation at once. So that for most of its length the film has nothing to be excited about. It has Miss Gordon bringing herbs and cookies and Miss Farrow eating or not eating them—nothing cumulative—to fill that time with suspense. But the good side of that is that you can see the movie, and like it, without risking terrors or nightmares; it opened yesterday at the Criterion and the Tower East.

—R.A., June 13, 1968

'ROUND MIDNIGHT

Directed by Bertrand Tavernier; written by David Rayfiel and Mr. Tavernier; director of photography, Bruno De Keyzer; edited by Armand

Pesenny: music by Herbie Hancock: production designer. Alexander Trauner: produced by Irwin Winkler: released by Warner Brothers. Running time: 133 minutes.

With: Dexter Gordon (Dale Turner). François Cluzet (Francis Borier). Gabrielle Haker (Berangère). Sandra Reaves-Phillips (Buttercup). Lonette McKee (Darcey Leigh). Christine Pascal (Sylvie) and Herbie Hancock (Eddie Wayne).

No actor could do what the great jazz saxophonist Dexter Gordon does in 'Round Midnight, Bertrand Tavernier's glowing tribute to the golden age of bebop. Mr. Gordon, who stars in the film as an expatriate American named Dale Turner, becomes the very embodiment of the music itself. It's in his heavy-lidded eyes, in his hoarse, smoky voice, in the way his long, graceful fingers seem to be playing silent accompaniment to his conversation. It's even in the way he habitually calls anyone or anything "Lady," as in "Well, Lady Sweets, are you ready for tonight?" In that instance, he's addressing his saxophone.

The film, with its lovely, elegiac pacing and its tremendous depth of feeling, was, according to an opening title, "inspired by incidents in the lives of Bud Powell and Francis Paudras," the American pianist and the French jazz enthusiast who befriended him. Drifting easily between French and English, it takes place largely in Paris in 1959, among the expatriate jazz musicians and the French aficionados they attracted. Dale Turner arrives there from New York, and has an instant caretaker in the form of Francis Borier (François Cluzet), who is his longtime admirer.

At first Dale is only interested in cadging drinks from this fan, but he quickly realizes that Francis's helpfulness will be far more substantial. Francis, who himself lives in straitened circumstances, nevertheless undertakes to make sure Dale is well looked after. He does what he can to keep the musician's self-destructiveness in check ("S'il vous plaît, I would like to have the same thing he had," Dale says to a bartender, after watching the man next to him keel over), and even begins to water down his wine. He takes Dale home, introduces him to his little daughter Berangère (Gabrielle Haker), and even borrows money from his estranged wife so as to rent a larger apartment. His present place, she points out, was

large enough for a family of three. But now Francis wants to look after Dale on a full-time basis and, as he puts it, "I want the greatest sax player to live decently."

'Round Midnight, which takes its title from a Thelonious Monk composition, doesn't have a great deal of narrative, and it moves with the leisurely feeling of a reverie—sometimes it even seems to drift forward in time, so that the vibrant, colorful images of Dale and Francis briefly turn into the black-and-white, home-movie memories they will someday become. Much of the film takes place in the Blue Note, a jazz club, and simply lets the audience experience the place and its atmosphere. Here, and in a recording studio, and in several other nightclub settings, Mr. Gordon plays with musicians including Herbie Hancock, Bobby Hutcherson, Wayne Shorter, and Tony Williams. The music is sublime.

Much of the film is purely atmospheric; the camera may move through an empty apartment as a saxophone plays lazily in the background and Dale, in voice-over, offers his thoughts. "You just don't go out and pick a style off a tree one day—the tree is inside you, growing naturally," he says at one point. "When you have to explore every night, even the most beautiful things you find can be the most painful," Mr. Hutcherson (in the role of a fellow musician and neighbor) explains. The screenplay, by Mr. Tavernier and David Rayfiel, is both rich and relaxed, with a style that perfectly matches the musicians'. Some of the talk may well be improvised, but nothing sounds improvised, nothing sounds forced, and the film remains effortlessly idiosyncratic all the way through.

Among the film's many memorable moments are a Billie Holiday number by Sandra Reaves-Phillips during a party scene, and Lonette McKee's brief appearance as Dale's old flame; there is also the sight of Mr. Gordon, as much of a giant physically as he is musically, wandering around Paris with his diminutive French friend, getting the lay of the land ("Very pretty town," he pronounces Paris, with typical sangfroid). Once the action shifts to New York, Martin Scorsese turns up as a club owner, and a very unlikely civic booster. "When you go back to Paris, you're going to be raving," he says, "just raving about how nice New Yorkers can be."

The off-and-on love affair between the New York Film Festival and the filmmakers of France is very much on this year. Mr. Tavernier's masterly tribute is a large part of the reason.

—*J.M., September 30, 1986*

RUGGLES OF RED GAP

Directed by Leo McCarey: written by Walter De Leon. Harlan Thompson and Humphrey Pearson. based on the novel and play by Harry Leon Wilson: cinematographer. Alfred Gilks: edited by Edward Dmytryk: music and lyrics by Ralph Rainger and Sam Coslow: art designers. Hans Dreier and Robert Odell: produced by Arthur Hornblow. Jr.: released by Paramount Pictures. Black and white. Running time: 76 minutes.

With: Charles Laughton (Ruggles). Mary Boland (Mrs. Effie Floud). Charlie Ruggles (Egbert Floud). ZaSu Pitts (Mrs. Judson). Roland Young (Earl of Burnstead). Leila Hyams (Nell Kenner) and Maude Eburne ("Ma" Pettingill).

If memory and the textbooks can be trusted, this is the third motion-picture history of Marmaduke Ruggles and his experiences with life in the raw as dished out in dripping hunks in the bustling community of Red Gap. Presented at the Paramount Theatre last evening, it bawled and capered with infant lustiness, and was rapturously funny. There are comic butlers and comic butlers, but Mr. Ruggles, the perfect gentleman's gentleman, is not of their tribe. An American edition of the admirable Crichton, he is, if you will forgive the expression, comparatively eternal, and he ought to go on freshly and ageless until such time as M. Trotsky's international dawn makes brothers of us all. This time he is brilliantly delineated by Charles Laughton. Ceasing his normal traffic with Dr. Freud and the devil, Mr. Laughton gives us a pudgy, droll, and quite irresistible Ruggles who reveals only the briefest taint of the Laughton pathology.

Since the presence of Charles Ruggles in the photoplay is likely to cause some confusion in the impressions hereinafter set down, let our well-beloved Charles be explained as the 1935 reincarnation of Cousin Egbert, the walrus-mustachioed sourdough whose yippees and yahoos form a minor theme in the symphony of Marmaduke's triumphs. Is it necessary to outline the events contained in *Ruggles of Red Gap*? Perhaps the younger members of this morning's breakfast group ought to be told that Marmaduke Ruggles became the property of Cousin Egbert as the result of a poker session in Paris, during which the Earl of Burnstead's three treys proved inferior to Cousin Egbert's straight flush.

The helpless valet was thereupon hurled into the frontier life of Red Gap, where he learned that man was created equal and that even the lowly gentleman's gentleman was privileged to get his left foot up on the rail of the corner saloon. He fell in love, was yanked frantically between Tradition and Environment, booted the superior Mr. Belknap-Jackson solidly in the seat, and by such gradations came at last to be the proprietor of an establishment which the present edition entitles the Anglo-American Grill.

Memory is briefer than laughter in the case of *Ruggles of Red Gap* and this column cannot decide what novelties the scenarists have confected for Harry Leon Wilson's original narrative. Certainly that splendid and touching scene is new in which Marmaduke recites the Gettysburg Address in the saloon to a hushed audience of barflies and maverick cowhands. But, new or old, Mr. Laughton makes the story uniquely his own. It is a privilege to watch Ruggles riding the Parisian carousel, getting pickled with Cousin Egbert, posing as the Colonel of the Coldstream Guards, and otherwise contributing to the cause of honest laughter in the cinema.

Although it is Mr. Laughton's picture, since he provides the element of understanding which raises buffoonery a peg out of slapstick, he has robust support from his fellows. Among the chief conspirators, there are the aforementioned Mr. Charles Ruggles as the democratic Egbert, Mary Boland as the socially ambitious wife, and Roland Young as the generous though impecunious Earl. Stifle a guffaw, too, for ZaSu Pitts, Lucien Littlefield and Maude Eburne.

—*A.S., March 7, 1935*

RULES OF THE GAME

Directed by Jean Renoir: written (in French. with English subtitles) by Mr. Renoir and Carl Koch. Camille François and the cast: cinematographer. Jean Bachelet: edited by Marguerite Renoir: music by Camille Saint-Saëns. Salabert E. Rose.

Vincent Scotto, Wolfgang Amadeus Mozart, Johann Strauss, Frédéric Chopin, Monsigny G. Claret. Ms. François and Delonnel Garnier: art designer, Eugène Lourié: released by Janus Films. Black and white. Running time: 110 minutes.

With: Marcel Dalio (Robert de la Chesnaye), Nora Gregor (Christine de la Chesnaye), Roland Toutain (André Jurieu), Jean Renoir (Octave) and Mila Parély (Geneviève de Marrast).

Exactly what Jean Renoir had in mind when he wrote, performed in, and directed *The Rules of the Game,* Saturday's French import at the Fifth Avenue Playhouse, is anybody's guess. This is the same M. Renoir, if you please, who gave us those notable imports, *Grand Illusion* and *The Human Beast,* not to mention *The Southerner,* from Hollywood. The new arrival, however, is really one for the buzzards.

Here we have a baffling mixture of stale sophistication, coy symbolism, and galloping slapstick that almost defies analysis. The distributors claim that the picture, made shortly before the war, was banned by the Occupation on grounds of immorality. Rest assured it wasn't immortality. And there's nothing particularly sizzling in this account of some addle-headed lounge lizards tangling up their amours on a weekend house party in the country.

One minute they're making sleek Noël Coward talk about art and free love, the next they're behaving like a Li'l Abner family reunion, chasing each other from pantry to boudoir to the din of wrecked furniture, yelling, and random gunfire. One carefully picturesque sequence, a rabbit hunt, may or may not be fraught with Renoir meaning, but the grand finale, in which everybody down to the cook joins in a hysterical conquest race, would shame the Keystone Kops.

In the juicy role of a family friend, M. Renoir acts as though it were his last day on earth. The other principals, Dalio, Nora Gregor, and Mila Parély, are right behind him. The picture ends abruptly with an unaccountable murder, whereupon one of the philanderers murmurs that the victim didn't learn the rules of the game. If the game is supposed to be life, love, or hide-and-seek, which makes more sense, it's M. Renoir's own secret. At any rate, the master has dealt his admirers a pointless, thudding punch below the belt.

—H.H.T., April 10, 1950

Twenty-two years after *The Rules of the Game* was made, and eleven years after a mutilated print was exhibited here, the full version of Jean Renoir's study of the manners and mores of prewar France opened yesterday at the Eighth Street Playhouse and completely justifies its European reputation.

This remarkable film was photographed in the Sologne valley, where a year later French armies were fighting their last battles against the Nazis. While the film was in production, Hitler's troops invaded Czechoslovakia. The film opened in Paris while the city was celebrating the 150th anniversary of the French Revolution.

All these factors are subtly evoked in M. Renoir's trenchant examination of the decaying social structure of France before its fall. His screenplay, loosely based on a modernized play by Alfred de Musset, deals with a house party given by a wealthy French aristocrat and his Viennese wife. Among the guests are his possessive mistress, a family friend who worships the wife from a distance, and her lover, a heroic aviator.

Downstairs, where the servants watch and imitate their employers, a parallel triangle develops among a flirtatious maid, her jealous gamekeeper husband, and an amorous poacher. The situation erupts into a wildly comic chase in the midst of a costume ball, when the masquerading lovers intermingle in the confusion and the marquis reluctantly discharges the distraught gamekeeper for taking potshots at his guests.

In an abrupt change of mood, reality intrudes upon the artificial surface, leaving the dazed and frightened guests gathered around the body of the only innocent victim, the man who broke the rules of a society founded upon a superficial display of manners by revealing the sincerity of his emotions. As a final coda, the marquis apologizes for the "accident," while a bystander remarks that "he has class—and, believe me, the race is dying out."

Entirely a director's film, *The Rules of the Game* is unevenly acted, although Dalio as the marquis, Carette as the poacher, and M. Renoir himself as the awkward family friend are fascinating to observe.

The technique is admirable throughout, with at least two sequences emerging as classics of their kind—a rabbit hunt, emphasizing the barbarity of the ritual, and a masquerade foreshadowing the finale, in which guests dressed as skeletons perform a grotesque dance of death.

Admirers of the director's work will not find the moving simplicity of his expression of a pacifist theme in *Grand Illusion* or the colorful decor of *The River*, but will discover instead a deeply personal statement of unusual richness and complexity. M. Renoir obviously set out to make a masterpiece, closely following the literary tradition of Beaumarchais—who also foreshadowed the fall of a decadent aristocracy on the eve of the French Revolution.

Janus Films is presenting the film in a complete, uncensored print equipped with intelligent English subtitles, which help to clarify the director's conception. For discerning audiences, *The Rules of the Game* affords a memorable experience.

—E.A., January 19, 1961

THE RULING CLASS

Directed by Peter Medak; written by Peter Barnes, adapted from his play; director of photography, Ken Hodges; edited by Ray Lovejoy; production designer, Peter Murton; music by John Cameron; produced by Jules Buck and Jack Hawkins; released by Avco Embassy Pictures. Running time: 154 minutes.

With: Peter O'Toole (Jack Arnold, 14th Earl of Gurney), Alastair Sim (Bishop Lampton), Arthur Lowe (Daniel Tucker), Harry Andrews (13th Earl of Gurney), Coral Browne (Lady Claire Gurney), Michael Bryant (Dr. Herder), Nigel Green (McKyle), William Mervyn (Sir Charles Gurney), Carolyn Seymour (Grace Shelley), James Villiers (Dinsdale), Hugh Burden (Matthew Peake), Graham Crowden (Truscott), Kay Walsh (Mrs. Piggot-Jones), Patsy Byrne (Mrs. Treadwell) and Joan Cooper (Nurse Brice).

When the 13th Earl of Gurney accidentally hangs himself wearing his usual night clothes (long underwear, sword, cocked hat and tutu), his will bequeaths £30,000 to his faithful manservant Tucker (Arthur Lowe), a secret Communist party member who limits his revolutionary activities to spitting furtively into the oxtail soup. The remainder of the earl's estate and his title go to his son Jack (Peter O'Toole), a cheerful, loving fellow who wears his hair

in long blonde curls that recall Barbara Stanwyck's wig in *Double Indemnity*.

The other members of the family are properly aghast. Jack is not simply eccentric. He believes that he is the Nameless One, Yaweh, Jehovah, God, Jesus, all things born and yet unborn, and that he is married to Marguerite Gautier.

While the rest of the family has its afternoon tea in the drawing room, Jack hovers over them, draped across the huge, stylishly carved wooden cross that was the sum total of his personal effects when he came home from the looney bin.

Jack is a paranoid-schizophrenic and the family's alternatives are to mate him quickly to obtain an heir (thus to be able to commit him permanently) or to bring him back to sanity. Both plans succeed and both plans backfire, in ways that are rudely predictable as soon as one recognizes the philosophy that is the spongy foundation of *The Ruling Class*, the new British film directed by Peter Medak (*A Day in the Death of Joe Egg*) and adapted by Peter Barnes from his own play.

As Philippe de Broca (or Jean Anouilh, or Kaufman and Hart) have written: because what passes for sanity today is lunacy, to be lunatic is to be sane. The rehabilitated Jack becomes supernormal, or, at least, Mr. Barnes's idea of supernormal in today's wretched world. The 14th Earl of Gurney who takes his seat in the House of Lords preaches law, order, discipline, fear and a return to capital punishment.

He also becomes a modern Jack the Ripper, and rather too garrulous for the good of a comedy that should trust itself. "Behavior that is looked upon as insanity in tradesmen," says Jack, "is mild eccentricity in the ruling class," or something to that effect. Jack, who gets away with literal murder, is a smash hit.

I use that phrase purposely, for Mr. Barnes has written *The Ruling Class*, and Mr. Medak has directed it, in a whiz-bang, vaudeville ("get 'em on and off quickly") style, employing songs, dances and gags that sometimes shock but never completely disguise the fundamental ordinariness of the ideas.

It is occasionally fun, as when Peter O'Toole breaks into an energetic chorus of "The Varsity Drag" before some church ladies, or when Arthur Lowe, as the newly wealthy butler, continues to serve his masters with total freedom to insult them and drink on the job. In very short takes it is inspirationally anti-Blimp.

Says Sir Charles Gurney when he finds his wife dead on the drawing-room carpet, her throat cut: "Who's the impudent clown who did this!" It's an exclamation, not a question.

Mr. O'Toole who, with each passing film, is coming to look more and more like a bloodhound with a particularly bizarre past, is splendid, but the chief joys of the film are opportunities to see—in such fine form—British character actors on the order of Mr. Lowe, Alastair Sim, Coral Browne, Harry Andrews, and James Villiers. In spite of the film's technical fanciness, which belabors every point, you may also be charmed by Carolyn Seymour, as the porcelain-faced doxy who is brought in to marry the crazy earl and stays on, foolishly to love him.

The Ruling Class opened yesterday at the Cinema I.
—*V.C., September 14, 1972*

RUSHMORE

Directed by Wes Anderson; written by Mr. Anderson and Owen Wilson; director of photography, Robert Yeoman; edited by David Moritz; music by Mark Mothersbaugh; production designer, David Wasco; produced by Barry Mendel and Paul Schiff; released by Touchstone Pictures. Running time: 93 minutes.

With: Jason Schwartzman (Max Fischer), Bill Murray (Mr. Blume), Olivia Williams (Miss Cross), Brian Cox (Dr. Guggenheim) and Seymour Cassel (Bert Fischer).

This guy looks awfully familiar. Don't we know him from somewhere? Is it the yearbook pictures, the ones that show him with the Piper Cub Club or leading the beekeepers's society? Is it the way he wrote and directed the school's most unbearable plays? Isn't he the crossing guard who used his job to hit on friends' mothers? Remember how he gave the orders and outsmarted the teachers? Probably he has grown up to be a captain of industry and loves reminiscing about his hard climb to the top.

This portrait of the mogul as a young man arrives courtesy of Wes Anderson, whose bright, spiky *Rushmore* has the brainstorm of envisioning a 15-year-old tycoon-wannabe as a schoolboy. At Rushmore Acad-

emy, in scenes filmed at the director's own Texas alma mater, horrid little Max Fischer (Jason Schwartzman) calls the shots. Oh, sure, the place has faculty, but none of the grown-ups has anything like Max's natural authority. Maybe one man on the scene, the steel tycoon and Rushmore benefactor played with all the right wiles by Bill Murray, is right on the same wavelength with Max.

While the film embroils Max and the mogul in pursuit of the same beautiful teacher (Olivia Williams), it's a particular treat for its skewed, hilarious memories of a cutthroat boyhood. Bespectacled Max, who's as much of a sight gag for the wide-angle lens as he is a flesh-and-blood character, starts off on top of the Rushmore world and experiences a wonderfully welcome comeuppance. He's meant to be mellowing along the way, but *Rushmore* wouldn't dare turn sentimental about that. As directed by Mr. Anderson and written by him with Owen Wilson (his partner on *Bottle Rocket*, which *Rushmore* far surpasses), it's too smart to be maudlin. Far better to show off Max's Vietnam play, with real explosives (earplugs and safety glasses available) or let him boast derangedly (in one especially funny dinner scene) about having a hit to his credit.

Casting notes about *Rushmore*, which also includes a sweet turn by Seymour Cassel as Max's father and a sputteringly indignant one from Brian Cox as the headmaster: of the many who auditioned for Max's role, some actors spontaneously showed up in preppy looking blazers. But Mr. Schwartzman earned the part by among other things being the only one who actually made a fake Rushmore patch. And since Ms. Williams's only other theatrical film credit is appearing opposite Kevin Costner in *The Postman*, this amounts to her feature debut.

—*J.M., October 9, 1998*

RUTHLESS PEOPLE

Directed by Jim Abrahams, David Zucker and Jerry Zucker; written by Dale Launer; director of photography, Jan DeBont; edited by Arthur Schmidt; music by Michel Colombier; art designer, Don Woodruff; produced by Michael Peyser; released by Touchstone Films. Running time: 93 minutes.

With: Danny DeVito (Sam Stone). Bette Midler (Barbara Stone). Judge Reinhold (Ken Kessler). Helen Slater (Sandy Kessler). Anita Morris (Carol). Bill Pullman (Earl). William G. Schilling (Police Commissioner). Art Evans (Lieutenant Bender) and Clarence Felder (Lieutenant Walters).

The most irresistible thing about the characters in *Ruthless People,* a conspicuously overconsuming, Beverly Hills update of O. Henry's classic *Ransom of Red Chief,* is that they all try with such earnestness to live up to their ruthless reputations.

However, they're not only doggedly mean, deceitful, and potentially murderous, they're also inefficient, fainthearted, and totally transparent. Yet they work without respite. If they devoted the same energies to the selling of cookies for the Girl Scouts of America, the G.S.A. could become the World Bank.

When first met, pint-sized Sam Stone (Danny DeVito), the Spandex miniskirt king, is having dinner in an elegant Los Angeles restaurant with Carol (Anita Morris), his tall, beautiful mistress, and planning the murder of his heiress-wife, Barbara (Bette Midler). Sam's loathing of Barbara knows no bounds. He becomes positively poetic when he talks about her as "that squeaky, corpulent broad. I even hate the way she licks stamps."

Sam gets so excited about the murder he's about to commit that he can't wait to finish dinner. He rushes home with his bottle of chloroform (he's going to drug her and toss the overweight body off a cliff) only to find that she's been kidnapped. One of the delights of this mostly barren movie season is to see the pleasure that creeps over Sam Stone's face as he listens to the kidnappers' telephoned instructions.

They demand half a million dollars in ransom and promise that Barbara will be tortured and murdered if the money isn't paid, as directed, and if the police are called in. Hoping for the worst, Sam immediately brings in the cops and every television reporter in Southern California.

The object of all this attention is as horrible as Sam describes her. Miss Midler's Barbara Stone enters *Ruthless People* kicking, clawing, and cursing, hidden inside the gunnysack in which she's been carried off by her kidnappers to their modest, spic-and-span, lower-middle-class hideaway.

The perpetrators are Ken and Sandy Kessler (Judge Reinhold and Helen Slater), a young, mousy, nonviolent couple who've been driven to this extreme action as a means of getting revenge on Sam, who stole Sandy's Spandex miniskirt idea and became a multimillionaire.

I don't want to oversell *Ruthless People,* which opens today at the Beekman and other theaters. It's the kind of movie that sounds a lot funnier than it sometimes plays. It has its arid patches.

It also has a uniformly splendid cast of comic actors—the best to be seen outside of any recent Blake Edwards movie. Its screenplay, by the newcomer Dale Launer, is packed with wonderfully vulgar, tasteless lines that perfectly reflect the sensibilities of Sam and Barbara Stone. (Says Sam at one point, when he should be grieving for his lost wife, "Let's face it—she's not Mother Teresa. Gandhi would have strangled her.")

The direction, which can most accurately be defined as enthusiastic, is by the team of Jim Abrahams, David Zucker and Jerry Zucker, who hit the target with *Airplane!,* which they also wrote, and then missed with their follow-up, *Top Secret.* Though *Ruthless People* has few moments to equal the inspired lunacies of *Airplane!* it's a true farce—uniformly, cheerily nasty, without any of the sentimental baggage that freights *Down and Out in Beverly Hills.*

I can't say enough good things about Mr. DeVito, who here is never allowed to "act cute," which has sabotaged his work in *Romancing the Stone* and *Jewel of the Nile,* or about Miss Midler, who starts off looking like a nightmare parody of Pia Zadora and winds up being a svelte if loud-mouthed kitten. "Do I understand this correctly?" she says on learning that her husband won't even pay $10,000 for her return. "I've been marked down? I've been kidnapped by K-Mart!"

Mr. Reinhold and Miss Slater (*Supergirl*) are almost as funny as the unlikely kidnappers who do their best to cater to the whims of their whimsical "guest." Also entering into the spirit of the film are Miss Morris and Bill Pullman, who plays "the stupidest person on the face of the earth," the handsome if eccentric-looking young man with whom Miss Morris is two-timing Sam Stone. William J. Schilling appears briefly, but memorably, as a distraught commissioner of the Los Angeles police.

Though unbilled, O. Henry lives on—in a time and a place and a vocabulary that would make him blush.

—*V.C., June 27, 1986*

SAHARA

Directed by Zoltan Korda; written by John Howard Lawson, James O'Hanlon and Mr. Korda, based on the story by Philip MacDonald about an incident in the Soviet screenplay *The Thirteen*; cinematographer, Rudolph Maté; edited by Charles Nelson; music by Miklos Rozsa; art designers, Lionel Banks and Eugène Lourié; produced by Harry Joe Brown; released by Columbia Pictures. Black and white. Running time: 97 minutes.

With: Humphrey Bogart (Sergeant Joe Gunn), Bruce Bennett (Waco Hoyt), Lloyd Bridges (Fred Clarkson), Rex Ingram (Tambul), J. Carrol Naish (Giuseppe), Dan Duryea (Jimmy Doyle), Richard Nugent (Captain Jason Halliday) and Patrick O'Moore (Ozzie Bates).

Those rugged, indomitable qualities which Humphrey Bogart has so masterfully displayed in most of his recent pictures—and even before, in his better gangster roles—have been doubled and concentrated in *Sahara,* a Columbia film about warfare in the Libyan desert, which came to the Capitol yesterday. And a capital picture it is, too—as rugged as Mr. Bogart all the way and in a class with that memorable picture which it plainly resembles, *The Lost Patrol.*

For this is a real he-man picture. There isn't a female in the cast, except for a monstrous M-3 tank which is affectionately called Lulubelle. And it tells of a grueling experience endured by a handful of men cut off from their lines in the desert and forced to fend for themselves. At the start, there are three American tankmen, one unit of the small American force which was fighting alongside the British in Libya in June of last year. But very soon they pick up six stranded allies—four Britishers, a South African, and a Frenchman—and a bit farther on they give tank room to a Sudanese corporal and a captured Italian.

And it is this tiny force of weary soldiers, depleted by one who dies and burdened with a captured Nazi flier, which reaches an abandoned desert well and there makes a stand against the Germans who endeavor to capture their waterhole. All the adversities of the desert—the heat, the thirst, and everlasting sand—are realized in the tortuous journey, but it is the fight against the Nazis which is rough. It is this which tests the endurance, the artifice, and the spunk of the handful of Allied soldiers. And it is this which makes a tense, exciting film.

Zoltan Korda, an old desert zealot (most of his pictures have been dusted with sand), has achieved a tremendous comprehension of wicked hardships and manly virtues in this film. He makes you feel grit beneath your eyelids, sweat rolling down your back, and the pitiful choking sensation of your tongue being swollen with thirst. His desert is cruelly realistic (most of the picture was made in the California wastes), and his tank rolling on across the sand dunes bangs and clatters with a true metallic din.

But it is in the fiber of the characters that Mr. Korda (and those who worked with him on the script) has accomplished some eloquent expression. And the performances are all on a par. Mr. Bogart is truly inspiring as the American sergeant who leads the little band. His toughness, his trenchant laconism and genius for using a poker face mark him as probably the best screen notion of the American soldier to date. Richard Nugent is splendidly reticent and cool as a British officer, while Carl Harbord gives a searching performance of a British soldier with a touch of churlishness. J. Carrol Naish brings bewilderment and pathos to the role of the Italian prisoner, and Kurt Krueger is impressively Teutonic as the Nazi flier brought to bay. Bruce Bennett and Dan Duryea are strictly hometown American soldiers to the core, and Rex Ingram plays the Sudanese quite nicely, even though his accent has a misplaced Dixie purr.

Sahara is a laudable conception of soldier fortitude in this war, and it is also a bang-up action picture, cut out to hold one enthralled.

—*B.C., November 12, 1943*

SALAAM BOMBAY!

Produced and directed by Mira Nair; written (in Hindi, with English subtitles) by Sooni Taraporevala, based on a story by Miss Nair and Miss Taraporevala; director of photography, Sandi Sissel; edited by Barry Alexander Brown; music by L. Subramaniam; production designer, Mitch Epstein; released by Cinecom Pictures. Running time: 113 minutes.

With: Shafiq Syed (Krishna/Chaipau), Sarfuddin Qurrassi (Koyla), Raju Barnad (Keera), Raghurbir Yadav (Chillum), Aneeta Kanwar (Rekha) and Nana Patekar (Baba).

Krishna, a small, spindly-legged ten-year-old country boy, is kicked out of the house by his mother and told not to return until he has 500 rupees to pay for a bicycle he has ruined. Krishna drifts to the nearest big city where, without effort, he is absorbed into Bombay's proliferating population of homeless street kids.

A concerned documentary would probably treat Krishna as one of the faceless mob, important mostly as a representation of a human condition. The film that contained him would be a general statement, and Krishna himself, old beyond his years, would remain unknowable, forever lost. How sad, we would be asked to say, and then, but that's India.

The achievement of *Salaam Bombay!*, Mira Nair's remarkably good first fiction feature, is that Krishna has his own identity. He's an utterly specific character. Krishna may be naive, but he quickly learns how to get along in a world of beggars, prostitutes, drug pushers, and vicious ripoff artists, some of whom are quite respectable.

For a film about such hopelessness, *Salaam Bombay!* is surprisingly cheering, not because Miss Nair has sentimentalized the scene but because, being Indian herself, she understands the particular reality of what appears, to us tourists, to be hopelessness. Seen close up, rather than from the window of a taxicab, despair is not so easily recognized. Life, lived always on the edge of disaster, is coped with, if not always with success.

Salaam Bombay! isn't exactly an upper, but neither is it a predigested social treatise. That the film is less nightmarish than Hector Babenco's riveting *Pixote* may have something to do with its being set in India rather than Brazil. There's a kind of ancient sophistication about the Bombay demimonde that is different from life in São Paulo, where widespread poverty and rootlessness are only a little older than the glass-and-steel high-rises of the very rich.

Salaam Bombay! will be shown at the New York Film Festival tonight and tomorrow. It opens its commercial engagement Sunday at the Lincoln Plaza 1.

Miss Nair, thirty-one, who was born and brought up in India and studied at Harvard as an undergraduate, has made four documentaries, all in India, which obviously helped prepare her for this work of fiction. One doesn't necessarily feed the other, however. *Salaam Bombay!* demonstrates this young director's extraordinary self-control when faced with fiction's manifold possibilities. The movie possesses a free-flowing exuberance not often associated with the documentary form.

Even more unusual is the director's success with her actors. Without the film's program notes, I'm not sure I'd be able to tell the professionals from the nonprofessionals.

The children, all nonprofessionals, are splendid, especially Shafiq Syed, the little boy who plays Krishna, and Hansa Vithal, as the tiny, stoic daughter of a Bombay prostitute and her pimp. The exceptionally good pro-actors include Aneeta Kanwar as the prostitute, Nana Patekar as the pimp, and Raghubir

Yadav as a godforsaken drug addict who, early on, befriends Krishna.

Salaam Bombay!, which was written by Sooni Taraporevala from a story by her and Miss Nair, is rich with self-explanatory incident. Action is character. Dialogue is spare. Even the camera is laconic. Though shot (beautifully by Sandi Sissel) entirely on location in Bombay, under conditions that could not have been easy, the film and its characters are never overwhelmed by local color.

Miss Nair sees Bombay less as a recognizable city than as the ever-present chaos surrounding Krishna and the people who move in and out of his life. Bombay is a place of noise, restless movement, and no privacy whatsover. It is squalor accepted as the natural order of things, and thus accommodated.

Miss Nair does not share this fatalism, but in *Salaam Bombay!* she allows us to examine it without panic, and without patronizing it. She is a new filmmaker to watch.

—*V.C., October 7, 1988*

SALESMAN

Produced and directed by Albert Maysles and David Maysles; cinematographer. Albert Maysles; edited by David Maysles and Charlotte Zwerin; released by Maysles Films. Black and white. Running time: 90 minutes.

With: Jamie Baker, Paul Brennan, Melbourne I. Feltman, Raymond Martos, Margaret McCarron, Charles McDevitt and Kennie Turner.

Albert and David Maysles's *Salesman,* which opened yesterday at the 68th Street Playhouse, is a documentary feature about four door-to-door Bible salesmen who move horizontally through the capitalistic dream. It's such a fine, pure picture of a small section of American life that I can't imagine its ever seeming irrelevant, either as a social document or as one of the best examples of what's called cinema verité or direct cinema.

Salesman is not a total movie—that is, a complete experience—as a fiction film may aspire to be. It is fact, photographed and recorded with extraordinarily mobile camera and sound equipment, and then edited and carefully shaped into a kind of cinematic mural of faces, words, motel rooms, parlors, kitchens, streets, television images, radio music—even weather.

The movie is a record of the adventures of four real-life, Boston-based representatives of the Mid-American Bible Company, filmed over a period of two months, first in and around Boston, then at a sales convention in Chicago, and finally during a sales tour in and around Miami. The focal point is Paul Brennan, a lean, bristly, professional Irish-American who, in the course of the movie, slowly comes to realize his inadequacy as a Bible pitchman. In a very gentle way, *Salesman* is Paul Brennan's voyage to personal defeat via rented automobile—a gallant Hickey in a Hertz.

Movie purists may object to some of the techniques employed by the Maysles brothers. They have eliminated from the film all evidence that the people being photographed—the salesmen and their customers—are aware of the presence of the camera. Obviously, they also photographed much more material than is included in the finished movie, allowing them to impose a certain narrative order on the events, and with that order, a point of view.

For one reason and another, I've seen *Salesman* three times, and each time I've been more impressed by what I can only describe as the decency of that point of view. The movie's lower-middle-class, Roman Catholic–oriented landscape is not particularly pretty, nor are the hard-sell tactics employed by the salesmen as they pitch their $49.95 Bibles to lonely widows, Cuban refugees, boozy housewives, and to one young couple that can't even pay its rent. "Be sure to have it blessed," a salesman reminds a customer to whom he's just made a sale, "or you won't get the full benefit from it."

However, everyone in the movie seems to be touched by the Maysleses' compassion, even the Mid-American Bible Company's pious "theological consultant," Melbourne I. Feltman, who, at the Chicago convention, urges the salesmen to go about their "Father's work," adding: "God grant you an abundant harvest." *Salesman* somehow transcends such surface mockery, partly, I think, because the salesmen really are no less vulnerable than their customers.

Giving the movie its comic and poignant dimension is Brennan's performance as Brennan, a cocky, beady-eyed drummer who finally succumbs to "negative thoughts" after a long period of being unable to make a sale. "I don't want to seem negative," he confesses to a colleague after a fruitless day, "but all I can see here is delinquent accounts." Brennan driving aimlessly through the fake Moorish architecture of Opa-Locka, Florida, where the streets are named after Sinbad and Ali Baba and the City Hall is shaped like a mosque, is an image of America as a worn-out Disneyland that is unforgettable.

Salesman is hardly a romantic movie, but in a curious way, it's just as exotic and strange a journey as any that the late Robert Flaherty (*Nanook of the North, Tabu*) ever took through the Arctic or the South Seas. It may not be the entire story of America or even of the salesmen themselves (whose private lives are barely touched), but it is a valuable and sometimes very funny footnote to contemporary history.

—*V.C., April 18, 1969*

SANJURO

Directed by Akira Kurosawa; written (in Japanese, with English subtitles) by Ryuzo Kikushima, Mr. Kurosawa and Hideo Oguni, based on the short story "Hibi Heian" by Shugoro Yamamoto; cinematographers, Fukuzo Koizumi and Koichi Saito; edited by Mr. Kurosawa; music by Masaru Sato; art designer, Yoshiro Muraki; produced by Mr. Kikushima and Tomoyuki Tanaka; released by the Toho Company. Black and white. Running time: 96 minutes.

With: Toshiro Mifune (Sanjuro), Tatsuya Nakadai (Murato), Takashi Shimura (Kurofori) and Reiko Dan (Kaigo).

The fans of Akira Kurosawa are due for an interesting surprise as they watch his new film, *Sanjuro*, which opened at the Toho Cinema yesterday.

So often have they been clobbered by the grand, violent, sword-swinging style of the Japanese director's samurai "Westerns" (*Yojimbo, The Magnificent Seven,* etc.) that they're likely to find themselves waiting somewhat restively to be socked again as this latest display of a samurai hero glides along toward its middle and nothing explodes.

The scene appears set for wild dramatics. A footloose samurai has turned up in a town where a cabal of nine young progressives is plotting to overthrow a corrupt regime. Boldly and brashly he has appeared among them while they have been fumbling for a plan and has haughtily taken over the ticklish task of directing them.

In an early encounter with armed retainers of one of the bosses of the corrupt regime, he has quickly and clearly demonstrated his superior technique with the sword by roundly routing his opponents. Here's the tip-off, it seems: this man is good.

Furthermore, he is played by none other than the grunting, swashbuckling Toshiro Mifune, the star in other Kurosawa "Westerns." So it should be only a matter of time, you think, before the picture explodes.

But it doesn't. And then as it slithers and almost dances deceptively into a strange lot of complicated plotting among the young busters on the one hand and the elderly bosses on the other, it slowly and entrancingly comes clear that this is not at all the sort of angry, wild, sword-swinging Kurosawa "Western" we have come to expect. This is a mischievous, sly, good-humored presentation of a crusty old samurai caught between two groups of plain incompetents, with a playful satiric point.

It is seen in the mechanized movements and facial expressions of the nine young men who could be kimono-clad duplications of a bunch of nitwits in gray flannel suits. It is seen in the snorting indignation and impatience of the old samurai, who just can't get over how stupid and unprofessional as conspirators these fellows are. And it is seen in the twittering of the bosses and in the clucking of a motherly type who comes in to chide the impatient old warrior, "Killing people at the slightest excuse is a bad habit, you know."

This is a new thing for Kurosawa, this making almost a joke of the heroic personality and the conventional conflicts in a samurai film. But while it is startling and refreshing, it isn't brought off with thorough success.

Amid the intensely graphic buildup of the devious complications of the plot—and, as usual, this is accomplished with brilliant blends of images and sounds—the clarity of the situation and a certain amount of interest are lost. It is awfully hard to follow who is conspiring against whom. One must simply accept the assumption that the old samurai is the "good guy" and all the rest are either stupid or bad.

Also, Kurosawa has not departed entirely from form. Sometimes he is kidding, sometimes he is not. When he has the magnificent Mifune lay about with his sword in one scene, sticking his leaping adversaries and slapping them soundly on their behinds, it is obvious that the aim is comic. But when he has the hero plunge his noble blade into the chest of a brave but wrongly allied adversary at the end, it appears that the sentiment is as fluid as the fountain of blood that gushes forth. Kurosawa can't abandon his feeling for the glory of the old samurai.

Even so, he has given us in *Sanjuro* a surprising, fetching, beautifully made film that fitly propounds the lesson of his own professionalism: "Never send a boy to do a man's work."

—*B.C., May 8, 1963*

SANSHO THE BAILIFF

Directed by Kenji Mizoguchi; written (in Japanese, with English subtitles) by Fuji Yahiro and Yahikata Yoda, based on the story "Sansho Dayu" by Ogai Mori; cinematographer, Kazuo Miyagawa; edited by Mitsuji Miyata; music by Fumio Hayasaka; art designer, Kasaku Ito; produced by Masaichi Nagata; released by Brandon Films. Black and white. Running time: 125 minutes.

With: Yoshiaki Hanayagi (Zushio), Kyoko Kagawa (Anju), Kinuyo Tanaka (Tamaki), Eitaro Shindo (Sansho), Akitaka Kono (Taro) and Masao Shimuzu (Masauji Taira).

The Bailiff, a Japanese film now playing at the New Yorker Theater, had its theatrical premiere at the Bleecker Street Cinema in September, at which time it was not reviewed. The present review intends to correct that omission and to reopen consideration of its director, the late Kenji Mizoguchi (1898–1956), whom film enthusiasts recognize as a supreme master but whom many intelligent moviegoers have never heard of. *The Bailiff* (more commonly known until now as *Sansho Dayu* or *Sansho the Bailiff*) dates from 1954, a year after *Ugetsu Monogatari*, the only Mizoguchi film at all well-known to local audiences—out of a career that extended back to 1923 and that includes more than forty movies in the sound period alone.

The film is set in eleventh-century Japan, when men could still own slaves. The bailiff of the title is such a slave owner, a powerful and cruel one, into whose hands fall Zushio and Anju, a young brother and sister, kidnapped children of a provincial governor, who has been exiled for his kindness to peasants.

The movie follows the children from before their kidnapping, through their ten years of servitude to the Bailiff Sansho, until Zushio escapes and Anju drowns herself—so she cannot be tortured into informing on her brother. Zushio makes his way to the capital, Kyoto, pleads his case, learns that his father (now dead) is honored for his humanity, and is appointed governor of the province where Sansho has his compound.

Zushio frees the slaves and then resigns his post so that he can search for his mother, who was sold into prostitution when her children were kidnapped. At the end he finds her, lame and blind, near a miserable hut on a distant island, sitting by the sea.

I have given the barest outline of the plot, which is immensely complicated and full of events—of a sensational and ultimately exemplary nature. It is typical of the method of *The Bailiff* that during their captivity Zushio and Anju should overhear a song, sung by a newly acquired slave girl, about two lost children named Zushio and Anju. The song is a device, familiar to fable, by which the children learn that their mother is alive and where she is. But it also suggests that the children have already entered folk literature, that their misery is also their glory, and, in a sense, their identity.

The Bailiff has a creed, the children's father's belief that "without mercy, man is like a beast," repeated many times in the subtitles and taken seriously by this very serious film. However, the film defines its characters as much by what they suffer as what they do, and its supreme quality, as in all the Mizoguchi I have seen, is its appreciation of lives lived by necessity rather than according to ideals.

In its two hours and five minutes, *The Bailiff* covers almost twenty years of family history. The expanse of time is necessary to accommodate the accretion of events that change people—not to define character so much as to let them submit, to become a part of their environment. In Mizoguchi's world, the end of living is to achieve minimal differentiation from the landscape—like the daughter walking to her watery death or the mother sitting at the edge of the sea.

859

The Bailiff is a film of breathtaking visual beauty, but the conditions of that beauty also change—from the ethereal delicacy of its beginning (before the kidnapping), through the dark masses of the Bailiff's compound, to the ordered perspectives of Kyoto and the governor's palace, and finally to the spare symbolic horizons at the end.

In effect, it moves from easy poetry to difficult poetry. Its impulses, which are profound but not transcendental, follow an esthetic program that is also a moral progression, and that emerges, with superb lucidity, only from the greatest art.

—*R.G., December 17, 1969*

SATURDAY NIGHT AND SUNDAY MORNING

Directed by Karel Reisz; written by Alan Sillitoe, based on his novel; cinematographer, Freddie Francis; edited by Seth Holt; music by John Dankworth; art designer, Ted Marshall; produced by Tony Richardson; released by Continental Distributing. Black and white. Running time: 90 minutes.

With: Albert Finney (Arthur), Shirley Anne Field (Doreen), Rachel Roberts (Brenda), Hylda Baker (Aunt Ada), Norman Rossington (Bert) and Bryan Pringle (Jack).

Another type of the youth of postwar Britain besides the "teddy boy" and the "angry young man" we've been seeing in some recent British pictures is portrayed fascinatingly in *Saturday Night and Sunday Morning,* which came to the Baronet yesterday.

He is a tough, robust, cheeky factory worker living (in this case) in midlands Nottingham, one of those great, sprawling, drab industrial cities that scar the landscape of Britain today. He is single and independent, rooms with his parents in their grubby worker's home, gripes about his low pay and harsh foreman, and spends his Saturday nights drinking beer in the pub.

Sure, he is skeptical and surly, sarcastic and rebellious toward certain things, including nasty old neighborhood women who get in his way and stick their noses into his affairs. But he is a fast, efficient worker—at his lathe and with the girls. He has confidence and a quiet determination. He can stand on his two feet in this world.

Maybe this sturdy young fellow, who is brilliantly realized and played by a fine young actor named Albert Finney, a new sensation of the British stage and screen, is a very exceptional specimen in the run of the working class. Maybe he has an uncommon share of humor, courage, pride, and dignity. But he certainly is a satisfying person and a happy, comforting relief from the devious, self-pitying rogues and weaklings we have seen in a lot of modern-day films.

So are most of the people around him in this remarkably graphic picture that Karel Reisz has directed and photographed in an impressively sharp, explicit, and often intimate "documentary" style. The young man's parents (Elsie Wagstaffe and Frank Pettitt) are sober, credible types—old folks, pretty well finished with the struggle and ready to sit in front of the "telly" and gaze. The young married woman (Rachel Roberts), with whom the young man is having a clandestine and shameless affair, and her machinist husband (Bryan Pringle) are reasonable and reassuring, too.

Our young man's friend (Norman Rossington) is a solid, slow, lantern-jawed midlands bloke, fine for a fishing companion and for listening to forthright, wholesome gripes. And the girl (Shirley Anne Field) he picks up at a pub and with whom he falls in love is a saucy, substantial, self-sufficient, and notably attractive kid.

In short, there is solid human fiber and a sense of hopefulness in this film, which Tony Richardson has produced with fine economy from a novel and screenplay by Alan Sillitoe. There is a confidence in the working class that is as matter-of-fact and severe as the long rows of workers' brick houses and the bank of beer spigots in the pub.

To be sure, a strong strain of melancholy, of regret that the freedom of man as a creature capable of having simple pleasures should be confined by ugly cities and machines, runs through the whole vivid picture. When Mr. Finney, in a sodden Saturday-night state, tries to keep the bobbies from nabbing a poor old bum who has heaved a rock, he is simply expressing resentment that life should be as it is; that an old man, lonely and frustrated, can only say so by breaking a pane of glass.

A smoldering of social rebellion, as well as sheer

lustfulness, is expressed in the sharp, sordid scenes with Mr. Finney and Miss Roberts as they conspire to make love or try bitterly to make some arrangement to get rid of an expected child. The camera, crowding them in these taut moments, shows the features of people cruelly trapped.

In the end, the sort of quiet accommodation that is compelled by life is made by the rugged people in a credible fashion, and they seem reasonably satisfied. The young man takes a beating for playing around with another man's wife and he discovers there's a hope of finding happiness with his young woman, played superbly by Miss Field. Within him there may always be resentment—an urge to "throw things," as he says in his last line—but he is not defeated or corrupted. You may be pretty sure he will survive.

Mr. Finney, with a grotesque Lancashire accent you have to keep your ears open to understand, is excitingly mobile and expressive, the outstanding person in the film. But all the others are richly authentic. They walk right out to you.

—*B.C., April 4, 1961*

SATURDAY NIGHT FEVER

Directed by John Badham; written by Norman Wexler, based on the magazine story "Tribal Rites of the New Saturday Night" by Nik Cohn; director of photography, Ralf D. Bode; edited by David Rawlins; music by Barry, Robin and Maurice Gibb, with David Shire; choreography by Lester Wilson; production designer, Charles Bailey; produced by Robert Stigwood; released by Paramount Pictures. Running time: 119 minutes.

With: John Travolta (Tony Manero), Karen Lynn Gorney (Stephanie), Barry Miller (Bobby C), Joseph Cali (Joey), Paul Pape (Double J) and Donna Pescow (Annette).

Tony is a handsome, bighearted guy with a lot more style than he knows what to do with. His job in a paint store doesn't call for much élan, but Tony supplies that anyway, charming the customers and strutting gamely down the street as he makes his deliveries. His room at home is dreary and his family even more so, but Tony has done what he can with Farrah and

Rocky and Pacino posters to give the place a little class. Even so, things can get him down—but just when they do, another week is over and it's time to hit the local disco. On the weekend, and on the dance floor, Tony is king.

Tony's whole life, as somebody else in *Saturday Night Fever* manages to point out, is "a cliché." But John Travolta is so earnestly in tune with the character that Tony becomes even more touching than he is familiar and a source of fierce, desperate excitement. The movie, which spends mercifully little time trying to explain Tony, has a violent energy very like his own.

This is best demonstrated during the dancing sequences, which take up much of the film's time. Tony is depicted as being better than most, but also one of many; everyone in the 2001 Odyssey disco in Bay Ridge, Brooklyn, seems possessed of a similar short-term vitality and pride. Their dancing is fluid, but it's also strictly, almost militaristically choreographed; people who stake everything on style can't afford to be sloppy, or even genuinely boisterous. Though the dancing is set to a blaring, contemporary score and often photographed in a red glow, the movie owes a lot more to *West Side Story* than it does to *Mean Streets*.

Mr. Travolta dances with a fine arrogance that follows naturally from the rest of his performance, and he has one solo number that stops the show. But John Badham, who previously directed another stylish, street-smart movie, *The Bingo Long Traveling All-Stars and Motor Kings*, isn't always content to let the simple energy of the music or the performances suffice. Too often, he cuts distractingly in the middle of a routine, and his efforts to aggrandize characters by shooting them at angles or from below are superfluous. If these kids weren't flamboyant enough on their own, no amount of camera tricks could cover for them.

Saturday Night Fever, which opens today at several theaters, begins to flag when, after an initial hour filled with high spirits and jubilant music, it settles down to tell its story; the effect is so deflating that it's almost as though another Monday has rolled around and it's time to get back to work.

It seems that Tony's friends, who are a lively but uninteresting lot, are so dead-ended that they're beginning to make him worry about his own future. And Stephanie (Karen Lynn Gorney), who has a job in Manhattan, is such a braggart that she has begun to give him notions of upward mobility.

Ten minutes into the movie, you can be sure that its ending will be at least partly upbeat and that whatever happens will be blunt. But that is still no preparation for all the gruesome tricks Norman Wexler's screenplay uses to get Tony out of Brooklyn.

Surely there are some people who make decisions without needing to be spurred on by a serious family trauma, an exceedingly ugly sexual episode, and a friend's leap off the Verrazano Bridge. Tony, from what we've seen of him, is too proud and sensitive to need this much disillusionment to get him moving, but the screenplay has a way of indirectly insulting the character by coddling him far more than he would ever coddle himself.

Mr. Travolta is deft and vibrant, and he never condescends to the character, not even in a scene that has Tony and Stephanie arguing about whose *Romeo and Juliet* it is, Zeffirelli's or Shakespeare's. (They also try to identify Sir Laurence Olivier, and then remember that he's the guy who sells cameras on television.) Miss Gorney uses a much thicker accent and many more mispronunciations, and too often she is transparent in playing dumb. Donna Pescow, as one of the many local girls whom Tony could have but doesn't want, stays much more comfortably within the boundaries of her role.

Among the movie's most influential principals—although they never appear on-screen—are the Bee Gees, who provided the most important parts of its score. It could be argued that the Bee Gees have been turning out the kinds of jaunty, formulaic disco hits that punctuate the movie for so long that they've lost any trace of originality. But it could also be argued that the group now has this kind of music down to a science, and that originality is not exactly a key ingredient in the disco mystique. In any case, at its best, the music moves with a real spring in its step, and the movie does too.

—*J.M., December 16, 1977*

SAVING PRIVATE RYAN

Directed by Steven Spielberg; written by Robert Rodat; director of photography, Janusz Kaminski; edited by Michael Kahn; music by John Williams; production designer, Tom Sanders; produced by Mr. Spielberg, Ian Bruce, Mark Gordon and Gary Levinsohn; released by Dreamworks Pictures and Paramount Pictures. Running time: 170 minutes.

With: Tom Hanks (Captain Miller), Tom Sizemore (Sergeant Horvath), Edward Burns (Private Reiben), Barry Pepper (Private Jackson), Adam Goldberg (Private Mellish), Vin Diesel (Private Caparzo), Giovanni Ribisi (T/4 Medic Wade), Jeremy Davies (Corporal Upham), Matt Damon (Private Ryan), Ted Danson (Captain Hamill), Paul Giamatti (Sergeant Hill), Dennis Farina (Lieutenant Colonel Anderson), Joerg Stadler (Steamboat Willie), Harve Presnell (General Marshall) and Harrison Young (Ryan as Old Man).

When soldiers are killed in *Saving Private Ryan*, their comrades carefully preserve any messages they left behind. Removed from the corpses of the newly dead, sometimes copied over to hide bloodstains, these writings surely describe some of the fury of combat, the essence of spontaneous courage, the craving for solace, the bizarre routines of wartime existence, the deep loneliness of life on the brink. Steven Spielberg's soberly magnificent new war film, the second such pinnacle in a career of magical versatility, has been made in the same spirit of urgent communication. It is the ultimate devastating letter home.

Since the end of World War II and the virtual death of the Western, the combat film has disintegrated into a showcase for swagger, cynicism, obscenely overblown violence, and hollow, self-serving victories. Now, with stunning efficacy, Mr. Spielberg turns back the clock. He restores passion and meaning to the genre with such whirlwind force that he seems to reimagine it entirely, dazzling with the breadth and intensity of that imagination. No received notions, dramatic or ideological, intrude on this achievement. This film simply looks at war as if war had not been looked at before.

Though the experience it recounts is grueling, the viscerally enthralling *Saving Private Ryan* is anything but. As he did in *Schindler's List*, Mr. Spielberg uses his preternatural storytelling gifts to personalize the unimaginable, to create instantly empathetic characters, and to hold an audience spellbound from the moment the action starts. Though the film essentially begins and ends with staggering, phenomenally agile battle sequences and contains isolated violent tragedies in between, its vision of combat is never allowed to grow numbing. Like the soldiers, viewers are made furiously alive to each new crisis and are never free to rest.

The film's immense dignity is its signal characteristic, and some of it is achieved through deliberate elision. We don't know anything about these men as they prepare to land at Omaha Beach on D-Day, which might make them featureless in the hands of a less intuitive filmmaker. Here, it means that any filter between audience and cataclysm has effectively been taken away.

The one glimmer of auxiliary information is the image of an elderly visitor at a military cemetery, which opens and closes the film (though these brief sequences lack the film's otherwise shattering verisimilitude). Whoever the man is, he sees the gravestones and drifts into D-Day memories. On the evidence of what follows, he can hardly have gone to sleep since June 6, 1944, without reliving these horrors in his dreams.

Though *Saving Private Ryan* is liable to be described as extremely violent for its battle reenactments, that is not quite the case. The battle scenes avoid conventional suspense and sensationalism; they disturb not by being manipulative but by being hellishly frank. Imagine Hieronymus Bosch with a Steadicam (instead of the immensely talented Janusz Kaminski) and you have some idea of the tableaux to emerge here, as the film explodes into panoramic yet intimate visions of bloodshed.

What's unusual about this, in both the D-Day sequence and the closing struggle, is its terrifying reportorial candor. These scenes have a sensory fullness (the soundtrack is boomingly chaotic yet astonishingly detailed), a realistic yet breakneck pace, a ceaseless momentum, and a vast visual scope. Artful, tumultuous warfare choreography heightens the intensity. So do editing decisions that balance the ordeal of the individual with the mass attack under way.

So somehow we are everywhere: aboard landing craft in the throes of anticipatory jitters; underwater where bullets kill near-silently and men drown under the weight of heavy equipment; on the shore with the man who flies upward in an explosion and then comes down minus a leg; moving inland with the Red Cross and the priest and the sharpshooter; reaching a target with the savagely vengeful troops who firebomb a German bunker and let the men burn. Most of all, we are with Captain John Miller (Tom Hanks) in heights of furious courage and then, suddenly, in an epiphany of shellshocked confusion. Never have Mr. Hanks's everyman qualities been more instantly effective than here.

When the battle finally ends, there are other unfamiliar sights, like the body of a soldier named Ryan washed up on the beach amid fish. (The film's bloody authenticity does not allow false majesty for the dead.) Next we are drawn into the incongruously small-scale drama of the Ryan family, with three sons killed and only one remaining, lost somewhere in Normandy. Miller and his unit, played with seamless ensemble spirit by actors whose preproduction bootcamp experience really shows here, are sent to find what the captain calls "a needle in a stack of needles" and bring him home alive.

In another beautifully choreographed sequence, shot with obvious freshness and alacrity, the soldiers talk while marching through the French countryside. On the way, they establish strong individual identities and raise the film's underlying questions about the meaning of sacrifice. Mr. Spielberg and the screenwriter, Robert Rodat, have a way of taking these standard-issue characters and making them unaccountably compelling.

Some of that can also be ascribed to the fine, indie-bred cast that includes Edward Burns (whose acting prospects match his directing talents) as the wise guy from Brooklyn; Tom Sizemore as the rock-solid second in command; Giovanni Ribisi as the thoughtful medic; Barry Pepper as the devout Southern sharpshooter; Jeremy Davies as the timid, desperately inadequate intellectual; Vin Diesel as the tough Italian; and Adam Goldberg as the tough Jew.

As the actors spar (coolly, with a merciful lack of glibness), the film creates a strong sense of just how different they are and just how strange it is for each man to find himself in this crucible. Yet *Saving Private Ryan,* unlike even the best films about the mind-bending disorientation of the Vietnam War, does not openly challenge the moral necessity of their being forced to fight. With a wonderfully all-embracing vision, it allows for patriotism, abject panic, and everything in between. The soldiers' decisions are never made easily, and sometimes they are fatally wrong. In this uncertainty, too, *Saving Private Ryan* tells an unexpected truth.

The film divides gracefully into a string of well-defined sequences that lead inexorably to Ryan. Inevitably, audiences will know that he is played by Matt Damon and thus will be found alive. But the film still manages to create considerable suspense about when and how he will appear. When it finally comes, Mr. Damon's entrance is one more tribute to Mr. Spielberg's ingenious staging, catching the viewer utterly off-guard. There's the same effect to Ryan's impassioned reaction, in one of many scenes that prompt deep emotion, to the news that he can go home.

Though *Saving Private Ryan* features Hollywood's most durable contemporary star in its leading role, there's nothing stellar about the way Mr. Hanks gives the film such substance and pride. As in *Apollo 13,* his is a modest, taciturn brand of heroism, and it takes on entirely new shadings here. In Miller, the film finds a plain yet gratifying complex focus, a decent, strong, fallible man who sustains his courage while privately confounded by the extent that war has now shaped him.

"Back home, I'd tell people what I do, they'd say, 'It figures,' " he explains to his men after an especially troubling encounter. "But over here, it's a big mystery, judging from the looks on your faces. I guess that means I've changed over here. I wonder sometimes if my wife is even going to recognize me, whenever it is I'm going to get back to her. And how I can possibly tell her about days like today."

Among the many epiphanies in *Saving Private Ryan* are some especially unforgettable ones: the anguished ordeal of Mr. Davies's mapmaker and translator in a staircase in the midst of battle; the tranquil pause in a bombed-out French village, to the strains of Edith Piaf; the brisk way the soldiers sift through a pile of dog tags, momentarily forgetting that each one signifies a death. A man driving a tank looks up for a split second before a Molotov cocktail falls on him. Two of the film's principals huddle against sandbags at a critical juncture; and then, suddenly, only one is still breathing.

The sparing use of John Williams's music sustains the tension in scenes, like these, that need no extra emphasis. But *Saving Private Ryan* does have a very few false notes. Like the cemetery scenes, the capture of a German soldier takes a turn for the artificial, especially when the man expresses his desperation through broad clowning. But in context, such a jarring touch is actually a relief. It's a reminder that, after all, *Saving Private Ryan* is only a movie. Only the finest war movie of our time.

—J.M., July 24, 1998

SAY ANYTHING

Written and directed by Cameron Crowe; director of photography, Laszlo Kovacs; edited by Richard Marks; music by Richard Gibbs and Anne Dudley; production designer, Mark Mansbridge; produced by Polly Platt; released by Twentieth Century Fox. Running time: 100 minutes.

With: John Cusack (Lloyd Dobler), Ione Skye (Diane Court), John Mahoney (James Court), Lili Taylor (Corey Flood), Amy Brooks (D. C.), Pamela Segall (Rebecca), Jason Gould (Mike Cameron), Loren Dean (Joe) and Glenn Walker Harris Jr. (Jason).

Can a nice guy named Lloyd, who has no plans for college, win the love of the beautiful ice princess who happens to be class valedictorian? Does anyone over the age of eighteen care? *Say Anything* has a prepackaged feel, with all the fuzzy-hearted warmth of a John Hughes film. But it was written and directed by Cameron Crowe, who wrote *Fast Times at Ridgemont High,* a tough-minded, sardonic film that makes Molly Ringwald's high school girls seem as realistic as Dorothy in Oz.

The predictable surface of *Say Anything* is constantly being cracked by characters who think and talk like real people and by John Cusack's terrifically natural, appealing Lloyd. Here is a film seriously at war with itself.

Lloyd's two best friends—girls named Corey and D. C.—warn him away from Diane, for his own good and with flawless reasoning. Lloyd spends his time practicing kick boxing—a combination of boxing and karate kicks he is convinced is the sport of the future. Diane is an overachieving, overprotected only child who lives with her divorced father and keeps a small model of a human brain in her bedroom. A jock and a brain; they're a hopeless match. But it is easy to see why Diane falls in love with Lloyd. He makes her feel as protected as her father but adds none of the pressure to be brilliant.

Mr. Cusack, who played the subdued, confused Buck Weaver in *Eight Men Out,* is one of the most accomplished, self-assured young actors around. Here he captures all of Lloyd's anxiety and determination. He fidgets and paces when he phones Diane but never looks mannered. Lloyd is so levelheaded and decent, so young and uncomplicated, that when he complains about his divorced sister's perpetual bad mood—"How hard is it to decide to be in a good mood and just be in a good mood?"—he almost makes sense.

Like many real-life teenagers, Lloyd and Diane have sex. Then Lloyd and his friends have conversations about sex. "You're an inspiration, Lloyd," D. C. tells him wistfully after he has slept with the presumably unattainable Diane. "You should go on *The 700 Club* or something."

John Mahoney, as Diane's father, is solid and opaque, exactly what he should be. When the I.R.S. investigates him for stealing money from patients in his nursing home, we can't tell, any more than his daughter can, whether his trustworthiness is an act. But we can see that Mr. Mahoney drives a car, sings "Rikki Don't Lose That Number" along with the radio, and manages not to lose his dignity.

Lili Taylor, who played the no-nonsense Jojo in *Mystic Pizza,* turns Corey into a major character. She once tried to commit suicide because her boyfriend left her (hinting at a more substantial subplot, as if some of Corey's scenes were chopped out). But she has survived to write sixty-five songs about him, one of which begins: "Joe lies. Joe lies. Joe lies."

Ione Skye looks beautiful as Diane, though she doesn't have the depth to convince us that behind those shiny love-struck eyes and that girlish voice is a brain that won a scholarship to England.

Say Anything, which opens today at the National and other theaters, resembles a first-rate production of a children's story. Its sense of parents and the summer after high school is myopic, presented totally from the teenagers' point of view. Yet its melodrama—Will Dad go to prison? Will Diane go to England?—distorts that perspective, so the film doesn't have much to offer an actual adult, not even a sense of what it's truly like to be just out of high school these days. The film is all charming performances and grace notes, but there are plenty of worse things to be.

—*C.J., April 14, 1989*

SAYONARA

Directed by Joshua Logan: written by Paul Osborn, based on the novel by James Michener: cinematographer, Ellsworth Fredericks: edited by Arthur Schmidt and Philip W. Anderson: music by Franz Waxman: art designer, Ted Haworth: produced by William Goetz: released by Warner Brothers. Running time: 147 minutes.

With: Marlon Brando (Major Gruver), Miiko Taka (Hana-ogi), Red Buttons (Kelly), Miyoshi Umeki (Katsumi), Patricia Owens (Eileen Webster) and Kent Smith (General Webster).

Now it is understandable why so much attention has been paid, in advertisements and publicity, to Marlon Brando's appearance in the film version of James A. Michener's *Sayonara,* which came to the Music Hall yesterday along with the Christmas stage show and the annual pageant of the Nativity.

It is Mr. Brando's Major Gruver, the Air Force hero who falls in love with a beautiful Japanese actress in this beautiful, sentimental tale, that gives eccentricity and excitement to a richly colorful film. It is Mr. Brando's offbeat acting of what could be a conventional role that spins what could be a routine romance into a lively and tense dramatic show.

Actually, Mr. Michener's story of a West Point champion who succumbs to the charm of a Kobe "girl opera" performer and secretly lives with her, at the risk of degrading his social status and harming his Air Force career, is a porously obvious modern rewrite of the old *Madame Butterfly* tale, fixed up with an easy happy ending. It could be as ho-hum as a yawn.

And Paul Osborn's screenplay does little to widen its scope, except call for the camera to be set up in situations that command nice atmosphere.

But into it booms Mr. Brando, not a warlike Westerner, as in the book—not a fiery-tongued patent-leather hero—but a shut-mah-mouf-talking Southerner with a good-humored sort of impish nature underneath his standard West Point-hardened crust.

Smartly controlled by Joshua Logan, he is not a hard-pants, decisive type. He thinks slowly. He ponders his problems. He slurs his ideas the way he slurs his words. His mind and emotions are untidy, so far as his own personal order is concerned. He may be a whiz of a jet pilot and a capable military man, but he's a kid at taking care of his own thinking. He's as emotionally immature as a teenage boy.

This is clearly conveyed by Mr. Brando in a gangling yet vigorous acting style, and it opens intriguing implications and possibilities in the rather simple tale. For the chink in his military armor is thus made more clear and logical, and it helps to make human, sympathetic, and even delicate his surrender to an unconventional love.

But Mr. Brando is not the whole picture. Mr. Logan, who directed for William Goetz, has harmonized many sensuous values in giving beauty and tenderness to the romance. He has got from an unskilled actress, Miiko Taka, a flute-like beauty—a really lovely, serene, and soothing impulse—as the vestal dancer who gives herself to the American.

In a frame of handsome Japanese surroundings— outdoor gardens, graceful, sliding-paneled homes, bare-walled theaters, and delicate teahouses, shown in colors of exceptional taste and blend—he has pictorially justified the jangle and the harmony of cultures in his tale. There are scenes that are visually poetic, and that's as good as can be said for such a film.

While the inserts of theater performances—the Matsubayashi Girl Revue (a sumptuous and ornate razzle-dazzle that looks like a Japanese Folies Bergère), the traditional Kabuki and No acting, and a quaint little puppet show—do not last long enough to give an idea of what they mean, they are colorful.

Also, Red Buttons is excellent as an Air Force sergeant who marries a Japanese girl and is championed by Major Gruver; Miyoshi Umeki is droll as the girl, Kent Smith is stolid as a general, and Patricia Owens is sleek as the hero's ex-fiancée. Ricardo Montalban is not up to giving the illusion of being a Japanese theater star, and two or three other fellows are Hollywood Army officers.

On the whole, the musical score of Franz Waxman suggests the crystal tinkling music of Japan and helps the moods. And then there's the title song number— you'll have to bear it—by Irving Berlin.

—B.C., December 6, 1957

SCENES FROM A MARRIAGE

Written (in Swedish, with English subtitles), produced and directed by Ingmar Bergman: cine-matographer. Sven Nykvist: edited by Siv Lundgren: art designer. Björn Thulin: released by Cinema V. Running time: 168 minutes.

With: Liv Ullmann (Marianne), Erland Josephson (Johan), Bibi Andersson (Katarina), Jan Malmsjö (Peter), Anita Wall (Mrs. Palm) and Gunnel Lindblom (Eva).

Ingmar Bergman's *Scenes from a Marriage,* starring the incomparable Liv Ullmann and Erland Josephson as lovers who don't always know it, is the first major film event of the autumn season. It's a movie of such extraordinary intimacy that it has the effect of breaking into mysterious components many things we ordinarily accept without thought, familiar and banal objects, faces, attitudes, and emotions, especially love.

A smile is a composite of pain, anger, affection, and creeping boredom. The surface of a double bed is a linen battleground. Later the rumpled white sheets suggest an abandoned Arctic landscape on a planet in a universe that might be contained within the head of a pin.

In *Scenes from a Marriage,* Mr. Bergman is examining the molecular structure of a human relationship. You think you've seen it before, but every time you see it, it's new, which is one of the things about love. Like a laboratory model of a molecule, the design is complex and beautiful in a purely abstract way, but the film is also intensely, almost unbearably moving.

The look of the film has something to do with this. The two-hour, forty-eight-minute movie, which opened yesterday at the Cinema I, is Mr. Bergman's theatrical version of a five-hour production he made for Swedish television last year. The director has not only edited the six original fifty-minute installments down to the present length, but he has blown up the 16mm negative to 35mm, which gives a kind of pointillist effect.

Then, too, the television film was mostly photographed (by Sven Nykvist) in tight close-ups that the masking of the theatrical screen, which is less square than the TV screen, emphasizes by cutting off chins and the tops of heads. A filmmaker really can't get much closer to his actors without using surgery.

Most ordinary films made for television seem empty when seen in a theater. There simply isn't enough visual and emotional detail to keep the mind occupied. It's like looking at a photomural in Grand Central Terminal, one of those elephantine enlargements of an Instamatic snap.

The absolute opposite is true of *Scenes from a Marriage*. Although we seldom see more than two persons at a time, and usually only one, the theater screen is bursting with information, associations, and contradictory feelings.

Mr. Bergman tells the story of Johan (Mr. Josephson) and Marianne (Miss Ullmann) in six seemingly arbitrary "chapters" that have titles such as "Innocence and Panic," "The Art of Sweeping Under the Rug," and "In the Middle of the Night in a Dark House."

When we first see them, Johan and Marianne are being interviewed about the perfection of their ten-year marriage as material for a drippy women's magazine. Johan appears to be smug, self-mocking. Marianne is uneasy. When pressed, she says that she thinks Johan is "awfully nice."

They've reached a kind of windless plateau in their marriage. Johan has a satisfying career as a university professor. Marianne is a lawyer specializing in family problems. They have two daughters (who always remain offscreen), in-laws who are fondly demanding, and an unstated agreement not to discuss real problems, including the fact that they no longer satisfy each other sexually. Marianne seems cold and at one point says that "sex isn't everything," but with hindsight we are able to recognize her desperation.

It is Johan who flies the coop—with an irritable, hugely jealous girl in her twenties named Paula, who also remains offscreen. In succeeding chapters of the film covering ten more years, *Scenes from a Marriage* tells of the divorce of Johan and Marianne, of the remarriage of each to other partners, and of their continuing meetings. They eventually forge a new relationship that isn't necessarily happy, although it marks a profound development in their capacities to understand and care for each other.

I suspect that if we met Johan or Marianne in real life neither would seem to be especially interesting. It is the accomplishment of the director and his actors that they reveal these humdrum characters in ways that usually aren't possible except in first-person prose, in ways that make them unique and important.

Under Mr. Bergman's direction and with his material, Miss Ullmann again establishes herself as one of the most fascinating actresses of our time, and if she seems to have the edge over her costar, it may well be because of the director's fascination with women. He can't help paying tribute to them.

Mr. Josephson gives an equally complex performance, but Johan seems to have been conceived with a certain amount of guilt. He's a not-quite-admirable character. As Marianne liberates herself, Johan drifts into unspectacular failure. Yet this is to oversimplify Bergman, and nothing in this film is cut and dried.

Toward the end, Johan and Marianne are having an illicit weekend at a country cabin. It is twenty years since they met, and Marianne still wonders whether she can love anyone. Johan cradles her as they sit in bed. After twenty years Johan is sleepy but not yet exhausted. He says: "I think I love you in my imperfect and rather selfish way. And I think you love me in your stormy, emotional way. In fact, I think that you and I love one another. In an earthly and imperfect way."

It is a happy ending, almost. And a superb film.

—*V.C., September 16, 1974*

SCHINDLER'S LIST

Directed by Steven Spielberg; written by Steve Zaillian, based on the novel by Thomas Keneally; director of photography, Janusz Kaminski; edited by Michael Kahn; music by John Williams; production designer, Allan Starski; produced by Mr. Spielberg, Gerald R. Molen and Branko Lustig; released by Universal Pictures. Black and white. Running time: 185 minutes.

With: Liam Neeson (Oskar Schindler), Ben Kingsley (Itzhak Stern), Ralph Fiennes (Amon Goeth), Caroline Goodall (Emilie Schindler), Jonathan Sagalle (Poldek Pfefferberg) and Embeth Davidtz (Helen Hirsch).

There is a real photographic record of some of the people and places depicted in *Schindler's List*, and it has a haunting history. Raimund Titsch, an Austrian Catholic who managed a uniform factory within the Plaszow labor camp in Poland, surreptitiously took pictures of what he saw. Fearful of having the pictures developed, he hid his film in a steel box, which he buried in a park outside Vienna and then did not disturb for nearly twenty years. Although it was sold secretly by Titsch when he was terminally ill, the film remained undeveloped until after his death.

The pictures that emerged, like so many visual representations of the Holocaust, are tragic, ghostly, and remote. The horrors of the Holocaust are often viewed from a similar distance, filtered through memory or insulated by grief and recrimination. Documented exhaustively or dramatized in terms by now dangerously familiar, the Holocaust threatens to become unimaginable precisely because it has been imagined so fully. But the film *Schindler's List,* directed with fury and immediacy by a profoundly surprising Steven Spielberg, presents the subject as if discovering it anew.

Schindler's List brings a preeminent pop mastermind together with a story that demands the deepest reserves of courage and passion. Rising brilliantly to the challenge of this material and displaying an electrifying creative intelligence, Mr. Spielberg has made sure that neither he nor the Holocaust will ever be thought of in the same way again. With every frame, he demonstrates the power of the filmmaker to distill complex events into fiercely indelible images. *Schindler's List* begins with the sight of Jewish prayer candles burning down to leave only wisps of smoke, and there can be no purer evocation of the Holocaust than that.

A deserted street littered with the suitcases of those who have just been rounded up and taken away. The look on the face of a captive Jewish jeweler as he is tossed a handful of human teeth to mine for fillings. A snowy sky that proves to be raining ashes. The panic of a prisoner unable to find his identity papers while he is screamed at by an armed soldier, a man with an obviously dangerous temper. These visceral scenes, and countless others like them, invite empathy as surely as Mr. Spielberg once made viewers wish E.T. would get well again.

But this time his emphasis is on the coolly Kafkaesque aspects of an authoritarian nightmare. Drawing upon the best of his storytelling talents, Mr. Spielberg has made *Schindler's List* an experience that is no less enveloping than his earlier works of pure entertainment. Dark, sobering, and also invigoratingly dramatic, *Schindler's List* will make terrifying sense to anyone, anywhere.

The big man at the center of this film is Oskar Schindler, a Catholic businessman from the Sudeten-

land who came to occupied Poland to reap the spoils of war. (You can be sure this is not the last time the words *Oscar* and *Schindler* will be heard together.) Schindler is also something of a cipher, just as he was for Thomas Keneally, whose 1982 book, *Schindler's List,* marked a daring synthesis of fiction and fact. Reconstructing the facts of Schindler's life to fit the format of a novel, Mr. Keneally could only draw upon the memories of those who owed their lives to the man's unexpected heroism. Compiling these accounts (in a book that included some of the Titsch photographs), Mr. Keneally told "the story of the pragmatic triumph of good over evil, a triumph in eminently measurable, statistical unsubtle terms."

The great strength of Mr. Keneally's book, and now of Mr. Spielberg's film, lies precisely in this pragmatism. Knowing only the particulars of Schindler's behavior, the audience is drawn into wondering about his higher motives, about the experiences that transformed a casual profiteer into a selfless hero.

Schindler's story becomes much more involving than a tale of more conventional courage might be, just as Mr. Spielberg's use of unfamiliar actors to play Jewish prisoners makes it hard to view them as stock movie characters (even when the real events that befall these people threaten to do just that). The prisoners' stories come straight from Mr. Keneally's factual account, which is beautifully recapitulated by Steven Zaillian's screenplay.

Oskar Schindler, played with mesmerizing authority by Liam Neeson, is unmistakably larger than life, with the panache of an old-time movie star. (The real Schindler was said to resemble George Sanders and Curt Jurgens.) From its first glimpse of Oskar as he dresses for a typically flamboyant evening socializing with German officers—and even from the way his hand appears, nonchalantly holding a cigarette and a bribe—the film studies him with rapt attention.

Mr. Neeson, captured so glamorously by Janusz Kaminski's richly versatile black-and-white cinematography, presents Oskar as an amalgam of canny opportunism and supreme, well-warranted confidence. Mr. Spielberg does not have to underscore the contrast between Oskar's life of privilege and the hardships of his Jewish employees.

Taking over a kitchenware factory in Cracow and benefiting from Jewish slave labor, Oskar at first is no hero. During a deft, seamless section of the film that depicts the setting up of this business operation, Oskar is seen happily occupying an apartment from which a wealthy Jewish couple has just been evicted. Meanwhile, the film's Jews are relegated to the Cracow ghetto. After the ghetto is evacuated and shut down, they are sent to Plaszow, which is overseen by a coolly brutal SS commandant named Amon Goeth.

Goeth, played fascinatingly by the English stage actor Ralph Fiennes, is the film's most sobering creation. The third of its spectacularly fine performances comes from Ben Kingsley as the reserved, wary Jewish accountant who becomes Oskar's trusted business manager, and who at one point has been rounded up by Nazi officers before Oskar saves him. "What if I got here five minutes later?" Oskar asks angrily, with the self-interest that keeps this story so startling. "*Then* where would I be?"

As the glossy, voluptuous look of Oskar's sequences gives way to a stark documentary-style account of the Jews' experience, *Schindler's List* witnesses a pivotal transformation. Oskar and a girlfriend, on horseback, watch from a hilltop as the ghetto is evacuated, and the image of a little girl in red seems to crystallize Oskar's horror.

But there is a more telling sequence later on, when Oskar is briefly arrested for having kissed a young Jewish woman during a party at his factory. Kissing women is, for Oskar, the most natural act in the world. And he is stunned to find it forbidden on racial grounds. All at once, he understands how murderous and irrational the world has become, and why no prisoners can be safe without the intervention of an Oskar Schindler.

The real Schindler saved more than a thousand Jewish workers by sheltering them in his factory, and even accomplished the unimaginable feat of rescuing some of them from Auschwitz. This film's moving coda, a full-color sequence, offers an unforgettable testimonial to Schindler's achievement.

The tension in *Schindler's List* comes, of course, from the omnipresent threat of violence. But here again, Mr. Spielberg departs from the familiar. The film's violent acts are relatively few, considering its subject matter, and are staged without the blatant sadism that might be expected. Goeth's hobby of playing sniper, casually targeting his prisoners with a high-powered rifle, is presented so matter-of-factly that it becomes much more terrible than it would be if given more lingering attention.

Mr. Spielberg knows well how to make such events truly shocking, and how to catch his audience off guard. Most of these shootings are seen from a great distance, and occur unexpectedly. When it appears that the film is leading up to the point-blank execution of a rabbi, the director has something else in store.

Goeth's lordly balcony, which overlooks the film's vast labor-camp set, presents an extraordinary set of visual possibilities, and Mr. Spielberg marshals them most compellingly. But the presence of huge crowds and an immense setting also plays to this director's weakness for staging effects en masse. *Schindler's List* falters only when the crowd of prisoners is reduced to a uniform entity, so that events no longer have the tumultuous variety of real life.

This effect is most noticeable in Schindler's last scene, the film's only major misstep, as a throng listens silently to Oskar's overwrought farewell. In a film that moves swiftly and urgently through its three-hour running time, this stagy ending—plus a few touches of fundamentally false uplift, most notably in a sequence at Auschwitz—amounts to a very small failing.

Among the many outstanding elements that contribute to *Schindler's List,* Michael Kahn's nimble editing deserves special mention. So does the production design by Allan Starski, which finds just the right balance between realism and drama. John Williams's music has a somber, understated loveliness. The soundtrack becomes piercingly beautiful as Itzhak Perlman's violin solos occasionally augment the score.

It should be noted, if only in passing, that Mr. Spielberg has this year delivered the most astounding one-two punch in the history of American cinema. *Jurassic Park,* now closing in on billion-dollar grosses, is the biggest movie moneymaker of all time. *Schindler's List,* destined to have a permanent place in memory, will earn something better.

—*J.M., December 15, 1993*

THE SCOUNDREL

Produced, written and directed by Ben Hecht and Charles MacArthur; cinematographer, Lee Garmes; edited by Arthur Ellis; music by Frank Tours; art designer, Walter E. Keller; released by Paramount Pictures. Black and white. Running time: 76 minutes.

With: Noël Coward (Anthony Mallare), Julie Haydon (Cora Moore), Stanley Ridges (Paul Decker), Martha Sleeper (Julia Vivian), Ernest Cossart (Jimmy Clay) and Alexander Woollcott (Vanderveer Veyden).

Ben Hecht and Charles MacArthur, the literary madmen of Long Island, have lured Noël Coward into their den and composed an enormously entertaining, witty, and bizarre photoplay called *The Scoundrel,* which the Radio City Music Hall presented yesterday. Regarding its merits there are likely to be many opinions, ranging the middle ground between the gentleman who stood up in his seat and shouted "Bravo! Bravo!" and the young woman who looked around defiantly after the lights went up and made an irreverent noise with her mouth. One thing is certain: it contains the most dazzling writing that this column has ever heard on the screen. A caustic and icily cynical essay in disillusion, topped off with some bogus mysticism that the boys doubtless tossed in for the herd to play with, it is a distinctly exhilarating event in the cinema regardless of whether you look upon it as art or spinach.

Originally it was entitled *Miracle in Forty-ninth Street,* which is a more illuminating title than *The Scoundrel.* In the magnificent half-tones of Lee Garmes's photography, the boys are presenting Mr. Coward as the New York publisher, Anthony Mallare, a man of brilliant surfaces and a bad case of elephantiasis of the ego. Mallare postures against a background of sick intellectuals, the degenerate literati who pose blearily in the warmth of their own wit and their superior disinterest in the world outside. Mallare himself functions as a "smirk of adjectives," an attitude, a gaudy and improbable mouthpiece for the malice of the Hecht-MacArthur typewriters.

He is Mr. Hecht's favorite hero, a thing of evil who destroys everything he touches. When Mallare betrays a naive young poetess, thereby driving her true love into the gutter, she calls down a frightful curse on him: that his plane may crash and that he may die with the thought that no tear will be shed for him when he is gone. When his plane actually crashes he finds his path into eternity barred by a divine voice which gives him one month in which to return to life and find someone who will mourn for him.

As a modern miracle play *The Scoundrel* suffers from the laborious sentimentality of its conclusion. It is a trifle difficult for us to be touched by the unlikely spectacle of Mr. Coward calling upon his God to perform a miracle in a shabby rooming house. We cannot escape the impression that the fadeout—the River Styx and Mr. Coward presumably journeying across it into the great beyond—was something the authors worked up in the malicious belief that movie audiences who remain untouched by the authentic merits of the picture will grasp at the mysticism as an example of art with a capital A. The devices which they employ to endow the resurrected Mallare with mystery are too routine for comfort, and that bit of symbolism about the seaweed has been lifted from Alexander Woollcott's ghost story.

Perhaps the secret of the picture is that Mallare, although presented as the most odious man on earth, really has the admiration of the Frankensteins who made him. Mallare did, after all, rattle six times like a snake before striking. He wore his ugliness and insincerity very plainly in his buttonhole and allowed the unhappy lady more premonitions of disaster than she had any right to expect. This column, sharing the authors' admiration for their fascinating gargoyle, thought it very ungracious of them to have Mallare become a repentant sinner like any ordinary mortal.

But as a suavely mannered portrait of decadence, *The Scoundrel* is a remarkably interesting motion picture. Mr. Coward is so perfectly attuned to the part that we cannot help suspecting that he contributed to the dialogue. He is a master at delivering the barbed epithet. You have to hear him reciting a line like "It reeks with morality"—stressing the r's so as to make it exquisitely funny—to know how good he can be. The other players, including Julie Haydon and Stanley Ridges as the lovers whom Mallare destroys, are thoughtfully repressed to the mood of the film. You will find Alexander Woollcott perishing languidly in a sea of tired epigrams and Hope Williams being sternly disillusioned. And, if you keep your eyes open, you will discover the Messrs. Hecht and MacArthur popping into the picture briefly as a pair of nondescript bums in the flophouse scene. Filmgoers who fail to see *The Scoundrel* are likely to be frozen out of after-dinner conversation for the next few weeks.

—*A.S., May 3, 1935*

THE SEARCH

Directed by Fred Zinnemann; written by Richard Schweizer, David Wechsler and Paul Jarrico; cinematographer, Emil Berna; edited by Herman Haller; music by Robert Blum; produced by Lazar Wechsler; released by Metro-Goldwyn-Mayer. Black and white. Running time: 105 minutes.

With: Montgomery Clift (Ralph Stevenson), Aline MacMahon (Mrs. Murray), Jarmila Novotna (Mrs. Malik), Wendell Corey (Jerry Fisher), Ivan Jande (Karel Malik) and Mary Patton (Mrs. Fisher).

Out of the stuff of one of the saddest and most arresting human dramas of our times—that is the fate of the children of Europe whose homes were wrecked and whose lives were damaged by the war—Lazar Wechsler, a Swiss film producer, has made a picture which may prudently be said to be as fine, as moving, and as challenging as any the contemporary screen provides. *The Search* is its American title, and it opened at the Victoria last night. Our earnest wish is that it might be seen by every adult in the United States.

For *The Search* is not only an absorbing and gratifying emotional drama of the highest sort, being a vivid and convincing representation of how one of the "lost children" of Europe is found, but it gives a graphic, overwhelming comprehension of the frightful cruelty to innocent children that has been done abroad. Within the framework of a basic human story—the tireless search of a displaced Czech mother for her little boy and the parallel efforts of others to help the nameless youngster and give him security after the war—it clearly lays out for us a problem facing western civilization today: what's to be done with this vast backwash of shattered children who will be grown-ups tomorrow?

Happily, the resolution of one unit of this problem is here found in the most desirable of all possible arrangements—the reunion of the mother and her little boy. And, indeed, it is not at all unlikely that, if this valid gratification were not used, the extension of the pathos that fills this picture would be well nigh unbearable. For Mr. Wechsler and his associates made their story triumph and spiritual justice is achieved.

In the visualization of this story, Mr. Wechsler's team, which included Richard Schweizer as scriptwriter, Fred Zinnemann as director, and writer Paul Jarrico, have worked for a naturalistic countenance which is brilliantly successful, in the main. Their film has the hard-focus contours of solid realities. Their cameras have looked at actual ruins, at the dry-eyed faces of children full of grief. And their neat presentation of the drama through a cast which speaks English when it should and other languages when they are in order (as in Mr. Wechsler's previous film, *The Last Chance*) makes not only for easy comprehension but for an illusion of absolute naturalness.

Unquestionably the remarkable performance of a little Czech lad named Ivan Jandl as the principal figure in the drama is vital to the spirit of the whole. For this youngster, who was found by Mr. Zinnemann in a school group in Prague, has such tragic expression in his slight frame, such poetry in his eyes and face, and such melting appeal in his thin voice that he is the ultimate embodiment of the sorrow-inflicted child.

As the American officer who "adopts" him, the young American actor, Montgomery Clift, gets precisely the right combination of intensity and casualness into the role, and Aline MacMahon is crisply professional yet compassionate as an UNRRA worker Wendell Corey, another American, is nice as a Military Government man who cautions against sentimentality and Jarmila Novotna, the opera singer, fills the role of the Czech mother with a weary sort of hopefulness that must be characteristic of Europeans today. Among the many lesser children in the picture, some of them actual war orphans, little Leopold Borkowski is outstanding as a Jewish lad who seeks sanctuary in the Catholic choir.

In fact, it is in such searching incidents as the one of the boy in the choir and the gauzy impulse of the little hero to seek his mother on the other side of a fence that the brilliant illumination of the tortured minds of Europe's children comes through. Here is exposed in shattering detail the terrible irony of religious and political bounds. And here, for the hearts of parents throughout the world, is a lesson of great truth.

The Search, in our estimation, is a major revelation in our times.

—B.C., March 24, 1948

THE SEARCHERS

Directed by John Ford: written by Frank S. Nugent. based on the novel by Alan LeMay: cinematographer. Winton C. Hoch: edited by Jack Murray: music by Max Steiner: art designers. Frank Hotaling and James Basevi: produced by Merian C. Cooper and C. V. Whitney: released by Warner Brothers. Running time: 119 minutes.

With: John Wayne (Ethan Edwards). Jeffrey Hunter (Martin Pawley). Vera Miles (Laurie Jorgensen). Ward Bond (Captain Reverend S. Clayton). Natalie Wood (Debbie Edwards). John Qualen (Lars Jorgensen). Olive Carey (Mrs. Jorgensen) and Henry Brandon (Chief Scar).

Appropriately, C. V. Whitney, the distinguished turfman, is making his debut as a producer of motion pictures with a horse opera, directed by John Ford. This, in the realm of motion pictures, is like having a favorite three-year-old going in the Kentucky Derby with Eddie Arcaro or Dave Erb up.

Thus, it is highly gratifying to be able to report that Mr. Whitney's first film, *The Searchers,* came thundering in a winner at the Criterion yesterday. And it is equally gratifying to notice that Mr. Ford hasn't lost his touch.

The Searchers, for all the suspicions aroused by excessive language in its ads, is really a ripsnorting Western, as brashly entertaining as they come. It starts with the tardy homecoming of a lean Texan from the Civil War and leaps right into a massacre by Comanches and the abduction of two white girls. And then it proceeds for almost two hours to detail the five-year search for the girls that is relentlessly conducted by the Texan, with the ultimate help of just one lad.

That is the story pattern on which Mr. Ford and his gang have plastered a wealth of Western action that has the toughness of leather and the sting of a whip. It bristles and howls with Indian fighting, goes into tense, nerve-rasping brawls between the Texan and his hunting companion, explodes with fiery comedy, and lays into some frontier heroics that make the welkin ring.

And when we distribute credit not only to Mr. Ford but to his gang, we do so with frank appreciation. For it is his familiar corps of actors, writers, etc., that helps to give the gusto to this film. From Frank S. Nugent, whose screenplay from the novel of Alan LeMay is a pungent thing, right on through the cast and technicians, it is the honest achievement of a well-knit team.

John Wayne is uncommonly commanding as the Texan whose passion for revenge is magnificently uncontaminated by caution or sentiment. Jeffrey Hunter is wonderfully callous and courageous as the lad who goes with him, and Ward Bond makes a dandy fighting parson in an old plug hat and a long linen coat.

John Qualen as a stolid Texas rancher, Olive Carey as his wife, Vera Miles as their militantly romantic daughter, Natalie Wood as one of the abducted girls, and a dozen or so other actors are great in supporting roles.

There are only two faults of minor moment that we can find in this slambang Western film. The first is that Mr. Ford, once started, doesn't seem to know when to stop. Episode is piled upon episode, climax upon climax, and corpse upon corpse until the whole thing appears to be taking a couple of turns around the course. The justification for it is that it certainly conveys the lengthiness of the hunt, but it leaves one a mite exhausted, especially with the speed at which it goes.

The other fault is that the director has permitted too many outdoor scenes to be set in the obviously synthetic surroundings of the studio stage. Mr. Ford's scenic stuff, shot in color and VistaVision, in the expanse of Monument Valley that he loves, has his customary beauty and grandeur, but some of those campfire scenes could have been shot in a sporting-goods store window. That isn't like Mr. Ford. And it isn't like most of this picture, which is as scratchy as genuine cockleburrs.

—B.C., May 31, 1956

SECRET HONOR

Produced and directed by Robert Altman: written by Donald Freed and Arnold M. Stone. based on their stage play *Secret Honor: The Last Will and Testament of Richard M. Nixon*: director of photography. Pierre Mignot: edited by Juliet Weber: music by George Burt: art designer. Steve Altman: released by Cinecom. Running time: 90 minutes.

With: Philip Baker Hall (Richard M. Nixon).

A dapperly dressed, fictional character named Richard M. Nixon, played by Philip Baker Hall, who sort of resembles the former President of the United States but certainly isn't a lookalike, comes into his wood-paneled study carrying a small wooden box, later revealed to contain a gun. He pours himself a brandy and, for about ten seconds, remains settled comfortably in a chair in front of the fire.

He abruptly gets up, changes into a natty maroon velvet smoking jacket, gets out a bottle of Chivas Regal, pours himself a serious drink, and starts fiddling with his tape recorder. "Testing, testing . . . one, two, three . . . and . . . and . . . oh . . . four," he says into the microphone, but when he plays it back, zilch. He tries again. Still nothing. He finds the instruction booklet. It turns out he's forgotten to insert the cassette.

This is more or less the beginning of one of the funniest, most unsettling, most imaginative, and most surprisingly affecting movies of its very odd kind I've ever seen. It's titled *Secret Honor* and has been adapted by Donald Freed and Arnold M. Stone from their monodrama that ran at the Provincetown Playhouse here two years ago. The director is none other than Robert Altman, the sometimes great filmmaker (*M*A*S*H, Nashville*) who has recently been dabbling in theater and in film adaptations of theater work.

Mr. Altman's screen version of *Come Back to the Five and Dime, Jimmy Dean, Jimmy Dean* was quite as foolish as it had been on the stage, while his screen version of *Streamers* successfully defused the explosive mechanism of David Rabe's play. Mr. Altman recoups his reputation with *Secret Honor,* a most unlikely work—a one-character movie, set entirely within a single set, unrelieved by flashbacks, fantasies, or cutaways of any sort.

The result is something of a cinematic tour de force, both for Mr. Altman and for the previously unknown to me Philip Baker Hall, whose contribution is a legitimate, bravura performance, not a *Saturday Night Live* impersonation.

Secret Honor, titled *Secret Honor: The Last Testament of Richard M. Nixon* when it was done on the stage, opens a two-day engagement today at the Thalia Theater. If this sort of thing interests you, you'll have to move quickly.

The film begins with a disclaimer that is utterly serious. *Secret Honor,* says an opening credit, "is not a work of history but of fiction." By calling itself "a political myth," the film may not forestall all criticism but, at least, it doesn't play the Costa-Gavras game—announcing that everything we're about to see is true and then going on to insert fiction at unidentified points.

It is, instead, a series of riffs—admittedly fictitious variations on recorded history—that have the unexpected effect of making Mr. Nixon, the only president ever to resign from office, a far more complicated, interesting, and almost likable figure than his severest critics are inclined to acknowledge. This film's Richard M. Nixon is not exactly a Lear or even a Richard II. He's not tragic. But he has some of the appeal of—and is as American as—the Duke in *Huckleberry Finn,* attempting to convince the members of a lynch party that they should elect him mayor.

Surrounded by the kind of mini-television cameras that banks use to photograph thieves, plus monitors so that he can watch his performance—and oil portraits of Washington, Lincoln, Wilson, and Kennedy, and one large photograph of Henry Kissinger, acting as witnesses—Mr. Hall delivers a ninety-minute monologue that mixes fact with fancy, and self-serving explanations with genuine insight into the American way.

Talking into his microphone, he begins by referring to himself in the third person, acting as his own defense attorney before an unseen judge, railing at the idea of "the pardon," and pointing out that there cannot be a pardon without a conviction for a crime. As the drinks and the memories accumulate, he often forgets the mike, speaks with increasing frequency in the first person, and seldom finishes sentences. He twists names, fumes about issues, large and small. His mind goes so much faster than his mouth that he seems to be approaching complete mental breakdown.

He's especially caustic about President Eisenhower ("He once introduced me as Nick Dixon!") and says that he never did see all the rooms in the White House "until Johnson was president." He's vicious about Dr. Kissinger: "They gave him a Nobel Peace Prize and accused me of stealing silver from the White House." Simultaneously, he is saddened when thinking of

Helen Gahagan Douglas—"I really liked her. I liked her looks," but "the committee" put him up to the things he said about her when he was running for office.

He recalls his heritage as "a loser" and manages to be moving as he recalls the death of his two brothers and other family members from tuberculosis. "Goddamn TB!" he says. "That's the reason we moved to California and they all died anyway." A little further on: "My old man sold the lemon grove, and *then* they discovered oil!" Hysteria mounts, but so do moments of self-awareness.

Finally he gets to "the reason behind the reasons," meaning Watergate, which involves that vague "committee," to which he sold his soul, he says, to win its backing. The ultimate revelation: "I orchestrated Watergate!" The reason: to divert attention from an even greater treason that, somehow, involved the committee, which wanted him to continue the Vietnam War for its private gain, which he absolutely refused to do.

There is more—much more—all far better analyzed by a political expert than a film critic. What is important here is that *Secret Honor* is a fascinating, funny, offbeat movie. The screenplay, whose coauthor, Mr. Freed, wrote the clumsily paranoid *Executive Action* and collaborated on the film adaptation, is an extremely skillful, witty, dramatic work with an extraordinary character at its center.

Mr. Altman serves it beautifully. He never undercuts the material or Mr. Hall's immense performance, which is as astonishing and risky—for the chances the actor takes and survives—as that of the Oscar-winning F. Murray Abraham in *Amadeus.*

Of special interest, Mr. Altman produced the film independently, shooting in Ann Arbor in cooperation with the University of Michigan Department of Communication and the Los Angeles Actors' Theater.

Also on the Thalia bill is the tired old kinescope of the Checkers speech, which, I think, is a mistake. It's become an easy laugh. *Secret Honor* is something of a different order. That is, good fiction.

—V.C., June 7, 1985

SECRETS AND LIES

Written and directed by Mike Leigh: director of photography. Dick Pope: edited by Jon Gregory: music by Andrew Dickson: production designers. Alison Chitty and Georgina Lowe: produced by Simon Channing-Williams: released by October Films. Running time: 136 minutes.

With: Brenda Blethyn (Cynthia). Marianne Jean-Baptiste (Hortense). Claire Rushbrook (Roxanne). Timothy Spall (Maurice) and Phyllis Logan (Monica).

The secrets that bring such immediacy to Mike Leigh's tender and wrenching new film are not confined to the screen. Mr. Leigh, celebrated for his patient, Olympian methods with actors, deliberately keeps those players in the dark as a way of capturing an essential inner light.

That light shines radiantly through the revelations of *Secrets and Lies,* which won the Palme d'Or at this year's Cannes International Film Festival and will now establish this once insular English filmmaker on a much broader commercial footing. It opens the 34th New York Film Festival tonight on a note of rare heart and soul.

When they began rehearsing this film's climactic, one-of-a-kind birthday party sequence, some of Mr. Leigh's actors experienced an extra jolt of surprise. Not all the white performers who play relatives of Cynthia Rose Purley, this film's unforgettable, big-hearted cockney heroine, understood that the character Hortense, Cynthia's long-lost daughter, would be black. So Hortense is seen arriving at the party as a true mystery guest, since others at the party are entirely unaware of her existence, let alone her race. She stays to prompt the crisis for which *Secrets and Lies* has methodically braced itself, as if awaiting a slow-moving storm.

By keeping blinders on his performers and withholding such a vital fact, Mr. Leigh assembles the makings of a histrionic bombshell. But the subtlety, sweetness, and generosity of *Secrets and Lies* are on a level where no bombshells are necessary. The racial difference between Cynthia and Hortense could have been the entire focus of a lesser film. Here, it's very nearly beside the point. There's just too much else to explore.

Brenda Blethyn's grand, heartrending performance as Cynthia ranks with David Thewlis's lacerating turn in Mr. Leigh's *Naked,* creating a central character so big and real she gives emotional life to an entire film. But Ms. Blethyn's lovely, tragicomic Cynthia is by far the more poignant figure, just as *Secrets and Lies* is a much gentler film than *Naked.* Too gentle, perhaps; this film's catharsis even finds one loving couple peaceably rubbing noses. In its last moments, it fires off more feel-good bromides than suit Mr. Leigh's usual brand of truth.

But everything else about this story unfolds beautifully, with a rueful, knowing intelligence that rises above easy assumptions. The audience is invited to watch the revealing ways in which these characters collide and to get out those handkerchiefs, too. When first seen, Cynthia is a wistfully lost soul, a fading beauty who works in a cardboard box factory and worriedly watches over the daughter she has brought up. The comically surly Roxanne (Claire Rushbrook, making her film debut as a perfect addition to Mr. Leigh's informal stock company) is approaching her twenty-first birthday, poised to repeat her mother's mistakes.

Mr. Leigh expertly introduces the film's other characters, all of whose paths will eventually intersect. Hortense, played with graceful reserve by Marianne Jean-Baptiste, is seen working as a capable optometrist. (The actress studied optometry for this role, in keeping with Mr. Leigh's consuming yet tightly disciplined method with his actors.) Hortense is also newly in mourning, in a film that is bracketed by the death of one mother and the hugely moving rebirth of another.

Secrets and Lies also introduces Maurice (Timothy Spall), the portrait photographer who is Cynthia's younger brother and who carries a great burden of guilt about his sister's unhappy life. Maurice is trapped in a fussy middle-class existence by his wife, Monica (Phyllis Logan), who has made it her business to keep Cynthia away. Like the people who pose for his photographs (in quick cameo appearances from actors seen in earlier Leigh films) and who work out their truces just before the flashbulbs pop, Maurice and Monica are not an easy fit. The film establishes this as effortlessly as it captures a closeness between Maurice and Cynthia that transcends all strain.

Early in the film, Maurice casually asks his tightly wound wife (who has her own sad secret) about the clothes she is wearing. Do the top and bottom make a suit? "If you think they do, they do," Monica answers.

"And if you think they don't, they don't." That's Mr. Leigh's casually deft way of describing the variously estranged relatives in *Secrets and Lies,* for whom family love is seen as a matter of will and choice.

The film's net carefully tightens once Hortense begins trying to find her birth mother and discovers what she thinks must be a mistake. The stages of this process are exquisitely rendered: the first phone call (Cynthia dissolves in weeping and terror), the shock of a face-to-face encounter, the long and lovely rendezvous in which mother and daughter begin seeing each other clearly. Ms. Blethyn conveys these developments so ferociously well that every nuance of emotion is visible on screen. In a performance that lurches thrillingly from grief to comedy to compassion, never losing its tart humor, her Cynthia rises up from the sodden mess of her life to face regret over the past and uncharacteristic hope for the future.

Soap opera? Never. Mr. Leigh's wry and magnanimous intelligence keeps *Secrets and Lies* determinedly unsentimental, helped immeasurably by Cynthia's fine, tough resilience and idiomatic verve. ("Shifty-lookin' bleeder!" she says of one character. Of another: "I wouldn't know 'im if 'e stood up in me soup!") And Ms. Blethyn, whose chirpy tones were used to comic effect in this director's 1980 *Grown-Ups* for BBC television and who managed to make herself look older then, undergoes an astonishing, tearful transformation without making a false or maudlin move.

Secrets and Lies gives shorter shrift to Hortense, who is asked to watch the other characters' outbursts with quiet chagrin. But Ms. Jean-Baptiste is impressively strong and dignified in this pivotal role. Mr. Spall, seen running a ridiculous French restaurant in Mr. Leigh's *Life Is Sweet,* makes Maurice so solid and decent that it comes as no surprise when he emerges as this film's voice of reason despite his absurd-looking lifestyle. This film's political concerns are much narrower than Mr. Leigh's have been in the past, expressed mostly through pity for Cynthia's and Roxanne's strapped circumstances and horror at Maurice's and Monica's home decor.

Secrets and Lies, which will open tomorrow in Manhattan for its commercial run, is accompanied by stately, melancholy chamber music and photographed by Dick Pope with a warm clarity suggesting that daylight is streaming in. In every sense, it is.

—*J.M., September 27, 1996*

SENSE AND SENSIBILITY

Directed by Ang Lee; written by Emma Thompson, based on the novel by Jane Austen; director of photography. Michael Coulter; edited by Tim Squyres; music by Patrick Doyle; production designer, Luciana Arrighi; produced by Lindsay Doran; released by Columbia Pictures. Running time: 135 minutes.

With: Emma Thompson (Elinor Dashwood), Alan Rickman (Colonel Brandon), Kate Winslet (Marianne Dashwood), Hugh Grant (Edward Ferrars) and Gemma Jones (Mrs. Dashwood).

In a banner year for movie-business mergers, one of the best-conceived collaborations takes place not in the boardroom but on the screen. The grandly entertaining *Sense and Sensibility* brings together Hollywood's new posthumous darling, Jane Austen, with Ang Lee, the director whose *Eat Drink Man Woman* had the irresistible good sense to combine Austen-like acuity with Chinese food.

Add to this inspired mix a team of production (Luciana Arrighi) and costume (Jenny Beavan and John Bright) designers who earned their tastefully muted stripes with Merchant-Ivory. They account for such charming distractions as carefully appointed country houses, bucolic flocks of sheep, and custom-made parchment used for the will, ledgers, and love letters that are so vital to this story. Also add Emma Thompson, who proves as crisp and indispensably clever a screenwriter as she is a leading lady. And Hugh Grant, as one of those genteel heartthrobs whose amiability and financial prospects can keep Miss Austen's heroines occupied throughout an entire book's worth of small talk.

The talk in this, the author's first published novel, is a shade less subtle and more achingly polite than the more rueful, sophisticated dialogue of her later work. And this film can't match the brilliant incisiveness of the more spartan *Persuasion,* still the most thoughtful new Austen adaptation. But Mr. Lee is after something more broadly accessible, a sparkling, colorful, and utterly contemporary comedy of manners. He achieves this so pleasantly that *Sense and Sensibility* matches the Austen-based *Clueless* for sheer fun. Not

bad, considering that these characters respond to any awkward social circumstance by talking about the weather.

But Mr. Lee and Ms. Thompson are not above winking at their audience over such musty, Regency-era conventions. Nor are they overly reverential about the text itself, which has been artfully pruned and sometimes modified to suit broader comic tastes. While it's not necessary to have John Dashwood (James Fleet) twitching so nervously at his father's deathbed, wincing over a promise to take financial care of his stepmother and half sisters, Mr. Lee often indulges in such bold strokes. In this case, it's as helpful a way as any of setting the story in motion.

Once John's wife, Fanny (Harriet Walter), has overruled her Milquetoast husband on any show of generosity, the Dashwood women are left to navigate shark-infested waters in their search for marriageable men. With the wonderfully self-possessed Ms. Thompson and Kate Winslet, another spirited and striking actress, playing these women, *Sense and Sensibility* needs no further outcry over the injustice of their plight. But it finds one anyway, in typically quick and sprightly style, with the youngest Dashwood daughter hiding in a treehouse. "Because houses go from father to son, dearest, not from father to daughter," says Elinor (Ms. Thompson), by way of explaining to little Margaret why the Dashwood women are being forced to leave their home. Margaret stays hidden, but she yanks up the treehouse ladder to show what she thinks of inheritance laws like that.

It doesn't take long for the older Dashwood girls (teenagers in Austen's version, but played gracefully and convincingly by more mature actresses) to attract enough suitors for a Harlequin romance. The most comically swashbuckling of these is John Willoughby (Greg Wise), whose matinee-idol qualities are treated as a source of amusement. He rescues Marianne from a rainstorm with an élan worthy of Gothic romance, and he never goes anywhere without a volume of Shakespeare's sonnets. (That marks one of Ms. Thompson's more felicitous changes; Austen's Willoughby admires William Cowper and Sir Walter Scott.)

When Marianne falls impetuously for Willoughby, the story underscores the dichotomy of the title. Marianne is the more passionate and impulsive of the two sisters, while Elinor has the greater composure and the more level head. Elinor's good sense guides her through a flirtation with Edward Ferrars, written as a decent but dull fellow and played with cheerfully incongruous *Four Weddings and a Funeral*-isms by Mr. Grant. Whatever this costs the film in terms of authenticity, it contributes obvious and welcome verve. And Mr. Grant, despite some overused fluttering and stammering, rises touchingly to the film's most straightforward and meaningful encounters.

Alan Rickman at first appears miscast as the oldest, most pained of the Dashwood girls' suitors. Overlooked at first, he lingers to remind audiences that in Austen's novels, patience and decency make for a winning hand. Surely that accounts for much of the author's current cinematic popularity, since it stands in contrast with so much of what Hollywood has offered lately. Here's a film in which sense and intelligence not only prevail but also create the most gratifying of happy endings.

In addition to emerging as the movies' most welcome new moralist, Jane Austen has also begun looking like the patron saint of supporting casts. Filling out the book's wealth of tartly etched secondary figures are Elizabeth Spriggs as an uproariously blunt matron, Gemma Jones as the Dashwood girls' gentle mother, Imogen Stubbs as the sweet young thing who slyly bedevils Elinor over Edward's attentions, and Robert Hardy as the country squire who assesses most issues in terms of money and hounds.

Hugh Laurie plays another of Austen's more memorable minor figures, the acerbic husband who buries himself in his newspaper except when making lacerating wisecracks. We need no further proof that this material is ageless.

—J.M., *December 13, 1995*

SERGEANT YORK

Directed by Howard Hawks; written by Abem Finkel, Harry Chandlee, Howard Koch and John Huston, based on the diary of Sergeant Alvin C. York; cinematographers, Sol Polita and Arthur Edeson; edited by William Holmes; music by Max Steiner; art designer, John Hughes; produced by Jesse L. Lasky and Hal B. Wallis; released by Warner Brothers. Black and white. Running time: 134 minutes.

With: Gary Cooper (Alvin C. York), Walter Brennan (Pastor Rosier Pile), Joan Leslie (Gracie Williams), Stanley Ridges (Major Buxton), George Tobias ("Pusher" Ross), Ward Bond (Ike Botkin) and Margaret Wycherly (Mother York).

At this time, when a great many people are thinking deep and sober thoughts about the possible involvement of our country in another deadly world war, Warner Brothers and a bewildering multiplicity of collaborative producers and writers have reflected propitiously upon the motives and influences which inspired America's No. 1 hero in the last war. And, in *Sergeant York*, which opened last night at the Astor, they have brought forth a simple and dignified screen biography of that famous Tennessee mountaineer who put aside his religious scruples against killing for what he felt was the better good of his country and the lasting benefit of mankind.

It is, in the light of what has happened, a strangely affecting account, this brave and sincerely wrought biography of the lanky Alvin C. York, who left his barren home way back in the Cumberland hills to travel across troubled waters and fight for what he hoped would be the best. It is an honest saga of a plain American who believed in fundamentals and acted with clean simplicity. And because the unmentioned sequel to the larger story has been so grim, the personal and well-earned triumph of Sergeant York acquires tragic overtones.

In outline, the film is no more than a straightaway narrative about a "fightin' an' hell-raisin'" mountain farmer named Alvin York who scrabbles a poor living from a piece of rocky high-ground in the Cumberlands and yearns for a "piece of bottom." Then he "gets religion" just about the time this country enters the World War and undergoes a terrific mental ordeal to decide whether he should fight. An American history book wins him over, and he goes on to Europe and to fame because of his single-handed capture of an incredible number of German soldiers. In the end, however, he returns to Tennessee and to a life of simple toil.

That is all there is to the story, but in the telling of it—of the first part, anyhow—the picture has all the flavor of true Americana, the blunt and homely humor of backwoodsmen and the raw integrity peculiar to simple folk. This phase of the picture is rich. The manner in which York is persuaded to join the fighting forces and the scenes of actual combat betray an unfortunate artificiality, however—in the battle scenes, especially; and the overly glamorized ending, in which York returns to a spotless little farm, jars sharply with the naturalness which has gone before. The suggestion of deliberate propaganda is readily detected here.

However, the performance of Gary Cooper in the title role holds the picture together magnificently, and even the most unfavorable touches are made palatable because of him. He is the gaunt, clumsy yokel, the American hayseed to the life—the proud, industrious, honest, simple citizen who marches in the forefront of this nation's ranks. Walter Brennan as a country parson and storekeeper is a perfect specimen of *Homo americanus,* too, while Robert Porterfield, Clem Bevans, Howard da Silva, and George Tobias make excellent "types." Margaret Wycherly as a pinched and inflexible hill-woman bears up too consciously under her manifold woes, and Joan Leslie plays a mountain beauty with little more than a bright smile, a phony accent, and a tight dress.

Sergeant York is good native drama, inspiring in parts and full of life. It is a little naive, perhaps, but so are the folks of which it tells. And, basically, it is as full of humility and pride as is the simple prayer which Mother York prays over a meager meal: "The Lord bless these victuals we got and help us to beholden to no one. Amen."

—B.C., July 13, 1941

SERPICO

Directed by Sidney Lumet; written by Waldo Salt and Norman Wexler; based on the book by Peter Maas; director of photography, Arthur J. Ornitz; edited by Dede Allen and Richard Marks; music by Mikis Theodorakis; production designer, Charles Bailey; produced by Martin Bregman; released by Paramount Pictures. Running time: 129 minutes.

With: Al Pacino (Serpico), John Randolph (Sidney Green), Tony Roberts (Bob Blair), Jack Kehoe (Tom Keough), Biff McGuire (Inspector McClain), Barbara Eda-Young (Laurie), Cornelia Sharpe (Leslie), John Medici (Pasquale) and Norman Ornelias (District Attorney Tauber).

Early in 1970, two New York City police officers, Detective Frank Serpico and Sergeant David Durk, put their careers and their lives on the line. After getting the runaround for months from their superiors, who preferred not to listen, they called on David Burnham, a reporter for *The New York Times,* to tell him their story of graft and corruption within the Police Department.

Detective Serpico and Sergeant Durk had places, dates, and names, information that, when published, prompted Mayor Lindsay to appoint the Knapp Commission to investigate the charges, leading eventually to the biggest shake-up in the Police Department's history.

In his book Serpico, published this year, Peter Maas recalls this story exclusively from the point of view of Detective Serpico, the bearded, bead-wearing, so-called hippie cop who, in February 1971, under circumstances that were puzzling, was shot in the face and critically wounded while attempting to make a narcotics arrest. When he recovered, Detective Serpico resigned from the department, exhausted and fearing for his life. Today he reportedly lives abroad, the bullet fragments still lodged a few centimeters below his brain.

Sidney Lumet's *Serpico,* which opened yesterday at the Baronet and Forum Theaters, is a galvanizing and disquieting film adapted from the Maas book by Waldo Salt and Norman Wexler. It is galvanizing because of Al Pacino's splendid performance in the title role and because of the tremendous intensity that Mr. Lumet brings to this sort of subject. The method—sudden contrasts in tempo, lighting, sound level—seems almost crude, but it reflects the quality of Detective Serpico's outrage, which, in our society, comes to look like an obsession bordering on madness.

The film is limited only by its form, which carries the limitations of the Maas book one step further. Only Detective Serpico and Mr. Burnham are identified by real names. Everyone else has a fictitious name, in consideration, I suppose, of potential suits for libel and invasion of privacy. I assume the filmmakers may also have been hampered by other people's consideration of personal gain. Why should a man give a movie company the rights to his life if he's likely to wind up playing a supporting role in someone else's film?

The use of fictitious names is not in itself disquieting, only the suspicion that we are getting the truth—

but sort of. One must suspect that Sergeant Durk played a much more important part in the Serpico story than is played by the character named Bob Blair (Tony Roberts) in the film.

The form also prevents Mr. Lumet and the screenwriters from much speculation about the motives that sustained Detective Serpico and made him the one officer in the precinct who refused even free meals, much less thousands of dollars in monthly payoffs from gamblers and numbers racketeers.

Detective Serpico is a driven character of Dostoyevskian proportions, an anti-cop cop. It's no accident, I suspect, that he has a great fondness for wild disguises, and that in his private life he adopts the look and manner of a flower child's vision of Christ.

Mr. Lumet and Mr. Pacino manage to suggest such a lot of things about Detective Serpico that one wishes they could have enjoyed even greater freedom in exploring the character of this unusual man who, like the worker priests in France, tried to change the system by working within it.

Serpico was photographed (by cameraman Arthur J. Ornitz) entirely in New York, a city that Mr. Lumet knows better than any other director working today. He also knows actors and has surrounded Mr. Pacino with a fine cast of supporting players of whom John Randolph, as an okay Bronx police captain, is the most prominent.

Aside from a couple of romantic interludes that threaten to bring things to a halt, the only major fault of the film is the absolutely terrible soundtrack score by Mikis Theodorakis. It is redundant and dumb, the way English subtitles might be.

If you can stop up your ears to this musical nonsense, which includes Neapolitan street airs whenever Detective Serpico's Italian immigrant parents threaten to appear, you should find the film most provocative, a remarkable record of one man's rebellion against the sort of sleaziness and second-rateness that has affected so much American life, from the ingredients of its hamburgers to the ethics of its civil servants and politicians.

—*V.C., December 6, 1973*

THE SERVANT

Directed by Joseph Losey: written by Harold Pinter, based on the novel by Robin Maugham: cine-matographer, Douglas Slocombe: edited by Reginald Mills: music by John Dankworth: production designer, Richard MacDonald: produced by Mr. Losey and Norman Priggen: released by the Landau Company. Black and white. Running time: 115 minutes.

With: Dirk Bogarde (Barrett), Sarah Miles (Vera), Wendy Craig (Susan), James Fox (Tony), Catherine Lacey (Lady Mounset), Richard Vernon (Lord Mounset) and Patrick Magee (Bishop).

If you think the Profumo scandals shed a seamy and shocking light on what is said to be a rather general crumbling of the British upper crust, wait until you see *The Servant,* an intrepid independent British film directed by the American Joseph Losey, which came to the Little Carnegie yesterday.

Its account of patrician degradation will cause you to blink your eyes. Although it is only fiction, it wafts a thick and acrid air of smoldering truth.

Written by Harold Pinter, the author of that strange, corrosive play, *The Caretaker,* which also reflected on British society, it tells of the slow degeneration of a wellborn young London bachelor under the cruelly calculated seductions of his gentleman's gentleman.

Politely and serenely, this servant comes into the not-yet-furnished home of the elegantly indolent hero, assists him with faultless taste in putting the place in handsome order with all that a genteel host could wish—splendid furniture, silverware, paintings, family portraits, napery, and books.

Then, without seeming intention, he ever so casually intrudes upon the master's intimate evenings with his competent fiancée, stirs a frustration between them, excites a strange ooze of jealousy, and then brings into the house a teasing trollop he pretends is to be a kitchen maid.

This trap for the carnal inclinations of the young master easily works. In no time at all, he is enmeshed in a sordid relation with the maid. And from this point on, the servant leads him relentlessly down a path of dissoluteness and abandon to a stage of complete decadence.

It is a flesh-creeping demonstration of human destructiveness that Mr. Pinter and Mr. Losey are presenting in this film, and it is made all the more horrifying by the genteel surroundings in which it occurs. Amid dignified intimations of the substance of a privileged, potent class, against paintings of lordly ancestors and British heroes performing gallant deeds, a handsome, undisciplined inheritor of a social tradition disintegrates. And the schemer who contributes to his downfall is, ironically, a descendant of loyal servitors to this tradition in the past.

There are here some shattering implications of many dismal things that have taken place in British and Continental society since World War II, and Mr. Losey and his cast convey them in vivid and subtle terms.

In the young master, played with dazzling whimsy and effeteness by James Fox, we are made to see the arrogance, impotence, and helplessness of those who are caught in the wreckage of a system that society will no longer support. And in the servant, played by Dirk Bogarde, we are made to see the bitter counterpart.

This man is the ugly representative of a professionally emasculated group, as feeble and obsolescent as the people they still pretend to serve and now possessed by a destructive sadism and vengefulness. He is as much a victim as the man he helps to destroy. Mr. Bogarde's performance, oily and insolent and cruel, conveys the entire range of weakness and wastage in his parallel decay.

As the stalwart and stubborn young woman who retains a certain pride and dignity in trying to save the hero, Wendy Craig is the strongest character. She trails the one strain of romantic pathos forlornly. Sarah Miles makes a shrill, saucy slattern—a strumpet of a universal breed who is but an incidental contributor to the fall of man.

The photography is worthy of special mention, and John Dankworth has provided a musical score that hits precisely the right note of melancholy for this decline in an old Georgian house in Chelsea, which could be the mausoleum of a class.

The Servant, incidentally, was one of the pictures shown at the first New York Film Festival last fall.

—B.C., March 17, 1964

THE SET-UP

Directed by Robert Wise; written by Art Cohn, based on the poem by Joseph Moncure March; cinematographer, Milton Krasner; edited by Roland Gross; music by C. Bakaleinikoff; art designers, Albert S. D'Agostino and Jack Okey; produced by Richard Goldstone; released by RKO Radio Pictures. Black and white. Running time: 72 minutes.

With: Robert Ryan (Stoker), Audrey Totter (Julie), George Tobias (Tiny), Alan Baxter (Little Boy), Wallace Ford (Gus), Percy Helton (Red), Hal Fieberling (Tiger Nelson), Darryl Hickman (Shanley) and Kenny O'Morrison (Moore).

The fight game can number its Stoker Thompsons by the dozens and practically any big city you care to name has its own counterpart of the Paradise Arena. The spectators are much of a kind, too; noisy, bloodthirsty men and women who check their inhibitions at the gate and for a couple of hours indulge their brutal cravings. The human animal has not changed much from the days of the Roman arena. The squared ring is an area where blood is expected to be spilled and when it is not the crowd yells its displeasure.

There is, we hear, a sporting as well as a seamy side to prizefighting. It is with the ugly aspects that *The Set-Up* is concerned. This RKO production, which opened yesterday at the Criterion, is a sizzling melodrama. The men who made it have nothing good to say about the sordid phase of the business under examination and their roving, revealing camera paints an even blacker picture of the type of fight fan who revels in sheer brutality.

The sweaty, stale-smoke atmosphere of an ill-ventilated small-time arena and the ringside types who work themselves into a savage frenzy have been put on the screen in harsh, realistic terms. And the great expectations and shattered hopes which are the drama of the dressing room also have been brought to vivid, throbbing life in the shrewd direction of Robert Wise and the understanding, colloquial dialogue written into the script by Art Cohn.

The Set-Up tells the story of a wheelhorse heavyweight who after twenty years still feels that the championship is just "one punch away." Stoker Thompson is an old, battered man at thirty-five, but he has a stubborn, fighting heart which won't allow his mind to acknowledge that he is through and hang up his gloves as his anxious wife pleads with him to do. It is, too, the story of how fights can be fixed by gangsters and the disastrous consequences which await the fighter who, without knowing that his manager has taken payment for him to go into "the tank," makes a desperate bid to justify his hopes of climbing back up the ladder and knocks out his rising opponent.

The fight scenes are lively and well staged, though they are not nearly as effectively handled as those in the earlier *Body and Soul*. The director cuts away too frequently from the action to provide ringside comment and this switching to and from the fighters gives a conventional quality to these episodes. The sound effects are striking and give added conviction to hard blows.

A small cast headed by Robert Ryan as Stoker Thompson; Audrey Totter as his wife; George Tobias as the manager; and Alan Baxter as a gangster give crisp, believable performances. And assorted secondary players as fighters and handlers fill their roles realistically. *The Set-Up* is a real dilly for those who go for muscular entertainment.

—*T.M.P., March 30, 1949*

SEVEN BEAUTIES

Written (in Italian, with English subtitles) and directed by Lina Wertmuller; director of photography, Tonino Delli Colli; edited by Franco Fraticelli; music by Enzo Jannacci; art designer, Enrico Job; produced by Ms. Wertmuller and Giancarlo Giannini; released by Cinema V. Running time: 115 minutes.

With: Giancarlo Giannini (Pasqualino Frafuso), Fernando Rey (Pedro), Shirley Stoler (Commandant), Elena Fiore (Concettina), Enzo Vitale (Don Raffaele), Piero di Orio (Francesco) and Ermelinad De Felice (Mother).

*S*even Beauties, the fifth Lina Wertmuller film to be released in this country in less than two years, is the finest, most ambitious work yet made by this gifted Italian director whose films appear to be inspired by irreconcilable contradictions.

Seven Beauties, which opened yesterday at the Cinema II, is a handbook for survival, a farce, a drama of almost shattering impact. It's a disorderly epic,

seductively beautiful to look at, as often harrowing as it is boisterously funny, though it has a solid substructure of common sense and precisely observed details from life.

It's the story of Pasqualino Frafuso (Giancarlo Giannini), a natty, small-time, completely self-absorbed Neapolitan dandy who had some notoriety shortly before World War II as "the monster of Naples." Pasqualino, to defend his sister's honor, had murdered her pimp, then chopped up the body and mailed the pieces to different parts of Italy. Pasqualino is a character whom Brecht might have found fascinating. He is a survivor, possessed of what someone calls that "thirst for life" that outruns ideas and ideals.

Miss Wertmuller's screenplay opens after the collapse of the Italian front when Pasqualino has deserted from the Italian army while being shipped through Germany to the Russian front. Picked up by the Germans, he is sent to a concentration camp where, to stay alive, he sets out to seduce the camp's ferocious female commandant—an uproariously funny and thoroughly doomed campaign. Counterpointing this story are flashbacks that tell a parallel story of that earlier time in Naples when Pasqualino, at his murder trial, had sacrificed honor to stay alive.

Summarized in this fashion, *Seven Beauties* (which is Pasqualino's nickname in Naples) sounds more schematic than the eccentric, surprising, and compassionate film that Miss Wertmuller has actually made.

Seven Beauties is the work of a filmmaker at the peak of her energies, so full of ideas and images that she can afford to throw away moments that other, less talented directors would tediously emphasize.

Typical is a moment during Pasqualino's preconcentration camp wanderings in rural Germany when he sees in the distance a small group of soldiers escorting what looks to be a funeral party of well-dressed mourners. Slowly, methodically, the mourners stop, take off their clothes and offer themselves to their firing squad.

Pasqualino's companion, an Italian socialist, is outraged at Italy's complicity in the Nazi terror. Pasqualino shrugs, and it's Pasqualino who lives to return home, not the socialist.

Miss Wertmuller states political positions bluntly. When Pasqualino is convicted of murder, he is sentenced to twelve years in prison, while a political prisoner receives twenty-eight years "for thinking." The female commandant (played by Shirley Stoler, the American actress) allows Pasqualino to make love to her, then sneers, "In Paris, a Greek made love to a goose . . . to eat, to live. That's why you'll survive . . . and our dreams for a master race [are] unattainable. . . ."

As are all of Miss Wertmuller's films, *Seven Beauties* is about choices, and the conditions that govern them. Though she states positions bluntly, she doesn't make films that are easily categorized for popular consumption as either optimistic or pessimistic. Pasqualino's survival is neither a triumph nor a tragedy, but simply the expression (as I take it) of the life force, whatever that may be.

The director is deeply committed to political action, which can alleviate intolerable social conditions, but her films are distinguished by an awareness that political action is always dependent upon the unpredictable human response. It's her awareness and her appreciation of this mystery that give her films their particular life.

They are also full of vitality and are marveously well acted. Giancarlo Giannini, superb as Pasqualino, receives especially effective support from Miss Stoler, Fernando Rey (as a fellow concentration camp prisoner), and Elena Fiore (as Pasqualino's elder sister, the would-be whore).

Seven Beauties deserves to be the first big hit of the new year.

—*V.C., January 22, 1976*

SEVEN BRIDES
FOR SEVEN BROTHERS

Directed by Stanley Donen; written by Albert Hackett, Frances Goodrich and Dorothy Kingsley, based on the story "The Sobbin' Women" by Stephen Vincent Benét; cinematographer, George Folsey; edited by Ralph E. Winters; music by Adolph Deutsch and Saul Chaplin; choreography by Michael Kidd; art designers, Cedric Gibbons and Urie McCleary; produced by Jack Cummings; released by Metro-Goldwyn-Mayer. Running time: 102 minutes.

With: Howard Keel (Adam), Jeff Richards (Benjamin), Matt Mattox (Caleb), Marc Platt (Daniel),

Jacques D'Amboise (Ephraim), Tommy Rall (Frank), Russ Tamblyn (Gideon), Jane Powell (Milly), Julie Newmeyer (Dorcas), Nancy Kilgas (Alice), Betty Carr (Sarah), Virginia Gibson (Liza), Ruta Kilmonts (Ruth), Norma Doggett (Martha), Ian Wolfe (Reverend Elcott), Russell Simpson (Mr. Bixby), Marjorie Wood (Mrs. Bixby) and Howard Petri (Pete Perkins).

M-G-M, a movie manufactory that has not been represented by any outstanding musicals in recent months, has delivered a wholly engaging, bouncy, tuneful, and panchromatic package labeled *Seven Brides for Seven Brothers* and deposited it at the Music Hall yesterday. A distant relation of *Oklahoma!* with such unrelated godfathers as Stephen Vincent Benét and Plutarch, this lively fable skillfully blends a warm and comic yarn about the rustic romances of a family of Oregonian pioneers with strikingly imaginative choreography and a melodic score several notches above standard. And an amiable and talented cast go to it with a will to make these cheerful ingredients infectious.

Perhaps it is not especially important to divine precisely what the author, or the scenarists who adopted his story, "The Sobbin' Women," had in mind. Suffice it to say that the results add up to a gay tale about seven strapping young farmers whose unkempt persons and filthy cabin have never been benefited by the tender distaff touch until, that is, the oldest brings home a comely bride.

That tiny but spirited lass not only changes their manners and habits but also, in typically feminine fashion, acts as Cupid's handmaiden by introducing them to Plutarch's legend about the Sabine women (Mr. Benét's "The Sobbin' Women"). So, hungering for companionship and love, our rugged Romeos raid the village according to the Latin tradition and return with six unwilling maidens, who, as might be expected, learn to like the arrangement even if their parents do not.

Call this a somewhat thin story line, but it has been enhanced by the contributions of Michael Kidd, whose dance creations are in keeping with the times (1850) and with the seemingly unbounded energy of the principals. He has provided them with a repertoire that could be exhausting. But such agile craftsmen as Jacques d'Amboise, Marc Platt, Tommy Rall, Russ

Tamblyn, Matt Mattox, and Jeff Richards give them a dizzying whirl. And, it might be noted specifically, that the combination of ballet, acrobatics, and a knockdown and drag-out fight he has conjured up to go with a barn-raising scene should leave audiences panting and cheering.

The eight songs fashioned by Gene de Paul and Johnny Mercer are fresh and lilting and keyed neatly into the speedy proceedings. Chances are that "When You're in Love," a ballad delivered in fine, romantic style by Howard Keel and Jane Powell, will be hitting the jukeboxes soon. "Spring, Spring, Spring," gaily warbled by both the "brothers" and "brides" of the title, and "Wonderful, Wonderful Day," to which Mr. Keel's pretty bride, Miss Powell, gives a smooth and tender rendition, are easy on the ears too. And "Sobbin' Women," a rhythmic, bouncy ditty, is done rousingly by Mr. Keel and his "brothers."

Stanley Donen, a director who is no stranger to M-G-M musicals, has kept the pace of this lark swift and in time with the tunes. And Mr. Keel, whose baritone is as big and impressive as his frame; Miss Powell, who sings and acts to the pioneer manner born; as well as their sturdy and energetic kinfolk—and this must include the nubile, dancing damsels they abduct—are lovely to look at and hear. Although the powers at M-G-M are deviating from the normal song-and-dance extravaganza in Seven Brides for Seven Brothers, it is a gamble that is paying rich rewards.

—A.W., July 23, 1954

SEVEN DAYS TO NOON

Directed by John Boulting; written by Roy Boulting and Frank Harvey, based on a story by Paul Dehn and James Bernard; cinematographers, Gilbert Taylor and Ray Sturgess; edited by Roy Boulting; music by John Addison; art designer, John Elphick; produced by Roy Boulting; released by Arthur Mayer-Edward Kingsley-Distinguished Films. Black and white. Running time: 93 minutes.

With: Barry Jones (Professor Willingdon), Olive Sloane (Goldie), André Morell (Superintendent Folland), Sheila Manahan (Ann Willingdon), Hugh Cross (Stephen Lane), Joan Hickson (Mrs. Peckett) and Ronald Adam (The Prime Minister).

An intensely absorbing contemplation—that of the crisis which would occur in the crowded city of London if a scientist with an atom bomb got loose and threatened to blow up the city unless atom bombs were outlawed—is pursued with superb pictorial clarity and ever-tightening dramatic suspense in a spanking new British melodrama, Seven Days to Noon. This terminally overwhelming picture, which John and Roy Boulting produced, opened yesterday at the Trans-Lux Theatre on Lexington Avenue at Fifty-second Street.

Let it be written on the record that a more exciting climax for a film than the one arrived at in this picture would be hard to invent today. For there is certainly no thought more oppressive to urban populations right now than that of an atom bomb exploding in their immediate midst. And the torment of fearfully waiting for a bomb to go off at a stated time, unless the man who controls it can be captured, is probably the most torturing to be conceived. This is the terrible anxiety that is patiently constructed in this film.

As the frightened officials in London, from the prime minister on down, prepare to cope with the problem and the people themselves begin to wonder as the rumors get around, there creeps in, too, a comprehension of the terrible responsibility which the control of the destructive forces of atomic energy presents. And the real implications of this picture are not so much in the crisis dramatized as they are in the image of destruction of civilization that this spectacle provokes.

From the moment that an innocent-looking letter is dropped through the prime minister's door and the city of London begins moving on an average Monday morning, the heat is on. To be sure, it glows fitfully and mildly (which is typically British) at the start, as Scotland Yard launches a checkup on the scientist from whom the letter comes. And it doesn't assume intense proportions even after the threat is verified and the hunt for the mad, elusive scientist has been going for several days.

Indeed, the midsection of this picture has an oddly pedestrian pace for a drama about a mounting crisis, and a flaw appears in the postulate. Assuming that the purpose of the officials is to apprehend the scientist at all costs, it would seem not only practical but forgivable to promise the madman his wish—at least, a consideration—to prevent him from firing his bomb.

The answer may be that this film is a parable on the whole social-political problem of the bomb and that such a promise would represent appeasement. Be that as it may, there is this hole in the plot.

However, the crisis—and the picture—assumes proportions of significance and suspense as the job of evacuating London entirely is decided upon and this major maneuver in transportation is represented on the screen. Here the Boulting brothers—their talents were spread throughout the film—have summoned and demonstrated their great passion for journalistic style. With London itself as their set, with its transportation system their props, and with its people as their actors, they have staged such a mass exodus, with all its attendant graphic details, as you would think only newsreel cameras could catch. And the ultimate search of the empty city by military units as the zero hour draws near is as tensely exciting and compelling as any realistic war scene ever filmed.

In this remarkable picture the Boultings have well employed a cast of uncommonly good actors whose names and faces are little known. Barry Jones, who plays the fugitive scientist, combines a frightening furtiveness with a poignant display of confusion and of despair over the "blindness" of men. Sheila Manahan is touching as his daughter and Olive Sloane does a picturesque job as a broken-down musical actress who innocently harbors the fugitive. André Morell as the Scotland Yard inspector and Ronald Adam as the prime minister well represent the coolness and determination of British officialdom.

To this reviewer, the most significant line in the picture comes when the scientist, unsuspected, overhears a man say in a pub that bombs should be dropped on the "enemy" before the enemy can drop his. Angrily and sadly the scientist says that the man "ought to be made to think about the things he says." As well as entertainment, this film provides something big to think about, too.

—B.C., December 19, 1950

THE SEVEN SAMURAI

Directed by Akira Kurosawa; written (in Japanese, with English subtitles) by Mr. Kurosawa, Shinobu Hashimoto and Hideo Oguni; cinematographer, Asakazu Nakai; edited by Mr. Kurosawa; music by Fumio Hayasaka; art designer, Takashi Matsuyama; produced by Shojiro Motoko; released by Toho Studios and Columbia Pictures. Black and white. Running time: 160 minutes.

With: Takashi Shimura (Kambei), Yoshio Inabe (Gorobei), Isao Kimura (Katsushiro), Seiji Miyaguchi (Kyuzo), Minoru Chiaki (Heihachi), Daisuke Kato (Shichiroji), Toshiro Mifune (Kikuchiyo), Yoshio Tsuchiya (Rikichi), Keiko Tsushima (Shino), Kamatari Fujiwara (Manzo), Bokuzen Hidari (Yohei) and Kuninori Kodo (Gisaku).

The Japanese film director Akira Kurosawa, who gave us that eerily exotic and fascinating picture *Rashomon,* is now, after five years, represented by another extraordinary film, which matches his first for cinema brilliance, but in another and contrasting genre. It is called *The Magnificent Seven,* though it was known in Japan and abroad as *Seven Samurai,* and it was put on public exhibition yesterday at the Guild.

To give you a quick, capsule notion of the nature of this unusual film, let us say it bears cultural comparison with our own popular western *High Noon.* That is to say, it is a solid, naturalistic, he-man outdoor action film, wherein the qualities of human strength and weakness are discovered in a crisis taut with peril. And although the occurrence of this crisis is set in the sixteenth century in a village in Japan, it could be transposed without surrendering a basic element to the nineteenth century and a town on our own frontier.

The drama, to put it briefly—which is not what Mr. Kurosawa does, since his film runs for two hours and thirty-eight minutes, after some considerable trimming, we understand—is concerned with the defense of a farming village against a horde of bandits by seven samurai (independent professional soldiers), who are hired by the poor farmers to do the job.

That is the sum and substance of it: seven warriors are persuaded to come in and guard the village against the fearful bandits who have warned they will return when the crops are ripe. Seven sword-swinging, bow-and-arrow footmen of varied courage and personality are on hand to oppose the forty mounted bandits when they come charging down from the hills.

But on that simple framework and familiar story

line, director Kurosawa has plastered a wealth of rich detail, which brilliantly illuminates his characters and the kind of action in which they are involved. He has loaded his film with unusual and exciting physical incidents and made the whole thing graphic in a hard, realistic Western style.

There are things about the picture to question and criticize. It is much too long for comfort or for the story it has to tell. The director is annoyingly repetitious. He shows so many shots of horses' feet tromping in the mud in the course of battle that you wonder if those horses have heads. And his use of modern music, which is as pointed as the ballad in *High Noon*, leads you to wonder whether this picture is any more authentic to its period of culture than is the average American Western film.

However, it sparkles with touches that would do honor to Fred Zinnemann or John Ford, particularly in close-ups of faces and in sudden changes of mood within scenes. There is one switch, for instance, from a couple making luxurious love in the woods to a blood-chilling indication that the bandits have returned.

And Mr. Kurosawa's actors are, in their métier, superb, beginning with Takashi Shimura as the cool, collected leader of the samurai and continuing through the one conspicuous female, Keiko Tsushima, as the frightened but ardent village girl. Outstanding for his rare command of humor, however, is Toshiro Mifune, who played the bandit in *Rashomon*. Here he is brilliant as a crazy but courageous samurai.

Again, as in his previous triumph, the director has got photography that is perfectly calculated and effected to evoke appropriate moods, from harshly realistic to poetic. It is in black and white. And the English subtitles for the Japanese dialogue are brief and to the point.
—*B.C., November 20, 1956*

7 UP

Prepared by Paul Almond with Michael Apted. Running time: 40 minutes.

With: Nicholas Hitchon, Paul Kligerman, Charles Furneaux, Andrew Brackfield, John Brisby, Peter Davies, Neil Hughes, Suzanne Lusk, Simon Basterfield, Tony Walker, Jackie Bassett, Lynn Johnson, Susan Davis and Bruce Balden.

28 UP

Directed by Michael Apted; photography by George Jesse Turner; edited by Orel Norrie Ottie and Kin Horton; produced by Mr. Apted and Margaret Bottomley; production company, Granada Television of England Productions. Running time: 136 minutes.

The twin documentaries *7 Up* and *28 Up*, which were shown last night at the New York Film Festival (and which open at the Film Forum 1 on October 16), constitute as fascinating a work of popular sociology as you may ever see. *7 Up*, which was first shown on British television in 1963, collected a group of seven-year-olds from different class strata and let them describe their values, their prejudices, and their hopes for the future. The same project takes on tremendous poignancy and a great deal more breadth in *28 Up*, a follow-up study consisting of much longer profiles of the same people, revealing how their dreams and aspirations have changed with time.

28 Up also draws upon two earlier documentaries, made when the subjects were fourteen and twenty-one. And during the course of this development, the apparent prescience of *7 Up*, in which several of the young subjects readily offer fully detailed outlines of their plans for careers, marriage, and schooling, gives way to numerous surprises. Some of the seven-year-olds have indeed grown up to be everything they said they would be. One, an aristocratic boy who at seven sang the virtues of private schooling and complained about the poor, has proven to be so accurate a reflection of his former self that he is seen fox-hunting at twenty-one, and at twenty-eight will not deign even to be interviewed. But several of the others, including a middle-class Liverpool boy who at seven was the most handsome, animated, and cheerful of children, and at twenty-eight is a homeless derelict, become living reminders of the uncertainty of fate.

Michael Apted, who directed *28 Up* (and worked as an assistant on the first film), interconnects the four different time frames very skillfully. Along with charting the growth and development of his subjects chronologically and telescoping their lives with startling speed, he also juxtaposes statements from one era with the contradictions or corroborations that came later. Mr. Apted is not interested in heavy ironics here, nor is he eager to reveal his subjects' failures. But the film, even at its most matter-of-fact, cannot help speaking volumes about the exuberance of childhood, the edginess and uncertainty of adolescence, the sweeping expectations of early adulthood, and the compromises that inevitably come later.

Almost all of the twenty-eight-year-olds have married, had children, and entered the trades and professions in which they will probably remain for a lifetime. Few express any desire for further accomplishment. When asked about the most exciting moments of their lives, several of those settled most firmly into middle-class family life mention sporting events seen on television.

But some of these people sound genuinely happy, particularly the ones who started out at either extreme on the socioeconomic spectrum. Suzi, who at seven was a smug, mirthless rich girl envisioning a future life with two children and a nanny, has gone through a rebellious adolescence and emerged as a contented-sounding wife and mother. In the latter capacity, living in the country and married to a prosperous lawyer, she is giving her two children a nanny-less upbringing after all.

Paul and Simon, who at seven lived in a state institution for orphaned or abandoned children, say they consider it a sizable achievement to be giving their own children stable homes. Each of these men flirted briefly, in his early twenties, with a life of more independence; Paul sold everything he owned to buy a van and travel through western Australia, and the twenty-one-year-old Simon declared he would never stay in his sausage-packing job for very long. But now Paul refers to himself and his wife as "Mr. and Mrs. Average." And Simon, the only black interviewee, says he finds it much easier to stay in the sausage factory and busy himself with his family than to hope for a change in his situation.

7 Up, by virtue of the outspokenness and candor of its young subjects, is a compendium of outrageous statements. "I like my newspaper because I've got shares in it, and I know every day what the shares are," says one wealthy boy. Another says his plans entail "going to Africa and trying to teach people who are not civilized to be more or less good." But in *28 Up,* the first of these subjects now looks back on himself as "a fairly precocious little brat." And the second has

become a teacher of immigrant children in a public school in London's East End.

The effect of *28 Up* is to bring a dimension of wisdom and insight to the earlier footage, and in doing this Mr. Apted has been subtle and selective. His film cannot presume to explain why each of these lives has followed the path it has; in the case of Neil, the extremely articulate and sympathetic man who has become a derelict, the limitations of the process are most apparent. But in tracing these lives so diligently, and in eliciting from his subjects the kind of frankness they display in all four interview stages, Mr. Apted has created an unforgettably vivid and revealing group portrait. Unmistakably, this is a work still in progress. It is to be hoped that, when the time comes, *35 Up* and other installments will be in the offing.

—J.M., October 6, 1985

THE SEVEN YEAR ITCH

Directed by Billy Wilder: written by Mr. Wilder and George Axelrod. based on the play by Mr. Axelrod: cinematographer. Milton Krasner: edited by Hugh S. Fowler: music by Alfred Newman: art designers: Lyle Wheeler and George W. Davis. produced by Charles K. Feldman and Mr. Wilder: released by Twentieth Century Fox. Running time: 105 minutes.

With: Marilyn Monroe (The Girl). Tom Ewell (Richard Sherman). Evelyn Keyes (Helen Sherman). Sonny Tufts (Tom McKenzie). Robert Strauss (Kruhulik). Oscar Homolka (Dr. Brubaker) and Marguerite Chapman (Miss Morris).

The primal urge in the male animal—particularly one who has been married for seven years when he finds himself left alone for the whole summer in the hot city, with a voluptuous young lady in the apartment upstairs—is one of the principal topics of *The Seven Year Itch* at Loew's State. The other, equally assertive and much more tangible, is Marilyn Monroe.

As the aforesaid voluptuous young lady who comes into close proximity with the highly susceptible male animal, adroitly played by Tom Ewell, Miss Monroe brings a special personality and a certain physical something or other to the film that may not be exactly what the playwright ordered but which definitely convey an idea.

From the moment she steps into the picture, in a garment that drapes her shapely form as though she had been skillfully poured into it (with about a quart and a half to spare), the famous screen star with the silver-blond tresses and the ingenuously wide-eyed stare emanates one suggestion. And that suggestion rather dominates the film. It is—well, why define it? Miss Monroe clearly plays the title role.

In a way, this is out of kilter. For George Axelrod, who wrote the stage play from which the picture is taken and collaborated with director Billy Wilder on the script, obviously meant that the dominating interest should be the comical anxieties of the character played by Mr. Ewell. The torments of this poor fellow, torn between the thought of his wife and the more immediate and pressing impulses of his libido and his highly fertile brain, are the principal substance of the stage play. They gave it lilt and character.

And they still have significance in the picture. As a publisher of paperbound books whose mind is drenched with lurid notions of sin and fatality, Mr. Ewell wrestles tensely with his urges and with his self-induced fantasies when the sexy number from upstairs becomes a real thing in his air-conditioned living room.

But the simple fact is that Mr. Wilder has permitted Miss Monroe, in her skin-fitting dresses and her frank gyrations, to overpower Mr. Ewell. She, without any real dimensions, is the focus of attention in the film.

This may be fortunate, however, as a factor of popularity, for there is a certain emptiness and eventual tedium to the anxieties of Mr. Ewell. Although some of his crises are explosive, in a far-fetched, farcical way, there is a sameness and repetition to the fixes he continuously finds himself in. And, it must be stated quite frankly, color and the CinemaScope screen do not lend an intriguing appearance to his plain and clownish phiz.

Also here is a further factor: in the play, as we recall, the wishful thoughts of the fellow toward the lady were finally realized. In the picture there is no such fulfillment. The rules of the Production Code have compelled a careful evasion that makes his ardor just a little absurd.

Thus it is that the undisguised performance of Miss Monroe, while it may lack depth, gives the show a caloric content that will not lose her any faithful fans. We merely commend her diligence when we say it leaves much—very much—to be desired.

In roles of minor importance Evelyn Keyes as Mr. Ewell's wife, Sonny Tufts as her darkly suspected suitor, Robert Strauss as a nosy janitor, and Oscar Homolka as an unsympathetic psychoanalyst do nicely in the rush of episodes. If they, too, seem to lack definition, that is the nature of the film.

—B.C., June 4, 1955

THE SEVENTH SEAL

Directed by Ingmar Bergman; written (in Swedish, with English subtitles) by Mr. Bergman, based on his play Tramalning; cinematographer. Gunnar Fischer; edited by Lennart Wallen; music by Erik Nordgren; choreography by Else Fischer; produced by Allan Ekelund; released by Janus Films. Black and white. Running time: 96 minutes.

With: Max von Sydow (Knight). Gunnar Björnstrand (Squire). Bengt Ekerot (Death). Nils Poppe (Jof). Inga Gill (Lisa). Bibi Andersson (Mia) and Maud Hansson (Witch).

Swedish director Ingmar Bergman, whose *Smiles of a Summer Night* proved him an unsuspected master of satiric comedy, surprises again in yet another even more neglected vein with his new self-written and self-directed allegorical film, *The Seventh Seal*.

This initially mystifying drama, known in Swedish as *Det Sjunde Inseglet*, opened yesterday at the Paris, and slowly turns out to be a piercing and powerful contemplation of the passage of man upon this earth. Essentially intellectual, yet emotionally stimulating, too, it is as tough—and rewarding—a screen challenge as the moviegoer has had to face this year.

The specified time of its action is the fourteenth century and the locale is apparently Sweden—or it could be any other medieval European country—in the fearful throes of the plague. A knight, just returned from the Crusades, meets black-robed Death on the beach and makes a bargain for time to do a good deed while the two of them play a sort of running game of chess.

While the game is in progress, the knight and his squire go forth to find the land full of trembling people who darkly await the Judgment Day. Some are led to self-pity and torturing themselves by their priests, who also have provided a symbol of wickedness in an innocent girl condemned as a "witch." Others are given to snatching a little fun while they may; and, recalling Mr. Bergman's last picture, you should guess what sort of fun that is.

But en route, the knight, who, significantly, was disillusioned by the Crusades and is still seeking God, comes across a little family of traveling actors who are as fresh and wholesome as the morning dew. Except that the young father of the little family has a way of seeing visions from time to time (to his pretty wife's tolerant amusement), the happy couple are as normal as their chubby child. And it is this little family that the sad knight, still uncertain, arranges to save when he and a gathering of weary wanderers, including his defiant squire, must submit to Death at the end of the game.

If this sounds a somewhat deep-dish drama, laden with obscurities and costumes, it is because the graphic style of Mr. Bergman does not glow in a summary. It is a provocative picture, filled with intimations that are true—some what you want to make of them and some as clear as the back of your hand.

For instance, it could be that Mr. Bergman means the plague to represent all mortal fears of threats beyond likely containment that hang over modern man. Certainly, there can be little question what he means when he shows the piteous herds of anguished and self-tormenting people driven by soldiers and priests.

But the profundities of the ideas are lightened and made flexible by glowing pictorial presentation of action that is interesting and strong. Mr. Bergman uses his camera and actors for sharp, realistic effects. Black-robed Death is as frank and insistent as a terrified girl being hustled to the stake. A beach and a cloudy sky are as literal and dramatic as a lusty woman's coquetries. Mr. Bergman hits you with it, right between the eyes.

And his actors are excellent, from Max von Sydow as the gaunt and towering knight, through Gunnar Björnstrand as his squire and Bengt Ekerot as Death,

to Maud Hansson as the piteous "witch." Nils Poppe as the strolling player and Bibi Andersson as his wife are warming and cheerful companions in an uncommon and fascinating film.

—B.C., October 14, 1958

SEX, LIES AND VIDEOTAPE

Written, edited and directed by Steven Soderbergh; director of photography, Walt Lloyd; music by Cliff Martinez; art designer, Joanne Schmidt; produced by Robert Newmyer and John Hardy; released by Miramax Films. Running time: 101 minutes.

With: James Spader (Graham), Andie MacDowell (Ann), Peter Gallagher (John), Laura San Giacomo (Cynthia) and Ron Vawter (Therapist).

A guileless beauty in a long flowered dress, Ann Millaney sits cross-legged on the couch in her psychiatrist's sunny office and describes her fear of the week: what will we do with all the garbage piling up in the world? Her soft southern voice floats over the image of Graham, her husband's straggly old friend, who stops for a shave in the men's room of Ray's Bait Shop and splashes a little water under his armpits before he drives on to Baton Rouge, Louisiana, and Ann's spacious white house.

Meanwhile, Ann's husband, John, spins his wedding ring on the desk in his law office, then heads off for a hot sexual interlude with Ann's sister, Cynthia. By the end of this opening sequence, when Graham takes his duffle bag and video camera from his trunk and walks through the Millaneys' door, the writer and director Steven Soderbergh has mapped out the bright wit, sinister undertone, and smooth, layered style that run through *Sex, Lies and Videotape.*

Mr. Soderbergh's astonishing first film is a *Liaisons Dangereuses* for the video age, a rich, absorbing tale of sexual greed and fear, love, and betrayal, in which Graham's camera becomes a central player. It is an intricate dance of constantly changing partners, whose connections are based on truth, self-denial, and outright deception. *Sex, Lies and Videotape,* which won the Grand Prize at this year's Cannes Film Festival,

888

comes loaded with advance praise that seems impossible to meet; amazingly, the film surpasses that.

Part of the video generation he is documenting, the twenty-six-year-old Mr. Soderbergh has an insider's sense of how his characters talk and think. Younger than television, he directs the camera as if it were the most natural storytelling device in the world. But his talent is clearly uncommon, for he has evoked four flawless performances.

Andie MacDowell's Ann is funny, confused, then smart at unexpected moments. She never turns coy, though she hides behind her good-girl demeanor. When the psychiatrist asks how things are with John, she says, "They're fine," adding almost as an afterthought. "But I'm kinda goin' through this thing where I don't want him to touch me." Her romantic look and flowing skirts hide a sexuality whose existence she can hardly admit.

Calling her sister "an extrovert, kind of loud," is a perfect Ann-like euphemism. Cynthia's nose is too long, she has a randy gap between her teeth, and her husky voice suggests "I don't care" with every word she spits out. Yet she is totally sexual and confident, advertising her perfect body in tight shirts and tiny skirts.

Her affair with John is built on rivalry and the thrill of deception as much as sexual heat. "The beautiful, the perfect Ann Bishop Millaney," Cynthia sneers about her sister, her voice dripping with contempt and ugly victory. Laura San Giacomo's amazing performance suggests a manic edge beneath Cynthia's self-possession.

John (Peter Gallagher) is meant to be a precise type. From his regulation yuppie wire-rim glasses and suspenders to his compulsive womanizing, he lacks imagination.

But Graham is Mr. Soderbergh's most disturbing, provocative, and perceptive creation, the video generation's nightmare child. Impotent whenever he is with another person, Graham's only physical satisfaction comes when he watches the tapes he has made of women answering his questions about their sexual histories and tastes.

James Spader, who won the Best Actor Award at Cannes, gives a tremendously subtle performance, playing Graham with a hesitant half-smile and tentative voice that makes him sweet and sinister at once, keeping everyone off-balance. He arrives at Ann's house and instantly starts questioning her, apologizing even as he pries. "Do you like being married? What do you like about it?" He is a cool observer so pained by his own detachment that the word voyeur never quite matches his perversity.

Ann responds to Graham sexually, sees in him a kindred repressed spirit, and runs from the friendship when she learns about the tapes. The film's one wholly sympathetic character, Ann sees in Graham a confusion of vulnerable and dangerous qualities.

Graham's video camera is the perfect metaphor for these people, who can only respond to one another as images and objects: Ann sees John as the Husband and he sees her as the Wife; Cynthia sees every male as a sex object; Graham distances everyone through his lens. But Mr. Soderbergh does not press this idea too hard.

We see the slightest glimpses of Graham's tapes, and just the teasing start when he interviews Cynthia. We learn how her tape ended later, when she phones her sister. "You didn't!" Ann says, "What if he beams it off some satellite?" (Mr. Soderbergh's funniest lines are dropped in at interludes, reminders that the murkiest lives are still ludicrous.) Mr. Soderbergh's camera, like Graham's, is more concerned with talk than sex, and he allows dialogue to carry the film's erotic charge.

It would have been more dramatic and predictable if this film had assumed Graham's distorted point of view. But Mr. Soderbergh's choices are more original, challenging, and subtle than that. His perspective resembles Graham's only in its style—that of a camera cutting fluidly from one pair to another, a haunting eye whose precision is funny and chilling. "I look around this town," Graham tells Ann toward the end, "and I see John and Cynthia and you, and I feel comparatively healthy."

They are all comparatively sick, of course, so eventually the dark deception of John and Cynthia is brought to light; the buried passion of Ann and Graham begins to emerge. Mr. Soderbergh's resolution is too clean for these very messy lives. And his characters' motives are sometimes too simple: Cynthia becomes sexy to set herself apart from Ann, and Ann rejects sex because that's how Cynthia thinks.

But these are small disappointments in a film whose enormous authority and intelligence extend to every detail. Even the bright windows that frequently frame the characters reinforce the idea of voyeurism while, more practically, they prevent this inbred drama from seeming too dark and claustrophobic. *Sex, Lies and Videotape,* which opens today at Cinema Studio 1 and 2, is one of the freshest American films of the decade.

—C.J., August 4, 1989

SEXY BEAST

Directed by Jonathan Glazer; written by Louis Mellis and David Scinto; director of photography, Ivan Bird; edited by John Scott and Sam Sneade; music by Roque Baños; production designer, Jan Houllevigue; produced by Jeremy Thomas; released by Fox Searchlight Pictures. Running time: 91 minutes.

With: Ray Winstone (Gal), Ben Kingsley (Don Logan/Malky Logan), Ian McShane (Teddy Bass), Amanda Redman (Deedee), Cavan Kendall (Aitch), Julianne White (Jackie), Álvaro Monje (Enrique) and James Fox (Harry).

At the start of *Sexy Beast,* Gal (Ray Winstone), a heavyset, middle aged English hoodlum, is enjoying a carefree retirement on the Mediterranean coast of Spain. Yes, a boulder has tumbled into his swimming pool, smashing the tilework and narrowly missing Gal himself, but this seems more like an inconvenience than an ill omen. Gal spends his time sunbathing on his patio, dining out with his friends, Aitch and Jackie (Cavan Kendall and Julianne White), and dancing in the moonlight with his beloved wife, Deedee (Amanda Redman). He's happy to have left England ("What a toilet!") and the dodgy life he led there.

But then one evening Aitch and Jackie arrive at Gal's favorite restaurant with stricken looks on their faces. What could be wrong? "Don Logan called from London."

Who is this Don Logan, you wonder, the mere mention of whose name can reduce the stoic, affable Gal to a state of sweaty panic? The answer arrives soon enough, in the terrifying person of Ben Kingsley whose performance jolts the movie like an exposed high-voltage wire.

It might be useful, with reference to Mr. Kingsley's most famous role, to think of Don Logan as the oppo-

site of Gandhi: he's pure violence, a sociopath who radiates menace even while sitting perfectly still mouthing pleasantries. His slightest pause or twitch freezes Gal, Jackie, and Aitch with terror. (Deedee turns out to be a bit tougher.) When he bursts into one of his frequent rages—reeling off profanity-laced cockney non sequiturs, absurd jokes and violent threats—you won't know whether to burst out laughing or hide under your seat.

Don's mission is job recruitment. A bunch of leathery London criminals led by the glowering Teddy Bass (Ian McShane, whose shiny jet-black hair sits atop his wrinkled, once-handsome face like a bad joke) is plotting an elaborate heist, which requires Gal's skill as an underwater safecracker. Gal says no, but Don's powers of persuasion are not to be underestimated.

Nor are the stylish, eye-popping pleasures to be found in *Sexy Beast.* The director, Jonathan Glazer, has come, like so many of his peers, to feature filmmaking from music videos and television commercials; he clearly has a knack for quick visual thinking and a snappy rhythmic sense.

The opening sequence of dazzling Spanish sunlight plays over the menacing growl of "Peaches" by the Stranglers. Mr. Glazer uses music—especially Roque Baños's paella-western score—both to italicize his images and to subvert them, but he also knows that sometimes the best sound effect is silence.

And while he clearly retains a fondness for the brevity and punch of a good thirty-second television commercial, he lets his story build slowly, with the haunting indirection of a Pinter play. At times he allows his discipline—most impressive in the break-in sequence, which is like a speeded-up, deep-water version of Jules Dassin's *Rififi*—to slip. The dream sequences, featuring a hairy rabbit-eared biped who dwells in Gal's unconscious, are jarring at first, but then just become puzzling.

In spite of Mr. Glazer's cleverness and panache, *Sexy Beast* tells the familiar story of an aging criminal dragged against his will into the life he's tried to escape. What makes the film an unusually satisfying genre exercise, apart from the director's youthful brio, is the gnarled authenticity of its cast.

Mr. Kingsley's explosive turn—which might overshadow the quieter work of Mr. Winstone, Ms. Redman, and Mr. Kendall—instead heightens your sense of their characters' vulnerable humanity. Mr. Winstone, with his bearish physique, his slowmoving sexual magnetism and his ability to convey tenderness and hurt at unexpected moments, might be James Gandolfini's East End cousin. The easy rapport he finds with Ms. Redman—rarely has the romance of middle-aged married love been depicted with such quiet heat—raises the film above its limitations. *Sexy Beast* delivers not only sensation but also, more remarkably, feeling.

—*A.O.S., June 13, 2001*

SHADOW OF A DOUBT

Directed by Alfred Hitchcock: written by Thornton Wilder, Sally Benson and Alma Reville, based on a story by Gordon McDonnell: cinematographer, Joseph Valentine: edited by Milton Carruth: music by Dimitri Tiomkin: art designers, John B. Goodman and Robert Boyle: produced by Jack H. Skirball: released by Universal Pictures. Black and white. Running time: 108 minutes.

With: Teresa Wright (Young Charlie), Joseph Cotten (Uncle Charlie), Macdonald Carey (Jack Graham), Patricia Collinge (Emma Newton), Henry Travers (Joseph Newton), Hume Cronyn (Herbie Hawkins) and Wallace Ford (Fred Saunders).

You've got to hand it to Alfred Hitchcock: when he sows the fearful seeds of mistrust in one of his motion pictures he can raise more goose pimples to the square inch of a customer's flesh than any other director of thrillers in Hollywood. He did it quite nicely in *Rebecca* and again in *Suspicion* about a year ago. And now he is bringing in another bumper crop of blue-ribbon shivers and chills in Jack Skirball's diverse production of *Shadow of a Doubt,* which came to the Rivoli last night.

Yes, the way Mr. Hitchcock folds suggestions very casually into the furrows of his film, the way he can make a torn newspaper or the sharpened inflection of a person's voice send ticklish roots down to the subsoil of a customer's anxiety, is a wondrous, enviable accomplishment. And the mental anguish he can thereby create, apparently in the minds of his characters but actually in the psyche of you, is of championship proportions and—being hokum, anyhow—a sheer delight.

But when Mr. Hitchcock and/or his writers start weaving allegories in his films or, worse still, neglect to spring surprises after the ground has apparently been prepared, the consequence is something less than cheering. And that is the principal fault—or rather, the sole disappointment—in *Shadow of a Doubt.* For this one suggests tremendous promise when a sinister character—a gentleman called Uncle Charlie—goes to visit with relatives, a typical American family, in a quiet California town. The atmosphere is charged with electricity when the daughter of the family, Uncle Charlie's namesake, begins to grow strangely suspicious of this moody, cryptic guest in the house. And the story seems loaded for fireworks and a beautiful explosion of surprise when the scared girl discovers that Uncle Charlie is really a murderer of rich, fat widows, wanted back East.

But from that point on the story takes a decidedly anticlimactic dip and becomes just a competent exercise in keeping a tightrope taut. It also becomes a bit too specious in making a moralistic show of the warmth of an American community toward an unsuspected rascal in its midst. We won't violate tradition to tell you how the story ends, but we will say that the moral is either antisocial or, at best, obscure. When Uncle Charlie's niece concludes quite cynically that the world is a horrible place and the young detective with whom she has romanced answers, "Sometimes it needs a lot of watching; seems to go crazy, every now and then, like Uncle Charlie," the bathos is enough to knock you down.

However, there is sufficient sheer excitement and refreshing atmosphere in the film to compensate in large measure for its few disappointing faults. Thornton Wilder, Sally Benson, and Alma Reville have drawn a graphic and affectionate outline of a small-town American family which an excellent cast has brought to life and Mr. Hitchcock has manifested completely in his naturalistic style. Teresa Wright is aglow with maiden spirit and subsequent emotional distress as the namesake of Uncle Charlie, and Patricia Collinge gives amazing flexibility and depth to the role of the patient, hard-working, sentimental mother of the house. Henry Travers is amusing as the father, Edna May Wonacott is fearfully precocious as "the brat," and Hume Cronyn makes a modest comic masterpiece out of the character of a literal-minded friend.

As the progressively less charming Uncle Charlie, Joseph Cotten plays with smooth, insinuating ease while injecting a harsh and bitter quality which nicely becomes villainy. He has obviously kept an eye on Orson Welles. And Macdonald Carey and Wallace Ford make an adequate pair of modern sleuths.

The flavor and "feel" of a small town have been beautifully impressed in this film by the simple expedient of shooting most of it in Santa Rosa, California, which leads to the obvious observation that the story should be as reliable as the sets.

—B.C., January 13, 1943

SHAFT

Directed by Gordon Parks: written by Ernest Tidyman and John D. F. Black. based on the novel by Mr. Tidyman: director of photography. Urs Furrer: edited by Hugh A. Robertson: art director. Emmanuel Gerard: music by Isaac Hayes and J.J. Johnson: produced by Joel Freeman: released by Metro-Goldwyn-Mayer. Running time: 100 minutes.

With: Richard Roundtree (John Shaft). Moses Gunn (Bumpy Jonas). Charles Cioffi (Vic Androzzi). Christopher St. John (Ben Buford). Gwenn Mitchell (Ellie Moore). Lawrence Pressman (Sergeant Tom Hannon). Victor Arnold (Charlie). Sherri Brewer (Marcy). Rex Robbins (Rollie). Camille Yarbrough (Dina Greene). Margaret Warncke (Linda). Joseph Leon (Byron Leibowitz). Arnold Johnson (Cul). Dominic Barto (Patsy) and George Strus (Carmen).

Shaft is a New York private eye with a shabby office in midtown, a duplex in the Village, a wad of bills (and no small change) to tip with, a working love-hate relation with the cops and friends all over the city. He is also black. When Bumpy Jonas, chief hood in Harlem, tells him that his teen-aged daughter has been kidnapped and he suspects that militants have done it, Shaft takes the case more for $50 an hour than for any love of Bumpy. The case turns out to be a bit complex, a major gang war with racial overtones, though, really, no racial undertones. But Shaft delivers Bumpy his girl. And to his pal, Police Lieut. Vic Androzzi, he delivers the still warm bodies of what seems to be virtually all the white half of East-coast organized crime.

Of course, everybody knows you can't make a private-eye movie anymore. But if you *could* make a private-eye movie, making it black might be a good idea. Not just for kicks, though there is nothing wrong with kicks, but for truth—or at least as much truth as you need to put into the genre. For who better than a black man to be both underdog and overlord, to understand everybody's motives including his own, to have that freedom of the city that is the point of the detective film and that, at least where many of us live, is no longer a right freely granted to anyone named Marlowe or Harper or even Madigan.

Gordon Parks's *Shaft*, which opened yesterday at the DeMille and the 72d Street Playhouse, has surely the best title of any of the one-name movies to have opened in recent years. And though it doesn't have too much else of the best, it has a kind of self-generated good will that makes you want to like it even when for scenes on end you know it is doing everything wrong.

Parks is a well-known and very classy still photographer, a composer, writer and general Renaissance man whose first feature, *The Learning Tree,* offered some moments of lovely, rather formal beauty amid vast stretches of conventional forms. *Shaft* demonstrates a similar respect for forms, and for formal good looks (though Parks is not this time his own cinematographer), so that much of the time it has the visual style of a *Life* magazine photographic essay—though its dramatic logic is all Flash Gordon.

Shaft really is wish-fulfillment: the pad, the girls (whom he treats none too well), the fancy leather clothes, the ability to put down absolutely everybody and be paid back in admiration, the instinct for danger, the physical prowess, the fantastic recuperative ability that has him up and around and feeling no pain an hour after taking three machine-gun slugs in the chest.

He is also New York's champion jaywalker and a kidder on all levels and master of enough character quirks to keep a whole series of detective movies going—and although Parks is not yet enough at ease in the medium to make these things work, he has ideas and a feeling for the form's more vulgar excitements that may in time allow him to overcome his own good taste.

He is at his worst in directing actors, or perhaps in cutting between actors, so that the strong cast (Richard Roundtree, Moses Gunn, Charles Gioffi) seems weak and without much sense of verbal rhythm. But, tin-eared and occasionally glass-eyed, he shows a grace in putting the horror of the city to the purposes of entertainment that seems especially welcome considering the options.

A.G., July 3, 1971

SHAKESPEARE IN LOVE

Directed by John Madden; written by Marc Norman and Tom Stoppard; director of photography, Richard Greatrex; edited by David Gamble; music by Stephen Warbeck; costumes by Sandy Powell; production designer, Martin Childs; produced by David Parritt, Donna Gigliotti, Harvey Weinstein, Edward Zwick and Mr. Norman; released by Miramax Films. Running time: 113 minutes.

With: Gwyneth Paltrow (Viola de Lesseps), Joseph Fiennes (Will Shakespeare), Geoffrey Rush (Philip Henslowe), Colin Firth (Lord Wessex), Ben Affleck (Ned Alleyn), Judi Dench (Queen Elizabeth), Rupert Everett (Christopher Marlowe), Simon Callow (Tilney, Master of the Revels), Jim Carter (Ralph Bashford), Martin Clunes (Richard Burbage), Antony Sher (Dr. Moth), Imelda Staunton (Nurse), Tom Wilkinson (Hugh Fennyman) and Mark Williams (Wabash).

Shakespeare meets Sherlock, and makes for pure enchantment in the inspired conjecture behind *Shakespeare in Love.* This film's exhilarating cleverness springs from its speculation about where the playwright might have found the beginnings of *Romeo and Juliet,* but it is not constrained by worries about literary or historical accuracy. (So what if characters talk about Virginia tobacco plantations before there was a Virginia?) Galvanized by the near-total absence of biographical data, it soars freely into the realm of invention, wittily weaving Shakespearean language and emotion into an intoxicatingly glamorous romance. No less marvelous are its imaginings of an Elizabethan theater fraught with the same backbiting and conniving we enjoy today.

Tom Stoppard's mark on the jubilant screenplay, which originated as the brainstorm of Marc Norman, harks back to the behind-the-scenes delights of his *Rosencrantz and Guildenstern Are Dead.* This is a world in which a therapist times his patient with an hourglass and a souvenir mug is inscribed "A Present from Stratford-Upon-Avon." Says the dashing young Shakespeare, played tempestuously well by Joseph Fiennes, about the more successful Christopher Marlowe (Rupert Everett): "Lovely waistcoat. Shame about the poetry." And there is the inevitable moment when someone asks who Shakespeare is, only to be told by a comically obtuse producer (Geoffrey Rush): "Nobody—that's the author."

Ingenious as the film's many inventions happen to be (from boatmen who behave like cabbies to its equivalent of Shakespearean outtakes—*One Gentleman of Verona* in the writing process), it could never have had so much energy without the right real-life Juliet to dazzle Will. Gwyneth Paltrow, in her first great, fully realized starring performance, makes a heroine so breathtaking that she seems utterly plausible as the playwright's guiding light. In a film steamy enough to start a sonnet craze, her Viola de Lesseps really does seem to warrant the most timeless love poems, and to speak Shakespeare's own elegant language with astonishing ease. *Shakespeare in Love* itself seems as smitten with her as the poet is, and as alight with the same love of language and beauty.

As directed by John Madden in much more rollicking, passionate style than his *Mrs. Brown, Shakespeare in Love* imagines Viola as the perfect muse: a literate, headstrong beauty who adores the theater and can use words like "anon" as readily as Shakespeare writes them. She comes into his life at a pivotal moment in his career, about which the film speculates with literary scholarship and Holmesian audacity. What if, before making the leap from his early works to the profound emotions of *Romeo and Juliet,* he had suffered both writer's block and a crisis in sexual confidence? ("It's as if my quill has broken," he tells his therapist.) What if such impotence could be cured only by a madly romantic liaison with a Juliet prototype, an unattainable woman with a habit of speaking from her balcony?

Enter Viola, who is so eager to work in the theater that she disguises herself as a boy, since women are forbidden to act. (Part of the film's great fun is its way of working such Shakespearean gambits into its own plot.) On her way to winning the role of Romeo, Viola finds herself suddenly enmeshed with the handsome playwright himself, and the film gives way to a heady brew of literature and ardor. In one transporting montage, the lovers embrace passionately while rehearsing dialogue that spills over into stage scenes, and the bond between tempestuous love and artistic creation is illustrated beautifully. The film is as bold in its romantic interludes as it is in historical second-guessing, leaving Ms. Paltrow and Mr. Fiennes enmeshed in frequent half-nude, hotblooded clinches in her boudoir.

Far richer and more deft than the other Elizabethan film in town (*Elizabeth*), this boasts a splendid, hearty cast of supporting players. (The actors in both films, like Mr. Fiennes, do notably better work here.) Colin Firth plays Viola's fiancé as a perfect Mr. Wrong. Mr. Rush's opportunistic producer is very funny, as is Ben Affleck's version of a big-egoed actor, Elizabethan style. (Cast as Mercutio, he is also hoodwinked by Will into thinking that "Mercutio" is the play's name.) Also most amusing is Tom Wilkinson as a financier who grows stagestruck, Jim Carter as the actor who looks silliest in a dress, Simon Callow as the Queen's censor, and Imelda Staunton as Viola's nurse. Judi Dench's shrewd, daunting Elizabeth is one of the film's utmost treats.

So are its costumes. The designer Sandy Powell has previous credits including *Orlando* and *The Wings of the Dove,* and she deserves to be remembered for her wonderfully inventive work this year. She contributes extravagantly to this film's visual allure and did the same for *Velvet Goldmine.* Gear-switching that extreme is no mean feat.

—*J.M., December 11, 1998*

SHANE

Produced and directed by George Stevens: written by A. B. Guthrie Jr. and Jack Sher, based on the novel by Jack Schaefer: cinematographer, Loyal Griggs: edited by William Hornbeck and Tom McAdoo: music by Victor Young: art designers. Hal Pereira and Walter Tyler: released by Paramount Pictures. Running time: 118 minutes.

With: Alan Ladd (Shane). Jean Arthur (Mrs. Starrett). Van Heflin (Mr. Starrett). Brandon de Wilde (Joey Starrett). Jack Palance (Wilson). Ben Johnson (Chris). Edgar Buchanan (Lewis). Emile Meyer (Tyker) and Elisha Cook Jr. (Torrey).

With *High Noon* so lately among us, it scarcely seems possible that the screen should so soon again come up with another great Western film. Yet that is substantially what has happened in the case of George Stevens's *Shane,* which made a magnificent appearance at the Music Hall yesterday. Beautifully filmed in Technicolor in the great Wyoming outdoors, under the towering peaks of the Grand Tetons, and shown on a larger screen that enhances the scenic panorama, it may truly be said to be a rich and dramatic mobile painting of the American frontier scene.

For *Shane* contains something more than beauty and the grandeur of the mountains and plains, drenched by the brilliant Western sunshine and the violent, torrential, black-browed rains. It contains a tremendous comprehension of the bitterness and passion of the feuds that existed between the new homesteaders and the cattlemen on the open range. It contains a disturbing revelation of the savagery that prevailed in the hearts of the old gunfighters, who were simply legal killers under the frontier code. And it also contains a very wonderful understanding of the spirit of a little boy amid all the tensions and excitements and adventures of a frontier home.

As a matter of fact, it is the concept and the presence of this little boy as an innocent and fascinated observer of the brutal struggle his elders wage that permits a refreshing viewpoint on material that's not exactly new. For it's this youngster's frank enthusiasms and naive reactions that are made the solvent of all the crashing drama in A. B. Guthrie Jr.'s script. And it's his youthful face and form, contributed by the precocious young Brandon de Wilde, that Mr. Stevens as director has most creatively worked with through the film.

There is tempestuous violence in a fistfight that a stranger and the youngster's father wage against a gang of cattlemen hoodlums in a plain-board frontier saloon, but the fight has a freshness about it because it is watched by the youngster from under a door. And there's novelty and charm in this stranger because he is hero-worshiped by the boy. Most particularly, there's eloquence and greatness in a scene of a frontier burial on a hill, but it gets its keenest punctuation when the boy wanders off to pet a colt.

The story Mr. Stevens is telling is simply that of the bold and stubborn urge of a group of modest homesteaders to hold on to their land and their homes against the threats and harassments of a cattle baron who implements his purpose with paid thugs. And it is brought to its ultimate climax when the stranger, who seeks peace on one of the farms, tackles an ugly gunfighter imported from Cheyenne to do a job on the leader of the homesteaders, the father of the boy.

This ultimate gunfight, incidentally, makes a beautiful, almost classic scene as Mr. Stevens has staged it in the dismal and dimly lit saloon, with characters slinking in the background as the antagonists, Alan Ladd and Jack Palance, face off in frigid silence before the fatal words fly and the guns blaze. It is a scene which, added to the many that Mr. Stevens has composed in this film, gives the whole thing the quality of a fine album of paintings of the frontier.

And in many respects the characters that Mr. Stevens's actors have drawn might be considered portraits of familiar frontier types. Van Heflin as the leading homesteader is outstanding among those played by Douglas Spencer, Elisha Cook, Jr., Edgar Buchanan, and Leonard Strong. Mr. Ladd, though slightly swashbuckling as a gunfighter wishing to retire, does well enough by the character, and Jean Arthur is good as the homesteader's wife. Mr. Palance as the mean, imported gunman; Emile Meyer as the cattleman boss; and Paul McVey as the frontier storekeeper give fine portrayals, too. But it is Master de Wilde with his bright face, his clear voice, and his resolute boyish ways who steals the affections of the audience and clinches *Shane* as a most unusual film.

—*B.C., April 24, 1953*

SHE WORE A YELLOW RIBBON

Directed by John Ford; written by Frank Nugent and Laurence Stallings, based on the *Saturday Evening Post* stories "War Party" and "The Big Hunt" by James Warner Bellah; cinematographer, Winton C. Hoch; edited by Jack Murray; music by Richard Hageman; art designer, James Basevi; produced by Mr. Ford and Merian C. Cooper; released by RKO Radio Pictures. Running time: 103 minutes.

With: John Wayne (Captain Brittles), Joanne Dru (Olivia), John Agar (Lieutenant Cohill), Ben Johnson (Tyree), Harry Carey Jr. (Lieutenant Pennell), Victor McLaglen (Sergeant Quincannon), Mildred Natwick (Mrs. Alishard) and George O'Brien (Major Alishard).

In whatever wisps of foliage are left on director John Ford's head, he wears a yellow ribbon—and, in the spirit of that rousing soldier song, he wears it with pride and affection for the old United States Cavalry. This you can see as plain as daylight and beyond the shadow of a bullet-scarred redoubt in Mr. Ford's grand *She Wore a Yellow Ribbon*, which came to the Capitol yesterday.

For in this big Technicolored Western Mr. Ford has superbly achieved a vast and composite illustration of all the legends of the frontier cavalryman. He has got the bold and dashing courage, the stout masculine sentiment, the grandeur of rear-guard heroism, and the brash bravado of the barrackroom brawl. And, best of all, he has got the brilliant color and vivid detail of those legendary troops as they ranged through the silent "Indian country" and across the magnificent western plains.

From the moment that Mr. Ford assembles the raw-boned troopers of Company C around the immortal guidon of the Seventh Cavalry at distant Fort Starke, thence to ride forth on a perilous mission under Captain Nathan Brittles's firm command, the rifles are held at ready and the scouts are flanked wide on alert, for somewhere out there in the vast plains a Cheyenne dog-party is on the prowl. Custer is dead at the Little Big Horn, the buffalo herds are coming north, and someone is making "big medicine" among the strangely emboldened Indian tribes. And with Mr. Ford being the admirer of the cavalry that he is, you may be sure that a'plenty happens before the mission is brought to a close.

That plenty includes a brace of brushes with the outriding Indians, a wild thunderstorm on the great plain, and an operation upon a wounded man. It also includes a dazzling stampede by whooping troopers through a startled Indian camp and a running romance between a shavetail and the major's beautiful niece. For the nimble scriptwriters, Frank Nugent and Laurence Stallings, scribbled diligently right alongside the bold director—or maybe one jump ahead—in the course of the headlong production of this obviously runaway film. And since they were snatching freely from two James Warner Bellah yarns, they scooped up some heterogeneous details with which the director could work.

And Mr. Ford has employed them to what is usually termed the best effect. His action is crisp and electric. His pictures are bold and beautiful. No one could make a troop of soldiers riding across the western plains look more exciting and romantic than this great director does. No one could get more emotion out of a thundering cavalry charge or an old soldier's farewell departure from the ranks of his comrades than he.

To be sure, he is ably assisted in his achievement by a fine outdoor cast, which boasts the experienced John Wayne in the tough Captain Brittles role. Mr. Wayne, his hair streaked with silver and wearing a dashing moustache, is the absolute image and ideal of the legendary cavalryman. A newcomer named Ben Johnson is likewise vivid as a trooper from the South and John Agar does very nicely as the lieutenant who loves the girl. The latter is brightly represented by the lovely Joanne Dru, and Midred Natwick is deliciously humorous as a hard-bitten Army wife.

Bulwarked with gay and spirited music and keyed to the colors of the plains, *She Wore a Yellow Ribbon* is a dilly of a cavalry picture. Yeehooooo!

—*B.C., November 18, 1949*

SHERMAN'S MARCH

Produced, edited and directed by Ross McElwee: director of photography. Mr. McElwee. Black and white. Running time: 155 minutes.

With: Mr. McElwee and various residents of the South.

At the beginning of Ross McElwee's *Sherman's March*, the filmmaker tells us that he had originally planned a documentary about the aftereffects, which are still to be found in Georgia and the Caroli-

nas, of the "total warfare" waged by General William Tecumseh Sherman during the final months of the Civil War.

Mr. McElwee, who was born and bred in Charlotte, North Carolina, is fascinated by the many ironies of Sherman's career. Not the least of these is that Sherman is more vividly remembered in the South, which he loved and laid waste, than in the North, where he'd once been a great hero.

In the course of Mr. McElwee's own march to the South from Boston, where he was then living, something devastating happened. On a stopover in New York, his girlfriend left him. It was a traumatic experience, he tells us on the soundtrack. He couldn't go on. He felt aimless, adrift. Yet he still had his camera and sound equipment, and the $9,000 grant to finance the film, as well as (and this is most important) his passion to make a film—any film.

Sherman's March, which opens today at the Bleecker Street Cinema, is the long (nearly three-hour) documentary that was finally produced by Mr. McElwee, whose dry vocal delivery and occasionally seen deadpan face are very much a part of his exceptionally comic filmmaking personality.

In *Sherman's March,* Mr. McElwee more or less follows Sherman's trail in that he visits Atlanta, Savannah, and Columbia, South Carolina. Occasionally he even stops off at a Civil War battlefield, fort, or monument. Primarily, though, he's picking up pretty, oddball young women or looking up old girlfriends, most of whom are now committed to other people. Quite early, he confides that the movie really is "a meditation on the possibility of romantic love in the South today." Or, to put it another way, is romantic love possible in an age of supermarkets, fast food, nuclear arms, and the sort of lightweight camera and sound equipment that allows anybody to film his own life?

During his journey, he has brief encounters with a sweetly dizzy actress, whose dearest wish is to meet Burt Reynolds; a somewhat more mature Atlanta interior designer, who introduces him to a group of conservative "survivalists" building private, underground bunkers in the mountains; a linguist, who looks like a Meryl Streep character and lives a hermit's life on an island off Savannah; and an aspiring rock singer, a Jacqueline Bisset look-alike, on her way to a career in New York.

In Charleston, there's also a young Mormon woman whose family is building its own fallout shelter. Her dowry, Mr. McElwee reports rather glumly, "is a better-than-average chance of survival in case of a nuclear attack."

Somewhere near the middle of these earnest non-adventures in romantic love, he looks up his friend and former teacher, Charleen, an ebullient, no-nonsense woman who thinks there's nothing seriously wrong with Ross that a good wife wouldn't cure. It's Charleen, the subject of Mr. McElwee's 1978 film *Charleen*, who introduces the filmmaker to the Mormon and is furious when Mr. McElwee insists on filming the introduction. "Will you stop?" Charleen screams at him. "This isn't art. It's life!"

Toward the end he seeks out Karen, now a lawyer and an active feminist with whom, he thought at one point, he might share his life. However, Karen, too, already has a man, but this doesn't stop the filmmaker. He follows her to a rally on behalf of the proposed equal rights amendment. "With consummate timing," he reports, "I insist on talking to Karen about our relationship in the midst of 10,000 angry women."

Though Mr. McElwee's timing with women is awful, he's a filmmaker-anthropologist with a rare appreciation for the eccentric details of our edgy civilization. *Sherman's March*, which was made in 1981, is a timely memoir of the eighties.

It's also a very cheerful recollection of the kind of self-searching, home-movie documentaries that Jim McBride, the director, and L. M. Kit Carson, the writer and actor, satirized so brilliantly in their fiction film, *David Holzman's Diary*.

In that 1967 classic, Mr. McBride and Mr. Carson were sending up the members of the so-called film generation—those restless graduates who came out of film schools with all of the proper equipment but with nothing much to say. In desperation, they filmed themselves searching for themselves, to the ultimate fury and scorn of everyone around them.

At one point, after the departure of one young woman and before the arrival of the next, Mr. McElwee says forlornly, "I think I'm devouring myself with the camera." That joke has worn a bit thin by the film's third hour. However, as Mr. McElwee fusses with himself for not getting on with his meditation on Sherman's March, and as the loose ends of his private life accumulate, a wonderfully goofy, pertinent movie comes into focus.

—*V.C., September 5, 1986*

SHE'S GOTTA HAVE IT

Written, edited and directed by Spike Lee; director of photography, Ernest Dickerson; music by Bill Lee; production designer, Tracy Wynn Thomas; produced by Shelton J. Lee; released by Island Pictures. Running time: 84 minutes.

With: Tracy Camilla Johns (Nola Darling), Tommy Redmond Hicks (Jamie Overstreet), John Canada Terrell (Greer Childs), Spike Lee (Mars Blackmon) and Raye Dowell (Opal Gilstrap).

Nola Darling, the heroine of *She's Gotta Have It*, a movie by the young black filmmaker Spike Lee, has too many men in her life. She doesn't think so, but each of her three lovers does. The situation is not entirely comic; while the film satirizes selfishness, sexual stereotypes, role-playing among black men, and other follies, its presentation of Nola turns serious, even poignant. In fact, the story is so good that I regret the film is sometimes technically messy and some of Mr. Lee's directing experiments ill-conceived.

Mr. Lee has said he wrote the film (he also directed and edited it and takes a leading role) with Tracy Camilla Johns in mind as Nola. No wonder. She is a luxury to look at, and in time she might become a real dramatic presence. She is not entirely convincing in every situation in this film, but her restrained and compassionate realization of a complex young woman is winning. Her Nola is too intelligent not to realize that her determination to be independent may isolate her from a world she wants only to embrace.

Nola is a graphic artist in Brooklyn who is loved by Greer Childs (John Canada Terrell), a successful actor enchanted with himself and who finds Nola a fabulous bit of decoration; Mars Blackmon (Mr. Lee), a nervous joker who seems not to like himself very much; and Jamie Overstreet (Tommy Redmond Hicks), who is emotionally mature—and very vulnerable. Since she will not choose one over the others, she becomes the battleground; the men don't challenge one another but try to change her. If all the potential of that dramatic device were realized, this could be a painful movie. The appeals for love and the many sexual couplings in the film are the cries and grapplings of people moving apart against their wills.

Mr. Hicks and Mr. Terrell are fairly versatile, and

they need to be. Every time it seems Mr. Terrell's Greer could not possibly love himself more, he reveals new levels of vanity and egotism in very funny scenes. Mr. Hicks gives Jamie a depth and passion that escapes the other men. It is telling that, when Jamie's patience gives out and he turns rather shockingly brutal to Nola, his violence seems natural and does not diminish interest in or sympathy with the character.

She's Gotta Have It was shot entirely in Brooklyn, and made on a budget smaller than those of some television commercials. Mr. Lee's decision to film it in black and white—except for one baffling color sequence—is unfortunate in some ways since inevitably a black and white film now appears arty. The impression of artiness is increased by Mr. Lee's use of collages of still shots at various points; he even turns one sex scene into a series of stills that is funny in ways he surely did not intend. And there are technical problems that seem to result at least as much from the relative inexperience of Mr. Lee and his director of photography, Ernest Dickerson, as from the tightness of their budget.

Yet the film probes important and intriguing questions, even if the characters are not explored as thoroughly as they might have been. Mr. Lee has said he worries about how black audiences will receive the film, which opens today at the Cinema Studio 1. He need not limit his concern to one audience; his characters will interest everyone. Stripped of some of the distractions of this presentation, their story has a touch of the classic. These people are not victims of blind forces; they make choices, defend them, and grow in understanding, not always happily, as a result. Their story would be more enjoyable in a more polished film, but it has a power that is not dissipated by this one's weaknesses.

—*D.J.R.B., August 8, 1986*

THE SHINING

Produced and directed by Stanley Kubrick; written by Mr. Kubrick and Diane Johnson, based on the novel by Stephen King; director of photography, John Alcott; edited by Ray Lovejoy; music by Béla Bartók, Wendy Carlos, Rachel Elking, Gyorgi Ligeti and Kryzysztof Penderecki; production designer, Roy Walker; released by Warner Brothers. Running time: 146 minutes.

With: Jack Nicholson (Jack Torrance), Shelly Duvall (Wendy Torrance), Danny Lloyd (Danny), Scatman Crothers (Halloran), Barry Dennen (Ullman), Philip Stone (Grady), Joe Turkel (Lloyd), Anne Jackson (Doctor) and Tony Burton (Durkin).

*T*he Shining, Stanley Kubrick's spellbinding foray into the realm of the horror film, is at its most gloriously diabolical as Jack and Wendy Torrance take the grand tour. They are being shown through the Overlook, the cavernous, isolated hotel where they and their young son Danny will be spending the winter as caretakers, supposedly without any company. Jack pronounces the place "Cozy!" But still everything in the Overlook signals trouble, trouble that unfolds at a leisurely pace almost as playful as it is hair-raising. Meticulously detailed and never less than fascinating, *The Shining* may be the first movie that ever made its audience jump with a title that simply says "Tuesday."

In the hotel, the Torrances find dozens of empty rooms, ominously huge windows, knives all over the kitchen, and a maze on the front lawn. As it later turns out, there are ghosts and more ghosts, and one of the elevators is full of blood. The Overlook would undoubtedly amount to one of the screen's scarier haunted houses even without its special feature, a feature that gives *The Shining* its richness and its unexpected intimacy. The Overlook is something far more fearsome than a haunted house—it's a home.

In *The Shining*, which opens today at the Sutton and other theaters, Mr. Kubrick tries simultaneously to unfold a story of the occult and a family drama. The domestic half of the tale is by far the more effective, partly because the supernatural story knows frustratingly little rhyme or reason, even by supernatural standards. Dead twins haunt Danny and then stop haunting him; a mirror reflects some things and not others; the ghosts aren't quite subjective and they aren't quite real. Even the film's most startling horrific images seem overbearing and perhaps even irrelevant, like Mr. Kubrick's celebrated monolith in *2001*.

Many of the film's more bewildering nightmarish touches are ill-explained holdovers from Stephen King's novel, upon which Mr. Kubrick and Diane

Johnson base their shrewd and economical screenplay. Most of their alterations in the story, which has been changed and improved considerably, have the effect of letting it run deeper. Mr. King has an episode, for instance, in which Danny is terrorized by a specter in one of the deserted rooms. After this, his father, Jack, returns to the same room to investigate.

Mr. Kubrick, aside from changing the room number from 217 to 237 for mysterious reasons of his own, entirely transforms the scene. In the book, what Danny sees is explicitly described, and his father catches a glimpse of the same creature. The film's Danny is silent after his encounter, which is not depicted. And his father, as the camera tracks slowly into the room in a frenzy of anticipation, is confronted by one of Mr. Kubrick's most heart-stopping inventions, an image halfway between eroticism and terror.

The Shining stands on the brink of a physicality that has been very much absent from Mr. Kubrick's other work, and that would surely have been welcome here. This is the story of a man gradually driven to destroy his wife and child, and it stops just short of pinpointing his rage. The marriage between Jack (Jack Nicholson) and Wendy (Shelly Duvall) is a listless one, and it is revealed obliquely: through the raggedness and dowdiness of Wendy's wardrobe, through Jack's constant irritation at her, through the immaculate cleanliness of the Overlook's bathrooms and kitchen, through the eerie way they turn this enormous building into something cramped and claustrophobic. This is as close as Mr. Kubrick has come to dealing with both female and male characters or to grappling with domesticity. There are occasional moments in *The Shining* when their union alone seems enough to drive Jack mad.

The "Gold Room," a clever amplification of the hotel ballroom in Mr. King's novel, becomes the place where Jack's rage about his fiscal and familial responsibilities is revealed. It's also the place where the movie begins to go wrong, lapsing into bright, splashy effects reminiscent of *A Clockwork Orange* (though the Gold Room sequences produce the film's closing shot, a startling photograph of Mr. Nicholson). *The Shining* begins, by this point, to show traces of sensationalism, and the effects don't necessarily pay off. The film's climactic chase virtually fizzles out before it reaches a resolution.

Mr. Nicholson's Jack is one of his most vibrant characterizations, furiously alive in every frame and fueled by an explosive anger. Mr. Nicholson is also devilishly funny, from his sarcastic edge at the film's beginning to his cry of "Heeere's Johnny!" as he chops down a bathroom door to get to Miss Duvall. Though Miss Duvall's Wendy at first seems a strange match for Mr. Nicholson, she eventually takes shape as an almost freakish cipher, her early banality making her terror all the more extreme. Danny Lloyd, as Danny, and Scatman Crothers, as the hotel chef who, like Danny, has psychic powers, both give keen, steady performances as the story's relatively naturalistic figures. Barry Nelson is a model of false assurance as the hotel manager.

Mr. Kubrick, using the works of various composers, has assembled another stunningly effective score. John Alcott's cinematography is lovely, although *The Shining* seems intentionally less glossy than Mr. Kubrick's other films. Like the characters, it has a certain ironic homeliness—as when Wendy sits in the hotel's elegant lobby, propped before a television screen during a blizzard. She's watching Jennifer O'Neill play the ultimate in sweetly mindless femininity, in *Summer of '42*.

—J.M., May 23, 1980

SHIP OF FOOLS

Produced and directed by Stanley Kramer; written by Abby Mann, based on the novel by Katherine Anne Porter; cinematographer, Ernest Laszlo; edited by Robert C. Jones; music by Ernest Gold; production designer, Robert Clatworthy; released by Columbia Pictures. Black and white. Running time: 149 minutes.

With: Vivien Leigh (Mary Treadwell), Simone Signoret (La Condesa), José Ferrer (Rieber), Lee Marvin (Tenny), Oskar Werner (Dr. Schumann), Elizabeth Ashley (Jenny), George Segal (David), José Greco (Pepe), Michael Dunn (Glocken) and Charles Korvin (Captain Thiele).

Out of Katherine Anne Porter's voluminous novel, *Ship of Fools,* which was a big prizewinning bestseller in 1962, the producer and director Stanley

Kramer has fetched a powerful, ironic film. It goes by the same name, and it opened yesterday at the Sutton and the Victoria.

Call it a *Grand Hotel*-type picture if you must have a quick descriptive tag for this multifaceted drama of an assortment of characters traveling in a German passenger vessel from Veracruz, Mexico, to Bremerhaven, Germany, in 1933. For it has the same interwoven pattern as that memorable star-crowded film, and it entertains in much the same manner with its crossplay of transient characters.

Likewise, it offers a full roster of older and younger stars in its fascinating medley of sharp and colorful roles. It has Vivien Leigh as a declining American divorcée, José Ferrer as a brazen Jew-baiting German businessman, Lee Marvin as a Texas baseball player, George Segal and Elizabeth Ashley as a pair of American artists and lovers, Simone Signoret as a fading Spanish countess, José Greco as the head of a troupe of ferocious Spanish dancers, plus others in lesser roles. And it has the same sort of casual ending as the archetypal *Grand Hotel.*

But there is such wealth of reflection upon the human condition in *Ship of Fools* and so subtle an orchestration of the elements of love and hate, achieved through an expert compression of the novel by Mr. Kramer and his script writer, Abby Mann, that it is really not fair to tag it with the label of any previous film. It has its own quiet distinction in the way it illuminates a theme.

Furthermore, it is notable that the actor who plays the key role is not a star—not yet, at least—in the reckoning of Hollywood magnitudes. He is Oskar Werner, the modest and much-accomplished European who is best known in this country from *Decision Before Dawn* and *Jules and Jim.* Yet it is his fine performance as the ship's doctor, a sad, tired, and disillusioned man, that pumps the main irony and pity into the troubled heart of this film.

It is the poignant figure of the doctor that Mr. Kramer and Mr. Mann have framed to symbolize the exhaustion of that old and cultivated German class that might have stopped the Nazis, had it possessed the wits and energy. And it is he whom they have clearly made the symbol of the helpless healer in this soul-sick ship of fools.

But mainly it is his involvement in a poignantly brief love affair with the tacitly doomed Spanish countess, whom Miss Signoret so finely plays, that makes for the focal implications and the major sympathy. For it is this love affair, so tender, understanding, and sad, between the two frustrated creatures of an obsolescent breed—he the uncommitted Junker, she the futilely committed aristocrat—that stands as the fading demonstration of human dignity and despair.

Around it swirl all the other distasteful and pathetic characters—the loud and noxious anti-Semite of scene-stealing Mr. Ferrer who spreads the foulness of hatred through the first-class saloon; the aging, man-hating, lonely woman of the beautifully decaying Miss Leigh; the comical cuss of Mr. Marvin, the story of whose life is compressed in his oft-repeated grumble that he can't hit a curve over the outside corner of the plate.

Around it, too, swirls the peevish and immature affair of Mr. Segal and Miss Ashley, neither of whom is very good; the cruelly contemptuous clattering of Mr. Greco's troupe; the stuffy and mawkish self-serving of several Germanic types; and the cryptic philosophizing of a cheerful dwarf, played superbly by Michael Dunn.

All of this is symbolic of the passage of foolish humanity into the maw of Nazism, if you chose to see it that way, and it may even be symbolic of the eternal folly and helplessness of man. Mr. Kramer has put it into motion at a leisurely, rolling pace that suggests the cyclical rhythm of a voyage across the sea—or across the horizonless stretches of a complacent world.

It is a perpetually engrossing and thought-provoking film that he has aptly put down at this moment, and it eminently deserves to be seen.

—B.C., July 29, 1965

SHOAH

Directed by Claude Lanzmann; in various languages, with English subtitles; directors of photography, Dominique Chapuis, Jimmy Glasberg and William Lubchansky; edited by Ziva Postec and Anna Ruiz; released by Les Films Aleph Historia Films, with the participation of the French Ministry of Culture. Black and white. Running time: Part 1, 273 minutes; Part 2, 290 minutes.

With: Holocaust survivors.

Abraham Bomba, a survivor of the Nazi death camp at Treblinka, stands in a busy Israeli barbershop, cutting a customer's hair and answering the questions of the offscreen interviewer. Mr. Bomba is a stocky man who seems to be in good health and is probably older than he looks. Initially his remarks about Treblinka have the manner of tales told so many times that they've lost their meaning.

As if by rote, he narrates the story of his arrival at the camp and about being assigned, with sixteen or seventeen other barbers, to cut the hair of women on their way into the gas chambers. The stories sound memorized—distanced—like recollections of wounds protected by thick scar tissue accumulated over the decades.

Almost accidently, he begins to remember in detail a friend of his, another Treblinka barber, who found himself confronting his wife and daughter in the "undressing" (also the haircutting) room just outside the gas chamber. Mr. Bomba is suddenly stricken, unable to talk. It's as if the rubber band, by which he'd held onto the past while keeping it as far away as possible, had snapped, stinging him back into the reality of the original moment.

He says he can't go on. The interviewer, Claude Lanzmann, says he must. "You know it," Mr. Lanzmann says. As Mr. Bomba continues in a far different voice, his expression no longer self-assured, something very particular happens. More than forty years disappear, the scar tissue is torn away, and something like the primal horror of the reality of Treblinka is revealed. The unspeakable is spoken.

This is the extraordinary accomplishment of *Shoah* (in Hebrew, *Annihilation*), Mr. Lanzmann's huge, almost nine-and-a-half hour oral history of the Holocaust, which is unlike any other Holocaust film ever made. This isn't a conventional documentary composed of newsreel footage from the archives. The images of *Shoah* prompt no preconditioned responses. Everything is of the present—the faces of the "witnesses" as well as the tranquil, neatly tended landscapes that once were the death camps. Where there'd once been railroad tracks leading to Treblinka, there's now only a path through a forest. In *Shoah,* that path suggests the roadbed of the River Styx.

Shoah, opening today at the Cinema Studio (Broadway and 66th Street), will be presented in two parts, which is the way I saw it and which neither lessens its power nor exhausts the audience. Part I (4 hours, 33 minutes) will be shown Wednesdays through Saturdays, and Part 2 (4 hours, 50 minutes) Sundays through Tuesdays.

Mr. Lanzmann, the French journalist and filmmaker (*Why Israel?* 1973) makes no attempt to recall the past with images recorded in the past, which have the effect of putting the past at a safe remove and reducing it to comprehensible proportions. Instead, *Shoah* is a voyage of discovery through memories that, because they are contemporary, bring the past back to us with a new, devastating clarity. Only Marcel Ophuls's *Sorrow and the Pity* is in any way comparable.

Shoah is journalism of an equally high order. It's history remembered by the survivors of Treblinka, Auschwitz, Chelmno, and the other extermination camps, by German civilians, by former Nazi officials and bureaucrats, by Polish peasants and members of the bourgeoisie, and by survivors of the 1943 uprising in the Warsaw ghetto.

Pulling all this together is the mostly offscreen presence of Mr. Lanzmann, a superb interviewer—persistent, informed, and patient—as well as a journalist who hears everything that's being said.

Among his more remarkable interviews is one with Franz Suchomel, a former SS Unterscharführer at Treblinka, who's surreptitiously photographed and recorded during interviews in Mr. Lanzmann's hotel. Mr. Suchomel carefully describes, for the sake of "history," the procedures at Treblinka.

With a certain amount of pride he cites facts and figures: 12,000 to 15,000 gassed a day at Treblinka, NOT the exaggerated figure of 18,000 that some Jews have reported. The entire operation, when things were running smoothly, took approximately two hours, from the arrival of the boxcars carrying the Jews until they had been incinerated in the ovens.

At one point, also in the interests of history, he sings for Mr. Lanzmann the Treblinka camp song, including the phrase, "All that matters to us now is Treblinka/It's our destiny." "Don't be sore at me," he says to Mr. Lanzmann. "You wanted history—I'm giving you history."

Equally astonishing are a number of other, similarly detailed recollections—of a man who was in charge of railroad traffic control for trains going to and from the death camps, of the former deputy to the

Nazi commissioner of the Warsaw ghetto, of a Polish peasant woman who smilingly admits that life for her is better without the Jews, and of a group of Polish villagers, who give a cheerful welcome home to Simon Srebnik, the now middle-aged survivor of Chelmno, as they stand in front of the Roman Catholic church where Jews were held until they could be hauled off in the gas vans.

In the middle of this company of well-wishers, Mr. Srebnick looks like someone who's won a Lotto prize he doesn't want, and doesn't comprehend.

Again and again the film returns to the specific procedures for extermination at the individual camps, described with unrelenting detail by the once young, now aging men who, because of their vitality and strength were picked to carry out tasks that today still numb the imagination: herding people into the gas chambers, cleaning up the gas chambers afterward, stoking the ovens, disposing of the ashes. Mr. Srebnik says at one point, "I didn't care about anything. I thought, 'If I survive, I just want one thing—five loaves of bread.' To eat. That's all."

Other survivors remember futile efforts at resistance, the politics within the camps, the tiny refinements intended to keep the truth from the victims until the last minute. The "undressing rooms," through which the victims passed to the gas chambers, thinking they were to be deloused, were fitted with hooks for the clothes, benches on which to sit and, on the walls, encouraging slogans, including "Clean Is Good," "Lice Can Kill."

Playing almost as important a part in the film's effectiveness as Mr. Lanzmann are the remarks of Raul Hilberg, the American historian, who examines the historical antecedent for the Nazi policies and finds that even the Final Solution, the Nazis' principal contribution to anti-Semitism, was really more of a refinement than an original impulse.

In opposition to the almost giggly testimony of a number of Polish peasants and villagers, who lived and worked near the death camps, or who benefited considerably by the sudden disappearance of Jewish neighbors, there are the desolate recollections of a railroad engineer, of a switchman, and of a man who, acting as a courier for the Polish government in exile, forced himself to go into the Warsaw ghetto in order to report to the outside world what was happening. These people are, however, in the minority.

Functioning as the film's leitmotif is the sound of overloaded boxcars moving slowly—over narrow-gauge railroad tracks—toward their destinations with a momentum that wasn't to diminish until the war ended.

Shoah itself has something of that awful power.

—*V.C., October 23, 1985*

SHOCK CORRIDOR

Written and directed by Samuel Fuller; director of photography, Stanley Cortez; edited by Jerome Thoms; art director, Eugene Lourie; music by Paul Dunlap; produced by Mr. Fuller, Sam Firks and Leon Fromkes; released by Allied Artists. Running time: 101 minutes.

With: Peter Breck (Johnny Barrett), Constance Towers (Cathy), Gene Evans (Boden), James Best (Stuart), Hari Rhodes (Trent), Larry Tucker (Pagliacci), Paul Dubov (Dr. J. L. Menkin), Chuck Roberson (Wilkes), Neyle Morrow (Psycho), John Matthews (Dr. L. G. Cristo), Bill Zuckert (Swanee Swanson), John Craig (Lloyd), Philip Ahn (Dr. Fong), Frank Gerstle (Lt. Kane) Rachel Romen (Singing Nympho).

Shock Corridor, which was exposed at the Palace Theater and at the 52d Street Trans-Lux Theater yesterday, begins and ends in a *Snake Pit* and should present few startling turns to the cinema psychiatrists. Life in bedlams is still no bed of roses, and Samuel Fuller, who wrote, produced and directed this movie descent into madness, certainly succeeds in shocking, if not particularly convincing, a logical moviegoer.

Mr. Fuller, who has made no secret of the fact that he was once a newspaperman (he worked at the old *World*) and who has turned to journalism themes before, now is concerned with a reporter fired with the idea of exposing the murderer of a patient in a mental hospital.

Our hero, it appears, prizes the Pulitzer Prize above all else, including his blond, curvaceous sweetheart, a striptease artiste with loads of affection and a towering I.Q. He persuades her to pose as his sister and have him committed to the mental hospital because of attempted incest so that he can dig the facts for his potential Pulitzer Prize story.

Are there tragic results? There are. And these are telegraphed in fairly obvious style. But Mr. Fuller's melodrama does describe—without probing too deeply into complex psyches—schizophrenia, dementia praecox, nymphomania and other aspects of the alternating worlds of fantasy and reality in which the patients live. His film expresses his opinion on some acute contemporary issues in the testimony of three witnesses to the crime—a Nobel Prize physicist now withdrawn into infantilism, a Negro student now violently anti-Negro and a brainwashed Korean war veteran who had defected to the Communists.

One is, however, plagued by lapses in the script's logic. How could a qualified hospital, psychiatrist be fooled by someone—feigning insanity even though the feigner has been coached by an expert? Why was the woman's simple assertion that she was the patient's sister taken at its face value?

There are other flaws, but if these do not disturb a viewer, he will find the performances of Peter Breck, as the reporter; Gene Evans, James Best, and Hari Rhodes, as the physicist, the turncoat, and the Negro respectively, and Constance Towers, as the stripper, hard, driving, and realistic.

In illustrating that journalism can be a hard way to make an honest dollar, Mr. Fuller and his dedicated cast also have made their *Shock Corridor* vividly shocking, if not a scientist's dream.

—*A.H.W., September 12, 1963*

SHOESHINE

Directed by Vittorio De Sica; written (in Italian, with English subtitles) by Sergio Amidei, Adolfo Franci, C. G. Viola and Cesare Zavattini, based on a story by Mr. Zavattini; cinematographer, Anchise Brizzi; music by Alessandro Cicognini; produced by Paolo W. Tamburella; released by Lopert Films. Black and white. Running time: 93 minutes.

With: Rinaldo Smordoni (Giuseppi), Franco Interlenghi (Pasquale), Aniello Mele (Raffaele), Bruno Ortensi (Arcangeli) and Francesco De Nicola (Ciriola).

The plight of Italy's homeless, hungry children in the days immediately after the downfall of fascism is recounted in harrowing pictorial terms in *Shoeshine.* This Italian-made drama, which had its premiere here last night at the Avenue Playhouse under the sponsorship of the New York Newspaper Guild, is not a pretty picture to contemplate nor is it by any means a well-made picture.

But *Shoeshine* mirrors the anguished soul of a starving, disorganized, and demoralized nation with such uncompromising realism that the roughness of its composition is overshadowed by its driving, emotional force. Quick transition of scenes tends to disturb the continuity, but in other respects the direction of Vittorio De Sica reveals keen and sympathetic understanding of the nature of embittered, frustrated youth.

Fascism's bequest to the children of Italy was a bitter cup of gall, and *Shoeshine* is an unrelenting study of the despair and corruption that seared the hearts and minds of so large a part of Italy's future manhood. Mr. De Sica got the inspiration for this film from the hordes of sickly, undernourished, and ill-clothed street urchins who followed American troops into Naples, Rome, and other cities with their shoeshine boxes, badgering the G.I.'s with their cries of "Shoosha, Joe." Some of these pathetic youngsters became pawns in the hands of unscrupulous black marketeers and, like Giuseppe and Pasquale, were tossed into jail to languish and lose whatever vestige of goodness remained in them while inefficient police authorities halfheartedly sought the real criminals.

It is against unjust incarceration and the inhuman handling of such unfortunate victims of war that *Shoeshine* cries out so eloquently. For where compassion should have been exercised, the big stick of authority was applied instead. The reform school in which Giuseppe and Pasquale are confined is a fine breeding place for criminals, for, in addition to suffering shocking physical discomforts, the boys are supervised by corrupt guards who steal from their meager food packages and are always open to bribes.

The complete hopelessness with which the film regards the future of these youths is cruelly dramatized by the brutal, though accidental, death Giuseppe meets at the hands of his friend, Pasquale, after a prison break. The only heartening thing about *Shoeshine* is the knowledge that this film was instrumental in bringing about reforms in the treatment of juvenile delinquents in Italian institutions, for the picture offers no solution to the problem it presents.

Director De Sica, working with boys who never before had faced a movie camera, much less acted, has done a masterful job in coaching his cast. Rinaldo Smordoni as Giuseppe and Franco Interlenghi as Pasquale are so genuine one never for a moment thinks of them as actors, and, indeed, they are not, for theirs are naturalistic performances devoid of any histrionic techniques. Moreover, Mr. De Sica has peppered the picture with the vulgar mannerisms typical of the street urchins, and the English title translations by Herman G. Weinberg preserve the earthy tone of their talk. *Shoeshine* is not an entertainment; rather, it is a brilliantly executed social document.

—*T.M.P., August 27, 1947*

SHOOT THE PIANO PLAYER

Written (in French, with English subtitles) and directed by François Truffaut: based on the novel *Down There* by David Goodis: cinematographer, Raoul Coutard: edited by Cécile Decugis: music by Georges Delarue: art designer, Jacques Mély: produced by Pierre Braunberger: released by Astor Pictures. Black and white. Running time: 92 minutes.

With: Charles Aznavour (Charlie Koller), Marie Dubois (Lena), Nicole Berger (Theresa), Michèle Mercier (Clarisse), Albert Rémy (Chico) and Jacques Asianian (Richard).

François Truffaut, the French director who showed in *The 400 Blows* that he had a rare talent for lacing pathos with slapstick comedy, pulled all the stops on that talent and let it run rampant when he made *Shoot the Piano Player,* which arrived at the Fifth Avenue Cinema yesterday.

Nuttiness, pure and simple—nuttiness of the sort that has a surly kidnapper in a presumably serious scene swearing to something on the life of his mother, whereupon there's a cut to the mother dropping dead—surges and swirls through the tangle of solemn intimations in this film until one finds it hard to see or figure what M. Truffaut is about.

Evidently he is asking that the audience pay gentle heed to the significance of the old barroom legend. "Don't shoot the piano player; he is doing the best he can." For his hero is a small piano player in a noisome Parisian bar who turns out to be a poignant victim of fate and his own timidity.

This little ivory-tickler, played by Charles Aznavour with an almost Buster Keaton-like insistence on the eloquence of the deadpan, is more than a tired and pallid jangler of popular ragtime tunes. Oh, yes. He is a former concert pianist with a brilliant and glamorous past. But for some unspecified reason he couldn't get along with his wife, who finally tells him she bought him his big chance with her virtue, and this dumps him into the bars.

Maybe, in this little fellow, M. Truffaut is trying to construct an arch example of a sentimental hero that he is subtly attempting to spoof. But if this is the case, why does he bear down on the little fellow's piety so hard and bring his seriocomic roughhouse to a mawkishly tearful end? Why does he scramble his satire with a madly melodramatic plot and have the little piano player kill a man in defense of a girl?

It looks, from where we are sitting, as though M. Truffaut went haywire in this film, which he made as his second feature picture, following the great success of *The 400 Blows*. It looks as though he had so many ideas for movies outpouring in his head, so many odd slants on comedy and drama and sheer clichés that he wanted to express, that he couldn't quite control his material, which he got from a novel by David Goodis called *Down There*.

Else why would he switch so abruptly from desperately serious scenes and moods to bits of irrelevant nonsense or blatant caricature? Why would he let Nicole Berger play a lengthy, heartbreaking scene in which she boldly explains to her husband how she was unfaithful to him, then turn around a few minutes later and put two gangsters through a frolic of farce?

It is a teasing and frequently amusing (or moving) film that M. Truffaut has made, but it simply does not hang together. It does not find a sufficiently firm line, even one of calculated spoof or mischief, on which to hang and thus be saved.

M. Aznavour is touching as the hero, when he is supposed to be, but his character is much too shallow and vagrant for substantiality. Marie Dubois is appealing as a young barmaid who tries to help him out, and Mlle. Berger is excellent in her brief role as his flashback wife. Several other fellows overact in various roles. The English subtitles do bare justice to the lusty colloquial French.

—B.C., July 24, 1962

THE SHOOTING PARTY

Directed by Alan Bridges; written by Julian Bond, based on the novel by Isabel Colegate; director of photography, Fred Tammes; edited by Peter Davies; music by John Scott; production designer, Morley Smith; produced by Geoffrey Reeve; released by European Classics. Running time: 97 minutes.

With: James Mason (Sir Randolph Nettleby), Dorothy Tutin (Lady Minnie Nettleby), Edward Fox (Lord Gilbert Hartlip), Cheryl Campbell (Lady Aline Hartlip), John Gielgud (Cornelius Cardew), Gordon Jackson (Tom Harker), Aharon Ipale (Sir Reuben Hergesheimer), Rupert Frazer (Lionel Stephens) and Robert Hardy (Lord Bob Lilburn).

Somewhere toward the middle of *The Shooting Party*, set on a great English estate in the autumn of 1913, Sir Randolph Nettleby (James Mason), the host for the fashionable country weekend, has a brief encounter with Cornelius Cardew (John Gielgud), a somewhat mad activist on behalf of the Doctrine of Universal Kinship.

In the midst of that morning's shoot, Cornelius has appeared out of the woods carrying a homemade placard proclaiming the Third Commandment. As Sir Randolph's startled guests, the gun-loaders, and the beaters look on, Cornelius marches manfully into the line of fire, wrestling with the unwieldy sign that says "Thou Shalt Not Kill." Cornelius, escorted over to Sir Randolph by a couple of the beaters, immediately charms the host when he produces his elegantly printed manifesto, "The Rights of Animals."

Sir Randolph admires the typeface and asks where Cornelius had the manifesto made up. Cornelius tells him about his printer, "an excellent man of anarchist views," in Dorking. Sir Randolph wants to know if Cornelius receives a discount and whether the printer would consent to do some work for him. Sir Ran-

dolph, himself something of a pamphleteer, is planning a short polemic on the ruin of rural England.

Cornelius asks if Sir Randolph could make it a diatribe. "Certainly," says Sir Randolph. The delighted old Cornelius bristles with excitement. He can see the pamphlet now. He looks almost blissful as the title rolls off his tongue, "'The Ruin of Rural England. A Diatribe'!" Before he leaves the field, he gives Sir Randolph his card, and Sir Randolph says that he'll be hearing from him. Knowing the quality of the Sir Randolph that Mr. Mason has so superbly created, you can be sure this is true.

The Shooting Party, which opens today at the Cinema One, is not a perfect movie but it's a most entertaining and civilized one, as demonstrated in that meeting—the only one they have in the film—of two remarkable actors and the characters they play.

In addition to Sir Randolph and Cornelius, *The Shooting Party* includes Lady Minnie Nettleby (Dorothy Tutin), Sir Randolph's wife, a former favorite of the late Edward VII; Lord and Lady Hartlip (Edward Fox and Cheryl Campbell), who have a very "civilized" marriage, meaning that each can go his/her own way if the other is in no way compromised; the young, sweet, and beautiful Lady Olivia Lilburn (Judi Bowker) who, though content with her stuffy husband, Lord Bob Lilburn (Robert Hardy), falls suddenly in love with the hugely romantic young Lionel Stephens (Rupert Frazer).

There are also the staggeringly rich Sir Reuben Hergesheimer (Aharon Ipale), fondly called "the Israelite" by his friend, Sir Randolph; an arrogant, French-speaking Hungarian count; assorted children; nannies; and dozens of servants, some lovesick and some doomed.

The Shooting Party is the kind of movie that you want to fall into, as into a magical, fictional world, though an underlying suspicion that the whole thing is slightly bogus inevitably breaks the spell. This, I suspect, originates with the novel.

The Shooting Party, directed by Alan Bridges (*The Return of the Soldier*) and adapted by Julian Bond, is, like Isabel Colegate's 1980 novel of the same title, only too self-consciously aware that it's about the end of an era. Twilight is the color of the film as well as its theme. The characters, immensely helped by the author's 20-20 hindsight, talk well and sometimes even with hope about the approaching Armageddon.

Sir Randolph thinks that it will cleanse England of its greed and endless pursuit of pleasure. As the old world, represented by these mostly careless people who put such store by proper form, is suddenly brought up short by a mindless act of violence during the shooting party, the movie does everything but treat us to the sounds of distant armies marching to battle. These are people for whom the events at Sarajevo the following June will come as no surprise.

When Chekhov wrote his gently apocalyptic comedies, the future still lay ahead—for him and his characters: Uncle Vanya's vision of the new Russia remains moving today, not because it is so prescient but because it is a leap into the darkness, illuminated by longings and informed by instinct, not by what the author already knew to have happened.

There is also a purely technical problem that Mr. Bond hasn't successfully dealt with. There are so many people in the film that some of them never do get sorted out. It comes as something of a shock late in the film to realize that one unidentified, uncharacterized woman is actually the daughter-in-law of Sir Randolph and Minnie. Because the movie is otherwise anything but slapdash, this amounts to a breach of etiquette.

The film's physical production is smashing, from the photography by Fred Tammes to the production design by Morley Smith and the pre-World War I costumes by Tom Rand.

As he showed in his direction of Glenda Jackson, Julie Christie, Ann-Margret, and Alan Bates in *The Return of the Soldier,* Mr. Bridges is especially good with his performers. There's not a weak member in this huge cast. Miss Bowker is especially charming as the innocent but unexpectedly strong-willed young woman who discovers a love she's never before known, and Miss Campbell a very witty, very desperate adulteress. Mr. Gielgud simply cannot do wrong.

More than to anyone else, however, *The Shooting Party* belongs to Mr. Mason, playing a role that was originally to be done by Paul Scofield, who had to drop out after a week of shooting because of a broken leg. Hindsight may well have something to do with it, but Mr. Mason's secure, wise, and utterly relaxed performance here ranks with the best work of his long, rich, increasingly productive film career, ended by his death last July at the age of seventy-five.

—*V.C., May 24, 1985*

THE SHOOTIST

Directed by Don Siegel; written by Miles Hood Swarthout and Scott Hale, based on the novel by Glendon Swarthout; cinematographer, Bruce Surtees; edited by Douglas Stewart; music by Elmer Bernstein; production designer, Robert Boyle; produced by M.J. Frankovich and William Self; released by Paramount Pictures. Black and white. Running time: 100 minutes.

With: John Wayne (J.B. Books), Lauren Bacall (Bond Rogers), Ron Howard (Gillam Rogers), James Stewart (Dr. Hostetler), Richard Boone (Sweeney), Hugh O'Brien (Pulford) and Bill McKinney (Cobb).

After the climactic shoot-out, the lone survivor marches out of the café into the sun's slanting light. It is a beautiful shot, hazy and golden, but it is all wrong. The shoot-out, we are told, takes place just before noon.

This is pretty symptomatic of the trouble with *The Shootist,* third in a wave of geriatric Westerns that have afforded new employment for the wrinkles and creases of John Wayne. It is not so much a question of dishonesty as of a confusion of purposes. Eleven A.M. is a taut *High-Noon*ish time for a showdown, but things look much prettier in the late afternoon. So you have both.

Don Siegel, the director, has used an ironic story about the new and old West, written by Glendon Swarthout, for his own unfocused purposes. Sometimes these run along the same lines of irony and incongruity as the book. Sometimes they are softened or speeded up, either for sentiment or for a traditional Western brand of excitement. The irony comes straight and coated in molasses.

This is not to say that *The Shootist* is a bad picture. It is often funny. It is sometimes telling. And John Wayne, James Stewart, and Lauren Bacall all possess that particular mystery of performance that allows them to touch us even when they are ridiculous. But Mr. Siegel's lack of form and fidelity to his own story means that as the movie proceeds, even those things that are charming turn to lead.

With a grizzled mustache, an aged nose, and a big stomach, and looking more like a conductor on the old

New Haven Railroad than any kind of Western hero, J. B. Books (Mr. Wayne) rides into town. In his prime as a lawman he gunned down thirty villains. What he is after, though, this day in 1902, is medical advice.

He has a backache, he tells the doctor. The doctor—James Stewart, old but apple-voiced—tells him he has terminal cancer. He settles down in a rooming house under an assumed name and waits to die peaceably.

He isn't a peaceable man, though. And the town, which has telephones, sewers, and horsedrawn tramcars, won't let him alone. He represents both the threat and the glamour of the violent past. A young boy adopts him as a hero-figure, a number of old badmen try to kill him, but most of the citizens of the new century figure him for a profit. A sleazy reporter wants to write his memoirs; an old girlfriend wants to marry him; an undertaker wants to handle his funeral; a barber sells his hair trimmings.

The doctor, seeing the physical agony that awaits Books, hints diffidently that he should kill himself. With no diffidence at all the town marshal—grossly overacted by Harry Morgan—gives the same advice, seeing in Books's presence a threat to peace and quiet.

Books devises his own solution—a shoot-out with three of the region's most sinister characters. The film's irony runs best and sharpest as he prepares himself for battle. He puts on his best suit—newly drycleaned—gets a haircut, orders a tombstone, and heads for the rendezvous. Not by horse, though: by tramcar.

That scene, funny and terrible, is the best thing in the movie. The medical consultation between the aged Messrs. Wayne and Stewart is poignant and near-devastating, though the reasons probably lie less in the film than in our own associations with the two actors. There is a lovely scene where Mr. Wayne goes for a buggy ride with his landlady—Lauren Bacall—their mutual decrepitude bundled beneath a lap robe.

These are the film's best points. Its weaknesses drag them down. None of the characters have any real precision, and after the first impact they wither. The attitude of Books toward his own passing—the crucial point in the whole structure—is quite unclear. Is the extinction of his own violent way of life something he accepts or resists? Mr. Siegel allows him to point both ways, and the ambiguity takes the bone out of the movie and it collapses.

—*R.E., August 12, 1976*

THE SHOP AROUND THE CORNER

Produced and directed by Ernst Lubitsch; written by Samson Raphaelson, based on the play *Parfumerie* by Nikolaus Laszlo; cinematographer, William Daniels; edited by Gene Ruggiero; music by Werner R. Heymann; art designers, Cedric Gibbons and Wade B. Rubottom; released by Metro-Goldwyn-Mayer. Black and white. Running time: 97 minutes.

With: Margaret Sullavan (Klara Novak), James Stewart (Alfred Kralik), Frank Morgan (Hugo Matuschek), Joseph Schildkraut (Ferencz Vadas), Sara Haden (Flora), Felix Bressart (Pirovitch), William Tracy (Pepi Katona) and Inez Courtney (Ilona).

Ernst Lubitsch is offering some attractive screen merchandise in *The Shop Around the Corner* which opened at the Music Hall yesterday. *Ninotchka* appears to have used up his supply of hearty comedy for the time at least, but his sense of humor is inexhaustible. He has employed it to brighten the shelves where his tidy Continental romance is stored and, among the bric-a-brac, there are several fragile scenes which he is handling with his usual delicacy and charm, assisted by a friendly staff of salespeople who are going under resoundingly Hungarian names, but remind us strangely of Margaret Sullavan, James Stewart, Frank Morgan, and Joseph Schildkraut. All told, they make *The Shop Around the Corner* a pleasant place to browse in.

The shop Mr. Lubitsch has opened, for his romantic-comedy purposes, is a very real one: Matuschek & Co. is its name; it seems to be in Budapest, and Mr. Morgan is not alone Matuschek, but the "& Co." as well. His clerks are most deferential. The ritual of each day's shop-opening is punctiliously observed. Less reverent, perhaps, is the circumstance that Clerk Vadas (Mr. Schildkraut) is having an affair with Madame Matuschek. Still more distressing is the fact that Matuschek suspects Clerk Kralik of the intrigue, while Kralik (being Mr. Stewart and therefore purer than Galahad) has been doing nothing worse than conducting an anonymous Lonelyheart correspondence with a dream girl who also happens to be working in the shop—although neither of them has the faintest notion that the other is the Dear Friend of the letters. In fact, Kralik and Miss Novak just don't get along at all.

So there it is, and a pretty kettle of bubbling brew it makes under Mr. Lubitsch's deft and tender management and with a genial company to play it gently, well this side of farce and well that side of utter seriousness. Possibly the most surprising part of it is the adaptability of the players to Mr. Lubitsch's Continental milieu whose splendid evocation is one of the nicest things of the picture. But they all have become natural figures against a natural background—even Mr. Stewart, who, on the face and speech of him, hardly could be called the Budapest type, and Mr. Morgan, who plays a benevolent dictator (in leather goods) with scarcely a trace of the comic fluster and bluster that have established him as one of Hollywood's most standardized funnymen.

Miss Sullavan, making one of her all-too-infrequent appearances, reminds us she still is one of our most piquant and delightful screen ladies, and there have been amusing contributing performances by Mr. Schildkraut as the unctuous rascal of the piece, by Felix Bressart as the timorous senior clerk, and by William Tracy as the epitome of all sassy (and much put-upon) errand boys. Mr. Lubitsch must set up shop soon again.

—F.S.N., January 26, 1940

THE SHOP ON MAIN STREET

Directed by Jan Kadar; written (in Slovak, with English subtitles) by Mr. Kadar, Elmar Klos and Ladislav Grosman, based on the story "Obchod Na Korze" by Mr. Grosman; cinematographer, Vladimir Novotny; edited by Jaromir Janacek; music by Zdenek Liska; art designer, Karel Skvor; produced by Jaromir Lukas and Jordan Balurov; released by Prominent Films. Black and white. Running time: 128 minutes.

With: Josef Kroner (Tono Brtko), Ida Kaminska (Rosalie Laufmann), Hana Slivkova (Evelina Brtko) and Frantisek Zvarik (Marcus Kolkotsky).

Except for a slight change in title, *The Shop on Main Street* (formerly High Street), which set up for eminently merited business at the 34th Street East yesterday, is the same stunning Czechoslovak picture that knocked us out of our chairs when it was unassumingly presented at the New York Film Festival last fall.

Nothing in it has been altered. Not a frame of it has been cut, even though there is room for trimming in some of its early and middle scenes—and there is some question, too, about the aptness of its fanciful happy epilogue. It still is for me, on second viewing, away from the crush of the festival, one of the most arresting and devastating pictures I've seen from Europe or anywhere else in several years.

The effectiveness of it is clearly in the honesty and simplicity with which it reckons with a great moral issue on the level of small human beings.

Its hero is an average little fellow—an amiable, dullish carpenter living in a small Slovak city in 1942. He doesn't hate anybody (except his nasty, big-mouthed brother-in-law who is the Nazi-installed gauleiter). Some of his best friends are Jews. And he thinks the new political disciplinarians are pompous and absurd.

Yet slowly, as a consequence of taking a favored appointment as the Aryan controller of a Jewish-owned shop in the hope of getting a rake-off from it, he becomes more and more involved in the gathering moral crisis of abuse and persecution of Jews.

Essentially, he is a good man, and when he finds that the elderly woman who owns the shop doesn't have any money—that she is being secretly supported, indeed, by the charity of the Jewish community—he accepts the fact with wry amusement and becomes the sweet little woman's helper and friend. But he heedlessly commits a cruel injustice by also taking money from the charitable group. And when the day finally comes when the Jewish population is to be transported (to the concentration camps, of course), the weak little man is confronted with the great decision of whether he will protect his helpless friend or betray her to save his own hide.

Out of this simple situation, Jan Kadar and Elmar Klos, who made this film, have constructed a human drama that is a moving manifesto of the dark dilemma that confronted all people who were caught as witnesses to Hitler's terrible crime. "Is one his brother's keeper?" is the thundering question the situation asks, and then, as supplement, "Are not all men brothers?" The answer given is a grim acknowledgment.

But the unfolding of the drama is simple, done in casual, homely, humorous terms—until the terrible, heartbreaking resolution of the issue at the end. The little man, played superbly by Josef Kroner, is a cross-cut of human good and bad, a sad and ironic combination of gentle virtues and tragic weaknesses. And the sweet old Jewish lady, played by Ida Kaminska, who is a leading light of the Polish Jewish theater, is a wondrous image of Old World innocence.

There are fine scenes and luminous moments in which the culture and social shape of the wartime Slovak city are vividly inscribed. And supporting roles are played as strongly and revealingly as the leads. Hana Slivkova as the carpenter's coarse and sensual wife, Frantisek Zvarik as the wicked Nazi-serving brother-in-law, Martin Holly as a benevolent elder citizen, and Martin Gregor as an earnest, patient Jew are unforgettable standouts in an excellent cast.

To my mind, the romantic transport that is tacked on at the end is an obvious and sentimental softening of the picture's intense reality. But it does serve a certain benevolent purpose. As Mr. Kadar was saying here the other day, it does provide him—and, he assumes, his countrymen—the balm of spiritual uplift and hope that the horrible injustices committed against innocent people may bring some realization of the need of brotherhood.

The dialogue is spoken in Slovak, with English subtitles.

—B.C., January 25, 1966

A SHOT IN THE DARK

Produced and directed by Blake Edwards; written by Mr. Edwards and William Peter Blatty, based on the play by Harry Kurnitz and Marcel Achard; cinematographer, Christopher Challis; edited by Bert Bates; music by Henry Mancini; production designer, Michael Stringer; released by United Artists. Black and white. Running time: 101 minutes.

With: Peter Sellers (Inspector Jacques Clouseau), Elke Sommer (Maria Gambrelli), George Sanders (Benjamin Ballon), Herbert Lom (Chief Inspector Charles Dreyfus), Tracy Reed (Dominique Ballon) and Graham Stark (Hercule Lajoy).

Close on the heels of *The Pink Panther,* which introduced Peter Sellers in the role of a bumbling Parisian detective, Inspector Jacques Clouseau, there comes another go-round with this explosively comical sleuth that makes his previous exposure seem like a warm-up for an out-of-town show. The title of this new adventure is *A Shot in the Dark,* and it opened yesterday at the Astor and the Trans-Lux East.

It's an utterly wacky entertainment, and if the title sounds familiar it's because it was plucked from the Broadway stage play, which was adapted from a French play by Marcel Achard. But, believe me, the title and the issue of a maid in a French family accused of murdering her Spanish lover are the only tangible ties to its nominal source.

For this is but vaguely the story of the naughty but nifty maid and of her whimsical attachment to her urbane employer. It is essentially the story—or let's just call it the vehicle—of the sleuth who is sent to find out who murdered that fellow lying dead on the floor.

With an output of comic invention that goes far beyond the matter of the style of the comparatively sophisticated trifle that was played here on the stage three years ago, Blake Edwards and William Peter Blatty have fashioned an out-and-out farce that puts no tax at all on the mentality but just plunges from gag to gag. And they have got Mr. Sellers to plunge with it in the joyously free and facile way that he has so carefully developed as his own special comedy technique.

No sooner does his stalwart-faced detective arrive on the murder scene, a handsome home in Paris, all set to nab the murderer in a moment, than he stumbles into a fountain and gets himself thoroughly drenched. And that's how he stays throughout the picture—figuratively, at least—all wet, while he fumbles and stumbles to unravel a progressively more remote mystery.

But the mystery doesn't matter. It is how Inspector Clouseau tackles it—and especially how he tackles Elke Sommer as the fantastically toothsome maid. Right off, he assumes she didn't do it. She's too pretty and comforting. His suspicions turn naturally to George Sanders, the wealthy owner of the place. In a hilarious billiards game with him, he gets all tangled up in cues and clues. Only all of the latter are as aimless as the warped cue with which he tries to play.

And while the detective is blundering all over the place—bumping into furniture, snagging crucial areas of his clothes, falling out of windows, pursuing Miss Sommer to a nudist camp—his nervous superior, Commissioner Dreyfus, played by Herbert Lom, is frantically trying to remove him—by murder, if need be—from the case. A series of near-miss encounters with a would-be killer in a succession of nightclubs to which the inspector and the maid go provides some of the liveliest action and some of the wildest humor in the show.

It is mad, but the wonderful dexterity and the air of perpetually buttressed dignity with which Mr. Sellers plays his role make what could quickly be monotonous enjoyable to the end. And the running gags are excellent, particularly one involving frequent bouts with an Oriental houseboy who is learning karate from him.

Miss Sommer is not only lovely. She also makes a bright comedy foil. And Mr. Sanders, Mr. Lom, and many others are apt and adroit in their roles, under Mr. Edwards's direction. The whole thing is colorful, gay—and Henry Mancini's music is as sassy and frivolous as the film.

—*B.C., June 24, 1964*

SHREK

Directed by Andrew Adamson and Vicky Jenson: written by Ted Elliott, Terry Rossio, Joe Stillman and Roger S.H. Schulman, based on the book by William Steig: edited by Sim Evan-Jones: music by Harry Gregson-Williams and John Powell: production designer, James Hegedus: produced by Aron Warner, John H. Williams and Jeffrey Katzenberg: released by DreamWorks Pictures. Running time: 89 minutes.

With the voices of: Mike Myers (Shrek), Eddie Murphy (Donkey), Cameron Diaz (Princess Fiona), John Lithgow (Lord Farquaad) and Vincent Cassel (Monsieur Hood).

The filmmaking team behind *Shrek* takes the bare bones of William Stieg's children's book about an ogre who thinks filthiness is next to godliness and glories in bad manners and ickiness and uses that as a taking-off point for a new animated film that rejoices in its own brand of perversity.

The opening sequence of the film—a DreamWorks movie directed by Andrew Adamson, and Vicky Jenson and written by Ted Elliot, Terry Rossio, Joe Stillman, and Roger S. H. Schulman—features the title monster (voiced by Mike Myers) enjoying a mud bath. It isn't merely because it will keep his glowing green skin supple and youthful; like the picture's young target audience, who love to display mouthfuls of half-chewed food to giggly friends and outraged adults, he loves creepy slop. (He garnishes his martinis with a human eye instead of an olive.) The movie itself is a giggly cocktail, though it's more foam than drink, a return to the frothy riffing on pop culture that started back on Bugs Bunny's watch in the Vitaphone days, before Disney created the fairy tales that were 90 percent merchandising and 10 percent boredom. *Shrek* maintains that beauty is on the inside, not the outside.

Mr. Myers subtly nudges his fans by giving *Shrek* a gentler version of the Scottish burr he employed for the least likable characters in *Austin Powers: The Spy Who Shagged Me* and *So I Married an Ax Murderer.* Eddie Murphy is also one of the voices in *Shrek,* playing a needy donkey who has been promoted from supporting character in the book to sidekick. It gives Mr. Murphy a chance to reprise his desperate-to-ingratiate character from *Mulan,* probably the subtlest of the film's many relentless jabs at the bland ubiquity of Disney's animated characters.

Shrek is just as desperate as the donkey, but it's because he wants to be alone. Lord Farquaad (John Lithgow) gives him the opportunity to return to his jolly, green hermetic state. If Shrek can deliver Princess Fiona (Cameron Diaz) for Farquaad to marry, Farquaad will ensure that Shrek's swamp is restored to its isolated status. The ogre sets off on his adventure with the donkey scampering behind, keen to help. Farquaad is responsible for Shrek's plight. He has assigned all of the magical creatures of the kingdom to "a designated resettlement facility" and many of them—the Three Little Pigs, Pinocchio and others—are on the run. They're using Shrek's mossy home as a hideout, which makes his mission all the more urgent.

Much of *Shrek* is scrappy, brash comedy, and the brio of the actors adds to the dynamism. The cycle of kiddie musicals typified by *Aladdin* seems to be drawing to a close, possibly because video stores have walls of these animated sing-along films already. Nonetheless, in a bleak nod to that tradition, Shrek himself has been saddled with a bit of pathos: he's only vile because he wants to preempt responses to his appearance. Fortunately, he doesn't break into song to explain his aching psyche, though he might as well.

In Mr. Steig's book, Shrek is unapologetic about his looks; for him, life is not trick or treat, it's trick and treat.

Like many movies nowadays, *Shrek* is a blistering race through pop culture, and what the movie represents is a way to bring the brash slob comedy of *The Simpsons* and *South Park*, as well as the institutional irreverence of *Saturday Night Live*, to a very young audience. This leads to some very funny scenes, like the torture of the Gingerbread Man. Such rambunctious heartlessness has become a way of life in children's animation, but television isn't equipped to do it as well as films can.

When *Shrek* is cooking, thanks to the writing as well the improvisational skills of stars like Mr. Myers and Mr. Murphy and the performance of Mr. Lithgow, the jokes have a bark. The film's co-producer, Jeffrey Katzenberg of DreamWorks, is taking cartoons back to their roots. They weren't originally created for children but were consigned to the early morning children's ghetto in the early days of television because they were colorful, imaginative and short.

Beating up on the irritatingly dainty Disney trademarks is nothing new; it's just that it has rarely been done with the demolition-derby zest of *Shrek*.

—E.M., May 16, 2001

SID AND NANCY

Directed by Alex Cox; written by Mr. Cox and Abbe Wool; director of photography, Roger Deakins; edited by David Martin; music by Pray for Rain, the Pogues and Joe Strummer; production designer, Andrew McAlpine; produced by Eric Fellner; released by Samuel Goldwyn Company. Running time: 111 minutes.

With: Gary Oldman (Sid Vicious), Chloe Webb (Nancy Spungen), Drew Schofield (Johnny Rotten), David Hayman (Malcolm McLaren), Debby Bishop (Phoebe), Tony London (Steve), Perry Benson (Paul) and Ann Lambton (Linda).

Few would have suspected, when Sid Vicious died of a heroin overdose in 1979 after having been charged with the stabbing death of his girlfriend Nancy Spungen several months earlier, that this story had the makings of a big-screen romance. Even now, there are those who wouldn't quite understand. But Alex Cox, who directed *Repo Man*, saw the Sid and Nancy story as the occasion for a sordid, intentionally ugly, and sometimes unexpectedly beautiful film, a pitch-black comedy about wasted love. At the very least, you have to admire his nerve.

It's not every filmmaker who credits special thanks to both Luis Buñuel and Dee Dee Ramone, but then Mr. Cox doesn't fit any recognizable mold. His decision to film the Sid and Nancy story (which has also been immortalized in at least one play, Denis Spedaliere's *Vicious*) is by no means the most idiosyncratic thing he has done. *Sid and Nancy* has a slow, almost lyrical shot of the title characters as they sit catatonically in bed, high on heroin, until the orangey light flickering across their faces lets the viewer know the room is on fire. There's another image, also lovely in its own weird way, in which they kiss in an alley while being showered with flying garbage. *Sid and Nancy* doesn't try to win its audience's sympathy in any conventional way, which is just as well, since that would have been a losing battle. But it does succeed in offering bleak, nasty, and sometimes hilarious glimpses of life in the punk demimonde.

The film could easily have concentrated on the story of the Sex Pistols, the punk group for which Sid Vicious played bass, and without which neither he nor Nancy Spungen would have achieved such notoriety, but it keeps the band's story on the sidelines. The lead singer Johnny Rotten (Drew Schofield) is portrayed as an ambitious figure who drops into and out of the film casually, having his head bandaged in one scene and showing himself to be an extremely messy eater in another; the group's manager, Malcolm McLaren (David Hayman), is the energetic huckster who pronounces Sid "a fabulous disaster." The group's brief story plays itself around Sid and Nancy, who meet when Sid and Johnny throw a brick through the apartment window of Linda, a friend of Nancy's who works as a dominatrix. Nancy, a groupie, is immediately interested, even though Johnny tells her sex is ugly and Sid tells her it's boring. Nancy doesn't really catch Sid's eye until she offers to find him drugs and slams herself against a brick wall. That, it turns out, is the sort of thing he understands.

It doesn't take long for Sid and Nancy (played vividly by Gary Oldman and Chloe Webb) to settle into their own version of domesticity. Nancy screams all the time (though this makes no discernible dent on Sid). They discuss things like their preferences in dolls, with Sid a G.I. Joe fan and Nancy declaring, "I'll never look like Barbie, Barbie doesn't have *bruises*!" They have matching dog collars and matching drug habits, and often find themselves in such dire straits that they'll say or do anything. At one point, Nancy calls her mother with the (fabricated) news that she and Sid have gotten married, using this as a ploy to ask for money. Within moments, the mother has turned down the request, Nancy has berated her at top volume, and the phone booth is a complete shambles.

Like Mr. Oldman's Sid, who comes through as furious but terminally vague, and Miss Webb's Nancy, who whines and squawks like a dying chicken, the film has a way of staggering uncertainly from one point to another. What it does best is to generate odd, unexpected images that epitomize the characters' affectlessness and rage; the glimpse of Nancy lying bleeding while Sid watches cartoons on television is only one of Mr. Cox's punk epiphanies, and the film's closing fantasy is indeed haunting. What is weakest, though, is the evocation of the punk ethos. These were doomed characters who lived entirely for the moment, and they can't easily be resurrected.

And Mr. Cox's efforts to graft romantic yearnings onto the characters often seem desperately out of place, as when Sid gives a violent rip to Nancy's black mesh stocking, then begins lovingly to caress her foot. Their tenderness for one another, short-lived as it is, becomes sentimental and even quaint in a film whose every line of dialogue contains one obscenity or another. The film changes its scale a lot too, going from cozy scenes amid the used Kentucky Fried Chicken buckets at Sid and Nancy's Chelsea Hotel room to broader, wilder moments like the reenactment of Sid's performance of "My Way." He lip-synchs the song, loses interest somewhere in the middle, and then shoots the rich, respectable know-nothings who make up his imaginary audience.

One more caveat about a film with a lot more cachet than the people who inspired it: *Sid and Nancy* is difficult to hear. Sid's Cockney accent is strong,

Nancy's wailing sometimes muddy, and there are times when even subtitles would have been welcome.

—*J.M., October 3, 1986*

THE SILENCE

Written (in Swedish, with English subtitles) and directed by Ingmar Bergman: cinematographer, Sven Nykvist: edited by Ulla Ryghe: music by Bo Nilsson and Johann Sebastian Bach: art designer, P. A. Lundgren: produced by Allan Ekelund: released by Janus Films. Black and white. Running time: 95 minutes.

With: Ingrid Thulin (Ester), Gunnel Lindblom (Anna), Hakan Jahnberg (Hotel Waiter), Birger Malmsten (Restaurant Waiter) and Jorgen Lindstrom (Johan).

The grapplings of Ingmar Bergman with loneliness, lust, and loss of faith, so weirdly displayed in his last two pictures, *Through a Glass Darkly,* and *Winter Light,* have plunged him at last into a tangle of brooding confusions and despairs in his latest film, which, he tells us, completes a trilogy begun with those previous films. It is titled appropriately *The Silence* and it opened yesterday at the Rialto (lately a house for striptease movies) and the Trans-Lux East.

What Mr. Bergman is trying to tell us is something each individual viewer must fathom and discover for himself. Or, indeed, one may reasonably question whether he is trying to give us anything save a grim philosophical observation of a tragic aspect of life.

For here, as in the previous pictures in his trilogy, he has fashioned his drama from the tensions of only a few people in a narrow frame. He has let his action develop in a casual, almost haphazard form. And he has brought it to a conclusion on a deliberately enigmatic note. What there is of commentary must be studiously inferred from dark psychological implications and heavy symbolic strokes.

Evidently the situation that Mr. Bergman presents is to be viewed as a singular speculation, a dramatic hypothesis. To a strange hotel in a strange city, he brings two women and one little boy, as though they were lonely wanderers and seekers in a stark, unfriendly world.

The women are obviously sisters and the tension between them seems to be over the latent predilection of the older to possess the younger one. She seems to want to clutch the younger in a sexual embrace that would include an emotional expression of their family associations and their youth. But the younger one, restless and resentful, resists her and takes revenge by finding a nameless lover and having a wild affair with him.

Meanwhile, the lonely youngster, the son of the younger woman, wanders in solemn desolation through the almost empty hotel. He has a briefly bright encounter with a theatrical troupe of dwarfs who entertain him with a bit of playful make-believe, until their leader comes along and calls it off. He hobnobs a bit with a nice old waiter who mutely attends his aunt, brings her bottles of brandy, and helps her when she has a racking cough. And, finally, the sad little fellow watches secretly while his mother embraces her lover and goes with him into a room.

Whether this strange amalgam of various states of loneliness and lust articulates a message may be questionable, but it does, at least, resolve into a vaguely affecting experience that moves one like a vagrant symphony. Mr. Bergman has ordered his images as though presenting a musical score, with separate themes projected and developed and with supplementary phrases struck.

It is notable, for instance, that he handles the poignant theme of the boy with an affecting use of close-ups that have deep emotional quality. Through the impersonal streets of the city, he suddenly rumbles an army tank, intruding a thought of menace in the alien community. Or down in the streets he shows his women an old junk wagon drawn by a nag, which calls up a contemplation of degeneration and death.

His actors are all superbly tempered and paced in their strange, allusive roles. Ingrid Thulin is sterile and anguished as the older sister who struggles in vain, and Gunnel Lindblom is earthy and arrogant as the younger one. Jorgen Lindstrom is touchingly spiritual yet entirely natural as the boy, and Hakan Jahnberg plays the old waiter as though he were a shadowy ghost from a happier age.

But, unfortunately, Mr. Bergman has not given us enough to draw on, to find the underlying meaning or emotional satisfaction in this film. They say when it was shown in Sweden, its several erotic scenes were so detailed and explicit that they literally shocked audiences. Perhaps these scenes are essential to a superheated mood required for the psychological context. But obviously these scenes have been cut or trimmed for this market. Here the whole thing is rather tame, mystifying, and morbid. *The Silence* is almost like death.

—B.C., February 4, 1964

THE SILENCE OF THE LAMBS

Directed by Jonathan Demme; written by Ted Tally; director of photography. Tak Fujimoto; edited by Craig McKay; music by Howard Shore; production designer. Kristi Zea; produced by Kenneth Utt. Edward Saxon and Ron Bozman; released by Orion Pictures. Running time: 120 minutes.

With: Jodie Foster (Clarice Starling). Anthony Hopkins (Dr. Hannibal Lecter). Scott Glenn (Jack Crawford). Ted Levine (Jame Gumb). Anthony Heald (Dr. Frederick Chilton). Brooke Smith (Catherine Martin). Diane Baker (Senator Ruth Martin). Kasi Lemmons (Ardelia Mapp) and Roger Corman (Hayden Burke).

All sorts of macabre things have gone on, and are still going on just offscreen, in Jonathan Demme's swift, witty new suspense thriller, *The Silence of the Lambs.*

Hannibal Lecter, a serial killer nicknamed Hannibal the Cannibal, once liked to feast on his victims, daintily, in a meal designed to complement the particular nature of the main dish. He would, for example, choose a "nice" Chianti to accompany a savory liver. A fine Bordeaux would compete.

Hannibal is a brilliant if bent psychiatrist, now under lock and key in a maximum-security facility.

Still at large, though, is a new serial killer, known as Buffalo Bill for reasons that can't be reported here. Bill's habit is to skin his victims.

At the beginning of *The Silence of the Lambs,* Jack Crawford (Scott Glenn), the F.B.I.'s man in charge of Bill's case, seeks the assistance of a bright young agent, Clarice Starling (Jodie Foster).

Her assignment: to interview Hannibal Lecter (Anthony Hopkins), arouse his interest, and secure his help in drawing a psychological profile of the new killer.

The principal concern of *The Silence of the Lambs* is the entrapment of Buffalo Bill before he can kill again. Yet the heart of the movie is the eerie and complex relationship that develops between Clarice and Hannibal during a series of prison interviews, conducted through inch-thick bulletproof glass.

Hannibal, as grandly played by Mr. Hopkins, is a most seductive psychopath, a fellow who listens to the "Goldberg Variations" and can sketch the Duomo from memory. It's not his elegant tastes that attract Clarice, and certainly not his arrogant manner or his death's-head good looks. His smile is frosty, and his eyes never change expression. It's his mind that draws her to him. It pierces and surprises. Hannibal is one movie killer who is demonstrably as brilliant and wicked as he is reported to be.

In their first interview, Hannibal sizes up Clarice from her expensive bag and cheap shoes, her West Virginia accent, and her furrow-browed, youthful determination not to appear intimidated. Hannibal isn't unkind to her.

He is at first skeptical and then amused. Finally he is seduced by her, at least to the extent that his egomania allows. She is flesh and blood and something more.

As played by Miss Foster, Clarice is as special in her way as Hannibal is in his. She is exceptionally pretty, but her appeal has more to do with her character, which is still in the process of being formed. She's unsure of herself, yet clear-headed enough to recognize her limitations.

Clarice has the charm of absolute honesty, something not often seen in movies or, for that matter, in life. She's direct, kind, always a bit on edge, and eager to make her way.

When Hannibal finally agrees to help Clarice, it's with the understanding that for every bit of information he gives her, she will tell him something about herself. Because Hannibal, by nature and by profession, is an expert in prying, the questions he asks, and the answers he receives, both frighten and soothe the young woman.

For Hannibal, they are a turn-on.

Through the bulletproof glass, in dizzy succession, Hannibal and Clarice become analyst and analysand, teacher and pupil, father and daughter, lover and beloved, while always remaining cat and mouse.

Miss Foster, in her first role since winning an Oscar for *The Accused,* and Mr. Hopkins, an actor of cool and eloquent precision, give exciting substance to the roles written by Ted Tally, who adapted the screenplay from a novel by Thomas Harris. An earlier Thomas novel, *Red Dragon,* in which the homicidal doctor also appears, was the basis of the 1986 film *Manhunter.*

Miss Foster and Mr. Hopkins are so good, in fact, that Clarice and Hannibal sometimes seem more important than the mechanics of *The Silence of the Lambs,* which is, otherwise, committed to meeting the obligations of a suspense melodrama.

Mr. Demme meets most of these obligations with great style. The buildup to the dread Hannibal's first scene is so effective that one almost flinches when he appears. Never after that, for good reason, does Hannibal become trusted, though he is always entertaining to have around.

Eventually, though, the demands of the plot begin to take precedence over people and plausibility. Hannibal not only can help with the Buffalo Bill case, but he also knows who Buffalo Bill is. About halfway through, so does the audience, at which point the movie shifts to a lower, more functional gear even as the pace increases.

The screenplay, which is very effective in detailing character, is occasionally hard pressed to feed the audience enough information so that it can follow the increasingly breathless manhunt without a road map.

I'm told it helps if one has read the book, but reading the book shouldn't be a requirement to enjoy the film. At a crucial point the audience must also accept, as perfectly reasonable and likely, some instant surgery that allows the story to continue moving forward.

This may be hairsplitting. *The Silence of the Lambs* is not meant to be a handy home guide to do-it-yourself face liftings. Yet the movie is so persuasive most of the time that the wish is that it be perfect.

Although the continuity is sometimes unclear, the movie is clearly the work of adults. The dialogue is tough and sharp, literate without being literary.

Mr. Demme is a director of both humor and subtlety. The gruesome details are vivid without being exploited. He also handles the big set pieces with skill. The final confrontation between Clarice and the man she has been pursuing is a knockout—a scene set in pitch dark, with Clarice being stalked by a killer who wears night-vision glasses.

Mr. Glenn is stalwart as Clarice's F.B.I. mentor, but the role is no match for those of his two costars.

The good supporting cast includes Anthony Heald, as another doctor who might be as nutty as Hannibal, and Ted Levine, as a fellow who spends more time making his own clothes than is entirely healthy. Roger Corman, the self-styled king of B-pictures, who gave Mr. Demme his start in filmmaking, appears briefly as the director of the F.B.I.

The Silence of the Lambs is pop filmmaking of a high order. It could well be the first big hit of the year.
—V.C., February 14, 1991

THE SILENT WORLD

Directed by Jacques-Yves Cousteau; written (in French, with English subtitles) by Mr. Cousteau; cinematographers, Philippe Agostini, Mr. Cousteau, Louis Malle and Edmond Séchan; edited by Georges Alépée; music by Yves Baudrier; produced by Société Filmad et Requins Associés. Running time: 86 minutes.

People who dote on real adventure in the ever-wondrous area of the sea are in for an hour and twenty-six minutes of pictorial (and piscatorial) marvels and thrills when they see the new film at the Paris, Captain Jacques-Yves Cousteau's *The Silent World*. For this account of oceanographic exploration on and below the surface of the sea is surely the most beautiful and fascinating documentary of its sort ever filmed.

With a sense of the awesome and the dramatic as well as with technical skill in surface and underwater exploration and color photography, Captain Cousteau and his team of skin divers have produced a marine adventure film that combines the experience of looking at marvels with a wonderful intimacy.

They have put the personnel of their research ship, the *Calypso*, as it ranges the Mediterranean and Red seas, the Persian Gulf, and the Indian Ocean, in contact with the creatures of the deep in such a way as to make the contrasts much more striking and wonderful than would be the mere fascinations if they were simply viewed objectively.

That is to say, the hardy divers and the operations of the compact little ship, a floating marine labora-

tory, are established clearly at the start of the film before the cameras are taken underwater to view the wonders and the beauties that are there. The personal perils as well as pleasures of free diving with the remarkable mechanism of the Aqua-Lung are brought to the attention of the audience before any extensive exploration is done. And the span of pictorial observation often is returned to the surface and to the ship, with the men maintained carefully in the foreground, as the picture flows along.

Thus we go from a brief introduction of divers moving with the phosphorus torches through blue-gray depths to the businesslike deck of the *Calypso*, where these magical creatures, emerging, are merely men in scanty swim trunks and grotesque apparatus that is dropped as they breathe open air. And then we go back into the water to look at fishes and lobsters and coral clumps and to feel a case of the "bends" with one of these divers, after we have been made acquainted with him.

This intimacy with the explorers, intelligently and humorously set up, is largely responsible for the vivid sense of participation one gets from this film. From the awesome experience of gazing into the purple coils of a sea anemone to the drama of thundering along the surface in a school of mammoth sperm whales, one is there as a breathless companion of the modern mariners in this tidy ship. At the end, you and Captain Cousteau, his crew, and their dachshund are friends.

You have been with the limber skindivers into the dark and haunted holds of a sunken ship and been dragged along with them by scooters, powered with batteries, that bore through the deeps. You have got a close view of racing porpoises from a portholed chamber in the prow of the ship and sat in a steel cage underwater and watched sharks attack the body of a dead whale.

All of this and much more, Captain Cousteau and his leading associate, Louis Malle, have filmed with an integrity of events and in colors that are irreproachable. Like true scientists, they've eschewed trickery. When the excellent music of Yves Baudrier is used, it is applied to scenes, however amazing, of authentic occurrence and continuity.

It should be noted that this picture is not a version of Captain Cousteau's book, *The Silent World*, but is a compilation of photographic material obtained on the *Calypso*-National Geographic expedition in 1954–55.

James Dugan prepared the narration, which is spoken in English, mostly by Captain Cousteau.

The only trouble with the whole thing is it makes you want to strap on an Aqua-Lung and go!

—B.C., September 25, 1956

SILK STOCKINGS

Directed by Rouben Mamoulian; written by Leonard Gershe, Harry Kurnitz and Leonard Spigelgass, based on the musical by George S. Kaufman, Leueen McGrath and Abe Burrows and the screenplay by Billy Wilder, Charles Brackett and Walter Reisch, adapted from *Ninotchka* by Melchior Lengyel; cinematographer, Robert Bronner; edited by Harold F. Kress; music by Cole Porter; choreography by Hermes Pan; art designers, William A. Horning and Randall Duell; produced by Arthur Freed; released by Metro-Goldwyn-Mayer. Running time: 117 minutes.

With: Fred Astaire (Steve Canfield), Cyd Charisse (Ninotchka), Janis Paige (Peggy Dainton), Peter Lorre (Brankov), Jules Munshin (Bibinski), Joseph Buloff (Ivanov), George Tobias (Commissar Vassili Markovich) and Wim Sonneveld (Peter Ilyitch Boroff).

There should be legislation requiring that Fred Astaire and Cyd Charisse appear together in a musical picture at least once every two years. Previously they were together in *The Band Wagon,* and the world was brightened. That was away back in 1953. Now they are together in *Silk Stockings,* and somebody should declare a holiday.

A week's holiday, for that matter—enough to give everybody time to see this delightful and amusing musical, which came to the Music Hall yesterday. It would sweeten the national disposition, embolden those hesitant toward romance, and possibly make us all feel easier about Soviet Russia, the butt of most of the kidding in this film.

For the simple fact is that this *Silk Stockings* is an all-round refreshing show, blessed with a bright book, delicious music, and the dancing of Miss Charisse and Mr. Astaire. Whether it would be as good without

them—without the two principals, that is—is a purely subversive speculation. They are in it, and you can take it from there.

The book is, of course, the clever adaptation that a trio of nimble wits derived from the old Greta Garbo film *Ninotchka* for the sake of a Broadway musical show. A few polished gags have been added by a couple of jokesmiths at Metro-Goldwyn-Mayer, but it is still pretty close to the lot of satire that was tossed upon the stage.

That, you'll remember, was the story of how an American movie man, in Paris to get a Soviet composer to write him a couple of songs, had to break down the ideological bulwarks and the forbiddingly sexless attitudes of a lady Communist sent to Paris to prevent the composer from going along. How he did it was elementary. It is still elementary—but charming—here.

Also—with two exceptions—the songs are the ones from the stage, those wonderful Cole Porter ditties that sing of Paris, silk stockings, and love. (They also sing of "Red blues" and Siberia in securely sardonic ways.)

But nowhere has yet been seen comparison to the performances of Miss Charisse and Mr. Astaire as the lady Communist who breaks down and the American movie man. They are both in delightful fettle when they testily spar with the words, but are off in the blissful empyrean when they rise on their dancing shoes.

First of their spinning numbers is done to "All of You." Miss Charisse is also expressive in a brilliant solo she does to the title song—an imaginative piece of choreography in which she gets out of those old Russian rags and into some nice Parisian things. And she unlimbers herself superbly with a gang of cutups doing "The Red Blues."

Mr. Astaire, too, has a bright solo (with chorus) to a new song, "The Ritz Roll and Rock," which, while synthetic, is not as inconsistent as it sounds. But the two of them together are best in a gay escapade spun off to "Fated to Be Mated" (a new song) and the reprises of two other ones.

All is not the principals, however. Janis Paige is delightfully droll as the American movie actress who is rather robustly involved. She does a great bit with "Silks and Satins" and also with "Stereophonic Sound." And Jules Munshin, Joseph Buloff, and Peter

Lorre are swell dialectical clowns as the three clumsy Russian agents who fall in love with Paris, women, and champagne. Likewise, George Tobias is fresh as a commissar.

Under the direction of Rouben Mamoulian the whole thing moves with a suave and graceful flow. And Arthur Freed's beautiful production is no less than the subject deserves.

—B.C., July 19, 1957

SILKWOOD

Directed by Mike Nichols; written by Nora Ephron and Alice Arlen; director of photography, Miroslav Ondricek; edited by Sam O'Steen; music by Georges Delarue; production designer, Patrizia von Brandenstein; produced by Mr. Nichols and Michael Hausman; released by Twentieth Century Fox. Running time: 131 minutes.

With: Meryl Streep (Karen Silkwood), Kurt Russell (Drew Stephens), Cher (Dolly Pelliker), Craig T. Nelson (Winston), Diana Scarwid (Angela), Fred Ward (Morgan), Ron Silver (Paul Stone), Charles Hallahan (Earl Lapin) and Josef Sommer (Max Richter).

Taking many of the facts of the life of Karen Silkwood, the young laboratory worker and union activist who, in 1974, died in an automobile crash that some believe to have been murder, Mike Nichols has directed a precisely visualized, highly emotional melodrama that's going to raise a lot of hackles.

Though far from perfect, *Silkwood* may be the most serious work Mr. Nichols has yet done in films, and that would include *Who's Afraid of Virginia Woolf?*, *The Graduate*, and *Catch-22*. Perhaps for the first time in a popular movie has America's petrochemical-nuclear landscape been dramatized, and with such anger and compassion.

Silkwood, which opens today at Loew's Tower East, also offers another stunning performance by Meryl Streep, who plays the title role. Having won her first Oscar for *Kramer vs. Kramer* and her second for *Sophie's Choice*, Miss Streep looks to be on what the Las Vegas people call "a roll."

Her portrait of the initially self-assured and free-living, then radicalized, and, finally, terrified Karen Silkwood is unlike anything she's done to date, except in its intelligence. It's a brassy, profane, gum-chewing tour de force, as funny as it is moving.

There are, however, problems, not unlike those faced by Costa-Gavras in his *State of Siege* and *Missing,* and they are major. Mr. Nichols and his writers, Nora Ephron and Alice Arlen, have attempted to impose a shape on a real-life story that, even as they present it, has no easily verifiable shape. We are drawn into the story of Karen Silkwood by the absolute accuracy and unexpected sweetness of its Middle American details and then, near the end, abandoned by a film whose images say one thing and whose final credit card another. The muddle of fact, fiction, and speculation almost, though not quite, denies the artistry of all that's gone before.

This much about Karen Silkwood's life apparently is not in dispute: she was born in Texas, went through one year of college, and had three children by a common-law husband, whom she left when she moved to Crescent, Oklahoma, to work in Kerr-McGee's Cimarron Plutonium Recycling Facility there. At Cimarron, she earned a reputation as someone who couldn't be pushed around.

She lived for a while with a young coworker named Drew Stephens and was known to drink and to pop pills. At the same time, she grew increasingly troubled by the sloppy safety conditions under which she and the other Cimarron employees worked when handling dangerous, highly radioactive plutonium.

One result was that she threw herself into union work and was herself "contaminated" by radioactive materials, though in ways that have never been satisfactorily explained. At the time of her death, she was alleged to have gathered evidence that would force the plant to close. On the night of the car crash, she was driving alone to Oklahoma City to meet David Burnham, a reporter for *The New York Times,* to tell her story.

Because of these circumstances, there are those who contend that she was murdered to keep her silent. At this point she had become almost as unpopular with many employees, who didn't want to lose their jobs, as she was with management. There are others who are convinced that her car crash was an accident, caused by her known use of tranquilizers and painkillers. They speculate further that her contaminations were, in fact, not accidents but self-inflicted, in a misguided attempt to dramatize the true gravity of conditions at the Cimarron facility, which, subsequently, was shut down.

Mr. Nichols and his writers attempt to acknowledge most of these theories and, in so doing, end their film in utter confusion. However, until these closing scenes, in which "Amazing Grace," heard on the soundtrack, is used as if it were caulking to plug the holes in a leaky boat, *Silkwood* is a very moving work about the raising of the consciousness of one woman of independence, guts, and sensitivity.

In the small-town atmosphere of Crescent, Miss Streep's Karen is, for understandable reasons, notorious. She shares a ramshackle house with her current lover, Drew (Kurt Russell), who's just as casual in his attachments as she is in hers, and with her best friend Dolly Pelliker (Cher), a practicing lesbian. At one point the more or less ménage à trois becomes four when they are joined by Dolly's newest lover, Angela (Diana Scarwid), who works as a beautician in a funeral parlor.

At the plant, Karen takes no lip from the company bosses and sounds off noisily about love, sex, and whatever else that comes to mind, to the shocked delight of her more conservative coworkers. That popularity begins to vanish, though, when she joins the battle over safety conditions.

If Miss Streep is superb, Mr. Russell and Cher are very, very good. After his years with Walt Disney and then in action-adventure films (*Escape from New York, The Thing*), Mr. Russell has become a star with the looks of a leading man and the substance and wit of a character player. Whether or not Cher is a great actress, I'm still not sure, but when you take away those wild wigs she wears on television, and substitute something a little less riveting for her crazy Bob Mackie gowns, there's an honest, complex screen presence underneath.

The entire cast is exceptional, especially Sudie Bond, as one of Karen's older coworkers; Craig T. Nelson, as a man who may be doctoring negatives for the company's protection; Josef Sommer and Ron Silver, as union executives; Bruce McGill, who must represent virtually the entire Kerr-McGee management team; and Graham Jarvis, as one of the specialists who alerts the union members to the dangers they face.

As the screenplay catches the Texas-Oklahoma speech rhythms, and as these rhythms are re-created by the members of the cast, the work of Miroslav Ondricek, the cameraman, is equally successful. It captures the essence of the contradictions that exist in the petrochemical-nuclear landscapes of Oklahoma and Texas, where huge, sophisticated industrial facilities are set upon vast plains, otherwise occupied only by isolated farms, small towns, and the sorts of roadhouses that haven't changed since the repeal of Prohibition.

I realize that films shouldn't be judged in bits and pieces, but it's difficult not to see *Silkwood* in that way. For most of its running time it is so convincing—and so sure of itself—that it seems a particular waste when it goes dangerously wrong. It's like watching a sky diver execute all sorts of graceful, breathtaking turns, as he appears to ignore gravity and fly on his own, only to have him smash to earth when the chute doesn't open.

—*V.C., December 14, 1983*

SINGIN' IN THE RAIN

Directed by Gene Kelly and Stanley Donen; written by Adolph Green and Betty Comden; cinematographer, Harold Rosson; edited by Adrienne Fazan; music by Nacio Herb Brown; art designers, Cedric Gibbons and Randall Duell; produced by Arthur Freed; released by Metro-Goldwyn-Mayer. Running time: 103 minutes.

With: Gene Kelly (Don Lockwood), Donald O'Connor (Cosmo Brown), Debbie Reynolds (Kathy Selden), Jean Hagen (Lina Lamont), Millard Mitchell (R. F. Simpson), Cyd Charisse (Guest Artist), Rita Moreno (Zelder Zanders), Douglas Fowley (Roscoe Dexter) and Madge Blake (Dora Bailey).

Spring came with a fresh and cheerful splatter to the Music Hall yesterday with the arrival of Metro's new musical, *Singin' in the Rain,* along with the Glory-of-Easter pageant and a vernal revue on the stage. Compounded generously of music, dance, color, spectacle, and a riotous abundance of Gene Kelly, Jean Hagen, and Donald O'Connor on the screen, all elements in this rainbow program are carefully contrived and guaranteed to lift the dolors of winter and put you in a buttercup mood.

Take as a token of the picture its title, *Singin' in the Rain*, which has no more to do with its story than it has to do with performing dogs. Of all things, this song-and-dance contrivance is an impudent, offhand comedy about the outlandish making of movies back in the sheik-and-flapper days when they were bridging the perilous chasm from silent to talking films. And its plot, if that's what you'd call it, concerns a silent film star who is linked with a slut-voiced leading lady while wooing a thrushy new young thing.

If anyone can tell us what all of the nonsense that goes on has to do with the title of the picture, we will buy him a new spring hat. But that doesn't make any difference, for the nonsense is generally good and at times it reaches the level of first-class satiric burlesque. Adolph Green and Betty Comden may have tossed off the script with their left hands, but occasionally they come through with powerful and hilarious round-house rights.

Take, for instance, the scene in which Miss Hagen as the guttersnipe silent queen is making her first acquaintance with the hidden microphone. No funnier lampoon of filmmaking has yet swum within our ken than this brief but side-splitting revelation of the battle with the machine. And some of the musical numbers that kid the old musical clichés, such as fashion parades and pinwheel chorus groups, are as mischievous as they come.

Also, we'll say for the authors—and for Mr. Kelly and Stanley Donen, who directed the show: they had the courage to kid Louella Parsons with a devastating take-off by Madge Blake. Under the protocol of Hollywood, this is lèse-majesté!

However, the pattern of the picture is such that a lot of room is made for singing and dancing in the liveliest Kelly-cum-all style. And it is in these elegant phases that the spirit is lightest and most gay. Mr. Kelly, who plays the silent film star up from burlesque and vaudeville, runs away, of course, with the dancing—and, as a matter of fact, with most of the songs.

His dance and duet with Debbie Reynolds to "You Were Meant for Me" is a sweet lump of Technicolored sugar, and his galloping through "Broadway Ballet" is a lot of eye-filling acrobatics against a mammoth production splurge. This is a combination of the oldies, "Broadway Rhythm" and "Broadway Melody," with

Cyd Charisse stepping out of nowhere to do a lovely dream dance with Mr. K. But by far his most captivating number is done to the title song—a beautifully soggy tap dance performed in the splashing rain.

Donald O'Connor, as Mr. Kelly's sidekick, also has a jolly romp in a battering and bruising slapstick number entitled "Make 'Em Laugh" and joins with the star in making "Moses" a lively thing.

—B.C., March 28, 1952

SITTING PRETTY

Directed by Walter Lang; written by F. Hugh Herbert, based on the novel *Belvedere* by Gwen Davenport; cinematographer, Norbert Brodine; edited by Harmon Jones; music by Alfred Newman; art designers, Lyle Wheeler and Leland Fuller; produced by Samuel G. Engel; released by Twentieth Century Fox. Black and white. Running time: 84 minutes.

With: Robert Young (Harry), Maureen O'Hara (Tacey), Clifton Webb (Lynn Belvedere), Richard Haydn (Mr. Appleton), Louise Allbritton (Edna Philby) and Randy Stuart (Peggy).

Since there is something spontaneously amusing about the very thought of Clifton Webb playing nurse to a brood of noisy children in an average American home, it is obvious that *Sitting Pretty*, which has this situation as its core, starts out with plenty in its favor—especially Mr. Webb. And since, around and about this situation, there is festooned a lot of lightweight fun, reeled off a script by F. Hugh Herbert and nimbly directed by Walter Lang, there's not much wanting to compel a flood of laughter in this rumpus from Twentieth Century Fox.

The screenplays from Mr. Herbert are not conspicuous for their tax upon the brain, and this effort, now showing at the Roxy, is no exception to the rule. It is a fiction derived from a novel entitled *Belvedere* by Gwen Davenport about a man who moves in with a family to serve as a "sitter" with the kids and swiftly assumes the proportions of a superior Trojan horse. The children are silenced by his hauteur, the parents are baffled by his noblesse oblige, and the neighbors are moved to chattering gossip by the scandal they think they perceive. In the end, of course, the haughty gentleman turns out to be the "genius" he claims—or, at least, an acceptable facsimile—and all mix-ups are settled happily.

Light in substance but solid in humor, this material is handled dexterously by all who come anywhere near it—and especially, as we say, by Mr. Webb. As the man who came to be a sitter and remains as a willful family friend, he plays the whole thing from an angle of observation well above his tilted nose. Whether it be a matter of removing oatmeal from his supercilious eye, splashed there by the less respectful baby, or of preaching to the parents on pride, he does it with elegant detachment and a chilling coolness toward the obvious common herd. Yet there slyly protrudes through his arrogance a flickering spoof of pomposity and a tentative benevolence toward humanity, of which he generously agrees to be one. A student of the fine shades of kidding will find a lot to admire in Mr. Webb.

Among those who bear his cool indulgence and his unqualified conceit, Robert Young and Maureen O'Hara are delightfully clever, too. As the husband and wife in the ménage of which he assumes command, they play with elaborate indignation, alternating with good-natured despair. Larry Olsen, Anthony Sydes, and Roddy McCaskill are properly explosive as the kids, while Richard Haydn is magnificently obnoxious as a neighbor with a clogged and snoopy nose.

Sitting Pretty is happily a picture which almost anyone should enjoy. For those of us who have faced the "sitter problem" and know its horrors, it's an oddly soothing balm.

—B.C., March 11, 1948

SLEEPER

Directed by Woody Allen; written by Mr. Allen and Marshall Brickman; director of photography, David M. Walsh; edited by Ralph Rosenblum; music by Mr. Allen; production designer, Dale Hennesy; produced by Jack Grossberg; released by United Artists. Running time: 88 minutes.

With: Woody Allen (Miles Monroe), Diane Keaton (Luna), John Beck (Erno), Marya Small (Dr. Nero), Bartlett Robinson (Dr. Orva) and Mary Gregory (Dr. Melik).

Miles Monroe (Woody Allen), the part-owner of the Happy Carrot Health Food Restaurant in Greenwich Village, has a major problem. He had gone into St. Vincent's Hospital in 1973 for a minor ulcer operation, only to wake up 200 years later, defrosted, having been wrapped in aluminum foil and frozen as hard as a South African lobster tail when the minor ulcer operation went somehow wrong.

Thus begins *Sleeper,* Woody's *2001* (actually, it's his *2173*), which confidently advances the Allen art into slapstick territory that I associate with the best of Laurel and Hardy. It's the kind of film comedy that no one in Hollywood has done with style in many years, certainly not since Jerry Lewis began to take himself seriously.

Sleeper is a comic epic that recalls the breathless pace and dizzy logic of the old two-reelers. The setting is an American police state, ruled by a terrible dictator who has the genial manners of your favorite TV anchorman, where Miles is enlisted to aid the forces of the antigovernment underground. Miles does his best to refuse. He is dirty-minded, mean-spirited, surreptitious, and incurably literate and cowardly. As he points out: "I was once beaten up by Quakers."

The world in which Miles finds himself is truly alarming, a half-analyzed paranoiac's worst dream come true. Automobiles look like giant plastic turtles. Chickens are twelve feet tall and banana skins are as long as canoes. There are robot servants and robot dogs, and at the end of a dinner party a hostess comments: "I think we should have had sex but there weren't enough people."

How did America get this way? Was there a ghastly war? Someone seems to remember that a man named Albert Shanker once got hold of a nuclear warhead.

Sleeper is Mr. Allen's fourth film as star, director, and writer (this time with Marshall Brickman) and it is, I'm sure, not only his most ambitious but also his best.

The fine madness of *Take the Money and Run* and *Bananas,* which were largely illustrated extensions of his nightclub routines, is now also apparent in the kind of slapstick comedy that can only be done in films.

When Woody wrestles with a butterscotch pudding mix that won't stop rising, when he runs afoul of an ill-fitting flying belt, or when he attempts to clone the entire body of the dead dictator from all that remains of the dictator (a nose), you realize that the stand-up comedian has at last made an unequivocal transition to the screen.

All of his original skills and humors remain intact. A fantasy in which Woody wins the Miss America contest, and another in which he plays Blanche Dubois to Diane Keaton's Stanley Kowalski, are vintage Allen.

As Woody continues to grow as a filmmaker, so does Diane Keaton (his costar in *Play It Again, Sam*) continue to develop as an elegant comedienne along the lines of Paula Prentiss and the late Kay Kendall. In *Sleeper,* Miss Keaton plays Luna, a beautiful, right-wing, absolutely awful poet whose metaphors are muddled by her inability to remember that caterpillars turn into butterflies, not the other way around. Through the love, aid, comfort, and cowardice of a very small man, Luna is finally liberated.

There are some comparatively calm spots in the film, here and there, but they don't count. If anything, they allow you to catch your breath. *Sleeper* is terrific.

—*V.C., December 18, 1973*

A SLIGHT CASE OF MURDER

Directed by Lloyd Bacon; written by Earl Baldwin and Joseph Schrank, based on the play by Damon Runyon and Howard Lindsay; cinematographer, Sid Hickox; edited by James Gibbon; music and lyrics by M.K. Jerome and Jack Scholl; art designer, Max Parker; produced by Samuel Bischoff; released by Warner Brothers. Black and white. Running time: 85 minutes.

With, Edward G. Robinson (Remy Marco), Jane Bryan (Mary Marco), Allen Jenkins (Mike), Ruth Donnelly (Nora Marco), Willard Parker (Dick Whitewood), John Litel (Post) and Edward Brophy (Lefty).

The Strand is enjoying *A Slight Case of Murder,* and we haven't laughed so much since Remy Marco's Mike found four parties shot to death in the back bedroom of the Saratoga house his boss had rented for the season.

The four parties, still clutching their poker hands, were No-Nose Cohen, Blackhead Gallagher, a stranger, and Little Dutch. Little Dutch was holding a king-high flush, which prompted Marco to growl, "Yeah, he always had the luck." Mrs. Marco was more indignant. With an outraged tenant's voice, she said the owners shouldn't have gone off leaving a room cluttered up that way. And Mike, Lefty, and Giuseppe thought it was inconsiderate of the four parties to get themselves bumped off in Remy's house just when the boss was going respectable.

That's the Damon Runyon approach to murder and if you can't look beyond a grisly joke and see only the joke, then the Strand's not your theater this week. But we hope it will be, for *A Slight Case of Murder* is just about the funniest show the new year has produced. Nothing subtle about it, of course. It goes after its laughs with Rabelaisian gusto, a dialogic scorn of the grammatical properties, and an impolite subscription to the dictum: de mortuis nil nisi mayhem. What happens to the four parties who got themselves so annoyingly rubbed out in the reformed beer baron's shack is plenty, but we can't go into it now.

After all, they constituted only a slight case of murder, and Remy Marco had more important things to worry about. He had a $500,000 note to pay before noon; he had a beer-drinking brat from his old alma mater, the orphanage, on his hands; and, worst of all, there was his daughter about to disgrace the Marco name by bringing a dilettante state trooper into the family. No wonder Mrs. Marco with wifely solicitude patted his brow and tenderly said, "Gee, Remy, you're sweatin' like a stuck hog."

We understand the Runyon-Howard Lindsay play was only moderately amusing; that the picture is immoderately so must be due, then, to Earl Baldwin's and Joseph Schrank's clever rewrite job, to Lloyd Bacon's impudently agile direction, and to the flavorsome performances of an unusually apt and well-chosen cast.

For a Runyonesque panel the casting director had the marvelous good fortune to find Edward G. Robinson and Ruth Donnelly to play Mr. and Mrs.; Bobby Jordan to be the problem child; Douglas Fairbanks, Rosenbloom; Allen Jenkins, Harold Huber, Eddie Brophy, and Joe Downing as assorted gunmen; Bert Hanlon to be the priceless bookie called Sad Sam. There are others, almost equally right. If you're not too squeamish, you should have a round of chuckles on the house.

—*F.S.N., February 28, 1938*

SMASH PALACE

Produced and directed by Roger Donaldson: written by Peter Hansard. Mr. Donaldson and Bruno Lawrence: cinematographer. Graeme Cowley: edited by Michael Horton: music by Sharon O'Neill: art designer, Reston Griffiths: released by Atlantic Releasing. Running time: 100 minutes.

With: Bruno Lawrence (Al Shaw). Anna Jemison (Jacqui Shaw). Greer Robson (Georgie Shaw). Keith Aberdein (Ray Foley) and Desmond Kelly (Tiny).

The "New Directors/New Films" series—which looks as if it will be particularly strong this year—gets off to a wonderful start with *Smash Palace,* Roger Donaldson's brisk, believable account of a marital breakup in New Zealand. An earlier film of Mr. Donaldson's, *Sleeping Dogs,* had its premiere in New York recently, and it demonstrated much the same command and crispness that distinguishes *Smash Palace.* (The film opens commercially April 30 at the Paris Theater.)

But this new film is by far the more substantial. Although films about divorce may be a commonplace right now, Mr. Donaldson's is something out of the ordinary—if not for any special wisdom or insight, then surely for the deft, intelligent, steadily surprising manner in which the story is told.

From its opening sequence, *Smash Palace* is clearly something unusual. A car hurtles dangerously across the New Zealand countryside, moving so fast that the driver loses control of the vehicle and the car flips over. Who was the driver? As we soon discover, it doesn't matter, because this film isn't his story. Instead, it's about Al and Jacqui Shaw, who run the wrecking yard to which the damaged car is taken. Al (Bruno Lawrence) and Jacqui (Anna Jemison) live in the midst of acres of wrecked cars, in a dreary, isolated landscape that has taken its toll on their marriage. When Jacqui left France to join Al in this backwoods setting, she never dreamed life could turn so dismal so soon.

Smash Palace is the name of the wrecking yard, and it's also a fine name for a film about Al and Jacqui's domestic warfare. Their daughter Georgie (Greer Robson), eight years old or so, is at the center of the quarrel. Mr. Donaldson provides idiosyncratic and cozy glimpses of the Shaw family early in the story, as they take their evening baths or as Georgie helps Al tinker with cars. The daughter's closeness to each of her parents is as well established as their estrangement from each other. One of Mr. Donaldson's many accomplishments here is to tell the story from no particular point of view and still etch each of the three principals with exceptional compassion and clarity.

One night, Jacqui goes to a local party at which yodeling is the chief entertainment. Mr. Donaldson doesn't need much more explanation than this to account for her restlessness. She becomes involved with Ray Foley (Keith Aberdein), a local policeman and friend of Al, who, without much preparation, finds himself in a morally indefensible position. Ray is perhaps even more astonished than anyone to find himself cuckolding the stolid, likable, and hardworking Al.

And Al is surprised to find himself rising to the occasion of his wife's desertion with some newly rebellious behavior of his own. After one last desperate sexual encounter in which all of the Shaws' rage and disappointment is expressed, Jacqui moves out and Al begins to badger her. One day, he arrives at Jacqui's house, where Ray is quietly lurking, and finds himself so frustrated that he shouts through the closed front door, "Tell you what, I'll give you the shirt off my back."

And more. Before Al knows it, he has torn off all his clothes and stuffed them through Jacqui's mail slot. Whatever one might have expected him to do when the scene began, it wasn't this. In Mr. Donaldson's films, the unexpected is about the only thing the audience can count on. That, and a sharply observed understanding of the way things look when they go wrong. As Georgie grows more and more upset, Mr. Donaldson doesn't devote much talk to her feelings. He just shows her cowering alone in her bedroom, obsessively clicking on and off a flashlight she has aimed at her eyes.

Though *Smash Palace* has the look of an intimate, domestic portrait, it's more an action film with an at-home setting than a character study. Mr. Donaldson doesn't have much insight into why the Shaws behave as they do, and his screenplay isn't particularly revealing. Jacqui's feelings are especially sketchy, and she never explains herself very well.

But the performances, most notably Mr. Lawrence's, are so strong that they fill in the screenplay's gaps. Mr. Lawrence makes Al real and recognizable every step of the way, so that even when his anger erupts into violence, he hasn't lost the audience's sympathy. Mr. Donaldson, according to the production notes, read a story like Al's in a newspaper, and in devising the film he worked backward from the man's fiercely funny climactic gesture to his days of relative serenity. This approach, not to mention Mr. Donaldson's overall forcefulness and originality, is enough to account for the film's eccentric, irresistible momentum.

—J.M., April 16, 1982

SMILE

Produced and directed by Michael Ritchie; written by Jerry Belson; director of photography, Conrad Hall; edited by Richard A. Harris; music by Daniel Osborn, Leroy Holmes and Charles Chaplin; choreography by Jim Bates; released by United Artists. Running time: 113 minutes.

With: Bruce Dern (Big Bob Freelander), Barbara Feldon (Brenda DiCarlo), Michael Kidd (Tommy French), Geoffrey Lewis (Wilson Shears), Nicholas Pryor (Andy DiCarlo), Joan Prather (Robin), Annette O'Toole (Doria), Maria O'Brien (Maria Gonzalez), Tito Vandis (Emile Eidelman) and Eric Shea (Little Bob Freelander).

Middle America is not exactly the fastest-moving target in the world. You don't have to be a sharpshooter to hit it. It just sits there like someone on a giant billboard, wearing an ear-to-ear grin, the eyes sparkling in anticipation of achieving some new plateau of pleasure, waiting to be defaced by anyone who has the price of a can of spray paint.

It's because Middle America is a pushover that Michael Ritchie's new comedy, *Smile,* about an annual beauty pageant in Santa Rosa, California, is such a pungent surprise, a rollicking satire that misses few of the obvious targets, but without dehumanizing the victims. It's an especially American kind of social comedy in the way that great good humor sometimes is used to reveal unpleasant facts instead of burying them.

Smile will be shown at the New York Film Festival tonight and again on Saturday night. No date has yet been set for its regular New York theater opening, though it has already played in several other cities around the country.

On its most general level, *Smile* is about a society in which optimism and positive thinking virtually amount to a political system, a guide to the making of choices, the principal goal of which is to have fun. A man who is on the brink of suicide is advised by his lifelong friend: "You've got to pull yourself together. Go out there and start having some fun." Fun is the operative word and, of course, fun is as illusive as a dim light in the dark. When you look at it directly, it disappears.

The pageant that is the center of *Smile* is fictitious, a statewide (California) Young American Miss contest that, one assumes, precedes the kind of national clambake that Bert Parks emcees annually. The film covers the four days of various trials in which the teenage contestants are graded on poise, beauty, zest for living, talent, and their concern for their fellow man.

They are coddled, threatened, and frightened into fakery with such questions as, "Marie, can you tell me why you want to go into missionary work?" and "Why do you play the flute, dear? In your own words . . ."

The kingpin of the affair is a local Santa Rosa booster, named Big Bob Freelander (Bruce Dern), a live-wire automobile salesman who, in the course of this particular pageant, begins to lose the smile that, until now, he had been convinced was making America great.

This is no big dramatic deal. *Smile* is not a film of explosive revelations. The soul-searching we do is our own. It's a comedy composed of dozens of vignettes—about Big Bob; about the pageant coordinator, Brenda DiCarlo, a pretty, silly, edgy woman beautifully played by Barbara Feldon; about Brenda's suicidal husband, Andy (Nicholas Pryor); about the other officials of the pageant; and especially about some of the contestants.

Unlike *Beauty Knows No Pain,* a comic and rude short subject made several years ago about the training of some drum majorettes in Texas, *Smile* treats its beauty contestants without condescension. The girls are sometimes hugely funny and foolish, but they are also decent and appealing in their earnest efforts to be the Ann-Margrets of tomorrow.

Three young actresses stand out in these roles: Maria O'Brien as a pushy, driving contestant who sells her Mexican-American heritage for all it's worth; Joan Prather, as the most levelheaded of the contestants; and Annette O'Toole, as the most desperate.

Jerry Belson wrote the excellent screenplay. *Smile,* which is Mr. Ritchie's best film to date (better than both *Downhill Racer* and *The Candidate*), questions the quality of our fun, while adding to it.

—V.C., October 9, 1975

SMILES OF A SUMMER NIGHT

Written (in Swedish, with English subtitles) and directed by Ingmar Bergman: cinematographer, Gunnar Fischer: edited by Oscar Rosander: music by Erik Nordgren: art designer, P.A. Lundgren: produced by Allen Ekelund: released by Rank Film Distributors. Black and white. Running time: 108 minutes.

With: Ulla Jacobsson (Anne Egerman), Eva Dahlbeck (Desirée Armfeldt), Harriet Anderson (Petra, the Maid), Margit Carlquist (Charlotte Malcolm), Gunnar Björnstrand (Fredrik Egerman), Bjorn Bjelvenstam (Henrik Egerman), Naima Wifstand (Madame Armfeldt), Ake Fridell (Frid, the Groom) and Jarl Kulle (Count Malcolm).

Who would have thought that august Sweden would be sending us a film comedy as witty and cheerfully candid about the complexities of love as any recent French essay on l'amour? Yet that is what Ingmar Bergman's *Smiles of a Summer Night* is—a delightfully droll contemplation of amorous ardors. It opened at the Sutton yesterday.

In a style of writing and direction more characteristic of the French or perhaps the prewar Hungarians than the usually solemn Swedes, Mr. Bergman skips us gaily through a mix-up of youthful and adult love affairs, which, while timed around the turn of the century, are as spicy as any such today.

Spicy, indeed, is the label to put on this charming film which logically ran away with comedy honors at the 1956 festival in Cannes. Its amorous incidents are spicy, in a thoroughly tasteful and elegant way, and its philosophical conclusions are made attractive with the most redolent of intellectual herbs. What is more, its involved situations are invariably comical and deft.

As is popular in European pictures (and seems to be becoming more so in those from Hollywood), Mr. Bergman is treating one of the conflicts between young and mature, experienced love. In his exquisite cast of characters are a polished Stockholm lawyer who is wed to a second wife many years his junior, this same man's serious and virginal son, his former mistress (a handsome, clever actress), her present lover (a pert dragoon), and the latter's wife. There is also a naughty little housemaid who knows her way around and an aged courtesan, the actress's mother, who has the pleasure of dropping wise epigrams.

The series of personal complications that makes up the content of the film begins when the lawyer seeks the counsel of his former mistress as to how to treat his young wife. This leads to surprising discoveries and developments of crisscrossed love. The young wife, while faithful to her husband, is drawn to his agonized son. The mistress still fancies the lawyer, while entertaining her jealous dragoon. The latter's wife wants her husband, yet is ready to seduce the lawyer to prove it can be done. All very complicated, sophisticated, and droll.

Mr. Bergman, whose previous pictures seen here have been on the deeply serious side, keeps this one light and intriguing with a fine blend of stylized high comedy and farce. His gentlemen are sternly pompous figures while his ladies are sweetly pliable. The matter most pointedly satirized is masculine dignity.

As the lawyer, Gunnar Björnstrand is elegantly stiff yet slyly droll and Jari Kulle is amusingly formal and arrogant as the dragoon. Ulla Jacobsson is delightfully nubile and naive as the young wife. Eva Dahlbeck is full-blown as the mistress and Margit Carlquist is brittle as the wife of the dragoon. Harriet Andersson is disarmingly breezy and lusty as the buxom maid. Bjorn Bjelvenstam is comical as the sad son and Naima Wifstrand is tart as the old courtesan. Ake Fridell is also good as a coachman who explains what the title means—there are three kinds of love that, according to legend, are possible on a summer night.

It is noticeable that the English subtitles do not translate some racy passages, but they are good, on the whole, along with a very lovely and effective musical score.

—B.C., December 24, 1957

924

THE SNAKE PIT

Directed by Anatole Litvak: written by Frank Partos and Millen Brand, based on the novel by Mary Jane Ward: cinematographer. Leo Tover: edited by Dorothy Spencer: music by Alfred Newman: art designers. Lyle Wheeler and Joseph C. Wright: produced by Mr. Litvak and Robert Bassler: released by Twentieth Century Fox. Black and white. Running time: 108 minutes.

With: Olivia de Havilland (Virginia Stuart Cunningham). Mark Stevens (Robert Cunningham). Leo Genn (Dr. Kik). Celeste Holm (Grace). Glenn Langan (Dr. Terry). Helen Craig (Miss Davis). Leif Erickson (Gordon) and Beulah Bondi (Mrs. Greer).

Mary Jane Ward's powerful novel, *The Snake Pit,* is hardly one which Hollywood might have been expected to choose for transcription to the screen. For it puts forth fully and frankly the case history of a young woman in a mental institute, wherein she proceeds through experiences which are not of the most beguiling sort. Yet it must be said to the credit of Anatole Litvak and Twentieth Century Fox (in the person of Darryl F. Zanuck) that they saw the special merit in this book and they had the imagination and temerity to buy and prepare it for the screen.

And, most particularly, it must be said to their credit that they approached this extraordinary job with a sense of responsibility to treat fairly a most delicate theme. They followed the book with rare fidelity. They stuck rigidly to documented facts, and they shunned the obvious temptation to melodramatize insanity. The consequence is that their picture, which opened at the Rivoli yesterday, is a true, illuminating presentation of the experiences of a psychotic in an institute. It is a cryptic but trenchant revelation of a crying need for better facilities for mental care. And although it is frequently harrowing, it is a fascinating and deeply moving film.

The most striking aspect of this picture is the forcefulness with which it makes us feel the dark confusion, distress, and anguished yearnings of a person who is mentally ill. And this it does from a literal, straightforward, and quietly objective point of view, with only one impressionistic intrusion, by catching the drama in the behavior of one thus torn. Without pointing or pounding at any details, it shows the myriad idiosyncrasies of "the sick" and draws them into a pattern which should expand and enlighten our lucid minds.

Telling the poignant story of a young married woman who is slowly returned to sanity from a mental derangement brought on by a complex of great depth, it goes with her through the experiences of electroshock treatment, narcosynthesis, hydrotherapy, and the revulsions of living in wards with the violently insane. And by following, through flashbacks, the drama of her earlier life, it gives a good Freudian explanation for her illness, on which to base her cure.

There are considerations which cannot be dismissed in a review. Though handled with great circumspection, this subject is dynamite. Faint or susceptible people might find it extremely hard to take, and children not baffled by it might be terrifically disturbed. Also, the macabre humor in the behavior of the insane, although treated with faithful realism, seems a poor thing at which one should laugh.

But it must be said, in this connection, that every one of the roles, even down to the smallest bit parts of the ward patients, is excellently played. It is impossible to mention all of them, from Beulah Bondi's flowery megalomaniac to Betsy Blair's manic depressive, but each adds a facet to the film.

In the chief roles, Olivia de Havilland does a brilliant, heartrending job as the central, guilt-ridden patient, and Leo Genn is remarkably fine as her shrewd, sympathetic psychiatrist who works beneath the benign portrait of Freud. Mark Stevens is gentle as her husband—a notably hard role to play—and Helen Craig gives a good, tough performance as a nurse who admires the doc. This latter fact, incidentally, is the only "Hollywood" touch that Millen Brand and Frank Partos have permitted to show in their superior script. And Mr. Litvak's direction is sure and rhythmic throughout.

The Snake Pit, while frankly quite disturbing, and not recommended for the weak, is a mature emotional drama on a rare and pregnant theme.

—B.C., November 5, 1948

SNOW WHITE AND THE SEVEN DWARFS

Directed by David Hand. Perce Pearce. Larry Morey. William Cottrell. Wilfred Jackson and Ben

Sharpsteen; written by Ted Sears, Otto Englander, Earl Hurd, Dorothy Ann Blank, Richard Creedon, Dick Richard, Merrill de Maris and Webb Smith, based on the fairy tale by the Brothers Grimm; music by Frank Churchill, Leigh Harline, Paul J. Smith and Larry Morey; art designers, Charles Philippi, Hugh Hennesy, Terrell Stapp, McLaren Stewart, Harold Miles, Tom Codrick, Gustaf Tenggren, Ken Anderson, Kendall O'Connor and Hazel Sewell; produced by Walt Disney; released by RKO Radio Pictures. Running time: 83 minutes.

With the voices of: Adriana Caselotti (Snow White), Harry Stockwell (Prince Charming), Lucille La Verne (The Queen), Moroni Olsen (Magic Mirror), Billy Gilbert (Sneezy), Pinto Colvig (Sleepy/Grumpy), Otis Harlan (Happy), Scotty Mattraw (Bashful) and Roy Atwell (Doc).

Sheer fantasy, delightful, gay, and altogether captivating, touched the screen yesterday when Walt Disney's long-awaited feature-length cartoon of the Grimm fairy tale, *Snow White and the Seven Dwarfs*, had its local premiere at the Radio City Music Hall. Let your fears be quieted at once: Mr. Disney and his amazing technical crew have outdone themselves. The picture more than matches expectations. It is a classic, as important cinematically as *The Birth of a Nation* or the birth of Mickey Mouse. Nothing quite like it has been done before; and already we have grown impolite enough to clamor for an encore. Another helping, please!

You can visualize it best if you imagine a child, with a wondrous, Puckish imagination, nodding over his favorite fairy tale and dreaming a dream in which his story would come true. He would see Snow White, victim of the wicked Queen's jealousy, dressed in rags, singing at her work quite unmindful of the Magic Mirror's warning to the Queen that the Princess, not she, was now the "fairest in the land." Then he would see Snow White's banishment from the castle, her fearful flight from the hobgoblins of the forest, her adoption by all the friendly little creatures of the wood, and her refuge at the home of the seven dwarfs.

And then, if this child had a truly marvelous imagination—the kind of impish imagination that Mr. Disney and his men possess—he might have seen the seven dwarfs as the picture sees them. There are Doc, who sputters and twists his words, and Happy, who is a rollicking little elf, and Grumpy, who is terribly grumpy—at first—and Sleepy, who drowses, and Sneezy, who acts like a volcano with hay fever, and Bashful, who blushes to the roots of his long white beard, and Dopey. Dopey really deserves a sentence all by himself. No, we'll make it a paragraph, because Dopey is here to stay.

Dopey is the youngest of the seven dwarfs. He is beardless, with a buttony nose, a wide mouth, beagle ears, cross-purpose eyes, and the most disarming, winning, helpless, puppy-dog expression that creature ever had. If we had to dissect him, we'd say he was one part little Benny of the comic strips, one part Worry-Wart of the same, and one part Pluto, of the Mickey Mouse Plutos. There may, too, be just a dash of Harpo Marx. But he's all Dopey, forever out of step in the dwarfs' processions, doomed to carry the red tail-light when they go to their jewel mines, and speechless. As Doc explains, "He never tried to talk."

So there they are, all seven of them, to protect the little Princess from her evil stepmother, the Queen, to dance and frolic and cavort—with the woodland creatures—in comic Disneyesque patterns, and ultimately to keep vigil at Snow White's glass-and-gold coffin until Prince Charming imprints "love's first kiss" upon her lips and so releases her from the sleeping death that claimed her after she ate the witch's poisoned apple. For this, you know, is partly the story of Sleeping Beauty.

But no child, of course, could dream a dream like this. For Mr. Disney's humor has the simplicity of extreme sophistication. The little bluebird who overreaches itself and hits a flat note to the horror of its parents; the way the animals help Snow White clean house, with the squirrels using their tails as dusters, the swallows scalloping pies with their feet, the fawns licking the plates clean, the chipmunks twirling cobwebs about their tails and pulling free; or the ticklish tortoise when the rabbits use his ribbed underside as a scrubbing board—all these are beyond a youngster's imagination, but not beyond his delight.

And technically it is superb. In some of the early sequences there may be an uncertainty of line, a jerkiness in the movements of the Princess; but it is corrected later and hand and lip movements assume an uncanny reality. The dwarfs and animals are flawless from the start. Chromatically, it is far and away the best Technicolor to date, achieving effects possible only to the cartoon, obtaining—through the multiplane camera—an effortless third dimension. You'll not, most of the time, realize you are watching animated cartoons. And if you do, it will be only with a sense of amazement.

Nor can any description overlook so important a Disney element as the score. There are eight songs—solos, duets, choruses—which perfectly counterpoint the action. In the traditional ballad manner are "The Wishing Well Song," "Some Day My Prince Will Come," and "One Song." Livelier is the dwarfs' theme, "Hi-Ho," "Whistle While You Work," "The Washing Song," and "Isn't This a Silly Song." We've lost one or two, but no great matter. They're gay and friendly and pleasant, all of them, and so is the picture. If you miss it, you'll be missing one of the ten best pictures of 1938. Thank you very much, Mr. Disney, and come again soon.

—*F.S.N., January 14, 1938*

SOME LIKE IT HOT

Produced and directed by Billy Wilder; written by Mr. Wilder and I. A. L. Diamond, based on the screenplay *Fanfares of Love* by Robert Thoeren and M. Logan; cinematographer, Charles Lang; edited by Arthur Schmidt; music by Adolph Deutsch; art designer, Ted Haworth; released by United Artists. Black and white. Running time: 120 minutes.

With: Marilyn Monroe (Sugar Kane), Tony Curtis (Joe/Josephine), Jack Lemmon (Jerry/Daphne), George Raft (Spats Colombo), Pat O'Brien (Mulligan), Joe E. Brown (Osgood Fielding 3d), Nehemiah Persoff (Little Bonaparte) and Joan Shawlee (Sue).

There should be no doubt this morning that the members of the happily irreverent film troupe that made *Some Like It Hot* have done something constructive about the old wheeze that begins, "Who was that lady I saw you with?" For, in fashioning this overlong, occasionally labored but often outrageously funny series of variations on an ancient gag, they have come up with a rare, rib-tickling lampoon that should keep them, the customers, and the management of the newly refurbished Loew's State, which reopened yesterday, chortling with glee.

Let's face it. Two hours is too long a time to harp on one joke. But Billy Wilder, who produced, directed, and collaborated with I. A. L. Diamond on this breeziest of scripts, proves once again that he is as professional as anyone in Hollywood. Mr. Wilder, abetted by such equally proficient operatives as Marilyn Monroe, Jack Lemmon, and Tony Curtis, surprisingly has developed a completely unbelievable plot into a broad farce in which authentically comic action vies with snappy and sophisticated dialogue.

It is quite possible also that this uninhibited team was inspired by Mack Sennett and *Charley's Aunt.* The slim story, to put it bluntly, simply deals with what happens to a pair of Prohibition-era musicians who witness a gangland murder in Chicago (strongly reminiscent of the St. Valentine's Day massacre) and who seek sanctuary masquerading as dames in an all-girl band in Florida.

But Mr. Wilder and company obviously are not bothered by this flimsy framework. *Some Like It Hot* is as constantly busy as picnickers fighting off angry wasps. Jack Lemmon has a torrid time guzzling gin at an impromptu party in a Pullman upper berth attended by Miss Monroe and the rest of the giddy band. Tony Curtis, switching disguises from bogus girl saxophonist to phony millionaire, amorously pursues Miss Monroe, and vice versa, aboard a "borrowed" yacht. The slightly addled playboy-owner of that ship, played in properly harebrained style by Joe E. Brown, chases Mr. Lemmon with nothing but honorable intentions. And Chicago's hoods, led by George Raft and Nehemiah Persoff, tear after Lemmon and Curtis, the witnesses to their foul deed, with equal determination.

Who gets whom is not particularly important. A viewer might question the taste of a few of the lines, situations, and the prolonged masquerade, but Mr. Wilder and his associates generally make their points with explosive effect. Besides the wild and wooly train sequence, one is reminded of such scenes as Miss Monroe's ardent and naive wooing of Mr. Curtis; Mr. Lemmon's gay fandango with Mr. Brown, a dopey pas-de-deux that ends in their becoming "engaged"; and Mr. Persoff's and Mr. Raft's caricatures of hoodlum big shots.

As the band's somewhat simple singer-ukulele player, Miss Monroe, whose figure simply cannot be overlooked, contributes more assets than the obvious ones to this madcap romp. As a pushover for gin and the tonic effect of saxophone players, she sings a couple of whispery old numbers ("Running Wild" and "I Wanna Be Loved by You") and also proves to be the epitome of a dumb blonde and a talented comedienne.

As has been noted, the sight of the Messrs. Curtis and Lemmon teetering around on high heels wears thin awfully quickly, as does Mr. Curtis's vocal imitation of a noted male movie star. But both take to slapstick, double takes, and mugging as though they were charter members of the Keystone Kops. They give vigorous, top-flight performances that add greatly to wacky goings-on.

Some Like It Hot does cool off considerably now and again, but Mr. Wilder and his carefree clowns keep it crackling and funny most of the time.

—*A.W., March 30, 1959*

THE SORROW AND THE PITY

Directed by Marcel Ophuls; written (in French, with English subtitles) by André Harris and Mr. Ophuls; cinematographers, André Gazut and Jürgen Thieme; edited by Claude Vadja; released by Norddeutscher Rundfunk, Télévision Rencontre and Télévision Suisse Romande. Black and white. Running time: 265 minutes.

With: Georges Bidault, Emile Coulaudon, Jacques Duclos, Robert Anthony Eden, Alexis Grave, Marius Klein, Pierre Le Calvez, Elmar Michel, Denis Rake, Madame Solange, Roger Tounze, Marcel Verdier and Walter Warlimont (Themselves).

A documentary that runs four-and-a-half hours (not including an intermission) should tire even the hardiest history or movie buff but, aside from its possible anatomical effects, *Le Chagrin et la Pitié*, which was unreeled last night at the New York Film Festival, makes a surprisingly educational and fascinating experience despite its inordinate length. As a studiously dispassionate but incisive inquiry into what both lowly and leading French citizens felt and did during the German attack on France in World War II

and during the occupation, it soberly spotlights history on impressively human, not pedantic, levels.

It should be noted that it is largely the result of the work of Marcel Ophuls, the son of the late French director, Max Ophuls, and André Harris, both reporters for French government-sponsored TV who were dismissed after the strike and student riots in 1968. Their film was completed last year with the help of Swiss and German government television and it since has been seen in several Parisian theaters (but not on French TV) and bought for showing on Swiss, German, Dutch, Belgian, Hungarian, and Swedish TV screens.

The producers also use 1939-through-1945 French and German newsreel footage of, among others, Hitler and of Vichy's Pierre Laval and Marshal Henri-Philippe Pétain, as well as fairly recent interviews with such involved V.I.P.'s as Lord Avon (Anthony Eden), Pierre Mendès-France, and Jacques Duclos, leader of the Communist Party.

These serve as counterpoint to their discussion with members of the Resistance, victims of both Nazis and the French Liberation groups, Rightists, and middle-of-the-roaders to spotlight glaringly a somber chapter of history dimmed by the passage of a quarter of a century.

They have, in short, concentrated their investigations on the industrial city of Clermont-Ferrand as exemplary (it is implied) of what most Frenchmen and invaders did then and how they feel about it now. And, with the aid of English voice-overs, which literally translate the French and German dialogue, its points, implied and otherwise, are made naturally and convincingly.

This viewer was especially impressed by the honesty of Marcel Verdier, the local pharmacist (who wasn't quite certain he was a bourgeois); Louis and Alexis Grave, two ex-Maquis farmers who good-naturedly continue to hate the Nazis who sent them to a concentration camp; Mendès-France's low-keyed memories of escape from a Nazi jail in his youth to fight with the Free French; and Captain Helmuth Tausend's bland evaluation of his role as a garrison commander.

Some of the important personages do stick in memory, too, such as the witty, cynical, late commander of the Resistance, Emanuel de la Vigier; Anthony Eden; and Count René de Chambrun, who, in legal style, defends his father-in-law, Pierre Laval. But they suffer by comparison with the straightforward accounts of the likes of Emile Caubaudon, Clermont-Ferrand's Resistance chief; the Rightist Christian de la Maziere, who fought with an SS regiment of Frenchmen; and even with the aging, unbilled hairdresser who was jailed as a collaborator.

One must agree with Anthony Eden, who notes that it is not right for the English, who were not invaded, to judge people who were. But this lengthy, complex, but entirely lucid insight into the minds of the occupied and the occupiers does give one the ability to judge from the participants' own views. *Le Chagrin et la Pitié* filled the more than 1,000 seats of the Vivian Beaumont last night, which indicates, if obliquely, that this special "nonentertainment" film might have a wider audience than this special one.

—*A.W., October 11, 1971*

THE SOUND OF MUSIC

Produced and directed by Robert Wise; written by Ernest Lehman, based on the stage musical by Richard Rodgers, Oscar Hammerstein 2d, Howard Lindsay and Russell Crouse; cinematographer, Ted McCord; edited by William Reynolds; music by Mr. Rodgers with lyrics by Mr. Hammerstein; production designer, Boris Leven; released by Twentieth Century Fox. Running time: 174 minutes.

With: Julie Andrews (Maria), Christopher Plummer (Captain Von Trapp), Eleanor Parker (Baroness), Richard Haydn (Max Detweiler), Peggy Wood (Mother Abbess), Charmian Carr (Liesl), Heather Menzies (Louisa) and Nicolas Hammond (Friedrich).

The fact that *The Sound of Music* ran for three and a half years on Broadway, despite the perceptible weakness of its quaintly old-fashioned book, was plainly sufficient assurance for the producer-director Robert Wise to assume that what made it popular in the theater would make it equally popular on the screen. That was a cheerful abundance of kirche-küche-kinder sentiment and the generally melodic felicity of the Richard Rodgers–Oscar Hammerstein 2d musical score.

As a consequence, the great-big color movie Mr. Wise has made from it, and which was given a great-big gala opening at the Rivoli last night, comes close to being a careful duplication of the show as it was done on the stage, even down to its operetta pattern, which predates the cinema age.

To be sure, Mr. Wise has used his cameras to set a magnificently graphic scene in and around the actual city of Salzburg that lies nestled in the Austrian Alps. By means of a helicopter, he zooms over the snow-capped peaks and down into the green and ochre region, just as he zoomed down into New York's crowded streets in his memorable film of *West Side Story* (which was considerably different from this).

He has used the handsome Frohnburg Castle to represent the exterior of the home of the ample Von Trapp family, whose prettified story is told, and he has also used such colorful landmarks as Nonnberg Abbey, the Mirabell Gardens, and the Mozart Bridge.

The scene of the music festival at the climax is the famous Felsenreitschule or Rocky Riding School, with its heavy arched tunnels cut out of the precipitous mountainside. And, of course, he has soared to those Alpine meadows with their dizzying and breathtaking views on occasions when there's a particularly joyous and air-filling song to be sung.

Furthermore, he has Julie Andrews to play—and sing—the role of the postulant nun who leaves the abbey to try her hand at being governess to the seven children of the widowed Captain Von Trapp—and remains, after the standard digressions, to become their stepmother. And it is she who provides the most apparent and fetching innovation in the film.

Miss Andrews, with her air of radiant vigor, her appearance of plain-Jane wholesomeness, and her ability to make her dialogue as vivid and appealing as she makes her songs, brings a nice sort of Mary Poppins logic and authority to this role, which is always in peril of collapsing under its weight of romantic nonsense and sentiment.

Despite the hopeless pretense of reality with which she and the others have to contend, especially in the last phase, when the Von Trapps are supposed to be fleeing from the Nazis and their homeland, Miss Andrews treats the whole thing with the same air of serenely controlled self-confidence that she has when we first come upon her trilling the title song on a mountain top.

Does she sense that it is really silly to find a chorus of twittering nuns considering what's to be done about her in a bright musical-comedy song? Does she feel her first exchanges with the children of the cruelly domineering Von Trapp to be conversational gambits that could only take place in a play? And does she know (as we do) that the business with the captain and the wealthy baroness is right out of Victor Herbert operetta, circa 1910?

Of course she does. And she also seems to realize that the whole thing is being staged by Mr. Wise in a cosy-cum-corny fashion that even theater people know is old hat. But she goes at it happily and bravely. She even pulls the pack of children into her bed and drowns out the noise of crashing thunder with the optimistic "My Favorite Things" and marches them through the streets of Salzburg happily howling the juvenile "Do-Re-Mi."

Miss Andrews is nothing daunted. She plays a more saccharine nanny than Mary Poppins, but it doesn't get her goat.

Her associates cannot be so commended. The septet of blond and beaming youngsters who have to act like so many Shirley Temples and Freddie Bartholomews when they were young do as well as could be expected with their assortedly artificial roles, but the adults are fairly horrendous, especially Christopher Plummer as Captain Von Trapp.

Looking as handsome and phony as a store-window Alpine guide, Mr. Plummer acts the hard-jawed, stiff-backed fellow with equal artificiality. And when he puts his expressions and his gestures to somebody else's singing of the wistful "Eidelweiss" (which, incidentally, was the last song that the late Mr. Hammerstein wrote), it is just a bit too painfully mawkish for the simple sentiments of that nice song.

Richard Haydn is conventionally histrionic with his grimaces and his rolling r's as the comical impresario who tries to sign the singing Von Trapps, and Eleanor Parker is highly enameled and just as brittle as the baroness. Peggy Wood as the mother abbess beams benignly beneath her cowl, but she blessedly turns away from the camera when somebody with a much younger voice—maybe Marni Nixon—sings "Climb Every Mountain" for her.

Incidentally, the famous Miss Nixon, who provides Audrey Hepburn's singing voice in *My Fair Lady,* turns up in this picture as one of the covey of singing nuns, all of whom act with the familiar cheeriness and poker-faced innocence of nuns in films. Charmian Carr as the oldest daughter, who has a crush on an embryo Nazi (Daniel Truhitte), dances rather sweetly but that's all to the "Sixteen Going on Seventeen" song.

Mentionable, too, is a pleasant little Bil and Cora Baird puppet show done to "The Lonely Goatherd," which was used for an Alpine ballet on the stage.

Even though a couple of new songs have been added (both forgettable), Mr. Wise seems to run out of songs toward the end of the picture and repeat two or three of the more familiar ones. But the same must be said of *The Sound of Music.* It repeats, in style—and in theme.

However, its sentiments are abundant. Business-wise, Mr. Wise is no fool.

—*B.C., March 3, 1965*

SOUND PACIFIC

SOUTH PACIFIC

Directed by Joshua Logan; written by Paul Osborn, based on the musical by Oscar Hammerstein 2d, Richard Rodgers and Mr. Logan, from the book *Tales of the South Pacific* by James A. Michener; cinematographer, Leon Shamroy; edited by Robert Simpson; music by Mr. Hammerstein and Mr. Rodgers; art designers, Lyle Wheeler and John DeCuir; produced by Buddy Adler; released by Twentieth Century Fox. Running time: 171 minutes.

With: Rossano Brazzi (Emile de Becque), Mitzi Gaynor (Nellie Forbush), John Kerr (Lieutenant Cable), Ray Walston (Luther Billis), Juanita Hall (Bloody Mary), France Nuyen (Liat), Russ Brown (Captain Brackett), Jack Mullaney (Professor), Ken Clark (Stewpot), Floyd Simmons (Harbison), Candace Lee (Nagana) and Warren Hsieh (Jerome).

Everyone who wished that *South Pacific* might be made into a large, luxurious film, glowing with literal scenic detail of lush green islands in blue tropical seas, bursting with a grand romantic story and brimming with stereophonic songs, need have no further anxiety. His wish has been fulfilled.

The screen version of the famous stage show, which

Twentieth Century Fox has produced and which opened last night at the Criterion with a benefit showing for the Police Athletic League, is a tremendously big picture. It runs for close to three hours and fills a huge arcing panel that goes with its projection process, Todd-AO.

It gives out with most of the enchantments of the Richard Rodgers–Oscar Hammerstein 2d musical. It is performed by a cast almost as winning as the one that played it on Broadway. And what it lacks in the more subtle values the show had upon the stage is balanced by frank spectacular features that will probably fascinate folks who go to films.

Most obvious and striking of these features is a photographic method used by Leon Shamroy, cameraman, that bathes in changing rainbow hues most of the scenes and settings in which the musical numbers are sung.

That is to say, when the soundtrack cues the performers into songs (which, incidentally, are sung for the most part by people other than those you see on the screen), waves of unnatural mists and colors blow across the scene, providing a sort of polychromatic aura for the various romantic words and melodies.

It is a theatrical concept and a plainly theatrical trick that is probably aimed to help the audience into the frankly deeper musical moods. And it does, in at least one instance. In the rendering of the haunting "Bali Ha'i," which comes along early in the picture and sets the tone for amorous magic ahead, the filtering of green and purple colors upon the natural beachfront scene brings in that unreal island off there in the distance with appropriate awe and mystery.

But the trick does become very obvious and stagy with some of the later songs, and quite inconsistent with the usual striking naturalness and beauty of the scenes. For instance, it is most disconcerting when Mitzi Gaynor and Rossano Brazzi in the roles of the Navy nurse Nellie Forbush and the French planter Emile de Becque drift into the lovely "Some Enchanted Evening" on a terrace facing a genuine, gorgeous view and the whole scene is slowly socked-in with a golden-yellow fog.

There are two or three other stagy features, such as the revels of natives on Bali Ha'i and the behavior of the "dealer," Luther Billis, when he enacts a "diversionary tactic" (not in the show), that tend to make the film version look less authentic than did the stage

musical. And Joshua Logan's direction, in the early part especially, strangely drags. The picture does not have the tempo and the bounce it should have in some scenes.

But let's not be too analytic, for it does have, by and large, a wonderful surge of charm and gusto that just keeps coming for hours and hours. While the love stories do not link too neatly—that is, the love story of the young lieutenant and the native girl and that of the Navy nurse and the French planter—each is touching and delightful in its way. And those Seabees down on the beach with Billis make an explosively raucous and comical Greek chorus.

Miss Gaynor is excellent as Nellie, Mr. Brazzi is handsome as de Becque, John Kerr wins the heart as the young lieutenant, and France Nuyen is a flowerlike thing as the native girl. Ray Walston makes a dandy good Billis and Juanita Hall happily returns as the realist, Bloody Mary. Jack Mullaney and Ken Clark are raffish gobs.

One good song, "My Girl Back Home," is added to the beautiful but loudly played score, and the script by Paul Osborn is faithful, though it does shuffle things around a lot. This and Mr. Logan's direction make *South Pacific* large, long, and loose on the screen.

—*B.C., March 20, 1958*

SPARTACUS

Directed by Stanley Kubrick; written by Dalton Trumbo, based on the novel by Howard Fast; cinematographers, Russell Metty and Clifford Stine; edited by Robert Lawrence, Robert Schulte and Fred Chulack; music by Alex North and Joseph Gershenson; production designer, Alexander Golitzen; produced by Edward Lewis; released by Universal Pictures. Running time: 196 minutes.

With: Kirk Douglas (Spartacus), Laurence Olivier (Crassus), Jean Simmons (Varinia), Charles Laughton (Gracchus), Peter Ustinov (Batistus), John Gavin (Caesar), Tony Curtis (Antoninus), Nina Foch (Helena) and Herbert Lom (Tigranes).

Every American schoolboy—at least, every American boy who went to school back in the days when it was fashionable to learn and recite heroic

931

verse—must have some recollection of the noble and flowery speech of "Spartacus to the Gladiators" (see Shoemaker's Best Selections, No. 1).

It rang with patriotic fervor ("Oh, Rome! Rome! thou hast been a tender nurse to me"). It spouted bloody tragedy ("Today I killed a man in the arena, and when I broke his helmet-clasps, behold! he was my friend"). And it happened—though this was seldom noticed—to be full of historical inaccuracies.

In a sense, the new motion picture, *Spartacus,* which Kirk Douglas's Bryna company has produced (in association with Universal-International) and which opened last night at the DeMille, is a modern-day cinematized-expansion of that lush and perfervid schoolboy's speech. For it is bursting with patriotic fervor, bloody tragedy, a lot of romantic fiddle-faddle, and historical inaccuracy. Also, it is pitched about to the level of a lusty schoolboy's taste.

There was a bit of amused speculation, when it was announced that Mr. Douglas was going to make a film about the Roman ex-slave, Spartacus, based on a novel by Howard Fast. The subject was obviously fitting for a spectacle-epic type of film, but it was also full of temptations to romanticize and elaborate. One could not help but remember what Mr. Douglas did in his over-romanticized *The Vikings* to the heroic legends of the Norse.

Well, he has not disappointed those who suspected he might let indiscretion be the better part of the valor displayed in this three-hour costume film—and this despite the fact that he surrounded himself in the title role with an elite cast (Jean Simmons, Laurence Olivier, Charles Laughton, and Peter Ustinov), got the aggressive Dalton Trumbo to write him a freedom-shouting script, and hired the very promising Stanley Kubrick (American "new wave") to direct.

His *Spartacus* is still heroic humbug—a vast, panoramic display of synthetic Rome and Romans, slaves and patricians, men and maids, at the time of the great slave rebellion in the first century B.C.; a grand show of gladiatorial combats and a beautiful big battle between the slaves under Mr. Douglas and the Roman legions under Mr. Olivier; a three-way stretch of romantic imagination in which the patrician, Mr. Olivier, vies with the slave leader, Mr. Douglas, for the affection of an emancipated slave girl, Miss Simmons; and an endless amount of simulation of political rivalry in Rome, in which the senators and generals are more confusing and less amusing than those in Washington.

It is a spotty, uneven drama in which the entire opening phase representing the basic-training program in a gladiatorial school is lively, exciting, and expressive, no matter how true to history it is, and the middle phase is pretentious and tedious, because it is concerned with the dull strife of politics.

Then comes a handsome, eye-filling reenactment of a battle between the slaves and the Roman legions, which matches the Battle of Agincourt in *Henry V.* (It has thousands of extras, hundreds of horses, shot on the rolling hills of Spain.) And it slides off into an anticlimax, wherein a great deal more is made of Miss Simmons's postwar predicament than of the crucifixion of 6,000 captive slaves.

Apparently, too many people, too many cooks had their ladles in this stew, and it comes out a romantic mishmash of a strange episode in history. The performances are equally uneven. Mr. Douglas sets his blunt, horse-opera style against the toga-clad precision of Mr. Laughton and the Roman-nosed gentility of Mr. Olivier. Tony Curtis as a former slave-boy minstrel contrasts in theatricality with the easy, accomplished clowning of a Romanized Mr. Ustinov.

Miss Simmons makes a very attractive slave girl—from Britannia, she explains, which somewhat accounts for her polish and her accent, obviously. And John Ireland, John Gavin, John Dall, Nina Foch, and Woody Strode make assorted American-looking gladiators, Roman senators, fancy ladies, and such.

The color is conspicuous, and the music score of Alex North is good and loud.

—B.C., October 7, 1960

SPELLBOUND

Directed by Alfred Hitchcock; written by Ben Hecht and Angus MacPhail, based on the novel *The House of Dr. Edwardes* by Francis Beeding; cinematographers, George Barnes and Rex Wimpy; edited by William Ziegler and Hal C. Kern; music by Miklos Rozsa; production designer, James Basevi; produced by David O. Selznick; released by United Artists. Black and white. Running time: 111 minutes.

With: Ingrid Bergman (Dr. Constance Peterson). Gregory Peck (J. B.). Jean Acker (Matron). Donald Curtis (Harry). Rhonda Fleming (Miss Carmichael). John Emery (Dr. Fleurot). Leo G. Carroll (Dr. Murchison). Norman Lloyd (Garmes) and Michael Chekhov (Dr. Alex Brutov).

This writer has had little traffic with practitioners of psychiatry or with the twilight abstractions of their science, so we are not in a position to say whether Ingrid Bergman, who plays one in her latest film, *Spellbound*, is typical of such professionals or whether the methods she employs would yield results. But this we can say with due authority: if all psychiatrists are as charming as she—and if their attentions to all their patients are as fruitful as hers are to Gregory Peck, who plays a victim of amnesia in this fine film which came to the Astor yesterday—then psychiatry deserves such popularity as this picture most certainly will enjoy.

For Miss Bergman and her brand of treatment, so beautifully demonstrated here, is a guaranteed cure for what ails you, just as much as it is for Mr. Peck. It consists of her winning personality, softly but insistently suffused through a story of deep emotional content; of her ardent sincerity, her lustrous looks, and her easy ability to toss off glibly a line of talk upon which most girls would choke.

In other words, lovely Miss Bergman is both the doctor and prescription in this film. She is the single stimulation of dramatic logic and audience belief. For the fact is the story of *Spellbound* is a rather obvious and often-told tale. And it depends, despite its truly expert telling, upon the illusion of the lady in the leading role.

It is the story of a female psychiatrist who falls suddenly and desperately in love with a man upon whom the dark suspicion of murder is relentlessly cast. All of the circumstantial evidence indicates that he has taken the dead man's place and is trying to assume his position—that is, until he prudently flees. But the lady, with full and touching confidence in the intuitive rightness of her love, is convinced that her adored one is most truly a victim of amnesia. And so she follows him to his place in hiding, begins the bold attempt to unlock his mind, and, always two jumps ahead of detectives, finally delves the gnawing secret of his past.

This story, we say, has relation to all the faith-healing films ever made, but the manner and quality of its telling is extraordinarily fine. The script, which was based on the novel of Francis Beeding, *The House of Dr. Edwardes,* was prepared by Ben Hecht and the director was Alfred Hitchcock, the old master of dramatic suspense. So the firm texture of the narration, the flow of continuity and dialogue, the shock of the unexpected, the scope of image—all are happily here.

But, in this particular instance, Mr. Hecht and Mr. Hitchcock have done more. They have fashioned a moving love story with the elements of melodramatic use. More than a literal "chase" takes place here—more than a run from the police. A "chase" of even more suspenseful moment is made through the mind of a man. And in this strange and indeterminate area the pursuer—and, partially, the pursued—is the girl with whom the victim is mutually in love. Mr. Hitchcock has used some startling images to symbolize the content of dreams—images designed by Salvador Dali. But his real success is in creating the illusion of love.

Miss Bergman, as we say, is his chief asset in accomplishing the sincerity of this film, but Mr. Peck is also a large contributor. His performance, restrained and refined, is precisely the proper counter to Miss Bergman's exquisite role. Michael Chekhov is likewise responsible for some of the excellent humor in this film, playing an elderly psychiatrist and an accomplice in Miss Bergman's mental "chase." Leo G. Carroll, Wallace Ford, and John Emery contribute excellent smaller roles.

Not to be speechless about it, David O. Selznick has a rare film in *Spellbound*.

—*B.C., November 2, 1945*

THE SPIRAL STAIRCASE

Directed by Robert Siodmak; written by Mel Dinelli, based on the novel *Some Must Watch* by Ethel Lina White; cinematographer. Nicholas Musuraca; edited by Harry Marker and Harry Gerstad; music by Roy Webb; art designers. Albert S. D'Agostino and Jack Okey; produced by Dore Schary; released by RKO Radio Pictures. Black and white. Running time: 83 minutes.

With: Dorothy McGuire (Helen Capel). George Brent (Professor Warren). Ethel Barrymore (Mrs.

Warren). Kent Smith (Dr. Parry). Rhonda Fleming (Blanche). Gordon Oliver (Steve Warren). Elsa Lanchester (Mrs. Oates). Sara Allgood (Nurse Barker). Rhys Williams (Mr. Oates) and James Bell (Constable).

Operating on the time-tested theory that moviegoers are seldom more satisfied than when a film causes them to experience cold chills, RKO Radio yesterday treated audiences at the Palace to a creepy melodrama called *The Spiral Staircase*. This is a shocker, plain and simple, and whatever pretentions it has to psychological drama may be considered merely as a concession to a currently popular fancy. It is quite evident by the technique director Robert Siodmak has employed to develop and sustain suspense—brooding photography and ominously suggestive settings—that he is at no time striving for narrative subtlety.

How could he have been when he has drawn upon practically every established device known to produce goose pimples? However, the only thing which really matters is that Mr. Siodmak has used the rumble and cracking of thunder, the flickering candlelight, the creaking door, and the gusts of wind from out of nowhere to startling advantage. For even though you are conscious that the tension is being built by obvious trickery, the effect is nonetheless telling. That Mr. Siodmak and his players, notably Dorothy McGuire, had a packed early-morning house under their spell most of the time was evident by the frequent spasms of nervous giggling and the audible, breathless sighs.

As a mute serving-girl in a sinister household, where family hatreds are deep and searing, Miss McGuire gives a remarkably lucid performance in pantomime. Her characterization of one who senses a dread shadow hovering over her but is incapable of communicating her fears, is restrained and effectively pathetic. In this day of much talk on the screen few actresses would dare to undertake a role which only permitted six words of speech. Miss McGuire is to be heartily commended for her adventurousness and the high degree of resourcefulness with which she has tackled the demanding and little used art of pantomime.

In relating this arresting tale about a psychopathic killer who terrorizes a New England town, circa 1906, director Siodmak has literally put the evil eye on the victims. For he has used his camera to give the specta-tor a close-up of the murderer's baleful eyes as they strike terror into his helpless victims, who, by the way, all are pretty, young girls. Whether *The Spiral Staircase* is a faithful translation of Ethel Lina White's novel *Some Must Watch* we are not in a position to say, but we do know that the film is likely to scare the daylights out of most of its audiences.

Ethel Barrymore, playing the matriarch of the Warren family, is always interesting even though her role as a cantankerous invalid is hardly deserving of her vast talents. Sara Allgood, George Brent, Rhys Williams, Gordon Oliver, Elsa Lanchester, and Kent Smith all do well by their respective characters.

—*T.M.P., February 7, 1946*

SPIRITED AWAY

Written and directed by Hayao Miyazaki: United States director. Kirk Wise: English language adaptation by Cindy Davis Hewitt and Donald H. Hewitt: music by Joe Hisaishi: produced by Toshio Suzuki (Japan) and Donald W. Ernst (United States): released by Walt Disney Studios. Running time: 125 minutes.

With the voices of: Daveigh Chase (Chihiro). Suzanne Pleshette (Yubaba, Zeniba). Jason Marsden (Haku). Susan Egan (Lin). David Ogden Stiers (Kamaji). Lauren Holly (Chihiro's Mother). Michael Chiklis (Chihiro's Father) and John Ratzenberger (Assistant Manager).

The title *Spirited Away* could refer to what Disney has done on a corporate level to the revered Japanese animation director Hayao Miyazaki's epic and marvelous new anime fantasy. The picture is being promoted as Disney's *Spirited Away,* although seeing just ten minutes of this English version of a hugely popular Japanese film will quickly disabuse any discerning viewer of the notion that it is a Disney creation. The towering, lost dreaminess at the heart of the film is an unmistakable obsession of this director. Actually, rather than Disney's *Spirited Away,* the movie could better be considered Mr. Miyazaki's *Through the Looking Glass*.

The picture's theme is dislocation. Chihiro (voice of Daveigh Chase), moving with her parents to a new neighborhood, is pouty about leaving her old friends and school behind. Her father's attempt to take a shortcut to their new town leads the family to a settlement that looks like what he calls an abandoned theme park: acres of beautifully designed kiosks, buildings, and statues.

Easily frightened and quick to voice her unhappiness, Chihiro wanders off while her parents gorge on a lunch from an unattended food stand. She encounters an apparition who warns her that she and her family have to leave before the sun goes down. But when she runs back to alert her mother and father, they've been turned into hogs, bursting out of their casual Friday garb and gobbling up everything before them.

Mr. Miyazaki's specialty is taking a primal wish of kids, transporting them to a fantasyland and then marooning them there. No one else conjures the phantasmagoric and shifting morality of dreams—that fascinating and frightening aspect of having something that seems to represent good become evil—in the way this master Japanese animator does.

For Chihiro each strange creature has the physical—and inevitably psychological—threat of a shark. Just because we know that they don't have a mean bone in their bodies doesn't make them seem any less dangerous to her. She doesn't know whom or what to trust. The initially friendly Haku, a boy with magical powers (Jason Marsden), advises Chihiro on navigating the new world. He helps her get a job at a bathhouse both staffed and frequented by strange creatures, including a bubbling, mountainous pile of foul-smelling liquid called the Stink God. But Haku becomes brusque, and Chihiro is warned that he's a sneak and cannot be trusted.

Keep in mind that much of the contradictory truth comes from Yubaba (Suzanne Pleshette), the witchy bathhouse owner whose greed is surpassed in size only by her head. Her grating voice alone could probably peel the filth from the Stink God. Haku's unwarranted shifts of personality reflect what distinguishes Mr. Miyazaki from Disney, or any other American animator. His movies are as much about moodiness as mood, and the prospect of animated figures' not being what they seem—either spiritually or physically—heightens the tension. *Spirited Away,* which opens nationwide today, deepens Chihiro's uncertainty by not defining the creatures that inhabit this spirit world in simple good-guy bad-guy terms, making them capricious and unintentionally treacherous.

Using his standard threat of the loss of self is a way that Mr. Miyazaki brings a sense of peril to Chihiro. During her adventures a little piece of Chihiro is chipped away at every turn. She's renamed by Yubaba and learns later that if she doesn't hide her real name away she'll lose her identity forever. And her whininess gradually disappears as she learns responsibility.

No big point is made of it, though fans of Mr. Miyazaki's "Princess Mononoke," which was promoted on a much larger scale, may be let down by the minor-chord fluidity of this film. *Spirited Away* is a marriage between the power of *Mononoke* and the lively pop-pop-pop of his film *My Friend Totoro.*

These storytelling subtleties were absorbed by John Lasseter of Pixar—the man behind the *Toy Story* movies—who also served as executive producer for this English-dubbed version. Undoubtedly something was lost in the translation; watching the parade of wild things flutter, stomp and crawl though the bathhouse will make you wonder what each represents in Japanese mythology. (At one point it's as if every item in the Japanese Sanrio line of toys has come to life.) The cultural weight that the picture bears partly explains why this was the biggest hit ever in Japan, outpacing *Titanic.*

The beauty of the animation, a skillful blend of handpainted foreground and well-placed computer background, works to generate the storytelling. It makes all the characters distinct in appearance and keeps them from looking as if they're drifting a couple of inches above the ground.

What the title really applies to is the director himself. After his struggle to get the career-capping "Mononoke" to the screen, Mr. Miyazaki retired but is said to have been sparked back to the drawing board after meeting a girl who inspired Chihiro. This child should accompany the director to Los Angeles for the Oscar nomination *Spirited Away* will probably receive. The world deserves a glimpse at the slacker-sprite behind so much magic.

—E.M., September 20, 2002

SPLENDOR IN THE GRASS

Produced and directed by Elia Kazan: written by William Inge: cinematographer. Boris Kaufman: edited by Gene Milford: music by David Amram:

art designer, Richard Sylbert; released by Warner Brothers. Running time: 124 minutes.

With: Natalie Wood (Wilma Dean Loomis), Warren Beatty (Bud Stamper), Pat Hingle (Ace Stamper), Audrey Christie (Mrs. Loomis), Zohra Lampert (Angelina), Fred Stewart (Del Loomis), Joanna Roos (Mrs. Stamper) and Jan Norris (Juanita Howard).

Sex and parental domineering again confound two romantic high-school youngsters in Elia Kazan's and William Inge's new film, *Splendor in the Grass*, which opened at the Victoria and the Trans-Lux Fifty-second Street yesterday.

But where these conventional homely hazards to the tranquility and freedom of youth have been frequently calculated to an obsessive degree in previous films, they are put rather fairly in focus and dramatic rationality in this. They are made to appear congenital forces that misshape the lives of two nice kids, played with amazing definition by Warren Beatty and Natalie Wood.

This is not to suggest that the hazards are hidden within a euphemistic haze or that the social and moral implications of their presence are tactfully glazed. Mr. Inge has written and Mr. Kazan has hurled upon the screen a frank and ferocious social drama that makes the eyes pop and the modest cheek burn.

Petting is not simply petting in this embarrassingly intimate film. It is wrestling and chewing and punching that end with clothes torn and participants spent. And boozing is not simply boozing with adults, and also with kids. It is swilling and reeling and hollering and getting disgustingly sick.

But where these might sound exaggerations and seem sensationalisms in other films, they are reasonable, plausible, convincing, and incisively significant here. For the turmoil of sex-starving youngsters is set within the socially isolated frame of a Kansas town in the late 1920's—a town raw, rich, and redolent with oil, with the arrogance of sweaty money grubbers and the platitudes of corn-belt puritans. The torment of two late-adolescents, yearning yet not daring to love, is played against the harsh backdrop of cheapness, obtuseness, and hypocrisy.

There are times when the heat gets too oppressive, when Mr. Kazan lays the purple on too thick, when you get a sneaking suspicion he is playing to the mob for effect. He has made a depraved flapper sister of the boy such an absolute mess that you cringe when she's flaming like a bonfire and are relieved when she disappears. Barbara Loden's performance is all fireworks and whirling razor blades.

But the milieu is generally terrific—right on the beam and down Main Street, ugly and vulgar and oppressive, comical at times, and sad. Pat Hingle gives a bruising performance as the oil-wealthy father of the boy, pushing and pounding and preaching, knocking the heart out of the lad. Audrey Christie is relentlessly engulfing as the sticky-sweet mother of the girl, and Fred Stewart, Joanna Roos, and John McGovern are excellent in other adult roles.

In the end, however, the authority and eloquence of the theme emerge in the honest, sensitive acting of Mr. Beatty and Miss Wood. The former, a surprising newcomer, shapes an amiable, decent, sturdy lad whose emotional exhaustion and defeat are the deep pathos in the film. Except that he talks like Marlon Brando and has some small mannerisms of James Dean, Mr. Beatty is a striking individual. He can purge himself, if he will.

And Miss Wood has a beauty and radiance that carry her through a role of violent passions and depressions with unsullied purity and strength. There is poetry in her performance, and her eyes in the final scene bespeak the moral significance and emotional fulfillment of this film.

The production is in excellent color and is scenically superb.

—*B.C., October 11, 1961*

STAGE DOOR

Directed by Gregory La Cava; written by Morrie Ryskind, Anthony Veiller and Mr. La Cava, based on the play by Edna Ferber and George S. Kaufman; cinematographer, Robert de Grasse; edited by William Hamilton; music by Roy Webb; art designers, Van Nest Polglase and Carroll Clark; produced by Pandro S. Berman; released by RKO Radio Pictures. Black and white. Running time: 92 minutes.

With: Katharine Hepburn (Terry Randall), Ginger Rogers (Jean Maitland), Adolphe Menjou

(Anthony Powell), Gail Patrick (Linda Shaw), Constance Collier (Catherine Luther), Andrea Leeds (Kaye Hamilton), Samuel S. Hinds (Henry Sims), Lucille Ball (Judy Canfield), Eve Arden (Eve) and Ann Miller (Annie).

The RKO-Radio version of *Stage Door,* which was opened at the Music Hall yesterday, is not merely a brilliant picture (although that should be enough), but happens as well to be a magnificently devastating reply on Hollywood's behalf to all the catty little remarks that George Kaufman and Edna Ferber had made about it in their play.

Those impolite playwrights, you remember, had filled the mouths of the aspirant Bernhardts of their Footlights Club with gall and wormwood whenever the Hollywood topic arose, which was fairly constantly. It was, we were told, a factory and a graveyard of art, a place of complete untalent and all-pervading witlessness, of sables for the body and starvation for the soul, etc.—all very wittily expressed and neatly packaged (through the courtesy of Metro-Goldwyn-Mayer, which had backed the show).

For a factory and a graveyard and other unpleasant institutions, Hollywood has done some rather incredible things with the Kaufman-Ferber contribution, not the least of them being the transformation of a fragile piece of theatrical wishful-willing into a far more soundly contrived comedy drama. Scriptwriters Morrie Ryskind and Anthony Veiller have taken the play's name, its setting, and part of its theme and have built a whole new structure which is wittier than the original, more dramatic than the original, more meaningful than the original, more cogent than the original.

Where the team of K & F (who really should have been ashamed) drew Hollywood as the leering man with the waxed black mustache, RKO has countered by showing that the villain of all serious acting fledglings is the Broadway producer who is too busy to look and listen. But with this premise, which was the whole sum of the stage's *Stage Door,* the film edition has only begun its narrative. Back it goes to the Footlights Club where the stagestruck maidens nurse their disappointments and sharpen their claws (on whatever victim is handy) and gossip betimes over the triangular sham battle being fought by Ginger Rogers, Katharine Hepburn, and Gail Patrick over and around Adolphe Menjou.

Miss Hepburn (to put this outburst into some sort of order) is the wealthy girl with stage notions and a serious outlook. Miss Rogers is the more realistic type. Miss Patrick has decided to play her producers off-stage. Mr. Menjou is the rake who has his better side. Miss Andrea Leeds, the real discovery of the picture, is the tortured young woman who has waited a year for the One Role. There are the other young ladies of the ensemble, and a cleverly individualized bevy they are, whose several destinies tragically or comically counterpoint those of the primary four.

The twists and turns of the narrative are sensibly motivated, the direction of Gregory La Cava has given it zest and pace and photographic eloquence, and the performances are amazingly good—considering that Mr. Kaufman's Hollywood is just a canning factory. Miss Hepburn and Miss Rogers, in particular, seemed to be acting so far above their usual heads that, frankly, we hardly recognized them. A round of curtain calls would demand a bow and smile from Constance Collier, Lucille Ball, Franklin Pangborn, Eve Arden, Ann Miller, Margaret Early, and Phyllis Kennedy, among the many others. And now, do we hear a retraction from Mr. Kaufman?

—*F.S.N., October 8, 1937*

STAGECOACH

Directed by John Ford; written by Dudley Nichols, based on the short story "Stage to Lordsburg" by Ernest Haycox; cinematographer, Bert Glennon; edited by Dorothy Spencer, Otho Lovering and Walter Reynolds; music by Richard Hageman, W. Franck Harling, Leo Shuken and John Leipold; art designer, Alexander Toluboff; produced by Walter Wanger; released by United Artists. Black and white. Running time: 97 minutes.

With: Claire Trevor (Dallas), John Wayne (Ringo Kid), Andy Devine (Buck), John Carradine (Hatfield), Thomas Mitchell (Doc Boone), Louise Platt (Lucy Mallory), George Bancroft (Curly Wilcox), Tim Holt (Lieutenant Blanchard), Berton Churchill (Gatewood) and Donald Meek (Peacock).

In one superbly expansive gesture, which we (and the Music Hall) can call *Stagecoach,* John Ford has swept aside ten years of artifice and talkie compromise and has made a motion picture that sings a song of camera. It moves, and how beautifully it moves, across the plains of Arizona, skirting the sky-reaching mesas of Monument Valley, beneath the piled-up cloud banks which every photographer dreams about, and through all the old-fashioned, but never really outdated, periods of prairie travel in the scalp-raising seventies, when Geronimo's Apaches were on the warpath. Here, in a sentence, is a movie of the grand old school, a genuine rib-thumper, and a beautiful sight to see.

Mr. Ford is not one of your subtle directors, suspending sequences on the wink of an eye or the precisely calculated gleam of a candle in a mirror. He prefers the broadest canvas, the brightest colors, the widest brush, and the boldest possible strokes. He hews to the straight narrative line with the well-reasoned confidence of a man who has seen that narrative succeed before. He takes no shadings from his characters: either they play it straight or they don't play at all. He likes his language simple and he doesn't want too much of it. When his Redskins bite the dust, he expects to hear the thud and see the dirt spurt up. Above all, he likes to have things happen out in the open, where his camera can keep them in view.

He has had his way in *Stagecoach* with Walter Wanger's benison, the writing assistance of Dudley Nichols, and the complete cooperation of a cast which had the sense to appreciate the protection of being stereotyped. You should know, almost without being told, the station in life (and in frontier melodrama) of the eight passengers on the Overland stage from Tonto to Lordsburg.

To save time, though, here they are: "Doc" Boone, a tipsy man of medicine; Major Hatfield, professional gambler, once a Southern gentleman and a gentleman still; Dallas, a lady of such transparently dubious virtue that she was leaving Tonto by popular request; Mrs. Mallory, who, considering her condition, had every reason to be hastening to her army husband's side; Mr. Gatewood, an absconding banker and windbag; Mr. Peacock, a small and timid whiskey salesman destined by Bacchus to be Doc Boone's traveling companion; Sheriff Wilcox; and his prisoner, the Ringo Kid. The driver, according to the rules, had to be Slim Summerville or Andy Devine; Mr. Devine got the call.

So onward rolls the stage, nobly sped by its six stout-hearted bays, and out there, somewhere behind the buttes and crags, Geronimo is lurking with his savage band, the United States Cavalry is biding its time to charge to the rescue, and the Ringo Kid is impatiently awaiting his cue to stalk down the frontier-town street and blast it out with the three Plummer boys. But foreknowledge doesn't cheat Mr. Ford of his thrills. His attitude, if it spoke its mind, would be: "All right, you know what's coming, but have you ever seen it done like this?" And once you've swallowed your heart again, you'll have to say: "No, sir! Not like this!"

His players have taken easily to their chores, all the way down the list from Claire Trevor's Dallas to Tom Tyler's Hank Plummer. But the cutest coach-rider in the wagon, to our mind, was little Donald Meek as Mr. Peacock, the whiskey-drummer. That, of course, is not meant as a slight to Thomas Mitchell as the toping Dr. Boone, to Louise Platt as the wan Mrs. Mallory, George Bancroft as the sheriff, or John Wayne as the Ringo Kid. They've all done nobly by a noble horse opera, but none so nobly as its director. This is one stagecoach that's powered by a Ford.

—F.S.N., *March 3, 1939*

STARWAY TO HEAVEN

Written, produced and directed by Michael Powell and Emeric Pressburger; cinematographer, Jack Cardiff; edited by Reginald Mills; music by Allan Gray; production designer, Alfred Junge; released by Universal International Pictures. Running time: 104 minutes;

With: David Niven (Peter Carter), Kim Hunter (June), Roger Livesey (Doctor Reeves), Robert Coote (Bob), Marius Goring (Conductor 71), Raymond Massey (Abraham Farlan), Kathleen Byron (An Angel) and Richard Attenborough (English Pilot).

Had you harked you would have heard the herald angels singing an appropriate paean of joy over a wonderful new British picture, *Stairway to Heaven*, which came to the Park Avenue Theatre yesterday. And if you will listen now to this reviewer you will hear that the delicate charm, the adult humor, and visual virtuosity of this Michael Powell—Emeric

Pressburger film render it indisputably the best of a batch of Christmas shows.

If you wished to be literal about it you might call it romantic fantasy with psychological tie-ins. But literally is not the way to take this deliciously sophisticated frolic in imagination's realm. For this is a fluid contemplation of a man's odd experiences in two worlds, one the world of the living and the other the world of his fantasies—which, in this particular instance, happens to be the great beyond. And the fact that the foreword advises, "any resemblance to any other worlds, known or unknown, is purely coincidental," is a cue to the nature and the mood.

We've no time for lengthy explanations—other than to remark that, by all the laws of probabilities, Squadron Leader Peter Carter should have been killed when he leapt from a burning bomber without a parachute over the Channel on May 2, 1945. And that is the natural assumption which revolves in the back of his injured mind. But, still alive after a freakish salvation and in love with a thoroughly mortal American Wac, he resists the hallucinatory "messenger" who keeps summoning him to the beyond. Indeed, he resists so strongly—in his disordered mind, that is—that he conceives an illusory "trial" in heaven in which his appeal to remain on earth is heard before a highly heterogeneous tribunal. And through this court (and by a brain operation), he is spared.

That gives you a slight indication of the substance and flavor of this film—and we haven't space at this writing to give you any more, except to say that the wit and agility of the producers, who also wrote and directed the job, is given range through the picture in countless delightful ways: in the use, for instance, of Technicolor to photograph the earthly scenes and sepia in which to vision the hygienic regions of the Beyond (so that the heavenly "messenger," descending, is prompted to remark, "Ah, how one is starved for Technicolor up there!").

We haven't space to credit the literate wit of the heavenly "trial" in which the right of an English flier to marry an American girl is discussed, with all the subtle ruminations of a cultivated English mind that it connotes, or the fine cinematic inventiveness and visual "touches" that sparkle throughout, notably in the exciting production designs of Alfred Junge.

Nor have we the space to say more than that David Niven is sensitive and real as the flier chap; that Roger Livesey is magnificent as his physician (and later advocate in the Beyond); that Kim Hunter is most appealing as his American sweetheart; and that many more do extremely well, including Raymond Massey, who plays the lawyer for the Court of Records at the heavenly "trial." (Mr. Massey represents the spirit of the first Boston patriot killed in the Revolutionary War.)

But we'll have much more to say later, when we've got Christmas out of our hair. Till then, take this recommendation: see *Stairway to Heaven*. It's a delight!
—B.C., December 26, 1946

STALAG 17

Produced and directed by Billy Wilder; written by Mr. Wilder and Edwin Blum, based on the play by Donald Bevan and Edmund Trzcinski; cinematographer, Ernest Laszlo; edited by Doane Harrison and George Tomasini; music by Franz Waxman; art designers, Hal Pereira and Franz Bachelin; released by Paramount Pictures. Black and white. Running time: 120 minutes.

With: William Holden (Sefton), Don Taylor (Lieutenant Dunbar), Otto Preminger (Oberst Von Scherbach), Robert Strauss (Stosh "Animal"), Harvey Lembeck (Harry), Richard Erdman (Hoffy), Peter Graves (Price), Neville Brand (Duke), Sig Ruman (Schulz), Michael Moore (Manfredi), Peter Baldwin (Johnson), Robinson Stone (Joey), Robert Shawley (Blondie), William Pierson (Marko) and Gil Stratton Jr. (Cookie)

A crackerjack movie entertainment has been made from *Stalag 17*, the play by Donald Bevan and Edmund Trzcinski that scored on Broadway two years ago. Produced and directed by Billy Wilder for the greater glory of Paramount and played by an all-male cast of experts, sparked by William Holden, Harvey Lembeck, and Robert Strauss, this film version of the comedy-drama of American airmen in a German prison camp becomes a humorous, suspenseful, disturbing, and rousing pastime on the Astor's screen.

Just like the play before it—which is faithfully followed, by the way—this film shows much more than the rompings of playful fellows that the ads might let you believe. Romping there is aplenty among the bored and restless prisoners battened down in the shabby and cluttered bunkhouse of Barrack 4 in Stalag 17. And the intensity of these rompings, which represent the normal spirits and grim despairs of healthy young men without incentives and without feminine companions, gives vitality to the film.

But the taut fascination of the offering is not in the comedy and the japes; it is in the unending conflicts among a campful of volatile men. And these conflicts are not confined only to the clashes between prisoners and guards; they extend with particular virulence within the group of supposed countrymen and friends.

As in the play, the tension resides in the knowledge that there is a "stool pigeon" doing his deadly mischief among the prisoners in Barrack 4—a "stoolie" who gives the fatal signal on a valiant endeavor to escape and slips to the guards damaging evidence against a new arrival in the camp. Suspected at first is one fellow who is a shrewd, calculating type—a cool, enterprising "operator"—whom one might naturally look at askance. But, again, the excitement is compounded when it is realized that he is not the man, and when this fellow, for vital self-protection, sets out to find the culprit—and does.

Although Mr. Wilder and his helper in preparing the script, Edwin Blum, have stuck pretty close to the original, they have also done several things that, in this corner's estimation, have considerably improved the play. For one, they have moved into the open of the camp compound for many scenes, achieving not only more color but more excitement in the episodes of escapes. One sequence, in which the two chief comics, Mr. Lembeck and Mr. Strauss, use the ruse of pretending to be painters to get into an adjacent camp, containing Russian women prisoners, is one of the funniest in the film.

But the major achievement of their revisions is in the character Mr. Holden plays—that of the clever "operator"—who becomes a positive and arresting force. Here he is not a pleasant fellow; he is strictly at bat for No. 1. He smokes cigars, scratches matches on others' clothing, and is acquisitive right down the line. He takes bets against his own companions and operates a makeshift racetrack and a whiskey still. But he has nerve, ingenuity, and a certain valor. Mr. Holden plays him exceedingly well.

Indeed, as a consequence of this character, there emerges something in this film that considerably underscores the drama. It is a cynical sort of display of effectiveness in a group dilemma of a selfish philosophy and approach. It isn't pretty, but it is realistic—another comment on the shabbiness of war. It goes with a certain hollow jesting about the Geneva conventions and the Red Cross.

As for the other performers—Mr. Lembeck as a Jewish wisecracker, Mr. Strauss as his oafish pal, Richard Erdman as chief of the barrack, Otto Preminger as warden of the camp, Don Taylor as the new arrival, Sig Ruman as a thick-headed guard, Peter Graves as the barrack security officer, and many, many more—they help weave the close and crackling fabric of what is certainly one of this year's most smashing films.

—B.C., July 2, 1953

A STAR IS BORN

Directed by William A. Wellman; written by Dorothy Parker, Alan Campbell, Robert Carson, David O. Selznick, Mr. Wellman, Ring Lardner Jr., Budd Schulberg and John Lee Mahin, based on a story by Mr. Wellman and Mr. Carson; cinematographer, W. Howard Greene; edited by James E. Newcom; music by Max Steiner; art designer, Lyle Wheeler; produced by Mr. Selznick; released by United Artists. Running time: 111 minutes.

With: Janet Gaynor (Esther Blodgett/Vicki Lester), Fredric March (Norman Maine), Adolphe Menjou (Oliver Niles), May Robson (Lettie), Andy Devine (Danny McGuire) and Lionel Stander (Libby).

It is not as dull a Spring as we had thought. Selznick International came to April's defense yesterday with one of the year's best shows, *A Star Is Born,* which probably will find the Music Hall's treasurer turning cartwheels in the streets this morning. For here, at least, is good entertainment by any standards, including the artistic, and convincing proof that Hollywood need not travel to Ruritania for its plots; there is drama aplenty in its own backyard.

A Star Is Born is a Hollywood story of, by, and for its people. It has the usual preface, attesting to the fictional quality of the characters and incidents depicted, but it is nonetheless the most accurate mirror ever held before the glittering, tinseled, trivial, generous, cruel, and ecstatic world that is Hollywood. That, in itself, guarantees its dramatic interest, for there is no place on this twentieth-century earth more fascinating—not even that enchanting make-believe republic which James Hilton called Shangri-La.

Looking at it objectively, one might argue that William Wellman, Robert Carson, Dorothy Parker, and Alan Campbell (who coined the plot) have been passing Confederate money. Their thesis is the old one about the rising star and the falling star in the theatrical firmament whose paths cross, create a pyrotechnic glow where they meet, then flame out tragically as one soars onward in her flight as the other dips sadly and dies. If this were all, then *A Star Is Born* would be no more than commonplace, a jaded repetition of a basic theatrical formula.

But there are vibrance and understanding in their writing, a feeling for telling detail and a sympathy for the people they are touching. It is not a maudlin picture— not nearly so heroic, let us say, as its dramatic corollary, *Stage Door*. Janet Gaynor's movie-struck Esther Blodgett is not a caricature; Fredric March's waning Norman Maine is not an outrageous "ham"; Adolphe Menjou's Oliver Niles (of Oliver Niles Productions) is no more—and no less—human than many producers are. They are honest, normal, well intentioned folk; different, of course, for Hollywood would make them so; but we can believe in them and understand them and be moved by their tragedy. Conviction can bring any formula to life.

So then, we have the story of little Esther Blodgett who came to Hollywood and stood beatifically in the concrete footprints of Norman Maine outside Grauman's Chinese Theatre; who somehow—by one of those 100,000-to-1 chances—became the sensational Vicki Lester and Mrs. Norman Maine; who could not arrest her husband's swift descent, nor protect him from being called Mr. Vicki Lester, nor stay him when he stepped gallantly from the scene. Little Esther Blodgett had her success in Hollywood, but she paid for it. *Stage Door* never took that into account.

It is, as we said before, a good picture. It has been capitally played all down the line. Its script is bright, inventive, and forceful. Mr. Wellman's direction is expert. Its color—we almost forgot to mention it, so casually was it used—proves Technicolor's value in a modern story, demonstrates that it need not, should not, be restricted to the gaudy costume dramas. Not even its three climaxes, one right after the other, are enough to alter our verdict. The Music Hall, after a long famine, is spreading a feast again.

—*F.S.N., April 23, 1937*

STAR TREK II: THE WRATH OF KHAN

Directed by Nicholas Meyer; written by Jack B. Sowards, based on a story by Mr. Sowards and Harve Bennett and on the television series *Star Trek*, created by Gene Roddenberry; director of photography, Gayne Rescher; edited by William Dornisch; music by James Horner; production designer, Joseph R. Jennings; produced by Robert Sallin; released by Paramount Pictures. Running time: 113 minutes.

With: William Shatner (Admiral Kirk), Leonard Nimoy (Mr. Spock), DeForest Kelley (Dr. Leonard "Bones" McCoy), James Doohan (Chief Engineer Montgomery Scott), Walter Koenig (Chekhov), George Takei (Sulu), Nichelle Nichols (Commander Uhura), Bibi Besch (Dr. Carol Marcus), Merritt Butrick (David), Paul Winfield (Terrell), Kirstie Alley (Saavik) and Ricardo Montalban (Khan).

Now *this* is more like it: after the colossal, big-budget bore that was *Star Trek: The Motion Picture,* here comes a sequel that's worth its salt. The second Star Trek movie is swift, droll, and adventurous, not to mention appealingly gadget-happy. It's everything the first one should have been and wasn't.

As its title suggests, *Star Trek II: The Wrath of Khan* has a much stronger plot than its predecessor. That helps, but it's not the only improvement. This film also has the gamesmanship that the first one lacked, a quality that helped win the *Star Trek* television series its amazingly devoted following. Maybe it's just that there are more and brighter blinking lights on the control panels of the Starship *Enterprise* this time, or that the costumes are so much cleverer, or that the special effects are so good they don't call undue attention to themselves. Perhaps it's the directorial switch from Robert Wise (*The Hindenburg* and *The Sound of Music*) to Nicholas Meyer (*Time After Time*) that has brought the material more pep. In any case, this time something has most assuredly gone right.

In addition to its derring-do, *Star Trek II,* which opens today at Loews State and other theaters, also has the quality of a sentimental journey. Here they are again—William Shatner, Leonard Nimoy, DeForest Kelley, and the rest of the crew—sixteen years older than they were when the television series began, still playing the roles for which they are best known.

Mr. Shatner's Captain Kirk is an admiral now, given to ribbing the young trainees and wistfully saying things like, "Galloping around the cosmos is a game for the young." Mr. Nimoy, a.k.a. Mr. Spock, now has a pointy-eared protégée, a staggeringly competent young woman named Saavik (Kirstie Alley), with whom he converses in their native tongue, which is Vulcan. Admiral Kirk, Saavik confides to Spock, isn't what she expected. "He's so—human," she says. "Nobody's perfect, Saavik," Spock replies. This passage is translated from the Vulcan by subtitles.

This film may not make a new Star Trek devotee out of anyone, but it's sure to delight the old ones. Mr. Shatner makes the grandest of grand entrances, surrounded by a halo of blue light. He proves immediately that he has regained his dry sense of humor, which was markedly absent the last time around. Here, on his birthday, he is given a bottle of blue firewater by Mr. Kelley, vintage A.D. 2283, and both characters remark on how long the stuff has aged. For his part, Spock presents Kirk with a copy of *A Tale of Two Cities,* saying, "I know of your fondness for antiques." The novel will later figure quite sentimentally in the plot, which is an odd blend of mawkishness, mysticism, high adventure, and remarks like, "I suppose it could be a particle of pre-animate matter, caught in the matrix." Even the mumbo jumbo of this latest *Star Trek* is fun.

Most fun of all is Khan himself, played as the classiest of comic-strip villains by Ricardo Montalban, who really is something to see. With his fierce profile, long white hair, manful décolletage, and space-age jewelry, Mr. Montalban looks like either the world's oldest rock star or its hippest Indian chief. Either way, he looks terrific, every bit as happily flamboyant as the first film's characters—notwithstanding the beautiful, bald Persis Khambatta—were drab.

It is not necessary to have followed Star Trek lore any too faithfully to understand some key things about Khan. He has been frozen cryogenically in the twentieth century, banished to a remote planet, and deprived of Mrs. Khan. He blames Kirk for all of these injuries and plans to get even with the aid of a secret weapon that, by the standards of movies like this one, has a modicum of nasty originality. You see, the one remaining life-form on the barren planet to which Khan was banished is some special-effects cross between a tortoise and a crustacean. It has scorpion-shaped babies that can be deposited, by someone as sadistic as Khan, in an enemy's ear. "Their young enter through the ears and wrap themselves around the cerebral cortex. This has the effect of rendering the victim *extremely* susceptible to suggestion." Khan says this with the greatest imaginable relish.

Star Trek II lasts a long time, and it ends on a note that will seem misty to those who are veteran fans of the series, corny to those who aren't. For those who find it corny, the movie may wear out its welcome after a while. But it's cheerful and ingenious most of the way through, with none of the overblown foolishness that spoiled the first film. The *Star Trek* television show lay no real claims to greatness. This movie can't either, and it doesn't really try. But on its own simple terms, those of pure escapism, it certainly succeeds.

—*J.M., June 24, 1982*

STAR WARS

Written and directed by George Lucas; director of photography, Gilbert Taylor; edited by Paul Hirsch, Marcia Lucas and Richard Chew; music by John Williams; production designer, John Barry; produced by Gary Kurtz; released by Twentieth Century Fox. Running time: 121 minutes.

With: Mark Hamill (Luke Skywalker), Harrison Ford (Han Solo), Carrie Fisher (Princess Leia), Peter Cushing (Grand Moff Tarkin), Alec Guinness (Ben Obi-Wan Kenobi), Anthony Daniels (See Threepio), Kenny Baker (Artoo-Deetoo), Peter Mayhew (Chewbacca) and David Prowse (Lord Darth Vader).

*S*tar Wars, George Lucas's first film since his terrifically successful *American Graffiti,* is the movie that the teenagers in *American Graffiti* would have broken their necks to see. It's also the movie that's going to entertain a lot of contemporary folk who have a soft spot for the virtually ritualized manners of comic-book adventure.

Star Wars, which opened yesterday at the Astor Plaza, Orpheum, and other theaters, is the most elaborate, most expensive, most beautiful movie serial ever made. It's both an apotheosis of *Flash Gordon* serials and a witty critique that makes associations with a variety of literature that is nothing if not eclectic: *Quo Vadis?, Buck Rogers, Ivanhoe, Superman, The Wizard of Oz, The Gospel According to St. Matthew,* the legend of King Arthur and the knights of the Round Table.

All of these works, of course, had earlier left their marks on the kind of science-fiction comic strips that Mr. Lucas, the writer as well as director of *Star Wars,* here remembers with affection of such cheerfulness that he avoids facetiousness. The way definitely not to approach *Star Wars,* though, is to expect a film of cosmic implications or to footnote it with so many references that one anticipates it as if it were a literary duty. It's fun and funny.

The time, according to the opening credit card, is "a long time ago" and the setting "a galaxy far far away," which gives Mr. Lucas and his associates total freedom to come up with their own landscapes, housing, vehicles, weapons, religion, politics—all of which are variations on the familiar.

When the film opens, dark times have fallen upon the galactic empire once ruled, we are given to believe, from a kind of space-age Camelot. Against these evil tyrants there is, in progress, a rebellion led by a certain Princess Leia Organa, a pretty round-faced young woman of old-fashioned pluck who, before you can catch your breath, has been captured by the guardians of the empire. Their object is to retrieve some secret plans that can be the empire's undoing.

That's about all the plot that anyone of voting age should be required to keep track of. The story of *Star Wars* could be written on the head of a pin and still leave room for the Bible. It is, rather, a breathless succession of escapes, pursuits, dangerous missions, unexpected encounters, with each one ending in some kind of defeat until the final one.

These adventures involve, among others, an ever-optimistic young man named Luke Skywalker (Mark Hamill), who is innocent without being naive; Han Solo (Harrison Ford), a free-booting freelance space-

ship captain who goes where he can make the most money; and an old mystic named Ben Kenobi (Alec Guinness), one of the last of the Old Guard, a fellow in possession of what's called "the force," a mixture of what appears to be ESP and early Christian faith.

Accompanying these three as they set out to liberate the princess and restore justice to the empire are a pair of Laurel-and-Hardyish robots. The thin one, who looks like a sort of brass woodman, talks in the polished phrases of a valet ("I'm adroit but I'm not very knowledgeable"), while the squat one, shaped like a portable washing machine, who is the one with the knowledge, simply squeaks and blinks his lights. They are the year's best new comedy team.

In opposition to these good guys are the imperial forces led by someone called the Grand Moff Tarkin (Peter Cushing) and his executive assistant, Lord Darth Vader (David Prowse), a former student of Ben Kenobi who elected to leave heaven sometime before to join the evil ones.

The true stars of *Star Wars* are John Barry, who was responsible for the production design, and the people who were responsible for the incredible special effects—spaceships, explosions of stars, space battles, hand-to-hand combat with what appear to be lethal neon swords. I have a particular fondness for the look of the interior of a gigantic satellite called the Death Star, a place full of the kind of waste space one finds today only in old Fifth Avenue mansions and public libraries.

There's also a very funny sequence in a low-life bar on a remote planet, a frontierlike establishment where they serve customers who look like turtles, apes, pythons, and various amalgams of same, but draw the line at robots. Says the bartender piously: "We don't serve their kind here."

It's difficult to judge the performances in a film like this. I suspect that much of the time the actors had to perform with special effects that were later added in the laboratory. Yet everyone treats his material with the proper combination of solemnity and good humor that avoids condescension. One of Mr. Lucas's particular achievements is the manner in which he is able to recall the tackiness of the old comic strips and serials he loves without making a movie that is, itself, tacky. *Star Wars* is good enough to convince the most skeptical eight-year-old sci-fi buff, who is the toughest critic.

—*V.C., May 26, 1977*

STARMAN

Directed by John Carpenter: written by Bruce A. Evans and Raynold Gideon: director of photography. Donald Morgan: edited by Marion Rothman: music by Jack Nitzsche: production designer. Daniel Lomino: produced by Larry Franco: released by Columbia Pictures. Running time: 115 minutes.

With: Jeff Bridges (Starman). Karen Allen (Jenny Hayden). Charles Martin Smith (Mark Shermin). Richard Jaeckel (George Fox). Robert Phalen (Major Bell) and Tony Edwards (Sergeant Lemon).

If *Starman* doesn't make a major difference in Jeff Bridges's career, Mr. Bridges is operating in the wrong galaxy. For a long time, in films ranging from *Winter Kills* to *Against All Odds,* Mr. Bridges has been shedding baby fat literally and figuratively, evolving into a wonderfully natural and sympathetic leading man. *Starman* provides him with a role that, played by anyone else, might seem preposterous. In Mr. Bridges's hands it becomes the occasion for a sweetly affecting characterization—a fine showcase for the actor's blend of grace, precision, and seemingly offhanded charm.

Starman, which opens today at the Coronet and other theaters, does a great deal for John Carpenter, too. Taking this, a project made notorious by Columbia's having chosen it rather than the thematically similar *E.T.,* Mr. Carpenter has elected to turn the material's familiar elements into assets. If this is a science fiction fable with sex appeal, where's the harm? Mr. Carpenter, making his own definitive leap out of the horror genre, gives the story a swift pace, a crisp look, and the kind of logic and coherence that, in any kind of material, are welcome.

Mr. Bridges makes quite an entrance in the film, materializing on the floor of a cabin in Wisconsin where a young widow named Jenny Hayden (Karen Allen) has been watching home movies of her late husband. Mr. Bridges, as a disembodied extraterrestrial sent to Earth in response to Voyager 2's invitation, chooses to become an exact replica of the dead man. The blue light, the hurtling spacecraft, even the quickly expanding organism (the alien grows from infant to adult in merely a minute) may be staples of this sort of story, but Mr. Carpenter gives them elements of originality all the same. The film sustains its slight but distinctive visual edge throughout, even giving new life to places like Las Vegas and Monument Valley. The latter, for once, is filmed snow-covered.

The Starman, like E.T., must return home quickly before he weakens and fades. He also shares with E.T. a beatific innocence and the ability to understand earthly customs with phenomenal alacrity. In the Starman's case, this means remembering everything perfectly but managing, through his comic obliviousness to nuance, to get things a little bit wrong. "I can't get no . . . satisfaction," he supposes from listening to a record carried by Voyager 2, is a conversational remark. Watching Jenny drive, after he insists that she take him to a rendezvous point in Arizona, he studies her response to traffic lights and deduces that the rule is "red light, stop; green light, go; yellow light, go very fast."

Starman is also a love story, tracing Jenny's growing attachment to this exact replica of her husband and the Starman's corresponding attraction to her (which he is able to act upon only after studying the beach scene in *From Here to Eternity* on the Late Show.) It works best where it might have been hokiest, depicting earthly customs as perceived by an alien who is utterly benign, even saintly. During the course of the story, it develops that the Starman can start a car with his fingertip and even revive the dead. He is unmistakably the product of a higher civilization, but neither Mr. Bridges nor Mr. Carpenter makes the mistake of overaccentuating that fact.

Mr. Bridges, at first using stiff, mechanical head movements and the gait of a giant toddler, moves into more comfortable human gestures by means of a deductive process that the audience can easily follow. And he remains oddly poised even when the character is clumsiest. Miss Allen, throaty and wide-eyed, melts convincingly from fear and disbelief into fondness. Richard Jaeckel and Charles Martin Smith figure in a somewhat gratuitous subplot about the government's efforts to catch the Starman and dissect him, but they bring conviction to their roles. Lu Leonard, as a sympathetic waitress Jenny meets in a truck stop, does a lot with a very small part.

The usual kudos go to Industrial Light & Magic for special visual effects, to visual consultant Joe Alves, and to Dick Smith, Stan Winston, and Rick Baker, who collaborated on Starman's transformation scene. If you'd ever like to blossom into a space creature, cat-eyed monster, or werewolf, these are the people to call.

—*J.M., December 14, 1984*

THE STARS LOOK DOWN

Directed by Carol Reed: written by J. B. Williams. based on the novel by A. J. Cronin: cinematographers. Ernest Palmer: Henry Harris and Mutz Greenbaum: edited by Reginald Beck: music by Hans May: art designer. James Carter: produced by Isadore Goldsmith: released by Metro-Goldwyn-Mayer. Black and white. Running time: 104 minutes.

With: Michael Redgrave (David Fenwick). Margaret Lockwood (Jennie Sunley). Emlyn Williams (Joe Gowlan). Nancy Price (Martha Fenwick). Allan Jeayes (Mr. Barras) and Linden Travers (Mrs. Laura Millington).

When there are reasons for anger, most films tread softly. Usually the producers count ten before speaking their minds. But now and again there comes along a film that seems to have been struck off at white heat, that surges with indignation, that says what it has to say with complete and undeviating honesty. *The Stars Look Down,* the English-made film which M-G-M has hesitantly brought into the Criterion after holding it for many a long month, is such a work.

As a story of catastrophe in a small Welsh mining town it is so stinging in its attack on those who made the disaster inevitable that one wonders how it came to be made at all. Fortunately it has more than indignation. Directed with brilliant restraint by Carol Reed, faithfully performed in even the smallest role, it has caught the slow anguish of its coal-blackened people in a splendid and overwhelming film.

For around Dr. Cronin's novel of men who go down into the pits and sometimes never return, director Reed has produced a study of English miners that has the breath of life in it, that has the hard actuality and often the sweep of tragedy. The men who work the seams of the Neptune No. 17 are a begrimed and tight-lipped crew. Their lives on the earth above are spent in the sleazy, dim hovels that stretch in an endless pattern of monotony across the town. The risks of their occupation they accept as readily as daily bread. And it is a mark of Mr. Reed's truthfulness as a director that they emerge as heroic without knowing it. With the possible exception of one moment when the agonized suspense of a handful of entombed miners is shattered by the ravings of a religious fanatic, Mr. Reed has never allowed the film to lapse into the exaggerated heroics of melodrama; its compassion runs too deep.

Perhaps Mr. Reed has sacrificed a little in the unity of the film by deviating too long into the domestic contretemps of the miners' younger spokesman, who jeopardizes his own career by marrying a little trollop who never loved him at all. In itself harshly revealing, the great emotional impact comes more from the wider story of the miners' strike against the dangers of the pit, the slow corrosion of their resolve through months of hunger, their betrayal alike by mine owner and corrupt union leaders, and finally their return to the pit to meet death as they had feared.

In the shots of idle men passing a cigarette from mouth to mouth, of the inchoate angers suddenly brought into focus by a stone through a butcher's window, in the grim panic of men caught in the underground labyrinths by a rush of flood water, Mr. Reed has recorded their struggle and their tragedy with sensitive camera shorthand.

But even these sequences are surpassed by the account of the vigil at the mine's mouth. In the silent relays of weary rescue workers, in the click-clack of pulmotors, and above all in the drawn white faces of the women waiting hour after uncertain hour, Mr. Reed has created one of the magnificent passages of screen realism. For he has caught here more than the surface grimness, he has touched life at its quick. Because of that his film has more of heart-filling beauty than most of the flat fictions that pass across our screens.

To single out the performers is almost an impertinence, and yet one must mention the bitter portrait of Michael Redgrave as the aspiring young spokesman; the pitiless accuracy of Margaret Lockwood as the cheap little busybody; Edward Rigby as the patient, wife-ridden father; and Nancy Price's grimly impassive mother, who can say after all hope of rescue is gone, "A disaster's a disaster." Emlyn Williams as a scheming young knave and Milton Rosmer as a friendly Member of Parliament are both excellent. Beyond them stand the people of Sleescale for whom the director has let the camera speak with candor and compassion. In *The Stars Look Down* Mr. Reed has made a film to be remembered in this or any other season.

—*T.S., July 24, 1941*

STATE FAIR

Directed by Henry King; written by Paul King and Sonya Levien, based on the novel by Phil Stong; cinematographer, Hal Mohr; edited by Robert Bischoff; music by Louis de Francesco; art designer, Duncan Cramer; produced by Winfield Sheehan; released by Twentieth Century Fox. Black and white. Running time: 80 minutes.

With: Janet Gaynor (Margy Frake), Will Rogers (Abel Frake), Lew Ayres (Pat Gilbert), Sally Eilers (Emily Joyce), Norman Foster (Wayne Frake), Louise Dresser (Melissa Frake), Frank Craven (The Storekeeper), Victor Jory (The Barker) and Frank Melton (Harry Ware).

Will Rogers, Janet Gaynor, and Frank Craven are supported most effectively in the interesting pictorial version of Phil Stong's novel, *State Fair,* by Blue Boy, a somewhat temperamental prize hog, who is presumed to prefer lolling in a pen to riding over the country in an automobile. As hogs go, he is a handsome specimen, his black coat being relieved by a band of white. No farmer could show greater pride in an animal than does Abel Frake in Blue Boy.

Frake, who is impersonated by Mr. Rogers, talks to the hog, adjuring Blue Boy to get up and show a little life. He watches over the huge animal, brushing Blue Boy's back and accusing the prize beast of being a quitter. Mr. Rogers is excellent in these sequences, for they give him a chance to air his dry humor; and, after all, a man talking to a hog is funny, but to hear a farmer virtually telling a hog that he does not believe that it is sick, but only shamming, is far more humorous.

Watching this film is almost as interesting as going to a State fair, for nothing seems to be neglected during the week in which it is supposed to take place. It is a homey tale, with many an intriguing bit. The out-

come of some of the incidents may be anticipated, but that does not militate against them. In fact, when Melissa Frake, Abel's sensible wife, wins first prizes with her pickles, jams, and mincemeat there was probably not a soul among those who crowded into the big theater yesterday who did not feel highly pleased, even though they well knew that Abel had poured brandy into the mincemeat and Mrs. Frake had flavored it still further with the same stimulant.

The Frakes joggle along in their station wagon from a small town some hundred and twenty miles distant to the big town where the fair is being held. In their car are Abel and his wife, their son, Wayne, and their daughter, Margy, and the hog in a sort of crate. After they are settled down on the fair grounds they hear the booming of a gun announcing the opening of the fair. By that time Abel is worried about Blue Boy, Wayne has promised to accompany his sister to the amusement section of the fair, Mrs. Frake is anxious over the outcome of her pickles, and so forth. The carnival tents are soon billowing in the breeze. There are pictures of the giant, the midget, the fat woman, the ventriloquist, and others.

Wayne Frake, played by Norman Foster, appears at the counter of a place where the owner defies customers to throw rings over certain objects. But Wayne has practiced indefatigably for several months and he has become so adept that the man who runs the place is eager to get rid of the young man. Here Wayne encounters Emily Joyce, an attractive girl, who poses as the daughter of an inspector of police. Wayne's heart begins to thump fast, and he agrees to meet her that night, notwithstanding that he has an engagement with his sister. Imagine his amazement when he discovers the girl he is enamored of is a trapeze artist!

Margy, acted by Janet Gaynor, is disappointed, but on the roller coaster she meets Pat Gilbert, a newspaper man, who later takes her to see the trotting races. It is a far more interesting romance than the ephemeral infatuation between the trapeze performer and Wayne. Miss Gaynor here gives her best performance in talking pictures.

An excellent sequence is that in which Mrs. Frake hears her name mentioned as winner for her condiments, and then comes the grand moment when Blue Boy shakes himself, staggers to his feet, and, guided by a light stick, consents to enter the prize ring. He grunts his disapproval of such things and looks generally surly, even more surly than the other hogs, which are supposed to be cheerful. But something seems to tell him that he had better put his best feet foremost and capture the prize, which he does when the laurels are about to be awarded to another animal.

And you get an idea of the life of a hog when the Frakes are returning to their home. Blue Boy grunts, but who cares? Frake certainly doesn't, for he says that what is a winner today may be ham tomorrow. More grunting from Blue Boy, but realizing that the noise he makes is almost drowned by that of the wagon, he sinks into a slumber.

The State fair over and the Frakes home, there is only one person who is gloomy and that is Margy. But everyone knows that Miss Gaynor must have a successful love affair in her pictures and *State Fair* is no exception.

Mr. Rogers is excellent in his role. Frank Craven supplies some well-spoken lines. Mr. Foster is a bit too intelligent to be convincing as the rustic Wayne. Louise Dresser is highly satisfactory as Mrs. Frake and Victor Jory is good as a barker. Lew Ayres is sympathetic as Gilbert.

—M.H., *January 27, 1933*

STEVIE

Produced and directed by Robert Enders: written by Hugh Whitemore. based on his play and the works of Stevie Smith. cinematographer. Freddie Young: edited by Peter Tanner: music by Patrick Gowers: art designer. Robert Jones: released by First Artists. Running time: 102 minutes.

With: Glenda Jackson (Stevie Smith). Mona Washbourne (Aunt). Alec McCowen (Freddy) and Trevor Howard (Man).

You'd better put on your running shoes if you don't want to miss the best performance by an actress to be seen in any film released so far this year. It's Glenda Jackson in *Stevie*, Hugh Whitemore's very good film adaptation of his play about the late Stevie Smith, the gallant, original, profoundly witty English poet who died in 1971 at the age of sixty-nine. Stevie, in Miss Jackson's splendid performance, is funny, fragile, demanding, suicidal, brave, and never at a loss for

the kind of words that light up the conventional world she clung to, even as those words turn the world upside down.

The only hitch: *Stevie* opens today at the Thalia on a double bill with *Mr. Forbush and the Penguins* and will close tomorrow. Incredible.

It's incredible that this English film, which was made in 1978, has not been released in New York until now, even under these foreshortened circumstances, and incredible that Mr. Whitemore's London play, with Miss Jackson in the title role, was never brought to New York. (The play did have a short run at the Manhattan Theater Club in 1979 with Roberta Maxwell in the title role.) This *Stevie*, directed by Robert Enders, who also directed Miss Jackson in the screen adaptation of her London production of *Hedda Gabler* with somewhat less success, is a knockout as a film that never for a minute attempts to disguise its theatrical roots. However, it uses those roots well. The camera italicizes a great stage performance. It also focuses our attention on the remarkable Stevie, whose poetry effectively connected the suburbs to the stars.

Miss Jackson has firmly established herself in the public consciousness as a fine comic actress (*Hopscotch, Nasty Habits, House Calls* and *A Touch of Class*) but not since *Sunday, Bloody Sunday* has she had a film role that so fully and efficiently utilizes the range of her intelligence and power as a dramatic actress. Watching her at work in *Stevie* is to see a special talent at the top of its form and to be aware of everything we've been missing in the junk films (*The Incredible Sarah, The Devil Is a Woman,* and *Mary Queen of Scots*) she's been doing to earn a living.

Whether or not Miss Jackson is physically like the real Stevie Smith, I've no idea. What's more important is that she communicates the passion and rueful wisdom of a singular personality and illuminates the language by which that personality came to some kind of truce with the human condition.

Though *Stevie* periodically cuts away to sepia-colored flashbacks, most of the film is set in the genteel parlor of the suburban Palmers Green house that Stevie shared most of her life with her aunt, marvelously well played by Mona Washbourne. Mr. Whitemore's screenplay makes use of a character identified only as the Man (Trevor Howard), who acts as a sort of master of ceremonies, introducing Stevie and her aunt, supplying exposition, commenting on Stevie's life and work, occasionally stepping in to play a subsidiary character, and, on several occasions, quoting from Stevie's poetry. It's proper and fitting that it's Mr. Howard, and not Stevie, who gives us her classic condensation of a life, "Not Waving but Drowning."

The only other character in the film is a fellow named Freddy (Alec McCowen), a young man to whom Stevie was engaged and with whom she has a brief affair, terminated quickly the night after their first and only sexual connection when Stevie asks, "Why, right in the middle of it, did you say, 'Are you enjoying it?'" Freddy, who carries a tennis racquet, is clearly no match for Stevie, who has no time for twits.

Stevie is not a movie for anyone not interested in language, particularly the uses to which Stevie could put it. Stevie's mind never lets anything be, and though she accepts "sensible" middle-class values, she never stops mocking them. "I am," she concedes at one point, "an Anglican agnostic." She carries on a constant war with Christianity.

As she says in the opening of "Thoughts About the Christian Doctrine of Eternal Hell," "Is it not interesting to see/How Christians continually/Try to separate themselves in vain/From the doctrine of eternal pain." Later, she suggests that if she had been the Virgin Mary, she would have replied with a firm, "No."

Miss Jackson and Stevie's poetry reveal the spirit inside the woman who avoided—and may well have been afraid of—any kind of romantic commitments, preferring instead less demanding but, for her, more fulfilling friendships. In the way of all artists, *Stevie* is always standing outside herself, even when she is experiencing pain. "They said," she tells us about her mother, "that she died in a minute. How long is a minute?"

She embraces the safety of the house in Palmers Green, speaking of "the orgy of boredom to which my soul is committed." "Housework," she says ironically, "is the most marvelous excuse for not working." Of the middle classes: "This Englishwoman is so refined/She has no bosom and no behind."

Stevie Smith died of a brain tumor that, before death, rendered her virtually mute. At that point, she wrote in typical Stevie fashion, "I cannot speech properly, but I do scramble well."

Stevie has only four characters in it, but it is a very big, beautiful film about a restlessly rambunctious soul. It deserves to stay around indefinitely.

—*V.C., June 19, 1981*

Directed by François Truffaut: written (in French, with English subtitles) by Mr. Truffaut, Bernard Revon and Claude de Givray: cinematographer, Denys Clerval: edited by Agnes Guillemot: music by Antoine Duhamel: art designer, Claude Pignot: produced by Marcel Berbert: released by Lopert Films. Running time: 90 minutes.

With: Jean-Pierre Léaud (Antoine Doinel), Delphine Seyrig (Madame Tabard), Michael Lonsdale (Monsieur Tabard), Claude Jade (Christine Darbon) and Harry Max (Monsieur Henri).

François Truffaut's *Stolen Kisses,* which opened yesterday at the Fine Arts Theater, is a movie so full of love that to define it may make it sound like a religious experience, which, of course, it is—but in a wonderfully unorthodox, cockeyed way. Truffaut loves his characters—the well-meaning misfit with the private integrity, even paranoids: he loves movies—the people who make them and the people who preserve them (this film is dedicated to Henri Langlois of the Cinémathèque Française); he loves the craft of movies, and he loves—or, at least he accepts—the mortality of love itself.

Everything Truffaut touches—bookburning (*Fahrenheit 451*), banal adultery (*The Soft Skin*), or monomaniacal revenge (*The Bride Wore Black*)—seems to be spontaneously invested with the lyricism that marks his greatest films, *Jules and Jim, Shoot the Piano Player,* and *The 400 Blows.*

Stolen Kisses is one of his best—strong, sweet, wise, and often explosively funny. It picks up the adolescent hero of *The 400 Blows* ten years later, after his discharge from the Army for being "temperamentally unfit," and details his chaotic adventures around Paris as a hotel night clerk and then as a private eye of spectacular ineptitude.

The movie at first seems to have a rather short focus, but because Truffaut is incapable of doing anything cheaply or flatly or vulgarly, it is soon apparent that *Stolen Kisses* is as humanistically complex as even *Shoot the Piano Player,* though more classically ordered in form. The focus is broad and deep and like all fine movies, *Stolen Kisses* has both social and political integrity that seem so casual as to appear unintentional.

Léaud, who has been playing lightweight versions of this role in other movies (most recently in Jerzy Skolimowski's *Le Départ*), is quite marvelous as Antoine, whose face is part predatory cartoon cat, part saint, and very, very French. Delphine Seyrig is the cool and beautiful older woman who seduces Antoine in one of the most erotic, nonsex scenes I've ever seen in a movie. Knowing that he has a crush on her she comes to his flat early one morning and points out, quite pragmatically, that since each of them is unique and exceptional, there is no reason they should not sleep together. He has to agree.

However, as in every Truffaut film, all the actors are so good one sometimes suspects that they, and not Truffaut, wrote their own lines. Michael Lonsdale is pricelessly funny as Miss Seyrig's husband, a shoe store owner who asks the detective agency to find out why everyone—waitresses, taxicab drivers, his employees, and his wife—detests him. He is curious because there can't possibly be any legitimate reason. Claude Jade, who looks like a dark-haired Catherine Deneuve, is Antoine's sometime fiancée, and Harry Max is an elderly detective who sponsors Antoine in the trade.

Antoine (whom Jean-Pierre Léaud plays here, as he did in *The 400 Blows*) is a kind of mid-sixties, Parisian Huckleberry Finn, committed to life if not to all of its rituals. Antoine, who is a physical and spiritual projection of Truffaut himself, is a constantly amazed observer and an enthusiastic participant, a fact that gives *Stolen Kisses* the perspective missing from so many other movies about youth seeking to connect.

With what can only be described as cinematic grace, Truffaut's point of view slips in and out of Antoine so that something that on the surface looks like a conventional movie eventually becomes as fully and carefully populated as a Balzac novel. There is not a silly or superfluous incident, character, or camera angle in the movie.

Truffaut, however, is the star of the film, always in control, whether the movie is ranging into the area of slapstick, lyrical romance or touching lightly on DeGaulle's France (a student demonstration on the TV screen). His love of old movies is reflected in plot devices (overheard conversations), incidental action (two children walking out of a drug store wearing Laurel and Hardy masks), and in the score, which takes Charles Trenet's 1943 song, known here as "I Wish You Love," and turns it into a joyous motif.

The ending—as in a Hitchcock movie—should not be revealed. It's a twist, all right, but not in plot. It simply italicizes everything that has gone before.

Stolen Kisses is a movie I'll cherish for a very long time, a lovely, human movie.

—V.C., March 4, 1969

STOP MAKING SENSE

Directed by Jonathan Demme: director of photography. Jordan Cronenweth: edited by Lisa Day: produced by Gary Goetzman: released by Cinecom International Films/Island Alive Releasing. Running time: 88 minutes.

With: The Talking Heads: David Byrne. Chris Frantz. Jerry Harrison. Tina Weymouth. Edna Holt. Lynn Mabry. Steve Scales. Alex Weir and Bernie Worrell.

From the opening frames of Jonathan Demme's *Stop Making Sense,* which opens today at the 57th Street Playhouse, it's apparent that this is a rock concert film that looks and sounds like no other. The sound is extraordinarily clear, thanks to the pioneering use of 24 track digital recording. And the film's visual style is as coolly iconoclastic as Talking Heads itself. Mr. Demme has captured both the look and the spirit of this live performance with a daring and precision that match the group's own.

It's worth noting some of the things that are *not* to be found here: screaming crowds, gaudy skintight costumes, candid scenes of the band members backstage. Talking Heads' performance style is unlike anything that has ever been captured by a standard concert film, and Mr. Demme is very well attuned to the group's eccentricities. Even the first image—the shadow of a guitar neck looming against a white wall—wittily suggests the menacing and mechanistic qualities of Talking Heads' music, as well as the clean, bold visual imagery they manage to make so surprising. The sight of this sexually and racially integrated nine-member ensemble, in white sneakers and neutral-colored playsuits, jogging in place as if practicing aerobics becomes at least as exciting as any standard rock spectacle.

The focus of both the film and the performance is

949

David Byrne, the lead singer, who is one of the group's four core members. With his hollow-eyed stare and bizarre gestures, Mr. Byrne is surely one of the oddest rock singers; he's also one of the most galvanizing. Mr. Byrne, or at least the sight of his sneakers, is initially seen alone, wandering onto the stage to perform the stark and rousing version of "Psycho Killer" that begins the show. (The other band members enter one at a time, a new one with each song, as a technical crew wanders conspicuously in their midst. Only in its latter half does the film build into an elaborately staged production, with Mr. Byrne in his Big Suit costume and words like "time clock" and "dustballs" flashing on a colored backdrop.)

Mr. Byrne's studied casualness is matched by a fierce intensity. Even his most peculiar gestures—darting his head and tongue like a lizard, or dancing with stiff, jerky motions and a perfectly immobile torso—have an originality and a mesmerizing strangeness.

And Mr. Byrne's vocals maintain their lucid, unsettling energy throughout the performance (the film actually draws upon four 1983 concerts at the Pantages theater in Hollywood). The film includes especially fine renditions of such Talking Heads classics as "Life During Wartime," "Heaven," "Once in a Lifetime," and "Burnin' Down the House."

Mr. Demme, in addition to avoiding any visual monotony, has gracefully tailored the film to suit the band's stage show. Using long, slow camera motions (the handsome cinematography is by Jordan Cronenweth), he captures the group members at close range without losing the overall visual effects they achieve on stage. The show's conception, which is both subtle and sophisticated, is credited to Mr. Byrne.

Stop Making Sense owes very little to the rock filmmaking formulas of the past. It may well help inspire those of the future.

—J.M., October 18, 1984

STORMY MONDAY

Written and directed by Mike Figgis: director of photography. Roger Deakins: edited by David Martin: music by Mr. Figgis: production designer. Andrew McAlpine: produced by Nigel Stafford-Clark: released by Atlantic Entertainment Group. Running time: 93 minutes.

With: Melanie Griffith (Kate). Tommy Lee Jones (Cosmo). Sting (Finney) and Sean Bean (Brendan).

Mike Figgis happens to be a fledgling director whose reach is more than matched by his grasp, which is very lucky, since his *Stormy Monday* might have amounted to overreaching had it been handled with anything less than Mr. Figgis's absolute assurance. Here is the kind of neo–film noir plot that could easily seem mannered; here is a fragmented story that could easily add up to less than the sum of its parts. Here is an idiosyncratic setting—the waterfront nightclub district of Newcastle, England—that could easily have grown claustrophobic if it had not been filmed with so much feeling and skill.

But Mr. Figgis, who is a musician as well as a filmmaker, brings the place, the plot, and the film's haunting characters vibrantly to life. What's more, he makes them irresistibly interesting. *Stormy Monday* is a sultry romantic thriller that holds its audience rapt with the promise of imminent danger, and is able to do this in an amazingly natural, unaffected way. Mr. Figgis, who wrote the film's original score, even manages to work some great blues songs into the jazz-tinged soundtrack, and to give the film a soulfulness matching that of the music.

As if this weren't enough, he's also gotten superb performances out of all four of his principals, who are fascinatingly mismatched. Despite this, the chemistry is there, for when Kate (Melanie Griffith) first meets Brendan (Sean Bean), she quite literally bowls him over. Kate, an American, has drifted into Newcastle at the behest of a powerful businessman named Cosmo (Tommy Lee Jones), who likes using her as a sexual lure in his dealings with other men, whereas Brendan has arrived in town with even less sense of purpose than that. Brendan gets a job in a nightclub run by the cool, insouciant Finney (Sting), and with this, the circle becomes complete. Cosmo has plans to pressure Finney to sell his club, and Kate and Brendan are caught between them. The narrative tightens slowly and inexorably, until it all most effectively comes together.

Stormy Monday, which opens today at the Embassy 72d Street and the Gemini, tells its story very well (Mr. Figgis also wrote the screenplay), but it isn't the plot for which this film will be remembered. It's the haunting, deeply evocative mood that's most impressive, and Mr. Figgis modulates it beautifully. His direction, which is intensely stylish without any effort or strain, has a way of prompting rather than forcing the audience's interest, and a gift for arousing the viewer's curiosity. This isn't a trick that's done with mirrors; it's done through characters who are, for a film of this genre, exceptionally substantial and real.

The stellar Miss Griffith, with her sexy, singular blend of kittenishness and strength, is entirely at home here, making an irrevocably strong impression. So does Sting, whose quietly menacing performance in a character role is perhaps the film's biggest surprise. Mr. Jones makes Cosmo dangerous in a much more direct way, and he turns the ugly-American role that is the screenplay's thinnest into much more than a mere caricature. Mr. Bean is a wonderfully sturdy yet unassuming hero, giving Brendan exactly the right mixture of sweetness and suspicion. In the end, each of these four principals is appreciably changed by the events that unfold here, which makes for a very satisfying story, and for a great deal of eye-opening in a relatively short time.

Also in *Stormy Monday* are the various musicians (including a Cracow Jazz Ensemble, comically out of place during Newcastle's week-long, gimmicky celebration of all things American) and thugs and functionaries who give the film its abundant background texture. That these minor details are as well chosen as the major ones is yet further proof of Mr. Figgis's commanding new talent.

—J.M., April 22, 1988

THE STORY OF ADÈLE H.

Directed by François Truffaut; written (in French, with English subtitles) by Mr. Truffaut, Jean Gruault, Suzanne Schiffman and Jan Dawson, based on the book *Le Journal d'Adèle Hugo* edited by Frances V. Guille; director of photography, Nestor Almendros; edited by Yann Dedet; music by Maurice Jaubert; art designer, Jean-Pierre Kohut-Svelko; produced by Marcel Berbert; released by New World. Running time: 97 minutes.

With: Isabelle Adjani (Adèle H.), Bruce Robinson (Lieutenant Pinson), Sylvia Marriott (Mrs. Saunders), Reubin Dorey (Mr. Saunders), Joseph Blatchley (Mr. Whistler) and M. White (Colonel).

In 1863 Adèle Hugo, the younger daughter of the great French poet and patriot, Victor Hugo, ran away from home on the Isle of Guernsey where her father was living in exile to follow a young English officer, a Lieutenant Pinson, to his new post in Halifax, Nova Scotia. Lieutenant Pinson was probably not a bad sort, not worse than most, but he wasn't very serious.

It's thought that the young, inexperienced Adèle had most likely been Lieutenant Pinson's mistress for a short time on Guernsey, and it's known that she wanted desperately to marry him, though her father disapproved. In any case, Lieutenant Pinson was not interested—a circumstance that Adèle was ill-equipped to understand or ever to support.

The Story of Adèle H., François Truffaut's profoundly beautiful new film, is about Adèle's journey, taken with measured steps, into a magnificent, isolating obsession, first to frozen Halifax and then, when Lieutenant Pinson is transferred to the West Indies, to Barbados, where Adèle sweeps through the tropical streets and alleys of Bridgetown talking to herself, wearing a heavy black cloak, and looking like some mad, benign witch of the north.

Unable to cope with the truth, and using her imagination and her feelings as carefully as someone writing a piece of fiction, Adèle created another world where she became Lieutenant Pinson's wife, where love was her religion (and no humiliation too great a sacrifice), and where she kept a coded journal, only recently deciphered. It is this journal that is the basis for Mr. Truffaut's most severe, most romantic meditation upon love.

The Story of Adèle H. was shown last night at Avery Fisher Hall to close the 13th New York Film Festival, which, despite one spectacular disappointment and several others of a lesser order, has been one of the best festivals in recent years. Without question the Truffaut entry was the surprising highlight, even to one who has admired the French director's films over the years.

One of the fascinations of the Truffaut career is in watching the way he circles and explores different aspects of the same subjects that dominate almost all of his films. However, *The Story of Adèle H.,* impeccably photographed by Nestor Almendros (*The Wild Child*), looks and sounds like no other Truffaut film you've ever seen.

The colors are deep, rich, and often dark, and the soundtrack is full of the noises that one associates with old costume films produced by M-G-M in its great days—carriages riding over cobblestones, pens scratching across vellum, servants arriving and departing with important messages, bells that tinkle over the doors of bookshops. More important, there is the fine background score by the late Maurice Jaubert (he died in 1940), who composed for Vigo and Clair among others. The film has the manner of a romance but it's a romance from which all the conventional concerns have been eliminated.

In the single-minded way in which the movie sticks to its subject, *The Story of Adèle H.* reminds one of *The Wild Child.* It's virtually a one-character film. It contemplates the classic beauty of Adèle, played with extraordinary grace by twenty-year-old Isabelle Adjani of the Comédie Française, much as Catherine Deneuve was admired by the camera in *Mississippi Mermaid,* and it appreciates the particularity of women in a fashion that recalls the erratic journey of Catherine to the crematorium in *Jules and Jim.*

The Story of Adèle H. is not a psychiatric case history, though all the facts seem to be there if one wants to accept it as such. Rather it's a poet's appreciation of the terrifying depth of Adèle's feelings, which, early on, drive her to lying to her family, to making life miserable for Lieutenant Pinson in Halifax (including canceling his engagement to someone else), to spying on him, happily, as he makes love to another woman. She's willful and spoiled and, the film understands, impossible to deal with. Yet the film makes us see both the madness and the grandeur of the passion.

It's this ability to allow us to see a subject from several different angles simultaneously that often proves most unsettling in a Truffaut film. Toughness and compassion get all mixed up. It's also this talent that separates his films from those of all other directors who are working in the humanist tradition today. *The Story of Adèle H.* is a film that I suspect Jean Renoir would much admire. He understands such things.

—*V.C., October 13, 1975*

THE STORY OF G.I. JOE

Directed by William A. Wellman: written by Leopold Atlas. Guy Endore and Philip Stevenson. based on the newspaper columns of Ernie Pyle: cinematographer. Russell Metty: edited by Otho Lovering and Al Joseph: music by Ann Ronell and Louis Applebaum: art designers. James Sullivan and David Hall: produced by Lester Cowan: released by United Artists. Black and white. Running time: 109 minutes.

With: Burgess Meredith (Ernie Pyle). Robert Mitchum (Captain Walker). Freddie Steele (Sergeant Warnicki). Wally Cassell (Private Dondaro). Jimmy Lloyd (Private Spencer). Jack Reilly (Private Murphy) and Bill Murphy (Private Mew).

The little men from a thousand different walks of life who were swept in the whirlpool of international discord to the battlefields of Europe and the Pacific—those tired, desperate infantrymen who fought bravely and spilled their lifeblood for the freedom of mankind—are projected in all their true glory in the eloquent motion picture *The Story of G.I. Joe.* This hard-hitting, penetrating drama of the footslogging soldier, which had a dual opening last night at the Globe and Gotham theaters, stems from the newspaper columns of the late Ernie Pyle. And the scenarists, the director, and the players have animated Mr. Pyle's chronicles in a manner that is truly inspired.

The Story of G.I. Joe has all the integrity and the uncompromising realism of those other great pictorial documents of the second World War, pictures like *The True Glory, San Pietro, Desert Victory,* and *Attack, the Battle of New Britain.* Being a personalized account of a small group of representative types—men whose lives we are permitted to share intimately for more than an hour—*The Story of G.I. Joe* moves across the screen with tremendous emotional impact. It is humorous, poignant, and tragic, an earnestly human reflection of a stern life and the dignity of man.

Director William A. Wellman's approach is starkly realistic. The documentary quality of the picture is enhanced by the frequent use of authentic Signal Corps footage of the North African and Italian campaigns, and the sparse, idiomatic dialogue. The opening scene shows a truckload of Eighteenth Infantry greenhorns, waiting to shove off toward Faid Pass and fondling a newly acquired mascot. "Get that pooch out of here," barks the lieutenant, "want to get him killed?" And much later, on a bleak, cold, and sodden

Christmas night in the shell-pocked valley below Cassino, the captain sums up his men's aspirations with simple eloquence: "If only we could create something good out of all this energy, all these men."

Ernie Pyle was an unobtrusive sidelines observer, more interested in the individual doughfoot than the strategic deployment of regimental power, and his *Story of G.I. Joe* depicts infantry action in the terms of rainsoaked, mud-caked, and desperately tired men. They are of all types. The tough sergeant who carries a carefully wrapped record of his baby's voice, the Brooklyn lothario who makes romantic capital out of his Italian heritage, the long-legged G.I. who was washed out as an air cadet because of his height and talks about cutting off his legs, and the taciturn captain, who understands his men better than he did his wife. As the wandering correspondent who brings all the threads into sharp focus, Burgess Meredith plays Ernie Pyle with the same humility and spirit of camaraderie which endeared the correspondent to so many G.I.'s.

His is not a big role, but it is impressively done. The meatiest roles fall to Robert Mitchum, the captain, and Freddie Steele, as the sergeant. Both give excellent characterizations, particularly Mr. Steele, who reveals a surprising degree of emotional flexibility. His performance is so well balanced one would think he had been acting for years, and only the most hardened will not experience a lump in the throat when this splendid soldier succumbs to battle fatigue.

When the men of the Fifth Army, many of whom participate in the picture, saw *The Story of G.I. Joe* in Italy, their verdict was "This is it." Lester Cowan, the producer, and all those others who contributed to this magnificent and so richly deserved tribute to the infantry soldier, could ask for no greater rewards.

—T.M.P., October 6, 1945

THE STORY OF QIU JU

Directed by Zhang Yimou; written (in Mandarin, with English subtitles) by Liu Heng, based on the novel *The Wan Family's Lawsuit* by Chen Yuanbin; directors of photography, Chi Xiaoling and Yu Xiao-qun; edited by Du Yuan; music by Zhao Jiping; art designer, Cao Jiuping; produced by Ma Fung-kwok; released by Sony Pictures Classics. Running time: 114 minutes.

With: Gong Li (Wan Qiu Ju), Lei Lao-sheng (Wang Shantang, the Village Head), Liu Pei-qi (Wan Qinglai, the Husband), Yang Liu-chun (Meizi), Ge Zhi-jun (Officer Li) and Zhu Qanqing (Cui Luowen).

Zhang Yimou is the superb Chinese filmmaker whose life sounds like the stuff of legend (he is said to have "sold his blood to buy his first camera") and whose rural historical dramas (among them *Raise the Red Lantern* and *Ju Dou*) would be accessible in any part of the globe. Now in *The Story of Qiu Ju*, which will be shown at the New York Film Festival tonight and on Sunday, Mr. Zhang has attempted something more modern and no less fascinating. With the simplicity of a folk tale or a fable, he tells of a farmer's wife and her search for justice, and in the process he provides a remarkably detailed view of contemporary Chinese life.

The principal performers in *The Story of Qiu Ju* are professional actors, most notably his familiar star, the beautiful Gong Li, who again emerges as a figure of astonishing fortitude. But this film's background figures are real people, caught unawares by Mr. Zhang's cameras as they travel and congregate in public settings. Without diminishing the film's dramatic interest, this realistic backdrop gives the film a documentary aspect, which is presented no less elegantly than the spare, historical details of the director's earlier films. Once again, it is Mr. Zhang's keen and universal view of human nature that raises his work far above its own visual beauty and into the realm of timeless storytelling.

The Story of Qiu Ju is, for Mr. Zhang, exceptionally down to earth. It tells of a very simple problem. The pregnant *Qiu Ju* (played by Gong Li) is incensed because her husband, Qinglai, has been kicked in the groin by a man named Wang, who is the head of the small village in which they all live. Qiu Ju wants to know exactly what happened; she wants justice, and she is not shy about saying so. "If we can't fix your plumbing, we're stuck with the single-child policy for good," she grouses to Qinglai as she pulls him in a cart so he can visit a local doctor. The doctor, when first seen, is splitting logs with a hatchet instead of treating patients.

Slowly but surely the film carries the stubborn Qiu Ju up the ladder of Chinese justice as she enlists ever-higher authorities to help her right this wrong. A local official, the smiling and compromise-minded Officer Li, initially suggests a monetary settlement to cover Qinglai's medical bills. He also advises the principals of the case: "I want both of you to do some self-criticism. Is that clear?" But Wang, who is gallingly amused by Qiu Ju's outrage, merely throws the financial settlement at her in cash, expecting her to retrieve it. "For each one you pick up," he says with a smile, "you bow your head to me."

Needless to say, Qiu Ju will have none of this. So she embarks on arduous journeys to see different officials, journeys that the film records with impressive attention to detail. In rural contemporary China, the viewer learns, a pregnant woman may travel sidesaddle on someone else's bicycle over icy roads if she wants badly to get to town. She may also haul a wagon filled with chili peppers if she thinks that can influence her case. Mr. Zhang, incidentally, still has a fine eye for the fastidious beauty of Chinese peasant customs. The simple farm dwellings of Qiu Ju's village are festooned with spectacular garlands of drying peppers and corn.

As Qiu Ju travels to ever more modern settings, the film overflows with interesting information. In town, the viewer can see how certain Western images, like pinups of Arnold Schwarzenegger, have infiltrated the indigenous culture. The film also observes Qiu Ju's reactions to such things as dishonest taxi drivers (the taxi is actually a bicycle-driven wagon) and loud, printed leggings.

Along the way, it also notes the behavior of public officials toward a woman of Qiu Ju's beauty and persistence, and it underscores some of the more basic inequities of Chinese life. The original fight between Wang and Qinglai had to do with Qinglai's impugning his rival's virility, since Wang is the father of four girls. "He cannot have sons, so he takes his frustrations out on us," a public letter-writer maintains on Qiu Ju's behalf. Though Qiu Ju is clearly the strongest character in this story (and Gong Li plays her as a real force of nature), she has no trouble with the thought that sons are preferable to daughters.

The Story of Qiu Ju manages to weave its dramatic spell while providing a clear, detailed picture of the way China works. From the petty graft at a cheap urban hotel (the rate is higher for those who want a receipt) to the way enemies, enmeshed in a bitter legal dispute, still sit down amicably to a meal of noodle soup, the film offers close and witty observations about Chinese daily life. The story's last moments, giving it an ending O. Henry would have appreciated, provide as much wisdom about Chinese hospitality and Chinese justice as what has come before.

The Story of Qiu Ju reaffirms Zhang Yimou's stature as storyteller and sociologist extraordinaire, and as a visual artist of exceptional delicacy and insight.

—*J.M., October 3, 1992*

STORY OF WOMEN

Directed by Claude Chabrol; written (in French, with English subtitles) by Colo Tavernier O'Hagan and Mr. Chabrol, based on the book *Une Affaire de Femmes* by Francis Szpiner; cinematographer, Jean Rabier; edited by Monique Fardoulis; music by Matthieu Chabrol; produced by Marin Karmitz; released by New Yorker Films. Running time: 110 minutes.

With: Isabelle Huppert (Marie), François Cluzet (Paul), Marie Trintignant (Lulu/Lucie) and Nils Tavernier (Lucien).

Isabelle Huppert has an uncanny ability to convey self-interest on the screen, a quality rendered even steelier by the utter indifference with which it is displayed. Pale and fine-boned though she is, Ms. Huppert never looks frail. The same strength of will that can transform her from a mousy, nondescript figure into a vibrant beauty is apparent in the blatant single-mindedness with which some of Ms. Huppert's most memorable characters command what they need. Ruthless pragmatists, they lead wholly unexamined lives, and they stop at nothing.

As Marie Latour in Claude Chambrol's icily haunting, beautifully delineated *Story of Women,* opening today at Cinema Studio 1, Ms. Huppert gives a performance that won her a well-deserved best-actress award at the Venice Film Festival last year, and she has one of her best roles. And Mr. Chabrol, whose career has had its distinct ups and downs and whose work has barely been shown here in recent years, makes a triumphant return to the kind of emblematic crime story that has long attracted him, in films as different as *Violette* (1978) and *Le Boucher* (1971).

Marie Latour, modeled on a woman who was guillotined for her activities during the German Occupation of France, is first seen in 1941 in the company of her two small children. She takes care of them more or less dutifully, but it's clear they are a burden. One night, typically, Marie leaves her son, who is perhaps seven years old, to mind his younger sister and goes out dancing. "I need to have fun," she reasons. "I'm still young, after all."

Marie is not outstandingly ambitious, but hard times do not agree with her. So when opportunity presents itself, in the form of a pregnant, unmarried neighbor, Marie is game. The neighbor has tried and failed to abort the baby by means of home remedies. Marie agrees to help, and in a chillingly businesslike sequence she performs an abortion in her own kitchen, on the floor. "It can't be harder than anything else," she says with a shrug. (*Story of Women,* which was a commercial success when it was released in France last year, has been controversial there, and the film's subject accounts for some of the delay in its American release.)

Marie, who loves music, is given a Victrola by her first grateful patient, and is delighted by the gift. She sees the beginnings of a career in this chance encounter. Meanwhile, the return from the war of Marie's husband, Paul (François Cluzet), whom she treats with contempt and regards as a loser, only strengthens her resolve to improve life for herself and, very secondarily, for her family. Performing abortions, for Marie, means that her children can eat cakes and jam. She does not see any irony in this, and the film, which resolutely avoids passing judgment, doesn't either.

As Marie's success begins to snowball—she eventually moves to a larger apartment, rents out rooms to prostitutes, performs abortions with the aid of an assistant, and even finds a lover to replace her despised husband—the film deliberately maintains its detachment. Marie's actions are seen as the result of overeager pragmatism, and perhaps of grotesque expediency, but not as moral transgressions. In keeping with the climate of the times, she's simply doing what is necessary to get by. Marie, like many around her, is careful to avoid taking the long view. When a Jewish friend is abruptly rounded up and deported, Marie's first reaction is misplaced surprise ("She's never been Jewish. She would've told me"). Later, neighbors deride her naïveté when she claims to be waiting for the friend's return.

"France has become a gigantic chicken coop," another character says of the Vichy years. In this atmosphere, a career like Marie's cannot help but backfire sooner or later. When it does, when a judge accuses her of "a certain cynicism, a certain abjection," Marie comes as close to genuine emotion as she has during any point in the story. She feels wronged and embittered, and she truly doesn't understand. The same climate that encouraged freewheeling opportunism in the interests of survival has now turned pious, developing a fondness for family values. Marie is monstrous in very different ways, having nothing to do with politics or platitudes.

Story of Women, vivid and handsome despite the drab, claustrophobic settings that are at the root of Marie's initial despair, has a fine supporting cast. Mr. Cluzet, as Paul, captures the helplessness and frustration of a man married to so single-minded a creature, and Marie Trintignant is both sharp-eyed and traffic-stopping as the prostitute who recognizes a kindred spirit behind Marie's housewifely airs.

Nils Tavernier, as the playboy and collaborator who catches Marie's eye, is first seen quite literally playing the Nazis' game, in a bit of local pageantry involving anti-Semitic props and the beheading of a goose. Like so much of the film, this episode is staged coolly, without fanfare, and with a keen eye for matter-of-fact horror.

—J.M., October 13, 1989

STORYTELLING

Written and directed by Todd Solondz; director of photography, Frederick Elmes; edited by Alan Oxman; music by Belle and Sebastian and Nathan Larson; production designer, James Chinlund; produced by Ted Hope and Christine Vachon; released by Fine Line Features. Running time: 87 minutes.

With: "Fiction": Selma Blair (Vi), Robert Wisdom (Mr. Scott) and Leo Fitzpatrick (Marcus). "Non-Fiction": Paul Giamatti (Toby Oxman), Mark Webber (Scooby Livingston), Noah Fleiss (Brady), John Goodman (Marty), Julie Hagerty (Fern), Jonathan Osser (Mickey) and Lupe Ontiveros (Consuelo).

"Don't worry, your movie's a hit." These are the last words of Todd Solondz's *Storytelling,* which will be shown tomorrow and Sunday in the 39th annual New York Film Festival. The line is spoken by Scooby Livingston (Mark Webber), a New Jersey high school student whose so-called life has been grist for a documentary grandiosely entitled "American Scooby" and made by a desperate nebbish named Toby Oxman (Paul Giamatti). With unsparing rigor and unsettling calculation, Mr. Solondz has made it unlikely that anyone, sarcastically or otherwise, will call his new movie a hit. It is, nonetheless, a bracing slap in the face—in several faces, really, including the director's own.

The two self-contained, asymmetrical stories that *Storytelling* comprises offer pointed provocations both to those who loathed *Welcome to the Dollhouse* and *Happiness,* Mr. Solondz's previous features, and to those who embraced them. But in defending himself from both his detractors and his fans and in attempting to clarify his methods and attitudes, the director is aiming at more than self-justification. The theme of both vignettes, called simply enough "Fiction" and "Non-Fiction," is the inevitable tendency of narrative to distort, exploit and wound. *Storytelling* is an ethically ambiguous undertaking, and Mr. Solondz seems almost unbearably aware, in every frame and line of dialogue, of the moral quicksand under his feet. He ventures into this morass knowing that each step he takes is open to misunderstanding and knowing that he is embroiled in paradoxes that no intelligence, even one as analytically exacting as his own, can resolve. This spiky integrity makes *Storytelling* worth taking seriously, a task only slightly impeded by the fact that it's awfully funny.

And I do mean awfully. Mr. Solondz's ear is preternaturally attuned to the self-deluding pieties and scrambled certainties that make up so much of the American idiom. His meticulous, deadpan sense of comedy shamelessly trawls for laughs and then turns laughter into shame. Each crisply written scene seems to play out for an extra squirming beat or two. Lighthearted moments suddenly turn dreadful; episodes of raw emotion are sealed with a jabbing punch line. But Mr. Solondz is after more than the avant-garde carnival trick of shocking us with our own mirth or the self-congratulatory pseudo-ironist's game of tossing dead fish into a barrel and taking aim with a toy gun.

Storytelling is an unabashedly manipulative movie, as most movies are, but manipulation is also its subject, and it scrambles our circuits and confuses our responses in the service not of mocking sensationalism but rather of satirical clarity.

The first section, "Fiction," chronicles the humiliation of a young woman named Vi (Selma Blair) by her African-American creative writing teacher, Mr. Scott (Robert Wisdom), a Pulitzer Prize–winning novelist whose sadistic tendencies are not confined to the classroom. At the center of the story is an excruciating, comicdreadful sex scene, impossible to describe in this newspaper and apparently impossible to show in this country without jeopardizing the film's R rating. A bright red rectangle has been superimposed on the screen to protect the eyes of the innocent, but the scene is disturbing as much for its feeling of emotional peril as for anything seen or said. Mr. Solondz folds the pornographic intensity of the encounter into what is, in the end, a short, sharp comedy of manners.

"Non-Fiction," which might be subtitled "The Making of 'American Scooby,'" is longer and a bit looser, weaving several subplots around the travails of the Livingston family and poor Toby, their would-be cinematic biographer. It might be described as an addendum to *Happiness*—further studies in suburban perversity—but it also seeks to elaborate, in a spirit of self-criticism, on that much-misinterpreted film's intentions. Many of the enemies of *Happiness* accused it of expressing a smug superiority to its unhappy characters, a view shared by many of the film's admirers, who enjoyed the film sealed in the complacent illusion that they were nothing like the grotesque suburban souls depicted on the screen. But the undeniable grotesquery of Mr. Solondz's characters—this is satire, after all—is a dimension of their humanity rather than the denial of it.

At one point in *Storytelling,* Scooby's mother (Julie Hagerty) muses that, since her family escaped Nazi Germany, she and her children should be considered Holocaust survivors. Scooby counters that since without the Nazis his forebears would have remained in Europe, "If it wasn't for Hitler, none of us would have been born." Scooby's father (John Goodman) responds to this by banishing his son from the dinner table. Mr. Solondz is drawn like a skeptical moth to the unspeakable: he wants to dispel both the taboos that make us hold our tongues and the well-meaning superstitions that inspire us to pour out reassuring nonsense.

His thorough and absolute disdain for sentimentality is not, however, a lack of sympathy. What makes *Storytelling* a genuinely and valuably painful experience (instead of a chicly uncomfortable one), is that Mr. Solondz cares for his characters even as he doesn't entertain illusions about their goodness or innocence. The idea that every individual is an unstable alloy of insight and obtuseness, of tenderness and cruelty, places exceptional demands on actors, and Mr. Solondz has once again coaxed and coerced an astonishing array of performances. Ms. Blair must, in the span of about twenty minutes, show us a young woman who is, as Mr. Scott says, "callow yet coy" and also one who is tough, reckless, sensible and terrified, available in short order for pity, ridicule and something like admiration. Mr. Webber, as the apparently brain-dead Scooby, must likewise evolve from a caricature of teenage slackerdom into a thoughtful and intuitive boy and leave us wondering whether the change was in Scooby himself or in our understanding of him. Lupe Ontiveros as the Livingstons' maid, Consuelo and Mr. Goodman, are brilliantly adept at simultaneously inhabiting the stereotypes their roles point toward and subverting them with nearly imperceptible subtleties of technique. And Mr. Giamatti, playing a desperately ridiculous character who is at once Mr. Solondz's foil and his alter ego, holds the movie together with his nervous energy.

Toby clings to an inchoate belief that his self-serving project, a film about real life in the suburbs, will somehow do some good. The most pleasing paradox in *Storytelling*—a determinedly paradoxical and, in spite of much of what I've said here, a genuinely pleasing movie is that it sets out to debunk this notion and ends up affirming it.

—*A.O.S., September 29, 2001*

LA STRADA

Directed by Federico Fellini; written (in Italian, with English subtitles) by Mr. Fellini, Tullio Pinelli and Ennio Flaiano, based on a story by Mr. Fellini and Mr. Pinelli; cinematographer, Otello Martelli; edited by Leo Catozzo and Lina Caterini; music by Nino Rota; art designer, Mario Ravasco; produced by Dino De Laurentiis and Carlo Ponti; released by Trans-Lux Films. Black and white. Running time: 115 minutes.

With: Anthony Quinn (Zampano), Giulietta Masina (Gelsomina), Richard Basehart (Matto the Fool) and Aldo Silvani (Colombaini).

Although Federico Fellini's talents as a director have not been displayed to advantage heretofore in these parts, his *La Strada* (*The Road*), which arrived at the Fifty-second Street Trans-Lux yesterday, is a tribute both to him and the Italian neo-realistic school of filmmaking.

His story of an itinerant strongman and the simple-minded girl who is his foil and helpmeet is a modern picaresque parable. Like life itself, it is seemingly aimless, disjointed on occasion, and full of truth and poetry. Like the principals, it wanders along a sad and sometimes comic path while accentuating man's loneliness and need for love.

We have no idea why *La Strada*, which won a prize at the 1954 Venice Film Festival, has not been exposed to American audiences until now. Perhaps it is because Signor Fellini's theme offers neither a happy ending so dear to the hearts of escapists nor a clear-cut and shiningly hopeful plot. Suffice it to say that his study of his principals is honest and unadorned, strikingly realistic and yet genuinely tender and compassionate. *La Strada* is a road well worth traveling.

The story, let it be said at the outset, is, like its protagonists, simplicity itself. A boorish and brutish strongman literally buys a happy but mentally incompetent lass from her impoverished mother to serve as his clown, cook, and concubine. She is replacing her sister, who has died. He teaches her some simple routines as they bowl along in his motorcycle-trailer—clowning and simple tunes on a cornet—to serve as a come-on to his pitifully corny act of breaking chains across his chest.

Although her timorousness fades into happiness as they play villages, fairs, and country weddings, her idyllic existence is broken when they join a small circus on the outskirts of Rome. Here a clown and high-wire artist goad her man, who is finally jailed for threatening the buffoon with a knife.

The clown, who has invited her to join him on the road, realizes that she is peculiarly dedicated to her hard master and advises her to wait for the bestial strongman.

"Everyone serves some purpose," he tells her, "and perhaps you must serve him."

Later, the pair meet the clown and the strongman beats and unwittingly kills him. Since the girl's constant whimpering serves as the strongman's conscience, he deserts his ill-fated companion. At the drama's climax, when he accidentally learns of her death, he breaks down in sudden and helpless realization of his solitude.

Despite this doleful outline, Signor Fellini has not handled his story in merely tragic or heavily dramatic fashion. In Giulietta Masina (Mrs. Fellini in private life) he has an extremely versatile performer who mirrors the simple passions and anxieties of the childlike girl with rare and acute perception. She is expert at pantomime, funny as the tow-headed, doe-eyed and trusting foil, and sentient enough to portray in wordless tension her fear of the man she basically loves.

Anthony Quinn is excellent as the growling, monosyllabic, and apparently ruthless strongman, whose tastes are primitive and immediate. But his characterization is sensitively developed so that his innate loneliness shows through the chinks of his rough exterior. As the cheerful and prescient clown, Richard Basehart, like the haunting background score by Nino Rota, provides a humorous but pointed counterpoint to the towering and basically serious delineations of the two princpals.

Signor Fellini has used his small cast, and, equally important, his camera, with the unmistakable touch of an artist. His vignettes fill his movie with beauty, sadness, humor, and understanding.

Although there are English subtitles and the voices of the Messrs. Quinn and Basehart have been dubbed into Italian, *La Strada* needs no fuller explanations. It speaks forcefully, poetically, and often movingly in a universal language.

—*A.W., July 17, 1956*

THE STRAIGHT STORY

Directed by David Lynch: written by John Roach and Mary Sweeney: director of photography. Freddie Francis: edited by Ms. Sweeney: music by Angelo Badalamenti: production designer. Jack Fisk: produced by Ms. Sweeney and Neal Edelstein: released by Walt Disney Pictures. Running time: 110 minutes.

With: Sissy Spacek (Rose). Richard Farnsworth (Alvin). Harry Dean Stanton (Lyle) and Wiley Harker (Verlyn Heller).

In 1994 an elderly man named Alvin Straight undertook a long Midwestern journey riding on a lawnmower. It was an arduous feat, but not nearly as daunting as what David Lynch sets out to do in *The Straight Story*: make a slow-moving, folksy-looking, profoundly spiritual film that can hold an audience in absolute thrall. As the least likely filmmaker on the planet to pull off such a G-rated miracle, Mr. Lynch rises to this challenge with exhilarating vigor. Switching gears radically, bravely defying conventional wisdom about what it takes to excite moviegoers, Mr. Lynch presents the flip side of *Blue Velvet* and turns it into a supremely improbable triumph.

Of course, this film's wholesome radiance and soothing natural beauty are distinctly at odds with the famously unwholesome Lynch imagination. The chasm between the ghoulish malevolence of the filmmaker's previous *Lost Highway* and the decent, forthright tone of *The Straight Story* is almost too huge to fathom. But the same bellwether quality that left *Blue Velvet* looking so prescient, and ushered in a whole cinematic wave of taboo-shattering, is at work once again. When a born unnaturalist like Mr. Lynch can bring such interest and emotion to one man's simple story, the realm of the ordinary starts looking like a new frontier.

It helps that *The Straight Story* is as precise and technically adept as Mr. Lynch's other work, and that its effects are achieved with the same exacting care. Indeed, the classic opening images of "Blue Velvet" are echoed at this film's start, as the camera takes in a seemingly ordinary house and lawn and Mr. Lynch uses sound, music and staging to build unnerving suspense. The house becomes eerily quiet and isolated until a sudden event introduces Alvin Straight, played without a trace of artifice by the veteran actor Richard Farnsworth. *The Straight Story* would not have been possible without Mr. Farnsworth's terse, no-nonsense honesty at its heart.

For a notion of just how far removed most American movies are from actual experience, consider the startling effect that Mr. Farnsworth has on screen. This actor, rancher, and former stunt man, enough of a film veteran to have driven a chariot in *The Ten Commandments,* cuts a startling figure as an unabashedly old man. Unshaven, infirm, scraggly haired, and without makeup, he automatically frees the film from any sense of artifice and delivers an amazingly stalwart performance that will not soon be forgotten.

Alvin lives with his daughter (played by Sissy Spacek) in Laurens, Iowa, a town where there's never any trouble finding a parking space on Main Street. His health is failing, and he knows that his life is about to change. A straightforward sequence, in which Alvin visits a doctor, quietly sizes up the ominous medical equipment and listens to dire predictions about his health, is enough to explain his subsequent behavior. Faced with a choice between aging helplessly in Laurens or having one more meaningful taste of freedom, Alvin decides to hit the road.

Ostensibly, he is on his way to Mount Zion, Wis., in hopes of finding his estranged brother, who has had a stroke. (The less a viewer knows about where this journey will lead, the better. The film builds real suspense about its outcome, and becomes extremely moving in its final scene.) But in fact Alvin's journey isn't much about a destination. Mr. Lynch, working from a lovely and succinct screenplay by John Roach and Mary Sweeney, invests each phase of the trip with resonance about Alvin's life and the lives of those he meets, so that each encounter takes on an unforced larger significance. *The Straight Story* has the curious disadvantage of being spoken in English and steeped in Americana. Its eloquent, contemplative spirit is much more indigenous to films from other parts of the world.

One of the many haunting images here finds Alvin moving along an open road on his mower, which he rides because he has no driver's license—and because he wants to make this one last voyage in his own way. The camera pans up, and Angelo Badalamenti's beautiful folk-influenced score rolls along, until the camera moves down again—and finds Alvin almost exactly where he was. *The Straight Story* is more about gazing at the sky, about experiencing each encounter to the fullest, than it is about getting anywhere in a hurry.

It's been too long since a great American movie dared to regard life that way.

—J.M., October 15, 1999

STRAIGHT TIME

Directed by Ulu Grosbard: written by Alvin Sargent. Edward Bunker and Jeffrey Boam, based on the novel *No Beast So Fierce* by Mr. Bunker: director of photography. Owen Roizman: edited by Sam O'Steen and Randy Roberts: music by David Shire: produced by Stanley Beck and Tim Zinnemann: released by Warner Brothers. Running time: 114 minutes.

With: Dustin Hoffman (Max Dembo). Theresa Russell (Jenny Mercer). Harry Dean Stanton (Jerry Schue). Gary Busey (Willy Darin). M. Emmet Walsh (Earl Frank). Sandy Baron (Manny). Kathy Bates (Selma Darin) and Edward Bunker (Mickey).

Max," says the parole officer, "I think you have a serious attitude problem." Just how serious is the dramatic substance of *Straight Time,* the grimly witty account of the decline of Max Dembo (Dustin Hoffman), an ex-con (six years for armed robbery) who would say that he pursues success though he measures his life in small failures and the treacheries of others. He knows the world is crooked and he behaves accordingly. Like millions of other people who live on the right side of the law, Max never questions the system. He simply tries to beat it in his own half-baked way.

Max is the sort of fellow who automatically lies when someone asks him how much rent he pays. It would make no difference if he told the truth, but Max has to keep in practice. The only time he can look someone in the eye with ease is when he stares through the slits in a face mask—during a holdup.

Max is shrewd, self-absorbed, tough in superficial ways, and doomed. He defines the meaning of recidivism. In real life you wouldn't trust him to hang up your coat. In *Straight Time,* in the person of Dustin Hoffman, he's a fascinating character, made romantic only to the extent that an actor of such stature invests him with importance that is otherwise denied. Max is strictly small-time.

Even though *Straight Time,* which opens today at

959

the Coronet Theater, has been tailored to Max's dimensions, it's not a small-time movie. Ulu Grosbard, the director, and Alvin Sargent, Edward Bunker, and Jeffrey Boam, who wrote the screenplay, have succeeded in making an uncommonly interesting film about a fellow whose significance is entirely negative. It's almost as if the real subject of the movie were all the things Max isn't.

This may be to invest *Straight Time* with more purpose than was ever intended, but it is such a leanly constructed, vividly staged film that one seeks to justify the way it compels the attention. The first words we hear in the movie are those of the guards as Max is getting out of prison—"Open the gates"—while the rest of the film is the detailed case history of a man doing his unconscious best to get back in.

The movie makes no attempt to explain Max. It simply says that this is the way he is. It requires us to fill in the gaps, and it's the measure of the film that we want to. In the meantime, we watch as Max has his early run-ins with his Los Angeles parole officer, a sadistic, patronizing redneck, marvelously well played by M. Emmet Walsh, and accept as inevitable his return to life as a holdup man.

The film's most surprising and involving sequences are the series of heists that Max carries out, at first solo, then in the company of an old associate, a fellow named Jerry Schue (Harry Dean Stanton), an ex-con, now a paint contractor apparently happily married, who is going out of his mind with the boredom of a settled life that involves a backyard swimming pool and barbecue pit.

Straight Time makes a concession to convention in the casting of Theresa Russell as the young woman who has a brief affair with Max. Miss Russell, who was so good in *The Last Tycoon,* is an extremely appealing actress, with a kind of contemporary authority, but she looks so classy, so understated-chic, that she suggests an upper-class girl whose path would cross Max's only at the beach, or maybe at a singles bar. The two really belong in different movies.

The film is beautifully acted by everyone, but especially by Mr. Hoffman, Mr. Walsh, Mr. Stanton, and Gary Busey, who plays a junkie friend of Max who cops out at the last minute of a crucial job. *Straight Time* is not a movie to raise the spirits. It is so cool it would leave a chill were it not done with such preci-

sion and control that we remain fascinated by a rat, in spite of ourselves.

—*V.C., March 18, 1978*

STRANGER THAN PARADISE

Written and directed by Jim Jarmusch; director of photography. Tom DiCillo; edited by Mr. Jarmusch and Melody London; music by John Lurie and Aaron Picht; produced by Sara Driver; released by the Samuel Goldwyn Company. Black and white. Running time: 90 minutes.

With: John Lurie (Willie), Eszter Balint (Eva), Richard Edson (Eddie), Cecillia Stark (Aunt Lottie), Danny Rosen (Billy), Tom DiCillo (Airline Agent) and Richard Boes (Factory Worker).

Jim Jarmusch's *Stranger than Paradise* looks as if it had been left on the windowsill too long. Shot in 16mm black-and-white, and now blown up to 35mm, its images appear to have been aged by the sun and by general neglect until they've faded into a uniform shade of gray. When, occasionally, there's a splotch of comparatively pure black or white, the effect is disorienting until you recognize what Mr. Jarmusch is up to—that is, discovering the ludicrously sublime in the supremely tacky. The film, a prize-winner at this year's Cannes festival, is something quite special.

Stranger than Paradise will be shown at the New York Film Festival at Alice Tully Hall tonight and tomorrow, and will open its regular commercial engagement at the Cinema Studio 2 on Monday. Among other things, it is one of the most original, wonderfully oddball, independent American films to turn up at the Lincoln Center festival in years, or at least since the showing of Eagle Pennell's *Last Night at the Alamo* last year.

The two films otherwise don't have much in common except their tiny budgets and each director's rare appreciation for the ridiculous. *Last Night at the Alamo* is a gregarious sort of comedy, full of oversize emotions and good humor. By comparison, *Stranger than Paradise* is inhibited, its visual manners almost as lazy as those of Rainer Werner Fassbinder's *Katzelmacher,* in which the camera often seems just too tired to follow a character as he walks offscreen, knowing full well that if it waits long enough, the character will walk back on.

Stranger than Paradise is a *Marty* that Jean-Paul Sartre might have appreciated, about hanging out, not in hell but in a permanent purgatory. This world sometimes looks like an eerily underpopulated New York City, a rundown but genteel working-class section of Cleveland, or that scrubby part of the east coast of Florida that has yet to be transformed into a vacation paradise, where the motels always have vacancies, even at the height of the season, and where the swimming pools are filled with weeds, not water.

Though Mr. Jarmusch's screenplay does contain a number of subsidiary roles, it's virtually a three-character piece. They are Willie (John Lurie), a thirty-ish, horse-faced fellow who, though Hungarian-born, has been in this country ten years and has no trace of any accent; his pal Eddie (Richard Edson), who looks like a condensed version of Willie, even down—or up—to the cheap fedoras they seldom remove, even to sleep; and Eva (Eszter Balint), Willie's pretty sixteen-year-old cousin from Budapest who is forced to spend ten days at Willie's grimy little New York room before going on to live with an elderly aunt in Cleveland.

Until the arrival of Eva, Willie appears to be perfectly content with his life on the outer fringes of capitalism. He has no visible means of support, and appears to make ends meet by playing the horses and occasionally cheating at cards. At first the presence of the taciturn, pony-tailed Eva seems a rude intrusion to Willie, especially when she asks why TV dinners are called TV dinners or what a quarterback does when his team is on defense.

She's a drag until she casually shoplifts food and cigarettes for them, at which point Willie begins to see her as a kindred spirit. He gets so carried away by what passes for affection in his life that he even buys her a present. When she opens the shopping bag and takes out the dress, her brow furrows. "Well?" says Willie. "I think it's kind of ugly," says Eva. They speak the same language.

Stranger than Paradise is about the curious, unspoken alliance of Willie, Eva, and Eddie and their adventures in New York, Cleveland, and, finally, Florida. They are as lost but also as quietly gallant in the American paradise as the three German misfits who seek their fortunes in Wisconsin in Werner Herzog's *Stroszek*. The film has no big scenes, and it takes a while to get the hang of it, but once you do, it's as funny as it is wise. Mr. Jarmusch isolates the film's series of tiny vignettes by extended blackouts that, at the beginning, seem to be an affectation, but then come to be the visual equivalent of the dead space that surrounds each character.

The quality of Mr. Jarmusch's humor is not easily described. It's there in the spare dialogue, as when Willie and Eddie, in a blinding snowstorm, are driving through Cleveland to find Eva, and Eddie asks, quite sincerely, if Cleveland looks like Budapest. "Of course not," says Willie. Later, when they are leaving Cleveland, Eddie muses, "You know, it's kind of funny. You're someplace new, and everything looks just the same."

Wherever they go, the world of Willie, Eva, and Eddie does look just the same. The Florida they find is not unlike a large vacant lot in Cleveland, though without the snow. Their adventures, however, are very particular, and the film ends on a note that slides without effort, like a piece of music, from the hilarious to the funny to the haunting.

The three lead performers are extremely good, never for a second betraying the film's consistently deadpan style. In a couple of short scenes, Cecillia Stark, as the elderly aunt in Cleveland, nearly walks off with the picture, but *Stranger than Paradise* is too much of an integrated piece of work for any one performer to steal it. Mention must also be made of Tom DiCillo's camera work, which is as funny and self-assured as the performances and Mr. Jarmusch's realization of his initial concept.

Here is one festival movie that should hang around for a good, long while.

—*V.C., September 29, 1984*

STRANGERS ON A TRAIN

Produced and directed by Alfred Hitchcock: written by Raymond Chandler. Czenzi Ormonde and Whitfield Cook. based on the novel by Patricia Highsmith: cinematographer. Robert Burks: edited by William Ziegler: music by Dimitri Tiomkin: art designer. Ted Haworth: released by

Warner Brothers. Black and white. Running time: 101 minutes.

With: Farley Granger (Guy Haines). Ruth Roman (Anna Morton). Robert Walker (Bruno Anthony). Leo G. Carroll (Senator Morton). Patricia Hitchcock (Barbara Morton). Laura Elliott (Miriam) and Marion Lorne (Mrs. Anthony).

It appears that Alfred Hitchcock is fascinated with the Svengali theme, as well as with his own dexterity in performing macabre tricks. His last picture, *Rope,* will be remembered as a stunt (which didn't succeed) involving a psychopathic murderer who induced another young man to kill for thrills. Now, in his latest effort, called *Strangers on a Train,* which served to reopen the Strand Theatre last night under its new name, the Warner, Mr. Hitchcock again is tossing a crazy murder story in the air and trying to con us into thinking that it will stand up without support.

And again his instigator of evil is a weirdly unbalanced young man who almost succeeds in enmeshing a young tennis star in a murder plot. This time the two individuals meet by seeming chance on a train, making what appears a devious journey from Washington to New York. And before the trip is over, the Svengali has hatched a scheme whereby he will do a murder for the athlete if the athlete will do one for him.

As a matter of fact, he doesn't even wait for the tennis star to agree to the scheme—or even to show an interest in it. He just goes out and murders the athlete's wife. And then he fast-talks the poor, scared fellow into thinking that he is somehow involved and keeping him in a state of terror and grave anxiety until the end of the film.

Perhaps there will be those in the audience who will likewise be terrified by the villain's darkly menacing warnings and by Mr. Hitchcock's sleekly melodramatic tricks. Certainly, Mr. Hitchcock is the fellow who can pour on the pictorial stuff and toss what are known as "touches" until they're flying all over the screen. From the slow, stalking murder of a loose girl in a tawdry amusement park to a "chase" and eventual calamity aboard a runaway merry-go-round, the nimble director keeps piling "touch" and stunt upon "touch." Indeed, his desire to produce them appears his main impulse in this film.

But, for all that, his basic premise of fear fired by menace is so thin and so utterly unconvincing that the story just does not stand. And the actors, as much as they labor, do not convey any belief—at least, not to this observer, who will give a Hitchcock character plenty of rope. Robert Walker as the diabolic villain is a caricature of silken suavity and Farley Granger plays the terrified catspaw (as he did in *Rope*) as though he were constantly swallowing his tongue. Ruth Roman holds herself in solemn tension as the latter's hopeful fiancée and Patricia Hitchcock, the daughter of the director, bounces about like a bespectacled tennis ball as the sister of Miss Roman and a convenience to the paternal "touch." Leo G. Carroll and Laura Elliott are others who jump and jig according to how Mr. Hitchcock arbitrarily yanks on the strings.

Also, it might be mentioned that there are a few inaccuracies in this film that may cause some knowing observers considerable skeptical pause—such as the evidence that you get to the Washington Union Station by going into Virginia over the Memorial Bridge. Also a purist might question how a tennis star could race around Washington half the night and then win three grueling sets of tennis in a Forest Hills tourney the next day.

Frankly, we feel that Mr. Hitchcock is "touching" us just a bit too much and without returning sufficient recompense in the sensation line.

—B.C., July 4, 1951

STRAW DOGS

Directed by Sam Peckinpah: written by David Zelag Goodman and Mr. Peckinpah, based on the novel *The Siege of Trencher's Farm* by Gordon M. Williams: cinematographer, John Coquillon: edited by Paul Davies, Roger Spottiswoode and Tony Lawson: music by Jerry Fielding: production designer, Ray Simm: produced by Daniel Melnick: released by Cinerama. Running time: 118 minutes.

With: Dustin Hoffman (David). Susan George (Amy). Peter Vaughn (Tom Hedden). T. P. McKenna (Major Scott). Del Henney (Venner) and Ken Hutchinson (Scott).

This is where I live," says David (Dustin Hoffman), the ordinarily loving, mild-mannered mathematician, to the thugs who want to invade his home. "This is me! I will not allow violence against this house!"

That pronunciamento, which sounds very much like the sort of thing that mild-mannered professors used to say in pre—Pearl Harbor, anti-Nazi films, as well as like the sort of thing that mild-mannered homesteaders still say in certain kinds of Western dramas, is not all there is in Sam Peckinpah's *Straw Dogs*. However, it comes close to being the entire point of Mr. Peckinpah's first non-Western—a contemporary melodrama set on the Cornish coast of England. And this is, I think, a major disappointment. When a movie can be summarized so easily, why make a movie at all? Why not release a greeting card instead?

After ninety minutes of filmed equivocation, during which David's cat has been strangled and hung in his closet, and his wife, Amy (Susan George), has been raped (not entirely against her will), David decides to make a stand when five local toughs try to enter his cottage. They want to carry off the local idiot (David Warner), suspected of molesting a teenage girl who (and this is important in Peckinpah's view of the world, and of women, too) asked to be molested in the first place.

For the next thirty minutes, David, the turned-worm, defends his home by, among other things, helping to shoot off one man's foot, heaving boiling oil (or is it vinegar?) in the faces of a couple of others, by throwing an antique man-trap around the neck of a fourth, and, at last, by persuading the fickle-hearted Amy to shoot the fifth through the chest with a shotgun.

Curiously enough, it's not really the violent climax that is objectionable about *Straw Dogs*. Although it is extremely explicit, it does serve a dramatic function in a film that seriously attempts to define the meaning of manhood in such terms. However, I was more than a little surprised by the poor quality of either the staging of or the editing of this final sequence, which results in total confusion as to who is doing what to whom and where, at any given moment. In movies about besieged fortresses, we always have a right to know where we are, and how the ammo supply is holding out.

A much greater problem with *Straw Dogs* is that nothing in the screenplay supports this extraordinary finale with conviction. Hoffman's David is a nice, clean-cut intellectual who, we are told early on, has refused to take stands, to be committed to anything,

and from the way he treats his wife ("Amy, I love you, but I want you to leave me alone") it's apparent that he's an embryo of one of those old-fashioned Western heroes to whom women are a necessary but lesser breed of being.

It is, further, very difficult to accept the quality of the hostility that greets the American mathematician and his English wife in the tiny Cornish community. It is, in fact, the kind of hostility that might be perfectly acceptable on a Western frontier but doesn't work very easily in a contemporary drama that pretends to be otherwise so realistic.

Even more difficult to accept in a contemporary setting is the almost Eve-like portrayal of women. Oddly, the best performance in the film is given by Miss George, who looks like a lovely young spin-off of Susannah York, yet I suspect this may be because the role is written with so much more venom, and contains the kind of contradictions that make characters interesting to watch.

Perhaps the toughest—and most erotic—scene in the film is the one in which she is raped by one of the thugs, an old boyfriend, an encounter that begins with the exercise of force and ends with the woman's complete and willing submission. This will not, I imagine, endear the director to something over half of this country's population.

Mr. Peckinpah has made some good films (*Ride the High Country*) and a couple of great films (*The Wild Bunch, The Ballad of Cable Hogue*)—which may be why *Straw Dogs* is a special disappointment. It is an intelligent movie, but interesting only in the context of his other works. His philosophy somehow belongs out West, either in the great spaces inhabited by Cable Hogue, or in those areas where the frontier is slowly being corrupted by civilization. I can't quarrel with the point of *Straw Dogs*. There are times when a man must take a position and maintain it. But the manner in which Dustin Hoffman, on the Cornish coast of England, does it reminds me of someone protecting his Jaguar with a flintlock.

—*V.C., January 20, 1972*

A STREETCAR NAMED DESIRE

Directed by Elia Kazan; written by Tennessee Williams and Oscar Saul, based on the play by Mr.

Williams: cinematographer. Harry Stradling: edited by David Weisbart: music by Alex North: art designer. Richard Day: produced by Charles K. Feldman: released by Warner Brothers. Black and white. Running time: 125 minutes.

With: Vivien Leigh (Blanche du Bois). Marlon Brando (Stanley Kowalski). Kim Hunter (Stella Kowalski). Karl Malden (Mitch). Rudy Bond (Steve). Nick Dennis (Pablo) and Peg Hillias (Eunice).

Out of Tennessee Williams's *A Streetcar Named Desire*, which gathered up most of the drama prizes that were awarded when it was playing on Broadway, director Elia Kazan and a simply superlative cast have fashioned a motion picture that throbs with passion and poignancy. Indeed, through the haunting performance England's great Vivien Leigh gives in the heartbreaking role of Mr. Williams's deteriorating Southern belle and through the mesmerizing moods Mr. Kazan has wreathed with the techniques of the screen, this picture, now showing at the Warner, becomes as fine, if not finer, than the play. Inner torments are seldom projected with such sensitivity and clarity on the screen.

Of course, the first factor in this triumph is Mr. Williams's play, which embraces, among its many virtues, an essential human conflict in visual terms. The last brave, defiant, hopeless struggle of the lonely and decaying Blanche du Bois to hold on to her faded gentility against the heartless badgering of her rough-neck brother-in-law is a tangible cat-and-dog set-to, marked with manifold physical episodes as well as a wealth of fluctuations of verbally fashioned images and moods. And all of these graphic components have been fully preserved in Oscar Saul's script and availed of by Mr. Kazan in his cinematic mounting of same.

Mélees, titanic and degrading, within the filthy New Orleans slum where Blanche comes to live with her sister and her low-born brother-in-law have been staged by the prescient director with such tumultuous energy that the screen fairly throbs with angry violence, before settling sharply into spent and aching quiet. Hate-oozing personal encounters between the lost lady and the brutish man have been filmed with such shrewd manipulation of the close-up that one feels the heat of them. And with lights and the move-ment of his people and the conjunction of a brilliant musical score with dialogue of real poetic richness, Mr. Kazan has wrought heartache and despair.

In this dramatic illustration, which makes vivid, of course, a great deal more than a fundamental clash of natures between a woman and a man—which transmits, indeed, a comprehension of a whole society's slow decay and the pathos of vain escapism in a crude and dynamic world—we say, in this dramatic illustration, Miss Leigh accomplishes more than a worthy repeat of the performance which Jessica Tandy gave on the stage.

Blessed with a beautifully molded and fluently expressive face, a pair of eyes that can flood with emotion, and a body that moves with spirit and style, Miss Leigh has, indeed, created a new Blanche du Bois on the screen—a woman of even greater fullness, torment, and tragedy. Although Mr. Williams's writing never precisely makes clear the logic of her disintegration before the story begins—why anyone of her breeding would become an undisciplined tramp—Miss Leigh makes implicitly cogent every moment of the lady on the screen.

Her mental confusions, her self-deceptions, the agonies of her lacerated nerves, and her final, unbearable madness, brought on by a brutal act of rape, are clearly conveyed by the actress with a tremendous concentration and economy of power. Likewise, her fumblings for affections are beautifully and poignantly done. And since Miss Leigh is present in virtually every scene or sequence of the film, the demands upon her vitality and her flexibility are great.

No less brilliant, however, within his area is Marlon Brando in the role of the loud, lusty, brawling, brutal, amoral Polish brother-in-law. Mr. Brando created the role in the stage play and he carries over all the energy and the steel-spring characteristics that made him vivid on the stage. But here, where we're so much closer to him, he seems that much more highly charged, his despairs seem that much more pathetic, and his comic moments that much more slyly enjoyed.

Others from the cast of the stage play—Kim Hunter as the torn young sister and wife, Karl Malden as a timid, boorish suitor, Nick Dennis as a pal, and all the rest—fill out the human pattern within a sleazy environment that is so fitly and graphically created that you can almost sense its sweatiness and smells. Alex North's incidental music deserves prominent commendation, too, as do all of the technical aspects of this film which Charles K. Feldman has produced.

But comments cannot do justice to the substance and the artistry of this film. You must see it to appreciate it. And that we strongly urge you to do.

—B.C., September 20, 1951

STROSZEK

Directed by Werner Herzog; written (in German, with English subtitles) by Mr. Herzog; cinematographers, Stefano Guidi, Wolfgang Knigge, Edward Lachmann and Thomas Mauch; edited by Beate Mainka-Jellinghaus; music by Chet Atkins and Sonny Terry; released by Werner Herzog Filmproduktion. Running time: 108 minutes.

With: Michael Gahr (Prisoner Hoss), Eva Mattes (Eva), Bruno S. (Stroszek), Clemens Scheitz (Scheitz), Vaclav Vojta (Doctor) and Ralph Wade (Auctioneer).

Werner Herzog, the young German director of *The Mystery of Kasper Hauser, The Great Ecstasy of the Sculptor Steiner,* and *Aguirre, the Wrath of God,* doesn't make movies that are easy to describe. *Kasper Hauser,* Mr. Herzog's variation on the "wild child" story, is a beautiful, ghostly movie, a parable almost too refined for mortal comprehension.

In his short film about Walter Steiner, Mr. Herzog demonstrates the ecstasy of the champion ski-jumper in sports footage so breathtaking, we see doom in every triumph.

Aguirre, about the mad, power-obsessed Spanish conquistador, is a meditation upon human futility photographed in Peru and Brazil in some of the world's most spectacular scenery. Among other things, Mr. Herzog visually dazzles us while he's pulling the rug from under our feet.

In a Herzog film we have to keep checking what we are hearing against what we're seeing. They are seldom the same things, but forcing us to reconcile contradictions is one of the ways in which he works.

Stroszek, which opened yesterday at the Cinema Studio, is described by Mr. Herzog as a ballad, which is probably as good a way as any to categorize it initially. It's a "road" picture. In some distant way it

reminds me of *Easy Rider,* but it's an *Easy Rider* without sentimentality or political paranoia. It's terrifically, spontaneously funny and, just as spontaneously, full of unexpected pathos.

Stroszek is the tale of three mismatched friends— each a loser—who set out from Berlin to find El Dorado in northern Wisconsin, in winter, with very little money and hardly any knowledge of English. It would be difficult to imagine three people less fit for such a journey.

Scheitz (Clemens Scheitz) is in his seventies, small, frail, modest, a fellow who seems always to be suffering from a chill. Eva (Eva Mattes) is a buxom but none-too-bright Berlin streetwalker, the sort that pimps can beat up and double-cross endlessly without seriously damaging her dogged dependence on them.

Most importantly there is Stroszek, played by Bruno S., the Berlin street musician who played the title role in *Kasper Hauser.* Stroszek, fortyish, is a worldly innocent who, when we first meet him, seems to be simple-minded. He is being released from prison by a not-unsympathetic warden who warns him to stay out of bars and to try to remember to shave and keep his fly zipped. It's not that Stroszek has tendencies. He simply doesn't pay attention to minor details. Something is missing from Stroszek, but what it is is not intelligence.

As an actor, Bruno S. is a found object. Much of the tension of the early scenes of *Stroszek* is created by our attempting to fit Bruno S. into some normal scheme of things. Is he acting? Is he following Mr. Herzog's directions like a trained dog? Is he improvising, sometimes with immense wit? I suspect it must be a combination of all three.

In whatever way the performance is created, it's an extraordinarily compelling one, and one that is virtually a physical manifestation of what the film is about. The Stroszek we get to know is a compassionate, patient, commonsensical man incapable of rage or physical assertiveness. This small, curious personality is imprisoned within a large, stocky, man-sized body that seems too big for him, a vehicle that can maneuver with only the utmost effort and concentration. When he glances around him, he looks like a child peering apprehensively out of the pilot's seat of a 747.

The adventures of these three contemporary pilgrims as they attempt to settle into what they believe to be the American way of life are both bleak and uproariously funny. Eva, who works as a waitress—for a while—and Stroszek, who gets a job as a mechanic, buy a huge mobile home of an indescribably fancy awfulness. Scheitz, who appears to shrink even smaller in the Wisconsin cold, becomes politely disoriented and decides he has discovered the means to measure "animal magnetism" by using a conventional ammeter.

Constantly working against Mr. Herzog's very cool view of the human condition is not only the humor—*Stroszek* contains one of the shortest, funniest holdups I've ever seen in a movie—but also the physical beauty of the landscapes, the cityscapes, and the squalid interiors. This visual lyricism, which at first seems at odds with the subject, eventually becomes a further celebration of Stroszek's survival.

That the pilgrims must eventually be disappointed is a foregone conclusion, but the way it happens is anything but predictable. Among the dozens of images in the film I'll remember for a very long time is one, near the end, of a chicken that can't stop dancing and another of a premature baby, hardly bigger than a man's hand, whose capacity to hang on is nothing less than ferocious. It's this mixture of feelings and attitudes that gives the Herzog works their haunting lives.

—V.C., July 13, 1977

SUDDENLY, LAST SUMMER

Directed by Joseph L. Mankiewicz; written by Gore Vidal and Tennessee Williams, based on the play by Mr. Williams; cinematographer, Jack Hildyard; edited by Thomas Stanford; music by Buxton Orr and Malcolm Arnold; art designer, William Kellner; produced by Sam Spiegel; released by Columbia Pictures. Black and white. Running time: 114 minutes.

With: Elizabeth Taylor (Catherine Holly), Katharine Hepburn (Mrs. Venable), Montgomery Clift (Dr. Dukrowicz), Albert Dekker (Dr. Hockstader) and Mercedes McCambridge (Mrs. Holly).

Whatever horrifying import there may have been in Tennessee Williams's short play *Suddenly, Last Summer,* when it was acted on the stage, has been drained out of it through tedious talking and

a terminal showdown that is irritatingly obscure in the close to two-hour film version of it that opened at the Criterion and the Sutton last night.

People who leap to conclusions may assume the trouble is that Sam Spiegel and his crew that made the picture were compelled to go easy with the ugly words. They may suspect that because the true nature of the most-talked-of character could not be tagged (he was obviously a homosexual, as well as a sadist of some sort, in the play) and because the precise and horrible details of his death could not be explained (he was literally eaten by urchins), the point of it all is missed.

There's no doubt that a great deal of the feeling of dank corruption that ran through the play has been lost or pitifully diluted by a tactful screening of the words. And certainly what should be thoroughly shocking in the flashback scenes of the focal character's death is only confusing and baffling, because you can't really see what's happening, and the lady who is describing the occasion is much less vivid and exact than she could be.

But, in this viewer's estimation, the main trouble with this picture is that an idea that is good for not much more than a blackout is stretched to exhausting length and, for all its fine cast and big direction, it is badly, pretentiously played.

In structure, as well as in content, the drama is a simple mystery, a psychological whodunit—or howdunit, to be exact. A touchy and skeptical young brain surgeon is patiently trying to find why a wealthy Louisiana dowager insists that her pretty young niece is insane and can be helped only by having a lobotomy, a section cut out of her brain.

After talking interminably to the dowager and later to the niece, then to both of them together and to other people at different times, he discovers there is friction between the females on account of the dowager's dead son. It seems the fellow was inseparable from his mother until he suddenly, last summer, took up with the niece and "died" while on a trip with her in Europe. How did the fellow die?

He died from being set upon by urchins. This fact eventually comes out when the niece, under the effects of a "truth serum" (like a character in a cheap thriller), blabs it out, shrieking and tossing in torment. This cures her and drives the dowager mad.

But this offers no valid solutions. It does not tell how the urchins killed the man, to justify frequent mention that it was "horrid and obscene." It does not tell why they did it, other than to suggest that they were "hungry," which is a feeble explanation and gastronomically far-fetched. And it certainly does not complete an image, made much of by the dowager early along, that vultures swooping down upon young turtles and devouring them reveal the cruel "face of God."

Mr. Williams and Gore Vidal, who helped him prepare his play for the screen, have indulged in sheer verbal melodramatics which have small effect on the screen and are barely elevated from tedium by some incidental scenes of inmates of a mental institution.

The acting is small compensation. Elizabeth Taylor is rightly roiled as the niece, but her wallow in agony at the climax is sheer histrionic showing off. Katharine Hepburn plays the arch and airy dowager with what looks like a stork's nest on her head and such bony and bumptious posturing that she acts a Mary Petty caricature. Montgomery Clift seems racked with pain and indifference as the brain surgeon; Albert Dekker growls and gropes as his dull boss; and Mercedes McCambridge and Gary Raymond do a routine—a vaudeville routine—as the mother and brother of the girl.

Joseph L. Mankiewicz's direction is strained and sluggish, as is, indeed, the whole conceit of the drama. It should have been left to the off-Broadway stage.

—B.C., December 23, 1959

THE SUGARLAND EXPRESS

Directed by Steven Spielberg; written by Hal Barwood and Matthew Robbins, based on a story by Mr. Spielberg, Mr. Barwood and Mr. Robbins; director of photography, Vilmos Zsigmond; edited by Edward Abroms and Verna Fields; music by John Williams; art designer, Joe Alves; produced by Richard D. Zanuck and David Brown; released by Universal Pictures. Running time: 109 minutes.

With: Goldie Hawn (Lou Jean), Ben Johnson (Captain Tanner), Michael Sacks (Slide) and William Atherton (Clovis).

Losers determined to win, nomads with a letch for roots, children hampered by adults' bodies: the young couple in *The Sugarland Express* is as American as pop-tops or the Grand Canyon. (The movie will be shown tonight in the New Directors series at the Museum of Modern Art and will open commercially tomorrow at Cinema II and the National Theater.) Both wife and husband (Goldie Hawn and William Atherton) have done time in Texas for petty larceny; she bullies him into a jailbreak because their small son has been put up for adoption by the Child Welfare Board. Frantically resolved to retrieve the baby, they hijack a highway patrol car and hold the patrolman as their hostage and chauffeur throughout several hundred miles.

A fleet of police cars hurtles after them across the Texas highways. Eventually, there are more than 200 vehicles in pursuit. Meanwhile, the naive outlaws bicker with their pleasant young captive and reject his warnings that the charges against them are formidable. Nonetheless, an offbeat bond of loyalty builds among them during the journey.

Thrilled crowds mass on the roadside to cheer and photograph them as they pass, while television crews scramble in their wake. (The movie is based on a real case in 1969, when many Texans were enthralled by a similar 300-mile chase.) The wife soars on their celebrity, queening it over the little kingdom of their car. But a police stakeout awaits them at their destination, and the husband is shot.

The movie has a casual craziness that seems especially native. From the drum majorettes who greet the fugitives to the press corps interviewing the gurgling baby, the narrative is studded with national lunacies, including the wife's passion for gold trading stamps. Above all, there's the familiar reek of overkill; the vast throngs of cars and cops and weapons that focus on one inefficient couple, and the fact that shooting the kidnappers is far more important to the authorities than preserving the hostage's life. The ending is a shock just because the movie isn't suspenseful—you don't expect these bunglers to draw the bullets reserved for Bonnie and Clyde.

Goldie Hawn has a manic concentration: no laws of any sort can girdle her, or prevent her from trying to regain her child. At moments, she's exasperation personified; at others, there's the sly, downward gaze we've seen before, plus the flaring sarcasm, the screams of pleasure. It's an extraordinary characterization of a defiant nature with an appetite for the conventions: make-up and hairspray are crucial for public appearances; autographs are eagerly collected. William Atherton has to be as helpless as seaweed in relation to her. It's a hard part, and he appears strained now and then. Yet he's touching as the child-man who can't control anything around him. Michael Sacks is excellent as the hostage, though Ben Johnson is somewhat ponderous as a fatherly police captain who seems just too noble to be true.

Steven Spielberg, the twenty-six-year-old director, has built up Texas as a major character in his movie. As the herd of cars races and heaves and crashes through the landscape, the state's personality surfaces like a sperm whale. Mr. Spielberg has also made marvelous use of many Texans, some of whom haven't acted before. And he has choreographed his cars in a way that almost makes me want to learn to drive.

Sugarland is a modest picture, even limited, and the gypsy couple doesn't have the emotional range or depth of the young pair in Robert Altman's *Thieves Like Us.* Here, the stress is on the story, on what happens to clumsy strays who lurch out of line and risk everything (including life) for their mistakes.

—N.S., March 30, 1974

SULLIVAN'S TRAVELS

Written and directed by Preston Sturges: cinematographer, John Seitz: edited by Stuart Gilmore: music by Leo Shuken: art designers, Hans Dreier and Earl Hedrick: produced by Paul Jones: released by Paramount Pictures. Black and white. Running time: 91 minutes.

With: Joel McCrea (John L. Sullivan), Veronica Lake (The Girl), Robert Warwick (Mr. LeBrand), William Demarest (Mr. Jones), Franklin Pangborn (Mr. Casalsis), Porter Hall (Mr. Hadrian), Eric Blore (Sullivan's Valet), Robert Greig (Sullivan's Butler) and Byron Foulger (Mr. Valdelle).

Preston Sturges need make no excuses for the dominance of comedy on the screen, since he has done more than anyone over the last two years to give brightness and bounce and authority to this general type of fare. But apparently he thinks it time that someone break a lance in the muse's defense—and maybe he also is anxious to quiet a still, small voice within himself. For his latest film, *Sullivan's Travels,* which rolled into the Paramount yesterday, is a beautifully trenchant satire upon "social significance" in pictures, a stinging slap at those fellows who howl for realism on the screen, and a deftly sardonic apologia for Hollywood make-believe.

Sardonic? How comes that word to creep in so slyly there? The answer is simple. Mr. Sturges is a charmingly sarcastic chap, and his pokes are not aimed exclusively at the "deep-dish" in screen attitudes. He also makes pointed sport, in his own blithely mischievous way, of Hollywood's lavish excesses, of baldly staged publicity stunts, and of motion picture producers whose notion of art is "a little sex." As a writer and director, Mr. Sturges believes in pictures which will make the customers laugh, but he obviously has his own opinions about the shams of showmanship. And thus this truly brilliant seriocomedy which makes fun of films with "messages" carries its own paradoxical morals and its note of tragedy. Laughter, it says, is "better than nothing in this cock-eyed caravan."

The hero of *Sullivan's Travels,* you see, is a film director, too—a sheltered and earnest young fellow who has been highly successful with frivolous fare (*So Long Sarong, Hey-Hey in the Hay* and *Ants in Your Plants of 1939*). But then he gets the notion that this is no time for comedy—that the public is not in a mood for cut-ups with things as they are. So he wants to make a grimly serious picture—*O Brother, Where Art Thou?*

To acquaint himself with hardship in order to do the job right, he puts on a trick tramp outfit and starts out solemnly to "see life." The fact that a studio retinue of publicity men follows close behind is but a minor annoyance. The fellow really thinks he's tramping the hard road. Nor are his illusions shattered when he picks up a despondent extra-girl and, with her as a cynical companion, makes a brief excursion among the down-and-outs. However, he truly finds trouble when a trick of fate robs him of identity—when his ties with a secure world are cut—and he learns about cruelty and poverty in a brutal convict camp. There he discovers that laughter is the only anodyne for grief—and subsequently returns to Hollywood, a gladder and wiser man.

This brief and sketchy outline of the story may—but should not—lead you to suspect that the film is heavy with "trouble" and bleak reality. Far from it. It has the blessing of Mr. Sturges's artful comic comment, and it crackles with extraordinary humor for most of its ninety-minute length. In the early part of the picture there is a wild, hilarious "chase" which outdoes any of the romping that Mack Sennett ever conceived, and even the "slumming" episodes are filled with ironic fun. The scenes in the prison camp are harsh and relentless, it is true, but they carry the point of the picture with sharp and incisive clarity.

One might wish that the ending had been a little more boldly conceived, for Mr. Sturges lets an obvious climax fall uncomfortably flat. He should have emphasized the bitter irony of Sullivan's return to Hollywood, of his willing acceptance of a mission which he had so elaborately eschewed. In short, Sullivan should have been more affected by his experience than he seems to be.

But that is a passing criticism of a picture which is expertly made and acted, under the direction of Mr. Sturges, with eminent artistry. Joel McCrea as the questing traveler is more of a human character than he has ever been in a film, and Veronica Lake as the little girl he picks up is a person when she comes out from behind her hair. William Demarest, Robert Warwick, Eric Blore, Robert Greig, and a host of Sturges puppets fill out the lesser roles superiorly.

Sullivan's Travels is one of the screen's more "significant" films. It is the best social comment made upon Hollywood since *A Star Is Born*. And that, we quietly suspect, is exactly what Mr. Sturges meant it to be.

—*B.C., January 29, 1942*

SUMMER

Written (in French, with English subtitles) and directed by Eric Rohmer; cinematographer, Sophie Maintigneux; edited by Marie-Luisa Garcia; music by Jean-Louis Valero; produced by Margaret Menegoz; released by Orion Classics. Running time: 98 minutes.

With: Marie Rivière (Delphine), Lisa Heredia (Manuella), Vincent Gauthier (Jacques), Béatrice Romand (Beatrice) and Carita (Lena).

Delphine (Marie Rivière), the Parisian secretary who's at the center of Eric Rohmer's exquisite new comedy, *Summer;* doesn't fit easily into a world of preconditioned responses. Like all of Mr. Rohmer's women, from Maud and Claire to Pauline, Delphine is unusually pretty and maddening in her steadfastness to her own decisions. She thinks for herself, which isn't easy for those around her. She's a pebble in everyone's shoe, particularly when she's a houseguest.

She doesn't eat meat, shellfish, or eggs—she prefers cereals and vegetables. When pressed by teasing companions, who suggest that even a salad means the death of a head of lettuce, she finds herself saying something to the effect that "lettuce is a friend." Greens "aerate" her. They make her feel refreshingly "light," which is the only way she can explain it.

She also becomes seasick on sailboats and dizzy on swings. When someone brings her a branch of apple blossoms, she says bluntly that she doesn't believe that such large branches should be torn from trees.

After the fact, it's not surprising that at the beginning of *Summer,* Delphine is being irrevocably dumped by the girlfriend with whom she'd planned to take her summer holiday in Greece. The girlfriend is going off with a boyfriend. Delphine offers to come along. The answer is no.

For all her whims and ways, and for all the trouble she causes her friends, Delphine is very good company at the Lincoln Plaza 1, where *Summer* opens today. Much like Delphine, *Summer* initially seems slight, but it's a movie of uncommon sensitivity and emotional reserves. Delphine is no great philosopher. Yet she's a woman who uses her mind, if only, sometimes, to go in self-searching circles. As played by Miss Rivière, she's funny, gallant, irritating, and terrifically romantic.

Delphine is the archetypal Rohmer heroine, a character who could exist only in a film. She's a remarkable, collaborative composition of the director's vision, the actress's personality, the settings through which she moves, and the sounds she hears, which, in addition to the words (not always kind) of her friends, include street noises, music, the passing of the occasional airplane, birds, even the wind in the trees.

People who say Mr. Rohmer's films aren't cinematic, because of the great amounts of dialogue they contain, simply aren't attending to the complete work. His dialogue is immensely important but, by itself, it doesn't add up to much. It's not epigrammatic.

In *Summer,* particularly, it tends to wander, then to turn back on itself. It's full of non sequiturs and of thoughts that just hang there, unfinished and forlorn, like Delphine when her self-assurance suddenly crumbles. However, unlike the dialogue of any other filmmaker, Mr. Rohmer's charts the course of characters who possess believable interior lives.

Summer is the picaresque tale of one woman's search for a holiday, in spite of her aversion to traveling by herself. Delphine turns down an invitation to go camping in Ireland with her sister's family. She decides, instead, to go to Cherbourg with a chum and the chum's boyfriend but, after several days of feeling out of it, returns to Paris.

She goes off, alone, to the Alps, stays just long enough (one afternoon) to climb one Alp and returns home that night. Finally, in desperation, she borrows the apartment of a friend in Biarritz. When last seen, she seems to be in the process of being rewarded for her stubbornness, though, as she has told a friend earlier, it's not she who's stubborn, but the world that's stubborn toward her.

Delphine's problems are not earthshaking. There are no major issues being solemnly debated to preconceived conclusions. What *Summer* celebrates—and this is important—is the independence of a singular mind. Delphine, a lonely woman who'd much prefer being in the company of a man she loved, refuses to play the conventional game.

She's appalled by the talk of Lena, a pretty, brassy young Swede she meets on the beach at Biarritz. Lena loves traveling on her own, picking up men, and moving on. "It's like a card game," says Lena. "You can't reveal your hand right off." Says Delphine, at the end of her rope (and holiday), "My hand is empty."

Summer, the fifth in Mr. Rohmer's series of "Comedies and Proverbs," is as romantic as Delphine, who, though she doesn't believe in astrology, does believe in what she calls her own superstitions. She believes in playing cards found by chance, and in the color green, which, she's been told, is her "color" for that year.

In Biarritz she becomes fascinated by an overheard conversation about Jules Verne's novel *Le Rayon Vert* (*The Green Ray*), which was the original title of the film in France. According to Verne, at the moment one sees that rare meteorological phenomenon (here known as the green flash)—when there's a burst of green light just as the top of the sun sinks below the horizon into the sea—one's own thoughts and those of others are magically revealed.

Though *Summer* seems resolutely pragmatic, it shares Delphine's appreciation for her own superstitions.

More than any other Rohmer film I've seen, *Summer* also sounds as if it had depended a lot on the improvisation of the players, Miss Rivière and the members of the large supporting cast. They all are quite wonderful, including the enchanting, now-grown Béatrice Romand, who played the young teenager in *Claire's Knee.*

An important technical note: *Summer,* looking as airy and ephemeral as a perfect summer afternoon, was photographed (by Sophie Maintigneux) in 16mm and then enlarged to 35. This is the sort of time- and cost-saving practice that allows Mr. Rohmer to make these very particular films so they don't have to appeal to a mass audience to be financially successful. Bravo.

—V.C., August 29, 1986

SUMMERTIME

Directed by David Lean; written by Mr. Lean and H. E. Bates, based on the play *The Time of the Cuckoo* by Arthur Laurents; cinematographer, Jack Hildyard; edited by Peter Taylor; music by Alessandro Cicognini; art designer, Vincent Korda; produced by Ilya Lopert; released by United Artists. Running time: 100 minutes.

With: Katharine Hepburn (Jane Hudson), Rossano Brazzi (Renato Di Rossi), Isa Miranda (Signora Fiorina), Darren McGavin (Eddie Jaeger), Mari Aldon (Phyl Jaeger), Jane Rose (Mrs. McIlhenny), MacDonald Parke (Mr. McIlhenny), Gaitano Audiero (Mauro), André Morell (Englishman), Jeremy Spenser (Vito) and Virginia Simeon (Giovanna).

The beautiful city of Venice, with its ancient buildings, its winding canals, its mingling of vivid sounds and colors and its bewitchingly romantic air comes off the principal performer in David Lean's and Ilya Lopert's *Summertime.* (The film opened last night at the Astor with a benefit showing for the American National Theatre and Academy "Salute to France.")

This is so, even though Katharine Hepburn and Rossano Brazzi are the picture's human stars and its cast includes Isa Miranda and several others of quality and charm.

The explanation is simple. In adapting for the screen Arthur Laurent's stage play *The Time of the Cuckoo,* Mr. Lean and H. E. Bates discarded most of the individual shadings and psychological subtleties of that romance. They reduced the complicated pondering of an American woman's first go at love with a middle-aged merchant of Venice to pleasingly elemental terms. And they let the evident inspiration for their heroine's emotional release be little more than the spell cast by the city upon her fitful and lonely state of mind.

The challenge thus set of making Venice the moving force in propelling the play has been met by Mr. Lean as the director with magnificent feeling and skill. Through the lens of his color camera, the wondrous city of spectacles and moods becomes a rich and exciting organism that fairly takes command of the screen. And the curious hypnotic fascination of that labyrinthine place beside the sea is brilliantly conveyed to the viewer as the impulse for the character's passing moods.

Miss Hepburn is clever and amusing as a spirited American old maid who turns up in Venice with her guide books and a romantic gleam in her eye. She makes a convincing summer tourist. And her breathlessly eager attitude is just right for the naive encounters and farcical mishaps that have been arranged.

But a sense of her wistful frustration and her loneliness in this city where she has dreamed she will find "a wonderful mystical magical miracle" does not take hold upon the mind until Mr. Lean has skillfully wrapped her in the haunting beauty of the place—until he has set her stringy figure against the impassive buildings, the moving crowds, and the great sweep of the Piazza St. Marco in the light of the setting sun.

Nor does the excitement of her meeting with a handsome Venetian come home until Mr. Lean has walked her with him through the shadows of the whispering arcades and let them reach for a fallen gardenia in the dark waters of a canal. It is Venice itself that gives the flavor and the emotional stimulation to this film.

For it can't be denied that the credibility of the brief love affair that occurs between the breathless old maid and the Venetian, whom Signor Brazzi nobly plays, is considerably strained in substance. Nor can it be honestly gainsaid that the breakup after a blissful go-round is abrupt and illogical. The youthfulness and handsomeness of Signor Brazzi precludes the reasonable excuse that the character offered in the play. And the producers have evidently been loath to have Miss Hepburn as mercenary as the original old maid.

These are weakness in structure. There are other minor weaknesses, too, in the scanty delineation of the Italian pensione-keeper whom Miss Miranda plays. But little Gaitano Audiero is beguiling as an enterprising boy of the canals, and Darren McGavin and Mari Aidon are likely as American newlyweds. The musical score of Sandro Cicognini has a lyrical quality.

And there is Venice, which itself defies logic!

Summertime is, indeed, a summer film.

—B.C., June 22, 1955

SUNDAY, BLOODY SUNDAY

Directed by John Schlesinger; written by Penelope Gilliatt; cinematographer, Billy Williams; edited by Richard Marden; music by Ron Geesin; production designer, Luciana Arrighi; produced by Joseph Janni; released by United Artists. Running time: 110 minutes.

With: Glenda Jackson (Alex Greville), Peter Finch (Dr. Daniel Hirsch), Murray Head (Bob Elkin), Peggy Ashcroft (Mrs. Greville), Tony Britton (Mr. Harding), Maurice Denham (Mr. Greville) and Bessie Love (Answering Service Woman).

Now tell me," says the voice from the black screen, "do you feel anything at all?"

When the lights come up we see a doctor (Peter Finch), probing the blubbery blue-white belly of a comically frightened, middle-aged man. The man, whose body is an anthology of small, harmless sags, the little remains of muscles that have given up, is convinced that he has cancer, not colitis, but he still would rather go to Frankfurt on business than face the gastrointestinal tests that would tell him he's all right. The man is scared half out of his mind and he'd prefer not to feel anything at all, though he does.

In this oblique fashion begins John Schlesinger's fine *Sunday, Bloody Sunday,* which is all about feelings of late twentieth-century love and desperation, recognized and embraced, but systematically channeled (some might say perverted) into safe areas where they can be controlled and then drawn from, like reservoirs of hope and despair.

Sunday, Bloody Sunday looks like a more or less unconventional triangle, but it's really two parallel love stories that happen to have a single love object. He's Bob Elkin (Murray Head), an artist in his early twenties who makes kinetic sculptures, which are created out of the glass and metal that house a see-through civilization, and that are set in motion by the same electricity that powers the telephones through which the timetables of his two affairs are kept remarkably untangled.

In what at first appears to be a perfect arrangement, agreed to by all, the boy divides his love and affection and physical presence between Dr. Daniel Hirsch (Finch), a successful London general practitioner in his forties, and Alex Greville (Glenda Jackson), a woman in her thirties, the survivor of a dull, middle-class marriage and the possessor of what someone describes, not too fondly, as "that piercing, educated mind."

The film is mostly about how these two intelligent people make do in what they both recognize as the final days of their affairs, during which Britain is wobbling along the edge of a financial crisis, and London itself sometimes seems to be on the verge of turning into a hallucination, as when we see groups of crazily dressed young people roller-skating through wet night streets in images that, like the feelings of Daniel and Alex, are vivid and mysterious and immensely sad.

At one point, when the boy has let it be known that he just might go to America, although he doesn't want to end the affair, Alex, in desperation, says that they have to pack it in. "I've had it with this business that anything is better than nothing," she screams, more at herself than at him. "There have to be times when nothing is better than anything!" And this, of course, is the cry of a time and a people for whom being sophisticated and controlled and cool is, ultimately, not enough.

Sunday, Bloody Sunday is Schlesinger's (*Darling, Midnight Cowboy*) wisest, least sentimental film, an almost perfect realization of Penelope Gilliatt's original screenplay, which is, I think, just about the best original screenplay since Eric Rohmer's *Claire's Knee.*

Like Rohmer, Miss Gilliatt, who is a novelist and short story writer as well as a film critic, has the extraordinary ability to create intelligent characters who don't sound like mouthpieces, to capture those looks and sounds of the surface of things that suggest the universes just beneath, and to write dialogue that is simultaneously rueful and funny, and as spontaneous as love itself.

It's a movie of unusual tensions and reserves, qualities reflected in the performances of both Finch, whose homosexual doctor has, at least, the stability of his large Jewish family, and Miss Jackson, who has come to be the movies' foremost actress of on-edge roles. As the bisexual boy, who is a sort of embodiment of the so-called new morality, which, in this case, amounts to enlightened selfishness, Murray Head is remarkably appealing, largely, I suspect, because the screenplay accepts him without tears or analysis.

There are, in the back of my mind, all sorts of questions about the relationship between the doctor and Alex, who meet in the film just once, in a scene of almost exquisite feeling. Does the awareness—each of the other—somehow enrich their affairs? I would suppose it does, but these questions are part of the film's complex underground that makes its serene surface so fascinating.

Sunday, Bloody Sunday opened yesterday at the Coronet Theater, where, I'm sure, it will remain for a long, long time.

—V.C., September 22, 1971

SUNDAYS AND CYBÈLE

Directed by Serge Bourguignon: written (in French, with English subtitles) by Mr. Bourguignon, Antoine Tudal and Bernard Eschassériaux, based on the novel *Les Dimanches de Ville d'Avray* by Mr. Eschassériaux: cinematographer, Henri Decae: edited by Leonide Azar: music by Maurice Jarre: art designer, Bernard Evein: produced by Romain Pines: released by Columbia Pictures. Black and white. Running time: 110 minutes.

With: Hardy Krüger (Pierre). Patricia Gozzi (Françoise "Cybèle"). Nicole Courcel (Madeleine). Daniel Ivernel (Carlos). Michel de Ré (Bernard) and André Oumansky (Nurse).

Heaven only knows for what rare virtue New York has been rewarded with the first public exhibition of a French motion-picture masterpiece. But so it has.

And, what's more, this work of beauty, known here as *Sundays and Cybèle,* which opened yesterday at the Fine Arts even before its opening in France, is almost by way of being a cinematic miracle. It is the first full-length production of a young writer-director, Serge Bourguignon.

How can one give a fair impression of the exquisite, delicate charm of this wondrous story of a magical attachment between a crash-injured young man who is suffering from amnesia and a lonely little twelve-year-old girl? By saying that it is what *Lolita* might conceivably have been had it been made by a poet and angled to be a rhapsodic song of innocence and not a smirking joke?

That doesn't begin to do it, because the circumstances that bring the young man and the child together and cause them to fall in love—into a kind of love that is exalting and consuming on the part of each—are nothing like the circumstances that fatefully impel the physically obsessed Humbert Humbert toward the treacherous nymphet in *Lolita.*

Here the man is drawn to the youngster when he sees her heartlessly left by her father at a convent in a village outside Paris where he lives. He presents himself as her father to take her out for walks on Sundays, when he discovers that the father does not intend to return. His feeling for her develops, and hers for him, as they weekly lose themselves in nature's vaulted cathedral of trees around a lake.

No, this is not close to *Lolita.* Yet the attachment that grows is not purely idyllic, either. It is clearly compounded of the sexual stirrings in the youngster, the psychic impulses that move her to grope for the male affection she has never had in a loveless, broken home—the faint intimations of womanhood that lead her to throbbing jealousy of the mistress of her hero and to flirting guilelessly with him.

The joyous release of the fellow when he is with the beautiful child is not a mere gush of sentiment, either. It is the poignant expression of a man whose hope and confidence are shattered and who seeks a way to begin his life anew.

How else, then, can one give an idea of the rare quality of this film? Perhaps best by giving an impression of the style of Mr. Bourguignon. It flows somewhere between the terse style of François Truffaut's *400 Blows* and the natural, serene lyricism of some of the films of Jean Renoir.

For a man whose career has been spent mainly in painting and making film shorts, Mr. Bourguignon has developed a remarkably sensitive camera eye and a taste that, in this film, is flawless. His sense of dramatic form—he helped write this screenplay from a novel by Bernard Eschassériaux, *Les Dimanches de Ville d'Avray*—is enhanced by a fine capacity to give subtle graphic expression and clarity to action and moods.

His images of misty Sunday mornings around the magical lake, of circular ripples on the water, at the heart of which the child perceives "our home," of symbolic objects and behavior that represent longings and fears, are as lovely and subtle and compelling as any sensitive being could wish.

The performances the director has evoked from his small but brilliant cast establish visions in the memory that one can surely never forget. Hardy Krüger is the listless young fellow shaken and vitalized into a weird kind of ecstatic vigor by the strength that flows to him from the child, and Patricia Gozzi is sheer magic as this nimble, refulgent-eyed tot.

Her wonderful changes of expression, her command of emotional states, her ways of suggesting amorous triumph or stabbing jealousy are far beyond the capacity of all but a few adult stars. This is one of the finest performances by a child we have ever seen.

Nicole Courcel is also brilliant as the tender, compassionate mistress of the young man. Her range from initial suspicion through awareness and jealousy to a sweet tolerance of the strange liaison and then to a state of gasping fear as to the social consequences of it is a full spread of drama in itself. Her reaction to the attachment is the reflection of true humanity.

Daniel Ivernel is also helpful as an understanding friend, and Michel de Ré does a fine job as a stubborn realist.

An additional element of beauty and eloquence is the musical score, ranging from Handel to Tibetan music and intruded as oblique suggestion of psychic shadows floating over emotional pools, plus wonderfully keen employment of precise and exquisite natural sounds. One place, in which the sing of pebbles skittering over the ice on a lake points a mood of faint depression, is unforgettable.

Finally, the gathering of anxiety and tension as the drama moves to a smashing, ironic climax completes the emotional purge. The fulfillment of the inevitable comes to the heart of tragedy. Here is truly a picture on a delicate, complicated theme that abides by the piercing adjuration of the mistress: it does not dirty something that is beautiful.

—*B.C., November 13, 1962*

SUNSET BOULEVARD

Directed by Billy Wilder; written by Mr. Wilder, Charles Brackett and D. M. Marshman Jr., based on the story "A Can of Beans" by Mr. Wilder and Mr. Brackett; cinematographer, John Seitz; edited by Doane Harrison and Arthur Schmidt; music by Franz Waxman; art designers Hans Dreier and John Meehan; produced by Mr. Brackett; released by Paramount Pictures. Black and white. Running time: 110 minutes.

With: William Holden (Joe Gillis), Gloria Swanson (Norma Desmond), Erich von Stroheim (Max Von Mayerling), Nancy Olson (Betty Schaefer), Fred Clark (Sheldrake) and Lloyd Gough (Morino).

A segment of life in Hollywood is being spread across the screen of the Music Hall in *Sunset Boulevard*. Using as the basis of their frank, caustic drama a scandalous situation involving a faded, aging silent screen star and a penniless, cynical young scriptwriter, Charles Brackett and Billy Wilder (with an assist from D. M. Marshman Jr.) have written a powerful story of the ambitions and frustrations that combine to make life in the cardboard city so fascinating to the outside world.

Sunset Boulevard is by no means a rounded story of Hollywood, past or present. But it is such a clever compound of truth and legend—and is so richly redolent of the past, yet so contemporaneous—that it seemingly speaks with great authority. *Sunset Boulevard* is that rare blend of pungent writing, expert acting, masterly direction, and unobtrusively artistic photography which quickly casts a spell over an audience and holds it enthralled to a shattering climax.

Gloria Swanson was coaxed out of long retirement to portray the pathetic, forgotten film queen, Norma Desmond, and now it can be said that it is inconceivable that anyone else might have been considered for the role. As the wealthy, egotistical relic desperately yearning to hear again the plaudits of the crowd, Miss Swanson dominates the picture. Even in those few scenes when she is not on-screen her presence is felt like the heavy scent of tuberoses which hangs over the gloomy, musty splendor of her memento-cluttered mansion in Beverly Hills.

Playing the part of Joe Gillis, the scriptwriter, William Holden is doing the finest acting of his career. His range and control of emotions never falters and he engenders a full measure of compassion for a character who is somewhat less than admirable. Hounded by collectors from the auto-finance company, the struggling, disillusioned writer grabs an opportunity to make some money by helping Norma Desmond to fashion a screenplay about Salome with which the hopeless egomaniac believes she will make a "return to the millions of people who have never forgiven me for deserting the screen."

Joe Gillis is indignant when Norma insists that he live in her house, but gradually his self-respect is corroded by easy comforts and he does nothing strenuous to thwart her unsubtle romantic blandishments. Before an attachment to a girl of his own age jolts him out of this dark abyss and rekindles his writing spark, Joe has become hopelessly entangled in the life of the psychopathic star who holds him down with lavish gifts and an attempted suicide.

With uncommon skill, Brackett and Wilder, who also produced and directed this splendid drama for Paramount Pictures, have kept an essentially tawdry romance from becoming distasteful and embarrassing. Aside from the natural, knowing tone of the dialogue, the realism of the picture is heightened by scenes set inside the actual iron-grilled gates of the Paramount Studio, where Norma Desmond goes for an on-the-set visit with her old comrade, Cecil B. DeMille himself. And the fantastic, Babylonian atmosphere of an incredible past is reflected sharply in the gaudy elegance of the decaying mansion in which Norma Desmond lives.

The hope that propels young people to try their luck in Hollywood is exemplified by Betty Schaefer, a studio reader with writing ambitions who is beautifully portrayed by Nancy Olson. Fred Clark makes a strong impression as a producer working for his second ulcer, and there is heartbreak in a simple card game scene where "the wax works," as Gillis cynically refers to Norma's friends, includes Buster Keaton, Anna Q. Nilsson and H. B. Warner.

Erich von Stroheim moves through *Sunset Boulevard* with a stiff, Prussian attitude that fits to a T his role as the devoted butler, who, in his day as a top director, discovered Norma as a young girl and became the first of her three husbands. But while all the acting is memorable, one always thinks first and mostly of Miss Swanson, of her manifestation of consuming pride, her forlorn despair, and a truly magnificent impersonation of Charlie Chaplin.

Sunset Boulevard is a great motion picture, marred only slightly by the fact that the authors permit Joe Gillis to take us into the story of his life after his bullet-ridden body is lifted out of Norma Desmond's swimming pool. That is a device completely unworthy of Brackett and Wilder, but happily it does not interfere with the success of *Sunset Boulevard*.

—T.M.P., August 11, 1950

SUSPICION

Directed by Alfred Hitchcock; written by Samson Raphaelson, Joan Harrison and Alma Reville, based on the novel *Before the Fact* by Francis Iles; cinematographer, Harry Stradling; edited by William Hamilton; music by Franz Waxman; art designers, Van Nest Polglase and Carroll Clark; released by RKO Radio Pictures. Black and white. Running time: 99 minutes.

With: Cary Grant (Johnnie Aysgarth), Joan Fontaine (Lina McLaidlaw), Sir Cedric Hardwicke (General McLaidlaw), Nigel Bruce (Beaky), Dame May Whitty (Mrs. McLaidlaw), Isabel Jeans (Mrs. Newsham), Heather Angel (Ethel) and Leo G. Carroll (Captain Melbeck).

I f Alfred Hitchcock were not the fine film director that he is, the chances are better than even that he would be a distinguished light at the (legal) bar. For very few lawyers are gifted with the special ability which is his to put a case together in the most innocent but subtle way, to plant prima facie evidence without rousing the slightest alarm and then suddenly to muster his assumptions and drive home a staggering attack. Mr. Hitchcock is probably the most artful sophist working for the films—and anyone who doesn't think so should see *Suspicion* at the Music Hall.

True, we should incidentally warn you that this is not Mr. Hitchcock at his best, for the clerical staff which helped him prepare his brief for this case did not provide too much in the way of material. Those highly intriguing complications which have featured in some of his previous masterworks are lacking in this instance. Rather, Mr. Hitchcock is compelled to construct his attack around a straight psychological progression: a shy, deeply sensitive English girl marries a charming rakehell in maiden innocence, and then, through accumulated evidence, begins to suspect him of dark and foul deeds, suspects him of murdering two dear people, and finally of having designs upon herself.

Clearly, Mr. Hitchcock's problem is to give this simple story great consequence—to build, out of slight suggestions and vague, uncertain thoughts, a mounting tower of suspicion which looms forbiddingly. And this he does magnificently with his customary casualness. An early remark dropped by the girl's father to the effect that her intended is a cheat, a scene in which the husband acts strangely indifferent to a friend when the latter is seized with a heart attack, a little squabble over a slight untruth—all are directed by Mr. Hitchcock so that they seem inconsequential at the time but still with a sinister undertone which grows as the tension mounts.

Much of his purpose is accomplished through the performance of Joan Fontaine, it must be said, and she, as well as Mr. Hitchcock, deserves unstinted praise. This young lady has unquestionably become one of the finest actresses on the screen, and one of the most beautiful, too; and her development in this picture of a fear-tortured character is fluid and compelling all the way. Cary Grant as the husband is provokingly irresponsible, boyishly gay and also oddly mysterious, as the role properly demands; and Nigel Bruce, Sir Cedric Hardwicke and Leo G. Carroll are fine in minor roles.

One must remark that the ending is not up to Mr. Hitchcock's usual style, and the general atmosphere of the picture is far less genuine than he previously has wrought. But still he has managed to bring through a tense and exciting tale, a psychological thriller which is packed with lively suspense and a picture that entertains you from beginning to—well, almost the end.

—B.C., November 21, 1941

THE SWEET HEREAFTER

Directed by Atom Egoyan: written by Mr. Egoyan, based on the novel by Russell Banks: director of photography, Paul Sarossy: edited by Susan Shipton: music by Mychael Danna: production designer, Philip Barker: produced by Mr. Egoyan and Camelia Frieberg: released by Fine Line Features. Running time: 110 minutes.

With: Ian Holm (Mitchell Stephens), Sarah Polley (Nicole Burnell), Bruce Greenwood (Billy Ansell), Tom McCamus (Sam Burnell), Gabrielle Rose (Dolores Driscoll), Arsinée Khanjian (Wanda Otto) and Alberta Watson (Risa Walker).

The lone special effects shot in *The Sweet Hereafter* is beautifully executed and terrible to see. A school bus skids off an icy road and sinks into a frozen lake, taking with it the children of a tiny, once neighborly Adirondack town. Presented midway through this latest, biggest and most wrenching film by the brilliantly analytical Atom Egoyan, this image becomes the basis for a many-faceted moral inquiry. In the aftermath of such calamity, how does life go on?

Not with the help of an ambulance-chasing lawyer, the people of this remote region at first agree. But Mitchell Stephens, Esq. (Ian Holm, expertly playing a stubbornly benighted character) arrives in the area with a self-appointed mission. "Let me direct your rage," he exhorts one prospective client, and he burns with self-serving indignation as he makes this plea. Mitchell is the voice of crass pragmatism in a situation that beggars all his notions of right and wrong.

Mitchell's is one of four voices that narrate *The Sweet Hereafter,* a book by Russell Banks, whose vivid and deeply felt moral tales are long overdue in reaching the screen. In a season of expertly adapted contemporary fiction (like *L.A. Confidential* and *The Ice Storm*), this fusion of Mr. Banks's and Mr. Egoyan's sensibilities stands as a particularly inspired mix. Both film and book are carefully fragmented, and both move indirectly toward the enlightenment they seek. But the book's built-in narrative strength helps to make this Mr. Egoyan's most accessible film.

Making this material very much his own, the filmmaker creates schematic, intuitive images that hauntingly crystallize the characters' situations. When first seen, for instance, Mitchell Stephens is trapped in a car wash, receiving a cellular phone call from his own lost child, a vituperative drug addict named Zoe. Stuck in a car being deluged with water, is he being washed clean or washed away? The film's perfect exactitude often provides such resonant images, as the town's life moves from the gaiety of a Ferris wheel to the wheel on a bus to the wheel on a chair. Mr. Egoyan also often invokes Robert Browning's poem *The Pied Piper of Hamelin,* with its mercenary piper and its children who disappear.

"The mind is kind," declares Mr. Banks, who has a fleeting cameo as a sweepingly optimistic doctor. And in a story that is ultimately cathartic, that eventually begins to be true. But first *The Sweet Hereafter,* which will be shown at the New York Film Festival as its centerpiece selection, must delve into this community's deep pain. Some has been caused by the accident, with contrasts underscored by a mosaic narrative that moves between pre- and post-crash time frames; parents are sometimes seen sending their children off to school, sometimes immersed in numbing grief.

Other matters, like the eerily serene love between the teenage Nicole Burnell (Sarah Polley) and her father (Tom McCamus), or the affair between widowed Billy Ansell (Bruce Greenwood) and unhappily married Risa Walker (Alberta Watson), meant trouble even before the crash. But the one common denominator is the completely transforming effect of the accident on everyone in this story, as its title suggests. Mr. Banks's book begins with a quotation from Emily Dickinson that suits this dark, contemplative film equally well: " 'Nothing' is the force that renovates the World."

Mr. Egoyan's keen compositional eye is well served by the film's wide-screen format, which works as handsomely in indoor scenes as in broad, lonely vistas. At one point, for instance, he sustains a marital spat in the background, a telephone call in the left foreground and a calendar on the right, indicating that this is December 1995, though the film's next scene is set in 1997 on an airplane. Transitions are utterly seamless, fluidly carrying the audience back and forth through memory. Mr. Egoyan's earlier films, among them *Exotica* and *The Adjuster,* depended heavily on the power of such contrasts, but *The Sweet Hereafter* works more straightforwardly. For all the suffering it describes, this eloquent film also carries the exhilaration of crystal-clear artistic vision.

Much of the cast belongs to the ensemble that has followed Mr. Egoyan through his ever more impressive career. Mr. Greenwood and Ms. Polley, both from *Exotica,* are particularly good here, and Arsinée Khanjian (the filmmaker's wife and frequent star) has a long, powerful scene as a shell-shocked mother. Gabrielle Rose, who goes back to the filmmaker's earlier *Speaking Parts* and *Family Viewing,* conveys much simple dignity as the woman who had the town's future in her hands and lost her grip. She plays the driver of the bus.

—*J.M., October 3, 1997*

SWEET SMELL OF SUCCESS

Directed by Alexander Mackendrick; written by Clifford Odets and Ernest Lehman, based on the short story "Tell Me About It Tomorrow" by Mr. Lehman; cinematographer, James Wong Howe; edited by Alan Crosland Jr.; music by Elmer Bernstein; art designer, Edward Carrere; produced by James Hill; released by United Artists. Black and white. Running time: 96 minutes.

With: Burt Lancaster (J. J. Hunsecker), Tony Curtis (Sidney Falco), Susan Harrison (Susan Hunsecker), Marty Milner (Steve Dallas), Sam Levene (Frank D'Angelo), Barbara Nichols (Rita), Jeff Donnell (Sally), Joseph Leon (Robard) and Edith Atwater (Mary).

The frenetic and often sordid machinations of a power-mad Broadway columnist, the unprincipled press agent who is his hatchet man and the avid coterie that surrounds them are savagely dissected in *Sweet Smell of Success,* which came to Lowe's State yesterday.

It is not a towering, universal theme the producers have developed in their indictment of this small, special segment of society operating in a tiny domain known intimately only to the cognoscenti. But pulsating dialogue, brisk direction, good performances, and photography that captures the sights and sounds of Manhattan's Bistro Belt make the meanness of this singular "success" story fascinating a good part of the way.

The adaptation by Clifford Odets and Ernest Lehman of the latter's fiction has caught the mannerisms and the language of the hustling guys and dolls in search of power, fame and a fast buck. But the basic motivation of J. J. Hunsecker, the columnist read by millions and sought after by the famous and infamous, remains unexplained. This is the film's major flaw.

What sort of love does the imperious Hunsecker have for his young sister? Is this exaggerated possessiveness psychological or something else? The only clue a viewer gets is Hunsecker's simple and uninformative admission to the thoroughly cowed lass, "You're all I've got in this whole wide world." And then he coldly sets in motion a plan to destroy the decent young jazz guitarist who wants to marry her.

Much clearer is the mental makeup of Sidney Falco, the publicist who has practically devoted body and soul to getting "items," muddy or otherwise, into Hunsecker's syndicated column. He is admittedly client-hungry and "fully up to the slimy tricks of the trade." Why? The "sweet smell of success" is a reality, he is convinced, and "Hunsecker is the golden ladder to where I want to get."

He squirms at his assignment—the planting of narcotics on the guileless guitarist, who is then nabbed by a detective also in thrall to the columnist—but coolly effects it because he cannot fight that drive toward success. That the diabolical schemers are upset is somewhat anticlimactic. The fact that justice is done and young love wins out eventually does not really solve the riddle that is Hunsecker.

Tony Curtis contributes a polished performance as the venal, double-talking, two-timing Falco, who is willing to go to extremes to do his gossip-dispensing Svengali's bidding. Nevertheless it is a disturbing portrait since he does not entirely emerge the black-hearted villain he is supposed to represent.

Burt Lancaster's delineation of Hunsecker is efficient but largely restrained. He is a seemingly bland, professorial type speaking in columnar clichés, who only explodes into violent emotion on rare occasions. It might be difficult for the uninitiate to understand why it is necessary to curry his favor but he gives the role its proper modicum of callousness.

Susan Harrison, a newcomer to films and a pert, appealing youngster, evokes sympathy as the columnist's distraught sister. Marty Milner is sincere and believable as her indomitable romantic vis-à-vis; and Barbara Nichols, as the voluptuous nightclub temptress Mr. Curtis uses in his schemes; Sam Levene, as an agent; Joe Frisco, as a comic; and Jeff Donnell, as Mr. Curtis's harried secretary add competent touches in their brief appearances.

Alexander Mackendrick, the British director, and James Wong Howe, his cinematographer, who shot a good part of their film hereabouts, have gotten a fair portion of our town's fast tempo, its night spots, and its sleazy aspects into their production. A viewer cannot blame Hunsecker too much when he happily exclaims, "I love this dirty old town." It's harder, of course, to fall for the characters in *Sweet Smell of Success.* They are mighty interesting but rarely lovable.

—A.W., June 28, 1957

SWEET SWEETBACK'S BAADASSSSS SONG

Written, edited and directed by Melvin Van Peebles; director of photography, Bob Maxwell; music by Mr. Van Peebles; released by Cinemation Industries. Running time: 97 minutes.

With: Melvin Van Peebles (Sweet Sweetback).

I think that Melvin Van Peebles has the talent, the intelligence and even the instincts of a good filmmaker—despite a growing body of evidence to the contrary. The latest exhibit, *Sweet Sweetback's Baadasssss Song,* Van Peebles's third and worst feature, opened yesterday at the Art and Cinerama theaters, and at the Loew's Victoria.

Van Peebles's first feature, *Story of a Three-Day Pass* (1967), was a gently ironic and very perceptive low-budget film about race relations, made in France and starring the late Nicole Berger. His second feature,

Watermelon Man (1970), concerned a middle-class white insurance agent who woke up one morning to find himself black—a predicament played as farcical situation comedy, which sounds like a better idea than, as acted by Estelle Parsons and Godfrey Cambridge, it turned out to be.

Indeed, ideas have saved Van Peebles several times when weak performances or no money or merely deadheaded directing have gotten in the way of realization. But in this movie the failure is so very nearly total that the ideas all turn into clichés and positively collaborate in taking things down.

Sweet Sweetback (played almost without dialogue by Van Peebles himself) performs in a black Southern California brothel until he is routinely picked up by the police one night and, driven by what they do to one of his brothers, he assaults a couple of cops and runs away. The subject, then, is Sweetback's flight to the border, and his adventures during flight; and at one level of artiness or another, it is almost all predictable formula material.

The film is being presented as searing racial indictment—which may be a reasonable enterprise, but I don't think it is Van Peebles's enterprise, even when he tries to make it so. He is, from everything I have seen, better at exploring relations and sophistications than he is at proclaiming separations and simplicities—and his man on the lam, whatever he stands for, comes to look like nothing much more than an academic exercise in advanced cinematography, characterized by double exposure, multiple screen and minimal feeling.

Melvin Van Peebles wrote, produced, directed and edited this work, as well as starring in it and composing the music—some of which is chanted a cappella by a chorus and is as aggressively bland and barren as anything that shows up on the screen.

Of course, such total control does not guarantee total commitment, and the moments in which I really sense Van Peebles as a valuable presence are few and fleeting. But there are such moments, mostly in the brothel near the beginning—Sweetback with his women, the way a pair of tired feet hit the floor, a quality of light felt and understood—that show the director at work in the kind of moviemaking I hope he'll someday complete.

—R.G., April 24, 1971

SWEPT AWAY
(BY AN UNUSUAL DESTINY IN THE BLUE SEA OF AUGUST)

Written (in Italian, with English subtitles) and directed by Lina Wertmuller; cinematographers, Giulio Battiferri, Stefano Ricciotti and Giuseppe Fornari; music by Piero Piccioni; art designer, Enrico Job; produced by Romano Cardarelli; released by Cinema V. Running time: 116 minutes.

With: Giancarlo Giannini (Gennarino) and Mariangela Melato (Raffaella).

Summer. A blue Mediterranean seascape seen through sunlit mist. In the distance a handsome white yawl moves with the light breeze. On the soundtrack we hear some jazzy instrumental music that recalls the score of every Italian film about the sweet life you've ever seen, but there's a point to it in the film. It pollutes air that once was as pure as it looked.

As the camera nears the yacht, the music gives way to the bickering of the yacht's well-heeled passengers. The mood that from a distance had seemed so serene turns suddenly, abrasively indolent—and furiously funny. People who have nothing to do, no visible responsibility to anything except tan skin, angrily debate capitalism, Communism, consumerism, the role of the Vatican in Italian life, while complaining about a crewman's smelly T-shirt.

This is the beginning of Lina Wertmuller's most entertaining new Italian comedy, Swept Away (By an Unusual Destiny in the Blue Sea of August), which opened yesterday at the Cinema II Theater.

Swept Away is Miss Wertmuller's fourth film to be released in this country. It follows The Lizards, which was shown in New York several years ago as part of a Festival of Women's Films, Love and Anarchy and The Seduction of Mimi, and it's played by the two actors, Giancarlo Giannini and Mariangela Melato, who were so remarkable in the latter two films. It's also by far the lightest, most successful fusion of Miss Wertmuller's two favorite themes, sex and politics, which are here so thoroughly and so successfully tangled that they become a single subject, like two people in love.

The shape of the film is as artificial as a fairy tale or a cartoon strip. Raffaella (Miss Melato), the rich, beautiful, acid-tongued Milanese who has chartered the yacht, and Gennarino (Giannini), the swarthy Sicilian deckhand whose T-shirts offend her, are marooned for several weeks on the only Mediterranean island not yet occupied by German tourists. They are Popeye and Olive Oyl locked in passionate combat.

The way Gennarino folds his pants and shirt—quickly, neatly, according to careful training that has become habit—you know he is a man who believes all things have their place, including women, who belong in the house with the children. Raffaella is an intelligent, selfish, superficially liberated slob who has never picked up anything in her life if there was an outside chance someone else would pick it up for her.

He is a Communist with the dedication of a first-century Christian. She is a capitalist because, for her, the system has paid off. More important, he is a man and she is a woman, for which there is hell to pay on both sides.

Swept Away is the story of their tumultuous, slapstick courtship, his systematic humiliation of her (as she sees it), until, suddenly, she submits to her love for him and becomes in the process truly liberated. Feminists, I suspect, will debate a number of plot points as if Miss Wertmuller had set out to write a treatise and not to make a love story, some of whose meanings are not easily translated into feminist agitprop.

More easily apparent are the director-writer's concerns about the Italian society that bred these two people and turned them into the mixed-up, wrongheaded characters they are, capable occasionally of unexpected, if imperfect, nobility. Her sympathies appear to be more with Gennarino than Raffaella, but that's a matter of politics, not sex, and he is, on the surface, a male chauvinist pig of a classic type.

Swept Away is less a film about ideas than about previous commitments, for which neither character can be held completely accountable. The enormous appeal of the comedy has to do with the way, briefly, each character is able to overcome those commitments.

It also has to do with the performances of Mr. Giannini and Miss Melato, who tear into their roles with a single-minded intensity that manages to be both hugely comic and believable, even in the most outrageous of situations. They are the best things to happen to Italian comedy since Marcello Mastroianni and Sophia Loren squared off in the 1960's.

—V.C., September 18, 1975

SWING TIME

Directed by George Stevens; written by Howard Lindsay and Allan Scott, based on a story by Erwin Gelsey; cinematographer, David Abel; edited by Henry Berman; music by Jerome Kern; art designers, Van Nest Polglase and Carroll Clark; produced by Pandro S. Berman; released by RKO Radio Pictures. Black and white. Running time: 105 minutes.

With: Fred Astaire (Lucky Garnett), Ginger Rogers (Penny Carroll), Victor Moore (Pop), Helen Broderick (Mabel), Eric Blore (Gordon), Betty Furness (Margaret Watson) and Georges Metaxa (Ricardo Romero).

That was no riot outside the Music Hall yesterday; it was merely the populace storming the Rockefeller's cinema citadel for a glimpse of the screen's nimblest song and dance team, Ginger Rogers and Fred Astaire, in their latest festival, *Swing Time.* Maybe they felt better about it than we did. We left the theater feeling definitely let down. The picture is good, of course. It would have to be with that dancing, with Victor Moore, Helen Broderick and Eric Blore. But after *Top Hat, Follow the Fleet* and the rest, it is a disappointment.

Blame it, primarily, upon the music. Jerome Kern has shadowboxed with swing, when he should have been trying to pick out a few companion pieces to "Smoke Gets in Your Eyes" and "I Won't Dance." Maybe we have no ear for music (do we hear cries of "No! No!"?) but right now we could not even whistle a bar of "A Fine Romance," and that's about the catchiest and brightest melody in the show. The others— "Pick Yourself Up," "Bojangles in Harlem," "The Way You Look Tonight," "Waltz in Swing Time" and "Never Gonna Dance"—are merely adequate, or worse. Neither good Kern nor good swing.

Elsewhere, though, you will find that the astute filmmakers at RKO Radio's studio have not forgotten their reliably entertaining formula for an Astaire-Rogers show. The plot is never permitted to weigh upon the shoulders of the cast; of comedy there is a generous portion; of romance the lightest sprinkling; of dancing, in solo, duet and ensemble, a brisk and debonair allotment. Add to these a handsomely modernistic, even impressionistic, series of sets, the usual appreciative photography and you have a picture that unquestionably will linger for a few weeks at the Music Hall.

Outlining it as briefly as we can, the story is that of Lucky Garnett, a dancer by profession, a gambler by avocation. Late for his wedding with a small-town girl, he is sent packing by her irate father with instructions not to return until he has accumulated $25,000—this serving as proof of his ability to support the young woman in proper style. With a lucky quarter and a man Friday, such being the incomparable Victor Moore, our hero comes to New York, meets a dancing instructress (Miss Rogers, of course) and strives thereafter, against Dame Fortune's constant smiles, to keep his wealth just below the fatally matrimonial $25,000.

If, by any chance, you are harboring any fears that Mr. Astaire and Miss Rogers have lost their magnificent sense of rhythm, be reassured. Their routines, although slightly more orthodox than usual, still exemplify ballroom technique at its best. And Mr. Astaire's solo tapping in the Bojangles number, with three giant silhouettes keeping step on the wall in the background, is one of the best things he has done.

If further eulogies are necessary, consider them uttered in behalf of Mr. Moore, his card tricks and his gallant attempt to dance with Miss Broderick; and for Miss Broderick's knack of making even an ordinary line seem to be a devastatingly witty Dorothy Parkerism; and for Mr. Blore for his brief—lamentably brief—appearance as the manager of the Gordon School of Dancing. These are solid virtues; nothing so intangible as a disappointing musical score should deter you from enjoying them to the Astaire-Rogers limit.

—F.S.N., August 28, 1936

THE TAKING OF PELHAM ONE TWO THREE

Directed by Joseph Sargent; written by Peter Stone, based on the novel by John Godey; director of photography, Owen Roizman; edited by Jerry Greenberg and Robert Q. Lovett; music by David Shire; art designer, Gene Rudolf; produced by Gabriel Katzka and Edgar J. Scherick; released by United Artists. Running time: 104 minutes.

With: Walter Matthau (Lieutenant Garber), Robert Shaw (Blue), Martin Balsam (Green), Hector Elizondo (Gray), Earl Hindman (Brown), James Broderick (Denny Doyle) and Lee Wallace (The Mayor).

It's been a while since we've had a movie that really catches the mood of New York and New Yorkers. The crisis mentality of what Henry James called "the vast hot pot"—which was revealed when numerous natives were convinced that they alone had caused the great November blackout of 1965—or the New York brand of logic that surfaced when a taxi driver shouted, "If we can get rid of Lindsay, we can get rid of the traffic!" is reflected in *The Taking of Pelham One Two Three*. The picture, directed by Joseph Sargent, opened yesterday at the 86th Street East and the Criterion Theater.

Four highly efficient hoods hijack an IRT subway car and hold eighteen people hostage for a million dollars; if the city doesn't pay within an hour, one hostage will be shot a minute. The Transit Authority, the Police Department, the Mayor and his colleagues all go into frenzied but coordinated action, while the film cuts most expertly between the stalled car and its passengers, the T.A. Command Center, Gracie Mansion and the city streets. Of course the subway system is soon backed up to the Bronx.

Walter Matthau's best caustic energies erupt as a Transit Authority lieutenant, and Peter Stone's script abounds with dialogue that's just right for this actor's benign bad temper. (Surely no one can say "Gesundheit!" to a sneezer quite so aggressively as Mr. Matthau.)

Martin Balsam and Robert Shaw—one glazed with a sleazy regret, the other endowed with a calm brutality—are all too likely as your typical rush-hour hijackers. Lee Wallace makes a pleasing, indecisive slob of a Mayor—aware that he'll be booed by any random crowd—and Tom Pedi is particularly good as an outraged official who can't tolerate a mess or a mystery in the subway. The bullying Deputy Mayor (Tony Roberts) unleashes a line that does sound just like home: "We're trying to run a city, not a goddam democracy!"

Throughout, there's a skillful balance between the vulnerability of New Yorkers and the drastic, provocative sense of comedy that thrives all over our sidewalks. And the hijacking seems like a perfectly probable event for this town. (Perhaps the only element of fantasy is the implication that the city's departments could function so smoothly together.) Meanwhile, the movie adds up to a fine piece of reporting—and it's the only action picture I've seen this year that has a rousing plot.

—*N.S., October 3, 1974*

TALK TO HER

Written (in Spanish, with English subtitles) and directed by Pedro Almodóvar; director of photography, Javier Aguirresarobe; edited by José Salcedo; music by Alberto Iglesias; production designer, Antxon Gómez; produced by Agustín Almodóvar; released by Sony Pictures Classics. Running time: 112 minutes.

With: Javier Cámara (Benigno), Darío Grandinetti (Marco), Leonor Watling (Alicia), Rosario Flores (Lydia), Geraldine Chaplin (Katarina), Mariola Fuentes (Rosa) and Lola Dueñas (Matilde).

Like all great doomed affairs, *Talk to Her,* the closing-night presentation of the New York Film Festival, is full of lovely, sweet suffering. And when it's over, the realization of how much the movie means to you really sinks in; you can't get it out of your heart.

Pedro Almodóvar has created a tragic comedy about need, its liberating and shackling powers. Movies haven't been so rapturous about characters plummeting to an awful end at least since the last Almodóvar film, *All About My Mother* (1999). But he doesn't mine the comic strip soap opera mystique so extravagantly here; everything falls into place with an almost surreal delicacy. The dense and deeply touching *Talk to Her* makes one think he has been listening to a lot of songs by the Smiths, those former postpunk potentates, particularly the band's classic, "Girlfriend in a Coma."

Benigno (Javier Cámara) is a nurse who sits patiently at the side of his unconscious girlfriend, Alicia (Leonor Watling), attending to her needs. What he does is talk to her, moving slowly, gently; his honeyed voice is a part of his physicality, going along with his meticulous, deliberate movement. He's a delicate, strangely assured stuffed animal of a man. And as in the compelling peculiarity of the Smiths—a sensibility that links the director and the band—the film takes fascinatingly soigné turns.

Initially the picture is about sympathy; Marco (Darío Grandinetti), taken by Benigno's lead, ministers to his own girlfriend, Lydia (Rosario Flores), who is also in a coma. Both women were intensely physical: Alicia was a dancer, and Lydia, a bullfighter, was gored.

With his placid face and caramel speaking tones, Benigno is the very center of the film, literally and spiritually. In terms of visual schemes, Mr. Almodóvar uses a dark, sweet richness and camera movements as deliberate and generous as Benigno. And we learn very slowly what depths of benign malice this apparently bland, kind man—and this superb filmmaker at the grown-up peak of his powers—is capable of. It is revealed that Benigno is an obsessive with no real ties to Alicia; she has become his after falling into unconsciousness, and the depth of his devotion becomes both a love story and a horror story. By the end of his story we're left as stunned and loyal as Marco.

By the end Mr. Almodóvar flips the script and demands not just sympathy but empathy for someone who you wouldn't think deserved it. It's a movie about being trapped in various kinds of prisons, spiritual, physical and finally literal. (His *All About My Mother* and the 1997 *Live Flesh* were also about being imprisoned.) And we see that *Talk to Her* is not about sympathy but about loyalty, and the picture with its crafty twists of fate earns our loyalty as well.

It's the most mature work this director has ever brought to the screen. His fearlessness used to lend itself to bizarre, wild plot turns that suggested he was out to tickle himself, a practical joker who loved giving his own pictures a hot foot.

The jabbering neuroses of his chattering characters grew out of Mr. Almodóvar himself; there was something lovable about his compulsive desire to entertain. Now the movies have the freakish, elegant calm of early Tennessee Williams, and the dramatic information is slipped into the movie with devastating panache: a love tap delivered with the force of a speeding car.

Mr. Almodóvar's purview started out as a lewd, slapstick version of the heightened melodrama of the 50's director Douglas Sirk: if *Magnificent Obsession* had starred a sexual Lucille Ball. But the director has moved past candy-colored Fassbinder with a sense of humor.

His plot turns are no longer as sharp and cruel, which was fun. (It's probably fitting that Marco Bellochio, who must also have influenced this director, was in the festival this year with *My Mother's Smile*.) Mr.

Almodóvar couldn't be more unhurried and assured about what he's doing; *Talk to Her* is evidence of his own evolving sensibility.

His movies have not lost their ability to startle, but the wayward ingenuity no longer gives vent to wild, delirious shocks. His metabolism has slowed; he doesn't cram in the lively excess for its own sake.

Yet the slippery mischievous streak remains, and *Talk to Her* shows how reliable he has become at marrying suspense, comedy and tragedy. He has become more capable than ever of not only shifting tones but also balancing several tones at once, answering questions and simultaneously deepening the mystery.

Mr. Almodóvar's appreciation of flesh—no other director photographs skin so lovingly—itself becomes a plot point. Benigno generously strokes Alicia, and the director evokes and subtly parodies movies like *Love Story.* Skin, and sex, are the heart of the trouble, and there's a grandly ludicrous scene about how deeply unavoidable sex is and the troubles it can raise. *Talk to Her* is totally in love with passion, and with love as we are—more than may be good for it.

—*E.M., October 12, 2002*

TAMPOPO

Written (in Japanese, with English subtitles) and directed by Juzo Itami; director of photography, Masaki Tamura; edited by Akira Suzuki; music by Kunihiko Murai; art designer, Takeo Kimura; produced by Yasushi Tamaoki; released by Itami Films. Running time: 114 minutes.

With: Tsutomu Yamazaki (Goro), Nobuko Miyamoto (Tampopo), Koji Yakusho (Man in White Suit), Ken Watanabe (Gun), Rikiya Yasuoka (Pisken), Kinzo Sakura (Shohei) and Mampei Iki-uchi (Tabo).

Tampopo, Juzo Itami's new Japanese film, is a satiric comedy about noodles—about their making, cooking, serving and consumption. It's about people who take noodles seriously, who read self-help books that, among other things, instruct the eater to regard the pork "affectionately" while "slurping" the noodles that have been "activated" by the soup.

In particular, the film is about Tampopo (the Japanese word for dandelion), a youngish widow who aspires to make, cook and serve the best noodles in any noodle shop in Tokyo, and about the people who help her on her way to the top. These include a truck driver–noodle connoisseur named Goro, who affects the mannerisms of Clint Eastwood, and a rich old man who loves noodles so much that, after he overindulges, a vacuum cleaner must be used to empty his stomach.

Though it's not consistently funny (at least not to someone who, with a clear conscience, buys his noodles in plastic bags), *Tampopo* is another example of the eccentric humor that has been showing up recently in Japanese films, most effectively in Yojiro Takita's *Comic Magazine* and Yoshimitsu Morita's *Family Game.*

Tampopo is buoyantly free in form. It's as much an essay as it is a narrative—always ready to digress into random gags and comic anecdotes. These may not have much bearing on Tampopo and her noodle education, but they all have to do with food and with the Japanese love of ritual that has made an art of slurping noodles, arranging flowers, drinking tea and committing suicide.

The film's writer-director, Mr. Itami, who's also an actor (he played the father in *The Family Game*), seems to have a special fondness for the solemnity of the prose used by connoisseurs. His principal characters and even the bit players converse by exchanging the sentiments of food critics.

Noodles that aren't great are described as "sincere," and when Tampopo is on the verge of a noodle breakthrough, her admirer must say, in all frankness, that "they're beginning to have substance, but they still lack depth." "Noodles," says a man searching for the perfect phrase, "are synergetic things." Early in the film, the sight of a bowl of noodles is compared to a Jackson Pollock painting.

Some of the best moments are only distantly related blackout sketches, including one about a father who urges his children, "Keep on eating! It's the last meal Mom cooked"—while Mom lies on the floor in the kitchen, having just committed suicide out of boredom.

Mr. Itami often strains after comic effects that remain elusive. The most appealing thing about *Tam-*

popo is that he never stops trying. A funny sensibility is at work here.

—V.C., May 22, 1987

TASTE OF CHERRY

Written (in Farsi, with English subtitles) and directed by Abbas Kiarostami; director of photography, Homayon Payvar; produced and edited by Mr. Kiarostami; released by Zeitgeist Films. Running time: 95 minutes.

With: Homayoun Ershadi (Mr. Badii), Abdolhossein Bagheri (Museum Guard), Afshin Khorshidbakhtair (Worker), Safar Ali Moradi (Soldier), Mir Hossein Noori (Seminarian), Ahman Ansari (Factory Guard), Hamid Massomi (Man in Phone Booth) and Elham Imani (Woman in Front of Museum).

For most people the will to live, even in hard times, is more than a determination to survive. It is an unquestioning, ebullient zest for being sensate in the world. This humanistic perception was the rockbottom insight of the great Iranian filmmaker Abbas Kiarostami's last two films, *And Life Goes On* and *Through the Olive Trees,* which were shown in the New York Film Festival in 1992 and '94. Both films portrayed Iranian farmers rolling with the punches of nature and almost cheerfully rebuilding their lives after a devastating earthquake.

In his exquisite new film, *Taste of Cherry,* which the festival is showing tomorrow at 4 P.M., Mr. Kiarostami contrasts the teeming vitality of Iranian working life with the suicidal inclination of a brooding, affluent middle-aged man identified only as Mr. Badii (Homayoun Ershadi).

Through most of the film, this character, whom Mr. Ershadi imbues with a quiet, smoldering bitterness, drives around the parched hills outside Teheran in a dusty white Range Rover, accosting strangers, interviewing them and asking them to assist him in a suicidal ritual. For a fee of 200,000 tomans (what a soldier would make in six months), he asks one man after another to accompany him to a predetermined grave site on the side of a hill and to return the next day to bury his dead body. In the unlikely possibility that Mr. Badii hasn't died from an overdose of sleeping pills taken the night before, the man designated to bury him is to help him to his feet.

If this grim scenario suggests one of Ingmar Bergman's bleaker cinematic meditations, *Taste of Cherry* is a long way from being a tormented probing into the soul's dark night. Mr. Badii's anguish is never explained, and he appears to be physically healthy and materially comfortable. He has just lost some instinctive knack.

Until he meets up with a wizened old taxidermist who tells him the story of his own failed suicide attempt decades earlier, Mr. Badii finds no takers for his scheme, despite the reward. His first prospective client is an impoverished young soldier who flees the Range Rover in terror when Mr. Badii makes his proposition. The second is an Afghan refugee who is a security guard at a lonely desert outpost. The third, another Afghan, is an articulate Islamic seminarian (Mir Hossein Noori) who lectures Mr. Badii calmly on the Muslim strictures against suicide.

Mr. Kiarostami, like no other filmmaker, has a vision of human scale that is simultaneously epic and precisely minuscule. While each of the men Mr. Badii approaches is a vivid, autonomous individual with a rich personal history and an innate sense of dignity, each is also seen as part of the human anthill.

The camera continually draws back for long shots of soldiers marching in formation over the harsh landscape and of workers moving enormous piles of red dirt and rock with heavy equipment. Dogs bark in the distance, the wind blows, flocks of crows circle and descend and rise. You feel the pulse and rhythms of earthly life on a grand scale. The breadth and fullness of this calm, orderly vision of people going about their business in a world that looks abundant, even beautiful, despite its aridity is idyllic if austere.

But it isn't until Mr. Badii meets the taxidermist, who is carrying a bunch of freshly killed quail for a natural-history museum class in stuffing birds, that the film finds a lyrical voice to match its powerful visual imagery. His gorgeous, rough-hewn soliloquy about regaining his zest for living after trying to hang himself from a mulberry tree is a simple, eloquent parable of the senses opening to the refreshment of life's simple pleasures.

—S.H., September 27, 1997

A TASTE OF HONEY

Produced and directed by Tony Richardson; written by Shelagh Delaney and Mr. Richardson, based on the play by Miss Delaney; cinematographer, Walter Lassally; edited by Anthony Gibbs; music by John Addison; art designer, Ralph Brinton; released by Continental Distributing. Black and white. Running time: 100 minutes.

With: Rita Tushingham (Jo), Dora Bryan (Helen), Murray Melvin (Geoffrey), Robert Stephens (Peter), Paul Danquah (Jimmy) and Maira Kaye (Doris).

Shelagh Delaney's *A Taste of Honey,* which justifiably drew theatergoers like flies to London and Broadway, is more memorable on film. The British-made drama, which was unveiled at the Paris Theatre yesterday, has been given specifically effective scope in the movie medium. Freed from the constricting confines of the stage, the shining honesty, the trials, the disenchantment of the drama's low-born Lancashire principals have become all the more striking and true. The dedicated producers have concocted a bitter *Honey* that is rare and travels well.

A Taste of Honey obviously is a labor of love. Tony Richardson, its producer-director, and Miss Delaney have been a team ever since it was staged here. Miss Delaney, it will be recalled, wrote the play when she was an astounding nineteen years old, out of conviction and the perceptions of an artist. Mr. Richardson, no less an artist, treated the work with appreciation of a shining and unusual talent. The result is a fittingly unadorned, sometimes drab, vehicle freighted with meaning and compassion that is universal despite its seemingly restrictive locale.

They and their sensitive cast have cleaved to the original story and to Miss Delaney's wry style. *A Taste of Honey* was and is less of a formalized narrative than it is a restrained, circuitous manner of presenting moods and moments of living. As such, Miss Delaney's slice of life evolves whole and with impact. It bursts with vitality against the sleazy environs of a North Country city slum, its dirty flats, dank docksides and the kaleidoscopic sights and the raucous, tinny sounds of Blackpool's fun fairs.

Having evoked complementary drama from a variety of sites, Mr. Richardson collaborated with Miss Delaney to keep her original lines intact. Her wide-eyed but worldly-wise teenager, who is constantly fighting loneliness and seeking affection she never gets from her man-chasing mother, meets an equally lonely Negro sailor and, after an idyllic interval, finds she is with child. After his tender departure for other ports, our heroine is all the more confused, frightened and unloved, especially when her brassy, roving mother marries a loud, free-spending type who plainly abhors the sight of the girl.

Since she is a resilient sort, she gives understanding and sanctuary to an effeminate youth from whom, for the first time, she receives tender care and tacit affection. But, as a realist, Miss Delaney finds life not only real and earnest but also hard. And, when childbirth is imminent, her mother, who has come to a parting of the ways with her spouse, returns to drive her delicate companion away. While she nominally takes up her maternal duties, a viewer is left with the idea that the daughter may yet be lonely and lovelorn.

As in the play, Miss Delaney is not compromising. One has the feeling that she chose abnormal characters to accent more forcefully society's indifference to its disenfranchised. They are neither angry nor lachrymose and they are, on occasion, a happy lot ready to laugh at themselves. Though they are involved in sordid circumstances, they manage to tug at the heart without breaking it.

Call it fateful or a matter of professionalism, but Mr. Richardson has been fortunate in finding Rita Tushingham, a nineteen-year-old newcomer to films, to portray Jo, the daughter. A plain Jane, she uses her saucer-eyed visage subtly to convey the pains and joys of her predicament, and her North Country accents, which may confuse some, beautifully transmit her humor and her self-protective cynicism. Mr. Richardson had a hand in shaping her performance but she is, nevertheless, a wondrous discovery.

Murray Melvin, who is repeating the role of the homosexual he created in the British play, handles this difficult assignment in muted but effective fashion. Like Miss Tushingham he is flesh and blood and not a caricature. Dora Bryan, a veteran of stage and screen comedy, is equally real as the hard and footloose mother. Paul Danquah in his movie debut as the

Negro sailor is gentle and subtle in a small but demanding role, and Robert Stephens is properly brash, vulgar and oafish as Miss Bryan's husband.

With the aid of Walter Lassally's expert camera work, which caught sooty, canal-lined Manchester exteriors, as well as grubby streets and happy, grubby, singing kids, Mr. Richardson and the company, who acted as though they lived there, have given a new dimension to an already sobering view of life among the lowly. In being transported out of the theater, this *Honey* has been enriched.

—A.W., May 1, 1962

TAXI DRIVER

Directed by Martin Scorsese; written by Paul Schrader; director of photography, Michael Chapman; edited by Marcia Lucas, Tom Rolf and Melvin Shapiro; music by Bernard Herrmann; art designer, Charles Rosen; produced by Michael Phillips and Julia Phillips; released by Columbia Pictures. Running time: 112 minutes.

With: Robert De Niro (Travis Bickle), Cybill Shepherd (Betsy), Jodie Foster (Iris), Harvey Keitel (Sport), Peter Boyle (Wizard), Leonard Harris (Charles Palantine), Albert Brooks (Tom) and Martin Scorsese (Passenger).

The steam billowing up around the manhole cover in the street is a dead giveaway. Manhattan is a thin cement lid over the entrance to hell, and the lid is full of cracks. Hookers, hustlers, pimps, pushers, frauds and freaks—they're all at large. They form a busy, faceless, unrepentant society that knows a secret litany. On a hot summer night the cement lid becomes a nonstop harangue written in neon: walk, stop, go, come, drink, eat, try, enjoy. Enjoy? That's the biggest laugh. Only the faceless ones—the human garbage—could enjoy it.

This is the sort of thing that Travis Bickle (Robert De Niro) might make note of in his diary. Travis, a loner who comes from somewhere else, drives a Manhattan cab at night. In the day he sleeps in short naps, pops pills to calm down, swigs peach brandy, which he sometimes pours on his breakfast cereal, and goes to porn films to relax. At one point he is aware that his headaches are worse and he suspects that he may have stomach cancer.

Travis Bickle is the hero of Martin Scorsese's flamboyant new film, *Taxi Driver,* which opened yesterday at the Coronet. He's as nutty as they come, a psychotic, but as played by Mr. De Niro he's a riveting character inhabiting a landscape that's as much his creation as he is the creation of it.

Taxi Driver is in many ways a much more polished film than Mr. Scorsese's other major Manhattan movie, *Mean Streets,* but its polish is what ultimately makes it seem less than the sum of its parts. The original screenplay by Paul Schrader, one of Hollywood's new young hopes (writers' division) imposes an intellectual scheme upon Travis's story that finally makes it seem too simple. It robs the film of mystery. At the end you may feel a bit cheated, as you do when the solution of a whodunit fails to match the grandeur of the crime.

But until those final moments *Taxi Driver* is a vivid, galvanizing portrait of a character so particular that you may be astonished that he makes consistent dramatic sense. Psychotics are usually too different, too unreliable, to be dramatically useful except as exotic decor.

Travis Bickle—the collaboration of writer, director and actor—remains fascinating throughout, probably because he is more than a character who is certifiably insane. He is a projection of all our nightmares of urban alienation, refined in a performance that is effective as much for what Mr. De Niro does as for how he does it. Acting of this sort is rare in films. It is a display of talent, which one gets in the theater, as well as a demonstration of behavior, which is what movies usually offer.

Were Mr. De Niro less an actor, the character would be a sideshow freak. The screenplay, of course, gives him plenty to work with. Until the final sequences, *Taxi Driver* has a kind of manic aimlessness that is a direct reflection of Travis's mind, capable of spurts of common sense and discipline that are isolated in his general confusion. Travis writes in his diary, "I don't believe that one should devote his life to morbid self-attention," and then sets about to make a name for himself by planning a political assassination.

Travis is an accumulation of self-destruct mechanisms. He makes friends with a pretty, intelligent campaign worker, played by Cybill Shepherd (who here recoups the reputation lost in *At Long Last Love*), but wonders why she is shocked when he takes her to the porn films he likes so much. His mind is full of crossed wires and short circuits.

The point of the film (which I can't talk about without giving away the plot), is, I feel, questionable, but the rest of it works. The supporting performances are fine, including those of Jodie Foster (whom I last saw as Becky Thatcher in *Tom Sawyer*) as a teenage hustler, Harvey Keitel as her pimp and Peter Boyle as a muddle-headed Manhattan cab driver.

You may want to argue with *Taxi Driver* at the end, and with good reason, but it won't be a waste of time.

—V.C., February 8, 1976

A TAXING WOMAN

Written (in Japanese, with English subtitles) and directed by Juzo Itami; director of photography, Yonezo Maeda; edited by Akira Suzuki; music by Toshiyuki Honda; produced by Yasushi Tamaoki and Seigo Hosogoe; released by Itami Films. Running time: 127 minutes.

With: Nobuko Miyamoto (Ryoko Itakura), Tsutomu Yamazaki (Hideki Gondo), Masahiko Tsugawa (Hanamura), Hideo Murota (Ishii), Shuji Otaki (Tsuyuguchi) and Daisuke Yamashita (Taro Gondo).

"Violence," says a Japanese gangster bidding a dramatic if temporary farewell to a confederate in handcuffs, "is obsolete. Today we go to prison for tax evasion."

The fine art of underreporting income, and the equally fine art of nabbing those who do, is the all-embracing subject of *A Taxing Woman,* the solemnly funny new satire by Juzo Itami, the Japanese director whose comic meditation on noodles, *Tampopo,* is still playing first-run here at the Cinema Studio.

A Taxing Woman will be shown at the New York Film Festival at Lincoln Center today and tomorrow.

It's now clear that Mr. Itami is one of the most original, most freewheeling sensibilities in movies today—either at home in Japan or abroad. He's robust

in a way that we seldom think of as characteristically Japanese. Like *Tampopo,* this new movie has a narrative of sorts, and several vividly sketched characters, but *A Taxing Woman* is as much a densely detailed essay on contemporary Japanese manners as it is conventional fiction.

Mr. Itami has the self-assurance and the eye of a born filmmaker and the mind of the kind of social critic who more often expresses himself in prose. In any other discipline it would be too much to call his work Swiftian, but in movies, where social criticism of this quality is virtually nonexistent, Mr. Itami's sarcasm deserves high praise.

At the center of *A Taxing Woman* is Ryoko Itakura (Nobuko Miyamoto), who, after her divorce, has gone to work in the Japanese equivalent of the Internal Revenue Service to support herself and her five-year-old son. A seemingly ordinary middle-class woman who wears her hair in a Louise Brooks bob and is self-conscious about her freckles, Ryoko suddenly finds her true calling as a tax inspector.

To all outward appearances, she's pretty, mild-mannered and shy, but on the trail of fraud she has the cool, unjudgmental tenacity of a bird dog with a nose for the second set of books. After serving her apprenticeship successfully terrorizing the aged proprietors of mom-and-pop stores, Ryoko moves into the big time: organized crime. She's promoted to an ultramodern task force whose principal target is Hideki Gondo (Tsutomu Yamazaki), a suave but gimpy fellow who operates what are called "adult motels" and who specializes in acquiring parcels of real estate from owners who don't want to sell. During the initial phases of the tax inquiry, Ryoko and Gondo are drawn to each other in a wacky variation on the sentimental movie about the cop who falls for the criminal. In Ryoko's case, however, it's evident that there could never be any real contest between infatuation and duty.

Mr. Itami is astonished by Japan's staggering affluence and by a materialism so unembarrassed and so aggressive that it has polarized society. On one side are those people—including moms, pops and hoodlums—whose sole interest is in hanging on to the money they've made. On the other side are those selfless, comradely functionaries dedicated to seeing that the government gets its cut of the melon. Nothing else matters.

The movie is thick with the inscrutably complex methods of tax evasion and with the high-tech methods of the law-enforcement officers. When, at long last, Ryoko and her fellow operatives close in on Gondo's empire, it's with enough precision, planning and Japanese-made electronic equipment to take not only Grenada but also Barbados and Tobago. The people in *A Taxing Woman* think small but on a grand scale.

The film is more witty than laugh-out-loud funny. *A Taxing Woman* doesn't possess the lyrically oddball footnotes that make *Tampopo* so special. Yet Mr. Itami is a man in touch with the world in which he lives and with the passions of his obsessed characters, which is why Ryoko and Gondo, though inflexible, are so appealing.

Miss Miyamoto (in private life, Mrs. Itami), who plays the ambitious noodle maker in *Tampopo,* and Mr. Yamazaki, the philosophizing, noodle-loving truck driver in the earlier film, are wonderfully single-minded and deadpan comics.

A Taxing Woman also looks terrific, from its arresting opening shot—an image of a dying old man, past all but infantile needs—to its final, bitter sequence in which Gondo and Ryoko meet for the last time. The setting is a great, deserted baseball park that, in the context of the rest of the movie, could possibly be the prototype for a brand-new export.

—V.C., September 26, 1987

A TAXING WOMAN'S RETURN

Written (in Japanese, with English subtitles) and directed by Juzo Itami; director of photography, Yonezo Maeda; edited by Akira Suzuki; music by Toshiyuki Honda; produced by Yasushi Tamaoki and Seigo Hosogoe; released by New Yorker Films. Running time: 127 minutes.

With: Nobuko Miyamoto (Ryoko Itakura), Rentaro Mikuni (Teppei Onizawa), Toru Masuoka (Inspector Mishima), Masahiko Tsugawa (Assistant Chief Inspector Hanamura), Tetsuro Tanba (Chief Inspector Sadohara), Koichi Ueda (Nekota) and Mansaku Fuwa (Shorty Masa).

Money is a living thing. It grows with time. Money is my child, my future life. When I am one with money, I am immortal."

So proclaims the seventy-year-old, exhausted-looking scalawag Onizawa (Rentaro Mikuni) in Juzo Itami's fine, scathing new comedy, *A Taxing Woman's Return,* which opens today at the Lincoln Plaza.

Onizawa, the self-styled Chief Elder of a bogus religious sect called Heaven's Path, has been brought in for questioning about some illicit real estate deals and a sizable amount of unreported income.

Having begun on a note of poetic confession, Onizawa seizes the banner of patriotism.

"I open land for Japan," he tells the startled tax investigators. "Tokyo must be an international center, but there isn't office space. We must build more buildings, but where? You'll never use eminent domain. That's why we must act."

The bureaucrats aren't ready for Onizawa's passion, but then they don't know Onizawa.

The old man works himself into a froth. "To revitalize Japan," he says, "someone must do the dirty work. Without us, Tokyo will be bypassed by Hong Kong and Seoul. Do you want that? Do you want Japan to become a second-rate power?"

He rises from the table and begins to bash his head furiously against the white wall. Blood drips from both the wall and Onizawa as he screams, "I'm being tortured! I'm being tortured!"

Onizawa, his head bandaged, his nostrils stuffed with cotton, returns home from the interview very pleased with himself.

Onizawa is a vicious, lecherous, crafty old rogue, who, when he must, deals in murder. That he also is unexpectedly engaging is due in part to the rich performance by Mr. Mikuni, a kind of Japanese Raimu, whose face is collapsing but whose eyes remain implacably fixed on the prize.

Mostly, though, the character is a reflection of the particular satiric talent of Mr. Itami, who wrote and directed *The Funeral, Tampopo, A Taxing Woman* and, now, *A Taxing Woman's Return.*

Mr. Itami plays against expectations. He loves having the wrong people say things the audience might think are right, or almost. In allowing Onizawa to be so persuasive, he gives folly and corruption a human face. Had this most witty and original of contemporary Japanese directors made *Mr. Smith Goes to Washington,* Mr. Smith would have been a secondary character. Mr. Itami is far less interested in celebrating virtue than in dissecting mendacity.

A Taxing Woman's Return is a sequel, but it's a very different kind of movie from the first, which introduced the "taxing woman," Ryoko (Nobuko Miyamoto), the former housewife who, after one setback and another, finds self-realization as a tax inspector.

In the new film, Ryoko is a fully formed character, one who functions much in the way of the lead of a television series. *A Taxing Woman's Return* is about Ryoko's further adventures, this time with Mishima (Toru Masuoka), a callow young Tokyo University graduate, as her partner.

Their immediate objective is the Heaven's Path religious cult, which is suspiciously rich for what looks to be a comparatively modest collection of fanatics. Their work isn't easy. It turns out that there are more registered religions in Tokyo than there are barbers.

Onizawa and his wife, the Holy Matriarch (Haruko Kato), drive around in his and hers Rolls-Royces. The Holy Matriarch has a special fondness for floor-length sable coats and Onizawa for women, especially for Nana, the pig-tailed sixteen-year-old who has been left with him as collateral on a loan.

The movie proceeds as a cat-and-mouse game as Ryoko and Mishima investigate the Heaven's Path cult and discover that Onizawa is, in fact, the front man for a group of crooked businessmen and corrupt members of the Diet.

This unholy alliance is changing the skyline of Tokyo, evicting tenants, buying land and putting up the sorts of spectacular high-rises that now dominate the city's western district of Shinjuku. The fruits of this real estate boom have nothing to do with the traditional Tokyo in which form has, until now, followed function. The "new" Tokyo could be the last Tokyo.

This is the subtext of the movie, which goes out of its way to disguise its serious concerns.

In *A Taxing Woman's Return,* Mr. Itami employs the mechanics of movie melodrama with unabashed gusto—stakeouts, car chases, disguises, secret chambers and even the kind of mysterious jewel that might turn up in an "Indiana Jones" adventure. With the exception of Onizawa, the movie is less interested in character than in scene, which is tumultuous and often Buñuelian.

Nothing could be more Buñuelian than the wintery love affair of Onizawa and the innocent Nana. She comes to adore the dirty old man who makes her pregnant and who then, as a sign of his undying love, proudly buys her a cemetery plot next to his mausoleum.

There is also something of Luis Buñuel in Mr. Itami's eagerness to disorient his audience with, perhaps, a sudden shot of a severed hand, or the lingering image of a corpse that's been some weeks in the water.

Representing the film's conscience are Ryoko, Mishima, and their comically gung-ho colleagues though, except for a parting glance at the end, they never betray their feelings in any overt fashion. Miss Miyamoto, in her Louise Brooks bob and wearing modishly baggy slacks, is a steadfast charmer, and a far more endearing crime buster than Batman.

As photographed by Yonezo Maeda and scored by Toshiyuki Honda (who is to Mr. Itami what Nino Rota was for Federico Fellini), *A Taxing Woman's Return* has the flashy look and romantic sound that have become the director's singular style.

However, don't be deceived by the cool, breezy manner of *A Taxing Woman's Return.* It scalds.

It's another major film from the man who is possibly the only true social satirist at work in movies today.

—*V.C., June 28, 1989*

TELL THEM WILLIE BOY IS HERE

Directed by Abraham Polonsky; written by Mr. Polonsky, based on the book *Willie Boy: A Desert Manhunt* by Harry Lawton; cinematographer, Conrad Hall; edited by Melvin Shapiro; music by Dave Grusin; art designers, Alexander Golitzen and Henry Bumstead; produced by Philip A. Waxman; released by Universal Pictures. Running time: 97 minutes.

With: Robert Redford (Cooper), Katharine Ross (Lola), Robert Blake (Willie), Susan Clark (Liz), Barry Sullivan (Calvert) and John Vernon (Hacker).

Abraham Polonsky directed his first movie, *Force of Evil,* in 1948. His second movie, *Tell Them Willie Boy Is Here,* opened yesterday at the Murray Hill Theater.

The intervening twenty years, apparently without directorial assignments and virtually without screen credits, perhaps the most wasteful injustice of the late 1940's Hollywood blacklisting, have invested Polonsky with considerable exemplary glamour and saddled him with a reputation no director of a second film should have to justify.

The reputation was well earned. *Force of Evil* is one of the best American movies, idiomatic to its period, evocative of its dense New York Jewish milieu, and resourceful in presenting a superb cast headed by the late John Garfield. And the reputation is now well maintained.

Tell Them Willie Boy Is Here is another one of the best American movies, and in its own way, equally idiomatic, evocative and resourceful.

Set in California near the beginning of the century, the story, based on fact, concerns a young Indian (Robert Blake) who after a long absence returns to his reservation and in self-defense kills the father of the girl (Katharine Ross) he loves. He flees with her into the mountains. Forced by the doctor (Susan Clark) in charge of the reservation, the local sheriff (Robert Redford) reluctantly organizes a posse to catch Willie Boy, whom he admires, and return the girl. Most of the film is devoted to the chase, the stupid intervention of an old Indian fighter (Barry Sullivan), the unexplained death of the girl and the ultimate confrontation between Willie Boy and the sheriff, ending in the killing and cremation of Willie Boy.

The film moves by cutting between the fugitives and their pursuers, sometimes enforcing sharp contrast, occasionally suggesting direct or ironic similarity (for example, the sheriff and the lady doctor engage in mutually humiliating sexual combat; Willie Boy and his girl make love) by means of sound bridges and parallel visual compositions. Polonsky treats his wide screen as space to be meaningfully filled, and one is aware of carefully considered effect, especially in the desert landscape, to a degree unusual in recent movies.

Tell Them Willie Boy Is Here can be read on two levels, and has already been so read by critics who are delighted or displeased according to how they feel about that liberal genre, the message Western.

Polonsky has his messages, tied to the white-Indian conflict, and they are delivered in a script that is not dialogue so much as a series of one-line monologues, to which characters may react but almost never effectively respond. With a moral victory or defeat registered every few minutes, the film is sometimes in danger of mistaking text for texture.

The danger is generally avoided. *Tell Them Willie Boy Is Here* lives most brilliantly on a third level, not unrelated to the action or the allegory, but deeper, more mysterious, more fully felt. I will not characterize this level except to note that it had to do with giving personal signs and signals, and that it informs every major gesture and image of the movie.

Because it is a chase movie, concerned with clues and tracks, all signs must be read. And because the film is interested in questions of personal identity, all signs are doubly relevant. But the nature of the signs changes in the course of the movie, becoming always more intimate, elusive, meaningful, impenetrable. Near the end, these signs include a dead girl's body, a scarecrow, a handprint, a ritual fire—images, in context, of exceptional resonance.

The four principal actors are wonderful. Robert Redford and Robert Blake meet physically only twice in the course of the film, but they constitute a superb ensemble. Susan Clark brings humanity to a schematized and sometimes melodramatic role. And Katherine Ross, whose character is the least accessible of all, suffers and finally submits without giving in to pathos or easy stylization.

—*R.G., December 19, 1969*

10

Written and directed by Blake Edwards; director of photography. Frank Stanley; edited by Ralph E. Winters; music by Henry Mancini; production designer. Rodger Maus; produced by Mr. Edwards and Tony Adams; released by Warner Brothers. Running time: 122 minutes.

With: Dudley Moore (George). Julie Andrews (Sam). Bo Derek (Jenny). Robert Webber (Hugh). Dee Wallace (Mary Lewis). Sam Jones (David). Brian Dennehy (Bartender) and Max Showalter (The Reverend).

George (Dudley Moore) is a very successful composer of popular songs, the kind that a member of the Pepsi generation calls "elevator music," though they've made him rich. He has a long-standing, apparently happy relationship with a good, intelligent woman named Sam (Julie Andrews), who has her own career as a singer. He lives in a lovely hilltop house in Los Angeles, lacks nothing and is thoroughly miserable. George is forty-two years old, and in Southern California you don't even have to be old to be ancient. Everything is too easy out there.

Blake Edwards's frequently hilarious new film, *10,* is the story of George's desperate efforts to come to terms with life in Southern California even though he knows he's inadequate. Everywhere he goes he sees youth, beauty and health. He drives casually down a street and feels assaulted by the sight of joggers. Nobody seems to drive anymore. They don't even walk. Everybody runs. It's as if their lives were on fire.

The movie *10,* a reference to the scale by which George rates beautiful women, is almost as much a celebration of the comedy talents of Dudley Moore as *Darling Lili* was a celebration of Mr. Edwards's admiration for his wife, Miss Andrews. Mr. Edwards, though deeply romantic, never lets that get in the way of comedy. Like George, he just can't help himself.

This is the biggest, fattest role Mr. Moore has yet had in American films. Though he's already delighted us in *Foul Play* and *Bedazzled,* and on the stage in *Beyond the Fringe* and, more recently, in *Good Evening,* the revue with Peter Cook, he's never done such a relatively straight role in a film before. He's not entirely comfortable as a romantic leading man, but then *10* doesn't play its romance straight very much of the time.

The frame of the film is George's pursuit of a phantom, a beautiful young woman he spots one day as her limousine pulls alongside his Rolls-Royce at a stoplight. The young woman, whom George rates conservatively as an "11," is dressed in a bridal gown and veil and is on her way to the church, which doesn't inhibit George. He sneaks into the ceremony, hides among the flowers and, just as the couple are exchanging vows, gets stung on the nose by a bee.

In Mr. Edwards's comic world, noses are meant to be stung, heads to have hangovers and beautiful women to be pursued at any cost.

Learning that the young woman's father is, as someone says importantly, "the most exclusive dentist in Beverly Hills," George allows himself to have eight teeth filled at one sitting to find out more about his mysterious, temporarily lost love. When the usually understanding Sam loses her temper at his unstable ways, George goes on an epic bender and follows the honeymoon couple to their Mexican resort, an overpoweringly picturesque place with a beach too hot to walk barefoot on, rum drinks that look like fancy garbage cans and rope bridges that aren't easily navigated by someone who's been drinking brandy and is loaded with painkillers.

George, who is short in stature compared to the rest of the population of Southern California, is most funny when most in peril, which is psychological as often as it's physical. His principal failing is to embark on an endeavor that, for one reason or another, he cannot complete. Success through failure, though, is the way comedies like *10* operate.

The movie belongs very much to Mr. Moore, who manages to be funny without ever having to appear stupid. Miss Andrews is on-screen for what seems like no time at all, though her no-nonsense presence is essential to much of the comedy, even when she doesn't participate in it. She is the light at the end of the tunnel of George's midlife crisis. A truly magnificent looking young woman named Bo Derek appears as George's phantom-mistress, and she turns out to be almost as funny as Mr. Moore, partly because the character she plays is the only person in the movie who has no doubts about herself.

The excellent supporting cast includes Robert Webber as George's songwriting partner, Dee Wallace as a lonely woman who tries to pick up George at the Mexican resort, Max Showalter as the pastor of a fancy Beverly Hills Protestant church, and a beautiful blonde named Deborah Rush, who plays the kind of assistant one might expect in the office of the most exclusive dentist in Beverly Hills. She doesn't handle the instruments or prepare the anesthetics. She just sits by the patient's chair and keeps up a running stream of sympathetic moans and winces as the dentist operates.

Mr. Edwards's comic gifts haven't been blunted by his recent series of *Pink Panther* hits with Peter Sellers. The film *10* is loaded with odd surprises. It also contains a routine about a nearly blind old lady serving tea, a variation on a routine that Mr. Moore did in his

Broadway show with Mr. Cook. It's classically funny no matter who does it.

—V.C., October 5, 1979

THE TEN COMMANDMENTS

Produced and directed by Cecil B. DeMille: written by Aeneas MacKenzie. Jesse Lasky Jr.. Jack Gariss and Fredric M. Frank. based on the novels *The Prince of Egypt* by Dorothy Clarke Wilson. *Pillar of Fire* by the Reverend J. H. Ingram and *On Eagle's Wings* by the Reverend G. E. Southon and on the text of the Bible and the ancient writings of Josephus. Eusebius. Philo and The Midrash: cinematographers. Loyal Griggs. John F. Warren. W. Wallace Kelley and Peverell Marley: edited by Anne Bauchens: music by Elmer Bernstein: art designers. Hal Pereira. Walter Tyler and Albert Nozaki: released by Paramount Pictures. Running time: 219 minutes.

With: Charlton Heston (Moses). Ann Baxter (Nefertiti). Yul Brynner (Rameses). Yvonne DeCarlo (Sephbra). Sir Cedric Hardwicke (Sethi). Debra Paget (Lilia). Edward G. Robinson (Dathan). John Derek (Joshua). Nina Foch (Bithiah). Judith Anderson (Memnet). John Carradine (Aaron). Vincent Price (Baka) and Martha Scott (Yochabel).

Against the raw news of modern conflict between Egypt and Israel—a conflict that has its preamble in the Book of Exodus—Cecil B. DeMille's *The Ten Commandments* was given its world premiere last night at the Criterion Theatre, and the coincidence was profound. For Mr. DeMille's latest rendering of Biblical literature in the spectacular framing and colloquial idiom of the screen tells an arresting story of Moses, the ancient Israelite who was a slave with his people in Egypt and who struggled to set them free.

As Mr. DeMille presents it in this three-hour-and-thirty-nine-minute film, which is by far the largest and most expensive that he has ever made, it is a moving story of the spirit of freedom rising in a man, under the divine inspiration of his Maker. And, as such, it strikes a ringing note today.

But aside from the timely arrival and contemporary context of this film, it is also a rather handsome romance in Mr. DeMille's best massive style. To the fundamental story of Moses, as told in the Old Testament and reflected in other ancient writings consulted by Mr. DeMille, he and his corps of screen playwrights have added some frank apocrypha which, while they may not be traceable in history (or even in legend), make for a robust tale.

In this imaginative recount, Moses is raised as a prince in the palace of Egypt's Pharaoh, after being found, as the Bible tells, by the Pharaoh's daughter in the bullrushes, where he was hidden by his mother, a Hebrew slave. And as a presumed Egyptian, he is a candidate for the Pharaoh's throne and a rival for the love of a luscious princess with the Pharaoh's own son, Rameses.

As one might well imagine, the plot-minded Mr. DeMille does not pass lightly or briefly over this phase of his tale. Moses, as played by Charlton Heston, is a handsome and haughty young prince who warrants considerable attention as a heroic man of the ancient world. And Anne Baxter as the sensual princess and Yul Brynner as the rival, Rameses, are unquestionably apt and complementary to a lusty and melodramatic romance.

But the story is brought back to contact with the Bible and with its inspirational trend when Moses discovers, acknowledges and is exiled from Egypt because of his Hebraic birth. Then Mr. DeMille, who, incidentally, acts as narrator for his film in many of its more exalted stretches, takes him into the wilderness and establishes his contact with his Maker, which leads to the Exodus and the Covenant on Mount Sinai.

In the latter phases of the drama, wherein the impulse to set his people free from the bondage of Egypt flames in Moses, the spiritual and supernatural surge comes somewhat bluntly in the picture, and the performance of such awesome miracles as the crossing of the Red Sea and the burning of the Ten Commandments into the tablets of stone may strike the less devout viewer as a bit mechanical and abrupt.

Also, and with all due regard for the technical difficulties besetting Mr. DeMille, we must say his special effects department was not up to sets or costumes. The parting of the Red Sea is an obvious piece of camera trickery in which two churning walls of water frame a course as smooth and dry as a racetrack. And the striking off of the Ten Commandments by successive thunderbolts, while a deep voice intones their contents, is disconcertingly mechanical.

However, in its other technical aspects—in its remarkable settings and decor, including an overwhelming facade of the Egyptian city from which the Exodus begins, and in the glowing Technicolor in which the picture is filmed—Mr. DeMille has worked photographic wonders. And his large cast of characters is very good, from Sir Cedric Hardwicke as a droll and urbane Pharaoh to Edward G. Robinson as a treacherous overlord. Yvonne DeCarlo as the Midianite shepherdess to whom Moses is wed is notably good in a severe role, as is John Derek as a reckless Joshua.

This is unquestionably a picture to which one must bring something more than a mere wish for entertainment in order to get a full effect from it. But for those to whom its fundamentalism will be entirely credible, it should be altogether thrilling and perhaps even spiritually profound.

—B.C., November 9, 1956

TENDER MERCIES

Directed by Bruce Beresford; written by Horton Foote; director of photography, Russell Boyd; edited by William Anderson; music by George Dreyfus, art designer Jeannine Oppewall; produced by Philip S. Hobel, Mary-Ann Hobel, Mr. Foote and Robert Duvall; released by Universal Pictures. Running time: 89 minutes.

With: Robert Duvall (Mac Sledge), Tess Harper (Rosa Lee), Betty Buckley (Dixie), Wilford Brimley (Harry), Ellen Barkin (Sue Anne), Allan Hubbard (Sonny) and Lenny Von Dohlen (Robert).

What better proof can there be of the distinctiveness of Australian filmmaking than *Tender Mercies,* a film by Bruce Beresford that manages to be thoroughly Australian though it features Texas settings and an American cast? Mr. Beresford, the director of *Breaker Morant,* has brought a hauntingly spare look to this story, which is set on a prairie as endless and barren as Australia's. And the characters are as silent and unyielding as the landscape. Indeed, *Tender Mercies* has a bleak handsomeness bordering on the arty, but it also has real delicacy and emotional power,

both largely attributable to a fine performance by Robert Duvall. Mr. Duvall's versatility seems to know no limit; in his role here as an over-the-hill country singer, he creates yet another quietly unforgettable character.

Mr. Beresford, working with less stiffly moralistic material than he did in *Breaker Morant,* has a lighter, easier touch this time. *Tender Mercies,* which was written by Horton Foote and opens today at Loews Tower East and other theaters, concerns a defeated-looking drunk who shows up at a remote, ramshackle motel one day and stays. At first, he lingers because he is broke and has offered to work off his debt to the pretty proprietor, Rosa Lee (Tess Harper). Soon he is staying for Rosa Lee herself, and without much ado or conversation, they are married. The gaunt, hollow-eyed Mac (Mr. Duvall) proposes this while helping Rosa Lee with her vegetable garden. Lonely, impoverished Rosa Lee says yes with almost more gratitude than excitement or surprise.

Only later does she learn that Mac used to be Mac Sledge, a famous country singer who drank himself out of a career at the top, and whose former wife was the still-successful country singer Dixie Lee (played by Betty Buckley, who doesn't much look or sound like a country star, but whose powerhouse voice makes any such discrepancies seem negligible). It's not clear whether Rosa Lee has heard of any of them before, but she hasn't had much time in her life for anything as frivolous as country music or its gaudy celebrities.

Though Mac's subsequent recovery of his strength would seem to lead toward a musical as well as a spiritual comeback, Mr. Foote's screenplay has its focus elsewhere. It follows Mac's relationships with his former wife, his daughter, his new bride and her son, weaving them into a sadly contemporary vision of family life and heading toward a final note of affirmation. This is a small, lovely and somewhat overloaded film about small-town life, loneliness, country music, marriage, divorce and parental love, and it deals with all of these things in equal measure. Still, the absence of a single, sharply dramatic story line is a relatively small price to pay for the plainness and clarity with which these other issues are defined.

Tender Mercies highlights Mr. Duvall, who is so thoroughly transformed into Mac that he even walks with a Texan's rolling gait, but it also features some superb supporting performances. Ellen Barkin, who was so good as the young wife in *Diner,* is even better as Mac's spoiled and troubled daughter, and Miss Harper brings a beautifully understated dignity to the role of a new wife who is not much older than her stepchild. Wilford Brimley is solid and durable as a music-business functionary, and Allen Hubbard does a convincing job as Rosa Lee's young son, whose father died in Vietnam. A great point is made of this, and it's probably one big issue more than a little film like *Tender Mercies* can handle. Like its laconic characters, the film itself seems to have more on its mind than it can manage to say.

—*J.M., March 4, 1983*

THE TENDER TRAP

Directed by Charles Walters; written by Julius Epstein, based on the play by Max Shulman and Robert Paul Smith; cinematographer, Paul C. Vogel; edited by John Dunning; music by Jeff Alexander; art designers, Cedric Gibbons and Arthur Lonergan; produced by Lawrence Weingarten; released by Metro-Goldwyn-Mayer. Running time: 110 minutes.

With: Debbie Reynolds (Julie Gillis), Frank Sinatra (Charlie Y. Reader), David Wayne (Joe McCall), Celeste Holm (Sylvia Crewes), Jarma Lewis (Jessica), Lola Albright (Poppy) and Joey Faye (Sol Z. Steiner).

It isn't very likely that Metro-Goldwyn-Mayer's *The Tender Trap,* which sprang with the joy of a low comedian into the Music Hall yesterday, is going to make marriage less attractive, but it certainly is going to do a lot to create a whole new respect for the joys and delights of bachelorhood. And, if a purely art-bent reviewer may introduce a commercial thought, it is likely to add a few fat digits to the credit of Metro-Goldwyn-Mayer.

For this comical dissertation on the fun a bright fellow can have merely by remaining single in the glutted marriage market of New York is a vastly beguiling entertainment, even for guys who already are hooked and for ladies of desperate disposition who have their traps out for any fair game. There is something here for all of us—in the way of amusement, that is.

True, the story is no *South Pacific,* any more than it was on the stage, where it turned up last year as a three-act roughhouse by Max Shulman and Robert Paul Smith. A thirty-five-year-old actors' agent with a terrace apartment on Sutton Place has to fight off the beautiful women who clamor to share their lives with him. To the wonder and consternation of an old and respected married friend who takes up temporary residence with him while on a tacit vacation from home, he lives like a self-indulgent sultan, until—ah, yes, you have guessed it!—until there comes into his life a stalwart maiden who treats him with elegant disdain.

What happens then, you can imagine. A romantic challenge is flung. The sultan is routed from his harem. Follow that camel, man! Our bachelor soon finds himself tangled in a couple of tender traps, one baited by the haughty maiden and the other the standing snare of an old friend. How he struggles to regain his freedom and by which trap he is eventually held are matters of exposition we strongly recommend that you attend.

Not for the exposition so much, but simply for all that's said and done, especially by Frank Sinatra as the bachelor and David Wayne as his envious married friend. These two gentlemen have a capacity to turn the crisp, idiomatic lines of Julius Epstein's adaptation into cheerfully sparkling repartée. And when it comes to such a thing as conveying the immensity of a celebrating brawl through the gloom and debris of the morning after, you'll not get it better than from these boys.

"Whoever said that Sue Danforth is stuffy?" Mr. Wayne fuzzily inquires. "There are not many girls that would let Charlie Fitzpatrick give them a crew haircut." So much for the brawl.

As the maiden who causes the confusion, Debbie Reynolds is all cuteness and spunk, and Celeste Holm is delightfully cool and casual as the one for whom the brawl is thrown. As other inhabitants of the harem, Jarma Lewis and Lola Albright are living dolls, and Joey Faye does a very funny short-take as something left over from the night before.

Charles Walters's direction is smooth and lively, the settings and costumes are chic and the whole thing looks very delicious in color and CinemaScope. A song sung twice over lightly by Miss Reynolds and the old-time Frankie-boy adds a lilt to the thematic soundtrack of a thoroughly diverting show.

—*B.C., November 11, 1955*

TERMS OF ENDEARMENT

Directed by James L. Brooks; written by Mr. Brooks, based on the novel by Larry McMurtry; director of photography, Andrzej Barkowiak; edited by Richard Marks and Sidney Wolinsky; music by Michael Gore; production designer, Polly Platt; produced by Mr. Brooks, Penny Finkelman and Martin Jurow; released by Paramount Pictures. Running time: 130 minutes.

With: Debra Winger (Emma Horton), Shirley MacLaine (Aurora Greenway), Jack Nicholson (Garrett Breedlove), Danny DeVito (Vernon Dahlert), Jeff Daniels (Flap Horton), John Lithgow (Sam Burns), Betty King (Rosie) and Lisa Hart Carroll (Patsy Clark).

*T*erms of Endearment is a funny, touching, beautifully acted film that covers more territory than it can easily manage. It's the thirty-year saga of a mother and daughter; the story of a charmingly eccentric woman who, in her fifties, finally permits herself to fall in love; and the chronicle of a troubled marriage between a young professor and his whimsical bride. It's a comedy, offbeat and lighthearted, then turns painfully and unexpectedly tragic in its final half hour.

A lesser movie might flail hopelessly between such drastic extremes, and *Terms of Endearment* does falter here and there. But it somehow manages to incorporate a great many dramatic threads. If it doesn't always do so with the most grace or economy, neither does it ever fail to be enormously appealing, thanks to the bright, witty, larger-than-life performances that James Brooks has elicited from his stars.

Terms of Endearment, which opens today at the Coronet, the Baronet, Loews Astor Plaza, and other theaters, is based on Larry McMurtry's novel of the same title. Mr. Brooks's screenplay doesn't follow the novel exactly, eliminating numerous incidental characters and adding at least one major figure, but it does echo the book's arch dialogue and its considerable sprawl. Mr. Brooks appears to have paid minimal attention to the pacing problems of the material, or to the fact that it frequently meanders. Instead, he concentrates on charm. And charm, at least on a scene-by-scene basis, is something *Terms of Endearment* has in abundance.

At the center of the movie is Aurora Greenway, a stern, fussy, wildly glamorous blond creature played with perfect composure by Shirley MacLaine. In the film's opening scene, Aurora awakens her infant daughter Emma to make sure the baby hasn't succumbed to crib death, and this mother-daughter dynamic persists long into Emma's adulthood. Emma, a beleaguered yet somehow radiant young woman played by Debra Winger, remains in her mother's orbit long after marrying Flap Horton (Jeff Daniels), whom Aurora despises, and bearing him three children. When the young Hortons tell Aurora that the first of these is on the way, she shrieks with typical delicacy, "Why should I be happy about being a grandmother?"

But grandmotherhood and the unavoidable fact of her own increasing age finally force Aurora into the arms of her wily next-door neighbor, a former astronaut named Garrett Breedlove. This is the character Mr. Brooks has added to the story, and as played by Jack Nicholson he becomes a masterly comic invention, with a magnificent repulsiveness that Mr. Nicholson turns into pure hilarity. Garrett is capable of making a mere lunch invitation sound amazingly obscene, and when he flirts with Aurora over the hedge that separates their houses, he threatens to ooze over into her yard. Miss MacLaine's deliberate coolness makes her a perfect foil for this sort of thing, and her scenes with Mr. Nicholson are among the film's most delightful.

Terms of Endearment, which affects a drily eccentric humor like Mr. McMurtry's particularly in its opening scenes, takes a while to get going; an audience may not realize that a bride and groom making love to show tunes (like "Gee, Officer Krupke") in their unpainted shack will evolve into characters who are genuinely affecting over the course of the story. After a while, though, the film seems to relax about establishing its own cleverness, and it moves on more comfortably to follow the characters and their lives.

By the time one of the women becomes ill—anyone who goes to this film expecting a light comic diversion had better bring along at least four hankies for the hospital scenes—the film has established its emotional base, and its ending is indeed wrenching. Miss MacLaine and Miss Winger bring great conviction to these final moments, just as they have brought buoyancy to what had come before. Miss MacLaine has one of her best roles in Aurora, and her performance is a lovely mixture of longing, stubbornness and reserve. Miss Winger again shows herself to be an astonishingly vital screen actress, able to imbue even the relatively drab Emma with urgency and passion.

There are some lovely supporting performances in *Terms of Endearment* too, most notably John Lithgow's as the bashful Iowa banker who becomes Emma's lover after encountering her in the supermarket. Mr. Lithgow plays this entire episode clutching a canned ham in his left arm, yet he manages to make this touch seem sweet rather than sardonic. Danny DeVito is also quite good as Vernon Dahlart, whose name captures the flavor of his character and who is one of the many Texan moths around Aurora's flame. As Flap, Mr. Daniels seems pleasant but ordinary, without the immense scale of the three other principals. This doesn't seem to be the fault of the performance, but rather that of the screenplay. As written, Flap is an indistinct character. It's never quite clear why Aurora can't stand him, or why Emma can.

Because the screenplay concentrates so heavily on the characters' wit and devotes so little attention to their backgrounds—no one who hasn't read Mr. McMurtry will have any idea how Aurora came by the Renoir she keeps in her bedroom, for instance—the film's production design is particularly important. As executed by Polly Platt, it is particularly good, giving a colorful but realistic sense of who the principals are and how they live. Andrzej Bartkowiak's handsome cinematography also contributes to the film's high gloss. And Mr. Brooks, even when struggling with the demands of his narrative, continues to bring out the best in this material: its humanity and its humor.

—*J.M., November 23, 1983*

LA TERRA TREMA

Directed by Luchino Visconti; written (in Italian, with English subtitles) by Mr. Visconti, based on the novel *I Malavoglia* by Giovanni Verga; cinematographer, G. R. Aldo; edited by Mario Serandrei; music by Willy Ferrero; produced by Salvo D'Angelo; released by Mario De Vecchi Pictures. Black and white. Running time: 160 minutes.

With: Luchino Visconti and Antonio Pietrangeli (Narrators).

Until yesterday, when it opened at the uptown New Yorker Theater, Luchino Visconti's early feature about Sicilian fishermen, *La Terra Trema* (*The Earth Will Tremble*), had not been shown anywhere in toto in a commercial theater since 1948, it is believed. This directorial tour de force, running almost three hours and resoundingly imprinted with a plea for social reform, was then compressed in half by its producers, over Mr. Visconti's protests, shown briefly in Italian theaters, and withdrawn.

With all due respect to the distinguished director of *Rocco and His Brothers* and *The Leopard,* and to the wonderful opening third of this seventeen-year-old work, his *Terra Trema* colleagues were probably right—after all these years.

Using the early neorealism format so triumphantly developed by Roberto Rossellini and Vittorio De Sica, and a cast and a coastal village of nonprofessional Sicilians, Mr. Visconti traces the doom and disintegration of one fishing family, after a rebel son tries to unite the village against traditional exploitation by wholesale merchants.

Two minutes after the picture starts—a predawn shore sequence with silhouetted fishermen pushing off in their boats—we recognize it as the work of a born moviemaker. In the selection of his uncredited players, especially the focal family, and the panoramic bleakness of his rough-hewn backgrounds, Mr. Visconti has evoked a simple, human landscape of potential power. But the die is cast, not only for the young hero, who perfectly personifies a lost cause, but for the bulk—and that's the word—of the film.

Most unfortunately, Mr. Visconti, who also wrote the scenario, has taken his spunky protagonist and literally drowned him in woes, even—let's face it— soapsuds.

Compared to this clan, the house of Job had a picnic. After foolishly wrecking his boat in a storm, their young leader abruptly becomes an outcast to the mean, cold, and abject villagers. Grandpa has a stroke.

The hero's young sister slinks out at night and he himself hits the bottle. His young brother is enticed into smuggling by a shadowy American, clad in black and handing out Lucky Strikes.

Yes, the mortgage is foreclosed on the old homestead, which looks ready to collapse at any moment. Mr. Visconti caps this with some sneering overlords badgering hungry job applicants, including the defeated hero, with bread.

Until he slices it too obviously, *La Terra Trema* is as real as the staff of life.

—*H.T., October 13, 1965*

TESS

Directed by Roman Polanski: written by Mr. Polanski, Gerard Brach and John Brownjohn, based on the novel *Tess of the d'Urbervilles* by Thomas Hardy: cinematographers, Geoffrey Unsworth and Ghislain Cloquet: edited by Alastair McIntyre and Tom Priestley: music by Philippe Sarde: production designer, Pierre Guffroy: produced by Claude Berri: released by Columbia Pictures. Running time: 170 minutes.

With: John Collin (John Durbeyfield), Leigh Lawson (Alec Durbeyfield), Tony Church (Parson Tringham), Nastassja Kinski (Tess) and Peter Firth (Angel Clare).

Thomas Hardy's *Tess of the D'Urbervilles,* which Roman Polanski has turned into a lovely, lyrical, unexpectedly delicate movie, might at first seem to be the wrong project for Mr. Polanski in every way. As a new biography of the director reports, when *Tess* was shown at the Cannes Film Festival, the press pointed nastily and repeatedly to the coincidence of Mr. Polanski's having made a film about a young girl's seduction by an older man, while he himself faced criminal charges for a similar offense. This would certainly seem to cast a pall over the project. So would the fact that Hardy's novel is so very deeply rooted in English landscapes, geographical and sociological, while Mr. Polanski was brought up in Poland.

Finally, *Tess of the D'Urbervilles* is so quintessentially Victorian a story that a believable version might seem well out of any contemporary director's reach. But if an elegant, plausible, affecting *Tess* sounds like more than might have been expected of Mr. Polanski, let's just say he has achieved the impossible. In fact, in the process of adapting his style to suit such a sweeping and vivid novel, he has achieved something very unlike his other work. Without Mr. Polanski's name

in the credits, this lush and scenic *Tess* could even be mistaken for the work of David Lean.

In a preface to the later editions of *Tess of the D'Urbervilles,* Mr. Hardy described the work as "an impression, not an argument." Mr. Polanski has taken a similar approach, removing the sting from both the story's morality and its melodrama. Tess Durbeyfield, the hearty country lass whose downfall begins when her father learns he had noble forebears, is sent to charm her rich D'Urberville relations. She learns that they aren't D'Urbervilles after all; instead, they have used their new money to purchase an old name.

Tess charms them anyhow, so much that Alec D'Urberville, her imposter cousin, seduces and impregnates her. The seduction, like many of the film's key scenes, is presented in a manner both earthy and discreet. In this case, the action is set in a forest, where a gentle mist arises from the ground and envelops Tess just around the time when she is enveloped by Alec.

Alec, as played by Leigh Lawson, is a slightly wooden character, unlike Angel Clare, Tess's later and truer lover, played with supreme radiance by Peter Firth. Long after Tess has borne and buried her illegitimate child, she finds and falls in love with this spirited soul mate. But when she marries Angel Clare and is at last ready to reveal the secret of her past, the story begins hurtling toward its final tragedy. When Tess becomes a murderer, the film offers its one distinctly Polanski-like moment—but even that scene has its fidelity to the novel. A housemaid listening at a door hears a "drip, drip, drip" sound, according to Hardy. Mr. Polanski has simply interpreted this with a typically mischievous flourish.

Of all the unlikely strong points of *Tess,* which opens today for a weeklong engagement at the Baronet and which will reopen next year, the unlikeliest is Nastassja Kinski, who plays the title role. Miss Kinski powerfully resembles the young Ingrid Bergman, and she is altogether ravishing. But she's an odd choice for Tess: not quite vigorous enough, and maybe even too beautiful. She's an actress who can lose her magnetism and mystery if she's given a great deal to do (that was the case in an earlier film called *Stay As You Are*). But here, Mr. Polanski makes perfect use of her. Instead of a driving force, she becomes an echo of the land and the society around her, more passive than Hardy's Tess but linked just as unmistakably with natural forces.

Miss Kinski's Tess has no inner life to speak of. But Mr. Polanski makes her surroundings so expressive that her placidity and reserve work very beautifully.

Even at its nearly three-hour running time, Mr. Polanski's *Tess* cannot hope for anything approaching the range of the novel. But the deletions have been made wisely, and though the story loses some of its resonance it maintains its momentum. There are episodes—like one involving Tess's shabby boots and Mercy Chant, the more respectable girl who expects to marry Angel—that don't make the sense they should, and the action is fragmented at times. That's a small price to pay for the movie's essential rightness, for its congruence with the mood and manner of the novel. Mr. Polanski had to go to Normandy and rebuild Stonehenge to stage his last scene, according to this same biography. As is the case throughout his *Tess,* the results were worth the trouble.

—*J.M., December 12, 1980*

THAT OBSCURE OBJECT OF DESIRE

Directed by Luis Buñuel; written (in French, with English subtitles) by Mr. Buñuel and Jean-Claude Carrière, based on the novel *La Femme et Le Pantin* by Pierre Louys; cinematographer, Edmond Richard; edited by Helene Plemiannikov; art designer, Pierre Guffroy; produced by Serge Silberman; released by First Artists. Running time: 100 minutes.

With: Fernando Rey (Mathieu), Carole Bouquet and Angela Molina (Conchita), Julien Bertheau (Judge), Andre Weber (Valet) and Milena Vukotic (Traveler).

Every film festival should end with a new film by the incomparable Luis Buñuel, whose latest work, the triumphantly funny and wise *That Obscure Object of Desire,* will be shown at Lincoln Center tonight to close the 15th New York Film Festival.

After one has sat through hours and hours of films by directors who don't know when to stop (and some who should never have started), seeing a work of such perfect control and precision has the effect of magically clearing the mind. It restores one's common sense and one's appreciation for the fantastic, and it reminds us of the profound possibilities of film in the hands of someone we now acknowledge to be an authentic master.

That Obscure Object of Desire is Buñuel's *Don Giovanni.* It combines the effervescence and gaiety of *The Discreet Charm of the Bourgeoisie* with the dark wit of *Tristana,* and though it continues to explore themes we recognize from these and other Buñuel films, it is something quite other.

Most obviously, I suppose, *That Obscure Object of Desire* is an upside-down romance in which love, Buñuel seems to be telling us, is "a devastating act of subversion." The setting is the easily recognizable contemporary world, but a world that is a half-degree off its axis and fast going to pieces, though everyone displays the fastidious manners of the members of a society that will last forever.

Just beyond the horizon of the film, which is set in Paris and in Seville, chaos reigns. Through newspaper headlines and radio broadcasts we learn that terrorism is rampant. Planes are being hijacked and innocents slaughtered. A mysterious virus is nearing Barcelona and a guerrilla group that calls itself the Revolutionary Army of the Infant Jesus has attempted to assassinate the Archbishop of Sienna. Even the Communists are outraged by the anarchic state of things.

Seemingly unruffled by all this (though he is impatient when a booby-trapped automobile in front of his explodes and forces his car to make a detour) is the charming, literate, wealthy Mathieu (Fernando Rey), Buñuel's Don, a French businessman whose life is in perfect order until the day that the beautiful Conchita enters it, dressed as a maid.

Though he has been a widower for seven years, Mathieu is no ordinary lecher. As he tells his brother, the judge (Julien Bertheau), Mathieu can count on the fingers of one hand the number of times he has ever made love to a woman whom he didn't love passionately. From the minute he sees Conchita, Mathieu is in the throes of an uncontrollable passion.

Conchita, though, is not someone whose measure he can get, and who eludes him even as he gets her into bed. Conchita flees his house, only to turn up a few months afterward traveling through Switzerland with a group of musicians. Later Mathieu makes a deal with Conchita's pious mother to set up Conchita as his mistress. Again she runs away. Each time they meet again, she leads him further into the recesses of his obsession, always promising him the moon (in the form of her virginity), then suddenly changing her mind.

As Mathieu sees her, Conchita is so changeable that Buñuel has cast two lovely new actresses to play her—Carole Bouquet, who looks a little like a young Rita Hayworth, as the coolly enigmatic Conchita, and Angela Molina as the earthy, flamenco-dancing Conchita whom he follows to Seville.

Poor old Mathieu. The night he succeeds in getting Conchita to his country house, where she has promised to be his mistress, the Conchita who goes into the bathroom to change, changes not only her clothes. Miss Bouquet goes in but Miss Molina comes out.

Mathieu huffs, puffs and groans in his agony. He leaves Conchita a dozen times but always is lured back. At one point he persuades her to live with him and to share his bed, though no sexual contact can be made. When the judge asks his brother why he doesn't marry her, Mathieu answers earnestly that if he married her, he would be helpless. At another point, when Mathieu upbraids Conchita for her maddening ways, she answers, "You only want what I refuse. That's not all of me. . . ."

Who really loves whom? Though Conchita at first seems to be the classic coquette, she becomes, as the film progresses, the true lover, while Mathieu becomes the coquette, a reversal of roles that is, nevertheless, not to be taken as the last word.

That Obscure Object of Desire is beautifully played by its small, impeccably chosen cast, beginning with Mr. Rey, who, at this point in his career, is virtually a projection of Buñuel's artistic personality—gentle, polite, self-aware, incapable of the superfluous gestures and driven. Miss Bouquet and Miss Molina are enchanting—I don't think Buñuel has ever before been so successful with neophyte actresses.

There are further delights in the performances of Mr. Bertheau (who played the "worker bishop" in *The Discreet Charm*); of Andre Weber, as Mathieu's all-wise valet; and of Pieral, a dwarf who plays the psychologist to whom Mathieu pours out his sad story on the train from Seville to Paris, which provides the frame for the film.

That Obscure Object of Desire is a lot more open-ended and surreal than I've indicated, but these are pleasures that one should discover for oneself. To attempt to interpret them in this sort of review would be as gross as giving away the ending of a whodunit.

One particular prop, though, I would suggest that you watch out for. It's an ordinary, but apparently well-stuffed burlap sack that the always-well-groomed Mathieu carries with him.

With an effortlessness matched by no other director today, Buñuel creates a vision of a world as logical as a theorem, as mysterious as a dream, and as funny as a vaudeville gag. I especially like the response of a waiter in a posh restaurant when an insect turns up in Mathieu's martini. "A fly," the waiter exclaims. "I've been after that one for days, and he had to fall into your glass!"

—*V.C., October 9, 1977*

THAT'S LIFE!

Directed by Blake Edwards; written by Milton Wexler and Mr. Edwards; cinematographer, Anthony Richmond; edited by Lee Rhoads; music by Henry Mancini; produced by Tony Adams; released by Columbia Pictures. Running time: 102 minutes.

With: Jack Lemmon (Harvey Fairchild), Julie Andrews (Gillian Fairchild), Sally Kellerman (Holly Parrish), Robert Loggia (Father Baragone), Jennifer Edwards (Megan Fairchild Bartlet), Rob Knepper (Steve Larwin) and Matt Lattanzi (Larry Bartlet).

When one considers "personal" films, one usually envisions something small and low-budget, photographed in a black and white that is solemn, self-effacing and artistic. Not Blake Edwards. He hasn't lived most of his life in and around the southern California movie community without coming to share many of its gaudy values, which he also enthusiastically ridicules.

Mr. Edwards's personal films are no less big, glittery, and comically irreverent than *Darling Lili,* his most romantic comedy, which was so expensive that it almost broke Paramount Pictures, and his classic farces, including *Victor/Victoria* and several of his Pink Panther films. Introspection needn't be a drag. Mr. Edwards likes Hollywood's style, both in his life and his movies.

That's Life!, which opens today at the Coronet and Guild Theaters, is so rich-looking—and so full of sunlight, warm feelings and wonderfully rude gags—that its worried psyche is obscured much of the time. Yet *That's Life!* may be this singular director's most somber comedy to date.

Its immediate antecedents are *10* (1979), in which the Edwards surrogate, an acclaimed Hollywood songwriter, faces spiritual decrepitude at age forty-two, and *S.O.B.* (1981), a merciless satire about a Hollywood producer made suicidal by his own megalomania and a series of box-office flops.

The Blake Edwards character in *That's Life!* is a successful southern California architect named Harvey Fairchild (Jack Lemmon), who's going to emotional pieces on the eve of his sixtieth birthday. As his children gather at his ultra-modern oceanside house to celebrate the occasion, Harvey edges toward the brink of total meltdown.

He whines about his car. He ridicules his clients. He's had to accept the fact that he isn't Frank Lloyd Wright. He tells Gillian (Julie Andrews), his remarkably patient wife of many years, that he's never accomplished what he wanted to do, and that time is running out.

He's also convinced that he's impotent, and possibly the host to any number of terminal diseases. All the people around him, including the medical doctor who's given him a clean bill of health, urge Harvey to seek psychiatric help, which only infuriates him more.

What Harvey doesn't realize, though the audience knows from the film's opening sequence, is that Gillian, who has her own career as a singer, is confronting the possibility that a small tumor in her throat is malignant. Having had a biopsy done on the Friday afternoon of the birthday weekend, Gillian won't receive the results until Monday. Thus, as Harvey behaves with increasing nastiness toward all those near and dear, it's Gillian who suffers most profoundly.

That's Life! is full of funny things, including Mr. Lemmon's legitimately comic performance as the impossible Harvey. He refuses to see a psychiatrist though he doesn't hesitate to seek aid from Madame Carrie, a roadside fortuneteller. At his wits' end, he goes to confession for the first time in decades, only to discover that the priest (Robert Loggia) is his old Notre Dame roommate, whose life and career seem in worse shape than Harvey's.

However, unlike Harvey, who's given to hysterical worry and fret, the priest sails blithely through his days, always a little drunk.

Though Mr. Lemmon's role is the flashiest in the film, it's Miss Andrews who dominates *That's Life!* in the same way that her Gillian keeps the other, overly indulged Fairchilds in some kind of semblance of a family unit. Like *Darling Lili* and *Victor/Victoria, That's Life!* is another Edwards celebration of the deepening talent and immaculate beauty of the actress who's also his wife.

The filmmaker has pulled off a fascinating trick here: though he focuses on Mr. Lemmon most of the time, Miss Andrews is always the heart of the movie. By the way the film is structured, she becomes its practical center, in a performance that skirts sentimentality to work in easy, amused counterpoint to Mr. Lemmon's.

That's Life! is very much a Hollywood "family" film. Appearing as the Fairchild children are Mr. Lemmon's son, Chris, playing a charmingly egocentric young man who's hit television stardom in a *Miami Vice* type of series, as well as Mr. Edwards's daughter, Jennifer, and Miss Andrews's daughter, Emma Walton. Felicia Farr, Mr. Lemmon's wife, plays Madame Carrie, the unorthodox fortuneteller who bestows gifts on her clients they hadn't expected. Everyone, including Sally Kellerman as a helpful next-door neighbor, is first-rate.

Though it contains a number of big, explosive laughs, and though it's so brightly colored you almost need sunglasses to watch it, *That's Life!* is considerably more contemplative than its manners initially suggest. According to Mr. Edwards, mortality, though inevitable, is as out of place and unsightly in southern California as surfers in gray flannel suits.

—*V.C., September 26, 1986*

THELMA AND LOUISE

Directed by Ridley Scott; written by Callie Khouri; director of photography, Adrian Biddle; edited by Thom Noble; music by Hans Zimmer; production designer, Norris Spencer; produced by Mr. Scott and Mimi Polk; released by Metro-Goldwyn-Mayer. Running time: 128 minutes.

With: Susan Sarandon (Louise), Geena Davis (Thelma), Harvey Keitel (Hal), Michael Madsen

(Jimmy), Christopher McDonald (Darryl), Stephen Tobolowsky (Max), Brad Pitt (J. D.) and Timothy Carhart (Harlan).

"I don't remember ever feeling this awake!" exclaims one of the two freewheeling runaways of Ridley Scott's hugely appealing new road movie, as they race ecstatically across the American Southwest. Funny, sexy and quick-witted, these two desperadoes have fled the monotony of their old lives and are making up new ones on a minute-by-minute basis. Their adventures, while tinged with the fatalism that attends any crime spree, have the thrilling, life-affirming energy for which the best road movies are remembered. This time there's a difference: this story's daring anti-heroes are beautiful, interesting women.

Mr. Scott's *Thelma and Louise*, with a sparkling screenplay by the first-time writer Callie Khouri, is a surprise on this and many other scores. It reveals the previously untapped talent of Mr. Scott (best known for majestically moody action films like *Alien, Blade Runner,* and *Black Rain*) for exuberant comedy, and for vibrant American imagery, notwithstanding his English roots. It reimagines the buddy film with such freshness and vigor that the genre seems positively new. It discovers unexpected resources in both its stars, Susan Sarandon and Geena Davis, who are perfectly teamed as the spirited and original title characters. Ms. Sarandon, whose Louise starts out as a waitress, seems to have walked right out of her *White Palace* incarnation into something much more fulfilling. Ms. Davis may have already won an Oscar (for *The Accidental Tourist*), but for her the gorgeous, dizzy, mutable Thelma still amounts to a career-making role.

Thelma and Louise, with a haunting dawn-to-nightfall title image that anticipates the story's trajectory, is immediately engaging. Even its relatively inauspicious opening scenes, which show the wise-cracking Louise planning a weekend getaway with Thelma, a desperately bored housewife who hates her husband, Darryl (Christopher McDonald), have self-evident flair.

"Are you at work?" Thelma asks when Louise telephones her from the coffee shop where she is employed, somewhere in Arkansas. "No, I'm callin' from the Playboy Mansion," snaps Louise, who goes on to propose a fishing trip to a friend's cabin. "I still don't know how to fish," Thelma muses, nibbling on a frozen candy bar. "Neither do I, sweetie, but Darryl does it," Louise answers. "How hard could it be?"

Soon the two of them have taken off in Louise's turquoise Thunderbird convertible, with Thelma dressed for the occasion in ruffles, denim and pearls. Eager to escape her stifling home life, she has left behind a note for Darryl and borrowed a little something in return: his gun. Later that same evening, when Thelma insists on stopping at a honky-tonk bar despite Louise's protestations, the gun comes in handy. It is used, by Louise, to settle a dispute between Thelma and a would-be rapist (Timothy Carhart) in the parking lot, and it forever changes the complexion of Thelma and Louise's innocent little jaunt. From this point on, they are killers on the run.

Ms. Khouri's screenplay never begins to provide the moral justification for Louise's violent act. But it does a remarkably smooth job of making this and other outlaw gestures at least as understandable as they would be in a traditional Western. It also invests them with a certain flair. When detectives investigate the slaying of this inveterate ladies' man, a local waitress says: "Has anyone asked his wife? She's the one I *hope* did it!" Later on, when cornering a truck driver who has pestered them on the highway, Louise furiously asks, "Where do you get off behavin' like that with women you don't know?"

That *Thelma and Louise* is able to coax a colorful, character-building escapade out of such relatively innocuous beginnings is a tribute to the grace of all concerned, particularly the film's two stars, whose flawless teamwork makes the story gripping and believable from start to finish. On the run, Louise evolves from her former fast-talking self into a much more moving and thoughtful figure, while Thelma outgrows her initial giddy hedonism and develops real grit. Their transformation, particularly in its final stages, gives the film its rich sense of openness and possibility even as the net around Thelma and Louise closes more tightly.

Some of what Thelma learns en route comes by way of a foxy young hitchhiker named J. D. (Brad Pitt), who eradicates the memory of Darryl and also gives a memorable lesson, with the help of a hair dryer, in how to rob a convenience store. "My goodness, you're so gentlemanly about it!" exclaims Thelma. "Well now, I've always believed that if done properly, armed robbery doesn't have to be a totally unpleasant experience," J. D. says.

Like any good road movie, *Thelma and Louise* includes a number of colorful characters who wander entertainingly in and out of the principals' lives. Among them, in this film's fine cast, are Mr. Pitt, who so convincingly wows Thelma; Michael Madsen, bringing shades of Elvis Presley to the role of Louise's once footloose and now devoted beau; and Harvey Keitel and Stephen Tobolowsky, as two of the detectives on Thelma and Louise's trail. Mr. Keitel, in a role resembling the one he has in *Mortal Thoughts,* has this time learned to say "mo-tel" in the spirit of the region, and conveys a great and touching concern for the renegades' well-being. His character alone, in a role that could have been perfunctory but is instead so full, gives an indication of how well developed this story is.

Among the film's especially memorable touches are those that establish its feminine side: the way Thelma insists on drinking her liquor from tiny bottles, or the way a weary Louise considers using lipstick after a few days in the desert but then disgustedly throws the thing away. "He's putting on his hat!" Louise confides to Thelma when a police officer stops them, which is surely not the kind of thing two male outlaws would notice. But the film's sense of freedom and excitement, as when the women exult in feeling the wind in their hair, goes well beyond sexual distinctions.

Thelma and Louise is greatly enhanced by a tough, galvanizing country-tinged score, and by Adrian Biddle's glorious cinematography, which gives a physical dimension to the film's underlying thought that life can be richer than one may have previously realized. At the story's end, as Thelma and Louise make their way through Monument Valley and to the Grand Canyon, the film truly lives up to its scenery.

"I guess I've always been a little crazy, huh?" Thelma muses in this majestic setting.

"You've always been crazy," Louise acknowledges. "This is just the first chance you've ever had to really express yourself."

—J.M., May 24, 1991

THESE THREE

Directed by William Wyler; written by Lillian Hellman, based on her play *The Children's Hour;* cinematographer, Gregg Toland; edited by Daniel Mandell; music by Alfred Newman; art designer, Richard Day; produced by Samuel Goldwyn; released by United Artists. Black and white. Running time: 93 minutes.

With: Miriam Hopkins (Martha Dobie), Merle Oberon (Karen Wright), Joel McCrea (Dr. Joseph Cardin), Catherine Doucet (Mrs. Mortar), Alma Kruger (Mrs. Tilford) and Bonita Granville (Mary Tilford).

The Hays office would not sanction a film of Lillian Hellman's *The Children's Hour,* but Miss Hellman had an idea for a different and acceptable treatment. Samuel Goldwyn thought well of it, and yesterday the considerably amended, but basically recognizable, version of her play opened at the Rivoli under the title *These Three.* Miss Hellman's job of literary carpentry is little short of brilliant. Upon the framework of her stage success she has constructed an absorbing, tautly written and dramatically vital screenplay. To it, in turn, a gifted cast headed by Merle Oberon, Miriam Hopkins and Joel McCrea has contributed lavishly of its talents, aided by superb direction and exceptionally fine photography. In its totality the picture emerges as one of the finest screen dramas in recent years.

There may be some dissatisfied comments from those who saw the play, for *These Three* lacks the biting, bitter tragedy of *The Children's Hour.* It chooses (or the censors chose for it) to ignore any implication of an abnormal relationship between the two women schoolteachers who are its chief adult characters, and it progresses to what must be considered a happy and romantic ending. Too, there is no Florence McGee to etch in acid the evil portrait of little Mary Tilford, who carries the play on her spiteful shoulders.

Yet the film has preserved, through the magic of Miss Hellman's adaptation, the very heart of the original—that quality of muddled helplessness which three persons experience when they find themselves struggling vainly to cut through the porous fabric of lies told by a venomous little girl. Whether the falsehood Mary Tilford tells is that Martha Dobie has an unnatural affection for Karen Wright or, as in *These Three,* that Karen's fiancé, Dr. Joe Cardin, has been "carrying on" with Martha Dobie is immaterial. The effect is still the same: because of an unreasoning lie, three lives have their courses changed and nothing can ever again be the same for any of them. Not even the film's happy ending can hide the realization that this is a tragedy.

Miss Hellman's story, in its screen form, is of the two young headmistresses of a school for small girls, both in love with the same man, Dr. Cardin, or, if you prefer, Joel McCrea. Miss Oberon has his heart, while Miss Hopkins is content to worship from afar. Then little Mary Tilford, a malevolent vixen who lies by preference and has a pathological hatred for her teachers, runs home to her grandmother and, to escape a punishment, whispers the venomous untruth about the misconduct of the doctor and his sweetheart's best friend.

The tale, confirmed by another little girl for reasons which must be seen to be believed, is accepted with horror and spread with indignation, and the three innocent victims of the slander are dragged through the dirt of public opinion, a suit for libel and—in the case of the fiancée—the torture of the hateful suspicion that the story might be true.

Strong, turbulent and caustic, *These Three* is an unusual picture and it has been brought to the screen with perception, beauty and a keen sense of drama. Miss Oberon gives one of her finest performances and Miss Hopkins and Mr. McCrea are no less impressive. But the honors really belong to Bonita Granville as Mary Tilford and to Marcia Mae Jones as Rosalie, her "vassal" among the schoolgirls. Both youngsters are splendid and, if our personal vote goes to little Miss Jones, then it may be because Florence McGee has branded the role of Mary indelibly in our memory as hers. Catherine Doucet is flawless in her presentation of Lily Mortar, the exasperating aunt of Martha Dobie, and Alma Kruger plays Mrs. Tilford with the proper dignity and outraged respectability.

In short, from story, through William Wyler's direction and Gregg Toland's photography to performances, *These Three* is capital. You can be reasonably certain that it will find its way into the ranks of the year's "best ten."

—*F.S.N., March 19, 1936*

THEY LIVE BY NIGHT

Directed by Nicholas Ray: written by Charles Schnee and Mr. Ray. based on the novel *Thieves Like Us* by Edward Anderson: cinematographer. George E. Diskant: edited by Sherman Todd: music by Woody Guthrie and Leigh Harline: art designers. Albert S. D'Agostino and Al Herman: produced by John Houseman and Dore Schary: released by RKO Radio Pictures. Black and white. Running time: 95 minutes.

With: Cathy O'Donnell (Keechie). Farley Granger (Bowie). Howard da Silva (Chicamaw). Jay C. Flippen (T-Dub). Helen Craig (Mattie). Will Wright (Mobley). Marie Bryant (Singer). Ian Wolfe (Hawkins). William Phipps (Young Farmer) and Harry Harvey (Hagenheimer).

A commonplace little story about a young escaped convict "on the lam" and his romance with a nice girl whom he picks up and marries is told with pictorial sincerity and uncommon emotional thrust in RKO's latest item, *They Live by Night,* at the Criterion. Although it—like others—is misguided in its sympathies for a youthful crook, this crime-and-compassion melodrama has the virtues of vigor and restraint.

Coming upon its young hero as he is escaping from a southwest prison farm with two older and tougher criminals, it takes him on a fast and desperate round of other criminal depredations and of deceptive maneuvers to avoid the police. And it also takes him gently into the arms of a tender farm girl with whom he is poignantly happy and grimly frightened until fate seals his doom.

Based on a novel by Edward Anderson, which, in turn, was no doubt inspired by the two or three real-life sagas that we've had of "boy bandits" and their brides, this well-designed motion picture derives what distinction it has from good, realistic production and sharp direction by Nicholas Ray. Mr. Ray has an eye for action details. His staging of the robbery of a bank, all seen by the lad in the pickup car, makes a fine clip of agitating film. And his sensitive juxtaposing of his actors against highways, tourist camps and bleak motels makes for a vivid comprehension of an intimate personal drama in hopeless flight.

As the young bandit, Farley Granger gives a genuine sense of nervous strain and is wistful and appealing in his brave approach to a piteous romance. Cathy O'Donnell, the girl who played the sweetheart of the handless sailor in *The Best Years of Our Lives,* is also sincerely affecting as his drab but intense little bride. Howard da Silva and Jay C. Flippen are impressive as hardened crooks, and Ian Wolfe is disturbingly shifty as a marrying parson in a Texas town.

They Live by Night has the failing of waxing sentimental over crime, but it manages to generate interest with its crisp dramatic movement and clear-cut types.

—*B.C., November 4, 1949*

THEY SHOOT HORSES, DON'T THEY?

Directed by Sydney Pollack; written by James Poe and Robert E. Thompson, based on the novel by Horace McCoy; cinematographer, Philip Lathrop; edited by Fredric Steinkamp; music by Johnny Green; choreography by Tom Panko; production designer, Harry Horner; produced by Irwin Winkler, Robert Chartoff and Mr. Pollack; released by Cinerama Releasing. Running time: 129 minutes.

With: Jane Fonda (Gloria), Michael Sarrazin (Robert), Susannah York (Alice), Gig Young (Rocky), Red Buttons (Sailor), Bonnie Bedelia (Ruby), Michael Conrad (Rollo), Bruce Dern (James), Al Lewis (Turkey) and Robert Fields (Joel).

"Can I get you something for your feet?" the nurse at the dance marathon asks Gloria (Jane Fonda) who, after approximately 700 hours of continuous dancing, looks like an exhausted Little Orphan Annie. Gloria asks in return: "How about a saw?" And, for a brief moment you can almost see Gloria, propped up on a grimy cot during her ten-minute break, purposefully dismembering her feet as an offscreen band plays something cheerful like "Japanese Sandman."

Gloria, a Typhoid Mary of existential despair, is the terrified and terrifying heroine of Sydney Pollack's *They Shoot Horses, Don't They?,* the film adaptation of Horace McCoy's Depression novel that opened yesterday at the Fine Arts Theater. The movie is far from being perfect, but it is so disturbing in such important ways that I won't forget it very easily, which is more than can be said of much better, more consistent films.

McCoy's novel, sometimes called "a minor classic" (a patronizing way of saying that something's good but not great), was written and published in its own time (1935). It's a spare, bleak parable about American life, which McCoy pictured as a Los Angeles dance marathon in the early thirties.

The setting is a shabby ballroom on an amusement pier at the edge of the Pacific. The narrator, Robert Syverton, is a gentle, passive nonentity who, as he is tried for Gloria's murder and then as he awaits execution, recalls the events leading up to the murder. When asked why he did it, he answers simply: "She asked me to," adding, "They shoot horses, don't they?" Robert Syverton is the sort of character who, fifteen years later, might have sought his fate in an exotic North Africa created by Paul Bowles.

There is, however, nothing exotic about McCoy's novel, which, although lean, is full of the kind of apocalyptic detail that both he and Nathanael West saw in life as lived on the Hollywood fringe.

Gloria, an Angel of Death who wears ankle socks and favors a marcel permanent wave, is too old, too bitter and too gross even to have gotten registered by Central Casting. Robert, who has fantasies of being a great director like von Sternberg and Mamoulian and Vidor, has only played a few "atmosphere bits." In desperation they enter the dance marathon, set, symbolically, at the edge of the Pacific Ocean, the last, impenetrable frontier.

Without actually changing the structure of the novel, told in flashbacks, the movie takes as its principal setting the marathon itself, and flashes forward to the trial in quick, subliminal, highly stylized cuts. Pollack, and his screenwriters, James Poe and Robert E. Thompson, have, necessarily, taken liberties in fleshing out a movie story. They have added characters, some of which, like Red Buttons (as an overage marathon contestant) and Susannah York (as a would-be Jean Harlow with delusions of grandeur), have their prototypes in the sort of 1930 B-picture microcosms set on submarines or in sorority houses.

Characters who existed in the book as little more than names have been given histories. Rocky, an aging, tank-town Ben Bernie (beautifully played by a no longer young Gig Young) who is the marathon's emcee, now has as much of a past (his father was a faith healer) as either Gloria or Robert (Michael Sarrazin). The effect of this is to blunt the edge of—and to overstate—the novel's single-minded nightmare-like qualities.

Even with all of the quite marvelous period touches—the songs, the settings, the costumes and the jargon—the movie always looks like a 1969 recapitulation of another time and place. The book, conceived as a contemporary tale, was not so encumbered with artifacts.

Nevertheless, the movie is by far the best thing that Pollack has ever directed (with the possible exception of *The Scalphunters*). While the cameras remain, as if they had been sentenced, within the ballroom, picking up the details of the increasing despair of the dancers, the movie becomes an epic of exhaustion and futility. The circular patterns of the dancers, the movement that leads nowhere, are the metaphors of the movie.

All of the performances are fine—Miss Fonda, Sarrazin, Young, Miss York and Bonnie Bedelia (as a little Okie girl who carries on in the seventh month of pregnancy).

The most disquieting thing is the movie's stated assumption that people are horses (I don't even think horses should be people, as in *Black Beauty*), an assumption that is somehow denied by the physical opulence (which, in some curious way, represents a kind of optimism) of the production itself.

—*V.C., December 11, 1969*

THEY WERE EXPENDABLE

Produced and directed by John Ford; written by Frank Wead, based on the book by William L. White; cinematographer, Joseph August; edited by Frank E. Hull and Douglas Biggs; music by Herbert Stothart; art designers, Cedric Gibbons and Malcolm Brown; released by Metro-Goldwyn-Mayer. Black and white. Running time: 135 minutes.

With: Robert Montgomery (Lieutenant John Brinkley), John Wayne (Lieutenant Rusty Ryan), Donna Reed (Lieutenant Sandy Davyss), Jack Holt (General Martin), Ward Bond (Boats Mulcahey), Marshall Thompson (Ensign Snake Gardner), Paul Langton (Ensign Andy Andrews), Murray Alper (Slug Mahan), Harry Tenbrook (Squarehead Larsen) and Leon Ames (Major James Morton).

It is in no wise depreciatory of Metro's *They Were Expendable* to say that if this film had been released last year—or the year before—it would have been a ringing smash. For then, while the war was still with us and the wave of victory was yet to break, the national impulse toward avengement, for which it cries out, would have been supremely stirred. Now, with the war concluded and the burning thirst for vengeance somewhat cooled, it comes as a cinematic postscript to the martial heat and passion of the last four years.

But, for all that, it is a stirring picture of a small but vital aspect of the war and, as now to be seen at the Capitol, it is a moving remembrance of things past. For, in two hours and fifteen minutes, it captures upon the screen all of the gallantry and daring of that handful of Navy men who threw their fast PT-boat squadron against the Japanese in the first days of the war, picked off the enemy shipping as it came down upon the Philippines and finally broke up in scattered remnants down in the islands, still slugging to the end. It tells the story substantially as related by William L. White in his book of the same title, with the exception that the names of the characters have been slightly changed.

Quite clearly, the making of this picture was a labor of understanding and love on the part of the men who produced it, from John Ford, the director, on down. Most of those who worked on it were active or recent Navy personnel. And the scenes of PT-boat action and all the "location" work was done with the service's help. From the shots of sleek killers racing grimly through the water to the scenes of personal life, complete authenticity and Navy "savvy" are notable throughout.

The most thrilling and electrifying passages in the film are those which show the torpedo-boat action—the midgets closing boldly on their prey, slamming their "fish" out of the raked tubes, then wheeling around in their white wakes. Mr. Ford and his watchful photographers have caught battle action at the full, even to the dying appearance of spent cartridge cases on the decks.

But the drama and essence of the story are most movingly refined in those scenes which compose the pattern of bravery and pathos implicit in the tale. Mr. Ford, and apparently his scriptwriter, Frank Wead, have a deep and true regard for men who stick to their business for no other purpose than to do their jobs. To hold on with dignity and courage, to improvise when resources fail, and to face the inevitable without flinching—those are the things which they have shown us how men do. Mr. Ford has made another picture which, in spirit, recalls his *Lost Patrol.* It is nostalgic, warm with sentiment, and full of fight in every foot.

It is hard to commend any actor above the rest. Each plays his part well. Robert Montgomery and John Wayne, however, are the most frequently and forcibly worked. Mr. Montgomery, who served in the Navy, makes a fine and laconic officer, and Mr. Wayne is magnificently robust as his tenacious executive. Donna Reed is extraordinarily touching in the role of an Army nurse who figures into the story in a brief romance which is most tastefully and credibly handled, by the way. And Ward Bond, Murray Alper and Harry Tenbrook are worthy of particular mention among the rest.

A bit of suspected sarcasm is notable in a sequence which recounts the dispatch of "The General," as he is called, from Corregidor. But the manner is not offensive. Indeed, it puts emphasis upon the boldness and bravery of all our people who were in there, looking forward, from the start.

—*B.C., December 21, 1945*

THEY WON'T FORGET

Produced and directed by Mervyn LeRoy; written by Aben Kandel and Robert Rossen, based on the novel *Death in the Deep South* by Ward Greene; cinematographer, Arthur Edeson; edited by Thomas Richards; music by Adolph Deutsch; art designer, Robert Haas; released by Warner Brothers. Black and white. Running time: 95 minutes.

With: Claude Rains (Andy Griffin), Edward Norris (Robert Hale), Allyn Joslyn (Bill Brook), Linda Perry (Imogene Mayfield), Cy Kendall (Detective Laneart), E. Alyn Warren (Carlisle P. Buxton) and Clifford Soubier (Jim Timberlake).

*T*hey Won't Forget, which the Warners presented at the Strand yesterday and which wears the fictional cloak of Ward Greene's novel, *Death in the Deep South,* reopens the Leo M. Frank case, holds it up for review, and, with courage, objectivity and simple elo-

quence, creates a brilliant sociological drama and a trenchant film editorial against intolerance and hatred.

In many ways it is superior to *Fury* and *Black Legion,* which have been milled from the same dramatic mine. Not so spectacular, or melodramatic, or strident perhaps, yet it is stronger, more vibrant than they through the quiet intensity of its narrative, the simplicity of Mervyn LeRoy's direction, its integrity of purpose, the even perfection of its cast. From Claude Rains and Allyn Joslyn and Gloria Dickson right on down the list of players heading this review, you will not find one whose performance does not deserve commendation. And, as one of the greatest factors in its favor, *They Won't Forget* cannot be dismissed as a Hollywood exaggeration of a state of affairs which once might have existed but exists no longer. Between the Frank trial at Atlanta and the more recent ones at Scottsboro is a bond closer than chronology indicates.

The picture's scene is Flodden, a small Southern city where Prosecutor Andy Griffin waits for his main chance and a spotlight that may dazzle the voters into sending him to the Senate. That chance comes when Mary Clay is murdered in the Buxton Business College on the afternoon of Confederate Memorial Day. Griffin scans his suspects. There is old Colonel Buxton, whose family, suh, has been untouched by the breath of scandal for three generations. There is Tump Redwine, the terrified Negro janitor who discovered the body in the elevator shaft and only could sob, "I didn't do it." There is millhand Joe Turner, Mary's boyfriend. There is Robert Hale, an instructor in the school, married, from up North, who stayed at the school that day—to correct examination papers, he said.

"I won't indict until I'm convinced the man is guilty," promises Prosecutor Griffin, but he knows there will be no political profit in convicting the Negro, little hope of weaving a circumstantial chain around Buxton, and—Hale was a stranger! Besides, there was evidence: he had been in the building, he had a blood spot on his coat (the barber had cut him, he insisted), Mary Clay's chum said the girl had been "crazy about him," he was thinking of leaving town (there had been that application for a new position). It added up and, to Griffin, it spelled opportunity.

The pace becomes staccato after that, with scene following scene in a mounting crescendo of hysteria, with the web spun ever more implacably, drawing ever more tightly the cords created by hatred and a fixed conviction of guilt. "We know how it'll end," the Clay boys say quietly, and Flodden nods its collective head. Headlines beat the drums. The North charges prejudice; the South interference. The New York detective is beaten; the New York attorney is stoned. Witnesses recant or enlarge. The "trial of the century" is conducted with due respect for the legal forms, but—like the Clay boys—we know how it'll end. There is a whiplash in the conclusion.

"Now that it's over, Andy, I wonder if Hale really did it," muses the reporter. And the prosecutor looks out the window and replies, almost absently, "I wonder."

That is all, and it is all the picture possibly could have done or said. For its perfection, chief credit must go to Mr. LeRoy for his remarkably skillful direction—there are a few touches as fine as anything the screen has done; to Aben Kandel and Robert Rossen for their excellent script; and to all the cast, but notably to Mr. Rains, for his savage characterization of the ambitious prosecutor; to Gloria Dickson (a newcomer) for her moving portrayal of Hale's wife; to Allyn Joslyn (late of Broadway's *Boy Meets Girl*) for his natural and sensible representation of a reporter.

A round-robin of appreciation must include mention of Edward Norris as Hale, Otto Kruger as his attorney, Elisha Cook, Jr. as Joe Turner, Trevor Bardette as Shattuck Clay, Paul Everton and Ann Shoemaker as the governor and his lady, and Clinton Rosemond as the Negro, Redwine.

—*F.S.N., July 15, 1937*

THE THIEF OF BAGDAD

Directed by Ludwig Berger and Michael Powell; written by Lajos Biro and Miles Malleson; cinematographer, Georges Périnal and Osmond Borradaile; edited by William Hornbeck and Charles Crichton; music by Miklos Rozsa; production designer, Vincent Korda; produced by Alexander Korda; released by United Artists. Running time: 106 minutes.

With: Conrad Veidt (Jaffar), Sabu (Abu), June Duprez (Princess), John Justin (Ahmad), Rex Ingram (Djinni), Miles Malleson (Sultan) and Morton Selten (The Old King).

It is all too seldom that the films, in their headlong quest of "escape," invade the happy realm of legends and fairy tales. Yet Alexander Korda, the eminent British producer, has dared to venture within the regions of fantastic make-believe, has been so bold as to spin a motion picture from the innocent stuff of daydreams. And, as a result, *The Thief of Bagdad*, which arrived yesterday at the Music Hall, ranks next to *Fantasia* as the most beguiling and wondrous film of this troubled season.

Remember, though, all of you adults who will surely be taking the youngsters to see it—you must purge your grown-up minds of all the logic which a literal world demands. You must be prepared to accept with an open and childlike faith a fabulous run of miracles performed amid oriental splendor. In short, you must take to heart the wise words of the white-bearded elder in the Land of Legend, to which the little thief goes. "Everything is possible," says he, "when seen through the eyes of youth." For everything—or most everything—that a child's imagination might conceive becomes perfectly simple and easy when seen through the eyes of Mr. Korda's cameras.

It is from the Arabian Nights stories that this colorful fantasy has been pieced—from the rich and suspenseful tales which Schéhérazade is supposed to have spun for a blasé sultan. And Miles Malleson has constructed it in the shape of a romantic adventure story of a handsome prince of Bagdad whose throne is usurped by his wicked Grand Vizier, of the little thief whom he meets in a dungeon cell and of the miraculous things which happen to both of them as the prince seeks the hand of a beautiful princess who dwells in the faraway city of Basra.

Woven into the story are such legends as that of the flying horse, which in this case the Grand Vizier constructs for the father of the princess; the fable of the giant djinni which the little thief releases from a bottle and which carries him over the world on extraordinary errands; the legend of the All-Seeing Eye; and finally that of the Magic Carpet, on which the little thief ultimately goes to the rescue of the prince and princess. All of these fanciful phenomena are represented upon the screen by means of trick photography which is accomplished with remarkable illusion, and credit for which is due in the main to William Cameron Menzies, the production designer.

But the particular glory of this film is its truly magnificent color. No motion picture to date has been so richly and eloquently hued, nor has any picture yet been so perfectly suited to it. Fairy tales are drenched in the mind with a pattern of colors, and here Mr. Menzies has filled the screen with a breathtaking succession of storybook illustrations—teeming bazaars, marble palaces glistening white against the deep blue sky, the red sails of ships against the sea, dream gardens, the gleam of jewels, and open terraces beneath the starry night. The color alone makes this picture a truly exciting entertainment.

But so, too, do the performances of Sabu, the Indian boy, as the little thief; of Conrad Veidt as the turbaned Grand Vizier with eyes of amazing potency; of John Justin as the handsome prince; June Duprez as the luscious princess; and Rex Ingram as the monstrous djinni with the lock of jet black hair. So the least one can do is recommend it as a cinematic delight, and thank Mr. Korda for reaching boldly into a happy world.

—B.C., December 6, 1940

THE THIN BLUE LINE

Directed and written by Errol Morris; directors of photography, Stefan Czapsky and Robert Chappell; edited by Paul Barnes; music by Philip Glass; production designer, Ted Bafaloukos; produced by Mark Lipson; released by Miramax Films. Running time: 101 minutes.

With: The principals in the case and, in reenactments, Adam Goldfine, Derek Horton, Ron Thornhill, Marianne Leone, Amanda Caprio and Michael Nicoll.

If Randall Adams and David Harris can agree on anything, it's that fate dealt them a terrible hand when, on Saturday, November 27, 1976, it threw them together. Mr. Adams knows that his whole life would have been different if he hadn't run out of gas that morning, if he hadn't been hitchhiking, and if

Mr. Harris hadn't picked him up. Mr. Harris, who gave Mr. Adams a ride in a car he had stolen a day earlier, wonders what would have happened if Mr. Adams, who was living in a seedy Dallas motel with his brother, hadn't refused to give him a place to sleep.

But the two men did meet and spend the day together, and they did wind up at a drive-in where a film called *Swinging Cheerleaders* was being shown. Mr. Adams, who was then a twenty-eight-year-old drifter, says he didn't like the movie and insisted on going home before it was over, leaving Mr. Harris to roam on his own. Mr. Harris, then a sixteen-year-old runaway, says the twosome were at the drive-in until midnight or so. The time is crucial, because at twelve-thirty A.M. a Dallas police officer named Robert Wood saw the stolen car moving with only its parking lights on. He signaled for the car to stop, walked over to talk to the driver and the driver killed him.

Errol Morris, the director of *The Thin Blue Line,* has fashioned a brilliant work of pulp fiction around this crime. Mr. Morris's film is both an investigation of the murder and a nightmarish meditation on the difference between truth and fiction, an alarming glimpse at the many distortions that have shaped Mr. Adams's destiny. Mr. Adams was tried for the murder, found guilty (in large part because of Mr. Harris's testimony) and given a death sentence that has since been commuted to life imprisonment. Mr. Harris, now on Death Row in connection with another murder, calmly acknowledges at the end of the film that he said what was necessary to save himself, even if it meant blaming a perfect stranger.

Aptly enough, Mr. Morris first approached this case through its most Kafkaesque figure, about whom he had planned to make a film. This was the psychiatrist nicknamed Dr. Death, a popular expert witness at capital trials who has regularly testified that defendants are sociopaths who will kill again. (In the Adams case, the defendant's lack of remorse became another damning element, though Mr. Adams claims that he feels no remorse because he didn't commit a crime.) In any case, this psychiatrist's approach to justice exemplifies the skewed but irrefutable logic that the film so hauntingly explores.

The Thin Blue Line, which opens today at the Lincoln Plaza, reinvents its story even as it reexamines it. Mr. Morris's graceful camera isolates witnesses and evidence against dark backgrounds, glides eerily through reenactments of certain episodes and selects and enlarges particular images (huge kernels of popcorn accompany a discussion of whether the drive-in's refreshment stand was really open as late as Mr. Harris said it was; in fact it closed early). In this deliberately artificial context, justice begins to feel as remote for the viewer as it undoubtedly feels to Mr. Adams.

Although actors are used in the reenactments, the people interviewed here are real participants in the case. But they, too, begin to sound like actors; everyone seems keenly aware of the camera. Mr. Harris in particular affects a beatific look and a candid manner that become all the more chilling as the film explores his lengthy criminal record. Indeed, the police in Mr. Harris's hometown of Vidor, Texas, know him so well by now that they speak of him rather fondly, despite the burglary, kidnapping and murder charges in his past. Though Mr. Morris avoids making obvious judgments, the section in which Mr. Harris describes his brother's accidental drowning becomes especially startling in view of his equally offhanded accounts of the criminal acts for which he has been convicted.

The Thin Blue Line is not really structured as an investigation. It's more like a reverie, filled with strangely exaggerated images and colored by the ominous hum of Philip Glass's score. This means that minor details sometimes assume undue importance, upstaging key facts of the case: Mr. Morris's slow-motion image of a milkshake flying through the air becomes much more memorable than the testimony of the policewoman who was drinking the shake, for example. Some striking shots of automobile taillights distract attention from the process whereby the killer's car was identified. The case itself is so complicated, and so fascinating, that there is reason to wish the facts emerged more clearly.

But Mr. Morris, to his credit, has created something larger and more compelling than the mere particulars. He explores this case and goes well beyond it, to the darker side of justice and to a vision that is both poetic and perverse. Hidden motives, withheld data and questionable interpretations of the facts are everywhere, and each interview invariably creates more questions than it answers. And the more maps, diagrams and key details the director assembles, the more frighteningly the truth slips away.

—*J.M., August 26, 1988*

THE THIN MAN

Directed by W. S. Van Dyke 2d; written by Albert Hackett and Frances Goodrich, based on the novel by Dashiell Hammett; cinematographer, James Wong Howe; edited by Robert J. Kern; music by William Axt; art designers, Cedric Gibbons and David Townsend; produced by Hunt Stromberg; released by Metro-Goldwyn-Mayer. Black and white. Running time: 93 minutes.

With: William Powell (Nick Charles), Myrna Loy (Nora Charles), Maureen O'Sullivan (Dorothy Wynant), Nat Pendleton (Guild), Minna Gombell (Mimi Wynant) and Porter Hall (MacCaulay).

Out of Dashiell Hammett's popular novel, *The Thin Man*, W. S. Van Dyke, one of Hollywood's most versatile directors, has made an excellent combination of comedy and excitement. It is another of those murder mysteries wherein the astute criminologist has many opportunities to chuckle over the work of the police and, as usual, it is virtually impossible for the onlooker to pick out the murderer.

William Powell, who by now is a past master in the art of sleuthing, is thoroughly in his element as Nick Charles, a retired detective, who undertakes to solve the series of crimes committed by an extraordinarily artful individual. Charles thinks fast and acts on the spur of the moment, occasionally trusting his wire-haired terrier to assist him.

Evidence points to Clyde Wynant, who is missing, as the murderer, but as the storyteller is so keen on having Wynant's name brought forth as the suspect, one knows, of course, that wherever he may be, he is innocent of the crimes. Charles appears to enjoy hunting the murderer and he revels in surprising the police and others. Nat Pendleton, who has recently been cast as No. 1 gangsters, in this production steps over to the side of the law, assuming the role of a police official.

Myrna Loy as Nora, Charles's wife, aids considerably in making this film an enjoyable entertainment. She speaks her lines effectively, frowns charmingly and is constantly wondering what her husband's next move will be. He goes off to Clyde Wynant's laboratory and office one night and makes an amazing discovery, chiefly through his terrier's keen scent. But this splendid animal draws the line at having to attack any criminal and when it is presumed to be confronted with a thug, the terrier hides under a table.

Charles believes in staging his final connection with the case effectively. In this instance he gives a dinner for all the curious persons involved in one way or another in the mystery. And it is at this neatly arranged banquet that the identity of the slayer is revealed.

Mr. Powell's performance is even better than his portrayals of Philo Vance in the S. S. Van Dine stories. He has good lines and he makes the most of them. Maureen O'Sullivan is attractive as Wynant's daughter and Henry Wadsworth is capital as her fiancé. Among others who serve the film well are Mr. Pendleton, Minna Gombell, Porter Hall and the wire-haired terrier.

—M.H., June 30, 1934

THE THIN RED LINE

Directed by Terrence Malick; written by Mr. Malick, based on the novel by James Jones; director of photography, John Toll; edited by Billy Weber and Leslie Jones; music by Hans Zimmer; production designer, Jack Fisk; produced by Robert Michael Geisler, John Roberdeau and Grant Hill; released by Twentieth Century Fox. Running time: 166 minutes.

With: Sean Penn (First Sergeant Edward Welsh), John Travolta (Barr), James Caviezel (Private Witt), Adrien Brody (Corporal Fife), Elias Koteas (Captain James Staros), Nick Nolte (Lieutenant Colonel Gordon Tall), Ben Chaplin (Private Bell), Dash Mihok (Private First Class Doll), Arie Verveen (Private Dale), David Harrod (Corporal Queen), John C. Reilly (Mess Sergeant Storm), John Cusack (Captain John Gaff), Larry Romano (Private Mazzi), Tim Blake Nelson (Private Tills), Woody Harrelson (Staff Sergeant Keck), Bill Pullman (McTae), George Clooney (Captain Charles Bosche) and John Savage (McCron).

A thrilling sense of déjà vu accompanies the lush Edenic images that provide *The Thin Red Line* with its prologue in paradise. Even if they could be watched without knowledge of their provenance, they would be instantly identifiable as the work of Terrence Malick, whose 1970's *Badlands* and *Days of Heaven* were the most beautiful and elusive films of their time. Mr. Malick's subsequent two decades in cinema limbo may have turned him into a figure of hype-inviting mystery, but it's immediately obvious that they have not dimmed his visual genius. It's as if a familiar voice had never left off speaking as, at long last, Mr. Malick's huge new opus begins.

His intoxication with natural beauty, fused so palpably and strangely with the psychic sleepwalking of his human characters, remains exactly as it was. So does the innate momentousness that has always come so easily to Mr. Malick's filmmaking.

Here is a visceral reminder of all that made his past work so hauntingly majestic, even if this movie's difficulties will soon announce themselves with equal clarity. Intermittently brilliant as it is, *The Thin Red Line* shows why being a great film director and directing a great film are not the same.

Having envisioned an adaptation of James Jones's famous Guadalcanal novel since at least 1988, Mr. Malick has had time to drift far afield of his original idea and into something hazier. Though its starting point was a book full of gut reactions and detailed particulars, Mr. Malick has moved the material to a different plane. Disjointed poetic effects and ravishing physical beauty now supplant the nuts and bolts of wartime experience, even if this film—like *Saving Private Ryan,* with which it happens so bizarrely to overlap—depicts a military landing on a beach and a terrifying assault on a hillside bunker. For all their surface similarities, Steven Spielberg's film was about character and Mr. Malick's is about spirit.

As *The Thin Red Line* contemplates mankind's self-destructiveness, the oneness of a company of soldiers, the rape of nature and the emptiness of Pyrrhic victory on the battlefield, it leaves behind any ordinary opportunities for individuals to emerge from the fray. Actors here, whether famous or unknown, are concealed behind helmets and grime as they move—often wordlessly—through the initially unspoiled landscape of this Pacific island. As filmed magnificently by John Toll (with the Daintree rain forest in Queensland, Australia, doubling for the actual site), *The Thin Red Line* seems to capture every blade of grass gloriously while also reminding the audience over two and three-quarter hours how very many blades of grass are here.

Though the United States–Japanese battle played out here was one of pivotal importance during World War II, its strategic value is not really the heart of the matter here. Indeed, the fury of battle often fades away as this film's indistinct principals venture into their own private thoughts. Hence the married man (Ben Chaplin) who faces battle thinking of his bride and reciting in typically dreamy voice-over: "Why should I be afraid to die? I belong to you. If I go first I'll wait for you on the other side of the dark waters. Be with me now." Mr. Malick can accompany even the most sentimental reveries with lofty phrasings and lovely imagery, like this man's visions of his sweetheart in summer dresses. She has purity, sensuality and lightness that would be rare in any film.

The Thin Red Line will as easily fascinate those attuned to Mr. Malick's artistry as it disappoints anyone in search of a plot. For all the marquee power of its stellar cast and the story's potential for high drama, remarkably little happens. As in *Saving Private Ryan,* violence erupts with shocking randomness for soldiers at the battle site, but it is interspersed with meditative passages, glimpses of the island's indigenous life and near-wordless passages propelled by the eloquent foreboding of Hans Zimmer's score. The way light filters through the canopy of the rain forest means at least as much here as the specifics of battle.

Nick Nolte, giving yet another ferocious performance in his own personal banner year (he can be seen to devastating effect in next week's *Affliction*), joins Sean Penn, Elias Koteas and Woody Harrelson (whose death scene here is among the film's most accessible, wrenching moments) as stars who manage to emerge with strong personalities intact. But no one here has a role with much continuity, since the film's editing shows off the performers to such poor advantage. *The Thin Red Line* is one more film that could have been helped by excising repetition and focusing performances, but it wanders almost randomly instead. The heart-piercing moments that punctuate its rambling are glimpses of what a tighter film might have been.

Among the unfamiliar actors in a position to make their marks here, James Caviezel supplies a handsome, beatific countenance to suit his character's fervent meditations on flawed humanity. ("How did we lose the good that was given us? Let it slip away. Scattered. Careless. What's keeping us from reaching out, touch-

ing the glory?") Red-haired Dash Mihok, as the private named Doll, provides the film's strongest visual sense of battlefield chaos. And Adrien Brody plays one of the novel's major figures, Corporal Fife, virtually without a peep. Like the film's leading Johns—Cusack as a Captain, Savage as a crazed Sergeant, and Travolta, believe it or not, as a brigadier general—he simply gets lost in the hubbub that surrounds him.

The glorious Melanesian scenes that provide both the film's divine serenity (and its signs of destruction) amount to nature photography as exquisite as it is redundant. Brilliantly colored birds, greenery in silhouette, shards of light and idyllic underwater swimming—not to mention a soundtrack layered with sounds of the rain forest—are among reasons to admire *The Thin Red Line* despite its habits of meandering. As was surely Mr. Malick's intent, those sensations matter as much as life or death here, to the point where they are inextricably intertwined. He brings that simple, essential message on his long-overdue return.

—*J.M., December 23, 1998*

THE THIRD GENERATION

Written (in German, with English subtitles) and directed by Rainer Werner Fassbinder; director of photography, Mr. Fassbinder; edited by Juliane Lorenz and Franz Wetsch; music by Peer Raben; released by New Yorker Films. Black and white. Running time: 111 minutes.

With: Eddie Constantine (P. J. Lurz), Hark Bohm (Gerhard Gest), Udo Kier (Edgar), Hanna Schygulla (Susanne) and Harry Baer (Rudolf Mann).

There no longer can be any doubt about it: Rainer Werner Fassbinder is the most dazzling, talented, provocative, original, puzzling, prolific and exhilarating filmmaker of his generation. Anywhere. I say this based partly on *The Third Generation,* his 1979 German film that opens today at the Public Theater and which is one of his best. Mostly, though, I'm thinking of the twenty-three Fassbinder features I've seen (including *Katzelmacher, The Bitter Tears of Petra Von Kant, Effi Briest, Fox and His Friends, Despair, The Marriage of Maria Braun* and *In a Year of 13 Moons*) of the thirty-five he has made since he turned to movies in 1965 at the age of nineteen.

There hasn't been a comparable phenomenon in films since Jean-Luc Godard came on the scene in the early sixties.

Mr. Fassbinder has demonstrated that he is quite capable of adapting his cinematic vision to fit the works of others (Fontane's *Effi Briest,* Nabokov's *Despair*), but it's his original screenplays that give the true measure of this great, unpredictable talent. He makes movies the way other, lesser directors talk about them—easily, quickly and precisely. When he shoots a film, he is speculating about the subject as well as about the craft of filmmaking, examining both as he goes along, freely, without being bound to arrive at some preset destination. His movies are the logbooks of an adventuring mind.

Some Fassbinder films are, of course, less successful than others, but that's beside the point. Each is a part of what can now be recognized as a single continuing work, and if one film ends in something of a muddle, there's always another coming along that may clear things up. A Fassbinder movie isn't necessarily an end in itself. It's a way of thinking.

Fassbinder films are so packed (visually and aurally) with information, references, asides, questions and unexpected connections (and, as a result so demanding) that most other contemporary movies look puny in comparison. Watching a good Fassbinder movie is like doing a Double-Crostic after too many games of ticktacktoe.

The Third Generation has you sitting on the edge of your seat even before you are sure what it's about. Scene: an elegant office high above a bustling city. We see a young woman, the secretary, watching a television set. A telephone rings. There's a mysterious, enigmatic message: "The world as will and idea." Cut to a cheap hotel room. The secretary of the earlier sequence is just getting out of bed after an assignation with an older man, who turns out to be not only a police inspector, but also her father-in-law. Cut to a rich, bourgeois home where an old man argues with his grandson about movies and war. Cut to a classroom. A student objects to the way the teacher is imposing her particular interpretation on history.

In this way, Mr. Fassbinder introduces the more than half-dozen principal characters of *The Third Generation,* a cruel, sometimes very funny comedy about terrorism, a subject he has treated with a certain amount of sympathy in the past but one that he now ridicules in a way that implicates virtually everyone, from the members of the New Left straight across to those of the New Right.

The film is about a cell of "third generation" terrorists, earnest, humorless, committed, largely middle-class boobs for whom terrorism has become a style of living without connections to political passions of any sort. They include Hilde (Bulle Ogier), the history teacher; Edgar (Udo Kier), a composer who doesn't compose very often; his wife, Susanne (Hanna Schygulla), the secretary; Rudolf Mann (Harry Baer), a clerk in a record store; Petra (Margit Castensen), a bored wife, and August (Volker Spengler), the always busy self-important leader of this particular cell of terrorists. They are small-timers with access to real explosives, and there's not a single coherent political idea among them.

It's not by chance that whenever we see the conspirators, either singly or in various combinations, we always see a television set flickering somewhere in the vicinity. What ideas they do possess have arrived predigested, second- or third-hand and have more to do with fashion than with intellect. They ridicule mercilessly a young man who comes into their midst with a suitcase loaded with books—books!—the weightier passages of which have been laboriously underlined with a pencil.

These people are mutations, distant spinoffs of the members of the notorious Bader-Meinhof gang. They are people for whom political commitment is a matter of secret passwords, disguises and assumed names. Unknown to them, but apparent to the audience early on, is that they are being manipulated by a rich, influential businessman, played by the venerable Eddie Constantine, who orchestrates their activities to increase his sales and to frighten the government into taking more repressive measures against the Left. The only character in the film who has the slightest suspicion about what's going on is the police inspector, played by Hark Bohm, who is himself an assassin of sorts.

The Third Generation is one of the richest looking and sounding films I've ever experienced. Like Mr. Godard, Mr. Fassbinder is extremely fond of printed titles, words seen on the screen as well as heard, and like Mr. Godard, he seems incapable of shooting a scene that isn't dense with detail, sometimes breath-takingly beautiful ones, which, in this case, serve to emphasize the deadly foolishness of the lives being lived in the foreground.

One especially stunning sequence is layered in sound, like a pousse-café meant to be heard rather than seen. As the conspirators meet to plan their next fruitless caper, we hear, simultaneously, two separate conversations, someone's reading from a book, a song being played on a guitar and sung and the voice of a man on the television screen. As one sound is no more or less important than another, an assignment to rob a bank or blow up a public building is accepted with no more thought of its importance than a request to go out for cigarettes.

The members of the Fassbinder "stock company" are in top form, and they're well complemented by Miss Ogier and Mr. Constantine. The photography, also by Mr. Fassbinder, recalls the ravishing work of Raoul Coutard when he was cameraman-in-residence to Mr. Godard.

The Third Generation is fascinating. It's also worry-ing. I keep wondering how long Mr. Fassbinder can continue this remarkable pace.

—V.C., September 9, 1980

THE THIRD MAN

Directed by Carol Reed; written by Graham Greene; cinematographer, Robert Krasker; edited by Oswald Hafenrichter; music by Anton Karas; production designers, Vincent Korda and Joseph Bato; produced by David O. Selznick; released by Korda-Selznick. Black and white. Running time: 104 minutes.

With: Joseph Cotten (Holly Martins), Alida Valli (Anna Schmidt), Orson Welles (Harry Lime), Trevor Howard (Major Calloway) and Ernst Deutsch (Kurtz).

The haunting music of a zither, the ring of Vienna's cobbled streets and a ghostly Graham Greene story about a manhunt in that seamy capital flow smoothly and beautifully together into one piece of top screen artifice in Carol Reed's most recent (and most touted) mystery-thriller-romance, *The Third Man.* Trailing Continental glories and faint echoes of that zither's weird refrains, this extraordinarily fasci-nating picture began a run at the Victoria yesterday.

But we feel we are bound to inform you that our key word is "artifice" in that thoroughly enthusiastic introductory paragraph. For the simple fact is that *The Third Man,* for all the awesome hoopla it has received, is essentially a first-rate contrivance in the way of melodrama—and that's all. It isn't a penetrating study of any European problem of the day (except that it skirts around black markets and the sinister anomalies of "zones"). It doesn't present any "message." It hasn't a point of view. It is just a bang-up melodrama, designed to excite and entertain. In the light of the buzz about it, this is something we feel you should know. Once it is understood clearly, there is no need for further asides.

For into this strangely offbeat story of a young American visitor's attempts to get to the bottom of the mystery of a friend's dubious "death" in Vienna's streets, Mr. Reed has brilliantly packaged the whole bag of his cinematic tricks, his whole range of inven-tive genius for making the camera expound. His emi-nent gifts for compressing a wealth of suggestion in single shots, for building up agonized tension and popping surprises are fully exercised. His devilishly mischievous humor also runs lightly through the film, touching the darker depressions with little glints of the gay or macabre.

To be sure, Mr. Greene has contributed conspicu-ously to the job with a script that is cleverly con-structed and pungently laced with dialogue. The smoothness and ease with which the edges of the mys-tery plot tongue and groove—with which the missing man's sweetheart joins the drama, the police build the case, and such as that, while all the while little bits of color and character are worked in—make for complete fascination. Except for one far-fetched allowance for poor police-craft (a dead man is not properly identi-fied) and a chase through the sewers for the climax (which is graphic but conventional) the script is tops.

So, too, are the performances of everyone in the cast—of Joseph Cotten as the American who blunders upon mystery and romance; of Valli, the cool Italian actress, who plays the refugee girl of the "dead" man; of Trevor Howard as a British police major, a beauti-fully crisp and seasoned gent; of Bernard Lee as his capable sergeant; and of several grand continental "types." Even our old and perennially villainous friend, Orson Welles, does a right nice job of shaping a dark and treacherous shadow as the "third man."

However, with all due allowance, top credit must go to Mr. Reed for molding all possible elements into a thriller of superconsequence. And especially must he be credited with the brilliant and triumphant device of using the music of a zither as the sole musical background in this film. This eerie and mesmerizing music, which is rhythmic and passionate and sad, becomes, indeed, the commentator—the genius loci—of the Viennese scene. Pulsing with hopefulness and longing, with "menace" and poignance and love, it thoroughly completes the illusions of a swift and intriguing romance.

—B.C., February 3, 1950

THE THIRTY-NINE STEPS

Directed by Alfred Hitchcock: written by Charles Bennett. Alma Reville and Ian Hay, based on the novel by John Buchan: cinematographer, Bernard Knowles: edited by Derek Twist: musical director. Louis Levy: production designers. Otto Wendorff and Albert Jullion: produced by Michael Balcon and Ivor Montagu: released by General Films. Black and white. Running time: 85 minutes.

With: Robert Donat (Hannay). Madeleine Carroll (Pamela). Godfrey Tearle (Professor Jordan). Helen Haye (Mrs. Jordan). Lucie Mannheim (Miss Smith). Peggy Ashcroft (Crofter's Wife). John Laurie (Crofter). Frank Cellier (The Sheriff). Wylie Watson (Mr. Memory) and Peggy Simpson (Maid).

Alfred Hitchcock, the gifted English screen director, has made one of the most fascinating pictures of the year in *The Thirty-nine Steps,* his new film at the Roxy Theatre. If the work has any single rival as the most original, literate and entertaining melodrama of 1935, then it must be *The Man Who Knew Too Much,* which is also out of Mr. Hitchcock's workshop. A master of shock and suspense, of cold horror and slyly incongruous wit, he uses his camera the way a painter uses his brush, stylizing his story and giving it values which the scenarists could hardly have suspected. By comparison with the sinister delicacy and urbane understatement of *The Thirty-nine Steps,* the best of our melodramas seem crude and brawling.

If you can imagine Anatole France writing a detective story, you will have some notion of the artistry that Mr. Hitchcock brings to this screen version of John Buchan's novel. Like *The Man Who Knew Too Much,* the photoplay immerses a quite normal human being in an incredible dilemma where his life is suddenly at stake and his enemies are mysterious, cruel and desperate. Richard Hannay, a young Canadian, is sitting in a London music hall when a man is killed, whereupon a young woman confesses to the murder to him and begs him for sanctuary. In his rooms she explains that she is playing a lone game of counterespionage against foreign spies who have stolen a valuable military secret and are preparing to take it out of the country. Then the enigmatic lady is herself murdered, leaving Hannay with the meager information that his own life is now in danger, that he will learn the secret of the Thirty-Nine Steps in a certain Scottish hamlet and that he must beware of a man whose little finger is amputated at the first joint.

That is the situation, and for the next four days Hannay finds himself in the most fantastic predicament of his life. The police are hunting him for the murder of the young woman and the spies are hunting him because he knows too much. His career is a murderous nightmare of chase and pursuit, in which he continually escapes by inches from the hangman's noose and the assassin's bullet. Mr. Hitchcock describes the remarkable chain of events in Hannay's flight across England and Scotland with a blend of unexpected comedy and breathless terror that is strikingly effective.

Perhaps the identifying hallmark of his method is its apparent absence of accent in the climaxes, which are upon the spectator like a slap in the face before he has set himself for the blow. In such episodes as the murder of the woman in Hannay's apartment, the icy ferocity of the man with the missing finger when he casually shoots Hannay or the brilliantly managed sequences on the train, the action progresses through seeming indifference to whiplike revelations. There is a subtle feeling of menace on the screen all the time in Mr. Hitchcock's low-slung, angled use of the camera. But the participants, both Hannay and his pursuers, move with a repressed excitement that adds significance to every detail of their behavior.

Robert Donat as the suavely desperate hero of the adventure is excellent both in the comic and the tragic phases of his plight. The lovely Madeleine Carroll, who begins by betraying him and believes his story when it is almost too late, is charming and skillful. All the players preserve that sureness of mood and that understanding of the director's intention which distinguished *The Man Who Knew Too Much.* There are especially fine performances by John Laurie as the treacherous Scot who harbors the fugitive, Peggy Ashcroft as his sympathetic wife, Godfrey Tearle as the man with the missing finger, and Wylie Watson as the memory expert of the music halls, who proves to be the hub of the mystery.

—A.S., September 14, 1935

THIRTY-TWO SHORT FILMS ABOUT GLENN GOULD

Directed by François Girard; written by Mr. Girard and Don McKellar; director of photography, Alain Dostie; edited by Gaétan Huot; music by various composers; produced by Niv Fichman; released by Samuel Goldwyn Company. Running time: 94 minutes.

With: Colm Feore as Glenn Gould.

In the control room of a recording studio, the engineers discuss the merits of taking cream in their coffee, only half-noticing the enraptured figure behind the soundproof glass. There, Glenn Gould (Colm Feore) begins by casually testing his blood pressure, then listens to a playback of his recording of Bach. To the sounds of the English Suite No. 2, he begins swaying and floating in the throes of esthetic ecstasy, his white shirt billowing in gravity-defying slow motion. Far removed from the engineers' prosaic talk, he seems truly to have passed into another dimension.

The audience for *Thirty-two Short Films About Glenn Gould,* a brilliant and transfixing cinematic portrait by François Girard, can look forward to enjoying much the same sensation. For an hour and a half, without repeating himself or resorting to tactics that are even slightly familiar, Mr. Girard, whose film opens today at the Lincoln Plaza Cinemas, thoughtfully holds the viewer in thrall.

Though it glancingly incorporates a great deal of biographical information, this carefully measured film does not choose to describe Gould in ordinary terms. Suffused as it is with the artist's musical sensibility, it doesn't even have to show him playing the piano. Instead, Mr. Girard explores and replicates his subject's eccentric thought processes in a remarkably visceral way, drawing the audience palpably into Gould's state of mind. This film works hypnotically, with great subtlety and grace, in ways that are gratifyingly consistent with Gould's own thoughts about his music and his life.

Mr. Girard's film is indeed a compilation of thirty-two glimpses, each of them instantly intelligible, some of them strung together in supremely delicate ways. The format makes dependable sense: this is hardly the first time the variations motif has been brought to bear in describing Gould. More than an homage to his triumphant recordings of Bach's "Goldberg" Variations, this multifaceted structure seems the only possible means of approaching such a complex individual. If it sounds defiantly arty, that suits the subject and his "academic owlishness" (in the words of his biographer Otto Friedrich) perfectly. If it sounds obscure and daunting, it most certainly is not.

If anything, *Thirty-two Short Films About Glenn Gould* should prove even more mesmerizing to those who know little about Gould's life than to those aware that he really did have tastes for ketchup, tranquilizers, arrowroot cookies and Petula Clark (not necessarily in that order). In its own quirky way, it assembles a surprisingly rigorous and illuminating portrait of the man. Defying any usual constraints of narrative or chronology, Mr. Girard can leap freely from Gould's boyhood to his mature work, from the hotel room to the concert stage, from the raptures of the music to silly questions asked by the press. The individual fragments are so meticulously realized that the whole becomes much greater than the sum of its parts.

Typically fascinating is "L.A. Concert," a fine example of how cannily Mr. Girard can present the facts of Gould's life. We first see the pianist backstage, poised over a sink, soaking his arms in steaming water five minutes before a concert is to begin. Pill bottles are conspicuously arrayed in front of him. Called to the stage, he next appears dressed and ready, maintaining a serene detachment as an aide tries to instruct him about the irritating show-business realities of the evening. Just before reaching the stage, he pauses to talk with a stagehand and winds up signing a program for the man. Only when the stagehand examines the autograph does he learn that Mr. Gould has decided to make this 1964 concert performance his last.

It would be difficult to think of a more adroit, economical way to convey all this information in such a relatively brief time. *Thirty-two Short Films About Glenn Gould,* which was written by Mr. Girard with Don McKellar, is also able to fuse the informative with the poetic, particularly in the passages that deal hauntingly with Gould's final days. (He died at fifty, in 1982.) One of the film's last images is of a Voyager satellite that went into space carrying aural souvenirs of Earth's culture, including Gould's recording of Bach's "Well-Tempered Clavier." The film's announcement that the two Voyager spacecraft left our solar system in 1987 and 1989, respectively, suits its lingering impression that Gould was never quite of this world.

Mr. Feore, a Canadian stage actor, does not overwhelmingly resemble Gould, but he becomes a commanding and believable presence all the same. With a voice that has been made to sound strangely disembodied, and with the ability to project brooding, playful intelligence, Mr. Feore enhances the film's sense of deep mystery. Equally lulling and seductive are Mr. Girard's fluid camera movements, which enable the film to prowl and survey with uncommon ease. In the end, his methods induce a complete and satisfying immersion into his many-faceted subject.

Among the individual glimpses that must be mentioned here: "Practice," in which Gould resonates to his own thrilling impression of Beethoven's "Tempest" Sonata without ever touching a keyboard; "Truck Stop," in which he hears and seems to orchestrate the voices of people around him; "Personal Ad," in which he toys with the language of the lovelorn, then chuckles at the thought of ever representing himself in that way; "Diary of One Day," a stunning compilation of formulas, medical notations, heartbeats, and detailed X rays of a person playing the piano. Even before the film reaches this last juncture, you will know that the heart and blood of the pianist have been captured on screen.

Also worth noting: some significant omissions. Mr. Girard knew better than to mention Gould's intense admiration for Barbra Streisand, or to use those sec-

tions of the "Goldberg" Variations that have powerfully evoked Dr. Hannibal Lecter ever since they were used to shocking effect in *The Silence of the Lambs.*
—J.M., April 14, 1994

THIS IS SPINAL TAP

Directed by Rob Reiner; written by Christopher Guest, Michael McKean, Harry Shearer and Mr. Reiner; director of photography, Peter Smokler; edited by Kent Beyda, Kim Secrist and Robert Leighton; music by Mr. Guest, Mr. McKean, Mr. Shearer and Mr. Reiner; production designer, Bryan Jones; produced by Karen Murphy; released by Embassy Pictures. Running time: 82 minutes.

With: Rob Reiner (Marty DiBerti), Michael McKean (David St. Hubbins), Christopher Guest (Nigel Tufnel), Harry Shearer (Derek Smalls), R. J. Parnell (Mick Shrimpton), David Kaff (Viv Savage), Tony Hendra (Ian Faith) and Bruno Kirby (Tommy Pischedda).

They are treading water in a sea of retarded sexuality and bad poetry," says one fictitious rock critic of the equally fictitious Spinal Tap, a British heavy-metal band. "That's just nitpicking, isn't it?" is one band member's calm rejoinder, but he's wrong. Spinal Tap *does* embody rock-and-roll at its most horrible, and yet *This Is Spinal Tap,* a mock-documentary following the band's American tour, isn't mean-spirited at all. It's much too affectionate for that. And it stays so wickedly close to the subject that it is very nearly indistinguishable from the real thing.

This Is Spinal Tap, which opens today at Loews New York Twin and other theaters, is a witty, mischievous satire, and it's obviously a labor of love. The four screenwriters—Christopher Guest, Michael McKean, Harry Shearer and Rob Reiner—all appear in the film, the first three as Spinal Tap members, and Mr. Reiner (who directed) as the filmmaker who is telling their story. Mr. Reiner introduces the film by explaining that Spinal Tap has earned "a distinguished place in rock history as one of England's loudest bands" and then presents the members of the group. Even their names are funny—David St. Hubbins, Nigel Tufnel, Mick Shrimpton, Viv Savage and Derek Smalls.

There's an in-joke quality to the film, one that will make it all the more hilarious to anyone at all knowledgeable about either the esthetic or the business aspects of pop music. However, you need not have heard a band like Spinal Tap to find its story highly amusing. The film traces the stages of its career, from early imitation-Beatle days (the musicians are seen on television, smiling sappily and wagging their hair) to a psychedelic period (they are seen flanked by go-go dancers and wearing beatific expressions) to the unfortunate present. Their American tour reveals them to be approaching their final stylistic incarnation, which involves screamingly loud solos, tight spandex pants and the use of a giant horned skull onstage.

"The Boston gig has been canceled. I wouldn't worry about it, though, it's not a big college town," says Ian Faith (Tony Hendra), the group's not-very-reassuring manager. Ian's duties involve running interference with the head of the group's record company, Sir Denis Eton-Hogg (Patrick MacNee), and quelling any backstage tantrums. (Nigel, played with fabulous stupidity by Mr. Guest, has one such fit about the provisions in his dressing room; the bread is the wrong shape for the cold cuts, and he can't make proper sandwiches.) And it is Ian, who, when asked if Spinal Tap's popularity might be slipping, explains coolly that "their appeal is becoming more selective."

Among the more inspired bits are several involving Spinal Tap's stage show. There is also a tender moment at Elvis Presley's grave, as the group's members try to sing "Heartbreak Hotel" in homage to the King and wind up quibbling over the harmony. And there is Spinal Tap's encounter with a rocker whose career, unlike theirs, is on the rise. "Listen, we'd love to stand around and chat," says Howard Hesseman, playing the other star's manager and delivering the perfect record business brushoff. "But we've got to sit down in the lobby and wait for the limo."

The most appealing thing about *This Is Spinal Tap*, aside from the obvious enthusiasm of all concerned, is the accompanying lack of condescension. Mr. Guest, in particular, does a wonderful job of capturing his character's sincere idiocy. Mr. McKean is also appealing as the group's most gullible member, who is under the spell of a girlfriend (June Chadwick) who can tell him on the telephone that he's been eating too much sugar ("she says my larynx is fat"), a girlfriend who winds up trying to manage the band with the help of

her astrological charts. And Mr. Shearer is quietly funny as the nondescript Tap member, the one who sees Nigel and David as "fire" and "ice" and thinks his own role is "to be in the middle of that, like lukewarm water."

One of the key problems with which the band grapples, during the course of the movie, is that its latest proposal for an album cover has been deemed unprintable by its record company. The musicians are furious when another artist gets permission to use a cover they think is almost equally obnoxious, until it is explained to them why their own illustration is worse. "It's such a fine line between stupid and . . ." "And clever," muse the band members collectively. It certainly is—and the delightful *This Is Spinal Tap* stays on the right side of that line.

—J.M., March 2, 1984

THIS MAN MUST DIE

Directed by Claude Chabrol; written (in French, with English subtitles) by Mr. Chabrol and Paul Gégauff, based on the novel *The Beast Must Die* by Nicholas Blake; director of photography, Jean Rabier; edited by Jacques Gaillard; music by Pierre Jansen; art designer, Guy Littaye; produced by André Génovès; released by Allied Artists. Black and white. Running time: 115 minutes.

With: Michel Duchaussoy (Charles Thenier), Jean Yanne (Paul), Caroline Cellier (Helene Lanson) and Lorraine Rainer (Jeanne).

Claude Chabrol's *Que la Bête Meure* is a revenge melodrama about a young father who sets out to discover and murder the hit-and-run killer of his little son. By providential chance he learns who was in the fatal car. He pursues first a television actress and then her brother-in-law, his intended victim, who, it turns out, is a monster whom everybody (except his own awful mother) would gladly see dead.

The title the American distributors have given the film, *This Man Must Die*, seriously mistranslates. Chabrol is not only characterizing his villain. He is also, by way of the first of Brahms's "Four Serious Songs," which furnishes a brooding musical motif to the action, referring to a passage in Ecclesiastes that

1017

reads "For that which befalleth the sons of men befalleth beasts; . . . as the one dieth, so dieth the other . . ." In the Chabrol world revenge is never simple, or without its own interdependencies and moral ambiguities.

In its preoccupations, its surprises, its dislocations, the glorious excesses and precise disclosures of its camera, *This Man Must Die* resembles earlier Chabrol, particularly in the revenge films (*The Third Lover* and *Ophelia*, both 1962). But in its working out it differs, not so much in technique, which is only more economical and more assured, or in insight, as in a certain thematic gravity by which character, always a curious element in Chabrol, sheds some of its protective ironic strangeness and becomes more direct, more normal in its actions and in its reactions, more sentimental.

It seems to me that as Chabrol loses some of its perversity he also loses some of his interest, and that *This Man Must Die*, like the even more recent *Le Boucher*, fails in almost exact ratio to its ultimate seriousness of purpose. Although its final images are very beautiful and rich, and clearly meant to be deeply felt (some critics have recalled the sea voyage at the end of Lang's *Moonfleet*), they are simply not as finely controlled as most of Chabrol, or, indeed, most of this film.

For on the whole, *This Man Must Die* adds wonderful moment to wonderful moment, from the fatal accident with which it begins, through the father's reserved and then ardent courting of the girl who will lead him to his prey, through his meeting with the beast's family and almost to the climax and its denouement.

There are the usual great Chabrol eating sequences, the usual unequaled ability visually to orchestrate a range of behavior among several people in any given scene and the usual superb capacity to implicate an entire countryside in the movements of his drama. This alone places Chabrol among the best directors of thrillers, and in *This Man Must Die* the sea and the Atlantic coast of France collaborate in a quest that is also an expression of universal doom.

Michel Duchaussoy as the avenging father is not one of Chabrol's strongest leading men, though he is pleasant to watch. But Jean Yanne as the beast provides an idiomatic performance, as likably hateful as any monster in this director's zoo. Caroline Cellier as the sister-in-law has the advantage of looking rather like the great Stéphane Audran (Chabrol's wife and favorite leading lady) while projecting an altogether sweeter, more pliantly vulnerable character. It is her personality that holds the film's disparate dramatic elements together, and very nearly makes the romantic plot succeed.

This Man Must Die, which opened yesterday at the 68th Street Playhouse, is surely one of the best new movies.

—*R.G., October 21, 1970*

THIS SPORTING LIFE

Directed by Lindsay Anderson: written by David Storey. based on his novel: cinematographer. Denys Coop: edited by Peter Taylor: music by Roberto Gerhard: art designer. Alan Withy: produced by Karel Reisz: released by Continental Distributing. Black and white. Running time: 129 minutes.

With: Richard Harris (Frank Machin). Rachel Roberts (Mrs. Margaret Hammond). Alan Badel (Weaver). William Hartnell (Johnson). Colin Blakely (Maurice Braithwaite). Vanda Godsell (Mrs. Weaver) and Anne Cunningham (Judith).

The past record only barely indicates that the comparatively untried team led by Richard Harris, its star; Lindsay Anderson, its director; Karel Reisz, its producer; and David Storey, its author-scenarist, would come up with a smashing victory in *This Sporting Life*.

But the British drama, which opened the newly built 84th Street East Theater last night and which will begin a concurrent run tomorrow at the Little Carnegie, translates the confusions and unrequited longings of the angry young men and women of our time into memorable universal truths.

Even though a dedicated moviegoer has been surfeited by the spate of films illustrating youth wallowing in the lower depths of kitchen-sink dramas, *This Sporting Life* gives this entire genre meaning and brilliance. But members of this troupe obviously are true to themselves and their audience and are not playing to the hearts and minds of escapists who adore the happy ending. Despite the thick Yorkshire dialect, these are easily recognizable, three-dimensional people seeking a place in the sun, or simply momentary surcease, who project their emotions honestly and effectively.

As a documentary director essaying his first feature film, Lindsay Anderson, and Karel Reisz, who previously directed the notable *Saturday Night and Sunday Morning,* have used a complicated stream-of-consciousness approach to their work, which, oddly enough, is only initially involved. It emerges as lucid, realistic stuff as tough and genuine as the rough rugby star on whom it is centered.

This Sporting Life, as Frank Machin, its brawny and inarticulate hero eventually learns, is as hard as the fickle fans whose cheers can turn to jeers. Kicked into gory semiconsciousness in the opening rugby scrimmage, his remembrance of things past reveals his first association with Mrs. Hammond, the widow with whom he lodges, and his growing desire for her affection and his disturbing need "to be wanted." He recalls his vicious attack of a football player to gain attention, his subsequent success with the team he makes and his unrelenting pursuit of money and fame through which he hopes to extricate himself from anonymity.

Success is shallow, however. The woman, racked by thoughts of a tragically ended marriage, only succumbs to him physically and the real roots he seeks are unattainable. She, in turn, goaded by her cloddish lover and bittersweet memories, shrieks her hatred and drives him out of her life. On his desperate, climactic return when he discovers she is dying and when he can speak tenderly to her for the first time, she is beyond caring. There is only the bleak prospect of a pointless, destructive "sporting life."

It is a "life" that is exotic, but despite the thickly accented dialogue these are people to whom a viewer can relate. Credit in good part must go to Richard Harris's portrait of the ravaged Frank Machin. He is a realistically rugged rugby player. The prognathous jaw, the overhanging brow, the dented Roman nose, piercing eyes and massively muscled torso are reminiscent of the early Marlon Brando. But, more importantly, this comparative newcomer (he previously was seen in *Mutiny on the Bounty*) projects in artistic, fumbling nuances and in rough, gentle and explosive terms, the terrible desperation he cannot overcome.

He certainly is not alone. As the driven widow with two children, Rachel Roberts, remembered for her fine performance in *Saturday Night and Sunday Morning,* contributes a striking delineation of a fading woman torn between the memory of happiness and a yearning for marriage and a love she cannot give. In effective, subsidiary roles are a covey of husky footballers to the life led by an amiable Colin Blakely, as the hero's sidekick, and William Hartnell, as a pitiful, aged scout for the team; Alan Badel and Arthur Lowe, as the rapacious rival owners of the club; and Vanda Godsell as Mr. Badel's designing wife.

With the aid of knowledgeable photography, Mr. Anderson's swift and decisive direction has captured in somber blacks and whites a sleazy mining town, flat, soggy football fields and roaring crowds and a few idyllic country vignettes. Above all they have caught in truly dramatic, poignant and vivid style a drab, universally recognizable world from which there is no escape.
—A.W., July 17, 1963

THREE COMRADES

Directed by Frank Borzage; written by F. Scott Fitzgerald and Edward E. Paramore, based on the novel by Erich Maria Remarque; cinematographer, Joseph Ruttenberg; edited by Frank Sullivan; music by Franz Waxman with lyrics by Bob Wright and Chet Forrest; art designers, Cedric Gibbons and Paul Groesse; produced by Joseph L. Mankiewicz; released by Metro-Goldwyn-Mayer. Black and white. Running time: 100 minutes.

With: Robert Taylor (Erich Lohkamp), Margaret Sullavan (Patricia Hoffman), Franchot Tone (Otto Koster), Robert Young (Gottfried Lenz), Guy Kibbee (Alfons), Lionel Atwill (Breuer), Henry Hull (Dr. Becker), Charley Grapewin (Local Doctor) and Monty Wooley (Dr. Jaffe).

Let us come to the point at once: the Metro-Goldwyn-Mayer version of Erich Maria Remarque's *Three Comrades,* which was presented at the Capitol yesterday, is a beautiful and memorable film. Faithful to the spirit and, largely, to the letter of the novel, it has been magnificently directed, eloquently written and admirably played. And in Margaret Sullavan's case, the word "admirably" is sheer understatement. Hers is a shimmering, almost unendurably lovely performance. We ask angrily why she hasn't been seen more often. Invite us now and you'll have us nominating her for Scarlett and Carlotta and every other prize role they are bidding for in Hollywood.

Remarque's novel was poignant in itself, the sorrowfully told tale of three war-shattered veterans in post-war, pre-Fascist Germany and of the frail and gallant young woman who loved one of them in the shadow of the white death, tuberculosis. It was a tale of which much or nothing might have been made. So little really happened. There were three comrades struggling for a living in their auto repair shop; there was the girl; there was a tragic honeymoon; and there was the horribly omnipresent doom. Look at it sourly and you find a twentieth-century *Camille*.

They haven't looked at it sourly, but with respect and appreciation. The adaptation by F. Scott Fitzgerald and Edward E. Paramore has kept Remarque's language, kept his characters, kept the slight but telling incidents the novel contained. And Frank Borzage, who directed it, has achieved once more the affecting simplicity that marked his *Seventh Heaven* (silent version) and *Farewell to Arms*. His cameras have evoked the tender mood, wooed the lovers in their wooing, imprisoned in swift bright images their helplessness and hopelessness and their ultimate brave triumph over death itself.

With the possible exception of Robert Taylor, who is good occasionally but more often is merely acceptable, Mr. Borzage has been fortunate in his cast. Miss Sullavan, of course, is the perfect Patricia. Franchot Tone has turned in a beautifully shaded portrait of Otto Koster, the loyal and devoted friend, and Robert Young is almost equally effective as the gay idealist, Gottfried. As the third of the comrades, Mr. Taylor has his moments of sincerity, but shares them with those suggesting again the charming, well fed, carefully hair-groomed leading man of the glamour school of cinema. That, possibly, is the picture's only weakness, and we are inclined to overlook it in celebrating its strength. It is a superlatively fine picture, obviously one of 1938's best ten, and not one to be missed.

—*F.S.N., June 3, 1938*

THREE DAYS OF THE CONDOR

Directed by Sydney Pollack: written by Lorenzo Semple Jr. and David Rayfiel, based on the novel *Six Days of the Condor* by James Grady: director of photography. Owen Roizman: edited by Fredric Steinkamp: music by Dave Grusin: production designer. Stephen Grimes: produced by Stanley Schneider: released by Paramount Pictures. Running time: 118 minutes.

With: Robert Redford (Turner). Faye Dunaway (Kathy). Cliff Robertson (Higgins). Max Von Sydow (Joubert). John Houseman (Mr. Wabash). Addison Powell (Atwood). Walter McGinn (Barber). Tina Chen (Janice) and Michael Kane (Wicks).

Turner (Robert Redford) is not your stereotypical Central Intelligence Agency operative, the short-haired, buttoned-down kind we've seen testifying live on television from time to time. Turner's hair is fashionably long. He wears blue jeans and shirts without ties and he rides to work on a motorcycle. He's an eccentric link in the C.I.A. chain of command.

Turner's "work" is on Manhattan's upper East Side, in a handsome old brownstone identified as the American Literary Historical Society, which is a blind for an esoteric C.I.A. research center where agents read and feed into a computer pertinent details from contemporary novels, short stories and journals of all sorts. The aim: to find out whether pending C.I.A. operations may have somehow been leaked, and to pick up pointers on spy methodology that may have been fantasized by hack fiction writers.

Turner is a C.I.A. "reader," which, like the job of a reader at a movie company, is about as unimportant as a job can be while still qualifying its incumbent as a member of the team.

Yet in Sydney Pollack's *Three Days of the Condor*, Turner, whose code name is Condor, comes close to wreaking more havoc on the C.I.A. in three days than any number of House and Senate investigating committees have done in years. (The film, based on James Grady's novel, *Six Days of the Condor*, has compressed the story's time span, necessitating the modification of title.)

Three Days of the Condor, which opened yesterday at Loews Astor Plaza and Tower East Theaters, is a good-looking, entertaining suspense film that is most effective when it's being most conventional, working variations on obligatory sequences of pursuit and flight, and on those sudden revelations that can reverse the roles of cat and mouse.

As a serious exposé of misdeeds within the C.I.A. the film is no match for stories that have appeared in your local newspaper. Indeed, one has to pay careful attention to figure out just what it is that who is doing to whom in *Three Days of the Condor* and, if I understood it correctly, it's never as horrifying as the real thing.

In the screenplay by Lorenzo Semple Jr. and David Rayfiel, Turner very early on stumbles upon the existence of a kind of super-C.I.A. within the C.I.A., after which his life is not worth a plug nickel. It doesn't do to analyze too closely the character Mr. Redford plays, that is, to ask why the bookish intellectual of the film's opening sequences would have joined the C.I.A. in the first place, or how he later manages so easily to become such a hotshot at tapping telephones and kidnapping very important persons.

The suspense of the film depends less on this kind of plausibility than on Mr. Redford's reputation (in a movie we accept the fact that he can do anything) and on the verve with which Mr. Pollack, the director, sets everything up. It also benefits from the presence of good actors, including Faye Dunaway (as the woman who befriends the fleeing Turner), Cliff Robertson, Max Von Sydow and John Houseman, though it's not a film to make particular demands on their talents.

At its best moments, *Three Days of the Condor* creates without effort or editorializing that sense of isolation—that far remove from reality—within which super-government agencies can operate with such heedless immunity. This point is implicit in the jargon the agents use. When a C.I.A. man speaks to Turner of "the community," he's not talking about a borough or a city or a state but about the brotherhood of intelligence people, who live in another dimension of time, place and expectation.

—V.C., September 25, 1975

THRONE OF BLOOD

Directed by Akira Kurosawa; written (in Japanese, with English subtitles) by Hideo Oguni, Shinobu Hashimoto, Ryuzo Kikushima and Mr. Kurosawa, based on the play *Macbeth* by William Shakespeare; cinematographer, Asaichi Nakai; edited by Mr. Kurosawa; music by Masaru Sato; art designer, Yoshiro Muraki; produced by Mr. Kurosawa and Sojiro Muraki; released by Brandon Films. Black and white. Running time: 110 minutes.

With: Toshiro Mifune (Taketoki), Isuzu Yamada (Asaji), Takashi Shimura (Noriyasu Odagura), Minoru Chiaki (Yoshiaki), Akira Kubo (Yoshiteru) and Takamaru Sasaki (Kuniharu).

If you think it would be amusing to see *Macbeth* done in Japanese, then pop around to the Fifth Avenue Cinema and see Akira Kurosawa's *Throne of Blood.* For a free Oriental translation of the Shakespeare drama is what this is, and amusing is the proper word for it. It opened yesterday.

We label it amusing because lightly is the only way to take this substantially serio-comic rendering of the story of an ambitious Scot into a form that combines characteristics of the Japanese No theater and the American Western film. Probably Mr. Kurosawa, who directed the classic *Rashomon,* did not intend it to be amusing for his formalistic countrymen, but its odd amalgamation of cultural contrasts hits the occidental funnybone.

Let us quickly remark that he has not attempted to employ the Shakespearean dialogue in even a sketchy translation, nor has he used all the Scottish characters, nor even the names of the characters in the original play. He has simply purloined the thread of the drama and used it as the plot of a film that splatters the screen with a wild horse-opera set in medieval Japan.

Now Macbeth is a Japanese warrior, returning home after helping to quell a revolt, who encounters a weird, white-faced soothsayer in a forest near his home. The soothsayer makes the prediction that he can become the chief warlord by seizing the opportunity for assassinations that will present itself.

This news is transmitted by the warrior to his waiting wife in a simple scene that is absolutely hypnotic in its theatrical austerity. Played in an architecturally bare room, which contrasts vividly with the scenes of outdoor violence and intensity that go before, it has the arresting compactness of a scene on the Japanese stage. It certainly presents a new conception of the scene between Macbeth and his wife.

But, for the most part, the action in this drama is grotesquely brutish and barbaric, reminiscent of the horse-opera business in Kurosawa's *The Magnificent Seven* with Toshiro Mifune as the warrior grunting and bellowing monstrously and making elaborately wild gestures to convey his passion and greed, while other of the warriors behave accordingly. To our western eyes, it looks fantastic and funny—that is all one can say—and the final scene, in which the hero is shot so full of arrows that he looks like a porcupine, is a pictorial extravagance that provides a conclusive howl.

Withal, Kurosawa's camera is handled with magnificent skill. There is exciting communication in its very movements and in the imagistic forms it evolves. And the soundtrack is interestingly filled with all sorts of harsh and eerie noises.

You should be strangely stimulated and have some fun at this film.

—B.C., November 23, 1961

TIGHT LITTLE ISLAND

Directed by Alexander Mackendrick; written by Compton Mackenzie and Angus MacPhail, based on the novel *Whiskey Galore* by Mr. Mackenzie; cinematographer, Gerald Gibbs; edited by Joseph Sterling; music by Ernest Irving; art designer, Jim Morahan; produced by Michael Balcon; released by Universal International Pictures. Black and white. Running time: 81 minutes.

With: Basil Radford (Captain Paul Waggett), Catherine Lacey (Mrs. Waggett), Bruce Seton (Sergeant Odd), Joan Greenwood (Peggy Macroon), Wylie Watson (Joseph Macroon), Gabrielle Blunt (Catriona Macroon) and Gordon Jackson (George Campbell).

Compton Mackenzie, who wrote *Tight Little Island* and also acts a small role in this new British film at the Trans-Lux Sixtieth Street Theatre, has a rare sense of humor. He is a lucky man, too. Mr. Mackenzie has written the most chucklesome comedy of the season in contemplating the great gloom that pervades the tiny Hebridean island of Todday when its wartime ration of whiskey runs out and the steamer from the mainland arrives without the anxiously awaited "water of life."

Mr. Mackenzie has been lucky because his wonderfully droll screenplay, adapted from his novel, *Whiskey Galore,* in collaboration with Angus MacPhail, has been visualized by a knowing group of performers under the skillful guidance of the director, Alexander Mackendrick. There can be no doubt that these people loved their work, and we have no doubt either that a lot of people over here are going to love this remarkable picture and go back to it again and again.

For *Tight Little Island* is another happy demonstration of that peculiar knack British moviemakers have for striking a rich and universally appealing comic vein in the most unexpected and seemingly insular situations. What more unlikely basis for a warm and gently satirical comedy than a group of people literally dying for want of a drink?

Without ever overstating the situation or cheapening the rock-ribbed respectability of the islanders, *Tight Little Island* draws grand fun out of a monumental thirst and the grave anxiety that prevails for twenty-four hours when a ship loaded with 50,000 cases of the precious liquid grounds on the rocks off Todday and is abandoned. Tired and dejected spirits are charged with excitement over prospects of looting the ship before it sinks, but before the islanders can get off the beach the village church clock heralds the arrival of the Sabbath. And being very proper people the islanders won't work on Sunday, even for a drink of whiskey.

What a day of waiting that turns out to be, with all eyes turned anxiously on the stricken vessel and consternation mounting when it becomes apparent that the fuddy-duddy British commandant of the Home Guard intends to protect the cargo. The strategy the islanders adopt in outwitting the perseveringly annoying Captain Waggett should not be spoiled by being robbed of surprise through mention in a review. But take our word for it, you will not be disappointed.

Aside from Basil Radford (Captain Waggett), who has the mentality if not the physical characteristics of Colonel Blimp, and Joan Greenwood, the players are not too well known here, by name at least, but they are all excellent. Wylie Watson deserves to be singled out because he happens to be more prominently featured than the others as becomes a postmaster.

—T.M.P., December 26, 1949

THE TIN DRUM

Directed by Volker Schlöndorff; written (in German, with English subtitles) by Jean-Claude Carrière, Mr. Schlöndorff, Franz Seitz and Günter Grass, based on the novel by Mr. Grass; director of photography, Igor Luther; edited by Suzanne Baron; music by Maurice Jarre; produced by Mr. Seitz and Anatole Dauman; released by New World Pictures. Running time: 142 minutes.

With: David Bennent (Oskar), Mario Adorf (Alfred Matzerath), Angela Winkler (Agnes Matzerath), Daniel Olbrychski (Jan Bronski), Katharina Tahlbach (Maria), Heinz Bennent (Greff) and Andrea Ferreol (Lina Greff).

Still in the womb with only seconds to go before birth, Oskar Matzerath stares out at a world to which he has no intention of submitting without protest. All around him is his sweet, warm, foolish mother Agnes, pushing hard and sweating in happy pain. Bustling around her are Alfred Matzerath, Oskar's "putative" father, a portly German shopkeeper with a fondness for cooking; Jan Bronski, Oskar's real father, a handsome young Pole who is Alfred's best friend; plus assorted relatives and midwives.

The joyous, noisy lower-middle-class confusion that attends his birth does not appeal to Oskar but, before he knows it, he's out and the umbilical cord has been cut. As Oskar tells us on the soundtrack, that act more or less settled the question of retreat.

This vivid, tumultuous sequence, which occurs near the beginning of *The Tin Drum,* efficiently introduces us to the extraordinary character who, as played by an extraordinary actor, dominates Volker Schlöndorff's screen version of Günter Grass's fantastic epic of a novel about Germany from the turn-of-the-century to after World War II.

If you've read *The Tin Drum* you'll remember that on the day of his birth Oskar Matzerath is promised a little tin drum for his third birthday present. When that day arrives, Oskar makes a firm decision not to grow any more, to remain forever at age three, banging away on his tin drum (to drown out the idiocies he hears around him) and, occasionally, lifting his voice in a scream than can shatter lightbulbs, thick glass jars and windows. To give his parents a logical reason for his unusual lack of growth, Oskar stages a fall down the cellar stairs. The accident results in an easily recognized head wound and brings an effective end to his increasingly drunken birthday party, which was amusing everyone except Oskar.

In reading *The Tin Drum* you might think that Oskar Matzerath is the sort of literary conceit that would be impossible to translate to film, the kind of character best seen in the privacy of the mind's eye. It's Mr. Schlöndorff's great good fortune to have David Bennent in this most unusual role. Mr. Bennent, who was twelve when the film was made, must in the course of the story age from a wisecracking, misanthropic, newborn babe to a man in his early twenties who still could pass for three.

What makes the performance so remarkable is that although the looks of the character don't change appreciably, the manners, the authority, the wit and the mind of Oskar do. It's the kind of transformation that makes you believe in the occult.

Mr. Bennent is no midget or dwarf. He's a small, sweet-looking child who tolerates adults with only the slightest hint of condescension. Oskar comes into the world as an angry, fully developed personality who elects to follow the only course open to anyone of sensibility when confronted with such obvious lunacies. In his child's disguise, he audits the world from a safe distance, now and then playing a terrible practical joke on the unsuspecting adults who are too self-absorbed to notice what's really going on.

It is through Oskar's cool eye that we watch his mother and Jan Bronski carry on their discreet affair under the nose of the jovial, cloddish Alfred. It's through Oskar's eyes, too, that we see Alfred become a Nazi stormtrooper and the free city of Danzig, where Oskar was born in 1924, gobbled up by Germany. Without batting an eyelash, Oskar looks on as his mother, to spite Alfred, embarks on a suicidal diet of nothing but fish. Later, Oskar runs away with a band of jolly midgets to entertain the Nazi troops manning the English Channel defenses. We are with Oskar, too, when the Soviet troops enter Berlin, when Alfred, to hide his Nazi pin, swallows it (with unfortunate effect) and when Oskar, for reasons that are obscure in the film, decides to resume his interrupted physical growth.

The screenplay, written by Mr. Schlöndorff, Jean-Claude Carrière (Luis Buñuel's favorite collaborator) and Franz Seitz, does not cover quite as much ground as Mr. Grass's novel, but it attempts to cover more than can be adequately comprehended in even a 142-minute film.

The Tin Drum, which opens today at the Cinema 1, is a seriously responsible adaptation of a gargantuan novel, but it's an adaptation that has no real life of its own. There are a number of things seen or said on the screen that, I suspect, will not make much sense to anyone who isn't familiar with the novel. An essential part of Oskar's makeup is his Kashubian heritage, his ties to that Slavic people settled near Danzig who never considered themselves either German or Polish and who were always at the mercy of one or the other.

Mr. Grass's narrative method is well-ordered chaos, the accumulation of events, legends, gossip, jokes, asides, dreams, fantastic speculation and the constant reevaluation of things we've already been told. Of necessity, I suppose, Mr. Schlöndorff has simplified and straightened things out but without making them especially clear. In adapting Vladimir Nabokov's *Despair* for the screen, Tom Stoppard found a screen style equivalent to Nabokov. *The Tin Drum* doesn't.

However, because the story it tells is so outsized, bizarre, funny and eccentric, the movie compels attention. There are several stunning sequences, including one in which little Oskar, beating a one-two-three, one-two-three tattoo on his drum, turns a Nazi rally into a waltz festival, and another in which the teenage Oskar seduces his "putative" father's future wife by pouring fizz powder onto her navel, which is the kind of aphrodisiac that only Mr. Grass might know about.

Mr. Bennent is the focal point of the picture from start to finish, but there are a number of other remarkable performances. Angela Winkler is marvelous as Oskar's beautiful, lost mother and Daniel Olbrychski, the star of Wajda's *Landscape After Battle* and *The Young Girls of Wilko,* is fine as the poetic, poor but always dapper Jan Bronski. Katharina Tahlbach is very funny as Oskar's mistress-stepmother. Charles Aznavour has a brief, not very satisfactory role as a Jewish shopkeeper. Fritz Hakl and Mariella Oliveri are terrifically appealing as Oskar's showbiz midget friends.

The Tin Drum is not a personal film, as are those of the other leaders in the New German Cinema. It's not even as personal as Mr. Schlöndorff's own *Young Torless,* which heralded the new era of Werner Herzog, Rainer Werner Fassbinder and Wim Wenders in German movies. *The Tin Drum* is a big, sweeping film that does its best to serve the torrential imagination of one of the most original, most gifted German writers of our day.

—V.C., April 11, 1980

TO BE OR NOT TO BE

Produced and directed by Ernst Lubitsch; written by Edwin Justus Mayer, based on a story by Mr. Lubitsch and Melchior Lengyel; cinematographer, Rudolph Maté; edited by Dorothy Spencer; music by Miklós Rózsa and Werner Heymann; production designer, Vincent Korda; released by United Artists. Black and white. Running time: 99 minutes.

With: Carole Lombard (Maria Tura), Jack Benny (Joseph Tura), Robert Stack (Lieutenant Stanislav Sobinski), Felix Bressart (Greenberg), Lionel Atwill (Rawitch), Stanley Ridges (Professor Siletsky) and Sig Rumann (Colonel Ehrhardt).

Hamlet's most famous soliloquy was a positive declaration when compared to the jangled moods and baffling humors of Ernst Lubitsch's new film, *To Be or Not to Be,* which opened yesterday at the Rivoli under delicate circumstances at best. For not only was this the last picture in which the late Carole Lombard played—and on which was therefore imposed an obligation of uncommon tact—but it happens to be upon a subject which is far from the realm of fun. And yet, in a spirit of levity, confused by frequent doses of shock, Mr. Lubitsch has set his actors to performing a spy-thriller of fantastic design amid the ruins and frightful oppressions of Nazi-invaded Warsaw. To say it is callous and macabre is understating the case.

Perhaps there are plenty of persons who can overlook the locale, who can still laugh at Nazi generals with pop eyes and bunglesome wits. Perhaps they can fancy Jack Benny, disguised behind goggles and beard, figuratively tweaking the noses of the best Gestapo sleuths. Those patrons will certainly relish the burlesque bravado of this film. And many more will enjoy the glib surprises and suspense of the plot. But it is hard to imagine how anyone can take, without batting an eye, a shattering air raid upon Warsaw right after a sequence of farce or the spectacle of Mr. Benny playing a comedy scene with a Gestapo corpse. Mr. Lubitsch had an odd sense of humor—and a tangled script—when he made this film.

As ever with Lubitsch pictures, it is unfair to give too much away. Suffice it to say that this time he is telling a fabulous tale about a company of Polish actors caught in Warsaw when it fell in the Fall of 1939 and of the way in which these enterprising thespians outsmart the dumb Gestapo. Conveniently, the company had been rehearsing an anti-Nazi play, so they are able to jump into roles and costumes which the exigencies demand.

As stars of the company, Mr. Benny and Miss Lombard—quite obviously the Polish Lunts—are called upon to assume the leading roles and the perils of the plot. And the tricks by which Miss Lombard entices the Nazi wolves and Mr. Benny, in a couple of disguises, pulls the wool right over their eyes, make for the comedy and grim excitement which Mr. Lubitsch has recklessly confused.

Miss Lombard, in this her last role, is very beautiful and comically adroit, and the feelings which one might imagine her presence would impose are never sensed. This is indeed a tribute to her glowing personality. But Mr. Benny, despite a successful endeavor to alter his style, still gives out too much of Jack Benny, the radio comedian, to be just right. Too many times does he bridle at reflections upon his talent. Too often does he pout or grow indignant or pull a double-take. Of course, the script encourages the old Benny legend of "ham." Once a German officer comments, laughing loudly, "What he did to Shakespeare we are doing now to Poland." That gives you a couple of ideas about this film.

In lesser roles, Sig Rumann is thick and blustering as a Nazi colonel, Stanley Ridges is suave and sinister as a Gestapo agent, Robert Stack is pleasantly youthful as a Polish flier, and Tom Dugan is funny to behold as a burlesque Hitler. Too bad a little more taste and a little more unity of mood were not put in this film. As it is, one has the strange feeling that Mr. Lubitsch is a Nero, fiddling while Rome burns.

—B.C., March 7, 1942

TO CATCH A THIEF

Produced and directed by Alfred Hitchcock: written by John Michael Hayes. based on the novel by David Dodge: cinematographer. Robert Burks: edited by George Tomasini: music by Lyn Murray: art designers. Hal Pereira and Joseph MacMillan Johnson: released by Paramount Pictures. Running time: 103 minutes.

With: Cary Grant (John Robie). Grace Kelly (Frances Stevens). Jessie Royce Landis (Mrs. Stevens). John Williams (H. H. Hughson). Charles Vanel (Bertani). Brigitte Auber (Danielle). Jean Martinelli (Foussard) and Georgette Anya (Germaine).

It takes a thief to catch a thief. That's the old saying, anyhow. And that's the thesis Alfred Hitchcock is exhibiting in his new mystery-thriller-romance at the Paramount. With Cary Grant playing the catcher and Grace Kelly playing—well, we won't say!—*To Catch a Thief* comes off completely as a hit in the old Hitchcock style.

We're not saying much about Miss Kelly, other than to observe that she is cool and exquisite and superior as a presumably rich American girl traveling with her mother in Europe in quest (her mother says) of a man. To say more might tip you as to whether she is what you suspect her to be—the jewel thief whom Mr. Grant is stalking through the lush gambling-rooms and gilded chambers of French Riviera villas, casinos, and hotels.

As a matter of fact, we shouldn't even tell you that you may rest entirely assured Mr. Grant himself is not the slick cat burglar he says he is out to catch, as a matter of self-protection and to help an insurance man from Lloyds. What with his being an acknowledged old gem thief, living in a villa high above Cannes and chumming with a covey of ex-convicts, he could be almost anything.

Well, he isn't the thief. That much we'll tell you. He's the fellow who genuinely tries to use his own knowledge of cat-burglary to nab the thief who has been terrorizing Cannes and causing hysterics and conniptions among the always ineffectual police. But then there are enough other suspects—ex-convicts, French thugs and pretty girls, not to mention that nervous Lloyds fellow—to let us write off Mr. Grant.

In his accustomed manner, Mr. Hitchcock has gone at this job with an omnivorous eye for catchy details and a dandy John Michael Hayes script. Most of his visual surprises are got this time with scenery—with the fantastic, spectacular vistas along the breathtaking Côte d'Azur.

As no one has ever done before him, Mr. Hitchcock has used that famous coast to form a pictorial backdrop that fairly yanks your eyes out of your head. Almost at the start, he gives you an automobile chase along roads that wind through cliff-hanging, seaside villages. The surprise is that it is seen from the air! If you have ever been on the Riviera, you can imagine how brilliant this is, in color and VistaVision, splashed on that giant screen.

All the way through the picture, he gets this sort of thing—shots from great heights down yawning chasms, glimpses of ruins high on hills, views across Mediterranean harbors and, usually in the background, the blue sea. And he winds up with a surge of production—a costume party at a villa outside Cannes—that should make the Marquis de Cuevas turn green.

True, there are times when the color is not always so good as it should be, and Mr. Hitchcock's cameraman (or somebody) has a bad time with slow dissolves and fades. He has not mastered VistaVision. It has almost mastered him.

But the script and the actors keep things popping, in a fast, slick, sophisticated vein. Mr. Grant and Miss Kelly do grandly, especially in one sly seduction scene. If you've never heard double entendre, you will hear it in this film. As the chap from Lloyds, John Williams is delightfully anxious and dry, and Jessie Royce Landis is most amusing as Miss Kelly's low-down American mom. Brigitte Auber is fetching and funny as a frightfully forward French girl, and Charles Vanel has the air of a rascal as a local restaurateur.

To Catch a Thief does nothing but give out a good, exciting time. If you'll settle for that at a movie, you should give it your custom right now.

—B.C., August 5, 1955

TO HAVE AND HAVE NOT

Produced and directed by Howard Hawks: written by Jules Furthman and William Faulkner. based on the novel by Ernest Hemingway: cinematographer. Sid Hickox: edited by Christian Nyby: music by Franz Waxman: art designer. Charles Novi: released by Warner Brothers. Black and white. Running time: 100 minutes.

With: Humphrey Bogart (Morgan). Walter Brennan (Eddie "The Rummy"). Lauren Bacall (Marie). Dolores Moran (Helene de Bursac). Hoagy Carmichael (Crickett). Sheldon Leonard (Lieutenant Coyo). Marcel Dalio (Gerard). Walter Sande (Johnson) and Dan Seymour (Captain Renard).

Having once cornered Humphrey Bogart in a Casablanca café and beheld his tremendous potential in that sultry and colorful spot, it was logical that the Warners should have wanted to get him there again—or in some place of similar nature, where the currents would flow much the same. A fellow like Mr. Bogart needs a well-coupled circuit, you know. Well, the desire has been accomplished with surprisingly comparable effect in Howard Hawks's production for that studio, *To Have and Have Not,* which came to the Hollywood yesterday.

Maybe they say that the story is based on Ernest Hemingway's tale of the same name, and maybe the locale is visually French Martinique four years ago. But there's no use dodging around it: *To Have and Have Not* is *Casablanca* moved west into the somewhat less hectic Caribbean but along the same basic parallel. And, although there are surface alterations in some of the characters, you will meet here substantially the same people as in that other geopolitical romance.

For what Mr. Hawks and his scriptwriters have done to Mr. Hemingway's tale is to shape it out of all recognition into a pattern of worldly intrigue. Now the professional sports fisherman, who was a brute in the original, is a much more tractable fellow where human destinies are involved and especially is he open to persuasion when a fascinating female waves in. And thus, while pursuing his profession in the region of Martinique, he is coerced to fish in the deep waters of pro- and anti-Vichy lawlessness by the push of his own moral suasion and the lure of a very fetching girl.

There is much more character than story in the telling of this tough and tight-lipped tale, and much more atmosphere than action of the usual muscular sort. And that—as was true with *Casablanca*—is generally just as well. For Mr. Bogart is best when his nature is permitted to smoulder in the gloom and his impulse to movement is restricted by a caution bred of cynical doubt. And those are his dispositions which Mr. Hawks has chiefly worked on in this film. As the hard-boiled professional fisherman who gives his ample ingenuity to a cause, Mr. Bogart is almost as impressive as he was as Rick, the Casablanca host.

And as the wistful bird of passage who moves dauntlessly into his life, Lauren Bacall, a blondish newcomer, is plainly a girl with whom to cope. Slumberous of eye and softly reedy along the lines of Veronica Lake, she acts in the quiet way of catnip and sings a song from deep down in her throat. Accompanied by Hoagy Carmichael, who plays a sweetly sleazy pianist in this film, she mumbles a song of his composing, "How Little We Know," in perfect low-down barroom style. Mr. Carmichael himself also does grandly by a sort of calypso song, which is strictly in keeping with the rambling and melancholy atmosphere.

Dan Seymour is powerfully sinister as a hyperthyroid gunman for Vichy and Walter Brennan gives an affecting performance (albeit pointless) as a drunk. A good many other ratty characters move in and out of the film—apparently the ones who kept on going when they passed through Casablanca some time back.

—B.C., October 12, 1944

TO KILL A MOCKINGBIRD

Directed by Robert Mulligan; written by Horton Foote, based on the novel by Harper Lee; cinematographer, Russell Harlan; edited by Aaron Stell; music by Elmer Bernstein; art designers, Alexander Golitzen and Henry Bumstead; art designers, Alexander Golitzen and Henry Bumstead; produced by Alan J. Pakula; released by Universal Pictures. Black and white. Running time: 129 minutes.

With: Gregory Peck (Atticus Finch), Mary Badham (Scout Finch), Philip Alford (Jem Finch), John Megna (Dill Harris), Frank Overton (Sheriff Tate), Brock Peters (Tom Robinson) and Robert Duvall (Boo Radley).

There is so much feeling for children in the film that has been made from Harper Lee's best-selling novel, *To Kill a Mockingbird* . . . so much delightful observation of their spirit, energy and charm as depicted by two superb discoveries, Mary Badham and Philip Alford—that it comes as a bit of a letdown at the end to realize that, for all the picture's feeling for children, it doesn't tell us very much of how they feel.

This is the one adult omission that is regretful in this fine film that Alan J. Pakula and Universal delivered to the Music Hall yesterday.

At the outset, it plops us down serenely in the comfort of a grubby Southern town at the time of the Great Depression, before "desegregation" was even a word. Here we are brought into contact with Scout Finch, a six-year-old girl who is a thoroughly beguiling tomboy; her ten-year-old brother, Jem; and their widowed father, Atticus, who is clearly the kindest man in town.

And for a fair spell it looks as though maybe we are going to be squeezed inside the skin of Scout and Jem as they go racing and tumbling around the neighborhood, shrieking with childish defiance at crusty old Mrs. Dubose, skirting with awe around the dark house where the mysterious Boo Radley lives.

So long as the film is on this level, the director, Robert Mulligan, achieves a bewitching indication of the excitement and thrill of being a child.

It is when the drama develops along the conventional line of a social crisis in the community—the charging of a Negro with the rape of a white woman—that the children are switched to the roles of lookers-on. They become but observers in the gallery as their father, played superbly by Gregory Peck, goes through a lengthy melodrama of defending the Negro in court and giving a strong but adult lesson of justice and humanity at work.

And their roles are still those of bystanders in a subsequent episode when they are attacked by a vengeful Negro-baiter and brought to realize that the strange Boo Radley is not a monster but a friend.

It is, in short, on the level of adult awareness of right and wrong, of good and evil, that most of the action in the picture occurs. And this detracts from the camera's observation of the point of view of the child.

While this still permits vivid melodrama and some touching observations of the children, especially in their relations with their father, which is the crucial relationship in the film, it leaves the viewer wondering precisely how the children feel. How have they really reacted to the things that affect our grown-up minds?

Horton Foote's script and the direction of Mr. Mulligan may not penetrate that deeply, but they do allow Mr. Peck and little Miss Badham and Master Alford to portray delightful characters. Their charming enactments of a father and his children in that close relationship that can occur at only one brief period are worth all the footage of the film.

Rosemary Murphy as a neighbor, Brock Peters as the Negro on trial, and Frank Overton as a troubled sheriff are good as locality characters, too. James Anderson and Collin Wilcox as Southern bigots are almost caricatures. But those are minor shortcomings in a rewarding film.

—B.C., February 15, 1963

TO LIVE

Directed by Zhang Yimou; written (in Mandarin, with English subtitles) by Yu Hua and Lu Wei, based on the novel by Mr. Yu; director of photography, Lu Yue; edited by Du Yuan; music by Zhao Jiping; produced by Chiu Fusheng; released by the Samuel Goldwyn Company. Running time: 129 minutes.

With: Ge You (Fugui), Gong Li (Jiazhen), Niu Ben (Town Chief), Guo Tao (Chungsheng), Jiang Wu (Er Xi), Ni Dabong (Long Er), Deng Fei (Youqing), Liu Tian Chi (Fengxia as adult), Zhang Lu (Fengxia as adolescent) and Xiao Cong (Fengxia as child).

In the gambling house where Fugui (Ge You) spends his nights, letting his family fortune slip from his grasp, he is treated like a young prince. The setting is China in the prerevolutionary 1940's, and after hours of gambling, Fugui is carried home at dawn through the streets of his small town on the back of a man who deposits him at his extravagant house. Fugui's wife, Jiazhen (Gong Li), begs him to stop gambling, for the sake of their small daughter and the child she is carrying.

Of course, he doesn't, and soon loses the family home to a bounder called Long Er. One of many great comic ironies in *To Live,* Zhang Yimou's family melodrama that sweeps through thirty years of Chinese history, is that this misfortune turns out to be a major piece of luck. When the revolution comes, the house is burned by the Communists and the landowning Long Er is executed. There, but for the grace of his gambling, goes Fugui.

"Your family's timber was first-rate," a good Communist tells him, describing how fast the house went up in flames. By then Fugui has developed a sense of survival that is by turns funny and heartbreaking and that expresses the very soul of this tragicomic film. "That wasn't my family's timber," he says. "That was counterrevolutionary timber."

To Live is purposefully more sentimental than anything Mr. Zhang has done before. After Fugui has lost the house, he takes over a traveling shadow puppet show. While he and his friend Chungsheng are on the road with their theater, they are captured by the losing Nationalist army. When Fugui returns to his much-changed town, he finds that Jiazhen earns a living by delivering water door to door. An illness has left their daughter, Fengxia, deaf. And their son, Youqing, is a spirited boy who becomes the victim of his father's desperate need to disguise his past as a wealthy man.

This film is also less sumptuously photographed than Mr. Zhang's other works; in the lives of these characters, touches of red on a gray uniform have to pass for glamour. Depicting the characters responding to Mao's changes, *To Live* brings to mind Chen Kaige's *Farewell, My Concubine,* though set among poor townspeople rather than against the rich backdrop of the Beijing Opera. In its emphasis on individuals, *To Live* has less in common with Mr. Zhang's earlier, less dramatic films, *Red Sorghum* and *Ju Dou,* than with his recent ones, the glorious soap opera *Raise the Red Lantern* and the comic tale of a rebellious woman, *The Story of Qiu Ju.* (All of them starring Gong Li.)

But the masterly Mr. Zhang knows he's creating melodrama and exaggerates to profound effect. The family tragedies in *To Live* demonstrate how China's politics scarred individuals who were treated as pawns in Mao's progress, and its sentimentality shows that ideology is no comfort in the face of personal anguish. In two magnificent performances, Gong Li carries the story's emotions and Ge You the weight of history. Gong Li is, as always, a powerful heroine. But Mr. Ge is a revelation, evoking sympathy and pity as a man whose weakness causes him to bend like a reed in the changing winds of Chinese politics and whose strength allows him to endure the consequences.

During the Great Leap Forward in the 1950's (the historical changes are explained clearly in succinct titles through the film), the entire town donates all metal objects to support steel production. Even the family's pans are taken away, and everyone eats at the communal kitchen. That is where the mischievous Youqing pours a huge amount of chili sauce on a big bowl of noodles, then calmly dumps it on the head of a boy who has been taunting his sister. For that, Fugui publicly spanks his son, agreeing that the little boy's gesture was a counterrevolutionary act meant to undermine the communal kitchen.

Irreverent though Mr. Zhang's take on Chinese history is, *To Live* is primarily a story of living with sadness. Fugui's old friend Chungsheng becomes a district leader and accidentally causes a death. "You owe us a life," Jiazhen screams at him, and the line becomes a refrain that resonates through the film.

In the sixties, during the Cultural Revolution, Fugui and Jiazhen hear that their prospective son-in-law, a committed Maoist, is tearing their house apart. They race home only to find him helpfully repairing the roof and painting huge murals of Mao on the walls. Throughout, Mr. Zhang creates an inescapable sense of the tension and fear that informs the characters' daily lives.

The Communist revolution is increasingly blamed for the family's tragedies. When someone dies because the reactionary doctors have been taken away from the hospital, leaving only inept students behind, there is no mistaking the political toughness of this melodrama's message.

This film has created serious problems for Mr. Zhang. The Chinese government was unhappy that *To Live* was entered in competition at this year's Cannes Film Festival, where Gong Li and Ge You were present and won best acting awards. In the last few weeks, the government has stopped production on Mr. Zhang's new movie, partly financed with French money, and barred him from working on foreign coproductions.

To Live will be shown at the New York Film Festival tonight and tomorrow night, and is scheduled to open commercially in November. It would be an extravagant and emotional film, even if it weren't a politically brave one too.

—*C.J., September 30, 1994*

TOKYO STORY

Directed by Yasujiro Ozu: written (in Japanese. with English subtitles) by Mr. Ozu and Kogo Noda: cinematographer. Yuharu Atsuta: edited by Yoshiyasu Hamamura: music by Kojun Saito: production designer. Tatsuo Hamada: produced by Takeshi Yamamoto: released by New Yorker Films. Black and white. Running time: 136 minutes.

With: Chishu Ryu (Old Father). Chiyeko Higashiyama (Old Mother). So Yamamura (Married Son). Haruko Sugimura (Married Daughter). Setsuko Hara (Widowed Daughter-in-Law). Kyoko Kagawa (Younger Daughter) and Shiro Osaka (Younger Son).

I am not sure how to introduce yet again a director who died nine years ago, whose name should be familiar to all film lovers, but who remains virtually unknown—except to say that *Tokyo Story*, another great movie by Yasujiro Ozu, opened yesterday at the New Yorker Theater. Made in 1952, it is the earliest of the three (out of more than fifty) Ozu features that have so far had local premieres.

Even on the basis of a limited exposure to his work, the story seems archetypal Ozu. An old couple living in the southern Japanese port city of Onomichi take their first trip to Tokyo, to visit their married children. The children—a neighborhood doctor and a beautician—are tolerant, but preoccupied and a little put out by the old folks' visit, and only a non-relation, the widowed daughter-in-law of their son lost in the war, makes them feel welcome.

After several days and a few small adventures, the parents return home. But on the train the mother takes sick, the children are summoned and shortly afterward she dies, surrounded by her family, "peacefully, without suffering and full of years," in the words of her somewhat disagreeable married daughter. The daughter-in-law stays the longest after the funeral, but eventually even she must leave, and the father settles quietly into the loneliness that is to be his life.

It is important to remark the characteristic look of the Ozu movies—the product of an almost immobile camera usually shooting from a low position, and the absolute rejection of such sleights of cinema as the fade or the dissolve—and to note that this look is in itself an example of the seemly patience the films mean to invoke. *Tokyo Story* really deals with three generations passing through life, but mostly with the generation that is passing out of it, and it understands that a calm reticence may be the true heroism of ordinary old age.

"Isn't life disappointing," observes the family's younger daughter, an unmarried schoolteacher who lives at home. "Yes, it is," answers the daughter-in-law, and the two of them smile with a cheerful, slightly embarrassed sense of misery. An anthology of Ozu's scenes of shared understanding between young women would constitute one of the glories of world cinema. But in context this scene, very near the end of *Tokyo Story*, essentially completes a view of normal life that is luminous in its freedom from the sentimentality or the satire that so often obscure an artist's vision of normal living.

Ozu will sometimes return to a room or a passageway, now empty, where, a few moments earlier, people had been seen. It is not nostalgia, so much as an acknowledgment that places are sanctified by people and that even when they have gone away, a bit of their presence lingers on.

Those people, at least in *Tokyo Story*, are marvelous and they are played by actors so wholly of their parts that it is all but impossible to think of them in other roles in other movies—though they do in fact make up part of an Ozu stock company.

Just for the record I should like to give credit to Setsuko Hara as the gracious daughter-in-law; Chiyeko Higashiyama as the mother; and Chishu Ryu, surely one of the most beautiful actors in Japanese film, as the father who lives so gently beyond his time.

—*R.G., March 14, 1972*

TOM JONES

Produced and directed by Tony Richardson; written by John Osborne, based on the novel by Henry Fielding; cinematographer, Walter Lassally; edited by Anthony Gibbs; music by John Addison; production designer, Ralph Brinton; released by Lopert Pictures. Running time: 135 minutes.

With: Albert Finney (Tom Jones), Susannah York (Sophie Western), Hugh Griffith (Squire Western), Dame Edith Evans (Miss Western), Joan Greenwood (Lady Bellaston), Diane Cilento (Molly) and Joyce Redman (Mrs. Waters).

Prepare yourself for what is surely one of the wildest, bawdiest and funniest comedies that a refreshingly agile filmmaker has ever brought to the screen. It is Tony Richardson's production of Henry Fielding's classic novel, *Tom Jones,* and it arrived yesterday for what I reckon should be at least a six-month run at Cinema 1.

But is it *Tom Jones?* Well, that voluminous and wonderfully entertaining tale of the social and amorous adventures of a young buck in England in the eighteenth century is the narrative source of the picture. And most of its major episodes recounting life in the beautiful west country and in fashionable London are packed into the film.

But in finding a means of cinema expression in which to convey most suitably to our age the deceptively fastidious rhetoric and ribald wit of the Fielding work, Mr. Richardson and his scenarist, John Osborne of *Angry Young Man* fame, have worked out a structure and a rhythm that constitute a major creative achievement in themselves.

Their attack on the lusty old novel is completely away from the line of a standard-movie treatment, with its usual endeavor to put a naturalistic reproduction of the original into pictorial terms. And they have whipped up a roaring entertainment that develops its own energy as much from its cinematic gusto as from the racy material it presents.

At the very beginning, for instance, before the main title comes on, they serve astonishing notice that this is to be a lark in movie terms. Home comes the righteous Squire Allworthy to find a bawling infant in his bed and the hint of an amatory scandal lurking somewhere below his stairs.

But do you think this conventional prologue is done in conventional style? Not at all! It is done in mock depictment of an old melodramatic silent film, with the action fast and the cutting frequent, printed titles instead of dialogue and a wild din of spinnet music setting an antique tone. And then, as the camera hits a close-up of the baby and as the title is superimposed, the voice of a primly sly narrator comes in to say, "Tom Jones, of whom the opinion of all was that he was born to be hanged."

Now it takes off, some years later, with Tom a lusty young man, played with a wonderfully open, guileless and raffish attitude by the brilliant new star, Albert Finney (who is now playing Martin Luther on Broadway), bounding through earthy adventures as Squire Allworthy's ward. And the breakneck pace set in the prologue is miraculously maintained to the measures of a highly contributive musical accompaniment composed by John Addison.

Mr. Addison's score, so full of mischief, instrumental and melodic, swings along with the breathtaking tempo of the action and with Mr. Richardson's camera techniques, which are really most apt revitalizations of flavorsome tricks and stunts.

For instance, he loves to cut an action with a fast across-the-frame or clock-hand wipe or to stop the action at a climactic moment for a split-second freeze before jumping on to the next scene. He will frame a character's face in an iris. He will even have his actors address the audience in "asides" as when Tom, suspicious of a woman innkeeper, turns to the audience and asks, "Did you see her take fifty pounds from me pocket?" At another point, when Tom is about to embrace the utterly abandoned Mrs. Waters, he considerately places his cap over the eye of the camera.

By such prankish devices, Mr. Richardson gives his film the speed and, indeed, somewhat the character of a Keystone comedy. He conveys, in these cinematic comments, an even fuller enjoyment of the absurd. His is a twentieth-century means of characterizing eighteenth-century manners and morals.

And what manners and morals he shows us, what characters and episodes! There's the big, brawling fight in the churchyard over Molly, the incorrigible slut (a word often used with rich expression). There's Squire Western's roaring deer hunt, with the camera handheld and pitching wildly in the midst of the huntsmen and hounds or flying over the scene (in a helicopter), surveying the madness below. There's the pell-mell explosion of characters, righteous and unrighteous, through the halls of the Upton inn after an irate husband has discovered a bit of scandalous going-on.

And what acting! We have mentioned Mr. Finney.

He is tops in the title role, but Hugh Griffith is his match as Squire Western, the snorting, cursing, barnyard-mannered goat. Mr. Griffith is everything that Fielding intended him to be—fire-eater, hypocrite, lecher—with a madcap style of his own.

Susannah York as his daughter—the lovely Sophie whom Tom hopes to wed—is a warm little package of passions; Diane Cilento is all teeth and claws as the insatiable Molly; Joyce Redman is brazen and bold as the naughty Mrs. Waters, and in one incomparable scene Mr. Richardson has her and Mr. Finney make eating a meal an act so lewd, yet so utterly clever and unassailable, that it is one of the highlights in the film.

Oh, there are a dozen others that should be mentioned—Joan Greenwood as Lady Bellaston, George Devine as Squire Allworthy, Dame Edith Evans as the sister of Squire Western, David Warner as the insidious Blifil, and many more. There's the excellent color photography and the amusing costuming that should be praised. There's even the new "cliff-hanger" ending that Fielding himself might have generously enjoyed.

Perhaps there will be those who will be embarrassed by so much bawdiness on the screen. But I find it too funny to be tasteless, too true to be artistically false. And, what's more, it should set a lot of people to reading that incomparable novel, *Tom Jones*.

—*B.C., October 8, 1963*

TOOTSIE

Directed by Sydney Pollack; written by Larry Gelbart and Murray Schisgal, based on a story by Don McGuire and Mr. Gelbart; director of photography, Owen Roizman; edited by Fredric Steinkamp and William Steinkamp; music by Dave Grusin; production designer, Peter Larkin; produced by Mr. Pollack and Dick Richards; released by Columbia Pictures. Running time: 110 minutes.

With: Dustin Hoffman (Michael Dorsey/Dorothy Michaels), Jessica Lange (Julie), Teri Garr (Sandy), Dabney Coleman (Ron), Charles Durning (Les), Bill Murray (Jeff), Sydney Pollack (George Fields), George Gaynes (John Van Horn), Geena Davis (April) and Doris Belack (Rita).

After twenty years as a mostly unemployed New York actor, Michael Dorsey (Dustin Hoffman) is desperate. He makes ends meet by teaching acting classes and then, in his spare time, auditioning for parts he never gets. Michael's worst problem is that he's "difficult." He insists on providing more subtext for a role than any director wants. He's the sort of actor who, when playing a tomato in a television commercial, angrily refuses to sit down because, as he insists, "tomatoes don't move."

At the beginning of Sydney Pollack's rollicking, hip new comedy, *Tootsie,* Michael Dorsey is at the end of his rope. When Sandy (Teri Garr), an actress friend, is turned down for a role on a television soap opera, Michael decides to prove just how great his talents are.

He goes home, applies some spectacular makeup, puts on a fussy reddish-brown wig, a suitable dress, high heels and harlequin glasses. Thus disguised, he looks like an efficient, middle-aged dietitian with a sense of style. He pushes his way into the audition and, affecting a slight Southern accent, not only wins the role on the soap, a hospital drama called *Southwest General,* but becomes an overnight star of daytime television.

This is the gimmick of *Tootsie,* and it's best gotten out of the way immediately because, unlike most such comedies, *Tootsie* has a lot more going for it than its gimmick. It's neither a drag show nor a knockabout comedy on the classic order of *Charley's Aunt.* Also, it shouldn't be compared to the elegant farce of Blake Edwards's *Victor/Victoria.*

Tootsie restores the original meaning to the term "situation comedy," free of the pejorative associations that have accrued over the years because of the glut of awful ones on television. Mr. Pollack and the writers of the screenplay, Larry Gelbart and Murray Schisgal, have taken a wildly improbable situation and found just about all of its comic possibilities, not by exaggerating the obvious, but by treating it with inspired common sense.

An important part of their success is Mr. Hoffman's grand performance as both the edgy, cantankerous Michael Dorsey and the serenely self-assured Dorothy Michaels, the stage name he takes on the soap, a character for whom the unappreciated Michael has obviously created a whole lifetime of subtext.

Dorothy does not wobble around on her high heels—she very carefully measures her small steps.

Her bra never gets knocked off-center, though she's rather tense when people get physical with her. When someone asks, not unkindly, why she wears such heavy makeup, she acknowledges that she has an unsightly mustache.

Dorothy is not a parody female. She's crazy idealization. She is almost frighteningly well groomed, as if she had followed every beauty hint ever given. She's also intelligent, understanding and not about to be pushed around by any male chauvinist pigs. Since Michael himself is a pig, this new, dual awareness of his gives the comedy unexpected sweetness.

There's a marvelous moment in the middle of the film when Michael, out of drag, admits to his friend Jeff (Bill Murray), a playwright, that he was at first disappointed when he realized his Dorothy Michaels would never be a beauty.

Dorothy may not be a beauty, but she possesses a bigness of heart and a no-nonsense approach to her life and career that Michael himself lacks. As she becomes a soap-opera personality, she also wins the friendship of one of her costars, Julie (Jessica Lange), who plays the trampish registered nurse on the show, and then rouses the passions of Julie's widowed father (Charles Durning). The fact that Michael-Dorothy has fallen in love with Julie provides the crisis that leads to the film's hilarious climax, played live to a nationwide audience.

Beginning with Mr. Pollack and Mr. Hoffman, no one connected with Tootsie has ever done anything quite like this before. Every member of the cast is splendid. Miss Lange is a total delight in a comedy role to which she brings the same sort of intelligent gravity that distinguishes her work in *Frances.* George Gaynes, known principally for his work on Broadway and television, is priceless as the seedy but tirelessly lecherous leading man on the soap.

Both Bill Murray and Teri Garr have had much larger, more flamboyant roles in other films, but neither has ever appeared to such rich advantage as in *Tootsie.* Doing what they've done before, but beautifully, are Mr. Durning and Dabney Coleman, who plays the highest-priced soap opera director in all television.

In addition to maintaining the discipline that keeps *Tootsie* on track from start to finish, Mr. Pollack also turns up in a small but vividly funny role as Michael's unfriendly agent.

Tootsie, which opens today at the Paramount and Loew's Tower East Theaters, is the best thing that's yet happened at this year end. It's a toot, a lark, a month in the country.

—*V.C., December 17, 1982*

TOP HAT

Directed by Mark Sandrich; written by Dwight Taylor and Allan Scott, based on the musical *The Gay Divorcee* by Mr. Taylor and Cole Porter and the play *The Girl Who Dared* by Alexander Farago; cinematographer, David Abel; edited by William Hamilton; music by Irving Berlin; choreography by Fred Astaire and Hermes Pan; art designer, Van Nest Polglase; produced by Pandro S. Berman; released by RKO Radio Pictures. Black and white. Running time: 101 minutes.

With: Fred Astaire (Jerry Travers), Ginger Rogers (Dale Tremont), Edward Everett Horton (Horace Hardwick), Helen Broderick (Madge Hardwick), Erik Rhodes (Alberto), Eric Blore (Bates) and Donald Meek (Curate).

Fred Astaire, the dancing master, and Miss Rogers, his ideal partner, bring all their joyous gifts to the new song and dance show at the Radio City Music Hall. Irving Berlin has written some charming melodies for the photoplay and the best of the current cinema teams does them agile justice on the dance floor. When *Top Hat* is letting Mr. Astaire perform his incomparable magic or teaming him with the increasingly dexterous Miss Rogers it is providing the most urbane fun that you will find anywhere on the screen. If the comedy itself is a little on the thin side, it is sprightly enough to plug those inevitable gaps between the shimmeringly gay dances.

Last year this column suggested that Miss Jessie Matthews would make a better partner for the debonair star than our own home girl. Please consider the matter dropped. Miss Rogers, improving magnificently from picture to picture, collaborates perfectly with Mr. Astaire in *Top Hat* and is entitled to keep the job for life. Their comic duet in the bandstand, danced to the lyric music of "Isn't This a Lovely Day," and their romantic adagio in the beautiful "Cheek to Cheek" song are among the major contributions of the show. In his solo flights, when he is abandoning his feet to the strains of "Fancy Free" or lulling Miss Rogers to sleep with the overpowering opiate of his sandman arrangement, Mr. Astaire is at his impeccable best. Then there is the "Top Hat, White Tie and Tails" number, which fortifies the star with a chorus of gentlemen of the evening and makes for a highly satisfying time.

The narrative complication which keeps the lovers apart for ninety minutes will have to go down as one of the most flimsily prolonged romantic misunderstandings of the season. Mr. Astaire, star of a London show, is occupying a hotel suite with his manager, the jittery Edward Everett Horton, at the time he falls in love with Miss Rogers. Somehow the lady becomes convinced, as ladies will, that Mr. Astaire is the one who is married to her friend, Helen Broderick, when all the time it is Mr. Horton. By a miracle of attenuation this mistaken identity persists in complicating matters all through the picture, causing Miss Rogers to slap Mr. Astaire's face vigorously every time he catches up with her, Miss Broderick to poke the unfortunate Mr. Horton in the eye and the passionate Latin, Erik Rhodes, to make terrifying lunges in all direction with a bared rapier. An amusing but largely undeveloped secondary theme in the film concerns Mr. Horton's feud with his manservant, Eric Blore, whereby the two manage not to be on speaking terms despite the intimacy of their life.

All the minor players are such skilled comedians that they are able to extract merriment from this none too original comedy of errors. Miss Broderick, that infamously funny lady, has too little support, though, from the script. *Top Hat,* after running almost its entire course with admirable restraint, collapses into one of those mammoth choral arrangements toward the end. It isn't worth ten seconds of the delightful Astaire-Rogers duet during the thunderstorm. Anyway, *Top Hat* is worth standing in line for. From the appearance of the lobby yesterday afternoon, you probably will have to.

—*A.S., August 30, 1935*

TOPAZ

Produced and directed by Alfred Hitchcock; written by Samuel Taylor, based on the novel by Leon

Uris: cinematographer. Jack Hildyard: edited by William Ziegler: music by Maurice Jarre: production designer. Henry Bumstead: released by Universal Pictures. Running time: 126 minutes.

With: Frederick Stafford (Andre Devereaux). Dany Robin (Nicole Devereaux). John Vernon (Rico Parra). Karin Dor (Juanita de Cordoba). Michel Piccoli (Jacques Granville). Philippe Noiret (Henri Jarre). Claude Jade (Michele Picard). Michel Subor (François Picard) and John Forsythe (Michael Nordstrom).

It's perfectly apparent from its opening sequence that no one except Alfred Hitchcock, the wise, round, supremely confident storyteller, is in charge of *Topaz,* the film that opened yesterday at the Cinerama Theater. *Topaz,* the code name for a Russian spy ring within the French government, is the film adaptation of the Leon Uris novel, which itself was based on a real-life espionage scandal that kept both sides of the Atlantic busy in 1962.

Hitchcock sets his scene in a first act that dramatizes the defection of a high Soviet intelligence officer to C.I.A. officials in Copenhagen. The sequence, which lasts approximately ten minutes and uses only a minimum of dialogue, is virtuoso Hitchcock, beginning with a dazzling, single-take pan shot outside the Soviet embassy, then detailing the flight, pursuit through, among other things, a ceramics factory and the final safe arrival of the irritable Soviet official and his family aboard an American plane headed for Wiesbaden. The Russian's only comment to the proud C.I.A. man: "We would have done it better."

Topaz is not a conventional Hitchcock film. It's rather too leisurely and the machinations of plot rather too convoluted to be easily summed up in anything except a very loose sentence. Being pressed, I'd say that it's about espionage as a kind of game, set in Washington, Havana and Paris at the time of the Cuban missile crisis, involving a number of dedicated people in acts of courage, sacrifice and death, after which the survivors find themselves pretty much where they were when they started, except that they are older, tired and a little less capable of being happy.

Topaz is, however, quite pure Hitchcock, a movie of beautifully composed sequences, full of surface tensions, ironies, absurdities (some hungry seagulls blow

the cover of two Allied agents), as well as of odd references to things such as Michelangelo's *Pietà,* only it's not a Mother holding her dead Son, but a middle-aged Cuban wife holding her dead husband, after they've been tortured in a Castro prison.

Hitchcock, who can barely tolerate actors, has been especially self-indulgent in the casting of *Topaz.* The film has no one on the order of James Stewart or Cary Grant on which to depend, although it does use some fine character actors (Michel Piccoli, Philippe Noiret) in small roles. Most of its performers are, if not entirely unknown, so completely subordinate to their roles that they seem, perhaps unfairly, quite forgettable.

Frederick Stafford, who plays a Washington-based French intelligence man (and is more or less the lead), and John Forsythe, his counterpart in the Central Intelligence Agency, have all the panache of well-tailored salesmen of electrical appliances. Dany Robin, cast as Stafford's worried wife, and Claude Jade, who was so lovely in Truffaut's *Stolen Kisses,* and who here plays Stafford's worried daughter, frown quite a lot.

The people one remembers are those who are employed for the effect of their looks (John Vernon as a bearded Castro aide with brilliant blue eyes; Carlos Rivas as his bodyguard, a Cuban with remarkably red hair), or who are bequeathed vivid images by the narrative (Karin Dor as a beautiful anti-Castro Cuban who is shot for her efforts and collapses onto a marble floor, her body framed by the brilliant purple of her dress).

The star of *Topaz* is Hitchcock, who, except for his brief, signature appearance, remains just off-screen, manipulating our emotions as well as our memories of so many other Hitchcock films, including *Foreign Correspondent, Saboteur* and *Torn Curtain,* all inferior to *Topaz.* This is a movie of superb sequences that lead from a magnificent Virginia mansion to the Hotel Theresa in Harlem, from an extraordinarily well-stocked Cuban hacienda to a small, claustrophobic, upstairs dining room in a Paris restaurant. Even architecture is important.

It's also a movie of classic Hitchcock effects. Exposition may be gotten across by being presented either as gossip or as incidental, postcoital small talk. Conversations are often seen—but not heard—through glass doors. A Cuban government minister, staying at the Theresa, finds a misplaced state document being used as a hamburger napkin.

The film is so free of contemporary cinematic clichés, so reassuring in its choice of familiar espionage gadgetry (remote control cameras, geiger counters), that it tends to look extremely conservative, politically. *Topaz,* however, is really above such things. It uses politics the way Hitchcock uses actors—for its own ends, without making any real commitments to it. *Topaz* is not only most entertaining. It is, like so many Hitchcock films, a cautionary fable by one of the most moral cynics of our time.

—*V.C., December 20, 1969*

TOPKAPI

Produced and directed by Jules Dassin; written (in French, with English subtitles) by Monja Danischewsky, based on the novel *The Light of Day* by Eric Ambler; cinematographer, Henri Alekan; edited by Roger Dwyre; music by Manos Hadjidakis; art designer, Max Douy; released by United Artists. Running time: 120 minutes.

With: Melina Mercouri (Elizabeth Lipp), Peter Ustinov (Arthur Simpson), Maximilian Schell (William Walter), Robert Morley (Cedric Page), Akim Tamiroff (Geven) and Gilles Segal (Giulio).

Imagine Jules Dassin's *Rififi* done in the spirit and style of his comical *Never on Sunday* and you have a good idea of the nature of his latest film, *Topkapi* (pronounced top-cappy), which breezed into the Astor and the Trans-Lux East yesterday. It is another adroitly plotted crime film, played this time for guffaws, and if you don't split something, either laughing or squirming in suspense, we'll be surprised.

We'll also be surprised if you're not dazzled by the extravagantly colorful decor and the brilliantly atmospheric setting, which happens to be Istanbul. This is the first time Mr. Dassin has used color on a film, and he is like a child with a new paint box. He has gone absolutely wild.

He starts with Melina Mercouri in a spotless, white tailored costume emerging like a figure in a waxworks out of a mélange of dancing colored lights to proclaim that she's a thief with a project, which is to rob the Topkapi Palace Museum in Istanbul. Then he cuts to an emerald-studded dagger, glittering golden and green, attached to the costume of a sultan that stands in a locked glass case in the museum. This is the object of her project, the goad to her desire.

Now she recruits her burglars. Out of a purple-blue mist on a Paris quai floats a handsome rascal, Maximilian Schell. He insists that their team be composed entirely of amateurs. It is nighttime and now we're in a boudoir, where red and lavender lights play.

Thus Mr. Dassin gets things started in an ambiance of colors that suggests elegance, richness, romance and—most of all—make-believe. Robert Morley, an English lord, is pulled in. He is an eccentric scientist, expert at building gadgets. He will attend to the machinery by which the burglars will drop from the ceiling of the museum and pluck the dagger from its case.

Two muscle men are recruited next. They are Gilles Segal and Jess Hahn. A tourist guide in a Greek seaport is roped in to drive a car. Bless them for picking this fellow, for he is Peter Ustinov, and he is the funniest, most delightful character. He is the salvation of the film.

Indeed, it is his misadventures and confusions and frights that truly make this picture something more than melodrama with a farcical edge. He makes it a joyous sort of travesty of the bad art of burglary. To see Mr. Ustinov sweating through his mischance encounters with the Turkish police, or playing the role of stool pigeon while running with the gang, or climbing about the roof of the palace under the heavy influence of vertigo, with the Golden Horn in the distance, is to see first-class comedy.

Mr. Morley is likewise amusing, but in a more obvious way, and Akim Tamiroff breaks in for a couple of wild scenes as a drunken and rowdy Russian cook. Mr. Schell plays the leader deftly, and Miss Mercouri is along for the ride. She is basically an indulgence and adornment, like those colored lights.

Being something of a musical-comedy pastiche, this is not one of Mr. Dassin's finer films. But it is a diverting entertainment.

Incidentally, it is based on an Eric Ambler tale.

—*B.C., September 18, 1964*

TOPSY-TURVY

Written and directed by Mike Leigh: director of photography. Dick Pope: edited by Robin Sales: music by Carl Davis, from the works of Arthur Sullivan: production designer. Eve Stewart: produced by Simon Channing-Williams: released by USA Films. Running time: 160 minutes.

With: Dorothy Atkinson (Jessie Bond), Jim Broadbent (W. S. Gilbert), Ron Cook (Richard D'Oyly Carte), Allan Corduner (Arthur Sullivan), Eleanor David (Fanny Ronalds), Shirley Henderson (Leonora Braham), Lesley Manville (Lucy Gilbert), Kevin McKidd (Durward Lely), Wendy Nottingham (Helen Lenoir), Martin Savage (George Grossmith), Timothy Spall (Richard Temple) and Alison Steadman (Madame Leon).

Mike Leigh's grandly entertaining *Topsy-Turvy* is one of those films that create a mix of erudition, pageantry and delectable acting opportunities, much as *Shakespeare in Love* did last year. Instead of a lovestruck young playwright, it presents the curiously matched personalities of the librettist William Schwenk Gilbert and the composer Arthur Sullivan in the midst of a robust, knowing, frequently hilarious look at the musical theater over which they held sway.

Mr. Leigh orchestrates this delightful film so well that he fittingly presents his own directorial credit just as Sullivan, preparing to conduct the new operetta *Princess Ida* in 1884, takes an introductory bow.

This is an interesting place for the story of *Topsy-Turvy* to start. Because when *Princess Ida* turns out to be a dud, it means a dead end for the Gilbert and Sullivan oeuvre and a challenge to these established hit-makers to reinvent themselves rather late in the game. Mr. Leigh and his large array of performers, who obviously lived and breathed their roles before filming (in keeping with the filmmaker's customary method), vigorously and amusingly explore what it means for an artist to renew his energies by returning to square one.

As the film begins, the newly knighted Sir Arthur Sullivan (the excellent Allan Corduner) has begun to turn away from the kind of comic operetta that won him wealth and celebrity. He has also grown so distant from the not-yet-titled Gilbert that the two men do not cross paths until well into the story. The dour Gilbert, played with wonderfully literate crankiness by Jim Broadbent, is too prim and stubborn to understand his partner's dissatisfaction. Only when the famous impresario Richard D'Oyly Carte (Ron Cook) tries to force his stars to settle their differences does Gilbert have to acknowledge a problem.

Though the differences between these two strong personalities are deftly captured, *Topsy-Turvy* (which takes its title from Sullivan's dismissive view of Gilbert's tidy plot contrivances) is much bigger than their story. Its aspirations are thrilling in their own right. Mr. Leigh's gratifyingly long view of life in the theater (Gilbert has a dentist who tells him *Princess Ida* could have been shorter) includes not only historical and biographical details but also the painstaking process of creating a Gilbert and Sullivan production from the ground up. The film details all this with the luxury of a leisurely pace, as opposed to a slow one.

The Gilbert and Sullivan turnaround begins with a lightning bolt of inspiration, in the form of a London exhibition on Japanese culture. Gilbert's wife (Lesley Manville) drags him to see this, and somewhere in the midst of the kimonos and Kabuki, *The Mikado* is born. The latter half of *Topsy-Turvy* describes everything about creating this operetta, as in a wonderful sequence that creates the famous fluttering and tippy-toeing to "Three Little Maids From School."

Then there are Gilbert's priceless ideas about how to direct actors. Mr. Broadbent's role is beautifully written ("I'm sure we shall reap the benefits of your remonstrations in the fullness of time," he tells one complainer), as is the actors' side of the story. One performer is heard to complain about management, "particularly when the management have difficulty in locating the various whereabouts" of the posterior and the elbow.

As *The Mikado* takes shape, the film offers exultant excerpts performed by actors who are as comfortable in full stage regalia as they are behind the scenes. Well trained by Gilbert to pronounce words like "persiflage" and "corroborative," the performers (a fine troupe including Timothy Spall, Shirley Henderson and familiar faces from earlier Leigh films) make it a palpable triumph. But for Gilbert, who calls his mother "the vicious woman who bore me into this ridiculous world," there are no happy endings.

"There's something inherently disappointing about success," he insists.

—J.M., October 2, 1999

TOTAL RECALL

Directed by Paul Verhoeven; written by Ronald Shusett, Dan O'Bannon and Gary Goldman, based on a story by Mr. Shusett, Mr. O'Bannon and Jon Povill and a short story "We Can Remember it for You Wholesale" by Philip K. Dick; director of photography, Jost Vacano; edited by Frank J. Urioste; music by Jerry Goldsmith; production designer, William Sandell; produced by Buzz Feitshans and Mr. Shusett; released by Tri-Star Pictures. Running time: 116 minutes.

With: Arnold Schwarzenegger (Quaid), Rachel Ticotin (Melina), Sharon Stone (Lori), Ronny Cox (Cohaagen), Michael Ironside (Richter), Marshall Bell (George/Kuato) and Mel Johnson Jr. (Benny).

In *Total Recall,* Arnold Schwarzenegger finds himself facing an existential quandary. It is the twenty-first century, and the technology of the day makes it possible for fully formed memories to be inserted into the minds of unsuspecting victims. So is Mr. Schwarzenegger actually a happily married construction worker named Doug Quaid? Or is Doug Quaid's whole identity a convenient fiction? Does he live on earth, as he appears to, or does he have another existence on Mars? Is he a person, or is he a dream?

Fifty million dollars' worth of exploding glass, blazing bullets, ear-splitting noises and sometimes clever, sometimes gut-wrenching special effects say that Mr. Schwarzenegger is no figment of anyone's imagination except, possibly, his own. *Total Recall* is a thunderous tribute to its star's determination to create, out of the unlikeliest raw materials, a patently synthetic yet surprisingly affable leading man. Melding the ever-more-workable Schwarzenegger mystique with a better-than-average science-fiction premise, the director Paul Verhoeven has come up with a vigorous, super-violent interplanetary thriller that packs in wallops with metronomic regularity. Mr. Verhoeven is much better at drumming up this sort of artificial excitement than he is at knowing when to stop.

Doug Quaid's troubles begin when he visits Rekall Inc., a space-age travel agency specializing in no-fuss, no-muss vacations. But when Doug, who is haunted by mysterious dreams of a red-hued life on Mars, agrees to buy two weeks' worth of Martian travel imagery that is "first-class" and "complete in every detail," something goes haywire. An apparently real set of memories is activated, throwing Doug's earthly existence into turmoil and eventually sending him to Mars to resolve his problems. Mars, he discovers, is a seamy, mutant-filled colony that is racked with rebellion and ruled by a tyrant (Ronny Cox) who charges exorbitant prices for air.

The first half of *Total Recall* (screenplay by Ronald Shusett, Dan O'Bannon and Gary Goldman from a story by Philip K. Dick) is the film's introductory phase, which toys ingeniously with gimmicks like household holograms and robot-driven taxis as it outlines the interesting confusion inside Quaid's mind. This culminates in a riveting scene, the film's best, in which a doctor (Roy Brocksmith) visits Quaid in his Martian hotel room and tells him that he is still dreaming, and still in fact at the Rekall offices. When Quaid fails to believe this, the doctor scathingly accuses him of being someone who imagines himself "the victim of an interplanetary conspiracy to make him think he's a lowly construction worker on earth." At this point, the film provides some helpful guidelines for differentiating flesh-and-blood doctors from imaginary ones.

Later on, though, *Total Recall* disintegrates into a string of gruesome shootouts, punctuated by interludes in the sleazy Martian hangouts that make this kiddie-minded film unsuitable for small children. A three-breasted whore is the film's idea of a witty mutation, and indeed all the malformed creatures populating this section of the film bespeak an off-putting fondness for the grotesque. By the time the story's number of plot reversals has become almost as astronomical as its body count, any audience may wind up repelled and exhausted. The attempts to leaven the story with humor, like the scene that shows Mr. Schwarzenegger in a dress, are not much help.

The visual style of *Total Recall,* which in its latter stages is loaded with gargantuan, grayish machine-shop imagery and filled with ever-more-sickening cosmetic touches, is wearing in its own way. Continually upping the special-effects ante, Mr. Verhoeven saves the eye-popping and hand-severing for last, not to mention a mutant character who appears as a slimy infant troll attached to another character's stomach. Showing a foot stepping on a bleeding, quivering corpse is more characteristic of the film's violence. This sort of thing happens early, and often.

Among the film's less than admirable aspects is its conception of the two principal women in the story. Sharon Stone as Quaid's earthly wife and Rachel Ticotin as his Martian sweetheart play hybrid hooker-commandos who eventually engage in a savage slug-out. Another is its concept of a nuclear reactor as something that can quite literally clean up the atmosphere, wipe out pollution and bring about blue skies. Have a nice day.

Total Recall, which can already be thought of as *Total Recall I,* includes an exceptionally large and fair-minded assortment of product plugs. Featured noticeably is Coca-Cola, the previous parent company of Tri-Star Pictures, which is the film's distributor. The new owner, Sony, gets a product plug, too.

—*J.M., June 1, 1990*

TOUCH OF EVIL

Directed by Orson Welles; written by Mr. Welles. based on the novel *Badge of Evil* by Whit Masterson; cinematographer, Russell Metty; edited by Virgil Vogel and Aaron Stell; music by Henry Mancini; art designers, Alexander Golitzen and Robert Clatworthy; produced by Alfred Zugsmith; released by Universal International Pictures. Running time: 95 minutes.

With: Charlton Heston (Ramon Vargas), Orson Welles (Hank Quinlan), Janet Leigh (Susan Vargas), Joseph Calleia (Pete Menzies), Akim Tamiroff (Uncle Joe Grandi), Ray Collins (Adair) and Dennis Weaver (Night Watchman).

Thanks to Orson Welles, nobody, and we mean nobody, will nap during *Touch of Evil,* which opened yesterday at RKO theaters. Just try.

The credits come on, for instance, to a sleepy, steady rumba rhythm as a convertible quietly plies the main street of a Mexican border town. The car is rigged with dynamite. And so, as a yarn-spinning

director, is the extremely corpulent Mr. Welles, who costars with Charlton Heston and Janet Leigh in this Universal release.

Mr. Welles also adapted the novel by Whit Masterson called *Badge of Evil* (which would have been more like it), helping himself to the juicy role of a fanatical Texas cop who frames a Mexican youth for murder, and clashes with an indignant Mexican sleuth, Mr. Heston. In addition to battling Mr. Welles, a psychopath who runs the town, Mr. Heston has to fend off a vengeful narcotics gang menacing his young bride, Miss Leigh.

Any other competent director might have culled a pretty good, well-acted melodrama from such material, with the suspense dwindling as justice begins to triumph (as happens here). Mr. Welles's is an obvious but brilliant bag of tricks. Using a superlative camera (manned by Russell Metty) like a black-snake whip, he lashes the action right into the spectator's eye.

The careful groupings of the cast, the overlapping of the speeches and other stylized trademarks of the director's Mercury Players unit are here. But the tempo, at least in the first half, is plain mercurial, as befits a thriller.

Where Mr. Welles soundly succeeds is in generating enough sinister electricity for three such yarns and in generally staging it like a wild, murky nightmare. Miss Leigh has the most bloodcurdling time of all in two sequences, one involving a strangulation in a hotel room. The other—her siege by some young punks in an isolated motel—should make any viewer leery of border accommodations for a long time to come.

However, while good versus evil remains the text, the lasting impression of this film is effect rather than substance, hence its real worth. The cunningly designed climax, for instance, barely alludes to the framed youth at the outset (in a fine, ironic twist, by the way). The entire unsavory supporting cast is excellent, including such people as Joseph Calleia, Akim Tamiroff and Ray Collins. Marlene Dietrich, as an incidental "guest star," wisely advises Mr. Welles to "lay off the candy bars."

Two questions—the first to Mr. Welles, who obviously savors his dominant, colorful role. Why would a villainous cop, having hoodwinked the taxpayers for some thirty years, suddenly buckle when a tourist calls his bluff? And why, Mr. Heston, pick the toughest little town in North America for a honeymoon with a nice morsel like Miss Leigh?

—*H.T., May 22, 1958*

TOY STORY

Directed by John Lasseter; written by Joss Whedon, Andrew Stanton, Joel Cohen and Alec Sokolow, based on an original story by Mr. Lasseter, Mr. Stanton, Pete Docter and Joe Ranft; supervising technical director, William Reeves; supervising animator, Mr. Docter; edited by Robert Gordon and Lee Unkrich; music by Randy Newman; produced by Ralph Guggenheim and Bonnie Arnold; released by Walt Disney Pictures. Running time: 81 minutes.

With the voices of: Tom Hanks (Woody), Tim Allen (Buzz Lightyear), Don Rickles (Mr. Potato Head), Jim Varney (Slinky), Wallace Shawn (Rex), John Ratzenberger (Hamm), Annie Potts (Bo Peep), John Morris (Andy), Erik Von Detten (Sid), Laurie Metcalf (Mrs. Davis), R. Lee Ermey (Sergeant), Sarah Freeman (Hannah) and Penn Jillette (Television Announcer).

Raised high above his humble station, Mr. Potato Head is now movie royalty, a star of the sweetest and savviest film of the year. The computer-animated *Toy Story*, a parent-tickling delight, is a work of incredible cleverness in the best two-tiered Disney tradition. Children will enjoy a new take on the irresistible idea of toys coming to life. Adults will marvel at a witty script and utterly brilliant anthropomorphism. And maybe no one will even mind what is bound to be a mind-boggling marketing blitz. After all, the toy tie-ins are to old friends.

It's a lovely joke that the film's toy characters are charmingly plain (Etch-a-Sketch, plastic soldiers, a dog made out of a Slinky) while its behind-the-scenes technology, under the inspired direction of John Lasseter, could not be more cutting edge. It's another joke that this film begins with human characters who have the flat, inexpressive look of toys. A boy named Andy is seen playing boisterously with Woody, his favorite cowboy, whose features remain innocently blank. Only after Andy gets bored and goes elsewhere does Woody spring magically to life.

With a voice supplied wonderfully by Tom Hanks, who leads this film's stellar vocal cast, Woody is instantly sympathetic. His prime spot in Andy's good graces has made him first among equals within the toy community, the civic leader who runs events like "Tuesday night's plastic corrosion awareness meeting." And all this has made him genially smug. Using a Tinkertoy canister for his podium, Woody enjoys the perks of his power, including the attraction it holds for a Little Bo Peep doll. "What do you say I get someone else to watch the sheep tonight?" she inquires.

But Woody gets a surprise with the opening of Andy's birthday presents, in an extended sequence that is one of the film's major marvels. The toys stage a reconnaissance mission to the living room, led by little soldiers who hide in the leaves of a houseplant as if this were a jungle. With the help of a walkie-talkie, data on the birthday gifts is relayed back to Woody, who isn't worried by Andy's new lunch box. However, Buzz Lightyear, the boastful new astronaut who takes over Woody's place on Andy's bed, is something else again.

With this buoyant introduction, *Toy Story* is off and running, spanning a remarkable range of moods and backdrops without ever venturing far from Andy's room. A Pizza Planet restaurant with a memorably clever vending machine (franchise alert: this is the niftiest theme restaurant since Jackrabbit Slim's in *Pulp Fiction*), a gas station, the house next door and some neighborhood streets are enough to keep this film constantly varied. In addition, *Toy Story* shows off a superb sense of utility as it spins out adventures attuned to each toy's individual talents. There's a terrific chase sequence in which the Slinky stretches, the radio car drives, the muscle man flexes, and so on.

As for the rivalry between Woody and Buzz, it too keeps the film sparkling in believable ways. When Woody starts feeling competitive with this new plastic sibling (and when Andy's cowboy bedspread subtly switches to an astronaut motif), it's easy to sympathize with his worries.

"Will Andy pick me?" he asks the eight ball, when Andy's mother decrees that only one toy can come on a car ride.

"Don't count on it," the eight ball typically replies.

Many a children's film would let the Buzz-Woody feud turn nasty, but *Toy Story* is better than that. It does an admirable job of exploring the tensions between these two, especially when both are captured by the fiendish boy next door, whose room has a heavy-metal decor. Even the mutant toys in this dark setting are eventually shown to be enchanting. And spending time in their presence is enough to drive Buzz to a creatively staged breakdown. Dressed in an apron for a little girl's tea party and addressed as "Mrs. Nesbit," he babbles hysterically in a Kirk Douglas voice that suits his big, dimpled chin. A joke like that plays cheerfully to adults without forgetting to amuse children.

The strong cast of *Toy Story* includes Tim Allen, posturing manfully as Buzz; Wallace Shawn as a neurotic and actorish dinosaur; John Ratzenberger as a wisecracking piggy bank; Jim Varney as the Slinky dog; R. Lee Ermey as commander of the toy soldiers; and Don Rickles (who also has a role in *Casino*) as the caustic Mr. Potato Head. Randy Newman and Lyle Lovett sing a genial duet over the closing credits, and Mr. Newman wrote the film's easygoing score. Thanks to exultant wit and so many distinctive voices, *Toy Story* is both an aural and visual delight.

—*J.M., November 22, 1995*

TRAFFIC

Directed by Steven Soderbergh; written by Stephen Gaghan, based on "Traffik" created by Simon Moore, originally produced by Carnival Films for Channel 4 Television (Britain); director of photography, Peter Andrews; edited by Stephen Mirrione; music by Cliff Martinez; production designer, Philip Messina; produced by Edward Zwick, Marshall Herskovitz and Laura Bickford; released by USA Films. Running time: 147 minutes.

With: Michael Douglas (Robert Wakefield), Don Cheadle (Montel Gordon), Benicio Del Toro (Javier Rodriguez), Luis Guzman (Ray Castro), Dennis Quaid (Arnie Metzger), Catherine Zeta-Jones (Helena Ayala), Steven Bauer (Carlos Ayala), Erika Christensen (Caroline Wakefield), Clifton Collins Jr. (Francisco Flores), Miguel Ferrer (Eduardo Ruiz), Topher Grace (Seth Abrahms), Amy Irving (Barbara Wakefield), Tomas Milian (General Arturo Salazar), Marisol Padilla Sanchez (Ana Sanchez), Jacob Vargas (Manolo Sanchez) and Albert Finney (Chief of Staff).

S teven Soderbergh's great, despairing squall of a film, *Traffic*, may be the first Hollywood movie

since Robert Altman's *Nashville* to infuse epic cinematic form with jittery new rhythms and a fresh, acid-washed palette.

The agitated pulse of the hand-held camerawork (by the director working under a pseudonym) that roughly elbows its way into the center of the action is perfectly suited to the film's hard-boiled subject, America's losing war on drugs. The color scheme sandwiches a few lush patches between sequences filmed in two hues—an icy blue and a sun-baked yellow-orange—that are as visually discordant as the forces doing battle.

Where Mr. Altman's masterpiece portrayed American culture as a jostling, twangy carnival of honky-tonk dreams, *Traffic* is a sprawling multicultural jazz symphony of clashing voices sounding variations of the same nagging discontent. The performances (in English and Spanish), by an ensemble from which not a false note issues, have the clarity and force of pithy instrumental solos insistently piercing through a dense cacophony.

The characters run the social gamut, from affluent United States government officials and wealthy drug lords on both sides of the United States border with Mexico and their fat-cat lawyers, to the foot soldiers doggedly toiling in a never-ending drug war.

The most indelible performances belong to Benicio Del Toro as a burly, eagle-eyed Mexican state policeman of pluck and resourcefulness who has the street smarts to wriggle out of almost any squeeze; Michael Douglas, as a conservative Ohio Supreme Court Justice who is appointed the country's new drug czar; and Erika Christensen, as his sullen drug-addicted teenage daughter. Catherine Zeta-Jones is also riveting as a wealthy, ruthless, Southern California matron who is unaware that her husband is a high-level drug smuggler until he is dragged out of their house by federal agents.

The movie, which jumps around from Tijuana to Cincinnati to Washington to San Diego, from a posh Ohio suburb to the inner city to the Mexican desert to the White House itself, offers a coolly scathing overview of the multibillion-dollar drug trade and the largely futile war being waged against it.

But as despairing as it is, *Traffic* is not cynical. It gives its isolated heroes in the trenches their due. One of these is Javier Rodriguez (Mr. Del Toro), a wily, good-hearted Mexican policeman who conspires with the Drug Enforcement Administration to bring down his own boss (Tomas Milian), a corrupt Mexican general who uses torture to get his way. Other heroes include a pair of D.E.A. undercover agents, Montel Gordon (Don Cheadle) and Ray Castro (Luis Guzman), who spend half their lives in cramped vans engaged in surveillance.

Traffic is an updated, Americanized version of a 1989 British television mini-series, *Traffik,* that followed the drug trade from Pakistan to Britain. From an ambiguous, paranoically-charged opening desert sequence (reminiscent of the crop-dusting scene in *North by Northwest*), in which Javier and his partner, Manolo (Jacob Vargas), surrender a newly captured truckload of cocaine to the corrupt general, to a late scene in which an American agent risks his life to plant a bug in a dealer's mansion, *Traffic* is an utterly gripping, edge-of-your-seat thriller. Or rather it is several interwoven thrillers, each with its own tense rhythm and explosive payoff.

What these stories add up to is something grander and deeper than a virtuosic adventure film.

Traffic is a tragic cinematic mural of a war being fought and lost. That failure, the movie suggests, has a lot to do with greed and economic inequity (third world drug cartels have endless financial resources to fight back). But the ultimate culprit, the movie implies, is human nature. Waging a war against drugs isn't just a matter of combating corruption but of eradicating the basic human desire to "take the edge off," as Mr. Douglas's character, Robert Wakefield, says in defense of his nightly drink of Scotch. "Otherwise, I'd be dying of boredom," he adds.

Traffic is no friend of the government. When Wakefield returns from Washington, where he has been briefed by the president's chief of staff (Albert Finney) and other major Beltway players in the war, he describes the experience to his wife, Barbara (Amy Irving), and daughter, Caroline (Ms. Christensen), as like being "in Calcutta, surrounded by beggars wearing $1,500 suits who don't say 'please' and 'thank you.'"

While Wakefield is exploring this new turf, Caroline is rapidly succumbing to crack addiction under the tutelage of her cynical boyfriend, Seth (Topher Grace), her classmate at the exclusive Cincinnati Country Day School and as a scary a contemporary teenager as you're likely to find in a recent movie. A high achiever who is sullen and angry beneath her preppy glass, Caroline quickly plummets to the bottom. Early scenes of her stoned friends sprawled around a fancy living room, drinking, sniffing cocaine and mumbling fuzzily about their discontents offer a devastating vision of youthful suburban ennui.

The movie does not shy away from portraying the pleasure of drugs, and Caroline's initiation into free-base cocaine by Seth is a voluptuous rush. Her head rolls back, and tears of joy trickle from her eyes as Seth repeats in a soothing voice, "You see? You see?" before making love to her. From that moment, Caroline is hooked, and she becomes a glazed-eyed baby-faced demon whose precipitous fall lands her in a seedy hotel under the thumb of the drug-dealing pimp who introduced her to heroin. As Wakefield tries desperately to wrest her from the gutter, this strand of the movie threatens to turn into a Charles Bronson–like vigilante drama. But the acting is so powerful that the scenes have documentary credibility.

A parallel strain of the demonic runs through the story of Helena Ayala (Ms. Zeta-Jones), whose comfortable world begins falling apart the moment her drug-dealing husband, Carlos (Steven Bauer), is arrested. Six months pregnant and the mother of a young son, she finds herself a social outcast, her finances frozen, her son's life threatened by Carlos's creditors. "I want my old life back," she declares furiously to her husband over a prison telephone. Then, with coldblooded determination, she sets about getting it back by any means necessary.

Her key to getting it back lies in forestalling the testimony of Eduardo Ruiz (Miguel Ferrer), a midlevel drug dealer busted by Montel and Ray who is being held in protective custody as the key witness in Carlos's trial. A harsh realist who knows his chances of survival aren't great, Eduardo bitterly scoffs at his captors for "knowing the futility of what you're doing and doing it anyway," and his words resound through the movie. The film's most exciting scenes demonstrate the efficiency of the drug cartels at penetrating the most heavily guarded inner sanctum.

If *Traffic* illustrates how the underfunded, red-tape-bound good guys are no match against the enemy's superior resources, what makes the film more than a powerful thriller is its unflinching contemplation of human frailty. From Helena's take-no-prisoners schemes to stay rich, to a hired assassin tracked down in a gay bar and seduced into a trap, to Carlos's two-faced lawyer (Dennis Quaid), who is tempted to steal from his boss while he is behind bars, the film understands the sheer, brutal force of human desire.

A theme that percolates throughout Stephen Gaghan's screenplay is a reflection on addiction and dependence. From Wakefield's nightly Scotch, to the two glasses of red wine Helena recommends to her friends over lunch at a fancy La Jolla restaurant, to Ray's chain smoking, to the druggy past of Wakefield's wife (was it experimentation or something more?), *Traffic* poses unanswerable questions about self-medication, pleasure, dependency and addiction. One character, who early in the movie invokes the slogan "In vino veritas" while plying a paid assassin with red wine to coax information out of him, later commits suicide by injecting heroin.

In the end, Wakefield, exhausted and demoralized after all he has been through, delivers the White House address he's been instructed to prepare in a weary, halfhearted voice, mumbling words like "courage," "perseverance" and "new ideas" before announcing a new "10-point plan." But as we've been shown, there are no new ideas. Wakefield's speech rings hollow until the moment he pauses and wonders out loud, "How can you wage a war against your own family?"

That family, *Traffic* implies, is not just his own drug-addicted daughter but also a culture devoted to instant gratification and quick-fix pain relief. The drugs, after all, don't flow out from the United States into the third world, they flow in. For this is a culture in which, at the end of the day, millions of people, just like Wakefield, find themselves "dying of boredom."

—*S.H., December 27, 2000*

THE TRAIN

Directed by John Frankenheimer; written by Rose Valland, Franklin Coen and Frank Davis, based on the book by Ms. Valland; cinematographers, Jean Tournier and Walter Wottitz; edited by David Bretherton; music by Maurice Jarre; production designer, Willy Holt; produced by Jules Bricken; released by United Artists. Black and white. Running time: 133 minutes.

With: Burt Lancaster (Labiche), Paul Scofield (Colonel Von Waldheim), Jeanne Moreau (Christine), Suzanne Flon (Miss Villard), Michel Simon (Papa Boule), Wolfgang Preiss (Herren) and Albert Rémy (Didont).

Such movement of railway equipment, chases and collisions with trains, throwing of switches, and derailments as used to make for vivid action in silent films is brought to mind with fondest feeling by John Frankenheimer's *The Train,* which piled up a beautiful, hissing tangle at the Astor and the Plaza yesterday.

Brought to mind, too, by this realistic and intensely engrossing account of the sabotaging of a Nazi endeavor to smuggle a trainload of art treasures out of France toward the end of World War II is that sizzling French war film, *Battle of the Rails,* which was made by Réné Clement and a company of chemin de fer workmen in 1945.

For here again is a re-creation in good, solid, documentary terms of the aspects, the spirit and the techniques of the French railway-workers' underground in putting up maddening resistance to the brazen invaders of their land in that system of communications where a thrown switch or a deliberately mistaken signal could result in magnificent harm.

Never mind that the mission of the heroes in this particular instance is just to keep that trainload of stolen treasures from being highballed out of France—a mission allegedly crucial to the maintenance of the nation's élan. No matter how much the Nazi colonel in charge of the smuggling job keeps insisting that the contents of the boxcars are more valuable than a trainload of men, or that the woman curator of the Paris museum—the Jeu de Paume—from which the treasures are grabbed, importunes the underground's assistance with lamentations that their loss would be most grave, the viewer—unless he is an owner—is not likely to be held in great suspense by the peril of a lot of paintings being lost from the private collections of the wealthy French.

One may feel the same skepticism about the urgency of the cause as Burt Lancaster, who plays the most active perpetrator of sabotage, says to a stubborn objector, "Do you know what's in that train? The national heritage! The pride of France!" And then, with a wry inflection, he adds, "Crazy, isn't it?"

No, the need of preserving the paintings is not

made so imperative and profound in the script of Franklin Coen and Frank Davis that it emotionally balances and justifies the staggering expense of life and effort that goes into the saving of the train. And this lack of strong involvement of the emotions in the cause itself is a weakness of the film.

But *The Train* certainly does not lack for action and the kind of hairtrigger suspense that accumulates in the pursuit of a deeply perilous and uncertain intent. Once the viewer is properly convinced of the personal commitment and resolve of Mr. Lancaster and his fellow railway workers to keep that train from going through—and it could be any train; the freight's a detail in the conflict of us and them—one gets thoroughly engrossed in the excitement of the melodramatic events.

There's the thrilling business of riding the train through the marshaling yards of Vaires in the midst of an air-raid that is shooting for a trainload of armaments on an adjacent track (and you must see what happens when that train—a real one—is finally hit)! There's the wickedly ingenious episode of the names of station boards being changed so that the Nazis guarding the art train think it's rolling right on to Germany when it is actually being routed in a wide swing that will bring it back almost to Paris.

And then there's a slickly planned collision, an extensive manhunt and chase and finally, Mr. Lancaster running ahead of the train, down the tracks, pulling spikes from the rails and risking that any-moment-bullet in the back so as to hold up the precious transport until the oncoming Allies arrive!

Sure, there are several far-fetched details, several points at which one might ask how this whole thing is being maneuvered. Who, outside of those we see, are clearing the tracks and running the railroad, no matter how inefficiently? And why should there be that hint of romance between the fleeing Mr. Lancaster and Jeanne Moreau, the tight-lipped and angry widow who keeps that little railroad-side hotel?

Never mind. It is a vivid melodrama through which Mr. Lancaster bolts with all that straight, strong, American sporting instinct and physical agility for which he is famous, vis-à-vis Paul Scofield's Nazi colonel who rants and rages because the train does not go through.

A full cast of excellent French actors pop in and out in small roles, which they play with as much authen-ticity as the settings in the railway yards of France. There's Suzanne Flon as the agonized curator of the ravished Jeu de Paume, Jacques Marin as a valorous stationmaster, Michel Simon as an aged engineer who deliberately burns a bearing on his engine and gets himself shot for it. And there are Charles Millot and Albert Rémy as sturdy enginemen, Wolfgang Preiss as a driving Nazi major, and several others who look their roles.

Mr. Frankenheimer's strong, resourceful camera gets some exciting shots that are all the more eloquent for this purpose by being in somber black-and-white. And Maurice Jarre has added an unobtrusive but nudging musical score, which is sparingly used in conjunction with excellent, realistic railroad sounds.

Of course, all the way through, one shudders, as one did through *Battle of the Rails,* at the thought of nonmilitary French people committing themselves so valiantly. And one wonders, at the end of this picture, at the irony of people giving up their lives for what seems like such a nonessential purpose. But that's really the point of the whole thing.

—*B.C., March 18, 1965*

TRAINSPOTTING

Directed by Danny Boyle: written by John Hodge. based on a novel by Irvine Welsh. director of photography. Brian Tufano: edited by Masahiro Hirakubo: production designer. Kave Quinn: produced by Andrew Macdonald: released by Miramax Films. Running time: 94 minutes.

With: Ewan McGregor (Renton). Ewen Bremner (Spud). Jonny Lee Miller (Sick Boy). Kevin McKidd (Tommy). Robert Carlyle (Begbie). Kelly Macdonald (Diane) and Shirley Henderson (Gail).

The needle goes in. The floorboards open. And Mark Renton (Ewan McGregor), the acidly attractive hero of *Trainspotting,* drifts into the druggy oblivion that this film depicts with such dead-on, calculating ingenuity. For better or worse, sometimes strictly for the sake of shock value, the stylish irreverence of *Trainspotting* mimics that drug high and delivers its own potent kick.

The young Scottish heroin addicts hurtling

through *Trainspotting* commit every misdeed they can think of, in ways intended to leave straitlaced audiences aghast. Mugging a tourist who attends the Edinburgh Festival is only one of their milder crimes. Yet the perversely irresistible *Trainspotting* is itself geared to the tourist trade, since it keeps a safely voyeuristic distance from the real dangers that go with its subject matter. Instead, it rocks to a throbbing beat and trains its jaundiced eye on some of the most lovable lowlifes ever to skulk across a screen.

If this reckless British hit has attracted an ardent following and spun off everything short of its own ice cream flavor (*Trainspotting* has also been a popular novel and a success onstage), then the wicked charisma of its mordant junkies really does explain why. These characters are funny, sharp, well played and fiercely memorable, whether cavorting Beatle-like for the camera or delivering sardonic commentary on one another. As Renton describes one drug-dealing friend, "We called him Mother Superior on account of the length of his habit."

At the heart of the *Trainspotting* phenomenon is a clever dissonance: the film's characters may be outlaws, but its directorial style is gleeful in slick, conventional ways. After their misanthropic first collaboration, *Shallow Grave*, Danny Boyle (the director), John Hodge (the screenwriter) and Andrew Macdonald (the producer) return with a much more exultant film and turn inexcusable merriment into a large part of its appeal. Dark as its subject matter is, this film manages the incredible trick of remaining jubilant and fresh. And in the face of AIDS, crib death, drug overdose and staggeringly vile bathroom jokes, that is no small feat.

As the cheerfully outrageous *Trainspotting* unfolds, loosely adapted from the dialect-heavy novel by Irvine Welsh, it introduces a tart and unforgettable crew of miscreants. Renton's comrades include the bleached blond Sick Boy (Jonny Lee Miller), who does a sly Sean Connery imitation borrowed from Mr. Welsh's book, and the serenely vacant, goggle-eyed Spud (Ewen Bremner, who originated the Renton role on stage). Spud is the film's most comically hapless character, whether arriving for a job interview in speedy overdrive or embarrassing himself at a girlfriend's house in ways that cannot begin to be described here. Don't even ask.

Also in this circle is Tommy (Kevin McKidd),

whose lapse into drug use is one of the film's few real plot developments. Then there's the electrifyingly dangerous Begbie, played with frightening intensity by Robert Carlyle (who could not seem more different from the gentle gay character he played in *Priest*). Scary and volatile, the short-fused Begbie rivets attention while also defining the limits of Renton's universe. Bounded on one side by the Thatcherite yuppie world into which Renton ventures briefly, it also stops at the psychotic extremes of Begbie's violent outbursts. Sooner or later, not even heroin will blind Renton to the bad-trip aspects of that behavior.

Episodic in structure but brisk and vigorous thanks to Mr. Boyle's buoyant direction, *Trainspotting* grapples repeatedly with Renton's problem of trying to kick heroin. In the sequence that stands as the film's biggest conversation piece, he finds himself diving into the Worst Toilet in Scotland (according to a printed caption) to retrieve drug suppositories he has lost. Compared with Mr. Welsh's stomach-turning written account, the film delivers what is practically the Martha Stewart version, though it will still have viewers gasping and laughing in disbelief. But what really makes the sequence work is the payoff that follows Renton's elaborate preparations and hideous misadventure. "And now I'm ready," he says, after all that.

Beyond a string of entertaining anecdotes and a handful of horrifying ones (the film's nastiest jolts involve the death of a baby), *Trainspotting* doesn't have much narrative holding it together. Nor does it really have the dramatic range to cope with such wild extremes. Most of it sticks to the same moderate pitch, with entertainment value enhanced by Mr. Boyle's savvy use of wide angles, bright colors, attractively clean compositions and a dynamic pop score. Deadpan humor is another solid asset, whether in Mr. Boyle's pitilessly funny glimpse of his characters loathing Scotland's great outdoors or in the sight of three characters staring patiently at the blank space in front of them. This is the spot where the television set used to be, before somebody stole it.

Mr. McGregor underplays Renton to dry perfection without letting viewers lose sight of the character's appeal. Comic timing is everything here, and Mr. Boyle elicits disarmingly droll performances all around. (Mr. Bremner's cartoonish Spud is especially amusing.) Also on hand, for those brief moments when the characters find themselves more interested in sex than in drugs, are Kelly Macdonald and Shirley Henderson as Renton and Spud's mates. When the women visit the bathroom in a nightclub, the mural on the wall depicts Jodie Foster's child prostitute from *Taxi Driver*. Within the context of *Trainspotting*, that becomes a memento of much more innocent times.

—J.M., July 19, 1996

TREASURE OF THE SIERRA MADRE

Directed by John Huston; written by Mr. Huston, based on the novel by Berwick Traven; cinematographer, Ted McCord; edited by Owen Marks; music by Max Steiner; art designer, John Hughes; produced by Henry Blanke; released by Warner Brothers. Black and white. Running time: 126 minutes.

With: Humphrey Bogart (Dobbs), Walter Huston (Howard), Tim Holt (Curtin), Bruce Bennett (Cody), Barton MacLane (McCormick), Alfonso Bedoya (Gold Hat), A. Soto Rangel (Presidente), Manuel Donde (El Jefe), Jose Torvay (Pablo), Margarito Luna (Pancho), Jacqueline Dalay (Flashy Girl) and Bobby Blake (Mexican Boy).

Greed, a despicable passion out of which other base ferments may spawn, is seldom treated in the movies with the frank and ironic contempt that is vividly manifested toward it in *Treasure of Sierra Madre*. And certainly the big stars of the movies are rarely exposed in such cruel light as that which is thrown on Humphrey Bogart in this new picture at the Strand. But the fact that this steel-springed outdoor drama transgresses convention in both respects is a token of the originality and maturity that you can expect of it.

Also, the fact that John Huston, who wrote and directed it from a novel by B. Traven, has resolutely applied the same sort of ruthless realism that was evident in his documentaries of war is further assurance of the trenchant and fascinating nature of the job.

Taking a story of three vagrants on "the beach" in Mexico who pool their scratchy resources and go hunting for gold in the desolate hills, Mr. Huston has shaped a searching drama of the collision of civilization's vicious greeds with the instinct for self-preservation in an environment where all the barriers are down. And, by charting the moods of his prospectors after they have hit a vein of gold, he has done a superb illumination of basic characteristics in men. One might almost reckon that he has filmed an intentional comment here upon the irony of avarice in individuals and in nations today.

But don't let this note of intelligence distract your attention from the fact that Mr. Huston is putting it over in a most vivid and exciting action display. Even the least perceptive patron should find this a swell adventure film. For the details are fast and electric from the moment the three prospectors start into the Mexican mountains, infested with bandits and beasts, until two of them come down empty-handed and the third one, the mean one, comes down dead. There are vicious disputes among them, a suspenseful interlude when a fourth man tries to horn in and some running fights with the banditi that will make your hair stand on end. And since the outdoor action was filmed in Mexico with all the style of a documentary camera, it has integrity in appearance, too.

Most shocking to one-tracked moviegoers, however, will likely be the job that Mr. Bogart does as the prospector who succumbs to the gnawing of greed. Physically, morally and mentally, this character goes to pot before our eyes, dissolving from a fairly decent hobo under the corroding chemistry of gold into a hideous wreck of humanity possessed with only one passion—to save his "stuff." And the final appearance of him, before a couple of roving bandits knock him off in a manner of supreme cynicism, is one to which few actors would lend themselves. Mr. Bogart's compensation should be the knowledge that his performance in this film is perhaps the best and most substantial that he has ever done.

Equally, if not more, important to the cohesion of the whole is the job done by Walter Huston, father of John, as a wise old sourdough. For he is the symbol of substance, of philosophy and fatalism, in the film, as well as an unrelenting image of personality and strength. And Mr. Huston plays this ancient with such humor and cosmic gusto that he richly suffuses the picture with human vitality and warmth. In the limited, somewhat negative role of the third prospector, Tim Holt is quietly appealing, while Bruce Bennett is intense as a prospecting lone wolf and Alfonso Bedoya is both colorful and revealing as an animalistic bandit chief.

To the honor of Mr. Huston's integrity, it should be finally remarked that women have small place in this picture, which is just one more reason why it is good.

—*B.C., January 24, 1948*

A TREE GROWS IN BROOKLYN

Directed by Elia Kazan; written by Tess Slesinger and Frank Davis, based on the novel by Betty Smith; cinematographer, Leon Shamroy; edited by Dorothy Spencer; music by Alfred Newman; art designer, Lyle Wheeler; produced by Louis D. Lighton; released by Twentieth Century Fox. Black and white. Running time: 128 minutes.

With: Dorothy McGuire (Katie), Joan Blondell (Aunt Sissy), James Dunn (Johnny Nolan), Lloyd Nolan (McShane), Peggy Ann Garner (Francie Nolan), Ted Donaldson (Neeley Nolan) and James Gleason (McGarrity).

The warm and compassionate story of a slum-pent family in Brooklyn's Williamsburg which was told with such rich and genuine feeling in *A Tree Grows in Brooklyn,* by Betty Smith, has received pictorial embodiment to a remarkably harmonious degree by Twentieth Century Fox in a fine film based on the novel which came to the Roxy yesterday. If some of the ripe descriptive detail of the original is missing, that is due to the time limitations of the picture. The essential substance has been maintained and presented in a manner which carries tremendous emotional punch.

For the producers have very bravely shunned the more felicitous course of making their film a humorous abstract of neighborhood folklore and folkways and have got to the core of the story which Miss Smith plainly tore from her own heart. That is the rare and tender story of a valiant and sensitive little girl reaching hopefully for spiritual fulfillment in a wretchedly meager home. It is the story of the wondrous love she gathered from a father who was a cheerful ne'er-do-well and of the painful peace she made with her brave mother after the adored father had died.

Where Miss Smith impinged her printed pages on a vast complex of human love and hope rooted wistfully in tenement surroundings, the camera has envisioned on the screen the outward and visible evidence of this inward and spiritual grace. Through a truly surpassing little actress, Peggy Ann Garner, on whom the camera mostly stays, the producers have ably provided a sensitive mirror for the reflection of childish moods and for all the personal comprehension of the pathos of poverty.

Little Miss Garner, with her plain face and lank hair, is Miss Smith's Francie Nolan to the life. And James Dunn plays her father, Johnny Nolan, with deep and sympathetic tenderness. In the radiant performance by these two actors of a dreamy adoration between father and child is achieved a pictorial demonstration of emotion that is sublimely eloquent. Perhaps the sequence representing the ambition of Francie to go to a better public school and the innocent conspiracy with her father to arrange it is the best in the film. Certainly the moment when Francie whispers joyously into her father's ear, "My cup runneth over," touched this reviewer as very few scenes ever have.

But, as well as the pathetic attachment between father and daughter, the film transmits a deeply affecting conception of the mother, Katie Nolan, whose life was a constant struggle against the family's only adversary, poverty. As Dorothy McGuire plays her, she gains strength and clarity through the film until a beautiful and rewarding understanding of her troubled, noble nature is revealed.

Joan Blondell's performance of Aunt Sissy, the family's "problem," is obviously hedged by the script's abbreviations and the usual "Hay's-office" restraints, but a sketchy conception of a warm character is plumply expanded by her. And Ted Donaldson is boyishly delightful as the healthy, literal tad of the brood. Lloyd Nolan is good as the policeman. James Gleason makes a vivid pub owner and Ferike Boros is fine as the grandmother in a generally excellent cast.

Elia Kazan has directed this picture, his first, with an easy naturalness that has brought out all the tone of real experience in a vastly affecting film.

—*B.C., March 1, 1945*

THE TREE OF WOODEN CLOGS

Written (in Italian, with English subtitles), edited and directed by Ermanno Olmi; director of photography, Mr. Olmi; music by Johann Sebastian

Bach: released by New Yorker Films. Running time: 185 minutes.

With: Luigi Ornaghi (Batisti). Francesca Moriggi (Batistina). Omar Brignoli (Minek). Antonio Ferrari (Tuni). Teresa Brescianini (Widow Runk) and Giuseppe Brignoli (Grandpa Anselmo).

The awkwardly titled *The Tree of Wooden Clogs,* Ermanno Olmi's fine Italian film (and winner of the top Cannes festival prize last year), has almost nothing going for it except that it may well be a masterpiece.

If the title doesn't put you off in the way it suggests tulip-time in Holland, Michigan, then the subject will. Here is a leisurely paced, appreciative, somberly beautiful movie, acted by non-professionals, about peasant life in northern Italy at the turn of the century. It's a movie in which no one dies and no one can see into the future, a movie with no particular narrative line and whose politics are never made explicit. Yet there's more political content in almost any one sequence of *The Tree of Wooden Clogs* than there is in all of Bernardo Bertolucci's grandiose *1900.*

Perhaps the worst handicap carried by the film is that it will be impossible to talk about in trend-conscious New York without sounding as if one had just discovered the joys of Rosa Bonheur. Someone is bound to say, "You can't be serious."

Like Terrence Malick's *Days of Heaven,* Mr. Olmi's film is almost too beautiful for its own good. In lesser films—and I'll probably be castigated for including some of Flaherty's work in this category—such density and clarity of image have a way of obscuring harsh subject matter or rendering it sentimental. Beauty is full of peril for the filmmaker. It can make reality seem exotic by putting it at a distance.

However, Mr. Olmi (*The Sound of Trumpets, The Fiancés,* etc.) is a rigorous director. He photographs his films straight-on, at eye-level. He admires these peasants without patronizing them or inflating the scope of their lives. Further, just as he chooses not to impose unlikely political consciousnesses on his characters, he refuses to use the tricks of melodrama to hold our attention. Instead, he has made a film that follows the lives of the farmers much as they follow the course of the seasons.

The film covers approximately a year and focuses on the members of three peasant families who live a communal existence on a large estate owned by a landlord who, though a resident, could not seem more absentee if he lived in Southern California. As they are faceless functions in the landlord's life, so is he the still unquestioned authority in theirs.

Mr. Olmi, who is his own cameraman as well as writer, director and editor, moves through these lives in the manner of someone remembering a long-gone past, though Mr. Olmi, who was born in 1931, could only be remembering the memories of others. Instead of shaping this material with hindsight, he allows us in the audience to interpret it ourselves. The movie thus involves us in ways far more moving than do those films that insist on telling us everything we are supposed to feel (and probably don't).

Though Mr. Olmi shoots his films at eye-level and always sticks closely to the details of specific events, the effect of the film is of knowledge gained obliquely. The movie, which runs slightly more than three hours, is an accumulation of dozens of experiences of children, adults, old people, village idiots, of harvest times and plantings, of moments of boredom and jealousy, celebrations, fatigue, brief pleasures and mysterious ones. It moves so effortlessly, often with great humor and always with compassion, that it seems much shorter than most ninety-minute films.

The quality of the performances of the huge cast is staggeringly good. The faces are beautiful without being pretty. You may be particularly taken by some of the children, all of whom look a bit underfed and undersized, and by the relationship of an especially tiny little girl and her ancient grandfather who grows tomatoes by his own secret formula. Near the end there's a sequence that more or less exemplifies Mr. Olmi's method. It's a day-long trip by riverboat to Milan where a young farm couple, on their honeymoon, witness a series of violent street demonstrations and never once question the reasons for the unrest. Politics are beyond them, though not Mr. Olmi.

The Tree of Wooden Clogs, which opens today at Cinema Studio I, is a profoundly serious film that stands outside time and fashion.

—*V.C., June 1, 1979*

THE TRIP TO BOUNTIFUL

Directed by Peter Masterson: written by Horton Foote, based on his play: director of photography.

Fred Murphy: edited by Jay Freund: music by J. A. C. Redford: production designer. Neil Spisak: produced by Sterling Vanwagenen and Mr. Foote: released by Island Pictures. Running time: 105 minutes.

With: Geraldine Page (Mrs. Watts). John Heard (Ludie Watts). Carlin Glynn (Jessie Mae). Richard Bradford (Sheriff). Rebecca De Mornay (Thelma). Kevin Cooney (Roy) and Mary Kay Mars (Rosella).

It's 1947. Carrie Watts is a well-meaning, loving old woman but, as her son, Ludie, and daughter-in-law, Jessie Mae, know from years of experience, living with Carrie in a tiny Houston apartment is no picnic. It's more like a Balkan truce.

When Carrie isn't butting into Ludie and Jessie Mae's business, she's singing hymns that, according to her daughter-in-law, "are going out of style." Even more irritating to Jessie Mae are the days when Carrie just stares out the window, "pouting." She also has "spells"—her heart is unreliable, though the doctor has assured her that it will last as long as she needs it.

Carrie is no more fond of the arrangement than Ludie and Jessie Mae are. She longs to go back to Bountiful, the small Texas town near the Gulf of Mexico where she was born, married, and raised her children, of whom only Ludie survives.

A return to Bountiful, however, is impossible. Nobody is certain that it even exists anymore, and there's the persistent problem of money. Times aren't great for Ludie and Jessie Mae, who are childless and approaching middle age with not much to show for it but each other.

On any average day, Jessie Mae will accuse Carrie of going through her dresser drawers, which is the one thing the refined Jessie Mae cannot stand. Carrie will respond by being rather imperially baffled by a woman who desires only to have her hair done or to go to the drug store to drink a Coke. Ludie, loving both women, satisfies neither.

One afternoon, while Ludie is at work and Jessie Mae is out sipping Coke, Carrie Watts makes a clean getaway. Wearing a hat that looks as if she always sat on it at the breakfast table, and her best dress, which sags in the wrong places, she takes off by bus for Bountiful. She travels light, carrying only an overnight bag, her pension check and some small change.

This is more or less the beginning of *The Trip to Bountiful,* Horton Foote's funny, exquisitely performed film adaptation of his own play, directed for the screen by Peter Masterson. *The Trip to Bountiful,* which opens today at Cinema 2, is almost as unstoppable as Carrie Watts.

First done in 1953 on the *Goodyear Television Playhouse* with Lillian Gish as Mrs. Watts, it was later expanded and produced on Broadway, again with Miss Gish. As fine as those productions are reported to have been, it's difficult to believe that this film version could be topped.

As Mrs. Watts, Geraldine Page has never been in better form, nor in more firm control of that complex, delicate mechanism that makes her one of our finest actresses, though one who occasionally finds herself whirling wildly in the wrong orbit.

Her Mrs. Watts is simultaneously hilarious and crafty, sentimental and unexpectedly tough. Having lived for years with her increasingly idealized memories of Bountiful, she doesn't hesitate—when her jig is up—to reconcile fantasy with reality. She's no quaint little old lady, a Texas-style Apple Mary, but a strong, shrewdly willful woman who also happens to be decent.

It's a wonderful role, and the performance ranks with the best things Miss Page has done on the screen, including her definitive Alexandra Del Lago in *Sweet Bird of Youth.*

The entire cast, however, is superb: John Heard, wearing the beginnings of a paunch, as Ludie; Carlin Glynn as Jessie Mae, whose patience is always nearing its end but always, somehow, being extended; Richard Bradford, as the country sheriff who becomes the unexpected ally of Carrie Watts during her flight; and Kevin Cooney, as the entire staff at a rural bus stop where Carrie is, for a while, brought to earth.

A particular treat is Rebecca De Mornay, first seen as the tireless hooker in *Risky Business,* who here plays the sympathetic, self-possessed young Army bride who befriends Mrs. Watts in the course of the bus trip. With immense good humor and seeming ease, Miss De Mornay holds her own with one of the great scene stealers of her age.

Though the narrative focus remains short and tight, Mr. Foote and Mr. Masterson have seen to it that the movie doesn't have the constricted manner of a play that's been filmed. Neither does it have the padded feeling of something that's been "opened up" to take advantage of what's called "the medium."

This *Trip to Bountiful* works perfectly as a small, richly detailed film that, in turn, realizes Mr. Foote's particular visions. The playwright's serene Southern landscapes are very different from those seen in Flannery O'Connor's gothic tales, yet neither vision denies the validity of the other. As Miss O'Connor's characters are less lost than their grotesque natures suggest, Mr. Foote's are in far more danger than is immediately made apparent by the circumstances in which they find themselves.

In *The Trip to Bountiful,* Carrie Watts, Ludie, and Jessie Mae keep their sanity. They make compromises and continue with their lives. Family loyalties are maintained—though at a certain price. Giving the film its edge is the unspoken awareness that these are the kinds of characters who, under other conditions, might become bag ladies, drunks or suicides, or run off to join tent shows. By chance, Mr. Foote is more interested in people who hang on.

—*V.C., December 20, 1985*

TRISTANA

Directed by Luis Buñuel; written (in Spanish, with English subtitles) by Mr. Buñuel and Julio Alejandro, based on the novel by Benito Pérez Galdós; cinematographer, José F. Aguayo; edited by Pedro del Rey; art designer, Enrique Alarcón; released by Maron Films. Running time: 95 minutes.

With: Catherine Deneuve (Tristana), Fernando Rey (Don Lope), Franco Nero (Horacio), Lola Gaos (Saturna), Jesús Fernández (Saturno) and Antonio Casas (Don Cosme).

Luis Buñuel, the Spanish director who has had to live and work most of his life in exile in France and Mexico, has been making movies since 1928 (*Un Chien Andalou*), but it wasn't until 1961 and the international critical success of *Viridiana* that he could pick his properties with any degree of independence. There has followed a kind of Buñuelian *age d'or,* nine years of extraordinarily rich moviemaking of the sort that most fine, idiosyncratic directors—probably unfortunately—pass through before they're fifty.

Since *Viridiana,* Buñuel, now seventy, has made *The Exterminating Angel, Diary of a Chambermaid, Simon of the Desert* and, starting in 1967, a series of "farewell" films that include *Belle de Jour, The Milky Way* and his latest, *Tristana,* which is nothing less than the quintessential Buñuel film of all time.

This is not quite the same thing as saying that *Tristana,* which closed the New York Film Festival last night and opens today at the Lincoln Art Theater, is Buñuel's best. Unlike Tristana, the virginal school girl whose transformation into grand demon Buñuel traces in his new film, I would hesitate to choose the better of two grapes, two bread crumbs or two snowflakes, to say nothing of two Buñuels.

Viridiana is his undoubted masterpiece, but *Tristana* is more pure and more consistent, less ambiguous and more complex. It has no "set pieces" to equal *Viridiana*'s tumultuous Last Supper, but the entire film moves so swiftly, with such uncompromising concern for the matters at hand, that anything on the order of a "set piece" would have destroyed its practically perfect symmetry.

The film is an adaptation by Buñuel and Julio Alejandro of a novel by Benito Pérez Galdós, the late nineteenth-century Spanish writer who also wrote the novel on which Buñuel and Alejandro based the screenplay for *Nazarin.* The time has been updated from 1892 to the early 1920's, and the setting is Toledo, the medieval city whose narrow streets and ancient courtyards (on which a certain amount of restoration is going on, but lethargically) correspond to the Buñuelian view of the social and political scene.

Don Lope (Fernando Rey) is an aging, aristocratic but financially impoverished free thinker, an enemy of all arbitrary authority (except his own) who believes in a gentleman's honor, in those commandments that do not have to do with sex and in the nobility of only the work that is done "with pleasure." When her mother, an old flame of Don Lope, dies, Tristana (Catherine Deneuve) comes to live with him.

Tristana is a dutiful girl who mopes around quite a lot and Don Lope, who is so astute in other ways, assumes that she is in mourning for her mother. Don Lope has compassion, but he is a man. He can't keep his hands off her and calls her "my adored child" with such feeling that it doesn't seem at all unlikely that he may well be her father. With very little fuss, Tristana becomes his mistress, and although she obviously doesn't love him, it is apparent that sex is immensely important to her.

Tristana is not the vacuum she has seemed to be. She puts into practice the freedom Don Lope preaches so loftily. "Smell the sickly odor of marital bliss," Don Lope sneers when they pass a pair of lovers in the street. When the opportunity comes, Tristana runs off with a young artist (Franco Nero), only to return some years later with a malignant tumor on her leg.

Don Lope, now rich with an inheritance, takes her in and nurses her back to health after her leg is amputated with such cheery thoughts as "some men would find you more attractive than ever now." Tristana does become more beautiful, as well as so imperiously perverse that, years later, after they have made "a sinful relationship holy" by marriage, and when he is an old, pathetic man, she can let him die without a gesture of pity.

In what amounts almost to a courtly gesture on his part, as the film's director, Buñuel underscores the terrible inevitability of the events at the very end with a series of quick replays of key moments from the film, unreeling the story backward in a kind of narrative zoom to our first meeting with Tristana, the first scene in the film in which the first words "spoken" are the sign language of deaf mutes.

On this simple tale, Buñuel has made a marvelously complex, funny and vigorously moral movie that also is, to me, his most perfectly cast film. Fernando Rey (Don Jaime of *Viridiana*) is splendid—vain, wise, proud, foolish. Catherine Deneuve is beautiful, of course, but never before has her beauty seemed more precise and enigmatic, so that while, at the beginning, there is just the slightest hint of the erotic woman inside the school girl, there is, at the end, an awareness of the saint that once lived within the majestically deformed woman.

Like all of Buñuel's films, *Tristana* is a vision of a very special, hermetically sealed world, and although it is fun to recognize familiar items of Buñueliana inside that world (a preoccupation with feet; earnest, misguided clerics; the kind of pragmatism that has Don Lope shout "Long live the living" after a funeral), the film is one that should fascinate even those coming into Buñuel's world for the first time.

The physical production, with color photography by José Aguayo, is uncommonly handsome, and its story is the work of an old master who has such command that he can tell a tale straightforward, without the sort of superficial subtleties and superfluous nuances that, in the work of lesser talents, take the place of primal substance.

—V.C., September 21, 1970

TROUBLE IN PARADISE

Produced and directed by Ernst Lubitsch; written by Grover Jones and Samson Raphaelson, based on the play *The Honest Finder* by Laszlo Aladar; cinematographer, Victor Milner; music by W. Franke Harling; art designer, Hans Dreier; released by Paramount Pictures. Black and white. Running time: 83 minutes.

With: Miriam Hopkins (Lily), Kay Francis (Marianne Colet), Herbert Marshall (Gaston Monescu), Charles Ruggles (The Major), Edward Everett Horton (François), C. Aubrey Smith (Giron) and Robert Greig (Jacques).

Surely *Trouble in Paradise*, a picture which was presented at the Rivoli yesterday, points no moral and the tale it tells is scant and innocuous, yet, because it was fashioned by the alert-minded Ernst Lubitsch, it is a shimmering, engaging piece of work. In virtually every scene the lively imagination of the German producer shines forth and it seems as though he were the only person in Hollywood who could have turned out such an effective entertainment from such a feathery story.

Mr. Lubitsch has drawn heavily upon Paramount's resources for his scenic designs, which are an important adjunct to this flippant film. Here the director has a flair for beautiful clocks of various types and in one sequence, while the voices of two players are heard carrying on their bantering, all one sees is a clock on a table. When the characters pass into another room, there is still another clock. Upstairs there is a modernistic grandfather clock and outside a window there is the tower from which chimes tell the hour. The settings are lovely and spacious with meticuluous attention to furnishings. No more inviting example of 1932 decorations has been offered on the screen.

This merry trifle, which was first spun as a play by Laszlo Aladar and arranged for a motion picture by

Grover Jones and Samson Raphaelson, deals, if you please, with those light-fingered gentry who rob and pick pockets. Imagine the charming Miriam Hopkins impersonating an ingratiating, capable thief! Then try to visualize Herbert Marshall as a delightful scoundrel who might look upon Alias Jimmy Valentine as a posing blunderer! They are such an interesting pair of crooks that it is not altogether astonishing that the other characters find them companionable.

First one has a glimpse of Venice with a refuse collector singing "O Sole Mio" as he steers his craft through the canals. The camera then introduces Gaston Monescu posing as a baron, and later Lily, whom Gaston calls his "little shoplifter" and "sweet little pickpocket."

This pair eventually turn their attention to Paris and Mme. Marianne Colet, the widow of a wealthy perfumery manufacturer. Marianne, impersonated by Kay Francis, has two suitors, neither of whom finds much favor with her. One is the Major, played by Charles Ruggles, who stays quite sober throughout the proceedings, and the other is François, who has been an easy victim for Gaston in the City of the Doges.

Through returning Mme. Colet's precious bag, which he had stolen, Gaston, after accepting the 20,000 francs' reward and explaining that he is one of the new poor, soon is ensconced in Marianne Colet's mansion as her secretary, and Lily, not long afterward, is employed as a typist. She has to sit on her hands when talking to Marianne Colet, for fear she might hurt the chances of stealing 100,000 francs in cash—cash being always better than jewelry—by pilfering one of the pieces of jewelry in a box.

As for Marianne Colet, one might say that her interest in Gaston is keener than most women who employ secretaries, and it prompts the fair but reprehensible Lily to tell Gaston that she admires him as a burglar and a thief, but she warns him not to sink to the low level of a gigolo.

After their fashion, they have a romantic and busy time at Marianne Colet's. There are moments when it looks as though Mr. Lubitsch were going to let fly a few ideas like René Clair's, but he stops himself and never for an instant can it be said that Lubitsch ever copies another director. Time and again in this feature he offers ideas which will undoubtedly be well imitated in Hollywood. He does not take this fable seriously at all, but he leaves nothing undone to make it

the sort of thing that will keep audiences in a constant state of chuckles.

Mr. Marshall is as smooth and easy as ever. He looks more the baron than the thief Gaston. It is not surprising that Marianne thinks of promoting him from secretary to husband. Miss Hopkins makes Lily a very interesting person, who steals as another girl might sing. Lily even steals her way out of the last scene in the film. Kay Francis is attractive and able as Marianne, whose sins consist of being too credulous and in being very fond of romantic adventures.

—M.H., November 9, 1932

THE TROUBLE WITH HARRY

Produced and directed by Alfred Hitchcock; written by John Michael Hayes, based on the novel by Jack Trevor Story; director of photography, Robert Burks; edited by Alma Macrorie; art directors, John Goodman and Hal Pereira; music by Bernard Herrmann; released by Paramount Pictures. Running time: 99 minutes.

With: Edmund Gwenn (Capt. Albert Wiles), John Forsythe (Sam Marlowe), Mildred Natwick (Miss Ivy Gravely), Mildred Dunnock (Mrs. Wiggs), Jerry Mathers (Arnie Rogers), Royal Dano (Deputy Sheriff Calvin Wiggs), Parker Fennelly (Millionaire), Barry Macollum (Tramp), Dwight Marfield (Dr. Greenbow) and Shirley MacLaine (Jennifer Rogers).

Let us state at the start that the misfortune of the title character in Alfred Hitchcock's *The Trouble With Harry,* which came to the Paris yesterday, is that he is slightly lifeless. In fact, he is dead.

He is that way at the start of the picture, when he is discovered exquisitely supine on a hilltop clad in autumn's foliage above a peaceful village in Vermont. And he is still that way at the finish—which may be what you would expect, but, because of the nature of this picture, comes as something of a surprise.

For this latest of Mr. Hitchcock's efforts is a curiously whimsical thing in which four characters take a most jaunty and unmorbid attitude towards the corpse. Each of them has a likely reason for wishing the state of the deceased to stay concealed, and each of them has no qualms whatever about shoving him into a nameless grave. So amiable is their indifference and so flexible is their handling of the deceased that you'd not be amazed if he should rise up and baffle them utterly.

There's the light-headed old sea captain, played by Edmund Gwenn, who thinks he has shot him accidentally while hunting rabbits on the hill. There's an old maid, played by Mildred Natwick, who thinks she conked poor Harry on the head while he was ruthlessly trying to attack her—and this she would not have revealed. There is Harry's estranged wife (now widow), played by Shirley MacLaine, who has recently clobbered him with a milk bottle and is quite relieved to have him dead. And finally, there's a debonair young artist, played by John Forsythe, who seems to get a great deal of innocent amusement out of juggling a corpse and helping his friends.

It is not a particularly witty or clever script that John Michael Hayes has put together from a novel by Jack Trevor Story, nor does Mr. Hitchcock's direction make it spin. The pace is leisurely, almost sluggish, and the humor frequently is strained. The whimsey inclines to be pretentious, such as Miss Natwick's cheery reply to Mr. Gwenn's expressed hope that her father's death was peaceful, "He was caught in a threshing-machine." Or again, when the two are out exhuming the freshly buried corpse, she says, "After we've dug him up, we'll go back to my place and I'll make you some hot chocolate."

That's the way it goes through the picture, to a rather obvious end. But it does possess mild and mellow merness about the manner of Miss MacLaine. Mildred Dunnock, Royal Dano and Parker Fennelly are dry Yankee types in other roles, and color and VistaVision reflect the rural beauty and quaintness of Vermont.

—B.C., October 18, 1955

TRUE GRIT

Directed by Henry Hathaway; written by Marguerite Roberts, based on the novel by Charles Portis; cinematographer, Lucien Ballard; edited by Warren Low; music by Elmer Bernstein; production designer, Walter Tyler; produced by Hal B. Wallis; released by Paramount Pictures. Running time: 128 minutes.

With: John Wayne (Rooster Cogburn), Glen Campbell (La Boeuf), Kim Darby (Mattie Ross), Jeremy Slate (Emmett Quincy), Robert Duvall (Ned Pepper), Dennis Hopper (Moon), Alfred Ryder (Goudy), Strother Martin (Mr. Stonehill) and Jeff Corey (Tom Chaney).

True Grit, which opened at the Radio City Music Hall yesterday, comes very close to being as good as we remember certain movies of our childhood to have been (but seldom are when we revisit them), a marvelously rambling frontier fable packed with extraordinary incidents, amazing encounters, noble characters and virtuous rewards.

Did somebody ask what it's about? Well, it's about this little fourteen-year-old girl, the kind who once would have been called plucky, whose father is murdered and who accompanies an eccentric old Federal marshal in pursuit of the killer into Choctaw country, and who gets captured by bandits, and has to shoot one of them, and who then falls into a pit of snakes, and so on and so forth.

I must say that I couldn't quite understand what all the fuss was about when the Charles Portis novel hit the best-selling lists last year. The book was strictly freeze-dried nostalgia, which imitated the flavor of nineteenth-century American writing without ever making you believe it was as good as the real thing (Mark Twain, Bret Harte).

The movie has its own formidable heritage with which it has to contend, but since the men who made it are the ones who contributed to that same heritage, *True Grit* seems more authentic as a film than as a piece of written literature.

It is the work of three of Hollywood's most enduring talents, and a triumph for each of them.

John Wayne is its star, a man who has been in movies for almost forty years and who has the best role of his career as the old, fat, one-eyed marshal. It was directed by Henry Hathaway who, at seventy-one, has made just about every kind of movie ever turned out on the Hollywood assembly line (*Lives of a Bengal Lancer, Kiss of Death, The Sons of Katie Elder*).

Mr. Hathaway's clear-eyed, no-nonsense approach to moviemaking has never been more effective, since he simply refuses to take the time to acknowledge the sentimentality in which the movie is really awash.

Equally important is the work of Lucien Ballard, the cinematographer whose career started over forty years ago and has embraced everything from the Dietrich-Von Sternberg *Morocco* and *The Devil Is a Woman* to the current *The Wild Bunch.* Anyone interested in what good cinematography means can compare Ballard's totally different contributions to *The Wild Bunch* and *True Grit,* In *The Wild Bunch,* camera work is hard and bleak and largely unsentimental. The images of *True Grit* are as romantic and autumnal as its landscapes, which, in the course of the story, turn with the season from the colors of autumn to the white of winter.

After *The Green Berets,* I never thought I'd be able to take John Wayne seriously again. The curious thing about *True Grit* is that although he still is playing a variation on the self-assured serviceman he has played so many times in the past, the character that seemed grotesque in Vietnam fits into this frontier landscape, emotionally—and perhaps politically too.

It's the kind of performance that I found myself beginning to remember quite fondly, even before the movie was over: Wayne riding the trail of the outlaw and getting increasingly, pleasantly drunk, finally falling off his horse and announcing to his party that that is where they'll camp for the night. There is a classic shoot-out in which the one-eyed marshal faces four outlaws, riding to meet them across a pastel-colored meadow, holding the reins of his horse in his teeth and shooting with both hands.

The last scene in the movie is so fine it will probably become Wayne's cinematic epitaph.

I was not particularly taken with Kim Darby, who is rather large and well-developed (both physically and as an actress) to be completely convincing as the fourteen-year-old Mattie Ross. Even her obvious, glossy professionalism is not entirely out of key with the Hollywood heritage. Glen Campbell, the country-and-western singer, is very pleasant as La Boeuf (which he pronounces "La Beef"), the Texas ranger who joins forces with Wayne and Miss Darby.

Marguerite Roberts wrote the screenplay, which differs from the original in several important ways, all to the good. The same cannot be said for the lacy, thumpy musical score contributed by Elmer Bernstein. Like some terrible, aural Chinese torture, it threat-

ens to overwhelm all the senses, and probably would have if the rest of the movie were not so good. This is only July, but I suspect that *True Grit* will stand as one of the major entertainments of the year.

—V.C., July 4, 1969

TRUE LOVE

Directed by Nancy Savoca; written by Ms. Savoca and Richard Guay; director of photography, Lisa Rinzler; edited by John Tintori; production designer, Lester W. Cohen; produced by Mr. Guay and Shelley Houis; released by United Artists. Running time: 100 minutes.

With: Annabella Sciorra (Donna), Ron Eldard (Michael), Aida Turturro (Grace), Roger Rignack (Dom) and Star Jasper (J. C.).

If *Moonstruck* had been made by, for, and about real people, it might have been a lot like *True Love,* Nancy Savoca's exuberant, raucously funny film about a big Italian-American wedding and all its abundant fallout. Ms. Savoca, a Bronx native and a first-time director making a delightful debut, knows her territory and knows much better than to treat it too kindly.

Not for her the hearts-and-flowers view of romance, not at all. This is a film in which the groom and his buddies cap off the bachelor party by driving to Atlantic City, making themselves thoroughly sick and mournfully discussing how to arrange the newlyweds' "Mediterranean" furniture suite as they watch the sun rise. It's a film in which the bride's aunts wish her well but instruct her in how to order her husband to "take gas"—i.e., stick his head in the oven—just in case.

True Love is piled high with all the rich silliness that goes into planning and executing a nuptial extravaganza. It's also loaded with sympathy for the nervous couple in danger of being buried beneath. Obviously, Donna (Annabella Sciorra) and Michael (Ron Eldard) wanted so much to get married that they were willing to tackle this, but that was then. This is now. This is time for sky-blue mashed potatoes ("Getatta here, I'm not eatin' any blue food!" Michael complains). It's time for things to be "classy," which is one of the caterer's favorite words. And it's time for trying to get a handle on exactly what marriage means—does it mean Michael can't go out with his friends after the wedding, if only for an hour or so? No one is quite sure.

True Love, which opens today at the Sutton, was written by Ms. Savoca with her husband, Richard Guay, and made on the kind of low budget that necessitates having a very good eye. Clearly, Ms. Savoca has one, not only for humorously real-looking settings but for unknown actors who manage to be utterly natural and uproariously funny at the same time. The big, bustling cast shares a uniformly over-the-top approach, but in this case that's ideal. Viewers will occasionally have to remind themselves that these are indeed actors, and that *True Love* is not a documentary.

Ms. Sciorra, with her gentle beauty and her hard-as-nails negotiating style, perfectly captures the mood of the film, and makes Donna fully and touchingly drawn. Mr. Eldard makes Michael a similar mix of contrasts, a sweet and decent fellow beneath all the bluster. Like most of the actors playing his friends, the brawny Mr. Eldard seems to do everything chest-first, and none of them finish a sentence without a certain indispensable, all-purpose modifier. The bride and her friends talk exactly the same way, and are probably a lot tougher.

The screenplay has a great ear for the local language. ("Just gimme a carton a Marlboros," says somebody at the deli where Michael works; "What'd ya do, hit the lottery?" he replies.) It's also adept at working a strain of real pathos into the mix, since Donna and Michael are both so young and scared. When Donna grills Michael with a magazine quiz asking whether couples are compatible, he says that his dream date is "a night at Dom's bar watchin' *The Honeymooners,* one of the original thirty-nine." His dream house is "a two-family house in the Bronx." He wants to wear black and white at his wedding, not pastels. He's an old-fashioned guy, and in one of the film's later scenes he expresses an old-fashioned worry: "I just don't wanna end up hating my life." Donna has the same fear, but it's not yet something these two are close enough to share.

True Love is never condescending. It has lots of affection for the specifically ethnic neighborhood touches that are the source of its humor. When one character offers an unusually candid and unprintable explanation for why he and a friend have shown up

late, the film can only stand by and marvel. In this it recalls the shaggy-dog Italian-American humor of films as diverse as *Mean Streets* and *Married to the Mob,* films with a happy appreciation of their characters' flamboyance and color. Like those films, *True Love* also makes apt and witty use of a well-chosen pop score.

—J.M., October 20, 1989

TRUST

Written and directed by Hal Hartley: director of photography. Mike Spiller: edited by Nick Gomez: music by Phil Reed: production designer. Daniel Ouellette: produced by Bruce Weiss: released by Fine Line Features. Running time: 90 minutes.

With: Adrienne Shelly (Maria Coughlin). Martin Donovan (Matthew Slaughter). Merritt Nelson (Jean Coughlin). John MacKay (Jim Slaughter) and Edie Falco (Peg Coughlin).

Putting on her purple lipstick one morning, a teenager tells her father she's pregnant. He calls her a slut, she slaps his face and the minute she stomps out the door he drops dead. Just as you were warned: if you break your father's heart, it will kill him. The situation is part nightmare, part bad joke and the perfect deadpan way to kick off Hal Hartley's *Trust.*

Mr. Hartley's two feature films—*The Unbelievable Truth* was released last year—share a droll, distinctive manner. He drops by suburban Long Island, finds a couple of young characters who have skewed but thoroughly sensible attitudes and lets them find each other. Like the films of this thirty-one-year-old writer and director, Mr. Hartley's characters look realistic, act cockeyed and turn out to be just right.

Maria, the pregnant teenager in a miniskirt and a high-school jacket, tells her boyfriend about the baby. He dumps her and goes to football practice. Back home, Maria's mother says she will never forgive her for killing her father and throws her out of the house. At the end of this luckless day, she finds shelter in an empty house and meets Matthew, potentially more lethal than she is and just the right guy to understand her.

When the film introduces Matthew, he is so disgusted with his job at a computer factory that he puts his boss's head in a vise and walks out. Mr. Hartley's control is so sure that we instantly know Matthew has made the right choice. He may be ten or so years older than Maria, but he is on the run from a sadistic parent himself. His father obsessively makes him clean the already spotless white bathroom. It is a true act of chivalry and self-sacrifice when Matthew takes Maria home.

Suddenly, it's a toss-up about who needs whom more. "I carry this with me at all times, just in case," Matthew says, showing Maria a hand grenade. "Are you emotionally disturbed?" she asks, cutting through politeness as if the superego had never been discovered. No, he answers. But they had been talking about how she killed her dad and thought about killing herself; he was trying to be sympathetic. Neither Maria nor Matthew is strong enough to escape alone, but each recognizes that the other needs to be dragged out of a suffocating situation.

Though this film's tone is more sober and weightier than the black humor of *The Unbelievable Truth,* Mr. Hartley has kept his sense that everyone seems screwy if you just look hard enough. As Maria and Matthew navigate toward each other, they keep bumping into characters who only seem normal.

A nurse at the abortion clinic is most sympathetic when she takes off her cap and pours a couple of glasses of Scotch for Maria and herself. Maria's sister is a flirty, gum-chomping waitress, a real type. She seems Neanderthal next to her younger sister, especially after Maria pulls back her hair, puts on her glasses and starts thinking about her life. "I am ashamed," this new Maria writes in a notebook. "I am ashamed of being young. I am ashamed of being stupid."

Surrounded by people who would agree with that wrenching self-description, she is lucky to find Matthew. As Maria says, their relationship is based on trust, admiration and respect. She is determined to convince him that those qualities add up to love, even if she has to jump off a bridge to prove it. This might be love, but not the kind usually seen on-screen. At the moment they seem about to kiss, Maria pulls back and says, "Give me your hand grenade."

Adrienne Shelly, who starred as another quick-to-grow-up teenager in *The Unbelievable Truth,* makes Maria's transformation from a smart-mouthed girl to a wise young woman both poignant and credible. Like Ms. Shelly, Martin Donovan (as Matthew) knows how to make Mr. Hartley's pared-down, stylized dialogue express the essence of his character. Though Mr. Hartley's films are richly detailed, there are no frills or grace notes. Such work risks being too blunt, but *Trust* comes through.

—C.J., July 26, 1991

TUNES OF GLORY

Directed by Ronald Neame; written by James Kennaway, based on his novel; cinematographer, Arthur Ibbetson; edited by Anne V. Coates; music by Malcolm Arnold; produced by Albert Fennell and Colin Lesslie; released by Lopert Films. Running time: 106 minutes.

With: Alec Guinness (Lieutenant Colonel Jock Sinclair), John Mills (Lieutenant Colonel Basil Barrow), Kay Walsh (Mary), Susannah York (Morag), Dennis Price (Major Charlie Scott), John Fraser (Colonel Piper Fraser) and Alan Cuthbertson (Captain Eric Simpson).

If ghostly echoes of Rudyard Kipling, *The Charge of the Light Brigade* and other voices respectfully intoning the traditions of the regiments seem to be heard through the new British film, *Tunes of Glory,* which came to the Little Carnegie yesterday, it figures. For this is a picture that gets around, at last, to saying some things about military traditions that haven't been said so aptly and eloquently for years.

It is also a film in which tradition itself is magnificently observed in acting that does full justice to the highest standards of an ancient British craft and merits all the honors it has already received. Not only do Alec Guinness and John Mills superlatively adorn the two top roles in this drama of professional military men, but also every actor, down to the walk-ons, acquits himself handsomely.

As in most first-rate dramas, whether of screen or stage, the theme of this one is not flung at you with a sign saying, "Here it is!" It is slowly and guardedly constructed after the foundation has been laid and even the vague facade of another structure appears to be taking shape. Then the sham facade is suddenly tumbled and the full structure of the solid theme is there to be viewed and contemplated, an achievement as well as a surprise.

So, when we have a smart new colonel arriving to take command of a crack battalion of a famous Scottish regiment and to supersede the present acting colonel, who is an amiable, up-from-the-ranks professional man, it appears that we are to be confronted with a conflict between two types, one the snobbish and frosty authoritarian and the other a good old solid pro.

Also, with Mr. Mills performing the "new boy" with a dandy, waspish air and Mr. Guinness making the tough old veteran a bluff and canny Scot, there seems to be no alternative for the disposal of our sympathies. The conspicuously egalitarian soldier is to be favored over the snob every time.

Other developments and aspects continue to twist our sympathies. The lesser officers of the battalion dispose themselves as you guess they would. The evident pipsqueaks and stinkers seem to gravitate to the "new boy," who cracks down with rigid training schedules and (horror of horrors!) does not drink booze. The stout fellows, true Scots and heroes, go along with the "old boy," who loves the bagpipes, likes to holler when he is happy and to do the old Scottish reels.

All the tides run in his direction. Even the casually planted facts that the new colonel is a son and grandson of former commanders of this glorious regiment and was himself kept from battle service only by being made a prisoner in World War II, seem paltry and negative details in the new colonel's pedigree. The "old boy" withers him adroitly with his comment, "From Oxford? Fancy that."

Then a terribly embarrassing thing happens: the "old boy" bops a young corporal in a pub when he catches the corporal with his daughter. This is a court-martial offense, a shameful violation of tradition as well as military law. And it looks as if the new colonel is going to have him up for it, until he, by a canny line of reasoning, dissuades the colonel in order to save his skin.

Now the theme emerges. Now the true structure appears. This is a drama about tradition and the kind of respect for it held by these two men. Suddenly the elements are assembled, the elements so skillfully contrived in the brilliant direction and color camera work of Ronald Neame—the characteristics of the peacetime soldiers in their old citadel on the high hill, the mellowness and casual spirit of the elegant officers' mess, the subtly planted notion that professional soldiers are not just fellows to please themselves but the guardians of a stern tradition and a selfless responsibility.

What happens to make the "old boy" eventually comprehend this, and how he behaves thereafter, are surprises we dare not dissipate, for they are shocking and moving, among the best things in the film written by James Kennaway.

As we say, the acting is brilliant. Mr. Mills is remarkably intense and tremendously revealing of an earnest, tormented man. Mr. Guinness, carrot-topped and commanding a delicious Scottish vocabulary and brogue, makes his characterization of the "old boy" a beautifully rich and humored thing and a fascinating contrast to his colonel in *The Bridge on the River Kwai*.

Dennis Price as a cool, laconic major, Gordon Jackson as a stalwart adjutant, John Fraser as a young bagpiper corporal, and Duncan MacRae as a canny pipe major stand out among many fine performers, while pretty Susannah York does well as Mr. Guinness's daughter and Kay Walsh is droll as his lady friend.

Glittering, snow-frosted settings and handsome kilts and uniforms, all in the very best of color, complete the visual score for a fine film. In a way, perhaps largely because of the acting, it reminds one of *In Which We Serve*.

—B.C., December 21, 1960

12 ANGRY MEN

Directed by Sidney Lumet; written by Reginald Rose, based on his television play; cinematographer, Boris Kaufman; edited by Carl Lerner; music by Kenyon Hopkins; art designer, Robert Markell; produced by Henry Fonda and Mr. Rose; released by United Artists. Black and white. Running time: 95 minutes.

With: Henry Fonda (Juror 8), Lee J. Cobb (Juror 3), Ed Begley (Juror 10), E. G. Marshall (Juror 4), Jack Warden (Juror 7), Martin Balsam (Juror 1), John Fiedler (Juror 2), Jack Klugman (Juror 5), Edward Binns (Juror 6), Joseph Sweeney (Juror 9), George Voskovec (Juror 11), Robert Webber (Juror 12), Rudy

Bond (Judge), James A. Kelly (Guard), Bill Nelson (Court Clerk) and John Savoca (Defendant).

Although cameras have been focused on jurors before, it is difficult to recall a more incisively revealing record of the stuff of which such "peers" can be made than is presented in *12 Angry Men.*

For Reginald Rose's excellent film elaboration of his fine television play of 1954, which arrived at the Capitol Saturday, is a penetrating, sensitive and sometimes shocking dissection of the hearts and minds of men who obviously are something less than gods. It makes for taut, absorbing and compelling drama that reaches far beyond the close confines of its jury room setting.

Credit the power of this lucid study to the fact that the attributes, failings, passions and prejudices of these talesmen are as striking and important as the awesome truth that they hold a boy's life in their hands. Director Sidney Lumet, who is making his debut in the movie medium with *12 Angry Men,* and Boris Kaufman, an Academy Award–winning cameraman, made expert use of a superb cast, which is ingeniously photographed in what normally would have been static situations. Above all, they have made full use of the trenchant words and ideas of the author to plumb the characters of their principals.

Mr. Rose's basic thought is that the somewhat terrifying legal ukase, "beyond a reasonable doubt," should not be regarded as just a flat phrase casually coined by the lawmakers. The defendant involved (whom we see only momentarily as the film opens) is a tough eighteen-year-old from a broken slum home charged with having stabbed his brutal father, an erstwhile convict. All but one of the veniremen are convinced this is an open-and-shut case. This juror does not assert that the boy is innocent but the conduct of the trial, especially that of the defense lawyer, has left him with gnawing doubts.

It is here that Mr. Rose begins delicately to expose the dissenter and his opponents. There is the self-made man who angrily remembers his son's defiance of authority. There is the garage owner seething with racial prejudice. There is the calm stockbroker who seriously has arrived at his verdict of guilty. There is the wisecracking salesman anxious to vote so as to be able to get out to the ball game. There is the handsome, vacillating Madison Avenue advertising man.

There is an old man, wise and benign with the years. And there is a refugee watchmaker who is appreciative of the ideals and freedoms of democracy.

Henry Fonda gives his most forceful portrayal in years as the open-minded juror whose logical reasoning implants facts and doubts into the minds of his colleagues so that they finally change their vote to not guilty. In being strikingly emotional he is both natural and effective. Strangely enough, the illogical aspect of the plot is embodied in his exclusive discoveries of evidence and improbabilities in the trial itself. Some of the other jurors appear capable of such perception too.

A viewer may assume, however, that Mr. Rose was interested solely in establishing the characters of his cast, which he has done admirably. Each of his performers has a "fat" part and they are convincingly played.

Lee J. Cobb, for example, is excellent as the vengeful self-made man tortured by the memory of a son who broke away from his rule. Ed Begley is properly warped and rabid as the prejudiced garage owner. And, to single out a few others, E. G. Marshall is fine as the unperturbed broker, as are Jack Warden, as the flip sport; George Voskovec, as the watchmaker; Joseph Sweeney, as the observant old man; and Robert Webber, as the vacuous advertising type.

Messrs. Rose, Lumet, Fonda, et al. have kept the fair sex out of their jury room. Although it may sound ungallant, these *12 Angry Men* are all right without distaff glamour. Their dramas are powerful and provocative enough to keep a viewer spellbound.

—A.W., April 15, 1957

TWELVE O'CLOCK HIGH

Directed by Henry King; written by Sy Bartlett and Beirne Lay Jr., based on their novel; cinematographer, Leon Shamroy; edited by Barbara McLean; music by Alfred Newman; art designers, Lyle Wheeler and Maurice Ransford; produced by Darryl F. Zanuck; released by Twentieth Century Fox. Black and white. Running time: 132 minutes.

With: Gregory Peck (General Savage), Hugh Marlowe (Lieutenant Colonel Ben Gately), Gary Merrill (Colonel Davenport), Millard Mitchell (General Pritchard), Dean Jagger (Major Stovall), Robert

Arthur (Sergeant McIlhenny), Paul Stewart (Captain Doc Kaiser) and John Kellogg (Lieutenant Bishop).

The saga of our Air Forces and their accomplishments in the recent war already has inspired a number of pictures—some fine, some not so good—in which contemplations have been focused upon individuals from sergeants to "top brass." But there hasn't yet been one from Hollywood which could compare in rugged realism and punch to *Twelve O'Clock High,* a top-flight drama which opened officially at the Roxy yesterday.

This tremendously vivid fictional story of a young general who, toward the end of 1942, takes command of a bomber group operating from a base in England and elevates it from bleak depression to a peak of aggressiveness and pride, has conspicuous dramatic integrity, genuine emotional appeal and a sense of the moods of an air base that absorb and amuse the mind. And it is beautifully played by a male cast, directed by Henry King and produced by Darryl F. Zanuck for Twentieth Century Fox.

Inevitably, this picture, since its hero is of the "brass" and its locale is centered and maintained at an Eighth Air Force bomber base, is bound to provoke comparisons with *Command Decision,* another fine film, released last year, which told the story of a general's bouts with the high command. The comparison should not be unflattering, but it is not really justified—and the main points of similarity are coincidental, no more.

For not only is the situation which confronts the hero in this film on a tactical, personnel level—not on the level of command—but it is a situation that compels his weight to be thrown at his subordinates, and not at the "brass." And the consequence of this dire necessity is tension of a much more personal sort and dramatic situations in which the emotional conflicts are close and direct.

Actually, the picture telegraphs its nature at the start, with a middle-aged American ex-major reminiscing at an old air base today, recalling in nostalgic sadness his experience at that same base during the war. And, on this note of tender sentiment, the heroic story is launched. This, in itself, is a provocation to a particular emotional response.

And the story of how this young general, put in command of a battered group, embarks upon a program of stern and ruthless discipline to test the point of "maximum effort" of his men likewise is loaded in favor of emotional incident. There is, for instance, the lieutenant colonel whom the general degrades at the start and who takes his medicine bravely, to emerge an obvious hero at the end. There is the quiet but rebellious young pilot who comes out for the general in the clutch. There is the middle-aged major (who does the musing), the washed-out colonel, the sad-eyed doctor—all rich types.

Placed credibly in a drama that has been crisply written by Beirne Lay, Jr., and Sy Bartlett, and surrounded with thrilling action, on the base and in the air, these men and their personal drama are brought to heroic heights. Except for a final situation, which appears both unlikely and contrived, the story has thorough integrity all the way down the line.

Wisely, the writers and director, Mr. King, have husbanded the potential of an illustrated mission for one big concentrated punch, and they have got into this major sequence great excitement and reality. The terrible tension of a bomber crew while on a mission, the breathless action of attack and repulse and even the anxiety of the ground crews are finely realized. Some fast actuality footage of attacking fighter planes has been discreetly used.

High and particular praise for Gregory Peck in the principal role is natural, since Mr. Peck does an extraordinarily able job in revealing the hardness and the softness of a general exposed to peril. But everyone else in the picture is equally good in carrying out his task—Dean Jagger as the middle-aged major, Hugh Marlowe as the lieutenant colonel who gets hazed, Gary Merrill as the displaced group commander, Millard Mitchell as a tough two-star general, Paul Stewart as the doctor, Bob Patten as the young pilot, and many more. They have helped to "cut" a bang-up good picture of aerial warfare and the ruggedness of men.

—*B.C., January 28, 1950*

TWENTIETH CENTURY

Produced and directed by Howard Hawks: written by Ben Hecht and Charles MacArthur. based on their play and the play *Napoleon on Broadway* by Charles Bruce Milholland: cinematographer.

Joseph August: edited by Gene Havlick: released by Columbia Pictures. Black and white. Running time: 91 minutes.

With: John Barrymore (Oscar Jaffe). Carole Lombard (Lily Garland). Walter Connolly (Oliver Webb). Roscoe Karns (Owen O'Malley). Charles Levison (Max Jacobs) and Etienne Girardot (Clark).

As a vainglorious stage producer, John Barrymore is in fine fettle in *Twentieth Century,* a pictorial adaptation of the Hecht-MacArthur play, which is now decorating the Radio City Music Hall screen. And if it be said that it is his best performance since the one he gave in the film *Reunion in Vienna* it is by no means casting any reflections on his work in the interim, but merely stating that here he has a role with which to conjure, one that calls for a definite characterization notwithstanding the farcical interludes. Even during the repetitious mad moments of the tale, Mr. Barrymore acts with such imagination and zest that he never fails to keep the picture thoroughly alive.

Messrs. Hecht and MacArthur, who in the first place based their stage offering on a play written by Charles Bruce Millholland, were also responsible for bringing the story to the screen. They have made certain changes in doing this task, but, as in the original work, it seems a pity that they were tempted to stray occasionally too far from the realm of restrained comedy and indulge their fancy for boisterous humor. Instead of having all the action occur on a train bound from Chicago for this city, as was the case in the play, nearly half of the picture is concerned with incidents in the theater run by the egomaniac Oscar Jaffe. This change is quite a good one, for although there is no gainsaying that the happenings on the train are frequently hilarious, the earlier glimpses have the virtue of being more effective through their relative restraint.

Oscar Jaffe's imperiousness is enough to rattle the brains of anybody working for him. He has his passing fancies, and his press agent and his manager are presumed to be able to guess what is in his mind. He decides that a girl who ventures backstage with the name of Mildred Plotka shall henceforth be known as Lily Garland. Oliver Webb and Owen O'Malley, respectively Jaffe's manager and press agent, evidently think that they have never looked upon a girl quite as gauche as this novice. On the other hand, the omnipotent impresario does not deign to harken to their advice and persists in instructing Lily in acting her role, drawing chalk lines and making figures on the floor to help her. It may not happen always so in life, but in this tale Lily wins histrionic laurels on her first night. A glistening star adorns her dressing room door and for three years Lily, as actress and mistress, endures Jaffe's idiosyncrasies.

Jaffe and Lily have their tempestuous moments, but they usually kiss and make up. Finally there is one outburst after which Lily vows she will have no more of the hysterical Jaffe, and she goes West, to Hollywood and fame. It is on the return journey some time later—after Lily Garland's blue eyes and blond hair have appeared on newsstands throughout the land—that Jaffe, accompanied by Webb and O'Malley, embarks at the Windy City for New York and discovers that the beauteous Lily is on the same train. Unfortunately, she is accompanied by her fiancé, for whom Jaffe expresses utter contempt.

A variety of characters aboard the flyer help to sustain the interest in the hectic doings. There is the lunatic with illusions of fabulous wealth, the excited conductors, porters and brakeman, and a couple of bearded players who hope to get into a Jaffe production, when actually the poor star maker has had to disguise himself to escape his creditors.

There is many a witty remark in this harum scarum adventure. Carole Lombard gives an able portrayal as Lily. Walter Connolly is excellent as Webb and Roscoe Karns, although he talks somewhat indistinctly, something which may be excused because of the bibulous nature of the character he plays, adds bright flashes to the film. Etienne Girardot is another asset.

—*M.H., May 4, 1934*

TWO ENGLISH GIRLS

Directed by François Truffaut: written (in French, with English subtitles) by Mr. Truffaut and Jean Gruault, based on the novel by Henri-Pierre Roché: cinematographer, Nestor Almendros: edited by Yann Dedet: music by Georges Delarue: art designer, Michel de Broin: produced by Claude Miler: released by Janus Films. Running time: 108 minutes.

With: Jean-Pierre Léaud (Claude Roc). Kika Markham (Anne Brown). Sylvia Marriott (Mrs. Brown). Marie Mansart (Madame Roc). Philippe Léotard (Djurka). Stacey Tendeter (Muriel Brown). Irene Tunc (Ruta) and Mark Peterson (Mr. Flint).

François Truffaut's *Two English Girls* is a film of such beautiful, charming and comic discretion that it isn't until the end that one realizes it's also immensely sad and even brutal, though in the nonbrutalizing way that truth can sometimes be.

The film was shown last night at the New York Film Festival at Alice Tully Hall and opens its commercial engagement Sunday at the Fine Arts Theater, where, I trust, it will remain through Thanksgiving, Christmas, and beyond.

The source material is *Les Deux Anglaises et Le Continent,* the second novel by Henri-Pierre Roché, who didn't get around to writing his first until he was seventy-four. That was *Jules et Jim,* which Truffaut adapted into his finest film in 1961.

A bit too much will probably be made of the fact that *Two English Girls* reverses the central situation of *Jules and Jim,* in which the two heroes spend their lives being turned on and off by the liberated Catherine.

The new film, like the earlier one, is set largely in an undefined past—that is, sometime in pre–World War I Paris, though the exact time is left fuzzy, as times usually are in fables. Instead of two young men, the victims (who are in great measure the mistresses of their fates) are two proper English girls, sisters, who share a profound attachment for the same young Frenchman.

In many ways, however, *Two English Girls* is more closely linked to such later (and dissimilar) Truffaut films as *The Soft Skin, Mississippi Mermaid* and *Stolen Kisses,* each a variation on the conflict between a love that is obsessive (sometimes called pure) and a mortal one that is always aware of compromise.

Jules and Jim touches on this. *Two English Girls* is about nothing else. *Jules and Jim* also has to do with a number of other things, including social satire, and is an ambitious work of a much younger director. *Two English Girls* is less lyric, more spare, completely preoccupied by not only the extremely complicated moral barriers to love, but also by the physical impediments.

In no other film he has made has Truffaut ever expressed the ruthless ecstasy of the scene in *Two En-*

glish Girls in which Claude (Jean-Pierre Léaud) finally takes the virginity of the pure Muriel (Stacey Tendeter). Unlike her sister Anne (Kika Markham, who accepts her sexuality, though with scarcely more happy results), Muriel, who manages to look like both Queen Elizabeth and Catherine Deneuve, behaves like a princess in a fairy tale. She hides behind dark glasses, as if she had suffered a wicked enchantment, and says such things as "I want all of Claude or nothing. If it's no, let it be like death."

The film covers seven years in the lives of the curious trio, much of it as if the film were the daily journal that was Roché's favorite literary form. The scenes are sometimes so short they are almost subliminal, with the voice of the narrator (Truffaut) often supplying a text. Purists, I expect, will again object to this tampering with the accepted relationship between image, which the purists think is paramount, and word, which has always been thought to be a lesser tool of cinema.

The effect, nevertheless, is lovely, and even appropriate, since fables begin with spoken words. The performances are fine. Léaud may well be—as Truffaut calls him—the greatest French actor of his generation. At least I think that explains why he seemed so off-putting—which he was supposed to—in *Bed and Board* and here, as the earnestly free-loving rake, so appealing.

The film is filled with wonderful things, but I especially remember the sequence in which Anne and Claude spend a week in a cabin on a lake in Switzerland. "They were more resolute than in love," says the narrator. "Their program was simple: live first and define it later." At the end of the week, we see them in a long-shot, rowing away from the island—in separate rowboats.

—*V.C., October 12, 1972*

THE TWO OF US

Directed by Claude Berri: written (in French, with English subtitles) by Mr. Berri and Gerard Brach: cinematographer. Jean Penzer: edited by Sophie Coussein and Denise Charvein: music by Georges Delarue: art designer. Georges Levy: produced by Paul Cadeac: released by Cinema V. Black and white. Running time: 86 minutes.

With: Michel Simon (Gramp), Luce Fabiole (Granny), Alain Cohen (Claude), Roger Carel (Victor) and Paul Preboist (Maxime).

The Two of Us, which opened last night at the Beekman Theater, is a lovely, sentimental reminiscence of childhood in wartime. The child is an eight-year-old Jewish boy in Paris in 1944; and one of the unstated themes of the movie is the degree to which even the most catastrophic political developments can leave personal lives, particularly the private lives of children, virtually untouched—or touched in quite mysterious ways.

The child, played with a wonderful balance of gravity and mischief by Alain Cohen, keeps getting into trouble right along with the other boys, and thereby threatening to blow the cover of his Jewish parents, who are trying to represent themselves in Paris as Alsatians. A Catholic friend of the family makes a suggestion. The boy is taught the Lord's Prayer, a new surname, and to call himself a Catholic. Then he is sent off to spend the remainder of the war with a lovable, but anti-Semitic old man in the country.

The old man is played by Michel Simon—who was already a great actor in 1934, when he starred in Jean Vigo's *L'Atalante* and in whose honor a festival of six films opened yesterday at the Museum of Modern Art. Michel Simon has grown in size, his face has more crevasses. He is still great. He breathes in a slow, underwater sort of way—so that the general impression is that of an immense, thoughtful, warmhearted and aquatic geological formation.

It is extraordinary to watch that live and serious child—with beautiful dark eyes and the marvelous dignity of children who are not trying to impress—playing against that enormous old genius. They grow to love each other. The boy shrewdly teases the old man about his anti-Semitism. The old man, in the context of his wife and provincial family, is an incarnation of everything.

He mutters. He listens to the BBC. He says, "In my house I decide who governs France." He listens to a German propaganda station. He dotes on his bronchitic dog Kinou, who languishes as the Allies advance. (In fact, the whole movie is based on a kind of reverse eddy from the war: every Allied advance brings the relationship nearer an end.)

The French movie, which is in black and white, is directed beautifully by Claude Berri, who also wrote the screenplay—and who directed the fine short film about a child and his rooster, *Le Poulet.* It is probably excellent for children who have seen more violent pictures about war. The story impinges on peacetime childhoods as well.

—*R.A., February 20, 1968*

2001: A SPACE ODYSSEY

Produced and directed by Stanley Kubrick; written by Mr. Kubrick and Arthur C. Clarke, based on the short story "The Sentinel" by Mr. Clarke; directors of photography, Geoffrey Unsworth and John Alcott; edited by Ray Lovejoy; art designer, John Hoesli; released by Metro-Goldwyn-Mayer. Running time: 139 minutes.

With: Keir Dullea (Bowman), Gary Lockwood (Poole), William Sylvester (Dr. Heywood Floyd), Dan Richter (Moonwatcher), Douglas Rain (Voice of HAL 9000), Leonard Rossiter (Smyslov), Margaret Tyzack (Elena), Robert Beatty (Halvorsen), Sean Sullivan (Michaels) and Frank Miller (Mission Controller).

Even the M-G-M lion is stylized and abstracted in Stanley Kubrick's *2001: A Space Odyssey,* a film in which infinite care, intelligence, patience, imagination and Cinerama have been devoted to what looks like the apotheosis of the fantasy of a precocious, early 1950's city boy. The movie, on which Kubrick collaborated with the British science-fiction author Arthur C. Clarke, is nominally about the finding, in the year 2001, of a camera-shy sentient slab on the moon and an expedition to the planet Jupiter to find whatever sentient being the slab is beaming its communications at.

There is evidence in the film of Clarke's belief that men's minds will ultimately develop to the point where they dissolve in a kind of world mind. There is a subplot in the old science-fiction nightmare of man at terminal odds with his computer. There is one ultimate science-fiction voyage of a man (Keir Dullea) through outer and inner space, through the phases of his own life in time thrown out of phase by some higher intelligence, to his death and rebirth in what looked like an intergalactic embryo.

But all this is the weakest side of a very complicated, languid movie—in which almost a half-hour passes before the first man appears and the first word is spoken, and an entire hour goes by before the plot even begins to declare itself. Its real energy seems to derive from that bespectacled prodigy reading comic books around the block. The whole sensibility is intellectual fifties child: chess games, body-building exercises, beds on the spacecraft that look like camp bunks, other beds that look like Egyptian mummies, Richard Strauss music, time games, Strauss waltzes, Howard Johnson's, birthday phone calls. In their space uniforms, the voyagers look like Jiminy Crickets. When they want to be let out of the craft they say, "Pod bay doors open," as one might say "Bomb bay doors open" in every movie out of World War II.

When the voyagers go off to plot against HAL, the computer, it might be HAL, the camper, they are ganging up on. When HAL is expiring, he sings "Daisy." Even the problem posed when identical twin computers, previously infallible, disagree is the kind of sentence-that-says-of-itself-I-lie paradox, which—along with the song and the nightmare of ganging up—belong to another age. When the final slab, a combination Prime Mover slab and coffin lid, closes in, it begins to resemble a fifties candy bar.

The movie is so completely absorbed in its own problems, its use of color and space, its fanatical devotion to science-fiction detail, that it is somewhere between hypnotic and immensely boring. (With intermission, it is three hours long.) Kubrick seems as occupied with the best use of the outer edge of the screen as any painter, and he is particularly fond of simultaneous rotations, revolving and straightforward motions—the visual equivalent of rubbing the stomach and patting the head. All kinds of minor touches are perfectly done: there are carnivorous apes that look real; when they throw their first bone weapon into the air, Kubrick cuts to a spacecraft; the amiable HAL begins most of his sentences with "Well," and his answer to "How's everything?" is, naturally, "Everything's under control."

There is also a kind of fanaticism about other kinds of authenticity: space travelers look as sickly and exhausted as travelers usually do; they are exposed in space stations to depressing canned music; the viewer is often made to feel that the screen is the window of a spacecraft; and as Kubrick introduces one piece of unfamiliar apparatus after another—a craft that looks, from one angle, like a plumber's helper with a fist on the end of it, a pod that resembles a limbed washing machine—the viewer is always made aware of exactly how it is used and where he is in it.

The special effects in the movie—particularly a voyage, either through Dullea's eye or through the slab and over the surface of Jupiter-Earth and into a period bedroom—are the best I have ever seen; and the number of ways in which the movie conveys visual information (there is very little dialogue) drives it to an outer limit of the visual.

And yet the uncompromising slowness of the movie makes it hard to sit through without talking—and people on all sides when I saw it were talking almost throughout the film. Very annoying. With all its attention to detail—a kind of reveling in its own I.Q.—the movie acknowledged no obligation to validate its conclusion for those, me for example, who are not science-fiction buffs. By the end, three unreconciled plot lines—the slabs, Dullea's aging, the period bedroom—are simply left there like a Rorschach, with murky implications of theology. This is a long step outside the convention, some extra scripts seem required and the all-purpose answer, "relativity," does not really serve unless it can be verbalized.

The movie opened yesterday at the Capitol.

—*R.A., April 4, 1968*

TWO WOMEN

Directed by Vittorio De Sica: written (in Italian, with English subtitles) by Cesare Zavattini and Mr. De Sica, based on the novel by Alberto Moravia: cinematographers, Gabor Pogany and Mari Capriotti: edited by Adriana Novelli: music by Armando Trovaioli: art designer, Gastone Medin: produced by Carlo Ponti: released by Embassy Pictures. Black and white. Running time: 105 minutes.

With: Sophia Loren (Cesira), Jean-Paul Belmondo (Michele), Eleanora Brown (Rosetta), Raf Vallone (Giovanni) and Renato Salvatori (Florindo).

A sharp change of pace for Sophia Loren from the generally slick and frivolous roles she has played during the last several years in American movies is most conspicuous and praiseworthy in her return to Italian films in *Two Women (La Ciociara),* which came to the Sutton yesterday. Suddenly, the decompressed Miss Loren demonstrates herself an actress again and, under the direction of Vittorio De Sica, takes a firm place in a simple, honest film.

It is not a momentous picture, not the sort that is likely to be recalled as one of the great neo-realist—or post-neo-realist—Italian films, for it is built upon a frame of little details that are collapsed by one cruel, climactic incident and it is so colloquial in so much of its content that it seems exclusively national. Furthermore, the English subtitles do such a poor job of translating the abundant and juicy Italian dialogue that the meaning and quality of the talk, which is so important, are lost for those who haven't the full Italian tongue.

For the first hour or so it is deceptive—deliberately so, no doubt, as a way of disarming the viewer for the shock and significance of its crushing episode. It is simply the easy, jolly story of a young widowed mother who cuts out of Rome after a series of heavy bombardments in 1943 and takes her thirteen-year-old daughter back to her own natal village in the hills of Ciociara.

Except for one ugly experience with a strafing plane on the way in and a brush with a couple of clumsy fascist police that is more amusing than unpleasant, the two get along quite nicely with the peasants back in the hills, sitting out the war in comparative safety and wanting only for an abundance of food and a little love. The latter is tentatively offered by a timid, bespectacled young man whom the mother lightly puts off as too feeble but the daughter wistfully worships from afar.

Then Italy is invaded by the Allies, the Germans grimly retreat, and mother and daughter fall in behind the Americans in what they hope will be an easy hike back to Rome. But one night, while seeking a little shelter alone in a bombed-out church, they are attacked and brutally ravished by a howling mob of Moroccan troops. It is a horrible, shattering experience, a destructive bolt out of the blue, and the mother's pathetic endeavors to correct the damage make up the remainder of the tale.

Evidently, the purpose of this suddenly tragic account, as originally written by Alberto Moravio and adapted by Cesare Zavattini for the screen, is to represent the disaster of those people—and, indeed, of Italy—who thought the war was a matter of playing it cozy and making do. The indication of Allied soldiers committing the devastating rape is the ultimate bitter dramatization and comment upon the tragedy of the war.

This is the comment of the picture, and it is suddenly, sharply put, but the beauty of Miss Loren's performance is in her illumination of a passionate mother role. She is happy, expansive, lusty in the early phases of the film, in tune with the gusto of the peasants, gentle with her child. But when disaster strikes, she is grave and profound. When she weeps for the innocence of her daughter, one quietly weeps with her.

The child is played with luminous sweetness and dignity by Eleanora Brown, and the Frenchman, Jean-Paul Belmondo (the thug of *Breathless*), is mildly amusing as the timid young man. Raf Vallone and Renato Salvatori are sturdy in very small roles.

Signor De Sica's direction has the qualities of fullness and momentum that are familiar and so compelling in his films.

—B.C., May 9, 1961

UGETSU

Directed by Kenji Mizoguchi; written (in Japanese, with English subtitles) by Matsutaro Kawaguchi and Yoshikata Yoda; based on the classic stories of Akinari Ueda; cinematographer, Kazuo Miyagawa; edited by Mitsuji Miyata; music by Fumio Hayasaka and Ichiro Saito; art designer, Kisaku Ito; produced by Masaichi Nagata; released by Daiei Films and Edward Harrison. Black and white. Running time: 96 minutes.

With: Machiko Kyo (Lady Wakasa), Masayuki Mori (Genjuro), Kinuyo Tanaka (Miyagi), Mitsuko Mito (Ohama) and Sakae Ozawa (Tobei).

Much more than the language that is spoken in *Ugetsu*, the Japanese film that opened last night at the Plaza, will be hard for American audiences to comprehend—hard for even the most attentive patron to grasp as it goes along. For both the theme and the style of exposition in this Venice award-winning film have a strangely obscure, inferential, almost studiedly perplexing quality.

Indeed, it is this peculiar vagueness and use of symbolism and subterfuge that give to this Oriental fable what it has of a sort of eerie charm. They vex you at first with their confusions, but if you have patience, and hold on, intent upon finding out what's cooking, you'll get flavor from this weird, exotic stew.

For the mélange of strange adventures of two peasants and their wives in feudal Japan—back in the sixteenth century, when war lords were ravaging the land—is composed of all manner of pictured violence, demoniac shapes and sounds, hypnotic wailing of voices and some beautiful images. Terror is caught in monstrous faces and wildly contorted human forms; quietness and peace are indicated in gorgeous pictorial harmonies. Kenji Mizoguchi, who directed, has a fantastic flexibility in using his actors and his camera, as witness his range in this film.

Perhaps it will help if we tell you, here and now, that the point of it all—as nearly as we could finally make out—is that social ambition and greed are vices which the Japanese peasant would do very well to avoid. This is eventually illustrated by the garbled misfortunes that befall the two somewhat reckless and disloyal husbands in the tale.

One of them, eager to be a soldier, an arrogant samurai, lets ambition lure him to such follies that he wholly neglects his poor wife and finally, in his moment of false triumph, discovers that she has been made a prostitute. The other, dreaming of riches, falls victim to a Japanese Lorelei, who seduces him away from his family and then turns out to be a ghost. This is a point of some confusion, since it isn't revealed until the end. Both fellows are stock fiction characters, and the lessons proved are banal.

It is this averageness of the stories that removes this legend-inspired film from a class with that previous artful and exciting Japanese picture *Rashomon*. But the imagery and the acting are no less intriguing here, and the use of sound for weird disturbance is notably rarefied. Machiko Kyo and Masayuki Mori, who played the wife and husband in *Rashomon,* are fine as the ghostly temptress and the man she vamps, to his chagrin. And Sakae Ozawa as the hotheaded fellow who wants to be a samurai has flamboyant airs.

We understand that *Ugetsu* means "pale and mysterious moon after the rain"—which is just about as revealing as a great deal else in this film.

—B.C., September 8, 1954

ULZANA'S RAID

Directed by Robert Aldrich; written by Alan Sharp; director of photography, Joseph Biroc; edited by Michael Luciano; music by Frank DeVol; art designer, James Vance; produced by Carter De Haven; released by Universal Pictures. Running time: 103 minutes.

With: Burt Lancaster (McIntosh), Bruce Davison (Lieutenant Garnet DeBuin), Jorge Luke (Ke-Ni-Tay), Richard Jaeckel (Sergeant), Joaquin Martinez (Ulzana), Lloyd Bochner (Captain Gates) and Karl Swenson (Rukeyser).

Because film reviews in newspapers are essentially news stories—that is, reports about what happened yesterday, to whom and where—one is required to describe at least something of the plot of Robert Aldrich's *Ulzana's Raid*.

However, I'll do it briefly because the very ordinary plot does not do justice to the complexity of the film itself. *Ulzana's Raid* is a Western whose conventional outlines have been rather violently and beautifully bent by Mr. Aldrich, an unreconstructed misogynist (*Whatever Happened to Baby Jane?*) even when he makes movies (such as *The Dirty Dozen*) dealing exclusively with men. On second thought, it may be that Mr. Aldrich doesn't really hate women. It could be that he feels they clutter up and, in effect, deny the dark side of the world where his most interesting films inevitably take place.

Ulzana's Raid, which opened yesterday at the Forum and other theaters around town, is the story of an ill-fated flight and almost equally ill-fated pursuit, about a tough old Indian fighter (Burt Lancaster) and a callow young cavalry lieutenant (Bruce Davison) and their mission to track down an Apache named Ulzana who, with nine braves, has fled the reservation to murder, rape and find the Indian equivalent of identity. Why, the lieutenant asks his Apache scout, do Apaches kill so cruelly and wantonly? Says the scout: "Man give up power when he die. Like fire and heat."

Like many Aldrich films, including the recent *The Grissom Gang,* the new film plays Russian roulette with itself, not with bullets but with ludicrous lines, and with violence that is so excessive that it comes close to self-parody. Aldrich fans tend either to be humorless (like his worst critics) or to admire (as I do) the daring with which he so consistently courts disaster by turning an ordinary story into (in this case) a winner-take-nothing parable.

Although *Ulzana's Raid* deals in the kind of narrative suspense and shock that would keep the most unsophisticated 42d Street audience awake, the film is as bleak as its Arizona landscapes. Much of the screenplay, written by Alan Sharp, depends on the pride and moral breakdown of the young lieutenant, an Eastern minister's son who is completely out of his element. Aldrich's West is a timeless place where noble motives lead to disastrous actions. Loyalties are hopelessly confused and the only possible satisfaction in life is behaving well for the immediate moment.

This Burt Lancaster does with ease, along with Bruce Davison, Richard Jaeckel, and the rest of the predominantly male cast. Of the three women I remember in the film, one is shot to death so she can't be raped by Indians, a second is raped and turned into a raving lunatic and the third, the Indian girl who plays Lancaster's mistress, is seen only from the eyes up. *Ulzana's Raid* has little time for sentiment.

—V.C., November 16, 1972

UMBERTO D.

Produced and directed by Vittorio De Sica; written (in Italian, with English subtitles) by Cesare Zavattini and Mr. De Sica, based on a story by Mr. Zavattini; cinematographer, Aldo Graziati; edited by Eraldo di Roma; music by Alessandro Cicognini; production designer, Virgilio Marchi; released by Harrison and Davison. Black and white. Running time: 89 minutes.

With: Carlo Battisti (Umberto D.), Maria Pia Casilio (Maria) and Lina Gennari (Landlady).

Vittorio De Sica's genius as a director of realistic films has already been evidenced in this country by his *Shoeshine* and *The Bicycle Thief*. But nothing of his that has yet been seen here has had quite the pure simplicity and almost unbearable candor and compassion of his current *Umberto D.*

This truly extraordinary picture, which is nothing more than a searching study of a lonely old man fighting a losing battle for existence on the piteous pension of a civil servant in Rome, is just now being offered in this country—it opened yesterday at the Guild—even though it has been finished for more than four years and has been shown considerably abroad.

The reason for this delay is to be suspected, once one has seen the film. It is an utterly heartbreaking picture, almost from the word go. The plight and destiny of the aging hero, who has only a mongrel dog and the casual friendship of a rooming-house slavey to comfort his loneliness, are plainly without prospect or hope. The only thing that could save the old gentleman is a happy contrivance of some sort. And this you may be sure that Signor De Sica, with his uncompromising integrity, will not invent.

The merchants obviously were anxious about the market for such a film.

But, hopeful or not, in comparison to the usual run of movie make-believe, this eloquent scan of a man's emotions under the most trying circumstances is a great and memorable achievement on the screen. It is an honest, noble study of human character with which few film exercises can compare.

The story, if such you can call it, that Signor De Sica and Cesare Zavattini tell is simply one of the old man's endeavors to sustain himself and his dog. The old man is about to be thrown out of his lodging by a proprietress who has no concern for him or his financial problem. He pitiably tries to sell his things to hang onto the room he has called home for the last twenty years. He goes to a charity hospital to try to save money. He loses his dog. He recovers the animal from the pound, but then is forced out of his room.

Weary, despondent and defeated, the gentle and dignified old man comes to the tragic extremity of attempting suicide, with his dog—which he has vainly attempted to give a good home—wrapped in his arms. But even that fails. The dog diverts him. At the plainly Charles Chaplinesque close, the old man is wistfully frolicking with his pet down an alley of autumnal trees.

But more than this simple continuity, the beautiful picture contains a comprehension of human feelings and fatalism that pierce the heart and mind. In Carlo Battisti, a college professor who never had acted before, Signor De Sica has a perfect reflector of the character of his lonely old man. Never have we seen shame and torment so clearly revealed on a man's face as when this old gentleman endeavors, unsuccessfully, to beg—or such absolute desolation as when he makes his decision to die. Signor De Sica has used him like a wonderfully mellow violin.

And the relations of the brave old fellow—who is not always cheerless, by the way—with the slavey, played gently by Maria Pia Casilio, give keen comment on the ages of man. For the young girl, too, has her troubles. She is pregnant and unwed. Her unwitting sense of the future as she comforts her old friend is deeply sad. Lina Gennari's landlady is an excellently etched character among the several minor persons that represent the flow of life in this film.

—*B. C., November 8, 1955*

THE UNBEARABLE LIGHTNESS OF BEING

Directed by Philip Kaufman; written by Jean-Claude Carrière and Mr. Kaufman, based on the novel by Milan Kundera; director of photography, Sven Nykvist; edited by Walter Murch; music by Mark Adler, Keith Richards and Leoš Janáček; production designer, Pierre Guffroy; produced by Saul Zaentz; released by Orion Pictures. Running time: 172 minutes.

With: Daniel Day-Lewis (Tomas), Juliette Binoche (Tereza), Lena Olin (Sabina), Derek de Lint (Franz) and Erland Josephson (The Ambassador).

Philip Kaufman's *Unbearable Lightness of Being* begins with much promise, as if it were a ribald fairy tale. "In Prague in 1968," says a title card, "there lived a young doctor named Tomas." Tomas (Daniel Day-Lewis) comes out of the operating room and goes straight to a pretty nurse waiting in the supply room.

"Take off your clothes," says Tomas. Forever altering one aspect of playing hard-to-get, the nurse does. On the other side of a frosted-glass window several other hospital employees watch Tomas's technique with admiration.

"But the woman who understood him best was Sabina," says a second title card. The film cuts to Tomas and Sabina (Lena Olin) in a frenzied, thoroughly satisfying coupling on the platform bed in her studio—she's a painter.

Tomas and Sabina share a passion for acrobatic, technically ingenious sex that excludes serious emotional commitment but not nonstop conversation. That's the wonder of Tomas and Sabina. They can enjoy everything they're doing while always remaining a little detached. Each is like a movie critic who goes through his job with one part of his mind on the movie, while the part that's safely outside it criticizes the critic's reactions and prepares to tell all at any minute.

In the midst of ecstasy, the sweating, exultant Sabina tells Tomas "You are the complete opposite of kitsch," though without defining the term. It makes no difference. It's clear that, to Sabina, whatever Tomas is doing, he's doing it right.

Tomas buzzes serenely through the world like a bumblebee, his eye on the next flower even before he has quite exhausted the one he's with.

A third title card: "Tomas was sent to a spa town to perform an operation." It's there that Tomas meets the exceptional young woman who changes the course of his existence, forever altering one aspect of what has seemed to be his lightness of being.

She is Tereza (Juliette Binoche), a romantic waitress who falls profoundly in love with Tomas without knowing anything about him. She follows him back to Prague and, before he's aware of the consequences, he's allowing her to sleep the entire night in his bed, something that has always been against his rules. Soon they are married.

After that, *The Unbearable Lightness of Being* settles down to recapitulate the superficial events of Milan Kundera's introspective, philosophical novel with fidelity and an accumulating heaviness, as well as at immense length—nearly three hours. It's possible to read the book in less time.

The film opens today at Loews Tower East.

The novel, by the celebrated Czechoslovak writer who now lives in Paris, was adapted by Mr. Kaufman and Jean-Claude Carrière. Mr. Carrière is the French writer whose screenplays (*Belle de Jour, The Discreet Charm of the Bourgeoisie,* among others) for Luis Buñuel exemplify the seamless collaboration possible when a brilliant director meets a brilliant writer who knows the director's mind better than the director possibly does. Mr. Kaufman's most recent work was the fine, underappreciated adaptation of Tom Wolfe's *Right Stuff.*

These credentials are worth noting. It's obvious that both Mr. Kaufman and Mr. Carrière understood the problems they faced in making a screen adaptation of a novel whose central character is really a never-seen, loquacious "I," representing the novelist spinning the tale. This "I" is both informally chatty and God-like. He doesn't participate in the story of Tomas, Sabina, Tereza and the others. He's looking down on them from a literary "above." When it suits him, he briefly enters the characters' minds and departs, a benign thief in the night.

Mr. Kundera entertains and instructs the reader. He also provokes responses that give point to commonplace misadventures set in momentous times. These are so unspeakably sad that the comic method seems the only civilized alternative to what would otherwise turn into kitsch, something sentimental and false.

Like brain surgeons removing a tumor, Mr. Kaufman and Mr. Carrière have excised the "I" from the screenplay. Whenever possible, they've saved bits and pieces of his observations, which have been reinserted as dialogue spoken by the characters, frequently with a good deal of awkwardness. The "voice" of the novel is gone. What remains is not exactly bowdlerized Kundera but, even with all the care, intelligence and eroticism that have gone into it, it's a bit zombielike. It would be difficult to recognize if one hadn't known it when it was alive.

Mr. Kundera, whose citizenship was revoked after he left Czechoslovakia, dislikes having his novels and stories parsed for their politics. Yet everything he writes inevitably has strong political meaning, especially in relation to Czechoslovakia, which, landlocked and periodically overrun and cut up by invaders through the centuries, has somehow maintained its own identity.

The Unbearable Lightness of Being opens in 1968

during the thaw known as the "Prague spring," when everything in politics and the arts seemed possible after the long repression of the Stalinist winter.

As Tomas is drawn against his will into commitment to Tereza, he's also, briefly, drawn into politics. He writes an ironic essay about the morality of Czechoslovak Communist politicians who admit the errors of their Stalinist days without, like Oedipus, feeling the necessity of purging their guilt.

After the Soviet invasion, Sabina drives off to Switzerland, followed by Tomas and Tereza. When Tereza, feeling bereft with her womanizing husband in a strange country, returns to Czechoslovakia, Tomas follows. He remains committed to Tereza, though still unfaithful. His essay on Oedipus is recalled to haunt him. Tomas becomes a true political activist by remaining resolutely passive. This is the bittersweet joke.

I'm not sure how much of this comes through in the movie since, if one has read the novel, the impulse is to fill in the gaps. Photographed by Sven Nykvist, the film looks beautiful and authentic, but it's so monotonously paced that it seems to have been edited with the aid of a metronome. Although a good deal of the narrative has been excised, nothing has been condensed. The details of the lives of Tomas, Sabina and Tereza, recalled without Mr. Kundera's comments, don't fill the huge landscape provided by the film's extraordinary running time. It's literal without even being literary.

Mr. Day-Lewis, Miss Binoche and Miss Olin (who was spectacular in Ingmar Bergman's *After the Rehearsal*) are surprisingly fine—both modest and intense as lovers whose private lives are defined by public events. The supporting cast includes Derek de Lint as one of Sabina's lovers, Erland Josephson in a tiny part, and (listed but unseen by me) Jan Nemec, the excellent Czechoslovak director whose *Report on the Party and Its Guests* came out during the "Prague spring."

Mr. Kaufman attempts to find a common denominator among the various accents by having everyone speak English with a Czechoslovak accent, but even these vary according to each actor's country of origin.

The *Unbearable Lightness of Being* is notably ambitious and it avoids kitsch. It understands Mr. Kundera, even as it fails to find picture-equivalents to his ideas.

CORRECTION

Because of a computer error, the film review of *The Unbearable Lightness of Being* in Weekend yesterday included a phrase erroneously in the second paragraph. The passage should have read: " 'Take off your clothes,' says Tomas. After three seconds of playing hard-to-get, the nurse does. On the other side of a frosted-glass window several other hospital employees watch Tomas's technique with admiration."

—*V.C., February 5, 1988*

UNFORGIVEN

Directed and produced by Clint Eastwood; written by David Webb Peoples; director of photography, Jack N. Green; edited by Joel Cox; music by Lennie Niehaus; production designer, Henry Bumstead; released by Warner Brothers. Running time: 130 minutes.

With: Clint Eastwood (Bill Munny), Gene Hackman (Little Bill Daggett), Morgan Freeman (Ned Logan), Richard Harris (English Bob), Jaimz Woolvett (Schofield Kid), Saul Rubinek (W. W. Beauchamp), Frances Fisher (Strawberry Alice), Anna Thomson (Delilah Fitzgerald), David Mucci (Quick Mike), Rob Campbell (Davey Bunting), Anthony James (Skinny DuBois), Tara Dawn Frederick (Little Sue), Beverley Elliott (Silky), Liisa Repo-Martell (Faith), Josie Smith (Crow Creek Kate), Shane Meier (Will Munny) and Aline Levasseur (Penny Munny).

Time has been good to Clint Eastwood. If possible, he looks even taller, leaner and more mysteriously possessed than he did in Sergio Leone's seminal *Fistful of Dollars* a quarter of a century ago. The years haven't softened him. They have given him the presence of some fierce force of nature, which may be why the landscapes of the mythic, late nineteenth-century West become him, never more so than in his new *Unforgiven*.

As written by David Webb Peoples and directed by Mr. Eastwood, *Unforgiven* is a most entertaining Western that pays homage to the great tradition of movie Westerns while surreptitiously expressing a certain amount of skepticism. Mr. Eastwood has learned a lot from his mentors, including the great Don Siegel

(*Two Mules for Sister Sara* and *The Beguiled,* among others), a director with no patience for sentimentality.

The time is the 1880's. The principal setting is Big Whiskey, a forlorn hamlet in that vast American no-man's-land of high plains edged by mountains, somewhere between St. Louis and San Francisco but not on any map.

Late one night a couple of cowboys are on the second floor of the saloon with the girls. Suddenly one of the cowboys whips out his knife and slashes the face of Delilah, the prostitute he's with. It seems that she made a rude comment about his anatomy. Instead of arresting the cowboys, Little Bill Daggett, the sheriff, allows them to get off with the understanding that they hand over six horses to the saloon keeper.

Strawberry Alice, the victim's best friend, is outraged. "We may be whores," she says, "but we aren't horses." Alice, Delilah, and the other girls pool their savings and offer a bounty of $1,000 to anybody who will murder the cowboys.

Thus *Unforgiven* becomes an epic about the revenge of whores. It's not sending up the women. Rather it's equating Old Western codes of honor with the handful of men who set out to collect the bounty, motivated in varying degrees by economic necessity, greed and half-baked notions of glory.

Chief among the bounty hunters is the aging Bill Munny (Mr. Eastwood), a widower trying to support his two young children on an unsuccessful hog farm. Munny has been keeping to himself in recent years. He's still trying to live down his notorious career as a gun-crazy outlaw, a man who used to shoot women, children—anybody—just for the hell of it.

There is something creepy about him now, especially about the way he keeps harping on how his wife "saved" him, his distaste for violence and his need to be true to his pledge never to pick up a gun again. He has something of the manner of the mild-mannered clerk who comes into the office on Monday morning and shoots everyone in sight.

When a young fellow who styles himself the Schofield Kid (Jaimz Woolvett) asks Munny to join him to win the bounty, Munny at first refuses. Then he changes his mind, apparently because he is desperately hard up, but with Munny you can't be sure. Along the way to Big Whiskey, they are joined by Ned Logan (Morgan Freeman), who rode with Munny in the outlaw days and appears to trust him.

Also en route to Big Whiskey for the same purpose is English Bob (Richard Harris). He's a dandyish former outlaw who, when first seen, is aboard a train, reading about the assassination of President James A. Garfield and explaining to anyone who will listen why America would be better off with a king. His admiring companion is W. W. Beauchamp (Saul Rubinek), whom English Bob introduces as "my biographer," the author of a penny dreadful about the outlaw titled *The Duke of Death.*

Little Bill Daggett (Gene Hackman) is ready for the bounty hunters as they arrive in Big Whiskey. He immediately spots English Bob as he gets off the stagecoach, gives him a sadistic beating and throws him in jail. Mr. Harris, who has a tendency to overpower his roles, has never been finer, funnier or more restrained than he is as English Bob, whom Daggett insists on calling "the Duck of Death."

Things turn far darker with the arrival of Munny, Ned and the Schofield Kid. Daggett suspects their purpose but is unable to prove anything. Just to let them know who runs Big Whiskey, Daggett beats up Munny as savagely as he has English Bob, but Munny appears to ask for it. Bleeding and only partly conscious, he crawls out of the saloon and into a muddy gutter.

It is a measure of how the film works that Munny's almost Christ-like acceptance of his beating is one of the film's scariest moments. There is a madness inside him waiting to emerge, but where and when? *Unforgiven,* which has no relation to *The Unforgiven,* the 1960 John Huston Western, never quite fulfills the expectations it so carefully sets up. It doesn't exactly deny them, but the bloody confrontations that end the film appear to be purposely muted, more effective theoretically than dramatically.

This, I suspect, is a calculated risk. Mr. Eastwood doesn't play it safe as a director, but there are times in *Unforgiven,* as in his jazz epic, *Bird,* that the sheer scope of the narrative seems to overwhelm him. It's not easy cramming so much information into a comparatively limited amount of time. Toward the end of *Bird,* he didn't seem to be telling the story of Charlie Parker as much as letting it unravel. That doesn't happen in *Unforgiven,* but the tone, so self-assured to begin with, becomes loaded with qualifications.

The film looks great, full of broad chilly landscapes and skies that are sometimes as heavy with portents as those in something by El Greco. It's corny but it works.

Photographed by Jack N. Green, who was the camera operator for Bruce Surtees, Mr. Eastwood's cinematographer for *Pale Rider, Unforgiven* favors the kind of backlighting that can add a sense of desolation and menace to even the most conventional moments. Seen against a bright background, faces turned to the camera are so hidden in shadow that they aren't immediately recognizable. It is a storyteller's gesture for the audience's benefit, since the other characters within the scene would not be so disadvantaged.

The cast is splendid, though some of the actors have more to do than others, including Mr. Freeman, whose role is not especially demanding. Mr. Hackman delights as Sheriff Daggett: no more Mr. Good Guy. Also worthy of particular note are Mr. Woolvett, who makes his feature film debut as the unreliable Schofield Kid; Mr. Rubinek as a city journalist out of his element out West; and Frances Fisher as Strawberry Alice, a woman who doesn't know when to shut up.

Yet the center of attention, from the moment he rises up out of a hog pen until the darkest fade-out in Western movie history, is Mr. Eastwood. This is his richest, most satisfying performance since the underrated, politically lunatic *Heartbreak Ridge*. There's no one like him.

—*V.C., August 7, 1992*

THE USUAL SUSPECTS

Directed by Bryan Singer; written by Christopher McQuarrie; director of photography. Newton Thomas Sigel; edited by John Ottman; music by Mr. Ottman; production designer. Howard Cummings; produced by Mr. Singer and Michael McDonnell; released by Gramercy Pictures. Running time: 105 minutes.

With: Stephen Baldwin (McManus). Gabriel Byrne (Keaton). Chazz Palminteri (Dave Kujan). Kevin Pollak (Hockney). Pete Postlethwaite (Kobayashi). Kevin Spacey (Verbal). Suzy Amis (Edie Finneran). Benicio Del Toro (Fenster) and Giancarlo Esposito (Jack Baer).

The tough guys of *The Usual Suspects* radiate confidence in their own movie-mythic possibilities, secure in the knowledge that they are this year's Reservoir Dogs. And it's not even a stretch, since Bryan Singer's immensely stylish film noir incorporates so many good masculine roles and such terse, literate conversational sparring. With these advantages, *The Usual Suspects* goes straight to cult status without quite touching one important base: the audience's emotions. This movie finally isn't anything more than an intricate feat of gamesmanship, but it's still quite something to see.

And it has been made to be seen twice, with a plot guaranteed to create minor bewilderment the first time around. Mr. Singer and the screenwriter, Christopher McQuarrie, whose collaboration on *Public Access* won the Grand Jury Prize at the Sundance Film Festival two years ago, include a great many hints and nuances that won't be noticeable until you know which Suspect bears the most watching. Suffice it to say that this film's trickiest role is handled with supreme slyness. And that acting of that caliber, plus a whopper of an ending, compensates for some inevitable head-scratching on the way home.

It's no surprise that this film's poster art, featuring five intriguing miscreants in a police lineup, was an important early aspect of its creation. Beyond following the demands of an unusually dense mystery plot, Mr. Singer and Mr. McQuarrie have also worked overtime at generating visual interest in their story. Even the jail cell looks eye-catchingly sleek when Keaton (Gabriel Byrne), McManus (Stephen Baldwin), Hockney (Kevin Pollak), Fenster (Benicio Del Toro) and Kevin Spacey (Verbal) are locked up together one fateful evening. "It was all the cops' fault," Verbal later remembers. "You don't put guys like that in a room together." Not unless you want the endless set of high-testosterone conversational standoffs that help keep *The Usual Suspects* perpetually on its toes.

The five New York cell mates, who seem to have been rounded up at random, are soon embroiled in a crime scheme that we know will lead, since the film is structured in flashback, to an explosion on a pier in California. In the aftermath of those fireworks, the story is being unraveled by three separate investigators (Chazz Palminteri, Dan Hedaya and Giancarlo Esposito), with the help of Verbal, who has survived to explicate the tale.

It involves figures as wildly mysterious as Keyser

Soze, the fierce, off-camera Hungarian who is referred to as "the devil himself" and whose very name seems to give the filmmakers a noirish thrill. Keyser Soze is as fabulously improbable as Pete Postlethwaite's Kobayashi, whose dark makeup and Pakistani accent just dare the viewer to call his bluff. It ultimately isn't best to do so, since *The Usual Suspects* has become so exhaustingly convoluted by the time it ends that some of its unraveled threads lead nowhere. But the film's secrets are also held together by dialogue of quiet ferocity: "Keyser always said, 'I believe in God and I'm afraid of Him.' Well, I believe in God and the only thing that scares me is Keyser Soze."

Mr. Singer has assembled a fine ensemble cast of actors who can parry such lines, and whose performances mesh effortlessly despite their exaggerated differences in demeanor. (Mr. Baldwin's mad-dog jokester, for instance, matches Mr. Byrne's elegant businessman without missing a beat.) Without the violence or obvious bravado of *Reservoir Dogs*, these performers still create strong and fascinatingly ambiguous characters. Mr. Spacey, so good in *Swimming with Sharks* this year, joins Mr. Palminteri to give the interrogation scenes a particular charge.

The Usual Suspects also benefits from Newton Thomas Sigel's handsome, moody cinematography, and from John Ottman's services as both editor and composer. His brooding score effectively summons Bernard Herrmann. And his editing of the film's finale is gratifyingly sensible, a lot more so than the secrets being revealed.

—*J.M., August 16, 1995*

VANYA ON 42ND STREET

Directed for the screen by Louis Malle; directed for the stage by André Gregory; written by David Mamet, based on the play *Uncle Vanya* by Anton Chekhov; director of photography, Declan Quinn; edited by Nancy Baker; music by Joshua Redman; production designer, Eugene Lee; produced by Fred Berner; released by Sony Pictures Classics. Running time: 119 minutes.

With: Wallace Shawn (Vanya), Julianne Moore (Yelena), Brooke Smith (Sonya), Larry Pine (Dr. Astrov), George Gaynes (Serybryakov), Lynn Cohen (Marian), Phoebe Brand (Marina), Jerry Mayer (Waffles), Madhur Jaffrey (Mrs. Chao) and André Gregory (Himself).

The actors and spectators for *Vanya on 42nd Street* make their entrances casually, drifting into one another at the New Amsterdam Theater and making idle conversation. That chitchat has evolved into Chekhov almost before a movie audience is ready to notice. By the time the viewer fully apprehends the grand, cavernous scale of this crumbling theater or the naturalness of the actors, the performance is under way. This is bare-bones Chekhov, though it is hardly Chekov without cachet.

Under the direction of André Gregory, this version of *Uncle Vanya* (filmed simply yet enthrallingly by Louis Malle) has a significant pedigree. Evolving over a period of years as a workshop production, and available only to small, select audiences, it developed the inevitable mystique, which is only heightened by Mr. Malle's participation. With Wallace Shawn in the title role and memories of *My Dinner with André* as a quirky, dazzling collaboration by these principals, *Vanya on 42nd Street* has a lot to live up to.

So the lack of fanfare in the film's opening moments amounts to a declaration. This *Vanya* is not so colorfully eccentric as *My Dinner with André,* but it is no less single-minded. It seeks to isolate the very essentials of the play, with an adaptation by David Mamet to expedite the task. Delving the despair of Chekhov's characters in what is actually quite a rarefied creative atmosphere, it incorporates its share of contradictions, in a way that recalls the most desolate Woody Allen films about privileged, luxuriantly introspective characters. On-screen, at intimately close range, a similarly refined angst emerges from *Uncle Vanya.*

But the elegant understatement of this production turns it into a livelier experiment, a fluent, gripping version of one of Chekhov's more elusive plays. There is no objective correlative of cherry orchard caliber here, no naturally riveting image that survives when the furniture and scenery are stripped away. Instead, there are only wayward emotions and deep regrets, the raw essentials of a psychodrama that has been coaxed forth here with illusory ease.

The actors wear street clothes. The props aren't more than tables, chairs and takeout coffee cups. The intent-looking audience consists only of Mr. Gregory and a few friends. And the absence of obvious artifice is used by Mr. Malle to focus attention entirely on a group of forthright, unmannered actors, with the camera appearing to gaze into their very souls. Exquisitely lighted and well served by the ravaged beauty of this unexpectedly photogenic old theater, *Vanya on 42nd Street* has a visual elegance that seems to isolate and purify its characters and their troubles.

Uncle Vanya is set at a rambling Russian country house, and Mr. Mamet has retained the atmospheric touches, right down to the samovars. But his neat, concise adaptation gives the dialogue a contemporary ring without noticeably departing from the text. (Mamet: "The people won't remember, but God will." Chekhov: "They don't need to remember. God remembers.") The convoluted problems of the household emerge that much more easily thanks to Mr. Mamet's unmannered adaptation.

The most peculiar aspect of this production comes with the casting, which reveals an oddly wavering approach to the play. Julianne Moore makes a sleek Yelena, the beautiful wife of a pompous, aging professor (George Gaynes), and a woman who stirs the yearnings of both Vanya, her brother-in-law (Mr. Shawn), and Astrov (Larry Pine), a country doctor with a worldly air. The history of this production goes back to 1989, so that it was Ms. Moore's appearance in *Uncle Vanya* that led Robert Altman to cast her memorably in *Short Cuts*.

But Ms. Moore's sly, delicately shaded performance, which is also made extraordinarily photogenic by careful lighting of her red hair, is in a very different key from Mr. Shawn's more comedic Vanya. That character's bitterness and frustration emerge very clearly, but the farcical side of Mr. Shawn is incongruous at times. When he tells Yelena passionately that she has mermaid's blood, he seems almost to be joking.

Mr. Gaynes, another actor known for humorous screen roles, is another surprising presence here, though both he and Mr. Shawn perform with obvious conviction. In a more straightforward vein, Mr. Pine plays Astrov with the rakishness of a younger Jason Robards. And Brooke Smith, memorable as that tough kidnapping victim in *The Silence of the Lambs,* makes a luminous and heartbreaking Sonya, the lonely young woman who adores Astrov but senses that her destiny is drearier than her aspirations.

Also in *Vanya on 42nd Street* are Phoebe Brand, the venerable teacher and Group Theater actress, as the household's reassuring Nanny; Lynn Cohen as Maman; Jerry Mayer as Waffles; and Madhur Jaffrey as one of the celebrityish guests chatting with Mr. Gregory during occasional breaks in the performance.

Declan Quinn's muted, precise cinematography adds one more grace note to an already graceful production.

—*J.M., October 19, 1994*

THE VERDICT

Directed by Sidney Lumet; written by David Mamet, based on the novel by Barry Reed; director of photography, Andrzej Bartkowiak; edited by Peter C. Frank; music by Johnny Mandel; production designer, Edward Pisoni; produced by Richard D. Zanuck; released by Twentieth Century Fox. Running time: 129 minutes.

With: Paul Newman (Frank Galvin), Charlotte Rampling (Laura Fischer), Jack Warden (Mickey Morrissey), James Mason (Ed Concannon), Milo O'Shea (Judge Hoyle), Edward Binns (Bishop Brophy), Julie Bovasso (Maureen Rooney), Lindsay Crouse (Kaitlin Costello Price), Roxanne Hart (Sally Doneghy) and James Handy (Dick Doneghy).

A solidly old-fashioned courtroom drama such as *The Verdict* could have gotten by with a serious, measured performance from its leading man, or it could have worked well with a dazzling movie-star turn. The fact that Paul Newman delivers both makes a clever, suspenseful, entertaining movie even better.

This is as good a role as Mr. Newman has ever had, and as shrewd and substantial a performance as he has ever given, although it may not be his most entirely credible. Mr. Newman begins the story as a lonely, washed-up, pathetic has-been lawyer. Not exactly typecasting, and not the sort of thing he does terribly convincingly. Of course, his luck is about to change. Mr. Newman plays Frank Galvin, first seen drinking, playing pinball in the daytime and bribing funeral-home operators to let him pass his business cards to the bereaved. Sidney Lumet's *The Verdict,* which opens today at the Gotham, Criterion Center and other theaters, watches him rise to an important challenge, shake off the cobwebs, resuscitate his law practice and fight furiously to help good triumph over evil. As near-miraculous transformations go, this one's not bad at all, considering the fact that it's accomplished in only slightly over two hours' screen time.

Frank's big case is a malpractice suit against a Roman Catholic hospital in Boston, and it has been his big case—his *only* case—for months before he remembers to get around to it. Suddenly, the court date is imminent, and it's time for Frank to meet his client, the sister of a now-comatose victim injured during childbirth. Frank tidies up his grimy-looking office, which has a semicircular window suggesting a setting sun. He locks it up, and leaves a note from his nonexistent secretary about a nonexistent lunch date with a judge. When he rushes back to greet the client, he does his best to look as if he has been busy. The client looks understandably doubtful.

What changes Frank? A look at the victim—Mr. Lumet has Frank take some bedside Polaroids and then lingers on Frank's feeling of slow realization as the pictures develop—and an offer from the church's prestigious law firm of a large out-of-court settlement. "If I take the money I'm lost," Frank says, suddenly realizing that he is not willing to be bought off. All we hear of his earlier record is that he has lost his handful of trial cases and was married to and was divorced by his boss's daughter. Arguing this case will be his chance of a lifetime to do something worthwhile.

David Mamet's terse screenplay for *The Verdict* is that of a David and Goliath story, as might be expected—why would anyone want to watch a loser risk everything for one more crushing defeat? But it's nonetheless full of surprises. Structurally, *The Verdict* is virtually a maze of a movie, because the audience can see at the outset where Frank Galvin ought to wind up but has no hint of how he might get there. Along the way, Mr. Mamet has supplied twists and obstacles of all sorts, and Mr. Lumet has provided a gallery of beautifully cast performers in supporting roles. Jack Warden is, as ever, dependably gruff, funny and bighearted as the former mentor who drops everything to help out Frank just one more time. James Mason does a wonderful job as the sleek, sarcastic mastermind behind the archdiocese's defense. And Milo O'Shea plays an obviously biased judge whose fondest wish is that Frank Galvin stop wasting everyone's time. The judge's hostility is only one of the numerous monkey wrenches that Mr. Mamet throws in Frank's path.

The movie provides him with a love interest, too, a stony young woman named Laura (Charlotte Rampling) who somehow seduces Frank by treating him as coldly as she possibly can. Although the extreme restraint of Miss Rampling's performance makes a bit more sense on second viewing than it does on first, both the character and the performance slow the movie down for no vital purpose. Even Mr. Lumet is uncharacteristically awkward in manipulating this part of the story, shooting the characters at a strangely long distance when they meet in a hotel room, or ending the film on an ambiguous note much like that on which Mr. Newman's performance in *Absence of Malice* also ended.

Mr. Lumet's best direction here is utterly unobtrusive, speeding the film along suspensefully and shading it in rich, dark tones. He falters so infrequently here that the rough spots are attention-getting, such as on the few occasions when the tale takes a melodramatic or preachy turn. Most of the film is swift and exciting, told in a style so measured that even the relatively far-fetched moments take on an air of plausibility.

When Mr. Newman delivers his climactic courtroom speech, Mr. Lumet begins with a shot of the entire room in late afternoon, with Mr. Newman only one of many figures in the tableau. This isn't the star treatment that other directors might have brought to the actor's big moment; it's not a particularly flattering shot, but it's one that keeps the star firmly and unswervingly in the service of the story. Should anyone in the audience drop a pin during these crucial, superbly staged moments, the rest of the audience is sure to hear.

—J.M., December 8, 1982

VERTIGO

Produced and directed by Alfred Hitchcock: written by Alec Coppel and Samuel Taylor, based on the novel by Pierre Boileau and Thomas Narcejac: cinematographer, Robert Burks: edited by George Tomasini: music by Bernard Herrmann: art designers, Hal Pereira and Henry Bumstead: released by Paramount Pictures. Running time: 127 minutes.

With: James Stewart (John Ferguson), Kim Novak (Madeleine/Judy), Barbara Bel Geddes (Midge) and Tom Helmore (Gavis Elster).

You might say that Alfred Hitchcock's latest mystery melodrama, *Vertigo,* is all about how a dizzy fellow chases after a dizzy dame, the fellow being an ex-detective and the dame being—well, you guess. That is as fair a thumbnail digest as we can hastily contrive to give you a gist of this picture without giving the secret away. And, believe us, that secret is so clever, even though it is devilishly far-fetched, that we wouldn't want to risk at all disturbing your inevitable enjoyment of the film.

If that recommendation is sufficient, read no further. *Vertigo* opened yesterday at the Capitol.

However, if you are a skeptic and want to know just a little more about this typically Hitchcock picture, which has James Stewart and Kim Novak as its stars, let us give you two hints that should be helpful.

The first hint is that the story begins with this long-legged ex-detective, a known sufferer from acrophobia (fear of heights), being hired by a San Francisco magnate to shadow his strangely acting wife. Seems that his chic and silent beauty, who the magnate says loves him very much, is given to mysterious wanderings in and about that dramatic city with the startling views—and, believe us, it is dramatic, as seen in color and Vista Vision in this film.

She goes to the Mission Dolores and places flowers on the grave of a famous San Francisco beauty who died years ago. Then she goes to the art museum, the Palace of the Legion of Honor in Golden Gate Park, and sits staring at the portrait of this beauty as though she were in a daze.

Slowly, the gumshoe realizes that, somehow, this dizzy dame has spells when she thinks she's animated by the personality of this tragic lady of the past. And he has no doubt about it when, one day at Old Fort Point, beneath the Golden Gate Bridge, she flings herself desperately and suicidally into the bay. Naturally, our fellow saves her and finds himself falling in love.

Still the mystery haunts him. What is this thing that invades the moody person of his loved one, the wife of another man? And how can he free her from this demon—and from her husband?

That's all we will tell you! Now—

Second hint: This fascinating mystery is based upon a tale written by the same fellows, Pierre Boileau and Thomas Narcejac, who wrote the story from which was taken that excellent French mystery, *Dia-bolique.* That film, if you remember, told of a terribly devious plot to simulate a murder that didn't happen.

There! No more hints! Coming or not?

What more's to say? Well, nothing, except that *Vertigo* is performed in the manner expected of all performers in Hitchcock films. Mr. Stewart, as usual, manages to act awfully tense in a casual way, and Miss Novak is really quite amazing in—well, here is a bit of a hint—dual roles. Tom Helmore is sleek as the husband and Barbara Bel Geddes is sweet as the nice girl who loves the detective and has to watch him drifting away.

One more thing: there is a big hole—a big question mark—at a critical point. It will stop you, if you're a quick thinker. But try not to be and enjoy the film.

—B.C., *May 29, 1958*

VICTOR/VICTORIA

Directed by Blake Edwards; written by Mr. Edwards, based on the film *Viktor und Viktoria* by Rheinhold Schuenzel and Hans Hoemburg; cinematographer, Dick Bush; edited by Ralph E. Winters; music by Henry Mancini; production designer, Rodger Maus; produced by Mr. Edwards and Tony Adams; released by United Artists. Running time: 133 minutes.

With: Julie Andrews (Victor/Victoria), James Garner (King), Robert Preston (Toddy), Lesley Ann Warren (Norma), Alex Karras (Squash) and John Rhys-Davies (Cassell).

Get ready, get set and go—*immediately*—to the Ziegfeld Theater, where Blake Edwards today opens his chef d'oeuvre, his cockeyed, crowning achievement, his *Duck Soup,* his *Charley's Aunt,* his *Hotel Paradiso,* his *Some Like It Hot,* his urban *As You Like It* and maybe even his *Citizen Kane,* which his film resembles in no way whatsoever.

It's called *Victor/Victoria,* and it stars Julie Andrews, Robert Preston and James Garner, each giving the performance of his and her career in a marvelous fable about mistaken identity, sexual role-playing, love, innocence and sight gags, including one that illustrates the dangers of balancing yourself on a champagne bottle on one finger within the range of a singing voice that shatters glass.

Victor/Victoria is a farce—a splendid one with music—of a timeless tradition, though its sensibilities are strictly of the 1980's and its own time is the far distant 1934. The setting is Paris, a magical, musical-comedy Paris. Its plot, much of which takes place in hotel rooms, in hotel beds, under them, in hotel closets, and outside hotel-room windows, peering in, is of a kind of blissful madness that recalls the work of Georges Feydeau, which is seldom seen in this country in the style to which it is accustomed.

It may be misleading, however, to associate *Victor/Victoria* with the work of other masters of comedy. Mr. Edwards is his own comic genius, as he has been demonstrating for years, sometimes only in bits and pieces, in his near-classic *Pink Panther* collaborations with the late Peter Sellers, in *The Party, Darling Lili* and more recently in *10* and *S.O.B.*

Victor/Victoria combines the sweetness of *Darling Lili* with the unbridled hilarity of *S.O.B.*, but without that comedy's bitterness. It is an unqualified hit.

Using as its inspiration Reinhold Schuenzel's 1933 German musical-comedy film, *Viktor und Viktoria,* released in New York in 1935, Mr. Edwards's screenplay is about a down-on-her-luck English actress (Miss Andrews) who finds herself starving in Depression Paris after her Gilbert and Sullivan troupe suddenly folds.

When just on the point of following a cockroach-strewn primrose path, she meets Toddy (Mr. Preston), the American master of ceremonies at a nightclub featuring transvestite entertainment. Toddy, too, is at the end of his rope. His male lovers are faithless. His career is at a standstill. Life has lost its charms.

It is Toddy who has the brilliant idea of presenting the actress as Victor, a Polish-born count and female impersonator known professionally as Victoria. With Toddy as her manager, Victor/Victoria becomes the toast of Paris, attracting particularly the attention of King Marchan (Mr. Garner), a Chicago mobster on a holiday in Paris with his peroxided mistress Norma (Lesley Ann Warren) and his taciturn bodyguard Squash (Alex Karras).

As happens in farce, everyone falls in love with everyone else, and because this is a liberated farce, the possible combinations are more than doubled—they're squared. Both Victor/Victoria and Toddy concede they have "feelings" for King Marchan, and the mobster is mortified to find himself drawn to the immaculately turned-out transvestite named Victor.

Norma, who sleeps with King, has one eye on Victor and another on Toddy, and would do anything within her considerable sexual powers to "cure" both of them. Squash, who never says very much, also becomes involved in a fashion that may not be an immense surprise, though it is immensely funny.

This is only the general outline of *Victor/Victoria.* However, I suspect it's more than enough to prompt a lot of lugubrious analyses designed to take the fun out of a film that, although it is more sexually outspoken than *Charley's Aunt,* is no less innocent. Just in passing, it should be noted that *Victor/Victoria* makes the two *Cage aux Folles* films look like failed television situation comedies.

Although *Victor/Victoria* preaches tolerance and understanding of homosexuality, and though it uses the word "gay" in a way that I doubt was much used in 1934 Paris, even in the demimonde portrayed in this film, the roots of the comedy are as ancient as the use of masks and disguises in the theater.

Far more indicative of what *Victor/Victoria* is all about are the wit and style of the performances and the production, which manages to be both romantic and bone-crushingly funny, frequently at the same time.

Mr. Edwards has never before treated Miss Andrews, his wife, with such confidence, admiration and generosity. She looks absolutely great and is at peak form both as a comedian and as a singer. Nothing she has done before, on the stage or on the screen, probably can match the exuberant charm of her switches between Victoria and Victor.

If she's not totally convincing as Victor, whose suits appear to have been carefully tailored to be a couple of sizes too big, that also is as it should be. She isn't meant to convince the movie audience she's a boy, only the characters within the film. The slightly eerie, androgynous purity of her singing voice also underscores the comedy of her masquerade. Her production numbers are knockouts, especially one called "Le Jazz Hot" and another, a sort of flamenco thing, which has been inserted, I suspect, for the principal purpose of allowing Mr. Preston to parody it at the film's finale.

If Mr. Preston doesn't get an Oscar for this film, he

never will. His Toddy is the richest, wisest, most rambunctious performance he's given since his triumph in
The Music Man. Most refreshing is the way he
embraces the character without condescending to it.
This is definitely not a camp turn. He also has three
show-stopping songs, "Gay Paree"; a duet with Miss
Andrews called—I think—"You and Me"; and the
flamenco-drag number. The music is by Henry
Mancini and the lyrics by Leslie Bricusse.

Mr. Garner's role is not as flamboyant as Mr. Preston's, but he makes a splendid straight man for the
others. Miss Warren's squeaky-voiced Norma is
enchantingly self-possessed and very comic in her one
production number. Mr. Karras here comes out of the
closet as a fine comic actor, and the contributions of
the huge supporting cast, including Graham Stark,
who plays a comedy waiter, are invaluable.

The production design by Rodger Maus is as elegant as anything we've seen this year. Unlike the production design for *One from the Heart,* Mr. Maus's
meets all the needs of the film without having also to
be its star.

Victor/Victoria is so good, so exhilarating, that the
only depressing thing about it is the suspicion that
Mr. Edwards is going to have a terrible time trying to
top it.

—*V.C., March 19, 1982*

VIDEODROME

Written and directed by David Cronenberg; director of photography, Mark Irwin; edited by Ronald
Sanders; art director, Carol Spier; music by
Howard Shore; produced by Claude Héroux;
released by Universal Pictures. Running time: 90
minutes.

With: James Woods (Max Renn), Sonja Smits
(Bianca O'Blivion), Deborah Harry (Nicki Brand),
Peter Dvorsky (Harlan), Leslie Carlson (Barry Con-
vex), Jack Creley (Brian O'Blivion), Lynne Gorman
(Masha), Julie Khaner (Bridey), Reiner Schwartz
(Moses), David Bolt (Raphael), Lally Cadeau (Rena
King) and Henry Gomez (Brolley).

When Max Renn, the hero of David Cronenberg's *Videodrome,* stumbles across a

Malaysian television station that appears to be broadcasting pure sex and brutality, he is stunned. "Torture, murder, mutilation!" he exclaims. "Brilliant!
Absolutely brilliant, and almost no production costs.
Where do they get actors who can do this?" Later on,
in a cooler moment, he contemplates this new form of
programming and murmurs, "I think it's what's next."

Max is a video entrepreneur, someone who considers it his business to give people what they want, however sordid or sleazy that may be. In Mr. Cronenberg's
universe, which is often very clever and inventive, this
doesn't make Max an evil man. It merely makes him
unprincipled, and therefore vulnerable to the wicked
machinations of others. In *Videodrome,* these abound.
So does poetic justice. Max is eventually turned into a
walking personification of the sexual, violent, media-
mad exploitation to which he has contributed.

It would be revealing the most eye-catching and
horrific secrets of *Videodrome,* which opens today at
the Rivoli and other theaters, to describe this physical
transformation in any detail. But Rick Baker, responsible for the film's special makeup effects, has devised
some tricks that are as droll as they are gruesome, even
if the gore does eventually become overpowering. He
and Mr. Cronenberg, while easily fulfilling the film's
horror requirements, try in addition for a more ironic,
satirical style, and at times they achieve it. Though
Videodrome finally grows grotesque and a little confused, it begins very well and sustains its cleverness for
a long while.

What Max quickly discovers, with the audience
way ahead of him, is that the sex-and-violence show
from Malaysia is neither staged nor a foreign import.
It originates in Pittsburgh, and it secretly emits a signal so powerful that the viewer is affected in unthinkable and irreversible ways. By the time Max figures
this out, he is already in the grip of Nicki, a seductive
and very kinky radio personality, played by Deborah
Harry. Radio personality?

Well, Nicki is heard giving advice on a self-help
show called "Emotional Rescue." Since she is also seen
putting out cigarettes on her body, the better to titil-
late Max, it's fair to wonder whether her on-the-air
advice is really of any use.

The other mystery woman in Mr. Cronenberg's
convoluted, intrigue-filled screenplay is one Bianca
O'Blivion (Sonja Smits), the daughter of a professor
who now exists entirely as a library of videotapes.

"The monologue is his preferred mode of discourse," Bianca says. Both she and Nicki, who represent opposing elements in Mr. Cronenberg's elaborate scheme, induce in Max the kind of hallucinations that are a special-effects-department's dream, as when a videocassette becomes throbbing, pulsating flesh, or when a television screen becomes a rounded, menacing mouth the size of a beach ball. Max is never sure where these visions leave off and reality begins; the viewer won't find it easy to tell, either. And there are times when it is dangerously unclear, in the midst of Max's lurid, sadomasochistic fantasies, whether *Videodrome* is far removed from the kind of sensationalism it seeks to satirize.

Mr. Cronenberg, who also directed *Scanners,* is developing a real genius for this sort of thing; one measure of the innovativeness of *Videodrome* is that it feels vaguely futuristic, even though it's apparently set in the present.

By far Mr. Cronenberg's most inspired touch is the casting of Mr. Woods, who brings an almost backhanded heroism to the horror genre. In villainous or sinister roles (in films like *The Onion Field* or *Split Image*), Mr. Woods has been startling, but that kind of casting is almost a redundancy. Here, his offhand wisecracking gives the performance a sharply authentic edge. And his jittery, insinuating manner even begins to look like a kind of innocence, in comparison with the calm, soothing attitudes of the video-crazed megalomaniacs he's up against.

—J.M., February 4, 1983

VIOLETTE

Directed by Claude Chabrol; written (in French, with English subtitles) by Odile Barski, Hervé Bromberger and Frederic Grendel, based on the book by Jean-Marie Fitere; director of photography, Jean Rabier; production designer, Jacques Brizzio; released by New Yorker Films. Running time: 123 minutes.

With: Isabelle Huppert (Violette Nozière), Stéphane Audran (Germaine Nozière), Jean Carmet (Baptiste Nozière), Jean-François Garreaud (Jean Dabin), Lisa Langlois (Maddy), Guy Hoffman (The Judge), Bernard Lajarrige (Andre de Pinguet) and Bernadette Lafont (Violette's Cell Mate).

From the very first moments of the new Claude Chabrol film, *Violette,* we are held spellbound by a combination of stunning artistry and brute suspense that never relaxes its grip until the final frame two hours later. This is an enthralling movie, virtually certain to become a classic, and in the performance of the title role it establishes Isabelle Huppert as one of the most enchanting actresses currently to be seen on the screen.

The story is based on a sensational murder case that caused a great stir in France in the 1930's. At the age of eighteen, Violette Nozière was put on trial for the murder of her father and the attempted murder of her mother. She was found guilty, and sentenced to death. (Later the sentence was changed to life imprisonment.) The time was 1933, and Violette Nozière became a heroine of the Left and a particular object of veneration by the Surrealists, who proclaimed her a symbol of liberation from "bourgeois" morals. Paul Eluard wrote a poem about her called "Violette Nozière's Complaint."

What had emerged in the course of the trial was a tale sordid enough to have been invented by Georges Simenon or James Cain. Violette Nozière had lived a double life. In the cramped tenement apartment she shared with her conventional, lower-class parents, she was a model of schoolgirl innocence—the very picture of a demure virgin unpracticed in the ways of the world. Unknown to her family, however, she was also living the loose life of a near-prostitute, on the prowl for men wherever she could find them.

In the course of this secret life, Violette acquired a ne'er-do-well lover for whom she began to steal from her parents. Eventually she plotted their murder in the hope of satisfying her lover's demands. Her mother survived, however, and sought retribution for her husband's murder.

From this once famous case Chabrol has fashioned an extraordinary movie that manages to make Violette a compelling character, utterly obsessed by the wayward appetites that govern her every action. Yet Chabrol does not for a moment subscribe to the misplaced political pieties once used to justify—and indeed, glorify—Violette's crime. He remains fascinated but detached, and in fact mocks this political response to her case as much as he ridicules the public's shameless absorption in the horror of the crime. About the motive of the murder he is completely clear-eyed, seeing it as plainly criminal. What really interests him is the character of the criminal and the special fate she had created for herself.

Where Chabrol excels in *Violette* is not only in the recreation of this curiously dour, obsessed character but in rendering the contrasting milieux in which she moves. The cramped flat in which Violette lives with her parents, without the least privacy or freedom, is itself a kind of prison from which her nocturnal escapades are a temporary liberation. (The first image we see on the screen is of iron bars—the gate to the building in which Violette lives with her parents, but also a forecast of the prison to which she will be condemned.)

Yet the cafés where she picks up her men, and the seedy hotel room to which she takes them, are almost as confining as her parents' flat. There is nothing of glamour or romance in Violette's secret life, but simply other forms of bondage. Only in prison does she find release, and a kind of freedom.

The Paris that we glimpse in this film—Paris in the 1930's—is very beautiful, but it is not dwelt on. The drama is mainly indoors, in the flat, the café and the hotel room, and we are made to feel the pressure of their claustral atmosphere tightening its hold until the final denouement. Interestingly, there is only one moment of real passion in the film, and it comes not in the love scenes or the murder but at the moment when Violette, having poisoned her parents and thinking them both dead, sits down to the dinner they were about to share and consumes it with an animal fury. It is a brief but chilling scene—utterly unforgettable.

In this, as in everything else she is called upon to do in this film, Isabelle Huppert shows herself to be a superb actress, able to convey in every gesture, in every utterance and facial expression, that special combination of passivity and violence that is the essential mark of Violette's personality. So persuasive is her performance of this role that even in those moments when she is most nakedly wicked, she continues to puzzle and even enchant us with her air of innocence and indifference.

But then, all the principals are superb in this film— Stéphane Audran, who plays the mother; Jean Carmet, who plays the father; and Jean-François Garreaud,

who plays the gutless lover who holds Violette in his power. It is the kind of film in which we feel the director totally in control of every detail and nuance, from the look of the bed in the seedy hotel room to the look in the eyes of Violette's mother when she awakens to her daughter's criminal act, and are yet caught up completely in the suspense of the action. *Violette* is a triumph for Chabrol, and may be the best film he has yet made.

Violette, which closes the New York Film Festival Sunday night, starts its regular commercial run Monday.

—H.K., October 7, 1978

VIRIDIANA

Directed by Luis Buñuel; written (in Spanish, with English subtitles) by Mr. Buñuel and Julio Alejandro, based on a story by Mr. Buñuel; cinematographer, José F. Agayo; edited by Pedro del Rey; music by Wolfgang Amadeus Mozart; art designer, Francisco Canet; produced by Ricardo Munoz Suay; released by Kingsley Films. Black and white. Running time: 90 minutes.

With: Silvia Pinal (Viridiana), Francisco Rabal (Jorge), Fernando Rey (Don Jaime), Margarita Lozano (Ramona) and Victoria Zinny (Lucia).

Luis Buñuel is presenting a variation on an ancient theme in his new Spanish film, *Viridiana,* which came to the Paris yesterday. The theme is that well-intended charity can often be badly misplaced by innocent, pious people. Therefore, beware of charity.

That is the obvious moral that forms in this grim and tumorous tale of a beautiful young religious novice who gets into an unholy mess when she gives up her holy calling to try to atone for a wrong she has done. But we strongly suspect that Señor Buñuel had more than this in mind when he made this intense and bitter picture, the first he's made in Spain in thirty years.

We sense all the way through this drama of the shocking education of this girl in the realities of passion and the grossness of most of mankind a stinging, unmerciful sarcasm directed at the piously insulated mind and a strong strain of guarded criticism of social conditions in Spain.

When his heroine, Viridiana, is violently and unhealthily repelled by the tendered affection of her uncle, who sees in her a perfect image of his long-dead wife, there is clearly implied recognition of the tangled libido of the girl and the pitiful confusion of the uncle in a bind of propriety, sentimentality and lust. That he hangs himself in remorse and anguish after the girl has fled reveals Señor Buñuel's recognition of the grotesqueness of the gentlemen's code.

And when the girl gives up her holy calling and returns to her dead uncle's farm with a rabble of derelicts and beggars to make amends for what she has done, there is stark evidence of his disgust at the pallid charitable gesture in the greed and meanness with which he has imbued these bums.

Señor Buñuel makes no bones about it. The most powerful stuff in his film are the macabre scenes of these people showing how vicious and contemptible they are. They snivel, cheat, steal, abuse one another, ostracize and brutalize one who has a foul disease and finally cut loose in a wild carouse that fairly wrecks the place. Played as a thundering obbligato to the milky generosity of the girl, these scenes carry the moralizing muscle and ironic punch of the film.

Following them, there is little more than drabness in the evidence that the girl ends up playing cards and listening to rock 'n' roll music with her uncle's robust illegitimate son.

Whether Señor Buñuel means his picture as a reflection of all people or just the people of Spain is not clear nor, indeed, is it essential. It is an ugly, depressing view of life. And, to be frank about it, it is a little old-fashioned, too. His format is strangely literary; his symbols are obvious and blunt, such as the revulsion of the girl toward milking or the display of a penknife built into a crucifix. And there is something just a bit corny about having his bums doing their bacchanalian dance to the thunder of the "Hallelujah Chorus."

However, it is stringently directed and expertly played. Silvia Pinal is lovely and precisely as stiff and forbidding as she should be as the misguided novice. Fernando Rey makes the uncle a poignant dolt and Francisco Rabal is aggressive and realistic as the illegitimate son. Margarita Lozano does a good job as a cowed and inhibited maid and Teresa Rabal is lively as the latter's nosy child.

As usual in Señor Buñuel's pictures, the black-and-white photography is artful and true, and the English subtitles do politely by the sometimes coarse Spanish dialogue.

—*B.C., March 20, 1962*

VIVA ZAPATA!

Directed by Elia Kazan; written by John Steinbeck, based on the novel *Zapata, the Unconquered* by Edgcumb Pichon; cinematographer, Joseph MacDonald; edited by Barbara McLean; music by Alex North; art designers, Lyle Wheeler and Leland Fuller; produced by Darryl F. Zanuck; released by Twentieth Century Fox. Black and white. Running time: 113 minutes.

With: Marlon Brando (Zapata), Jean Peters (Josefa), Anthony Quinn (Eufemio), Joseph Wiseman (Fernando), Arnold Moss (Don Nacio), Alan Reed (Pancho Villa) and Margo (Soldadera).

Whatever vague and misty memory the rest of the world may have of Emiliano Zapata, the Mexican Indian who led wild revolts of hungry peasants in the south of his country while Pancho Villa was doing the same in the north, a very strong recollection of him is in the mind of Twentieth Century Fox. In that studio's *Viva Zapata!*, which came to the Rivoli yesterday in as lively a swirl of agitation as has been stirred in quite a time, the Mexican rebel leader, whom Marlon Brando plays, is recalled as a man of savage passion devoted to the poor and the oppressed. He is also recalled as a champion of matchless integrity, unswerving in his belief in the people—a romantic ideal in every way.

This fervent conception of Zapata may not agree in all details with the little that is really known about him, nor may John Steinbeck's hotly penned account of his troubles with noisome politicians be consistent with history. There is some question from the record whether Zapata was quite the selfless soul, devoutly domesticated, that he is made to appear in this film. But certainly this ardent portrait of him throbs with a rare vitality, and a masterful picture of a nation in revolutionary torment has been got by director Elia Kazan.

Indeed, the best features of this drama are the vivid

aspects it presents of social injustice and unbalance in a primitive and misgoverned land. From the earliest scenes of ragged peasants in the ornate palace of President Diaz, pleading with him to assist them in recovering their stolen lands, to the last poignant shot of toil-worn women pawing feebly over their murdered leader's corpse, there emerges a stark illumination of the tragic state of disordered Mexico.

Mr. Kazan is eloquent with a camera, and all of his individual shots, as well as his sequences, describing the brutal slaughter of hungry peasants in ripe cornfields, ambuscades, rebel fights, assassinations and even the crowding of people in dusty streets are pregnant with character and meaning and the wind-scoured dessication of the land. Most of the outdoor action was filmed in Mexico.

Actually the progression of the drama is toward the tragic frustration of a man who is hampered by ignorance and impatience in his zeal to assist his fellow men. And in the construction of this drama, Mr. Steinbeck has spent a lot of time, along with a lot of ponderous verbiage, on the intricacies and deceits of politics.

When Mr. Brando and Mr. Kazan are in the midst of these devious details of changing governments and changing personalities under the pressure of necessity and power, the picture becomes a bit sluggish, as it does when Mr. Kazan takes too long to trifle with romantic byplay, such as the hero's prenuptial parley with his bride. And it is in these clumsy exchanges that Mr. Brando is not at his best. His acting of a baffled, tongue-tied Indian does not carry too much force.

But when this dynamic young performer is speaking his anger or his love for a fellow revolutionary, or when he is charging through the land at the head of his rebel soldiers or walking bravely into the trap of his doom, there is power enough in his portrayal to cause the screen to throb. And throb it does, in particular, in the last tragic, heartbreaking scene, when the rebel leader is shot down, the victim of his own unfailing trust.

As the wild, weak-willed brother of Zapata, Anthony Quinn does a dandy, raw-boned job and Joseph Wiseman is wonderfully steel-springed as a dark, vicious revolutionist. Lou Gilbert as a temporizing associate and Harold Gordon as the feeble president, Madero, also contribute to the picturesque character of the film. Alan Reed appears briefly as Villa, the famous rebel who was played some years ago with a slightly different emphasis by the late Wallace Beery. Many more do splendidly in small roles, while Jean Peters is as good as she can be as the proper young lady of the village who hooks up with the wild man of the hills.

—B.C., February 8, 1952

THE VOICE OF THE TURTLE

Directed by Irving Rapper; written by John van Druten and Charles Hoffman, based on his play; cinematographer, Sol Polito; edited by Rudi Fehr; music by Max Steiner; art designer, Robert Haas; produced by Mr. Hoffman; released by Warner Brothers. Black and white. Running time: 103 minutes.

With: Ronald Reagan (Sergeant Bill Page), Eleanor Parker (Sally Middleton), Eve Arden (Olive Lashbrooke), Wayne Morris (Commander Ned Burling), Kent Smith (Kenneth Bartlett), John Emery (George Harrington), Erskine Sanford (Storekeeper) and John Holland (Henry Atherton).

It does not often happen that a hit play and its film version run concurrently on Broadway, and, generally speaking, it is true that most bright theatrical achievements lose considerable luster in the process of their screen adaptations. The Warner Brothers' picturization of *The Voice of the Turtle* is a very happy exception, and, in fact, the film, which opened yesterday at the Warner Theatre, is in many ways much more satisfying than the John van Druten comedy, which, after five years, still is going along nicely at the Hudson Theatre.

Mr. van Druten is entitled to take as many bows as he pleases this morning, for he also wrote the screenplay. With slight variations here and there, but with no appreciable alteration of the play's spirit, he has circumvented its censorable aspects and made the romantic weekend shared by Sally Middleton and Sergeant Bill Page morally wholesome and ideally romantic. The author makes delicate use of innuendo, which may be interpreted as narrowly or as broadly as the individual spectator may see fit. But the greatest triumph scored by *The Voice of the Turtle* is its reassurance that there is nothing wrong with the boy-meets-girl formula that a deft presentation cannot overcome.

Although the framework of the play has been expanded so that characters only mentioned on the stage become living personalities on the screen, *The Voice of the Turtle* still is essentially a three-character story. And those principals are most attractively portrayed by Eleanor Parker and Ronald Reagan and by Eve Arden as the hardshelled, wisecracking friend whose promiscuity is, surprisingly enough, more amusing than vulgar. Miss Parker is altogether winning as the naive young actress who reluctantly falls in love while nursing the hurt of a newly shattered first romance with a theatrical producer. Miss Parker is consciously aping Margaret Sullavan's conception of the role, but she brings to it the innocence and bewilderment of youth that is so essential and in this respect she is even more successful than was Miss Sullavan.

The Voice of the Turtle is, in short, a very pleasant entertainment and proof sufficient that Hollywood can, when it wills, do anything as well as the theater can and, perhaps, even somewhat better.

—*T.M.P., December 26, 1947*

THE WAGES OF FEAR

Produced and directed by Henri-Georges Clouzot; written (in French, with English subtitles) by Mr. Clouzot and Jerome Geronimi, based on the novel by Georges Arnaud; cinematographer, Armand Thirard; edited by Henri Rust, Madeleine Gug and Etienne Muse; music by Georges Auric; production designer, Rene Renoux; released by International Affiliates. Black and white. Running time: 140 minutes.

With: Yves Montand (Mario), Charles Vanel (Jo), Vera Clouzot (Linda), Folco Lulli (Luigi), Peter Van Eyck (Bimba), William Tubbs (Bill O'Brien) and Dario Moreno (Hernandez).

As heavy a charge of nitroglycerine as a motion picture may legally contain is figuratively—and literally—transported in the French film, *The Wages of Fear* (*Le Salaire de la Peur*), which opened at the Paris yesterday.

At the outset, this lethally laden thriller looks as though it is taking off to be a squalid and mordant contemplation of the psychological problems of a group of men, stuck without hope of salvation in a fetid South American oil town. And, in this area, the prospect of achievement grows progressively dim, as H. G. Clouzot's screenplay of Georges Arnaud's novel goes wandering down slimy back alleys and gives evidence of having been trimmed.

There's a vague bit about a young Frenchman who lives with a fat Italian, then mocks and deserts him to latch onto an older Frenchman who blows into town.

What lies in this cryptic liaison is never clarified. It smacks of some noisome perversion, but the matter has obviously been cut. The film ran for two hours and a half in the original. It runs for an hour and forty-five minutes here.

There is also a towheaded German knocking around the town, being oddly sarcastic and mysterious. He, too, remains a blur.

Further—and this is most bewildering—there are hints of resentment and fear on the part of these men and the natives against the American oil company that runs the town. Suggestions of hard-boiled exploitation dangle barrenly here and there. But nothing is ever made of them.

The show looks ragged at the end of a half hour.

Then there's a sudden concentration. An oil well takes fire back in the field, and two truckloads of nitroglycerine have to be sent there to blow it out. The mission will be intensely dangerous, over rocky and winding mountain roads. Volunteers to drive the death-charged vehicles will be paid $2,000 a man.

Whereupon our four characters—the Italian, the German and the two Frenchmen—are chosen as separate teams to man the two trucks on the journey, at the end of which liberation lies. The wages of their fears will be salvation.

Now the excitement begins.

For M. Clouzot, who directed this thriller as well as wrote the script, goes all out in setting situations that fairly shiver with ice-cold suspense. He shows the deadliness of the explosive by having a drop of it hit the floor and boom with a mighty detonation. The frightfulness of the cargo is plain. Then he starts building up the ominous menace by dispatching the trucks in the dawn, with lights blinking and warning horns hooting. Thus he goes to work on the nerves.

First test of the courage of the characters—and the audience—is a hairpin curve, to take which the trucks must be backed up onto a rickety platform that hangs over a mountainous drop. This standard cliff-hanging maneuver is executed with hairbreadth teetering on the edge, and proves too much for the older Frenchman, who is played intensely by Charles Vanel.

Next a huge rock in the road becomes a barrier, until the German, played by Peter Van Eyck, devises a way to remove it with an improvised charge of nitroglycerine. The performance of this operation is fearsomely visualized by M. Clouzot.

And, finally, there's a gruesome, nightmare sequence of getting one of the trucks through an obstructing pool of oil.

It would not be fair to mention how this picture ends, other than to say that the conclusion is a deliberate and arbitrary irony.

Yves Montand does appear hard-grained and ruthless as the one Frenchman who survives, and Folco Lulli is vulgar and nerveless as the Italian who gets killed. Vera Clouzot, the wife of the director, is unbelievable as a beauteous slavey in the oil town, and William Tubbs is tough and rasping as the American manager of the oil company. But the characteristics of the people are not the absorbing thing in this film.

The excitement derives entirely from the awareness of nitroglycerine and the gingerly, breathless handling of it. You sit there waiting for the theater to explode.

—B.C., February 17, 1955

WAKING LIFE

Written and directed by Richard Linklater; director of photography, Mr. Linklater and Tommy Pallotta; edited by Sandra Adair; music score by Glover Gill, performed by Tosca Tango Orchestra; production designer, Bob Sabiston; produced by Palmer West, Jonah Smith, Mr. Pallotta and Anne Walker-McBay; released by Fox Searchlight Pictures. Running time: 99 minutes.

With: Wiley Wiggins, Julie Delpy, Adam Goldberg, Timothy (Speed) Levitch, Ethan Hawke and Steven Soderbergh.

There are those who will insist that the best way of approaching *Waking Life,* Richard Linklater's witty cosmic wow of a movie, is in a chemically altered state, and it's easy to see why.

The screenplay for *Waking Life,* which the New York Film Festival is showing tonight and tomorrow at Alice Tully Hall, blithely tosses out a bouquet of theories about human consciousness—some intellectually rigorous, others ludicrous crackpot riffs—whose cumulative impact suggests a stoned-out Big Bang of human thought.

With all the jostling philosophic notions tumbling from the mouths of everyday people, one response might be to lie back and go with the flow of mind-teasing what-if's without trying to piece them together or even to remember what's been said.

But I would urge you to resist the temptation to swoon into *Waking Life* as though it were a dizzy millennial throwback to a 60's trip movie. The film, which opens commercially next week, is so verbally dexterous and visually innovative that you can't absorb it unless you have all your wits about you. And even then, you may want to see it again to enjoy its subtle humor and warm humanity.

Visually, *Waking Life* is a technological coup: it transforms photographed reality into a sophisticated cartoon world by superimposing brightly hued digital animation on live-action digital video. (Bob Sabiston, who supervised the film's animation team, developed the software used in *Waking Life.*) Mr. Linklater's stroke of brilliance is his application of this technique to an open-ended fable about perception itself. I can't imagine a more powerful visual metaphor for the suspension between waking and dreaming evoked by the movie than this surreal merging of photography and animation.

In the expressionistic landscape of *Waking Life,* nothing is static. The images are continually rippling and heaving in a way that lends an extra meaning to the concept of animation by suggesting how the universe and all matter are in ceaseless flux. Depending on the image, what is on the screen varies in appearance from the lurid panels of an action cartoon (the angry scarlet face of a prisoner behind bars fantasizing about torturing his enemies to death) to a dazzling van Gogh–like canvas (New York City at night).

At the center of all this frantic activity, an unidentified protagonist played by Wiley Wiggins experiences a metaphysical identity crisis: he awakens in a dream in which he levitates, rides the highway in a boat and has other peculiar adventures. Like many of the people in Mr. Linklater's 1991 film, *Slacker,* Mr. Wiggins's laid-back character has the look and attitude of a perennial college student postponing any commitments as he drifts through life accumulating information without applying it to any goal.

The story is a record of his random encounters with teachers, students, street people and television personalities, all eagerly spouting their theories. Like *Slacker,* the film moves from one character to the next to the next before finally circling back to where it started.

Midway in his circuitous journey, he begins to realize that every time he thinks he has awakened, he has only entered another chapter of an ongoing dream. One recurrent indication is that the fragmented digital numbers on a bedside clock don't come into focus. The digitized faces delivering philosophical spiels, pet theories and tall tales include actors from earlier Linklater films, like Ethan Hawke and Julie Delpy (both from *Before Sunrise*) reunited, and the director Steven Soderbergh. The sources cited range from the philosopher Jean-Paul Sartre to the film critic André Bazin to the science-fiction writer Philip K. Dick.

Many of the spiels revolve around aphorisms and riddles. "I believe reincarnation is just a poetic expression of what collective memory really is," one commentator declares.

Another says, "I'd rather be a gear in a big deterministic physical machine than just some random swerving," and his face turns into a giant gray gear as he talks.

Some characters, like a white-haired man who asks, "Which is the most universal human characteristic, fear or laziness?," are pessimists. Others, like the coffeehouse Existentialist who declares, "Your life is yours to create," and backs it up quite eloquently, are optimists. And some, like the man who declares that dreams are fun and that "fun rules," are dingbats.

Mr. Linklater's pose of political and philosophical objectivity occasionally crumbles, as in a scene in which two enthusiastic gun advocates senselessly shoot each other in a bar. Although the screenplay shies away from overtly preferring one vision to another, the perspective of a pinball player who appears near the end of the film might come closest to the director's,

since he is played by Mr. Linklater: "There's only one instant, and it's right now, and it's eternity."

What might it mean that *Waking Life* is the third American feature film in this year's festival to eschew realism for fantasy? After David Lynch's Hollywood nightmare, *Mulholland Drive,* and Wes Anderson's nostalgic Salinger-esque fantasy of a bygone New York, *The Royal Tenenbaums,* the animated universe of *Waking Life* appears to carry us even further outside the realm of realism.

But that appearance is deceiving. If the faces of his characters are cartoonish, the digital animation paradoxically heightens their reality by making them more visually distinct from one another, and their remarks assume a cartoon-balloon significance that makes their words seem at once lighter and more distilled. *Waking Life,* unlike the two other films mentioned, leaves you buoyed and a little awestruck at the crazy quilt of human experience. It feels like a hearty cinematic slice of America's dream life as it really is.

—S.H., *October 12, 2001*

WALKABOUT

Directed by Nicolas Roeg; written by Edward Bond, adapted from a novel by James Vance Marshall; director of photography, Mr. Roeg; edited by Antony Gibbs and Alan Pattillo; production designer, Brian Eatwell; music by John Barry; produced by Si Litvinoff; released by twentieth Century Fox. Running time: 100 minutes.

With: Jenny Agutter (Girl), Lucien John (Boy), David Gumpilil (Aborigine) and John Meillon (Father).

Nicholas Roeg's *Walkabout,* which opened yesterday at the Plaza Theater, is a very sincere movie that evokes—especially, I suspect, in the minds of sophisticates—nostalgia for an innocence that probably never existed. Its sympathies are with the simple folk, but the techniques by which those sympathies are demonstrated are so fancy they remind me of things like heated swimming pools and safaris in air-conditioned Cadillacs.

The film takes its title from the Australian aborigine ritual that separates the men from the boys. When the aborigine youth reaches adolescence, he is sent out from his tribe to survive as best he can, for a period of months, on the flora and fauna of the bush.

Walkabout, shot entirely on location in Australia, is actually the story of two, quite different rites of passage, those of a cheerful aborigine boy and of a sweet, very self-possessed English girl whom he meets, along with her six-year-old brother, at the foot of a sand dune in the middle of a primeval wilderness. The girl and her brother had earlier been abandoned by their father, an archetypal urban breakdown, who drove into the outback with his children, attempted to shoot them and, having failed, set fire to his Volkswagen and put a bullet through his brain.

A movie that celebrates life, but is framed by suicides, is clearly not a simple movie. The journey—the walkabout—of the three children is full of lovely things, of unexpected understandings, of comradeship and, between the aborigine boy and the English schoolgirl, of a love that is neither understood, nor articulated, since neither one can speak the language of the other.

Unfortunately, Roeg, who made his directorial debut as co-director (with Donald Cammell) of *Performance* and who both directed and photographed *Walkabout,* never allows character, incident or even landscape to speak for itself. Extraordinarily beautiful rock formations become, through the director-photographer's eye, abstract patterns for us to marvel at. The camera often looks at the children from the vantage point of wombats, or desert lizards, or scorpions, who pass warily before us in "Living Desert" close-ups. When a sun goes down, or a moon rises, it may be accompanied by a full symphony orchestra and a choir of what I take to be heavenly voices, recorded in the comfort of a soundproof studio.

This is too bad because the film has a very decent screenplay by Edward Bond, the young Royal Court playwright (*Saved*) who adapted James Vance Marshall's novel with what seems to be fine restraint, even to its final, sad ironies. Exposition is kept to a minimum in favor of action, and individual incidents are as funny and to the point as the little boy's announcing, after two days of tramping through an exotic land: "I'm fed up."

The performances—those of Jenny Agutter, as the girl, Lucien John, as her brother (he is Roeg's youngest son) and David Gumpilil, as the aborigine boy—have all of the directness and simplicity the film itself seems to eschew, although Miss Agutter, especially in her nude scenes, appears to be remarkably well developed to be the 14-year-old girl my program notes say she's supposed to be.

Even though she is a charming actress, her figure thus helps to add to the credibility gap between the innocence that *Walkabout* says it's about, and the anything-but-innocent film techniques employed.
—*V.C., July 2, 1971*

A WALK IN THE SUN

Produced and directed by Lewis Milestone; written by Robert Rossen, based on the novel by Harry Brown; cinematographer, Russell Harlan; edited by Duncan Mansfield; music by Freddie Rich; art designer, Max Bertisch; released by Twentieth Century Fox. Black and white. Running time: 117 minutes.

With: Dana Andrews (Sergeant Tyne), Richard Conte (Rivera), Sterling Holloway (McWilliams), George Tyne (Friedman), John Ireland (Windy), Herbert Rudley (Porter), Richard Benedict (Tranella), Norman Lloyd (Archimbeau), Lloyd Bridges (Sergeant Ward) and Huntz Hall (Carraway).

Your response to Lewis Milestone's brave film version of Harry Brown's classic war story, *A Walk in the Sun,* will likely depend, proportionally speaking, on whether you have read the book. And if you haven't had the rare experience of absorbing the original, then you will surely find this film at the Victoria a swiftly overpowering piece of work. For Mr. Milestone, producing and directing, has followed Mr. Brown's intense report of a small beachhead maneuver near Salerno in a literal reproduction of episodes.

He has picked up the platoon of American infantry, which is the collective protagonist of the tale, at precisely the point that Mr. Brown did—as its landing barge drives toward the beach. He has faithfully recorded with his camera the calamity which befell the lieutenant, the confusion of the sergeants and their dilemma as they go ashore. And then, in a sequence of vignettes which include the subsequent actions and talk of twenty of the men, he has followed the platoon as it probes inland toward a farmhouse—its perilous "walk in the sun."

"The book was my script," said Mr. Milestone to someone the other day, and that is substantially evident. For virtually every detail, with a few technical alterations, has been photographed sequentially from the book. As a consequence and in a manner which achieves the fullest from the photograph, he has captured in illustration the complex tensions of that desperate, ravaging "walk." He has given a completely graphic picture of the natures and responses of the various men, their humors and whims and nerve reflexes as they move in isolation toward the unknown.

In this, Mr. Milestone has been aided by a generally superlative cast—a score of speaking actors who play infantry men credibly. Most impressive is Dana Andrews, who makes of Corporal (here Sergeant) Tyne an intelligent, acute and sensitive leader of the pathetically confused but stubborn group. Richard Conte is robustly endearing as a cheeky machine gunner, and Sterling Holloway, George Tyne, and Lloyd Bridges are variously appealing in other roles. A bit of theatrical ostentation is in Herbert Rudley's Sergeant Porter (he's the one who cracks up) and Norman Lloyd is plainly acting as the cold and cryptic Archimbeau. However, the performance in toto is consistent with the film's authentic tone.

But readers of the book are almost certain to find the picture falls considerably short of the cumulative force of the original—and that is, perhaps, inevitable. It is patent that the camera's observation cannot lay bare the insides of the men as did Mr. Brown's lean, unvarnished and thoroughly comprehending prose. The terrible uncertainty of the soldiers, the oppressive sense of lurking peril and doom, all the inner stress suggested in the writing is but surfacely envisioned on the screen. And the transcendent bomb-burst of emotion which forms the climax of the book is not achieved.

Mr. Milestone has hopefully endeavored to lift the audience to a high, reflective plane from time to time by handing the soundtrack to a singer of heroic ballad-verse. The music and words are disturbing but the device does not come off too well, mainly because it encroaches upon the illusion of the literal scene. Mr.

Milestone should not have attempted to mix real and expressionistic styles. His picture is most effective when it dramatically documents.

However, don't let these side discourses deter you from seeing the film. *A Walk in the Sun* is unquestionably one of the fine, sincere pictures about the war.

—B.C., January 12, 1946

THE WAR GAME

Written and directed by Peter Watkins: cinematographer. Peter Barlett: produced by the British Broadcasting System. Running time: 47 minutes.

The War Game, you may have heard, is the forty-seven-minute film that was originally made for the British Broadcasting Corporation and then withheld from showing on the air because it was considered too grisly and gruesome for indiscriminate projection into homes.

Its fearful and forceful nature was reported in this paper from London by Jack Gould on March 28, and its showing now in this festival is but a token of the talk and controversy its subsequent showing in a few British theaters has caused.

The film was made by a young man, Peter Watkins, in hand-held-camera style and at a pace that endows its grim, on-the-spot enactments with the seeming truth of a documentary film. It gives us a minute-by-minute rundown of cumulating horrors in an area of Kent from the time the first off-course Soviet bomb explodes in the region until the better part of the landscape and population are laid waste.

While the horrors it shows, such as firestorms, the melting of children's eyes and the mercy shooting by police of rows of victims who are too badly burned to be helped, are based upon actual experiences in Hiroshima and in German cities in World War II, the monstrous piling up of these horrors in one picture seems a calculated showing of the worst.

And the fact that no immediate way to avoid this is suggested to the audience by the film makes it, for most, a sheer frustrating excitement of morbidity and dread.

Mr. Watkins, whom I talked to in London after seeing his film there in June, said he hopes it will agitate people to demand the elimination of nuclear bombs. But one might guess it will serve that purpose only if shown in connection with some concrete and widespread campaign. Otherwise it is no more than a powerful, isolated horror film.

—*B.C., September 14, 1966*

THE WAR OF THE ROSES

Directed by Danny DeVito; written by Michael Leeson, based on the novel by Warren Adler; director of photography, Stephen H. Burum; edited by Lynzee Klingman; music by David Newman; production designer, Ida Random; produced by James L. Brooks and Arnon Milchan; released by Twentieth Century Fox. Running time: 116 minutes.

With: Michael Douglas (Oliver Rose), Kathleen Turner (Barbara Rose), Danny DeVito (Gavin D'Amato), Marianne Sägebrecht (Susan), Sean Astin (Josh at 17), Heather Fairfield (Carolyn at 17), G. D. Spradlin (Harry Thurmont) and Peter Donat (Larrabee).

Barbara and Oliver Rose (Kathleen Turner and Michael Douglas) started out as young lovebirds, ready to scrimp and save and struggle their way toward a rosy future. But by the time that future arrived, bringing with it two kids, two pets, two cars and a big house with a lighted, glassed-in shoe closet, they hated each other like poison. Why did this happen? Danny DeVito, who directed and costars in *The War of the Roses,* is hardly one to take the June-moon-spoon view of romance. It is Mr. DeVito's opinion, on the evidence of this film and his earlier *Throw Momma From the Train,* that love and rottenness are two sides of a single coin.

And since Mr. DeVito happens to have more of a taste for gleeful malice than any cinematic figure this side of Freddy Kruger (old Needs-a-Manicure, from the *Nightmare on Elm Street* movies), the Roses don't limit themselves to empty threats. Once their battle is under way, no holds are barred. *The War of the Roses* becomes a deliriously mean-spirited free-for-all in which nothing—not the pets, not the shoes, not the cars, and certainly not the principals themselves—is

sacred. This much should surely be said about *The War of the Roses:* it promises to take the gloves off, and it delivers.

The film's outstanding nastiness, which is often diabolically funny until a poorly staged final battle sequence simply takes things too far, has something real and recognizable at its core. The Roses may be caricatures, but the rise and fall of their romance and the viciousness of their fighting will be elements that many viewers can understand. One peculiarity: neither of the Roses, once the gauntlet has been thrown down, moves out of the house or bothers to become involved with another partner so that both remain free to concentrate singlemindedly on inflicting connubial misery. This makes the film slightly less believable than it might otherwise be, but it gives it a tighter focus.

Mr. DeVito narrates the story of the Roses as he plays Gavin D'Amato, Oliver's friend and lawyer. Throughout the film, Mr. DeVito is seen telling a silent young client about the Roses' problems. This looks so much like an extended setup for a final punch line that it's surprising when the payoff never comes. But *The War of the Roses* is never fully certain just how satirical or serious it means to be.

The film's tone may be slightly shaky at times, but when its humor works, it's very funny indeed. Mr. Douglas and Ms. Turner have never been more comfortable a team, and each of them is at his or her comic best when being as awful as both are required to be here. Ms. Turner plays Barbara as a blithe, breezy college girl whose streak of spontaneity evolves into something a lot scarier as she grows ever more disgusted with Oliver. Mr. Douglas, who continues to be a great comic embodiment of pure overweening ambition, makes Oliver the kind of self-congratulatory careerist who never notices his wife's disaffection until she fails to show up at the hospital on the day when he thinks he's dying. His little mishap, Barbara later tells Oliver dreamily, really took her by surprise. She had no idea she'd be so happy at the thought of getting rid of him.

Among the film's funnier images is one of Oliver holed up in his bedroom surrounded by dozens of the beloved Staffordshire figurines he thinks Barbara might try to break, once the orgy of antique-bashing and general house-wrecking is under way. Among its more extreme acts are Oliver's doing his utmost to wreck one of Barbara's dinner parties, Barbara's barricading Oliver in the sauna, a sexual interlude to end all sexual interludes, and the events leading up to the death of a pet. The film becomes merrily vulgar at some of these moments, but it seldom loses its sense of humor.

In addition to Mr. Douglas and Ms. Turner, both of whom are evilly enchanting, and Mr. DeVito, a welcome presence even in his master of ceremonies capacity, the film also features the German actress Marianne Sägebrecht (of *Baghdad Cafe* and *Sugarbaby*) as the plump, patient housekeeper who is privy to the Roses' worst moments. Mr. DeVito's direction is distinctively odd (with a lot of low-angle shots looking up at things), enjoyably mischievous, and always somehow mindful that there may be, at the heart of all this comic mayhem, something substantial going on.

—J.M., December 8, 1989

THE WARRIORS

Directed by Walter Hill; written by Mr. Hill and David Shaber, based on the novel by Sol Yurick; director of photography, Andrew Laszlo; edited by David Holden; music by Barry De Vorzon; art director, Don Swanagan; produced by Lawrence Gordon; released by Paramount Pictures. Running time: 93 minutes.

With: Michael Beck (Swan), James Remar (Ajax), Dorsey Wright (Cleon), Brian Tyler (Snow), David Harris (Cochise), Tom McKitterick (Cowboy), Marcelino Sanchez (Rembrandt), Terry Michos (Vermin), Thomas G. Waites (Fox), Deborah Van Valkenburgh (Mercy), Roger Hill (Cyrus), David Patrick Kelly (Luther) and Lynne Thigpen (Radio Deejay).

The Warriors are the artiest street gang you've ever seen. And what a surprise they'll be for anyone who's misled by the ads for *The Warriors*, which opened yesterday at Loews State and other theaters, and goes to the film expecting good old-fashioned head-bashing on a grand scale. There is head-bashing, of course, but it tends to be oddly fastidious. And the Warriors, when they aren't getting into fights, stand around very solemnly and only speak one at a time. Their diction is impeccable.

But Walter Hill, who co-wrote and directed *The Warriors,* is onto something, provided an audience is willing to meet him halfway. The film is as handsome to watch as it is preposterous to listen to, full of gorgeous nocturnal city images that splash blaring neon colors against filthy, rain-slicked gray. Mr. Hill uses subways, jukeboxes, spectacularly eerie costumes and deserted streets to create a stark yet extravagant visual style, and a grimy little world in which everything looks curiously brand-new. Thanks to a lot of wipes and slow-motion shots, you are never in danger of forgetting that somebody clever is at the helm.

Mr. Hill, who was a screenwriter before directing his first film, *Hard Times,* with Charles Bronson, can be exasperating in his fidelity to genre-movie conventions—last year, he worked so hard at making a *film noir* out of *The Driver* that he came up with *film gris.* This time, Mr. Hill has by no means relinquished his pretensions, but he is far more attentive to the demands of his story, which comes from a novel by Sol Yurick. Were it not for all those pregnant pauses, *The Warriors* might pass for a swift, streamlined adventure film in something like a futuristic cowboys-and-Indians mode.

At the start of the movie, The Warriors and a hundred other gangs have each sent nine delegates to a rally in the Bronx. Each group of nine wears its own set of matching outfits, making the rally sequence the most stunning of the film's inventive set-pieces.

At the rally, the leader of the Gramercy Riffs is assassinated; this is most unfortunate, because there are about 200 Gramercy Riffs and they're all impassive-looking blacks who carry hockey sticks and know karate. The Warriors didn't kill him—a lunatic named Luther, with a cry like a banshee's, did—but everyone's after them. The subway trip back to their home turf of Coney Island is a long one, punctuated by ingeniously plotted fights with other gangs and tight, portentous shots of the mouth of a woman disk jockey, who taunts the Warriors and plays songs like "Nowhere To Run" in their honor.

Along the way, Mr. Hill stages some wonderful-looking encounters, including a confrontation with a gang on roller skates and a love scene in the path of an oncoming train. A particularly strong sequence is set in Riverside Park, where the Warriors are attacked by the

Furies, who wear baseball uniforms and carry bats. The Furies also wear black and brightly colored face makeup reminiscent of *Clockwork Orange* but when a Warrior punches a Fury, he doesn't get paint on his fist. That's the magic of movies.

Most of the actors in *The Warriors* seem likely to have given wooden performances even if Mr. Hill hadn't directed them to. But a few of them—notably Michael Beck, James Remar and Brian Tyler—hold the screen even when they're affecting the most stoical of attitudes. Deborah Van Valkenburgh, as the obligatory pouty pick-up, and David Patrick Kelly, as crazy Luther, lend an unexpected humanity to Mr. Hill's glossy scheme. Thomas Waites is a promising actor who's as miscast here as he is in *On The Yard*. Mr. Waites plays tough guys in both films, and in both he seems much less formidable than his surroundings.

—J.M., February 10, 1979

WATCH ON THE RHINE

Directed by Herman Shumlin; written by Dashiell Hammett and Lillian Hellman, based on the play by Ms. Hellman; cinematographers, Merritt Gerstad and Hal Mohr; edited by Rudi Fehr; music by Max Steiner; art designer, Carl Jules Weyl; produced by Hal B. Wallis; released by Warner Brothers. Black and white. Running time: 114 minutes.

With: Bette Davis (Sara Muller), Paul Lukas (Kurt Muller), Geraldine Fitzgerald (Marthe de Brancovis), Lucile Watson (Fanny Farrelly), Beulah Bondi (Anise), George Coulouris (Teck de Brancovis), Donald Woods (David Farrelly), Henry Daniell (Phil von Ramme), Donald Buka (Joshua), Eric Roberts (Bodo) and Janis Wilson (Babette).

Out of Lillian Hellman's stirring play, *Watch on the Rhine,* which Herman Shumlin presented here in the spring of 1941, Warner Brothers and Mr. Shumlin have made a distinguished film—a film full of sense, power and beauty—which came to the Strand yesterday. Its sense resides firmly in its facing one of civilization's most tragic ironies, its power derives from the sureness with which it tells a mordant tale, and its beauty lies in its disclosures of human courage and dignity. It is meager praise to call it one of the fine adult films of these times.

For the irony Miss Hellman was pointing out back there before we entered this war—entered it formally, that is—was the fact that some people of goodwill were still blind to the barbaric nature of a conflict that has shaken the world. She was showing complacent Americans, serene in their neat security, that the spreading disease called fascism was not remote from our shores and that it wasn't an academic problem to be met with good intentions and smug outrage. She brought the essential conflict right into a soft American home and revealed that this modern barbarism could only be checked through force and sacrifice.

Basically, her story is just as pertinent today as it was then, since the conflict still calls for great endurance and its nature is not always too well perceived. It is still—and always is—of vital moment for people to see clearly that the fundamental clash in civilization is between those bent on self-aggrandizement and those who are not and that "it doesn't pay in money to fight for that in which we believe."

Miss Hellman's play—and this picture—point that moral through a German patriot, an anti-Nazi "underground" leader, who, in 1940, brings his wife and children to the American home of his mother-in-law. After years of fighting and hiding in Europe, he is thankful to deposit his loved ones in this peaceful sanctuary where the war seems fantastic and remote. But here, in this quiet home by the Potomac, he encounters the Nazi tentacles. A ratty Rumanian opportunist, a guest in the mother-in-law's house, discovers his "underground" connections, discovers that he is in America to raise funds and threatens to disclose him to the Nazis unless a price is paid. The manner in which the patriot meets this crisis and the awakening it gives his relatives is the shattering dramatic climax of this powerful, heart-stirring tale.

Through an almost literal adaptation by Dashiell Hammett, Miss Hellman's play tends to be somewhat static in its early stretches on the screen. With much of the action confined to one room in the American home, development depends largely on dialogue—which is dangerous in films. But the prose of Miss Hellman is so lucid, her characters so surely conceived, and Mr. Shumlin has directed for such fine tension in this his first effort for the screen that movement is not essential. The characters propel themselves.

Paul Lukas as the anti-Nazi German shapes a character of superb magnificence—a man worn with fighting and suffering, full of sorrow and humility, yet whose heart burns with human compassion and whose spirit is invincible. His love for his wife and his children, his great tenderness toward them—especially in the scene of their parting—is mingled so trenchantly with his grim determination in his mission that one perceives him as an enviable ideal.

There is dignity and strength, too, in the character of the wife as Bette Davis plays her—a gentle restraint and warm devotion such as Miss Davis has seldom revealed. And Lucile Watson repeats her stage performance of the mother-in-law with gracious charm. George Coulouris is a devastating villain, hard and implacably cruel, while Geraldine Fitzgerald, Donald Woods and Beulah Bondi are very good in minor roles. So too, are Donald Buka, Janis Wilson and Eric Roberts as the children, although the latter's loquacity as a prodigy is somewhat hard to take.

An ending has been given the picture which advances the story a few months and shows the wife preparing to let her older son follow his father back to Europe. This is dramatically superfluous, but the spirit is good in these times. And it adds just that much more heroism to a fine, sincere, outspoken film.

—B.C., August 28, 1943

THE WATERDANCE

Directed by Neal Jimenez and Michael Steinberg; written by Mr. Jimenez; director of photography, Mark Plummer; edited by Jeff Freeman; music by Michael Convertino; production designer, Robert Ziembicki; produced by Gale Anne Hurd and Marie Cantin; released by the Samuel Goldwyn Company. Running time: 106 minutes.

With: Eric Stoltz (Joel Garcia), Helen Hunt (Anna), William Allen Young (Les), James Roach (Man in Electronic Wheelchair), Elizabeth Peña (Rosa), Henry Harris (Mr. Gibson), Tony Genaro (Victor), Eva Rodriguez (Victor's Wife), Erick Vigil and Edgar Rodriguez (Victor's Sons) and Angelica Castell (Victor's Daughter).

In 1984 Neal Jimenez, the screenwriter (*The River's Edge, Something for the Boys*), was left with his legs permanently paralyzed after breaking his neck on a camping trip. Now he has written and codirected, with Michael Steinberg, *The Waterdance*, a good, tightly constructed film about the kind of intense physical and psychological therapy that he himself went through during long months at a rehabilitation center.

It's easy to understand why *The Waterdance* was named the audience's favorite film at the Sundance Film Festival in January. Though small in scale, it is big in feelings expressed with genuine passion and a lot of gutsy humor. Also, because of the kind of movie it is, there's never much doubt that these paraplegics will somehow come through. *The Waterdance*, set mostly in a hospital ward, is occasionally harrowing, but it doesn't mean to expose anything except the human spirit's capacity to triumph over adversity.

The excellent cast is headed by Eric Stoltz, Wesley Snipes and William Forsythe. Mr. Stoltz is Joel Garcia, Mr. Jimenez's surrogate, a young but already successful writer who, at the time of his accident, was involved in a serious affair with Anna (Helen Hunt), married, unfortunately, to someone else. Though Joel's origins are Hispanic, he doesn't look it and pays little attention to ethnic roots.

One of the contradictions of Mr. Stoltz's career is that he made his biggest splash in *Mask*, but he was disguised under so many prosthetic devices that audiences could never be sure of recognizing him again. There will be no such problem after *The Waterdance*. It's a fine, self-assured, carefully measured performance that is the conscience of the film.

Mr. Forsythe plays Bloss, a beefy, bigoted white biker who hates black, Hispanic and Asian people, which gives him a lot to complain about since the ward is so demographically balanced. It's one of the film's funnier touches that Bloss, the would-be social outlaw, is about the only patient whose mother is a steady, doting visitor.

Mr. Snipes, who can also be seen currently in *White Men Can't Jump*, has the film's richest role and wastes none of it. He is Raymond Hill, a quick-witted, fast-talking, womanizing young black man who, in the course of the therapy, must acknowledge the accumulation of emotional debts owed to his no-longer sympathetic wife (Fay Hauser).

Mr. Jimenez's screenplay is so packed with incident and so cannily paced that it has the somewhat breathless feeling of a certain genre of upbeat Broadway play. It's not dishonest, but there is such a symmetry to it that the revelations, confrontations, and resolutions become predictable. Yet the dialogue and the performances surprise even when the story does not.

There is a moving and doomily funny sequence in which Raymond suddenly explodes in hopeless fury during a group discussion about the sexual possibilities available to paraplegics. Raymond focuses his anger on the particular practices suggested by the discussion leader. He says he's shocked, but it's the life forever denied him that prompts the outburst. These sexual adjustments are pursued further in an inevitably sad encounter between Joel and Anna in a motel room.

The film's subsidiary characters are as finely drawn as the major ones. Ms. Hunt's Anna is a woman of unusual sensibility but not unlimited patience. Also good are Elizabeth Peña and William Allen Young as the ward nurses, and Grace Zabriskie as Bloss's chatty mother.

The exact significance of the title is not spelled out, but it apparently alludes to the miraculous self-assurance required of these paraplegics if they are to survive and keep their sanity: it's like dancing on water. The film is notable as much for all the bathos it manages to avoid as for its consistent common sense and seriously good humor.

—V.C., May 13, 1992

THE WAY WE WERE

Directed by Sydney Pollack: written by Arthur Laurents: director of photography. Harry Stradling Jr.: edited by John F. Burnett: music by Marvin Hamlisch: produced by Ray Stark: released by Columbia Pictures. Running time: 118 minutes.

With: Barbra Streisand (Katie Morosky). Robert Redford (Hubbell Gardner). Bradford Dillman (J. J.). Lois Chiles (Carol Ann). Patrick O'Neal (George Bissinger). Viveca Lindfors (Paula). Allyn Ann McLerie (Rhea Edwards). Murray Hamilton (Brooks Carpenter). Herb Edelman (Bill Verso). Diana Ewing (Vicki Bissinger). Sally Kirkland (Pony Dunbar) and Marcia Mae Jones (Peggy Vanderbilt).

The only thing that limits Barbra Streisand as a movie superstar is that she's not really an actress, not even much of a comedienne. She's an impersonator. When the impersonation fits the contours of the public personality—tough, driving, ambitious, shrewd, self-mocking—the performance can be effective as it was in *Funny Girl,* and as it is for a short space of time in her new film, Sydney Pollack's *The Way We Were.* The movie opened yesterday at the Loews State I and Tower East Theaters.

The Way We Were, adapted by Arthur Laurents from his novel, looks like a 747 built around an elephant. It seems to have been constructed of prefabricated parts that were then bolted together as best they could, considering the nature of the cargo.

The Streisand talent is huge, eccentric and intractable. When she goes one way and the movie goes another, it's no contest. The movie is turned into junk.

Mr. Laurents's story, charmingly told in his novel, is about Katie Morosky (Miss Streisand), a humorlessly determined political activist, and her lifelong love for good causes and a WASP of the sort that can only be true in romantic movies, Hubbell Gardiner (Robert Redford), so blond and talented that when Katie calls him America the Beautiful you know she isn't kidding.

Katie and Hubbell meet in college in the mid-nineteen-thirties. Katie, her hair a wild souvenir of the era of the electric curling iron, is president of the Young Communists League, spokesperson for the Spanish loyalists and implacable foe of the overprivileged, which means Hubbell. He not only has a roadster and is the top campus athlete but he also possesses the kind of writing talent Katie would like to have but never will.

These early sequences of the movie are not at all bad. The period detail, though heavily laid on, is funny and evocative. More importantly it's easy to understand why these two mismatched people could be so drawn to each other. Miss Streisand's furious determination is never very appealing but it is comprehensible, as is Redford's essential weakness, which carries with it a good deal of unrecognized cruelty.

The love affair, the movie and Miss Streisand's performance all go wrong when the story follows the now-married couple to post-war Hollywood, where Hubbell sells his soul for second-rate success and Katie, still fighting fascism, becomes a target of the House Un-American Activities Committee's witchhunt.

The Way We Were may have some historical value as the first Hollywood film I can think of to employ the red scare of the late forties and early fifties as a plot device of no more believeability than an auto accident. An extraordinary and very sad chapter in American politics is thus cheaply and futilely exploited.

Because both Pollack and Laurents have done good work in the past, I'm not at all sure they are fully responsible for the stylistic gaffs and narrative discontinuities in the finished film. Miss Streisand is a formidable star. It's difficult enough to accept her as a wronged wife, and it's ludicrous when the movie presents her photographed in the sentimental manner once used on lovelorn movie heroines of forty years ago.

By some peculiar alchemy, *The Way We Were* turns into the kind of compromised claptrap that Hubbell is supposed to be making within the film and that we're meant to think is a sellout. It is.

—*V.C., October 18, 1973*

WEEKEND

Written (in French, with English subtitles) and directed by Jean-Luc Godard: cinematographer, Raoul Coutard, edited by Agnes Guillemot; music by Antoine Duhamel and Wolfgang Amadeus Mozart; released by Grove Press. Running time: 103 minutes.

With: Mireille Darc (Corinne). Jean Yanne (Roland). Jean-Pierre Kalfon (Leader of the F.L.S.O.). Valerie Lagrange (His Moll). Jean-Pierre Léaud (Saint-Just/Man in Phone Booth) and Yves Benneyton (Member of the F.L.S.O.).

Jean-Luc Godard's *Weekend,* which was shown last night at the New York Film Festival, is a fantastic film, in which all of life becomes a weekend, and the weekend is a cataclysmic, seismic traffic jam—with cars running pedestrians and cyclists off the road, only to collide and leave blood and corpses everywhere.

In one tremendously long take, the camera passes along a highway where traffic is stopped by a long line of dead, smashed, burned and stalling vehicles—oil trucks, Renaults, sports cars, Mercedeses, a zoo truck with two llamas in it, recumbent tigers, people playing ball through the tops of their stalled Deux Chevaux, people playing cards, playing chess, honking horns, making gestures, quarreling, crying and ignoring the fact that there is mayhem everywhere. The conception of the movie is very grand. It is as though the violent quality of life had driven Godard into and through insanity, and he had caught it and turned it into one of the most important and difficult films he has ever made.

There are plot fragments at the beginning, betrayals, dire conspiracies to murder, detailed, intimate (and highly comic) sexual anecdotes. They lead nowhere. There are a couple (Mireille Darc and Jean Yanne), who, like refugees from the world of Samuel Beckett, are always looking for a gas station, and later for a town. A lot of the movie is like Beckett, the despair (if this can be imagined) not as it is on stage, simplified and austere, but rich, overloaded, really epic. At one point, as the couple sit by the side of the road, the woman is casually raped in a ditch. No one even bothers to mention it. This would not work in the theater or in prose. It works on film.

The movie is interspersed with little essays, idylls, jokes, a Mozart sonata, a frantic love song sung by Jean-Pierre Léaud in a telephone booth, noise, rituals, battles with paint sprayers and tennis balls. It ends in slaughter and cannibalism. There are a lot of infantile pretentious touches, punning flashcards (Anal . . . lyse, Faux . . . tographie) and the subtitles seem to have caught a bit of this. "La Paresse" (laziness) is regularly translated as "press."

There is a moment near the end when the movie cracks up—long, dogmatic, motionless diatribes on behalf of Africa and the Arab countries with a peroration against black nonviolence, which keeps one thinking Biafra, Biafra, and wanting to walk out. (In fact, it might be advisable to walk out when the speeches begin for a cup of coffee and a cigarette.) It's unprofessional, like a musician stopping a concert to deliver a bit of invective to a captive audience. But perhaps, like any serious artist, Godard cannot help including all his preoccupations raw right now, even if they bring his movie down.

But the film must be seen, for its power, ambition, humor and scenes of really astonishing beauty. There are absurdist characters from Lewis Carroll, from Fellini, from *La Chinoise,* from Buñuel. At many moments the movie, which is in color, captures the precise sense one has about the world, when one is in a city or in a rush, when one reads the headlines or obituary columns, when one drives, when one sets out, for that matter, on a weekend. It is as though the apocalypse had somehow registered on a sensibility calibrated very fine. It is an appalling comedy. There is nothing like it at all. It is hard to take.

—*R.A., September 28, 1968*

WELCOME TO THE DOLLHOUSE

Written and directed by Todd Solondz; director of photography, Randy Drummond; edited by Alan Oxman; music by Jill Wisoff; production designer, Susan Block; produced by Ted Skillman and Mr. Solondz; released by Sony Pictures Classics. Running time: 87 minutes.

With: Heather Matarazzo (Dawn Wiener), Eric Mabius (Steve Rodgers), Brendan Sexton Jr. (Brandon McCarthy), Daria Kalinina (Missy), Angela Pietropinto (Mrs. Wiener) and Matthew Faber (Mark Wiener).

Remembering perfectly is the best revenge, as Todd Solondz demonstrates so beautifully in *Welcome to the Dollhouse,* his mordantly hilarious suburban comedy about the torments endured by an awkward young girl. With a fine vengeance along with flashes of great, unexpected tenderness, Mr. Solondz lethally evokes every petty humiliation that his seventh-grade heroine can't wait to forget.

Amazingly, he captures these experiences with both junior high school immediacy and the knowing, novelistic hindsight of a wry adult sensibility. And come to think of it, these may not be such different perspectives. Will getting older make life easier, eleven-year-old Dawn Wiener (Heather Matarazzo) plaintively

asks her brother. Well, no, not exactly. "They call you names, but not as much to your face," he replies.

Welcome to the Dollhouse, which brings new insight to name-calling and many other preadolescent agonies, won a well-deserved Grand Prize at this year's Sundance Film Festival. Tonight, it glowingly inaugurates the New Directors/New Films series at the Museum of Modern Art, which is cosponsored by the Film Society of Lincoln Center. The best of an unusual abundance of bright American comedies on this year's schedule, *Welcome to the Dollhouse* displays wrenching emotional acuity beneath a veneer of devilishly funny surface details. Even the fact that Dawn's parents are called Harv and Marj becomes mischievously revealing, somehow.

Then there's Dawn herself: squinting, bespectacled, breathing through an open mouth as if the world won't allow her enough air. (Her biography says that the poised and wonderfully deadpan Miss Matarazzo "is now thirteen years old and very happy to have finished seventh grade.") Dawn is a model of geekiness, looking permanently perplexed and decked out in a wardrobe that only enhances her social problems. The charitable thought is that her mother picks out her clothes.

Nobody likes Dawn, or at least nobody would be caught dead admitting it. At school, she's picked on by popular girls with names like Lolita and barely tolerated by her teacher. At home, she has a pretty, tutu-wearing kid sister named Missy (played by Daria Kalinina, a shrewd little actress and a real ballerina) who capers adorably and is everybody's pet. Their mother (Angela Pietropinto) claims not to favor Missy, but this film's characters have an interesting way of saying one thing and doing another. Mr. Solondz, who wrote, directed and helped produce his film, knows exactly how that process works.

Everyone in *Welcome to the Dollhouse* speaks in some sort of dissembling code, most notably Brandon McCarthy (Brendan Sexton Jr.), the schoolroom bully who is one of Dawn's chief tormentors. One of the film's delights is watching Dawn realize that this relationship is more loaded than it looks. Brandon does devote an awful lot of energy to harassing her, after all. And his threats, shockingly nasty as they are, have a double-edged aspect. When Brandon threatens to rape Dawn, he gives her a time and location and sounds strangely like somebody making a date. "Tomorrow, same time, same place," he tells her. "You get raped. Be there."

Because life is no simpler in the seventh grade than at any other time, Dawn is too distracted to appreciate Brandon's backhanded courtship. She is dazzled by Steve Rodgers (Eric Mabius), the local Fabio in this New Jersey suburb, who has been recruited as lead singer in the rock band led by Dawn's brother, Mark (Matthew Faber). Mark is such a computer nerd that the band is named for a type of equation (the Quadratics) and includes a clarinet, which isn't much help when they try to play "Satisfaction." The trio has recruited Steve in a desperate stab at cool.

Steve certainly dazzles Dawn, who plies him with home cooking (fish sticks and Pop-Tarts) and wants him so badly she almost reaches out and touches him (she is wearing ridiculous pajamas at the time). Steve, made hunky and comically moronic by Mr. Mabius, seems to represent everything that could save Dawn from her miseries.

Mr. Solondz has said that *Welcome to the Dollhouse* isn't a coming-of-age film because he doesn't believe anyone truly grows up in seventh grade, but in fact it has all the bittersweet wisdom that genre requires. Deftly and caustically, the film brings Steve into sharp focus for Dawn while also capturing, in excruciatingly funny detail, her every misguided effort to win him over. She makes a shrine to Steve using candles and his ID card. She elicits advice (and some sexual information that Dawn misunderstands, rather mortifyingly) from the town tramp, who is seen regaling her admirers while lying on a car hood. Dawn even dresses up in midriff-baring splendor for Harv and Marj's anniversary party, for which Steve has been hired to sing hora numbers and a personalized love song.

"Mommy, let's watch it again!" exclaims Missy, because the entire event, featuring one of Dawn's many humiliations, has been captured on videotape. Anyone who has ever felt as Dawn does when she sneaks that tape outside in the middle of the night and smashes it with a hammer will find *Welcome to the Dollhouse* a brilliantly malevolent treat.

Though Mr. Solondz now finds himself in the brightest limelight of the New Directors series, he is not quite new. A decade ago, he had three-picture writing contracts with both Twentieth Century Fox and Columbia Pictures. "Unfortunately, the only thing I really liked about these deals was telling everyone I had them," he has written.

After making another short and acting in his little-noticed first feature, *Fear, Anxiety and Depression* (1989), he left filmmaking and taught English as a second language to Russian immigrants for several years before reviving *Welcome to the Dollhouse,* one of his early screenplays. Mr. Solondz, small, nervous and bespectacled, bearing a more than passing resemblance to Dawn Wiener, can regard his own reversal of fortune as proof of his film's premise. When losers persevere this cleverly, they win.

—*J.M., March 22, 1996*

THE WELL-DIGGER'S DAUGHTER

Written (in French, with English subtitles), produced and directed by Marcel Pagnol; edited by Charles Clement; music by Vincent Scotto; released by Siritzky International Pictures. Black and white. Running time: 124 minutes.

With: Raimu (Pascal), Fernandel (Felipe), Josette Day (Patricia), Charpin (Mr. Mazel) and George Grey (Jacques Mazel).

Good news should not be unnecessarily delayed in the telling, so let's come right to the point of this notice. *The Well-digger's Daughter* is just about the most delightful French comedy-drama that has come this way since the memorable *The Baker's Wife.* In fact, it might even be said without the slightest intention of detracting from the ample merit of this new film, which had its premiere on Saturday at the new Avenue Playhouse, Avenue of the Americas and Forty-seventh Street, that the motivation of both pictures is far from dissimilar. For Raimu is again playing a simple French peasant whose honor and dignity is compromised by a feminine indiscretion, committed in this instance by one of his six motherless daughters.

That this should be so is not surprising, considering that *The Well-digger's Daughter* was written, directed and produced by Marcel Pagnol, also of *The Baker's Wife* cinematic fame. Raimu, who died recently in Paris, once said in an interview that he liked working with Pagnol because "his genius lies in his ability to take the public from laughter to tears and back again in a flash." And that is just what *The Well-digger's Daughter* manages with wondrous dexterity, after a rather halting beginning. The story is no great shakes in outline, being simply a tale about an innocent country maiden who is seduced and left with child by the dashing son of a prosperous merchant. The young man goes off to war as an aviator and the girl is turned out by her outraged father to protect the innocence of his other little girls.

It is the way this framework has been embellished by the facile writing of M. Pagnol and the brilliant acting of Raimu that makes *The Well-digger's Daughter* a distinguished accomplishment. For Raimu, no less than Pagnol, had a genius for turning with complete naturalness from laughter to tears. His characterization of Pascal, the master well-digger, is expertly proportioned and runs the gamut of emotions. The quiet dignity of his speech and manner as he confronts the aviator's parents on the subject of his daughter's condition is one of the most compassionate and moving scenes ever filmed. And it will indeed be a hard heart that will not give vent to a tear when Pascal, his honor finally restored, receives the boy's parents with great dignity and formality when they come to apologize and ask his daughter's hand in marriage.

We suspect it is the frankness with which the situation is presented and discussed by the characters that gives the film its nobility of purpose. *The Well-digger's Daughter* runs close to two hours and, as we said away back, it has a tendency to drag because it takes Mr. Pagnol some time to get his story under way. But after that, the rest is a sheer delight. Josette Day is appealing as the erring daughter and Fernandel, as a distant suitor and family friend, has several deliciously comic scenes. George Grey as the young man and Charpin as his father contribute well-rounded performances, as do several others in lesser roles.

With its few faults—the photography is bad here and there—*The Well-digger's Daughter* still is one of the very best pictures to come out of France and, indeed, this spectator does not hesitate to place it on a par with *The Baker's Wife*.

—*T.M.P., September 30, 1946*

WEST SIDE STORY

Directed by Robert Wise and Jerome Robbins: written by Ernest Lehman. based on the play by Arthur Laurents. from a conception by Mr. Robbins. inspired by *Romeo and Juliet* by William Shakespeare: cinematographer. Daniel Fapp: edited by Thomas Stanford: music by Leonard Bernstein: choreography by Mr. Robbins: production designer. Boris Leven: produced by Mr. Wise: released by United Artists. Running time: 155 minutes.

With: Natalie Wood (Maria). Richard Beymer (Tony). Russ Tamblyn (Riff). Rita Moreno (Anita). George Chakiris (Bernardo). Tucker Smith (Ice). Tony Mordente (Action). David Winters (Arab). Eliot Feld (Baby John). Bert Michaels (Snowboy) and Sue Oakes (Anybodys).

What they have done with *West Side Story* in knocking it down and moving it from stage to screen is to reconstruct its fine material into nothing short of a cinema masterpiece.

In every respect, the recreation of the Arthur Laurents-Leonard Bernstein musical in the dynamic forms of motion pictures is superbly and appropriately achieved. The drama of *New York* juvenile gang war, which cried to be released in the freer and less restricted medium of the mobile photograph, is now given range and natural aspect on the large Panavision color screen, and the music and dances that expand it are magnified as true sense-experiences.

The strong blend of drama, dance and music folds into a rich artistic whole. It may be seen at the Rivoli Theatre, where it had its world premiere last night.

Perhaps the most striking aspect of it is the sweep and vitality of the dazzling Jerome Robbins dances that the kids of the seamy West Side do. Here is conveyed the wild emotion that burns in these youngsters' tough, lithe frames. Here are the muscle and the rhythm that bespeak a collective energy.

From the moment the camera swings grandly down out of the sky at the start of the film and discovers the Jets, a gang of tough kids, twitching restlessly in a playground park, bodies move gracefully and fiercely in frequent spontaneous bursts of dance, and even the movements of the characters in the drama have the grace of actors in a ballet.

This pulsing persistence of rhythm all the way through the film—in the obviously organized dances, such as the arrogant show-offs of the Jets, that swirl through playgrounds, alleys, school gymnasiums and parking lots, and in the less conspicuous stagings, such as that of the "rumble" (battle) of the two kids—gives an overbeat of eloquence to the graphic realism of this film and sweeps it along, with Mr. Bernstein's potent music, to the level of an operatic form.

Against, or within, this flow of rhythm is played the tender drama of two nice kids, a Puerto Rican girl and a Polish boy, who meet and fall rapturously in love, despite the hatred and rivalry of their respective ethnic groups, and are plunged to an end that is tragic, just like Romeo and Juliet.

Every moment of the drama has validity and integrity, got from skillful, tasteful handling of a universal theme. Ernest Lehman's crackling screenplay, taken from Arthur Laurents's book, and Robert Wise's incisive direction are faithful and cinema-wise, and the performances are terrific except in one major role.

Richard Beymer's characterization of the boy who meets and loves the girl is a little thin and pretty-pretty, but Natalie Wood is full of luster and charm as the nubile Puerto Rican who is poignantly drawn to him. Rita Moreno is a spitfire as Miss Wood's faithful friend, and George Chakiris is proud and heroic as her sweetheart and leader of the rival gang.

Excellent as young toughs (and dancers) in a variety of characterizations are Russ Tamblyn, Tucker Smith, Tony Mordente, Jose De Vega, Jay Norman and many more, and outstanding girls are Gina Trikonis, Yvonne Othon, Suzie Kaye and Sue Oakes.

Although the singing voices are, for the most part, dubbed by unspecified vocal performers, the device is not noticeable and detracts not one whit from the beauty and eloquence of the songs.

In the end, of course, the moral of the tragedy comes through in the staggering sense of wastage of the energies of kids. It is screamed by the candy-store owner, played trenchantly by Ned Glass, when he flares, "You kids make this world lousy! When will you stop?"

It is a cry that should be heard by thoughtful people—sympathetic people—all over the land.

—*B.C., October 19, 1961*

THE WHALES OF AUGUST

Directed by Lindsay Anderson; written by David Berry, based on his play; director of photography, Mike Fash; edited by Nicolas Gaster; music by Alan Price; production designer, Jocelyn Herbert; produced by Carolyn Pfeiffer and Mike Kaplan; released by Alive. Running time: 90 minutes.

With: Bette Davis (Libby Strong), Lillian Gish (Sarah Webber), Vincent Price (Mr. Maranov), Ann Sothern (Tisha Doughty), Harry Carey Jr. (Joshua Brackett), Frank Grimes (Mr. Beckwith), Frank Pitkin (Old Randall), Mike Bush (Young Randall), Margaret Ladd (Young Libby), Tisha Sterling (Young Tisha) and Mary Steenburgen (Young Sarah).

Busy, busy, busy," says Libby (Bette Davis), the elder of two ancient, widowed sisters who are sharing what could be their last summer on the Maine coast.

The target of Libby's sarcasm is Sarah (Lillian Gish), the sweet-natured younger sister who takes care of Libby, brushes her long white hair, lays out her clothes, finds her shoes, does the cooking, tends to the cottage, weeds the garden and, in her spare time, makes little cloth dolls shaped like koala bears to be sold at the end-of-summer benefit.

Sarah is a living saint, but her saintliness is of the unremitting kind that might drive anyone crazy, especially the way she inserts an insistent "dear" as a preface or postscript to every sentence directed to her older sister.

Says Libby after a long silence, "I wish we were back in Philadelphia." "But, dear," says Sarah, "it would be hot in Philadelphia." Says Sarah, "It would keep you from being so busy."

Sarah can be sarcastic too. When Libby comes out with yet another nasty remark, Sarah acknowledges it with a deadpan, serene, "As you like to say, dear." Sarah's sarcasm is muted, casual. Unlike Libby, she has memories of a happy, sexually satisfying marriage. She's not caged in an arid darkness.

With its two beautiful, very different, very characteristic performances by Miss Gish and Miss Davis, who, together, exemplify American films from 1914 to the present, Lindsay Anderson's *Whales of August* is a cinema event, though small in scale and commonplace in detail. It's as moving for all the history it recalls as for anything that happens on the screen. Yet what happens on the screen is not to be underrated.

It's possible that *The Whales of August,* opening today at Cinema 2, could not have been made by anyone except Mr. Anderson, the English director (*This Sporting Life, If, Britannia Hospital*) whose profound appreciation (and knowledge) of screen history is commanded by a rigorous sensibility. This is no *On Golden Pond,* the kind of sentimental sitcom that reaches for laughs by having its old folk talk the jargon of the young.

In its way, *The Whales of August* is tough, but it has a major flaw in that David Berry's adaptation of his stage play isn't strong enough for the treatment it receives from the director and his extraordinary actors. In addition to the film's two icons, the cast includes Ann Sothern, wonderful as the sisters' resilient, full-blooded Maine neighbor, and Vincent Price, as an old, mannerly (and broke) White Russian refugee, who may be as fraudulent as the skeptical Libby suspects.

Mr. Berry is no American Chekhov. Though minutely observed, the lives of Libby and Sarah evoke no landscape larger than this tiny Maine island to which they've been returning every summer since they were girls. There are references to lost childhoods, dead husbands, wars survived, and estranged children, but the references are more obligatory than enriching. There's nothing really at stake in the course of the day we see in almost documentary detail, except the possibility that Libby will not eat fish for dinner. There's even some confusion about time.

The film opens with a black-and-white prologue in which the sisters and their best friend, eventually to be played by Miss Sothern, are introduced as teenage girls. They later refer to friendships lasting fifty years. But if the old ladies are in their eighties—at least— that would mean they'd started coming to the island in their comparatively mature thirties.

Because the film operates most effectively by being literal, the raising of such basic questions obscures one's commitment to it.

The pleasure of *The Whales of August* comes from watching how Mr. Anderson keeps his two stars working in unison, though each works by totally different methods. Miss Gish, intuitive like Sarah, appears to be without guile, still something of the silent-screen innocent, but there's not a gesture or a line-reading that doesn't reflect her nearly three-quarters of a century in front of a camera. Scenes are not purloined when she's on-screen.

Miss Davis is more than up to the competition, which comes to look like harmony. Her elegantly sculptured features rivet the attention. When she barks out an uncalled-for, rudely welcome comment, the familiar voice, an echo from both *The Little Foxes* and *Beyond the Forest,* cuts through the stasis, not to overwhelm Miss Gish but to give her something to act with and against.

Much in the way that Libby and Sarah come to terms with their edgy, precarious existence, *The Whales of August* records the reconciliation of the cinema of D. W. Griffith (and its idealized view of women) and that of Hollywood's golden era, when women could be far less than perfect and great actresses could be heard as well as seen.

Appearing in supporting roles are Harry Carey Jr., identified with the films of John Ford (one of Mr. Anderson's favorite American directors), as a Maine handyman, and Frank Grimes, who plays a cameo role as a real-estate salesman. Mary Steenburgen, Tisha Sterling (Miss Sothern's daughter) and Margaret Ladd are seen in the film's prologue.

The Whales of August takes its time. One has to accept its pacing, which is deliberate and careful, the way someone with brittle bones walks across a rocky patch of earth. Its rewards are unexpected and quite marvelous. When Miss Gish sits in front of a mirror, doing up her hair, we're seeing a character named Sarah girding herself for further battle with an impossibly demanding sister, as well a demonstration of how a movie works on all the memories we bring to it.

—*V.C., October 16, 1987*

WHATEVER HAPPENED TO BABY JANE?

Produced and directed by Robert Aldrich; written by Lukas Heller; cinematographer, Ernest Haller; edited by Michael Luciano; music by Frank DeVol; art designer, William Glasgow; released by Seven Arts/Warner Brothers. Black and white. Running time: 132 minutes.

With: Bette Davis (Jane Hudson), Joan Crawford (Blanche Hudson), Victor Buono (Edwin Flagg).

Marjorie Bennett (Della Flagg), Maidie Norman (Elvira Stitt), Anna Lee (Mrs. Bates), Barbara Merrill (Liza Bates), Julie Allred (Baby Jane as a Child) and Dave Willock (Ray Hudson).

Joan Crawford and Bette Davis make a couple of formidable freaks in the new Robert Aldrich melodrama *Whatever Happened to Baby Jane?* But we're afraid this unique conjunction of the two one-time top-ranking stars in a story about two aging sisters who were once theatrical celebrities themselves does not afford either opportunity to do more than wear grotesque costumes, make up to look like witches and chew the scenery to shreds.

As this pair of profoundly jealous has-beens who live alone in an old Hollywood house, where one of them (Miss Crawford), a cripple, is confined to a wheelchair as the result of a long-ago vindictive "accident," they do get off some amusing and eventually blood-chilling displays of screaming sororal hatred and general monstrousness.

Especially Miss Davis. As the mobile one who is slowly torturing to death the helpless sister whose fame as a movie actress eclipsed her own as a child vaudeville star, she shrieks and shrills in brazen fashion, bats her huge mascaraed eyes with evil glee, snarls at the charitable neighbors and acts like a maniac. Indeed, it is only as a maniac that her character can be credited here—a sadly demented creature who is simply working out an ancient spite.

If you see her as that and see this picture, which opened yesterday in several score neighborhood theaters, as a "chiller" of the old-fashioned type—as a straight exercise in studied horror—you may find it a fairly gripping film.

The feeble attempts that Mr. Aldrich has made to suggest the irony of two once idolized and wealthy females living in such depravity and the pathos of their deep-seated envy having brought them to this, wash out very quickly under the flood of sheer grotesquerie. There is nothing particularly moving or significant about these two.

Miss Crawford does have the less malevolent and more sympathetic role. As a poor thing stuck in a wheelchair, unable to counter or resist her diabolic sister when she delivers a dinner tray bearing a dead pet canary or a scalded rat, she might earn one's gentle compassion. But she is such a sweetly smiling fraud,

such an artlessly helpless ninny, that one feels virtually nothing for her. No wonder her crazy sister finds her a deadly bore.

Of course, she does have her big chance to chew some scenery when she has to drag herself to the telephone and when she later thrashes about in pop-eyed terror with her hands tied and tape across her mouth.

Victor Buono gets a nice chance to do some elaborate acting, too. He plays a fat piano player who is invited into the house. But his weirdly epicene intruder is little more than a colorful buffoon, a bit of comic relief in the proceedings. He takes a fast powder toward the end.

Maidie Norman also gets in for a few tense scenes as an anxious maid, and Anna Lee burbles occasionally as the woman who lives next door.

Of course, we won't tell you how it comes out. But the revelation at the end would be enough to tag the whole thing synthetic and a contrivance, if nothing else did—which it does.

—B.C., *November 7, 1962*

WHAT'S EATING GILBERT GRAPE?

Directed by Lasse Hallstrom; written by Peter Hedges, based on his novel; director of photography, Sven Nykvist; edited by Andrew Mondshein; music by Alan Parker and Bjorn Isfalt; production designer, Bernt Capra; produced by Meir Teper, Bertil Ohlsson and David Matalon; released by Paramount Pictures. Running time: 117 minutes.

With: Johnny Depp (Gilbert Grape), Leonardo DiCaprio (Arnie Grape), Juliette Lewis (Becky), Darlene Cates (Momma), Mary Steenburgen (Betty Carver) and Crispin Glover (Mortician).

It's hard to describe the many eccentricities of *What's Eating Gilbert Grape* without making the film sound as if it had a case of terminal whimsy. Better to say that this is the work of Lasse Hallstrom, the Swedish director of *My Life as a Dog*, whose gentle, rueful style can accommodate vast amounts of quirkiness in enchanting ways. Mr. Hallstrom is also adept at viewing the world from the perspective of troubled young characters. And Gilbert Grape, the hero and narrator of this story, has troubles to spare.

Gilbert lives in Endora, Iowa, a town so flat and featureless that all of its energy seems to have turned inward, particularly where the Grape family is concerned. The Grape household is dominated by 500-pound Momma (Darlene Cates), who hasn't ventured outside in so long that local children sneak up to the Grape windows to stare at her. Gilbert helps them.

The household, which also includes two quarrelsome sisters, is kept in a constant state of emergency by Arnie (Leonardo DiCaprio), Gilbert's retarded younger brother. Arnie enjoys heights, and he has a way of climbing to the top of the local water tower whenever Gilbert forgets to watch him.

Gilbert himself has a career as a delivery boy, working in the small, outmoded grocery store where few Endorans shop now that a big, modern supermarket has come to town. (The fact that the supermarket has a tank containing live lobsters has created a considerable stir.) Gilbert has been making very special deliveries to Mrs. Betty Carver (Mary Steenburgen) for a long time. "Uh, get out," Betty says to her two small children when Gilbert comes over. "Go outside and play right now."

Betty may see some urgency in these meetings, but Gilbert has begun to grow bored. Everything in Endora bores him a little, until flirty, diffident Becky (Juliette Lewis) comes to town. To the extent that this offbeat, slyly deadpan film has any forward momentum, it has to do with how Becky's arrival raises Endora's energy level a little. It's also about how Arnie and Momma's various problems finally bring Gilbert to the brink of change.

What's Eating Gilbert Grape is based on a somewhat darker, more acerbic first novel by Peter Hedges, who also wrote the screenplay. Like a lot of first novels, this one is much stronger on texture and character than on plot, and the film has inherited the same problem. But the screen version of *What's Eating Gilbert Grape* also has a lot to recommend it. Particularly impressive are the sweet, weirdly idyllic tone of Mr. Hallstrom's direction and Johnny Depp's tender, disarming performance as the long-suffering Gilbert Grape.

In films like *Edward Scissorhands* and *Benny and Joon*, Mr. Depp has made a specialty of playing gentle outsiders, and doing so with enormous charm. He brings much the same soulfulness and strength to this role, even though for once he is cast as a pillar of the community. This particular community needs every

pillar it can find, as does the Grape house itself, which sags badly under the spot where Momma holds court in the living room. Momma so seldom leaves the sofa that her children bring the kitchen table over to her at mealtimes.

Mr. Hallstrom, working much more comfortably in an American setting than he did in the 1990 *Once Around* (which took place in the Boston area), has done a particularly canny job of casting this film. The impossible role of Momma is ideally played by Ms. Cates, who was spotted on a *Sally Jessy Raphaël* episode about overweight women who never leave home. Ms. Cates, believable and emphatic, has done herself and the film a big favor by getting out of the house for this. Some of the film's minor characters are also very well etched, particularly the avid young mortician (Crispin Glover) who takes his work a little too seriously and likes to talk about it over lunch.

Ms. Lewis is seductively good as someone obviously bemused by what goes on in Endora, and by Gilbert himself. But the film's real show-stopping turn comes from Mr. DiCaprio, who makes Arnie's many tics so startling and vivid that at first he is difficult to watch. Mr. DiCaprio, who also had a prominent role in *This Boy's Life* earlier this year, winds up capturing the enormous range of Arnie's raw emotions, and making it clear why the Grape brothers share such an unbreakable bond. The performance has a sharp, desperate intensity from beginning to end.

What's Eating Gilbert Grape has been given an invitingly bucolic glow by Sven Nykvist's cinematography, which makes the antics of the Grapes that much more colorfully incongruous. The film's hairdresser, apparently thinking like a Grape herself, gives Ms. Lewis a spiky-looking brush cut while letting Mr. Depp fit one of Gilbert's lines from the novel: "My hair is so long that it's beginning to eat my head."

—J.M., December 17, 1993

WHAT'S UP, DOC?

Produced and directed by Peter Bogdanovich; written by Buck Henry, David Newman and Robert Benton, based on a story by Mr. Bogdanovich; cinematographer, Laszlo Kovacs; edited by Verna Fields; music by Artie Butler;

production designer, Polly Platt; released by Warner Brothers. Running time: 94 minutes.

With: Barbra Streisand (Judy Maxwell), Ryan O'Neal (Howard Bannister), Kenneth Mars (Hugh Simon), Madeline Kahn (Eunice Burns), Austin Pendleton (Frederick Larabee), Sorrell Booke (Harry) and Mabel Albertson (Mrs. Van Hoskins).

Because screwball comedy is as much a part of the 1930's as Franklin D. Roosevelt, Jafsie, Wrong Way Corrigan, and the Works Progress Administration, it may be that Peter Bogdanovich is doing himself a disservice by emphasizing his totally cheerful new film's association with a kind of movie that would be as out-of-date today as a 1972 Model-A Ford.

What's Up, Doc? is, admittedly, stuffed with references to the comedies of the thirties (as well as to some of the twenties and forties), by Hawks, McCarey and a number of lesser directors. It also recalls their marvelously inane concerns for mistaken identities and motives, and their great character actors who made the landscapes of these films as immediately familiar to us as those in the Bugs Bunny cartoons, which gave Bogdanovich's farce its title.

However, *What's Up, Doc?* is no more a fake antique than is his *The Last Picture Show.* It has a soul of its own, which reflects the changes, for good and evil, in American life in the last forty years.

What's Up, Doc? takes place in the classless, homogenized society that television imagines to be at hand, here and now, and the things it doesn't notice (blacks, Vietnam, you name it) give the film an intentional lack of relevance that, in a backhanded way, makes it seem completely contemporary.

That is the dark, unseen side of the picture. On the screen itself is a beautifully disordered farce set in San Francisco and involving the mix-up of four identical red plaid overnight cases. It also involves, among other things, some stolen Top Secret documents, a couple of pounds of diamonds, a lot of ordinary clothing, some igneous rocks, a convention of musicologists, an absent-minded professor (Ryan O'Neal), and a girl named Judy Maxwell (Barbra Streisand), who has total recall of every course she ever took at all five or six universities she's attended to date.

Not the least of Bogdanovich's triumphs is his success in scaling down Miss Streisand's superstar personality to fit the dimensions of farce. Although she never lets us forget the power that seems always to be held in uncertain check, she is surprisingly appealing, more truly comic than she's ever before been on film. Bogdanovich has also had the good sense to allow her to sing at least twice, once under the titles (a smashing arrangement of Porter's "You're the Top") and once in the film itself ("As Time Goes By").

O'Neal is even better in an equally tough assignment, that of the so-called Cary Grant role, which it isn't really. It's apparent that double-takes, helpless stares and slow dawnings of light do not come too easily to him, but they are the gestures of another era.

The people who give the film its particular style are the superb (and largely unknown to me) new character actors, including Austin Pendleton, as the eccentric young head of something called the Larrabee Foundation; Kenneth Mars, as a mean, nasty, Croatian musicologist named Simon (who probably only wants love and affection); Liam Dunn, as the harassed judge of the night court ("Let's get this horror show on the road") where all of the confusions end; and, most especially, Madeline Kahn.

Miss Kahn, who has a voice that sounds as if it had been filtered through a ceramic nose, just about walks off with the movie as O'Neal's impossibly square fiancée. It should also be noted that each of the actors in the film has an identifiable equivalent (Ralph Bellamy, Franklin Pangborn, Edgar Kennedy) in the old comedies from which Bogdanovich, in a very loose sense, is quoting.

What's Up, Doc? opened yesterday at the Radio City Music Hall, which seems a perfect place for it if the audience with which I saw it is any indication. There were lots of children on hand to fall apart with laughter during the chases and the hoverings on hotel ledges seventeen floors above the street, but the real mean age of most of the others was, I'd estimate, about fifty-two and three months. With their pearl earrings and crunchy, purple-hued beehives, they didn't always laugh as much as they might, but they did feel secure in the evocation of a past remembered as innocent.

—V.C., March 10, 1972

WHEN HARRY MET SALLY . . .

Directed by Rob Reiner: written by Nora Ephron: director of photography. Barry Sonnenfeld: edited by Robert Leighton: production designer. Jane Musky: produced by Mr. Reiner and Andrew Scheinman: released by Castle Rock Entertainment. Running time: 95 minutes.

With: Billy Crystal (Harry Burns). Meg Ryan (Sally Albright). Carrie Fisher (Marie). Bruno Kirby (Jess). Steven Ford (Joe). Lisa Jane Persky (Alice) and Michelle Nicastro (Amanda).

The opening credits feature Woody Allen's trademark white letters on a black background, with a jaunty version of "It Had to Be You" on the soundtrack. The score is rich with Gershwin, the camera infatuated with Manhattan, the dialogue obsessed with love, sex and death. Altogether, Rob Reiner's *When Harry Met Sally . . .* is the most blatant bow from one director to another since Mr. Allen imitated Ingmar Bergman in *Interiors.*

On and off for eleven years, Harry (Billy Crystal) and Sally (Meg Ryan) ostensibly debate whether men and women can be nonsexual friends. But that issue instantly evaporates and the question becomes: When will they realize they were made for each other? What Harry and Sally do in the meantime—the true focus of this often funny but amazingly hollow film—is saunter through the romanticized lives of intelligent, successful, neurotic New Yorkers.

Harry and Sally's version of the city offers constant jolts of recognition, as it dwells on carefully specified landmarks and echoes *Annie Hall* and *Manhattan.* At the Temple of Dendur in the Metropolitan Museum of Art, they discuss dating. In autumn, they stroll by gloriously bright trees in Central Park (Sally wears an Annie Hall hat) and describe their recurring sex dreams. They walk by the glittering Christmas display at Rockefeller Center and the decorated windows at Saks Fifth Avenue. And when Harry and Sally join their two best friends at a SoHo restaurant, half of the people at that table write for *New York* magazine.

Mr. Allen can get away with such a rarefied vision because, as he put it in *Manhattan:* "He adored New York City. He idolized it all out of proportion." Gen-

tly mocking his own romanticism, Mr. Allen gives his films depth and a believable, astringent undertone. But Mr. Reiner has a simple faith in fated love, which makes his film cute and sentimental rather than romantic and charming. *When Harry Met Sally . . .* is like the sitcom version of a Woody Allen film, full of amusing lines and scenes, all infused with an uncomfortable sense of déjà vu.

When Harry and Sally first meet, in 1977, they are University of Chicago graduates driving to New York together. Harry seems carefree, but is pessimistic enough to read the last page of a book first; in case he dies, he says, at least he'll know how it ends. And know-it-all Sally insists that Ingrid Bergman really wanted to leave Humphrey Bogart. "I don't want to spend the rest of my life in Casablanca with a guy who owns a bar," she argues, in a line that nails precisely who she is at that moment. Ten years later, after Harry's wife has left him and Sally has broken up with her boyfriend, they become best friends.

Mr. Crystal and Ms. Ryan are appealing and sometimes even unpredictable. Mr. Crystal has the wittiest lines and snappiest delivery, but he also shows Harry to be remarkably gentle, a sensitive mensch. Ms. Ryan has the more subdued role, and the two most volatile scenes. She hilariously and loudly fakes an orgasm in a crowded deli, and goes on a truly mournful crying jag when she learns that her former boyfriend is getting married.

Yet in Mr. Reiner's conception, and in Nora Ephron's screenplay, Harry and Sally are defined by their witty, epigrammatic dialogue and so never become more than types. Sally is a journalist who occasionally sits at her home computer and stares into space; Harry's job as a political consultant is even more shadowy. As their best friends, Carrie Fisher and Bruno Kirby are at least meant to be types, and both bring some flair to their roles. She is a marriage-starved woman who totes around an index file of men's names and he is a woman-shy man. Miraculously, these two are also perfect for each other.

And Mr. Reiner's belief in miracles goes far beyond their comic pairing. Throughout the film, he inserts mock-documentary scenes in which long-married couples face the camera and briefly tell their stories of love at first sight, or of love lost and later found. It is much too blunt a way of pointing to Harry and Sally's future.

Oddly, Mr. Reiner's best, most inventive films— *The Sure Thing* and *This Is Spinal Tap*—have precisely the sly edge and sardonic tone that *Harry Met Sally* needs. His most recent films, *Stand by Me* and *The Princess Bride,* are softer and more nostalgic. And like a sitcom with too much canned laughter, *When Harry Met Sally . . . ,* which opens today at the Beekman and other theaters, is a perfectly pleasant Woody Allen wannabe, full of canned romance.

—*C.J., July 12, 1989*

WHITE HEAT

Directed by Raoul Walsh; written by Ivan Goff and Ben Roberts, based on a story by Virginia Kellogg; cinematographer, Sid Hickox; music by Max Steiner; produced by Louis F. Edelman; released by Warner Brothers. Black and white. Running time: 114 minutes.

With: James Cagney (Cody Jarrett), Virginia Mayo (Verna Jarrett), Edmond O'Brien (Hank Fallon), Margaret Wycherly (Ma Jarrett), Steve Cochran ("Big Ed" Somers), John Archer (Philip Evans), Wally Cassell (Cotton Valetti), Mickey Knox (Het Kohler), Fred Clark (The Trader), G. Pat Collins (The Reader), Paul Guilfoyle (Roy Parker), Fred Coby (Happy Taylor), Ford Rainey (Zuckie Hommell) and Robert Osterloh (Tommy Ryley).

Warner Brothers weren't kidding when they put the title *White Heat* on the new James Cagney picture, which came to the Strand yesterday. They might have gone several points higher in the verbal caloric scale and still have understated the thermal intensity of this film. For the simple fact is that Mr. Cagney has made his return to a gangster role in one of the most explosive pictures that he or anyone has ever played.

If that is inviting information to the cohorts of thriller fans, whose eagerness this reviewer can readily understand, let us soberly warn that *White Heat* is also a cruelly vicious film and that its impact upon the emotions of the unstable or impressionable is incalcu-

lable. That is an observation which might fairly be borne in mind by those who would exercise caution in supporting such matter on the screen.

For there is no blinking the obvious: the Warners have pulled all the stops in making this picture the acme of the gangster-prison film. They have crammed it with criminal complications—some of them old, some of them glittering new—pictured to technical perfection in a crisp documentary style. And Mr. Cagney has played it in a brilliantly graphic way, matching the pictorial vigor of his famous *Public Enemy* job.

Indeed, as the ruthless gang-leader in this furious and frightening account of train-robbery, prison-break, gang war and gun fighting with the police, Mr. Cagney achieves the fascination of a brilliant bull-fighter at work, deftly engaged in the business of doing violence with economy and grace. His movements are supple and electric, his words are as swift and sharp as swords and his whole manner carries the conviction of confidence, courage and power.

If you think Mr. Cagney looked brutal when he punched Mae Clark in the face with a ripe grapefruit in *Public Enemy,* you should see the sweet and loving things he does to handsome Virginia Mayo, who plays his low-grade wife in this film. Or you should scan the exquisite indifference with which he "lets a little air" into the trunk compartment of an auto in which is locked a treacherous "friend."

And Mr. Cagney's performance is not the only one in this film. Director Raoul Walsh has gathered vivid acting from his whole cast. Miss Mayo, in fact, is excellent as the gangster's disloyal spouse— brassy, voluptuous and stupid to just the right degree. And Edmund O'Brien does a slick job as a Treasury Department T-man who gets next to the gang boss in prison and works into a place of favor in his mob. Steve Cochran is ugly as an outlaw, John Archer is stout as a Treasury sleuth, and Margaret Wycherly is darkly invidious as the gangster's beloved old "ma."

Perhaps her inclusion in the story is its weakest and most suspected point, for the notion of Mr. Cagney being a "mama's boy" is slightly remote. And this motivation for his cruelty, as well as for his frequent howling fits, is convenient, perhaps, for novel action but not entirely convincing as truth.

However, impeccable veracity is not the first purpose of this film. It was made to excite and amuse people. And that it most certainly does.

—B.C., September 3, 1949

WHO FRAMED ROGER RABBIT

Directed by Robert Zemeckis; written by Jeffrey Price and Peter S. Seaman, based on the book *Who Censored Roger Rabbit?* by Gary K. Wolf; director of photography, Dean Cundey; edited by Arthur Schmidt; music by Alan Silvestri; production designers, Elliot Scott and Roger Cain; special effects by Peter Biggs, Brian Morrison Lince, Tony Dunsterville and Brain Warner; produced by Robert Watts and Frank Marshall; released by Buena Vista Pictures. Running time: 103 minutes.

With: Bob Hoskins (Eddie Valiant), Christopher Lloyd (Judge Doom), Joanna Cassidy (Dolores), Charles Fleischer (Voice of Roger Rabbit), Stubby Kaye (Marvin Acme), Kathleen Turner (Voice of Jessica Rabbit) and Alan Tilvern (R. K. Maroon).

In a parallel universe near a Hollywood movie studio, the Toons make the rules. Toons are movie actors who also happen to be cartoon characters, second-class citizens by Hollywood standards but a force to be reckoned with just the same. They have their own laws of physics, their own laws of gravity, and their own distinctive sense of humor. So a Toon who's under the influence is apt to change color and spiral upward until he hits the ceiling. A Toon sent flying through a window leaves an exact silhouette. Toon shoes, if unpacked by accident, start to dance.

At the movie studio, where Toon stars like Dumbo work "for peanuts," in the words of one mogul who employs them, the collision between Toon attitudes and those of the so-called real world leads to countless surprises. It also makes *Who Framed Roger Rabbit* a film whose best moments are so novel, so deliriously funny, and so crazily unexpected that they truly must be seen to be believed.

Although this isn't the first time that cartoon characters have shared the screen with live actors, it's the first time they've done it on their own terms. So the Toons have one way of viewing the world, the humans another—and the director Robert Zemeckis,

as the mastermind presiding over this wizardry, has an all-important overview. Mr. Zemeckis has directed a number of comedies about ordinary individuals who take that thrilling step into another dimension, from *Back to the Future* to *Romancing the Stone* and *I Wanna Hold Your Hand*. Though it's long been clear that he's as much innovator as entertainer, Mr. Zemeckis has never before concocted anything quite as dizzying as this.

Who Framed Roger Rabbit, which opens today at the Ziegfeld and other theaters, should be a delight for children of all ages except, perhaps, the ages of real children. It's hard to know what very young viewers will make of the Toons' refusal to maintain their lovable, parent-pleasing demeanor when the movie company's cameras cease to roll. The film's brilliant opening episode finds Roger Rabbit, a very Bugs-like invention, starring with a gurgling infant named Baby Herman in an animated sequence that's an inspired, hellish parody of the kind of cartoon that finds its humor in wanton destruction. Chasing the baby through a kitchen that expands unnervingly as the action becomes more frantic, Roger risks electrocution, flying knives and the many other insane hazards built into his line of work.

Then comes the cry of "Cut!" and the real film begins, with a live director berating Roger for seeing little birds when he should have seen little stars. Baby Herman speaks up in his real voice, a deep, masculine growl. And the camera follows Roger from the brightly colored cartoon set into the real world of 1947 Hollywood, making this transition with the supreme ease that is this film's greatest achievement. However wildly inventive the Toon-human interchanges become, they are executed with the utmost sangfroid.

Roger has a problem, and his boss at the studio has a solution: Eddie Valiant (Bob Hoskins), a private detective, will be engaged to find out whether Roger's wife, Jessica, has been misbehaving. It is one small measure of the film's cleverness that Jessica, an animated bombshell who is a Rabbit only by marriage, looks and sounds so sultry (an uncredited Kathleen Turner supplies her speaking voice) that Roger and Eddie find her equally alluring. In any case, Eddie's search for clues about Jessica sends him stumbling onto something even bigger: a *Chinatown* scheme to corrupt an Eden of a Los Angeles, which according to the screenplay once had the greatest public transportation system in the world before a villain named Judge Doom (Christopher Lloyd) envisioned "wonderful, wonderful billboards reaching as far as the eye can see" beside the first freeway.

The film's only problem, and it's a minor one, is that the gumshoe plot of the screenplay by Jeffrey Price and Peter S. Seaman is relatively ordinary. Nothing else about the film can be described that way: not the startling visual tricks, not the Toon-related wit, and not the remarkable Mr. Hoskins, who spends the entire film essentially talking to himself and still manages to give a performance that is foolproof. His Eddie is a gruff, lovable lug who nurses a terrible secret: a Toon killed his brother. "Just like a Toon to drop a safe on a guy's head," says another character sympathetically.

Talking to Toons, visiting the Toon universe (where everything sings) and even playing long scenes with the animated Roger handcuffed to his wrist, Mr. Hoskins makes his own very matter-of-factness funny. Another source of humor is his constant irritation with the Toons' odd habits, as when he shouts angrily at Roger, "Do you mean to tell me you could've taken your hand out of that cuff at any time?" "No, not any time," Roger explains patiently, "Only when it was funny."

Who Framed Roger Rabbit is a film with many, many stars. Some are animated, making cameo appearances the way Betty Boop does, waiting tables at a nightspot where a human clientele watches Toons like Daffy and Donald Duck perform their stage show. ("Work's been kinda slow since cartoons went to color, but I still got it, Eddie," she confides.) Some are live actors, like Mr. Lloyd and Joanna Cassidy, who bring amusing conviction to the most improbable of roles. And many are offscreen: the hundreds of painters, animators, special effects technicians, and other ingenious contributors whose work has been made to look so blissfully effortless. That's the most magical illusion of all.

—*J.M., June 22, 1988*

WHO'S AFRAID OF VIRGINIA WOOLF?

Directed by Mike Nichols; written by Ernest Lehman, based on the play by Edward Albee; cinematographer, Haskell Wexler; edited by Sam O'Steen; music by Alex North; production designer, Richard Sylbert; produced by Mr. Lehman; released by Warner Brothers. Black and white. Running time: 129 minutes.

With: Elizabeth Taylor (Martha), Richard Burton (George), George Segal (Nick) and Sandy Dennis (Honey).

Edward Albee's *Who's Afraid of Virginia Woolf?*, the best American play of the last decade and a violently candid one, has been brought to the screen without pussy-footing. (It is now at the Criterion and Loew's Tower East.) This in itself makes it a notable event in our film history. About the film as such, there is more to be said.

First things first. The most pressing question—since we already know a great deal about the play and the two stars—is the direction. Mike Nichols, after a brilliant and too-brief career as a satirist, proved to be a brilliant theatrical director of comedy. This is his debut as a film director, and it is a successful Houdini feat.

Houdini, you remember, was the magician who was chained hand and foot, bound in a sack, dumped in a river and then appeared some minutes later on the surface. You do not expect Olympic swimming form in a Houdini: the triumph is just to come out alive.

Which Mr. Nichols has done. He was given two world-shaking stars, the play of the decade, and the auspices of a large looming studio. What more inhibiting conditions could be imagined for a first film, if the director is a man of talent? But Mr. Nichols has at least survived. The form is not Olympic, but he lives.

Any transference of a good play to film is a battle. (Which is why the best film directors rarely deal with good plays.) The better the play, the harder it struggles against leaving its natural habitat, and Mr. Albee's extraordinary comedy-drama has put up a stiff fight.

Ernest Lehman, the screen adapter, has broken the play out of its one living-room setting into various rooms in the house and onto the lawn, which the play accepts well enough. He has also placed one scene in a roadhouse, which is a patently forced move for visual variety. These changes and some minor cuts, including a little inconsequential blue-penciling, are about the sum of his efforts. The real job of "filmizing" was left to the director.

With no possible chance to cut loose cinematically (as, for example, Richard Lester did in his film of the stage comedy *The Knack*), Mr. Nichols has made the most of two elements that were left to him—intimacy and acting.

He has gone to school to several film masters (Kurosawa among them, I would guess) in the skills of keeping the camera close, indecently prying; giving us a sense of his characters' very breath, bad breath, held breath; tracking a face—in the rhythm of the scene—as the actor moves, to take us to other faces; punctuating with sudden withdrawals to give us a brief, almost dispassionate respite; then plunging us in close again to one or two faces, for lots of pores and bile.

There is not much that is original in Mr. Nichols's camerawork, no sense of the personality that we got in his stage direction. In fact, the direction is weakest when he gets a bit arty: electric signs flashing behind heads or tilted shots from below to show passion and abandon (both of them hallmarks of the college cinema virtuoso). But he has minimized the "stage" feeling, and he has given the film an insistent presence, good phrasing and a nervous drive. It sags toward the end, but this is because the third act of the play sags.

As for the acting, Mr. Nichols had Richard Burton as George. To refresh us all, George is a fortyish history professor, married to Martha, the daughter of the president of a New England college. They return home from a party at one thirty a.m., slightly sozzled, drenched in their twenty-year-old marital love-hate ambivalence. A young faculty couple come over for drinks, and the party winds viciously on until dawn. In the course of it, Martha sleeps with the young man as an act of vengeance on George. The play ends with George's retribution—the destruction of their myth about a son they never had.

Mr. Burton was part of the star package with which this film began, but—a big but—Mr. Burton is also an actor. He has become a kind of specialist in sensitive self-disgust, as witness the latter scenes of *Cleopatra* and all of *The Spy Who Came In from the Cold,* and he does it well. He is not in his person the George we might imagine, but he is utterly convincing as a man with a great lake of nausea in him, on which he sails with regret and compulsive amusement.

On past evidence, Mr. Nichols had relatively little

work to do with Mr. Burton. On past evidence, he had a good deal to do with Elizabeth Taylor, playing Martha. She has shown previously, in some roles, that she could respond to the right director and could at least flagellate herself into an emotional state (as in *Suddenly, Last Summer*). Here, with a director who knows how to get an actor's confidence and knows what to do with it after he gets it, she does the best work of her career, sustained and urgent.

Of course, she has an initial advantage. Her acceptance of gray hair and her use of profanity make her seem to be acting even (figuratively) before she begins. ("Gee, she let them show her looking old! Wow, she just said 'Son of a bitch'! A star!") It is not the first time an American star has gotten mileage out of that sort of daring. Miss Taylor does not have qualities that, for instance, Uta Hagen had in the Broadway version, no suggestion of endlessly coiled involutions. Her venom is nearer the surface. But, under Mr. Nichols's hand, she gets vocal variety, never relapses out of the role, and she charges it with the utmost of her powers—which is an achievement for any actress, great or little.

As the younger man, George Segal gives his usual good terrier performance, lithe and snapping, with nice bafflement at the complexities of what he thought was simply a bad marriage. As his bland wife, Sandy Dennis is credibly bland.

Mr. Albee's play looks both better and a little worse under the camera's magnification. A chief virtue for me is that it is not an onion-skin play—it does not merely strip off layers, beginning at the surface with trifles and digging deeper as it proceeds. Of course, we learn more about the characters as we go, and almost all of it is fascinating, but, like its giant forebear, Strindberg's *Dance of Death,* the play begins in hell, and all the revelations and reactions take place within that landscape.

What does not wear well in the generally superb dialogue is the heavy lacing of vaudeville cross-talk, particularly facile non sequiturs. (Also, in Mr. Lehman's version, so much shouting and slamming takes place on the front lawn at four in the morning that we keep wondering why a neighbor doesn't wake up and complain.)

More serious is the heightened impression that the myth of the son is irrelevant to the play. It seems a device that the author tacked on to conclude matters as the slash and counterslash grew tired; a device that he then went back and planted earlier. Else why would Martha have told the other woman the secret of the son so glibly—not when she was angry or drunk—if she knew she was breaching an old and sacred compact with her husband? It obtrudes as an arbitrary action to justify the ending.

The really relevant unseen character is not the son: it is Martha's father, the president of the college. It is he whom she idolizes and measures her husband against, it is his presence George has to contend with in and out of bed. It is Daddy's power, symbolic in Martha, that keeps the visiting couple from leaving, despite circumstances that would soon have driven them out of any other house.

Awareness—of this truth about Daddy, of multiple other truths about themselves and their world—is the theme of this play; not the necessity of narcotic illusion about the son, but naked, peeled awareness. Under the vituperation and violence, under Martha's aggressive and self-punishing infidelities, this is the drama of a marriage flooded with more consciousness than the human psyche is at present able to bear.

Their world is too much with them, their selves are much too clear. It is the price to be paid for living in a cosmos of increasing clarity—which includes a clearer view of inevitable futilities. And, fundamentally, it is this desperation—articulated in a childless, broken-hearted, demonically loving marriage—that Mr. Albee has crystallized in his flawed but fine play.

And in its forthright dealing with the play, this becomes one of the most scathingly honest American films ever made. Its advertisements say, "No one under 18 will be admitted unless accompanied by his parent." This may safeguard the children; the parents must take their chances.

—S.K., June 30, 1966

THE WILD BUNCH

Directed by Sam Peckinpah; written by Walon Green and Mr. Peckinpah, based on story by Mr. Green and Roy N. Sickner; cinematographer, Lucien Ballard; edited by Lou Lombardo; music by Jerry Fielding; art designer, Edward Carrere; produced by Phil Feldman; released by Warner Brothers. Running time: 145 minutes.

With: William Holden (Pike), Ernest Borgnine (Dutch), Robert Ryan (Thornton), Edmond O'Brien (Sykes), Warren Oates (Lyle Gorch), Jaime Sanchez (Angel) and Ben Johnson (Tector Gorch).

Sam Peckinpah's *The Wild Bunch* is about the decline and fall of one outlaw gang at what must be the bleeding end of the frontier era, 1913, when Pancho Villa was tormenting a corrupt Mexican Government while the United States watched cautiously from across the border.

The movie, which opened yesterday at the Trans-Lux East and West Theaters, is very beautiful and the first truly interesting American-made Western in years. It's also so full of violence—of an intensity that can hardly be supported by the story—that it's going to prompt a lot of people who do not know the real effect of movie violence (as I do not) to write automatic condemnations of it.

The Wild Bunch begins on a hot, lazy afternoon as six United States soldiers ride into a small Texas border town with all the aloofness of an army of benign occupation. Under a makeshift awning, the good bourgeoisie of San Rafael is holding a temperance meeting. Gentle spinsters, sweating discreetly, vow to abstain from all spirits.

The "soldiers" pass on to the railroad office, which they quietly proceed to rob of its cash receipts. Down the street, a group of children giggle as they watch a scorpion being eaten alive by a colony of red ants. A moment later, the town literally explodes in the ambush that has been set for the outlaws.

Borrowing a device from *Bonnie and Clyde,* Peckinpah suddenly reduces the camera speed to slow motion, which at first heightens the horror of the mindless slaughter, and then—and this is what really carries horror—makes it beautiful, almost abstract, and finally into terrible parody.

The audience, which earlier was appalled at the cynical detachment with which the camera watched the death fight of the scorpion, is now in the position of the casually cruel children. The face of a temperance parade marcher erupts in a fountain of red. Bodies, struck by bullets, make graceful arcs through the air before falling onto the dusty street, where they seem to bounce, as if on a trampoline.

This sort of choreographed brutality is repeated to excess, but in excess, there is point to a film in which realism would be unbearable. *The Wild Bunch* takes the basic elements of the Western movie myth, which once defined a simple, morally comprehensible world, and by bending them turns them into symbols of futility and aimless corruption.

The screenplay, by Peckinpah and Walon Green, follows the members of the *Wild Bunch* from their disastrous, profitless experience at San Rafael to Mexico, where they become involved with a smilingly sadistic Mexican general fighting Villa. Although the movie's conventional and poetic action sequences are extraordinarily good and its landscapes beautifully photographed (lots of dark foregrounds and brilliant backgrounds) by Lucien Ballard, who did *Nevada Smith,* it is most interesting in its almost jolly account of chaos, corruption and defeat. All personal relationships in the movie seem somehow perverted in odd mixtures of noble sentimentality, greed and lust.

Never satisfactorily resolved is the conflict between William Holden, as the aging leader of the Wild Bunch, and Robert Ryan, as his former friend who, with disdain, leads the bounty hunters in pursuit of the gang. An awkward flashback shows the two men, looking like characters out of a silent movie, caught in an ambush in a bordello from which only Holden escapes.

The ideals of masculine comradeship are exaggerated and transformed into neuroses. The fraternal bonds of two brothers, members of the Wild Bunch, are so excessive they prefer having their whores in tandem. A feeling of genuine compassion prompts the climactic massacre that some members of the film trade are calling, not without reason, "the blood ballet."

Peckinpah also has a way of employing Hollywood life to dramatize his legend. After years of giving bored performances in boring movies, Holden comes back gallantly in *The Wild Bunch.* He looks older and tired, but he has style, both as a man and as a movie character who persists in doing what he's always done, not because he really wants the money but because there's simply nothing else to do.

Ryan, Ernest Borgnine, and Edmond O'Brien add a similar kind of resonance to the film. O'Brien is a special shock, looking like an evil Gabby Hayes, a foul-mouthed, cackling old man who is the only member of the Wild Bunch to survive.

In two earlier Westerns, *Ride the High Country* (1962) and *Major Dundee* (1965), Peckinpah seemed to be creating comparatively gentle variations on the genre about the man who walks alone—a character about as rare in a Western as a panhandler on the Bowery.

In *The Wild Bunch,* which is about men who walk together, but in desperation, he turns the genre inside out. It's a fascinating movie and, I think I should add, when I came out of it, I didn't feel like shooting, knifing or otherwise maiming any of Broadway's often hostile pedestrians.

—*V.C., June 26, 1969*

THE WILD CHILD

Directed by François Truffaut; written (in French, with English subtitles) by Mr. Truffaut and Jean Gruault, based on the book *Mémoires et rapports sur le sauvage de l'Aveyron* by Jean-Marc Gaspard; cinematographer, Nestor Almendros; edited by Agnes Guillemot; music by Antonio Vivaldi; art designer, Jean Mandaroux; produced by Marcel Berbert; released by United Artists. Black and white. Running time: 90 minutes.

With: Jean-Pierre Cargol (Victor, the Boy), François Truffaut (Dr. Jean Itard), Jean Dasté (Professor Philippe Pinel), Françoise Seigner (Madame Guerin), Paul Ville (Remy) and Claude Miler (Monsieur Lemeri).

As if to satisfy the increasing curiosity about Natural Man, that is, man uncontaminated by civilization, there began to be found throughout Europe in the seventeenth and eighteenth centuries all sorts of "wild children," boys and girls who had apparently been raised in messy but graceful states by wolves and bears, and by just about everything except kangaroos, which aren't often found in Europe in any state.

Between 1544 and 1731, no fewer than ten such wild children were reported. However, it wasn't until 1799, the year seven by *le calendrier républicain* (itself the product of a revolution that attempted to make reason a religion), that anyone tried to systematically study and educate one of these creatures whom Carolus Linnaeus, the Swedish scientist, had earlier classified as a distinct human species (*Homo ferus*).

In that year, Jean-Marc-Gaspard Itard, a doctor at

the National Institute for the Deaf and Dumb in Paris, was given custody of a boy, between ten and twelve years old, who had been found living wild in the forests of Aveyron in southern France. With immense skill, patience and love, and with more than a little pride, the doctor set out to prove what he took to be the beliefs of Locke and Condillac, that the total content of the human mind is supplied by experience. The doctor assumed that Victor, as his wild child came to be called, had a mind capable of using experience.

Itard failed. At least, he never succeeded in transforming Victor into a completely normal, rational being, but he succeeded triumphantly in establishing procedures and techniques of teaching that survive today in the Montessori method. It is the doctor's account of his work (*Mémoires et rapports sur le sauvage de l'Aveyron*) that François Truffaut has used as the source material for his ninth feature, in many ways his most mature, most radical, most lovely film to date.

The Wild Child (*L'Enfant Sauvage*), which opened the Eighth New York Film Festival at Philharmonic Hall last night and begins its regular commercial run at the Festival Theater today looks almost as if it had been designed to answer those critics who have been finding all of Truffaut's post–*Jules and Jim* films either too romantic or too charming—both quite superficial qualities (but never the true substance of Truffaut) that have been rigorously suppressed in *The Wild Child.*

The new film bears some vague resemblances to the director's first film, *The 400 Blows,* in that it was photographed in black and white (which seems almost eccentric today) and is about an adolescent boy. However, where the first film had to do with the making of a boy into a man, *The Wild Child* is about nothing less than the evolution of beast into human, a really epic theme that Truffaut obstinately refuses to emphasize in any showy or sentimental way.

Like all of Truffaut's films, however, *The Wild Child* is concerned with the promise and the pain of human experience, here reduced, or refined, to the essentials that begin with hunger and fear, which humans share with animals, and go on to include affection, love and what the doctor confidently calls moral intelligence.

The film is almost painfully austere, a series of two character confrontations between Victor, who is played by a black-eyed gypsy boy, Jean-Pierre Cargol,

and Itard, who is played by Truffaut, who thus becomes the metteur en scène within his own mise en scène.

It is interesting that Truffaut dedicates the movie to Jean-Pierre Léaud, the young actor who has been the Truffaut surrogate in the director's films à clef, beginning with *The 400 Blows* and most recently in the just-completed *Domicile Conjugal.* That is, however, about the only interior cinema reference in the entire film.

The Wild Child is very pure, ascetic Truffaut. Also, it almost seems shy. It focuses tightly on the minute details of Victor's education as if to avoid announcing the fact that it's about Larger Matters. Truffaut treats us, the audience, much in the manner that Itard treats Victor, never quite letting us become sentimental about Victor's triumphs—his first tears, the day he invents a chalk holder, or the day Itard punishes Victor unjustly to force the child into making a moral distinction.

Victor never learns to say more than one word ("*lait*"), but he eventually does respond to the education and love to the extent that once, having run away, he returns of his own accord.

There are, in the film, some unanswered questions that bother both the doctor and us. Is Victor subnormal, and was he born that way or is his seeming subnormality the result of his long isolation? Is his ultimate surrender to the doctor really a triumph for humanity, or a kind of wicked victory that has turned the wild child, who could cope in the forests, into a semicivilized moron?

The movie that looks so simple on its surface is dense with such questions, with feelings expressed obliquely and with moments of tenderness that are as surprising in the film as they are in Itard's formal reports. The movie has been consciously distanced from the present by Truffaut's fondness for such silent-screen techniques as lap dissolves and the irising in and out of scenes, and he uses a flat, rapid voice-over narration (here spoken in English) that makes it all seem like a sort of medical fairy tale. The ultimate effect of this, however, is not necessarily one of distance, but one of the kind of closeness that comes when you must reach into a film and discover it for yourself.

The Wild Child is not the sort of movie in which individual performances can be easily separated from the rest of the film, but young Cargol, who early in the film looks and sounds like a Mediterranean Patty Duke, responds with marvelous, absolute faith to his costar and director, Truffaut, who himself performs with humane, just slightly self-conscious cool.

Everyone—Truffaut, us, Itard—seems to have had their lives enriched by the child. The real-life Victor remained with Itard five years, but not much is reported about him after that except that he died, around the age of forty, without ever having become (says one account) "a normal human being."

—*V.C., September 11, 1970*

WILD REEDS

Directed by Andre Techine; written (in French, with English subtitles) by Mr. Techine, Gilles Taurand and Olivier Massart; director of photography, Jeanne Lapoirie and Germain Desmoulins; edited by Martine Giordano; sound by Jean-Paul Mugel; produced by Georges Benayoun and Alain Sarde; released by Strand. Running time: 110 minutes.

With: Elodie Bouchez (Maite), Gael Morel (Francois), Stephane Rideau (Serge), Frederic Gorny (Henri), Michele Moretti (Mme. Alvarez) and Jacques Nolot (Mr. Morelli).

Wild Reeds is Andre Techine's delicate, lovingly photographed, strongly acted coming-of-age story in which a smart, sensitive boy named Francois falls in love with his classmate, a peasant boy named Serge. Set in the French countryside in 1962, at the end of the Algerian war, the film is more successful at making Francois an evocative character than it is in its lukewarm attempt to make politics an integral part of the story.

In a discreet scene at school one night, Francois and Serge sleep together. It is clear that for Serge, this is an adolescent experiment, done for lack of any females around. But Francois falls painfully in love, and has no idea what to do about it.

In the film's most vivid scene, Francois decides to go to the owner of the local shoe store, a man he has heard is a homosexual, too. With touching naivete, he decides to ask the man for advice. "It's not about my shoes," he tells the bewildered stranger. "It's about my destiny."

Yet too much of *Wild Reeds* seems stilted. Francois's best friend and confidante is a girl named Maite, who is unbelievably wise beyond her years and well ahead of her time. "I slept with a boy," Francois tells her, and she calmly replies, "I don't care what you do with others."

Henri, an Algerian schoolmate of Francois and Serge, is meant to carry the weight of the political theme, his sense of Algerian oppression being the counterpart to Francois's unacceptable status as a homosexual. Yet politics seems a veneer laid over the film. Mr. Techine gives short shrift to a more intriguing aspect of that theme. Maite's mother refuses to help a young man avoid the war, then falls apart because she feels responsible for his fate.

Wild Reeds will be shown as part of the New York Film Festival tonight at 9 and tomorrow at noon. Like Mr. Techine's *Scene of the Crime*, which was shown at the festival in 1986, it is too tepid to generate much excitement.

It will be preceded by Lara Shapiro's six-minute *Crawl*, a brightly colored tale in which a young woman goes to a swimming pool, makes eye contact with a handsome man, and becomes disillusioned. Ms. Shapiro creates an ominous sense of foreboding and playfully demonstrates a theme her film shares with Mr. Techines: that the ideal object of your affection is not always the person in your direct line of vision.

—*C.J., October 7, 1994*

WILD STRAWBERRIES

Written (in Swedish, with English subtitles) and directed by Ingmar Bergman; cinematographers, Gunnar Fischer and Bjorn Thermenius; edited by Oscar Rosander; music by Erik Nordgren; art designer, Gittan Gustafsson; produced by Allan Ekelund; released by Janus Films. Black and white. Running time: 90 minutes.

With: Victor Sjostrom (Professor Isak Borg), Bibi Andersson (Sara), Ingrid Thulin (Marianne), Gunnar Björnstrand (Evald), Jullan Kindahl (Agda), Folke Sundquist (Anders) and Bjorn Bjelvenstam (Viktor).

If any of you thought you had trouble understanding what Ingmar Bergman was trying to convey in his beautifully poetic and allegorical Swedish film, *The Seventh Seal,* wait until you see his *Wild Strawberries* (*Smultron-Stallet*), which came to the Beekman yesterday. This one is so thoroughly mystifying that we wonder whether Mr. Bergman himself knew what he was trying to say.

As nearly as we can make out—and, frankly, we found *The Seventh Seal* a tough but comparatively lucid and extraordinarily stimulating film—the purpose of Mr. Bergman in this virtually surrealist exercise is to get at a comprehension of the feelings and the psychology of an aging man.

His hero is a seventy-eight-year-old doctor—whether a physician or a scientist is not made clear—who is going from his place of retirement to the university at Lund to be honored on an anniversary. Before he starts out, he has a shocking and plainly depressing dream in which he sees his own mournerless funeral and his own corpse trying to pull him into the grave. This rather ill prepares him for an admission made a few hours later by his daughter-in-law, who accompanies him on the journey, that she and her husband consider him a cold and egotistical old man.

Therefore, the journey becomes a series of actual and dream experiences of encounters with mortal beings and with ghosts and fantasies, in which the old man runs a recapitulation of many events and phases of his life, and apparently comes to the conclusion that he has been admired but not loved. The consensus of those who have known him, including his still-living mother and his dead and faithless wife, seems to be that he has been standoffish and emotionally cold.

This is as close as we can make it in the way of a general résumé, but this doesn't give an explanation of several details that we still don't dig. And it also doesn't carry much conviction in the light of the sweet and charming character of the old man portrayed by Victor Seastrom (Sjostrom), one of the great actors and directors of Swedish films.

Mr. Seastrom, whom we older moviegoers remember from the silent films as the visiting director of such fine American pictures as Lon Chaney's *He Who Gets Slapped* and Lillian Gish's *The Scarlet Letter* and *The Wind,* is wonderfully warm and expressive as the old gentleman who finds the wild strawberry patch where his first love fatefully forsook him and then goes off from there. He is so real and sensitive and poignant, so

winning of sympathy in every way, that Mr. Bergman's apparent explanation doesn't make sense.

This is not to say, however, that the film doesn't have its brilliant scenes and its beautifully touching moments, its tatters of sheer nostalgia. These, with Mr. Seastrom, are most rewarding. So are the straight performances of Ingrid Thulin as the daughter-in-law and Bibi Andersson as a modern girl who is a duplicate of an old love. Mr. Bergman, being a poet with the camera, gets some grand, open, sensitive images, but he has not conveyed full clarity in this film. And the English subtitles are not much help.

—B.C., June 23, 1959

WILSON

Directed by Henry King; written by Lamar Trotti; cinematographer. Leon Shamroy; edited by Barbara McLean; music by Alfred Newman; art designers. Wiard Ihnen and James Basevi; produced by Darryl F. Zanuck; released by Twentieth Century Fox. Black and white. Running time: 154 minutes.

With: Alexander Knox (Woodrow Wilson). Geraldine Fitzgerald (Edith Galt Wilson) Cedric Hardwicke (Henry Cabot Lodge). Charles Coburn (Professor Holmes). Thomas Mitchell (Joseph Tumulty). Ruth Nelson (Ellen Axson Wilson). Vincent Price (William G. McAdoo) and William Eythe (George Felton).

The life of a man and his significance in history cannot be described with clear and judicious definition in broadly pictorial terms—especially when the subject is one of great depth and scope. Yet within the capacious framework of a predominant spectacle-film, producer Darryl F. Zanuck and Twentieth Century Fox have managed a commanding screen biography of Woodrow *Wilson,* the twenty-eighth president of the United States. In their film, simply titled *Wilson,* which came to the Roxy last night, they have imaged the salient nature of the leader to a remarkable degree, and they have pictured the man against his period with uncommon dignity and good taste.

One must not expect in this picture a keen analysis of the World War president, of his rare and complex disposition, nor of the historic battles that he fought. Historians themselves are still disputing the ambiguities of the things that Wilson did, and the memories of personal encounters with him are borne by living men. The era of Woodrow Wilson merges closely with the one in which we live. So a searching biography of him could hardly be presumed on the screen. But for sheer admiration of the champion of a higher social ideal; for a stirring, eye-filling panorama of the hot political world in which he lived; and for a warm appreciation of his humanity, it would be hard to beat this glowing film.

For Mr. Zanuck and all who worked with him have packed onto the screen a rich and colorful record of high points in Wilson's career, from his presidency at Princeton to the tragic close of his public life. They have pictured with humor and understanding his unique entrance upon the political scene, his bold elevation to the White House and his rigorous efforts to keep this country out of the first World War. They have manifested in merest outline, but with stirring pictorial display, his final acceptance of the German challenge, his battle for the peace—and for the League—and his defeat.

Against this broad and dominant canvas they have cameoed some intimate scenes of Wilson in his role as husband and father—and especially as the suitor of his second wife. They have indicated his dependence upon the judgment and support of the wife he lost, and with delicate emphasis upon his loneliness they have explained his marriage to Edith Bolling Galt. This careful and tasteful representation of Wilson's private life is constantly set in contrast to the strife of his public position, and draws the human sympathy upon which the characterization depends.

There are obvious omissions in the story, some forgivable and some less so. A little less time spent on spectacle in this two-hour-and-thirty-four-minute film might have allowed for a clearer definition of Wilson's historic battle for the League. As it now stands, the League is but a symbol of international accord, and the opposition to it—with Senator Lodge as the villain—is just an inchoate obstructive force. Wilson's refusal to ask assistance from his Senatorial enemies in framing the peace is covered in his righteous pronouncement that "too many treaties have been written by practical men." And his epic encounters with Clemenceau at Paris are disappointingly played down. More searching dramatization of this phase might be of profit to the public just now.

But the general construction of the picture is expert in every way, and its production in Technicolor enhances its picturesque displays. The enactment of the Baltimore convention which nominated Wilson in 1912 is a rare gem of screen picturization, full of American flavor and gusto. And the immediately contrasting announcement to Wilson of his election at his Princeton home brings a striking suggestion of the dignity and integrity of the man. Lamar Trotti's script is beautifully written; the musical score is compounded of pulsing tunes; and the design of the whole production amply indicates taste and expense.

Much of the film's exceptional quality is due to the performance of Alexander Knox in the title role. Mr. Knox, under Henry King's direction, draws a character that is full of inner strength—honest, forceful and intelligent, yet marked by a fine reserve. And he also makes a startling facsimile of Wilson, lacking the length of the latter's head. It is good to hear speeches spoken—especially Wilson's—with a clear and resonant voice. The casting of Mr. Knox, a comparative unknown, in this role was truly inspired.

Sir Cedric Hardwicke concentrates a distillation of bitterness and icy contempt in his brief but telling performance of Senator Lodge, and Geraldine Fitzgerald makes a remarkably understanding woman of the second Mrs. Wilson. A large cast of prominent actors do exceptionally well in minor roles, and generally are made up superbly to imitate their real-life counterparts.

Coming at this time, the picture *Wilson* should inspire millions of people throughout this land to renewed appreciation of its subject's ideals and especially of his trials, which may be ours.

—B.C., August 2, 1944

WINGS OF DESIRE

Directed by Wim Wenders: written (in German and French. with English subtitles) by Mr. Wenders and Peter Handke: director of photography. Henri Alekan: edited by Peter Przygodda: music by Jürgen Knieper: production designer. Heidi Ludi: produced by Mr. Wenders and Anatole Dauman: released by Orion Classics. Running time: 130 minutes.

With: Bruno Ganz (Damiel), Solveig Dommartin (Marion), Otto Sander (Cassiel), Curt Bois (Homer) and Peter Falk (Himself).

Men have envisioned angels in many forms, but who besides Wim Wenders has seen them as sad, sympathetic, long-haired men in overcoats, gliding through a beautiful black-and-white Berlin on the lookout for human suffering? Like so many existential Clark Kents, the angels of *Wings of Desire* are mild-mannered, all-seeing individuals poised to assist those in need.

Some earthly beings can sense their presence, the children most keenly, but none really see or hear them as they perform their duties. A potential suicide with an angel draped compassionately against his shoulder may very well suppose he is alone. If the angels appear downcast, this partly results from a certain ineffectualness that is built into the job, since they cannot change fate but can only witness what it does to individual lives. It is this helplessness, as well as a longing for corporeal sensation, that ultimately gives an angel named Damiel (Bruno Ganz) the celestial equivalent of seven-year itch.

Wings of Desire, which opens today at the Cinema Studio 1, has a loveliness of conception that, for a time, keeps it as feathery as an angel's wing. The early parts of the film trace the ordinary details of Damiel's working day, and the responsibilities he shares with a sort of teammate named Cassiel (Otto Sander). These angels may ride the subway, and listen in on each commuter's thought process, or they may find themselves in traffic, listening to a woman talk to the dog in her car. They may comfort a pregnant woman on her way to the hospital, or cradle the head of a wounded man.

They may also visit the library, which serves as a sort of headquarters, for the sheer pleasure of tuning in the cacophony of ideas to be found there. The most alluring thing about *Wings of Desire* is its vision of these angels as silent partners in almost all forms of human experience, be they physical or cerebral, violent or serene. In outlining the range of these angels' participatory role in the human sphere, Mr. Wenders presents the Berlin they inhabit as a stark, forbidding urban setting haunted by its own past, and brought warmly to life by the existence of this extra dimension. On those few occasions when Damiel's thoughts nearly turn him human, the black-and-white cinematography by the venerable Henri Alekan (who has worked with Charlie Chaplin, Abel Gance and Jean Cocteau) bursts into color.

The underlying conception of *Wings of Desire* is enchanting, but Mr. Wenders allows it to become terribly overripe. In a screenplay written by the director with Peter Handke, his earlier collaborator (on *The Goalie's Anxiety at the Penalty Kick*), the angels deliver an incessant flow of voice-over meditations, and so do the film's other characters—even Peter Falk, who plays himself in the uncharacteristically windy process of contemplating his own acting career.

Mr. Falk, supposedly in Berlin to make a World War II film, worries about whether he understands his role deeply enough, makes sketches, and broods in the screenplay's typically overblown fashion. While drawing an extra on the film set, he exclaims, "What a dramatic nostril!" Looking at an actor in costume, he muses, "Yellow star means death. Why did they pick yellow? Sunflowers. Van Gogh killed himself. This drawing stinks . . ." Throughout the screenplay, there's a lot more where that came from.

The worst offender is a trapeze artist named Marion (Solveig Dommartin), the woman who at long last tempts Damiel to hang up his wings. Though her ultimate effect is to trivialize the film, Marion speaks loftily ("Where did time begin, and where does space begin?") and never seems to stop, except on those occasions when the camera lingers endlessly on her high-wire acrobatics. Marion embodies the sentimental, ponderously playful streak that is relatively recent in Mr. Wenders's films, and that does a lot to diminish the beauty of this one. When the characters quite literally wear wings, and when the director is willing to end a scene with a glimpse of someone juggling, the film's fundamental airiness turns very heavy indeed.

Startlingly original at first, *Wings of Desire* is in the end damagingly overloaded. The excesses of language, the ceaseless camera movement, the unyielding whimsy have the ultimate effect of wearing the audience down. The flashes of real delight that spring out of Mr. Wenders's visionary methods grow fewer and fewer as the film proceeds, and they are long gone by the time it nominally comes to life. Mr. Ganz, who conveys great yearning before reaching his decision "to take the plunge" and a charming eagerness thereafter, is left in a kind of limbo, and the film is, too. This comes as a relief of sorts, but it's also far less effective than must have been intended.

Wings of Desire is Mr. Wenders's most ambitious effort yet, and certainly radiates immense promise. But there's a relentlessness to the direction, which won the best-director award at Cannes last year, that keeps it earthbound.

—J.M., April 29, 1988

WISE BLOOD

Directed by John Huston; written by Benedict Fitzgerald, based on the novel by Flannery O'Connor; cinematographer, Gerry Fisher; edited by Roberto Silvi; music by Alex North; art designer, Sally Fitzgerald; produced by Michael Fitzgerald and Kathy Fitzgerald; released by Anthea Films/New Line Cinema. Running time: 108 minutes.

With: Brad Dourif (Hazel Motes), Ned Beatty (Hoover Shoates), Harry Dean Stanton (Asa Hawks), Daniel Shor (Enoch Emery), Amy Wright (Sabbath Lilly), Mary Nell Santacroce (Landlady) and John Huston (Grandfather).

Wise Blood, based on Flannery O'Connor's 1952 novel about an inside-out religious fanatic of the rural South, is one of John Huston's most original, most stunning movies. It is so eccentric, so funny, so surprising and so haunting that it is difficult to believe it is not the first film of some enfant terrible instead of the thirty-third feature by a man who is now in his seventies and whose career has had more highs and lows than a decade of weather maps.

Mr. Huston's affection for misfits has never been more profoundly expressed than in this uproarious tale about Hazel Motes, a young Army veteran who returns home from the wars—one assumes Vietnam—obsessed with the idea of founding a Church of Christ without Christ. Hazel Motes is no Elmer Gantry and *Wise Blood* is no exposé of well-paying religious fakery, although it is about salvation.

Hazel's success as a preacher is minimal, even in a region where the crazier the homemade religion, the more likely it is to be popular. Small crowds do listen to Hazel as he stands on the hood of his battered car,

and some people are taken by his creed: "I'm a member and preacher to that church where the blind don't see and the lame don't walk and what's dead stays that way." But Hazel is too preoccupied with his own visions to organize his church and reap the financial rewards. He is ruled by fears and furies of the unloving Jesus of his childhood, when his grandfather was a hellfire-and-brimstone preacher.

Wise Blood will be shown at the New York Film Festival today and tomorrow. Its commercial opening has not been set.

Mr. Huston's best films have always been about misfits of one sort or another, from the early ones, *The Maltese Falcon* and *The Treasure of Sierra Madre,* through *The Asphalt Jungle* and *The African Queen* to his most recent production, *The Man Who Would Be King,* in 1975.

The New York Festival's program makes a mistake, I think, in saying that *Wise Blood* marks a return by the director to the "hardheaded" style of his *Fat City.* As much as I admired *Fat City,* it seems to me that *Wise Blood* is more evocative of *Beat the Devil,* the slapdash comedy classic written by Truman Capote. The seriously lunatic characters in *Wise Blood* are much closer kin to the would-be thieves in *Beat the Devil* than they are to the losers in the gritty, realistic *Fat City.*

Like all fine fiction writers, Miss O'Connor created a self-contained world that was immediately recognizable although very bizarre. No matter how odd the characters and how grotesque the events, one believes in her world because, among other things, it is consistent within itself.

This is one of the achievements of *Wise Blood,* which is lyrically mad and absolutely compelling even when we don't fully comprehend it. Shot in the South, the film presents us with familiar landscapes in which, however, all the people appear to be just slightly removed from the reality we know. This applies equally to casual passersby and to someone like the county sheriff, who appears in one brief, hilarious scene, and to the principal characters.

In addition to Hazel Motes, beautifully played by Brad Dourif (the stuttering kid in *One Flew Over the Cuckoo's Nest*), these include Sabbath Lilly Hawks (Amy Wright), a libidinous teenager who looks as if she had grown up drinking Cokes and eating french fries and never coming near a green vegetable; Asa

Hawks (Harry Dean Stanton), her evil-tempered father, a conventionally fraudulent sidewalk preacher; Enoch Emery (Daniel Shor), a crazy country boy who finds a "new" Jesus at the local museum in the form of the tiny corpse of a shrunken South American Indian; Hoover Shoates (Ned Beatty), a fast-talking promoter who wants to manage Hazel's career as a prophet; and Hazel's landlady (Mary Nell Santacroce), the lonely, middle-aged woman who falls in love with Hazel. They're all splendid. Mr. Huston himself appears in several lividly pink fantasy sequences as Hazel's grandfather.

The screenplay by Benedict Fitzgerald is not neat by usual movie standards. Characters wander off never to be heard of again. The movie delights in the odd moment that doesn't obviously carry the story forward. Yet it's always alive. Mr. Fitzgerald also seems to have preserved a lot of Miss O'Connor's dialogue. Nowhere else might you hear someone say, "Her hair was so thin it looked like ham gravy trickling down her skull," or another character, Hazel, defend himself and his second-hand wreck of an automobile with the statement, "Nobody with a good car needs to be justified."

Hazel's journey toward salvation is terrifying, tortured and bloody; yet the end effect of the film is exhilarating, as it always is when you see something so well and seemingly so effortlessly realized. Mr. Huston is in top form.

—*V.C., September 29, 1979*

THE WIZARD OF OZ

Directed by Victor Fleming; written by Noel Langley, Florence Ryerson and Edgar Allan Woolf, based on the book by L. Frank Baum; cinematographer, Harold Rosson; edited by Blanche Sewell; music by Herbert Stothart, with songs by Harold Arlen and lyrics by E. Y. Harburg; choreography by Bobby Connolly; art designer, Cedric Gibbons; produced by Mervyn LeRoy; released by Metro-Goldwyn-Mayer. Running time: 101 minutes.

With: Judy Garland (Dorothy), Frank Morgan (Professor Marvel/The Wizard), Ray Bolger (Hunk/The Scarecrow), Bert Lahr (Zeke/The Cowardly Lion), Jack Haley (Hickory/The Tin Woodman), Billie Burke (Glinda, the Good Witch), Margaret Hamilton (Miss Gulch/The Wicked Witch), Charles Grapewin (Uncle Henry) and Clara Blandick (Auntie Em).

By courtesy of the wizards of Hollywood, *The Wizard of Oz* reached the Capitol's screen yesterday as a delightful piece of wonder-working which had the youngsters' eyes shining and brought a quietly amused gleam to the wiser ones of the oldsters. Not since Disney's *Snow White* has anything quite so fantastic succeeded half so well. A fairybook tale has been told in the fairybook style, with witches, goblins, pixies, and other wondrous things drawn in the brightest colors and set cavorting to a merry little score. It is all so well-intentioned, so genial and so gay that any reviewer who would look down his nose at the fun-making should be spanked and sent off, supperless, to bed.

Having too stout an appetite to chance so dire a punishment, we shall merely mention, and not dwell upon, the circumstance that even such great wizards as those who lurk in the concrete caverns of California are often tripped in their flights of fancy by trailing vines of piano wire and outcroppings of putty noses. With the best of will and ingenuity, they cannot make a Munchkin or a Flying Monkey that will not still suggest, however vaguely, a Singer's midget in a Jack Dawn masquerade. Nor can they, without a few betraying jolts and split-screen overlappings, bring down from the sky the great soap bubble in which the Good Witch rides and roll it smoothly into place. But then, of course, how can anyone tell what a Munchkin, a Flying Monkey or a witch-bearing bubble would be like and how comport themselves under such remarkable circumstances?

And the circumstances of Dorothy's trip to Oz are so remarkable, indeed, that reason cannot deal with them at all. It blinks, and it must wink, too, at the cyclone that lifted Dorothy and her little dog, Toto, right out of Kansas and deposited them, not too gently, on the conical cap of the Wicked Witch of the East who had been holding Oz's Munchkins in thrall. Dorothy was quite a heroine, but she did want to get back to Kansas and her Aunt Em; and her only hope of that, said Glinda, the Good Witch of the North, was to see the Wizard of Oz who, as everyone knows, was a whiz of a Wiz if ever a Wiz there was. So Dorothy sets off for the Emerald City, hexed by the broomstick-riding sister of the late Wicked Witch and accompanied, in due time, by three of Frank Baum's most enchanting creations, the Scarecrow, the Tin Woodman and the Cowardly Lion.

Judy Garland's Dorothy is a pert and fresh-faced miss with the wonder-lit eyes of a believer in fairy tales, but the Baum fantasy is at its best when the Scarecrow, the Woodman and the Lion are on the move. The Scarecrow, with the elastic, dancing legs of Ray Bolger, joins the pilgrimage in search of brains; the Woodman, an armor-plated Jack Haley, wants a heart; the Cowardly Lion, comicalest of all, is Bert Lahr with an artistically curled mane, a threshing tail, and a timid heart. As he mourns in one of his ballads, his Lion hasn't the prowess of a mow-ess; he can't sleep for brooding; he can't even count sheep because he's scared of sheep. And what he wants is courage to make him king of the forest so that even being afraid of a rhinocerus would be imposerus. Mr. Lahr's lion is fion.

There, in a few paragraphs, are most of the elements of the fantasy. We haven't time for the rest, but we must mention the talking trees that pelt the travelers with apples, the witch's sky-written warning to the Wizard, the enchanted poppy field, the magnificent humbuggery of Frank Morgan's whiz of a Wiz, and the marvel of the chameleonlike "horse of another color." They are entertaining conceits all of them, presented with a naive relish for their absurdity and out of an obvious—and thoroughly natural—desire on the part of their fabricators to show what they could do. It is clear enough that Mr. Dawn, the makeup wizard, Victor Fleming, the director-wizard, Arnold Gillespie, the special effects wizard, and Mervyn LeRoy, the producing wizard, were pleased as Punches with the tricks they played. They have every reason to be.

—F.S.N., August 18, 1939

WOMAN IN THE DUNES

Directed by Hiroshi Teshigahara: written (in Japanese, with English subtitles) by Kobo Abe, based on the novel *Suna no Onna* by Mr. Abe: cinematographer. Hiroshi Segawa: edited by F. Susui: music by Toru Takemitsu: produced by Kiichi Ichikawa: released by Pathè Pictures. Black and white. Running time: 123 minutes.

With: Eiji Okada (The Teacher) and Kyoko Kishida (The Woman).

The first of five Japanese pictures to be shown among the twenty-six feature entries in the second New York Film Festival went on for the second show last night in Philharmonic Hall. It proved to be a strongly allegorical, strangely engrossing film.

Based on a novel by Kobo Abe called *Woman in the Dunes* (also the title of the picture), it is a long, leaden, grueling account of the arguing and quarreling and lovemaking of a man and a woman trapped in a shack at the bottom of a sand pit amid some remote and desolate dunes. Despite its drabness and some tedium, it grips and agitates the mind.

It begins with the man, an entomologist collecting beetles on the dunes, being directed to the shack by anonymous people from whom he has sought shelter for the night. They lower him into the sand pit with a crude block-and-fall, and there he finds the shabby woman who willingly provides him with bed and board.

But when he is ready to leave the next morning, he finds he cannot get out without having a rope lowered to him by the people above. And they are either absent or are scornful and unwilling to help.

Then the woman tells him that they are eternally caught—or, at least, must remain there at the will of the people above, who send them water and food. She explains, too, that she is resigned to existence under these circumstances. "Last year," she says, "a storm swallowed up my husband and child."

Further, she shows him the necessity of working hard every day to shovel out the sand that has fallen into the shack during the night.

Of course, the man is indignant. He rages and refuses to help. But slowly he makes his adjustment to this frustrating fate. As the picture progresses, he, too, becomes used to the pit, and at the end he does not want to leave it when he has a chance.

This is the barest outline of the plot of this more than two-hour film, which is crowded with harsh and subtle details of the personal relations of the two. But it is in the projection of these details, which have strong emotional and psychological significances, that the director, Hiroshi Teshigahara, has packed a bewitching poetry and power.

In describing, for instance, the manner in which the man becomes seduced by the physical presence of the woman, he works such subtle pictorial change that the bare body of the drab widow has a warm and attractive glow; and the physical act is suggested with such closeups of faces and limbs that a strong emanation of passion surges from the screen.

He also draws from his performers, Eiji Okada as the man (he played the lover in *Hiroshima, Mon Amour*) and Kyoko Kishida as the woman, some sharp and devastating glints of anger, sadness, compassion, gratefulness and despair. In a starkly atmospheric setting and with an eerie musical score, this drama develops an engulfing sense of spiritual discouragement and decay.

Obviously, it is intended to symbolize the absorption of man and the alienation of his spirit by all the demands and oppressions of his environment. The soul of the individual is clearly challenged in this existentialist realm, and it is reduced to resignation and surrender. Not a happy but a hypnotic film.

Woman in the Dunes took the Special Jury Prize at this year's Cannes festival and will be distributed in this country by Pathé-Contemporary. No theater booking in New York is yet set.

—*B.C., September 17, 1964*

WOMAN OF THE YEAR

Directed by George Stevens; written by Ring Lardner Jr. and Michael Kanin; cinematographer, Joseph Ruttenberg; edited by Frank Sullivan; music by Franz Waxman; art designers, Cedric Gibbons and Randall Duell; produced by Joseph L. Mankiewicz; released by Metro-Goldwyn-Mayer. Black and white. Running time: 112 minutes.

With: Spencer Tracy (Sam Craig), Katharine Hepburn (Tess Harding), Fay Bainter (Ellen Whitcomb), Reginald Owen (Clayton), Minor Watson (William J. Harding), William Bendix ("Pinkie" Peters) and Gladys Blake (Flo Peters).

For the first time in months, this critical spectator feels like tossing his old hat into the air and weaving a joyous snake dance over the typewriter keys in celebration of Metro's triumphant *Woman of the Year,* which brought sunshine and glee to the Music Hall in spite of the weather yesterday. For here is the jolliest screen comedy that's come along since *The Lady Eve* – a cheering, delightful combination of tongue-tip wit and smooth romance, a picture of surface brilliance designed unreservedly "pour le sport" but with enough of a homely little moral to make it quite comforting in these times. It's as warming as a Manhattan cocktail and as juicy as a porterhouse steak.

Since the picture opens on a session of *Information Please* heard over a bar, we will here pop a leading question. What are the two current topics most frequently discussed by your average American citizen? Why, war and sports, of course. One is grave and depressing, the other is frivolous and fun. So the very clever authors of this picture, Ring Lardner Jr. and Michael Kanin, have let a famous woman writer on international matters and an easy-going New York sports columnist fall in love, get married and then thrash out the comparative importance of their respective jobs. Only one guess as to which wins.

Of course, that is the crux by implication. The tangible conflict is along more obvious lines. The wife is so giddily preoccupied with the international situation—always grabbing the transocean telephone, hanging breathless over teletype machines—that her husband, a plain, old-fashioned fellow, can't be sure whether he is married to her or General De Gaulle. Why, their bedroom is even invaded by a Yugoslav refugee on their wedding night. But the blow-off comes when the great lady—the "outstanding woman of the year"—permits a little Greek boy she has adopted to languish, unmothered and unloved, in their apartment. Then the good old American sportswriter stands up on his hind feet; then Mrs. Outstanding Woman discovers what a wife should really be—and she ends by breaking into her husband's kitchen and fixing, or attempting to fix, breakfast for him.

A picture more carefully designed to stimulate the emotions and flatter the egos of the average American citizen, man or woman, has seldom been made. It frankly does nothing more than give an old story a significant, contemporary twist. *Young Man of Manhattan,* for instance, had pretty much the same background and plot. But it has been written with such charming adroitness—smart dialogue and neatly ranged scenes; it has been directed by George Stevens so smoothly and with such appreciation of character; and it is played so brilliantly by everyone, especially Katharine Hepburn and Spencer Tracy in the top roles, that it has the freshness of something entirely new.

Miss Hepburn was the perfect actress to play this *Woman of the Year,* and she does so with authority and feeling. She also projects a surprising warmth which she has not heretofore seemed to possess. But her best scene is the one in which she tries to make breakfast in a terrifying modern kitchen, all thumbs and confusion. Honestly, Mr. Stevens has put her beautifully through some farce hoops. This is certainly a scene over which the ladies are going to gloat. Mr. Tracy is at his top form as the rugged sports columnist—cool, deliberate and sensible—and other very flavorsome performances are given by William Bendix, Dan Tobin, Minor Watson and, briefly, Roscoe Karns.

If you are one of those wasters who secretly prefer the sports pages to the Harvard Classics you'll have a great time at this film. And even the fans of Anne O'Hare McCormick and Dorothy Thompson will be thoroughly satisfied.

—*B.C., February 6, 1942*

THE WOMEN

Directed by George Cukor; written by Anita Loos and Jane Murfin, based on the play by Clare Boothe; cinematographers Oliver T. Marsh and Joseph Ruttenberg; edited by Robert J. Kern; music by Edward Ward and David Snell; art designers Cedric Gibbons and Wade B. Rubottom; produced by Hunt Stromberg; released by Metro-Goldwyn-Mayer. Running time: 132 minutes.

With: Norma Shearer (Mary, Mrs. Stephen Haines), Joan Crawford (Crystal Allen), Rosalind Russell (Sylvia, Mrs. Howard Fowler), Mary Boland (The Countess de Lave), Paulette Goddard (Miriam Aarons), Phyllis Povah (Edith, Mrs. Phelps Potter), Joan Fontaine (Peggy, Mrs. John Day), Virginia Weidler (Little Mary), Lucile Watson (Mrs. Morehead), Florence Nash (Nancy Blake) and Muriel Hutchinson (Jane).

The tonic effect of Metro-Goldwyn-Mayer's film of Clare Boothe's *The Women* is so marvelous we believe every studio in Hollywood should make at least one thoroughly nasty picture a year. The saccharine is too much with us; going and coming to syrupy movies we lose our sense of balance. Happily, Miss Boothe hasn't. She has dipped her pen in venom and written a comedy that would turn a litmus paper pink. Metro, without alkalizing it too much, has fed it to a company of actresses who normally are so sweet that butter (as the man says) wouldn't melt in their mouths. And, instead of gasping and clutching at their throats, the women—bless 'em—have downed it without blinking, have gone on a glorious cat-clawing rampage and have turned in one of the merriest pictures of the season.

Her comedy, which Metro's Anita Loos and Jane Murfin have adapted remarkably well, is in the nature of a sociological investigation of the scalpel-tongued Park Avenue set, entirely female, who amputate their best friends' reputations at luncheon, dissect their private lives at the beauty salon, and perform the postmortems over the bridge table, while the victims industriously carve away at their surgeons. It is a ghoulish and disillusioning business and the drama critics, when first they saw the play, turned away in chivalrous horror, wondering—no doubt—whether they, too, had a Mrs. Hyde under their roofs.

Possibly some of that venom has been lost in the screen translation. Edith Potter's "glorious motherhood"—do you remember the scene in the play when she blew the cigarette ashes off her infant's nose?—has not been satirized so bitingly. A few of the blunt words have been softened. The omissions are not terribly important and some of the new sequences are so good Miss Boothe might have thought of them herself. Among these, however, we do not include a style show in Technicolor which may be lovely—at least that's what most of the women around us seemed to think—but has no place in the picture. Why not a diving exhibition or a number by the Rockettes? It is the only mark against George Cukor's otherwise shrewd and sentient direction.

The most heartening part of it all, though, aside from the pleasure we derive from hearing witty lines crackle on the screen, is the way Norma Shearer, Joan Crawford, Rosalind Russell, Paulette Goddard, and the others have leaped at the chance to be vixens. Miss Shearer, as the Mary Stephens whose divorce and matrimonial comeback keep the catfight going, is virtually the only member of the all-feminine cast who behaves as one of Hollywood's leading ladies is supposed to. And even Miss Shearer's Mary sharpens her talons finally and joins the birds of prey. It is, parenthetically, one of the best performances she has given.

Rosalind Russell, who usually is sympathetic as all-get-out, is flawless—by which we mean as good as Ilka Chase was—as the arch-prowler in the Park Avenue jungle. Miss Crawford is hard as nails in the Crystal Allen role, which is as it should be; and Miss Goddard as a frank house-wrecker, Mary Boland as a shameless buyer in the love mart, Virginia Weidler as Miss Shearer's daughter, Lucile Watson as Mrs. Morehead, Marjorie Main as the realist from Reno are all so knowing, so keen on their jobs and so successful in bringing them off that we don't know when we've ever seen such a terrible collection of women. They're really appallingly good, and so is their picture.

—F.S.N., September 22, 1939

WOMEN IN LOVE

Directed by Ken Russell: written by Larry Kramer. based on the novel by D. H. Lawrence: cinematographer, Billy Williams: edited by Michael Bradsell: music by Georges Delarue and Peter Ilich Tchaikovsky: art designer, Ken Jones: produced by Mr. Kramer: released by United Artists. Running time: 130 minutes.

With: Alan Bates (Rupert Birkin). Oliver Reed (Gerald Crich). Glenda Jackson (Gudrun Brangwen). Jennie Linden (Ursula Brangwen). Eleanor Bron (Hermione Roddice). Alan Webb (Thomas Crich). Vladek Sheybal (Loerke) and Catherine Willmer (Mrs. Crich).

If you think of D. H. Lawrence's novel, *Women in Love,* as a kind of metaphysical iceberg, then you can accept the film version, which opened yesterday at the Fine Arts Theater, as a loving, faithful, intelligent, visual representation of that part of the iceberg that can be seen above the water. It looks right, and it sounds right, but you can only guess at its actual dimensions.

Lawrence's rhapsodic polemic on behalf of a new form of consciousness, which would allow man to fulfill his sexual nature (and which struck me, when I was in college, as nothing less than Revealed Truth), is now, in this reduced form, an intensely romantic love story about four people and their curiously desperate struggles for sexual power. The polemics can still be heard, but as dim, eccentric echoes.

Because time has served to cool my passion for Lawrence, and especially for *Women in Love,* I must admit that, for me, the movie is not a sacrilege.

Ken Russell, the director, and Larry Kramer, who wrote and produced it, have transformed the novel-of-ideas into a movie-of-action that is almost as romantic as something by a Brontë sister. By retaining the original locale (provincial England) and the era (circa World War I), they have made a movie that is steeped in nostalgia that has very little to do with the work of a novelist who was ahead of his time—or, at least, thought to be.

The story remains that of two sets of cross-cutting loves, focusing principally on Birkin (the Lawrence figure), an untidy, moody school inspector who aspires to "a free proud singleness" in love, seeking "pure" relationships both with woman and man. Ursula, a sweet schoolmistress, is the somewhat baffled object of his conventional attentions; Gerald, his best friend, is the wealthy son of the local mine owner, and the man to whom he once suggests, quite seriously, a pact of blood brotherhood; and Gudrun, Ursula's liberated sister, is Gerald's love, who completes the quartet.

In the novel, the four are not so much characters as points of view that are constantly shifting. In the film, they remain fixed as they enact various Lawrentian parables about the war between the sexes that can sometimes end in death. Gerald refuses Birkin's overtures to spiritual intimacy and thus winds up in fatal combat with Gudrun, the Female Rampant who is unable to love a man without defeating him.

Although the novel's ideas are necessarily simplified onscreen, the movie does capture a feeling of nature and of physical contact between people, and between people and nature, that is about as sensuous as anything you've probably ever seen in a film. Also faithful to Lawrence is the feeling that the relationship between the two men, though unfulfilled, is somehow cleaner, less messy, than the relationships of the men with their women. When Birkin first makes love to Ursula, a frantic assignation in the woods, it's a sort of mad scramble of garters, buttons and lust. When, however, he and Gerald strip to the buff to wrestle—in the movie's loveliest sequence—there is a sense of positive grace in the eroticism.

The movie, like the novel, seems to be propagandizing for a kind of bisexuality that looks terribly confused, at least in any Freudian context. Is Birkin, or isn't he? You never really find out. The film, however, evinces a bias in the fact that female nudity is never presented with the same kind of decent simplicity as is male.

I liked all of the performances, although Alan Bates, as Birkin, and Glenda Jackson, as Gudrun, stand out as the two most vivid characters. Oliver Reed, all black brows and piercing eyes, is fine as Gerald, and Jennie Linden, who momentarily threw me because she looks so much like Debbie Reynolds, is a lovely, intelligent Ursula.

Russell sometimes gets carried away with his lyric camera, but he shoots, for the most part, directly, letting the scenes play themselves without editorial comment by the camera.

Although this *Women in Love,* is not the complete *Women in Love,* it is such an appealing movie that I'm not going to worry why someone felt the compulsion to put on-screen something that was not made for it. I prefer to think that Russell and Kramer were simply caught up in a passion for a complex novel—a passion they could not control. That, of course, is as romantic a notion as any in the film.

—V.C., March 26, 1970

WOMEN ON THE VERGE OF A NERVOUS BREAKDOWN

Written (in Spanish, with English subtitles) and directed by Pedro Almodóvar; director of photography, José Luis Alcaine; edited by José Salcedo; music by Bernardo Bonezzi; produced by Agustín Almodóvar; released by Orion Classics. Running time: 88 minutes.

With: Carmen Maura (Pepa Marcos), Antonio Banderas (Carlos), Julieta Serrano (Lucia), Maria Bar-ranco (Candela), Rossy De Palma (Marisa), Fernando Guillen (Ivan) and Guillermo Montesinos (Taxi Driver).

It hasn't been Pepa's day, or even week. Ivan, her longtime lover and a male-chauvinist rat, walks out on her, leaving only a bland message on her answering machine. Planning suicide, Pepa spikes a blenderful of garden-fresh gazpacho with sleeping pills, but forgets to drink it.

Pepa's suicide quickly takes on the aspects of a dental checkup: it keeps getting sidetracked.

Saying she really shouldn't smoke, Pepa lights a cigarette and sets her bed ablaze. Her best friend, Candela, who has been having a blissful affair with a man she didn't realize was a Shiite terrorist, comes by looking for refuge from the police.

The first couple to look at Pepa's apartment, which she has put on the market, are Carlos, Ivan's grown son, whom Pepa had never known about, and Marisa, Carlos's toothy girlfriend. When Pepa seeks legal advice, the lawyer happens to be Ivan's newest mistress.

These are only some of the delirious ingredients in this most entertaining, deliberately benign new Spanish farce, *Women on the Verge of a Nervous Breakdown.* The director is Pedro Almodóvar, better known here for his deliberately scandalous dark comedies (*Matador, Law of Desire* and *What Have I Done to Deserve This?*) in which anything goes, provided that it may offend *somebody's* sensibility.

In *Women on the Verge of a Nervous Breakdown,* Mr. Almodóvar sets out to charm rather than shock. That he succeeds should not come as a surprise. The common denominator of all Almodóvar films, even the ones that wind up in an ecstatic murder-suicide pact, is their great good humor.

Women on the Verge of a Nervous Breakdown will be shown tonight at Alice Tully Hall to begin the 26th New York Film Festival.

In what may be one of the most cheering programming decisions in the festival's quarter-century, tonight's show begins with *Night of the Living Duck.* This is an all-new Merrie Melodies cartoon in which Daffy Duck, who has too long played second fiddle to Disney's Donald, makes a memorable Lincoln Center debut, the first Hollywood cartoon character to be so honored.

In his brisk eight minutes on screen, Daffy sets a

pace for priceless nuttiness that is impossible for any feature to follow with complete security.

However, Mr. Almodóvar is not a filmmaker who can be easily upstaged by a near-classic cartoon. At its best, *Women on the Verge of a Nervous Breakdown* has much of the cheeringly mad intensity of animated shorts produced in Hollywood before the television era.

This is exemplified in Carmen Maura's grand performance as Pepa. Miss Maura, who looks a bit like Jeanne Moreau, is to Mr. Almodóvar's cinema what Anna Magnani once was to Roberto Rossellini's. This comparison would come to mind even if the director hadn't said publicly that the inspiration for *Women on the Verge* was Jean Cocteau's short, one-character play *The Human Voice,* which was acted by Miss Magnani in the Rossellini screen adaptation.

Though Mr. Almodóvar apparently adores *The Human Voice,* or did at one time, his new film is a fiendishly funny sendup of Cocteau's fustian portrait of a desperate woman who, abandoned by her lover, uses the telephone as a blunt instrument just by talking into it. As written and performed, Pepa is every bracing thing that the self-pitying Cocteau character is not.

Miss Maura is wonderful as a woman who simply cannot resist fighting back. The actress has a big, no-nonsense screen personality that perfectly fits Mr. Almodóvar's raffishly deadpan comic method. Watching *Women on the Verge* while remembering *The Human Voice,* one experiences the same sense of liberation that Bob Hoskins feels when he leaves Los Angeles and enters Toontown in *Who Framed Roger Rabbit.*

Women on the Verge takes place in its own, very special farcical universe, where outrageous coincidences are the norm and where logic dictates that a forgotten blender full of spiked gazpacho will be drunk by the wrong person. It's also a place where a television anchor is a sweet old grandmother instead of a barely literate sex symbol, and where Pepa, an actress, appears in a commercial for a detergent guaranteed to get the blood out of your killer son's shirt and trousers.

Though feminist in its sympathies, *Women on the Verge* is far from being a tract of any sort. The characters Mr. Almodóvar has written and directed keep asserting idiosyncrasies that do not allow them, or the film, to be so humorlessly categorized.

The pace sometimes flags, and there are scenes in which the comic potential appears to be lost only because the camera is in the wrong place. Farce isn't easy to pull off, but Mr. Almodóvar is well on his way to mastering this most difficult of all screen genres.

For the record, credit should be given also to the auteurs responsible for *Night of the Living Duck,* including Greg Ford and Terry Lennon, who did the story and direction. The venerable Mel Blanc is heard as Daffy. Mel Tormé provides Daffy's singing voice and the song "Monsters Lead Such Interesting Lives (They Don't Live 9 to 5)" was written by Virg Dzurinko and Mr. Ford. Pure funniness.

—*V.C., September 23, 1988*

WOODSTOCK

Directed by Michael Wadleigh; cinematographers, Don Lenzer, David Meyers, Richard Pearce, Mr. Wadleigh and Al Wertheimer; edited by Jere Huggins, Thelma Schoonmaker, Martin Scorsese, Mr. Wadleigh, Stanley Warnow and Yeu-Bun Yee; produced by Dale Bell and Bob Maurice; released by Warner Brothers. Running time: 184 minutes.

With: Richie Havens, Joan Baez, the Who (Roger Daltrey, Pete Townshend, John Entwistle and Keith Moon), Joe Cocker, David Crosby, Graham Nash, Stephen Stills, Country Joe McDonald, Arlo Guthrie, Jimi Hendrix, John Sebastian, Carlos Santana, Jerry Garcia, Janis Joplin, Sylvester Stone and Johnny Winter.

*W*oodstock is a record of an extraordinary event, the rock festival that last August drew nearly half a million young people to a 600-acre farm near Bethel, New York, for three days of music, mud, grass, love, milk, skinny-dipping, acid, Cokes, hot dogs, love, meth, music, and, for those who would stand in line, *Port-O-San* sanitary facilities.

In effect, the festival is still going on—with stunning good humor and relentlessly—in this movie, which opened yesterday at the Trans-Lux East Theater, and which could become the totem for the benign collectivists who want to save America's soul before worrying about the garbage gap.

The movie, directed by Michael Wadleigh, produced by Bob Maurice and photographed by

Wadleigh and twelve other cameramen, is somewhat less extraordinary than the event it preserves—that is, in comparison with a documentary that transforms its subject into cinematic art that is its own justification.

Woodstock, I think, couldn't care less about such considerations. It is designed, as an entertainment film, to present the performances of its stars—Joan Baez, Country Joe and the Fish, Sly and the Family Stone, Jimi Hendrix, Arlo Guthrie, and the rest—in the context of the event. To this end, it uses a lot of fancy optical effects, including split screens and superimpositions, in aggressive, largely superfluous attempts to interpret performers who are themselves interpreters.

The movie spends, I'd estimate, not quite a third of its time recording the offstage events at what comes to look like Calvary (minus the last act, of course) as it might be staged by a stoned Cecil B. De Mille. An interviewer listens as one totally drenched young man castigates "the fascist pigs" in the helicopters for having seeded the clouds. A pretty little girl, with a face as blank as a pancake, marvels at how beautiful it all is, though she hasn't seen her sister in twenty-four hours and she must find her to get her to court on Monday morning.

Words fail just about everybody, including the interviewer who comments on a statement by one young man by saying: "Great—er, I mean—groovy." An elderly man in Bethel says: "The last time we saw anything like this was at the Rose Bowl Parade." And one lady in the early stages of hysteria pleads for someone to get her out of there—there are just too many people. "We're the third largest city in the world!" exults another girl, and the communicants make love in the bushes, do yoga exercises, say how groovy it all is (thus, perhaps, to protect more private fears), and splash around a nearby pond with (of all things to be found in Bethel, New York) a surfboard.

I can only assume that the film follows the chronology of the festival in the presentation of its stars, who come on for comparatively brief sets in endless procession. Some are better than others. Miss Baez is treated beautifully, without cinematic distortions, singing "Joe Hill" and "Swing Low, Sweet Chariot," as is Jimi Hendrix, who manufactures his own optical effects as he rocks "The Star-Spangled Banner" to close the festival.

In between are such things as the driving rock of

the Who ("Summertime Blues"), Joe Cocker ("With a Little Help from My Friends"), and Sly and the Family Stone ("Higher"). The sheer length of the film (three hours, four minutes), as well as the monotony of its visual rhythm, eventually produces a kind of fatigue that is, I suspect, as close to the feeling of being at an almost nonstop, three-day, togetherness orgy as can be prompted by a film. This effect is magnified, rather than diminished, by those moments when the musicians really do seem to take off for special, secret moments, as when Country Joe sings his Vietnam lament, "Fixin' to Die Rag." There have to be low points if there are any that are high.

Wadleigh and Maurice employ various devices to stimulate a feeling of participation on the part of the theater audience. In addition to split screens, which may show a single performer from two or three different angles simultaneously, they use auditorium speakers for "surround" effects. (The sound quality is great, much better, in fact, than that of the 35mm film that has been blown up from 16.)

Although the film never really gave me a sense of experiencing the public ecstasy experienced by those who were at Woodstock, it did make me feel comparatively benign. When a woman sitting in my row got up for the third time to go to the ladies' room, and stepped squarely on my toe with a high heel, I said simply: "Peace."

—V.C., *March 27, 1970*

WORKING GIRL

Directed by Mike Nichols: written by Kevin Wade: director of photography. Michael Ballhaus: edited by Sam O'Steen: music by Carly Simon: production designer. Patrizia Von Brandenstein: produced by Douglas Wick: released by Twentieth Century Fox. Running time: 115 minutes.

With: Harrison Ford (Jack Trainer). Sigourney Weaver (Katharine Parker). Melanie Griffith (Tess McGill). Alec Baldwin (Mick Dugan). Joan Cusack (Cyn). Philip Bosco (Oren Trask) and Nora Dunn (Ginny).

In *Working Girl,* Tess McGill (Melanie Griffith) first appears wearing the hairdo that Farrah forgot: a teased, bleached, badly outdated coiffure that immediately places her at the bottom of the corporate totem pole. Tess is a secretary who lives on Staten Island, works in Manhattan, and has no idea how large a gulf exists, at least in this film's scheme of things, between the states of mind represented by those two places.

But she's about to find out. *Working Girl* presents Tess with one of the best opportunities for wish fulfillment this side of "Cinderella," an opportunity that's conceived in contemporary terms and goes well beyond Prince Charming. Tess is given a chance to prove herself in the professional arena, undergo a much-needed fashion overhaul and move up from a romance based on animal magnetism to one that very pointedly mixes business with pleasure. Though it isn't likely that an innocent like Tess could accomplish all this in a few weeks' time, *Working Girl* is enjoyable even when it isn't credible, which is most of the time. The film, like its heroine, has a genius for getting by on pure charm.

Working Girl, which opens today at the Coronet and other theaters, derives a lot of its charm from the performance of Melanie Griffith, the baby-voiced bombshell who gives Tess an unbeatable mixture of street smarts, business sense and sex appeal. Tess's crazy-like-a-fox approach to career advancement is demonstrated early in the story when she rejects a pass from an obnoxious arbitrager and spitefully impugns the manliness of one boss with a gesture that none of her coworkers could possibly miss.

Yet under the right circumstances, Tess can become the very essence of cooperation. Her big mistake in *Working Girl* is to suppose that her new boss, a thrillingly flirtatious and encouraging female executive, is deserving of all the helpfulness and loyalty a good secretary can give.

The first half-hour of the film, which also establishes Tess's dismal home life on Staten Island—with a tattooed boyfriend, played amusingly by Alec Baldwin, who never manages to give Tess anything she can wear outside the bedroom—works wonderfully. This is especially true of the delightful sequence that has Tess being bowled over by Katharine Parker (Sigourney Weaver), who soon after hiring Tess breezily quotes Coco Chanel and makes it known that she is younger than her secretary, if only by two weeks.

Under Katharine's tutelage, Tess comes up with new ideas, like a suggestion that dim sum be served at a business reception. "I'd love to help you," Katharine whispers smoothly to the perspiring Tess, "but we can't busy the quarterback with passing out the Gatorade."

It's essential to *Working Girl* that Tess quickly find reason to reassess her admiration for Katharine, and that Katharine quite literally break a leg. With this, the film's fairy tale aspects are set in motion. Tess decides to masquerade as an executive in order to sell the idea she thinks Katharine was stealing, and she arranges a head-to-toe overnight transformation without needing help from a fairy godmother.

Thanks to Katharine's trust, Tess even has access to the right wardrobe, though viewers would do well to ignore the fact that Miss Griffith and Miss Weaver aren't remotely the same size. Or that no one in the office spots Tess wearing Katharine's clothes, commandeering her desk, and using a very nonsecretarial manner to answer the telephone.

The screenplay, by Kevin Wade, has a sly wit, but it is also surprisingly primitive. So the plot contains distracting holes, and the details of Tess's scheme to succeed seem crude, even for a film as lighthearted as this. Mike Nichols, who directed *Working Girl,* also displays an uncharacteristically blunt touch, and in its later stages the story remains lively but seldom has the perceptiveness or acuity of Mr. Nichols's best work. When Tess crashes the wedding of a C.E.O.'s daughter to help promote her idea, for instance, the C.E.O. is made gullible, the guests unattractive, and the party so full of fake tropical scenery that it looks much more idiotic than it has to.

Working Girl combines romance with satire when it introduces Tess to Jack Trainer (Harrison Ford), an executive who wears so many hats here that he serves the screenplay as a kind of all-purpose generic male. Mr. Ford, who plays Jack in a foggy and rather faraway manner, never sets off many sparks with Miss Griffith, but perhaps that's not the point. One of the many things that mark *Working Girl* as an eighties creation is its way of regarding business and sex as almost interchangeable pursuits and suggesting that life's greatest happiness can be achieved by combining the two.

Working Girl, always fun even when at its most frivolous, has the benefit of the cinematographer Michael Ballhaus's sharp visual sense of boardroom chic, and of supporting characters who help carry its class distinctions beyond simple caricature. Chief among these, along with Mr. Baldwin, is Joan Cusack as the no-nonsense Staten Island girlfriend who lets Tess know that she takes a dim view of magical transformations. "Sometimes I sing and dance around the house in my underwear," she says witheringly. "Doesn't make me Madonna. Never will."

—J.M., December 21, 1988

THE WORLD OF APU

Produced and directed by Satyajit Ray: written (in Bengali. with English subtitles) by Mr. Ray. based on the novel *Aparajita* by Bibhutibhushan Bandyopadhyaa: cinematographer. Subrata Mitra: edited by Dulal Dutta: music by Ravi Shankar: art designer. Banshi Chandra Gupta: released by Harrison Films. Black and white. Running time: 103 minutes.

With: Soumitra Chatterjee (Apu). Sharmila Tagore (Aparna). Alok Chakravarty (Katol) and Swapan Mukherji (Pulu).

The cycle of life in India that filmmaker Satyajit Ray determined to make graphic and poetic in an uncommon film trilogy is finally brought full circle in *The World of Apu* (*Apur Sansar*), which opened yesterday at the Fifth Avenue Cinema. The fulfillment honors the screen.

For with this beautiful picture, which completes the story of the Hindu lad we first met as a boy in *Pather Panchali* and saw grow into a raw young man in the succeeding *Aparajito,* an impressive capstone is put not only upon a touching human drama but also upon the development of a genuine artist's skill. Mr. Ray, whose grasp of the cinema medium was uncertain in *Pather Panchali,* his first film, demonstrates in *The World of Apu* that he is master of a complex craft and style.

Here he is telling us what happens to Apu, the lad of his previous films, when he has completed his skimpy education and gone out into the cold and challenging world. It is helpful to know about Apu, his broken family and his boyhood trials from the previous films. But it isn't essential or even vital, for this is a complete and rounded drama in itself.

It is the drama of a young man, shy and lonely, who is drawn into marriage with a girl, whom he doesn't know, out of regard for friendship and for a Hindu custom that is patently absurd; of his quick realization of love for her and their blissful happiness together for one year, until she dies in childbirth and he is left desolate, the stricken father of an unwanted child.

Through all of this tender experience, Mr. Ray pursues the story and constructs the film with an attention to the finer spiritual values that is extraordinarily sensitive and rare. Being a man who won't be hurried—or, at least, will not allow the tempo of a placid, pensive people to be stepped up to suit the custom of the screen—he follows the life stream of his hero with elaborate serenity, observing his world with close attention and delicately molding the beauties along the way.

Life is an everlasting poem in the canon observed by Mr. Ray. It is a slow flow of sensuous experience, surrounded by esthetic qualities. A man comes home in disappointment after having failed to get a job; he pensively shuts the windows, lies on his bed, and plays a flute. A bride adorned in all her finery dares nothing more than a soft smile and whatever delight shows in her large eyes to express her gratitude at being wed. A woman goes home to have a baby; a message comes that she is dead.

Mr. Ray conveys in simple symbols the inexorable swing of life and death.

But the climax and triumph of his picture is its final phase in which the hero, the husband of the dead wife, the father of the unwanted child, goes into a period of several years of wandering and seeking for peace, finally to return to pick up his youngster and start another cycle of Apu.

Mr. Ray's command of the telling image and of tempo is superior in this film, and he seems to have elicited from his actors as fine performances as he has ever had. In the role of Apu, Soumitra Chatterjee is timid, tender, sad, serene, superb. He is the perfect extension of Apu as a man. Sharmila Tagore is an idol—an animated idol—as his bride, and Swapan Mukherji is striking as his modern, educated, practical friend. An incredibly slight and sad-eyed youngster named Alok Chakravarty is heartbreaking as the child.

A lovely musical score by Ravi Shankar complements the imagery of Mr. Ray. English subtitles apparently give us the gist of the conglomerate dialogue.

—B.C., October 5, 1960

THE WORLD OF HENRY ORIENT

Directed by George Roy Hill: written by Nora Johnson and Nunnally Johnson, based on the novel by Nora Johnson: cinematographer, Boris Kaufman: edited by Stuart Gilmore: music by Elmer Bernstein: production designer, James Sullivan: produced by Jerome Hellman: released by United Artists. Running time: 106 minutes.

With: Peter Sellers (Henry Orient), Paula Prentiss (Stella), Tippy Walker (Valerie Boyd), Merrie Spaeth (Marian Gilbert), Angela Lansbury (Isabel Boyd), Tom Bosley (Frank Boyd) and Phyllis Thaxter (Mrs. Gilbert).

Should you be one who worries about the sanity of those teenagers who carry on like crazy about the Beatles, you should have your confidence happily restored by going to see *The World of Henry Orient*, which opened yesterday as the Easter attraction at the Music Hall.

You should even get a lot of comfort from it, whether you worry about the youngsters or not, because it is one of the most joyous and comforting movies about teenagers that we've had in a long time. And it introduces two delightful youngsters, Tippy Walker and Merrie Spaeth, who are the nicest proofs since Hayley Mills that little girls are made of sugar and spice.

Don't let that make you think it's icky. It is anything but. It is a juicily tart and sassy go-round with believably robust youngsters. It also has Peter Sellers playing a cheerfully rakish role—that of a predaceous concert pianist. So don't worry, it won't stick in your teeth.

What it does, in essence, is give a picture of two fourteen-year-old New York girls, students at one of the snazzier private schools on the upper East Side, who get a wild crush on this conceited and highly affected pianist and drive him almost to distraction with their relentless, adoring pursuit.

They park across the street from his apartment when he is slyly entertaining another man's wife. They peer at him through the front window of a Greenwich Village restaurant. They bump into him when he is racing to make a fast getaway with a girl. They even have the temerity, finally, to knock on his apartment door.

What they find there—well, it is something you had better see for yourself. Just let me say it casts much more discredit on the behavior of adults than of teenagers.

That is habitual with this picture, which comes from the writing machines of Nora Johnson and her father, Nunnally Johnson, and has been directed well by George Roy Hill. It has a great deal more regard for the solidity and integrity of girls than it has for the qualities of their parents, which are a little worn and frazzled with the years.

The youngsters may be thoroughly harum-scarum. They may live in their private, secret worlds—at this point, the world of Henry Orient, which they gleefully invent and fabricate. But their values are wholesome and decent, their loyalties are true and their flights from reality are not so buoyant that they can't be suddenly bumped to the ground.

More fetching of the two is the screwball that the agile Miss Walker plays—a fey girl whose parents have all but deserted her and who consequently lives for the most part in a mink coat. She is a wonderfully hoydenish creature, equally forthright and strong, whether vaulting fire hydrants along the curbstone or playing Debussy on the Steinway in her living room. Her period of adjustment with her parents is the most touching thing in the film, and Miss Walker plays her part with sensitivity.

Miss Spaeth is the softer, the quieter and the less aggressive of the two. She is a credible product of a broken but still loving home. Perhaps you could say she plays the straight-girl to the more flamboyant friend.

As for Mr. Sellers, he is beautifully voluble and droll on a level of comic exposition that is just a wee bit above burlesque. His Henry Orient, the pianist, is a poseur, a popinjay, a fraud—an arch deceiver of women. But he is great and ever-surprising fun.

High scores are also in order for Phyllis Thaxter and Bibi Osterwald as the mother and aunt of the quieter youngster and for Angela Lansbury and Tom Bosley as the parents of the one who lives in the mink coat and is oh-so-nervous and anxious when they come home. Indeed, Mr. Bosley, in his slow way, injects the most sensitive note of adult appreciation and responsibility in the film.

A frisky musical score by Elmer Bernstein flows comfortably into the softer moods. Like the whole film, it leaves one feeling (as one of the girls says) awfully happy in a sad way.

—B.C., March 20, 1964

WRITTEN ON THE WIND

Directed by Douglas Sirk: written by George Zuckerman. based on the novel by Robert Wilder: director of photography. Russell Metty: edited by Russell F. Schoengarth: art directors. Robert Clatworthy and Alexander Golitzen: music by Frank Skinner and Victor Young: produced by Albert Zugsmith: released by Universal Pictures. Running time: 99 minutes.

With: Rock Hudson (Mitch Wayne). Lauren Bacall (Lucy Moore Hadley). Robert Stack (Kyle Hadley). Dorothy Malone (Marylee Hadley). Robert Keith (Jasper Hadley). Grant Williams (Biff Miley). Robert J. Wilke (Dan Willis). Edward Platt (Doctor Paul Cochrane). John Larch (Roy Carter). Joseph Granby (R. J. Courtney) and Roy Glenn (Sam).

Those Texas millionaires whose sad psychoses are subject for frequent literary concern come in for another harsh inspection in Universal's *Written on the Wind*. At least one of them does in this picture, which came to the Capitol yesterday. He is a miserable unfortunate who has only about $10,000,000 to his name and is married to a gracious young lady who looks and acts just like Lauren Bacall.

The trouble with this young fellow, who is bleakly portrayed by Robert Stack, is that he can't measure up to his best friend, whom Rock Hudson manfully plays. (There is no relation between this Texan and the one Mr. Hudson plays in *Giant*.)

Where Mr. Hudson is stalwart, disciplined, able and serene, Mr. Stack is weak, irresponsible, incompetent and as flighty as a bird. And where Mr. Hudson is clearly a first-class ladies' man, Mr. Stack is something of a wash-out—or so it would appear. (Why Miss

Bacall ever marries him is known only to George Zuckerman, who wrote the screenplay, and maybe to Robert Wilder, who wrote the book on which it is based.)

Thus, it is not much wonder that Mr. Stack has suspicions dark and dire when he learns, to his utter amazement, that his wife is going to have a child. Could it be Mr. Hudson has been carrying friendship a little too far? The idea is not ridiculous to the Texas millionaire. And especially since his sister, played by Dorothy Malone, has been acting the role of Iago, he can't get it out of his head.

Anyhow, after close to ninety minutes of everyone trying hard to keep Mr. Stack from boozing and blubbering into his beer, he starts a little action by grabbing a pistol and threatening Mr. Hudson. In the scuffle, he himself gets killed and Mr. Hudson, as innocent as a daisy, gets the emancipated Miss Bacall.

The trouble with this romantic picture—among other minor things, including Mr. Stack's absurd performance and another even more so by Miss Malone—is that nothing really happens, the complications within the characters are never clear and the sloppy, self-pitying fellow at the center of the whole thing is a bore.

Outside of that, it is luxurious and the color is conspicuously strong, even though it gets no closer to Texas—either geographically or in spirit—than a few locations near Hollywood.

—B.C., January 12, 1957

WUTHERING HEIGHTS

Directed by William Wyler: written by Ben Hecht and Charles MacArthur. based on the novel by Emily Brontë: cinematographer. Gregg Toland: edited by Daniel Mandell: music by Alfred Newman: art designer. James Basevi: produced by Samuel Goldwyn: released by United Artists. Black and white. Running time: 103 minutes.

With: Merle Oberon (Cathy). Laurence Olivier (Heathcliff). David Niven (Edgar). Flora Robson (Ellen Dean). Donald Crisp (Dr. Kenneth). Hugh Williams (Hindley). Geraldine Fitzgerald (Isabella). Leo G. Carroll (Joseph) and Cecil Humphreys (Judge Linton).

After a long recess, Samuel Goldwyn has returned to serious screen business again with his film *Wuthering Heights*, which had its premiere at the Rivoli last night. It is Goldwyn at his best, and better still, Emily Brontë at hers. Out of her strange tale of a tortured romance Mr. Goldwyn and his troupe have fashioned a strong and somber film, poetically written as the novel not always was, sinister and wild as it was meant to be, far more compact dramatically than Miss Brontë had made it. During December's dusty researches we expect to be filing it away among the year's best ten; in April it is a living thing, vibrant as the wind that swept Times Square last night.

One of the most incredible aspects of it is the circumstance that the story has reached the screen through the agency of Ben Hecht and Charles MacArthur, as un-Brontian a pair of infidels as ever danced a rigadoon upon a classicist's grave. But be assured: as Alexander Wollcott was saying last week, they've done right by our Emily. It isn't exactly the faithful transcription, which would have served neither Miss Brontë nor the screen—whatever the Brontë societies may think about it. But it is a faithful adaptation, written reverently and well, which goes straight to the heart of the book, explores its shadows and draws dramatic fire from the savage flints of scene and character hidden there.

And it has been brilliantly played. Laurence Olivier's Heathcliff is the man. He has Heathcliff's broad lowering brow, his scowl, the churlishness, the wild tenderness, the bearing, speech and manner of the demon-possessed. Charlotte Brontë, in her preface to her sister's novel, said Heathcliff never loved Cathy; the only claim he might have had to humanity was his lukewarm regard for Hareton Earnshaw; take that away, she said, and Heathcliff is demon, ghoul or Afreet. Hecht and MacArthur have taken Hareton away. In fact, they have removed the novel's entire second generation, have limited the story to Heathcliff and Cathy, to Edgar and Isabella Linton and their servants, dogs and the desolate moor where their drama is played. But Heathcliff is no demon and he loved Cathy, in the film as in the novel.

To the sheltered Brontës, it must have seemed that a passion so consuming, violent, and destructive—of itself and what it touched—must have been diabolic. Even now on the Rivoli's screen there is something overwhelming in the tumult of the drama's pulse, the sweep and surge of Heathcliff's love and hate, their crushing before them of all the softness of that Yorkshire world a century ago, their brave defiance of heaven and hell and death itself. No wonder Charlotte recoiled in holy horror and exclaimed "Afreet!" and that Emily, like Mrs. Shelley with her *Frankenstein,* only dimly sensed the potent force she was wielding.

So Mr. Olivier has played Heathcliff, and Merle Oberon, as Cathy, has matched the brilliance of his characterization with hers. She has perfectly caught the restless, changeling spirit of the Brontë heroine who knew she was not meant for heaven and broke her heart and Heathcliff's in the synthetic paradise of her marriage with gentle Edgar Linton. The Lintons, so pallid, so namby-pamby in the novel, have been more charitably reflected in the picture. David Nivens's Edgar, Geraldine Fitzgerald's Isabella are dignified and poignant characterizations of two young people whose tragedy was not in being weak themselves but in being weaker than the abnormal pair whose destinies involved their destruction. And, in Flora Robson's Ellen (Nellie in the novel), in Miles Mander's Mr. Lockwood, Hugh Williams's sottish Hindley, and the others, Mr. Goldwyn has provided a flawless supporting cast.

William Wyler has directed it magnificently, surcharging even his lighter scenes with an atmosphere of suspense and foreboding, keeping his horror-shadowed narrative moving at a steadily accelerating pace, building absorbingly to its tragic climax. It is, unquestionably, one of the most distinguished pictures of the year, one of the finest ever produced by Mr. Goldwyn and one you should decide to see.

—*F.S.N., April 14, 1939*

YANKEE DOODLE DANDY

Directed by Michael Curtiz; written by Robert
Buckner and Edmund Joseph, based on a story by
Mr. Buckner; cinematographer, James Wong
Howe; edited by George Amy; music and lyrics by
George M. Cohan; choreography by LeRoy Prinz,
Seymour Felix and John Boyle; art designer, Carl
Jules Weyl; produced by William Cagney, Hal B.
Wallis and Jack L. Warner; released by Warner
Brothers. Black and white. Running time: 126
minutes.

With: James Cagney (George M. Cohan), Joan
Leslie (Mary Cohan), Walter Huston (Jerry Cohan),
Richard Whorf (Sam Harris), Irene Manning (Fay
Templeton), George Tobias (Dietz) and Rosemary
DeCamp (Nellie Cohan).

Yankee Doodle Dandy rode into town last night on a
whole lot more than a pony; it rode on the star-
spangled crest of one of the fanciest buildups that
Broadway has ever known, not to mention the glowing
reputation of one of "the Street's" most beloved sons.
Folks who are looking for something propitious to
decorate today would do well to try for a seat at the
Hollywood Theatre. For there, at the scene of last
night's "$5,000,000 premiere," you will find as warm
and delightful a musical picture as has hit the screen in
years, a corking good entertainment and as affectionate, if not as accurate, a film biography as has ever—
yes, ever—been made.

No need to tell anybody who the subject of this
sparkling picture is. The public has been well advised

for months that Warner Brothers were filming the life
of George M. Cohan, with all the old Cohan songs
and bits from his memorable shows. And the fact that
cocky James Cagney would play the leading role has
been a matter of common knowledge and of joyous
anticipation all around. So the only news this morning
is that all has come out fine. The picture magnificently
matches the theatrical brilliance of Mr. Cohan's
career, packed as it is with vigorous humor and honest
sentiment. And the performance of Mr. Cagney as the
one and original Song-and-Dance Man is an unbelievably faithful characterization and a piece of playing
that glows with energy.

True, Robert Buckner and Edmund Joseph, the
scriptwriters, have taken some liberties with Mr.
Cohan's life. They have juggled facts rather freely to
construct a neat, dramatic story line, and they have let
slip a few anachronisms which the wise ones will gleefully spot. But, as the late Sigmund Lubin once put it,
they're yours at no extra cost. And, of course, Mr.
Cohan had the last word. He said okay, let them go.

And the story as now presented is that of a lusty
trouper, a showman who earned in the theater a lasting place in our nation's Hall of Fame. Indeed, the
picture begins with Cohan being called to Washington
while playing the role of President Roosevelt in the
musical show *I'd Rather Be Right*. At the White House
he meets the president (an unprecedented trick for the
screen) and to him is told, in flashback, the wonderful
story of this Yankee dandy's life.

And it is a hummer of a life! It starts on July 4,
1878, in Providence, Rhode Island, when the red and
squalling Georgie first hitched his wagon to the stars
and stripes. And it follows the fortunes of the Cohan

family—the famous Four Cohans, vaudeville specialists—through their picturesque trouping around the country, the first break of saucy George as *Peck's Bad Boy,* his teaming with Sam H. Harris and the production of *Little Johnny Jones,* and it traces his rising fortune to the World War and the writing of "Over There." Then it digresses pleasantly into the fictitious afternoon of the family's life, and takes up for a climax with Cohan receiving the Congressional Medal of Honor from President Roosevelt.

Without question, the most solidly entertaining portion of the film is that which has to do with Cohan's early bouts with the stage and the sumptuous reproductions of bits from his early shows. Here Mr. Cagney excels, both in characterization and jubilant song and dance. His handling of "Yankee Doodle Boy" and "Give My Regards to Broadway," from *Little Johnny Jones,* must be—with all due respect—quite as buoyant as Mr. Cohan's own. And one priceless dialogue he plays with Eddie Foy, Jr., representing the elder Foy, couldn't have been better if Mr. Cohan had played it—and written it—himself.

But the complementary intimate family story is also appealing, too, largely because of the warmhearted portrayal of the elder Cohan by Walter Huston. He and Mr. Cagney, as father and son, create the image of a deep attachment which has the very breath of life in it. And the episode wherein is recounted Mr. Cohan's composition of "Over There" is tremendously moving in its simplicity. There is not a maudlin note struck in the film. And the only elaborate flag-waving is done in one gaudy production sequence based on the song, "You're a Grand Old Flag."

The abundance of further pleasures is endless. There is Irene Manning playing Fay Templeton and singing "Mary Is a Grand Old Name" and "So Long, Mary," fit to make any oldster cry. There are the excellent performances of Joan Leslie as Cohan's romantic prompter, Rosemary DeCamp as his mother, Richard Whorf as Sam H. Harris, and countless others, not to forget Captain Jack Young's tastefully restrained and surprisingly realistic impersonation of the president. Indeed, there is so much in this picture and so many persons that deserve their meed of praise that everyone connected with it can stick a feather in his hat and take our word—it's dandy!

—*B.C., May 30, 1942*

THE YEAR OF LIVING DANGEROUSLY

Directed by Peter Weir; written by David Williamson, Mr. Weir and C.J. Koch, based on the novel by Mr. Koch; director of photography, Russell Boyd; edited by Bill Anderson; music by Maurice Jarre; art designer, Herbert Pinter; produced by James McElroy; released by Metro-Goldwyn-Mayer/United Artists. Running time: 114 minutes.

With: Mel Gibson (Guy Hamilton), Sigourney Weaver (Jill Bryant), Linda Hunt (Billy Kwan), Michael Murphy (Pete Curtis), Noel Ferrier (Wally O'Sullivan), Paul Sonkkila (Kevin Condon), Bill Kerr (Colonel Henderson), Mike Emperio (Sukarno) and Bembol Roco (Kumar).

Peter Weir's *The Year of Living Dangerously* is a good, romantic melodrama that suffers more than most good, romantic melodramas in not being much better than it is. This film should be some kind of epic. It's set in and around Jakarta in 1965, in the last months of the flamboyant, one-man rule of President Sukarno, the Indonesian nationalist hero who aspired to be a Third World leader abroad, to reconcile left and right at home, and to be the playboy of the Eastern world.

The international intrigue that surrounded Sukarno, the economic chaos he caused and the terrible poverty of the people to whom he gave identity—all this is the sort of material one associates with Graham Greene's stories of power and nobly crossed purposes amid the steamy squalor of emerging nations.

Mr. Weir, who adapted C.J. Koch's Australian novel with Mr. Koch and David Williamson (who wrote *Don's Party*), has all the correct impulses but no real grasp of the humane irony that separates sincere fiction from possibly great fiction.

As it stands, *The Year of Living Dangerously,* which opens today at the Cinema I, is an entertaining tale about an ambitious young Australian journalist, Guy Hamilton (Mel Gibson), who comes to Jakarta on his first overseas assignment determined to make a name for himself. The times are ripe for such opportunistic advancement.

Every day there is a new rumor of an impending coup. Sukarno, to placate the Communists, offers to sanction a Communist army. The right-wing Moslem generals, supported by the West, resist. Peking is sending a shipload of arms to its Indonesian supporters. Bureaucratic corruption is the order of the day and, in the streets, people are starving to death.

As Guy Hamilton moves through this desperate world, he has the assistance of an extraordinary little man named Billy Kwan, a newsreel cameraman and photographer, half Chinese and half Australian, whose mixed blood and midget size are a life sentence to be an outsider.

Though one can never entirely escape the suspicion that Billy is as much a theatrical device as a character, he's a fascinating, bristly, androgynous figure. The fact that he is played—marvelously well—by a woman, an American actress named Linda Hunt, only works to the film's advantage. It's Billy's fate to play God, and gods are, if not androgynous, then not necessarily condemned to a single sexual identity.

Billy Kwan provides Guy with contacts that enable him to obtain stories his colleagues cannot. He attempts to transform Guy into an activist-journalist, one who, as I. F. Stone once instructed, remembers to consider the victims when he covers a terrifically exciting disaster story. It's also Billy who introduces Guy to Jill Bryant (Sigourney Weaver), an assistant to the military attaché at the British embassy. Because Billy loves but cannot have Jill, a bright, unusually intelligent young woman, he presents her to Guy.

In each Weir film I've ever seen —*Picnic at Hanging Rock, The Last Wave* and *Gallipoli*, the Australian director has shown great imagination and style in the setting up of situations that somehow always fall short of one's expectations at the payoff. Now, with *The Year of Living Dangerously*, this problem seems to be not an accident but almost a personal idiosyncracy. One yearns for *The Year of Living Dangerously* to reach heights or depths that, perhaps, Mr. Weir never intended.

The film's physical production, much of it shot on location in the Philippines, is superb, as is the director's handling of the big, crowded scenes of civil turmoil. Best of all are his performers.

If this film doesn't make an international star of Mr. Gibson (*Gallipoli, The Road Warrior*), then nothing will. He possesses both the necessary talent and the screen presence. Though Miss Weaver has less to work with, she's an equally compelling film personality, one who brings to a role a distinctive manner that fills a lot of the holes left by the writers.

It's one of the odd—and effective—ways in which Mr. Weir works that the film's only erotic love scene is played not on a bed, or even in a clinch, but when the two about-to-be lovers, running out on an embassy dinner party, drive at high speed—just for the hell of it—through a heavily armed roadblock. That, friends, is heat.

Heading the fine supporting cast are Michael Murphy and Noel Ferrier, as two of Guy Hamilton's colleagues, and Bembol Roco, as Guy Hamilton's Indonesian assistant.

Not exactly dominating these performances, but providing the film with its dramatic center, is Miss Hunt's haunted Billy Kwan, who keeps detailed files on everyone he loves, weeps at the purity of the voice of Kiri Te Kanawa and, when the chips are down, is capable of the film's single grand gesture.

—*V. C., January 21, 1983*

THE YEARLING

Directed by Clarence Brown; written by Paul Osborn, based on the novel by Marjorie Kinnan Rawlings; cinematographers, Charles Rosher, Leonard Smith and Arthur E. Arling; edited by Harold F. Kress; music by Herbert Stothart; art designers, Cedric Gibbons and Paul Groesse; produced by Sidney Franklin; released by Metro-Goldwyn-Mayer. Running time: 134 minutes.

With: Gregory Peck (Penny Baxter), Jane Wyman (Ma Baxter), Claude Jarman Jr. (Jody Baxter), Chill Wills (Buck Forrester), Clem Bevans (Pa Forrester), Margaret Wycherly (Ma Forrester), Henry Travers (Mr. Boyles), Forrest Tucker (Lem Forrester), Matt Willis (Gabby Forrester) and Donn Gift (Fodderwing).

It isn't very often that there is realized upon the screen the innocence and trust and enchantment that are in the nature of a child or the yearning love and anxiety that a father feels for his boy. These are human emotions which are a little too sensitive and fine for easy comprehension in the usually artificial terms of films. But we've got to hand it to Metro and to everyone who helped to visualize *The Yearling* from Marjorie Kinnan Rawlings's great novel of that name; they have caught these rare sentiments and beauties in this picture which came to the Music Hall yesterday.

And they have also caught much of the feeling which a lonesome lad has for wild things, expressed with such tenderness and eloquence in Mrs. Rawlings's classic work. They have caught, too, the adult pain and struggle in a frontier farmer's life, the humor and spunk of rawboned rustics, and the strength that derives from patient toil. All these they have richly compounded in this Technicolor film which provides such a wealth of satisfaction as few pictures ever attain.

In less loving hands, Mrs. Rawlings's story of a backwoods Florida boy whose heart wells with wild and magic torrents might have become quite a mawkish thing. For it is one of those delicate stories which depends entirely upon restraint in visualization and purity of mood. The strong bond of trust and wistful longing which exists between the boy and his "Pa" required the most sensitive tuning in order to ring sharp and true. The love of the lad for a pet fawn, which his father understands, had to be tenderly developed to appear wholly genuine. And the ultimate tragic necessity to destroy the yearling deer compelled the most sure dramatic handling to avoid the pit of bathos.

But Clarence Brown, who directed for Metro from Paul Osborn's excellent script, has revealed both his heart and his intelligence in keeping the whole thing restrained. By simple pictorial indications, devoid of gestures or "gush," he has shown the fabric and its shading which bind the father, the mother, and the boy. Yet vitality and zest flow through the whole film. The many vivid incidents in the book—the bear hunt, the dog swap, the snake bite and the fight with the Forrester boys—are played with abundance of tension and great richness of graphic detail.

There's no denying that the fitness of the picture is due in large measure to the incredibly fine performance which little Claude Jarman Jr. gives. As Jody, the towheaded farm boy, this youngster who had never acted before achieves a child characterization as

haunting and appealing as any we've ever seen. Spindly, delicate of features and possessed of a melting Southern voice, he makes not a single sound or movement which does not seem completely genuine. And his confident handling of the animals reveals him plainly as their natural, primal friend.

Equally important, however, is the performance of Gregory Peck as Penny, the warm and gentle father who knows that "a boy ain't a boy fer long." Although he measures several inches taller than Mrs. Rawlings's original "Pa," he fills out every one of them with simple dignity and strength. And Jane Wyman, while she does not have the physical characteristics of the original "Ma," compels credulity and sympathy for a woman of stern and Spartan stripe. Chill Wills, Clem Bevans and Margaret Wycherly are robust as Forresters and little Donn Gift is pathetic and disturbing as crippled Fodderwing, the child of distant moods.

To be sure, there are two or three moments when the Aurora Borealis is turned on and the heavenly choir starts singing. With those we could willingly dispense. Jody's hysterics at the climax, when he shoots the deer, seem also overlong. But, those aside, all of *The Yearling* is a cheerful and inspiring film about the coming to manhood of a youngster. As Jody says to his father, "I seen a sight today!"

—B.C., January 24, 1947

YELLOW SUBMARINE

Directed by George Dunning; written by Lee Minoff, Al Brodax, Erich Segal and Jack Mendelsohn, based on the song by John Lennon and Paul McCartney; cinematographer, John Williams; animation by Jack Stokes; edited by Brian J. Bishop; music by George Martin; art designer, Heinz Edelmann; produced by Mr. Brodax; released by United Artists. Running time: 85 minutes.

With: Sgt. Pepper's Lonely Hearts Club Band.

Yellow Submarine, which opened yesterday at the Forum and Tower East, is the Beatles' first feature-length cartoon, designed, for the most part beautifully, by Heinz Edelmann, in styles ranging through Steinberg, Arshile Gorky, Bob Godfrey (of the short film *The Do It Yourself Cartoon Kit*), the *Sgt. Pepper* album cover, and day comic strip. The Phantom appears. So do many other pop art and comics characters. (Dick Tracy's inspired Moon Maid would not have been out of place.)

The story concerns the kingdom of Pepperland, invaded by the Blue Meanies, the only antidote to whom is music. There are twelve songs, most of them from *Sgt. Pepper's Lonely Hearts Club Band,* and it becomes clear throughout the film not only that the rhythm of movie direction (by George Dunning) and the rhythms of music are meant for each other, but also that any human occasion demands—before pictures, before prose even—something in music.

"Do you ever get the feeling . . . ?"

"Yeah."

"That things are not as rosy as they appear to be underneath the surface?"

"There's a cyclops?"; "But he's got two eyes?" A bicyclops; "Black, Blue, White, Red. Can I take my friend to bed" ("Can I bring my friend to tea" is another refrain); "Tell us where we're at," The Socratic question—the whole movie, alternately washed and hard edge, art nouveau, and full of flowering shrubs and thistles, is full of enfolded meanings, jokes, puns—some of them lemon-infantile, none of them aggressive, pretentious or self-indulgent—that would delight a child, or a head, or anybody who loves and admires the Beatles, even though this is a film in which they either redo old songs or appear once, in person, briefly, in one of their worst acted appearances ever. "Come on, The whole world is being attacked"; "Hook up, and otherwise commingle"; "All together now"—these are the lines in which the Beatles, with their special talent, life and energy, launch their unfrenetic, unhardsell, upbeat message to the world.

There are completely lovely visual ideas: a fish with hands, which swims breast stroke; a consumer creature with a trumpet snout, who ingests the whole world, decanting people out of a glass ball, by means of a hole that has been picked up from an op polka-dot field of right-side up and upside-down holes; a submarine that is convertible into a bravely smiling fish; a fort that disgorges a cavalry charge against Indians; and a cigarette lighter. The Dantesque landscape of otherworldly types; the Alice in Wonderland snails; mushrooms; trains emerging from under sinks; bleachings of color from hyperactive corridors; teeny weeny Meanies; and particularly the thistles are drawn

with such care and amiability by Heinz Edelmann. (He is not so good on people or anthropomorphic types: they tend to Popeye distortions below the waist, and undistinguished faces above.) Not a great film, after all, but truly nice.

Yellow Submarine is a family movie in the truest sense—something for the little kids who watch the same sort of punning stories, infinitely less nonviolent and refined, on television; something for the older kids, whose musical contribution to the arts and longings for love and gentleness and color could hardly present a better case; something for parents, who can see the best of what being newly young is all about. *Hard Day's Night* and *Help!* were more serious, and more truly Beatle saturated. But *Yellow Submarine,* with its memories of Saturday morning at the movies, and its lovely Oswald the Rabbit in Candyland graphics, makes the hooking up and otherwise commingling very possible. When invited to, the whole audience picks up the "All together now" refrain and sings.

—*R.A., November 14, 1968*

YI YI: A ONE AND A TWO

Written and directed by Edward Yang; in Mandarin, with English subtitles; director of photography, Yang Weihan; edited by Chen Bowen; music and production design by Peng Kaili, produced by Shinya Kawai and Naoko Tsukeda; released by Winstar Cinema. Running time: 173 minutes.

With: Jonathan Chang (Yang-Yang) Yupang Chang (Fatty), Chen Xisheng (A-Di), Elaine Jin (Min-Min), Ke Suyun (Sherry Chang-Breitner), Kelly Lee (Ting-Ting), Adrian Lin (Lili), Issey Ogata (Mr. Ota), Tang Ruyun (Grandma), Michael Tao (Da-Da), Wu Nienjen (NJ Jian), Xiao Shushen (Xiao Yan), Xu Shuyuan (Lili's Mother) and Zeng Xinyi (Yun-Yun).

Midway through *Yi Yi,* a morose, skeletally thin teenager (whose nickname is Fatty) tells his date: "Movies are lifelike. That's why we like them." In his view, movies don't only resemble the world we live in—they expand it. "We live three times," he declares, his passion overwhelming his arithmetic. "Two times as much life at the movies!" After watching this lovely, absorbing film you'll be inclined to agree. In exchange for three hours of your time, *Yi Yi* will give you more life.

Edward Yang, the Taiwanese filmmaker who wrote and directed this intimate epic of a middle-class Taipei family's everyday struggles, knows that for a movie to be full of life, it must above all concern itself with specific lives. *Yi Yi* begins with the chaotic bustle of wedding preparations—a portrait of the bride and groom is hung upside down, the groom's jilted girl-friend arrives uninvited and makes a scene—and ends with the somber calm of a funeral.

In the long interval between these events, the members of the Jian family collectively and individually traverse what feels like the full spectrum of human experience, from the mundane to the catastrophic. NJ (Wu Nienjen), the wiry, sad-eyed patriarch, must deal with setbacks at his software company and a midlife crisis triggered by the reappearance of Sherry (Ke Suyun), his high-school sweetheart. NJ's wife, Min-Min (Elaine Jin), despondent over her mother's crippling stroke, retreats first into depression and then into a religious cult. Their teenage daughter, Ting-Ting (Kelly Lee), undergoes her own identity crisis, caught between loyalty to her troubled best friend and the slightly dangerous appeal of Fatty (Yupang Chang). There is a birth, a suicide attempt and a murder. Friendships are made and broken. Ting-Ting's runty younger brother, Yang-Yang (Jonathan Chang), is harassed at school by a gang of bigger girls. There is a lot of music (NJ's passion), eating and drinking, all of it set amid the sleek cosmopolitan kineticism of Taipei and, briefly, Tokyo, where NJ goes in search of an investor to save his business and a second chance with Sherry, who is now married to an American businessman.

But *Yi Yi* is more than a soap opera, which is to say it's less. The mood is restrained and gentle and the narrative rhythm fluid and easy, meandering from story to story. Although it rises on occasion to a high pitch of intensity, this movie never feels overwrought or melodramatic. The title is nothing more than the Chinese word for "one" repeated twice; the Chinese characters, which appear in the opening titles, look like birds in flight seen from afar. The English translation, "A One and a Two," suggests a bandleader counting off, and *Yi Yi*, composed with the meticulous discipline of a symphony, nonetheless has the swing and spontaneity of group improvisation.

It's no accident that the eight-year-old Yang-Yang shares his name with the filmmaker, since he functions within the film as a kind of alter ego, a watcher and recorder of the world's enigmas. In the privacy of his bath Yang-Yang conducts elaborate experiments with funnels and bottles and wanders from scene to scene with a camera. He's a half-pint philosopher, complaining to his father: "I can't see what you see and you can't see what I see. So how can I know what you see?" To remedy this condition, he takes pictures of the backs of people's heads.

As a filmmaker, Mr. Yang is like a wiser, less anxious version of this boy. He uses the limitations of visual perspective to convey chaos without succumbing to it. He likes to shoot people in groups at medium range, allowing sound and movement to spill in from outside of the frame. He also likes to shoot through glass, and even to aim his camera at closed doors, as though to suggest both the transparency and the opacity of experience. The film's most extraordinary shot is of a woman weeping alone in a hotel room. The camera is outside the window, and the woman is barely visible through the reflected phantoms of skyscrapers and passing traffic.

None of this feels gimmicky or contrived. Mr. Yang's style is like a novelist's prose—lucid, unobtrusive and absorbing. Mr. Yang's earlier films, especially *A Brighter Summer Day,* his exquisite, disturbing 1991 story of adolescence in Taiwan, have gained him a passionate following among critics and international festivalgoers. *Yi Yi,* the first of his movies to be released commercially in the United States (it will open at the Film Forum on Friday, after being shown at the New York Film Festival tonight), is the work of a master in full command of the resources of his art. Movies are an inherently, sometimes cheaply emotional medium, but it takes a lot to make a grown critic cry. As I watched the final credits of *Yi Yi* through bleary eyes, I struggled to identify the overpowering feeling that was making me tear up. Was it grief? Joy? Mirth? Yes, I decided, it was all of these. But mostly, it was gratitude.

—*A.O.S., October 4, 2000*

YOJIMBO

Produced and directed by Akira Kurosawa: written (in Japanese. with English subtitles) by Mr. Kurosawa. Ryuzo Kikushima and Hideo Oguni: cinematographer. Kazuo Miyagawa: music by Masaru Sato: art designer. Yoshiro Maraki: released by Seneca International. Black and white. Running time: 110 minutes.

With: Toshiro Mifune (Sanjuro). Eijiro Tono (Genji). Seizaburo Kawazu (Seibei). Isuzu Yamada (Orin. his wife). Hiroshi Tachikawa (Yoichiro) and Tatsuya Nakadai (Nosuke).

Akira Kurosawa's obvious taste for American Western films, manifested most clearly in his *Magnificent Seven* (known in Japan as *Seven Samurai*), is evident again in his *Yojimbo,* which opened yesterday at the Carnegie Hall Cinema. Underneath its Japanese kimonos lurk the aspects of a *High Noon* or *Shane.*

Consider simply its story. A jobless and vagrant samurai (a mercenary or sword fighter) comes into a nineteenth-century Japanese town where two lawless and vicious factions are battling for control. He goes to the local tavern, orders sake (counterpart for "red eye"), gets briefed on the local situation and offers his sword for hire. He will work as a bodyguard (yojimbo) for the side that makes the better bid.

This leads to considerable contention. Both sides are suspicious of him, yet neither wants the other to get him because he is so fast and powerful on the draw. There's a good deal of back-and-forth jockeying, in which the awesome samurai (who is really a peace-loving fellow) works the factions into a standoff spot.

Then into town charges the brother of the leader of one of the gangs. He is a wicked and reckless young fellow and he brandishes a Colt .45. This changes the situation. Swords would appear obsolete. The power of the old sword fighter would appear irrevocably doomed.

And it is—for a while. Caught off guard in the performance of a sentimental act, he is beaten up by the henchmen of the gunman and presumably rendered null and void. But he crawls into a hideout, slowly gets back his strength and finally sallies forth to challenge the gunman, sword (and heroism) versus gun. He meets him and faces off with him, right out in the middle of the windy, empty street. Needless to say, the old sword fighter—all canniness and heroism—wins.

As he leaves, with the warring factions scattered and himself in a mood of disgust, he remarks (according to the English subtitle), "Now it will be quiet in this town."

So help us, that is the melodrama that occurs in this Japanese film—and we leave you to reckon how closely it reflects the historical and cultural features of Japan. It is, beyond any question, a straight transposition of Western film clichés, which in turn may be dubious reflections of the historical and cultural truth of our frontier. Still, they stem from our tradition, not that of the Japanese.

But despite the sometime appearance of the whole thing as a forthright travesty, it does have stretches of excitement and cinematic power. Kurosawa is a master director. He can work up a melodramatic scene, such as that final street fight (as in *High Noon* or *Red River*), so that it gets you, kimonos and all. Or he can catch a close-up of his hero's battered face in a deep shadow, with one good eye lit by a beam of light that fires it with invincible savage defiance.

Also, Toshiro Mifune, who plays the leading role, is always an interesting actor, commanding and apt at imaging strain. He passes well in this picture for a Japanese Gary Cooper or John Wayne. Tatsuya Nakadai plays the fellow with the gun in broad, wild style, and Seizaburo Kawazu is knotty as the leader of one of the gangs.

However, as in most Westerns, the dramatic penetration is not deep, and the plot complications are many and hard to follow in Japanese. Kurosawa is here showing more virtuosity than strength. *Yojimbo* is a long way (in the wrong direction) from his brilliant *Rashomon.*

—*B.C., October 16, 1962*

YOU CAN COUNT ON ME

Written and directed by Kenneth Lonergan: director of photography. Stephen Kazmierski: edited by Anne McCabe: music by Lesley Barber: production designer. Michael Shaw: produced by John N. Hart. Jeffrey Sharp. Larry Meistrich and

Barbara De Fina: released by Paramount Classics. Running time: 111 minutes.

With: Laura Linney (Sammy), Mark Ruffalo (Terry), Matthew Broderick (Brian), Jon Tenney (Bob), Rory Culkin (Rudy), J. Smith-Cameron (Mabel), Josh Lucas (Rudy Sr.), Gaby Hoffmann (Sheila) and Adam LeFevre (Sheriff Darryl).

For all the bullying inspirational slogans hurled at us about never giving up on your dream, following your bliss and today being the first day of the rest of your life, the fact remains that most people's lives run on fairly narrow tracks. And in the real world, as opposed to self-help fantasyland, once you find yourself on a track, it's awfully hard to get off, even if it's headed nowhere in particular.

The way so many lives coast along on familiar but frustrating paths is one of the themes of *You Can Count on Me,* the perfectly pitched directorial debut of the playwright (*This Is Your Youth*) and screenwriter (*Analyze This!*) Kenneth Lonergan.

Because it arrives near the end of one of the most dismal film seasons in memory, this melancholy little gem of a movie, which won two major awards at the Sundance Festival, qualifies as one of the two or three finest American films released this year. If nothing better comes along between now and the end of December, it could reap some more honors.

What distinguishes *You Can Count on Me* from almost every other recent American film is its modesty. Although visually handsome, it is about the furthest thing from an event movie and would fit as comfortably on television as it does on the big screen. Its biggest strength is a steadfast integrity that sharpens as the story goes along. Steering clear of the shrill melodramatic confrontations and kitschy spiritual uplift that Hollywood routinely confuses with profundity, it proposes no pat solutions for its characters' problems. One significant character, a likable but cautious young boy, is the refreshing antithesis of the psychically gifted, problem-solving superchild that is becoming one of Hollywood's most obnoxious cliches.

You Can Count on Me is an exquisitely observed slice of upstate New York life that reminds us there are still plenty of American communities where the pace is more human than computer-driven. The movie dares to portray small-town middle-class life in America as somewhat drab and predictable. Without ever condescending to its characters, it trusts that the everyday problems of ordinary people, if portrayed with enough knowledge, empathy and insight, can be as compelling as the most bizarre screaming carnival on "The Jerry Springer Show."

The two main characters, Samantha and Terry Prescott (Laura Linney and Mark Ruffalo), are a grown-up brother and sister who reunite after not having seen each other for some time. Samantha (known as Sammy), a single mother with an eight-year-old son, Rudy (Rory Culkin), works as a loan officer in a bank in the fictional New York town of Scottsville. A quiet, slightly wilted place with a sleepy main street whose vitality hasn't entirely been co-opted by shopping malls, it is a typical middle-to-working-class New York State community. Country music dominates the local jukeboxes, and the soundtrack serves up a generous helping of Steve Earle's country-rock.

Samantha and Terry share a childhood trauma, recalled in the film's opening scenes, of having lost both parents in a car accident when they were very young. In remembering this event the film exercises a stunning restraint. We see the parents having a banal conversation in the car moments before the accident and then the looming disaster. Cut to an anxious policeman about to bear the horrible news to the children who have been waiting at home. Sparing us their reaction, the movie cuts to the sermon at the parents' funeral service, where we see the priest's lips moving while no words are heard on the soundtrack except for the ethereal cry of a children's choir.

These early scenes demonstrate an unerring sense (one shared by the best screenplays) of when it is best to leave things to the imagination. And as Ms. Linney's and Mr. Ruffalo's grown-up Samantha and Terry reunite, quarrel and reminisce, you retain a lingering image of the two of them as children, silently clinging to each other, still mute with shock.

In their beautifully harmonized performances, Ms. Linney and Mr. Ruffalo evoke this sibling bond with an astounding depth and subtlety. Ms. Linney's Samantha may be a responsible mother and churchgoing Catholic, but we learn that she was a wild teenager who has had to choke back her rebellious instincts in order to bring up her son. Even now, her innate rebelliousness still manifests itself in ways both small (she secretly smokes cigarettes) and large (she recklessly initiates an affair with her new boss, a persnickety straight arrow with a pregnant wife).

Mr. Ruffalo's Terry is a classic overgrown adolescent. A good-hearted drifter with a perversely self-destructive streak, he has recently spent time in prison after a bar brawl and has also impregnated a suicidally inclined girlfriend in Worcester, Mass. The main reason for his visit to Scottsville is to borrow money from his sister to deal with the situation. Samantha is furious and disappointed by her brother's lack of direction and behavioral sloppiness. He in turn is contemptuous of her for remaining stuck in Scottsville, whose small-town atmosphere he finds suffocating.

Terry stays on longer than he had planned and further infuriates Samantha with his irresponsible treatment of Rudy, who instantly gravitates toward him as a father figure. One evening, as a boyish prank, they sneak out to a pool hall while Samantha is away; later they are caught lying about it.

Samantha, in the meantime, finds herself torn between a sudden marriage proposal from her on-again, off-again boyfriend Bob (Jon Tenney) and her foolish affair with her boss, Brian (Matthew Broderick), who is instantly besotted. On the job Brian is a gray-faced, passive-aggressive company man and stickler for rules who is so obsessed with appearances that he issues an edict forbidding his employees to use loud colors on their computer screens.

The culminating event, an excruciating, brilliantly executed scene of emotional chaos as old personal wounds are ripped open, is Terry's impulsive, ill-advised decision to take Rudy on a surprise visit to meet his roughneck biological father (Josh Lucas) whom Samantha has built up as a hero to the boy. Mr. Ruffalo's star-making performance deserves to be added to the list of charismatic, grownup lost boys that includes the Marlon Brando of *A Streetcar Named Desire* and the Jack Nicholson of *Easy Rider*.

Talking in a slightly dazed drawl, bursts of anger occasionally flashing through a manner that suggests the defensive, semi-apologetic attitude of a boy trying to please his strict mother, Terry is a softer, contemporary version of this archetype. He is the kind of man women instinctively want to rescue, only to discover a maddening obstinacy lurking beneath his appealing boyish surface.

You Can Count on Me makes some slight missteps. In an otherwise scrupulously realistic movie, Mr.

Broderick's Brian borders uncomfortably on caricature. But in countless other small but telling ways, the movie gets its characters and their world exactly and indelibly right.

—*S.H., November 10, 2000*

YOU ONLY LIVE ONCE

Directed by Fritz Lang; written by Gene Towne and Graham Baker; based on a story by Mr. Towne; cinematographer, Leon Shamroy; edited by Daniel Mandell; music by Alfred Newman; art designer, Alexander Toluboff; produced by Walter Wanger; released by United Artists. Black and white. Running time: 86 minutes.

With: Sylvia Sidney (Joan Graham), Henry Fonda (Eddie Taylor), Barton MacLane (Stephen Whitney), Jean Dixon (Bonnie Graham), William Gargan (Father Dolan), Warren Hymer (Muggsy) and Charles "Chic" Sale (Ethan).

Fritz Lang's *You Only Live Once,* now at the Rivoli, is not the dynamic and powerful photoplay his *Fury* was, but, within the somewhat theatrical limits of its script, it is an intense, absorbing and relentlessly pursued tragedy which owes most of its dignity to the eloquence of its direction. In less gifted hands, it might have been the merest melodrama; Mr. Lang's intuitive sense of camera angle, pace and mood raises it to dramatic stature, even though it does not become the convincing social document its producers obviously meant it to be.

Here, as in *Fury,* the story is that of two young people dogged inexorably by the hounds of fate to a tragic destiny. But here, unlike *Fury,* the roots of their tragedy are within themselves, not grafted, flowering, upon them by a cruel and insensate society. We accept their life story, then, as the somber biography of two persons born under a dark star. They may have our sympathy, but it is sympathy unmixed with self-reproach. The picture tries vagrantly to blame society for their tragedy, but its arguments are none too persuasive.

Eddie Taylor, when we find him, is a three-time loser, a convict completing his third term for felony. One more offense, the warden warns him as he sets him free, and he will be returned to prison for life. Taylor, we are assured, is not a bad sort. He has made his mistakes, but he has paid for them. Now he asks no more of life than a job, a home for the girl who has been waiting for him, a family. He gets the job, he marries the girl, he makes a down payment on a little house—then the onslaught begins.

He loses his job, and a hat, bearing the initials "E. T.," found at the scene of a fatal bank robbery, is enough to convince a jury of his guilt. Sentenced to die, he breaks out of the death-house and fights his way to freedom just as his innocence has been established and his pardon comes through. With a gun prodding the back of a hostage, Taylor hears the warden read the pardon message. "Lies!" he says, and kills the prison chaplain who barred his path. From that step there was no retreat. Destiny had closed in upon the Taylors; their flight could have but one end.

Mr. Lang's direction is his usual brilliant compound of suspense and swift action, heightened always by his complete command of lights and cameras in pointing and counterpointing his scenes. The dismal rain at the bank holdup, the swirling fog during the prison break, the black-and-white contrast of the death-house, the photographic crescendo of Taylor's flight—these are ready and perfect illustrations of directorial imagination.

The performances are less conspicuous, although Sylvia Sidney's portrayal is poignantly real. Henry Fonda's characterization of Taylor is unidimensional, making us guess at—rather than realize—the inner honesty and goodness he is supposed to possess. Barton MacLane is, as usual, inflexible as the public defender and Jean Dixon is the stereotype of the sympathetic sister. More helpful are William Gargan as the chaplain, Jerome Cowan as the prison doctor, and Warren Hymer as an inmate. Essentially, it's a one-man job; that one being the director.

—*F.S.N., February 1, 1937*

YOUNG FRANKENSTEIN

Directed by Mel Brooks; written by Gene Wilder and Mr. Brooks, based on the novel *Frankenstein* by Mary Wollstonecraft Shelley; director of photography, Gerald Hirschfeld; edited by John Howard; music by John Morris; art designer, Dale Hennesy; produced by Michael Gruskoff; released by Twentieth Century Fox. Running time: 104 minutes.

With: Gene Wilder (Dr. Frankenstein), Peter Boyle (Monster), Marty Feldman (Igor), Madeline Kahn (Elizabeth), Cloris Leachman (Frau Blucher), Teri Garr (Inga), Kenneth Mars (Inspector Kemp), Richard Haydn (Herr Falkenstein) and Gene Hackman (Blind Man).

He's young. He's clean-cut. He's all-American. You are certain he uses the correct deodorants and aftershave lotions. He has a fiancée who's so fussy about her makeup that when they say good-bye, they don't kiss, they gently rub elbows. The young man is a brain surgeon named Dr. Frankenstein, but when a medical student calls him that, he has a fit. "No, no," he screams, "it's pronounced Fron-ken-shteen!" He doesn't want to be confused with his infamous grandfather.

As played by Gene Wilder in Mel Brooks's funniest, most cohesive comedy to date, this Dr. Frankenstein is a marvelous addled mixture of young Tom Edison, Winnie-the-Pooh and your average *Playboy* reader with a keen appreciation of beautiful bosoms.

At this point in time it isn't easy to make fun of Mary Shelley's durable old chestnut about the visionary doctor and the monster to whom he gave life. All of the jokes would seem to have been told. Hammer Productions' *Frankenstein* movies employ deadpan humor. *Andy Warhol's Frankenstein,* released this year, was an all-out assault that used wild anachronisms and grotesque special effects.

It would be misleading to describe *Young Frankenstein,* written by Mr. Wilder and Mr. Brooks, as astoundingly witty, but it's a great deal of low fun of the sort that Mr. Brooks specializes in.

Although it hasn't as many roof-raising boffs as *Blazing Saddles,* it is funnier over the long run because it is more disciplined. The anarchy is controlled. Mr. Brooks sticks to the subject, recalling the clichés of horror films of the 1930's as lovingly as someone remembering the small sins of youth.

Perhaps the nicest thing about *Young Frankenstein* is that one can laugh with it and never feel as if the target film, James Whale's 1931 classic that starred Boris Karloff, is being rudely used.

The new movie, which has Young Frankenstein returning to the family castle and bringing to life a monster played by Peter Boyle, is a horror film composed almost entirely of hilarious interruptions, including the doctor's near-fatal encounter with one of those mysterious bookcases that hides a secret door. It keeps turning around and hitting him in the back.

The doctor is helped in his endeavors by his loyal hunchback servant, Igor, pronounced Eye-gor, played by a nervily funny newcomer to films named Marty Feldman; by a pretty blond laboratory assistant (Teri Garr) who recalls (intentionally) every blond starlet who never quite made the big time; and, of course, by Mr. Boyle in monster-drag.

Madeline Kahn, one of the best things in *Blazing Saddles,* is in top form as the doctor's bossy fiancée who eventually finds sexual fulfillment in the arms of the monster, and Gene Hackman turns up in a pricelessly funny bit as the blind man who befriends the monster and after offering him a cigar carefully lights the monster's thumb.

The high point of the film is a sequence in which the young doctor takes his monster to a medical convention in Bucharest and demonstrates his accomplishment by joining the monster for several choruses of "Puttin' on the Ritz," both dressed nattily in white tie and tails.

Young Frankenstein, which opened yesterday at the Sutton, was photographed in black and white with fastidious attention to the kind of slightly fake details you'll find only in a studio-made movie over which tremendous care has been taken. It has an affectionate look to it, especially in the laboratory equipment that is said to be a reproduction of the stuff used in the Whale film.

Some of the gags don't work, but fewer than in any previous Brooks film that I've seen, and when the jokes are meant to be bad, they are riotously poor. What more can one ask of Mel Brooks?

—*V.C., December 16, 1974*

YOUNG MR. LINCOLN

Directed by John Ford: written by Lamar Trotti: cinematographers. Bert Glennon and Arthur Miller: edited by Walter Thompson: music by Alfred Newman: art designers. Richard Day and Mark-Lee Kirk: produced by Darryl F. Zanuck and Kenneth MacGowan: released by Twentieth Century Fox. Black and white. Running time: 100 minutes.

With: Henry Fonda (Abraham Lincoln). Alice Brady (Abagail Clay). Marjorie Weaver (Mary Todd). Arleen Whelan (Hannah Clay). Eddie Collins (Efe). Pauline Moore (Ann Rutledge). Richard Cromwell (Matt Clay). Donald Meek (John Felder) and Spencer Charters (Judge Herbert A. Bell).

One of the most human and humorous of the Lincoln biographies is *Young Mr. Lincoln,* which Twentieth Century Fox presented at the Roxy yesterday. Without a trace of self-consciousness or an interlinear hint that its subject is a man of destiny, it has followed young Abe through his early years in Illinois, chuckling over his gangliness and folksy humor, sympathizing with him in his melancholy, grinning from ear to ear with—and at—him as he goes to court in Springfield before a pipe-smoking judge and a jury of prairie-raised pundits. These were the happy years, before he got into politics; the picture is happier for ending before the long shadows came creeping up.

Henry Fonda's characterization is one of those once-in-a-blue-moon things: a crossroads meeting of nature, art and a smart casting director. Nature gave Mr. Fonda long legs and arms, a strong and honest face, and a slow smile; the makeup man added a new nose bridge, the lank brown hair, the frock coat, and stove-pipe hat (the beard hadn't begun to sprout in those days) and the trace of a mole. Mr. Fonda supplied the rest—the warmth and kindliness, the pleasant modesty, the courage, resolution, tenderness, shrewdness and wit that Lincoln, even young Mr. Lincoln, must have possessed. His performance kindles the film, makes it a moving unity, at once gentle and quizzically comic.

And yet, while his Lincoln dominates the picture, director John Ford and scriptwriter Lamar Trotti never have permitted it to stand out too obviously against its background—the Midwestern frontier. Scene and minor character have their place, and an important one. The prairie types have been skillfully drawn. One knows, somehow, that they are Lincoln's kind of people, that they think as he does, laugh at the same jokes, appreciate the same kind of horseplay. Had they been less carefully presented, Abe himself would have seemed less natural, would have been a stranger in his own community. Alice Brady's frontier mother, Donald Meek's spellbinding prosecutor, Spencer Charters's circuit judge, Eddie Collins's Efe—they all fit into the picture, give Mr. Fonda's colorful Lincoln the protection of their coloration.

The result of it, happily, is not merely a natural and straightforward biography, but a film which indisputably has the right to be called Americana. It isn't merely part of a life that has been retold, but part of a way of living when government had advanced little beyond the town meeting stage, when every man knew his neighbor's business and meddled in it at times, when a municipal high spot was a pie-judging contest, the parade of the Silver Cornets and a tug of war on the principal thoroughfare. Against that background and through events more melodramatic and humorous than nationally eventful, Twentieth Century's *Young Mr. Lincoln* passes; and it is a journey most pleasant to share.

—F.S.N., June 3, 1939

Y TU MAMA TAMBIEN

Directed by Alfonso Cuarón: written (in Spanish, with English subtitles) by Alfonso Cuarón and Carlos Cuarón: director of photography, Emmanuel Lubezki: edited by Alfonso Cuarón and Alex Rodriguez: music by Liza Richardson and Annette Fradera: art directors. Miguel Alvarez and Sandra Solarres: produced by Jorge Vergara: released by IFC Films. Running time: 105 minutes.

With: Maribel Verdú (Luisa). Diego Luna (Tenoch). Gael García Bernal (Julio) and Juan Carlos Remolina (Jano).

Y Tu Mama Tambien—the phrase translates from Spanish as "And your mama, too"—is one of those Bildungsroman films that could begin or end with the phrase, "And my life was never the same again." (The movie uses a voice-over narration, which it mercifully relies on less and less to explicate the inner lives of the characters.) But the director, Alfonso

Cuarón, works with a quicksilver fluidity, and the movie, which plays today and tomorrow at the New York Film Festival, is fast, funny, unafraid of sexuality and finally devastating.

Mostly, *Mama* happily brings to mind the rough-and-tumble male friendships and dangerous sexual alliances that Bertrand Blier explored in his film tributes to the volatility of lust, movies like *Going Places* and *Trop Belle Pour Toi* (*Too Beautiful for You*). Mr. Cuarón has a propensity for turning the tables and imbuing scenes with a kind of lyric reality, a different feel from Blier's voluble straightforwardness; *Mama* is more *Jules and Jim* in the age of Ecstasy.

His first film, *Solo con Tu Pareja* (*Love in the Time of Hysteria,* 1991), is very close in tone to *Trop Belle,* though his ability to depict the allure of flesh on screen can be both shocking and comic. In *Great Expectations* (1998), in which a little girl teases a shy, backward boy, the kids are like flirting colts until they touch tongues at a water fountain, and lust is unleashed in a moment of hilarious and potentially scary virtuosity.

In *Mama,* which takes place in Mexico, the hormonally consumed teenage boys Julio (Gael García Bernal) and Tenoch (Diego Luna) are backward, too. These guys think of themselves as worldly sophisticates attending to their appetites, despite their sneaking into the bedrooms of their girlfriends for sex and their furious fanning of weed fumes so that their overprotective parents can't smell their indulgences.

Mr. Cuarón wickedly establishes the middle-class cocoon his characters are swathed in. And their infantile macho games (they compete on every level, even conducting an onanists' Olympics on side-by-side diving boards) seem more like baby steps than ever when they meet Luisa (Maribel Verdú). This sad-eyed young woman is married to Tenoch's older cousin Jano (Juan Carlos Remolina), who's even more of a poseur than the boys. Tenoch and Julio come on to Luisa by promising her a tour of the wondrous beach called Heaven's Mouth. Many of its wonders stem from its nonexistence. Julio and Tenoch are lonely and bored because their girlfriends are touring Europe; they view Luisa as a respite from their thumb-twiddling summer vacations.

Mama is finally a story of maturation, as Julio and Tenoch learn truths about themselves that they're not happy to face, and Mr. Cuaron twists the narrative to peer at the latent homoeroticism that drives teenage sex-drive stories like *American Pie*—something boys-to-men movies never deal with explicitly.

The director's lucid storytelling skills and his instinct for getting at unsettling emotional states are huge parts of this film's power. Luisa's willingness to join Julio and Tenoch on their journey to utopia is apparently motivated by her husband's betrayal of their marriage. But there are other, more somber reasons for her decision. She takes it upon herself to educate these squalling teenagers, and there's always a trace of sadness in her brimming eyes.

Even when throwing herself into the sexual games that become part of the trip—and are an almost pro forma element of this genre—Ms. Verdú sinks her teeth into her role, and devours it. Oddly enough, her forcefulness plays as a layer of unspoken virility; she's far more intent than the pups in her care.

The sex is also a way to trigger the feelings that Julio and Tenoch can never express because they're too busy talking and thinking about sex. They're gifted at chatter, too—they talk so heatedly about everything that it seems as if they actually conjure the resort area of their dreams. The trio find a real Heaven's Mouth, and for a while *Mama* becomes dreamy, bathed in lusciousness; the picture takes on the unhurried carnality of a 70's film.

Once sated, though, Julio and Tenoch have to deal with their empty ambitions. The self-knowledge they gain adds a grim context to the narration, which becomes both more detached and more informative as a result of its distanced quality.

Ms. Verdú's suppleness is astounding, and she matches the daring of Mr. Bernal and Mr. Luna. In contrast to the competitiveness of their characters, these actors can't undercut each other. They have to support each other's work or they would be unbearable to watch. Mr. Cuaron creates an atmosphere of emotional intimacy so efficiently that the bouncy-bouncy between Julio, Tenoch and Luisa seems less exploitative and part of the wild orchestration of comedy and melodrama.

It's in the final moments of *Mama,* when the three-some are roused out of their dreams, that Mr. Cuaron's offhand ability to startle finishes off the happy-ending expectations. He harnesses the boyish jumpiness of Julio and Tenoch to his own need to subvert the easy and irresponsible conclusions of the teenage sex movie genre. Instead of telling this story with excited exclamation points, Mr. Cuaron provides a climax that's a question mark.

By the end of *Y Tu Mama Tambien,* Julio and Tenoch are left with their eyes wide open; they'll never sleep as easily again. Those in the audience will have seen something unforgettable, too.

—*F.M., October 6, 2002*

Z

Directed by Costa-Gavras: written in French with English subtitles by Costa-Gavras and Jorge Semprun. based on the novel by Vassilis Vassilikos: director of photography. Raoul Coutard: edited by Francoise Bonnoi: production designer. Jacques D'Ovidio: music by Mikis Theodorakis: produced by Jacques Perrin and Hamed Rachedi: released by Cinema V Distributing. Running time: 127 minutes.

With: Yves Montand (the Deputy). Irene Papas (Helene). Jean-Louis Trintignant (The Examining Magistrate). Jacques Perrin (Photojournalist). Charles Denner (Manuel). François Perier (Public Prosecutor). Pierre Dux (The General). Georges Gret (Nick) Bernard Fresson (Matt). Marcel Bozzuffi (Vago) and Julien Guiomar (The Colonel).

Costa-Gavras's *Z*, the French film that won the Jury Prize (in effect, the third prize) at this year's Cannes Festival, is an immensely entertaining movie—a topical melodrama that manipulates our emotional responses and appeals to our best prejudices in such satisfying ways that it is likely to be mistaken as a work of fine—rather than popular—movie art.

The film, which opened last night at the Beekman, is based on Vassilis Vassilikos's novel, which, in turn, is a lightly fictionalized account of the 1963 assassination in Salonika of Gregarios Lambrakis, a professor of medicine at the University of Athens and a leader of the forces opposing the placement of Polaris missiles in Greece. There is a kind of momentum to democratic processes, and the official investigation of that murder, instigated with some reluctance by the Government, eventually uncovered a plot involving high Government officials as well as a secret right-wing organization of patriotic goons.

In the course of the scandal, the Greek Government fell and the men morally and directly responsible for the murder were brought to trial. Within four years, there was a military coup d'état, after which almost everyone connected with the assassination was conveniently "rehabilitated."

The story of the Lambrakis affair is one of national sorrow, of idealism, of bravery, of defeat, of terrible irony. The movie is not one of ideas or ideals, but of sensations—horror, anger, frustration and suspense.

These are communicated—sometimes with all of the subtlety of a hypodermic needle stuck in a nerve—through the extraordinary color camerawork of Raoul Coutard, the man who has photographed just about every important French film of the nineteen-sixties, including Démy's *Lola*, Truffaut's *Jules and Jim* and Godard's *Weekend*.

Coutard may be unique among cinematographers in the manner in which he adapts himself to the individual demands of his directors without losing his own identity. His work on *Z*, shot entirely in an Algiers designed to suggest Salonika, is largely responsible for Costa-Gavras's realization of what is, actually, a dazzling, super-*Dragnet* film, a sort of remarkable newsreel record of events rather than people.

Costa-Gavras, the Greek-born French director (*The Sleeping Car Murder*) laborated with Jorge Semprun (*La Guerre Est Finie*) on a screen adaptation that quite consciously subordinates characterization to vivid incident. The cast is large and excellent: Yves Montand as the assassinated doctor, Jean-Louis Trintignant (*Ma Nuit Chez Maud*) as the government's investigator, Jacques Perrin as a totally dispassionate newspaper reporter, Pierre Dux and Julien Guiomar as right-wing leaders, and Renato Salvatori and Marcel Bozzufi as the assassins whose patriotism is for hire.

A small part of me, however, tends to rebel against the film's carefully programed responses, including the sight of Irene Papas, who can be a very fine actress, as the doctor's widow. The film thus employs for easy effect Miss Papa's professional image of perpetual bereavement. Without telling us much of what the assassinated doctor believes (except that he is against missiles and for peace), the film makes us grieve by shocking us with graphic details of brutal beatings and civil disorders.

Just as the fascists in the film appeal to their audiences by oversimplification, by generalities, by fear, so does the film appeal to us by its use of the techniques of rather ordinary suspense drama—a car speeding crazily down a sidewalk in an attempt to run over a witness. Ever since the days of the swastika, I've been leery of symbols designed to elicit automatic emotional responses—even leery of the peace symbol and of "Z" itself, which, I'm told, stands for the Greek words "he is alive" and is employed by the assassinated doctor's followers in the film.

These are not meant to be major reservations, but I mention them because I think they restrict the film to a genre that is perfectly respectable but incapable of greatness. A lot of people are going to become emotionally unstuck about *Z*, seeing it as a strong political statement, which is an unnecessary ruse to ennoble sheer entertainment.

—*V.C., December 9, 1969*

"the 10 best"

1931–2002

Times critics usually named 10 best films at the end of the year, but occasionally there were more or fewer than 10 if the critics so deemed. From 1991 through 1994, moreover, the "10 Best" designation was dropped in favor of more broad-based year-end roundups.

It should also be noted that not every best 10 choice is included in the book's 1,000 reviews. Some have been displaced by other titles that from a current critical vantage point seem more important.

1931

Arrowsmith
Bad Girl
La Chienne (The Bitch)
City Lights
A Connecticut Yankee
Frankenstein
The Guardsman
Private Lives
Skippy
The Smiling Lieutenant
Tabu

1932

A Bill of Divorcement
Dr. Jekyll and Mr. Hyde
The Doomed Battalion
Grand Hotel
Maedchen in Uniform
The Mouthpiece
One Hour with You
Der Raub der Mona Lisa
Reserved for Ladies
Trouble in Paradise

1933

Berkeley Square
Cavalcade
Dinner at Eight
His Double Life
The Invisible Man
Little Women
Morgenrot
The Private Life of Henry VIII
Reunion in Vienna
State Fair

1934

The Battle
Catherine the Great
The First World War
The House of Rothschild
It Happened One Night
The Lost Patrol
Man of Aran
One Night of Love
Our Daily Bread
The Thin Man

1935

Chapayev
David Copperfield
The Informer
Lives of a Bengal Lancer
Love Me Forever
The Man Who Knew Too Much
Les Misérables
Ruggles of Red Gap
The Scoundrel
Sequoia

1936

Carnival in Flanders (La Kermesse Héroique)
Dodsworth
Fury
The Ghost Goes West
The Great Ziegfeld
The Green Pastures
Mr. Deeds Goes to Town
Romeo and Juliet
The Story of Louis Pasteur
These Three
Winterset

1937

Camille
Captains Courageous
The Good Earth
I Met Him in Paris
The Life of Emile Zola
Lost Horizon
Make Way for Tomorrow
Stage Door
A Star Is Born
They Won't Forget

1938

The Adventures of Robin Hood
The Citadel
Four Daughters
The Lady Vanishes
A Man to Remember
Pygmalion
A Slight Case of Murder
Snow White and the Seven Dwarfs
Three Comrades
To the Victor

1939

Dark Victory
Gone With the Wind
Goodbye, Mr. Chips
Juarez
Made for Each Other
Mr. Smith Goes to Washington
Ninotchka
Stagecoach
The Women
Wuthering Heights

1940

The Baker's Wife
Fantasia
The Grapes of Wrath
The Great Dictator
The Great McGinty
The Long Voyage Home
The Mortal Storm
Our Town
Pride and Prejudice
Rebecca

1941

Citizen Kane
Dumbo
Here Comes Mr. Jordan
How Green Was My Valley
The Lady Eve
Major Barbara
One Foot in Heaven
Sergeant York
The Stars Look Down
Target for Tonight

1942

Casablanca
The Gold Rush
In Which We Serve
Journey for Margaret
Mrs. Miniver
One of Our Aircraft Is Missing
Sullivan's Travels
Wake Island
Woman of the Year
Yankee Doodle Dandy

1943

Air Force
Corvette K-225
Desert Victory
For Whom the Bell Tolls
Madame Curie
The More the Merrier
The Ox-Bow Incident
Report from the Aleutians
Sahara
Watch on the Rhine

1944

Destination Tokyo
Going My Way
Hail the Conquering Hero
Meet Me in St. Louis
The Miracle of Morgan's Creek
National Velvet
None but the Lonely Heart
The Purple Heart
Thirty Seconds Over Tokyo
Wilson

1945

Anchors Aweigh
The House on 92nd Street
The Last Chance
The Lost Weekend

Pride of the Marines
Spellbound
The Story of G.I. Joe
They Were Expendable
A Tree Grows in Brooklyn
The Way Ahead

1946

The Best Years of Our Lives
Brief Encounter
The Green Years
Henry V
My Darling Clementine
Notorious
Open City
Road to Utopia
Stairway to Heaven
The Well-Digger's Daughter

1947

The Bishop's Wife
Crossfire
The Fugitive
Gentleman's Agreement
Great Expectations
Life with Father
Miracle on 34th Street
Shoeshine
To Live in Peace
The Yearling

1948

Apartment for Peggy
A Foreign Affair
Hamlet
Johnny Belinda
Louisiana Story
The Pearl
The Red Shoes
The Search
The Snake Pit
The Treasure of the Sierra Madre

1949

All the King's Men
Battleground
Command Decision
The Fallen Idol
The Heiress
Intruder in the Dust
A Letter to Three Wives
Lost Boundaries
Pinky
The Quiet One

1950

All About Eve
The Asphalt Jungle
Born Yesterday
Destination Moon
Father of the Bride
The Men
Sunset Boulevard
Titan: The Story of Michelangelo
Trio
Twelve O'Clock High

1951

An American in Paris
The Brave Bulls
Death of a Salesman
Decision Before Dawn
Detective Story
Fourteen Hours
Oliver Twist
People Will Talk
A Place in the Sun
A Streetcar Named Desire

1952

Breaking Through the Sound Barrier
Come Back, Little Sheba
Cry, the Beloved Country
Five Fingers

The Greatest Show on Earth
High Noon
Ivanhoe
Limelight
The Quiet Man
Viva Zapata!

1953

The Conquest of Everest
From Here to Eternity
Julius Caesar
Lili
Man on a Tightrope
Martin Luther
Moulin Rouge
Roman Holiday
Shane
Stalag 17

1954

The Country Girl
Genevieve
The Glenn Miller Story
Knock on Wood
The Little Kidnappers
Mr. Hulot's Holiday
On the Waterfront
Romeo and Juliet
Sabrina
Seven Brides for Seven Brothers

1955

Bad Day at Black Rock
The Bridges at Toko-Ri
The Great Adventure
It's Always Fair Weather
A Man Called Peter
Marty
Mister Roberts
Oklahoma!
The Phenix City Story
The Prisoner

1956

Anastasia
Around the World in 80 Days
Bus Stop
Friendly Persuasion
Giant
The King and I
Lust for Life
Moby Dick
Richard III
The Silent World

1957

The Bridge on the River Kwai
Funny Face
The Great Man
The Green Man
A Hatful of Rain
Les Girls
Love in the Afternoon
Sayonara
Silk Stockings
12 Angry Men

1958

Cat on a Hot Tin Roof
Damn Yankees
The Defiant Ones
Gigi
The Goddess
God's Little Acre
The Horse's Mouth
I Want to Live
A Night to Remember
Teacher's Pet

1959

Anatomy of a Murder
Ben-Hur
The Diary of Anne Frank
A Hole in the Head

North by Northwest
The Nun's Story
On the Beach
Pillow Talk
Porgy and Bess
Room at the Top

1960

The Angry Silence
The Apartment
Elmer Gantry
The Entertainer
Exodus
I'm All Right, Jack
Inherit the Wind
Psycho
Sunrise at Campobello
Tunes of Glory

1961

Ashes and Diamonds
Breathless
The Bridge
La Dolce Vita
Don Quixote
Girl with a Suitcase
The Hustler
Judgment at Nuremberg
One, Two, Three
Purple Noon
A Raisin in the Sun
Rocco and His Brothers
Saturday Night and Sunday Morning
A Summer to Remember
Two Women
West Side Story

1962

Divorce—Italian Style
Electra
Freud
Last Year at Marienbad

Long Day's Journey Into Night
The Longest Day
Lover Come Back
Sundays and Cybèle
A Taste of Honey
Whistle Down the Wind

Ship of Fools
Thunderball
To Die in Madrid

1966

Alfie
Blow-Up
Born Free
Georgy Girl
The Gospel According to St. Matthew
Loves of a Blonde
A Man for All Seasons
Morgan!
The Professionals
The Shop on Main Street
Who's Afraid of Virginia Woolf?

1963

America, America
Any Number Can Win
Cleopatra
8½
Heavens Above!
Hud
It's a Mad, Mad, Mad, Mad World
The L-shaped Room
The Sound of Trumpets
Tom Jones

1967

Closely Watched Trains
Cool Hand Luke
Elvira Madigan
Father
The Graduate
La Guerre Est Finie
The Hunt
In Cold Blood
In the Heat of the Night
Ulysses

1964

The Americanization of Emily
Dr. Strangelove or: How I Learned to Stop
    Worrying and Love the Bomb
A Hard Day's Night
Marriage—Italian Style
Mary Poppins
My Fair Lady
One Potato, Two Potato
The Servant
That Man from Rio
Woman in the Dunes

1968

Belle de Jour
The Bride Wore Black
Les Carabiners
Charlie Bubbles
Faces
The Fifth Horseman Is Fear
Petulia
A Report on the Party and the Guests
Rosemary's Baby
The Two of Us

1965

Darling
The Eleanor Roosevelt Story
Juliet of the Spirits
Kwaidan
The Pawnbroker
Red Desert
Repulsion

1969

Alice's Restaurant
The Damned
La Femme Infidèle
If . . .
Midnight Cowboy
Stolen Kisses
Topaz
True Grit
The Wild Bunch
Z

1970

The Ballad of Cable Hogue
Catch-22
Fellini Satyricon
Little Big Man
Loving
M*A*S*H
My Night at Maud's
The Passion of Anna
Tristana
The Wild Child

1971

Bed and Board
Le Boucher
Carnal Knowledge
Claire's Knee
A Clockwork Orange
The Conformist
Derby
The French Connection
The Last Picture Show
Sunday, Bloody Sunday

1972

Chloë in the Afternoon
Cries and Whispers
The Discreet Charm of the Bourgeoisie
Fat City
Frenzy
The Godfather
The Heartbreak Kid
Tokyo Story
Traffic
Two English Girls

1973

American Graffiti
Day for Night
Heavy Traffic
Last Tango in Paris
The Long Goodbye
Love
Mean Streets
Memories of Underdevelopment
Playtime
Sleeper

1974

Amarcord
Badlands
California Split
Claudine
Daisy Miller
Harry & Tonto
Lacombe, Lucien
Man Is Not a Bird
Le Petit Théâtre de Jean Renoir
The Phantom of Liberty
Scenes from a Marriage

1975

Alice Doesn't Live Here Anymore
Barry Lyndon
Distant Thunder
Hearts and Minds
Love and Death
The Magic Flute
Nashville
Shampoo
The Story of Adèle H.

Swept Away (By an Unusual Destiny in the
    Blue Sea of August)

1976

All the President's Men
Face to Face
The Memory of Justice
Network
Seven Beauties
The Seven-Per-Cent Solution
Taxi Driver

1977

Annie Hall
Close Encounters of the Third Kind
Effi Briest
The Goalie's Anxiety at the Penalty Kick
Handle with Care
The Late Show
The Man Who Loved Women
Star Wars
Stroszek
That Obscure Object of Desire

1978

California Suite
Days of Heaven
The Deer Hunter
A Geisha
Movie Movie
Perceval le Gallois
Pretty Baby
A Slave of Love
Straight Time
Violette

1979

Breaking Away
Escape from Alcatraz
Fedora

Hair
Kramer vs. Kramer
Love on the Run
Manhattan
The Marriage of Maria Braun
10
The Tree of Wooden Clogs

1980

Airplane!
Dressed to Kill
Every Man for Himself
Melvin and Howard
Mon Oncle d'Amérique
Ordinary People
Raging Bull
Stardust Memories
The Third Generation
Wise Blood

1981

Arthur
Atlantic City
Body Heat
Four Friends
Pixote
Raiders of the Lost Ark
Reds
Stevie
True Confessions
The Woman Next Door

1982

Le Beau Mariage
Chan Is Missing
E.T. the Extra-Terrestrial
Fitzcarraldo
Gregory's Girl
Lola
Missing
Smash Palace
Tootsie
Victor/Victoria

1983

Berlin Alexanderplatz
Betrayal
The Big Chill
Fanny and Alexander
Heart Like a Wheel
The King of Comedy
Local Hero
The Right Stuff
Tender Mercies
Zelig

1984

The Bostonians
Broadway Danny Rose
Entre Nous
The Family Game
Greystoke: The Legend of Tarzan, Lord of
    the Apes
A Love in Germany
A Passage to India
Places in the Heart
Stranger than Paradise
This Is Spinal Tap

1985

Desperately Seeking Susan
Kiss of the Spider Woman
Prizzi's Honor
The Purple Rose of Cairo
Ran
Secret Honor
7 Up/28 Up
Shoah
The Trip to Bountiful

1986

Blue Velvet
The Color of Money
Down by Law
Hannah and Her Sisters

Ménage
My Beautiful Laundrette
Platoon
A Room with a View
Smooth Talk
Summer

1987

Barfly
The Dead
Empire of the Sun
Full Metal Jacket
House of Games
Housekeeping
Radio Days
Tampopo
Tin Men
The Untouchables

1988

Au Revoir Les Enfants
Hotel Terminus: The Life and Times of Klaus
    Barbie
Married to the Mob
Mississippi Burning
Patty Hearst
A Taxing Woman
Things Change
Who Framed Roger Rabbit
Women on the Verge of a Nervous Breakdown
Working Girl

1989

Chocolat
Crimes and Misdemeanors
Do the Right Thing
Enemies, A Love Story
High Hopes
Little Vera
Mystery Train
Roger & Me
Sex, Lies and Videotape
True Love

1990

Akira Kurosawa's Dreams
Alice
Dick Tracy
Goodfellas
The Grifters
Metropolitan
Mr. and Mrs. Bridge
My 20th Century
Reversal of Fortune
Sweetie

1991

Instead of one 10 Best list, several *Times* critics cited films that impressed them for a variety of reasons. Here are some of them.

Barton Fink
Beauty and the Beast
Bugsy
Cape Fear
The Fisher King
Life Is Sweet
My Own Private Idaho
The Silence of the Lambs
Thelma and Louise

1992

As in 1991, there was no 10 Best list, but *Times* critics cited the following films as the most noteworthy.

The Crying Game
A Few Good Men
Gas Food Lodging
Howards End
Malcolm X
The Match Factory Girl
One False Move
Reservoir Dogs
Savage Nights
The Story of Qiu Ju

1993

Some of the films praised by *Times* critics, who again named no 10 Best.

Belle Époque
Farewell My Concubine
The Joy Luck Club
Much Ado About Nothing
The Piano
Remains of the Day
Schindler's List

1994

Times critics especially liked these films, while naming no 10 Best.

Crumb
Four Weddings and a Funeral
Hoop Dreams
I Like It Like That
The Madness of King George
Nobody's Fool
Il Postino (The Postman)
Pulp Fiction
Red
Vanya on 42nd Street

1995

Apollo 13
Before the Rain
Dead Man Walking
Lamerica
Leaving Las Vegas
Living in Oblivion
Persuasion
To Die For
Toy Story

1996

Breaking the Waves
The Crucible

The English Patient
Fargo
Flirting with Disaster
Jerry Maguire
Lone Star
Looking for Richard
The People vs. Larry Flynt
Secrets and Lies

1997

The Apostle
Boogie Nights
Deconstructing Harry
In the Company of Men
L.A. Confidential
The Pillow Book
Ponette
The Sweet Hereafter
Titanic
Ulee's Gold

1998

The Butcher Boy
The Celebration
The General
Happiness
Henry Fool
Life Is Beautiful
The Opposite of Sex
Saving Private Ryan
Shakespeare in Love
A Simple Plan
The Thin Red Line

1999

All About My Mother (Spain)
American Movie
Being John Malkovich
Boys Don't Cry
The Dreamlife of Angels (France)
Eyes Wide Shut

The Insider
The Straight Story
The Talented Mr. Ripley
Topsy-Turvy

2000

Beautiful People
Before Night Falls
Calle 54
Chicken Run
The Decalogue 1987 (Poland) reviewed in 2000
Hamlet
Traffic
Yi Yi: A One and a Two (China)
You Can Count on Me

2001

A.I.
Amores Perros (Mexico) reviewed in 2000
Ghost World
The Gleaners and I (France)
Gosford Park
In the Bedroom
The Man Who Wasn't There
Monsters, Inc.
Sexy Beast
Shrek

2002

About Schmidt
Adaptation
Chicago
Far From Heaven
The Fast Runner (Atanarjuat) (Inuit)
Gangs of New York
The Hours
The Pianist
Spirited Away (Japan)
Talk To Her (Spain)
Y Tu Mama Tambien (Mexico)

films by category

ACTION/ADVENTURE

King Kong 1933	516
The Lives of a Bengal Lancer 1935	568
Captains Courageous 1937	163
The Adventures of Robin Hood 1938	9
Gunga Din 1939	417
The Wizard of Oz 1939	1117
The Thief of Bagdad 1940	1007
Sahara 1943	855
Sanjuro 1963 (Japan)	858
Yojimbo 1962 (Japan)	1137
Goldfinger 1964	393
Operation Crossbow 1965	726
The Dirty Dozen 1967	258
The Day of the Jackal 1973	230
Close Encounters of the Third Kind 1977	191
Star Wars 1977	942
Mad Max 1980	600
Raiders of the Lost Ark 1981	800
The Road Warrior 1982	836
Back to the Future 1985	67
Die Hard 1988	254
Total Recall 1990	1037
Apollo 13 1995	52

ANIMATED

Snow White and the Seven Dwarfs 1938	925
Fantasia 1940	322
Pinocchio 1940	764
Dumbo 1941	288
Bambi 1942	73
Yellow Submarine 1968	1134
Heavy Traffic 1973	438
Who Framed Roger Rabbit 1988; also Comedy	1106
Beauty and the Beast 1991	84
Aladdin 1992	18
Toy Story 1995	1039
Chicken Run 2000	178
Monsters, Inc. 2001	658
Shrek 2001	910
Spirited Away 2002	934

COMEDY

Trouble in Paradise 1932	1050
Dinner at Eight 1933	256
Duck Soup 1933	286
It Happened One Night 1934	493
It's a Gift 1934	494
The Thin Man 1934	1009
Twentieth Century 1934	1058
Ruggles of Red Gap 1935	849
The Scoundrel 1935	869
Mr. Deeds Goes to Town 1936	651
My Man Godfrey 1936	681
The Awful Truth 1937	62
Easy Living 1937	293
Bringing Up Baby 1938	146
A Slight Case of Murder 1938	921
Love Affair 1939	587
Midnight 1939	640
Ninotchka 1939	698

CRIME/MYSTERY/SUSPENSE

DOCUMENTARY

DRAMA

foreign films by country of origin

GERMANY
(FEDERAL REPUBLIC OF GERMANY)

GREECE

HUNGARY

INDIA